cev youth **bible**

Contemporary English Version

CARE operates across the UK, caring, campaigning and communicating. CARE works for the well-being of all in society but particularly the most vulnerable and needy. www.care.org.uk

Credit Action is a national money education charity. It has a wide range of material and speakers to help teach on these subjects. www.creditaction.org.uk

Christians in Sport encourage, equip and support Christians to share the good news of Jesus with their sporting friends. www.christiansinsport.org.uk

Christian Solidarity Worldwide is a human rights charity working on behalf of those persecuted for their Christian beliefs and also promoting religious liberty for all. www.csw.org.uk

Churches' Criminal Justice Forum is drawn from all churches. It upholds Christian values in the field of criminal justice, stresses the relevance of criminal justice to Christian teaching and encourages people to get involved in useful ways. www.ccjf.org.uk

Damaris helps people develop a firm grasp of the Bible, a clear understanding of contemporary popular culture, and the ability to connect one to the other. www.damaris.org

Discovery is the youth and schools ministry of Agapé. Telling teenagers about Jesus, helping them grow in their faith and teaching them how to tell others about Jesus too. www.agape.org.uk

exalt.co.uk

Exalt helps to connect faith with life. Exalt is a large web community where you can read, chat, engage in debate, shop, download music or use our charity based ISP. www.exalt.co.uk

Hope UK is a Christian drugs prevention/education charity working to prevent drug-related harm and promote drug-free choices. Encouraging children and young people to live healthy lives, making their own decisions and fulfilling their potential. www.hopeuk.org

Open Doors is an organisation working for justice and freedom, combating persecution against Christians. www.opendoorsuk.org

Soul Survivor has run festival-style conferences since 1993 for young people wanting to give their whole lives in worship to Jesus. www.soulsurvivor.com

Tearfund is a Christian relief and development charity which works through local partners to bring help and hope to communities in need around the world. www.tearfund.org

THROWSTAR

Throwstar is a Birmingham-based art movement intent on worshipping God through the arts and serving creative people. They sponsor thought-provoking events and innovative collaborations while loving and challenging local artists and musicians. www.throwstar.com.

Wycliffe aims, by 2025 and together with partners worldwide, to see a Bible translation project begun in all the remaining languages that need one. That is about 2707 languages. www.wycliffe.org.uk

We have also been helped by Graham Kendrick.

cev youth **bible**

Contemporary English Version

Collins is a divitsion of HarperCollins*Publishers*
77–85 Fulham Palace Road, London W6 8JB
www.collins.co.uk

CEV Youth Bible
Contemporary English Version

Title	ISBN
CEV Youth Bible Hardback	0 00 716960 4

BFBS/20M/2004/2.9a

CEV Text design by Martin Richards.
Typeset in Stone Serif 8/9pt using Corel Ventura 9 by The British and Foreign Bible Society.
Production arranged by The British and Foreign Bible Society. www.biblesociety.org.uk
Cover design by HarperCollins*Publishers*
Printed in Great Britain by The Bath Press, Bath.

For permission to use excerpts of the CEV please contact:
Permissions, The British and Foreign Bible Society, Stonehill Green, Westlea, Swindon SN5 7DG

Contents

Books of the Bible in alphabetical order

Acts	Acts	NT	1205	Judges	Judg	OT	226
Amos	Amos	OT	880	Kings 1	1 King	OT	326
Chronicles 1	1 Chron	OT	389	Kings 2	2 King	OT	357
Chronicles 2	2 Chron	OT	419	Lamentations	Lam	OT	788
Colossians	Col	NT	1329	Leviticus	Lev	OT	92
Corinthians 1	1 Cor	NT	1275	Luke	Luke	NT	1115
Corinthians 2	2 Cor	NT	1293	Malachi	Mal	OT	931
Daniel	Dan	OT	846	Mark	Mark	NT	1085
Deuteronomy	Deut	OT	156	Matthew	Matt	NT	1031
Ecclesiastes	Ecc	OT	638	Micah	Mic	OT	896
Ephesians	Eph	NT	1314	Nahum	Nah	OT	904
Esther	Esth	OT	481	Nehemiah	Neh	OT	465
Exodus	Exod	OT	51	Numbers	Num	OT	120
Ezekiel	Ezek	OT	796	Obadiah	Obad	OT	891
Ezra	Ezra	OT	454	Peter 1	1 Pet	NT	1384
Galatians	Gal	NT	1305	Peter 2	2 Pet	NT	1391
Genesis	Gen	OT	1	Philemon	Phlm	NT	1360
Habakkuk	Hab	OT	908	Philippians	Phil	NT	1323
Haggai	Hag	OT	917	Proverbs	Prov	OT	609
Hebrews	Heb	NT	1362	Psalms	Psa	OT	520
Hosea	Hos	OT	862	Revelation	Rev	NT	1407
Isaiah	Isa	OT	654	Romans	Rom	NT	1254
James	Jam	NT	1378	Ruth	Ruth	OT	255
Jeremiah	Jer	OT	722	Samuel 1	1 Sam	OT	260
Job	Job	OT	489	Samuel 2	2 Sam	OT	296
Joel	Joel	OT	875	Song of Songs	Song	OT	647
John	John	NT	1167	Thessalonians 1	1 Thes	NT	1336
John 1	1 John	NT	1395	Thessalonians 2	2 Thes	NT	1341
John 2	2 John	NT	1401	Timothy 1	1 Tim	NT	1345
John 3	3 John	NT	1402	Timothy 2	2 Tim	NT	1351
Jonah	Jon	OT	893	Titus	Titus	NT	1356
Joshua	Josh	OT	198	Zechariah	Zech	OT	920
Jude	Jude	NT	1404	Zephaniah	Zeph	OT	912

The Bible...

What is it?

The boring, missing the main point version

The Bible is a collection of books written by many different authors, across thousands of years. It contains 66 books, including books of history, prophecy, poetry, letters and biographies of Jesus. It's very, very old and very, very big.

The exciting, why you should read it answer

The Bible is the most amazing book ever written. It's like no other book, because this is a book that speaks to you. Let me explain: Christians believe that the Bible is inspired by God. Which means that the people who wrote it were passing on messages from God – messages which were not only for the people of their time, but for all people, everywhere and in any time.

Think about that for a minute: if you read this book, you'll be hearing from God. Yes, it has 66 books in it, written in different styles; yes it's very old. But the key thing about the Bible is that it's the word of God. There are passages in the Bible that lift and inspire – and there are parts which disgust and shock. The Bible is challenging, unsettling, comforting and encouraging. What we have to do is explore it for ourselves.

The Bible...

Six myths about the Bible

1. It's written in a weird, old language

Wrong. The Bible was originally written in two main languages: Hebrew and Greek. Most of us have to read it, therefore, in translation. And what people mean when they say 'it's in an old language' is that they've been reading a translation done a long time ago. The version you're holding is a modern translation, designed specifically to make the language simple to understand.

2. Only experts can understand it

Mostly wrong. Most of the Bible speaks in pretty straightforward language. I mean, you don't need a degree in Ancient Assyrian to understand the words: 'Love your enemies.' Jesus famously boiled down the whole of the Old Testament into two commandments: 'Love the Lord your God with all your heart, soul, and mind' and 'Love others as much as you love yourself' (Matthew 22.36–40). That's not exactly brain surgery, is it? It's not easy to do, admittedly, but it's pretty easy to understand.

There are some difficult bits of the Bible, it's true. There are some bits where we need an expert to give us a bit of help. But mostly the thing to do is to concentrate on doing the things we can understand.

3. It takes too much time

Wrong. You don't have to read the whole thing in one go! In fact, you don't have to read the whole thing at all – although it's not a bad thing to do. You can get a good grip of what the Bible is all about by reading it for five or ten minutes a day. That's probably less than the time you spend watching adverts on TV!

4. It's boring

Occasionally right. Parts of it are a bit dull to a modern reader. Lists of families, long lists of laws, all those strange names of people and countries... (Actually some cultures do find this stuff interesting, they're just not our thing). But along with all this, you get great poetry, stirring stories, thought-provoking wisdom, life-changing truths. You get love, sex, violence, faithfulness, bravery, cowardice, triumph and disaster. You get astonishing miracles, amazing insights, stirring speeches, startling facts and inspiring examples. Most of all, you get to hear from God. If you think that's boring then you're probably dead from the neck up.

5. It's too big

Partly right. It does contain around 750,000 words. So take it a bit at a time. After all, we don't give up eating because there's 'too much food in the world'. Instead we take it one meal and one bite at a time. Which is exactly why the Bible is organised into books, chapters and verses. Choose bite size chunks.

6. It's not relevant

Completely wrong. Totally and utterly wrong. Wrong, wrong, wrong, wrong, wrong... well, I think you get the point.

The Bible is all about the big issues in life. It tells us why we're here, what we're supposed to be doing on earth, where we all came from. It tells us how we should live our lives and how we should treat other people. It talks about real people with real problems – and although they lived a long time ago, they faced exactly the same kind of problems that we face today.

Most of all, it tells us how we can have a relationship with God and live forever. And that's relevant to everyone on earth.

The Bible is the most revolutionary, most exciting, most important book ever written. What more do you need to know?

The Bible...

How did we get it?

The Hebrew Scriptures

The Old Testament is made up of the Hebrew Scriptures, the holy books of the Jews. They arrange the books in three sections: Law, Prophets and Writings. The early Church used the Jewish Scriptures, probably singing from the Psalms and reading the prophets to see how they pointed to Jesus. But they also told stories and shared memories of Jesus's life and teaching, passing on these memories from group to group.

Writings of the early church

After a while the church had grown and the original eyewitnesses began to die. So various people began to write down their own accounts, drawing on a range of material and their own observations. At the same time, leaders such as Paul, Peter or John wrote to different churches helping them to solve problems and offering spiritual advice. These letters were collected and copied and passed around the early Church.

True or false

The trouble was that, along with these true documents, fake gospels began to circulate, full of bizarre details and false teaching. So various church leaders began to draw up their lists of 'recommended' reading. In 376AD, Bishop Athanasius wrote to the churches in his region, with his list of what constituted 'Holy Scripture'. He listed books which were attributed to apostles or people closely associated with Jesus. His list was eventually confirmed by two councils, one in Rome in 382 and one in Carthage in 397 and that is the New Testament that we have today.

It's a surprising fact that, although individual books date from as early as 50AD, the collection of books that we know as 'The Bible' was not agreed until around 400.

The Bible...

Bible languages

We read the whole thing in English, but the Bible was originally written in several different kinds of languages, depending on who was writing and the time it was written.

Hebrew

The language of the Old Testament (apart from a bit of Daniel which was written in Aramaic). After the exile, it was replaced by Aramaic in common use, but it continued to be the 'religious language' used in religious ritual and, of course, when reading the Hebrew scriptures.

Aramaic

The Aramaic language was used throughout most of the Assyrian and Persian empire. After the restoration of the Jews, Aramaic was adopted as the common language. This was the language that Jesus spoke. Aramaic words which appear in the New Testament include 'Abba' (Mark 14.36) and 'Talitha, koum' (Mark 5.41), which many translations leave as they are.

Greek

The New Testament is written in Greek. But this is not the Greek of classical literature. This is what is known as koine or common Greek. This was the language used by ordinary people throughout the Roman empire, the language used for trade and commerce. Even in Rome, most people spoke Greek, with Latin being reserved for official use, or used by the upper classes. Paul and the Gospel writers used Greek, because everybody spoke it. It's worth remembering that the New Testament was not written in posh language, but the language of the ordinary, working man and woman of the time.

Latin

Latin only occurs in the New Testament in a handful of places, mostly to do with official terms such as census, Centurion or denarius. Most people spoke Aramaic or Greek. However, Latin became widely used in the medieval church and the first translations of the Bible were into Latin.

The Bible...

A bit about divine inspiration

Christians talk about the Bible as being 'divinely inspired'. They take this idea from verses such as 2 Timothy 3.16 which says, 'Everything in the Scriptures is God's Word. All of it is useful for teaching and helping people and for correcting them and showing them how to live.' In fact, the phrase Paul uses of the Scriptures is 'God-breathed' which Christians interpret as meaning that the Scriptures are not merely the production of men, but of men working under the command of God.

Some people believe in what is called verbal inspiration – the idea that every word in the Bible came directly from God. At its extreme, followers of this view believe that everything in the Bible is free from error, not only in terms of religion, but also in terms of history and science. Others believe that the writers were prompted and inspired by the Holy Spirit, but the words they used were their own. God gave them the message, but they passed it on using their own style. This view is called 'plenary inspiration'.

Perhaps the key factor here is what we mean by 'inspire'. The word comes from two Latin words: spirare meaning 'breathe', and in meaning... um... 'in'. Inspire literally means, to breathe in. To read the Bible is to breathe in something of God; to feel what he feels, hear his words, feel his life within us.

The Bible...

How is it organised?

Old and New Testaments

The Bible is split into two parts, the Old and New Testaments. The Old Testament also forms the Jewish scriptures. For this reason some people call the Old Testament the Hebrew Scriptures.

Sections

The Old Testament is split into four different sections: History, Prophecy, Wisdom and what some people call 'the Pentateuch' or 'the Books of the Law'.

The New Testament is divided into three sections: the Gospels, the book of Acts, and the Letters, from people such as Paul, John and Peter.

Books

Each of these sections is made up of different numbers of books. The Law, for example, consists of five books: Genesis, Exodus, Leviticus, Numbers, Deuteronomy. The Gospels, in the New Testament, are Matthew, Mark, Luke and John. Some books are huge, some are just one page long. They are written in different styles. The Psalms, for instance, are collections of poems; Kings is a long history.

Chapters

Each book of the Bible is broken down into chapters. Some bits of these appear in more than one book; Chronicles and Kings share a lot of the same content, as do Matthew, Mark and John.

Verses

Finally the chapters are split into individual, numbered verses. Again, some verses are found in more than one book of the Bible.

Bible references

To find our way around the Bible we use 'Bible references' – a bit like an address. Here's how those 'addresses' are used in this Bible:

John 3.16 means 'the book of John, chapter 3, verse 16.

Genesis 1.1–17 means the book of Genesis, chapter one, verses 1 to 17.

James 4.13,15; 5.6 means read James chapter 4, verse 13, verse 15 and chapter 5, verse 6.

The Bible...

How do we read it?

The reason we find it difficult to read the Bible is that we don't approach it in the right way. We approach it like going to the dentist's. We have to do it for our own good, but no-one really enjoys it.

Well, I don't think the Bible is like that. It's more like exploring another country. We should approach the Bible with the spirit of pioneers, 'boldly going' into brave new chapters, seeking to understand the natives and to learn from their wisdom.

So here are some tips to help you get the most out of your visit to 'Bible-land'.

Ask questions

This is the most important thing you can do. A lot of people feel like they shouldn't ask questions about the Bible, as if it's somehow being sinful or unbelieving, but in fact, the Bible is full of people who asked God challenging questions. If they weren't afraid, then neither should we be. If you don't ask, you won't find out.

Work to a plan

It helps to have a plan of action to help you explore. The *CEV Youth Bible* contains over 150 mini reading plans, called 'Footsteps', which suggest readings on a wide range of topics. You can work through a particular book, or follow a particular person and study their life. Or you could study a topic such as 'prayer', or 'forgiveness' or 'justice'.

Move slowly

Take your time. You can't see anywhere clearly if you're zooming through it at 120 miles per hour. Read carefully and you'll find loads to fascinate you.

Read it aloud

It often helps to read the passage aloud. Don't be embarrassed. This version of the Bible is specifically designed to be read aloud – you'll find it easy to understand.

Write notes

Keep a traveller's journal as you visit each part of Bible-land. Make your own maps. Draw your own pictures. Write down your thoughts and observations. You might like to keep a separate book for the purpose or you might like to scribble on your Bible. Personalise your Bible with pictures, post-it notes, letters and things to pray about. Underline bits which you find important and write down how God has spoken to you.

Look around you

Try not to concentrate on just one verse, but look around at the passages that surround it. Find out about the time it was written and the situation of the writer.

Use some guidebooks

When I go travelling I take some reference materials – like guidebooks, maps and phrasebooks. You'll find a lot of help in this Bible, but if you want to go deeper, you can use Bible guides and commentaries to help you delve into a lot more detail.

Learn about the history

If there is one thing that really helps people understand the Bible, it's a broad understanding of the history. Each book of the Bible was written at a particular point in history and understanding this can help our understanding of the entire book.

Understand the culture

They did things differently in Bible times. They had different attitudes to war, women, families, relationships and other such things. If you spend a little time trying to grasp the culture it will help you understand the passage a lot better.

Get to know the locals

The people of Bible times faced the same problems we do today. So take time to get to know the lives of the people. The problems that people like David and Paul and Elijah grappled with will help us understand and cope with the problems in our life.

Don't expect to understand everything

Here's a secret: nobody understands all the Bible, except God. There are bits in the Bible that even the experts don't understand. So if you find a difficult bit, work at it, ask questions and then, if it's still baffling, move on. Just because we don't understand one bit, doesn't mean we should stop exploring.

Don't worry about the pronunciation

A lot of people get very hung up on the names. But the truth is no-one really knows for sure how they were pronounced. I mean, for all we know, Zerubbabel might have been called 'Zubble' by his mates.

Use your commonsense

God has given us wisdom. Some of us could do with a little more, admittedly, but we all have it. So, when you read the Bible, try to use the wisdom God has given you. Don't fly off into fanciful theories and ideas based on one verse. Try to identify when people are speaking metaphorically or literally. Use your common sense.

The Bible...

How do I help others to read it?

It may be that you're asked to lead a Bible study or a housegroup. So how do you help people get into the Bible? Here are a few 'do's and don'ts.'

Don't pretend

Don't pretend that you're some kind of spiritual hero or an academic expert. Be honest if you don't know the answer to questions. Try and find the answer together.

Prepare

Do your preparation. Organise yourself. Do some background reading. Pray it through.

Make it real

It really helps to know the history and context of the passage – and many people find the history fascinating. But we want people to meet God through the Bible. So look for lessons that can be applied to real life.

Be inventive

You don't have to make people sit in a circle listening to a lecture! Use different methods. Steal approaches that have worked in training sessions at your school or college. Get people moving. You can get people to retell the story in a number of ways – through drama, by drawing a comic book version, by creating a newspaper...

Make them think

Don't tell them what to think, get them thinking for themselves. Ask questions, and listen to the answers. Get them to ask questions as well. Try to ask open questions – questions which don't just need a 'yes' or 'no' answer.

Look around you

Use the newspaper, movies or TV programmes to provide material. Show a scene from a movie as a way in to one of the Bible issues.

Don't put pressure on people

Not everyone feels comfortable reading aloud (in fact not everyone can read). So be sensitive. Few things put people off more than being forced to stand up and recite.

Create an atmosphere

Get the environment right. Make it small and intimate if possible. Maybe pick a theme. Are you looking at Jonah? Move the furniture in the room around to resemble a boat. People will really remember it if they learn in an unusual environment.

Get them moving

Give people a chance to move around. Research shows that people remember a lot more if they move about a bit.

Be enthusiastic

If you're bored with the topic, they'll be bored with what you're doing. Share your enthusiasm and interest. Even if the subject is difficult, the journey can be fascinating.

The Bible...

How to use the cev youth bible

This Bible has loads of extra features to help you find out more about the Bible and understand what God is saying to you.

Life Files

Mini-biogs of all the major figures in the Bible; their life stories, and the lessons we can learn. From David to Daniel, from Jacob to Jesus.

Big Ideas

Major themes of the Bible covering ideas like forgiveness, sin, God's love, suffering, creation, justice, and judgment.

Footsteps

Over 150 short reading plans to guide you through the Bible. Follow a theme or the life of a person, work your way through a book or check out the history.

Helplines

Thoughts on the issues that fill our lives. Friendship, love, families, education, work, college... if you're in need of help, you'll find something here.

Holy History

All the background info you need. Find out what was going on, and what life was like. What clothes they wore, what food they ate, who killed who and who did what. It's history, but it's also interesting.

Real Life

Real issues from a book that's all about reality. Adoption, abortion, the poor, racism, sex, genetic engineering, civil disobedience... features from Christian organisations who know what they're talking about.

Viewpoints

Real young people writing about the Bible. What do people like you get out of 'the good book'? 60 comments written by young people, for young people.

Being Christian

What does it mean to be a Christian? What are we supposed to do? A whole range of features taking you through the obligations, attitudes and actions that come from being Christian.

Introductions

The main introduction to each book of the Bible sets the scene and sums up the story, giving you what you need to know.

Anorak corner

Fascinating facts that you can quietly drop in to enliven any conversation! Quizzes, lists, everything the self-respecting anorak should know.

Maps

Assyria, Galilee, Palestine: find your way around the ancient world with these easy to use maps.

Big Index

Want to find a particular passage, or look up a topic or event? Search here first.

Quickstart

Some readings to get you going. Where to go in the Bible if you're feeling angry, sad, rejected, worried, skint...

The Bible...

What's the big story?

Creation and the early times

God creates the heavens and the earth. He creates a world that is good. He creates men and women and gives them a garden to inhabit. They are only given one rule to obey, but they choose to disobey, to give into temptation and turn away from God. The result is that they're thrown out of the garden. Sin and evil have polluted God's creation.

And it doesn't stop there. As humanity spreads throughout the earth, so does evil. Eventually God decides to start again, by wiping out all human beings. Well... not quite all. Noah is a good man and he and his family are saved from the flood. Noah is given the task of repopulating the earth. God makes a solemn promise to Noah never to destroy humanity again.

The ancestors

Evil has not gone away, however. God begins a new approach. He decides to choose a nation to work through, and, to father this nation, he chooses Abraham. God promises Abraham that his descendants will be a great nation and they will inhabit the land of Canaan. He also promises that all of humanity will be blessed by Abraham's descendants.

This promise to Abraham looks dodgy, since Abraham is in his nineties. But God keeps his promises, and Abraham's wife Sarah gives birth to Isaac. Isaac is the father to twins, Esau and Jacob, and the line progresses through the younger son, Jacob. Jacob has twelve children, one of whom, Joseph, ends up in Egypt after annoying his brothers. In the end the rest of the family flee to Egypt to escape famine where they are reunited with Joseph. Jacob changes his name to Israel, and it is by this name that the people will henceforth be known.

In Egypt, the Israelites start to multiply and by the time a few hundred years have passed, the good news is that the promise has come true – Abraham's descendants have become a nation. The bad news is that the entire nation is in slavery.

The exodus

God selects a leader called Moses, who commands the Egyptian king to let the Israelites go. After a series of disasters, the Israelites escape. They make their way back to Canaan. On the way God gives them commandments and detailed instructions on how they should live and how they should worship their God. However, when they get to the borders of Canaan, they are too scared to cross into the land. God punishes this lack of faith, by making them wander in the desert.

Forty years on, and Moses dies on a mountain overlooking Canaan. He hands over leadership to Joshua, under whose command the Israelites cross the River Jordan and invade the land. However, God gave his people explicit instructions to conquer all the land, but the people compromise. Some of the old inhabitants – the Canaanites – remain and, with them, their own ways of worship. For the next 800 years Israel's history is a battle between the worship of God and the worship of false gods.

The judges

First there is the period of the judges – a period when the country was filled with lawlessness and violence and when 'each man did what he thought was right'. The judges – leaders like Deborah and Gideon and Samson – bring only occasional light into the darkness.

The united kingdom

The Israelites ask for a king. Although God says they don't need one, in the end he gives in and Saul becomes the first king of Israel. Saul is a brave, but foolish, leader and he's succeeded by David, Israel's greatest king. Under the leadership of David and his son Solomon, Israel achieves the height of its power and influence. David defeats the enemies of Israel and Solomon builds a magnificent temple in Jerusalem.

The divided kingdom

It was not to last. On Solomon's death, the country falls into civil war, and the 'promised land' splits into two countries; Israel in the north and Judah in the south. The next 300 years are a long, slow descent into destruction. The two nations are constantly attacked by powerful enemies, while they are led astray by a series of evil kings who follow false gods. In an attempt to turn them around, God sends a series of messengers – the prophets – who challenge, criticise and warn the kingdoms what will happen to them if they don't change. It doesn't do much good. In 722BC the northern kingdom of Israel is captured and the inhabitants taken into captivity in Assyria. They are never heard of again. A hundred years later, the southern kingdom of Judah falls to another mighty empire, the Babylonians, and the people are taken captive in Babylon. Yet not all hope is lost. In the years before and during the exile, the prophets talked of a Messiah – a 'chosen one' – a mighty leader whom God would send to save his people.

The exile and return

Their exile lasts seventy years, before the Babylonian empire falls and the exiles return to Israel. Despite opposition, they rebuild Jerusalem and the temple. But the glory days have gone. God sends no more prophets and Israel remains at the mercy of invading nations, first the Greeks and then the mighty Roman empire. Increasingly, the people of Israel place their hopes in the long-awaited Messiah.

Jesus

The promise given centuries before to Abraham was to come true in a remarkable way. A poor young woman called Mary falls pregnant with a son, a son whose father is God himself. This son Jesus is born in poverty and raised in obscurity in an unremarkable town in northern Israel.

Jesus' public work begins when he is around 30 years old. After a short spell in the desert, he travels through Israel preaching, teaching and performing miracles. He starts to make claims for himself; claims that go beyond those of a teacher or even a prophet. He forgives people their sins and raises the dead; he challenges the establishment. With his small band of followers he enters Jerusalem in triumph. Then it all seems to go wrong. Betrayed by one of his followers, Jesus is tried by the authorities, taken outside the city and executed.

Three days later, his followers start to make remarkable claims. They claim that Jesus has risen from the dead, that he has appeared to many of his followers. More, they claim that Jesus is the Messiah, that his death has changed the world, and that he has sent them a new helper, the Holy Spirit, to empower and inspire them. These followers spread the message far and wide.

The early church

As the message catches hold, the followers face persecution from the Jewish and Roman authorities. New leaders emerge: Peter, the fisherman who was one of Jesus' first followers; Paul, who began his career persecuting Jesus' followers and who, after a dramatic vision of Jesus, becomes one of its most outspoken followers. Gradually the stories about Jesus are written down and sent around the world. The followers set up local groups – called churches. People of all nationalities start to believe in this Messiah.

The future

In exile on a small island, John, one of Jesus' earliest followers, has a vision of the end of time. Jesus will return and gain the final victory over darkness. The world will end as it began – with creation, with God creating a new heaven and a new earth, where all his followers will live in peace.

Quickstart

Where to find help when you're...

Afraid
Psalms 34.4-6; Isaiah 12.1-5;
Matthew 10.28-31; 1 Peter 3.13-14

Angry
Matthew 5.22; Ephesians 4.25-27;
1 Timothy 2.8

Ashamed
Psalms 32.1-11; 51.1-19; Proverbs 17.9;
Isaiah 55.7-13; Micah 7.18; Acts 13.38-39

Bitter
Proverbs 3.11-12; Ephesians 4.31-32;
James 3.13-18

Confused
Psalms 25.4-5; 32.8-9; Proverbs 3.1-6;
Isaiah 42.16; Ephesians 5.1-2

Depressed
Psalms 34.1-22; Isaiah 35.1-2

Discouraged
Psalms 23.1-6; 41.5-11; 55.22; 150.6;
Matthew 5.11-12; 2 Corinthians 4.8-18;
Philippians 4.4-7

Discriminated against
Matthew 7.1-5,12; Acts 10.34-36;
Galatians 3.26-29; Ephesians 2.11-22;
Colossians 3.5-11; James 2.1-13

Doubting
Matthew 8.23-27; John 20.24-29;
Jude 1.21-22

Feeling a failure
Psalms 73.25-26; 136.1-19;
Jeremiah 30.18-22; Romans 8.31-39

Feeling let down by people
Luke 17.3-4; Romans 12.14-21

Feeling rejected
Psalm 86.1-17; 136.1-26;
Romans 8.28,38-39

Grieving
Psalms 119.49-52; Matthew 5.4

Hating yourself
Psalm 139; 1 Corinthians 1:26-31;
Colossians 3.12

Impatient
Proverbs 14.29; 19.11; 29.11;
Romans 12.11-12; Galatians 5.22-23;
Hebrews 10.36

In need of protection
Numbers 6.23-26; Psalms 27.1-6,14;
56.8-13; 91.1-16; Nahum 1.7;
Malachi 3.17-18

Leading others
1 Timothy 3.1-7; 2 Timothy 2.14-26;
Titus 1.5-9

Lonely
Psalm 22, 23.1-6, 40.1-3; 68.5-6;
Hebrews 13.5,6

Needing peace
Luke 1.78-79; John 14.27-29;
Romans 5.1-5; Philippians 4.6-7

Running out of time
Proverbs 12.11; 28.19; Ecclesiastes 3.1-8;
Luke 21.34-36; Titus 3.14

Sad
Psalms 51.1-19; Isaiah 53.3-10; 61.1-7;
Jeremiah. 31.15-17; Matthew 5.4;
2 Corinthians 1.3-4; Revelation 21.3-4

Sick or in pain
Psalms 38.1-22; Proverbs 18.14;
Matthew 14.34-36; James 5.14-15

Skint

Ecclesiastes 5.10–20; Matthew 6.24–34;
Luke 12.13–21; 1 Timothy 6.6–10

Starting a new job

Proverbs 11.3; Ecclesiastes 10.4;
Romans 12.3–11;
1 Thessalonians 5.12–18;
2 Thessalonians 3.6–13

Suffering

Psalm 102; 2 Corinthians 12.9–10;
Colossians 1.24–2.5; 1 Peter 4.12–13,19

Tempted

Psalms 1.1–6; 139.23–24;
1 Corinthians 10.12–13;
Hebrews 2.14–18; James 4.7;
2 Peter 3.17–18

Thankful

Psalms 100.1–5; 118.27–29;
Philippians 4.6; Colossians 3.16;
1 Thessalonians 5.18

Under pressure

Exodus 18.17–23; 1 Samuel 30:6;
Job 19.1–27; Psalms 43.1–4

Weary

Matthew 11.28–30; 1 Corinthians 15.58;
Galatians 6.9–10

Worried

Psalms 46.1–11; 94.18–19;
Matthew 6.19–34; John 14.27;
Philippians 4.6; 1 Peter 5.6–7

Quickstart

Where is it in the Bible? Some famous Bible bits

Creation and fall: Genesis 2.4–3.24
Noah and the flood: Genesis 6.1–9.17
The call of Abraham: Genesis 12.1–9
Abraham and Isaac: Genesis 22.1–19
The burning bush: Exodus 3.1–22
The ten commandments: Exodus 20.1–17;
Deuteronomy 5.1–21
David v. Goliath: 1 Samuel 17.1–54
David and Jonathan: 1 Samuel 20.1–42
David brings the ark to Jerusalem:
2 Samuel 6.1–23
David and Bathsheba: 2 Samuel 11.1–27
Wisdom of Solomon: 1 Kings 2.12—11.43
Elijah fights the prophets of Baal:
1 Kings 18.1–46
Elijah meets God in the wilderness:
1 Kings 19.1–18

A new agreement: Jeremiah 31.31–40
Isaiah's vision of heaven: Isaiah 65.17–25
True worship: Isaiah 58.6–12
The beatitudes: Matthew 5.3–11;
Luke 6.20–26
The golden rule: Matthew 7.12; Luke 6.31
The vital commandment:
Matthew 22.37–39: Mark 12.29–31;
Luke 10.27
The sermon on the mount: Matthew 5–7
The Lord's prayer: Matthew 6.9–13
Mary's song: Luke 1.46–55
The great commission: Matthew 28.16–20
The last supper: Matthew 26.17–30
The greatest gift: 1 Corinthians 13

Quickstart

The Parables of Jesus

Two builders: Matthew 7.24–27
The sower: Matthew 13.3–23; Mark 4.1–9;
Luke 8.5–15
Weeds among the wheat:
Matthew 13.24–30,36–43
Mustard-seed: Matthew 13.31,32;
Mark 4.30–32; Luke 13.18
Yeast: Matthew 13.33; Luke 13.19
Hidden treasure: Matthew 13.44
The pearl: Matthew 13.45,46
The fishing net: Matthew 13.47–50
Unforgiving official: Matthew 18.23–35
Workers in a vineyard: Matthew 20.1–16
Two sons: Matthew 21.28–32
Tenants of the vineyard: Matthew 21.33–45;
Mark 12.1–12; Luke 20.9–19
Great banquet: Matthew 22.2–14;
Luke 14.15–23
Faithful, and unfaithful servants:
Matthew 24.45–51
Ten girls: Matthew 25.1–13
Three servants (the Talents):
Matthew 25.14–30; Luke 19.12–27
Seeds growing: Mark 4.26–29
Man taking a journey: Mark 13.34–37
Good samaritan: Luke 10.30–37
The friend in the night: Luke 11.5–9
The rich fool: Luke 12.16–21
The fig-tree: Luke 13.6–9
Lost sheep: Matthew 18.12–14; Luke 15.3–7
One coin: Luke 15.8–10
Prodigal son: Luke 15.11–32
Dishonest manager: Luke 16.1–8
Lazarus and the rich man: Luke 16.19–31
Widow and the judge: Luke 18.1–8
Pharisee and tax-collector: Luke 18.9–14
The good shepherd: John 10.1–6

The Miracles of Jesus

Water into wine: John 2.1–11
Feeding loads of people:
Matthew 14.13–21; 15.32–39;
Mark 6.30–44; 8.1–10; Luke 9.10–17;
John 6.1–15
Calming the storm: Matthew 8.23–27;
Mark 4.35–41; Luke 8.22–25
Great catch of fish: Luke 5.1–11
Walking on water: Matthew 14.22–33;
Mark 6.45–52; John 6.16–21
Healing people with leprosy:
Matthew 8.1–4; Mark 1.40–45;
Luke 5.12–16; 17.11–19
Casting out demons: Matthew 8.28–34;
12.22–37; 17.14–21; Mark 1.21–28;
3.20–30; 5.1–20; 9.14–29; Luke 4.31–37;
8.26–39; 9.37–43; 11.14–23
Healing the blind: Matthew 9.27–31;
20.29–34; Mark 10.46–52; Luke 18.35–43
Healing the deaf: Mark 7.31–37
Healing the crippled: Matthew 12.9–14;
9.1–8; Mark 2.1–12; 3.1–6; Luke 5.17–26;
6.6–11; 14.1–6; John 5.1–9
Healing many women: Matthew 9.18–26;
15.21–28; Mark 5.21–43; 7.24–30;
Luke 8.1–3; 8.40–56; 13.10–17
Healing an army officer's servant:
Matthew 8.5–13; Luke 7.1–10
Healing Peter's mother–in–law:
Matthew 8.14–15; Mark 1.29–31;
Luke 4.38–39
Bringing the official's daughter back to life:
Matthew 9.18–26; Mark 5.21–42;
Luke 8.40–56
Bringing the widow's son back to life:
Luke 7.11–17
Bringing Lazarus back to life: John 11.1–44

Quickstart

Life files

Real life

Quickstart

Being Christian

Maps

quickstart

Big ideas

Quickstart

Helplines

Help! God seems to talk to everyone else but me p.589

Help! How do I know it's God and not my emotions? p.300

Help! How do I stop my friends doing wrong? p.1312

Help! I can't be bothered with homework p.719

Help! I can't cope with revision p.1011

Help! I can't make friends p.714

Help! I can't stand my brothers or sisters p.349

Help! I can't stop feeling guilty p.993

Help! I can't stop masturbating p.1339

Help! I don't know what to do in my gap year p.692

Help! I don't want to go to college p.591

Help! I feel like I've failed p.837

Help! I feel stuck p.762

Help! I hate myself! p.1332

Help! I haven't been called p.1352

Help! I haven't got a boyfriend or girlfriend p.722

Help! I know I have been saved, but somehow I don't feel that way p.742

Help! I want to go out with a non-Christian p.280

Help! I want to leave home p.395

Help! I want to pay someone back p.1127

Help! I'm being bullied p.603

Help! I'm bored with my church p.715

Help! I'm confused about my sexuality p.1280

Help! I'm in trouble with the police p.378

Help! I'm praying but God isn't doing anything p.619

Help! I'm scared p.662

Help! I'm struggling with lust p.954

Help! I'm the only Christian in my home p.1090

Help! I've got doubts about my faith p.1201

Help! I've messed up really badly p.347

Help! It wasn't my fault! p.652

Help! My best friends don't want to know me any more p.616

Help! My Dad's never around p.187

Help! My friends slag off other people p.694

Help! My parents are letting me down p.598

Help! My parents oppose my faith p.1143

Help! My parents have favourites p.42

Help! My parents won't give me any freedom p.683

Help! Other people are better Christians than me p.1350

Help! People are saying horrible things about me p.822

Help! Someone I care about has die p.223

Help! They're really annoying me p.1381

Help! Why should I bother with marriage? p.1320

Quickstart

Holy History

'Viewpoints' are taken from www.eattheword.net – daily Bible bites for young people by young people.

Each day you can grab a bite-sized chunk about the Bible, cooked up by writers just like you. You can view the articles on the website, or sign up to receive a daily bite in your inbox.

www.eattheword.net is brought to you by underground (the youth division of Open Doors) and WYnet (the Wycliffe youth network).

Quickstart

Viewpoints

The Old Testament

Big ideas

The Old Testament

The title comes from two words: 'Testament', meaning 'agreement' or 'promise', and 'Old' meaning... er... 'old'. So we call this part of the Bible the 'Old Testament' not because of the age of the writings (although most of them are very old indeed) but because it's about the 'old' promise; the promise that God made with Israel before Jesus came along. If we were to translate the word into today's language, the two parts of the Bible should really be called 'The Old Promise' and 'The New Promise'.

The Old Testament contains a huge mixture of different kinds of writing. There are adventure stories and love poems, there are hymns of praise and howls of despair. Much of the Old Testament is uplifting and inspiring; but some bits are weird and even disgusting. The Old Testament appears, at times, to be, well, not very *Christian*. There are several very good reasons for this.

It wasn't written by Christians, and the people in it weren't Christian.

You can't expect the people in the Old Testament to behave like Christians – they lived thousands of years before Jesus arrived. They were great people of faith and there is a lot that we can learn from their experiences and their lives. They too were exploring, finding things out as they went along. But they weren't Christians. They didn't have the whole picture.

It's about real people

One of the reasons why the people in the Old Testament behave so badly is that they are real. And real people sometimes do stupid, dumb, dangerous and evil things. Sometimes they just make mistakes, sometimes they do them deliberately; but this stuff happens. (In fact, pick up your paper, and you'll find some pretty Old Testament type of behaviour in there today. So maybe they're not so different to us.)

It's set in a very different culture

The Old Testament spans a wide range of cultures and took around 1,500 years to put together. Abraham, for example, lived around 4,000 years ago. Things were very different then. The culture of the time had very different values and ways of behaving.

So when we read the Old Testament we will find stuff that is hard to understand. But the good news is that we'll find loads of stuff that is just brilliant. Ideas of love, justice, mercy, compassion, faith, trust – and many other important themes are found throughout the Old Testament. There may be some things that we find confusing, but there is loads of stuff that we will find inspiring, moving and encouraging.

Most importantly, the Old Testament tells the story of God's relationship with human beings. It's the story of how humans were created by God, how they rebelled against him and how he saved them. You can't understand what happened in the New Testament unless you get a grip on what happened in the Old Testament.

👟 Footsteps

Two weeks on the Old Testament

The story of creation: Genesis 1.1–31
The origin of sin: Genesis 2.1–24
The promise of God: Genesis 17.1–27
Moses meets with God: Exodus 3 .1–22
Escape from Egypt: Exodus 12.31–41
The Ten Commandments:
Exodus 19.1–20.21
Entering the Promised Land: Joshua 1.1–16
The people ask for a king: 1 Samuel 8.1–22
Samuel anoints David: 1 Samuel 16.1–13
The Lord's promise to David:
2 Samuel 7.1–29
Elijah and the prophets: 1 Kings 18.1–46
A cry for justice: Amos 5.10–15
The coming king: Isaiah 11.1–9
A new agreement: Jeremiah 31.31–40

Genesis

The basics

What's the point? To explain where we all came from and why we are all here.

What happens? God makes everything. Humans rebel against God. Things get so bad, God sends a flood to kill everyone except Noah and his family. After the flood, people spread out again. God tells Abram that his descendants will be a special nation. The line continues through Jacob and his twelve sons. At the end of the book, the clan are living in Egypt where one of Jacob's sons had become governor.

What should I remember? 1.1 'In the beginning God created the heavens and the earth.'

More detail

Setting the scene We're at the very beginning. Nothing exists. Just blackness. Then God starts to speak...

What's it all about? Genesis is about origins. It tells the readers where we came from and why we are here. In the opening chapters of Genesis there are all the themes that will fill the rest of the Bible – creation, sin and rebellion; love, grace and mercy.

It's about people Genesis is structured around the lives of several key figures. These are important people, people who will be referred to again and again in the Bible and whose relationship with God sets the pattern for much of the action that is to follow.

They include Adam and Eve, Noah, Abraham, Jacob and Joseph. These are known as the patriarchs, which means 'the fathers'. They are the fathers of the Israelite nation, but they are also our spiritual, and in the case of Adam and Eve, physical, ancestors. Their stories tell us much about the relationship between God and man.

Because that's the thing about Genesis – it's all about the relationship between the being who created the world and the people he made. In Genesis, God – the creator of the universe – is a personal God. He speaks with people, makes promises to them, even argues with them. He punishes them and protects them. This is not some impersonal 'life-force', this is a 'someone', a being who wants to communicate with the world he has created.

Most importantly, he makes promises to his people. He promises Noah that he will never again wipe out the human race – and he gives Noah the rainbow as a sign. He promises Abraham that, even though he is old and childless, he will be the father of a mighty nation. These promises – or covenants as they are often known – underpin God's relationship with his people throughout the rest of the Bible. God has promised to be with them and he will keep his promises.

Footsteps

Creation: 1.1–2.4
Adam & Eve: 2.7–25
First sin: 3.1–24
Noah is called: 6.5–7.24
After the flood: 8.1–9.17
Abram: Genesis 12.1–7; 13.2–18
The promise: 15.7–21
a.k.a. Abraham: 17.1–27
Abraham's faith: 22.1–19
Esau and Jacob: 25.19–34; 27.1–45
Jacob becomes Israel: 32.1–31
Joseph: 37.1–36; 39.1–21
Joseph becomes governor: 41.1–42.5
Family reunion: 45.1–13; 47.1–12; 50.22–26

And another thing

Genesis is a real book of firsts. Not only does it contain the first human beings, it also contains the first farmer, the first musician and the first metalworker (Genesis 4.20–22). Not to mention Noah, who was the first person to plant a vineyard (Genesis 9.20). Cheers!

The story of creation

CHAPTER 1

¹ In the beginning God
created the heavens
and the earth.*
² The earth was barren,
with no form of life;◆
it was under a roaring ocean
covered with darkness.
But the Spirit of God◆
was moving over the water.

The first day

³ God said, "I command light to shine!" And light started shining. ⁴ God looked at the light and saw that it was good. He separated light from darkness ⁵ and named the light "Day" and the darkness "Night". Evening came and then morning — that was the first day.*

The second day

⁶ God said, "I command a dome to separate the water above it from the water below it." ⁷ And that's what happened. God made the dome ⁸ and named it "Sky". Evening came and then morning — that was the second day.

The third day

⁹ God said, "I command the water under the sky to come together in one place, so there will be dry ground." And that's what happened. ¹⁰ God named the dry ground "Land", and he named the water "Sea". God looked at what he had done and saw that it was good. ¹¹ God said, "I command the earth to produce all kinds of plants, including fruit trees and grain." And that's what happened.

1.1 the heavens and the earth: "The heavens and the earth" stood for the universe.

1.5 the first day: A day was measured from evening to evening.

See also: 1.3: 2 Cor 4.6. 1.6–8: 2 Pet 3.5.

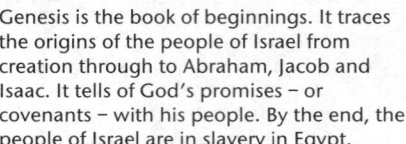

Big ideas

The Books of the Law

Genesis is the book of beginnings. It traces the origins of the people of Israel from creation through to Abraham, Jacob and Isaac. It tells of God's promises – or covenants – with his people. By the end, the people of Israel are in slavery in Egypt.

Exodus tells of the Israelites' escape from Egypt and ends with Moses receiving the Ten Commandments and the instructions for building the tabernacle.

Leviticus is mainly about the laws that Israel was to follow to show they were true followers of God. Many people find it a difficult book, but there are gems such as the amazing Jubilee legislation.

Numbers is so called because it's full of numbers. Amazing. But, along with a record of how many Israelites left Egypt, it tells how Israel rebelled against God and ended up spending forty years in the wilderness.

Deuteronomy is a kind of summary of the other books. It's Moses' farewell speech, given just before his death and before the Israelites' entry to the promised land.

 Anorak corner

The posh name for the first five books of the Bible is the Pentateuch, from the Greek word *pentateuchos*, meaning 'five-volumed book'.

 Footsteps

Two Weeks in the Pentateuch

Creation: Genesis 1.1–2.4
First sin: Genesis 3.1–24
The promise to Abraham: Genesis 15.7–21
The slavery of Israel: Exodus 1.1–14
The burning bush: Exodus 3.1–21
Passover and escape: Exodus 12.1–42
Ten Commandments: Exodus 19.16–20.17
Key commandment: Deuteronomy 6.1–25
The Sacred Tent and Chest: Exodus 25.1–22
The Jubilee: Leviticus 25.1–55
The twelve spies: Numbers 13.1–33
Punishment: Numbers 14.1–45
Journey to Canaan: Numbers 33.1–56
Against false gods:
Deuteronomy 12.29–13.18

Big ideas

Creation

Genesis starts with God creating the whole universe (1.1). Then, over a period of six days, God creates and populates the earth.

The first four days prepare the place – the universe, the land, the seas, the energy source. The last two days populate that place, with animals, birds, fish and, of course, humans.

Genesis is not a science manual. It's not a book that describes how God did what he did. It's a book that is about why he did it. Genesis is about cause rather than process. It's about who made the universe, not how he did it.

So whether you believe that God made the whole thing in six 24-hour days, or whether you believe that 'day' here means 'a period of time', the key message is that we did not come about by accident. Whatever scientific process brought about the existence of man and the universe – and whatever processes still keep the thing going – Genesis says that God's hand was behind the whole thing.

And remember, even the literal interpretation of the book of Genesis is not opposed by scientific facts, but by scientific theories. Nobody really knows how the universe was created; scientists have a number of theories to explain it. The big bang is a theory. Nobody was there with a video camera to record it. Some of these theories make a lot of sense, but they are still theories, nevertheless.

Genesis says that God made everything. It does not explain how he did it. It just says that he did.

More...

Environment p.6
Genetic engineering p.577
New heaven & new earth p.1427
God – he takes your breath away p.567

[12] The earth produced all kinds of vegetation. God looked at what he had done, and it was good. [13] Evening came and then morning — that was the third day.

The fourth day

[14] God said, "I command lights to appear in the sky and to separate day from night and to show the time for seasons, special days, and years. [15] I command them to shine on the earth." And that's what happened. [16] God made two powerful lights, the brighter one to rule the day and the other* to rule the night. He also made the stars. [17] Then God put these lights in the sky to shine on the earth, [18] to rule day and night, and to separate light from darkness. God looked at what he had done, and it was good. [19] Evening came and then morning — that was the fourth day.

The fifth day

[20] God said, "I command the sea to be full of living creatures, and I command birds to fly above the earth." [21] So God made the giant sea monsters and all the living creatures that swim in the sea. He also made every kind of bird. God looked at what he had done, and it was good. [22] Then he gave the living creatures his blessing — he told the sea creatures to live everywhere in the sea and the birds to live everywhere on earth. [23] Evening came and then morning — that was the fifth day.

The sixth day

[24] God said, "I command the earth to give life to all kinds of tame animals, wild animals, and reptiles." And that's what happened. [25] God made every one of them. Then he looked at what he had done, and it was good.

[26] God said, "Now we will make humans, and they will be like us. We will let them rule the fish, the birds, and all other living creatures."

[27] So God created humans to be like himself; he made men and women. [28] God gave them his blessing and said:

Have a lot of children! Fill the earth with people and bring it under your control.

---

*1.16 the brighter . . . the other: The sun and the moon. But they are not called by their names, because in Old Testament times some people worshipped the sun and the moon as though they were gods.

See also: **1.26:** 1 Cor 11.7. **1.27,28:** Gen 5.1-2.
1.27: Matt 19.4; Mark 10.6.

Real life

Art

Contributed by Throwstar

In early 2000, the National Gallery in London ran an exhibition called 'Seeing Salvation. The Image of Christ'. Neil MacGregor, then director of the National Gallery, was quoted as saying 'our visual tradition has been, overwhelmingly, determined by Christianity.' However, the entire 'Seeing Salvation' exhibition only included ONE positive painting of Jesus done since the turn of the century – Stanley Spencer's 'Resurrection at Cookham' (1921–3).

In Christian circles these days, creativity is often only nurtured and valued if it has a clear and functional use. It's brilliant to be a musician if you help lead the choruses on Sunday mornings. It's wonderful to be a fine artist if you paint something pretty (usually with sheep and rainbows) for the church hall. And you'll definitely be in the good books if you direct the children's Christmas play.

But what if you write a song about something beautiful that has moved you? What if you paint something that isn't pretty, but communicates how you feel? What if you want to make a short film that challenges people to think? Can God still be honoured by your creativity?

The answer to this question is YES! You need only read the first chapter of Genesis to see how amazingly creative God is. He created all of nature and didn't just make it functional – he made it beautiful. God focused on details like the range of the human voice and outrageous fish swimming in the deepest parts of the ocean where most humans will never even see them. God delights in his own creation.

And the exciting thing is that Genesis 1.27 says 'God created man in his own image.' This means that not only are we a part of his exquisite handiwork – a living piece of art based on the Great Artist himself – but this instinct for creativity is placed within each of us. God is lavish and innovative in his own creation, and we can be as well! In fact, the very act of creating can be worship to God.

Think

What creative arts do you like doing? How can you worship God through them?
Does your church or youth group provide opportunities for art and creativity as a part of teaching or worship? If not, why not?
What would you really like to say to God? How could you communicate this through an artistic pursuit that you enjoy?

Act

Write a poem or short story
Paint or sculpt something unusual
Make up a song about something that happened today
Audition for a play
Take photos for no reason at all
Design a pair of trainers
Or even bake a cake
...and then thank God for making you in his image and giving you this divinely inspired ability to create!

Check

Exodus 25 & 26 – God had an opulent design for the Tabernacle – he demanded excellence and beauty in his house, and certainly put the artists to work.
Psalm 40.3 – God even made David, a musician and poet, king!
Revelation 15.2–3 – Art doesn't stop in heaven!

More...

Creation p.3
Media p.1235
Movies p.1297
Finding God every day p.660
Prayer p.1002

Rule over the fish in the sea, the birds in the sky, and every animal on the earth.

²⁹ I have provided all kinds of fruit and grain for you to eat. ³⁰ And I have given the green plants as food for everything else that breathes. These will be food for animals, both wild and tame, and for birds.

³¹ God looked at what he had done. All of it was very good! Evening came and then morning — that was the sixth day.

CHAPTER 2

¹ So the heavens and the earth and everything else were created.

The seventh day

² By the seventh day God had finished his work, and so he rested. ³ God blessed the seventh day and made it special because on that day he rested from his work.

⁴ That's how God created the heavens and the earth.

The Garden of Eden

When the LORD God made the heavens and the earth, ⁵ no grass or plants were growing anywhere. God had not yet sent any rain, and there was no one to work the land. ⁶ But streams⁺ came up from the ground and watered the earth.

⁷ The LORD God took a handful of soil and made a man.* God breathed life into the man, and the man started breathing. ⁸ The LORD made a garden in a place called Eden, which was in the east, and he put the man there.

⁹ The LORD God placed all kinds of beautiful trees and fruit trees in the garden. Two other trees were in the middle of the garden. One of the trees gave life — the other gave the power to know the difference between right and wrong.

¹⁰ From Eden a river flowed out to water the garden, then it divided into four rivers. ¹¹ The first one is the River Pishon that flows through the land of Havilah, ¹² where pure gold, rare perfumes, and precious stones are found. ¹³ The second is the River Gihon that winds through Ethiopia.* ¹⁴ The River Tigris

*2.7 man: In Hebrew "man" comes from the same word as "soil".
*2.13 Ethiopia: The Hebrew text has "Cush", which was a region south of Egypt that included parts of the present countries of Ethiopia and Sudan.
See also: 2.2,3: Exod 20.11.   2.2: Heb 4.4,10.
2.7: 1 Cor 15.45.   2.9: Rev 2.7; 22.2,14.

Life files

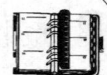

Adam and Eve

Name: Adam
Background: Created by God. The original.

What's the story?

Adam was told to look after the garden. With just one rule: not to eat from one specific tree. It was a question of obedience. The fruit gave the knowledge of good and evil. Leaving it says, 'I'll obey God.' Eating it says 'I'm going to make my own decisions.'

In the end he ate the apple, and the world changed. Adam and Eve's disobedience got them expelled from the garden.

Work will now be hard (Genesis 3.17–19). He will not live forever. The man made from soil will return there. More than that, Adam and Eve's action brought sin into the world. Creation was never the same.

What's the point?

Adam had it all. But he chose to follow his own desires, and that meant leaving the garden and infecting the whole of creation.

Name: Eve
Background: The second human. Her name sounds like the Hebrew word for living.

What's the story?

Eve was created to be Adam's partner. She gave into temptation, disobeyed God, persuaded Adam to do the same and, like him, was banished from the garden.

What's the point?

Eve gave into sin. Her actions and her husband's brought sin into the world.

 **Footsteps**

Five days with Adam and Eve
Happy birthday: Genesis 2.7–22
Disobedience: Genesis 3.1–8
Excuses, excuses: Genesis 3.9–24
Adam's children: Genesis 4.1–19; 5.1–5
Adam and Christ: Romans 5.12–21

More...
Sin p.1261

Real life

Environment

This world is in a bad shape. Humans are always better at taking than giving; we're always greedy for more, more, more. We've hunted species to extinction just to make some quack remedy. Rainforests have been decimated so that we can have nice garden furniture. We've filled the air with exhaust fumes to save a ten minute walk. We've driven a hole through the ozone layer, just so our armpits can smell nice.

It's not what we're supposed to do. Adam was put in the garden to 'take care of it and look after it' (Genesis 2.15). The Bible makes it clear that this is God's world, not man's. He's the owner; we're the caretakers.

So humans are not supposed to exhaust the earth. The jubilee legislation said that the earth should have every seventh year off to recover. We're supposed to protect the rights of the poor – which means not ruining the land where they live just to make a profit. And above all it means remembering that we don't own this earth; we're just leasing it from the owner.

And one day he's going to come back...

Think

What does it mean to be a caretaker of the world?
In what ways can we give something back to the earth?
Can individuals really make a difference?

Act

Make sure that you use environmentally-friendly products
Cut down on your consumption. One way to help the earth is to use less.
Buy fairly traded goods.
Give money to an environmental agency.
Just go for a walk. Isn't the world fantastic?

Check

Deuteronomy 10.14; Psalms 19.1–6; 104.1–35; Jeremiah 10.11–13

More...

Creation p.3
Materialism p.1141

that flows east of Assyria is the third, and the fourth is the River Euphrates.

¹⁵ The LORD God put the man in the Garden of Eden to take care of it and to look after it. ¹⁶ But the LORD told him, "You may eat fruit from any tree in the garden, ¹⁷ except the one that has the power to let you know the difference between right and wrong. If you eat any fruit from that tree, you will die before the day is over!"

¹⁸ The LORD God said, "It isn't good for the man to live alone. I need to make a suitable partner for him." ¹⁹⁻²⁰ So the LORD took some soil and made animals and birds. He brought them to the man to see what names he would give each of them. Then the man named the tame animals and the birds and the wild animals. That's how they got their names.

None of these was the right kind of partner for the man. ²¹ So the LORD God made him fall into a deep sleep, and he took out one of the man's ribs. Then after closing the man's side, ²² the LORD made a woman out of the rib.

The LORD God brought her to the man, ²³ and the man exclaimed,

> "Here is someone like me!
> She is part of my body,
>   my own flesh and bones.
> She came from me, a man.
>   So I will name her Woman!"*

²⁴ That's why a man will leave his own father and mother. He marries a woman, and the two of them become like one person.

²⁵ Although the man and his wife were both naked, they were not ashamed.

The first sin and the first murder

CHAPTER 3

The first sin

¹ The snake was more cunning than any of the other wild animals that the LORD God had made. One day it came to the woman and asked, "Did God tell you not to eat fruit from any tree in the garden?"

² The woman answered, "God said we could eat fruit from any tree in the garden,

---

*2.23 a man . . . Woman: In Hebrew the words "man" and "woman" are similar.

See also: 2.24: Matt 19.5; Mark 10.7–8; 1 Cor 6.16; Eph 5.31. 3.1: Rev 12.9; 20.2.

³ except the one in the middle. He told us not to eat fruit from that tree or even to touch it. If we do, we will die."

⁴ "No, you won't!" the snake replied. ⁵ "God understands what will happen on the day you eat fruit from that tree. You will see what you have done, and you will know the difference between right and wrong, just as God does."

⁶ The woman stared at the fruit. It looked beautiful and tasty. She wanted the wisdom that it would give her, and she ate some of the fruit. Her husband was there with her, so she gave some to him, and he ate it too. ⁷ Straight away they saw what they had done, and they realized they were naked. Then they sewed fig leaves together to make something to cover themselves.

⁸ Late in the afternoon a breeze began to blow, and the man and woman heard the LORD God walking in the garden. They were frightened and hid behind some trees.

The trouble with sin

⁹ The LORD called out to the man and asked, "Where are you?"

¹⁰ The man answered, "I was naked, and when I heard you walking through the garden, I was frightened and hid!"

¹¹ "How did you know you were naked?" God asked. "Did you eat any fruit from that tree in the middle of the garden?"

¹² "It was the woman you put here with me," the man said. "She gave me some of the fruit, and I ate it."

¹³ The LORD God then asked the woman, "What have you done?"

"The snake tricked me," she answered. "And I ate some of that fruit."

¹⁴ So the LORD God said to the snake:

"Because of what you have done,
   you will be the only animal
      to suffer this curse —
for as long as you live,
   you will crawl on your stomach
      and eat dust.
¹⁵ You and this woman
   will hate each other;
your descendants and hers
   will always be enemies.
One of hers will strike you
   on the head,
and you will strike him
   on the heel."

¹⁶ Then the LORD said to the woman:

"You will suffer terribly
   when you give birth.
But you will still desire
   your husband,
   and he will rule over you."

¹⁷ The LORD said to the man:

"You listened to your wife
   and ate fruit from that tree.
And so, the ground
   will be under a curse
   because of what you did.
As long as you live,
   you will have to struggle
   to grow enough food.
¹⁸ Your food will be plants,
   but the ground will produce
      thorns and thistles.
¹⁹ You will have to sweat
   to earn a living;
you were made out of soil,
   and you will once again
      turn into soil."

²⁰ The man Adam* named his wife Eve* because she would become the mother of all who live.

²¹ Then the LORD God made clothes out of animal skins for the man and his wife.

²² The LORD said, "These people now know the difference between right and wrong, just as we do. But they must not be allowed to eat fruit from the tree that lets them live for ever." ²³ So the LORD God sent them out of the Garden of Eden, where they would have to work the ground from which the man had been made. ²⁴ Then God put winged creatures at the entrance to the garden and a flaming, flashing sword to guard the way to the life-giving tree.

CHAPTER 4

Cain murders Abel

¹ Adam* and Eve had a son. Then Eve said, "I'll name him Cain because I got* him with the help of the LORD." ² Later she had another son and named him Abel.

---

*3.20 The man Adam: In Hebrew "man" and "Adam" are the same.
*3.20 Eve: In Hebrew "Eve" sounds like "living".
*4.1 Adam: See the note at 3.20.
*4.1 Cain . . . got: In Hebrew "Cain" sounds like "got".

See also: 3.13: 2 Cor 11.3; 1 Tim 2.14.   3.15: Rev 12.17.   See also: 3.17–18: Heb 6.8.   3.22: Rev 22.14.

Abel became a sheep farmer, but Cain farmed the land. ³ One day, Cain gave part of his harvest to the LORD, ⁴ and Abel also gave an offering to the LORD. He killed the firstborn lamb from one of his sheep and gave the LORD the best parts of it. The LORD was pleased with Abel and his offering, ⁵ but not with Cain and his offering. This made Cain so angry that he could not hide his feelings.

⁶ The LORD said to Cain:

What's wrong with you? Why do you have such an angry look on your face? ⁷ If you had done the right thing, you would be smiling.' But you did the wrong thing, and now sin is waiting to attack you like a lion. Sin wants to destroy you, but don't let it!

⁸ Cain said to his brother Abel, "Let's go for a walk."' And when they were out in a field, Cain killed him.

⁹ Afterwards the LORD asked Cain, "Where is Abel?"

"How should I know?" he answered. "Am I supposed to look after my brother?"

¹⁰ Then the LORD said:

Why have you done this terrible thing? You killed your own brother, and his blood flowed on to the ground. Now his blood is calling out for me to punish you. ¹¹ And so, I'll put you under a curse. Because you killed Abel and made his blood run out on the ground, you will never be able to farm the land again. ¹² If you try to farm the land, it won't produce anything for you. From now on, you'll be without a home, and you'll spend the rest of your life wandering from place to place.

¹³ "This punishment is too hard!" Cain said. ¹⁴ "You're making me leave my home and live far from you.* I will have to wander about without a home, and anyone could kill me."

¹⁵ "No!"' the LORD answered. "Anyone who kills you will be punished seven times worse than I am punishing you." So the LORD put a mark on Cain to warn everyone not to kill him. ¹⁶ But Cain had to go far from the LORD and live in the Land of Wandering,' which is east of Eden.

Descendants of Adam before the flood

More and more people

¹⁷ Later, Cain and his wife had a son named Enoch. At the time Cain was building a town, and so he named it Enoch after his son.
¹⁸ Then Enoch had a son named Irad, who had a son named Mehujael, who had a son named Methushael, who had a son named Lamech.
¹⁹ Lamech married Adah, then Zillah.
²⁰⁻²¹ Lamech and Adah had two sons, Jabal and Jubal. Their son Jabal was the first to live in tents and raise sheep and goats. Jubal was the first to play harps and flutes.
²² Lamech and Zillah had a son named Tubal Cain who made tools out of bronze and iron. They also had a daughter, whose name was Naamah.
²³ One day, Lamech said to his two wives, "A young man wounded me, and I killed him. ²⁴ Anyone who tries to get even with me will be punished ten times more than anyone who tries to get even with Cain."
²⁵ Adam and his wife had another son. They named him Seth, because they said, "God has given* us a son to take the place of Abel, who was killed by his brother Cain." ²⁶ Later, Seth had a son and named him Enosh.

About this time people started worshipping the LORD.'

CHAPTER 5

Descendants of Adam

¹⁻² God created men and women to be like himself. He gave them his blessing and called them human beings. This is a list of the descendants of Adam, the first man:
³⁻⁴ When Adam was one hundred and thirty, he had a son who was just like him, and he named him Seth. Adam had more children ⁵ and died at the age of nine hundred and thirty.
⁶ When Seth was one hundred and five, he had a son named Enosh. ⁷ Seth had more children ⁸ and died at the age of nine hundred and twelve.
⁹ When Enosh was ninety, he had a son named Kenan. ¹⁰ Enosh had more children ¹¹ and died at the age of nine hundred and five.

---

*4.14 live . . . you: At this time it was believed that the LORD was with his people only in their own land.
See also: 4.4: Heb 11.4.   4.8: Matt 23.35; Luke 11.51; 1 John 3.12.   4.10: Heb 12.24.

*4.25 Seth . . . given: In Hebrew "Seth" sounds like "given".
See also: 5.1–2: Gen 1.27–28.   5.2: Matt 19.4; Mark 10.6.

¹² When Kenan was seventy, he had a son named Mahalalel. ¹³ Kenan had more children ¹⁴ and died at the age of nine hundred and ten.

¹⁵ When Mahalalel was sixty-five, he had a son named Jared. ¹⁶ Mahalalel had more children ¹⁷ and died at the age of eight hundred and ninety-five.

¹⁸ When Jared was one hundred and sixty-two, he had a son named Enoch. ¹⁹ Jared had more children ²⁰ and died at the age of nine hundred and sixty-two.

²¹ When Enoch was sixty-five, he had a son named Methuselah, ²² and during the next three hundred years he had more children. Enoch truly loved God, ²³⁻²⁴ and God took him away at the age of three hundred and sixty-five.

²⁵ When Methuselah was one hundred and eighty-seven, he had a son named Lamech. ²⁶ Methuselah had more children ²⁷ and died at the age of nine hundred and sixty-nine.

²⁸ When Lamech was one hundred and eighty-two, he had a son. ²⁹ Lamech said, "I'll name him Noah because he will give us comfort,* as we struggle hard to make a living on this land that the LORD has put under a curse." ³⁰ Lamech had more children ³¹ and died at the age of seven hundred and seventy-seven.

³² After Noah was five hundred years old, he had three sons and named them Shem, Ham, and Japheth.

Noah and the flood

CHAPTER 6

The LORD will send a flood

¹⁻² More and more people were born, until finally they spread all over the earth. Some of their daughters were so beautiful that supernatural beings⟩ came down and married the ones they wanted. ³ Then the LORD said, "I won't let my life-giving breath remain in anyone for ever.⟩ No one will live for more than one hundred and twenty years."⟩

⁴ The children of the supernatural beings who had married these women became famous heroes and warriors. They were called Nephilim and lived on the earth at that time and even later.

---

*5.29 Noah . . . comfort: In Hebrew "Noah" sounds like "comfort".
See also: 5.24: Heb 11.5; Jude 14.   6.1–4: Job 1.6; 2.1.
6.4: Num 13.33.

Life files

Noah

Background: Son of Lamech. Wife and three boys.

What's the story?

Noah was a righteous person (Genesis 6.9). Despite the culture around him, despite the way that the world was going, Noah trusted God and did what he wanted.

And what God wanted was for him to build a boat. Well, I say boat. The word usually used is 'ark' and that means box. After all, Noah didn't need to steer the thing; God would do that. He didn't need any power, because all it needed to do was float. All it needed to be was a huge, waterproof box full of animals.

 Anorak corner

Noah was not only a pretty good sailor, he also invented wine. Not that it did him much good (Genesis 9.20–27).

What's the point?

Noah's faith is what matters. He went against the world in doing what he did. He refused to give up on God.

 Footsteps

Five days with Noah

Noah's birth: Genesis 5.28–32
A flood is coming: Genesis 6.1–22
Forty days at sea: Genesis 7.1–24
Back on dry land: Genesis 8.1–19
'Never again – I promise':
Genesis 8.20—9.17

More...

Covenant p.17
Alcohol p.700
Going against the crowd p.1045
Is God calling you to be a rebel? p.1342

⁵ The LORD saw how bad the people on earth were and that everything they thought and planned was evil. ⁶ He was very sorry that he had made them, ⁷ and he said, "I'll destroy every living creature on earth! I'll wipe out people, animals, birds, and reptiles. I'm sorry I ever made them."

⁸ But the LORD was pleased with Noah, ⁹ and this is the story about him. Noah was the only person who lived right and obeyed God. ¹⁰ He had three sons: Shem, Ham, and Japheth.

¹¹⁻¹² God knew that everyone was terribly cruel and violent. ¹³ So he told Noah:

Cruelty and violence have spread everywhere. Now I'm going to destroy the whole earth and all its people. ¹⁴ Get some good timber and build a boat. Put rooms in it and cover it with tar inside and out. ¹⁵ Make it one hundred and thirty-three metres long, twenty-two metres wide, and thirteen metres high. ¹⁶ Build a roof' on the boat and leave a space of about forty-four centimetres between the roof and the sides.' Make the boat three storeys high and put a door on one side.

¹⁷ I'm going to send a flood that will destroy everything on earth! Nothing will be left alive. ¹⁸ But I solemnly promise that you, your wife, your sons, and your daughters-in-law will be kept safe in the boat.'

¹⁹⁻²⁰ Bring into the boat with you a male and a female of every kind of animal and bird, as well as a male and a female of every reptile. I don't want them to be destroyed. ²¹ Store up enough food both for yourself and for them.

²² Noah did everything the LORD told him to do.

CHAPTER 7

The flood

¹ The LORD told Noah:

Take your whole family with you into the boat, because you are the only one on this earth who pleases me. ² Take seven pairs of every kind of animal that can be used for sacrifice* and one pair of all others. ³ Also

take seven pairs of every kind of bird with you. Do this so there will always be animals and birds on the earth. ⁴ Seven days from now I will send rain that will last for forty days and nights, and I will destroy all other living creatures I have made.

⁵⁻⁷ Noah was six hundred years old when he went into the boat to escape the flood, and he did everything the LORD had told him to do. His wife, his sons, and his daughters-in-law all went inside with him. ⁸⁻⁹ He obeyed God and took a male and a female of each kind of animal and bird into the boat with him. ¹⁰ Seven days later a flood began to cover the earth.

¹¹⁻¹² Noah was six hundred years old when the water under the earth started gushing out everywhere. The sky opened like windows, and rain poured down for forty days and nights. All this began on the seventeenth day of the second month of the year. ¹³ On that day Noah and his wife went into the boat with their three sons, Shem, Ham, and Japheth, and their wives. ¹⁴ They took along every kind of animal, tame and wild, including the birds. ¹⁵ Noah took a male and a female of every living creature with him, ¹⁶ just as God had told him to do. And when they were all in the boat, God closed the door.

¹⁷⁻¹⁸ For forty days the rain poured down without stopping. And the water became deeper and deeper, until the boat started floating high above the ground. ¹⁹⁻²⁰ Finally, the mighty flood was so deep that even the highest mountain peaks were about seven metres below the surface of the water. ²¹ Not a bird, animal, reptile, or human was left alive anywhere on earth. ²²⁻²³ The LORD destroyed everything that breathed. Nothing was left alive except Noah and the others in the boat. ²⁴ A hundred and fifty days later, the water started going down.

CHAPTER 8

The water goes down

¹ God did not forget about Noah and the animals with him in the boat. So God made a wind blow, and the water started going down. ² God stopped up the places where the water had been gushing out from under the earth. He also closed up the sky, and the rain stopped. ³ For one hundred and fifty days the water slowly went down. ⁴ Then on the seventeenth day of the seventh month of the

---

*7.2 animal . . . for sacrifice: Hebrew "clean animals". Animals that could be used for sacrifice were called "clean", and animals that could not be used were called "unclean".

See also: 6.5–8: Matt 24.37; Luke 17.26; 1 Pet 3.20.
6.9: 2 Pet 2.5.   **6.22:** Heb 11.7.

See also: 7.7: Matt 24.38–39; Luke 17.27.   7.11: 2 Pet 3.6.

year, the boat came to rest somewhere in the Ararat mountains. 5 The water kept going down, and the mountain tops could be seen on the first day of the tenth month.

6-7 Forty days later Noah opened a window to send out a raven, but it kept flying around until the water had dried up. 8 Noah wanted to find out if the water had gone down, and he sent out a dove. 9 Deep water was still everywhere, and the dove could not find a place to land. So it flew back to the boat. Noah held out his hand and helped it back in.

10 Seven days later Noah sent the dove out again. 11 It returned in the evening, holding in its beak a green leaf from an olive tree. Noah knew that the water was finally going down. 12 He waited seven more days before sending the dove out again, and this time it did not return.

13 Noah was now six hundred and one years old. And by the first day of that year, almost all the water had gone away. Noah made an opening in the roof of the boat* and saw that the ground was getting dry. 14 By the twenty-seventh day of the second month, the earth was completely dry.

15 God said to Noah, 16 "You, your wife, your sons, and your daughters-in-law may now leave the boat. 17 Let out the birds, animals, and reptiles, so they can mate and live all over the earth." 18 After Noah and his family had gone out of the boat, 19 the living creatures left in groups of their own kind.

The LORD's promise for the earth

20 Noah built an altar where he could offer sacrifices to the LORD. Then he offered on the altar one of each kind of animal and bird that could be used for a sacrifice.* 21 The smell of the burning offering pleased God, and he said:

> Never again will I punish the earth for the sinful things its people do. All of them have evil thoughts from the time they are young, but I will never destroy everything that breathes, as I did this time.

> 22 As long as the earth remains,
> there will be planting
> and harvest,
> cold and heat;
> winter and summer,
> day and night.

CHAPTER 9

God's promise to Noah

1 God said to Noah and his sons:

> I am giving you my blessing. Have a lot of children and grandchildren, so people will live everywhere on this earth. 2 All animals, birds, reptiles, and fish will be afraid of you. I have placed them under your control, 3 and I have given them to you for food. From now on, you may eat them, as well as the green plants that you have always eaten. 4 But life is in the blood, and you must not eat any meat that still has blood in it. 5-6 I created humans to be like me, and I will punish any animal or person that takes a human life. If an animal kills someone, that animal must die. And if a person takes the life of another, that person must be put to death.

> 7 I want you and your descendants to have many children, so people will live everywhere on earth.

8 Again, God said to Noah and his sons:

> 9 I am going to make a solemn promise to you and to everyone who will live after you. 10 This includes the birds and the animals that came out of the boat. 11 I promise every living creature that the earth and those living on it will never again be destroyed by a flood.

> 12-13 The rainbow that I have put in the sky will be my sign to you and to every living creature on earth. It will remind you that I will keep this promise for ever. 14 When I send clouds over the earth, and a rainbow appears in the sky, 15 I will remember my promise to you and to all other living creatures. Never again will I let flood waters destroy all life. 16 When I see the rainbow in the sky, I will always remember the promise that I have made to every living creature. 17 The rainbow will be the sign of that solemn promise.

Noah and his family

18 Noah and his sons, Shem, Ham, and Japheth, came out of the boat. Ham later had a son named Canaan. 19 All people on earth are descendants of Noah's three sons.

20 Noah farmed the land and was the first to plant a vineyard. 21 One day he got drunk and

---

*8.20 animal . . . sacrifice: See the note at 7.2.

See also: 9.1: Gen 1.28. 9.4: Lev 7.26–27; 17.10–14; 19.26; Deut 12.16,23; 15.23. 9.6: Exod 20.13; Gen 1.26. 9.7: Gen 1.28.

Viewpoints 👁

People look for God in many places – where's he to be found?

Contributed by Ben R

'The rainbow will be the sign of that solemn promise.'

In the world we live in it is sometimes hard to see God. Pick up any newspaper on any day of the week and you are likely to see stories of abuse, murder, war, drugs – the list goes on. In this world we need to keep focused on Christ, to remember the compassion and love he has shown us in the past and he is continuing to show us.

God tries to make this easy for us. Rainbows are just one example of things in which we can see God and remember him by. I once met a Kenyan man who was living in England for about a year as part of an exchange programme. He told me that he saw God in the rain; he saw God when the leaves fell off the trees; he saw God in the snow.

This man appreciated these things so much more as he had never seen them before – God was showing him completely new amazing things and they were touching his heart and making him realise just how wonderful our God is. Our trouble is that we see these things so often we take them for granted. Take a fresh look around you today. See all the wonderful things God has given us. God has given them to us as he wants us to enjoy them and to enjoy life – his creativity and his love are overflowing from heaven onto earth. Make the most of it.

More...

Covenant p.17
Creation p.3
Finding God every day p.660

was lying naked in his tent. ²² Ham entered the tent and saw him naked, then went back outside and told his brothers. ²³ Shem and Japheth put a robe over their shoulders and walked backwards into the tent. Without looking at their father, they placed it over his body.

²⁴ When Noah woke up and learnt what his youngest son Ham had done, ²⁵ he said,

"I now put a curse on Canaan!
He will be the lowest slave
    of his brothers.
²⁶ I ask the LORD my God
    to bless Shem
    and make Canaan his slave.
²⁷ I pray that the LORD
    will give Japheth
    more and more* land
    and let him take over
        the territory of Shem.
May Canaan be his slave."

²⁸ Noah lived three hundred and fifty years after the flood ²⁹ and died at the age of nine hundred and fifty.

The descendants of Noah and the tower of Babel

CHAPTER 10

The descendants of Noah

¹ After the flood Shem, Ham, and Japheth had many descendants.

The descendants of Japheth

²⁻⁵ Japheth's descendants had their own languages, tribes, and land. They were Gomer, Magog, Madai, Javan, Tubal, Meshech, and Tiras.

Gomer was the ancestor of Ashkenaz, Riphath, and Togarmah.

Javan was the ancestor of Elishah, Tarshish, Kittim, and Dodanim,› who settled along the coast.

The descendants of Ham

⁶⁻²⁰ Ham's descendants had their own languages, tribes, and land. They were Ethiopia,* Egypt, Put, and Canaan. Cush*

---

*9.27 more and more: In Hebrew "Japheth" sounds like "more and more".
*10.6–20 Ethiopia: See the note at 2.13.
*10.6–20 Cush: See the note at 2.13.

was the ancestor of Seba, Havilah, Sabtah, Raamah, and Sabteca.

Raamah was the ancestor of Sheba and Dedan.

Cush was also the ancestor of Nimrod, a mighty warrior whose strength came from the LORD. Nimrod is the reason for the saying, "You hunt like Nimrod with the strength of the LORD!" Nimrod first ruled in Babylon, Erech, and Accad, all of' which were in Babylonia.' From there Nimrod went to Assyria and built the great city of Nineveh. He also built Rehoboth-Ir and Calah, as well as Resen, which is between Nineveh and Calah.

Egypt was the ancestor of Ludim, Anamim, Lehabim, Naphtuhim, Pathrusim, Casluhim, and Caphtorim, the ancestor of the Philistines.'

Canaan's sons were Sidon and Heth. He was also the ancestor of the Jebusites, the Amorites, the Girgashites, the Hivites, the Arkites, the Sinites, the Arvadites, the Zemarites, and the Hamathites.

Later the Canaanites spread from the territory of Sidon and went as far as Gaza in the direction of Gerar. They also went as far as Lasha in the direction of Sodom, Gomorrah, Admah, and Zeboiim.

The descendants of Shem

21-31 Shem's descendants had their own languages, tribes, and land. He was the elder brother of Japheth and the ancestor of the tribes of Eber.

Shem was the ancestor of Elam, Asshur, Arpachshad, Lud, and Aram.

Aram was the ancestor of Uz, Hul, Gether, and Mash.

Arpachshad was the father of Shelah and the grandfather of Eber, whose first son was named Peleg,* because it was during his time that tribes divided up the earth. Eber's second son was Joktan.

Joktan was the ancestor of Almodad, Sheleph, Hazarmaveth, Jerah, Hadoram, Uzal, Diklah, Obal, Abimael, Sheba, Ophir, Havilah, and Jobab. Their land reached from Mesha in the direction of Sephar, the hill country in the east.

32 This completes the list of Noah's descendants. After the flood their descendants became nations and spread all over the world.

CHAPTER 11

The tower of Babel

1 At first everyone spoke the same language, 2 but after some of them moved from the east' and settled in Babylonia,' 3-4 they said:

Let's build a city with a tower that reaches to the sky! We'll use hard bricks and tar instead of stone and mortar. We'll become famous, and we won't be scattered all over the world.

5 But when the LORD came down to look at the city and the tower, 6 he said:

These people are working together because they all speak the same language. This is just the beginning. Soon they will be able to do anything they want. 7 Come on! Let's go down and confuse them by making them speak different languages — then they won't be able to understand each other.

8-9 So the people had to stop building the city, because the LORD confused their language and scattered them all over the earth. That's how the city of Babel* got its name.

The descendants of Shem

10-11 Two years after the flood, when Shem was one hundred, he had a son named Arpachshad. He had more children and died at the age of six hundred. This is a list of his descendants:

12 When Arpachshad was thirty-five, he had a son named Shelah. 13 Arpachshad had more children and died at the age of four hundred and thirty-eight.

14 When Shelah was thirty, he had a son named Eber. 15 Shelah had more children and died at the age of four hundred and thirty-three.

16 When Eber was thirty-four, he had a son named Peleg. 17 Eber had more children and died at the age of four hundred and sixty-four.

18 When Peleg was thirty, he had a son named Reu. 19 Peleg had more children and died at the age of two hundred and thirty-nine.

20 When Reu was thirty-two he had a son named Serug. 21 Reu had more children and died at the age of two hundred and thirty-nine.

---

*10.21-31 Peleg: In Hebrew "Peleg" means "divided".

*11.8-9 Babel: In Hebrew "Babel" sounds like "confused".

²² When Serug was thirty, he had a son named Nahor. ²³ Serug had more children and died at the age of two hundred and thirty.

²⁴ When Nahor was twenty-nine, he had a son named Terah. ²⁵ Nahor had more children and died at the age of one hundred and forty-eight.

The descendants of Terah

²⁶⁻²⁸ After Terah was seventy years old, he had three sons: Abram, Nahor, and Haran, who became the father of Lot. Terah's sons were born in the city of Ur in Chaldea,* and Haran died there before the death of his father. The following is the story of Terah's descendants.

²⁹⁻³⁰ Abram married Sarai, but she was not able to have any children. And Nahor married Milcah, who was the daughter of Haran and the sister of Iscah.

³¹ Terah decided to move from Ur to the land of Canaan. He took along Abram and Sarai and his grandson Lot, the son of Haran. But when they came to the city of Haran,* they decided to settle there instead. ³² Terah lived to be two hundred and five years old and died in Haran.

The Lord chooses Abram

CHAPTER 12

¹ The LORD said to Abram:

Leave your country, your family, and your relatives and go to the land that I will show you. ² I will bless you and make your descendants into a great nation. You will become famous and be a blessing to others. ³ I will bless anyone who blesses you, but I will put a curse on anyone who puts a curse on you. Everyone on earth will be blessed because of you.'

⁴⁻⁵ Abram was seventy-five years old when the LORD told him to leave the city of Haran. He obeyed and left with his wife Sarai, his nephew Lot, and all the possessions and slaves they had got while in Haran.

---

*11.26–28 Ur in Chaldea: Chaldea was a region at the head of the Persian Gulf. Ur was on the main trade routes from Mesopotamia to the Mediterranean Sea.
*11.31 Haran: About 885 kilometres north-west of Ur.
See also: 12.1: Acts 7.2–3; Heb 11.8.   12.3: Gal 3.8.

Life files

Abraham (a.k.a. Abram)

Background: Son of Terah. Wife Sarah (formerly Sarai).

What's the story?

Abram was living in Haran when God called him. Childless at 75, God promises to make Abram a 'great nation' (Genesis 12.2).

He travels to Canaan where God repeats his promise (Genesis 15 and 17) and seals it with a covenant. In Genesis 17, Abram has his name changed, to Abraham. And he has to mark his allegiance by circumcision.

Abraham 'believed the LORD and the LORD was pleased with him' (Genesis 15.6). He left home and travelled far away when God told him to. He believed that he would have a son, despite his age. He was even prepared to give up that son if God asked. He had faith that God would do what he said he would. (Of course, sometimes he was not so sure – like when he passed his wife off as his sister; but nobody's perfect.)

What's the point?

Abraham is *the* man of faith of the Old Testament. Think about it: he had no prior experience on which to base his faith, no Bible, no historical books to examine.

Faith in God means acting on his commands. Abraham didn't just believe in God, he started walking. Even when God's hands were tough and hard to obey.

footsteps

A week with Abraham

Origins: Genesis 11.26–31; 12.1–9
Abram in Egypt Genesis 12.10—13.1
Abram and Lot: Genesis 13.2–18
Abram to Abraham: Genesis 17.1–27
Arguing with God: Genesis 18.16–33
Abraham has a son: Genesis 18.1–15; 21.1–8
Abraham's faith: Genesis 22.1–19

More...

Faith p.1373
Covenant p.17
Circumcisio p.1259

When they came to the land of Canaan, ⁶ Abram went as far as the sacred tree of Moreh in a place called Shechem. The Canaanites were still living in the land at that time, ⁷ but the LORD appeared to Abram and promised, "I will give this land to your family for ever." Abram then built an altar there for the LORD.

⁸ Abram travelled to the hill country east of Bethel and camped between Bethel and Ai, where he built another altar and worshipped the LORD. ⁹ Later, Abram started out towards the Southern Desert.

Abram in Egypt

¹⁰⁻¹¹ The crops failed, and there was no food anywhere in the land. So Abram and his wife Sarai went to live in Egypt for a while. But just before they got there, he said, "Sarai, you are really beautiful! ¹² When the Egyptians see how lovely you are, they will murder me because I am your husband. But they won't kill you. ¹³ Please save my life by saying that you are my sister."

¹⁴ As soon as Abram and Sarai arrived in Egypt, the Egyptians noticed how beautiful she was. ¹⁵ The king's' officials told him about her, and she was taken to his house. ¹⁶ The king was good to Abram because of Sarai, and Abram was given sheep, cattle, donkeys, slaves, and camels.

¹⁷ Because of Sarai, the LORD struck the king and everyone in his palace with terrible diseases. ¹⁸ Finally, the king sent for Abram and said to him, "What have you done to me? Why didn't you tell me Sarai was your wife? ¹⁹ Why did you make me believe she was your sister? Now I've married her. Take her and go! She's your wife."

²⁰ So the king told his men to let Abram and Sarai take their possessions and leave.

Abram and Lot

CHAPTER 13

Abram and Lot separate

¹ Abram and Sarai took everything they owned and went to the Southern Desert. Lot went with them.

² Abram was very rich. He owned many cattle, sheep, and goats, and had a lot of silver and gold. ³ Abram moved from place to place in the Southern Desert. And finally, he went north and set up his tents between Bethel and

Ai, ⁴ where he had earlier camped and built an altar. There he worshipped the LORD.

⁵ Lot, who was travelling with him, also had sheep, goats, and cattle, as well as his own family and slaves. ⁶⁻⁷ At this time the Canaanites and the Perizzites were living in the same area, and so there wasn't enough pasture land left for Abram and Lot with all their animals. Besides this, the men who took care of Abram's animals and the ones who took care of Lot's animals started quarrelling.

⁸ Abram said to Lot, "We are close relatives. We shouldn't argue, and our men shouldn't be fighting one another. ⁹ There is plenty of land for you to choose from. Let's separate. If you go north, I'll go south; if you go south, I'll go north."

¹⁰ This happened before the LORD had destroyed the cities of Sodom and Gomorrah. And when Lot looked around, he saw there was plenty of water in the Jordan Valley. All the way to Zoar the valley was as green as the garden of the LORD or the land of Egypt. ¹¹ So Lot chose the whole Jordan Valley for himself, and as he started towards the east, he and Abram separated. ¹² Abram stayed in the land of Canaan. But Lot settled near the cities of the valley and put up his tents not far from Sodom, ¹³ where the people were evil and sinned terribly against the LORD.

Abram moves to Hebron

¹⁴ After Abram and Lot had gone their separate ways, the LORD said to Abram:

Look around to the north, south, east, and west. ¹⁵ I will give you and your family all the land you can see. It will be theirs for ever! ¹⁶ I will give you more descendants than there are specks of dust on the earth, and some day it will be easier to count the specks of dust than to count your descendants. ¹⁷ Now walk back and forth across the land, because I am giving it to you.

¹⁸ Abram took down his tents and went to live near the sacred trees of Mamre at Hebron, where he built an altar in honour of the LORD.

CHAPTER 14

Abram rescues Lot

¹ About this time, King Amraphel of Babylonia,' King Arioch of Ellasar, King Chedorlaomer of Elam, and King Tidal

---

See also: **12.7:** Acts 7.5; Gal 3.16. **12.13:** Gen 20.2; 26.7.   **See also:** **13.10:** Gen 2.10. **13.15:** Acts 7.5.

of Goiim [2] attacked King Bera of Sodom, King Birsha of Gomorrah, King Shinab of Admah, King Shemeber of Zeboiim, and the king of Bela, also known as the city of Zoar. [3-4] King Chedorlaomer and his allies had ruled these last five kings for twelve years, but in the thirteenth year the kings rebelled and came together in Siddim Valley, which is now covered by the southern part of the Dead Sea.

[5] A year later King Chedorlaomer and his allies attacked and defeated the Rephaites in Ashteroth-Karnaim, the Zuzites in Ham, and the Emites in Shaveh-Kiriathaim. [6] They also defeated the Horites in the hill country of Edom,' as far as El-Paran, near the desert.

[7] They went back to the city of Enmishpat, better known as Kadesh. Then they captured all the land that belonged to the Amalekites, and they defeated the Amorites who were living in Hazazon-Tamar.

[8-9] At Siddim Valley, the armies of the kings of Sodom, Gomorrah, Admah, Zeboiim, and Bela fought the armies of King Chedorlaomer of Elam, King Tidal of Goiim, King Amraphel of Babylonia, and King Arioch of Ellasar. The valley [10] was full of tar pits, and when the troops from Sodom and Gomorrah started running away, some of them fell into the pits. Others escaped to the hill country. [11] Their enemies took everything of value from Sodom and Gomorrah, including their food supplies. [12] They also captured Abram's nephew Lot, who lived in Sodom. They took him and his possessions and then left.

[13] At this time Abram the Hebrew was living near the oaks that belonged to Mamre the Amorite. Mamre and his brothers Eshcol and Aner were Abram's friends. Someone who had escaped from the battle told Abram [14] that his nephew Lot had been taken away. Three hundred and eighteen of Abram's servants were fighting men, so he took them and followed the enemy as far north as the city of Dan. [15] That night, Abram divided up his troops, attacked from all sides, and won a great victory. But some of the enemy escaped to the town of Hobah north of Damascus, [16] and Abram went after them. He brought back his nephew Lot, together with Lot's possessions and the women and everyone else who had been captured.

Abram is blessed by Melchizedek

[17] Abram returned after he had defeated King Chedorlaomer and the other kings. Then the king of Sodom went to meet Abram in Shaveh Valley, which is also known as King's Valley.

[18] King Melchizedek of Salem was a priest of God Most High. He brought out some bread and wine [19] and said to Abram:

> "I bless you in the name
>   of God Most High,
>   Creator of heaven and earth.
> [20] All praise belongs
>   to God Most High
>   for helping you defeat
>   your enemies."

Then Abram gave Melchizedek a tenth of everything.

[21] The king of Sodom said to Abram, "All I want are my people. You can keep everything else."

[22] Abram answered:

> The LORD God Most High made the heavens and the earth. And I have promised him [23] that I won't keep anything of yours, not even a sandal strap or a piece of thread. Then you can never say that you are the one who made me rich. [24] Let my share be the food that my men have eaten. But Aner, Eshcol, and Mamre went with me, so give them their share of what we brought back.

The Lord's promises to Abram

CHAPTER 15

[1] Later the LORD spoke to Abram in a vision, "Abram, don't be afraid! I will protect you and reward you greatly."

[2] But Abram answered, "LORD All-Powerful, you have given me everything I could ask for, except children. And when I die, Eliezer of Damascus will get all I own.' [3] You have not given me any children, and this servant of mine will inherit everything."

[4] The LORD replied, "No, he won't! You will have a son of your own, and everything you have will be his." [5] Then the LORD took Abram outside and said, "Look at the sky and see if you can count the stars. That's how many descendants you will have."

See also: **14.18–20:** Heb 7.1–10. **15.5:** Rom 4.18; Heb 11.12.

[6] Abram believed the LORD, and the LORD was pleased with him.

The LORD makes another promise to Abram

[7] The LORD said to Abram, "I brought you here from Ur in Chaldea, and I gave you this land."

[8] Abram asked, "LORD God, how can I know the land will be mine?"

[9] Then the LORD told him, "Bring me a three-year-old cow, a three-year-old female goat, a three-year-old ram, a dove, and a young pigeon."

[10] Abram obeyed the LORD. Then he cut' the animals in half and laid the two halves of each animal opposite each other on the ground. But he did not cut the doves and pigeons in half. [11] And when birds came down to eat the animals, Abram chased them away.

[12] As the sun was setting, Abram fell into a deep sleep, and everything became dark and frightening. [13-15] Then the LORD said:

Abram, you will live to an old age and die in peace.

But I solemnly promise that your descendants will live as foreigners in a land that doesn't belong to them. They will be forced into slavery and abused for four hundred years. But I will terribly punish the nation that enslaves them, and they will leave with many possessions.

[16] Four generations later,* your descendants will return here and take this land, because only then will the people who live here' be so sinful that they deserve to be punished.

[17] Some time after sunset, when it was very dark, a smoking cooking pot* and a flaming fire went between the two halves of each animal. [18] At that time the LORD made an agreement with Abram and told him:

I will give your descendants the land east of the River Shihor* on the border of Egypt as far as the River Euphrates. [19] They will

---

*15.16 Four generations later: This may refer to the "four hundred years" of verses 13–15.
*15.17 smoking cooking pot: One possible meaning for the difficult Hebrew text. The smoke and fire represent the presence of the LORD.
*15.18 River Shihor: See Joshua 13.2–7.
See also: 15.6: Rom 4.3; Gal 3.6; Jam 2.23.
15.12: Job 4.13–14.   15.13: Exod 1.1–14; Acts 7.6.
15.14: Exod 12.40–41; Acts 7.7.   15.18: Acts 7.5.

Big ideas

Covenant

The solemn promise that God makes to Abraham is what was called a covenant.

A covenant was a legally binding agreement. In the Bible it refers to the agreement God has made with mankind.

After the flood, God made an agreement with Noah never to destroy humanity in that way again (Genesis 6.18). God then promised Abraham that he would make a great nation our of Abraham's descendants. It's sealed by circumcision (Genesis 15; 17).

After rescuing the Israelites from Egypt, God makes a covenant with Moses. If the people obey, they will be his people. God gives the Law, written on two large stones. These are kept in 'the ark of the covenant', a special acacia wood chest.

The New Agreement

Problem. The Israelites never kept to the agreement. They worshipped false gods and broke the law. So God said he would draw up a new agreement, not of rituals, sacrifices and circumcision, but written on people's hearts and minds (Jeremiah 31.31–4).

This new agreement was brought into being through Jesus. He established it at the last supper (Mark 14.24) and sealed it with his death (Hebrews 8.8–13).

Anorak corner

This idea is picked up in the two sections of the Bible, which use the word Testamentum – Latin for 'covenant'. So the Bible is really the Old and New Agreements.

Footsteps

A week with Covenants

The promise to Noah: Genesis 9.7–17
The promise to Abraham: Genesis 17.1–22
The promise to Moses: Exodus 19.1–8
A new agreement: Jeremiah 31.31–34
Jesus is the new agreement: Luke 22.14–20
More about it: 1 Corinthians 11.23–29
And even more: 2 Corinthians 3.4–11

More...

Communion p.1285

possess the land of the Kenites, the Kenizzites, the Kadmonites, 20 the Hittites, the Perizzites, the Rephaites, 21 the Amorites, the Canaanites, the Girgashites, and the Jebusites.

Abram, Hagar, and Ishmael

CHAPTER 16

1 Abram's wife Sarai had not been able to have any children. But she owned a young Egyptian slave woman named Hagar, 2 and Sarai said to Abram, "The LORD has not given me any children. Sleep with my slave, and if she has a child, it will be mine."* Abram agreed, 3 and Sarai gave him Hagar to be his wife. This happened after Abram had lived in the land of Canaan for ten years. 4 Later, when Hagar knew she was going to have a baby, she became proud and was hateful to Sarai.

5 Then Sarai said to Abram, "It's all your fault!ˑ I gave you my slave woman, but she has been hateful to me ever since she found out she was pregnant. You have done me wrong, and you will have to answer to the LORD for this."

6 Abram said, "All right! She's your slave, and you can do whatever you want with her." But Sarai began treating Hagar so harshly that she finally ran away.

7 Hagar stopped to rest at a spring in the desert on the road to Shur. While she was there, the angel of the LORD came to her 8 and asked, "Hagar, where have you come from, and where are you going?"

She answered, "I'm running away from Sarai, my owner."

9 The angel said, "Go back to Sarai and be her slave. 10-11 I will give you a son, who will be called Ishmael,* because I have heard your cry for help. And later I will give you so many descendants that no one will be able to count them all. 12 But your son will live far from his relatives; he will be like a wild donkey, fighting everyone, and everyone fighting him."

13 Hagar thought, "Have I really seen God and lived to tell about it?"ˑ So from then on she called him, "The God who Sees Me".ˑ 14 That's why people call the well between

Kadesh and Bered, "The Well of the Living One who Sees Me".ˑ

15-16 Abram was eighty-six years old when Hagar gave birth to their son, and he named him Ishmael.

God changes Abram's name to Abraham and promises him a son

CHAPTER 17

1 Abram was ninety-nine years old when the LORD appeared to him again and said, "I am God All-Powerful. If you obey me and always do right, 2 I will keep my solemn promise to you and give you more descendants than can be counted." 3 Abram bowed with his face to the ground, and God said:

4-5 I promise that you will be the father of many nations. That's why I now change your name from Abram to Abraham.* 6 I will give you a lot of descendants, and in the future they will become great nations. Some of them will even be kings.

7 I will always keep the promise I have made to you and your descendants, because I am your God and their God. 8 I will give you and them the land in which you are now a foreigner. I will give the whole land of Canaan to your family for ever, and I will be their God.

9 Abraham, you and all future members of your family must promise to obey me. 10-11 As the sign that you are keeping this promise, you must circumcise every man and boy in your family. 12-13 From now on, your family must circumcise every baby boy when he is eight days old. You must even circumcise any man or boy you have as a slave, both those born in your homes and those you buy from foreigners. This will be a sign that my promise to you will last for ever. 14 Any man who isn't circumcised hasn't kept his promise to me and cannot be one of my people.

15 Abraham, your wife's name will now be Sarah instead of Sarai. 16 I will bless her, and you will have a son by her. She will become the mother of nations, and some of her descendants will even be kings.

16.2 Sleep . . . mine: It was the custom for a wife who could not have children to let her husband sleep with one of her slave women. The children of the slave would belong to the wife.

16.10–11 Ishmael: In Hebrew "Ishmael" sounds like "God hears".

17.4–5 Abraham: In Hebrew "Abraham" sounds like "father of many nations".

See also: 16.15: Gal 4.22. 17.5: Rom 4.17. 17.7: Luke 1.55. 17.8: Acts 7.5. 17.10: Acts 7.8; Rom 4.11.

¹⁷ Abraham bowed with his face to the ground and thought, "I am almost a hundred years old. How can I become a father? And Sarah is ninety. How can she have a child?" So he started laughing. ¹⁸ Then he asked God, "Why not let Ishmael* inherit what you have promised me?"

¹⁹ But God answered:

No! You and Sarah will have a son. His name will be Isaac,* and I will make an everlasting promise to him and his descendants.

²⁰ I have heard what you asked me to do for Ishmael, and so I will also bless him with many descendants. He will be the father of twelve princes, and I will make his family a great nation. ²¹ But your son Isaac will be born about this time next year, and the promise I am making to you and your family will be for him and his descendants for ever.

²² God finished speaking to Abraham and then left. ²³⁻²⁷ On that same day Abraham obeyed God by circumcising Ishmael. Abraham was also circumcised, and so were all other men and boys in his household, including his servants and slaves. He was ninety-nine years old at the time, and his son Ishmael was thirteen.

CHAPTER 18

The LORD promises Abraham a son

¹ One hot summer afternoon Abraham was sitting by the entrance to his tent near the sacred trees of Mamre, when the LORD appeared to him. ² Abraham looked up and saw three men standing nearby. He quickly ran to meet them, bowed with his face to the ground, ³ and said, "Please come to my home where I can serve you. ⁴ I'll have some water brought, so you can wash your feet, then you can rest under the tree. ⁵ Let me get you some food to give you strength before you leave. I would be honoured to serve you."

"Thank you very much," they answered. "We accept your offer."

⁶ Abraham quickly went to his tent and said to Sarah, "Hurry! Get a large sack of flour and make some bread." ⁷ After saying this, he rushed off to his herd of cattle and picked out one of the best calves, which his servant quickly prepared. ⁸ He then served his guests some yoghurt and milk together with the meat.

While they were eating, he stood near them under the trees, ⁹ and they asked, "Where is your wife Sarah?"

"She is there in the tent," Abraham answered.

¹⁰ One of the guests was the LORD, and he said, "I'll come back about this time next year, and when I do, Sarah will already have a son."

Sarah was behind Abraham, listening at the entrance to the tent. ¹¹ Abraham and Sarah were very old, and Sarah was well past the age for having children. ¹² So she laughed and said to herself, "Now that I am worn out and my husband is old, will I really know such happiness?"*

¹³ The LORD asked Abraham, "Why did Sarah laugh? Does she doubt that she can have a child in her old age? ¹⁴ I am the LORD! There is nothing too difficult for me. I'll come back next year at the time I promised, and Sarah will already have a son."

¹⁵ Sarah was so frightened that she lied and said, "I didn't laugh."

"Yes, you did!" he answered.

Abraham, Lot, Sodom, and Gomorrah

Abraham prays for Sodom

¹⁶ When the three men got ready to leave, they looked down towards Sodom, and Abraham walked part of the way with them.

¹⁷ The LORD said to himself, "I should tell Abraham what I am going to do, ¹⁸ since his family will become a great and powerful nation that will be a blessing to all other nations on earth.▸ ¹⁹ I have chosen him to teach his family to obey me for ever and to do what is right and fair. Then I will give Abraham many descendants, just as I promised."

²⁰ The LORD said, "Abraham, I have heard that the people of Sodom and Gomorrah are doing all kinds of evil things. ²¹ Now I am going down to see for myself if those people really are that bad. If they aren't, I want to know about it."

---

*17.18 Ishmael: Ishmael was the son of Sarah's slave Hagar (see 16.1–16).

*17.19 Isaac: In Hebrew "Isaac" sounds like "laugh".

See also: 18.2a: Heb 13.2.

*18.12 know such happiness: Either the joy of making love or the joy of having children.

See also: 18.10: Rom 9.9. 18.12: 1 Pet 3.6.
18.14: Luke 1.37.

Life files

Lot

Background: Son of Haran, nephew of Abraham. Married with children.

What's the story?

Lot journeyed with his Uncle Abram from Haran to Canaan. Given first choice, he chose to settle in the fertile Jordan valley. First he pitched his tents not far from Sodom, later he moved inside the city. This was not a good career move, since the city was full of people who 'were evil and sinned terribly against the LORD' (Genesis 13.13).

He then had to be rescued twice: once by his Uncle Abraham (Genesis 14.11–16) and then by God when Sodom was destroyed.

Frankly, Lot never knew when he was well off. His moral weakness can be seen when he tried to persuade the Sodom mob to have his daughters rather than rape the angels! Even when the angels offered him the chance of escape, he argued that the hills were too far away and asked if he could escape somewhere nearer. His family weren't any better. Despite being warned not to look back at the destruction, his wife sneaked a look and was transformed into a pillar of salt. His daughters, scared that they would not have children, got their father drunk and slept with him. This is not what you'd call an intelligent family.

What's the point?

Lot is a curious character. 2 Peter 2.7 describes him as a 'good man' who 'lived right'; yet he was also capable of acts of foolishness. He made bad choices, he compromised with the world around him, but ultimately he was saved by the mercy of God.

 Footsteps

Five days with Lot

[22] The men turned and started towards Sodom. But the LORD stayed with Abraham, [23] who asked, "LORD, when you destroy the evil people, are you also going to destroy those who are good? [24] Wouldn't you spare the city if there are only fifty good people in it? [25] You surely wouldn't let them be killed when you destroy the evil ones. You are the judge of all the earth, and you do what is right."

[26] The LORD replied, "If I find fifty good people in Sodom, I will save the city to keep them from being killed."

[27] Abraham answered, "I am nothing more than the dust of the earth. Please forgive me, LORD, for daring to speak to you like this. [28] But suppose there are only forty-five good people in Sodom. Would you still wipe out the whole city?"

"If I find forty-five good people," the LORD replied, "I won't destroy the city."

[29] "Suppose there are just forty good people?" Abraham asked.

"Even for them," the LORD replied, "I won't destroy the city."

[30] Abraham said, "Please don't be angry, LORD, if I ask you what you will do if there are only thirty good people in the city."

"If I find thirty," the LORD replied, "I still won't destroy it."

[31] Then Abraham said, "I don't have any right to ask you, LORD, but what would you do if you find only twenty?"

"Because of them, I won't destroy the city," was the LORD's answer.

[32] Finally, Abraham said, "Please don't get angry, LORD, if I speak just once more. Suppose you find only ten good people there."

"For the sake of ten good people," the LORD told him, "I still won't destroy the city."

[33] After speaking with Abraham, the LORD left, and Abraham went back home.

CHAPTER 19

The evil city of Sodom

[1] That evening the two angels* arrived in Sodom, while Lot was sitting near the city gate.* When Lot saw them, he got up, bowed down low, [2] and said, "Gentlemen, I am your servant. Please come to my home. You can wash your feet, spend the night, and be on your way in the morning."

***19.1 two angels:** The two men of 18.22.
***19.1 near the city gate:** In a large area where the people would gather for community business and for meeting with friends.

They told him, "No, we'll spend the night in the city square." ³ But Lot kept insisting, until they finally agreed and went home with him. He baked some bread,* cooked a meal, and they ate.

⁴ Before Lot and his guests could go to bed, every man in Sodom, young and old, came and stood outside his house ⁵ and started shouting, "Where are your visitors? Send them out, so we can have sex with them!"

⁶ Lot went outside and shut the door behind him. ⁷ Then he said, "Friends, please don't do such a terrible thing! ⁸ I have two daughters who have never been married. I'll bring them out, and you can do what you want with them. But don't harm these men. They are guests in my home."

⁹ "Don't get in our way," the crowd answered. "You're an outsider. What right do you have to order us around? We'll do worse things to you than we're going to do to them."

The crowd kept arguing with Lot. Finally, they rushed towards the door to break it down. ¹⁰ But the two angels in the house reached out and pulled Lot safely inside. ¹¹ Then they struck everyone in the crowd blind, and none of them could even find the door.

¹²⁻¹³ The two angels said to Lot, "The Lᴏʀᴅ has heard many terrible things about the people of Sodom, and he has sent us here to destroy the city. Take your family and leave. Take every relative you have in the city, as well as the men your daughters are going to marry."

¹⁴ Lot went to the men who were engaged to his daughters and said, "Hurry and get out of here! The Lᴏʀᴅ is going to destroy this city." But they thought he was joking, and they laughed at him.

¹⁵ Early the next morning the two angels tried to make Lot hurry and leave. They said, "Take your wife and your two daughters and get out of here as fast as you can! If you don't, every one of you will be killed when the Lᴏʀᴅ destroys the city." ¹⁶ At first, Lot just stood there. But the Lᴏʀᴅ wanted to save him. So the angels took Lot, his wife, and his two daughters by the hand and led them out of the city. ¹⁷ When they were outside, one of the angels said, "Run for your lives! Don't

even look back. And don't stop in the valley. Run to the hills, where you will be safe."

¹⁸⁻¹⁹ Lot answered, "You have done us a great favour, sir. You have saved our lives, but please don't make us go to the hills. That's too far away. The city will be destroyed before we can get there, and we will be killed when it happens. ²⁰ There's a town near here. It's only a small place, but my family and I will be safe, if you let us go there."

²¹ "All right, go there," he answered. "I won't destroy that town. ²² Hurry! Run! I can't do anything until you are safely there."

The town was later called Zoar* because Lot had said it was small.

Sodom and Gomorrah are destroyed

²³ The sun was coming up as Lot reached the town of Zoar, ²⁴ and the Lᴏʀᴅ sent burning sulphur down like rain on Sodom and Gomorrah. ²⁵ He destroyed those cities and everyone who lived in them, as well as their land and the trees and grass that grew there.

²⁶ On the way, Lot's wife looked back and was turned into a block of salt.

²⁷ That same morning Abraham got up and went to the place where he had stood and spoken with the Lᴏʀᴅ. ²⁸ He looked down towards Sodom and Gomorrah and saw smoke rising from all over the land — it was like a flaming furnace.

²⁹ When God destroyed the cities of the valley where Lot lived, he remembered his promise to Abraham and saved Lot from the terrible destruction.

Moab and Ammon

³⁰ Lot was afraid to stay on in Zoar. So he took his two daughters and moved to a cave in the hill country. ³¹ One day his elder daughter said to her sister, "Our father is old, and there are no men anywhere for us to marry. ³² Let's get our father drunk! Then we can sleep with him and have children." ³³ That night they got their father drunk, and the elder daughter got in bed with him, but he was too drunk even to know she was there.

³⁴ The next day the elder daughter said to her sister, "I slept with my father last night. We'll get him drunk again tonight, so you can go to bed with him, and we can each have a child." ³⁵ That night they got their father drunk, and this time the younger sister

---

*19.3 bread: The Hebrew text has "bread without yeast", which could be prepared quickly when guests came without warning.
See also: 19.5–8: Judg 19.22–24. 19.11: 2 King 6.18. 19.16: 2 Pet 2.7.

*19.22 Zoar: In Hebrew "Zoar" sounds like "small".
See also: 19.24,25: Matt 10.15; 11.23–24; Luke 10.12; 17.29; 2 Pet 2.6. 19.26: Luke 17.32.

slept with him. But once again he was too drunk even to know she was there.
³⁶ That's how Lot's two daughters had their children. ³⁷ The elder daughter named her son Moab,* and he is the ancestor of the Moabites. ³⁸ The younger daughter named her son Benammi,* and he is the ancestor of the Ammonites.

Abraham, Sarah, and Isaac

CHAPTER 20

Abraham and Sarah at Gerar

¹ Abraham moved to the Southern Desert, where he settled between Kadesh and Shur. Later he went to Gerar, and while there ² he told everyone that his wife Sarah was his sister. So King Abimelech of Gerar had Sarah brought to him. ³ But God came to Abimelech in a dream and said, "You have taken a married woman, and for this you will die!"

⁴⁻⁵ Abimelech said to the Lord, "Don't kill me! I haven't slept with Sarah. Didn't they say they were brother and sister? I am completely innocent."

⁶ God spoke to Abimelech in another dream and said:

I know you are innocent. That's why I kept you from sleeping with Sarah and doing anything wrong. ⁷ Her husband is a prophet. Let her go back to him, and his prayers will save you from death. But if you don't return her, you and all your people will die.

⁸ Early the next morning Abimelech sent for his officials, and when he told them what had happened, they were frightened. ⁹ Abimelech then called in Abraham and said:

Look what you've done to us! What have I ever done to you? Why did you make me and my nation guilty of such a terrible sin? ¹⁰ What were you thinking when you did this?

¹¹ Abraham answered:

I did it because I didn't think any of you respected God, and I was sure that someone would kill me to get my wife. ¹² Besides, she is my half-sister. We have the same father, but different mothers.

¹³ When God made us leave my father's home and start wandering, I told her, "If you really love me, you will tell everyone that I am your brother."

¹⁴ Abimelech gave Abraham some sheep, cattle, and slaves. He sent Sarah back ¹⁵ and told Abraham that he could settle anywhere in his country. ¹⁶ Then he said to Sarah, "I have given your brother a thousand pieces of silver as proof to everyone that you have done nothing wrong."

¹⁷⁻¹⁸ Meanwhile, God had kept Abimelech's wife and slaves from having children. But Abraham prayed, and God let them start having children again.

CHAPTER 21

Sarah has a son

¹ The LORD was good to Sarah and kept his promise. ² Although Abraham was very old, Sarah had a son exactly at the time God had said. ³ Abraham named his son Isaac, ⁴ and when the boy was eight days old, Abraham circumcised him, just as the LORD had commanded.

⁵ Abraham was a hundred years old when Isaac was born, ⁶ and Sarah said, "God has made me laugh.* Now everyone will laugh with me. ⁷ Who would have dared to tell Abraham that some day I would have a child? But in his old age, I have given him a son."

⁸ The time came when Sarah no longer had to nurse Isaac,* and on that day Abraham gave a big feast.

Hagar and Ishmael are sent away

⁹⁻¹⁰ One day, Sarah noticed Hagar's son Ishmael* playing,ᵇ and she said to Abraham, "Get rid of that Egyptian slave woman and her son! I don't want him to inherit anything. It should all go to my son."*

---

*21.6 God has made me laugh: In Hebrew "Isaac" sounds like "laugh".
*21.8 no longer had to nurse Isaac: In ancient Israel mothers nursed their children until they were about three years old. Then there was a family celebration.
*21.9–10 Ishmael: The son of Abraham and Hagar, who was Sarah's slave woman (see 16.1–16).
*21.9–10 Get rid . . . son: When Abraham accepted Ishmael as his son, it gave Ishmael the right to inherit part of what Abraham owned. But slaves who were given their freedom lost the right to inherit such property.

See also: 21.2: Heb 11.11.   21.4: Gen 17.12; Acts 7.8.
21.10: Gal 4.29–30.

---

*19.37 Moab: In Hebrew "Moab" sounds like "from (my) father".
*19.38 Benammi: In Hebrew "Benammi" means "son of my relative".

See also: 20.2: Gen 12.13; 26.7.

Life files

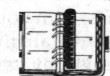

Hagar

a.k.a. Not known, but she must have had another name. 'Hagar' is a Hebrew name, and she was Egyptian.
Background: An Egyptian slave in the household of Abraham

What's the story?

Abraham and Sarai have no children, so Sarai suggests that Hagar should become a kind of surrogate mother. (In Old Testament times, men whose wives could not have children would sleep with a slave. The child would then be adopted by the wife.)

But Hagar and Sarah fall out. Although pregnant, Hagar is driven away. God meets her and promises great things for her son, Ishmael. He will also be the father of many descendants, although, unlike the promise to Abram, God does not promise that blessing will come through them. So Hagar returns.

Later, when Ishmael is older, the rivalry flares up again and Sarah forces Abraham to exile Hagar and Ishmael. Alone in the desert, Hagar crawls away to leave her child to die. But God rescues them from death and renews his promise to Hagar.

His promise to Hagar comes true. The Ishmaelites – a nomadic tribe – appear later in the Bible, and it is part of Islamic theology that all Arabs are descended from Ishmael. Ishmael's name means 'God has heard'.

What's the point?

Hagar is remarkable. Although she was an Egyptian slave, she met God. God comforts and rescues her, he makes promises to her. God's decided to work through the descendants of Abraham, but he still cares for his other children.

 Footsteps

Four days with Hagar

Hagar sees God: Genesis 16.1–16
God's promise to Ishmael: Genesis 17.17–27
God rescues Hagar: Genesis 21.9–21
The descendants of Ishmael:
Genesis 25.7–17

[11] Abraham was worried about Ishmael. [12] But God said, "Abraham, don't worry about your slave woman and the boy. Just do what Sarah tells you. Isaac will inherit your family name, [13] but the son of the slave woman is also your son, and I will make his descendants into a great nation."

[14] Early the next morning Abraham gave Hagar an animal skin full of water and some bread. Then he put the boy on her shoulder and sent them away.

They wandered around in the desert near Beersheba, [15] and after they had run out of water, Hagar put her son under a bush. [16] Then she sat down a long way off, because she could not bear to watch him die. And she cried bitterly.

[17] When God heard the boy crying, the angel of God called out to Hagar from heaven and said, "Hagar, why are you worried? Don't be afraid. I have heard your son crying. [18] Help him up and hold his hand, because I will make him the father of a great nation." [19] Then God let her see a well. So she went to the well and filled the skin with water, then gave some to her son.

[20-21] God blessed Ishmael, and as the boy grew older, he became an expert with his bow and arrows. He lived in the Paran Desert, and his mother chose an Egyptian woman for him to marry.

A peace treaty

[22] About this time Abimelech and his army commander Phicol said to Abraham, "God blesses everything you do! [23] Now I want you to promise in the name of God that you will always be loyal to me and my descendants, just as I have always been loyal to you in this land where you have lived as a foreigner." [24] And so, Abraham promised.

[25] One day, Abraham told Abimelech, "Some of your servants have taken over one of my wells."

[26] "This is the first I've heard about it," Abimelech replied. "Why haven't you said something before? I don't have any idea who did it." [27] Abraham gave Abimelech some sheep and cattle, and then the two men made a peace treaty.

[28] Abraham separated seven female lambs from his flock of sheep, [29] and Abimelech asked, "Why have you done this?"

[30] Abraham told him, "I want you to accept these seven lambs as proof that I dug this

---

See also: 21.12: Rom 9.7; Heb 11.18. 21.22: Gen 26.26.

well." ³¹ So they called the place Beersheba,*
because they made a treaty there.
³² When the treaty was completed,
Abimelech and his army commander Phicol
went back to the land of the Philistines.
³³ Abraham planted a tamarisk tree* in
Beersheba and worshipped the eternal LORD
God. ³⁴ Then Abraham lived a long time as a
foreigner in the land of the Philistines.

CHAPTER 22

The LORD tells Abraham to offer Isaac as a sacrifice

¹ Some years later God decided to test
Abraham, so he spoke to him.
Abraham answered, "Here I am, LORD."
² The LORD said, "Go and get Isaac, your
only son, the one you dearly love! Take him
to the land of Moriah, and I will show you a
mountain where you must sacrifice him to
me on the fires of an altar." ³ So Abraham got
up early the next morning and chopped
wood for the fire. He put a saddle on his
donkey and left with Isaac and two servants
for the place where God had told him to go.
⁴ Three days later Abraham looked into the
distance and saw the place. ⁵ He told his
servants, "Stay here with the donkey, while
my son and I go over there to worship. We
will come back."
⁶ Abraham put the wood on Isaac's
shoulder, but he carried the hot coals and the
knife. As the two of them walked along,
⁷⁻⁸ Isaac said, "Father, we have the coals and
the wood, but where is the lamb for the
sacrifice?"
"My son," Abraham answered, "God will
provide the lamb."
The two of them walked on, and ⁹ when
they reached the place that God had told him
about, Abraham built an altar and placed the
wood on it. Next, he tied up his son and put
him on the wood. ¹⁰ He then took the knife
and got ready to kill his son. ¹¹ But the LORD's
angel shouted from heaven, "Abraham!
Abraham!"
"Here I am!" he answered.
¹² "Don't hurt the boy or harm him in any
way!" the angel said. "Now I know that you

truly obey God, because you were willing to
offer him your only son."
¹³ Abraham looked up and saw a ram
caught by its horns in the bushes. So he took
the ram and sacrificed it in place of his son.
¹⁴ Abraham named that place "The LORD
will Provide". And even now people say, "On
the mountain of the LORD it will be
provided."ʼ
¹⁵ The LORD's angel called out from heaven
a second time:

¹⁶ You were willing to offer the LORD your
only son, and so he makes you this solemn
promise, ¹⁷ "I will bless you and give you
such a large family, that some day your
descendants will be more numerous than
the stars in the sky or the grains of sand
along the beach. They will defeat their
enemies and take over the cities where
their enemies live. ¹⁸ You have obeyed me,
and so you and your descendants will be a
blessing to all nations on earth."

¹⁹ Abraham and Isaac went back to the
servants who had come with him, and they
returned to Abraham's home in Beersheba.

The children of Nahor

²⁰⁻²³ Abraham's brother Nahor had married
Milcah, and Abraham was later told that they
had eight sons. Uz was their firstborn; Buz
was next, and then there was Kemuel who
became the father of Aram; their other five
sons were: Chesed, Hazo, Pildash, Jidlaph,
and Bethuel, who became the father of
Rebekah. ²⁴ Nahor also had another wife.*
Her name was Reumah, and she had four
sons: Tebah, Gaham, Tahash, and Maacah.

CHAPTER 23

Sarah's death and burial

¹⁻² When Sarah was one hundred and
twenty-seven years old, she died in
Kiriath-Arba, better known as Hebron, in the
land of Canaan. After Abraham had mourned
for her, ³ he went to the Hittites and said,
⁴ "I live as a foreigner in your land, and I
don't own any property where I can bury my
wife. Please let me buy a piece of land."

---

*21.31 Beersheba: Meaning "Well of Good Fortune"
or "Peace Treaty Well".
*21.33 tamarisk tree: A tall shade tree that has deep
roots and needs little water.
See also: 22.1–13: Heb 11.17–19. 22.2: 2 Chron 3.1.
22.9: Jam 2.21.

*22.24 another wife: This translates a Hebrew word
for a woman who was legally bound to a man, but
without the full privileges of a wife.
See also: 22.16–17: Heb 6.13–14. 22.17: Heb 11.12.
22.18: Acts 3.25. 23.4: Heb 11.9,13; Acts 7.16.

5-6 "Sir," they answered, "you are an important man. Choose the best place to bury your wife. None of us would refuse you a resting place for your dead."

7 Abraham bowed down 8 and replied, "If you are willing to let me bury my wife here, please ask Zohar's son Ephron 9 to sell me Machpelah Cave at the end of his field. I'll pay what it's worth, and all of you can be witnesses."

10 Ephron was sitting there near the city gate, when Abraham made this request, and he answered, 11 "Sir, the whole field, including the cave, is yours. With my own people as witnesses, I freely give it to you as a burial place for your dead."

12 Once again, Abraham bowed down 13 and said to Ephron, "In front of these witnesses, I offer you the full price, so I can bury my wife. Please accept my offer."

14-15 "But sir," the man replied, "the property is worth only four hundred pieces of silver. Why should we haggle over such a small amount? Take the land. It's yours."

16-18 Abraham accepted Ephron's offer and paid him the four hundred pieces of silver in front of everyone at the city gate. That's how Abraham got Ephron's property east of Hebron,⁑ which included the field with all its trees, as well as Machpelah Cave at the end of the field. 19 So Abraham buried his wife Sarah in Machpelah Cave that was in the field 20 he had bought from the Hittites.

Rebekah, a wife for Isaac

CHAPTER 24

1 Abraham was now a very old man. The LORD had made him rich, and he was successful in everything he did. 2 One day, Abraham called in his most trusted servant and said to him, "Solemnly promise me 3 in the name of the LORD, who rules heaven and earth, that you won't choose a wife for my son Isaac from the people here in the land of Canaan. 4 Instead, go back to the land where I was born and find a wife for him from among my relatives."

5 But the servant asked, "What if the young woman I choose refuses to leave home and come here with me? Should I send Isaac there to look for a wife?"

6 "No!" Abraham answered. "Don't ever do that, no matter what. 7 The LORD who rules heaven brought me here from the land where I was born and promised that he would give this land to my descendants for ever. When you go back there, the LORD will send his angel ahead of you to help you find a wife for my son. 8 If the woman refuses to come along, you don't have to keep this promise. But don't ever take my son back there." 9 So the servant gave Abraham his word that he would do everything he had been told to do.

10 Soon after that, the servant loaded ten of Abraham's camels with valuable gifts. Then he set out for the city in northern Syria,⁑ where Abraham's brother Nahor lived.

11 When he got there, he let the camels rest near the well outside the city. It was late afternoon, the time when the women came out for water. 12 The servant prayed:

You, LORD, are the God my master Abraham worships. Please keep your promise to him and let me find a wife for Isaac today. 13 The young women of the city will soon come to this well for water, 14 and I'll ask one of them for a drink. If she gives me a drink and then offers to get some water for my camels, I'll know she is the one you have chosen and that you have kept your promise to my master.

15-16 While he was still praying, a beautiful unmarried young woman came by with a water jar on her shoulder. She was Rebekah, the daughter of Bethuel, the son of Abraham's brother Nahor and his wife Milcah. Rebekah walked past Abraham's servant, then went over to the well, and filled her water jar. When she started back, 17 Abraham's servant ran to her and said, "Please let me have a drink of water."

18 "I'll be glad to," she answered. Then she quickly took the jar from her shoulder and held it while he drank. 19-20 After he had finished, she said, "Now I'll give your camels all the water they want." She quickly poured out water for them, and she kept going back for more, until his camels had drunk all they wanted. 21 Abraham's servant did not say a word, but he watched everything Rebekah did, because he wanted to know for certain if this was the woman the LORD had chosen.

22 The servant had brought along an expensive gold ring and two large gold bracelets. When Rebekah had finished bringing the water, he gave her the ring for her nose* and the bracelets for her arms. 23 Then he said, "Please tell me who your

---

*24.22 ring for her nose: Nose-rings were popular jewellery items, as were earrings.

father is. Does he have room in his house for me and my men to spend the night?"

²⁴ She answered, "My father is Bethuel, the son of Nahor and Milcah. ²⁵ We have a place where you and your men can stay, and we also have enough straw and feed for your camels."

²⁶ Then the servant bowed his head and prayed, ²⁷ "I thank you, LORD God of my master Abraham! You have led me to his relatives and kept your promise to him."

²⁸ Rebekah ran straight home and told her family everything. ²⁹⁻³⁰ Her brother Laban heard her tell what the servant had said, and he saw the ring and the bracelets she was wearing. So Laban ran out to Abraham's servant, who was standing by his camels at the well. ³¹ Then Laban said, "The LORD has brought you safely here. Come home with me. There's no need for you to keep on standing outside. I have a room ready for you in our house, and there's also a place for your camels."

³² Abraham's servant went home with Laban, where Laban's servants unloaded his camels and gave them straw and feed. Then they brought water into the house, so Abraham's servant and his men could wash their feet. ³³ After that, they brought in food. But the servant said, "Before I eat, I must tell you why I have come."

"Go ahead and tell us," Laban answered.

³⁴ The servant explained:

I am Abraham's servant. ³⁵ The LORD has been good to my master and has made him very rich. He has given him many sheep, goats, cattle, camels, and donkeys, as well as a lot of silver and gold, and many slaves. ³⁶ Sarah, my master's wife, didn't have any children until she was very old. Then she had a son, and my master has given him everything. ³⁷ I solemnly promised my master that I would do what he said. And he told me, "Don't choose a wife for my son from the women in this land of Canaan. ³⁸ Instead, go back to the land where I was born and find a wife for my son from among my relatives."

³⁹ I asked my master, "What if the young woman refuses to come with me?"

⁴⁰ My master answered, "I have always obeyed the LORD, and he will send his angel to help you find my son a wife from among my own relatives. ⁴¹ But if they refuse to let her come back with you, then you are freed from your promise."

Life files

Isaac

Background: The long-awaited son of Abraham.

What's the story?

A story of triumph over obstacles. Isaac was the son promised to Abraham when he and his wife were in their old age. His name may refer to Sarah's reaction to God's promise (Genesis 17.17).

Having only just made it into life, he nearly made a quick exit, when God commanded Abraham to sacrifice his son as a test of faith. Having had a miraculous birth, he then had a miraculous marriage, when a servant sent by his father returns with Rebekah. However, once again childbirth proves tricky and Isaac has to call out to God.

Rebekah eventually gives birth to twins: Esau and Jacob. Jacob tricks his ageing father into handing over the blessing, an action which leads to antagonism between Rebekah and Isaac.

What's the point?

Isaac's life is testimony to the continuing promise of God. God said to Abraham that he would be the father of great nations and, even when things looked unlikely, he kept that promise.

Footsteps

Five days with Isaac

The birth of Isaac: Genesis 21.1–7
Abraham's test of faith: Genesis 22.1–19
Isaac and Rebekah: 24.1–67
The birth of Esau and Jacob:
Genesis 25.19–26
Jacob tricks Isaac: Genesis 27.1–40

More...

Abraham p.14
Covenant p.17

⁴² When I came to the well today, I silently prayed, "You, LORD, are the God my master Abraham worships, so please lead me to a wife for his son ⁴³ while I am here at the well. When a young woman comes out to get water, I'll ask her to give me a drink. ⁴⁴ If she gives me a drink and offers to get some water for my camels, I'll know she is the one you have chosen."

⁴⁵ Even before I had finished praying, Rebekah came by with a water jar on her shoulder. When she had filled the jar, I asked her for a drink. ⁴⁶ She quickly lowered the jar from her shoulder and said, "Have a drink. Then I'll get water for your camels." So I drank, and after that she got some water for my camels. ⁴⁷ I asked her who her father was, and she answered, "My father is Bethuel the son of Nahor and Milcah." Straight away I put the ring in her nose and the bracelets on her arms. ⁴⁸ Then I bowed my head and gave thanks to the God my master Abraham worships. The LORD had led me straight to my master's relatives, and I had found a wife for his son.

⁴⁹ Now please tell me if you are willing to do the right thing for my master. Will you treat him fairly, or do I have to look for another young woman?

⁵⁰ Laban and Bethuel answered, "The LORD has done this. We have no choice in the matter. ⁵¹ Take Rebekah with you; she can marry your master's son, just as the LORD has said." ⁵² Abraham's servant bowed down and thanked the LORD. ⁵³ Then he gave clothing, as well as silver and gold jewellery, to Rebekah. He also gave expensive gifts to her brother and her mother.

⁵⁴ Abraham's servant and the men with him ate and drank, then spent the night there. The next morning they got up, and the servant told Rebekah's mother and brother, "I would like to go back to my master now."

⁵⁵ "Let Rebekah stay with us for a week or ten days," they answered. "Then she may go."

⁵⁶ But he said, "Don't make me stay any longer. The LORD has already helped me find a wife for my master's son. Now let us return."

⁵⁷ They answered, "Let's ask Rebekah what she wants to do." ⁵⁸ They called her and asked, "Are you willing to leave with this man at once?"

"Yes," she answered.

⁵⁹ So they agreed to let Rebekah and an old family servant woman* leave immediately with Abraham's servant and his men. ⁶⁰ They gave Rebekah their blessing and said, "We pray that God will give you many children and grandchildren and that he will help them defeat their enemies." ⁶¹ Afterwards, Rebekah and the young women who were to travel with her prepared to leave. Then they got on camels and left with Abraham's servant and his men.

⁶² At that time Isaac was living in the southern part of Canaan near a place called "The Well of the Living One who Sees Me".ᵛ ⁶³⁻⁶⁵ One evening he was walking out in the fields, when suddenly he saw a group of people approaching on camels. So he started towards them. Rebekah saw him coming; she got down from her camel, and asked, "Who is that man?"

"He is my master Isaac," the servant answered. Then Rebekah covered her face with her veil.*

⁶⁶ The servant told Isaac everything that had happened.

⁶⁷ Isaac took Rebekah into the tent* where his mother had lived before she died, and Rebekah became his wife. He loved her and was comforted over the loss of his mother.

The death of Abraham

CHAPTER 25

Abraham marries Keturah

¹ Abraham married Keturah, ² and they had six sons: Zimran, Jokshan, Medan, Midian, Ishbak, and Shuah. ³ Later, Jokshan became the father of Sheba and Dedan, and when Dedan grew up, he had three sons: Asshurim, Letushim, and Leummim. ⁴ Midian also had five sons: Ephah, Epher, Hanoch, Abida, and Eldaah.

⁵⁻⁶ While Abraham was still alive, he gave gifts to the sons of Hagar and Keturah. He also sent their sons to live in the east far from

---

*24.59 old family servant woman: Probably Deborah, who had taken care of Rebekah from the time she was born (see 35.8).
*24.63–65 covered . . . veil: Since the veiling of a bride was part of the wedding ceremony, this probably means that she was willing to become the wife of Isaac.
*24.67 took . . . tent: This shows that Rebekah is now the wife of Isaac and the successor of Sarah as the leading woman in the tribe.

his son Isaac, and when Abraham died, he left everything to Isaac.

The death of Abraham

7-8 Abraham died at the ripe old age of one hundred and seventy-five. 9-10 His sons Isaac and Ishmael buried him east of Hebron* in Machpelah Cave that was part of the field Abraham had bought from Ephron son of Zohar the Hittite. Abraham was buried there beside his wife Sarah. 11 God blessed Isaac after this, and Isaac moved to a place called "The Well of the Living One who Sees Me".*

Ishmael's descendants

12 Ishmael was the son of Abraham and Hagar, the slave woman of Sarah. 13 Ishmael had twelve sons, in this order: Nebaioth, Kedar, Adbeel, Mibsam, 14 Mishma, Dumah, Massa, 15 Hadad, Tema, Jetur, Naphish, and Kedemah. 16 Each of Ishmael's sons was a tribal chief, and a village was named after each of them.

17-18 Ishmael had settled in the land east of his brothers, and his sons* settled everywhere from Havilah to Shur, east of Egypt on the way to Asshur.* Ishmael was one hundred and thirty-seven when he died.

Isaac and his family

The birth of Esau and Jacob

19 Isaac was the son of Abraham, 20 and he was forty years old when he married Rebekah, the daughter of Bethuel. She was also the sister of Laban, the Aramean from northern Syria.*

Almost twenty years later, 21 Rebekah still had no children. So Isaac asked the LORD to let her have a child, and the LORD answered his prayer.

22 Before Rebekah gave birth, she knew she was going to have twins, because she could feel them inside her, fighting each other. She thought, "Why is this happening to me?" Finally, she asked the LORD why her twins were fighting, 23 and he told her:

> "Your two sons will become
>   two separate nations.*
> The younger of the two
>   will be stronger,
> and the elder son
>   will be his servant."

---

*25.17-18 Havilah to Shur . . . Asshur: The exact location of these places is not known.
See also: 25.10: Gen 23.3-16. 25.23: Rom 9.12.

Life files

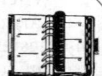

Esau

a.k.a. Edom (Genesis 36.1). The name means 'hairy', referring to his abundant red hair.
Background: Eldest son of Isaac. Grandson of Abraham.

What's the story?

Esau fought with his brother from before he was born. He was a hairy hunter, a red-headed, hot-tempered man of action. His heart ruled his head, such as when he gave away his birthright simply because he fancied a bowl of stew. That may have been his fault, but later he was the innocent party, tricked out of his father's blessing by his scheming twin brother. No wonder he lost his temper; no wonder he vowed to kill Jacob, forcing the younger brother to flee.

Time, as they say, is a great healer. Many years go by and Jacob finally returns to Canaan. Even without his father's blessing, Esau has prospered, and far from punishing Jacob, he runs towards him and kisses him and burst into tears (Genesis 33.4). He then moved to the hill country, where his ancestors were to live.

What's the point?

Esau was the ancestor of the Edomites, and the tricks played by his brother form the background to the animosity between the Edomites and the Israelites. Later Esau becomes a symbol of all those who throw away God's blessings for the sake of their own comfort (Hebrews 12.15–17). For whatever reason, God chose Jacob to continue his line (Malachi 1.2–3). Even though Esau was not chosen, he still prospered. Whatever the strangeness and injustice of it all, Esau still ended up with a lot of riches. Not to mention a lot of sheep.

24 When Rebekah gave birth, 25 the first baby was covered with red hair, so he was named Esau.* 26 The second baby grabbed his brother's heel, so they named him Jacob.* Isaac was sixty years old when they were born.

Esau sells his rights as the firstborn son

27 As Jacob and Esau grew older, Esau liked the outdoors and became a good hunter, while Jacob settled down and became a shepherd. 28 Esau would take the meat of wild animals to his father Isaac, and so Isaac loved him more, but Jacob was his mother's favourite son.

29 One day, Jacob was cooking some stew, when Esau came home hungry 30 and said, "I'm starving to death! Give me some of that red stew at once!" That's how Esau got the name "Edom".*

31 Jacob replied, "Sell me your rights as the firstborn son."*

32 "I'm about to die," Esau answered. "What good will those rights do me?"

33 But Jacob said, "Promise me your birthrights, here and now!" And that's what Esau did. 34 Jacob then gave Esau some bread and some of the bean stew, and when Esau had finished eating and drinking, he just got up and left, showing how little he thought of his rights as the firstborn.

CHAPTER 26

Isaac and Abimelech

1 Once during Abraham's lifetime, the fields had not produced enough grain, and now the same thing happened. So Isaac went to King Abimelech of the Philistines in the land of Gerar, 2 because the LORD had appeared to Isaac and said:

> Isaac, stay away from Egypt! I will show you where I want you to go. 3 You will live there as a foreigner, but I will be with you and bless you. I will keep my promise to your father Abraham by giving this land to you and your descendants.

> 4 I will give you as many descendants as there are stars in the sky, and I will give your descendants all this land. They will be

---

*25.25 Esau: In Hebrew "Esau" sounds like "hairy".
*25.26 Jacob: In Hebrew "Jacob" sounds like "heel".
*25.30 Edom: In Hebrew "Edom" sounds like "red".
*25.31 rights . . . son: The firstborn son inherited the largest amount of property, as well as the leadership of the family.
See also: 25.33: Heb 12.16. 26.3–4: Gen 22.16–18.

Life files

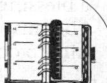

Jacob a.k.a. Israel

Background: Son of Isaac. Brother of Esau. Had twelve famous sons and some girls too. His name means 'he grasps the heel', which is an ancient way of saying 'trickster' – we might say 'he pulls your leg'.)

What's the story?

Jacob starts as a cheat, tricking his brother out of his birthright and his blessing – then fleeing for his life. While running away he dreams of a ladder to heaven with angels on it. God speaks to him, repeating the promise he gave to Abraham. Jacob stays with his uncle, who tricks him into marrying the wrong woman. The trickster is tricked.

Eventually he heads home. He wrestles with a stranger in the night, who dislocates his hip, but Jacob holds him and demands a blessing. Following this he gets a new name, Israel, which means 'he struggles with God'.

He ends his life in Egypt, where his son Joseph is a major player. He gives Joseph's sons a special blessing, preferring the younger to the elder. Where have we seen that before?

What's the point?

Jacob learnt that trust is better than trickery. The twelve tribes who were to descend from his children took on his name, but also his character – a people who struggle with God.

 footsteps

A week with Jacob

Birth and birthrights: Genesis 25.19–34
He steals Esau's blessing: Genesis 27.1–45
Jacob's ladder: Genesis 28.10–22
Jacob's wives: Genesis 29.1–35
Jacob goes home: Genesis 32.1–21
Jacob fights God: Genesis 32.22–32
Final years: Genesis 46.1–4; 48.8–21

More...

The twelve tribes p.56
Joseph p.46
Birthright & blessings p.31
Names p.66
Appearances of God p.99

a blessing to every nation on earth,'
⁵ because Abraham did everything I told
him to do.

⁶ Isaac moved to Gerar ⁷ with his beautiful
wife Rebekah. He was afraid that someone
might kill him to get her, and so he told
everyone that Rebekah was his sister. ⁸ After
Isaac had been there a long time, King
Abimelech looked out of a window and
saw Isaac hugging and kissing Rebekah.
⁹ Abimelech called him in and said, "Rebekah
must be your wife! Why did you say she is
your sister?"

"Because I thought someone would kill
me," Isaac answered.

¹⁰ "Don't you know what you've done?"
Abimelech exclaimed. "If someone had slept
with her, you would have made our whole
nation guilty!" ¹¹ Then Abimelech warned his
people that anyone who even touched Isaac
or Rebekah would be put to death.

¹² Isaac planted grain and had a good
harvest that same year. The LORD blessed him,
¹³ and Isaac was so successful that he became
very rich. ¹⁴ In fact, the Philistines were jealous
of the large number of sheep, goats, and slaves
that Isaac owned, ¹⁵ and they stopped up the
wells that Abraham's servants had dug before
his death. ¹⁶ Finally, Abimelech said, "Isaac,
I want you to leave our country. You have
become too powerful to stay here."

¹⁷ Isaac left and settled in Gerar Valley,
¹⁸ where he cleaned out those wells that the
Philistines had stopped up. Isaac also gave
each of the wells the same name* that
Abraham had given to them. ¹⁹ While his
servants were digging in the valley, they
found a spring-fed well. ²⁰ But the shepherds
of Gerar Valley quarrelled with Isaac's
shepherds and claimed the water belonged to
them. So the well was named "Quarrel",
because they had quarrelled with Isaac.

²¹ Isaac's servants dug another well, and
the shepherds also quarrelled about it. So
that well was named "Jealous". ²² Finally,
they dug one more well. There was no
quarrelling this time, and the well was
named "Lots of Room", because the LORD
had given them room and would make them
very successful.

²³ Isaac went on to Beersheba, ²⁴ where the
LORD appeared to him that night and told
him, "Don't be afraid! I am the God who was

worshipped by your father Abraham, my
servant. I will be with you and bless you, and
because of Abraham I will give you many
descendants." ²⁵ Isaac built an altar there and
worshipped the LORD. Then he set up camp,
and his servants started digging a well.

²⁶ Meanwhile, Abimelech had left Gerar and
was taking his adviser Ahuzzath and his army
commander Phicol to see Isaac. ²⁷ When they
arrived, Isaac asked, "Why are you here?
Didn't you send me away because you
hated me?"

²⁸ They answered, "We now know for
certain that the LORD is with you, and we
have decided there needs to be a peace treaty
between you and us. So let's make a solemn
agreement ²⁹ not to harm each other.
Remember, we have never hurt you, and
when we sent you away, we let you go in
peace. The LORD has truly blessed you."

³⁰ Isaac gave a big feast for them, and
everyone ate and drank. ³¹ Early the next
morning Isaac and the others made a solemn
agreement, then he let them go in peace.

³² Later that same day Isaac's servants came
and said, "We've struck water!" ³³ So Isaac
named the well Shibah,* and the town is still
called Beersheba.*

Esau's foreign wives

³⁴ When Esau was forty, he married Judith
the daughter of Beeri the Hittite and
Basemath the daughter of Elon the Hittite.
³⁵ But these two women brought a lot of grief
to his parents Isaac and Rebekah.

CHAPTER 27

Isaac blesses Jacob

¹ After Isaac had become old and almost
blind, he called in his firstborn son Esau, who
asked him, "Father, what can I do for you?"

² Isaac replied, "I am old and might die at
any time. ³ So take your bow and arrows, then
go out in the fields, and kill a wild animal.
⁴ Cook some of that tasty food that I love so
much and bring it to me. I want to eat it once
more and give you my blessing before I die."

⁵ Rebekah had been listening, and as soon
as Esau left to go hunting, ⁶ she said to Jacob,
"I heard your father tell Esau ⁷ to kill a wild
animal and cook some tasty food for your

*26.18 gave . . . same name: By doing this Isaac
claimed ownership of the wells.
See also: 26.7: Gen 12.13; 20.2.

*26.33 Shibah: In Hebrew "Shibah" sounds
something like "good luck" and "promise".
*26.33 Beersheba: See the note at 21.31.
See also: 26.26: Gen 21.22.

father before he dies. Your father said this because he wants to bless your brother with the LORD as his witness. ⁸ Now, my son, listen carefully to what I want you to do. ⁹ Go and kill two of your best young goats and bring them to me. I'll cook the tasty food that your father loves so much. ¹⁰ Then you can take it to him, so he can eat it and give you his blessing before he dies."

¹¹ "My brother Esau is a hairy man," Jacob reminded her. "And I am not. ¹² If my father touches me and realizes I am trying to trick him, he will put a curse on me instead of giving me a blessing."

¹³ Rebekah insisted, "Let his curse fall on me! Just do what I say and bring me the meat." ¹⁴ So Jacob brought the meat to his mother, and she cooked the tasty food that his father liked. ¹⁵ Then she took Esau's best clothes and put them on Jacob. ¹⁶ She also covered the smooth part of his hands and neck with goatskins ¹⁷ and gave him some bread and the tasty food she had cooked.

¹⁸ Jacob went to his father and said, "Father, here I am."

"Which one of my sons are you?" his father asked.

¹⁹ Jacob replied, "I am Esau, your firstborn, and I have done what you told me. Please sit up and eat the meat I have brought. Then you can give me your blessing."

²⁰ Isaac asked, "My son, how did you find an animal so quickly?"

"The LORD your God was kind to me," Jacob answered.

²¹ "My son," Isaac said, "come closer, where I can touch you and find out if you really are Esau." ²² Jacob went closer. His father touched him and said, "You sound like Jacob, but your hands feel hairy like Esau's." ²³ And so Isaac blessed Jacob, thinking he was Esau.

²⁴ Isaac asked, "Are you really my son Esau?"

"Yes, I am," Jacob answered.

²⁵ So Isaac told him, "Serve me the wild meat, and I can give you my blessing."

Jacob gave him some meat, and he ate it. He also gave him some wine, and he drank it. ²⁶ Then Isaac said, "Son, come over here and kiss me." ²⁷ While Jacob was kissing him, Isaac caught the smell of his clothes and said:

"The smell of my son
is like a field
the LORD has blessed.

See also: 27.27–29: Heb 11.20.

Holy history

Birthright & blessings

When the father died, his property was divided among the surviving sons. However, the eldest boy always got a larger share – usually a double portion (Deuteronomy 21.17).

Birthright was about more than property. The eldest son became the 'head of the household', with authority over his brothers and sisters. He also had other responsibilities, such as looking after his mother or any unmarried sisters. Daughters did not inherit from their father unless there were no surviving sons.

Birthright, however, was not automatic. Esau swapped his birthright for a meat stew (Genesis 25.29–34). Later, his grandson Reuben lost his birthright because he committed incest with his father's concubine (Genesis 35.22; 49.3–4).

By the time of the New Testament, things had changed. Greeks and Romans used wills to pass on their property, as we do today. Still, Paul uses the theme of birthright to show how all Christians are 'heirs' to God. We will all share equally in his glory (Romans 8.16–17).

Blessings

When Jacob tricks his brother out of his blessing, the modern reader is a bit confused. Why doesn't Isaac just say 'Oops. Wrong one. Let's start again'? Why can't he just press the rewind button and re-record the blessing into the right microphone?

In the Old Testament world, words had power. A blessing like this was a legally binding announcement, an official 'handover' which Isaac could not withdraw. That's why Isaac shakes with shock when he finds out the truth; he knows that the promise could not be taken back. By giving his blessing he had officially given Jacob power over Esau, making him 'lord' over his brother (Genesis 27.27–29).

28 God will bless you, my son,
    with dew from heaven
and with fertile fields,
    rich with grain and grapes.
29 Nations will be your servants
    and bow down to you.
You will rule over your brothers,
    and they will kneel
        at your feet.
Anyone who curses you
    will be cursed;
anyone who blesses you
    will be blessed."

30 Straight after Isaac had given Jacob his blessing and Jacob had gone, Esau came back from hunting. 31 He cooked the tasty food, brought it to his father, and said, "Father, please sit up and eat the meat I have brought you, so you can give me your blessing."

32 "Who are you?" Isaac asked.

"I am Esau, your firstborn son."

33 Isaac started trembling and said, "Then who brought me some wild meat just before you came in? I ate it and gave him a blessing that cannot be taken back."

34 Esau cried loudly and begged, "Father, give me a blessing too!"

35 Isaac answered, "Your brother tricked me and stole your blessing."

36 Esau replied, "My brother deserves the name Jacob,* because he has already cheated me twice. The first time he cheated me out of my rights as the firstborn son, and now he has cheated me out of my blessing." Then Esau asked his father, "Don't you still have any blessing left for me?"

37 "My son," Isaac answered, "I have made Jacob the ruler over you and your brothers, and all of you will be his servants. I have also promised him all the grain and grapes that he needs. There's nothing left that I can do for you."

38 "Father," Esau asked, "don't you have more than one blessing? You can surely give me a blessing too!" Then Esau started crying again.

39 So his father said:

"Your home will be far
    from that fertile land,
where dew comes down
    from the heavens.

40 You will live by the power
    of your sword
    and be your brother's slave.
But when you decide to be free,
    you will break loose."

41 Esau hated his brother Jacob because he had stolen the blessing that was supposed to be his. So he said to himself, "Just as soon as my father dies, I'll kill Jacob."

42 When Rebekah found out what Esau planned to do, she sent for Jacob and told him, "Son, your brother Esau is just waiting for the time when he can kill you. 43 Now listen carefully and do what I say. Go to the home of my brother Laban in Haran 44 and stay with him for a while. When Esau stops being angry 45 and forgets what you have done to him, I'll send for you to come home. Why should I lose both of my sons on the same day?"*

46 Rebekah later told Isaac, "Those Hittite wives of Esau are making my life miserable! If Jacob marries a Hittite woman, I'd be better off dead."

CHAPTER 28

Isaac's instructions to Jacob

1 Isaac called in Jacob, then gave him a blessing, and said:

Don't marry any of those Canaanite women. 2 Go at once to your mother's father Bethuel in northern Syria' and choose a wife from one of the daughters of Laban, your mother's brother. 3 I pray that God All-Powerful will bless you with many descendants and let you become a great nation. 4 May he bless you with the land he gave Abraham, so that you will take over this land where we now live as foreigners.

5 Isaac then sent Jacob to stay with Rebekah's brother Laban, the son of Bethuel the Aramean.

Esau marries the daughter of Ishmael

6 Esau found out that his father Isaac had blessed Jacob and had warned him not to marry any of the Canaanite women. He also learnt that Jacob had been sent to find a wife in northern Syria' 7 and that he had obeyed

---

*27.36 Jacob: In Hebrew "Jacob" sounds like "cheat".
See also: 27.29: Gen 12.3. 27.36: Gen 25.29–34.
27.38: Heb 12.17. 27.39–40: Heb 11.20.

*27.45 lose . . . day: Esau would be hunted down as a murderer if he killed Jacob, and so Rebekah would lose both of her sons.
See also: 27.40: Gen 36.8; 2 King 8.20. 28.4: Gen 17.4–8.

his father and mother. 8 Esau already had several wives, but he realized at last how much his father hated the Canaanite women. 9 So he married Ishmael's daughter Mahalath, who was the sister of Nebaioth* and the granddaughter of Abraham.

Jacob and his family

Jacob's dream at Bethel

10 Jacob left the town of Beersheba and started out for Haran. 11 At sunset he stopped for the night and went to sleep, resting his head on a large rock. 12 In a dream he saw a ladder' that reached from earth to heaven, and God's angels were going up and down on it.

13 The LORD was standing beside the ladder' and said:

I am the LORD God who was worshipped by Abraham and Isaac. I will give to you and your family the land on which you are now sleeping. 14 Your descendants will spread over the earth in all directions and will become as numerous as the specks of dust. Your family will be a blessing to all people.' 15 Wherever you go, I will watch over you, then later I will bring you back to this land. I won't leave you — I will do all I have promised.

16 Jacob woke up suddenly and thought, "The LORD is in this place, and I didn't even know it." 17 Then Jacob became frightened and said, "This is a fearsome place! It must be the house of God and the ladder' to heaven."

18 When Jacob got up early the next morning, he took the rock that he had used for a pillow and stood it up for a place of worship. Then he poured olive oil on the rock to dedicate it to God, 19 and he named the place Bethel.* Before that it had been named Luz.

20 Jacob solemnly promised God, "If you go with me and watch over me as I travel, and if you give me food and clothes 21 and bring me safely home again, you will be my God. 22 This rock will be your house, and I will give back to you a tenth of everything you give me."

28.9 Nebaioth: Ishmael's eldest son (see 25.13).
28.19 Bethel: In Hebrew "Bethel" means "House of God".
See also: 28.12: John 1.51. 28.13: Gen 13.14–15. 28.14: Gen 12.3; 22.18.

CHAPTER 29

Jacob arrives at Laban's home

1 As Jacob continued on his way to the east, 2 he looked out in a field and saw a well where shepherds took their sheep for water. Three flocks of sheep were lying around the well, which was covered with a large rock. 3 Shepherds would roll the rock away when all their sheep had gathered there. Then after the sheep had been watered, the shepherds would roll the rock back over the mouth of the well.

4 Jacob asked the shepherds, "Where are you from?"

"We're from Haran," they answered.

5 Then he asked, "Do you know Nahor's grandson Laban?"

"Yes we do," they replied.

6 "How is he?" Jacob asked.

"He's fine," they answered. "And here comes his daughter Rachel with the sheep."

7 Jacob told them, "Look, the sun is still high up in the sky, and it's too early to bring in the rest of the flocks. Water your sheep and take them back to the pasture."

8 But they replied, "We can't do that until they all get here, and the rock has been rolled away from the well."

9 While Jacob was still talking with the men, his cousin Rachel came up with her father's sheep. 10 When Jacob saw her and his uncle's sheep, he rolled the rock away and watered the sheep. 11 He then kissed Rachel and started crying because he was so happy. 12 He told her that he was the son of her aunt Rebekah, and she ran and told her father about him.

13 As soon as Laban heard the news, he ran out to meet Jacob. He hugged and kissed him and brought him to his home, where Jacob told him everything that had happened. 14 Laban said, "You are my nephew, and you are like one of my own family."

Jacob marries Leah and Rachel

After Jacob had been there for a month, 15 Laban said to him, "You shouldn't have to work without pay, just because you are a relative of mine. What do you want me to give you?"

16–17 Laban had two daughters. Leah was older than Rachel, but her eyes didn't sparkle,' while Rachel was beautiful and had a good figure. 18 Since Jacob was in love with Rachel, he answered, "If you will let me marry Rachel, I'll work seven years for you."

19 Laban replied, "It's better for me to let you marry Rachel than for someone else to

have her. So stay and work for me." ²⁰ Jacob worked seven years for Laban, but the time seemed like only a few days, because he loved Rachel so much.

²¹ Jacob said to Laban, "The time is up, and I want to marry Rachel now!" ²² So Laban gave a big feast and invited all their neighbours. ²³ But that evening he brought Leah to Jacob, who married her and spent the night with her. ²⁴ Laban also gave Zilpah to Leah as her servant woman.

²⁵ The next morning Jacob found out that he had married Leah, and he asked Laban, "Why did you do this to me? Didn't I work to get Rachel? Why did you trick me?"

²⁶ Laban replied, "In our country the elder daughter must get married first. ²⁷ After you spend this week* with Leah, you may also marry Rachel. But you will have to work for me another seven years."

²⁸⁻³⁰ At the end of the week of celebration, Laban let Jacob marry Rachel, and he gave her his servant woman Bilhah. Jacob loved Rachel more than he did Leah, but he had to work another seven years for Laban.

³¹ The LORD knew that Jacob loved Rachel more than he did Leah, and so he gave children to Leah, but not to Rachel. ³² Leah gave birth to a son and named him Reuben,* because she said, "The LORD has taken away my sorrow. Now my husband will love me more than he does Rachel." ³³ She had a second son and named him Simeon,* because she said, "The LORD has heard that my husband doesn't love me." ³⁴ When Leah's third son was born, she said, "Now my husband will hold me close." So this son was named Levi.* ³⁵ She had one more son and named him Judah,* because she said, "I'll praise the LORD!"

CHAPTER 30

Problems between Rachel and Leah

¹ Rachel was very jealous of Leah for having children, and she said to Jacob, "I'll die if you don't give me some children!"

² But Jacob became upset with Rachel and answered, "Don't blame me! I'm not God."

³ "Here, take my servant Bilhah," Rachel told him. "Have children by her, and I'll let them be born on my knees to show that they are mine."

⁴ Then Rachel let Jacob marry Bilhah, ⁵ and they had a son. ⁶ Rachel named him Dan,* because she said, "God has answered my prayers. He has judged me and given me a son." ⁷ When Bilhah and Jacob had a second son, ⁸ Rachel said, "I've struggled hard with my sister, and I've won!" So she named the boy Naphtali.*

⁹ When Leah realized she could not have any more children, she let Jacob marry her servant Zilpah, ¹⁰ and they had a son. ¹¹ "I'm really lucky," Leah said, and she named the boy Gad.* ¹² When they had another son, ¹³ Leah exclaimed, "I'm happy now, and all the women will say how happy I am." So she named him Asher.*

Love flowers

¹⁴ During the time of the wheat harvest, Reuben found some love flowers* and took them to his mother Leah. Rachel asked Leah for some of them, ¹⁵ but Leah said, "It's bad enough that you stole my husband! Now you want my son's love flowers too."

"All right," Rachel answered. "Let me have the flowers, and you can sleep with Jacob tonight."

¹⁶ That evening when Jacob came in from the fields, Leah told him, "You're sleeping with me tonight. I hired you with my son's love flowers."

They slept together that night, ¹⁷ and God answered Leah's prayers by giving her a fifth son. ¹⁸ Leah shouted, "God has rewarded me for letting Jacob marry my servant," and she named the boy Issachar.*

¹⁹ When Leah had another son, ²⁰ she exclaimed, "God has given me a wonderful

---

*29.27 this week: The wedding feast lasted for seven days (see Judges 14.12,17).
*29.32 Reuben: In Hebrew "Reuben" means "Look, a son!"
*29.33 Simeon: In Hebrew "Simeon" sounds like "someone who hears".
*29.34 hold me close . . . Levi: In Hebrew "Levi" sounds like "hold (someone) close".
*29.35 Judah: In Hebrew "Judah" sounds like "praise".

*30.6 Dan: In Hebrew "Dan" means "judge".
*30.8 Naphtali: In Hebrew "Naphtali" means "struggle" or "contest".
*30.11 Gad: In Hebrew "Gad" means "lucky".
*30.13 Asher: In Hebrew "Asher" means "happy".
*30.14 love flowers: Also called "mandrakes", a flowering plant that was thought to give sexual powers.
*30.18 Issachar: In Hebrew "Issachar" sounds like "reward".

gift, and my husband will praise me for giving him six sons." So she named the boy Zebulun.* ²¹ Later, Leah had a daughter and named her Dinah.

²²⁻²³ Finally, God remembered Rachel — he answered her prayer by giving her a son. "God has taken away my disgrace," she said. ²⁴ "I'll name the boy Joseph,* and I'll pray that the LORD will give me another son."

Jacob and Laban

²⁵ After Joseph was born, Jacob said to Laban, "Release me from our agreement* and let me return to my own country. ²⁶ You know how hard I've worked for you, so let me take my wives and children and leave."

²⁷⁻²⁸ But Laban told him, "If you really are my friend, stay on, and I'll pay whatever you ask. I'm sure' the LORD has blessed me because of you."

²⁹ Jacob answered:

You've seen how hard I've worked for you, and you know how your flocks and herds have grown under my care. ³⁰ You didn't have much before I came, but the LORD has blessed everything I have ever done for you. Now it's time for me to start looking after my own family.

³¹ "How much do you want me to pay you?" Laban asked.

Then Jacob told him:

I don't want you to pay me anything. Just do one thing, and I'll take care of your sheep and goats. ³² Let me go through your flocks and herds and take the sheep and goats that are either spotted or speckled* and the black lambs. That's all you need to give me. ³³ In the future you can easily find out if I've been honest. Just look and see if my animals are either spotted or speckled, or if the lambs are black. If they aren't, they've been stolen from you.

³⁴ "I agree to that," was Laban's response. ³⁵ Before the end of the day, Laban had separated his spotted and speckled animals and the black lambs from the others and had put his sons in charge of them. ³⁶ Then Laban made Jacob keep the rest of the sheep and goats at a distance of three days' journey.

³⁷ Jacob cut branches from some poplar trees and from some almond and evergreen trees. He peeled off part of the bark and made the branches look spotted and speckled. ³⁸ Then he put the branches where the sheep and goats would see them* while they were drinking from the water trough. The goats mated there ³⁹ in front of the branches, and their young were spotted and speckled.

⁴⁰ Some of the sheep that Jacob was keeping for Laban were already spotted. And when the others were ready to mate, he made sure that they faced in the direction of the spotted and black ones. In this way, Jacob built up a flock of sheep for himself and did not put them with the other sheep.

⁴¹ When the stronger sheep were mating near the drinking place, Jacob made sure that the spotted branches were there. ⁴² But he would not put out the branches when the weaker animals were mating. So Jacob got all the healthy animals, and Laban got what was left. ⁴³ Jacob soon became rich and successful. He owned many sheep, goats, camels, and donkeys, as well as a lot of slaves.

CHAPTER 31

Jacob runs from Laban

¹ Jacob heard that Laban's sons were complaining, "Jacob is now a rich man, and he got everything he owns from our father." ² Jacob also noticed that Laban was not as friendly as he had been before. ³ One day the LORD said, "Jacob, go back to your relatives in the land of your ancestors, and I will bless you."

⁴ Jacob sent for Rachel and Leah to meet him in the field where he kept his sheep, ⁵ and he told them:

Your father isn't as friendly with me as he used to be, but the God my ancestors worshipped has been on my side. ⁶ You

---

*30.20 Zebulun: In Hebrew "Zebulun" sounds like "give" and "praise".
*30.24 Joseph: In Hebrew "Joseph" sounds like "take away" and "add".
*30.25 Release . . . agreement: Jacob had agreed to work seven years for each of Laban's two daughters (see 29.18).
*30.32 spotted or speckled: In ancient times sheep were usually white, and goats were usually black or dark brown; only a few sheep would have black spots, and only a few goats would have white spots.

---

*30.38 would see them: It was believed by some that what sheep and goats saw at the time of breeding would determine the colour of their young.

know that I have worked hard for your father [7] and that he keeps cheating me by changing my wages time after time. But God has protected me. [8] When your father said the speckled sheep would be my wages, all of them were speckled. And when he said the spotted ones would be mine, all of them were spotted. [9] That's how God has taken sheep and goats from your father and given them to me.

[10] Once, when the flocks were mating, I dreamed that all the rams were either spotted or speckled. [11] Then God's angel called me by name. I answered, [12] and he said, "Notice that all the rams are either spotted or speckled. I know everything Laban is doing to you, [13] and I am the God you worshipped at Bethel,' when you poured olive oil on a rock and made a promise to me. Leave here straight away and return to the land where you were born."

[14] Rachel and Leah said to Jacob:

There's nothing left for us to inherit from our father. [15] He treats us like foreigners and has even cheated us out of the bride price* that should have been ours. [16] Now do whatever God tells you to do. Even the property God took from our father and gave to you really belongs to us and our children.

[17] Then Jacob, his wives, and his children got on camels and left [18] for the home of his father Isaac in Canaan. Jacob took all the flocks, herds, and other property that he had got in northern Syria.'

[19] Before Rachel left, she stole the household idols* while Laban was out shearing his sheep. [20] Jacob tricked Laban the Aramean' by not saying that he intended to leave. [21] When Jacob crossed the River Euphrates and headed for the hill country of Gilead, he took with him everything he owned.

Laban catches up with Jacob

[22] Three days later Laban found out that Jacob had gone. [23] So he took some of his relatives along and chased after Jacob for seven days, before catching up with him in the hill country of Gilead. [24] But God appeared to Laban in a dream that night and warned, "Don't say a word to Jacob. Don't make a threat or a promise."

[25] Jacob had set up camp in the hill country of Gilead, when Laban and his relatives came and set up camp in another part of the hill country. Laban went to Jacob [26] and said:

Look what you've done! You've tricked me and run off with my daughters like a kidnapper. [27] Why did you sneak away without telling me? I would have given you a going-away party with singing and with music on tambourines and harps. [28] You didn't even give me a chance to kiss my own grandchildren and daughters goodbye. That was really foolish. [29] I could easily hurt you, but the God your father worshipped has warned me not to make any threats or promises.

[30] I can understand why you were eager to return to your father, but why did you have to steal my idols?

[31] Jacob answered, "I left secretly because I was afraid you would take your daughters from me by force. [32] If you find that any one of us has taken your idols, I'll have that person killed. Let your relatives be witnesses. Show me what belongs to you, and you can take it back." Jacob did not realize that Rachel had stolen the household idols.

[33] Laban searched the tents of Jacob, Leah, and the two servant women,* but did not find the idols. Then he started for Rachel's tent. [34] She had already hidden them in the cushion she used as a saddle and was sitting on it. Laban searched everywhere and did not find them. [35] Rachel said, "Father, please don't be angry with me for not getting up; I am having my period." Laban kept on searching, but still did not find the idols.

[36] Jacob became very angry and said to Laban:

What have I done wrong? Have I committed some crime? Is that why you hunted me down? [37] After searching through everything I have, did you find anything of yours? If so, put it here, where

---

*31.15 bride price: Usually the husband-to-be paid a bride price to the father of the bride. But Jacob didn't pay Laban a bride price for either Rachel or Leah. Instead he was tricked into working fourteen years to get the bride he loved. So there was no money for either of Laban's daughters.

*31.19 household idols: These were thought to protect the household from danger. It is also possible that the person who had them would inherit the family property.

See also: 31.13: Gen 28.18–22.

*31.33 two servant women: Bilhah and Zilpah (see 30.4,9).

your relatives and mine can see it. Then we can decide what to do.

³⁸ In all the twenty years that I've worked for you, not one of your sheep or goats has had a miscarriage, and I've never eaten even one of your rams. ³⁹ If a wild animal killed one of your sheep or goats, I paid for it myself. In fact, you demanded the full price, whether the animal was killed during the day or at night.* ⁴⁰ I sweated every day, and I couldn't sleep at night because of the cold.

⁴¹ I had to work fourteen of these twenty long years to earn your two daughters and another six years to buy your sheep and goats. During that time you kept changing my wages. ⁴² If the fearsome God* worshipped by Abraham and my father Isaac had not been on my side, you would have sent me away without a thing. But God saw my hard work, and he knew the trouble I was in, so he helped me. Then last night he told you how wrong you were.

Jacob and Laban make an agreement

⁴³ Laban said to Jacob, "Leah and Rachel are my daughters, and their children belong to me. All these sheep you are taking are really mine too. In fact, everything you have belongs to me. But there is nothing I can do to keep my daughters and their children. ⁴⁴ So I am ready to make an agreement with you, and we will pile up some large rocks here to remind us of the agreement."

⁴⁵ After Jacob had set up a large rock, ⁴⁶ he told his men to get some more rocks and pile them up next to it. Then Jacob and Laban ate a meal together beside the rocks. ⁴⁷ Laban named the pile of rocks Jegar Sahadutha.* But Jacob named it Galeed.* ⁴⁸ Laban said to Jacob, "This pile of rocks will remind us of our agreement." That's why the place was named Galeed. ⁴⁹ Laban also said, "This pile of rocks means that the LORD will watch us both while we are apart from each other." So the place was also named Mizpah.*

⁵⁰ Then Laban said:

---

*31.39 you demanded . . . night: A shepherd was not responsible for sheep and goats killed by wild animals, if the shepherd could supply proof of how they were killed.
*31.47 Jegar Sahadutha: In Aramaic "Jegar Sahadutha" means "a pile of rocks to remind us".
*31.47 Galeed: In Hebrew "Galeed" means "a pile of rocks to remind us".
*31.49 Mizpah: In Hebrew "Mizpah" sounds like "a place from which to watch".

If you ill-treat my daughters or marry other women, I may not know about it, but remember, God is watching us! ⁵¹⁻⁵² Both this pile of rocks and this large rock have been set up between us as a reminder. I must never go beyond them to attack you, and you must never go beyond them to attack me. ⁵³ My father Nahor, your grandfather Abraham, and their ancestors all worshipped the same God, and he will make sure that we each keep the agreement.

Then Jacob made a promise in the name of the fearsome God* his father Isaac had worshipped. ⁵⁴ Jacob killed an animal and offered it as a sacrifice there on the mountain, and he invited his men to eat with him. After the meal they spent the night on the mountain. ⁵⁵ Early the next morning, Laban kissed his daughters and his grandchildren goodbye, then he left to go back home.

CHAPTER 32

Jacob gets ready to meet Esau

¹ As Jacob was on his way back home, some of God's angels came and met him. ² When Jacob saw them, he said, "This is God's camp." So he named the place Mahanaim.*

³ Jacob sent messengers on ahead to Esau, who lived in the land of Seir, also known as Edom. ⁴ Jacob told them to say to Esau, "Master, I am your servant! I have lived with Laban all this time, ⁵ and now I own cattle, donkeys, and sheep, as well as many slaves. Master, I am sending these messengers in the hope that you will be kind to me."

⁶ When the messengers returned, they told Jacob, "We went to your brother Esau, and now he is heading this way with four hundred men."

⁷ Jacob was so frightened that he divided his people, sheep, cattle, and camels into two groups. ⁸ He thought, "If Esau attacks one group, perhaps the other can escape."

⁹ Then Jacob prayed:

You, LORD, are the God who was worshipped by my grandfather Abraham and by my father Isaac. You told me to return home to my family, and you promised to be with me and make me successful. ¹⁰ I don't deserve all the good things you have done for me, your servant.

---

*32.2 Mahanaim: In Hebrew "Mahanaim" means "two camps".

When I first crossed the Jordan, I had only my walking stick, but now I have two large groups of people and animals. ¹¹ Please rescue me from my brother. I am afraid he will come and attack not only me, but my wives and children as well. ¹² But you have promised that I would be a success and that some day it will be as hard to count my descendants as it is to count the stars in the sky.

¹³ After Jacob had spent the night there, he chose some animals as gifts for Esau: ¹⁴⁻¹⁵ two hundred female goats and twenty males, two hundred female sheep and twenty males, thirty female camels with their young, forty cows and ten bulls, and twenty female donkeys and ten males.

¹⁶ Jacob put servants in charge of each herd and told them, "Go ahead of me and keep a space between each herd." ¹⁷ Then he said to the servant in charge of the first herd, "When Esau meets you, he will ask whose servant you are. He will want to know where you are going and who owns those animals in front of you. ¹⁸ So tell him, 'They belong to your servant Jacob, who is coming this way. He is sending them as a gift to his master Esau.' "

¹⁹ Jacob also told the men in charge of the second and third herds and those who followed to say the same thing when they met Esau. ²⁰ And Jacob told them to be sure to say that he was just behind them. Jacob hoped the gifts would make Esau friendly, so Esau would be glad to see him when they met. ²¹ Jacob's men took the gifts on ahead of him, but he spent the night in camp.

Jacob's name is changed to Israel

²²⁻²³ Jacob got up in the middle of the night and took his wives, his eleven children, and everything he owned across to the other side of the River Jabbok for safety. ²⁴ Afterwards, Jacob went back and spent the rest of the night alone.

A man came and fought with Jacob until just before daybreak. ²⁵ When the man saw that he could not win, he struck Jacob on the hip and threw it out of joint. ²⁶ They kept on wrestling until the man said, "Let go of me! It's almost daylight."

"You can't go until you bless me," Jacob replied.

²⁷ Then the man asked, "What is your name?"

"Jacob," he answered.

²⁸ The man said, "Your name will no longer be Jacob. You have wrestled with God and with men, and you have won. That's why your name will be Israel."*

²⁹ Jacob said, "Now tell me your name."

"Don't you know who I am?" he asked. And he blessed Jacob.

³⁰ Jacob said, "I have seen God face to face, and I am still alive." So he named the place Peniel.* ³¹ The sun was coming up as Jacob was leaving Peniel. He was limping because he had been struck on the hip, ³² and the muscle on his hip joint had been injured. That's why even today the people of Israel don't eat the hip muscle of any animal.

CHAPTER 33

Jacob meets Esau

¹ Later that day Jacob met Esau coming with his four hundred men. So Jacob made his children walk with their mothers. ² The two servant women, Zilpah and Bilhah, together with their children went first, followed by Leah and her children, then by Rachel and Joseph. ³ Jacob himself walked in front of them all, bowing to the ground seven times as he came near his brother.

⁴ But Esau ran towards Jacob and hugged and kissed him. Then the two brothers started crying.

⁵ When Esau noticed the women and children he asked, "Whose children are these?"

Jacob answered, "These are the ones the Lord has been kind enough to give to me, your servant."

⁶ Then the two servant women and their children came and bowed down to Esau. ⁷ Next, Leah and her children came and bowed down; finally, Joseph and Rachel also came and bowed down.

⁸ Esau asked Jacob, "What did you mean by these herds I met along the road?"

"Master," Jacob answered, "I sent them so that you would be friendly to me."

⁹ "But, brother, I already have plenty," Esau replied. "Keep them for yourself."

¹⁰ "No!" Jacob said. "Please accept these gifts as a sign of your friendship for me. When you welcomed me and I saw your face, it was like seeing the face of God. ¹¹ Please

*32.28 Israel: In Hebrew one meaning of "Israel" is "a man who wrestles with God".
*32.30 Peniel: In Hebrew "Peniel" means "face of God".

See also: 32.28: Gen 35.10. 32.29: Judg 13.17–18.

accept these gifts I brought to you. God has been good to me, and I have everything I need." Jacob kept insisting until Esau accepted the gifts.

¹² "Let's get ready to travel," Esau said. "I'll go along with you."

¹³ But Jacob answered, "Master, you know travelling is hard on children, and I have to look after the sheep and goats that are nursing their young. If my animals travel too much in one day, they will all die. ¹⁴ Why don't you go on ahead and let me travel along slowly with the children, the herds, and the flocks. We can meet again in the country of Edom."

¹⁵ Esau replied, "Let me leave some of my men with you."

"You don't have to do that," Jacob answered. "I am happy, simply knowing that you are friendly to me."

¹⁶ So Esau left for Edom. ¹⁷ But Jacob went to Succoth,* where he built a house for himself and set up shelters for his animals. That's why the place is called Succoth.

Jacob arrives at Shechem

¹⁸ After leaving northern Syria,ᵇ Jacob arrived safely at Shechem in Canaan and set up camp outside the city. ¹⁹ The land where he camped was owned by the descendants of Hamor, the father of Shechem. So Jacob paid them one hundred pieces of silverᵇ for the property, ²⁰ then he set up his tents and built an altar there to honour the God of Israel.

CHAPTER 34

Dinah is raped

¹ Dinah, the daughter of Jacob and Leah, went to visit some of the women who lived there. ² She was seen by Hamor's son Shechem, the leader of the Hivites, and he grabbed her and raped her. ³ But Shechem was attracted to Dinah, so he told her how much he loved her. ⁴ He even asked his father to get her for his wife.

⁵ Meanwhile, Jacob heard what had happened. But his sons were out in the fields with the cattle, so he did not do anything at the time. ⁶ Hamor arrived at Jacob's home ⁷ just as Jacob's sons were coming in from work. When they learnt that their sister had been raped, they became furiously angry.

Nothing is more disgraceful than rape, and it should not be tolerated in Israel.

⁸ Hamor said to Jacob and his sons:

My son Shechem really loves Dinah. Please let him marry her. ⁹ Why don't you start letting your families marry into our families and ours marry into yours? ¹⁰ You can share this land with us. Move freely about until you find the property you want; then buy it and settle down here.

¹¹ Shechem added, "Do this favour for me, and I'll give whatever you want. ¹² Ask anything, no matter how expensive. I'll do anything, just let me marry Dinah."

¹³ Jacob's sons wanted to get even with Shechem and his father because of what had happened to their sister. ¹⁴ So they tricked them by saying:

You're not circumcised!* It would be a disgrace for us to let you marry Dinah now. ¹⁵ But we will let you marry her, if you and the other men in your tribe get circumcised. ¹⁶ Then your families can marry into ours, and ours can marry into yours, and we can live together like one nation. ¹⁷ But if you don't agree to get circumcised, we'll take Dinah and leave this place.

¹⁸ Hamor and Shechem liked what was said. ¹⁹ Shechem was the most respected person in his family, and he was so in love with Dinah that he hurried off to get everything done. ²⁰ The two men met with the other leaders of their city and told them:

²¹ These people really are friendly. Why not let them move freely about until they find the property they want? There's enough land here for them and for us. Then our families can marry into theirs, and theirs can marry into ours.

²² We have to do only one thing before they will agree to stay here and become one nation with us. Our men will have to be circumcised like their men. ²³ Just think! We'll get their property, as well as their flocks and herds. All we have to do is to agree, and they will live here with us.

²⁴ Every grown man followed this advice and got circumcised.

*33.17 Succoth: In Hebrew "Succoth" means "shelters".
See also: 33.19: Josh 24.32; John 4.5.

*34.14 You're not circumcised: Israelite boys were circumcised when they were eight days old, and no uncircumcised man could be part of the people of Israel.

Dinah's brothers take revenge

25 Three days later the men who had been circumcised were still weak from pain. So Simeon and Levi,* two of Dinah's brothers, attacked with their swords and killed every man in town, 26 including Hamor and Shechem. Then they took Dinah and left. 27 Jacob's other sons came and took everything they wanted. All this was done because of the horrible thing that had happened to their sister. 28 They took sheep, goats, donkeys, and everything else that was in the town or the fields. 29 After taking everything of value from the houses, they dragged away the wives and children of their victims.

30 Jacob said to Simeon and Levi, "Look what you've done! Now I'm in real trouble with the Canaanites and Perizzites who live around here. There aren't many of us, and if they attack, they'll kill everyone in my household."

31 They answered, "Was it right to let our own sister be treated that way?"

CHAPTER 35

Jacob returns to Bethel

1 God told Jacob, "Return to Bethel, where I appeared to you when you were running from your brother Esau. Make your home there and build an altar for me."

2 Jacob said to his family and to everyone else who was travelling with him:

Get rid of your foreign gods! Then make yourselves acceptable to worship God and put on clean clothes. 3 Afterwards, we'll go to Bethel. I will build an altar there for God, who answered my prayers when I was in trouble and who has always been at my side.

4 So everyone gave Jacob their idols and their earrings,* and he buried them under the oak tree near Shechem.

5 While Jacob and his family were travelling through Canaan, God terrified the people in the towns so much that no one dared bother them. 6 Finally, they reached Bethel, also known as Luz. 7 Jacob built an altar there and called it "God of Bethel", because that was the place where God had appeared to him when

he was running from Esau. 8 While they were there, Rebekah's personal servant Deborah* died. They buried her under an oak tree and called it "Weeping Oak".

God blesses Jacob at Bethel

9-11 After Jacob came back to the land of Canaan, God appeared to him again. This time he gave Jacob a new name and blessed him by saying:

I am God All-Powerful, and from now on your name will be Israel* instead of Jacob. You will have many children. Your descendants will become nations, and some of the men in your family will even be kings. 12 I will give you the land that I promised Abraham and Isaac, and it will belong to your family for ever.

13 After God had gone, 14 Jacob set up a large rock, so that he would remember what had happened there. Then he poured wine and olive oil on the rock to show that it was dedicated to God, 15 and he named the place Bethel.*

Benjamin is born

16 Jacob and his family had left Bethel and were still a long way from Ephrath, when the time came for Rachel's baby to be born. 17 She was having a rough time, but the woman who was helping her said, "Don't worry! It's a boy." 18 Rachel was at the point of death, and just before dying, she said, "I'll name him Benoni."* But Jacob called him Benjamin.*

19 Rachel was buried beside the road to Ephrath, which is also called Bethlehem. 20 Jacob set up a tombstone over her grave, and it is still there. 21 Jacob, also known as Israel, travelled to the south of Eder Tower, where he set up camp. 22 During their time there, Jacob's eldest son Reuben slept with Bilhah, who was one of Jacob's other wives.* And Jacob found out about it.

---

*34.25 Simeon and Levi: Dinah's full brothers.
*35.4 earrings: These would have had symbols of foreign gods on them.
See also: 35.1: Gen 28.11-17.

*35.8 Deborah: See 24.59 and the note there.
*35.9-11 Israel: See the note at 32.28.
*35.15 Bethel: See the note at 28.19.
*35.18 Benoni: In Hebrew "Benoni" means "Son of my Sorrow".
*35.18 Benjamin: In Hebrew "Benjamin" can mean "Son at my Right Side" (the place of power).
*35.22 other wives: See the note at 22.24. Bilhah had been Rachel's servant woman (see 29.28-30).
See also: 35.9-11: Gen 32.28. 35.11-12: Gen 17.4-8. 35.14-15: Gen 28.18-19. 35.22: Gen 49.4.

Jacob's twelve sons

23-26 Jacob had twelve sons while living in northern Syria.' His firstborn Reuben was the son of Leah, who later gave birth to Simeon, Levi, Judah, Issachar, and Zebulun. Leah's servant Zilpah had two sons: Gad and Asher.

Jacob and his wife Rachel had Joseph and Benjamin. Rachel's servant woman Bilhah had two more sons: Dan and Naphtali.

Isaac dies

27 Jacob went to his father Isaac at Hebron, also called Mamre or Kiriath-Arba, where Isaac's father Abraham had lived as a foreigner. 28-29 Isaac died at the ripe old age of one hundred and eighty, then his sons Esau and Jacob buried him.

Esau and his family

CHAPTER 36

1 Esau, also known as Edom, had many descendants. 2 He married three Canaanite women: the first was Adah, the daughter of Elon the Hittite; the second was Oholibamah, the daughter of Anah and the granddaughter of Zibeon the Hivite; 3 the third was Basemath, who was Ishmael's daughter and Nebaioth's sister.

4-5 Esau and his three wives had five sons while in Canaan. Adah's son was Eliphaz; Basemath's son was Reuel; Oholibamah's three sons were Jeush, Jalam, and Korah.

6 Esau took his children and wives, his relatives and servants, his animals and possessions he had got while in Canaan, and moved far from Jacob. 7 He did this because the land was too crowded and could not support him and his brother with their flocks and herds. 8 That's why Esau made his home in the hill country of Seir.

9-14 Esau lived in the hill country of Seir and was the ancestor of the Edomites. Esau had three wives: Adah, Basemath, and Oholibamah. Here is a list of his descendants: Esau and Adah had a son named Eliphaz, whose sons were Teman, Omar, Zepho, Gatam, and Kenaz. Timna was the other wife* of Esau's son Eliphaz, and she had a son named Amalek.

Esau and Basemath had a son named Reuel, whose sons were Nahath, Zerah, Shammah, and Mizzah.

Esau and Oholibamah had three sons: Jeush, Jalam, and Korah.

Chiefs and leaders in Edom

15 Esau and Adah's eldest son was Eliphaz, and the clans that descended from him were Teman, Omar, Zepho, Kenaz, 16 Korah, Gatam, and Amalek. These and Esau's other descendants lived in the land of Edom.

17 The clans that descended from Esau and Basemath's son Reuel were Nahath, Zerah, Shammah, and Mizzah.

18 The clans that descended from Esau and Oholibamah the daughter of Anah were Jeush, Jalam, and Korah. 19 All of these clans descended from Esau, who was known as Edom.

20 Seir was from the Horite tribe that had lived in Edom before the time of Esau. The clans that had descended from him were Lotan, Shobal, Zibeon, Anah, 21 Dishon, Ezer, and Dishan.

22 Lotan's sons were Hori and Heman; his sister was Timna.

23 Shobal's sons were Alvan, Manahath, Ebal, Shepho, and Onam.

24 Zibeon's sons were Aiah and Anah — the same Anah who found an oasis' in the desert while taking the donkeys of his father out to pasture.

25 Anah's children were Dishon and Oholibamah.

26 Dishon's sons were Hemdan, Eshban, Ithran, and Cheran.

27 Ezer's sons were Bilhan, Zaavan, and Akan.

28 Dishan's sons were Uz and Aran.

29 The clans of the Horites were Lotan, Shobal, Zibeon, Anah, 30 Dishon, Ezer, and Dishan, and they lived in the land of Seir.

31-39 Before there were kings in Israel, the following kings ruled Edom one after another:

> Bela son of Beor from Dinhabah;
> Jobab son of Zerah from Bozrah;
> Husham from the land of Teman;
> Hadad son of Bedad from Avith (Bedad had defeated the Midianites in Moab);
> Samlah from Masrekah;
> Shaul from the city of Rehoboth on the River Euphrates;
> Baalhanan son of Achbor;
> Hadar from the city of Pau (his wife Mehetabel was the daughter of Matred and the granddaughter of Mezahab).

---

*36.9–14 other wife: See the note at 22.24.

See also: 35.27: Gen 13.18. 36.2: Gen 26.34.
36.3: Gen 28.9.

40 The clans that descended from Esau took their names from their families and the places where they lived. They are Timna, Alvah, Jetheth, 41 Oholibamah, Elah, Pinon, 42 Kenaz, Teman, Mibzar, 43 Magdiel, and Iram. These clans descended from Esau, who was known as Edom, the father of the Edomites. They took their names from the places where they settled.

Joseph is sold by his brothers as a slave

CHAPTER 37

Joseph and his brothers

1 Jacob lived in the land of Canaan, where his father Isaac had lived, 2 and this is the story of his family.

When Jacob's son Joseph was seventeen years old, he took care of the sheep with his brothers, the sons of Bilhah and Zilpah.* But he was always telling his father all sorts of bad things about his brothers.

3 Jacob loved Joseph more than he did any of his other sons, because Joseph was born after Jacob was very old. Jacob had given Joseph a fine coat 4 to show that he was his favourite son, and so Joseph's brothers hated him and would not be friendly to him.

5 One day, Joseph told his brothers what he had dreamed, and they hated him even more. 6 Joseph said, "Let me tell you about my dream. 7 We were out in the field, tying up bundles of wheat. Suddenly my bundle stood up, and your bundles gathered around and bowed down to it."

8 His brothers asked, "Do you really think you are going to be king and rule over us?" Now they hated Joseph more than ever because of what he had said about his dream.

9 Joseph later had another dream, and he told his brothers, "Listen to what else I dreamed. The sun, the moon, and eleven stars bowed down to me."

10 When he told his father about this dream, his father became angry and said, "What's that supposed to mean? Are your mother and I and your brothers all going to come and bow down in front of you?" 11 Joseph's brothers were jealous of him, but his father kept wondering about the dream.

*37.2 Bilhah and Zilpah: See 30.1–13.
See also: 37.11: Acts 7.9.

Helpline

Help! My parents have favourites

'I get picked on and criticised, while the rest of my family get let off. My parents have got it in for me!'

It's shocking, isn't it? Aren't parents supposed to love their children equally?

In some families one child gets treated differently to the rest. Either they're the favourite, or they're not as good as the others. Even someone as close to God as Jacob still played favourites; he treated Joseph better than the rest of his sons – and they took their revenge!

Maybe you feel as though you get the raw deal in your family. Or maybe you're the favourite? First, check whether you're right. Sometimes it's not really favouritism, we just don't like the way we're being treated.

But maybe it is true. Maybe they do treat you differently. Can you do anything about it? Talk to them and explain how you feel. Don't get angry, don't get emotional (if you can help it). Explain why it is that you feel like this. If you don't feel you're getting through to them, talk to your youth leader or church leader.

And try to avoid taking it out on your brother or sister. Chances are they're not aware of it, or they might even be embarrassed by it. It may not be their fault.

Three things

Check

Check out whether it's true or imagined. Be honest.

Talk

Talk to someone about it. They'll be able to help.

Children

Remember God loves all his children equally. Whatever your relationship is like with your earthly parents, your heavenly father thinks you are fantastic.

More...

Families p.1224
Help! My parents are letting me down! p.598

Joseph is sold and taken to Egypt

¹² One day when Joseph's brothers had taken the sheep to a pasture near Shechem, ¹³ his father Jacob said to him, "I want you to go to your brothers. They are with the sheep near Shechem."

"Yes, sir," Joseph answered.

¹⁴ His father said, "Go and find out how your brothers and the sheep are doing. Then come back and let me know." So he sent him from Hebron Valley.

Joseph was near Shechem ¹⁵ and wandering through the fields, when a man asked, "What are you looking for?"

¹⁶ Joseph answered, "I'm looking for my brothers who are watching the sheep. Can you tell me where they are?"

¹⁷ "They're not here any more," the man replied. "I overheard them say they were going to Dothan."

Joseph left and found his brothers in Dothan. ¹⁸ But before he got there, they saw him coming and made plans to kill him. ¹⁹ They said to one another, "Look, here comes the hero of those dreams! ²⁰ Let's kill him and throw him into a pit and say that some wild animal ate him. Then we'll see what happens to those dreams."

²¹ Reuben heard this and tried to protect Joseph from them. "Let's not kill him," he said. ²² "Don't murder him or even harm him. Just throw him into a dry well out here in the desert." Reuben planned to rescue Joseph later and take him back to his father.

²³ When Joseph came to his brothers, they pulled off his fine coat ²⁴ and threw him into a dry well.

²⁵ As Joseph's brothers sat down to eat, they looked up and saw a caravan of Ishmaelites coming from Gilead. Their camels were loaded with all kinds of spices that they were taking to Egypt. ²⁶ So Judah said, "What will we gain if we kill our brother and hide his body? ²⁷ Let's sell him to the Ishmaelites and not harm him. After all, he is our brother." And the others agreed.

²⁸ When the Midianite merchants came by, Joseph's brothers took him out of the well, and for twenty pieces of silver they sold him to the Ishmaelites who took him to Egypt.

²⁹ When Reuben returned to the well and did not find Joseph there, he tore his clothes in sorrow. ³⁰ Then he went back to his brothers and said, "The boy is gone! What am I going to do?"

³¹ Joseph's brothers killed a goat and dipped Joseph's fine coat in its blood. ³² After this, they took the coat to their father and said, "We found this! Look at it carefully and see if it belongs to your son."

³³ Jacob knew it was Joseph's coat and said, "It's my son's coat! Joseph has been torn to pieces and eaten by some wild animal."

³⁴ Jacob mourned for Joseph a long time, and to show his sorrow he tore his clothes and wore sackcloth.* ³⁵ All Jacob's children came to comfort him, but he refused to be comforted. "No," he said, "I will go to my grave, mourning for my son." So Jacob kept on grieving.

³⁶ Meanwhile, the Midianites had sold Joseph in Egypt to a man named Potiphar, who was the king's official in charge of the palace guard.

Judah and Tamar

CHAPTER 38

¹ About that time Judah left his brothers in the hill country and went to live near his friend Hirah in the town of Adullam. ² While there he met the daughter of Shua, a Canaanite man. Judah married her, ³ and they had three sons. He named the first one Er; ⁴ she named the next one Onan. ⁵ The third one was born when Judah was in Chezib, and she named him Shelah.

⁶ Later, Judah chose Tamar as a wife for Er, his eldest son. ⁷ But Er was very evil, and the LORD took his life. ⁸ So Judah told Onan, "It's your duty to marry Tamar and have a child for your brother."*

⁹ Onan knew the child would not be his,* and when he had sex with Tamar, he made sure that she would not get pregnant. ¹⁰ The LORD wasn't pleased with Onan and took his life too.

*37.34 sackcloth: A rough dark-coloured cloth made from goat or camel hair and used to make grain sacks. It was worn in times of trouble or sorrow.
*38.8 It's your duty . . . child . . . brother: If a man died without having children, his brother was to marry the dead man's wife and have a child, who was to be considered the child of the dead brother (see Deuteronomy 25.5–6).
*38.9 the child . . . not be his: When Judah died, Onan would get his dead brother's share of the inheritance, but if his dead brother had a son, the inheritance would go to him instead.

See also: 37.28: Acts 7.9.

Life files

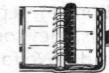

Judah

Background: Fourth son of Jacob. His name means 'praise'.

What's the story?

Although he was not the eldest son, Judah took a leading role among his brothers. It was Judah who decided to sell Joseph to the slave-traders (Genesis 37.26–7); and later it was Judah who tried to negotiate with Joseph in Egypt (Genesis 44.16–18).

For some time, Judah left his brothers to live among the Canaanites. His eldest son, Er, marries a woman called Tamar. When Er dies, by custom, his brother Onan takes Tamar as his wife. Onan, however, refuses to do his duty and never fully consummates the marriage. This is seen as a great sin and, in consequence, he dies. By now, Judah is fearing for the life of the rest of his sons, so he refuses to marry Shelah to Tamar.

Tamar takes matters into her own hands. Disguising herself as a prostitute, she sleeps with Judah, taking his seal as a pledge of payment. (The seal was the way Judah would sign and seal legal documents, the ancient equivalent of an ID Card, or PIN number.) When Tamar is discovered to be pregnant, she reveals who the father is, and Judah realises that it is he who has been in the wrong (Genesis 38.1–30). Judah 'never slept with her again'.

What's the point?

Judah gave his name to more than a tribe. When Israel split into two after the death of Solomon, ten tribes formed the northern country, which was still called Israel. But the southern country was called Judah, and it was through the land of Judah that the line of kings continued which led to Jesus.

More...

Israel and Judah p.385
Marriage p.205
The twelve tribes p.56

[11] Judah did not want the same thing to happen to his son Shelah, and he told Tamar, "Go home to your father and live there as a widow until my son Shelah is grown up." So Tamar went to live with her father.

[12] Some years later Judah's wife died, and he mourned for her. He then went with his friend Hirah to the town of Timnah, where his sheep were being sheared. [13] Tamar found out that her father-in-law Judah was going to Timnah to shear his sheep. [14] She also realized that Shelah was now a grown man, but she had not been allowed to marry him. So she decided to dress in something other than her widow's clothes and to cover her face with a veil. After this, she sat outside the town of Enaim on the road to Timnah.

[15] When Judah came along, he did not recognize her because of the veil. He thought she was a prostitute [16] and asked her to sleep with him. She asked, "What will you give me if I do?"

[17] "One of my young goats," he answered.
"What will you give me to keep until you send the goat?" she asked.

[18] "What do you want?" he asked in return.
"The ring on that cord around your neck," was her reply. "I also want the special walking stick* you have with you." He gave them to her, they slept together, and she became pregnant.

[19] After returning home, Tamar took off the veil and dressed in her widow's clothes again.

[20] Judah sent his friend Hirah to take a goat to the woman, so he could get back the ring and walking stick, but she wasn't there.
[21] Hirah asked the people of Enaim, "Where is the prostitute who sat along the road outside your town?"

"There's never been one here," they answered.

[22] Hirah went back and told Judah, "I couldn't find the woman, and the people of Enaim said no prostitute had ever been there."

[23] "If you couldn't find her, we'll just let her keep the things I gave her," Judah answered. "And we'd better forget about the goat, or else we'll look like fools."

---

*38.18 ring . . . walking stick: The ring was shaped like a cylinder and could be rolled over soft clay as a way of sealing special documents. The walking stick was probably a symbol of power and the sign of leadership in the tribe, though it may have been a shepherd's rod.

24 About three months later someone told Judah, "Your daughter-in-law Tamar has behaved like a prostitute, and now she's pregnant!"

"Drag her out of town and burn her to death!" Judah shouted.

25 As Tamar was being dragged off, she sent someone to tell her father-in-law, "The man who gave me this ring, this cord, and this walking stick is the one who got me pregnant."

26 "Those are mine!" Judah admitted. "She's a better person than I am, because I broke my promise to let her marry my son Shelah." After this, Judah never slept with her again.

27-28 Tamar later gave birth to twins. But before either of them was born, one of them stuck a hand out of her womb. The woman who was helping tied a red thread around the baby's hand and explained, "This one came out first."

29 Straight away his hand went back in, and the other child was born first. The woman then said, "What an opening you've made for yourself!" So they named the baby Perez.* 30 When the brother with the red thread came out, they named him Zerah.*

Joseph in Egypt

CHAPTER 39

Joseph and Potiphar's wife

1 The Ishmaelites took Joseph to Egypt and sold him to Potiphar, the king's* official in charge of the palace guard. 2-3 So Joseph lived in the home of Potiphar, his Egyptian owner.

Soon Potiphar realized that the LORD was helping Joseph to be successful in whatever he did. 4 Potiphar liked Joseph and made him his personal assistant, putting him in charge of his house and all his property. 5 Because of Joseph, the LORD began to bless Potiphar's family and fields. 6 Potiphar left everything up to Joseph, and with Joseph there, the only decision he had to make was what he wanted to eat.

Joseph was well-built and handsome, 7 and Potiphar's wife soon noticed him. She asked him to make love to her, 8 but he refused and said, "My master isn't worried about anything in his house, because he has placed me in charge of everything he owns. 9 No one in my master's house is more important than I am. The only thing he hasn't given me is you, and that's because you are his wife. I won't sin against God by doing such a terrible thing as this." 10 She kept begging Joseph day after day, but he refused to do what she wanted or even to go near her.

11 One day, Joseph went to Potiphar's house to do his work, and none of the other servants were there. 12 Potiphar's wife grabbed hold of his coat and said, "Make love to me!" Joseph ran out of the house, leaving her hanging on to his coat.

13 When this happened, 14 she called in her servants and said, "Look! This Hebrew has come just to make fools of us. He tried to rape me, but I screamed for help. 15 And when he heard me scream, he ran out of the house, leaving his coat with me."

16 Potiphar's wife kept Joseph's coat until her husband came home. 17 Then she said, "That Hebrew slave of yours tried to rape me! 18 But when I screamed for help, he left his coat and ran out of the house."

19 Potiphar became very angry 20 and threw Joseph in the same prison where the king's prisoners were kept.

While Joseph was in prison, 21 the LORD helped him and was good to him. He even made the jailer like Joseph so much that 22 he put him in charge of the other prisoners and of everything that was done in the jail. 23 The jailer did not worry about anything, because the LORD was with Joseph and made him successful in all that he did.

CHAPTER 40

Joseph tells the meaning of the prisoners' dreams

1-3 While Joseph was in prison, both the king's* personal servant* and his chief cook made the king angry. So he had them thrown into the same prison with Joseph. 4 They spent a long time in prison, and Potiphar, the official in charge of the palace guard, made Joseph their servant.

5 One night each of the two men had a dream, but their dreams had different

---

*38.29 Perez: In Hebrew "Perez" sounds like "opening".
*38.30 Zerah: In Hebrew "Zerah" means "bright", probably referring to the red thread.
See also: 39.2: Acts 7.9.

*40.1-3 personal servant: The Hebrew text has "cup bearer", an important and trusted official in the royal court, who personally served wine to the king.
See also: 39.21: Acts 7.9.

meanings. ⁶ The next morning, when Joseph went to see the men, he could tell they were upset, ⁷ and he asked, "Why are you so worried today?"

⁸ "We each had a dream last night," they answered, "and there is no one to tell us what they mean."

Joseph replied, "Doesn't God know the meaning of dreams? Now tell me what you dreamed."

⁹ The king's personal servant told Joseph, "In my dream I saw a vine ¹⁰ with three branches. As soon as it budded, it blossomed, and its grapes became ripe. ¹¹ I held the king's cup and squeezed the grapes into it, then I gave the cup to the king."

¹² Joseph said:

This is the meaning of your dream. The three branches stand for three days, ¹³ and in three days the king will pardon you. He will make you his personal servant again, and you will serve him his wine, just as you used to do. ¹⁴ But when these good things happen, please don't forget to tell the king about me, so I can get out of this place. ¹⁵ I was kidnapped from the land of the Hebrews, and here in Egypt I haven't done anything to deserve being thrown in jail.

¹⁶ When the chief cook saw that Joseph had given a good meaning to the dream, he told Joseph, "I also had a dream. In it I was carrying three breadbaskets stacked on top of my head. ¹⁷ The top basket was full of all kinds of baked things for the king, but birds were eating them."

¹⁸ Joseph said:

This is the meaning of your dream. The three baskets are three days, ¹⁹ and in three days the king will cut off your head. He will hang your body on a pole, and birds will come and peck at it.

²⁰ Three days later, while the king was celebrating his birthday with a dinner for his officials, he sent for his personal servant and the chief cook. ²¹ He put the personal servant back in his old job ²² and had the cook put to death.

Everything happened just as Joseph had said it would, ²³ but the king's personal servant completely forgot about Joseph.

Life files

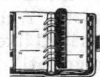

Joseph (a.k.a. Lord Zaphenath Paneah, Genesis 41.45)

Background: Jacob's eleventh – and favourite – son.

What's the story?

Joseph's dreams, and his lack of tact, really irritate his brothers. They fake his murder and sell him into slavery. He ends up in Egypt, where, in one of the earliest cases of sexual harassment in the workplace, the mistress of the house tries to seduce him. He rejects her and is thrown into prison.

In prison he interprets the dreams of a baker and a butler. When the King has nightmares, the butler remembers Joseph. Joseph interprets the King's dreams: there'll be seven good years, then seven years of famine. He is made governor of Egypt.

Due to Joseph's foresight, the Egyptians are OK during the famine. But in Canaan, things are bad and Joseph's brothers set out for Egypt. There follows a cat and mouse game, as Joseph teases them. Finally he reveals who he is, there is a tearful reunion and the whole family settles in Egypt.

What's the point?

To become somebody, you have to be a nobody first. Jacob, Joseph, Moses – all of them had to become outcasts in order to find God. God is at work. As Joseph says, 'you weren't really the ones who sent me here – it was God' Genesis 45.8.

footsteps

A week with Joseph

Dreams cause his downfall: Genesis 37.1–36
Joseph at Potiphar's house: Genesis 39.1–23
Joseph in jail: Genesis 40.1–23
Joseph and the King: Genesis 41.1–57
Joseph's brothers come and go: 42.1–38
Joseph comes clean: 45.1–15
Joseph dies: 50.15–26

More...

Dreams and visions p.1410
Guidance p.685

CHAPTER 41

Joseph interprets the king's dreams

[1] Two years later the king' of Egypt dreamed he was standing beside the River Nile. [2] Suddenly, seven fat, healthy cows came up from the river and started eating grass along the bank. [3] Then seven ugly, skinny cows came up out of the river and [4] ate the fat, healthy cows. When this happened, the king woke up.

[5] The king went back to sleep and had another dream. This time seven full heads of grain were growing on a single stalk. [6] Later, seven other heads of grain appeared, but they were thin and scorched by the east wind. [7] The thin heads of grain swallowed the seven full heads. Again the king woke up, and it had only been a dream.

[8] The next morning the king was upset. So he called in his magicians and wise men and told them what he had dreamed. None of them could tell him what the dreams meant.

[9] The king's personal servant said:

Now I remember what I was supposed to do. [10] When you were angry with me and your chief cook, you threw us both in jail in the house of the captain of the guard. [11] One night we both had dreams, and each dream had a different meaning. [12] A young Hebrew, who was a servant of the captain of the guard, was there with us at the time. When we told him our dreams, he explained what each of them meant, [13] and everything happened just as he said it would. I got my job back, and the cook was put to death.

[14] The king sent for Joseph, who was quickly brought out of jail. He shaved, changed his clothes, and went to the king. [15] The king said to him, "I had a dream, yet no one can explain what it means. I am told that you can interpret dreams."

[16] "Your Majesty," Joseph answered, "I can't do it myself, but God can give a good meaning to your dreams."

[17] The king told Joseph:

I dreamed I was standing on the bank of the River Nile. [18] I saw seven fat, healthy cows come up out of the river, and they began feeding on the grass. [19] Next, seven skinny, bony cows came up out of the river. I have never seen such terrible looking cows anywhere in Egypt. [20] The skinny cows ate the fat ones. [21] But you couldn't tell it, because these skinny cows were just as skinny as they were before. Straight away, I woke up.

[22] I also dreamed that I saw seven heads of grain growing on one stalk. The heads were full and ripe. [23] Then seven other heads of grain came up. They were thin and scorched by a wind from the desert. [24] These heads of grain swallowed the full ones. I told my dreams to the magicians, but none of them could tell me the meaning of the dreams.

[25] Joseph replied:

Your Majesty, both of your dreams mean the same thing, and in them God has shown what he is going to do. [26] The seven good cows stand for seven years, and so do the seven good heads of grain. [27] The seven skinny, ugly cows that came up later also stand for seven years, as do the seven bad heads of grain that were scorched by the east wind. The dreams mean there will be seven years when there won't be enough grain.

[28] It is just as I said — God has shown what he intends to do. [29] For seven years Egypt will have more than enough grain, [30] but that will be followed by seven years when there won't be enough. The good years of plenty will be forgotten, and everywhere in Egypt people will be starving. [31] The famine will be so bad that no one will remember that once there had been plenty. [32] God has given you two dreams to let you know that he has definitely decided to do this and that he will do it soon.

[33] Your Majesty, you should find someone who is wise and will know what to do, so that you can put him in charge of all Egypt. [34] Then appoint some other officials to collect one-fifth of every crop harvested in Egypt during the seven years when there is plenty. [35] Give them the power to collect the grain during those good years and to store it in your cities. [36] It can be stored until it is needed during the seven years when there won't be enough grain in Egypt. This will keep the country from being destroyed because of the lack of food.

Joseph is made governor over Egypt

[37] The king' and his officials liked this plan. [38] So the king said to them, "No one could

See also: 41.8: Dan 2.2.

possibly handle this better than Joseph, since the Spirit of God is with him."

³⁹ The king told Joseph, "God is the one who has shown you these things. No one else is as wise as you are or knows as much as you do. ⁴⁰ I'm putting you in charge of my palace, and everybody will have to obey you. No one will be over you except me. ⁴¹ You are now governor of all Egypt!"

⁴² Then the king took off his royal ring and put it on Joseph's finger. He gave him fine clothes to wear and placed a gold chain around his neck. ⁴³ He also let him ride in the chariot next to his own, and people shouted, "Make way for Joseph!" So Joseph was governor of Egypt.

⁴⁴ The king told Joseph, "Although I'm king, no one in Egypt is to do anything without your permission." ⁴⁵ He gave Joseph the Egyptian name Zaphenath Paneah. And he let him marry Asenath, the daughter of Potiphera, a priest in the city of Heliopolis.' Joseph travelled all over Egypt.

⁴⁶ Joseph was thirty when the king made him governor, and he went everywhere for the king. ⁴⁷ For seven years there were big harvests of grain. ⁴⁸ Joseph collected and stored up the extra grain in the cities of Egypt near the fields where it was harvested. ⁴⁹ In fact, there was so much grain that they stopped keeping record, because it was like counting the grains of sand along the beach.

⁵⁰ Joseph and his wife had two sons before the famine began. ⁵¹ Their first son was named Manasseh, which means, "God has let me forget all my troubles and my family back home." ⁵² His second son was named Ephraim, which means "God has made me a success' in the land where I suffered."'

⁵³ Egypt's seven years of plenty came to an end, ⁵⁴ and the seven years of famine began, just as Joseph had said. There was not enough food in other countries, but all over Egypt there was plenty. ⁵⁵ When the famine finally struck Egypt, the people asked the king for food, but he said, "Go to Joseph and do what he tells you to do."

⁵⁶ The famine became bad everywhere in Egypt, so Joseph opened the storehouses and sold the grain to the Egyptians. ⁵⁷ People from all over the world came to Egypt, because the famine was severe in their countries.

Joseph and his brothers

CHAPTER 42

Joseph's brothers go to Egypt to buy grain

¹ When Jacob found out there was grain in Egypt, he said to his sons, "Why are you just sitting here, staring at one another? ² I have heard there is grain in Egypt. Now go down and buy some, so we won't starve to death."

³ Ten of Joseph's brothers went to Egypt to buy grain. ⁴ But Jacob did not send Joseph's younger brother Benjamin with them; he was afraid that something might happen to him. ⁵ So Jacob's sons joined others from Canaan who were going to Egypt because of the terrible famine.

⁶ Since Joseph was governor of Egypt and in charge of selling grain, his brothers came to him and bowed with their faces to the ground. ⁷⁻⁸ They did not recognize Joseph, but straight away he knew who they were, though he pretended not to know. Instead, he spoke harshly and asked, "Where do you come from?"

"From the land of Canaan," they answered. "We've come here to buy grain."

⁹ Joseph remembered what he had dreamed about them and said, "You're spies! You've come here to find out where our country is weak."

¹⁰ "No sir," they replied. "We're your servants, and we have only come to buy grain. ¹¹ We're honest men, and we come from the same family — we're not spies."

¹² "That isn't so!" Joseph insisted. "You've come here to find out where our country is weak."

¹³ But they explained, "Sir, we come from a family of twelve brothers. The youngest is still with our father in Canaan, and one of our brothers is dead."

¹⁴ Joseph replied:

It's just like I said. You're spies, ¹⁵ and I'm going to find out who you really are. I swear by the life of the king that you won't leave this place until your youngest brother comes here. ¹⁶ Choose one of you to go after your brother, while the rest of you stay here in jail. That will show whether you are telling the truth. But if you are lying, I swear by the life of the king that you are spies!

See also: 41.40: Acts 7.10. 41.42: Dan 5.29.
41.54: Acts 7.11. 41.55: John 2.5.

See also: 42.2: Acts 7.12. 42.9: Gen 37.5–10.

17 Joseph kept them all under guard for three days, 18 before saying to them:

Since I respect God, I'll give you a chance to save your lives. 19 If you are honest men, one of you must stay here in jail, and the rest of you can take the grain back to your starving families. 20 But you must bring your youngest brother to me. Then I'll know that you are telling the truth, and you won't be put to death.

Joseph's brothers agreed 21 and said to one another, "We're being punished because of Joseph. We saw the trouble he was in, but we refused to help him when he begged us. That's why these terrible things are happening."

22 Reuben spoke up, "Didn't I tell you not to harm the boy? But you wouldn't listen, and now we have to pay the price for killing him."

23 They did not know that Joseph could understand them, since he was speaking through an interpreter. 24 Joseph turned away from them and cried, but soon he turned back and spoke to them again. Then he had Simeon tied up and taken away while they watched.

Joseph's brothers return to Canaan

25 Joseph gave orders for his brothers' grain sacks to be filled with grain and for their money* to be put in their sacks. He also gave orders for them to be given food for their journey home. After this was done, 26 they each loaded the grain on their donkeys and left.

27 When they stopped for the night, one of them opened his sack to get some grain for his donkey, and straight away he saw his money bag. 28 "Here's my money!" he told his brothers. "Right here in my sack."

They were trembling with fear as they stared at one another and asked themselves, "What has God done to us?"

29 When they returned to the land of Canaan, they told their father Jacob everything that had happened to them:

30 The governor of Egypt was rude and treated us like spies. 31 But we told him, "We're honest men, not spies. 32 We come from a family of twelve brothers. The youngest is still with our father in Canaan, and the other is dead."

33 Then the governor of Egypt told us, "I'll find out if you really are honest. Leave one of your brothers here with me, while you take the grain to your starving families. 34 But bring your youngest brother to me, so I can be certain that you are honest men and not spies. After that, I'll let your other brother go free, and you can stay here and trade."

35 When the brothers started emptying their sacks of grain, they found their money bags in them. They were frightened, and so was their father Jacob, 36 who said, "You have already taken my sons Joseph and Simeon from me. And now you want to take away Benjamin! Everything is against me."

37 Reuben spoke up, "Father, if I don't bring Benjamin back, you can kill both of my sons. Trust me with him, and I will bring him back."

38 But Jacob said, "I won't let my son Benjamin go down to Egypt with the rest of you. His brother is already dead, and he is the only son I have left.* I am an old man, and if anything happens to him on the way, I'll die from sorrow, and all of you will be to blame."

CHAPTER 43

Joseph's brothers return to Egypt with Benjamin

1 The famine in Canaan got worse, 2 until finally, Jacob's family had eaten all the grain they had bought in Egypt. So Jacob said to his sons, "Go back and buy some more grain."

3-5 Judah replied, "The governor strictly warned us that we would not be allowed to see him unless we brought our youngest brother with us. If you let us take Benjamin along, we will go and buy grain. But we won't go without him!"

6 Jacob asked, "Why did you cause me so much trouble by telling the governor you had another brother?"

7 They answered, "He asked a lot of questions about us and our family. He wanted to know if you were still alive and if we had any more brothers. All we could do was answer his questions. How could we know he would tell us to bring along our brother?"

---

*42.25 money: Probably in the form of small pieces of silver and/or other precious or semi-precious metals; there were no coins or paper money at this time.

See also: 42.22: Gen 37.21-22.

---

*42.38 only son I have left: Jacob had only two sons by Rachel, his favourite wife.

8 Then Judah said to his father, "Let Benjamin go with me, and we will leave straight away, so that none of us will starve to death. 9 I promise to bring him back safely, and if I don't, you can blame me as long as I live. 10 If we had not wasted all this time, we could already have been there and back twice."

11 Their father said:

If Benjamin must go with you, take the governor a gift of some of the best things from our own country, such as perfume, honey, spices, pistachio nuts, and almonds.* 12 Also take along twice the amount of money for the grain, because there must have been some mistake when the money was put back in your sacks. 13 Take Benjamin with you and leave right away.

14 When you go in to see the governor, I pray that God All-Powerful will be good to you and that the governor will let your other brother and Benjamin come back home with you. If I must lose my children, I suppose I must.

15 The brothers took the gifts, twice the amount of money, and Benjamin. Then they hurried off to Egypt. When they stood in front of Joseph, 16 he saw Benjamin and told the servant in charge of his house, "Take these men to my house. Slaughter an animal and cook it, so they can eat with me at midday."

17 The servant did as he was told and took the brothers to Joseph's house. 18 But on the way they got worried and started thinking, "We are being taken there because of the money that was put back in our sacks last time. He will arrest us, make us his slaves, and take our donkeys."

19 So when they arrived at Joseph's house, they said to the servant in charge, 20 "Sir, we came to Egypt once before to buy grain. 21 But when we stopped for the night, we each found in our grain sacks the exact amount we had paid. We have brought that money back, 22 together with enough money to buy more grain. We don't know who put the money in our sacks."

23 "It's all right," the servant replied. "Don't worry. The God you and your father worship must have put the money there,

because I received your payment in full." Then he brought Simeon out to them.

24 The servant took them into Joseph's house and gave them water to wash their feet. He also tended their donkeys. 25 The brothers got their gifts ready to give to Joseph at midday, since they had heard they were going to eat there.

26 When Joseph came home, they gave him the gifts they had brought, and they bowed down to him. 27 After Joseph had asked how they were, he said, "What about your elderly father? Is he still alive?"

28 They answered, "Your servant our father is still alive and well." And again they bowed down to Joseph.

29 When Joseph looked around and saw his brother Benjamin, he said, "This must be your youngest brother, the one you told me about. God bless you, my son."

30 Straight away he rushed off to his room and cried because of his love for Benjamin. 31 After washing his face and returning, he was able to control himself and said, "Serve the meal!"

32 Joseph was served at a table by himself, and his brothers were served at another. The Egyptians sat at yet another table, because Egyptians felt it was disgusting to eat with Hebrews. 33 To the surprise of Joseph's brothers, they were seated in front of him according to their ages, from the eldest to the youngest. 34 They were served food from Joseph's table, and Benjamin was given five times as much as each of the others. So Joseph's brothers drank with him and had a good time.

CHAPTER 44

The missing cup

1-2 Later, Joseph told the servant in charge of his house, "Fill the men's grain sacks with as much as they can hold and put their money in the sacks. Also put my silver cup in the sack of the youngest brother." The servant did as he was told.

3 Early the next morning, the men were sent on their way with their donkeys. 4 But they had not gone far from the city when Joseph told the servant, "Go after those men! When you catch them, say, 'My master has been good to you. So why have you stolen his silver cup? 5 Not only does he drink from his cup, but he also uses it to learn about the future. You have done a terrible thing.' "

---

*43.11 honey, spices, pistachio nuts, and almonds: Some of these foods were still available in Canaan, but the main food was bread, and there was no grain to make bread.

[6] When the servant caught up with them, he said exactly what Joseph had told him to say. [7] But they replied, "Sir, why do you say such things? We would never do anything like that! [8] We even returned the money we found in our grain sacks when we got back to Canaan. So why would we want to steal any silver or gold from your master's house? [9] If you find that one of us has the cup, then kill him, and the rest of us will become your slaves."

[10] "Good!" the man replied, "I'll do what you have said. But only the one who has the cup will become my slave. The rest of you can go free."

[11] Each of the brothers quickly put his sack on the ground and opened it. [12] Joseph's servant started searching the sacks, beginning with the one that belonged to the eldest brother. When he came to Benjamin's sack, he found the cup. [13] This upset the brothers so much that they began tearing their clothes in sorrow. Then they loaded their donkeys and returned to the city.

[14] When Judah and his brothers got there, Joseph was still at home. So they bowed down to Joseph, [15] who asked them, "What have you done? Didn't you know I could find out?"

[16] "Sir, what can we say?" Judah replied. "How can we prove we are innocent? God has shown that we are guilty. And now all of us are your slaves, especially the one who had the cup."

[17] Joseph told them, "I would never punish all of you. Only the one who was caught with the cup will become my slave. The rest of you are free to go home to your father."

Judah pleads for Benjamin

[18] Judah went over to Joseph and said:

Sir, you have as much power as the king' himself, and I am only your slave. Please don't get angry if I speak. [19] You asked us if our father was still alive and if we had any more brothers. [20] So we told you, "Our father is a very old man. In fact, he was already old when Benjamin was born. Benjamin's brother is dead. Now Benjamin is the only one of the two brothers who is still alive, and our father loves him very much."

[21] You ordered us to bring him here, so you could see him for yourself. [22] We told you that our father would die if Benjamin left him. [23] But you warned us that we could never see you again, unless our youngest brother came with us. [24] So we returned to our father and reported what you had said.

[25] Later our father told us to come back here and buy more grain. [26] But we answered, "We can't go back to Egypt without our youngest brother. We will never be let in to see the governor, unless he is with us."

[27] Sir, our father then reminded us that his favourite wife had given birth to two sons. [28] One of them was already missing and had not been seen for a long time. My father thinks the boy was torn to pieces by some wild animal, [29] and he said, "I am an old man. If you take Benjamin from me, and something happens to him, I will die of a broken heart."

[30] That's why Benjamin must be with us when I go back to my father. He loves him so much [31] that he will die if Benjamin doesn't come back with me. [32] I promised my father that I would bring him safely home. If I don't, I told my father he could blame me the rest of my life.

[33] Sir, I am your slave. Please let me stay here in place of Benjamin and let him return home with his brothers. [34] How can I face my father if Benjamin isn't with me? I couldn't bear to see my father in such sorrow.

CHAPTER 45

Joseph tells his brothers who he is

[1] Since Joseph could no longer control his feelings in front of his servants, he sent them out of the room. When he was alone with his brothers, he told them, "I am Joseph." [2] Then he cried so loudly that the Egyptians heard him and told about it in the king's' palace.

[3] Joseph asked his brothers if his father was still alive, but they were too frightened to answer. [4] Joseph told them to come closer to him, and when they did, he said:

Yes, I am your brother Joseph, the one you sold into Egypt. [5] Don't worry or blame yourselves for what you did. God is the one who sent me ahead of you to save lives.

[6] There has already been a famine for two years, and for five more years no one will plough fields or harvest grain. [7] But God sent me on ahead of you to keep your families alive and to save you in this wonderful way. [8] After all, you weren't

---

See also: 45.1: Acts 7.13.

really the ones who sent me here — it was God. He made me the highest official in the king's court and placed me over all Egypt.

⁹ Now hurry back and tell my father that his son Joseph says, "God has made me ruler of Egypt. Come here as quickly as you can. ¹⁰ You will live near me in the region of Goshen with your children and grandchildren, as well as with your sheep, goats, cattle, and everything else you own. ¹¹ I will take care of you there during the next five years of famine. But if you don't come, you and your family and your animals will starve to death."

¹² All of you, including my brother Benjamin, can tell by what I have said that I really am Joseph. ¹³ Tell my father about my great power here in Egypt and about everything you have seen. Hurry and bring him here.

¹⁴ Joseph and Benjamin hugged each other and started crying. ¹⁵ Joseph was still crying as he kissed each of his other brothers. After this, they started talking with Joseph.

¹⁶ When it was told in the palace that Joseph's brothers had come, the king and his officials were happy. ¹⁷ So the king said to Joseph:

Tell your brothers to load their donkeys and return to Canaan. ¹⁸ They must bring their father and their families here. I will give them the best land in Egypt, and they can eat and enjoy everything that grows on it. ¹⁹ Also tell your brothers to take some wagons from Egypt for their wives and children to ride in. And they must be sure to bring their father. ²⁰ They can leave their possessions behind, because they will be given the best of everything in Egypt.

²¹ Jacob's sons agreed to do what the king had said. And Joseph gave them wagons and food for their trip home, just as the king had ordered. ²² Joseph gave some new clothes to each of his brothers, but to Benjamin he gave five new outfits and three hundred pieces of silver. ²³ To his father he sent ten donkeys loaded with the best things in Egypt, and ten other donkeys loaded with grain and bread and other food for the return trip. ²⁴ Then he sent his brothers off and told them, "Don't argue on the way home!"

²⁵ Joseph's brothers left Egypt, and when they arrived in Canaan, ²⁶ they told their father that Joseph was still alive and was the ruler of Egypt. But their father was so surprised that he could not believe them. ²⁷ Then they told him everything Joseph had said. When he saw the wagons Joseph had sent, he felt much better ²⁸ and said, "Now I can believe you! My son Joseph must really be alive, and I will get to see him before I die."

Jacob and his family go to Egypt

CHAPTER 46

¹ Jacob packed up everything he owned and left for Egypt. On the way he stopped near the town of Beersheba and offered sacrifices to the God his father Isaac had worshipped. ² That night, God spoke to him and said, "Jacob! Jacob!"

"Here I am," Jacob answered.

³ God said, "I am God, the same God your father worshipped. Don't be afraid to go to Egypt. I will give you so many descendants that one day they will become a nation. ⁴ I will go with you to Egypt, and later I will bring your descendants back here. Your son Joseph will be at your side when you die."

⁵⁻⁷ Jacob and his family set out from Beersheba and headed for Egypt. His sons put him in the wagon that the kingʼ had sent for him, and they put their small children and their wives in the other wagons. Jacob's whole family went to Egypt, including his sons, his grandsons, his daughters, and his granddaughters. They took along their animals and everything else they owned.

⁸⁻¹⁵ When Jacob went to Egypt, his children who were born in northern Syriaʼ also went along with their families.

Jacob and his wife Leah had a total of thirty-three children, grandchildren, and great-grandchildren, but two of their grandchildren had died in Canaan.

Their eldest son Reuben took his sons Hanoch, Pallu, Hezron, and Carmi.

Their son Simeon took his sons Jemuel, Jamin, Ohad, Jachin, Zohar, and Shaul, whose mother was a Canaanite.

Their son Levi took his sons Gershon, Kohath, and Merari.

Their son Judah took his sons Shelah, Perez, and Zerah. Judah's sons Er and Onan had died in Canaan. Judah's son Perez took his sons Hezron and Hamul.

Their son Issachar took his sons Tola, Puvah, Jashub,⸱ and Shimron.

Their son Zebulun took his sons Sered, Elon, and Jahleel.

Their daughter Dinah also went.

16–18 Jacob and Zilpah, the servant woman Laban had given his daughter Leah, had a total of sixteen children, grandchildren, and great-grandchildren.

Their son Gad took his sons Ziphion, Haggi, Shuni, Ezbon, Eri, Arodi, and Areli.

Their son Asher took his sons Imnah, Ishvah, Ishvi, and Beriah, who took his sons Heber and Malchiel.

Serah, the daughter of Asher, also went.

19–22 Jacob and Rachel had fourteen children and grandchildren.

Their son Joseph was already in Egypt, where he had married Asenath, daughter of Potiphera, the priest of Heliopolis.⸱ Joseph and Asenath had two sons Manasseh and Ephraim.

Jacob and Rachel's son Benjamin took his sons Bela, Becher, Ashbel, Gera, Naaman, Ehi, Rosh, Muppim, Huppim, and Ard.

23–25 Jacob and Bilhah, the servant woman Laban had given his daughter Rachel, had seven children and grandchildren.

Their son Dan took his son Hushim.

Their son Naphtali took his sons Jahzeel, Guni, Jezer, and Shillem.

26 Sixty-six members of Jacob's family went to Egypt with him, not counting his daughters-in-law. 27 Jacob's two grandsons who were born there made it a total of seventy members of Jacob's family in Egypt.

28 Jacob had sent his son Judah ahead of him to ask Joseph to meet them in Goshen. 29 So Joseph got in his chariot and went to meet his father. When they met, Joseph hugged his father around the neck and cried for a long time. 30 Jacob said to Joseph, "Now that I have seen you and know you are still alive, I am ready to die."

31 Then Joseph said to his brothers and to everyone who had come with them:

I must go and tell the king⸱ that you have arrived from Canaan. 32 I will tell him that you are shepherds and that you have

brought your sheep, goats, cattle, and everything else you own. 33 The king will call you in and ask what you do for a living. 34 When he does, be sure to say, "We are shepherds. Our families have always raised sheep." If you tell him this, he will let you settle in the region of Goshen.

Joseph wanted them to say this to the king, because the Egyptians did not like to have anything to do with people who raised sheep.

CHAPTER 47

1–2 Joseph took five of his brothers to the king and told him, "My father and my brothers have come from Canaan. They have brought their sheep, goats, cattle, and everything else they own to the region of Goshen."

Then he introduced his brothers to the king, 3 who asked them, "What do you do for a living?"

"Sir, we are shepherds," was their answer. "Our families have always raised sheep. 4 But in our country all the pastures are dried up, and our sheep have no grass to eat. So we, your servants, have come here. Please let us live in the region of Goshen."

5 The king said to Joseph, "It's good that your father and brothers have arrived. 6 I will let them live anywhere they choose in the land of Egypt, but I suggest that they settle in Goshen, the best part of our land. I would also like your finest shepherds to look after my own sheep and goats."

7 Then Joseph brought his father Jacob and introduced him to the king. Jacob gave the king his blessing, 8 and the king asked him, "How old are you?"

9 Jacob answered, "I have lived only a hundred and thirty years, and I have had to move from place to place. My parents and my grandparents also had to move from place to place. But they lived much longer, and their life was not as hard as mine." 10 Then Jacob gave the king his blessing once again and left. 11 Joseph obeyed the king's orders and gave his father and brothers some of the best land in Egypt near the city of Rameses. 12 Joseph also provided food for their families.

A famine in Egypt

13 The famine was bad everywhere in Egypt and Canaan, and the people were suffering terribly. 14 So Joseph sold them the grain that had been stored up, and he put the money*

in the king's' treasury. ¹⁵ But when everyone had run out of money, the Egyptians came to Joseph and demanded, "Give us more grain! If you don't, we'll soon be dead, because our money's all gone."

¹⁶ "If you don't have any money," Joseph answered, "give me your animals, and I'll let you have some grain." ¹⁷ From then on, they brought him their horses and donkeys and their sheep and goats in exchange for grain.

Within a year Joseph had collected every animal in Egypt. ¹⁸ Then the people came to him and said:

Sir, there's no way we can hide the truth from you. We are broke, and we don't have any more animals. We have nothing left except ourselves and our land. ¹⁹ Don't let us starve and our land be ruined. If you'll give us grain to eat and seed to plant, we'll sell ourselves and our land to the king. We'll become his slaves.

²⁰ The famine became so severe that Joseph finally bought every piece of land in Egypt for the king ²¹ and made everyone the king's slaves,' ²² except the priests. The king gave the priests a regular food allowance, so they did not have to sell their land. ²³ Then Joseph said to the people, "You and your land now belong to the king. I'm giving you seed to plant, ²⁴ but one-fifth of your crops must go to the king. You can keep the rest as seed or as food for your families."

²⁵ "Sir, you have saved our lives!" they answered. "We are glad to be slaves of the king." ²⁶ Then Joseph made a law that one-fifth of the harvest would always belong to the king. Only the priests did not lose their land.

Jacob becomes an old man

²⁷ The people of Israel made their home in the land of Goshen, where they became prosperous and had large families. ²⁸ Jacob himself lived there for seventeen years, before dying at the age of one hundred and forty-seven. ²⁹ When Jacob knew he did not have long to live, he called in Joseph and said, "If you really love me, you must make a solemn promise not to bury me in Egypt. ³⁰ Instead, bury me in the place where my ancestors are buried."

"I will do what you have asked," Joseph answered.

³¹ "Will you give me your word?" Jacob asked.

"Yes, I will," Joseph promised. After this, Jacob bowed down and prayed at the head of his bed.

Jacob blesses his family and dies

CHAPTER 48

Jacob blesses Joseph's two sons

¹ Joseph was told that his father Jacob had become very sick. So Joseph went to see him and took along his two sons, Manasseh and Ephraim. ² When Joseph arrived, someone told Jacob, "Your son Joseph has come to see you." Jacob sat up in bed, but it took almost all his strength.

³ Jacob told Joseph:

God All-Powerful appeared to me at Luz in the land of Canaan, where he gave me his blessing ⁴ and promised, "I will give you a large family with many descendants that will grow into a nation. And I am giving you this land that will belong to you and your family for ever."

⁵ Then Jacob went on to say:

Joseph, your two sons Ephraim and Manasseh were born in Egypt, but I accept them as my own, just as Reuben and Simeon are mine. ⁶ Any children you have later will be considered yours, but their inheritance will come from Ephraim and Manasseh. ⁷ Unfortunately, your mother Rachel died in Canaan after we had left northern Syria' and before we reached Bethlehem.' And I had to bury her along the way.

⁸⁻¹⁰ Jacob was very old and almost blind. He did not recognize the two boys, and so he asked Joseph, "Who are these boys?"

Joseph answered, "They are my sons. God has given them to me here in Egypt."

"Bring them to me," Jacob said. "I want to give them my blessing." Joseph brought the boys to him, and he hugged and kissed them.

¹¹ Jacob turned to Joseph and told him, "For many years I thought you were dead and that I would never see you again. But now God has even let me live to see your children." ¹² Then Joseph made his sons

See also: 47.29–30: Gen 49.29–32; 50.6.

See also: 48.3–4: Gen 28.13–14.   48.7: Gen 35.16–19.

move away from Jacob's knees,* and Joseph bowed down in front of him with his face to the ground.

¹³ After Joseph got up, he brought his two sons over to Jacob again. He led his younger son Ephraim to the left side of Jacob and his elder son Manasseh to the right. ¹⁴ But before Jacob gave them his blessing, he crossed his arms, putting his right hand on the head of Ephraim and his left hand on the head of Manasseh. ¹⁵ Then he gave Joseph his blessing and said:

My grandfather Abraham and my father Isaac worshipped the LORD God. He has been with me all my life, ¹⁶ and his angel has kept me safe. Now I pray that he will bless these boys and that my name and the names of Abraham and Isaac will live on because of them. I ask God to give them many children and many descendants as well.

¹⁷ Joseph did not like it when he saw his father place his right hand on the head of the younger son. So he tried to move his father's right hand from Ephraim's head and place it on Manasseh. ¹⁸ Joseph said, "Father, you have made a mistake. This is the elder boy. Put your right hand on him."

¹⁹ But his father said, "Son, I know what I am doing. It's true that Manasseh's family will some day become a great nation. But Ephraim will be even greater than Manasseh, because his descendants will become many great nations."

²⁰ Jacob told him that in the future the people of Israel would ask God's blessings on one another by saying, "I pray for God to bless you as much as he blessed Ephraim and Manasseh." Jacob put Ephraim's name first to show that he would be greater than Manasseh. ²¹ After that, Jacob said, "Joseph, you can see that I won't live much longer. But God will be with you and will lead you back to the land he promised our family long ago. ²² Meanwhile, I'm giving you the hillside▸ I captured from the Amorites."

CHAPTER 49

Jacob blesses his sons

¹⁻² Jacob called his sons together and said:

My sons, I am Jacob,
   your father Israel.
Come, gather around,
   as I tell your future.

³ Reuben, you are my eldest,
   born at the peak of my powers;
   you were an honoured leader.
⁴ Uncontrollable as a flood,
   you slept with my wife
   and disgraced my bed.
And so you no longer deserve
   the place of honour.

⁵ Simeon and Levi, you are brothers,
   each a gruesome sword.
⁶ I never want to take part
   in your plans or deeds.
You slaughtered people
   in your anger,
and you crippled cattle
   for no reason.
⁷ Now I place a curse on you
because of your fierce anger.
Your descendants
   will be scattered
   among the tribes of Israel.

⁸ Judah, you will be praised
   by your brothers;
they will bow down to you,
   as you defeat your enemies.
⁹ My son, you are a lion
   ready to eat your victim!
You are terribly fierce;
   no one will bother you.
¹⁰ You will have power and rule
   until nations obey you▸
   and come bringing gifts.
¹¹ You will tie your donkey
   to a choice grapevine
and wash your clothes
   in wine from those grapes.
¹² Your eyes are darker than wine,
   your teeth whiter than milk.

¹³ Zebulun, you will settle
   along the seashore
and provide safe harbours
   as far north as Sidon.

¹⁴ Issachar, you are a strong donkey
   resting in the meadows.▸

Holy history

The twelve tribes

Jacob's sons become the twelve tribes of Israel. Well, not quite all his sons. Because of their involvement with the massacre of the inhabitants of Shechem (Genesis 34.1–31), Simeon is disinherited, and Levi is not allowed to have any land. Simeon's place is taken by two of Jacob's grandsons: Ephraim and Manasseh, the sons of Joseph. Levi's tribe was never given any land for their own, becoming the priestly tribe. Reuben is also disinherited, losing his birthright to Joseph; this is because he slept with one of his father's wives (Genesis 35.22).

On his deathbed, Jacob describes the characteristics of the people who would descend from his sons, and the kinds of territories they would inhabit. The tribe of Zebulun will live closest to the sea, Asher will dwell in rich and fertile farmland. The tribe of Benjamin will behave like a savage wolf – a reference to their wild and savage behaviour in later years (Judges 19–21).

So, the twelve tribes of Israel are named after ten of Jacob's sons, and two of his grandsons.
The sons: Judah, Reuben, Levi, Asher, Dan, Zebulun, Issachar, Gad, Naphtali, Benjamin
The grandsons: Manasseh and Ephraim

More...

Israel and Judah p.385
Jacob p.29
Birthright & blessings p.31

Anorak corner

Crazy name, crazy peoples – the ten strangest names of peoples in the Bible

Netophathites (1 Chronicles 2.54)
Jerahmeelites (1 Samuel 30.27)
Cherethites (1 Samuel 30.14)
Eshtaolites (1 Chronicles 2.53)
Sucathites (1 Chronicles 2.55)
Uzzielites (Numbers 3.27)
Arvadites (Genesis 10.6)
Zemarites (Genesis 10.6)

15 You found them so pleasant
   that you worked too hard
      and became a slave.
16 Dan,* you are the tribe
   that will bring justice
      to Israel.
17 You are a snake that bites
   the heel of a horse,
      making its rider fall.
18 Our LORD, I am waiting
   for you to save us.
19 Gad,* you will be attacked,
   then attack your attackers.
20 Asher, you will eat food
   fine enough for a king.
21 Naphtali, you are a wild deer
   with lovely fawns.›
22 Joseph, you are a fruitful vine
   growing near a stream
      and climbing a wall.›
23 Enemies attacked with arrows,
   refusing to show mercy.
24 But you stood your ground,
      swiftly shooting back
   with the help of Jacob's God,
      the All-Powerful One —
   his name is the Shepherd,
      Israel's mighty rock.*
25 Your help came from the God
   your father worshipped,
      from God All-Powerful.
   God will bless you with rain
      and streams from the earth;
   he will bless you
      with many descendants.
26 My son, the blessings I give
   are better than the promise
      of ancient mountains
      or eternal hills.›
   Joseph, I pray these blessings
   will come to you,
   because you are the leader
      of your brothers.
27 Benjamin, you are a fierce wolf,
   destroying your enemies
      morning and evening.

---

*49.16 Dan: In Hebrew "Dan" means "justice" or "judgment".
*49.19 Gad: In Hebrew "Gad" sounds like "attack".
*49.24 mighty rock: The Hebrew text has "rock", which is sometimes used in poetry to compare the LORD to a mountain where his people can run for protection from their enemies.

[28] These are the twelve tribes of Israel, and this is how Jacob gave each of them their proper blessings.

Jacob's death

[29-31] Jacob told his sons:

Soon I will die, and I want you to bury me in Machpelah Cave. Abraham bought this cave as a burial place from Ephron the Hittite, and it is near the town of Mamre in Canaan. Abraham and Sarah are buried there, and so are Isaac and Rebekah. I buried Leah there too. [32] Both the cave and the land that goes with it were bought from the Hittites.

[33] When Jacob had finished giving these instructions to his sons, he lay down on his bed and died.

CHAPTER 50

[1] Joseph started crying, then leaned over to hug and kiss his father.

[2] Joseph gave orders for Jacob's body to be embalmed, [3] and it took the usual forty days. The Egyptians mourned seventy days for Jacob. [4] When the time of mourning was over, Joseph said to the Egyptian leaders, "If you consider me your friend, please speak to the king’ for me. [5] Just before my father died, he made me promise to bury him in his burial cave in Canaan. If the king will give me permission to go, I will come back here."

[6] The king answered, "Go to Canaan and keep your promise to your father."

[7-9] When Joseph left Goshen with his brothers, his relatives, and his father's relatives to bury Jacob, many of the king's highest officials and even his military chariots and cavalry went along. The Israelites left behind only their children, their cattle, and their sheep and goats.

[10] After crossing the River Jordan and reaching Atad's threshing place, Joseph made everyone mourn and weep seven days for his father. [11] The Canaanites saw this and said, "The Egyptians are in great sorrow." Then they named the place "Egypt in Sorrow".‣

[12] So Jacob's sons did just as their father had instructed. [13] They took him to Canaan and buried him in Machpelah Cave, the burial place Abraham had bought from Ephron the Hittite.

[14] After the funeral, Joseph, his brothers, and everyone else returned to Egypt.

Joseph dies

Joseph's promise to his brothers

[15] After Jacob died, Joseph's brothers said to each other, "What if Joseph still hates us and wants to get even with us for all the cruel things we did to him?"

[16] So they sent this message to Joseph:

Before our father died, [17] he told us, "You did some cruel and terrible things to Joseph, but you must ask him to forgive you."

Now we ask you to forgive the terrible things we did. After all, we serve the same God that your father worshipped.

When Joseph heard this, he started crying.

[18] At once, Joseph's brothers came and bowed down to the ground in front of him and said, "We are your slaves."

[19] But Joseph told them, "Don't be afraid! I have no right to change what God has decided. [20] You tried to harm me, but God made it turn out for the best, so that he could save all these people, as he is now doing. [21] Don't be afraid! I will take care of you and your children." After Joseph said this, his brothers felt much better.

Joseph's death

[22] Joseph lived in Egypt with his brothers until he died at the age of one hundred and ten. [23] Joseph lived long enough to see Ephraim's children and grandchildren. He also lived to see the children of Manasseh's son Machir, and he welcomed them into his family. [24] Before Joseph died, he told his brothers, "I won't live much longer. But God will take care of you and lead you out of Egypt to the land he promised Abraham, Isaac, and Jacob. [25] Now promise me that you will take my body with you when God leads you to that land."

[26] So Joseph died in Egypt at the age of one hundred and ten; his body was embalmed and put in a coffin.

See also: 49.30: Gen 23.3–20.   **49.31:** a Gen 25.9–10; b Gen 35.29.   **49.33:** Acts 7.15.   **50.5:** Gen 47.29–31. **50.13:** Acts 7.16.

See also: **50.25:** Exod 13.19; Josh 24.32; Heb 11.22.

Additional Notes

›**1.1–2 In . . . life:** Or "When God began to create the heavens and the earth, the earth was barren with no form of life."

›**1.2 the Spirit of God:** Or "a mighty wind".

›**2.6 streams:** Or "mist".

›**4.7 you would be smiling:** Or "I would have accepted your offering."

›**4.8 Cain said to his brother Abel, "Let's . . . walk":** Most ancient translations; Hebrew "Cain spoke to his brother Abel."

›**4.15 No:** Three ancient translations; Hebrew "Very well!"

›**4.16 Wandering:** The Hebrew text has "Nod", which means "wandering".

›**4.26 worshipping the LORD:** Or "worshipping in the name of the LORD."

›**6.1,2 supernatural beings:** Or "angels".

›**6.3 I won't . . . for ever:** One possible meaning for the difficult Hebrew text.

›**6.3 No one . . . years:** Or "In fact, they will all be destroyed in about one hundred years" (that is, at the time of the flood).

›**6.16 roof:** Or "window".

›**6.16 leave . . . sides:** One possible meaning for the difficult Hebrew text.

›**6.18 boat:** One possible meaning for the difficult Hebrew text of verse 18.

›**8.13 made . . . boat:** One possible meaning for the difficult Hebrew text.

›**10.2–5 Dodanim:** Most Hebrew manuscripts; some Hebrew manuscripts and one ancient translation have "Rodanim".

›**10.6–20 and Accad, all of:** Or "Accad, and Calneh".

›**10.6–20 Babylonia:** The Hebrew text has "Shinar", another name for Babylonia.

›**10.6–20 Casluhim, and Caphtorim, the ancestor of the Philistines:** Hebrew "Caphtorim, and Casluhim, the ancestor of the Philistines". The Philistines were from Caphtor (see Jeremiah 47.4; Amos 9.7), better known as Crete.

›**11.2 from the east:** Or "to the east".

›**11.2 Babylonia:** See the note at 10.6–20.

›**12.3 Everyone . . . you:** Or "Everyone on earth will ask me to bless them as I have blessed you."

›**12.15 the king's:** The Hebrew text has "Pharaoh's", a Hebrew word sometimes used for the king of Egypt.

›**14.1 Babylonia:** See the note at 10.6–20.

›**14.6 Edom:** The Hebrew text has "Seir", another name for Edom.

›**15.2 And . . . own:** One possible meaning for the difficult Hebrew text.

›**15.10 cut:** In Hebrew "cut" sounds something like "agreement". What follows shows that the LORD is making an agreement with Abram.

›**15.16 people who live here:** The Hebrew text has "Amorites", a name sometimes used of the people who lived in Palestine before the Israelites.

›**16.5 It's . . . fault:** Or "I hope you'll be punished for what you did to me!"

›**16.13 Have . . . it:** One possible meaning for the difficult Hebrew text.

›**16.13 The God who Sees Me:** Or "The God I have Seen".

›**16.14 The Well . . . Me:** Or "Beer-Lahai-Roi" (see 25.11).

›**18.18 that will be . . . on earth:** Or "and all other nations on earth will ask me to bless them as I have blessed his family."

›**20.16 as proof . . . wrong:** One possible meaning for the difficult Hebrew text.

›**21.9–10 playing:** Hebrew; one ancient translation "playing with her son Isaac".

›**22.14 The LORD will Provide . . . it will be provided:** Or "The LORD will be Seen . . . the LORD will be seen" or "It (a ram) will be Seen . . . it (a ram) will be seen".

›**23.16–18 Hebron:** The Hebrew text has "Mamre", a place just north of Hebron.

›**24.10 northern Syria:** The Hebrew text has "Aram-Naharaim", probably referring to the land around the city of Haran (see also "Paddan-Aram" in 25.20; 28.2,6; 31.18,20; 33.18; 35.23–26; 46.8–15; and "Paddan" in 48.7).

›**24.62 who Sees Me:** Or "I Have Seen".

›**25.9–10 Hebron:** See the note at 23.16–18.

›**25.11 The Well . . . Sees Me:** Or "Beer-Lahai-Roi" (see 16.14).

›**25.17,18 sons:** Or "descendants".

›**25.20 northern Syria:** See the note at 24.10.

›**25.23 two separate nations:** Or "two nations always in conflict".

›**26.4 They . . . on earth:** Or "All nations on earth will ask me to bless them."

›**28.2 northern Syria:** See the note at 24.10.

›**28.6 northern Syria:** See the note at 24.10.

›**28.12 ladder:** Or "stairway".

›**28.13 the ladder:** Or "Jacob" or "the stairway" (see the note at 28.12).

›**28.14 Your family . . . people:** Or "All people will ask me to bless them as I have blessed your family."

›**28.17 ladder:** See the note at 28.12.

›**29.16–17 but her eyes didn't sparkle:** Or "and her eyes sparkled".

›**30.27–28 I'm sure:** The Hebrew text means to find out by some kind of magic, such as fortune-telling.

›**31.13 you . . . Bethel:** Or "who appeared to you at Bethel".

›**31.18 northern Syria:** See the note at 24.10.

›**31.20 the Aramean:** Meaning someone from northern Syria (see the note at 24.10).

›**31.42 fearsome God:** One possible meaning for the difficult Hebrew text.

›**31.53 fearsome God:** See the note at 31.42.

›**33.18 northern Syria:** See the note at 24.10.

›**33.19 pieces of silver:** Or "lambs" or "cattle".

›**35.23–26 northern Syria:** See the note at 24.10.

›**36.24 an oasis:** One possible meaning for the difficult Hebrew text.

›**37.3 fine coat:** Or "a coat of many colours" or "a coat with long sleeves".

›**37.23 fine coat:** See the note at 37.3.

›37.28 Midianite . . . Ishmaelites: According to 25.1–2,12 both the Midianites and the Ishmaelites were descendants of Abraham, and in Judges 8.22–24 the two names are used of the same people. It is possible that in this passage "Ishmaelite" has the meaning "nomadic traders", while "Midianite" refers to their ethnic origin.

›37.36 the king's: See the note at 12.15.

›39.1 the king's: See the note at 12.15.

›40.1–3 the king's: See the note at 12.15.

›41.1 the king: See the note at 12.15.

›41.37 The king: See the note at 12.15.

›41.45 Heliopolis: The Hebrew text has "On", which is better known by its Greek name "Heliopolis".

›41.52 God has made me a success: Or "God has given me children".

›41.52 Ephraim . . . suffered: In Hebrew "Ephraim" actually means either "fertile land" or "pasture land".

›44.18 the king: See the note at 12.15.

›45.2 the king's: See the note at 12.15.

›46.5–7 the king: See the note at 12.15.

›46.8–15 northern Syria: See the note at 24.10.

›46.8–15 Jashub: The Samaritan Hebrew Text and one ancient translation; the Standard Hebrew Text "Iob".

›46.19–22 Heliopolis: See the note at 41.45.

›46.31 the king: See the note at 12.15.

›47.14 the king: See the note at 12.15.

›47.21 made . . . slaves: One ancient translation and the Samaritan Hebrew Text; the Standard Hebrew Text "made everyone move to the cities".

›48.7 northern Syria: See the note at 24.10.

›48.7 Bethlehem: The Hebrew text has "Ephrath, that is, Bethlehem".

›48.22 the hillside: Or "a larger share than your brothers, the land".

›49.10 until . . . you: One possible meaning for the difficult Hebrew text.

›49.14 resting . . . meadows: One possible meaning for the difficult Hebrew text.

›49.21 with lovely fawns: Or "speaking lovely words".

›49.22 wall: One possible meaning for the difficult Hebrew text.

›49.26 eternal hills: One possible meaning for the difficult Hebrew text.

›50.4 the king: See the note at 12.15.

›50.11 Egypt in Sorrow: Or "Abel-Mizraim".

Exodus

The basics

What's the point? Exodus shows how God keeps his promises. He promised to lead the Israelites to their freedom, and that's exactly what happens.

What happens? The book deals with the escape of the Israelites from slavery in Egypt. It also includes a great deal of religious rite and ceremony and legal issues.

What should I remember? 3.14–15 'I am the eternal God. So tell them that the Lord, whose name is "I Am", has sent you. This is my name for ever, and it is the name that people must use from now on.'

More detail

Setting the scene The people who came to Egypt in the time of Joseph have grown into a large nation, and they are now enslaved by the Egyptians. But God wants them to leave...

What's it all about? Exodus means, literally, 'exit'. Which is really what the book is about: how God helped the Israelites to escape from slavery in Egypt.

In the many years after the time of Joseph two significant things have happened: first, people have forgotten who Joseph was and what he did for them; second, the Israelites are now a slave nation, oppressed and abused by their Egyptian masters.

Exodus centres around Moses, the Israelite raised as an Egyptian, the first freedom fighter. God meets with Moses in the desert and empowers him to go and lead the people out of slavery. The first section deals with God choosing Moses to lead his people out of Egypt. Moses presents God's demands to the Egyptian king, who refuses to listen. Finally, after a series of plagues and disasters, the king

sees sense and the Israelites are set free. The second section shows the journey of the Israelites to Mount Sinai. Despite attacks from the Egyptians and other problems, the Lord protects the Israelites and provides for them.

And the third section... It starts well. At Mount Sinai God gives his people the laws for them to follow. This includes the Ten Commandments and many other laws for regulating their daily life and worship. But even while God is laying down the rules on the mountain, down at ground level the people are disobeying him and setting up their own gods to worship. It doesn't bode well for the future.

Exodus is more than the history of the Israelites' rescue – even though that history is miraculous in the extreme. It also contains some of the deepest and most mysterious passages of the Bible; passages which give us a unique insight into what God is like and what relationship he wants to have with his followers. Moses' meetings with God reveal a lot about who God is and the kind of relationship he wants to have with his people. He is not a distant, remote God, but one who cares for his people, who rescues them and who wants to show them how best to live.

Footsteps

The slavery of Israel: 1.1–14
The birth of Moses: 1.15–2.10
Moses commits murder: 2.11–25
The burning bush: 3.1–21
Moses is given his instructions: 4.1–17
Moses and Aaron confront the king: 5.1–21
The first few plagues: 7.14–8.32
The final punishment of the Egyptians: 11.1–10; 12.29–30
The Passover: 12.1–28
The escape: 12.31–42

Crossing the sea: 14.1–31
The Lord sends food: 16.1–26
The Ten Commandments: 19.16—20.17
The Sacred Tent and Sacred Chest: 25.1–22

The people of Israel become slaves

CHAPTER 1

The people of Israel suffer

¹⁻⁵ When Jacob went to Egypt, his son Joseph was already there. So Jacob took his eleven other sons and their families. They were: Reuben, Simeon, Levi, Judah, Issachar, Zebulun, Benjamin, Dan, Naphtali, Gad, and Asher. Altogether, Jacob had seventy children, grandchildren, and great-grandchildren* who went with him.

⁶ After Joseph, his brothers, and everyone else in that generation had died, ⁷ the people of Israel became so numerous that the whole region of Goshen was full of them.

⁸ Many years later a new king came to power. He did not know what Joseph had done for Egypt, ⁹ and he told the Egyptians:

There are too many of those Israelites in our country, and they are becoming more powerful than we are. ¹⁰ If we don't outsmart them, their families will keep growing larger. And if our country goes to war, they could easily fight on the side of our enemies and escape from Egypt.

¹¹ The Egyptians put slave bosses in charge of the people of Israel and tried to wear them down with hard work. Those bosses forced them to build the cities of Pithom and Rameses,* where the king' could store his supplies. ¹² But even though the Israelites were ill-treated, their families grew larger, and they took over more land. Because of this, the Egyptians hated them more than before ¹³ and made them work so hard ¹⁴ that

---

*1.1–5 seventy children . . . great-grandchildren:
See Genesis 46.8–27.
*1.11 Pithom and Rameses: This is the only mention of Pithom in the Bible; its exact location is unknown, though it was probably in the northern Delta of Egypt. Rameses is the famous Delta city that was the home of Rameses II; its exact location is also unknown.

See also: 1.1–4: Gen 46.8–27. 1.7: Acts 7.17.
1.8: Acts 7.18. 1.10: Acts 7.19.

Life files

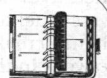

Moses

Background: Adopted by Egyptian princess

What's the story?

Moses' life falls into three neat sections: Egyptian prince (aged 1–40); shepherd (41–80); leader of the Israelites (81–120).

His mother set the baby Moses afloat on the Nile to avoid his death. He was found by an Egyptian princess, and raised in the royal household. But he never forgot his origins. He killed a guard for abusing a Hebrew slave, fled and spent years in the desert, working as a shepherd. There he met God, in a burning bush. God told Moses to lead his people out of Egypt, and gave him the Law for the people to live by.

However, the people lacked faith in God, who punished them by making them wander in the wilderness. Even Moses never made it to the Promised Land.

What's the point?

Moses is one of the great figures of the Bible. He battled against the Israelites' lack of faith (and constant moaning) leading them to the very edge of the promised land.

Footsteps

Ten days with Moses

The birth and the boat trip: Exodus 2.1–10
Murder and escape: Exodus 2.11–25
The burning bush: Exodus 3.1–22
The first few plagues: Exodus 5.1–5; 7.1–25
Final disaster, Passover: Exodus 11.1—12.30
The Red Sea: Exodus 14
Food from heaven: Exodus 16
Ten Commandments: Exodus 19.1—20.21
The golden calf: Exodus 32
Last days: Deuteronomy 31.1–13; 34.1–8

More...

Can people tell when you've been spending time with God? p.101
Aaron p.159
The golden calf p.191
Ark of the Covenant p.104
The Tabernacle: the Sacred Tent p.107
The Law p.127

their lives were miserable. The Egyptians were cruel to the people of Israel and forced them to make bricks and to mix mortar and to work in the fields.

15 Finally, the king called in Shiphrah and Puah, the two women who helped the Hebrew* mothers when they gave birth. 16 He told them, "If a Hebrew woman gives birth to a girl, let the child live. If the baby is a boy, kill him!"

17 But the two women were faithful to God and did not kill the boys, even though the king had told them to. 18 The king called them in again and asked, "Why are you letting those baby boys live?"

19 They answered, "Hebrew women have their babies much quicker than Egyptian women. By the time we arrive, their babies are already born." 20-21 God was good to the two women because they truly respected him, and he blessed them with children of their own.

The Hebrews kept increasing 22 until finally, the king gave a command to everyone in the nation, "As soon as a Hebrew boy is born, throw him into the River Nile! But you can let the girls live."

Moses is born and grows up

CHAPTER 2

1 A man from the Levi tribe married a woman from the same tribe, 2 and she later had a baby boy. He was a beautiful child, and she kept him inside for three months. 3 But when she could no longer keep him hidden, she made a basket out of reeds and covered it with tar. She put him in the basket and placed it in the tall grass along the edge of the River Nile. 4 The baby's elder sister* stood at a distance to see what would happen to him.

5 About that time one of the king's﹢ daughters came down to take a bath in the river, while her servant women walked along the river bank. She saw the basket in the tall grass and sent one of the young women to pull it out of the water. 6 When the king's daughter opened the basket, she saw the baby and felt sorry for him because he was crying. She said, "This must be one of the Hebrew babies."

7 At once the baby's elder sister came up and asked, "Do you want me to get a Hebrew woman to take care of the baby for you?"

8 "Yes," the king's daughter answered.

So the girl brought the baby's mother, 9 and the king's daughter told her, "Take care of this child, and I will pay you."

The baby's mother carried him home and took care of him. 10 And when he was old enough, she took him to the king's daughter, who adopted him. She named him Moses* because she said, "I pulled him out of the water."

Moses escapes from Egypt

11 After Moses had grown up, he went out to where his own people were hard at work, and he saw an Egyptian beating one of them. 12 Moses looked around to see if anyone was watching, then he killed the Egyptian and hid his body in the sand.

13 When Moses went out the next day, he saw two Hebrews fighting. So he went to the man who had started the fight and asked, "Why are you beating up one of your own people?"

14 The man answered, "Who put you in charge of us and made you our judge? Are you planning to kill me, just as you killed that Egyptian?"

This frightened Moses because he was sure that people must have found out what had happened. 15 When the king﹢ heard what Moses had done, the king wanted to kill him. But Moses escaped and went to the land of Midian.

One day, Moses was sitting there by a well, 16 when the seven daughters of Jethro, the priest of Midian,﹢ came up to water their father's sheep and goats. 17 Some shepherds tried to chase them away, but Moses came to their rescue and watered their animals.

18 When Jethro's daughters returned home, their father asked, "Why have you come back so early today?"

19 They answered, "An Egyptian rescued us from the shepherds, and he even watered our sheep and goats."

20 "Where is he?" Jethro asked. "Why did you leave him out there? Invite him to eat with us."

---

*1.15 Hebrew: An earlier term for "Israelite".
*2.4 elder sister: Miriam, the sister of Moses and Aaron.
See also: 1.22: Acts 7.19. 2.2: Acts 7.20; Heb 11.23.

*2.10 Moses: In Hebrew "Moses" sounds like "pull out".
See also: 2.10: Acts 7.21. 2.11-14: Acts 7.23-28.
2.11: Heb 11.24. 2.15: Acts 7.29; Heb 11.27.

Real life

Fostering and adoption

Contributed by Care

Moses' mother had a choice to make regarding her son. She could have hidden Moses and brought him up as a slave under the Egyptian regime; or she could have given him up to a soldier with a sword. Instead she placed him in a basket on the river, allowing God to determine his future. Moses' adoption by a princess was part of God's purpose for him to become a leader of Israel. Samuel. Esther, even Jesus himself, were adopted. It was part of their destiny. When we become Christians, we too are adopted by the Father (Romans 8.23) who restores our broken lives and changes our destiny.

There are many reasons why, throughout the centuries, children have required the support and care of adults outside their own family, but their basic needs – security, significance and self-worth – have remained the same.

In Britain, during the late 18th and 19th centuries, many Christians helped children at risk, by providing food and shelter. In the 20th Century, the State took over this role, and still does today. In fact, the demand for substitute care is increasing; local authorities have been overwhelmed by the need and many Independent Foster Care Agencies have been formed to meet the shortfall. Care Fostering Service (CFS) is one such agency which has, in recent years, been providing care for young people involved in criminal activities, and sibling groups who are unable to remain within their own families.

Good quality foster care makes a huge difference to broken and hurting lives, especially when it's underpinned by a living Christian faith, and carers who will sticks with young people, even when the 'going gets (very) tough'. Homes like this provide a safe, nurturing and stimulating environment where children can make sense of past hurts, develop positive friendships, have fun, and fulfil their potential. Many young lives have been turned around by daily practical expressions of 'love in action' in ordinary family settings. So, with prayer, a child can be healed of the separation from its natural mother, bond with new parents and grow into wholeness.

But it's not just the children. The birth mother often feels ashamed of placing her child for adoption, but with prayer and support, adoption can be a redeeming process for her too. The adopters may have already suffered loss and grief through infertility. Adoption is a way of bringing healing, joy and sense of purpose to them too.

With adoption, everybody can win.

Think

Have you any experience of fostering or adoption?
Would you consider fostering or adopting a child?
How does being adopted by God change your life?

Act

Listen to the stories of those who've been fostered or adopted.
Pray for any foster parents you may know – it's not an easy task!

Check

Exodus 2.1–10; Luke 18.15–16; Ephesians 1.1–6

More...

Families p.1224
Help! My Dad's never around p.187
Help! My parents are letting me down! p.598
Divorce p.1281

Real life

School

Contributed by Discovery

Here's the scene: the alarm goes off... your brain takes a few minutes to enter the real world... your heart sinks as you gradually register that the day is Monday, and you have 5 days of school ahead of you! What's the point anyway? You hate half your subjects, the teachers are from another planet, and really you're just counting down the days until the weekend when you'll have your freedom back again.

Does any of this sound familiar? What does the thought of school stir up in you? 5 days a week for most of the year, for at least 12 years of your life...probably more! Is it really necessary?

Let's bring in a guy called Moses. Maybe he can throw some light on the subject. Read Exodus 2.1–11 and Acts 7.20–25.

Actually, not much is written in the Bible about Moses' growing up years. In fact, between verses 10 and 11 of Exodus 2, Moses jumps from being a young lad to suddenly being all grown up and living as an adult. So what happened in between? Well, what we do know is that because Moses was adopted into the king's family, he was given the best education that money could buy. He became a very powerful man. He learnt about the ways of the Egyptians and their beliefs, which God later used when rescuing the Israelites from Egypt.

Those growing up years were vitally important to God, Moses, and the Israelites. God used that time to create foundations in Moses that would shape his life and character, and in turn would have a great effect on his thinking, attitudes and actions. God would have used the situations and circumstances around Moses to do this...not just in his lessons, but in the time he spent with friends, and solving problems that came his way. His time in education was a part of making him who he was, and helped prepare him for the calling that God had upon his life... and what an amazing calling it was!

'His power at work in us can do far more than we dare ask or imagine.'
Ephesians 3.20

Just think: your time in school, and all that it entails, may be the key to the mind-blowing plan that God has for your life... now can YOU answer the question: 'What's the point?'

Think

What might God be preparing you for during your school days?
What impact are you having on your friends and teachers while you're there?
What could you be learning from them?
Do you see school as a chore, or a God-given training ground?

Act

Find a (positive) way to surprise friends or teachers this week.
Keep asking, why is it important to learn this subject, lesson, rule? (It's not a bad question for teachers to be trying to answer, too!)

Check

Job 23.9; Proverbs 12.27; 16.26; Ecclesiastes 3.9–11; 8.6–7; Jeremiah 29.11; Hebrews 3.5

More...

Help! I can't be bothered with homework p.719
Help! I can't cope with revision p.1011
Help! I don't know what to do in my gap year p.692
Help! I don't want to go to college p.591
Sharing with your friends p.1198
Sharing your faith p.1082

21 Moses agreed to stay on with Jethro, who later let his daughter Zipporah marry Moses. 22 And when she had a son, Moses said, "I will name him Gershom,* since I am a foreigner in this country."

23 After the death of the king of Egypt, the Israelites still complained because they were forced to be slaves. They cried out for help, 24 and God heard their loud cries. He did not forget the promise he had made to Abraham, Isaac, and Jacob, 25 and because he knew what was happening to his people, he felt sorry for them.

God sends Moses to speak to the king of Egypt

CHAPTER 3

God speaks to Moses

1 One day, Moses was taking care of the sheep and goats of his father-in-law Jethro, the priest of Midian, and Moses decided to lead them across the desert to Sinai,♦ the holy mountain. 2 There an angel of the LORD appeared to him from a burning bush. Moses saw that the bush was on fire, but it was not burning up. 3 "This is strange!" he said to himself. "I'll go over and see why the bush isn't burning up."

4 When the LORD saw Moses coming near the bush, he called him by name, and Moses answered, "Here I am."

5 God replied, "Don't come any closer. Take off your sandals — the ground where you are standing is holy. 6 I am the God who was worshipped by your ancestors Abraham, Isaac, and Jacob."

Moses was afraid to look at God, and so he hid his face.

7 The LORD said:

I have seen how my people are suffering as slaves in Egypt, and I have heard them beg for my help because of the way they are being ill-treated. I feel sorry for them, 8 and I have come down to rescue them from the Egyptians.

I will bring my people out of Egypt into a country where there is good land, rich with milk and honey. I will give them the land where the Canaanites, Hittites, Amorites, Perizzites, Hivites, and Jebusites now live.

Big ideas

Names of God

Many names and images are used to describe God.

Yahweh

Always written in Scriptures as YHWH, and never uttered by the Jews out of reverence for God. There is a lot of dispute about what the name means. Some experts believe that it doesn't, in fact, mean anything. Others believe that it means 'he causes to be what exists' and refers to God as creator. Instead of printing Yahweh or YHWH, most modern Bibles use 'the LORD'.

This is the name that God gives to Moses in Exodus 3.14, where it is linked with God calling himself 'I Am'.

Elohim

Usually rendered 'God'. Although the word is actually plural (i.e. 'Gods'), it is commonly used of God as the one, supreme deity.

El

The singular of 'Elohim'. It is usually used before another term, for example 'El Elyon' which means 'God Most High' (Genesis 14.18) or El Shaddai, which is translated 'God Almighty'.

Images used to describe God

The Bible uses loads of images to describe what God is like. Examples include a rock (Exodus 7.1–7), a shepherd (Psalms 23.1), a stronghold (Psalms 18.2), a refuge (Psalms 37.39), and a redeemer (Isaiah 41.14).

Jesus uses perhaps the most potent image, which is that of a father.

More...

Names p.66
Holiness p.1386

---

*2.22 Gershom: In Hebrew "Gershom" sounds like "foreigner".

See also: 2.24: Gen 15.13–14.   3.2–10: Acts 7.30–34.

Holy history

Names

In the Bible, names are important. Your name was more than just something that sounded nice, or something that people called you; it said something about your character. To know someone's name was to know their nature.

Thus, when Moses asks God what his name is, he is doing far more than just introducing himself; he is seeking to know something crucial about God. Something vital. And here's the really amazing bit: God tells him.

God could have told Moses to go away. He could have refused to answer him. After all, who was this insignificant mortal to ask his name? But God didn't do that. Instead he answered Moses.

'So tell them that the LORD, whose name is "I Am," has sent you. This is my name forever, and it is the name that people must use from now on' (Exodus 3.14).

God is in the present tense. He has no beginning and no end, he simply is. And more than that, he has allowed us to glimpse something of his nature through his name.

That's why God changes people's names in the Bible. Their change of name reflects a new purpose in their life, or a significant event. So Abram becomes Abraham; Jacob becomes Israel. To change someone's name also reflected a change of ownership. Later on in the Old Testament, when the kingdom of Judah is taken into captivity, their new owners, the Babylonians, change their names. It signifies complete control.

So. Names are important. Names have meaning. If God was renaming you, what name would he choose?

More...

Names of God p.65

[9] My people have begged for my help, and I have seen how cruel the Egyptians are to them. [10] Now go to the king! I am sending you to lead my people out of his country.

[11] But Moses said, "Who am I to go to the king and lead your people out of Egypt?"

[12] God replied, "I will be with you. And you will know that I am the one who sent you, when you worship me on this mountain after you have led my people out of Egypt."▸

[13] Moses answered, "I will tell the people of Israel that the God their ancestors worshipped has sent me to them. But what should I say, if they ask me your name?"

[14-15] God said to Moses:

I am the eternal God. So tell them that the LORD,* whose name is "I Am", has sent you. This is my name for ever, and it is the name that people must use from now on.

[16] Call together the leaders of Israel and tell them that the God who was worshipped by Abraham, Isaac, and Jacob has appeared to you. Tell them I have seen how terribly they are being treated in Egypt, [17] and I promise to lead them out of their troubles. I will give them a land rich with milk and honey, where the Canaanites, Hittites, Amorites, Perizzites, Hivites, and Jebusites now live.

[18] The leaders of Israel will listen to you. Then you must take them to the king of Egypt and say, "The LORD God of the Hebrews has appeared to us. Let us walk three days into the desert, where we can offer a sacrifice to him." [19] But I know that the king of Egypt won't let you go unless something forces him to. [20] So I will use my mighty power to perform all kinds of miracles and strike down the Egyptians. Then the king will send you away.

[21] After I punish the Egyptians, they will be so afraid of you that they will give you anything you want. You are my people, and I will let you take many things with you when you leave the land of Egypt. [22] Every Israelite woman will go to her Egyptian neighbours or to any Egyptian woman living in her house. She will ask them for gold and silver jewellery and for their finest

*3.14-15 LORD: The Hebrew text has "Yahweh", which is usually translated "LORD" in the CEV. Since it seems related to the word translated "I Am", it may mean "I am the one who is" or "I will be what I will be" or "I am the one who brings into being".

See also: 3.13: Exod 6.2-3.   3.14: Rev 1.4,8.
3.21-22: Exod 12.35-36.

clothes. The Egyptians will give them to you, and you will put these fine things on your sons and daughters. You will carry all this away when you leave Egypt.

CHAPTER 4

The LORD gives great power to Moses

¹ Moses asked the LORD, "Suppose everyone refuses to listen to my message, and no one believes that you really appeared to me?"

² The LORD answered, "What's that in your hand?"

"A walking stick," Moses replied.

³ "Throw it down!" the LORD commanded. So Moses threw the stick on the ground. It immediately turned into a snake, and Moses jumped back.

⁴ "Pick it up by the tail!" the LORD told him. And when Moses did this, the snake turned back into a walking stick.

⁵ "Do this," the LORD said, "and the Israelites will believe that you have seen me, the God who was worshipped by their ancestors Abraham, Isaac, and Jacob."

⁶ Next, the LORD commanded Moses, "Put your hand inside your shirt." Moses obeyed, and when he took it out, his hand had turned white as snow — like someone with leprosy.*

⁷ "Put your hand back inside your shirt," the LORD told him. Moses did so, and when he took it out again, it was as healthy as the rest of his body.

⁸⁻⁹ Then the LORD said, "If no one believes either of these miracles, take some water from the River Nile and pour it on the ground. The water will immediately turn into blood."

¹⁰ Moses replied, "I have never been a good speaker. I wasn't one before you spoke to me, and I'm not one now. I am slow at speaking, and I can never think of what to say."

¹¹ But the LORD answered, "Who makes people able to speak or makes them deaf or unable to speak? Who gives them sight or makes them blind? Don't you know that I am the one who does these things? ¹² Now go! When you speak, I will be with you and give you the words to say."

¹³ Moses begged, "LORD, please send someone else to do it."

¹⁴ The LORD became irritated with Moses and said:

What about your brother Aaron, the Levite? I know he is a good speaker. He is already on his way here to visit you, and he will be happy to see you again. ¹⁵⁻¹⁶ Aaron will speak to the people for you, and you will be like me, telling Aaron what to say. I will be with both of you as you speak, and I will tell each of you what to do. ¹⁷ Now take this walking stick and use it to perform miracles.

Moses returns to Egypt

¹⁸ Moses went to his father-in-law Jethro and asked, "Please let me return to Egypt to see if any of my people are still alive."

"All right," Jethro replied. "I hope all goes well."

¹⁹ But even before this, the LORD had told Moses, "Leave the land of Midian and return to Egypt. Everyone who wanted to kill you is dead." ²⁰ So Moses put his wife and sons on donkeys and headed for Egypt, holding the walking stick that had the power of God.

²¹ On the way the LORD said to Moses:

When you get to Egypt, go to the king and work the miracles I have shown you. But I will make him so stubborn that he will refuse to let my people go. ²² Then tell him that I have said, "Israel is my firstborn son, ²³ and I commanded you to release him, so he could worship me. But you refused, and now I will kill your firstborn son."

Zipporah's son is circumcised

²⁴ One night while Moses was in camp, the LORD was about to kill him. ²⁵ But Zipporah* circumcised her son with a flint knife. She touched his* legs with the skin she had cut off and said, "My dear son, this blood will protect you."▸ ²⁶ So the LORD did not harm Moses. Then Zipporah said, "Yes, my dear, you are safe because of this circumcision."▸

Aaron is sent to meet Moses

²⁷ The LORD sent Aaron to meet Moses in the desert. So Aaron met Moses at Mount Sinai▸ and greeted him with a kiss. ²⁸ Moses told Aaron what God had sent him to say; he also told him about the miracles God had given him the power to perform.

²⁹ Later they brought together the leaders of Israel, ³⁰ and Aaron told them what the

*4.6 leprosy: The word translated "leprosy" was used for many different kinds of skin diseases.

*4.25 Zipporah: The wife of Moses (see 2.16–21).
*4.25 his: Either Moses or the boy.
See also: 4.23: Exod 12.29.

LORD had sent Moses to say. Then Moses worked the miracles for the people, 31 and everyone believed. They bowed down and worshipped the LORD because they knew that he had seen their suffering and was going to help them.

CHAPTER 5

Moses and Aaron go to the king of Egypt

1 Moses and Aaron went to the king⟩ of Egypt and told him, "The LORD God says, 'Let my people go into the desert, so they can honour me with a celebration there.' "

2 "Who is this LORD and why should I obey him?" the king replied. "I refuse to let you and your people go!"

3 They answered, "The LORD God of the Hebrews has appeared to us. Please let us walk three days into the desert where we can offer sacrifices to him. If you don't, he may strike us down with terrible troubles or with war."

4-5 The king said, "Moses and Aaron, why are you keeping these people from working? Look how many you are keeping from doing their work. Now everyone get back to work!"

6 That same day the king gave orders to his slave bosses and to the men directly in charge of the Israelite slaves. He told them:

7 Don't give the slaves any more straw* to put in their bricks. Force them to find their own straw wherever they can, 8 but they must make the same number of bricks as before. They are lazy, or else they would not beg me to let them go and sacrifice to their God. 9 Make them work so hard that they won't have time to listen to these lies.

10 The slave bosses and the men in charge of the slaves went out and told them, "The king says he will not give you any more straw. 11 Go and find your own straw wherever you can, but you must still make as many bricks as before."

12 The slaves went all over Egypt, looking for straw. 13 But the slave bosses were hard on them and kept saying, "Each day you have to make as many bricks as you did when you were given straw." 14 The bosses beat the men in charge of the slaves and said, "Why didn't you force the slaves to make as many bricks yesterday and today as they did before?"

15 Finally, the men in charge of the slaves went to the king and said, "Why are you treating us like this? 16 No one brings us any straw, but we are still ordered to make the same number of bricks. We are beaten with whips, and your own people are to blame."

17 The king replied, "You are lazy — nothing but lazy! That's why you keep asking me to let you go and sacrifice to your LORD. 18 Get back to work! You won't be given straw, but you must still make the same number of bricks."

19 The men knew they were in deep trouble when they were ordered to make the same number of bricks each day. 20 After they left the king, they went to see Moses and Aaron, who had been waiting for them. 21 Then the men said, "We hope the LORD will punish both of you for making the king and his officials hate us. Now they even have an excuse to kill us."

The LORD's promise to Moses

22 Moses left them and prayed, "Our LORD, why have you brought so much trouble on your people? Is that why you sent me here? 23 Ever since you told me to speak to the king,⟩ he has caused nothing but trouble for these people. And you haven't done a thing to help."

CHAPTER 6

1 The LORD God told Moses:

Soon you will see what I will do to the king. Because of my mighty power, he will let my people go, and he will even chase them out of his country.

2 My name is the LORD.* 3 But when I appeared to Abraham, Isaac, and Jacob, I came as God All-Powerful and did not use my name. 4 I made an agreement and promised them the land of Canaan, where they were living as foreigners. 5 Now I have seen how the people of Israel are suffering because of the Egyptians, and I will keep my promise.

6 Here is my message for Israel: "I am the LORD! And with my mighty power I will punish the Egyptians and free you from slavery. 7 I will accept you as my people, and I will be your God. Then you will

---

*5.7 straw: The straw made the mud bricks stronger and kept them from shrinking, cracking, or losing their shape.

*6.2 My name is the LORD: See the note at 3.14−15. See also: 6.2−3: Gen 17.1; 28.3; 35.11; Exod 3.13−15.

know that I was the one who rescued you from the Egyptians. [8] I will bring you into the land that I solemnly promised Abraham, Isaac, and Jacob, and it will be yours. I am the LORD!"

[9] When Moses told this to the Israelites, they were too discouraged and ill-treated to believe him.

[10] Then the LORD told Moses [11] to demand that the king of Egypt let the Israelites leave. [12] But Moses replied, "I'm not a powerful speaker. If the Israelites won't listen to me, why should the king of Egypt?" [13] But the LORD sent Aaron and Moses with a message for the Israelites and for the king; he also ordered Aaron and Moses to free the people from Egypt.

Family record of Aaron and Moses

[14] The following men were the heads of their ancestral clans:

The sons of Reuben, Jacob's' eldest son, were Hanoch, Pallu, Hezron, and Carmi. [15] The sons of Simeon were Jemuel, Jamin, Ohad, Jachin, Zohar, and Shaul, the son of a Canaanite woman.

[16] Levi lived to be one hundred and thirty-seven; his sons were Gershon, Kohath, and Merari.

[17] Gershon's sons were Libni and Shimei. [18] Kohath lived to be one hundred and thirty-three; his sons were Amram, Izhar, Hebron, and Uzziel.

[19] Merari's sons were Mahli and Mushi. All of the above were from the Levi tribe.

[20] Amram lived to be one hundred and thirty-seven. He married his father's sister Jochebed, and they had two sons, Aaron and Moses.

[21] Izhar's sons were Korah, Nepheg, and Zichri.

[22] Uzziel's sons were Mishael, Elzaphan, and Sithri.

[23] Aaron married Elisheba. She was the daughter of Amminadab and the sister of Nahshon; they had four sons, Nadab, Abihu, Eleazar, and Ithamar.

[24] Korah's sons were Assir, Elkanah, and Abiasaph.

[25] Aaron's son Eleazar married one of Putiel's daughters, and their son was Phinehas. This ends the list of those who were the heads of clans in the Levi tribe.

[26] The LORD had commanded Aaron and Moses to lead every family and tribe of Israel out of Egypt, [27] and so they ordered the king of Egypt to set the people of Israel free.

The LORD commands Moses and Aaron to speak to the king

[28] When the LORD spoke to Moses in the land of Egypt, [29] he said, "I am the LORD. Tell the king' of Egypt everything I say to you."

[30] But Moses answered, "You know I am a very poor speaker, and the king will never listen to me."

The first nine disasters

CHAPTER 7

[1] The LORD said:

I am going to let your brother Aaron speak for you. He will tell your message to the king, just as a prophet speaks my message to the people. [2] Tell Aaron everything I say to you, and he will order the king to let my people leave his country. [3-4] But I will make the king so stubborn that he won't listen to you. He won't listen even when I do many terrible things to him and his nation. Then I will bring a final punishment on Egypt, and the king will let Israel's families and tribes go. [5] When this happens, the Egyptians will know that I am the LORD.

[6] Moses and Aaron obeyed the LORD [7] and spoke to the king. At the time, Moses was eighty years old, and Aaron was eighty-three.

A stick turns into a snake

[8-9] The LORD said, "Moses, when the king' asks you and Aaron to perform a miracle, command Aaron to throw his walking stick down in front of the king, and it will turn into a snake."

[10] Moses and Aaron went to the king and his officials and did exactly as the LORD had commanded — Aaron threw the stick down, and it turned into a snake. [11] Then the king called in the wise men and the magicians, who used their secret powers to do the same thing — [12] they threw down sticks that turned into snakes. But Aaron's snake swallowed theirs. [13] The king behaved just as the LORD had said and stubbornly refused to listen.

See also: **6.16–19:** Num 3.17–20; 26.57–58; 1 Chron 6.16–19.

See also: **7.3:** Acts 7.36.

The River Nile turns into blood

14 The LORD said to Moses:

The Egyptian king' stubbornly refuses to change his mind and let the people go. 15 Tomorrow morning take the stick that turned into a snake, then wait beside the River Nile for the king. 16 Tell him, "The LORD God of the Hebrews sent me to order you to release his people, so they can worship him in the desert. But until now, you have paid no attention.

17 "The LORD is going to do something to show you that he really is the LORD. I will strike the Nile with this stick, and the water will turn into blood. 18 The fish will die, the river will stink, and none of you Egyptians will be able to drink the water."

19 Moses, then command Aaron to hold his stick over the water. And when he does, every drop of water in Egypt will turn into blood, including rivers, canals, ponds, and even the water in buckets and jars.

20 Moses and Aaron obeyed the LORD. Aaron held out his stick, then struck the Nile, as the king and his officials watched. The river turned into blood, 21 the fish died, and the water smelt so bad that none of the Egyptians could drink it. Blood was everywhere in Egypt.

22 But the Egyptian magicians used their secret powers to do the same thing. The king did just as the LORD had said — he stubbornly refused to listen. 23 Then he went back to his palace and never gave it a second thought. 24 The Egyptians had to dig holes along the banks of the Nile for drinking water, because water from the river was unfit to drink.

Frogs

25 Seven days after the LORD had struck the Nile,

CHAPTER 8

1 he said to Moses:

Go to the palace and tell the king' of Egypt that I order him to let my people go, so they can worship me. 2 If he refuses, I will cover his entire country with frogs. 3 Warn the king that the Nile will be full of frogs, and from there they will spread into the royal palace, including the king's bedroom and even his bed. Frogs will enter the homes of his officials and will find their way into ovens and into the bowls of bread dough. 4 Frogs will be crawling on everyone — the king, his officials, and every citizen of Egypt."

5 Moses, now command Aaron to hold his stick over the water. Then frogs will come from all rivers, canals, and ponds in Egypt, and they will cover the land.

6 Aaron obeyed, and suddenly frogs were everywhere in Egypt. 7 But the magicians used their secret powers to do the same thing.

8 The king sent for Moses and Aaron and told them, "If you ask the LORD to take these frogs away from me and my people, I will let your people go and offer sacrifices to him."

9 "All right," Moses answered. "You choose the time when I am to pray for the frogs to stop bothering you, your officials, and your people, and for them to leave your houses and be found only in the river."

10 "Do it tomorrow!" the king replied.

"As you wish," Moses agreed. "Then everyone will discover that there is no god like the LORD, 11 and frogs will no longer be found anywhere, except in the Nile."

12 After Moses and Aaron left the palace, Moses begged the LORD to do something about the frogs he had sent as punishment for the king. 13 The LORD listened to Moses, and frogs died everywhere — in houses, yards, and fields. 14 The dead frogs were placed in piles, and the whole country began to stink. 15 But when the king saw that things were now better, he again did just as the LORD had said and stubbornly refused to listen to Moses and Aaron.

Gnats

16 The LORD said to Moses, "Command Aaron to strike the ground with his walking stick, and everywhere in Egypt the dust will turn into gnats." 17 They obeyed, and when Aaron struck the ground with the stick, gnats started swarming on people and animals. In fact, every speck of dust in Egypt turned into a gnat. 18 When the magicians tried to use their secret powers to do this,' they failed, and gnats stayed on people and animals.

19 The magicians told the king,' "God has done this."

But, as the LORD had said, the king was too stubborn to listen.

Holy history

Plagues

Exodus chapters 7–10 describe the plagues or disasters that God sends on Egypt. (The final, terrible disaster is described in 11.4–8 and 12.29–30.) They occur, roughly, in three groups of three, with the final plague – death of the first-born children – on its own. They can also be traced within a calendar year, beginning with the floods in late summer and early autumn and the resulting plagues of infestation and diseases. Each group is introduced when Moses confronts Pharaoh early in the morning (7.14; 8.20; 9.13).

The important thing to remember about the plagues is that they are not just randomly selected punishments. In Exodus 12.12, God says, 'I am the LORD, and I will punish the gods of Egypt.'

The Egyptian gods took the forms of nature, so the disasters show up how ineffectual the gods of Egypt are. The Nile was an object of worship, frogs were fertility symbols, livestock such as rams, goats and bulls were sacred animals. All these were attacked. Ra, the sun-god, is entirely eclipsed by God's darkness.

Most significantly, Pharaoh himself was seen as a god. But he cannot save his people, or even his own family, from the wrath of God (Exodus 12.29).

More...

Foreign gods p.262
Destruction p.236

 Anorak corner

Five gruesome deaths from the Bible

Jezebel is defenestrated (2 Kings 9.30–33)
Sisera pegs out (Judges 4.21)
Abimelech and the millstone
(Judges 9.52–54)
Eglon gets a sword gut (Judges 3.19–25)
Herod is eaten by worms (Acts 12.23)

Flies

20 The LORD said to Moses:

Early tomorrow morning, while the king' is on his way to the river, go and say to him, "The LORD commands you to let his people go, so they can worship him. 21 If you don't, he will send swarms of flies to attack you, your officials, and every citizen of your country. Houses will be full of flies, and the ground will crawl with them.

22-23 "The LORD's people in Goshen won't be bothered by flies, but your people in the rest of the country will be tormented by them. That's how you will know that the LORD is here in Egypt. This miracle will happen tomorrow."

24 The LORD kept his promise — the palace and the homes of the royal officials swarmed with flies, and the rest of the country was infested with them as well. 25 Then the king sent for Moses and Aaron and told them, "Go and sacrifice to your God, but stay here in Egypt."

26 "That's impossible!" Moses replied. "Any sacrifices we offer to the LORD our God would disgust the Egyptians, and they would stone us to death. 27 No indeed! The LORD has ordered us to walk three days into the desert before offering sacrifices to him, and that's what we have to do."

28 Then the king told him, "I'll let you go into the desert to offer sacrifices, if you don't go very far. But in the meantime, pray for me."

29 "Your Majesty," Moses replied, "I'll pray for you as soon as I leave, and by tomorrow the flies will stop bothering you, your officials, and the citizens of your country. Only make sure that you're telling the truth this time and that you really intend to let our people offer sacrifices to the LORD."

30 After leaving the palace, Moses prayed, 31 and the LORD answered his prayer. Not a fly was left to pester the king, his officials, or anyone else in Egypt. 32 But the king turned stubborn again and would not let the people go.

CHAPTER 9

Dead animals

1 The LORD sent Moses with this message for the king' of Egypt:

The LORD God of the Hebrews commands you to let his people go, so they can worship him. 2 If you keep refusing, 3 he will bring a terrible disease on your horses and donkeys, your camels and cattle, and your sheep and goats. ⁴ But the LORD will protect the animals that belong to the people of Israel, and none of theirs will die. ⁵ Tomorrow is the day the LORD has set to do this.

⁶ It happened the next day — all the animals belonging to the Egyptians died, but the Israelites did not lose even one. ⁷ When the king found out, he was still too stubborn to let the people go.

Sores

⁸ The LORD said to Moses and Aaron:

Take a few handfuls of ashes from a stove and let Moses throw them into the air. Be sure the king is watching. ⁹ The ashes will blow across the land of Egypt, causing sores to break out on people and animals.

¹⁰ So they took a few handfuls of ashes and went to the king.' Moses threw them into the air, and sores immediately broke out on the Egyptians and their animals. ¹¹ The magicians were suffering so much from the sores, that they could not even come to Moses. ¹² Everything happened just as the LORD had told Moses — he made the king too stubborn to listen to Moses and Aaron.

Hailstones

¹³ The LORD told Moses to get up early the next morning and say to the king:'

The LORD God of the Hebrews commands you to let his people go, so they can worship him! ¹⁴ If you don't, he will send his worst plagues to strike you, your officials, and everyone else in your country. Then you will find out that no one can oppose the LORD. ¹⁵ In fact, he could already have sent a terrible disease and wiped you from the face of the earth. ¹⁶ But he has kept you alive, just to show you his power and to bring honour to himself everywhere in the world.

¹⁷ You are still determined not to let the LORD's people go. ¹⁸ All right. At this time tomorrow, he will bring on Egypt the worst hailstorm in its history. ¹⁹ You had better give orders for every person and every animal in Egypt to take shelter. If they don't, they will die.

Viewpoints 👁

Why does God sometimes do things that seem completely loopy?

Contributed by Lucy C S

'But he has kept you alive, just to show you his power and to bring honour to himself everywhere in the world.'

This verse is part of a message to Pharaoh, which God gave to Moses just before releasing the seventh of the ten plagues on Egypt. Before giving a warning of the next plague, God points out that he could have completely wiped out Pharaoh and the entire Egyptian race before then. Then comes this verse.

Moses and the Israelites may have been wondering why God didn't wipe out Pharaoh and the Egyptians. After all, Pharaoh didn't seem likely to free them but God could easily get rid of him. Surely that was the easiest option! No. God had a better plan. God knew that if he let Pharaoh live, ultimately he and his people would have to admit how powerful God is. The Israelites would be freed; Pharaoh would learn that he could not set himself up in competition against God; and the whole event would show God's glory and power.

God knew what he was doing, even if the Israelites had thought that other options would be better. Sometimes God does things for us that we don't understand, or we think our prayers aren't being answered when perhaps the right time hasn't come yet. We need to trust God about these things – he's in control, he won't let us down. Some time we'll look back and understand what God was doing.

More...

Guidance p.685

See also: 9.10: Rev 16.2.   9.16: Rom 9.17.

20 Some of the king's officials were frightened by what the LORD had said, and they hurried off to make sure their slaves and animals were safe. 21 But others paid no attention to his threats and left their slaves and animals out in the open.

22 Then the LORD told Moses, "Stretch your arm towards the sky, so that hailstones will fall on people, animals, and crops in the land of Egypt." 23-24 Moses pointed his walking stick towards the sky, and hailstones started falling everywhere. Thunder roared, and lightning flashed back and forth, striking the ground. This was the worst storm in the history of Egypt. 25 People, animals, and crops were pounded by the hailstones, and bark was stripped from trees. 26 Only Goshen, where the Israelites lived, was safe from the storm.

27 The king sent for Moses and Aaron and told them, "Now I have really sinned! My people and I are guilty, and the LORD is right. 28 We can't stand any more of this thunder and hail. Please ask the LORD to make it stop. Your people can go — you don't have to stay in Egypt any longer."

29 Moses answered, "As soon as I leave the city, I will lift my arms in prayer. When the thunder and hail stop, you will know that the earth belongs to the LORD. 30 But I am certain that neither you nor your officials really fear the LORD God."

31 Meanwhile, the flax and barley crops had been destroyed by the storm because they were ready to ripen. 32 But the wheat crops ripen later, and they were not damaged.

33 After Moses left the royal palace and the city, he lifted his arms in prayer to the LORD, and the thunder, hail, and drenching rain stopped. 34 When the king realized that the storm was over, he disobeyed once more. He and his officials were so stubborn 35 that he refused to let the Israelites go. This was exactly what the LORD had said would happen.

CHAPTER 10

Locusts

1 The LORD said to Moses:

> Go back to the king. I have made him and his officials stubborn, so that I could work these miracles. 2 I did this because I want you to tell your children and your grandchildren about my miracles and about my harsh treatment of the Egyptians. Then all of you will know that I am the LORD.

3 Moses and Aaron went to the king and told him that the LORD God of the Hebrews had said:

> How long will you stubbornly refuse to obey? Release my people so they can worship me. 4 Do this by tomorrow, or I will cover your country with so many locusts* 5 that you won't be able to see the ground. Most of your crops were ruined by the hailstones, but these locusts will destroy what little is left, including the trees. 6 Your palace, the homes of your officials, and all other houses in Egypt will overflow with more locusts than have ever been seen in this country.

After Moses left the palace, 7 the king's officials asked, "Your Majesty, how much longer is this man going to be a trouble-maker? Why don't you let the people leave, so they can worship the LORD their God? Don't you know that Egypt is a disaster?"

8 The king had Moses and Aaron brought back, and he said, "All right, you may go and worship the LORD your God. But first tell me who will be going."

9 "Everyone, young and old," Moses answered. "We will even take our sheep, goats, and cattle, because we want to hold a celebration in honour of the LORD."

10 The king replied, "The LORD had better watch over you on the day I let you leave with your families! You're up to no good. 11 Do you want to worship the LORD? All right, take only the men and go." Then Moses and Aaron were chased out of the palace.

12 The LORD told Moses, "Stretch your arm towards Egypt. Swarms of locusts will come and eat everything left by the hail."

13 Moses held out his walking stick, and the LORD sent an east wind that blew across Egypt the rest of the day and all that night. By morning, locusts 14 were swarming everywhere. Never before had there been so many locusts in Egypt, and never again will there be so many. 15 The ground was black with locusts, and they ate everything left on the trees and in the fields. Nothing green remained in Egypt — not a tree or a plant.

See also: 9.24: Rev 8.7; 16.21.

***10.4 locusts:** A type of grasshopper that comes in swarms and causes great damage to crops.

See also: 10.14–15: Rev 9.2–3.

16 At once the king sent for Moses and Aaron. He told them, "I have sinned against the LORD your God and against you. 17 Forgive me one more time and ask the LORD to stop these insects from killing every living plant." 18 Moses left the palace and prayed. 19 Then the LORD sent a strong west wind' that swept the locusts into the Red Sea.* Not one locust was left anywhere in Egypt, 20 but the LORD made the king so stubborn that he still refused to let the Israelites go.

Darkness

21 The LORD said to Moses, "Stretch your arm towards the sky, and everything will be covered with darkness thick enough to touch." 22 Moses stretched his arm towards the sky, and Egypt was covered with darkness for three days. 23 During that time, the Egyptians could not see each other or leave their homes, but there was light where the Israelites lived.

24 The king' sent for Moses and told him, "Go and worship the LORD! And take your families with you. Just leave your sheep, goats, and cattle."

25 "No!" Moses replied. "You must let us offer sacrifices to the LORD our God, 26 and we won't know which animals we will need until we get there. That's why we can't leave even one of them here."

27 This time the LORD made the king so stubborn 28 that he said to Moses, "Get out and stay out! If you ever come back, you're dead!"

29 "Have it your way," Moses answered. "You won't see me again."

The last disaster and the first Passover

CHAPTER 11

Moses warns the Egyptians that the LORD will kill their firstborn sons

1 The LORD said to Moses:

I am going to punish the king' of Egypt and his people one more time. Then the

king will gladly let you leave his land, so that I will stop punishing the Egyptians. He will even chase you out. 2 Now go and tell my people to ask their Egyptian neighbours for gold and silver jewellery.

3 So the LORD made the Egyptians greatly respect the Israelites, and everyone, including the king and his officials, considered Moses an important leader.

4 Moses went to the king and said:

I have come to let you know what the LORD is going to do. About midnight he will go through the land of Egypt, 5 and wherever he goes, the firstborn son in every family will die. Your own son will die, and so will the son of the lowest slave woman. Even the firstborn males of cattle will die. 6 Everywhere in Egypt there will be loud crying. Nothing like this has ever happened before or will ever happen again. 7 But there won't be any need for the Israelites to cry. Things will be so quiet that not even a dog will be heard barking. Then you Egyptians will know that the LORD is good to the Israelites, even while he punishes you. 8 Your leaders will come and bow down, begging me to take my people and leave your country. Then we will leave.

Moses was very angry; he turned and left the king.

9 What the LORD had earlier said to Moses came true. He had said, "The king of Egypt won't listen. Then I will perform even more miracles." 10 So the king of Egypt saw Moses and Aaron work miracles, but the LORD made him stubbornly refuse to let the Israelites leave his country.

CHAPTER 12

The Passover

1 Some time later the LORD said to Moses and Aaron:

2 This month* is to be the first month of the year for you. 3 Tell the people of Israel that on the tenth day of this month the head of each family must choose a lamb or a young goat for his family to eat. 4-5 If any family is too small to eat the whole animal, they must share it with their next-door

---

*10.19 Red Sea: Hebrew *yam suph*, here referring to the Gulf of Suez, since the term is extended to include the north-western arm of the Red Sea (see also the note at 13.18).
See also: 10.22: Psa 105.28; Rev 16.10.

*12.2 This month: Abib (also called Nisan), the first month of the Hebrew calendar, from about mid-March to mid-April.
See also: 12.1–13: Lev 23.5; Num 9.1–5; 28.16; Deut 16.1–2.

neighbours. Choose either a sheep or a goat, but it must be a one-year-old male that has nothing wrong with it. And it must be large enough for everyone to have some of the meat.

⁶ Each family must take care of its animal until the evening of the fourteenth day of the month, when the animals are to be killed. ⁷ Some of the blood must be put on the two doorposts and above the door of each house where the animals are to be eaten. ⁸ That night the animals are to be roasted and eaten, together with bitter herbs and thin bread made without yeast. ⁹ Don't eat the meat raw or boiled. The entire animal, including its head, legs, and insides, must be roasted. ¹⁰ Eat what you want that night, and the next morning burn whatever is left. ¹¹ When you eat the meal, be dressed and ready to travel. Have your sandals on, carry your walking stick in your hand, and eat quickly. This is the Passover Festival in honour of me, your LORD.

¹² That same night I will pass through Egypt and kill the firstborn son in every family and the firstborn male of all animals. I am the LORD, and I will punish the gods of Egypt. ¹³ The blood on the houses will show me where you live, and when I see the blood, I will pass over you. Then you won't be bothered by the terrible disasters I will bring on Egypt.

¹⁴ Remember this day and celebrate it each year as a festival in my honour. ¹⁵ For seven days you must eat bread made without yeast. And on the first of these seven days, you must remove all yeast from your homes. If you eat anything made with yeast during this festival, you will no longer be part of Israel. ¹⁶ Meet together for worship on the first and seventh days of the festival. The only work you are allowed to do on either of these two days is that of preparing the bread.

¹⁷ Celebrate this Festival of Thin Bread as a way of remembering the day that I brought your families and tribes out of Egypt. And do this each year. ¹⁸ Begin on the evening of the fourteenth day of the first month by eating bread made without yeast. Then continue this celebration until the evening of the twenty-first day.

¹⁹ During these seven days no yeast is allowed in anyone's home, whether they are native Israelites or not. If you are caught eating anything made with yeast, you will no longer be part of Israel. ²⁰ Stay away from yeast, no matter where you live. No one is allowed to eat anything made with yeast!

²¹ Moses called the leaders of Israel together and said:

Each family is to pick out a sheep and kill it for Passover. ²² Make a brush from a few small branches of a hyssop plant and dip the brush in the bowl that has the blood of the animal in it. Then brush some of the blood above the door and on the posts at each side of the door of your house. After this, everyone is to stay inside.

²³ During that night the LORD will go through the country of Egypt and kill the firstborn son in every Egyptian family. He will see where you have put the blood, and he will not come into your house. His angel that brings death will pass over and not kill your firstborn sons.

²⁴⁻²⁵ After you have entered the country promised to you by the LORD, you and your children must continue to celebrate Passover each year. ²⁶ Your children will ask you, "What are we celebrating?" ²⁷ And you will answer, "The Passover animal is killed to honour the LORD. We do these things because on that night long ago the LORD passed over the homes of our people in Egypt. He killed the firstborn sons of the Egyptians, but he saved our children from death."

After Moses finished speaking, the people of Israel knelt down and worshipped the LORD. ²⁸ Then they left and did what Moses and Aaron had told them to do.

Death for the firstborn sons

²⁹ At midnight the LORD killed the firstborn son of every Egyptian family, from the son of the king᾿ to the son of every prisoner in jail. He also killed the firstborn male of every animal that belonged to the Egyptians.

³⁰ That night the king, his officials, and everyone else in Egypt got up and started crying bitterly. In every Egyptian home, someone was dead.

See also: **12.14–20:** Exod 23.15; 34.18; Lev 23.6–8; Num 28.17–25; Deut 16.3–8.

See also: **12.23:** Heb 11.28. **12.29:** Exod 4.22–32.

Big ideas

Passover

God tells Moses that he will pass through the country, and the first-born of the Egyptians will die. (Even their cattle.)

But there are safety rules that the Hebrews must follow. They are given detailed instructions to prepare their houses: every household is to take a lamb, slaughter it and then paint their doorposts with blood and eat the meat together. Houses marked in this way will be protected, they will be 'passed over' by the devastation.

These instructions form the basis for Passover – a festival which is still celebrated today among Jewish families. Passover is followed by the Feast of Thin Bread, which is a week-long festival commemorating the speed with which the Israelites had to leave Egypt. These festivals are supposed to remind the Jews of the way in which God punished a proud nation and rescued his people from slavery.

Although there were long periods when the Israelites did not celebrate Passover, by the time of Jesus it had become a significant ritual. At first, the Passover was held in peoples' homes, but in New Testament times people went to Jerusalem to celebrate it at the temple.

Anorak corner

The Hebrew name for Passover is 'Pesach'.

Footsteps

Five days on Passover

The First Passover: Exodus 12.1–28
Passover in the Promised Land:
Joshua 5.2–11
Passover is celebrated after a long absence:
2 Chronicles 34.29–35.18
Passover after the Exile: Ezra 6.15–22
Jesus celebrates Passover with the disciples:
Luke 22.14–30

More...

Feasts and festivals p.134
The Last Supper p.1157
Exodus – the route p.78

The people of Israel escape from Egypt

31 During the night the king' sent for Moses and Aaron and told them, "Get your people out of my country and leave us alone! Go and worship the LORD, as you have asked. 32 Take your sheep, goats, and cattle, and get out. But ask your God to be kind to me."

33 The Egyptians did everything they could to get the Israelites to leave their country fast. They said, "Please hurry and leave. If you don't, we will all be dead." 34 So the Israelites quickly made some bread dough and put it in pans. But they did not mix any yeast in the dough to make it rise. They wrapped cloth around the pans and carried them on their shoulders.

35 The Israelites had already done what Moses had told them to do. They had gone to their Egyptian neighbours and asked for gold and silver and for clothes. 36 The LORD had made the Egyptians friendly towards the people of Israel, and they gave them whatever they asked for. In this way they carried away the wealth of the Egyptians when they left Egypt.

37 The Israelites walked from the city of Rameses to the city of Succoth. There were about six hundred thousand of them, not counting women and children. 38 Many other people went with them as well, and there were also a lot of sheep, goats, and cattle. 39 They left Egypt in such a hurry that they did not have time to prepare any food except the bread dough made without yeast. So they baked it and made thin bread.

40-41 The LORD's people left Egypt exactly four hundred and thirty years after they had arrived. 42 On that night the LORD kept watch for them, and on this same night each year Israel will always keep watch in honour of the LORD.

Instructions for Passover

43 The LORD gave Moses and Aaron the following instructions for celebrating Passover:

No one except Israelites may eat the Passover meal.

44 Your slaves may eat the meal if they have been circumcised, 45 but no foreigners who work for you are allowed to have any.

See also: 12.35–36: Exod 3.21–22.   12.40: Gen 15.13; Gal 3.17.

⁴⁶ The entire meal must be eaten inside, and no one may leave the house during the celebration.

No bones of the Passover lamb may be broken. ⁴⁷ And all Israelites must take part in the meal.

⁴⁸ If anyone who isn't an Israelite wants to celebrate Passover with you, every man and boy in that family must first be circumcised. Then they may join in the meal, just like native Israelites. No uncircumcised man or boy may eat the Passover meal! ⁴⁹ This law applies both to native Israelites and to those foreigners who live among you.

⁵⁰ The Israelites obeyed everything the LORD had commanded Moses and Aaron to tell them. ⁵¹ And on that same day the LORD brought Israel's families and tribes out of Egypt.

CHAPTER 13

Dedication of the firstborn

¹ The LORD said to Moses, ² "Dedicate to me the firstborn son of every family and the firstborn males of your flocks and herds. These belong to me."

The Festival of Thin Bread

³⁻⁴ Moses said to the people:

Remember this day in the month of Abib.* It is the day when the LORD's mighty power rescued you from Egypt, where you were slaves. Do not eat anything made with yeast. ⁵ The LORD promised your ancestors that he would bring you into the land of the Canaanites, Hittites, Amorites, Hivites, and Jebusites. It is a land rich with milk and honey.

Each year during the month of Abib, celebrate these events in the following way: ⁶ for seven days you are to eat bread made without yeast, and on the seventh day you are to celebrate a festival in honour of the LORD. ⁷ During those seven days, you must not eat anything made with yeast or even have yeast anywhere near your homes. ⁸ Then on the seventh day you must explain to your children that you do this because the LORD brought you out of Egypt.

⁹ This celebration will be like wearing a sign on your hand or on your forehead, because then you will pass on to others the teaching of the LORD, whose mighty power brought you out of Egypt. ¹⁰ Celebrate this festival each year at the same time.

¹¹ The LORD will give you the land of the Canaanites, just as he promised you and your ancestors. ¹² From then on, you must give him every firstborn son from your families and every firstborn male from your animals, because these belong to him. ¹³ You can save the life of a firstborn donkey* by sacrificing a lamb; if you don't, you must break the donkey's neck. You must save every firstborn son.

¹⁴ In the future your children will ask what this ceremony means. Explain it to them by saying, "The LORD used his mighty power to rescue us from slavery in Egypt. ¹⁵ The king' stubbornly refused to set us free, so the LORD killed the firstborn male of every animal and the firstborn son of every Egyptian family. This is why we sacrifice to the LORD every firstborn male of every animal and save every firstborn son."

¹⁶ This ceremony will serve the same purpose as a sign on your hand or on your forehead to tell how the LORD's mighty power rescued us from Egypt.

The LORD leads his people

¹⁷ After the king' had finally let the people go, the LORD did not lead them through Philistine territory,* though that was the shortest way. God had said, "If they are attacked, they may decide to return to Egypt." ¹⁸ So he led them around through the desert and towards the Red Sea.*

The Israelites left Egypt, prepared for battle.

---

*13.13 donkey:** This was the only "unclean" animal that had to be saved; the firstborn of all "clean" animals (sheep, goats, cattle) had to be sacrificed. Donkeys were important because they were the basic means of transport.
*13.17 Philistine territory:** The shortest land route from the Nile Delta to Canaan; it was the southern section of the major road that led to Megiddo and then on to Mesopotamia by way of Asia Minor.
*13.18 Red Sea:** Hebrew *yam suph* "Sea of Reeds", one of the marshes or fresh water lakes, near the eastern part of the Nile Delta. This identification is based on Exodus 13.17—14.9, which lists the towns on the route of the Israelites before crossing the sea. In the Greek translation of the Scriptures made about 200 BC, the "Sea of Reeds" was named "Red Sea".
See also: 13.12: Exod 34.19–20; Luke 2.23.

---

*13.3–4 Abib:** Or Nisan, the first month of the Hebrew calendar, from about mid-March to mid-April.
See also: 12.46: Num 9.12; John 19.36. **13.2:** Num 3.13; Luke 2.23.

The Exodus from Egypt

It's difficult to trace their journey, because many of the places named in the story have disappeared. (That's the way with deserts. You get one big sandstorm and all the dunes shift and you don't know where everything is any more.) However, we can identify some of the key points where the action took place...

The Israelites didn't actually cross the red sea. The words in Hebrew are 'Yam Suph', which means 'sea of reeds' (see note Exodus 13.18). The Egyptians probably weren't worried what sea it was. All that mattered was that there was a lot of it. And it was falling on them.

On leaving Egypt, the Israelites followed the 'way of the sea'. The main trading routes ran north through Philistine country but the 'way of the sea' led south, through the mining districts around Mount Sinai.

As they wander in the desert, the Israelites start to moan about the catering. So God provides manna and quails for the Israelites to eat (Exodus 16), and fresh water for them to drink (Exodus 17).

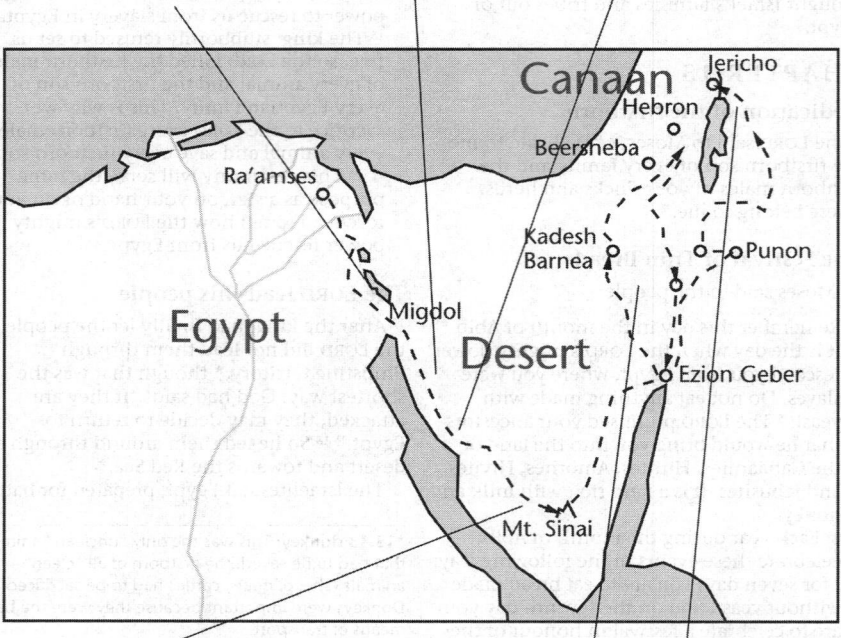

At Mount Sinai, Israel received the law from God and the instructions about the tabernacle. At Mount Sinai they also made their own god in the shape of a calf.

Only eleven days after leaving Sinai, the Israelites reach Hebron. Moses sent spies into Canaan. When the spies report back, the people decide they won't invade. As punishment, they spend the next forty years wandering in the eastern wilderness of the Sinai Peninsular.

Eventually, they moved up to the east of the Dead Sea, crossing the Jordan to Jericho.

¹⁹ Moses made them take along the bones of Joseph, whose dying words had been, "God will come to your rescue, and when he does, be sure to take along my bones."

²⁰ The people of Israel left Succoth and camped at Etham at the border of Egypt near the desert. ²¹⁻²² During the day the LORD went ahead of his people in a thick cloud, and during the night he went ahead of them in a flaming fire. That way the LORD could lead them at all times, whether day or night.

The people cross the Red Sea

CHAPTER 14

¹ At Etham the LORD said to Moses:

² Tell the people of Israel to turn back and camp across from Pi-Hahiroth near Baal-Zephon, between Migdol and the Red Sea.ʼ ³ The kingʼ will think they were afraid to cross the desert and that they are wandering around, trying to find another way to leave the country. ⁴ I will make the king stubborn again, and he will try to catch you. Then I will destroy him and his army. People everywhere will praise me for my victory, and the Egyptians will know that I really am the LORD.

The Israelites obeyed the LORD and camped where he told them.

⁵ When the king of Egypt heard that the Israelites had finally left, he and his officials changed their minds and said, "Look what we have done! We let them get away, and they will no longer be our slaves."

⁶ The king got his war chariot and army ready. ⁷ He commanded his officers in charge of his six hundred best chariots and all his other chariots to start after the Israelites. ⁸ The LORD made the king so stubborn that he went after them, even though the Israelites proudlyʼ went on their way. ⁹ But the king's horses and chariots and soldiers caught up with them while they were camping by the Red Sea near Pi-Hahiroth and Baal-Zephon.

¹⁰ When the Israelites saw the king coming with his army, they were frightened and begged the LORD for help. ¹¹ They also complained to Moses, "Wasn't there enough room in Egypt to bury us? Is that why you brought us out here to die in the desert? Why did you bring us out of Egypt anyway?

¹² While we were there, didn't we tell you to leave us alone? We would rather be slaves in Egypt than die in this desert!"

¹³ But Moses answered, "Don't be afraid! Be brave, and you will see the LORD save you today. These Egyptians will never bother you again. ¹⁴ The LORD will fight for you, and you won't have to do a thing."

¹⁵ The LORD said to Moses, "Why do you keep calling out to me for help? Tell the Israelites to move forward. ¹⁶ Then hold your walking stick over the sea. The water will open up and make a road where they can walk through on dry ground. ¹⁷ I will make the Egyptians so stubborn that they will go after you. Then I will be praised because of what happens to the king and his chariots and cavalry. ¹⁸ The Egyptians will know for sure that I am the LORD."

¹⁹ All this time God's angel had gone ahead of Israel's army, but now he moved behind them. A large cloud had also gone ahead of them, ²⁰ but now it moved between the Egyptians and the Israelites. The cloud gave light to the Israelites, but made it dark for the Egyptians, and during the night they could not come any closer.

²¹ Moses stretched his arm over the sea, and the LORD sent a strong east wind that blew all night until there was dry land where the water had been. The sea opened up, ²² and the Israelites walked through on dry land with a wall of water on each side.

²³ The Egyptian chariots and cavalry went after them. ²⁴ But before daylight the LORD looked down at the Egyptian army from the fiery cloud and made them panic. ²⁵ Their chariot wheels got stuck,ʼ and it was hard for them to move. So the Egyptians said to one another, "Let's leave these people alone! The LORD is on their side and is fighting against us."

²⁶ The LORD told Moses, "Stretch your arm towards the sea — the water will cover the Egyptians and their cavalry and chariots." ²⁷ Moses stretched out his arm, and at daybreak the water rushed towards the Egyptians. They tried to run away, but the LORD drowned them in the sea. ²⁸ The water came and covered the chariots, the cavalry, and the whole Egyptian army that had followed the Israelites into the sea. Not one of them was left alive. ²⁹ But the sea had made a wall of water on each side of the Israelites; so they walked through on dry land.

See also: 13.19: Gen 50.25; Josh 24.32.

See also: 14.22: 1 Cor 10.1–2; Heb 11.29.

30 On that day, when the Israelites saw the bodies of the Egyptians washed up on the shore, they knew that the LORD had saved them. 31 Because of the mighty power he had used against the Egyptians, the Israelites worshipped him and trusted him and his servant Moses.

CHAPTER 15

The song of Moses

1 Moses and the Israelites sang this song in praise of the LORD:

> I sing praises to the LORD
> for his great victory!
> He has thrown the horses
> and their riders into the sea.
> 2 The LORD is my strength,
> the reason for my song,
> because he has saved me.
> I praise and honour the LORD —
> he is my God and the God
> of my ancestors.
> 3 The LORD is his name,
> and he is a warrior!
> 4 He threw the chariots and army
> of Egypt's king*
> into the Red Sea,*
> and he drowned the best
> of the king's officers.
> 5 They sank to the bottom
> just like stones.
>
> 6 With the tremendous force
> of your right arm, our LORD,
> you crushed your enemies.
> 7 What a great victory was yours,
> as you defeated everyone
> who opposed you.
> Your fiery anger wiped them out,
> as though they were straw.
> 8 You were so furious
> that the sea piled up like a wall,
> and the ocean depths
> curdled like cheese.
>
> 9 Your enemies boasted
> that they would
> pursue and capture us,
> divide up our possessions,
> treat us as they wished,
> then take out their swords
> and kill us there.
> 10 But when you got furious,

> they sank like lead,
> swallowed by ocean waves.
> 11 Our LORD, no other gods
> compare with you —
> Majestic and holy!
> Fearsome and glorious!
> Miracle worker!
> 12 When you signalled
> with your right hand,
> your enemies were swallowed
> deep into the earth.
>
> 13 The people you rescued
> were led by your powerful love
> to your holy place.
> 14 Nations learnt of this and trembled —
> Philistines shook with horror.
> 15 The leaders of Edom and of Moab
> were terrified.
> Everyone in Canaan fainted,
> 16 struck down by fear.
> Our LORD, your powerful arm
> kept them still as a rock
> until the people you rescued
> for your very own had marched by.
>
> 17 You will let your people settle
> on your chosen mountain,
> where you built your home
> and your temple.
> 18 Our LORD, you will rule for ever!

The song of Miriam

19 The LORD covered the royal Egyptian cavalry and chariots with the sea, after the Israelites had walked safely through on dry ground. 20 Miriam the sister of Aaron was a prophet. So she took her tambourine and led the other women out to play their tambourines and to dance. 21 Then she sang to them:

> "Sing praises to the LORD
> for his great victory!
> He has thrown the horses
> and their riders into the sea."

Moses leads the people to Mount Sinai

Bitter water at Marah

22 After the Israelites left the Red Sea,* Moses led them through the Shur Desert for three days, before finding water. 23 They did find water at Marah, but it was bitter, which is

---

*15.4 Red Sea: See the note at 13.18.
See also: 15.1: Rev 15.3. 15.2: Psa 118.14; Isa 12.2.

*15.22 Red Sea: See the note at 13.18.

how that place got its name.* 24 The people
complained and said, "Moses, what are we
going to drink?"

25 Moses asked the LORD for help, and the
LORD told him to throw a piece of wood into
the water. Moses did so, and the water
became fit to drink.

At Marah the LORD tested his people and
also gave them some laws and teachings.
26 Then he said, "I am the LORD your God,
and I cure your diseases. If you obey me by
doing right and by following my laws and
teachings, I won't punish you with the
diseases I sent on the Egyptians."

27 Later the Israelites came to Elim, where
there were twelve springs and seventy palm
trees. So they camped there.

CHAPTER 16

The LORD sends food from heaven

1 On the fifteenth day of the second month
after the Israelites had escaped from Egypt,
they left Elim and started through the
western edge of the Sinai Desert in the
direction of Mount Sinai. 2 There in the
desert they started complaining to Moses and
Aaron, 3 "We wish the LORD had killed us in
Egypt. When we lived there, we could at least
sit down and eat all the bread and meat we
wanted. But you have brought us out here
into this desert, where we are going to
starve."

4 The LORD said to Moses, "I will send
bread* down from heaven like rain. Each day
the people can go out and gather only
enough for that day. That's how I will see if
they obey me. 5 But on the sixth day of each
week they must gather and cook twice as
much."

6 Moses and Aaron told the people, "This
evening you will know that the LORD was the
one who rescued you from Egypt. 7 And in
the morning you will see his glorious power,
because he has heard your complaints against
him. Why should you grumble to us? Who
are we?"

8 Then Moses continued, "You will know it
is the LORD when he gives you meat each
evening and more than enough bread each
morning. He is really the one you are

complaining about, not us — we are
nobodies — but the LORD has heard your
complaints."

9 Moses turned to Aaron and said, "Bring
the people together, because the LORD has
heard their complaints."

10 Aaron was speaking to them, when
everyone looked out towards the desert and
saw the bright glory of the LORD in a cloud.
11 The LORD said to Moses, 12 "I have heard
my people complain. Now tell them that
each evening they will have meat and each
morning they will have more than enough
bread. Then they will know that I am the
LORD their God."

13 That evening a lot of quails came and
landed everywhere in the camp, and the next
morning dew covered the ground. 14 After the
dew had gone, the desert was covered with
thin flakes that looked like frost. 15 The
people had never seen anything like this, and
they started asking each other, "What is it?"*

Moses answered, "This is the bread that the
LORD has given you to eat. 16 And he orders
you to gather about two litres for each person
in your family — that should be more than
enough."

17 They did as they were told. Some
gathered more and some gathered less,
18 according to their needs, and none was left
over.

19 Moses told them not to keep any
overnight. 20 Some of them disobeyed, but the
next morning what they kept was stinking
and full of worms, and Moses was angry.

21 Each morning everyone gathered as
much as they needed, and in the heat of the
day the rest melted. 22 However, on the sixth
day of the week, everyone gathered enough
to have four litres, instead of two. When the
leaders reported this to Moses, 23 he told
them that the LORD had said, "Tomorrow is
the Sabbath, a sacred day of rest in honour of
me. So gather all you want to bake or boil,
and make sure you save enough for
tomorrow."

24 The people obeyed, and the next
morning the food smelt fine and had no
worms. 25 "You may eat the food," Moses
said. "Today is the Sabbath in honour of the
LORD, and there won't be any of this food on
the ground today. 26 You will find it there for
the first six days of the week, but not on the
Sabbath."

*15.23 Marah . . . name: In Hebrew "Marah" means
"bitter".
*16.4 bread: This was something like a thin wafer,
and it was called "manna", which in Hebrew means,
"What is it?"
See also: 16.4: John 6.31.

*16.15 What is it: See the note at 16.4.
See also: 16.15: 1 Cor 10.3. 16.18: 2 Cor 8.15.
16.23: Exod 20.8–11.

81

²⁷ A few of the Israelites did go out to look for some, but there was none. ²⁸ Then the LORD said, "Moses, how long will you people keep disobeying my laws and teachings? ²⁹ Remember that I was the one who gave you the Sabbath. That's why on the sixth day I provide enough bread for two days. Everyone is to stay at home and rest on the Sabbath." ³⁰ And so they rested on the Sabbath.

³¹ The Israelites called the bread manna.* It was white like coriander seed and delicious as wafers made with honey. ³² Moses told the people that the LORD had said, "Store up two litres of this manna, because I want future generations to see the food I gave you during the time you were in the desert after I rescued you from Egypt."

³³ Then Moses told Aaron, "Put some manna in a jar and store it in the place of worship for future generations to see."

³⁴ Aaron followed the LORD's instructions and put the manna in front of the sacred chest for safekeeping. ³⁵⁻³⁶ The Israelites ate manna for forty years, before they came to the border of Canaan that was a settled land.᾿

CHAPTER 17

The LORD gives water from a rock

This is also told in Numbers 20.1–13

¹ The Israelites left the desert and moved from one place to another each time the LORD ordered them to. Once they camped at Rephidim,* but there was no water for them to drink.

² The people started complaining to Moses, "Give us some water!"

Moses replied, "Why are you complaining to me and trying to put the LORD to the test?"

³ But the people were thirsty and kept on complaining, "Moses, did you bring us out of Egypt just to let us and our families and our animals die of thirst?"

⁴ Then Moses prayed to the LORD, "What am I going to do with these people? They are about to stone me to death!"

⁵ The LORD answered, "Take some of the leaders with you and go ahead of the rest of the people. Also take along the walking stick you used to strike the River Nile, ⁶ and when

you get to the rock at Mount Sinai,᾿ I will be there with you. Strike the rock with the stick, and water will pour out for the people to drink." Moses did this while the leaders watched.

⁷ The people had complained and tested the LORD by asking, "Is the LORD really with us?" So Moses named that place Massah, which means "testing" and Meribah, which means "complaining".

Israel defeats the Amalekites

⁸ When the Israelites were at Rephidim, they were attacked by the Amalekites. ⁹ So Moses told Joshua, "Have some men ready to attack the Amalekites tomorrow. I will stand on a hilltop, holding this walking stick that has the power of God."

¹⁰ Joshua led the attack as Moses had commanded, while Moses, Aaron, and Hur stood on the hilltop. ¹¹ The Israelites out-fought the Amalekites as long as Moses held up his arms, but they started losing whenever he had to lower them. ¹² Finally, Moses was so tired that Aaron and Hur got a rock for him to sit on. Then they stood beside him and supported his arms in the same position until sunset. ¹³ That's how Joshua defeated the Amalekites.

¹⁴ Afterwards, the LORD said to Moses, "Write an account of this victory and read it to Joshua. I want the Amalekites to be forgotten for ever."

¹⁵ Moses built an altar and named it "The LORD Gives me Victory". ¹⁶ Then Moses explained, "This is because I depended on the LORD.᾿ But in future generations, the LORD will have to fight the Amalekites again."

CHAPTER 18

Jethro visits Moses

¹ Jethro was the priest of Midian and the father-in-law of Moses. And he heard what the LORD God had done for Moses and his people, after rescuing them from Egypt.

²⁻⁴ In the meantime, Moses had sent his wife Zipporah and her two sons to stay with Jethro, and he had welcomed them. Moses was still a foreigner in Midian when his first son was born, and so Moses said, "I'll name him Gershom."*

---

*16.31 manna: See the note at 16.4.
*17.1 Rephidim: The last stopping place for the Israelites between the Red Sea and Mount Sinai; the exact location is not known.

See also: 16.31: Num 11.7,8. **16.33:** Heb 9.4.
16.35: Josh 5.12. **17.1–7:** Num 20.2–13.

*18.2–4 Gershom: See the note at 2.22.
See also: 17.14: Deut 25.17–19; 1 Sam 15.2–9.
18.2–3: Exod 2.21–22. **18.3:** Acts 7.29.

When his second son was born, Moses said, "I'll name him Eliezer,* because the God my father worshipped has saved me from the king of Egypt."*

5-6 While Israel was camped in the desert near Mount Sinai,' Jethro sent Moses this message: "I am coming to visit you, and I am bringing your wife and two sons."

7 When they arrived, Moses went out and bowed down in front of Jethro, then kissed him. After they had greeted each other, they went into the tent, 8 where Moses told him everything the LORD had done to protect Israel against the Egyptians and their king. He also told him how the LORD had helped them in all their troubles.

9 Jethro was so pleased to hear this good news about what the LORD had done, 10 that he shouted, "Praise the LORD! He rescued you and the Israelites from the Egyptians and their king. 11 Now I know that the LORD is the greatest God, because he has rescued Israel from their arrogant enemies." 12 Jethro offered sacrifices to God. Then Aaron and Israel's leaders came to eat with Jethro there at the place of worship.

Judges are appointed

This is also told in Deuteronomy 1.9–18

13 The next morning Moses sat down at the place where he decided legal cases for the people, and everyone crowded around him until evening. 14 Jethro saw how much Moses had to do for the people, and he asked, "Why are you the only judge? Why do you let these people crowd around you from morning till evening?"

15 Moses answered, "Because they come here to find out what God wants them to do. 16 They bring their complaints to me, and I make decisions on the basis of God's laws."

17 Jethro replied:

That isn't the best way to do it. 18 You and the people who come to you will soon be worn out. The job is too much for one person; you can't do it alone. 19 God will help you if you follow my advice. You should be the one to speak to God for the people, 20 and you should teach them God's laws and show them what they must do to live right.

21 You will need to appoint some competent leaders who respect God and are trustworthy and honest. Then put them over groups of ten, fifty, a hundred, and a thousand. 22 These judges can handle the ordinary cases and bring the more difficult ones to you. Having them to share the load will make your work easier. 23 This is the way God wants it done. You won't be under nearly as much stress, and everyone else will return home feeling satisfied.

24 Moses followed Jethro's advice. 25 He chose some competent leaders from every tribe in Israel and put them over groups of ten, fifty, a hundred, and a thousand. 26 They served as judges, deciding the easy cases themselves, but bringing the more difficult ones to Moses.

27 After Moses and his father-in-law Jethro had said goodbye to each other, Jethro returned home.

The Ten Commandments and other laws

CHAPTER 19

At Mount Sinai

1-2 The Israelites left Rephidim.* Then two months after leaving Egypt, they arrived at the desert near Mount Sinai, where they set up camp at the foot of the mountain.

3 Moses went up the mountain to meet with the LORD God, who told him to say to the people:

4 You saw what I did in Egypt, and you know how I brought you here to me, just as a mighty eagle carries its young. 5 Now if you will faithfully obey me, you will be my very own people. The whole world is mine, 6 but you will be my holy nation and serve me as priests.

Moses, that is what you must tell the Israelites.

7 After Moses went back, he reported to the leaders what the LORD had said, 8 and they promised, "We will do everything the LORD has commanded." So Moses told the LORD about this.

9 The LORD said to Moses, "I will come to you in a thick cloud and let the people hear me speak to you. Then they will always trust

---

*18.2–4 Eliezer: In Hebrew "Eliezer" means "God has helped me".

*18.2–4 saved . . . Egypt: See 2.1–15.

*19.1–2 Rephidim: See the note at 17.1.

See also: 19.5–6: 1 Pet 2.9. 19.5: Deut 4.20; 7.6; 14.2; 26.18; Titus 2.14. 19.6: Rev 1.6; 5.10.

you." Again Moses reported to the people what the LORD had told him.

¹⁰ Once more the LORD spoke to Moses:

Go back and tell the people that today and tomorrow they must get themselves ready to meet me. They must wash their clothes ¹¹ and be ready by the day after tomorrow, when I will come down to Mount Sinai, where all of them can see me.

¹² Warn the people that they are forbidden to touch any part of the mountain. Anyone who does will be put to death, ¹³ either with stones or arrows, and no one must touch the body of a person killed in this way. Even an animal that touches this mountain must be put to death. You may go up the mountain only after a signal is given on the trumpet.

¹⁴ After Moses went down the mountain, he gave orders for the people to wash their clothes and make themselves acceptable to worship God. ¹⁵ He told them to be ready in three days and not to have sex in the meantime.

The LORD comes to Mount Sinai

¹⁶ On the morning of the third day there was thunder and lightning. A thick cloud covered the mountain, a loud trumpet blast was heard, and everyone in camp trembled with fear. ¹⁷ Moses led them out of the camp to meet God, and they stood at the foot of the mountain.

¹⁸ Mount Sinai was covered with smoke because the LORD had come down in a flaming fire. Smoke poured out of the mountain just like a furnace, and the whole mountain shook. ¹⁹ The trumpet blew louder and louder. Moses spoke, and God answered him with thunder.

²⁰ The LORD came down to the top of Mount Sinai and told Moses to meet him there. ²¹ Then he said, "Moses, go and warn the people not to cross the boundary that you set at the foot of the mountain. They must not cross it to come and look at me, because if they do, many of them will die. ²² Only the priests may come near me, and they must obey strict rules before I let them. If they don't, they will be punished."

²³ Moses replied, "The people cannot come up the mountain. You warned us to stay away because it is holy."

²⁴ Then the LORD told Moses, "Go down and bring Aaron back here with you. But the priests and people must not try to push their way through, or I will rush at them like a flood!"

²⁵ After Moses had gone back down, he told the people what the LORD had said.

CHAPTER 20

The Ten Commandments

This is also told in Deuteronomy 5.1–21

¹ God said to the people of Israel:

² I am the LORD your God, the one who brought you out of Egypt where you were slaves.

³ Do not worship any god except me.

⁴ Do not make idols that look like anything in the sky or on earth or in the sea under the earth. ⁵ Don't bow down and worship idols. I am the LORD your God, and I demand all your love. If you reject me, I will punish your families for three or four generations. ⁶ But if you love me and obey my laws, I will be kind to your families for thousands of generations.

⁷ Do not misuse my name.* I am the LORD your God, and I will punish anyone who misuses my name.

⁸ Remember that the Sabbath Day belongs to me. ⁹ You have six days when you can do your work, ¹⁰ but the seventh day of each week belongs to me, your God. No one is to work on that day — not you, your children, your slaves, your animals, or the foreigners who live in your towns. ¹¹ In six days I made the sky, the earth, the seas, and everything in them, but on the seventh day I rested. That's why I made the Sabbath a special day that belongs to me.

¹² Respect your father and your mother, and you will live a long time in the land I am giving you.

¹³ Do not murder.

---

*20.7 misuse my name: Probably includes breaking promises, telling lies after swearing to tell the truth, using the LORD's name as a curse word or a magic formula, and trying to control the LORD by using his name.

See also: 20.4–5: Exod 34.17; Lev 19.4; 26.1; Deut 4.15–18; 27.15. 20.5–6: Exod 34.6–7; Num 14.18; Deut 7.9–10. 20.7: Lev 19.12. 20.8: Exod 16.23–30; 31.12–14. 20.9–10: Exod 23.12; 31.15; 34.21; 35.2; Lev 23.3. 20.11: Gen 2.1–3; Exod 31.17. 20.12: a Deut 27.16; Matt 15.4; 19.19; Mark 7.10; 10.19; Luke 18.20; Eph 6.2; b Eph 6.3. 20.13: Gen 9.6; Lev 24.17; Matt 5.21; 19.18; Mark 10.19; Luke 18.20; Rom 13.9; Jam 2.11.

See also: 19.12–13: Heb 12.18–20. 19.16: Rev 4.5. 19.16–18: Deut 4.11–12.

Big ideas

Ten Commandments

The Ten Commandments form the basis for most of the legal systems of our world. Not bad for something written on the top of a mountain 3,500 years ago!

When Moses repeats these commandments (Deuteronomy 5.1–21) he calls them an 'agreement' between God and Israel. And that's what they are – a covenant promise, just like the one that Abraham made with God.

They begin with a bit of history: 'I am the Lord your God, the one who brought you out of Egypt where you were slaves' (Exodus 20.2). This is crucial. God is not promising to rescue the Israelites if they are good boys and girls. He has already rescued them. Obedience to God is therefore a response to his love and concern for us.

The root of all theses commandments is the first one: 'Do not worship any god except me' (Exodus 20.3). No god, either real or imagined, is to take the place of the one true God, whether ancient gods like Zeus or Baal or Dagon, or 'modern' gods of our world, like money, success or sex.

Most of the commands are pretty straightforward, but some need a little more interpretation. 'Respecting' your father and mother, means 'honouring', 'prizing highly', or 'caring about' your parents. It doesn't mean they're always right, it means that we have obligations towards them. And 'misusing the Lord's name' means more than not using 'God' or 'Jesus' as any kind of exclamation or swearword. It means not swearing falsely on God's name in court; nor using it as some kind of cheap magic formula. God demands to be taken seriously. And that means not using his name in wrong ways.

More...

Help! My parents are letting me down! p.598
Foreign gods p.262
The Law p.127
Ark of the Covenant p.104
Sabbath p.97

14 Be faithful in marriage.
15 Do not steal.
16 Do not tell lies about others.
17 Do not want to take anything that belongs to someone else. Don't want to take anyone's house, wife or husband, slaves, oxen, donkeys or anything else.

The people are afraid

This is also told in Deuteronomy 5.23–33

18 The people trembled with fear when they heard the thunder and the trumpet and saw the lightning and the smoke coming from the mountain. They stood a long way off 19 and said to Moses, "If you speak to us, we will listen. But don't let God speak to us, or we will die!"

20 "Don't be afraid!" Moses replied. "God has come only to test you, so that by obeying him you won't sin." 21 But when Moses went near the thick cloud where God was, the people stayed a long way off.

Idols and altars

22 The LORD told Moses to say to the people of Israel:

With your own eyes, you saw me speak to you from heaven. 23 So you must never make idols of silver or gold to worship in place of me.'

24 Build an altar out of earth, and offer on it your sacrifices* of sheep, goats, and cattle. Wherever I choose to be worshipped, I will come down to bless you. 25 If you ever build an altar for me out of stones, do not use any tools to chisel the stones, because that would make the altar unfit. 26 And don't build an altar that requires steps; you might expose yourself when you climb up.

*20.24 sacrifices: The Hebrew text mentions two types of sacrifices: sacrifices to please the LORD (traditionally called "whole burnt offerings") and sacrifices to ask the LORD's blessing (traditionally called "peace offerings").

See also: 20.14: Lev 20.10; Matt 5.27; 19.18; Mark 10.19; Luke 18.20; Rom 13.9; Jam 2.11. 20.15: Lev 19.11; Matt 19.18; Mark 10.19; Luke 18.20; Rom 13.9. 20.16: Exod 23.1; Matt 19.18; Mark 10.19; Luke 18.20. 20.17: Rom 7.7; 13.9. 20.18–19: Heb 12.18–19. 20.25: Deut 27.5–7; Josh 8.31.

CHAPTER 21

Hebrew slaves

This is also told in Deuteronomy 15.12–18

¹ The LORD gave Moses the following laws for his people:

² If you buy a Hebrew slave, he must remain your slave for six years. But in the seventh year you must set him free, without cost to him. ³ If he was single at the time you bought him, he alone must be set free. But if he was married at the time, both he and his wife must be given their freedom. ⁴ If you give him a wife, and they have children, only the man himself must be set free; his wife and children remain the property of his owner.

⁵ But suppose the slave loves his wife and children so much that he won't leave without them. ⁶ Then he must stand beside either the door or the doorpost at the place of worship,' while his owner punches a small hole through one of his ears with a sharp metal rod. This makes him a slave for life.

⁷ A young woman who was sold by her father doesn't gain her freedom in the same way that a man does. ⁸ If she doesn't please the man who bought her to be his wife, he must let her be bought back.* He cannot sell her to foreigners; this would break the contract he made with her. ⁹ If he selects her as a wife for his son, he must treat her as his own daughter.

¹⁰ If the man later marries another woman, he must continue to provide food and clothing for the one he bought and to treat her as a wife. ¹¹ If he fails to do any of these things, she must be given her freedom without cost.

Murder and other violent crimes

The LORD said:

¹² Death is the punishment for murder. ¹³ But if you did not intend to kill someone, and I, the LORD, let it happen anyway, you may run for safety to a place that I have set aside. ¹⁴ If you plan in advance to murder someone, there's no escape, not even by holding on to my altar.* You will be dragged off and killed.

¹⁵ Death is the punishment for attacking your father or mother.
¹⁶ Death is the punishment for kidnapping. If you sell the person you kidnapped, or if you are caught with that person, the penalty is death.
¹⁷ Death is the punishment for cursing your father or mother.
¹⁸ Suppose two of you are arguing, and you hit the other with either a rock or your fist, without causing a fatal injury. If the victim has to stay in bed, ¹⁹ and later has to use a stick when walking outside, you must pay for the loss of time and do what you can to help until the injury is completely healed. That's your only responsibility.
²⁰ Death is the punishment for beating to death any of your slaves. ²¹ However, if the slave lives a few days after the beating, you are not to be punished. After all, you have already lost the services of that slave who was your property.
²² Suppose a pregnant woman suffers a miscarriage' as the result of an injury caused by someone who is fighting. If she isn't badly hurt, the one who injured her must pay whatever fine her husband demands and the judges approve. ²³ But if she is seriously injured, the payment will be life for life, ²⁴ eye for eye, tooth for tooth, hand for hand, foot for foot, ²⁵ burn for burn, cut for cut, and bruise for bruise.
²⁶ If you hit one of your slaves and cause the loss of an eye, the slave must be set free. ²⁷ The same law applies if you knock out a slave's tooth — the slave goes free.
²⁸ A bull that kills someone with its horns must be killed and its meat destroyed, but the owner of the bull isn't responsible for the death.
²⁹ Suppose you own a bull that has been in the habit of attacking people, but you have refused to keep it fenced in. If that bull kills someone, both you and the bull must be put to death by stoning. ³⁰ However, you may save your own life by paying whatever fine is demanded. ³¹ This same law applies if the bull gores someone's son or daughter.
³² If the bull kills a slave, you must pay the slave owner thirty pieces of silver for the loss of the slave, and the bull must be killed by stoning.
³³ Suppose someone's ox or donkey is killed by falling into an open pit that you dug or left uncovered on your property.

---

*21.8 bought back: Either by her family or by another Israelite who wanted to marry her.
*21.14 altar: As a rule, anyone who ran to the altar was safe from the death penalty, until proved guilty.
See also: 21.2–6: Lev 25.39–46. 21.12: Lev 24.17.
21.13: Num 35.10–34; Deut 19.1–13; Josh 20.1–9.

See also: 21.16: Deut 24.7. 21.17: Lev 20.9; Matt 15.4;
Mark 7.10. 21.24: Lev 24.19–20; Deut 19.21; Matt 5.38.

³⁴ You must pay for the dead animal, and it becomes yours.

³⁵ If your bull kills someone else's, yours must be sold. Then the money from your bull and the meat from the dead bull must be divided equally between you and the other owner.

³⁶ If you refuse to fence in a bull that is known to attack others, you must pay for any animal it kills, but the dead animal will belong to you.

CHAPTER 22

Property laws

The LORD said:

¹ If you steal an ox and slaughter or sell it, you must replace it with five oxen; if you steal a sheep and slaughter it or sell it, you must replace it with four sheep. ²⁻⁴ But if you cannot afford to replace the animals, you must be sold as a slave to pay for what you have stolen. If you steal an ox, donkey, or sheep, and are caught with it still alive, you must pay the owner double.

If you happen to kill a burglar who breaks into your home after dark, you are not guilty. But if you kill someone who breaks in during the day, you are guilty of murder.

⁵ If you allow any of your animals to stray from your property and graze▸ in someone else's field or vineyard, you must repay the damage from the best part of your own harvest of grapes and grain.

⁶ If you carelessly let a fire spread from your property to someone else's, you must pay the owner for any crops or fields destroyed by the fire.

⁷ Suppose a neighbour asks you to keep some silver or other valuables, and they are stolen from your house. If the thief is caught, the thief must repay double. ⁸ But if the thief isn't caught, some judges▸ will decide if you are the guilty one.

⁹ Suppose two people claim to own the same ox or donkey or sheep or piece of clothing. Then the judges▸ must decide the case, and the guilty person will pay the owner double.

¹⁰ Suppose a neighbour who is going to be away asks you to keep a donkey or an ox or a sheep or some other animal, and it dies or gets injured or is stolen while no one is looking. ¹¹ If you swear with me as your witness that you did not harm the animal, you do not have to replace it. Your word is enough. ¹² But if the animal was stolen

while in your care, you must replace it. ¹³ If the animal was attacked and killed by a wild animal, and you can show the remains of the dead animal to its owner, you do not have to replace it.

¹⁴ Suppose you borrow an animal from a neighbour, and it gets injured or dies while the neighbour isn't around. Then you must replace it. ¹⁵ But if something happens to the animal while the owner is present, you do not have to replace it. If you had leased the animal, the money you paid the owner will cover any harm done to it.

Laws for everyday life

The LORD said:

¹⁶ Suppose a young woman has never been married and isn't engaged. If a man talks her into having sex, he must pay the bride price* and marry her. ¹⁷ But if her father refuses to let her marry the man, the bride price must still be paid.

¹⁸ Death is the punishment for witchcraft.

¹⁹ Death is the punishment for having sex with an animal.

²⁰ Death is the punishment for offering sacrifices to any god except me.

²¹ Do not ill-treat or abuse foreigners who live among you. Remember, you were foreigners in Egypt.

²² Do not ill-treat widows or orphans. ²³ If you do, they will beg for my help, and I will come to their rescue. ²⁴ In fact, I will get so angry that I will kill your men and make widows of their wives and orphans of their children.

²⁵ Don't charge interest when you lend money to any of my people who are in need. ²⁶ Before sunset you must return any coat taken as security for a loan, ²⁷ because that is the only cover the poor have when they sleep at night. I am a merciful God, and when they call out to me, I will come to help them.

²⁸ Don't speak evil of me▸ or of the ruler of your people.

²⁹ Don't fail to give me the offerings of grain and wine that belong to me.▸

---

*22.16 bride price: It was the custom for a man to pay his wife's family a bride price before the actual wedding ceremony took place.

See also: 22.16–17: Deut 22.28–29. 22.18: Deut 18.10–11. 22.19: Lev 18.23; 20.15–16; Deut 27.21. 22.20: Deut 17.2–7. 22.21–22: Exod 23.9; Lev 19.33–34; Deut 24.17–18; 27.19. 22.25: Lev 25.35–38; Deut 15.7–11; 23.19–20. 22.26–27: Deut 24.10–13. 22.28: Acts 23.5.

Dedicate to me your firstborn sons [30] and the firstborn of your cattle and sheep. Let the animals stay with their mothers for seven days, then on the eighth day give them to me, your God.

[31] You are my chosen people, so don't eat the meat of any of your livestock that was killed by a wild animal. Instead, feed the meat to dogs.

CHAPTER 23

Equal justice for all

The LORD said:

[1] Don't spread harmful rumours or help a criminal by giving false evidence.

[2] Always tell the truth in court, even if everyone else is' dishonest and stands in the way of justice. [3] And don't favour the poor, simply because they are poor.

[4] If you find an ox or a donkey that has wandered off, take it back where it belongs, even if the owner is your enemy.

[5] If a donkey is overloaded and falls down, you must do what you can to help, even if it belongs to someone who doesn't like you.'

[6] Make sure that the poor are given equal justice in court. [7] Don't bring false charges against anyone or sentence an innocent person to death. I won't forgive you if you do.

[8] Don't accept bribes. Judges are blinded and justice is twisted by bribes.

[9] Don't ill-treat foreigners. You were foreigners in Egypt, and you know what it is like.

Laws for the Sabbath

The LORD said:

[10] Plant and harvest your crops for six years, [11] but let the land rest during the seventh year. The poor are to eat what they want from your fields, vineyards, and olive trees during that year, and when they have all they want from your fields, leave the rest for wild animals.

[12] Work the first six days of the week, but rest and relax on the seventh day. This law is not only for you, but for your oxen,

See also: 22.31: Lev 17.15. **23.1:** Exod 20.16; Lev 19.11–12; Deut 5.20. **23.3:** Lev 19.15. **23.4,5:** Deut 22.1–4. **23.6–8:** Lev 19.15; Deut 16.19. **23.9:** Exod 22.21; Lev 19.33–34; Deut 24.17–18; 27.19. **23.10,11:** Lev 25.1–7. **23.12:** Exod 20.9–11; 31.15; 34.21; 35.2; Lev 23.3; Deut 5.13–14.

Big ideas

Justice

The Bible is full of God's concern for the poor, the refugee, the outcast, the prisoner, the despised, the hungry.

The Israelites must feed the poor and look after immigrants (Deuteronomy 24.19–22). They are to care for orphans and widows (Deuteronomy 14.28–29). They are not to steal land (Deuteronomy 19.14), nor tamper with scales so as to make more money (Leviticus 19.35). And in the Jubilee year everything was supposed to be restored to the original owners.

But they weren't very good at obeying these instructions, leading to harsh criticism from prophets such as Amos and Isaiah.

This concern was picked up by Jesus, who healed the sick, had parties with tax collectors and prostitutes, and spoke with respect to children and women. In his home town, he chose a passage on social justice from Isaiah to explain why he had come (Luke 4.18–19). And he warned us that we would be judged on how much our faith affected our lives (Matthew 25.31–46).

The early Church followed his example. They welcomed outcasts to their shared meals and shared all their possessions. Today Christians are working with the poor and the dispossessed, showing that God cares for the poor. He cares about justice.

 ## footsteps

Ten days on Justice

The cries of the slaves: Exodus 3.1–10
The Year of Jubilee: Leviticus 25.1–34
Rules for the poor: Deuteronomy 24.6–22
Justice in court: Exodus 23.1–9
True worship: Isaiah 58.1–14
I hate your religion: Amos 5.10–24
See that justice is done: Micah 6.1–16
Good news for the poor: Luke 4.16–30
God blesses the poor: Luke 6.20–26
Alive and dead faith: James 2.1–17

More...

Jubilee – the year of celebration p.137
Fair trade p.923
Prisons and criminal justice p.876

donkeys, and slaves, as well as for any foreigners among you. [13] Make certain that you obey everything I have said. Don't pray to other gods or even mention their names.

Three annual festivals

This is also told in Exodus 34.18–26; Deuteronomy 16.1–17

The LORD said:

[14] Celebrate three festivals each year in my honour.

[15] Celebrate the Festival of Thin Bread by eating bread made without yeast, just as I have commanded.* Do this at the proper time during the month of Abib,* because it is the month when you left Egypt. And make certain that everyone brings the proper offerings.

[16] Celebrate the Harvest Festival* each spring when you start harvesting your wheat, and celebrate the Festival of Shelters* each autumn when you pick your fruit.

[17] Your men must come to these three festivals each year to worship me.

[18] Do not offer bread made with yeast when you sacrifice an animal to me. And make sure that the fat of the animal is burnt that same day.

[19] Each year bring the best part of your first harvest to the place of worship.

Don't boil a young goat in its mother's milk.

A promise and a warning

The LORD said:

[20] I am sending an angel to protect you and to lead you into the land I have ready for you. [21] Carefully obey everything the angel says, because I am giving him complete authority, and he won't tolerate rebellion.

[22] If you faithfully obey him, I will be a fierce enemy of your enemies. [23] My angel will lead you into the land of the Amorites, Hittites, Perizzites, Canaanites, Hivites, and Jebusites, and I will wipe them out. [24] Don't worship their gods or follow their customs. Instead, destroy their idols and shatter their stone images.

[25] Worship only me, the LORD your God! I will bless you with plenty of food and water and keep you strong. [26] Your women will give birth to healthy children, and everyone will live a long life.

[27] I will terrify those nations and make your enemies so confused that they will run from you. [28] I will make the Hivites, Canaanites, and Hittites panic as you approach. [29] But I won't do all this in the first year, because the land would become poor, and wild animals would be everywhere. [30] Instead, I will force out your enemies little by little and give your nation time to grow strong enough to take over the land.

[31] I will see that your borders reach from the Red Sea* to the River Euphrates and from the Mediterranean Sea to the desert. I will let you defeat the people who live there, and you will force them out of the land. [32] But you must not make any agreements with them or with their gods. [33] Don't let them stay in your land. They will trap you into sinning against me and worshipping their gods.

CHAPTER 24

The people agree to obey God

[1] The LORD said to Moses, "Come up to me on this mountain. Bring along Aaron, as well as his two sons Nadab and Abihu, and seventy of Israel's leaders. They must worship me at a distance, [2] but you are to come near. Don't let anyone else come up."

[3] Moses gave the LORD's instructions to the people, and they promised, "We will do everything the LORD has commanded!" [4] Then Moses wrote down what the LORD had said.

The next morning Moses got up early. He built an altar at the foot of the mountain and set up a large stone for each of the twelve tribes of Israel. [5] He also sent some young

---

*23.15 as I have commanded: See 12.14–20.
*23.15 Abib: See the note at 13.3–4.
*23.16 Harvest Festival: Traditionally called the "Festival of Weeks" and known in New Testament times as "Pentecost".
*23.16 Festival of Shelters: The Hebrew text has "Festival of Ingathering" (so also in 34.22), which was the final harvesting of crops and fruits before the autumn rains began. But the usual name was "Festival of Shelters".

See also: 23.15: Exod 12.14–20; Lev 23.6–8; Num 28.17–25. 23.16: a Lev 23.15–21; Num 28.26–31; b Lev 23.39–43. 23.19: Deut 26.2; Exod 34.26; Deut 14.21.

*23.31 Red Sea: Hebrew *yam suph*, here referring to the Gulf of Aqaba, since the term is extended to include the north-eastern arm of the Red Sea (see also the note at 13.18).

men to burn offerings and to sacrifice bulls as special offerings* to the LORD. 6 Moses put half of the blood from the animals into bowls and sprinkled the rest on the altar. 7 Then he read aloud the LORD's commands and promises, and the people shouted, "We will obey the LORD and do everything he has commanded!"

8 Moses took the blood from the bowls and sprinkled it on the people. Next, he told them, "With this blood the LORD makes his agreement with you."

9 Moses and Aaron, together with Nadab and Abihu and the seventy leaders, went up the mountain 10 and saw the God of Israel. Under his feet was something that looked like a pavement made out of sapphire,* and it was as bright as the sky.

11 Even though these leaders of Israel saw God, he did not punish them. So they ate and drank.

Moses on Mount Sinai

12 The LORD said to Moses, "Come up on the mountain and stay here for a while. I will give you the two flat stones on which I have written the laws that my people must obey."
13 Moses and Joshua his assistant got ready, then Moses started up the mountain to meet with God.

14 Moses had told the leaders, "Wait here until we come back. Aaron and Hur will be with you, and they can settle any arguments while we are away."

15 When Moses went up on Mount Sinai, a cloud covered it, 16 and the bright glory of the LORD came down and stayed there. The cloud covered the mountain for six days, and on the seventh day the LORD told Moses to come into the cloud. 17-18 Moses did so and stayed there forty days and nights. To the people, the LORD's glory looked like a blazing fire on top of the mountain.

Instructions for the sacred tent, its furnishings, and the sacred chest

CHAPTER 25

The sacred tent
This is also told in Exodus 35.4–9

1 The LORD said to Moses:

2 Tell everyone in Israel who wants to give gifts that they must bring them to you.
3 Here is a list of what you are to collect: gold, silver, and bronze; 4 blue, purple, and red wool; fine linen; goat hair; 5 tanned ram skins; fine leather; acacia wood; 6 olive oil for the lamp; sweet-smelling spices to mix with the oil for dedicating the tent and ordaining the priests; 7 and onyx* stones for the sacred apron and the breastpiece. 8 I also want them to build a special place where I can live among my people. 9 Make it and its furnishings exactly like the pattern I will show you.

The sacred chest
This is also told in Exodus 37.1–9

The LORD said to Moses:

10 Tell the people to build a chest of acacia wood one hundred and ten centimetres long, sixty-six centimetres wide, and sixty-six centimetres high. 11 Cover it inside and out with pure gold and put a gold edging around the lid. 12 Make four gold rings and fasten one of them to each of the four legs of the chest. 13 Make two poles of acacia wood. Cover them with gold 14 and put them through the rings, so the chest can be carried by the poles. 15 Don't ever remove the poles from the rings. 16 When I give you the Ten Commandments written on two flat stones, put them inside the chest.

17 Cover the lid of the chest with pure gold. 18-19 Then hammer out two winged creatures of pure gold and fasten them to the lid at the ends of the chest. 20 The creatures must face each other with their wings spread over the chest. 21 Inside it place the two flat stones with the Ten Commandments and put the gold lid on

---

24.5 special offerings: Often translated "peace offerings", which were to make peace between God and his people, who ate certain parts of the sacrificed animal.
24.10 sapphire: A precious stone, blue in colour.
See also: 24.8: a Matt 26.28; Mark 14.24; Luke 22.20; 1 Cor 11.25; Heb 10.29; b Heb 9.19–20. 24.18: Deut 9.9.

25.7 onyx: A precious stone with bands of different colours.
See also: 25.17: Heb 9.5.

top of the chest. ²² I will meet you there*
between the two creatures and tell you what
my people must do and what they must not
do.

The table for the sacred bread

This is also told in Exodus 37.10–16

The LORD said:

²³ Make a table of acacia wood eighty-eight
centimetres long, forty-four centimetres
wide, and sixty-six centimetres high.
²⁴⁻²⁵ Cover it with pure gold and put a gold
edging around it with a border seventy-five
millimetres wide.▸ ²⁶ Make four gold rings
and attach one to each of the legs ²⁷⁻²⁸ near
the edging. The poles for carrying the table
are to be placed through these rings and
are to be made of acacia wood covered with
gold. ²⁹⁻³⁰ The table is to be kept in the holy
place, and the sacred loaves of bread must
always be put on it. All bowls, plates, jars,
and cups for wine offerings are to be made
of pure gold and set on this table.

The lampstand

This is also told in Exodus 37.17–24

The LORD said:

³¹ Make a lampstand of pure gold. The
whole lampstand, including its decorative
flowers, must be made from a single piece
of hammered gold ³² with three branches
on each of its two sides. ³³ There are to be
three decorative almond blossoms on each
branch ³⁴ and four on the stem. ³⁵ There
must also be a blossom where each pair of
branches comes out from the stem. ³⁶ The
lampstand, including its branches and
decorative flowers, must be made from a
single piece of hammered pure gold. ³⁷ The
lamp on the top and those at the end of
each of its six branches must be made so as
to shine towards the front of the
lampstand. ³⁸ The tongs and trays for
taking care of the lamps are to be made of
pure gold. ³⁹ The lampstand and its
equipment will require thirty-five
kilogrammes of pure gold, ⁴⁰ and they must
be made according to the pattern I showed
you on the mountain.

---

*25.22 I will meet you there: It was believed that God
had his earthly throne on the lid of the sacred chest.
See also: 25.30: Lev 24.5–8. 25.40: Acts 7.44; Heb 8.5.

CHAPTER 26

Curtains and coverings for the sacred tent

This is also told in Exodus 36.8–19

The LORD said to Moses:

¹ Furnish the sacred tent with curtains
made from ten pieces of the finest linen.
They must be woven with blue, purple,
and red wool and embroidered with figures
of winged creatures. ² Make each piece
twelve metres long and two metres wide
³ and sew them together into two curtains
with five sections each. ⁴⁻⁶ Put fifty loops
of blue cloth along one of the wider sides of
each curtain, then fasten the two curtains
at the loops with fifty gold hooks.

⁷⁻⁸ As the material for the tent, use goat
hair to weave eleven sections thirteen
metres by two metres each. ⁹ Sew five of
the sections together to make one panel.
Then sew the other six together to make a
second panel, and fold the sixth section
double over the front of the tent. ¹⁰ Put
fifty loops along one of the wider sides of
each panel ¹¹ and fasten the two panels at
the loops with fifty bronze hooks. ¹²⁻¹³ The
panel of goat hair will be a metre longer
than the tent itself, so fold fifty centimetres
of the material behind the tent and on
each side as a protective covering. ¹⁴ Make
two more coverings — one with ram skins
dyed red and the other with fine leather.

The framework for the sacred tent

This is also told in Exodus 36.20–34

The LORD said:

¹⁵ Build a framework of acacia wood for the
walls of the sacred tent. ¹⁶ Each frame is to
be four metres high and sixty-six
centimetres wide ¹⁷ with two wooden pegs
near the bottom. ¹⁸⁻²¹ Place two silver
stands under each frame with sockets for
the pegs, so the frames can be joined
together. Twenty of these frames are to be
used along the south side and twenty more
along the north. ²² For the back wall along
the west side use six frames ²³⁻²⁴ with two
more at the south-west and north-west
corners. Make certain that these corner
frames are joined from top to bottom.
²⁵ Altogether, this back wall will have eight
frames with two silver stands under each
one.

26-27 Make five crossbars for each of the wooden frames, 28 with the centre crossbar running the full length of the wall. 29 Cover the frames and the crossbars with gold and attach gold rings to the frames to run the crossbars through. 30 Then set up the tent in the way I showed you on the mountain.

The curtain inside the sacred tent

This is also told in Exodus 36.35–38

The LORD said:

31-33 Make a curtain to separate the holy place from the most holy place. Use fine linen woven with blue, purple, and red wool, and embroidered with figures of winged creatures. Cover four acacia wood posts with gold and set them each on a silver stand. Then fasten gold hooks to the posts and hang the curtain there.

34 Inside the most holy place, you must put the sacred chest that has the place of mercy on its lid.* 35 Outside the curtain put the table for the sacred bread on the right side and the gold lampstand on the left.

36 For the entrance to the tent, use a piece of fine linen woven with blue, purple, and red wool and embroidered with fine needlework. 37 Cover five acacia wood posts with gold and set them each on a bronze stand. Then put gold hooks on the posts and hang the curtain there.

CHAPTER 27

The altar for offering sacrifices

This is also told in Exodus 38.1–7

The LORD said to Moses:

1 Use acacia wood to build an altar two and a quarter metres square and one and a third metres high, 2 and make each of the four top corners stick up like the horn of a bull. Then cover the whole altar with bronze, including the four horns. 3 All the equipment for the altar must also be made of bronze — the pans for the hot ashes, the shovels, the sprinkling bowls, the meat forks, and the fire pans. 4-5 Half-way up the altar build a ledge around it, and cover the

bottom half of the altar with a decorative bronze grating. Then attach a bronze ring beneath the ledge at the four corners of the altar. 6-7 Cover two acacia wood poles with bronze and put them through the rings for carrying the altar. 8 Construct the altar in the shape of an open box, just as you were shown on the mountain.

The courtyard around the sacred tent

This is also told in Exodus 38.9–20

The LORD said:

9-15 Surround the sacred tent with a courtyard forty-four metres long on the south and north and twenty-two metres wide on the east and west. Use twenty bronze posts on bronze stands for the south and north and ten for the west. Then hang a curtain of fine linen on the posts along each of these three sides by using silver hooks and rods.

Place three bronze posts on each side of the entrance at the east and hang a curtain six and two thirds metres wide on each set of posts. 16 Use four more of these posts for the entrance way, then hang on them an embroidered curtain of fine linen nine metres long and woven with blue, purple, and red wool.

17-18 The curtains that surround the courtyard must be two and a quarter metres high and are to be hung from the bronze posts with silver hooks and rods. 19 The rest of the equipment for the sacred tent must be made of bronze, including the pegs for the tent and for the curtain surrounding the courtyard.

The oil for the lamp in the holy place

This is also told in Leviticus 24.1–4

The LORD said to Moses:

20 Command the people of Israel to supply you with the purest olive oil. Do this so the lamp will keep burning 21 in front of the curtain that separates the holy place from the most holy place, where the sacred chest is kept. Aaron and his sons are responsible for keeping the lamp burning every night in the sacred tent. The Israelites must always obey this command.

---

*26.34 place of mercy on its lid:** It was believed that God had his earthly throne on the lid of the sacred chest, and from this place he showed mercy to his people.
See also: 26.33: Heb 6.19; 9.3–5.

Instructions for priests, sacrifices, and the Sabbath

CHAPTER 28

The clothes for the high priest

This is also told in Exodus 39.1–7

The LORD said to Moses:

¹ Send for your brother Aaron and his sons Nadab, Abihu, Eleazar, and Ithamar. They are the ones I have chosen from Israel to serve as my priests. ² Make Aaron some beautiful clothes that are worthy of a high priest. ³ Aaron is to be dedicated as my high priest, and his clothes must be made only by persons who possess skills that I have given them. ⁴ Here are the items that need to be made: a breastpiece, a priestly apron, a robe, an embroidered shirt, a turban, and a sash. These sacred clothes are to be made for your brother Aaron and his sons who will be my priests. ⁵ Only gold and fine linen, woven with blue, purple, and red wool, are to be used for making these clothes.

The apron for the high priest

This is also told in Exodus 39.2–7

The LORD said:

⁶⁻⁸ The entire priestly apron must be made of fine linen skilfully woven with blue, purple, and red wool, and decorated with gold. It is to have two shoulder straps to support it and a sash that fastens around the waist.

⁹⁻¹² Put two onyx* stones in gold settings, then attach one to each of the shoulder straps. On one of these stones engrave the names of Israel's first six sons in the order of their birth. And do the same with his remaining six sons on the other stone. In this way Aaron will always carry the names of the tribes of Israel when he enters the holy place, and I will never forget my people.

¹³⁻¹⁴ Attach two gold settings to the shoulder straps and fasten them with two braided chains of pure gold.

The breastpiece for the high priest

This is also told in Exodus 39.8–21

The LORD said:

¹⁵ From the same costly material make a breastpiece for the high priest to use in learning what I want my people to do. ¹⁶ It is to be twenty-two centimetres square and folded double ¹⁷ with four rows of three precious stones: in the first row put a carnelian, a chrysolite, and an emerald; ¹⁸ in the second row a turquoise, a sapphire, and a diamond; ¹⁹ in the third row a jacinth, an agate, and an amethyst; ²⁰ and in the fourth row a beryl, an onyx, and a jasper.* Mount the stones in delicate gold settings ²¹ and engrave on each of them the name of one of the twelve tribes of Israel.

²²⁻²⁵ Attach two gold rings to the upper front corners of the breastpiece and fasten them with two braided gold chains to gold settings on the shoulder straps. ²⁶ Attach two other gold rings to the lower inside corners next to the apron ²⁷ and two more near the bottom of the shoulder straps just above the sash. ²⁸ Then take a blue cord and tie the two lower rings on the breastpiece to those on the apron. This will keep the breastpiece in place.

²⁹ In this way Aaron will have the names of the twelve tribes of Israel written on his heart each time he enters the holy place, and I will never forget my people. ³⁰ He must also wear on his breastpiece the two small objects* that he uses to receive answers from me.

The other high-priestly clothes

This is also told in Exodus 39.22–26,30–31

The LORD said:

³¹ Under his apron Aaron must wear a robe of blue wool ³² with an opening in the centre for his head. Be sure to bind the material around the collar to keep it from fraying. ³³⁻³⁴ Along the hem of the robe weave pomegranates* of blue, purple, and red wool with a gold bell between each of

---

*28.20 jasper:** The stones mentioned in verses 17–20 are of different colours: *carnelian* is deep red or reddish white; *chrysolite* is olive green; *emerald* is green; *turquoise* is blue or blue green; *sapphire* is blue; *diamond* is colourless or white; *jacinth* is reddish orange; *agate* has circles of brown and white; *amethyst* is deep purple; *beryl* is green or bluish green; *onyx* has bands of different colours; and *jasper* is usually green or clear.

*28.30 two small objects:** The Hebrew text has "urim and thummim", which may have been made of wood, stone, or metal, and were used in some way to receive answers from God.

*28.33–34 pomegranates:** A bright red fruit that looks like an apple.

See also: 28.30: Num 27.21; Deut 33.8; Ezra 2.63; Neh 7.65.

*28.9–12 onyx:** See the note at 25.7.

them. 35 If Aaron wears these clothes when he enters the holy place as my high priest, the sound of the bells will be heard, and his life will not be in danger.

36 On a narrow strip of pure gold engrave the words: "Dedicated to the LORD".

37 Fasten it to the front of Aaron's turban with a blue cord, 38 so he can wear it on his forehead. This will show that he will take on himself the guilt for any sins the people of Israel commit in offering their gifts to me, and I will forgive them.

39 Make Aaron's robe and turban of fine linen and decorate his sash with fine needlework.

The clothes for the other priests

This is also told in Exodus 39.27–29

The LORD said:

40 Since Aaron's sons are priests, they should also look dignified. So make robes, sashes, and special caps for them. 41 Then dress Aaron and his sons in these clothes, pour olive oil on their heads, and ordain them as my priests.

42 Make linen shorts for them that reach from the waist down to the thigh, so they won't expose themselves. 43 Whenever they enter the sacred tent or serve at the altar or enter the holy place, they must wear these shorts, or else they will be guilty and die. This same rule applies to any of their descendants who serve as priests.

CHAPTER 29

Instructions for ordaining priests

This is also told in Leviticus 8.1–36

The LORD said to Moses:

1 When you ordain one of Aaron's sons as my priest, choose a young bull and two rams that have nothing wrong with them. 2 Then from your finest flour make three batches of dough without yeast. Shape some of it into larger loaves, some into smaller loaves mixed with olive oil, and the rest into thin wafers brushed with oil. 3 Put all this bread in a basket and bring it when you come to sacrifice the three animals to me.

4 Bring Aaron and his sons to the entrance of the sacred tent and make them wash themselves. 5 Dress Aaron in the priestly shirt, the robe that goes under the sacred apron, the apron itself, the breastpiece, and the sash. 6 Put on his turban with its narrow strip of engraved gold 7 and then ordain him by pouring olive oil on his head.

8 Next, dress Aaron's sons in their special shirts 9 and caps and their sashes, then ordain them, because they and their descendants will always be priests.

10 Lead the bull to the entrance of the sacred tent, where Aaron and his sons will lay their hands on its head. 11 Kill the bull near my altar in front of the tent. 12 Use a finger to smear some of its blood on each of the four corners of the altar and pour out the rest of the blood on the ground next to the altar. 13 Then take the fat from the animal's insides, as well as the lower part of the liver and the two kidneys with their fat, and send them up in smoke on the altar. 14 But the meat, the skin, and the food still in the bull's stomach must be burnt outside the camp as an offering to ask forgiveness for the sins of the priests.*

15 Bring one of the rams to Aaron and his sons and make them lay their hands on its head. 16 Kill the ram and splatter its blood against all four sides of the altar. 17 Cut up the ram, wash its insides and legs, and lay all its parts on the altar, including the head. 18 Then make sure that the whole animal goes up in smoke with a smell that pleases me.

19 Bring the other ram to Aaron and his sons and make them lay their hands on its head. 20 Kill the ram and place some of its blood on Aaron's right ear lobe, his right thumb, and the big toe of his right foot. Do the same for each of his sons and splatter the rest of the blood against the four sides of the altar. 21 Then take some of the blood from the altar, mix it with the oil used for ordination, and sprinkle it on Aaron and his clothes, and also on his sons and their clothes. This will show that they and their clothes have been dedicated to me.

22 This ram is part of the ordination service. So remove its right hind leg,* its fat tail, the fat on its insides, as well as the lower part of the liver and the two kidneys with their fat. 23 Take one loaf of each kind of bread* from the basket, 24 and put this

---

*29.14 for the sins of the priests: When a sacrifice for the forgiveness of sins was made for someone other than priests, the part that was not burnt on the altar could be eaten by the priests (see Leviticus 5.13; 6.26).

*29.22 right hind leg: This was usually given to the officiating priest (see Leviticus 7.33).

*29.23 each kind of bread: See verses 2–3.

See also: 29.18: Eph 5.2; Phil 4.18.

bread, together with the meat, into the hands of Aaron and his sons. Then they will lift it all up' to show that it is dedicated to me. ²⁵ After this, the meat and bread are to be placed on the altar and sent up in smoke with a smell that pleases me.

²⁶ You may eat the choice ribs from this second ram, but you must first lift them up' to show that this meat is dedicated to me.

²⁷⁻²⁸ In the future, when anyone from Israel offers the ribs and a hind leg of a ram either to ordain a priest or to ask for my blessing, the meat belongs to me, but it may be eaten by the priests. This law will never change.

²⁹⁻³⁰ After Aaron's death, his priestly clothes are to be handed down to each descendant who succeeds him as high priest, and these clothes must be worn during the seven-day ceremony of ordination.

³¹ Boil the meat of the ordination ram in a sacred place, ³² then Aaron and his sons are to eat it together with the three kinds of bread* at the entrance to the sacred tent. ³³ At their ordination, a ceremony of forgiveness was performed for them with this sacred food, and only they have the right to eat it. ³⁴ If any of the sacred food is left until morning, it must be burnt up.

³⁵ Repeat this ordination ceremony for Aaron and his sons seven days in a row, just as I have instructed you. ³⁶ Each day you must offer a bull as a sacrifice for sin and as a way of purifying the altar. In addition, you must smear the altar with olive oil to make it completely holy. ³⁷ Do this for seven days, and the altar will become so holy that anyone who touches it will become holy.

Daily sacrifices

This is also told in Leviticus 6.8–13; Numbers 28.1–8

The LORD said:

³⁸ Each day you must sacrifice two lambs a year old, ³⁹ one in the morning and one in the evening. ⁴⁰⁻⁴¹ With each lamb offer one kilogramme of your finest flour mixed with a litre of pure olive oil, and also pour out a litre of wine as an offering. The smell of this sacrifice on the fires of the altar will be pleasing to me. ⁴²⁻⁴³ You and your descendants must always offer this sacrifice on the altar at the entrance to the sacred tent.

People of Israel, I will meet and speak with you there, and my shining glory will make the place holy. ⁴⁴ Because of who I am, the tent will become sacred, and Aaron and his sons will become worthy to serve as my priests. ⁴⁵ I will live among you as your God, ⁴⁶ and you will know that I am the LORD your God, the one who rescued you from Egypt, so that I could live among you.

CHAPTER 30

The altar for burning incense

This is also told in Exodus 37.25–28

The LORD said to Moses:

¹ Build an altar of acacia wood where you can burn incense. ² Make it forty-five centimetres square and ninety centimetres high, and make each of its four corners stick up like the horn of a bull. ³ Cover it with pure gold and put a gold edging around it. ⁴ Then below the edging on opposite sides attach two gold rings through which you can put the poles for carrying the altar. ⁵ These poles are also to be made of acacia wood covered with gold.

⁶ Put the altar in front of the inside curtain of the sacred tent. The chest with the place of mercy* is kept behind that curtain, and I will talk with you there. ⁷⁻⁸ From now on, when Aaron tends the lamp each morning and evening, he must burn sweet-smelling incense to me on the altar. ⁹ Burn only the proper incense on the altar and never use it for grain sacrifices or animal sacrifices or drink offerings. ¹⁰ Once a year Aaron must purify the altar by smearing on its four corners* the blood of an animal sacrificed for sin, and this practice must always be followed. The altar is sacred because it is dedicated to me.

The money for the sacred tent

¹¹ The LORD said to Moses:

¹² Find out how many grown men there are in Israel and require each of them to pay me to keep him safe from danger while you are counting them. ¹³⁻¹⁵ Each man over nineteen, whether rich or poor, must pay me the same amount of money, weighed according to the official standards. ¹⁶ This money is to be used for the upkeep of the sacred tent, and because of it, I will never forget my people.

*30.6 place of mercy: See the note at 26.34.
*30.10 four corners: See 27.2; 30.2.
See also: 30.13: Exod 38.25–26; Matt 17.24.

*29.32 three kinds of bread: See verses 2–3.

The large bronze bowl

This is also told in Exodus 38.8

[17] The LORD said to Moses:

[18-21] Make a large bronze bowl and a bronze stand for it. Then put them between the altar for sacrifice and the sacred tent, so the priests can wash their hands and feet before entering the tent or offering a sacrifice on the altar. Each priest in every generation must wash himself in this way, or else he will die there.

The oil for dedication and ordination

This is also told in Exodus 37.29

[22] The LORD said to Moses:

[23-25] Mix four litres of olive oil with the following costly spices: six kilogrammes of myrrh, three kilogrammes of cinnamon, three kilogrammes of cane, and six kilogrammes of cassia. Measure these according to the official standards. Then use this sacred mixture [26] for dedicating the tent and chest, [27] the table with its equipment, the lampstand with its equipment, the incense altar with all its utensils, [28] the altar for sacrifices, and the large bowl with its stand. [29] By dedicating them in this way, you will make them so holy that anyone who even touches them will become holy.

[30] When you ordain Aaron and his sons as my priests, sprinkle them with some of this oil, [31] and say to the people of Israel: "This oil must always be used in the ordination service of a priest. It is holy because it is dedicated to the LORD. [32] So treat it as holy! Don't ever use it for everyday purposes or mix any for yourselves. [33] If you do, you will no longer belong to the LORD's people."

The sweet-smelling incense

The LORD said:

[34-35] Mix equal amounts of the costly spices stacte, onycha, galbanum, and pure frankincense, then add salt to make the mixture pure and holy. [36] Pound some of it into powder and sprinkle it in front of the sacred chest, where I meet with you. Be sure to treat this incense as something very holy. [37] It is truly holy because it is dedicated to me, so don't ever make any for yourselves. [38] If you ever make any of it to use as perfume, you will no longer belong to my people.

CHAPTER 31

The LORD chooses Bezalel and Oholiab

This is also told in Exodus 35.30—36.1

[1] The LORD said to Moses:

[2] I have chosen Bezalel' from the Judah tribe to make the sacred tent and its furnishings. [3-5] Not only have I filled him with my Spirit, but I have given him wisdom and made him a skilled craftsman who can create objects of art with gold, silver, bronze, stone, and wood. [6] I have appointed Oholiab' from the tribe of Dan to work with him, and I have also given skills to those who will help them make everything exactly as I have commanded you: [7-11] the sacred tent with its furnishings, the sacred chest with its place of mercy, the table with all that is on it, the lamp with its equipment, the incense altar, the altar for sacrifices with its equipment, the bronze bowl with its stand, the beautiful priestly clothes for Aaron and his sons, the oil for dedication and ordination services, and the sweet-smelling incense for the holy place.

Laws for the Sabbath

[12-13] Moses told the Israelites that the LORD had said:

The Sabbath belongs to me. Now I command you and your descendants always to obey the laws of the Sabbath. By doing this, you will know that I have chosen you as my own. [14-15] Keep the Sabbath holy. You have six days to do your work, but the Sabbath is mine, and it must remain a day of rest. If you work on the Sabbath, you will no longer be part of my people, and you will be put to death.

[16] Every generation of Israelites must respect the Sabbath. [17] This day will always serve as a reminder, both to me and to the Israelites, that I made the heavens and the earth in six days, then on the seventh day I rested and relaxed.

[18] When God had finished speaking to Moses on Mount Sinai, he gave him the two flat stones on which he had written all his laws with his own hand.

See also: **31.15:** Exod 20.8-11; 23.12; 34.21; 35.2; Lev 23.3; Deut 5.12-14.   **31.17:** Exod 20.11.

See also: **30.18:** Exod 38.8.   **30.22-38:** Exodus 37.29.

Big ideas

Sabbath

The word means 'to stop work' and that's the basic point: it's a time to rest. In today's 24/7 culture, working every hour we can is seen as a kind of macho thing to do. But the reality is, it's against God's rules.

The Sabbath is also about reflection. The Sabbath gives us space to think about God, to look at our lives, to worship God. By deciding not to work on the Sabbath, by choosing to spend it in worshipping God, it shows who is really in control. That's why the prophets were so strong in their insistence on observing the Sabbath. It was a sign of what was important.

However, there is a danger that we go the other way. Over time, the laws about what Jews could, or couldn't do on the Sabbath became so complex that the focus of the day switched away from God and onto the rules themselves. It was this attitude which was challenged by Jesus (Mark 2.28).

The Sabbath principle was applied across years as well. God ordered that every seventh year the land was allowed to lie fallow, to recover. Sabbath is not just about humans, it's about creation as well.

The Jews were instructed to observe the Sabbath on the seventh day of the week. From very early on Christians chose to move their Sabbath to the first day of the week, in honour of Jesus rising again on a Sunday (1 Corinthians 16.2).

Footsteps

A week with the Sabbath

God rests: Genesis 1.31—2.3
God institutes the Sabbath: Exodus 20. 8–11
The Sabbath year: Leviticus 25.1–6
Nehemiah's reminder: Nehemiah 13.31
Isaiah's warning: Isaiah 56.1–7
Jesus replies to his critics: Matthew 12.1–12
The move to Sunday: 1 Corinthians 16.1–4

More...

Ten Commandments p.85
Work p.1343
Jubilee – the year of celebration p.137
The Law p.127

The people make an idol

CHAPTER 32

This is also told in Deuteronomy 9.6–29

[1] After the people saw that Moses had been on the mountain for a long time, they went to Aaron and said, "Make us an image of a god who will lead and protect us. Moses brought us out of Egypt, but nobody knows what has happened to him."

[2] Aaron told them, "Bring me the gold earrings that your wives and sons and daughters are wearing." [3] Everybody took off their earrings and brought them to Aaron, [4] then he melted them and made an idol in the shape of a young bull.

All the people said to one another, "This is the god who brought us out of Egypt!"

[5] When Aaron saw what was happening, he built an altar in front of the idol and said, "Tomorrow we will celebrate in honour of the LORD." [6] The people got up early the next morning and killed some animals to be used for sacrifices and others to be eaten. Then everyone ate and drank so much that they began to carry on like wild people.

[7] The LORD said to Moses:

Hurry back down! Those people you led out of Egypt are acting like fools. [8] They have already stopped obeying me and have made themselves an idol in the shape of a young bull. They have bowed down to it, offered sacrifices, and said that it is the god who brought them out of Egypt. [9] Moses, I have seen how stubborn these people are, [10] and I'm angry enough to destroy them, so don't try to stop me. But I will make your descendants into a great nation.

[11] Moses tried to get the LORD God to change his mind:

Our LORD, you used your mighty power to bring these people out of Egypt. Now don't become angry and destroy them. [12] If you do, the Egyptians will say that you brought your people out here into the mountains just to get rid of them. Please don't be angry with your people. Don't destroy them!

[13] Remember the solemn promise you made to Abraham, Isaac, and Jacob. You promised that some day they would have

See also: 32.1: Acts 7.40. **32.4:** 1 King 12.28; Acts 7.41. **32.6:** 1 Cor 10.7. **32.11–14:** Num 14.13–19. **32.13:** Gen 22.16–17; Gen 17.8.

as many descendants as there are stars in the sky and that you would give them land.

¹⁴ So even though the LORD had threatened to destroy the people, he changed his mind and let them live.

¹⁵⁻¹⁶ Moses went back down the mountain with the two flat stones on which God had written all his laws with his own hand, and he had used both sides of the stones.

¹⁷ When Joshua heard the noisy shouts of the people, he said to Moses, "A battle must be going on down in the camp."

¹⁸ But Moses replied, "It doesn't sound like they are shouting because they have won or lost a battle. They are singing wildly!"

¹⁹ As Moses got closer to the camp, he saw the idol, and he also saw the people dancing around. This made him so angry that he threw down the stones and broke them to pieces at the foot of the mountain. ²⁰ He melted the idol the people had made, and he ground it into powder. He scattered it in their water and made them drink it. ²¹ Moses asked Aaron, "What did these people do to harm you? Why did you make them sin in this terrible way?"

²² Aaron answered:

Don't be angry with me. You know as well as I do that they are determined to do evil. ²³ They even told me, "That man Moses led us out of Egypt, but now we don't know what has happened to him. Make us a god to lead us." ²⁴ Then I asked them to bring me their gold earrings. They took them off and gave them to me. I threw the gold into a fire, and out came this bull.

²⁵ Moses knew that the people were out of control and that it was Aaron's fault. And now they had made fools of themselves in front of their enemies. ²⁶ So Moses stood at the gate of the camp and shouted, "Everyone who is on the LORD's side come over here!"

Then the men of the Levi tribe gathered around Moses, ²⁷ and he said to them, "The LORD God of Israel commands you to strap on your swords and go through the camp, killing your relatives, your friends, and your neighbours."

²⁸ The men of the Levi tribe followed his orders, and that day they killed about three thousand men. ²⁹ Moses said to them, "You obeyed the LORD and did what was right, and so you will serve as his priests for the people of Israel. It was hard for you to kill your own sons and brothers, but the LORD has blessed you and made you his priests today."

³⁰ The next day Moses told the people, "This is a terrible thing you have done. But I will go back to the LORD to see if I can do something to keep this sin from being held against you."

³¹ Moses returned to the LORD and said, "The people have committed a terrible sin. They have made a gold idol to be their god. ³² But I beg you to forgive them. If you don't, please wipe my name out of your book."*

³³ The LORD replied, "I will wipe out of my book the name of everyone who has sinned against me. ³⁴ Now take my people to the place I told you about, and my angel will lead you. But when the time comes, I will punish them for this sin."

³⁵ So the LORD punished the people of Israel with a terrible disease for talking Aaron into making the gold idol.

The Lord makes promises, renews his agreement, and gives more laws to Israel

CHAPTER 33

The LORD tells Israel to leave Mount Sinai

¹ The LORD said to Moses:

You led the people of Israel out of Egypt. Now get ready to lead them to the land I promised their ancestors Abraham, Isaac, and Jacob. ²⁻³ It is a land rich with milk and honey, and I will send an angel to force out those people who live there — the Canaanites, the Amorites, the Hittites, the Perizzites, the Hivites, and the Jebusites. I would go with my people, but they are so rebellious that I would destroy them before they get there.

⁴⁻⁵ Even before the LORD said these harsh things, he had told Moses, "These people really are rebellious, and I would kill them at once, if I went with them. But tell them to take off their jewellery, then I'll decide what to do with them." So the people started mourning, ⁶ and after leaving Mount Sinai,ᵇ they stopped wearing jewellery.

---

*32.32 your book: The people of Israel believed that the LORD kept a record of the names of his people, and anyone whose name was removed from that book no longer belonged to the LORD.

See also: 32.32: Psa 69.28; Rev 3.5. **33.1: a** Gen 12.7; **b** Gen 26.3; **c** Gen 28.13.

The LORD is with his people

7 Moses used to set up a tent far from camp. He called it the "meeting tent", and whoever needed some message from the LORD would go there. 8 Each time Moses went out to the tent, everyone would stand at the entrance to their own tents and watch him enter. 9-11 Then they would bow down because a thick cloud would come down in front of the tent, and the LORD would speak to Moses face to face, just like a friend. Afterwards, Moses would return to camp, but his young assistant Joshua' would stay at the tent.

The LORD promises to be with his people

12 Moses said to the LORD, "I know that you have told me to lead these people to the land you promised them. But you have not told me who my assistant will be. You have said that you are my friend and that you are pleased with me. 13 If this is true, let me know what your plans are, then I can obey and continue to please you. And don't forget that you have chosen this nation to be your own."

14 The LORD said, "I will go with you and give you peace."

15 Then Moses replied, "If you aren't going with us, please don't make us leave this place. 16 But if you do go with us, everyone will know that you are pleased with your people and with me. That way, we will be different from the rest of the people on earth."

17 So the LORD told him, "I will do what you have asked, because I am your friend and I am pleased with you."

18 Then Moses said, "I pray that you will let me see you in all your glory."

19 The LORD answered:

All right. I am the LORD, and I show mercy and kindness to anyone I choose. I will let you see my glory and hear my holy name, 20 but I won't let you see my face, because anyone who sees my face will die. 21 There is a rock not far from me. Stand beside it, 22 and before I pass by in all my shining glory, I will put you in a large crack in the rock. I will cover your eyes with my hand until I have passed by. 23 Then I will take my hand away, and you will see my back. You will not see my face.

See also: **33.19:** Rom 9.15.

Big ideas

Appearances of God

When Moses asks to see what God really looks like, God refuses his request, because he knows that the reality would destroy Moses. Even Moses cannot see God 'full on'. He does allow Moses to see his back, and that is enough to make Moses' face glow; such is the power of the reflected glory of God. However, God does make a lot of appearances in the Old Testament, and he appears in different forms.

The Angel of the LORD

In some computer chatrooms, you can choose an image to represent you; a cartoon, an icon or a drawing. It's not you, it's not even what you look like; it is how you want to appear in that world. The angel of the LORD is a bit like that. He is a human figure who acts for God, speaks as God, but is only the way that God chooses to appear in this instance.

The burning bush

The Angel of the LORD doesn't always appear in human form. Moses's first encounter with God is as a bush, which is consumed with fire, but does not burn up. When Moses sees the burning bush he claims he has seen the Angel of the LORD.

The cloud in the Temple

The presence of God is often indicated by a cloud. The cloud covers the top of Mount Sinai, when Moses speaks with God. When Solomon opens the Temple, it is filled with a cloud.

What does God look like? It's an interesting question, but we can't answer it. For now, if we want to see what God looks like, the best thing is to look at Jesus.

More...

Names of God p.65
We may not see him like Moses did, but God hasn't changed p.154
Angels p.412

CHAPTER 34

The second set of commandments

This is also told in Deuteronomy 10.1–5

¹ One day the LORD said to Moses, "Cut two flat stones like the first ones I made, and I will write on them the same commandments that were on the two you broke. ² Be ready tomorrow morning to come up Mount Sinai and meet me at the top. ³ No one is to come with you or to be on the mountain at all. Don't even let the sheep and cattle graze at the foot of the mountain." ⁴ So Moses cut two flat stones like the first ones, and early the next morning he carried them to the top of Mount Sinai, just as the LORD had commanded.

⁵ The LORD God came down in a cloud and stood beside Moses there on the mountain. God spoke his holy name, "the LORD".* ⁶ Then he passed in front of Moses and called out, "I am the LORD God. I am merciful and very patient with my people. I show great love, and I can be trusted. ⁷ I keep my promises to my people for ever, but I also punish anyone who sins. When people sin, I punish them and their children, and also their grandchildren and great-grandchildren."

⁸ Moses quickly bowed down to the ground and worshipped the LORD. ⁹ He prayed, "LORD, if you really are pleased with me, I pray that you will go with us. It is true that these people are sinful and rebellious, but forgive our sin and let us be your people."

A promise and its demands

This is also told in Exodus 23.14–19;
Deuteronomy 7.1–5; 16.1–17

¹⁰ The LORD said:

I promise to perform miracles for you that have never been seen anywhere on earth. Neighbouring nations will stand in fear and know that I was the one who did these marvellous things. ¹¹ I will force out the Amorites, the Canaanites, the Hittites, the Perizzites, the Hivites, and the Jebusites, but you must do what I command you today. ¹² Don't make treaties with any of those people. If you do, it will be like falling into a trap. ¹³ Instead, you must destroy their altars and tear down the sacred poles* they use in the worship of the goddess Asherah. ¹⁴ I demand your complete loyalty — you must not worship any other god! ¹⁵ Don't make treaties with the people there, or you will soon find yourselves worshipping their gods and taking part in their sacrificial meals. ¹⁶ Your men will even marry their women and be influenced to worship their gods.

¹⁷ Don't make metal images of gods.

¹⁸ Don't fail to observe the Festival of Thin Bread in the month of Abib.* Obey me and eat bread without yeast for seven days during Abib, because that is the month you left Egypt.

¹⁹ The firstborn males of your families and of your flocks and herds belong to me. ²⁰ You can save the life of a firstborn donkey* by sacrificing a lamb; if you don't, you must break the donkey's neck. You must save every firstborn son.

Bring an offering every time you come to worship.

²¹ Do your work in six days and rest on the seventh day, even during the seasons for ploughing and harvesting. ²² Celebrate the Harvest Festival* each spring when you start harvesting your wheat, and celebrate the Festival of Shelters* each autumn when you pick your fruit.

²³ Your men must come to worship me three times a year, because I am the LORD God of Israel. ²⁴ I will force the nations out of your land and enlarge your borders. Then no one will try to take your property when you come to worship me these three times each year.

²⁵ When you sacrifice an animal on the altar, don't offer bread made with yeast. And don't save any part of the Passover meal for the next day.

²⁶ I am the LORD your God, and you must bring the first part of your harvest to the place of worship.

Don't boil a young goat in its mother's milk.

---

*34.5 the LORD: See the note at 3.14–15.
*34.13 sacred poles: Or "trees", used as symbols of Asherah, the goddess of fertility.
See also: 34.6–7: Exod 20.5–6; Num 14.18; Deut 5.9–10; 7.9–10. 34.13: Deut 16.21.

*34.18 Abib: See the note at 13.3–4.
*34.20 donkey: See the note at 13.13.
*34.22 Harvest Festival: See the note at 23.16.
*34.22 Festival of Shelters: See the note at 23.16.
See also: 34.17: Exod 20.4; Lev 19.4; Deut 5.8; 27.15.
34.18: Exod 12.14–20; Lev 23.6–8; Num 28.16–25.
34.19: Exod 13.2. 34.20: Exod 13.13. 34.21: Exod 20.9–10;
23.12; 31.15; 35.2; Lev 23.3; Deut 5.13,14.
34.22: a Lev 23.15–21; Num 28.26–31; b Lev 23.39–43.
34.25: Exod 12.10. 34.26: a Deut 26.2; b Deut 14.21.

Viewpoints 👁

Can people tell when you've been spending time with God?

Contributed by Sam R

'His face was shining brightly because the LORD had been speaking to him. But Moses did not know at first that his face was shining.'

Moses must have been really aware that in talking to the LORD face to face, he had an awesome privilege! At a time when being admitted into God's presence involved animal sacrifice, priests and curtains, Moses is up on the mountain having a chat with him! WOW! And when he came down, everyone could see that he'd been with God, because his face glowed.

Amazingly, our relationship with God is exactly like that of Moses. We have the privilege of spending time with him. So should our faces shine like Moses' did? I'm not talking literally here. We shouldn't all be going round with lightbulbs for heads. But an encounter with God changes people. The people who knew Moses saw in his face when he had been with God.

I don't know about you, but there are Christians I know, and you can just see they are head over heels in love with Jesus. When they talk about him, there's an excitement that shines out of their eyes. You can see that they've been spending time with him.

It says in this verse that Moses 'wasn't aware' that his face glowed. So this isn't about putting on your best crinkly Christian smile and thinking 'Man, I look SUPER-holy today.' But the point is that if we spend time with God, if we get to know him, then the world will see and take notice. It'll just be obvious. And I think that's a pretty awesome thought!

More...

Moses p.61
Appearances of God p.99
Holiness p.1386

27 The LORD told Moses to put these laws in writing, as part of his agreement with Israel. 28 Moses stayed on the mountain with the LORD for forty days and nights, without eating or drinking. And he wrote down the Ten Commandments, the most important part of God's agreement with his people.

Moses comes down from Mount Sinai

29 Moses came down from Mount Sinai, carrying the Ten Commandments. His face was shining brightly because the LORD had been speaking to him. But Moses did not know at first that his face was shining. 30 When Aaron and the others looked at Moses, they saw that his face was shining, and they were afraid to go near him. 31 Moses called out for Aaron and the leaders to come to him, and he spoke with them. 32 Then the rest of the people of Israel gathered around Moses, and he gave them the laws that the LORD had given him on Mount Sinai.

33 The face of Moses kept shining, and after he had spoken with the people, he covered his face with a veil. 34 Moses would always remove the veil when he went into the sacred tent to speak with the LORD. And when he came out, he would tell the people everything the LORD had told him to say. 35 They could see that his face was still shining. So after he had spoken with them, he would put the veil back on and leave it on until the next time he went to speak with the LORD.

CHAPTER 35

Laws for the Sabbath

1 Moses called together the people of Israel and told them that the LORD had said:

> 2 You have six days in which to do your work. But the seventh day must be dedicated to me, your LORD, as a day of rest. Whoever works on the Sabbath will be put to death. 3 Don't even build a cooking fire at home on the Sabbath.

See also: 34.29–35: 2 Cor 3.7–16. **35.2:** Exod 20.8–11; 23.12; 31.15; 34.21; Lev 23.3; Deut 5.12–14.

Offerings and gifts for the sacred tent and the priestly clothes

Offerings for the sacred tent

This is also told in Exodus 25.1–9; 35.10–19

⁴ Moses told the people of Israel that the LORD had said:

⁵ I would welcome an offering from anyone who wants to give something. You may bring gold, silver, or bronze; ⁶ blue, purple, or red wool; fine linen; goat hair; ⁷ tanned ram skin or fine leather; acacia wood; ⁸ olive oil for the lamp; sweet-smelling spices for the oil of dedication and for the incense; or ⁹ onyx* stones or other gems for the sacred apron and breastpiece.

¹⁰ If you have any skills, you should use them to help make what I have commanded: ¹¹ the sacred tent with its covering and hooks, its framework and crossbars, and its post and stands; ¹² the sacred chest with its carrying poles, its place of mercy, and the curtain in front of it; ¹³ the table with all that goes on it, including the sacred bread; ¹⁴ the lamp with its equipment and oil; ¹⁵ the incense altar with its carrying poles and sweet-smelling incense; the ordination oil; the curtain for the entrance to the sacred tent; ¹⁶ the altar for sacrifices with its bronze grating, its carrying poles, and its equipment; the large bronze bowl with its stand; ¹⁷ the curtains with the posts and stands that go around the courtyard; ¹⁸ the pegs and ropes for the tent and the courtyard; ¹⁹ and the finely woven priestly clothes for Aaron and his sons.

Gifts for the LORD

²⁰ Moses finished speaking, and everyone left. ²¹ Then those who wanted to bring gifts to the LORD, brought them to be used for the sacred tent, the worship services, and the priestly clothes. ²² Men and women came willingly and gave all kinds of gold jewellery such as pins, earrings, rings, and necklaces. ²³ Everyone brought their blue, purple, and red wool, their fine linen, and their cloth made of goat hair, as well as their ram skins dyed red and their fine leather. ²⁴ Anyone who had silver or bronze or acacia wood brought it as a gift to the LORD. ²⁵ The women who were good at weaving cloth brought the blue, purple, and red wool and the fine linen they had made. ²⁶ And the women who knew how to make cloth from goat hair were glad to do so.

²⁷ The leaders brought different kinds of jewels to be sewn on the special clothes and the breastpiece for the high priest. ²⁸ They also brought sweet-smelling spices to be mixed with the incense and olive oil that were for the lamps and for ordaining the priests. ²⁹ Moses had told the people what the LORD wanted them to do, and many of them decided to bring their gifts.

Bezalel and Oholiab

This is also told in Exodus 31.1–11

³⁰ Moses said to the people of Israel:

The LORD has chosen Bezalelᵖ of the Judah tribe. ³¹⁻³³ Not only has the LORD filled him with his Spirit, but he has given him wisdom and made him a skilled craftsman who can create objects of art with gold, silver, bronze, stone, and wood. ³⁴ The LORD is urging him and Oholiabᵖ from the tribe of Dan to teach others. ³⁵ And he has given them all kinds of artistic skills, including the ability to design and embroider with blue, purple, and red wool and to weave fine linen.

CHAPTER 36

Moses said:

¹ The LORD has given to Bezalel, Oholiab, and others the skills needed for building a place of worship, and they will follow the LORD's instructions.

² Then Moses brought together these workers who were eager to work, ³ and he gave them the money that the people of Israel had donated for building the place of worship. In fact, so much money was being given each morning, ⁴ that finally everyone stopped working ⁵ and said, "Moses, there is already more money than we need for what the LORD has assigned us to do." ⁶ So Moses sent word for the people to stop giving, and they did. ⁷ But there was already more than enough to do what needed to be done.

---

*35.9 onyx: See the note at 25.7.

Skilled workers make the sacred tent and its furnishings

The curtains and coverings for the sacred tent

This is also told in Exodus 26.1-14

8-9 The skilled workers got together to make the sacred tent and its linen curtains woven with blue, purple, and red wool and embroidered with figures of winged creatures. Each of the ten panels was twelve metres long and two metres wide, 10 and they were sewn together to make two curtains with five panels each. 11-13 Then fifty loops of blue cloth were put along one of the wider sides of each curtain, and the two curtains were fastened together at the loops with fifty gold hooks.

14-15 As the material for the tent, goat hair was used to weave eleven sections thirteen metres by two metres each. 16 These eleven sections were joined to make two panels, one with five and the other with six sections. 17 Fifty loops were put along one of the wider sides of each panel, 18 and the two panels were fastened at the loops with fifty bronze hooks. 19 Two other coverings were made — one with fine leather and the other with ram skins dyed red.

The framework for the sacred tent

This is also told in Exodus 26.15-30

20 Acacia wood was used to build the framework for the walls of the sacred tent. 21 Each frame was four metres high and sixty-six centimetres wide 22-26 with two wooden pegs near the bottom. Then two silver stands were placed under each frame with sockets for the pegs, so they could be joined together. Twenty of these frames were used along the south side and twenty more along the north. 27 Six frames were used for the back wall along the west side 28-29 with two more at the south-west and north-west corners. These corner frames were joined from top to bottom. 30 Altogether, along the back wall there were eight frames with two silver stands under each of them.

31-33 Five crossbars were made for each of the wooden frames, with the centre crossbar running the full length of the wall. 34 The frames and crossbars were covered with gold, and gold rings were attached to the frames to run the crossbars through.

The inside curtain for the sacred tent

This is also told in Exodus 26.31-37

35 They made the inside curtain* of fine linen woven with blue, purple, and red wool, and embroidered with figures of winged creatures. 36 They also made four acacia wood posts and covered them with gold. Then gold rings were fastened to the posts, which were set on silver stands.

37 For the entrance to the tent, they used a curtain of fine linen woven with blue, purple, and red wool and embroidered with fancy needlework. 38 They made five posts, covered them completely with gold, and set them each on a gold-covered bronze stand. Finally, they attached hooks for the curtain.

CHAPTER 37

The sacred chest

This is also told in Exodus 25.10-22

1 Bezalel built a chest of acacia wood one hundred and ten centimetres long, sixty-six centimetres wide, and sixty-six centimetres high. 2 He covered it inside and out with pure gold and put a gold edging around the top. 3 He made four gold rings and fastened one of them to each of the four legs of the chest. 4 Then he made two poles of acacia wood, covered them with gold, 5 and put them through the rings, so the chest could be carried by the poles.

6 The entire lid of the chest, which was also covered with pure gold, was the place of mercy.* 7-9 On each of the two ends of the chest he made a winged creature of hammered gold. They faced each other, and their wings covered the place of mercy.

The table for the sacred bread

This is also told in Exodus 25.23-30

10 Bezalel built a table of acacia wood eighty-eight centimetres long, forty-four centimetres wide, and sixty-six centimetres high. 11-12 He covered it with pure gold and put a gold edging around it with a border seventy-five millimetres wide.' 13 He made four gold rings and attached one to each of the legs 14 near the edging. The poles for carrying the table were placed through these rings 15 and were made of acacia wood

---

*36.35 inside curtain: Separating the holy place from the most holy place.
*37.6 place of mercy: See the note at 26.34.

The Ark of the covenant

Basically, it was a very posh box. This Bible calls it the 'Sacred Chest'; other Bibles use the phrase 'Ark of the Covenant'. (Ark is an old English word for box.)

It was made of gold-covered acacia wood and contained the tablets of stone on which God had written the Ten Commandments. The lid had the figures of two angels with their wings outstretched. The box could be carried by long poles, which were put through metal rings.

While the Israelites were in the desert, it was stored in the most holy place in the tabernacle. After the conquest of Canaan, it was kept at Bethel (Judges 20.27) and then Shiloh (1 Samuel 1.3). Eventually David brought it to Jerusalem, where his son, Solomon, installed it in the 'holy of holies' in his temple.

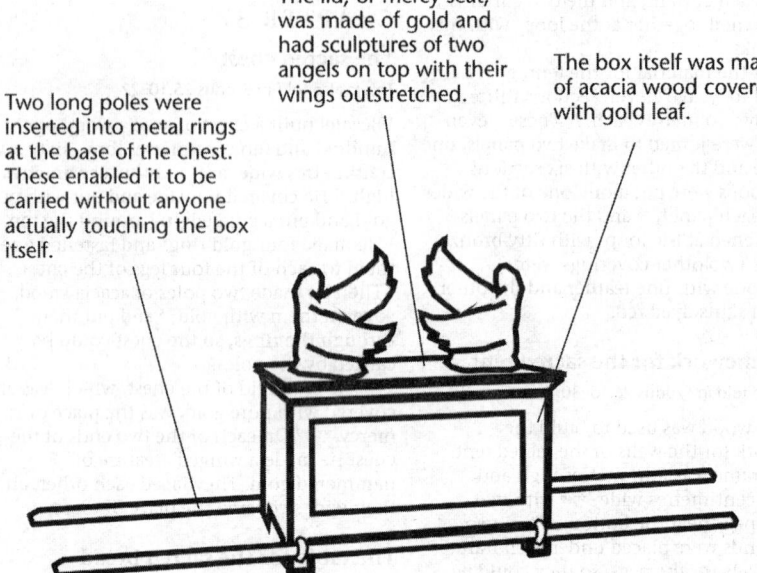

The lid, or mercy seat, was made of gold and had sculptures of two angels on top with their wings outstretched.

The box itself was made of acacia wood covered with gold leaf.

Two long poles were inserted into metal rings at the base of the chest. These enabled it to be carried without anyone actually touching the box itself.

The ark was a dangerous, unsettling object. It could not be touched directly, and it was associated with various strange, powerful happenings. It was as if it contained some kind of raw power and it had to be handled with care.

Its fate is unknown. It was probably lost during the Babylonian siege of Jerusalem in 587BC.

covered with gold. ¹⁶ Everything that was to be set on the table was made of pure gold — the bowls, plates, jars, and cups for wine offerings.

The lampstand
This is also told in Exodus 25.31–40

¹⁷ Bezalel made a lampstand of pure gold. The whole lampstand, including its decorative flowers, was made from a single piece of hammered gold, ¹⁸ with three branches on each of its two sides. ¹⁹ There were three decorative almond blossoms on each branch ²⁰ and four on the stem. ²¹ There was also a blossom where each pair of branches came out from the stem. ²² The lampstand, including its branches and decorative flowers, was made from a single piece of hammered pure gold. ²³⁻²⁴ The lamp and its equipment, including the tongs and trays, were made of about thirty-five kilogrammes of pure gold.

The altar for burning incense
This is also told in Exodus 30.1–5

²⁵ For burning incense, Bezalel made an altar of acacia wood. It was forty-five centimetres square and ninety centimetres high with each of its four corners sticking up like the horn of a bull. ²⁶ He covered it with pure gold and put a gold edging around it. ²⁷ Then below the edging on opposite sides he attached two gold rings through which he put the poles for carrying the altar. ²⁸ These poles were also made of acacia wood and covered with gold.

The oil for dedication and the incense
This is also told in Exodus 30.22–38

²⁹ Bezalel mixed the oil for dedication and the sweet-smelling spices for the incense.

CHAPTER 38

The altar for offering sacrifices
This is also told in Exodus 27.1–8

¹ Bezalel built an altar of acacia wood for offering sacrifices. It was two and a quarter metres square and one and a third metres high ² with each of its four corners sticking up like the horn of a bull, and it was completely covered with bronze. ³ The equipment for the altar was also made of bronze — the pans for the hot ashes, the

shovels, the meat forks, and the fire pans. ⁴ Half-way up the altar he built a ledge around it and covered the bottom half of the altar with a decorative bronze grating. ⁵ Then he attached a bronze ring beneath the ledge at the four corners to put the poles through. ⁶ He covered two acacia wood poles with bronze and ⁷ put them through the rings for carrying the altar, which was shaped like an open box.

The large bronze bowl
This is also told in Exodus 30.18–21

⁸ Bezalel made a large bowl and a stand out of bronze from the mirrors of the women who helped at the entrance to the sacred tent.

The courtyard around the sacred tent
This is also told in Exodus 27.9–19

⁹⁻¹⁷ Around the sacred tent Bezalel built a courtyard forty-four metres long on the south and north and twenty-two metres wide on the east and west. He used twenty bronze posts on bronze stands for the south and north and ten for the west. Then he hung a curtain of fine linen on the posts along each of these three sides by using silver hooks and rods. He placed three bronze posts on each side of the entrance at the east and hung a curtain six and two thirds metres wide on each set of posts.

¹⁸⁻¹⁹ For the entrance to the courtyard, Bezalel made a curtain nine metres long, which he hung on four bronze posts that were set on bronze stands. This curtain was the same height as the one for the rest of the courtyard and was made of fine linen embroidered and woven with blue, purple, and red wool. He hung the curtain on the four posts, using silver hooks and rods. ²⁰ The pegs for the tent and for the curtain around the tent were made of bronze.

The sacred tent
²¹⁻²³ Bezalel had worked closely with Oholiab,ᵇ who was an expert at designing and engraving, and at embroidering blue, purple, and red wool. The two of them completed the work that the LORD had commanded.

Moses made Aaron's son Ithamar responsible for keeping record of the metals used for the sacred tent. ²⁴ According to the official weights, the amount of gold given was a thousand kilogrammes, ²⁵ and the

See also: 37.29: Exod 30.22–38.   See also: 38.8: Exod 30.18. 38.25–26: Exod 30.11–16.

105

silver that was collected when the people were counted* came to three thousand four hundred and thirty kilogrammes. 26 Everyone who was counted paid the required amount, and there was a total of 603,550 men who were twenty years old or older.

27 Thirty-four kilogrammes of the silver were used to make each of the one hundred stands for the sacred tent and the curtain. 28 The remaining thirty kilogrammes of silver were used for the hooks and rods and for covering the tops of the posts.

29 Two thousand four hundred and twenty-five kilogrammes of bronze were given. 30 And it was used to make the stands for the entrance to the tent, the altar and its grating, the equipment for the altar, 31 the stands for the posts that surrounded the courtyard, including those at the entrance to the courtyard, and the pegs for the tent and the courtyard.

The priestly clothes are made

CHAPTER 39

Making the priestly clothes

This is also told in Exodus 28.1–14

1 Beautiful priestly clothes were made of blue, purple, and red wool for Aaron to wear when he performed his duties in the holy place. This was done exactly as the LORD had commanded Moses.

2-3 The entire priestly apron was made of fine linen, woven with blue, purple, and red wool. Thin sheets of gold were hammered out and cut into threads that were skilfully woven into the apron. 4-5 It had two shoulder straps to support it and a sash that fastened around the waist. 6 Onyx* stones were placed in gold settings, and each one was engraved with the name of one of Israel's sons. 7 Then these were attached to the shoulder straps of the apron, so the LORD would never forget his people. Everything was done exactly as the LORD had commanded Moses.

The breastpiece

This is also told in Exodus 28.15–30

8 The breastpiece was made with the same materials and designs as the priestly apron. 9 It was twenty-two centimetres square and folded double 10 with four rows of three precious stones: a carnelian, a chrysolite, and an emerald were in the first row; 11 a turquoise, a sapphire, and a diamond were in the second row; 12 a jacinth, an agate, and an amethyst were in the third row; 13 and a beryl, an onyx, and a jasper* were in the fourth row. They were mounted in a delicate gold setting, 14 and on each of them was engraved the name of one of the twelve tribes of Israel.

15-18 Two gold rings were attached to the upper front corners of the breastpiece and fastened with two braided gold chains to gold settings on the shoulder straps. 19 Two other gold rings were attached to the lower inside corners next to the apron, 20 and two more near the bottom of the shoulder straps just above the sash. 21 To keep the breastpiece in place, a blue cord was used to tie the two lower rings on the breastpiece to those on the apron. These things were done exactly as the LORD had commanded Moses.

The clothes for the priests

This is also told in Exodus 28.31–43

22 The priestly robe was made of blue wool 23 with an opening in the centre for the head. The material around the collar was bound so as to keep it from fraying. 24-26 Along the hem of the robe were woven pomegranates* of blue, purple, and red wool with a bell of pure gold between each of them. This robe was to be worn by Aaron when he performed his duties.

27-29 Everything that Aaron and his sons wore was made of fine linen woven with blue, purple, and red wool, including their robes and turbans, their fine caps and underwear, and even their sashes that were embroidered with needlework.

30 "Dedicated to the LORD" was engraved on a narrow strip of pure gold, 31 which was fastened to Aaron's turban. These things were done exactly as the LORD had commanded Moses.

---

*38.25 counted: See 30.11–16; Numbers 1.
*39.6 Onyx: See the note at 25.7.
See also: 38.26: Matt 17.24.

*39.13 jasper: For the stones mentioned in verses 10–13, see the note at 28.20.
*39.24–26 pomegranates: See the note at 28.33–34.

The Tabernacle/Sacred Tent

The Sacred Tent or Tabernacle was, simply, a huge tent, a kind of flat-pack temple.

The tent was made from embroidered linen (Exodus 26.1–6), covered with layers of goat hair (Exodus 26.7–13) and an 'outer tent' of waterproof leather (Exodus 26.14). Inside, a large curtain divided the space into two 'rooms': 'the holy place' and 'the most holy place' (Exodus 26.31–35). Only the high priest could enter the most holy place. This pattern was the basis for later, more permanent structures, such as the temples.

The holy place contained a table, on which was the sacred bread, a lampstand representing the glory of the Lord and an altar, where the high priest would burn incense.

The only thing in the most holy place was the sacred chest or ark of the covenant. This was a special box containing the stones on which the Ten Commandments were written.

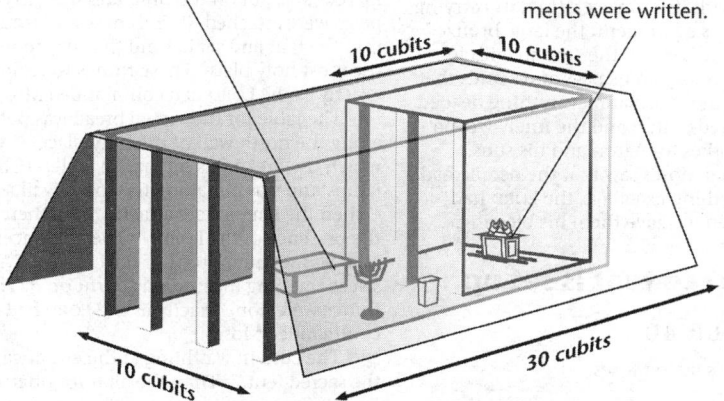

The tabernacle was situated in a large, fenced area. It contained, along with the sacred tent, an altar on which the offerings were burned and a huge bronze basin in which the priests could wash themselves before entering the tent.

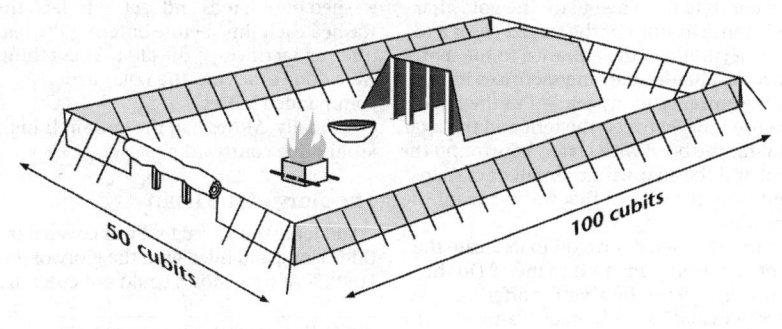

The work is completed

This is also told in Exodus 35.10–19

[32] So the people of Israel finished making everything the LORD had told Moses to make. [33] Then they brought it all to Moses: the sacred tent and its equipment, including the hooks, the framework and crossbars, and its posts and stands; [34] the covering of tanned ram skins and fine leather; the inside curtain; [35] the sacred chest with its carrying poles and the place of mercy; [36] the table with all that goes on it, including the sacred bread; [37] the lampstand of pure gold, together with its equipment and oil; [38] the gold-covered incense altar; the ordination oil and the sweet-smelling incense; the curtain for the entrance to the tent; [39] the bronze altar for sacrifices with its bronze grating, its carrying poles, and its equipment; the large bronze bowl with its stand; [40] the curtain with its posts and cords, and its pegs and stands that go around the courtyard; everything needed for the sacred tent; [41] and the finely woven priestly clothes for Aaron and his sons.

[42-43] When Moses saw that the people had done everything exactly as the LORD had commanded, he gave them his blessing.

The sacred tent is set up

CHAPTER 40

[1] The LORD said to Moses:

[2] Set up my tent on the first day of the year* [3] and put the chest with the Ten Commandments behind the inside curtain* of the tent. [4] Bring in the table and set on it those things that are made for it. Also bring in the lampstand and attach the lamps to it. [5] Then place the gold altar of incense in front of the sacred chest and hang a curtain at the entrance to the tent. [6] Set the altar for burning sacrifices in front of the entrance to my tent. [7] Put the large bronze bowl between the tent and the altar and fill the bowl with water. [8] Surround the tent and the altar with the wall of curtains and hang the curtain that was made for the entrance.

[9] Use the sacred olive oil to dedicate the tent and everything in it to me. [10] Do the same thing with the altar for offering sacrifices and its equipment [11] and with the

bowl and its stand. [12] Bring Aaron and his sons to the entrance of the tent and make them wash themselves. [13] Dress Aaron in the priestly clothes, then use the sacred olive oil to ordain him and dedicate him to me as my priest. [14] Put the priestly robes on Aaron's sons [15] and ordain them in the same way, so they and their descendants will always be my priests.

[16] Moses followed the LORD's instructions. [17] And on the first day of the first month* of the second year, the sacred tent was set up. [18] The posts, stands, and framework were put in place, [19] then the two layers of coverings were hung over them. [20] The stones with the Ten Commandments written on them were stored in the sacred chest, the place of mercy* was put on top of it, and the carrying poles were attached. [21] The chest was brought into the tent and set behind the curtain in the most holy place. These things were done exactly as the LORD had commanded Moses.

[22] The table for the sacred bread was put along the north wall of the holy place, [23] after which the bread was set on the table. [24] The lampstand was put along the south wall, [25] then the lamps were attached to it there in the presence of the LORD. [26] The gold incense altar was set up in front of the curtain, [27] and sweet-smelling incense was burnt on it. These things were done exactly as the LORD had commanded Moses.

[28] The curtain was hung at the entrance to the sacred tent. [29] Then the altar for offering sacrifices was put in front of the tent, and animal sacrifices and gifts of grain were offered there. [30] The large bronze bowl was placed between the altar and the entrance to the tent. It was filled with water, [31] then Moses and Aaron, together with Aaron's sons, washed their hands and feet. [32] In fact, they washed each time before entering the tent or offering sacrifices at the altar. These things were done exactly as the LORD had commanded Moses.

[33] Finally, Moses had the curtain hung around the courtyard.

The glory of the LORD

[34] Suddenly the sacred tent was covered by a thick cloud and filled with the glory of the LORD. [35] And so, Moses could not enter the

*40.17 first month: See the note at 12.2.
*40.20 place of mercy: See the note at 26.34.
See also: 40.34: 1 King 8.10–11; Isa 6.4; Ezek 43.4–5; Rev 15.8.

*40.2 first day of the year: See the note at 12.2.
*40.3 inside curtain: See the note at 36.35.

108

tent. ³⁶ Whenever the cloud moved from the tent, the people would break camp and follow; ³⁷ then they would set up camp and stay there, until it moved again. ³⁸ No matter where the people travelled, the LORD was with them. Each day his cloud was over the tent, and each night a fire could be seen in the cloud.

Additional notes

›**1.11 the king:** The Hebrew text has "Pharaoh", a Hebrew word sometimes used for the title of the king of Egypt.
›**2.5 the king's:** See the note at 1.11.
›**2.15 the king:** See the note at 1.11.
›**2.16 Jethro, the priest of Midian:** Hebrew "the priest of Midian". But see 3.1; 4.18; 18.1,2–4 where his name is given. In the Hebrew of verse 18 he is spoken of as "Reuel", which may have been the name of the tribe to which Jethro belonged.
›**3.1 Sinai:** The Hebrew text has "Horeb", another name for Sinai.
›**3.12 I will be with you . . . out of Egypt:** Or "I will be with you. This bush is a sign that I am the one sending you, and it is a promise that you will worship me on this mountain after you have led my people out of Egypt."
›**4.25 My dear son . . . you:** Or "My dear husband, you are a man of blood" (meaning Moses).
›**4.26 you are . . . circumcision:** Or "you are a man of blood."
›**4.27 Mount Sinai:** Hebrew "the mountain of God".
›**5.1 the king:** See the note at 1.11.
›**5.23 the king:** See the note at 1.11.
›**6.14 Jacob:** The Hebrew text has "Israel", Jacob's name after God renamed him.
›**6.29 the king:** See the note at 1.11.
›**7.8–9 the king:** See the note at 1.11.
›**7.14 The Egyptian king:** See the note at 1.11.
›**8.1 the king:** See the note at 1.11.
›**8.18 to do this:** Or "to get rid of the gnats".
›**8.19 the king:** See the note at 1.11.
›**8.20 the king:** See the note at 1.11.
›**9.1 the king:** See the note at 1.11.
›**9.10 the king:** See the note at 1.11.
›**9.13 the king:** See the note at 1.11.
›**9.32 wheat crops:** The Hebrew text mentions two kinds of wheat.
›**10.1 the king:** See the note at 1.11.
›**10.19 west wind:** The Hebrew text has "wind from the sea", referring to the Mediterranean Sea (see verse 13).
›**10.24 The king:** See the note at 1.11.
›**11.1 the king:** See the note at 1.11.
›**12.29 the king:** See the note at 1.11.
›**12.31 the king:** See the note at 1.11.
›**13.15 The king:** See the note at 1.11.
›**13.17 the king:** See the note at 1.11.

›**14.2 Red Sea:** Hebrew *hayyam* "the Sea", understood as *yam suph*, "Sea of Reeds" (see also the note at 13.18).
›**14.3 The king:** See the note at 1.11.
›**14.8 proudly:** Or "victoriously".
›**14.25 stuck:** The Samaritan Hebrew text and two ancient translations; Hebrew "came off".
›**15.4 Egypt's king:** See the note at 1.11.
›**16.1 the western edge of the Sinai Desert:** Hebrew "the Sin Desert".
›**16.35–36 land:** The Hebrew text adds, "An omer is one tenth of an ephah." In the CEV "omer" is usually translated "two litres".
›**17.6 Sinai:** See the note at 3.1.
›**17.16 This . . . LORD:** One possible meaning for the difficult Hebrew text.
›**18.5–6 Mount Sinai:** See the note at 4.27.
›**20.23 in place of me:** Or "together with me".
›**21.6 at the place of worship:** The Hebrew text has "in the presence of God", which probably refers to the place where God was worshipped.
›**21.22 suffers a miscarriage:** Or "gives birth before her time".
›**22.5 graze:** Or "eat everything".
›**22.8 some judges:** Or "I".
›**22.9 the judges:** Or "I".
›**22.28 me:** Or "your judges".
›**22.29 Don't fail . . . me:** One possible meaning for the difficult Hebrew text.
›**23.2 everyone else is:** Or "the authorities are".
›**23.5 you:** One possible meaning for the difficult Hebrew text of verse 5.
›**25.24–25 a gold edging . . . wide:** Or "a gold edging around it seventy-five millimetres wide".
›**29.9 their sashes:** One ancient translation; Hebrew "the sashes of Aaron and his sons".
›**29.24 lift it all up:** Or "wave it all".
›**29.26 lift them up:** Or "wave them".
›**31.2 Bezalel:** Hebrew "Bezalel, son of Uri and grandson of Hur".
›**31.6 Oholiab:** Hebrew "Oholiab son of Ahisamach".
›**33.6 Mount Sinai:** See the notes at 3.1 and 4.27.
›**33.9–11 Joshua:** Hebrew "Joshua son of Nun".
›**35.30 Bezalel:** See the note at 31.2.
›**35.34 Oholiab:** See the note at 31.6.
›**37.11–12 a gold edging . . . wide:** See the note at 25.24–25.
›**38.21–23 Bezalel . . . Oholiab:** Hebrew "Bezalel son of Uri and grandson of Hur of the Judah tribe had worked closely with Oholiab son of Ahisamach from the tribe of Dan."

Leviticus

The basics

What's the point? Provides rules for the Israelites which were intended to keep them holy.

What happens? The book starts after the escape of the Israelites from slavery in Egypt. It also includes a great deal of religious rite and ceremony and legal issues.

What should I remember? 20.7-8 'Dedicate yourselves to me and be holy because I am the Lord your God. I have chosen you as my people, and I expect you to obey my laws.'

More detail

Setting the scene In the desert, Moses passes on from God the laws that are to set Israel apart from the other nations. Lots of laws. Lots and lots of laws...

What's it all about? Leviticus takes its name from the tribe of Levi – the tribe which supplied all the priests for Israel. It's really their manual – a book of rules which they and the people are supposed to follow, covering subjects such as worship, ritual, behaviour, criminal justice, health and safety, food production and even clothing manufacture.

So, there is a lot in Leviticus that is no longer applicable to Christians. But there is also a lot that is. There are simple things like behaving honestly, not making fun of blind or deaf people and respecting the elderly (19.13-17,23).

Footsteps

The Priests are ordained: 8.1–36
The first sacrifice: 9.1–24
Clean and unclean animals: 11.1–47
Good ways to behave: 19.9–37
The festivals: 23.1–44
The Jubilee: 25.1–55

And another thing

Along with all the sacrifice stuff, Leviticus also contains radical laws to help the poor. Like the jubilee laws where slaves were freed and the land returned to the original owners. Amazing!

Laws about sacrifices

CHAPTER 1

1-3 The LORD spoke to Moses from the sacred tent and gave him instructions for the community of Israel to follow when they offered sacrifices.

Sacrifices to please the LORD

The LORD said:

Sacrifices to please me* must be completely burnt on the bronze altar.*

Bulls or rams or goats’ are the animals to be used for these sacrifices. If the animal is a bull, it must not have anything wrong with it. Lead it to the entrance of the sacred tent, and I will let you know if it is’ acceptable to me. 4 Lay your hand on its head, and I will accept the animal as a sacrifice for taking away your sins.

5 After the bull is killed in my presence, some priests from Aaron's family will offer

---

*1.1–3 Sacrifices to please me: These sacrifices have traditionally been called "whole burnt offerings" because the whole animal was burnt on the altar. A main purpose of such sacrifices was to please the LORD with the smell of the sacrifice, and so in the CEV they are often called "sacrifices to please the LORD".
*1.1–3 bronze altar: This altar for offering sacrifices was in front of the entrance to the sacred tent; it was made of acacia wood covered with bronze. A smaller altar for offering incense was inside the tent; it was made of acacia wood covered with gold.

its blood to me by splattering it against the four sides of the altar.

⁶ Skin the bull and cut it up, ⁷ while the priests pile wood on the altar fire to make it start blazing. ⁸⁻⁹ Wash the bull's insides and hind legs, so the priests can lay them on the altar with the head, the fat, and the rest of the animal. A priest will then send all of it up in smoke with a smell that pleases me.

¹⁰ If you sacrifice a ram or a goat, it must not have anything wrong with it. ¹¹ Lead the animal to the north side of the altar, where it is to be killed in my presence. Then some of the priests will splatter its blood against the four sides of the altar.

¹²⁻¹³ Cut up the animal and wash its insides and hind legs. A priest will put these parts on the altar with the head, the fat, and the rest of the animal. Then he will send all of it up in smoke with a smell that pleases me.

¹⁴ If you offer a bird for this kind of sacrifice, it must be a dove or a pigeon. ¹⁵ A priest will take the bird to the bronze altar, where he will wring its neck and put its head on the fire. Then he will drain out its blood on one side of the altar, ¹⁶ remove the bird's craw with what is in it,⟩ and throw them on the ash heap at the east side of the altar.* ¹⁷ Finally, he will take the bird by its wings, tear it partially open,⟩ and send it up in smoke with a smell that pleases me.

CHAPTER 2

Sacrifices to give thanks to the LORD

The LORD said:

¹ When you offer sacrifices to give thanks to me,* you must use only your finest flour. Put it in a dish, sprinkle olive oil and incense on the flour, ² and take it to the priests from Aaron's family. One of them will scoop up the incense together with a handful of the flour and oil. Then, to show that the whole offering belongs to me, the priest will lay this part on the bronze altar and send it up in smoke with a smell that pleases me. ³ The rest of this sacrifice is for the priests; it is very holy because it was offered to me.

⁴ If you bake bread in an oven for this sacrifice, use only your finest flour, but without any yeast. You may make the flour into a loaf mixed with olive oil, or you may make it into thin wafers and brush them with oil.

⁵ If you cook bread in a shallow pan for this sacrifice, use only your finest flour. Mix it with olive oil, but do not use any yeast. ⁶ Then break the bread into small pieces and sprinkle them with oil. ⁷ If you cook your bread in a pan with a lid on it, you must also use the finest flour mixed with oil.

⁸ You may prepare sacrifices to give thanks in any of these three ways. Bring your sacrifice to a priest, and he will take it to the bronze altar*. ⁹ Then, to show that the whole offering belongs to me, the priest will lay part of it on the altar and send it up in smoke with a smell that pleases me. ¹⁰ The rest of this sacrifice is for the priests; it is very holy because it was offered to me.

¹¹ Yeast and honey must never be burnt on the altar, so don't ever mix either of these in a grain sacrifice. ¹² You may offer either of them separately,⟩ when you present the first part of your harvest to me, but they must never be burnt on the altar.

¹³ Salt is offered when you make an agreement with me, so sprinkle salt on these sacrifices.

¹⁴ Freshly cut grain, either roasted or coarsely ground,⟩ must be used when you offer the first part of your grain harvest. ¹⁵ You must mix in some olive oil and put incense on top, because this is a grain sacrifice. ¹⁶ A priest will sprinkle all the incense and some of the grain and oil on the altar and send them up in smoke to show that the whole offering belongs to me.

CHAPTER 3

Sacrifices to ask the LORD's blessing

The LORD said:

¹ When you offer sacrifices to ask my blessing,* you may offer either a bull or a

---

*1.16 ash heap at the east side of the altar: Ashes were piled here, then once a day they were taken to the ash heap outside the camp (see 4.11–12; 6.10–11).
*2.1 sacrifices to give thanks to me: These sacrifices have traditionally been called "grain offerings". A main purpose of such sacrifices was to thank the LORD with a gift of grain, and so in the CEV they are sometimes called "sacrifices to give thanks to the LORD".

*2.8 bronze altar: See the note at 1.1–3.
*3.1 sacrifices to ask my blessing: These sacrifices have traditionally been called "peace offerings" or "offerings of well-being". A main purpose was to ask for the LORD's blessing, and so in the CEV they are sometimes called "sacrifices to ask the LORD's blessing".

cow, but there must be nothing wrong with the animal. ² Lead it to the entrance of the sacred tent, lay your hand on its head, and have it killed there. A priest from Aaron's family will splatter its blood against the four sides of the altar.

³ Offer all the fat on the animal's insides, ⁴ as well as the lower part of the liver and the two kidneys with their fat. ⁵ Some of the priests will lay these pieces on the altar and send them up in smoke with a smell that pleases me, together with the sacrifice that is offered to please me.*

⁶ Instead of a bull or a cow, you may offer any sheep or goat that has nothing wrong with it. ⁷ If you offer a sheep, you must present it to me at the entrance to the sacred tent. ⁸ Lay your hand on its head and have it killed there. A priest will then splatter its blood against the four sides of the altar.

⁹ Offer the fat on the tail, the tailbone, and the insides, ¹⁰ as well as the lower part of the liver and the two kidneys with their fat. ¹¹ One of the priests will lay these pieces on the altar and send them up in smoke as a food offering for me.

¹² If you offer a goat, you must also present it to me ¹³ at the entrance to the sacred tent. Lay your hand on its head and have it killed there. A priest will then splatter its blood against the four sides of the altar.

¹⁴ Offer all the fat on the animal's insides, ¹⁵ as well as the lower part of the liver and the two kidneys with their fat. ¹⁶ One of the priests will put these pieces on the altar and send them up in smoke as a food offering with a smell that pleases me.

All fat belongs to me. ¹⁷ So you and your descendants must never eat any fat or any blood, not even in the privacy of your own homes.' This law will never change.

CHAPTER 4

Sacrifices for sin

This is also told in Leviticus 6.24–30

¹ The LORD told Moses ² to say to the community of Israel:

Offer a sacrifice to ask forgiveness when you sin by accidentally doing something I have told you not to do.

When the high priest sins

The LORD said:

³ When the high priest sins, he makes everyone else guilty too. And so, he must sacrifice a young bull that has nothing wrong with it. ⁴ The priest will lead the bull to the entrance of the sacred tent, lay his hand on its head, and kill it there. ⁵ He will take a bowl of the blood inside the tent, ⁶ dip a finger in the blood, and sprinkle some of it seven times towards the sacred chest behind the curtain. ⁷ Then, in my presence, he will smear some of the blood on each of the four corners of the incense altar, before pouring out the rest at the foot of the bronze altar* near the entrance to the tent.

⁸⁻¹⁰ The priest will remove the fat from the bull, just as he does when he sacrifices a bull to ask my blessing.* This includes the fat on the insides, as well as the lower part of the liver and the two kidneys with their fat. He will then send it all up in smoke.

¹¹⁻¹² The skin and flesh of the bull, together with its legs, insides, and the food still in its stomach, are to be taken outside the camp and burnt on a wood fire near the ash heap.*

When the whole nation sins

The LORD said:

¹³ When the nation of Israel disobeys me without meaning to, the whole nation is still guilty. ¹⁴ Once you realize what has happened, you must sacrifice a young bull to ask my forgiveness. Lead the bull to the entrance of the sacred tent, ¹⁵ where your tribal leaders will lay their hands on its head, before having it killed in my presence.

¹⁶ The priest will take a bowl of the animal's blood inside the sacred tent, ¹⁷ dip a finger in the blood, and sprinkle some of it seven times towards the sacred chest behind the curtain. ¹⁸ Then, in my presence, he must smear some of the blood on each of the four corners of the incense altar, before pouring out the rest at the foot of the bronze altar* near the entrance to the tent. ¹⁹⁻²¹ After this, the priest will remove the fat from the bull and send it

*4.7,18 incense altar . . . bronze altar: See the note at 1.1–3.
*4.8–10 to ask my blessing: See the note at 3.1.
*4.11–12 ash heap: See the note at 1.16.

*3.5 sacrifice . . . to please me: See the note at 1.1–3.

up in smoke on the altar. Finally, he will burn its remains outside the camp, just as he did with the other bull. By this sacrifice the sin of the whole nation will be forgiven.

When a tribal leader sins

The LORD God said:

²² Any tribal leader who disobeys me without meaning to is still guilty. ²³ As soon as the leader realizes what has happened, he must sacrifice a goat⁾ that has nothing wrong with it. ²⁴ This is a sacrifice for sin. So he will lay his hand on the animal's head, before having it killed in my presence at the north side of the bronze altar. ²⁵ The priest will dip a finger in the blood, smear some of it on each of the four corners of the altar, and pour out the rest at the foot of the altar. ²⁶ Then he must send all the fat up in smoke, just as he does when a sacrifice is offered to ask my blessing.* By this sacrifice the leader's sin will be forgiven.

When ordinary people sin

The LORD said:

²⁷ When any of you ordinary people disobey me without meaning to, you are still guilty. ²⁸ As soon as you realize what you have done, you must sacrifice a female goat that has nothing wrong with it. ²⁹ Lead the goat to the north side of the bronze altar and lay your hand on its head, before having it killed. ³⁰ Then a priest will dip a finger in the blood; he will smear some of it on each of the four corners of the altar and pour out the rest at the foot of the altar. ³¹ After this, the priest will remove all the fat, just as he does when an animal is sacrificed to ask my blessing.* The priest will then send the fat up in smoke with a smell that pleases me. This animal is sacrificed so that I will forgive you ordinary people when you sin.

³² If you offer a lamb instead of a goat as a sacrifice for sin, it must be a female that has nothing wrong with it. ³³ Lead the lamb to the altar and lay your hand on its head, before having it killed. ³⁴ The priest will dip a finger in the blood, smear some of it on each of the four corners of the

altar, and pour out the rest at the foot of the altar. ³⁵ After this, all the fat must be removed, just as when an animal is sacrificed to ask my blessing. Then the priest will send it up in smoke to me, together with a food offering, and your sin will be forgiven.

CHAPTER 5

The LORD said:

¹ If you refuse to testify in court about something you saw or know has happened, you have sinned and can be punished.

² You are guilty and unfit to worship me, if you accidentally touch the dead body of any kind of unclean animal.

³ You are guilty if you find out that you have accidentally touched any waste that comes from a human body.

⁴ You are guilty the moment you realize that you have made a hasty promise to do something good or bad.

⁵ As soon as you discover that you have committed any of these sins, you must confess what you have done. ⁶ Then you must bring a female sheep or goat to me as the price for your sin. A priest will sacrifice the animal, and you will be forgiven.

⁷ If you are poor and cannot afford to bring an animal, you may bring two doves or two pigeons. One of these will be a sacrifice to ask my forgiveness, and the other will be a sacrifice to please me.

⁸ Give both birds to the priest, who will offer one as a sacrifice to ask my forgiveness. He will wring its neck without tearing off its head, ⁹ splatter some of its blood on one side of the bronze altar, and drain out the rest at the foot of the altar. ¹⁰ Then he will follow the proper rules for offering the other bird as a sacrifice to please me.

You will be forgiven when the priest offers these sacrifices as the price for your sin.

¹¹ If you are so poor that you cannot afford doves or pigeons, you may bring one kilogramme of your finest flour. This is a sacrifice to ask my forgiveness, so don't sprinkle olive oil or sweet-smelling incense on it. ¹² Give the flour to a priest, who will scoop up a handful and send it up in smoke together with the other offerings. This is a reminder that all the flour belongs to me. ¹³ By offering this sacrifice, the

---

*4.26,31 sacrifice . . . blessing: See the note at 3.1.
See also: 4.27–31: Num 15.27–28.

priest pays the price for any of these sins you may have committed. The priest gets the rest of the flour, just as he does with grain sacrifices.

Sacrifices to make things right

This is also told in Leviticus 7.1–10

14-15 The LORD told Moses what the people must do to make things right when they find out they have cheated the LORD without meaning to:

> If this happens, you must either sacrifice a ram that has nothing wrong with it or else pay the price of a ram with the official money used by the priests. 16 In addition, you must pay what you owe plus a fine of twenty per cent. Then the priest will offer the ram as a sacrifice to make things right, and you will be forgiven.
>
> 17-19 If you break any of my commands without meaning to, you are still guilty, and you can be punished. When you realize what you have done, you must either bring to the priest a ram that has nothing wrong with it or else pay him for one. The priest will then offer it as a sacrifice to make things right, and you will be forgiven.

CHAPTER 6

Other sins that need sacrifices or payments

This is also told in Numbers 5.5–10

1-3 The LORD told Moses what the people must do when they commit other sins against the LORD:

> You have sinned if you rob or cheat someone, if you keep back money or valuables left in your care, or if you find something and claim not to have it.
>
> 4 When this happens, you must return what doesn't belong to you 5 and pay the owner a fine of twenty per cent. 6-7 In addition, you must either bring to the priest a ram that has nothing wrong with it or else pay him for one. The priest will then offer it as a sacrifice to make things right, and you will be forgiven for what you did wrong.

Daily sacrifices

This is also told in Exodus 29.38–43; Numbers 28.1–8

8-9 The LORD told Moses to tell Aaron and his sons how to offer the daily sacrifices that are sent up in smoke to please the LORD:*

> You must put the animal for the sacrifice on the altar in the evening and let it stay there all night. But make sure the fire keeps burning. 10 The next morning you will dress in your priestly clothes, including your linen underwear. Then clean away the ashes left by the sacrifices and pile them beside the altar. 11 Change into your everyday clothes, take the ashes outside the camp, and pile them in the special place.*
>
> 12 The fire must never go out, so put wood on it each morning. After this, you are to lay an animal on the altar next to the fat that you sacrifice to ask my blessing.* Then send it all up in smoke to me.
>
> 13 The altar fire must always be kept burning — it must never go out.

Sacrifices to give thanks to the LORD

The LORD said:

> 14 When someone offers a sacrifice to give thanks to me,* the priests from Aaron's family must bring it to the front of the bronze altar, 15 where one of them will scoop up a handful of the flour and oil, together with all the incense on it. Then, to show that the whole offering belongs to me, he will lay all of this on the altar and send it up in smoke with a smell that pleases me. 16-17 The rest of it is to be baked without yeast and eaten by the priests in the sacred courtyard of the sacred tent. This bread is very holy, just like the sacrifices for sin or for making things right, and I have given this part to the priests from what is offered to me on the altar.
>
> 18 Only the men in Aaron's family are allowed to eat this bread, and they must go through a ceremony to be made holy before touching it.᾿ This law will never change.

---

*6.8–9 to please the LORD: See the note at 1.1–3.
*6.11 ashes . . . in the special place: See the note at 1.16.
*6.12 sacrifice to ask my blessing: See the note at 3.1.
*6.14 a sacrifice to give thanks to me: See the note at 2.1.

See also: 6.1–7: Num 5.5–8.

When priests are ordained

¹⁹ The LORD spoke to Moses ²⁰ and told him what sacrifices the priests must offer on the morning and evening of the day they are ordained:

It is the same as the regular morning and evening sacrifices — half a kilogramme of flour ²¹ mixed with olive oil and cooked in a shallow pan. The bread must then be crumbled into small pieces⁾ and sent up in smoke with a smell that pleases me.

²²⁻²³ Each of Aaron's descendants who is ordained as a priest must perform this ceremony and make sure that the bread is completely burnt on the altar. None of it may be eaten!

Sacrifices for sin

This is also told in Leviticus 4.1–2

²⁴ The LORD told Moses ²⁵ how the priests from Aaron's family were to offer the sacrifice for sin:

This sacrifice is very sacred, and the animal must be killed in my presence at the north side of the bronze altar. ²⁶ The priest who offers this sacrifice must eat it in the sacred courtyard of the sacred tent, ²⁷ and anyone or anything that touches the meat will be holy.⁾ If any of the animal's blood is splattered on the clothes of the priest, they must be washed in a holy place. ²⁸ If the meat was cooked in a clay pot, the pot must be destroyed,* but if it was cooked in a bronze pot, the pot must be scrubbed and rinsed with water.

²⁹ This sacrifice is very holy, and only the priests may have any part of it. ³⁰ None of the meat may be eaten from the sacrifices for sin that require blood to be brought into the sacred tent.* These sacrifices must be completely burnt.

CHAPTER 7

Sacrifices to make things right

This is also told in Leviticus 5.14–19

The LORD said:

¹ The sacrifice to make things right is very sacred. ² The animal must be killed in the same place where the sacrifice to please

me* is killed, and the animal's blood must be splattered against the four sides of the bronze altar. ³ Offer all the animal's fat, including the fat on its tail and on its insides, ⁴ as well as the lower part of the liver and the two kidneys with their fat. ⁵ One of the priests will lay these pieces on the altar and send them up in smoke to me. ⁶ This sacrifice for making things right is very holy. Only the priests may eat it, and they must eat it in a holy place.*

⁷ The ceremony for this sacrifice and the one for sin are alike, and the meat may be eaten only by the priest who performs this ceremony of forgiveness.

⁸ In fact, the priest who offers a sacrifice to please me* may keep the skin of the animal, ⁹ just as he may eat the bread from a sacrifice to give thanks to me.* ¹⁰ All other grain sacrifices — with or without olive oil in them — are to be divided equally among the priests of Aaron's family.

Sacrifices to ask the LORD's blessing

The LORD said:

¹¹ Here are the instructions for offering a sacrifice to ask my blessing:* ¹² If you offer it to give thanks, you must offer some bread together with it. Use the finest flour to make three kinds of bread without yeast — two in the form of loaves mixed with olive oil and one in the form of thin wafers brushed with oil. ¹³ You must also make some bread with yeast. ¹⁴ Give me one loaf or wafer from each of these four kinds of bread, after which they will belong to the priest who splattered the blood against the bronze altar.

¹⁵ When you offer an animal to ask a blessing from me or to thank me, the meat belongs to you, but it must be eaten the same day. ¹⁶ It is different with the sacrifices you offer when you make me a promise or voluntarily give me something. The meat from those sacrifices may be kept and eaten the next day, ¹⁷⁻¹⁸ but any that is left must be destroyed. If you eat any after the second day, your sacrifice will be useless and unacceptable, and you will be both disgusting and guilty.

6.28 clay pot . . . destroyed: Juice from the meat cannot be completely cleaned from a clay pot.
6.30 that require blood . . . tent: See 4.1–21.

7.2,8 sacrifice to please me: See the note at 1.1–3.
7.6 holy place: The courtyard of the sacred tent (see 6.16–17).
7.9 sacrifice to give thanks to me: See the note at 2.1.
7.11 sacrifice to ask my blessing: See the note at 3.1.

¹⁹ Don't eat any of the meat that touches something unclean. Instead, burn it. The rest of the meat may be eaten by anyone who is clean and acceptable to me. ²⁰⁻²¹ But don't eat any of this meat if you have become unclean by touching something unclean from a human or an animal or from any other creature. If you do, you will no longer belong to the community of Israel.

²² The LORD told Moses ²³ to say to the people:

Don't eat the fat of cattle, sheep, or goats. ²⁴ If one of your animals dies or is killed by some wild animal, you may do anything with its fat except eat it. ²⁵ If you eat the fat of an animal that can be used as a sacrifice to me, you will no longer belong to the community of Israel. ²⁶ And no matter where you live, you must not eat the blood of any bird or animal, ²⁷ or you will no longer belong to the community of Israel.

²⁸ The LORD also told Moses ²⁹⁻³⁰ to say to the people of Israel:

If you want to offer a sacrifice to ask my blessing, you must bring the part to be burnt and lay it on the bronze altar. But you must first lift up▸ the choice ribs with their fat to show that the offering is dedicated to me. ³¹ A priest from Aaron's family will then send the fat up in smoke, but the ribs belong to the priests. ³²⁻³³ The upper joint of the right hind leg is for the priest who offers the blood and the fat of the animal. ³⁴ I have decided that the people of Israel must always give the choice ribs and the upper joint of the right hind leg to Aaron's descendants ³⁵ who have been ordained as priests to serve me. ³⁶ This law will never change. I am the LORD!

³⁷ These are the ceremonies for sacrifices to please the LORD, to give him thanks, and to ask his blessing or his forgiveness, as well as the ceremonies for those sacrifices that demand a payment and for the sacrifices that are offered when priests are ordained. ³⁸ While Moses and the people of Israel were in the desert at Mount Sinai, the LORD commanded them to start offering these sacrifices.

Ordaining the priests

CHAPTER 8

This is also told in Exodus 29.1–37

¹ The LORD said to Moses:

² Send for Aaron and his sons, as well as their priestly clothes, the oil for ordination, the bull for the sin offering, the two rams, and a basket of bread made without yeast. ³ Then bring the whole community of Israel together at the entrance to the sacred tent.

⁴ Moses obeyed the LORD, and when everyone had come together, ⁵ he said, "We are here to follow the LORD's instructions."

⁶ After Moses told Aaron and his sons to step forward, he made them wash themselves. ⁷ He put the priestly shirt and robe on Aaron and wrapped the sash around his waist. Then he put the sacred apron on Aaron and fastened it with the finely woven belt. ⁸ Next, he put on Aaron the sacred breastpiece that was used in learning what the LORD wanted his people to do. ⁹ He placed the turban on Aaron's head, and on the front of the turban was the narrow strip of thin gold as a sign of his dedication to the LORD.

¹⁰ Moses then dedicated the sacred tent and everything in it to the LORD by sprinkling them with some of the oil for ordination. ¹¹ He sprinkled the bronze altar seven times, and he sprinkled its equipment, as well as the large bronze bowl and its base. ¹² He also poured some of the oil on Aaron's head to dedicate him to the LORD. ¹³ At last, Moses dressed Aaron's sons in their shirts, then tied sashes around them and put special caps on them, just as the LORD had commanded.

¹⁴ Moses led out the bull that was to be sacrificed for sin, and Aaron and his sons laid their hands on its head. ¹⁵ After it was killed, Moses dipped a finger in the blood and smeared some of it on each of the four corners of the bronze altar, before pouring out the rest at the foot of the altar. This purified the altar and made it a fit place for offering the sacrifice for sin. ¹⁶ Moses then took the fat on the bull's insides, as well as the lower part of the liver and the two kidneys with their fat, and sent them up in smoke on the altar fire. ¹⁷ Finally, he took the skin and the flesh of the bull, together with the food

See also: 7.26–27: Gen 9.4; Lev 17.10–14; 19.26; Deut 12.16,23; 15.23.

Big ideas

Priests

Aaron was the first high priest of Israel (Exodus 28–9) and from then on, all priests of Israel were supposed to come from his descendants, assisted by other members of the tribe of Levi.

Their main job was to offer sacrifices. In the early days of Israel they also taught the Law. It was not an easy job – at least in the early times. If you didn't obey the instructions exactly, it meant death (Leviticus 10). They began at the age of 25, and retired at 50 (Numbers 8.24–6).

Priests wore special uniforms with a two piece 'apron' called an ephod, and a chest-piece inset with twelve precious stones, representing the twelve tribes of Israel. The chest-piece had a pocket over the priest's heart, which contained the Urim and the Thummim (Exodus 28.30). No one really knows how these worked, but experts think they were some kind of stones, which were thrown to find out God's will. A bit like throwing dice.

Only the high priest could enter the Holy of Holies, the sacred inner room, and then only for one day a year – on the Day of Atonement. Priests were the go-betweens between God and the people. Once Jesus arrived, there was no need for priests or sacrifices as such. Jesus was the sacrifice, once and for all (Hebrews 7.27–8). After Jesus, all Christians are described as a 'royal priesthood' (1 Peter 2.9).

Footsteps

A week with Priests

Moses and the priesthood: Leviticus 8.1–36
The staff uniform: Exodus 28.1–43
A dangerous job: Leviticus 10.1–20
Unfaithful priests: Ezekiel 22.23–31
Ezra reinstates the Priesthood: Ezra 8.15–30
Jesus' warning: Matthew 21.33–46
Jesus is the real priest: Hebrews 7.22–28

More...

Aaron p.159
The Tabernacle: the Sacred Tent p.107
Pharisees, Sadducees and the rest p.1097

still in its stomach, and burnt them outside the camp, just as the LORD had commanded.

18 Moses led out the ram for the sacrifice to please the LORD.* After Aaron and his sons had laid their hands on its head, 19 Moses killed the ram and splattered its blood against the four sides of the altar. 20-21 Moses had the animal cut up, and he washed its insides and hind legs. Then he laid the head, the fat, and the rest of the ram on the altar and sent them up in smoke with a smell that pleased the LORD. All this was done just as the LORD had commanded.

22 Moses led out the ram for the ceremony of ordination. Aaron and his sons laid their hands on its head, 23 and it was killed. Moses smeared some of its blood on Aaron's right ear lobe, some on his right thumb, and some on the big toe of his right foot. 24 Moses did the same thing for Aaron's sons, before splattering the rest of the blood against the four sides of the altar. 25 He took the animal's fat tail, the fat on its insides, and the lower part of the liver and the two kidneys with their fat, and the right hind leg. 26 Then he took from a basket some of each of the three kinds of bread* that had been made without yeast and had been dedicated to the LORD.

27 Moses placed the bread on top of the meat and gave it all to Aaron and his sons, who lifted it up' to show that it was dedicated to the LORD. 28 After this, Moses placed it on the fires of the altar and sent it up in smoke with a smell that pleased the LORD. This was part of the ordination ceremony. 29 Moses lifted up' the choice ribs of the ram to show that they were dedicated to the LORD. This was the part that the LORD had said Moses could have.

30 Finally, Moses sprinkled the priestly clothes of Aaron and his sons with some of the oil for ordination and with some of the blood from the altar. So Aaron and his sons, together with their priestly clothes, were dedicated to the LORD.

31 Moses said to Aaron and his sons:

The LORD told me that you must boil this meat at the entrance to the sacred tent and eat it there with the bread. 32 Burn what is left over 33 and stay near the entrance to the

---

*8.18 sacrifice to please the LORD: See the note at 1.1–3.

*8.26 three kinds of bread: Made from the finest wheat flour; olive oil was mixed into part of the dough, and some of it was made into thin wafers brushed with oil (see Exodus 29.2–3).

sacred tent until the ordination ceremony ends seven days from now. [34] We have obeyed the LORD in everything that has been done today, so that your sins may be forgiven.' [35] The LORD has told me that you must stay near the entrance to the tent for seven days and nights, or else you will die.

[36] Aaron and his sons obeyed everything that the LORD had told Moses they must do.

Aaron's first sacrifices

CHAPTER 9

[1] Eight days later Moses called together Aaron, his sons, and Israel's leaders. [2] Then he said to Aaron:

Find a young bull and a ram that have nothing wrong with them. Offer the bull to the LORD as a sacrifice for sin and the ram as a sacrifice to please him.*

[3] Tell the people of Israel that they must offer sacrifices as well. They must offer a goat' as a sacrifice for sin, and a bull and a ram as a sacrifice to please the LORD. The bull and the ram must be a year old and have nothing wrong with them. [4] Then the people must offer a bull and a ram as a sacrifice to ask the LORD's blessing* and also a grain sacrifice* mixed with oil. Do this, because the LORD will appear to you today.

[5] After the animals and the grain had been brought to the front of the sacred tent, and the people were standing there in the presence of the LORD, [6] Moses said:

The LORD has ordered you to do this, so that he may appear to you in all his glory. [7] Aaron, step up to the altar and offer the sacrifice to please the LORD, then offer the sacrifices for the forgiveness of your sins and for the sins of the people, just as the LORD has commanded.

[8] Aaron stepped up to the altar and killed the bull that was to be the sacrifice for his sins. [9] His sons brought him the blood. He dipped a finger in it, smeared some on the four corners of the bronze altar, and poured out the rest at its foot. [10] But he sent up in smoke the fat, the kidneys, and the lower part of the

liver, just as the LORD had commanded Moses. [11] Then Aaron burnt the skin and the flesh outside the camp.

[12] After Aaron had killed the ram that was sacrificed to please the LORD, Aaron's sons brought him the blood, and he splattered it against all four sides of the altar. [13] They brought him each piece of the animal, including the head, and he burnt them all on the altar. [14] He washed the insides and the hind legs and also sent them up in smoke.

[15] Next, Aaron sacrificed the goat for the sins of the people, as he had done with the sacrifice for his own sins. [16] And so, he burnt this sacrifice on the altar in the proper way. [17] He also presented the grain sacrifice and burnt a handful of the flour on the altar as part of the morning sacrifice.

[18] At last, he killed the bull and the ram as a sacrifice to ask the LORD's blessing on the people. Aaron's sons brought him the blood, and he splattered it against the four sides of the altar. [19] His sons placed all the fat, as well as the kidneys and the lower part of the liver [20] on top of the choice ribs. [21] Then Aaron burnt the fat on the altar and lifted up' the ribs and the right hind leg to show that these were dedicated to the LORD. This was done just as the LORD had instructed Moses.

[22] Aaron held out his hand and gave the people his blessing, before coming down from the bronze altar where he had offered the sacrifices. [23] He and Moses went into the sacred tent, and when they came out, they gave the people their blessing. Then the LORD appeared to the people in all his glory. [24] The LORD sent fiery flames that burnt up everything on the altar, and when everyone saw this, they shouted and fell to their knees to worship the LORD.

Two priests are killed

CHAPTER 10

Nadab and Abihu

[1] Nadab and Abihu were two of Aaron's sons, but they disobeyed the LORD by burning incense to him on a fire pan, when they were not supposed to.' [2] Suddenly the LORD sent fiery flames and burnt them to death. [3] Then Moses told Aaron that this was exactly what the LORD had meant when he said:

"I demand respect
from my priests,

---

*9.2 sacrifice to please him:** See the note at 1.1–3.
*9.4 to ask the LORD's blessing:** See the note at 3.1.
*9.4 grain sacrifice:** To give thanks to the LORD (see the note at 2.1).

See also: 9.7: Heb 7.27.

See also: 9.18: Lev 3.1–11. 9.22: Num 6.22–26.

and I will be praised
by everyone!"

Aaron was speechless.

⁴ Moses sent for Mishael and Elzaphan, the two sons of Aaron's uncle Uzziel. Then he told them, "Take these two dead relatives of yours outside the camp far from the entrance to the sacred tent." ⁵ So they dragged the dead men away by their clothes.

⁶ Then Moses told Aaron and his other two sons, Eleazar and Ithamar:

Don't show your sorrow by leaving your hair uncombed and tearing your priestly clothes, or the LORD will get angry. He will kill the three of you and punish everyone else. It's all right for your relatives, the people of Israel, to mourn for those he destroyed by fire. ⁷ But you are the LORD's chosen priests, and you must not leave the sacred tent, or you will die.

Aaron and his two sons obeyed Moses.

⁸ The LORD said to Aaron:

⁹ When you or your sons enter the sacred tent, you must never drink beer or wine. If you do, you will die there! This law will never change. ¹⁰ You must learn the difference between what is holy and what isn't holy and between the clean and the unclean. ¹¹ You must also teach the people of Israel everything that I commanded Moses to say to them.

¹² Moses told Aaron and his two sons, Eleazar and Ithamar:

The grain sacrifice that was offered to give thanks to the LORD* is very holy. So make bread without yeast from the part that wasn't sent up in smoke and eat it beside the altar. ¹³ The LORD has said that this belongs to you and your sons, and that it must be eaten in a holy place. ¹⁴⁻¹⁵ But the choice ribs and the hind leg that were lifted up⸆ may be eaten by your entire family, as long as you do so in an acceptable place.* These parts are yours from the sacrifices that the people offer to ask the LORD's blessing.* This is what the LORD has commanded, and it will never change.

¹⁶ When Moses asked around and learnt that the ram for the sin sacrifice had already been burnt on the altar, he became angry with Eleazar and Ithamar and said, ¹⁷ "Why didn't you eat the meat from this sacrifice in an acceptable place? It is very holy, and the LORD has given you this sacrifice to remove Israel's sin and guilt. ¹⁸ Whenever an animal's blood isn't brought into the sacred tent, I commanded you to eat its meat in an acceptable place, but you burnt it instead."

¹⁹ Their father Aaron replied, "Today two of my sons offered the sacrifice for sin and the sacrifice to please the LORD, and look what has happened to me! Would the LORD have approved if I had eaten the sacrifice for sin?"

²⁰ Moses was satisfied with Aaron's reply.

Laws about what is clean and unclean

CHAPTER 11

Clean and unclean animals

This is also told in Deuteronomy 14.3–21

¹ The LORD told Moses and Aaron ² to say to the community of Israel:

You may eat ³ any animal that has divided hoofs and chews the cud.* ⁴⁻⁸ But you must not eat animals such as camels, rock badgers, and rabbits that chew the cud but don't have divided hoofs. And you must not eat pigs — they have divided hoofs, but don't chew the cud. All these animals are unclean,* and you are forbidden even to touch their dead bodies.

⁹⁻¹² You may eat anything that lives in water and has fins and scales. But it would be disgusting for you to eat anything else that lives in water, and you must not even touch their dead bodies.

---

*11.3 chews the cud: Some animals that eat grass and leaves have more than one stomach and chew their food a second time after it has been partly digested in the first stomach. This partly digested food is called the "cud".
*11.4–8 unclean: In the Old Testament "clean" and "unclean" refer to whatever makes a person, animal, or object acceptable or unacceptable to God. For example, a person became unclean by eating certain foods, touching certain objects, and having certain kinds of diseases and bodily discharges.
See also: 10.17: Lev 6.24–26.

---

*10.12 grain sacrifice . . . to give thanks to the LORD: See the note at 2.1.
*10.14–15 acceptable place: See 6.24–30.
*10.14–15 to ask the LORD's blessing: See the note at 3.1.
See also: 10.12–13: Lev 6.14–18. 10.14–15: Lev 7.30–34.

¹³⁻¹⁹ Eagles, vultures, buzzards, crows, ostriches, hawks, seagulls, owls, pelicans, storks, herons, hoopoes,' and bats are also disgusting, and you are forbidden to eat any of them.

²⁰⁻²³ The only winged insects you may eat are locusts, grasshoppers, and crickets. All other winged insects that crawl are too disgusting for you to eat.

²⁴⁻²⁸ Don't even touch the dead bodies of animals that have divided hoofs but don't chew the cud. And don't touch the dead bodies of animals that have paws. If you do, you must wash your clothes, but you are still unclean until evening.

²⁹⁻³⁰ Moles, rats, mice, and all kinds of lizards are unclean. ³¹ Anyone who touches their dead bodies or anything touched by their dead bodies becomes unclean until evening. ³² If something made of wood, cloth, or leather touches one of their dead bodies, it must be washed, but it is still unclean until evening. ³³ If any of these animals is found dead in a clay pot, the pot must be broken to pieces, and everything in it becomes unclean. ³⁴ If you pour water from this pot on any food, that food becomes unclean, and anything drinkable in the pot becomes unclean.

³⁵ If the dead body of one of these animals touches anything else, including ovens and stoves, that thing becomes unclean and must be destroyed. ³⁶ A spring or a cistern where one of these dead animals is found is still clean, but anyone who touches the animal becomes unclean. ³⁷ If the dead body of one of these animals is found lying on seeds that have been set aside for planting, the seeds remain clean. ³⁸ But seeds that are soaking in water become unclean, if the dead animal is found in the water.

³⁹ If an animal that may be eaten happens to die, and you touch it, you become unclean until evening. ⁴⁰ If you eat any of its meat or carry its body away, you must wash your clothes, but you are still unclean until evening.

⁴¹⁻⁴² Don't eat any of those disgusting little creatures that crawl or walk close to the ground. ⁴³ If you eat any of them, you will become just as disgusting and unclean as they are. ⁴⁴ I am the LORD your God, and you must dedicate yourselves to me and be holy, just as I am holy. Don't become disgusting by eating any of these unclean

Holy history

Clean and unclean

'You must learn the difference between what is holy and what isn't holy and between the clean and the unclean.' (Leviticus 10.10)

The law placed a great emphasis on the idea of clean and unclean. Various things made a person unclean:

Contact with a dead person (Numbers 19.11–22)

For the early Israelites the dead body represented the ultimate consequences of sin. So touching a dead body made someone unclean.

Leprosy or other skin diseases (Leviticus 13–14)

Any disease which affected the skin, or even the house or clothing of someone rendered them unclean.

Bodily functions

Certain natural functions, or discharges of the body made someone unclean.

Eating an unclean animal

Food was separated into the clean and the unclean, mostly on the issue of hygiene. Certain foods like shellfish or pork – foods which even today have to be cooked carefully to avoid food poisoning. For a nomadic people it was particularly important to keep healthy.

How to get rid of it

Generally, the cure for uncleanness was bathing of the body and washing the clothes, or by undergoing ritual healing, involving sacrifice and prayer.

More...

The Law p.127
Social and moral laws p.130
Ten Commandments p.85
Leprosy p.410
Gentiles p.1232

See also: 11.44: Lev 19.2; 1 Pet 1.16.

creatures. [45] I brought you out of Egypt so that I could be your God. Now you must become holy, because I am holy!

[46-47] I have given these laws so that you will know what animals, birds, and fish are clean and may be eaten, and which ones are unclean and may not be eaten.

CHAPTER 12

What women must do after giving birth

[1] The LORD told Moses [2] to say to the community of Israel:

If a woman gives birth to a son, she is unclean for seven days, just as she is during her monthly period. [3] Her son must be circumcised on the eighth day, [4] but her loss of blood keeps her from being completely clean for another thirty-three days. During this time she must not touch anything holy or go to the place of worship. [5] Any woman who gives birth to a daughter is unclean for two weeks, just as she is during her period. And she won't be completely clean for another sixty-six days.

[6] When the mother has completed her time of cleansing, she must come to the front of the sacred tent and bring to the priest a year-old lamb as a sacrifice to please me* and a dove or a pigeon as a sacrifice for sin. [7] After the priest offers the sacrifices to me, the mother will become completely clean from her loss of blood, whether her child is a boy or a girl. [8] If she cannot afford a lamb, she can offer two doves or two pigeons, one as a sacrifice to please me and the other as a sacrifice for sin.

CHAPTER 13

Skin diseases

[1] The LORD told Moses and Aaron to say to the people:

[2] If sores or boils or a skin rash should break out and start spreading on your body, you must be brought to Aaron or to one of the other priests. [3] If the priest discovers that the hair in the infected area has turned white and that the infection

seems more than skin deep, he will say, "This is leprosy* — you are unclean."

[4] But if the infected area is white and only skin deep, and if the hair in it hasn't turned white, the priest will order you to stay away from everyone else for seven days. [5] If the disease hasn't spread by that time, he will order you to stay away from everyone else for another seven days. [6] Then if the disease hasn't got any worse or spread, the priest will say, "You are clean. It was only a sore. After you wash your clothes, you may go home."

[7] However, if the disease comes back, you must return to the priest. [8] If it is discovered that the disease has started spreading, he will say, "This is leprosy — you are unclean."

[9] Any of you with a skin disease must be brought to a priest. [10] If he discovers that the sore spot is white with pus and that the hair around it has also turned white, [11] he will say, "This is leprosy. You are unclean and must stay away from everyone else."

[12-13] But if the disease has run its course and only the scars remain, he will say, "You are clean." [14-15] If the sores come back and turn white with pus, he will say, "This is leprosy — you are unclean."

[16-17] However, if the sores heal and only white spots remain, the priest will say, "You are now clean."

[18-19] If you have a sore that either swells or turns reddish-white after it has healed, then you must show it to a priest. [20] If he discovers that the hair in the infected area has turned white and that the infection seems more than skin deep, he will say, "This is leprosy — you are unclean." [21] But if the white area is only on the surface of the skin and hasn't got any worse, and if the hair in it hasn't turned white, he will make you stay away from everyone else for seven days.

[22] If the sore begins spreading during this time, the priest will say, "You are unclean because you have a disease." [23] But if it doesn't spread, and only a scar remains, he will say, "You are now clean."

[24] If you have a burn that gets infected and turns red or reddish-white, [25] a priest must examine it. Then if he discovers that the hair in the infected area has turned white and that the infection seems more than skin deep, he will say, "The burn has turned into leprosy, and you are unclean."

---

*12.6 sacrifice to please me: See the note at 1.1–3.
See also: 12.3: Gen 17.12; Luke 2.21. 12.8: Luke 2.24.

*13.3 leprosy: The word translated "leprosy" was used for many different kinds of skin diseases.

26 But if the priest finds that the hair in the infected area hasn't turned white and that the sore is only skin deep and it is healing, he will make you stay away from everyone else for seven days. 27 On the seventh day the priest will examine you again, and if the infection is spreading, he will say, "This is leprosy — you are unclean." 28 However, if the infection hasn't spread and has begun to heal, and if only a scar remains, he will say, "Only a scar remains from the burn, and you are clean."

29 If you have a sore on your head or chin, 30 it must be examined by a priest. If the infection seems more than skin deep, and the hair in it has thinned out and lost its colour, he will say, "This is leprosy — you are unclean." 31 On the other hand, if he discovers that the itchy spot is only skin deep, but that the hair still isn't healthy, he will order you to stay away from everyone else for seven days. 32 By that time, if the itch hasn't spread, if the hairs seem healthy, and if the itch is only skin deep, 33 you must shave off the hairs around the infection, but not those on it. Then the priest will tell you to stay away from everyone else for another seven days. 34 By that time, if the itch hasn't spread and seems no more than skin deep, he will say, "You are clean; now you must wash your clothes."

35-36 Later, if the itch starts spreading, even though the hair is still healthy, the priest will say, "You are unclean." 37 But if he thinks you are completely well, he will say, "You are clean."

38 If white spots break out on your skin, 39 but the priest discovers that it is only a rash, he will say, "You are clean."

40-41 If you become bald on any part of your head, you are still clean. 42-43 But if a priest discovers that a reddish-white sore has broken out on the bald spot and looks like leprosy, he will say, 44 "This is leprosy — you are unclean."

45 If you ever have leprosy, you must tear your clothes, leave your hair uncombed, cover the lower part of your face, and go around shouting, "I'm unclean! I'm unclean!" 46 As long as you have the disease, you are unclean and must live alone outside the camp.

47-50 If a greenish or reddish spot* appears anywhere on any of your clothing or on anything made of leather, you must let the priest examine the clothing or the leather. He will put it aside for seven days, 51 and if the mildew has spread in that time, he will say, "This is unclean 52 because the mildew has spread." Then he will burn the clothing or the piece of leather.

53 If the priest discovers that the mildew hasn't spread, 54 he will tell you to wash the clothing or leather and put it aside for another seven days, 55 after which he will examine it again. If the spot hasn't spread, but is still greenish or reddish, the clothing or leather is unclean and must be burnt. 56 But if the spot has faded after being washed, he will tear away the spot. 57 Later, if the spot reappears elsewhere on the clothing or the leather, you must burn it. 58 Even if the spot completely disappears after being washed, it must be washed again before it is clean.

59 These are the rules for deciding if clothing is clean or unclean after a spot appears on it.

CHAPTER 14

The ceremony for people healed of leprosy

1 The LORD told Moses to say to the people:

2-3 After you think you are healed of leprosy,* you must ask for a priest to come outside the camp and examine you. And if you are well, 4 he will order someone to bring out two live birds that are acceptable for sacrifice, together with a stick of cedar wood, a piece of red yarn, and a branch from a hyssop plant. 5 The priest will order someone to kill one of the birds over a clay pot of spring water. 6 Then he will dip the other bird, the cedar, the red yarn, and the hyssop in the blood of the dead bird. 7 Next, he will sprinkle you seven times with the blood and say, "You are now clean." Finally, he will release the bird and let it fly away.

8 After this you must wash your clothes, shave your entire body, and take a bath before you are completely clean. You may move back into camp, but you must not enter your tent for seven days. 9 Then you must once again shave your head, face, and eyebrows, as well as the hair on the rest of your body. Finally, wash your

---

*13.47–50 spot: The Hebrew word translated "spot" and "mildew" in verses 47–59 is the same one translated "leprosy" earlier in the chapter.

*14.2–3 leprosy: See the note at 13.3.
See also: 14.2: Matt 8.4; Mark 1.44; Luke 5.14; 17.14.

clothes and take a bath, and you will be completely clean.

¹⁰ On the eighth day you must bring to the priest two rams and a year-old female lamb that have nothing wrong with them; also bring a third of a litre of olive oil and three kilogrammes of your finest flour mixed with oil. ¹¹ Then the priest will present you and your offerings to me at the entrance to my sacred tent. ¹² There he will offer one of the rams, together with the one third of a litre of oil, as a sacrifice to make things right.* He will also lift them up' to show that they are dedicated to me. ¹³ This sacrifice is very holy. It belongs to the priest and must be killed in the same place where animals are killed as sacrifices for sins and as sacrifices to please me.*

¹⁴ The priest will smear some of the blood from this sacrifice on your right ear lobe, some on your right thumb, and some on the big toe of your right foot. ¹⁵ He will then pour some of the olive oil into the palm of his left hand, ¹⁶ dip a finger of his right hand into the oil, and sprinkle some of it seven times towards the sacred tent. ¹⁷ Next, he will smear some of the oil on your right ear lobe, some on your right thumb, and some on the big toe of your right foot, ¹⁸⁻²⁰ and pour the rest of the oil from his palm on your head. Then he will offer the other two animals — one as a sacrifice for sin and the other as a sacrifice to please me, together with a grain sacrifice. After this you will be completely clean.

²¹ If you are poor and cannot afford to offer this much, you may offer a ram as a sacrifice to make things right, together with a third of a litre of olive oil and one kilogramme of flour mixed with oil as a grain sacrifice. The priest will then lift these up' to dedicate them to me. ²² Depending on what you can afford, you must also offer either two doves or two pigeons, one as a sacrifice for sin and the other as a sacrifice to please me. ²³ The priest will offer these to me in front of the sacred tent on the eighth day.

²⁴⁻²⁵ The priest will kill this ram for the sacrifice to make things right, and he will lift it up' with the olive oil in dedication to me. Then he will smear some of the blood on your right ear lobe, some on your right thumb, and some on the big toe of your right foot.

²⁶ The priest will pour some of the olive oil into the palm of his left hand, ²⁷ then dip a finger of his right hand in the oil and sprinkle some of it seven times towards the sacred tent. ²⁸ He will smear some of the oil on your right ear lobe, some on your right thumb, and some on the big toe of your right foot, just as he did with the blood of the sacrifice to make things right. ²⁹⁻³¹ And he will pour the rest of the oil from his palm on your head.

Then, depending on what you can afford, he will offer either the doves or the pigeons together with the grain sacrifice. One of the birds is the sacrifice for sin, and the other is the sacrifice to please me. After this you will be completely clean.

³² These are the things you must do if you have leprosy and cannot afford the usual sacrifices to make you clean.

When mildew is in a house

³³ The LORD told Moses and Aaron to say to the people:

³⁴ After I have given you the land of Canaan as your permanent possession, here is what you must do, if I ever put mildew* on the walls of any of your homes. ³⁵ First, you must say to a priest, "I think mildew is on the wall of my house."

³⁶ The priest will reply, "Empty the house before I inspect it, or else everything in it will be unclean."

³⁷ If the priest discovers greenish or reddish spots that go deeper than the surface of the walls, ³⁸ he will have the house closed for seven days. ³⁹ Then he will return and check to see if the mildew has spread. ⁴⁰⁻⁴¹ If so, he will order someone to scrape the plaster from the walls, remove the filthy stones, then haul everything off and dump it in an unclean place outside the town. ⁴² Afterwards the wall must be repaired with new stones and fresh plaster.

⁴³ If the mildew appears a second time, ⁴⁴ the priest will come and say, "This house is unclean. It's covered with mildew that can't be removed." ⁴⁵ Then he will have the house torn down and every bit of wood, stone, and plaster hauled off to an unclean place outside the town. ⁴⁶ Meanwhile, if any of you entered the house while it was closed, you will be unclean until evening.

---

*14.12 sacrifice to make things right: See 7.1–10.
*14.13 sacrifices to please me: See the note at 1.1–3.

*14.34 mildew: The Hebrew word translated "mildew" is the same one translated "leprosy" and "spot" in chapter 13.

⁴⁷ And if you either slept or ate in the house, you must wash your clothes.

⁴⁸ On the other hand, if the priest discovers that mildew hasn't reappeared after the house was newly plastered, he will say, "This house is clean — the mildew has gone." ⁴⁹ Then, to show that the house is now clean, he will get two birds, a stick of cedar wood, a piece of red yarn, and a branch from a hyssop plant and bring them to the house. ⁵⁰ He will kill one of the birds over a clay pot of spring water ⁵¹⁻⁵² and let its blood drain into the pot. Then he will dip the cedar, the hyssop, the yarn, and the other bird into the mixture of blood and water. Next, he will sprinkle the house seven times with the mixture, then the house will be completely clean. ⁵³ Finally, he will release the bird and let it fly away, ending the ceremony for purifying the house.

⁵⁴⁻⁵⁷ These are the things you must do if you discover that you are unclean because of an itch or a sore, or that your clothing or house is unclean because of mildew.

CHAPTER 15

Sexual uncleanness

¹ The LORD told Moses and Aaron ² to say to the community of Israel:

Any man with an infected penis is unclean, ³ whether it is stopped up or keeps dripping. ⁴ Anything that he rests on or sits on is also unclean, ⁵⁻⁷ and if you touch either these or him, you must wash your clothes and take a bath, but you still remain unclean until evening.

⁸ If you are spat on by the man, you must wash your clothes and take a bath, but you still remain unclean until evening. ⁹⁻¹⁰ Any saddle or seat on which the man sits is unclean. And if you touch or carry either of these, you must wash your clothes and take a bath, but you still remain unclean until evening. ¹¹ If the man touches you without first washing his hands, you must wash your clothes and take a bath, but you still remain unclean until evening. ¹² Any clay pot that he touches must be destroyed, and any wooden bowl that he touches must be washed.

¹³ Seven days after the man gets well, he will be considered clean, if he washes his clothes and takes a bath in spring water. ¹⁴ On the eighth day he must bring either two doves or two pigeons to the front of my sacred tent and give them to a priest. ¹⁵ The priest will offer one of the birds as a sacrifice for sin and the other as a sacrifice to please me,* then I will consider the man completely clean.

¹⁶ Any man who has a flow of semen must take a bath, but he still remains unclean until evening. ¹⁷ If the semen touches anything made of cloth or leather, these must be washed, but they still remain unclean until evening. ¹⁸ After having sex, both the man and the woman must take a bath, but they still remain unclean until evening.

¹⁹ When a woman has her monthly period, she remains unclean for seven days, and if you touch her, you must take a bath, but you remain unclean until evening. ²⁰⁻²³ Anything that she rests on or sits on is also unclean, and if you touch either of these, you must wash your clothes and take a bath, but you still remain unclean until evening. ²⁴ Any man who has sex with her during this time becomes unclean for seven days, and anything he rests on is also unclean.

²⁵ Any woman who has a flow of blood outside her regular monthly period is unclean until it stops, just as she is during her monthly period. ²⁶ Anything that she rests on or sits on during this time is also unclean, just as it would be during her period. ²⁷ If you touch either of these, you must wash your clothes and take a bath, but you still remain unclean until evening.

²⁸ Seven days after the woman gets well, she will be considered clean. ²⁹ On the eighth day, she must bring either two doves or two pigeons to the front of my sacred tent and give them to a priest. ³⁰ He will offer one of the birds as a sacrifice for sin and the other as a sacrifice to please me; then I will consider the woman completely clean.

³¹ When any of you are unclean, you must stay away from the rest of the community of Israel. Otherwise, my sacred tent will become unclean, and the whole nation will die.

³²⁻³³ These are the things you men must do if you become unclean because of an infected penis or if you have a flow of semen. And these are the things you women must do when you become unclean either because of your monthly period or an unusual flow of blood. This is

---

*15.15 sacrifice to please me: See the note at 1.1–3.

also what you men must do if you have sex with a woman who is unclean.

Laws about the Great Day of Forgiveness

CHAPTER 16

¹⁻² Two of Aaron's sons had already lost their lives for disobeying the LORD,* so the LORD told Moses to say to Aaron:

I, the LORD, appear in a cloud over the place of mercy on the sacred chest, which is behind the inside curtain* of the sacred tent. And I warn you not to go there except at the proper time. Otherwise, you will die!

³ Before entering this most holy place, you must offer a bull as a sacrifice for your sins* and a ram as a sacrifice to please me.* ⁴ You will take a bath and put on the sacred linen clothes, including the underwear, the robe, the sash, and the turban. ⁵ Then the community of Israel will bring you a ram and two goats, both of them males. The goats are to be used as sacrifices for sin, and the ram is to be used as a sacrifice to please me.

⁶ Aaron, you must offer the bull as a sacrifice of forgiveness for your own sins and for the sins of your family. ⁷ Then you will lead the two goats into my presence at the front of the sacred tent, ⁸ where I will show you* which goat will be sacrificed to me and which one will be sent into the desert to the demon Azazel.* ⁹ After you offer the first goat as a sacrifice for sin, ¹⁰ the other one must be presented to me alive, before you send it into the desert to take away the sins of the people.

¹¹ You must offer the bull as a sacrifice to ask forgiveness for your own sins and for the sins of your family. ¹² Then you will take a fire pan of live coals from the bronze altar, together with two handfuls of finely

ground incense, into the most holy place. ¹³ There you will present them to me by placing the incense on the coals, so that the place of mercy will be covered with a cloud of smoke. Do this, or you will die there! ¹⁴ Next, use a finger to sprinkle some of the blood on the place of mercy, which is on the lid of the sacred chest; then sprinkle blood seven times in front of the chest.

¹⁵ Aaron, you must next sacrifice the goat for the sins of the people, and you must sprinkle its blood inside the most holy place, just as you did with the blood of the bull. ¹⁶ By doing this, you will take away the sins that make both the most holy place and the people of Israel unclean. Do the same for the sacred tent, which is here among the people. ¹⁷ Only you are allowed in the sacred tent from the time you enter until the time you come out. ¹⁸ After leaving the tent, you will purify the bronze altar by smearing each of its four corners with some of the blood from the bull and from the goat. ¹⁹ Use a finger to sprinkle the altar seven times with the blood, and it will be completely clean from the sins of the people.

²⁰ After you have purified the most holy place, the sacred tent, and the bronze altar, you must bring the live goat to the front of the tent. ²¹ There you will lay your hands on its head, while confessing every sin the people have committed, and you will appoint someone to lead the goat into the desert, so that it can take away their sins. ²² Finally, this goat that carries the heavy burden of Israel's sins must be released deep in the desert.

²³⁻²⁴ Aaron, after this you must go inside the sacred tent, take a bath, put on your ordinary priestly clothes, and leave there the clothes you put on before entering the most holy place. Then you will come out and offer sacrifices to please me and sacrifices for your sins and for the sins of the people. ²⁵ The fat from these sacrifices for sin must be sent up in smoke on the bronze altar.

²⁶ The one who led the goat into the desert and sent it off to the demon Azazel must take a bath and wash his clothes before coming back into camp. ²⁷ The remains of the bull and the goat whose blood was taken into the most holy place must be taken outside the camp and burnt.

*16.1–2 lost . . . disobeying the LORD: See 10.1,2.
*16.1–2 inside curtain: That separated the holy place from the most holy place.
*16.3 for your sins: See 4.3–12.
*16.3 sacrifice to please me: See the note at 1.1–3.
*16.8 I will show you: The Hebrew text has "you must cast lots to find out". Pieces of wood or stone (called "lots") were used to find out what God wanted his people to do.
*16.8 Azazel: It was believed that a demon named Azazel lived in the desert.
See also: 16.2: Heb 6.19. 16.3: Heb 9.7.

See also: 16.15: Heb 9.12. 16.23: Ezek 44.19. 16.27: Heb 13.11.

²⁸ And whoever does this must take a bath and change clothes before coming back into camp.

The LORD told Moses to say to the people:

²⁹ On the tenth day of the seventh month* of each year, you must go without eating to show sorrow for your sins, and no one, including foreigners who live among you, is allowed to work. ³⁰ This is the day on which the sacrifice for the forgiveness of your sins will be made in my presence, ³¹ and from now on, it must be celebrated each year. Go without eating and make this a day of complete rest just like the Sabbath. ³² The high priest must offer the sacrifices for cleansing from sin, while wearing the sacred linen clothes. ³³ He will offer these sacrifices for the most holy place, the sacred tent, the bronze altar, all the priests, and for the whole community. ³⁴ You must celebrate this day each year — it is the Great Day of Forgiveness* for all the sins of the people of Israel.

Moses did exactly as the LORD had commanded.

Laws on various subjects

CHAPTER 17

Where to offer sacrifices

¹ The LORD told Moses ² to tell Aaron, his sons, and everyone else in Israel:

³⁻⁴ Whenever you kill any of your cattle, sheep, or goats as sacrifices to me, you must do it at the entrance to the sacred tent. If you don't, you will be guilty of pouring out blood, and you will no longer belong to the community of Israel. ⁵ And so, when you sacrifice an animal to ask my blessing,* it must not be done out in a field, ⁶ but in front of the sacred tent. Then a priest can splatter its blood against the bronze altar and send its fat up in smoke with a smell that pleases me. ⁷ Don't ever

turn from me again and offer sacrifices to goat-demons. This law will never change.

⁸ Remember! No one in Israel, including foreigners, is to offer a sacrifice anywhere ⁹ except at the entrance to the sacred tent. If you do, you will no longer belong to my people.

Do not eat blood

The LORD said:

¹⁰ I will turn against any of my people who eat blood. This also includes any foreigners living among you. ¹¹ Life is in the blood, and I have given you the blood of animals to sacrifice in place of your own. ¹² That's also why I have forbidden you to eat blood. ¹³ Even if you should hunt and kill a bird or an animal, you must drain out the blood and cover it with soil.

¹⁴ The life of every living creature is in its blood. That's why I have forbidden you to eat blood and why I have warned you that anyone who does will no longer belong to my people.

¹⁵ If you happen to find a dead animal and eat it, you must take a bath and wash your clothes, but you are still unclean until evening. ¹⁶ If you don't take a bath, you will suffer for what you did wrong.

CHAPTER 18

Forbidden sex

¹ The LORD told Moses ² to tell the people of Israel:

I am the LORD your God! ³ So don't follow the customs of Egypt where you used to live or those of Canaan where I am bringing you. ⁴ I am the LORD your God, and you must obey my teachings. ⁵ Obey them and you will live. I am the LORD.

⁶ Don't have sex with any of your close relatives, ⁷ especially your own mother. This would disgrace your father. ⁸ And don't disgrace him by having sex with any of his other wives. ⁹ Don't have sex with your sister or stepsister, whether you grew up together or not. ¹⁰ Don't disgrace yourself by having sex with your granddaughter ¹¹ or half-sister ¹²⁻¹³ or a sister of your father or mother. ¹⁴ Don't

---

*16.29 seventh month: Tishri (also called Ethanim), the seventh month of the Hebrew calendar, from about mid-September to mid-October.

*16.34 Great Day of Forgiveness: Traditionally known as the Day of Atonement.

*17.5 sacrifice . . . to ask my blessing: See the note at 3.1.

See also: 16.29–34: Lev 23.26–32; Num 29.7–11.

See also: 17.10: Gen 9.4; Lev 7.26–27; 19.26; Deut 12.16,23; 15.23. 17.11: Heb 9.22. 18.5: Neh 9.29; Ezek 18.9; 20.11–13; Luke 10.28; Rom 10.5; Gal 3.12. 18.8: Lev 20.11; Deut 22.30; 27.20. 18.9: Lev 20.17; Deut 27.22. 18.12–14: Lev 20.19–20.

Big ideas

The Law

When we read these laws and regulations, one simple question arises: why? Why all these regulations? What's the point? Why were they necessary?

Justice

The law was intended to ensure that society operated justly. It contains many regulations designed to protect the poor and oppressed. It talks about caring for refugees (Exodus 22.21); it talks about leaving food for those who have no land of their own (Leviticus 19.9–10); it talks about caring for widows and orphans (Exodus 22.22–4). The law provides for fair treatment for all, regardless of wealth or status.

One of the most astonishing of its decrees was the jubilee provision, which declared a 'Sabbath' for the land and, once every fifty years, a complete reset of society to what was fair and right.

Health & hygiene

These include things like dealing with skin diseases and avoiding eating foods such as pork and seafood. This also includes laws on what to do with people who are unclean or who have horrible infections (Leviticus 13)!

Family & society

Many laws deal with how the Israelites should behave towards one another. They deal with crime and punishment, with sexual relationships and with respecting different areas of society. It covers how you treat your slaves, lending money to people in need, even what to do if you borrow a donkey and it gets stolen (Exodus 22.10).

Worship

There are many laws about sacrifices and worship and which go into a huge amount of detail about the activities (and design) of temple and tabernacle. Israel was not supposed to act in the same way as the nations around it. At least part of the reason for the laws about the priestly functions was about keeping Israel focused on God.

Forgiveness

A lot of the law is about offering sacrifice to say 'sorry' for different types of sins. There is also a great day of forgiveness, a time when the whole nation would ask forgiveness for their sins (Leviticus 16.1–34).

Identity

The law was supposed to make Israel distinctive. It was through obeying God's commands that Israel found unity and purpose. The Law was what distinguished the people of Israel from the 'lawless' nations surrounding them.

Warning: take the culture into account

Some of the laws are not what you'd call 'politically correct'. When it comes to women and their periods, for example, it's not very fair to call them 'unclean'. But we have to take into account the prevailing culture of the times. We might wish that God had gently corrected everyone and ushered in a new era of political correctness, but God works through the culture of the people he is dealing with. So a large chunk of the Law reflects the culture and expectations of the times.

Anorak corner

The law covers stuff like having sex with animals (Exodus 22.19) and even where to build your toilet (Deuteronomy 23.12–13). Who says the Bible isn't about real life?

More...

Ten Commandments p.85
Ark of the Covenant p.104
Jubilee – the year of celebration p.137
Social and moral laws p.130
Clean and unclean p.120

disgrace your uncle by having sex with his wife. ¹⁵ Don't have sex with your daughter-in-law ¹⁶ or sister-in-law. ¹⁷ And don't have sex with the daughter or granddaughter of any woman that you have earlier had sex with. You may be having sex with a relative, and that would make you unclean. ¹⁸ As long as your wife is alive, don't cause trouble for her by taking one of her sisters as a second wife.

¹⁹ When a woman is having her monthly period, she is unclean, so don't have sex with her.

²⁰ Don't have sex with another man's wife — that would make you unclean.

²¹ Don't sacrifice your children on the altar fires to the god Molech. I am the LORD your God, and that would disgrace me.

²² It is disgusting for a man to have sex with another man.

²³ Anyone who has sex with an animal is unclean.

²⁴ Don't make yourselves unclean by any of these disgusting practices of those nations that I am forcing out of the land for you. They made themselves ²⁵ and the land so unclean, that I punished the land because of their sins, and I made it vomit them up. ²⁶⁻²⁷ Now don't do these sickening things that make the land filthy. Instead, obey my laws and teachings. ²⁸ Then the land won't become sick of you and vomit you up, just as it did them. ²⁹⁻³⁰ If any of you do these vulgar, disgusting things, you will be unclean and no longer belong to my people. I am the LORD your God, and I forbid you to follow their sickening way of life.

CHAPTER 19

Moral and religious laws

¹ The LORD told Moses ² to say to the community of Israel:

I am the LORD your God. I am holy, and you must be holy too! ³⁻⁴ Respect your father and your mother, honour the Sabbath, and don't make idols or images. I am the LORD your God.

⁵ When you offer a sacrifice to ask my blessing,* be sure to follow my instructions. ⁶ You may eat the meat either on the day of the sacrifice or on the next day, but you must burn anything left until the third day. ⁷ If you eat any of it on the third day, the sacrifice will be disgusting to me, and I will reject it. ⁸ In fact, you will be punished for not respecting what I say is holy, and you will no longer belong to the community of Israel.

⁹ When you harvest your grain, always leave some of it standing along the edges of your fields and don't pick up what falls on the ground. ¹⁰ Don't strip your grapevines clean or gather the grapes that fall off the vines. Leave them for the poor and for those foreigners who live among you. I am the LORD your God.

¹¹ Do not steal or tell lies or cheat others.

¹² Do not misuse my name by making promises you don't intend to keep. I am the LORD your God.

¹³ Do not steal anything or cheat anyone, and don't fail to pay your workers at the end of each day.*

¹⁴ I am the LORD your God, and I command you not to make fun of the deaf or to cause a blind person to stumble.

¹⁵ Be fair, no matter who is on trial — don't favour either the poor or the rich.

¹⁶ Don't be a gossip, but never hesitate to speak up in court, especially if your testimony can save someone's life.'

¹⁷ Don't hold grudges. On the other hand, it's wrong not to correct someone who needs correcting. ¹⁸ Stop being angry and don't try to take revenge. I am the LORD, and I command you to love others as much as you love yourself.

¹⁹ Breed your livestock animals only with animals of the same kind, and don't plant two kinds of seed in the same field or wear clothes made of different kinds of material.

²⁰ If a man has sex with a slave woman who is promised in marriage to someone else, he must pay a fine, but they are not to

---

19.5 to ask my blessing: See the note at 3.1.
19.13 to pay . . . end of each day: Day labourers needed their wages to buy food for their evening meal, which was the main meal of the day.

See also: **18.15:** Lev 20.12. **18.16:** Lev 20.21. **18.17:** Lev 20.14; Deut 27.23. **18.19:** Lev 20.18. **18.20:** Lev 20.10. **18.21:** Lev 20.1–5. **18.22:** Lev 20.13. **18.23:** Exod 22.19; Lev 20.15–16; Deut 27.21. **19.2:** Lev 11.44–45; 1 Pet 1.16. **19.3: a** Exod 20.12; Deut 5.16; **b** Exod 20.8; Deut 5.12. **19.4: a** Lev 26.1; **b** Exod 20.23; 34.17; Deut 17.25.

See also: **19.9–10:** Lev 27.15; Deut 24.19–22. **19.11: a** Exod 20.15; Deut 5.19; **b** Exod 20.16; Deut 5.20. **19.12:** Exod 20.7; Deut 5.11; Matt 5.33. **19.13:** Deut 24.14–15. **19.14:** Deut 27.18. **19.15:** Exod 23.6–8; Deut 16.19. **19.17:** Matt 18.15. **19.18:** Matt 5.43; 19.19; 22.39; Mark 12.31; Luke 10.27; Rom 13.9; Gal 5.14; Jam 2.8. **19.19:** Deut 22.9–11.

Real life

Refugees

Refugees get a bad press. They're portrayed as scroungers, sneaking into the country illegally and taking what they shouldn't.

Funny to think that Jesus was a refugee. His family had to flee to Egypt to escape persecution. Moses was a refugee in the desert. When Joseph's brothers came into Egypt looking for food, they were economic migrants. Paul had to escape Damascus in a basket. Lots of refugees in the Bible...

Perhaps that's why the Bible is very clear on our obligations to the poor and dispossessed. The law that God gave to Israel commands the Jews to be welcoming to strangers in their midst. The Jews had been refugees in Egypt; they were supposed to remember that.

God doesn't see people as refugees or natives. He just sees them as children. So we should try to understand what makes people flee their country. We should treat people with compassion. And we should resist the urge to label people, to put them in a box and to look on them with hatred.

After all, we're all refugees. We're staying here on earth for a while, but our real home is in heaven.

Think

Why do people flee from their countries in the first place?
Is it fair that refugees should come here?
How does God look at them?

Act

Are there refugees in your church? How can you help them?
Find out what Christian agencies are doing with refugees and see how you can help.

Check

Exodus 22.21; Leviticus 19.33–34; Deuteronomy 10.16–19; Isaiah 14.1–2; 56.3–8; Jeremiah 7.1–7; Ezekiel 22.27–29; Ephesians 2.14–22; 1 Peter 2.11–12

More...

Racism p.1308
Homelessness p.1386

be put to death. After all, she was still a slave at the time.ᵇ ²¹⁻²² The man must bring a ram to the entrance of the sacred tent and give it to a priest, who will then offer it as a sacrifice to me, so the man's sins will be forgiven.

²³ After you enter the land, you will plant fruit trees, but you are not to eat any of their fruit for the first three years. ²⁴ In the fourth year the fruit must be set apart, as an expression of thanks ²⁵ to me, the LORD God. Do this, and in the fifth year, those trees will produce an abundant harvest of fruit for you to eat.

²⁶ Don't eat the blood of any animal. Don't practise any kind of witchcraft.

²⁷⁻²⁸ I forbid you to shave any part of your head or beard or to cut and tattoo yourself as a way of worshipping the dead.

²⁹ Don't let your daughters serve as temple prostitutes — this would bring disgrace both to them and the land.

³⁰ I command you to respect the Sabbath and the place where I am worshipped.

³¹ Don't make yourselves disgusting to me by going to people who claim they can talk to the dead.

³² I command you to show respect for older people and to obey me with fear and trembling.

³³ Don't ill-treat any foreigners who live in your land. ³⁴ Instead, treat them as well as you treat citizens and love them as much as you love yourself. Remember, you were once foreigners in the land of Egypt. I am the LORD your God.

³⁵⁻³⁶ Use honest scales and don't cheat when you weigh or measure anything.

I am the LORD your God. I rescued you from Egypt, ³⁷ and I command you to obey my laws.

CHAPTER 20

Penalties for disobeying God's laws

¹ The LORD told Moses ² to say to the community of Israel:

Death by stoning is the penalty for any citizens or foreigners in the country who

See also: 19.26: a Gen 9.4; Lev 7.26–27; 17.10–14; Deut 12.16,23; 15.23; **b** Deut 18.10. **19.27–28:** Lev 21.5; Deut 14.1. **19.29:** Deut 23.17. **19.30:** Lev 26.2. **19.31:** Deut 18.11; 1 Sam 28.3; 2 King 23.4; Isa 8.19. **19.33–34:** Exod 22.21; Deut 24.17–18; 27.19. **19.35–36:** Deut 25.13–16; Prov 20.10; Ezek 45.10.

Holy history

Social and moral laws

Leviticus is often seen as a book full of religious ritual. But many of the laws it contains are concerned with the way the Israelites were supposed to behave to one another, and the values they were to hold as a society. Here are some examples.

Leave some food for the poor and refugees (Leviticus 19.9–10)

Respecting the disabled (Leviticus 9.14)

Fair justice for all (Leviticus 9.15)

Respect the elderly (Leviticus 9.32)

Treat refugees fairly (Leviticus 9.33–34)

Don't cheat your customers! (Leviticus 9.35–6)

Don't take bribes (Deuteronomy 16.19–19)

Make your roofs safe (Deuteronomy 22.8)

Pay people on time (Deuteronomy 24.14–15)

Care for the powerless (Deuteronomy 24.17–18)

So, you see, the law was about a lot more than just worship and sacrifices. It told Israel the way to live as a society. And, although as Christians we don't have to follow the religious ritual any more, the social laws still have a lot to teach us.

More...

The Law p.127
The poor p.991
Jubilee – the year of celebration p.137
Refugees p.129
Homelessness p.789

sacrifice their children to the god Molech. ³ They have disgraced both the place where I am worshipped and my holy name, and so I will turn against them and no longer let them belong to my people. ⁴ Some of you may let them get away with human sacrifice, ⁵ but not me. If any of you worship Molech, I will turn against you and your entire family, and I will no longer let you belong to my people.

⁶ I will be your enemy if you go to someone who claims to speak with the dead, and I will destroy you from among my people. ⁷ Dedicate yourselves to me and be holy because I am the LORD your God. ⁸ I have chosen you as my people, and I expect you to obey my laws.

⁹ If you curse your father or mother, you will be put to death, and it will be your own fault.

¹⁰ If any of you men have sex with another man's wife, both you and the woman will be put to death.

¹¹ Having sex with one of your father's wives disgraces him. So both you and the woman will be put to death, just as you deserve. ¹² It isn't natural to have sex with your daughter-in-law, and both of you will be put to death, just as you deserve. ¹³ It's disgusting for men to have sex with one another, and those who do will be put to death, just as they deserve. ¹⁴ It isn't natural for a man to marry both a mother and her daughter, and so all three of them will be burnt to death. ¹⁵⁻¹⁶ If any of you have sex with an animal, both you and the animal will be put to death, just as you deserve.

¹⁷ If you marry one of your sisters, you will be punished, and the two of you will be disgraced by being openly forced out of the community. ¹⁸ If you have sex with a woman during her monthly period, both you and the woman will be cut off from the people of Israel. ¹⁹ The sisters of your father and mother are your own relatives, and you will be punished for having sex with any of them. ²⁰ If you have sex with your uncle's wife, neither you nor she will ever have any children. ²¹ And if you marry

See also: 20.9: Exod 21.17; Matt 15.4; Mark 7.10.
20.10: Exod 20.14; Lev 18.20; Deut 5.18.   **20.11:** Lev 18.8; Deut 22.30; 27.20.   **20.12:** Lev 18.15.   **20.13:** Lev 18.22.
20.14: Lev 18.17; Deut 27.23.   **20.15–16:** Exod 22.19; Lev 18.23; Deut 27.21.   **20.17:** Lev 18.9; Deut 27.22.
20.18: Lev 18.19.   **20.19–20:** Lev 18.12–14.
20.21: Lev 18.16.

your sister-in-law, neither of you will ever have any children.*

²² Obey my laws and teachings. Or else the land I am giving you will become sick of you and throw you out. ²³ The nations I am chasing out did these disgusting things, and I hated them for it, so don't follow their example. ²⁴ I am the LORD your God, and I have promised you their land that is rich with milk and honey. I have chosen you to be different from other people. ²⁵ That's why you must make a difference between animals and birds that I have said are clean and unclean* — this will keep you from becoming disgusting to me. ²⁶ I am the LORD, the holy God. You have been chosen to be my people, and so you must be holy too.

²⁷ If you claim to receive messages from the dead, you will be put to death by stoning, just as you deserve.

Rules for priests to follow

CHAPTER 21

¹ The LORD gave Moses these instructions for Aaron's sons, the priests:

Touching a dead body will make you unclean. So don't go near a dead relative, ² except your mother, father, son, daughter, brother, ³ or an unmarried sister, who has no husband to take care of her. ⁴ Don't make yourself unclean by attending the funeral of someone related to you by marriage.ᴵ ⁵ Don't shave any part of your head or trim your beard or cut yourself to show that you are mourning. ⁶ I am the LORD your God, and I have chosen you alone to offer sacrifices of food to me on the altar. That's why you must keep yourselves holy. ⁷ Don't marry a divorced woman or a woman who has served as a temple prostitute. You are holy, ⁸ because I am holy. And so, you must be treated with proper respect, since you offer food sacrifices to me, the God of holiness.

⁹ If any of you priests has a daughter who disgraces you by serving as a temple prostitute, she must be burnt to death.

¹⁰ If you are the high priest, you must not leave your hair uncombed or tear your clothes in order to mourn for the dead. ¹¹ Don't make yourself unclean by going near a dead body, not even that of your own father or mother. ¹² If you leave the sacred place to attend a funeral, both you and the sacred place become unclean, because you are the high priest.

¹³ If you are the high priest, you must marry only a virgin ¹⁴ from your own tribe. Don't marry a divorced woman or any other woman who has already had sex, including a temple prostitute. ¹⁵ In this way, your descendants will be qualified to serve me. Remember — I am the LORD, and I have chosen you.

¹⁶ The LORD told Moses ¹⁷⁻¹⁸ to say to Aaron:

No descendant of yours can ever serve as my priest if he is blind or lame, if his face is disfigured, if one leg is shorter than the other, ¹⁹ if either a foot or a hand is crippled, ²⁰ if he is a hunchback or a dwarf, if an eye or his skin is diseased, or if his testicles have been damaged. ²¹ These men may not serve as my priests and burn sacrifices to me. ²² They may eat the food offerings presented to me, ²³ but they may not enter the sacred place or serve me at the altar. Remember — I am the LORD, the one who makes a priest holy.

²⁴ Moses told all this to Aaron, his sons, and the people of Israel.

CHAPTER 22

The offerings are holy

¹ The LORD told Moses ² to say to Aaron and his sons:

I am the LORD God, and I demand that you honour my holy name by showing proper respect for the offerings brought to me by the people of Israel. ³ If any of you are unclean when you accept an offering for me, I will no longer let you serve as a priest. ⁴ None of you may take part in the sacred meals while you have a skin disease or an infected penis, or after you have been near a dead body or have had a flow of semen, ⁵ or if you have touched an unclean creature of any sort, including an unclean person. ⁶⁻⁷ Once you are unclean, you must

*20.21 And . . . children: According to Deuteronomy 25.5–6 a man was supposed to marry his brother's widow if his brother had died without having children. Otherwise, such marriages were forbidden (see also Matthew 22.23–33; Mark 12.18–27; Luke 20.27–40).
*20.25 clean and unclean: See the note at 11.4–8.
See also: 21.5: Lev 19.27–28; Deut 14.1.

take a bath, but you still cannot eat any of the sacred food until evening. ⁸ I command you not to eat anything that is killed by a wild animal or dies a natural death. This would make you unclean. ⁹ Obey me, or you will die on duty for disgracing the place of worship. Remember — I am the LORD, the one who makes a priest holy.

¹⁰ Only you priests and your families may eat the food offerings; these are too sacred for any of your servants. ¹¹ However, any slave that you own, including those born into your household, may eat this food. ¹² If your daughter marries someone who isn't a priest, she can no longer have any of this food. ¹³ But if she returns to your home, either widowed or divorced, and has no children, she may join in the meal. Only members of a priestly family can eat this food, ¹⁴ and anyone else who accidentally does so, must pay for the food plus a fine of twenty per cent.

¹⁵ I warn you not to treat lightly the offerings that are brought by the people of Israel. ¹⁶ Don't let them become guilty of eating this sacred food. Remember — I am the LORD, the one who makes these offerings holy.

Acceptable sacrifices

¹⁷ The LORD told Moses ¹⁸ to tell Aaron and his sons and everyone else the rules for offering sacrifices. He said:

The animals that are to be completely burnt on the altar ¹⁹⁻²⁰ must have nothing wrong with them, or else I won't accept them. Bulls or rams or goats' are the animals to be used for these sacrifices.

²¹ When you offer a sacrifice to ask my blessing,* there must be nothing wrong with the animal. This is true, whether the sacrifice is part of a promise or something you do voluntarily. ²² Don't offer an animal that is blind or injured or that has an infection or a skin disease. ²³ If one of your cattle or lambs has a leg that is longer or shorter than the others, you may offer it voluntarily, but not as part of a promise. ²⁴ As long as you live in this land, don't offer an animal with injured testicles. ²⁵ And don't bring me animals you bought from a foreigner. I won't accept them,

because they are no better than one that has something wrong with it.

²⁶ The LORD told Moses to say:

²⁷ Newborn cattle, sheep, or goats must remain with their mothers for seven days, but on the eighth day, you may send them up in smoke to me, and I will accept the offering. ²⁸ Don't sacrifice a newborn animal and its mother on the same day.

²⁹ When you offer a sacrifice to give thanks* to me, you must do it in a way that is acceptable. ³⁰ Eat all the meat that same day and don't save any for the next day. I am the LORD your God!

³¹ Obey my laws and teachings — I am the LORD. ³²⁻³³ I demand respect from the people of Israel, so don't disgrace my holy name. Remember — I am the one who chose you to be priests and rescued all of you from Egypt, so that I would be your LORD.

Instructions for religious festivals

CHAPTER 23

¹ The LORD told Moses ² to say to the community of Israel:

I have chosen certain times for you to come together and worship me.

³ You have six days when you can do your work, but the seventh day of each week is holy because it belongs to me. No matter where you live, you must rest on the Sabbath and come together for worship. This law will never change.

Passover and the Festival of Thin Bread

This is also told in Numbers 28.16-25

The LORD said:

⁴⁻⁵ Passover is another time when you must come together to worship me, and it must be celebrated on the evening of the fourteenth day of the first month* of each year.

⁶ The Festival of Thin Bread begins on the fifteenth day of that same month; it lasts

---

*22.29 sacrifice to give thanks: See 7.12.
*23.4-5 first month: Abib (also called Nisan), the first month of the Hebrew calendar, from about mid-March to mid-April.

See also: 23.3: Exod 20.8-10; 23.12; 31.15; 34.21; 35.2; Deut 5.12-14. 23.5: Exod 12.1-13; Deut 16.1-2. 23.6-8: Exod 12.14-20; 23.15; 34.18; Deut 16.3-8.

---

*22.21 sacrifice to ask my blessing: See the note at 3.1.
See also: 22.20: Deut 17.1.

seven days, and during this time you must honour me by eating bread made without yeast. ⁷ On the first day of this festival you must rest from your work and come together for worship. ⁸ Each day of this festival you must offer sacrifices. Then on the final day you must once again rest from your work and come together for worship.

Offering the first part of the harvest

⁹ The LORD told Moses ¹⁰ to say to the community of Israel:

After you enter the land I am giving you, the first bundle of wheat from each crop must be given to me. So bring it to a priest ¹¹ on the day after the Sabbath. He will lift it up⁾ in dedication to me, and I will accept you. ¹² You must also offer a sacrifice to please me.* So bring the priest a one-year-old lamb that has nothing wrong with it ¹³ and two kilogrammes of your finest flour mixed with olive oil. Then he will place these on the bronze altar and send them up in smoke with a smell that pleases me. Together with these, you must bring a litre of wine as a drink offering. ¹⁴ I am your God, and I forbid you to eat any new grain or anything made from it until you have brought these offerings. This law will never change.

The Harvest Festival

This is also told in Numbers 28.26–31

The LORD said:

¹⁵ Seven weeks after you offer this bundle of grain, each family must bring another offering of new grain. ¹⁶ Do this exactly fifty days later, which is the day following the seventh Sabbath. ¹⁷ Bring two loaves of bread to be lifted up⁾ in dedication to me. Each loaf is to be made with yeast and with two kilogrammes of the finest flour from the first part of your harvest. ¹⁸ At this same time, the entire community of Israel must bring seven lambs that are a year old, a young bull, and two rams. These animals must have nothing wrong with them, and they must be offered as a sacrifice to please me.* You must also offer the proper grain and wine sacrifices with each animal.* ¹⁹ Offer a

goat⁾ as a sacrifice for sin, and two rams a year old as a sacrifice to ask my blessing.* ²⁰ The priest will lift up⁾ the rams together with the bread in dedication to me. These offerings are holy and are my gift to the priest. ²¹ This is a day of celebration and worship, a time of rest from your work. You and your descendants must obey this law.

²² When you harvest your grain, always leave some of it standing around the edges of your fields and don't pick up what falls on the ground. Leave it for the poor and for those foreigners who live among you. I am the LORD your God!

The Festival of Trumpets

This is also told in Numbers 29.1–6

²³ The LORD told Moses ²⁴⁻²⁵ to say to the people of Israel:

The first day of the seventh month* must be a day of complete rest. Then at the sound of the trumpets, you will come together to worship and to offer sacrifices on the altar.

The Great Day of Forgiveness

This is also told in Numbers 29.7–11

²⁶ The LORD God said to Moses:

²⁷ The tenth day of the seventh month* is the Great Day of Forgiveness.* It is a solemn day of worship; everyone must go without eating to show sorrow for their sins, and sacrifices must be burnt. ²⁸ No one is to work on that day — it is the Great Day of Forgiveness, when sacrifices will be offered to me, so that I will forgive your sins. ²⁹ I will destroy anyone who refuses to go without eating. ³⁰⁻³¹ None of my people are ever to do any work on that day — not now or in the future. And I will wipe out those who do! ³² This is a time of complete rest just like the Sabbath, and everyone must go without eating from the evening of the ninth to the evening of the tenth.

23.12,18 sacrifice to please me: See the note at 1.1–3.
23.18 proper grain . . . animal: See Numbers 15.1–16.
See also: 23.15–21: Exod 23.16; 34.22; Deut 16.9–12.

23.19 sacrifice to ask my blessing: See the note at 3.1.
23.24–25,27 seventh month: See the note at 16.29.
23.27 Great Day of Forgiveness: See the note at 16.34.
See also: 23.22: Lev 19.9–10; Deut 24.19–22.
23.26–32: Lev 16.29–34.

Holy history

Feasts and festivals

Leviticus 16 and 23 list a number of festivals. These formed the backbone of the Israelite calendar. There were three main festivals: Passover, Pentecost and Atonement. The following list is in calendar order.

Passover (Leviticus 23.4–5)

What's it for? Commemorating the rescuing of the Israelites from Egypt.

How long does it last? One evening.

When does it take place? First month.

What do I have to do? Cook lamb and eat it.

Festival of Thin Bread (Leviticus 23.6–8)

What's it for? Commemorating the speedy exit of the Israelites from Egypt.

How long does it last? Seven days.

When does it take place? First month, starting the day after Passover.

What do I have to do? Eat unleavened bread.

First Harvest (Leviticus 23.9–14)

a.k.a. First Fruits

What's it for? Commemorating the LORD's provision for his people.

How long does it last? One day.

When does it take place? The first Sabbath after the wheat harvest.

What do I have to do? Bring the first bundle of wheat from the harvest and dedicate it to the LORD. Sacrifice a lamb, four pounds of flour and some wine.

Harvest Festival (Leviticus 23.15–22; Numbers 28.26–31)

a.k.a. Pentecost; The Feast of Weeks

What's it for? Celebrating the main harvest.

How long does it last? One day.

When does it take place? Fifty days after the First Harvest.

What do I have to do? Bring two loaves of bread and dedicate them to the LORD. The entire community of Israel has to sacrifice seven lambs, a young bull and two rams. Plus some wine. Plus a goat as a sacrifice for in and two rams for God's blessing.

The Festival of Trumpets (Leviticus 23.23–25)

What's it for? A third harvest festival, later in the year, commemorating the LORD's provision.

How long does it last? One day.

When does it take place? First day of the seventh month.

What do I have to do? Rest, then, when the trumpets sound, join with others to worship the LORD.

The Great Day of Forgiveness (Leviticus 16.1–34; 23.26–32)

a.k.a. the Day of Atonement

What's it for? Asking for forgiveness of Israel's sins. A day of national fasting and repentance.

How long does it last? One day.

When does it take place? Tenth day, seventh month.

What do I have to do? Fast and repent. Offer sacrifices for forgiveness of sins.

Festival of Shelters (Leviticus 23.33–44)

a.k.a. The Feast of Tabernacles

What's it for? A thanksgiving and celebration of Israel's wanderings in the desert.

How long does it last? 8 days.

When does it take place? The seventh month.

What do I have to do? Live in a tent for seven days and offer up the best fruit from your trees.

More...

Passover p.76

The Festival of Shelters
This is also told in Numbers 29.12–40

33 The LORD told Moses 34 to say to the community of Israel:

Beginning on the fifteenth day of the seventh month,* and continuing for seven days, everyone must celebrate the Festival of Shelters in honour of me. 35 No one is to do any work on the first day of the festival — it is a time when everyone must come together for worship. 36 For seven days, sacrifices must be offered on the altar. The eighth day is also to be a day of complete rest, as well as a time of offering sacrifices on the altar and of coming together for worship.

37 I have chosen these festivals as times when my people must come together for worship and when animals, grain, and wine are to be offered on the proper days. 38 These festivals must be celebrated in addition to the Sabbaths and the times when you offer special gifts or sacrifices to keep a promise or as a voluntary offering.

39 Remember to begin the Festival of Shelters on the fifteenth day of the seventh month after you have harvested your crops. Celebrate this festival for seven days in honour of me and don't do any work on the first day or on the day following the festival. 40 Pick the best fruit from your trees' and cut leafy branches to use during the time of this joyous celebration in my honour. 41 I command you and all your descendants to celebrate this festival during the seventh month of each year. 42 For seven days every Israelite must live in a shelter, 43 so future generations will know that I made their ancestors live in shelters when I brought them out of Egypt. I am the LORD your God.

44 This is how Moses instructed the people of Israel to celebrate the LORD's festivals.

CHAPTER 24

Caring for the lamps
This is also told in Exodus 27.20–21

1 The LORD told Moses 2 to say to the community of Israel:

You must supply the purest olive oil for the lamps in the sacred tent, so they will keep burning. 3-4 Aaron will set up the gold lampstand in the holy place of the sacred tent. Then he will light the seven lamps that must be kept burning there in my presence, every night from now on. This law will never change.

The sacred bread
The LORD said:

5 Use your finest flour to bake twelve loaves of bread about two kilogrammes each, 6 then take them into the sacred tent and lay them on the gold table in two rows of six loaves. 7 Beside each row put some pure incense that will be sent up by fire in place of the bread as an offering to me. 8 Aaron must lay fresh loaves on the table each Sabbath, and priests in all generations must continue this practice as part of Israel's agreement with me. 9 This bread will always belong to Aaron and his family; it is very holy because it was offered to me, and it must be eaten in a holy place.*

Punishment for cursing the LORD
10-11 Shelomith, the daughter of Dibri from the tribe of Dan, had married an Egyptian, and they had a son. One day their son got into a fight with an Israelite man in camp and cursed the name of the LORD. So the young man was dragged off to Moses, 12 who had him guarded while everyone waited for the LORD to tell them what to do.

13 Finally, the LORD said to Moses:

14 This man has cursed me! Take him outside the camp and make the witnesses lay their hands on his head. Then command the whole community of Israel to stone him to death. 15-16 And warn the others that everyone else who curses me will die in the same way, whether they are Israelites by birth or foreigners living among you.

17 Death is also the penalty for murder, 18 but the killing of an animal that belongs to someone else requires only that the animal be replaced. 19 Personal injuries to others must be dealt with in keeping with the crime — 20 a broken bone for a broken bone, an eye for an eye, or a tooth for a

*24.9 holy place:** See the note at 7.6.
See also: 24.5–6: Exod 25.30. 24.9: Matt 12.4; Mark 2.26; Luke 6.4. 24.17: Exod 21.12. 24.20: Exod 21.23–25; Deut 19.21; Matt 5.38.

*23.34 seventh month:** See the note at 16.29.
See also: 23.33–36: Deut 16.13–15.

tooth. ²¹ It's possible to pay the owner for an animal that has been killed, but death is the penalty for murder. ²² I am the LORD your God, and I demand equal justice both for you Israelites and for those foreigners who live among you.

²³ When Moses finished speaking, the people did what the LORD had told Moses, and they stoned to death the man who had cursed the LORD.

CHAPTER 25

The seventh year

This is also told in Deuteronomy 15.1–11

¹ When Moses was on Mount Sinai, the LORD told him ² to say to the community of Israel:

After you enter the land that I am giving you, it must be allowed to rest one year out of every seven. ³ You may raise grain and grapes for six years, ⁴ but the seventh year you must let your fields and vineyards rest in honour of me, your LORD. ⁵ This is to be a time of complete rest for your fields and vineyards, so don't harvest anything they produce. ⁶⁻⁷ However, you and your slaves and your hired workers, as well as any domestic or wild animals, may eat whatever grows on its own.

The Year of Celebration

The LORD said to his people:

⁸ Once every forty-nine years ⁹ on the tenth day of the seventh month,* which is also the Great Day of Forgiveness,* trumpets are to be blown everywhere in the land. ¹⁰ This fiftieth year* is sacred — it is a time of freedom and of celebration when everyone will receive back their original property, and slaves will return home to their families. ¹¹ This is a year of complete celebration, so don't plant any seed or harvest what your fields or vineyards produce. ¹² In this time of sacred celebration you may eat only what grows on its own.

¹³ During this year, all property must go back to its original owner. ¹⁴⁻¹⁵ So when you buy or sell farmland, the price is to be determined by the number of crops it can produce before the next Year of Celebration. Don't try to cheat. ¹⁶ If it is a long time before the next Year of Celebration, the price will be higher, because what is really being sold are the crops that the land can produce. ¹⁷ I am the LORD your God, so obey me and don't cheat anyone.

¹⁸⁻¹⁹ If you obey my laws and teachings, you will live safely in the land and enjoy its abundant crops. ²⁰ Don't ever worry about what you will eat during the seventh year when you are forbidden to plant or harvest. ²¹ I will see to it that you harvest enough in the sixth year to last for three years. ²² In the eighth year you will live on what you harvested in the sixth year, but in the ninth year you will eat what you plant and harvest in the eighth year.

²³ No land may be permanently bought or sold. It all belongs to me — it isn't your land, and you only live there for a little while.

²⁴ When property is being sold, the original owner must be given the first chance to buy it.

²⁵ If any of you Israelites become so poor that you are forced to sell your property, your closest relative must buy it back, ²⁶ if that relative has the money. Later, if you can afford to buy it, ²⁷ you must pay enough to make up for what the present owner will lose on it before the next Year of Celebration, when the property would become yours again. ²⁸ But if you don't have the money to pay the present owner a fair price, you will have to wait until the Year of Celebration, when the property will once again become yours.

²⁹ If you sell a house in a walled city, you have only one year in which to buy it back. ³⁰ If you don't buy it back before that year is up, it becomes the permanent property of the one who bought it, and it will not be returned to you in the Year of Celebration. ³¹ But a house out in a village may be bought back at any time just like a field. And it must be returned to its original owner in the Year of Celebration. ³² If any Levites own houses inside a walled city, they will always have the right to buy them back. ³³ And any houses that they do not buy back will be returned to them in the Year of Celebration, because these homes

---

*25.9 seventh month: See the note at 16.29.
*25.9 Great Day of Forgiveness: See the note at 16.34.
*25.10 fiftieth year: The year following seven periods of seven years.

See also: 24.22: Num 15.16. 25.1–7: Exod 23.10–11.

are their permanent property among the people of Israel. [34] No pasture land owned by the Levi tribe can ever be sold; it is their permanent possession.

Help for the poor

The LORD said:

[35] If any of your people become poor and unable to support themselves, you must help them, just as you are supposed to help foreigners who live among you. [36-37] Don't take advantage of them by charging any kind of interest or selling them food for profit. Instead, honour me by letting them stay where they now live. [38] Remember — I am the LORD your God! I rescued you from Egypt and gave you the land of Canaan, so that I would be your God.

[39] Suppose some of your people become so poor that they have to sell themselves and become your slaves. [40] Then you must treat them as servants, rather than as slaves. And in the Year of Celebration they are to be set free, [41] so they and their children may return home to their families and property. [42] I brought them out of Egypt to be my servants, not to be sold as slaves. [43] So obey me, and don't be cruel to the poor.

[44] If you want slaves, buy them from other nations [45] or from the foreigners who live in your own country, and make them your property. [46] You can own them, and even leave them to your children when you die, but do not make slaves of your own people or be cruel to them.

[47] Even if some of you Israelites become so much in debt that you must sell yourselves to foreigners in your country, [48] you still have the right to be set free by a relative, such as a brother [49] or uncle or cousin, or some other family member. In fact, if you ever get enough money, you may buy your own freedom [50] by paying your owner for the number of years you would still be a slave before the next Year of Celebration. [51-52] The longer the time until then, the more you will have to pay. [53] And even while you are the slaves of foreigners in your own country, your people must make sure that you are not ill-treated. [54] If you cannot gain your freedom in any of these ways, both you and your children will still be set free in

See also: **25.35:** Deut 15.7–8. **25.37:** Exod 22.25; Deut 23.19–20. **25.39–46:** Exod 21.2–6; Deut 15.12–18.

Big ideas

Jubilee – the year of celebration

Leviticus contains one of the most amazing pieces of social law in history. Every seven years the land was allowed a year off. And every fiftieth year – that is, after seven lots of seven years – the entire social structure of Israel was to be reset.

The Seventh Year

This was a chance for the land to recover. All gardeners and farmers know that you have to let the land recover, you can't just keep growing the same stuff and taking nourishment from the soil forever.

The seven-year rule also applied to other things. Hebrew slaves were only to be kept for six years; in the seventh year they were to be freed (Exodus 21.2). Debts were also to be cancelled (Deuteronomy 15.1–11).

The year of celebration

And then after fifty years, it was time for the big celebration. A kind of 'Sabbath of Sabbaths', in which most of the property (although not houses inside walled cities) was to revert to its original owners (Leviticus 25.18–34). Slaves would be released and could return to their homes. Everyone, no matter what their status, would have the chance to start again. No matter how life had treated them or what misfortune had happened to them, in the jubilee year they could wipe the slate clean and start again. It's like pressing the reset button on your computer. It sets everything back to how it was when you first unpacked the thing.

Not surprisingly, this rule was hardly ever obeyed. The only time in the Bible that it is reported as occurring, the slaves were freed – and then immediately taken back into slavery (Jeremiah 34.8–22).

More...

Ten Commandments p.85
Sabbath p.97
Globalisation p.199
Fair trade p.923
Environment p.6

the Year of Celebration. 55 People of Israel, I am the LORD your God, and I brought you out of Egypt to be my own servants.

Blessings and punishments

CHAPTER 26

Blessings for obeying the LORD

The LORD said:

1 I am the LORD your God! So don't make or worship any sort of idols or images. 2 Respect the Sabbath and honour the place where I am worshipped, because I am the LORD. 3 Faithfully obey my laws, 4 and I will send rain to make your crops grow and your trees produce fruit. 5 Your harvest of grain and grapes will be so abundant, that you won't know what to do with it all. You will eat and be satisfied, and you will live in safety. 6 I will bless your country with peace, and you will rest without fear. I will wipe out the dangerous animals and protect you from enemy attacks. 7 You will chase and destroy your enemies, 8 even if there are only five of you and a hundred of them, or only a hundred of you and ten thousand of them. 9 I will treat you with such kindness that your nation will grow strong, and I will also keep my promises to you. 10 Your barns will overflow with grain each year. 11 I will live among you and never again look on you with disgust. 12 I will walk with you — I will be your God, and you will be my people. 13 I am the LORD your God, and I rescued you from Egypt, so that you would never again be slaves. I have set you free; now walk with your heads held high.

Punishment for disobeying the LORD

The LORD said:

14-15 If you disobey me and my laws, and if you break our agreement, 16 I will punish you terribly, and you will be ruined. You will be struck with incurable diseases and with fever that leads to blindness and depression. Your enemies will eat the crops you plant, 17 and I will turn from you and let you be destroyed by your attackers. You will even run at the very rumour of attack.

18 Then, if you still refuse to obey me, I will punish you seven times for each of your sins, 19 until your pride is completely crushed. I will hold back the rain, so the sky above you will be like iron, and the ground beneath your feet will be like copper. 20 All your hard work will be for nothing — and there will be no harvest of grain or fruit.

21 If you keep rebelling against me, I'll punish you seven times worse, just as your sins deserve! 22 I'll send wild animals to attack you, and they will gobble up your children and livestock. So few of you will be left that your roads will be deserted.

23 If you remain my enemies after this, 24 I'll remain your enemy and punish you even worse. 25 War will break out because you broke our agreement, and if you escape to your walled cities, I'll punish you with horrible diseases, and you will be captured by your enemies. 26 You will have such a shortage of bread, that ten women will be able to bake their bread in the same oven. Each of you will get only a few crumbs, and you will go hungry.

27 Then if you don't stop rebelling, 28 I'll really get furious and punish you terribly for your sins! 29 In fact, you will be so desperate for food that you will eat your own children. 30 I'll destroy your shrines and tear down your incense altars, leaving your dead bodies piled on top of your idols. And you will be disgusting to me. 31 I'll wipe out your towns and your places of worship and will no longer be pleased with the smell of your sacrifices. 32 Your land will become so desolate that even your enemies who settle there will be shocked when they see it. 33 After I destroy your towns and ruin your land with war, I'll scatter you among the nations.

34-35 While you are prisoners in foreign lands, your own land will enjoy years of rest and refreshment, as it should have done each seventh year when you lived there. 36-37 In the land of your enemies, you will tremble at the rustle of a leaf, as though it were a sword. And you will become so weak that you will stumble and fall over each other, even when no one is chasing you. 38 Many of you will die in foreign lands, 39 and others of you will waste away in sorrow as the result of your sins and the sins of your ancestors.

40-41 Then suppose you realize that I turned against you and brought you to the

See also: 26.1: a Lev 19.4; b Exod 20.4; Deut 5.8; 16.21–22; 27.1. 26.3–5: Deut 11.13–15; 28.1–14. 26.12: 2 Cor 6.16. 26.14–33: Deut 28.15–68.

Viewpoints

He's beside you in good times and bad

Contributed by Megan T

'I will walk with you – I will be your God, and you will be my people.'

Verses like this always blow me away; I love the idea of God as a father figure who is welcoming us to him, telling us that we are his people, his children. It's really mind-boggling that a God so holy, so pure, so righteous would call us his children and accept us as his people. I don't know about you, but reading this verse makes me feel so privileged that we, out of all God's creations, we're chosen to be his people, we are his chosen ones! How exciting is that?! And this applies to each and every one of us, it applies to YOU.

So often we can read verses and we think, 'Wow, that's really cool, but it's not for me' and yet God meant it for all of us, for you. He wants you, personally, to be one of his people and he wants to walk with you and be involved with you. He wants to walk with you! Think about it people, this is God we are talking about here... GOD!! The Creator of the Universe wants and desires a relationship with you, he wants to be beside you through the good and the bad, to walk with you hand-in-hand.

Now ask yourself this; do you want the same relationship with him? Do you want to walk hand-in-hand with the creator of the universe?! I know I do!

More...

Suffering p.555
Ever had those days when you just can't keep going? p.528
God's love p.958

land of your enemies because both you and your ancestors had stubbornly sinned against me. If you humbly confess what you have done and start living right, 42 I'll keep the promise I made to your ancestors Abraham, Isaac, and Jacob. I will bless your land 43 and let it rest during the time that you are in a foreign country, paying for your rebellion against me and my laws.

44 No matter what you have done, I am still the LORD your God, and I will never completely reject you or become absolutely disgusted with you there in the land of your enemies. 45 While nations watched, I rescued your ancestors from Egypt so that I would be their God. Yes, I am your LORD, and I will never forget our agreement.

46 Moses was on Mount Sinai when the LORD gave him these laws and teachings for the people of Israel.

Laws about promises and offerings to the Lord

CHAPTER 27

Making promises to the LORD

1 The LORD told Moses 2 to say to the community of Israel:

If you ever want to free someone who has been promised to me, 3-7 you may do so by paying the following amounts, weighed according to the official standards:

fifty pieces of silver for men
  aged twenty to sixty,
and thirty pieces for women;
twenty pieces of silver
  for young men
  aged five to twenty,
and ten pieces
  for young women;
fifteen pieces of silver for men
  aged sixty and above
  and ten pieces for women;
five pieces of silver for boys
  aged one month to five years,
  and three pieces for girls.

8 If you have promised to give someone to me and can't afford to pay the full amount for that person's release, you will be taken

See also: 26.42: a Gen 28.13–14; **b** Gen 26.3–4; **c** Gen 17.7–8.

to a priest, and he will decide how much you can afford.

⁹ If you promise to sacrifice an animal to me, it becomes holy, and there is no way you can set it free. ¹⁰ If you try to substitute any other animal, no matter how good, for the one you promised, they will both become holy and must be sacrificed. ¹¹ Donkeys are unfit for sacrifice, so if you promise me a donkey,* you must bring it to the priest, ¹² and let him determine its value. ¹³ But if you want to buy it back, you must pay an additional twenty per cent.

¹⁴ If you promise a house to me, a priest will set the price, whatever the condition of the house. ¹⁵ But if you decide to buy it back, you must pay an additional twenty per cent.

¹⁶ If you promise part of your family's land to me, its value must be determined by the amount of seed needed to plant the land, and the rate will be ten pieces of silver for every twenty kilogrammes of seed. ¹⁷ If this promise is made in the Year of Celebration,* the land will be valued at the full price. ¹⁸ But any time after that, the price will be worked out according to the number of years before the next Year of Celebration. ¹⁹ If you decide to buy back the land, you must pay the price plus an additional twenty per cent, ²⁰ but you cannot buy it back once someone else has bought it. ²¹ When the Year of Celebration comes, the land becomes holy because it belongs to me, and it will be given to the priests.

²² If you promise me a field that you have bought, ²³ its value will be decided by a priest, according to the number of years before the next Year of Celebration, and the money you pay will be mine. ²⁴ However, on the next Year of Celebration, the land will go back to the family of its original owner. ²⁵ Every price will be set by the official standards.

Various offerings

The LORD said:

²⁶ All firstborn animals of your flocks and herds are already mine, and so you cannot promise any of them to me. ²⁷ If you promise me a donkey,* you may buy it back by adding an additional twenty per cent to its value. If you don't buy it back, it can be sold to someone else for whatever a priest has said it is worth.

²⁸ Anything that you completely dedicate to me must be completely destroyed.* It cannot be bought back or sold. Every person, animal, and piece of property that you dedicate completely is only for me. ²⁹ In fact, any humans who have been promised to me in this way must be put to death.

³⁰ Ten per cent of everything you harvest is holy and belongs to me, whether it grows in your fields or on your fruit trees. ³¹ If you want to buy back this part of your harvest, you may do so by paying what it is worth plus an additional twenty per cent.

³² When you count your flocks and herds, one out of ten of every newborn animal' is holy and belongs to me, ³³ no matter how good or bad it is. If you substitute one animal for another, both of them become holy, and neither can be bought back.

³⁴ Moses was on Mount Sinai when the LORD gave him these laws for the people of Israel.

---

*27.27 donkey: See the note at verse 11.
*27.28 completely dedicate . . . completely destroyed: In order to show that something belonged completely to the LORD and could not be used by anyone else, it was destroyed. This law most often applied to towns and people captured in war (see Joshua 6.16–17).
See also: 27.28: Num 18.14. 27.30–33: Num 18.21; Deut 14.22–29.

Additional notes

'1.1–3 goats: Hebrew "male goats".
'1.1–3 if it is: Or "if you are".
'1.16 with what is in it: One possible meaning for the difficult Hebrew text.
'1.17 tear it partially open: Or "tear it open without pulling off the wings".
'2.12 You . . . separately: One possible meaning for the difficult Hebrew text.
'2.14 either . . . ground: Or "roasted and coarsely ground".
'3.17 not even . . . homes: Or "no matter where you live".
'4.23 goat: See the note at 1.1–3.
'6.18 and they . . . touching it: One possible meaning for the difficult Hebrew text.
'6.21 crumbled . . . pieces: One possible meaning for the difficult Hebrew text.

---

*27.11 Donkeys . . . donkey: The Hebrew text has "If you promise me an unclean animal", which probably refers to a donkey (see Exodus 13.13; 34.20).
*27.17 Year of Celebration: See 25.8–34.

›**6.27 that touches . . . holy:** One possible meaning for the difficult Hebrew text.
›**7.29–30 lift up:** Or "wave".
›**8.27 lifted it up:** See the note at 7.29–30.
›**8.29 lifted up:** See the note at 7.29–30.
›**8.34 forgiven:** One possible meaning for the difficult Hebrew text of verse 34.
›**9.3 goat:** See the note at 1.1–3.
›**9.21 lifted up:** See the note at 7.29–30.
›**10.1 when they . . . to:** One possible meaning for the difficult Hebrew text.
›**10.14–15 lifted up:** See the note at 7.29–30.
›**11.13–19 Eagles . . . hoopoes:** Some of the birds in this list are difficult to identify.
›**14.12 lift them up:** See the note at 7.29–30.
›**14.21 lift these up:** See the note at 7.29–30.
›**14.24–25 lift it up:** See the note at 7.29–30.
›**19.16 but never . . . someone's life:** One possible meaning for the difficult Hebrew text.
›**19.20 time:** One possible meaning for the difficult Hebrew text of verse 20.
›**21.4 marriage:** One possible meaning for the difficult Hebrew text of verse 4.
›**22.19–20 goats:** See the note at 1.1–3.
›**23.11 lift it up:** See the note at 7.29–30.
›**23.17 lifted up:** See the note at 7.29–30.
›**23.19 goat:** See the note at 1.1–3.
›**23.20 lift up:** See the note at 7.29–30.
›**23.40 best fruit from your trees:** One possible meaning for the difficult Hebrew text.
›**27.32 one out of ten of every newborn animal:** Or "one out of every ten animals".

Numbers

The basics

What's the point? Rebellion against God will always leave you in the wilderness.

What happens? Israel's lack of faith culminates in their failure to believe that God will help them win the Promised Land. Accordingly, they are punished by God and they spend forty years wandering in the desert. The book ends with them on the brink of the Promised Land again.

What should I remember? 14.22–3 'I swear that not one of these Israelites will enter the land I promised to give their ancestors. These people have seen my power in Egypt and in the desert, but they will never see Canaan. They have disobeyed and tested me too many times.'

More detail

Setting the scene Numbers takes up the action immediately after Israel has escaped from Egypt. After the giving of the Law and the creation of the tabernacle at Sinai, the Israelites marched out to conquer the Promised Land. Or not...

What's it all about? It's a book of numbers. And here are a few to get you started: 6,42,317, the square root of 97.2...

Oh all right, it's not those kind of numbers. But the title does tell you most of what you need to know. This is largely a book of statistics and accounts. It's a list of families and tribes, of how many people there were in them and even the order in which they were marching.

At times, therefore, reading this book is a bit like browsing through a telephone directory, but it's worth persevering, because there are lots of exciting bits in there. No, really. And one of the key points to remember about this book – and about all of the Bible – is that it comes from God. Nearly every section of Numbers begins 'The LORD said,' or 'The LORD told Moses'. This book is about how God stayed with his people and continued to guide them in the wilderness.

Because most of this book takes place in the desert. Perhaps the Hebrew title 'Bemidbar' is more exciting; it means, 'in the desert'. Along with all the statistics, Numbers tells the story of Israel's journey to the edge of the promised land.

Along the way we see their initial failure, their grumbling and moaning and God's judgement on their faithlessness and disobedience. We see the jealousy of Moses' family, the conflict with the Moabites and the strange tale of Balaam and his incredible talking donkey.

We see the people travel quickly to the very edge of the land God had promised them, before chickening out – a lack of nerve which resulted in them spending years in the desert. We even see Moses' disobedience, and God's decision that he, too, will not enter the Promised Land.

They got their act together in the end, though. Exodus tells us how the Israelites became worshippers; Numbers shows us how they became warriors. Because the third bit of the book – after all those lists and after their rebellion on the border – tells of the Israelites' conquering the land to the east of the Jordan river, fighting battles against enemies such as the Moabites, and preparing at last to enter the promised land.

So there is a lot more in Numbers than just, well, a load of numbers.

And another thing

There is a lot of debate about the numbers in the book. The problem is that, if the figures are correct, then the Israelites would have had a total population of over 2,000,000 people – a bit tricky considering the fact that they were marching through the desert. Some argue that these numbers are literally true; some that the numbers represent the total number of people born since leaving Egypt. Other experts argue that the numbers are symbolic. Whatever the answer, we can be certain of two things: this was a nation on the move and God was looking after them.

Footsteps

The people of Israel are counted

CHAPTER 1

¹ The people of Israel had left Egypt and were living in the Sinai Desert. Then on the first day of the second month* of the second year, Moses was in the sacred tent when the LORD said:

²⁻³ I want you and Aaron to find out how many people are in each of Israel's clans and families. And make a list of all the men twenty years and older who are able to fight in battle. ⁴⁻¹⁵ The following twelve family leaders, one from each tribe, will help you:

Elizur son of Shedeur from Reuben,
Shelumiel son of Zurishaddai
  from Simeon,
Nahshon son of Amminadab
  from Judah,

*1.1 second month: Ziv, the second month of the Hebrew calendar, from about mid-April to mid-May.
See also: 1.1–46: Num 26.1–51.

Nethanel son of Zuar from Issachar,
Eliab son of Helon from Zebulun,
Elishama son of Ammihud
  from Ephraim,
Gamaliel son of Pedahzur
  from Manasseh,
Abidan son of Gideoni from Benjamin,
Ahiezer son of Ammishaddai from Dan,
Pagiel son of Ochran from Asher,
Eliasaph son of Deuel from Gad,
and Ahira son of Enan from Naphtali.

¹⁶⁻¹⁷ Moses and Aaron, together with these twelve tribal leaders, ¹⁸ called together the people that same day. They were counted according to their clans and families. Then Moses and the others listed the names of the men twenty years and older, ¹⁹ just as the LORD had commanded. ²⁰⁻⁴⁶ The number of men from each tribe who were at least twenty years old and strong enough to fight in Israel's army was as follows:

46,500 from Reuben,
  the eldest son of Jacob,'
59,300 from Simeon,
45,650 from Gad,
74,600 from Judah,
54,400 from Issachar,
57,400 from Zebulun,
40,500 from Ephraim,
32,200 from Manasseh,
35,400 from Benjamin,
62,700 from Dan,
41,500 from Asher,
53,400 from Naphtali.

The total number of men registered by Moses, Aaron, and the twelve leaders was 603,550. ⁴⁷ But those from the Levi tribe were not included ⁴⁸ because the LORD had said to Moses:

⁴⁹ When you count the Israelites, do not include those from the Levi tribe. ⁵⁰⁻⁵¹ Instead, give them the job of caring for the sacred tent, its furnishings, and the objects used for worship. They will camp around the tent, and whenever you move, they will take it down, carry it to the new camp, and set it up again. Anyone else who tries to go near it must be put to death. ⁵² The rest of the Israelites will camp in their own groups and under their own banners. ⁵³ But the Levites will camp around the sacred tent to make sure that no one goes near it and makes me furious with the Israelites.

[54] The people of Israel did everything the LORD had commanded.

CHAPTER 2

Instructions for setting up Israel's camp

[1] The LORD told Moses and Aaron [2] how the Israelites should arrange their camp:

Each tribe must set up camp under its own banner and under the flags of its ancestral families. These camps will be arranged around the sacred tent, but not close to it.

[3-4] Judah and the tribes that march with it must set up camp on the east side of the sacred tent, under their own banner. The 74,600 troops of the tribe of Judah will be arranged by divisions and led by Nahshon son of Amminadab. [5-6] On one side of Judah will be the tribe of Issachar, with Nethanel son of Zuar as the leader of its 54,400 troops. [7-8] On the other side will be the tribe of Zebulun, with Eliab son of Helon as the leader of its 57,400 troops. [9] These 186,400 troops will march into battle first.

[10-11] Reuben and the tribes that march with it must set up camp on the south side of the sacred tent, under their own banner. The 46,500 troops of the tribe of Reuben will be arranged by divisions and led by Elizur son of Shedeur. [12-13] On one side of Reuben will be the tribe of Simeon, with Shelumiel son of Zurishaddai as the leader of its 59,300 troops. [14-15] On the other side will be the tribe of Gad, with Eliasaph son of Deuel as the leader of its 45,650 troops. [16] These 151,450 troops will march into battle second.

[17] Marching behind Reuben will be the Levites, arranged in groups, just as they are camped. They will carry the sacred tent and their own banners.

[18-19] Ephraim and the tribes that march with it must set up camp on the west side of the sacred tent, under their own banner. The 40,500 troops of the tribe of Ephraim will be arranged by divisions and led by Elishama son of Ammihud. [20-21] On one side of Ephraim will be the tribe of Manasseh, with Gamaliel son of Pedahzur as the leader of its 32,200 troops. [22-23] On the other side will be the tribe of Benjamin, with Abidan son of Gideoni as the leader of its 35,400 troops. [24] These 108,100 troops will march into battle third.

[25-26] Dan and the tribes that march with it must set up camp on the north side of the sacred tent, under their own banner. The 62,700 troops of the tribe of Dan will be arranged by divisions and led by Ahiezer son of Ammishaddai. [27-28] On one side of Dan will be the tribe of Asher, with Pagiel son of Ochran as the leader of its 41,500 troops. [29-30] On the other side will be the tribe of Naphtali with Ahira son of Enan as the leader of its 53,400 troops. [31] These 157,600 troops will march into battle last.

[32] So all the Israelites in the camp were counted according to their ancestral families. The troops were arranged by divisions and totalled 603,550. [33] The only Israelites not included were the Levites, just as the LORD had commanded Moses.

[34] Israel did everything the LORD had told Moses. They arranged their camp according to clans and families, with each tribe under its own banner. And that was the order by which they marched into battle.

CHAPTER 3

The sons of Aaron

[1] When the LORD talked with Moses on Mount Sinai, [2] Aaron's four sons, Nadab, Abihu, Eleazar, and Ithamar, [3] were the ones to be ordained as priests. [4] But the LORD killed Nadab and Abihu in the Sinai Desert when they used fire that was unacceptable' in their offering to the LORD.* And because Nadab and Abihu had no sons, only Eleazar and Ithamar served as priests with their father Aaron.

The duties of the Levites

[5] The LORD said to Moses:

[6] Assign the Levi tribe to Aaron the priest. They will be his assistants [7] and will work at the sacred tent for him and for all the Israelites. [8] The Levites will serve the community by being responsible for the furnishings of the tent. [9] They are assigned to help Aaron and his sons, [10] who have been appointed to be priests. Anyone else who tries to perform the duties of a priest must be put to death.

[11-13] Moses, I have chosen these Levites from all Israel, and they will belong to me in a special way. When I killed the

---

*3.4 the LORD killed Nadab and Abihu . . . to the LORD: See Leviticus 10.1-2.

See also: 3.2: Num 26.60. 3.4: Lev 10.1-2; Num 26.61. 3.13: Exod 13.2.

firstborn sons of the Egyptians, I decided that the firstborn sons in every Israelite family and the firstborn males of their flocks and herds would be mine.* But now I accept these Levites in place of the firstborn sons of the Israelites.

The Levites are counted

¹⁴ In the Sinai Desert the LORD said to Moses, ¹⁵ "Now I want you to count the men and boys in the Levi tribe by families and by clans. Include every one at least a month old." ¹⁶ So Moses obeyed and counted them.

¹⁷ Levi's three sons, Gershon, Kohath, and Merari, had become the heads of their own clans. ¹⁸ Gershon's sons were Libni and Shimei. ¹⁹ Kohath's sons were Amram, Izhar, Hebron, and Uzziel. ²⁰ And Merari's sons were Mahli and Mushi. These were the sons and grandsons of Levi, and they had become the leaders of the Levite clans.

²¹ The two Gershon clans were the Libnites and Shimeites, ²² and they had seven thousand five hundred men and boys at least one month old. ²³ The Gershonites were to camp on the west side of the sacred tent, ²⁴ under the leadership of Eliasaph son of Lael. ²⁵ Their duties at the tent included taking care of the tent itself, along with its outer covering, the curtain for the entrance, ²⁶ the curtains hanging inside the courtyard around the tent, as well as the curtain and ropes for the entrance to the courtyard and its altar. The Gershonites were responsible for setting these things up and taking them down.

²⁷ The four Kohath clans were the Amramites, Izharites, Hebronites, and the Uzzielites, ²⁸ and they had eight thousand six hundred᾿ men and boys at least one month old. ²⁹ The Kohathites were to camp on the south side of the sacred tent, ³⁰ under the leadership of Elizaphan son of Uzziel. ³¹ Their duties at the tent included taking care of the sacred chest, the table for the sacred bread, the lampstand, the altars, the objects used for worship, and the curtain in front of the most holy place. The Kohathites were responsible for setting these things up and taking them down.

³² Eleazar son of Aaron was the head of the Levite leaders, and he made sure that the work at the sacred tent was done.

³³ The two Merari clans were the Mahlites and the Mushites, ³⁴ and they had six thousand two hundred men and boys at least one month old. ³⁵ The Merarites were to camp on the north side of the sacred tent, under the leadership of Zuriel son of Abihail. ³⁶⁻³⁷ Their duties included taking care of the tent frames and the pieces that held the tent up: the bars, the posts, the stands, and its other equipment. They were also in charge of the posts that supported the courtyard, as well as their stands, tent pegs, and ropes. The Merari clans were responsible for setting these things up and taking them down.

³⁸ Moses, Aaron, and his sons were to camp in front of the sacred tent, on the east side, and to make sure that the Israelites worshipped in the proper way. Anyone else who tried to do the work of Moses and Aaron was to be put to death.

³⁹ So Moses and Aaron obeyed the LORD and counted the Levites by their clans. The total number of Levites at least one month old was twenty-two thousand.

The Levites are accepted as substitutes for the firstborn sons

⁴⁰ The LORD said to Moses, "Make a list and count the firstborn sons at least one month old in each of the Israelite families. ⁴¹ They belong to me, but I will accept the Levites as substitutes for them, and I will accept the Levites' livestock as substitutes for the Israelites' firstborn livestock."

⁴² Moses obeyed the LORD and counted the firstborn sons; ⁴³ there were 22,273 of them.

⁴⁴ Then the LORD said, ⁴⁵ "The Levites will belong to me and will take the place of the firstborn sons; their livestock will take the place of the Israelites' firstborn livestock. ⁴⁶ But since there are more firstborn sons than Levites, the extra two hundred and seventy-three men and boys must be bought back from me. ⁴⁷ For each one, you are to collect five pieces of silver, weighed according to the official standards. ⁴⁸ This money must then be given to Aaron and his sons."

⁴⁹ Moses collected the silver from the extra two hundred and seventy-three firstborn men and boys, ⁵⁰ and it amounted to one thousand three hundred and sixty-five pieces of silver, weighed according to the official standards. ⁵¹ Then he gave it to Aaron and his sons, just as the LORD had commanded.

---

*3.11–13 When I killed . . . mine: See Exodus 13.1–2,11–16.

CHAPTER 4

The duties of the Kohathite clans

¹ The LORD told Moses and Aaron:

²⁻³ Find out how many men between the ages of thirty and fifty are in the four Levite clans of Kohath. Count only those who are able to work at the sacred tent.

⁴ The Kohathites will be responsible for carrying the sacred objects used in worship at the sacred tent. ⁵ When the Israelites are ready to move their camp, Aaron and his sons will enter the tent and take down the curtain that separates the sacred chest from the rest of the tent. They will cover the chest with this curtain, ⁶ and then with a piece of fine leather, and cover it all with a solid blue cloth. After this they will put the carrying poles in place.

⁷ Next, Aaron and his sons will use another cloth to cover the table for the sacred bread.* On the cloth they will place the dishes, the bowls for incense, the cups, the jugs for wine, as well as the bread itself. ⁸ They are to cover all of this with a bright red cloth, and then with a piece of fine leather, before putting the carrying poles in place.

⁹ With another blue cloth they will cover the lampstand, along with the lamps, the lamp snuffers, the fire pans, and the jars of oil for the lamps. ¹⁰ All of this will then be covered with a piece of fine leather and placed on a carrying frame.

¹¹ The gold incense altar* is to be covered with a blue cloth, and then with a piece of fine leather, before its carrying poles are put in place.

¹² Next, Aaron and his sons will take blue cloth and wrap all the objects used in worship at the sacred tent. These will need to be covered with a piece of fine leather, then placed on a carrying frame.

¹³ They are to remove the ashes from the bronze altar and cover it with a purple cloth. ¹⁴ On that cloth will be placed the utensils used at the altar, including the fire pans, the meat forks, the shovels, and the sprinkling bowls. All of this will then be covered with a piece of fine leather, before the carrying poles are put in place.

¹⁵ When the camp is ready to be moved, the Kohathites will be responsible for carrying the sacred objects and the furnishings of the sacred tent. But Aaron and his sons must have already covered those things so the Kohathites won't touch them and die.

¹⁶ Eleazar son of Aaron the priest will be in charge of the oil for the lamps, the sweet-smelling incense, the grain for the sacrifices, and the olive oil used for dedications and ordinations. Eleazar is responsible for seeing that the sacred tent, its furnishings, and the sacred objects are taken care of.

¹⁷⁻²⁰ The Kohathites must not go near or even look at the sacred objects until Aaron and his sons have covered those objects. If they do, their entire clan will be wiped out. So make sure that Aaron and his sons go into the tent with them and tell them what to carry.

The duties of the Gershonite clans

²¹ The LORD said to Moses:

²²⁻²³ Find out how many men between the ages of thirty and fifty are in the two Levite clans of Gershon. Count only those who are able to work at the sacred tent.

²⁴ The Gershonites will be responsible ²⁵ for carrying the curtains of the sacred tent, its two outer coverings,* the curtain for the entrance to the tent, ²⁶ the curtains hanging around the courtyard of the tent, and the curtain and ropes for the entrance to the courtyard. The Gershonites are to do whatever needs to be done to take care of these things, ²⁷ and they will carry them wherever Aaron and his sons tell them to. ²⁸ These are the duties of the Gershonites at the sacred tent, and Ithamar son of Aaron will make sure they do their work.

The duties of the Merarite clans

²⁹⁻³⁰ The LORD said:

Moses, find out how many men between thirty and fifty are in the two Levite clans of Merari, but count only those who are able to work at the sacred tent.

---

*4.7 sacred bread: This bread was offered to the LORD and was a symbol of his presence in the sacred tent. It was put out on a special table and was replaced with fresh bread each Sabbath (Leviticus 24.5–9).
*4.11 gold incense altar: This altar for offering incense was inside the sacred tent; it was made of acacia wood covered with gold. A large altar for offering sacrifices was in front of the entrance to the tent; it was made of acacia wood covered with bronze (see verse 13).

*4.25 two outer coverings: See Exodus 26.14.

31 The Merarites will be responsible for carrying the frames of the tent and its other pieces, including the bars, the posts, the stands, 32 as well as the posts that support the courtyard, together with their stands, tent pegs, and ropes. The Merarites are to be told exactly what objects they are to carry, 33 and Ithamar son of Aaron will make sure they do their work.

The Levites are counted again

34-49 Moses, Aaron, and the other Israelite leaders obeyed the LORD and counted the Levi tribe by families and clans, to find out how many men there were between the ages of thirty and fifty who could work at the sacred tent. There were two thousand seven hundred and fifty Kohathites, two thousand six hundred and thirty Gershonites, and three thousand two hundred Merarites, making a total of eight thousand five hundred and eighty. Then they were all assigned their duties.

Various laws and the dedication of the Levites

CHAPTER 5

People are sent outside the camp

1 The LORD told Moses 2-3 to say to the people of Israel, "Put out of the camp everyone who has leprosy* or a bodily discharge or who has touched a dead body. Now that I live among my people, their camp must be kept clean."
4 The Israelites obeyed the LORD's instructions.

The penalty for committing a crime

This is also told in Leviticus 6.1-7

5 The LORD told Moses 6 to say to the community of Israel:

If any of you commit a crime against someone, you have sinned against me. 7 You must confess your guilt and pay the victim in full for whatever damage has been done, plus a fine of twenty per cent. 8 If the victim has no relative who can accept this money, it belongs to me and will be paid to the priest. In addition to that payment, you must take a ram for the priest to sacrifice so your sin will be forgiven.
9-10 When you make a donation to the sacred tent, that money belongs only to the priest, and each priest will keep what is given to him.

A suspicious husband

11 The LORD told Moses 12-14 to say to the people of Israel:

Suppose a man becomes jealous and suspects that his wife has been unfaithful, but he has no proof. 15 He must take his wife to the priest, together with one kilogramme of ground barley as an offering to find out if she is guilty. No olive oil or incense is to be put on that offering.
16 The priest is to make the woman stand at my altar, 17 where he will pour sacred water into a clay jar and stir in some dust from the floor of the sacred tent. 18-22 Next, he will remove her veil, then hand her the barley offering, and say, "If you have been faithful to your husband, this water won't harm you. But if you have been unfaithful, it will bring down the LORD's curse — you will never be able to give birth to a child, and everyone will curse your name."
Then the woman will answer, "If I am guilty, let it happen just as you say."
23 The priest will write these curses on special paper and wash them off into the bitter water, 24 so that when the woman drinks this water, the curses will enter her body. 25 He will take the barley offering from her and lift it up' in dedication to me, the LORD. Then he will place it on my altar 26 and burn part of it as a sacrifice. After that, the woman must drink the bitter water.
27 If the woman has been unfaithful, the water will immediately make her unable to have children, and she will be a curse among her people. 28 But if she is innocent, her body will not be harmed, and she will still be able to have children.
29-30 This is the ceremony that must take place at my altar when a husband suspects that his wife has been unfaithful. The priest must make the woman stand in my presence and carefully follow these instructions. 31 If the husband is wrong, he will not be punished; but if his wife is guilty, she will be punished.

---

*5.2-3 leprosy: The word translated "leprosy" was used for many different kinds of skin diseases.
See also: 5.5-8: Lev 6.1-7.

CHAPTER 6

Rules for Nazirites

¹ The LORD told Moses ² to say to the people of Israel:

If any of you want to dedicate yourself to me by vowing to become a Nazirite, ³ you must no longer drink any wine or beer or use any kind of vinegar. Don't drink grape juice or eat grapes or raisins — ⁴ not even the seeds or skins.

⁵ Even the hair of a Nazirite is sacred to me, and as long as you are a Nazirite, you must never cut your hair.

⁶ During the time that you are a Nazirite, you must never go close to a dead body, ⁷⁻⁸ not even that of your father, mother, brother, or sister. That would make you unclean. Your hair is the sign that you are dedicated to me, so remain holy.

⁹ If someone suddenly dies near you, your hair is no longer sacred, and you must shave it seven days later during the ceremony to make you clean. ¹⁰ Then on the next day, bring two doves or two pigeons to the priest at the sacred tent. ¹¹ He will offer one of the birds as a sacrifice for sin and the other as a sacrifice to please me.* You will then be forgiven for being too near a dead body, and your hair will again become sacred. ¹² But the dead body made you unacceptable, so you must make another vow to become a Nazirite and be dedicated once more. Finally, a year- old ram must be offered as the sacrifice to make things right.

¹³ When you have completed your promised time of being a Nazirite, go to the sacred tent ¹⁴ and offer three animals that have nothing wrong with them: a year-old ram as a sacrifice to please me, a year-old female lamb as a sacrifice for sin, and a full-grown ram as a sacrifice to ask my blessing.* ¹⁵ Wine offerings and grain sacrifices must also be brought with these

---

*6.11 sacrifice to please me: This sacrifice has traditionally been called a "whole burnt offering", because the whole animal was burnt on the altar. A main purpose of such a sacrifice was to please the LORD with the smell of the sacrifice, and so in the CEV it is often called "a sacrifice to please the LORD".
*6.14 sacrifice to ask my blessing: This sacrifice has traditionally been called a "peace offering" or an "offering of well-being". A main purpose of such a sacrifice was to ask the LORD's blessing, and so in the CEV it is often called a "sacrifice to ask the LORD's blessing".

See also: 6.3: Luke 1.15. 6.13–21: Acts 21.23–24.

Holy history

Nazirites

What's the story?

The Nazirites are a special group who took strict vows of purity. Indeed, the word Nazirite means 'vowed'. They were the monks and nuns of ancient Israel, people who chose to devote their lives to the Lord. In a way they were like the priests, but unlike the priesthood, both men and women could be Nazirites. They did not cut their hair, drank no alcohol and had no contact with dead bodies – not even their parents'. The vow could be perpetual, or for a set period.

What's the point?

The Nazirite vow showed that anyone could choose to be totally devoted to God. Although the priests all came from the family of Aaron, anyone, if they felt called, could be a Nazirite. So, the Nazirite vow showed that anyone could choose extreme holiness, if they wanted. It also points ahead to certain special figures in Israel's history. Famous Nazirites included Samson, Samuel and John the Baptist.

More...

Going against the crowd p.1045
Samson p.277
Samuel p.298
John the Baptist p.1121

 Anorak corner

Illness

1. What was wrong with Mephibosheth?
2. Why did sick people gather by the Bethzatha pool?
3. When Jesus healed ten lepers, how many returned to say thanks?
4. How did a crippled man's friends get his bed through the crowds to Jesus?
5. Who was it who saw people like trees walking around?
(Answers on p.1431)

animals. Finally, you are to bring a basket of bread made with your finest flour and olive oil, but without yeast. Also bring some thin wafers brushed with oil.

¹⁶ The priest will take these gifts to my altar and offer them, so that I will be pleased and will forgive you. ¹⁷ Then he will sacrifice the ram and offer the wine, grain, and bread.

¹⁸ After that, you will stand at the entrance to the sacred tent, shave your head, and put the hair in the fire where the priest has offered the sacrifice to ask my blessing.

¹⁹ Once the meat from the ram's shoulder has been boiled, the priest will take it, along with one loaf of bread and one wafer brushed with oil, and give them to you. ²⁰ You will hand them back to the priest, who will lift them up⁾ in dedication to me. Then he can eat the meat from the ram's shoulder, its choice ribs, and its hind leg, because this is his share of the sacrifice. After this, you will no longer be a Nazirite and will be free to drink wine.

²¹ These are the requirements for Nazirites. However, if you can afford to offer more, you must do so.

The blessing for the people

²² The LORD told Moses, ²³ "When Aaron and his sons bless the people of Israel, they must say:

²⁴ I pray that the LORD
     will bless and protect you,
²⁵ and that he will show you mercy
     and kindness.
²⁶ May the LORD be good to you
     and give you peace."

²⁷ Then the LORD said, "If Aaron and his sons ask me to bless the Israelites, I will give them my blessing."

CHAPTER 7

The leaders bring gifts to the sacred tent

¹ When Moses had finished setting up the sacred tent, he dedicated it to the LORD, together with its furnishings, the altar, and its equipment. ² Then the twelve tribal leaders of Israel, the same men who had been in charge of counting the people,* came to the tent ³ with gifts for the LORD. They

brought six strong carts and twelve oxen — one ox from each leader and a cart from every two.

⁴ The LORD said to Moses, ⁵ "Accept these gifts, so the Levites can use them here at the sacred tent for carrying the sacred things."

⁶ Then Moses took the carts and oxen and gave them to the Levites, ⁷⁻⁸ who were under the leadership of Ithamar son of Aaron. Moses gave two carts and four oxen to the Gershonites for their work, and four carts and eight oxen to the Merarites for their work. ⁹ But Moses did not give any to the Kohathites, because they were in charge of the sacred objects that had to be carried on their shoulders.

¹⁰ On the day the altar was dedicated, the twelve leaders brought offerings for its dedication. ¹¹ The LORD said to Moses, "Each day one leader is to give his offering for the dedication."

¹²⁻⁸³ So each leader brought the following gifts:

a silver bowl that weighed one and a half kilogrammes and a silver sprinkling bowl weighing almost a kilogramme, both of them filled with flour and olive oil as grain sacrifices and weighed according to the official standards;

a small gold dish filled with incense;

a young bull, a full-grown ram, and a year-old ram as sacrifices to please the LORD;*

a goat⁾ as a sacrifice for sin;

and two bulls, five full-grown rams, five goats, and five rams a year old as sacrifices to ask the LORD's blessing.*

The tribal leaders brought their gifts and offerings in the following order:

On the first day Nahshon from Judah,
on the second day Nethanel
     from Issachar,
on the third day Eliab from Zebulun,
on the fourth day Elizur from Reuben,
on the fifth day Shelumiel from Simeon,
on the sixth day Eliasaph from Gad,
on the seventh day Elishama
     from Ephraim,
on the eighth day Gamaliel
     from Manasseh,
on the ninth day Abidan from Benjamin,
on the tenth day Ahiezer from Dan,

*7.2 the same men . . . the people: See 1.1–19.

*7.12–83 sacrifices to please the LORD: See the note at 6.11.
*7.12–83 sacrifices to ask the LORD's blessing: See the note at 6.14.

on the eleventh day Pagiel from Asher,
on the twelfth day Ahira from Naphtali.

84-88 And so when the altar was dedicated to the LORD, these twelve leaders brought the following gifts:

twelve silver bowls and twelve silver sprinkling bowls, weighing a total of almost twenty-eight kilogrammes, according to the official standards;

twelve gold dishes filled with incense and weighing over a kilogramme;

twelve bulls, twelve full-grown rams, and twelve rams a year old as sacrifices to please the LORD, along with the proper grain sacrifices;

twelve goats as sacrifices for sin;

and twenty-four bulls, sixty full-grown rams, sixty goats, and sixty rams a year old as sacrifices to ask the LORD's blessing.

89 Whenever Moses needed to talk with the LORD, he went into the sacred tent, where he heard the LORD's voice coming from between the two winged creatures above the lid of the sacred chest.

CHAPTER 8

Aaron puts the gold lamps in place

1 The LORD said to Moses, 2 "Tell Aaron to put the seven lamps on the lampstand so they shine towards the front."

3 Aaron obeyed and placed the lamps as he was told. 4 The lampstand was made of hammered gold from its base to the decorative flowers on top, exactly like the pattern the LORD had described to Moses.

Instructions for ordaining the Levites

5 The LORD said to Moses:

6 The Levites must be acceptable to me before they begin working at the sacred tent. So separate them from the rest of the Israelites 7 and sprinkle them with the water that washes away their sins. Then tell them to shave their entire bodies and wash their clothes.

8 They are to bring a bull and its proper grain sacrifice of flour mixed with olive oil. And they must bring a second bull as a sacrifice for sin.

9 Then you, Moses, will call together all the people of Israel and make the Levites go to my sacred tent, 10 where the people will place their hands on them. 11 Aaron

will present the Levites to me as a gift from the people, so that the Levites will do my work.

12 After this, the Levites are to place their hands on the heads of the bulls. Then one of the bulls will be sacrificed for the forgiveness of sin, and the other to make sure that I am pleased. 13 The Levites will stand at my altar in front of Aaron and his sons, who will then dedicate the Levites to me.

14 This ceremony will show that the Levites are different from the other Israelites and belong to me in a special way. 15 After they have been made acceptable and have been dedicated, they will be allowed to work at my sacred tent. 16 They are mine and will take the place of the firstborn Israelite sons. 17 When I killed the eldest sons of the Egyptians, I decided that the firstborn sons in each Israelite family would be mine, as well as every firstborn male from their flocks and herds. 18 But now I have chosen these Levites as substitutes for the firstborn sons, 19 and I have given them as gifts to Aaron and his sons to serve at the sacred tent. I will hold them responsible for what happens to anyone who gets too close to the sacred tent.'

The Levites are dedicated to the LORD

20 Moses, Aaron, and the other Israelites made sure that the Levites did everything the LORD had commanded. 21 The Levites sprinkled themselves with the water of forgiveness and washed their clothes. Then Aaron brought them to the altar and offered sacrifices to forgive their sins and make them acceptable to the LORD. 22 After this, the Levites worked at the sacred tent as assistants to Aaron and his sons, just as the LORD had commanded.

23 The LORD also told Moses, 24-25 "Levites who are between the ages of twenty-five and fifty can work at my sacred tent. But once they turn fifty, they must retire. 26 They may help the other Levites in their duties, but they must no longer be responsible for any work themselves. Remember this when you assign their duties."

See also: 8.1–4: Exod 25.31–40; 37.17–24.

See also: 8.17: Exod 13.2.

Passover is celebrated and a cloud covers the sacred tent

CHAPTER 9

Regulations for celebrating Passover

¹ During the first month of Israel's second year in the Sinai Desert,* the LORD had told Moses ² to say to the people, "Celebrate Passover ³ in the evening of the fourteenth day of this month* and do it by following all the regulations." ⁴⁻⁵ Moses told the people what the LORD had said, and they celebrated Passover there in the desert in the evening of the fourteenth day of the first month.

⁶ Some people in Israel's camp had touched a dead body and had become unfit to worship the LORD, and they could not celebrate Passover. But they asked Moses and Aaron, ⁷ "Even though we have touched a dead body, why can't we celebrate Passover and offer sacrifices to the LORD at the same time as everyone else?"

⁸ Moses said, "Wait here while I go into the sacred tent and find out what the LORD says about this."

⁹ The LORD then told Moses ¹⁰ to say to the community of Israel:

If any of you or your descendants touch a dead body and become unfit to worship me, or if you are away on a long journey, you may still celebrate Passover. ¹¹ But it must be done in the second month,* in the evening of the fourteenth day. Eat the Passover lamb with thin bread and bitter herbs, ¹² and don't leave any of it until morning or break any of the animal's bones. Be sure to follow these regulations.

¹³ But if any of you refuse to celebrate Passover when you are not away on a journey, you will no longer belong to my people. You will be punished because you did not offer sacrifices to me at the proper time.

¹⁴ Anyone, including foreigners who live among you, can celebrate Passover, if they follow all the regulations.

The cloud over the sacred tent

This is also told in Exodus 40.34–38

¹⁵⁻¹⁶ As soon as the sacred tent was set up,* a thick cloud appeared and covered it. The cloud was there each day, and during the night, a fire could be seen in it. ¹⁷⁻¹⁹ The LORD used this cloud to tell the Israelites when to move their camp and where to set it up again. As long as the cloud covered the tent, the Israelites did not break camp. But when the cloud moved, they followed it, and wherever it stopped, they camped and stayed there, ²⁰⁻²² whether it was only one night, a few days, a month, or even a year. As long as the cloud remained over the tent, the Israelites stayed where they were. But when the cloud moved, so did the Israelites. ²³ They obeyed the LORD's commands and went wherever he directed Moses.

The people begin their journey

CHAPTER 10

The silver trumpets

¹ The LORD told Moses:

² Have two trumpets made out of hammered silver. These will be used to call the people together and to give the signal for moving your camp. ³ If both trumpets are blown, everyone is to meet with you at the entrance to the sacred tent. ⁴ But if just one is blown, only the twelve tribal leaders need to come together.

⁵⁻⁶ Give a signal on a trumpet when it is time to break camp. The first blast will be the signal for the tribes camped on the east side, and the second blast will be the signal for those on the south. ⁷ But when you want everyone to come together, sound a different signal on the trumpet. ⁸ The priests of Aaron's family will be the ones to blow the trumpets, and this law will never change.

---

*9.1 first month . . . Sinai Desert: The book of Numbers begins in the second month of the second year (see 1.1), so 9.1–5 refers to a Passover celebration that had already taken place.
*9.3 this month: Abib (also called Nisan), the first month of the Hebrew calendar, from about mid-March to mid-April.
*9.11 second month: See the note at 1.1.
See also: 9.1–5: Exod 12.1–13. 9.12: Exod 12.46; John 19.36.

---

*9.15–16 As soon as the sacred tent was set up: According to Exodus 40.17, this took place "on the first day of the first month of the second year" of the Israelites' stay in the desert.

⁹ Whenever you go into battle against an enemy attacking your land, give a warning signal on the trumpets. Then I, the LORD, will hear it and rescue you. ¹⁰ During the celebration of the New Moon Festival and other religious festivals, sound the trumpets while you offer sacrifices. This will be a reminder that I am the LORD your God.

The Israelites begin their journey

¹¹ On the twentieth day of the second month* of that same year, the cloud over the sacred tent moved on. ¹² So the Israelites broke camp and left the Sinai Desert. And some time later, the cloud stopped in the Paran Desert.* ¹³ This was the first time the LORD had told Moses to command the people of Israel to move on.

¹⁴ Judah and the tribes that camped beside it marched out first, carrying their banner. Nahshon son of Amminadab was the leader of the Judah tribe, ¹⁵ Nethanel son of Zuar was the leader of the Issachar tribe, ¹⁶ and Eliab son of Helon was the leader of the Zebulun tribe.

¹⁷ The sacred tent had been taken down, and the Gershonites and the Merarites carried it, marching behind the Judah camp.

¹⁸ Reuben and the tribes that camped beside it marched out second, carrying their banner. Elizur son of Shedeur was the leader of the Reuben tribe, ¹⁹ Shelumiel son of Zurishaddai was the leader of the Simeon tribe, ²⁰ and Eliasaph son of Deuel was the leader of the Gad tribe.

²¹ Next were the Kohathites, carrying the objects for the sacred tent, which was to be set up before they arrived at the new camp.

²² Ephraim and the tribes that camped beside it marched next, carrying their banner. Elishama son of Ammihud was the leader of the Ephraim tribe, ²³ Gamaliel son of Pedahzur was the leader of the Manasseh tribe, ²⁴ and Abidan son of Gideoni was the leader of the Benjamin tribe.

²⁵ Dan and the tribes that camped beside it were to protect the Israelites against an attack from behind, and so they marched last, carrying their banner. Ahiezer son of Ammishaddai was the leader of the tribe of Dan, ²⁶ Pagiel son of Ochran was the leader of the Asher tribe, ²⁷ and Ahira son of Enan was the leader of the Naphtali tribe.

²⁸ This was the order in which the Israelites marched each time they moved their camp.

²⁹ Hobab⸌ the Midianite, the father-in-law of Moses, was there. And Moses said to him, "We're leaving for the place the LORD has promised us. He has said that all will go well for us. So come along, and we will make sure that all goes well for you."

³⁰ "No, I won't go," Hobab answered. "I'm returning home to be with my own people."

³¹ "Please go with us!" Moses said. "You can be our guide because you know the places to camp in the desert. ³² Besides that, if you go, we will give you a share of the good things the LORD gives us."

³³ The people of Israel began their journey from Mount Sinai.⸌ They travelled three days, and the Levites who carried the sacred chest led the way, so the LORD could show them where to camp. ³⁴ And the cloud always stayed with them.

³⁵ Each day as the Israelites began their journey, Moses would pray, "Our LORD, defeat your enemies and make them run!" ³⁶ And when they stopped to set up camp, he would pray, "Our LORD, stay close to Israel's thousands and thousands of people."

The people complain

CHAPTER 11

¹ One day the Israelites started complaining about their troubles. The LORD heard them and became so angry that he destroyed the outer edges of their camp with fire.

² When the people begged Moses to help, he prayed, and the fire went out. ³ They named the place "Burning",⸌ because in his anger the LORD had set their camp on fire.

The people grumble about being hungry

⁴ One day some worthless foreigners among the Israelites became greedy for food, and even the Israelites themselves began moaning, "We don't have any meat! ⁵ In Egypt we could eat all the fish we wanted, and there were cucumbers, melons, onions, and garlic. ⁶ But we're starving out here, and the only food we have is this manna."

⁷ The manna was like small whitish seeds ⁸⁻⁹ and tasted like something baked with sweet olive oil. It appeared at night with the

---

*10.11 second month: See the note at 1.1.
*10.12 the Paran Desert: Probably a general name for the northernmost part of the Sinai Desert.

See also: 10.35: Psa 68.1. 11.7–8: Exod 16.31.
11.9: Exod 16.13–15.

dew. In the morning the people would collect the manna, grind or crush it into flour, then boil it and make it into thin wafers.

¹⁰ The Israelites stood around their tents complaining. Moses heard them and was upset that they had made the LORD angry. ¹¹ He prayed:

I am your servant, LORD, so why are you doing this to me? What have I done to deserve this? You've made me responsible for all these people, ¹² but they're not my children. You told me to nurse them along and to carry them to the land you promised their ancestors. ¹³ They keep whining for meat, but where can I get meat for them? ¹⁴ This job is too much for me. How can I take care of all these people by myself? ¹⁵ If this is the way you're going to treat me, just kill me now and end my miserable life!

Seventy leaders are chosen to help Moses

¹⁶ The LORD said to Moses:

Choose seventy of Israel's respected leaders and go with them to the sacred tent. ¹⁷ While I am talking with you there, I will give them some of your authority, so they can share responsibility for my people. You will no longer have to care for them by yourself.

¹⁸ As for the Israelites, I have heard them complaining about not having meat and about being better off in Egypt. So tell them to make themselves acceptable to me, because tomorrow they will have meat. ¹⁹⁻²⁰ In fact, they will have meat day after day for a whole month — not just a few days, or even ten or twenty. They turned against me and wanted to return to Egypt. Now they will eat meat until they get sick of it.

²¹ Moses replied, "At least six hundred thousand grown men are here with me. How can you say there will be enough meat to feed them and their families for a whole month? ²² Even if we butchered all our sheep and cattle, or caught every fish in the sea, we wouldn't have enough to feed them."

²³ The LORD answered, "I can do anything! Watch and you'll see my words come true."

²⁴ Moses told the people what the LORD had said. Then he chose seventy respected leaders and went with them to the sacred tent. While the leaders stood in a circle around the tent,

Moses went inside, ²⁵ and the LORD spoke with him. Then the LORD took some authority⁺ from Moses and gave it to the seventy leaders. And when the LORD's Spirit took control of them, they started shouting like prophets. But they did it only this one time.

²⁶ Eldad and Medad were two leaders who had not gone to the tent. But when the Spirit took control of them, they began shouting like prophets there in camp. ²⁷ A boy ran to Moses and told him about Eldad and Medad.

²⁸ Joshua⁺ was there helping Moses, as he had done since he was young. And he said to Moses, "Sir, you must stop them!"

²⁹ But Moses replied, "Are you concerned what this might do to me? I wish the LORD would give his Spirit to all his people so everyone could be a prophet." ³⁰ Then Moses and the seventy leaders went back to camp.

The LORD sends quails

³¹ Some time later the LORD sent a strong wind that blew quails in from the sea until Israel's camp was completely surrounded with birds, piled up about a metre high for miles in every direction. ³² The people picked up quails for two days — each person collected at least a thousand kilogrammes. Then they spread them out to dry. ³³ But before the meat could be eaten, the LORD became angry and sent a disease through the camp.

³⁴ After they had buried the people who had been so greedy for meat, they called the place "Graves for the Greedy".⁺

³⁵ Israel then broke camp and travelled to Hazeroth.

Miriam and Aaron are jealous of Moses

CHAPTER 12

¹⁻³ Although Moses was the most humble person in all the world, Miriam and Aaron started complaining, "Moses had no right to marry that woman from Ethiopia!* Who does he think he is? The LORD has spoken to us, not just to him."

The LORD heard their complaint ⁴ and told Moses, Aaron, and Miriam to come to the entrance of the sacred tent. ⁵ There the LORD appeared in a cloud and told Aaron and

---

*12.1–3 Ethiopia: The Hebrew text has "Cush", which was a region south of Egypt that included parts of the present countries of Ethiopia and Sudan.

Viewpoints

We may not see him like Moses did, but God hasn't changed

Contributed by Sam R

'He sees me face to face, and everything I say to him is perfectly clear.'

When you're praying, do you ever think: 'If only I could actually see God sitting in the room across from me, look him in the eye, feel like I was having a "proper" conversation, then this would be so much easier.'

Or wish that God would be just a little bit clearer. I mean, I don't expect much. An angel choir, maybe. Some writing on a wall somewhere. A message etched in the clouds. Anything that will show me that I'm involved in a conversation with something other than the ceiling (I don't know about you, but I've not found ceilings to be all that responsive).

And because of that, I find it really hard to get my head round this verse. This is God speaking here. Talking about Moses; telling the people of Israel that he speaks to him face to face. Moses sees God as he is – something that as Christians we're promised, but not till we get to heaven! It's quite an accolade. I suspect Moses didn't struggle with those kind of questions (although he had enough of his own, let's face it). I have to confess to just a bit of envy!

What an amazing idea – that God really did speak face to face with this man, appearing to him tangibly, sharing his heart. Well, he does that with us too! We may not have seen a burning bush walking down the high street the other day. But God hasn't changed. He still speaks to us. He still shares his heart with us. He wants to involve us in his plans for the world. Keep your eyes and ears open!

More...

Moses p.61
Appearances of God p.99
Prayer p.1002

Miriam to come closer. [6] Then after commanding them to listen carefully, he said:

> "I, the LORD, speak to prophets
> in visions and dreams.
> [7] But my servant Moses
> is the leader of my people.
> [8] He sees me face to face,
> and everything I say to him
> is perfectly clear.
> You have no right to criticize
> my servant Moses."

[9] The LORD became angry with Aaron and Miriam. And after the LORD left [10] and the cloud disappeared from over the sacred tent, Miriam's skin turned white with leprosy.* When Aaron saw what had happened to her, [11] he said to Moses, "Sir, please don't punish us for doing such a foolish thing. [12] Don't let Miriam's flesh rot away like a child born dead!"

[13] Moses prayed, "LORD God, please heal her."

[14] But the LORD replied, "Miriam would be disgraced for seven days if her father had punished her by spitting in her face. So make her stay outside the camp for seven days, before coming back."

[15] The people of Israel did not move their camp until Miriam returned seven days later. [16] Then they left Hazeroth and set up camp in the Paran Desert.

Twelve men are sent into Canaan

CHAPTER 13

This is also told in Deuteronomy 1.19–33

[1] The LORD said to Moses, [2] "Choose a leader from each tribe and send them into Canaan to explore the land I am giving you."

[3] So Moses sent twelve tribal leaders from Israel's camp in the Paran Desert [4-16] with orders to explore the land of Canaan. And here are their names:

> Shammua son of Zaccur from Reuben,
> Shaphat son of Hori from Simeon,
> Caleb son of Jephunneh from Judah,
> Igal son of Joseph from Issachar,

---

*12.10 leprosy: See the note at 5.2–3.
See also: 12.7: Heb 3.2. 12.14: Num 5.2–3.

Joshua son of Nun from Ephraim,*
Palti son of Raphu from Benjamin,
Gaddiel son of Sodi from Zebulun,
Gaddi son of Susi from Manasseh,
Ammiel son of Gemalli from Dan,
Sethur son of Michael from Asher,
Nahbi son of Vophsi from Naphtali,
and Geuel son of Machi from Gad.

17 Before Moses sent them into Canaan, he said:

After you go through the Southern Desert of Canaan, continue north into the hill country 18 and find out what those regions are like. Be sure to remember how many people live there, how strong they are, 19-20 and if they live in open towns or walled cities. See if the land is good for growing crops and find out what kinds of trees grow there. It's time for grapes to ripen, so try to bring back some of the fruit that grows there.

21 The twelve men left to explore Canaan from the Zin Desert in the south all the way to the town of Rehob near Lebo-Hamath in the north. 22 As they went through the Southern Desert, they came to the town of Hebron, which was seven years older than the Egyptian town of Zoan. In Hebron, they saw the three Anakim* clans of Ahiman, Sheshai, and Talmai. 23-24 When they got to Bunch Valley,* they cut off a branch with such a huge bunch of grapes, that it took two men to carry it on a pole. That's why the place was called Bunch Valley. Along with the grapes, they also took back pomegranates* and figs.

The men report back to the people

25 After exploring the land of Canaan for forty days, 26 the twelve men returned to Kadesh in the Paran Desert and told Moses, Aaron, and the people what they had seen. They showed them the fruit 27 and said:

Look at this fruit! The land we explored is rich with milk and honey. 28 But the people who live there are strong, and their cities are large and walled. We even saw the three Anakim* clans. 29 Besides that, the Amalekites live in the Southern Desert; the Hittites, Jebusites, and Amorites are in the

hill country; and the Canaanites* live along the Mediterranean Sea and the River Jordan.

30 Caleb calmed down the crowd and said, "Let's go and take the land. I know we can do it!"
31 But the other men replied, "Those people are much too strong for us." 32 Then they started spreading rumours and saying, "We won't be able to grow anything in that soil. And the people are like giants. 33 In fact, we saw the Nephilim who are the ancestors of the Anakim. They were so big that we felt as small as grasshoppers."

The people rebel and are punished

CHAPTER 14

The Israelites rebel against Moses

1 After the Israelites heard the report from the twelve men who had explored Canaan, the people cried all night 2 and complained to Moses and Aaron, "We wish we had died in Egypt or somewhere out here in the desert! 3 Is the LORD leading us into Canaan, just to have us killed and our women and children captured? We'd be better off in Egypt." 4 Then they said to one another, "Let's choose our own leader and go back."

5 Moses and Aaron bowed down to pray in front of the crowd. 6 Joshua and Caleb tore their clothes in sorrow 7 and said:

We saw the land ourselves, and it's very good. 8 If we obey the LORD, he will surely give us that land rich with milk and honey. 9 So don't rebel. We have no reason to be afraid of the people who live there. The LORD is on our side, and they won't stand a chance against us!

10 The crowd threatened to stone Moses and Aaron to death. But just then, the LORD appeared in a cloud at the sacred tent.

Moses prays for the people

11 The LORD said to Moses, "I have done great things for these people, and they still reject me by refusing to believe in my power. 12 So they will no longer be my people. I will

---

*13.22,28 Anakim: Perhaps a group of people of great stature (see Deuteronomy 2.10–11,20–21).
*13.23–24 pomegranates: A bright red fruit that looks like an apple.

*13.29 Amalekites . . . Hittites . . . Jebusites . . . Amorites . . . Canaanites: These people lived in Canaan before the Israelites.
See also: 13.33: Gen 6.4. 14.9: Heb 3.16.

destroy them, but I will make you the ancestor of a nation even stronger than theirs."

¹³⁻¹⁶ Moses replied:

With your mighty power you rescued your people from Egypt, so please don't destroy us here in the desert. If you do, the Egyptians will hear about it and tell the people of Canaan. Those Canaanites already know that we are your people, and that we see you face to face. And they have heard how you lead us with a thick cloud during the day and flaming fire at night. But if you kill us, they will claim it was because you weren't powerful enough to lead us into Canaan as you promised.

¹⁷ Show us your great power, LORD. You promised ¹⁸ that you love to show mercy and kindness. And you said that you are very patient, but that you will punish everyone guilty of doing wrong — not only them but their children and grandchildren as well.

¹⁹ You are merciful, and you treat people better than they deserve. So please forgive these people, just as you have forgiven them ever since they left Egypt.

²⁰ Then the LORD said to Moses:

In answer to your prayer, I do forgive them. ²¹ But as surely as I live and my power has no limit, ²²⁻²³ I swear that not one of these Israelites will enter the land I promised to give their ancestors. These people have seen my power in Egypt and in the desert, but they will never see Canaan. They have disobeyed and tested me too many times.

²⁴ But my servant Caleb isn't like the others. So because he has faith in me, I will allow him to cross into Canaan, and his descendants will settle there.

²⁵ Now listen, Moses! The Amalekites and the Canaanites live in the valleys of Canaan.* And tomorrow morning, you'll need to turn round and head back into the desert towards the Red Sea.*

---

*14.25 The Amalekites and the Canaanites . . .
valleys of Canaan: That is, all possible ways into Canaan were blocked.
*14.25 **Red Sea:** Hebrew *yam suph*, here referring to the Gulf of Aqaba, since the term is extended to include the north-eastern arm of the Red Sea (see also the note at Exodus 13.18).
See also: 14.13–19: Exod 32.11–14. 14.18: Exod 20.5–6; 34.6–7; Deut 5.9–10; 7.9–10. 14.21–23: Heb 3.18. 14.24: Josh 14.9–12.

The Israelites are punished for complaining

²⁶ The LORD told Moses and Aaron ²⁷⁻²⁸ to give this message to the people of Israel:

You sinful people have complained against me too many times! Now I swear by my own life that I will give you exactly what you wanted.* ²⁹ You will die here in the desert, and your dead bodies will cover the ground. You have insulted me, and none of you men who are over twenty years old ³⁰ will enter the land that I solemnly promised to give you as your own — only Caleb and Joshua' will go in.

³¹ You were worried that your own children would be captured. But I, the LORD, will let them enter the land you have rejected. ³² You will die here in the desert! ³³ Your children will wander around in this desert forty years, suffering because of your sins, until all of you are dead. ³⁴ I will cruelly punish you every day for the next forty years — one year for each day that the land was explored. ³⁵ You sinful people who ganged up against me will die here in the desert.

³⁶ Ten of the men sent to explore the land had brought back bad news and had made the people complain against the LORD. ³⁷ So he sent a deadly disease that killed those men, ³⁸ but he let Joshua and Caleb live.

The Israelites fail to enter Canaan

This is also told in Deuteronomy 1.41–45

³⁹ The people of Israel were very sad after Moses gave them the LORD's message. ⁴⁰ So they got up early the next morning and got ready to head towards the hill country of Canaan. They said, "We were wrong to complain about the LORD. Let's go into the land that he promised us."

⁴¹ But Moses replied, "You're disobeying the LORD! Your plan won't work, ⁴²⁻⁴³ so don't even try it. The LORD refuses to help you, because you turned your backs on him. The Amalekites and the Canaanites are your enemies, and they will attack and defeat you."

⁴⁴ But the Israelites ignored Moses' and marched towards the hill country, even though the sacred chest and Moses did not go with them. ⁴⁵ The Amalekites and the

---

*14.27–28 **wanted:** See verse 2.
See also: 14.29: Heb 3.17. 14.33: Acts 7.36.

Canaanites came down from the hill country, defeated the Israelites, and chased them as far as the town of Hormah.

Laws and punishments

CHAPTER 15

Laws about sacrifices

¹ The LORD told Moses ² to give the Israelites the following laws about offering sacrifices:

³ Bulls or rams or goats' are the animals that you may burn on the altar as sacrifices to please me.* You may also offer sacrifices voluntarily or because you made a promise, or because they are part of your regular religious ceremonies. The smell of the smoke from these sacrifices is pleasing to me.

⁴⁻⁵ If you sacrifice a young ram or goat, you must also offer a kilogramme of your finest flour mixed with a litre of olive oil as a grain sacrifice. A litre of wine must also be poured on the altar.

⁶⁻⁷ And if the animal is a full-grown ram, you must offer two kilogrammes of flour mixed with one and a half litres of olive oil. One and a half litres of wine must also be poured on the altar. The smell of this smoke is pleasing to me.

⁸ If a bull is offered as a sacrifice to please me or to ask my blessing,* ⁹ you must offer three kilogrammes of flour mixed with two litres of olive oil. ¹⁰ Two litres of wine must also be poured on the altar. The smell of this smoke is pleasing to me.

¹¹⁻¹³ If you are a native Israelite, you must obey these rules each time you offer a bull, a ram, or a goat as a sacrifice. ¹⁴ And the foreigners who live among you must also follow these rules. ¹⁵⁻¹⁶ This law will never change. I am the LORD, and I consider all people the same, whether they are Israelites or foreigners living among you.

¹⁷⁻¹⁹ When you eat food in the land that I am giving you, remember to set aside some of it as an offering to me. ²⁰ From the first batch of bread dough that you make after each new grain harvest, make a loaf of bread and offer it to me, just as you offer grain. ²¹ All your descendants must follow this law and offer part of the first batch of bread dough.

²²⁻²³ The LORD also told Moses to tell the people what must be done if they ever disobey his laws:

²⁴ If all of you disobey one of my laws without meaning to, you must offer a bull as a sacrifice to please me, together with a grain sacrifice, a wine offering, and a goat as a sacrifice for sin. ²⁵ Then the priest will pray and ask me to forgive you. And since you did not mean to do wrong, and you offered sacrifices, ²⁶ the sin of everyone — both Israelites and foreigners among you — will be forgiven.

²⁷ But if one of you does wrong without meaning to, you must sacrifice a year-old female goat as a sacrifice for sin. ²⁸ The priest will then ask me to forgive you, and your sin will be forgiven.

²⁹ The law will be the same for anyone who does wrong without meaning to, whether an Israelite or a foreigner living among you.

³⁰⁻³¹ But if one of you does wrong on purpose, whether Israelite or foreigner, you have sinned against me by disobeying my laws. You will be sent away and will no longer live among the people of Israel.

A man put to death for gathering firewood on the Sabbath

³² Once, while the Israelites were travelling through the desert, a man was caught gathering firewood on the Sabbath.* ³³ He was taken to Moses, Aaron, and the rest of the community. ³⁴ But no one knew what to do with him, so he was not allowed to leave.

³⁵ Then the LORD said to Moses, "Tell the people to take that man outside the camp and stone him to death!" ³⁶ So he was killed, just as the LORD had commanded Moses.

The tassels on the people's clothes

³⁷ The LORD told Moses ³⁸ to say to the people of Israel, "Sew tassels on to the bottom edge of your clothes and tie a purple string to each tassel. ³⁹⁻⁴⁰ These will remind you that you must obey my laws and teachings. And when you do, you will be dedicated to me and won't follow your own sinful desires. ⁴¹ I am the LORD your God who led you out of Egypt."

---

*15.3 **sacrifices to please me:** See the note at 6.11.
*15.8 **to ask my blessing:** See the note at 6.14.
See also: 15.16: Lev 24.22.

*15.32 **a man . . . Sabbath:** No work was to be done on the Sabbath (see Exodus 31.12–17).
See also: 15.27–28: Lev 4.27–31.   **15.38:** Deut 22.12.

The people rebel

CHAPTER 16

Korah, Dathan, and Abiram lead a rebellion

1-2 Korah son of Izhar was a Levite from the Kohathite clan. One day he called together Dathan, Abiram, and On' from the Reuben tribe, and the four of them decided to rebel against Moses. So they asked two hundred and fifty respected Israelite leaders for their support, and together they went to Moses 3 and Aaron and said, "Why do you think you're so much better than anyone else? We're part of the LORD's holy people, and he's with all of us. What makes you think you're the only ones in charge?"

4 When Moses heard this, he knelt down to pray.' 5 Then he said to Korah and his followers:

Tomorrow morning the LORD will show us the person he has chosen to be his priest, and that man will faithfully serve him.

6-7 Korah, now here is what you and your followers must do: get some fire pans, fill them with coals and incense, and place them near the sacred tent. And the man the LORD chooses will be his priest.* Korah, this time you Levites have gone too far!

8-9 You know that the God of Israel has chosen you Levites from all Israel to serve him by being in charge of the sacred tent and by helping the community to worship in the proper way. What more do you want? 10 The LORD has given you a special responsibility, and now, Korah, you think you should also be his priest. 11 You and your followers have rebelled against the LORD, not against Aaron.

12 Then Moses sent for Dathan and Abiram, but they sent back this message: "We won't come! 13 It's bad enough that you took us from our rich farmland in Egypt to let us die here in the desert. Now you also want to boss us around! 14 You keep promising us rich farmlands with fertile fields and vineyards — but where are they? Stop trying to trick these people. No, we won't come to see you."

15 Moses was very angry and said to the LORD, "Don't listen to these men! I haven't done anything wrong to them. I haven't taken as much as a donkey."

16 Then he said to Korah, "Tomorrow you and your followers must go with Aaron to the LORD's sacred tent. 17 Each of you take along your fire pan with incense in it and offer the incense to the LORD."

18 The next day the men placed incense and coals in their fire pans and stood with Moses and Aaron at the entrance to the sacred tent. 19 Meanwhile, Korah had convinced the rest of the Israelites to rebel against their two leaders.

When that happened, the LORD appeared in all his glory 20 and said to Moses and Aaron, 21 "Get away from the rest of the Israelites so I can kill them at once!"

22 But the two men bowed down and prayed, "Our God, you gave these people life. Why would you punish everyone here when only one man has sinned?"

23 The LORD answered Moses, 24 "Tell the people to stay away from the tents of Korah, Dathan, and Abiram."

25 Moses walked over to Dathan and Abiram, and the other leaders of Israel followed. 26 Then Moses warned the people, "Get away from the tents of these sinful men! Don't touch anything that belongs to them or you'll be wiped out." 27 So everyone moved away from those tents, except Korah, Dathan, Abiram, and their families.

28 Moses said to the crowd, "The LORD has chosen me and told me to do these things — it wasn't my idea. And here's how you will know: 29 if these men die a natural death, it means the LORD hasn't chosen me. 30 But suppose the LORD does something that has never been done before. For example, what if a huge crack appears in the ground, and these men and their families fall into it and are buried alive, together with everything they own? Then you will know they have turned their backs on the LORD!"

31 As soon as Moses said this, the ground under the men opened up 32-33 and swallowed them alive, together with their families and everything they owned. Then the ground closed back up, and they were gone.

34 The rest of the Israelites heard their screams, so they ran off, shouting, "We don't want that to happen to us!"

---

*16.6-7 get some fire pans . . . his priest: Only priests could offer incense at the sacred altar; anyone else who tried would be killed. In this case, the man who lived would be the one the LORD had chosen.
See also: 16.1: Jude 11.

35 Suddenly the LORD sent a fire that burnt up the two hundred and fifty men who had offered incense to him.

36 Then the LORD said to Moses, 37 "Tell Aaron's son Eleazar to take the fire pans from the smouldering fire and scatter the coals. The pans are now sacred, 38 because they were used for offering incense to me. Have them hammered into a thin layer of bronze as a covering for the altar. Those men died because of their sin, and now their fire pans will become a warning for the rest of the community."

39 Eleazar collected the pans and had them hammered into a thin layer of bronze as a covering for the altar, 40 just as the LORD had told Moses. The pans are a warning to the Israelites that only Aaron's descendants would be allowed to offer incense to the LORD. Anyone else who tried would be punished like Korah and his followers.

The Israelites rebel and are punished

41 The next day the people of Israel again complained against Moses and Aaron, "The two of you killed some of the LORD's people!"

42 As the people crowded around them, Moses and Aaron turned towards the sacred tent, and the LORD appeared in his glory in the cloud covering the tent. 43 So Moses and Aaron walked to the front of the tent, 44 where the LORD said to them, 45 "Stand back! I am going to wipe out these Israelites once and for all."

They immediately bowed down and prayed. 46 Then Moses told Aaron, "Grab your fire pan and fill it with hot coals from the altar. Put incense in it, then quickly take it to where the people are and offer it to the LORD, so they can be forgiven. The LORD is very angry, and people have already started dying!"

47-48 Aaron did exactly what he had been told. He ran over to the crowd of people and stood between the dead bodies and the people who were still alive. He placed the incense on the pan, then offered it to the LORD and asked him to forgive the people's sin. The disease immediately stopped spreading, and no one else died from it. 49 But fourteen thousand seven hundred Israelites were dead, not counting those who had died with Korah and his followers.

50 Aaron walked back and stood with Moses at the sacred tent.

Life files

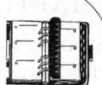

Aaron

Background: Brother of Moses. Acted as his brother's spokesman before the King of Egypt.

What's the story?

Aaron acted as Moses' spokesman and second-in-command. Once the Israelites escaped from Egypt, Aaron was appointed High Priest.

Obviously he had a lot of good qualities. He was specifically chosen by God (Numbers 17.1–13) for what was a difficult and even dangerous job. He didn't flinch from the task.

But what is amazing about Aaron is that he broke the law. When the people wanted to build a false idol to worship, Aaron went along with it. Perhaps he was scared, perhaps he didn't know what else to do, but he clearly disobeys God. Then he goes and criticises Moses and seems to get away with it (Numbers 12.1–16), although his sister is punished.

Perhaps the truth is that Aaron was punished, but in a less obvious way. Like Moses, he never got to the Promised Land. And his two sons died as a result of not obeying the Lord's commands precisely (Leviticus 10.1–3). Perhaps, too, he recognises his sins and repents. Maybe his failing was that he was too easily led.

What's the point?

Aaron's role is significant in the Bible. As the first High Priest, and the ancestor of the priestly tribe of Levi, he had a significant role. He made mistakes; he did things wrong. But he served God faithfully as well.

More...

Priests p.117
Surprise! God sees you as a super-holy priest... p.1387
Moses p.61
Holiness p.1386
Sacrifice p.1368

CHAPTER 17

Aaron's walking stick blooms and produces almonds

[1] The LORD told Moses:

[2-3] Call together the twelve tribes of Israel and tell the leader of each tribe to write his name on the walking stick he carries as a symbol of his authority. Make sure Aaron's name is written on the one from the Levi tribe, then collect all the sticks.

[4] Place these sticks in the tent in front of the sacred chest where I appear to you. [5] I will then choose a man to be my priest, and his stick will sprout. After that happens, I won't have to listen to any more complaints about you.

[6] Moses told the people what the LORD had commanded, and they gave him the walking sticks from the twelve tribal leaders, including Aaron's from the Levi tribe. [7] Moses took them and placed them in the LORD's sacred tent.

[8] The next day when Moses went into the tent, flowers and almonds were already growing on Aaron's stick. [9] Moses brought the twelve sticks out of the tent and showed them to the people. Each of the leaders found his own and took it.

[10] But the LORD told Moses, "Put Aaron's stick back! Let it stay near the sacred chest as a warning to anyone who might think about rebelling. If these people don't stop their grumbling about me, I will wipe them out." [11] Moses did what he was told.

[12] The Israelites cried out to Moses, "We're done for [13] and doomed if we even get near the sacred tent!"

Priests and Levites

CHAPTER 18

The duties of the priests and Levites

[1] The LORD said to Aaron:

You, your sons, and the other Levites of the Kohath clan, are responsible for what happens at the sacred tent.ᵇ And you and your sons will be responsible for what the priests do. [2] The Levites are your relatives and are here to help you in your service at the tent. [3] You must see that they perform their duties. But if they go near any of the

sacred objects or the altar, all of you will die. [4] No one else is allowed to take care of the sacred tent or to do anything connected with it. [5] Follow these instructions, so I won't become angry and punish the Israelites ever again.

[6] I alone chose the Levites from all the other tribes to belong to me, and I have given them to you as your helpers. [7] But only you and your sons can serve as priests at the altar and in the most holy place. Your work as priests is a gift from me, and anyone else who tries to do that work must be put to death.

The priests' share of offerings given to the LORD

This is also told in Deuteronomy 18.1–8

[8-9] The LORD said to Aaron:

I have put you in charge of the sacred gifts and sacrifices that the Israelites bring to me. And from now on, you, your sons, and your descendants will receive part of the sacrifices for sin, as well as part of the grain sacrifices, and the sacrifices to make things right. Your share of these sacrifices will be the parts not burnt on the altar. [10] Since these things are sacred, they must be eaten near the sacred tent, but only men are allowed to eat them.

[11] You will also receive part of the special gifts and offerings that the Israelites bring to me. Any member of your family who is clean and acceptable for worship can eat these things. [12] For example, when the Israelites bring me the first batches of oil, wine, and grain, you can have the best parts of those gifts. [13] And the first part of the crops from their fields and vineyards also belongs to you. The people will offer this to me, then anyone in your family who is clean may have some of it.

[14] Everything in Israel that has been completely dedicated to me* will now belong to you.

[15] The firstborn son in every Israelite family, as well as the firstborn males of their flocks and herds, belong to me. But a firstborn son and every firstborn

---

18.14 that has been completely dedicated to me: This translates a Hebrew word that describes property and things that were taken away from humans and given to God for ever. Sometimes such things had to be completely destroyed (see Joshua 6.15–19).

See also: 18.14: Lev 27.28.

donkey* must be bought back from me.
¹⁶ The price for a firstborn son who is at
least one month old will be five pieces of
silver, weighed according to the official
standards. ¹⁷ However, all firstborn cattle,
sheep, and goats belong to me and cannot
be bought back. Splatter their blood on the
altar and send their fat up in smoke, so I
can smell it and be pleased. ¹⁸ You are
allowed to eat the meat of those animals,
just as you can eat the choice ribs and the
right hind leg of the special sacrifices.

¹⁹ From now on, the sacred offerings that
the Israelites give to me will belong to you,
your sons, and your daughters. This is my
promise to you and your descendants, and
it will never change.

²⁰ You will not receive any land in Israel
as your own. I am the LORD, and I will give
you whatever you need.

What the Levites receive

The LORD said to Aaron:

²¹ Ten per cent of the Israelites' crops and
one out of every ten of their newborn
animals belong to me. But I am giving all
this to the Levites as their pay for the work
they do at the sacred tent. ²²⁻²³ They are the
only ones allowed to work at the tent, and
they must not let anyone else come near it.
Those who do must be put to death, and
the Levites will also be punished. This law
will never change.

Since the Levites won't be given any land
in Israel as their own, ²⁴ they will be given
the crops and newborn animals that the
Israelites offer to me.

What the Levites must give

²⁵ The LORD told Moses ²⁶ to say to the
Levites:

When you receive from the people of Israel
ten per cent of their crops and newborn
animals, you must offer a tenth of that to
me. ²⁷ Just as the Israelites give me part of
their grain and wine, you must set aside
part of what you receive ²⁸ as an offering to
me. That amount must then be given to
Aaron, ²⁹ so the best of what you receive
will be mine.

³⁰ After you have dedicated the best parts
to me, you can eat the rest, just as the
Israelites eat part of their grain and wine
after offering them to me.' ³¹ Your share
may be eaten anywhere by anyone in your
family, because it is your pay for working at
the sacred tent. ³² You won't be punished
for eating it, as long as you have already
offered the best parts to me.

The gifts and sacrifices brought by the
people must remain sacred, and if you eat
any part of them before they are offered to
me, you will be put to death.

Becoming clean

CHAPTER 19

The ceremony to wash away sin

¹⁻² The LORD gave Moses and Aaron the
following law:

The people of Israel must bring Moses a
reddish-brown cow that has nothing wrong
with it and that has never been used for
ploughing. ³ Moses will give it to Eleazar
the priest, then it will be led outside the
camp and killed while Eleazar watches. ⁴ He
will dip his finger in the blood and
sprinkle it seven times in the direction of
the sacred tent. ⁵ Then the whole cow,
including its skin, meat, blood, and insides
must be burnt. ⁶ A priest' is to throw a stick
of cedar wood, a hyssop* branch, and a
piece of red yarn into the fire.

⁷ After the ceremony, the priest is to take
a bath and wash his clothes. Only then can
he go back into the camp, but he remains
unclean and unfit for worship until
evening. ⁸ The man who burnt the cow
must also wash his clothes and take a bath,
but he is also unclean until evening.

⁹ A man who isn't unclean must collect
the ashes of the burnt cow and store them
outside the camp in a clean place. The
people of Israel can mix these ashes with
the water used in the ceremony to wash
away sin. ¹⁰ The man who collects the ashes
must wash his clothes, but will remain
unclean until evening. This law must
always be obeyed by the people of Israel
and the foreigners living among them.

---

*18.15 donkey: The Hebrew text has "unclean
animal", which probably refers to a donkey (see
Exodus 13.13; 34.20).
See also: 18.21: Lev 27.30–33; Deut 14.22–29.

*19.6 hyssop: A plant with small clusters of blue
flowers and sweet-smelling leaves.
See also: 19.9: Heb 9.13.

What must be done after touching a dead body

The LORD said:

¹¹ If you touch a dead body, you will be unclean for seven days. ¹² But if you wash with the water mixed with the cow's ashes on the third day and again on the seventh day, you will be clean and acceptable for worship. You must wash yourself on those days; if you don't, you will remain unclean. ¹³ Suppose you touch a dead body, but refuse to be made clean by washing with the water mixed with ashes. You will be guilty of making my sacred tent unclean and will no longer belong to the people of Israel.

¹⁴ If someone dies in a tent while you are there, you will be unclean for seven days. And anyone who later enters the tent will also be unclean. ¹⁵ Any open jar in the tent is unclean.

¹⁶ If you touch the body of someone who was killed or who died of old age, or if you touch a human bone or a grave, you will be unclean for seven days.

¹⁷⁻¹⁸ Before you can be made clean, someone who is clean must take some of the ashes from the burnt cow and stir them into a pot of spring water. That same person must dip a hyssop branch in the water and ashes, then sprinkle it on the tent and everything in it, including everyone who was inside. If you have touched a human bone, a grave, or a dead body, you must be sprinkled with that water. ¹⁹ If this is done on the third day and on the seventh day, you will be clean. Then after you take a bath and wash your clothes, you can worship that evening.

²⁰ If you are unclean and refuse to be made clean by washing with the water mixed with ashes, you will be guilty of making my sacred tent unclean, and you will no longer belong to the people of Israel. ²¹ These laws will never change.

The man who sprinkled the water and the ashes on you when you were unclean must also wash his clothes. And whoever touches this water is unclean until evening. ²² When you are unclean, everything you touch becomes unclean, and anyone who touches you will be unclean until evening.

On the way to Moab

CHAPTER 20

Water from a rock

This is also told in Exodus 17.1–7

¹ The people of Israel arrived at the Zin Desert during the first month* and set up camp near the town of Kadesh. It was there that Miriam died and was buried.

² The Israelites had no water, so they went to Moses and Aaron ³ and complained, "Moses, we'd be better off if we had died along with the others in front of the LORD's sacred tent.* ⁴ You brought us into this desert, and now we and our livestock are going to die! ⁵ Egypt was better than this horrible place. At least there we had grain and figs and grapevines and pomegranates.* But now we don't even have any water."

⁶ Moses and Aaron went to the entrance to the sacred tent, where they bowed down. The LORD appeared to them in all his glory ⁷⁻⁸ and said, "Moses, get your walking stick.* Then you and Aaron call the people together and command that rock to give you water. That's how you will provide water for the people of Israel and their livestock."

⁹ Moses obeyed and took his stick from the sacred tent. ¹⁰ After he and Aaron had gathered the people around the rock, he said, "Look, you rebellious people, and you will see water flow from this rock!" ¹¹ He raised his stick in the air and struck the rock two times. At once, water gushed from the rock, and the people and their livestock had water to drink.

¹² But the LORD said to Moses and Aaron, "Because you refused to believe in my power, these people did not respect me. And so, you will not be the ones to lead them into the land I have promised."

¹³ The Israelites had complained against the LORD, and he had shown them his holy power by giving them water to drink. So they named the place Meribah, which means "Complaining".

---

*20.1 first month: See the note at 9.3.
*20.3 if we had died . . . sacred tent: See 16.41–49.
*20.5 pomegranates: See the note at 13.23–24.
*20.7–8 walking stick: A symbol of his authority.
See also: 20.2–13: Exod 17.1–7.

Israel isn't allowed to go through Edom

14 Moses sent messengers from Israel's camp near Kadesh with this message for the king of Edom:

We are Israelites, your own relatives, and we're sure you have heard the terrible things that have happened to us. 15 Our ancestors settled in Egypt and lived there a long time. But later the Egyptians were cruel to us, 16 and when we begged our LORD for help, he answered our prayer and brought us out of that land.

Now we are camped at the border of your territory, near the town of Kadesh. 17 Please let us go through your country. We won't go near your fields and vineyards, and we won't drink any water from your wells. We will stay on the main road* until we leave your territory.

18 But the Edomite king answered, "No, I won't let you go through our country! And if you try, we will attack you."

19 Moses sent back this message: "We promise to stay on the main road, and if any of us or our livestock drink your water, we will pay for it. We just want to pass through."

20 But the Edomite king insisted, "You can't go through our land!"

Then Edom sent out its strongest troops 21 to keep Israel from passing through its territory. So the Israelites had to go in another direction.

Aaron dies

22 After the Israelites had left Kadesh and had gone as far as Mount Hor 23 on the Edomite border, the LORD said, 24 "Aaron, this is where you will die. You and Moses disobeyed me at Meribah, and so you will not enter the land I promised the Israelites. 25 Moses, go with Aaron and his son Eleazar to the top of the mountain. 26 Then take Aaron's priestly robe from him and place it on Eleazar. Aaron will die there."

27 Moses obeyed, and everyone watched as he and Aaron and Eleazar walked to the top of Mount Hor. 28 Moses then took the priestly robe from Aaron and placed it on Eleazar. Aaron died there.

When Moses and Eleazar came down, 29 the people knew that Aaron had died, and they mourned his death for thirty days.

CHAPTER 21

Israel defeats the Canaanites at Hormah

1 The Canaanite king of Arad lived in the Southern Desert of Canaan, and when he heard that the Israelites were on their way to the village of Atharim, he attacked and took some of them hostage.

2 The Israelites prayed, "Our LORD, if you will help us defeat these Canaanites, we will completely destroy their towns and everything in them, to show that they belong to you."*

3 The LORD answered their prayer and helped them wipe out the Canaanite army and completely destroy their towns. That's why one of the towns is named Hormah, which means "Destroyed Place".

Moses makes a bronze snake

4 The Israelites had to go around the territory of Edom, so when they left Mount Hor, they headed south towards the Red Sea.* But along the way, the people became so impatient 5 that they complained against God and said to Moses, "Did you bring us out of Egypt, just to let us die in the desert? There's no water out here, and we can't stand this awful food!"

6 Then the LORD sent poisonous snakes that bit and killed many of them.

7 Some of the people went to Moses and admitted, "It was wrong of us to insult you and the LORD. Now please ask him to make these snakes go away."

Moses prayed, 8 and the LORD answered, "Make a snake out of bronze and place it on top of a pole. Anyone who gets bitten can look at the snake and won't die."

9 Moses obeyed the LORD. And all of those who looked at the bronze snake lived, even

---

*20.17 the main road: The Hebrew text has "the King's Highway", which was an important trade route through what is today the country of Jordan. It connected the city of Damascus in Syria with the Gulf of Aqaba in southern Jordan.

See also: 20.28: Exod 29.29; Num 33.38; Deut 10.6.

*21.2 completely destroy . . . belong to you: The complete destruction of a town and everything in it, including its people and animals, showed that the town belonged to the LORD and could no longer be used by humans.

*21.4 Red Sea: See the note at 14.25.

See also: 21.1: Num 33.40. 21.4: Deut 2.1. 21.5-6: 1 Cor 10.9. 21.9: 2 King 18.4; John 3.14.

though they had been bitten by the poisonous snakes.

Israel's journey to Moab

¹⁰ As the Israelites continued their journey to Canaan, they camped at Oboth, ¹¹ then at Iye-Abarim in the desert east of Moab, ¹² and then in the Zered Gorge. ¹³ After that, they crossed the gorge of the River Arnon and camped in the Moabite desert bordering Amorite territory. The Arnon was the border between the Moabites and the Amorites.
¹⁴ A song in *The Book of the LORD's Battles** mentions the town of Waheb with its creeks in the territory of Suphah. It also mentions the River Arnon, ¹⁵ with its valleys that lie beside the Moabite border and extend to the town of Ar.
¹⁶ From the Arnon, the Israelites went to the well near the town of Beer, where the LORD had said to Moses, "Call the people together, and I will give them water to drink."
¹⁷ That's also the same well the Israelites sang about in this song:

> Let's celebrate!
> The well has given us water.
> ¹⁸ With their royal sceptres,
> our leaders pointed out
> where to dig the well.

The Israelites left the desert and camped near the town of Mattanah, ¹⁹ then at Nahaliel, and then at Bamoth. ²⁰ Finally, they reached Moabite territory, where they camped near Mount Pisgah* in a valley overlooking the desert north of the Dead Sea.

Israel defeats King Sihon the Amorite

This is also told in Deuteronomy 2.26–37

²¹ The Israelites sent this message to King Sihon of the Amorites:

> ²² Please let us pass through your territory. We promise to stay away from your fields and vineyards, and we won't drink any water from your wells. As long as we're in your land, we won't get off the main road.*

²³ But Sihon refused to let Israel travel through his land. Instead, he called together his entire army and marched into the desert to attack Israel near the town of Jahaz. ²⁴ Israel defeated them and took over the Amorite territory from the gorge of the River Arnon in the south to the gorge of the River Jabbok in the north. Beyond the Jabbok was the territory of the Ammonites, who were much stronger than Israel.
²⁵ The Israelites settled in the Amorite towns, including the capital city of Heshbon with its surrounding villages. ²⁶ King Sihon had ruled from Heshbon, after defeating the Moabites and taking over their land north of the Arnon gorge. ²⁷ That's why the Amorites had written this poem about Heshbon:

> Come and rebuild Heshbon,
>   King Sihon's capital city!
> ²⁸ His armies marched out
>   like fiery flames,
>   burning down the town of Ar
>   and destroying⁾ the hills
>   along the River Arnon.
> ²⁹ You Moabites are done for!
>   Your god Chemosh
>   deserted your people;
>   they were captured, taken away
>   by King Sihon the Amorite.
> ³⁰ We completely defeated Moab.
>   The towns of Heshbon and Dibon,
>   of Nophah and Medeba
>   are ruined and gone.⁾

³¹ After the Israelites had settled in the Amorite territory, ³² Moses sent some men to explore the town of Jazer. Later, the Israelites captured the villages surrounding it and forced out the Amorites who lived there.

Israel defeats King Og of Bashan

This is also told in Deuteronomy 3.1–11

³³ The Israelites headed towards the region of Bashan, where King Og ruled, and he led his entire army to Edrei to meet Israel in battle.
³⁴ The LORD said to Moses, "Don't be afraid of Og. I will help you defeat him and his army, just as you did King Sihon who ruled in Heshbon. Og's territory will be yours."
³⁵ So the Israelites wiped out Og, his family, and his entire army — there were no survivors. Then Israel took over the land of Bashan.

---

*21.14 The Book of the LORD's Battles: This may have been a collection of ancient war songs.
*21.20 Mount Pisgah: This probably refers to the highest peak in the Abarim Mountains in Moab.
*21.22 the main road: See the note at 20.17.

See also: 21.28–29: Jer 48.45–46.

The messages of Balaam

CHAPTER 22

¹ Israel moved from there to the hills of Moab, where they camped across the River Jordan from the town of Jericho.

King Balak of Moab hires Balaam to curse Israel

²⁻³ When King Balak* of Moab and his people heard how many Israelites there were and what they had done to the Amorites, he and the Moabites were terrified and panicked. ⁴ They said to the Midianite leaders, "Those Israelites will wipe out everything in sight, like a bull eating grass in a field."

So King Balak ⁵ sent a message to Balaam son of Beor who lived among his relatives in the town of Pethor near the River Euphrates. It said:

I need your help. A huge group of people has come here from Egypt and settled near my territory. ⁶ They are too powerful for us to defeat, so would you come and place a curse on them? Perhaps then we can drive them out. I know that anyone you bless will be successful, but anyone you curse will fail.

⁷ The leaders of Moab and Midian left and took along money to pay Balaam for his work. When they got to his house, they gave him Balak's message.

⁸ "Spend the night here," Balaam replied, "and tomorrow I will tell you the LORD's answer." So the officials stayed at his house.

⁹ During the night, God asked Balaam, "Who are these people at your house?"

¹⁰ "They are messengers from King Balak of Moab," Balaam answered. "He sent them ¹¹ to ask me to go to Moab and place a curse on the people who have come there from Egypt. They have settled everywhere around him, and he wants to drive them out."

¹² But God replied, "Don't go with Balak's messengers. I have blessed those people who have come from Egypt, so don't curse them."

¹³ The next morning, Balaam said to Balak's officials, "Go back home. The LORD says I cannot go with you."

¹⁴ The officials left and told Balak that Balaam refused to come.

Life files

Balaam

What's the story?

Alarmed at their success, the king of Moab asks Balaam to curse the Israelites. (In those days a curse was thought to have great power.) Balaam asks God whether he should go. Eventually, God says 'yes', providing he does exactly what the LORD says.

Balaam sets out, only to have his donkey break down on him. It swerves off the path, crushes Balaam's leg against the wall and finally sinks to the ground, leaving Balaam beating it in frustration. The donkey then has a right go at Balaam, at which Balaam's eyes are opened and he sees an angel standing in the way with drawn sword to bar his passage. The so-called 'holy man' cannot see the angel, but the 'dumb' beast can. In the end Balaam goes to Balak but, instead of cursing Israel, he blesses them, and delivers a prophecy that, in the far future a 'king of Israel will appear like a star'.

Later Balaam appears to have stayed among the Midianites where he seems to have persuaded the Midianite women to infiltrate the Israelites and seduce them into worshipping Baal (Numbers 31.16). Balaam is killed in the war.

What's the point?

Angels, talking donkeys, curses – this is a seriously strange story. Perhaps the key to it lies in the story of Balaam's death. This was a prophet who never seemed to know his own mind. God warned him to do what he was told, but perhaps he was tempted to earn money from the king of Moab. One thing is sure, if your donkey starts behaving strangely, pay attention; it might be the LORD!

*22.2–3 **Balak**: Hebrew "Balak son of Zippor".
See also: 22.5: Num 31.8; 2 Pet 2.15–16.

165

15 Then Balak sent a larger group of officials, who were even more important than the first ones. 16 They went to Balaam and told him that Balak had said, "Balaam, if you come to Moab, 17 I'll pay you very well and do whatever you ask. Just come and place a curse on these people."

18 Balaam answered, "Even if Balak offered me a palace full of silver or gold, I wouldn't do anything to disobey the LORD my God. 19 You are welcome to spend the night here, just as the others did. I will find out if the LORD has something else to say about this."

20 That night, God said, "Balaam, I'll let you go to Moab with Balak's messengers, but do only what I say."

21 So Balaam got up the next morning and saddled his donkey, then left with the Moabite officials.

Balaam and his donkey meet an angel

22 Balaam was riding his donkey to Moab, and two of his servants were with him. But God was angry that Balaam had gone, so one of the LORD's angels stood in the road to stop him. 23 When Balaam's donkey saw the angel standing there with a sword, it walked off the road and into an open field. Balaam had to beat the donkey to get it back on the road.

24 Then the angel stood between two vineyards, in a narrow path with a stone wall on each side. 25 When the donkey saw the angel, it walked so close to one of the walls that Balaam's foot scraped against the wall. Balaam beat the donkey again.

26 The angel moved once more and stood in a spot so narrow that there was no room for the donkey to go around. 27 So it just lay down. Balaam lost his temper, then picked up a stick and hit the donkey.

28 When that happened, the LORD told the donkey to speak, and it asked Balaam, "What have I done to you that made you beat me three times?"

29 "You made me look stupid!" Balaam answered. "If I had a sword, I'd kill you here and now!"

30 "But you're my owner," replied the donkey, "and you've ridden me many times. Have I ever done anything like this before?"

"No," Balaam admitted.

31 Just then, the LORD let Balaam see the angel standing in the road, holding a sword, and Balaam bowed down.

32 The angel said, "You had no right to treat your donkey like that! I was the one who blocked your way, because I don't think

you should go to Moab.' 33 If your donkey had not seen me and stopped those three times, I would have killed you and let the donkey live."

34 Balaam replied, "I was wrong. I didn't know you were trying to stop me. If you don't think I should go, I'll return home at once."

35 "It's all right for you to go," the LORD's angel answered. "But you must say only what I tell you." So Balaam went on with Balak's officials.

King Balak meets Balaam

36 When Balak heard that Balaam was coming, he went to meet him at the town of Ir, which is on the northern border of Moab. 37 Balak asked, "Why didn't you come when I invited you the first time? Did you think I wasn't going to pay you?"

38 "I'm here now," Balaam answered. "But I will say only what God tells me to say."

39 They left and went to the town of Kiriath-Huzoth, 40 where Balak sacrificed cattle and sheep and gave some of the meat to Balaam and the officials who were with him.

41 The next morning, Balak took Balaam to the town of Bamoth-Baal. From there, Balaam could see some of the Israelites.*

CHAPTER 23

Balaam's first message

1 Balaam said to Balak, "Build seven altars here, then bring seven bulls and seven rams."

2 After Balak had done this, they sacrificed a bull and a ram on each altar. 3 Then Balaam said, "Wait here beside your offerings, and I'll go somewhere to be alone. Perhaps the LORD will appear to me. If he does, I will tell you everything he says." And he left.

4 When God appeared to him, Balaam said, "I have built seven altars and have sacrificed a bull and a ram on each one."

5 The LORD gave Balaam a message, then sent him back to tell Balak. 6 When Balaam returned, he found Balak and his officials standing beside the offerings.

7 Balaam said:

"King Balak of Moab brought me
   from the hills of Syria
to curse Israel
   and announce its doom.

---

*22.41 Balaam could see some of the Israelites: For a curse to work, the people or thing being cursed had to be seen.

8 But I can't go against God!
He did not curse
or condemn Israel.

9 "From the mountain peaks,
I look down and see Israel,
the obedient people of God.
10 They are living alone in peace.
And though they are many,
they don't bother
the other nations.

"I hope to obey God
for as long as I live
and to die in such peace."

11 Balak said, "What are you doing? I asked you to come and place a curse on my enemies. But you have blessed them instead!"
12 Balaam answered, "I can say only what the LORD tells me."

Balaam's second message

13 Balak said to Balaam, "Let's go somewhere else. Perhaps if you see a smaller part of the Israelites, you will be able to curse them for me." 14 So he took Balaam to a field on top of Mount Pisgah where lookouts were stationed.' Then he built seven altars there and sacrificed a bull and a ram on each one.
15 "Wait here beside your offerings," Balaam said. "The LORD will appear to me over there."
16 The LORD appeared to Balaam and gave him another message, then he told him to go and tell Balak. 17 Balaam went back and saw him and his officials standing beside the offerings.
Balak asked, "What did the LORD say?"
18 Balaam answered:

"Pay close attention to my words —
19 God is no mere human!
He doesn't tell lies
or change his mind.
God always keeps his promises.

20 "My command from God
was to bless these people,
and there's nothing I can do
to change what he has done.
21 Israel's king is the LORD God.
He lives there with them
and intends them no harm.
22 With the strength of a wild ox,
God led Israel out of Egypt.
23 No magic charms can work
against them —

just look what God has done
for his people.
24 They are like angry lions
ready to attack;
and they won't rest
until their victim is gobbled up."

25 Balak shouted, "If you're not going to curse Israel, then at least don't bless them."
26 "I've already told you," Balaam answered. "I will say only what the LORD tells me."

Balaam's third message

27 Balak said to Balaam, "Come on, let's try another place. Perhaps God will let you curse Israel from there." 28 So he took Balaam to Mount Peor overlooking the desert north of the Dead Sea.
29 Balaam said, "Build seven altars here, then bring me seven bulls and seven rams."
30 After Balak had done what Balaam asked, he sacrificed a bull and a ram on each altar.

CHAPTER 24

1 Balaam was sure that the LORD would tell him to bless Israel again. So he did not use any magic to find out what the LORD wanted him to do, as he had the first two times. Instead, he looked out towards the desert 2 and saw the tribes of Israel camped below. Just then, God's Spirit took control of him, 3 and Balaam said:

"I am the son of Beor,
and my words are true,'
so listen to my message!
4 It comes from the LORD,
the God All-Powerful.
I bowed down to him
and saw a vision of Israel.

5 "People of Israel,
your camp is lovely.
6 It's like a grove of palm trees'
or a garden beside a river.
You are like tall aloe trees
that the LORD has planted,
or like cedars
growing near water.
7 You and your descendants
will prosper like an orchard
beside a stream.
Your king will rule with power

and be a greater king
than Agag the Amalekite.*
[8] With the strength of a wild ox,
God led you out of Egypt.
You will defeat your enemies,
shooting them with arrows'
and crushing their bones.
[9] Like a lion you lie down,
resting after an attack.
Who would dare disturb you?

"Anyone who blesses you
will be blessed;
anyone who curses you
will be cursed."

[10] When Balak heard this, he was so furious
that he pounded his fist against his hand and
said, "I called you here to place a curse on my
enemies, and you've blessed them three
times. [11] Leave now and go home! I told you I
would pay you well, but since the LORD
didn't let you do what I asked, you won't be
paid." [12] Balaam answered, "I told your
messengers [13] that even if you offered me a
palace full of silver or gold, I would still obey
the LORD. And I explained that I would say
only what he told me. [14] So I'm going back
home, but I'm leaving you with a warning
about what the Israelites will some day do to
your nation."

Balaam's fourth message

[15] Balaam said:

"I am the son of Beor,
and my words are true,'
so listen to my message!
[16] My knowledge comes
from God Most High,
the LORD All-Powerful.
I bowed down to him
and saw a vision of Israel.

[17] "What I saw in my vision
hasn't happened yet.
But some day, a king of Israel
will appear like a star.
He will wipe out you Moabites'
and destroy' those tribes
who live in the desert.'

[18] Israel will conquer Edom
and capture the land
of that enemy nation.
[19] The king of Israel will rule
and destroy the survivors
of every town there.'

[20] "And I saw this vision
about the Amalekites:*
Their nation is now great,
but it will some day
disappear for ever.'

[21] "And this is what I saw
about the Kenites:*
They think they're safe,
living among the rocks,
[22] but they will be wiped out
when Assyria conquers them.'

[23] "No one can survive
if God plans destruction.'
[24] Ships will come from Cyprus,
bringing people who will invade
the lands of Assyria and Eber.
But finally, Cyprus itself
will be ruined."

[25] After Balaam finished, he started home,
and Balak also left.

The people are unfaithful

CHAPTER 25

The Israelites worship Baal

[1] While the Israelites were camped at Acacia,
some of the men had sex with Moabite
women. [2] These women then invited the men
to ceremonies where sacrifices were offered to
their gods. The men ate the meat from the
sacrifices and worshipped the Moabite gods.
[3] The LORD was angry with Israel because
they had worshipped the god Baal-Peor. [4] So
he said to Moses, "Take the Israelite leaders
who are responsible for this and have them
killed in front of my sacred tent where
everyone can see. Perhaps then I will stop
being angry with the Israelites."
[5] Moses told Israel's officials,* "Each of you
must put to death any of your men who
worshipped Baal."

---

*24.7 Agag the Amalekite: The Amalekites were
long-time enemies of the Israelites (see
Exodus 17.8–16), and Agag was one of their most
powerful kings.
See also: 24.9: a Gen 49.9; b Gen 12.3.

*24.20 the Amalekites: See the note at 24.7.
*24.21 the Kenites: A group of people who lived in
the desert south of Israel.
*25.5 officials: These were special leaders who were
probably responsible for an entire tribe or part of a
tribe.

6 Later, Moses and the people were at the sacred tent, crying, when one of the Israelite men brought a Midianite* woman to meet his family. 7 Phinehas, the grandson of Aaron' the priest, saw the couple and left the crowd. He found a spear 8 and followed the man into his tent, where he ran the spear through the man and into the woman's stomach. The LORD immediately stopped punishing Israel with a deadly disease, 9 but twenty-four thousand Israelites had already died.

10 The LORD said to Moses, 11 "In my anger, I would have wiped out the Israelites if Phinehas had not been faithful to me. 12-13 But instead of punishing them, I forgave them. So because of the loyalty that Phinehas showed, I solemnly promise that he and his descendants will always be my priests."

14 The Israelite man that was killed was Zimri son of Salu, who was one of the leaders of the Simeon tribe. 15 And the Midianite woman killed with him was Cozbi, the daughter of a Midianite clan leader named Zur.

16 The LORD told Moses, 17-18 "The Midianites are now enemies of Israel, so attack and defeat them! They tricked the people of Israel into worshipping their god at Peor, and they are responsible for the death of Cozbi, the daughter of one of their own leaders."

The people of Israel are counted a second time

CHAPTER 26

1 After the LORD had stopped the deadly disease from killing the Israelites, he said to Moses and Eleazar son of Aaron, 2 "I want you to find out how many Israelites are in each family. And list every man twenty years and older who is able to serve in Israel's army."

3 Israel was now camped in the hills of Moab across the River Jordan from the town of Jericho. Moses and Eleazar told them 4 what the LORD had said about counting the men twenty years and older, just as Moses and their ancestors had done when they left Egypt.'

5-7 There were 43,730 men from the tribe of Reuben, the eldest son of Jacob.' These men were from the clans of Hanoch, Pallu, Hezron, and Carmi. 8 Pallu was the father of Eliab 9 and the grandfather of Nemuel, Dathan, and Abiram. These are the same Dathan and Abiram who had been chosen by the people, but who followed Korah and rebelled against Moses, Aaron, and the LORD. 10 That's when the LORD made the earth open up and swallow Dathan, Abiram, and Korah. At the same time, fire destroyed two hundred and fifty men as a warning to the other Israelites.* 11 But the Korahite clan wasn't destroyed.

12-14 There were 22,200 men from the tribe of Simeon; they were from the clans of Nemuel, Jamin, Jachin, Zerah, and Shaul.

15-18 There were 40,500 men from the tribe of Gad; they were from the clans of Zephon, Haggi, Shuni, Ozni, Eri, Arod, and Areli.

19-22 There were 76,500 men from the tribe of Judah; they were from the clans of Shelah, Perez, Zerah, Hezron, and Hamul. Judah's sons Er and Onan had died in Canaan.*

23-25 There were 64,300 men from the tribe of Issachar; they were from the clans of Tola, Puvah, Jashub, and Shimron.

26-27 There were 60,500 men from the tribe of Zebulun; they were from the clans of Sered, Elon, and Jahleel.

28-34 There were 52,700 men from the tribe of Manasseh son of Joseph; they were from the clan of Machir, the clan of Gilead his son, and the clans of his six grandsons: Iezer, Helek, Asriel, Shechem, Shemida, and Hepher. Zelophehad son of Hepher had no sons, but he had five daughters: Mahlah, Noah, Hoglah, Milcah, and Tirzah.*

35-37 There were 32,500 men from the tribe of Ephraim son of Joseph; they were from the clans of Shuthelah, Becher, Tahan, and Eran the son of Shuthelah.

38-41 There were 45,600 men from the tribe of Benjamin; they were from the clans of Bela, Ashbel, Ahiram, Shephupham, Hupham, as well as from Ard and Naaman, the two sons of Bela.

42-43 There were 64,400 men from the tribe of Dan; they were all from the clan of Shuham.

---

*25.6 Midianite: Used here as a general term for various peoples who lived east of the River Jordan. Some of these people were probably ruled by the Moabite king (see Genesis 36.35).

See also: 26.1-51: Num 1.1-46.

*26.10 Israelites: See 16.1-35.
*26.19-22 Judah's sons . . . Canaan: See Genesis 38.1-10.
*26.28-34 Zelophehad . . . Tirzah: See also 27.1-11; 36.1-12.

⁴⁴⁻⁴⁷ There were 53,400 men from the tribe of Asher; they were from the clans of Imnah, Ishvi, and Beriah, and from the two clans of Heber and Malchiel, the sons of Beriah. Asher's daughter was Serah.

⁴⁸⁻⁵⁰ There were 45,400 men from the tribe of Naphtali; they were from the clans of Jahzeel, Guni, Jezer, and Shillem.

⁵¹ The total number of Israelite men listed was 601,730.

⁵² The LORD said to Moses, ⁵³ "Divide the land of Canaan among these tribes, according to the number of people in each one, ⁵⁴ so the larger tribes have more land than the smaller ones. ⁵⁵⁻⁵⁶ I will show you* what land to give each tribe, and they will receive as much land as they need, according to the number of people in it."

⁵⁷ The tribe of Levi included the clans of the Gershonites, Kohathites, Merarites, ⁵⁸ as well as the clans of Libni, Hebron, Mahli, Mushi, and Korah. Kohath the Levite was the father of Amram, ⁵⁹ the husband of Levi's daughter Jochebed, who was born in Egypt. Amram and Jochebed's three children were Aaron, Moses, and Miriam. ⁶⁰ Aaron was the father of Nadab, Abihu, Eleazar, and Ithamar. ⁶¹ But Nadab and Abihu had died when they offered fire that was unacceptable to the LORD.*

⁶² In the tribe of Levi there were 23,000 men and boys at least a month old. They were not listed with the other tribes, because they would not receive any land in Canaan.

⁶³ Moses and Eleazar counted the Israelites while they were camped in the hills of Moab across the River Jordan from Jericho. ⁶⁴ None of the people that Moses and Aaron had counted in the Sinai Desert were still alive, ⁶⁵ except Caleb son of Jephunneh and Joshua son of Nun. The LORD had said that everyone else would die there in the desert.*

---

*26.55–56 I will show you:** The Hebrew text has "Cast lots to find out". Pieces of wood or stone (called "lots") were used to find out what the LORD wanted his people to do.
*26.61 Nadab and Abihu . . . the LORD:** See 3.1–4 and Leviticus 10.1–2.
*26.64–65 None of the people . . . the desert:** See 14.26–30.
See also: 26.52–56: Num 34.13; Josh 14.1–2.
26.60: Num 3.2. 26.61: Lev 10.1–2; Num 3.4.
26.65: Num 14.26–35.

The daughters of Zelophehad are given land

CHAPTER 27

¹ Zelophehad' was from the Manasseh tribe, and he had five daughters, whose names were Mahlah, Noah, Hoglah, Milcah, and Tirzah.

² One day his daughters went to the sacred tent, where they met with Moses, Eleazar, and some other leaders of Israel, as well as a large crowd of Israelites. The young women said:

³ You know that our father died in the desert. But it was for something he did wrong, not for joining with Korah in rebelling against the LORD.

Our father left no sons ⁴ to carry on his family name. But why should his name die out for that reason? Give us some land like the rest of his relatives in our clan, so our father's name can live on.

⁵ Moses asked the LORD what should be done, ⁶ and the LORD answered:

⁷ Zelophehad's daughters are right. They should each be given part of the land their father would have received.

⁸ Tell the Israelites that when a man dies without a son, his daughter will inherit his land. ⁹ If he has no daughter, his brothers will inherit the land. ¹⁰ But if he has no brothers, his father's brothers will inherit the land. ¹¹ And if his father has no brothers, the land must be given to his nearest relative in the clan. This is my law, and the Israelites must obey it.

Joshua is appointed Israel's leader

This is also told in Deuteronomy 31.1–8

¹² The LORD said to Moses, "One day you will go up into the Abarim Mountains, and from there you will see the land I am giving the Israelites. ¹³ After you have seen it, you will die,* just like your brother Aaron, ¹⁴ because both of you disobeyed me at

---

*27.12–13 One day . . . you will die:** The story of Moses' death is in Deuteronomy 34.1–8.
See also: 27.7: Num 36.2. 27.12–14: Deut 3.23–27; 32.48–52.

Meribah near the town of Kadesh in the Zin Desert. When the Israelites insulted me there, you didn't believe in my holy power."*

15 Moses replied, 16 "You are the LORD God, and you know what is in everyone's heart. So I ask you to appoint a leader for Israel. 17 Your people need someone to lead them into battle, or else they will be like sheep wandering around without a shepherd."

18 The LORD answered, "Joshua son of Nun can do the job. Place your hands on him to show that he is the one to take your place. 19 Then go with him and make him stand in front of Eleazar the priest and the Israelites. Appoint Joshua as their new leader 20 and tell them they must now obey him, just as they obey you. 21 But Joshua must depend on Eleazar to find out from me' what I want him to do as he leads Israel into battle."

22 Moses followed the LORD's instructions and took Joshua to Eleazar and the people, 23 then he placed his hands on Joshua and appointed him Israel's leader.

Various laws and sacrifices for Israel's festivals

CHAPTER 28

Regular daily sacrifices

This is also told in Exodus 29.38–43; Leviticus 6.8–13

1 The LORD told Moses 2 to say to the people of Israel:

Offer sacrifices to me at the appointed times of worship, so that I will smell the smoke and be pleased.

3 Each day offer two rams a year old as sacrifices to please me.* The animals must have nothing wrong with them; 4 one will be sacrificed in the morning, and the other in the evening. 5 Along with each of them, one kilogramme of your finest flour mixed with a litre of olive oil must be offered as a grain sacrifice. 6 This sacrifice to please me was first offered on Mount Sinai. 7 Finally, along with each of these two sacrifices, a litre of wine must be poured on the altar as a drink offering. 8 The second ram will be

sacrificed that evening, along with the other offerings, just like the one sacrificed that morning. The smell of the smoke from these sacrifices will please me.

The sacrifice on the Sabbath

The LORD said:

9-10 On the Sabbath, in addition to the regular daily sacrifices,* you must sacrifice two rams a year old to please me.* These rams must have nothing wrong with them, and they will be sacrificed with a drink offering and two kilogrammes of your finest flour mixed with olive oil.

The sacrifices on the first day of the month

The LORD said:

11 On the first day of each month, bring to the altar two bulls, one full-grown ram, and seven rams a year old that have nothing wrong with them. Then offer these as sacrifices to please me.* 12 Three kilogrammes of your finest flour mixed with olive oil must be offered with each bull as a grain sacrifice. Two kilogrammes of flour mixed with oil must be offered with the ram, 13 and one kilogramme of flour mixed with oil must be offered with each of the young rams. The smell of the smoke from these sacrifices will please me.

14-15 Offer two litres of wine as a drink offering with each bull, one and a half litres with the ram, and one litre with each of the young rams.

Finally, you must offer a goat' as a sacrifice for sin.

These sacrifices are to be offered on the first day of each month, in addition to the regular daily sacrifices.*

The sacrifices during Passover and the Festival of Thin Bread

This is also told in Leviticus 23.4–8

The LORD said:

16 Celebrate Passover in honour of me on the fourteenth day of the first month* of each year. 17 The following day will begin

---

*27.14 both of you . . . my holy power: See 20.1–13.
*28.3 sacrifices to please me: See the note at 6.11.

See also: 27.17: 1 King 22.17; Ezek 34.5; Matt 9.36; Mark 6.34. 27.18: Exod 24.13. 27.21: Exod 28.30; 1 Sam 14.41; 28.6. 27.23: Deut 31.23.

*28.9-10,14-15 regular daily sacrifices: See 28.1-8.
*28.9-10,11 sacrifice(s) . . . to please me: See the note at 6.11.
*28.16 first month: See the note at 9.3.

See also: 28.16: Exod 12.1–13; Deut 16.1–2.
28.17–25: Exod 12.14–20; 23.15; 34.18; Deut 16.3–8.

the Festival of Thin Bread, which will last for a week. During this time you must honour me by eating bread made without yeast.

18 On the first day of this festival, you must rest from your work and come together for worship. 19 Bring to the altar two bulls, one full-grown ram, and seven rams a year old that have nothing wrong with them. And then offer these as sacrifices to please me.* 20 Three kilogrammes of your finest flour mixed with olive oil must be offered with each bull as a grain sacrifice. Two kilogrammes of flour mixed with oil must be offered with the ram, 21 and one kilogramme of flour mixed with oil must be offered with each of the young rams. 22 Also offer a goat' as a sacrifice for the sins of the people. 23-24 All of these are to be offered in addition to the regular daily sacrifices,* and the smoke from them will please me. 25 Then on the last day of the festival, you must once again rest from work and come together for worship.

The sacrifices during the Harvest Festival

This is also told in Leviticus 23.15–22

The LORD said:

26 On the first day of the Harvest Festival, you must rest from your work, come together for worship, and bring a sacrifice of new grain. 27 Offer two young bulls, one full-grown ram, and seven rams a year old as sacrifices to please me.* 28 Three kilogrammes of your finest flour mixed with olive oil must be offered with each bull as a grain sacrifice. Two kilogrammes of flour mixed with oil must be offered with the ram, 29 and one kilogramme of flour mixed with oil must be offered with each of the young rams. 30 Also offer a goat' as a sacrifice for sin. 31 The animals must have nothing wrong with them and are to be sacrificed along with the regular daily sacrifices.*

CHAPTER 29
The sacrifices at the Festival of Trumpets

This is also told in Leviticus 23.23–25

The LORD said:

1 On the first day of the seventh month,* you must rest from your work and come together to celebrate at the sound of the trumpets. 2 Bring to the altar one bull, one full-grown ram, and seven rams a year old that have nothing wrong with them. And then offer these as sacrifices to please me.* 3 Three kilogrammes of your finest flour mixed with olive oil must be offered with the bull as a grain sacrifice. Two kilogrammes of flour mixed with oil must be offered with the ram, 4 and one kilogramme of flour mixed with oil must be offered with each of the young rams. 5 You must also offer a goat' as a sacrifice for sin. 6 These sacrifices will be made in addition to the regular daily sacrifices* and the sacrifices for the first day of the month.* The smoke from these sacrifices will please me.

The sacrifices on the Great Day of Forgiveness

This is also told in Leviticus 23.26–32

The LORD said:

7 The tenth day of the seventh month* is the Great Day of Forgiveness.* On that day you must rest from all work and come together for worship. Show sorrow for your sins by going without food, 8 and bring to the altar one young bull, one full-grown ram, and seven rams a year old that have nothing wrong with them. Then offer these as sacrifices to please me.* 9 Three kilogrammes of your finest flour mixed with olive oil must be offered with the bull as a grain sacrifice. Two kilogrammes of flour mixed with oil must be offered with the ram, 10 and one kilogramme of flour mixed with oil must be offered with each of

---

*29.1,7 seventh month: Tishri (also called Ethanim), the seventh month of the Hebrew calendar, from about mid-September to mid-October.
*29.2,8 sacrifices to please me: See the note at 6.11.
*29.6 regular daily sacrifices: See 28.1–8.
*29.6 sacrifices . . . month: See 28.11–15.
*29.7 Great Day of Forgiveness: Traditionally known as the Day of Atonement.
See also: 29.7–11: Lev 16.29–34.

---

*28.19,27 sacrifices to please me: See the note at 6.11.
*28.23–24,31 regular daily sacrifices: See 28.1–8.
See also: 28.26–31: Exod 23.16; 34.22; Deut 16.9–12.

the young rams. ¹¹ A goat‣ must also be sacrificed for the sins of the people. You will offer these sacrifices in addition to the sacrifice to ask forgiveness and the regular daily sacrifices.*

The sacrifices during the Festival of Shelters

This is also told in Leviticus 23.33–44

The LORD said:

¹² Beginning on the fifteenth day of the seventh month* and continuing for seven days, everyone must celebrate the Festival of Shelters in honour of me.

¹³ On the first day, you must rest from your work and come together for worship. Bring to the altar thirteen bulls, two full-grown rams, and fourteen rams a year old that have nothing wrong with them. Then offer these as sacrifices to please me.*

¹⁴ Three kilogrammes of your finest flour mixed with olive oil must be offered with each bull as a grain sacrifice. Two kilogrammes of flour mixed with oil must be offered with each of the rams, ¹⁵ and one kilogramme of flour mixed with oil must be offered with each of the young rams. ¹⁶ You must also offer a goat‣ as a sacrifice for sin. These are to be offered in addition to the regular daily sacrifices.*

¹⁷⁻³⁴ For the next six days of the festival, you will sacrifice one less bull than the day before, so that on the seventh day, seven bulls will be sacrificed. The other sacrifices and offerings must remain the same for each of these days.

³⁵ On the eighth day, you must once again rest from your work and come together for worship. ³⁶ Bring to the altar one bull, one full-grown ram, and seven rams a year old that have nothing wrong with them. Then offer these as sacrifices to please me. ³⁷ You must also offer the proper grain sacrifices and drink offerings of wine with each animal. ³⁸ And offer a goat‣ as the sacrifice to ask forgiveness for the people. These sacrifices are made in addition to the regular daily sacrifices.*

³⁹ You must offer all these sacrifices to me at the appointed times of worship, together with any offerings that are voluntarily given or given because of a promise.

⁴⁰ Moses told the people of Israel everything the LORD had told him about the sacrifices.

CHAPTER 30

Making promises to the LORD

¹ The LORD told Moses to say to Israel's tribal leaders:

² When one of you men makes a promise to the LORD,* you must keep your word.

³ Suppose a young woman who is still living with her parents makes a promise to the LORD. ⁴ If her father hears about it and says nothing, she must keep her promise. ⁵ But if he hears about it and objects, then she no longer has to keep her promise. The LORD will forgive her, because her father did not agree with the promise.

⁶⁻⁷ Suppose a woman makes a promise to the LORD and then gets married. If her husband later hears about the promise but says nothing, she must do what she said, whether she meant it or not. ⁸ But if her husband hears about the promise and objects, she no longer has to keep it, and the LORD will forgive her.

⁹ Widows and divorced women must keep every promise they make to the LORD.

¹⁰ Suppose a married woman makes a promise to the LORD. ¹¹ If her husband hears about the promise and says nothing, she must do what she said. ¹² But if he hears about the promise and does object, she no longer has to keep it. The LORD will forgive her, because her husband would not allow her to keep the promise. ¹³ Her husband has the final say about any promises she makes to the LORD. ¹⁴ If her husband hears about a promise and says nothing about it for a whole day, she must do what she said — since he did not object, the promise must be kept. ¹⁵ But if he waits until the next day to stop her from keeping her promise, he is the one who must be punished.

¹⁶ These are the laws that the LORD gave Moses about husbands and wives, and about young daughters who still live at home.

---

*29.11,16,38 regular daily sacrifices: See 28.1–8.
*29.12 seventh month: See the note at 29.1.
*29.13 sacrifices to please me: See the note at 6.11.
See also: 29.12–38: Lev 23.34; Deut 16.13–15.

*30.2 a promise to the LORD: Either the promise of a gift or the promise to do something.
See also: 30.2: Deut 23.21–23; Matt 5.33.

Israel defeats Midian and prepares to cross the River Jordan

CHAPTER 31

Israel's war against Midian

[1] The LORD said to Moses, [2] "Before you die, make sure that the Midianites are punished for what they did to Israel."*

[3] Then Moses told the people, "The LORD wants to punish the Midianites. So tell our men to prepare for battle. [4] Each tribe will send a thousand men to fight."

[5] Twelve thousand men were picked from the tribes of Israel, and after they were prepared for battle, [6] Moses sent them off to war. Phinehas the son of Eleazar went with them and took along some things from the sacred tent* and the trumpets for sounding the battle signal.

[7] The Israelites fought against the Midianites, just as the LORD had commanded Moses. They killed all the men, [8] including Balaam son of Beor and the five Midianite kings, Evi, Rekem, Zur, Hur, and Reba. [9] The Israelites captured every woman and child, then led away the Midianites' cattle and sheep, and took everything else that belonged to them. [10] They also burnt down the Midianite towns and villages.

[11] Israel's soldiers gathered together everything they had taken from the Midianites, including the captives and the animals. [12-13] Then they returned to their own camp in the hills of Moab across the River Jordan from Jericho, where Moses, Eleazar, and the other Israelite leaders met the troops outside camp.

[14] Moses became angry with the army commanders [15] and said, "I can't believe you let the women live! [16] They are the ones who followed Balaam's advice and invited our people to worship the god Baal-Peor. That's why the LORD punished us by killing so many of our people. [17] You must put to death every boy and all the women who have ever had sex. [18] But do not kill the young women who have never had sex. You may keep them for yourselves."

[19] Then Moses said to the soldiers, "If you killed anyone or touched a dead body, you are unclean and have to stay outside the camp for seven days. On the third and seventh days, you must go through a ceremony to make yourselves and your captives clean. [20] Then wash your clothes and anything made from animal skin, goat's hair, or wood."

[21-23] Eleazar then explained, "If you need to purify something that won't burn, such as gold, silver, bronze, iron, tin, or lead, you must first place it in a hot fire. After you take it out, sprinkle it with the water that purifies. Everything else should only be sprinkled with the water. Do all of this, just as the LORD commanded Moses. [24] Wash your clothes on the seventh day, and after that, you will be clean and may return to the camp."

Everything taken from the Midianites is divided

[25] The LORD told Moses:

[26-27] Make a list of everything taken from the Midianites, including the captives and the animals. Then divide them between the soldiers and the rest of the people. Eleazar the priest and the family leaders will help you.

[28-29] From the half that belongs to the soldiers, set aside for the LORD one out of every five hundred people or animals and give these to Eleazar.

[30] From the half that belongs to the people, set aside one out of every fifty and give these to the Levites in charge of the sacred tent.

[31] Moses and Eleazar followed the LORD's instructions [32-35] and listed everything that had been taken from the Midianites. The list included 675,000 sheep and goats, 72,000 cattle, 61,000 donkeys, and 32,000 young women who had never had sex.

[36-47] Each half included 337,500 sheep and goats, 36,000 cattle, 30,500 donkeys, and 16,000 young women. From the half that belonged to the soldiers, Moses counted out 675 sheep and goats, 72 cattle, 61 donkeys, and 32 women and gave them to Eleazar to be dedicated to the LORD. Then from the half that belonged to the people, Moses set aside one out of every fifty animals and women, as the LORD had said, and gave them to the Levites.

[48] The army commanders went to Moses [49] and said, "Sir, we have counted our troops,

---

*31.2 Midianites . . . to Israel: See 25.1–18.

*31.6 Phinehas . . . sacred tent: Phinehas would serve as the priest during the battle, so he took along the things needed to ask God what he wanted done.

See also: 31.16: Num 25.1–9.

and not one soldier is missing. [50] So we want to give the LORD all the gold jewellery we took from the Midianites. It's our gift to him for watching over us and our troops."

[51] Moses and Eleazar accepted the jewellery from the commanders, [52] and its total weight was nearly two hundred kilogrammes. [53] This did not include the things that the soldiers had kept for themselves. [54] So Moses and Eleazar placed the gold in the LORD's sacred tent to remind Israel of what had happened.'

CHAPTER 32

Land east of the River Jordan is settled

This is also told in Deuteronomy 3.12–22

[1] The tribes of Reuben and Gad owned a lot of cattle and sheep, and they saw that the regions of Jazer and Gilead had good pasture land. [2] So they went to Moses, Eleazar, and the other leaders of Israel and said, [3-4] "The LORD has helped us capture the land around the towns of Ataroth, Dibon, Jazer, Nimrah, Heshbon, Elealeh, Sebam, Nebo, and Beon. That's good pasture land, and since we own cattle and sheep, [5] would you let us stay here east of the River Jordan and have this land as our own?"

[6] Moses answered:

You mean you'd stay here while the rest of the Israelites go into battle? [7] If you did that, it would discourage the others from crossing over into the land the LORD promised them. [8] This is exactly what happened when I sent your ancestors from Kadesh-Barnea to explore the land. [9] They went as far as Eshcol Valley, then returned and told the people that we should not enter it. [10] The LORD became very angry. [11] And he said that no one who was twenty years or older when they left Egypt would enter the land he had promised to Abraham, Isaac, and Jacob. Not one of those people believed in the LORD's power, [12] except Caleb and Joshua.' They remained faithful to the LORD, [13] but he was so angry with the others that he forced them to wander around in the desert forty years. By that time everyone who had sinned against him had died.

[14] Now you people of Reuben and Gad are doing the same thing and making the LORD even angrier. [15] If you reject the LORD, he will once again abandon his people and leave them here in the desert. And you will be to blame!

[16] The men from Reuben and Gad replied:

Let us build places to keep our sheep and goats, and towns for our wives and children, [17] where they can stay and be safe. Then we'll prepare to fight and lead the other tribes into battle. [18] We will stay with them until they have settled in their own tribal lands. [19] The land on this side of the River Jordan will be ours, so we won't expect to receive any on the other side.

[20] Moses said:

You promised that you would be ready to fight for the LORD. [21] You also agreed to cross the Jordan and stay with the rest of the Israelites, until the LORD forces our enemies out of the land. If you do these things, [22] then after the LORD helps Israel capture the land, you can return to your own land. You will no longer have to stay with the others. [23] But if you don't keep your promise, you will sin against the LORD and be punished.

[24] Go ahead and build towns for your wives and children, and places for your sheep and goats. Just be sure to do what you have promised.

[25] The men from Reuben and Gad answered:

Sir, we will do just what you have said. [26] Our wives and children and sheep and cattle will stay here in the towns in Gilead. [27] But those of us who are prepared for battle will cross the Jordan and fight for the LORD.

[28] Then Moses said to Eleazar, Joshua, and the family leaders, [29] "Make sure that the tribes of Gad and Reuben prepare for battle and cross the River Jordan with you. If they do, then after the land is in your control, give them the region of Gilead as their tribal land. [30] But if they break their promise, they will receive land on the other side of the Jordan, like the rest of the tribes."

[31] The tribes of Gad and Reuben replied, "We are your servants and will do whatever the LORD has commanded. [32] We will cross the River Jordan, ready to fight for the LORD in Canaan. But the land we will inherit as our own will be on this side of the river."

[33] So Moses gave the tribes of Gad, Reuben, and half of Manasseh' the territory and towns that King Sihon the Amorite had ruled, as

---

See also: **32.8–9**: Num 13.17–33. **32.10–13**: Num 14.26–35.   See also: **32.28–32**: Josh 1.12–15.

well as the territory and towns that King Og of Bashan had ruled.'

³⁴ The tribe of Gad rebuilt the towns of Dibon, Ataroth, Aroer, ³⁵ Atroth-Shophan, Jazer, Jogbehah, ³⁶ Beth-Nimrah, and Beth-Haran. They built walls around them and also built places to keep their sheep and goats.

³⁷ The tribe of Reuben rebuilt Heshbon, Elealeh, Kiriathaim, ³⁸ Sibmah, as well as the towns that used to be known as Nebo and Baal-Meon. They renamed all those places.

³⁹ The clan of Machir from the tribe of East Manasseh went to the region of Gilead, captured its towns, and forced out the Amorites. ⁴⁰ So Moses gave the Machirites the region of Gilead, and they settled there.

⁴¹ Jair from the Manasseh tribe captured villages and renamed them "Villages of Jair".'

⁴² Nobah captured the town of Kenath with its villages and renamed it Nobah.

CHAPTER 33

Israel's journey from Egypt to Moab

¹ As Israel travelled from Egypt under the command of Moses and Aaron, ² Moses kept a list of the places where they camped, just as the LORD had instructed. Here is the record of their journey:

³⁻⁴ Israel left the Egyptian city of Rameses on the fifteenth day of the first month.* This was the day after the LORD had punished Egypt's gods by killing the firstborn sons in every Egyptian family. So while the Egyptians were burying the bodies, they watched the Israelites proudly' leave their country.

⁵ After the Israelites left Rameses, they camped at Succoth, ⁶ and from there, they moved their camp to Etham on the edge of the desert. ⁷ Then they turned back towards Pi-Hahiroth, east of Baal-Zephon, and camped near Migdol. ⁸ They left Pi-Hahiroth,' crossed the Red Sea,* then walked three days into the Etham Desert and camped at Marah. ⁹ Next, they camped at Elim, where there were twelve springs of water and seventy palm trees. ¹⁰ They left Elim and camped near the Red Sea,* ¹¹ then turned east and camped

along the western edge of the Sinai Desert.'

¹²⁻¹⁴ From there they went to Dophkah, Alush, and Rephidim, where they had no water.* ¹⁵ They left Rephidim and finally reached the Sinai Desert.

¹⁶⁻³⁶ As Israel travelled from the Sinai Desert to Kadesh in the Zin Desert, they camped at Kibroth-Hattaavah, Hazeroth, Rithmah, Rimmon-Perez, Libnah, Rissah, Kehelathah, Mount Shepher, Haradah, Makheloth, Tahath, Terah, Mithkah, Hashmonah, Moseroth, Bene-Jaakan, Hor-Haggidgad, Jotbathah, Abronah, Ezion-Geber, and finally Kadesh. ³⁷ When they left Kadesh, they came to Mount Hor, on the border of Edom.

³⁸ That's where the LORD commanded Aaron the priest to go to the top of the mountain. Aaron died there on the first day of the fifth month,* forty years after the Israelites left Egypt. ³⁹ He was one hundred and twenty-three years old at the time.

⁴⁰ It was then that the Canaanite king of Arad, who lived in the Southern Desert of Canaan, heard that Israel was headed that way.

⁴¹⁻⁴⁷ The Israelites left Mount Hor and headed towards Moab. Along the way, they camped at Zalmonah, Punon, Oboth, Iye-Abarim in the territory of Moab, Dibon-Gad, Almon-Diblathaim, at a place near Mount Nebo in the Abarim Mountains, ⁴⁸ and finally in the lowlands of Moab across the River Jordan from Jericho. ⁴⁹ Their camp stretched from Beth-Jeshimoth to Acacia.

The LORD's command to conquer Canaan

⁵⁰ While Israel was camped in the lowlands of Moab across the River Jordan from Jericho, the LORD told Moses ⁵¹ to give the people of Israel this message:

When you cross the River Jordan and enter Canaan, ⁵² you must force out the people living there. Destroy their idols and tear down their altars. ⁵³ Then settle in the land — I have given it to you as your own.

⁵⁴ I will show you* how to divide the land among the tribes, according to the

---

*33.3–4 first month: See the note at 9.3.
*33.8 Red Sea: Hebrew *hayyam* "the Sea", understood as *yam suph*, "Sea of Reeds" (see also the note at Exodus 13.18).
*33.10 Red Sea: Hebrew *yam suph*, here referring to the Gulf of Suez, since the term is extended to include the north-western arm of the Red Sea (see also the note at Exodus 13.18).

*33.12–14 Rephidim . . . no water: See Exodus 17.1–7.
*33.38 fifth month: Ab, the fifth month of the Hebrew calendar, from about mid-July to mid-August.
*33.54 I will show you: See the note at 26.55–56.
See also: 33.38: Num 20.22–28; Deut 10.6; 32.50. 33.40: Num 21.1. 33.54: Num 26.54–56.

number of clans in each one, so that the larger tribes will have more land than the smaller ones.

⁵⁵ If you don't force out all the people there, they will be like pointed sticks in your eyes and thorns in your back. They will always be trouble for you, ⁵⁶ and I will treat you as cruelly as I planned to treat them.

CHAPTER 34

Israel's borders

¹ The LORD told Moses ² to tell the people of Israel that their land in Canaan would have the following borders:

³ The southern border will be the Zin Desert and the north-west part of Edom. This border will begin at the south end of the Dead Sea. ⁴ It will go west from there, but will turn southward to include Scorpion Pass, the village of Zin, and the town of Kadesh-Barnea. From there, the border will continue to Hazar-Addar and on to Azmon. ⁵ It will run along the Egyptian Gorge and end at the Mediterranean Sea.

⁶ The western border will be the Mediterranean Sea.

⁷ The northern border will begin at the Mediterranean, then continue eastward to Mount Hor.* ⁸ After that, it will run to Lebo-Hamath and across to Zedad, which is the northern edge of your land. ⁹ From Zedad, the border will continue east to Ziphron and end at Hazar-Enan.

¹⁰ The eastern border will begin at Hazar-Enan in the north, then run south to Shepham, ¹¹ and on down to Riblah on the east side of Ain. From there, it will go south to the eastern hills of Lake Galilee, ¹² then follow the River Jordan down to the north end of the Dead Sea.

The land within those four borders will belong to you.

¹³ Then Moses told the people, "You will receive the land inside these borders. It will be yours, but the LORD has commanded you to divide it among the nine and a half tribes. ¹⁴ The tribes of Reuben, Gad, and East Manasseh have already been given their land ¹⁵ across from Jericho, east of the River Jordan."

The leaders who will divide the land

¹⁶ The LORD said to Moses, ¹⁷ "Eleazar the priest and Joshua son of Nun will divide the land for the Israelites. ¹⁸ One leader from each tribe will help them, ¹⁹⁻²⁸ and here is the list of their names:

Caleb son of Jephunneh from Judah,
Shemuel son of Ammihud from Simeon,
Elidad son of Chislon from Benjamin,
Bukki son of Jogli from Dan,
Hanniel son of Ephod from Manasseh,
Kemuel son of Shiphtan from Ephraim,
Elizaphan son of Parnach from Zebulun,
Paltiel son of Azzan from Issachar,
Ahihud son of Shelomi from Asher,
and Pedahel son of Ammihud
  from Naphtali."

²⁹ These are the men the LORD commanded to help Eleazar and Joshua divide the land for the Israelites.

CHAPTER 35

The towns for the Levites

¹ While the people of Israel were still camped in the lowlands of Moab across the River Jordan from Jericho, the LORD told Moses ² to say to them:

When you receive your tribal lands, you must give towns and pastures to the Levi tribe. ³ That way, the Levites will have towns to live in and pastures for their animals. ⁴⁻⁵ The pasture around each of these towns must be in the shape of a square, with the town itself in the centre. The pasture is to measure nine hundred metres on each side, with four hundred and fifty metres of land outside each of the town walls. This will be the Levites' pasture land.

⁶ Six of the towns you give them will be Safe Towns where a person who has accidentally killed someone can run for protection. But you will also give the Levites forty-two other towns, ⁷ so they will have a total of forty-eight towns with their surrounding pastures.

⁸ Since the towns for the Levites must come from Israel's own tribal lands, the larger tribes will give more towns than the smaller ones.

---

*34.7 Mount Hor: Not the same as in 33.37.
See also: 34.13: Num 26.52–56. 34.13–15: Josh 14.1–5.

See also: 35.1–8: Josh 21.1–42.

The Safe Towns

This is also told in Deuteronomy 19.1–13; Joshua 20.1–9

⁹ The Lord then told Moses ¹⁰ to tell the people of Israel:

> After you have crossed the River Jordan and are settled in Canaan, ¹¹ choose Safe Towns, where a person who has accidentally killed someone can run for protection. ¹² If the victim's relatives think it was murder, they might try to take revenge.* Anyone accused of murder can run to one of these Safe Towns for protection and not be killed before a trial is held.
>
> ¹³ There are to be six of these Safe Towns, ¹⁴ three on each side of the River Jordan. ¹⁵ They will be places of protection for anyone who lives in Israel and accidentally kills someone.

Laws about murder and accidental killing

The Lord said:

> ¹⁶⁻¹⁸ Suppose you hit someone with a piece of iron or a large stone or a dangerous wooden tool. If that person dies, then you are a murderer and must be put to death ¹⁹ by one of the victim's relatives.* He will take revenge for his relative's death as soon as he finds you.
>
> ²⁰⁻²¹ Or suppose you get angry and kill someone by pushing or hitting or by throwing something. You are a murderer and must be put to death by one of the victim's relatives.
>
> ²²⁻²⁴ But if you are not angry and accidentally kill someone in any of these ways, the townspeople must hold a trial and decide if you are guilty. ²⁵ If they decide that you are innocent, you will be protected from the victim's relative and sent to stay in one of the Safe Towns until the high priest dies. ²⁶ But if you ever leave the Safe Town ²⁷ and are killed by the victim's relative, he cannot be punished for killing you. ²⁸ You must stay inside the town until the high priest dies; only then can you go back home.
>
> ²⁹ The community of Israel must always obey these laws.

³⁰ Death is the penalty for murder. But no one accused of murder can be put to death unless there are at least two witnesses to the crime. ³¹ You cannot give someone money to escape the death penalty; you must pay with your own life! ³² And if you have been proved innocent of murder and are living in a Safe Town, you cannot pay to go back home; you must stay there until the high priest dies.

³³⁻³⁴ I, the Lord, live among you people of Israel, so your land must be kept pure. But when a murder takes place, blood pollutes the land, and it becomes unclean. If that happens, the murderer must be put to death, so the land will be clean again. Keep murder out of Israel!

CHAPTER 36

The laws about married women and land

¹ One day the family leaders from the Gilead clan of the Manasseh tribe went to Moses and the other family leaders of Israel ² and said, "Sir, the Lord has said that he will show* what land each tribe will receive as their own. And the Lord has commanded you to give the daughters of our relative Zelophehad* the land that he would have received. ³ But if they marry men from other tribes of Israel, the land they receive will become part of that tribe's inheritance and will no longer belong to us. ⁴ Even when land is returned to its original owner in the Year of Celebration,* we will not get back Zelophehad's land — it will belong to the tribe into which his daughters married."

⁵ So Moses told the people that the Lord had said:

> These men from the Manasseh tribe are right. ⁶ I will allow Zelophehad's daughters to marry anyone, as long as those men belong to one of the clans of the Manasseh tribe.
>
> ⁷ Tribal land must not be given to another tribe — it will remain the property

---

*35.12 the victim's relatives . . . revenge: At this time in Israel's history, the clan would appoint the closest male relative to find and kill a person who had killed a member of their clan.

*35.19 one of the victim's relatives: See the note at 35.12.

See also: 35.9–28: Deut 19.2–4; Josh 20.1–9.

*36.2 that he will show: See the note at 26.55–56.

*36.2 Zelophehad: See also 26.28–34; 27.1–11.

*36.4 Year of Celebration: This was a sacred year for Israel, traditionally called the "Year of Jubilee". During this year, all property had to go back to its original owner. But here, the property was not sold; it became part of the other tribe's land when the daughter who owned it married into that tribe. So the property could not be returned even during this year.

See also: 35.30: Deut 17.6; 19.15. 36.2: Num 27.7.

of the tribe that received it. [8-9] In the future, any daughter who inherits land must marry someone from her own tribe. Israel's tribal land is never to be passed from one tribe to another.

[10-11] Mahlah, Tirzah, Hoglah, Milcah, and Noah the daughters of Zelophehad obeyed the LORD and married their uncles' sons [12] and remained part of the Manasseh tribe. So their land stayed in their father's clan.

[13] These are the laws that the LORD gave to Moses and the Israelites while they were camped in the lowlands of Moab across the River Jordan from Jericho.

Additional notes

[1.20-46] Jacob: The Hebrew text has "Israel", Jacob's name after God renamed him.

[3.4] fire that was unacceptable: One possible meaning for the difficult Hebrew text.

[3.28] eight thousand six hundred: Hebrew; some manuscripts of one ancient translation "eight thousand three hundred".

[5.25] lift it up: Or "wave it".

[6.20] lift them up: See the note at 5.25.

[7.12-83] goat: Hebrew "male goat".

[8.19] I will hold . . . sacred tent: One possible meaning for the difficult Hebrew text.

[10.29] Hobab: Hebrew "Hobab son of Reuel".

[10.33] Mount Sinai: Hebrew "the LORD's mountain."

[11.3] Burning: Or "Taberah".

[11.25] some authority: Or "some of the Spirit's power".

[11.28] Joshua: Hebrew "Joshua son of Nun".

[11.34] Graves for the Greedy: Or "Kibroth-Hattaavah".

[13.4-16] Joshua . . . Ephraim: Hebrew "Hoshea son of Nun from Ephraim; Moses renamed him Joshua."

[13.23-24] Bunch Valley: Or "Eshcol Valley".

[14.30] Caleb and Joshua: Hebrew "Caleb son of Jephunneh and Joshua son of Nun".

[14.44] ignored Moses: One possible meaning for the difficult Hebrew text.

[15.3] goats: See the note at 7.12-83.

[16.1-2] Dathan, Abiram, and On: Hebrew "Dathan and Abiram the sons of Eliab, and On son of Peleth".

[16.4] he knelt down to pray: Or "he fell to his knees in sorrow."

[18.1] are responsible . . . sacred tent: Or "are to make sure that no one gets near the sacred tent."

[18.30] just as the Israelites . . . to me: One possible meaning for the difficult Hebrew text.

[19.6] A priest: Or "Eleazar".

[21.28] destroying: One ancient translation; Hebrew "the rulers of".

[21.30] gone: One possible meaning for the difficult Hebrew text of verse 30.

[22.32] I don't think you should go to Moab: One possible meaning for the difficult Hebrew text.

[23.14] a field . . . where lookouts were stationed: Or "Zophim Field on the top of Mount Pisgah."

[24.3] my words are true: One possible meaning for the difficult Hebrew text.

[24.6] grove of palm trees: Or "green valley".

[24.8] shooting them with arrows: One possible meaning for the difficult Hebrew text.

[24.15] my words are true: See the note at 24.3.

[24.17] you Moabites: Or "the territories of Moab".

[24.17] destroy: The Standard Hebrew Text; the Samaritan Hebrew Text "the skulls of".

[24.17] those tribes . . . desert: The Hebrew text has "the descendants of Sheth", which probably refers to the people who lived in the desert areas of Canaan before the Israelites.

[24.19] every town there: Or "Ir in Moab".

[24.20] but . . . for ever: One possible meaning for the difficult Hebrew text.

[24.22] them: One possible meaning for the difficult Hebrew text of verse 22.

[24.23] destruction: One possible meaning for the difficult Hebrew text of verse 23.

[25.7] Phinehas . . . Aaron: Hebrew "Phinehas, son of Eleazar and grandson of Aaron".

[26.4] just as . . . Egypt: One possible meaning for the difficult Hebrew text.

[26.5-7] Jacob: See the note at 1.20-46.

[27.1] Zelophehad: Hebrew "Zelophehad son of Hepher son of Gilead son of Machir son of Manasseh son of Joseph". See also 26.28-34; 36.1-12.

[27.21] from me: The Hebrew text has "by the urim", something used by the priests to get answers from the LORD.

[28.14-15] goat: See the note at 7.12-83.

[28.22] goat: See the note at 7.12-83.

[28.30] goat: See the note at 7.12-83.

[29.5] goat: See the note at 7.12-83.

[29.11] goat: See the note at 7.12-83.

[29.16] goat: See the note at 7.12-83.

[29.38] goat: See the note at 7.12-83.

[31.54] to remind . . . happened: Or "so the LORD would continue to help Israel."

[32.12] Caleb and Joshua: Hebrew "Caleb son of Jephunneh the Kenizzite and Joshua son of Nun".

[32.33] half of Manasseh: Or "East Manasseh".

[32.33] ruled: One possible meaning for the difficult Hebrew text of verse 33.

[32.41] Villages of Jair: Or "Havvoth-Jair".

[33.3-4] proudly: Or "bravely".

[33.8] Pi-Hahiroth: Two ancient translations and the Samaritan Hebrew Text; the Standard Hebrew Text "a place near Hahiroth".

[33.11] the western edge of the Sinai Desert: Hebrew "the Sin Desert".

[34.11] Lake Galilee: The Hebrew text has "Lake Chinnereth", an earlier name for Lake Galilee.

Deuteronomy

The basics

What's the point? To remind Israel of all that God has done for them.

What happens? Moses gives a series of speeches to the people of Israel.

What should I remember? 30.15 'Today I am giving you a choice. You can choose life and success or death and disaster.'

More detail

Setting the scene After forty years wandering in the wilderness, it's finally time for the Israelites to enter the promised land. On the eve of invasion, Moses speaks to them...

What's it all about? The name 'Deuteronomy' means 'repetition of the law' and that's what happens: Moses reminds people of the laws they are to obey. But he also reminds them of the whole story; of the way that God has brought them out of slavery and – despite their own lack of faith – has brought them to the verge of the promised land. Moses reminds the people of how God has provided for them. In all their wanderings they have never gone hungry, their clothes haven't worn out and they didn't even get swollen feet (8.1–9)!

This, you see, is a goodbye speech. Moses is old, he's handed over the leadership to Joshua, he knows he isn't going to make it into the promised land. So these speeches are his farewell gifts to the people that he has led all these years. He can't go with them. He can't fight their battles any more; but he can remind them of who God is and all that he has done for them.

He issues promises and warnings as well; promises of blessings if Israel obeys God, and dire warnings of the consequences should they

disobey. These warnings look far ahead, to a time when the Israelites would be in exile and when all the dreams of a promised land seemed to have turned to dust. Yet they also offer signs of hope; the Lord warns of punishment, but he also promises that he will bring his people back (30.1–10).

Footsteps

The first speech: 1.1–46
Moses is refused entry: 3.1–29
The Ten Commandments: 5.1–33
The most important commandment: 6.1–25
The stones and the chest: 10.1–9
Against the Canaanite gods: 12.29—13.18
A promise of blessings: 28.1–14
Joshua is appointed leader: 31.1–8
The song of Moses: 31.30—32.47
The death of Moses: 34.1–12

CHAPTER 1

The final speeches of Moses

[1-5] This book contains the speeches that Moses made while Israel was in the land of Moab, camped near the town of Suph in the desert east of the River Jordan. The town of Paran was in one direction from their camp, and the towns of Tophel, Laban, Hazeroth, and Dizahab* were in the opposite direction.

Earlier, Moses had defeated the Amorite King Sihon of Heshbon. Moses had also defeated King Og of Bashan, who used to live in Ashtaroth for part of the year and in Edrei for the rest of the year.

---

*1.1–5 Suph . . . Paran . . . Tophel, Laban, Hazeroth, and Dizahab:** The exact location of these towns is not known.
See also: 1.4: Num 21.21–35.

Although it takes only eleven days to walk from Mount Sinai' to Kadesh-Barnea by way of the Mount Seir road, these speeches were not made until forty years after Israel left Egypt.*

THE FIRST SPEECH: MOSES REVIEWS THE PAST

The LORD's command at Mount Sinai

The LORD had given Moses his laws for the people of Israel. And on the first day of the eleventh month,* Moses began explaining those laws by saying:

6 People of Israel, when we were in our camp at Mount Sinai,' the LORD our God told us:

You have stayed here long enough. 7 Leave this place and go into the land that belongs to the Amorites and their neighbours the Canaanites. This land includes the valley of the River Jordan, the hill country, the western foothills, the Southern Desert, the Mediterranean coast, the Lebanon Mountains, and all the territory as far as the River Euphrates. 8 I give you this land, just as I promised your ancestors Abraham, Isaac, and Jacob. Now you must go and take the land.

Leaders were appointed

This is also told in Exodus 18.13–27

Moses said:

9 Straight after the LORD commanded us to leave Mount Sinai,' I told you:

Israel, being your leader is too big a job for one person. 10 The LORD our God has blessed us, and so now there are as many of us as there are stars in the sky. 11 God has even promised to bless us a thousand times more, and I pray that he will. 12 But I cannot take care of all your problems and settle all your arguments alone. 13 Each tribe must choose some experienced men who are known for their wisdom and understanding, and I will make those men the official leaders of their tribes.

14 You answered, "That's a good idea!"
15 Then I took these men, who were already wise and respected leaders, and I appointed them as your official leaders. Some of them became military officers in charge of groups of a thousand, or a hundred, or fifty, or ten, 16 and others became judges. I gave these judges the following instructions:

When you settle legal cases, your decisions must be fair. It doesn't matter if the case is between two Israelites, or between an Israelite and a foreigner living in your community. 17 And it doesn't matter if one is helpless and the other is powerful. Don't be afraid of anyone! No matter who comes to your court, God will help you make a fair decision.

If any case is too hard for you, bring the people to me, and I will make the decision.

18 After I gave these instructions to the judges, I taught you the LORD's commands.

Men were sent to explore the hill country

This is also told in Numbers 13.1–33

Moses said to Israel:

19 The LORD had commanded us to leave Mount Sinai' and go to the hill country that belonged to the Amorites, so we started out into the huge desert. You remember how frightening it was, but soon we were at Kadesh-Barnea, 20-21 and I told you, "We have reached the hill country. It belongs to the Amorites now, but the LORD our God is giving it to us. He is the same God our ancestors worshipped, and he has told us to go in and take this land, so don't hesitate and be afraid."

22 Then all of you came to me and said, "Before we go into the land, let's send some men to explore it. When they come back, they can tell us about the towns we will find and what roads we should take to get there."

23 It seemed like a good idea, so I chose twelve men, one from each tribe. 24 They explored the hill country as far as Bunch Valley* 25 and even brought back some of the fruit. They said, "The LORD our God is giving us good land."

---

*1.1–5 Egypt: The Israelites would soon enter Canaan, but they would have entered the land of Canaan from Kadesh-Barnea forty years earlier if they had not rebelled against God (see verses 6–40).
*1.1–5 eleventh month: Shebat, the eleventh month of the Hebrew calendar, from about mid-January to mid-February.

---

*1.24 Bunch Valley: Or "Eshcol Valley", famous for its large bunches of grapes.

Israel refused to obey the LORD

This is also told in Numbers 14.1–45

Moses said to Israel:

26 You did not want to go into the land, and you refused to obey the LORD your God.
27 You stayed in your tents and grumbled, "The LORD must hate us — he brought us out of Egypt, just so he could hand us over to the Amorites and get rid of us. 28 We are afraid, because the men who explored the land told us that the cities are large, with walls that reach to the sky. The people who live there are taller and stronger than we are,' and some of them are Anakim.* We have nowhere to go."

29 Then I said, "Don't worry! 30 The LORD our God will lead the way. He will fight on our side, just as he did when we saw him do all those things to the Egyptians. 31 And you know that the LORD has taken care of us the whole time we've been in the desert, just as you might carry one of your children."

32 But you still would not trust the LORD, 33 even though he had always been with us in the desert. During the daytime, the LORD was in the cloud, leading us in the right direction and showing us where to camp. And at night, he was there in the fire.*

34 You had made the LORD angry, and he said:

35 You people of this generation are evil, and I refuse to let you go into the good land that I promised your ancestors.
36 Caleb son of Jephunneh is the only one of your generation that I will allow to go in. He obeyed me completely, so I will give him and his descendants the land he explored.

37 The LORD was even angry with me because of you people, and he said, "Moses, I won't let you go into the land either. 38 Instead, I will let Joshua' your assistant lead Israel to conquer the land. So encourage him."

39 Then the LORD spoke to you again:

People of Israel, you said that your innocent young children would be taken prisoner in the battle for the land. But some day I will let them go into the land, and with my help they will conquer it and live there.
40 Now, turn round and go back into the desert by way of Red Sea* Road.

41 Then you told me, "We disobeyed the LORD our God, but now we want to obey him. We will go into the hill country and fight, just as he told us to do." So you picked up your weapons, thinking it would be easy to take over the hill country.

42 But the LORD said, "Moses, warn them not to go into the hill country. I won't help them fight, and their enemies will defeat them."

43 I told you what the LORD had said, but you paid no attention. You disobeyed him and went into the hill country anyway. You thought you were so great! 44 But when the Amorites in the hill country attacked from their towns, you ran from them as you would run from a swarm of bees. The Amorites chased your troops into Seir* as far as Hormah, killing them as they went. 45 Then you came back to the place of worship at Kadesh-Barnea and wept, but the LORD would not listen to your prayers.

Israel spent years in the desert

Moses said to Israel:

46 After we had been in Kadesh for a few months, we obeyed the LORD and headed back into the desert by way of Red Sea* Road.

CHAPTER 2

1 We spent many years wandering around outside the hill country of Seir,* 2 until the LORD said:

Moses, 3 Israel has wandered in these hills long enough. Turn and go north. 4 And give the people these orders: "Be very careful, because you will soon go through the land that belongs to your relatives, the

---

1.28 Anakim: Perhaps a group of people of great stature that lived in or near Palestine before the Israelites. See also 2.10–11,20–21; Numbers 13.33.
1.33 the cloud . . . the fire: See Exodus 40.34–38; Numbers 9.15–23.
See also: 1.26: Deut 9.23; Heb 3.16. 1.31: Acts 13.18. 1.32: Heb 3.19. 1.34–35: Heb 3.18.

1.40 Red Sea: Hebrew *yam suph*, here referring to the Gulf of Aqaba, since the term is extended to include the north-eastern arm of the Red Sea (see also the note at 11.4).
1.44 Seir: An area of hills and mountains that was part of the territory of Edom.
1.46 Red Sea: See the notes at 1.40; 11.4.
2.1 hill country of Seir: See the note at 1.44.
See also: 2.1: Num 21.4. 2.4: Gen 36.8.

descendants of Esau.* They are afraid of you, [5] but don't start a war with them. I have given them the hill country of Seir, so I won't give any of it to you, not even enough to set a foot on. [6] And as you go through their land, you will have to buy food and water from them."

[7] The LORD has helped us and taken care of us during the past forty years that we have been in this huge desert. We've had everything we needed, and the LORD has blessed us and made us successful in whatever we have done.

[8] We went past the territory that belonged to our relatives, the descendants of Esau.* We followed Arabah Road that starts in the south at Elath and Ezion-Geber, then we turned on to the desert road that leads to Moab.

[9] The LORD told me, "Don't try to start a war with Moab. Leave them alone, because I gave the land of Ar* to them,* and I will not let you have any of it."

Tribes that lived near Canaan

[10] Before the LORD gave the Moabites their land, a large and powerful tribe lived there. They were the Emim, and they were as tall as the Anakim. [11] The Moabites called them Emim, though others sometimes used the name Rephaim* for both the Anakim and the Emim.

[12] The Horites used to live in Seir, but the Edomites* took over that region. They killed many of the Horites and forced the rest of

them to leave, just as Israel did to the people in the land that the LORD gave them.

Israel crossed the Zered Gorge

Moses said to Israel:

[13] When we came to the Zered Gorge along the southern border of Moab, the LORD told us to cross the gorge into Moab, and we did. [14] This was thirty-eight years after we left Kadesh-Barnea, and by that time all the men who had been in the army at Kadesh-Barnea had died, just as the LORD had said they would. [15-16] The LORD kept getting rid of* them until finally none of them were left.

[17] Then the LORD told me, [18] "Moses, now go past the town of Ar and cross Moab's northern border [19] into Ammon. But don't start a war with the Ammonites. I gave them* their land, and I won't give any of it to Israel."

More nations that lived near Canaan

[20] Before the Ammonites conquered the land that the LORD had given them, some of the Rephaim used to live there, although the Ammonites called them Zamzummim. [21] The Zamzummim were a large and powerful tribe and were as tall as the Anakim.* But the LORD helped the Ammonites, and they killed many of the Zamzummim and forced the rest to leave. Then the Ammonites settled there. [22] The LORD helped them as he had helped the Edomites,* who killed many of the Horites in Seir and forced the rest to leave before settling there themselves.

[23] A group called the Avvim used to live in villages as far south as Gaza, but the Philistines* killed them and settled on their land.

Israel crossed the Arnon Gorge

Moses said:

[24] After we went through Ammon, the LORD told us:

2.4 your relatives, the descendants of Esau: Esau was the brother of Jacob, the ancestor of the nation of Israel. Esau's descendants were also known as the nation of Edom.

2.8 We went past . . . Esau: According to Numbers 20.14–21, the king of Edom did not let the Israelites go through his land.

2.9 Ar: One of the main cities of Moab (see Numbers 21.28); sometimes it may have stood for the whole territory of Moab.

2.9 them: The Hebrew text has "the descendants of Lot"; the nation of Moab descended from Moab, who was the son of Lot, the nephew of Abraham.

2.10–11 Emim . . . Anakim . . . Rephaim: These may refer to a group or groups of people of great stature that lived in or near Palestine before the Israelites (see also Numbers 13.33).

2.12 Edomites: The Hebrew text has "the descendants of Esau", who became the nation of Edom.

See also: 2.9: Gen 19.37.

2.19 them: The Hebrew text has "descendants of Lot"; the nation of Ammon descended from Benammi, who was the son of Lot, the nephew of Abraham.

2.21 Anakim: See the notes at 1.28; 2.10–11.

2.22 Edomites: See the note at 2.12.

2.23 Philistines: The Hebrew text has "the Caphtorim from Caphtor", probably referring to the Philistines who originally came from Crete.

See also: 2.14: Num 14.28–35. 2.19: Gen 19.38.

Israel, pack up your possessions, take down your tents, and cross the gorge of the River Arnon.* The territory of the Amorite King Sihon of Heshbon lies on the other side of the river, but I now give you his land. So attack and take it! 25 Today I will start making all other nations afraid of you. They will tremble with fear when anyone mentions you, and they will be terrified when you appear.

The defeat of King Sihon of Heshbon

This is also told in Numbers 21.21-30

Moses said to Israel:

26 After we had crossed the Arnon and had set up camp in the Kedemoth Desert, I sent messengers to King Sihon of Heshbon, telling him that his nation and ours could be at peace. I said:

27 Please let Israel go across your country. We will walk straight through, without turning off the road. 28-29 You can even sell us food and water, and we will pay with silver. We need to reach the River Jordan and cross it, because the LORD our God is giving us the land on the west side. The Edomites and Moabites' have already let us cross their land. Please let us cross your land as well.

30-31 But Sihon refused to let us go across his country, because the LORD made him stubborn and eager to fight us. The LORD told me, "I am going to help you defeat Sihon and take his land, so attack him!"

32 We met Sihon and his army in battle at Jahaz, 33 and the LORD our God helped us defeat them. We killed Sihon, his sons, and everyone else in his army. 34 Then we captured and destroyed every town in Sihon's kingdom, killing everyone, 35 but keeping the livestock and everything else of value. 36 The LORD helped us capture every town from the gorge of the River Arnon north to the boundary of Gilead, including the town of Aroer on the edge of the gorge and the town in the middle of the gorge. 37 However, we stayed away from all the Ammonite towns, both in the hill country and near the River Jabbok, just as the LORD had commanded.

CHAPTER 3

The defeat of King Og of Bashan

This is also told in Numbers 21.31-35

Moses said to Israel:

1 When we turned on to the road that leads to Bashan, King Og of Bashan led out his whole army to fight us at Edrei. 2 But the LORD told me, "Moses, don't be afraid of King Og. I am going to help you defeat him and his army and take over his land. Destroy him and his people, just as you did with the Amorite King Sihon of Heshbon."

3-6 The LORD our God helped us destroy Og and his army and conquer his entire kingdom of Bashan, including the Argob region. His kingdom had lots of villages and sixty towns with high walls and gates that locked with bars. We completely destroyed* them all, killing everyone, 7 but keeping the livestock and everything else of value.

8 Sihon and Og had ruled Amorite kingdoms east of the River Jordan. Their land stretched from the gorge of the River Arnon in the south to Mount Hermon in the north, and we captured it all. 9 Mount Hermon is called Mount Sirion by the people of Sidon, and it is called Mount Senir by the Amorites. 10 We captured all the towns in the highlands, all of Gilead, and all of Bashan as far as Salecah and Edrei, two of the towns that Og had ruled.

Og's coffin

11 King Og was the last of the Rephaim,* and his coffin' is in the town of Rabbah in Ammon. It is made of hard black rock* and is four metres long and almost two metres wide.

The land east of the River Jordan is divided

This is also told in Numbers 32.1-42

Moses said to Israel:

12-17 I gave some of the land and towns we captured to the tribes of Reuben and Gad. Their share started at the gorge of the River

---

*3.3-6 completely destroyed: The Hebrew word means that the town was given completely to the LORD, and since it could not be used for normal purposes any more, it had to be destroyed. Every person was killed and sometimes all the animals as well.
*3.11 Rephaim: See the note at 2.10,11.
*3.11 hard black rock: The Hebrew text has "iron", which probably refers to basalt, a hard black rock.

---

*2.24 gorge of the River Arnon: The northern boundary of Moab's territory and the southern boundary of Sihon's kingdom.

Arnon in the south, took in the town of Aroer on the edge of the gorge, and went far enough north to include the southern half of the Gilead region. The northern part of their land went as far east as the upper gorge of the River Jabbok, which formed their border with the Ammonites.* I also gave them the eastern side of the valley of the River Jordan, from Lake Galilee⟩ south to the Dead Sea⟩ below the slopes of Mount Pisgah.

I gave the northern half of Gilead and all of the Bashan region to half the tribe of Manasseh.⟩ Bashan had belonged to King Og, and the Argob region in Bashan used to be called the Land of the Rephaim. Jair from the Manasseh tribe conquered the Argob region as far west as the kingdoms of Geshur and Maacah. The Israelites even started calling Bashan by the name "Villages of Jair",⟩ and that is still its name. I gave the northern half of Gilead to the Machir clan.⟩

18-19 At that time I told the men of Reuben, Gad, and East Manasseh:

The LORD our God told me to give you this land with its towns, and that's what I have done. Now your wives and children can stay here with your large flocks of sheep and goats and your large herds of cattle. But all of you men who can serve in our army must cross the River Jordan and help the other tribes, because they are your relatives. 20 The LORD will let them defeat the enemy nations on the west side of the Jordan and take their land. Afterwards, you can come back here to the land I gave you.

21-22 Then I told Joshua, "You saw how the LORD our God helped us destroy King Sihon and King Og. So don't be afraid! Wherever you go, the LORD will fight on your side and help you destroy your enemies."

God refused to let Moses enter Canaan

Moses said to Israel:

23 At that time I prayed and begged, 24 "Our LORD, it seems that you have just begun to show me your great power. No other god in the sky or on earth is able to do the mighty things that you do. 25 The land west of the Jordan is such good land. Please let me cross the Jordan and see the hills and the Lebanon Mountains."

26 But the LORD was angry with me because of you people,* and he refused to listen. "That's enough!" he said. "I don't want to hear any more. 27 Climb to the top of Mount Pisgah and look north, south, east, and west. Take a good look, but you are not going to cross the River Jordan. 28 Joshua will lead Israel across the Jordan to take the land, so help him be strong and brave and tell him what he must do."

29 After this we stayed in the valley at Beth-Peor.

CHAPTER 4

Israel must obey God

Moses said:

1 Israel, listen to these laws and teachings! If you obey them, you will live, and you will go in and take the land that the LORD is giving you. He is the God your ancestors worshipped, 2 and now he is your God. I am telling you everything he has commanded, so don't add anything or take anything away.

3 You saw how he killed everyone who worshipped the god Baal-Peor.* 4 But all of you who were faithful to the LORD your God are still alive today.

5-8 No other nation has laws that are as fair as the ones the Lord my God told me to give you. If you faithfully obey them when you enter the land, you will show other nations how wise you are. In fact, everyone who hears about your laws will say, "That great nation certainly is wise!" And what makes us greater than other nations? We have a God who is close to us and answers our prayers.

9 You must be very careful not to forget the things you have seen God do for you. Keep reminding yourselves, and tell your children and grandchildren as well. 10 Do you remember the day you stood in the LORD's presence at Mount Sinai?⟩ The LORD said, "Moses, bring the people of Israel here. I want to speak to them so they will

---

3.12-17 The northern part . . . border with the Ammonites: The River Jabbok flowed from south to north, then it turned west and formed the northern border of the land belonging to the Reuben and Gad tribes.
See also: 3.18-20: Josh 1.12-15. 3.23-27: Num 27.12-14; Deut 32.48-52.

3.26 But the LORD . . . people: See 1.37.
4.3 Baal-Peor: See Numbers 25.1-9.
See also: 4.2: Rev 22.18-19. 4.3: Num 25.1-9.

obey me as long as they live, and so they will teach their children to obey me too."

11 Mount Sinai* was surrounded by deep dark clouds, and fire went up to the sky. You came to the foot of the mountain, 12 and the LORD spoke to you from the fire. You could hear him and understand what he was saying, but you couldn't see him. 13 The LORD said he was making an agreement with you, and he told you that your part of the agreement is to obey the Ten Commandments. Then the LORD wrote these Commandments on two flat stones.

14 That's when the LORD commanded me to give you the laws and teachings you must obey in the land that you will conquer west of the River Jordan.

Don't worship idols

Moses said to Israel:

15 When God spoke to you from the fire, he was invisible. So be careful 16 not to commit the sin of worshipping idols. Don't make idols to be worshipped, whether they are shaped like men, women, 17 animals, birds, 18 reptiles, or fish. 19 And when you see the sun or moon or stars, don't be tempted to bow down and worship them. The LORD put them there for all the other nations to worship. 20 But you are the LORD's people, because he led you through fiery trials and rescued you from Egypt.

21 The LORD was angry with me because of what you said,* and he told me that he would not let me cross the River Jordan into the good land that he is giving you.* 22 So I must stay here and die on this side of the Jordan, but you will cross the river and take the land.

23 Always remember the agreement that the LORD your God made with you, and don't make an idol in any shape or form. 24 The LORD will be angry if you worship other gods, and he can be like a fire destroying everything in its path.

25-26 Soon you will cross the River Jordan and settle down in the land. Then in the years to come, you will have children, and they will give you grandchildren. After many years, you might lose your sense of right and wrong and make idols, even though the LORD your God hates them. So I am giving you fair warning today, and I call the earth and the sky as witnesses. If you ever make idols, the LORD will be angry, and you won't have long to live, because the LORD will let you be wiped out. 27 Only a few of you will survive, and the LORD will force you to leave the land and will scatter you among the nations. 28 There you will have to worship gods made of wood and stone, and these are nothing but idols that can't see or hear or eat or smell.

29-30 In all your troubles, you may finally decide that you want to worship only the LORD. And if you turn back to him and obey him completely, he will again be your God. 31 The LORD your God will have mercy — he won't destroy you or desert you. The LORD will remember his promise, and he will keep the agreement he made with your ancestors.

32-34 When the LORD your God brought you out of Egypt, you saw how he fought for you and showed his great power by performing terrifying miracles. You became his people, and at Mount Sinai you heard him talking to you out of fiery flames. And yet you are still alive! Has anything like this ever happened since the time God created humans? No matter where you go or who you ask, you will get the same answer. No one has ever heard of another god even trying to do such things as the LORD your God has done for you.

35-36 The LORD wants you to know he is the only true God, and he wants you to obey him. That's why he let you see his mighty miracles and his fierce fire on earth, and why you heard his voice from that fire and from the sky.

37 The LORD loved your ancestors and decided that you would be his people. So the LORD used his great power to bring you out of Egypt. 38 Now you face other nations more powerful than you are, but the LORD has already started forcing them out of their land and giving it to you.

39 So remember that the LORD is the only true God, whether in the sky above or on the earth below. 40 Today I am explaining his laws and teachings. And if you always obey them, you and your descendants will live long and be successful in the land the LORD is giving you.

---

*4.21 The LORD was angry . . . giving you: See 1.37; 3.26.

See also: **4.11-12:** Exod 19.16-18; Heb 12.18-19. **4.13:** Exod 31.18; 34.28; Deut 9.10. **4.14:** Exod 21.1. **4.16:** Exod 20.4; Lev 26.1; Deut 5.8; 27.15. **4.17-18a:** Rom 1.23. **4.20:** Exod 19.5; Deut 7.6; 14.2; 26.18; Titus 2.14; 1 Pet 2.9. **4.21:** Num 20.12. **4.24:** Heb 12.29.

See also: **4.27-28:** Deut 28.36. **4.29:** Jer 29.13. **4.35:** Mark 12.32.

Safe Towns

⁴¹⁻⁴³ Moses said, "People of Israel, you must set aside the following three towns east of the River Jordan as Safe Towns: Bezer in the desert highlands belonging to the Reuben tribe; Ramoth in Gilead, belonging to the Gad tribe; and Golan in Bashan, belonging to the Manasseh tribe. If you kill a neighbour without meaning to, and if you had not been angry with that person, you can run to one of these towns and find safety."*

THE SECOND SPEECH: MOSES TELLS WHAT THE LORD DEMANDS

Israel at Beth-Peor

⁴⁴⁻⁴⁶ The Israelites had come from Egypt and were camped east of the River Jordan near Beth-Peor, when Moses gave these laws and teachings. The land around their camp had once belonged to King Sihon of Heshbon. But Moses and the Israelites defeated him ⁴⁷ and King Og of Bashan, and took their lands. These two Amorite kings had ruled the territory east of the River Jordan ⁴⁸ from the town of Aroer on the edge of the gorge of the River Arnon, north to Mount Hermon.⸵ ⁴⁹ Their land included the eastern side of the Jordan valley, as far south as the Dead Sea⸵ below the slopes of Mount Pisgah.

CHAPTER 5

The Ten Commandments

This is also told in Exodus 20.1–17

¹ Moses called together the people of Israel and said:

Today I am telling you the laws and teachings that you must follow, so listen carefully. ² The LORD our God made an agreement with our nation at Mount Sinai.⸵ ³ That agreement wasn't only with⸵ our ancestors but with us, who are here today. ⁴ The LORD himself spoke to you out of the fire, ⁵ but you were afraid of the fire and refused to go up the mountain. So I spoke with the LORD for you, then I told you that he had said:

⁶ I am the LORD your God, the one who brought you out of Egypt where you were slaves.

---

*4.41–43 find safety: From the victim's clan, who might appoint one of their men to track down and put to death the killer (see also 19.1–13).
See also: 4.41–43: Josh 20.8–9.

Helpline

Help! My Dad's never around

'I never see him. He doesn't want to know me. The Bible says I should honour him, but how can I if he's never there?'

'Respect your father and mother', it says in the Ten Commandments (Deuteronomy 5.16). Which is all very well, but what if one of them isn't around to respect? It's difficult to honour someone who doesn't seem to care much about you.

But there are some ways in which we can show that person respect and love – even if they're unaware of it. Pray for them. Ask God to bless them.

And ask God to help you to deal with your own feelings. You probably won't feel any better straight away – but forgiveness of this kind, when we are dealing with deep hurts – needs to be worked at.

Remember, God is the perfect father. He's always there for you and he will never abandon you. Whatever has happened on earth, we know that our father is in heaven.

Three things

Release

It's perfectly natural to feel resentment, anger and even a sense of injustice, but if you hold on to these feelings, they'll infect your life. Let them go and try to hold onto the things of God instead.

Time

Deep hurts need deep healing. Don't expect an overnight cure. But the more you pray, the more you let go of the bad feelings, the less power this thing will have in your life.

Support

You will need others to help you. You will need the support and prayers of your youth leaders and friends.

More...
Ten Commandments p.85
Help! My parents are letting me down! p.598
Forgiveness p.614

⁷ Do not worship any god except me.
⁸ Do not make idols that look like anything in the sky or on earth or in the ocean under the earth. ⁹ Don't bow down and worship idols. I am the LORD your God, and I demand all your love. If you reject me and worship idols, I will punish your families for three or four generations. ¹⁰ But if you love me and obey my laws, I will be kind to your families for thousands of generations.

¹¹ Do not misuse my name.* I am the LORD your God, and I will punish anyone who misuses my name.

¹² Show respect for the Sabbath Day — it belongs to me. ¹³ You have six days when you can do your work, ¹⁴ but the seventh day of the week belongs to me, your God. No one is to work on that day — not you, your children, your oxen or donkeys or any other animal, not even those foreigners who live in your towns. And don't make your slaves do any work. ¹⁵ This special day of rest will remind you that I reached out my mighty arm and rescued you from slavery in Egypt.

¹⁶ Respect your father and mother, and you will live a long and successful life in the land I am giving you.

¹⁷ Do not murder.

¹⁸ Be faithful in marriage.

¹⁹ Do not steal.

²⁰ Do not tell lies about others.

²¹ Do not want to take anything that belongs to someone else. Don't want to take anyone's wife or husband, house, land, slaves, oxen, donkeys, or anything else.

²² When we were gathered on the mountain, the LORD spoke to us in a loud voice from the dark fiery cloud. The LORD gave us these commands, and only these. Then he wrote them on two flat stones and gave them to me.

The people were afraid

This is also told in Exodus 20.18–21

Moses said to Israel:

²³ When fire blazed from the mountain, and you heard the voice coming from the darkness, your tribal leaders came to me ²⁴ and said:

Today the LORD our God has shown us how powerful and glorious he is. He spoke to us from the fire, and we learnt that people can live, even though God speaks to them. ²⁵ But we don't want to take a chance on being killed by that terrible fire, and if we keep on hearing the LORD's voice, we will die. ²⁶ Has anyone else ever heard the only true God speaking from fire, as we have? And even if they have, would they live to tell about it? ²⁷ Moses, go up close and listen to the LORD. Then come back and tell us, and we will do everything he says.

²⁸ The LORD heard you and said:

Moses, I heard what the people said to you, and I approve. ²⁹ I wish they would always worship me with fear and trembling and be this willing to obey me! Then they and their children would always enjoy a successful life.

³⁰ Now, tell them to return to their tents, ³¹ but you come back here to me. After I tell you my laws and teachings, you will repeat them to the people, so they can obey these laws in the land I am giving them.

Moses said:

³² Israel, you must carefully obey the LORD's commands. ³³ Follow them, because they make a path that will lead to a long successful life in the land the LORD your God is giving you.

CHAPTER 6

The most important commandment

Moses said to Israel:

¹ The LORD told me to give you these laws and teachings,‣ so you can obey them in the land he is giving you. Soon you will cross the River Jordan and take that land. ² And if you and your descendants want to live a long time, you must always worship the LORD and obey his laws. ³ Pay attention,

---

5.11 misuse my name: Probably includes breaking promises, telling lies after swearing to tell the truth, using the LORD's name as a curse word or a magic formula, and trying to control the LORD by using his name.

See also: **5.8–9:** Lev 26.1; Deut 4.15–18; 27.15.
5.9–10: Exod 34.6–7; Num 14.18; Deut 7.9–10.
5.11: Lev 19.12. **5.12:** Exod 16.23–30; 31.12–14.
5.13–14: Exod 23.12; 31.15; 34.21; 35.2; Lev 23.3.
5.16: a Deut 27.16; Matt 15.4; 19.19; Mark 7.10; 10.19;
Luke 18.20; Eph 6.2; **b** Eph 6.3. **5.17:** Gen 9.6; Lev 24.17;
Matt 5.21; 19.18; Mark 10.19; Luke 18.20; Rom 13.9;
Jam 2.11. **5.18:** Lev 20.10; Matt 5.27; 19.18; Mark 10.19;
Luke 18.20; Rom 13.9; Jam 2.11. **5.19:** Lev 19.11; Matt 19.18;
Mark 10.19; Luke 18.20; Rom 13.9. **5.20:** Exod 23.1;
Matt 19.18; Mark 10.19; Luke 18.20. **5.21:** Rom 7.7; 13.9.
5.22–27: Heb 12.18–19.

Israel! Our ancestors worshipped the LORD, and he promised to give us this land that is rich with milk and honey. Be careful to obey him, and you will become a successful and powerful nation.

[4] Listen, Israel! The LORD our God is the only true God![b] [5] So love the LORD your God with all your heart, soul, and strength. [6] Memorize his laws [7] and tell them to your children over and over again. Talk about them all the time, whether you're at home or walking along the road or going to bed at night, or getting up in the morning. [8] Write down copies and tie them to your wrists and foreheads to help you obey them. [9] Write these laws on the door frames of your homes and on your town gates.

Worship only the LORD

Moses said to Israel:

[10] The LORD promised your ancestors Abraham, Isaac, and Jacob that he would give you this land. Now he will take you there and give you large towns, with good buildings that you didn't build, [11] and houses full of good things that you didn't put there. The LORD will give you wells* that you didn't have to dig, and vineyards and olive orchards that you didn't have to plant. But when you have eaten so much that you can't eat any more, [12] don't forget it was the LORD who set you free from slavery and brought you out of Egypt. [13] Worship and obey the LORD your God with fear and trembling, and promise that you will be loyal to him.

[14] Don't have anything to do with gods that are worshipped by the nations around you. [15] If you worship other gods, the LORD will be furious and wipe you off the face of the earth. The LORD your God is with you, [16] so don't try to make him prove that he can help you, as you did at Massah.*
[17] Always obey the laws that the LORD has given you [18-19] and live in a way that pleases him. Then you will be able to go in and take this good land from your enemies, just as he promised your ancestors.

[20] Some day your children will ask, "Why did the LORD give us these laws and teachings?"
[21] Then you will answer:

We were slaves of the king of Egypt, but the LORD used his great power and set us free. [22] We saw him perform miracles and make horrible things happen to the king, his officials, and everyone else. [23] The LORD rescued us from Egypt, so he could bring us into this land, as he had promised our ancestors. [24-25] That's why the LORD our God demands that we obey his laws and worship him with fear and trembling. And if we do, he will protect us and help us be successful.

CHAPTER 7

Force the other nations out of the land

This is also told in Exodus 34.11–16

Moses said:

[1] People of Israel, the LORD your God will help you take the land of the Hittites, the Girgashites, the Amorites, the Canaanites, the Perizzites, the Hivites, and the Jebusites. These seven nations have more people and are stronger than Israel, but when you attack them, [2] the LORD will force them out of the land. Then you must destroy them without mercy. Don't make any peace treaties with them, [3] and don't let your sons and daughters marry any of them. [4] If you do, those people will lead your descendants to worship other gods and to turn their backs on the LORD. That will make him very angry, and he will quickly destroy Israel.

[5] So when you conquer these nations, tear down the altars where they worship their gods. Break up their sacred stones, cut down the poles* that they use in worshipping the goddess Asherah, and throw their idols in the fire.

The LORD's chosen people

Moses said:

[6] Israel, you are the chosen people of the LORD your God. There are many nations on this earth, but he chose only Israel to be his very own. [7] You were the weakest of all nations, [8] but the LORD chose you because

---

*6.11 wells: Cisterns cut into the rock to collect rainwater.
*6.16 Massah: See Exodus 17.1–7; Numbers 20.2–13.
See also: 6.4: Mark 12.29. 6.5: Matt 22.37; Mark 12.30; Luke 10.27. 6.6-9: Deut 11.18-20. 6.10: a Gen 12.7; b Gen 26.3; c Gen 28.13. 6.13: Matt 4.10; Luke 4.8. 6.16: a Matt 4.7; Luke 4.12; b Exod 17.1-7.

*7.5 poles: Or "trees", used as symbols of Asherah, the goddess of fertility.
See also: 7.1: Acts 13.19. 7.5: Deut 12.3. 7.6: Exod 19.5; Deut 4.20; 14.2; 26.18; Titus 2.14; 1 Pet 2.9.

he loves you and because he had made a promise to your ancestors. Then with his mighty arm, he rescued you from the king of Egypt, who had made you his slaves.

⁹ You know that the LORD your God is the only true God. So love him and obey his commands, and he will faithfully keep his agreement with you and your descendants for a thousand generations. ¹⁰ But if you turn against the LORD, he will quickly destroy you. ¹¹ So be sure to obey his laws and teachings I am giving you today.

The LORD will bless you if you obey

This is also told in Deuteronomy 28.1–14; Leviticus 26.3–13

Moses said to Israel:

¹² If you completely obey these laws, the LORD your God will be loyal and keep the agreement he made with you, just as he promised our ancestors. ¹³ The LORD will love you and bless you by giving you many children and plenty of food, wine, and olive oil. Your herds of cattle will have many calves, and your flocks of sheep will have many lambs. ¹⁴ God will bless you more than any other nation — your families will grow and your livestock increase. ¹⁵ You will no longer suffer with the same horrible diseases that you sometimes had in Egypt. You will be healthy, but the LORD will make your enemies suffer from those diseases.

Destroy the nations and their gods

Moses said to Israel:

¹⁶ When the LORD helps you defeat your enemies, you must destroy them without pity! And don't get trapped into worshipping their gods.

¹⁷ You may be thinking, "How can we destroy these nations? They are more powerful than we are." ¹⁸ But stop worrying! Just remember what the LORD your God did to Egypt and its king. ¹⁹ You saw how the LORD used his tremendous power to work great miracles and bring you out of Egypt. And he will again work miracles for you when you face these enemies you fear so much. ²⁰ Some of them may try to survive by hiding from you, but the LORD will make them panic, and soon they will be dead.᾿ ²¹ So don't be frightened when you meet them in battle. The LORD your God is great and fearsome, and he will fight at your side.

²² As you attack these nations, the LORD will force them out little by little. He won't let you get rid of them all at once — if he did, there wouldn't be enough people living in the land to keep down the number of wild animals. ²³⁻²⁴ But when you attack your enemies, the LORD will make them panic, and you will easily destroy them. You will defeat them one after another until they are gone, and no one will remember they ever lived.

²⁵ After you conquer a nation, burn their idols. Don't get trapped into wanting the silver or gold on an idol. Even the metal on an idol is disgusting to the LORD, ²⁶ so destroy it. If you bring it home with you, both you and your house will be destroyed. Stay away from those disgusting idols!

CHAPTER 8

The LORD takes care of you

Moses said:

¹ Israel, do you want to go into the land the LORD promised your ancestors? Do you want to capture it, live there, and become a powerful nation? Then be sure to obey every command I am giving you.

² Don't forget how the LORD your God has led you through the desert for the past forty years. He wanted to find out if you were truly willing to obey him and depend on him, ³ so he made you go hungry. Then he gave you manna,* a kind of food that you and your ancestors had never even heard about. The LORD was teaching you that people need more than food to live — they need every word that the LORD has spoken.

⁴ Over the past forty years, your clothing hasn't worn out, and your feet haven't swollen. ⁵ So keep in mind that the LORD has been correcting you, just as parents correct their children. ⁶ Obey the commands the LORD your God has given you and worship him with fear and trembling.

⁷ The LORD your God is bringing you into a good land with streams that flow from springs in the valleys and hills. ⁸⁻⁹ You can dig for copper in those hills, and the stones

---

See also: **7.9–10:** Exod 20.5–6; 34.6–7; Num 14.18; Deut 5.9–10. **7.12–16:** Deut 11.13–17.

*8.3 manna: See Exodus 16.1–36.
See also: **8.3:** Matt 4.4; Luke 4.4.

are made of iron ore. And you won't go hungry. Wheat and barley fields are everywhere, and so are vineyards and orchards full of fig, pomegranate,* and olive trees, and there is plenty of honey.

Don't forget the LORD

Moses said to Israel:

¹⁰ After you eat and are full, give praise to the LORD your God for the good land he gave you. ¹¹ Make sure that you never forget the LORD or disobey his laws and teachings that I am giving you today. If you always obey them, ¹² you will have plenty to eat, and you will build good houses to live in. ¹³ You will get more and more cattle, sheep, silver, gold, and other possessions.

¹⁴ But when all this happens, don't be proud! Don't forget that you were once slaves in Egypt and that it was the LORD who set you free. ¹⁵ Remember how he led you in that huge and frightening desert where poisonous snakes and scorpions live. There was no water, but the LORD split open a rock, and water poured out so you could drink. ¹⁶ He also gave you manna,* a kind of food your ancestors had never even heard about. The LORD was testing you to make you trust him, so that later on he could be good to you.

¹⁷ When you become successful, don't say, "I'm rich, and I've earned it all myself." ¹⁸ Instead, remember that the LORD your God gives you the strength to make a living. That's how he keeps the promise he made to your ancestors.

¹⁹⁻²⁰ But I'm warning you — if you forget the LORD your God and worship other gods, the LORD will destroy you, just as he destroyed the nations you fought.

CHAPTER 9

Why the LORD will help Israel

Moses said:

¹ Israel, listen to me! You will soon cross the River Jordan and go into the land to force out the nations that live there. They are more powerful than you are, and the walls around their cities reach to the sky. ² Some of these nations are descendants of

---

*8.8–9 **pomegranate**: A bright red fruit that looks like an apple.
*8.16 **manna**: See the note at 8.3.
See also: 8.11–16: Hos 13.5–6.

Holy history

The golden calf

What's the story?

The Israelites, thinking that Moses had disappeared, made a new god. Possibly they were copying the Egyptians, and making their own version of the Egyptian bull-god Apis. Or maybe they just liked cows. Either way, they celebrate in a drunken orgy.

It's astonishing when you think about it. Only a few weeks before the Israelites had been rescued from slavery by God. Only 40 days earlier they agreed to abide by the Ten Commandments – which specifically banned worshipping other gods. Now, while Moses is up the mountain speaking to the real thing, they make a fake god!

And if that isn't shocking enough, Aaron – Moses' brother and the High priest of Israel – agrees to their demands and joins in.

Moses zooms down the mountain, smashes the stone tablets, crushes the calf, scatters the powder on water, and forces the people to drink it. Now that's what you call making the punishment fit the crime!

Then those who remained faithful go through the camp killing the worst offenders. Moses offers to take the responsibility, but God decides that each individual must bear their own guilt. As punishment, a plague sweeps through the camp (32.31–35).

What's the point?

Throughout their history the Israelites were tempted by false gods. God told them at the start that he was the only true God, but time after time they disobeyed him. Truth to tell, we're all tempted in the same way. Money, sex, power, possessions – we can end up worshipping all of these things. But beware, they're no more real gods than the golden calf.

More...
Foreign gods p.262

the Anakim.* You know how tall and strong they are, and you've heard that no one can defeat them in battle. ³ But the LORD your God has promised to go ahead of you, like a raging fire burning everything in its path. So when you attack your enemies, it will be easy for you to destroy them and take their land.

⁴⁻⁶ After the LORD helps you wipe out these nations and conquer their land, don't think he did it because you are such good people. You aren't good — you are stubborn! No, the LORD is going to help you, because the nations that live there are evil, and because he wants to keep the promise he made to your ancestors Abraham, Isaac, and Jacob.

When Israel made an idol

This is also told in Exodus 32

Moses said to Israel:

⁷ Don't ever forget how you kept rebelling and making the LORD angry the whole time you were in the desert. You rebelled from the day you left Egypt until the day you arrived here.

⁸ At Mount Sinai' you made the LORD so angry that he was going to destroy you. ⁹⁻¹¹ It happened during those forty days and nights that I was on the mountain, without anything to eat or drink. He had told me to come up there so he could give me the agreement he made with us. And this agreement was actually the same Ten Commandments' he had announced to you when he spoke from the fire on the mountain. The LORD had written them on two flat stones with his own hand. But after giving me the two stones, ¹² he said:

Moses, hurry down the mountain to those people you led out of Egypt. They have already disobeyed me and committed the terrible sin of making an idol.

¹³ I've been watching the Israelites, and I've seen how stubborn and rebellious they are. ¹⁴ So don't try to stop me! I am going to wipe them out, and no one on earth will remember they ever lived. Then I will let your descendants become an even bigger and more powerful nation than Israel.

Moses said:

¹⁵ Fire was raging on the mountaintop as I went back down, carrying the two stones

with the commandments on them. ¹⁶ I saw how quickly you had sinned and disobeyed the LORD your God. There were, worshipping the metal idol you had made in the shape of a calf. ¹⁷ So I threw down the two stones and smashed them before your very eyes.

¹⁸⁻²⁰ I bowed down at the place of worship and prayed to the LORD, without eating or drinking for forty days and nights. You had committed a terrible sin by making that idol, and the LORD hated what you had done. He was angry enough to destroy all of you and Aaron as well. So I prayed for you and Aaron as I had done before, and this time the LORD answered my prayers.*

²¹ It was a sin for you to make that idol, so I threw it into the fire to melt it down. Then I took the lump of gold, ground it into powder, and threw the powder into the stream flowing down the mountain.

²² You also made the LORD angry when you were staying at Taberah,* at Massah,* and at Kibroth-Hattaavah.* ²³ Then at Kadesh-Barnea the LORD said, "I am giving you the land, so go ahead and take it!" But since you didn't trust the LORD, you rebelled and disobeyed his command.* ²⁴ In fact, you've rebelled against the LORD for as long as he has' known you.

²⁵ After you had made the idol in the shape of a calf, the LORD said he was going to destroy you. So I bowed down in front of the sacred tent for forty days and nights, ²⁶ and I prayed:

Our LORD, please don't wipe out your people. You used your great power to rescue them from Egypt and to make them your very own. ²⁷ Israel's ancestors Abraham, Isaac, and Jacob obeyed you faithfully. Think about them, and not about Israel's stubbornness, evil, and sin. ²⁸ If you destroy your people, the Egyptians will say, "The LORD promised to give Israel land, but he wasn't powerful enough to keep his promise. In fact, he hated them so

---

*9.18–20 as I had done before . . . prayers:** This may refer to Moses' praying for Israel before he came down from the mountain (see Exodus 32.11–14).
*9.22 Taberah:** See Numbers 11.1–3.
*9.22 Massah:** See the note at 6.16.
*9.22 Kibroth-Hattaavah:** See Numbers 11.31–34.
*9.23 Kadesh-Barnea . . . you rebelled and disobeyed his command:** See Numbers 13,14.

See also: 9.19: Heb 12.21. 9.22: a Num 11.3; b Exod 17.7; c Num 11.34. 9.23: a Num 13.17; b Deut 1.21; c Num 13.31; Deut 1.26; Heb 3.16.

---

*9.2 Anakim:** See the notes at 1.28; 2.10–11.
See also: 9.9: Exod 24.18.

much that he took them into the desert and killed them." ²⁹ But you, our LORD, chose the people of Israel to be your own, and with your mighty power you rescued them from Egypt.

CHAPTER 10

The second set of commandments

This is also told in Exodus 34.1–10

Moses said to the people:

¹ The LORD told me to chisel out two flat stones, just like the ones he had given me earlier. He also commanded me to make a wooden chest, then come up the mountain and meet with him. ² He told me that he would write on the new stones the same words that he had written on the ones I broke, and that I could put these stones in this sacred chest.

³ So I made a chest out of acacia wood, and I chiselled two flat stones like the ones I broke. Then I carried the stones up the mountain, ⁴ where the LORD wrote the Ten Commandments on them, just as he had done the first time. The commandments were exactly what he had announced from the fire, when you were gathered at the mountain.

After the LORD returned the stones to me, ⁵ I took them down the mountainside and put them in the chest, just as he had commanded. And they are still there.

Aaron died

This is also told in Numbers 20.22–29

Moses said to Israel:

⁶ Later we set up camp at the wells belonging to the descendants of Jaakan.' Then we moved on and camped at Moserah, where Aaron died and was buried, and his son Eleazar became the priest. ⁷ Next, we camped at Gudgodah and then at Jotbathah, where there are flowing streams.

The Levites were appointed to carry the chest

Moses said to Israel:

⁸ After I put the two stones in the sacred chest,' the LORD chose the tribe of Levi, not only to carry the chest, but also to serve as his priests at the place of worship and to bless the other tribes in his name. And they

still do these things. ⁹ The LORD promised that he would always provide for the tribe of Levi, and that's why he won't give them any land, when he divides it among the other tribes.

The LORD answered the prayers of Moses

This is also told in Exodus 34.9–10,27–29

Moses said to Israel:

¹⁰ When I had taken the second set of stones up the mountain, I spent forty days and nights there, just as I had done before. Once again, the LORD answered my prayer and did not destroy you. ¹¹ Instead, he told me, "Moses, get ready to lead the people into the land that I promised their ancestors."*

What the LORD wants

Moses said:

¹² People of Israel, what does the LORD your God want from you? The LORD wants you to respect and follow him, to love and serve him with all your heart and soul, ¹³ and to obey his laws and teachings that I am giving you today. Do this, and all will go well for you.

¹⁴ Everything belongs to the LORD your God, not only the earth and everything on it, but also the sky and the highest heavens. ¹⁵ Yet the LORD loved your ancestors and wanted them to belong to him. So he chose them and their descendants rather than any other nation, and today you are still his people.

¹⁶ Remember your agreement with the LORD and stop being so stubborn. ¹⁷ The LORD your God is more powerful than all other gods and lords, and his tremendous power is to be feared. His decisions are always fair, and you cannot bribe him to change his mind. ¹⁸ The LORD defends the rights of orphans and widows. He cares for foreigners and gives them food and clothing. ¹⁹ And you should also care for them, because you were foreigners in Egypt.

²⁰ Respect the LORD your God, serve only him, and make promises in his name alone. ²¹ Offer your praises to him, because you

---

*10.11 lead . . . ancestors:** The LORD would later tell Moses that he would not be allowed to enter the land (see 1.37; 3.23–28; Numbers 20.10–12).

See also: 10.10: Exod 34.28.   **10.17:** 1 Tim 6.15; Rev 17.14; 19.16; Acts 10.34; Rom 2.11; Gal 2.6; Eph 6.9.

See also: 10.6: Num 20.28; 33.38.   **10.8:** Num 3.5–8.

Viewpoints 👁

As a child of God, you're different too...

Contributed by Tim B

'The LORD defends the rights of orphans and widows. He cares for foreigners and gives them food and clothing.'

God's talking about the weird kid, the one with no friends; the tramp on the street, the poor one who everyone laughs at because he's got holes in his socks and speaks funny. The person no-one cares about except God. Foreigners in the time this was written (while Moses was around, remember – big plagues, Red Sea, pillar of fire) weren't treated very well at all, they were strangers with weird and strange ways who spoke differently and had no one to stick up for them – which meant that it was seen as OK to kick them occasionally and be generally unpleasant to them.

The orphan, reduced to a life of scavenging if not taken in: friendless, uneducated and smelly. But God cares about all these people; the God who created the heavens and the earth loves them, he won't kick them just because they're down and can't kick back, he loves them even if no-one else does. Despite their flaws and apparent strangeness, God cares for them, and so should we.

Even if everyone else jeers and mocks we shouldn't join in, because we are different and we should act differently: we are God's chosen people. We should be friends of the friendless.

More...

Homelessness p.789
Refugees p.129
Racism p.1308

have seen him work such terrifying miracles for you.

22 When your ancestors went to live in Egypt, there were only seventy of them. But the LORD has blessed you, and now there are more of you than there are stars in the sky.

CHAPTER 11

If you are loyal to the LORD, he will bless you

Moses said to Israel:

1 The LORD is your God, so you must always love him and obey his laws and teachings. 2 Remember, he corrected you and not your children. You are the ones who saw the LORD use his great power 3 when he worked miracles in Egypt, making terrible things happen to the king and all his people. 4 And when the Egyptian army chased you in their chariots, you saw the LORD drown them and their horses in the Red Sea.* Egypt still suffers from that defeat!

5 You saw what the LORD did for you while you were in the desert, right up to the time you arrived here. 6 And you saw how the LORD made the ground open up in the middle of our camp underneath the tents of Dathan and Abiram,' who were swallowed up along with their families, their animals, and their tents.

7 With your own eyes, you saw the LORD's mighty power do all these things.

8 Soon you will cross the River Jordan, and if you obey the laws and teachings I'm giving you today, you will be strong enough to conquer the land 9 that the LORD promised your ancestors and their descendants. It's rich with milk and honey, and you will live there and enjoy it for a long time. 10 It's better land than you had in Egypt, where you had to struggle just to water your crops.' 11 But the hills and valleys in the promised land are

---

*11.4 **Red Sea**: Hebrew *yam suph* "Sea of Reeds", one of the marshes or fresh water lakes near the eastern part of the Nile Delta. This identification is based on Exodus 13.7—14.9, which lists towns on the route of the Israelites before crossing the sea. In the Greek translation of the Scriptures made about 200 BC, the "Sea of Reeds" was named "Red Sea".

See also: 10.22: a Gen 46.27; b Gen 15.5; 22.17.
11.3: Exod 7.8—12.13.   11.4: Exod 14.28.
11.6: Num 16.31—32.

watered by rain from heaven,* ¹² because the LORD your God keeps his eye on this land and takes care of it all year long.

¹³ The LORD your God commands you to love him and to serve him with all your heart and soul. If you obey him, ¹⁴⁻¹⁵ he will send rain at the right seasons,* so you will have more than enough food, wine, and olive oil, and there will be plenty of grass for your cattle.

¹⁶ But watch out! You will be tempted to turn your backs on the LORD. And if you worship other gods, ¹⁷ the LORD will become angry and keep the rain from falling. Nothing will grow in your fields, and you will die and disappear from the good land that the LORD is giving you.

¹⁸ Memorize these laws and think about them. Write down copies and tie them to your wrists and your foreheads to help you obey them. ¹⁹ Teach them to your children. Talk about them all the time — whether you're at home or walking along the road or going to bed at night, or getting up in the morning. ²⁰ Write them on the door frames of your homes and on your town gates. ²¹ Then you and your descendants will live a long time in the land that the LORD promised your ancestors. Your families will live there as long as the sky is above the earth.

²² Love the LORD your God and obey all the laws and teachings that I'm giving you today. If you live the way the LORD wants, ²³ he will help you take the land. And even though the nations there are more powerful than you, the LORD will force them to leave when you attack. ²⁴ You will capture the land everywhere you go, from the Southern Desert to the Lebanon Mountains, and from the River Euphrates west to the Mediterranean Sea. ²⁵ No one will be able to stand up to you. The LORD will make everyone terrified of you, just as he promised.

²⁶ You have a choice — do you want the LORD to bless you, or do you want him to put a curse on you? ²⁷ Today I am giving you his laws, and if you obey him, he will bless you. ²⁸ But if you disobey him and worship those gods that have never done anything for you, the LORD will put a curse on you.

²⁹ After the LORD your God helps you take the land, you must have a ceremony where you announce his blessings from Mount Gerizim and his curses from Mount Ebal. ³⁰ You know that these two mountains are west of the River Jordan in land now controlled by the Canaanites living in the Jordan valley. The mountains are west of the road near the sacred trees of Moreh on the other side of Gilgal. ³¹ Soon you will cross the River Jordan to conquer the land that the LORD your God is giving you. And when you have settled there, ³² be careful to obey his laws and teachings that I am giving you today.

CHAPTER 12

Only one place to worship the LORD

Moses said to Israel:

¹ Now I'll tell you the laws and teachings that you have to obey as long as you live. Your ancestors worshipped the LORD, and he is giving you this land. ² But the nations that live there worship other gods. So after you capture the land, you must completely destroy their places of worship — on mountains and hills or in the shade of large trees. ³ Wherever these nations worship their gods, you must tear down their altars, break their sacred stones, burn the sacred poles* used in worshipping the goddess Asherah, and smash their idols to pieces. Destroy these places of worship so completely that no one will remember they were ever there. ⁴ Don't worship the LORD your God in the way those nations worship their gods.

⁵⁻¹⁹ Soon you will cross the Jordan, and the LORD will help you conquer your enemies and let you live in peace, there in the land he has given you. But after you are settled, life will be different. You must not offer sacrifices anywhere you want to. Instead, the LORD will choose a place somewhere in Israel where you must go to worship him. All your sacrifices and offerings must be taken there, including

---

*11.10–11 to water your crops . . . rain from heaven:** Egypt was flat and had very little rain. All water for crops had to come from the River Nile.
*11.14–15 rain . . . seasons:** In Palestine, almost all the rain for the year comes during the months from October to April.
See also: 11.13–17: Lev 26.3–5; Deut 7.12–16; 28.1–14. 11.18–20: Deut 6.6–9. 11.24–25: Josh 1.3–5.

*12.3 sacred poles:** See the note at 7.5.
See also: 11.29: Deut 27.11–14; Josh 8.33–35. 12.3: Deut 7.5. 12.16: Gen 9.4; Lev 7.26–27; 17.10–14; 19.26; Deut 15.23.

sacrifices to please the LORD* and any gift
you promise or voluntarily give him. That's
where you must also take one tenth of your
grain, wine, and olive oil,* as well as the
firstborn of your cattle, sheep, and goats.*
You and your family and servants will eat
your gifts and sacrifices* and celebrate
there at the place of worship, because the
LORD your God has made you successful in
everything you have done. And since
Levites will not have any land of their own,
you must ask some of them to come along
and celebrate with you.

Sometimes you may want to kill an
animal for food and not as a sacrifice. If the
LORD has blessed you and given you
enough cows or sheep or goats, then you
can butcher one of them where you live.
You can eat it just like the meat from a deer
or gazelle that you kill when you go
hunting. And even those people who are
unclean and unfit for worship can have
some of the meat. But you must not eat the
blood of any animal — let the blood drain
out on the ground.

20-21 The LORD has promised that later on
he will give Israel more land, and some of
you may not be able to travel all the way
from your homes to the place of worship
each time you are hungry for meat.* But
the LORD will give you cattle, sheep, and
goats, and you can butcher any of those
animals at home and eat as much as you
want. 22 It is the same as eating the meat
from a deer or a gazelle that you kill when
you go hunting. And in this way, anyone

who is unclean and unfit for worship can
have some of the meat.*

23-24 But don't eat the blood. It is the life
of the animal, so let it drain out on the
ground before you eat the meat. 25 Do you
want the LORD to make you successful? Do
you want your children to be successful
even after you are gone? Then do what
pleases the LORD and don't eat blood.

26-27 All sacrifices and offerings to the
LORD must be taken to the place where he
chooses to be worshipped. If you offer a
sacrifice to please the LORD, all of its meat
must be burnt on the altar. You can eat the
meat from certain kinds of sacrifices, but
you must always pour out the animal's
blood on the altar.

28 If you obey these laws, you will be
doing what the LORD your God says is right
and good. Then he will help you and your
descendants be successful.

Worship the LORD in the right way

Moses said:

29 Israel, as you go into the land and attack
the nations that are there, the LORD will get
rid of them, and you can have their land.

30 But that's when you must be especially
careful not to ask, "How did those nations
worship their gods? Shouldn't we worship
the LORD in the same way?" 31 No, you
should not! The LORD hates the disgusting
way those nations worship their gods,
because they even burn their sons and
daughters as sacrifices.

32 Obey all the laws and teachings I am
giving you. Don't add any, and don't take
any away.

CHAPTER 13

Don't worship other gods

Moses said to Israel:

1-2 Some day a prophet' may come along
who is able to perform miracles or tell what
will happen in the future. Then the prophet
may say, "Let's start worshipping some new
gods — some gods that we know nothing
about." 3 If the prophet says this, don't
listen! The LORD your God will be watching
to find out whether or not you love him

---

*12.5-19 sacrifices to please the LORD: These
sacrifices have traditionally been called "whole burnt
offerings" because the whole animal was burnt on
the altar. A main purpose of such sacrifices was to
please the LORD with the smell of the sacrifice, and so
in the CEV they are often called "sacrifices to please
the LORD".
*12.5-19 one tenth of your grain, wine, and olive
oil: The Israelites had to give one tenth of their
harvest of these products to the LORD each year (see
14.22-29; 26.12-13; Leviticus 27.30-33).
*12.5-19 the firstborn of your cattle, sheep, and
goats: The Israelites had to sacrifice these to the LORD
(see 15.19-22).
*12.5-19 sacrifices: Some sacrifices were completely
burnt on the altar; in other sacrifices, part of the
animal was burnt and part was given to the priests,
but most of the meat was eaten by the worshippers
as a sacred meal.
*12.20-21 meat: Usually eaten only on special
occasions, such as during a sacred meal when
sacrifices were offered to the LORD.

*12.22 anyone . . . the meat: Only those who were
properly prepared for worship, or "clean", could eat a
sacred meal, but anyone could eat this kind of meat.
See also: 12.23-24: Lev 17.10-14. 12.32: Deut 4.2;
Rev 22.18-19.

with all your heart and soul. ⁴ You must be completely faithful to the LORD. Worship and obey only the LORD and do this with fear and trembling, ⁵ because he rescued you from slavery in Egypt.

If a prophet tells you to disobey the LORD your God and to stop worshipping him, then that prophet is evil and must be put to death.

⁶⁻¹⁰ Someone else may say to you, "Let's worship other gods." That person may be your best friend, your brother or sister, your son or daughter, or your own dear wife or husband. But you must not listen to people who say such things. Instead, you must stone them to death. You must be the first to throw the stones, then others from the community will finish the job. Don't show any pity.

The gods worshipped by other nations have never done anything for you or your ancestors. People who ask you to worship other gods are trying to get you to stop worshipping the LORD, who rescued you from slavery in Egypt. So put to death anyone who asks you to worship another god. ¹¹ And when the rest of Israel hears about it, they will be afraid, and no one else will ever do such an evil thing again.

¹² After the LORD your God gives you towns to live in, you may hear a rumour about one of the towns. ¹³ You may hear that some worthless people have talked everyone there into worshipping other gods, even though these gods had never done anything for them. ¹⁴ You must carefully find out if the rumour is true. Then if the people of that town have actually done such a disgusting thing in your own country, ¹⁵ you must take your swords and kill every one of them, and their livestock too. ¹⁶⁻¹⁷ Gather all the possessions of the people who lived there, and pile them up in the market place, without keeping anything for yourself. Set the pile and the whole town on fire, and don't ever rebuild the town. The whole town will be a sacrifice to the LORD your God. Then he won't be angry any more, and he will have mercy on you and make you successful, just as he promised your ancestors. ¹⁸ That's why you must do what the LORD your God says is right. I am giving you his laws and teachings today, and you must obey them.

CHAPTER 14

Don't mourn like other nations

Moses said:

¹ People of Israel, you are the LORD's children, so when you mourn for the dead, you must not cut yourselves or shave your forehead.⸆ ² Out of all the nations on this earth, the LORD your God chose you to be his own. You belong to the LORD, so don't behave like those who worship other gods.

Animals that can be eaten

This is also told in Leviticus 11.1–47

Moses said:

³ Don't eat any disgusting animals.
⁴⁻⁵ You may eat the meat of cattle, sheep, and goats; wild sheep and goats; and gazelles, antelopes, and all kinds of deer. ⁶ It is all right to eat meat from any animals that have divided hoofs and also chew the cud.*

⁷ But don't eat camels, rabbits, and rock badgers. These animals chew the cud but do not have divided hoofs. You must treat them as unclean. ⁸ And don't eat pork, since pigs have divided hoofs, but they do not chew their cud. Don't even touch a dead pig!

⁹ You can eat any fish that has fins and scales. But there are other creatures that live in the water, ¹⁰ and if they do not have fins and scales, you must not eat them. Treat them as unclean.

¹¹ You can eat any clean bird. ¹²⁻¹⁸ But don't eat the meat of any of the following birds: eagles, vultures, falcons, kites, ravens, ostriches, owls, seagulls, hawks, pelicans, ospreys, cormorants, storks, herons, and hoopoes.⸆ You must not eat bats. ¹⁹ Swarming insects are unclean, so don't eat them. ²⁰ However, you are allowed to eat certain kinds of winged insects.*

²¹ You belong to the LORD your God, so if you happen to find a dead animal, don't eat

---

*14.6 chew the cud: Some animals that eat grass and leaves have more than one stomach, and they chew their food a second time, after it has been partly digested in the first stomach. This partly digested food is called "cud".

*14.20 certain kinds of winged insects: These were locusts, crickets, and grasshoppers; see Leviticus 11.21–22.

See also: 14.1: Lev 19.28; 21.5. 14.2: Exod 19.5–6; Deut 4.20; 7.6; 26.18; Titus 2.14; 1 Pet 2.9. 14.21: Exod 23.19; 34.26.

its meat. You may give it to foreigners who live in your town or sell it to foreigners who are visiting your town.

Don't boil a young goat in its mother's milk.

Give the LORD ten per cent of your harvest

Moses said:

22 People of Israel, every year you must set aside ten per cent of your grain harvest. 23 Also set aside ten per cent of your wine and olive oil, and the firstborn of every cow, sheep, and goat. Take these to the place where the LORD chooses to be worshipped, and eat them there. This will teach you to always respect the LORD your God.

24 But suppose you can't carry that ten per cent of your harvest to the place where the LORD chooses to be worshipped. If you live too far away, or if the LORD gives you a big harvest, 25 then sell this part and take the money there instead. 26 When you and your family arrive, spend the money on food for a big celebration. Buy cattle, sheep, goats, wine, beer, and if there are any other kinds of food that you want, buy those too. 27 And since people of the Levi tribe won't own any land for growing crops, remember to ask the Levites to celebrate with you.

28 Every third year, instead of using the ten per cent of your harvest for a big celebration, bring it into town and put it in a community storehouse. 29 The Levites have no land of their own, so you must give them food from the storehouse. You must also give food to the poor who live in your town, including orphans, widows, and foreigners. If they have enough to eat, then the LORD your God will be pleased and make you successful in everything you do.

CHAPTER 15

Loans

This is also told in Leviticus 25.1–7

Moses said:

1-2 Every seven years you must announce, "The LORD says loans do not need to be paid back." Then if you have loaned money to another Israelite, you can no longer ask

for payment.* 3 This law applies only to loans you have made to other Israelites. Foreigners will still have to pay back what you have loaned them.

4-6 No one in Israel should ever be poor. The LORD your God is giving you this land, and he has promised to make you very successful, if you obey his laws and teachings that I'm giving you today. You will lend money to many nations, but you won't have to borrow. You will rule many nations, but they won't rule you.

7 After the LORD your God gives land to each of you, there may be poor Israelites in the town where you live. If there are, then don't be mean and selfish with your money. 8 Instead, be kind and lend them what they need. 9 Be careful! Don't say to yourself, "Soon it will be the seventh year, and then I won't be able to get my money back." It would be horrible for you to think that way and to be so selfish that you refuse to help the poor. They are your relatives, and if you don't help them, they may ask the LORD to decide whether you have done wrong. And he will say that you are guilty. 10 You should be happy to give the poor what they need, because then the LORD will make you successful in everything you do.

11 There will always be some Israelites who are poor and needy. That's why I am commanding you to be generous with them.

Setting slaves free

This is also told in Exodus 21.1–11

Moses said to Israel:

12 If any of you buy Israelites as slaves, you must set them free after six years. 13 And don't just tell them they are free to leave — 14 give them sheep and goats and a good supply of grain and wine. The more the LORD has given you, the more you should give them. 15 I am commanding you to obey the LORD as a reminder that you were slaves in Egypt before he set you free. 16 But one of your slaves may say, "I love you and your family, and I would be better off staying with you, so please don't make me

---

15.1–2 The LORD says . . . no longer ask for payment: Or " 'The LORD says loans do not need to be paid back this year.' Then if you have loaned money to another Israelite, you cannot ask for payment until the next year."

See also: 15.7–8: Lev 25.35. 15.11: Matt 26.11; Mark 14.7; John 12.8. 15.12–18: Lev 25.39–46.

See also: 14.22–29: Lev 27.30–33; Num 18.21.

Real Life

Globalisation

Globalisation is on the march. There has been a rapid increase in international trade, and data flows across borders via the internet, satellite and telephone. People travel further and more often than ever before – on business, as tourists, or as refugees. The food on your table has travelled thousands of miles, whether it's tea from Kenya or bananas from the Windward Islands. Your clothes may be designed in London, Paris or New York, but they're often made in the developing world. The person on the end of a customer support line may well be sitting in an office in India. The football you kick into the goal has been stitched by a worker in Pakistan.

Many people are not happy with these developments, and argue that the rules which govern international trade are written purely for the benefit of multinational corporations. An increased share of the world economy is controlled by them, and the export of cultural influences (e.g. Hollywood movies) leads to a reduction in global cultural diversity – what some call the 'MacDonaldisation' of the world. Global economic summits have seen mass protests about these changes.

Globalisation. It's such a 'modern' phenomenon. So what does the Bible say?

First it talks about the need to avoid exploiting the poor. Globalisation is about money. At its best it is about sharing the world's wealth around. At its worst it's about getting the best possible price and cheapest labour. Let's face it, huge multinational companies set up factories or open up branches in the developing world because labour is cheap or because there is money to be made. They bring jobs and employment, but what about the working conditions of the workers, and the effects on the environment? The Bible calls on us to help people out of poverty, not to exploit their poverty to enhance our profits.

The big multinational companies wield enormous power. They control the prices of goods. Decisions taken by boards in London or New York can make or break towns and communities on the other side of the world. Sometimes it seems as though one day everyone will speak English, buy the same kind of fast food, drink the same soft drinks (and even support the same football teams!)

There is nothing wrong with trade, or providing jobs and buying goods from other nations. But the Bible is quite clear on the need for fairness and the responsibility of those with money and power to protect the poor and helpless. As Christians we should ensure that people are being treated fairly; that globalisation does not wipe out other cultures or exploit workers; that it is about sharing money around the world, rather than making the rich richer and the poor poorer. Globalisation should lead to genuine freedom and choice.

Think

What are the benefits of globalisation? Do these outweigh the negative effects?
Is it possible to uphold the Sabbath principle? How do you spend Sundays? Is this any different to how you spend the rest of week?
What would the world look like if nation states were eclipsed by economic powers? Picture your high street. Is it any different to high streets in other towns – or other countries?

Act

Plan to spend next Sunday in accord with what the Bible says about Sabbath. Protest about an issue that is important to you and is in line with Biblical principles.

Check

Exodus 21.2; Leviticus 25; Deuteronomy 15.1–11; 1 Chronicles 29.14–18; Nehemiah 10.31

More...

Sabbath p.97
Jubilee – the Year of Celebration p.137
Fair Trade p.923 Materialism p.1141
Civil disobedience p.1247

leave." ¹⁷ Take the slave to the door of your house and push a sharp metal rod through one ear lobe and into the door. Such slaves will belong to you for life, whether they are men or women.

¹⁸ Don't complain when you have to set a slave free. After all, you got six years of service at half the cost of hiring someone to do the work.'

Firstborn animals

This is also told in Leviticus 27.26–27; Numbers 18.15–18

Moses said to Israel:

¹⁹ If the firstborn animal of a cow or sheep or goat is a male, it must be given to the LORD. Don't put firstborn cattle to work or cut wool from firstborn sheep. ²⁰ Instead, each year you must take the firstborn of these animals to the place where the LORD your God chooses to be worshipped. You and your family will sacrifice them to the LORD and then eat them as part of a sacred meal.

²¹ But if the animal is lame or blind or has something else wrong with it, you must not sacrifice it to the LORD your God. ²² You can butcher it where you live, and eat it just like the meat of a deer or gazelle that you kill while hunting. Even those people who are unclean and unfit for worship can have some. ²³ But you must never eat the blood of an animal — let it drain out on the ground.

CHAPTER 16

Passover

This is also told in Exodus 12.1–20; Leviticus 23.4–8

Moses said:

¹ People of Israel, you must celebrate Passover in the month of Abib,* because one night in that month years ago, the LORD your God rescued you from Egypt. ² The Passover sacrifice must be a cow, a sheep, or a goat, and you must offer it at the place where the LORD chooses to be worshipped. ³⁻⁴ Eat all the meat of the Passover sacrifice that same night. But don't

serve bread made with yeast at the Passover meal. Serve the same kind of thin bread that you ate when you were slaves suffering in Egypt' and when you had to leave Egypt quickly. As long as you live, this thin bread will remind you of the day you left Egypt.

For seven days following Passover,* don't make any bread with yeast. In fact, there should be no yeast anywhere in Israel.

⁵ Don't offer the Passover sacrifice in any town where you happen to live. ⁶ It must be offered at the place where the LORD chooses to be worshipped. Kill the sacrifice at sunset, the time of day when you left Egypt.' ⁷ Then cook it and eat it there at the place of worship, returning to your tents the next morning.

⁸ Eat thin bread for the next six days. Then on the seventh day, don't do any work. Instead, come together and worship the LORD.

The Harvest Festival

This is also told in Exodus 34.22; Leviticus 23.15–21

Moses said to Israel:

⁹ Seven weeks after you start your grain harvest, ¹⁰⁻¹¹ go to the place where the LORD chooses to be worshipped and celebrate the Harvest Festival* in honour of the LORD your God. Bring him an offering as large as you can afford, depending on how big a harvest he has given you. Be sure to take along your sons and daughters and all your servants. Also invite the poor, including Levites, foreigners, orphans, and widows. ¹² Remember that you used to be slaves in Egypt, so obey these laws.

The Festival of Shelters

This is also told in Leviticus 23.33–43; Numbers 29.12–38

Moses said to Israel:

¹³⁻¹⁵ After you have finished the grain harvest and the grape harvest,* take your

---

*16.1 in the month of Abib: Abib (also called Nisan), the first month of the Hebrew calendar, from about mid-March to mid-April. Passover was celebrated on the evening of the fourteenth of Abib (see Exodus 12.6; Leviticus 23.4–5).

See also: 15.19: Exod 13.12. 15.23: Gen 9.4; Lev 7.26–27; 17.10–14; 19.26; Deut 12.16,23. 16.1–8: Exod 12.1–20; Lev 23.5–8; Num 28.16–25.

*16.3–4 seven days following Passover: This period was called the Festival of Thin Bread (see also verse 16).
*16.10–11 Harvest Festival: Traditionally called the "Festival of Weeks", and known in New Testament times as "Pentecost".
*16.13–15 After you . . . harvest: Leviticus 23.34 gives the exact date as the fifteenth day of the seventh month of the Hebrew calendar, which would be early in October.

See also: 16.9–12: Lev 23.15–21; Num 28.26–31. 16.13–15: Lev 23.33–36,39–43; Num 29.12–38.

sons and daughters and all your servants to the place where the LORD chooses to be worshipped. Celebrate the Festival of Shelters for seven days. Also invite the poor, including Levites, foreigners, orphans, and widows.

The LORD will give you big harvests and make you successful in everything you do. You will be completely happy, so celebrate this festival in honour of the LORD your God.

Three festivals at the place of worship
This is also told in Exodus 23.14–17

Moses said:

16 Each year there are three festivals when all Israelite men must go to the place where the LORD chooses to be worshipped. These are the Festival of Thin Bread, the Harvest Festival,* and the Festival of Shelters. And don't forget to take along a gift for the LORD. 17 The bigger the harvest the LORD gives you, the bigger your gift should be.

Treat everyone with justice

Moses said to Israel:

18-19 After you are settled in the towns that you will receive from the LORD your God, the people in each town must appoint judges and other officers. Those of you who become judges must be completely fair when you make legal decisions, even if someone important is involved. Don't take bribes to give unfair decisions. Bribes keep people who are wise from seeing the truth and turn honest people into liars.'

20 People of Israel, if you want to enjoy a long and successful life, make sure that everyone is treated with justice in the land the LORD is giving you.

Don't set up sacred poles or stones

Moses said to Israel:

21 When you build the altar for offering sacrifices to the LORD your God, don't set up a sacred pole* for the worship of the goddess Asherah. 22 And don't set up a sacred stone! The LORD hates these things.

CHAPTER 17
Sacrifices that have something wrong with them
Moses said to Israel:

1 If an ox or a sheep has something wrong with it, don't offer it as a sacrifice to the LORD your God — he will be disgusted!

Put to death people who worship idols
Moses said to Israel:

2-3 The LORD your God is giving you towns to live in. But later, a man or a woman in your town may start worshipping other gods, or even the sun, moon, or stars.* I have warned you not to worship other gods, because whoever worships them is disobeying the LORD and breaking the agreement he made with you. 4 So when you hear that someone in your town is committing this disgusting sin, you must carefully find out if that person really is guilty. 5-7 But you will need two or three witnesses — one witness isn't enough to prove a person guilty.

Get rid of those who are guilty of such evil. Take them outside your town gates and let everyone stone them to death. But the witnesses must be the first to throw stones.

Difficult cases
Moses said to Israel:

8-12 It may be difficult to find out the truth in some legal cases in your town. You may not be able to decide if someone was killed accidentally or murdered. Or you may not be able to tell whether an injury or some property damage was done by accident or on purpose. If the case is too difficult, take it to the court at the place where the LORD your God chooses to be worshipped.

This court will be made up of one judge and several priests* who serve at the LORD's altar. They will explain the law to you and give you their decision about the case. Do exactly what they tell you, or you will be put to death. 13 When other Israelites hear about it, they will be afraid and obey the decisions of the court.

---

*17.2–3 sun, moon, or stars: Some people thought these were gods and worshipped them.
*17.8–12 several priests: The Hebrew text has "the priests, the Levites"; priests belonged to the Levi tribe.
See also: 17.3: Exod 22.20. 17.6: Num 35.30; Deut 19.15; Matt 18.16; 2 Cor 13.1; 1 Tim 5.19; Heb 10.28.
17.7: 1 Cor 5.13.

---

*16.16 Harvest Festival: See the note at 16.10–11.
*16.21 sacred pole: See the note at 7.5.
See also: 16.19: Exod 23.6–8; Lev 19.15.
16.21: Exod 34.13. 16.22: Lev 26.1.

The king

Moses said:

14 People of Israel, after you capture the land the LORD your God is giving you, and after you settle on it, you will say, "We want a king, just like the nations around us."

15 Go ahead and appoint a king, but make sure that he is an Israelite and that he is the one the LORD has chosen.

16 The king should not have many horses, especially those from Egypt. The LORD has said his people are never to go back there again. 17 And the king must not have a lot of wives — they might tempt him to be unfaithful to the LORD.* Finally, the king must not try to get huge amounts of silver and gold.

18 The official copy of God's laws' will be kept by the priests of the Levi tribe. So, as soon as anyone becomes king, he must go to the priests and write out a copy of these laws while they watch. 19 Each day the king must read and obey these laws, so that he will learn to worship the LORD with fear and trembling 20 and not think that he's better than everyone else.

If the king completely obeys the LORD's commands, he and his descendants will rule Israel for many years.

CHAPTER 18

Special privileges for priests and Levites

This is also told in Numbers 18.8–32

Moses said to Israel:

1 The people of the Levi tribe, including the priests, will not receive any land. Instead, they will receive part of the sacrifices that are offered to the LORD, 2 because he has promised to provide for them in this way.

3 When you sacrifice a bull or sheep, the priests will be given the shoulder, the jaws, and the stomach.* 4 In addition, they will receive the first part of your grain harvest and part of your first batches of wine and olive oil.* You must also give them the first wool that is cut from your sheep each year. 5 Give these gifts to the priests, because the LORD has chosen them and their descendants out of all the tribes of Israel to be his special servants at the place of worship.

6 Any Levite can leave his home town, and go to the place where the LORD chooses to be worshipped, 7 and then be a special servant of the LORD' there, just like all the other Levites. 8 Some Levites may have money from selling family possessions, and others may not. But all Levites serving at the place of worship will receive the same amount of food from the sacrifices and gifts brought by the people.

Don't do disgusting things

Moses said to Israel:

9 Soon you will go into the land that the LORD your God is giving you. The nations that live there do things that are disgusting to the LORD, and you must not follow their example. 10-11 Don't sacrifice your son or daughter. And don't try to use any kind of magic or witchcraft to tell fortunes* or to cast spells or to talk with spirits of the dead.

12 The LORD is disgusted with anyone who does these things, and that's why he will help you destroy the nations that are in the land. 13 Never be guilty of doing any of these disgusting things!

A prophet like Moses

Moses said to Israel:

14 You will go in and take the land from nations that practise magic and witchcraft. But the LORD your God won't allow you to do those things. 15 Instead, he will choose one of your own people to be a prophet just like me, and you must do what that prophet says. 16 You were asking for a prophet the day you were gathered at

---

*17.17 a lot of wives . . . unfaithful to the LORD: A king would often marry the daughter of another king whom he was making a treaty with. These foreign women would naturally want to worship their own gods, and would want their husband the king to do so as well.

*18.3 stomach: Certain portions of the stomach were considered a delicacy.

See also: 17.14: 1 Sam 8.5. 17.16: 1 King 10.28; 2 Chron 1.16; 9.28. 17.17: a 1 King 11.1–8; b 1 King 10.14–22,27; 2 Chron 1.15; 9.27. 18.2: Num 18.20.

*18.4 grain . . . olive oil: An Israelite was supposed to offer the first part of the harvest as a gift to the LORD (see Leviticus 23.10–11).

*18.10–11 tell fortunes: Fortune-tellers thought they could learn secrets or learn about the future by watching the flight of birds or looking at the livers of animals or in many other ways.

See also: 18.10: a Lev 19.26; b Exod 22.18. 18.11: Lev 19.31. 18.13: Matt 5.48. 18.15: Acts 3.22; 7.37.

Mount Sinai* and said to the LORD, "Please don't let us hear your voice or see this terrible fire again — if we do, we will die!"

¹⁷ Then the LORD told me:

Moses, they have said the right thing. ¹⁸ So when I want to speak to them, I will choose one of them to be a prophet like you. I will give my message to that prophet, who will tell the people exactly what I have said. ¹⁹ Since the message comes from me, anyone who doesn't obey the message will have to answer to me.

²⁰ But if I haven't spoken, and a prophet claims to have a message from me, you must kill that prophet, and you must also kill any prophet who claims to have a message from another god.

Moses said to Israel:

²¹ You may be asking yourselves, "How can we tell if a prophet's message really comes from the LORD?" ²² You will know, because if the LORD says something will happen, it will happen. And if it doesn't, you will know that the prophet was falsely claiming to speak for the LORD. Don't be afraid of any prophet whose message doesn't come from the LORD.

CHAPTER 19

Safe Towns

This is also told in Numbers 35.9–28; Joshua 20.1–9

Moses said to Israel:

¹ Soon you will go into the land and attack the nations. The LORD your God will destroy them and give you their lands, towns, and homes. Then after you are settled, ²⁻⁴ you must choose three of your towns to be Safe Towns. Divide the land into three regions with one Safe Town near the middle of each, so that a Safe Town can be easily reached from anywhere in your land.

Then, if one of you accidentally kills someone, you can run to a Safe Town and find protection from being put to death. But you must not have been angry with the person you killed.

⁵ For example, suppose you and a friend go into the forest to cut wood. You are chopping down a tree with an axe, when the axe head slips off the handle, hits your friend, and kills him. You can run to one of

the Safe Towns and save your life. ⁶ You don't deserve to die, since you did not mean to harm your friend. But he did get killed, and his relatives might be very angry. They might even choose one of the men from their family to track you down and kill you. If it is too far to one of the Safe Towns, the victim's relative might be able to catch you and kill you. ⁷ That's why I said there must be three Safe Towns.

⁸⁻⁹ Israel, the LORD your God has promised that if you obey his laws and teachings I'm giving you, and if you always love him, then he will give you the land he promised your ancestors. When that happens, you must name three more Safe Towns in the new territory. ¹⁰ You will need them, so innocent people won't be killed on your land while they are trying to reach a Safe Town that is too far away. You will be guilty of murder, if innocent people lose their lives because you didn't name enough Safe Towns in the land the LORD your God will give you.

¹¹ But what if you really do commit murder? Suppose one of you hates a neighbour. So you wait in a deserted place, kill the neighbour, and run to a Safe Town. ¹² If that happens, the leaders of your town must send messengers to bring you back from the Safe Town. They will hand you over to one of the victim's relatives, who will put you to death.

¹³ Israel, for the good of the whole country, you must kill anyone who murders an innocent person. Never show mercy to a murderer!

Boundary marks

Moses said to Israel:

¹⁴ In the land the LORD is giving you, there are already stones set up to mark the boundaries between fields. So don't move those stones.

Witnesses must tell the truth

Moses said to Israel:

¹⁵ Before you are convicted of a crime, at least two witnesses must be able to testify that you did it.

¹⁶ If you accuse someone of a crime, but seem to be lying, ¹⁷⁻¹⁸ then both you and the accused must be taken to the court at

See also: **19.14:** Deut 27.17. **19.15:** Num 35.30; Deut 17.6; Matt 18.16; John 8.17; 2 Cor 13.1; 1 Tim 5.19; Heb 10.28.

203

the place where the LORD is worshipped. There the priests and judges will find out if you are lying or telling the truth.

If you are lying and the accused is innocent, ¹⁹⁻²¹ then you will be punished without mercy. You will receive the same punishment the accused would have received if found guilty, whether it means losing an eye, a tooth, a hand, a foot, or even your life.

Israel, the crime of telling lies in court must be punished. And when people hear what happens to witnesses that lie, everyone else who testifies in court will tell the truth.

CHAPTER 20

Laws for going to war

Moses said to Israel:

¹ If you have to go to war, you may find yourselves facing an enemy army that is bigger than yours and that has horses and chariots. But don't be afraid! The LORD your God rescued you from Egypt, and he will help you fight. ² Before you march into battle, a priest will go to the front of the army ³ and say, "Soldiers of Israel, listen to me! Today when you go into battle, don't be afraid of the enemy, and when you see them, don't panic. ⁴ The LORD your God will fight beside you and help you win the battle."

⁵ Then the tribal officials will say to the troops:

If any of you have built a new house, but haven't yet moved in, you may go home. It isn't right for you to die in battle and for somebody else to live in your new house.

⁶ If any of you have planted a vineyard but haven't had your first grape harvest, you may go home. It isn't right for you to die in battle and for somebody else to enjoy your grapes.

⁷ If any of you are engaged to be married, you may go back home and get married. It isn't right for you to die in battle and for somebody else to marry the woman you are engaged to.

⁸ Finally, if any of you are afraid, you may go home. We don't want you to discourage the other soldiers.

⁹ When the officials have finished giving these orders, they will appoint officers to be in command of the army.

¹⁰⁻¹⁵ Before you attack a town that is far from your land, offer peace to the people who live there. If they surrender and open their town gates, they will become your slaves. But if they reject your offer of peace and try to fight, surround their town and attack. Then, after the LORD helps you capture it, kill all the men. Take the women and children as slaves and keep the livestock and everything else of value.

¹⁶ Whenever you capture towns in the land the LORD your God is giving you, be sure to kill all the people and animals. ¹⁷ He has commanded you to completely wipe out the Hittites, the Amorites, the Canaanites, the Perizzites, the Hivites, and the Jebusites. ¹⁸ If you allow them to live, they will persuade you to worship their disgusting gods, and you will be unfaithful to the LORD.

¹⁹ When you are attacking a town, don't chop down its fruit trees, not even if you have had the town surrounded for a long time. Fruit trees aren't your enemies, and they produce food that you can eat, so don't cut them down. ²⁰ You may need wood to make ladders and towers to help you get over the walls and capture the town. But use only trees that you know are not fruit trees.

CHAPTER 21

Unsolved murder

Moses said to Israel:

¹ Suppose the body of a murder victim is found in a field in the land the LORD your God is giving you, and no one knows who the murderer is. ² The judges and other leaders from the towns around there must find out what town is the closest to where the body was found. ³ The leaders from that town will go to their cattle herds and choose a young cow that has never been put to work.* ⁴⁻⁵ They and some of the priests will take this cow to a nearby valley where there is a stream, but no crops. Once they reach the valley, the leaders will break the cow's neck.

The priests must be there, because the LORD your God has chosen them to be his special servants at the place of worship. The LORD has chosen them to bless the people in his name and to be judges in

See also: 19.21: Exod 21.23–25; Lev 24.19–20; Matt 5.38.

204

*__*21.3 young cow . . . work:__ Cows and oxen pulled ploughs and wagons.*

all legal cases, whether property or injury is involved.

⁶ The town leaders will wash their hands over the body of the dead cow ⁷ and say, "We had no part in this murder, and we don't know who did it. ⁸⁻⁹ But since an innocent person was murdered, we beg you, our LORD, to accept this sacrifice and forgive Israel. We are your people, and you rescued us. Please don't hold this crime against us."

If you obey the LORD and do these things, he will forgive Israel.

Marrying a woman taken prisoner in war

Moses said to Israel:

¹⁰ From time to time, you men will serve as soldiers and go off to war. The LORD your God will help you defeat your enemies, and you will take many prisoners. ¹¹⁻¹³ One of these prisoners may be a beautiful woman, and you may want to marry her. But first you must bring her into your home, and she must shave her head, cut her nails, get rid of her foreign clothes, and start wearing Israelite clothes. She will mourn a month for her father and mother, then you can marry her.

¹⁴ Later on, if you are not happy with the woman, you can divorce her, and she can go free. But you have slept with her as your wife, so you cannot sell her as a slave or make her into your own slave.

Rights of a firstborn son

Moses said to Israel:

¹⁵⁻¹⁷ Suppose a man has two wives and loves one more than the other. The first son of either wife is the man's firstborn son, even if the boy's mother is the wife the man doesn't love. Later, when the man is near death and is dividing up his property, he must give a double share to his firstborn son, simply because he was the first to be born.

A son who rebels

Moses said to Israel:

¹⁸ A father and a mother may have a stubborn and rebellious son who refuses to obey them even after he has been punished. ¹⁹ If a son is like that, his parents must drag him to the town gate, where the leaders of the town hold their meetings.

Holy history

Marriage

Marriage was very different in Bible times.

For a start, most marriages were arranged. None of this 'I'll choose who I want stuff.' No, your parents sorted it out.

Not that love didn't come into the equation. Rebekah fell in love with Isaac. And Samson chose his bride. But he still asked his parents to arrange things (Judges 14.1–3).

Engagements were then a matter of drawing up the contract. The bride was usually purchased by the groom's family – usually by paying a 'bride-price' which was supposed to compensate the bride's family for the loss of a useful worker. Brides could also be captured in wars (Deuteronomy 21.10–14) or even gained as the result of seduction (Exodus 22.16).

Brides were heavily veiled on the wedding day – which is why Jacob could be fooled into marrying the wrong woman (Genesis 29.21–28).

If the husband died, it was customary for widows to marry their dead husband's nearest living relative, usually the brother (Deuteronomy 25.5–6.) This is the marriage custom behind the story of Ruth (Ruth 4.1–8) and the Sadducees question to Jesus (Luke 20.27–36). It's also why Tamar goes to such great lengths; she is asserting her rights as a woman of the time. Her actions were rewarded with twins, the eldest of whom would be an ancestor of King David, and, ultimately, Jesus. Tamar is one of the few women mentioned in the family tree of Christ (Matthew 1.3).

More...

Sex p.727
Help! I want to go out with a non-Christian p.280
Divorce p.1281

²⁰ The parents will tell the leaders, "This son of ours is stubborn and never obeys. He spends all his time drinking and feasting."

²¹ The men of the town will stone that son to death, because they must get rid of the evil he brought into the community. Everyone in Israel will be afraid when they hear how he was punished.

The body of a criminal

Moses said to Israel:

²² If a criminal is put to death, and you hang the dead body on a tree, ²³ you must not let it hang there overnight. Bury it the same day, because the dead body of a criminal will bring God's curse on the land. The LORD your God is giving this land to you, so don't make it unclean by leaving the bodies of executed criminals on display.

CHAPTER 22

Helping others

Moses said to Israel:

¹ If you see a cow or sheep wandering around lost, take the animal back to its owner. ² If the owner lives too far away, or if you don't know who the owner is, take the animal home with you and take care of it. The owner will come looking for the animal, and then you can give it back. ³ That's what you should do if you find anything that belongs to someone else. Do whatever you can to help, whether you find a cow or sheep or donkey or some clothing.

⁴ Oxen and donkeys that carry heavy loads can stumble and fall, and be unable to get up by themselves. So as you walk along the road, help anyone who is trying to get an ox or donkey back on its feet.

Don't pretend to be the opposite sex

Moses said to Israel:

⁵ Women must not pretend to be men, and men must not pretend to be women.' The LORD your God is disgusted with people who do that.

Don't take a mother bird

Moses said to Israel:

⁶⁻⁷ As you walk along the road, you might see a bird's nest in a tree or on the ground. If the mother bird is in the nest with either her eggs or her baby birds, you are allowed to take the baby birds or the eggs, but not the mother bird. Let her go free, and the LORD will bless you with a long and successful life.

Put a wall around your flat roof

Moses said to Israel:

⁸ If you build a house, make sure to put a low wall around the edge of the flat roof.* Then if someone falls off the roof and is killed, it won't be your fault.

Laws against mixing different things

Moses said to Israel:

⁹ If you plant a vineyard, don't plant any other fruit tree or crop in it. If you do plant something else there, you must bring to the place of worship everything you harvest from the vineyard.

¹⁰ Don't hitch an ox and a donkey to your plough at the same time.

¹¹ When you weave cloth for clothing, you can use thread made of flax* or wool, but not both together. ¹² And when you make a coat, sew a tassel on each of the four corners.

When a husband accuses his wife

Moses said to Israel:

¹³ Suppose a man starts hating his wife soon after they are married. ¹⁴ He might tell ugly lies about her, and say, "I married this woman, but when we slept together, I found out she wasn't a virgin."

¹⁵ If this happens, the bride's father and mother must go to the town gate to show the town leaders the proof that the woman was a virgin. ¹⁶ Her father will say, "I let my daughter marry this man, but he started hating her ¹⁷ and accusing her of not being a virgin. But he is wrong, because here is proof that she was a virgin!" Then the bride's parents will show them the bed sheet from the woman's wedding night.

---

*22.8 flat roof: Houses usually had flat roofs. In hot dry weather, it was cooler on the roof than in the house, and so roofs were used for sleeping and living quarters, and for entertaining guests.
*22.11 flax: The stalks of flax plants were harvested, soaked in water, and dried, then their fibres were separated and spun into thread, which was woven into linen cloth.

See also: 21.23: Gal 3.13. 22.1–4: Exod 23.4–5.   See also: 22.9–11: Lev 19.19. 22.12: Num 15.37–41.

¹⁸ The town leaders will beat the man with a whip ¹⁹ because he accused his bride of not being a virgin. He will have to pay her father one hundred pieces of silver and will never be allowed to divorce her.

²⁰ But if the man was right and there is no proof that his bride was a virgin, ²¹ the men of the town will take the woman to the door of her father's house and stone her to death.

This woman brought evil into your community by sleeping with someone before she got married, and you must get rid of that evil by killing her.

Laws about illegal sex

Moses said:

²² People of Israel, if a man is caught having sex with someone else's wife, you must put them both to death. That way, you will get rid of the evil they have done in Israel.

²³⁻²⁴ If a man is caught in town having sex with an engaged woman who isn't screaming for help, they both must be put to death. The man is guilty of having sex with a married woman.* And the woman is guilty because she didn't call for help, even though she was inside a town and people were nearby. Take them both to the town gate and stone them to death. You must get rid of the evil they brought into your community.

²⁵ If an engaged woman is raped out in the country, only the man will be put to death. ²⁶ Do not punish the woman at all; she has done nothing wrong, and certainly nothing deserving death. This crime is like murder, ²⁷ because the woman was alone out in the country when the man attacked her. She screamed, but there was no one to help her.

²⁸ Suppose a woman isn't engaged to be married, and a man talks her into sleeping with him. If they are caught, ²⁹ they will be forced to get married. He must give her father fifty pieces of silver as a bride price and᾿ can never divorce her.

³⁰ A man must not marry a woman who was married to his father. This would be a disgrace to his father.

CHAPTER 23

Who cannot become one of the LORD's people

Moses said to Israel:

¹ If a man's private parts have been crushed or cut off,* he cannot fully belong to the LORD's people.

² No one born outside a legal marriage, or any of their descendants for ten generations, can fully belong to the LORD's people.

³ No Ammonites or Moabites, or any of their descendants for ten generations, can become part of Israel, the LORD's people. ⁴ This is because when you came out of Egypt, they refused to provide you with food and water. And besides, they hired Balaam᾿ to put a curse on you. ⁵ But the LORD your God loves you, so he refused to listen to Balaam and turned Balaam's curse into a blessing. ⁶ Don't even think of signing a peace treaty with Moab or Ammon.

⁷ But Edomites are your relatives, and you lived as foreigners in the country of Egypt. Now you must be kind to Edomites and Egyptians ⁸ and let their great-grandchildren become part of Israel, the LORD's people.

Keep the army camp acceptable

Moses said to Israel:

⁹ When you men go off to fight your enemies, make sure your camp is acceptable to the LORD.

¹⁰ For example, if something happens at night that makes a man unclean and unfit for worship, he᾿ must go outside the camp and stay there ¹¹ until late afternoon. Then he must take a bath, and at sunset he can go back into camp.

¹² Set up a place outside the camp to be used as a toilet area. ¹³ And make sure that you have a small shovel in your equipment. When you go out to the toilet area, use the shovel to dig a hole. Then, after you relieve yourself, bury the waste in the hole. ¹⁴ You must keep your camp clean of filthy and disgusting things. The LORD is always

---

*22.23–24 engaged woman . . . married woman: An engaged woman was legally married, but had not yet slept with her husband or started living with him. See also: 22.28–29: Exod 22.16–17. 22.30: Lev 18.8; 20.11; Deut 27.20.

*23.1 a man's private parts have been crushed or cut off: This was sometimes done to show devotion to pagan gods. See also: 23.3–5: Neh 13.1–2. 23.4: Num 22.1–6. 23.5: Num 23.7–24.9.

present in your camp, ready to rescue you and give you victory over your enemies. But if he sees something disgusting in your camp, he may turn around and leave.

Runaway slaves from other countries

Moses said:

15 When runaway slaves from other countries come to Israel and ask for protection, you must not hand them back to their owners. 16 Instead, you must let them choose which one of your towns they want to live in. Don't be cruel to runaway slaves.

Temple prostitutes

Moses said:

17 People of Israel, don't any of you ever be temple prostitutes.* 18 The LORD your God is disgusted with men and women who are prostitutes of any kind, and he will not accept a gift from them, even if it had been promised to him.

Interest on loans

Moses said:

19 When you lend money, food, or anything else to another Israelite, you are not allowed to charge interest. 20 You can charge a foreigner interest. But if you charge other Israelites interest, the LORD your God will not let you be successful in the land you are about to take.

Sacred promises to the LORD

Moses said:

21 People of Israel, if you make a sacred promise to give a gift to the LORD, then do it as soon as you can. If the LORD has to come looking for the gift you promised, you will be guilty of breaking that promise. 22 On the other hand, if you never make a sacred promise, you can't be guilty of breaking it. 23 You must keep whatever promises you make to the LORD. After all, you are the one who chose to make the promises.

Eating someone else's produce

Moses said:

24 If you go into a vineyard that belongs to someone else, you are allowed to eat as many grapes as you want while you are there. But don't take any with you when you leave. 25 In the same way, if you are in a grain field that belongs to someone else, you can pick heads of grain and eat the kernels. But don't cut down the stalks of grain and take them with you.

CHAPTER 24

A law about divorce

Moses said to Israel:

1 Suppose a woman was divorced by her first husband because he found something disgraceful about her.' He wrote out divorce papers, gave them to her, and sent her away. 2 Later she married another man, 3 who then either divorced her in the same way or died. 4 Since she has slept with her second husband, she cannot marry her first husband again. Their marriage would pollute the land that the LORD your God is giving you, and he would be disgusted.

Newlyweds

Moses said to Israel:

5 If a man and a woman have been married less than one year, he must not be sent off to war or sent away to do forced labour. He must be allowed to stay home for a year and be happy with his wife.

Loans

Moses said to Israel:

6 When you lend money to people, you are allowed to keep something of theirs as a guarantee that they will pay back the loan. But don't take one or both of their millstones, or else they may starve. They need these stones for grinding grain into flour to make bread.

Kidnapping

Moses said to Israel:

7 If you are guilty of kidnapping Israelites and forcing them into slavery, you will be

---

*23.17 temple prostitutes: Some Canaanites worshipped by going to their temples and having sex with prostitutes who represented their gods.

See also: 23.17: Lev 19.29. 23.19–20: Exod 22.25; Lev 25.36–37; Deut 15.7–11. 23.21: Num 30.1–16; Matt 5.33.

See also: 24.1: Matt 5.31; 19.7; Mark 10.4. 24.7: Exod 21.16.

put to death to remove this evil from the community.

Skin diseases

Moses said to Israel:

8 I have told the priests* what to do if any of you have leprosy,* so do exactly what they say. 9 And remember what the LORD your God did to Miriam* after you left Egypt.

Loans

Moses said to Israel:

10 When you lend money to people, you are allowed to keep something of theirs as a guarantee that the money will be paid back. But you must not go into their house to get it. 11 Wait outside, and they will bring out the item you have agreed on.

12 Suppose someone is so poor that a coat is the only thing that can be offered as a guarantee on a loan. Don't keep the coat overnight. 13 Instead, give it back before sunset, so the owner can keep warm and sleep and ask the LORD to bless you. Then the LORD your God will notice that you have done the right thing.

Poor people's wages

Moses said:

14 If you hire poor people to work for you, don't hold back their pay,’ whether they are Israelites or foreigners who live in your town. 15 Pay them their wages at the end of each day, because they live in poverty and need the money to survive. If you don't pay them on time, they will complain about you to the LORD, and he will punish you.

The death penalty

Moses said to Israel:

16 Parents must not be put to death for crimes committed by their children, and children must not be put to death for crimes committed by their parents. Don't put anyone to death for someone else's crime.

Don't ill-treat the powerless

Moses said to Israel:

17 Make sure that orphans and foreigners are treated fairly. And if you lend money to a widow and want to keep something of hers to guarantee that she will pay you back, don't take any of her clothes. 18 You were slaves in Egypt until the LORD your God rescued you. That's why I am giving you these laws.

Leave some of your harvest for the poor

Moses said to Israel:

19 If you forget to bring in a stack of harvested grain, don't go back in the field to get it. Leave it for the poor, including foreigners, orphans, and widows, and the LORD will make you successful in everything you do.

20 When you harvest your olives, don't try to get them all for yourself, but leave some for the poor. 21 And when you pick your grapes, go over the vines only once, then let the poor have what is left. 22 You lived in poverty as slaves in Egypt until the LORD your God rescued you. That's why I am giving you these laws.

CHAPTER 25

Whipping as punishment for a crime

Moses said to Israel:

1-2 Suppose you and someone else each accuse the other of doing something wrong, and you go to court, where the judges decide you are guilty. If your punishment is to be beaten with a whip,’ one of the judges will order you to lie down, and you will receive the number of lashes you deserve. 3 Forty lashes is the most that you can be given, because more than that might make other Israelites think you are worthless.

Don't muzzle an ox

Moses said to Israel:

4 Don't muzzle an ox while it is threshing grain.*

---

*24.8 the priests:** See the note at 17.8–12.
*24.8 leprosy:** The word "leprosy" was used for many different kinds of skin diseases.
*24.9 what the LORD your God did to Miriam:** See Numbers 12.1–16.
See also: 24.8: Lev 13.1–14.54. 24.9: Num 12.10.
24.10-13: Exod 22.26–27. 24.14–15: Lev 19.13.
24.16: 2 King 14.6; 2 Chron 25.4; Ezek 18.20.

---

*25.4 threshing grain:** Oxen were used at the threshing place to walk on heads of grain, or pull heavy slabs of wood over it, to separate the kernels from the husks.
See also: 24.17–18: Exod 23.9; Lev 19.33–34; Deut 27.19.
24.19-21: Lev 19.9–10; 23.22. 25.3: 2 Cor 11.24.
25.4: 1 Cor 9.9; 1 Tim 5.18.

Real life

Choices

Contributed by Tearfund

Living in the fourth-richest country in the world gives us plenty of choices. It also gives us plenty of responsibilities. How will we rise to the challenge?

Justice

The Bible says that we should use honest weights and measures (Deuteronomy 25.13–16) meaning that we should not take advantage of others. With all the wealth at our disposal, it can be easy for the west to come off best when trading with poorer countries: money makes money, it is said. But it's not just about financial wealth: for some, the lack of basic education leaves them unable to read or write, and therefore potentially far more vulnerable to being stitched up by unscrupulous traders. Jesus said that 'workers deserve their wages' (Luke 10.7).

Responsibility

God commanded the Israelites to build a protective wall around the roof of their house so that they would not be guilty of bloodshed on their property if someone were to fall (check out Deuteronomy 22.8 for more DIY tips). So what's the message? We are responsible for the safety of others, even if they happen to be making our clothes thousands of miles from our home. If we're paying for something, we're acting as an employer.

Choices

If we want to buy cheap, we can't simply leave our conscience at the check-out. James 5.4 points out that 'the wages you have failed to pay the workers who mowed your fields are crying out against you.' Products have to be paid for, and the cheap ones often cost less because at some point someone has been paid less for their work. The voiceless are the ones who often get squeezed out of the fair wages, and James is right to make a link between the treatment of others and our conscience. Buying Fair trade says 'no' to the system that abuses others and says 'yes' to a decent wage for a decent job. The choice is ours.

Equality

The age of the multi-national company is well and truly upon us – the same products get sold all around the world – but this principle is strangely familiar to many of the Bible writers. As well as Micah 2.2 and Habbakuk 2.6–10, take a look at Isaiah 5.8. There we read that the prophet condemns those who 'add house to house and join field to field till no space is left...' Ring any bells?

How about those businesses who dominate the world markets? What about the familiar situation where power is held by only a few people? This desire to control an ever greater part of the market, to put profit above all other priorities can bring about a whole load of problems. How should we respond? We might not be able to cause a change of heart at the top of a skyscraper, but we can support local businesses, ones where decent wages are paid and decent profit go back to help that community.

Think

For whom and for what are you responsible? What advantages have you been given in life? How can you share those advantages? Do you know of any group or individual whose hard work you take advantage of? How can you redress the balance?

Act

Find out which companies you buy from act ethically towards their workers and the community. Support the ones whose values you admire.

Check

Deuteronomy 22.8; 25.13–16; Isaiah 5.8; Micah 2.2; Habbakuk 2.6–10; Luke 10.7; James 5.4

More...

Guidance p.685
Fair trade p.923
Shopping p.973
Materialism p.1141
Living truthfully p.1070

A son for a dead brother

Moses said to Israel:

5-6 Suppose two brothers are living on the same property, when one of them dies without having a son to carry on his name. If this happens, his widow must not marry anyone outside the family. Instead, she must marry her late husband's brother, and their first son will be the legal son of the dead man.

7 But suppose the brother refuses to marry the widow. She must go to a meeting of the town leaders at the town gate and say, "My husband died without having a son to carry on his name. And my husband's brother refuses to marry me so I can have a son."

8 The leaders will call the living brother to the town gate and try to persuade him to marry the widow. But if he doesn't change his mind and marry her, 9 she must go over to him while the town leaders watch. She will pull off one of his sandals and spit in his face, while saying, "That's what happens to a man who won't help provide descendants for his dead brother." 10 From then on, that man's family will be known as "the family of the man whose sandal was pulled off".

When two men fight

Moses said to Israel:

11 If two men are fighting, and the wife of one man tries to rescue her husband by grabbing the other man's private parts, 12 you must cut off her hand. Don't have any mercy.

Be honest in business

Moses said to Israel:

13-14 Don't try to cheat people by having two sets of weights or measures, one to get more when you are buying, and the other to give less when you are selling. 15 If you weigh and measure things honestly, the LORD your God will let you enjoy a long life in the land he is giving you. 16 But the LORD is disgusted with anyone who cheats or is dishonest.

Wipe out Amalek

Moses said:

17 People of Israel, do you remember what the Amalekites did to you after you came out of Egypt? 18 You were tired, and they followed along behind, attacking those who could not keep up with the others. This showed that the Amalekites have no respect for God.

19 The LORD your God will help you capture the land, and he will give you peace. But when that day comes, you must wipe out Amalek so completely that no one will remember they ever lived.

CHAPTER 26

Give the LORD the first part of your harvest

Moses said to Israel:

1 The LORD is giving you the land, and soon you will conquer it, settle down, 2 and plant crops. And when you begin harvesting each of your crops, the very first things you pick must be put in a basket. Take them to the place where the LORD your God chooses to be worshipped, 3 and tell the priest, "Long ago the LORD our God promised our ancestors that he would give us this land. And today, I thank him for keeping his promise and giving me a share of the land."

4 The priest will take the basket and set it in front of the LORD's altar. 5 Then, standing there in front of the place of worship, you must pray:

My ancestor was homeless,
an Aramean who went to live in Egypt.
There were only a few
    in his family then,
but they became great and powerful,
    a nation of many people.

6 The Egyptians were cruel
    and had no pity on us.
They ill-treated our people
    and forced us into slavery.
7 We called out for help
    to you, the LORD God of our ancestors.
You heard our cries;
    you knew we were in trouble
    and abused.

See also: 25.5–6: Matt 22.24; Mark 12.19; Luke 20.28.
25.7–10: Ruth 4.7–8.   25.13–16: Lev 19.35–36.

See also: 25.17–19: Exod 17.8–14; 1 Sam 15.2–9.
26.2: Exod 23.19.

⁸ Then you terrified the Egyptians
  with your mighty miracles
    and rescued us from Egypt.
⁹ You brought us here
  and gave us this land
    rich with milk and honey.
¹⁰ Now, LORD, I bring to you
  the best of the crops
    that you have given me.

After you say these things, place the basket in front of the LORD's altar and bow down to worship him.
¹¹ Then you and your family must celebrate by eating a meal at the place of worship to thank the LORD your God for giving you such a good harvest. And remember to invite the Levites and the foreigners who live in your town.

Ten per cent of the harvest

Moses said to Israel:

¹² Every year you are to give ten per cent of your harvest to the LORD.* But every third year,* this ten per cent must be given to the poor who live in your town, including Levites, foreigners, orphans, and widows. That way, they will have enough to eat.
¹³ Then you must pray:

Our LORD and our God, you have said that ten per cent of my harvest is sacred. I have obeyed your command and given this to the poor, including the Levites, foreigners, orphans, and widows.
¹⁴ I have not eaten any of this sacred food while I was in mourning; in fact, I never touched it when I was unclean.* And none of it has been offered as a sacrifice to the spirits of the dead. I have done everything exactly as you commanded.
¹⁵ Our LORD, look down from your temple in heaven and bless your people Israel. You promised our ancestors that you would give us this land rich with milk and honey, and you have kept your promise.

The LORD is your God, and you are his people

Moses said to Israel:

¹⁶ Today the LORD your God has commanded you to obey these laws and teachings with all your heart and soul.
¹⁷ In response, you have agreed that the LORD will be your God, that you will obey all his laws and teachings, and that you will listen when he speaks to you.
¹⁸ Since you have agreed to obey the LORD, he has agreed that you will be his people and that you will belong to him, just as he promised.
¹⁹ The LORD created all nations, but he will make you more famous than any of them, and you will receive more praise and honour. You will belong only to the LORD your God, just as he promised.

CHAPTER 27

Build an altar on Mount Ebal

¹ Moses stood together with the leaders and told the people of Israel:

Obey all the laws and teachings that I am giving you today. ²⁻⁴ Soon you will enter the land that the LORD your God is giving to you. He is the God your ancestors worshipped, and he has promised that this land is rich with milk and honey.

After you cross the River Jordan, go to Mount Ebal. Set up large slabs of stone, then cover them with white plaster and write on them a copy of these laws.
⁵ At this same place, build an altar for offering sacrifices to the LORD your God. But don't use stones that have been cut with iron tools. ⁶ Look for stones that can be used without being cut. Then offer sacrifices to please the LORD,* burning them completely on the altar. ⁷ Next, offer sacrifices to ask the LORD's blessing,* and serve the meat at a sacred meal where you will celebrate in honour of the LORD.

---

*26.12 Every year . . . LORD:** See 14.22–29.
*26.12 every third year:** Probably the third and sixth years of the seven-year cycle described in 15.1–11 and Leviticus 25.1–7.
*26.14 in mourning . . . unclean:** Touching a dead body made a person unclean and unfit to worship God. Ten per cent of the harvest belonged to God, and was not to be touched by an unclean person.
See also: 26.12: Deut 14.28–29.

*27.6 sacrifices to please the LORD:** See the note at 12.5–19.
*27.7 sacrifices to ask the LORD's blessing:** These sacrifices have traditionally been called "peace offerings" or "offerings of well-being". A main purpose was to ask for the LORD's blessing, and so in the CEV they are sometimes called "sacrifices to ask the LORD's blessing".
See also: 26.18: Exod 19.5; Deut 4.20; 7.6; 14.2; Titus 2.14; 1 Pet 2.9.   **27.2–8:** Josh 8.30–32.   **27.5–6:** Exod 20.25.

8 Don't forget to write out a copy of these laws on the stone slabs that you are going to set up. Make sure that the writing is easy to read.

Curses on those who disobey

9 Moses stood together with the priests* and said, "Israel, be quiet and listen to me! Today you have become the people of the LORD your God.* 10 So you must obey his laws and teachings that I am giving you."

11 That same day, Moses gave them the following instructions:

12-13 After you cross the River Jordan, you will go to Mount Gerizim and Mount Ebal.* The tribes of Simeon, Levi, Judah, Issachar, Ephraim, Manasseh,* and Benjamin will go up on Mount Gerizim, where they will bless the people of Israel. The tribes of Reuben, Gad, Asher, Zebulun, Dan, and Naphtali will go up on Mount Ebal where they will agree to the curses.

14-26 The people of the Levi tribe will speak each curse in a loud voice, then the rest of the people' will agree to that curse by saying, "Amen!" Here are the curses:

We ask the LORD to put a curse on anyone who makes an idol or worships idols, even secretly. The LORD is disgusted with idols.

We ask the LORD to put a curse on all who do not show respect for their father and mother.

We ask the LORD to put a curse on anyone who moves the rocks that mark boundaries.

We ask the LORD to put a curse on anyone who tells blind people to go the wrong way.

We ask the LORD to put a curse on anyone who keeps the poor from getting justice, whether these poor are foreigners, widows, or orphans.

We ask the LORD to put a curse on any man who sleeps with his father's wife; that man has shown no respect for his father's marriage.

We ask the LORD to put a curse on anyone who has sex with an animal.

We ask the LORD to put a curse on any man who sleeps with his sister or his half-sister or his mother-in-law.

We ask the LORD to put a curse on anyone who commits murder, even when there are no witnesses to the crime.

We ask the LORD to put a curse on anyone who accepts money to murder an innocent victim.

We ask the LORD to put a curse on anyone who refuses to obey his laws.

And so, to each of these curses, the people will answer, "Amen!"

CHAPTER 28

The LORD will bless you if you obey

Moses said to Israel:

1-2 Today I am giving you the laws and teachings of the LORD your God. Always obey them, and the LORD will make Israel the most famous and important nation on earth, and he will bless you in many ways.

3 The LORD will make your businesses and your farms successful.

4 You will have many children. You will harvest large crops, and your herds of cattle and flocks of sheep and goats will produce many young.

5 You will have plenty of bread* to eat.

6 The LORD will make you successful in your daily work.

7 The LORD will help you defeat your enemies and make them scatter in all directions.

8 The LORD your God is giving you the land, and he will make sure you are successful in everything you do. Your harvests will be so large that your storehouses will be full.

9 If you follow and obey the LORD, he will make you his own special people, just as he promised. 10 Then everyone on earth will know that you belong to the LORD, and they will be afraid of you.

11 The LORD will give you a lot of children and make sure that your animals give birth to many young. The LORD promised your

---

27.9 priests: See the note at 17.8–12.
27.9 Today you have become the people of the LORD your God: As a result of the agreement that the LORD had made with them, recorded in 26.16–19.
27.12–13 Mount Gerizim and Mount Ebal: These mountains were separated by a valley.
27.12–13 Ephraim, Manasseh: The Hebrew text has "Joseph"; the descendants of Joseph formed the two tribes of Ephraim and Manasseh.

See also: 27.12: Deut 11.29; Josh 8.33–35.
27.15: Exod 20.4; 34.17; Lev 19.4; 26.1; Deut 4.15–18; 5.8.
27.16: Exod 20.12; Deut 5.16.   27.17: Deut 19.14.
27.18: Lev 19.14.   27.19: Exod 22.21; 23.9; Lev 19.33–34;
Deut 24.17–18.   27.20: Lev 18.8; 20.11; Deut 22.30.
27.21: Exod 22.19; Lev 18.23; 20.15.   27.22: Lev 18.9; 20.17.
27.23: Lev 18.17; 20.14.   27.26: Gal 3.10.

28.5 bread: The main food of the Israelites.
See also: 28.1–14: Deut 11.13–17.

ancestors that this land would be yours, and he will make it produce large crops for you.

¹² The LORD will open the storehouses of the skies where he keeps the rain, and he will send rain on your land at just the right times. He will make you successful in everything you do. You will have plenty of money to lend to other nations, but you won't need to borrow any yourself.

¹³ Obey the laws and teachings that I'm giving you today, and the LORD your God will make Israel a leader among the nations, and not a follower. Israel will be wealthy and powerful, not poor and weak. ¹⁴ But you must not reject any of his laws and teachings or worship other gods.

The LORD will put curses on you if you disobey

This is also told in Leviticus 26.14–46

Moses said:

¹⁵ Israel, today I am giving you the laws and teachings of the LORD your God. And if you don't obey them all, he will put many curses on you.

¹⁶ Your businesses and farms will fail.

¹⁷ You won't have enough bread* to eat.

¹⁸ You'll have only a few children, your crops will be small, and your herds of cattle and flocks of sheep and goats won't produce many young.

¹⁹ The LORD will make you fail in everything you do.

²⁰ No matter what you try to accomplish, the LORD will confuse you, and you will feel his anger. You won't last long, and you may even meet with disaster, all because you rejected the LORD.

²¹⁻²³ The LORD will send terrible diseases to attack you, and you will never be well again. You will suffer with burning fever and swelling and pain until you die somewhere in the land that you captured.

The LORD will make the sky overhead seem like a bronze roof that keeps out the rain, and the ground under your feet will become as hard as iron. Your crops will be scorched by the hot east wind or ruined by mildew. ²⁴ He will send dust and sandstorms instead of rain, and you will be wiped out.

²⁵ The LORD will let you be defeated by your enemies, and you will scatter in all directions. You will be a horrible sight for the other nations to see, ²⁶ and no one will disturb the birds and wild animals while they eat your dead bodies.

²⁷ The LORD will make you suffer with diseases that will cause oozing sores or crusty itchy patches on your skin or boils like the ones that are common in Egypt. And there will be no cure for you! ²⁸ You will become insane and go blind. The LORD will make you so confused, ²⁹ that even in bright sunshine you will have to feel your way around like a blind person, who cannot tell day from night. For the rest of your life, people will beat and rob you, and no one will be able to stop them.

³⁰ A man will be engaged to a woman, but before they can get married, she will be raped by enemy soldiers. Some of you will build houses, but never get to live in them. If you plant a vineyard, you won't be around long enough to enjoy the first harvest. ³¹ Your cattle will be killed while you watch, but you won't get to eat any of the meat. Your donkeys and sheep will be stolen from you, and no one will be around to force your enemies to give them back. ³² Your sons and daughters will be dragged off to a foreign country, while you stand there helpless. And even if you watch for them until you go blind, you will never see them again.

³³ You will work hard on your farms, but everything you harvest will be eaten by foreigners, who will ill-treat you and abuse you for the rest of your life.

³⁴ What you see will be so horrible that you will go insane, ³⁵ and the LORD will punish you from head to toe with boils that never heal.

³⁶ The LORD will let you and your king be taken captive to a country that you and your ancestors have never even heard of, and there you will have to worship idols* made of wood and stone. ³⁷ People of nearby countries will shudder when they see your terrible troubles, but they will still make fun of you.

³⁸ You will plant a lot of seed, but gather a small harvest, because locusts* will eat your crops. ³⁹ You will plant vineyards and work hard at taking care of them, but you

---

28.36 have to worship idols: It was sometimes thought that only the gods of a country could be worshipped within the borders of that country.
28.38 locusts: A type of grasshopper that comes in swarms and causes great damage to plant life.

28.17 bread: See the note at 28.5.

won't gather any grapes, much less get any wine, and the vines themselves will be eaten by worms. 40 Even if your olive trees grow everywhere in your country, the olives will fall off before they are ready, and there won't be enough olive oil for combing your hair.*

41 Even your infant sons and daughters will be taken as prisoners of war.

42 Locusts* will eat your crops and strip your trees of leaves and fruit.

43 Foreigners in your towns will become wealthy and powerful, while you become poor and powerless. 44 You will be so short of money that you will have to borrow from these foreigners. They will be the leaders in the community, and you will be the followers.

More curses for disobedience

Moses said:

45 Israel, if you don't obey the laws and teachings that the LORD your God is giving you, he will send these curses to chase, attack, and destroy you. 46 Then everyone will look at you and your descendants and realize that the LORD has placed you under a curse.

47 If the LORD makes you wealthy, but you don't joyfully worship and honour him, 48 he will send enemies to attack you and make you their slaves. Then you will live in poverty with nothing to eat, drink, or wear, and your owners will work you to death.

49 Foreigners who speak a strange language will be sent to attack you without warning, just like an eagle swooping down. 50 They won't show any mercy, and they will have no respect for old people or pity for children. 51 They will take your cattle, sheep, goats, grain, wine, and olive oil, then leave you to starve.

52 All over the land that the LORD your God gave you, the enemy army will surround your towns. You may feel safe inside your town walls, but the enemy will tear them down, 53 while you wait in horror. Finally, you will get so hungry that you will eat the sons and daughters that the LORD gave you. 54-55 Because of hunger, a man who had been gentle and kind will eat his own children and refuse to share the meal with his brother or wife or with his other children. 56-57 A woman may have grown up in such luxury that she never had to put a foot on the ground. But times will be so bad that she will secretly eat both her newborn baby and the afterbirth, without sharing any with her husband or her other children.

Disobedience brings destruction

Moses said to Israel:

58 You must obey everything in *The Book of God's Law*. Because if you don't respect the LORD, 59 he will punish you and your descendants with incurable diseases, 60 like those you were so afraid of in Egypt. 61 Remember! If the LORD decides to destroy your nation, he can use any disease or disaster, not just the ones written in *The Book of God's Law*.

62 There are as many of you now as the stars in the sky, but if you disobey the LORD your God, only a few of you will be left. 63 The LORD is happy to make you successful and to help your nation grow while you conquer the land. But if you disobey him, he will be just as happy to pull you up by your roots.

64 Those of you who survive will be scattered to every nation on earth, and you will have to worship stone and wood idols* that never helped you or your ancestors. 65 You will be restless — always longing for home, but never able to return. 66 You will live in constant fear of your life. 67 Each morning you will wake up to such terrible sights that you will say, "I wish it were night!" But at night you will be terrified and say, "I wish it were day!"

68 I told you never to go back to Egypt. But now the LORD himself will load you on ships and send you back. Then you will even try to sell yourselves as slaves, but no one will be interested.

CHAPTER 29

The agreement in Moab

1 So Moses finished telling the Israelites what they had to do in order to keep the agreement the LORD was making with them in Moab, which was in addition to the one the LORD had made with them at Mount Sinai.◊

---

*28.40 olive oil . . . hair: Olive oil was used for combing the hair.
*28.42 Locusts: See the note at 28.38.

*28.64 have to worship . . . idols: See the note at 28.36.
See also: 28.57: 2 King 6.28-29; Lam 4.10.

THE THIRD SPEECH: ISRAEL MUST KEEP ITS AGREEMENT WITH THE LORD

The LORD is your God

²⁻³ Moses called the nation of Israel together and told them:

When you were in Egypt, you saw the LORD perform great miracles that caused trouble for the king, his officials, and everyone else in the country. ⁴⁻⁶ He has even told you, "For forty years I, the LORD, led you through the desert, but your clothes and your sandals didn't wear out, and I gave you special food.ᵇ I did these things so you would realize that I am your God."

But the LORD must give you a change of heart before you truly understand what you have seen and heard.

⁷ When we first camped here, King Sihon of Heshbon and King Og of Bashan attacked, but we defeated them. ⁸ Then we captured their land and divided it among the tribes of Reuben, Gad, and East Manasseh.

Keep the agreement

Moses said:

⁹ Israel, the LORD has made an agreement with you, and if you keep your part, you will be successful in everything you do. ¹⁰⁻¹² Today everyone in our nation is standing here in the LORD's presence, including leaders and officials, parents and children, and even those foreigners who cut wood and carry water for us. We are at this place of worship to promise that we will keep our part of the agreement with the LORD our God.

¹³⁻¹⁵ In this agreement, the LORD promised that you would be his people and that he would be your God. He first made this promise to your ancestors Abraham, Isaac, and Jacob, and today the LORD is making this same promise to you. But it isn't just for you; it is also for your descendants.

¹⁶⁻¹⁷ When we lived in Egypt, you saw the Egyptians worship disgusting idols of wood, stone, silver, and gold. Then as we travelled through other nations, you saw those people worship other disgusting idols. ¹⁸ So make sure that everyone in your tribe remains faithful to the LORD and never starts worshipping gods of other nations.

If even one of you worships idols, you will be like the root of a plant that produces bitter, poisonous fruit. ¹⁹ You may be an Israelite and know all about the LORD's agreement with us, but he won't bless you if you rebel against him. You may think you can get away with it, but you will cause the rest of Israel to be punished along with you.ᶜ ²⁰⁻²¹ The LORD will be furious, and instead of forgiving you, he will separate you from the other tribes. Then he will destroy you, by piling on you all the curses in *The Book of God's Law*, and you will be forgotten for ever.

²² The LORD will strike your country with diseases and disasters. Your descendants and foreigners from distant countries will see that your land ²³ has become a scorching desert of salt and sulphur, where nothing is planted, nothing sprouts, and nothing grows. It will be as lifeless as the land around the cities of Sodom, Gomorrah, Admah, and Zeboiim, after the LORD became angry and destroyed them.*

²⁴ People from other nations will ask, "Why did the LORD destroy this country? Why was he so furious?"

²⁵ And they will be given this answer:

Our ancestors worshipped the LORD, but after he brought them out of Egypt and made an agreement with them, they rejected the agreement ²⁶ and decided to worship gods that had never helped them. The LORD had forbidden Israel to worship these gods, ²⁷⁻²⁸ and so he became furious and punished the land with all the curses in *The Book of God's Law*. Then he pulled up Israel by the roots and tossed them into a foreign country, where they still are today.

²⁹ The LORD our God hasn't explained the present or the future, but he has commanded us to obey the laws he gave to us and our descendants.

CHAPTER 30

The LORD will bring you back

Moses said to Israel:

¹ I have told you everything the LORD your God will do for you, and I've also told you the curses he will put on you if you reject

---

See also: 29.7: a Num 21.21–30; b Num 21.31–35.
29.8: Num 32.33. 29.18: Heb 12.15.

*29.23 Sodom . . . destroyed them: See Genesis 18.16–28.
See also: 29.23: Gen 19.24–25.

him. He will scatter you in faraway countries, but when you realize that he is punishing you, [2] return to him with all your heart and soul and start obeying the commands I have given to you today. [3-4] Then he will stop punishing you and treat you with kindness. He may have scattered you to the furthest countries on earth, but he will bring you back [5] to the land that had belonged to your ancestors and make you even more successful and powerful than they ever were.

[6] You and your descendants are stubborn, but the LORD will make you willing to obey him and love him with all your heart and soul, and you will enjoy a long life.

[7] Then the LORD your God will remove the curses from you and put them on those enemies who hate and attack you.

[8] You will again obey the laws and teachings of the LORD, [9] and he will bless you with many children, large herds and flocks, and abundant crops. The LORD will be happy to do good things for you, just as he did for your ancestors. [10] But you must decide once and for all to worship him with all your heart and soul and to obey everything in *The Book of God's Law.*

Choose life, not death

Moses said to Israel:

[11] You know God's laws, and it isn't impossible to obey them. [12] His commands aren't in heaven, so you can't excuse yourselves by saying, "How can we obey the LORD's commands? They are in heaven, and no one can go up to get them, then bring them down and explain them to us." [13] And you can't say, "How can we obey the LORD's commands? They are across the sea, and someone must go across, then bring them back and explain them to us." [14] No, these commands are nearby and you know them by heart. All you have to do is obey!

[15] Today I am giving you a choice. You can choose life and success or death and disaster. [16-18] I am commanding you to be loyal to the LORD, to live the way he has told you, and to obey his laws and teachings. You are about to cross the River Jordan and take the land that he is giving you. If you obey him, you will live and become successful and powerful.

On the other hand, you might choose to disobey the LORD and reject him. So I'm

warning you that if you bow down and worship other gods, you won't have long to live.

[19] Now I call the sky and the earth to be witnesses that I am offering you this choice. Will you choose for the LORD to make you prosperous and give you a long life? Or will he put you under a curse and kill you? Choose life! [20] Be completely faithful to the LORD your God, love him, and do whatever he tells you. The LORD is the only one who can give life, and he will let you live a long time in the land that he promised to your ancestors Abraham, Isaac, and Jacob.

CHAPTER 31

FINAL SPEECHES AND THE DEATH OF MOSES

Joshua is appointed the leader of Israel

[1] Moses again spoke to the whole nation of Israel:

[2] I am a hundred and twenty years old, and I am no longer able to be your leader. And besides that, the LORD your God has told me that he won't let me cross the River Jordan. [3-5] But he has promised that he and Joshua will lead you across the Jordan to attack the nations that live on the other side. The LORD will destroy those nations just as he destroyed Sihon and Og, those two Amorite kings. Just remember — whenever you capture a place, kill everyone who lives there.

[6] Be brave and strong! Don't be afraid of the nations on the other side of the Jordan. The LORD your God will always be at your side, and he will never abandon you.

[7] Then Moses called Joshua up in front of the crowd and said:

Joshua, be brave and strong as you lead these people into their land. The LORD made a promise long ago to Israel's ancestors that this land would some day belong to Israel. That time has now come, and you must divide up the land among the people. [8] The LORD will lead you into the land. He will always be with you and help you, so don't ever be afraid of your enemies.

See also: 30.12–14: Rom 10.6–8.

See also: 30.20: a Gen 12.7; **b** Gen 26.3; **c** Gen 28.13.
31.2: Num 20.12.   **31.4:** Num 21.21–35.   **31.8:** Josh 1.5; Heb 13.5.

Read these laws

9 Moses wrote down all these laws and teachings and gave them to the priests and the leaders of Israel. The priests were from the Levi tribe, and they carried the sacred chest that belonged to the LORD. 10-11 Moses told these priests and leaders:

Each year the Israelites must come together to celebrate the Festival of Shelters at the place where the LORD chooses to be worshipped. You must read these laws and teachings to the people at the festival every seventh year, the year when loans do not need to be repaid.* 12-13 Everyone must come — men, women, children, and even the foreigners who live in your towns. And each new generation will listen and learn to worship the LORD their God with fear and trembling and to do exactly what is said in God's Law.

Israel will reject the Lord

14 The LORD told Moses, "You will soon die, so bring Joshua to the sacred tent, and I will appoint him the leader of Israel."

Moses and Joshua went to the sacred tent, 15 and the LORD appeared in a thick cloud right over the entrance to the tent. 16 The LORD said:

Moses, you will soon die. But Israel is going into a land where other gods are worshipped, and Israel will reject me and start worshipping these gods. The people will break the agreement I made with them, 17 and I will be so furious that I will abandon them and ignore their prayers. I will send disasters and suffering that will nearly wipe them out. Finally, they will realize that the disasters happened because I abandoned them. 18 They will pray to me, but I will ignore them because they were evil and started worshipping other gods.

19 Moses and Joshua, I am going to give you the words to a new song. Write them down and teach the song to the Israelites. If they learn it, they will know what I want them to do, and so they will have no excuse for not obeying me. 20 I am bringing them into the land that I promised their ancestors. It is a land rich with milk and honey, and the Israelites will have more

than enough food to eat. But they will get fat and turn their backs on me and start worshipping other gods. The Israelites will reject me and break the agreement that I made with them.

21 When I punish the Israelites and their descendants with suffering and disasters, I will remind them that they know the words to this song, so they have no excuse for not obeying me.

I will give them the land that I promised, but I know the way they are going to live later on.

22 Moses wrote down the words to the song* straight away, and he taught it to the Israelites.

23 The LORD told Joshua, "Be brave and strong! I will help you lead the people of Israel into the land that I have promised them."

24 Moses wrote down all these laws and teachings in a book, 25 then he went to the Levites who carried the sacred chest and said:

26 This is *The Book of God's Law*. Keep it beside the sacred chest that holds the agreement the LORD your God made with Israel. This book is proof that you know what the LORD wants you to do. 27 I know how stubborn and rebellious you and the rest of the Israelites are. You have rebelled against the LORD while I have been alive, and it will only get worse after I am gone. 28 So call together the leaders and officials of the tribes of Israel. I will bring this book and read every word of it to you, and I will call the sky and the earth as witnesses that all of you know what you are supposed to do.

29 I am going to die soon, and I know that in the future you will stop caring about what is right and what is wrong, and so you will disobey the LORD and stop living the way I told you to live. The LORD will be angry, and terrible things will happen to you.

The song of Moses

30 Moses called a meeting of all the people of Israel, so he could teach them the words to the song that the LORD had given him. And here are the words:

---

*31.10–11 every seventh year . . . repaid: See 15.1–2 and the note there.
See also: 31.10: a Deut 15.12; b Deut 16.13–15.

*31.22 the words to the song: See 32.1–43.
See also: 31.23: Num 27.23; Josh 1.6.

Viewpoints 👁

How does God's love support us?

Contributed by Tom R

'The LORD is a mighty rock, and he never does wrong. God can always be trusted to bring justice.'

The Rock? What does that mean? His work is perfect? Everything he does is just and fair? Well, what about all the rubbish in the world then? What's perfect about that? How is it fair that there are people starving, being murdered, raped, kidnapped?

He is the Rock. HIS work is perfect. Everything HE does is just and fair. If you look at the amount of food in the world, there's plenty. But have we shared it out properly? When people get attacked, God promises he will have his revenge, so just keep praying. God's vengeance is greater than anything we can do. The verse says that everything God does is perfect. Well it is. It's just that we have chosen to make this world what it is – we have spoilt it; it was perfect at the beginning.

And when things go wrong for Christians (which no one will deny they do) God is our Rock, a foundation under our feet to stand on, to cling to. He'll bail us out in his own way. And when it seems like God is against us, just remember this verse. Everything he does is just and fair, and he WILL have his vengeance. So hold onto him no matter what you're going through because he loves you more than anyone else in the universe and he will catch you when you fall.

More...

Coping with suffering p.1391
Suffering p.555

CHAPTER 32

¹ Earth and Sky, listen to what I say!
² Israel, I will teach you.
My words will be like gentle rain
on tender young plants,
or like dew on the grass.

³ Join with me in praising
the wonderful name
of the LORD our God.
⁴ The LORD is a mighty rock,*
and he never does wrong.
God can always be trusted
to bring justice.
⁵ But you lie and cheat
and are unfaithful to him.
You have disgraced yourselves
and are no longer worthy
to be his children.›
⁶ Israel, the LORD is your Father,
the one who created you,
but you repaid him
by being foolish.
⁷ Think about past generations.
Ask your parents
or any of your elders.
They will tell you
⁸ that God Most High
gave land to every nation.
He assigned a guardian angel
to each of them,›
⁹ but the LORD himself
takes care of Israel.›

¹⁰ Israel, the LORD discovered you
in a barren desert
filled with howling winds.
God became your fortress,
protecting you as though
you were his own eyes.
¹¹ The LORD was like an eagle
teaching its young to fly,
always ready to swoop down
and catch them on its back.
¹² Israel, the LORD led you,
and without the aid
of a foreign god,
¹³ he helped you capture the land.
Your fields were rich with grain.
Olive trees grew in your stony soil,

---

*32.4 **mighty rock:** The Hebrew text has "rock", which is sometimes used in poetry to compare the LORD to a mountain where his people can run for protection from their enemies.
See also: 32.8: Acts 17.26.

and honey was found
   among the rocks.
¹⁴ Your flocks and herds
   produced milk and yoghurt,
and you got choice meat
   from your sheep and goats
   that grazed in Bashan.
Your wheat was the finest,
   and you drank the best wine.

¹⁵ Israel,' you grew fat and rebelled
   against God, your Creator;
you rejected the Mighty Rock,*
   your only place of safety.
¹⁶ You made God jealous and angry
   by worshipping disgusting idols
   and foreign gods.
¹⁷ You offered sacrifices
   to demons, those useless gods*
   that never helped you,
new gods that your ancestors
   never worshipped.
¹⁸ You turned away
   from God, your Creator;
you forgot the Mighty Rock,*
   the source of your life.
¹⁹ You were the LORD's children,
   but you made him angry.
Then he rejected you ²⁰ and said,
"You are unfaithful
   and can't be trusted.
So I won't answer your prayers;
   I'll just watch and see
   what happens to you.
²¹ You worshipped worthless idols,
   and made me jealous and angry!
Now I will send a cruel'
   and worthless nation
   to make you jealous and angry.

²² "My people, I will breathe out fire
   that sends you down
   to the world of the dead.
It will scorch your farmlands
   and burn deep down
   under the mountains.
²³ I'll send disaster after disaster
   to strike you like arrows.
²⁴ You'll be struck by starvation
   and deadly diseases,
by the fangs of wild animals
   and poisonous snakes.

²⁵ Young and old alike
   will be killed in the streets
   and terrified at home.

²⁶ "I wanted to scatter you,
   so no one would remember
   that you had ever lived.
²⁷ But I dreaded the sound
   of your enemies saying,
'We defeated Israel with no help
   from the LORD.' "

²⁸ People of Israel, that's what the LORD
   has said to you.
But you don't have good sense,
   and you never listen to advice.
²⁹ If you did, you could see
   where you are headed.
³⁰ How could one enemy soldier
   chase a thousand of Israel's troops?
Or how could two of theirs
   pursue ten thousand of ours?
It can only happen if the LORD
   stops protecting Israel
   and lets the enemy win.
³¹ Even our enemies know
   that only our God is a Mighty Rock.*

³² Our enemies are grapevines
   rooted in the fields
   of Sodom and Gomorrah.*
The grapes they produce
   are full of bitter poison;
³³ their wine is more deadly
   than cobra venom.
³⁴ But the LORD has written
   a list of their sins
   and locked it in his vault.
³⁵ Soon our enemies will get
   what they deserve' —
suddenly they will slip,
   and total disaster will quickly follow.

³⁶ When only a few
   of the LORD's people remain,
when their strength is gone,
   and some of them are slaves,
the LORD will feel sorry for them
   and give them justice.

³⁷ But first the LORD will say,
"You ran for safety to other gods —
   couldn't they help you?

---

*32.15,18 Mighty Rock: See the note at 32.4.
*32.16-17 disgusting idols . . . foreign
gods . . . demons . . . those useless gods: Different
ways of referring to gods of other nations.
See also: 32.17: 1 Cor 10.20. 32.21: a 1 Cor 10.22;
b Rom 10.19.

*32.31 Mighty Rock: See the note at 32.4.
*32.32 Sodom and Gomorrah: Two cities that the
LORD destroyed because their people were so evil
(see Genesis 18.16—19.28).
See also: 32.35: Rom 2.19; Heb 10.30. 32.36a: Psa 135.14.

[38] You offered them wine
   and your best sacrifices.
Can't those gods help you now
   or give you protection?
[39] Don't you understand?
   I am the only God;
   there are no others.
I am the one who takes life
   and gives it again.
I punished you with suffering.
But now I will heal you,
   and nothing can stop me!

[40] "I make this solemn promise:
   just as I live for ever,
[41] I will take revenge
   on my hateful enemies.
I will sharpen my sword
   and let it flash like lightning.
[42] My arrows will get drunk
   on enemy blood;
my sword will taste the flesh
   and the blood of the enemy.
It will kill prisoners,
   and cut off the heads
   of their leaders."'

[43] Tell the heavens to celebrate
   and all gods to bow down
   to the LORD,'
because he will take revenge
   on those hateful enemies
   who killed his people.
He will forgive the sins of Israel
   and purify their land.'

[44-45] Moses spoke the words of the song so that all the Israelites could hear, and Joshua' helped him. When Moses had finished, [46] he said, "Always remember this song I have taught you today. And let it be a warning that you must teach your children to obey everything written in *The Book of God's Law*. [47] The Law isn't empty words. It can give you a long life in the land that you are going to take."

Moses sees the land and blesses the tribes of Israel

Moses will see the land

[48] Later that day the LORD said to Moses:

[49] Go up into the Abarim Mountain range here in Moab across the Jordan valley from Jericho. And when you reach the top of Mount Nebo, you will be able to see the land of Canaan, which I am giving to Israel. [50] Then you will die and be buried on the mountaintop, just as your brother Aaron died and was buried on Mount Hor. [51] Both of you were unfaithful to me at Meribah Spring near Kadesh in the Zin Desert.* I am God, but there in front of the Israelites, you did not treat me with the honour and respect I deserve. [52] So I will give the land to the people of Israel, but you will only get to see it from a distance.

CHAPTER 33

Moses blesses the tribes of Israel

[1] Moses was a prophet, and before he died, he blessed the tribes of Israel by saying:

[2] The LORD came from Mount Sinai.
   From Edom, he gave light
   to his people,
and his glory was shining
   from Mount Paran.
Thousands of his warriors
   were with him, and fire
   was at his right hand.'
[3] The LORD loves the tribes of Israel,'
   and he protects his people.
They listen to his words
   and worship at his feet.
[4-5] I called a meeting
   of the tribes of Israel'
   and gave you God's Law.
Then you and your leaders
   made the LORD your king.

[6] Tribe of Reuben, you will live,
even though your tribe
   will always be small.'

[7] The LORD will listen to you,
   tribe of Judah, as you beg
   to come safely home.
You fought your enemies alone;'
   now the LORD will help you.

[8] At Massah and Meribah Spring,*
   the LORD tested you, tribe of Levi.
You were faithful,'
   and so the priesthood' belongs
   to the Levi tribe.

---

*32.51 Both of you were unfaithful . . . the Zin Desert: See Numbers 20.1–13.
*33.8 Massah and Meribah Spring: See Exodus 17.1–7; Numbers 20.1–13.

See also: 32.43: Rom 5.10; Rev 19.2.
32.48–52: Num 27.12–14; Deut 3.23–27.

See also: 33.8: a Exod 28.30; b Exod 17.7; c Exod 17.7; Num 20.13.

221

9 Protecting Israel's agreement
   with the LORD
was more important to you
than the life of your father or mother,
or brothers or sisters,
   or your own children.*

10 You teach God's laws to Israel,'
   and at the place of worship
you offer sacrifices and burn incense.
11 I pray that the LORD will bless
   everything you do,
and make you strong enough
   to crush your enemies.

12 The LORD Most High' loves you,
   tribe of Benjamin.
He will live among your hills
   and protect you.

13 Descendants of Joseph,
   the LORD will bless you
with precious water
   from deep wells
and with dew from the sky.
14 Month by month, your fruit
   will ripen in the sunshine.
15 You will have a rich harvest
   from the slopes of the ancient hills.
16 The LORD who appeared
   in the burning bush
wants to give you the best
   the land can produce,
and it will be a princely crown
   on Joseph's head.

17 The armies of Ephraim and Manasseh
   are majestic and fierce
like a bull or a wild ox.
They will run their spears
   through faraway nations.

18 Be happy, Zebulun,
   as your boats set sail;
be happy, Issachar, in your tents.
19 The sea will make you wealthy,
   and from the sandy beach
   you will get treasure.*
So invite the other tribes'
to celebrate with you
   and offer sacrifices to God.

20 Tribe of Gad,
   the LORD will bless you
   with more land.

So shout his praises!
Your tribe is like a lion
   ripping up its victim.
21 Your leaders met together
and chose the best land
   for your tribe,
but you obeyed the LORD
   and helped the other tribes.*

22 Tribe of Dan, you are like a lion cub,
   startled by a snake.'

23 The LORD is pleased with you,
   people of Naphtali.
He will bless you
and give you the land
   to the west and the south.'

24 The LORD's greatest blessing
   is for you, tribe of Asher.
You will be the favourite
   of all the other tribes.
You will be rich with olive oil
25 and have strong town gates
   with bronze and iron bolts.
Your people will be powerful
   for as long as they live.

26 Israel,' no other god is like ours —
   the clouds are his chariot
as he rides across the skies
   to come and help us.
27 The eternal God
   is our hiding place;
   he carries us in his arms.
When God tells you
to destroy your enemies,
   he will make them run.
28 Israel, you will live in safety;
   your enemies will be gone.'
The dew will fall from the sky,
and you will have plenty
   of grain and wine.
29 The LORD has rescued you
and given you more blessings
   than any other nation.
He protects you like a shield
   and is your majestic sword.
Your enemies will bow in fear,
and you will trample on their backs.

---

*33.9 Protecting Israel's agreement . . . your own
children: See Exodus 32.25–29.
*33.19 sandy beach . . . treasure: Possibly a
reference to glass made from sand; glass was rare and
very valuable.

*33.21 tribes: One possible meaning for the difficult
Hebrew text of verse 21. The Gad tribe asked for
some of the land east of the River Jordan, but
promised that their warriors would cross the Jordan
and help the other tribes take over the land west of
the Jordan (see Numbers 32.1–33; Joshua 4.10–13).

The death of Moses

CHAPTER 34

¹ Some time later, Moses left the lowlands of Moab. He went up Mount Pisgah to the peak of Mount Nebo,* which is across the River Jordan from Jericho. The LORD showed him all the land as far north as Gilead and the town of Dan. ² He let Moses see the territories that would soon belong to the tribes of Naphtali, Ephraim, Manasseh, and Judah, as far west as the Mediterranean Sea. ³ The LORD also showed him the land in the south, from the valley near the town of Jericho, known as The City of Palm Trees, down to the town of Zoar.

⁴ The LORD said, "Moses, this is the land I was talking about when I solemnly promised Abraham, Isaac, and Jacob that I would give land to their descendants. I have let you see it, but you will not cross the Jordan and go in."

⁵ And so, Moses the LORD's servant died there in Moab, just as the LORD had said. ⁶ The LORD buried him in a valley near the town of Beth-Peor, but even today no one knows exactly where. ⁷ Moses was a hundred and twenty years old when he died, yet his eyesight was still good, and his body was strong.

⁸ The people of Israel stayed in the lowlands of Moab, where they mourned and grieved thirty days for Moses, as was their custom.

Joshua becomes the leader of Israel

⁹ Before Moses died, he had placed his hands on Joshua, and the LORD had given Joshua wisdom. The Israelites paid attention to what Joshua said and obeyed the commands that the LORD had given Moses.

Moses was a great prophet

¹⁰ There has never again been a prophet in Israel like Moses. The LORD spoke face to face with him ¹¹ and sent him to perform powerful miracles in the presence of the king of Egypt and his entire nation. ¹² No one else has ever had the power to do such great things as Moses did for everyone to see.

---

*34.1 Mount Pisgah . . . Mount Nebo: Mount Nebo was probably one peak of the ridge known as Mount Pisgah.

See also: 34.4: a Gen 12.7; b Gen 26.3; c Gen 28.13. 34.10: Exod 33.11.

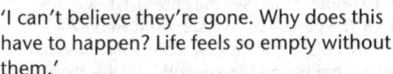

Helpline

Help! Someone I care about has died!

'I can't believe they're gone. Why does this have to happen? Life feels so empty without them.'

What must the Israelites have felt when Moses died? Here was someone who seemed to have been around forever, who had always looked after them. And now he was gone. It's a strange thing to say, but death is part of life. Sooner or later, we all encounter it; losing someone we love or care about, either through illness, accident or old age.

The first thing to remember is that it wasn't supposed to be that way. God never intended death to be a part of his creation, but man's choice to disobey him brought it in. This is why Jesus cried at the death of his mate Lazarus. It wasn't because Lazarus had died – Jesus knew he would be back – it was death itself that made Jesus cry. He knew it was wrong.

Which is why God has fixed it. Because of Jesus we know death has lost its power. It's not the end for Christians. We feel it now, but there will come a time when death itself will be dead and all the tears will be wiped away (Isaiah 65.17–20).

Three things

Grieve

You need to grieve. It's not wrong to miss someone – it shows how much they meant to you. Allow God to comfort you.

Hope

Remember that God has overcome death. Don't be scared of death, but put your hope in God.

Support

Get the support of friends and families, don't grieve on your own. If you know someone who is grieving, get alongside them. There's not a lot you can say, just being there is often enough.

Additional notes

1.1–5 Mount Sinai: The Hebrew text has "Horeb", another name for Mount Sinai.

1.6 Mount Sinai: See the note at 1.1–5.

1.9 Mount Sinai: See the note at 1.1–5.

1.19 Mount Sinai: See the note at 1.1–5.

1.28 The people . . . we are: Most Hebrew manuscripts; a few Hebrew manuscripts and one ancient translation "The people who live there are stronger than we are, and there are more of them than there are of us."

1.38 Joshua: Hebrew "Joshua son of Nun".

2.15–16 getting rid of: Or "sending diseases on".

2.28–29 Edomites and Moabites: Hebrew "descendants of Esau, who live in Seir and Moabites who live in Ar".

3.11 coffin: Or "bed".

3.12–17 Lake Galilee: The Hebrew text has "Lake Chinnereth", an earlier name.

3.12–17 the Dead Sea: Hebrew "the Sea of the Arabah, the Salt Sea".

3.12–17 half the tribe of Manasseh: Or "East Manasseh".

3.12–17 Villages of Jair: Or "Havvoth-Jair".

3.12–17 Machir clan: One of the clans of the Manasseh tribe.

4.10 Mount Sinai: See the note at 1.1–5.

4.11 Mount Sinai: See the note at 1.1–5.

4.21 what you said: Or "you people".

4.48 Hermon: The Hebrew text also includes the name "Sion", probably another form of "Sirion", the name used by the Sidonians.

4.49 the Dead Sea: Hebrew "the Sea of the Arabah".

5.2 Mount Sinai: See the note at 1.1–5.

5.3 wasn't only with: Hebrew "wasn't with".

6.1 these laws and teachings: Or "the following commandment with its laws and teachings" (see 6.4,5).

6.4 The LORD . . . true God: Or "Only the LORD is our God."

7.20 make them . . . dead: Or "send hornets to kill them".

9.8 Mount Sinai: See the note at 1.1–5.

9.9–11 Ten Commandments: Hebrew "commandments".

9.24 he has: The Samaritan Hebrew Text and one ancient translation; the Standard Hebrew Text "I have".

10.6 the wells . . . Jaakan: Or "Beeroth Bene-Jaakan".

10.8 After . . . chest: Or "After Israel reached Jotbathah".

11.6 Dathan and Abiram: Hebrew "Dathan and Abiram, the sons of Eliab from the Reuben tribe".

11.10 where . . . crops: One possible meaning for the difficult Hebrew text.

13.1–2 a prophet: Hebrew adds "or a dreamer of dreams", another name for a prophet.

14.1 when you mourn . . . forehead: Or "you must not worship Baal, cutting yourselves and shaving your forehead."

14.12–18 eagles . . . hoopoes: Some of the birds in this list are difficult to identify.

15.18 six years . . . work: Or "six years of service, and it cost you no more than if you had hired someone to do the work"; or "six years of service, for what you would have had to pay a worker for two years."

16.3–4 the same kind . . . in Egypt: One possible meaning for the difficult Hebrew text.

16.6 sunset, the time of day when you left Egypt: Or "sunset on the same date as when you left Egypt".

16.18–19 turn . . . liars: Or "keep innocent people from getting justice".

17.18 God's laws: Or "God's laws for the king".

18.7 a special servant of the LORD: Or "one of the LORD's priests".

18.16 Mount Sinai: See the note at 1.1–5.

22.5 pretend to be men . . . pretend to be women: Or "wear men's clothing . . . wear women's clothing".

22.28–29 talks her into sleeping with him . . . bride price and: Or "forces her to have sex. 29 Then if they are caught, he will have to marry her. He must give her father fifty pieces of silver as a bride price and".

23.4 Balaam: Hebrew "Balaam son of Beor from Pethor".

23.10 if something . . . worship, he: Or "if a man has a flow of semen at night, he is unclean and unfit for worship, and he".

24.1 something disgraceful about her: One possible meaning for the difficult Hebrew text.

24.14 don't hold back their pay: The Dead Sea Scrolls; the Standard Hebrew Text "treat them right".

25.1–2 whip: Or "rod".

27.14–26 the rest of the people: Or "all the people who are standing on Mount Ebal".

29.1 Mount Sinai: See the note at 1.1–5.

29.4–6 I gave . . . food: Hebrew "you didn't eat bread or drink any wine or beer."

29.19 you will cause the rest of Israel to be punished along with you: Hebrew "The mud will be swept away as well as the dust."

32.5 and are unfaithful . . . children: One possible meaning for the difficult Hebrew text.

32.8 He assigned . . . them: The Dead Sea Scrolls and one ancient translation; the Standard Hebrew Text "So there were as many nations as Israel (that is, Jacob) had children".

32.9 Israel: The Hebrew text has "Jacob", another name for Israel's ancestor.

32.15 Israel: The Standard Hebrew Text has "Jeshurun", a rare name for Israel related to a word meaning "honest". The Samaritan Hebrew Text and one ancient translation also use "Jacob", another name for the ancestor of the nation of Israel.

32.21 cruel: One possible meaning for the difficult Hebrew text.

32.35 our enemies . . . deserve: The Samaritan Hebrew Text and one ancient translation; the Standard Hebrew Text "I will pay them back".

›**32.42 leaders:** Or "long-haired warriors", who let their hair grow to show that they had made sacred promises to their gods.

›**32.43 Tell . . . LORD:** The Dead Sea Scrolls and one ancient translation; the Standard Hebrew Text "Let the nations, his people, celebrate".

›**32.43 because he will . . . land:** One possible meaning for the difficult Hebrew text.

›**32.44–45 Joshua:** The Hebrew text has "Hoshea", another form of Joshua's name.

›**33.2 Thousands . . . right hand:** One possible meaning for the difficult Hebrew text.

›**33.3 the tribes of Israel:** Or "the nations".

›**33.4–5 Israel:** The Hebrew text also uses the name "Jeshurun", a rare name for "Israel".

›**33.6 even though . . . small:** One possible meaning for the difficult Hebrew text.

›**33.7 beg . . . alone:** One possible meaning for the difficult Hebrew text.

›**33.8 the LORD tested you, tribe of Levi. You were faithful:** Or "the LORD tested me. I was faithful" or "the LORD tested Aaron and me. We were faithful".

›**33.8 priesthood:** The Hebrew text has "your thummim and your urim", objects that were used by priests to get answers from God.

›**33.10 Israel:** See the note at 32.9.

›**33.12 Most High:** One possible meaning for the difficult Hebrew text.

›**33.19 other tribes:** Or "nations".

›**33.22 startled by a snake:** Or "jumping out from the forest of Bashan."

›**33.23 land to the west and the south:** Or "land south as far as Lake Galilee."

›**33.26 Israel:** See the note at 33.4.

›**33.28 your enemies will be gone:** One possible meaning for the difficult Hebrew text.

Joshua

The basics

What's the point? To show how Israel came to conquer Canaan.

What happens? The Israelites invade. There is lots of fighting. They settle the land, but the job is never completed.

What should I remember? 21.43 'The LORD gave the Israelites the land he had promised their ancestors, and they captured it and settled in it.'

More detail

Setting the scene After their years of wandering in the desert, the Israelites finally make it across the River Jordan and start to take the land which God has given them...

What's it all about? The first half of this book (up to chapter 12) tells of the invasion of Canaan by the Israelites. In this, they are helped by God – sometimes miraculously, as in the defeat of Jericho and the battle at Gibeon where the Amorites are hail-stoned to death (10.1–15)! In many cases, the Israelites had to follow God's commands exactly, and there are stories in this book about what happens when the people are disobedient.

The second part of the book tells of how the Israelites came to settle the land. Each tribe is allocated territory to live in, with the exception of the Levites, who are given towns scattered throughout the country.

Some towns were safe towns – places which offered sanctuary for people who had accidentally killed someone. All those who were applying for refuge had to have their case tried by the citizens, but at least it meant that the country wasn't torn apart by blood feuds and revenge.

So Joshua tells the story of how the Israelites finally conquered the promised land. But their victory is not quite the triumph it seems. God always intended the Israelites to completely conquer the land and to kick out the gods worshipped by the other races.

But the Israelites never completed the job; some of the previous inhabitants remained, and many towns and cities were still occupied by Canaanite tribes; cities like Jebus where the Jebusites lived (and which was later to become Jerusalem); or Gibeon where the Gibeonites tricked the Israelites into signing a peace treaty with them (Joshua 9). These people might have lived among the Israelites, but they didn't follow Israelite practice. They continued to worship their own gods and these gods would be a temptation and a downfall to Israel for many years to come.

And another thing

Many of us have prayed for more hours in the day; only Joshua ever got an answer! During a battle the sun doesn't go 'down for a whole day'. Some argue that God literally did this, others that what this really means is that the weather remained overcast, allowing the Israelites to fight through the scorching heat of the afternoon. Whateverthe case, it was proof positive that God was on the side of the Israelites.

Footsteps

God's instructions: 1.1–16
Rahab helps the spies: 2.1–24
The fall of Jericho: 6.1–27
Achan's folly: 5.1–26
Israel takes over the land: 10.40–43; 11.12–20
The safe towns: 20.1–9
Joshua's farewell: 23.1–16; 24.29–33

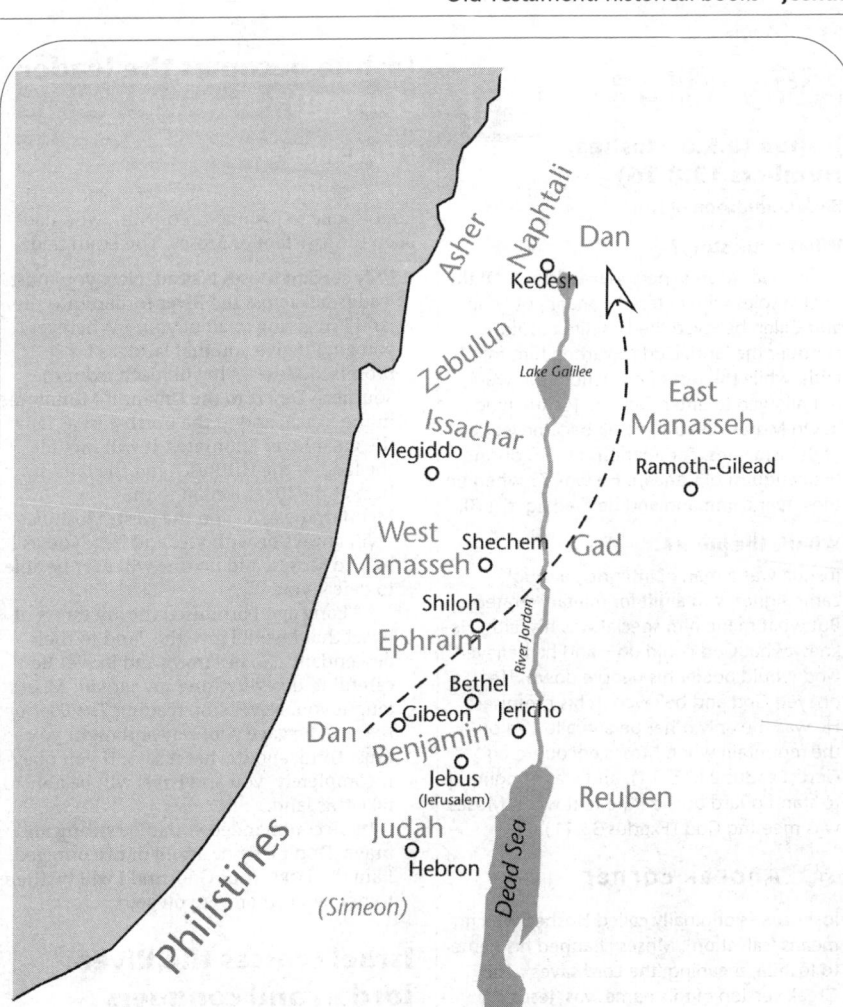

Asher
Naphtali
Dan
Kedesh
Zebulun
Lake Galilee
Issachar
East Manasseh
Megiddo
Ramoth-Gilead
West Manasseh
Shechem
Gad
Shiloh
River Jordan
Ephraim
Bethel
Gibeon
Jericho
Dan
Benjamin
Jebus (Jerusalem)
Reuben
Judah
Dead Sea
Hebron
Philistines
(Simeon)

The Tribes of Israel

After the conquest, the tribes of Israel were allotted regions of land. Levi does not appear on this map, because the Levites were a tribe of priests and did not own land as such. Instead they were given 48 towns with land around them (Joshua 21.41).

The tribe of Dan started in the south, but migrated north, to escape enemy attacks (Joshua 19.47).

Although the Israelites were supposed to completely conquer the land, they didn't complete the job. The result was that there were still Canaanites living in cities such as Gibeon, Jebus and Megiddo, and the Israelites continually gave in to the temptation to follow their gods (Judges 1.21,27–36).

Life files

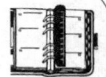

Joshua (a.k.a. Hoshea, Numbers 13.8,16)

Background: Son of Nun

What's the story?

Joshua was Moses' personal assistant. Of the twelve spies who entered Canaan, only he and Caleb believed the Israelites could conquer the land. God rewarded him for his faith: while the rest of his generation were not allowed to enter Canaan, Joshua made it. On Moses' death, Joshua became leader of the Israelites, commanding them during the conquest of Canaan. He was 75 when he took over command and he died aged 110.

What's the point?

Joshua was a man of integrity, a tough campaigner with a gift for military strategy. But what made him special was his faith. He knew what God could do – and he believed God would not let his people down. He obeyed God and believed in his promises. He was the only other person allowed on the mountain when Moses encountered God (Exodus 24.13–14), and was appointed to stand guard outside the tent when Moses was meeting God (Exodus 33.11).

Anorak corner

Joshua was originally called Hoshea which means 'salvation'. Moses changed his name to Joshua, meaning 'the Lord saves'. The Greek version of this name was 'Jesus'.

Footsteps

A week with Joshua

Exploring Canaan: Numbers 13.1–33
Joshua's faith: Numbers 14.1–38
Appointed leader: Numbers 27.12–23
God's promise to Joshua: Joshua 1.1–9
Across the river: Joshua 3.7–4.14
The capture of Jericho: Joshua 5.13–6.27
Joshua's final message: Joshua 24.1–31

More...

Canaanites p.241
Destruction p.236
Warfare and armour p.309

Joshua becomes the leader of Israel

CHAPTER 1

[1] Moses, the LORD's servant, was dead. So the LORD spoke to Joshua son of Nun, who had been the assistant of Moses. The LORD said:

[2] My servant Moses is dead. Now you must lead Israel across the River Jordan into the land I'm giving to all of you. [3] Wherever you go, I'll give you that land, as I promised Moses. [4] It will reach from the Southern Desert to the Lebanon Mountains in the north, and to the north-east as far as the great River Euphrates. It will include the land of the Hittites,* and the land from here at the River Jordan to the Mediterranean Sea on the west. [5] Joshua, I will always be with you and help you as I helped Moses, and no one will ever be able to defeat you.

[6-8] Long ago I promised the ancestors of Israel that I would give this land to their descendants. So be strong and brave! Be careful to do everything my servant Moses taught you. Never stop reading *The Book of the Law* he gave you. Day and night you must think about what it says. If you obey it completely, you and Israel will be able to take this land.

[9] I've commanded you to be strong and brave. Don't ever be afraid or discouraged! I am the LORD your God, and I will be there to help you wherever you go.

Israel crosses the River Jordan and conquers Jericho

The eastern tribes promise to help

[10] Joshua ordered the tribal leaders [11] to go through the camp and tell everyone:

In a few days we will cross the River Jordan to take the land that the LORD our God is giving us. So prepare as much food as you'll need for the march into the land.

---

*1.4 the land . . . Hittites: This refers to the northern part of Syria, which had been the southernmost part of the Hittite Empire.

See also: 1.3–5: Deut 11.24–25.   **1.5:** Deut 31.6,8; Heb 13.5.   **1.6:** Deut 31.6–7,23.

¹² Joshua told the men of the tribes of Reuben, Gad, and East Manasseh:*

¹³⁻¹⁴ The LORD's servant Moses said that the LORD our God has given you land here on the east side of the River Jordan, where you could live in peace. Your wives and children and your animals can stay here in the land Moses gave you. But all of you who can serve in our army must pick up your weapons and lead the men of the other tribes across the River Jordan. They are your relatives, so you must help them ¹⁵ conquer the land that the LORD is giving them. The LORD will give peace to them as he has given peace to you, and then you can come back and settle here in the land that Moses promised you.

¹⁶ The men answered:

We'll cross the River Jordan and help our relatives. We'll fight anywhere you send us. ¹⁷⁻¹⁸ If the LORD our God will help you as he helped Moses, and if you are strong and brave, we will obey you as we obeyed Moses. We'll even put to death anyone who rebels against you or refuses to obey you.

CHAPTER 2

Rahab helps the Israelite spies

¹ Joshua chose two men as spies and sent them from their camp at Acacia with these instructions: "Go across the river and find out as much as you can about the whole region, especially about the town of Jericho."

The two spies left the Israelite camp at Acacia and went to Jericho, where they decided to spend the night at the house of a prostitute* named Rahab.

² But someone found out about them and told the king of Jericho, "Some Israelite men came here tonight, and they are spies." ³⁻⁷ So the king sent soldiers to Rahab's house to arrest the spies.

Meanwhile, Rahab had taken the men up to the flat roof of her house and had hidden them under some piles of flax plants* that she had put there to dry.

---

*1.12 East Manasseh: The half of Manasseh that settled east of the River Jordan.
*2.1 prostitute: Rahab was possibly an innkeeper.
*2.3–7 flax plants: The stalks of flax plants were harvested, soaked in water, and dried, then their fibres were separated and spun into thread, which was woven into linen cloth.
See also: 1.12–15: Num 32.28–32; Deut 3.18–20; Josh 22.1–6. 2.1: Heb 11.31; Jam 2.25.

Life files

Rahab

Background: Prostitute in Jericho

What's the story?

Rahab was a prostitute in Jericho, who hid two spies from Israel. When the Jericho police came to investigate, she tricked them and sent them off on a false trail, allowing the spies to escape.

In the ancient world there were two main kinds of prostitute. Temple prostitutes performed sex as part of their 'worship', or to make money to support the temples of false gods. These are always condemned in the Bible.

'Ordinary' prostitutes stood on street corners, or worked in brothels. Generally the Bible disapproves of these as well, although in early times, when kings themselves had many courtesans, it was less frowned upon. Proverbs, for example, is full of warnings to young men not to get ensnared into this kind of 'trap'. Rahab was the second kind of prostitute. She was an ordinary 'working girl' who, given that she owned a house, may even have combined prostitution with running an inn.

What's the point?

You might be surprised to find that a prostitute is one of the heroines of the Bible story. But Rahab's actions made her a heroine for the Israelites. She is even mentioned in the family tree of Jesus – one of only four women to be mentioned. She might have been a hooker, but she believed in God and the New Testament praises her faith (Hebrews 11.31) and her good works (James 2.25). The issue of her job is, apparently, less important than her role in helping to establish God's kingdom.

Footsteps

Four days with Rahab

Rahab helps the spies: Joshua 2.1–24
Rahab escapes the destruction:
Joshua 6.12–25
Rahab in Jesus's family tree: Matthew 1.2–6
Rahab's faith: Hebrews 11.30–31

The soldiers came to her door and demanded, "Let us have the men who are staying at your house. They are spies."

She answered, "Some men did come to my house, but I didn't know where they had come from. They left about sunset, just before it was time to close the town gate.* I don't know where they were going, but if you hurry, perhaps you can catch them."

The guards at the town gate let the soldiers leave Jericho, but they closed the gate again as soon as the soldiers went through. Then the soldiers headed towards the River Jordan to look for the spies at the place where people cross the river.

⁸ Rahab went back up to her roof. The spies were still awake, so she told them:

⁹ I know that the LORD has given Israel this land. Everyone shakes with fear because of you. ¹⁰ We heard how the LORD dried up the Red Sea* so you could leave Egypt. And we heard how you destroyed Sihon and Og, those two Amorite kings east of the River Jordan. ¹¹ We know that the LORD your God rules heaven and earth, and we've lost our courage and our will to fight.

¹² Please promise me in the LORD's name that you will be as kind to my family as I have been to you. Do something to show ¹³ that you won't let your people kill my father and mother and my brothers and sisters and their families.

¹⁴ "Rahab," the spies answered, "if you keep quiet about what we're doing, we promise to be kind to you when the LORD gives us this land. We pray that the LORD will kill us if we don't keep our promise!"

¹⁵ Rahab's house was built into the town wall,* and one of the windows in her house faced outside the wall. She gave the spies a rope, showed them the window, and said,

"Use this rope to let yourselves down to the ground outside the wall. ¹⁶ Then hide in the hills. The men who are looking for you won't be able to find you there. They'll give up and come back after a few days, and you can be on your way."

¹⁷⁻²⁰ The spies said:

You made us promise to let you and your family live. We will keep our promise, but you can't tell anyone why we were here. You must tie this red rope on your window when we attack, and your father and mother, your brothers, and everyone else in your family must be here with you. We'll take the blame if anyone who stays in this house gets hurt. But anyone who leaves your house will be killed, and it won't be our fault.

²¹ "I'll do exactly what you said," Rahab promised. Then she sent them on their way and tied the red rope to the window.

²² The spies hid in the hills for three days while the king's soldiers looked for them along the roads. As soon as the soldiers gave up and returned to Jericho, ²³ the two spies went down into the Jordan Valley and crossed the river. They reported to Joshua and told him everything that had happened. ²⁴ "We're sure the LORD has given us the whole country," they said. "The people there shake with fear every time they think of us."

CHAPTER 3

Israel crosses the River Jordan

¹ Early the next morning, Joshua and the Israelites packed up and left Acacia. They went to the River Jordan and camped there that night. ² Two days later᾽ their leaders went through the camp, ³⁻⁴ shouting, "When you see some of the priests᾽ carrying the sacred chest, you'll know it is time to cross to the other side. You've never been there before, and you won't know the way, unless you follow the chest. But don't get too close! Stay about a kilometre back."

⁵ Joshua told the people, "Make yourselves acceptable* to worship the LORD, because he is going to do some amazing things for us."

⁶ Then Joshua turned to the priests and said, "Take the chest and cross the River Jordan ahead of us." So the priests picked

---

*2.3–7 gate: Many towns and cities had walls with heavy gates that were closed at night for protection.
*2.10 Red Sea: Hebrew *yam suph* "Sea of Reeds", one of the marshes or fresh water lakes near the eastern part of the Nile Delta. This identification is based on Exodus 13.17—14.9, which lists the towns on the route of the Israelites before crossing the sea. In the Greek translation of the Scriptures made about 200 BC, the "Sea of Reeds" was named "Red Sea".
*2.15 wall: In ancient times, cities and larger towns had high walls around them to protect them against attack. Sometimes houses were built against the wall so that the city wall formed one wall of the house. This added strength to the city wall.
See also: 2.10: a Exod 14.21; b Num 21.21–35.

*3.5 Make yourselves acceptable: People had to do certain things to make themselves acceptable to worship the LORD (see Leviticus 7.20–21; 15.2,33; 22.4–8; Deuteronomy 23.10–11).

up the chest by its carrying poles and went on ahead.

⁷ The LORD told Joshua, "Beginning today I will show the people that you are their leader, and they will know that I am helping you as I helped Moses. ⁸ Now, tell the priests who are carrying the chest to go a little way into the river and stand there."

⁹ Joshua spoke to the people:

Come here and listen to what the LORD our God said he will do! ¹⁰ The Canaanites, the Hittites, the Hivites, the Perizzites, the Girgashites, the Amorites, and the Jebusites control the land on the other side of the river. But the living God will be with you and will force them out of the land when you attack. And now, God is going to prove that he's powerful enough to force them out. ¹¹⁻¹³ Just watch the sacred chest that belongs to the LORD, the ruler of the whole earth. As soon as the priests carrying the chest step into the Jordan, the water will stop flowing and pile up as if someone had built a dam across the river.

The LORD has also said that each of the twelve tribes should choose one man to represent it.

¹⁴ The Israelites packed up and left camp. The priests carrying the chest walked in front, ¹⁵ until they came to the River Jordan. The water in the river had risen over its banks, as it often does in springtime.* But as soon as the feet of the priests touched the water, ¹⁶⁻¹⁷ the river stopped flowing, and the water started piling up at the town of Adam near Zarethan. No water flowed towards the Dead Sea, and the priests stood in the middle of the dry river bed near Jericho while everyone else crossed over.

CHAPTER 4

The people set up a monument

¹ After Israel had crossed the Jordan, the LORD said to Joshua:

²⁻³ Tell' one man from each of the twelve tribes to pick up a large rock from where the priests are standing. Then tell the men to set up those rocks as a monument at the place where you camp tonight.

⁴ Joshua chose twelve men; he called them together, ⁵ and told them:

Go to the middle of the river bed where the sacred chest is, and pick up a large rock. Carry it on your shoulder to our camp. There are twelve of you, so there will be one rock for each tribe. ⁶⁻⁷ Some day your children will ask, "Why are these rocks here?" Then you can tell them how the water stopped flowing when the chest was being carried across the river. These rocks will always remind our people of what happened here today.

⁸ The men followed the instructions that the LORD had given Joshua. They picked up twelve rocks, one for each tribe, and carried them to the camp, where they put them down.

⁹ Joshua told some other men to set up a monument next to the place where the priests were standing. This monument was also made of twelve large rocks, and it is still there in the middle of the river.

The people of Israel set up camp at Gilgal

¹⁰⁻¹³ The army got ready for battle and crossed the Jordan. They marched quickly past the sacred chest* and into the desert near Jericho. Forty thousand soldiers from the tribes of Reuben, Gad, and East Manasseh' led the way, as Moses had ordered.*

The priests stayed where they were until the army had followed the orders that the LORD had given Moses and Joshua. Then the army watched as the priests carried the chest the rest of the way across.

¹⁴⁻¹⁸ "Joshua," the LORD said, "tell the priests to come up from the Jordan and bring the chest with them." So Joshua went over to the priests and told them what the LORD had said. And as soon as the priests carried the chest past the highest place that the flood waters of the Jordan had reached, the river flooded its banks again.

That's how the LORD showed the Israelites that Joshua was their leader.* For the rest of Joshua's life, they respected him as they had respected Moses.

---

*4.10–13 the sacred chest: The Hebrew text has "the LORD". The army was marching past the sacred chest, which was a symbol of God's throne on earth (see 1 Samuel 4.4 and Exodus 25.10–22; 37.1–9).
*4.10–13 Moses . . . ordered: See Numbers 32.16–32; Joshua 1.12–16.
*4.14–18 leader: See 3.7.

*3.15 springtime: Or "harvest time"; the grain harvest was in late spring.

¹⁹ It was the tenth day of the first month* of the year when Israel crossed the River Jordan. They set up camp at Gilgal, which was east of the land controlled by Jericho. ²⁰ The men who had carried the twelve rocks from the Jordan brought them to Joshua, and they made them into a monument. ²¹ Then Joshua told the people:

Years from now your children will ask you why these rocks are here. ²²⁻²³ Tell them, "The LORD our God dried up the River Jordan so we could walk across. He did the same thing here for us that he did for our people at the Red Sea,* ²⁴ because he wants everyone on earth to know how powerful he is. And he wants us to worship only him."

CHAPTER 5

¹ The Amorite kings west of the River Jordan and the Canaanite kings along the Mediterranean Sea lost their courage and their will to fight, when they heard how the LORD had dried up the River Jordan to let Israel go across.

Israel gets ready to celebrate Passover

² While Israel was camped at Gilgal, the LORD said, "Joshua, make some flint knives* and circumcise the rest of the Israelite men and boys."*

³ Joshua made the knives, then circumcised those men and boys at Haaraloth Hill.ᵇ ⁴⁻⁷ This had to be done, because none of Israel's baby boys had been circumcised during the forty years that Israel had wandered through the desert after leaving Egypt.

And why had they wandered for forty years? It was because straight after they left Egypt, the men in the army had disobeyed the LORD. And the LORD had said, "None of you men will ever live to see the land that I promised Israel. It is a land rich with milk and honey, and some day your children will live there, but not before you die here in the desert."

⁸ Everyone who had been circumcised needed time to heal, and they stayed in camp.

⁹ The LORD told Joshua, "It was a disgrace for my people to be slaves in Egypt, but now I have taken away that disgrace." So the Israelites named the place Gilgal,* and it still has that name.

¹⁰ Israel continued to camp at Gilgal in the desert near Jericho, and on the fourteenth day of the same month,* they celebrated Passover.

¹¹⁻¹² The next day, God stopped sending the Israelites manna* to eat each morning, and they started eating food grown in the land of Canaan. They ate roasted grain* and thin bread* made of the barley they had gathered from nearby fields.

Israel captures Jericho

¹³ One day, Joshua was near Jericho when he saw a man standing some distance in front of him. The man was holding a sword, so Joshua walked up to him and asked, "Are you on our side or on our enemies' side?"

¹⁴ "Neither," he answered. "I am here because I am the commander of the LORD's army."

Joshua fell to his knees and bowed down to the ground. "I am your servant," he said. "Tell me what to do."

¹⁵ "Take off your sandals," the commander answered. "This is a holy place."

So Joshua took off his sandals.

CHAPTER 6

¹ Meanwhile, the people of Jericho had been locking the gates in their town wall because

---

*5.9 Gilgal: In Hebrew "Gilgal" sounds like "take away".

*5.10 the same month: See the note at 4.19.

*5.11–12 manna: The special food that God provided for the Israelites while they were in the desert for forty years. It was about the size of a small seed, and it appeared on the ground during the night, except on the Sabbath. It was gathered early in the morning, ground up, and then baked or boiled (see Exodus 16.13–35; Numbers 11.4–9).

*5.11–12 roasted grain: Roasted grain was made by cooking the grain in a dry pan or on a flat rock, or by holding a bunch of grain stalks over a fire.

*5.11–12 thin bread: Bread made without yeast. Israelites were not supposed to eat bread made with yeast for the week following Passover. That week is called the Festival of Thin Bread (see Exodus 12.14–20; 13.3–7).

See also: 5.10: Exod 12.1–13. 5.12: Exod 16.35.

---

*4.19 first month: Abib (also called Nisan), the first month of the Hebrew calendar, from about mid-March to mid-April.

*4.22–23 Red Sea: See the note at 2.10.

*5.2 flint knives: Flint is a stone that can be chipped until it forms a very sharp edge.

*5.2 circumcise . . . men and boys: They could not celebrate Passover unless they were circumcised (see Exodus 12.43–49).

See also: 5.6: Num 14.28–35.

Holy history

Cities and towns

Unlike modern towns and cities – at least in the western world – cities in the Bible were cramped and confined.

Cities had to be defended. Many were built on a hill. They couldn't spread out, they had to be surrounded by a wall. The earliest walls were mud brick, but later towns and cities had stone walls, with observation towers.

If you have walls, you need gates. The gates were the busiest parts of the city, where the streets were wider and where everyone was coming and going. Gates often housed markets (such as the Fish Gate in Jerusalem) and prophets often delivered their announcements at the gates (1 Kings 21.10; Acts 7.58). Gates were closed every night, and secured with iron bars. Streets were not paved, except in the richest cities.

Cities usually had a citadel or palace which was the main administrative centre, where the king or governor lived. Cities also had market areas and even industrial zones, where 'smelly' industries such as cloth-dying or leather-tanning were put. If you were well-off, you lived on the western side of the city, or on the higher ground, where the ventilation was better. Poorer homes were generally in the lower regions of the city.

No indoor plumbing, of course. All water had to be carried in large clay jars or drawn from a well. Some sophisticated cities like Jerusalem had water tunnels, aqueducts and pools. In Roman times water might even be distributed through clay pipes.

 Anorak corner

The outside of the wall was often covered with chalk to make it too slippery to climb.

More...
Houses p.408
Food and drink p.355
Destruction p.236

they were afraid of the Israelites. No one could go out or come in.

2-3 The LORD said to Joshua:

With my help, you and your army will defeat the king of Jericho and his army, and you will capture the town. Here is how to do it: march slowly around Jericho once a day for six days. 4 Take along the sacred chest and make seven priests walk in front of it, carrying trumpets.*

But on the seventh day, march slowly around the town seven times while the priests blow their trumpets. 5 Then the priests will blast on their trumpets, and everyone else will shout. The wall will fall down, and your soldiers can go straight in from every side.

6 Joshua called the priests together and said, "Take the chest and make seven priests carry trumpets and march ahead of it."

7-10 Next, he gave the army their orders: "March slowly around Jericho. A few of you will go ahead of the chest to guard it, but most of you will follow it. Don't shout the battle cry or yell or even talk until the day I tell you to. Then let out a shout!"

As soon as Joshua finished giving the orders, the army started marching. One group of soldiers led the way, with some priests marching behind them and blowing trumpets. Then came the priests carrying the chest, followed by the rest of the soldiers. 11 They obeyed Joshua's orders and carried the chest once around the town before returning to camp for the night.

12-14 Early the next morning, Joshua and everyone else started marching around Jericho in the same order as the day before. One group of soldiers was in front, followed by the seven priests with trumpets and the priests who carried the chest. The rest of the army came next. The seven priests blew their trumpets while everyone marched slowly around Jericho and back to camp. They did this once a day for six days.

15 On the seventh day, the army got up at daybreak. They marched slowly around Jericho as they had done for the past six days, except on this day they went around seven times. 16 Then the priests blew the trumpets, and Joshua yelled:

Get ready to shout! The LORD will let you capture this town. 17 But you must destroy

---

*6.4 trumpets: These were hollowed-out ram's horns.

it and everything in it, to show that it now belongs to the LORD.* The woman Rahab helped the spies we sent,* so protect her and the others who are inside her house. But kill everyone else in the town. 18-19 The silver and gold and everything made of bronze and iron belong to the LORD and must be put in his treasury. Be careful to follow these instructions, because if you see something you want and take it, the LORD will destroy Israel. And it will be all your fault.'

20 The priests blew their trumpets again, and the soldiers shouted as loud as they could. The walls of Jericho fell flat. Then the soldiers rushed up the hill, went straight into the town, and captured it. 21-25 They killed everyone, men and women, young and old, everyone except Rahab and the others in her house. They even killed every cow, sheep, and donkey.

Joshua said to the two men who had been spies, "Rahab kept you safe when I sent you to Jericho. We promised to protect her and her family, and we will keep that promise. Now go into her house and bring them out."

The two men went into Rahab's house and brought her out, along with her father and mother, her brothers, and her other relatives. Rahab and her family had to stay in a place just outside the Israelite army camp.* But later they were allowed to live among the Israelites, and her descendants still do.

The Israelites took the silver and gold and the things made of bronze and iron and put them with the rest of the treasure that was kept at the LORD's house.* Finally, they set fire to Jericho and everything in it.

26 After Jericho was destroyed, Joshua warned the people, "Some day a man will rebuild Jericho, but the LORD will put a curse on him, and the man's eldest son will die when he starts to build the town wall. And by the time he finishes the wall and puts gates in it, all his children will be dead."'

27 The LORD helped Joshua in everything he did, and Joshua was famous everywhere in Canaan.

Achan disobeys the Lord

CHAPTER 7

1 The LORD had said that everything in Jericho belonged to him.* But Achan' from the Judah tribe took some of the things from Jericho for himself. And so the LORD was angry with the Israelites, because one of them had disobeyed him.*

2 While Israel was still camped near Jericho, Joshua sent some spies with these instructions: "Go to the town of Ai' and find out whatever you can about the region around the town."

The spies left and went to Ai, which is east of Bethel and near Beth-Aven. 3 They went back to Joshua and reported, "You don't need to send the whole army to attack Ai — two or three thousand troops will be enough. Why bother the whole army for a town that small?"

4-5 Joshua sent about three thousand soldiers to attack Ai. But the men of Ai fought back and chased the Israelite soldiers away from the town gate and down the hill to the stone quarries.' Thirty-six Israelite soldiers were killed, and the Israelite army felt discouraged.

6 Joshua and the leaders of Israel tore their clothes and put dust on their heads to show their sorrow. They lay face down on the ground in front of the sacred chest until sunset. 7 Then Joshua said:

Our LORD, did you bring us across the River Jordan just so the Amorites could destroy us? This wouldn't have happened if we had agreed to stay on the other side of the Jordan. 8 I don't even know what to say to you, since Israel's army has turned and run from the enemy. 9 Everyone will think you weren't strong enough to protect your people. Now the Canaanites and everyone else who lives in the land will surround us and wipe us out.

---

*6.17 destroy . . . now belongs to the LORD: Destroying a city and everything in it, including its people and animals, showed that it belonged to the LORD and could no longer be used by humans.
*6.17 sent: See 2.1,21.
*6.21-25 camp: Rahab and her family were Canaanites and were considered unclean. If they stayed in the Israelite army camp, the Lord would not help the Israelite army in battle (see Deuteronomy 23.9-14). However, Rahab and her family later became part of Israel.
*6.21-25 the LORD's house: A name for the place of worship, which at that time was the sacred tent.
See also: 6.20: Heb 11.30. 6.25: Heb 11.31.
6.26: 1 King 16.34.

*7.1 belonged to him: See the note at 6.17.
*7.1 the LORD was angry . . . disobeyed him: Even though only one person had disobeyed, it meant that the LORD's instructions to the people of Israel had not been followed, and the whole nation was held responsible.

¹⁰ The LORD answered:

Stop lying there on the ground! Get up!
¹¹ I said everything in Jericho belonged to
me and had to be destroyed. But the
Israelites have kept some of the things for
themselves. They stole from me and hid
what they took. Then they lied about it.
¹² What they stole was supposed to be
destroyed, and now Israel itself must be
destroyed. I cannot help you any more
until you do exactly what I have said.
That's why Israel turns and runs from its
enemies instead of standing up to them.

¹³ Tell the people of Israel, "Tomorrow
you will meet with the LORD your God, so
make yourselves acceptable to worship
him. The LORD says that you have taken
things that should have been destroyed.
You won't be able to stand up to your
enemies until you get rid of those things.

¹⁴ "Tomorrow morning everyone must
gather near the place of worship. You will
come forward tribe by tribe, and the LORD
will show which tribe is guilty. Next, the
clans in that tribe must come forward, and
the LORD will show which clan is guilty.
The families in that clan must come, and
the LORD will point out the guilty family.
Finally, the men in that family must come,
¹⁵ and the LORD will show who stole what
should have been destroyed. That man
must be put to death, his body burnt, and
his possessions thrown into the fire. He has
done a terrible thing by breaking the sacred
agreement that the LORD made with Israel."

¹⁶ Joshua got up early the next morning and
brought each tribe to the place of worship,
where the LORD showed that the Judah tribe
was guilty. ¹⁷ Then Joshua brought the clans
of Judah to the LORD, and the LORD showed
that the Zerah clan was guilty. One by one he
brought the leader of each family in the
Zerah clan to the LORD, and the LORD showed
that Zabdi's family was guilty. ¹⁸ Finally,
Joshua brought each man in Zabdi's family to
the LORD, and the LORD showed that Achan
was the guilty one.

¹⁹ "Achan," Joshua said, "the LORD God of
Israel has decided that you are guilty. Is this
true? Tell me what you did, and don't try to
hide anything."

²⁰ "It's true," Achan answered. "I sinned
and disobeyed the LORD God of Israel.
²¹⁻²² While we were in Jericho, I saw a
beautiful Babylonian robe, two hundred
pieces of silver, and a gold bar that weighed

the same as fifty pieces of gold. I wanted
them for myself, so I took them. I dug a hole
under my tent and hid the silver, the gold,
and the robe."

Joshua told some people to run to Achan's
tent, where they found the silver, the gold,
and the robe. ²³ They brought them back and
put them in front of the sacred chest, so
Joshua and the rest of the Israelites could see
them. ²⁴ Then everyone took Achan and the
things he had stolen to Trouble Valley.ʼ They
also took along his sons and daughters, his
cattle, donkeys, and sheep, his tent, and
everything else that belonged to him.

²⁵ Joshua said, "Achan, you caused us a lot
of trouble. Now the LORD is paying you back
with the same kind of trouble."

The people of Israel then stoned to death
Achan and his family. They made a fire and
burnt the bodies, together with what Achan
had stolen, and all his possessions. ²⁶ They
covered the remains with a big pile of rocks,
which is still there. Then the LORD stopped
being angry with Israel.

That's how the place came to be called
Trouble Valley.

The battle at Ai

CHAPTER 8

Israel destroys the town of Ai

¹⁻² The LORD told Joshua:

Don't be afraid, and don't be discouraged
by what happened at the town of Ai. Take
the army and attack again. But first, make
part of the army set up an ambush on the
other side of the town. I will help you
defeat the king of Ai and his army, and you
will capture the town and the land around
it. Destroy Ai and kill its king as you did at
Jericho. But you may keep the livestock
and everything else you want.

³⁻⁴ Joshua quickly got the army ready to
attack Ai. He chose thirty thousand of his
best soldiers and gave them these orders:

Tonight, while it is dark, march to Ai and
take up a position behind the town. Get as
close to the town as you can without being
seen, but be ready to attack.
⁵⁻⁶ The rest of the army will come with
me and attack near the gate. When the
people of Ai come out to fight, we'll run
away and let them chase us. They will
think we are running from them just like

the first time. But when we've let them chase us far enough away, ⁷ you come out of hiding. The LORD our God will help you capture the town. ⁸ Then set it on fire, as the LORD has told us to do. Those are your orders, ⁹ now go!

The thirty thousand soldiers went to a place on the west side of Ai, between Ai and Bethel, where they could hide and wait to attack.

That night, Joshua stayed in camp with the rest of the army. ¹⁰ Early the next morning he got his troops ready to move out, and he and the other leaders of Israel led them to Ai. ¹¹ They set up camp in full view of the town, across the valley to the north. ¹² Joshua had already sent five thousand soldiers to the west side of the town to hide and wait to attack. ¹³ Now all his troops were in place. Part of the army was in the camp to the north of Ai, and the others were hiding to the west, ready to make a surprise attack. That night, Joshua went into the valley.*

¹⁴⁻¹⁵ The king of Ai saw Joshua's army, so the king and his troops hurried out early the next morning to fight them. Joshua and his army pretended to be beaten, and they let the men of Ai chase them towards the desert. The king and his army were facing the Jordan Valley as Joshua had planned.

The king did not realize that some Israelite soldiers were hiding behind the town. ¹⁶⁻¹⁷ So he called out every man in Ai to go after Joshua's troops. They all rushed out to chase the Israelite army, and they left the town gates wide open. Not one man was left in Ai or in Bethel.ʼ

Joshua let the men of Ai chase him and his army further and further away from Ai. ¹⁸ Finally, the LORD told Joshua, "Point your swordʼ at the town of Ai, because now I am going to help you defeat it!"

As soon as Joshua pointed his sword at the town, ¹⁹ the soldiers who had been hiding got up and ran into the town. They captured it and set it on fire.

²⁰⁻²¹ When Joshua and his troops saw smoke rising from the town, they knew that the other part of their army had captured it. So they turned and attacked.

The men of Ai looked back and saw smoke rising from their town. But they could not escape, because the soldiers they had been chasing had suddenly turned and started fighting. ²²⁻²⁴ Meanwhile, the other Israelite

---

Holy history

Destruction

Joshua describes Israel's triumphant conquest of Canaan, but it also includes commands which, to our eyes, seem shocking. Israel is ordered not only to defeat their enemies, but to wipe them out entirely. Which raises some pretty big questions.

God is the God of peace and love. But he's also the God of judgment. And in Joshua he is judging the Canaanites, who worshipped false and terrible gods and who engaged in practices such as human sacrifice. So the destruction of cities like Jericho is also a judgment on the people of that city. And when Israel followed the same false gods, they were treated just as harshly.

And we have to remember that God was establishing a kingdom. Israel faced a choice: fight or die. And the riches they obtained through victory were to be distributed as God saw fit. They didn't really own the land. It was God's land and they were only tenants.

But we still have to face the fact that innocent men, women and children – people who had no say in their country's government or in their state religion – were killed. There's no easy answer to this. All we can say is that God is just and merciful and that everyone will be judged fairly. The Bible teaches us that death is not the end, so who knows what happened to these people? It's up to God.

Now, of course, things are different. The kind of warfare listed in Joshua isn't necessary any more. Jesus has commanded us to go out and make disciples of every nation. We're still called to establish a kingdom, but this time in peoples' hearts.

More...

Joshua p.228
Canaanites p.241
Foreign gods p.262
Other nations p.259

---

*8.13 valley: This may refer either to the Jordan Valley or to the valley between the Israelite camp and Ai.

soldiers had come from the town and attacked the men of Ai from the rear. The Israelites captured the king of Ai and brought him to Joshua. They also chased the rest of the men of Ai into the desert and killed them.◆

The Israelite army went back to Ai and killed everyone there. 25-26 Joshua kept his sword pointed at the town of Ai until every last one of Ai's twelve thousand people was dead. 27 But the Israelites took the animals and the other possessions of the people of Ai, because this was what the LORD had told Joshua to do.

28-29 Joshua made sure every building in Ai was burnt to the ground. He told his men to kill the king of Ai and hang his body on a tree. Then at sunset he told the Israelites to take down the body,* throw it in the gateway of the town, and cover it with a big pile of rocks. Those rocks are still there, and the town itself has never been rebuilt.

Joshua reads the blessings and curses
This is also told in Deuteronomy 27.1–26

30-32 One day, Joshua led the people of Israel to Mount Ebal, where he told some of his men, "Build an altar for offering sacrifices to the LORD. And use stones that have never been cut with iron tools,* because that is what Moses taught in *The Book of the Law*."◆

Joshua offered sacrifices to please the LORD* and to ask his blessing.* Then with the Israelites still watching, he copied parts of *The Book of the Law*◆ of Moses on to stones.

33-35 Moses had said that everyone in Israel was to go to the valley between Mount Ebal and Mount Gerizim, where they were to be blessed. So everyone went there, including the foreigners, the leaders, officials, and judges. Half of the people stood on one side of the valley, and half on the other side, with the priests from the Levi tribe standing in the middle with the sacred chest. Then in a loud voice, Joshua read the blessings and curses from *The Book of the Law* of Moses.◆

The people of Gibeon trick the leaders of Israel

CHAPTER 9

1-2 The kings west of the River Jordan heard about Joshua's victories, and so they got together and decided to attack Joshua and Israel. These kings were from the hill country and from the foothills to the west, as well as from the Mediterranean coast as far north as the Lebanon Mountains. Some of them were Hittites, others were Amorites or Canaanites, and still others were Perizzites, Hivites, or Jebusites.

3 The people of Gibeon had also heard what Joshua had done to Jericho and Ai. 4 So they decided that some of their men should pretend to be messengers to Israel from a faraway country.◆ The men put worn-out bags on their donkeys and found some old wineskins that had cracked and had been sewn back together. 5 Their sandals were old and patched, and their clothes were worn out. They even took along some dry and crumbly bread. 6 Then they went to the Israelite camp at Gilgal, where they said to Joshua and the men of Israel, "We have come from a country that is far from here. Please make a peace treaty with us."

7-8 The Israelites replied, "But perhaps you really live near us. We can't make a peace treaty with you if you live nearby."*

The Gibeonites◆ said, "If you make a peace treaty with us, we will be your servants."

"Who are you?" Joshua asked. "Where do you come from?"

They answered:

9 We are your servants, and we live far from here. We came because the LORD your God is so famous. We heard what the LORD did in Egypt 10 and what he did to those two Amorite kings on the other side of the Jordan: King Og of Bashan, who lived in Ashtaroth, and King Sihon of Heshbon. 11 Our leaders and everyone who lives in our country told us to meet with you and

---

*8.28–29 take down the body: See Deuteronomy 21.22–23.
*8.30–32 use stones . . . iron tools: See Exodus 20.25.
*8.30–32 sacrifices to please the LORD: These sacrifices have been traditionally called "whole burnt offerings" because the whole animal was burnt on the altar. A main purpose of such sacrifices was to please the LORD with the smell of the sacrifice, and so in the CEV they are often called "sacrifices to please the LORD".
*8.30–32 to ask his blessing: These sacrifices have traditionally been called "peace offerings", or "offerings of well-being". A main purpose was to ask for the LORD's blessing, and so in the CEV they are often called "sacrifices to ask the LORD's blessing".
See also: 8.30–32: Deut 27.2–8. 8.31: Exod 20.25.
8.33–35: Deut 11.29; 27.11–14.

*9.7–8 nearby: See Deuteronomy 20.10–18.
See also: 9.7: Exod 23.32; 34.12; Deut 7.2.
9.10: Num 21.21–35.

tell you that all of us are your servants. They said to ask you to make a peace treaty with our people. They told us to be sure and take along enough food for our journey. 12 See this dry, crumbly bread of ours? It was hot out of the oven when we packed the food on the day we left our homes. 13 These cracked wineskins were new when we filled them, and our clothes and sandals are worn out because we have travelled so far.

14 The Israelites tried some of the food,* but they did not ask the LORD if he wanted them to make a treaty. 15 So Joshua made a peace treaty with the messengers and promised that Israel would not kill their people. Israel's leaders swore that Israel would keep this promise.

16-17 A couple of days later,' the Israelites found out that these people actually lived in the nearby towns of Gibeon, Chephirah, Beeroth, and Kiriath-Jearim.* So the Israelites left the place where they had camped and arrived at the four towns two days later.' 18 But they did not attack the towns, because the Israelite leaders had sworn in the name of the LORD that they would let these people live.

The Israelites complained about their leaders' decision not to attack, 19-21 but the leaders reminded them, "We promised these people in the name of the LORD God of Israel that we would let them live, so we must not harm them. If we break our promise, God will punish us. We'll let them live, but we'll make them cut wood and carry water for our people."

22 Joshua told some of his soldiers, "I want to meet with the Gibeonite leaders. Bring them here."

When the Gibeonites came, Joshua said, "You live close to us. Why did you lie by claiming you lived far away? 23 Now you are under a curse, and your people will have to send workers to cut wood and carry water for the place of worship."'

24 The Gibeonites answered, "The LORD your God told his servant Moses that you were to kill everyone who lives here and take their land for yourselves. We were afraid you would kill us, and so we tricked you into making a peace treaty. But we agreed to be

your servants, 25 and you are strong enough to do anything to us that you want. We just ask you to do what seems right."

26 Joshua did not let the Israelites kill the Gibeonites, 27 but he did tell the Gibeonites that they would have to be servants of the nation of Israel. They would have to cut firewood and bring it for the priests to use for burning sacrifices on the LORD's altar, wherever the LORD decided the altar would be. The Gibeonites would also have to carry water for the priests. And that is still the work of the Gibeonites.

Joshua commands the sun to stand still

CHAPTER 10

1 King Adonizedek of Jerusalem* heard that Joshua had captured and destroyed the town of Ai, and then killed its king as he had done at Jericho. He also learnt that the Gibeonites had signed a peace treaty with Israel. 2 This frightened Adonizedek and his people. They knew that Gibeon was a large town, as big as the towns that had kings, and even bigger than the town of Ai had been. And all the men of Gibeon were warriors. 3 So Adonizedek sent messages to the kings of four other towns: King Hoham of Hebron, King Piram of Jarmuth, King Japhia of Lachish, and King Debir of Eglon. The messages said, 4 "The Gibeonites have signed a peace treaty with Joshua and the Israelites. Come and help me attack Gibeon!"

5 When these five Amorite kings called their armies together and attacked Gibeon, 6 the Gibeonites sent a message to the Israelite camp at Gilgal: "Joshua, please come and rescue us! The Amorite kings from the hill country have joined together and are attacking us. We are your servants, so don't let us down. Please hurry!"

7 Joshua and his army, including his best warriors, left Gilgal. 8 "Joshua," the LORD said, "don't be afraid of the Amorites. They will run away when you attack, and I will help you defeat them."

9 Joshua marched all night from Gilgal to Gibeon and made a surprise attack on the Amorite camp. 10 The LORD made the enemy panic, and the Israelites started killing them right and left. They' chased the Amorite

---

*9.14 tried . . . food: Probably to see if it really was old or to show that they wanted peace.
*9.16-17 Gibeon, Chephirah, Beeroth, and Kiriath-Jearim: These towns were thirty to fifty kilometres west of the Israelite camp at Gilgal.

*10.1 Jerusalem: Jerusalem was not an Israelite city at this time.

troops up the road to Beth-Horon and kept on killing them, until they reached the towns of Azekah and Makkedah.* [11] And while these troops were going down through Beth-Horon Pass,* the LORD made huge hailstones fall on them all the way to Azekah. More of the enemy soldiers died from the hail than from the Israelite weapons.

[12-13] The LORD was helping the Israelites defeat the Amorites that day. So about midday, Joshua prayed to the LORD loud enough for the Israelites to hear:

> "Our LORD, make the sun stop
>   in the sky over Gibeon,
> and the moon stand still
>   over Aijalon Valley."*
> So the sun and the moon
>   stopped and stood still
> until Israel defeated its enemies.

This poem can be found in *The Book of Jashar.** The sun stood still and didn't go down for about a whole day. [14] Never before and never since has the LORD done anything like that for someone who prayed. The LORD was really fighting for Israel.

[15] After the battle, Joshua and the Israelites went back to their camp at Gilgal.

Israel takes over much of the land of Canaan

Joshua kills the five enemy kings

[16] While the enemy soldiers were running from the Israelites, the five enemy kings ran away and hid in a cave near Makkedah. [17] Joshua's soldiers told him, "The five kings have been found in a cave near Makkedah." [18] Joshua answered, "Roll some big stones over the mouth of the cave and leave a few soldiers to guard it. [19] But you and everyone else must keep following the enemy troops, because they will be safe if they reach their walled towns. Don't let them get away! The LORD our God is helping us get rid of them." [20] So Joshua and the Israelites almost wiped out the enemy soldiers. Only a few safely reached their walled towns.

[21] The Israelite army returned to their camp at Makkedah, where Joshua was waiting for them. No one around there dared say anything bad about the Israelites. [22] Joshua told his soldiers, "Now, move the rocks from the entrance to the cave and bring those five kings to me."

[23] The soldiers opened the entrance to the cave and brought out the kings of Jerusalem, Hebron, Jarmuth, Lachish, and Eglon. [24] After Joshua had called the army together, he forced the five kings to lie down on the ground. Then he called his officers forward and told them, "You fought these kings along with me, so put your feet on their necks." The officers did, [25] and Joshua continued, "Don't ever be afraid or discouraged. Be brave and strong. This is what the LORD will do to all your enemies."

[26] Joshua killed the five kings and told his men to hang each body on a tree. Then at sunset [27] he told some of his troops, "Take the bodies down and throw them into the cave where the kings were found. Cover the entrance to the cave with big rocks."

Joshua's troops obeyed his orders, and those rocks are still there.

Joshua continues the fighting

[28] Later that day, Joshua captured Makkedah and killed its king and everyone else in the town, just as he had done at Jericho.

[29] Joshua and his army left Makkedah and attacked the town of Libnah. [30] The LORD let them capture the town and its king, and they killed the king and everyone else, just as they had done at Jericho.

[31] Joshua then led his army to Lachish, and they set up camp around the town. They attacked, [32] and the next day the LORD let them capture the town. They killed everyone, as they had done at Libnah. [33] King Horam of Gezer arrived to help Lachish, but Joshua and his troops attacked and destroyed him and his army.

[34] From Lachish, Joshua took his troops to Eglon, where they set up camp surrounding the town. They attacked, [35] captured it that same day, then killed everyone, as they had done at Lachish.

[36] Joshua and his army left Eglon and attacked Hebron. [37] They captured the town and the nearby villages, then killed everyone, including the king. They destroyed Hebron in the same way they had destroyed Eglon.

---

*10.10 Makkedah: A total distance of about forty kilometres.

*10.11 Beth-Horon Pass: A three-kilometre long, steeply-sloping valley between the towns of Upper Beth-Horon and Lower Beth-Horon.

*10.12-13 Aijalon Valley: A valley south-west of Beth-Horon Pass.

*10.12-13 Book of Jashar: This book may have been a collection of ancient war songs.

See also: 10.13: 2 Sam 1.18.

38 Joshua and the Israelite army turned and attacked Debir. 39 They captured the town, and its nearby villages. Then they destroyed Debir and killed its king, together with everyone else, just as they had done with Hebron and Libnah.

40 Joshua captured towns everywhere in the land: in the central hill country and the foothills to the west, in the Southern Desert and the region that slopes down towards the Dead Sea. Whenever he captured a town, he would kill the king and everyone else, as the LORD God of Israel had commanded.

41 Joshua wiped out towns from Kadesh-Barnea to Gaza, everywhere in the region of Goshen,* and as far north as Gibeon.

42-43 The LORD fought on Israel's side, so Joshua and the Israelite army were able to capture these kings and take their land. They fought one battle after another, then they went back to their camp at Gilgal after capturing all that land.

CHAPTER 11

Joshua captures towns in the north

1 King Jabin of Hazor heard about Joshua's victories, so he sent messages to many nearby kings and asked them to join him in fighting Israel. He sent these messages to King Jobab of Madon, the kings of Shimron and Achshaph, 2 the kings in the northern hill country and in the valley of the River Jordan south of Lake Galilee,' and the kings in the foothills and in Naphath-Dor to the west.
3 He sent messages to the Canaanite kings in the east and the west, to the Amorite, Hittite, Perizzite, and Jebusite kings in the hill country, and to the Hivite kings in the region of Mizpah, near the foot of Mount Hermon.*

4-5 The kings and their armies went to Merom Pond,' where they set up camp, and got ready to fight Israel. It seemed as though there were more soldiers and horses and chariots than there are grains of sand on a beach.

6 The LORD told Joshua:

Don't let them frighten you! I'll help you defeat them, and by this time tomorrow they will be dead.

When you attack, the first thing you have to do is to cripple their horses. Then after the battle is over,' burn their chariots.

7 Joshua and his army made a surprise attack against the enemy camp at Merom Pond 8-9 and crippled the enemies' horses.' Joshua followed the LORD's instructions, and the LORD helped Israel defeat the enemy. The Israelite army even chased enemy soldiers as far as Misrephoth-Maim to the north-west,' the city of Sidon to the north, and Mizpeh Valley to the north-east.* None of the enemy soldiers escaped alive. The Israelites came back after the battle and burnt the enemy's chariots.

10 Up to this time, the king of Hazor had controlled the kingdoms that had joined together to attack Israel, so Joshua led his army back and captured Hazor. They killed its king 11 and everyone else, then they set the town on fire.

12-15 Joshua captured all the towns where the enemy kings had ruled. These towns were built on small hills,* and Joshua did not set fire to any of these towns, except Hazor. The Israelites kept the animals and everything of value from these towns, but they killed everyone who lived in them, including their kings. That's what the LORD had told his servant Moses to do, that's what Moses had told Joshua to do, and that's exactly what Joshua did.

16 Joshua and his army took control of the northern and southern hill country, the foothills to the west, the Southern Desert, the whole region of Goshen,* and the Jordan valley. 17-18 They took control of the land from Mount Halak near the country of Edom in the south to Baal-Gad in Lebanon Valley at the foot of Mount Hermon in the north. Joshua and his army were at war with the kings in this region for a long time, but finally they captured and put to death the last king.

19-20 The LORD had told Moses that he wanted the towns in this region destroyed and their people killed without mercy. That's

---

*10.41 Goshen: A region between the hill country of Judah and the desert further south. Not the same Goshen as in Genesis 47.4–6.
*11.3 Mizpah, near the foot of Mount Hermon: Probably the same region as Mizpeh Valley in verses 8–9, but different from the two other places named Mizpeh in 15.37–41; 18.25–28, and also different from the Mizpah mentioned in Genesis 31.49 and Judges 10.17.

*11.8–9 north-east: These three areas were thirty to fifty-five kilometres north of Merom.
*11.12–15 small hills: Towns were often built on top of the ruins of a previous town that had been destroyed. When this happened many times at one place, a hill was formed.
*11.16 Goshen: See the note at 10.41.
See also: 11.20: Deut 7.16.

why the LORD made the people in the towns stubborn and determined to fight Israel. The only town that signed a peace treaty with Israel was the Hivite town of Gibeon. The Israelite army captured the rest of the towns in battle.

²¹ During this same time, Joshua and his army killed the Anakim* from the northern and southern hill country. They also destroyed the towns where the Anakim had lived, including Hebron, Debir, and Anab. ²² There were not any Anakim left in the regions where the Israelites lived, although there were still some in Gaza, Gath, and Ashdod.*

²³ That's how Joshua captured the land, just as the LORD had commanded Moses, and Joshua divided it up among the tribes.

Finally, there was peace in the land.

CHAPTER 12

The kings defeated by the Israelites

¹ Before Moses died, he and the people of Israel had defeated two kings east of the River Jordan. These kings had ruled the region from the gorge of the River Arnon in the south to Mount Hermon in the north, including the eastern side of the Jordan valley.

² The first king whom Moses and the Israelites defeated was an Amorite, King Sihon of Heshbon.* The southern border of his kingdom ran down the middle of the Arnon gorge, taking in the town of Aroer on the northern edge of the gorge. The River Jabbok separated Sihon's kingdom from the Ammonites on the east. Then the Jabbok turned west and became his northern border, so his kingdom included the southern half of the region of Gilead. ³ Sihon also controlled the eastern side of the Jordan valley from Lake Galilee› south to Beth-Jeshimoth and the Dead Sea. In addition to these regions, he ruled the town called Slopes of Mount Pisgah› and the land south of there at the foot of the hill.

⁴ Next, Moses and the Israelites defeated King Og of Bashan,* who lived in the town of

---

*11.21 Anakim: Perhaps a group of people of great stature that lived in Palestine before the Israelites (see Numbers 13.33 and Deuteronomy 2.10–11,20–21).
*11.22 Gaza, Gath, and Ashdod: Towns in Philistia.
*12.2 King Sihon of Heshbon: See Numbers 21.21–31.
*12.4 King Og of Bashan: See Numbers 21.33–35.
See also: 12.1–5: Num 21.21–35; Deut 2.26–3.11.

Holy history

Canaanites

The Canaanites are first mentioned in Genesis, where they are the descendants of Canaan, the son of Ham and grandson of Noah (Genesis 10.15–18).

Canaan, however, is a general term for all the different tribes and peoples who lived in the land that God gave to the Israelites. It includes such tribes as the Jebusites, Amorites, Hivites, and others. They mainly lived in independent towns such as Megiddo, Jericho and, of course, Jerusalem.

They were an agricultural nation, with an advanced culture which had a huge influence on the Israelites after the conquest of the promised land. However, this influence also included Israel taking on some aspects of Canaanite religion, including the worship of false gods such as Baal, the setting up of altars and even, on occasions, human sacrifice. When they entered the promised land, the Israelites were supposed to get rid of all Canaanite influences, but they never did complete the task, and the Canaanites continued to have an influence over the Israelites for many centuries.

More...
Other nations p.259
Foreign gods p.262

 Anorak corner

False Gods
1. Who worshipped Dagon?
2. Who destroyed the priests of Baal?
3. What happened when the sacred chest was put in a Philistine temple?
4. What was repulsive about the god Molech?
5. What goddess was a source of profit for the silversmiths in Ephesus?
(Answers on p.1431)

Ashtaroth part of each year and in Edrei the rest of the year. Og was one of the last of the Rephaim.* 5 His kingdom stretched north to Mount Hermon, east to the town of Salecah, and included the land of Bashan as far west as the borders of the kingdoms of Geshur and Maacah. He also ruled the northern half of Gilead.

6 Moses, the LORD's servant, had led the people of Israel in defeating Sihon and Og. Then Moses gave their land to the tribes of Reuben, Gad, and East Manasseh.

7-8 Later, Joshua and the Israelites defeated many kings west of the River Jordan, from Baal-Gad in Lebanon Valley in the north to Mount Halak near the country of Edom in the south. This region included the hill country and the foothills, the Jordan valley and its western slopes, and the Southern Desert. Joshua and the Israelites took this land from the Hittites, the Amorites, the Canaanites, the Perizzites, the Hivites, and the Jebusites. Joshua divided up the land among the tribes of Israel.

The Israelites defeated the kings of the following towns west of the River Jordan:

9-24 Jericho, Ai near Bethel, Jerusalem, Hebron, Jarmuth, Lachish, Eglon, Gezer, Debir, Geder, Hormah, Arad, Libnah, Adullam, Makkedah, Bethel, Tappuah, Hepher, Aphek, Lasharon,' Madon, Hazor, Shimron-Meron, Achshaph, Taanach, Megiddo, Kedesh, Jokneam on Mount Carmel, Dor in Naphath-Dor, Goiim in Galilee,' and Tirzah.'

There were thirty-one of these kings in all.

Land that Israel did not take over

CHAPTER 13

1 Many years later, the LORD told Joshua:

Now you are very old, but there is still a lot of land that Israel has not yet taken. 2-7 First, there is the Canaanite territory that starts at the River Shihor just east of Egypt and goes north to Ekron. The southern part of this region belongs to the

Avvites and the Geshurites,* and the land around Gaza, Ashdod, Ashkelon, Gath, and Ekron belongs to the five Philistine rulers.

The other Canaanite territory is in the north. Its northern border starts at the town of Arah, which belongs to the Sidonians. From there, it goes to Aphek,* then along the Amorite border' to Hamath Pass.' The eastern border starts at Hamath Pass and goes south to Baal-Gad at the foot of Mount Hermon, and its southern boundary runs west from there to Misrephoth-Maim.' This northern region includes the Lebanon Mountains and the land that belongs to the Gebalites' and the Sidonians who live in the hill country from the Lebanon Mountains to Misrephoth-Maim.

With my help, Israel will capture these Canaanite territories and force out the people who live there. But you must divide up the land from the River Jordan to the Mediterranean Sea' among the nine tribes and the half of Manasseh that don't have any land yet. Then each tribe will have its own land.

Tribal lands that Moses had assigned east of the Jordan

8 Moses had already given land east of the River Jordan to the tribes of Reuben, Gad, and half of Manasseh. 9 This region stretched north from the town in the middle of the valley of the River Arnon, and included the town of Aroer on the northern edge of the valley. It covered the flat lands of Medeba north of Dibon, 10 and took in the towns that had belonged to Sihon, the Amorite king of Heshbon. Some of these towns were as far east as the Ammonite border.

11-12 Geshur and Maacah were part of this region, and so was the whole territory that King Og had ruled, that is, Gilead, Mount Hermon, and all of Bashan as far east as Salecah. Og had lived in Ashtaroth part of each year, and he had lived in Edrei the rest of the year. Og had been one of the last of the Rephaim,* but Moses had defeated Sihon

---

*12.4 Rephaim: Perhaps a group of people of great stature that lived in Palestine before the Israelites (see Deuteronomy 2.10–11,20–21).
See also: 12.6: Num 32.33; Deut 3.12. 13.6: Num 33.54.

*13.2–7 Geshurites: Not the same Geshur as in 12.5 and 13.11. One ancient translation has "Gezerites". Gezer was a town north of Ekron that the Israelites did not capture (see Judges 1.29).
*13.2–7 Aphek: Not the same Aphek as in 12.9–24.
*13.11–12 Rephaim: See the note at 12.4.
See also: 13.8: Num 32.33; Deut 3.12.

and Og and their people' and had forced them to leave their land. [13] However, the Israelites did not force the people of Geshur and Maacah to leave, and they still live there among the Israelites.

Moses did not give land to the Levi tribe

[14] Moses did not give any land to the Levi tribe, because the LORD God of Israel had told them, "Instead of land, you will receive the sacrifices offered at my altar."

Moses gave land to the Reuben tribe

[15] Moses gave land to each of the clans in the Reuben tribe. [16] Their land started in the south at the town in the middle of the valley of the River Arnon, took in the town of Aroer on the northern edge of the valley, and went as far north as the flat lands around Medeba. [17-21] The Amorite King Sihon had lived in Heshbon and had ruled the towns in the flat lands. Now Heshbon belonged to Reuben, and so did the following towns in the flat lands: Dibon, Bamoth-Baal, Beth-Baal-Meon, Jahaz, Kedemoth, Mephaath, Kiriathaim, Sibmah, Zereth-Shahar on the hill in the valley, Beth-Peor, Slopes of Mount Pisgah, and Beth-Jeshimoth.

Moses defeated Sihon and killed him and the Midianite chiefs who ruled parts of his kingdom for him. Their names were Evi, Rekem, Zur, Hur, and Reba. [22] The Israelites also killed Balaam the son of Beor, who had been a fortune-teller.

[23] This region with its towns and villages was the land for the Reuben tribe, and the River Jordan was its western border.

Moses gave land to the Gad tribe

[24] Moses also gave land to each of the clans in the Gad tribe. [25] It included the town of Jazer, and in the Gilead region their territory took in the land and towns as far east as the town of Aroer* just west of Rabbah.* This was about half of the land that had once belonged to the Ammonites. [26] The land given to Gad stretched from Heshbon in the south to Ramath-Mizpeh and Betonim in the north, and even further north to Mahanaim and Lidebor.' [27] Gad also received the eastern

half of the Jordan valley, which had been ruled by King Sihon of Heshbon. This territory stretched as far north as Lake Galilee,' and included the towns of Beth-Haram, Beth-Nimrah, Succoth, and Zaphon. [28] These regions with their towns and villages were given to the Gad tribe.

Moses gave land to half of the Manasseh tribe

[29] Moses gave land east of the River Jordan to half of the clans from the Manasseh tribe. [30-31] Their land started at Mahanaim and took in the region that King Og of Bashan had ruled, including Ashtaroth and Edrei, the two towns where he had lived. The villages where the Jair clan settled were part of Manasseh's land, and so was the northern half of the region of Gilead. The clans of this half of Manasseh had sixty towns in all.

The Manasseh tribe is sometimes called the Machir tribe, after Manasseh's son Machir.

[32] That was how Moses divided up the Moab Plains to the east of Jericho on the other side of the River Jordan, so these two and a half tribes would have land of their own. [33] But Moses did not give any land to the Levi tribe, because the LORD had promised that he would always provide for them.

Tribal lands west of the Jordan

CHAPTER 14

[1-5] Nine and a half tribes still did not have any land, although two and a half tribes had already received land east of the River Jordan. Moses had divided that land among them, and he had also said that the Levi tribe would not receive a large region like the other tribes. Instead, the people of Levi would receive towns and the nearby pastures for their sheep, goats, and cattle. And since the descendants of Joseph had become the two tribes of Ephraim and Manasseh, there were still nine and a half tribes that needed land. The LORD had told Moses that he would show those tribes* how to divide up the land of Canaan.

*14.1-5 he would show those tribes: The Hebrew text has "those tribes must cast lots to find out." Pieces of wood or stone (called "lots") were used to find out what God wanted his people to do.
See also: 13.33: Num 18.20; Deut 18.2.
14.2: Num 26.52-56; 34.13. 14.3,4: Num 32.33; 34.14-15; Deut 3.12-17.

*13.25 Aroer: Not the same town as the Aroer in verse 16.
*13.25 Rabbah: The capital city of Ammon.
See also: 13.14: Deut 18.1.

When the priest Eleazar, Joshua, and the leaders of the families and tribes of Israel met to divide up the land of Canaan, the LORD showed them how to do it.

Joshua gives Hebron to Caleb

⁶ One day while the Israelites were still camped at Gilgal, Caleb the son of Jephunneh went to talk with Joshua. Caleb belonged to the Kenaz clan, and many other people from the Judah tribe went with Caleb. He told Joshua:

You know that back in Kadesh-Barnea the LORD talked to his prophet Moses about you and me. ⁷ I was forty years old at the time Moses sent me from Kadesh-Barnea into Canaan as a spy. When I came back and told him about the land, everything I said was true. ⁸ The other spies said things that made our people afraid, but I completely trusted the LORD God. ⁹ The same day I came back, Moses told me, "Since you were faithful to the LORD God, I promise that the places where you went as a spy will belong to you and your descendants for ever."

¹⁰ Joshua, it was forty-five years ago that the LORD told Moses to make that promise, and now I am eighty-five. Even though Israel has moved from place to place in the desert, the LORD has kept me alive all this time as he said he would. ¹¹ I'm just as strong today as I was then, and I can still fight as well in battle.

¹² So I'm asking you for the hill country that the LORD promised me that day. You were there. You heard the other spies talk about that part of the hill country and the large, walled towns where the Anakim* live. But perhaps the LORD will help me take their land, just as he promised.

¹³ Joshua prayed that God would help Caleb, then he gave Hebron to Caleb and his descendants. ¹⁴ And Hebron still belongs to Caleb's descendants, because he was faithful to the LORD God of Israel.

¹⁵ Hebron used to be called Arba's Town,* because Arba had been one of the greatest* of the Anakim.

There was peace in the land.

CHAPTER 15

Judah's land

¹ The clans of the Judah tribe were given land that went south along the border of Edom, and at its furthest point south it even reached the Zin Desert. ² Judah's southern border started at the south end of the Dead Sea. ³ As it went west from there, it ran south of Scorpion Pass* to Zin, and then came up from the south to Kadesh-Barnea. It continued past Hezron up to Addar, turned towards Karka, ⁴ and ran along to Azmon. After that, it followed the Egyptian Gorge and ended at the Mediterranean Sea. This was also Israel's southern border.

⁵ Judah's eastern border ran the full length of the Dead Sea.

The northern border started at the northern end of the Dead Sea.* ⁶ From there it went west up to Beth-Hoglah, continued north of Beth-Arabah, and went up to the Monument of Bohan,* who belonged to the Reuben tribe. ⁷ From there, it went to Trouble Valley* and Debir,* then turned north and went to Gilgal,* which is on the north side of the valley across from Adummim Pass. It continued on to Enshemesh, Enrogel, ⁸ and up through Hinnom Valley on the land sloping south from Jerusalem. The city of Jerusalem itself belonged to the Jebusites.

Next, the border went up to the top of the mountain on the west side of Hinnom Valley and at the north end of Rephaim Valley. ⁹ At the top of the mountain it turned and went to Nephtoah Spring and then to the ruins* on Mount Ephron. From there, it went to Baalah, which is now called Kiriath-Jearim.

¹⁰ From Baalah the northern border curved west to Mount Seir and then ran along the northern ridge of Mount Jearim, where Chesalon is. Then it went down to Beth-Shemesh* and over to Timnah.

¹¹ It continued along to the hillside north of Ekron, curved around to Shikkeron, and then went to Mount Baalah. After going to Jabneel, the border finally ended at the Mediterranean Sea, ¹² which was Judah's western border.

The clans of Judah lived within these borders.

---

*14.12 Anakim: See the note at 11.21.

See also: 14.6: Num 14.30. 14.7: Num 13.1-30. 14.9: Num 14.24.

*15.7 Debir: Not the same town as in 10.38-39.
*15.7 Gilgal: Not the same Gilgal as in 4.19.

Caleb's land

This is also told in Judges 1.12–15

13 Joshua gave Caleb some land among the people of Judah, as God had told him to do. Caleb's share was Hebron, which at that time was known as Arba's Town,' because Arba was the famous ancestor of the Anakim.*

14 Caleb attacked Hebron and forced the three Anakim clans of' Sheshai, Ahiman, and Talmai to leave. 15 Next, Caleb started a war with the town of Debir, which at that time was called Kiriath-Sepher. 16 He told his men, "The man who captures Kiriath-Sepher can marry my daughter Achsah."

17 Caleb's nephew Othniel' captured Kiriath-Sepher, and Caleb let him marry Achsah. 18 Straight after the wedding, Achsah started telling Othniel that he' ought to ask her father for a field. She went to see her father, and while she was getting down from' her donkey, Caleb asked her, "What's bothering you?"

19 She answered, "I need your help. The land you gave me is in the Southern Desert, so I really need some spring-fed ponds' for a water supply."

Caleb gave her a couple of small ponds, named Higher Pond and Lower Pond.'

Towns in Judah's land

20 The following is a list of the towns in each region given to the Judah clans:

21-32 The first region was in the Southern Desert along the border with Edom, and it had the following twenty-nine towns with their surrounding villages:

Kabzeel, Eder, Jagur, Kinah, Dimonah, Aradah,' Kedesh, Hazor of Ithnan,' Ziph, Telem, Bealoth, Hazor-Hadattah, Kerioth-Hezron, which is also called Hazor, Amam, Shema, Moladah, Hazar-Gaddah, Heshmon, Beth-Pelet, Hazar-Shual, Beersheba and its surrounding villages,' Baalah, Iim, Ezem, Eltolad, Chesil, Hormah, Ziklag, Madmannah, Sansannah, Lebaoth, Shilhim, and Enrimmon.'

33-36 The second region was in the northern part of the lower foothills, and it had the following fourteen towns with their surrounding villages:

Eshtaol, Zorah, Ashnah, Zanoah, En-Gannim, Tappuah, Enam, Jarmuth,

Adullam, Socoh, Azekah, Shaaraim, Adithaim, Gederah, and Gederothaim.

37-41 The third region was in the southern part of the lower foothills, and it had the following sixteen towns with their surrounding villages:

Zenan, Hadashah, Migdalgad, Dilan, Mizpeh, Joktheel, Lachish, Bozkath, Eglon, Cabbon, Lahmas,' Chitlish, Gederoth, Beth-Dagon, Naamah, and Makkedah.

42-44 The fourth region was in the central part of the lower foothills, and it had the following nine towns with their surrounding villages:

Libnah, Ether, Ashan, Iphtah, Ashnah, Nezib, Keilah, Achzib, and Mareshah.

45-47 The fifth region was along the Mediterranean coast, and it had the following towns with their surrounding settlements and villages:

Ekron and the towns between there and the coast, Ashdod and the larger towns nearby, Gaza, the towns from Gaza to the Egyptian Gorge, and the towns along the coast of the Mediterranean Sea.

48-51 The sixth region was in the south-western part of the hill country, and it had the following eleven towns with their surrounding villages:

Shamir, Jattir, Socoh, Dannah, Kiriath-Sannah, which is now called Debir, Anab, Eshtemoh,' Anim, Goshen, Holon, and Giloh.

52-54 The seventh region was in the south-central part of Judah's hill country, and it had the following nine towns with their surrounding villages:

Arab, Dumah,' Eshan, Janim, Beth-Tappuah, Aphekah, Humtah, Kiriath-Arba, which is now called Hebron, and Zior.

55-57 The eighth region was in the south-eastern part of the hill country, and it had the following ten towns with their surrounding villages:

Maon, Carmel, Ziph, Juttah, Jezreel,* Jokdeam,' Zanoah, Kain, Gibeah,* and Timnah.

---

*15.55–57 Jezreel: Not the same Jezreel as in 19.17–23.

*15.55–57 Gibeah: Not the same Gibeah as in 18.25–28.

*15.13 Anakim: See the note at 11.21.

See also: 15.13–14: Judg 1.20.

58-59 The ninth region was in the central part of Judah's hill country, and it had the following six towns with their surrounding villages:

Halhul, Beth-Zur, Gedor, Maarath, Beth-Anoth, and Eltekon.

The tenth region was in the north-central part of Judah's hill country, and it had the following eleven towns with their surrounding villages:

Tekoa, Ephrath, which is also called Bethlehem, Peor, Etam, Culon, Tatam, Shoresh, Kerem, Gallim, Bether, and Manahath.ʼ

60 The eleventh region was in the northern part of Judah's hill country, and it had the following two towns with their surrounding villages:

Rabbah, and Kiriath-Baal, which is also called Kiriath-Jearim.

61-62 The twelfth region was in the desert along the Dead Sea, and it had the following six towns with their surrounding villages:

Beth-Arabah, Middin, Secacah, Nibshan, Salt Town, and En-Gedi.

The Jebusites

63 The Jebusites lived in Jerusalem, and the people of the Judah tribe could not capture the city and get rid of them. That's why Jebusites still live in Jerusalem along with the people of Judah.*

CHAPTER 16

Ephraim's land

1-4 Ephraim and Manasseh are the two tribes descended from Joseph, and the following is a description of the land they received. The southern border of their land started at the River Jordan east of the spring at Jericho. From there it went west through the desert up to the hill country around Bethel. From Bethel it went to Luz and thenʼ to the border of the Archites in Ataroth.* It continued west down to the land that belonged to the Japhlet

clan, then went on to Lower Beth-Horon, Gezer, and the Mediterranean Sea.

5 The following is a description of the land that was divided among the clans of the Ephraim tribe. Their southern border started at Ataroth-Addar and went west to Upper Beth-Horon 6-8 and the Mediterranean Sea. Their northern border started on the east at Janoah, curved a little to the north, then came back south to Michmethath and Tappuah, where it followed the Kanah Gorge west to the Mediterranean Sea.

The eastern border started on the north near Janoah and went between Janoah on the south-west and Taanath-Shiloh on the north-east. Then it went south to Ataroth, Naarah, and on as far as the edge of the land that belonged to Jericho. At that point it turned east and went to the River Jordan. The clans of Ephraim received this region as their tribal land. 9 Ephraim also had some towns and villages that were inside Manasseh's tribal land.

10 Ephraim could not force the Canaanites out of Gezer, so there are still some Canaanites who live there among the Israelites. But now these Canaanites have to work as slaves for the Israelites.

CHAPTER 17

Manasseh's land west of the River Jordan

1-6 Manasseh was Joseph's eldest son, and Machir was Manasseh's eldest son. Machir had a son named Gilead, and some of his descendants had already received the regions of Gilead and Bashan because they were good warriors. The other clans of the Manasseh tribe descended from Gilead's sons Abiezer, Helek, Asriel, Shechem, Hepher, and Shemida. The following is a description of the land they received.

Hepher's son Zelophehad did not have any sons, but he did have five daughters: Mahlah, Noah, Hoglah, Milcah, and Tirzah. One day the clans that were descendants of Zelophehad's five daughters went to the priest Eleazar, Joshua, and the leaders of Israel. The people of these clans said, "The LORD told Moses to give us land just as he gave land to our relatives."*

Joshua followed the LORD's instructions and gave land to these five clans, as he had given

---

*15.63 Jebusites . . . Judah: Israel captured Jerusalem in King David's time, but even then the Jebusites were not forced to leave.

*16.1–4 Ataroth: This is the same Ataroth as Ataroth-Addar in verse 5, but a different Ataroth from the one in verses 6–8.

See also: 15.63: Judg 1.21; 2 Sam 5.6; 1 Chron 11.4.

*17.1–6 The LORD told Moses . . . relatives: See Numbers 27.1–11; 36.1–12.

See also: 16.10: Judg 1.29. 17.4: Num 27.1–7.

land to the five clans that had descended from Hepher's brothers.' So Manasseh's land west of the River Jordan was divided into ten parts.

⁷ The land of the Manasseh tribe went from its northern border with the Asher tribe south to Michmethath, which is to the east of Shechem. The southern border started there, but curved even further south to include the people who lived around Tappuah Spring.'
⁸ The town of Tappuah was on Manasseh's border with Ephraim. Although the land around Tappuah belonged to Manasseh, the town itself belonged to Ephraim.

⁹⁻¹⁰ Then the border went west to the Kanah Gorge and ran along the northern edge of the gorge to the Mediterranean Sea. The land south of the gorge belonged to Ephraim. And even though there were a few towns that belonged to Ephraim north of the gorge, the land north of the gorge belonged to Manasseh.

The western border of Manasseh was the Mediterranean Sea, and the tribe shared a border with the Asher tribe on the north-west and with the Issachar tribe on the north-east.

¹¹ Manasseh was supposed to have the following towns with their surrounding villages inside the borders of Issachar's and Asher's tribal lands:

Beth-Shan, Ibleam, Endor, Taanach, Megiddo, and Dor, which is also called Naphath.'

¹² But the people of Manasseh could not capture these towns, so the Canaanites kept on living in them. ¹³ When the Israelites grew stronger, they made the Canaanites in these towns work as their slaves, though they never did force them to leave.

Joseph's descendants ask for more land

¹⁴ One day the Joseph tribes* came to Joshua and asked, "Why didn't you give us more land? The LORD has always been kind to us, and we have too many people for this small region."

¹⁵ Joshua replied, "If you have so many people that you don't have enough room in the hill country of Ephraim, then go into the forest that belonged to the Perizzites and the Rephaim.* Clear out the trees and make more room for yourselves there."

¹⁶ "Even if we do that," they answered, "there still won't be enough land for us in the hill country. And we can't move down into Jezreel Valley, because the Canaanites who live in Beth-Shan and in other parts of the valley have iron chariots."

¹⁷ "Your tribes do have a lot of people," Joshua admitted. "I'll give you more land. Your tribes are powerful, ¹⁸ so you can have the rest of the hill country, but it's a forest, and you'll have to cut down the trees and clear the land. You can also have Jezreel Valley. Even though the Canaanites there are strong and have iron chariots, you can force them to leave the valley."

CHAPTER 18

Joshua gives out the rest of the land

¹ After Israel had captured the land, they met at Shiloh and set up the sacred tent.' ² There were still seven tribes without any land, ³⁻⁷ so Joshua told the people:

The Judah tribe has already settled in its land in the south, and the Joseph tribes* have settled in their land in the north. The tribes of Gad, Reuben, and East Manasseh already have the land that the LORD's servant Moses gave them east of the River Jordan. And the people of Levi won't get a single large region of the land like the other tribes. Instead, they will serve the LORD as priests.

But the rest of you haven't done a thing to take over any land. The LORD God who was worshipped by your ancestors has given you the land, and now it's time to go ahead and settle there.

Seven tribes still don't have any land. Each of these tribes should choose three men, and I'll send them to explore the remaining land. They will divide it into seven regions, write a description of each region, and bring these descriptions back to me. I will find out* from the LORD our God what region each tribe should get.

⁸ Just before the men left camp, Joshua repeated their orders: "Explore the land and write a description of it. Then come back to Shiloh, and I will find out from the LORD how to divide the land."

⁹ The men left and went across the land, dividing it into seven regions. They wrote

---

*17.14 Joseph tribes: Ephraim and the half of Manasseh that lived west of the River Jordan.
*17.15 Rephaim: See the note at 12.4.
See also: 17.12–13: Judg 1.27–28.

*18.3–7 Joseph tribes: See the note at 17.14.
*18.3–7 find out: Hebrew "cast lots to find out" (see the note at 14.1–5).

down a description of each region, town by town, and returned to Joshua at the camp at Shiloh. [10] Joshua found out from the LORD how to divide the land, and he told the tribes what the LORD had decided.

Benjamin's land

[11] Benjamin was the first tribe chosen to receive land. The region for its clans lay between the Judah tribe on the south and the Joseph tribes* on the north. [12] Benjamin's northern border started at the River Jordan and went up the ridge north of Jericho, then on west into the hill country as far as the Beth-Aven Desert. [13-14] From there it went to Luz, which is now called Bethel. The border ran along the ridge south of Luz, then went to Ataroth-Orech' and on as far as the mountain south of Lower Beth-Horon. At that point it turned south and became the western border. It went as far south as Kiriath-Baal, a town in Judah now called Kiriath-Jearim.

[15] Benjamin's southern border started at the edge of Kiriath-Jearim and went east to the ruins' and on to Nephtoah Spring. [16] From there it went to the bottom of the hill at the northern end of Rephaim Valley. The other side of this hill faces Hinnom Valley, which is on the land that slopes south from Jerusalem.' The border went down through Hinnom Valley until it reached Enrogel.

[17] At Enrogel the border curved north and went to Enshemesh and on east to Geliloth,' which is across the valley from Adummim Pass. Then it went down to the Monument of Bohan,' who belonged to the Reuben tribe. [18] The border ran along the hillside north of Beth-Arabah,' then down into the Jordan Valley. [19] Inside the valley it went south as far as the northern hillside of Beth-Hoglah. The last section of the border went from there to the northern end of the Dead Sea,' at the mouth of the River Jordan. [20] The River Jordan itself was Benjamin's eastern border.

These were the borders of Benjamin's tribal land, where the clans of Benjamin lived.

[21-24] One region of Benjamin's tribal land had twelve towns with their surrounding villages. Those towns were Jericho, Beth-Hoglah, Emek-Keziz, Beth-Arabah, Zemaraim, Bethel, Avvim, Parah, Ophrah, Chephar-Ammoni, Ophni, and Geba.

[25-28] In the other region there were the following fourteen towns with their

surrounding villages: Gibeon, Ramah, Beeroth, Mizpeh, Chephirah, Mozah, Rekem, Irpeel, Taralah, Zelah, Haeleph, Gibeah, Kiriath-Jearim,' and Jerusalem, which is also called Jebusite Town.

These regions are the tribal lands of Benjamin.

CHAPTER 19

Simeon's land

[1] Simeon was the second tribe chosen to receive land, and the region for its clans was inside Judah's borders. [2-6] In one region of Simeon's tribal land there were the following thirteen towns with their surrounding villages:

Beersheba, Shema,' Moladah, Hazar-Shual, Balah, Ezem, Eltolad, Bethul, Hormah, Ziklag, Beth-Marcaboth, Hazar-Susah, Beth-Lebaoth, and Sharuhen.

[7] In another region, Simeon had the following four towns with their surrounding villages:

Enrimmon,' Tachan,' Ether, and Ashan.

[8] Simeon's land also included all the other towns and villages as far south as Baalath-Beer, which is also called Ramah of the South.

[9] Simeon's tribal land was actually inside Judah's territory. Judah had received too much land for the number of people in its tribe, so part of Judah's land was given to Simeon.

Zebulun's land

[10-12] Zebulun was the third tribe chosen to receive land. The southern border for its clans started in the west at the edge of the gorge near Jokneam. It went east to the edge of the land that belongs to the town of Dabbesheth, and continued on to Maralah and Sarid. It took in the land that belongs to Chislothtabor, then ended at Daberath.

The eastern border went up to Japhia [13] and continued north to Gath-Hepher, Ethkazin, and Rimmonah,' where it curved' towards Neah [14] and became the northern border. Then it curved south around Hannathon and went as far west as Iphtahel Valley.

[15] Zebulun had twelve towns with their surrounding villages. Some of these were

Kattath, Nahalal, Shimron, Jiralah,' and Bethlehem.*

16 This is the tribal land, and these are the towns and villages of the Zebulun clans.

Issachar's land

17-23 Issachar was the fourth tribe chosen to receive land. The northern border for its clans went from Mount Tabor east to the River Jordan. Their land included the following sixteen towns with their surrounding villages:

Jezreel, Chesulloth, Shunem, Hapharaim, Shion, Anaharath, Debirath,' Kishion, Ebez, Remeth, En-Gannim, Enhaddah, Beth-Pazzez, Tabor,' Shahazumah and Beth-Shemesh.*

Asher's land

24-26 Asher was the fifth tribe chosen to receive land, and the region for its clans included the following towns:

Helkath, Hali, Beten, Achshaph, Allammelech, Amad, and Mishal.

Asher's southern border ran from the Mediterranean Sea south-east along the River Shihor-Libnath at the foot of Mount Carmel, 27 then east to Beth-Dagon. On the south-east, Asher shared a border with Zebulun along the Iphtahel Valley. On the eastern side their border ran north to Beth-Emek, went east of Cabul, and then on to Neiel, 28 Abdon,' Rehob, Hammon, Kanah, and as far north as the city of Sidon. 29-31 Then it turned west to become the northern border and went to Ramah* and the fortress-city of Tyre.* Near Tyre it turned towards Hosah and ended at the Mediterranean Sea.

Asher had a total of twenty-two towns with their surrounding villages, including Mahalab,' Achzib, Acco,' Aphek, and Rehob.

Naphtali's land

32-34 Naphtali was the sixth tribe chosen to receive land. The southern border for its

clans started in the west, where the tribal lands of Asher and Zebulun meet near Hukkok. From that point it ran east and south-east along the border with Zebulun as far as Aznoth-Tabor. From there the border went east to Heleph, Adami-Nekeb, Jabneel,* then to the town called Oak in Zaanannim,' and Lakkum. The southern border ended at the River Jordan, at the edge of the town named Jehudah.' Naphtali shared a border with Asher on the west.

35-39 The Naphtali clans received this region as their tribal land, and it included nineteen towns with their surrounding villages. The following towns had walls around them:

Ziddim, Zer, Hammath, Rakkath, Chinnereth, Adamah, Ramah,* Hazor, Kedesh, Edrei,* Enhazor, Iron, Migdalel, Horem, Beth-Anath, and Beth-Shemesh.*

Dan's land

40-46 Dan was the seventh tribe chosen to receive land, and the region for its clans included the following towns:

Zorah, Eshtaol, Ir-Shemesh,* Shaalabbin, Aijalon, Ithlah, Elon, Timnah, Ekron, Eltekeh, Gibbethon, Baalath, Jehud, Azor,' Beneberak, Gath-Rimmon, Mejarkon, and Rakkon.

Dan's tribal land' went almost as far as Joppa. 47-48 Its clans received this land and these towns with their surrounding villages.

Later, when enemies* forced them to leave their tribal land, they went to the town of Leshem. They attacked the town, captured it, and killed the people who lived there. Then they settled there themselves and renamed the town Dan after their ancestor.

Joshua's land

49-51 The Israelites were still gathered in Shiloh in front of the sacred tent,' when Eleazar the priest, Joshua, and the family leaders of Israel

---

*19.15 Bethlehem: This town is different from the Bethlehem in 15.58-59.
*19.17-23 Beth-Shemesh: Not the same Beth-Shemesh as in 15.10 or 19.35-39.
*19.29-31 Ramah: Not the same Ramah as in 18.25-28 or 19.35-39.
*19.29-31 fortress-city of Tyre: Tyre was a walled city built on an island about a kilometre from shore.

*19.32-34 Jabneel: This town is not the same Jabneel as in 15.11.
*19.35-39 Ramah: See the note at 19.29-31.
*19.35-39 Edrei: Not the same Edrei as the town in Bashan east of the River Jordan where King Og had lived (see 12.4; 13.11-12,30-31).
*19.35-39 Beth-Shemesh: Not the same Beth-Shemesh as in 15.10 or 19.17-23.
*19.40-46 Ir-Shemesh: Possibly the same town as the Beth-Shemesh of 15.10.
*19.47-48 enemies: Probably the Philistines.
See also: 19.47: Judg 18.27-29.

finished giving out the land to the tribes. The LORD had told the people to give Joshua whatever town he wanted. So Joshua chose Timnath-Serah in the hill country of Ephraim, and the people gave it to him. Joshua went to Timnath-Serah, rebuilt it, and lived there.

Towns for protecting people accused of murder

CHAPTER 20

The Safe Towns

This is also told in Numbers 35.9–15; Deuteronomy 19.1–13

¹ One day the LORD told Joshua:

² When Moses was still alive, I told him to tell the Israelites about the Safe Towns. Now you tell them that it is time to set up these towns. ³⁻⁴ If a person accidentally kills someone and the victim's relatives say it was murder, they might try to take revenge.* Anyone accused of murder can run to one of the Safe Towns and be safe from the victim's relatives. The one needing protection will stand at the entrance to the town gate and explain to the town leaders what happened. Then the leaders will bring that person in and provide a place to live in their town.

⁵ One of the victim's relatives might come to the town, looking for revenge. But the town leaders must not simply hand over the person accused of murder. After all, the accused and the victim had been neighbours, not enemies. ⁶ The citizens of that Safe Town must come together and hold a trial. They may decide that the victim was killed accidentally and that the accused is not guilty of murder.

Everyone found not guilty* must still live in the Safe Town until the high priest dies. Then they can go back to their own towns and their homes that they had to leave behind.

⁷ The Israelites decided that the following three towns west of the River Jordan would be Safe Towns:

Kedesh in Galilee in Naphtali's hill country, Shechem in Ephraim's hill country, and Kiriath-Arba in Judah's hill country. Kiriath-Arba is now called Hebron.

⁸ The Israelites had already decided on the following three towns east of the River Jordan:

Bezer in the desert flat lands of Reuben, Ramoth in Gilead, which was a town that belonged to Gad, and Golan in Bashan, which belonged to Manasseh.

⁹ These Safe Towns were set up, so that if Israelites or even foreigners who lived in Israel accidentally killed someone, they could run to one of these towns. There they would be safe until a trial could be held, even if one of the victim's relatives came looking for revenge.

Towns for the Levi tribe

CHAPTER 21

¹⁻² While the Israelites were still camped at Shiloh in the land of Canaan, the family leaders of the Levi tribe went to speak to the priest Eleazar, Joshua, and the family leaders of the other Israelite tribes. The leaders of Levi said, "The LORD told Moses that you have to give us towns and provide pastures for our animals."*

³ Since the LORD had said this, the leaders of the other Israelite tribes agreed to give some of the towns and pastures from their tribal lands to Levi. ⁴ The leaders asked the LORD to show them* in what order the clans of Levi would be given towns, and which towns each clan would receive.

The Kohath clans were first. The descendants of Aaron, Israel's first priest, were given thirteen towns from the tribes of Judah, Simeon, and Benjamin. ⁵ The other members of the Kohath clans received ten towns from the tribes of Ephraim, Dan, and West Manasseh. ⁶ The clans that were descendants of Gershon were given thirteen towns from the tribes of Issachar, Asher, Naphtali, and East Manasseh. ⁷ The clans that

---

*20.3–4 revenge: At this time in Israel's history, the clan could appoint a close male relative to find and kill a person who had killed a member of their clan.

*20.6 not guilty: If the person was found to be guilty of murder, the citizens of the Safe Town were to let the victim's relatives kill the murderer (see Deuteronomy 19.11–13).

See also: 20.1–9; Num 35.9–34; Deut 4.41–43; 19.1–13.

---

*21.1–2 The LORD told Moses . . . animals: See Numbers 35.1–8.

*21.4 asked the LORD to show them: Hebrew "cast lots to find out". See the note at 14.1–5.

See also: 21.2: Num 35.1–8.

were descendants of Merari* received twelve towns from the tribes of Reuben, Gad, and Zebulun.

8 The LORD had told Moses that he would show the Israelites which towns and pastures to give to the clans of Levi, and he did.

Towns from Judah, Simeon, Benjamin

9-19 The descendants of Aaron from the Kohath clans of Levi were priests, and they were chosen to receive towns first. They were given thirteen towns and the pasture land around them. Nine of these towns were from the tribes of Judah and Simeon and four from Benjamin.

Hebron, Libnah, Jattir, Eshtemoa, Holon, Debir, Ashan,' Juttah, and Beth-Shemesh were from Judah and Simeon. Hebron, in the hill country of Judah, was earlier called Arba's Town.' It had been named after Arba, the ancestor of the Anakim.* Hebron's pasture lands went along with the town, but its farmlands and the villages around it had been given to Caleb.* Hebron was also one of the Safe Towns for people who had accidentally killed someone.

Gibeon, Geba, Anathoth, and Almon were from Benjamin.

Towns from Ephraim, Dan, West Manasseh

20-26 The rest of the Kohath clans of the Levi tribe received ten towns and the pasture land around them. Four of these towns were from the tribe of Ephraim, four from Dan, and two from West Manasseh.

Shechem, Gezer, Kibzaim, and Beth-Horon were from Ephraim. Shechem was in the hill country, and it was also one of the Safe Towns for people who had accidentally killed someone.

Elteke, Gibbethon, Aijalon, and Gath-Rimmon were from Dan.

Taanach and Jibleam' were from West Manasseh.

Towns from East Manasseh, Issachar, Asher, Naphtali

27-33 The clans of Levi that were descendants of Gershon received thirteen towns and the pasture land around them. Two of these towns were from the tribe of East Manasseh, four from Issachar, four from Asher, and three from Naphtali.

Golan in Bashan and Beeshterah were from East Manasseh.

Kishion, Daberath, Jarmuth, and En-Gannim were from Issachar.

Mishal, Abdon, Helkath, and Rehob were from Asher.

Kedesh in Galilee, Hammothdor, and Kartan were from Naphtali. Golan in Bashan and Kedesh in Galilee were also Safe Towns for people who had accidentally killed someone.

Towns from Zebulun, Reuben, Gad

34-40 The rest of the Levi clans were descendants of Merari, and they received twelve towns with the pasture land around them. Four towns were from the tribe of Zebulun, four from Reuben, and four from Gad.

Jokneam, Kartah, Rimmonah,' and Nahalal were from Zebulun.

Bezer, Jazah, Kedemoth, and Mephaath were from Reuben. Bezer was in the desert flat lands east of the River Jordan across from Jericho.'

Ramoth in Gilead, Mahanaim, Heshbon, and Jazer were from Gad.

Bezer and Ramoth in Gilead were Safe Towns' for people who had accidentally killed someone.

41-42 The people of the Levi tribe had a total of forty-eight towns within Israel, and they had pastures around each one of their towns.

Israel settles in the land

43 The LORD gave the Israelites the land he had promised their ancestors, and they captured it and settled in it. 44 There still were enemies around Israel, but the LORD kept his promise to let his people live in peace. And whenever the Israelites did have to go to war, no enemy could defeat them. The LORD always helped Israel win. 45 The LORD promised to do many good things for Israel, and he kept his promise every time.

The eastern tribes return home

CHAPTER 22

The two and a half tribes return home

1 Joshua called the men of the tribes of Reuben, Gad, and East Manasseh to a meeting, and he told them:

2-3 You have obeyed every command of the LORD your God and of his servant Moses.

---

*21.4-7 Kohath . . . Gershon . . . Merari: Sons of Levi, the ancestor of the tribe of Levi.
*21.9-19 Anakim: See the note at 11.21.
*21.9-19 Caleb: See 14.6-14.

See also: 22.2: Num 32.20-32; Jam 1.12-15.

And you have done everything I've told you to do. It's taken a long time, but you have stayed and helped your relatives. 4 The LORD promised to give peace to your relatives, and that's what he has done. Now it's time for you to go back to your own homes in the land that Moses gave you east of the River Jordan.

5 Moses taught you to love the LORD your God, to be faithful to him, and to worship and obey him with your whole heart and with all your strength. So be very careful to do everything Moses commanded.

6-9 You've become rich from what you've taken from your enemies. You have big herds of cattle, lots of silver, gold, bronze, and iron, and plenty of clothes. Take everything home with you and share it with the people of your tribe.

I pray that God will be kind to you. You are now free to go home.

The tribes of Reuben and Gad started back to Gilead, their own land. Moses had given the land of Bashan to the East Manasseh tribe, so they started back along with Reuben and Gad. God had told Moses that these two and a half tribes should conquer Gilead and Bashan, and they had done so.

Joshua had given land west of the River Jordan to the other half of the Manasseh tribe, so they stayed at Shiloh in the land of Canaan with the rest of the Israelites.

10-11 The tribes of Reuben, Gad, and East Manasseh reached the western side of the Jordan Valley' and built a huge altar there beside the river.

When the rest of the Israelites heard what these tribes had done,* 12 the Israelite men met at Shiloh to get ready to attack the two and a half tribes. 13 But first they sent a priest, Phinehas the son of Eleazar, to talk with the two and a half tribes. 14 Each of the tribes at Shiloh sent the leader of one of its families along with Phinehas.

15 Phinehas and these leaders went to Gilead and met with the tribes of Reuben, Gad, and East Manasseh. They said:

16 All the LORD's people have gathered together and have sent us to find out why you are unfaithful to our God. You have turned your backs on the LORD by building that altar. Why are you rebelling against him? 17 Wasn't our people's sin at Peor* terrible enough for you? The LORD punished us by sending a horrible sickness that killed many of us, and we still suffer because of that sin.' 18 Now you are turning your backs on the LORD again.

If you don't stop rebelling against the LORD at once, he will be angry with the whole nation. 19 If you don't think your land is a fit place to serve God, then move across the Jordan and live with us in the LORD's own land, where his sacred tent is. But don't rebel against the LORD our God or against us by building another altar besides the LORD's own altar.' 20 Don't you remember what happened when Achan was unfaithful* and took some of the things that belonged to God? This made God angry with the entire nation. Achan died because he sinned, but he also caused the death of many others.

21 The tribes of Reuben, Gad, and East Manasseh answered:

22 The LORD is the greatest God! We ask him to be our witness, because he knows whether or not we were rebellious or unfaithful when we built that altar. If we were unfaithful, then we pray that God won't rescue us today. Let us tell you why we built that altar, 23 and we ask the LORD to punish us if we are lying. We didn't build it so we could turn our backs on the LORD. We didn't even build it so we could offer animal or grain sacrifices to please the LORD or ask his blessing.

24-25 We built that altar because we were worried. Some day your descendants might tell our descendants, "The LORD made the River Jordan the boundary between us Israelites and you people of Reuben and Gad. The LORD is Israel's God, but you're not part of Israel, so you can't take part in worshipping the LORD."

Your descendants might say that and try to make our descendants stop worshipping and obeying the LORD. 26 That's why we decided to build the altar. It isn't for offering sacrifices, not even sacrifices to please the LORD.* 27-29 To build another altar for offering sacrifices would be the same as

---

*22.10–11 built a huge altar . . . tribes had done:
According to Deuteronomy 12.5–14, the LORD wanted the Israelites to have only one altar for offering sacrifices. To build another altar would be to disobey the LORD.

See also: 22.16: Deut 12.13–14.

*22.17 our people's sin at Peor: See Numbers 25.
*22.20 Achan was unfaithful: See 7.1–26.
*22.26 sacrifices to please the LORD: See the note at 8.30–32.

See also: 22.17: Num 25.1–9. 22.20: Josh 7.1–26.

turning our backs on the LORD and rebelling against him. We could never do that! No, we built the altar to remind us and you and the generations to come that we will worship the LORD. And so we will keep bringing our sacrifices to the LORD's altar, there in front of his sacred tent. Now your descendants will never be able to say to our descendants, "You can't worship the LORD."

But if they do say this, our descendants can answer back, "Look at this altar our ancestors built! It's like the LORD's altar, but it isn't for offering sacrifices. It's here to remind us and you that we belong to the LORD, just as much as you do."

30-31 Phinehas and the clan leaders were pleased when they heard the tribes of Reuben, Gad, and East Manasseh explain why they had built the altar. Then Phinehas told them, "Today we know that the LORD is helping us. You have not been unfaithful to him, and this means that the LORD will not be angry with us."

32 Phinehas and the clan leaders left Gilead and went back to Canaan to tell the Israelites about their meeting with the Reuben and Gad tribes. 33 The Israelites were happy and praised God. There was no more talk about going to war and wiping out the tribes of Reuben and Gad.

34 The people of Reuben and Gad named the altar "A Reminder to us all that the LORD is our God".⟩

Joshua's farewell speeches and death

CHAPTER 23

1 The LORD let Israel live in peace with its neighbours for a long time, and Joshua lived to a ripe old age. 2 One day he called a meeting of the leaders of the tribes of Israel, including the old men, the judges, and the officials. Then he told them:

I am now very old. 3 You have seen how the LORD your God fought for you and helped you defeat the nations who lived in this land. 4-5 There are still some nations left, but the LORD has promised you their land. So when you attack them, he will make them run away. I have already divided their land among your tribes, as I did with the land of the nations I defeated between the River Jordan and the Mediterranean Sea.

6 Be sure that you carefully obey everything written in *The Book of the Law*⟩ of Moses and do exactly what it says.

7 Don't have anything to do with the nations that live around you. Don't worship their gods or pray to their idols or make promises in the names of their gods. 8 Be as faithful to the LORD as you have always been.

9 When you attacked powerful nations, the LORD made them run away, and no one has ever been able to stand up to you. 10 Any one of you can defeat a thousand enemy soldiers, because the LORD God fights for you, just as he promised. 11 Be sure to love the LORD your God always.

12-13 Don't ever turn your backs on him by marrying people from the nations that are left in the land. Don't even make friends with them. I tell you that if you are friendly with those nations, the LORD won't chase them away when you attack. Instead, they'll be like a trap for your feet, a whip on your back, and thorns in your eyes. And finally, none of you will be left in this good land that the LORD has given you.

14 I will soon die, as everyone must. But deep in your hearts you know that the LORD has kept every promise he ever made to you. Not one of them has been broken. 15-16 Yes, when the LORD makes a promise, he does what he has promised. But when he makes a threat, he will also do what he has threatened. The LORD is our God. He gave us this wonderful land and made an agreement with us that we would worship only him. But if you worship other gods, it will make the LORD furious. He will start getting rid of you, and soon not one of you will be left in this good land that he has given you.

CHAPTER 24

We will worship and obey the LORD

1 Joshua called the tribes of Israel together for a meeting at Shechem. He made the leaders, including the old men, the judges, and the officials, come up and stand near the sacred tent.⟩ 2 Then Joshua told everyone to listen to this message from the LORD, the God of Israel:

Long ago your ancestors lived on the other side of the River Euphrates, and they worshipped other gods. This continued

See also: **23.10:** a Deut 32.30; b Deut 3.22.
24.2: Gen 11.27.

until the time of your ancestor Terah and his two sons, Abraham and Nahor. ³ But I brought Abraham across the River Euphrates and led him through the land of Canaan. I blessed him by giving him Isaac, the first in a line of many descendants. ⁴ Then I gave Isaac two sons, Jacob and Esau. I let Esau live in the hill country of Mount Seir, but your ancestor Jacob and his children went to live in Egypt.

⁵⁻⁶ Later I sent Moses and his brother Aaron to help your people, and I made all those horrible things happen to the Egyptians. I brought your ancestors out of Egypt, but the Egyptians got in their chariots and on their horses and chased your ancestors, catching up with them at the Red Sea.* ⁷ Your people cried to me for help, so I put a dark cloud between them and the Egyptians. Then I opened up the sea and let your people walk across on dry ground. But when the Egyptians tried to follow, I commanded the sea to swallow them, and they drowned while you watched.

You lived in the desert for a long time, ⁸ then I brought you into the land east of the River Jordan. The Amorites were living there, and they fought you. But with my help, you defeated them, wiped them out, and took their land. ⁹ King Balak decided that his nation Moab would go to war against you, so he asked Balaam′ to come and put a curse on you. ¹⁰ But I wouldn't listen to Balaam, and I rescued you by making him bless you instead of curse you.

¹¹ You crossed the River Jordan and came to Jericho. The rulers of Jericho fought you, and so did the Amorites, the Perizzites, the Canaanites, the Hittites, the Girgashites, the Hivites, and the Jebusites. I helped you defeat them all. ¹² Your enemies ran from you, but not because you had swords and bows and arrows. I made your enemies panic and run away, as I had done with the two Amorite kings east of the River Jordan.

¹³ You didn't have to work for this land — I gave it to you. Now you live in towns you didn't build, and you eat grapes and olives from vineyards and trees you didn't plant.

¹⁴ Then Joshua told the people:

Worship the LORD, obey him, and always be faithful. Get rid of the idols your ancestors worshipped when they lived on the other side of the River Euphrates and in Egypt. ¹⁵ But if you don't want to worship the LORD, then choose now! Will you worship the same idols your ancestors did? Or since you're living on land that once belonged to the Amorites, perhaps you'll worship their gods. I won't. My family and I are going to worship and obey the LORD!

¹⁶ The people answered:

We could never worship other gods or stop worshipping the LORD. ¹⁷ The LORD is our God. We were slaves in Egypt as our ancestors had been, but we saw the LORD work miracles to set our people free and to bring us out of Egypt. Even though other nations were all around us, the LORD protected us wherever we went. ¹⁸ And when we fought the Amorites and the other nations that lived in this land, the LORD made them run away. Yes, we will worship and obey the LORD, because the LORD is our God.

¹⁹ Joshua said:

The LORD is fearsome; he is the one true God, and I don't think you are able to worship and obey him in the ways he demands. You would have to be completely faithful, and if you sin or rebel, he won't let you get away with it. ²⁰ If you turn your backs on the LORD and worship the gods of other nations, the LORD will turn against you. He will make terrible things happen to you and wipe you out, even though he had been good to you before.

²¹ But the people shouted, "We won't worship any other gods. We will worship and obey only the LORD!"

²² Joshua said, "You have heard yourselves say that you will worship and obey the LORD. Isn't that true?"

"Yes, it's true," they answered.

²³ Joshua said, "But you still have some idols, like those the other nations worship. Get rid of your idols! You must decide once and for all that you really want to obey the LORD God of Israel."

---

*24.5-6 Red Sea: See the note at 2.10.

See also: 24.3: a Gen 12.1–9; b Gen 21.1–3.
24.4: a Gen 25.24–26; b Gen 36.8; Deut 2.5; c Gen 46.1–7.
24.5: Exod 3.1—12.42. 24.6,7: Exod 14.1–31.
24.8: Num 21.21–35. 24.9,10: Num 22.1—24.25.
24.11: a Josh 3.14–17; b Josh 6.1–21. 24.12: Exod 23.28;
Deut 7.20. 24.13: Deut 6.10–11.

²⁴ The people said, "The LORD is our God, and we will worship and obey only him."

²⁵ Joshua helped Israel make an agreement with the LORD that day at Shechem. Joshua made laws for Israel ²⁶ and wrote them down in *The Book of the Law*⸋ of God. Then he set up a large stone under the oak tree at the place of worship in Shechem ²⁷ and told the people, "Look at this stone. It has heard everything that the LORD has said to us. Our God can call this stone as a witness if we ever reject him."

²⁸ Joshua sent everyone back to their homes.

Joshua, Joseph, and Eleazar are buried

²⁹ Not long afterwards, the LORD's servant Joshua died at the age of one hundred and ten. ³⁰ The Israelites buried him in his own land at Timnath-Serah, north of Mount Gaash in the hill country of Ephraim.

³¹ As long as Joshua lived, Israel worshipped and obeyed the LORD. There were other leaders old enough to remember everything that the LORD had done for Israel. And for as long as these men lived, Israel continued to worship and obey the LORD.

³² When the people of Israel left Egypt, they brought the bones of Joseph along with them. They took the bones to the town of Shechem and buried them in the field that Jacob had bought for one hundred pieces of silver⸋ from Hamor, the founder of Shechem. The town and the field both⸋ became part of the land belonging to the descendants of Joseph.

³³ When Eleazar the priest⸋ died, he was buried in the hill country of Ephraim on a hill that belonged to his son Phinehas.

See also: 24.30: Josh 19.49–50. **24.32:** Gen 33.19; 50.24–25; Exod 13.19; John 4.5; Acts 7.16.

Additional notes

⸋**1.6–8 the Law:** Or "Teachings".
⸋**2.14 We pray . . . promise:** Or "If you save our lives, we will save yours!"
⸋**3.2 Two days later:** The Hebrew text has "At the end of three days", two days after they had set up camp.
⸋**3.3–4 the priests:** The Hebrew text has "the priests, the Levites"; priests belonged to the tribe of Levi.
⸋**4.1–3 Joshua . . . Tell:** Or "Joshua, you and the other leaders must tell".
⸋**4.10–13 Forty thousand soldiers from the tribes of Reuben, Gad, and East Manasseh:** Or "There were forty thousand soldiers altogether, and those from the tribes of Reuben, Gad, and East Manasseh".

⸋**5.3 Haaraloth Hill:** Or "Foreskin Hill".
⸋**6.18–19 Be careful . . . fault:** One ancient translation; Hebrew "Don't keep any of it for yourself. If you do, the LORD will destroy both you and Israel."
⸋**6.26 by the time . . . dead:** Or "when he puts gates into the town wall, his youngest son will die."
⸋**7.1 Achan:** The Hebrew text has "Achan, son of Carmi, grandson of Abdi, and great-grandson of Zerah".
⸋**7.2 of Ai:** Or "called The Ruins".
⸋**7.4–5 stone quarries:** Or "Shebarim".
⸋**7.24 Trouble Valley:** Or "Achor Valley".
⸋**8.16–17 Ai or in Bethel:** Hebrew; one ancient translation "Ai".
⸋**8.18 sword:** Or "spear".
⸋**8.22–24 Joshua. They also chased . . . them:** Or "Joshua. The men of Ai had chased the Israelites into the desert, but the Israelites killed them there."
⸋**8.30–32 taught . . . Law:** Or "commanded . . . Teachings".
⸋**8.30–32 Law:** See the note at 1.6–8.
⸋**8.33–35 the blessings . . . Moses:** Or "all of *The Book of the Law* of Moses, including the blessings and the curses."
⸋**9.4 So . . . country:** One possible meaning for the difficult Hebrew text.
⸋**9.7–8 Gibeonites:** Hebrew "Hivites".
⸋**9.16–17 A couple . . . later:** The Hebrew text has "At the end of three days", meaning two days after the day the treaty was made.
⸋**9.16–17 A couple of days . . . later:** Or "A couple of days later, the Israelites moved their camp to the area near the towns of Gibeon, Chephirah, Beeroth, and Kiriath-Jearim. When they arrived, they realized that they had made a peace treaty with the people of these nearby towns!"
⸋**9.23 the place of worship:** The Hebrew text has "God's house", which at that time was the sacred tent.
⸋**10.10 They:** Or "The LORD".
⸋**11.2 Lake Galilee:** The Hebrew text has "Lake Chinnereth", an earlier name.
⸋**11.4–5 Pond:** Or "Gorge".
⸋**11.6 When . . . over:** Or "After the battle is over, cripple their horses and burn their chariots."
⸋**11.8–9 and crippled the enemies' horses:** It is also possible that the Israelites crippled the enemies' horses after the battle at the same time they burnt the enemies' chariots; see the note at 11.6.
⸋**11.8–9 Misrephoth-Maim . . . north-west:** Or "the town of Misrephoth to the north-west" or "the River Misrephoth".
⸋**12.3 Lake Galilee:** See the note at 11.2.
⸋**12.3 the town called Slopes of Mount Pisgah:** Or "the slopes of Mount Pisgah".
⸋**12.9–24 Aphek, Lasharon:** Or "Aphek in the Sharon Plain".
⸋**12.9–24 Galilee:** One ancient translation; Hebrew "Gilgal".
⸋**12.9–24 Jericho . . . Tirzah:** There are some differences in this list between the Hebrew and several ancient translations.

›**13.2–7 Amorite border:** What had been the southern border of the old Amorite kingdom of Amurru.

›**13.2–7 Hamath Pass:** Or "Lebo-Hamath".

›**13.2–7 Misrephoth-Maim:** Or "Misrephoth" or "the River Misrephoth".

›**13.2–7 Gebalites:** Gebal was another name for Byblos.

›**13.2–7 from . . . Sea:** One ancient translation; the Hebrew text does not have these words.

›**13.11–12 Sihon . . . people:** Or "the Rephaim".

›**13.26 Lidebor:** This may be another name for Lodebar, a town a few kilometres east of the River Jordan and about sixteen kilometres south of Lake Galilee.

›**13.27 Lake Galilee:** See the note at 11.2.

›**14.15 Arba's Town:** Or "Kiriath-Arba".

›**14.15 Arba's Town, because . . . greatest:** Hebrew; one ancient translation "Arba's Town. It was one of the main towns."

›**15.3 Scorpion Pass:** Or "Akrabbim Pass".

›**15.5 at . . . Dead Sea:** One possible meaning for the difficult Hebrew text.

›**15.6 Monument of Bohan:** Or "Bohan Rock", possibly a natural rock formation.

›**15.7 Trouble Valley:** See the note at 7.24.

›**15.9 ruins:** Hebrew; one ancient translation "towns".

›**15.10 Beth-Shemesh:** Probably the same town as the Ir-Shemesh of 19.41–46. Two other towns were also named Beth-Shemesh (see 19.17–23 and 19.35–39).

›**15.13 Arba's Town:** See the note at 14.15.

›**15.14 clans of:** Or "warriors".

›**15.17 Caleb's nephew Othniel:** Hebrew "Othniel the son of Caleb's brother Kenaz".

›**15.18 Achsah . . . Othniel . . . he:** Hebrew; one manuscript of one ancient translation and two ancient translations of the parallel in Judges 1.14 "Othniel . . . Achsah . . . she".

›**15.18 getting down from:** One possible meaning for the difficult Hebrew text.

›**15.19 spring-fed ponds:** Or "wells".

›**15.19 small ponds . . . Pond . . . Pond:** Or "wells . . . Well . . . Well".

›**15.21–32 Aradah:** One possible meaning for the difficult Hebrew text.

›**15.21–32 Hazor of Ithnan:** One ancient translation; Hebrew "Hazor and Ithnan".

›**15.21–32 its . . . villages:** One ancient translation; Hebrew "Biziothiah".

›**15.21–32 Enrimmon:** One ancient translation; Hebrew "Ain and Rimmon".

›**15.37–41 Lahmas:** Most Hebrew manuscripts; many other Hebrew manuscripts and one manuscript of one ancient translation "Lahmam".

›**15.48–51 Eshtemoh:** Another spelling for the name Eshtemoa (see 21.9–19).

›**15.52–54 Dumah:** Most Hebrew manuscripts; some Hebrew manuscripts and one ancient translation "Rumah".

›**15.55–57 Jokdeam:** Hebrew; one ancient translation "Jorkeam".

›**15.58–59 The tenth region . . . Manahath:** One ancient translation; the Hebrew text does not have these words.

›**16.1–4 it . . . then:** Or "which is also called Luz, it went".

›**17.1–6 the clans that were descendants of Zelophehad's five daughters . . . Hepher's brothers:** Or "Zelophehad's five daughters went to the priest Eleazar, Joshua, and the leaders of Israel. The five sisters said, 'The Lord told Moses to give us land just as he gave land to our relatives.' Joshua followed the Lord's instructions and gave land to these five sisters, as he had given land to Hepher's brothers."

›**17.7 to include . . . Tappuah Spring:** Hebrew; one ancient translation "to Jassiben-Tappuah" or "and turns towards Tappuah Spring".

›**17.11 Dor . . . Naphath:** One possible meaning for the difficult Hebrew text.

›**18.1 sacred tent:** Or "meeting tent".

›**18.13–14 Ataroth-Orech:** One ancient translation; Hebrew "Ataroth-Addar".

›**18.15 the ruins:** One possible meaning for the difficult Hebrew text.

›**18.16 Jerusalem:** Hebrew "the Jebusite town."

›**18.17 Geliloth:** Probably another name for Gilgal.

›**18.17 Monument of Bohan:** See the note at 15.6.

›**18.18 hillside north of Beth-Arabah:** One ancient translation (see also the border description in 15.6); Hebrew "the northern hillside overlooking the Jordan Valley".

›**18.19 northern . . . Dead Sea:** One possible meaning for the difficult Hebrew text.

›**18.25–28 Kiriath-Jearim:** One ancient translation; Hebrew "Kiriath".

›**19.2–6 Shema:** One ancient translation and some manuscripts of another ancient translation (see also the list at 15.21–32); Hebrew and some manuscripts of one ancient translation "Sheba". The list in 1 Chronicles 4.28 does not have either "Shema" or "Sheba".

›**19.7 Enrimmon:** Some Hebrew manuscripts and one ancient translation; most Hebrew manuscripts "Ain, Rimmon".

›**19.7 Tachan:** Some manuscripts of one ancient translation; the Hebrew text does not have this word.

›**19.13 Rimmonah:** Or "Rimmon".

›**19.13 Rimmonah . . . curved:** One possible meaning for the difficult Hebrew text.

›**19.15 Jiralah:** Some Hebrew manuscripts and two ancient translations; most Hebrew manuscripts "Idalah".

›**19.17–23 Debirath:** One ancient translation; Hebrew "Rabbith". Debirath is probably the same place as Daberath in verse 12.

›**19.17–23 Mount Tabor . . . Tabor:** In Hebrew the name "Tabor" is used only once. It was probably intended as the name of a town at the foot of Mount Tabor and which formed one point on the northern border of Issachar.

›**19.28 Abdon:** A few Hebrew manuscripts and one ancient translation; most Hebrew manuscripts "Ebron".

'19.29–31 **Mahalab:** One possible meaning for the difficult Hebrew text.

'19.29–31 **Acco:** One ancient translation; Hebrew "Ummah".

'19.32–34 **the town . . . Zaanannim:** Or "the oak tree in the town of Zaanannim".

'19.32–34 **at . . . Jehudah:** One possible meaning for the difficult Hebrew text.

'19.40–46 **Azor:** Some manuscripts of one ancient translation; the Hebrew text does not have this word.

'19.40–46 **Gath-Rimmon, Mejarkon, and Rakkon. Dan's tribal land:** Or "Gath-Rimmon, and Rakkon. Dan's tribal land also included the River Yarkon and".

'19.49–51 **sacred tent:** See the note at 18.1.

'21.4 **The descendants . . . priest:** Hebrew text; three ancient translations "The priests, the descendants of Aaron". The male descendants of Aaron would also be priests.

'21.9–19 **Ashan:** One ancient translation and the parallel in 1 Chronicles 6.59; Hebrew "Ain".

'21.9–19 **Arba's Town:** See the note at 14.15.

'21.20–26 **Jibleam:** One ancient translation and the parallel in 1 Chronicles 6.70; Hebrew "Gath-Rimmon".

'21.34–40 **Rimmonah:** One possible meaning for the difficult Hebrew text.

'21.34–40 **Bezer . . . Jericho:** One possible meaning for the difficult Hebrew text.

'21.34–40 **Bezer and Ramoth in Gilead were Safe Towns:** One ancient translation; Hebrew "Ramoth in Gilead was a Safe Town".

'22.10–11 **western . . . valley:** Or "the town of Geliloth, which is in the land of Canaan near the River Jordan".

'22.17 **we still . . . sin:** Or "There are still people in Israel who want to worship other gods."

'22.19 **or against . . . altar:** Or "by building another altar besides the LORD's own altar. That would even make us into rebels along with you."

'22.34 **named . . . God:** Or "gave a name to the altar. They explained, 'This altar is here to remind us all that the LORD is our God' "; most Hebrew manuscripts. A few Hebrew manuscripts and one ancient translation "named the altar 'Reminder'. They explained, 'This altar is here to remind us all that the LORD is our God.' "

'23.6 **Law:** See the note at 1.6–8.

'24.1 **near . . . tent:** Or "in front of the sacred chest"; Hebrew "in the presence of God".

'24.9 **King Balak . . . Balaam:** The Hebrew text has "King Balak the son of Zippor . . . Balaam the son of Beor".

'24.26 **Law:** See the note at 1.6–8.

'24.32 **pieces of silver:** One possible meaning for the difficult Hebrew word.

'24.32 **town . . . both:** One possible meaning for the difficult Hebrew text.

'24.33 **Eleazar the priest:** Hebrew "Eleazar the son of Aaron".

Judges

The basics

What's the point? A society without rules is not freedom, but anarchy.

What happens? God sends a series of judges to rescue his people history of the violent early – even though they are disobedient.

What should I remember? 17.6 'This was before kings ruled Israel, so all the Israelites did whatever they thought was right.'

More detail

Setting the scene The Israelites have conquered the land. But, offered the choice of following God, or following the gods of Canaan, they choose to follow the false gods...

What's it all about? The book takes its name from 2.16, 'From time to time, the LORD would choose special leaders known as judges...' These judges were not only war-leaders, they also decided legal cases and in some cases performed religious rituals.

They were needed, because the country was so violent. Judges starts with a captured king having his thumbs and big toes cut off (1.6–7) and goes downhill from there. It's more like a horror movie than a holy book!

Judges is about a society that abandons God. Events follow the same pattern: the people turn away from God; God sends a foreign nation to punish them; the people cry out to God for help; God sends a 'judge' to help them. Then the people turn away again...

It's not all despair. There are heroes like Samson, Deborah and Gideon. Many of these heroes, like the people around them, fall away from God, but then again, Judges is not only about the faithlessness of the people, it's also about the faithfulness of God.

Footsteps

Israel captures only part of the land

CHAPTER 1

The tribes of Judah and Simeon fight the Canaanites

1 After the death of Joshua, the Israelites asked the LORD, "Which of our tribes should attack the Canaanites first?"

2 "Judah!" the LORD answered. "I'll help them take the land."

3 The people of Judah went to their relatives, the Simeon tribe, and said, "Canaanites live in the land God gave us. Help us fight them, and we will help you."

Troops from Simeon came to help Judah. 4-5 Together they attacked an army of ten thousand Canaanites and Perizzites at Bezek, and the LORD helped Judah defeat them. During the battle, Judah's army found out where the king of Bezek' was, and they attacked there. 6 Bezek tried to escape, but soldiers from Judah caught him. They cut off his thumbs and big toes, 7 and he said, "I've cut off the thumbs and big toes of seventy kings and made those kings crawl around under my table for scraps of food. Now God is paying me back."

The army of Judah took the king of Bezek along with them to Jerusalem, where he died.

Holy history

Other nations

Midianites

Nomads and travellers who lived in the desert regions. According to Genesis, they were descended from Midian, the son of Abraham by his wife Keturah.

Moses went to Midian after fleeing from Egypt. He worked for Jethro, who was a Midianite priest, and married Zipporah, one of his daughters (Exodus 2). It was while working for Jethro that Moses met God in the shape of a burning bush. Jethro might have been friendly, but he was an exception. Finally, after much conflict, Gideon defeated the Midianites (Judges 6).

Arameans or Syrians

Neighbours of Israel to the northeast. Genesis says that the nation was descended from Aram, the son of Shem. The Arameans were a confederation of small, independent city states like Damascus, which attacked Israel frequently during the time of the kings (1 Kings 20). The Arameans were finally destroyed by the Assyrians.

Edomites

Next door neighbours of the Israelites, living south of Moab. They were the descendants of Esau, hard, tough people who lived in a hard, tough, mountainous land. They frequently fought against Israel, and, although they were conquered and almost wiped out by David, they remained brutal and fierce opponents. They defeated Judah during the reign of Ahaz (2 Chronicles 28.17) but they were then conquered by the Assyrians and the Babylonians.

Moabites

The Moabites descended from Moab, the son of Lot, who had had sex with his oldest daughter (Genesis 19.30–38). This is not what you'd call a promising start, but they became a large nation, living to the east of Israel, beyond the Dead Sea. Israel and Moab were often at war and seem to have hated each other. There were exceptions, however, and one of the important facts about Ruth is that she was a Moabitess who became David's great-grandmother (Ruth 4.17). They were eventually destroyed by the Babylonians.

Hittites

The Hittites came from Asia Minor (modern day Turkey) and invaded northern Syria and Lebanon, where they established a series of small city states. Solomon had Hittite wives (1 Kings 11.1) and David had an affair, and later married Bathsheba, wife of Uriah the Hittite (2 Samuel 11), who was a general in David's army. Eventually the Hittites were absorbed by the Assyrians and Babylonians.

Phoenicians

The Phoenicians lived along the coast, to the north of Israel. They called themselves Canaanites and their language was very close to Old Testament Hebrew. They were sea-traders who travelled throughout the Mediterranean as far as Spain. They traded in wood, pottery and in purple cloth – in fact the name 'Phoenician' comes from the Greek word meaning purple dye.

The Israelites generally had good relations with the Phoenicians. There was even a colony of Phoenician merchants living just outside Jerusalem (Zephaniah 1.11). One Phoenician king, Hiram of Tyre, supplied a huge amount of materials and craftsmanship for the temple (1 Kings 5).

However, the Phoenicians also sent Israel their gods, Baal and his female partner Astarte. The notorious Queen Jezebel, was a Phoenician princess and she was an enthusiastic evangelist for these gods, much to the disgust of prophets like Elijah.

More...

Foreign gods p.262
Canaanites p.241

8 They attacked Jerusalem,* captured it, killed everyone who lived there, and then burnt it to the ground.

9 Judah's army fought the Canaanites who lived in the hill country, the Southern Desert, and the foothills to the west. 10 After that, they attacked the Canaanites who lived at Hebron, defeating the three clans called꞊ Sheshai, Ahiman, and Talmai. At that time, Hebron was called Kiriath-Arba.

11 From Hebron, Judah's army went to attack Debir, which at that time was called Kiriath-Sepher. 12 Caleb* told his troops, "The man who captures Kiriath-Sepher can marry my daughter Achsah."

13 Caleb's nephew Othniel captured Kiriath-Sepher, so Caleb let him marry Achsah. Othniel was the son of Caleb's younger brother Kenaz.꞊ 14 Straight after the wedding, Achsah started telling Othniel that he꞊ ought to ask her father for a field. She went to see her father, and while she was getting down from꞊ her donkey, Caleb asked, "What's bothering you?"

15 She answered, "I need your help. The land you gave me is in the Southern Desert, so please give me some spring-fed ponds for a water supply."

Caleb gave her a couple of small ponds named Higher Pond and Lower Pond.꞊

16 The people who belonged to the Kenite clan were the descendants of the father-in-law of Moses. They left Jericho꞊ with the people of Judah and settled near Arad in the Southern Desert of Judah not far from the Amalekites.꞊

17 Judah's army helped Simeon's army attack the Canaanites who lived at Zephath. They completely destroyed* the town and renamed it Hormah.*

18-19 The LORD helped the army of Judah capture Gaza, Ashkelon, Ekron, and the land near those towns. They also took the hill country. But the people who lived in the valleys had iron chariots, so Judah was not able to make them leave or to take their land.

20 The tribe of Judah gave the town of Hebron to Caleb, as Moses had told them to do. Caleb defeated the three Anakim* clans꞊ and took over the town.

The Benjamin tribe does not capture Jerusalem

21 The Jebusites were living in Jerusalem, and the Benjamin tribe did not defeat them or capture the town. That's why Jebusites still live in Jerusalem along with the people of Benjamin.

The Ephraim and Manasseh tribes capture Bethel

22-23 The Ephraim and Manasseh tribes* were getting ready to attack Bethel, which at that time was called Luz. And the LORD helped them when they sent spies to find out as much as they could about Bethel. 24 While the spies were watching the town, a man came out, and they told him, "If you show us how our army can get into the town,* we will make sure that you aren't harmed." 25 The man showed them, and the two Israelite tribes attacked Bethel, killing everyone except the man and his family. The two tribes made the man and his family leave, 26 so they went to the land of the Hittites,* where he built a town. He named the town Luz, and that is still its name.

Israel does not get rid of all the Canaanites

27-28 Canaanites lived in the towns of Beth-Shan, Taanach, Dor, Ibleam, Megiddo, and all the villages nearby. The Canaanites were determined to stay, and the Manasseh

---

*1.8 Jerusalem: This probably refers to towns and villages belonging to Jerusalem but lying in Judah's territory south of the city wall. Jerusalem itself was just inside Benjamin's territory, but was not captured by Israel at this time (see verse 21; Joshua 15.5–9; 18.15–18).

*1.12 Caleb: One of the leaders of Judah; see Joshua 14.6–14 and Numbers 13.6,30; 14.6,10,20–24. For verses 12–15, see Joshua 15.13–19.

*1.17 completely destroyed: The Hebrew word means that the town was given completely to the LORD, and since it could not be used for normal purposes any more, it had to be destroyed.

*1.17 Hormah: In Hebrew "Hormah" sounds like "completely destroyed".

*1.20 Anakim: Perhaps a group of people of great stature that lived in Palestine before the Israelites (see Numbers 13.33 and Deuteronomy 2.10–11,20–21).

*1.22–23 The Ephraim and Manasseh tribes: The Hebrew text has "The Joseph family", which was divided into these two tribes named after Joseph's sons.

*1.24 If you . . . town: Sometimes there were small doors in the town wall that could be opened from the inside even when the main town gates were shut and locked.

*1.26 land of the Hittites: The Hittites had an empire centred in what is now Turkey. At one time their empire reached south into Syria, north of Israel.

See also: 1.20: Josh 15.13–14. 1.21: Josh 15.63; 2 Sam 5.6; 1 Chron 11.4. 1.27–28: Josh 17.11–13.

tribe never did get rid of them. But later on, when the Israelites grew more powerful, they made slaves of the Canaanites.

²⁹ The Ephraim tribe did not get rid of the Canaanites who lived in Gezer, so the Canaanites lived there with Israelites all around them.

³⁰ The Zebulun tribe did not get rid of the Canaanites who lived in Kitron and Nahalol, and the Canaanites stayed there with Israelites around them. But the people of Zebulun did force the Canaanites into slave labour.

³¹⁻³² The Asher tribe did not get rid of the Canaanites who lived in Acco, Sidon, Ahlab, Achzib, Helbah, Aphik, and Rehob, and the Asher tribe lived with Canaanites all around them.

³³ The Naphtali tribe did not get rid of the Canaanites who lived in Beth-Shemesh and Beth-Anath, but they did force the Canaanites into slave labour. The Naphtali tribe lived with Canaanites around them.

³⁴ The Amorites* were strong enough to keep the tribe of Dan from settling in the valleys, so Dan had to stay in the hill country.

³⁵ The Amorites on Mount Heres and in Aijalon and Shaalbim were also determined to stay. Later on, as Ephraim and Manasseh grew more powerful, they forced those Amorites into slave labour.

The Amorite-Edomite border

³⁶ The old Amorite-Edomite border used to go from Sela through Scorpion Pass▸ into the hill country.▸

The Lord chooses judges for Israel

CHAPTER 2

The Lord's angel speaks to Israel

¹ The Lord's angel went from Gilgal to Bochim* and gave the Israelites this message from the Lord:

I promised your ancestors that I would give this land to their families, and I brought your people here from Egypt. We made an agreement that I promised never to break, ² and you promised not to make any peace

treaties with the other nations that live in the land. Besides that, you agreed to tear down the altars where they sacrifice to their idols. But you didn't keep your promise.

³ And so, I'll stop helping you defeat your enemies. Instead, they will be there to trap▸ you into worshipping their idols.

⁴ The Israelites started crying loudly, ⁵ and they offered sacrifices to the Lord. From then on, they called that place "Crying".*

Israel stops worshipping the Lord

⁶⁻⁹ Joshua had been faithful to the Lord. And after Joshua sent the Israelites to take the land they had been promised, they remained faithful to the Lord until Joshua died at the age of one hundred and ten. He was buried on his land in Timnath-Heres, in the hill country of Ephraim north of Mount Gaash. Even though Joshua was gone, the Israelites were faithful to the Lord during the lifetime of those men who had been leaders with Joshua and who had seen the wonderful things the Lord had done for Israel.

¹⁰ After a while the people of Joshua's generation died, and the next generation did not know the Lord or any of the things he had done for Israel. ¹¹⁻¹³ The Lord had brought their ancestors out of Egypt, and they had worshipped him. But now the Israelites stopped worshipping the Lord and worshipped the idols of Baal and Astarte, as well as the idols of other gods from nearby nations.

The Lord was so angry ¹⁴⁻¹⁵ with the Israelites that he let other nations raid Israel and steal their crops and other possessions. Enemies were everywhere, and the Lord always let them defeat Israel in battle. The Lord had warned Israel he would do this, and now the Israelites were miserable.

The Lord chooses leaders for Israel

¹⁶ From time to time, the Lord would choose special leaders known as judges.* These judges would lead the Israelites into battle and defeat the enemies that made raids on them. ¹⁷ In years gone by, the Israelites had been faithful to the Lord, but now they were quick to be unfaithful and to refuse even to

---

1.34 Amorites: Used in the general sense of nations that lived in Canaan before the Israelites.
2.1 Bochim: In Hebrew "Bochim" means "crying" (see verse 5).
See also: 1.29: Josh 16.10. 2.2: Exod 34.12–13; Deut 7.2–5.

2.5 Crying: Or "Bochim".
2.16 special leaders known as judges: The Hebrew text has "judges". In addition to leading Israelites in battle, these special leaders also decided legal cases and sometimes performed religious duties.
See also: 2.9: Josh 19.49–50.

listen to these judges. The Israelites would disobey the LORD, and instead of worshipping him, they would worship other gods.

¹⁸ When enemies made life miserable for the Israelites, the LORD would feel sorry for them. He would choose a judge and help that judge rescue Israel from its enemies. The LORD would be kind to Israel as long as that judge lived. ¹⁹ But afterwards, the Israelites would become even more sinful than their ancestors had been. The Israelites were stubborn — they simply would not stop worshipping other gods or following the teachings of other religions.

The LORD lets enemies test Israel

²⁰ The LORD was angry with Israel and said:

The Israelites have broken the agreement I made with their ancestors. They won't obey me, ²¹ so I'll stop helping them defeat their enemies. Israel still had a lot of enemies when Joshua died, ²² and I'm going to let those enemies stay. I'll use them to test Israel, because then I can find out if Israel will worship and obey me as their ancestors did.

²³ That's why the LORD had not let Joshua get rid of all those enemy nations straight away.

CHAPTER 3

¹⁻² And the LORD had another reason for letting these enemies stay. The Israelites needed to learn how to fight in war, just as their ancestors had done. Each new generation would have to learn by fighting ³ the Philistines and their five rulers, as well as the Canaanites, the Sidonians, and the Hivites who lived in the Lebanon Mountains from Mount Baal-Hermon to Hamath Pass.ʼ

⁴ Moses had told the Israelites what the LORD had commanded them to do, and now the LORD was using these nations to find out if Israel would obey. ⁵⁻⁶ But they refused. And it was because of the Canaanites, Hittites, Amorites, Perizzites, Hivites, and Jebusites who lived all around them. Some of the Israelites married the people of these nations, and that's how they started worshipping foreign gods.

Othniel, Ehud, and Shamgar

Othniel

⁷ The Israelites sinned against the LORD by forgetting him and worshipping idols of Baal

Holy history

Foreign gods

One of the most dangerous and serious failings of the people of Israel was their addiction to foreign gods. Often this was because their leaders – the kings and priests – became followers of different gods and they passed this religion onto the people. However, it has to be said that the people didn't seem to object. These gods were mainly 'imported' from the nations surrounding Israel. Gods were often linked to specific topics: you might have a sun god for heat, a storm god for rain, nature gods to provide crops and plants; fertility gods to help with having babies.

In the Bible probably the best known of these gods is Baal. (The name actually means 'lord'.) Baal was a Canaanite god who was responsible for storms and nature. He was supposed to bring rain to make the crops grow. Which is why Elijah challenged the priests of Baal to a rain-making contest – he wanted to show how useless Baal was. There was also Asherah, a female deity who was probably some kind of fertility goddess. The Canaanites set up many 'Asherah poles', which were local shrines.

The worship of foreign gods was often repulsive. Some gods demanded human sacrifices. Many shrines had male and female prostitutes who would have sex with the followers and give the money to the shrine priests.

Who you worshipped was important, so important, that, in the Bible, kings are ranked not according to their wealth or military prowess, but according to whether or not they stayed faithful to the one true God.

More...

The golden calf p.191
Other nations p.259
All the kings of Israel p.419
All the kings of Judah p.434

and Astarte. 8 This made the LORD angry, so
he let Israel be defeated by King Cushan
Rishathaim of northern Syria,' who ruled
Israel eight years and made everyone pay
taxes. 9 The Israelites begged the LORD for
help, and he chose Othniel to rescue them.
Othniel was the son of Caleb's younger
brother Kenaz.' 10 The Spirit of the LORD took
control of Othniel, and he led Israel in a war
against Cushan Rishathaim. The LORD gave
Othniel victory, 11 and Israel was at peace
until Othniel died about forty years later.

Ehud

12 Once more the Israelites started disobeying
the LORD. So he let them be defeated by King
Eglon of Moab, 13 who had joined forces with
the Ammonites and the Amalekites to attack
Israel. Eglon and his army captured Jericho.'
14 Then he ruled Israel for eighteen years and
forced the Israelites to pay heavy taxes.

15-16 The Israelites begged the LORD for help,
and the LORD chose Ehud' from the Benjamin
tribe to rescue them. They put Ehud in charge
of taking the taxes to King Eglon, but before
Ehud went, he made a double-edged dagger.
Ehud was left-handed, so he strapped the
dagger to his right thigh, where it would be
hidden under his robes.

17-18 Ehud and some other Israelites took
the taxes to Eglon, who was a very fat man. As
soon as they gave the taxes to Eglon, Ehud
said it was time to go home.

19-20 Ehud went with the other Israelites as
far as the statues* at Gilgal.* Then he turned
back and went upstairs to the cool room*
where Eglon had his throne. Ehud said, "Your
Majesty, I need to talk with you in private."

Eglon replied, "Don't say anything yet!"
His officials left the room, and Eglon stood
up as Ehud came closer.

"Yes," Ehud said, "I have a message for you
from God!" 21 Ehud pulled out the dagger
with his left hand and shoved it so far into
Eglon's stomach 22-23 that even the handle
was buried in his fat. Ehud left the dagger
there. Then after closing and locking the
doors to the room, he climbed through a
window on to the porch' 24 and left.

When the king's officials came back and
saw that the doors were locked, they said,
"The king is probably inside relieving
himself." 25 They stood there waiting until
they felt foolish, but Eglon never opened the
doors. Finally, they unlocked the doors and
found King Eglon lying dead on the floor.
26 But by that time, Ehud had already escaped
past the statues.*

Ehud went to the town of Seirah 27-28 in the
hill country of Ephraim and started blowing a
signal on a trumpet. The Israelites came
together, and he shouted, "Follow me! The
LORD will help us defeat the Moabites."

The Israelites followed Ehud down to the
Jordan Valley, and they captured the places
where people cross the river on the way to
Moab. They would not let anyone go across,
29 and before the fighting was over, they killed
about ten thousand Moabite warriors — not
one escaped alive.

30 Moab was so badly defeated that it was a
long time before they were strong enough to
attack Israel again. And Israel was at peace for
eighty years.

Shamgar

31 Shamgar the son of Anath was the next to
rescue Israel. In one battle, he used a sharp
wooden pole* to kill six hundred Philistines.

Deborah, Barak, and Jael

CHAPTER 4

Deborah and Barak

1 After the death of Ehud, the Israelites again
started disobeying the LORD. 2 So the LORD let
the Canaanite King Jabin of Hazor conquer
Israel. Sisera, the commander of Jabin's army,
lived in Harosheth-Ha-Goiim. 3 Jabin's army
had nine hundred iron chariots, and for
twenty years he made life miserable for the
Israelites, until finally they begged the LORD
for help.

4 Deborah the wife of Lappidoth was a
prophet and a leader* of Israel during those
days. 5 She would sit under Deborah's Palm
Tree between Ramah and Bethel in the hill
country of Ephraim, where Israelites would
come and ask her to settle their legal cases.

*3.19–20 statues: Or "stone idols" or "stone
monuments".
*3.19–20 Gilgal: About two and a half kilometres from
Jericho, where Eglon probably was (see verse 13).
*3.19–20 upstairs . . . cool room: Houses usually had
flat roofs, and sometimes a room was built on one
corner of the roof where it could best catch the
breeze and be kept cooler than the rest of the house.

*3.26 statues: See the note at 3.19–20.
*3.31 sharp wooden pole: The Hebrew text has
"cattle-prod", a pole with a sharpened tip or metal
point at one end.
*4.4 leader: See 2.16 and the note there.

⁶ One day, Barak the son of Abinoam was in Kedesh in Naphtali, and Deborah sent word for him to come and talk with her. When he arrived, she said:

I have a message for you from the LORD God of Israel! You are to get together an army of ten thousand men from the Naphtali and Zebulun tribes and lead them to Mount Tabor. ⁷ The LORD will trick Sisera into coming out to fight you at the River Kishon. Sisera will be leading King Jabin's army as usual, and they will have their chariots, but the LORD has promised to help you defeat them.

⁸ "I'm not going unless you go!" Barak told her.

⁹ "All right, I'll go!" she replied. "But I'm warning you that the LORD is going to let a woman defeat Sisera, and no one will honour you for winning the battle."

Deborah and Barak left for Kedesh, ¹⁰ where Barak called together the troops from Zebulun and Naphtali. Ten thousand soldiers gathered there, and Barak led them out from Kedesh. Deborah went too.

¹¹ At this time, Heber of the Kenite clan was living near the village of Oak in Zaanannim, not far from Kedesh. The Kenites were descendants of Hobab, the father-in-law of Moses, but Heber had moved and had set up his tents away from the rest of the clan.

¹² When Sisera learnt that Barak had led an army to Mount Tabor, ¹³ he called his troops together and got all nine hundred iron chariots ready. Then he led his army away from Harosheth-Ha-Goiim to the River Kishon.

¹⁴ Deborah shouted, "Barak, it's time to attack Sisera! Because today the LORD is going to help you defeat him. In fact, the LORD has already gone on ahead to fight for you."

Barak led his ten thousand troops down from Mount Tabor. ¹⁵ And during the battle, the LORD confused Sisera, his chariot drivers, and his whole army. Everyone was so afraid of Barak and his army, that even Sisera jumped down from his chariot and tried to escape.
¹⁶ Barak's forces went after Sisera's chariots and army as far as Harosheth-Ha-Goiim.

Sisera's entire army was wiped out. ¹⁷ Only Sisera escaped. He ran to Heber's camp, because Heber and his family had a peace treaty with the king of Hazor. Sisera went to the tent that belonged to Jael, Heber's wife. ¹⁸ She came out to greet him and said, "Come in, sir! Please come on in. Don't be afraid."

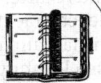

Life files

Deborah

Background: Wife of Lappidoth

What's the story?

Deborah is a prophet, wise woman and leader in Israel. Her 'office' was under a palm tree, and there she would settle disputes and dispense her advice.

One day, Barak comes to see her and she tells him that he is to raise an army and fight against the invaders. He insists that Deborah accompany him, which she does, although this lack of faith means that Barak does not get the full honour. Sisera is defeated – partly because his army gets bogged down in a flood – and Deborah sings a famous song.

What's the point?

In one way Deborah was a traditional judge: she gave out advice and sorted out disputes. But she was also a powerful prophet and when Barak comes calling on her she gives him a command from the LORD.

 Anorak corner

Deborah's song – a powerful, moving description of the battle – is probably one of the oldest passages in the Bible.

 Footsteps

Two days with Deborah

Deborah calls Barak: Judges 4.1–24
Deborah's song: Judges 5.1–31

More...

Other nations p.259
Destruction p.236
Arms and warfare p.309
Prophecy p.730

After they had gone inside, Sisera lay down, and Jael covered him with a blanket.
19 "Could I have a little water?" he asked. "I'm thirsty."

Jael opened a leather bottle and poured him some milk, then she covered him up again.

20 "Stand at the entrance to the tent," Sisera told her. "If someone comes by and asks if anyone is inside, tell them 'No.' "

21 Sisera was exhausted and soon fell fast asleep. Jael took a hammer and drove a tent-peg through his head into the ground, and he died.

22 Meanwhile, Barak had been following Sisera, and Jael went out to meet him. "The man you're looking for is inside," she said. "Come in and I'll show him to you."

They went inside, and there was Sisera — dead and stretched out with a tent-peg through his skull.

23 That same day the Israelites defeated the Canaanite King Jabin, and his army was no longer powerful enough to attack the Israelites. 24 Jabin grew weaker while the Israelites kept growing stronger, and at last the Israelites destroyed him.

CHAPTER 5

Deborah and Barak sing for the LORD

1 After the battle was over that day, Deborah and Barak sang this song:

2 We praise you, LORD!
Our soldiers volunteered,
ready to follow you.
3 Listen, kings and rulers,
while I sing for the LORD,
the God of Israel.

4-5 Our LORD, God of Israel,
when you came from Seir,
where the Edomites live,
rain poured from the sky,
the earth trembled,
and mountains shook.

6 In the time of Shamgar son of Anath,
and now again in Jael's time,
roads were too dangerous
for caravans.
Travellers had to take the back roads,
7 and villagers couldn't work
in their fields.'
Then Deborah' took command,
protecting Israel as a mother
protects her children.

8 The Israelites worshipped other gods,
and the gates of their towns
were then attacked.'
But they had no shields
or spears to fight with.
9 I praise you, LORD,
and I am grateful
for those leaders and soldiers
who volunteered.
10 Listen, everyone!
Whether you ride a donkey
with a padded saddle
or have to walk.
11 Even those who carry water'
to the animals will tell you,
"The LORD has won victories,
and so has Israel."

Then the LORD's people marched
down to the town gates
12 and said, "Deborah, let's go!
Let's sing as we march.
Barak, capture our enemies."

13 The LORD's people who were left
joined with their leaders
and fought at my side.'
14 Troops came from Ephraim,
where Amalekites once lived.
Others came from Benjamin;
officers and leaders came
from Machir and Zebulun.
15 The rulers of Issachar
came along with Deborah,
and Issachar followed Barak
into the valley.

But the tribe of Reuben
was no help at all!'
16 Reuben, why did you stay
among your sheep pens?'
Was it to listen to shepherds
whistling for their sheep?
No one could understand
why Reuben wouldn't come.'
17 The people of Gilead stayed
across the Jordan.
Why did the tribe of Dan
remain on their ships
and the tribe of Asher
stay along the coast
near the harbours?

18 But soldiers of Zebulun and Naphtali
risked their lives
to attack the enemy.'
19 Canaanite kings fought us
at Taanach by the stream
near Megiddo' —

See also: 5.4–5: Exod 19.18.

but they couldn't rob us of our silver.*

20 From their pathways in the sky
   the stars* fought Sisera,
21 and his soldiers were swept away
   by the ancient River Kishon.

I will march on and be brave.

22 Sisera's horses galloped off,
   their hoofs thundering in retreat.

23 The LORD's angel said,
   "Put a curse on Meroz Town!
   Its people refused
   to help the LORD fight
   his powerful enemies."

24 But honour Jael, the wife of Heber
   from the Kenite clan.
   Give more honour to her
   than to any other woman
   who lives in tents.
   Yes, give more honour to her
   than to any other woman.
25 Sisera asked for water,
   but Jael gave him milk —
   cream in a fine cup.
26 She reached for a tent-peg
   and held a hammer
   in her right hand.
   And with a blow to the head,
   she crushed his skull.
27 Sisera sank to his knees
   and fell dead at her feet.

28 Sisera's mother looked out
   through her window.
   "Why is he taking so long?"
   she asked.
   "Why haven't we heard
   his chariots coming?"
29 She and her wisest women
   gave the same answer:
30 "Sisera and his troops
   are finding treasures to bring back —
   a woman, or perhaps two,
   for each man,
   and beautiful dresses
   for those women to wear."

31 Our LORD, we pray
   that all your enemies
   will die like Sisera.
   But let everyone who loves you
   shine brightly like the sun at dawn.

---

*5.19 rob us of our silver: The army that won a
battle would take everything of value from the dead
enemy soldiers.
*5.20 stars: In ancient times, the stars were
sometimes regarded as supernatural beings.

Gideon

CHAPTER 6

Midian steals everything from Israel

There was peace in Israel for about forty years.
1 Then once again the Israelites started
disobeying the LORD, so he let the nation of
Midian control Israel for seven years. 2 The
Midianites were so cruel that many Israelites
ran to the mountains and hid in caves.

3 Every time the Israelites would plant crops,
the Midianites invaded Israel together with
the Amalekites and other eastern nations.
4-5 They rode in on their camels, set up their
tents, and then let their livestock eat the crops
as far as the town of Gaza. The Midianites stole
food, sheep, cattle, and donkeys. Like a swarm
of locusts,* they could not be counted, and
they ruined the land wherever they went.

6-7 The Midianites took almost everything
that belonged to the Israelites, and the
Israelites begged the LORD for help. 8-9 Then
the LORD sent a prophet to them with this
message:

I am the LORD God of Israel, so listen to
what I say. You were slaves in Egypt, but I
set you free and led you out of Egypt into
this land. And when nations here made life
miserable for you, I rescued you and
helped you get rid of them and take their
land. 10 I am your God, and I told you not
to worship Amorite gods, even though you
are living in the land of the Amorites. But
you refused to listen.

The LORD chooses Gideon

11 One day an angel from the LORD went to
the town of Ophrah and sat down under the
big tree that belonged to Joash, a member of
the Abiezer clan. Joash's son Gideon was
nearby, threshing grain in a shallow pit,
where he could not be seen by the Midianites.

12 The angel appeared and spoke to Gideon,
"The LORD is helping you, and you are a
strong warrior."

13 Gideon answered, "Please don't take this
wrong, but if the LORD is helping us, then why
have all these awful things happened? We've
heard how the LORD performed miracles and
rescued our ancestors from Egypt. But those
things happened long ago. Now the LORD has
abandoned us to the Midianites."

---

*6.4-5 locusts: Insects like grasshoppers that travel in
swarms and cause great damage to crops.

Life files

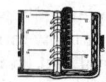

Gideon
(a.k.a. Jerubbaal, Judges 6.32)

Background: Son of Joash

What's the story?

The Israelites were oppressed by the Midianites. Gideon was called upon by an angel to rescue his people from oppression. He was reluctant at first and insisted on testing God's call. His first act was to pull down one of the altars of Baal. Then he led an army – which God deliberately kept down to only 300 men – to attack the Midianites. The Midianites were routed and Israel lived in peace.

Because of his success, Gideon was asked to become king, but he refused, believing that only the LORD should rule Israel. However, he took the gold that he had won home and made it into statues which he later worshipped.

What's the point?

Gideon is one of the greatest judges of Israel. A member of the poor tribe of Manasseh, he routs the enemy with only a small force and brings peace to the land.

However, he was never that sure of himself. It took several 'tests' for him to really believe that God would be with him. And at the end of his life, he starts worshipping statues – exactly the behaviour that got Israel in trouble in the first place! In some ways Gideon's story is like Israel's: when he believed and trusted God great things happened, but after that, he forgot about God and turned away. We should always be vigilant.

 Footsteps

Three days with Gideon

Gideon is called: Judges 6.1–32
The Midianites defeated: Judges 6.33—7.22
Gideon refuses to be king: Judges 8.22–35

More...

Other nations p.259
Foreign gods p.262
Canaanites p.241

---

[14] Then the LORD himself said, "Gideon, you will be strong, because I am giving you the power to rescue Israel from the Midianites."

[15] Gideon replied, "But how can I rescue Israel? My clan is the weakest one in Manasseh, and everyone else in my family is more important than I am."

[16] "Gideon," the LORD answered, "you can rescue Israel because I am going to help you! Defeating the Midianites will be as easy as beating up one man."

[17] Gideon said, "It's hard to believe that I'm actually talking to the LORD. Please do something so I'll know that you really are the LORD. [18] And wait here until I bring you an offering."

"All right, I'll wait," the LORD answered.

[19] Gideon went home and killed a young goat, then started boiling the meat. Next, he opened a big sack of flour and made it into thin bread.* When the meat was done, he put it in a basket and poured the broth into a clay cooking pot. He took the meat, the broth, and the bread and placed them under the big tree.

[20] God's angel said, "Gideon, put the meat and the bread on this rock, and pour the broth over them." Gideon did as he was told. [21] The angel was holding a walking stick, and he touched the meat and the bread with the end of the stick. Flames jumped from the rock and burnt up the meat and the bread.

When Gideon looked, the angel was gone. [22] Gideon realized that he had seen one of the LORD's angels. "Oh!" he moaned. "Now I'm going to die."*

[23] "Calm down!" the LORD told Gideon. "There's nothing to be afraid of. You're not going to die."

[24] Gideon built an altar for worshipping the LORD and called it "The LORD Calms our Fears". It still stands there in Ophrah, a town in the territory of the Abiezer clan.

Gideon tears down Baal's altar

[25] That night the LORD spoke to Gideon again:

> Get your father's second-best bull, the one that's seven years old. Use it to pull down the altar where your father worships Baal

---

*6.19 thin bread: Bread made without yeast, since there was no time for the dough to rise.

*6.22 Now I'm going to die: The Hebrew text has "I have seen an angel of the LORD face to face." Some people believed that if they saw one of the LORD's angels, they would die (see 13.22).

and cut down the sacred pole* next to the altar. ²⁶ Then build an altar for worshipping me on the highest part of the hill where your town is built. Use layers of stones for my altar, not just a pile of rocks. Cut up the wood from the pole, make a fire, kill the bull, and burn it as a sacrifice to me.

²⁷ Gideon chose ten of his servants to help him, and they did everything God had said. But since Gideon was afraid of his family and the other people in town, he did it all at night. ²⁸ When the people of the town got up the next morning, they saw that Baal's altar had been knocked over, and the sacred pole next to it had been cut down. Then they noticed the new altar covered with the remains of the sacrificed bull.

²⁹ "Who could have done such a thing?" they asked. And they kept on asking, until finally someone told them, "Gideon the son of Joash did it."

³⁰ The men of the town went to Joash and said, "Your son Gideon knocked over Baal's altar and cut down the sacred pole next to it. Hand him over, so we can kill him!"

³¹ The crowd pushed closer and closer, but Joash replied, "Are you trying to take revenge for Baal? Are you trying to rescue Baal? If you are, you will be the ones who are put to death, and it will happen before another day dawns. If Baal really is a god, let him take his own revenge on someone who tears down his altar."

³² That same day, Joash changed Gideon's name to Jerubbaal, explaining, "He tore down Baal's altar, so let Baal take revenge himself."*

Gideon defeats the Midianites

³³ All the Midianites, Amalekites, and other eastern nations got together and crossed the River Jordan. Then they invaded the land of Israel and set up camp in Jezreel Valley. ³⁴ The LORD's Spirit took control of Gideon, and Gideon blew a signal on a trumpet to tell the men in the Abiezer clan to follow him. ³⁵ He also sent messengers to the tribes of Manasseh, Asher, Zebulun, and Naphtali, telling the men of these tribes to come and join his army. Then they set out towards the enemy camp.

³⁶⁻³⁷ Gideon prayed to God, "I know that you promised to help me rescue Israel, but I need proof. Tonight I'll put some wool on the stone floor of that threshing-place over there. If you really will help me rescue Israel, then tomorrow morning let there be dew on the wool, but let the stone floor be dry."

³⁸ And that's just what happened. Early the next morning, Gideon got up and checked the wool. He squeezed out enough water to fill a bowl. ³⁹ But Gideon prayed to God again. "Don't be angry with me," Gideon said. "Let me try this just one more time, so I'll really be sure you'll help me. Only this time, let the wool be dry and the stone floor be wet with dew."

⁴⁰ That night, God made the stone floor wet with dew, but he kept the wool dry.

CHAPTER 7

¹ Early the next morning, Gideon and his army got up and moved their camp to Fear Spring.ᵇ The Midianite camp was to the north, in the valley at the foot of Moreh Hill.*

² The LORD said, "Gideon, your army is too big. I can't let you win with this many soldiers. The Israelites would think that they had won the battle all by themselves and that I didn't have anything to do with it. ³ So call your troops together and tell them that anyone who is really afraid can leave Mount Gilead* and go home."

Twenty-two thousand men returned home, leaving Gideon with only ten thousand soldiers.

⁴ "Gideon," the LORD said, "you still have too many soldiers. Take them down to the spring and I'll test them. I'll tell you which ones can go along with you and which ones must go back home."

⁵ When Gideon led his army down to the spring, the LORD told him, "Watch how each man gets a drink of water. Then divide them into two groups — those who lap the water like a dog and those who kneel down to drink."

⁶ Three hundred men scooped up water in their hands and lapped it, and the rest knelt to get a drink. ⁷ The LORD said, "Gideon, your army will be made up of everyone who lapped the water from their hands. Send the others home. I'm going to rescue Israel by helping you and your army of three hundred defeat the Midianites."

6.25 sacred pole: Or "sacred tree", used as a symbol of Asherah, the Canaanite goddess of fertility.
6.32 Jerubbaal . . . take revenge himself: In Hebrew, "Jerubbaal" means "Let Baal take revenge".

7.1 Moreh Hill: About 8 kilometres north of Fear Spring.
7.3 Mount Gilead: Usually "Gilead" refers to an area east of the River Jordan, but in this verse it refers to a place near Jezreel Valley west of the Jordan.
See also: 7.3: Deut 20.8.

⁸ Then Gideon gave these orders, "You three hundred men stay here. The rest of you may go home, but leave your food and trumpets with us."

Gideon's army camp was on top of a hill overlooking the Midianite camp in the valley. ⁹ That night, the LORD said to Gideon. "Get up! Attack the Midianite camp. I am going to let you defeat them, ¹⁰ but if you're still afraid, you and your servant Purah should sneak down to their camp. ¹¹ When you hear what the Midianites are saying, you'll be brave enough to attack."

Gideon and Purah worked their way to the edge of the enemy camp, where soldiers were on guard duty. ¹² The camp was huge. The Midianites, Amalekites, and other eastern nations covered the valley like a swarm of locusts.* And it would be easier to count the grains of sand on a beach than to count their camels. ¹³ Gideon overheard one enemy guard telling another, "I had a dream about a flatᵇ loaf of barley bread that came tumbling into our camp. It hit the headquarters tent,ᵇ and the tent tipped over and fell down."

¹⁴ The other soldier answered, "Your dream must have been about Gideon, the Israelite commander. It means God will let him and his army defeat the Midianite army and everyone else in our camp."

¹⁵ As soon as Gideon heard about the dream and what it meant, he bowed down to praise God. Then he went back to the Israelite camp and shouted, "Let's go! The LORD is going to let us defeat the Midianite army."

¹⁶ Gideon divided his little army into three groups of one hundred men, and he gave each soldier a trumpet and a large clay jar with a burning torch inside. ¹⁷⁻¹⁸ Gideon said, "When we get to the enemy camp, spread out and surround it. Then wait for me to blow a signal on my trumpet. As soon as you hear it, blow your trumpets and shout, 'Fight for Gideon!' "

¹⁹ Gideon and his group reached the edge of the enemy camp a few hours after dark, just after the new guards had come on duty.* Gideon and his soldiers blew their trumpets

and smashed the clay jars that were hiding the torches. ²⁰ The rest of Gideon's soldiers blew the trumpets they were holding in their right hands. Then they smashed the jars and held the burning torches in their left hands. Everyone shouted, "Fight with your swords for the LORD and for Gideon!"

²¹ The enemy soldiers started yelling and tried to run away. Gideon's troops stayed in their positions surrounding the camp ²² and blew their trumpets again. As they did, the LORD made the enemy soldiers pull out their swords and start fighting each other.

The enemy army tried to escape from the camp. They ran to Acacia Tree Town, towards Zeredah,ᵇ and as far as the edge of the land that belonged to the town of Abel-Meholah near Tabbath.*

²³ Gideon sent word for more Israelite soldiers to come from the tribes of Naphtali, Asher, and both halves of Manasseh* to help fight the Midianites. ²⁴ He also sent messengers to tell all the men who lived in the hill country of Ephraim, "Come and help us fight the Midianites! Put guards at every spring, stream, and well, as far as Beth-Barah before the Midianites can get to them. And guard the River Jordan."

Troops from Ephraim did exactly what Gideon had asked, ²⁵ and they even helped chase the Midianites on the east side of the River Jordan. These troops captured Raven and Wolf,ᵇ the two Midianite leaders. They killed Raven at a large rock that has come to be known as Raven Rock, and they killed Wolf near a wine-pit that has come to be called Wolf Wine-pit.ᵇ

The men of Ephraim brought the heads of the two Midianite leaders to Gideon.

CHAPTER 8

¹ But the men were really upset with Gideon and complained, "When you went to war with Midian, you didn't ask us to help! Why did you treat us like that?"

² Gideon answered:

Don't be upset! Even though you came later, you were able to do much more than I did. It's just like the grape harvest: the grapes your tribe doesn't even bother to

---

*7.12 locusts: See the note at 6.4–5.
*7.19 a few hours after dark, just . . . duty: The Hebrew text has "at the beginning of the second watch, just . . . duty." The night was divided into three periods called "watches", each about four hours long, and different guards would come on duty at the beginning of each watch. The first watch began at sunset, so the beginning of the second watch would have been shortly after 10:00 PM.

*7.22 Acacia Tree Town . . . Zeredah . . . Abel-Meholah near Tabbath: These were places east of the River Jordan.
*7.23 both halves of Manasseh: Half of Manasseh lived east of the River Jordan, and the other half lived on the west.

pick are better than the best grapes my family can grow. ³ Besides, God chose you to capture Raven and Wolf. I didn't do a thing compared to you.

By the time Gideon had finished talking, the men of Ephraim had calmed down and were no longer angry with him.

Gideon finishes destroying the Midianite army

⁴ After Gideon and his three hundred troops had chased the Midianites as far as the River Jordan, they were exhausted. ⁵ The town of Succoth was nearby, so he went there and asked, "Please give my troops some food. They are worn out, but we have to keep chasing Zebah and Zalmunna, the two Midianite kings."

⁶ The town leaders of Succoth answered, "Why should we feed your army? We don't know if you really will defeat Zebah and Zalmunna."

⁷ "Just wait!" Gideon said. "After the LORD helps me defeat them, I'm coming back here. I'll make a whip out of thorns and rip the flesh from your bones."

⁸ After leaving Succoth, Gideon went to Penuel and asked the leaders there for some food. But he got the same answer as he had got at Succoth. ⁹ "I'll come back safe and sound," Gideon said, "but when I do, I'm going to tear down your tower!"*

¹⁰ Zebah and Zalmunna were in Karkor* with an army of fifteen thousand troops. They were all that was left of the army of the eastern nations, because one hundred and twenty thousand of their warriors had been killed in the battle.

¹¹ Gideon reached the enemy camp by going east along Nomad* Road past Nobah and Jogbehah. He made a surprise attack, ¹² and the enemy panicked. Zebah and Zalmunna tried to escape, but Gideon chased and captured them.

¹³ After the battle, Gideon set out for home. As he was going through Heres Pass, ¹⁴ he caught a young man who lived in Succoth. Gideon asked him who the town officials of Succoth were, and the young man wrote down seventy-seven names.

¹⁵ Gideon went to the town officials and said, "Here are Zebah and Zalmunna. Remember how you made fun of me? You said, 'We don't know if you really will defeat those two Midianite kings. So why should we feed your worn-out army?' "

¹⁶ Gideon made a whip from thorn plants and used it to beat the town officials. ¹⁷ Afterwards he went to Penuel, where he tore down the tower and killed all the town officials* there.

¹⁸ Then Gideon said, "Zebah and Zalmunna, tell me about the men you killed at Tabor."

"They were a lot like you," the two kings answered. "They were dignified, almost like royalty."

¹⁹ "They were my very own brothers!" Gideon said. "I swear by the living LORD that if you had let them live, I would let you live."

²⁰ Gideon turned to Jether, his eldest son. "Kill them!" Gideon said.

But Jether was young,* and he was too afraid even to pull out his sword.

²¹ "What's the matter, Gideon?" Zebah and Zalmunna asked. "Do it yourself, if you're not too much of a coward!"

Gideon jumped up and killed them both. Then he took the fine gold ornaments from the necks of their camels.

The Israelites ask Gideon to be their king

²² After the battle with the Midianites, the Israelites said, "Gideon, you rescued us! Now we want you to be our king. Then after your death, your son and then your grandson will rule."

²³ "No," Gideon replied, "I won't be your king, and my son won't be king either. Only the LORD is your ruler. ²⁴ But I will ask you to do one thing: give me all the earrings you took from the enemy."

The enemy soldiers had been Ishmaelites,* and they wore gold earrings.

²⁵ The Israelite soldiers replied, "Of course we will give you the earrings." Then they spread out a robe on the ground and tossed

---

*8.9 tower: Towers were often part of a town wall.
*8.10 Karkor: About 160 kilometres east of the Dead Sea.
*8.11 Nomad: A person who lives in a tent and moves from place to place.
See also: 8.3–5: Psa 83.11.

*8.20 young: Gideon wanted to insult the kings by having them killed by a young boy.
*8.24 Ishmaelites: According to Genesis 25.1–2,12, both Ishmaelites and Midianites were descendants of Abraham. It is possible that in this passage "Ishmaelites" has the meaning "nomadic traders", while "Midianites" (verses 22,26–29) refers to their ethnic origin.

the earrings on it. 26 The total weight of this gold was nearly twenty kilogrammes. In addition, there was the gold from the camels' ornaments and from the beautiful jewellery worn by the Midianite kings. Gideon also took their purple robes.

27-29 Gideon returned to his home in Ophrah and had the gold made into a statue, which the Israelites soon started worshipping. They became unfaithful to God, and even Gideon and his family were trapped into worshipping the statue.‣

The Midianites had been defeated so badly that they were no longer strong enough to attack Israel. And so Israel was at peace for the remaining forty years of Gideon's life.

Gideon dies

30 Gideon had many wives and seventy sons. 31 He even had a wife* who lived at Shechem.* They had a son, and Gideon named him Abimelech.

32 Gideon lived to be an old man. And when he died, he was buried in the family tomb in his home town of Ophrah, which belonged to the Abiezer clan.

33 Soon after Gideon's death, the Israelites turned their backs on God again. They set up idols of Baal and worshipped Baal Berith‣ as their god. 34 The Israelites forgot that the LORD was their God, and that he had rescued them from the enemies who lived around them. 35 Besides all that, the Israelites were unkind to Gideon's family, even though Gideon had done so much for Israel.

Abimelech

CHAPTER 9

Abimelech tries to be king

1 Abimelech the son of Gideon‣ went to Shechem. While there, he met with his mother's relatives 2 and told them to say to the leaders of Shechem, "Do you think it would be good to have all seventy of Gideon's sons ruling us? Wouldn't you rather have just one man as king? Abimelech would make a good king, and he's related to us."

3 Abimelech's uncles talked it over with the leaders of Shechem who agreed, "Yes, it would be better for one of our relatives to be king." 4 Then they gave Abimelech seventy pieces* of silver from the temple of their god Baal Berith.‣

Abimelech used the silver to hire a gang of rough soldiers who would do anything for money. 5 Abimelech and his soldiers went to his father's home in Ophrah and brought out Gideon's other sons to a large rock, where they murdered all seventy. Gideon's youngest son Jotham hid from the soldiers, but he was the only one who escaped.

6 The leaders of Shechem, including the priests and the military officers,‣ met at the tree next to the sacred rock‣ in Shechem to crown Abimelech king. 7 Jotham heard what they were doing. So he climbed to the top of Mount Gerizim and shouted down to the people who were there at the meeting:

> Leaders of Shechem,
>   listen to me,
> and perhaps God
>   will listen to you.

8 Once the trees searched
    for someone to be king;
they asked the olive tree,
    "Will you be our king?"
9 But the olive tree replied,
"My oil brings honour
    to people and gods.
I won't stop making oil,
    just so my branches can wave
        above the other trees."

10 Then they asked the fig tree,
    "Will you be our king?"
11 But the fig tree replied,
"I won't stop growing
    my delicious fruit,
just so my branches can wave
    above the other trees."

12 Next they asked the grape vine,
    "Will you be our king?"
13 But the grape vine replied,
"My wine brings cheer
    to people and gods.
I won't stop making wine,
    just so my branches can wave
        above the other trees."

14 Finally, they went
    to the thorn bush and asked,
    "Will you be our king?"

---

*8.31 wife: This translates a Hebrew word for a woman who was legally bound to a man, but without the full privileges of a wife.
*8.31 who lived at Shechem: Sometimes marriages were arranged so that the wife lived with her parents, and the husband visited her from time to time.

---

*9.4 seventy pieces: Nearly 800 grammes.

¹⁵ The thorn bush replied,
"If you really want me
    to be your king,
then come into my shade
    and I will protect you.
But if you're deceiving me,
    I'll start a fire
that will spread out and destroy
    the cedars of Lebanon."*

After Jotham had finished telling this story, he said:

¹⁶⁻¹⁸ My father Gideon risked his life for you when he fought to rescue you from the Midianites. Did you reward Gideon by being kind to his family? No, you did not! You attacked his family and killed all seventy of his sons on that rock.

And was it right to make Abimelech your king? He's merely the son of my father's slave girl.* But just because he's your relative, you made him king of Shechem.

¹⁹ So, you leaders of Shechem, if you treated Gideon and his family the way you should have, then I hope you and Abimelech will make each other very happy. ²⁰ But if it was wrong to treat Gideon and his family the way you did, then I pray that Abimelech will destroy you with fire, and I pray that you will do the same to him.

²¹ Jotham ran off and went to live in the town of Beer, where he could be safe from his brother Abimelech.

Abimelech destroys Shechem

²² Abimelech had been a military commander of Israel for three years, ²³⁻²⁴ when God decided to punish him and the leaders of Shechem for killing Gideon's seventy sons.

So God turned the leaders of Shechem against Abimelech. ²⁵ Then they sent some men to hide on the hilltops and watch for Abimelech and his troops, while they sent others to rob everyone who went by on the road. But Abimelech found out what they were doing.

²⁶ One day, Gaal son of Ebed went to live in Shechem. His brothers moved there too, and soon the leaders of Shechem started trusting him.

²⁷ The time came for the grape harvest, and the people of Shechem went into their

vineyards and picked the grapes. They put the grapes in their wine-pits and walked on them to squeeze out the juice in order to make wine. Then they went into the temple of their god and threw a big party. There was a lot of eating and drinking, and before long they were cursing Abimelech.

²⁸ Gaal said:

Hamor was the founder of Shechem, and one of his descendants should be our ruler. But Abimelech's father was Gideon, so Abimelech isn't really one of us. He shouldn't be our king, and we shouldn't have to obey him or Zebul, who rules Shechem for him. ²⁹ If I were the ruler of Shechem, I'd get rid of that Abimelech. I'd tell him, "Get yourself an even bigger army, and we will still defeat you."

³⁰ Zebul was angry when he found out what Gaal had said. ³¹ And so he sent some messengers to Abimelech. But they had to pretend to be doing something else, or they would not have been allowed to leave Shechem.' Zebul told the messengers to say:

Gaal the son of Ebed has come to Shechem along with his brothers, and they have persuaded the people to let Gaal rule Shechem instead of you. ³² This is what I think you should do. Lead your army here during the night and hide in the fields.

³³ Get up the next morning at sunrise and rush out of your hiding places to attack the town. Gaal and his followers will come out to fight you, but you will easily defeat them.

³⁴ So one night, Abimelech led his soldiers to Shechem. He divided them into four groups, and they all hid near the town.

³⁵ The next morning, Gaal went out and stood in the opening of the town gate. Abimelech and his soldiers left their hiding places, ³⁶ and Gaal saw them. Zebul was standing there with Gaal, and Gaal remarked, "Zebul, that looks like a crowd of people coming down from the mountaintops."

"No," Zebul answered, "it's just the shadows of the mountains. It only looks like people moving."

³⁷ "But Zebul, look over there," Gaal said. "There's a crowd coming down from the sacred mountain,' and another group is coming along the road from the tree where people talk with the spirits of the dead."

³⁸ Then Zebul replied, "What good is all your boasting now? You were the one who said Abimelech shouldn't be the ruler of

*9.15 cedars of Lebanon: The cedars that grew in the Lebanon mountains were some of the largest trees in that part of the world.
*9.16-18 son of . . . slave girl: See 8.31.

Shechem. Out there is the army that you made fun of. So go out and fight them!"

³⁹ Gaal and the leaders of Shechem went out and fought Abimelech. ⁴⁰ Soon the people of Shechem turned and ran back into the town. However, Abimelech and his troops were close behind and killed many of them along the way.

⁴¹ Abimelech stayed at Arumah,* and Zebul forced Gaal and his brothers out of Shechem.

⁴² The next morning, the people of Shechem were getting ready to work in their fields as usual, but someone told Abimelech about it. ⁴³ Abimelech divided his army into three groups and set up an ambush in the fields near Shechem. When the people came out of the town, he and his army rushed out from their hiding places and attacked.

⁴⁴ Abimelech and the troops with him ran to the town gate and took control of it, while two other groups attacked and killed the people who were in the fields. ⁴⁵ He and his troops fought in Shechem all day, until they had killed everyone in town. Then he and his men tore down the houses and buildings and scattered salt* everywhere.

⁴⁶ Earlier that day, the leaders of the temple of El Berith⸕ at Shechem had heard about the attack. So they went into the temple fortress, ⁴⁷ but Abimelech found out where they were. ⁴⁸ He led his troops to Mount Zalmon, where he took an axe and chopped off a tree branch. He lifted the branch on to his shoulder and shouted, "Hurry! Cut off a branch just as I did."

⁴⁹ When they all had branches, they followed Abimelech back to Shechem. They piled the branches against the fortress and set them on fire, burning down the fortress and killing about one thousand men and women.

⁵⁰ After destroying Shechem, Abimelech went to Thebez. He surrounded the town and captured it. ⁵¹ But there was a tall fortress in the middle of the town, and the town leaders and everyone else went inside. Then they barred the gates and went up to the flat roof.

⁵² Abimelech and his army rushed to the fortress and tried to force their way inside. Abimelech himself was about to set the heavy wooden doors on fire, ⁵³ when a woman on the roof dropped a large rock* on his head

and cracked his skull. ⁵⁴ The soldier who carried his weapons was nearby, and Abimelech told him, "Take out your sword and kill me. I don't want people to say that I was killed by a woman!"

So the soldier ran his sword through Abimelech. ⁵⁵ And when the Israelite soldiers saw that their leader was dead, they went back home.

⁵⁶ That's how God punished Abimelech for killing his brothers and bringing shame on his father's family. ⁵⁷ God also punished the people of Shechem for helping Abimelech.⸕ Everything happened just as Jotham's curse said it would.

Tola, Jair, and Jephthah

CHAPTER 10

Tola

¹ Tola was the next person to rescue Israel. He belonged to the Issachar tribe, but he lived in Shamir, a town in the hill country of Ephraim. His father was Puah, and his grandfather was Dodo. ² Tola was a leader* of Israel for twenty-three years, then he died and was buried in Shamir.

Jair

³ The next leader* of Israel was Jair, who lived in Gilead. He was a leader for twenty- two years. ⁴ He had thirty sons, and each son had his own mule* and was in charge of one town in Gilead. Those thirty towns are still called The Settlements of Jair.⸕ ⁵ When he died, he was buried in the town of Kamon.

Israel is unfaithful again

⁶ Before long, the Israelites began disobeying the LORD by worshipping Baal, Astarte, and gods from Syria, Sidon, Moab, Ammon, and Philistia.

⁷ The LORD was angry with Israel and decided to let Philistia and Ammon conquer them. ⁸ So the same year that Jair died, Israel's army was crushed by these two nations. For eighteen years, Ammon was cruel to the Israelites who lived in Gilead, the region east of the River Jordan that had once belonged to the Amorites. ⁹ Then the Ammonites began crossing the Jordan and

---

*9.41 **Arumah:** About eight kilometres from Shechem.
*9.45 **scattered salt:** This may have been part of a ceremony to place a curse on the town.
*9.53 **large rock:** One that was used in the grinding of grain.
See also: 9.53: 2 Sam 11.21.

*10.2,3 **leader:** See 2.16 and the note there.
*10.4 **each son had his own mule:** A sign that the family was wealthy.

attacking the tribes of Judah, Benjamin, and Ephraim. Life was miserable for the Israelites. 10 They begged the LORD for help and confessed, "We were unfaithful to you, our LORD. We stopped worshipping you and started worshipping idols of Baal."

11-12 The LORD answered:

In the past when you came crying to me for help, I rescued you. At one time or another I've rescued you from the Egyptians, the Amorites, the Ammonites, the Philistines, the Sidonians, the Amalekites, and the Maonites.⁰ 13-14 But I'm not going to rescue you any more! You've left me and gone off to worship other gods. If you're in such big trouble, go and cry to them for help!

15 "We have been unfaithful," the Israelites admitted. "If we must be punished, do it yourself, but please rescue us from the Ammonites."

16 Then the Israelites got rid of the idols of the foreign gods, and they began worshipping only the LORD. Finally, there came a time when the LORD could no longer stand to see them suffer.

The Ammonites invade Gilead

17 The rulers of Ammon called their soldiers together and led them to Gilead, where they set up camp.

The Israelites gathered at Mizpah* and set up camp there. 18 The leaders of Gilead asked each other, "Who can lead an attack on the Ammonites?" Then they agreed, "If we can find someone who can lead the attack, we'll make him the ruler of Gilead."

CHAPTER 11

Jephthah

1-5 The leaders of the Gilead clan decided to ask a brave warrior named Jephthah son of Gilead to lead the attack against the Ammonites.

Even though Jephthah belonged to the Gilead clan, he had earlier been forced to leave the region where they had lived. Jephthah was the son of a prostitute, but his half-brothers were the sons of his father's wife.

One day his half-brothers told him, "You don't really belong to our family, so you can't have any of the family property." Then they forced Jephthah to leave home.

Jephthah went to the country of Tob, where he was joined by a number of men who would do anything for money.

So the leaders of Gilead went to Jephthah and said, 6 "Please come back to Gilead! If you lead our army, we will be able to fight off the Ammonites."

7 "Didn't you hate me?" Jephthah replied. "Weren't you the ones who forced me to leave my family? You're coming to me now, just because you're in trouble."

8 "But we do want you to come back," the leaders said. "And if you lead us in battle against the Ammonites, we will make you the ruler of Gilead."

9 "All right," Jephthah said. "If I go back with you and the LORD lets me defeat the Ammonites, will you really make me your ruler?"

10 "You have our word," the leaders answered. "And the LORD is a witness to what we have said."

11 So Jephthah went back to Mizpah* with the leaders of Gilead. The people of Gilead gathered at the place of worship and made Jephthah their ruler. Jephthah also made promises to them.

12 After the ceremony, Jephthah sent messengers to say to the king of Ammon, "Are you trying to start a war? You have invaded my country, and I want to know why!"

13 The king of Ammon replied, "Tell Jephthah that the land really belongs to me, all the way from the River Arnon in the south, to the River Jabbok in the north, and west to the River Jordan. When the Israelites came out of Egypt, they stole it. Tell Jephthah to return it to me, and there won't be any war."

14 Jephthah sent the messengers back to the king of Ammon, 15 and they told him that Jephthah had said:

Israel hasn't taken any territory from Moab or Ammon. 16 When the Israelites came from Egypt, they travelled in the desert to the Red Sea* and then to Kadesh. 17 They sent messengers to the king of Edom and

---

*11.11 Mizpah: See the note at 10.17.
*11.16 Red Sea: Hebrew *yam suph*, here referring to the Gulf of Aqaba, since the term is extended to include the north-eastern arm of the Red Sea (see also the note at Exodus 13.18).
See also: 11.17: Num 20.14-21.

---

*10.17 Mizpah: In chapters 10—12, Mizpah is the name of a town in Gilead (see 11.29), not the same town as the Mizpah of chapters 20,21.

said, "Please, let us go through your country." But the king of Edom refused. They also sent messengers to the king of Moab, but he wouldn't let them cross his country either. And so the Israelites stayed at Kadesh.

18 A little later, the Israelites set out into the desert, going east of Edom and Moab, and camping on the eastern side of the gorge of the River Arnon. The Arnon is the eastern border of Moab, and since the Israelites didn't cross it, they didn't even set foot in Moab.

19 The Israelites sent messengers to the Amorite King Sihon of Heshbon. "Please," they said, "let our people go through your country to get to our own land."

20 Sihon didn't think the Israelites could be trusted, so he called his army together. They set up camp at Jahaz, then they attacked the Israelite camp. 21 But the LORD God helped Israel defeat Sihon and his army. Israel took over all of the Amorite land where Sihon's people had lived, 22 from the River Arnon in the south to the River Jabbok in the north, and from the desert in the east to the River Jordan in the west.

23 The messengers also told the king of Ammon that Jephthah had said:

The LORD God of Israel helped his nation get rid of the Amorites and take their land. Now do you think you're going to take over that same territory? 24 If Chemosh your god* takes over a country and gives it to you, don't you have a right to it? And if the LORD takes over a country and gives it to us, the land is ours!

25 Are you better than Balak the son of Zippor? He was the king of Moab, but he didn't quarrel with Israel or start a war with us.

26 For three hundred years, Israelites have been living in Heshbon and Aroer and the nearby villages, and in the towns along the Arnon gorge. If the land really belonged to you Ammonites, you wouldn't have waited until now to try to get it back.

27 I haven't done anything to you, but it's certainly wrong of you to start a war. I pray that the LORD will show whether Israel or Ammon is in the right.

28 But the king of Ammon paid no attention to Jephthah's message.

29 Then the LORD's Spirit took control of Jephthah, and Jephthah went through Gilead and Manasseh, raising an army. Finally, he arrived at Mizpah in Gilead, where 30 he promised the LORD, "If you will let me defeat the Ammonites 31 and come home safely, I will sacrifice to you whoever comes out to meet me first."

32 From Mizpah, Jephthah attacked the Ammonites, and the LORD helped him defeat them.

33 Jephthah and his army destroyed the twenty towns between Aroer and Minnith, and others as far as Abel-Keramim. After that, the Ammonites could not invade Israel any more.

Jephthah's daughter

34 When Jephthah returned to his home in Mizpah, the first one to meet him was his daughter. She was playing a tambourine and dancing to celebrate his victory, and she was his only child.

35 "Oh!" Jephthah cried. Then he tore his clothes in sorrow and said to his daughter, "I made a sacred promise to the LORD, and I must keep it. Your coming out to meet me has broken my heart."

36 "Father," she said, "you made a sacred promise to the LORD, and he let you defeat the Ammonites. Now, you must do what you promised, even if it means I must die. 37 But first, please let me spend two months, wandering in the hill country with my friends. We will cry together, because I can never get married and have children."

38 "Yes, you may have two months," Jephthah said.

She and some other girls left, and for two months they wandered in the hill country, crying because she could never get married and have children. 39 Then she went back to her father. He did what he had promised, and she never got married.

That's why 40 every year, Israelite girls walk around for four days, weeping for⁾ Jephthah's daughter.

---

*11.24 Chemosh your god: Chemosh was actually the national god of Moab, not Ammon. The land that Ammon was trying to take over had belonged to the Moabites before belonging to the Amorites (see Numbers 21.26). So the Ammonites may have thought that Chemosh controlled it.

See also: **11.18**: Num 21.4. **11.19–22**: Num 21.21–24. **11.25**: Num 22.1–6.

See also: **11.35**: Num 30.2.

CHAPTER 12

The Ephraim tribe fights Jephthah's army

¹ The men of the Ephraim tribe got together an army and went across the River Jordan to Zaphon to meet with Jephthah. They said, "Why did you go to war with the Ammonites without asking us to help? Just for that, we're going to burn down your house with you inside!"

² "But I did ask for your help," Jephthah answered. "That was back when the people of Gilead and I were having trouble with the Ammonites, and you wouldn't do a thing to help us. ³ So when we realized you weren't coming, we risked our lives and attacked the Ammonites. And the LORD let us defeat them. There's no reason for you to come here today to attack me."

⁴ But the men from Ephraim said, "You people of Gilead are nothing more than refugees from Ephraim. You even live on land that belongs to the tribes of Ephraim and Manasseh."'

So Jephthah called together the army of Gilead, then they attacked and defeated the army from Ephraim. ⁵ The army of Gilead also posted guards at all the places where the soldiers from Ephraim could cross the River Jordan to return to their own land.

Whenever one of the men from Ephraim would try to cross the river, the guards would say, "Are you from Ephraim?"

"No," the man would answer, "I'm not from Ephraim."

⁶ The guards would then tell them to say "Shibboleth", because they knew that people of Ephraim could say "Sibboleth", but not "Shibboleth".

If the man said "Sibboleth", the guards would grab him and kill him there. Altogether, forty-two thousand men from Ephraim were killed in the battle and at the Jordan.

⁷ Jephthah was a leader* of Israel for six years, before he died and was buried in his home town Mizpah' in Gilead.

Ibzan, Elon, and Abdon

Ibzan

⁸ Ibzan, the next leader* of Israel, came from Bethlehem. ⁹ He had thirty daughters and thirty sons, and he let them all marry outside his clan.

Ibzan was a leader for seven years, ¹⁰ before he died and was buried in Bethlehem.

Elon

¹¹ Elon from the Zebulun tribe was the next leader* of Israel. He was a leader for ten years, ¹² before he died and was buried in Aijalon that belonged to the Zebulun tribe.

Abdon

¹³⁻¹⁵ Abdon the son of Hillel was the next leader* of Israel. He had forty sons and thirty grandsons, and each one of them had his own donkey.* Abdon was a leader for eight years, before he died and was buried in his home town of Pirathon, which is in the part of the hill country of Ephraim where Amalekites used to live.

Samson

CHAPTER 13

Samson is born

¹ Once again the Israelites started disobeying the LORD. So he let the Philistines take control of Israel for forty years.

² Manoah from the tribe of Dan lived in the town of Zorah. His wife was not able to have children, ³⁻⁵ but one day an angel from the LORD appeared to her and said:

> You have never been able to have any children, but very soon you will be pregnant and have a son. He will belong to God* from the day he is born, so his hair must never be cut. And even before he is born, you must not drink any wine or beer or eat any food forbidden by God's laws.
>
> Your son will begin to set Israel free from the Philistines.

⁶ She went to Manoah and said, "A prophet who looked like an angel of God came and talked to me. I was so frightened, that I didn't

---

*12.11,13–15 leader: See 2.16 and the note there.
*12.13–15 each . . . donkey: A sign that the family was wealthy.
*13.3–5 belong to God: The Hebrew text has "be a Nazirite of God". Nazirites were dedicated to God and had to follow special rules to stay that way (see Numbers 6.1,21).
See also: 13.5: Num 6.1–5.

---

*12.7,8 leader: See 2.16 and the note there.

even ask where he was from. He didn't tell me his name, [7] but he did say that I'm going to have a baby boy. I'm not supposed to drink any wine or beer or eat any food forbidden by God's laws. Our son will belong to God for as long as he lives."

[8] Then Manoah prayed, "Our LORD, please send that prophet again and let him tell us what to do for the son we are going to have."

[9] God answered Manoah's prayer, and the angel went back to Manoah's wife while she was resting in the fields. Manoah wasn't there at the time, [10] so she found him and said, "That same man is here again! He's the one I saw the other day."

[11] Manoah went with his wife and asked the man, "Are you the one who spoke to my wife?"

"Yes, I am," he answered.

[12] Manoah then asked, "When your promise comes true, what rules must he obey and what will be his work?"

[13] "Your wife must be careful to do everything I told her," the LORD's angel answered. [14] "She must not eat or drink anything made from grapes. She must not drink wine or beer or eat anything forbidden by God's laws. I told her exactly what to do."

[15] "Please," Manoah said, "stay here with us for just a little while, and we'll prepare a young goat for you to eat." [16] Manoah didn't realize that he was really talking to one of the LORD's angels.

The angel answered, "I can stay for a little while, although I won't eat any of your food. But if you would like to offer the goat as a sacrifice to the LORD, that would be fine."

[17] Manoah said, "Tell us your name, so we can honour you after our son is born."

[18] "No," the angel replied. "You don't need to know my name. And if you did, you couldn't understand it."

[19] So Manoah took a young goat over to a large rock he had chosen for an altar, and he built a fire on the rock. Then he killed the goat, and offered it with some grain as a sacrifice to the LORD. But then an amazing thing happened. [20] The fire blazed up towards the sky, and the LORD's angel went up towards heaven in the fire. Manoah and his wife bowed down low when they saw what happened.

[21] The angel was gone, but Manoah and his wife realized that he was one of the LORD's

Life files

Samson

What's the story?

From an early age, Samson was dedicated to God. He was granted superhuman strength, provided he followed the rules of the Nazirites and never cut his hair. This strength helped Samson battle the Philistines. Unfortunately, Samson had a weakness for a pretty face, not to mention the rest of the body, and he fell in love with a woman called Delilah. Delilah was paid a lot of money by the Philistines to find out Samson's secret. After a few false starts, she found out the secret, cut his hair while he was sleeping and he was captured.

The Philistines brought him out for entertainment at a banquet, but they made a mistake: they had let his hair grow back. Mustering his strength, he pulled down a pillar holding up the roof, killing himself and about 3,000 of the enemy.

What's the point?

Samson's legendary strength – and faith in God – enabled him to achieve great victories over the enemy. But his love of women lured him into more and more compromises. He was almost captured when he slept with prostitutes in Gaza. And his infatuation with Delilah proved fatal.

Samson is a flawed hero. He was dedicated to God, but he kept breaking the rules. In the end he asked God for one final blessing. And God heard him. He might have been blind at the end, but maybe, for the first time in his life, he saw things clearly.

Footsteps

Five days with Samson

Birth and dedication: Judges 13.1–25
Samson's bride: Judges 14.1–20
Samson's revenge: Judges 15.1–20
Samson and Delilah: Judges 16.1–22
Samson's death: Judges 16.23–31

More...

Nazirites p.148
Sex p.727
Philistines p.282

angels. ²² Manoah said, "We have seen an angel.' Now we're going to die."*

²³ "The LORD isn't going to kill us," Manoah's wife responded. "The LORD accepted our sacrifice and grain offering, and he let us see something amazing. Besides, he told us that we're going to have a son."

²⁴ Later, Manoah's wife did give birth to a son, and she named him Samson. As the boy grew, the LORD blessed him. ²⁵ Then, while Samson was staying at Dan's Camp' between the towns of Zorah and Eshtaol, the Spirit of the LORD took control of him.

CHAPTER 14

Samson gets married

¹ One day, Samson went to Timnah, where he saw a Philistine woman. ² When he got back home, he told his parents, "I saw a Philistine woman in Timnah, and I want to marry her. Get her for me!"*

³ His parents answered, "There are a lot of women in our clan and even more in the rest of Israel. Those Philistines are pagans. Why would you want to marry one of their women?"

"She looks good to me," Samson answered. "Get her for me!"

⁴ At that time, the Philistines were in control of Israel, and the LORD wanted to stir up trouble for them. That's why he made Samson desire that woman.

⁵ As Samson and his parents reached the vineyards near Timnah, a fierce young lion suddenly roared and attacked Samson. ⁶ But the LORD's Spirit took control of Samson, and with his bare hands he tore the lion apart, as though it had been a young goat. His parents didn't know what he had done, and he didn't tell them.

⁷ When they got to Timnah, Samson talked to the woman, and he was sure that she was the one for him.

⁸ Later,' Samson returned to Timnah for the wedding. And when he came near the place where the lion had attacked, he left the road to see what was left of the lion. He was surprised to see that bees were living in the lion's skeleton, and that they had made some honey. ⁹ He scooped up the honey in his hands and ate some of it as he walked along.

When he got back to his parents, he gave them some of the honey, and they ate it too. But he didn't tell them he had found the honey in the skeleton of a lion.*

¹⁰ While Samson's father went to make the final arrangements with the bride and her family, Samson threw a big party,* as grooms' usually did. ¹¹ When the Philistines saw what Samson was like, they told thirty of their young men to stay with him at the party.

¹² Samson told the thirty young men, "This party will last for seven days. Let's make a bet: I'll tell you a riddle, and if you can tell me the right answer before the party is over, I'll give each one of you a shirt and a full change of clothing. ¹³ But if you can't tell me the answer, then each of you will have to give me a shirt and a full change of clothing."

"It's a bet!" the Philistines said. "Tell us the riddle."

¹⁴ Samson said:

> Once so strong and mighty —
>   now so sweet and tasty!

Three days went by, and the Philistine young men had not come up with the right answer. ¹⁵ Finally, on the seventh' day of the party they went to Samson's bride and said, "You had better trick your husband into telling you the answer to his riddle. Have you invited us here just to rob us? If you don't find out the answer, we will burn you and your family to death."

¹⁶ Samson's bride went to him and started crying in his arms. "You must really hate me," she sobbed. "If you loved me at all, you would have told me the answer to your riddle."

"But I haven't even told my parents the answer!" Samson replied. "Why should I tell you?"

¹⁷ For the entire seven days of the party, she had been whining and trying to get the answer from him. But that seventh day she put so much pressure on Samson that he finally gave in and told her the answer. She went straight to the young men and told them.

¹⁸ Before sunset that day, the men of the town went to Samson with this answer:

---

*13.22 We have seen an angel. Now we're going to die: Some people believed that if they saw the LORD or one of the LORD's angels, they would die.
*14.2 Get her for me: At that time, parents arranged marriages for their children.

*14.9 But he didn't tell them . . . skeleton of a lion: To eat anything that had touched a skeleton was against God's laws (see Leviticus 11.27–40).
*14.10 party: The Hebrew term means a party that involved a lot of drinking.

A lion is the strongest —
honey is the sweetest!

Samson replied,

This answer you have given me
doubtless came
from my bride-to-be.

19 Then the LORD's Spirit took control of
Samson. He went to Ashkelon,* where he
killed thirty men and took their clothing.
Samson then gave it to the thirty young men
at Timnah and stormed back home to his own
family.

20 The father of the bride made Samson's
wife marry one of the thirty young men who
had been at Samson's party.'

CHAPTER 15

1 Later, during the wheat harvest, Samson
went to visit the young woman he thought
was still his wife.* He brought along a young
goat as a gift and said to her father, "I want to
go into my wife's bedroom."

"You can't do that," he replied. 2 "When
you left the way you did, I thought you were
divorcing* her. So I arranged for her to marry
one of the young men who were at your
party. But my younger daughter is even
prettier, and you can have her as your wife."

3 "This time," Samson answered, "I have a
good reason for really hurting some
Philistines."

Samson takes revenge

4 Samson went out and caught three hundred
foxes and tied them together in pairs with
oil-soaked rags around their tails. 5 Then
Samson took the foxes into the Philistine
wheat fields that were ready to be harvested.
He set the rags on fire and let the foxes go.
The wheat fields went up in flames, and so
did the stacks of wheat that had already been
cut. Even the Philistine vineyards and olive
orchards burnt.

6 Some of the Philistines started asking
around, "Who could have done such a thing?"

"It was Samson," someone told them. "He
married the daughter of that man in Timnah,
but then the man gave Samson's wife to one
of the men at the wedding."

The Philistine leaders went to Timnah and
burnt to death Samson's wife and her father.'

7 When Samson found out what they had
done, he went to them and said, "You killed
them! And I won't rest until I get even with
you." 8 Then Samson started hacking them to
pieces with his sword.'

Samson left Philistia and went to live in
the cave at Etam Rock. 9 But it wasn't long
before the Philistines invaded Judah* and set
up a huge army camp at Jawbone.'

10 The people of Judah asked, "Why have
you invaded our land?"

The Philistines answered, "We've come to
get Samson. We're going to do the same
things to him that he did to our people."

11 Three thousand men from Judah went
to the cave at Etam Rock and said to Samson,
"Don't you know that the Philistines rule
us, and they will punish us for what you
did?"

"I was only getting even with them,"
Samson replied. "They did the same things to
me first."

12 "We came here to tie you up and turn
you over to them," said the men of Judah.

"I won't put up a fight," Samson answered,
"but you have to promise not to hurt me
yourselves."

13-14 "We promise," the men said. "We will
only tie you up and turn you over to the
Philistines. We won't kill you." Then they
tied up his hands and arms with two
brand-new ropes and led him away from
Etam Rock.

When the Philistines saw that Samson was
being brought to their camp at Jawbone, they
started shouting and ran towards him. But
the LORD's Spirit took control of Samson, and
Samson broke the ropes, as though they were
pieces of burnt cloth. 15 Samson glanced
around and spotted the jawbone of a donkey.
The jawbone had not yet dried out, so it was
still hard and heavy. Samson grabbed it and
started hitting Philistines — he killed a
thousand of them! 16 After the fighting was
over, he made up this poem about what he
had done to the Philistines:

I used a donkey's jawbone
to kill a thousand men;
I beat them with this jawbone
over and over again.'

---

*14.19 Ashkelon: Another Philistine town.
*15.1 Samson went to visit . . . his wife: See the note
at 8.31.
*15.2 divorcing: It was often very easy for a husband
to divorce his wife.

*15.9 Judah: Samson belonged to the Dan tribe, but
his hide-out in the cave at Etam Rock was in Judah, a
few kilometres south-west of Bethlehem.

¹⁷ Samson tossed the jawbone on the ground and decided to call the place Jawbone Hill.' It is still called that today.

¹⁸ Samson was so thirsty that he prayed, "Our LORD, you helped me win a battle against a whole army. Please don't let me die of thirst now. Those heathen Philistines will carry off my dead body."

¹⁹ Samson was tired and weary, but God sent water gushing from a rock.' Samson drank some and felt strong again.

Samson named the place Caller Spring,' because he had called out to God for help. The spring is still there at Jawbone.

²⁰ Samson was a leader* of Israel for twenty years, but the Philistines were still the rulers of Israel.

CHAPTER 16

Samson carries off the gates of Gaza

¹ One day while Samson was in Gaza, he saw a prostitute and went to her house to spend the night. ² The people who lived in Gaza found out he was there, and they decided to kill him at sunrise. So they went to the city gate and waited all night in the guardrooms on each side of the gate.*

³ But Samson got up in the middle of the night and went to the town gate. He pulled the gate doors and doorposts out of the wall and put them on his shoulders. Then he carried them all the way to the top of the hill that overlooks Hebron,* where he set the doors down, still closed and locked.

Delilah tricks Samson

⁴ Some time later, Samson fell in love with a woman named Delilah, who lived in Sorek Valley. ⁵ The Philistine rulers* went to Delilah and said, "Trick Samson into telling you what makes him so strong and what can make him weak. Then we can tie him up so he can't get away. If you find out his secret, we will each give you eleven hundred pieces of silver."*

⁶ The next time Samson was at Delilah's house, she asked, "Samson, what makes you

---

*15.20 leader:** See 2.16 and the note there.
*16.2 guardrooms . . . gate:** The gate was often in a part of the town wall that was thicker and taller than the rest of the wall, and that had rooms where guards stayed when they were on duty.
*16.3 Hebron:** About sixty-five kilometres from Gaza.
*16.5 Philistine rulers:** There were five rulers, each one controlling part of Philistia.
*16.5 silver:** About 60 kilogrammes of silver altogether.

Helpline

Help! I want to go out with a non-Christian

'Things just clicked. We seem so right together. Everything's perfect. Except they're not a Christian...'

This is a really difficult area. On the face of it, it shouldn't matter. After all, shouldn't love conquer everything?

The problem is that, however well you get on, your lives are based on different things. You base your life on what God wants; your prospective boyfriend or girlfriend doesn't have that restriction: they can do what they please. You live in the light of God, they live in a different light altogether.

It's not a question of not having non-Christian friends; it's different when you're sharing with someone on the very deepest level. Ultimately, any long-term relationship relies on both people travelling in the same direction. But this is very difficult if you have different goals, dreams and passions.

In the end, of course, every relationship is different. But beware. The Bible is full of people who married people with other faiths. And more often than not, they found themselves dragged off-course from their relationship with God.

Three things

Decide

What is the most important thing in your life? How will this relationship affect this?

Talk

You have to talk this through with others. Talk to your friends and youth leaders. They'll help you with these kind of difficult decisions.

Pray

Pray about it. See what God wants. Go in with your eyes open.

More...

Sex p.727
Marriage p.205
Help! I haven't got a boyfriend or girlfriend p.722

so strong? How can I tie you up so you can't get away? Come on, you can tell me."

⁷ Samson answered, "If someone ties me up with seven new bowstrings that have never been dried,* it will make me just as weak as anyone else."

⁸⁻⁹ The Philistine rulers gave seven new bowstrings to Delilah. They also told some of their soldiers to go to Delilah's house and hide in the room where Samson and Delilah were. If the bowstrings made Samson weak, they would be able to capture him.

Delilah tied up Samson with the bowstrings and shouted, "Samson, the Philistines are attacking!"

Samson snapped the bowstrings, as though they were pieces of scorched string. The Philistines had not found out why Samson was so strong.

¹⁰ "You lied and made me look like a fool," Delilah said. "Now tell me. How can I really tie you up?"

¹¹ Samson answered, "Use some new ropes. If I'm tied up with ropes that have never been used, I'll be just as weak as anyone else."

¹² Delilah got new ropes and again some Philistines hid in the room. Then she tied up Samson's arms and shouted, "Samson, the Philistines are attacking!"

Samson snapped the ropes as if they were threads.

¹³ "You're still lying and making a fool of me," Delilah said. "Tell me how I can tie you up!"

"My hair is in seven braids," Samson replied. "If you weave my braids into the threads on a loom* and nail the loom to a wall, then I will be as weak as anyone else."

¹⁴ While Samson was asleep, Delilah wove his braids into the threads on a loom and nailed the loom to a wall.' Then she shouted, "Samson, the Philistines are attacking!"

Samson woke up and pulled the loom free from its posts in the ground and from the nails in the wall. Then he pulled his hair free from the woven cloth.

¹⁵ "Samson," Delilah said, "you claim to love me, but you don't mean it! You've made me look like a fool three times now, and you still haven't told me why you are so strong."

¹⁶ Delilah started nagging and pestering him day after day, until he couldn't stand it any longer.

¹⁷ Finally, Samson told her the truth. "I have belonged to God* ever since I was born, so my hair has never been cut. If it were ever cut off, my strength would leave me, and I would be as weak as anyone else."

¹⁸ Delilah realized that he was telling the truth. So she sent someone to tell the Philistine rulers, "Come to my house one more time. Samson has finally told me the truth."

The Philistine rulers went to Delilah's house, and they brought along the silver they had promised her. ¹⁹ Delilah had lulled Samson to sleep with his head resting in her lap. She signalled to one of the Philistine men as she began cutting off Samson's seven braids. And by the time she had finished, Samson's strength was gone. Delilah tied him up ²⁰ and shouted, "Samson, the Philistines are attacking!"

Samson woke up and thought, "I'll break loose and escape, just as I always do." He did not realize that the LORD had stopped helping him.

²¹ The Philistines grabbed Samson and put out his eyes. They took him to the prison in Gaza and chained him up. Then they put him to work, turning a millstone to grind grain. ²² But they didn't cut his hair any more, so it started growing back.

²³ The Philistine rulers threw a big party and sacrificed a lot of animals to their god Dagon. The rulers said:

> Samson was our enemy,
> but our god Dagon
>   helped us capture him!

²⁴⁻²⁵ Everyone there was having a good time, and they shouted, "Bring out Samson — he's still good for a few more laughs!"

The rulers had Samson brought from the prison, and when the people saw him, this is how they praised their god:

> Samson ruined our crops
>   and killed our people.
> He was our enemy,
> but our god helped us
>   capture him.

They made fun of Samson for a while, then they told him to stand near the columns that supported the roof. ²⁶ A young man was leading Samson by the hand, and Samson

---

*16.7 new bowstrings . . . dried: The string for a bow was often made from sinews or internal organs of animals. These strings were made while the animal tissues were still moist, and they became much stronger, once they were dry.
*16.13 loom: A large wooden frame on which cloth is woven.

*16.17 belonged to God: See the note at 13.3–5.

said to him, "I need to lean against something. Take me over to the columns that hold up the roof."

27 The Philistine rulers were celebrating in a temple packed with people and with three thousand᾽ more on the flat roof. They had all been watching Samson and making fun of him.*

28 Samson prayed, "Please remember me, LORD God. The Philistines put out my eyes, but make me strong one last time, so I can take revenge for at least one of my eyes!"᾽

29 Samson was standing between the two middle columns that held up the roof. He felt around and found one column with his right hand, and the other with his left hand. 30 Then he shouted, "Let me die with the Philistines!" He pushed against the columns as hard as he could, and the temple collapsed with the Philistine rulers and everyone else still inside. Samson killed more Philistines when he died than he had killed during his entire life.

31 His brothers and the rest of his family went to Gaza and took his body back home. They buried him in his father's tomb,* which was between Zorah and Eshtaol.

Samson was a leader* of Israel for twenty years.

The tribe of Dan and their place of worship

CHAPTER 17

Micah makes idols and hires a priest

1 Micah᾽ belonged to the Ephraim tribe and lived in the hill country. 2 One day he told his mother, "Do you remember those eleven hundred pieces of silver* that were stolen from you? I was there when you put a curse on whoever stole them. Well, I'm the one who did it."

His mother answered, "I pray that the LORD will bless* you, my son."

3-4 Micah returned the silver to his mother, and she said, "I give this silver to the LORD, so my son can use it to make an idol."

---

*16.27 They . . . him: Samson may have been in a courtyard visible from the roof.
*16.31 buried him in his father's tomb: Several family members were often buried in one tomb.
*16.31 leader: See 2.16 and the note there.
*17.2 eleven hundred . . . silver: About 13 kilogrammes.
*17.2 curse . . . bless: A curse could not be taken back, but it could be made powerless by a blessing.

Holy history

Philistines

The Philistines have had a pretty bad press in the past. If you want to insult someone, you call them an 'ignorant philistine'. But the Philistines were actually quite cultured. They produced fine pottery and art. They had metalworking before the Israelites.

They lived in the coastal region of Philistia. They were sea-going people, who worshipped the gods Dagon, Ashtoreth and Baalzebub. Philistia had five major cities: Gaza, Ashkelon, and Ashdod on the coast; Ekron and Gath inland. Unlike many of the other nations around them, the Philistines did not practice circumcision; which is why the Israelites, rather scornfully, called them 'the uncircumcised'.

Philistia as a power declined after the reign of David. They were eventually defeated by the Babylonian armies.

 Anorak corner

The Philistines were the only neighbouring nation to Israel that were not defeated by the judges.

More...
Other nations p.259
David p.314
Samson p.277

 Anorak corner

Places

1. Where did Jonah head for to escape from God?
2. Where was Paul going when he met Jesus?
3. Where did the walls fall down?
4. Who made Jerusalem the capital city of Israel?
5. Where was Jesus when he was arrested?
(Answers on p.1431)

Turning to her son, she said, "Micah, now the silver belongs to you."

But Micah handed it back to his mother. She took two hundred pieces* of the silver and gave them to a silver worker, who made them into an idol.* They kept the idol in Micah's house. 5 He had a shrine for worshipping God there at his home, and he had made some idols and a sacred priestly apron. Micah chose one of his own sons to be the priest for his shrine.

6 This was before kings ruled Israel, so all the Israelites did whatever they thought was right.

7-8 One day a young Levite came to Micah's house in the hill country of Ephraim. He had been staying with one of the clans of Judah in Bethlehem, but he had left Bethlehem to find a new place to live* where he could be a priest.'

9 "Where are you from?" Micah asked.

"I am a Levite from Bethlehem in Judah," the man answered, "and I'm on my way to find a new place to live."

10 Micah said, "Why don't you stay here with me? You can be my priest and tell me what God wants me to do. Every year I'll give you ten pieces of silver and one complete set of clothes, and I'll provide all your food."

The young man went for a walk, 11-12 then he agreed to stay with Micah and be his priest. He lived in Micah's house, and Micah treated him like one of his own sons. 13 Micah said, "I have a Levite as my own priest. Now I know that the LORD will be kind to me."

CHAPTER 18

1 These things happened before kings ruled Israel.

The tribe of Dan takes Micah's priest and idols

About this time, the tribe of Dan was looking for a place to live. The other tribes had land, but the people of Dan did not really have any to call their own. 2 The tribe chose five warriors to represent their clans and told them, "Go and find some land where we can live."

The warriors left the area of Zorah and Eshtaol and went into the hill country of Ephraim. One night they stayed at Micah's house, 3 because they heard the young Levite talking, and they knew from his accent that he was from the south. They asked him, "What are you doing here? Who brought you here?"

4 The Levite replied, "Micah hired me as his priest." Then he told them how well Micah had treated him.

5 "Please talk to God for us," the men said. "Ask God if we will be successful in what we are trying to do."

6 "Don't worry," answered the priest. "The LORD is pleased with what you are doing."

7 The five men left and went to the town of Laish, whose people were from Sidon,' but Sidon was too far away to protect them. Even though their town had no walls, the people thought they were safe from attack. So they had not asked anyone else' for protection, which meant that the tribe of Dan could easily take over Laish.'

8 The five men went back to Zorah and Eshtaol, where their relatives asked, "Did you find any land?"

9-10 "Let's go!" the five men said. "We saw some very good land with enough room for all of us, and it has everything we will ever need. What are you waiting for? Let's attack and take it. You'll find that the people think they're safe, but God is giving the land to us."

11 Six hundred men from the tribe of Dan strapped on their weapons and left Zorah and Eshtaol with their families.' 12 One night they camped near Kiriath-Jearim in the territory of Judah, and that's why the place just west of Kiriath-Jearim is still known as Dan's Camp.' 13 Then they went into the hill country of Ephraim.

When they came close to Micah's house, 14 the five men who had been spies asked the other warriors, "Did you know that someone in this village has several idols and a sacred priestly apron? What do you think we should do about it?"

15-18 The six hundred warriors left the road and went to the house on Micah's property where the young Levite priest lived. They stood at the gate and greeted the priest. Meanwhile, the five men who had been there before went into Micah's house and took the sacred priestly apron and the idols.

"Hey!" the priest shouted. "What do you think you're doing?"

---

*17.3–4 two hundred pieces: About 2 kilogrammes.
*17.3–4 idol: Probably carved from wood and covered with the silver.
*17.7–8 place to live: The people of the Levi tribe did not have a large area of land like the other tribes.

See also: 17.6: Judg 21.25.

[19] "Quiet!" the men said. "Keep your mouth shut and listen. Why don't you come with us and be our priest, so you can tell us what God wants us to do? You could stay here and be a priest for one man's family, but wouldn't you rather be the priest for a clan or even a whole tribe of Israel?"

[20] The priest really liked that idea. So he took the apron and the idols and joined the others [21] from the tribe of Dan. Then they turned and left, after putting their children, their cattle, and the rest of their other possessions in front.

[22] They had travelled for some time, before Micah asked his neighbours to help him get his things back. He and his men caught up with the people of Dan [23] and shouted for them to stop.

They turned to face him and asked, "What's wrong? Why did you bring all these men?"

[24] Micah answered, "You know what's wrong. You stole the gods⟩ I made, and you took my priest. I don't have anything left."

[25] "We don't want to hear any more about it," the people of Dan said. "And if you make us angry, you'll only get yourself and your family killed." [26] After saying this, they turned and left.

Micah realized there was no way he could win a fight with them, and so he went back home.

The tribe of Dan captures Laish

[27-28] The tribe of Dan took Micah's priest and the things Micah had made, and headed for Laish, which was in a valley controlled by the town of Beth-Rehob. Laish was defenceless, because it had no walls and was too far from Sidon for the Sidonians to help defend it. The leaders of Laish had not even asked nearby towns to help them in case of an attack.

The warriors from Dan made a surprise attack on Laish, killing everyone and burning it down. Then they rebuilt the town and settled there themselves. [29] But they named it Dan, after one of Israel's* sons, who was the ancestor of their tribe.

[30-31] Even though the place of worship* was in Shiloh, the people of Dan set up the idol Micah had made. They worshipped the idol,

and the Levite was their priest. His name was Jonathan, and he was a descendant of Gershom the son of Moses.⟩ His descendants served as priests for the tribe of Dan, until the people of Israel were taken away as prisoners by their enemies.

Civil war against the tribe of Benjamin

CHAPTER 19

A woman is murdered

[1] Before kings ruled Israel, a Levite* was living deep in the hill country of the Ephraim tribe. He married* a woman from Bethlehem in Judah, [2] but she was unfaithful and went back to live with her family in Bethlehem.

Four months later [3] her husband decided to try and talk her into coming back. So he went to Bethlehem, taking along a servant and two donkeys. He talked with his wife, and she invited him into her family's home. Her father was glad to see him [4] and did not want him to leave. So the man stayed three days, eating and drinking with his father-in-law.

[5] When everyone got up on the fourth day, the Levite started getting ready to go home. But his father-in-law said, "Don't leave until you have a bite to eat. You'll need strength for your journey."

[6] The two men sat down together and ate a big meal. "Come on," the man's father-in-law said. "Stay tonight and have a good time."

[7] The Levite tried to leave, but his father-in-law insisted, and he spent one more night. [8] On the fifth day, the man got up early to leave, but his wife's father said, "You need to keep up your strength! Why don't you leave straight after lunch?" So the two of them started eating.

[9] Finally, the Levite got up from the meal, so he and his wife and servant could leave. "Look," his father-in-law said, "it's already late afternoon, and if you leave now, you won't get very far before dark. Stay with us one more night and enjoy yourself. Then you can get up early tomorrow morning and start home."

[10] But the Levite decided not to spend the night there again. He had the saddles put on his two donkeys, then he and his wife and servant travelled as far as Jebus, which is now called Jerusalem. [11] It was beginning to get

---

18.29 Israel's: Israel was another name for Jacob, the father of the twelve ancestors of the tribes of Israel.

18.30–31 place of worship: The Hebrew text has "house of God", which at this time was probably the sacred tent.

19.1 a Levite: Someone from the Levi tribe, which had no tribal lands of its own.

19.1 married: See the note at 8.31.

dark, and the man's servant said, "Let's stop and spend the night in this town where the Jebusites live."

12 "No," the Levite answered. "They aren't Israelites, and I refuse to spend the night there. We'll stop for the night at Gibeah, 13 because we can make it to Gibeah or perhaps even to Ramah* before dark."

14 They walked on and reached Gibeah in the territory of Benjamin just after sunset. 15 They left the road and went into Gibeah. But the Levite couldn't find a house where anyone would let them spend the night, and they sat down in the open area just inside the town gates.

16 Soon an old man came in through the gates on his way home from working in the fields. Most of the people who lived in Gibeah belonged to the tribe of Benjamin, but this man was originally from the hill country of Ephraim. 17 He noticed that the Levite was just in town to spend the night. "Where are you going?" the old man asked. "Where did you come from?"

18 "We've come from Bethlehem in Judah," the Levite answered. "We went there on a visit. Now we're going to the place where the LORD is worshipped, and later we will return to our home in the hill country of Ephraim. But no one here will let us spend the night* in their home. 19 We brought food for our donkeys and bread and wine for ourselves, so we don't need anything except a place to sleep."

20 The old man said, "You are welcome to spend the night in my home and to be my guest, but don't stay out here!"

21 The old man brought them into his house and fed their donkeys. Then he and his guests washed their feet* and began eating and drinking. 22 They were having a good time, when some worthless men of that town surrounded the house and started banging on the door and shouting, "A man came to your house tonight. Send him out, so we can have sex with him!"

23 The old man went outside and said, "My friends, please don't commit such a horrible crime against a man who is a guest in my house. 24 Let me send out my daughter instead. She's a virgin. And I'll even send out the man's wife.* You can rape them or do whatever else you want, but please don't do such a horrible thing to this man."

25 The men refused to listen, so the Levite grabbed his wife and shoved her outside. The men raped her and abused her all night long. Finally, they let her go just before sunrise, 26 and it was almost daybreak when she went back to the house where her husband* was staying. She collapsed at the door and lay there until sunrise.

27 About that time, her husband woke up and got ready to leave. He opened the door and went outside, where he found his wife lying at the door with her hands on the doorstep. 28 "Get up!" he said. "It's time to leave."

But his wife didn't move.⟩

He lifted her body on to his donkey and left. 29 When he got home, he took a butcher's knife and cut her body into twelve pieces. Then he told some messengers, "Take one piece to each tribe of Israel 30 and ask everyone if anything like this has ever happened since Israel left Egypt. Tell them to think about it, talk it over, and tell us what should be done."

Everyone who saw a piece of the body said, "This is horrible! Nothing like this has ever happened since the day Israel left Egypt."⟩

CHAPTER 20

Israel gets ready for war

1-3 The Israelites called a meeting of the nation. And since they were God's people, the meeting was held at the place of worship in Mizpah. Men who could serve as soldiers came from everywhere in Israel — from Dan in the north, Beersheba in the south, and Gilead east of the River Jordan. Four hundred thousand of them came to Mizpah, and they each felt the same about what those men from the tribe of Benjamin had done.

News about the meeting at Mizpah reached the tribe of Benjamin.

---

*19.13 **Gibeah . . . Ramah:** It was about five kilometres from Jerusalem to Gibeah, and another five kilometres to Ramah.
*19.18 **spend the night:** People usually considered it a duty to ask travellers to spend the night in their homes, since there were often no other places to stay.
*19.21 **washed their feet:** This was a custom, since people wore open sandals and their feet would be dirty after walking on the earth roads or working in the fields.
See also: **19.22-24:** Gen 19.5-8.

*19.24 **wife:** See the note at 8.31.
*19.26 **husband:** Or "owner"; the Hebrew word may mean that she was his slave and had no legal rights.
See also: **19.29:** 1 Sam 11.7.

As soon as the leaders of the tribes of Israel took their places, the Israelites said, "How could such a horrible thing happen?"

4 The husband of the murdered woman answered:

My wife* and I went into the town of Gibeah in Benjamin to spend the night. 5 Later that night, the men of Gibeah surrounded the house. They wanted to kill me, but instead they raped and killed my wife. 6 It was a terrible thing for Israelites to do! So I cut up her body and sent pieces everywhere in Israel.

7 You are the people of Israel, and you must decide today what to do about the men of Gibeah.

8 The whole army was in agreement, and they said, "None of us will go home. 9-10 We'll send one tenth of the men from each tribe to get food for the army. And we'll ask God* who should attack Gibeah, because those men' deserve to be punished for committing such a horrible crime in Israel."

11 Everyone agreed that Gibeah had to be punished.

12 The tribes of Israel sent messengers to every town and village in Benjamin. And wherever the messengers went, they said, "How could those worthless men in Gibeah do such a disgusting thing? 13 We can't allow such a terrible crime to go unpunished in Israel! Hand the men over to us, and we will put them to death."

But the people of Benjamin refused to listen to the other Israelites. 14 Men from towns all over Benjamin's territory went to Gibeah and got ready to fight Israel. 15 The Benjamin tribe had twenty-six thousand soldiers, not counting the seven hundred who were Gibeah's best warriors. 16 In this army there were seven hundred left-handed experts who could sling a stone* at a target the size of a hair and hit it every time.

17 The other Israelite tribes organized their army and found they had four hundred thousand experienced soldiers. 18 So they went to the place of worship at Bethel' and asked God, "Which tribe should be the first to attack the people of Benjamin?"

"Judah," the LORD answered.

19 The next morning the Israelite army moved its camp to a place near Gibeah. 20 Then they left their camp and got into position to attack the army of Benjamin.

The war between Israel and Benjamin

21 Benjamin's soldiers came out of Gibeah and attacked, and when the day was over, twenty-two thousand Israelite soldiers lay dead on the ground.

22-24 The people of Israel went to the place of worship and cried until sunset. Then they asked the LORD, "Should we attack the people of Benjamin again, even though they are our relatives?"

"Yes," the LORD replied, "attack them again!"

The Israelite soldiers encouraged each other to be brave and to fight hard. Then the next day they went back to Gibeah and took up the same positions as they had before.

25 That same day, Benjamin's soldiers came out of Gibeah and attacked, leaving another eighteen thousand Israelite soldiers dead on the battlefield.

26-28 The people of Israel went to the place of worship at Bethel,' where the sacred chest was being kept. They sat on the ground, crying and not eating for the rest of the day. Then about sunset, they offered sacrifices to please the LORD and to ask his blessing.* Phinehas' the priest then prayed, "Our LORD, the people of Benjamin are our relatives. Should we stop fighting or attack them again?"

"Attack!" the LORD answered. "Tomorrow I will let you defeat them."

29 The Israelites surrounded Gibeah, but stayed where they could not be seen. 30 Then the next day, they took the same positions as twice before, 31-41 but this time they had a different plan. They said, "When the men of Benjamin attack, we will run off and let them chase us away from the town and into the country roads."

The soldiers of Benjamin attacked the Israelite army and started pushing it back from the town. They killed about thirty Israelites in the fields and along the road between Gibeah and Bethel. The men of Benjamin were thinking, "We're mowing them down like we did before."

The Israelites were running away, but they headed for Baal-Tamar, where they regrouped. They had set an ambush, and they were sure it

---

*20.4 wife: See the note at 8.31.
*20.9–10 ask God: The Hebrew text has "use lots to decide"; small pieces of wood or stone called "lots" were used to find out what God wanted his people to do.
*20.16 sling a stone: By using a sling made from a leather strap.

*20.26–28 sacrifices . . . blessing: See Leviticus 1—3.

would work. Ten thousand of Israel's best soldiers had been hiding west of Gibeah,' and as soon as the men of Benjamin chased the Israelites into the countryside, these ten thousand soldiers made a surprise attack on the town gates. They dashed in and captured Gibeah, killing everyone there. Then they set the town on fire, because the smoke would be the signal for the other Israelite soldiers to turn and attack the soldiers of Benjamin.

The fighting had been so heavy around the soldiers of Benjamin, that they did not know the trouble they were in. But then they looked back and saw clouds of smoke rising from the town. They looked in front and saw the soldiers of Israel turning to attack. This terrified them, because they realized that something horrible was happening. And it was horrible — over twenty-five thousand' soldiers of Benjamin died that day, and those who were left alive knew that the LORD had given Israel the victory.

⁴² The men of Benjamin headed down the road towards the desert, trying to escape from the Israelites. But the Israelites stayed just behind them, keeping up their attack. Men even came out of the nearby towns to help kill the men of Benjamin, ⁴³ who were having to fight on all sides. The Israelite soldiers never let up their attack.' They chased and killed the warriors of Benjamin as far as a place directly east of Gibeah,' ⁴⁴ until eighteen thousand of these warriors lay dead.

⁴⁵ Some other warriors of Benjamin turned and ran down the road towards Rimmon Rock in the desert. The Israelites killed five thousand of them on the road, then chased the rest until they had killed' two thousand more.
⁴⁶ Twenty-five thousand soldiers of Benjamin died that day, all of them experienced warriors.
⁴⁷ Only six hundred of them finally made it into the desert to Rimmon Rock, where they stayed for four months.
⁴⁸ The Israelites turned back and went to every town in Benjamin's territory, killing all the people and animals, and setting the towns on fire.

CHAPTER 21

Wives for the men of Benjamin

¹ When the Israelites had met at Mizpah before the war with Benjamin,* they had made this sacred promise: "None of us will ever let our daughters marry any man from Benjamin."

² After the war with Benjamin, the Israelites went to the place of worship at Bethel and sat there until sunset. They cried loudly and bitterly ³ and prayed, "Our LORD, you are the God of Israel. Why did you let this happen? Now one of our tribes is almost gone."
⁴ Early the next morning, the Israelites built an altar and offered sacrifices to please the LORD and to ask his blessing.* ⁵ Then they asked each other, "Did any of the tribes of Israel fail to come to the place of worship? We made a sacred promise that anyone who didn't come to the meeting at Mizpah would be put to death."
⁶ The Israelites were sad about what had happened to the Benjamin tribe, and they said, "One of our tribes was almost wiped out. ⁷ Only a few men of Benjamin weren't killed in the war. We need to get wives for them, so the tribe won't completely disappear. But how can we do that, after promising in the LORD's name that we wouldn't let them marry any of our daughters?"
⁸⁻⁹ Again the Israelites asked, "Did any of the tribes stay away from the meeting at Mizpah?"

After asking around, they discovered that no one had come from Jabesh in Gilead.
¹⁰⁻¹¹ So they sent twelve thousand warriors with these orders: "Attack Jabesh in Gilead and kill everyone, except the women who have never been married."
¹² The warriors attacked Jabesh in Gilead, and returned to their camp in Canaan* with four hundred young women.
¹³ The Israelites met and sent messengers to the men of Benjamin at Rimmon Rock, telling them that the Israelites were willing to make peace with them. ¹⁴ So the men of Benjamin came back from Rimmon Rock, and the Israelites let them marry the young women from Jabesh. But there weren't enough women.
¹⁵ The Israelites were very sad, because the LORD had almost wiped out one of their tribes. ¹⁶ Then their national leaders said:

All the women of the Benjamin tribe were killed. How can we get wives for the men of Benjamin who are left? ¹⁷ If they don't have children, one of the Israelite tribes will die out. ¹⁸ But we can't let the men of Benjamin marry any of our daughters. We made a

---

*21.1 the Israelites . . . Benjamin: See 20.1-3.

*21.4 sacrifices . . . blessing: See the note at 20.26–28.

*21.12 in Canaan: Jabesh was in Gilead, across the River Jordan from the land of Canaan.

sacred promise not to do that, and if we break our promise, we will be under our own curse.

19 Then someone suggested, "What about the LORD's Festival that takes place each year in Shiloh? It's held north of Bethel, south of Lebonah, and just east of the road that goes from Bethel to Shechem."

20 The leaders told the men of Benjamin who still did not have wives:

Go to Shiloh and hide in the vineyards near the festival. 21 Wait there for the young women of Shiloh to come out and perform their dances. Then rush out and grab one of the young women, then take her home as your wife. 22 If the fathers or brothers of these women complain about this, we'll say, "Be kind enough to let those men keep your daughter. After all, we couldn't get enough wives for all the men of Benjamin in the battle at Jabesh. And because you didn't give them permission to marry your daughters, you won't be under the curse we earlier agreed on.'

23 The men of Benjamin went to Shiloh and hid in the vineyards. The young women soon started dancing, and each man grabbed one of them and carried her off. Then the men of Benjamin went back to their own land and rebuilt their towns and started living in them again.

24 Afterwards, the rest of the Israelites returned to their homes and families.

Israel was not ruled by a king

25 In those days Israel wasn't ruled by a king, and everyone did what they thought was right.

See also: 21.25: Judg 17.6.

Additional notes

›1.4–5 king of Bezek: Or "Adoni-Bezek".
›1.10 clans called: Or "warriors".
›1.13 Othniel was the son of . . . Kenaz: Or "Othniel and Caleb both belonged to the Kenaz clan, but Othniel was younger than Caleb."
›1.14 Achsah . . . Othniel . . . he: Hebrew; two ancient translations "Othniel . . . Achsah . . . she".
›1.14 getting down from: One possible meaning for the difficult Hebrew text.
›1.15 spring-fed ponds . . . small ponds . . . Higher Pond and Lower Pond: Or "wells . . . wells . . . Higher Well and Lower Well."
›1.16 Jericho: The Hebrew text has "Town of Palm Trees", another name for Jericho.

›1.16 not far . . . Amalekites: One possible meaning for the difficult Hebrew text.
›1.20 clans: See the note at 1.10.
›1.36 Scorpion Pass: Or "Akrabbim Pass".
›1.36 country: One possible meaning for the difficult Hebrew text of verse 36.
›2.3 trap: One possible meaning for the difficult Hebrew text.
›3.3 Hamath Pass: Or "Lebo-Hamath".
›3.8 northern Syria: The Hebrew text has "Aram-Naharaim", probably referring to the land around the city of Haran (see Genesis 24.10; 25.20; 28.2,6; 31.18,20; 33.18; 35.23–26; 46.8–15; 48.7).
›3.9 Othniel was the son of . . . Kenaz: See the note at 1.13.
›3.13 Jericho: See the note at 1.16.
›3.15–16 Ehud: Hebrew "Ehud the son of Gera".
›3.22–23 he climbed . . . porch: One possible meaning for the difficult Hebrew text.
›4.11 the village . . . Zaanannim: Or "the oak tree in the town of Zaanannim".
›5.7 villagers . . . fields: One possible meaning for the difficult Hebrew text.
›5.7 Deborah: Or "I, Deborah".
›5.8 The Israelites . . . attacked: One possible meaning for the difficult Hebrew text.
›5.11 Even . . . water: One possible meaning for the difficult Hebrew text.
›5.13 side: One possible meaning for the difficult Hebrew text of verse 13.
›5.15 But . . . at all: Or "But the people of Reuben couldn't make up their minds."
›5.16 sheep pens: Or "campfires".
›5.16 No . . . come: See the note at 5.15.
›5.18 to attack the enemy: One possible meaning for the difficult Hebrew text.
›5.19 stream near Megiddo: Probably refers to one of the streams that flow into the River Kishon.
›5.30 and beautiful . . . wear: One possible meaning for the difficult Hebrew text.
›7.1 Fear Spring: Or "Harod Spring".
›7.13 flat: Or "mouldy".
›7.13 the headquarters tent: Or "a tent".
›7.22 Zeredah: Some Hebrew manuscripts; most Hebrew manuscripts "Zererah"; these may be different names for the town of Zarethan in the Jordan Valley.
›7.25 Raven and Wolf: Or "Oreb and Zeeb".
›7.25 Raven Rock . . . Wolf Wine-pit: Or "Oreb Rock . . . Zeeb Wine-pit".
›8.17 all . . . officials: Or "every man in town".
›8.27–29 statue . . . statue: Or "sacred priestly apron . . . apron".
›8.33 Baal Berith: Or "Baal of the Agreement" or "the Lord of the Agreement".
›9.1 Gideon: The Hebrew text has "Jerubbaal", another name for Gideon (see 6.32).
›9.4 Baal Berith: See the note at 8.33.

9.6 including the priests and the military officers: The Hebrew text has "and the Millo house", another name for the temple of Baal Berith. It probably also served as a military fortress.

9.6 tree . . . rock: One ancient translation; Hebrew "propped-up sacred tree".

9.31 But . . . Shechem: One possible meaning for the difficult Hebrew text.

9.37 sacred mountain: The Hebrew text has "the navel of the land", which probably refers to Mount Gerizim as a sacred mountain linking heaven and earth.

9.46 temple of El Berith: The Hebrew text also calls all or part of this temple the "Fortress of Shechem". El Berith, "the God of the Agreement", was also known as Baal Berith, "the Lord of the Agreement" (see also 8.33; 9.4).

9.57 helping Abimelech: Hebrew "their evil" (see 9.3–4).

10.4 The Settlements of Jair: Or "Havvoth-Jair".

10.11–12 Maonites: Hebrew; one ancient translation "Midianites".

11.40 weeping for: Or "remembering".

12.4 You people of Gilead . . . Ephraim and Manasseh: One possible meaning for the difficult Hebrew text.

12.7 his home town Mizpah: One possible meaning for the difficult Hebrew text.

13.22 angel: The Hebrew text has "god", which can be used of God or of other supernatural beings.

13.25 Dan's Camp: Or "Mahaneh-Dan".

14.8 Later: Or "The following year".

14.10 grooms: Or "warriors".

14.15 Finally, on the seventh: Hebrew; three ancient translations "on the fourth".

14.20 one . . . at Samson's party: One possible meaning for the difficult Hebrew text.

15.6 and her father: Most Hebrew manuscripts; many Hebrew manuscripts and two ancient translations "and her family".

15.8 hacking . . . sword: One possible meaning for the difficult Hebrew text.

15.9 Jawbone: Or "Lehi" (see verse 17).

15.16 I beat . . . again: One possible meaning for the difficult Hebrew text.

15.17 Jawbone Hill: Or "Ramath-Lehi".

15.19 God sent . . . a rock: One possible meaning for the difficult Hebrew text.

15.19 Caller Spring: Or "Enhakkore".

16.13–14 If you weave . . . to a wall: Some manuscripts of one ancient translation; Hebrew "Weave my braids into the threads on a loom. She nailed the loom to a wall."

16.27 three thousand: Hebrew; some manuscripts of one ancient translation "seven hundred".

16.28 one of my eyes: Or "my eyes".

17.1 Micah: The Hebrew also uses the longer form "Micaiah".

17.7–8 to find . . . priest: Or "and was on his way to find a new place to live."

18.7 whose people . . . Sidon: One possible meaning for the difficult Hebrew text.

18.7 anyone else: Hebrew; one ancient translation has "the Arameans", who were a short distance to the north.

18.7 which . . . Laish: One possible meaning for the difficult Hebrew text.

18.11 Eshtaol with their families: Hebrew "Eshtaol" (see verse 21).

18.12 Dan's Camp: See the note at 13.25.

18.24 gods: Or "god".

18.30–31 Moses: Some manuscripts of two ancient translations; the Standard Hebrew Text has "Manasseh", but written in a special way that tells the reader "Moses" had been changed to "Manasseh".

19.28 move: Hebrew; one ancient translation "move. She was dead."

19.29–30 he told some messengers . . . since Israel left Egypt: One ancient translation; Hebrew "he told some messengers, 'Take one piece to each tribe of Israel.' Everyone who saw a piece of the body said, 'This is horrible! Nothing like this has ever happened since the day Israel left Egypt. Think of it! Let's talk it over and decide what to do.' "

20.9–10 those men: One Hebrew manuscript and one ancient translation; The Standard Hebrew Text "the men of Geba".

20.18 place . . . Bethel: The Hebrew text has "beth-el", which means "house of God". This could refer to the town of Bethel, to the place of worship at Mizpah, or to the sacred tent at Shiloh (see 18.30–31).

20.26–28 place . . . Bethel: See at the note at 20.18.

20.26–28 Phinehas: Hebrew "Phinehas the son of Eleazar the son of Aaron".

20.31–41 west of Gibeah: Three ancient translations; Hebrew "in a field at Geba".

20.31–41 over twenty-five thousand: Hebrew "twenty-five thousand one hundred".

20.42–43 Men even came out . . . their attack: One possible meaning for the difficult Hebrew text.

20.43 Gibeah: Or "Geba".

20.45 until . . . killed: Or "as far as Gidom, killing".

21.22 on: One possible meaning for the difficult Hebrew text of verse 22.

Ruth

The basics

What's the point? God is a God for all nations and all people.

What happens? Ruth the Moabitess shows her loyalty to her family and her faith in the God of Israel.

What should I remember? 1.16 'Please don't tell me to leave you and return home! I will go where you go, I will live where you live; your people will be my people, your God will be my God.'

More detail

Setting the scene This book is set in the time of the judges, during a period of peace between Israel and Moab. Naomi, a woman from Bethlehem, has moved to Moab during a time of famine. After the death of her two sons, she decides to move back to her home town. She is accompanied by her daughter-in-law Ruth, who, although not an Israelite, decides to follow the God of the Israelites.

What's it all about? Ruth is a book about duty, affection and friendship. The important thing to remember about Ruth, the heroine of this story, is that she is not an Israelite. She's a Moabitess – a woman from a despised and hated enemy of Israel. Yet her goodness and love shine through. She is a prime example of how participation in the kingdom of God is nothing to do with nationality, but a matter of loving God and following his commands.

The other hero of this story is Boaz, who protects Ruth, provides for her and eventually marries her. From this marriage comes the family which a few generations later is to lead to King David and then, eventually, to Jesus. So this is a story of Jesus's ancestors – indeed, Ruth is so honoured that this foreign woman

found a mention in the family tree of Christ (Matthew 1.2).

Footsteps

Naomi and Ruth go to Bethlehem: 1.1–22
Ruth meets Boaz: 2.1–23
Naomi's plan: 3.1–18
Ruth and Boaz are married: 4.1–22

Ruth is loyal to Naomi

CHAPTER 1

¹⁻² Before Israel was ruled by kings, Elimelech from the tribe of Ephrath lived in the town of Bethlehem. His wife was named Naomi, and their two sons were Mahlon and Chilion. But when their crops failed, they moved to the country of Moab.* And while they were there, ³ Elimelech died, leaving Naomi with only her two sons.

⁴ Later, Naomi's sons married Moabite women. One was named Orpah and the other Ruth. About ten years later, ⁵ Mahlon and Chilion also died. Now Naomi had no husband or sons.

⁶⁻⁷ When Naomi heard that the LORD had given his people a good harvest, she and her two daughters-in-law got ready to leave Moab and go to Judah. As they were on their way there, ⁸ Naomi said to them, "Don't you want to go back home to your own mothers? You were kind to my husband and sons, and you have always been kind to me. I pray that the LORD will be just as kind to you. ⁹ May he

---

*1.1–2 Moab: The people of Moab worshipped idols and were usually enemies of the people of Israel.

give each of you another husband and a home of your own."

Naomi kissed them. They cried [10] and said, "We want to go with you and live among your people."

[11] But she replied, "My daughters, why don't you return home? What good will it do you to go with me? Do you think I could have more sons for you to marry?* [12] You must go back home, because I am too old to marry again. Even if I got married tonight and later had more sons, [13] would you wait for them to become old enough to marry? No, my daughters! Life is harder for me than it is for you, because the Lord has turned against me."▸

[14] They cried again. Orpah kissed her mother-in-law goodbye, but Ruth held on to her. [15] Naomi then said to Ruth, "Look, your sister-in-law is going back to her people and to her gods! Why don't you go with her?"

[16] Ruth answered,

"Please don't tell me
to leave you and return home!
I will go where you go,
I will live where you live;
your people will be my people,
your God will be my God.
[17] I will die where you die
and be buried beside you.
May the Lord punish me
if we are ever separated,
even by death!"▸

[18] When Naomi saw that Ruth had made up her mind to go with her, she stopped urging her to go back.

[19] They reached Bethlehem, and the whole town was excited to see them. The women who lived there asked, "Can this really be Naomi?"

[20] Then she told them, "Don't call me Naomi any longer! Call me Mara,* because God has made my life bitter. [21] I had everything when I left, but the Lord has brought me back with nothing. How can you still call me Naomi, when God has turned against me and made my life so hard?"

[22] The barley harvest was just beginning when Naomi and Ruth, her Moabite daughter-in-law, arrived in Bethlehem.

*1.11 for you to marry: When a married man died and left no children, it was the custom for one of his brothers to marry his widow. Any children they had would then be thought of as those of the dead man, so that his family name would live on.
*1.20 Mara: In Hebrew "Naomi" means "pleasant", and "Mara" means "bitter".

Ruth meets Boaz

CHAPTER 2

[1-3] One day, Ruth said to Naomi, "Let me see if I can find someone who will let me pick up the grain left in the fields by the harvest workers."*

Naomi answered, "Go ahead, my daughter." So straight away, Ruth went out to pick up grain in a field owned by Boaz. He was a relative of Naomi's husband Elimelech, as well as a rich and important man.

[4] When Boaz left Bethlehem and went out to his field, he said to the harvest workers, "The Lord bless you!"

They replied, "And may the Lord bless you!"

[5] Then Boaz asked the man in charge of the harvest workers, "Who is that young woman?"

[6] The man answered, "She is the one who came back from Moab with Naomi. [7] She asked if she could pick up grain left by the harvest workers, and she has been working all morning without a moment's rest."▸

[8] Boaz went over to Ruth and said, "I think it would be best for you not to pick up grain in anyone else's field. Stay here with the women [9] and follow along behind them, as they gather up what the men have cut. I have warned the men not to bother you, and whenever you are thirsty, you can drink from the water jars they have filled."

[10] Ruth bowed down to the ground and said, "You know I come from another country. Why are you so good to me?"

[11] Boaz answered, "I've heard how you've helped your mother-in-law ever since your husband died. You even left your own father and mother to come and live in a foreign land among people you don't know. [12] I pray that the Lord God of Israel will reward you for what you have done. And now that you have come to him for protection, I pray that he will bless you."

[13] Ruth replied, "Sir, it's good of you to speak kindly to me and make me feel so welcome. I'm not even one of your servants."

[14] At mealtime Boaz said to Ruth, "Come, eat with us. Have some bread and dip it in the sauce." Straight away she sat down with the

*2.1-3 grain left . . . workers: It was the custom at harvest time to leave some grain in the field for the poor to pick up (see Leviticus 19.10; 23.22).
See also: 2.2: Lev 19.9-10; Deut 24.19.

Big ideas

Redemption

Ruth is all about redemption, which is an old fashioned word which means paying the price to save someone from evil.

In ancient times – and actually even up until the seventeenth century – it was common for people who were captured as slaves to be redeemed by their families. Their families would pay a price to buy them back, to free them from slavery.

This theme runs throughout the book of Ruth. Through the selfless love of Ruth and Boaz, Naomi is redeemed; brought back from hunger and homelessness to security and contentment, given a grandson, and through that, a future.

Boaz buys back the family property. He is described by Naomi as 'one of those who is supposed to look after us' (2.20) and the phrase literally means a kinsman-redeemer, someone who is supposed to rescue his relatives.

This concept is a very important one in the Bible because it describes what God does for all humans through Jesus. Through the death of Jesus we are bought back, redeemed, from slavery to sin and evil. God has paid the price. The way in which Boaz recognises his obligations is an echo of the way in which God keeps his promises. And it is through another descendant of David – Jesus – that God was truly to bring his people back to him.

Footsteps

Seven days with Redemption

Redemption from slavery: Exodus 6.6–8
Slaves, property, people: Leviticus 25.25–55
Saving those who call: Psalms 34.15–22
Prophecies of redemption: Isaiah 52.3–10
Jesus will rescue us: Luke 1.67–79
Faith redeems us: Galatians 3.10–14
Jesus to the rescue: Ephesians 1.7–14

More...

Saying sorry p.1258
Starting again p.1172
Help! I've messed up really badly p.347

workers, and Boaz handed her some roasted grain. Ruth ate all she wanted and had some left over.

[15] When Ruth got up to start picking up grain, Boaz told his men, "Don't stop her, even if she picks up grain from where it is stacked. [16] Be sure to pull out some stalks of grain from the bundles and leave them on the ground for her. And don't speak harshly to her!"

[17] Ruth worked in the field until evening. Then after she had pounded the grain off the stalks, she had a large basket full of grain. [18] She took the grain to town and showed Naomi how much she had picked up. Ruth also gave her the food left over from her lunch.

[19] Naomi said, "Where did you work today? Whose field was it? God bless the man who treated you so well!" Then Ruth told her that she had worked in the field of a man named Boaz.

[20] "The LORD bless Boaz!" Naomi replied. "He* has shown that he is still loyal to the living and to the dead. Boaz is a close relative, one of those who is supposed to look after us."

[21] Ruth told her, "Boaz even said I could stay in the field with his workers until they had finished gathering all his grain."

[22] Naomi replied, "My daughter, it's good that you can pick up grain beside the women who work in his field. Who knows what might happen to you in someone else's field!" [23] And so, Ruth stayed close to the women, while picking up grain in his field.

Ruth worked in the fields until the barley and wheat were harvested. And all this time she lived with Naomi.

Naomi makes plans for Ruth

CHAPTER 3

[1] One day, Naomi said to Ruth:

It's time I found you a husband, who will give you a home and take care of you. [2] You have been picking up grain beside the women who work for Boaz, and you know he is a relative of ours. Tonight he will be threshing the grain. [3] Now take a bath and put on some perfume, then dress in your best clothes. Go where he is working, but don't let him see you until he

See also: 2.20: Lev 25.25.

has finished eating and drinking. ⁴ Watch where he goes to spend the night, then when he is asleep, lift the cover and lie down at his feet.* He will tell you what to do.

⁵ Ruth answered, "I'll do whatever you say." ⁶ She went out to the place where Boaz was working and did what Naomi had told her.

⁷ After Boaz finished eating and drinking and was feeling happy, he went over and fell asleep near the pile of grain. Ruth slipped over quietly. She lifted the cover and lay down near his feet.

⁸ In the middle of the night, Boaz suddenly woke up and was shocked to see a woman lying at his feet. ⁹ "Who are you?" he asked.

"Sir, I am Ruth," she answered, "and you are the relative who is supposed to take care of me. So spread the edge of your cover over me."*

¹⁰ Boaz replied:

The LORD bless you! This shows how truly loyal you are to your family. You could have looked for a younger man, either rich or poor, but you didn't. ¹¹ Don't worry, I'll do what you have asked. You are respected by everyone in town.

¹² It's true that I am one of the relatives who is supposed to take care of you, but there is someone who is an even closer relative. ¹³ Stay here until morning, then I will find out if he is willing to look after you. If he isn't, I promise by the living God to do it myself. Now go back to sleep until morning.

¹⁴ Ruth lay down again, but she got up before daylight, because Boaz did not want anyone to know she had been there. ¹⁵ Then he told her to spread out her cape. And he filled it with a lot of grain and placed it on her shoulder.

When Ruth got back to town, ¹⁶ Naomi asked her⁺ what had happened, and Ruth told her everything. ¹⁷ She also said, "Boaz gave me this grain, because he didn't want me to come back without something for you."

¹⁸ Naomi replied, "Just be patient and don't worry about what will happen. He won't rest until everything is settled today!"

3.4 lift the cover . . . feet: To ask for protection and possibly for marriage.
3.9 So . . . me: To show that he would protect and take care of her.
See also: 3.12: Ruth 2.20.

Holy history

Harvest

Harvest was vitally important. If food went short, the people would starve. They couldn't just nip down to the supermarket and pick up a packet of fish fingers.

The harvest usually took place around April and May. Barley was the first crop to be harvested, followed by wheat a few weeks later.

Men would cut the crops with sickles, followed by women who would gather up the cuttings into sheaves. Then people would go through again, doing what was called 'gleaning' which means collecting the stalks which had been missed. According to the law, gleaning had to be left to the poor; the owners were not to take absolutely everything.

The wheat was taken to the threshing floor, where it would be winnowed – tossed or thrown in the air, either by hand or with winnowing forks. Threshing floors were wide open spaces which allowed the wind to get in and blow away the straw, while the grains would simply fall to the ground. The wheat would then be sifted to remove any other impurities, put into bags and then either stored or taken to be milled into flour.

For the people of those days, a successful harvest was the most important economic event of the year. It was their pay day. So it's significant that the best of their harvest was supposed to be presented to God – a symbolic reminder of who it was who gave them the harvest in the first place.

The ancient Israelites knew something that we often forget: that harvests are given by God, not purchased in the supermarket.

More...
Farming p.494
Feasts and festivals p.134

Ruth and Boaz get married

CHAPTER 4

¹ Meanwhile, Boaz had gone to the meeting place at the town gate and was sitting there when the other close relative came by. So Boaz invited him to come over and sit down, and he did. ² Then Boaz got ten of the town leaders and also asked them to sit down. After they had sat down, ³ he said to the man:

Naomi has come back from Moab and is selling the land that belonged to her husband Elimelech. ⁴ I am telling you about this, since you are his closest relative and have the right to buy the property. If you want it, you can buy it now. These ten men and the others standing here can be witnesses. But if you don't want the property, let me know, because I am next in line.

The man replied, "I will buy it!"
⁵ "If you do buy it from Naomi," Boaz told him, "you must also marry Ruth. Then if you have a son by her, the property will stay in the family of Ruth's first husband."
⁶ The man answered, "If that's the case, I don't want to buy it! That would make problems with the property I already own.* You may buy it yourself, because I cannot."
⁷ To make a sale legal in those days, one person would take off a sandal and give it to the other. ⁸ So after the man had agreed to let Boaz buy the property, he took off one of his sandals and handed it to Boaz.
⁹ Boaz told the town leaders and everyone else:

All of you are witnesses that today I have bought from Naomi the property that belonged to Elimelech and his two sons, Chilion and Mahlon. ¹⁰ You are also witnesses that I have agreed to marry Mahlon's widow Ruth, the Moabite woman. This will keep the property in his family's name, and he will be remembered in this town.

¹¹ The town leaders and the others standing there said:

We are witnesses to this. And we pray that the LORD will give your wife many children, just as he did Leah and Rachel, the wives of Jacob. May you be a rich man in the tribe of Ephrath and an important man in Bethlehem. ¹² May the children you have by this young woman make your family as famous as the family of Perez,* the son of Tamar and Judah.

¹³ Boaz married Ruth, and the LORD blessed her with a son. ¹⁴ After his birth, the women said to Naomi:

Praise the LORD! Today he has given you a grandson to take care of you. We pray that the boy will grow up to be famous everywhere in Israel. ¹⁵ He will᾽ make you happy and take care of you in your old age, because he is the son of your daughter-in-law. And she loves you more than seven sons of your own would love you.

¹⁶ Naomi loved the boy and took good care of him. ¹⁷ The neighbourhood women named him Obed, but they called him "Naomi's Boy".
When Obed grew up he had a son named Jesse, who later became the father of King David. ¹⁸⁻²² Here is a list of the ancestors of David: Jesse, Obed, Boaz, Salmon, Nahshon, Amminadab, Ram, Hezron, and Perez.

---

*4.12 Perez: One of the sons of Judah; he was an ancestor of Boaz and of many others who lived in Bethlehem.
See also: 4.12: Gen 38.27–30.

Additional notes

᾽1.13 Life . . . me: Or "I'm sorry that the LORD has turned against me and made life so hard for you."
᾽1.17 even by death: Or "by anything but death".
᾽2.7 she has . . . rest: One possible meaning for the difficult Hebrew text.
᾽2.20 He: Or "The LORD".
᾽3.15–16 When . . . her: Some Hebrew manuscripts and two ancient translations; most Hebrew manuscripts "Boaz went back to town. ¹⁶ Naomi asked Ruth".
᾽4.14–15 We pray that . . . famous . . . ¹⁵ He will: Or "We pray that the LORD will be praised everywhere in Israel. ¹⁵ Your grandson will".

---

*4.6 property . . . own: This property would then have to be shared with Ruth and her children as well as with his own family.
See also: 4.7–8: Deut 25.9.   4.10: Deut 25.5–6.
4.11: Gen 29.31.

1 Samuel

The basics

What's the point?   God wants obedience, not just good intentions.

What happens?   The people ask the prophet Samuel for a king. God gives them a king. Then God gives them another king, because the first king turns out wrong.

What should I remember?   15.22 'Does the Lord really want sacrifices and offerings? No! He doesn't want your sacrifices. He wants you to obey him.'

More details

Setting the scene   By the end of the period of the judges, the people of Israel were desperate for strong, stable leadership. So they asked the prophet Samuel to find them a king. This is the story of the first two kings, Saul and David.

What's it all about?   1 and 2 Samuel cover about one hundred years, from the close of the time of the judges to the establishment of the kingdom under David.

The first book of Samuel is a tale of three people:

First we have Samuel, one of the great prophets of Israel, and the man given the job of appointing the kings of Israel. It is Samuel who the people come to for help and who they go to with their demands and requests.

Then we have Saul, the first king of Israel, a man who should have had it all, but who persistently relies on his own judgement, rather than obeying God's commands. Saul's problem was that he could never obey simple commands; he always wanted to add something, to do his own thing. Saul starts well, but as the book continues, he becomes an increasingly unstable figure, prone to wild mood swings and ever more desperate to hold

on to his kingdom. In the end his disobedience seems to have tipped him over into a kind of madness.

And nothing – or should we say nobody – made Saul lose it more than David, the third major figure in this book. David is the real thing – a man who was passionate about God and about his country. This young shepherd/harpist/giant-slayer was the man chosen by God – and anointed by Samuel to replace Saul.

Saul can see what's going to happen, and this knowledge, along with David's success and popularity makes him drive David out of the kingdom and into exile. For his part, David had chances to kill Saul but chose to let the king live. He knew that it was not his job to 'help God out' by doing things his way. Instead he was content to obey God, to trust him and to let God work things out as he wanted.

If only Saul could have learned that lesson.

Footsteps

The calling of Samuel: 3.1–21
The people ask for a king: 8.1–22
Saul becomes king: 10.1–27
The Lord rejects Saul: 13.1–16
The Lord chooses David: 16.1–13
David v. Goliath: 17.1–58
Saul v. David: 18.6–30
David lets Saul live: 24.1–22
Saul talks to a ghost: 28.1–25
Saul dies: 31.1–13

And another thing

1 and 2 Samuel is actually one book, which is divided into two parts for the simple reason that you couldn't fit the whole thing onto one scroll.

The book was probably compiled from a number of sources which no longer survive; like the 'Book of Jashar' (2 Samuel 1.18), the 'Book of the Annals of King David' (1 Chronicles 27.24), the 'Records of Samuel the Seer', the 'Records of Nathan the Prophet' and the 'Records of Gad the Seer' (1 Chronicles 29.29).

The birth and early childhood of Samuel

CHAPTER 1

Hannah asks the LORD for a child

¹ Elkanah lived in Ramah,ʼ a town in the hill country of Ephraim. His great-great-grandfather was Zuph, so Elkanah was a member of the Zuph clan of the Ephraim tribe. Elkanah's father was Jeroham, his grandfather was Elihu, and his great-grandfather was Tohu.

² Elkanah had two wives,* Hannah and Peninnah. Although Peninnah had children, Hannah did not have any.

³ Once a year Elkanah travelled from his home town to Shiloh, where he worshipped the LORD All-Powerful and offered sacrifices. Eli was the LORD's priest there, and his two sons Hophni and Phinehas served with him as priests.ʼ

⁴ Whenever Elkanah offered a sacrifice, he gave some of the meat* to Peninnah and some to each of her sons and daughters. ⁵ But he gave Hannah even more, because he loved Hannah very much, even though the LORD had kept her from having children of her own.

⁶ Peninnah liked to make Hannah feel miserable about not having any children, ⁷ especially when the family went to the house of the LORD* each year.

One day, Elkanah was there offering a sacrifice, when Hannah began crying and refused to eat. ⁸ So Elkanah asked, "Hannah, why are you crying? Why won't you eat? Why

---

*1.2 two wives: Having more than one wife was allowed in those times.

*1.4 meat: For some sacrifices, like this one, only part of the meat was burnt. Some was given to the priest, and the rest was eaten by the family and guests of the worshipper (see Leviticus 3.1–17; 7.11–18).

*1.7 house of the LORD: Another name for the place of worship at Shiloh, which may still have been the sacred tent at this time.

Holy history

Temples and shrines

Temples were where gods 'lived'. Usually, the temple contained a statue of the god, as well as an altar for people's offerings. Although God didn't need a house in which to dwell, and had no statue, the Bible lists a number of different buildings built in his honour, and where he spoke to people.

Tabernacle or Sacred Tent

The tabernacle was a huge tent which was transported from place to place. It had an altar, candles, tables and an inner room where God could be consulted.

Shrines

In Canaan the Israelites put up the sacred tent at Shiloh (Joshua 18.1). It became a famous shrine.

Temple

King David wanted to build a temple in Jerusalem, but the work was completed by his son, Solomon. This magnificent building followed the same shape as the Tabernacle.

The shrine at Bethel

After the split, Israel's kings set up their own religious centre in Bethel, to compete with Jerusalem. This became a place of false worship (Hosea 10.15) until destroyed by King Josiah of Judah (2 Kings 23.15–20).

Footsteps

Five days with Temples and shrines

Making the sacred tent: Exodus 36.8–38
The temple in Jerusalem: 1 Kings 6.1–38
The shrine at Bethel: 1 Kings 12.26–33; 2 Kings 23.15–20
Destruction of the temple: 2 Kings 25.8–21
The second temple: Ezra 3.1–13

More...

The Tabernacle: the Sacred Tent p.107
David p.314
Solomon p.370
Ezra p.517

do you feel so bad? Don't I mean more to you than ten sons?"

⁹ When the sacrifice had been offered, and they had eaten the meal, Hannah got up and went to pray. Eli was sitting in his chair near the door to the place of worship. ¹⁰ Hannah was brokenhearted and was crying as she prayed, ¹¹ "LORD All-Powerful, I am your servant, but I am so miserable! Please let me have a son. I will give him to you for as long as he lives, and his hair will never be cut."*

¹²⁻¹³ Hannah prayed silently to the LORD for a long time. But her lips were moving, and Eli thought she was drunk. ¹⁴ "How long are you going to stay drunk?" he asked. "Sober up!"

¹⁵⁻¹⁶ "Sir, please don't think I'm no good!" Hannah answered. "I'm not drunk, and I haven't been drinking. But I do feel miserable and terribly upset. I've been praying all this time, telling the LORD about my problems."

¹⁷ Eli replied, "You may go home now and stop worrying. I'm sure the God of Israel will answer your prayer."

¹⁸ "Sir, thank you for being so kind to me," Hannah said. Then she left, and after eating something, she felt much better.

Samuel is born

¹⁹ Elkanah and his family got up early the next morning and worshipped the LORD. Then they went back home to Ramah. Later the LORD blessed Elkanah and Hannah ²⁰ with a son. She named him Samuel because she had asked the LORD for him.*

Hannah gives Samuel to the LORD

²¹ The next time Elkanah and his family went to offer their yearly sacrifice, he took along a gift that he had promised to give to the LORD. ²² But Hannah stayed at home, because she had told Elkanah, "Samuel and I won't go until he's old enough for me to stop nursing him. Then I'll give him to the LORD, and he can stay there at Shiloh for the rest of his life."

²³ "You know what's best," Elkanah said. "Stay here until it's time to stop nursing him. I'm sure the LORD will help you do what you

have promised."‣ Hannah did not go to Shiloh until she stopped nursing Samuel.

²⁴⁻²⁵ When it was the time of year to go to Shiloh again, Hannah and Elkanah‣ took Samuel to the LORD's house. They brought along a three-year-old bull,‣ a sack containing about nine kilogrammes of flour, and a clay jar full of wine. Hannah and Elkanah offered the bull as a sacrifice, then brought the little boy to Eli.

²⁶ "Sir," Hannah said, "a few years ago I stood here beside you and asked the LORD ²⁷ to give me a child. Here he is! The LORD gave me just what I asked for. ²⁸ Now I am giving him to the LORD, and he will be the LORD's servant for as long as he lives."

CHAPTER 2

Hannah prays

Elkanah‣ worshipped the LORD there at Shiloh, and ¹ Hannah prayed:

You make me strong
  and happy, LORD.
You rescued me.
Now I can be glad
  and laugh at my enemies.

² No other god‣ is like you.
We're safer with you
  than on a high mountain.‣
³ I can tell those proud people,
  "Stop your boasting!
Nothing is hidden from the LORD,
  and he judges what we do."

⁴ Our LORD, you break
  the bows of warriors,
but you give strength
  to everyone who stumbles.
⁵ People who once had plenty to eat
  must now hire themselves out
  for only a piece of bread.
But you give the hungry more
  than enough to eat.
A woman did not have a child,
  and you gave her seven,
but a woman who had many
  was left with none.
⁶ You take away life,
  and you give life.
You send people down
  to the world of the dead
  and bring them back again.

⁷ Our LORD, you are the one
  who makes us rich or poor.

---

*1.11 his hair . . . cut: Never cutting the child's hair would be a sign that he would belong to the LORD (see Numbers 6.1,21, especially verse 5).
*1.20 him: In Hebrew "Samuel" sounds something like "Someone from God" or "The name of God" or "His name is God".
See also: 1.11: Num 6.5.

See also: 2.1–10: Luke 1.46–55.

Life files

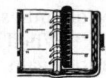

Samuel

Background: Son of Hannah and Elkanah

What's the story?

Samuel was born as a result of prayer. His mother dedicated him to the LORD at an early age and sent him to serve in the shrine at Shiloh. He became the chief prophet of Israel, and the last of the judges (1 Samuel 7.13–17).

When the people of Israel asked him for a king, Samuel told them what the LORD thought of the idea, but then anointed first Saul and then David. He gave a farewell speech when he was old, but he still lived long enough to condemn Saul and anoint David. After his death, Saul called up his ghost – much to the dead prophet's annoyance.

What's the point?

It was Samuel who oversaw the transition of Israel from the judges to the Kings. He saw the country through a time of change and difficulty, calling the people to return to the true worship of God and even leading Israel in battle against the Philistines (1 Samuel 7.3–13).

The people looked to Samuel to tell them what God wanted. He was not the King; he was the man who anointed the kings. It was a sign that even though Israel had kings now, God was still in charge, and what his prophets said overruled the words even of a king.

 Footsteps

A week with Samuel

The birth of Samuel: 1 Samuel 1.1–20
God speaks to Samuel: 1 Samuel 3.1–4.1
Samuel leads Israel: 1 Samuel 7.3–17
The people ask for a King: 1 Samuel 8.1–22
Samuel anoints Saul: 1 Samuel 10.1–8
Samuel condemns Saul: 1 Samuel 15.10–35
Samuel anoints David: 1 Samuel 16.1–13

More...

Saul p.305
David p.314

You put some in high positions
  and bring disgrace on others.
⁸ You lift the poor and homeless
  out of the rubbish dump
and give them places of honour
  in royal palaces.

You set the world on foundations,
  and they belong to you.
⁹ You protect your loyal people,
  but everyone who is evil
    will die in darkness.

We cannot win a victory
  by our own strength.
¹⁰ Our LORD, those who attack you
    will be broken in pieces
  when you fight back
    with thunder from heaven.
You will judge the whole earth
  and give power and strength
    to your chosen king.

Samuel at the sacred tent

Samuel stays with Eli

¹¹ Elkanah and Hannah went back home to Ramah, but the boy Samuel stayed to help Eli serve the LORD.

Eli's sons

¹²⁻¹³ Eli's sons were priests, but they were dishonest and refused to obey the LORD. So, while people were boiling the meat from their sacrifices, these priests would send over a servant with a large, three-pronged fork. ¹⁴ The servant would stick the fork into the cooking pot, and whatever meat came out on the fork was taken back to the priests. That is how these two priests treated every Israelite who came to offer sacrifices in Shiloh. ¹⁵ Sometimes, when people were offering sacrifices, the servant would come over, even before the fat had been cut off and sacrificed to the LORD.*

Then the servant would tell them, "The priest doesn't want his meat boiled! Give him some raw meat that he can roast!"

¹⁶ Usually the people answered, "Take what you want. But first, let us sacrifice the fat to the LORD."

"No," the servant would reply. "If you don't give it to me now, I'll take it by force."

---

*2.15 sacrificed to the LORD: The fat belonged to the LORD and was supposed to be burnt as a sacrifice before the rest of the animal was cooked and eaten (see Leviticus 3.3–4,9–10,14–15).

¹⁷ Eli's sons did not show any respect for the sacrifices that the people offered. This was a terrible sin, and it made the LORD very angry.

Hannah visits Samuel

¹⁸ The boy Samuel served the LORD and wore a special linen garment* ¹⁹ and the clothes* his mother made for him. She would bring new clothes every year, when she and her husband came to offer sacrifices at Shiloh.
²⁰ Eli would always bless Elkanah and his wife and say, "Samuel was born in answer to your prayers. Now you have given him to the LORD. I pray that the LORD will bless you with more children to take his place." After Eli had blessed them, Elkanah and Hannah would return home.
²¹ The LORD was kind to Hannah, and she had three more sons and two daughters. But Samuel grew up at the LORD's house in Shiloh.

Eli warns his sons

²² Eli was now very old, and he heard what his sons were doing to the people of Israel.◆
²³⁻²⁴ "Why are you doing these awful things?" he asked them. "I've been hearing nothing but complaints about you from all the LORD's people. ²⁵ If you harm another person, God can help make things right between the two of you. But if you commit a crime against the LORD, no one can help you!"
But the LORD had already decided to kill them. So he kept them from listening to their father.

A prophet speaks to Eli

²⁶ Each day the LORD and his people liked Samuel more and more.
²⁷ One day a prophet came to Eli and gave him this message from the LORD:

When your ancestors were slaves of the king of Egypt, I came and showed them who I am. ²⁸⁻²⁹ Out of all the tribes of Israel, I chose your family to be my priests. I wanted them to offer sacrifices and burn

incense to me and to find out from me what I want my people to do. I commanded everyone to bring their sacrifices here where I live, and I allowed you and your family to keep those that were not offered to me on the altar.
But you honour your sons instead of me! You don't respect◆ the sacrifices and offerings that are brought to me, and you've all got fat from eating the best parts.
³⁰ I am the LORD, the God of Israel. I promised to let your family serve me as priests for ever, but now I tell you that I cannot do this any longer! I honour anyone who honours me, but I put a curse on anyone who hates me. ³¹ The time will come when I will kill you and everyone else in your family. Not one of you will live to an old age.
³² Your family◆ will have a lot of trouble. I will be kind to Israel,◆ but everyone in your family will die young. ³³ If I let anyone from your family be a priest, his◆ life will be full of sadness and sorrow. But most of the men in your family will die a violent death!◆ ³⁴ To prove to you that I will do these things, your two sons, Hophni and Phinehas, will die on the same day.
³⁵ I have chosen someone else to be my priest, someone who will be faithful and obey me. I will always let his family serve as priests and help my chosen king. ³⁶ But if anyone is left from your family, he will come to my priest and beg for money or a little bread. He may even say to my priest, "Please let me be a priest, so I will at least have something to eat."

CHAPTER 3

The LORD speaks to Samuel

¹⁻² Samuel served the LORD by helping Eli the priest, who was by that time almost blind. In those days, the LORD hardly ever spoke directly to people, and he did not appear to them in dreams very often. But one night, Eli was asleep in his room, ³ and Samuel was sleeping on a mat near the sacred chest in the LORD's house. They had not been asleep very long* ⁴ when the LORD called out Samuel's name.
"Here I am!" Samuel answered. ⁵ Then he ran to Eli and said, "Here I am. What do you want?"

---

*2.18 a special linen garment: Either a loin cloth or a jacket or an apron worn only by priests.
*2.19 clothes: The Hebrew word means a sleeveless coat or robe that was worn by priests. Samuel was a small child, but his mother made him clothes just like those worn by priests.
See also: **2.26:** Luke 2.52. **2.28:** a Exod 28.1-4; b Lev 7.35-36.

*3.3 They . . . long: The Hebrew text has "The lamp was still burning". An olive oil lamp would go out after a few hours if the wick was not adjusted.
See also: **2.34:** 1 Sam 4.11.

"I didn't call you," Eli answered. "Go back to bed."

Samuel went back.

⁶ Again the LORD called out Samuel's name. Samuel got up and went to Eli. "Here I am," he said. "What do you want?"

Eli told him, "Son, I didn't call you. Go back to sleep."

⁷ The LORD had not spoken to Samuel before, and Samuel did not recognize the voice. ⁸ When the LORD called out his name for the third time, Samuel went to Eli again and said, "Here I am. What do you want?"

Eli finally realized that it was the LORD who was speaking to Samuel. ⁹ So he said, "Go back and lie down! If someone speaks to you again, answer, 'I'm listening, LORD. What do you want me to do?' "

Once again Samuel went back and lay down. ¹⁰ The LORD then stood beside Samuel and called out as he had done before, "Samuel! Samuel!"

"I'm listening," Samuel answered. "What do you want me to do?"

¹¹ The LORD said:

Samuel, I am going to do something in Israel that will shock everyone who hears about it! ¹² I will punish Eli and his family, just as I promised. ¹³ He knew that his sons refused to respect me,' and he let them get away with it, even though I said I would punish his family for ever. ¹⁴ I warned Eli that sacrifices or offerings could never make things right! His family has done too many disgusting things.

¹⁵ The next morning, Samuel got up and opened the doors of the LORD's house. He was afraid to tell Eli what the LORD had said. ¹⁶ But Eli told him, "Samuel, my boy, come here!"

"Here I am," Samuel answered.

¹⁷ Eli said, "What did God say to you? Tell me everything. I pray that God will punish you terribly if you don't tell me every word he said!"

¹⁸ Samuel told Eli everything. Then Eli said, "He is the LORD, and he will do what's right."

The LORD helps Samuel

¹⁹ As Samuel grew up, the LORD helped him and made everything Samuel said come true. ²⁰ From the town of Dan in the north to the town of Beersheba in the south, everyone in the country knew that Samuel was truly the LORD's prophet. ²¹ The LORD often appeared to Samuel at Shiloh and told him what to say.

Helpline

Help! How do I know it's God and not my emotions?

'I heard this speaker and now I'm all fired up! But is it me? Or is it God?'

Sometimes you get these feelings. You're in church and you get enthused. You're watching TV and you want to respond. You read the Bible and things just seem to leap out at you. You want to do something.

But can your feelings be trusted? Like Samuel in this story, you don't know if you've heard God's voice, or someone else's (1 Samuel 3.7).

Christianity is based on facts. But at the same time, God does want us to get fired up about the things that really matter in this world. He wants us to be excited about our faith, thrilled by his love, awestruck at his power. He wants us to be appalled by suffering, outraged by injustice and angry about evil.

So emotions are necessary. What we have to do is bring the two sides together.

Three things

Time

Don't rush into things. One of the surest tests of whether it was 'just your emotions speaking' is whether you still feel as strongly about it tomorrow morning, or next week, or next month. If the feelings persist, that's a clue it could be from God.

Check

Talk to others about how you feel. Samuel needed to talk to Eli before he knew what was happening. Pray with them. If they feel that you're letting your emotions run away with you, listen to their wisdom.

Light

See what the Bible has to say. Look at your feelings in the light of the Bible. Are there verses to back up what you feel? Is God speaking to you through a certain passage in the Bible?

More...

Guidance p.685

CHAPTER 4

[1] Then Samuel would speak to the whole nation of Israel.

The sacred chest is captured and returned

The Philistines capture the sacred chest

One day the Israelites went out to fight the Philistines. They set up camp near Ebenezer, and the Philistines camped at Aphek. [2] The Philistines made a fierce attack. They defeated the Israelites and killed about four thousand of them.

[3] The Israelite army returned to their camp, and the leaders said, "Why did the LORD let us lose to the Philistines today? Let's get the sacred chest where the LORD's agreement with Israel is kept. Then the LORD' will help us and rescue us from our enemies."

[4] The army sent some soldiers to bring back the sacred chest from Shiloh, because the LORD All-Powerful has his throne on the winged creatures on top of the chest.

As Eli's two sons, Hophni and Phinehas, [5] brought the chest into camp, the army cheered so loudly that the ground shook. [6] The Philistines heard the noise and said, "What are those Hebrews shouting about?"

When the Philistines learnt that the sacred chest had been brought into the camp, [7] they were scared to death and said:

The gods have come into their camp. Now we're in real trouble! Nothing like this has ever happened to us before. [8] We're in big trouble! Who can save us from these powerful gods? They're the same gods who made all those horrible things happen to the Egyptians in the desert.

[9] Philistines, be brave and fight hard! If you don't, those Hebrews will rule us, just as we've been ruling them. Fight and don't be afraid.

[10] The Philistines did fight. They killed thirty thousand Israelite soldiers, and all the rest ran off to their homes. [11] Hophni and Phinehas were killed, and the sacred chest was captured.

Eli dies

[12] That same day a soldier from the tribe of Benjamin ran from the battlefront to Shiloh. He had torn his clothes and put earth on his

See also: 4.4: Exod 25.22.

head to show his sorrow. [13] He went into town and told the news about the battle, and everyone started crying.

Eli was afraid that something might happen to the sacred chest. So he was sitting on his chair beside the road, just waiting. [14-15] He was ninety-eight years old and blind, but he could hear everyone crying, and he asked, "What's all that noise?"

The soldier hurried over and told Eli, [16] "I escaped from the fighting today and ran here."

"Young man, what happened?" Eli asked.

[17] "Israel ran away from the Philistines," the soldier answered. "Many of our people were killed, including your two sons, Hophni and Phinehas. But worst of all, the sacred chest was captured."

[18] Eli was still sitting on a chair beside the wall of the town gate. And when the man said that the Philistines had taken the sacred chest, Eli fell backwards. He was a very heavy old man, and the fall broke his neck and killed him. He had been a leader* of Israel for forty years.

[19] The wife of Phinehas was about to give birth. And soon after she heard that the sacred chest had been captured and that her husband and his father had died, her baby came. The birth was very hard, [20] and she was dying. But the women taking care of her said, "Don't be afraid — it's a boy!"

She didn't pay any attention to them. [21-22] Instead she kept thinking about losing her husband and her father-in-law. So she said, "My son will be named Ichabod,* because the glory of Israel left our country when the sacred chest was captured."

CHAPTER 5

God causes trouble for the Philistines

[1] The Philistines took the sacred chest from near Ebenezer to the town of Ashdod. [2] They brought it into the temple of their god Dagon and put it next to the statue of Dagon, which they worshipped.

[3] When the people of Ashdod got up early the next morning, they found the statue lying face down on the floor in front of the sacred chest. They put the statue back where it belonged. [4] But early the next morning, it had fallen over again and was lying face

---

*4.18 leader: The Hebrew word means that Eli may have been an army commander, a judge, and a priest.
*4.21–22 Ichabod: Ichabod means "where is the glory?" or "there is no glory".

down on the floor in front of the chest. The body of the statue was still in one piece, but its head and both hands had broken off and were lying on the stone floor in the doorway. ⁵ This is the reason the priests and everyone else step over that part of the doorway when they enter the temple of Dagon in Ashdod.

⁶ The LORD caused a lot of trouble for the people of Ashdod and their neighbours. He made sores break out all over their bodies,' and everyone was in a panic.' ⁷ Finally, they said, "The God of Israel did this. He is the one who caused all this trouble for us and our god Dagon. We've got to get rid of this chest."

⁸ The people of Ashdod called all the Philistine rulers to Ashdod, and they asked them, "What can we do with the sacred chest that belongs to the God of Israel?"

"Send it to Gath," the rulers answered. But after they took it there, ⁹ the LORD made sores break out on everyone in town. The people of Gath were frightened, ¹⁰ so they sent the sacred chest to Ekron. But before they could take it through the town gates, the people of Ekron started screaming, "They've brought the sacred chest that belongs to the God of Israel! It will kill us and our families too!"

The Philistines send back the sacred chest

¹¹ The people of Ekron called for another meeting of the Philistine rulers and told them, "Send this chest back where it belongs. Then it won't kill us."

Everyone was in a panic, because God was causing a lot of people to die, ¹² and those who had survived were suffering from the sores. They all cried to their gods for help.

CHAPTER 6

¹ After the sacred chest had been in Philistia for seven months,' ² the Philistines called in their priests and fortune-tellers, and asked, "What should we do with this sacred chest? Tell us how to send it back where it belongs!"

³ "Don't send it back without a gift," the priests and fortune-tellers answered. "Send along something to Israel's God to make up for taking the chest in the first place. Then you will be healed, and you will find out why the LORD was causing you so much trouble."

⁴ "What should we send?" the Philistines asked.

The priests and fortune-tellers answered:

There are five Philistine rulers, and they all have the same disease that you have. ⁵ So make five gold models of the sores and five gold models of the rats that are wiping out your crops. If you honour the God of Israel with this gift, perhaps he will stop causing trouble for you and your gods and your crops. ⁶ Don't be like the Egyptians and their king. They were stubborn, but when Israel's God had finished with them, they had to let Israel go.

⁷ Get a new cart and two cows that have young calves and that have never pulled a cart. Hitch the cows to the cart, but take the calves back to their barn. ⁸ Then put the chest on the cart. Put the gold rats and sores into a bag and put it on the cart next to the chest. Then send it on its way.

⁹ Watch to see if the chest goes on up the road to the Israelite town of Beth-Shemesh. If it goes back to its own country, you will know that it was the LORD who made us suffer so badly. But if the chest doesn't go back to its own country, then the LORD had nothing to do with the disease that hit us — it was simply bad luck.

¹⁰ The Philistines followed their advice. They hitched up the two cows to the cart, but they kept their calves in a barn. ¹¹ Then they put the chest on the cart, along with the bag that had the gold rats and sores in it.

¹² The cows went straight up the road towards Beth-Shemesh, mooing as they went. The Philistine rulers followed them until they got close to Beth-Shemesh.

¹³ The people of Beth-Shemesh were harvesting their wheat* in the valley. When they looked up and saw the chest, they were so happy that they stopped working and started celebrating.

¹⁴⁻¹⁵ The cows left the road and pulled the cart into a field that belonged to Joshua from Beth-Shemesh, and they stopped beside a huge rock. Some men from the tribe of Levi were there. So they took the chest off the cart and placed it on the rock, and then they did the same thing with the bag of gold rats and sores. A few other people chopped up the cart and made a fire. They killed the cows and burnt them as sacrifices to the LORD. After that, they offered more sacrifices.

¹⁶ When the five rulers of the Philistines saw what had happened, they went back to Ekron that same day.

---

*6.13 wheat: The wheat harvest took place in May and June.

17 That is how the Philistines sent gifts to the LORD to make up for taking the sacred chest. They sent five gold sores, one each for their towns of Ashdod, Gaza, Ashkelon, Gath, and Ekron. 18 They also sent one gold rat for each walled town and for every village that the five Philistine rulers controlled. The huge stone' where the Levites set the chest is still there in Joshua's field as a reminder of what happened.

The sacred chest is sent to Kiriath-Jearim

19 Some of the men of Beth-Shemesh looked inside the sacred chest, and the LORD God killed seventy' of them. This made the people of Beth-Shemesh very sad, 20 and they started saying, "No other God is like the LORD! Who can go near him and still live? We'll have to send the chest away from here. But where can we send it?"

21 They sent messengers to tell the people of Kiriath-Jearim, "The Philistines have sent back the sacred chest. Why don't you take it and keep it there with you?"

CHAPTER 7

1 The people of Kiriath-Jearim got the chest and took it to Abinadab's house, which was on a hill in their town. They chose his son Eleazar to take care of it, 2 and it stayed there for twenty years.

During this time everyone in Israel was very sad and begged the LORD for help.'

Samuel as the leader of Israel

The people of Israel turn back to the LORD

3 One day, Samuel told all the people of Israel, "If you really want to turn back to the LORD, then prove it. Get rid of your foreign idols, including the ones of the goddess Astarte. Turn to the LORD with all your heart and worship only him. Then he will rescue you from the Philistines."

4 The people got rid of their idols of Baal and Astarte and began worshipping only the LORD.

5 Then Samuel said, "Tell everyone in Israel to meet together at Mizpah, and I will pray to the LORD for you."

6 The Israelites met together at Mizpah with Samuel as their leader. They drew water from the well and poured it out as an offering to the LORD. On that same day they went without eating to show their sorrow, and they confessed they had been unfaithful to the LORD.

The Philistines attack Israel

7 When the Philistine rulers found out about the meeting at Mizpah, they sent an army there to attack the people of Israel.

The Israelites were afraid when they heard that the Philistines were coming. 8 "Don't stop praying!" they told Samuel. "Ask the LORD our God to rescue us."

9-10 Samuel begged the LORD to rescue Israel, then he sacrificed a young lamb to the LORD. Samuel had not even finished offering the sacrifice when the Philistines started to attack. But the LORD answered his prayer and made thunder crash all around them. The Philistines panicked and ran away. 11 The men of Israel left Mizpah and went after them as far as the hillside below Beth-Car, killing every enemy soldier they caught.

12-13 The Philistines were so badly beaten that it was quite a while before they attacked Israel again. After the battle, Samuel set up a monument between Mizpah and the rocky cliffs. He named it "Help Monument" to remind Israel how much the LORD had helped them.

For as long as Samuel lived, the LORD helped Israel fight the Philistines. 14 The Israelites were even able to recapture their towns and territory between Ekron and Gath.

Israel was also at peace with the Amorites.*

Samuel is a leader in Israel

15 Samuel was a leader* in Israel all his life. 16 Every year he would go around to the towns of Bethel, Gilgal, and Mizpah where he served as judge for the people. 17 Then he would go back to his home in Ramah and do the same thing there. He also had an altar built for the LORD at Ramah.

*7.14 Amorites: In this verse, the non-Israelite peoples of Canaan.
*7.15 leader: The Hebrew word could mean an army commander, a judge, and a religious leader.

See also: 7.1: 2 Sam 6.2–4; 1 Chron 13.5–7.

Saul, the first king of Israel

CHAPTER 8

The people of Israel want a king

1-2 Samuel had two sons. The elder one was Joel, and the younger one was Abijah. When Samuel was getting old, he let them be leaders* at Beersheba. 3 But they were not like their father. They were dishonest and accepted bribes to give unfair decisions.

4 One day the nation's leaders came to Samuel at Ramah 5 and said, "You are an old man. You set a good example for your sons, but they haven't followed it. Now we want a king to be our leader,* just like all the other nations. Choose one for us!"

6 Samuel was upset to hear the leaders say they wanted a king, so he prayed about it. 7 The LORD answered:

Samuel, do everything they want you to do. I am really the one they have rejected as their king. 8 Ever since the day I rescued my people from Egypt, they have turned from me to worship idols. Now they are turning away from you. 9 Do everything they ask, but warn them and tell them how a king will treat them.

10 Samuel told the people who were asking for a king what the LORD had said:

11 If you have a king, this is how he will treat you. He will force your sons to join his army. Some of them will ride in his chariots, some will serve in the cavalry, and others will run ahead of his own chariot.* 12 Some of them will be officers in charge of a thousand soldiers, and others will be in charge of fifty. Still others will have to farm the king's land and harvest his crops, or make weapons and parts for his chariots. 13 Your daughters will have to make perfume or do his cooking and baking.

14 The king will take your best fields, as well as your vineyards and olive orchards, and give them to his own officials. 15 He will also take a tenth of your grain and grapes and give it to his officers and officials.

16 The king will take your slaves and your best young men and your donkeys and make them do his work. 17 He will also take a tenth of your sheep and goats. You will become the king's slaves, 18 and you will finally cry out for the LORD to save you from the king you wanted. But the LORD won't answer your prayers.

19-20 The people would not listen to Samuel. "No!" they said. "We want to be like other nations. We want a king to rule us and lead us in battle."

21 Samuel listened to them and then told the LORD exactly what they had said. 22 "Do what they want," the LORD answered. "Give them a king."

Samuel told the people to go back to their homes.

CHAPTER 9

Saul meets Samuel

1 Kish was a wealthy man who belonged to the tribe of Benjamin. His father was Abiel, his grandfather was Zeror, his great-grandfather was Becorath, and his great-great-grandfather was Aphiah. 2 Kish had a son named Saul, who was better looking and more than a head taller than anyone else in all Israel.

3 Kish owned some donkeys, but they had run off. So he told Saul, "Take one of the servants and go and look for the donkeys."

4 Saul and the servant went through the hill country of Ephraim and the territory of Shalishah, but they could not find the donkeys. Then they went through the territories of Shaalim and Benjamin, but still there was no sign of the donkeys. 5 Finally they came to the territory where the clan of Zuph* lived. "Let's go back home," Saul told his servant. "If we don't go back soon, my father will stop worrying about the donkeys and start worrying about us!"

6 "Wait!" the servant answered. "There's a man of God who lives in a town near here. He's amazing! Everything he says comes true. Let's talk to him. Perhaps he can tell us where to look."

7 Saul said, "How can we talk to the prophet when I don't have anything to give him? We don't even have any bread left in our sacks. What can we give him?"

8 "I have a small piece of silver," the servant answered. "We can give him that, and then he will tell us where to look for the donkeys."

---

*8.1-2 leaders: See the note at 7.15.
*8.5 leader: See the note at 7.15.
*8.11 others . . . chariot: These men were probably his bodyguards.
See also: 8.5: Deut 17.14.

*9.5 Zuph: Samuel's father Elkanah was from the Zuph clan.

Life files

Saul

Background: Son of Kish

What's the story?

Saul was Israel's first king. A handsome, tall warrior, he was selected by Samuel at the prompting of the Lord. He too had the gift of prophecy, but his disobedience to the LORD meant that, two years after he had become king, Samuel told him that the LORD had a replacement lined up.

That replacement was David, and from then on, Saul became obsessed with his rival. He tried to kill David, then fought a civil war against him. When the Philistines attacked again, Saul visited a witch to try to speak to the dead spirit of Samuel. In the end, he and his sons died on the slopes of Mount Gilboa, killed by the Philistines.

What's the point?

Saul's reign is a bit baffling. God chooses him and then, two years later, rejects him. The problem was Saul's attitude. He was capable of prophecy, but he was incapable of understanding. He never did just as the LORD commanded, he was always trying to take things into his own hands. And later his hatred and jealousy of David drove him to ever more stupid and evil actions.

Perhaps the point about Saul is that it is one thing to be chosen, it is another thing to obey. Saul was anointed as the first king of Israel, but he did not live up to the task. God gave him the opportunity to lead Israel, but he simply would not listen.

Footsteps

A week with Saul

Saul is chosen: 1 Samuel 9.1–10.8
Early successes: 1 Samuel 11.1–15
Saul disobeys God: 1 Samuel 15.1–35
Saul tries to kill David: 1 Samuel 18.6–11
Samuel's ghost: 1 Samuel 28.1–25
The death of Saul: 1 Samuel 31.1–13

More...

Samuel p.298
David p.314

9-10 "Great!" Saul replied. "Let's go to the man who can see visions!" He said this because in those days God would answer questions by giving visions to prophets.

Saul and his servant went to the town where the prophet lived. 11 As they were going up the hill to the town, they met some young women coming out to get water,* and the two men said to them, "We're looking for the man who can see visions. Is he in town?"

12 "Yes, he is," they replied. "He's in town today because there's going to be a sacrifice and a sacred meal at the place of worship. In fact, he's just ahead of you. Hurry 13 and you should find him just inside the town gate. He's on his way out to the place of worship to eat with the invited guests. They can't start eating until he blesses the sacrifice. If you go now, you should find him."

14 They went to the town, and just as they were going through the gate, Samuel was coming out on his way to the place of worship.

15 The day before Saul came, the LORD had told Samuel, 16 "I've seen how my people are suffering, and I've heard their call for help. About this time tomorrow I'll send you a man from the tribe of Benjamin, who will rescue my people from the Philistines. I want you to pour olive oil* on his head to show that he will be their leader."

17 Samuel looked at Saul, and the LORD told Samuel, "This is the man I told you about. He's the one who will rule Israel."

18 Saul went over to Samuel in the gateway and said, "A man who can see visions lives here in town. Could you tell me the way to his house?"

19 "I am the one who sees visions!" Samuel answered. "Go on up to the place of worship. You will eat with me today, and in the morning I'll answer your questions. 20 Don't worry about your donkeys that ran off three days ago. They've already been found. Everything of value in Israel now belongs to you and your family."

21 "Why are you telling me this?" Saul asked. "I'm from Benjamin, the smallest tribe in Israel, and my clan is the least important in the tribe."

---

*9.11 water: Towns were often built on a hill near a source of water, which would often be down in the valley outside the town. It was usually the job of women to get water for their family.

*9.16 olive oil: Olive oil was poured on the head of someone who was chosen to be a priest, a prophet, or a king.

Saul eats with Samuel and stays at his house

22 Samuel took Saul and his servant into the dining room at the place of worship. About thirty people were there for the dinner, but Samuel gave Saul and his servant the places of honour. 23-24 Then Samuel told the cook, "I gave you the best piece of meat and told you to set it aside. Bring it here now."

The cook brought the meat over and set it down in front of Saul. "This is for you," Samuel told him. "Go ahead and eat it. I had this piece saved especially for you, and I invited these guests to eat with you."

After Saul and Samuel had finished eating, 25 they went down from the place of worship and back into town. A bed was set up for Saul on the flat roof* of Samuel's house, 26 and Saul slept there.

About sunrise the next morning,' Samuel called up to Saul on the roof, "Time to get up! I'll help you get started on your way."

Saul got up. He and Samuel left together 27 and had almost reached the edge of town when Samuel stopped and said, "Tell your servant to go on. Stay here with me for a few minutes, and I'll tell you what God has told me."

Samuel tells Saul he will be king

After the servant had gone,

CHAPTER 10

1 Samuel took a small jar of olive oil and poured it on Saul's head. Then he kissed* Saul and told him:

The LORD has chosen you to be the leader and ruler of his people.' 2 When you leave me today, you'll meet two men near Rachel's tomb at Zelzah in the territory of Benjamin. They'll tell you, "The donkeys you've been looking for have been found. Your father has forgotten about them, and now he's worrying about you! He's wondering how he can find you."

3 Go on from there until you reach the big oak tree at Tabor, where you'll meet three men on their way to worship God at Bethel. One of them will be leading three young goats, another will be carrying three round loaves of bread, and the last one will be carrying a clay jar of wine. 4 After they greet you, they'll give you two loaves of bread.

5 Next, go to Gibeah,' where the Philistines have an army camp. As you're going into the town, you'll meet a group of prophets coming down from the place of worship. They'll be going along prophesying while others are walking in front of them, playing small harps, small drums, and flutes.

6 The Spirit of the LORD will suddenly take control of you.' You'll become a different person and start prophesying along with them. 7 After these things happen, do whatever you think is right! God will help you.

8 Then you should go to Gilgal. I'll come a little later, so wait for me. It may even take a week for me to get there, but when I come, I'll offer sacrifices and offerings to the LORD. I'll also tell you what to do next.

Saul goes back home

9 As Saul turned around to leave Samuel, God made Saul feel like a different person. That same day, everything happened just as Samuel had said. 10 When Saul arrived at Gibeah, a group of prophets met him. The Spirit of God suddenly took control of him,' and there in the middle of the group he began prophesying.

11 Some people who had known Saul for a long time saw that he was speaking and behaving like a prophet. They said to each other, "What's happened? How can Saul be a prophet?"

12 "Why not?" one of them answered. "Saul has as much right to be a prophet as anyone else!"' That's why everyone started saying, "How can Saul be a prophet?"

13 After Saul stopped prophesying, he went to the place of worship.

14 Later, Saul's uncle asked him, "Where have you been?"

Saul answered, "Looking for the donkeys. We couldn't find them, so we went to talk with Samuel."

15 "And what did he tell you?" Saul's uncle asked.

16 Saul answered, "He told us the donkeys had been found." But Saul didn't mention that Samuel had chosen him to be king.

---

*9.25 roof: Guests often slept on the flat roof of their host's house, where it was cool and breezy.

*10.1 kissed: Relatives or close friends often greeted one another with a kiss. But this may have been a ceremonial kiss after Samuel poured oil on Saul's head to show that he was to be the king.

See also: 10.12: 1 Sam 19.23-24.

The LORD shows Israel that Saul will be king

17 Samuel sent messengers to tell the Israelites to come to Mizpah and meet with the LORD. 18 When everyone had arrived, Samuel said:

The LORD God of Israel told me to remind you that he had rescued you from the Egyptians and from the other nations that abused you.

19 God has rescued you from your troubles and hard times. But you have rejected your God and have asked for a king. Now each tribe and clan must come near the place of worship so the LORD can choose a king.

20 Samuel brought each tribe, one after the other, to the altar, and the LORD chose the Benjamin tribe. 21 Next, Samuel brought each clan of Benjamin there, and the LORD chose the Matri clan. Finally, Saul the son of Kish was chosen. But when they looked for him, he was nowhere to be found.

22 The people prayed, "Our LORD, is Saul here?"

"Yes," the LORD answered, "he is hiding behind the baggage."

23 The people ran and got Saul and brought him into the middle of the crowd. He was more than a head taller than anyone else. 24 "Look closely at the man the LORD has chosen!" Samuel told the crowd. "There is no one like him!"

The crowd shouted, "Long live the king!"

25 Samuel explained the rights and duties of a king and wrote them all in a book. He put the book in a temple building at one of the places where the LORD was worshipped. Then Samuel sent everyone home.

26 God had encouraged some young men to become followers of Saul, and when he returned to his home town of Gibeah, they went with him. 27 But some worthless fools said, "How can someone like Saul rescue us from our enemies?" They did not want Saul to be their king, and so they didn't bring him any gifts. But Saul kept calm.

CHAPTER 11

Saul rescues the town of Jabesh in Gilead

1 About this time,' King Nahash of Ammon came with his army and surrounded the town of Jabesh in Gilead. The people who lived there told Nahash, "If you will sign a peace treaty with us, you can be our ruler, and we will pay taxes to you."

2 Nahash answered, "Certainly, I'll sign a treaty! But not before I insult Israel by putting out the right eye of every man who lives in Jabesh."

3 The town leaders said, "Give us seven days so we can send messengers everywhere in Israel to ask for help. If no one comes here to save us, we will surrender to you."

4 Some of the messengers went to Gibeah, Saul's home town. They told what was happening at Jabesh, and everyone in Gibeah started crying. 5 Just then, Saul came in from the fields, walking behind his oxen.

"Why is everyone crying?" Saul asked.

They told him what the men from Jabesh had said. 6 Then the Spirit of God suddenly took control of Saul and made him furious. 7 Saul killed two of his oxen, cut them up in pieces, and gave the pieces to the' messengers. He told them to show the pieces to everyone in Israel and say, "Saul and Samuel are getting an army together. Come and join them. If you don't, this is what will happen to your oxen!"

The LORD made the people of Israel terribly afraid. So all the men came together 8 at Bezek. Saul had them organized and counted. There were three hundred thousand from Israel and thirty thousand' from Judah.

9 Saul and his officers sent the messengers back to Jabesh with this promise: "We will rescue you tomorrow afternoon." The messengers went back to the people at Jabesh and told them that they were going to be rescued.

Everyone was encouraged! 10 So they told the Ammonites, "We will surrender to you tomorrow, and then you can do whatever you want to."

11 The next day, Saul divided his army into three groups and attacked before daylight. They started killing Ammonites and kept it up until afternoon. A few Ammonites managed to escape, but they were scattered far from each other.

12 The Israelite soldiers went to Samuel and demanded, "Where are the men who said they didn't want Saul to be king? Bring them to us, and we will put them to death!"

13 "No you won't!" Saul told them. "The LORD rescued Israel today, and no one will be put to death."

Saul is accepted as king

14 "Come on!" Samuel said. "Let's go to Gilgal and make an agreement that Saul will continue to be our king."

15 Everyone went to the place of worship at Gilgal, where they agreed that Saul would be their king. Saul and the people sacrificed animals to ask for the LORD's blessing,* and they had a big celebration.

Samuel's farewell speech

CHAPTER 12

1 Samuel told the Israelites:

I have given you a king, just as you asked. 2 You have seen how I have led you ever since I was a young man. I'm already old. My hair is grey, and my own sons are grown up. Now you must see how well your king will lead you.

3 Let me ask this. Have I ever taken anyone's ox or donkey or forced you to give me anything? Have I ever hurt anyone or taken a bribe to give an unfair decision? Answer me so the LORD and his chosen king can hear you. And if I have done any of these things, I will give it all back.

4 "No," the Israelites answered. "You've never cheated us in any way!"

5 Samuel said, "The LORD and his chosen king are witnesses to what you have said."

"That's true," they replied.

6 Then Samuel told them:

The LORD brought your ancestors out of Egypt and chose Moses and Aaron to be your leaders. 7 Now the LORD will be your judge. So stand here and listen, while I remind you how often the LORD has saved you and your ancestors from your enemies.

8 After Jacob went to Egypt, your ancestors cried out to the LORD for help, and he sent Moses and Aaron. They led your ancestors out of Egypt and settled them in this land. 9 But your ancestors forgot the LORD, so he let them be defeated by the Philistines, the king of Moab, and Sisera, the commander of Hazor's army.

10 Again your ancestors cried out to the LORD for help. They said, "We have sinned! We stopped worshipping you, our

LORD, and started worshipping Baal and Astarte. But now, if you rescue us from our enemies, we will worship you."

11 The LORD sent Gideon,ᵇ Bedan, Jephthah, and Samuel to rescue you from your enemies, and you didn't have to worry about being attacked. 12 Then you saw that King Nahash of Ammon was going to attack you. And even though the LORD your God is your king, you told me, "This time it's different. We want a king to rule us!"

13 You asked for a king, and you chose one. Now he stands here where all of you can see him. But it was really the LORD who made him your king. 14 If you and your king want to be followers of the LORD, you must worship himᵇ and do what he says. Don't be stubborn! 15 If you're stubborn and refuse to obey the LORD, he will turn against you and your king.ᵈ

16 Just stand here and watch the LORD show his mighty power. 17 Isn't this the dry season?* I'm going to ask the LORD to send a thunderstorm. When you see it, you will realize how wrong you were to ask for a king.

18 Samuel prayed, and that same day the LORD sent a thunderstorm. Everyone was afraid of the LORD and of Samuel. 19 They told Samuel, "Please, pray to the LORD your God for us! We don't want to die. We have sinned many times in the past, and we were very wrong to ask for a king."

20 Samuel answered:

Even though what you did was wrong, you don't need to be afraid. But you must always follow the LORD and worship him with all your heart. 21 Don't worship idols! They don't have any power, and they can't help you or save you when you're in trouble. 22 But the LORD has chosen you to be his own people. He will always take care of you so that everyone will know how great he is.

23 I would be disobeying the LORD if I stopped praying for you! I will always teach you how to live right. 24 You also must obey the LORD — you must worship him with all your heart and remember the great things he has done for you. 25 But if you and your king do evil, the LORD will wipe you out.

---

*11.15 sacrificed . . . blessing: This kind of sacrifice is described in Leviticus 3; 7.11–36; 19.5–8. People who offered these sacrifices were allowed to eat most of the meat, and they could invite others to share it with them.

See also: **12.6:** Exod 6.26. **12.8:** Exod 2.23. **12.9:** a Judg 4.2; b Judg 13.1; c Judg 3.12. **12.10:** Judg 10.10–15.

*12.17 the dry season: The Hebrew text has "time for wheat harvest", which was usually in the spring, the beginning of the dry season.

See also: **12.11:** a Judg 7.1; b Judg 4.6; c Judg 11.29; d 1 Sam 3.20. **12.12:** 1 Sam 8.19.

Holy history

Arms and warfare

There's a lot of warfare in the Bible. Sometimes it's open warfare – where two armies meet on a battlefield; sometimes it was a siege, where one army attacks a fortified city. There are also many surprise attacks (Joshua was good at these – see Joshua 6). Even while wandering in the desert, the Israelites had some sort of military force. But there was no official, standing army until after the first king.

Saul had a band of 3000 (1 Samuel 13.2). David had around 600 core troops, as well as a large army, of which 24,000 were on duty each month. According to the Law, you could be released from military service if you had just built a house, got engaged, planted a vineyard or were just a bit scared (Deuteronomy 20.5–8). Which gives most people a get-out, really.

Swords were usually hung round the waist and were the size of a large dagger. There were spears and bows and some fighters were experts in using the sling, which could throw a stone as large as an orange with a lot of accuracy. (And the big advantage of slings is there's always a lot of ammo lying around.) Helmets were originally made of leather and then later of bronze or iron. Breastplates were generally pieces of metal sewn onto shirts. King Uzziah was the first king to issue helmets to his troops (2 Chronicles 26.14). Most shields were small, but important soldiers would have a large shield, carried by a shield-bearer.

Chariots didn't come into common use in Israel until after Solomon's time. They were lightweight carts pulled by one or two horses.

More...

Joshua p.228
David p.314
Destruction p.236

Saul disobeys the Lord, and the Lord rejects him as king

CHAPTER 13

1 Saul was a young man' when he became king, and he ruled Israel for two years.
2 Then' he chose three thousand men from Israel to be full-time soldiers and sent everyone else* home. Two thousand of these troops stayed with him in the hills around Michmash and Bethel. The other thousand were stationed with Jonathan* at Gibeah* in the territory of Benjamin.
3 Jonathan led an attack on the Philistine army camp at Geba.* The Philistine camp was destroyed, but' the other Philistines heard what had happened. Then Saul told his messengers, "Go to every village in the country. Give a signal with the trumpet, and when the people come together, tell them what has happened."
4 The messengers then said to the people of Israel, "Saul has destroyed the Philistine army camp at Geba.' Now the Philistines really hate Israel, so every town and village must send men to join Saul's army at Gilgal."
5 The Philistines called their army together to fight Israel. They had three thousand' chariots, six thousand cavalry, and as many foot soldiers as there are grains of sand on the beach. They went to Michmash and set up camp there east of Beth-Aven.*
6 The Israelite army realized that they were outnumbered and were going to lose the battle. Some of the Israelite men hid in caves or in clumps of bushes,' and some ran to places where they could hide among large rocks. Others hid in tombs* or in deep

---

*13.2 **everyone else:** People who were not full-time soldiers, but fought together with the army when the nation was in danger.
*13.2 **Jonathan:** Saul's son (see verse 16).
*13.2 **Michmash . . . Bethel . . . Gibeah:** These three towns form a triangle, with Bethel to the north.
*13.3 **Geba:** Geba was between Gibeah and Michmash.
*13.5 **Beth-Aven:** This Beth-Aven was probably about one and a half kilometres south-west of Michmash, between Michmash and Geba.
*13.6 **tombs:** The Hebrew word may mean a room cut into solid rock and used as a burial place, or it may mean a cellar.

dry pits. ⁷ Still others* went to Gad and Gilead on the other side of the River Jordan.

Saul stayed at Gilgal. His soldiers were shaking with fear, ⁸ and they were starting to run off and leave him. Saul waited there seven days, just as Samuel had ordered him to do,* but Samuel did not come. ⁹ Finally, Saul commanded, "Bring me some animals, so we can offer sacrifices to please the LORD and ask for his help."

Saul killed one of the animals, ¹⁰ and just as he was placing it on the altar, Samuel arrived. Saul went out to welcome him.

¹¹ "What have you done?" Samuel asked.

Saul answered, "My soldiers were leaving in all directions, and you didn't come when you were supposed to. The Philistines were gathering at Michmash, ¹² and I was worried that they would attack me here at Gilgal. I hadn't offered a sacrifice to ask for the LORD's help, so I forced myself to offer a sacrifice on the altar fire."

¹³ "That was stupid!" Samuel said. "You didn't obey the LORD your God. If you had obeyed him, someone from your family would always have been king of Israel. ¹⁴ But no, you disobeyed, and so the LORD won't choose anyone else from your family to be king. In fact, he has already chosen the one he wants to be the next leader of his people." ¹⁵ Then Samuel left Gilgal.

Part of Saul's army had not deserted him, and he led them to Gibeah in Benjamin to join his other troops. Then he counted them' and found that he still had six hundred men. ¹⁶ Saul, Jonathan, and their army set up camp at Geba in Benjamin.

Jonathan attacks the Philistines

The Philistine army was camped at Michmash. ¹⁷ Each day they sent out patrols to attack and rob villages and then destroy them. One patrol would go north along the road to Ophrah in the region of Shual. ¹⁸ Another patrol would go west along the road to Beth-Horon. A third patrol would go east towards the desert on the road to the ridge that overlooks Zeboim Valley.

¹⁹ The Philistines would not allow any Israelites to learn how to make iron tools. "If

we allowed that," they said, "those worthless Israelites would make swords and spears."

²⁰⁻²¹ Whenever the Israelites wanted to get an iron point put on a cattle prod,* they had to go to the Philistines. Even if they wanted to sharpen plough-blades, picks, axes, sickles,' and pitchforks' they still had to go to them. And the Philistines charged high prices. ²² So, whenever the Israelite soldiers had to go into battle, none of them had a sword or a spear except Saul and his son Jonathan. ²³ The Philistines moved their camp to the pass at Michmash,

CHAPTER 14

¹⁻³ and Saul was in Geba' with his six hundred men. Saul's own tent was set up under a fruit tree* by the threshing place' at the edge of town. Ahijah was serving as priest, and one of his jobs was to get answers from the LORD for Saul. Ahijah's father was Ahitub, and his father's brother was Ichabod. Ahijah's grandfather was Phinehas, and his great-grandfather Eli had been the LORD's priest at Shiloh.

One day, Jonathan told the soldier who carried his weapons that he wanted to attack the Philistine camp on the other side of the valley. So they slipped out of the Israelite camp without anyone knowing it. Jonathan didn't even tell his father he was leaving.

⁴⁻⁵ Jonathan decided to get to the Philistine camp by going through the pass that led between Shiny Cliff and Michmash to the north and Thorn Bush Cliff' and Geba to the south.

⁶ Jonathan and the soldier who carried his weapons talked as they went towards the Philistine camp. "It's just the two of us against all those godless men," Jonathan said. "But the LORD can help a few soldiers win a battle just as easily as he can help a whole army. Perhaps the LORD will help us win this battle."

⁷ "Do whatever you want," the soldier answered. "I'll be with you."

⁸ "This is what we will do," Jonathan said. "We will go across and let them see us. ⁹ If they agree to come down the hill and fight where we are, then we won't climb up to their camp. ¹⁰ But we will go if they tell us to

---

*13.7 Still others: This translates a Hebrew word which may be used of wandering groups of people who sometimes became outlaws or hired soldiers (see also 14.21).
*13.8 Samuel . . . to do: See 10.8.
See also: 13.8: 1 Sam 10.8. 13.14: Acts 13.22.

*13.20–21 cattle prod: A pole used to poke cattle and make them move.
*14.1–3 fruit tree: Hebrew "pomegranate tree". A pomegranate is a bright red fruit that looks like an apple.

come up the hill and fight. That will mean the LORD is going to help us win."

¹¹⁻¹² Jonathan and the soldier stood at the bottom of the hill where the Philistines could see them. The Philistines said, "Look! Those worthless Israelites have crawled out of the holes where they've been hiding." Then they yelled down to Jonathan and the soldier, "Come up here, and we will teach you a thing or two!"

Jonathan turned to the soldier and said, "Follow me! The LORD is going to let us win."

¹³ Jonathan crawled up the hillside with the soldier following him. When they got to the top, Jonathan killed the Philistines who attacked from the front, and the soldier killed those who attacked from behind.' ¹⁴ Before they had gone thirty metres,' they had killed about twenty Philistines.

¹⁵ The whole Philistine army panicked — those in camp, those on guard duty, those in the fields, and those on raiding patrols. All of them were afraid and confused. Then God sent an earthquake, and the ground began to tremble.'

Israel defeats the Philistines

¹⁶ Saul's lookouts at Geba' saw that the Philistine army was running in every direction, like melted wax. ¹⁷ Saul told his officers, "Call the roll and find out who left our camp." When they had finished, they found out that Jonathan and the soldier who carried his weapons were missing.

¹⁸ At that time, Ahijah was serving as priest for the army of Israel, and Saul told him, "Come over here! Let's ask God what we should do."' ¹⁹ Just as Saul finished saying this, he could see that the Philistine army camp was getting more and more confused, and he said, "Ahijah, never mind!"

²⁰ Saul quickly called his army together, then led them to the Philistine camp. By this time the Philistines were so confused that they were killing each other.

²¹ There were also some hired soldiers* in the Philistine camp, who now switched to Israel's side and fought for Saul and Jonathan.

²² Many Israelites had been hiding in the hill country of Ephraim. And when they heard that the Philistines were running away, they came out of hiding and joined in chasing the Philistines.

²³⁻²⁴ So the LORD helped Israel win the battle that day.

Saul's curse on anyone who eats

Saul had earlier told his soldiers, "I want to get even with those Philistines by sunset. If any of you eat before then, you will be under a curse!" So he made them swear not to eat.

By the time the fighting moved past Beth-Aven,* the Israelite troops were weak from hunger. ²⁵⁻²⁶ The army and the people who lived nearby had gone into a forest, and they came to a place where honey was dripping on the ground.' But no one ate any of it, because they were afraid of being put under the curse.

²⁷ Jonathan did not know about Saul's warning to the soldiers. So he dipped the end of his walking stick in the honey and ate some with his fingers. He felt stronger and more alert. ²⁸ Then a soldier told him, "Your father swore that anyone who ate food today would be put under a curse, and we agreed not to eat. That's why we're so weak."

²⁹ Jonathan said, "My father has caused you a lot of trouble. Look at me! I had only a little of this honey, but already I feel strong and alert. ³⁰ I wish you had eaten some of the food the Philistines left behind. We would have been able to kill a lot more of them."

³¹ By evening the Israelite army was exhausted from killing Philistines all the way from Michmash to Aijalon.* ³² They grabbed the food they had captured from the Philistines and started eating. They even killed sheep and cows and calves right on the ground and ate the meat without draining the blood.* ³³ Someone told Saul, "Look! The army is disobeying the LORD by eating meat before the blood drains out."

"You're right," Saul answered. "They are being unfaithful to the LORD! Hurry! Roll a big rock over here.' ³⁴ Then tell everyone in camp to bring their cattle and lambs to me. They can kill the animals on this rock,* then

---

*14.23⁻24 Beth-Aven: See the note at 13.5.

*14.31 Aijalon: About 30 kilometres west of Michmash.

*14.32 blood: The Israelites were supposed to drain the blood from a butchered animal before the meat was cooked and eaten (see Genesis 9.4; Leviticus 17.11; Deuteronomy 12.23).

*14.34 kill . . . rock: That is, up off the ground so the blood could drain out.

See also: 14.33: Gen 9.4; Lev 7.26–27; 17.10–14; 19.26; Deut 12.16,23; 15.23.

---

*14.21 hired soldiers: See the note at 13.7.

eat the meat. That way no one will disobey the LORD by eating meat with blood still in it."

That night the soldiers brought their cattle over to the big rock and killed them there. ³⁵ It was the first altar Saul had built for offering sacrifices to the LORD.*

The army rescues Jonathan

³⁶ Saul said, "Let's attack the Philistines again while it's still dark. We can fight them all night. Let's kill them and take everything they own!"

The people answered, "We will do whatever you want."

"Wait!" Ahijah the priest said. "Let's ask God what we should do."

³⁷ Saul asked God, "Should I attack the Philistines? Will you help us win?"

This time God did not answer. ³⁸ Saul called his army officers together and said, "We have to find out what sin has kept God from answering. ³⁹ I swear by the living LORD that whoever sinned must die, even if it turns out to be my own son Jonathan."

No one said a word.

⁴⁰ Saul told his army, "You stand on that side of the priest, and Jonathan and I will stand on the other side."

Everyone agreed.

⁴¹ Then Saul prayed, "Our LORD, God of Israel, why haven't you answered me today? Please show us who sinned. Was it my son Jonathan and I, or was it your people Israel?"ᐟ

The answer came back that Jonathan or Saul had sinned, not the army. ⁴² Saul told Ahijah, "Now ask the LORD to decide between Jonathan and me."

The answer came back that Jonathan had sinned. ⁴³ "Jonathan," Saul exclaimed, "tell me what you did!"

"I dipped the end of my walking stick in some honey and ate a little. Now you say I have to die!"

⁴⁴ "Yes, Jonathan. I swear to God that you must die."

⁴⁵ "No!" the soldiers shouted. "God helped Jonathan win the battle for us. We won't let you kill him. We swear to the LORD that we won't let you kill him or even lay a hand on him!" So the army kept Saul from killing Jonathan.

⁴⁶ Saul stopped hunting down the Philistines, and they went home.

Saul fights his enemies

⁴⁷⁻⁴⁸ When Saul became king, the Moabites, the Ammonites, the Edomites, the kings of Zobah, the Philistines, and the Amalekites had all been robbing the Israelites. Saul fought back against these enemies and stopped them from robbing Israel. He was a brave commander and always won his battles.ᐟ

Saul's family

⁴⁹⁻⁵¹ Saul's wife was Ahinoam, the daughter of Ahimaaz. They had three sons: Jonathan, Ishvi,* and Malchishua. They also had two daughters: the elder one was Merab, and the younger one was Michal.

Abner, Saul's cousin, was the commander of the army. Saul's father Kish and Abner's father Ner were sons of Abiel.

War with the Philistines

⁵² Saul was at war with the Philistines for as long as he lived. Whenever he found a good warrior or a brave man, Saul made him join his army.

CHAPTER 15

Saul disobeys the LORD

¹ One day, Samuel told Saul:

The LORD made me choose you to be king of his people, Israel. Now listen to this message from the LORD: ² "When the Israelites were on their way out of Egypt, the nation of Amalek attacked them. I am the LORD All-Powerful, and now I am going to make Amalek pay!

³ "Go and attack the Amalekites! Destroy them and all their possessions. Don't have any pity. Kill their men, women, children, and even their babies. Slaughter their cattle, sheep, camels, and donkeys."

⁴ Saul sent messengers who told every town and village to send men to join the army at Telaim. There were two hundred and ten thousand troops in all, and ten thousand of these were from Judah. Saul organized them,

---

*14.35 offering sacrifices to the LORD: Even when animals were killed for food, it was often done as a sacrifice to the LORD.

See also: 14.41: Num 27.21; 1 Sam 28.6.

*14.49-51 Ishvi: Also known as Eshbaal (see 1 Chronicles 8.33; 9.39) and Ishbosheth (see 2 Samuel 2.8–13; 3.8–15; 4.5–12).

See also: 15.1: 1 Sam 10.1. 15.2: Exod 17.8–14; Deut 25.17–19.

5 then led them to a valley near one of the towns in' Amalek, where they got ready to make a surprise attack. 6 Some Kenites lived nearby, and Saul told them, "Your people were kind to our nation when we left Egypt, and I don't want you to get killed when I wipe out the Amalekites. Leave here and stay away from them."

The Kenites left, 7 and Saul attacked the Amalekites from Havilah' to Shur, which is just east of Egypt. 8 Every Amalekite was killed except King Agag. 9 Saul and his army let Agag live, and they also spared the best sheep and cattle. They didn't want to destroy anything of value, so they only killed the animals that were worthless or weak.'

The LORD rejects Saul

10 The LORD told Samuel, 11 "Saul has stopped obeying me, and I'm sorry that I made him king."

Samuel was angry, and he cried out in prayer to the LORD all night. 12 Early the next morning he went to talk with Saul. Someone told him, "Saul went to Carmel, where he had a monument built so everyone would remember his victory. Then he left for Gilgal."

13 Samuel finally caught up with Saul,' and Saul told him, "I hope the LORD will bless you! I have done what the LORD told me."

14 "Then why," Samuel asked, "do I hear sheep and cattle?"

15 "The army took them from the Amalekites," Saul explained. "They kept the best sheep and cattle, so they could sacrifice them to the LORD your God. But we destroyed everything else."

16 "Stop!" Samuel said. "Let me tell you what the LORD told me last night."

"All right," Saul answered.

17 Samuel continued, "You may not think you're very important, but the LORD chose you to be king, and you are in charge of the tribes of Israel. 18 When the LORD sent you on this mission, he told you to wipe out those worthless Amalekites. 19 Why didn't you listen to the LORD? Why did you keep the animals and make him angry?"

20 "But I did listen to the LORD!" Saul answered. "He sent me on a mission, and I went. I captured King Agag and destroyed his nation. 21 All the animals were going to be destroyed* anyway. That's why the army

---

15.21 animals . . . destroyed: The Hebrew means things that were set aside for God. They could not be used for anything else, so they had to be destroyed.

brought the best sheep and cattle to Gilgal as sacrifices to the LORD your God."

22 "Tell me," Samuel said. "Does the LORD really want sacrifices and offerings? No! He doesn't want your sacrifices. He wants you to obey him. 23 Rebelling against God or disobeying him because you are proud is just as bad as worshipping idols or asking them for advice. You refused to do what God told you, so God has decided that you can't be king."

24 "I have sinned," Saul admitted. "I disobeyed both you and the LORD. I was afraid of the army, and I listened to them instead. 25 Please forgive me and come back with me so I can worship the LORD."

26 "No!" Samuel replied, "You disobeyed the LORD, and I won't go back with you. Now the LORD has said that you can't be king of Israel any longer."

27 As Samuel turned to go, Saul grabbed the edge of Samuel's robe. It tore! 28 Samuel said, "The LORD has torn the kingdom of Israel away from you today, and he will give it to someone who is better than you. 29 Besides, the eternal' God of Israel isn't a human being. He doesn't tell lies or change his mind."

30 Saul said, "I did sin, but please honour me in front of the leaders of the army and the people of Israel. Come back with me, so I can worship the LORD your God."

31 Samuel followed Saul back, and Saul worshipped the LORD. 32 Then Samuel shouted, "Bring me King Agag of Amalek!"

Agag came in chains,' and he was saying to himself, "Surely they won't kill me now."'

33 But Samuel said, "Agag, you have snatched children from their mothers' arms and killed them. Now your mother will be without children." Then Samuel chopped Agag to pieces at the place of worship in Gilgal.

34 Samuel went home to Ramah, and Saul returned to his home in Gibeah. 35 Even though Samuel felt sad about Saul, Samuel never saw him again.

The Lord chooses David to be the next king

The LORD was sorry he had made Saul the king of Israel.

CHAPTER 16

1 One day he said, "Samuel, I've rejected Saul, and I refuse to let him be king any

---

See also: 15.27–28: 1 Sam 28.17; 1 King 11.30–31.

Life files

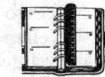

David

Background: Son of Jesse, grandson of Ruth and Boaz

What's the story?

David was the shepherd boy who became a king. Chosen by God to replace Saul, he showed his courage in numerous battles (not to mention when facing Saul's increasingly bizarre behaviour). He fought Saul and eventually became king after Saul's death. After reigning for seven years at Hebron, he captured the city of Jerusalem and made it his capital, bringing the sacred chest into the city and planning a glorious temple to the LORD. So close was his relationship to the city that it became known as the City of David. Under his rule, Israel's borders spread to their furthest-ever extent. He brought success to the country and defeated their enemies.

Then it all went wrong. He committed adultery with Bathsheba, tried to cover it up with lies and ended up committing murder. He was confronted with the truth by the prophet Naaman, and confessed his sins. God forgave him, but he had to live with the consequences.

After that things were never quite the same. His family rebelled against him and behaved terribly towards each other. He wanted to build a temple to God, but it was not to be and it was left to his son Solomon to complete the task.

What's the point?

David is celebrated as Israel's greatest king. He was a brave warrior, a great poet and a man who made Israel great.

But what makes David so important as a king is his relationship with God. David trusted in God, and sought to serve and obey him. At first it all went well, and God blessed him, but then he managed to muck things up quite spectacularly. He was guilty of adultery. He was directly responsible for the deaths of people such as Uriah, Joab and Shimei. His favouritism towards his eldest son caused murder and rebellion within the family.

So why should such a man be so celebrated? Because he admitted his sins and he sought forgiveness from God. You can see the real David in the many Psalms that bear his name. There, we find him in many different moods; scared, full of joy, sad, remorseful, triumphant, hesitant, desperate – above all honest. That's what makes David so special. Despite the actions of himself and others, he truly loved God. (He never could hide his feelings. When the Ark returned to Jerusalem he threw off his clothes and danced for joy, despite the disapproving looks of his wife.)

God responded to David's faith by promising him that his descendants would always reign on the throne of Israel. Which is why the Messiah was to come from his line – from the house of David. Ultimately, David was not special because he won more battles or reigned for more years; he was special because he truly loved God and trusted in his promises.

Footsteps

Two weeks with David

Samuel anoints David: 1 Samuel 16.1–13
David v. Goliath: 1 Samuel 17.1–54
Saul becomes jealous of David:
1 Samuel 18.6–30
Jonathan helps David: 1 Samuel 20.1–42
David spares Saul's life: 1 Samuel 24.1–22
David mourns Saul's death:
2 Samuel 1.1–2.7
The ark is brought to Jerusalem:
2 Samuel 6.1–23
The LORD's covenant promise to David:
2 Samuel 7.1–29
David and Bathsheba: 2 Samuel 11.1–27
Nathan confronts David: 2 Samuel 12.1–25
The Rape of Tamar: 2 Samuel 13.1–38
Absalom's rebellion: 2 Samuel 14.25—15.22
Death of Absalom: 2 Samuel 18.7—19.8
Death of David: 1 Kings 1.1–4; 2.1–12

More...

Help! I've messed up really badly p.347
Forgiveness p.614
Help! I'm struggling with lust p.954
Musical instruments p.644

longer. Stop feeling sad about him. Put some olive oil* in a small container* and go and visit a man named Jesse, who lives in Bethlehem. I've chosen one of his sons to be my king."

² Samuel answered, "If I do that, Saul will find out and have me killed."

"Take a calf with you," the LORD replied. "Tell everyone that you've come to offer it as a sacrifice to me, ³ then invite Jesse to the sacrifice.* When I show you which one of his sons I have chosen, pour the olive oil on his head."

⁴ Samuel did what the LORD told him and went to Bethlehem. The town leaders went to meet him, but they were terribly afraid and asked, "Is this a friendly visit?"

⁵ "Yes, it is!" Samuel answered. "I've come to offer a sacrifice to the LORD. Get yourselves ready* to take part in the sacrifice and come with me." Samuel also invited Jesse and his sons to come to the sacrifice, and he got them ready to take part.

⁶ When Jesse and his sons arrived, Samuel noticed Jesse's eldest son, Eliab. "He must be the one the LORD has chosen," Samuel said to himself.

⁷ But the LORD told him, "Samuel, don't think Eliab is the one just because he's tall and handsome. He isn't the one I've chosen. People judge others by what they look like, but I judge people by what is in their hearts."

⁸ Jesse told his son Abinadab to go over to Samuel, but Samuel said, "No, the LORD hasn't chosen him."

⁹ Next, Jesse sent his son Shammah to him, and Samuel said, "The LORD hasn't chosen him either."

¹⁰ Jesse sent all seven of his sons over to Samuel. Finally, Samuel said, "Jesse, the LORD hasn't chosen any of these young men. ¹¹ Do you have any more sons?"

"Yes," Jesse answered. "My youngest son David is out taking care of the sheep."

"Send for him!" Samuel said. "We won't start the ceremony until he gets here."

¹² Jesse sent for David. He was a healthy, good-looking boy with a sparkle in his eyes.

As soon as David came, the LORD told Samuel, "He's the one! Get up and pour the olive oil on his head."*

¹³ Samuel poured the oil on David's head while his brothers watched. At that moment, the Spirit of the LORD took control of David and stayed with him from then on.

Samuel returned home to Ramah.

David plays the harp for Saul

¹⁴ The Spirit of the LORD had left Saul, and an evil spirit from the LORD was terrifying him. ¹⁵ "It's an evil spirit from God that's frightening you," Saul's officials told him. ¹⁶ "Your Majesty, let us go and look for someone who is good at playing the harp. He can play for you whenever the evil spirit from God bothers you, and you'll feel better."

¹⁷ "All right," Saul answered. "Find me someone who is good at playing the harp and bring him here."

¹⁸ "A man named Jesse who lives in Bethlehem has a son who can play the harp," one official said. "He's a brave warrior, he's good-looking, he can speak well, and the LORD is with him."

¹⁹ Saul sent a message to Jesse: "Tell your son David to leave your sheep and come here to me."

²⁰ Jesse loaded a donkey with bread and a goatskin full of wine,* then he told David to take the donkey and a young goat to Saul. ²¹ David went to Saul and started working for him. Saul liked him so much that he put David in charge of carrying his weapons. ²² Not long after this, Saul sent another message to Jesse: "I really like David. Please let him stay with me."

²³ Whenever the evil spirit from God bothered Saul, David would play his harp. Saul would relax and feel better, and the evil spirit would go away.

David kills Goliath

CHAPTER 17

Goliath challenges Israel's army

¹ The Philistines got ready for war and brought their troops together to attack the

---

*16.1 olive oil: See the note at 9.16.
*16.1 small container: Hebrew "horn"; animal horns were sometimes hollowed out and used as containers.
*16.3 sacrifice: A sacrifice often involved a dinner where the meat from the sacrificed animal would be served.
*16.5 Get yourselves ready: The people of Israel sometimes had to perform certain ceremonies to make themselves acceptable to God.

---

*16.12 olive oil on his head: See the note at 9.16.
*16.20 wine: Wine was sometimes kept in bottles made of goatskin sewn up with the fur on the outside.

town of Socoh in Judah. They set up camp at Ephes-Dammim, between Socoh and Azekah.* 2-3 King Saul and the Israelite army set up camp on a hill overlooking Elah Valley, and they got ready to fight the Philistine army that was on a hill on the other side of the valley.

4 The Philistine army had a hero named Goliath who was from the town of Gath and was about three metres' tall. 5-6 He wore a bronze helmet and had bronze armour to protect his chest and legs. The chest armour alone weighed about fifty-seven kilogrammes. He carried a bronze sword strapped on his back, 7 and his spear was so big that the iron spearhead alone weighed about seven kilogrammes. A soldier always walked in front of Goliath to carry his shield.

8 Goliath went out and shouted to the army of Israel:

Why are you lining up for battle? I'm the best soldier in our army, and all of you are in Saul's army. Choose your best soldier to come out and fight me! 9 If he can kill me, our people will be your slaves. But if I kill him, your people will be our slaves. 10 Here and now I challenge Israel's whole army! Choose someone to fight me!

11 Saul and his men heard what Goliath said, but they were so frightened of Goliath that they couldn't do a thing.

David Decides To Challenge Goliath

12 David's father Jesse was an old man, who belonged to the Ephrath clan and lived in Bethlehem in Judah. Jesse had eight sons: 13-14 the eldest was Eliab, the next was Abinadab, and Shammah was the third. The three of them had gone off to fight in Saul's army.

David was Jesse's youngest son. 15 He took care of his father's sheep, and he went back and forth between Bethlehem and Saul's camp.

16 Goliath came out and gave his challenge every morning and every evening for forty days.

17 One day, Jesse told David, "Hurry and take this sack of roasted grain and these ten loaves of bread to your brothers at the army camp. 18 And here are ten large chunks of cheese to take to their commanding officer. Find out how your brothers are doing and

bring back something that shows that they're all right. 19 They're with Saul's army, fighting the Philistines in Elah Valley."

20 David obeyed his father. He got up early the next morning and left someone else in charge of the sheep; then he loaded the supplies and started off. He reached the army camp just as the soldiers were taking their places and shouting the battle cry. 21 The army of Israel and the Philistine army stood there facing each other.

22 David left his things with the man in charge of supplies and ran up to the battle line to ask his brothers if they were well. 23 While David was talking with them, Goliath came out from the line of Philistines and started boasting as usual. David heard him.

24 When the Israelite soldiers saw Goliath, they were scared and ran off. 25 They said to each other, "Look how he keeps coming out to insult us. The king is offering a big reward to the man who kills Goliath. That man will even get to marry the king's daughter, and no one in his family will ever have to pay taxes again."

26 David asked some soldiers standing nearby, "What will a man get for killing this Philistine and stopping him from insulting our people? Who does that worthless Philistine think he is? He's making fun of the army of the living God!"

27 The soldiers told David what the king would give the man who killed Goliath.

28 David's eldest brother Eliab heard him talking with the soldiers. Eliab was angry with him and said, "What are you doing here, anyway? Who's taking care of that little flock of sheep out in the desert? You spoilt brat! You came here just to watch the fighting, didn't you?"

29 "Now what have I done?" David answered. "Can't I even ask a question?" 30 Then he turned and asked another soldier the same thing he had asked the others, and he got the same answer.

31 Some soldiers overheard David talking, so they told Saul what David had said. Saul sent for David, and David came. 32 "Your Majesty," he said, "this Philistine shouldn't turn us into cowards. I'll go out and fight him myself!"

33 "You don't have a chance against him," Saul replied. "You're only a boy, and he's been a soldier all his life."

34 But David told him:

Your Majesty, I take care of my father's sheep. And when one of them is dragged off by a lion or a bear, 35 I go after it and beat

---

*17.1 Socoh and Azekah: Socoh was controlled by the Israelites, while Azekah was in Philistine hands.

the wild animal until it lets the sheep go. If the wild animal turns and attacks me, I grab it by the throat and kill it.

[36] Sir, I have killed lions and bears that way, and I can kill this worthless Philistine. He shouldn't have made fun of the army of the living God! [37] The LORD has rescued me from the claws of lions and bears, and he will keep me safe from the hands of this Philistine.

"All right," Saul answered, "go ahead and fight him. And I hope the LORD will help you."

[38] Saul had his own military clothes and armour put on David, and he gave David a bronze helmet to wear. [39] David strapped on a sword and tried to walk around, but he was not used to wearing those things.

"I can't move with all this stuff on," David said. "I'm just not used to it."

David took off the armour [40] and picked up his shepherd's stick. He went out to a stream and picked up five smooth stones and put them in his leather bag. Then with his sling in his hand, he went straight towards Goliath.

David kills Goliath

[41] Goliath came towards David, walking behind the soldier who was carrying his shield. [42] When Goliath saw that David was just a healthy, good-looking boy, he made fun of him. [43] "Do you think I'm a dog?" Goliath asked. "Is that why you've come after me with a stick?" He cursed David in the name of the Philistine gods [44] and shouted, "Come on! When I'm finished with you, I'll feed you to the birds and wild animals!"

[45] David answered:

You've come out to fight me with a sword and a spear and a dagger. But I've come out to fight you in the name of the LORD All-Powerful. He is the God of Israel's army, and you have insulted him too!

[46] Today the LORD will help me defeat you. I'll knock you down and cut off your head, and I'll feed the bodies of the other Philistine soldiers to the birds and wild animals. Then the whole world will know that Israel has a real God. [47] Everybody here will see that the LORD doesn't need swords or spears to save his people. The LORD always wins his battles, and he will help us defeat you.

[48] When Goliath started forward, David ran towards him. [49] He put a stone in his sling and swung the sling around by its straps. When he

let go of one strap, the stone flew out and hit Goliath on the forehead. It cracked his skull, and he fell face down on the ground. [50] David defeated Goliath with a sling and a stone. He killed him without even using a sword.

[51] David ran over and pulled out Goliath's sword. Then he used it to cut off Goliath's head.

When the Philistines saw what had happened to their hero, they started running away. [52] But the soldiers of Israel and Judah let out a battle cry and went after them as far as Gath' and Ekron. The bodies of the Philistines were scattered all along the road from Shaaraim to Gath and Ekron.

[53] When the Israelite army returned from chasing the Philistines, they took what they wanted from the enemy camp. [54] David took Goliath's head to Jerusalem, but he kept Goliath's weapons in his own tent.

David becomes one of Saul's officers

[55] After King Saul had watched David go out to fight Goliath, Saul turned to the commander of his army and said, "Abner, who is that young man?"

"Your Majesty," Abner answered, "I swear by your life that I don't know."

[56] "Then find out!" Saul told him.

[57] When David came back from fighting Goliath, he was still carrying Goliath's head. Abner took David to Saul, [58] and Saul asked, "Who are you?"

"I am David the son of Jesse, a loyal Israelite from Bethlehem."

CHAPTER 18

[1] David and Saul finished talking, and soon David and Jonathan* became best friends. Jonathan thought as much of David as he did of himself. [2] From that time on, Saul kept David in his service and would not let David go back to his own family.

[3] Jonathan liked David so much that they promised they would always be loyal friends. [4] Jonathan took off the robe that he was wearing and gave it to David. He also gave him his military clothes,* his sword, his bow and arrows, and his belt.

[5] David was a success in everything that Saul sent him to do, and Saul made him a high officer in his army. That pleased everyone, including Saul's other officers.

---

*18.1 Jonathan: See the note at 13.2.
*18.4 military clothes: Or "armour".
See also: 17.50: 2 Sam 21.19.   17.51: 2 Sam 21.29.

Saul tries to kill David

Saul becomes David's enemy

6 David had killed Goliath, the battle was over, and the Israelite army set out for home. As the army went along, women came out of each Israelite town to welcome King Saul. They were singing happy songs and dancing to the music of tambourines and harps. 7 They sang:

Saul has killed
  a thousand enemies;
David has killed
  ten thousand enemies!

8 This song made Saul very angry, and he thought, "They are saying that David has killed ten times more enemies than I ever did. Next they will want to make him king." 9 Saul never again trusted David.

10 The next day the LORD let an evil spirit take control of Saul, and he began acting like a mad man inside his house. David came to play the harp for Saul as usual, but this time Saul had a spear in his hand. 11 Saul thought, "I'll pin David to the wall." He threw the spear at David twice, but David dodged and got away both times.

12 Saul was afraid of David, because the LORD was helping David and was no longer helping him. 13 Saul put David in charge of a thousand soldiers and sent him out to fight. 14 The LORD helped David, and he and his soldiers always won their battles. 15 This made Saul even more afraid of David. 16 But everyone else in Judah and Israel was loyal to▸ David, because he led the army in battle.

17 One day, Saul told David, "If you'll be brave and fight the LORD's battles for me, I'll let you marry my eldest daughter Merab." But Saul was really thinking, "I don't want to kill David myself, so I'll let the Philistines do it for me."

18 David answered, "How could I possibly marry your daughter? I'm not very important, and neither is my family."

19 But when the time came for David to marry Saul's daughter Merab, Saul told her to marry Adriel from the town of Meholah.

20 Saul had another daughter. Her name was Michal, and Saul found out that she was in love with David. This made Saul happy, 21 and he thought, "I'll tell David he can marry Michal, but I'll set it up so that the Philistines will kill him." He told David, "I'm

going to give you a second chance to marry one of my daughters."

22-23 Saul ordered his officials to speak to David in private, so they went to David and said, "Look, the king likes you, and all his officials are loyal to you. Why not ask the king if you can marry his daughter Michal?"

"I'm not rich* or famous enough to marry Princess Michal!" David answered.

24 The officials went back to Saul and told him exactly what David had said. 25 Saul was hoping that the Philistines would kill David, and he told his officials to tell David, "The king doesn't want any silver or gold. He only wants to get even with his enemies. All you have to do is to bring back proof that you have killed a hundred Philistines!"* 26 The officials told David, and David wanted to marry the princess.

King Saul had set a time limit, and before it ran out, 27 David and his men left and killed two hundred Philistines. He brought back the proof and showed it to Saul, so he could marry Michal. Saul agreed to let David marry Michal. 28 Saul knew that she loved David,▸ and he also realized that the LORD was helping David. 29 But knowing those things made Saul even more afraid of David, and he was David's enemy for the rest of his life.

30 The Philistine rulers kept coming to fight Israel, but whenever David fought them, he won. He was famous because he won more battles against the Philistines than any of Saul's other officers.

Jonathan, Michal, Samuel, and Ahimelech help David

CHAPTER 19

Saul tries to have David killed

1 One day, Saul told his son Jonathan and his officers to kill David. But Jonathan liked David a lot, 2-3 and he warned David, "My father is trying to have you killed, so be very careful. Hide in a field tomorrow morning, and I'll bring him there. Then I'll talk to him

---

*18.22–23 not rich: It was the custom for a man to give the bride's father some silver or gold in order to marry his daughter, and it would take a large amount to marry the daughter of the king.
*18.25 proof . . . Philistines: Hebrew "one hundred Philistine foreskins". In ancient times soldiers would sometimes cut off body parts of their dead enemies to prove how many they had killed.

See also: 18.7: 1 Sam 21.11; 29.5.

about you, and if I find out anything, I'll let you know."

⁴⁻⁵ The next morning, Jonathan reminded Saul about the many good things David had done for him. Then he said, "Why do you want to kill David? He hasn't done anything to you. He has served in your army and has always done what's best for you. He even risked his life to kill Goliath. The LORD helped Israel win a great victory that day, and it made you happy."

⁶ Saul agreed and promised, "I swear by the living LORD that I won't have David killed!"

⁷ Jonathan called to David and told him what Saul had said. Then he brought David to Saul, and David served in Saul's army just as he had done before.

⁸ The next time there was a war with the Philistines, David fought hard and forced them to retreat.

Michal helps David escape

⁹⁻¹⁰ One night, David was in Saul's home, playing the harp for him. Saul was sitting there, holding a spear, when an evil spirit from the LORD took control of him. Saul tried to pin David to the wall with the spear, but David dodged, and it stuck in the wall. David ran out of the house and escaped.

¹¹ Saul sent guards to watch David's house all night and then to kill him in the morning. Michal, David's wife, told him, "If you don't escape tonight, they'll kill you tomorrow!" ¹² She helped David go through a window and climb down to the ground.* As David ran off, ¹³ Michal put a statue in his bed. She put goat hair on its head and dressed it in some of David's clothes.

¹⁴ The next morning, Saul sent guards to arrest David. But Michal told them, "David is sick."

¹⁵ Saul sent the guards back and told them, "Get David out of his bed and bring him to me, so I can have him killed."

¹⁶ When the guards went in, all they found in the bed was the statue with the goat hair on its head.

¹⁷ "Why have you tricked me this way?" Saul asked Michal. "You helped my enemy get away!"

She answered, "He said he would kill me if I didn't help him escape!"

Samuel helps David escape

¹⁸ Meanwhile, David went to Samuel at Ramah and told him what Saul had done. Then Samuel and David went to Prophets Village* and stayed there.

¹⁹ Someone told Saul, "David is at Prophets Village in Ramah."

²⁰ Saul sent a few soldiers to bring David back. They went to Ramah and found Samuel in charge of a group of prophets who were all prophesying. Then the Spirit of God took control of the soldiers and they started prophesying too.

²¹ When Saul heard what had happened, he sent another group of soldiers, but they prophesied the same way. He sent a third group of soldiers, but the same thing happened to them. ²² Finally, Saul left for Ramah himself. He went as far as the deep pit* at the town of Secu, and he asked, "Where are Samuel and David?"

"At Prophets Village in Ramah," the people answered.

²³ Saul left for Ramah. But as he walked along, the Spirit of God took control of him, and he started prophesying. Then, when he reached Prophets Village, ²⁴ he stripped off his clothes and prophesied in front of Samuel. He dropped to the ground and lay there naked all day and night. That's how the saying started, "Is Saul now a prophet?"

CHAPTER 20

Jonathan helps David escape

¹ David escaped from Prophets Village. Then he ran to see Jonathan and asked, "Why does your father Saul want to kill me? What have I done wrong?"

² "My father can't be trying to kill you! He never does anything without telling me about it. Why would he hide this from me? It can't be true!"

³ "Jonathan, I swear it's true! But your father knows how much you like me, and he didn't want to break your heart. That's why he didn't tell you. I swear by the living LORD and by your own life that I'm only one step ahead of death."

⁴ Then Jonathan said, "Tell me what to do, and I'll do it."

⁵ David answered:

19.12 ground: The house was probably built into the town wall, allowing David to come down outside the wall.
See also: 19.11: Psa 59 Title.

19.22 pit: A cistern, a large pit dug down into the rock and used for storing rainwater.
See also: 19.24: 1 Sam 10.11–12. 20.5: Num 28.11.

Tomorrow is the New Moon Festival,* and I'm supposed to have dinner with your father. But instead, I'll hide in a field until the evening of the next day. ⁶ If Saul wonders where I am, tell him, "David asked me to let him go to his home town of Bethlehem, so he could take part in a sacrifice his family makes there every year."

⁷ If your father says it's all right, then I'm safe. But if he gets angry, you'll know he wants to harm me. ⁸ Be kind to me. After all, it was your idea to promise the LORD that we would always be loyal friends. If I've done anything wrong, kill me yourself, but don't hand me over to your father.

⁹ "Don't worry," Jonathan said. "If I find out that my father wants to kill you, I'll certainly let you know."

¹⁰ "How will you do that?" David asked.

¹¹ "Let's go out to this field, and I'll tell you," Jonathan answered.

When they got there, ¹² Jonathan said:

I swear by the LORD God of Israel, that two days from now I'll know what my father is planning. Of course I'll let you know if he's friendly towards you. ¹³ But if he wants to harm you, I promise to tell you and help you escape. And I ask the LORD to punish me severely if I don't keep my promise.

I pray that the LORD will bless you, just as he used to bless my father. ¹⁴⁻¹⁵ Some day the LORD will wipe out all your enemies. Then if I'm still alive, please be as kind to me as the LORD has been. But if I'm dead, be kind to my family.

¹⁶ Jonathan and David made an agreement that even David's descendants would have to keep.ᵉ Then Jonathan said, "I pray that the LORD will take revenge on your descendants if they break our promise."ᵉ

¹⁷ Jonathan thought as much of David as he did of himself, so he asked David to promise once more that he would be a loyal friend. ¹⁸ After this Jonathan said:

Tomorrow is the New Moon Festival, and people will wonder where you are, because your place will be empty. ¹⁹ By the day after tomorrow, everyone will think you've been gone a long time.ᵉ Then go to the place where you hid before and stay beside

Going-Away Rock.ᵉ ²⁰ I'll shoot three arrows at a target off to the side of the rock, ²¹ and send my servant to find the arrows.

You'll know if it's safe to come out by what I tell him. If it is safe, I swear by the living LORD that I'll say, "The arrows are on this side of you! Pick them up!" ²² But if it isn't safe, I'll say to the boy, "The arrows are further away!" This will mean that the LORD wants you to leave, and you must go. ²³ But he will always watch us to make sure that we keep the promise we made to each other.

²⁴ So David hid there in the field.

During the New Moon Festival, Saul sat down to eat ²⁵ by the wall, just as he always did. Jonathan sat across from him,ᵉ and Abner sat next to him. But David's place was empty. ²⁶ Saul didn't say anything that day, because he was thinking, "Something must have happened to make David unfit to be at the Festival.* Yes, something must have happened."

²⁷ The day after the New Moon Festival, when David's place was still empty, Saul asked Jonathan, "Why hasn't that son of Jesse come to eat with us? He wasn't here yesterday, and he still isn't here today!"

²⁸⁻²⁹ Jonathan answered, "The reason David hasn't come to eat with you is that he begged me to let him go to Bethlehem. He said, 'Please let me go. My family is offering a sacrifice, and my brother told me I have to be there. Do me this favour and let me slip away to see my brothers.' "

³⁰ Saul was furious with Jonathan and yelled, "You're no son of mine, you traitor! I know you've chosen to be loyal to that son of Jesse. You should be ashamed of yourself! And your own mother should be ashamed that you were ever born. ³¹ You'll never be safe, and your kingdom will be in danger as long as that son of Jesse is alive. Turn him over to me now! He deserves to die!"

³² "Why do you want to kill David?" Jonathan asked. "What has he done?"

³³ Saul threw his spear at Jonathan and tried to kill him. Then Jonathan was sure that his father really did want to kill David. ³⁴ Jonathan was angry that his father had

---

*20.5 New Moon Festival: The first day of the month, when Israelites offered special sacrifices to the LORD and had special sacred meals.
See also: 20.15: 2 Sam 9.1.

*20.26 unfit . . . Festival: During the New Moon Festival a sacred meal was served that could only be eaten by people who were properly prepared. Some of the things that could make a person unfit are listed in Leviticus 7.20–21; 15.2,31; 22.4–8; Deuteronomy 23.10–11.

insulted David' so terribly. He got up, left the table, and didn't eat anything all that day.
³⁵ In the morning, Jonathan went out to the field to meet David. He took a servant boy along ³⁶ and told him, "When I shoot the arrows, you run and find them for me."

The boy started running, and Jonathan shot an arrow so that it would go beyond him. ³⁷ When the boy got near the place where the arrow had landed, Jonathan shouted, "Isn't the arrow on past you?" ³⁸ Jonathan shouted to him again, "Hurry up! Don't stop!"

The boy picked up the arrows and brought them back to Jonathan, ³⁹ but he had no idea about what was going on. Only Jonathan and David knew. ⁴⁰ Jonathan gave his weapons to the boy and told him, "Take these back into town."

⁴¹ After the boy had gone, David got up from beside the mound' and bowed very low three times. Then he and Jonathan kissed* each other and cried, but David cried louder. ⁴² Jonathan said, "Take care of yourself. And remember, we have each asked the LORD to watch and make sure that we and our descendants keep our promise for ever."

David left and Jonathan went back to town.

CHAPTER 21

Ahimelech helps David

¹ David went to see Ahimelech, a priest who lived in the town of Nob. Ahimelech was trembling with fear as he came out to meet David. "Why are you alone?" Ahimelech asked. "Why isn't anyone else with you?"

² "I'm on a mission for King Saul," David answered. "He ordered me not to tell anyone what the mission is all about, so I told my soldiers to stay somewhere else. ³ Do you have any food you can give me? Could you spare five loaves of bread?"

⁴ "The only bread I have is the sacred bread," the priest told David. "You can have it if your soldiers didn't sleep with women last night."*

⁵ "Of course we didn't sleep with women," David answered. "I never let my men do that when we're on a mission. They have to be acceptable to worship God even when we're

on an ordinary mission, and today we're on a special mission."

⁶ The only bread the priest had was the sacred bread that he had taken from the place of worship after putting out the fresh loaves. So he gave it to David.

⁷ It so happened that one of Saul's officers was there, worshipping the LORD that day. His name was Doeg the Edomite,* and he was the strongest of' Saul's shepherds.

⁸ David asked Ahimelech, "Do you have a spear or a sword? I had to leave so quickly on this mission for the king that I didn't bring along my sword or any other weapons."

⁹ The priest answered, "The only sword here is the one that belonged to Goliath the Philistine. You were the one who killed him in Elah Valley, and so you can take his sword if you want to. It's wrapped in a cloth behind the statue."

"It's the best sword there is," David said. "I'll take it!"

David runs from Saul

David tries to find safety in Gath

¹⁰ David kept on running from Saul that day until he came to Gath,* where he met with King Achish. ¹¹ The officers of King Achish were also there, and they asked Achish, "Isn't David a king back in his own country? Don't the Israelites dance and sing,

> "Saul has killed
> a thousand enemies;
> David has killed
> ten thousand enemies?"

¹² David thought about what they were saying, and it made him afraid of Achish. ¹³ So in front of everyone, he pretended to be insane. He acted confused and scratched on the doors of the town gate, while drooling in his beard.

¹⁴ "Look at him!" Achish said to his officers. "You can see he's mad. Why did you bring him to me? ¹⁵ I have enough mad people without your bringing another one here. Keep him away from my palace!"

---

*20.41 kissed: A common way of greeting or saying goodbye in biblical times (see Mark 14.44).
*21.4 night: Having sex was one of the things that would make someone temporarily unfit to take part in worship or a sacred meal (see Exodus 19.15; Leviticus 15.18).
See also: 21.1-6: Matt 12.3-4; Mark 2.25-26; Luke 6.3.

*21.7 Edomite: A person from the country of Edom, to the south of Israel.
*21.10 Gath: One of the five main Philistine towns.
See also: 21.6: Lev 24.5-9. 21.9: 1 Sam 17.51. 21.11: 1 Sam 18.7; 29.5. 21.12: Psa 56 Title. 21.13: Psa 34 Title.

CHAPTER 22

People join David

[1] When David escaped from the town of Gath, he went to Adullam Cave. His brothers and the rest of his family found out where he was, and they followed him there. [2] A lot of other people joined him too. Some were in trouble, others were angry or in debt, and David was soon the leader of four hundred men.

[3] David left Adullam Cave and went to the town of Mizpeh in Moab, where he talked with the king of Moab. "Please," David said, "let my father and mother stay with you until I find out what God will do with me." [4] So he brought his parents to the king of Moab, and they stayed with him while David was in hiding.

[5] One day the prophet Gad told David, "Don't stay here! Go back to Judah." David then left and went to Hereth Forest.

Saul kills the priests of the Lord

[6] Saul was sitting under a small tree on top of the hill at Gibeah when he heard that David and his men had been seen. Saul was holding his spear, and his officers were standing in front of him. [7] He told them:

Listen to me! You belong to the Benjamin tribe,* so if that son of Jesse ever becomes king, he won't give you fields or vineyards. He won't make you officers in charge of thousands or hundreds as I have done. [8] But you're all plotting against me! Not one of you told me that my own son Jonathan had made an agreement with him. Not one of you cared enough to tell me that Jonathan had helped one of my officers* rebel. Now that son of Jesse is trying to ambush me.

[9] Doeg the Edomite was standing with the other officers and spoke up, "When I was in the town of Nob, I saw that son of Jesse. He was visiting the priest Ahimelech the son of Ahitub. [10] Ahimelech talked to the LORD for

him, then gave him food and the sword that had belonged to Goliath the Philistine."

[11] Saul sent a message to Ahimelech and his whole family of priests at Nob, ordering them to come to him. When they came, [12] Saul told them, "Listen to me, you son of Ahitub."

"Certainly, Your Majesty," Ahimelech answered.

[13] Saul demanded, "Why did you plot against me with that son of Jesse? You helped him rebel against me by giving him food and a sword, and by talking with God for him. Now he's trying to ambush me!"

[14] "Your Majesty, none of your officers is more loyal than David!" Ahimelech replied. "He's your son-in-law and the captain of your bodyguard. Everyone in your family respects him. [15] This isn't the first time I've talked with God for David, and it's never made you angry before! Please don't accuse me or my family like this. I have no idea what's going on!"

[16] "Ahimelech," Saul said, "you and your whole family are going to die."

[17] Saul shouted to his bodyguards, "These priests of the LORD helped David! They knew he was running away, but they didn't tell me. Kill them!"

But the king's officers would not attack the priests of the LORD.

[18] Saul turned to Doeg, who was from Edom, and said, "Kill the priests!"

On that same day, Doeg killed eighty-five priests. [19] Then he attacked the town of Nob, where the priests had lived, and he killed everyone there — men, women, children, and babies. He even killed their cattle, donkeys, and sheep.

Only Abiathar escapes from Nob

[20] Ahimelech's son Abiathar was the only one who escaped. He ran to David [21] and told him, "Saul has murdered the priests at Nob!"

[22] David answered, "That day when I saw Doeg, I knew he would tell Saul! Your family died because of me. [23] Stay here. Isn't the same person trying to kill both of us? Don't worry! You'll be safe here with me."

David refuses to kill Saul

CHAPTER 23

David rescues the town of Keilah

[1] One day some people told David, "The Philistines keep attacking the town of Keilah and stealing grain from the threshing place."

---

*22.7 You . . . Benjamin tribe: David was from the Judah tribe and would have given special privileges to the people of his own tribe rather than to those of Benjamin.

*22.7–8 son of Jesse . . . officers: That is, David. Saul avoids even saying David's name.

See also: 22.1: Psa 57 Title; Psa 142 Title.
22.9–10: 1 Sam 21.7–9; Psa 52 Title.

² David asked the LORD, "Should I attack these Philistines?"

"Yes," the LORD answered. "Attack them and rescue Keilah."

³ But David's men said, "Look, even here in Judah we're afraid of the Philistines. We will be terrified if we try to fight them at Keilah!"*

⁴ David asked the LORD about it again. "Leave at once," the LORD answered. "I will give you victory over the Philistines at Keilah."

⁵ David and his men went there and fiercely attacked the Philistines. They killed many of them, then led away their cattle, and rescued the people of Keilah.

⁶⁻⁸ Meanwhile, Saul heard that David was in Keilah. "God has let me catch David," Saul said. "David is trapped inside a walled town where the gates can be locked." Saul decided to go there and surround the town, in order to trap David and his men. He sent messengers who told the towns and villages, "Send men to serve in Saul's army!"

By this time, Abiathar had joined David in Keilah and had brought along everything he needed to get answers from God.

⁹ David heard about Saul's plan to capture him, and he told Abiathar, "Let's ask God what we should do."

¹⁰ David prayed, "LORD God of Israel, I was told that Saul is planning to come here. What should I do? Suppose he threatens to destroy the town because of me. ¹¹ Would the leaders of Keilah turn me over to Saul? Or is he really coming? Please tell me, LORD."

"Yes, he will come," the LORD answered.

¹² David asked, "Would the leaders of Keilah hand me and my soldiers over to Saul?"

"Yes, they would," the LORD answered.

¹³ David and his six hundred men got out of there fast and started moving from place to place. Saul heard that David had left Keilah, and he decided not to go after him.

Jonathan says David will be king

¹⁴ David stayed in hide-outs in the hill country of Ziph Desert. Saul kept searching, but God never let Saul catch him.

¹⁵ One time, David was at Horesh in Ziph Desert. He was afraid because' Saul had come to the area to kill him. ¹⁶ But Jonathan went to see David, and God helped him encourage David. ¹⁷ "Don't be afraid," Jonathan said. "My father Saul will never get his hands on you. In fact, you're going to be the next king of Israel, and I'll be your highest official. Even my father knows it's true."

¹⁸ They both promised the LORD that they would always be loyal to each other. Then Jonathan went home, but David stayed at Horesh.

David escapes from Saul

¹⁹ Some people from the town of Ziph went to Saul at Gibeah and said, "Your Majesty, David has a hide-out not far from us! It's near Horesh, somewhere on Mount Hachilah south of Jeshimon.* ²⁰ If you come, we will help you catch him."

²¹ Saul told them:

You've done me a big favour, and I pray that the LORD will bless you. ²² Now please do just a little more for me. Find out exactly where David is, as well as where he goes, and who has seen him there. I've been told that he's very cunning. ²³ Find out where all his hiding places are and come back when you're sure. Then I'll go with you. If he is still in the area, or anywhere among the clans of Judah, I'll find him.

²⁴ The people from Ziph went back ahead of Saul, and they found out that David and his men were still south of Jeshimon in the Maon Desert. ²⁵ Saul and his army set out to find David. But David heard that Saul was coming, and he went to a place called The Rock, one of his hide-outs in Maon Desert.

Saul found out where David was and started closing in on him. ²⁶ Saul was going around a hill on one side, and David and his men were on the other side, trying to get away. Saul and his soldiers were just about to capture David and his men, ²⁷ when a messenger came to Saul and said, "Come quickly! The Philistines are attacking Israel and taking everything."

²⁸ Saul stopped going after David and went back to fight the Philistines. That's why the place is called "Escape Rock".

²⁹ David left and went to live in the hide-outs at En-Gedi.

---

*23.3 Keilah: Keilah was probably not controlled by Israelites at this time.

*23.19 Jeshimon: A place in the desert near the southern border of Judah.

See also: 23.18: 1 Sam 18.3.   23.19: Psa 54 Title.

CHAPTER 24

David lets Saul live

¹ When Saul got back from fighting off the Philistines, he heard that David was in the desert around En-Gedi. ² Saul led three thousand of Israel's best soldiers out to look for David and his men near Wild Goat Rocks at En-Gedi. ³ There were some sheep pens along the side of the road, and one of them was built around the entrance to a cave. Saul went into the cave to relieve himself.

David and his men were hiding at the back of the cave. ⁴ They whispered to David, "The LORD told you he was going to let you defeat your enemies and do whatever you want with them. This must be the day the LORD was talking about."

David sneaked over and cut off a small piece˒ of Saul's robe, but Saul didn't notice a thing. ⁵ Afterwards, David was sorry that he had even done that, ⁶⁻⁷ and he told his men, "Stop talking foolishly. We're not going to attack Saul. He's my king, and I pray that the LORD will keep me from doing anything to harm his chosen king."

Saul left the cave and started down the road. ⁸ Soon, David also got up and left the cave. "Your Majesty!" he shouted from a distance.

Saul turned around to look. David bowed down very low ⁹ and said:

Your Majesty, why do you listen to people who say that I'm trying to harm you? ¹⁰ You can see for yourself that the LORD gave me the chance to catch you in the cave today. Some of my men wanted to kill you, but I wouldn't let them do it. I told them, "I will not harm the LORD's chosen king!" ¹¹ Your Majesty, look at what I'm holding. You can see that it's a piece of your robe. If I could cut off a piece of your robe, I could have killed you. But I let you live, and that should prove I'm not trying to harm you or to rebel. I haven't done anything to you, and yet you keep trying to ambush and kill me.

¹² I'll let the LORD decide which one of us has done right. I pray that the LORD will punish you for what you're doing to me, but I won't do anything to you. ¹³ An old proverb says, "Only evil people do evil things," and so I won't harm you.

¹⁴ Why should the king of Israel be out chasing me, anyway? I'm as worthless as a dead dog or a flea. ¹⁵ I pray that the LORD will help me escape and show that I am in the right.

¹⁶ "David, my son — is that you?" Saul asked. Then he started crying ¹⁷ and said:

David, you're a better person than I am. You treated me with kindness, even though I've been cruel to you. ¹⁸ You've told me how you were kind enough not to kill me when the LORD gave you the chance. ¹⁹ If you really were my enemy, you wouldn't have let me leave here alive. I pray that the LORD will give you a big reward for what you did today.

²⁰ I realize now that you will be the next king, and a powerful king at that. ²¹ Promise me with the LORD as your witness, that you won't wipe out my descendants. Let them live to keep my family name alive.

²² So David promised, and Saul went home. David and his men returned to their hide-out.

CHAPTER 25

Samuel dies

¹ Samuel died, and people from all over Israel gathered to mourn for him when he was buried at his home* in Ramah. Meanwhile, David moved his camp to Paran Desert.˒

Abigail keeps David from killing innocent people

²⁻³ Nabal was a very rich man who lived in Maon. He owned three thousand sheep and a thousand goats, which he kept at Carmel.* His wife Abigail was sensible and beautiful, but he was from the Caleb clan˒ and was rough and mean.

⁴ One day, Nabal was in Carmel, while his servants cut the wool from his sheep. David was in the desert when he heard about it. ⁵⁻⁶ So he sent ten men to Carmel with this message for Nabal:

---

*25.1 at his home: Hebrew "in his house". Family tombs were sometimes underneath the house or in the courtyard of the home.

*25.2–3 Carmel: About one and a half kilometres north of Maon in the Southern Desert of Judah.

See also: 24.14: 1 Sam 26.20.

See also: 24.3: Psa 57 Title; Psa 142 Title.
24.6: 1 Sam 26.11.

I hope that you and your family are healthy and that all is going well for you. [7] I've heard that you are cutting the wool from your sheep.

When your shepherds were with us in Carmel, we didn't harm them, and nothing was ever stolen from them. [8] Ask your shepherds, and they'll tell you the same thing.

My servants are your servants, and you are like a father to me. This is a day for celebrating,* so please be kind and share some of your food with us.

[9] David's men went to Nabal and gave him David's message, then they waited for Nabal's answer.

[10] This is what he said:

Who does this David think he is? That son of Jesse is just one more slave on the run from his master, and there are too many of them these days. [11] What makes you think I would take my bread, my water, and the meat that I've had cooked for my own servants* and give it to you? Besides, I'm not sure that David sent you!›

[12] The men returned to their camp and told David everything Nabal had said.

[13] "Everybody get your swords!" David ordered.

They all strapped on their swords. Two hundred men stayed behind to guard the camp, but the other four hundred followed David.

[14-16] Meanwhile, one of Nabal's servants told Abigail:

David's men were often nearby while we were taking care of the sheep in the fields. They were very good to us, they never hurt us, and nothing was ever stolen from us while they were nearby. With them around day or night, we were as safe as we would have been inside a walled city.

David sent some messengers from the desert to wish our master well, but he shouted insults at them. [17] He's a bully who won't listen to anyone.

Isn't there something you can do? Please think of something! Or else our master and his family and everyone who works for him are all doomed.

[18] Abigail quickly got together two hundred loaves of bread, two large clay jars of wine, the meat from five sheep, a large sack of roasted grain, a hundred handfuls of raisins, and two hundred handfuls of dried figs. She loaded all the food on donkeys [19] and told her servants, "Take this on ahead, and I'll catch up with you." She didn't tell her husband Nabal what she was doing.

[20] Abigail was riding her donkey on the path that led around the hillside, when suddenly she met David and his men heading straight at her.

[21] David had just been saying, "I wasted my time guarding Nabal's things in the desert and keeping them from being stolen! I was good to him, and now he pays me back with insults. [22] I swear that by morning, there won't be a man or boy left from his family or his servants' families. I pray that God will punish me› if I don't do it!"

[23] Abigail quickly got off her donkey and bowed down in front of David. [24] Then she said:

Sir, please let me explain! [25] Don't pay any attention to that good-for-nothing Nabal. His name means "fool", and it really fits him!

I didn't see the men you sent, [26-27] but please take this gift of food that I've brought and share it with your followers. The LORD has kept you from taking revenge and from killing innocent people. But I hope your enemies and anyone else who wants to harm you will end up like Nabal. I swear this by the living LORD and by your life.

[28] Please forgive me if I say a little more. The LORD will always protect you and your family, because you fight for him. I pray that you won't ever do anything evil as long as you live. [29] The LORD your God will keep you safe when your enemies try to kill you. But he will snatch away their lives quicker than you can throw a stone from a sling.

[30] The LORD has promised to do many good things for you, even to make you the ruler of Israel. The LORD will keep his promises to you, [31] and now your conscience will be clear, because you won't be guilty of taking revenge and killing innocent people.

When the LORD does all those good things for you, please remember me.

[32] David told her:

I praise the LORD God of Israel! He must have sent you to meet me today. [33] And you

---

25.8 celebrating: Cutting the wool from the sheep was a time for celebrating as well as for working.
25.11 servants: Hebrew "shearers", the servants who cut the wool from the sheep.

should also be praised. Your good sense kept me from taking revenge and killing innocent people. [34] If you hadn't come to meet me so quickly, every man and boy in Nabal's family and in his servants' families would have been killed by morning. I swear by the living LORD God of Israel who protected you that this is the truth.

[35] David accepted the food Abigail had brought. "Don't worry," he said. "You can go home now. I'll do what you asked."

[36] Abigail went back home and found Nabal throwing a party fit for a king. He was very drunk and feeling good, so she didn't tell him anything that night. [37] But when he sobered up the next morning, Abigail told him everything that had happened. Nabal had a heart attack, and he lay in bed as still as a stone. [38] Ten days later, the LORD took his life.

[39-40] David heard that Nabal had died. "I praise the LORD!" David said. "He has judged Nabal guilty for insulting me. The LORD kept me from doing anything wrong, and he made sure that Nabal hurt only himself with his own evil."

David and Abigail are married

Abigail was still at Carmel. So David sent messengers to ask her if she would marry him. [41] She bowed down and said, "I would willingly be David's slave and wash his servants' feet."

[42] Abigail quickly got ready and went back with David's messengers. She rode on her donkey, while five of her servant women walked beside her. She and David were married as soon as she arrived.

[43] David had earlier married Ahinoam from the town of Jezreel, so both she and Abigail were now David's wives.* [44] Meanwhile, Saul had arranged for Michal* to marry Palti the son of Laish, who came from the town of Gallim.

CHAPTER 26

David again lets Saul live

[1] Once again,* some people from Ziph went to Gibeah to talk with Saul. "David has a hide-out on Mount Hachilah near Jeshimon out in the desert," they told him.

[2] Saul took three thousand of Israel's best soldiers and went to look for David there in Ziph Desert. [3] Saul set up camp on Mount Hachilah, which is across the road from Jeshimon. But David was hiding out in the desert.

When David heard that Saul was following him, [4] he sent some spies to find out if it was true. [5] Then he sneaked up to Saul's camp. He noticed that Saul and his army commander Abner the son of Ner were sleeping in the middle of the camp, with soldiers sleeping all around them. [6] David asked Ahimelech the Hittite and Joab's brother Abishai,* "Which one of you will go with me into Saul's camp?"

"I will!" Abishai answered.

[7] That same night, David and Abishai crept into the camp. Saul was sleeping, and his spear was stuck in the ground not far from his head. Abner and the soldiers were sound asleep all around him.

[8] Abishai whispered, "This time God has let you get your hands on your enemy! I'll pin him to the ground with one thrust of his own spear."

[9] "Don't kill him!" David whispered back. "The LORD will punish anyone who kills his chosen king. [10] As surely as the LORD lives, the LORD will kill Saul, or Saul will die a natural death or be killed in battle. [11] But I pray that the LORD will keep me from harming his chosen king. Let's grab his spear and his water jar and get out of here!"

[12] David took the spear and the water jar, then left the camp. None of Saul's soldiers knew what had happened or even woke up — the LORD had made all of them fall sound asleep. [13] David and Abishai crossed the valley and went to the top of the next hill, where they were at a safe distance. [14] "Abner!" David shouted towards Saul's army. "Can you hear me?"

Abner shouted back. "Who dares disturb the king?"

[15] "Abner, what kind of a man are you?" David replied. "Aren't you supposed to be the best soldier in Israel? Then why didn't you protect your king? Anyone who went into your camp could have killed him tonight.*
[16] You're a complete failure! I swear by the living LORD that you and your men deserve to die for not protecting the LORD's chosen king.

---

*25.43 wives: See the note at 1.2.
*25.44 Michal: David's first wife (see 18.20—19.17).
*26.1 again: See 23.19.
See also: 25.44: 2 Sam 3.14–16. 26.1: Psa 54 Title.

*26.6 Abishai: Hebrew "Abishai the son of Zeruiah". Zeruiah was David's elder sister, so Abishai and Joab were David's nephews (see 1 Chronicles 2.12–17; 2 Samuel 17.25 and the note there).
See also: 26.11: 1 Sam 24.26.

Look and see if you can find the king's spear and the water jar that were near his head."

[17] Saul could tell it was David's voice, and he called out, "David, my son! Is that you?"

"Yes it is, Your Majesty. [18] Why are you after me? Have I done something wrong, or have I committed a crime? [19] Please listen to what I have to say. If the LORD has turned you against me, perhaps a sacrifice will make him change his mind. But if some people have turned you against me, I hope the LORD will punish them! They have forced me to leave the land that belongs to the LORD and have told me to worship foreign gods.* [20] Don't let me die in a land far away from the LORD. I'm no more important than a flea! Why should the king of Israel hunt me down as if I were a bird in the mountains?"

[21] "David, you had the chance to kill me today. But you didn't. I was very wrong about you. It was a terrible mistake for me to try to kill you. I've acted like a fool, but I'll never try to harm you again. You're like a son to me, so please come back."

[22] "Your Majesty, here's your spear! Let one of your soldiers come and get it. [23] The LORD put you in my power today, but you are his chosen king and I wouldn't harm you. The LORD rewards people who are faithful and live right. [24] I saved your life today, and I pray that the LORD will protect me and keep me safe."

[25] "David, my son, I pray that the Lord will bless you and make you successful!"

David in Philistia

CHAPTER 27

Saul went back home. David also left, [1] but he thought to himself, "One of these days, Saul is going to kill me. The only way to escape from him is to go to Philistia. Then I'll be outside Israel, and Saul will give up trying to catch me."

[2-3] David and his six hundred men went across the border to stay in Gath with King Achish the son of Maoch. His men brought their families with them. David brought his wife Ahinoam whose home town was Jezreel, and he also brought his wife Abigail who had been married to Nabal from Carmel. [4] When Saul found out that David had run off to Gath, he stopped trying to catch him.

[5] One day, David was talking with Achish and said, "If you are happy with me, then let me live in one of the towns in the countryside. I'm not important enough to live here with you in the royal city."

[6] Achish gave David the town of Ziklag that same day, and Ziklag has belonged to the kings of Judah ever since.

[7] David was in Philistia for a year and four months. [8] The Geshurites, the Girzites, and the Amalekites lived in the area from Telam to Shur' and on as far as Egypt, and David often attacked their towns. [9] Whenever David and his men attacked a town, they took the sheep, cattle, donkeys, camels, and the clothing, and killed everyone who lived there.

After he returned from a raid, David always went to see Achish, [10] who would ask, "Where did you attack today?"'

David would answer, "Oh, we attacked some desert town that belonged to the Judah tribe." Sometimes David would say, "Oh, we attacked a town in the desert where the Jerahmeel clan lives" or "We attacked a town in the desert where the Kenites* live." [11] That's why David killed everyone in the towns he attacked. He thought, "If I let any of them live, they might come to Gath and tell what I've really been doing."

David made these raids all the time he was in Philistia. [12] But Achish trusted David and thought, "David's people must be furious with him. From now on he will have to take orders from me."

Saul talks with Samuel's ghost

CHAPTER 28

[1-3] Samuel had died some time earlier,* and people from all over Israel had attended his funeral in his home town of Ramah.

Meanwhile, Saul had been trying to get rid of everyone who spoke with the spirits of the dead.* But one day the Philistines brought their soldiers together to attack Israel.

---

*26.19 gods: In ancient times it was often believed that gods (even the God of Israel) could only be properly worshipped in their own countries, and only a country's gods should be worshipped in that country.

*27.10 Jerahmeel . . . Kenites: These were clans of the Judah tribe.

*28.1–3 earlier: See 25.1.

*28.1–3 dead: Many people believed that it was possible to talk to spirits of the dead, and that these spirits could tell the future.

See also: 28.1: 1 Sam 25.1.

Achish told David, "Of course, you know that you and your men must fight as part of our Philistine army."

David answered, "That will give you a chance to see for yourself just how well we can fight!"

"In that case," Achish said, "you and your men will always be my bodyguards."

⁴ The Philistines went to Shunem and set up camp. Saul called the army of Israel together, and they set up their camp in Gilboa. ⁵ Saul took one look at the Philistine army and started shaking with fear. ⁶ So he asked the LORD what to do. But the LORD would not answer, either in a dream or by a priest or a prophet. ⁷ Then Saul told his officers, "Find me a woman who can talk to the spirits of the dead. I'll go to her and find out what's going to happen."

His servants told him, "There's a woman at Endor who can talk to spirits of the dead."

⁸ That night, Saul put on different clothing so nobody would recognize him. Then he and two of his men went to the woman, and asked, "Will you bring up the ghost of someone for us?"

⁹ The woman said, "Why are you trying to trick me and get me killed? You know King Saul has got rid of everyone who talks to the spirits of the dead!"

¹⁰ Saul replied, "I swear by the living LORD that nothing will happen to you because of this."

¹¹ "Who do you want me to bring up?" she asked.

"Bring up the ghost of Samuel," he answered.

¹² When the woman saw Samuel, she screamed. Then she turned to Saul and said, "You've tricked me! You're the king!"

¹³ "Don't be afraid," Saul replied. "Just tell me what you see."

She answered, "I see a spirit rising up out of the ground."

¹⁴ "What does it look like?"

"It looks like an old man wearing a robe."

Saul knew it was Samuel, so he bowed down low.

¹⁵ "Why are you bothering me by bringing me up like this?" Samuel asked.

"I'm terribly worried," Saul answered. "The Philistines are about to attack me. God has turned his back on me and won't answer any more by prophets or by dreams. What should I do?"

See also: 28.6: Num 27.21. 28.7: Lev 20.27; Deut 18.10–11.

Real life

Occult

The Bible condemns occult practices. Christians in the early Church used to 'renounce the works of the Devil' at their baptism and they had to destroy any occult objects that they owned (Acts 19.19). Involvement in the occult means putting your faith in other forces than God. We shouldn't need to check our stars, our future is in God's hands.

Obviously when there's 'magic' in books or TV shows, most people can differentiate between fact and fiction. But take care. You might enjoy dressing as a Goth or listening to extreme heavy metal music, but a lot of this stuff is 'nihilistic', anti-life: celebrating despair and hopelessness and death.

A small percentage of people go further, getting heavily into serious occult practices – often with tragic results. Many are drawn into witchcraft; there have been incidents of people taking their own lives as a kind of sacrifice to Satan, or of killing others as part of some kind of 'vampire' cult.

The occult is dangerous. We should not put our faith in dead spirits and constellations and magic charms. If you want to be counter-culture and rebellious, put your faith in the living God and let him guide your future.

Think

Why is the occult wrong?
How do we protect ourselves from occult influences?

Act

Been involved in the occult? Ask God to forgive you, protect you and set you free.
Still feel 'caught'? Talk and pray with your youth leader or church leaders.
Get rid of any occult paraphernalia such as ouija boards or tarot cards.

Check

Deuteronomy 4.19; 18.9–12;
1 Samuel 28.1–25; Isaiah 44.25; 47.12;
Jeremiah 10.2; 27.8–11; Ezekiel 13.17–19;
Micah 5.12; Zephaniah 1.5;
Galatians 5.20–21

16 Samuel said:

If the LORD has turned away from you and is now your enemy, don't ask me what to do. 17 I've already told you: the LORD has sworn to take the kingdom from you and give it to David. And that's just what he's doing! 18 When the LORD was angry with the Amalekites, he told you to destroy them, but you didn't do it. That's why the LORD is doing this to you. 19 Tomorrow the LORD will let the Philistines defeat Israel's army, then you and your sons will join me down here in the world of the dead.

20 At once, Saul collapsed and lay stretched out on the floor, terrified at what Samuel had said. He was weak because he had not eaten anything since the day before.

21 The woman came over to Saul, and when she saw that he was completely terrified, she said, "Your Majesty, I listened to you and risked my life to do what you asked. 22 Now please listen to me. Let me get you a little something to eat. It will give you strength for your walk back to camp."

23 "No, I won't eat!"

But his officers and the woman kept on urging Saul, until he finally agreed. He got up off the floor and sat on the bed. 24 Straight away the woman killed a calf that she had been fattening up. She cooked part of the meat and baked some thin bread.* 25 Then she served the food to Saul and his officers, who ate and left before daylight.

David rescues the families of his troops

CHAPTER 29

The Philistines send David back

1 The Philistines had brought their whole army to Aphek,* while Israel's army was camping near Jezreel Spring. 2-3 The Philistine rulers and their troops were marching past the Philistine army commanders in groups of a hundred and a thousand. When David and his men marched by at the end with Achish, the commanders said, "What are these worthless Israelites doing here?"

"They are David's men," Achish answered. "David used to be one of Saul's officers, but he left Saul and joined my army a long time ago. I've never had even one complaint about him."

4 The Philistine army commanders were angry and shouted:

Send David back to the town you gave him. We won't have him going into the battle with us. He could turn and fight against us! Saul would take David back as an officer if David brought him the heads of our soldiers. 5 The Israelites even dance and sing,

"Saul has killed
  a thousand enemies;
David has killed
  ten thousand enemies!"

6 Achish called David over and said:

I swear by the living LORD that you've been honest with me, and I want you to fight by my side. I don't think you've done anything wrong from the day you joined me until this very moment. But the other Philistine rulers don't want you to come along. 7 Go back home and try not to upset them.

8 "But what have I done?" David asked. "Do you know of anything I've ever done that would keep me from fighting the enemies of my king?"*

9 Achish said:

I believe that you're as good as an angel of God, but our army commanders have decided that you can't fight in this battle. 10 You and your troops will have to go back to the town I gave you.' Get up and leave tomorrow morning as soon as it's light. I am pleased with you, so don't let any of this bother you.'

11 David and his men got up early in the morning and headed back towards Philistia, while the Philistines left for Jezreel.

CHAPTER 30

David rescues his soldiers' families

1 It took David and his men three days to reach Ziklag. But while they had been away, the Amalekites had been raiding in the desert

---

*28.24 thin bread:** Bread made without yeast, since there was no time for the bread to rise.
*29.1 Aphek:** The events of chapter 29 probably took place as the Philistine army was on its way to Shunem, which they reached in 28.4.
See also: **28.17:** 1 Sam 15.28. **28.18:** 1 Sam 15.3–9.

*29.8 my king:** David may be referring to either Saul or Achish.
See also: **29.5:** 1 Sam 18.7; 21.11.

around there. They had attacked Ziklag, burnt it to the ground, ² and had taken away the women and children. ³ When David and his men came to Ziklag, they saw the burnt-out ruins and learnt that their families had been taken captive. ⁴ They started crying and kept it up until they were too weak to cry any more. ⁵ David's two wives, Ahinoam and Abigail, had been taken captive with everyone else.

⁶ David was desperate. His soldiers were so upset over what had happened to their sons and daughters that they were thinking about stoning David to death. But he felt the LORD God giving him strength, ⁷ and he said to the priest, "Abiathar, let's ask God what to do."

Abiathar brought everything he needed to get answers from God, and he went over to David. ⁸ Then David asked the LORD, "Should I go after the people who raided our town? Can I catch up with them?"

"Go after them," the LORD answered. "You will catch up with them, and you will rescue your families."

⁹⁻¹⁰ David led his six hundred men to Besor Gorge, but two hundred of them were too tired to go across. So they stayed behind, while David and the other four hundred men crossed the gorge.

¹¹ Some of David's men found an Egyptian out in a field and took him to David. They gave the Egyptian some bread, and he ate it. Then they gave him a drink of water, ¹² some dried figs, and two handfuls of raisins. This was the first time in three days he had tasted food or water. Now he felt much better.

¹³ "Who is your master?" David asked. "And where do you come from?"

"I'm from Egypt," the young man answered. "I'm the servant of an Amalekite, but he left me here three days ago because I was sick. ¹⁴ We had attacked some towns in the desert where the Cherethites live, in the area that belongs to Judah, and in the desert where the Caleb clan lives. And we burnt down Ziklag."

¹⁵ "Will you take me to those Amalekites?" David asked.

"Yes, I will, if you promise with God as a witness that you won't kill me or hand me over to my master."

¹⁶ He led David to the Amalekites. They were eating and drinking everywhere, celebrating because of what they had taken from Philistia and Judah. ¹⁷ David attacked just before sunrise the next day and fought

See also: 30.5: 1 Sam 25.42–43.   30.7: 1 Sam 22.20–23.

Viewpoints

Is God's strength just for spiritual heroes?

Contributed by Marc W

David was desperate. His soldiers were so upset over what had happened to their sons and daughters that they were thinking about stoning David to death. But he felt the LORD God giving him strength.

David, Daniel, and Paul did it. And they're not the only ones. Now it's our turn. Our turn to get our strength from the LORD. David did it more than once. He found himself messed up, worried and facing huge problems (let's face it, they don't come a lot bigger than Goliath!) What he did though is something that I find very hard to do.

So did Daniel. He was told not to pray to his God, but he still did. The penalty… death by lions. Daniel put his faith in the LORD, however, and came out of it alive. And then there's Paul. He got in trouble everywhere he went. He'd changed from his old ways, giving himself totally to God, and as a result, no-one liked him. And they liked what he was saying even less. They really had a go at him.

All three of them found a way of dealing with their situations. They asked God if he would take over the situation, and he did: David beat Goliath and won the war, Daniel survived and became the King's mate, and Paul kept preaching.

When things don't go my way, and I'm in a muddle, I find it hard to keep my cool. Luckily though, I know someone who can help. God can give us strength to show who we really are: people of God.

More…

Help! I've messed up really badly p.347
Prayer p.1002
Persecution p.1215
Going against the crowd p.1045

until sunset.' Four hundred Amalekites rode away on camels, but they were the only ones who escaped.

¹⁸ David rescued his two wives and everyone else the Amalekites had taken from Ziklag. ¹⁹ No one was missing — young or old, sons or daughters. David brought back everything that had been stolen, ²⁰ including their livestock.

David also took the sheep and cattle that the Amalekites had with them, but he kept these separate from the others. Everyone agreed that these would be David's reward.

²¹ On the way back, David went to the two hundred men he had left at Besor Gorge, because they had been too tired to keep up with him. They came towards David and the people who were with him. When David was close enough, he greeted the two hundred men and asked how they were doing.

²² Some of David's men were good-for-nothings, and they said, "Those men didn't go with us to the battle, so they don't get any of the things we took back from the Amalekites. Let them take their wives and children and go!"

²³ But David said:

My friends, don't be so greedy with what the LORD has given us! The LORD protected us and gave us victory over the people who attacked. ²⁴ Who would pay attention to you, anyway? Soldiers who stay behind to guard the camp get as much as those who go into battle.

²⁵ David made this a law for Israel, and it has been the same ever since.

²⁶ David went back to Ziklag with everything they had taken from the Amalekites. He sent some of these things as gifts to his friends who were leaders of Judah, and he told them, "We took these things from the LORD's enemies. Please accept them as a gift."

²⁷⁻³¹ This is a list of the towns where David sent gifts: Bethel,* Ramoth in the Southern Desert, Jattir, Aroer, Siphmoth, Eshtemoa, Racal, the towns belonging to the Jerahmeelites and the Kenites, Hormah, Bor-Ashan, Athach, and Hebron. He also sent gifts to the other towns where he and his men had travelled.

Saul and his sons die in battle against the Philistines

CHAPTER 31

¹ Meanwhile, the Philistines were fighting Israel at Mount Gilboa. Israel's soldiers ran from the Philistines, and many of them were killed. ² The Philistines closed in on Saul and his sons, and they killed his sons Jonathan, Abinadab, and Malchishua. ³ The fighting was fierce around Saul, and he was badly wounded by enemy arrows.

⁴ Saul told the soldier who carried his weapons, "Kill me with your sword! I don't want those worthless Philistines to torture me and make fun of me." But the soldier was afraid to kill him.

Saul then took out his own sword; he stuck the blade into his stomach, and fell on it. ⁵ When the soldier knew that Saul was dead, he killed himself in the same way.

⁶ Saul was dead, his three sons were dead, and the soldier who carried his weapons was dead. They and all his soldiers died on that same day. ⁷ The Israelites on the other side of Jezreel Valley* and the other side of the Jordan learnt that Saul and his sons were dead. They saw that the Israelite army had run away. So they ran away too, and the Philistines moved into the towns the Israelites had left behind.

⁸ The day after the battle, when the Philistines returned to the battlefield to take the weapons of the dead Israelite soldiers, they found Saul and his three sons lying dead on Mount Gilboa. ⁹⁻¹⁰ The Philistines cut off Saul's head and pulled off his armour. Then they put his armour in the temple of the goddess Astarte, and they nailed his body to the city wall of Beth-Shan. They also sent messengers everywhere in Philistia to spread the good news in the temples of their idols and among their people.

¹¹ The people who lived in Jabesh in Gilead heard what the Philistines had done to Saul's body. ¹² So one night, some brave men from Jabesh went to Beth-Shan. They took down the bodies of Saul and his sons, then brought them back to Jabesh and burnt them. ¹³ They buried the bones under a small tree in Jabesh, and for seven days, they went without eating to show their sorrow.

---

*30.27–31 Bethel: Or "Bethuel" (see Joshua 19.4).

*31.7 Jezreel Valley: Hebrew "valley". Shunem (see 28.4) and Gilboa (see verse 1) were across the Jezreel Valley from each other.

Holy history

Funerals

The scariest thing of all was not to be buried.

When you died, you had to be buried. Not to be buried was a punishment and a scandal (Deuteronomy. 28.26; 1 Kings 14.11; Jeremiah 22.19). That's why Jacob asked his family to ensure he was buried in his family tomb (Genesis 49.30; 50.5) and why the people of Jabesh in Gilead risked so much to rescue the body of Saul (1 Samuel 31.8–13).

Tombs were often made out of existing caves and were places where all the family were buried. Abraham bought the cave of Machpelah for his family, including Sarah, Abraham, Isaac, Rebekah, Leah and Jacob. Big tombs usually had a deep tunnel, leading into a square or oval burial chamber. The opening was sealed with rocks to stop animals or grave-robbers. Later tombs were often multi-chambered and cut into rocks, with ledges cut into the walls where the dead were placed.

Cremation was not practised by the Jews or early Christians. In fact, burning was considered shameful and was inflicted as a death penalty for criminals (Leviticus 20.14; 21.9). But coffins were rarely used. Instead the body was simply wrapped in a cloth. Later on, after the body had decomposed, the bones were collected and put into a box (called an ossuary) which was placed in another area of the same tomb.

Jesus was placed in a Roman-style tomb, which had a burial chamber containing one or more benches where the body would be laid. The more elaborate tombs had a stone which rolled in a groove, like a kind of sliding door to seal the entrance.
Not that it worked...

More...

Heaven p.1412
Hell p.1148

Additional notes

›1.1 Ramah: The Hebrew has "Ramathaim", a longer form of "Ramah" (see verse 19).

›1.3 Eli . . . priests: One ancient translation; Hebrew "Hophni and Phinehas, the two sons of Eli, served the LORD as priests."

›1.23 the LORD . . . promised: The Dead Sea Scrolls and two ancient translations; the Standard Hebrew Text "the LORD will do what he said."

›1.24–25 When it was the time of year to go to Shiloh again, Hannah and Elkanah: The Dead Sea Scrolls and one ancient translation; the Standard Hebrew Text "she".

›1.24–25 a three-year-old bull: The Dead Sea Scrolls and two ancient translations; the Standard Hebrew Text "three bulls".

›1.28 Elkanah: Or "They" or "Samuel".

›2.2 god: The Hebrew text has "holy one", a term for supernatural beings or gods.

›2.2 mountain: One possible meaning for the difficult Hebrew text of verse 2.

›2.22 Israel: The Dead Sea Scrolls and one ancient translation; the Standard Hebrew Text adds "He heard that his sons were even sleeping with the women who worked at the entrance to the sacred tent."

›2.28–29 don't respect: The Standard Hebrew Text; the Dead Sea Scrolls and one ancient translation "are greedy for".

›2.32 Your family: Or "My house of worship".

›2.31–32 Not one . . . to Israel: The Standard Hebrew Text; the Dead Sea Scrolls and one ancient translation do not have these words.

›2.33 his: The Dead Sea Scrolls and one ancient translation; the Standard Hebrew Text "your".

›2.33 die a violent death: The Dead Sea Scrolls and one ancient translation; the Standard Hebrew Text "die".

›3.13 refused . . . me: Or "were insulting everyone".

›4.3 LORD: Or "chest".

›5.6 sores . . . bodies: Or "He struck them with bubonic plague".

›5.6 panic: Two ancient translations add "Rats came from their ships, and people were dying right and left."

›6.1 months: One ancient translation adds "and rats were everywhere" or "and rats ate the crops".

›6.18 stone: A few Hebrew manuscripts; most Hebrew manuscripts "meadow" or "stream".

›6.19 seventy: A few Hebrew manuscripts; most Hebrew manuscripts "seventy men, fifty thousand men".

›7.2 Israel . . . help: Or "Israel turned to the Lord and begged him for help."

›7.12–13 Help Monument: Or "Ebenezer".

›9.20 Everything . . . family: Or "You and your family are what all Israel wants."

›9.25–26 was set . . . morning: One ancient translation; Hebrew "Samuel spoke with Saul on the flat roof of his house. They got up early the next morning, around sunrise, and . . . ".

›**10.1 people:** One ancient translation adds "You will rule the Lord's people and save them from their enemies who are all around them. These things will prove that what I say is true."

›**10.5 Gibeah:** The Hebrew text has "Gibeah of God", which may or may not have been the same Gibeah as Saul's home town.

›**10.6 take . . . you:** Or "will take control of you in a powerful way."

›**10.10 suddenly . . . him:** Or "came over him in a powerful way".

›**10.12 Why not . . . anyone else:** Or "He certainly is! He's probably the leader of the prophets!" or "How can he be? Those prophets are nobodies!"

›**10.27—11.1 But Saul . . . time:** The Standard Hebrew Text; the Dead Sea Scrolls add "King Nahash of Ammon was making the people of Gad and Reuben miserable. He was putting out everyone's right eye, and no one in Israel could stop him. He had put out the right eye of every Israelite man who lived east of the River Jordan. Only seven thousand men had escaped from the Ammonites, and they had gone into the town of Jabesh in Gilead. About a month later . . . ".

›**11.7 the:** Or "some other".

›**11.8 three hundred thousand . . . thirty thousand:** The Dead Sea Scrolls and some ancient translations have different numbers.

›**12.11 Gideon:** The Hebrew text has "Jerubbaal", another name for "Gideon".

›**12.14 If . . . him:** Or "If you and your king want things to go well for you, then you must worship the LORD."

›**12.15 and your king:** One ancient translation; Hebrew "and your ancestors" or "as he was against your ancestors".

›**13.1 a young man:** One possible meaning for the difficult Hebrew text; several manuscripts of one ancient translation have "thirty years old".

›**13.1-2 for . . . Then:** One possible meaning for the difficult Hebrew text.

›**13.3 led an attack . . . destroyed, but:** Or "killed the Philistine military governor who lived at Geba, and . . . ".

›**13.4 destroyed . . . Geba:** Or "killed the Philistine military governor who lived at Geba".

›**13.5 three thousand:** Some ancient translations; Hebrew "thirty thousand".

›**13.6 in . . . bushes:** Or "in cracks in the rocks".

›**13.15 Then Samuel . . . counted them:** Two ancient translations; Hebrew "Then Samuel left Gilgal and went to Gibeah in Benjamin. Saul counted his army".

›**13.20-21 sickles:** One ancient translation; Hebrew "plough-blades".

›**13.20-21 pitchforks:** One possible meaning for the difficult Hebrew text.

›**14.1-3 Geba:** Or "Gibeah". In 13.16 and 14.5 the name "Geba" is used, while 14.2,16 have "Gibeah". In ancient Hebrew writing there is only one letter different between the two words.

›**14.1-3 threshing place:** Or "in Migron".

›**14.4-5 Shiny Cliff . . . Thorn Bush Cliff:** Or "Bozez Cliff . . . Seneh Cliff".

›**14.13 Jonathan killed . . . from behind:** Or "Jonathan attacked the Philistines with his sword, and the soldier killed those who fell to the ground wounded."

›**14.14 thirty metres:** One possible meaning for the difficult Hebrew text.

›**14.15 Then . . . tremble:** Or "Then the ground began to tremble, and everyone was in a terrible panic." Or "Then the ground began to tremble, and God made them all panic."

›**14.16 Geba:** See the note at 14.1-3.

›**14.18 At that time . . . should do:** One ancient translation; Hebrew "Saul told Ahijah, 'Bring the sacred chest,' because at that time it was with the army of Israel."

›**14.25-26 The army . . . ground:** One possible meaning for the difficult Hebrew text.

›**14.33 over here:** One ancient translation; Hebrew "today".

›**14.41 why . . . Israel:** One ancient translation; Hebrew "give me an answer."

›**14.47-48 won his battles:** One ancient translation; Hebrew "hurt them".

›**15.5 one . . . in:** Or "the town of".

›**15.7 from Havilah:** Or "from the valley" (see 15.5).

›**15.9 animals . . . weak:** One possible meaning for the difficult Hebrew text.

›**15.13 Saul:** One ancient translation adds "Saul had sacrificed to the LORD the best animals they had taken from Amalek, when Samuel came up to him . . . ".

›**15.29 eternal:** Or "glorious".

›**15.32 in chains:** One possible meaning for the difficult Hebrew text.

›**15.32 Surely . . . now:** Hebrew; one ancient translation "It would have been better to die in battle!"

›**17.4 about three metres:** The Standard Hebrew Text; the Dead Sea Scrolls and some manuscripts of one ancient translation have "about two metres".

›**17.52 Gath:** One ancient translation; Hebrew "a valley".

›**18.16 was loyal to:** Or "loved".

›**18.28 she . . . David:** Hebrew; one ancient translation "all Israel was loyal to David".

›**19.18 Prophets Village:** Or "Naioth".

›**20.16 Jonathan . . . keep:** Or, continuing Jonathan's statement to David, "You and your descendants must not kill off my descendants."

›**20.16 I pray . . . promise:** Or "I pray that the LORD take revenge on you if you break our promise!"

›**20.19 By . . . time:** One possible meaning for the difficult Hebrew text.

›**20.19 Going-Away Rock:** Or "Ezel Rock"; one ancient translation "that mound" (see 20.41).

›**20.25 sat . . . him:** One ancient translation; Hebrew "stood up".

›**20.34 insulted David:** Or "insulted him" (that is, Jonathan).

›**20.41 the mound:** One ancient translation; Hebrew "from the south side".

›**21.7 the strongest of:** Or "in charge of".

›**23.15 He . . . because:** Or "He saw that".

›**24.4 small piece:** Hebrew "corner" or "lower hem".

›**25.1 Paran Desert:** Hebrew; some manuscripts of one ancient translation "Maon Desert".

›**25.2–3 from the Caleb clan:** Or "behaved like a dog".

›**25.11 I'm not sure . . . sent you:** Or "I don't know where you come from."

›**25.22 me:** One ancient translation; Hebrew "my enemies".

›**26.15 Anyone . . . tonight:** Or "Someone went into your camp to kill him tonight."

›**27.8 lived . . . Shur:** One ancient translation; Hebrew "had lived for a long time in Shur".

›**27.10 Where . . . today:** A few Hebrew manuscripts, the Dead Sea Scrolls, and three ancient translations; most Hebrew manuscripts "Didn't you make a raid today?"

›**29.10 go . . . you:** One ancient translation; these words are not in the Hebrew text.

›**29.10 I am . . . bother you:** One ancient translation; these words are not in the Hebrew text.

›**30.17 just . . . sunset:** Or "at dusk, and fought until sunset on the next day."

2 Samuel

The basics

What's the point? Sin has consequences, but God will always forgive us if we ask.

What happens? David becomes king. He unifies the kingdom, defeats foreign enemies, but also commits a terrible sin and has to face the consequences. God forgives David, and even promises that his family will reign forever in Israel.

What should I remember? 7.11–13 'Now I promise that you and your descendants will be kings. I'll choose one of your sons to be king when you reach the end of your life and are buried in the tomb of your ancestors. I'll make him a strong ruler, and no one will be able to take his kingdom away from him. He will be the one to build a temple for me.'

More details

Setting the scene Saul, the first king of Israel, is dead. Now the crown passes to David, the young hero of the first part of the story. But Saul still has his supporters. First David must defeat them, then he must defeat Israel's enemies. And once he is king, he finds that the pressures are hard to resist...

What's it all about? This is the story of David's triumph – and his downfall. It's the tale of how Israel's greatest king gained control of the kingdom, only to lose control of himself and his family.

The first seven years of David's reign are spent in civil war. David battles against Saul's supporters, led by the late king's son, Ishbosheth. Finally, David defeats Ishbosheth, captures Jerusalem from the Jebusites, and becomes king of the United Kingdom of Israel.

But he doesn't leave it there. He goes on to defeat the enemy nations around Israel and develop the nation into a kind of small empire.

He transforms Jerusalem into the capital of the country, instals the ark of the covenant in place and starts to plan a magnificent temple.

And then it all goes wrong. David commits adultery, tries to cover it up with murder and his family is torn apart by the consequences. Faced with his own actions, he throws himself on God's mercy. Perhaps that's the key message of 2 Samuel. Yes, it's about national success and glory, but it's also about personal failure and forgiveness. David defeated Israel's enemies, but he also discovered more about Israel's God – a God who promised that his family would reign in the land for ever more.

And another thing

It was David who made Jerusalem the capital city of Israel. He captured the city by sending his troops up through underground water tunnels (2 Samuel 5.6–12).

Footsteps

David becomes king and brings the sacred chest to Jerusalem: 5.1–12; 6.1–23
God's promise to David: 7.1–29
David and Bathsheba: 11.1–27
Nathan reveals the truth: 12.1–23
Absalom rebels against his father: 15.1–31
Absalom is killed: 18.1–33
David's final sin: 24.1–25

David mourns for Saul

CHAPTER 1

David finds out about Saul's death

[1] Saul was dead.

Meanwhile, David had defeated the Amalekites and returned to Ziklag. [2] Three days later, a soldier came from Saul's army. His clothes were torn, and earth was on his head.* He went to David and knelt down in front of him.

³ David asked, "Where did you come from?"

The man answered, "From Israel's army. I barely escaped with my life."

⁴ "Who won the battle?" David asked.

The man said, "Our army turned and ran, but many were wounded and died. Even King Saul and his son Jonathan are dead."

⁵ David asked, "How do you know Saul and Jonathan are dead?"

⁶ The young man replied:

I was on Mount Gilboa and saw King Saul leaning on his spear. The enemy's war chariots and cavalry were closing in on him. ⁷ When he turned round and saw me, he called me over. I went and asked what he wanted.

⁸ Saul asked me, "Who are you?"

"An Amalekite," I answered.

⁹ Then he said, "Kill me! I'm dying, and I'm in terrible pain."ʼ

¹⁰ So I killed him. I knew he was too badly wounded to live much longer. Then I took his crown and his arm-band, and I brought them to you, Your Majesty. Here they are.

¹¹ Straight away, David and his soldiers tore their clothes in sorrow. ¹² They cried all day long and would not eat anything. Everyone was sad because Saul, his son Jonathan, and many of the LORD's people had been killed in the battle.

¹³ David asked the young man, "Where is your home?"

The man replied, "My father is an Amalekite, but we live in Israel."

¹⁴⁻¹⁶ David said to him, "Why weren't you afraid to kill the LORD's chosen king? And you even told what you did. It's your own fault that you're going to die!"

Then David told one of his soldiers, "Come here and kill this man!"

David sings in memory of Saul

¹⁷ David sang a song in memory of Saul and Jonathan, ¹⁸ and he ordered his men to teach the song to everyone in Judah. He called it "The Song of the Bow", and it can be found in *The Book of Jashar.** This is the song:

¹⁹ Israel, your famous hero
lies dead on the hills,
and your mighty warriors
have fallen!
²⁰ Don't tell it in Gath
or spread the news
in the streets of Ashkelon.
The godless Philistine women
will be happy
and jump for joy.
²¹ Don't let dew or rain fall
on the hills of Gilboa.
Don't let its fields
grow offerings for God.
There the warriors' shields
were smeared with mud,
and Saul's own shield
was left unpolished.*

²² The arrows of Jonathan struck,
and warriors died.
The sword of Saul cut
the enemy apart.

²³ It was easy to love Saul
and Jonathan.
Together in life,
together in death,
they were faster than eagles
and stronger than lions.

²⁴ Women of Israel, cry for Saul.
He brought you fine red cloth
and jewellery made of gold.
²⁵ Our warriors have fallen
in the heat of battle,
and Jonathan lies dead
on the hills of Gilboa.

²⁶ Jonathan, I miss you most!
I loved you like a brother.
You were truly loyal to me,
more faithful than a wife
to her husband.ʼ

²⁷ Our warriors have fallen,
and their weapons*
are destroyed.

---

*1.2 His clothes . . . his head:** People tore their clothes and put earth on their heads to show they were sad because someone had died.
See also: 1.6–10: 1 Sam 31.1–6; 1 Chron 10.1–6.
1.18: Josh 10.13.

*1.18 The Book of Jashar:** This book may have been a collection of ancient war songs.
*1.21 unpolished:** Some shields were made of leather and were polished with olive oil.
*1.27 weapons:** This may refer to Saul and Jonathan.

David, king of Judah

CHAPTER 2

[1] Later, David asked the LORD, "Should I go back to one of the towns of Judah?"

The LORD answered, "Yes."

David asked, "Which town should I go to?"

"Go to Hebron," the LORD replied.

[2] David went to Hebron with his two wives, Ahinoam and Abigail. Ahinoam was from Jezreel, and Abigail was the widow of Nabal from Carmel. [3] David also took his men and their families to live in the villages near Hebron.

[4] The people of Judah met with David at Hebron and poured olive oil on his head to show that he was their new king. Then they told David, "The people from Jabesh in Gilead buried Saul."

[5] David sent messengers to tell them:

The LORD bless you! You were kind enough to bury Saul your ruler, [6] and I pray that the LORD will be kind and faithful to you. I will be your friend because of what you have done. [7] Saul is dead, but the tribe of Judah has made me their king. So be strong and have courage.

Ishbosheth becomes king of Israel

[8] Abner the son of Ner* had been the general of Saul's army. He took Saul's son Ishbosheth* across the River Jordan to Mahanaim [9] and made him king of Israel,* including the areas of Gilead, Asher,* Jezreel, Ephraim, and Benjamin. [10] Ishbosheth was forty years old at the time, and he ruled for two years. But the tribe of Judah made David their king, [11] and he ruled from Hebron for seven and a half years.

The war between David and Ishbosheth

[12] One day, Abner and the soldiers of Ishbosheth* left Mahanaim and went to Gibeon. [13] Meanwhile, Joab the son of Zeruiah* was leading David's soldiers, and the two groups met at the pool in Gibeon.* Abner and his men sat down on one side of the pool, while Joab and his men sat on the other side. [14] Abner yelled to Joab, "Let's get some of our best soldiers to stand up and fight each other!"

Joab agreed, [15] and twelve of Ishbosheth's men from the tribe of Benjamin got up to fight twelve of David's men. [16] They grabbed each other by the hair and stabbed each other in the side with their daggers. They all died there! That's why the place in Gibeon is called "Field of Daggers".▸ [17] Then everyone started fighting. Both sides fought very hard, but David's soldiers defeated Abner and the soldiers of Israel.

[18] Zeruiah's three sons were there: Joab, Abishai, and Asahel. Asahel could run as fast as a deer in an open field, [19] and he ran straight after Abner, without looking to the right or to the left.

[20] When Abner turned and saw him, he said, "Is that you, Asahel?"

Asahel answered, "Yes it is."

[21] Abner said, "There are soldiers all around. Stop chasing me and fight one of them! Kill him and take his clothes and weapons for yourself."

But Asahel refused to stop.

[22] Abner said, "If you don't turn back, I'll have to kill you! Then I could never face your brother Joab again."

[23] But Asahel would not turn back, so Abner struck him in the stomach with the back end of his spear. The spear went all the way through and came out of his back. Asahel fell down and died. Everyone who saw Asahel lying dead just stopped and stood still. [24] But Joab and Abishai went after Abner.

---

*2.8 son of Ner: Abner was Saul's cousin (see 1 Samuel 14.50).
*2.8 Ishbosheth: One ancient translation has "Ishbaal" (see also 1 Chronicles 8.33). In Hebrew "baal" means "lord" and was used as the name of a Canaanite god. The people of Israel often changed "baal" to "bosheth" (which means "shame") in personal names. Ishbosheth was probably called Ishvi or Ishyo in 1 Samuel 14.49.
*2.9 Israel: Sometimes "Israel" means the northern tribes and does not include the tribes of Judah and Simeon. That is how it is used in this verse.
*2.9 Asher: The Hebrew text has "Ashur", which is the Hebrew name for the Assyrians. It may be another spelling for Asher (one of the tribes of Israel) or it may refer to Geshur (a small area between Gilead and Jezreel, east of Lake Galilee).
See also: 2.2: 1 Sam 25.42–43. 2.4: 1 Sam 31.11–13.

*2.12 Ishbosheth: See the note at 2.8.
*2.13 the son of Zeruiah: Zeruiah was David's elder sister, so Joab was David's nephew (see 1 Chronicles 2.12–17 and the note at 2 Samuel 17.25).
*2.13 pool in Gibeon: This pool was just inside the city wall and was used for storing water. It was in the shape of a circle and was about 11 metres wide and about 11 metres deep.

Finally, about sunset, they came to the hill of Ammah, not far from Giah on the road to Gibeon Desert. 25 Abner brought the men of Benjamin together in one group on top of a hill, and they got ready to fight.

26 Abner shouted to Joab, "Aren't we ever going to stop killing each other? Don't you know that the longer we keep on doing this, the worse it's going to be when it's all over? When are you going to order your men to stop chasing their own relatives?"

27 Joab shouted back, "I swear by the living God, if you hadn't spoken, my men would have chased their relatives all night!" 28 Joab took his trumpet and blew the signal for his soldiers to stop chasing the soldiers of Israel. Straight away, the fighting stopped.

29 Abner and his troops marched through the Jordan Valley all that night. Then they crossed the river and marched all morning' until they arrived back at Mahanaim.

30 As soon as Joab stopped chasing Abner, he got David's troops together and counted them. There were nineteen missing besides Asahel. 31 But David's soldiers had killed 360 of Abner's men from the tribe of Benjamin. 32 Joab and his troops carried Asahel's body to Bethlehem and buried him in the family burial place. Then they marched all night and reached Hebron before sunrise.

CHAPTER 3

1 This battle was the beginning of a long war between the followers of Saul and the followers of David. Saul's power grew weaker, but David's grew stronger.

David's sons born in Hebron

This is also told in 1 Chronicles 3.1–4

2–5 Several of David's sons were born while he was living in Hebron. His eldest son was Amnon, whose mother was Ahinoam from Jezreel. David's second son was Chileab, whose mother was Abigail, who had been married to Nabal from Carmel. Absalom was the third. His mother was Maacah, the daughter of King Talmai of Geshur. The fourth was Adonijah, whose mother was Haggith. The fifth was Shephatiah, whose mother was Abital. The sixth was Ithream, whose mother was Eglah, another one of David's wives.

Abner decides to help David

6 As the war went on between the families of David and Saul, Abner was gaining more power than ever in Saul's family. 7 He had even slept with a wife* of Saul by the name of Rizpah the daughter of Aiah. But Saul's son Ishbosheth* told Abner, "You shouldn't have slept with one of my father's wives!"

8 Abner was very angry at what Ishbosheth had said, and he told Ishbosheth:

Am I some kind of worthless dog from Judah? I've always been loyal to your father's family and to his relatives and friends. I haven't turned you over to David. And yet you talk to me as if I've committed a crime with this woman.

9 I ask God to punish me if I don't help David get what the LORD promised him! 10 God said that he wouldn't let anyone in Saul's family ever be king again and that David would be king instead. He also said that David would rule both Israel and Judah, all the way from Dan in the north to Beersheba in the south.*

11 Ishbosheth was so afraid of Abner that he could not even answer.

12 Abner sent some of his men to David with this message: "You should be the ruler of the whole nation.' If you make an agreement with me, I will persuade everyone in Israel to make you their king."

13 David sent this message back: "Good! I'll make an agreement with you. But before I will even talk with you about it, you must get Saul's daughter Michal back for me."

14 David sent a few of his officials to Ishbosheth to give him this message: "Give me back my wife Michal! I killed a hundred Philistines so I could marry her."*

15 Ishbosheth sent some of his men to take Michal away from her new husband, Paltiel the son of Laish. 16 Paltiel followed Michal and the men all the way to Bahurim, crying as he walked. But he went back home after Abner ordered him to leave.

17 Abner talked with the leaders of the tribes of Israel and told them, "You've wanted to make David your king for a long time now. 18 So do it! After all, God said he

---

*3.7 wife: This translates a Hebrew word for a woman who was legally bound to a man, but without the full privileges of a wife.

*3.7 Ishbosheth: See the note at 2.8.

*3.10 from . . . south: Hebrew "from Dan to Beersheba". This was one way of describing all of the Israelite land, from north to south.

*3.14 I killed . . . marry her: See 1 Samuel 18.20–27.

See also: 3.10: 1 Sam 15.28. 3.14: 1 Sam 18.27.

would use his servant David to rescue his people Israel from their enemies, especially from the Philistines."

¹⁹ Finally, Abner talked with the tribe of Benjamin. Then he left for Hebron to tell David everything that the tribe of Benjamin and the rest of the people of Israel wanted to do. ²⁰ Abner took twenty soldiers with him, and when they got to Hebron, David gave a big feast for them.

²¹ After the feast, Abner said, "Your Majesty, let me leave now and bring Israel here to make an agreement with you. You'll be king of the whole nation, just as you've been wanting."

David told Abner he could leave, and he left without causing any trouble.

Joab kills Abner

²² Soon after Abner had left Hebron, Joab and some of David's soldiers came back, bringing a lot of things they had taken from an enemy village. ²³ Just after they arrived, someone told Joab, "Abner visited the king, and the king let him go. Abner even left without causing any trouble."

²⁴ Joab went to David and said, "What have you done? Abner came to you, and you let him go. Now he's long gone! ²⁵ You know Abner — he came to trick you. He wants to find out how strong your army is and to know everything you're doing."

²⁶ Joab left David, then he sent some messengers to catch up with Abner. They brought him back from the well at Sirah,' but David did not know anything about it. ²⁷ When Abner returned to Hebron, Joab pretended he wanted to talk privately with him. So he took Abner into one of the small rooms that were part of the town gate and stabbed him in the stomach. Joab killed him because Abner had killed Joab's brother Asahel.

Abner's funeral

²⁸ David heard how Joab had killed Abner, and he said, "I swear to the LORD that I am completely innocent of Abner's death! ²⁹ Joab and his family are the guilty ones. I pray that Joab's family will always be sick with sores and other skin diseases. May they all be cowards,' and may they die in war or starve to death."

³⁰ Joab and his brother Abishai killed Abner because he had killed their brother Asahel in the battle at Gibeon.

³¹ David told Joab and everyone with him, "Show your sorrow by tearing your clothes and wearing sackcloth!* Walk in front of Abner's body and cry!"

David walked behind the stretcher on which Abner's body was being carried. ³² Abner was buried in Hebron, while David and everyone else stood at the tomb and cried loudly. ³³ Then the king sang a funeral song about Abner:

> Abner, why should you
>   have died like an outlaw?'
> ³⁴ No one tied your hands
>   or chained your feet,
>   yet you died as a victim
>   of murderers.

Everyone started crying again. ³⁵ Then they brought some food to David and told him he would feel better if he had something to eat. It was still daytime, and David said, "I swear to God that I'll not take a bite of bread or anything else until sunset!"

³⁶ Everyone noticed what David did, and they liked it, just as they always liked what he did. ³⁷ Now the people of Judah and Israel were certain that David had nothing to do with killing Abner.

³⁸ David said to his officials, "Don't you realize that today one of Israel's great leaders has died? ³⁹ I am the chosen king, but Joab and Abishai have more power than I do. So God will have to pay them back' for the evil thing they did."

CHAPTER 4

Ishbosheth is killed

¹ Ishbosheth' felt like giving up after he heard that Abner had died in Hebron. Everyone in Israel was terrified.

² Ishbosheth had put the two brothers Baanah and Rechab in charge of the soldiers who raided enemy villages. Rimmon was their father, and they were from the town of Beeroth, which belonged to the tribe of Benjamin. ³ The people who used to live in Beeroth had run away to Gittaim, and they still live* there.

---

*3.31 sackcloth: Sackcloth was a rough, dark-coloured cloth made from goat or camel hair and was used to make grain sacks. People wore sackcloth or tore their clothes in times of trouble or sorrow.
*4.3 live: The Hebrew word means that they did not have the full legal rights of citizens.

⁴ Saul's son Jonathan had a son named Mephibosheth,* who had not been able to walk since he was five years old. It happened when someone from Jezreel told his nurse that Saul and Jonathan had died.* She hurried off with the boy in her arms, but he fell and injured his legs.

⁵ One day about midday, Rechab and Baanah went to Ishbosheth's house. It was a hot day, and he was resting ⁶⁻⁷ in his bedroom. The two brothers went into the house, pretending to get some flour. But once they were inside, they stabbed Ishbosheth in the stomach and killed him. Then they cut off his head and took it with them.

Rechab and Baanah walked through the Jordan valley all night long. ⁸ Finally they turned west and went to Hebron. They went in to see David and told him, "Your Majesty, here is the head of Ishbosheth, the son of your enemy Saul who tried to kill you! The LORD has let you get even with Saul and his family."

⁹ David answered:

I swear that only the LORD rescues me when I'm in trouble! ¹⁰ When a man came to Ziklag and told me that Saul was dead, he thought he deserved a reward for bringing good news. But I grabbed him and killed him.

¹¹ You evil men have done something much worse than he did. You've killed an innocent man in his own house and on his own bed. I'll make you pay for that. I'll wipe you from the face of the earth!

¹² Then David said to his troops, "Kill these two brothers! Cut off their hands and feet and hang their bodies by the pool in Hebron. But bury Ishbosheth's head in Abner's tomb near Hebron." And they did.

David, king of all Israel

CHAPTER 5

David becomes king of Israel
This is also told in 1 Chronicles 11.1–3

¹ Israel's leaders met with David at Hebron and said, "We are your relatives. ² Even when Saul was king, you led our nation in battle. And the LORD promised that some day you would rule Israel and take care of us like a shepherd."

³ During the meeting, David made an agreement with the leaders and asked the LORD to be their witness. Then the leaders poured olive oil on David's head to show that he was now the king of Israel.

⁴ David was thirty years old when he became king, and he ruled for forty years. ⁵ He lived in Hebron for the first seven and a half years and ruled only Judah. Then he moved to Jerusalem, where he ruled both Israel and Judah for thirty-three years.

How David captured Jerusalem
This is also told in 1 Chronicles 11.4–9; 14.1,2

⁶ The Jebusites lived in Jerusalem, and David led his army there to attack them. The Jebusites did not think he could get in, so they told him, "You can't get in here! We could drive you away, even if we couldn't see or walk!"

⁷⁻⁹ David told his troops, "You will have to go up through the water tunnel to get those Jebusites. I hate people like them who can't walk or see."➤

That's why there is still a rule that says, "Only people who can walk and see are allowed in the temple."➤

David captured the fortress on Mount Zion, then he moved there and named it David's City. He had the city rebuilt, starting with the landfill to the east. ¹⁰ David became a great and strong ruler, because the LORD All-Powerful was on his side.

¹¹ King Hiram of Tyre sent some officials to David. Carpenters and stone workers came with them, and they brought cedar logs so they could build David a palace.

¹² David knew that the LORD had made him king of Israel and that he had made him a powerful ruler for the good of his people.

David's sons born in Jerusalem
This is also told in 1 Chronicles 14.3–7

¹³ After David left Hebron and moved to Jerusalem, he married many women* from Jerusalem,➤ and he had a lot of children. ¹⁴ His sons who were born there were

---

4.4 Mephibosheth: Some manuscripts of one ancient translation have "Mephibaal". In 1 Chronicles 8.34 and 9.40 he is called "Meribbaal". See the note on "baal" and "bosheth" at 2.8.
4.4 Saul . . . died: See 1 Samuel 31.1–6.
See also: 4.4: 2 Sam 9.3. 4.10: 2 Sam 1.1–16.

5.13 married many women: Some of these women were second-class wives (see the note at 3.7).
See also: 5.4,5: 1 King 2.11; 1 Chron 3.4; 29.27.
5.6: Josh 15.63; Judg 1.21.

Shammua, Shobab, Nathan, Solomon, 15 Ibhar, Elishua, Nepheg, Japhia, 16 Elishama, Eliada,* and Eliphelet.

David fights the Philistines

This is also told in 1 Chronicles 14.8–17

17 The Philistines heard that David was now king of Israel, and they came into the hill country to try and capture him. But David found out and went into his fortress.* 18 So the Philistines camped in Rephaim Valley.*

19 David asked the LORD, "Should I attack the Philistines? Will you let me win?"

The LORD told David, "Attack! I will let you win."

20 David attacked the Philistines and defeated them. Then he said, "I watched the LORD break through my enemies like a mighty flood." So he named the place "The Lord Broke Through".ʼ 21 David and his troops also carried away the idols that the Philistines had left behind.

22 Some time later, the Philistines came back into the hill country and camped in Rephaim Valley. 23 David asked the LORD what he should do, and the LORD answered:

Don't attack them from the front. Circle around behind and attack from among the balsamʼ trees. 24 Wait until you hear a sound like troops marching through the tops of the trees. Then attack quickly! That sound will mean I have marched out ahead of you to fight the Philistine army.

25 David obeyed the LORD and defeated the Philistines. He even chased them all the way from Geba to the entrance to Gezer.

CHAPTER 6

David brings the sacred chest back to Jerusalem

This is also told in 1 Chronicles 13.1–14; 15.1–16.3,43

1 David brought together thirty thousand of Israel's best soldiers and 2 led them to Baalah in Judah, which was also called

Kiriath-Jearim. They were going thereʼ to get the sacred chest and bring it back to Jerusalem. The throne of the LORD All-Powerful is above the winged creatures* on top of this chest, and he is worshipped there.ʼ

3 They put the sacred chest on a new ox cart and started bringing it down the hill from Abinadab's house. Abinadab's sons Uzzah and Ahio were guiding the ox cart, 4 with Ahioʼ walking in front of it. 5 Some of the people of Israel were playing music on small harps and other stringed instruments, and on tambourines, castanets, and cymbals. David and the others were happy, and they danced for the LORD with all their might.

6 But when they came to Nacon's threshing-floor, the oxen stumbled, so Uzzah reached out and took hold of the sacred chest. 7 The LORD God was very angry with Uzzah for doing this, and he killed Uzzah there beside the chest.

8 David got angry with God for killing Uzzah. He named that place "Bursting Out Against Uzzah",ʼ and that's what it's still called.

9 David was afraid of the LORD and thought, "Should I really take the sacred chest to my city?" 10 He decided not to take it there. Instead, he turned off the road and took it to the home of Obed-Edom, who was from Gath.ʼ

11-12 The chest stayed there for three months, and the LORD greatly blessed Obed-Edom, his family, and everything he owned. Then someone told King David, "The LORD has done this because the sacred chest is in Obed-Edom's house."

Straight away, David went to Obed-Edom's house to get the chest and bring it to David's City. Everyone was celebrating. 13 The people carrying the chest walked six steps, then David sacrificed an ox and a choice cow. 14 He was dancing for the LORD with all his might, but he wore only a linen cloth.* 15 He and everyone else were celebrating by shouting and blowing horns while the chest was being carried along.

---

*5.16 Eliada: See 1 Chronicles 3.8. 1 Chronicles 14.7 has "Baalyada".
*5.17 fortress: Probably the fortress of Adullam, which was David's former hide-out (see 1 Samuel 22.1,4; 24.22). Or it could refer to the older walled city of Jerusalem, called the "fortress on Mount Zion" in verses 7–9.
*5.18 Rephaim Valley: A few kilometres south-west of Jerusalem.
See also: 6.2: Exod 25.22.

*6.2 winged creatures: Two golden statues of winged creatures were on top of the sacred chest and were symbols of the LORD's throne on earth (see Exodus 25.18).
*6.14 only a linen cloth: The Hebrew word is "ephod", which can mean either a piece of clothing like a skirt that went from the waist to the knee or a garment like an apron or a jacket that only the priests wore.
See also: 6.3: 1 Sam 7.1–2. 6.11: 1 Chron 26.4–5.

Viewpoints

Are we too cool to show our feelings about God?

Contributed by Bethan P

'The LORD chose me, and I was celebrating in honour of him.'

Are you willing to be mocked, derided, or ignored for the sake of God? In this society, it's not cool to be enthusiastic about ANYthing, let alone about God, but we should be. See how David is – he's so excited about how great God is that he's dancing around like a mad man.

It's not the actions that matter so much; it's the attitude. Are you so consumed by God that at times you can't help but express it? No? Let's take some time to look at God and see why we should be so enthusiastic.

Romans 11.33 shows us what a wonderful God we have! He's just too big for us to even grasp. You can explore and explore, and never reach the end of Him, but that makes it all the more exciting!

And his love – his love is just so amazing. Paul prays in Ephesians 3.18 that they would grasp just how high, long and wide Jesus' love is. But then he goes on to say it is 'too wonderful to be measured'. Sometimes we take God's love for granted, but think how hard it is for you to love someone who has annoying tendencies, or someone who has in the past upset you... and then multiply that a million times over – and you still will not be near how much God loves us.

I've hardly begun to delve into God's greatness, but look for yourself, look through the Bible, and ask him to help you to understand it. Discover for yourself, through the help of the Holy Spirit, just how brilliant God is!

More...

Living the truth of God's power in your life p.1251
Living truthfully p.1070
God's love p.958

---

16 Saul's daughter Michal looked out of her window and watched the chest being brought into David's City. But when she saw David jumping and dancing for the LORD, she was disgusted.

17 They put the chest inside a tent that David had set up for it. David worshipped the LORD by sacrificing animals and burning them on an altar,* 18 then he blessed the people in the name of the LORD All-Powerful. 19 He gave all the men and women in the crowd a small loaf of bread, some meat, and a handful of raisins, and everyone went home.

Michal talks to David

20 David went home so he could ask the LORD to bless his family. But Saul's daughter Michal went out and started yelling at him. "You were really great today!" she said. "You acted like a dirty old man, dancing around half-naked in front of your servants' slave-girls."

21 David told her, "The LORD didn't choose your father or anyone else in your family to be the leader of his people. The LORD chose me, and I was celebrating in honour of him. 22 I'll show you just how great I can be! I'll even be disgusting to myself. But those slave-girls you talked about will still honour me!"

23 Michal never had any children.

The Lord's promise to David

CHAPTER 7

The LORD's message to David

This is also told in 1 Chronicles 17.1–15

1 King David moved into his new palace, and the LORD let his kingdom be at peace. 2 Then one day, as David was talking with Nathan the prophet, David said, "Look around! I live in a palace made of cedar, but the sacred chest has to stay in a tent."

3 Nathan replied, "The LORD is with you, so do what you want!"

4 That night, the LORD told Nathan 5 to go to David and give him this message:

David, you are my servant, so listen to what I say. Why should you build a temple for me? 6 I didn't live in a temple when I

---

*6.17 sacrificing . . . altar: The Hebrew mentions two kinds of sacrifices. In one kind of sacrifice, the whole animal was burnt on the altar. In the other kind, only part was burnt, and the worshippers ate the rest, as in verse 19 (see Leviticus 1.2–17; 3.1–17).

See also: 6.19–20: 1 Chron 16.43.

brought my people out of Egypt, and I don't live in one now. A tent has always been my home wherever I have gone with them. [7] I chose leaders and told them to be like shepherds for my people Israel. But did I ever say anything to even one of them about building a cedar temple for me?

[8] David, this is what I, the LORD All-Powerful, say to you. I brought you in from the fields where you took care of sheep, and I made you the leader of my people. [9] Wherever you went, I helped you and destroyed your enemies right in front of your eyes. I have made you one of the most famous people in the world.

[10] I have given my people Israel a land of their own where they can live in peace, and they won't have to tremble with fear any more. Evil nations won't bother them, as they did [11] when I let judges rule my people. And I have kept your enemies from attacking you.

Now I promise that you and your descendants will be kings. [12] I'll choose one of your sons to be king when you reach the end of your life and are buried in the tomb of your ancestors. I'll make him a strong ruler, [13] and no one will be able to take his kingdom away from him. He will be the one to build a temple for me. [14] I will be his father, and he will be my son.

When he does wrong, I'll see that he is corrected, just as children are corrected by their parents. [15] But I will never put an end to my agreement with him, as I put an end to my agreement with Saul, who was king before you. [16] I will make sure that one of your descendants will always be king.

[17] Nathan told David exactly what he had heard in the vision.

David gives thanks to the LORD

This is also told in 1 Chronicles 17.16–27

[18] David went into the tent he had set up for the sacred chest. Then he sat there and prayed:

LORD All-Powerful, my family and I don't deserve what you have already done for us, [19] and yet you have promised to do even more. Is this the way you usually treat people?ᵇ [20] I am your servant, and you know my thoughts, so there is nothing more that I need to say. [21] You have done

this wonderful thing, and you have let me know about it, because you wanted to keep your promise.

[22] LORD All-Powerful, you are greater than all others. No one is like you, and you alone are God. Everything we have heard about you is true. [23] And there is no other nation on earth like Israel, the nation you rescued from slavery in Egypt to be your own. You became famous by using great and wonderful miracles to force other nations and their gods out of your land, so your people could live here.ᵇ [24] You have chosen Israel to be your people for ever, and you have become their God.

[25] And now, LORD God, please do what you have promised me and my descendants. [26] Then you will be famous for ever, and everyone will say, "The LORD God All-Powerful rules Israel, and David's descendants are his chosen kings." [27] After all, you really are Israel's God, the LORD All-Powerful. You've told me that you will let my descendants be kings. That's why I have the courage to pray to you like this, even though I am only your servant.

[28] LORD All-Powerful, you are God. You have promised me some very good things, and you can be trusted to do what you promise. [29] Please bless my descendants and let them always be your chosen kings. You have already promised, and I'm sure that you will bless my family for ever.

The wars of King David

CHAPTER 8

A list of David's victories in war

This is also told in 1 Chronicles 18.1–13

[1] Later, David attacked and badly defeated the Philistines. Israel was now free from their control.ᵇ

[2] David also defeated the Moabites. Then he made their soldiers lie down on the ground, and he measured them off with a rope. He would measure off two lengths of the rope and have those men killed, then he would measure off one length and let those men live. The people of Moab had to accept David as their ruler and pay taxes to him.

[3] David set out for the River Euphrates to build a monument* there. On his way,ᵇ he

---

See also: 7.12: Psa 89.3–4; 132.11; John 7.42; Acts 2.30.
7.14: Psa 89.26–27; 2 Cor 6.18; Heb 1.5.   **7.16:** Psa 89.36–37.

*8.3 monument: Kings sometimes set up monuments in lands they had conquered.
See also: 7.23: Deut 4.34.

defeated the king of Zobah, whose name was Hadadezer the son of Rehob. ⁴ In the battle, David captured seventeen hundred cavalry▸ and twenty thousand foot soldiers. He also captured war chariots, but he destroyed all but one hundred of them.▸ ⁵ When troops from the Aramean kingdom of Damascus came to help Hadadezer, David killed twenty thousand of them. ⁶ He left some of his soldiers in Damascus, and the Arameans had to accept David as their ruler and pay taxes to him.

Everywhere David went, the LORD helped him win battles.

⁷ Hadadezer's officers had carried their arrows in gold cases hung over their shoulders, but David took these cases▸ and brought them to Jerusalem. ⁸ He also took a lot of bronze from the cities of Betah and Berothai, which had belonged to Hadadezer.

⁹⁻¹⁰ King Toi of Hamath and King Hadadezer had been enemies. So when Toi heard that David had attacked and defeated▸ Hadadezer's whole army, he sent his son Joram to praise and congratulate David. Joram also brought him gifts made of silver, gold, and bronze. ¹¹ David gave these to the LORD, just as he had done with the silver and gold that he had captured from ¹² Edom,▸ Moab, Ammon, Philistia, and from King Hadadezer of Zobah.

¹³ David fought the Edomite▸ army in Salt Valley and killed eighteen thousand of their soldiers. When he returned, he built a monument.▸ ¹⁴ David left soldiers all through Edom, and the people of Edom had to accept him as their ruler.

Wherever David went, the LORD helped him.

A list of David's officials

This is also told in 1 Chronicles 18.14–17

¹⁵ David ruled all Israel with fairness and justice.

¹⁶ Joab the son of Zeruiah was the commander in chief of the army.

Jehoshaphat the son of Ahilud kept the government records.

¹⁷ Zadok the son of Ahitub, and Abiathar the son of Ahimelech,▸ were the priests.

Seraiah was the secretary.

¹⁸ Benaiah the son of Jehoiada was the commander of▸ David's bodyguard.▸

David's sons were priests.

CHAPTER 9

David is kind to Mephibosheth

¹ One day, David thought, "I wonder if any of Saul's family are still alive. If they are, I will be kind to them, because I made a promise to Jonathan." ² David called in Ziba, one of the servants of Saul's family. David said, "So you are Ziba."

"Yes, Your Majesty, I am."

³ David asked, "Are any of Saul's family still alive? If there are, I want to be kind to them."

Ziba answered, "One of Jonathan's sons is still alive, but he can't walk."

⁴ "Where is he?" David asked.

Ziba replied, "He lives in Lo-Debar with Machir the son of Ammiel."

⁵⁻⁶ David sent some servants to bring Jonathan's son from Lo-Debar. His name was Mephibosheth,* and he was the grandson of Saul. He came to David and knelt down.

David asked, "Are you Mephibosheth?"

"Yes, I am, Your Majesty."

⁷ David said, "Don't be afraid. I'll be kind to you because Jonathan was your father. I'm going to give you back the land that belonged to your grandfather Saul. Besides that, you will always eat with me at my table."

⁸ Mephibosheth knelt down again and said, "Why should you care about me? I'm worth no more than a dead dog."

⁹ David called in Ziba, Saul's chief servant, and told him, "Since Mephibosheth is Saul's grandson, I've given him back everything that belonged to your master Saul and his family. ¹⁰ You and your fifteen sons and twenty servants will work for Mephibosheth. You will farm his land and bring in his crops, so that Saul's family and servants▸ will have food. But Mephibosheth will always eat with me at my table."

¹¹⁻¹³ Ziba replied, "Your Majesty, I will do exactly what you tell me to do." So Ziba's family and servants worked for Mephibosheth.

Mephibosheth was lame, but he lived in Jerusalem and ate at David's▸ table, just like one of David's own sons. And he had a young son of his own, named Mica.

---

*9.5–6 Mephibosheth: Or "Mephibaal" (see the note at 4.4).

See also: 9.1: 1 Sam 20.15–17. 9.3: 2 Sam 4.4.

See also: 8.13: Psa 60 Title.

CHAPTER 10
Israel fights Ammon
This is also told in 1 Chronicles 19.1–19

¹ Some time later, King Nahash of Ammon died, and his son Hanun became king. ² David said, "Nahash was kind to me, and I will be kind to his son." So he sent some officials to the country of Ammon to tell Hanun how sorry he was that his father had died.

³ But Hanun's officials told him, "Do you really believe David is honouring your father by sending these people to comfort you? He probably sent them to spy on our city, so he can destroy it." ⁴ Hanun arrested David's officials and had their beards shaved off on one side of their faces. He had their robes cut off just below the waist, and then he sent them away. ⁵ They were terribly ashamed.

When David found out what had happened to his officials, he sent a message and told them, "Stay in Jericho until your beards grow back. Then you can come home."

⁶ The Ammonites realized that they had made David very angry, so they hired more foreign soldiers. Twenty thousand of them were foot soldiers from the Aramean cities of Beth-Rehob and Zobah, one thousand were from the king of Maacah, and twelve thousand were from the region of Tob. ⁷ David heard what they had done, and he sent out Joab with all his well-trained soldiers.

⁸ The Ammonite troops came out and got ready to fight in front of the gate to their city. The Arameans from Zobah and Rehob and the soldiers from Tob and Maacah formed a separate group in the nearby fields.

⁹ Joab saw that he had to fight in front and behind at the same time, and he picked some of the best Israelite soldiers to fight the Arameans. ¹⁰ He put his brother Abishai in command of the rest of the army and made them fight the Ammonites. ¹¹ Joab told his brother, "If the Arameans are too much for me to handle, you can come and help me. If the Ammonites are too strong for you, I'll come and help you. ¹² Be brave and fight hard to protect our people and the cities of our God. I pray that the LORD will do whatever pleases him."

¹³ Joab and his soldiers attacked the Arameans, and the Arameans ran from them. ¹⁴ When the Ammonite soldiers saw that the Arameans had run away, they ran from Abishai's soldiers and went back into their own city. Joab stopped fighting the Ammonites and returned to Jerusalem.

¹⁵ The Arameans realized they had lost the battle, so they brought all their troops together again. ¹⁶ Hadadezer sent messengers to call in the Arameans who were on the other side of the River Euphrates. Then Shobach, the commander of Hadadezer's army, led them to the town of Helam.

¹⁷ David found out what the Arameans were doing, and he brought Israel's whole army together. They crossed the River Jordan and went to Helam, where the Arameans were ready to meet them. ¹⁸ The Arameans attacked, but then they ran from Israel. David killed seven hundred chariot drivers and forty thousand cavalry.* He also killed Shobach, their commander.

¹⁹ When the kings who had been under Hadadezer's rule saw that Israel had beaten them, they made peace with Israel and accepted David as their ruler. The Arameans were afraid to help Ammon any more.

David's affair with Bathsheba
CHAPTER 11
David and Bathsheba
This is also told in 1 Chronicles 20.1a

¹ It was now spring, the time when kings go to war.* David sent out the whole Israelite army under the command of Joab and his officers. They destroyed the Ammonite army and surrounded the capital city of Rabbah, but David stayed in Jerusalem.

²⁻⁴ Late one afternoon, David got up from a nap and was walking around on the flat roof of his palace. A beautiful young woman was down below in her courtyard, bathing as her religion required.* David happened to see her, and he sent one of his servants to find out who she was.

The servant came back and told David, "Her name is Bathsheba. She is the daughter of Eliam, and she is the wife of Uriah the Hittite."

David sent some messengers to bring her to his palace. She came to him, and he slept with her. Then she returned home. ⁵ But later, when she found out that she was going to have a baby, she sent someone to David with this message: "I'm pregnant!"

---
*11.2–4 as . . . required: This bathing was often a requirement for worshipping God.
See also: 11.1: 1 Chron 20.1.

⁶ David sent a message to Joab: "Send Uriah the Hittite to me."

Joab sent Uriah ⁷ to David's palace, and David asked him, "Is Joab well? How is the army doing? And how about the war?" ⁸ Then David told Uriah, "Go home and clean up."* Uriah left the king's palace, and David had dinner sent to Uriah's house. ⁹ But Uriah didn't go home. Instead, he slept outside the entrance to the royal palace, where the king's guards slept.

¹⁰ Someone told David that Uriah had not gone home. So the next morning David asked him, "Why didn't you go home? Haven't you been away for a long time?"

¹¹ Uriah answered, "The sacred chest and the armies of Israel and Judah are camping out somewhere in the fields⸳ with our commander Joab and his officers and troops. Do you really think I would go home to eat and drink and sleep with my wife? I swear by your life that I would not!"

¹² Then David said, "Stay here in Jerusalem today, and I will send you back tomorrow."

Uriah stayed in Jerusalem that day. Then the next day, ¹³ David invited him for dinner. Uriah ate with David and drank so much that he got drunk, but he still did not go home. He went out and slept on his mat near the palace guards. ¹⁴ Early the next morning, David wrote a letter and told Uriah to deliver it to Joab. ¹⁵ The letter said: "Put Uriah on the front line where the fighting is the worst. Then pull the troops back from him, so that he will be wounded and die."

¹⁶ Joab had been carefully watching the city of Rabbah, and he put Uriah in a place where he knew there were some of the enemy's best soldiers. ¹⁷ When the men of the city came out, they fought and killed some of David's soldiers — Uriah the Hittite was one of them.

¹⁸ Joab sent a messenger to tell David everything that was happening in the war. ¹⁹ He gave the messenger these orders:

When you finish telling the king everything that has happened, ²⁰ he may get angry and ask, "Why did you go so near the city to fight? Didn't you know they would shoot arrows from the wall? ²¹ Don't you know how Abimelech the son of Gideon⸳ was killed at Thebez? Didn't a woman kill him by dropping a large rock from the top of the city wall? Why did you go so close to the city walls?"

Then you tell him, "One of your soldiers who was killed was Uriah the Hittite."

²² The messenger went to David and reported everything Joab had told him. ²³ He added, "The enemy chased us from the wall and out into the open fields. But we pushed them back as far as the city gate. ²⁴ Then they shot arrows at us from the top of the wall. Some of your soldiers were killed, and one of them was Uriah the Hittite."

²⁵ David replied, "Tell Joab to cheer up and not to be upset about what happened. You never know who will be killed in a war. Tell him to strengthen his attack against the city and break through its walls."⸳

²⁶ When Bathsheba heard that her husband was dead, she mourned for him. ²⁷ Then after the time for mourning was over, David sent someone to bring her to the palace. She became David's wife, and they had a son.

CHAPTER 12

The LORD's message for David

The LORD was angry at what David had done, ¹ and he sent Nathan the prophet to tell this story to David:

A rich man and a poor man lived in the same town. ² The rich man owned a lot of sheep and cattle, ³ but the poor man had only one little lamb that he had bought and raised. The lamb became a pet for him and his children. He even let it eat from his plate and drink from his cup and sleep on his lap. The lamb was like one of his own children.

⁴ One day someone came to visit the rich man, but the rich man didn't want to kill any of his own sheep or cattle and serve it to the visitor. So he stole the poor man's little lamb and served it instead.

⁵ David was furious with the rich man and said to Nathan, "I swear by the living LORD that the man who did this deserves to die! ⁶ And because he didn't have any pity on the poor man, he will have to pay four times what the lamb was worth."

⁷ Then Nathan told David:

You are that rich man! Now listen to what the LORD God of Israel says to you: "I chose you to be the king of Israel. I kept you safe from Saul ⁸ and even gave you his house and his wives. I let you rule Israel and Judah, and if that had not been enough, I would have given you much more. ⁹ Why

---

11.8 and clean up: Or "and sleep with your wife".
See also: **11.21:** Judg 9.53.

See also: **12.1:** Psa 51 Title.

did you disobey me and do such a horrible thing? You murdered Uriah the Hittite by letting the Ammonites kill him, so you could take his wife.

¹⁰ Because you wouldn't obey me and took Uriah's wife for yourself, your family will never live in peace. ¹¹ Someone from your own family will cause you a lot of trouble, and I will take your wives and give them to another man before your very eyes. He will go to bed with them while everyone looks on. ¹² What you did was in secret, but I will do this in the open for everyone in Israel to see.

¹³⁻¹⁴ David said, "I have disobeyed the LORD."

"Yes, you have!" Nathan answered. "You showed you didn't care what the LORD wanted.' He has forgiven you, and you won't die. But your newborn son will." ¹⁵ Then Nathan went back home.

David's young son dies

The LORD made David's young son very sick.

¹⁶ So David went without eating to show his sorrow, and he begged God to make the boy well. David would not sleep on his bed, but spent each night lying on the floor. ¹⁷ His officials stood beside him and tried to talk him into getting up. But he would not get up or eat with them.

¹⁸ After the child had been sick for seven days, he died, but the officials were afraid to tell David. They said to each other, "Even when the boy was alive, David wouldn't listen to us. How can we tell him his son is dead? He might do something terrible!"

¹⁹ David noticed his servants whispering, and he knew the boy was dead. "Has my son died?" he asked his servants.

"Yes, he has," they answered.

²⁰ David got up off the floor; he took a bath, combed his hair, and dressed. He went into the LORD's tent and worshipped, then he went back home. David asked for something to eat, and when his servants brought him some food, he ate it.

²¹ His officials said, "What are you doing? You went without eating and cried for your son while he was alive! But now that he's dead, you're up and eating."

²² David answered:

While he was still alive, I went without food and cried because there was still hope.

See also: **12.11-12:** 2 Sam 16.22.

Helpline

Help! I've messed up really badly

'I didn't mean it. Everything went wrong. I've done some really stupid things...'

In 2 Samuel 12 we see the outcome of David's affair with Bathsheba, where he got her pregnant and then have her husband 'removed'. David's remorse is obvious; he refuses to eat, goes without sleep...

And God forgives him.

Even though we're Christians we all do things we shouldn't. Sometimes we mess things up so badly that there seems no way back. Maybe we've cheated on a partner or said something incredibly hurtful. Maybe we've gone way too far in a relationship, stolen or lied or... well, it could be anything.

But God is there for us – whatever we've done. So ask him for forgiveness first. He will restore the relationship. Simple as that.

But, he won't change history. Whatever you did, you'll have to live with the consequences. David's child died; he had to live with the consequences of his sin for the rest of his reign. So talk things through with friends, family or youth leaders. Work out what you're going to do about all this. Do you need to make it up with people? Do you need to make decisions? Get some advice.

Three things

Sorry

Ask for forgiveness. Say sorry to God for what you did.

Know

Know that God loves you. Whatever you're going through, God is still your father and he still cares for you.

Plan

Talk and plan. Talk to people you trust and work out what you can do about the situation. Pray with them and listen to their wisdom and advice.

More...

Forgiveness p.614
Saying sorry p.1258

I said to myself, "Who knows? Perhaps the LORD will have pity on me and let the child live." ²³ But now that he's dead, why should I go without eating? I can't bring him back! Some day I will join him in death, but he can't return to me."

Solomon is born

²⁴ David comforted his wife Bathsheba and slept with her. Later on, she gave birth to another son and named him Solomon. The LORD loved Solomon ²⁵ and sent Nathan the prophet to tell David, "The LORD will call him Jedidiah."*

The end of the war with Ammon

This is also told in 1 Chronicles 20.1b–3

²⁶ Meanwhile, Joab had been in the country of Ammon, attacking the city of Rabbah. He captured the royal fortress ²⁷ and sent a messenger to tell David:

I have attacked Rabbah and captured the fortress guarding the city water supply. ²⁸ Call the rest of the army together. Then surround the city, and capture it yourself. If you don't, everyone will remember that I captured the city.

²⁹ David called the rest of the army together and attacked Rabbah. He captured the city ³⁰ and took the crown from the statue of their god Milcom.' The crown was made of about thirty-five kilogrammes of gold, and there was a valuable jewel on it. David put the jewel on his own crown.' He also carried off everything else of value. ³¹ David made the people of Rabbah tear down the city walls' with iron picks and axes, and then he put them to work making bricks. He did the same thing with all the other Ammonite cities.

David went back to Jerusalem, and the people of Israel returned to their homes.

Violence in David's family: Tamar, Amnon, and Absalom

CHAPTER 13

Amnon disgraces Tamar

¹ David had a beautiful daughter named Tamar, who was the sister of Absalom. She was also the half-sister of Amnon,* who fell in love with her. ² But Tamar was a virgin, and Amnon could not think of a way to be alone with her. He was so upset about it that he made himself sick.

³ Amnon had a friend named Jonadab, who was the son of David's brother Shimeah. Jonadab always knew how to get what he wanted, ⁴ and he said to Amnon, "What's the matter? You're the king's son! You shouldn't have to go around feeling sorry for yourself every morning."

Amnon said, "I'm in love with Tamar, my brother Absalom's sister."

⁵ Jonadab told him, "Lie down on your bed and pretend to be sick. When your father comes to see you, ask him to send Tamar, so you can watch her cook something for you. Then she can serve you the food."

⁶ So Amnon went to bed and pretended to be sick. When the king came to see him, Amnon said, "Please, ask Tamar to come over. She can make some special bread' while I watch, and then she can serve me the bread."

⁷ David told Tamar, "Go over to Amnon's house and prepare him some food." ⁸ When she got there, he was lying in bed. She mixed the dough, made the loaves, and baked them while he watched. ⁹ Then she took the bread out of the pan and put it on his plate, but he refused to eat it.

Amnon said, "Send the servants out of the house." After they had gone, ¹⁰ he said to Tamar, "Serve the food in my bedroom."

Tamar picked up the bread that she had made and brought it into Amnon's bedroom. ¹¹ But as she was taking it over to him, he grabbed her and said, "Come to bed with me!"

¹² She answered, "No! Please don't force me! This sort of thing isn't done in Israel. It's too disgusting! ¹³ Think of me. I'll be disgraced for ever! And think of yourself. Everyone in Israel will say you're nothing but a load of rubbish! Just ask the king, and he will let you marry me."

¹⁴ But Amnon would not listen to what she said. He was stronger than she was, so he overpowered her and raped her. ¹⁵ Then Amnon hated her even more than he had loved her before. So he told her, "Get up and get out!"

¹⁶ She said, "Don't send me away! That would be worse than what you have already done."

---

*12.25 Jedidiah: In Hebrew this name means "Loved by the LORD".

*13.1 Tamar . . . Absalom . . . Amnon: David was their father, but Amnon had a different mother.

Helpline

Help! I can't stand my brothers or sisters

'They wind me up so much! I never wanted brothers and sisters in the first place!'

Families give us stability, love and support... and quite frequently grief as well.

I doubt that your family behaves the same as David's (if it does, get out – quick.) But all families have arguments. Sometimes it's just one of those things. Words are said, doors slammed. And sometimes, it's a war. Maybe it's rivalry, maybe it's not feeling understood; but the grudge is always there.

Either way, give it some time. Think about who you're angry with, and why. Maybe later, when things have chilled a bit, you can talk about the situation with your family and find out why it happened.

But if the arguments descend into physical violence don't hesitate. Tell someone about it. The same goes for emotional abuse. If you're being systematically picked on, tell someone. Don't try to fight it all on your own.

Three things

Understand

What it is that you're really angry about? Try talking to someone about things to get the whole situation in perspective. Pray with someone to get some godly insight.

Sacrifice

Christians are people of sacrifice. Be prepared to sacrifice your desires sometimes. Be the first to apologise. (Or, if you think that an apology would just open things up again, take it easy and let it fade.)

Trust

Your parents love and respect you (even if sometimes they don't show it!) So talk to them about it. Let them know how you feel. Don't strut in and demand an audience, don't be strident and aggressive, just explain, as calmly as you can, how you feel.

More...

Help! They're really annoying me p.1381

But Amnon would not listen. ¹⁷ He called in his servant and said, "Throw this woman out and lock the door!"

¹⁸ The servant made her leave, and he locked the door behind her.

The king's unmarried daughters used to wear long robes with sleeves.' ¹⁹ Tamar tore the robe she was wearing and put ashes on her head. Then she covered her face with her hands and cried loudly as she walked away.

Absalom kills Amnon

²⁰ Tamar's brother Absalom said to her, "How could Amnon have done such a terrible thing to you! But since he's your brother, don't tell anyone what happened. Just try not to think about it."

Tamar soon moved into Absalom's house, but she was always sad and lonely. ²¹ When David heard what had happened to Tamar, he was very angry. But Amnon was his eldest son and also his favourite, and David would not do anything to make Amnon unhappy.'

²² Absalom treated Amnon as though nothing had happened, but he hated Amnon for what he had done to his sister Tamar.

²³ Two years later, Absalom's servants were cutting wool from his sheep in Baal-Hazor near the town of Ephraim, and Absalom invited all the king's sons to be there.* ²⁴ Then he went to David and said, "My servants are cutting the wool from my sheep. Please come and join us!"

²⁵ David answered, "No, my son, we won't go. It would be too expensive for you." Absalom tried to get him to change his mind, but David did not want to go. He only said that he hoped they would have a good time.

²⁶ Absalom said, "If you won't go, at least let my brother Amnon come with us."

David asked, "Why should he go with you?" ²⁷ But Absalom kept on insisting, and finally David let Amnon and all his other sons go with Absalom.

Absalom prepared a banquet fit for a king.' ²⁸ But he told his servants, "Keep an eye on Amnon. When he gets a little drunk from the wine and is feeling good, I'll give the signal. Then kill him! I've commanded you to do it, so don't be afraid. Be strong and brave."

²⁹ Absalom's servants killed Amnon, just as Absalom had told them. The rest of the king's sons quickly rode away on their mules to escape from Absalom.

---

*13.23 invited . . . there: Cutting the wool from sheep was a time for celebrating as well as working.

30 While they were on their way to Jerusalem, someone told David, "Absalom has killed all your sons! Not even one is left."
31 David got up, and in his sorrow he tore his clothes and lay down on the ground. His servants remained standing, but they tore their clothes too.
32 Then David's nephew⟩ Jonadab said, "Your Majesty, not all your sons were killed! Only Amnon is dead. On the day that Amnon raped Tamar, Absalom decided to kill him.
33 Don't worry about the report that all your sons were killed. Only Amnon is dead, 34 and Absalom has run away."

One of the guards noticed a lot of people coming along the hillside on the road to Horonaim.⟩ He went and told the king, "I saw some men coming along Horonaim Road."⟩
35 Jonadab said, "Your Majesty, look! Here come your sons now, just as I told you."
36 No sooner had he said it, than David's sons came in. They were weeping out loud, and David and all his officials cried just as loudly. 37-38 David was sad for a long time because Amnon was dead.

David lets Absalom come home

Absalom had run away to Geshur, where he stayed for three years with King Talmai* the son of Ammihud. 39 David still felt so sad over the loss of Amnon that he wanted to take his army there and capture Absalom.⟩

CHAPTER 14

1 Joab knew that David couldn't stop thinking about Absalom, 2-3 and he sent someone to bring in the wise woman who lived in Tekoa. Joab told her, "Put on funeral clothes and don't use any make-up. Go to the king and pretend you have spent a long time mourning the death of a loved one." Then he told her what to say.
4 The woman from Tekoa went to David. She bowed very low and said, "Your Majesty, please help me!"
5 David asked, "What's the matter?"
She replied:

My husband is dead, and I'm a widow.
6 I had two sons, but they got into a fight out in a field where there was no one to pull them apart, and one of them killed the other. 7 Now all my relatives have come to

me and said, "Hand over your son! We're going to put him to death for killing his brother." But what they really want is to get rid of him, so they can take over our land.

Please don't let them put out my only flame of hope! There won't be anyone left on this earth to carry on my husband's name.

8 "Go home," David told her. "I'll take care of this matter for you."
9 The woman said, "I hope your decision doesn't cause any problems for you. But if it does, you can blame me."⟩
10 He said, "If anyone gives you any trouble, bring them to me, and it won't happen again!"
11 "Please," she replied, "swear by the LORD your God that no one will be allowed to kill my son!"
He said, "I swear by the living LORD that no one will touch even a hair on his head!"
12 Then she asked, "Your Majesty, may I say something?"
"Yes," he answered.
13 The woman said:

Haven't you been hurting God's people? Your own son had to leave the country. And when you judged in my favour, it was the same as admitting that you should have let him come back. 14 We each must die and disappear like water poured out on the ground. But God doesn't take our lives.⟩ Instead, he finds ways of bringing us back when we run away.
15 Your Majesty, I came here to tell you about my problem, because I was afraid of what someone might do to me. I decided to come to you, because I thought you could help. 16 In fact, I knew that you would listen and save my son and me from those who want to take the land that God gave us.⟩
17 I can rest easy now that you have given your decision. You know the difference between right and wrong just like an angel of God, and I pray that the LORD your God will be with you.

18 Then David said to the woman, "Now I'm going to ask you a question, and don't try to hide the truth!"
The woman replied, "Please go ahead, Your Majesty."
19 David asked, "Did Joab put you up to this?"

---

*13.37–38 King Talmai: Absalom's grandfather (see 3.3).
See also: 13.37: 2 Sam 3.3.

See also: 14.17: 2 Sam 19.27.

The woman answered, "Your Majesty, I swear by your life that no one can hide the truth from you. Yes, Joab did tell me what to say, ²⁰ but only to show you the other side of this problem. You must be as wise as the angel of God to know everything that goes on in this country."

²¹ David turned to Joab and said, "It seems that I have already given my decision. Go and bring Absalom back."

²² Joab bowed very low and said, "Your Majesty, I thank you for giving your permission. It shows that you approve of me."

²³ Joab went to Geshur to get Absalom. But when they came back to Jerusalem, ²⁴ David told Joab, "I don't want to see my son Absalom. Tell him to stay away from me." So Absalom went to his own house without seeing his father.

Absalom was handsome

²⁵ No one in all Israel was as handsome and well-built as Absalom. ²⁶ He got his hair cut once a year, and when the hair was weighed, it came to over two kilogrammes.

²⁷ Absalom had three sons. He also had a daughter named Tamar, who grew up to be very beautiful.

Absalom finally sees David

²⁸ Absalom lived in Jerusalem for two years without seeing his father. ²⁹ He wanted Joab to talk to David for him. So one day he sent a message asking Joab to come over, but Joab refused. Absalom sent another message, but Joab still refused. ³⁰ Finally, Absalom told his servants, "Joab's barley field is next to mine. Go and set it on fire!" And they did.

³¹ Joab went to Absalom's house and demanded, "Why did your servants set my field on fire?"

³² Absalom answered, "You didn't pay any attention when I sent for you. I want you to ask my father why he told me to come back from Geshur. I was better off there. I want to see my father now! If I'm guilty, let him kill me."

³³ Joab went to David and told him what Absalom had said. David sent for Absalom, and Absalom came. He bowed very low, and David leaned over and kissed him.

Absalom leads a rebellion

CHAPTER 15

¹ Some time later, Absalom got himself a chariot with horses to pull it, and he had fifty men to run in front. ² He would get up early each morning and wait by the side of the road that led to the city gate.' Anyone who had a complaint to bring to King David would have to go that way, and Absalom would ask each of them, "Where are you from?"

If they said, "I'm from a tribe in the north," ³ Absalom would say, "You deserve to win your case. But the king doesn't have anyone to hear complaints like yours. ⁴ I wish someone would make me the judge around here! I would be fair to everyone."

⁵ Whenever anyone would come to Absalom and start bowing down, he would reach out and hug and kiss them. ⁶ That's how he treated everyone from Israel who brought a complaint to the king. Soon everyone in Israel liked Absalom better than they liked David.

⁷ Four years' later, Absalom said to David, "Please, let me go to Hebron. I have to keep a promise that I made to the LORD, ⁸ when I was living with the Arameans in Geshur. I promised that if the LORD would bring me back to live in Jerusalem, I would worship him in Hebron."'

⁹ David gave his permission, and Absalom went to Hebron. ¹⁰⁻¹² He took two hundred men from Jerusalem with him, but they had no idea what he was going to do. Absalom offered sacrifices in Hebron and sent someone to Gilo to tell David's adviser Ahithophel to come.

More and more people were joining Absalom and supporting his plot. Meanwhile, Absalom had secretly sent some messengers to the northern tribes of Israel. The messengers told everyone, "When you hear the sound of the trumpets, you must shout, 'Absalom now rules as king in Hebron!' "

David has to leave Jerusalem

¹³ A messenger came and told David, "Everyone in Israel is on Absalom's side!"

¹⁴ David's officials were in Jerusalem with him, and he told them, "Let's get out of here! We'll have to leave soon, or none of us will escape from Absalom. Hurry! If he moves fast, he could catch us while we're still here. Then he will kill us and everyone else in the city."

¹⁵ The officials said, "Your Majesty, we'll do whatever you say."

16-17 David left behind ten of his wives* to take care of the palace, but the rest of his family and his officials and soldiers went with him.

They stopped at the last house at the edge of the city. 18 Then David stood there and watched while his regular troops and his bodyguards' marched past. The last group was the six hundred soldiers who had followed him from Gath.* Their commander was Ittai.

19 David spoke to Ittai and said, "You're a foreigner from the town of Gath. You don't have to leave with us. Go back and join the new king! 20 You haven't been with me very long, so why should you have to follow me, when I don't even know where I'm going? Take your soldiers and go back. I pray that the Lord will be' kind and faithful to you."

21 Ittai answered, "Your Majesty, just as surely as you and the LORD live, I will go where you go, no matter if it costs me my life."

22 "Then come on!" David said.

So Ittai and all his men and their families walked on past David.

David sends the sacred chest back to Jerusalem

23 The people of Jerusalem were crying and moaning as David and everyone with him passed by. He led them across Kidron Valley* and along the road towards the desert.

24 Zadok and Abiathar the priests were there along with several men from the tribe of Levi who were carrying the sacred chest. They set the chest down, and left it there until David and his followers had gone out of the city.

25 Then David said:

Zadok, take the sacred chest back to Jerusalem. If the LORD is pleased with me, he will bring me back and let me see it and his tent again. 26 But if he says he isn't pleased with me, then let him do what he knows is best.

27 Zadok, you are a good judge of things,' so return to the city and don't cause any trouble. Take your son Ahimaaz with you. Abiathar and his son Jonathan will also go back. 28 I'll wait at the river crossing in the desert until I hear from you.

29 Zadok and Abiathar took the sacred chest back into Jerusalem and stayed there.

30 David went on up the slope of the Mount of Olives. He was barefoot and crying, and he covered his head to show his sorrow. Everyone with him was crying, and they covered their heads too.

31 Someone told David, "Ahithophel is helping Absalom plot against you!"

David said, "Please, LORD, keep Ahithophel's plans from working!"

David sends Hushai back as a spy

32 When David reached the top of the Mount of Olives, he met Hushai the Archite* at a place of worship. Hushai's robe was torn, and dust was on his head.* 33 David told him:

If you come with me, you might slow us down.* 34 Go back into the city and tell Absalom, "Your Majesty, I am your servant. I will serve you now, just as I served your father in the past."

Hushai, if you do that, you can help me ruin Ahithophel's plans. 35 Zadok and Abiathar the priests will be there with you, and you can tell them everything you hear in the palace. 36 Then they can send their sons Ahimaaz and Jonathan to tell me what you've heard.

37 David's adviser Hushai slipped back into Jerusalem, just about the same time that Absalom was coming in.

CHAPTER 16

Ziba gives food to David

1 David had started down the other side of the Mount of Olives, when he was met by Ziba, the chief servant of Mephibosheth.* Ziba had two donkeys that were carrying two hundred loaves of bread, a hundred handfuls of raisins, a hundred figs,' and some wine.

2 "What's all this?" David asked.

Ziba said, "The donkeys are for your family to ride. The bread and fruit are for the people to eat, and the wine is for them to drink in the desert when they are tired out."

3 "And where is Mephibosheth?" David asked.

Ziba answered, "He stayed in Jerusalem, because he thinks the people of Israel want him to rule the kingdom of his grandfather Saul."

⁴ David then told him, "Everything that used to belong to Mephibosheth is now yours."

Ziba said, "Your Majesty, I am your humble servant, and I hope you will be pleased with me."

Shimei curses David

⁵ David was near the town of Bahurim when a man came out and started cursing him. The man was Shimei the son of Gera, and he was one of Saul's distant relatives. ⁶ He threw stones at David, at his soldiers, and at everyone else, including the bodyguards who walked on each side of David.

⁷ Shimei was yelling at David, "Get out of here, you murderer! You good-for-nothing, ⁸ the LORD is paying you back for killing so many in Saul's family. You stole his kingdom, but now the LORD has given it to your son Absalom. You're a murderer, and that's why you're in such big trouble!"

⁹ Abishai said, "Your Majesty, this man is as useless as a dead dog! He shouldn't be allowed to curse you. Let me go over and chop off his head."

¹⁰ David replied, "What will I ever do with you and your brother Joab? If Shimei is cursing me because the LORD has told him to, then who are you to tell him to stop?"

¹¹ Then David said to Abishai and all his soldiers:

My own son is trying to kill me! Why shouldn't this man from the tribe of Benjamin want me dead even more? Let him curse all he wants. Perhaps the LORD did tell him to curse me. ¹² But if the LORD hears these curses and sees the trouble I'm in, perhaps he will have pity on me instead.

¹³ David and the others went on down the road. Shimei went along the hillside by the road, cursing and throwing stones and earth at them. ¹⁴ When David and those with him came to the River Jordan, they were tired out. But after they rested, they' felt much better.

Hushai meets Absalom

¹⁵ By this time, Absalom, Ahithophel, and the others had reached Jerusalem. ¹⁶ David's friend Hushai came to Absalom and said, "Long live the king! Long live the king!"

¹⁷ But Absalom asked Hushai, "Is this how you show loyalty to your friend David? Why didn't you go with him?"

¹⁸ Hushai answered, "The LORD and the people of Israel have chosen you to be king. I can't leave. I have to stay and serve the one they've chosen. ¹⁹ Besides, it seems right for me to serve you, just as I served your father."

Ahithophel's advice

²⁰ Absalom turned to Ahithophel and said, "Give us your advice! What should we do?"

²¹ Ahithophel answered, "Some of your father's wives* were left here to take care of the palace. You should have sex with them. Then everyone will find out that you have publicly disgraced your father. This will make you and your followers even more powerful."

²² Absalom had a tent set up on the flat roof of the palace, and everyone watched as he went into the tent with his father's wives.

²³ Ahithophel gave such good advice in those days that both Absalom and David thought it came straight from God.

CHAPTER 17

¹ Ahithophel said to Absalom:

Let me choose twelve thousand men and attack David tonight, ² while he is tired and discouraged. He will panic, and everyone with him will run away. I won't kill anyone except David, ³ since he's the one you want to get rid of. Then I'll bring the whole nation back to you like a bride coming home to her husband.' This way there won't be a civil war.

Hushai fools Absalom

⁴ Absalom and all the leaders of the tribes of Israel agreed that Ahithophel had a good plan. ⁵ Then Absalom said, "Bring in Hushai the Archite. Let's hear what he has to say."

⁶ Hushai came in, and Absalom told him what Ahithophel had planned. Then Absalom said, "Should we do what he says? And if we shouldn't, can you come up with anything better?"

⁷ Hushai said:

This time Ahithophel's advice isn't so good. ⁸ You know that your father and his followers are real warriors. Now they are as fierce as a mother bear whose cubs have

---

*16.21 wives: See the note at 3.7.
See also: 16.22: 2 Sam 12.11–12.

just been killed. Besides, your father has a lot of experience in fighting wars, and he won't be spending the night with the others. ⁹ He has probably already found a hiding place in a cave or somewhere else.

As soon as anyone hears that some of your soldiers have been killed, everyone will think your whole army has been destroyed. ¹⁰ Then even those who are as brave as a lion will lose their courage. All Israel knows what a great warrior your father is and what brave soldiers he has.

¹¹ My advice is to gather all the fighting men of Israel from the town of Dan in the north down to the town of Beersheba in the south. You will have more soldiers than there are grains of sand on the seashore. Absalom, you should lead them yourself, ¹² and we will all go to fight David wherever he is. We will fall on him just as dew falls and covers the ground. He and all his soldiers will die! ¹³ If they go into a walled town, we will put ropes around that town and drag it into the river. We won't leave even one small piece of a stone.

¹⁴ Absalom and the others liked Hushai's plan better than Ahithophel's plan. This was because the LORD had decided to keep Ahithophel's plan from working and to cause trouble for Absalom.

Jonathan and Ahimaaz tell David the news

¹⁵ Straight away, Hushai went to Zadok and Abiathar. He told them what advice Ahithophel had given to Absalom and to the leaders of Israel. He also told them about the advice he had given. ¹⁶ Then he said, "Hurry! Send someone to warn David not to spend the night on this side of the river. He must get across the river, so he and the others won't be wiped out!"

¹⁷ Jonathan and Ahimaaz* had been waiting at Rogel Spring* because they did not want to be seen in Jerusalem. A servant girl went to the spring and gave them the message for David. ¹⁸ But a young man saw them and went to tell Absalom. So Jonathan and Ahimaaz left and hurried to the house of a man who lived in Bahurim. Then they climbed down into a well in the courtyard. ¹⁹ The man's wife put the cover on the well

and poured grain on top of it, so the well could not be seen.*

²⁰ Absalom's soldiers came to the woman and demanded, "Where are Ahimaaz and Jonathan?"

The woman answered, "They went across the stream."

The soldiers went off to look for the two men. But when they did not find the men, they went back to Jerusalem.

²¹ After the soldiers had gone, Jonathan and Ahimaaz climbed out of the well. They went to David and said, "Hurry! Get ready to cross the river!" Then they told him about Ahithophel's plan.

²² David and the others got ready and started crossing the River Jordan. By sunrise all of them were on the other side.

Ahithophel kills himself

²³ When Ahithophel saw that Absalom and the leaders of Israel were not going to follow his advice, he saddled his donkey and rode back to his home in Gilo. He told his family and servants what to do. Then he hanged himself, and they buried him in his family's burial place.

Absalom puts Amasa in charge of the army

²⁴ David went to the town of Mahanaim, and Absalom crossed the River Jordan with the army of Israel. ²⁵ Absalom put Amasa in Joab's place as commander of the army. Amasa's father was Ithra⁕ from the family of Ishmael,⁕ and his mother was Abigal,* the daughter of Nahash and the sister of Joab's mother Zeruiah. ²⁶ The Israelites under Absalom's command set up camp in the region of Gilead.

Friends bring supplies to David

²⁷ After David came to the town of Mahanaim, Shobi the son of Nahash came from Rabbah in Ammon,* Machir the son of

---

*17.19 The man's wife . . . seen: Everyone would have thought that the woman was drying grain on a mat that she had spread on the ground.

*17.25 Amasa . . . Abigal: Abigal and Zeruiah (Joab's mother) were full sisters, and David was evidently their half-brother with the same mother, but a different father. This made Amasa one of David's nephews (see 1 Chronicles 2.12–17).

*17.27 Shobi . . . Ammon: Shobi was probably the new king of the Ammonites whom David had appointed after he captured Rabbah (see 2 Samuel 10.1–3; 12.26–31).

---

*17.17 Jonathan and Ahimaaz: See 15.27.

*17.17 Rogel Spring: South of Jerusalem in Kidron Valley.

Holy history

Food and drink

Almost all the family's food was grown and prepared at home. Preparing meals took a long time, so the main meal was in the evening.

The basic daily food was vegetables cooked with herbs and eaten with bread. Common herbs were cumin, garlic and onion, so food was probably quite spicy. And Jewish food laws meant no blood and nothing 'unclean', such as pork or seafood.

Here's a typical shopping list.

Bread

Made from wheat or barley flour, with olive oil and yeast to make it rise; baked on a flat oven floor, or on a tray over the fire.

Olive Oil

A multi-purpose ingredient. You fried food in it, used it as a dressing – and in lamps.

Meat

Generally only for special occasions and mostly boiled. Most people ate goat or mutton. You could eat doves, or chickens, or, if you were desperate, fried locusts.

Fish

If you lived near the sea, or Galilee, then fish would have been a common part of your diet. Jerusalem had a 'Fish Gate' where fresh and dried fish were sold.

Vegetables and Fruit

Lentils, beans, cucumbers, leeks, onions and garlic were all cheap and filling. Fruit included figs, pomegranates and grapes.

Drinks

Water was readily available but often unhealthy. So most people drank wine, or vinegar mixed with water.

Dairy Products

Milk was drunk and used to make butter and cheese. They also made yoghurt. Most cheese was made from goat's milk.

Ammiel came from Lo-Debar, and Barzillai the Gileadite came from Rogelim. 28-29 Here is a list of what they brought: sleeping mats, blankets, bowls, pottery jars, wheat, barley, flour, roasted grain, beans, lentils, honey, yoghurt, sheep, and cheese.

They brought the food for David and the others because they knew that everyone would be hungry, tired, and thirsty from being out in the desert.

CHAPTER 18

David gets ready for battle

¹ David divided his soldiers into groups of a hundred and groups of a thousand. Then he chose officers to be in command of each group. ² He sent out one-third of his army under the command of Joab, another third under the command of Abishai the son of Zeruiah, and the rest under the command of Ittai from Gath. He told the soldiers, "I'm going into battle with you."

³ But the soldiers said, "No, don't go into battle with us! It won't matter to our enemies if they make us all run away, or even if they kill half of us. But you are worth ten thousand of us. It would be better for you to stay in town and send help if we need it."

4-6 David said, "All right, if you think I should."

Then in a voice loud enough for everyone to hear, he said, "Joab! Abishai! Ittai! For my sake, be sure that Absalom comes back unharmed."

David stood beside the town gate as his army marched past in groups of a hundred and in groups of a thousand.

Joab kills Absalom

The war with Israel took place in Ephraim Forest. 7-8 Battles were being fought all over the forest, and David's soldiers were winning. Twenty thousand soldiers were killed▸ that day, and more of them died from the dangers of the forest than from the fighting itself.

⁹ Absalom was riding his mule under a huge tree when his head▸ caught in the branches. The mule ran off and left Absalom hanging in mid-air. Some of David's soldiers happened to pass by, ¹⁰ and one of them went and told Joab, "I saw Absalom hanging in a tree!"

¹¹ Joab said, "You saw Absalom? Why didn't you kill him? I would have given you ten pieces of silver and a special belt."

12 The man answered, "Even if you paid me a thousand pieces of silver here and now, I still wouldn't touch the king's son. We all heard King David tell you and Abishai and Ittai not to harm Absalom. 13 He always finds out what's going on. I would have been risking my life to kill Absalom, because you would have let me take the blame."

14 Joab said, "I'm not going to waste any more time on you!"

Absalom was still alive, so Joab took three spears and stuck them through Absalom's chest. 15 Ten of Joab's bodyguards came over and finished him off. 16 Then Joab blew a trumpet to signal his troops to stop chasing Israel's soldiers. 17 They threw Absalom's body into a deep pit in the forest and put a big pile of rocks over it.

Meanwhile, the people of Israel had all run back to their own homes.

18 When Absalom was alive, he had set up a stone monument for himself in King's Valley. He explained, "I don't have any sons* to keep my name alive." He called it Absalom's Monument, and that is the name it still has today.*

Ahimaaz wants to tell David

19 Ahimaaz the son of Zadok said, "Joab, let me run and tell King David that the LORD has rescued him from his enemies."

20 Joab answered, "You're not the one to tell the king that his son is dead. You can take him a message some other time, but not today."

21 Someone from Ethiopia* was standing there, and Joab told him, "Go and tell the king what you have seen." The man knelt down in front of Joab and then got up and started running.

22 Ahimaaz spoke to Joab again, "No matter what happens, I still want to run. And besides, the Ethiopian has already left."

Joab said, "Why should you run? You won't get a reward for the news you have!"

23 "I'll run no matter what!" Ahimaaz insisted.

"All right then, run!" Joab said.

Ahimaaz took the road through the Jordan Valley and outran the Ethiopian.

24 Meanwhile, David was sitting between the inner and outer gates* in the city wall. One of his soldiers was watching from the roof of the gate-tower. He saw a man running towards the town 25 and shouted down to tell David.

David answered, "If he's alone, he must have some news."

The runner was getting closer, 26 when the soldier saw someone else running. He shouted down to the gate, "Look! There's another runner!"

David said, "He must have some news too."

27 The soldier on the roof shouted, "The first one runs just like Ahimaaz the son of Zadok."

This time David said, "He's a good man. He must have some good news."

28 Ahimaaz called out, "We won! We won!" Then he bowed low to David and said, "Your Majesty, praise the LORD your God! He has given you victory over your enemies."

29 "Is my son Absalom all right?" David asked.

Ahimaaz said, "When Joab sent your personal servant and me, I saw a noisy crowd. But I don't know what it was all about."

30 David told him, "Stand over there and wait."

Ahimaaz went over and stood there. 31 The Ethiopian came and said, "Your Majesty, today I have good news! The LORD has rescued you from all your enemies!"

32 "Is my son Absalom all right?" David asked.

The Ethiopian replied, "I wish that all Your Majesty's enemies and everyone who tries to harm you would end up like him!"

David cries for Absalom

33 David started trembling. Then he went up to the room above the city gate to cry. As he went, he kept saying, "My son Absalom! My son, my son Absalom! I wish I could have died instead of you! Absalom, my son, my son!"

CHAPTER 19

1 Someone told Joab, "The king is crying because Absalom is dead."

---

*18.18 I don't have any sons: According to 14.27, Absalom had three sons. But they could have died young or been put to death for Absalom's murder of Amnon.

*18.18 today: That is, at the time of writing. This monument is not the same as the structure now known as "Absalom's Tomb", which was built at least 600 years later.

*18.21 Ethiopia: The Hebrew text has "Cush", which was a region south of Egypt that included parts of the present countries of Ethiopia and Sudan.

*18.24 between . . . gates: The city gate was often like a tower in the city wall, with one gate on the outside of the wall and another gate on the inside of the wall.

² David's army found out he was crying because his son had died, and their day of victory suddenly turned into a day of sadness. ³ The troops were sneaking into Mahanaim, just as if they had run away from a battle and were ashamed.

⁴ David held his hands over his face and kept on crying loudly, "My son, Absalom! Absalom, my son, my son!"

⁵ Joab went to the house where David was staying and told him:

You've made your soldiers ashamed! Not only did they save your life, they saved your sons and daughters and wives as well. ⁶ You're more loyal to your enemies than to your friends. What you've done today has shown your officers and soldiers that they don't mean a thing to you. You would be happy if Absalom was still alive, even if the rest of us were dead.

⁷ Now get up! Go out there and thank them for what they did. If you don't, I swear by the LORD that you won't even have one man left on your side tomorrow morning. You may have had a lot of troubles in the past, but this will be the worst thing that has ever happened to you!

⁸ David got up and went to the town gate and sat down. When the people heard that he was sitting there, they came to see him.

Israel and Judah want David back

After Israel's soldiers had all returned home, ⁹⁻¹⁰ everyone in Israel started arguing. They were saying to each other, "King David rescued us from the Philistines and from our other enemies. But then we chose Absalom to be our new leader, and David had to leave the country to get away. Absalom died in battle, so why hasn't something been done to bring David back?"

¹¹ When David found out what they were saying, he sent a message to Zadok and Abiathar the priests. It said:

Say to the leaders of Judah, "Why are you the last tribe to think about bringing King David back home? ¹² He is your brother, your own relative! Why haven't you done anything to bring him back?"

¹³ And tell Amasa, "You're my nephew, and with God as a witness, I swear I'll make you commander of my army instead of Joab."

¹⁴ Soon the tribe of Judah again became followers of David, and they sent him this message: "Come back, and bring your soldiers with you."

David starts back for Jerusalem

¹⁵ David started back and had gone as far as the River Jordan when he met the people of Judah. They had gathered at Gilgal and had come to help him cross the river.

¹⁶ Shimei* the son of Gera was there with them. He had hurried from Bahurim to meet David. Shimei was from the tribe of Benjamin, and ¹⁷ a thousand others from Benjamin had come with him.

Ziba, the chief servant of Saul's family, also came to the River Jordan. He and his fifteen sons and twenty servants waded across⁺ to meet David. ¹⁸ Then they brought David's family and servants back across the river, and they did everything he wanted them to do.

Shimei meets with David

Shimei crossed the River Jordan and bowed down in front of David. ¹⁹ He said, "Your Majesty, I beg you not to punish me! Please, forget what I did when you were leaving Jerusalem. Don't even think about it. ²⁰ I know I was wrong. That's why I wanted to be the first one from the northern tribes to meet you."

²¹ But Abishai shouted, "You should be killed for cursing the LORD's chosen king!"

²² David said, "Abishai, whatever will I do with you and your brother Joab? Is it your job to tell me who has done wrong? I've been made king of all Israel today, and no one will be put to death!" ²³ Then David promised Shimei that he would not be killed.

Mephibosheth meets with David

²⁴ Mephibosheth, the grandson of Saul, also came to meet David. He had missed David so much that he had not taken a bath or trimmed his beard or washed his clothes the whole time David was gone.

²⁵ After they had gone back to Jerusalem, Mephibosheth came to see David, who asked him, "Why didn't you go with me?"

²⁶ He answered, "Your Majesty, you know I can't walk. I told my servant to saddle a donkey for me⁺ so I could go with you. But my servant left without me, and ²⁷ then he lied about me. You're as wise as an angel of

---

*19.16 Shimei: See 16.5–13.

See also: 19.16: 2 Sam 16.5–13. 19.24: 2 Sam 9.1–13; 16.1–4.

God, so do what you think is right. ²⁸ After all, you could have killed my whole family and me. But instead, you let me eat at your own table. Your Majesty, what more could I ask?"

²⁹ David answered, "You've said enough! I've decided to divide the property* between you and Ziba."

³⁰ Mephibosheth replied, "He can have it all! I'm just glad you've come home safely."

Barzillai returns home

³¹ Barzillai came from Rogelim in Gilead to meet David at the River Jordan and go across with him. ³² Barzillai was eighty years old. He was very rich and had sent food to David in Mahanaim.

³³ David said to him, "Cross the river and go to Jerusalem with me. I will take care of you."

³⁴ Barzillai answered:

Your Majesty, why should I go to Jerusalem? I don't have much longer to live. ³⁵ I'm already eighty years old, and my body is almost numb. I can't taste my food or hear the sound of singing, and I would be nothing but a burden. ³⁶ I'll cross the river with you, but I'll only go a little way on the other side. You don't have to be so kind to me. ³⁷ Just let me return to my home town, where I can some day be buried near my father and mother. My servant Chimham' can go with you, and you can treat him as your own.

³⁸ David said, "I'll take Chimham with me, and whatever you ask me to do for him, I'll do. And if there's anything else you want, I'll also do that."

³⁹ David's soldiers went on across the river, while he stayed behind to say goodbye to Barzillai and to wish him well. Barzillai returned home, but ⁴⁰ Chimham crossed the river with David.

Israel and Judah argue

All of Judah's army and half of Israel's army were there to help David cross the river. ⁴¹ The soldiers from Israel came to him and said, "Why did our relatives from Judah sneak you and your family and your soldiers across the Jordan?"

⁴² The people of Judah answered, "Why are you so angry? We are the king's relatives. He

didn't give us any food, and we didn't take anything for ourselves!"

⁴³ Those from Israel said, "King David belongs to us ten times more than he belongs to you.* Why didn't you think we were good enough to help you? After all, we were the first ones to think of bringing him back!"

The people of Judah spoke more harshly than the people of Israel.

CHAPTER 20

Sheba rebels against David

¹ A troublemaker from the tribe of Benjamin was there. His name was Sheba the son of Bichri, and he blew a trumpet to get everyone's attention. Then he said, "People of Israel, David the son of Jesse doesn't belong to us! Let's go home."

² So they stopped following David and went off with Sheba. But the people of Judah stayed close to David all the way from the Jordan to Jerusalem.

David's ten wives

³ David had left ten of his wives in Jerusalem to take care of his palace. But when he came back, he had them taken to another house, and he placed soldiers there to guard them. He gave them whatever they needed, but he never slept with any of them again.* They had to live there for the rest of their lives as if they were widows.

The army goes after Sheba

⁴ David said to Amasa, "Three days from now I want you and all of Judah's army to be here!"

⁵ Amasa started bringing the army together, but it was taking him more than three days. ⁶ So David said to Abishai, "Sheba will hurt us more than Absalom ever did. Take my best soldiers and go after him. We don't want him to take over any walled cities and get away from us."'

Joab kills Amasa

⁷ Abishai left Jerusalem to try and capture Sheba. He took along Joab and his soldiers, as

---

*19.29 the property: The property that had belonged to Saul (see 9.7; 16.4).
See also: 19.31: 2 Sam 17.27-29.

*19.43 King David . . . you: In this verse "Israel" stands for the ten northern tribes and does not include the tribe of Judah in the south.
*20.3 he . . . again: Because of what Absalom had done (see 16.21-22).
See also: 20.1: 1 King 12.16; 2 Chron 10.16.
20.3: 2 Sam 16.22.

well as David's bodyguard' and best troops.
⁸ They had gone as far as the big rock at
Gibeon when Amasa caught up with them.
Joab had a dagger strapped around his waist
over his military uniform, but it fell out as he
started towards Amasa.

⁹ Joab said, "Amasa, my cousin, how are
you?" Then Joab took hold of Amasa's beard
with his right hand, so that he could greet
him with a kiss. ¹⁰ Amasa did not see the
dagger in Joab's other hand. Joab stuck it in
Amasa's stomach, and his insides spilt out on
the ground. Joab only struck him once, but
Amasa was dying.

Joab and his brother Abishai went off to
chase Sheba. ¹¹ One of Joab's soldiers stood
by Amasa and shouted, "If any of you like
Joab, and if you are for David, then follow
Joab!"

¹² Amasa was still rolling in his own blood
in the middle of the road. The soldier who
had shouted noticed that everyone who
passed by would stop, so he dragged Amasa
off the road and covered him with a blanket.
¹³ After this, no one else stopped. They all
walked straight past him on their way to help
Joab capture Sheba.

Sheba hides out in the town of Abel

¹⁴ Sheba had gone through all the tribes of
Israel when he came to the town of Abel
Beth-Maacah. All his best soldiers' met him
there and followed him into the town.

¹⁵ Joab and his troops came and
surrounded Abel, so that no one could go in
or come out. They made an earth ramp up to
the town wall and then started to use a
battering ram to knock the wall down.

A wise woman saves the town

¹⁶ A wise woman shouted from the top of the
wall,' "Listen to me! Listen to me! I have to
talk to Joab! Tell him to come here!" ¹⁷ When
he came, the woman said, "Are you Joab?"

"Yes, I am," he answered.

She said, "Please, listen to what I have to
say."

"All right," he said. "I'll listen."

¹⁸ She said, "Long ago people used to say,
'If you want good advice, go to the town of
Abel to get it.' The answers they got here was
all that was needed to settle any problem.
¹⁹ We are Israelites, and we want peace! You
can trust us. Why are you trying to destroy a
town that's like a mother in Israel? Why do
you want to wipe out the LORD's people?"

²⁰ Joab answered, "No, no! I'm not trying
to wipe you out or destroy your town!
²¹ That's not it at all. There's a man in your
town from the hill country of Ephraim. His
name is Sheba, and he is the leader of a
rebellion against King David. Turn him
over to me, and we will leave your town
alone."

The woman told Joab, "We will throw his
head over the wall."

²² She went to the people of the town and
talked them into doing it. They cut off
Sheba's head and threw it to Joab.

Joab blew a signal on his trumpet, and the
soldiers returned to their homes. Joab went
back to David in Jerusalem.

Another list of David's officials*

²³ Joab was the commander of Israel's entire
army.

Benaiah the son of Jehoiada was in
command of David's bodyguard.'

²⁴ Adoram' was in charge of the
slave-labour force.

Jehoshaphat the son of Ahilud kept
government records.

²⁵ Sheva was the secretary.

Zadok and Abiathar were the priests.

²⁶ Ira from Jair was David's priest.

Other events from David's rule

CHAPTER 21

The Gibeonites hang Saul's descendants

¹ While David was king, there were three
years in a row when the nation of Israel could
not grow enough food. So David asked the
LORD for help, and the LORD answered, "Saul
and his family are guilty of murder, because
he had the Gibeonites killed."

² The Gibeonites were not Israelites; they
were descendants of the Amorites. The people
of Israel had promised not to kill them,* but
Saul had tried to kill them because he wanted
Israel and Judah to control all the land.

David called the Gibeonites to him, and he
talked with them. ³ He said, "What can I do to

---

*20.23 Another list of David's officials: See also the
list in 8.16–17.
*21.2 promised . . . them: See Joshua 9.3–27.
See also: 21.2: Josh 9.3–15.

make up for what Saul did, so that you'll ask the LORD to be kind to his people again?"*

⁴ The Gibeonites answered, "Silver and gold from Saul and his family are not enough. On the other hand, we don't have the right to put any Israelite to death."

David said, "I'll do whatever you ask."ᵇ

⁵ They replied, "Saul tried to kill all our people so that none of us would be left in the land of Israel. ⁶ Give us seven of his descendants. We will hangᵇ these men near the place where the LORD is worshipped in Gibeah, the home town of Saul, the LORD's chosen king."

"I'll give them to you," David said.

⁷ David had made a promise to Jonathan with the LORD as his witness, so he spared Jonathan's son Mephibosheth, the grandson of Saul. ⁸ But Saul and Rizpah the daughter of Aiah had two sons named Armoni and Mephibosheth. Saul's daughter Merab* had five sons whose father was Adriel the son of Barzillai from Meholah.ᵇ David took Rizpah's two sons and Merab's five sons and ⁹ turned them over to the Gibeonites, who hangedᵇ all seven of them on the mountain near the place where the LORD was worshipped. This happened right at the beginning of the barley harvest.*

Rizpah takes care of the bodies

¹⁰ Rizpah spread out some sackcloth* on a nearby rock. She wouldn't let the birds land on the bodies during the day, and she kept the wild animals away at night. She stayed there from the beginning of the harvest until it started to rain.*

---

*21.3 ask . . . again: Saul's guilt had become a curse on Israel that had resulted in famine. For the effects of this curse to be removed, the Gibeonites would have to ask the LORD to be kind to Israel.
*21.8 Merab: Some Hebrew manuscripts and some manuscripts of one ancient translation. Most other manuscripts have "Michal", Saul's daughter who was one of David's wives, but she never had any children (see 2 Samuel 6.23). According to 1 Samuel 18.19, Merab was Saul's daughter, and she married Adriel from Meholah.
*21.9 This . . . harvest: This would have been late in April.
*21.10 sackcloth: See the note at 3.31.
*21.10 started to rain: This may have been the beginning of the rainy season in September or October. It usually didn't rain from May to September. Or, it may have been a sign that now there would be enough rain again.
See also: 21.7: 1 Sam 20.15–17; 2 Sam 9.1–7. 21.8: 1 Sam 18.19.

The burial of Saul and his descendants

¹¹⁻¹² Earlier the Philistines had killed Saul and Jonathan on Mount Gilboa and had hung their bodies in the town square at Beth-Shan. The people of Jabesh in Gilead had secretly taken the bodies away, but David found out what Saul's wife* Rizpah had done, and he went to the leaders of Jabesh to get the bones of Saul and his son Jonathan. ¹³⁻¹⁴ David had their bones taken to the land of Benjamin and buried in a side room in Saul's family burial place. Then he gave orders for the bones of the men who had been hangedᵇ to be buried there. It was done, and God answered prayers to bless the land.

The descendants of the Rephaim

This is also told in 1 Chronicles 20.4–8

¹⁵ One time David got very tired when he and his soldiers were fighting the Philistines. ¹⁶ One of the Philistine warriors was Ishbibenob, who was a descendant of the Rephaim,* and he tried to kill David. Ishbibenob was armed with a new sword,ᵇ and his bronze spearheadᵇ alone weighed about three and a half kilogrammes. ¹⁷ But Abishai* came to the rescue and killed the Philistine.

David's soldiers told him, "We can't let you risk your life in battle any more! You give light to our nation, and we want that flame to keep burning."

¹⁸ There was another battle with the Philistines at Gob, where Sibbecai from Hushah killed a descendant of the Rephaim named Saph.

¹⁹ There was still another battle with the Philistines at Gob. A soldier named Elhanan killed Goliath* from Gath, whose spear shaft was like a weaver's beam.* Elhanan's father was Jariᵇ from Bethlehem.

²⁰ There was another war, this time in Gath. One of the enemy soldiers was a

---

*21.11–12 wife: See the note at 3.7.
*21.16 Rephaim: This may refer to a group of people of great stature that lived in Palestine before the Israelites.
*21.17 Abishai: David's nephew, the brother of Joab.
*21.19 Goliath: According to 1 Chronicles 20.5, Elhanan killed the brother of Goliath.
*21.19 weaver's beam: When a weaver made cloth, one set of threads was tied on to a large wooden rod that was known as a weaver's beam.
See also: 21.12: 1 Sam 31.8–13. 21.17: 1 King 11.36; Psa 132.17.

descendant of the Rephaim. He was as big as a giant and had six fingers on each hand and six toes on each foot. [21] But when he made fun of Israel, David's nephew Jonathan killed him. Jonathan was the son of David's brother Shimei.

[22] David and his soldiers killed these four men who were descendants of the Rephaim from Gath.

Two poems by David

CHAPTER 22

David sings to the LORD

This is also told in Psalm 18.1–50

[1] David sang a song to the LORD after the LORD had rescued him from his enemies, especially Saul. These are the words to David's song:

[2] Our LORD and our God,
  you are my mighty rock,*
    my fortress, my protector.
[3] You are the rock where I am safe.
  You are my shield,
  my powerful weapon,'
    and my place of shelter.

  You rescue me and keep me
    from being hurt.
[4] I praise you, our LORD!
  I prayed to you,
  and you rescued me
    from my enemies.
[5] Death, like ocean waves,
    surrounded me,
  and I was almost swallowed
    by its flooding waters.

[6] Ropes from the world
  of the dead had coiled around me,
  and death had set a trap in my path.
[7] I was in terrible trouble
    when I called out to you,
  but from your temple you heard me
    and answered my prayer.
[8] Earth shook and shivered!
  The columns supporting the sky*
    rocked back and forth.

  You were angry
[9] and breathed out smoke.
  Scorching heat and fiery flames
    spewed from your mouth.

[10] You opened the heavens
  like curtains,
  and you came down
  with storm clouds under your feet.
[11] You rode on the backs
  of flying creatures.*
  You appeared' with the wind as wings.
[12] Darkness was your tent!
  Thunderclouds filled the sky,
    hiding you from sight.
[13] Fiery coals lit up the sky
    in front of you.

[14] LORD Most High, your voice
    thundered from the heavens.
[15] You scattered your enemies
    with arrows of lightning.
[16] You roared at the sea,
  and its deepest channels could be seen.
  You snorted,
  and the earth shook
    to its foundations.

[17] You reached down from heaven,
  and you lifted me
    from deep in the ocean.
[18] You rescued me from enemies
  who were hateful
    and too powerful for me.
[19] On the day disaster struck,
  they came and attacked,
    but you defended me.
[20] When I was fenced in,
  you freed and rescued me
    because you love me.
[21] You are good to me, LORD,
    because I do right,
  and you reward me
    because I am innocent.
[22] I do what you want
    and never turn to do evil.
[23] I keep your laws in mind
  and never turn away
    from your teachings.
[24] I obey you completely
    and guard against sin.
[25] You have been good to me
    because I do right;
  you have rewarded me
  for being innocent
    by your standards.

---

*22.2 mighty rock: The Hebrew text has "rock", which is sometimes used in poetry to compare the LORD to a mountain where his people can run for protection from their enemies.
*22.8 columns . . . sky: The sky was sometimes described as a dome that was held up by a foundation or pillars.

---

*22.11 flying creatures: These were supernatural beings (see the note at 6.2).

26 You are always loyal
      to your loyal people,
   and you are faithful to the faithful.
27 With all who are sincere
      you are sincere,
   but you treat the unfaithful
      as their deeds deserve.
28 You rescue the humble,
   but you look for ways
      to put down the proud.

29 Our LORD and God,
      you are my lamp.
   You turn darkness to light.
30 You help me defeat armies
      and capture cities.

31 Your way is perfect, LORD,
      and your word is correct.
   You are a shield for those
      who run to you for help.
32 You alone are God!
      Only you are a mighty rock.*
33 You are my strong fortress,
      and you set me free.
34 You make my feet run as fast
      as those of a deer,
   and you help me stand
      on the mountains.

35 You teach my hands to fight
      and my arms to use
      a bow of bronze.
36 You alone are my shield,
      and by coming to help me,
      you have made me famous.
37 You clear the way for me,
      and now I won't stumble.

38 I kept chasing my enemies
      until I caught them
      and destroyed them.
39 I destroyed them!
   I stuck my sword
      through my enemies,
   and they were crushed
      under my feet.
40 You helped me win victories
      and forced my attackers
      to fall victim to me.

41 You made my enemies run,
      and I killed them.
42 They cried out for help,
      but no one saved them;
   they called out to you,
      but there was no answer.

43 I ground them to dust,
   and I squashed them
      like mud in the streets.

44 You rescued me
      from my stubborn people
   and made me the leader
      of foreign nations,
   who are now my slaves.
45 They obey and come crawling.
46   They have lost all courage
      and from their fortresses
      they come trembling.

47 You are the living LORD!
   I will praise you!
   You are a mighty rock.*
   I will honour you
      for keeping me safe.
48 You took revenge for me,
   and you put nations in my power.
49 You protected me
      from violent enemies,
   and you made me much greater
      than all of them.

50 I will praise you, LORD,
   and I will honour you
      among the nations.
51 You give glorious victories
      to your chosen king.
   Your faithful love for David
   and for his descendants will never end.

CHAPTER 23

David's last words

1 These are the last words
      of David the son of Jesse.
   The God of Jacob chose David
      and made him a great king.
   The Mighty God of Israel loved him.ᵇ
   When God told him to speak,
      David said:
2 The Spirit of the LORD
      has told me what to say.
3 Our Mighty Rock,*
      the God of Jacob, told me,
   "A ruler who obeys God
      and does right
4 is like the sunrise
      on a cloudless day,
   or like rain that sparkles
      on the grass."ᵇ

---

*22.32 mighty rock: See the note at 22.2.
See also: 22.34: Hab 3.19.

*22.47; 23.3 mighty rock: See the note at 22.2.
See also: 22.50: Rom 15.9.

⁵ I have ruled this way,
   and God will never break
      his promise to me.
God's promise is complete
   and unchanging;
he will always help me
   and give me what I hope for.
⁶ But evil people are pulled up
   like thorn bushes.
   They are not dug up by hand,
⁷ but with a sharp spear
   and are burnt on the spot.

David's warriors

The Three Warriors
This is also told in 1 Chronicles 11.10–19

⁸ These are the names of David's warriors:
   Ishbosheth* the son of Hachmon' was the leader of the Three Warriors.* In one battle, he killed eight hundred men with his spear.'
   ⁹ The next one of the Three Warriors was Eleazar the son of Dodo the Ahohite. One time when the Philistines were at war with Israel, he and David dared the Philistines to fight them. Every one of the Israelite soldiers turned and ran, ¹⁰ except Eleazar. He killed Philistines until his hand was cramped, and he couldn't let go of his sword. When Eleazar finished, all the Israelite troops had to do was come back and take the enemies' weapons and armour. The LORD gave Israel a great victory that day.
   ¹¹ Next was Shammah the son of Agee the Hararite. One time the Philistines brought their army together to destroy a crop of peas growing in a field near Lehi. The rest of Israel's soldiers ran away from the Philistines, ¹² but Shammah stood in the middle of the field and killed the Philistines. The crops were saved, and the LORD gave Israel a great victory.
   ¹³ One year at harvest time, the Three Warriors' went to meet David at Adullam Cave.* The Philistine army had set up camp in Rephaim Valley ¹⁴ and had taken over

Bethlehem. David was in his fortress, ¹⁵ and he was very thirsty. He said, "I wish I had a drink from the well by the gate at Bethlehem."
   ¹⁶ The Three Warriors' sneaked into the Philistine camp and got some water from the well near Bethlehem's gate. But after they brought the water back to David, he refused to drink it. Instead, he poured it out as a sacrifice ¹⁷ and said to the LORD, "I can't drink this water! It's like the blood of these men who risked their lives to get it for me."
   The Three Warriors did these brave deeds.

The Thirty Warriors
This is also told in 1 Chronicles 11.20–47

¹⁸ Joab's brother Abishai was the leader of the Thirty Warriors,* and in one battle he killed three hundred men with his spear. He was as famous as the Three Warriors ¹⁹ and certainly just as famous as the rest of the Thirty Warriors. He was the commander of the Thirty Warriors, but he still did not become one of the Three Warriors.
   ²⁰ Benaiah the son of Jehoiada was a brave man from Kabzeel who did some amazing things. He killed two of Moab's best fighters,' and on a snowy day he went down into a pit and killed a lion. ²¹ Another time, he killed an Egyptian, as big as a giant.' The Egyptian was armed with a spear, but Benaiah only had a club. Benaiah grabbed the spear from the Egyptian and killed him with it. ²²⁻²³ Benaiah did these things. He never became one of the Three Warriors, but he was just as famous as they were and certainly just as famous as the rest of the Thirty Warriors. David made him the leader of his bodyguard.
   ²⁴⁻³⁹ Some of the Thirty Warriors were:

   Asahel the brother of Joab
   Elhanan the son of Dodo from Bethlehem
   Shammah from Harod
   Elika from Harod
   Helez the Paltite
   Ira the son of Ikkesh from Tekoa
   Abiezer from Anathoth
   Mebunnai' the Hushathite
   Zalmon the Ahohite
   Maharai from Netophah
   Heleb the son of Baanah from Netophah
   Ittai the son of Ribai from Gibeah of the
      tribe of Benjamin
   Benaiah from Pirathon

---

*23.8 Ishbosheth: Hebrew "Josheb Bashebeth", which seems to be another spelling of Ishbosheth. See the note at 2.8, although this is a different Ishbosheth.
*23.8 the Three Warriors: The most honoured group of warriors. They may have been part of the Thirty Warriors. "Three" and "thirty" are spelt almost the same in Hebrew, so there is some confusion in the manuscripts as to which group is being talked about in some places in the following lists.
*23.13 Adullam Cave: This may have happened during the time that David was an outlaw (see 1 Samuel 22.1–6).

*23.18 the Thirty Warriors: The second most honoured group of warriors. They may have also been officers in the army (see the note at 23.8).

Hiddai from the streams on Mount Gaash
Abialbon from Beth-Arabah
Azmaveth from Bahurim'
Eliahba from Shaalbon
Jashen'
Jonathan the son of Shammah the
  Hararite'
Ahiam the son of Sharar the Hararite
Eliphelet the son of Ahasbai from Maacah
Eliam the son of Ahithophel from Gilo
Hezro from Carmel
Paarai the Arbite
Igal the son of Nathan from Zobah
Bani the Gadite
Zelek from Ammon
Naharai from Beeroth, who carried the
  weapons of Joab the son of Zeruiah
Ira the Ithrite
Gareb the Ithrite
Uriah the Hittite

There were thirty-seven in all.

David counts the people of Israel, and Israel is punished

CHAPTER 24

David counts the people

This is also told in 1 Chronicles 21.1–6

1 The LORD was angry with Israel again, and he made David think it would be a good idea to count the people in Israel and Judah. 2 So David told Joab and the army officers,' "Go to every tribe in Israel, from the town of Dan in the north all the way south to Beersheba, and count everyone who can serve in the army. I want to know how many there are."

3 Joab answered, "I hope the LORD your God will give you a hundred times more soldiers than you already have. I hope you will live to see that day! But why do you want to do a thing like this?"

4 But when David refused to change his mind, Joab and the army officers went out and started counting the people. 5 They crossed the River Jordan and began with' Aroer and the town in the middle of the river valley. From there they went towards Gad and on as far as Jazer. 6 They went to Gilead and to Kadesh in Syria.' Then they went to Dan, Ijon,' and on towards Sidon. 7 They came to the fortress of Tyre, then went through every town of the Hivites and the Canaanites. Finally, they went to Beersheba in the Southern Desert of Judah. 8 After they

had gone through the whole land, they went back to Jerusalem. It had taken them nine months and twenty days.

9 Joab came and told David, "In Israel there are eight hundred thousand who can serve in the army, and in Judah there are five hundred thousand."

The LORD punishes David

This is also told in 1 Chronicles 21.7–17

10 After David had everyone counted, he felt guilty and told the LORD, "What I did was stupid and terribly wrong. LORD, please forgive me."

11 Before David even got up the next morning, the LORD had told David's prophet Gad 12-13 to take a message to David. Gad went to David and told him:

> You must choose one of three ways for the LORD to punish you: will there be seven' years when the land won't grow enough food for your people? Or will your enemies chase you and make you run from them for three months? Or will there be three days of horrible disease in your land? Think about it and decide, because I have to give your answer to God, who sent me.

14 David was really frightened and said, "It's a terrible choice to make! But the LORD is kind, and I'd rather be punished by him than by anyone else."

15-16 So that morning, the LORD sent an angel to spread a horrible disease everywhere in Israel, from Dan to Beersheba. And before it was over, seventy thousand people had died.

When the angel was about to destroy Jerusalem, the LORD felt sorry for all the suffering he had caused and told the angel, "That's enough! Don't touch them." This happened at the threshing place that belonged to Araunah the Jebusite.

17 David saw the angel killing everyone and told the LORD, "These people are like sheep with me as their shepherd.' I have sinned terribly, but they have done nothing wrong. Please, punish me and my family instead of them!"

David buys Araunah's threshing place

This is also told in 1 Chronicles 21.18–22.1

18-19 That same day the prophet Gad came and told David, "Go to the threshing place that belongs to Araunah and build an altar there for the LORD."

So David went.

²⁰ Araunah looked and saw David and his soldiers coming up towards him. He went over to David, bowed down low, ²¹ and said, "Your Majesty! Why have you come to see me?"

David answered, "I've come to buy your threshing place. I have to build the LORD an altar here, so this disease will stop killing the people."

²² Araunah said, "Take whatever you want and offer your sacrifice. Here are some oxen for the sacrifice. You can use the threshing-boards* and the wooden yokes for the fire. ²³ Take them — they're yours! I hope the LORD your God will be pleased with you."

²⁴ But David answered, "No! I have to pay you what they're worth. I can't offer the LORD my God a sacrifice that I got for nothing." So David bought the threshing place and the oxen for fifty pieces of silver. ²⁵ Then he built an altar for the LORD. He sacrificed animals and burnt them on the altar.

The LORD answered the prayers of the people, and no one else died from the terrible disease.

*24.22 threshing-boards: Heavy boards with bits of rock or metal on the bottom. They were dragged across the grain to separate the husks from the kernels.

Additional notes

›1.9 in terrible pain: Or "very weak".
›1.26 You . . . husband: Or "You loved me more than a wife could possibly love her husband."
›2.16 Field of Daggers: Or "Field of Opponents" or "Battlefield".
›2.29 all morning: One possible meaning for the difficult Hebrew text.
›3.12 You . . . nation: Or "I like you."
›3.26 well at Sirah: Or "oasis of Sirah" or "cistern at Sirah".
›3.29 cowards: One possible meaning for the difficult Hebrew text.
›3.33 outlaw: Or "fool".
›3.39 God . . . back: Or "I pray that God will pay them back."
›4.1 Ishbosheth: Hebrew "The son of Saul".
›5.7–9 You will . . . or see: One possible meaning for the difficult Hebrew text.
›5.7–9 temple: Or "palace".
›5.13 from Jerusalem: Or "in Jerusalem".
›5.20 The Lord Broke Through: Or "Baal-Perazim".
›5.23 balsam: One possible meaning for the difficult Hebrew text.
›6.2 to Baalah . . . there: The Dead Sea Scrolls and 1 Chronicles 13.6; the Standard Hebrew Text "from Baalah in Judah. They had gone there".

›6.2 he is worshipped there: Or "the chest belongs to him."
›6.3–4 Ahio . . . Ahio: Or "his brother . . . his brother".
›6.8 Bursting . . . Uzzah: Or "Perez-Uzzah".
›6.10 Gath: Or perhaps "Gittaim".
›7.19 Is this . . . people: One possible meaning for the difficult Hebrew text.
›7.23 You . . . here: One possible meaning for the difficult Hebrew text.
›8.1 Israel . . . control: Or "David also took the town of Metheg-Ammah away from them."
›8.3 David . . . way: One possible meaning for the difficult Hebrew text. It may have been Hadadezer who was going to the River Euphrates. And he may have gone there either to build a monument or to put down a rebellion.
›8.4 seventeen hundred cavalry: Hebrew; one ancient translation and 1 Chronicles 18.4 "a thousand chariots and seven thousand cavalry".
›8.4 He also captured . . . them: Or "He crippled all but one hundred of the horses."
›8.7 Hadadezer's . . . cases: Or "Hadadezer's soldiers carried gold shields, but David took these shields".
›8.9–10 defeated: Or "killed".
›8.12 Edom: Some Hebrew manuscripts and two ancient translations (see also 1 Chronicles 18.11); most Hebrew manuscripts "Aram". In Hebrew the words for "Edom" and "Aram" look almost alike.
›8.13 Edomite: Some Hebrew manuscripts and two ancient translations (see also 1 Chronicles 18.12); most Hebrew manuscripts "Aramean". In Hebrew the words for "Edomite" and "Aramean" look almost alike.
›8.13 built a monument: Or "was famous".
›8.17 Abiathar the son of Ahimelech: One ancient translation and 1 Samuel 22.11–23; Hebrew "Ahimelech the son of Abiathar".
›8.18 was the commander of: Not in the Hebrew text of this verse, but see 1 Chronicles 18.17.
›8.18 David's bodyguard: The Hebrew text has "the Cherethites and the Pelethites", who were foreign soldiers hired by David to be his bodyguard.
›9.10 Saul's family and servants: Some manuscripts of one ancient translation; Hebrew "the son of your master".
›9.11–13 David's: Hebrew "my".
›10.18 cavalry: The Hebrew manuscripts and ancient translations differ as to how many and what kind of soldiers were killed.
›11.1 when . . . war: Or "when the messengers had gone to Ammon" (see 10.2) or "the time when the kings had gone to war" (see 10.6–8).
›11.11 somewhere in the fields: Or "at Succoth".
›11.21 Gideon: The Hebrew text has Jerubbesheth, which stands for "Jerubbaal", another name for Gideon. See Judges 6.32 and the note on "bosheth" at 2.8 ("besheth" means the same as "bosheth").
›11.25 break . . . walls: Or "destroy it."
›12.13–14 what . . . wanted: One manuscript of one ancient translation; one Hebrew manuscript "what the LORD had said"; most Hebrew manuscripts "what the enemies of the LORD would think".

›**12.30 the statue of their god Milcom:** Or "their king."

›**12.30 David . . . crown:** Or "and David wore the crown."

›**12.31 tear . . . walls:** One possible meaning for the difficult Hebrew text.

›**13.6 special bread:** Or "heart-shaped bread" or "dumplings".

›**13.18 long . . . sleeves:** One possible meaning for the difficult Hebrew text.

›**13.21 But Amnon . . . unhappy:** The Dead Sea Scrolls and one ancient translation; these words are not in the Standard Hebrew Text.

›**13.27 Absalom prepared . . . king:** One ancient translation; these words are not in the Hebrew text.

›**13.32 David's nephew:** The Hebrew text has "the son of David's brother Shimeah".

›**13.34 the road to Horonaim:** Or "the road behind him" or "the road to the west".

›**13.34 He . . . Road:** One ancient translation; these words are not in the Hebrew text.

›**13.39 David . . . Absalom:** Or "David was comforted over the loss of Amnon, and he no longer wanted to take his army there to capture Absalom."

›**14.9 I hope . . . me:** Or "May I speak some more?"

›**14.14 take our lives:** Or "make any exceptions".

›**14.16 take . . . us:** Or "make sure we have no part in God's people."

›**15.2 the city gate:** Or "the entrance to the king's palace."

›**15.7 Four years:** The Hebrew text has "forty years".

›**15.8 in Hebron:** Some manuscripts of one ancient translation; these words are not in the Hebrew text.

›**15.18 bodyguards:** See the note at 8.18.

›**15.20 I pray . . . be:** One ancient translation; these words are not in the Hebrew text.

›**15.27 you . . . things:** Or "You are a prophet" or "You are not a prophet".

›**16.1 figs:** Or "pomegranates", a bright red fruit that looks like an apple.

›**16.14 they:** Hebrew "he".

›**17.3 back to you . . . husband:** One ancient translation; Hebrew "back to you. The man you are chasing is like bringing back the whole nation."

›**17.25 Ithra:** Or "Jether".

›**17.25 the family of Ishmael:** Some manuscripts of one ancient translation; other manuscripts of the same translation "the town of Jezreel"; Hebrew "the people of Israel".

›**18.7-8 Twenty . . . killed:** This may refer to the total number or to the number of Absalom's soldiers who were killed.

›**18.9 head:** Or "hair".

›**18.33 son:** In Hebrew, this verse is 19.1.

›**19.17 waded across:** Or "rushed".

›**19.26 I told . . . me:** Two ancient translations; Hebrew, "I said, 'I will saddle a donkey for myself.' "

›**19.37 My servant Chimham:** Or "My son Chimham".

›**20.6 get . . . us:** One possible meaning for the difficult Hebrew text.

›**20.7 bodyguard:** See the note at 8.18.

›**20.14 best soldiers:** One ancient translation; the difficult Hebrew text may mean either "Berites" or "Bichrites", Sheba's relatives.

›**20.16 the top of the wall:** Or "the town".

›**20.23 David's bodyguard:** See the note at 8.18.

›**20.24 Adoram:** One ancient translation "Adoniram" (see 1 Kings 4.1–6; 5.14).

›**21.4 I'll . . . ask:** Or "What are you asking me to do for you?"

›**21.6 hang:** One possible meaning for the difficult Hebrew text.

›**21.8 Meholah:** Also known as Abel-Meholah.

›**21.9 hanged:** One possible meaning for the difficult Hebrew text.

›**21.13-14 hanged:** See the note at 21.9.

›**21.16 new sword:** One possible meaning for the difficult Hebrew text.

›**21.16 spearhead:** Or "helmet".

›**21.19 Jari:** Or "Jaare".

›**22.3 powerful weapon:** The Hebrew text has "the horn", which refers to the horn of a bull, one of the most powerful animals in ancient Palestine.

›**22.11 appeared:** Most Hebrew manuscripts; some Hebrew manuscripts "swooped down" (see Psalm 18.10).

›**23.1 The Mighty . . . him:** Or "He wrote Israel's favourite songs."

›**23.4 sparkles . . . grass:** Or "makes the grass grow."

›**23.8 the son of Hachmon:** Or "the Tahchemonite" (see 1 Chronicles 11.11).

›**23.8 with . . . spear:** One possible meaning for the difficult Hebrew text (see 1 Chronicles 11.11).

›**23.13 the Three Warriors:** Or "three warriors"; Hebrew "three of the thirty most important".

›**23.16 the Three Warriors:** Or "three warriors".

›**23.20 Moab's best fighters:** Or "big lions in Moab"; one ancient translation "sons of Ariel from Moab".

›**23.21 Egyptian . . . giant:** 1 Chronicles 11.23; in this verse the Hebrew text has "good-looking Egyptian."

›**23.24-39 Mebunnai:** Or "Sibbecai" (see 1 Chronicles 11.26–47).

›**23.24-39 Bahurim:** Or "Barhum".

›**23.24-39 Jashen:** Hebrew "sons of Jashen".

›**23.24-39 Jonathan . . . Hararite:** Some manuscripts of one ancient translation (see 1 Chronicles 26—47). In the Hebrew text Jonathan and Shammah are separate members of the list.

›**24.2 Joab . . . officers:** Some manuscripts of one ancient translation (see 24.4); 1 Chronicles 21.2; Hebrew "Joab, the officer of the army".

›**24.5 began with:** Some manuscripts of one ancient translation; Hebrew "set up camp in".

›**24.6 Kadesh in Syria:** Or "the lower slopes of Mount Hermon."

›**24.6 Dan, Ijon:** Or "Danjaan", an unknown place.

›**24.12-13 seven:** Hebrew; some manuscripts of one ancient translation "three" (see 1 Chronicles 21.12).

›**24.17 as their shepherd:** The Dead Sea Scrolls, and some manuscripts of two ancient translations (see 1 Chronicles 21.17); these words are not in the Standard Hebrew Text of this verse.

1 Kings

The basics

What's the point?   Kings explains why things went wrong for Israel. It wasn't economic problems, it wasn't military failure, it was the disobedience and unfaithfulness of the kings and the people.

What happens?   David dies. Solomon starts well then loses it. The kingdom splits into two. God raises up prophets to challenge the disobedience of the kings and the people.

What should I remember?   18.21 'Elijah stood in front of them and said, "How much longer will you try to have things both ways? If the LORD is God, worship him! But if Baal is God, worship him!" The people did not say a word.'

More details

Setting the scene   King David is dying. On his deathbed he reaffirms his promise to hand the kingdom to Solomon, his son by Bathsheba. But can Solomon defeat the other claimants to the throne? And what will happen to Israel after Solomon himself dies?

What's it all about?   The book of Kings is, you will not be surprised to hear, about a load of kings.

Like Samuel and Chronicles it was originally one book, but was too big to fit on one scroll. So it got split into two parts. The first part concentrates on the reign of Solomon and the split of the kingdom after his death.

Solomon begins his reign magnificently. Marked out by his wisdom, he builds the kingdom into a powerful force and builds a magnificent temple of God in Jerusalem. But his reign ends badly. He has married literally hundreds of foreign women and they have lured him into worshipping foreign gods.

He has also caused a split between the tribes by the way that he used some tribes as forced labour in the building of the temple.

So, after his death, the kingdom of Israel splits into two. The southern section is called Judah, and is made up of the two tribes. The northern half is made up of the other ten tribes and retains the name Israel.

The second part of 1 Kings describes the kings of these two kingdoms. Each king is given a kind of approval rating by the writer, rated as 'good' or 'bad'. What decides their rating is not the kinds of things that we might judge a king or a leader on. They aren't given points for political achievments, or military conquests, or even for building prosperous economies. The only thing that matters is their faithfulness to God. And most of the kings fail this test. They forget God and choose to worship a range of foreign gods.

So God sends a load of prophets – the other major characters in this book. The prophets are tempestuous, passionate, stroppy, God-filled people who God sends to challenge the behaviour of the kings and the people.

In particular, 1 Kings introduces two mighty prophets: Elijah and Elisha. Elijah opposes King Ahab and Queen Jezebel of Israel – the northern kingdom. At the time he seems almost a lone voice; it's Elijah v. the Rest.

Elijah's life shows what a difficult job it was to be a prophet. At times he was a lone voice in the face of huge opposition. It took courage, commitment and huge faith in God to confront wickedness and speak out for God in a world that did not wish to hear what its maker had to say.

Footsteps

Solomon becomes king

CHAPTER 1

David in his old age

¹ King David was now an old man, and he always felt cold, even under a lot of blankets. ² His officials said, "Your Majesty, we will look for a young woman to take care of you. She can lie down beside you and keep you warm." ³⁻⁴ They looked everywhere in Israel until they found a very beautiful young woman named Abishag, who lived in the town of Shunem.* They brought her to David, and she took care of him. But David did not have sex with her.

Adonijah tries to become king

⁵⁻⁶ Adonijah was the son of David and Haggith. He was Absalom's younger brother* and was very handsome. One day, Adonijah started boasting, "I'm going to make myself king!" So he got some chariots and horses, and he hired fifty men as bodyguards. David did not want to hurt his feelings, so he never asked Adonijah why he was doing these things.

⁷ Adonijah met with Joab the son of Zeruiah and Abiathar the priest and asked them if they would help him become king. Both of them agreed to help. ⁸ But Zadok the priest, Benaiah the son of Jehoiada, Nathan the prophet, Shimei, Rei,' and David's bodyguards all refused.

⁹ Adonijah invited his brothers and David's officials from Judah to go with him to Crawling Rock' near Rogel Spring, where he sacrificed some sheep, cattle, and fat calves.* ¹⁰ But he did not invite Nathan, Benaiah, David's bodyguards, or his own brother Solomon.

¹¹ When Nathan heard what had happened, he asked Bathsheba, Solomon's mother:

Have you heard that Adonijah the son of Haggith has made himself king? But David doesn't know a thing about it. ¹² You and your son Solomon will be killed, unless you do what I tell you. ¹³ Go and say to David, "You promised me that Solomon would be the next king. So why is Adonijah now king?"

¹⁴ While you are still talking to David, I'll come in and tell him that everything you said is true.

¹⁵ Meanwhile, David was in his bedroom where Abishag was taking care of him because he was so old. Bathsheba went in ¹⁶ and bowed down.

"What can I do for you?" David asked.
¹⁷ Bathsheba answered:

Your Majesty, you promised me in the name of the LORD your God that my son Solomon would be the next king. ¹⁸ But Adonijah has already been made king, and you didn't know anything about it. ¹⁹ He sacrificed a lot of cattle, calves, and sheep. And he invited Abiathar the priest, Joab your army commander, and all your sons to be there, except Solomon, your loyal servant.

²⁰ Your Majesty, everyone in Israel is waiting for you to announce who will be the next king. ²¹ If you don't, they will say that Solomon and I have rebelled. They will treat us like criminals and kill us as soon as you die.

²² Just then, Nathan the prophet arrived. ²³ Someone told David that he was there, and Nathan came in. He bowed with his face to the ground ²⁴ and said:

Your Majesty, did you say that Adonijah would be king? ²⁵ Earlier today, he sacrificed a lot of cattle, calves, and sheep. He invited the army commanders, Abiathar, and all your sons to be there. Now they are eating and drinking and shouting,

---

*1.3–4 Shunem: A town in northern Israel, just north of Jezreel Valley.
*1.5–6 brother: Since Absalom was dead, Adonijah was now David's eldest living son and would be next in line to be king.
See also: 1.5: 2 Sam 3.4.

*1.9 sacrificed . . . calves: This was part of a ceremony where Adonijah was made the new king.
See also: 1.11: 2 Sam 12.24.

"Long live King Adonijah!" ²⁶ But he didn't invite me or Zadok the priest or Benaiah or Solomon. ²⁷ Did you say they could do this without telling the rest of us who would be the next king?

Solomon becomes king

²⁸ David said, "Tell Bathsheba to come here." She came and stood in front of him. ²⁹⁻³⁰ Then he said, "The living LORD God of Israel has kept me safe. And so today, I will keep the promise I made to you in his name: Solomon will be the next king!"

³¹ Bathsheba bowed with her face to the ground and said, "Your Majesty, I pray that you will live a long time!"

³² Then David said, "Tell Zadok, Nathan, and Benaiah to come here."

When they arrived, ³³ he told them:

Take along some of my officials and let Solomon ride my own mule to Gihon Spring. ³⁴ When you get there, Zadok and Nathan will make Solomon the new king of Israel. Then after the ceremony* is over, make someone blow a trumpet and tell everyone to shout, "Long live King Solomon!" ³⁵ Bring him back here, and he will take my place as king. He is the one I have chosen to rule Israel and Judah.

³⁶ Benaiah answered, "We will do it, Your Majesty. I pray that the LORD your God will let it happen. ³⁷ The LORD has always watched over you, and I pray that he will now watch over Solomon. May the LORD help Solomon to be an even greater king than you."

³⁸ Zadok, Nathan, and Benaiah left and took along the two groups of David's special bodyguards.ᵌ Solomon rode on David's mule as they led him to Gihon Spring. ³⁹ Zadok the priest brought some olive oil from the sacred tent and poured it on Solomon's head to show that he was now king. A trumpet was blown and everyone shouted, "Long live King Solomon!" ⁴⁰ Then they played flutes and celebrated as they followed Solomon back to Jerusalem. They made so much noise that the ground shook.

⁴¹ Adonijah and his guests had almost finished eating when they heard the noise. Joab also heard the trumpet and asked, "What's all that noise about in the city?"

⁴² Just then, Jonathan son of Abiathar came running up. "Come in," Adonijah said. "An important man like you must have some good news."

⁴³ Jonathan answered:

No, I haven't! David has just announced that Solomon will be king. ⁴⁴⁻⁴⁵ Solomon rode David's own mule to Gihon Spring, and Zadok, Nathan, Benaiah, and David's special bodyguardsᵌ went with him. When they got there, Zadok and Nathan made Solomon king. Then everyone celebrated all the way back to Jerusalem. That's the noise you hear in the city. ⁴⁶ Solomon is now king.

⁴⁷ And listen to this! David's officials told him, "We pray that your God will help Solomon to be an even greater king!"

David was in his bed at the time, but he bowed ⁴⁸ and prayed, "I praise you, LORD God of Israel. You have made my son Solomon king and have let me live to see it."

⁴⁹ Adonijah's guests shook with fear when they heard this news, and they left as fast as they could. ⁵⁰ Adonijah himself was afraid of what Solomon might do to him, so he ran to the sacred tent and grabbed hold of the corners of the altar for protection.*

⁵¹ Someone told Solomon, "Adonijah is afraid of you and is holding on to the corners of the altar. He wants you to promise that you won't kill him."

⁵² Solomon answered, "If Adonijah doesn't cause any trouble, I won't hurt him. But if he does, I'll have him killed." ⁵³ Then he sent someone to the altar to get Adonijah.

After Adonijah came and bowed down, Solomon said, "Adonijah, go home."

David's final words and his death

CHAPTER 2

David's instructions to Solomon

¹ Not long before David died, he told Solomon:

² My son, I will soon die, as everyone must. But I want you to be strong and brave. ³ Do what the LORD your God commands and

---

*1.34 the ceremony: Part of this ceremony was pouring olive oil on Solomon's head to show that he was now king.

*1.50 the corners . . . for protection: The four corners of some ancient altars looked like animal horns. Since the entire altar was sacred, anyone holding on to its corners was supposed to be safe from being killed.

follow his teachings. Obey everything written in the Law of Moses. Then you will be a success, no matter what you do or where you go. ⁴ You and your descendants must always faithfully obey the LORD. If you do, he will keep the solemn promise he made to me that someone from our family will always be king of Israel.

⁵ Solomon, don't forget what Joab did to me by killing Abner son of Ner and Amasa son of Jether, the two commanders of Israel's army. He killed them as if they were his enemies in a war, but he did it when there was no war.* He is guilty, and now it's up to you to punish him ⁶ in the way you think best. Whatever you do, don't let him die peacefully in his old age.

⁷ The sons of Barzillai from Gilead helped me when I was running from your brother Absalom.* Be kind to them and let them eat at your table.

⁸ Be sure to do something about Shimei son of Gera from Bahurim in the territory of Benjamin. He cursed and insulted me the day I went to Mahanaim. But later, when he came to meet me at the River Jordan, I promised that I wouldn't kill him.* ⁹ Now you must punish him. He's an old man, but you're wise enough to know that you must have him killed.

David dies

¹⁰⁻¹¹ David was king of Israel forty years. He ruled seven years from Hebron and thirty-three years from Jerusalem. Then he died and was buried in Jerusalem.᾿ ¹² His son Solomon became king and took control of David's kingdom.

Solomon takes control of the kingdom

Adonijah is killed

¹³ One day, Adonijah went to see Bathsheba, Solomon's mother, and she asked, "Is this a friendly visit?"

"Yes. ¹⁴ I just want to talk with you."

"All right," she told him, "go ahead."

---

*2.5 war: See 2 Samuel 3.22–27 and 20.7–10.
*2.7 Absalom: See 2 Samuel 17.27–29.
*2.8 him: See 2 Samuel 16.5–14 and 19.16–23.

See also: 2.5: a 2 Sam 3.27; b 2 Sam 20.10.
2.7: 2 Sam 17.27–29. 2.8: 2 Sam 16.5–13; 19.16–23.
2.11: 2 Sam 5.4–5; 1 Chron 3.4. 2.12: 1 Chron 29.23.

Life files

Solomon

Background: Son of David and Bathsheba.

What's the story?

Solomon succeeded his father to the throne of Israel. God appeared to him in a dream and offered to grant him one request; so Solomon asked for wisdom – which shows he was pretty wise to begin with.

And he got it – he became the wisest man in the world (1 Kings 4.29). He solved individual disputes as well as bigger problems facing his nation. Under his leadership, the United Kingdom of Israel reached its most prosperous (1 Kings 4.20–27). He also built a temple to God in Jerusalem, not to mention a huge palace.

Then things went wrong. Solomon married around a thousand women, and was led astray. Amazingly, the man who built the temple in Jerusalem ended up building shrines to 'disgusting' gods such as Molech and Chemosh (1 Kings 11.7). In the building of the temple, some of the other tribes of Israel had been used as forced labour, and huge taxes had been charged – and this led to civil war after his death.

What's the point?

Solomon was the wisest person of his day, but he ended his life doing stupid things. Obedience to God and faithfulness to his commands are the wisest course. Solomon was given everything, yet he threw it all away. Maybe he wasn't so clever after all.

Footsteps

A week with Solomon

Solomon becomes King: 1 Kings 2.13–46
The wisdom of Solomon: 1 Kings 3.1–28
Solomon's reputation: 1 Kings 4.29–34
The building of the temple: 1 Kings 6.1–38
The opening of the temple: 1 Kings 8.1–66
The Queen of Sheba: 1 Kings 10.1–29
The foolishness of Solomon: 1 Kings 11.1–43

More...

David p.314
Wisdom p.548

[15] "You know that I was king for a little while," Adonijah replied. "And everyone in Israel accepted me as their ruler. But the LORD wanted my brother to be king, so now things have changed. [16] Would you do me a favour?"

"What do you want?" Bathsheba asked.

[17] "Please ask Solomon to let me marry Abishag. He won't say no to you."

[18] "All right," she said. "I'll ask him."

[19] When Bathsheba went to see Solomon, he stood up to meet her, then bowed low. He sat back down and had another throne brought in, so his mother could sit at his right side.* [20] Bathsheba sat down and then asked, "Would you do me a small favour?"

Solomon replied, "Mother, just tell me what you want, and I will do it."

[21] "Allow your brother Adonijah to marry Abishag," she answered.

[22] Solomon said:

What? Let my elder brother marry Abishag? You may as well ask me to let him rule the kingdom! And why don't you ask such favours for Abiathar and Joab?▸

[23] I swear in the name of the LORD that Adonijah will die because he asked for this! If he doesn't, I pray that God will severely punish me. [24] The LORD made me king in my father's place and promised that the kings of Israel would come from my family. Yes, I swear by the living LORD that Adonijah will die today.

[25] "Benaiah," Solomon shouted, "go and kill Adonijah." So Adonijah died.

Abiathar is sent back home

[26] Solomon sent for Abiathar the priest and said:

Abiathar, go back home to Anathoth! You ought to be killed too, but I won't do it now. When my father David was king, you were in charge of the sacred chest, and you went through a lot of hard times with my father. [27] But I won't let you be a priest of the LORD any more.

And so the promise that the LORD had made at Shiloh about the family of Eli came true.*

Joab is killed

[28] Joab had not helped Absalom try to become king, but he had helped Adonijah. So when Joab learnt that Adonijah had been killed, he ran to the sacred tent and grabbed hold of the corners of the altar for protection.* [29] When Solomon heard about this, he sent someone to ask Joab, "Why did you run to the altar?"

Joab sent back his answer, "I was afraid of you, and I ran to the LORD for protection."▸

Then Solomon shouted, "Benaiah, go and kill Joab!"

[30] Benaiah went to the sacred tent and yelled, "Joab, the king orders you to come out!"

"No!" Joab answered. "Kill me right here."

Benaiah went back and told Solomon what Joab had said.

[31-32] Solomon replied:

Do what Joab said. Kill him and bury him! Then my family and I won't be responsible for what he did to Abner the commander of Israel's army and to Amasa the commander of Judah's army. He killed those innocent men without my father knowing about it. Both of them were better men than Joab. Now the LORD will make him pay for those murders. [33] Joab's family will always suffer because of what he did, but the LORD will always bless David's family and his kingdom with peace.

[34] Benaiah went back and killed Joab. His body was taken away and buried near his home in the desert.

[35] Solomon put Benaiah in Joab's place as army commander, and he put Zadok in Abiathar's place as priest.

Shimei is killed

[36] Solomon sent for Shimei and said, "Build a house here in Jerusalem and live in it. But whatever you do, don't leave the city! [37] If you ever cross Kidron Valley and leave Jerusalem, you will be killed. And it will be your own fault."

[38] "That's fair, Your Majesty," Shimei answered. "I'll do that." So Shimei lived in Jerusalem from then on.

[39] About three years later, two of Shimei's servants ran off to King Achish in Gath. When Shimei found out where they were, [40] he saddled his donkey and went after them. He found them and brought them back to Jerusalem.

---

*2.19 at his right side: The place of honour.

*2.27 the promise . . . came true: See 1 Samuel 2.27–34.

See also: 2.17: 1 King 1.3–4. 2.26: a 2 Sam 15.24; b 1 Sam 22.20–23. 2.27: 1 Sam 2.27–36.

---

*2.28 the corners . . . for protection: See the note at 1.50.

[41] Someone told Solomon that Shimei had gone to Gath and was back. [42] Solomon sent for him and said:

Shimei, you promised in the name of the LORD that you would never leave Jerusalem. I warned you that you would die if you did. You agreed that this was fair, didn't you? [43] You have disobeyed me and have broken the promise you made to the LORD.

[44] I know you remember all the cruel things you did to my father David. Now the LORD is going to punish you for what you did. [45] But the LORD will bless me and make my father's kingdom strong for ever.

[46] "Benaiah," Solomon shouted, "kill Shimei." So Shimei died.

Solomon was now in complete control of his kingdom.

Solomon's wisdom and his officials

CHAPTER 3

The LORD makes Solomon wise

This is also told in 2 Chronicles 1.1–13

[1] Solomon signed a treaty with the king of Egypt and married his daughter. She lived in the older part of Jerusalem' until the palace, the LORD's temple, and the wall around Jerusalem were completed.

[2] At that time, there was no temple for worshipping the LORD, and everyone offered sacrifices at the local shrines.' [3] Solomon loved the LORD and followed his father David's instructions, but Solomon also offered sacrifices and burnt incense at the shrines.

[4] The most important shrine was in Gibeon, and Solomon had offered more than a thousand sacrifices on that altar.

[5] One night while Solomon was in Gibeon, the LORD God appeared to him in a dream and said, "Solomon, ask for anything you want, and I will give it to you."

[6] Solomon answered:

My father David, your servant, was honest and did what you commanded. You were always loyal to him, and you gave him a son who is now king. [7] LORD God, I'm your servant, and you've made me king in my father's place. But I'm very young and know so little about being a leader. [8] And now I must rule your chosen people, even though there are too many of them to count.

[9] Please make me wise and teach me the difference between right and wrong. Then I will know how to rule your people. If you don't, there is no way I could rule this great nation of yours.

[10-11] God said:

Solomon, I'm pleased that you asked for this. You could have asked to live a long time or to be rich. Or you could have asked for your enemies to be destroyed. Instead, you asked for wisdom to make right decisions. [12] So I'll make you wiser than anyone who has ever lived or ever will live.

[13] I'll also give you what you didn't ask for. You'll be rich and respected as long as you live, and you'll be greater than any other king. [14] If you obey me and follow my commands, as your father David did, I'll let you live a long time.

[15] Solomon woke up and realized that God had spoken to him in the dream. He went back to Jerusalem and stood in front of the sacred chest, where he offered sacrifices to please the Lord* and sacrifices to ask his blessing.* Then Solomon gave a feast for his officials.

Solomon makes a difficult decision

[16] One day two women' came to King Solomon, [17] and one of them said:

Your Majesty, this woman and I live in the same house. Not long ago my baby was born at home, [18] and three days later her baby was born. Nobody else was there with us.

[19] One night while we were all asleep, she rolled over on her baby, and he died. [20] Then while I was still asleep, she got up and took my son out of my bed. She put him in her bed, then she put her dead baby next to me.

[21] In the morning when I got up to feed my son, I saw that he was dead. But when I looked at him in the light, I knew he wasn't my son.

[22] "No!" the other woman shouted. "He was your son. My baby is alive!"

"The dead baby is yours," the first woman yelled. "Mine is alive!"

---

*3.15 sacrifices to please the Lord: See Leviticus 1.1–17.
*3.15 sacrifices to ask his blessing: See Leviticus 3.1–17.

They argued back and forth in front of Solomon, ²³ until finally he said, "Both of you say this live baby is yours. ²⁴ Someone bring me a sword."

A sword was brought, and Solomon ordered, ²⁵ "Cut the baby in half! That way each of you can have part of him."

²⁶ "Please don't kill my son," the baby's mother screamed. "Your Majesty, I love him very much, but give him to her. Just don't kill him."

The other woman shouted, "Go ahead and cut him in half. Then neither of us will have the baby."

²⁷ Solomon said, "Don't kill the baby." Then he pointed to the first woman, "She is his real mother. Give the baby to her."

²⁸ Everyone in Israel was amazed when they heard how Solomon had made his decision. They realized that God had given him wisdom to judge fairly.

CHAPTER 4

Solomon's officials

¹⁻⁶ Here is a list of Solomon's highest officials while he was king of Israel:

Azariah son of Zadok was the priest;
Elihoreph and Ahijah sons of Shisha were the secretaries;
Jehoshaphat son of Ahilud kept the government records;
Benaiah son of Jehoiada was the army commander;
Zadok and Abiathar were priests;
Azariah son of Nathan was in charge of the regional officers;
Zabud son of Nathan was a priest and the king's adviser;
Ahishar was the prime minister;
Adoniram son of Abda was in charge of the forced labour.

⁷ Solomon chose twelve regional officers, who took turns bringing food for him and his household. Each officer provided food from his region for one month of the year. ⁸ These were the twelve officers:

The son of Hur was in charge of the hill country of Ephraim.

⁹ The son of Deker was in charge of the towns of Makaz, Shaalbim, Beth-Shemesh, and Elon-Beth-Hanan.

¹⁰ The son of Hesed was in charge of the towns of Arubboth and Socoh, and the region of Hepher.

¹¹ The son of Abinadab was in charge of Naphath-Dor and was married to Solomon's daughter Taphath.

¹² Baana son of Ahilud was in charge of the towns of Taanach and Megiddo. He was also in charge of the whole region of Beth-Shan near the town of Zarethan, south of Jezreel from Beth-Shan to Abel-Meholah to the other side of Jokmeam.

¹³ The son of Geber was in charge of the town of Ramoth in Gilead and the villages in Gilead belonging to the family of Jair, a descendant of Manasseh. He was also in charge of the region of Argob in Bashan, which had sixty walled towns with bronze bars on their gates.

¹⁴ Ahinadab son of Iddo was in charge of the territory of Mahanaim.

¹⁵ Ahimaaz was in charge of the territory of Naphtali and was married to Solomon's daughter Basemath.

¹⁶ Baana son of Hushai was in charge of the territory of Asher and the town of Bealoth.

¹⁷ Jehoshaphat son of Paruah was in charge of the territory of Issachar.

¹⁸ Shimei son of Ela was in charge of the territory of Benjamin.

¹⁹ Geber son of Uri was in charge of Gilead, where King Sihon of the Amorites and King Og of Bashan had lived.

And one officer was in charge of the territory of Judah.▸

The size of Solomon's kingdom

²⁰ There were so many people living in Judah and Israel while Solomon was king that they seemed like grains of sand on a beach. Everyone had enough to eat and drink, and they were happy. ²¹ Solomon ruled every kingdom between the River Euphrates and the land of the Philistines down to Egypt. These kingdoms paid him taxes as long as he lived.

²² Every day, Solomon needed five thousand litres of fine flour, ten thousand litres of coarsely-ground flour, ²³ ten grain-fed cattle, twenty pasture-fed cattle, one hundred sheep, as well as deer, gazelles, and geese.

²⁴ Solomon ruled the whole region west of the River Euphrates, from Tiphsah to Gaza, and he was at peace with all the countries around him. ²⁵ Everyone living in Israel, from the town of Dan in the north to Beersheba in the south, was safe as long as Solomon lived.

See also: **4.21:** Gen 15.18; 2 Chron 9.26.

Each family sat undisturbed beneath its own grape vines and fig trees.

26 Solomon had forty thousand stalls of chariot horses and twelve thousand chariot soldiers.

27 Each of the twelve regional officers brought food to Solomon and his household for one month of the year. They provided everything he needed, 28 as well as barley and straw for the horses.

Solomon's wisdom

29 Solomon was brilliant. God had blessed him with insight and understanding. 30-31 He was wiser than anyone else in the world, including the wisest people of the east and of Egypt. He was even wiser than Ethan the Ezrahite, and Mahol's three sons, Heman, Calcol, and Darda. Solomon became famous in every country around Judah and Israel. 32 Solomon wrote three thousand wise sayings and composed more than a thousand songs. 33 He could talk about all kinds of plants, from large trees to small bushes, and he taught about animals, birds, reptiles, and fish. 34 Kings all over the world heard about Solomon's wisdom and sent people to listen to him teach.

Building and dedication of the Jerusalem temple

CHAPTER 5

Solomon asks Hiram to help build the temple

This is also told in 2 Chronicles 2.1–16

1 King Hiram of Tyre* had always been friends with Solomon's father David. When Hiram learnt that Solomon was king, he sent some of his officials to meet with Solomon.

2 Solomon sent a message back to Hiram:

3 Remember how my father David wanted to build a temple where the LORD his God could be worshipped? But enemies kept attacking my father's kingdom, and he never had the chance. 4 Now, thanks to the LORD God, there is peace in my kingdom and no trouble or threat of war anywhere.

5 The LORD God promised my father that when his son became king, he would build a temple for worshipping the LORD. So I've decided to do that.

6 I'd like you to send your workers to cut down cedar trees in Lebanon for me. I will pay them whatever you say and will even make my workers help them. We both know that your workers are more experienced than anyone else at cutting timber.

7 Hiram was so happy when he heard Solomon's request that he said, "I am grateful that the LORD gave David such a wise son to be king of that great nation!" 8 Then he sent back his answer:

I received your message and will give you all the cedar and pine logs you need. 9 My workers will carry them down from Lebanon to the Mediterranean Sea. They will tie the logs together and float them along the coast to wherever you want them. Then they will untie the logs, and your workers can take them from there.

To pay for the logs, you can provide the grain I need for my household.

10 Hiram gave Solomon all the cedar and pine logs he needed. 11 In return, Solomon gave Hiram two thousand tonnes of wheat and four hundred thousand litres of pure olive oil each year.

12 The LORD kept his promise and made Solomon wise. Hiram and Solomon signed a treaty and never went to war against each other.

Solomon's workers

13 Solomon ordered thirty thousand people from all over Israel to cut logs for the temple, 14 and he put Adoniram in charge of these workers. Solomon divided them into three groups of ten thousand. Each group worked one month in Lebanon and had two months off at home.

15 He also had eighty thousand workers to cut stone in the hill country of Israel, seventy thousand workers to carry the stones, 16 and over three thousand assistants to keep track of the work and to supervise the workers. 17 He ordered the workers to cut and shape large blocks of good stone for the foundation of the temple.

*5.1 Tyre: The most important city in Phoenicia. It was on the coast of the Mediterranean Sea north of Israel, in what is today southern Lebanon.

See also: 4.26: 1 King 10.26; 2 Chron 1.14; 9.25. 4.31: Psa 89 Title. 4.32: Prov 1.1; 10.1; 25.1; Song 1.1.

See also: 5.5: 2 Sam 7.12–13; 1 Chron 17.11–12. 5.14: 1 King 12.18.

¹⁸ Solomon's and Hiram's men worked with men from the city of Gebal,* and together they got the stones and logs ready for the temple.

CHAPTER 6

The outside of the temple is completed

¹ Solomon's workers started building the temple during Ziv,* the second month of the year. It had been four years since Solomon became king of Israel, and four hundred and eighty years since the people of Israel left Egypt.

² The inside of the LORD's temple was twenty-seven metres long, nine metres wide, and thirteen and a half metres high.

³ A four-and-a-half-metre porch went all the way across the front of the temple. ⁴ The windows were narrow on the outside but wide on the inside.

⁵⁻⁶ Along the sides and back of the temple, there were three levels of storage rooms. The rooms on the bottom level were just over two metres wide, the rooms on the middle level were over two and a half metres wide, and those on the top level were just over three metres wide. There were ledges on the outside of the temple that supported the beams of the storage rooms, so that nothing was built into the temple walls.

⁷ Solomon did not want the noise of hammers and axes to be heard at the place where the temple was being built. So he made the workers shape the blocks of stone at the quarry.

⁸ The entrance to the bottom storage rooms was on the south side of the building, and stairs to the other rooms were also there. ⁹ The roof of the temple was made out of beams and cedar boards.

The workers finished building the outside of the temple. ¹⁰ Storage rooms just over two metres high were all around the temple, and they were attached to the temple by cedar beams.

¹¹ The LORD told Solomon:

¹²⁻¹³ If you obey my commands and do what I say, I will keep the promise I made to your father David. I will live among my people Israel in this temple you are building, and I will not desert them.

¹⁴ So Solomon's workers finished building the temple.

The inside of the temple is furnished

This is also told in 2 Chronicles 3.8–14

¹⁵ The floor of the temple was made out of pine, and the walls were lined with cedar from floor to ceiling.›

¹⁶ The most holy place was in the back of the temple, and it was nine metres square. Cedar boards standing from floor to ceiling› separated it from the rest of the temple.

¹⁷ The temple's main room was eighteen metres long, and it was in front of the most holy place.

¹⁸ The inside walls were lined with cedar to hide the stones, and the cedar was decorated with carvings of gourds and flowers.

¹⁹ The sacred chest was kept in the most holy place. ²⁰⁻²² This room was nine metres long, nine metres wide, and nine metres high, and it was lined with pure gold. There were also gold chains across the front of the most holy place. The inside of the temple, as well as the cedar altar in the most holy place, was covered with gold.

²³ Solomon had two statues of winged creatures* made from olive wood to put in the most holy place. Each creature was four and a half metres tall ²⁴⁻²⁶ and four and a half metres across. They had two wings, and the wings were just over two metres long. ²⁷ Solomon put them next to each other in the most holy place. Their wings were spread out and reached across the room. ²⁸ The creatures were also covered with gold.

²⁹ The walls of the two rooms were decorated with carvings of palm trees, flowers, and winged creatures. ³⁰ Even the floor was covered with gold.

³¹⁻³² The two doors to the most holy place were made out of olive wood and were decorated with carvings of palm trees, flowers, and winged creatures. The doors and the carvings were covered with gold. The door frame came to a point at the top.

³³⁻³⁴ The two doors to the main room of the temple were made out of pine, and each one had two sections› so they could fold open. The door frame was shaped like a rectangle and was made out of olive wood. ³⁵ The doors were covered with gold and were decorated with carvings of palm trees, flowers, and winged creatures.

---

*5.18 Gebal: Later known as Byblos.
*6.1 Ziv: The second month of the Hebrew calendar, from about mid-April to mid-May.

*6.23 statues of winged creatures: These were symbols of the LORD's throne on earth (see Exodus 25.18–22).

See also: 6.16: Exod 26.33–34. 6.22: Exod 30.1–3.
6.23–28: Exod 25.18–20.

36 The inner courtyard of the temple had walls made out of three layers of cut stones with one layer of cedar beams.

37 Work began on the temple during Ziv,* the second month of the year, four years after Solomon became king of Israel. 38 Seven years later the workers finished building it during Bul,* the eighth month of the year. It was built exactly as it had been planned.

CHAPTER 7

Solomon's palace is built

1 Solomon's palace took thirteen years to build.

2-3 Forest Hall was the largest room in the palace. It was forty-four metres long, twenty-two metres wide, and thirteen and a half metres high, and was lined with cedar from Lebanon. It had four rows of cedar pillars, fifteen in a row, and they held up forty-five cedar beams. The ceiling was covered with cedar. 4 Three rows of windows on each side faced each other, 5 and there were three doors on each side near the front of the hall.

6 Pillar Hall was twenty-two metres long and thirteen and a half metres wide. A covered porch supported by pillars went all the way across the front of the hall.

7 Solomon's throne was in Justice Hall, where he judged cases. This hall was completely lined with cedar.

8 The section of the palace where Solomon lived was behind Justice Hall and looked exactly like it. He had a similar place built for his wife, the daughter of the king of Egypt.

9 From the foundation all the way to the top, these buildings and the courtyard were made out of the best stones' carefully cut to size, then smoothed on every side with saws. 10 The foundation stones were huge, good stones — some of them four and a half metres long and others three and a half metres long. 11 The cedar beams and other stones that had been cut to size were on top of these foundation stones. 12 The walls around the palace courtyard were made out of three layers of cut stones with one layer of cedar beams, just like the front porch and the inner courtyard of the temple.

Hiram makes the bronze furnishings

This is also told in 2 Chronicles 3.15–17; 4.1–10

13-14 Hiram was a skilled bronze worker from the city of Tyre.* His father was now dead, but he also had been a bronze worker from Tyre, and his mother was from the tribe of Naphtali.

King Solomon asked Hiram to come to Jerusalem and make the bronze furnishings to use for worship in the LORD's temple, and he agreed to do it.

15 Hiram made two bronze columns eight metres tall and almost two metres across. 16 For the top of each column, he also made a bronze cap just over two metres high. 17 The caps were decorated with seven rows of designs that looked like chains,' 18 with two rows of designs that looked like pomegranates.*

19 The caps for the columns of the porch were almost two metres high and were shaped like lilies.'

20 The chain designs on the caps were just above the rounded tops of the two columns, and there were two hundred pomegranates in rows around each cap. 21 Hiram placed the two columns on each side of the main door of the temple. The column on the south side was called Jachin,* and the one on the north was called Boaz.*

22 The lily-shaped caps were on top of the columns.

This completed the work on the columns.

23 Hiram also made a large bowl called the Sea. It was just over two metres deep, about four and a half metres across, and thirteen and a half metres around. 24 Two rows of bronze gourds were around the outer edge of the bowl, ten gourds to about every forty-five centimetres. 25 The bowl itself sat on top of twelve bronze bulls with three bulls facing outwards in each of four directions. 26 The sides of the bowl were seventy-five millimetres thick, and its rim was like a cup that curved outwards like flower petals. The bowl held about forty thousand litres.

27 Hiram made ten moveable bronze stands, each one over a metre high, almost

---

*6.37 Ziv: See the note at 6.1.
*6.38 Bul: The eighth month of the Hebrew calendar, from about mid-October to mid-November.
See also: 7.8: 1 King 3.1.

*7.13–14 Hiram . . . city of Tyre: This is not the same person as "King Hiram of Tyre" (see 5.1).
*7.18 pomegranates: One possible meaning for the difficult Hebrew text of verse 18. A pomegranate is a bright red fruit that looks like an apple. In ancient times, it was a symbol of life.
*7.21 Jachin: Or "He makes secure".
*7.21 Boaz: Or "He is strong."

two metres long, and almost two metres wide. 28-29 The sides were made with panels attached to frames decorated with flower designs. The panels themselves were decorated with figures of lions, bulls, and winged creatures. 30-31 Each stand had four bronze wheels and axles and a round frame sixty-eight centimetres across, held up by four supports forty-five centimetres high. A small bowl rested in the frame. The supports were decorated with flower designs, and the frame with carvings.

The side panels of the stands were square, 32 and the wheels and axles were underneath them. The wheels were about sixty-eight centimetres high 33 and looked like chariot wheels. The axles, rims, spokes, and hubs were made out of bronze.

34-35 Around the top of each stand was a twenty-two-centimetre strip, and there were four braces* attached to the corners of each stand. The panels and the supports were attached to the stands, 36 and the stands were decorated with flower designs and figures of lions, palm trees, and winged creatures. 37 Hiram made the ten bronze stands from the same mould, so they were exactly the same size and shape.

38 Hiram also made ten small bronze bowls, one for each stand. The bowls were almost two metres across and could hold about eight hundred litres.

39 He put five stands on the south side of the temple, five stands on the north side, and the large bowl at the south-east corner of the temple. 40 Hiram made pans for hot ashes, and also shovels and sprinkling bowls.

A list of everything inside the temple

This is also told in 2 Chronicles 4.11—5.1

This is a list of the bronze items that Hiram made for the LORD's temple: 41 two columns; two bowl-shaped caps for the tops of the columns; two chain designs on the caps; 42 four hundred pomegranates* for the chain designs; 43 ten moveable stands; ten small bowls for the stands; 44 a large bowl; twelve bulls that held up the bowl; 45 pans for hot ashes, and also shovels and sprinkling bowls.

Hiram made these bronze things for Solomon 46 near the River Jordan between

Succoth and Zarethan by pouring melted bronze into clay moulds.

47 There were so many bronze things that Solomon never bothered to weigh them, and no one ever knew how much bronze was used.

48 Solomon gave orders to make the following temple furnishings out of gold: the altar; the table that held the sacred loaves of bread;* 49 ten lampstands that went in front of the most holy place; flower designs; lamps and tongs; 50 cups, lamp snuffers, and small sprinkling bowls; dishes for incense; fire pans; and the hinges for the doors to the most holy place and the main room of the temple.

51 After the LORD's temple was finished, Solomon put into its storage rooms everything that his father David had dedicated to the LORD, including the gold and the silver.

CHAPTER 8

Solomon brings the sacred chest to the temple

This is also told in 2 Chronicles 5.2—6.2

1-2 The sacred chest had been kept on Mount Zion, also known as the city of David. But Solomon decided to have the chest moved to the temple while everyone was in Jerusalem, celebrating the Festival of Shelters during Ethanim,* the seventh month of the year.

Solomon called together the important leaders of Israel. 3-4 Then the priests and the Levites carried to the temple the sacred chest, the sacred tent, and the objects used for worship. 5 Solomon and a crowd of people walked in front of the chest, and along the way they sacrificed more sheep and cattle than could be counted.

6 The priests carried the chest into the most holy place and put it under the winged creatures, 7 whose wings covered the chest and the poles used for carrying it. 8 The poles were so long that they could be seen from just outside the most holy place, but not from anywhere else. And they stayed there from then on.

---

*7.34-35 braces:** Or "handles".
*7.42 pomegranates:** See the note at 7.18.
See also: 7.38: Exod 30.17-21.

*7.48 sacred loaves of bread:** This bread was offered to the LORD and was a symbol of the LORD's presence in the temple. It was put out on a special table, and was replaced with fresh bread each week (see Leviticus 24.5-9).
*8.1-2 Ethanim:** The seventh month of the Hebrew calendar, from about mid-September to mid-October.
See also: 7.48: a Exod 30.1-3; b Exod 25.23-30.
7.49: Exod 25.31-40. 7.51: 2 Sam 8.11; 1 Chron 18.11.
8.1: 2 Sam 6.12-16; 1 Chron 15.25-29. 8.2: Lev 23.34.

Helpline

Help! I'm in trouble with the police

'I didn't think. I couldn't resist. I just went along... And now I've been caught.'

Sometimes we mess up big time. We lose our temper, return to habits we thought we'd kicked or see an opportunity we just can't resist. Whatever the situation, we have to face up to it. We've done wrong. We need to admit our guilt, own up to whatever part we played in the affair.

Ask God for forgiveness. Solomon asks God to forgive his people 'no matter how much they have sinned' (1 Kings 8.50). The great news is, that's what God does. He forgives all who are sorry for what they've done.

See if there's any practical way you can make amends. Have you damaged someone's property? Maybe you can repair or replace it. Get the advice of people you trust. Talk to the police and the probation service and see what they can suggest.

Sometimes there's nothing we can really do to make amends. But then it's even more important to ask God to forgive you and to accept whatever punishment you deserve.

Three things

Honest

Be honest about what you've done. Are you to blame? Don't pretend it never happened.

Confess

Seek forgiveness. Ask God to forgive you and he will. See if there's any way in which you can make it up to the person, or community that your actions have affected.

Restart

Move on. We all mess up. But that doesn't mean that we can't start again. With God there are always new starts and new opportunities to serve.

More...

Help! I've messed up really badly p.347
Sin p.1261
Forgiveness p.614
Saying sorry p.1258

9 The only things kept in the chest were the two flat stones Moses had put there when the LORD made his agreement with the people of Israel at Mount Sinai,' after bringing them out of Egypt.

10 Suddenly a cloud filled the temple as the priests were leaving the most holy place. 11 The LORD's glory was in the cloud, and the light from it was so bright that the priests could not stay inside to do their work. 12 Then Solomon prayed:

> "Our LORD, you said that you
>   would live in a dark cloud.
> 13 Now I have built a glorious temple
>   where you can live for ever."

Solomon speaks to the people
This is also told in 2 Chronicles 6.3–11

14 Solomon turned towards the people standing there. Then he blessed them 15-16 and said:

> Praise the LORD God of Israel! Long ago he brought his people out of Egypt. He later kept his promise to make my father David the king of Israel. The LORD also said that he had not chosen the city where his temple would be built.
> 17 So when David wanted to build a temple for the LORD God of Israel, 18 the LORD said, "It's good that you want to build a temple where I can be worshipped. 19 But you're not the one to do it. Your son will build a temple to honour me."
> 20 The LORD has done what he promised. I am the king of Israel like my father, and I've built a temple for the LORD our God. 21 I've also made a place in the temple for the sacred chest. And in that chest are the two flat stones on which is written the solemn agreement the LORD made with our ancestors when he led them out of Egypt.

Solomon prays at the temple
This is also told in 2 Chronicles 6.12–42

22 Solomon stood facing the altar with everyone standing behind him. Then he lifted his arms towards heaven 23 and prayed:

> LORD God of Israel, no other god in heaven or on earth is like you!

See also: 8.9: Deut 10.5. 8.10,11: Exod 40.34–35.
8.12: Psa 18.11; 97.2. 8.16: 2 Sam 7.4–11; 1 Chron 17.3–10.
8.17–18: 2 Sam 7.1–3; 1 Chron 17.1–2. 8.19: 2 Sam 7.12–13;
1 Chron 17.11–12.

You never forget the agreement you made with your people, and you are loyal to anyone who faithfully obeys your teachings. [24] My father David was your servant, and today you have kept every promise you made to him.

[25] LORD God of Israel, you promised my father that someone from his family would always be king of Israel, if they do their best to obey you, just as he did. [26] Please keep this promise you made to your servant David.

[27] There's not enough room in all of heaven for you, LORD God. How could you possibly live on earth in this temple I have built? [28] But I ask you to answer my prayer. [29] This is the temple where you have chosen to be worshipped. Please watch over it day and night and listen when I turn towards it and pray. [30] I am your servant, and the people of Israel belong to you. So whenever any of us look towards this temple and pray, answer from your home in heaven and forgive our sins.

[31] Suppose someone accuses a person of a crime, and the accused has to stand in front of the altar in your temple and say, "I swear I am innocent!" [32] Listen from heaven and decide who is right. Then punish the guilty person and let the innocent one go free.

[33] Suppose your people Israel sin against you, and then an enemy defeats them. If they come to this temple and beg for forgiveness, [34] listen from your home in heaven. Forgive them and bring them back to the land you gave their ancestors.

[35] Suppose your people sin against you, and you punish them by holding back the rain. If they turn towards this temple and pray in your name and stop sinning, [36] listen from your home in heaven and forgive them. The people of Israel are your servants, so teach them to live right. And please send rain on the land you promised them for ever.

[37] Sometimes the crops may dry up or rot or be eaten by locusts* or grasshoppers, and your people will be starving. Sometimes enemies may surround their towns, or your people will become sick with deadly diseases. [38] Listen when anyone in Israel truly feels sorry and sincerely prays with arms lifted towards your temple. [39] You know what is in everyone's heart. So from your home in heaven answer their prayers, according to the way they live and what is in their hearts. [40] Then your people will worship and obey you for as long as they live in the land you gave their ancestors.

[41-42] Foreigners will hear about you and your mighty power, and some of them will come to live among your people Israel. If any of them pray towards this temple, [43] listen from your home in heaven and answer their prayers. Then everyone on earth will worship you, just like your people Israel, and they will know that I have built this temple to honour you.

[44] Our LORD, sometimes you will order your people to attack their enemies. Then your people will turn towards this temple I have built for you in your chosen city, and they will pray to you. [45] Answer their prayers from heaven and give them victory.

[46] Everyone sins. But when your people sin against you, suppose you get angry enough to let their enemies drag them away to foreign countries. [47-49] Later, they may feel sorry for what they did and ask your forgiveness. Answer them when they pray towards this temple I have built for you in your chosen city, here in this land you gave their ancestors. From your home in heaven, listen to their sincere prayers and do what they ask. [50] Forgive your people no matter how much they have sinned against you. Make the enemies who defeated them be kind to them. [51] Remember, they are the people you chose and rescued from Egypt that was like a blazing fire to them.

[52] I am your servant, and the people of Israel belong to you. So listen when any of us pray and cry out for your help. [53] When you brought our ancestors out of Egypt, you told your servant Moses to say to them, "From all people on earth, the LORD God has chosen you to be his very own."

Solomon blesses the people

[54] When Solomon finished his prayer at the altar, he was kneeling with his arms lifted towards heaven. He stood up, [55] turned towards the people, blessed them, and said loudly:

[56] Praise the LORD! He has kept his promise and given us peace. Every good thing he promised to his servant Moses has happened.

---

*8.37 locusts: A type of grasshopper that comes in swarms and causes great damage to plant life.

See also: 8.25: 1 King 2.4.   8.27: 2 Chron 2.6.
8.29: Deut 12.11.

See also: 8.56: Deut 12.10; Josh 21.44–45.

⁵⁷ The LORD our God was with our ancestors to help them, and I pray that he will be with us and never abandon us. ⁵⁸ May the LORD help us obey him and follow all the laws and teachings he gave our ancestors.

⁵⁹ I pray that the LORD our God will remember my prayer day and night. May he help everyone in Israel each day, in whatever way we need it. ⁶⁰ Then every nation will know that the LORD is the only true God.

⁶¹ Obey the LORD our God and follow his commands with all your heart, just as you are doing today.

Solomon dedicates the temple

This is also told in 2 Chronicles 7.4–10

⁶²⁻⁶³ Solomon and the people dedicated the temple to the LORD by offering twenty-two thousand cattle and one hundred and twenty thousand sheep as sacrifices to ask the LORD's blessing.* ⁶⁴ On that day, Solomon dedicated the courtyard in front of the temple and made it acceptable for worship. He offered the sacrifices there because the bronze altar in front of the temple was too small.

⁶⁵ Solomon and the huge crowd celebrated the Festival of Shelters at the temple for seven days.' There were people from as far away as the Egyptian Gorge in the south and Lebo-Hamath in the north. ⁶⁶ Then on the eighth day, he sent everyone home. They said goodbye and left, very happy because of all the good things the LORD had done for his servant David and his people Israel.

Other events during Solomon's rule

CHAPTER 9

The LORD appears to Solomon again

This is also told in 2 Chronicles 7.11–22

¹ The LORD's temple and Solomon's palace were now finished, and Solomon had built everything he wanted. ² Some time later the LORD appeared to him again in a dream, just as he had done at Gibeon. ³ The LORD said:

I heard your prayer and what you asked me to do. This temple you have built is where I will be worshipped for ever. It belongs to me, and I will never stop watching over it.

⁴ You must obey me, as your father David did, and be honest and fair. Obey my laws and teachings, ⁵ and I will keep my promise to David that someone from your family will always be king of Israel.

⁶ But if you or any of your descendants disobey my commands or start worshipping foreign gods, ⁷ I will no longer let my people Israel live in this land I gave them. I will desert this temple where I said I would be worshipped. Then people everywhere will think this nation is only a joke and will make fun of it. ⁸ This temple will become a pile of rocks!' Everyone who walks by will be shocked, and they will ask, "Why did the LORD do such a terrible thing to his people and to this temple?" ⁹ Then they will answer, "We know why the LORD did this. The people of Israel rejected the LORD their God, who rescued their ancestors from Egypt, and they started worshipping other gods."

Other things Solomon did

This is also told in 2 Chronicles 8.1–18

¹⁰ It took twenty years for the LORD's temple and Solomon's palace to be built. ¹¹ Later, Solomon gave King Hiram of Tyre twenty towns in the region of Galilee to repay him for the cedar, pine, and gold he had given Solomon.

¹² When Hiram went to see the towns, he did not like them. ¹³ He said, "Solomon, my friend, are these the kind of towns you want to give me?" So Hiram called the region Cabul because he thought it was worthless.* ¹⁴ He sent Solomon only five thousand kilogrammes of gold in return.

¹⁵ After Solomon's workers had finished the temple and the palace, he ordered them to fill in the land on the east side of Jerusalem,* to build a wall around the city, and to rebuild the towns of Hazor, Megiddo, and Gezer. ¹⁶ Earlier, the king of Egypt had captured the town of Gezer; he burnt it to the ground and killed the Canaanite people living there. Then he gave it to his daughter as a wedding

---

*9.13 Cabul . . . worthless: Cabul sounds like the Hebrew word for "worthless".
*9.15 fill . . . Jerusalem: The Hebrew text has "build the Millo", which probably refers to a landfill to strengthen and extend the hill where the city was built.
See also: 9.5: 1 King 2.4. 9.8: 2 King 25.9; 2 Chron 36.19.

*8.62–63 sacrifices to ask the LORD's blessing: See Leviticus 3.1–17.
See also: 9.2: 1 King 3.5; 2 Chron 1.7.

present when she married Solomon. 17 So Solomon had the town rebuilt.

Solomon made his workers rebuild Lower Beth-Horon, 18 Baalath, and Tamar in the desert of Judah. 19 They also built towns where he could keep his supplies and his chariots and horses. Solomon made them build whatever he wanted in Jerusalem, Lebanon, and anywhere in his kingdom.

20-22 Solomon did not force the Israelites to do his work. They were his soldiers, officials, leaders, commanders, chariot captains, and chariot drivers. But he did make slaves of the Amorites, Hittites, Perizzites, Hivites, and Jebusites who were living in Israel. These were the descendants of those foreigners the Israelites could not destroy, and they remained Israel's slaves.

23 Solomon appointed five hundred and fifty officers to be in charge of his workers and to watch over his building projects.

24 Solomon's wife, the daughter of the king of Egypt, moved from the older part of Jerusalem' to her new palace. Then Solomon had the land on the east side of Jerusalem filled in.*

25 Three times a year, Solomon burnt incense and offered sacrifices to the LORD on the altar he had built.

Solomon had now finished building the LORD's temple.

26 He also had a lot of ships at Ezion-Geber, a town in Edom near Eloth on the Red Sea.*

27-28 King Hiram let some of his experienced sailors go to the country of Ophir* with Solomon's own sailors, and they brought back about fourteen thousand kilogrammes of gold for Solomon.

CHAPTER 10

The Queen of Sheba visits Solomon

This is also told in 2 Chronicles 9.1–12

1 The Queen of Sheba heard how famous Solomon was, so she went to Jerusalem to test him with difficult questions. 2 She took along several of her officials, and she loaded her camels with gifts of spices, jewels, and gold. When she arrived, she and Solomon talked about everything she could think of. 3 He answered every question, no matter how difficult it was.

4-5 The Queen was amazed at Solomon's wisdom. She was breathless when she saw his palace, the food on his table, his officials, his servants in their uniforms, the people who served his food, and the sacrifices he offered at the LORD's temple. 6 She said:

Solomon, in my own country I had heard about your wisdom and all you've done. 7 But I didn't believe it until I saw it with my own eyes! And there's so much I didn't hear about. You are wiser and richer than I was told. 8 Your wives' and officials are lucky to be here where they can listen to the wise things you say.

9 I praise the LORD your God. He is pleased with you and has made you king of Israel. The LORD loves Israel, so he has given them a king who will rule fairly and honestly.

10 The Queen of Sheba gave Solomon more than four thousand kilogrammes of gold, many jewels, and more spices than anyone had ever brought into Israel.

11-13 In return, Solomon gave her the gifts he would have given any other ruler, but he also gave her everything else she wanted. Then she and her officials went back to their own country.

Solomon's wealth

This is also told in 2 Chronicles 9.13–28

King Hiram's ships brought gold, juniper wood, and jewels from the country of Ophir. Solomon used the wood to make steps' for the temple and palace, and harps and other stringed instruments for the musicians. It was the best juniper wood anyone in Israel had ever seen.

14 Solomon received almost twenty-three thousand kilogrammes of gold a year. 15 The merchants and traders, as well as the kings of Arabia and rulers from Israel, also gave him gold.

16 Solomon made two hundred gold shields and used almost seven kilogrammes of gold for each one. 17 He also made three hundred smaller gold shields, using almost two kilogrammes for each one, and he put the shields in his palace in Forest Hall.

18 His throne was made of ivory and covered with pure gold. 19-20 The back of the throne was rounded at the top, and it had

---

*9.24 the land . . . filled in: See the note at 9.15.
*9.26 Red Sea: Hebrew yam suph, here referring to the Gulf of Aqaba, since the term is extended to include the north-eastern arm of the Red Sea (see also the note at Exodus 13.11).
*9.27–28 Ophir: The location of this place is not known.
See also: 9.25: Exod 23.17; 34.23; Deut 16.16.
10.1–10: Matt 12.42; Luke 11.31.

Viewpoints

Honour and obey
God through your actions and
he will be glorified

Contributed by Deborah F

'I praise the LORD your God. He is pleased with you and has made you king of Israel.'

The queen of Sheba was visiting Solomon to test his wisdom that she had heard so much about. She asked him everything she could think of and no matter how hard it was, he answered it.

God had given Solomon the wisdom which he asked for and because he chose his gift wisely God blessed him tremendously with riches, respect and a long life, provided that Solomon obeyed God and followed his commands. God made him 'greater than any other king'.

Solomon pleased God with his actions and the LORD was pleased with him. Through Solomon, the Lord was honoured as the queen of Sheba praised him.

In the same way, when we honour and obey God through our actions, he will bless us and he will be glorified. Our actions have consequences and if we choose wisely, other people will praise God because of them and we too will receive so much blessing from God.

More...

Wisdom p.548
Choices p.210
Living truthfully p.1070

 Anorak corner

The temple

1. What was in the most holy place?
2. What was kept in the sacred chest?
3. What was torn when Jesus died?
4. What age was Jesus when he was found teaching in the temple?
5. What did Jesus do to the temple traders?
(Answers on p.1431)

arm rests on each side. There was a statue of a lion on both sides of the throne, and there was a statue of a lion at both ends of each of the six steps leading up to the throne. No other throne in the world was like Solomon's.

²¹ Since silver was almost worthless in those days, everything was made of gold, even the cups and dishes used in Forest Hall.

²² Solomon had a lot of seagoing ships.* Every three years he sent them out with Hiram's ships to bring back gold, silver, and ivory, as well as monkeys and peacocks.♦

²³ He was the richest and wisest king in the world. ²⁴ People from every nation wanted to hear the wisdom God had given him. ²⁵ Year after year people came and brought gifts of silver and gold, as well as clothes, weapons, spices, horses, or mules.

²⁶ Solomon had one thousand four hundred chariots and twelve thousand horses that he kept in Jerusalem and other towns.

²⁷ While he was king, there was silver everywhere in Jerusalem, and cedar was as common as ordinary sycamore trees in the foothills.

²⁸⁻²⁹ Solomon's merchants bought his horses and chariots in the regions of Musri and Kue.* They paid about six hundred pieces of silver for a chariot and a hundred and fifty pieces of silver for a horse. They also sold horses and chariots to the Hittite and Syrian kings.

Solomon's unfaithfulness, enemies, and death

CHAPTER 11

Solomon disobeys the LORD

¹⁻² The LORD did not want the Israelites to worship foreign gods, so he had warned them not to marry anyone who was not from Israel.

Solomon loved his wife, the daughter of the king of Egypt. But he also loved some

---

*10.22 seagoing ships: The Hebrew text has "ships of Tarshish", which may have been a Phoenician city in Spain. "Ships of Tarshish" probably means large, seagoing ships.
*10.28–29 Musri and Kue: Hebrew "Egypt and Kue". Musri and Kue were regions in what is today south-east Turkey.

See also: 10.26: 1 King 4.26. 10.27: Deut 17.17.
10.28: Deut 17.16. 11.1: Deut 17.17. 11.2: Exod 34.16;
Deut 7.3–4.

women from Moab, Ammon, and Edom, and others from Sidon and the land of the Hittites. 3-4 Seven hundred of his wives were daughters of kings, but he also married three hundred other women.*

As Solomon got older, some of his wives led him to worship their gods. He wasn't like his father David, who had worshipped only the LORD God. 5 Solomon also worshipped Astarte the goddess of Sidon, and Milcom the disgusting god of Ammon. 6 Solomon's father had obeyed the LORD with all his heart, but Solomon disobeyed and did what the LORD hated.

7 Solomon built shrines on a hill east of Jerusalem to worship Chemosh the disgusting god of Moab, and Molech the disgusting god of Ammon. 8 In fact, he built a shrine for each of his foreign wives, so all of them could burn incense and offer sacrifices to their own gods.

9-10 The LORD God of Israel had appeared to Solomon twice and warned him not to worship foreign gods. But Solomon disobeyed and did it anyway. This made the LORD very angry, 11 and he said to Solomon:

You did what you wanted and not what I told you to do. Now I'm going to take your kingdom from you and give it to one of your officials. 12 But because David was your father, you will remain king as long as you live. I will wait until your son becomes king, then I will take the kingdom from him. 13 When I do, I will still let him rule one tribe, because I have not forgotten that David was my servant and Jerusalem is my city.

Hadad becomes an enemy of Solomon

14 Hadad was from the royal family of Edom, and here is how the LORD made him Solomon's enemy:

15-16 Some time earlier, when David conquered the nation of Edom,* Joab his army commander went there to bury those who had died in battle. Joab and his soldiers stayed in Edom six months, and during that time they killed every man and boy who lived there.

17-19 Hadad was a boy at the time, but he escaped to Midian with some of his father's officials. At Paran some other men joined

them, and they went to the king of Egypt. The king liked Hadad and gave him food, some land, and a house, and even let him marry the sister of Queen Tahpenes. 20 Hadad and his wife had a son named Genubath, and the queen let the boy grow up in the palace with her own children.

21 When Hadad heard that David and Joab were dead, he said to the king, "Your Majesty, please let me go back to my own country."

22 "Why?" asked the king. "Do you want something I haven't given you?"

"No, I just want to go home."

Rezon becomes an enemy of Solomon

23 Here is how God made Rezon son of Eliada an enemy of Solomon:

Rezon had run away from his master, King Hadadezer of Zobah. 24-25 He formed his own small army and became its leader after David had defeated Hadadezer's troops.* Then Rezon and his army went to Damascus, where he became the ruler of Syria and an enemy of Israel.

Both Hadad and Rezon were enemies of Israel while Solomon was king, and they caused him a lot of trouble.

The LORD makes a promise to Jeroboam

26 Jeroboam was from the town of Zeredah in Ephraim. His father Nebat had died, but his mother Zeruah was still alive. Jeroboam was one of Solomon's officials, but even he rebelled against Solomon. 27 Here is how it happened:

While Solomon's workers were filling in the land on the east side of Jerusalem* and repairing the city walls, 28 Solomon noticed that Jeroboam was a hard worker. So he put Jeroboam in charge of the work force from Manasseh and Ephraim.

29-30 One day when Jeroboam was leaving Jerusalem, he met Ahijah, a prophet from Shiloh. No one else was anywhere around. Suddenly, Ahijah took off his new coat and ripped it into twelve pieces. 31 Then he said:

Jeroboam, take ten pieces of this coat and listen to what the LORD God of Israel says to you. "Jeroboam, I am the LORD God, and I am about to take Solomon's kingdom from him and give you ten tribes

---

*11.3-4 other women: This translates a Hebrew word for a woman who was legally bound to a man, but without the full privileges of a wife.
*11.15-16 Edom: See 2 Samuel 8.13-14.

*11.24-25 troops: See 2 Samuel 8.3-6.
*11.27 filling . . . Jerusalem: See the note at 9.15.

to rule. [32] But Solomon will still rule one tribe,* since he is the son of David my servant, and Jerusalem is my chosen city.

[33] "Solomon and the Israelites are not like their ancestor David. They will not listen to me, obey me, or do what is right. They have turned from me to worship Astarte the goddess of Sidon, Chemosh the god of Moab, and Milcom the god of Ammon.

[34] "Solomon is David's son, and David was my chosen leader, who did what I commanded. So I will let Solomon be king until he dies. [35] Then I will give you ten tribes to rule, [36] but Solomon's son will still rule one tribe. This way, my servant David will always have a descendant ruling in Jerusalem, the city where I have chosen to be worshipped.

[37] "You will be king of Israel and will rule every nation you want. [38] I'll help you if you obey me. And if you do what I say, as my servant David did, I will always let someone from your family rule in Israel, just as someone from David's family will always rule in Judah. The nation of Israel will be yours.

[39] "I will punish the descendants of David, but not for ever."

[40] When Solomon learnt what the LORD had told Jeroboam, Solomon tried to kill Jeroboam. But he escaped to King Shishak of Egypt and stayed there until Solomon died.

Solomon dies

This is also told in 2 Chronicles 9.29–31

[41] Everything else Solomon did while he was king is written in the book about him and his wisdom. [42] After he had ruled forty years from Jerusalem, [43] he died and was buried there in the city of his father David. His son Rehoboam then became king.

The northern tribes of Israel rebel against King Rehoboam

CHAPTER 12

Some of the people rebel against Rehoboam

This is also told in 2 Chronicles 10.1–19

[1] Rehoboam went to Shechem where everyone was waiting to crown him king.

[2] Jeroboam son of Nebat heard what was happening, and he stayed in Egypt,' where he had gone to hide from Solomon. [3] But the people from the northern tribes of Israel sent for him. Then together they went to Rehoboam and said, [4] "Your father Solomon forced us to work very hard. But if you make our work easier, we will serve you and do whatever you ask."

[5] "Give me three days to think about it," Rehoboam replied, "then come back for my answer." So the people left.

[6] Rehoboam went to some leaders who had been his father's senior officials, and he asked them, "What should I tell these people?"

[7] They answered, "If you want them to serve and obey you, then you should do what they ask today. Tell them you will make their work easier."

[8] But Rehoboam refused their advice and went to the younger men who had grown up with him and were now his officials. [9] He asked, "What do you think I should say to these people who asked me to make their work easier?"

[10] His younger advisers said:

Here's what we think you should say to them: "Compared to me, my father was weak.' [11] He made you work hard, but I'll make you work even harder. He punished you with whips, but I'll use whips with pieces of sharp metal!"

[12] Three days later, Jeroboam and the others came back. [13] Rehoboam ignored the advice of the older advisers. [14] He spoke bluntly and told them exactly what his own advisers had suggested: "My father made you work hard, but I'll make you work even harder. He punished you with whips, but I'll use whips with pieces of sharp metal!"

---

*11.31–32 ten tribes . . . one tribe: By this time the tribe of Simeon had become part of the tribe of Judah. "One tribe" refers to Judah. Instead of "one tribe", one ancient translation has "two tribes".

Big ideas

Israel and Judah

In a strange way, one of Solomon's greatest triumphs was also the kingdom's ruin.

When he built the temple, Solomon used some tribes a lot more harshly than others. He imposed unjust taxes and used some Israelites as forced labour. And people resented his extravagance. When Solomon's son Rehoboam took over, they wanted assurances that things would change.

Rehoboam refused. In fact, he said he'd be even harder on them than his father. Which goes to show that he hadn't inherited any of his father's wisdom. Immediately the 10 northern tribes split away from the 2 southern tribes.

The northern kingdom remained as Israel, while the southern kingdom called itself Judah, after its biggest tribe. (So, from here on in the Old Testament, when you read of Israel, it mainly refers to the northern kingdom – the ten tribes. And Judah means the southern kingdom – the two tribes.)

Judah

The southern kingdom was based around the territory originally assigned to the tribes of Judah and Benjamin. The capital was the city of Jerusalem – David's city – with its temple and palace. Judah's kings all came from the royal line of David, although that didn't stop many of them being thoroughly evil. Judah was the poorer of the two nations, especially after the wealth that Solomon had piled up in Jerusalem was carried away by the Egyptians.

Israel

Israel's capital was first Bethel, and then Samaria. Israel was always the more unstable of the two countries, with a history of palace revolts, bloodfeuds, assassinations and masses of very bad kings. A number of different families seizing the throne.

More...

15-19 When the people realized that Rehoboam would not listen to them, they shouted: "We don't have to be loyal to David's family. We can do what we want. Come on, people of Israel, let's go home! Rehoboam can rule his own people."

Adoniram' was in charge of the forced labour, and Rehoboam sent him to talk to the people. But they stoned him to death. Then Rehoboam ran to his chariot and hurried back to Jerusalem.

So the people from the northern tribes of Israel went home, leaving Rehoboam to rule only the people from the towns in Judah. Ever since that day, the people of Israel have opposed David's family in Judah. All this happened just as the LORD's prophet Ahijah had told Jeroboam.

20 When the Israelites heard that Jeroboam was back, they called everyone together. Then they sent for Jeroboam and made him king of Israel. Only the people from the tribe of Judah* remained loyal to David's family.

Shemaiah warns Rehoboam

This is also told in 2 Chronicles 11.1–4

21 After Rehoboam returned to Jerusalem, he decided to attack Israel and take control of the whole country. So he called together one hundred and eighty thousand soldiers from the tribes of Judah and Benjamin.

22 Meanwhile, God told Shemaiah the prophet **23** to give Rehoboam and everyone from Judah and Benjamin this warning: **24** "Don't go to war against the people from Israel — they are your relatives. Go home! I am the LORD, and I made these things happen."

Rehoboam and his army obeyed the LORD and went home.

King Jeroboam of Israel makes two gold statues of calves

25 Jeroboam rebuilt Shechem in Ephraim and made it a stronger town, then he moved there. He also fortified the town of Penuel.

26-27 One day, Jeroboam started thinking, "Everyone in Israel still goes to the temple in

---

*12.20 Israelites ... Israel ... Judah:** From this time on, "Israel" usually refers to the northern kingdom, and "Israelites" refers to the people who lived there. The southern kingdom is called "Judah".

See also: 12.16: 2 Sam 20.1.

Jerusalem to offer sacrifices to the LORD. What if they become loyal to David's family again? They will kill me and accept Rehoboam as their king."

28 Jeroboam asked for advice and then made two gold statues of calves. He showed them to the people and said, "Listen everyone! You won't have to go to Jerusalem to worship any more. Here are your gods' who rescued you from Egypt." 29-30 Then he put one of the gold calves in the town of Bethel. He put the other one in the town of Dan, and the crowd walked out in front as the calf was taken there.' What Jeroboam did was a terrible sin.

31 Jeroboam built small places of worship at the shrines' and appointed men who were not from the tribe of Levi to serve as priests. 32-33 He also decided to start a new festival for the Israelites on the fifteenth day of the eighth month, just like the one in Judah.* On that day, Jeroboam went to Bethel and offered sacrifices on the altar to the gold calf he had put there. Then he assigned the priests their duties.

Prophets condemn Jeroboam

CHAPTER 13

A prophet condemns the altar at Bethel

1-2 One day, Jeroboam was standing at the altar in Bethel, ready to make an offering. Suddenly one of God's prophets' arrived from Judah and shouted:

> The LORD sent me with a message about this altar. A child named Josiah will be born into David's family. He will sacrifice on this altar the priests who make offerings here, and human bones will be burnt on it.

> 3 You will know that the LORD has said these things when the altar splits in half, and the ashes on it fall to the ground.

4 Jeroboam pointed at the prophet and shouted, "Grab him!" But straight away, Jeroboam's hand became stiff, and he could not move it. 5 The altar split in half, and the ashes fell to the ground, just as the prophet had warned.

6 "Please pray to the LORD your God and ask him to heal my hand," Jeroboam begged.

The prophet prayed, and Jeroboam's hand was healed.

7 "Come home with me and eat something," Jeroboam said. "I want to give you a gift for what you have done."

8 "No, I wouldn't go with you, even if you offered me half of your kingdom. I won't eat or drink here either. 9 The LORD said I can't eat or drink anything and that I can't go home the same way I came." 10 Then he started home down a different road.

An old prophet from Bethel

11 At that time an old prophet lived in Bethel, and one of his sons told him what the prophet from Judah had said and done.

12 "Show me which way he went," the old prophet said, and his sons pointed out the road. 13 "Put a saddle on my donkey," he told them. After they did, he got on the donkey 14 and rode off to look for the prophet from Judah.

The old prophet found him sitting under an oak tree and asked, "Are you the prophet from Judah?"

"Yes, I am."

15 "Come home with me," the old prophet said, "and have something to eat."

16 "I can't go back with you," the prophet replied, "and I can't eat or drink anything with you. 17 The LORD warned me not to eat or drink or to go home the same way I came."

18 The old prophet said, "I'm a prophet too. One of the LORD's angels told me to take you to my house and give you something to eat and drink."

The prophet from Judah did not know that the old prophet was lying, 19 so he went home with him and ate and drank.

20 During the meal the LORD gave the old prophet 21 a message for the prophet from Judah:

> Listen to the LORD's message. You have disobeyed the LORD your God. 22 He told you not to eat or drink anything here, but you came home and ate with me. And so, when you die, your body won't be buried in your family tomb.

23 After the meal the old prophet got a donkey ready, 24 and the prophet from Judah left. Along the way, a lion attacked and killed him, and the donkey and the lion stood there beside his dead body.

---

*12.32–33 the one in Judah:** This probably refers to the Festival of Shelters.

See also: 12.28: Exod 32.4.   **12.32–33:** Lev 23.33–34. **13.2:** 2 King 23.15–16.

Before and after the split

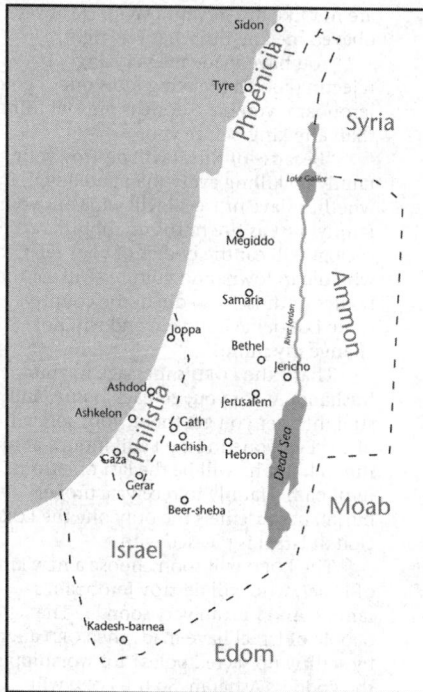

Under David and Solomon, the kingdom of Israel reached its biggest extent.

David captured Jerusalem and established it as his capital city. He also extended Israel's boundaries east of the Jordan, subdued the Philistines and forced surrounding countries such as Edom, Syria and Moab to pay tribute money.

Solomon instigated lavish and expensive building projects, which he paid for by raising taxes. This caused some resentment among the northern tribes – especially when they noticed that Judah, Solomon's tribe, paid a lot less than the others.

After Solomon's death, the northern tribes rebelled against Solomon's son and the kingdom split into two. Solomon's son Rehoboam became the king of Judah, the southern kingdom. The northern kingdom retained the name Israel and was ruled by Jeroboam.

The two countries lived alongside each other for the next 200 years or so. Under subsequent kings the countries diminished in size and lost their power and influence, not least because they turned away from God and worshipped false idols. Israel was eventually destroyed by the Assyrians, while Judah struggled on for another 150 years before it was conquered by the Babylonians.

25 Some people walked by and saw the body with the lion standing there. They ran into Bethel, telling everyone what they had seen.

26 When the old prophet heard the news, he said, "That must be the prophet from Judah. The LORD warned him, but he disobeyed. So the LORD sent a lion to kill him."

27 The old prophet told his sons to saddle his donkey, and when it was ready, 28 he left. He found the body lying on the road, with the donkey and lion standing there. The lion had not eaten the body or attacked the donkey. 29 The old prophet picked up the body, put it on his own donkey, and took it back to Bethel, so he could bury it and mourn for the prophet from Judah.

30 He buried the body in his own family tomb and cried for the prophet. 31 He said to his sons, "When I die, bury my body next to this prophet. 32 I'm sure that everything he said about the altar in Bethel and the shrines in Samaria will happen."

33 But Jeroboam kept on doing evil things. He appointed men to be priests at the local shrines, even if they were not Levites. In fact, anyone who wanted to be a priest could be one. 34 This sinful thing led to the downfall of his kingdom.

CHAPTER 14

Jeroboam's son dies

1 About the same time, Abijah son of Jeroboam got sick. 2-3 Jeroboam told his wife:

Disguise yourself so no one will know you're my wife, then go to Shiloh, where the prophet Ahijah lives. Take him ten loaves of bread, some small cakes, and honey, and ask him what will happen to our son. He can tell you, because he's the one who told me I would become king.

4 She got ready and left for Ahijah's house in Shiloh.

Ahijah was now old and blind, 5 but the LORD told him, "Jeroboam's wife is coming to ask about her son. I will tell you what to say to her."

Jeroboam's wife came to Ahijah's house, pretending to be someone else. 6 But when Ahijah heard her walking up to the door, he said:

Come in! I know you're Jeroboam's wife — why are you pretending to be someone else? I have some bad news for you. 7 Give your husband this message from the LORD God of Israel: "Jeroboam, you know that I, the LORD, chose you over anyone else to be the leader of my people Israel. 8 I even took David's kingdom away from his family and gave it to you. But you are not like my servant David. He always obeyed me and did what was right.

9 "You have made me very angry by rejecting me and making idols out of gold. Jeroboam, you have done more evil things than any king before you.

10 "Because of this, I will destroy your family by killing every man and boy in it, whether slave or free. I will wipe out your family, just as fire burns up rubbish. 11 Dogs will eat the bodies of your relatives who die in town, and vultures will eat the bodies of those who die in the country. I, the LORD, have spoken and will not change my mind!"

12 That's the LORD's message to your husband. As for you, go back home, and straight after you get there, your son will die. 13 Everyone in Israel will mourn at his funeral. But he will be the last one from Jeroboam's family to receive a proper burial, because he's the only one the LORD God of Israel is pleased with.

14 The LORD will soon choose a new king of Israel, who will destroy Jeroboam's family. And I mean very soon.' 15 The people of Israel have made the LORD angry by setting up sacred poles* for worshipping the goddess Asherah. So the LORD will punish them until they shake like grass in a stream. He will take them out of the land he gave to their ancestors, then scatter them as far away as the River Euphrates. 16 Jeroboam sinned and caused the Israelites to sin. Now the LORD will desert Israel.

17 Jeroboam's wife left and went back home to the town of Tirzah. As soon as she set foot in her house, her son died. 18 Everyone in Israel came and mourned at his funeral, just as the LORD's servant Ahijah had said.

Jeroboam dies

19 Everything else Jeroboam did while he was king, including the battles he won, is written in *The History of the Kings of Israel*. 20 He was king of Israel for twenty-two years, then he died, and his son Nadab became king.

---

*14.15 sacred poles: Or "trees", used as symbols of Asherah, the goddess of fertility.
See also: 14.10: 1 King 15.29.

Kings of Judah and Israel

King Rehoboam of Judah

This is also told in 2 Chronicles 11.5–12.16

²¹ Rehoboam son of Solomon was forty-one years old when he became king of Judah, and he ruled seventeen years from Jerusalem, the city where the LORD had chosen to be worshipped. His mother Naamah was from Ammon.

²² The people of Judah disobeyed the LORD and made him even angrier than their ancestors had. ²³ They also built their own local shrines⟩ and stone images of foreign gods, and they set up sacred poles* for worshipping the goddess Asherah on every hill and in the shade of large trees. ²⁴ Even worse, they allowed prostitutes* at the shrines, and followed the disgusting customs of the foreign nations that the LORD had forced out of Canaan.

²⁵ After Rehoboam had been king for four years, King Shishak of Egypt attacked Jerusalem. ²⁶ He took everything of value from the temple and the palace, including Solomon's gold shields.

²⁷ Rehoboam had bronze shields made to replace the gold ones, and he ordered the guards at the city gates to keep them safe. ²⁸ Whenever Rehoboam went to the LORD's temple, the guards carried the shields. But they always took them back to the guardroom as soon as he had finished.

²⁹ Everything else Rehoboam did while he was king is written in *The History of the Kings of Judah*. ³⁰ He and Jeroboam were constantly at war. ³¹ Rehoboam's mother Naamah was from Ammon, but when Rehoboam died, he was buried beside his ancestors in Jerusalem.⟩ His son Abijam then became king.

CHAPTER 15

King Abijam of Judah

This is also told in 2 Chronicles 13.1–22

¹ Abijam became king of Judah in Jeroboam's eighteenth year as king of Israel, ² and he ruled from Jerusalem for three years. His mother was Maacah the daughter of Abishalom.

³ Abijam did not truly obey the LORD his God as his ancestor David had done. Instead, he was sinful just like his father Rehoboam. ⁴⁻⁵ David had always obeyed the LORD's commands by doing right, except in the case of Uriah.* And since Abijam was David's great-grandson, the LORD kept Jerusalem safe and let Abijam have a son who would be the next king.

⁶⁻⁷ The war that had broken out between Rehoboam and Jeroboam continued during the time that Abijam was king.

Everything else Abijam did while he was king is written in *The History of the Kings of Judah*. ⁸ Abijam died and was buried in Jerusalem,⟩ and his son Asa became king.

King Asa of Judah

This is also told in 2 Chronicles 15.16–16.6,11–13

⁹ Asa became king of Judah in the twentieth year of Jeroboam's rule in Israel, ¹⁰ and he ruled forty-one years from Jerusalem. His grandmother was Maacah the daughter of Abishalom.

¹¹ Asa obeyed the LORD, as David had done. ¹² He forced the prostitutes* at the shrines to leave the country, and he got rid of the idols his ancestors had made. ¹³ His own grandmother Maacah had made an idol of Asherah, and Asa took it and burnt it in Kidron Valley. Then he removed Maacah from her position as queen mother.*

¹⁴ As long as Asa lived, he was completely faithful to the LORD, even though he did not destroy the local shrines. ¹⁵ He placed in the temple all the silver and gold objects that he and his father had dedicated to the LORD.

¹⁶ Asa was always at war with King Baasha of Israel. ¹⁷ One time, Baasha invaded Judah and captured the town of Ramah. He started making the town stronger, so he could put troops there to stop people from going in and out of Judah.

¹⁸ When Asa heard about this, he took the silver and gold from his palace and from the

---

*14.23 sacred poles: See the note at 14.15.

*14.24 prostitutes: Men and women sometimes served at the local shrines as prostitutes in the worship of Canaanite gods, but the LORD had forbidden the people of Israel to worship in this way (see Deuteronomy 23.17–18).

See also: 14.23: 2 King 17.9–10. 14.24: Deut 23.17. 14.25: 2 Chron 12.2–8. 14.26: 1 King 10.16–17; 2 Chron 9.15–16.

---

*15.4–5 Uriah: A Hittite who served in David's army; David had him killed so he could marry his wife Bathsheba (see 2 Samuel 11.1–27).

*15.12 prostitutes: See the note at 14.24.

*15.13 queen mother: Or "the mother of the king", an important position in biblical times (see 2.19).

See also: 15.4: 1 King 11.36. 15.5: 2 Sam 11.1–27. 15.6: 2 Chron 13.3–21. 15.12: 2 Chron 15.8–15.

LORD's temple. He gave it to some of his officials and sent them to Damascus with this message for King Benhadad' of Syria: ¹⁹ "Our fathers signed a peace treaty. Why don't we do the same thing? This silver and gold is a present for you. So, would you please break your treaty with Baasha and force him to leave my country?"

²⁰ Benhadad did what Asa asked and sent the Syrian army into Israel. They captured the towns of Ijon, Dan, and Abel-Bethmaacah, and the territories of Chinneroth and Naphtali. ²¹ When Baasha heard about it, he left Ramah and went back to Tirzah.

²² Asa ordered everyone in Judah to carry away the stones and wood Baasha had used to strengthen the town of Ramah. Then he used these same stones and wood to fortify the town of Geba in the territory of Benjamin and the town of Mizpah.

²³ Everything else Asa did while he was king, including his victories and the towns he rebuilt, is written in *The History of the Kings of Judah*. When he got older, he had a foot disease. ²⁴ Asa died and was buried in the tomb of his ancestors in Jerusalem.' His son Jehoshaphat then became king.

King Nadab of Israel

²⁵ Nadab son of Jeroboam became king of Israel in Asa's second year as king of Judah, and he ruled two years. ²⁶ Nadab disobeyed the LORD by following the evil example of his father, who had caused the Israelites to sin.

²⁷⁻²⁸ Baasha son of Ahijah was from the tribe of Issachar, and he made plans to kill Nadab. When Nadab and his army went to attack the town of Gibbethon in Philistia, Baasha killed Nadab there. So in the third year of Asa's rule, Baasha became king of Israel.

²⁹ The LORD's prophet Ahijah had earlier said, "Not one man or boy in Jeroboam's family will be left alive." And, as soon as Baasha became king, he killed everyone in Jeroboam's family, ³⁰ because Jeroboam had made the LORD God of Israel angry by sinning and causing the Israelites to sin.

³¹ Everything else Nadab did while he was king is written in *The History of the Kings of Israel*.

³² King Asa of Judah and King Baasha of Israel were always at war.

King Baasha of Israel

³³ Baasha son of Ahijah became king of Israel in Asa's third year as king of Judah, and he ruled twenty-four years from Tirzah.

³⁴ Baasha also disobeyed the LORD by acting like Jeroboam, who had caused the Israelites to sin.

CHAPTER 16

¹ The LORD sent Jehu son of Hanani to say to Baasha:

² Nobody knew who you were until I, the LORD, chose you' to be the leader of my people Israel. And now you're acting exactly like Jeroboam by causing the Israelites to sin. What you've done has made me so angry ³ that I will destroy you and your family, just as I did the family of Jeroboam. ⁴ Dogs will eat the bodies of your relatives who die in town, and vultures will eat the bodies of those who die in the country.

⁵⁻⁷ Baasha made the LORD very angry, and that's why the LORD gave Jehu this message for Baasha and his family. Baasha constantly disobeyed the LORD by following Jeroboam's sinful example — but even worse, he killed everyone in Jeroboam's family!

Everything else Baasha did while he was king, including his brave deeds, is written in *The History of the Kings of Israel*. Baasha died and was buried in Tirzah, and his son Elah became king.

King Elah of Israel

⁸ Elah son of Baasha became king of Israel after Asa had been king of Judah for twenty-five years, and he ruled from Tirzah for two years.

⁹ Zimri commanded half of Elah's chariots, and he made plans to kill Elah.

One day, Elah was in Tirzah, getting drunk at the home of Arza, his prime minister, ¹⁰ when Zimri went there and killed Elah. So Zimri became king in the twenty-seventh year of Asa's rule in Judah.

¹¹ As soon as Zimri became king, he killed everyone in Baasha's family. Not one man or boy in his family was left alive — even his close friends were killed. ¹² Baasha's family was completely wiped out, just as the LORD's prophet Jehu had warned. ¹³ Baasha and Elah sinned and caused the Israelites to sin, and they made the LORD angry by worshipping idols.

See also: 15.29: 1 King 14.10.

Life files

Elijah

Background: Not known. Came from Tishbe, which was probably in Israel.

What's the story?

Elijah is the first great prophet of the divided kingdoms. With his rough garments and wild appearance, he was a kind of throwback – a reminder to Israel of the authentic faith they had thrown aside.

He predicted a drought for Israel – a sign of God's anger – and then left the country, perhaps indicating that God was 'leaving' Israel. After staying with a widow and performing miracles, he returned to Israel for a showdown between God and Baal at Mount Carmel. After that he was forced to flee, but God cared for him in the wilderness. In the end, Elijah didn't just die, God came to collect him.

What's the point?

Elijah's name means 'the LORD is my God,' which more or less sums up his message. His life was a fight between the forces of evil and the God of justice and love. Elijah presented the people of Israel with a stark choice: serve God or serve Baal. In his actions he demonstrated the power and presence of God, in contrast to the empty, barren Baal worship, but by doing so he made himself very unpopular. Queen Jezebel, who was responsible for much of the popularity of Baal worship, hated him, while King Ahab couldn't bear to meet him.

Elijah was an aggressive warrior for the Lord, and is not above humiliating and mocking his opponents. When the prophets at Mount Carmel cannot raise fire he suggests it is because their god has gone for a walk, or is sitting on the toilet (1 Kings 18.27). Elijah was a kind of spiritual successor to Moses. Just like Moses, he spent time in the wilderness (40 days in fact). Just like Moses, he 'sees' God on the mountain.

Elijah's presence in the country is an indication of God's presence. When he goes to live in the ravine at Kerith it is a sign that God himself has left Israel. Many of his miracles take place outside Israel – a sign that God's favour is resting on other nations. Elijah demonstrates God's power through a series of miracles. The most spectacular one was probably the raising of the widow's son at Zarephath, the first recorded instance of the raising of the dead in Scripture (1 Kings 17.7–24).

In spite of all this, Elijah is a very human figure. He got depressed and scared; he worried that his best wasn't good enough. But God worked through Elijah in powerful ways; and few figures in the Bible have had as close a relationship with God as this strange, hairy man from Tishbe.

Footsteps

A week with Elijah

Elijah predicts the drought: 1 Kings 17.1–7
Elijah helps the widow: 1 Kings 17.8–24
Elijah fights the prophets of Baal:
1 Kings 18.1–46
Elijah meets God in the wilderness:
1 Kings 19.1–18
Elijah appoints a successor:
1 Kings 19.19–21
Elijah condemns king Ahaziah:
2 Kings 1.1–18
Elijah is taken away by God: 2 Kings 2.1–18

More...

Prophecy p.730
All the kings of Israel p.419
Israel and Judah p.385
Elisha p.404

¹⁴ Everything else Elah did while he was king is written in *The History of the Kings of Israel.*

King Zimri of Israel

¹⁵⁻¹⁶ Zimri became king of Israel in Asa's twenty-seventh year as king of Judah, but he ruled only seven days from Tirzah.

Israel's army was camped near Gibbethon in Philistia under the command of Omri. The soldiers heard that Zimri had killed Elah, and they made Omri their king that same day. ¹⁷ At once, Omri and his army marched to Tirzah and attacked. ¹⁸ When Zimri saw that the town was captured, he ran into the strongest part of the palace and killed himself by setting it on fire. ¹⁹ Zimri had disobeyed the LORD by following the evil example of Jeroboam, who had caused the Israelites to sin.

²⁰ Everything else Zimri did while he was king, including his rebellion against Elah, is written in *The History of the Kings of Israel.*

King Omri of Israel

²¹ After Zimri died, some of the Israelites wanted Tibni son of Ginath to be king, but others wanted Omri. ²² Omri's followers were stronger than Tibni's, so Tibni was killed, and Omri became king of Israel ²³ in the thirty-first year of Asa's rule in Judah.

Omri ruled Israel for twelve years. The first six years he ruled from Tirzah, ²⁴ then he bought the hill of Samaria from Shemer for six thousand pieces of silver. He built a town there and named it Samaria, after Shemer who had owned the hill.

²⁵ Omri did more evil things than any king before him. ²⁶ He acted just like Jeroboam and made the LORD God of Israel angry by causing the Israelites to sin and to worship idols.

²⁷ Everything else Omri did while he was king, including his brave deeds, is written in *The History of the Kings of Israel.* ²⁸ Omri died and was buried in Samaria, and his son Ahab became king.

King Ahab of Israel

²⁹ Ahab son of Omri became king of Israel in the thirty-eighth year of Asa's rule in Judah, and he ruled twenty-two years from Samaria. ³⁰ Ahab did more things to disobey the LORD than any king before him. ³¹ He acted just like Jeroboam. Even worse, he married Jezebel the daughter of King Ethbaal of Sidon* and started worshipping Baal. ³² Ahab built an altar and temple for Baal in Samaria ³³ and set up a sacred pole* for worshipping the goddess Asherah. Ahab did more to make the LORD God of Israel angry than any king of Israel before him.

³⁴ While Ahab was king, a man from Bethel named Hiel rebuilt the town of Jericho. But while Hiel was laying the foundation for the town wall, his eldest son Abiram died. And while he was finishing the gates, his youngest son Segub died. This happened just as the LORD had told Joshua to say many years ago.*

Elijah the prophet

CHAPTER 17

Elijah stops the rain

¹ Elijah was a prophet from Tishbe in Gilead.' One day he went to King Ahab and said, "I'm a servant of the living LORD, the God of Israel. And I swear in his name that it won't rain until I say so. There won't even be any dew on the ground."

² Later, the LORD said to Elijah, ³ "Leave and go across the River Jordan so you can hide near Cherith Brook. ⁴ You can drink water from the brook, and eat the food I've told the ravens to bring you."

⁵ Elijah obeyed the LORD and went to live near Cherith Brook. ⁶ Ravens brought him bread and meat twice a day, and he drank water from the brook. ⁷ But after a while, it dried up because there was no rain.

Elijah helps a widow in Zarephath

⁸ The LORD told Elijah, ⁹ "Go to the town of Zarephath in Sidon and live there. I've told a widow in that town to give you food."

¹⁰ When Elijah came near the town gate of Zarephath, he saw a widow gathering sticks for a fire. "Would you please bring me a cup of water?" he asked. ¹¹ As she left to get it, he asked, "Would you also please bring me a piece of bread?"

---

*16.31 Sidon: One of the most important cities in Phoenicia. It was on the coast of the Mediterranean Sea, north of Israel, in what is today southern Lebanon.
*16.33 sacred pole: See the note at 14.15.
*16.34 a man from Bethel . . . ago: See Joshua 6.26.
See also: 16.34: Josh 6.26.   17.1: Jam 5.17.
17.9: Luke 4.25–26.

¹² The widow answered, "In the name of the living LORD your God, I swear that I don't have any bread. All I have is a handful of flour and a little olive oil. I'm on my way home now with these few sticks to cook what I have for my son and me. After that, we will starve to death."

¹³ Elijah said, "Everything will be fine. Do what you said. Go home and prepare something for yourself and your son. But first, please make a small piece of bread and bring it to me. ¹⁴ The LORD God of Israel has promised that your jar of flour won't run out and your bottle of oil won't dry up before he sends rain for the crops."

¹⁵ The widow went home and did exactly what Elijah had told her. She and Elijah and her family had enough food for a long time. ¹⁶ The LORD kept the promise that his prophet Elijah had made, and she did not run out of flour or oil.

Elijah brings a boy back to life

¹⁷ Several days later, the son of the woman who owned the house* got sick, and he kept getting worse, until finally he died.

¹⁸ The woman shouted at Elijah, "What have I done to you? I thought you were God's prophet. Did you come here to cause the death of my son as a reminder that I've sinned against God?"*

¹⁹ "Bring me your son," Elijah said. Then he took the boy from her arms and carried him upstairs to the room where he was staying. Elijah laid the boy on his bed ²⁰ and prayed, "LORD God, why did you do such a terrible thing to this woman? She's letting me stay here, and now you've let her son die." ²¹ Elijah stretched himself out over the boy three times, while praying, "LORD God, bring this boy back to life!"

²² The LORD answered Elijah's prayer, and the boy started breathing again. ²³ Elijah picked him up and carried him downstairs. He gave the boy to his mother and said, "Look, your son is alive."

²⁴ "You are God's prophet!" the woman replied. "Now I know that you really do speak for the LORD."

---

*17.17 the woman who owned the house: This may or may not be the same woman as the widow in verses 8–16.

*17.18 Did you . . . God: In ancient times people sometimes thought that if they sinned, something terrible would happen to them.

See also: 17.21: 2 King 4.34–35.

CHAPTER 18

Elijah proves he is the LORD's prophet

¹⁻² For three years no rain fell in Samaria, and there was almost nothing to eat anywhere. The LORD said to Elijah, "Go and meet with King Ahab. I will soon make it rain." So Elijah went to see Ahab.

³⁻⁴ At that time Obadiah was in charge of Ahab's palace, but he faithfully worshipped the LORD. In fact, when Jezebel was trying to kill the LORD's prophets, Obadiah hid a hundred of them in two caves and gave them food and water.

Ahab sent for Obadiah ⁵ and said, "We have to find something for our horses and mules to eat. If we don't, we will have to kill them. Let's look around every brook and spring in the country for some grass. ⁶ You go one way, and I'll go the other." Then they left in separate directions.

⁷ As Obadiah was walking along, he met Elijah. Obadiah recognized him, bowed down, and asked, "Elijah, is it really you?"

⁸ "Yes. Go and tell Ahab I'm here."

⁹ Obadiah replied:

King Ahab would kill me if I told him that. And I haven't even done anything wrong. ¹⁰ I swear to you in the name of the living LORD your God that the king has looked everywhere for you. He sent people to look in every country, and when they couldn't find you, he made the leader of each country swear that you were not in that country. ¹¹ Do you really want me to tell him you're here?

¹² What if the LORD's Spirit takes you away as soon as I leave? When Ahab comes to get you, he won't find you. Then he will surely kill me.

I have worshipped the LORD since I was a boy. ¹³ I even hid a hundred of the LORD's prophets in caves when Jezebel was trying to kill them. I also gave them food and water. ¹⁴ Do you really want me to tell Ahab you're here? He will kill me!

¹⁵ Elijah said, "I'm a servant of the living LORD All-Powerful, and I swear in his name that I will meet with Ahab today."

¹⁶ Obadiah left and told Ahab where to find Elijah.

Ahab went to meet Elijah, ¹⁷ and when he saw him, Ahab shouted, "There you are, the biggest troublemaker in Israel!"

¹⁸ Elijah answered:

You're the troublemaker — not me! You and your family have disobeyed the LORD's commands by worshipping Baal.

¹⁹ Call together everyone from Israel to meet me on Mount Carmel. Be sure to bring along the four hundred and fifty prophets of Baal and the four hundred prophets of Asherah who eat at Jezebel's table.

²⁰ Ahab got everyone together, then they went to meet Elijah on Mount Carmel. ²¹ Elijah stood in front of them and said, "How much longer will you try to have things both ways? If the LORD is God, worship him! But if Baal is God, worship him!"

The people did not say a word.

²² Then Elijah continued:

I am the LORD's only prophet, but Baal has four hundred and fifty prophets.

²³ Bring us two bulls. Baal's prophets can take one of them, kill it, and cut it into pieces. Then they can put the meat on the wood without lighting the fire. I will do the same thing with the other bull, and I won't light a fire under it either.

²⁴ The prophets of Baal will pray to their god, and I will pray to the LORD. The one who answers by starting the fire is God.

"That's a good idea," everyone agreed.

²⁵ Elijah said to Baal's prophets, "There are more of you, so you go first. Pick out a bull and get it ready, but don't light the fire. Then pray to your god."

²⁶ They chose their bull, then they got it ready and prayed to Baal all morning, asking him to start the fire. They danced around the altar and shouted, "Answer us, Baal!" But there was no answer.

²⁷ At midday, Elijah began making fun of them. "Pray louder!" he said. "Baal must be a god. Perhaps he's daydreaming or using the toilet or travelling somewhere. Or perhaps he's asleep, and you have to wake him up."

²⁸ The prophets kept shouting louder and louder, and they cut themselves with swords and knives until they were bleeding. This was the way they worshipped, ²⁹ and they kept it up all afternoon. But there was no answer of any kind.

³⁰ Elijah told everyone to gather around him while he repaired the LORD's altar. ³¹⁻³² Then he used twelve stones to build an altar in honour of the LORD. Each stone stood for one of the tribes of Israel, which was the name the LORD had given to their ancestor Jacob. Elijah dug a ditch around the altar, large enough to hold almost fourteen litres. ³³ He placed the wood on the altar, then they cut the bull into pieces and laid the meat on the wood.

He told the people, "Fill four large jars with water and pour it over the meat and the wood." After they did this, ³⁴ he told them to do it two more times. They did exactly as he said ³⁵ until finally, the water ran down the altar and filled the ditch.

³⁶ When it was time for the evening sacrifice, Elijah prayed:

Our LORD, you are the God of Abraham, Isaac, and Israel. Now, prove that you are the God of this nation,' and that I, your servant, have done this at your command. ³⁷ Please answer me, so these people will know that you are the LORD God, and that you will turn their hearts back to you.'

³⁸ The LORD immediately sent fire, and it burnt up the sacrifice, the wood, and the stones. It scorched the ground everywhere around the altar and dried up every drop of water in the ditch. ³⁹ When the crowd saw what had happened, they all bowed down and shouted, "The LORD is God! The LORD is God!"

⁴⁰ Just then, Elijah said, "Grab the prophets of Baal! Don't let any of them get away."

So the people captured the prophets and took them to the River Kishon, where Elijah killed every one of them.

It starts to rain

⁴¹ Elijah told Ahab, "Get something to eat and drink. I hear a heavy rain coming."

⁴² Ahab left, but Elijah climbed back to the top of Mount Carmel. Then he stooped down with his face almost to the ground ⁴³ and said to his servant, "Look towards the sea."

The servant left. And when he came back, he said, "I looked, but I didn't see anything." Elijah told him to look seven more times.

⁴⁴ After the seventh time the servant replied, "I see a small cloud coming this way. But it's no bigger than a fist."

Elijah told him, "Tell Ahab to get his chariot ready and start home now. Otherwise, the rain will stop him."

⁴⁵⁻⁴⁶ A few minutes later, it got very cloudy and windy, and rain started pouring down. So Elijah wrapped his coat around himself, and the LORD gave him strength to run all the way to Jezreel. Ahab followed him.

See also: 18.31: Gen 32.28; 35.10.

See also: 18.42–45: Jam 5.18.

Helpline

Help! I want to leave home

'It's time for me to go! I want independence! I want my freedom!'

I wonder what Elisha's Mum and Dad thought when he told them he was leaving?

Sooner or later, most of us will leave home. Sometimes it's because things at home are difficult and it would be better to leave. Sometimes it's simply a question of independence. Sometimes, like Elisha, there's the chance to do something exciting.

It's a big decision, so don't rush it. Stop and think. Talk it over with your parents. It's often an exciting prospect and we might even see it as the end to our problems. But will it really be that way? You might be keen to leave, but moving out might not be the catch-all solution that you think it is.

And recognise that independence has its upsides and its downsides. Yes, you get a certain amount of freedom, but you also have extra responsibilities.

Three things

Gentle

For you it's exciting. For your parents it can be depressing and sad. So be gentle and thoughtful. It can be upsetting for parents to say 'goodbye' to someone they've looked after and cared for for many years.

Peace

Try to leave on good terms with people. Storming out and 'slamming the door behind you' might not be the best move; for a start, if things go wrong, it will be very hard for you to move back in again.

Realism

It's your life now. No safety net any more. There will be no one to wake you up if you oversleep. And you're going to have to do your own washing up and laundry!

More...

Families p.1224
Help! My parents won't give me any freedom p.683

CHAPTER 19

Elijah runs away from Ahab and Jezebel

¹ Ahab told his wife Jezebel what Elijah had done and that he had killed the prophets. ² She sent a message to Elijah: "You killed my prophets. Now I'm going to kill you! I pray that the gods will punish me even more severely if I don't do it by this time tomorrow."

³ Elijah was afraid when he got her message, and he ran to the town of Beersheba in Judah. He left his servant there, ⁴ then walked another whole day into the desert. Finally, he came to a large bush and sat down in its shade. He begged the LORD, "I've had enough. Just let me die! I'm no better off than my ancestors." ⁵ Then he lay down in the shade and fell asleep.

Suddenly an angel woke him up and said, "Get up and eat." ⁶ Elijah looked around, and by his head was a jar of water and some baked bread. He sat up, ate and drank, then lay down and went back to sleep.

⁷ Soon the LORD's angel woke him again and said, "Get up and eat, or else you'll get too tired to travel." ⁸ So Elijah sat up and ate and drank.

The food and water made him strong enough to walk forty more days. At last, he reached Mount Sinai,' the mountain of God, ⁹ and he spent the night there in a cave.

The LORD appears to Elijah

While Elijah was on Mount Sinai, the LORD asked, "Elijah, why are you here?"

¹⁰ He answered, "LORD God All-Powerful, I've always done my best to obey you. But your people have broken their solemn promise to you. They have torn down your altars and killed all your prophets, except me. And now they are even trying to kill me!"

¹¹ "Go out and stand on the mountain," the LORD replied. "I want you to see me when I pass by."

All at once, a strong wind shook the mountain and shattered the rocks. But the LORD was not in the wind. Next, there was an earthquake, but the LORD was not in the earthquake. ¹² Then there was a fire, but the LORD was not in the fire.

Finally, there was a gentle breeze,' ¹³ and when Elijah heard it, he covered his face with his coat. He went out and stood at the entrance to the cave.

See also: 19.4: Jon 4.3. 19.10: Rom 11.3.

The LORD' asked, "Elijah, why are you here?"

¹⁴ Elijah answered, "LORD God All-Powerful, I've always done my best to obey you. But your people have broken their solemn promise to you. They have torn down your altars and killed all your prophets, except me. And now they are even trying to kill me!"

¹⁵ The LORD said:

Elijah, you can go back to the desert near Damascus. And when you get there, appoint* Hazael to be king of Syria. ¹⁶ Then appoint Jehu son of Nimshi to be king of Israel, and Elisha son of Shaphat' to take your place as my prophet.

¹⁷ Hazael will start killing the people who worship Baal. Jehu will kill those who escape from Hazael, and Elisha will kill those who escape from Jehu.

¹⁸ But seven thousand Israelites have refused to worship Baal, and they will live.

Elisha becomes Elijah's assistant

¹⁹ Elijah left and found Elisha ploughing a field with a pair of oxen. There were eleven other men in front of him, and each one was also ploughing with a pair of oxen. Elijah went over and put his own coat on Elisha.*

²⁰ Elisha stopped ploughing and ran after him. "Let me kiss my parents goodbye, then I'll go with you," he said.

"You can go," Elijah said. "But remember what I've done for you."

²¹ Elisha left and took his oxen with him. He killed them and boiled them over a fire he had made with the wood from his plough. He gave the meat to the people who were with him, and they ate it. Then he left with Elijah and became his assistant.

King Ahab and Queen Jezebel

CHAPTER 20

Syria attacks Israel

¹ King Benhadad of Syria* called his army together. He was joined by thirty-two other kings with their horses and chariots, and together they marched to Samaria and attacked. ² Benhadad sent a messenger to tell King Ahab of Israel, ³ "Ahab, give me your silver and gold, your wives,* and your strongest sons!"

⁴ "Your Majesty," Ahab replied, "everything I have is yours, including me."

⁵ Later, Benhadad sent another messenger to say to Ahab, "I have already told you to give me your silver and gold, your wives, and your children. ⁶ But tomorrow at this time, I will send my officials into your city to search your palace and the houses of your officials. They will take everything else that you' own."

⁷ Ahab called a meeting with the leaders of Israel and said, "Benhadad is causing real trouble. He told me to give him my wives and children, as well as my silver and gold. And I agreed."

⁸ "Don't listen to him!" they answered. "You don't have to do what he says."

⁹ So Ahab sent someone to tell Benhadad, "Your Majesty, I'll give you my silver and gold, and even my wives and children. But I won't let you have anything else."

When Benhadad got his answer, ¹⁰ he replied, "I'll completely destroy Samaria! There won't even be enough of it left for my soldiers to carry back in their hands. If I don't do it, I pray that the gods will punish me terribly."

¹¹ Ahab then answered, "Benhadad, don't boast before the fighting even begins. Wait and see if you live through it."

¹² Meanwhile, Benhadad and the other kings had been drinking in their tents. But when Ahab's reply came, he ordered his soldiers to prepare to attack Samaria, and they all got ready.

¹³ At that very moment, a prophet ran up to Ahab and said, "You can see that Benhadad's army is very strong. But the LORD has

---

*19.15 appoint: This would have included a ceremony in which olive oil would be poured on his head to show that he was now king.
*19.19 put . . . Elisha: This was a sign that Elijah wanted Elisha to follow him and become a prophet.
See also: 19.14: Rom 11.3. 19.15: 2 King 8.7–13. 19.16: 2 King 9.1–6. 19.18: Rom 11.4.

---

*20.1 King Benhadad of Syria: This is probably not the same Benhadad mentioned in 15.18–21.
*20.3 wives: Having more than one wife was allowed in those times.

promised to help you defeat them today. Then you will know that the LORD is in control."

¹⁴ "Who will fight the battle?" Ahab asked.

The prophet answered, "The young bodyguards who serve the district officials."

"But who will lead them into battle?" Ahab asked.

"You will!" the prophet replied.

¹⁵ So Ahab called together the two hundred and thirty-two young soldiers and the seven thousand troops in Israel's army, and he got them ready to fight the Syrians.

Israel defeats the Syrians

¹⁶⁻¹⁷ At midday, King Ahab and his Israelite army marched out of Samaria, with the young soldiers in front.

King Benhadad of Syria and the thirty-two kings with him were drunk when the scouts he had sent out ran up to his tent, shouting, "We just now saw soldiers marching out of Samaria!"

¹⁸ "Take them alive!" Benhadad ordered. "I don't care if they have come out to fight or to surrender."

¹⁹ The young soldiers led Israel's troops into battle, ²⁰ and each of them attacked and killed an enemy soldier. The rest of the Syrian army turned and ran, and the Israelites went after them. Benhadad and some others escaped on horses, ²¹ but Ahab and his soldiers followed them and captured* their horses and chariots.

Ahab and Israel's army crushed the Syrians.

²² Later, the prophet* went back and warned Ahab, "Benhadad will attack you again next spring. Build up your troops and make sure you have some good plans."

Syria attacks Israel again

²³ Meanwhile, Benhadad's officials went to him and explained:

Israel's gods are mountain gods. We fought Israel's army in the hills, and that's why they defeated us. But if we fight them on flat land, there's no way we can lose.

²⁴ Here's what you should do. First, get rid of those thirty-two kings and put army commanders in their places. ²⁵ Then get more soldiers, horses, and chariots, so your army will be as strong as it was before. We'll fight Israel's army on flat land and wipe them out.

Benhadad agreed and did what they suggested.

²⁶ In the spring, Benhadad got his army together, and they marched to the town of Aphek to attack Israel. ²⁷ The Israelites also prepared to fight. They marched out to meet the Syrians, and the two armies camped facing each other. The Syrians covered the whole area, but the Israelites looked like two little flocks of goats.

²⁸ The prophet went to Ahab and said, "The Syrians think the LORD is a god of the hills and not of the valleys. So he has promised to help you defeat their powerful army. Then you will know that the LORD is in control."

²⁹ For seven days the two armies stayed in their camps, facing each other. Then on the seventh day the fighting broke out, and before sunset the Israelites had killed one hundred thousand Syrian troops. ³⁰ The rest of the Syrian army ran back to Aphek, but the town wall fell and crushed twenty-seven thousand of them.

Benhadad also escaped to Aphek and hid in the back room of a house. ³¹ His officials said, "Your Majesty, we've heard that Israel's kings keep their agreements. We will wrap sackcloth around our waists, put ropes around our heads, and ask Ahab to let you live."

³² They dressed in sackcloth and put ropes on their heads, then they went to Ahab and said, "Your servant Benhadad asks you to let him live."

"Is he still alive?" Ahab asked. "Benhadad is like a brother to me."

³³ Benhadad's officials were trying to understand what Ahab was thinking, and when he said "brother," they quickly replied, "You're right! You and Benhadad are like brothers."

"Go and get him," Ahab said.

When Benhadad came out, Ahab asked him to climb up into his chariot.

³⁴ Benhadad said, "I'll give back the towns my father took from your father. And you can have shops in Damascus, just as my father had in Samaria."

Ahab replied, "If you do these things, I'll let you go free." Then they signed a peace treaty, and Ahab let Benhadad go.

A prophet condemns Ahab

³⁵ About this time the LORD commanded a prophet to say to a friend, "Hit me!" But the friend refused, ³⁶ and the prophet told him, "You disobeyed the LORD, and as soon as you walk away, a lion will kill you." The friend left, and suddenly a lion killed him.

---

*20.22 the prophet: See verse 13.

See also: 20.36: 1 King 13.24.

37 The prophet found someone else and said, "Hit me!" So this man beat him up.
38 The prophet left and put a bandage over his face to disguise himself. Then he went and stood beside the road, waiting for Ahab to pass by.
39 When Ahab went by, the prophet shouted, "Your Majesty, right in the heat of battle, someone brought a prisoner to me and told me to guard him. He said if the prisoner got away, I would either be killed or forced to pay three thousand pieces of silver.
40 But I got busy doing other things, and the prisoner escaped."

Ahab answered, "You will be punished just as you have said."
41 The man quickly tore the bandage off his face, and Ahab saw that he was one of the prophets. 42 The prophet said, "The LORD told you to kill Benhadad, but you let him go. Now you will die in his place, and your people will die in place of his people."
43 Ahab went back to Samaria, angry and depressed.

CHAPTER 21

Jezebel has Naboth killed

1 Naboth owned a vineyard in Jezreel near King Ahab's palace.
2 One day, Ahab said, "Naboth, your vineyard is near my palace. Give it to me so I can turn it into a vegetable garden. I'll give you a better vineyard or pay whatever you want for yours."
3 Naboth answered, "This vineyard has always been in my family. I won't let you have it."
4 So Ahab went home, angry and depressed because of what Naboth had told him. He lay on his bed, just staring at the wall and refusing to eat a thing.
5 Jezebel his wife came in and asked, "What's wrong? Why won't you eat?"
6 "I asked Naboth to sell me his vineyard or to let me give him a better one," Ahab replied. "And he told me I couldn't have it."
7 "Aren't you the king of Israel?" Jezebel asked. "Get out of bed and eat something! Don't worry, I'll get Naboth's vineyard for you."
8-10 Jezebel wrote a letter to each of the leaders of the town where Naboth lived. In the letters she said:

Call everyone together and tell them to go without eating* today. When they come together, give Naboth a seat at the front. Get two liars to sit facing him and swear that Naboth has cursed God and the king. Then take Naboth outside and stone him to death!

She signed Ahab's name to the letters and sealed them with his seal. Then she sent them to the town leaders.
11 After receiving her letters, they did exactly what she had asked. 12 They told the people that it was a day to go without eating, and when they all came together, they seated Naboth at the front. 13 The two liars came in and sat facing Naboth. Then they accused him of cursing God and the king, so the people dragged Naboth outside and stoned him to death.
14 The leaders of Jezreel sent a message back to Jezebel that said, "Naboth is dead."
15 As soon as Jezebel got their message, she told Ahab, "Now you can have the vineyard Naboth refused to sell. He's dead." 16 Ahab got up and went to take over the vineyard.

Elijah condemns Ahab

17 The LORD said to Elijah the prophet,
18 "King Ahab of Israel is in Naboth's vineyard right now, taking it over. 19 Go and tell him that I say, 'Ahab, you murdered Naboth and took his property. And so, in the very spot where dogs licked up Naboth's blood, they will lick up your blood.' "

When Elijah found him, 20 Ahab said, "So, my enemy, you've found me at last."

Elijah answered:

Yes, I have! Ahab, you have managed to do everything the LORD hates. 21 Now you will be punished. You and every man and boy in your family will die, whether slave or free. 22 Your whole family will be wiped out, just like the families of King Jeroboam and King Baasha. You've made the LORD very angry by sinning and causing the Israelites to sin.
23 And as for Jezebel, dogs will eat her body there in Jezreel. 24 Dogs will also eat the bodies of your relatives who die in town, and vultures will eat the bodies of those who die in the country.

---

*21.8-10 to go without eating: People sometimes came together to worship and to go without eating to show that they were sorry for their sins.
See also: 21.23: 2 King 9.36.

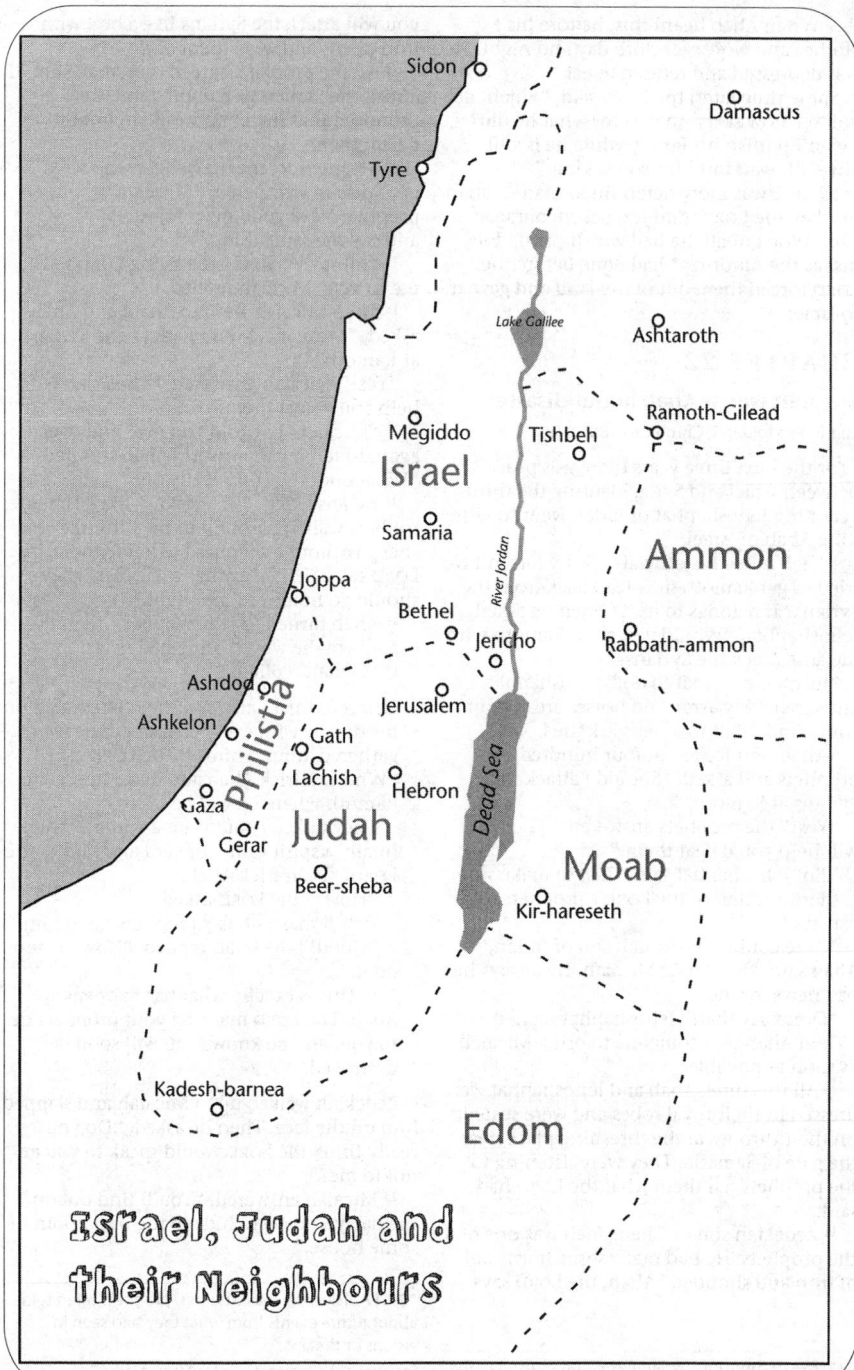

Israel, Judah and their Neighbours

25-29 When Ahab heard this, he tore his clothes and wore sackcloth day and night. He was depressed and refused to eat.

Some time later, the LORD said, "Elijah, do you see how sorry Ahab is for what he did? I won't punish his family while he is still alive. I'll wait until his son is king."

No one was more determined than Ahab to disobey the LORD. And Jezebel encouraged him. Worst of all, he had worshipped idols, just as the Amorites* had done before the LORD forced them out of the land and gave it to Israel.

CHAPTER 22

Micaiah warns Ahab about disaster

This is also told in 2 Chronicles 18.2–27

¹ For the next three years there was peace between Israel and Syria. ² During the third year King Jehoshaphat of Judah went to visit King Ahab of Israel.

³ Ahab asked his officials, "Why haven't we tried to get Ramoth in Gilead back from the Syrians? It belongs to us." ⁴ Then he asked Jehoshaphat, "Would you go to Ramoth with me and attack the Syrians?"

"Just tell me what to do," Jehoshaphat answered. "My army and horses are at your command. ⁵ But first, let's ask the LORD."

⁶ Ahab sent for about four hundred prophets and asked, "Should I attack the Syrians at Ramoth?"

"Yes!" the prophets answered. "The Lord will help you defeat them."

⁷ But Jehoshaphat said, "Just to make sure, is there another of the LORD's prophets we can ask?"

⁸ "We could ask Micaiah son of Imlah," Ahab said. "But I hate Micaiah. He always has bad news for me."

"Don't say that!" Jehoshaphat replied.
⁹ Then Ahab sent someone to bring Micaiah as soon as possible.

¹⁰ All this time, Ahab and Jehoshaphat were dressed in their royal robes and were seated on their thrones at the threshing place near the gate of Samaria. They were listening to the prophets tell them what the LORD had said.

¹¹ Zedekiah son of Chenaanah was one of the prophets. He had made some horns out of iron and shouted, "Ahab, the LORD says you will attack the Syrians like a bull with iron horns and wipe them out!"

¹² All the prophets agreed that Ahab should attack the Syrians at Ramoth, and they promised that the LORD would help him defeat them.

¹³ Meanwhile, the messenger who went to get Micaiah whispered, "Micaiah, all the prophets have good news for Ahab. Now go and say the same thing."

¹⁴ "I'll say whatever the living LORD tells me to say," Micaiah replied.

¹⁵ Then Micaiah went to Ahab, and Ahab asked, "Micaiah, should I attack the Syrians at Ramoth?"

"Yes!" Micaiah answered. "The LORD will help you defeat them."

¹⁶ "Micaiah, I've told you over and over again to tell me the truth!" Ahab shouted. "What does the LORD really say?"

¹⁷ He answered, "In a vision* I saw Israelite soldiers walking around in the hills like sheep without a shepherd to guide them. The LORD said, 'This army has no leader. They should go home and not fight.' "

¹⁸ Ahab turned to Jehoshaphat and said, "I told you he would bring bad news!"

¹⁹ Micaiah replied:

Listen to this! I also saw the LORD seated on his throne with every creature in heaven gathered around him. ²⁰ The LORD asked, "Who can trick Ahab and make him go to Ramoth where he will be killed?"

They talked about it for a while, ²¹ then finally a spirit came forward and said to the LORD, "I can trick Ahab."

"How?" the LORD asked.

²² "I'll make Ahab's prophets lie to him."

"Good!" the LORD replied. "Now go and do it."

²³ This is exactly what has happened, Ahab. The LORD made all your prophets lie to you, and he knows you will soon be destroyed.

²⁴ Zedekiah walked up to Micaiah and slapped him on the face. Then he asked, "Do you really think the LORD would speak to you and not to me?"

²⁵ Micaiah answered, "You'll find out on the day you have to hide in the back room of some house."

*22.17 vision: In ancient times, prophets often told about future events from what they had seen in visions or dreams.
See also: 22.17: Num 27.17; Matt 9.36; Mark 6.34. 22.19: Job 1.6; Isa 6.1.

²⁶ Ahab shouted, "Arrest Micaiah! Take him to Prince Joash and Governor Amon of Samaria. ²⁷ Tell them to put him in prison and to give him nothing but bread and water until I come back safely."

²⁸ Micaiah said, "If you do come back, I was wrong about what the LORD wanted me to say." Then he told the crowd, "Don't forget what I said!"

Ahab dies at Ramoth

This is also told in 2 Chronicles 18.28–34

²⁹ Ahab and Jehoshaphat led their armies to Ramoth in Gilead. ³⁰ Before they went into battle, Ahab said, "Jehoshaphat, I'll disguise myself, but you wear your royal robe." Then Ahab disguised himself and went into battle.

³¹ The king of Syria had ordered his thirty-two chariot commanders to attack only Ahab. ³² So when they saw Jehoshaphat in his robe, they thought he was Ahab and started to attack him. But when Jehoshaphat shouted out to them, ³³ they realized he wasn't Ahab, and they left him alone.

³⁴ However, during the fighting a soldier shot an arrow without even aiming, and it hit Ahab where two pieces of his armour joined. He shouted to his chariot driver, "I've been hit! Get me out of here!"

³⁵ The fighting lasted all day, with Ahab propped up in his chariot so he could see the Syrian troops. He bled so much that the bottom of the chariot was covered with blood, and by evening he was dead.

³⁶ As the sun was going down, someone in Israel's army shouted to the others, "Retreat! Go back home!"

³⁷ Ahab's body was taken to Samaria and buried there. ³⁸ Some workers washed his chariot near a spring in Samaria, and prostitutes washed themselves in his blood.◗ Dogs licked Ahab's blood off the ground, just as the LORD had warned.

³⁹ Everything else Ahab did while he was king, including the towns he strengthened and the palace he built and furnished with ivory, is written in *The History of the Kings of Israel*. ⁴⁰ Ahab died, and his son Ahaziah became king.

King Jehoshaphat of Judah and King Ahaziah of Israel

King Jehoshaphat of Judah

This is also told in 2 Chronicles 20.31–21.1

⁴¹ Jehoshaphat son of Asa became king of Judah in Ahab's fourth year as king of Israel. ⁴² Jehoshaphat was thirty-five years old when he became king, and he ruled from Jerusalem for twenty-five years. His mother was Azubah daughter of Shilhi.

^{43–46} Jehoshaphat obeyed the LORD, just as his father Asa had done, and during his rule he was at peace with the king of Israel.

He got rid of the rest of the prostitutes* from the local shrines, but he did not destroy the shrines, and they were still used as places for offering sacrifices.

Everything else Jehoshaphat did while he was king, including his brave deeds and military victories, is written in *The History of the Kings of Judah*.

⁴⁷ The country of Edom had no king at the time, so a lower official ruled the land.

⁴⁸ Jehoshaphat had seagoing ships* built to sail to Ophir for gold. But they were wrecked at Ezion-Geber and never sailed. ⁴⁹ Ahaziah son of Ahab offered to let his sailors go with Jehoshaphat's sailors, but Jehoshaphat refused.

⁵⁰ Jehoshaphat died and was buried beside his ancestors in Jerusalem,◗ and his son Jehoram became king.

King Ahaziah of Israel

⁵¹ Ahaziah son of Ahab became king of Israel in the seventeenth year of Jehoshaphat's rule in Judah, and he ruled two years from Samaria.

⁵² Ahaziah disobeyed the LORD, just as his father, his mother, and Jeroboam had done. They all led Israel to sin. ⁵³ Ahaziah worshipped Baal and made the LORD God of Israel very angry, just as his father had done.

---

*22.43–46 prostitutes: See the note at 14.24.
*22.48 seagoing ships: See the note at 10.22.

Additional notes

◗1.8 Shimei, Rei: Or "Shimei his adviser".
◗1.9 Crawling Rock: Or "Zoheleth Rock".
◗1.38 the two . . . bodyguards: The Hebrew text has "the Cherethites and the Pelethites", who were foreign soldiers hired by David to be part of his bodyguard.

‹1.44-45 David's special bodyguards: See the note at 1.38.

‹2.10-11 Jerusalem: Hebrew "the city of David".

‹2.22 And why . . . Joab: One possible meaning for the difficult Hebrew text.

‹2.29 he sent someone . . . for protection: One ancient translation; these words are not in the Hebrew text.

‹3.1 the older . . . Jerusalem: Hebrew "the city of David".

‹3.2 local shrines: The Hebrew text has "high places", which were local places to worship God or foreign gods.

‹3.16 women: Hebrew "prostitutes".

‹4.19 of Judah: One ancient translation; these words are not in the Hebrew text.

‹6.15 from floor to ceiling: One possible meaning for the difficult Hebrew text.

‹6.16 standing . . . ceiling: One possible meaning for the difficult Hebrew text.

‹6.33-34 two sections: One possible meaning for the difficult Hebrew text.

‹7.9 From . . . best stones: One possible meaning for the difficult Hebrew text.

‹7.17 seven rows . . . chains: One possible meaning for the difficult Hebrew text.

‹7.19 lilies: One possible meaning for the difficult Hebrew text of verse 19.

‹8.9 Sinai: Hebrew "Horeb".

‹8.65 seven days: One ancient translation; Hebrew "seven days and seven more days, fourteen days in all."

‹9.8 a pile of rocks: Some ancient translations; Hebrew "high".

‹9.24 the older . . . Jerusalem: See the note at 3.1.

‹10.8 wives: Two ancient translations; Hebrew "men".

‹10.11-13 steps: Or "stools" or "railings".

‹10.22 peacocks: Or "baboons".

‹12.2 he stayed in Egypt: Hebrew; two ancient translations "he returned from Egypt" (see also 2 Chronicles 10.2).

‹12.10 Compared . . . weak: Hebrew "My little finger is bigger than my father's waist."

‹12.15-19 Adoniram: Two ancient translations (see also 4.6 and 5.14); Hebrew "Adoram".

‹12.28 Here are your gods: Or "Here is your God".

‹12.29-30 the crowd . . . taken there: One possible meaning for the difficult Hebrew text.

‹12.31 shrines: See the note at 3.2.

‹13.1-2 one of God's prophets: Hebrew "a man of God".

‹14.14 And I mean very soon: One possible meaning for the difficult Hebrew text.

‹14.23 local shrines: See the note at 3.2.

‹14.31 Jerusalem: See the note at 2.10-11.

‹15.8 Jerusalem: See the note at 2.10-11.

‹15.18 Benhadad: Hebrew "Benhadad son of Tabrimmon son of Hezion".

‹15.24 Jerusalem: See the note at 2.10-11.

‹16.2 Nobody . . . you: Hebrew "I pulled you up out of the dust".

‹17.1 from Tishbe in Gilead: Or "from the settlers in Gilead".

‹18.36 this nation: Hebrew "Israel".

‹18.37 will turn . . . to you: One possible meaning for the difficult Hebrew text.

‹19.8 Sinai: See the note at 8.9.

‹19.12 a gentle breeze: Or "a soft whisper" or "hardly a sound".

‹19.13 The Lord: Hebrew "A voice".

‹19.16 Shaphat: Hebrew "Shaphat from Abel-Meholah".

‹20.6 you: Hebrew; three ancient translations "they".

‹20.21 captured: One ancient translation; Hebrew "attacked".

‹22.38 prostitutes . . . blood: Or "they cleaned his weapons".

‹22.50 Jerusalem: See the note at 2.10-11.

2 Kings

The basics

What's the point? 2 Kings shows God's judgment on Israel and Judah. It tells of the godlessness of the people, and the eventual destruction of the two kingdoms.

What happens? A lot of kings – mainly bad – are warned by God to change their ways. They don't. So the Assyrians and the Babylonians destroy their countries and take the people into captivity.

What should I remember? 24.20 'The people of Judah and Jerusalem had made the LORD so angry that he finally turned his back on them. That's why these horrible things were happening.'

More details

Setting the scene The second part of Kings opens just before Elijah's departure. Elijah passes on the role of 'main prophet' to Elisha. And he carries on where his teacher left off...

What's it all about? The second book of Kings continues the story of the long plunge to disaster. The first few chapters are the story of Elisha, who goes around condemning ungodly kings, performing all manner of miracles and even defeating an entire army single-handed. (Well, not quite single-handed. He had the aid of an army of angels.) But even Elisha can't bring the nations back to the straight and narrow, and after he departs from the scene Israel and Judah more or less go into free-fall. King after king ignores God and follows false and evil gods. Despite the many warnings from the prophets, they refuse to change their ways.

They're not all bad though. Among the 36 or so kings of Judah and Israel after Solomon,

there are a couple of glimmers of hope in the form of King Hezekiah and King Josiah. However, they're more or less the only two good ones. And two out of 36 is not a good ratio.

The first kingdom to fall is Israel – the northern kingdom. In 722BC the Assyrians invade and completely conquer the kingdom. The capital city of Samaria is demolished and all the people taken into captivity. They are never heard of again.

Judah, the southern kingdom, staggers on for another 150 years or so. But in 586BC another huge and powerful empire – the Babylonians – invade and systematically dismantle the entire country. Jerusalem is completely destroyed and the majority of the population taken away to Babylon.

During this period prophets such as Isaiah, Jeremiah, Ezekiel, Amos and Hosea were at work. Although they are rarely mentioned in the text of Kings, we can supplement the tale told here, by looking at the writings they left behind.

Footsteps

Elijah departs: 2.1–18
Elisha, Naaman and Gehazi: 5.1–27
Elisha v. the Syrian Army: 6.8–23
The tears of a prophet: 8.7–15
The death of Jezebel: 9.1–37
Elisha dies: 13.14–21
The destruction of Israel: 17.1–23
King Hezekiah: 18.1–4; 19.1–37
King Josiah and the Law: 22.1–20; 23.21–3
The destruction of Jerusalem: 25.1–30

Elijah the prophet condemns King Ahaziah of Israel

CHAPTER 1

1-2 Soon after King Ahab of Israel died, the country of Moab rebelled against his son King Ahaziah.*

One day, Ahaziah fell through the wooden slats around the porch on the flat roof of his palace in Samaria, and he was badly injured. So he sent some messengers to the town of Ekron* with orders to ask the god Baalzebub if he would get well.

3 About the same time, an angel from the LORD sent Elijah the prophet from Tishbe to say to the king's messengers, "Ahaziah has rejected Israel's own God by sending you to ask Baalzebub about his injury. 4 Tell him that because he has done this, he's on his deathbed!" And Elijah did what he was told.

5 When the messengers returned to Ahaziah, he asked, "Why are you back so soon?"

6 "A man met us along the road with a message for you from the LORD," they answered. "The LORD wants to know why you sent us to ask Baalzebub about your injury and why you don't believe there's a God in Israel. The man also told us that the LORD says you're going to die."

7 "What did the man look like?" Ahaziah asked.

8 "He was hairy⋅ and had a leather belt around his waist," they answered.

"It must be Elijah!" replied Ahaziah. 9 So at once he sent an army officer and fifty soldiers to meet Elijah.

Elijah was sitting on top of a hill* at the time. The officer went up to him and said, "Man of God,* the king orders you to come down and talk with him."

10 "If I am a man of God," Elijah answered, "God will send down fire on you and your fifty soldiers." Fire immediately came down from heaven and burnt up the officer and his men.

---

*1.1-2 the country . . . King Ahaziah: The story of Moab's rebellion is in 3.4-27.
*1.1-2 Ekron: An important Philistine town about sixty-five kilometres south-west of Samaria.
*1.9 a hill: Probably Mount Carmel.
*1.9 Man of God: Another name for a prophet of the LORD.

See also: 1.8: Matt 3.4; Mark 1.6. 1.10: Luke 9.54.

Life files

Elisha

Background: Son of a farmer. Apprentice, then successor, to Elijah.

What's the story?

His acts are similar to those of his master Elijah. He provides a widow with a miraculous supply of oil (2 Kings 4.1–7); he brings a lad back from the dead (2 Kings 4.8–37); he provides for one hundred people using twenty loaves and some grain (Mark 6.35–43). He was an international prophet, working in Syria as well as Israel.

He was God's secret weapon. When the Syrian king sent an army to capture him, Elisha took all the Syrian army into captivity.

What's the point?

Elisha's miracles vary from the impressive (raising the dead) to the somewhat 'domestic' (fixing a stew, making an axe-head float). But Elisha didn't distinguish between 'ordinary' life and 'religious' life. God is concerned with all aspects of our lives.

Elisha's life shows that God is in command of the whole world. God allows Hazael to become king of Syria. And God will use Hazael to punish his people.

 Anorak corner

Elisha was bald. When some kids mocked his appearance he called a load of bears to attack them (2 Kings 2.23–25). So be careful what you say around holy baldies...

 Footsteps

A week with Elisha

Elisha is appointed: 1 Kings 19.19–21
Elisha and Elijah: 2 Kings 2.1–18
Some miracles: 2 Kings 4.1–44
Naaman Healed: 2 Kings 5.1–27
Elisha stops an army: 2 Kings 6.8–23
Elisha visits Syria: 2 Kings 8.7–15
The death of Elisha: 2 Kings 13.14–21

More...

All the kings of Israel p.419
Prophecy p.730

¹¹ Ahaziah sent another officer and fifty more soldiers to Elijah. The officer said, "Man of God, the king orders you to come and see him at once."

¹² "If I am a man of God," Elijah answered, "fire will destroy you and your fifty soldiers." And God sent down fire* from heaven on the officer and his men.

¹³ Ahaziah sent a third army officer and fifty more soldiers. This officer went up to Elijah, then he got down on his knees and begged, "Man of God, please be kind to me and these fifty servants of yours. Let us live! ¹⁴ Fire has already wiped out the other officers and their soldiers. Please don't let it happen to me."

¹⁵ The angel from the LORD said to Elijah, "Go with him and don't be afraid." So Elijah got up and went with the officer.

¹⁶ When Elijah arrived, he told Ahaziah, "The LORD wants to know why you sent messengers to Ekron to ask Baalzebub about your injury. Don't you believe there's a God in Israel? Ahaziah, because you did that, the LORD says you will die."

¹⁷ Ahaziah died, just as the LORD had said. But since Ahaziah had no sons, Joram* his brother* then became king. This happened in the second year that Jehoram son of Jehoshaphat was king of Judah.* ¹⁸ Everything else Ahaziah did while he was king is written in *The History of the Kings of Israel.*

Elisha the prophet

CHAPTER 2

The LORD takes Elijah away

¹ Not long before the LORD took Elijah up into heaven in a strong wind, Elijah and Elisha* were leaving Gilgal. ² Elijah said to Elisha, "The LORD wants me to go to Bethel, but you must stay here."

Elisha replied, "I swear by the living LORD and by your own life that I will stay with you no matter what!" And he went with Elijah to Bethel.

³ A group of prophets who lived there asked Elisha, "Do you know that today the LORD is going to take away your master?"

"Yes, I do," Elisha answered. "But don't remind me of it."

⁴ Elijah then said, "Elisha, now the LORD wants me to go to Jericho, but you must stay here."

Elisha replied, "I swear by the living LORD and by your own life, that I will stay with you no matter what!" And he went with Elijah to Jericho.

⁵ A group of prophets who lived there asked Elisha, "Do you know that today the LORD is going to take away your master?"

"Yes, I do," Elisha answered. "But don't remind me of it."

⁶ Elijah then said to Elisha, "Now the LORD wants me to go to the River Jordan, but you must stay here."

Elisha replied, "I swear by the living LORD and by your own life that I will never leave you!" So the two of them walked on together.

⁷ Fifty prophets followed Elijah and Elisha from Jericho, then stood at a distance and watched as the two men walked towards the river. ⁸ When they got there, Elijah took off his coat, then he rolled it up and struck the water with it. At once a path opened up through the river, and the two of them walked across on dry ground.

⁹ After they had reached the other side, Elijah said, "Elisha, the LORD will soon take me away. What can I do for you before that happens?"

Elisha answered, "Please give me twice as much of your power as you give the other prophets, so I can be the one who takes your place as their leader."

¹⁰ "It won't be easy," Elijah answered. "It can happen only if you see me as I am being taken away."

¹¹ Elijah and Elisha were walking along and talking, when suddenly there appeared between them a flaming chariot pulled by fiery horses. Straight away, a strong wind took Elijah up into heaven. ¹² Elisha saw this and shouted, "Israel's cavalry and chariots have taken my master away!"* After Elijah had gone, Elisha tore his clothes in sorrow.

¹³ Elijah's coat had fallen off, so Elisha picked it up and walked back to the River Jordan. ¹⁴ He struck the water with the coat and wondered, "Will the LORD perform miracles for me as he did for Elijah?" As soon as Elisha did this, a dry path opened up through the water, and he walked across.

*1.17 This happened . . . Judah: According to 3.1, this was also the eighteenth year of Jehoshaphat's rule in Judah. In biblical times, a father and son would sometimes rule as kings at the same time. This way, when the father died, the son would already have control of the kingdom (see also 8.16).
See also: 1.12: Luke 9.54.

See also: 2.9: Deut 21.17. 2.12: 2 King 13.14.

15 When the prophets from Jericho saw what happened, they said to each other, "Elisha now has Elijah's power."

They walked over to him, bowed down, 16 and said, "There are fifty strong men here with us. Please let them go and look for your master. Perhaps the Spirit of the LORD carried him off to some mountain or valley."

"No," Elisha replied, "they won't find him." 17 They kept begging until he was embarrassed to say no. He finally agreed, and the prophets sent the men out. They looked three days for Elijah but never found him. 18 They returned to Jericho, and Elisha said, "I told you that you wouldn't find him."

Elisha makes the water pure at Jericho

19 One day the people of Jericho said, "Elisha, you can see that our city is in a good spot. But the water from our spring is so bad that it even keeps our crops from growing."

20 He replied, "Put some salt in a new bowl and bring it to me."

They brought him the bowl of salt, 21 and he carried it to the spring. He threw the salt into the water and said, "The LORD has made this water pure again. From now on you'll be able to grow crops, and no one will starve."

22 The water has been fine ever since, just as Elisha said.

Some boys make fun of Elisha

23 Elisha left and headed towards Bethel. Along the way some boys started making fun of him by shouting, "Go away, baldy! Get out of here!"

24 Elisha turned round and stared at the boys. Then he cursed them in the name of the LORD. Straight away two bears ran out of the woods and ripped to pieces forty-two of the boys.

25 Elisha went up to Mount Carmel, then returned to Samaria.

CHAPTER 3

King Joram of Israel

1 Joram* son of Ahab became king of Israel in Jehoshaphat's eighteenth year as king of Judah.* Joram ruled twelve years from Samaria 2 and disobeyed the LORD by doing wrong. He tore down the stone image his father had made to honour Baal, and so he wasn't as sinful as his parents. 3 But he kept doing the sinful things that Jeroboam son of Nebat had led Israel to do.*

The country of Moab rebels against Israel

4 For many years the country of Moab had been controlled by Israel and was forced to pay taxes to the kings of Israel. King Mesha of Moab raised sheep, so he paid the king of Israel one hundred thousand lambs and the wool from one hundred thousand rams. 5 But soon after the death of Ahab, Mesha rebelled against Israel.

6 One day, Joram left Samaria and called together Israel's army. 7 He sent this message to King Jehoshaphat of Judah, "The king of Moab has rebelled. Will you go with me to attack him?"

"Yes, I will," Jehoshaphat answered. "I'm on your side, and my soldiers and horses are at your command. 8 But which way should we go?"

"We will march through Edom Desert," Joram replied.

9 So Joram, Jehoshaphat, and the king of Edom led their troops out. But seven days later, there was no drinking water left for them or their animals. 10 Joram cried out, "This is terrible! The LORD must have led us out here to be captured by Moab's army."

11 Jehoshaphat said, "Which of the LORD's prophets is with us? We can find out from him what the LORD wants us to do."

One of Joram's officers answered, "Elisha son of Shaphat is here. He was one of Elijah's closest followers."

12 Jehoshaphat replied, "He can give us the LORD's message."

The three kings went over to Elisha, 13 and he asked Joram, "Why did you come to me? Go and talk to the prophets of the foreign gods your parents worshipped."*

"No," Joram answered. "It was the LORD who led us out here, so that Moab's army could capture us."

*3.1 **Joram:** See the note at 1.17 and additional note 1.17.
*3.1 **Joram . . . Judah:** See 1.17 and 8.16 and the notes there.

*3.3 **the sinful things . . . to do:** When Jeroboam became king of Israel, he made two gold statues of calves and put them in the towns of Bethel and Dan, so the people of Israel could worship them (see 1 Kings 12.26–30).
*3.13 **the prophets . . . worshipped:** These were prophets of the Canaanite god Baal and the goddess Asherah (see 1 Kings 16.30–33; 18.19).

Holy history

Human sacrifice

Many of the nations around Israel engaged in human sacrifice, but the Israelites were forbidden to do so. It was one of the things which marked Israel out from their neighbours.

The idea was to appease the gods by sacrificing your most precious possession. For example, when King Meshua of Moab sacrifices his son to try to stop the Israelite army (2 Kings 3.27). (Actually it worked, but only because the Israelites were so horrified by the act they went home.)

Later in the Bible, the Israelites sank so low that they engaged in the practice. King Ahaz and King Manasseh of Judah sacrificed their own sons to foreign gods (2 Kings 16.3; 21.6).

And it wasn't just the kings. Jeremiah accused the people of sacrificing their children to Baal (Jeremiah 7.30–33). The place where they did this, was outside Jerusalem and was known as Slaughter Valley or the Valley of Hinnom. Later the Jews used this phrase in the word Gehenna – their word for hell.

Today, human sacrifice and ritual murder is still found in some extreme cults and religions. Perhaps there's a less obvious equivalent as well. How many children are still sacrificed in the sweatshops of this world? How many children are sold into slavery or prostitution by desperate parents? Child sacrifice is still abhorrent to God, whether it's done in the valley of Hinnom or on the streets of Thailand.

More...

Foreign gods p.262
Sacrifice p.1368
Other nations p.259
Hell p.1148

¹⁴ Elisha said to him, "I serve the LORD All-Powerful, and as surely as he lives, I swear I wouldn't even look at you if I didn't respect King Jehoshaphat." ¹⁵ Then Elisha said, "Send for someone who can play the harp."

The harpist began playing, and the LORD gave Elisha this message for Joram:

¹⁶ The LORD says that this dry river bed will be filled with water.' ¹⁷ You won't feel any wind or see any rain, but there will be plenty of water for you and your animals.

¹⁸ That simple thing isn't all the LORD is going to do. He will also help you defeat Moab's army. ¹⁹ You will capture all their walled cities and important towns. You will chop down every good tree and stop up every spring of water, then ruin their fertile fields by covering them with rocks.

²⁰ The next morning, while the sacrifice was being offered, water suddenly started flowing from the direction of Edom, and it flooded the land.

²¹ Meanwhile, the people of Moab had heard that the three kings were coming to attack them. They had called together all their fighting men, from the youngest to the oldest, and these troops were now standing at their border, ready for battle. ²² When they got up that morning, the sun was shining across the water, making it look red. The Moabite troops took one look ²³ and shouted, "Look at that blood! The armies of those kings must have fought and killed each other. Come on, let's go and take what's left in their camp."

²⁴ But when they arrived at Israel's camp, the Israelite soldiers came out and attacked them, until they turned and ran away. Israel's army chased them all the way back to Moab, and even there they kept up the attack.' ²⁵ The Israelites destroyed the Moabite towns. They chopped down the good trees and stopped up the springs of water, then covered the fertile fields with rocks.

Finally, the only city left standing was Kir-Hareseth, but soldiers armed with slings surrounded and attacked it. ²⁶ King Mesha of Moab saw that he was about to be defeated. So he took along seven hundred soldiers with swords and tried to break through the front line where the Edomite troops were positioned. But he failed. ²⁷ He then grabbed his eldest son who was to be the next king and sacrificed him as an offering on the city wall. The Israelite troops were so horrified that' they left the city and went back home.

CHAPTER 4

Elisha helps a poor widow

¹ One day the widow of one of the LORD's prophets said to Elisha, "You know that before my husband died, he was a follower of yours and a worshipper of the LORD. But he owed a man some money, and now that man is on his way to take my two sons as his slaves."

² "Perhaps there's something I can do to help," Elisha said. "What do you have in your house?"

"Sir, I have nothing but a small bottle of olive oil."

³ Elisha told her, "Ask your neighbours for their empty jars. And after you've borrowed as many as you can, ⁴ go home and shut the door behind you and your sons. Then begin filling the jars with oil and set each one aside as you fill it." ⁵ The woman left.

Later, when she and her sons were back inside their house, the two sons brought her the jars, and she began filling them.

⁶ At last, she said to one of her sons, "Bring me another jar."

"We don't have any more," he answered, and the oil stopped flowing from the small bottle.

⁷ After she told Elisha what had happened, he said, "Sell the oil and use part of the money to pay what you owe the man. You and your sons can live on what is left."

Elisha brings a rich woman's son back to life

⁸ Once, while Elisha was in the town of Shunem,* he met a rich woman who invited him to her home for dinner. After that, whenever he was in Shunem, he would have a meal there with her and her husband.

⁹ Some time later the woman said to her husband, "I'm sure the man who comes here so often is a prophet of God. ¹⁰ Why don't we build him a small room on the flat roof of our house? We can put a bed, a table and chair, and an oil lamp in it. Then whenever he comes, he can stay with us."

¹¹ The next time Elisha was in Shunem, he stopped at their house and went up to his room to rest. ¹²⁻¹³ He said to his servant Gehazi, "This woman has been very helpful. Ask her to come up here to the roof for a moment." She came, and Elisha told Gehazi to say to her, "You've gone to a lot of trouble

---

*4.8 **Shunem:** A town in Israel, about forty kilometres north of Samaria.

Holy history

Houses

The first Israelites lived in tents. Each family within the tribe would have had a big tent which was made from goat skins or goat hair. (Goatskins have good insulating properties: warm and dry in winter, relatively cool in summer.)

In the summer they may have moved to higher ground to catch what breeze there was, in the winter they would have used the shelter of the mountains, while avoiding the valley floor in case of flooding. Channels would have been dug around the edge of the tent for drainage and briars and twigs laid around to stop animals and snakes entering.

Most homes in Bible times followed a similar pattern: one or two storey houses, with storage and workrooms on the ground floor and living accommodation above. Several homes would have been clustered around a central courtyard, where the food would have been prepared.

Homes had their own water reservoirs to collect and store rainwater. Doors and windows were very small, so the houses were dark inside. Light would have been provided by oil-lamps, fuelled by olive oil.

Most homes were furnished simply with stools, a table and beds. (When Elijah stayed with the Shunammite widow, his room contained a table, chair, bed and lamp – see 2 Kings 4.10).

Most people slept on the floor or on a mattress made of animal skins or reeds. Or they might use their clothes as a mattress and blanket. Some richer people had beds which could double as couches, on which people reclined to eat. Tables were normally owned only by the rich. Everyone else sat on the floor, with their food laid out on a sort of picnic mat made out of animal skin or cloth.

More...
Cities and towns p.233

for us, and we want to help you. Is there something we can request the king or army commander to do?"*

The woman answered, "With my relatives nearby, I have everything I need."

¹⁴ "Then what can we do for her?" Elisha asked Gehazi.

Gehazi replied, "I do know that her husband is old, and that she doesn't have a son."

¹⁵ "Ask her to come here again," Elisha told his servant. He called for her, and she came and stood in the doorway of Elisha's room.

¹⁶ Elisha said to her, "Next year at this time, you'll be holding your own baby son in your arms."

"You're a man of God," the woman replied. "Please don't lie to me."

¹⁷ But a few months later, the woman got pregnant. She gave birth to a son, just as Elisha had promised.

¹⁸ One day while the boy was still young, he was out in the fields with his father, where the workers were harvesting the crops. ¹⁹ Suddenly he shouted, "My head hurts. It hurts a lot!"

"Carry him back to his mother," the father said to his servant. ²⁰ The servant picked up the boy and carried him to his mother. The boy lay on her lap all morning, and by midday he was dead. ²¹ She carried him upstairs to Elisha's room and laid him across the bed. Then she walked out and shut the door behind her.

²² The woman called to her husband, "I need to see the prophet. Let me use one of the donkeys. Send a servant along with me, and let me leave now, so I can get back quickly."

²³ "Why do you need to see him today?" her husband asked. "It's not the Sabbath or time for the New Moon Festival."

"That's all right," she answered. ²⁴ She saddled the donkey and said to her servant, "Let's go. And don't slow down unless I tell you to." ²⁵ She left at once for Mount Carmel* to talk with Elisha.

When Elisha saw her coming, he said, "Gehazi, look! It's the woman from Shunem. ²⁶ Run and meet her. And ask her if everything is all right with her and her family."

"Everything is fine," she answered Gehazi. ²⁷ But as soon as she got to the top of the mountain, she went over and grabbed Elisha by the feet.

Gehazi started towards her to push her away, when Elisha said, "Leave her alone! Don't you see how sad she is? But the LORD hasn't told me why."

²⁸ The woman said, "Sir, I begged you not to get my hopes up, and I didn't even ask you for a son."

²⁹ "Gehazi, get ready and go to her house," Elisha said. "Take along my walking stick, and when you get there, lay it on the boy's face. Don't stop to talk to anyone, even if they try to talk to you."

³⁰ But the boy's mother said to Elisha, "I swear by the living LORD and by your own life that I won't leave without you." So Elisha got up and went with them.

³¹ Gehazi ran on ahead and laid Elisha's walking stick on the boy's face, but the boy didn't move or make a sound. Gehazi ran back to Elisha and said, "The boy didn't wake up."

³² Elisha arrived at the woman's house and went straight to his room, where he saw the boy's body on his bed. ³³ He walked in, shut the door, and prayed to the LORD. ³⁴ Then he got on the bed and stretched out over the dead body, with his mouth on the boy's mouth, his eyes on his eyes, and his hand on his hands. As he lay there, the boy's body became warm. ³⁵ Elisha got up and walked back and forth in the room, then he went back and leaned over the boy's body. The boy sneezed seven times and opened his eyes.

³⁶ Elisha called out to Gehazi, "Ask the boy's mother to come here." Gehazi did, and when she was at the door, Elisha said, "You can take your son."

³⁷ She came in and bowed down at Elisha's feet. Then she picked up her son and left.

Elisha makes some stew taste better

³⁸ Later, Elisha went back to Gilgal, where there was almost nothing to eat, because the crops had failed.

One day while the prophets who lived there were meeting with Elisha, he said to his servant, "Prepare a big pot of stew for these prophets."

³⁹ One of them went out into the woods to gather some herbs. He found a wild vine and picked as much of its fruit as he could carry,

---

4.12–13 request the king . . . do: Elisha may have meant that he could ask these leaders to lower her taxes.

4.25 Mount Carmel: About forty kilometres from Shunem.

See also: 4.16: Gen 18.4.

See also: 4.34–35: 1 King 17.21.

but he didn't know that the fruit was very sour. When he got back, he cut up the fruit and put it in the stew.

⁴⁰ The stew was served, and when the prophets started eating it, they shouted, "Elisha, this stew tastes terrible! We can't eat it."

⁴¹ "Bring me some flour," Elisha said. He sprinkled the flour in the stew and said, "Now serve it to them." And the stew tasted fine.

Elisha feeds a hundred people

⁴² A man from the town of Baal-Shalishah* brought Elisha some freshly cut grain and twenty loaves of bread made from the first barley that was harvested. Elisha said, "Give it to the people so they can eat."

⁴³ "There's not enough here for a hundred people," his servant said.

"Just give it to them," Elisha replied. "The LORD has promised there will be more than enough."

⁴⁴ So the servant served the bread and grain to the people. They ate and still had some left over, just as the LORD had promised.

CHAPTER 5

Elisha heals Naaman

¹ Naaman was the commander of the Syrian army. The LORD had helped him and his troops defeat their enemies, so the king of Syria respected Naaman very much. Naaman was a brave soldier, but he had leprosy.*

² One day while the Syrian troops were raiding Israel, they captured a girl, and she became a servant of Naaman's wife. ³ Some time later the girl said, "If your husband Naaman would go to the prophet in Samaria, he would be cured of his leprosy."

⁴ When Naaman told the king what the girl had said, ⁵ the king replied, "Go ahead! I will give you a letter to take to the king of Israel."

Naaman left and took along thirty thousand pieces of silver, six thousand pieces of gold, and ten new outfits. ⁶ He also carried the letter to the king of Israel. It said, "I am sending my servant Naaman to you. Would you cure him of his leprosy?"

Holy history

Leprosy

Leprosy was one of the most dreaded diseases in the Bible. It was a skin disease, usually identified by white patches or spots under the skin (Leviticus 13.3–4). It was enormously contagious.

There are many instances of leprosy in the Bible. Sometimes it occurs as a punishment, as in the case of Miriam (Numbers 12.10,15) and Gehazi (2 Kings 5.27). Often it is the occasion of a miraculous cure or a demonstration of God's power such as in the case of Moses (Exodus 4.6–7) or Naaman (2 Kings 5.1–14).

Lepers were considered to be unclean. They were forced to live in isolation, not allowed inside the camp or inside cities and towns. They had to wear mourning clothes and to shout 'Unclean! Unclean!' It was a kind of alarm, a warning sign to people to keep their distance.

So leprosy meant more than just being ill. It was a kind of living death; incurable, untreatable and leaving the sufferer excluded from society and alienated from the people around. When Jesus healed people of leprosy he was bringing them back to life. More, the fact that leprosy could only be cured through God's intervention showed clearly who Jesus really was (Luke 17.15–19).

Today, Christians are still at work against leprosy, using modern methods and modern medicine to control the disease, but still showing Christ's love and compassion.

More...
Serving others p.1190

---

*4.42 Baal-Shalishah: The exact location of this town is not known, but it was probably somewhere near Shechem.
*5.1 leprosy: The word translated "leprosy" was used for many different kinds of skin diseases.
See also: 5.1–14: Luke 4.27.

7 When the king of Israel read the letter, he tore his clothes in fear and shouted, "That Syrian king believes I can cure this man of leprosy! Does he think I'm God with power over life and death? He must be trying to pick a fight with me."

8 As soon as Elisha the prophet' heard what had happened, he sent the Israelite king this message: "Why are you so afraid? Send the man to me, so that he will know there is a prophet in Israel."

9 Naaman left with his horses and chariots and stopped at the door of Elisha's house. 10 Elisha sent someone outside to say to him, "Go and wash seven times in the River Jordan. Then you'll be completely cured."

11 But Naaman stormed off, grumbling, "Why couldn't he come out and talk to me? I thought he would be sure to stand in front of me and pray to the LORD his God, then wave his hand over my skin and cure me. 12 What about the River Abana' or the River Pharpar? Those rivers in Damascus are just as good as any river in Israel. I could have washed in them and been cured."

13 His servants went over to him and said, "Sir, if the prophet had told you to do something difficult, you would have done it. So why don't you do what he said? Go and wash and be cured."

14 Naaman walked down to the Jordan; he waded out into the water and stooped down in it seven times, just as Elisha had told him. Straight away, he was cured, and his skin became as smooth as a child's.

15 Naaman and his officials went back to Elisha. Naaman stood in front of him and announced, "Now I know that the God of Israel is the only God in the whole world. Sir, would you please accept a gift from me?"

16 "I am a servant of the living LORD," Elisha answered, "and I swear that I will not take anything from you."

Naaman kept begging, but Elisha kept refusing. 17 Finally Naaman said, "If you won't accept a gift, then please let me take home as much soil as two mules can pull in a wagon. Sir, from now on I will offer sacrifices only to the LORD.* 18 But I pray that the LORD will forgive me when I go into the temple of the god Rimmon and bow down there with the king of Syria."

19 "Go home, and don't worry about that," Elisha replied. Then Naaman left.

Elisha places a curse on Gehazi

After Naaman had gone only a short distance, 20 Gehazi said to himself, "Elisha let that Syrian off too easily. He should have taken Naaman's gift. I swear by the living LORD that I will talk to Naaman myself and get something from him." 21 So he hurried after Naaman.

When Naaman saw Gehazi running after him, he got out of his chariot to meet him. Naaman asked, "Is everything all right?"

22 "Yes," Gehazi answered. "But my master has sent me to tell you about two young prophets from the hills of Ephraim. They came asking for help, and now Elisha wants to know if you would give them three thousand pieces of silver and some new clothes?"

23 "Certainly," Naaman replied. "But why don't you take twice that amount of silver?" He convinced Gehazi to take it all, then put the silver in two bags. He handed the bags and the clothes to his two servants, and they carried them for Gehazi.

24 When they reached the hill where Gehazi lived, he took the bags from the servants and placed them in his house, then sent the men away. After they had gone, 25 Gehazi went in and stood in front of Elisha, who asked, "Gehazi, where have you been?"

"Nowhere, sir," Gehazi answered.

26 Elisha asked, "Don't you know that my spirit was there when Naaman got out of his chariot to talk with you? Gehazi, you have no right to accept money or clothes, olive orchards or vineyards, sheep or cattle, or servants. 27 Because of what you've done, Naaman's leprosy* will now be on you and your descendants for ever!"

Suddenly, Gehazi's skin became white with leprosy, and he left.

CHAPTER 6

Elisha makes an axe head float

1 One day the prophets said to Elisha, "The place where we meet with you is too small. 2 Why don't we build a new meeting place near the River Jordan? Each of us could get some wood, then we could build it."

"That's a good idea," Elisha replied, "get started."

3 "Aren't you going with us?" one of the prophets asked.

"Yes, I'll go," Elisha answered, 4 and he left with them.

---

*5.17 let me take . . . the LORD: It was believed that the LORD had to be worshipped in Israel or on soil taken from Israel.

*5.27 leprosy: See the note at 5.1.

Big ideas

Angels

The word 'angel' comes from the Greek word for 'messenger', and that's one of the main jobs they do: they're God's couriers.

Angels also act on behalf of God; they were active in the destruction of Sodom (Genesis 19), they brought food to Elijah (1 Kings 19.5–7), and even gave military assistance (2 Kings 19).

Angels are created beings and we know they are capable of moral judgment, because some chose to rebel against God.

As to what they look like, well, let's just say that the nice, chubby-cheeked cherubs that you see in most paintings can't be accurate. While angels can look just like humans, they can also appear as dazzling creatures of light, who strike terror into the hearts of those who see them.

The Angel of the Lord (a.k.a. Gabriel)

This angel is so closely identified with God that, at times, it's as if he were a direct extension of God's personality. He is God's representative, his 'spokes-angel' (e.g. Genesis 16.7; Exodus 3.2). At other times he is distinguished from God (2 Samuel 26.16). In the New Testament he is specifically identified as Gabriel.

Fallen Angels

A group of angels who, led by Satan, rebelled against God and were cast out of heaven (Matthew 25.41; Revelation 12.9; Luke 10.18). They fight against the forces of good, but will one day be totally defeated.

Footsteps

Five days with the angels

The angels destroy Sodom: Genesis 19.1–29
An angelic army: 2 Kings 6.8–23
Gabriel talks to Mary: Luke 1.26–38
An angel organises a jailbreak: Acts 5.17–24
God's plans: Revelation 10.1–11

More...

Appearances of God p.99
Demonic powers p.1131

They went to the River Jordan and began chopping down trees. ⁵ While one of the prophets was working, his axe head fell off and dropped into the water. "Oh!" he shouted. "Sir, I borrowed this axe."

⁶ "Where did it fall in?" Elisha asked. The prophet pointed to the place, and Elisha cut a stick and threw it into the water at that spot. The axe head floated to the top of the water.

⁷ "Now get it," Elisha told him. And the prophet reached in and grabbed it.

Elisha stops an invasion of the Syrian army

⁸ Time after time, when the king of Syria was at war against the Israelites, he met with his officers and announced, "I've decided where we will set up camp."

⁹ Each time, Elisha would send this warning to the king of Israel: "Don't go near there. That's where the Syrian troops have set up camp."▸ ¹⁰ So the king would warn the Israelite troops in that place to be on guard.

¹¹ The king of Syria was furious when he found out what was happening. He called in his officers and asked, "Which one of you has been telling the king of Israel our plans?"

¹² "None of us, Your Majesty," one of them answered. "It's an Israelite named Elisha. He's a prophet, so he can tell his king everything — even what you say in your own room."

¹³ "Find out where he is!" the king ordered. "I'll send soldiers to bring him here."

They learnt that Elisha was in the town of Dothan* and reported it to the king. ¹⁴ He ordered his best troops to go there with horses and chariots. They marched out during the night and surrounded the town.

¹⁵ When Elisha's servant got up the next morning, he saw that Syrian troops had the town surrounded. "Sir, what are we going to do?" he asked.

¹⁶ "Don't be afraid," Elisha answered. "There are more troops on our side than on theirs." ¹⁷ Then he prayed, "LORD, please help him to see." And the LORD let the servant see that the hill* was covered with fiery horses and flaming chariots all around Elisha.

¹⁸ As the Syrian army came closer, Elisha prayed, "LORD, make those soldiers blind!" And the LORD blinded them with a bright light.

---

*6.13 Dothan: About fifteen kilometres north of Samaria.
*6.17 the hill: The hill on which the town was built.

¹⁹ Elisha told the enemy troops, "You've taken the wrong road and are in the wrong town. Follow me. I'll lead you to the man you're looking for." Elisha led them straight to the capital city of Samaria.

²⁰ When all the soldiers were inside the city, Elisha prayed, "LORD, now let them see again." The LORD let them see that they were standing in the middle of Samaria.

²¹ The king of Israel saw them and asked Elisha, "Should I kill them, sir?"

²² "No!" Elisha answered. "You didn't capture these troops in battle, so you have no right to kill them. Instead, give them something to eat and drink and let them return to their leader."

²³ The king ordered a huge meal to be prepared for Syria's army, and when they finished eating, he let them go.

For a while, the Syrian troops stopped invading Israel's territory.

King Benhadad of Syria attacks Samaria

²⁴ Some time later, King Benhadad of Syria* called his entire army together, then they marched to Samaria and attacked. ²⁵ They kept up the attack until there was nothing to eat in the city. In fact, a donkey's head cost about eighty pieces of silver, and a small bowl of pigeon droppings* cost five pieces of silver.

²⁶ One day as the king of Israel* was walking along the top of the city wall, a woman shouted to him, "Please, Your Majesty, help me!"

²⁷ "Let the LORD help you!" the king said. "Do you think I have grain or wine to give you?" ²⁸ Then he asked, "What's the matter anyway?"

The woman answered, "Another woman and I were so hungry that we agreed to eat our sons. She said if we ate my son one day, we could eat hers the next day. ²⁹ So yesterday we cooked my son and ate him. But today when I went to her house to eat her son, she had hidden him."

³⁰ The king tore off his clothes in sorrow, and since he was on top of the city wall, the people saw that he was wearing sackcloth underneath. ³¹ He said, "I pray that God will punish me terribly, if Elisha's head is still on his shoulders by this time tomorrow." ³² Then he sent a messenger to Elisha.

Elisha was at home at the time, and the important leaders of Israel were meeting with him. Even before the king's messenger arrived, Elisha told the leaders, "That murderer* is sending someone to cut off my head. When you see him coming, shut the door and don't let him in. I'm sure the king himself will be just behind him."

³³ Before Elisha finished talking, the messenger* came up and said, "The LORD has made all these terrible things happen to us. Why should I think he will help us now?"

CHAPTER 7

¹ Elisha answered, "I have a message for you. The LORD promises that tomorrow here in Samaria, you will be able to buy a large sack of flour or two large sacks of barley for almost nothing."

² The chief officer there with the king replied, "I don't believe it! Even if the LORD sent a rainstorm, it couldn't produce that much grain by tomorrow."

"You will see it happen, but you won't eat any of the food," Elisha warned him.

The Syrian army stops its attack

³ About the same time, four men with leprosy* were just outside the gate of Samaria. They said to each other, "Why should we sit here, waiting to die? ⁴ There's nothing to eat in the city, so we would starve if we went inside. But if we stay out here, we will die for certain. Let's sneak over to the Syrian army camp and surrender. They might kill us, but they might not." ⁵⁻⁸ That evening the four men got up and left for the Syrian camp.

As they walked towards the camp, the Lord caused the Syrian troops to hear what sounded like the roar of a huge force of cavalry. The soldiers said to each other, "Listen! The king of Israel must have hired Hittite and Egyptian troops to attack us. Let's get out of here!" So they ran out of their camp that night, leaving their tents and horses and donkeys.

---

*6.24 King Benhadad of Syria: This may or may not be the same Benhadad mentioned in 1 Kings 20.1. Several of the Syrian kings were named Benhadad.

*6.25 pigeon droppings: This may have been used for food or to burn for fuel. It also may have been a popular name for roasted beans or the shells of certain seeds.

*6.26 the king of Israel: Probably either Jehoahaz or Jehoash, but possibly even Joram.

See also: 6.29: Deut 28.57; Lam 4.10.

*6.33 messenger: Or "king" (see 7.2,18); the two Hebrew words are very similar.

*7.3 leprosy: See the note at 5.1.

When the four men with leprosy reached the edge of the Syrian camp, no one was there. They walked into one of the tents, where they ate and drank, before carrying off clothes, as well as silver and gold. They hid all this, then walked into another tent; they took what they wanted and hid it too.

9 They said to each other, "This isn't right. Today is a day to celebrate, and we haven't told anyone else what has happened. If we wait until morning, we will be punished. Let's go to the king's palace straight away and tell the good news."

10 They went back to Samaria and shouted up to the guards at the gate, "We've just come from the Syrian army camp, and all the soldiers are gone! The tents are empty, and the horses and donkeys are still tied up. We didn't see or hear anybody."

11 The guards reported the news to the king's palace. 12 The king got out of bed and said to his officers, "I know what those Syrians are doing. They know we're starving, so they're hiding in the fields, hoping we will go out to look for food. When we do, they can capture us and take over our city."

13 One of his officers replied, "We have a few horses left — why don't we let some men take five of them and go to the Syrian camp and see what's happening? We're going to die anyway like those who have already died."▸ 14 They found two chariots, and the king commanded the men to find out what had happened to the Syrian troops.

15 The men rode as far as the River Jordan. All along the way they saw clothes and equipment that the Syrians had thrown away as they escaped. Then they went back to the king and told him what they had seen.

16 At once the people went to the Syrian camp and carried off what was left. They took so much that a large sack of flour and two large sacks of barley sold for almost nothing, just as the LORD had promised.

17 The king of Israel had put his chief officer in charge of the gate, but he died when the people trampled him as they rushed out of the city. 18 Earlier, when the king was at Elisha's house, Elisha had told him that flour or barley would sell for almost nothing. 19 But the officer refused to believe that even the LORD could do that. So Elisha warned him that he would see it happen, but would not eat any of the food. 20 And that's exactly what happened — the officer was trampled to death.

CHAPTER 8

The woman from Shunem is given back her land

1 Elisha told the woman whose son he had brought back to life,* "The LORD has warned that there will be no food here for seven years. Take your family and go and live somewhere else for a while." 2 The woman did exactly what Elisha had said and went to live in Philistine territory.

She and her family lived there seven years. 3 Then she returned to Israel and immediately begged the king to give back her house and property.

4 Meanwhile, the king was asking Gehazi the servant of Elisha about the amazing things Elisha had been doing. 5 While Gehazi was telling him that Elisha had brought a dead boy back to life, the woman and her son arrived.

"Here's the boy, Your Majesty," Gehazi said. "And this is his mother."

6 The king asked the woman to tell her story, and she told him everything that had happened. He then said to one of his officials, "I want you to make sure that this woman gets back everything that belonged to her, including the money her crops have made since the day she left Israel."

Hazael kills Benhadad

7 Some time later Elisha went to the capital city of Damascus to visit King Benhadad of Syria, who was sick. And when Benhadad was told he was there, 8 he said to Hazael,* "Go and see Elisha the man of God and get him to ask the LORD if I will get well. And take along a gift for him."

9 Hazael left with forty camel loads of the best things made in Damascus as a gift for Elisha. He found the prophet and said, "Your servant, King Benhadad, wants to know if he will get well."

10 "Tell him he will," Elisha said to Hazael. "But the LORD has already told me that Benhadad will definitely die." 11 Elisha stared at him until Hazael was embarrassed, then Elisha began crying.▸

12 "Sir, why are you crying?" Hazael asked.

Elisha answered, "Because I know the terrible things you will do to the people of Israel. You will burn down their walled cities and slaughter their young men. You will even

---

*8.1 Elisha . . . life: See 4.8–37.
*8.8 Hazael: Probably one of Benhadad's officials.
See also: 8.1: 2 King 4.8–37.

crush the heads of their babies and rip open their pregnant women."

¹³ "How could I ever do anything like that?" Hazael replied. "I'm only a servant and don't have that kind of power."

"Hazael, the LORD has told me that you will be the next king of Syria."

¹⁴ Hazael went back to Benhadad and told him, "Elisha said that you will get well."
¹⁵ But the very next day, Hazael got a thick blanket; he soaked it in water and held it over Benhadad's face until he died. Hazael then became king.

Kings of Judah and Israel

King Jehoram of Judah

This is also told in 2 Chronicles 21.2–20

¹⁶ Jehoram son of Jehoshaphat became king of Judah in Joram's fifth year as king of Israel, while Jehoshaphat was still king of Judah.*
¹⁷ Jehoram was thirty-two years old when he became king, and he ruled eight years from Jerusalem.
¹⁸ Jehoram disobeyed the LORD by doing wrong. He married Ahab's daughter and was as sinful as Ahab's family and the kings of Israel. ¹⁹ But the LORD refused to destroy Judah, because he had promised his servant David that someone from his family would always rule in Judah.
²⁰ While Jehoram was king, the people of Edom rebelled and chose their own king.
²¹ So Jehoram' and his cavalry marched to Zair, where the Edomite army surrounded him and his commanders. During the night he attacked the Edomites, but he was defeated, and his troops escaped to their homes.' ²² Judah was never able to regain control of Edom. Even the town of Libnah* rebelled at that time.
²³ Everything else Jehoram did while he was king is written in *The History of the Kings of Judah.* ²⁴ Jehoram died and was buried beside his ancestors in Jerusalem.' His son Ahaziah then became king.

King Ahaziah of Judah

This is also told in 2 Chronicles 22.1–6

²⁵ Ahaziah son of Jehoram became king of Judah in the twelfth year of Joram's rule in Israel. ²⁶ Ahaziah was twenty-two years old when he became king, and he ruled from Jerusalem for only one year. His mother was Athaliah, a granddaughter of King Omri of Israel. ²⁷ Since Ahaziah was related to Ahab's family,* he acted just like them and disobeyed the LORD by doing wrong.
²⁸ Ahaziah went with King Joram of Israel to attack King Hazael and the Syrian troops at Ramoth in Gilead. Joram was wounded in that battle, ²⁹ so he went to the town of Jezreel to recover. Ahaziah went there to visit him.

CHAPTER 9

Jehu becomes king of Israel

¹ One day, Elisha called for one of the other prophets and said:

Take this bottle of olive oil and get ready to go to the town of Ramoth in Gilead. ² When you get there, find Jehu son of Jehoshaphat and grandson of Nimshi. Take him to a place where the two of you can be alone, ³ then pour olive oil on his head to show that he is the new king. Say to him, "The LORD has chosen you to be king of Israel." Then leave quickly — don't wait for anything!

⁴ The young prophet left for Ramoth. ⁵ When he arrived, the army officers were meeting together. "Sir, I have a message for you," he said.

"For which one of us?" Jehu asked.

"You, sir," the prophet answered. ⁶ So Jehu got up and went inside.* The prophet poured olive oil on Jehu's head and told him:

The LORD God of Israel has this message for you: "I am the LORD, and I have chosen you to be king of my people Israel. ⁷ I want you to wipe out the family of Ahab, so Jezebel will be punished for killing the prophets and my other servants. ⁸ Every man and boy in Ahab's family must die, whether slave or free. ⁹ His whole family

---

*8.16 while Jehoshaphat . . . Judah: In biblical times, a father and son would sometimes rule as kings at the same time. That way, when the father died, his son would already have control of the kingdom.
*8.22 Even the town of Libnah: This was a town on the border between Philistia and Judah, which means that Jehoram was facing rebellion on two sides of his kingdom.
See also: 8.13: 1 King 19.15. 8.19: 1 King 11.36. 8.20: Gen 27.40.

*8.27 Since . . . family: Ahaziah's mother was Ahab's daughter (see verse 18).
*9.6 went inside: The officers were probably meeting outside in an open courtyard of some building.
See also: 9.6: 1 King 19.16.

must be destroyed, just like the families of Jeroboam son of Nebat and Baasha son of Ahijah. ¹⁰ As for Jezebel, her body will be eaten by dogs in the town of Jezreel. There won't be enough left of her to bury."

Then the young prophet opened the door and ran out.

¹¹ Jehu went back to his officers, and one of them asked, "What did that mad prophet want? Is everything all right?"

"You know him and how he talks," Jehu answered.

¹² "No, we don't. What did he say?" they asked.

"He had a message from the LORD," Jehu replied. "He said that the LORD has chosen me to be the next king of Israel."

¹³ They quickly grabbed their coats and spread them out on the steps where Jehu was standing. Someone blew a trumpet, and everyone shouted, "Jehu is king!"

Jehu kills Joram and Ahaziah

¹⁴⁻¹⁶ King Joram⸌ of Israel had been badly wounded in the battle at Ramoth, trying to defend it against King Hazael and the Syrian army. Joram was now recovering in Jezreel, and King Ahaziah of Judah was there, visiting him.

Meanwhile, Jehu was in Ramoth, making plans to kill Joram. He said to his officers, "If you want me to be king, then don't let anyone leave this town. They might go to Jezreel and tell Joram." Then Jehu got in his chariot and rode to Jezreel.

¹⁷ When the guard in the watchtower at Jezreel saw Jehu and his men riding up, he shouted to the king, "I see some men coming this way."

Joram ordered, "Send someone out to ask them if this is a friendly visit."

¹⁸ One of the soldiers rode out and said to Jehu, "King Joram wants to know if this is a friendly visit."

"What's it to you?" Jehu asked. "Just stay behind me with the rest of my troops!"

About the same time the guard in the watchtower said, "Your Majesty, the rider got there, but he isn't coming back."

¹⁹ So Joram sent out another rider, who rode up to Jehu and said, "The king wants to know if this is a friendly visit."

"What's it to you?" Jehu asked. "Just get behind me with the rest of my troops!"

²⁰ The guard in the watchtower said, "Your Majesty, the rider got there, but he isn't coming back either. Wait a minute! That one man is a reckless chariot driver — it must be Jehu!"

²¹ Joram commanded, "Get my chariot ready." Then he and Ahaziah got in their chariots and rode out to meet Jehu. They all met on the land that had belonged to Naboth.*
²² Joram asked, "Jehu, is this a peaceful visit?"

"How can there be peace?" Jehu asked. "Your mother Jezebel has caused everyone to worship idols and practise witchcraft."

²³ "Ahaziah, let's get out of here!" Joram yelled. "It's a trap!" As Joram tried to escape, ²⁴ Jehu shot an arrow. It hit Joram between his shoulders, then it went through his heart and came out of his chest. He fell over dead in his chariot.

²⁵⁻²⁶ Jehu commanded his assistant Bidkar, "Get Joram's body and throw it in the field that Naboth once owned. Do you remember when you and I used to ride side by side behind Joram's father Ahab? It was then that the LORD swore to Ahab that he would be punished in the same field where he had killed Naboth and his sons. So throw Joram's body there, just as the LORD said."

²⁷ Ahaziah saw all this happen and tried to escape to the town of Beth-Haggan, but Jehu caught up with him and shouted, "Kill him too!" So his troops shot Ahaziah with an arrow while he was on the road to Gur near Ibleam. He went as far as Megiddo, where he died. ²⁸ Ahaziah's officers put his body in a chariot and took it back to Jerusalem, where they buried him beside his ancestors.

²⁹ Ahaziah had become king of Judah in the eleventh year of the rule of Ahab's son Joram.

Jehu kills Jezebel

³⁰ Jehu headed towards Jezreel, and when Jezebel heard he was coming, she put on eye shadow and brushed her hair. Then she stood at the window, waiting for him to arrive. ³¹ As he walked through the city gate, she shouted down to him, "Why did you come here, you murderer? To kill the king? You're no better than Zimri!"*

³² He looked up towards the window and asked, "Is anyone up there on my side?" A few

---

*9.21 the land . . . Naboth: See 1 Kings 21.
*9.31 Zimri: An Israelite king who killed King Elah and his family so he could become king, but who ruled only seven days (see 1 Kings 16.8–20).

See also: 9.10: 1 King 21.23.

See also: 9.26: 1 King 21.19.

palace workers stuck their heads out of a window, ³³ and Jehu shouted, "Throw her out of the window!" They threw her down, and her blood splattered on the walls and on the horses that trampled her body.'

³⁴ Jehu left to get something to eat and drink. Then he told some workers, "Even though she was evil, she was a king's daughter,* so make sure she has a proper burial."

³⁵ But when they went out to bury her body, they found only her skull, her hands, and her feet. ³⁶ They reported this to Jehu, and he said, "The Lord told Elijah the prophet that Jezebel's body would be eaten by dogs here in Jezreel. ³⁷ And he warned that her bones would be spread all over the ground like manure, so that no one could tell who it was."

CHAPTER 10

Jehu kills all of Ahab's descendants

¹ Ahab still had seventy descendants living in Samaria. So Jehu wrote a letter to each of the important leaders and officials of the town,' and to those who supported Ahab. In the letters he wrote:

² Your town is strong, and you're protected by chariots and an armed cavalry. And I know that King Ahab's descendants live there with you. So as soon as you read this letter, ³ choose the best person for the job and make him the next king. Then be prepared to defend Ahab's family.

⁴ The officials and leaders read the letters and were very frightened. They said to each other, "Jehu has already killed King Joram and King Ahaziah! We have to do what he says." ⁵ The prime minister, the mayor of the city, as well as the other leaders and Ahab's supporters, sent this answer to Jehu, "We are your servants, Your Majesty, and we will do whatever you tell us. But it's not our place to choose someone to be king. You do what you think is best."

⁶ Jehu then wrote another letter which said, "If you are on my side and will obey me, then prove it. Bring me the heads of the descendants of Ahab! And be here in Jezreel by this time tomorrow."

The seventy descendants of King Ahab were living with some of the most important people of the city. ⁷ And when these people read Jehu's second letter, they called together all seventy of Ahab's descendants. They killed them, put their heads in baskets, and sent them to Jezreel.

⁸ When Jehu was told what had happened, he said, "Put the heads in two piles at the city gate, and leave them there until morning."

⁹ The next morning, Jehu went out and stood where everyone could hear him, and he said, "You people are not guilty of anything. I'm the one who plotted against Joram and had him killed. But who killed all these men? ¹⁰ Listen to me. Everything the Lord's servant Elijah promised about Ahab's family will come true."*

¹¹ Then Jehu killed the rest of Ahab's relatives living in Jezreel, as well as his highest officials, his priests, and his closest friends. No one in Ahab's family was left alive in Jezreel.

¹²⁻¹³ Jehu left for Samaria, and along the way, he met some relatives of King Ahaziah of Judah at a place where shepherds meet.' He asked, "Who are you?"

"We are relatives of Ahaziah," they answered. "We're going to visit his family."

¹⁴ "Take them alive!" Jehu said to his officers. So they grabbed them and led them to the well near the shepherds' meeting place, where they killed all forty-two of them.

¹⁵ As Jehu went on, he saw Jehonadab son of Rechab' coming to meet him. Jehu greeted him, then said, "Jehonadab, I'm on your side. Are you on mine?"

"Yes, I am."

"Then give me your hand," Jehu answered. He helped Jehonadab into his chariot ¹⁶ and said, "Come with me and see how faithful I am to the Lord."

They rode together in Jehu's chariot ¹⁷ to Samaria. Jehu killed everyone there who belonged to Ahab's family, as well as all his officials. Everyone in his family was now dead, just as the Lord had promised Elijah.

Jehu kills all the worshippers of Baal

¹⁸ Jehu called together the people in Samaria and said:

King Ahab sometimes worshipped Baal, but I will be completely faithful to Baal. ¹⁹ I'm going to offer a huge sacrifice to him. So invite his prophets and priests, and be sure everyone who worships him is there. Anyone who doesn't come will be killed.

---

*9.34 she . . . daughter: Her father was King Ethbaal of Sidon (see 1 Kings 16.31).
See also: 9.36: 1 King 21.23.

*10.10 Everything . . . come true: See 1 Kings 21.17–24.
See also: 10.11: Hos 1.4.

But this was a trick — Jehu was really planning to kill the worshippers of Baal. [20] He said, "Announce a day of worship for Baal!" After the day had been announced, [21] Jehu sent an invitation to everyone in Israel. All the worshippers of Baal came, and the temple was filled from one end to the other. [22] Jehu told the official in charge of the sacred robes to make sure that everyone had a robe to wear.

[23] Jehu and Jehonadab went into the temple, and Jehu said to the crowd, "Look around and make sure that only the worshippers of Baal are here. No one who worships the LORD is allowed in." [24] Then they began to offer sacrifices to Baal.

Earlier, Jehu had ordered eighty soldiers to wait outside the temple. He had warned them, "I will get all these worshippers here, and if any of you let even one of them escape, you will be killed instead!"

[25] As soon as Jehu finished offering the sacrifice, he told the guards and soldiers, "Come in and kill them! Don't let anyone escape." They slaughtered everyone in the crowd and threw the bodies outside. Then they went back into the temple [26] and carried out the image of Baal. They burnt it [27] and broke it into pieces, then they completely destroyed Baal's temple. And since that time, it's been nothing but a public toilet.'

[28] That's how Jehu stopped the worship of Baal in Israel. [29] But he did not stop the worship of the gold statues of calves at Dan and Bethel that Jeroboam had made for the people to worship.*

[30] Later the LORD said, "Jehu, you have done right by destroying Ahab's entire family, just as I had planned. So I will make sure that the next four kings of Israel will come from your own family."

[31] But Jehu did not completely obey the commands of the LORD God of Israel. Instead, he kept doing the sinful things that Jeroboam had caused the Israelites to do.

Jehu dies

[32] In those days the LORD began to reduce the size of Israel's territory. King Hazael of Syria defeated the Israelites and took control [33] of the regions of Gilead and Bashan east of the River Jordan and north of the town of Aroer near the River Arnon. This was the land where the tribes of Gad, Reuben, and Manasseh had once lived. [34] Everything else Jehu did while he was king, including his brave deeds, is written in *The History of the Kings of Israel*. [35] Jehu died and was buried in Samaria, and his son Jehoahaz became king. [36] Jehu had ruled Israel twenty-eight years from Samaria.

CHAPTER 11

Queen Athaliah of Judah

This is also told in 2 Chronicles 22.10–12

[1] As soon as Athaliah heard that her son King Ahaziah was dead, she decided to kill any relative who could possibly become king. She would have done that, [2] but Jehosheba rescued Joash son of Ahaziah just as he was about to be murdered. Jehosheba, who was Jehoram's' daughter and Ahaziah's half-sister, hid her nephew Joash and his personal servant in a bedroom in the LORD's temple where he was safe from Athaliah. [3] Joash hid in the temple with Jehosheba* for six years while Athaliah ruled as queen of Judah.

Jehoiada makes Joash king of Judah

This is also told in 2 Chronicles 23.1–21

[4] Joash son of Ahaziah had hidden in the LORD's temple six years. Then in the seventh year, Jehoiada the priest sent for the commanders of the king's special bodyguards' and the commanders of the palace guards. They met him at the temple, and he asked them to make a promise in the name of the LORD. Then he brought out Joash [5] and said to them:

Here's what I want you to do. Three of your guard units will be on duty on the Sabbath. I want one unit to guard the palace. [6] Another unit will guard Sur Gate, and the third unit will guard the palace gate and relieve the palace guards.

[7] The other two guard units are supposed to be off duty on the Sabbath. But I want both of them to stay here at the temple and protect King Joash. [8] Make sure they follow him wherever he goes, and tell them to keep their swords ready to kill anyone who tries to get near him.

10.29 gold statues . . . to worship: See 1 Kings 12.26–30.

See also: 10.29: 1 King 12.28–30.

11.3 Jehosheba: Jehosheba was the wife of Jehoiada the priest (see 2 Chronicles 22.11), which is why she could hide Joash in one of the private bedrooms used only by the priests.

Holy history

All the kings of Israel

Jeroboam (1 Kings 12.25—14.20)
Did not obey God. Set up shrines to rival Jerusalem.

Nadab (1 Kings 15.25–32)
Only reigned for two years, but in that time managed to kill all the rest of his family. He was assassinated.

Baasha (1 Kings 15.33—16.7)
A soldier who, after killing Nadab, carried on a long conflict with Judah and its king Asa.

Elah (1 Kings 16.8–14)
Son of Baasha who only reigned for two years before he was killed while drunk at the home of his prime minister.

Zimri (1 Kings 16.15–20)
Zimri assassinated Elah and then, a week later, besieged by Omri, killed himself by setting fire to the palace.

Omri (2 Kings 16.21–8)
After seeing off Zimri, Omri established the city of Samaria as his capital.

Ahab (1 Kings 16.29—22.40)
Ahab's reign forms the backdrop to the activities of the great prophet Elijah. He was an evil man who, along with his wife Jezebel, organised Baal worship, persecuted true followers and killed prophets. He came to a sticky end, bleeding to death after a battle. His chariot is washed with a whore's bath water, and the dogs lick off his blood.

Ahaziah (1 Kings 22.51–3; 2 Kings 1.1–18)
The son of Ahab and as bad as his dad.

Joram (2 Kings 3.1–27)
Another son of Ahab's and not much improvement.

Jehu (2 Kings 9.1—10.35)
An army officer who kills not only Joram, but also Ahaziah, King of Judah. Then he kills Jezebel, takes Samaria, and removes the rest of Ahab's family. He wipes out the rest of the prophets of Baal by inviting them to a sacrifice. They file into the temple and the guards kill them. Simple, but effective.

Jehoahaz (2 Kings 13.1–9)
A bad man and appalling military leader, his army was decimated by the Syrians.

Jehoash (2 Kings 13.10–19)
Weak and ineffective. Defeated the Syrians and recaptured the territory they had taken, although that was only through Elisha.

Jeroboam II (2 Kings 14.23–9)
He oversaw a time of prosperity and military success, as well as a time of hypocrisy and wealthy cynicism. The prophets Amos and Hosea offer a true perspective on this reign.

Zechariah (2 Kings 15.8–12)
Zechariah only ruled for six months before he was assassinated by…

Shallum (2 Kings 15.13–16)
No time to tell if he was good or bad, since he only made it to one month before he was killed by…

Menahem (2 Kings 15.17–22)
A violent, bloody murderer who even attacked pregnant women.

Pekahiah (2 Kings 5.23–26)
A bad king who was assassinated. His killer was one of his officials, a man called…

Pekah (2 Kings 15.27–31)
He ruled for twenty years, but eventually he was attacked by the Assyrians. They took over huge portions of Israel and took many of the inhabitants into captivity. In the end he was assassinated by…

Hoshea (2 Kings 17.1–41)
When Hoshea rebelled against the Assyrians, the kingdom of Israel was simply wiped out, and all the inhabitants were carted away into captivity in Assyria.

More...
Israel and Judah p.385
Elijah p.391
Elisha p.404

9 The commanders followed Jehoiada's orders. Each one called together his guards — those coming on duty and those going off duty. 10 Jehoiada brought out the swords and shields that had belonged to King David and gave them to the commanders. 11 Then they gave the weapons to their guards, who took their positions around the temple and the altar to protect Joash on every side.

12 Jehoiada brought Joash outside, where he placed the crown on his head and gave him a copy of instructions for ruling the nation. Olive oil was poured on his head to show that he was now king, while the crowd clapped and shouted, "Long live the king!"

13 Queen Athaliah heard the crowd and went to the temple. 14 There she saw Joash standing by one of the columns, which was the usual place for the king. The singers' and the trumpet players were standing next to him, and the people were celebrating and blowing trumpets. Athaliah tore her clothes in anger and shouted, "You betrayed me, you traitors!"

15 Straight away, Jehoiada said to the army commanders, "Kill her! But don't do it anywhere near the LORD's temple. Take her out in front of the troops and kill anyone who is with her!" 16 So the commanders dragged her to the gate where horses are led into the palace, and they killed her there.

17 Jehoiada the priest asked King Joash and the people to promise that they would be faithful to each other and to the LORD. 18 Then the crowd went to the temple built to honour Baal and tore it down. They smashed the altars and idols and killed Mattan the priest of Baal in front of the altars.

After Jehoiada had placed guards around the LORD's temple, 19 he called together all the commanders, the king's special bodyguards,' the palace guards, and the people. They led Joash from the temple, through the Guards' Gate, and into the palace. He took his place on the throne and became king of Judah. 20 Everyone celebrated because Athaliah had been killed and Jerusalem was peaceful again. 21 Joash was only seven years old when this happened.

CHAPTER 12

King Joash of Judah

This is also told in 2 Chronicles 24.1–16

1 Joash' became king of Judah in Jehu's seventh year as king of Israel, and he ruled forty years from Jerusalem. His mother Zibiah was from the town of Beersheba.

2 Jehoiada the priest taught Joash what was right, and so for the rest of his life Joash obeyed the LORD. 3 But even Joash did not destroy the local shrines,' and they were still used as places for offering sacrifices.

4 One day, Joash said to the priests, "Collect all the money that has been given to the LORD's temple, whether from taxes or gifts, 5 and use it to repair the temple. You priests can contribute your own money too."'

6 But the priests never started repairing the temple. So in the twenty-third year of his rule, 7 Joash called for Jehoiada and the other priests and said, "Why aren't you using the money to repair the temple? Don't take any more money for yourselves. It is only to be used to pay for the repairs." 8 The priests agreed that they would not collect any more money or be in charge of the temple repairs.

9 Jehoiada found a wooden box; he cut a hole in the top of it and set it on the right side of the altar where people went into the temple. Whenever someone gave money to the temple, the priests guarding the entrance would put it into this box. 10 When the box was full of money, the king's secretary and the chief priest would count the money and put it in bags. 11 Then they would give it to the men supervising the repairs to the temple. Some of the money was used to pay the builders, the woodworkers, 12 the stonecutters, and the men who built the walls. And some was used to buy wood and stone and to pay any other costs for repairing the temple.

13 While the repairs were being made, the money that was given to the temple was not used to make silver bowls, lamp snuffers, small sprinkling bowls, trumpets, or anything gold or silver for the temple. 14 It went only to pay for repairs. 15 The men in charge were honest, so no one had to keep track of the money.

16 The fines that had to be paid along with the sacrifices to make things right and the sacrifices for sin did not go to the temple. This money belonged only to the priests.

See also: **11.14:** 2 King 23.3.

See also: **12.4:** Exod 30.11–16. **12.15:** 2 King 22.7. **12.16:** Lev 7.7.

¹⁷ About the same time, King Hazael of Syria attacked the town of Gath and captured it. Next, he decided to attack Jerusalem. ¹⁸ So Joash collected everything he and his ancestors Jehoshaphat, Jehoram, and Ahaziah had dedicated to the LORD, as well as the gold in the storage rooms in the temple and palace. He sent it all to Hazael as a gift, and when Hazael received it, he ordered his troops to leave Jerusalem.

¹⁹ Everything else Joash did while he was king is written in *The History of the Kings of Judah*. ²⁰⁻²¹ At the end of his rule, some of his officers rebelled against him. Jozabad▸ son of Shimeath and Jehozabad son of Shomer murdered him in a building where the land was filled in on the east side of Jerusalem,* near the road to Silla. Joash was buried beside his ancestors in Jerusalem,▸ and his son Amaziah became king.

CHAPTER 13

King Jehoahaz of Israel

¹ Jehoahaz son of Jehu became king of Israel in the twenty-third year of Joash's rule in Judah. Jehoahaz ruled seventeen years from Samaria ² and disobeyed the LORD by doing wrong. He never stopped following the example of Jeroboam, who had caused the Israelites to sin.

³ The LORD was angry with the Israelites, so he let King Hazael of Syria and his son Benhadad rule over them for a long time. ⁴ Jehoahaz prayed to the LORD for help, and the LORD saw how terribly Hazael was treating the Israelites. He answered Jehoahaz ⁵ by sending Israel a leader who rescued them from the Syrians,* and the Israelites lived in peace as they had before. ⁶⁻⁷ But Hazael had defeated Israel's army so badly that Jehoahaz had only ten chariots, fifty cavalry troops, and ten thousand regular soldiers left in his army.

The Israelites kept sinning and following the example of Jeroboam's family. They did not tear down the sacred poles* that had been set up in Samaria for the worship of the goddess Asherah.

⁸ Everything else Jehoahaz did while he was king, including his brave deeds, is written in *The History of the Kings of Israel*. ⁹ Jehoahaz died and was buried in Samaria, and his son Jehoash became king.

King Jehoash of Israel

¹⁰ Jehoash became king of Israel in the thirty-seventh year of Joash's rule in Judah, and he ruled sixteen years from Samaria. ¹¹ He disobeyed the LORD by doing just like Jeroboam, who had caused the Israelites to sin.

¹² Everything else Jehoash did while he was king, including his war against King Amaziah of Judah, is written in *The History of the Kings of Israel*. ¹³ Jehoash died and was buried in Samaria beside the other Israelite kings. His son Jeroboam then became king.

Elisha the prophet dies

¹⁴ Some time before the death of King Jehoash, Elisha the prophet was very sick and about to die. Jehoash went in and stood beside him, crying. He said, "Master, what will Israel's chariots and cavalry be able to do without you?"▸

¹⁵⁻¹⁶ "Grab a bow and some arrows," Elisha told him, "and hold them in your hand." Jehoash grabbed the bow and arrows and held them. Elisha placed his hand on the king's hand ¹⁷ and said, "Open the window facing east." When it was open, Elisha shouted, "Now shoot!" Jehoash shot an arrow and Elisha said, "That arrow is a sign that the LORD will help you completely defeat the Syrian army at Aphek."

¹⁸ Elisha said, "Pick up the arrows and hit the ground with them." Jehoash grabbed the arrows and hit the ground three times, then stopped. ¹⁹ Elisha became angry with the king and exclaimed, "If you had struck it five or six times, you would completely wipe out the Syrians. Now you will defeat them only three times."

²⁰ Elisha died and was buried.

Every year in the spring, Moab's leaders sent raiding parties into Israel. ²¹ Once, while some Israelites were burying a man's body, they saw a group of Moabites. The Israelites quickly threw the body into Elisha's tomb and ran away. As soon as the man's body touched the bones of Elisha, the man came back to life and stood up.

---

*12.20–21 where . . . Jerusalem: The Hebrew text has "on the Millo", which probably refers to a landfill to strengthen and extend the hill where the city was built.
*13.5 by sending . . . the Syrians: The name of this leader is not given, but it may refer to Elisha the prophet, King Jehoash of Israel, or his son King Jeroboam.
*13.6–7 sacred poles: Or "trees", used as symbols of Asherah, the goddess of fertility.

See also: 13.14: 2 King 2.12.

Israel defeats Syria

22 Israel was under the power of King Hazael of Syria during the entire rule of Jehoahaz. 23 But the LORD was kind to the Israelites and showed them mercy because of his solemn agreement with their ancestors Abraham, Isaac, and Jacob. In fact, he has never turned his back on them or let them be completely destroyed.

24 Hazael died, and his son Benhadad then became king of Syria. 25 King Jehoash of Israel attacked and defeated the Syrian army three times. He took back from Benhadad all the towns Hazael had captured in battle from his father Jehoahaz.

CHAPTER 14

King Amaziah of Judah

This is also told in 2 Chronicles 25.1–24

1 Amaziah son of Joash became king of Judah in the second year of Jehoash's rule in Israel. 2 Amaziah was twenty-five years old when he became king, and he ruled twenty-nine years from Jerusalem, which was also the home town of his mother Jehoaddin.

3 Amaziah followed the example of his father Joash by obeying the LORD and doing right. But he was not as faithful as his ancestor David. 4 Amaziah did not destroy the local shrines*, and they were still used as places for offering sacrifices.

5 As soon as Amaziah had control of Judah, he arrested and killed the officers who had murdered his father. 6 But the children of those officers were not killed. The LORD had commanded in the Law of Moses that only the people who sinned were to be punished, not their parents or children.*

7 While Amaziah was king, he killed ten thousand Edomite soldiers in Salt Valley. He captured the town of Sela and renamed it Joktheel, which is still its name.

8 One day, Amaziah sent a message to King Jehoash of Israel: "Come out and face me in battle!"

9 Jehoash sent back this reply:

Once upon a time, a small thorn bush in Lebanon announced that his son was going to marry the daughter of a large cedar tree. But a wild animal came along and trampled the small bush.

10 Amaziah, you think you're so powerful because you defeated Edom. Go ahead and celebrate — but stay at home. If you cause any trouble, both you and your kingdom of Judah will be destroyed.

11 But Amaziah refused to listen. So Jehoash and his troops marched to the town of Beth-Shemesh in Judah to attack Amaziah and his troops. 12 During the battle, Judah's army was crushed. Every soldier from Judah ran back home, 13 and Jehoash captured Amaziah.

Jehoash then marched to Jerusalem and broke down the city wall from Ephraim Gate to Corner Gate, a section nearly two hundred metres long. 14 He took the gold and silver, as well as everything of value from the LORD's temple and the king's treasury. He took hostages, then returned to Samaria.

15 Everything else Jehoash did while he was king, including his brave deeds and how he defeated King Amaziah of Judah, is written in *The History of the Kings of Israel.* 16 Jehoash died and was buried in Samaria beside the other Israelite kings. His son Jeroboam then became king.

17 Fifteen years after Jehoash died, 18-20 some people in Jerusalem plotted against Amaziah. He was able to escape to the town of Lachish, but another group of people caught him and killed him there. His body was taken back to Jerusalem on horseback and buried beside his ancestors.

Everything else Amaziah did while he was king is written in *The History of the Kings of Judah.* 21 After his death the people of Judah made his son Azariah king, even though he was only sixteen at the time. 22 Azariah was the one who later recaptured and rebuilt the town of Elath.

King Jeroboam the Second of Israel

23 Jeroboam son of Jehoash became king of Israel in the fifteenth year of Amaziah's rule in Judah. Jeroboam ruled forty-one years from Samaria. 24 He disobeyed the LORD by following the evil example of Jeroboam son of Nebat, who had caused the Israelites to sin.

25 Jeroboam extended the boundaries of Israel from Lebo-Hamath in the north to the Dead Sea in the south, just as the LORD had promised his servant Jonah son of Amittai, who was a prophet from Gath-Hepher. 26 The LORD helped Jeroboam do this because he had seen how terribly the Israelites were

*14.6 The LORD had commanded . . . children: See Deuteronomy 24.16.

See also: 14.6: Deut 24.16.

See also: 14.25: Jon 1.1.

suffering, whether slave or free, and no one was left to help them. [27] And since the LORD had promised that he would not let Israel be completely destroyed, he helped Jeroboam rescue them.

[28] Everything else Jeroboam did while he was king, including his brave deeds and how he recaptured the towns of Damascus and Hamath,' is written in *The History of the Kings of Israel*. [29] Jeroboam died and was buried, and his son Zechariah became king.

CHAPTER 15

King Azariah of Judah

This is also told in 2 Chronicles 26.1–23

[1] Azariah son of Amaziah became king of Judah in Jeroboam's twenty-seventh year as king of Israel. [2] He was only sixteen years old when he became king, and he ruled fifty-two years from Jerusalem, which was also the home town of his mother Jecoliah.

[3] Azariah obeyed the LORD by doing right, as his father Amaziah had done. [4] But Azariah did not destroy the local shrines,' and they were still used as places for offering sacrifices.

[5] The LORD punished Azariah with leprosy* for the rest of his life. He wasn't allowed to live in the royal palace, so his son Jotham lived there and ruled in his place.

[6] Everything else Azariah did while he was king is written in *The History of the Kings of Judah*. [7] Azariah died and was buried beside his ancestors in Jerusalem. His son Jotham then became king.

King Zechariah of Israel

[8] Zechariah son of Jeroboam became king of Israel in the thirty-eighth year of Azariah's rule in Judah, but he ruled only six months from Samaria. [9] Like his ancestors, Zechariah disobeyed the LORD by following the evil ways of Jeroboam son of Nebat, who had caused the Israelites to sin.

[10] Shallum son of Jabesh plotted against Zechariah and killed him in public.' Shallum then became king. [11-12] So the LORD had kept his promise to Jehu that the next four kings of Israel would come from his family.*

Everything else Zechariah did while he was king is written in *The History of the Kings of Israel*.

King Shallum of Israel

[13] Shallum became king of Israel in the thirty-ninth year of Azariah's' rule in Judah. But only one month after Shallum became king, [14-16] Menahem son of Gadi came to Samaria from Tirzah and killed him. Menahem then became king. The town of Tiphsah would not surrender to him, so he destroyed it and all the surrounding towns as far as Tirzah. He killed everyone living in Tiphsah, and with his sword he even ripped open pregnant women.

Everything else Shallum did while he was king, including his plot against Zechariah, is written in *The History of the Kings of Israel*.

King Menahem of Israel

[17] Menahem became king of Israel in Azariah's thirty-ninth year as king of Judah, and he ruled Israel ten years from Samaria. [18] He constantly disobeyed the LORD by following the example of Jeroboam son of Nebat, who had caused the Israelites to sin.

[19] During Menahem's rule, King Tiglath Pileser* of Assyria invaded Israel. He agreed to help Menahem keep control of his kingdom, if Menahem would pay him thirty-four thousand kilogrammes of silver. [20] So Menahem ordered every rich person in Israel to give him fifty pieces of silver, and he gave it all to Tiglath Pileser, who stopped his attack and left Israel.

[21] Everything else Menahem did while he was king is written in *The History of the Kings of Israel*. [22] Menahem died, and his son Pekahiah became king.

King Pekahiah of Israel

[23] Pekahiah became king of Israel in the fiftieth year of Azariah's rule in Judah, and he ruled two years from Samaria. [24] He disobeyed the LORD and caused the Israelites to sin, just as Jeroboam son of Nebat had done.

[25] Pekah son of Remaliah was Pekahiah's chief officer, but he made plans to kill the king. So he and fifty men from Gilead broke into the strongest part of the palace in Samaria and murdered Pekahiah, together with Argob and Arieh.' Pekah then became king.

[26] Everything else Pekahiah did while he was king is written in *The History of the Kings of Israel*.

---

*15.5 **leprosy:** See the note at 5.1.
*15.11–12 **So the LORD . . . family:** See 10.28–31.
See also: 15.7: Isa 6.1. 15.12: 2 King 10.30.

*15.19 **Tiglath Pileser:** The Hebrew text has "Pul", another name for Tiglath Pileser, who ruled Assyria from 745 to 727 BC.

King Pekah of Israel

27 Pekah son of Remaliah became king of Israel in Azariah's fifty-second year as king of Judah, and he ruled twenty years from Samaria. 28 He disobeyed the LORD and followed the evil example of Jeroboam son of Nebat, who had caused the Israelites to sin.

29 During Pekah's rule, King Tiglath Pileser of Assyria marched into Israel. He captured the territories of Gilead and Galilee, including the towns of Ijon, Abel-Bethmaacah, Janoah, Kedesh, and Hazor, as well as the entire territory of Naphtali. Then he took Israelites from those regions to Assyria as prisoners.*

30 In the twentieth year of Jotham's rule in Judah, Hoshea son of Elah plotted against Pekah and murdered him. Hoshea then became king of Israel.

31 Everything else Pekah did while he was king is written in *The History of the Kings of Israel.*

King Jotham of Judah

This is also told in 2 Chronicles 27.1–9

32 Jotham son of Azariah' became king of Judah in the second year of Pekah's rule in Israel. 33 Jotham was twenty-five years old when he became king, and he ruled sixteen years from Jerusalem. His mother Jerusha was the daughter of Zadok.

34 Jotham followed the example of his father by obeying the LORD and doing right. 35 It was Jotham who rebuilt the Upper Gate that led into the court around the LORD's temple. But the local shrines' were not destroyed, and they were still used as places for offering sacrifices.

36 Everything else Jotham did while he was king is written in *The History of the Kings of Judah.* 37 During his rule, the LORD let King Rezin of Syria and King Pekah of Israel start attacking Judah. 38 Jotham died and was buried beside his ancestors in Jerusalem, and his son Ahaz became king.

CHAPTER 16

King Ahaz of Judah

This is also told in 2 Chronicles 28.1–27

1 Ahaz son of Jotham became king of Judah in the seventeenth year of Pekah's rule in Israel.

2 He was twenty years old at the time, and he ruled from Jerusalem for sixteen years.

Ahaz wasn't like his ancestor David. Instead, he disobeyed the LORD 3 and was even more sinful than the kings of Israel. He sacrificed his own son, which was a disgusting custom of the nations that the LORD had forced out of Israel. 4 Ahaz offered sacrifices at the local shrines', as well as on every hill and in the shade of large trees.

5-6 While Ahaz was ruling Judah, the king of Edom recaptured the town of Elath from Judah and forced out the people of Judah. Edomites' then moved into Elath, and they still live there.

About the same time, King Rezin of Syria and King Pekah of Israel marched to Jerusalem and attacked, but they could not capture it.

7 Ahaz sent a message to King Tiglath Pileser of Assyria that said, "Your Majesty, King Rezin and King Pekah are attacking me, your loyal servant. Please come and rescue me." 8 Along with the message, Ahaz sent silver and gold from the LORD's temple and from the palace treasury as a gift for the Assyrian king.

9 As soon as Tiglath Pileser received the message, he and his troops marched to Syria. He captured the capital city of Damascus, then he took the people living there to the town of Kir as prisoners and killed King Rezin.*

10 Later, Ahaz went to Damascus to meet Tiglath Pileser. And while Ahaz was there, he saw an altar and sent a model of it back to Uriah the priest, along with the plans for building one. 11 Uriah followed the plans and built an altar exactly like the one in Damascus, finishing it just before Ahaz came back.

12 When Ahaz returned, he went to see the altar and to offer sacrifices on it. He walked up to the altar 13 and poured wine over it. Then he offered sacrifices to please the LORD, to give him thanks, and to ask for his blessings.* 14 After that, he had the bronze altar moved aside,' so his new altar would be right in front of the LORD's temple. 15 He told Uriah the priest:

---

*16.9 King Rezin: This probably took place around 734 BC, before the events in 15.29.

*16.13 offered . . . blessings: In traditional translations, these sacrifices are usually called "whole burnt offerings", "grain offerings", and "peace offerings". These are described in Leviticus 1–3.

See also: 16.3: Deut 12.31. 16.5: Isa 7.1. 16.14: Exod 27.1–2; 2 Chron 4.1.

---

*15.29 prisoners: The events in this verse probably took place around 733 BC.

From now on, the morning and evening sacrifices as well as all gifts of grain and wine are to be offered on this altar. The sacrifices for the people and for the king must also be offered here. Sprinkle the blood from all the sacrifices on it, but leave the bronze altar for me to use for prayer and finding out what God wants me to do.

¹⁶ Uriah did everything Ahaz told him.

¹⁷ Ahaz also had the side panels and the small bowls taken off the moveable stands in the LORD's temple. He had the large bronze bowl, called the Sea, removed from the bronze bulls on which it rested and had it placed on a stand made of stone. ¹⁸ He took down the special tent that was used for worship on the Sabbath⁺ and closed up the private entrance that the kings of Judah used for going into the temple. He did all these things to please Tiglath Pileser.

¹⁹ Everything else Ahaz did while he was king is written in *The History of the Kings of Judah*. ²⁰ Ahaz died and was buried beside his ancestors in Jerusalem,⁺ and his son Hezekiah became king.

King Hoshea of Israel and the defeat of the northern kingdom

CHAPTER 17

¹ Hoshea son of Elah became king of Israel in the twelfth year of Ahaz's rule in Judah, and he ruled nine years from Samaria. ² Hoshea disobeyed the LORD and sinned, but not as much as the earlier Israelite kings had done.

³ During Hoshea's rule, King Shalmaneser of Assyria⁎ invaded Israel; he took control of the country and made Hoshea pay taxes. ⁴ But later, Hoshea refused to pay the taxes and asked King So of Egypt to help him rebel. When Shalmaneser found out, he arrested Hoshea and put him in prison.

Samaria is destroyed and the Israelites are taken to Assyria

⁵ Shalmaneser invaded Israel and attacked the city of Samaria for three years, ⁶ before capturing it in the ninth year of Hoshea's

---

17.3 King Shalmaneser of Assyria: The son of Tiglath Pileser, who ruled Assyria from 727 to 722 BC.
See also: 16.17: 1 King 7.23–39; 2 Chron 4.2–6.
16.20: Isa 14.28.

Holy history

The fate of Israel

Israel was vulnerable to attack from the east. Which would have been OK, were it not for the fact that the greatest power of the time was Assyria. Which lay in the east.

The first invasion was led by King Tiglath Pileser, but King Menahem of Israel paid him off with 34 tons of silver (2 Kings 15.19–20). This was always going to be a temporary measure and Tiglath-Pileser returned under the reign of King Pekah, capturing several cities (2 Kings 16.29).

Ironically, the next time Israel was invaded by the Assyrians they were called in by Judah. King Pekah, in alliance with Syria, invaded Judah. So Ahaz King of Judah called the Assyrians to Judah's rescue. Ahaz was a real fan of the Assyrians. He even copied their religious equipment (2 Kings 16.10–18).

For Israel, the end finally came under King Hoshea. He rebelled against Assyrian taxes, but the plan went disastrously wrong. The Assyrians, angered by the rebellion, marched in, took over the country and took the people into captivity.

According to Assyrian records, 27,290 people were deported from Israel to Assyria. They were replaced by foreign settlers, who the Assyrians sent to Israel to take over the homes and towns. Many of these settled in Samaria, the region between Israel and Judah. They became the Samaritans that we read about in the New Testament. They developed their own version of Judaism, and built their own temple on Mount Gerazim. The Samaritans were never viewed as 'proper Jews' by those in Judah. Instead they regarded them as half-breeds, and hated them with a passion which was to last for centuries.

More...

Assyria p.500
Suffering p.555
Messiah p.770

rule. The Assyrian king* took the Israelites away to Assyria as prisoners. He forced some of them to live in the town of Halah, others to live near the River Habor in the territory of Gozan, and still others to live in towns where the Median people lived.

⁷ All of this happened because the people of Israel had sinned against the LORD their God, who had rescued them from Egypt, where they had been slaves. They worshipped foreign gods, ⁸ followed the customs of the nations that the LORD had forced out of Israel, and were just as sinful as the Israelite kings. ⁹ Even worse, the Israelites tried to hide their sins from the LORD their God. They built their own local shrines everywhere in Israel — from small towns to large, walled cities. ¹⁰ They also built stone images of foreign gods and set up sacred poles* for the worship of Asherah on every hill and under every shady tree. ¹¹ They offered sacrifices at the shrines,' just as the foreign nations had done before the LORD forced them out of Israel. They did sinful things that made the LORD very angry.

¹² Even though the LORD had commanded the Israelites not to worship idols,* they did it anyway. ¹³ So the LORD made sure that every prophet warned Israel and Judah with these words: "I, the LORD, command you to stop doing sinful things and start obeying my laws and teachings! I gave them to your ancestors, and I told my servants the prophets to repeat them to you."

¹⁴ But the Israelites would not listen; they were as stubborn as their ancestors who had refused to worship the LORD their God. ¹⁵ They ignored the LORD's warnings and commands, and they rejected the solemn agreement he had made with their ancestors. They worshipped worthless idols and became worthless themselves. The LORD had told the Israelites not to do the things that the foreign nations around them were doing, but Israel became just like them.

¹⁶ The people of Israel disobeyed all the commands of the LORD their God. They made two gold statues of calves and set up a sacred pole for Asherah; they also worshipped the

stars and the god Baal. ¹⁷ They used magic and witchcraft and even sacrificed their own children. The Israelites were determined to do whatever the LORD hated. ¹⁸ The LORD became so furious with the people of Israel that he allowed them to be carried away as prisoners.

Only the people living in Judah were left, ¹⁹ but they also disobeyed the LORD's commands and acted like the Israelites. ²⁰ So the LORD turned his back on everyone in Israel and Judah' and let them be punished and defeated until no one was left.

²¹ Earlier, when the LORD took the northern tribes away from David's family,* the people living in northern Israel chose Jeroboam son of Nebat as their king. Jeroboam caused the Israelites to sin and to stop worshipping the LORD. ²² The people kept on sinning like Jeroboam, ²³ until the LORD got rid of them, just as he had warned his servants the prophets.

That's why the people of Israel were taken away as prisoners to Assyria, and that's where they remained.

Foreigners are resettled in Israel

²⁴ The king of Assyria took people who were living in the cities of Babylon, Cuthah, Avva, Hamath, and Sepharvaim, and forced them to move to Israel. They took over the towns where the Israelites had lived, including the capital city of Samaria.

²⁵ At first these people did not worship the LORD, so he sent lions to attack them, and the lions killed some of them. ²⁶ A messenger told the king of Assyria, "The people you moved to Israel don't know how to worship the god of that country. So he sent lions that have attacked and killed some of them."

²⁷ The king replied, "Get one of the Israelite priests we brought here and send him back to Israel. He can live there and teach them about the god of that country." ²⁸ One of the Israelite priests was chosen to go back to Israel. He lived in Bethel and taught the people how to worship the LORD.

²⁹ But in towns all over Israel, the different groups of people made statues of their own gods, then they placed these idols in local Israelite' shrines. ³⁰ The people from Babylonia made the god Succoth-Benoth; those from Cuthah made the god Nergal;

17.6 The Assyrian king: Probably Sargon, Shalmaneser's successor. Shalmaneser died after the city of Samaria was captured (722 BC) but before the people were taken away as prisoners (720 BC). Sargon ruled Assyria from 721 to 705 BC.
17.12 the LORD . . . idols: See Exodus 20.4–5.
See also: 17.10: 1 King 14.23. 17.16: 1 King 12.28.

17.21 when the LORD . . . family: See 1 Kings 11.29–39.
See also: 17.17: Deut 18.10.

those from Hamath made Ashima; ³¹ those from Avva made Nibhaz and Tartak; and the people from Sepharvaim sacrificed their children to their own gods Adrammelech and Anammelech. ³²⁻³³ They worshipped their own gods, just as they had before they were taken away to Israel. They also worshipped the LORD, but they chose their own people to be priests at the shrines. ³⁴ Everyone followed their old customs. None of them worshipped only the LORD, and they refused to obey the laws and commands that the LORD had given to the descendants of Jacob, the man he named Israel. ³⁵ At the time when the LORD had made his solemn agreement with the people of Israel, he told them:

Do not worship any other gods! Do not bow down to them or offer a sacrifice. ³⁶ Worship only me! I am the one who rescued you from Egypt with my mighty power. Bow down to me and offer sacrifices. ³⁷ Never worship any other god, always obey my laws and teachings, ³⁸ and remember the solemn agreement between us.

I will say it again: do not worship any god ³⁹ except me. I am the LORD your God, and I will rescue you from all your enemies.

⁴⁰ But the people living in Israel ignored that command and kept on following their old customs. ⁴¹ They did worship the LORD, but they also worshipped their own idols. Their descendants did the same thing.

King Hezekiah of Judah and the Assyrian invasion

CHAPTER 18

King Hezekiah of Judah

This is also told in 2 Chronicles 29.1,2; 31.1

¹ Hezekiah son of Ahaz became king of Judah in the third year of Hoshea's rule in Israel. ² Hezekiah was twenty-five years old when he became king, and he ruled twenty-nine years from Jerusalem. His mother Abi was the daughter of Zechariah. ³ Hezekiah obeyed the LORD, just as his ancestor David had done. ⁴ He destroyed the local shrines', then tore down the images of foreign gods and cut down the sacred pole*

for worshipping the goddess Asherah. He also smashed the bronze snake Moses had made. The people had named it Nehushtan* and had been offering sacrifices to it.

⁵ Hezekiah trusted the LORD God of Israel. No other king of Judah was like Hezekiah, either before or after him. ⁶ He was completely faithful to the LORD and obeyed the laws the LORD had given to Moses for the people. ⁷ The LORD helped Hezekiah, so he was successful in everything he did. He even rebelled against the king of Assyria, refusing to be his servant. ⁸ Hezekiah defeated the Philistine towns as far away as Gaza — from the smallest towns to the large, walled cities.

⁹ During the fourth year of Hezekiah's rule, which was the seventh year of Hoshea's rule in Israel, King Shalmaneser of Assyria led his troops to Samaria, the capital city of Israel. They attacked ¹⁰ and captured it three years later,* in the sixth year of Hezekiah's rule and the ninth year of Hoshea's rule. ¹¹ The king of Assyria* took the Israelites away as prisoners; he forced some of them to live in the town of Halah, others to live near the River Habor in the territory of Gozan, and still others to live in towns where the Median people lived. ¹² All of that happened because the people of Israel had not obeyed the LORD their God. They rejected the solemn agreement he had made with them, and they ignored everything that the LORD's servant Moses had told them.

King Sennacherib of Assyria invades Judah

This is also told in 2 Chronicles 32.1–19; Isaiah 36.1–22

¹³ In the fourteenth year of Hezekiah's rule in Judah, King Sennacherib of Assyria invaded the country and captured every walled city,* except Jerusalem. ¹⁴ Hezekiah sent this message to Sennacherib, who was in the town of Lachish: "I know I am guilty of rebellion. But I will pay you whatever you want, if you stop your attack."

---

*18.4 sacred pole: See the note at 13.6–7.

See also: 17.34: Gen 32.28; 35.10. 17.35: Exod 20.5; Deut 5.9. 17.36: Deut 6.13. 18.4: Num 21.9.

*18.4 the bronze snake . . . Nehushtan: See Numbers 21.8–9. "Nehushtan" is a nickname that sounds like the Hebrew words for "snake" and "bronze".
*18.10 three years later: When the Israelites measured time, part of a year could be counted as a whole year.
*18.11 The king of Assyria: Probably Sargon, Shalmaneser's successor (see the note at 17.6).
*18.13 King Sennacherib . . . walled city: Sennacherib ruled Assyria 705–681 BC, and this event probably took place in 701 BC.

Sennacherib told Hezekiah to pay ten thousand kilogrammes of silver and a thousand kilogrammes of gold. ¹⁵ So Hezekiah collected all the silver from the LORD's temple and the royal treasury. ¹⁶ He even stripped the gold that he had used to cover the doors and doorposts' in the temple. He gave it all to Sennacherib.

¹⁷ The king of Assyria ordered his three highest military officers to leave Lachish and take a large army to Jerusalem. When they arrived, the officers stood on the road near the cloth makers' shops along the canal from the upper pool. ¹⁸ They called out to Hezekiah, and three of his highest officials came out to meet them. One of them was Hilkiah's son Eliakim, who was the prime minister. The other two were Shebna, assistant to the prime minister, and Joah son of Asaph, keeper of the government records.

¹⁹ One of the Assyrian commanders told them:

I have a message for Hezekiah from the great king of Assyria. Ask Hezekiah why he feels so sure of himself. ²⁰ Does he think he can plan and win a war with nothing but words? Who is going to help him, now that he has turned against the king of Assyria? ²¹ Is he depending on Egypt and its king? That's the same as leaning on a broken stick, and it will go right through his hand.

²² Is Hezekiah now depending on the LORD your God? Didn't Hezekiah tear down all except one of the LORD's altars and places of worship?* Didn't he tell the people of Jerusalem and Judah to worship at that one place?

²³ The king of Assyria wants to make a bet with you people. He will give you two thousand horses, if you have enough troops to ride them. ²⁴ How could you even defeat our lowest ranking officer, when you have to depend on Egypt for chariots and cavalry? ²⁵ Don't forget that it was the LORD who sent me here with orders to destroy your nation!

²⁶ Eliakim, Shebna, and Joah said, "Sir, we don't want the people listening from the city wall to understand what you are saying. So please speak to us in Aramaic instead of Hebrew."

²⁷ The Assyrian army commander answered, "My king sent me to speak to everyone, not just to you leaders. These people will soon have to eat their own body waste and drink their own urine! And so will the three of you."

²⁸ Then, in a voice loud enough for everyone to hear, he shouted in Hebrew:

Listen to what the great king of Assyria says! ²⁹ Don't be fooled by Hezekiah. He can't save you. ³⁰ Don't trust him when he tells you that the LORD will protect you from the king of Assyria. ³¹ Stop listening to Hezekiah! Pay attention to my king. Surrender to him. He will let you keep your own vineyards, fig trees, and cisterns ³² for a while. Then he will come and take you away to a country just like yours, where you can plant vineyards, raise your own grain, and have plenty of olive oil and honey. Believe me, you won't starve there.

Hezekiah claims the LORD will save you. But don't be fooled by him. ³³ Were any other gods able to defend their land against the king of Assyria? ³⁴ What happened to the gods of Hamath and Arpad? What about the gods of Sepharvaim, Hena, and Ivvah? Were the gods of Samaria able to protect their land against the Assyrian forces? ³⁵ None of these gods kept their people safe from the king of Assyria. Do you think the LORD your God can do any better?

³⁶⁻³⁷ Eliakim, Shebna, and Joah had been warned by King Hezekiah not to answer the Assyrian commander. So they tore their clothes in sorrow and reported to Hezekiah everything the commander had said.

CHAPTER 19

Hezekiah asks Isaiah the prophet for advice

This is also told in Isaiah 37.1–13

¹ As soon as Hezekiah heard the news, he tore off his clothes in sorrow and put on sackcloth. Then he went into the temple of the LORD. ² He told Prime Minister Eliakim, Assistant Prime Minister Shebna, and the senior priests to dress in sackcloth and tell the prophet Isaiah:

³ These are difficult and disgraceful times. Our nation is like a woman too weak to give birth, when it's time for her baby to be born. ⁴ Please pray for those of us who are left alive. The king of Assyria sent his army

---

*18.22 worship: Hezekiah actually had torn down the places where idols were worshipped, and he had told the people to worship the LORD at the one place of worship in Jerusalem. But the Assyrian leader was confused and thought these were also places where the LORD was supposed to be worshipped.

commander to insult the living God. Perhaps the LORD heard what he said and will do something, if you will pray.

5 When these leaders went to Isaiah, 6 he told them that the LORD had this message for Hezekiah:

I am the LORD. Don't worry about the insulting things that have been said about me by these messengers from the king of Assyria. 7 I will upset him with rumours about what's happening in his own country. He will go back, and there I will make him die a violent death.

8 Meanwhile, the commander of the Assyrian forces heard that his king had left the town of Lachish and was now attacking Libnah. So he went there.
9 About this same time the king of Assyria learnt that King Tirhakah of Ethiopia* was on his way to attack him. Then the king of Assyria sent some messengers with this note for Hezekiah:

10 Don't trust your God or be fooled by his promise to defend Jerusalem against me. 11 You have heard how we Assyrian kings have completely wiped out other nations. What makes you feel so safe? 12 The Assyrian kings before me destroyed the towns of Gozan, Haran, Rezeph, and everyone from Eden who lived in Telassar. What good did their gods do them? 13 The kings of Hamath, Arpad, Sepharvaim, Hena, and Ivvah have all disappeared.

Hezekiah prays
This is also told in Isaiah 37.14–20

14 After Hezekiah had read the note from the king of Assyria, he took it to the temple and spread it out for the LORD to see. 15 He prayed:

LORD God of Israel, your throne is above the winged creatures.* You created the heavens and the earth, and you alone rule the kingdoms of this world. 16 But just look how Sennacherib has insulted you, the living God.

17 It is true, our LORD, that Assyrian kings have turned nations into deserts. 18 They destroyed the idols of wood and stone that the people of those nations had made and worshipped. 19 But you are our LORD and our God! We ask you to keep us safe from the Assyrian king. Then everyone in every kingdom on earth will know that you are the only God.

The LORD's answer to Hezekiah
This is also told in Isaiah 37.21–35

20 Isaiah went to Hezekiah and told him that the LORD God of Israel had said:

Hezekiah, I heard your prayer about King Sennacherib of Assyria. 21 Now this is what I say to that king:

The people of Jerusalem
hate and make fun of you;
they laugh behind your back.

22 Sennacherib, you cursed,
shouted, and sneered at me,
the holy God of Israel.
23 You let your officials
insult me, the Lord.
And here is what you
have said about yourself,
"I led my chariots
to the highest heights
of Lebanon's mountains.
I went deep into its forest,
cutting down the best cedar
and cypress trees.
24 I dried up every stream
in the land of Egypt,
and I drank water from wells I had dug."

25 Sennacherib, now listen
to me, the Lord.
I planned all this long ago.
And you don't even realize
that I alone am the one
who decided that you
would do these things.
I let you make ruins of fortified cities.
26 Their people became weak,
terribly confused.
They were like wild flowers
or tender young grass
growing on a flat roof,
scorched before it matures.*

---

*19.9 Ethiopia: The Hebrew text has "Cush", which was a region south of Egypt that included parts of the present countries of Ethiopia and Sudan.
*19.15 winged creatures: Two winged creatures made of gold were on the top of the sacred chest and were symbols of the LORD's throne on earth (see Exodus 25.18; 2 Samuel 6.2).
See also: 19.15: Exod 25.22.

*19.26 tender young grass . . . matures: Many of the houses had roofs made of packed earth. Grass would sometimes grow out of the roof, but would die quickly because of the sun and hot winds.

27 I know all about you,
   even how fiercely angry
      you are with me.
28 I have seen your pride
   and the tremendous hatred
      you have for me.
   Now I will put a hook in your nose,
      a bit in your mouth,*
   then I will send you back
      to where you came from.

29 Hezekiah, I will tell you what's going to happen. This year you will eat crops that grow on their own, and the next year you will eat whatever springs up where those crops grew. But the third year you will plant grain and vineyards, and you will eat what you harvest. 30 Those who survive in Judah will be like a vine that puts down deep roots and bears fruit. 31 I, the LORD All-Powerful, will see to it that some who live in Jerusalem will survive.

32 I promise that the king of Assyria won't get into Jerusalem, or shoot an arrow into the city, or even surround it and prepare to attack. 33 As surely as I am the LORD, he will return by the way he came and will never enter Jerusalem. 34 I will protect it for myself and for my servant David.

The death of King Sennacherib

This is also told in Isaiah 37.36–38

35 That same night the LORD sent an angel to the camp of the Assyrians, and he killed one hundred and eighty-five thousand of them. And so the next morning, the camp was full of dead bodies. 36 After this King Sennacherib went back to Assyria and lived in the city of Nineveh. 37 One day he was worshipping in the temple of his god Nisroch, when his sons, Adrammelech and Sharezer, killed him with their swords. They escaped to the land of Ararat, and his son Esarhaddon became king.*

CHAPTER 20

Hezekiah gets sick and almost dies

This is also told in 2 Chronicles 32.24–26;
Isaiah 38.1–8,2–22

1 About this time, Hezekiah got sick and was almost dead. Isaiah the prophet went in and

told him, "The LORD says you won't ever get well. You are going to die, so you had better start doing what needs to be done."

2 Hezekiah turned towards the wall and prayed, 3 "Don't forget that I have been faithful to you, LORD. I have obeyed you with all my heart, and I do whatever you say is right." After this, he cried hard.

4 Before Isaiah got to the middle court of the palace, 5 the LORD sent him back to Hezekiah with this message:

Hezekiah, you are the ruler of my people, and I am the LORD God, who was worshipped by your ancestor David. I heard you pray, and I saw you cry. I will heal you, so that three days from now you will be able to worship in my temple.
6 I will let you live fifteen years more, while I protect you and your city from the king of Assyria. I will defend this city as an honour to me and to my servant David.

7 Then Isaiah said to the king's servants, "Bring some mashed figs and place them on the king's open sore. He will then get well."

8 Hezekiah asked Isaiah, "Can you prove that the LORD will heal me, so that I can worship in his temple in three days?"

9 Isaiah replied, "The LORD will prove to you that he will keep his promise. Will the shadow made by the setting sun on the stairway go forward ten steps or back ten steps?"

10 "It's normal for the sun to go forward," Hezekiah answered. "But how can it go back?"

11 Isaiah prayed, and the LORD made the shadow go back ten steps on the stairway built for King Ahaz.▶

The LORD is still with Hezekiah

This is also told in Isaiah 39.1–8

12 Merodach▶ Baladan, the son of Baladan, was now king of Babylonia.* And when he learnt that Hezekiah had been sick, he sent messengers with letters and a gift for him. 13 Hezekiah welcomed▶ the messengers and showed them all the silver, the gold, the spices, and the fine oils that were in his storehouse. He even showed them where he kept his weapons. Nothing in his palace or in his entire kingdom was kept hidden from them.

---

*19.28 I will put . . . your mouth: This is how the Assyrians treated their prisoners, and now the LORD will treat Sennacherib the same way.
*19.37 Esarhaddon became king: Ruled Assyria 681–669 BC.

*20.12 Merodach Baladan . . . Babylonia: Ruled Babylonia 722–710 and 704–703 BC.

14 Isaiah asked Hezekiah, "Where did these men come from? What did they want?"

"They came all the way from Babylonia," Hezekiah answered.

15 "What did you show them?" Isaiah asked.

Hezekiah answered, "I showed them everything in my kingdom."

16 Then Isaiah told Hezekiah:

I have a message for you from the LORD. 17 One day everything you and your ancestors have stored up will be taken to Babylonia. The LORD has promised that nothing will be left. 18 Some of your own sons will be taken to Babylonia, where they will be disgraced and made to serve in the king's palace.

19 Hezekiah thought, "At least our nation will be at peace for a while." So he told Isaiah, "The message you brought me from the LORD is good."

Hezekiah dies

This is also told in 2 Chronicles 32.32-33

20 Everything else Hezekiah did while he was king, including how he made the upper pool and tunnel to bring water into Jerusalem, is written in *The History of the Kings of Judah*. 21 Hezekiah died, and his son Manasseh became king.

Two evil kings of Judah: Manasseh and Amon

CHAPTER 21

King Manasseh of Judah

This is also told in 2 Chronicles 33.1-20

1 Manasseh was twelve years old when he became king of Judah, and he ruled fifty-five years from Jerusalem. His mother was Hephzibah. 2 Manasseh disobeyed the LORD by following the disgusting customs of the nations that the LORD had forced out of Israel. 3 He rebuilt the local shrines⸴ that his father Hezekiah had torn down. He built altars for the god Baal and set up a sacred pole* for worshipping the goddess Asherah, just as King Ahab of Israel had done. And he faithfully worshipped the stars in heaven.

4 In the temple, where only the LORD was supposed to be worshipped, Manasseh built altars for pagan gods 5 and for the stars. He placed these altars in both courts of the temple, 6-7 and even set up the pole for Asherah there. Manasseh practised magic and witchcraft; he asked fortune-tellers for advice and sacrificed his own son. He did many sinful things and made the LORD very angry.

Years ago the LORD had told David and his son Solomon:

Jerusalem is the place I prefer above all others in Israel. It belongs to me, and there I will be worshipped for ever. 8 If my people will faithfully obey all the commands in the Law of my servant Moses, I will never make them leave the land I gave to their ancestors.

9 But the people of Judah disobeyed the LORD. They listened to Manasseh and did even more sinful things than the nations the LORD had wiped out.

10 One day the LORD said to some of his prophets:

11 King Manasseh has done more disgusting things than the Amorites,* and he has led my people to sin by forcing them to worship his idols. 12 Now I, the LORD God of Israel, will destroy both Jerusalem and Judah! People will hear about it but won't believe it. 13 Jerusalem is as sinful as Ahab and the people of Samaria were. So I will wipe out Jerusalem and be done with it, just as someone wipes water off a plate and turns it over to dry.

14 I will even get rid of my people who survive. They will be defeated and robbed by their enemies. 15 My people have done what I hate and have not stopped making me angry since their ancestors left Egypt.

16 Manasseh was guilty of causing the people of Judah to sin and disobey the LORD. He also refused to protect innocent people — he even let so many of them be killed⸴ that their blood filled the streets of Jerusalem.

17 Everything else Manasseh did while he was king, including his terrible sins, is written in *The History of the Kings of Judah*. 18 He died and was buried in Uzza Garden near his palace, and his son Amon became king.

---

*21.3 sacred pole: See the note at 13.6-7.
See also: 20.17: 2 King 24.13; 2 Chron 36.10.
20.18: 2 King 24.14-15; Dan 1.1-7. 21.2: Jer 15.4.

*21.11 Amorites: Here used in the general sense of nations that lived in Canaan before the Israelites.
See also: 21.4: 2 Sam 7.13. 21.7-8: 1 King 9.3-5; 2 Chron 7.12-18.

King Amon of Judah

This is also told in 2 Chronicles 33.21–25

19 Amon was twenty-two years old when he became king of Judah, and he ruled from Jerusalem for two years. His mother Meshullemeth was the daughter of Haruz from Jotbah. 20 Amon disobeyed the LORD, just as his father Manasseh had done. 21 Amon worshipped the idols Manasseh had made and 22 refused to be faithful to the LORD, the God his ancestors had worshipped.

23 Some of Amon's officials plotted against him and killed him in his palace. 24-26 He was buried in Uzza Garden. Soon after that, the people of Judah killed the murderers of Amon, then they made his son Josiah king.

Everything else Amon did while he was king is written in *The History of the Kings of Judah*.

The rule of King Josiah and "The Book of God's Law"

CHAPTER 22

King Josiah of Judah

This is also told in 2 Chronicles 34.1–2

1 Josiah was eight years old when he became king of Judah, and he ruled thirty-one years from Jerusalem. His mother Jedidah was the daughter of Adaiah from Bozkath. 2 Josiah always obeyed the LORD, just as his ancestor David had done.

Hilkiah finds *The Book of God's Law*

This is also told in 2 Chronicles 34.8–28

3 After Josiah had been king for eighteen years, he told Shaphan,' one of his highest officials:

> Go to the LORD's temple 4 and ask Hilkiah the high priest to collect from the guards all the money that the people have donated. 5 Tell Hilkiah to give it to the men supervising the repairs to the temple. They can use some of the money to pay 6 the workers, and with the rest of it they can buy wood and stone for the repair work. 7 They are honest, so we won't ask them to keep track of the money.

8 While Shaphan was at the temple, Hilkiah handed him a book and said, "Look what I found here in the temple — *The Book of God's Law*."

Shaphan read it, 9 then went back to Josiah and reported, "Your officials collected the money in the temple and gave it to the men supervising the repairs. 10 But there's something else, Your Majesty. The priest Hilkiah gave me this book." Then Shaphan read it out loud.

11 When Josiah heard what was in *The Book of God's Law*, he tore his clothes in sorrow. 12 At once he called together Hilkiah, Shaphan, Ahikam son of Shaphan, Achbor son of Micaiah, and his own servant Asaiah. He said, 13 "The LORD must be furious with me and everyone else in Judah, because our ancestors did not obey the laws written in this book. Go and find out what the LORD wants us to do."

14 The five men left straight away and went to talk with Huldah the prophet. Her husband was Shallum,' who was in charge of the king's clothes. Huldah lived in the northern part of Jerusalem, and when they met in her home, 15 she said:

> You were sent here by King Josiah, and this is what the LORD God of Israel says to him: 16 "Josiah, I am the LORD! And I will see to it that this country and everyone living in it will be destroyed. It will happen just as this book says. 17 The people of Judah have rejected me. They have offered sacrifices to foreign gods and have worshipped their own idols. I cannot stand it any longer. I am furious.
>
> 18 "Josiah, listen to what I am going to do. 19 I noticed how sad you were when you read that this country and its people would be completely wiped out. You even tore your clothes in sorrow, and I heard you cry. 20 So I will let you die in peace, before I destroy this place."

The men left and took Huldah's answer back to Josiah.

CHAPTER 23

Josiah reads *The Book of God's Law*

This is also told in 2 Chronicles 34.29–33

1 King Josiah called together the older leaders of Judah and Jerusalem. 2 Then he went to the LORD's temple, together with the people of Judah and Jerusalem, the priests, and the prophets. Finally, when everybody was there,

---

See also: 22.1: Jer 3.6.   22.7: 2 King 12.15.

he read aloud *The Book of God's Law** that had been found in the temple.

³ After Josiah had finished reading, he stood by one of the columns. He asked the people to promise in the LORD's name to obey the LORD faithfully and to follow his commands. The people agreed to do everything written in the book.

Josiah follows the teachings of God's Law

This is also told in 2 Chronicles 34.3–7

⁴ Josiah told Hilkiah the priest, the assistant priests, and the guards at the temple door to go into the temple and bring out the things used to worship Baal, Asherah, and the stars. Josiah had these things burnt in Kidron Valley just outside Jerusalem, and he had the ashes carried away to the town of Bethel.

⁵ Josiah also got rid of the pagan priests at the local shrines' in Judah and around Jerusalem. These were the men whom the kings of Judah had appointed to offer sacrifices to Baal and to the sun, moon, and stars. ⁶ Josiah had the sacred pole* for Asherah brought out of the temple and taken to Kidron Valley, where it was burnt. He then had its ashes ground into dust and scattered over the public cemetery there. ⁷ He had the buildings torn down where the male prostitutes* lived next to the temple, and where the women wove sacred robes* for the idol of Asherah.

⁸ In almost every town in Judah, priests had been offering sacrifices to the LORD at local shrines.' Josiah brought these priests to Jerusalem and had their shrines made unfit for worship — every shrine from Geba just north of Jerusalem to Beersheba in the south. He even tore down the shrine at Beersheba that was just to the left of Joshua Gate, which was named after the highest official of the city. ⁹ Those local priests could not serve at the LORD's altar in Jerusalem, but they were allowed to eat sacred bread,* just like the priests from Jerusalem.

¹⁰ Josiah sent some men to Hinnom Valley just outside Jerusalem with orders to make the altar there unfit for worship. That way, people could no longer use it for sacrificing their children to the god Molech. ¹¹ He also got rid of the horses that the kings of Judah used in their ceremonies to worship the sun, and he destroyed the chariots along with them. The horses had been kept near the entrance to the LORD's temple, in a courtyard' close to where an official named Nathan-Melech lived.

¹² Some of the kings of Judah, especially Manasseh, had built altars in the two courts of the temple and in the room that Ahaz had built on the palace roof. Josiah had these altars torn down and smashed to pieces, and he had the pieces thrown into Kidron Valley, just outside Jerusalem. ¹³ After that, he closed down the shrines that Solomon had built east of Jerusalem and south of Spoil Hill to honour Astarte the disgusting goddess of Sidon, Chemosh the disgusting god of Moab, and Milcom the disgusting god of Ammon.* ¹⁴ He tore down the stone images of foreign gods and cut down the sacred pole used in the worship of Asherah. Then he had the whole area covered with human bones.*

¹⁵ But Josiah had not finished yet. At Bethel he destroyed the shrine and the altar that Jeroboam son of Nebat had built and that had caused the Israelites to sin. Josiah had the shrine and the Asherah pole burnt and ground into dust. ¹⁶ As he looked around, he saw graves on the hillside. He had the bones in them dug up and burnt on the altar, so that it could no longer be used. This happened just as God's prophet had said when Jeroboam was standing at the altar, celebrating a festival.*

---

*23.2 **The Book of God's Law**: The Hebrew text has "The Book of God's Agreement", which is the same as "The Book of God's Law" in 22.8,11. In traditional translations this is called "The Book of the Covenant".
*23.6 **sacred pole**: See the note at 13.6–7.
*23.7 **male prostitutes**: Young men or boys sometimes served as prostitutes in the worship of Canaanite gods, but the LORD had forbidden the people of Israel and Judah to worship in this way (see Deuteronomy 23.17–18).
*23.7 **sacred robes**: Or "coverings".
See also: 23.4–6: 2 King 21.3; 2 Chron 33.3.

*23.9 **sacred bread**: The Hebrew text has "thin bread", which may be either the pieces of thin bread made without yeast to be eaten during the Passover Festival (see verses 21–23) or the baked flour used in sacrifices to give thanks to the LORD (see Leviticus 2.4–5).
*23.13 **the shrines . . . Ammon**: See 1 Kings 11.5–7.
*23.14 **Then he . . . human bones**: This made the whole area unfit for the worship of any god.
*23.16 **just . . . festival**: See 1 Kings 13.1–2.
See also: 23.10: a Jer 7.31; 19.1–6; 32.35; b Lev 18.21.
23.12: 2 King 21.5; 2 Chron 33.5.   23.13: 1 King 11.7.
23.15: 1 King 12.33.   23.16: 1 King 13.2.

Holy history

All the kings of Judah

Rehoboam (1 Kgs 12.1–24; 14.21–31; 2 Chr 10–12)
Set up shrines to Asherah and allowed temple prostitutes.

Abijam/Abijah (1 Kgs 1–8; 2 Chr 13.1–22)
Kings calls him Abijam; Chronicles, Abijah. A mix of good and bad king.

Asa (1 Kgs 15.9–24; 2 Chr 14.1–16.14)
Cleared out evil practices and restored the temple. But didn't entirely trust the Lord.

Jehoshaphat (1 Kgs 22.41–50; 2 Chr 17.1–21.1)
Toured the country convincing people to turn back to God (2 Chronicles 19.4).

Jehoram (2 Kgs 8.16–4; 2 Chr 21.2–20)
Ruled at the same time as his father Jehoshaphat, maybe because his dad was ill.

Ahaziah (2 Kgs 8.25–9; 2 Chr 22.1–6)
A bad king, killed by Jehu, King of Israel.

Queen Athaliah of Judah (2 Kgs 11.1–21; 2 Chr 22.10–23.21)
Murdered her family and took over. Joash, her grandson, was hidden and brought out six years later. Athaliah came to investigate and was killed (2 Kings 11.13–16).

Joash (2 Kgs 12.1–21; 2 Chr 24.1–16)
A good king, but when Jehoida dies, Joash worshipped Astarte. He was assassinated.

Amaziah (2 Kgs 14.1–22; 2 Chr 25.1–24)
Started well, then grew arrogant, turned against God and he, too, was assassinated.

Azariah/Uzziah (2 Kgs 15.7; 2 Chr 26.1–23)
A good king who loved farming and reorganised the army, but tried to act as a priest and was punished with leprosy.

Jotham (2 Kgs 15.32–8; 2 Chr 27.1–9)
Obeyed God, but didn't destroy the shrines.

Ahaz (2 Kgs 16.1–20; 2 Chr 28.1–27)
Probably the worst. Worshipped at pagan shrines and sacrificed his own son (16.2–4).

Hezekiah (2 Kgs 18.1–20.21; Is 37.1–39.8; 2 Chr 32.24–33)
One of the best. Trusted the Lord and God destroyed the Assyrians when they invaded.

Manasseh (2 Kgs 21.1–18; 2 Chr 33.1–20)
He worshipped 'Astarte and the stars in heaven' (21.3) and practised witchcraft.

Amon (2 Kgs 21.19–26; 2 Chr 33.21–5)
Manasseh's son continued his father's wicked ways. He only reigned for two years before being assassinated by his officials.

Josiah (2 Kgs 22.1–30; 2 Chr 34.29–36.1)
A good king. The Book of God's Law (probably Deuteronomy) was discovered during temple renovations, Josiah promised to obey its commands (23.2).

Jehoahaz (2 Kgs 23.31–4; 2 Chr 36.2–4)
Josiah's son had no real military power and was captured by Pharaoh Neco.

Jehoiakim (2 Kgs 23.35–24.7; 2 Chr 36.5–8)
Jehoahaz's brother had his name changed to Jehoiakim. He rebelled against the Babylonians, dying before they hit back.

Jehoiachin (2 Kgs 24.8–17; 25.27–30; 2 Chr 36.9–10; Jer 52.31–4)
Served only three months before surrendering to the Babylonians. Taken to Babylon, along with most of his people.

Zedekiah (2 Kgs 24.18–25.21; 2 Chr 36.17–21; Jer 52.3–30)
Rebelled against Babylon. After months of suffering, Jerusalem was taken, the king captured and saw his sons' killed. Then Nebuchadnezzar had him blinded.

Gedaliah (2 Kgs 25.22–26; Jer 40.7–9; 41.1–3)
Appointed to govern what was left of the country. He was assassinated.

Then Josiah saw the grave of the prophet who had said this would happen [17] and he asked,' "Whose grave is that?"

Some people who lived nearby answered, "It belongs to the prophet from Judah who told what would happen to this altar."

[18] Josiah replied, "Then leave it alone. Don't dig up his bones." So they did not disturb his bones or the bones of the old prophet from Israel who had also been buried there.*

[19] Some of the Israelite kings had made the LORD angry by building pagan shrines all over Israel. So Josiah sent troops to destroy these shrines just as he had done to the one in Bethel. [20] He killed the priests who served at them and burnt their bones on the altars.

After all that, Josiah went back to Jerusalem.

Josiah and the people of Judah celebrate Passover

This is also told in 2 Chronicles 35.1–19

[21] Josiah told the people of Judah, "Celebrate Passover in honour of the LORD your God, just as it says in *The Book of God's Law*."*

[22] This festival had not been celebrated in this way since kings ruled Israel and Judah. [23] But in Josiah's eighteenth year as king of Judah, everyone came to Jerusalem to celebrate Passover.

The LORD is still angry with the people of Judah

[24] Josiah got rid of every disgusting person and thing in Judah and Jerusalem — including magicians, fortune-tellers, and idols. He did his best to obey every law written in the book that the priest Hilkiah found in the LORD's temple. [25] No other king before or after Josiah tried as hard as he did to obey the Law of Moses.

[26] But the LORD was still furious with the people of Judah because Manasseh had done so many things to make him angry. [27] The LORD said, "I will desert the people of Judah, just as I deserted the people of Israel. I will reject Jerusalem, even though I chose it to be mine. And I will abandon this temple built to honour me."

Josiah dies in battle

This is also told in 2 Chronicles 35.20—36.1

[28] Everything else Josiah did while he was king is written in *The History of the Kings of Judah*. [29] During Josiah's rule, King Neco of Egypt led his army north to the River Euphrates to help the king of Assyria. Josiah led his troops north to fight Neco, but when they met in battle at Megiddo, Josiah was killed.* [30] A few of Josiah's servants put his body in a chariot and took it back to Jerusalem, where they buried it in his own tomb. Then the people of Judah found his son Jehoahaz and poured olive oil on his head to show that he was their new king.

The last kings of Judah

King Jehoahaz of Judah

This is also told in 2 Chronicles 36.2–4

[31] Jehoahaz was twenty-three years old when he became king of Judah, and he ruled from Jerusalem only three months. His mother Hamutal was the daughter of Jeremiah from Libnah. [32] Jehoahaz disobeyed the LORD, just as some of his ancestors had done.

[33] King Neco of Egypt had Jehoahaz arrested and put in prison at Riblah* near Hamath. Then he forced the people of Judah to pay him three thousand four hundred kilogrammes of silver and thirty-four kilogrammes of gold as taxes. [34] Neco appointed Josiah's son Eliakim king of Judah, and changed his name to Jehoiakim. He took Jehoahaz as a prisoner to Egypt, where he died.

[35] Jehoiakim forced the people of Judah to pay higher taxes, so he could give Neco the silver and gold he demanded.

King Jehoiakim of Judah

This is also told in 2 Chronicles 36.5–8

[36] Jehoiakim was twenty-five years old when he was appointed king, and he ruled

---

*23.29 killed: At this time, King Neco of Egypt (609–595 BC) was fighting on the side of the Assyrians. He marched north to fight the Babylonian army and help Assyria keep control of its land. Since Josiah considered Assyria an enemy, he set out to stop Neco and the Egyptian troops.
*23.33 Riblah: An important town in Syria on the River Orontes.
See also: 23.34: Jer 22.11–12.   23.36: Jer 22.18–19; 26.1–6; 35.1–19.

---

*23.18 old prophet . . . there: See 1 Kings 13.11–32.
*23.21 *The Book of God's Law*: See the note at verse 2.
See also: 23.17: 1 King 13.30–32.

eleven years from Jerusalem. His mother Zebidah was the daughter of Pedaiah from Rumah. [37] Jehoiakim disobeyed the LORD by following the example of his ancestors.

CHAPTER 24

[1] During Jehoiakim's rule, King Nebuchadnezzar of Babylonia* invaded and took control of Judah. Jehoiakim obeyed Nebuchadnezzar for three years, but then he rebelled.

[2] At that time, the LORD started sending troops to rob and destroy towns in Judah. Some of these troops were from Babylonia, and others were from Syria, Moab, and Ammon. The LORD had sent his servants the prophets to warn Judah about this, [3] and now he was making it happen. The country of Judah was going to be wiped out, because Manasseh had sinned [4] and caused many innocent people to die. The LORD would not forgive this.

[5] Everything else Jehoiakim did while he was king is written in *The History of the Kings of Judah*. [6] Jehoiakim died, and his son Jehoiachin became king.

[7] King Nebuchadnezzar defeated King Neco of Egypt and took control of his land from the Egyptian Gorge all the way north to the River Euphrates. So Neco never invaded Judah again.*

King Jehoiachin of Judah is taken to Babylon

This is also told in 2 Chronicles 36.9,10

[8] Jehoiachin was eighteen years old when he became king of Judah, and he ruled only three months from Jerusalem. His mother Nehushta was the daughter of Elnathan from Jerusalem. [9] Jehoiachin disobeyed the LORD, just as his father Jehoiakim had done.

[10] King Nebuchadnezzar of Babylonia sent troops to attack Jerusalem soon after Jehoiachin became king. [11] During the attack, Nebuchadnezzar himself arrived at the city. [12] Jehoiachin immediately

surrendered, together with his mother and his servants, as well as his army officers and officials. Then Nebuchadnezzar had Jehoiachin arrested. These things took place in the eighth year of Nebuchadnezzar's rule in Babylonia.*

[13] The LORD had warned* that some day the treasures would be taken from the royal palace and from the temple, including the gold objects that Solomon had made for the temple. And that's exactly what Nebuchadnezzar ordered his soldiers to do. [14] He also led away as prisoners the Jerusalem officials, the military leaders, and the skilled workers — ten thousand in all. Only the very poorest people were left in Judah.

[15] Nebuchadnezzar took Jehoiachin to Babylon, along with his mother, his wives, his officials, and the most important leaders of Judah. [16] He also led away seven thousand soldiers, one thousand skilled workers, and anyone who would be useful in battle.

[17] Then Nebuchadnezzar appointed Jehoiachin's uncle Mattaniah king of Judah and changed his name to Zedekiah.

King Zedekiah of Judah

This is also told in 2 Chronicles 36.11–16; Jeremiah 52.1–3

[18] Zedekiah was twenty-one years old when he was appointed king of Judah, and he ruled from Jerusalem for eleven years. His mother Hamutal was the daughter of Jeremiah from Libnah. [19] Zedekiah disobeyed the LORD, just as Jehoiakim had done. [20] It was Zedekiah who finally rebelled against Nebuchadnezzar.

The people of Judah and Jerusalem had made the LORD so angry that he finally turned his back on them. That's why these horrible things were happening.

---

*24.1 King Nebuchadnezzar of Babylonia: Ruled Babylonia 605–562 BC.
*24.7 again: Nebuchadnezzar defeated the Egyptian army in 605 BC at the town of Carchemish. But a few years later, he was forced to retreat all the way back to Babylonia, which allowed Jehoiakim to rebel (see verse 1).

See also: 24.1: Jer 25.1–38; Dan 1.1–2. 24.12: Jer 22.24–30; 24.1–10; 29.1–2.

*24.12 Babylonia: These events took place in 597 BC.
*24.13 warned: See 20.16–18.

See also: 24.15: Ezek 17.12. 24.17: Jer 37.1; Ezek 17.13. 24.18: Jer 27.1–22; 28.1–17. 24.20: Ezek 17.15.

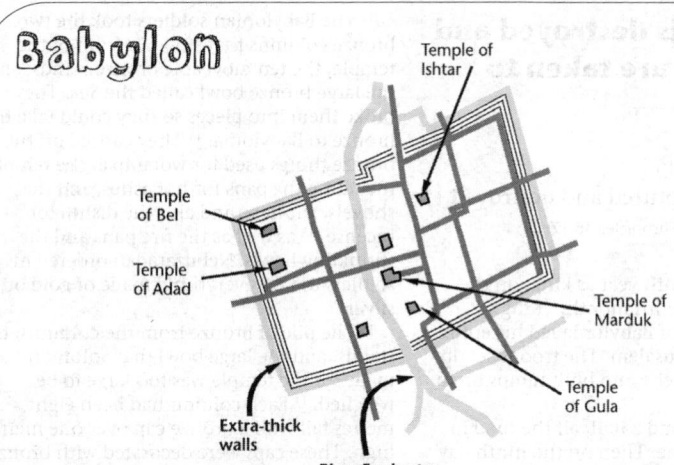

Babylon was the capital city of the Babylonian empire. It was a vast city, with walls so huge than you could drive chariots around them. Not so much a wall, more like a ring-road!

The walls were tiled with blue enamelled bricks, and surrounded by a moat channelled from the River Euphrates. Inside the city there were temples and towers at almost every corner.

The Babylonians reached the height of their strength under Nebuchadnezzar. He defeated Pharaoh Necho at Carchemish in 605BC (Jeremiah 46.2) and under his reign, the Babylonian empire stretched through Syria and Palestine to the Egyptian border. When the kings of Judah rebelled against Babylon, he destroyed Jerusalem and took the inhabitants of the country into exile.

Both Ezekiel and Daniel were captives in Babylon. The Jews remained captive in Babylon until Cyrus of Persia defeated the Babylonian empire 70 years later.

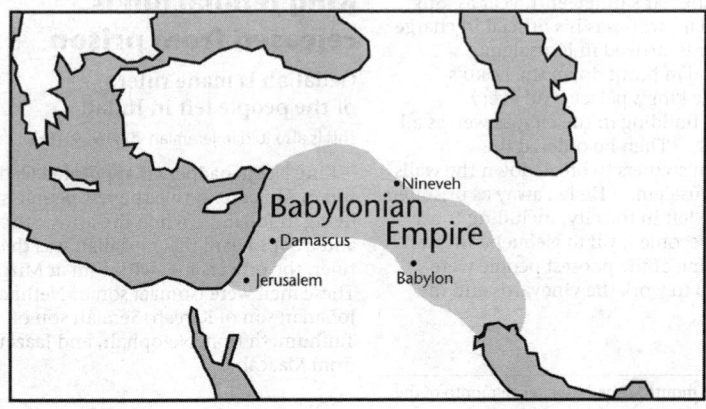

Jerusalem is destroyed and the people are taken to Babylonia

CHAPTER 25

Jerusalem is captured and destroyed

This is also told in 2 Chronicles 36.17–21; Jeremiah 52.3–30

[1] In Zedekiah's ninth year as king, on the tenth day of the tenth month,* King Nebuchadnezzar of Babylonia led his entire army to attack Jerusalem. The troops set up camp outside the city and built ramps up to the city walls.

[2-3] After a year and a half, all the food in Jerusalem was gone. Then on the ninth day of the fourth' month, [4] the Babylonian troops broke through the city wall.* That same night, Zedekiah and his soldiers tried to escape through the gate near the royal garden, even though they knew the enemy had the city surrounded. They headed towards the desert, [5] but the Babylonian troops caught up with them near Jericho. They arrested Zedekiah, but his soldiers scattered in every direction.

[6] Zedekiah was taken to Riblah, where Nebuchadnezzar put him on trial and found him guilty. [7] Zedekiah's sons were killed right in front of him. His eyes were then put out, and he was put in chains and dragged off to Babylon.

[8] About a month later,' in Nebuchadnezzar's nineteenth year as king, Nebuzaradan, who was his official in charge of the guards, arrived in Jerusalem. [9] Nebuzaradan burnt down the LORD's temple, the king's palace, and every important building in the city, as well as all the houses. [10] Then he ordered the Babylonian soldiers to break down the walls around Jerusalem. [11] He led away as prisoners the people left in the city, including those who had become loyal to Nebuchadnezzar. [12] Only some of the poorest people were left behind to work the vineyards and the fields.

[13] The Babylonian soldiers took the two bronze columns that stood in front of the temple, the ten moveable bronze stands, and the large bronze bowl called the Sea. They broke them into pieces so they could take the bronze to Babylonia. [14] They carried off the bronze things used for worship at the temple, including the pans for hot ashes, and the shovels, snuffers, and also the dishes for incense, [15] as well as the fire pans and the sprinkling bowls. Nebuzaradan ordered his soldiers to take everything made of gold or silver.

[16] The pile of bronze from the columns, the stands, and the large bowl that Solomon had made for the temple was too large to be weighed. [17] Each column had been eight metres tall with a bronze cap over one metre high. These caps were decorated with bronze designs — some of them like chains and others like pomegranates.*

[18] Next, Nebuzaradan arrested Seraiah the chief priest, Zephaniah his assistant, and three temple officials. [19] Then he arrested one of the army commanders, the king's five personal advisers, and the officer in charge of gathering the troops for battle. He also found sixty more soldiers who were still in Jerusalem. [20] Nebuzaradan led them all to Riblah [21] near Hamath, where Nebuchadnezzar had them killed.

The people of Judah no longer lived in their own country.

Gedaliah is made ruler and King Jehoiachin is released from prison

Gedaliah is made ruler of the people left in Judah

This is also told in Jeremiah 40.7–9; 41.1–3

[22] King Nebuchadnezzar appointed Gedaliah son of Ahikam' to rule the few people still living in Judah. [23] When the army officers and troops heard that Gedaliah was their ruler, the officers met with him at Mizpah. These men were Ishmael son of Nethaniah, Johanan son of Kareah, Seraiah son of Tanhumeth from Netophah, and Jaazaniah from Maacah.

---

*25.1 tenth month: Tebeth, the tenth month of the Hebrew calendar, from about mid-December to mid-January.
*25.4 wall: Jerusalem was destroyed in 586 BC.
See also: 25.1: Jer 21.1–10; 34.1–5; Ezek 24.2. 25.4: Ezek 33.21. 25.7: Ezek 12.13. 25.9: 1 King 9.8.

*25.17 pomegranates: A bright red fruit that looks like an apple.
See also: 25.13: a 1 King 7.15–26; 2 Chron 3.15–17; b 1 King 7.23–26; 2 Chron 4.2–5. 25.14: 1 King 7.45; 2 Chron 4.16. 25.22–24: Jer 40.7–9.

²⁴ Gedaliah said to them, "Everything will be fine, I promise. We don't need to be afraid of the Babylonian rulers, if we live here peacefully and do what Nebuchadnezzar says."

²⁵ Ishmael⟩ was from the royal family. And about two months after Gedaliah began his rule,⟩ Ishmael and ten other men went to Mizpah. They killed Gedaliah and his officials, including those from Judah and those from Babylonia. ²⁶ After that, the army officers and all the people in Mizpah, whether important or not, were afraid of what the Babylonians might do. So they left Judah and went to Egypt.

Jehoiachin is set free

This is also told in Jeremiah 52.31-34

²⁷ Jehoiachin was a prisoner in Babylon for thirty-seven years. Then Evil-Merodach became king of Babylonia,* and in the first year of his rule, on the twenty-seventh day of the twelfth month,* he let Jehoiachin out of prison. ²⁸ Evil-Merodach was kind to Jehoiachin and honoured him more than any of the other kings held prisoner there. ²⁹ Jehoiachin was even allowed to wear his own clothes, and he ate at the king's table every day. ³⁰ As long as Jehoiachin lived, he was paid a daily allowance to buy whatever he needed.

---

*25.27 Evil-Merodach . . . Babylonia: The son of Nebuchadnezzar, who ruled Babylonia from 562 to 560 BC.
*25.27 twelfth month: Adar, the twelfth month of the Hebrew calendar, from about mid-February to mid-March.
See also: 25.25: Jer 41.1-3. 25.26: Jer 43.5-7.

Additional notes

⟩1.8 hairy: Or "wearing a furry coat".
⟩1.12 God sent down fire: Or "A mighty fire came down".
⟩1.17 Joram: The Hebrew text has "Jehoram", another spelling of the name.
⟩1.17 his brother: Some ancient translations (see also 3.1); these words are not in the Hebrew text.
⟩2.1 Elisha: Hebrew "the man of God".
⟩2.12 Israel's . . . away: Or "Master, you were like cavalry and chariots for the people of Israel!"
⟩3.16 that . . . water: Or "you must dig holes everywhere in this river bed."
⟩3.24 chased . . . attack: One possible meaning for the difficult Hebrew text.

⟩3.27 The Israelite . . . that: One possible meaning for the difficult Hebrew text.
⟩5.8 the prophet: Hebrew "the man of God".
⟩5.12 River Abana: Most Hebrew manuscripts; some Hebrew manuscripts and two ancient translations "River Amana".
⟩6.9 have set up camp: Or "are going".
⟩6.32 That murderer: Hebrew "That murderer's son".
⟩7.13 We're going . . . died: One possible meaning for the difficult Hebrew text.
⟩8.11 Elisha stared . . . crying: Or "Hazael stared at him until Elisha was embarrassed and began to cry."
⟩8.21 Jehoram: The Hebrew text has "Joram", another spelling of the name.
⟩8.21 he attacked . . . homes: One possible meaning for the difficult Hebrew text.
⟩8.24 Jerusalem: Hebrew "the city of David".
⟩9.14-16 Joram: See the note at 1.17.
⟩9.33 horses . . . her body: Two ancient translations; Hebrew "horses. Then Jehu trampled her body."
⟩10.1 the town: Two ancient translations; Hebrew "Jezreel".
⟩10.12-13 at a place where shepherds meet: Or "at Betheked of the Shepherds".
⟩10.15 Jehonadab son of Rechab: Or "Jehonadab the chariot driver".
⟩10.27 public toilet: Or "rubbish dump".
⟩11.2 Jehoram's: The Hebrew text has "Joram's", another spelling of the name.
⟩11.4 the king's special bodyguards: The Hebrew text has "the Carites", who were probably foreign soldiers hired to serve as royal bodyguards.
⟩11.14 singers: Two ancient translations; Hebrew "commanders".
⟩11.19 the king's special bodyguards: See the note at 11.4.
⟩12.1 Joash: The Hebrew text has "Jehoash", another spelling of the name.
⟩12.3 local shrines: The Hebrew text has "high places", which were local places to worship God or foreign gods.
⟩12.5 You priests . . . money too: One possible meaning for the difficult Hebrew text.
⟩12.20-21 Jozabad: Some manuscripts of the Hebrew text; other manuscripts "Jozacar".
⟩12.20-21 Jerusalem: See the note at 8.24.
⟩13.14 Master . . . without you: Or "Master, you were like chariots and cavalry for Israel!"
⟩14.4 local shrines: See the note at 12.3.
⟩14.28 how he recaptured . . . Hamath: One possible meaning for the difficult Hebrew text.
⟩15.4 local shrines: See the note at 12.3.
⟩15.10 in public: Hebrew; some manuscripts of one ancient translation "in Ibleam".
⟩15.13 Azariah's: The Hebrew text has "Uzziah's", another spelling of the name.
⟩15.25 together with Argob and Arieh: One possible meaning for the difficult Hebrew text.
⟩15.32 Azariah: See the note at 15.13.
⟩15.35 local shrines: See the note at 12.3.
⟩16.4 local shrines: See the note at 12.3.

'16.5–6 the king of Edom . . . Edomites: The Hebrew text has "King Rezin of Syria . . . Syrians"; in Hebrew, there is only one letter difference between "Edom" and "Aram", which is the usual Hebrew name for Syria in the Bible (see also 2 Chronicles 28.17).

'16.14 aside: Hebrew "to the north".

'16.18 the special tent . . . Sabbath: One possible meaning for the difficult Hebrew text.

'16.20 Jerusalem: See the note at 8.24.

'17.11 shrines: See the note at 12.3.

'17.20 Israel and Judah: Or "Israel", that is, the northern kingdom only.

'17.29 Israelite: The Hebrew text has "Samaritan", which is a later word to describe the people who lived in northern Israel at this time.

'18.4 local shrines: See the note at 12.3.

'18.16 doorposts: One possible meaning for the difficult Hebrew text.

'20.9 Will . . . steps: One possible meaning for the difficult Hebrew text.

'20.11 the shadow . . . Ahaz: One possible meaning for the difficult Hebrew text.

'20.12 Merodach: The Hebrew text has "Berodach", another spelling of the name.

'20.13 welcomed: Or "listened to".

'21.3 local shrines: See the note at 12.3.

'21.16 He also refused . . . killed: Or "He killed so many innocent people".

'22.3 Shaphan: Hebrew "Shaphan son of Azaliah son of Meshullam".

'22.14 Shallum: Hebrew "Shallum son of Tikvah son of Harhas".

'23.5 local shrines: See the note at 12.3.

'23.8 local shrines: See the note at 12.3.

'23.11 in a courtyard: One possible meaning for the difficult Hebrew text.

'23.16–17 said when Jeroboam . . . asked: One ancient translation; Hebrew "said. ¹⁷ Then Josiah asked".

'25.2–3 fourth: This word is not in the Hebrew text here, but see the parallel in Jeremiah 52.5–6.

'25.8 About a month later: Hebrew "On the seventh day of the fifth month".

'25.22 Ahikam: Hebrew "Ahikam son of Shaphan".

'25.25 Ishmael: Hebrew "Ishmael son of Nethaniah son of Elishama".

'25.25 about two months . . . his rule: Hebrew "in the seventh month".

1 Chronicles

The basics

What's the point? It's the history of Israel, showing how God has been with their kings in the past.

What happens? We start with a load of family trees, then there is an account of the life of King David.

What should I remember? 17.14 'I will make sure that your son and his descendants will rule my people and my kingdom forever.'

More details

Setting the scene Chronicles starts at the beginning; the very beginning. It begins with Adam and takes us right through to the death of Saul. Then the real action starts...

What's it all about? Chronicles aims to answer a simple question: 'Does God care about Israel any more?'

It was probably written just after the Jews returned from exile in Babylon. They must have been feeling like it was all over; as though they would never see their homeland again. But Chronicles argues that God hasn't finished with Israel yet. By telling the great story of King David and the building of the temple, the book argues that Israel is still alive and kicking, and that God has a plan. God has been with Israel in the past, so he will still be with Israel in the future.

A lot of 1 Chronicles is found in 1 Samuel too. Both books tell the story of King David, although from a slightly different perspective. In 1 Chronicles, David is given the hero's treatment. He's the person who made Jerusalem great, who planned the temple and who brought the Sacred Chest into the city. He's powerful because he trusts in the LORD.

Maybe one of the reasons why Chronicles misses out the grubby bits of David's life is that it's trying to stir the people, to inspire them. We're always more inspired by our heroes' successes, than by their failures.

And another thing

A lot of Chronicles is made up of lists and family trees, tracing the descendants of Adam right down to Saul and David. These make for less-than-exciting reading, but they serve a purpose; they show that God was continuing his purpose from generation to generation. This is important because, as Chronicles was written after the people had been in exile; the writer wanted to show that, despite all that had happened to them, God was still with them, just as he had been with Adam, all those centuries ago.

And *another* another thing

Like Kings and Samuel, Chronicles is really one book, split into two because it was too big to fit on a single scroll.

And *yet another* another thing

Chronicles may have been written by Ezra. The first lines of the book of Ezra are identical to the last lines of 2 Chronicles.

Footsteps

The death of Saul: 10.1–14
David becomes king: 11.1–9
The return of the Sacred Chest: 15.1–29
David's song: 16.7–36
'Your descendants will be kings': 17.1–26
The plans for the temple: 28.1–21
Solomon takes over: 29.21–30

Descendants of Adam until the time of King Saul

CHAPTER 1

The descendants of Adam

This is also told in Genesis 5.1–32; 10.1–32; 11.10–32

[1-4] Adam was the father of Seth, and his descendants were Enosh, Kenan, Mahalalel, Jared, Enoch, Methuselah, Lamech, and Noah, who had three sons: Shem, Ham, and Japheth.

[5] Japheth was the father of Gomer, Magog, Madai, Javan, Tubal, Meshech, and Tiras, and they were the ancestors of the kingdoms named after them. [6] Gomer was the ancestor of Ashkenaz, Riphath,' and Togarmah. [7] Javan was the ancestor of Elishah, Tarshish, Kittim, and Dodanim.'

[8] Ham was the father of Ethiopia,* Egypt, Put, and Canaan, and they were the ancestors of the kingdoms named after them. [9] Ethiopia was the ancestor of Seba, Havilah, Sabta, Raamah, and Sabteca. Raamah was the ancestor of Sheba and Dedan. [10] Ethiopia was also the father of Nimrod, the world's first mighty warrior. [11] Egypt was the ancestor of Ludim, Anamim, Lehabim, Naphtuhim, [12] Pathrusim, Casluhim, and Caphtorim, the ancestor of the Philistines.' [13] Canaan's eldest son was Sidon; his other son was Heth. [14-16] Canaan was also the ancestor of the Jebusites, the Amorites, the Girgashites, the Hivites, and Arkites, the Sinites, the Arvadites, the Zemarites, and the Hamathites.

[17] Shem was the ancestor of Elam, Asshur, Arpachshad, Lud, Aram, Uz, Hul, Gether, and Meshech;' they were the ancestors of the kingdoms named after them. [18] Arpachshad was Shelah's father and Eber's grandfather. [19] Eber named his first son Peleg,* because in his time the earth was divided into tribal regions. Eber's second son was Joktan, [20-23] the ancestor of Almodad, Sheleph, Hazarmaveth, Jerah, Hadoram, Uzal, Diklah, Ebal, Abimael, Sheba, Ophir, Havilah, and Jobab. [24-27] Shem's descendants included Arpachshad, Shelah, Eber, Peleg, Reu, Serug, Nahor, Terah, and Abram, later renamed Abraham.

Abraham's family

This is also told in Genesis 25.1–4,12–16

[28] Abraham was the father of Isaac and Ishmael.

[29-31] Ishmael had twelve sons, who were born in the following order: Nebaioth, Kedar, Adbeel, Mibsam, Mishma, Dumah, Massa, Hadad, Tema, Jetur, Naphish, and Kedemah. [32] Abraham and his slave woman Keturah had six sons: Zimran, Jokshan, Medan, Midian, Ishbak, and Shuah. Jokshan was the father of Sheba and Dedan. [33] Midian was the father of Ephah, Epher, Hanoch, Abida, and Eldaah.

Esau's family

This is also told in Genesis 36.1–14

[34] Abraham's son Isaac was the father of Esau and Jacob.' [35] Esau was the father of Eliphaz, Reuel, Jeush, Jalam, and Korah. [36] Eliphaz was the father of Teman, Omar, Zephi, Gatam, Kenaz, Timna, and Amalek. [37] Reuel was the father of Nahath, Zerah, Shammah, and Mizzah.

The first Edomites and their kings

This is also told in Genesis 36.20–43

[38] Seir was the father of Lotan, Shobal, Zibeon, Anah, Dishon, Ezer, and Dishan. [39] Lotan was the father of Hori and Homam; Lotan's sister was Timna. [40] Shobal was the father of Alvan,' Manahath, Ebal, Shephi, and Onam. Zibeon was the father of Aiah and Anah. [41] Anah was the father of Dishon and the grandfather of Hemdan,' Eshban, Ithran, and Cheran. [42] Ezer was the father of Bilhan, Zaavan, and Jaakan.' Dishan' was the father of Uz and Aran.

[43] Before kings ruled in Israel, Bela son of Beor ruled the country of Edom from its capital of Dinhabah. [44] After Bela's death, Jobab son of Zerah from Bozrah became king. [45] After Jobab's death, Husham from the land of Teman became king. [46] After Husham's death, Hadad son of Bedad became king and ruled from Avith. Earlier, Bedad had defeated the Midianites in the territory of Moab. [47] After Hadad's death, Samlah from Masrekah became king; [48] after Samlah's death, Shaul from the town of Rehoboth on the River Euphrates became king; [49] and after Shaul's death, Baal Hanan son of Achbor became king. [50] After Baal Hanan's death, Hadad ruled from Pai. His wife was Mehetabel, the daughter of Matred and granddaughter of Mezahab.

---

*1.8 Ethiopia: The Hebrew text has "Cush", which was a region south of Egypt that included parts of the present countries of Ethiopia and Sudan.
*1.19 Peleg: In Hebrew "Peleg" means "divided".

⁵¹ The Edomite clans' were Timna, Alvah,' Jetheth, ⁵² Oholibamah, Elah, Pinon, ⁵³ Kenaz, Teman, Mibzar, ⁵⁴ Magdiel, and Iram.

CHAPTER 2

The descendants of Judah

¹⁻² Jacob' was the father of twelve sons: Reuben, Simeon, Levi, Judah, Issachar, Zebulun, Dan, Joseph, Benjamin, Naphtali, Gad, and Asher.

³ Judah and his Canaanite wife Bathshua had three sons: Er, Onan, and Shelah. But the LORD had Er put to death, because he disobeyed and did what the LORD hated. ⁴ Judah and his daughter-in-law Tamar also had two sons: Perez and Zerah.

⁵ Perez was the father of Hezron and Hamul. ⁶ Zerah was the father of Zimri, Ethan, Heman, Calcol, and Darda.' ⁷ Achan,* who was a descendant of Zerah and the son of Carmi, caused trouble for Israel, because he kept for himself things that belonged only to the LORD.* ⁸ Ethan's son was Azariah.

The ancestors of King David

⁹ Hezron was the father of Jerahmeel, Ram, and Caleb.' ¹⁰ Ram was the father of Amminadab and the grandfather of Nahshon, a tribal leader of Judah. ¹¹ Nahshon's descendants included Salma, Boaz, ¹² Obed, and Jesse. ¹³⁻¹⁵ Jesse had seven sons, who were born in the following order: Eliab, Abinadab, Shimea, Nethanel, Raddai, Ozem, and David. ¹⁶ Jesse also had two daughters: Zeruiah and Abigail. Zeruiah was the mother of Abishai, Joab, and Asahel. ¹⁷ Abigail's husband was Jether, who was a descendant of Ishmael, and their son was Amasa.

The descendants of Hezron

¹⁸ Hezron's son Caleb married Azubah, and their daughter was Jerioth,' the mother of Jesher, Shobab, and Ardon. ¹⁹ After the death of Azubah, Caleb married Ephrath. Their son Hur ²⁰ was the father of Uri and the grandfather of Bezalel.

²¹ When Hezron was sixty years old, he married the daughter of Machir, who settled the region of Gilead. Their son Segub ²² was the father of Jair, who ruled twenty-three villages in the region of Gilead. ²³ Some time later the

nations of Geshur and Aram captured sixty towns in that region, including the villages that belonged to Jair, as well as the town of Kenath and the nearby villages. Everyone from the region of Gilead was a descendant of Machir. ²⁴ After the death of Hezron, Caleb married Ephrath, his father's wife. Their son was Ashhur,' who later settled the town of Tekoa.

The descendants of Jerahmeel

²⁵ Jerahmeel, Hezron's eldest son, was the father of Ram, Bunah, Oren, Ozem, and Ahijah. ²⁶ Jerahmeel had a second wife, Atarah, who gave birth to Onam. ²⁷ Ram was the father of Maaz, Jamin, and Eker. ²⁸ Onam was the father of Shammai and Jada.

Shammai was the father of Nadab and Abishur. ²⁹ Abishur married Abihail, and their two sons were Ahban and Molid. ³⁰ Nadab was the father of Seled and Appaim. Seled had no children; ³¹ Appaim's son was Ishi, the father of Sheshan and the grandfather of Ahlai. ³² Jada was the father of Jether and Jonathan. Jether had no children, ³³ but Jonathan had two sons: Peleth and Zaza.

³⁴⁻³⁵ Sheshan had no sons, and so he let one of his daughters marry Jarha, his Egyptian slave. Their son was Attai, ³⁶ the father of Nathan and the grandfather of Zabad. ³⁷⁻⁴¹ Zabad's descendants included Ephlal, Obed, Jehu, Azariah, Helez, Eleasah, Sismai, Shallum, Jekamiah, and Elishama.

The descendants of Caleb

⁴² Caleb, Jerahmeel's brother, had the following descendants: Mesha,' Ziph, Mareshah,' Hebron, ⁴³ and Hebron's four sons, Korah, Tappuah, Rekem, and Shema. ⁴⁴ Shema was the father of Raham and the grandfather of Jorkeam. Rekem was the father of Shammai, ⁴⁵ the grandfather of Maon, and the great-grandfather of Bethzur.

⁴⁶ Ephah was one of Caleb's wives,* and their sons were Haran, Moza, and Gazez. Haran named his son after his brother Gazez. ⁴⁷ Ephah was the daughter of Jahdai, who was also the father of Regem, Jotham, Geshan, Pelet, and Shaaph.'

⁴⁸ Maacah was another of Caleb's wives,* and their sons were Sheber and Tirhanah. ⁴⁹ Later, they had two more sons: Shaaph the father of Madmannah, and Sheva the father of Machbenah and Gibea. Caleb's daughter was

---

*2.7 **Achan:** The Hebrew text has "Achar", which means "trouble".
*2.7 **Achan . . . the LORD:** See Joshua 7.1–26.
See also: 2.7: Josh 7.1.

*2.46,48 **wives:** This translates a Hebrew word for women who were legally bound to a man, but without the full privileges of a wife.

Achsah. ⁵⁰⁻⁵¹ All of these were Caleb's descendants.

Hur, the eldest son of Caleb and Ephrath, had three sons: Shobal, Salma, and Hareph, who settled the town of Beth-Gader. ⁵² Shobal, who settled the town of Kiriath-Jearim, was the ancestor of Haroeh, half of the Menuhoth clan, ⁵³ and the clans that lived near Kiriath-Jearim; they were the Ithrites, the Puthites, the Shumathites, and the Mishraites. The Zorathites and the Eshtaolites were descendants of the Mishraites.

⁵⁴ Salma settled the town of Bethlehem and was the ancestor of the Netophathites, the people of Atroth-Bethjoab, half of the Manahathite clan, and the Zorites. ⁵⁵ Salma was also the ancestor of the clans in Jabez that kept the court and government records; they were the Tirathites, the Shimeathites, and the Sucathites. These clans were the descendants of Hammath the Kenite, who was also the ancestor of the Rechabites.

CHAPTER 3

The descendants of King David

¹⁻⁴ King David ruled from Hebron for seven years and six months, and during that time he had six sons, who were born in the following order: Amnon, Daniel, Absalom, Adonijah, Shephatiah, and Ithream. Ahinoam from Jezreel was the mother of Amnon; Abigail from Carmel was the mother of Daniel; Maacah daughter of King Talmai of Geshur was the mother of Absalom; Haggith was the mother of Adonijah; Abital was the mother of Shephatiah; and Eglah was the mother of Ithream.

David then ruled from Jerusalem for thirty-three years, ⁵ and during that time, he had thirteen more sons. His wife Bathsheba᾽ daughter of Ammiel gave birth to Shimea, Shobab, Nathan, and Solomon. ⁶⁻⁸ David's other sons included Ibhar, Elishua,᾽ Eliphelet, Nogah, Nepheg, Japhia, Elishama, Eliada, and Eliphelet. ⁹ David's other wives* also gave birth to sons. Tamar was his daughter.

The descendants of King Solomon

¹⁰⁻¹⁵ Solomon's descendants included the following kings: Rehoboam, Abijah, Asa, Jehoshaphat, Jehoram,᾽ Ahaziah, Joash, Amaziah, Azariah, Jotham, Ahaz, Hezekiah, Manasseh, Amon, and Josiah and his four

sons, Johanan, Jehoiakim, Zedekiah, and Jehoahaz.᾽ ¹⁶ Jehoiakim was the father of Jehoiachin and Zedekiah.

¹⁷ Jehoiachin, who was taken to Babylon as a prisoner, had seven sons: Shealtiel, ¹⁸ Malchiram, Pedaiah, Shenazzar, Jekamiah, Hoshama, and Nedabiah. ¹⁹ Pedaiah had two sons: Zerubbabel and Shimei. Zerubbabel was the father of Meshullam, Hananiah, and Shelomith their sister. ²⁰ He also had five other sons: Hashubah, Ohel, Berechiah, Hasadiah, and Jushabhesed. ²¹ Hananiah's descendants were Pelatiah, Jeshaiah, Rephaiah, Arnan, Obadiah, and Shecaniah,᾽ ²² the father of Shemaiah and the grandfather of Hattush, Igal, Bariah, Neariah, and Shaphat. ²³ Neariah was the father of Elioenai, Hizkiah, and Azrikam. ²⁴ Elioenai was the father of Hodaviah, Eliashib, Pelaiah, Akkub, Johanan, Delaiah, and Anani.

CHAPTER 4

The descendants of Judah

¹ Judah was the father of five sons: Perez, Hezron, Carmi, Hur, and Shobal. ² Shobal was the father of Reaiah, the grandfather of Jahath, and the great-grandfather of Ahumai and Lahad. These men all belonged to the Zorathite clan.

³⁻⁴ Hur was the eldest son of Caleb and Ephrath. Some of his descendants settled the town of Bethlehem. Hur's other descendants included Etam, Penuel, and Ezer. Etam's sons᾽ were Jezreel, Ishma, and Idbash, and his daughter was Hazzelelponi. Penuel settled the town of Gedor, and Ezer settled the town of Hushah.

⁵ Ashhur, who settled the town of Tekoa, had two wives: Helah and Naarah. ⁶ Ashhur and Naarah were the parents of Ahuzzam, Hepher, Temeni, and Haahashtari. ⁷ Ashhur and Helah were the parents of Zereth, Izhar, and Ethnan.

⁸ Koz, the father of Anub and Zobebah, was also the ancestor of the clans of Aharhel, the son of Harum.

⁹ Jabez was a man who got his name because of the pain he caused his mother during birth.* But he was still the most respected son in his family. ¹⁰ One day he prayed to Israel's God, "Please bless me and give me a lot of land. Be with me so I will be safe from harm."᾽ And God did just what Jabez had asked.

---

*3.9 other wives: See the note at 2.46,48.
See also: 3.4: 2 Sam 5.4–5; 1 King 2.11; 1 Chron 29.27.
3.5: 2 Sam 11.3.

---

*4.9 Jabez . . . pain . . . birth: In Hebrew "Jabez" sounds like "pain".

¹¹ Chelub was the brother of Shuhah and the father of Mehir. Later, Mehir had a son, Eshton, ¹² whose three sons were Bethrapha, Paseah, and Tehinnah. It was Tehinnah who settled the town of Nahash.▸ These men and their families lived in the town of Recah.

¹³ Kenaz was the father of Othniel and Seraiah. Othniel had two sons: Hathath and Meonothai,▸ ¹⁴ who was the father of Ophrah. Seraiah was the father of Joab, who settled a place called "Valley of Crafts"▸ because the people who lived there were experts in making things.

¹⁵ Caleb son of Jephunneh had three sons: Iru, Elah, and Naam. Elah was the father of Kenaz.

¹⁶ Jehallel was the father of Ziph, Ziphah, Tiria, and Asarel.

¹⁷⁻¹⁸ Ezrah was the father of Jether, Mered, Epher, and Jalon. Mered was married to Bithiah the daughter of the king of Egypt. They had a daughter named Miriam and two sons: Shammai and Ishbah. It was Ishbah who settled the town of Eshtemoa. Mered was also married to a woman from the tribe of Judah, and their sons were Jered, Heber, and Jekuthiel. Jered settled the town of Gedor; Heber settled the town of Soco; and Jekuthiel settled the town of Zanoah.

¹⁹ A man named Hodiah was married to the sister of Naham. Hodiah's descendants included Keilah of the Garmite clan and Eshtemoa of the Maacathite clan.

²⁰ Shimon was the father of Amnon, Rinnah, Benhanan, and Tilon.
Ishi was the father of Zoheth and Benzoheth.

²¹⁻²² Judah also had a son named Shelah, whose descendants included Jokim and the people of the town of Cozeba, as well as Er who settled the town of Lecah and Laadah who settled the town of Mareshah. The people who lived in Beth-Ashbea were also descendants of Shelah, and they were experts in weaving cloth. Shelah was the ancestor of Joash and Saraph, two men who married Moabite women and then settled near Bethlehem▸ — but these family records are very old. ²³ The members of these clans were the potters who lived in the towns of Netaim and Gederah and worked for the king.

The descendants of Simeon

²⁴ Simeon had five sons: Nemuel, Jamin, Jarib, Zerah, and Shaul. ²⁵ The descendants of Shaul included his son Shallum, his grandson Mibsam, and his great-grandson

Mishma. ²⁶ The descendants of Mishma included his son Hammuel, his grandson Zaccur, and his great-grandson Shimei. ²⁷ Shimei had sixteen sons and six daughters. But his brothers did not have as many children, so the Simeon tribe was smaller than the Judah tribe.

²⁸⁻³¹ Before David became king, the people of the Simeon tribe lived in the following towns: Beersheba, Moladah, Hazar-Shual, Bilhah, Ezem, Tolad, Bethuel, Hormah, Ziklag, Beth-Marcaboth, Hazarsusim, Bethbiri, and Shaaraim. ³² They also lived in the five villages of Etam, Ain, Rimmon, Tochen, and Ashan, ³³ as well as in the nearby villages as far as the town of Baal. These are the places where Simeon's descendants had settled, according to their own family records.

³⁴⁻³⁸ As their families and clans became larger, the people of Simeon had the following leaders: Meshobab, Jamlech, Joshah son of Amaziah, Joel, Jehu,▸ Elioenai, Jaakobah, Jeshohaiah, Asaiah, Adiel, Jesimiel, Benaiah, and Ziza.▸ ³⁹ When the people needed more pasture land for their flocks and herds, they looked as far as the eastern side of the valley where the town of Gerar▸ is, ⁴⁰ and they found a lot of good pasture land that was quiet and undisturbed. This had once belonged to the Hamites, ⁴¹ but when Hezekiah was king of Judah, the descendants of Simeon attacked and forced the Hamites and Meunites off the land, then settled there.

⁴² Some time later, five hundred men from the Simeon tribe went into Edom▸ under the command of Pelatiah, Neariah, Rephaiah, and Uzziel the sons of Ishi. ⁴³ They killed the last of the Amalekites and lived there from then on.

CHAPTER 5

The descendants of Reuben

¹ Reuben was the eldest son of Jacob,▸ but he lost his rights as the firstborn son* because he slept with one of his father's wives.* The honour of the firstborn son was then given to Joseph, ² even though it was the Judah tribe that became the most powerful and produced a leader.

---

*5.1 rights as the firstborn son: The firstborn son inherited the largest amount of property, as well as the leadership of the family.
*5.1 wives: See Genesis 35.22; 49.3–4.
See also: 4.28–33: Josh 19.2–8. 5.1: Gen 35.22; 49.3–4.
5.2: Gen 49.8–10.

³ Reuben had four sons: Hanoch, Pallu, Hezron, and Carmi.

⁴⁻⁶ The descendants of Joel included Shemaiah, Gog, Shimei, Micah, Reaiah, Baal, and Beerah, a leader of the Reuben tribe. Later, King Tiglath Pileser of Assyria took Beerah away as prisoner.

⁷⁻⁸ The family records also include Jeiel, who was a clan leader, Zechariah, and Bela son of Azaz and grandson of Shema of the Joel clan. They lived in the territory around the town of Aroer, as far north as Nebo and Baal-Meon, ⁹ and as far east as the desert just west of the River Euphrates. They needed this much land because they owned too many cattle to keep them all in Gilead.

¹⁰ When Saul was king, the Reuben tribe attacked and defeated the Hagrites, then took over their land east of Gilead.

The descendants of Gad

¹¹ The tribe of Gad lived in the region of Bashan, north of the Reuben tribe. Gad's territory extended all the way to the town of Salecah. ¹² Some of the clan leaders were Joel, Shapham, Janai, and Shaphat. ¹³ Their relatives included Michael, Meshullam, Sheba, Jorai, Jacan, Zia, and Eber.

¹⁴ They were all descendants of Abihail, whose family line went back through Huri, Jaroah, Gilead, Michael, Jeshishai, Jahdo, and Buz. ¹⁵ Ahi, the son of Abdiel and the grandson of Guni, was the leader of their clan.

¹⁶ The people of Gad lived in the towns in the regions of Bashan and Gilead, as well as in the pasture land of Sharon. ¹⁷ Their family records were written when Jotham was king of Judah and Jeroboam was king of Israel.

¹⁸ The tribes of Reuben, Gad, and East Manasseh had 44,760 soldiers trained to fight in battle with shields, swords, bows, and arrows. ¹⁹ They fought against the Hagrites and the tribes of Jetur, Naphish, and Nodab. ²⁰ Whenever these soldiers went to war against their enemies, they prayed to God and trusted him to help. That's why the tribes of Reuben, Gad, and East Manasseh defeated the Hagrites and their allies.

²¹ These Israelite tribes captured fifty thousand camels, two hundred and fifty thousand sheep, two thousand donkeys, and one hundred thousand people. ²² Many of the Hagrites died in battle, because God was fighting this battle against them. The tribes of Reuben, Gad, and East Manasseh lived in that territory until they were taken as prisoners to Assyria.*

The tribe of East Manasseh

²³ East Manasseh was a large tribe, so its people settled in the northern region of Bashan, as far north as Baal-Hermon,* Senir, and Mount Hermon. ²⁴ Epher, Ishi, Eliel, Azriel, Jeremiah, Hodaviah, and Jahdiel were their clan leaders; they were well-known leaders and brave soldiers.

The tribes of Reuben, Gad, and East Manasseh are defeated

²⁵ The people of the tribes of Reuben, Gad, and East Manasseh were unfaithful to the God their ancestors had worshipped, and they started worshipping the gods of the nations that God had forced out of Canaan. ²⁶ So God sent King Tiglath Pileser⁽ᵇ⁾ of Assyria to attack these Israelite tribes. The king led them away as prisoners to Assyria, and from then on, he forced them to live in Halah, Habor, Hara, and near the River Gozan.

CHAPTER 6

The descendants of Levi

¹ Levi was the father of Gershon, Kohath, and Merari.

² Kohath was the father of Amram, Izhar, Hebron, and Uzziel. ³ Amram was the father of Aaron, Moses, and Miriam.

Aaron had four sons: Nadab, Abihu, Eleazar, and Ithamar.

⁴⁻¹⁴ Eleazar's descendants included Phinehas, Abishua, Bukki, Uzzi, Zerahiah, Meraioth, Amariah, Ahitub, Zadok, Ahimaaz, Azariah, Johanan, Azariah the priest who served in the temple built by King Solomon, Amariah, Ahitub, Zadok, Shallum, Hilkiah, Azariah, Seraiah, and Jehozadak. ¹⁵ King Nebuchadnezzar of Babylonia took Jehozadak to Babylon as prisoner when the LORD let the people of Judah and Jerusalem be dragged from their land.*

---

*5.22 **they were taken as prisoners to Assyria:** See 2 Kings 15.29; 17.5–23.

*5.23 **Baal-Hermon:** The location of this place is unknown.

*6.15 **King Nebuchadnezzar . . . dragged from their land:** See 2 Kings 24.8–17; 25.1–21.

See also: 5.26: a 2 Kings 15.19; b 2 Kings 15.29; c 2 Kings 17.6.

16 Levi's three sons had sons of their own.
17 Gershon was the father of Libni and Shimei.
18 Kohath was the father of Amram, Izhar, Hebron, and Uzziel. 19 Merari was the father of Mahli and Mushi. These descendants of Levi each became leaders of their own clans.

20-21 Gershon's descendants included Libni, Jahath, Zimmah, Joah, Iddo, Zerah, and Jeatherai.

22-24 Kohath's descendants included Amminadab, Korah, Assir, Elkanah, Ebiasaph, Assir, Tahath, Uriel, Uzziah, and Shaul.

25 Elkanah was the father of Amasai and Ahimoth. 26-27 Ahimoth's descendants included Elkanah, Zophai, Nahath, Eliab, Jeroham, and Elkanah.

28 Samuel was the father of Joel* and Abijah, born in that order.

29-30 Merari's descendants included Mahli, Libni, Shimei, Uzzah, Shimea, Haggiah, and Asaiah.

The temple musicians

31 After King David had the sacred chest moved to Jerusalem, he appointed musicians from the Levi tribe to be in charge of the music at the place of worship. 32 These musicians served at the sacred tent and later at the LORD's temple that King Solomon built.

33-38 Here is a list of these musicians and their family lines:

Heman from the Kohathite clan was the director. His ancestors went all the way back to Jacob and included Joel, Samuel, Elkanah, Jeroham, Eliel, Toah, Zuph, Elkanah, Mahath, Amasai, Elkanah, Joel, Azariah, Zephaniah, Tahath, Assir, Ebiasaph, Korah, Izhar, Kohath, and Levi.

39-43 Asaph was Heman's relative and served as his assistant. Asaph's ancestors included Berechiah, Shimea, Michael, Baaseiah, Malchijah, Ethni, Zerah, Adaiah, Ethan, Zimmah, Shimei, Jahath, Gershon, and Levi.

44-47 Ethan was also Heman's relative and served as his assistant. Ethan belonged to the Merari clan, and his ancestors included Kishi, Abdi, Malluch, Hashabiah, Amaziah, Hilkiah, Amzi, Bani, Shemer, Mahli, Mushi, Merari, and Levi.

48 The rest of the Levites were appointed to work at the sacred tent.

The descendants of Aaron

49 Only Aaron and his descendants were allowed to offer sacrifices and incense on the two altars at the sacred tent.* They were in charge of the most holy place and the ceremonies to forgive sins, just as God's servant Moses had commanded.

50-53 Aaron's descendants included his son Eleazar, Phinehas, Abishua, Bukki, Uzzi, Zerahiah, Meraioth, Amariah, Ahitub, Zadok, and Ahimaaz.

The towns for the Levites

This is also told in Joshua 21.1-42

54 Aaron's descendants belonged to the Levite clan of Kohath, and they were the first group chosen to receive towns to live in. 55 They received the town of Hebron in the territory of Judah and the pasture land around it. 56 But the farmland and villages around Hebron were given to Caleb son of Jephunneh. 57-59 So Aaron's descendants received the following Safe Towns* and the pasture land around them: Hebron, Libnah, Jattir, Eshtemoa, Hilen, Debir, Ashan, and Beth-Shemesh.
60 From the Benjamin tribe they were given the towns of Geba, Alemeth, and Anathoth and the pasture land around them. Thirteen towns were given to Aaron's descendants.

61 The rest of the Levite clan of Kohath received ten towns from West Manasseh.

62 The Levite clan of Gershon received thirteen towns from the tribes of Issachar, Asher, Naphtali, and East Manasseh in Bashan.

63 The Levite clan of Merari received twelve towns from the tribes of Reuben, Gad, and Zebulun.

64 So the people of Israel gave the Levites towns to live in and the pasture land around them. 65 All the towns were chosen with the LORD's help,* including those towns from the tribes of Judah, Simeon, and Benjamin.

66 Some of the families of the Kohath clan received their towns from the tribe of Ephraim. 67-69 These families received the following Safe Towns and the pasture land around them: Shechem in the hill country, Gezer, Jokmeam, Beth-Horon, Aijalon, and Gath-Rimmon. 70 And from West Manasseh they received Aner and Bileam, together with their pasture land.

---

*6.57-59 Safe Towns:** These were special towns set aside where a person who had accidentally killed someone could run for protection from the victim's relatives (see Numbers 35.9-15; Deuteronomy 19.1-13; Joshua 20.1-9).
*6.65 with the LORD's help:** The Hebrew text has "by lot". Pieces of wood or stone (called "lots") were used to find out what God wanted his people to do.

See also: 6.16-19: Exod 6.16-19.

71 The Gershonite clan received two towns from the tribe of East Manasseh: Golan in Bashan and Ashtaroth, including the pasture land around them. 72–73 The Gershonites also received four towns from the tribe of Issachar: Kedesh, Daberath, Ramoth, and Anem, including the pasture land around them. 74–75 The Gershonites received four towns from the tribe of Asher: Mashal, Abdon, Hukok, and Rehob, including the pasture land around them. 76 Finally, the Gershonites received three towns from the tribe of Naphtali: Kedesh in Galilee, Hammon, and Kiriathaim, including the pasture land around them.

77 The rest of the Merari clan received the towns of Rimmono and Tabor and their pasture land from the tribe of Zebulun. 78–79 They also received four towns east of the River Jordan from the tribe of Reuben: Bezer in the flat lands, Jahzah, Kedemoth, and Mephaath, including the pastures around them. 80–81 And from the tribe of Gad the Merarites received the towns of Ramoth in Gilead, Mahanaim, Heshbon, and Jazer, including the pasture land around them.

CHAPTER 7

The descendants of Issachar

1 Issachar was the father of four sons: Tola, Puah, Jashub, and Shimron.

2 Tola was the father of Uzzi, Rephaiah, Jeriel, Jahmai, Ibsam, and Shemuel, who were all brave soldiers and family leaders in their clan. There were 22,600 people in Tola's family by the time David became king.

3 Uzzi was the father of Izrahiah and the grandfather of Michael, Obadiah, Joel, and Isshiah, who were also family leaders. 4 Their families were so large that they had 36,000 soldiers in their clans. 5 In fact, according to family records, the tribe of Issachar had a total of 87,000 warriors.

The descendants of Benjamin and Dan

6 Benjamin was the father of three sons: Bela, Becher, and Jediael.

7 Bela was the father of Ezbon, Uzzi, Uzziel, Jerimoth, and Iri. They were all brave soldiers and family leaders in their father's clan. The number of soldiers in their clan was 22,034.

8 Becher was the father of Zemirah, Joash, Eliezer, Elioenai, Omri, Jeremoth, Abijah, Anathoth, and Alemeth. 9 The official family records listed 20,200 soldiers in the families of this clan, as well as their family leaders.

10 Jediael was the father of Bilhan and the grandfather of Jeush, Benjamin, Ehud, Chenaanah, Zethan, Tarshish, and Ahishahar. 11 They were family leaders in their clan, which had 17,200 soldiers prepared to fight in battle. 12 Ir was the father of Shuppim and Huppim, who also belonged to this clan.

Dan' was the father of Hushim.

The descendants of Naphtali

13 Naphtali's mother was Bilhah,* and he was the father of Jahziel, Guni, Jezer, and Shallum.

The descendants of Manasseh

14 Manasseh and his Syrian wife* were the parents of Asriel and Machir the father of Gilead. 15 Machir found a wife for Huppim and one for Shuppim. Machir had a sister named Maacah.

Zelophehad was also a descendant of Manasseh, and he had five daughters.'

16 Machir and his wife Maacah were the parents of Peresh and Sheresh. Peresh was the father of Ulam and Rekem. 17 Ulam was the father of Bedan. These were all descendants of Gilead, the son of Machir and the grandson of Manasseh.

18 Gilead's sister Hammolecheth was the mother of Ishhod, Abiezer, and Mahlah.

19 Shemida, another descendant of Manasseh, was the father of Ahian, Shechem, Likhi, and Aniam.

The descendants of Ephraim

20 Ephraim was the father of Shuthelah and the ancestor of Bered, Tahath, Eleadah, Tahath, 21 Zabad, and Shuthelah.

Ephraim had two other sons, Ezer and Elead. But they were killed when they tried to steal livestock from the people who lived in the territory of Gath. 22 Ephraim mourned for his sons a long time, and his relatives came to comfort him. 23 Some time later his wife gave birth to another son, and Ephraim named him Beriah, because he was born during a time of misery.*

24 Ephraim's daughter was Sheerah. She built the towns of Lower Beth-Horon, Upper Beth-Horon, and Uzzen-Sheerah.

---

*7.13 Bilhah: One of Jacob's wives and the mother of Dan and Naphtali (see Genesis 46.23–25).
*7.14 wife: See the note at 2.46,48.
*7.23 Beriah . . . misery: In Hebrew "Beriah" sounds like "in misery".

25 Ephraim also had a son named Rephah, and his descendants included Resheph, Telah, Tahan, 26 Ladan, Ammihud, Elishama, 27 Nun, and Joshua.

28 The descendants of Ephraim took over the territory as far south as Bethel, as far east as Naaran, and as far west as Gezer. Their territory included all the villages around these towns, as well as Shechem, Ayyah, and the nearby villages.

29 The descendants of Manasseh settled in the territory that included Beth-Shan, Taanach, Megiddo, Dor, and the nearby villages.

The descendants of Joseph' lived in these towns and villages.

The descendants of Asher

30 Asher had four sons, Imnah, Ishvah, Ishvi, and Beriah, and one daughter, Serah.

31 Beriah was the father of Heber and Malchiel the father of Birzaith. 32 Heber was the father of three sons, Japhlet, Shomer, and Hotham, and one daughter, Shua. 33 Japhlet was the father of Pasach, Bimhal, and Ashvath. 34 Shomer was the father of Ahi, Rohgah, Hubbah, and Aram. 35 And Japhlet's brother Hotham' was the father of Zophah, Imna, Shelesh, and Amal. 36 Zophah was the father of Suah, Harnepher, Shual, Beri, Imrah, 37 Bezer, Hod, Shamma, Shilshah, Ithran, and Beera. 38 Jether was the father of Jephunneh, Pispa, and Ara.

39 Ulla was the father of Arah, Hanniel, and Rizia.

40 These were the descendants of Asher, and they were all respected family leaders and brave soldiers. The tribe of Asher had a total of 26,000 soldiers.

CHAPTER 8

More descendants of Benjamin

1 Benjamin had five sons, who were born in the following order: Bela, Ashbel, Aharah, 2 Nohah, and Rapha. 3 Bela was the father of Addar, Gera, Abihud, 4 Abishua, Naaman, Ahoah, 5 Gera, Shephuphan, and Huram.

6-7 Ehud was the father of Naaman, Ahijah, and Gera. They were clan leaders in the town of Geba, but were later forced to move to the town of Manahath, and Gera led the way. He had two sons: Uzza and Ahihud.

8-11 Shaharaim and his wife Hushim had two sons: Abitub and Elpaal. But Shaharaim later divorced her and his other wife, Baara. Then he moved to the country of Moab and married Hodesh, and they had seven sons:

Jobab, Zibia, Mesha, Malcam, Jeuz, Sachia, and Mirmah. They were all family leaders in his clan. 12 Elpaal was the father of Eber, Misham, and Shemed, who settled the towns of Ono and Lod, as well as the nearby villages.

13 Beriah and Shema were family leaders in the clan that lived in the town of Aijalon and that forced out the people of Gath.

14-16 Beriah's descendants included Ahio, Shashak, Jeremoth, Zebadiah, Arad, Eder, Michael, Ishpah, and Joha. 17-18 Elpaal's descendants included Zebadiah, Meshullam, Hizki, Heber, Ishmerai, Izliah, and Jobab. 19-21 Shimei's descendants included Jakim, Zichri, Zabdi, Elienai, Zillethai, Eliel, Adaiah, Beraiah, and Shimrath. 22-25 Shashak's descendants included Ishpan, Eber, Eliel, Abdon, Zichri, Hanan, Hananiah, Elam, Anthothijah, Iphdeiah, and Penuel. 26-27 Jeroham's descendants included Shamsherai, Shehariah, Athaliah, Jaareshiah, Elijah, and Zichri. 28 These were the family leaders in their ancestor's clan, and they and their descendants lived in Jerusalem.

29 Jeiel' settled the town of Gibeon. He and his wife Maacah lived there 30 along with their sons, who were born in the following order: Abdon, Zur, Kish, Baal, Ner,' Nadab, 31 Gedor, Ahio, Zecher, 32 and Mikloth the father of Shimeah. Some of them went to live in Jerusalem near their relatives.

The descendants of King Saul

33 Ner was the father of Kish and the grandfather of King Saul.

Saul had four sons: Jonathan, Malchishua, Abinadab, and Eshbaal.* 34 Jonathan was the father of Meribbaal,* the grandfather of Micah, 35 and the great-grandfather of Pithon, Melech, Tarea, and Ahaz. 36 Saul's other descendants were Jehoaddah, Alemeth, Azmaveth, Zimri, Moza, 37 Binea, Raphah, Eleasah, Azel, 38 as well as Azel's six sons: Azrikam, Bocheru, Ishmael, Sheariah, Obadiah, and Hanan. 39 Azel's brother Eshek was the father of Ulam, Jeush, and Eliphelet. 40 Ulam's sons were brave soldiers who were experts at using a bow and arrows. They had a total of one hundred and fifty children and grandchildren.

All of these belonged to the tribe of Benjamin.

---

*8.33 Eshbaal: Also called "Ishbosheth" (see 2 Samuel 2.8 and the note there).

*8.34 Meribbaal: Also called "Mephibosheth" (see 2 Samuel 4.4 and the note there).

CHAPTER 9

The people who returned from Babylonia and settled in Jerusalem

¹ Everyone in Israel was listed in the official family records that were included in the history of Israel's kings.

The people of Judah were taken to Babylonia as prisoners because they sinned against the LORD. ² And the first people to return to their towns included priests, Levites, temple workers, and other Israelites. ³ People from the tribes of Judah, Benjamin, Ephraim, and Manasseh settled in Jerusalem.

⁴⁻⁶ There were six hundred and ninety people from the Judah tribe who settled in Jerusalem. They were all descendants of Judah's three sons: Perez, Shelah, and Zerah. Their leaders were Uthai, Asaiah, and Jeuel. Uthai was the son of Ammihud and a descendant of Omri, Imri, Bani, and Perez. Asaiah was a descendant of Shelah; Jeuel was a descendant of Zerah.

⁷⁻⁹ There were also nine hundred and fifty-six family leaders from the Benjamin tribe who settled in Jerusalem. They included: Sallu son of Meshullam, grandson of Hodaviah, and great-grandson of Hassenuah; Ibneiah son of Jeroham; Elah son of Uzzi and grandson of Michri; Meshullam son of Shephatiah, grandson of Reuel, and great-grandson of Ibnijah.

The priests who settled in Jerusalem

¹⁰⁻¹² Here is a list of priests who settled in Jerusalem: Jedaiah; Jehoiarib; Jachin; Azariah, who was a temple official, and whose ancestors included Hilkiah, Meshullam, Zadok, Meraioth, and Ahitub; Adaiah son of Jeroham, whose ancestors included Pashhur and Malchijah; Maasai son of Adiel, whose ancestors included Jahzerah, Meshullam, Meshillemith, and Immer.

¹³ There was a total of 1,760 priests, all of them family leaders in their clan and trained in the work at the temple.

The Levites who settled in Jerusalem

¹⁴⁻¹⁶ Here is a list of Levites who settled in Jerusalem: Shemaiah from the Merari clan, whose ancestors included Hasshub, Azrikam, and Hashabiah; Bakbakkar; Heresh; Galal; Mattaniah son of Mica, whose ancestors included Zichri and Asaph; Obadiah son of Shemaiah, whose ancestors included Galal and Jeduthun; Berechiah son of Asa and

grandson of Elkanah, who had lived in the villages near the town of Netophah.

The temple guards who settled in Jerusalem

¹⁷ Shallum, Akkub, Talmon, Ahiman, and their relatives were the guards at the temple gates. Shallum was the leader of this clan, ¹⁸ and for a long time they had been the guards at the King's Gate on the east side of the city. Before that, their ancestors guarded the entrance to the Levite camp.

¹⁹ Shallum son of Kore,⋆ as well as the other men in the Korahite clan, guarded the entrance to the temple, just as their ancestors had guarded the entrance to the sacred tent. ²⁰ Phinehas son of Eleazar had supervised their work because the LORD was with him.

²¹ Zechariah son of Meshelemiah was also one of the guards at the temple.

²² There was a total of two hundred and twelve guards, all of them listed in the family records in their towns. Their ancestors had been chosen by King David and by Samuel the prophet to be responsible for this work, ²³ and now they guarded the temple gates.

²⁴ There was one full-time guard appointed to each of the four sides of the temple. ²⁵ Their assistants lived in the villages outside the city, and every seven days a group of them would come into the city and take their turn at guard duty. ²⁶ The four full-time guards were Levites, and they supervised the other guards and were responsible for the rooms in the temple and the supplies kept there. ²⁷ They guarded the temple day and night and opened its doors every morning.

The duties of the Levites

²⁸ Some of the Levites were responsible for the equipment used in worship at the temple, and they had to count everything before and after it was used. ²⁹ Others were responsible for the temple furnishings and its sacred objects, as well as the flour, wine, olive oil, incense, and spices. ³⁰ But only the priests could mix the spices. ³¹ Mattithiah, Shallum's eldest son, was a member of the Levite clan of Korah, and he was in charge of baking the bread used for offerings.⋆ ³² The Levites from the Kohath clan were in charge of baking the sacred loaves of bread for each Sabbath.⋆

⋆9.31 the bread used for offerings: See Leviticus 2.4–7.
⋆9.32 the sacred loaves of bread for each Sabbath: See Leviticus 24.5–9.

See also: 9.2–3; Ezra 2.27; Neh 7.73.

33 The Levite family leaders who were the musicians also lived at the temple. They had no other responsibilities, because they were on duty day and night.

34 All these men were family leaders in the Levi tribe and were listed that way in their family records. They lived in Jerusalem.

King Saul's family

This is also told in 1 Chronicles 8.29–38

35 Jeiel had settled the town of Gibeon, where he and his wife Maacah lived. 36 They had ten sons, who were born in the following order: Abdon, Zur, Kish, Baal, Ner, Nadab, 37 Gedor, Ahio, Zechariah, and Mikloth 38 the father of Shimeam. Some of them went to live in Jerusalem near their relatives.

39 Ner was the father of Kish and the grandfather of King Saul.

Saul had four sons: Jonathan, Malchishua, Abinadab, and Eshbaal.* 40-41 Jonathan was the father of Meribbaal,* the grandfather of Micah, and the great-grandfather of Pithon, Melech, Tahrea, and Ahaz.› 42-44 The descendants of Ahaz included Jarah, Alemeth, Azmaveth, Zimri, Moza, Binea, Rephaiah, Eleasah, and Azel and his six sons: Azrikam, Bocheru, Ishmael, Sheariah, Obadiah, and Hanan.

The death of Saul and his sons

CHAPTER 10

This is also told in 1 Samuel 31.1–13

1 The Philistines fought against Israel in a battle at Mount Gilboa. Israel's soldiers ran from the Philistines, and many of them were killed. 2 The Philistines closed in on Saul and his sons and killed three of them: Jonathan, Abinadab, and Malchishua. 3 The fighting was fierce around Saul, and he was badly wounded by enemy arrows.

4 Saul told the soldier who carried his weapons, "Kill me with your sword! I don't want those godless Philistines to torture and make fun of me."

But the soldier was afraid to kill him. Then Saul stuck himself in the stomach with his own sword and fell on the blade. 5 When the soldier realized that Saul was dead, he killed himself in the same way.

6 Saul, three of his sons, and all his male relatives were dead. 7 The Israelites who lived in Jezreel Valley› learnt that their army had run away and that Saul and his sons were dead. They ran away too, and the Philistines moved into the towns the Israelites left behind.

8 The next day the Philistines came back to the battlefield to carry away the weapons of the dead Israelite soldiers. When they found the bodies of Saul and his sons on Mount Gilboa, 9 they took Saul's weapons, pulled off his armour, and cut off his head. Then they sent messengers everywhere in Philistia to spread the news among their people and to thank the idols of their gods. 10 They put Saul's armour in the temple of their gods and hung his head in the temple of their god Dagon.

11 When the people who lived in Jabesh in Gilead heard what the Philistines had done to Saul, 12 some brave men went to get his body and the bodies of his three sons. The men brought the bodies back to Jabesh, where they buried them under an oak tree. Then for seven days, they went without eating to show their sorrow.

13 Saul died because he was unfaithful and disobeyed the Lord. He even asked advice from a woman who talked to spirits of the dead, 14 instead of asking the Lord. So the Lord had Saul killed and gave his kingdom to David, the son of Jesse.

David becomes king of Israel and captures Jerusalem

CHAPTER 11

David becomes king of Israel

This is also told in 2 Samuel 5.1–3

1 Israel's leaders met with David at Hebron and said, "We are your relatives, 2 and we know that you have led our army into battle, even when Saul was still our king. The Lord God has promised that you would rule our country and take care of us like a shepherd. 3 So we have come to crown you king of Israel."

David made an agreement with the leaders and asked the Lord to be their witness. Then the leaders poured olive oil on David's head

---

*9.39 Eshbaal: See the note at 8.33.
*9.40–41 Meribbaal: See the note at 8.34.

See also: 10.13: a 1 Sam 13.8-14; 15.1–24; b Lev 19.31; 20.6; 1 Sam 28.7-8.

to show that he was now king of Israel. This happened just as the LORD's prophet Samuel had said.

David captures Jerusalem

This is also told in 2 Samuel 5.6–10

⁴ Jerusalem was called Jebus at the time, and David led Israel's army to attack the town. ⁵ The Jebusites said, "You won't be able to get in here!" But David captured the fortress of Mount Zion, which is now called the City of David.

⁶ David had told his troops, "The first soldier to kill a Jebusite will become my army commander." And since Joab son of Zeruiah attacked first, he became commander.

⁷ Later, David moved to the fortress — that's why it's called the City of David. ⁸ He had the city rebuilt, starting at the landfill on the east side.* Meanwhile, Joab supervised the repairs to the rest of the city.

⁹ David became a great and strong ruler, because the LORD All-Powerful was on his side.

David's warriors

The Three Warriors

This is also told in 2 Samuel 23.8–17

¹⁰ The LORD had promised that David would become king, and so everyone in Israel gave David their support. Certain warriors also helped keep his kingdom strong.

¹¹ The first of these warriors was Jashobeam the son of Hachmoni, the leader of the Three Warriors.* In one battle he killed three hundred men with his spear.

¹² Another one of the Three Warriors was Eleazar son of Dodo the Ahohite. ¹³ During a battle against the Philistines at Pas-Dammim, all the Israelite soldiers ran away, ¹⁴ except Eleazar, who stayed with David. They took

their positions in a nearby barley field and defeated the Philistines! The LORD gave Israel a great victory that day.

¹⁵ One time the Three Warriors' went to meet David among the rocks at Adullam Cave. The Philistine army had set up camp in Rephaim Valley ¹⁶ and had taken over Bethlehem. David was in a fortress, ¹⁷ and he said, "I'm very thirsty. I wish I had a drink of water from the well by the gate to Bethlehem."

¹⁸ The Three Warriors sneaked through the Philistine camp and got some water from the well near Bethlehem's gate. They took it back to David, but he refused to drink it. Instead, he poured out the water as a sacrifice to the LORD ¹⁹ and said, "Drinking this water would be like drinking the blood of these men who risked their lives to get it for me."

The Three Warriors did these brave deeds.

The Thirty Warriors

This is also told in 2 Samuel 23.18–39

²⁰ Joab's brother Abishai was the leader of the Thirty Warriors,* and in one battle he killed three hundred men with his spear. He was just as famous as the Three Warriors ²¹ and was more famous than the rest of the Thirty Warriors. He was their commander, but he never became one of the Three Warriors.'

²² Benaiah the son of Jehoiada was a brave man from Kabzeel who did some amazing things. One time he killed two of Moab's best fighters, and one snowy day he went into a pit and killed a lion. ²³ Another time he killed an Egyptian who was over two metres tall and was armed with a spear. Benaiah only had a club, so he grabbed the spear from the Egyptian and killed him with it. ²⁴ Benaiah did things like that; he was just as brave as the Three Warriors, ²⁵ even though he never became one of them. And he was certainly as famous as the rest of the Thirty Warriors. So David made him the leader of his own bodyguard.

²⁶⁻⁴⁷ Here is a list of the other famous warriors:

Asahel the brother of Joab; Elhanan the son of Dodo from Bethlehem; Shammoth from Haror; Helez from Pelon; Ira the son of

---

*11.8 the landfill on the east side: The Hebrew text has "the Millo", which probably refers to a landfill to strengthen and extend the hill where the city was built.

*11.11 Three Warriors: One ancient translation and 2 Samuel 23.8; Hebrew "Thirty Warriors". The "Three Warriors" was the most honoured group of warriors and may have also been officers in the army and part of the Thirty Warriors. "Three" and "thirty" are spelt almost the same in Hebrew, so there is some confusion in the manuscripts as to which group is being talked about in some places in the following lists.

See also: 11.4: Josh 15.63; Judg 1.21.

*11.20 Thirty Warriors: One ancient translation; Hebrew "Three Warriors". The "Thirty Warriors" was the second most honoured group of warriors and they may have also been officers in the army.

Ikkesh from Tekoa; Abiezer from Anathoth; Sibbecai the Hushathite; Ilai' the Ahohite; Maharai from Netophah; Heled the son of Baanah from Netophah; Ithai the son of Ribai from Gibeah in Benjamin; Benaiah from Pirathon; Hurai' from near the streams on Mount Gaash; Abiel from Arbah; Azmaveth from Baharum; Eliahba from Shaalbon; Hashem' the Gizonite; Jonathan the son of Shagee from Harar; Ahiam the son of Sachar the Hararite; Eliphal the son of Ur; Hepher from Mecherah; Ahijah from Pelon; Hezro from Carmel; Naarai the son of Ezbai; Joel the brother of Nathan; Mibhar the son of Hagri; Zelek from Ammon; Naharai from Beeroth who carried Joab's weapons; Ira the Ithrite; Gareb the Ithrite; Uriah the Hittite; Zabad the son of Ahlai; Adina the son of Shiza, a leader in the Reuben tribe, and thirty of his soldiers; Hanan the son of Maacah; Joshaphat from Mithan; Uzzia from Ashterah; Shama and Jeiel the sons of Hotham from Aroer; Jediael and Joha the sons of Shimri from Tiz; Eliel from Mahavah; Jeribai and Joshaviah the sons of Elnaam; Ithmah from Moab; Eliel, Obed, and Jaasiel from Mezobah.

CHAPTER 12

David's men at Ziklag

¹ Some time earlier, David had gone to live in the town of Ziklag to escape from King Saul. While David was there, several brave warriors joined him to help fight his battles.*

Warriors from the Benjamin tribe

² Several of these warriors were from King Saul's own tribe of Benjamin. They were experts at using a bow and arrows, and they could shoot an arrow or sling a stone with either hand. ³⁻⁷ Their leaders were Ahiezer and Joash, the sons of Shemaah from Gibeah. Here is a list of those men from Benjamin: Jeziel and Pelet the sons of Azmaveth; Beracah and Jehu from Anathoth; Ishmaiah from Gibeon, who was the leader of the Thirty Warriors; Jeremiah, Jahaziel, Johanan, and Jozabad from Gederah; Eluzai, Jerimoth, Bealiah, Shemariah, and Shephatiah from

Haruph; Elkanah, Isshiah, Azarel, Joezer, and Jashobeam from the Korah clan; Joelah and Zebadiah the sons of Jeroham from Gedor.

Warriors from the Gad tribe

⁸ Men from the tribe of Gad also joined David at his fortress in the desert and served as his warriors. They were also brave soldiers — fierce as lions and quick as gazelles. They were always prepared to fight with shields and spears. ⁹⁻¹³ There were eleven of them, ranked in the following order: Ezer the leader, then Obadiah, Eliab, Mishmannah, Jeremiah, Attai, Eliel, Johanan, Elzabad, Jeremiah, and Machbannai.

¹⁴ All these men were army officers; some were high-ranking officers over a thousand troops, and others were officers over a hundred troops. ¹⁵ Earlier, they had crossed the River Jordan when it flooded, and they chased out the people who lived in the valleys on each side of the river.

Warriors from the Benjamin and Judah tribes

¹⁶ One time a group of men from the tribes of Benjamin and Judah went to the fortress where David was staying. ¹⁷ David met them outside and said, "If you are coming as friends to fight on my side, then stay and join us. But if you try to turn me over to my enemies, the God our ancestors worshipped will punish you, because I have done nothing wrong."

¹⁸ Amasai, who later became the leader of the Thirty Warriors, was one of these men who went to David. God's Spirit took control of him, and he said, "We will join you, David son of Jesse! You and your followers will always be successful, because God fights on your side."

So David agreed to let them stay, and he even put them in charge of his soldiers who raided enemy villages.

Warriors from the Manasseh tribe

¹⁹ Some of the warriors who joined David were from the tribe of Manasseh. They had earlier gone with David when he agreed to fight on the side of the Philistines against King Saul. But as soon as the Philistine rulers realized that David might turn against them and rejoin Saul, they sent David away to the town of Ziklag. ²⁰ That's when the following men from Manasseh joined him: Adnah, Jozabad, Jediael, Michael, Jozabad, Elihu, and Zillethai. They had all been

---

*12.1 David had gone . . . battles: Ziklag was the Philistine town that King Achish of Gath gave David in return for his loyalty (see 1 Samuel 27.6). This happened during the time when David was living as an outlaw, so the events in this chapter actually took place before chapter 11 when David became king of Israel.

commanders in Saul's army [21] and brave soldiers, and so David made them officers in his army. They fought on his side when enemy troops attacked.

[22] Day after day, new men came to join David, and soon he had a large, powerful army.

David's men at Hebron

[23-37] The kingdom of Israel had been taken away from Saul, and it now belonged to David. He was ruling from Hebron, and thousands of well-trained soldiers from each tribe went there to crown David king of all Israel, just as the LORD had promised. These soldiers, who were always prepared for battle, included: 6,800 from Judah, who were armed with shields and spears; 7,100 from Simeon; 4,600 from Levi, including Jehoiada, who was a leader from Aaron's descendants, and his 3,700 men, as well as Zadok, who was a brave soldier, and 22 of his relatives, who were also officers; 3,000 from Benjamin, because this was Saul's own tribe and most of the men had remained loyal to him; 20,800 from Ephraim, who were not only brave, but also famous in their clans; 18,000 from West Manasseh, who had been chosen to help make David king; 200 leaders from Issachar, along with troops under their command — these leaders knew the right time to do what needed to be done; 50,000 from Zebulun, who were not only loyal, but also trained to use any weapon; 1,000 officers from Naphtali and 37,000 soldiers armed with shields and spears; 28,600 from Dan; 40,000 from Asher; and 120,000 from the tribes of Reuben, Gad, and East Manasseh, who were armed with all kinds of weapons.

[38] All these soldiers voluntarily came to Hebron because they wanted David to become king of Israel. In fact, everyone in Israel wanted the same thing. [39] The soldiers stayed in Hebron three days, eating and drinking what their relatives had prepared for them. [40] Other Israelites from as far away as the territories of Issachar, Zebulun, and Naphtali brought cattle and sheep to slaughter for food. They also brought donkeys, camels, mules, and oxen that were loaded down with flour, dried figs, wine, and olive oil.

Everyone in Israel was very happy.

The sacred chest is moved to Jerusalem

CHAPTER 13

David moves the sacred chest to Jerusalem

This is also told in 2 Samuel 6.1–12a

[1] Some time later, David talked with his army commanders, [2-3] and then announced to the people of Israel:

> While Saul was king, the sacred chest was ignored. But now it's time to bring the chest to Jerusalem. We will invite everyone in Israel to come here, including the priests and the Levites in the towns surrounded by pasture land. But we will do these things only if you agree, and if the LORD our God wants us to.

[4] The people agreed this was the right thing to do.

[5] David gathered everyone from the River Shihor in Egypt to Lebo-Hamath in the north. [6] Then he led them to Baalah in Judah, which was also called Kiriath-Jearim. They went there to get the sacred chest and bring it to Jerusalem, because it belonged to the LORD God, whose throne is above the winged creatures* on the lid of the chest.

[7] The sacred chest was still at Abinadab's house,* and when David and the crowd arrived there, they brought the chest outside and placed it on a new ox cart. Abinadab's sons† Uzzah and Ahio guided the cart, [8] while David and the crowd danced and sang praises to the LORD with all their might. They played music on small harps and other stringed instruments, and on tambourines, cymbals, and trumpets.

[9] But when they came to Chidon's threshing place, the oxen stumbled, and Uzzah reached out and took hold of the chest to stop it from falling. [10] The LORD God was very angry at Uzzah for doing this, and he killed Uzzah there beside the chest.

[11] David then got angry with God for killing Uzzah. So he named that place

---

*13.6 winged creatures: Two golden statues of winged creatures were on top of the sacred chest and were symbols of the LORD's throne on earth (see Exodus 25.18).

*13.7 The sacred chest . . . Abinadab's house: See 1 Samuel 6.19—7.2.

See also: 13.5: 1 Sam 7.1–2.   13.6: Exod 25.22.

"Attack on Uzzah",⸜ and it's been called that ever since.

¹² David was afraid of what the LORD might do to him, and he asked himself, "Should I really be the one to take care of the sacred chest?" ¹³ So instead of taking it to Jerusalem, David decided to take it to the home of Obed-Edom, who lived in the town of Gath.

¹⁴ The chest stayed there for three months, and the LORD blessed Obed-Edom, his family, and everything he owned.

CHAPTER 14

David's palace in Jerusalem
This is also told in 2 Samuel 5.11–16

¹ King Hiram of Tyre sent some officials to David. They brought along carpenters and stone workers, and enough cedar logs to build David a palace. ² David now knew that the LORD had made him a powerful king of Israel for the good of his people.

³ After David moved to Jerusalem, he married more women and had more sons and daughters. ⁴⁻⁷ His children born there were Shammua, Shobab, Nathan, Solomon, Ibhar, Elishua, Elpelet, Nogah, Nepheg, Japhia, Elishama, Beeliada,⸜ and Eliphelet.

David defeats the Philistines
This is also told in 2 Samuel 5.17–25

⁸ When the Philistines heard that David had become king of Israel, they came to capture him. But David heard about their plan and marched out to meet them in battle. ⁹ The Philistines had already camped in Rephaim Valley and were raiding the nearby villages.

¹⁰ David asked God, "Should I attack the Philistines? Will you help me win?"

The LORD told David, "Yes, attack them! I will give you victory."

¹¹ David and his army marched to Baal-Perazim, where they attacked and defeated the Philistines. He said, "I defeated my enemies because God broke through them like a mighty flood." So he named the place "The Lord Broke Through".⸜ ¹² Then David ordered his troops to burn the idols that the Philistines had left behind.

¹³ Some time later, the Philistines came back into the hill country and camped in Rephaim Valley. ¹⁴ David asked God what he should do, and God answered, "Don't attack them from the front. Circle around behind them where the balsam⸜ trees are. ¹⁵ Wait there until you hear the treetops making the sound of marching troops. That sound will mean I have marched out ahead of you to fight the Philistine army. So you must then attack quickly!"

¹⁶ David obeyed God and he defeated the Philistines. He even chased them all the way from Gibeon to the entrance to Gezer.

¹⁷ From then on, David became even more famous, and the LORD made all the nations afraid of him.

CHAPTER 15

David gets ready to bring the sacred chest to Jerusalem

¹ David had several buildings built in Jerusalem, and he had a tent set up where the sacred chest would be kept. ² He said, "Only Levites will be allowed to carry the chest, because the LORD has chosen them to do that work and to serve him for ever."

³ Next, David invited everyone to come to Jerusalem and watch the sacred chest being carried to the place he had set up for it. ⁴ He also sent for Aaron's descendants and for the Levites. The Levites who came were: ⁵ Uriel, the leader of the Kohath clan, and one hundred and twenty of his relatives; ⁶ Asaiah, the leader of the Merari clan, and two hundred and twenty of his relatives; ⁷ Joel, the leader of the Gershon clan, and one hundred and thirty of his relatives; ⁸ Shemaiah, the leader of the Elizaphan clan, and two hundred of his relatives; ⁹ Eliel, the leader of the Hebron clan, and eighty of his relatives; and ¹⁰ Amminadab, the leader of the Uzziel clan, with one hundred and twelve of his relatives.

¹¹ David called together these six Levites and the two priests, Zadok and Abiathar. ¹² He said to them, "You are the leaders of the clans in the Levi tribe. You and your relatives must first go through the ceremony to make yourselves clean and acceptable to the LORD. Then you may carry the sacred chest that belongs to the LORD God of Israel and bring it to the place I have prepared for it. ¹³ The first time we tried to bring the chest to Jerusalem, we didn't ask the LORD what he wanted us to do. He was angry with us, because you Levites weren't there to carry the chest."

¹⁴ The priests and the Levites made themselves clean. They were now ready to carry the sacred chest ¹⁵ on poles that rested

See also: **13.14:** 1 Chron 26.4–5.

See also: **15.2:** Deut 10.8. **15.15:** Exod 25.14.

on their shoulders, just as the LORD had told Moses to do.

¹⁶ David then told the leaders to choose some Levites to sing and play music on small harps, other stringed instruments, and cymbals. ¹⁷⁻²¹ The men chosen to play the cymbals were Heman the son of Joel, his relative Asaph the son of Berechiah, and Ethan the son of Kushaiah from the Merari clan. Some of their assistants played the smaller harps: they were Zechariah, Aziel, Shemiramoth, Jehiel, Unni, Eliab, Maaseiah, and Benaiah. Others played the larger harps: they were Mattithiah, Eliphelehu, Mikneiah, Azaziah, and two of the temple guards, Obed-Edom and Jeiel.

²² Chenaniah was chosen to be the music director, because he was a skilled musician.

²³⁻²⁴ Four Levites were then appointed to guard the sacred chest. They were Berechiah, Elkanah, Obed-Edom, and Jehiah.

Finally, David chose priests to walk in front of the sacred chest and blow trumpets. They were Shebaniah, Joshaphat, Nethanel, Amasai, Zechariah, Benaiah, and Eliezer.

The sacred chest is brought to Jerusalem

This is also told in 2 Samuel 6.12–22

²⁵ David, the leaders of Israel, and the army commanders were very happy as they went to Obed-Edom's house to get the sacred chest. ²⁶ God gave the Levites the strength they needed to carry the chest, and so they sacrificed seven bulls and seven rams.

²⁷ David, the Levites, Chenaniah the music director, and all the musicians were wearing linen robes, and David was also wearing a linen cloth.* ²⁸ While the sacred chest was being carried into Jerusalem, everyone was celebrating by shouting and playing music on horns, trumpets, cymbals, harps, and other stringed instruments.

²⁹ Saul's daughter Michal* looked out of her window and watched the chest being brought into David's City. But when she saw David jumping and dancing in honour of the LORD, she was disgusted.

---

*15.27 a linen cloth: The Hebrew word is "ephod", which can mean either a piece of clothing like a skirt that went from the waist to the knee or a garment like an apron or jacket that only the priests wore.
*15.29 Michal: One of David's wives.

CHAPTER 16

¹ They put the sacred chest inside the tent that David had set up for it, then they offered sacrifices to please the LORD* and sacrifices to ask his blessing.* ² After David had finished, he blessed the people in the name of the LORD ³ and gave every person in the crowd a small loaf of bread, some meat, and a handful of raisins.

⁴ David appointed some of the Levites to serve at the sacred chest; they were to play music and sing praises to the LORD God of Israel. ⁵ Asaph was their leader, and Zechariah was his assistant. Jeiel, Shemiramoth, Jehiel, Mattithiah, Eliab, Benaiah, Obed-Edom, and another man named Jeiel were appointed to play small harps and stringed instruments. Asaph himself played the cymbals, ⁶ and the two priests Benaiah and Jahaziel were to blow trumpets every day in front of the sacred chest.

David's song of praise

This is also told in Psalms 105.1–15; 96.1–13; 106.1,47–48

⁷ That same day, David instructed Asaph and his relatives for the first time to sing these praises to the LORD:

⁸ Praise the LORD
and pray in his name!
Tell everyone what he has done.
⁹ Sing praises to the LORD!
Tell about his miracles.
¹⁰ Celebrate and worship
his holy name with all your heart.

¹¹ Trust the LORD
and his mighty power.
Worship him always.
¹² Remember his miracles
and all his wonders
and his fair decisions.
¹³ You belong to the family
of Israel, his servant;

---

*16.1 sacrifices to please the LORD: These sacrifices have traditionally been called "whole burnt offerings" because the whole animal was burnt on the altar. A main purpose of such sacrifices was to please the LORD with the smell of the sacrifice, and so in the CEV they are often called "sacrifices to please the LORD".
*16.1 sacrifices to ask his blessing: These sacrifices have traditionally been called "peace offerings" or "offerings of well-being". A main purpose was to ask for the LORD's blessing, and so in the CEV they are sometimes called "sacrifices to ask the LORD's blessing".

you are his chosen ones,
   the descendants of Jacob.

14 The LORD is our God,
   bringing justice everywhere on earth.
15 We must never forget
   his agreement and his promises,
   not in thousands of years.
16-17 God made an eternal promise
   to Abraham, Isaac, and Jacob
18 when he said, "I'll give you
   the land of Canaan."

19 At the time there were
   only a few of us,
   and we were homeless.
20 We wandered from nation to nation,
   from one country to another.
21 God did not let anyone
   ill-treat our people.
   Instead he protected us
   by punishing rulers
22 and telling them,
   "Don't touch my chosen leaders
   or harm my prophets!"

23 Everyone on this earth,
   sing praises to the LORD.
   Day after day announce,
   "The LORD has saved us!"
24 Tell every nation on earth,
   "The LORD is wonderful
   and does marvellous things!
25 The LORD is great and deserves
   our greatest praise!
   He is the only God
   worthy of our worship.
26 Other nations worship idols,
   but the LORD created the heavens.
27 Give honour and praise to the LORD,
   whose power and beauty
   fill his holy temple."

28 Tell everyone of every nation,
   "Praise the glorious power of the LORD.
29 He is wonderful! Praise him
   and bring an offering
   into his temple.
   Worship the LORD,
   majestic and holy.
30 Everyone on earth, now tremble!"

   The world stands firm,
   never to be shaken.
31 Tell the heavens and the earth
   to be glad and celebrate!

And announce to the nations,
   "The LORD is King!"
32 Command the ocean to roar
   with all its creatures
   and the fields to rejoice
   with all their crops.
33 Then every tree in the forest
   will sing joyful songs to the LORD.
   He is coming to judge
   all people on earth.

34 Praise the LORD
   because he is good to us,
   and his love never fails.
35 Say to him, "Save us, LORD God!
   Bring us back from among the nations.
   Let us celebrate and shout
   in praise of your holy name.
36 LORD God of Israel,
   you deserve to be praised
   for ever and ever."

After David finished, the people shouted,
"Amen! Praise the LORD!"

David appoints worship leaders at Jerusalem and Gibeon

37 David chose Asaph and the Levites in his clan to be in charge of the daily worship at the place where the sacred chest was kept. 38 Obed-Edom and sixty-eight of his relatives were their assistants, and Hosah and Obed-Edom the son of Jeduthun were the guards. 39 David also chose Zadok the priest and his relatives who were priests to serve at the LORD's sacred tent at Gibeon. 40 They were to offer sacrifices on the altar every morning and evening, just as the LORD had commanded in the Law he gave Israel. 41 Heman and Jeduthun were their assistants, as well as the other men who had been chosen to praise the LORD for his never-ending love. 42 Heman and Jeduthun were also responsible for blowing the trumpets, and for playing the cymbals and other instruments during worship at the tent. The Levites in Jeduthun's clan were the guards at Gibeon.
43 After that, everyone went home, and David went home to his family.

See also: **16.16:** a Gen 12.7; b Gen 26.3.
16.16-18: Gen 28.13. **16.21-22:** Gen 20.3-7.

See also: **16.34:** 2 Chron 5.13; 7.3; Ezra 3.11; Psa 100.5; 106.1; 107.1; 118.1; 136.1; Jer 33.11. **16.43:** 2 Sam 6.19-20.

Solomon will build the Lord's temple

CHAPTER 17

The LORD's message to David

This is also told in 2 Samuel 7.1–17

[1] Soon after David moved into his new palace, he said to Nathan the prophet, "Look around! I live in a palace made of cedar, but the sacred chest is kept in a tent."

[2] Nathan replied, "The LORD is with you — do what you want."

[3] That night, the LORD told Nathan [4] to go to David and tell him:

David, you are my servant, so listen carefully: you are not the one to build a temple for me. [5] I didn't live in a temple when I brought my people out of Egypt, and I don't live in one now. A tent has always been my home wherever I have gone with them. [6] I chose special leaders and told them to be like shepherds for my people Israel. But did I ever say anything to even one of them about building a cedar temple for me?

[7] David, this is what I, the LORD All-Powerful, say to you. I brought you in from the fields where you took care of sheep, and I made you the leader of my people. [8] Wherever you went, I helped you and destroyed your enemies right in front of your eyes. I have made you one of the most famous people in the world.

[9] I have given my people Israel a land of their own where they can live in peace. They will no longer have to tremble with fear — evil nations won't bother them, as they did [10] when I let judges rule my people, and I will keep your enemies from attacking you.

Now I promise that like you, your descendants will be kings. [11] I'll choose one of your sons to be king when you reach the end of your life and are buried beside your ancestors. I'll make him a strong ruler, [12] and no one will be able to take his kingdom away from him. He will be the one to build a temple for me. [13] I will be like a father to him, and he will be like a son to me. I will never put an end to my agreement with him, as I put an end to my agreement with Saul, who was king before you. [14] I will make sure that your son and

See also: 17.13: 2 Cor 6.18; Heb 1.5.

Viewpoints 👁

A relationship with God is filled with God's generosity

Contributed by Laura C

'LORD God, my family and I don't deserve what you have already done for us.'

One of the awe-inspiring wonders of God's love is the way that his loving us can make us feel so small. David has just been told that the Messiah will come from his line, and despite being King of Israel he still feels humbled and amazed at the privilege and honour God has granted him.

A relationship with God is filled with God's generosity; David's importance in God's plan is not because of David's diligence or flawless character but because of God's love and grace to his children. Often when we take time in our prayer life to reflect on 'who we are' and what we have been 'brought through', there may well be pain, hurt and fear: David spent years fleeing for his life, being attacked by Saul and thrust into warfare; but when we can commit this to God and listen to his promises to us, we know the grace, patience and undeserved love that keeps us buoyant despite our weaknesses.

The fact is that God says in 1 Chronicles 17.8, 'Wherever you went, I helped you', and he works out his promises through us, despite the dangers we go through, and the weaknesses and sins these circumstances expose in us.

More...

Messiah p.770
God's love p.958

his descendants will rule my people and my kingdom for ever.

¹⁵ Nathan told David exactly what the LORD had said.

David gives thanks to the LORD

This is also told in 2 Samuel 7.18–29

¹⁶ David went into the tent he had set up for the sacred chest. He sat there and prayed:

LORD God, my family and I don't deserve what you have already done for us, ¹⁷ and yet you have promised to do even more for my descendants. You are treating me as if I am a very important person.' ¹⁸ I am your servant, and you know my thoughts. What else can I say, except that you have honoured me? ¹⁹ It was your choice to do these wonderful things for me and to make these promises.

²⁰ No other god is like you, LORD — you alone are God. Everything we have heard about you is true. ²¹ And there is no other nation on earth like Israel, the nation you rescued from slavery in Egypt to be your own. You became famous by using great and wonderful miracles to force other nations and their gods out of your land, so that your people could live here. ²² You have chosen Israel to be your people for ever, and you have become their God.

²³ LORD God, please do what you promised me and my descendants. ²⁴ Then you will be famous for ever, and everyone will say, "The LORD All-Powerful rules Israel and is their God."

My kingdom will be strong, ²⁵ because you are my God, and you have promised that my descendants will be kings. That's why I have the courage to pray to you like this, even though I am only your servant. ²⁶ You are the LORD God, and you have made this good promise to me. ²⁷ Now please bless my descendants for ever, and let them always be your chosen kings. You have already blessed my family, and I know you will bless us for ever.

David's military victories

CHAPTER 18

A list of David's victories in war

This is also told in 2 Samuel 8.1–14

¹ Later, David attacked and defeated the Philistines. He captured their town of Gath and the nearby villages.

² David also defeated the Moabites, and so they had to accept him as their ruler and pay taxes to him.

³ While King Hadadezer of Zobah was trying to gain control of the territory near the River Euphrates, David met him in battle at Hamath and defeated him. ⁴ David captured one thousand chariots, seven thousand chariot drivers, and twenty thousand soldiers. And he crippled all but one hundred of the horses.

⁵ When troops from the Syrian kingdom of Damascus came to help Hadadezer, David killed twenty-two thousand of them. ⁶ Then David stationed some of his troops in Damascus, and the people there had to accept David as their ruler and pay taxes to him.

Everywhere David went, the LORD helped him win battles.

⁷ Hadadezer's officers had carried gold shields, but David took these shields and brought them back to Jerusalem. ⁸ He also took a lot of bronze from the cities of Tibhath and Cun, which had belonged to Hadadezer. Later, Solomon used this bronze to make the large bowl called the Sea, and to make the pillars and other furnishings for the temple.

⁹⁻¹⁰ King Tou of Hamath and King Hadadezer had been enemies. So when Tou heard that David had defeated Hadadezer's whole army, he sent his son Hadoram to congratulate David on his victory. Hadoram also brought him gifts made of gold, silver, and bronze. ¹¹ David gave these gifts to the LORD, just as he had done with the silver and gold he had captured from Edom, Moab, Ammon, Philistia, and Amalek.

¹² Abishai the son of Zeruiah defeated the Edomite army in Salt Valley and killed eighteen thousand of their troops. ¹³ Then he stationed troops in Edom, and the people there had to accept David as their ruler.

Everywhere David went, the LORD gave him victory in war.

A list of David's officials

This is also told in 2 Samuel 8.15–18

¹⁴ David ruled all Israel with fairness and justice.

¹⁵ Joab the son of Zeruiah was the commander in chief of the army.

Jehoshaphat the son of Ahilud kept the government records.

See also: 18.8: 1 King 7.40–47; 2 Chron 4.11–18.
18.12: Psa 60 Title.

16 Zadok the son of Ahitub and Ahimelech the son of Abiathar were the priests.

Shavsha was the secretary.

17 Benaiah the son of Jehoiada was the commander of David's bodyguard.'

David's sons were his highest-ranking officials.

CHAPTER 19

Israel fights Ammon and Syria

This is also told in 2 Samuel 10.1–19

1 Some time later, King Nahash of Ammon died, and his son Hanun became king. 2 David said, "Nahash was kind to me, so I will be kind to his son." He sent some officials to Ammon to tell Hanun how sorry he was that his father had died.

But when David's officials arrived at Ammon, 3 the Ammonite leaders said to Hanun, "Do you really believe King David is honouring your father by sending these men to comfort you? He probably sent them to spy on our country, so he can come and destroy it."

4 Hanun arrested David's officials and had their beards shaved off and their robes cut off just below the waist, and then he sent them away. 5 They were terribly ashamed.

When David found out what had happened to his officials, he sent a message that told them, "Stay in Jericho until your beards grow back. Then you can come home."

6 The Ammonites realized they had made David furious. So they paid thirty-four thousand kilogrammes of silver to hire chariot troops from Mesopotamia and from the Syrian kingdoms of Maacah and Zobah. 7 Thirty-two thousand troops, as well as the king of Maacah and his army, came and camped near Medeba. The Ammonite troops also left their towns and came to prepare for battle.

8 David heard what was happening, and he sent out Joab with his army. 9 The Ammonite troops marched to the entrance of the city* and prepared for battle, while the Syrian troops took their positions in the open fields.

10 Joab saw that the enemy troops were lined up on both sides of him. So he picked some of the best Israelite soldiers to fight the Syrians. 11 Then he put his brother Abishai in command of the rest of the army and told

them to fight against the Ammonites. 12 Joab told his brother, "If the Syrians are too much for me to handle, come and help me. And if the Ammonites are too strong for you, I'll come and help you. 13 Be brave and fight hard to protect our people and the towns of our LORD God. I pray he will do whatever pleases him."

14 Joab and his soldiers attacked the Syrians, and the Syrians ran from them. 15 When the Ammonite troops saw that the Syrians had run away, they ran from Abishai's soldiers and went back into their own city. Joab then returned to Jerusalem.

16 As soon as the Syrians realized they had been defeated, they sent for their troops that were stationed on the other side of the River Euphrates. Shophach, the commander of Hadadezer's army, led these troops to Ammon.

17 David found out what the Syrians were doing, and he brought Israel's entire army together. They crossed the River Jordan, and he commanded them to take their positions facing the Syrian troops.

Soon after the fighting began, 18 the Syrians ran from Israel. David killed seven thousand chariot troops and forty thousand regular soldiers. He also killed Shophach, their commander.

19 When the kings who had been under Hadadezer's rule saw that Israel had defeated them, they made peace with David and accepted him as their new ruler. The Syrians never helped the Ammonites again.

CHAPTER 20

The end of the war with Ammon

This is also told in 2 Samuel 11.1; 12.26–31

1 The next spring, the time when kings go to war, Joab marched out in command of the Israelite army and destroyed towns all over the country of Ammon. He attacked the capital city of Rabbah and left it in ruins. But David stayed in Jerusalem.

2 Later, David himself went to Rabbah, where he took the crown from the statue of their god Milcom.' The crown was made of about thirty-four kilogrammes of gold, and there was a valuable jewel on it. David put the jewel on his crown,' then carried off everything else of value. 3 He forced the people of Rabbah to work with saws, iron picks, and axes. He also did the same

---

*19.9 the city: Probably Rabbah, the capital city of Ammon.

See also: 20.1: 2 Sam 11.1.

thing with the people in all the other Ammonite towns.

David then led Israel's army back to Jerusalem.

The descendants of the Rephaim

This is also told in 2 Samuel 21.15–22

⁴ Some time later, Israel fought a battle against the Philistines at Gezer. During this battle, Sibbecai from Hushah killed Sippai, a descendant of the Rephaim,* and the Philistines were defeated.

⁵ In another battle against the Philistines, Elhanan the son of Jair killed Lahmi the brother of Goliath from Gath, whose spear shaft was like a weaver's beam.*

⁶ Another one of the Philistine soldiers who was a descendant of the Rephaim was as big as a giant and had six fingers on each hand and six toes on each foot. During a battle at Gath, ⁷ he made fun of Israel, so David's nephew Jonathan' killed him.

⁸ David and his soldiers killed these three men from Gath who were descendants of the Rephaim.

David's preparations for building the temple

CHAPTER 21

David counts the people

This is also told in 2 Samuel 24.1–9

¹ Satan decided to cause trouble for Israel by making David think it was a good idea to find out how many people there were in Israel and Judah. ² David told Joab and the army commanders, "Count everyone in Israel, from the town of Beersheba in the south all the way north to Dan. Then I will know how many people can serve in my army."

³ Joab answered, "Your Majesty, even if the LORD made your kingdom a hundred times larger, you would still rule everyone in it. Why do you need to know how many soldiers there are? Don't you think that would make the whole nation angry?"

⁴ But David would not change his mind. And so Joab went everywhere in Israel and Judah and counted the people. He returned to Jerusalem ⁵ and told David that the total number of men who could serve in the army was one million one hundred thousand in Israel and four hundred and seventy thousand in Judah. ⁶ Joab refused to include anyone from the tribes of Levi and Benjamin, because he still disagreed with David's orders.

God punishes Israel

This is also told in 2 Samuel 24.10–17

⁷ David's order to count the people made God angry, and he punished Israel. ⁸ David prayed, "I am your servant. But what I did was stupid and terribly wrong. Please forgive me."

⁹ The LORD said to Gad, one of David's prophets, ¹⁰ "Tell David that I will punish him in one of three ways. But he will have to choose which one it will be."

¹¹ Gad went to David and told him:

You must choose how the LORD will punish you: ¹² Will there be three years when the land won't grow enough food for its people? Or will your enemies constantly defeat you for three months? Or will the LORD send a horrible disease to strike your land for three days? Think about it and decide, because I have to give your answer to God who sent me.

¹³ David was miserable and said, "It's a terrible choice to make! But the LORD is kind, and I'd rather be punished by him than by anyone else."

¹⁴ So the LORD sent a horrible disease on Israel, and seventy thousand Israelites died. ¹⁵ Then he sent an angel to destroy the city of Jerusalem. But just as the angel was about to do that, the LORD felt sorry for all the suffering he had caused the people, and he told the angel, "Stop! They have suffered enough." This happened at the threshing place that belonged to Araunah' the Jebusite.

¹⁶ David saw the LORD's angel in the air, holding a sword over Jerusalem. He and the leaders of Israel, who were all wearing sackcloth,* bowed with their faces to the ground, ¹⁷ and David prayed, "It's my fault! I sinned by ordering the people to be

---

*20.4 Rephaim: This may refer to a group of people of great stature that lived in Palestine before the Israelites.

*20.5 weaver's beam: When a weaver made cloth, one set of threads was tied on to a large wooden rod that was known as a weaver's beam.

See also: 20.5: 1 Sam 17.4–7.

---

*21.16 sackcloth: A rough, dark-coloured cloth made from goat or camel hair and used to make grain sacks. It was worn in times of trouble or sorrow.

counted. They have done nothing wrong —
they are innocent sheep. LORD God, please
punish me and my family. Don't let the
disease wipe out your people."

David buys Araunah's threshing place

This is also told in 2 Samuel 24.18-25

¹⁸ The LORD's angel told the prophet Gad to
tell David that he must go to Araunah's
threshing place and build an altar in honour
of the LORD. ¹⁹ David followed the LORD's
instructions.

²⁰ Araunah and his four sons were
threshing wheat at the time, and when they
saw the angel, the four sons ran to hide.
²¹ Just then, David arrived, and when
Araunah saw him, he stopped his work and
bowed down.

²² David said, "Would you sell me your
threshing place, so I can build an altar on it
to the LORD? Then this disease will stop
killing the people. I'm willing to pay
whatever you say it's worth."

²³ Araunah answered, "Take it, Your
Majesty, and do whatever you want with it.
I'll even give you the oxen for the sacrifice
and the wheat for the grain sacrifice. And you
can use the threshing-boards* for the fire. It's
all yours!"

²⁴ But David replied, "No! I want to pay
you what they're worth. I can't just take
something from you and then offer the LORD
a sacrifice that cost me nothing."

²⁵ So David paid Araunah six hundred gold
coins for his threshing place. ²⁶ David built
an altar and offered sacrifices to please the
LORD* and sacrifices to ask his blessing.*
David prayed, and the LORD answered him by
sending fire down on the altar. ²⁷ Then the
LORD commanded the angel to put the sword
away.*

²⁸ When David saw that the LORD had
answered his prayer, he offered more
sacrifices there at the threshing place,
²⁹⁻³⁰ because he was afraid of the angel's
sword and did not want to go all the way to

Gibeon. That's where the sacred tent that
Moses had made in the desert was kept, as
well as the altar where sacrifices were offered
to the LORD.

CHAPTER 22

¹ David said, "The temple of the LORD God
must be built here at this threshing place.
And the altar for offering sacrifices will also
be here."

David prepares to build the temple

² David ordered the foreigners living in Israel
to come to Jerusalem. Then he assigned some
to cut blocks of stone for building the
temple. ³ He got a large supply of iron to
make into nails and hinges for the doors, and
he provided so much bronze that it could not
be weighed. ⁴ He also had cedar logs brought
in from the cities of Sidon and Tyre.

⁵ He said, "The temple for the LORD must
be great, so that everyone in the world will
know about it. But since my son Solomon is
young and has no experience, I will make
sure that everything is ready for the temple to
be built."

That's why David did all these things
before he died.

David instructs Solomon to build the temple

⁶ David sent for his son Solomon and told
him to build a temple for the LORD God of
Israel. ⁷ He said:

My son, I wanted to build a temple where
the LORD my God would be worshipped.
⁸ But some time ago, he told me, "David,
you have killed too many people and have
fought too many battles. That's why you
are not the one to build my temple. ⁹ But
when your son becomes king, I will give
him peace throughout his kingdom. His
name will be Solomon, because during his
rule I will keep Israel safe and peaceful.*
¹⁰ Solomon will build my temple. He will
be like a son to me, and I will be like a
father to him. In fact, one of his
descendants will always rule in Israel."

¹¹ Solomon, my son, I now pray that the
LORD your God will be with you and keep
his promise to help you build a temple for

---

*21.23 threshing-boards: Heavy boards with bits of
rock or metal on the bottom. They were dragged
across the grain to separate the husks from the
kernels.
*21.26 sacrifices to please the LORD: See the note
at 16.1.
*21.26 sacrifices to ask his blessing: See the note
at 16.1.
*21.27 the LORD commanded the angel to put the
sword away: See verse 16.

*22.9 Solomon . . . safe and peaceful: In Hebrew
"Solomon" sounds like "peace".
See also: 22.7-10: 2 Sam 7.1-16; 1 Chron 17.1-14.

him. ¹² May he give you wisdom and knowledge, so that you can rule Israel according to his Law. ¹³ If you obey the laws and teachings that the LORD gave Moses, you will be successful. Be strong and brave and don't get discouraged or be afraid of anything.

¹⁴ I have all the supplies you'll need to build the temple: you have more than three thousand tonnes of gold and over thirty-four thousand tonnes of silver. There's also plenty of wood, stone, and more bronze and iron than I could weigh. Ask for anything else you need. ¹⁵ I have also assigned men who will cut and lay the stone. And there are carpenters and people who are experts in working with ¹⁶ gold, silver, bronze, and iron. You have plenty of workers to do the job. Now get started, and I pray that the LORD will be with you in your work.

¹⁷ David then gave orders for the leaders of Israel to help Solomon. ¹⁸ David said:

The LORD our God has helped me defeat all the people who lived here before us, and he has given you peace from all your enemies. Now this land belongs to the LORD and his people. ¹⁹ Obey the LORD your God with your heart and soul. Begin work on the temple to honour him, so that the sacred chest and the things used for worship can be kept there.

CHAPTER 23

David assigns the Levites their duties

¹ David was old when he chose his son Solomon to be king of Israel. ² Some time later, David called together all of Israel's leaders, priests, and Levites. ³ He then counted the Levite men who were at least thirty years old, and the total was thirty-eight thousand. ⁴ He said, "Twenty-four thousand of the Levites will be in charge of the temple, six thousand will be temple officials and judges, ⁵ four thousand will be guards at the temple, and four thousand will praise the LORD by playing the musical instruments I have given them."

⁶ David then divided the Levites into three groups according to the clans of Levi's sons, Gershon, Kohath, and Merari.

⁷ Gershon had two sons: Ladan and Shimei. ⁸ Ladan was the father of Jehiel, Zetham, and Joel. ⁹ They were all family leaders among their father's descendants. Shimei was the father of Shelomoth, Haziel, and Haran. ¹⁰⁻¹¹ Later, Shimei had four more sons, in the following order: Jahath, Zina, Jeush, and Beriah. But Jeush and Beriah didn't have many children, so their descendants were counted as one family.

¹² Kohath had four sons: Amram, Izhar, Hebron, and Uzziel. ¹³ Amram was the father of Aaron and Moses. Aaron and his descendants were chosen to be in charge of all the sacred things. They served the LORD by offering sacrifices to him and by blessing the people in his name. ¹⁴⁻¹⁵ Moses, the man of God, was the father of Gershom and Eliezer, and their descendants were considered Levites. ¹⁶ Gershom's eldest son was Shebuel. ¹⁷ Rehabiah, who was Eliezer's only son, had many children. ¹⁸ The second son born to Kohath was Izhar, and his eldest son was Shelomith. ¹⁹ Hebron, the third son of Kohath, was the father of Jeriah, Amariah, Jahaziel, and Jekameam. ²⁰ Kohath's youngest son, Uzziel, was the father of Micah and Isshiah.

²¹ Merari had two sons: Mahli and Mushi. Mahli was the father of Eleazar and Kish. ²² Eleazar had no sons, only daughters, and they married their uncle's sons. ²³ Mushi the second son of Merari, was the father of Mahli, Eder, and Jeremoth.

²⁴ These were the clans and families of the tribe of Levi. Those who were twenty years and older were assigned to work at the LORD's temple.

²⁵ David said:

The LORD God of Israel has given his people peace, and he will live in Jerusalem for ever. ²⁶ And so, the Levites won't need to move the sacred tent and the things used for worship from place to place.

²⁷ From now on, all Levites at least twenty years old ²⁸ will serve the LORD by helping Aaron's descendants do their work at the temple, by keeping the courtyards and rooms of the temple clean, and by making sure that everything used in worship stays pure. ²⁹ They will also be in charge of the sacred loaves of bread, the flour for the grain sacrifices, the thin wafers, any offerings to be baked, and the flour mixed with olive oil. These Levites will weigh and measure these offerings.

See also: **22.13:** Josh 1.6–9. **23.1:** 1 King 1.1–40.

See also: **23.13:** Exod 28.1. **23.26:** Deut 10.8. **23.28–32:** Num 3.5–9.

[30] Every morning and evening, the Levites are to give thanks to the LORD and sing praises to him. [31] They must also give thanks and sing praises when sacrifices are offered on each Sabbath, as well as during New Moon Festivals and other religious feasts. There must always be enough Levites on duty at the temple to do everything that needs to be done. [32] They were once in charge of taking care of the sacred tent; now they are responsible for the temple and for helping Aaron's descendants.

CHAPTER 24

David assigns the priests their duties

[1] Aaron's descendants were then divided into work groups. Aaron had four sons: Nadab, Abihu, Eleazar, and Ithamar. [2] But Nadab and Abihu died long before their father, without having any sons. That's why Eleazar and Ithamar served as priests.

[3] David divided Aaron's descendants into groups, according to their assigned work. Zadok, one of Eleazar's descendants, and Ahimelech, one of Ithamar's descendants, helped David.

[4] Eleazar's descendants were divided into sixteen groups, and Ithamar's were divided into eight groups, because Eleazar's family included more family leaders. [5] However, both families included temple officials and priests, and so to make sure the work was divided fairly, David asked God what to do.*

[6] As each group was assigned their duties, Shemaiah the son of Nethanel the Levite wrote down the name of the family leader in charge of that group. The witnesses were David and his officials, as well as Zadok the priest, Ahimelech the son of Abiathar, and the family leaders from the clans of the priests and the Levites.

[7-18] Each group of priests went by the name of its family leader, and they were assigned their duties in the following order: Jehoiarib, Jedaiah, Harim, Seorim, Malchijah, Mijamin, Hakkoz, Abijah, Jeshua, Shecaniah, Eliashib, Jakim, Huppah, Jeshebeab, Bilgah, Immer, Hezir, Happizzez, Pethahiah, Jehezkel, Jachin, Gamul, Delaiah, Maaziah. [19] These men were assigned their duties at the temple, just as the LORD God of Israel had commanded their ancestor Aaron.

The rest of the Levites are assigned their duties

[20] Here is a list of the other descendants of Levi:

Amram was the ancestor of Shubael and Jehdeiah.
[21] Rehabiah was the ancestor of Isshiah, the eldest son in his family.
[22] Izhar was the father of Shelomoth and the grandfather of Jahath.
[23] Hebron had four sons, in the following order: Jeriah, Amariah, Jahaziel, and Jekameam.
[24] Uzziel was the father of Micah and the grandfather of Shamir.
[25] Isshiah, Micah's brother, was the father of Zechariah.
[26] Merari was the father of Mahli, Mushi, and Jaaziah.

[27] Jaaziah had three sons: Shoham, Zaccur, and Ibri. [28-29] Mahli was the father of Eleazar and Kish. Eleazar had no sons, but Kish was the father of Jerahmeel. [30] Mushi had three sons: Mahli, Eder, and Jerimoth.

These were the descendants of Levi, according to their clans. [31] Each one was assigned his duties in the same way that their relatives the priests had been assigned their duties. David, Zadok, Ahimelech, and the family leaders of the priests and Levites were the witnesses.

CHAPTER 25

David assigns the temple musicians their duties

[1] David and the temple officials chose the descendants of Asaph, Heman, and Jeduthun to be in charge of music. They were to praise the LORD by playing cymbals, harps, and other stringed instruments. Here is a list of the musicians and their duties:

[2] Asaph's four sons, Zaccur, Joseph, Nethaniah, and Asarelah, were under the direction of their father and played music whenever the king told them to.

[3] Jeduthun's six sons, Gedaliah, Zeri, Jeshaiah, Shimei,' Hashabiah, and Mattithiah, were under the direction of their father and played harps and sang praises to the LORD.

[4] Heman had fourteen sons: Bukkiah, Mattaniah, Uzziel, Shebuel, Jerimoth, Hananiah, Hanani, Eliathah, Giddalti, Romamtiezer, Joshbekashah, Mallothi, Hothir, Mahazioth. [5] Heman was one of the

---

*24.5 asked God what to do: The Hebrew text has "cast lots" (see the note at 6.65).

See also: 24.2: Lev 10.1-2.

king's prophets, and God honoured Heman by giving him fourteen sons and three daughters. [6] His sons were under his direction and played cymbals, harps, and other stringed instruments during times of worship at the temple.

Asaph, Jeduthun, and Heman took their orders directly from the king.

[7] There were two hundred and eighty-eight of these men, and all of them were skilled musicians. [8] David assigned them their duties by asking the LORD what he wanted.* Everyone was responsible for something, whether young or old, teacher or student.

[9-31] The musicians were divided into twenty-four groups of twelve, and each group went by the name of their family leader. They were assigned their duties in the following order: Joseph, Gedaliah, Zaccur, Zeri, Nethaniah, Bukkiah, Asarelah, Jeshaiah, Mattaniah, Shimei, Uzziel, Hashabiah, Shebuel, Mattithiah, Jerimoth, Hananiah, Joshbekashah, Hanani, Mallothi, Eliathah, Hothir, Giddalti, Mahazioth, and Romamtiezer.

CHAPTER 26

The temple guards are assigned their duties

[1] The temple guards were also divided into groups according to clans.

Meshelemiah son of Kore was from the Korah clan and was a descendant of Asaph. [2] He had seven sons, who were born in the following order: Zechariah, Jediael, Zebadiah, Jathniel, [3] Elam, Jehohanan, and Eliehoenai.

[4-5] Obed-Edom had been blessed with eight sons: Shemaiah, Jehozabad, Joah, Sachar, Nethanel, Ammiel, Issachar, and Peullethai. [6-7] Shemaiah was the father of Othni, Rephael, Obed, Elzabad, Elihu, and Semachiah. They were all respected leaders in their clan. [8] There were sixty-two descendants of Obed-Edom who were strong enough to be guards at the temple.

[9] Eighteen descendants of Meshelemiah were chosen for this work.

[10-11] Hosah, from the Merari clan, was the father of Shimri, Hilkiah, Tebaliah, and Zechariah. Hosah had made Shimri the family leader, even though he was not the eldest son. Thirteen men from Hosah's family were chosen to be temple guards.

[12] The guards were divided into groups, according to their family leaders, and they were assigned duties at the temple, just like the other Levites. [13] Each group, no matter how large or small, was assigned a gate to guard, and they let the LORD show them what he wanted done.*

[14] Shelemiah' was chosen to guard the East Gate. Zechariah his son was a wise man and was chosen to guard the North Gate. [15] Obed-Edom was then chosen to guard the South Gate, and his sons were chosen to guard the storerooms. [16] Shuppim and Hosah were chosen to guard the West Gate and the Shallecheth Gate on the upper road.

The guards were assigned the following work schedule: [17] each day six guards were on duty on the east side of the temple, four were on duty on the north side, and four were on duty on the south side. Two guards were stationed at each of the two storerooms, [18] four were stationed along the road leading to the west courtyard,' and two guards stayed in the court itself.

[19] These were the guard duties assigned to the men from the clans of Korah and Merari.

Guards are assigned to the treasury

[20] The Levites who were relatives of the Korahites and the Merarites were' in charge of guarding the temple treasury and the gifts that had been dedicated to God.

[21] Ladan was from the Gershon clan and was the father of Jehieli. Many of his other descendants were family leaders in the clan.' [22] Jehieli was the father of Zetham and Joel, and they were responsible for guarding the treasury.

[23] Other guards at the treasury were from the Kohathite clans of Amram, Izhar, Hebron, and Uzziel.

[24] Shebuel was a descendant of Gershom the son of Moses. He was the chief official in charge of the temple treasury. [25] The descendants of Gershom's brother Eliezer included Rehabiah, Jeshaiah, Joram, Zichri, and Shelomoth.

[26] Shelomoth and his relatives were in charge of all the gifts that were dedicated to the LORD. These included the gifts that King David had dedicated, as well as those dedicated by the family leaders, army

---

*25.8 asking the LORD what he wanted: The Hebrew text has "casting lots" (see the note at 6.65).
See also: 26.4–5: 2 Sam 6.11; 1 Chron 13.14.

*26.13 they let the LORD show them what he wanted done: The Hebrew text has "they cast lots to find out what the LORD wanted done" (see the note at 6.65).

officers, and army commanders. ²⁷ And whenever valuable things were captured in battle, these men brought some of them to the temple. ²⁸ Shelomoth and his relatives were responsible for any gifts that had been given to the temple, including those from Samuel the prophet, King Saul the son of Kish, Abner the son of Ner,* and Joab the son of Zeruiah.

Other officers are assigned their duties

²⁹ Chenaniah from the Izhar clan and his sons were government officials and judges. They did not work at the temple.

³⁰ Hashabiah from the Hebron clan and one thousand seven hundred of his skilled relatives were the officials in charge of all religious and government business in the Israelite territories west of the River Jordan.

³¹⁻³² Jerijah was the leader of the Hebron clan. David assigned him and two thousand seven hundred of his relatives, who were all respected family leaders, to be the officials in charge of all religious and government business in the tribes of Reuben, Gad, and East Manasseh. David found out about these men during the fortieth year of his rule, when he had a list made of all the families in the Hebron clan. They were from the town of Jazer in the territory of Gilead.

CHAPTER 27

David assigns army commanders

¹ Each month a group of twenty-four thousand men served as soldiers in Israel's army. These men, who included the family leaders, army commanders, and officials of the king, were under the command of the following men, arranged by the month of their service:

² In the first month, Jashobeam the son of Zabdiel, ³ a descendant of Perez;

⁴ in the second month, Dodai the Ahohite, whose assistant was Mikloth;⁰

⁵ in the third month, Benaiah the son of Jehoiada the priest, ⁶ who was the leader of the Thirty Warriors,* and whose son Ammizabad was also an army commander;⁰

⁷ in the fourth month, Asahel the brother of Joab, whose son Zebadiah took over command after him;

⁸ in the fifth month, Shamhuth from the Izrah clan;

⁹ in the sixth month, Ira the son of Ikkesh from Tekoa;

¹⁰ in the seventh month, Helez from Pelon in the territory of Ephraim;

¹¹ in the eighth month, Sibbecai from Hushah of the Zerah clan;

¹² in the ninth month, Abiezer from Anathoth in the territory of Benjamin;

¹³ in the tenth month, Maharai from Netophah of the Zerah clan;

¹⁴ in the eleventh month, Benaiah from Pirathon in the territory of Ephraim;

¹⁵ in the twelfth month, Heldai from Netophah, who was a descendant of Othniel.

David assigns tribal leaders

¹⁶⁻²² Here is a list of the leaders of each tribe in Israel:

Eliezer son of Zichri was over Reuben; Shephatiah son of Maacah was over Simeon; Hashabiah son of Kemuel was over the Levites, and Zadok the priest was over the descendants of Aaron; Elihu the brother of David was over Judah; Omri son of Michael was over Issachar; Ishmaiah son of Obadiah was over Zebulun; Jerimoth son of Azriel was over Naphtali; Hoshea son of Azaziah was over Ephraim; Joel son of Pedaiah was over West Manasseh; Iddo son of Zechariah was over East Manasseh; Jaasiel son of Abner was over Benjamin; Azarel son of Jeroham was over Dan.

²³ When David decided to count the people of Israel, he gave orders not to count anyone under twenty years of age, because the LORD had promised long ago that Israel would have as many people as there are stars in the sky. ²⁴ Joab the son of Zeruiah had begun to count the people, but he stopped when the LORD began punishing Israel. So the total number was never included in David's official records.

Officials in charge of the king's property

²⁵ Azmaveth the son of Adiel was in charge of the king's personal storage rooms. Jonathan the son of Uzziah was in charge of the king's other storerooms that were in the towns, the villages, and the defence towers in Israel.

²⁶ Ezri the son of Chelub was in charge of the workers who farmed the king's land.

²⁷ Shimei from Ramah was in charge of the vineyards, and Zabdi from Shepham was in charge of storing the wine.

---

*26.28 Abner the son of Ner:** Abner was King Saul's uncle (see 9.39).

*27.6 Thirty Warriors:** See the note at 11.20.

See also: 27.23: Gen 15.5; 22.17; 26.4. **27.24:** 2 Sam 24.15; 1 Chron 21.1–14.

²⁸ Baal Hanan from Geder was in charge of the olive and sycamore trees in the western foothills, and Joash was in charge of storing the olive oil.

²⁹ Shitrai from Sharon was responsible for the cattle that were kept in Sharon Plain, and Shaphat son of Adlai was responsible for those kept in the valleys.

³⁰ Obil the Ishmaelite was in charge of the camels, Jehdeiah from Meronoth was in charge of the donkeys, and Jaziz the Hagrite was in charge of the sheep and goats.

³¹ These were the men in charge of David's royal property.

David's personal advisers

³² David's uncle Jonathan was a wise and intelligent adviser. He and Jehiel the son of Hachmoni taught David's sons.

³³ Ahithophel and Hushai the Archite were two of David's advisers. ³⁴ Jehoiada the son of Benaiah was the king's adviser after Ahithophel, and later, Abiathar was his adviser.

Joab was commander of Israel's army.

CHAPTER 28

David gives Solomon the plans for the temple

¹ David called a meeting in Jerusalem for all Israel's leaders, including the tribal leaders, the government officials, the army commanders, the officials in charge of the royal property and livestock, the palace officials, and the brave warriors.

² After everyone was there, David stood up and said:

Listen to me, my people. I wanted to build a place where the sacred chest would be kept, so we could go there and worship the LORD our God. I have prepared all the supplies for building a temple, ³ but the LORD has refused to let me build it, because he said I have killed too many people in battle.

⁴ The LORD God chose Judah to be the leading tribe in Israel. Then from Judah, he chose my father's family, and from that family, he chose me to be the king of Israel, and he promised that my descendants will also rule as kings. ⁵ The LORD has blessed me with many sons, but he chose my son Solomon to be the next king of Israel. ⁶ The LORD said to me, "Your son Solomon will build my temple, and it will honour me.

Solomon will be like a son to me, and I will be like a father to him. ⁷ If he continues to obey my laws and commands, his kingdom will never end."

⁸ My friends, you are the LORD's people. And now, with God as your witness, I want you to promise that you will do your best to obey everything the LORD God has commanded us. Then this land will always belong to you and your descendants.

⁹ Solomon, my son, worship God and obey him with all your heart and mind, just as I have done. He knows all your thoughts and your reasons for doing things, and so if you turn to him, he will hear your prayers. But if you ignore him, he will reject you for ever. ¹⁰ The LORD has chosen you to build a temple for worshipping him. Be confident and do the work you have been assigned.

¹¹ After David finished speaking, he gave Solomon the plans for building the main rooms of the temple, including the porch, the storerooms, the rooms upstairs and downstairs, as well as the most holy place. ¹² He gave Solomon his plans for the courtyards and the open areas around the temple, and for the rooms to store the temple treasures and gifts that had been dedicated to God.

¹³ David also gave Solomon his plans for dividing the priests and the Levites into groups, as well as for the work that needed to be done at the temple and for taking care of the objects used for worship. ¹⁴ He told Solomon how much gold and silver was to be used in making the sacred objects, ¹⁵ including the lampstands and lamps, ¹⁶ the gold table which held the sacred loaves of bread, the tables made of silver, ¹⁷ the meat forks, the bowls and cups, ¹⁸ the gold incense altar, and the gold statue of a chariot for the winged creatures* which were on the lid of the sacred chest.

¹⁹ David then said to Solomon:

The LORD showed me how his temple is to be built. ²⁰ But you must see that everything is done according to these plans. Be confident, and never be afraid of anything or get discouraged. The LORD my God will help you do everything needed to finish the temple, so it can be used for worshipping him. ²¹ The priests and Levites have been assigned their duties, and all the skilled workers are prepared to do their work. The people and their leaders will do anything you tell them.

See also: **28.2–7:** 2 Sam 7.1–16; 1 Chron 17.1–14.

*28.18 winged creatures: See the note at 13.6.

The people bring gifts for building the temple

CHAPTER 29

¹ David told the crowd:

> God chose my son Solomon to build the temple, but Solomon is young and has no experience. This is not just any building — this is the temple for the LORD God! ² That's why I have done my best to get everything Solomon will need to build it — gold, silver, bronze, iron, wood, onyx, turquoise, coloured gems, all kinds of precious stones, and marble.
>
> ³ Besides doing all that, I have promised to give part of my own gold and silver as a way of showing my love for God's temple. ⁴ More than a hundred tonnes of my finest gold and almost two hundred and forty tonnes of my silver will be used to decorate its walls ⁵ and to make the gold and silver objects. Now, who else will show their dedication to the LORD by giving gifts for building his temple?

⁶ After David finished speaking, the family leaders, the tribal leaders, the army commanders, and the government officials voluntarily gave gifts ⁷ for the temple. These gifts included more than a hundred and seventy tonnes of gold, over three hundred and forty tonnes of silver, six hundred and twenty tonnes of bronze, and more than three thousand four hundred tonnes of iron. ⁸ Everyone who owned precious stones also donated them to the temple treasury, where Jehiel from the Levite clan of Gershon guarded them. ⁹ David and the people were very happy that so much had been given to the LORD, and they all celebrated.

David praises the LORD

¹⁰ Then, in front of everyone, David sang praises to the LORD:

> I praise you for ever, LORD! You are the God our ancestor Jacob' worshipped. ¹¹ Your power is great, and your glory is seen everywhere in heaven and on earth. You are king of the entire world, ¹² and you rule with strength and power. You make people rich and powerful and famous. ¹³ We thank you, our God, and praise you.

See also: 29.1–2: 1 Chron 22.5.   **29.11:** Matt 6.13.

Viewpoints

God is more than a friend – he's a best friend.

Contributed by Tosin O

'You know what is in everyone's heart, and you are pleased when people are honest.'

You can try and keep things secret. If you don't voice it, it can be easy to believe that it's OK to keep that bad feeling of envy, hate or bitterness in your heart. This is not the case. This verse makes it clear that God examines our hearts – others may not know our true feelings, but God does.

If there is a lot of anger and bitterness in our hearts it is not very comforting to know that God, who wants us to be about love, can see that we are about a lot less.

However, we can be comforted in this; God examines our hearts, which means God knows us better than anyone else. This is a great fact in having a relationship with God. In knowing our weaknesses and failures he wants us to be better, to have better feelings, to have integrity, and when we are able to do so through his grace, he rejoices. He is happy and full of joy. This is really good to think about as it helps us to remember that God is our friend as he only wants what is best for us. In fact, God is more than a friend – he's a best friend.

More...

Help! I can't make friends p.714
Help! I want to pay someone back p.1127
Forgiving others p.1162

 Anorak corner

Rulers

1. How long did David rule Israel?
2. What happened to Israel after Solomon's death?
3. Which king was fond of farming?
4. Why did Israel want a king?
5. Which Jewish girl became Queen of Persia?
(Answers on p.1431)

¹⁴ But why should we be happy that we have given you these gifts? They belong to you, and we have only given back what is already yours. ¹⁵ We are only foreigners living here on earth for a while, just as our ancestors were. And we will soon be gone, like a shadow that suddenly disappears.

¹⁶ Our LORD God, we have brought all these things for building a temple to honour you. They belong to you, and you gave them to us. ¹⁷ But we are happy, because everyone has voluntarily given you these things. You know what is in everyone's heart, and you are pleased when people are honest.

¹⁸ Always make us eager to give, and help us be faithful to you, just as our ancestors Abraham, Isaac, and Jacob faithfully worshipped you. ¹⁹ And give Solomon the desire to obey your laws and teachings completely, and the desire to build the temple for which I have provided these gifts.

²⁰ David then said to the people, "Now it's your turn to praise the LORD, the God your ancestors worshipped!" So everyone praised the LORD, and they bowed down to honour him and David their king.

Solomon is crowned king

²¹ The next day, the Israelites slaughtered a thousand bulls, a thousand rams, and a thousand lambs, and they offered them as sacrifices to please the LORD,* along with offerings of wine. ²² The people were very happy, and they ate and drank there at the LORD's altar.

That same day, Solomon was crowned king. The people celebrated and poured olive oil on Solomon's head to show that he would be their next king. They also poured oil on Zadok's head to show that he was their priest.

²³ So Solomon became king after David his father. Solomon was successful, and everyone in Israel obeyed him. ²⁴ Every official and every soldier, as well as all David's other sons, were loyal to him. ²⁵ The LORD made Solomon a great king, and the whole nation was amazed at how famous he was. In fact, no other king of Israel was as great as Solomon.

The death of David

²⁶ David the son of Jesse was king of Israel ²⁷ for forty years. He ruled from Hebron for seven years and from Jerusalem for thirty-three years. ²⁸ David was rich and respected and lived to be an old man. Then he died, and his son Solomon became king.

²⁹ Everything David did while he was king is included in the history written by the prophets Samuel, Nathan, and Gad. ³⁰ They wrote about his powerful rule and about the things that happened not only to him, but also to Israel and the other nations.

See also: 29.27: 2 Sam 5.4–5; 1 Chron 3.4.

Additional notes

›**1.6 Riphath:** Most Hebrew manuscripts and two ancient translations (see also Genesis 10.2–5); some Hebrew manuscripts "Diphath". In Hebrew the letters "d" and "r" look almost exactly the same.
›**1.7 Dodanim:** Most Hebrew manuscripts and one ancient translation (see also Genesis 10.2–5); some Hebrew manuscripts "Rodanim". In Hebrew the letters "d" and "r" look almost exactly the same.
›**1.12 Casluhim, and Caphtorim, the ancestor of the Philistines:** The Hebrew text has "Casluhim, the ancestor of the Philistines, and Caphtorim"; but see Jeremiah 47.4 and Amos 9.7.
›**1.17 Meshech:** Most Hebrew manuscripts; a few Hebrew manuscripts and some manuscripts of one ancient translation "Mash" (see also Genesis 10.21–31).
›**1.34 Jacob:** The Hebrew text has "Israel", which was Jacob's name after God renamed him.
›**1.40 Alvan:** Or "Alian".
›**1.41 Hemdan:** Most Hebrew manuscripts and some manuscripts of one ancient translation (see also Genesis 36.26); other Hebrew manuscripts "Hamran".
›**1.42 Jaakan:** Or "Akan" (see Genesis 36.27).
›**1.42 Dishan:** The Hebrew text has "Dishon", another spelling of the name (see Genesis 36.28).
›**1.51 The Edomite clans:** Or "The leaders of the Edomite clans".
›**1.51 Alvah:** Or "Aliah".
›**2.1–2 Jacob:** See the note at 1.34.
›**2.6 Darda:** Most Hebrew manuscripts and two ancient translations (see also 1 Kings 4.30–31); some Hebrew manuscripts "Dara".
›**2.9 Caleb:** The Hebrew text has "Chelubai", another form of the name.
›**2.18 married Azubah . . . Jerioth:** One possible meaning for the difficult Hebrew text.
›**2.24 After the death of Hezron . . . Ashhur:** Two ancient translations; Hebrew "After Hezron died in Caleb-Ephrath, Abijah his wife gave birth to Ashhur."

*__*29.21 sacrifices to please the LORD:__ See the note at 16.1.
See also: 29.23: 1 King 2.12.

›2.42 Mesha: Hebrew; one ancient translation "Mareshah".

›2.42 following descendants . . . Mareshah: One possible meaning for the difficult Hebrew text.

›2.47 Shaaph: One possible meaning for the difficult Hebrew text of verse 47.

›3.5 Bathsheba: Two ancient translations (see also 2 Samuel 11); Hebrew "Bathshua".

›3.6–8 Elishua: Some Hebrew manuscripts and some manuscripts of one ancient translation (see also 2 Samuel 5.14,15); most Hebrew manuscripts "Elishama".

›3.10–15 Jehoram: The Hebrew text has "Joram", another spelling of the name.

›3.10–15 Jehoahaz: The Hebrew text has "Shallum", probably another name for Jehoahaz (see also 2 Kings 23.30).

›3.21 Shecaniah: One possible meaning for the difficult Hebrew text of verse 21.

›4.3–4 Etam's sons: Some manuscripts of one ancient translation; Hebrew "Etam's ancestors".

›4.10 I . . . harm: Or "keep me from harm, so I won't cause any pain."

›4.12 who settled the town of Nahash: Or "who was the father of Irnahash."

›4.13 and Meonothai: Two ancient translations; these words are not in the Hebrew text.

›4.14 Valley of Crafts: Hebrew "Geharashim".

›4.21–22 who married Moabite women and then settled near Bethlehem: Or "who ruled in Moab and Jashubi-Lahem" or "who ruled in Moab but then returned to Lahem".

›4.34–38 Jehu: Hebrew "Jehu son of Joshibiah son of Seraiah son of Asiel".

›4.34–38 Ziza: Hebrew "Ziza son of Shiphi son of Allon son of Jedaiah son of Shimri son of Shemaiah".

›4.39 Gerar: One ancient translation; Hebrew "Gedor".

›4.42 Edom: The Hebrew text has "Mount Seir", a common name for the nation of Edom.

›5.1 Jacob: See the note at 1.34.

›5.26 King Tiglath Pileser: The Hebrew text also includes "King Pul", another name by which he was known.

›6.28 Joel: Two ancient translations (see also verse 33 and 1 Samuel 8.1–2); this name is not in the Hebrew text.

›6.49 the two altars at the sacred tent: The Hebrew text mentions two different altars: a large altar for offering sacrifices, and a smaller altar for offering incense.

›7.12 Dan: The Hebrew text has "Aher", which can mean "someone else" (see Genesis 46.23–25).

›7.15 Zelophehad . . . daughters: One possible meaning for the difficult Hebrew text (see also Numbers 26.28–33).

›7.29 Joseph: Hebrew "Joseph son of Israel".

›7.35 Hotham: The Hebrew text has "Helem", another spelling of the name.

›8.29 Jeiel: One ancient translation and 9.35; the Hebrew text does not have this name.

›8.30 Ner: One ancient translation and 9.36; the Hebrew text does not have this name.

›9.19 Shallum son of Kore: Hebrew "Shallum son of Kore, grandson of Ebiasaph, and great-grandson of Korah".

›9.40–41 and Ahaz: Most ancient translations and 8.35; the Hebrew text does not have this name.

›10.7 Jezreel Valley: Hebrew "the valley".

›11.15 the Three Warriors: Hebrew "three of the thirty most important warriors".

›11.20–21 Warriors: One possible meaning for the difficult Hebrew text of these verses.

›11.26–47 Ilai: Or "Zalmon" (see 2 Samuel 23.24–39).

›11.26–47 Hurai: Or "Hiddai" (see 2 Samuel 23.24–39).

›11.26–47 Hashem: One ancient translation; Hebrew "the sons of Hashem".

›13.7 Abinadab's sons: These words are not in the Hebrew text, but see 2 Samuel 6.3.

›13.11 Attack on Uzzah: Or "Perez-Uzzah".

›14.4–7 Beeliada: Or "Eliada" (see 3.6–8).

›14.11 The Lord Broke Through: Or "Baal-Perazim".

›14.14 balsam: One possible meaning for the difficult Hebrew text.

›17.17 You are treating me . . . person: One possible meaning for the difficult Hebrew text.

›18.17 David's bodyguard: The Hebrew text has "the Cherethites and the Pelethites", who were foreign soldiers hired by David to be his bodyguard.

›20.2 the statue of their god Milcom: Or "their king."

›20.2 David put the jewel on his crown: Or "David put the crown on his head."

›20.7 David's nephew Jonathan: Hebrew "Jonathan son of Shimea, David's brother".

›21.15 Araunah: The Hebrew text has "Ornan", another spelling of Araunah (see 2 Samuel 24.16).

›24.26,27 Ibri: One possible meaning for the difficult Hebrew text of verses 26–27.

›25.3 Shimei: One Hebrew manuscript and two ancient translations; other Hebrew manuscripts do not have this name.

›26.14 Shelemiah: Another spelling for Meshelemiah.

›26.18 courtyard: One possible meaning for the difficult Hebrew text.

›26.20 The Levites . . . were: One ancient translation; Hebrew "Ahijah the Levite was".

›26.21 Many of his other . . . clan: One possible meaning for the difficult Hebrew text.

›27.4 whose . . . Mikloth: One possible meaning for the difficult Hebrew text.

›27.6 whose son Ammizabad . . . army commander: One possible meaning for the difficult Hebrew text.

›29.10 Jacob: See the note at 1.34.

2 Chronicles

The basics

What's the point? To show how God has been with the Israelites and how, despite their behaviour, he has not forgotten them.

What happens? Solomon builds the temple. A lot of other kings do mainly bad things. Jerusalem is destroyed and the people taken into captivity. But in the end, Cyrus releases them to go home.

What should I remember? 7.19–20 'But if you or any of the people of Israel disobey my laws or start worshipping foreign gods, I will pull you out of this land I gave you. I will desert this temple where I said I would be worshipped, so that people everywhere will think it is only a joke and will make fun of it.'

More details

Setting the scene 2 Chronicles continues the story begun in 1 Chronicles. David has died. Solomon is king. The work on the temple can begin.

What's it all about? 2 Chronicles is mainly about the life of Solomon and the building of the temple. It also gives us accounts of kings like those we get in 1 and 2 Samuel.

Mainly, this is a book about the temple. When you read the book, it's hard to avoid the impression that the bloke who wrote it is a bit of a temple anorak. He's obsessed with the rites and rituals, the details of who did what and when.

This is also a book about holiness. The writer is concerned that the LORD should be worshipped properly, that the people should obey his instructions. That's why he praises kings like Hezekiah and Josiah; two kings who obeyed the Lord, stayed close to him and made every effort to reform their kingdoms and see that things were done in the right way. God had called Israel to be a holy nation, and that meant following God's commands.

Part of the reason why this is so important is that the writer was probably writing for an audience who had just returned from Babylon and who were struggling to rebuild their kingdom. They were trying to rebuild the temple, to start things over again. Chronicles shows them how it used to be done and inspires them to stay holy.

So we get a lot of detail about the first temple, because they were trying to rebuild it. The writer is giving them a pattern to follow, something to aim at. The temple was the symbol that God was with Israel and Israel worshipped God. No wonder he thought it was so important.

That's also why we get so many names and tribes. To the people who had returned from exile they needed to know the role which their ancestors, their tribe, had played. Thus the history was personalised for them. They were urged to continue the work which had been given to their ancestors.

Footsteps

The wealth of Solomon: 1.1–17
The building begins: 3.1–17
Solomon dedicates the temple: 7.1–22
The Queen of Sheba: 9.1–12
The split: 10.1–19
King Uzziah: 26.1–23
Hezekiah and renewal: 31.1–21
Josiah and the law: 34.1–33
Passover: 35.1–19
An end and a beginning 36.17–23

Solomon's wisdom and wealth

CHAPTER 1

The LORD makes Solomon wise

This is also told in 1 Kings 3.1–15

[1] King Solomon, the son of David, was now in complete control of his kingdom, because the LORD God had blessed him and made him a powerful king.

[2-5] At that time, the sacred tent that Moses the servant of the LORD had made in the desert was still kept at Gibeon, and in front of the tent was the bronze altar that Bezalel' had made.

One day, Solomon told the people of Israel, the army commanders, the officials, and the family leaders, to go with him to the place of worship at Gibeon, even though his father King David had already moved the sacred chest from Kiriath-Jearim to the tent that he had set up for it in Jerusalem. Solomon and the others went to Gibeon to worship the LORD, [6] and there at the bronze altar, Solomon offered a thousand animals as sacrifices to please the LORD.*

[7] God appeared to Solomon that night in a dream and said, "Solomon, ask for anything you want, and I will give it to you."

[8] Solomon answered:

LORD God, you were always loyal to my father David, and now you have made me king of Israel. [9] I am supposed to rule these people, but there are as many of them as there are specks of dust on the ground. So keep the promise you made to my father [10] and make me wise. Give me the knowledge I'll need to be the king of this great nation of yours.

[11] God replied:

Solomon, you could have asked me to make you rich or famous or to let you live a long time. Or you could have asked for your enemies to be destroyed. Instead, you asked for wisdom and knowledge to rule

my people. [12] So I will make you wise and intelligent. But I will also make you richer and more famous than any king before or after you.

[13] Solomon then left Gibeon and returned to Jerusalem, the capital city of Israel.

Solomon's wealth

This is also told in 1 Kings 10.26–29

[14] Solomon had a force of one thousand four hundred chariots and twelve thousand horses that he kept in Jerusalem and other towns.

[15] While Solomon was king of Israel, there was silver and gold everywhere in Jerusalem, and cedar was as common as ordinary sycamore trees in the foothills.

[16-17] Solomon's merchants bought his horses and chariots in the regions of Musri and Kue.* They paid six hundred pieces of silver for a chariot and a hundred and fifty pieces of silver for a horse. They also sold horses and chariots to the Hittite and Syrian kings.

Building and dedication of the Jerusalem temple

CHAPTER 2

Solomon asks Hiram to help build the temple

This is also told in 1 Kings 5.1–12

[1] Solomon decided to build a temple where the LORD would be worshipped, and also to build a palace for himself. [2] He assigned seventy thousand men to carry building supplies and eighty thousand to cut stone from the hills. And he chose three thousand six hundred men to supervise these workers.

[3] Solomon sent the following message to King Hiram of Tyre:

Years ago, when my father David was building his palace, you supplied him with cedar logs. Now will you send me supplies? [4] I am building a temple where the LORD my God will be worshipped. Sweet-smelling incense will be burnt there, and sacred bread will be offered to him. Worshippers will offer sacrifices to the LORD every

---

*1.6 sacrifices to please the LORD: These sacrifices have traditionally been called "whole burnt offerings", because the whole animal was burnt on the altar. A main purpose of such sacrifices was to please the LORD with the smell of the sacrifice, and so in the CEV they are often called "sacrifices to please the LORD".
See also: 1.4: 2 Sam 6.1–17; 1 Chron 13.5–14; 15.25—16.1. 1.5: Exod 38.1–7. 1.9: Gen 13.16; 28.14.

*1.16-17 Musri and Kue: Hebrew "Egypt and Kue". Musri and Kue were regions in what is today south-east Turkey.
See also: 1.14: 1 King 4.26. 1.16: Deut 17.16.

morning and evening, every Sabbath, and on the first day of each month, as well as during all our religious festivals. These things will be done for all time, just as the LORD has commanded.

⁵ This will be a great temple, because our God is greater than all other gods. ⁶ No one can ever build a temple large enough for God — even the heavens are too small a place for him to live in! All I can do is build a place where we can offer sacrifices to him.

⁷ Send me a worker who can not only carve, but who can work with gold, silver, bronze, and iron, as well as make brightly-coloured cloth. The person you send will work here in Judah and Jerusalem with the skilled workers that my father has already hired.

⁸ I know that you have workers who are experts at cutting timber in Lebanon. So would you please send me some cedar, pine, and juniper logs? My workers will be there to help them, ⁹ because I'll need a lot of timber to build such a large and glorious temple. ¹⁰ I will pay your woodcutters two thousand tonnes of wheat, the same amount of barley, four hundred thousand litres of wine, and that same amount of olive oil.

¹¹ Hiram sent his answer back to Solomon:

I know that the LORD must love his people, because he has chosen you to be their king. ¹² Praise the LORD God of Israel who made heaven and earth! He has given David a son who is not only wise and clever, but who has the knowledge to build a temple for the LORD and a palace for himself.

¹³ I am sending Huram Abi to you. He is very bright. ¹⁴ His mother was from the Israelite tribe of Dan, and his father was from Tyre. Not only is Huram an expert at working with gold, silver, bronze, iron, stone, and wood, but he can also make coloured cloth and fine linen. And he can carve anything if you give him a pattern to follow. He can help your workers and those hired by your father King David.

¹⁵ Go ahead and send the wheat, barley, olive oil, and wine you promised to pay my workers. ¹⁶ I will tell them to start cutting down trees in Lebanon. They will cut as many as you need, then tie them together into rafts, and float them down along the coast to Joppa. Your workers can take them to Jerusalem from there.

Solomon's work force

¹⁷ Solomon counted all the foreigners who were living in Israel, just as his father David had done when he was king, and the total was 153,600. ¹⁸ He assigned 70,000 of them to carry building supplies and 80,000 of them to cut stone from the hills. He chose 3,600 others to supervise the workers and to make sure the work was completed.

CHAPTER 3

The temple is built

This is also told in 1 Kings 6.1–38

¹⁻² Solomon's workers began building the temple in Jerusalem on the second day of the second month,* four years after Solomon had become king of Israel. It was built on Mount Moriah where the LORD had appeared to David at the threshing place that had belonged to Araunah⁰ from Jebus.

³ The inside of the temple was twenty-seven metres long and nine metres wide, according to the older standards.*
⁴ Across the front of the temple was a porch nine metres wide and nine metres⁰ high. The inside walls of the porch were covered with pure gold.

⁵ Solomon had the inside walls of the temple's main room panelled first with pine and then with a layer of gold, and he had them decorated with carvings of palm trees and designs that looked like chains. ⁶ He used precious stones to decorate the temple, and he used gold imported from Parvaim* ⁷ to decorate the ceiling beams, the doors, the door frames, and the walls. Solomon also made the workers carve designs of winged creatures into the walls.

⁸ The most holy place was nine metres square, and its walls were covered with over twenty tonnes of fine gold. ⁹ Five hundred and seventy grammes of gold was used to cover the heads of the nails. The walls of the small storage rooms were also covered with gold.⁰

---

*3.1–2 second month:** Ziv, the second month of the Hebrew calendar, from about mid-April to mid-May.
*3.3 according to the older standards:** There were possibly two different standards of measurement during Israel's history.
*3.6 Parvaim:** An unknown place.

See also: 3.1: Gen 22.22. 3.8: Exod 26.33–34.

Solomon's Temple

King David made Jerusalem the capital of Israel and brought the ark of the covenant into the city. David wanted to build a temple, but the work was completed by his son, Solomon. It was a magnificent building, but still basically followed the same shape as the Tabernacle with a main room (the holy place) and a smaller inner sanctuary (the most holy place or 'holy of holies'). Only the high priest was allowed in the most holy place – and then only once a year.

The building was made of plain stone, with rooms panelled with cedar wood. It was two storeys high and contained priests' rooms along the side walls.

The holy place contained the incense table for the sacred bread and ten lampstands.

The most holy place – or 'holy of holies' – was a cubic room (20x20x20 cubits) containing the ark of the covenant and two large, decorative angels on the rear wall.

Outside were the large main altar and a huge bronze basin for ritual washing.

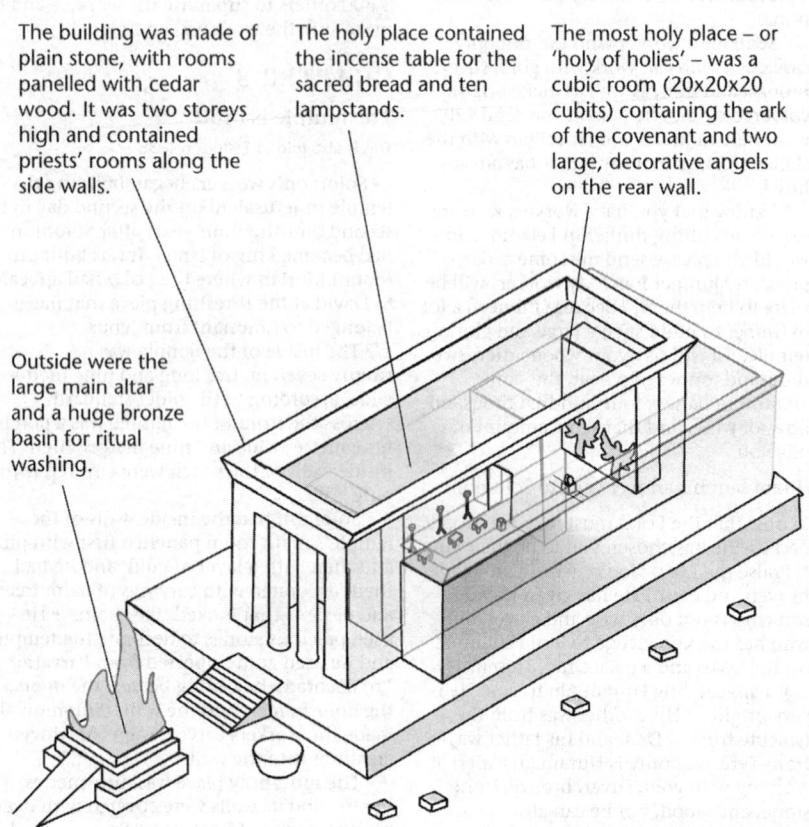

Future temples

Solomon's temple was only the first of several in Jerusalem. The original was destroyed by the Babylonians in 587BC. It was rebuilt seventy years later and lasted around 500 years until it was massively redeveloped by Herod the Great. Herod did so many alterations to the temple that the work carried on for many decades – the temple was still under construction during the life of Jesus. Herod's temple – the third temple – was finally completed in AD64, but it only stood for 6 years. It was completely destroyed by the Romans in AD70, following a Jewish uprising. There was never a temple in Israel again.

¹⁰ Solomon had two statues of winged creatures* made to put in the most holy place, and he covered them with gold. ¹¹⁻¹³ Each creature had two wings and was four and a half metres from the tip of one wing to the tip of the other wing. Solomon set them next to each other in the most holy place, facing the doorway. Their wings were spread out and reached all the way across the nine-metre room.

¹⁴ A curtain* was made of fine linen woven with blue, purple, and red wool, and embroidered with designs of winged creatures.

The two columns

This is also told in 1 Kings 7.15–22

¹⁵ Two columns were made for the entrance to the temple. Each one was five and a half metres tall and had a cap on top that was over two metres high. ¹⁶ The top of each column was decorated with designs that looked like chains' and with a hundred carvings of pomegranates.* ¹⁷ Solomon had one of the columns placed on the south side of the temple's entrance; it was called Jachin.* The other one was placed on the north side of the entrance; it was called Boaz.*

CHAPTER 4

The furnishings for the temple

This is also told in 1 Kings 7.23–51

¹ Solomon had a bronze altar made that was nine metres square and four and a half metres high. ² He also gave orders to make a large metal bowl called the Sea. It was four and a half metres across, just over two metres deep, and thirteen and a half metres around. ³ Its outer edge was decorated with two rows of carvings of bulls, ten bulls to about every forty-five centimetres, all made from the same piece of metal as the bowl. ⁴ The bowl itself sat on top of twelve bronze bulls, with

three bulls facing outwards in each of four directions. ⁵ The sides of the bowl were seventy-five millimetres thick, and its rim was in the shape of a cup that curved outwards like flower petals. The bowl held about sixty thousand litres.

⁶ He also made ten small bowls and put five on each side of the large bowl. The small bowls were used to wash the animals that were burnt on the altar as sacrifices, and the priests used the water in the large bowl to wash their hands.

⁷ Ten gold lampstands were also made according to the plans. Solomon placed these lampstands inside the temple, five on each side of the main room. ⁸ He also made ten tables and placed them in the main room, five on each side. And he made a hundred small gold sprinkling bowls.

⁹ Solomon gave orders to build two courtyards: a smaller one that only priests could use and a larger one. The doors to these courtyards were covered with bronze. ¹⁰ The large bowl called the Sea was placed near the south-east corner of the temple.

¹¹ Huram made shovels, sprinkling bowls, and pans for hot ashes. Here is a list of the other furnishings he made for God's temple: ¹² two columns, two bowl-shaped caps for the tops of these columns, two chain designs on the caps, ¹³ four hundred pomegranates* for the chain designs, ¹⁴ the stands and the small bowls, ¹⁵ the large bowl and the twelve bulls that held it up, ¹⁶ pans for hot ashes, as well as shovels and meat forks.

Huram made all these things out of polished bronze ¹⁷ by pouring melted bronze into the clay moulds he had set up near the River Jordan, between Succoth and Zeredah.

¹⁸ There were so many bronze furnishings that no one ever knew how much bronze it took to make them.

¹⁹ Solomon also gave orders to make the following temple furnishings out of gold: the altar, the tables that held the sacred loaves of bread,* ²⁰ the lampstands and the lamps that burnt in front of the most holy place, ²¹ flower designs, lamps and tongs, ²² lamp snuffers, small sprinkling bowls, ladles, fire

---

*3.10 statues of winged creatures: These were symbols of the Lord's throne on earth (see Exodus 25.18–22).
*3.14 A curtain: To separate the most holy place from the main room of the temple.
*3.16 pomegranates: A pomegranate is a small red fruit that looks like an apple. In ancient times, it was a symbol of life.
*3.17 Jachin: Or "He (God) makes secure."
*3.17 Boaz: Or "He (God) is strong."
See also: 3.10–13: Exod 25.18–20. 3.14: Exod 26.31. 4.1: Exod 27.1–2.

*4.13 pomegranates: See the note at 3.16.
*4.19 sacred loaves of bread: This bread was offered to the Lord and was a symbol of the Lord's presence in the temple. It was put out on special tables, and was replaced with fresh bread every week (see Leviticus 24.5–9).
See also: 4.6: Exod 30.17–21. 4.7: Exod 25.31–40. 4.8: Exod 25.23–30.

pans, and the doors to the most holy place and the main room of the temple.

CHAPTER 5

¹ After the LORD's temple was finished, Solomon put in its storage rooms everything that his father David had dedicated to the LORD, including the gold and silver, and the objects used in worship.

Solomon brings the sacred chest to the temple

This is also told in 1 Kings 8.1–13

²⁻³ The sacred chest had been kept on Mount Zion, also known as the City of David. But Solomon decided to have the chest moved to the temple while everyone was in Jerusalem to celebrate the Festival of Shelters during the seventh month.*

Solomon called together all the important leaders of Israel. ⁴⁻⁵ Then the priests and the Levites picked up the sacred chest, the sacred tent, and the objects used for worship, and they carried them to the temple. ⁶ Solomon and a crowd of people walked in front of the chest, and along the way they sacrificed more sheep and cattle than could be counted.

⁷ The priests carried the chest into the most holy place and put it under the winged creatures,* ⁸ whose wings covered the chest and the poles used for carrying it. ⁹ The poles were so long that they could be seen from just outside the most holy place, but not from anywhere else. And they stayed there from then on.

¹⁰ The only things kept in the chest were the two flat stones Moses had put there when the LORD made his agreement with the people of Israel at Mount Sinai,› after bringing them out of Egypt.

¹¹⁻¹³ The priests of every group had gone through the ceremony to make themselves clean and acceptable to the LORD. The Levite musicians, including Asaph, Heman, Jeduthun, and their sons and relatives, were wearing robes of fine linen. They were standing on the east side of the altar, playing cymbals, small harps, and other stringed

instruments. One hundred and twenty priests were with these musicians, and they were blowing trumpets.

They were praising the LORD by playing music and singing:

"The LORD is good,
   and his love never ends."

Suddenly a cloud filled the temple as the priests were leaving the holy place. ¹⁴ The LORD's glory was in that cloud, and the light from it was so bright that the priests could not stay inside to do their work.

CHAPTER 6

¹ Solomon prayed:

"Our LORD, you said that you
   would live in a dark cloud.
² Now I've built a glorious temple
   where you can live for ever."

Solomon speaks to the people

This is also told in 1 Kings 8.14–21

³ Solomon turned towards the people standing there. Then he blessed them ⁴⁻⁶ and said:

Praise the LORD God of Israel! He brought his people out of Egypt long ago and later kept his promise to make my father David the king of Israel. The LORD also promised him that Jerusalem would be the city where his temple will be built, and now that promise has come true.

⁷ When my father wanted to build a temple for the LORD God of Israel, ⁸ the LORD said, "It's good that you want to build a temple where I can be worshipped. ⁹ But you're not the one to do it. Your son will build the temple to honour me."

¹⁰ The LORD has done what he promised. I am now the king of Israel, and I've built a temple for the LORD our God. ¹¹ I've also put the sacred chest in the temple. And in that chest are the two flat stones on which is written the solemn agreement the LORD made with our ancestors when he rescued them from Egypt.

Solomon prays at the temple

This is also told in 1 Kings 8.22–53

¹²⁻¹³ Earlier, Solomon had a bronze platform made that was about two metres square and

---

*5.2–3 seventh month: Tishri (also called Ethanim), the seventh month of the Hebrew calendar, from about mid-September to mid-October.
*5.7 winged creatures: See the note at 3.10.
See also: 5.1: 2 Sam 8.11; 1 Chron 18.11.
5.2: 2 Sam 6.12–15; 1 Chron 15.25–28. 5.10: Deut 10.5.
5.13: 1 Chron 16.34; 2 Chron 7.3; Ezra 3.11; Psa 100.5; 106.1; 107.1; 118.1; 136.1; Jer 33.11. 5.13–14: Exod 40.34–35.

See also: 6.4–9: 2 Sam 7.1–13; 1 Chron 17.1–12.

over a metre high, and he put it in the centre of the outer courtyard near the altar. Solomon stood on the platform facing the altar with everyone standing behind him. Then he lifted his arms towards heaven; he knelt down 14 and prayed:

LORD God of Israel, no other god in heaven or on earth is like you!

You never forget the agreement you made with your people, and you are loyal to anyone who faithfully obeys your teachings. 15 My father David was your servant, and today you have kept every promise you made to him.

16 You promised that someone from his family would always be king of Israel, if they do their best to obey you, just as he did. 17 Please keep this promise you made to your servant David. 18 There's not enough room in all of heaven for you, LORD God. How could you possibly live on earth in this temple I have built? 19 But I ask you to answer my prayer. 20 This is the temple where you have chosen to be worshipped. Please watch over it day and night and listen when I turn towards it and pray. 21 I am your servant, and the people of Israel belong to you, and so whenever any of us look towards this temple and pray, answer from your home in heaven and forgive our sins.

22 Suppose someone accuses a person of a crime, and the accused has to stand in front of the altar in your temple and say, "I swear I am innocent!" 23 Listen from heaven and decide who is right. Then punish the guilty person and let the innocent one go free.

24 Suppose your people Israel sin against you, and then an enemy defeats them. If they come to this temple and beg for forgiveness, 25 listen from your home in heaven. Forgive them and bring them back to the land you gave their ancestors.

26 Suppose your people sin against you, and you punish them by holding back the rain. If they stop sinning and turn towards this temple to pray in your name, 27 listen from your home in heaven and forgive them. The people of Israel are your servants, so teach them to live right. And send rain on the land you promised them for ever.

28 Sometimes the crops may dry up or rot or be eaten by locusts* or grasshoppers, and your people will be starving. Sometimes enemies may surround their towns, or your people will become sick with deadly diseases. 29 Please listen when anyone in Israel truly feels sorry and sincerely prays with arms lifted towards your temple. 30 You know what is in everyone's heart. So from your home in heaven answer their prayers, according to what they do and what is in their hearts. 31 Then your people will worship you and obey you for as long as they live in the land you gave their ancestors.

32 Foreigners will hear about you and your mighty power, and some of them will come to live among your people Israel. If any of them pray towards this temple, 33 listen from your home in heaven and answer their prayers. Then everyone on earth will worship you, just as your own people Israel do, and they will know that I have built this temple in your honour.

34 Sometimes you will order your people to attack their enemies. Then your people will turn towards this temple I have built for you in your chosen city, and they will pray to you. 35 Answer their prayers from heaven and give them victory.

36 Everyone sins. But when your people sin against you, suppose you get angry enough to let their enemies drag them away to foreign countries. 37-39 Later, they may feel sorry for what they did and ask your forgiveness. Answer them when they pray towards this temple I have built for you in your chosen city, here in this land you gave their ancestors. From your home in heaven, listen to their sincere prayers and forgive your people who have sinned against you.

40 LORD God, hear us when we pray in this temple. 41 Come to your new home, where we have already placed the sacred chest, which is the symbol of your strength. I pray that when the priests announce your power to save people, those who are faithful to you will celebrate what you've done for them. 42 Always remember the love you had for your servant David,' so that you will not reject your chosen kings.

---

*6.28 locusts: A type of grasshopper that comes in swarms and causes great damage to crops.
See also: **6.41-42:** Psa 132.8-10.

CHAPTER 7

Solomon dedicates the temple

This is also told in 1 Kings 8.62–66

[1] As soon as Solomon finished praying, fire came down from heaven and burnt up the offerings. The LORD's dazzling glory then filled the temple, [2] and the priests could not go in.

[3] When the crowd of people saw the fire and the LORD's glory, they knelt down and worshipped the LORD. They prayed:

"The LORD is good,
and his love never ends."

[4-5] Solomon and the people dedicated the temple to the LORD by sacrificing twenty-two thousand cattle and one hundred and twenty thousand sheep. [6] Everybody stood up during the ceremony. The priests were in their assigned places, blowing their trumpets. And the Levites faced them, playing the musical instruments that David had made for them to use when they praised the LORD for his never-ending love.

[7] On that same day, Solomon dedicated the courtyard in front of the temple and got it ready to be used for worship. The bronze altar he had made was too small, so he used the courtyard to offer sacrifices to please the LORD* and grain sacrifices, and also to send up in smoke the fat from the other offerings.

[8] For seven days, Solomon and the crowd celebrated the Festival of Shelters, and people came from as far away as the Egyptian Gorge in the south and Lebo-Hamath in the north. [9] Then on the next day, everyone came together for worship. They had celebrated a total of fourteen days, seven days for the dedication of the altar and seven more days for the festival. [10] Then on the twenty-third day of the seventh month,* Solomon sent everyone home. They left very happy because of all the good things the LORD had done for David and Solomon, and for his people Israel.

The LORD appears to Solomon again

This is also told in 1 Kings 9.1–9

[11] The LORD's temple and Solomon's palace were now finished. In fact, everything Solomon had planned to do was completed.

[12] Some time later, the LORD appeared to Solomon in a dream and said:

I heard your prayer, and I have chosen this temple as the place where sacrifices will be offered to me. [13] Suppose I hold back the rain or send locusts* to eat the crops or make my people suffer with deadly diseases. [14] If my own people will humbly pray and turn back to me and stop sinning, then I will answer them from heaven. I will forgive them and make their land fertile once again. [15] I will hear the prayers made in this temple, [16] because it belongs to me, and this is where I will be worshipped for ever. I will never stop watching over it.

[17] Your father David obeyed me, and now, Solomon, you must do the same. Obey my laws and teachings, [18] and I will keep my solemn promise to him that someone from your family will always be king of Israel.

[19] But if you or any of the people of Israel disobey my laws or start worshipping foreign gods, [20] I will pull you out of this land I gave you. I will desert this temple where I said I would be worshipped, so that people everywhere will think it is only a joke and will make fun of it. [21] This temple is now magnificent. But when these things happen, everyone who walks by it will be shocked and will ask, "Why did the LORD do such a terrible thing to his people and to this temple?" [22] Then they will answer, "It was because the people of Israel rejected the LORD their God, who rescued their ancestors from Egypt, and they started worshipping other gods."

Other events during Solomon's rule

CHAPTER 8

Other things Solomon did

This is also told in 1 Kings 9.10–28

[1] It took twenty years for the LORD's temple and Solomon's palace to be built. [2] After that, Solomon's workers rebuilt the towns that Hiram had given him. Then Solomon sent Israelites to live in those towns.

[3] Solomon attacked and captured the town of Hamath-Zobah. [4] He made his workers

---

*7.7 sacrifices to please the LORD: See the note at 1.6.
*7.10 seventh month: See the note at 5.2–3.
See also: 7.1: Lev 9.23–24. 7.3: 1 Chron 16.34; 2 Chron 5.13; Ezra 3.11; Psa 100.5; 106.1; 107.1; 118.1; 136.1; Jer 33.11.

*7.13 locusts: See the note at 6.28.
See also: 7.18: 1 King 2.4.

build the town of Tadmor in the desert and some towns in Hamath where he could keep his supplies. ⁵ He strengthened Upper Beth-Horon and Lower Beth-Horon by adding walls and gates that could be locked. ⁶ He did the same thing to the town of Baalath and to the cities where he kept supplies, chariots, and horses. Solomon made his workers build whatever he wanted in Jerusalem, Lebanon, and anywhere else in his kingdom.

⁷⁻⁹ Solomon did not force the Israelites to do his work. Instead, they were his soldiers, officers, army commanders, and cavalry troops. But he did make slaves of the Hittites, Amorites, Perizzites, Hivites, and Jebusites who were living in Israel. These were the descendants of those foreigners the Israelites did not destroy, and they remained Israel's slaves.

¹⁰ Solomon appointed two hundred and fifty officers to be in charge of his workers.

¹¹ Solomon's wife, the daughter of the king of Egypt, moved from the part of Jerusalem called David's City to her new palace that Solomon had built. The sacred chest had been kept in David's City, which made his palace sacred, and so Solomon's wife could no longer live there.

¹² Solomon offered sacrifices to the LORD on the altar he had built in front of the temple. ¹³ He followed the requirements that Moses had given for sacrifices offered on the Sabbath, on the first day of each month, the Festival of Thin Bread, the Harvest Festival, and the Festival of Shelters.

¹⁴ Solomon then assigned the priests and the Levites their duties at the temple, and he followed the instructions that his father David had given him. Some of the Levites were to lead music and help the priests in their duties, and others were to guard the temple gates ¹⁵ and the storage rooms. The priests and Levites followed these instructions exactly.

¹⁶ Everything Solomon had planned to do was now finished — from the laying of the temple's foundation to its completion.

¹⁷ Solomon went to Ezion-Geber and Eloth, two Edomite towns on the Red Sea.* ¹⁸ Hiram sent him ships and some of his experienced sailors. They went with Solomon's own sailors to the country of Ophir* and brought

back more than fifteen thousand kilogrammes of gold for Solomon.

CHAPTER 9

The Queen of Sheba visits Solomon

This is also told in 1 Kings 10.1–13

¹ The Queen of Sheba heard how famous Solomon was, so she went to Jerusalem to test him with difficult questions. She took along several of her officials, and she loaded her camels with gifts of spices, jewels, and gold. When she arrived, she and Solomon talked about everything she could think of. ² He answered every question, no matter how difficult it was.

³⁻⁴ The Queen was amazed at Solomon's wisdom. She was breathless when she saw his palace,› the food on his table, his officials, all his servants in their uniforms, and the sacrifices he offered at the LORD's temple. ⁵ She said:

Solomon, in my own country I had heard about your wisdom and all you've done. ⁶ But I didn't believe it until I saw it with my own eyes! And there's so much I didn't hear about. You are greater than I was told. ⁷ Your people and officials are lucky to be here where they can listen to the wise things you say.

⁸ I praise the LORD your God. He is pleased with you and has made you king of Israel. God loves the people of this country and will never desert them, so he has given them a king who will rule fairly and honestly.

⁹ The Queen of Sheba gave Solomon more than four thousand kilogrammes of gold, a large amount of jewels, and the best spices anyone had ever seen.

¹⁰⁻¹² In return, Solomon gave her everything she wanted — even more than she had given him. Then she and her officials went back to their own country.

Solomon's wealth

This is also told in 1 Kings 10.14–29

Hiram's and Solomon's sailors brought gold, juniper wood, and jewels from the country of Ophir. Solomon used the wood to make steps› for the temple and palace, and harps and other stringed instruments for the musicians. Nothing like these had ever been made in Judah.

---

*8.17 Red Sea: Hebrew *yam suph*, here referring to the Gulf of Aqaba, since the term is extended to include the north-eastern arm of the Red Sea (see also the note at Exodus 13.18).
*8.18 Ophir: The location of this place is not known.
See also: 8.13: a Num 28.9–10; b Num 28.11–15; c Exod 23.14–17; 34.22–23; Num 28.16–29.39; Deut 16.16.

See also: 9.1–9: Matt 12.42; Luke 11.31.

13 Solomon received almost twenty-three thousand kilogrammes of gold each year, 14 not counting what the merchants and traders brought him. The kings of Arabia and the leaders of Israel also gave him gold and silver.

15 Solomon made two hundred gold shields that weighed over three kilogrammes each. 16 He also made three hundred smaller gold shields that weighed almost two kilogrammes, and he put these shields in his palace in Forest Hall.

17 His throne was made of ivory and covered with pure gold. 18 It had a gold footstool attached to it and arm rests on each side. There was a statue of a lion on each side of the throne, 19 and there were two lion statues on each of the six steps leading up to the throne. No other throne in the world was like Solomon's.

20 Solomon's cups and dishes in Forest Hall were made of pure gold, because silver was almost worthless in those days.

21 Solomon had a lot of seagoing ships.* Every three years he sent them out with Hiram's ships to bring back gold, silver, and ivory, as well as monkeys and peacocks.'

22 Solomon was the richest and wisest king in the world. 23-24 Year after year, other kings came to hear the wisdom God had given him. And they brought gifts of silver and gold, as well as clothes, weapons, spices, horses, and mules.

25 Solomon had four thousand stalls for his horses and chariots, and he owned twelve thousand horses that he kept in Jerusalem and other towns.

26 He ruled all the nations from the River Euphrates in the north to the land of Philistia in the south, as far as the border of Egypt.

27 While Solomon was king, there was silver everywhere in Jerusalem, and cedar was as common as the sycamore trees in the western foothills. 28 Solomon's horses were brought in from other countries, including Musri.*

The death of Solomon

This is also told in 1 Kings 11.41–43

29 Everything else Solomon did while he was king is written in the records of Nathan the prophet, Ahijah the prophet from Shiloh, and Iddo the prophet who wrote about Jeroboam son of Nebat. 30 After Solomon had ruled forty years from Jerusalem, 31 he died and was buried in the city of his father David. His son Rehoboam then became king.

The northern tribes of Israel rebel against King Rehoboam

CHAPTER 10

This is also told in 1 Kings 12.1–20

1 Rehoboam went to Shechem where everyone was waiting to crown him king.

2 Jeroboam son of Nebat heard what was happening, and he returned from Egypt, where he had gone to hide from Solomon. 3 The people from the northern tribes of Israel sent for him. Then together they went to Rehoboam and said, 4 "Your father Solomon forced us to work very hard. But if you make our work easier, we will serve you and do whatever you ask."

5 Rehoboam replied, "Come back in three days for my answer." So the people left.

6 Rehoboam went to some leaders who had been his father's senior officials, and he asked them, "What should I tell these people?"

7 They answered, "If you want them to serve and obey you, then you should be kind and promise to make their work easier."

8 But Rehoboam refused their advice and went to the younger men who had grown up with him and were now his officials. 9 He asked, "What do you think I should say to these people who asked me to make their work easier?"

10 His younger advisers said:

Here's what we think you should say to them: "Compared to me, my father was weak.' 11 He made you work hard, but I'll make you work even harder. He punished you with whips, but I'll use whips with pieces of sharp metal!"

---

*9.21 seagoing ships: The Hebrew text has "ships of Tarshish", which may have been a Phoenician city in Spain. "Ships of Tarshish" probably means large, seagoing ships.
*9.28 Musri: See the note at 1.16–17.
See also: 9.25: 1 King 4.26. 9.26: Gen 15.18; 1 King 4.21. 9.28: Deut 17.16.

12 Three days later, Jeroboam and the others came back. 13 Rehoboam ignored the advice of the older advisers. He spoke bluntly 14 and told them exactly what his own advisers had suggested. He said: "My father made you work hard, but I'll make you work even harder. He punished you with whips, but I'll use whips with pieces of sharp metal!"

15-19 When the people realized that Rehoboam would not listen to them, they shouted: "We don't have to be loyal to David's family. We can do what we want. Come on, people of Israel, let's go home! Rehoboam can rule his own people."

Adoniram' was in charge of the work force, and Rehoboam sent him to talk to the people. But they stoned him to death. Then Rehoboam ran to his chariot and hurried back to Jerusalem.

Everyone from Israel's northern tribes went home, leaving Rehoboam to rule only the people from Judah. And since that day, the people of Israel have been opposed to David's descendants in Judah.* All this happened just as Ahijah the LORD's prophet from Shiloh had told Jeroboam.

Kings of Judah

CHAPTER 11

Shemaiah the prophet warns Rehoboam

This is also told in 1 Kings 12.21-24

1 After Rehoboam returned to Jerusalem, he decided to attack Israel and regain control of the whole country. So he called together one hundred and eighty thousand soldiers from the tribes of Judah and Benjamin.

2 Meanwhile, the LORD had told Shemaiah the prophet 3 to tell Rehoboam and everyone from Judah and Benjamin, 4 "The LORD warns you not to go to war against the people from the northern tribes — they are your relatives. Go home! The LORD is the one who made these things happen."

Rehoboam and his army obeyed the LORD's message and did not attack Jeroboam and his troops.

Rehoboam fortifies cities in Judah

5 Rehoboam ruled from Jerusalem, and he had several cities in Judah turned into fortresses so he could use them to defend his country. These cities included 6 Bethlehem, Etam, Tekoa, 7 Beth-Zur, Soco, Adullam, 8 Gath, Mareshah, Ziph, 9 Adoraim, Lachish, Azekah, 10 Zorah, Aijalon, and Hebron. After he had fortified these cities in the territories of Judah and Benjamin, 11 he assigned an army commander to each of them and stocked them with supplies of food, olive oil, and wine, 12 as well as with shields and spears. He used these fortified cities to keep control of Judah and Benjamin.

The priests and the Levites support Rehoboam

13 The priests and Levites from the northern tribes of Israel gave their support to King Rehoboam. 14 And since Jeroboam and the kings of Israel who followed him would not allow any Levites to serve as priests, most Levites left their towns and pasture lands in Israel and moved to Jerusalem and other towns in Judah. 15 Jeroboam chose his own priests to serve at the local shrines' in Israel and at the places of worship where he had set up statues of goat-demons and of calves.

16 But some of the people from Israel wanted to worship the LORD God, just as their ancestors had done. So they followed the priests and Levites to Jerusalem, where they could offer sacrifices to the LORD. 17 For the next three years, they lived in Judah and were loyal to Rehoboam and his kingdom, just as they had been loyal to David and Solomon.

Rehoboam's family

18 Rehoboam married Mahalath, whose father was Jerimoth son of David, and whose mother was Abihail the daughter of Eliab and granddaughter of Jesse. 19 Rehoboam and Mahalath had three sons: Jeush, Shemariah, and Zaham. 20 Then Rehoboam married Maacah the daughter of Absalom. Their sons were Abijah, Attai, Ziza, and Shelomith.

21 Rehoboam had eighteen wives, but he also married sixty other women,* and he was the father of twenty-eight sons and sixty

---

*10.15–19 the people of Israel have been opposed . . . Judah: From this time on, "Israel" usually refers only to the northern kingdom. The southern kingdom is called "Judah".
See also: 10.16: 2 Sam 20.1.

*11.21 other women: This translates a Hebrew word for women who were legally bound to a man, but without the full privileges of a wife.
See also: 11.15: 1 King 12.31.

daughters. Rehoboam loved his wife Maacah the most, 22 so he chose their eldest son Abijah to be the next king. 23 Rehoboam was wise enough to put one of his sons in charge of each fortified city in his kingdom. He gave them all the supplies they needed and found wives for every one of them.

CHAPTER 12

King Shishak of Egypt invades Judah

This is also told in 1 Kings 14.25–28

1 Soon after Rehoboam had control of his kingdom, he and everyone in Judah stopped obeying the LORD. 2 So in the fifth year of Rehoboam's rule, the LORD punished them for their unfaithfulness and allowed King Shishak of Egypt to invade Judah. 3 Shishak attacked with his army of one thousand two hundred chariots and sixty thousand cavalry troops, as well as Egyptian soldiers from Libya, Sukkoth, and Ethiopia.* 4 He captured every one of the fortified cities in Judah and then marched to Jerusalem.

5 Rehoboam and the leaders of Judah had gone to Jerusalem to escape Shishak's invasion. And while they were there, Shemaiah the prophet told them, "The LORD says that because you have disobeyed him, he has now abandoned you. The LORD will not help you against Shishak!"

6 Rehoboam and the leaders were sorry for what they had done and admitted, "The LORD is right. We have deserted him."

7 When the LORD heard this, he told Shemaiah:

The people of Judah are truly sorry for their sins, and so I won't let Shishak completely destroy them. But because I am still angry, 8 he will conquer and rule them.

Then my people will know what it's like to serve a foreign king instead of serving me.

9 Shishak attacked Jerusalem and took all the valuable things from the temple and from the palace, including Solomon's gold shields.

10 Rehoboam had bronze shields made to replace the gold ones, and he ordered the guards at the city gates to keep them safe.
11 Whenever Rehoboam went to the LORD's temple, the guards carried the shields. But

they always took them back to the guardroom as soon as he had finished worshipping.

12 Rehoboam turned back to the LORD, and so the LORD did not let Judah be completely destroyed, and Judah was prosperous again.

Rehoboam's rule in Judah

This is also told in 1 Kings 14.21,29–31

13 Rehoboam was forty-one years old when he became king, and he ruled seventeen years from Jerusalem, the city where the LORD had chosen to be worshipped. His mother Naamah was from Ammon. Rehoboam was a powerful king, 14 but he still did wrong and refused to obey the LORD.

15 Everything else Rehoboam did while he was king, including a history of his family, is written in the records of the two prophets, Shemaiah and Iddo. During Rehoboam's rule, he and King Jeroboam of Israel were constantly at war. 16 When Rehoboam died, he was buried beside his ancestors in Jerusalem, and his son Abijah became king.

CHAPTER 13

King Abijah of Judah

This is also told in 1 Kings 15.1–8

1 Abijah' became king of Judah in Jeroboam's eighteenth year as king of Israel, 2 and he ruled from Jerusalem for three years. His mother was Micaiah the daughter of Uriel from Gibeah.

Some time later, Abijah and King Jeroboam of Israel went to war against each other.
3 Abijah's army had four hundred thousand troops, and Jeroboam met him in battle with eight hundred thousand troops.

4 Abijah went to the top of Mount Zemaraim* in the hills of Ephraim and shouted:

Listen, Jeroboam and all you Israelites!
5 The LORD God of Israel has made a solemn promise that every king of Israel will be from David's family. 6 But Jeroboam, you were King Solomon's official, and you rebelled. 7 Then straight after Rehoboam became king, you and your bunch of worthless followers challenged Rehoboam, who was too young to know how to stop you.

---

*12.3 Ethiopia: The Hebrew text has "Cush", which was a region south of Egypt that included parts of the present countries of Ethiopia and Sudan.
See also: 12.9: 1 King 10.16–17; 2 Chron 9.15–16.

*13.4 Mount Zemaraim: Probably on the northern border of the territory of Benjamin.

⁸ Now you and your powerful army think you can stand up to the kingdom that the LORD has given to David's descendants. The only gods you have are those gold statues of calves that Jeroboam made for you. ⁹ You don't even have descendants of Aaron on your side, because you forced out the LORD's priests and Levites. In their place, you appoint ordinary people to be priests, just as the foreign nations do. In fact, anyone who brings a bull and seven rams to the altar can become a priest of your so-called gods.

¹⁰ But we have not turned our backs on the LORD God! Aaron's own descendants serve as our priests, and the Levites are their assistants. ¹¹ Twice every day they offer sacrifices and burn incense to the LORD. They set out the sacred loaves of bread on a table that has been purified, and they light the lamps in the gold lampstand every day at sunset. We follow the commands of the LORD our God — you have rejected him! ¹² That's why God is on our side and will lead us into battle when the priests sound the signal on the trumpets. It's no use, Israelites. You might as well give up. There's no way you can defeat the LORD, the God your ancestors worshipped.

¹³ But while Abijah was talking, Jeroboam had sent some of his troops to attack Judah's army from behind, while the rest attacked from the front. ¹⁴ Judah's army realized they were trapped, and so they prayed to the LORD. The priests blew the signal on the trumpet, ¹⁵ and the troops let out a battle cry. Then with Abijah leading them into battle, God defeated Jeroboam and Israel's army. ¹⁶ The Israelites ran away, and God helped Judah's soldiers slaughter ¹⁷ five hundred thousand enemy troops. ¹⁸ Judah's army won because they had trusted the LORD God of their ancestors.

¹⁹ Abijah kept up his attack on Jeroboam's army and captured the Israelite towns of Bethel, Jeshanah, and Ephron, as well as the villages around them.

²⁰ Jeroboam never regained his power during the rest of Abijah's rule. The LORD punished Jeroboam, and he died, but Abijah became more powerful. ²¹ Abijah had a total of fourteen wives, twenty-two sons, and sixteen daughters. ²² Everything Abijah said and did while he was king is written in the records of Iddo the prophet.

CHAPTER 14

King Asa of Judah

¹ Abijah died and was buried in Jerusalem. Then his son Asa became king, and Judah had ten years of peace.

² Asa obeyed the LORD his God and did right. ³ He destroyed the local shrines' and the altars to foreign gods. He smashed the stone images of gods and cut down the sacred poles* used in worshipping the goddess Asherah. ⁴ Then he told everyone in Judah to worship the LORD God, just as their ancestors had done, and to obey his laws and teachings. ⁵ He destroyed every local shrine and incense altar in Judah.

⁶ The LORD blessed Judah with peace while Asa was king, and so during that time, Asa fortified many of the towns. ⁷ He said to the people, "Let's build walls and defence towers for these towns, and put in gates that can be locked with bars. This land still belongs to us, because we have obeyed the LORD our God. He has given us peace from all our enemies." The people did everything Asa had suggested.

⁸ Asa had a large army of brave soldiers: three hundred thousand of them were from the tribe of Judah and were armed with shields and spears; two hundred and eighty thousand were from Benjamin and were armed with bows and arrows.

Judah defeats Ethiopia's army

⁹ Zerah from Ethiopia* led an army of a million soldiers and three hundred chariots to the town of Mareshah* in Judah. ¹⁰ Asa met him there, and the two armies prepared for battle in Zephathah Valley.

¹¹ Asa prayed:

LORD God, only you can help a powerless army defeat a stronger one. So we depend on you to help us. We will fight against this powerful army to honour your name, and we know that you won't be defeated. You are the LORD our God.

¹² The LORD helped Asa and his army defeat the Ethiopians. The enemy soldiers ran away, ¹³ but Asa and his troops chased them as far as Gerar. It was a total defeat — the Ethiopians could not even fight back!'

---

*14.3 sacred poles: Or "trees", used as symbols of Asherah, the goddess of fertility.
*14.9 Ethiopia: See the note at 12.3.
*14.9 Mareshah: About forty kilometres south-west of Jerusalem.

The soldiers from Judah took everything that had belonged to the Ethiopians. ¹⁴ The people who lived in the villages around Gerar learnt what had happened and were afraid of the LORD. So Judah's army easily defeated them and carried off everything of value that they wanted from these towns. ¹⁵ They also attacked the camps where the shepherds lived and took a lot of sheep, goats, and camels. Then they went back to Jerusalem.

CHAPTER 15

Asa destroys the idols in Judah

¹ Some time later, God spoke to Azariah son of Oded. ² At once, Azariah went to Asa and said:

Listen to me, King Asa and you people of Judah and Benjamin. The LORD will be with you and help you, as long as you obey and worship him. But if you disobey him, he will desert you.

³ For a long time, the people of Israel did not worship the true God or listen to priests who could teach them about God. They refused to obey God's Law. ⁴ But whenever trouble came, Israel turned back to the LORD their God and worshipped him.

⁵ There was so much confusion in those days that it wasn't safe to go anywhere in Israel. ⁶ Nations were destroying each other, and cities were wiping out other cities, because God was causing trouble and unrest everywhere.

⁷ So you must be brave. Don't give up! God will honour you for obeying him.

⁸ As soon as Asa heard what Azariah the prophet said, he gave orders for all the idols in Judah and Benjamin to be destroyed, including those in the towns he had captured in the territory of Ephraim. He also repaired the LORD's altar that was in front of the temple porch.

⁹ Asa called together the people from Judah and Benjamin, as well as the people from the territories of Ephraim, West Manasseh, and Simeon who were living in Judah. Many of these people were now loyal to Asa, because they had seen that the LORD was with him. ¹⁰ In the third month of the fifteenth year of Asa's rule, they all met in Jerusalem. ¹¹ That same day, they took seven hundred bulls and seven thousand sheep and goats from what they had brought back from Gerar and sacrificed them as offerings to the LORD.

¹² They made a solemn promise to faithfully worship the LORD God their ancestors had worshipped, ¹³ and to put to death anyone who refused to obey him. ¹⁴ The crowd solemnly agreed to keep their promise to the LORD, then they celebrated by shouting and blowing trumpets and horns. ¹⁵ Everyone was happy because they had made this solemn promise, and in return, the LORD blessed them with peace from all their enemies.

¹⁶ Asa's grandmother Maacah had made a disgusting idol of the goddess Asherah, so he cut it down, crushed it, and burnt it in Kidron Valley. Then he removed Maacah from her position as queen mother.* ¹⁷ As long as Asa lived, he was faithful to the LORD, even though he did not destroy the local shrines⋄ in Israel. ¹⁸ He placed in the temple all the silver and gold objects that he and his father had dedicated to God.

¹⁹ There was peace in Judah until the thirty-fifth year of Asa's rule.

CHAPTER 16

King Baasha of Israel invades Judah

This is also told in 1 Kings 15.16–22

¹ In the thirty-sixth year of Asa's rule, King Baasha of Israel invaded Judah and captured the town of Ramah. He started making the town stronger, and he put troops there to stop people from going in and out of Judah.

² When Asa heard about this, he took the silver and gold from his palace and from the LORD's temple. Then he sent it to Damascus with this message for King Benhadad of Syria: ³ "I think we should sign a peace treaty, just as our fathers did. This silver and gold is a present for you. Would you please break your treaty with King Baasha of Israel and force him to leave my country?"

⁴ Benhadad did what Asa asked and sent the Syrian army into Israel. They captured the towns of Ijon, Dan, Abel-Maim,⋄ and all the towns in Naphtali where supplies were kept. ⁵ When Baasha heard about it, he stopped his work on the town of Ramah.

⁶ Asa ordered everyone in Judah to carry away the stones and wood Baasha had used to fortify Ramah. Then he fortified the towns of Geba and Mizpah with these same stones and wood.

---

*15.16 queen mother: Or "the mother of the king", which was an important position in biblical times (see 1 Kings 2.19).

Viewpoints

Are you ready to move in faith? Really ready?

Contributed by Fiona H

'The LORD is constantly watching everyone, and he gives strength to those who faithfully obey him.'

Moving in faith, tough or easy? I can testify even now that it is not easy! Asa, the king mentioned here, didn't rate moving in faith very highly.

Moving in faith often means enduring the valley lows that come with the mountain peaks. There will be times, when you are perhaps 'moving in faith' most, that you feel lost in the valley, grounded, alone, weary and weak, and your heart feels worn very low.

There will be times when you wonder where you will find the strength to carry you, as you are moving in faith, and roughing it on a hard road that cuts directly through the deepest parts of a painful valley, but let me tell you, you will never be left to stand alone in the 'journey of faith'.

The amazing thing about moving in faith, about being a Christian, is that we are not called to find our own strength.

We are called to be committed, but not to be strong in ourselves. If we faithfully persevere the trials that are refining us and carrying us further and deeper in faith, and if we remain committed to him when the going becomes toughest, then that is when and where we will find an almost supernatural strength of heart, that cannot come from anywhere but God. A strength that builds our hearts up in insight, understanding, wisdom and most importantly love.

More...

Staying committed p.1327
Faith p.1373
Coping with suffering p.1391

Hanani the prophet condemns Asa

⁷ Soon after that happened, Hanani the prophet went to Asa and said:

You depended on the king of Syria instead of depending on the LORD your God. And so, you will never defeat the Syrian army. ⁸ Remember how powerful the Ethiopian* and Libyan army was, with all their chariots and cavalry troops! You trusted the LORD to help you then, and you defeated them. ⁹ The LORD is constantly watching everyone, and he gives strength to those who faithfully obey him. But you have done a foolish thing, and your kingdom will never be at peace again.

¹⁰ When Asa heard this, he was so angry that he put Hanani in prison. Asa was also cruel to some of his people.'

Asa dies

This is also told in 1 Kings 15.23–24

¹¹ Everything Asa did while he was king is written in *The History of the Kings of Judah and Israel*. ¹² In the thirty-ninth year of his rule, he got a very bad foot disease, but he relied on doctors and refused to ask the LORD for help. ¹³ He died two years later.

¹⁴ Earlier, Asa had his own tomb cut out of a rock hill in Jerusalem. So he was buried there, and the tomb was filled with spices and sweet-smelling oils. Then the people built a bonfire in his honour.

CHAPTER 17

King Jehoshaphat of Judah

¹ Jehoshaphat son of Asa became king and strengthened his defences against Israel. ² He assigned troops to the fortified cities in Judah, as well as to other towns in Judah and to those towns in Ephraim that his father Asa had captured.

³⁻⁴ When Jehoshaphat's father had first become king of Judah, he was faithful to the LORD and refused to worship the god Baal as the kings of Israel did. Jehoshaphat followed his father's example and obeyed and worshipped the LORD. And so the LORD blessed Jehoshaphat ⁵ and helped him keep firm control of his kingdom. The people of Judah brought gifts to Jehoshaphat, but even after he became very rich and respected, ⁶ he remained completely faithful to the LORD. He

---

*16.8 Ethiopian: See the note at 12.3.

destroyed all the local shrines' in Judah, including the places where the goddess Asherah was worshipped.

7 In the third year of Jehoshaphat's rule, he chose five officials and gave them orders to teach the LORD's Law in every city and town in Judah. They were Benhail, Obadiah, Zechariah, Nethanel, and Micaiah. 8 Their assistants were the following nine Levites: Shemaiah, Nethaniah, Zebadiah, Asahel, Shemiramoth, Jehonathan, Adonijah, Tobijah, and Tob-Adonijah. Two priests, Elishama and Jehoram, also went along. 9 They carried with them a copy of the LORD's Law wherever they went and taught the people from it.

10 The nations around Judah were afraid of the LORD's power, so none of them attacked Jehoshaphat. 11 Philistines brought him silver and other gifts to keep peace. Some of the Arab people brought him seventy-seven hundred rams and the same number of goats.

12 As Jehoshaphat became more powerful, he built fortresses and cities 13 where he stored supplies. He also kept in Jerusalem some experienced soldiers 14 from the Judah and Benjamin tribes. These soldiers were grouped according to their clans.

Adnah was the commander of the troops from Judah, and he had three hundred thousand soldiers under his command. 15 Jehohanan was second in command, with two hundred and eighty thousand soldiers under him. 16 Amasiah son of Zichri, who had volunteered to serve the LORD, was third in command, with two hundred thousand soldiers under him.

17 Eliada was a brave warrior who commanded the troops from Benjamin. He had two hundred thousand soldiers under his command, all of them armed with bows and shields. 18 Jehozabad was second in command, with one hundred and eighty thousand soldiers under him. 19 These were the troops who protected the king in Jerusalem, not counting those he had assigned to the fortified cities throughout the country.

CHAPTER 18

Micaiah warns King Ahab of Israel

This is also told in 1 Kings 22.1–28

1 Jehoshaphat was now very rich and famous. He signed a treaty with King Ahab of Israel by arranging the marriage of his son and Ahab's daughter.

2 One day, Jehoshaphat went to visit Ahab in his capital city of Samaria. Ahab slaughtered sheep and cattle and prepared a big feast to honour Jehoshaphat and the officials with him. Ahab talked about attacking the city of Ramoth in Gilead,* 3 and finally asked, "Jehoshaphat, would you go with me to attack Ramoth?"

"Yes," Jehoshaphat answered. "My army is at your command. 4 But first let's ask the LORD what to do."

5 Ahab sent for four hundred prophets and asked, "Should I attack the city of Ramoth?"

"Yes!" the prophets answered. "God will help you capture the city."

6 But Jehoshaphat said, "Just to make sure, is there another of the LORD's prophets we can ask?"

7 "We could ask Micaiah son of Imlah," Ahab said. "But I hate Micaiah. He always has bad news for me."

"Don't say that!" Jehoshaphat replied. 8 Then Ahab sent someone to bring Micaiah as soon as possible.

9 All this time, Ahab and Jehoshaphat were dressed in their royal robes and were seated on their thrones at the threshing place near the gate of Samaria, listening to the prophets tell them what the LORD had said.

10 Zedekiah son of Chenaanah was one of the prophets. He had made some horns out of iron and shouted, "Ahab, the LORD says you will attack the Syrians like a bull with iron horns and wipe them out!"

11 All the prophets agreed that Ahab should attack the Syrians at Ramoth and promised that the LORD would help him defeat them.

12 Meanwhile, the messenger who went to get Micaiah whispered, "Micaiah, all the prophets have good news for Ahab. Now go and say the same thing."

13 "I'll say whatever the living LORD my God tells me to say," Micaiah replied.

14 Then Micaiah went up to Ahab, who asked, "Micaiah, should we attack Ramoth?"

"Yes!" Micaiah answered. "The LORD will help you capture the city."

15 Ahab shouted, "Micaiah, I've told you over and over again to tell me the truth! What does the LORD really say?"

---

*18.2 attacking the city of Ramoth in Gilead: The Syrians had taken control of Ramoth (see 1 Kings 22.3–4).

16 Micaiah answered, "In a vision* I saw Israelite soldiers wandering around, lost in the hills like sheep without a shepherd. The LORD said, 'These troops have no leader. They should go home and not fight.' "

17 Ahab turned to Jehoshaphat and said, "I told you he would bring me bad news!"

18 Micaiah replied:

I then saw the LORD seated on his throne with every creature in heaven gathered around him. 19 The LORD asked, "Who can trick Ahab and make him go to Ramoth where he will be killed?"

They talked about it for a while, 20 then finally a spirit came forward and said to the LORD, "I can trick Ahab."

"How?" the LORD asked.

21 "I'll make Ahab's prophets lie to him."

"Good!" the LORD replied. "Now go and do it. You will be successful."

22 Ahab, this is exactly what has happened. The LORD made all your prophets lie to you, and he knows you will soon be destroyed.

23 Zedekiah walked over and slapped Micaiah on the face. Then he asked, "Do you really think the LORD would speak to you and not to me?"

24 Micaiah answered, "You'll find out on the day you have to hide in the back room of some house."

25 Ahab shouted, "Arrest Micaiah! Take him to Prince Joash and Governor Amon of Samaria. 26 Tell them to put him in prison and to give him nothing but bread and water until I come back safely."

27 Micaiah said, "If you do come back, I was wrong about what the LORD wanted me to say." Then he told the crowd, "Don't forget what I said!"

Ahab dies at Ramoth
This is also told in 1 Kings 22.29–35

28 Ahab and Jehoshaphat led their armies to Ramoth in Gilead. 29 Before they went into battle, Ahab said, "Jehoshaphat, I'll disguise myself, but you wear your royal robe." Ahab disguised himself and went into battle.

30 The king of Syria had ordered his chariot commanders to attack only Ahab. 31 So when they saw Jehoshaphat in his robe, they thought he was Ahab and started to attack him. But Jehoshaphat prayed, and the LORD made the Syrian soldiers stop. 32 And when they realized he wasn't Ahab, they left him alone.

33 However, during the fighting a soldier shot an arrow without even aiming, and it hit Ahab between two pieces of his armour. He shouted to his chariot driver, "I've been hit! Get me out of here!"

34 The fighting lasted all day, with Ahab propped up in his chariot so he could see the Syrian troops. He stayed there until evening, and by sundown he was dead.

CHAPTER 19

1 Jehoshaphat returned safely to his palace in Jerusalem. 2 But the prophet Jehu son of Hanani met him and said:

By helping that wicked Ahab, you have made friends with someone who hates the LORD. Now the LORD God is angry with you! 3 But not everything about you is bad. You destroyed the sacred poles* used in worshipping the goddess Asherah — that shows you have tried to obey the LORD.

Jehoshaphat appoints judges to settle cases

4 Jehoshaphat lived in Jerusalem, but he often travelled through his kingdom, from Beersheba in the south to the edge of the hill country of Ephraim in the north. He talked with the people and convinced them to turn back to the LORD God and worship him, just as their ancestors had done.

5 He assigned judges to each of the fortified cities in Judah 6 and told them:

Be careful when you make your decisions in court, because these are the LORD's people, and he will know what you decide. 7 So do your work in honour of him and know that he won't allow you to be unfair to anyone or to take bribes.

8 Jehoshaphat also chose some Levites, some priests, and some of the family leaders, and he appointed them to serve as judges in Jerusalem. 9 He told them:

Faithfully serve the LORD! 10 The people of Judah will bring you legal cases that involve every type of crime, including murder. You must settle these cases and

*18.16 vision: In ancient times, prophets often told about future events from what they had seen in visions or dreams.
See also: 18.16: Num 27.17; Ezek 34.5; Matt 9.36; Mark 6.34.

*19.3 sacred poles: See the note at 14.3.

warn the people to stop sinning against the LORD, so that he won't get angry and punish Judah. Remember, if you follow these instructions, you won't be held responsible for anything that happens.

¹¹ Amariah the high priest will have the final say in any religious case. And Zebadiah, the leader⸳ of the Judah tribe, will have the final say in all other cases. The rest of the Levites will serve as your assistants. Be brave, and I pray that the LORD will help you do right.

CHAPTER 20

Moab and Ammon are defeated

¹ Some time later, the armies of Moab and Ammon, together with the Meunites,⸳ went to war against Jehoshaphat. ² Messengers told Jehoshaphat, "A large army from Edom⸳ east of the Dead Sea has invaded our country. They have already reached En-Gedi."*

³ Jehoshaphat was afraid, so he asked the LORD what to do. He then told the people of Judah to go without eating to show their sorrow. ⁴ They immediately left for Jerusalem to ask for the LORD's help.

⁵ After everyone from Judah and Jerusalem had come together at the LORD's temple, Jehoshaphat stood in front of the new courtyard ⁶ and prayed:

You, LORD, are the God our ancestors worshipped, and from heaven you rule every nation in the world. You are so powerful that no one can defeat you. ⁷ Our God, you forced out the nations who lived in this land before your people Israel came here, and you gave it to the descendants of your friend Abraham for ever. ⁸ Our ancestors lived in this land and built a temple to honour you. ⁹ They believed that whenever this land is struck by war or disease or famine, your people can pray to you at the temple, and you will hear their prayer and save them.

¹⁰ You can see that the armies of Ammon, Moab, and Edom are attacking us! Those are the nations you would not let our ancestors invade on their way from Egypt, so these nations were not destroyed. ¹¹ Now they are coming to take back the

land you gave us. ¹² Aren't you going to punish them? We won't stand a chance when this army attacks. We don't know what to do — we are begging for your help.

¹³ While every man, woman, and child of Judah was standing there at the temple, ¹⁴ the LORD's Spirit suddenly spoke to Jahaziel, a Levite from the Asaph clan.⸳ ¹⁵ Then Jahaziel said:

Your Majesty and everyone from Judah and Jerusalem, the LORD says that you don't need to be afraid or let this powerful army discourage you. God will fight on your side! ¹⁶ So here's what you must do. Tomorrow the enemy armies will march through the desert around the town of Jeruel. March down and meet them at the town of Ziz as they come up the valley. ¹⁷ You won't even have to fight. Just take your positions and watch the LORD rescue you from your enemy. Don't be afraid. Just do as you're told. And as you march out tomorrow, the LORD will be there with you.

¹⁸ Jehoshaphat bowed low to the ground and everyone worshipped the LORD. ¹⁹ Then some Levites from the Kohath and Korah clans stood up and shouted praises to the LORD God of Israel.

²⁰ Early the next morning, as everyone got ready to leave for the desert near Tekoa, Jehoshaphat stood up and said, "Listen my friends, if we trust the LORD God and believe what these prophets have told us, the LORD will help us, and we will be successful." ²¹ Then he explained his plan and appointed men to march in front of the army and praise the LORD for his holy power by singing:⸳

"Praise the LORD!
His love never ends."

²² As soon as they began singing, the LORD confused the enemy camp, ²³ so that the Ammonite and Moabite troops attacked and completely destroyed those from Edom. Then they turned against each other and fought until the entire camp was wiped out! ²⁴ When Judah's army reached the tower that overlooked the desert, they saw that every soldier in the enemy's army was lying dead on the ground. ²⁵ So Jehoshaphat and his troops went into the camp to carry away everything of value. They found a large herd of livestock,⸳ a lot of equipment, clothes,⸳ and other valuable things. It took them three days to carry it all away, and there was still some left over.

---

*20.2 En-Gedi: The Hebrew text has "Hazazon-Tamar, also known as En-Gedi", a city on the west shore of the Dead Sea, about forty kilometres south-east of Jerusalem.

See also: 20.7: Isa 41.8; Jam 2.23.   20.10: Deut 2.4–19.

See also: 20.15–17: Deut 20.1–4.   20.17: Exod 14.13–14.

26 Then on the fourth day, everyone came together in Beracah Valley and sang praises to the LORD. That's why that place was called Praise Valley.*

27-28 Jehoshaphat led the crowd back to Jerusalem. And as they marched, they played harps and blew trumpets. They were very happy because the LORD had given them victory over their enemies, so when they reached the city, they went straight to the temple.

29 When the other nations heard how the LORD had fought against Judah's enemies, they were too afraid 30 to invade Judah. The LORD let Jehoshaphat's kingdom be at peace.

Jehoshaphat dies

This is also told in 1 Kings 22.41-50

31 Jehoshaphat was thirty-five years old when he became king of Judah, and he ruled from Jerusalem for twenty-five years. His mother was Azubah daughter of Shilhi. 32 Jehoshaphat obeyed the LORD, just as his father Asa had done, 33 but he did not destroy the local shrines.' So the people still worshipped foreign gods, instead of faithfully serving the God their ancestors had worshipped.

34 Everything else Jehoshaphat did while he was king is written in the records of Jehu son of Hanani that are included in *The History of the Kings of Israel.*

35 While Jehoshaphat was king, he signed a peace treaty with Ahaziah the wicked king of Israel. 36 They agreed to build several seagoing ships* at Ezion-Geber. 37 But the prophet Eliezer' warned Jehoshaphat, "The LORD will destroy these ships because you have supported Ahaziah." The ships were wrecked and never sailed.

CHAPTER 21

1 Jehoshaphat died and was buried beside his ancestors in Jerusalem, and his son Jehoram became king.

King Jehoram of Judah

This is also told in 2 Kings 8.16-24

2 King Jehoshaphat had seven sons: Jehoram, Azariah, Jehiel, Zechariah, Azariah, Michael, and Shephatiah. 3 Jehoshaphat gave each of them silver and gold, as well as other

valuable gifts. He also put them in charge of the fortified cities in Judah, but he had chosen his eldest son Jehoram to succeed him as king.

4 After Jehoram had taken control of Judah, he had his brothers killed, as well as some of the nation's leaders. 5 He was thirty-two years old when he became king, and he ruled eight years from Jerusalem.

6 Jehoram married Ahab's daughter and followed the sinful example of Ahab's family and the other kings of Israel. He disobeyed the LORD by doing wrong, 7 but because the LORD had made a solemn promise to King David that someone from his family would always rule in Judah, he refused to wipe out David's descendants.

8 While Jehoram was king, the people of Edom rebelled and chose their own king. 9 Jehoram, his officers, and his cavalry marched to Edom, where the Edomite army surrounded them. He escaped during the night, 10 but Judah was never able to regain control of Edom. Even the town of Libnah* rebelled at that time.

Those things happened because Jehoram had turned away from the LORD, the God his ancestors had worshipped. 11 Jehoram even built local shrines' in the hills of Judah and let the people sin against the LORD by worshipping foreign gods.

12 One day, Jehoram received a letter from Elijah the prophet that said:

I have a message for you from the LORD God your ancestor David worshipped. He knows that you have not followed the example of Jehoshaphat your father or Asa your grandfather. 13 Instead you have acted like those sinful kings of Israel and have encouraged the people of Judah to stop worshipping the LORD, just as Ahab and his descendants did. You even murdered your own brothers, who were better men than you.

14 Because you have done these terrible things, the LORD will severely punish the people in your kingdom, including your own family, and he will destroy everything you own. 15 You will be struck with a painful stomach disease and suffer until you die.

---

*21.10 Even the town of Libnah:** This was a town on the border between Philistia and Judah, which means that Jehoram was facing rebellion on both sides of his kingdom.

See also: 21.7: 1 King 11.36. **21.8:** Gen 27.40.

---

*20.26 Beracah Valley . . . sang praises . . . Praise Valley:** In Hebrew the name "Beracah" means "praise".
*20.36 seagoing ships:** See the note at 9.21.

¹⁶ The LORD later caused the Philistines and the Arabs who lived near the Ethiopians* to become angry with Jehoram. ¹⁷ They invaded Judah and stole the royal property from the palace, and they led Jehoram's wives and sons away as prisoners. The only one left behind was Ahaziah,' his youngest son.

¹⁸ After this happened, the LORD struck Jehoram with an incurable stomach disease. ¹⁹ About two years later, Jehoram died in terrible pain. No bonfire was built to honour him, even though the people had done this for his ancestors.

²⁰ Jehoram was thirty-two years old when he became king, and he ruled eight years from Jerusalem. He died, and no one even felt sad. He was buried in Jerusalem, but not in the royal tombs.

CHAPTER 22

King Ahaziah of Judah

This is also told in 2 Kings 8.25–29; 9.21,27–28

¹ Earlier, when the Arabs led a raid against Judah, they killed all of Jehoram's sons, except Ahaziah, the youngest one. So the people of Jerusalem crowned him their king. ² He was twenty-two' years old at the time, and he ruled only one year from Jerusalem.

Ahaziah's mother was Athaliah, a granddaughter of King Omri of Israel, ³ and she encouraged her son to sin against the LORD. He followed the evil example of King Ahab and his descendants. ⁴ In fact, after his father's death, Ahaziah sinned against the LORD by appointing some of Ahab's relatives to be his advisers.

Their advice led to his downfall. ⁵ He listened to them and went with King Joram of Israel to attack King Hazael and the Syrian troops at Ramoth in Gilead. Joram was wounded in that battle, ⁶ and he went to the town of Jezreel to recover. And Ahaziah later went there to visit him. ⁷ It was during that visit that God had Ahaziah put to death.

When Ahaziah arrived at Jezreel, he and Joram went to meet with Jehu, grandson of Nimshi. The LORD had already told Jehu to kill every male in Ahab's family, ⁸ and while Jehu was doing that, he saw some of Judah's leaders and Ahaziah's nephews who had come with Ahaziah. Jehu killed them on the spot, ⁹ then gave orders to find Ahaziah. Jehu's officers found him hiding in Samaria. They brought Ahaziah to Jehu, who immediately put him to death. They buried Ahaziah only because they respected Jehoshaphat his grandfather, who had done his best to obey the LORD.

There was no one from Ahaziah's family left to become king of Judah.

Queen Athaliah of Judah

This is also told in 2 Kings 11.1–3

¹⁰ As soon as Athaliah heard that her son King Ahaziah was dead, she decided to kill any relative who could possibly become king. She would have done just that, ¹¹ but Jehosheba' rescued Joash son of Ahaziah just as the others were about to be murdered. Jehosheba, who was Jehoram's daughter and Ahaziah's half-sister, was married to Jehoiada the priest. So she was able to hide her nephew Joash and his personal servant in a bedroom in the LORD's temple where he was safe from Athaliah. ¹² Joash hid in the temple with them for six years while Athaliah ruled as queen of Judah.

CHAPTER 23

Jehoiada makes Joash king of Judah

This is also told in 2 Kings 11.4–21

¹ After Ahaziah's son Joash had hidden in the temple for six years, Jehoiada the priest knew that something had to be done. So he made sure he had the support of several army officers. They were Azariah son of Jeroham, Ishmael son of Jehohanan, Azariah son of Obed, Maaseiah son of Adaiah, and Elishaphat son of Zichri. ² These five men went to the towns in Judah and called together the Levites and the clan leaders. They all came to Jerusalem ³ and gathered at the temple, where they agreed to help Joash.

Jehoiada said to them:

Joash will be our next king, because long ago the LORD promised that one of David's descendants would always be king. ⁴ Here is what we will do. Three groups of priests and Levites will be on guard duty on the Sabbath — one group will guard the gates of the temple, ⁵ one will guard the palace, and the other will guard Foundation Gate. The rest of you will stand guard in the temple courtyards. ⁶ Only the priests and Levites who are on duty will be able to enter the temple, because they will be the only ones who have gone through the

---

ceremony to make themselves clean and acceptable. The others must stay outside in the courtyards, just as the LORD has commanded. 7 You Levites must protect King Joash. Don't let him out of your sight! And keep your swords ready to kill anyone who comes into the temple.

8 The Levites and the people of Judah followed Jehoiada's orders. The guards going off duty were not allowed to go home, and so each commander had all his guards available — those going off duty as well as those coming on duty. 9 Jehoiada went into the temple and brought out the swords and shields that had belonged to King David, and he gave them to the commanders. 10 They gave the weapons to the guards, and Jehoiada then made sure that the guards took their positions around the temple and the altar to protect the king on every side.

11 Jehoiada and his sons brought Joash outside, where they placed the crown on his head and gave him a copy of the instructions for ruling the nation. Olive oil was poured on his head to show that he was now king, and the crowd cheered and shouted, "Long live the king!"

12 As soon as Queen Athaliah heard the crowd cheering for Joash, she went to the temple. 13 There she saw Joash standing by one of the columns near the entrance, which was the usual place for the king. The commanders and the trumpet players were standing next to him, and the musicians were playing instruments and leading the people as they celebrated and blew trumpets. Athaliah tore her clothes in anger and shouted, "You betrayed me, you traitors!"

14 Straight away, Jehoiada said to the army commanders, "Don't kill her near the LORD's temple. Take her out in front of the troops, and be sure to kill all her followers!" 15 She tried to escape, but the commanders caught and killed her near the gate where horses are led into the palace.

16 Jehoiada asked King Joash and the people to join with him in being faithful to the LORD. They agreed, 17 then rushed to the temple of the god Baal and tore it down. They smashed the altars and the idols and killed Mattan the priest of Baal in front of the altars.

18 Jehoiada assigned the priests and Levites their duties at the temple, just as David had done. They were in charge of offering sacrifices to the LORD according to the Law of Moses, and they were responsible for leading the celebrations with singing. 19 Jehoiada

ordered the guards at the temple gates to keep out anyone who was unclean.

20 Finally, Jehoiada called together the army commanders, the most important citizens of Judah, and the government officials. The crowd of people followed them as they led Joash from the temple, through the Upper Gate, and into the palace, where he took his place as king of Judah.

21 Everyone celebrated because Athaliah had been killed and Jerusalem was peaceful again.

CHAPTER 24

King Joash of Judah

This is also told in 2 Kings 12.1–16

1 Joash was only seven years old when he became king of Judah, and he ruled forty years from Jerusalem. His mother Zibiah was from the town of Beersheba.

2 While Jehoiada the priest was alive, Joash obeyed the LORD by doing right. 3 Jehoiada even chose two women for Joash to marry so he could have a family.

4 Some time later, Joash decided it was time to repair the temple. 5 He called together the priests and Levites and said, "Go everywhere in Judah and collect the annual tax from the people. I want this done straight away — we need that money to repair the temple."

But the Levites were in no hurry to follow the king's orders. 6 So he sent for Jehoiada the high priest and asked, "Why didn't you send the Levites to collect the taxes? The LORD's servant Moses and the people agreed long ago that this tax would be collected and used to pay for the upkeep of the sacred tent. 7 And now we need it to repair the temple because the sons of that evil woman Athaliah came in and wrecked it. They even used some of the sacred objects to worship the god Baal."

8 Joash gave orders for a wooden box to be made and had it placed outside, near the gate of the temple. 9 He then sent letters everywhere in Judah and Jerusalem, asking everyone to bring their taxes to the temple, just as Moses had required their ancestors to do.

10 The people and their leaders agreed, and they brought their money to Jerusalem and placed it in the box. 11 Each day, after the Levites took the box into the temple, the king's secretary and the high priest's assistant would take out the money and count it. Then the empty box would be taken back outside.

See also: 24.6: Exod 30.11–16.

This happened day after day, and soon a large amount of money was collected. [12] Joash and Jehoiada turned the money over to the men who were supervising the repairs to the temple. They used the money to hire stonecutters, carpenters, and experts in working with iron and bronze.

[13] These workers went straight to work repairing the temple, and when they had finished, it looked as good as new. [14] They did not use all the tax money for the repairs, so the rest of it was handed over to Joash and Jehoiada, who then used it to make dishes and other gold and silver objects for the temple.

Sacrifices to please the LORD* were offered regularly in the temple for as long as Jehoiada lived. [15] He died at the ripe old age of one hundred and thirty years, [16] and he was buried in the royal tombs in Jerusalem, because he had done so much good for the people of Israel, for God, and for the temple.

Joash turns away from the LORD

[17] After the death of Jehoiada the priest, the leaders of Judah went to Joash and talked him into doing what they wanted. [18] Straight away, the people of Judah stopped worshipping in the temple of the LORD God, and they started worshipping idols and the symbols of the goddess Asherah. These sinful things made the LORD God angry with the people of Judah and Jerusalem, [19] but he still sent prophets who warned them to turn back to him. The people refused to listen.

[20] God's Spirit spoke to Zechariah son of Jehoiada the priest, and Zechariah told everyone that God was saying: "Why are you disobeying me and my laws? This will only bring punishment! You have deserted me, so now I will desert you."

[21-22] King Joash forgot that Zechariah's father had always been a loyal friend. So when the people of Judah plotted to kill Zechariah, Joash joined them and gave orders for them to stone him to death in the courtyard of the temple. As Zechariah was dying, he said, "I pray that the LORD will see this and punish all of you."

Joash is killed

[23] In the spring of the following year, the Syrian army invaded Judah and Jerusalem,

killing all the nation's leaders. They collected everything of value that belonged to the people and took it back to their king in Damascus. [24] The Syrian army was very small, but the LORD let them defeat Judah's large army, because he was punishing Joash and the people of Judah for turning away from him.

[25-26] Joash was severely wounded during the battle, and as soon as the Syrians left Judah, two of his officials, Zabad and Jehozabad,' decided to avenge the death of Zechariah. They plotted and killed Joash while he was in bed, recovering from his wounds. Joash was buried in Jerusalem, but not in the royal tombs. [27] *The History of the Kings* also tells more about the sons of Joash, what the prophets said about him, and how he repaired the temple. Amaziah son of Joash became king after his father's death.

CHAPTER 25

King Amaziah of Judah

This is also told in 2 Kings 14.1–6

[1] Amaziah was twenty-five years old when he became king, and he ruled twenty-nine years from Jerusalem, the home town of his mother Jehoaddin.'

[2] Even though Amaziah obeyed the LORD by doing right, he refused to be completely faithful. [3] For example, as soon as he had control of Judah, he arrested and killed the officers who had murdered his father. [4] But the children of those officers were not killed; the LORD had commanded in the Law of Moses that only the people who sinned were to be punished.*

Edom is defeated

This is also told in 2 Kings 14.7

[5] Amaziah sent a message to the tribes of Judah and Benjamin and called together all the men who were twenty years old and older. Three hundred thousand men went to Jerusalem, all of them ready for battle and able to fight with spears and shields. Amaziah grouped these soldiers according to their clans and put them under the command of his army officers. [6] Amaziah also paid about three thousand four hundred kilogrammes of silver to hire one hundred thousand soldiers from Israel.

---

*24.14 Sacrifices to please the LORD: See the note at 1.6.
See also: 24.20–21: Matt 23.35; Luke 11.51.

*25.4 the LORD had commanded . . . punished: See Deuteronomy 24.16.

7 One of God's prophets said, "Your Majesty, don't let these Israelite soldiers march into battle with you. The LORD has refused to help anyone from the northern kingdom of Israel, 8 and so he will let your enemies defeat you, even if you fight hard. He is the one who brings both victory and defeat."

9 Amaziah replied, "What am I supposed to do about all the silver I paid those troops?"

"The LORD will give you back even more than you paid," the prophet answered.

10 Amaziah ordered the troops from Israel to go home, but when they left, they were furious with the people of Judah.

11 After Amaziah got his courage back, he led his troops to Salt Valley, where he killed ten thousand Edomite soldiers in battle. 12 He captured ten thousand more soldiers and dragged them to the top of a high cliff. Then he pushed them over the side, and they were all killed on the rocks below.

13 Meanwhile, the Israelite troops that Amaziah had sent home raided the towns in Judah between Samaria and Beth-Horon. They killed three thousand people and carried off their possessions.

14 After Amaziah had defeated the Edomite army, he returned to Jerusalem. He took with him the idols of the Edomite gods and set them up. Then he bowed down and offered them sacrifices. 15 This made the LORD very angry, and he sent a prophet to ask Amaziah, "Why would you worship these foreign gods that couldn't even save their own people from your attack?"

16 But before the prophet finished speaking, Amaziah interrupted and said, "You're not one of my advisers! Don't say another word, or I'll have you killed."

The prophet stopped. But then he added, "First you sinned and now you've ignored my warning. It's clear that God has decided to punish you!"

Israel defeats Judah

This is also told in 2 Kings 14.8–14

17 King Amaziah of Judah talked with his officials, then sent a message to King Jehoash▸ of Israel: "Come out and face me in battle!"

18 Jehoash sent back a reply that said:

Once upon a time, a small thorn bush in Lebanon arranged the marriage between his son and the daughter of a large cedar tree. But a wild animal came along and trampled the small bush.

19 Amaziah, you think you're so powerful because you defeated Edom. But stay at home and do your celebrating. If you cause any trouble, both you and your kingdom of Judah will be destroyed.

20 God made Amaziah stubborn because he was planning to punish him for worshipping the Edomite gods. Amaziah refused to listen to Jehoash's warning, 21 so Jehoash led his army to the town of Beth-Shemesh in Judah to attack Amaziah and his troops. 22 During the battle, Judah's army was crushed. Every soldier from Judah ran back home, 23 and Jehoash captured Amaziah.

Jehoash took Amaziah with him when he went to attack Jerusalem. Jehoash broke down the city wall from Ephraim Gate to Corner Gate, a section nearly two hundred metres long. 24 He carried away the gold, the silver, and all the valuable furnishings from God's temple where the descendants of Obed-Edom stood guard. He robbed the king's treasury, took hostages, then returned to Samaria.

Amaziah is killed

This is also told in 2 Kings 14.15–20

25 Amaziah lived fifteen years after Jehoash died. 26 Everything else Amaziah did while he was king is written in *The History of the Kings of Judah and Israel.*

27 As soon as Amaziah started disobeying the LORD, some people in Jerusalem plotted against Amaziah. He was able to escape to the town of Lachish, but another group of people caught him and killed him there. 28 His body was taken to Jerusalem on horseback and buried beside his ancestors.

CHAPTER 26

King Uzziah of Judah

This is also told in 2 Kings 14.21–22; 15.1–7

1-3 After the death of King Amaziah, the people of Judah crowned his son Uzziah▸ king, even though he was only sixteen at the time. Uzziah ruled fifty-two years from Jerusalem, the home town of his mother Jecoliah. During his rule, he recaptured and rebuilt the town of Elath.

4 He obeyed the LORD by doing right, as his father Amaziah had done. 5 Zechariah was Uzziah's adviser and taught him to obey God. And so, as long as Zechariah was alive, Uzziah was faithful to God, and God made him successful.

Holy history

Farming

Farming was one of the main occupations of ancient times. There were no shops as we know them; you couldn't nip to the out-of-Jerusalem superstore; you had to grow stuff. So most families kept some livestock and grew some crops. Even kings like King Uzziah got involved (2 Chronicles 26.10).

Livestock

The main livestock were goats and sheep. The Israelites, because of the restrictions on them in the Law, did not eat pigs. Farmers also had oxen, donkeys and mules to help with ploughing and transport. They also had some geese and ducks, but chickens only arrived in the 6th century BC, when they were brought back from the Babylonian captivity.

Arable

Basic crops included wheat and barley. Farmers also grew vegetables, such as leeks, onions, cucumbers and melons; fruit trees like pomegranates, dates and figs; olive and nut trees and herbs such as hyssop, dill, mint and cumin. Walls were often built around fields to keep animals such as goats out.

Vineyards

Wine was a basic part of the ancient diet. Then, as today, wine was made by crushing grapes in a press, and letting the juice ferment. According to Genesis, Noah was the first person to make wine (Genesis 9.20). Stone watchtowers were often built in the vineyards and farmers often slept in the tower, on constant watch to protect the crop from predators such as birds and foxes.

More...

Food and drink p.355

---

⁶ While Uzziah was king, he started a war against the Philistines. He smashed the walls of the cities of Gath, Jabneh, and Ashdod, then rebuilt towns around Ashdod and in other parts of Philistia. ⁷ God helped him defeat the Philistines, the Arabs living in Gur-Baal, and the Meunites. ⁸ Even the Ammonites paid taxes to Uzziah. He became very powerful, and people who lived as far away as Egypt heard about him.

⁹ In Jerusalem, Uzziah built fortified towers at the Corner Gate, the Valley Gate, and the place where the city wall turned inward.⸀
¹⁰ He also built defence towers out in the desert.

He owned such a large herd of livestock in the western foothills and in the flat lands, that he had cisterns dug there to catch the rainwater. He loved farming, so he had crops and vineyards planted in the hill country wherever there was fertile soil, and he hired farmers to take care of them.

¹¹ Uzziah's army was always ready for battle. Jeiel and Maaseiah were the officers who kept track of the number of soldiers, and these two men were under the command of Hananiah, one of Uzziah's officials.
¹²⁻¹³ There were 307,500 trained soldiers, all under the command of 2,600 clan leaders. These powerful troops protected the king against any enemy. ¹⁴ Uzziah supplied his army with shields, spears, helmets, armour, bows, and stones used for slinging. ¹⁵ Some of his skilled workers invented machines that could shoot arrows and sling large stones. Uzziah set these up in Jerusalem at his defence towers and at the corners of the city wall.

God helped Uzziah become more and more powerful, and he was famous all over the world.

Uzziah becomes too proud

¹⁶ Uzziah became proud of his power, and this led to his downfall.

One day, Uzziah disobeyed the LORD his God by going into the temple and burning incense as an offering to him.* ¹⁷ Azariah the priest and eighty other brave priests followed Uzziah into the temple ¹⁸ and said, "Your Majesty, this isn't right! You are not allowed to burn incense to the LORD. That must be

---

*26.16 going into the temple and burning incense as an offering to him: This was to be done only by priests (see Exodus 30.1–10; Numbers 16.39–40).
See also: 26.18: Exod 30.7–8; Num 3.10.

done only by priests who are descendants of Aaron. You will have to leave! You have sinned against the LORD, and so he will no longer bless you."

¹⁹ Uzziah, who was standing next to the incense altar at the time, was holding the incense burner, ready to offer incense to the LORD. He became very angry when he heard Azariah's warning, and leprosy* suddenly appeared on his forehead! ²⁰ Azariah and the other priests saw it and immediately told him to leave the temple. Uzziah realized that the LORD had punished him, so he hurried to get outside.

²¹ Uzziah had leprosy for the rest of his life. He was no longer allowed in the temple or in his own palace. That's why his son Jotham lived there and ruled in his place.

²² Everything else Uzziah did while he was king is in the records written by the prophet Isaiah son of Amoz. ²³ Since Uzziah had leprosy, he could not be buried in the royal tombs. Instead, he was buried in a nearby cemetery that the kings owned. His son Jotham then became king.

CHAPTER 27

King Jotham of Judah

This is also told in 2 Kings 15.32–38

¹ Jotham was twenty-five years old when he became king of Judah, and he ruled from Jerusalem for sixteen years. Jerushah his mother was the daughter of Zadok.

² Jotham obeyed the LORD and did right. He followed the example of his father Uzziah, except he never burnt incense in the temple as his father had done. But the people of Judah kept sinning against the LORD.

³ Jotham rebuilt the Upper Gate of the temple and did a lot of work to repair the wall near Mount Ophel. ⁴ He built towns in the mountains of Judah and built fortresses and defence towers in the forests.

⁵ During his rule he attacked and defeated the Ammonites. Then every year for the next three years, he forced them to pay three thousand four hundred kilogrammes of silver, one thousand tonnes of wheat, and one thousand tonnes of barley.

⁶ Jotham remained faithful to the LORD his God and became a very powerful king.

⁷ Everything else Jotham did while he was king, including the wars he fought, is written in *The History of the Kings of Israel and Judah.* ⁸ After he had ruled Judah sixteen years, he died at the age of forty-one. ⁹ He was buried in Jerusalem, and his son Ahaz became king.

CHAPTER 28

King Ahaz of Judah

This is also told in 2 Kings 16.1–4

¹ Ahaz was twenty years old when he became king of Judah, and he ruled from Jerusalem for sixteen years.

Ahaz was nothing like his ancestor David. Ahaz disobeyed the LORD ² and was as sinful as the kings of Israel. He made idols of the god Baal, ³ and he offered sacrifices in Hinnom Valley. Worst of all, Ahaz sacrificed his own sons, which was a disgusting custom of the nations that the LORD had forced out of Israel. ⁴ Ahaz offered sacrifices at the local shrines,◦ as well as on every hill and in the shade of large trees.

Syria and Israel attack Judah

This is also told in 2 Kings 16.5–6

⁵⁻⁶ Ahaz and the people of Judah sinned and turned away from the LORD, the God their ancestors had worshipped. So the LORD punished them by letting their enemies defeat them.

The king of Syria attacked Judah and took many of its people to Damascus as prisoners. King Pekah◦ of Israel later defeated Judah and killed one hundred and twenty thousand of its bravest soldiers in one day. ⁷ During that battle, an Israelite soldier named Zichri killed three men from Judah: Maaseiah the king's son; Azrikam, the official in charge of the palace; and Elkanah, the king's second in command. ⁸ The Israelite troops captured two hundred thousand women and children and took them back to their capital city of Samaria, along with a large amount of their possessions. They did these things even though the people of Judah were their own relatives.

Oded the prophet condemns Israel

⁹ Oded lived in Samaria and was one of the LORD's prophets. He met Israel's army on their way back from Judah and said to them:

---

*26.19 leprosy: The word translated "leprosy" was used for many different kinds of skin diseases.
See also: 26.23: Isa 6.1.

See also: 28.5–6: 2 King 16.5; Isa 7.1.

The LORD God of your ancestors let you defeat Judah's army only because he was angry with them. But you should not have been so cruel! ¹⁰ If you make slaves of the people of Judah and Jerusalem, you will be as guilty as they are of sinning against the LORD.

¹¹ Send these prisoners back home — they are your own relatives. If you don't, the LORD will punish you in his anger.

¹² About the same time, four of Israel's leaders arrived. They were Azariah son of Johanan, Berechiah son of Meshillemoth, Jehizkiah son of Shallum, and Amasa son of Hadlai. They agreed with Oded that the Israelite troops were wrong, ¹³ and they said:

If you bring these prisoners into Samaria, that will be one more thing we've done to sin against the LORD. And he is already angry enough with us.

¹⁴ So in front of the leaders and the crowd, the troops handed over their prisoners and the property they had taken from Judah. ¹⁵ The four leaders took some of the stolen clothes and gave them to the prisoners who needed something to wear. They later gave them all a new change of clothes and shoes, then provided something for them to eat and drink, and cleaned their wounds with olive oil. They gave donkeys to those who were too weak to walk, and led all of them back to Jericho, the city known for its palm trees. The leaders then returned to Samaria.

Ahaz asks the king of Assyria for help
This is also told in 2 Kings 16.7–9

¹⁶⁻¹⁸ Some time later, the Edomites attacked the eastern part of Judah again and carried away prisoners. And at the same time, the Philistines raided towns in the western foothills and in the Southern Desert. They conquered the towns of Beth-Shemesh, Aijalon, Gederoth, Soco, Timnah, and Gimzo, including the villages around them. Then some of the Philistines went to live in these places.

Ahaz sent a message to King Tiglath Pileser of Assyria and begged for help. ¹⁹ But God was punishing Judah with these disasters, because Ahaz had disobeyed him and refused to stop Judah from sinning. ²⁰ So Tiglath Pileser came to Judah, but instead of helping, he made things worse. ²¹ Ahaz gave him gifts from the LORD's temple and the king's palace, as well as from the homes of

Israel's other leaders. The Assyrian king still refused to help Ahaz.

The final sin of Ahaz and his death

²² Even after all these terrible things happened to Ahaz, he sinned against the LORD even worse than before. ²³ He said to himself, "The Syrian gods must have helped their kings defeat me. Perhaps if I offer sacrifices to those gods, they will help me." That was the sin that finally led to the downfall of Ahaz, as well as to the destruction of Judah.

²⁴ Ahaz collected all the furnishings of the temple and smashed them to pieces. Then he locked the doors to the temple and set up altars to foreign gods on every street corner in Jerusalem. ²⁵ In every city and town in Judah he built local shrines* to worship foreign gods. All this made the LORD God of his ancestors very angry.

²⁶ Everything else Ahaz did while he was king is written in *The History of the Kings of Judah and Israel.* ²⁷ Ahaz died and was buried in Jerusalem, but not in the royal tombs. His son Hezekiah then became king.

King Hezekiah and the Assyrian invasion
CHAPTER 29
King Hezekiah of Judah
This is also told in 2 Kings 18.1–3

¹ Hezekiah was twenty-five years old when he became king of Judah, and he ruled twenty-nine years from Jerusalem. His mother was Abijah daughter of Zechariah. ² Hezekiah obeyed the LORD by doing right, just as his ancestor David had done.

The temple is purified

³ In the first month* of the first year of Hezekiah's rule, he unlocked the doors to the LORD's temple and had them repaired.* ⁴ Then he called the priests and Levites to the east courtyard of the temple ⁵ and said:

---

*29.3 first month: Abib (also called Nisan), the first month of the Hebrew calendar, from about mid-March to mid-April.
*29.3 he unlocked the doors . . . repaired: King Ahaz had locked the doors and stopped everyone from worshipping the LORD (see 28.24–25).
See also: 28.27: Isa 14.28.

It's time to purify the temple of the LORD God of our ancestors. You Levites must first go through the ceremony to make yourselves clean, then go into the temple and bring out everything that is unclean and unacceptable to the LORD. ⁶ Some of our ancestors were unfaithful and disobeyed the LORD our God. Not only did they turn their backs on the LORD, but they also completely ignored his temple. ⁷ They locked the doors, then let the lamps go out and stopped burning incense and offering sacrifices to him. ⁸ The LORD became terribly angry with the people of Judah and Jerusalem, and everyone was shocked and horrified at what he did to punish them. Not only were ⁹ our ancestors killed in battle, but our own children and wives were taken captive.

¹⁰ So I have decided to renew our agreement with the LORD God of Israel. Perhaps then he will stop being so angry with us. ¹¹ Let's not waste any time, my friends. You are the ones who were chosen to be the LORD's priests and to offer him sacrifices.

¹²⁻¹⁴ When Hezekiah finished talking, the following Levite leaders went to work:

Mahath son of Amasai and Joel son of Azariah from the Kohath clan; Kish son of Abdi and Azariah son of Jehallelel from the Merari clan; Joah son of Zimmah and Eden son of Joah from the Gershon clan; Shimri and Jeuel from the Elizaphan clan; Zechariah and Mattaniah from the Asaph clan; Jehuel and Shimei from the Heman clan; Shemaiah and Uzziel from the Jeduthun clan.

¹⁵ These leaders gathered together the rest of the Levites, and they all went through the ceremony to make themselves clean. Then they began to purify the temple according to the Law of the LORD, just as Hezekiah had commanded.

¹⁶ The priests went into the temple and carried out everything that was unclean. They put these things in the courtyard, and from there, the Levites carried them outside the city to Kidron Valley.

¹⁷ The priests and Levites began their work on the first day of the first month.* It took them one week to purify the courtyards of the temple and another week to purify the temple. So on the sixteenth day of that same month ¹⁸ they went back to Hezekiah and said:

Your Majesty, we have finished our work. The entire temple is now pure again, and so

*29.17 first month: See the note at 29.3.

Viewpoints

Why can't we just go to heaven as soon as we become Christians?

Contributed by Sharon B

'Let's not waste any time, my friends. You are the ones who were chosen to be the LORD's priests and to offer him sacrifices.'

Mission is not the ultimate goal of the church. Worship is.

What are we doing here? Why, when we become Christians, doesn't God just whisk us away to join him in eternity since, when we die, that's where we're going anyway? We're left here to bring glory to God and worship him. But couldn't we do that equally well in heaven? Yes! But being here on earth we can call ALL the nations to God's praise, tell others about him and his greatness. The sound of people worshipping God will just get louder and louder.

God has chosen us to worship him – I find it pretty hard to think that anything I do or say will ever be worthy of God. It's all just an understatement compared to his majesty and power. Yet this verse reminds us that he loves it when we worship him, to tell him we love him because of who he is. He loves it even more when we bring other people to a place where they too can worship him. After all, that's all worship leading really is; it's not about being the person up front with a microphone, but about taking people to the throne room of God for the sake of his glory and fame.

More...

Worshipping God p.622
Heaven p.1412

is the altar and its utensils, as well as the table for the sacred loaves of bread and its utensils. ¹⁹ And we have brought back all the things that King Ahaz took from the temple during the time he was unfaithful to God. We purified them and put them back in front of the altar.

Worship in the temple

²⁰ Straight away, Hezekiah called together the officials of Jerusalem, and they went to the temple. ²¹ They brought with them seven bulls, seven rams, seven lambs, and seven goats* as sacrifices to take away the sins of Hezekiah's family and of the people of Judah, as well as to purify the temple. Hezekiah told the priests, who were descendants of Aaron, to sacrifice these animals on the altar.

²² The priests killed the bulls, the rams, and the lambs, then splattered the blood on the altar. ²³ They took the goats to Hezekiah and the worshippers, and they laid their hands on the animals. ²⁴ The priests then killed the goats and splattered the blood on the altar as a sacrifice to take away the sins of everyone in Israel, because Hezekiah had commanded that these sacrifices be made for all the people of Israel.

²⁵ Next, Hezekiah assigned the Levites to their places in the temple. He gave them cymbals, harps, and other stringed instruments, according to the instructions that the LORD had given King David and the two prophets, Gad and Nathan. ²⁶ The Levites were ready to play the instruments that had belonged to David; the priests were ready to blow the trumpets.

²⁷ As soon as Hezekiah gave the signal for the sacrifices to be burnt on the altar, the musicians began singing praises to the LORD and playing their instruments, ²⁸ and everyone worshipped the LORD. This continued until the last animal was sacrificed.

²⁹ After that, Hezekiah and the crowd of worshippers knelt down and worshipped the LORD. ³⁰ Then Hezekiah and his officials ordered the Levites to sing the songs of praise that David and Asaph the prophet had written. And so they bowed down and joyfully sang praises to the LORD.

³¹ Hezekiah said to the crowd, "Now that you are once again acceptable to the LORD, bring sacrifices and offerings to give him thanks."

The people did this, and some of them voluntarily brought animals to be offered as sacrifices. ³² Seventy bulls, one hundred rams, and two hundred lambs were brought as sacrifices to please the LORD;* ³³ six hundred bulls and three thousand sheep were brought as sacrifices to ask the LORD's blessing.* ³⁴ There were not enough priests to skin all these animals, because many of the priests had not taken the time to go through the ceremony to make themselves clean. However, since all the Levites had made themselves clean, they helped the priests until the last animal was skinned. ³⁵ Besides all the sacrifices that were burnt on the altar, the fat from the other animal sacrifices was burnt, and the offerings of wine were poured over the altar.

So the temple was once again used for worshipping the LORD. ³⁶ Hezekiah and the people of Judah celebrated, because God had helped them make this happen so quickly.

CHAPTER 30

Hezekiah prepares to celebrate Passover

¹⁻⁴ Passover wasn't celebrated in the first month,* which was the usual time, because many of the priests were still unclean and unacceptable to serve, and because not everyone in Judah had come to Jerusalem for the festival. So Hezekiah, his officials, and the people agreed to celebrate Passover in the second month.*

Hezekiah sent a message to everyone in Israel and Judah, including those in the territories of Ephraim and West Manasseh, inviting them to the temple in Jerusalem for the celebration of Passover in honour of the LORD God of Israel. ⁵ Everyone from Beersheba in the south to Dan in the north was invited. This was the largest crowd of people that had ever celebrated Passover, according to the official records.

⁶ Hezekiah's messengers went everywhere in Israel and Judah with the following letter:

***29.32 sacrifices to please the LORD:** See the note at 1.6.

***29.33 sacrifices to ask the LORD's blessing:** These sacrifices have traditionally been called "peace offerings" or "offerings of well-being". A main purpose was to ask for the LORD's blessing, and so in the CEV they are sometimes called "sacrifices to ask the LORD's blessing".

***30.1-4 first month:** See the note at 29.3.

***30.1-4 second month:** See the note at 3.1-2.

See also: 30.1-4: Num 9.9-11.

People of Israel, now that you have survived the invasion of the Assyrian kings,* it's time for you to turn back to the LORD God our ancestors Abraham, Isaac, and Jacob worshipped. If you do this, he will stop being angry. 7 Don't follow the example of your ancestors and your Israelite relatives in the north. They were unfaithful to the LORD, and he punished them horribly. 8 Don't be stubborn like your ancestors. Decide now to obey the LORD our God! Come to Jerusalem and worship him in the temple that will belong to him for ever. Then he will stop being angry, 9 and the enemies who have captured your families will show pity and send them back home. The LORD God is kind and merciful, and if you turn back to him, he will no longer turn his back on you.

10 The messengers went to every town in Ephraim and West Manasseh as far north as the territory of Zebulun, but everyone laughed and insulted them. 11 Only a few people from the tribes of Asher, West Manasseh, and Zebulun were humble and went to Jerusalem. 12 God also made everyone in Judah eager to do what Hezekiah and his officials had commanded.

Passover is celebrated

13 In the second month,* a large crowd of people gathered in Jerusalem to celebrate the Festival of Thin Bread.* 14 They took all the foreign altars and incense altars in Jerusalem and threw them into Kidron Valley.

15-17 Then, on the fourteenth day of that same month, the Levites began killing the lambs for Passover, because many of the worshippers were unclean and were not allowed to kill their own lambs. Meanwhile, some of the priests and Levites felt ashamed because they had not gone through the ceremony to make themselves clean. They immediately went through that ceremony and went to the temple, where they offered sacrifices to please the LORD.* Then the priests and Levites took their positions, according to the Law of Moses, the servant of God.

As the Levites killed the lambs, they handed some of the blood to the priests, who splattered it on the altar.

18-19 Most of the people who came from Ephraim, West Manasseh, Issachar, and Zebulun had not made themselves clean, but they ignored God's Law and ate the Passover lambs anyway. Hezekiah found out what they had done and prayed, "LORD God, these people are unclean according to the laws of holiness. But they are worshipping you, just as their ancestors did. So, please be kind and forgive them." 20 The LORD answered Hezekiah's prayer and did not punish them.

21 The worshippers in Jerusalem were very happy and celebrated the Festival for seven days. The Levites and priests sang praises to the LORD every day and played their instruments. 22 Hezekiah thanked the Levites for doing such a good job, leading the celebration.

The worshippers celebrated for seven days by offering sacrifices, by eating the sacred meals, and by praising the LORD God of their ancestors. 23 Everyone was so excited that they agreed to celebrate seven more days. 24 So Hezekiah gave the people one thousand bulls and seven thousand sheep to be offered as sacrifices and to be used as food for the sacred meals. His officials gave one thousand bulls and ten thousand sheep, and many more priests agreed to go through the ceremony to make themselves clean. 25 Everyone was very happy, including those from Judah and Israel, the priests and Levites, and the foreigners living in Judah and Israel. 26 It was the biggest celebration in Jerusalem since the days of King Solomon, the son of David. 27 The priests and Levites asked God to bless the people, and from his home in heaven, he did.

CHAPTER 31

The people destroy the local shrines

This is also told in 2 Kings 18.4

1 After the Festival, the people went to every town in Judah and smashed the stone images of foreign gods and cut down the sacred poles* for worshipping the goddess Asherah. They destroyed all the local shrines' and foreign altars in Judah, as well as those in the territories of Benjamin, Ephraim, and West Manasseh. Then everyone went home.

---

*30.6 the invasion of the Assyrian kings: See 2 Kings 17.1–22.
*30.13 second month: See the note at 3.1–2.
*30.13 the Festival of Thin Bread: The celebration of this Festival began one day after Passover. And so these two festivals were often referred to as one.
*30.15–17 sacrifices to please the LORD: See the note at 1.6.

*31.1 sacred poles: See the note at 14.3.

499

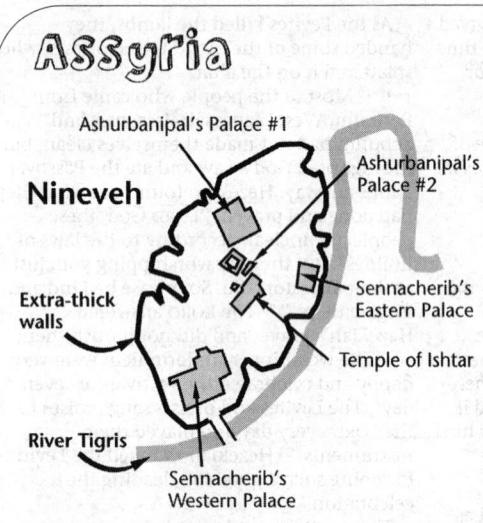

Assyria

Ashurbanipal's Palace #1

Nineveh

Ashurbanipal's Palace #2

Sennacherib's Eastern Palace

Extra-thick walls

Temple of Ishtar

River Tigris

Sennacherib's Western Palace

Assyria was one of the most powerful empires that the world has ever seen. It was a powerful, often brutal regime, noted for the efficiency with which it would conquer countries and take their inhabitants into exile.

Which is what happened with Israel. Although Israel managed to buy Assyria off by paying protection money (2 Kings 15.20) this was a temporary solution. Eventually the Assyrian emperor Shalmaneser V invaded, destroyed the city of Samaria and took away some 27,000 of the residents, replacing them with foreigners. It was the end of the northern kingdom.

God used Assyria, but he did not approve of it. Assyria also attacked Judah, but God intervened and the siege of Jerusalem was miraculously lifted (2 Kings 19). Prophets like Zephaniah and Nahum predicted what was going to happen to the empire. 'Nineveh is like a pond,' wrote Nahum, 'with leaking water. Shouts of "Stop! Don't go!" can be heard everywhere. But everyone is leaving' (Nahum 2.8). He was not speaking in pictures either. When the end finally came for Assyria in 612BC, their enemies flooded the city of Nineveh and tore the walls down (2 Kings 19.36). The once mighty empire was gone and its greatest city was a huge, ruined pond.

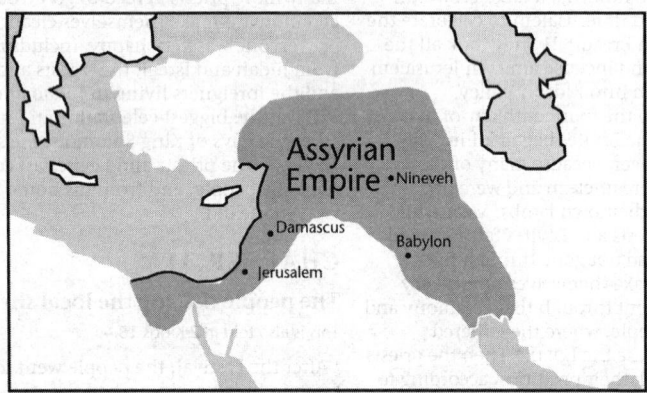

Assyrian Empire •Nineveh

•Damascus

Babylon •

• Jerusalem

Assyria today is in modern Iraq. The remains of Nineveh can be found near modern Mosul. It was discovered in 1847 by a young British explorer, Austen Henry Layard. He discovered the palace of Sennacherib, which contained a sculpture depicting Sennacherib's own account of his siege of Jerusalem and the capture of cities like Lachish. Many of these objects are in London's British Museum, so go there if you really want to see what Assyria was like.

Offerings for the priests and Levites

2 Hezekiah divided the priests and Levites into groups, according to their duties. Then he assigned them the responsibilities of offering sacrifices to please the LORD* and sacrifices to ask his blessing.* He also appointed people to serve at the temple and to sing praises at the temple gates. 3 Hezekiah provided animals from his own herds and flocks to use for the morning and evening sacrifices, as well as for the sacrifices during the Sabbath celebrations, the New Moon Festivals, and the other religious feasts required by the Law of the LORD.

4 He told the people of Jerusalem to bring the offerings that were to be given to the priests and Levites, so that they would have time to serve the LORD with their work. 5 As soon as the people heard what the king wanted, they brought a tenth of everything they owned, including their best grain, wine, olive oil, honey, and other crops. 6 The people from the other towns of Judah brought a tenth of their herds and flocks, as well as a tenth of anything they had dedicated to the LORD. 7 The people started bringing their offerings to Jerusalem in the third month,* and the last ones arrived four months later. 8 When Hezekiah and his officials saw these offerings, they thanked the LORD and the people.

9 Hezekiah asked the priests and Levites about the large amount of offerings. 10 The high priest at the time was Azariah, a descendant of Zadok, and he replied, "Ever since the people have been bringing us their offerings, we have had more than enough food and supplies. The LORD has certainly blessed his people. Look at how much is left over!"

11 So the king gave orders for storerooms to be built in the temple, and when they were completed, 12-13 all the extra offerings were taken there. Hezekiah and Azariah then appointed Conaniah the Levite to be in charge of these storerooms. His brother Shimei was his assistant, and the following Levites worked with them: Jehiel, Azaziah, Nahath, Asahel, Jerimoth, Jozabad, Eliel, Ismachiah, Mahath, and Benaiah. 14 Kore son of Imnah was assigned to guard the East Gate, and he was put in charge of receiving the offerings voluntarily

given to God and of dividing them among the priests and Levites. 15-16 He had six assistants who were responsible for seeing to it that all the priests in the other towns of Judah also got their share of these offerings. They were Eden, Miniamin, Jeshua, Shemaiah, Amariah, and Shecaniah.

Every priest and every Levite over thirty' years old who worked daily in the temple received part of these offerings, according to their duties. 17 The priests were listed in the official records by clans, and the Levites twenty years old and older were listed by their duties. 18 The official records also included their wives and children, because they had also been faithful in keeping themselves clean and acceptable to serve the LORD.

19 Hezekiah also appointed other men to take food and supplies to the priests and Levites whose homes were in the pasture land around the towns of Judah. But the priests had to be descendants of Aaron, and the Levites had to be listed in the official records.

20-21 Everything Hezekiah did while he was king of Judah, including what he did for the temple in Jerusalem, was right and good. He was a successful king, because he obeyed the LORD God with all his heart.

CHAPTER 32

King Sennacherib of Assyria invades Judah

This is also told in 2 Kings 18.13–37; Isaiah 36.1–22

1 After King Hezekiah had faithfully obeyed the LORD's instructions by doing these things, King Sennacherib of Assyria invaded Judah. He attacked the fortified cities and thought he would capture every one of them. 2 As soon as Hezekiah learnt that Sennacherib was planning to attack Jerusalem, 3-4 he and his officials worked out a plan to cut off the supply of water outside the city, so that the Assyrians would have no water when they came to attack. The officials got together a large work force that stopped up the springs and streams near Jerusalem.

5 Hezekiah's workers also repaired the broken sections of the city wall. Then they built defence towers and an outer wall to help protect the one already there. The landfill on the east side* of David's City was also strengthened.

---

*31.2 sacrifices to please the LORD: See the note at 1.6.
*31.2 sacrifices to ask his blessing: See the note at 29.33.
*31.7 third month: Sivan, the third month of the Hebrew calendar, from about mid-May to mid-June.
See also: 31.3: Num 28.1–29.39. 31.4–5: Num 18.12–13,21.

*32.5 The landfill on the east side: The Hebrew text has "the Millo", which probably refers to a landfill to strengthen and extend the hill where the city was built.

He gave orders to make a large supply of weapons and shields, 6 and he appointed army commanders over the troops. Then he gathered the troops together in the open area in front of the city gate and said to them:

7 Be brave and confident! There's no reason to be afraid of King Sennacherib and his powerful army. We are much more powerful, 8 because the LORD our God fights on our side. The Assyrians must rely on human power alone.

These words encouraged the army of Judah.
9 When Sennacherib and his troops were camped at the town of Lachish, he sent a message to Hezekiah and the people in Jerusalem. It said:

10 I am King Sennacherib of Assyria, and I have Jerusalem surrounded. Do you think you can survive my attack? 11 Hezekiah your king is telling you that the LORD your God will save you from me. But he is lying, and you'll die of hunger and thirst. 12 Didn't Hezekiah tear down all except one of the LORD's altars and places of worship?* And didn't he tell you people of Jerusalem and Judah to worship at that one place?
13 You've heard what my ancestors and I have done to other nations. Were the gods of those nations able to defend their land against us? 14 None of those gods kept their people safe from the kings of Assyria. Do you really think your God can do any better? 15 Don't be fooled by Hezekiah! No god of any nation has ever been able to stand up to Assyria. Believe me, your God cannot keep you safe!

16 The Assyrian officials said terrible things about the LORD God and his servant Hezekiah. 17 Sennacherib's letter even made fun of the LORD. It said, "The gods of other nations could not save their people from Assyria's army, and neither will the God that Hezekiah worships." 18 The officials said all these things in Hebrew, so that everyone listening from the city wall would understand and be terrified and surrender. 19 The officials talked about the LORD God as if he were nothing but an ordinary god or an idol that someone had made.

---

*32.12 worship: Hezekiah actually had torn down the places where idols were worshipped, and he had told the people to worship the LORD at the one place of worship in Jerusalem. But the Assyrian leader was confused and thought these were also places where the LORD was supposed to be worshipped.

The death of King Sennacherib

This is also told in 2 Kings 19.14-19,35-37; Isaiah 37.14-20; 37.36-38

20 Hezekiah and the prophet Isaiah son of Amoz asked the LORD for help, 21 and he sent an angel who killed every soldier and commander in the Assyrian camp.

Sennacherib returned to Assyria, completely disgraced. Then one day he went into the temple of his god where some of his sons killed him.
22 The LORD rescued Hezekiah and the people of Jerusalem from Sennacherib and also protected them from other enemies. 23 People brought offerings to Jerusalem for the LORD and expensive gifts for Hezekiah, and from that day on, every nation on earth respected Hezekiah.

Hezekiah gets sick and almost dies

This is also told in 2 Kings 20.1-11; Isaiah 38.1-8

24 About this same time, Hezekiah got sick and was almost dead. He prayed, and the LORD gave him a sign that he would recover. 25 But Hezekiah was so proud that he refused to thank the LORD for everything he had done for him. This made the LORD angry, and he punished Hezekiah and the people of Judah and Jerusalem. 26 Hezekiah and the people later felt sorry and asked the LORD to forgive them. So the LORD did not punish them as long as Hezekiah was king.

Hezekiah's wealth

This is also told in 2 Kings 20.12-19; Isaiah 39.1-8

27 Hezekiah was very rich, and everyone respected him. He built special rooms to store the silver, the gold, the precious stones and spices, the shields, and the other valuable possessions. 28 Storehouses were also built for his supply of grain, wine, and olive oil; barns were built for his cattle, and pens were put up for his sheep. 29 God made Hezekiah extremely rich, so he bought even more sheep, goats, and cattle. And he built towns where he could keep all these animals.

30 It was Hezekiah who built a tunnel that carried the water from Gihon Spring into the city of Jerusalem. In fact, everything he did was successful! 31 Even when the leaders of Babylonia sent messengers to ask Hezekiah about the sign God had given him, God let Hezekiah give his own answer to test him and to see if he would remain faithful.

Hezekiah dies

This is also told in 2 Kings 20.20,21

32 Everything else Hezekiah did while he was king, including how faithful he was to the LORD, is included in the records kept by Isaiah the prophet. These are written in *The History of the Kings of Judah and Israel.* 33 When Hezekiah died, he was buried in the section of the royal tombs that was reserved for the most respected kings,' and everyone in Judah and Jerusalem honoured him. His son Manasseh then became king.

King Manasseh and King Amon

CHAPTER 33

King Manasseh of Judah

This is also told in 2 Kings 21.1–9,17–18

1 Manasseh was twelve years old when he became king of Judah, and he ruled fifty-five years from Jerusalem. 2 Manasseh disobeyed the LORD by following the disgusting customs of the nations that the LORD had forced out of Israel. 3 He rebuilt the local shrines' that his father Hezekiah had torn down. He built altars for the god Baal and set up sacred poles* for worshipping the goddess Asherah. And he faithfully worshipped the stars in the sky.

4 In the temple, where only the LORD was supposed to be worshipped, Manasseh built altars for pagan gods 5 and for the stars. He placed these altars in both courtyards of the temple 6–7 and even set up a stone image of a foreign god. Manasseh practised magic and witchcraft; he asked fortune-tellers for advice and sacrificed his own sons in Hinnom Valley. He did many other sinful things and made the LORD very angry.

Years ago, God had told David and Solomon:

Jerusalem is the place I prefer above all others in Israel. It belongs to me, and there in the temple I will be worshipped for ever. 8 If my people will faithfully obey all the laws and teaching I gave to my servant Moses, I will never again force them to leave the land I gave to their ancestors.

9 But the people of Judah and Jerusalem listened to Manasseh and did even more sinful things than the nations the LORD had wiped out.

10 The LORD tried to warn Manasseh and the people about their sins, but they ignored the warning. 11 So he let Assyrian army commanders invade Judah and capture Manasseh. They put a hook in his nose and tied him up in chains, and they took him to Babylon. 12 While Manasseh was held captive there, he asked the LORD God to forgive him and to help him. 13 The LORD listened to Manasseh's prayer and saw how sorry he was, and so he let him go back to Jerusalem and rule as king. Manasseh knew from then on that the LORD was God.

14 Later, Manasseh rebuilt the eastern section of Jerusalem's outer wall and made it taller. This section went from Gihon Valley north to Fish Gate and around the part of the city called Mount Ophel. He also assigned army officers to each of the fortified cities in Judah.*

15 Manasseh also removed the idols and the stone image of the foreign god from the temple, and he gathered the altars he had built near the temple and in other parts of Jerusalem. He threw all these things outside the city. 16 Then he repaired the LORD's altar and offered sacrifices to thank him and sacrifices to ask his blessing.* He gave orders that everyone in Judah must worship the LORD God of Israel. 17 The people obeyed Manasseh, but they worshipped the LORD at their own shrines.

18 Everything else Manasseh did while he was king, including his prayer to the LORD God and the warnings from his prophets, is written in *The History of the Kings of Israel.* 19 Hozai' wrote a lot about Manasseh, including his prayer and God's answer. But Hozai also recorded the evil things Manasseh did before turning back to God, as well as a list of places where Manasseh set up idols, and where he built local shrines and places to worship Asherah. 20 Manasseh died and was buried near the palace, and his son Amon became king.

---

*33.14 fortified cities in Judah:** At this time, Judah was under the control of Assyria. The fortifications mentioned in this verse may have been done under orders from Assyrian officials, hoping to strengthen their southern border against the rising power of Egypt.
*33.16 sacrifices to ask his blessing:** See the note at 29.33.

---

*33.3 sacred poles:** See the note at 14.3.
See also: 33.2: Jer 15.4. 33.4: 2 Chron 6.6.
33.6–8: 1 King 9.3–5; 2 Chron 7.12–18.

King Amon of Judah

This is also told in 2 Kings 21.19–26

21 Amon was twenty-two years old when he became king of Judah, and he ruled from Jerusalem for two years. 22 Amon disobeyed the LORD, just as his father Manasseh had done, and he worshipped and offered sacrifices to the idols his father had made. 23 Manasseh had turned back to the LORD, but Amon refused to do that. Instead, he sinned even more than his father.

24 Some of Amon's officials plotted against him and killed him in his palace. 25 But the people of Judah killed the murderers of Amon and made his son Josiah king.

King Josiah and "The Book of God's Law"

CHAPTER 34

King Josiah of Judah

This is also told in 2 Kings 22.1–2

1 Josiah was eight years old when he became king of Judah, and he ruled thirty-one years from Jerusalem. 2 He followed the example of his ancestor David and always obeyed the LORD.

Josiah stops the worship of foreign gods

This is also told in 2 Kings 23.4–20

3 When Josiah was only sixteen years old he began worshipping God, just as his ancestor David had done. Then, four years later, he decided to destroy the local shrines' in Judah and Jerusalem, as well as the sacred poles* for worshipping the goddess Asherah and the idols of foreign gods. 4 He watched as the altars for the worship of the god Baal were torn down, and as the nearby incense altars were smashed. The Asherah poles, the idols, and the stone images were also smashed, and the pieces were scattered over the graves of their worshippers. 5 Josiah then had the bones of the pagan priests burnt on the altars.*

And so Josiah got rid of the worship of foreign gods in Judah and Jerusalem. 6 He did the same things in the towns and ruined villages' in the territories of West Manasseh, Ephraim, and Simeon, as far as the border of Naphtali. 7 Everywhere in the northern kingdom of Israel, Josiah tore down pagan altars and Asherah poles; he crushed idols to dust and smashed incense altars.

Then Josiah went back to Jerusalem.

Hilkiah finds *The Book of God's Law*

This is also told in 2 Kings 22.3–20

8 In the eighteenth year of Josiah's rule in Judah, after he had got rid of all the sinful things from the land and from the LORD's temple, he sent three of his officials to repair the temple. They were Shaphan son of Azaliah, Governor Maaseiah of Jerusalem, and Joah son of Joahaz, who kept the government records.

9 These three men went to Hilkiah the high priest. They gave him the money that the Levite guards had collected from the people of West Manasseh, Ephraim, and the rest of Israel, as well as those living in Judah, Benjamin, and Jerusalem. 10 Then the money was turned over to the men who supervised the repairs to the temple. They used some of it to pay the workers, 11 and they gave the rest of it to the carpenters and builders, who used it to buy the stone and wood they needed to repair the other buildings that Judah's kings had not taken care of.

12 The workers were honest, and their supervisors were Jahath and Obadiah from the Levite clan of Merari, and Zechariah and Meshullam from the Levite clan of Kohath. Other Levites, who were all skilled musicians, 13 were in charge of carrying supplies and supervising the workers. Other Levites were appointed to stand guard around the temple.

14 While the money was being given to these supervisors, Hilkiah found the book that contained the laws that the LORD had given to Moses. 15 Hilkiah handed the book to Shaphan the official and said, "Look what I found here in the temple — *The Book of God's Law*."

16 Shaphan took the book to Josiah and reported, "Your officials are doing everything you wanted. 17 They have collected the money from the temple and have given it to the men supervising the repairs. 18 But there's something else, Your Majesty. The priest Hilkiah gave me this book." Then Shaphan read it aloud.

---

*34.3 sacred poles: See the note at 14.3.
*34.5 the bones of the pagan priests burnt on the altars: This made the altars unclean, so that they could not be used in worshipping any god.

See also: 34.1: Jer 3.6. 34.4: 2 King 21.3; 2 Chron 33.3. 34.5: 1 King 13.2.

¹⁹ When Josiah heard what was in *The Book of God's Law*, he tore his clothes in sorrow. ²⁰ At once he called together Hilkiah, Shaphan, Ahikam son of Shaphan, Abdon son of Micah,⁕ and his own servant Asaiah. He said, ²¹ "The LORD must be furious with me and everyone else in Israel and Judah, because our ancestors did not obey the laws written in this book. Go and find out what the LORD wants us to do."

²² Hilkiah and the four other men left straight away and went to talk with Huldah the prophet. Her husband was Shallum,⁕ who was in charge of the king's clothes. Huldah lived in the northern part of Jerusalem, and when they met in her home, ²³ she said:

You were sent here by King Josiah, and this is what the LORD God of Israel says to him: ²⁴ "Josiah, I am the LORD! And I intend to punish this country and everyone in it, just as this book says. ²⁵ The people of Judah and Israel have rejected me. They have offered sacrifices to foreign gods and have worshipped their own idols. I can't stand it any longer. I am furious.

²⁶⁻²⁷ "Josiah, listen to what I am going to do. I noticed how sad you were when you heard that this country and its people would be completely wiped out. You even tore your clothes in sorrow, and I heard you cry. ²⁸ So before I destroy this place, I will let you die in peace."

The men left and reported to Josiah what Huldah had said.

Josiah reads *The Book of God's Law*
This is also told in 2 Kings 23.1–3

²⁹ King Josiah called together the leaders of Judah and Jerusalem. ³⁰ Then he went to the LORD's temple, together with all the people of Judah and Jerusalem, the priests, and the Levites.

Finally, when everybody was there, he read aloud *The Book of God's Law*⁕ that had been found in the temple.

³¹ After Josiah had finished reading, he stood in the place reserved for the king. He promised in the LORD's name to obey the LORD faithfully and to follow his laws and teachings that were written in the book.

³² Then he asked the people of Jerusalem and Benjamin to make that same promise and to obey the God their ancestors had worshipped.

³³ Josiah destroyed all the idols in the territories of Israel, and he commanded everyone in Israel to worship only the LORD God. The people did not turn away from the LORD God of their ancestors for the rest of Josiah's rule as king.

CHAPTER 35

Passover is celebrated
This is also told in 2 Kings 23.21–23

¹ Josiah commanded that Passover be celebrated in Jerusalem to honour the LORD. So, on the fourteenth day of the first month,⁕ the lambs were killed for the Passover celebration.

² On that day, Josiah made sure the priests knew what duties they were to do in the temple. ³ He called together the Levites who served the LORD and who taught the people his laws, and he said:

No longer will you have to carry the sacred chest from place to place. It will stay in the temple built by King Solomon son of David, where you will serve the LORD and his people Israel. ⁴ Get ready to do the work that David and Solomon assigned to you, according to your clans. ⁵ Divide yourselves into groups, then arrange yourselves throughout the temple so that each family of worshippers will be able to get help from one of you.⁕ ⁶ When the people bring you their Passover lamb, you must kill it and prepare it to be sacrificed to the LORD. Make sure the people celebrate according to the instructions that the LORD gave Moses, and don't do anything to make yourselves unclean and unacceptable.

⁷ Josiah donated thirty thousand sheep and goats, and three thousand bulls from his own flocks and herds for the people to offer as sacrifices. ⁸ Josiah's officials also voluntarily gave some of their animals to the people, the priests, and the Levites as sacrifices. Hilkiah, Zechariah, and Jehiel, who were the officials in charge of the temple, gave the priests twenty-six hundred sheep and lambs and three hundred bulls to sacrifice during the Passover celebration. ⁹ Conaniah, his two

---

⁕**34.30** *The Book of God's Law*: The Hebrew text has "The Book of God's Agreement", which is the same as *The Book of God's Law* in verses 15 and 19. In traditional translations this is called "The Book of the Covenant".

⁕**35.1 first month:** See the note at 29.3.
See also: 35.4: 2 Chron 8.14.

brothers Shemaiah and Nethanel, as well as Hashabiah, Jeiel, and Jozabad were leaders of the Levites, and they gave the other Levites five thousand sheep and goats, and five hundred bulls to offer as sacrifices.

[10] When everything was ready to celebrate Passover, the priests and the Levites stood where Josiah had told them. [11] Then the Levites killed and skinned the Passover lambs, and they handed some of the blood to the priests, who splattered it on the altar. [12] The Levites set aside the parts of the animal that the worshippers needed for their sacrifices to please the LORD,* just as the Law of Moses required. They also did the same thing with the bulls. [13] They sacrificed the Passover animals on the altar and boiled the meat for the other offerings in pots, kettles, and pans. Then they quickly handed the meat to the people so they could eat it.

[14] All day long, the priests were busy offering sacrifices and burning the animals' fat on the altar. And when everyone had finished, the Levites prepared Passover animals for themselves and for the priests.

[15] During the celebration some of the Levites prepared Passover animals for the musicians and the guards, so that the Levite musicians would not have to leave their places, which had been assigned to them according to the instructions of David, Asaph, Heman, and Jeduthun the king's prophet. Even the guards at the temple gates did not have to leave their posts.

[16] So on that day, Passover was celebrated to honour the LORD, and sacrifices were offered on the altar to him, just as Josiah had commanded. [17] The worshippers then celebrated the Festival of Thin Bread for the next seven days.

[18] People from Jerusalem and from towns all over Judah and Israel were there. Passover had not been observed like this since the days of Samuel the prophet. In fact, this was the greatest Passover celebration in Israel's history! [19] All these things happened in the eighteenth year of Josiah's rule in Judah.

Josiah dies in battle

This is also told in 2 Kings 23.28–30

[20] Some time later, King Neco of Egypt led his army to the city of Carchemish on the River Euphrates. And Josiah led his troops north to meet the Egyptians in battle.*

[21] Neco sent the following message to Josiah:

> I'm not attacking you, king of Judah! We're not even at war. But God has told me to attack my enemy quickly. God is on my side, so if you try to stop me, he will punish you.

[22] But Josiah ignored Neco's warning, even though it came from God! Instead, he disguised himself and marched into battle against Neco in the valley near Megiddo. [23] During the battle an Egyptian soldier shot Josiah with an arrow. Josiah told his servants, "Get me out of here! I've been hit." [24] They carried Josiah out of his chariot, then put him in the other chariot he had there and took him back to Jerusalem, where he soon died. He was buried beside his ancestors, and everyone in Judah and Jerusalem mourned his death.

[25] Jeremiah the prophet wrote a funeral song in honour of Josiah. And since then, anyone in Judah who mourns the death of Josiah sings that song. It is included in the collection of funeral songs.

[26] Everything else Josiah did while he was king, including how he faithfully obeyed the LORD, [27] is written in *The History of the Kings of Israel and Judah*.

The last kings of Judah

CHAPTER 36

King Jehoahaz of Judah

This is also told in 2 Kings 23.30–35

[1] After the death of Josiah, the people of Judah crowned his son Jehoahaz their new king. [2] He was twenty-three years old at the time, and he ruled only three months from Jerusalem. [3] King Neco of Egypt captured Jehoahaz and forced Judah to pay three thousand four hundred kilogrammes of silver and thirty-four kilogrammes of gold as taxes. [4] Then Neco appointed Jehoahaz's brother Eliakim king of Judah and changed his name to Jehoiakim. He led Jehoahaz away to Egypt as his prisoner.

35.12 sacrifices to please the LORD: See the note at 1.6.

See also: **35.13:** Exod 12.8–9. **35.15:** 1 Chron 25.1. **35.17:** Exod 12.1–20.

35.20 battle: At this time, King Neco of Egypt (609–595 BC) was fighting on the side of the Assyrians. He marched north to fight the Babylonian army and help Assyria keep control of its land. Since Josiah considered Assyria an enemy, he set out to stop Neco and the Egyptian troops.

See also: **36.4:** Jer 22.11–12.

King Jehoiakim of Judah

This is also told in 2 Kings 23.36—24.7

⁵ Jehoiakim was twenty-five years old when he was appointed king, and he ruled eleven years from Jerusalem. Jehoiakim disobeyed the LORD his God by doing evil.

⁶ During Jehoiakim's rule, King Nebuchadnezzar of Babylonia invaded Judah. He arrested Jehoiakim and put him in chains, and he sent him to the capital city of Babylon. ⁷ Nebuchadnezzar also carried off many of the valuable things in the LORD's temple, and he put them in his palace in Babylon.

⁸ Everything else Jehoiakim did while he was king, including all the disgusting and evil things, is written in *The History of the Kings of Israel and Judah*. His son Jehoiachin then became king.

King Jehoiachin of Judah

This is also told in 2 Kings 24.8-17

⁹ Jehoiachin was eighteen' years old when he became king of Judah, and he ruled only three months and ten days from Jerusalem. Jehoiachin also disobeyed the LORD by doing evil. ¹⁰ In the spring of the year, King Nebuchadnezzar of Babylonia had Jehoiachin arrested and taken to Babylon, along with more of the valuable items in the temple. Then Nebuchadnezzar appointed Zedekiah king of Judah.

King Zedekiah of Judah

This is also told in 2 Kings 24.18-20; Jeremiah 52.1-3

¹¹ Zedekiah was twenty-one years old when he was appointed king of Judah, and he ruled from Jerusalem for eleven years. ¹² He disobeyed the LORD his God and refused to change his ways, even after a warning from Jeremiah, the LORD's prophet.

¹³ King Nebuchadnezzar of Babylonia had forced Zedekiah to promise in God's name that he would be loyal. Zedekiah was stubborn and refused to turn back to the LORD God of Israel, so he rebelled against Nebuchadnezzar. ¹⁴ The people of Judah and even the priests who were their leaders became more unfaithful. They followed the disgusting example of the nations around them and made the LORD's holy temple unfit for worship. ¹⁵ But the LORD God felt sorry for his people, and instead of destroying the

temple, he sent prophets who warned the people over and over again about their sins. ¹⁶ But the people only laughed and insulted these prophets. They ignored what the LORD God was trying to tell them, until he finally became so angry that nothing could stop him from punishing Judah and Jerusalem.

Jerusalem is destroyed and the people are taken to Babylonia

This is also told in 2 Kings 25.1-21; Jeremiah 52.3-30

¹⁷ The LORD sent King Nebuchadnezzar of Babylonia to attack Jerusalem. Nebuchadnezzar killed the young men who were in the temple, and he showed no mercy to anyone, whether man or woman, young or old. God let him kill everyone in the city. ¹⁸ Nebuchadnezzar carried off everything that was left in the temple; he robbed the treasury and the personal storerooms of the king and his officials. He took everything back to Babylon.

¹⁹ Nebuchadnezzar's troops burnt down the temple and destroyed every important building in the city. Then they broke down the city wall. ²⁰ The survivors were taken to Babylonia as prisoners, where they were slaves of the king and his sons, until Persia became a powerful nation.

²¹ Judah was an empty desert, and it stayed that way for seventy years, to make up for all the years it was not allowed to rest. These things happened just as Jeremiah the LORD's prophet had said.*

King Cyrus of Persia lets the Jews return to Judah

Cyrus lets the Jews return home

This is also told in Ezra 1.1-4

²² In the first year that Cyrus was king of Persia,* the LORD told Cyrus to send a message to all parts of his kingdom. This happened just

---

36.21 not allowed to rest . . . Jeremiah . . . said: Jeremiah 25.11-12; 29.10. According to the Law, the people had to allow the land to rest one out of every seven years (see Leviticus 25.1-7).
36.22 the first year that Cyrus was king of Persia: Probably 539 BC, when Cyrus captured Babylonia. He had actually ruled Persia since 549 BC.

See also: **36.17:** Jer 21.1-10; 34.1-5. **36.19:** 1 King 9.8. **36.21:** Jer 25.11; 29.10.

See also: **36.5:** Jer 22.18-19; 26.1-6; 35.1-19.
36.6: Jer 25.1-38; 36.1-32; 45.1-5; Dan 1.1,2.
36.10: a Jer 22.24-30; 24.1-10; 29.1-2; Ezek 17.12; **b** Jer 37.1; Ezek 17.13. **36.11:** Jer 27.1-22; 28.1-17. **36.13:** Ezek 17.15.

as Jeremiah the LORD's prophet had promised.
²³ The message said:

> I am King Cyrus of Persia.
> The LORD God of heaven has made me the ruler of every nation on earth. He has also chosen me to build a temple for him in Jerusalem, which is in Judah. The LORD God will watch over any of his people who want to go back to Judah.

See also: 36.23: Isa 44.28.

Additional notes

›1.2–5 Bezalel: Hebrew "Bezalel son of Uri son of Hur".

›3.1–2 Araunah: The Hebrew text has "Ornan", another spelling of the name (see 2 Samuel 24.18–25; 1 Chronicles 21.18—22.1).

›3.4 nine metres: Some manuscripts of two ancient translations; Hebrew "fifty-four metres".

›3.9 The walls . . . gold: One possible meaning for the difficult Hebrew text.

›3.16 designs that looked like chains: One possible meaning for the difficult Hebrew text.

›5.10 Sinai: Hebrew "Horeb".

›6.42 the love you had for your servant David: Or "how loyal your servant David was to you".

›9.3–4 his palace: Or "the temple".

›9.10–12 steps: Or "stools" or "railings".

›9.21 peacocks: Or "baboons".

›10.10 Compared . . . weak: Hebrew "My little finger is bigger than my father's waist."

›10.15–19 Adoniram: The Hebrew text has "Hadoram", another spelling of the name.

›11.15 local shrines: The Hebrew text has "high places", which were local places to worship foreign gods.

›13.1 Abijah: In 1 Kings 15.1–8 his name is spelt "Abijam".

›14.3 local shrines: See the note at 11.15.

›14.13 the Ethiopians could not even fight back: Or "not one of the Ethiopians survived!"

›15.17 local shrines: See the note at 11.15.

›16.4 Abel-Maim: Also called "Abel-Bethmaacah" (see 1 Kings 15.20).

›16.10 Asa was also cruel . . . people: Or "Asa also started being cruel to some of his people."

›17.6 local shrines: See the note at 11.15.

›19.11 Zebadiah, the leader: Hebrew "Zebadiah son of Ishmael, who is the leader".

›20.1 Meunites: One ancient translation (see also 26.7); Hebrew "Ammonites".

›20.2 Edom: The Hebrew text has "Syria"; in Hebrew there is only one letter difference between "Edom" and "Aram", which is the usual Hebrew name for Syria in the Bible.

›20.14 Jahaziel, a Levite from the Asaph clan: Hebrew "Jahaziel son of Zechariah son of Benaiah son of Jeiel son of Mattaniah, who was a Levite from the Asaph clan."

›20.21 to march in front . . . singing: Or "to put on their sacred robes, lead the army into battle, and praise the LORD by singing".

›20.25 a large herd of livestock: One ancient translation; Hebrew "among the bodies a large herd of".

›20.25 clothes: One ancient translation; Hebrew "dead bodies".

›20.33 local shrines: See the note at 11.15.

›20.37 Eliezer: Hebrew "Eliezer son of Dodavahu from Mareshah".

›21.11 local shrines: See the note at 11.15.

›21.17 Ahaziah: The Hebrew text has "Jehoahaz", another spelling of the name.

›22.2 twenty-two: One ancient translation (see also 2 Kings 8.26); Hebrew "forty-two".

›22.11 Jehosheba: The Hebrew text has "Jehoshabeath", another spelling of the name.

›24.25–26 Zabad and Jehozabad: Hebrew "Zabad son of Shimeath from Ammon and Jehozabad son of Shimrith from Moab".

›25.1 Jehoaddin: The Hebrew text has "Jehoaddan", another spelling of the name.

›25.17 King Jehoash: The Hebrew text has "King Joash son of Jehoahaz son of Jehu"; Jehoash is another spelling for the name Joash.

›26.1–3 Uzziah: In the parallel passages in 2 Kings, he is called "Azariah" (see also 1 Chronicles 3.10–15). He is also called "Uzziah" in 2 Kings 15.13; Isaiah 1.1; Hosea 1.1; and Amos 1.1. One of these names was probably his birth name, while the other was his name after he became king.

›26.9 the place where the city wall turned inward: One possible meaning for the difficult Hebrew text.

›28.4 local shrines: See the note at 11.15.

›28.5–6 Pekah: Hebrew "Pekah son of Remaliah".

›28.25 local shrines: See the note at 11.15.

›29.21 goats: Hebrew "male goats".

›31.1 local shrines: See the note at 11.15.

›31.15–16 thirty: The Hebrew text has "three" instead of "thirty"; in Hebrew, these two words look almost exactly the same (see also Numbers 4.3; 1 Chronicles 23.3).

›32.33 in the section . . . reserved for the most respected kings: One possible meaning for the difficult Hebrew text.

›33.3 local shrines: See the note at 11.15.

›33.19 Hozai: Or "The prophets".

›34.3 local shrines: See the note at 11.15.

›34.6 ruined villages: One possible meaning for the difficult Hebrew text.

›34.20 Abdon son of Micah: Also called "Achbor son of Micaiah" (see 2 Kings 22.12).

›34.22 Shallum: Hebrew "Shallum son of Tokhath son of Hasrah".

›35.5 each family of worshippers . . . you: One possible meaning for the difficult Hebrew text.

›36.9 eighteen: Some manuscripts of one ancient translation (see also 2 Kings 24.8); Hebrew "eight".

Ezra

The basics

What's the point? To show how God brought his people back to Jerusalem from captivity in Babylon.

What happens? Cyrus the Persian defeats the Babylonians and allows the Jews to return to Jerusalem. They return in several groups, and devote themselves to rebuilding the temple.

What should I remember? 3.11–12 'They praised the Lord and gave thanks as they took turns singing: "The LORD is good! His faithful love for Israel will last forever." Everyone started shouting and praising the LORD because work on the foundation of the temple had begun. Many of the older priests and Levites and the heads of families cried aloud because they remembered seeing the first temple years before. But others were so happy that they celebrated with joyful shouts.'

More details

Setting the scene Cyrus has swept into Babylon and released the Jews from captivity. They return home and set to work...

What's it all about? Ezra carries on where 2 Chronicles leaves off. It tells of the return of the Jews from Babylon and how God's promises were fulfilled. God promised the people would return and to achieve this he uses a mix of people including foreign kings (Cyrus, Darius and Artaxerxes), Jewish leaders (Joshua, Zerubbabel, Ezra and Nehemiah) and prophets (Haggai and Zechariah).

Ezra tells how the Jews returned to Jerusalem and started rebuilding. But the rebuilding is opposed by some of the people who had settled in the area while the Jews were in exile and gradually their enthusiasm dims. Ezra calls them back to a 100% focus on God.

And another thing

The chronology of Ezra leaps about a bit. Here's the right chronological order:

The return: 1.1—4.5
Work stops: 4.24
Work starts again: 4.24—6.22
Work stops again: 4.6–23
Ezra returns to Jerusalem: 7.1–10.44

Footsteps

Return: 1.1–11
Rebuilding and opposition: 3.7–4.5
Haggai gets them going again: 5.1–6.5
The temple and the Passover: 6.13–22
Ezra returns: 7.1–27
The problem: 9.1–15
The solution: 10.1–17

The Jews return home from exile

CHAPTER 1

¹ Years ago the LORD sent Jeremiah with a message about a promise* for the people of Israel. Then in the first year that Cyrus was king of Persia,* the LORD kept his promise by telling Cyrus to send this official message to all parts of his kingdom:

---

*1.1 a promise: That the people of Israel would be set free from Babylonia after seventy years (see Jeremiah 25.11; 29.10).
*1.1 the first year that Cyrus was king of Persia: Probably 539 BC, when Cyrus captured Babylonia. He had actually ruled Persia since 549 BC.
See also: 1.1: Jer 25.11; 29.10.

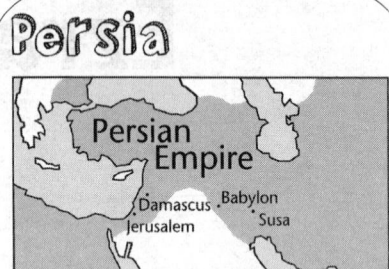

Persia

Persian Empire

Damascus · Babylon
Jerusalem · · Susa

First there were the Assyrians, then there were the Babylonians, then there were the Persians.

Under the leadership of Cyrus the Great, the Persian empire swept away the Babylonians in 539BC, capturing the capital and taking over the empire.

Persia was a huge empire, stretching all the way from Greece in the west to India in the east. Perhaps the size of the empire gave them a bigger perspective, because they had a much more relaxed religious policy than the Babylonians. They decided to give back all the religious objects that the Babylonians had looted from throughout their empire. So, all the precious objects that the Babylonians stole from the temple were returned.

Most importantly, Cyrus allowed the Jews to return to Judah. Under their king Zerubbabel, the Jews were authorised to return to their homeland and begin the rebuilding of Jerusalem and the temple.

God had promised the Jews he would rescue them (again). He kept his promise, using the Persians to achieve his aims.

Not all the Jews rushed back. Some even went further away, travelling to Susa, the Persian capital. This was a luxurious city, noted for the work of the jewellers and goldsmiths. This luxury is reflected in the book of Esther which is set amongst the Jewish community in Susa and where the action takes place in one of the royal palaces built by Darius.

2–3 I am King Cyrus of Persia.

The LORD God of heaven, who is also the God of Israel, has made me the ruler of all nations on earth. And he has chosen me to build a temple for him in Jerusalem, which is in Judah. The LORD God will watch over and encourage any of his people who want to go back to Jerusalem and help build the temple.

4 Everyone else must provide what is needed. They must give money, supplies, and animals, as well as gifts for rebuilding God's temple.

5 Many people felt that the LORD God wanted them to help rebuild his temple, and they made plans to go to Jerusalem. Among them were priests, Levites, and leaders of the tribes of Judah and Benjamin. 6 The others helped by giving silver articles, gold, personal possessions, cattle, and other valuable gifts, as well as offerings for the temple.

7 King Cyrus gave back the things that Nebuchadnezzar* had taken from the LORD's temple in Jerusalem and had put in the temple of his own gods. 8 Cyrus placed Mithredath, his chief treasurer, in charge of these things. Mithredath counted them and gave a list to Sheshbazzar, the governor of Judah. 9–10 Included among them were: 30 large gold dishes; 1,000 large silver dishes; 29 other dishes;' 30 gold bowls; 410 silver bowls; and 1,000 other articles.

11 Altogether, there were 5,400 gold and silver dishes, bowls, and other articles. Sheshbazzar took them with him when he and the others returned to Jerusalem from Babylonia.

CHAPTER 2

A list of people who returned from exile

This is also told in Nehemiah 7.4–73

1 King Nebuchadnezzar* of Babylonia had captured many of the people of Judah and had taken them as prisoners to Babylonia. Now they were on their way back to Jerusalem and to their own towns everywhere in Judah.

2–20 Zerubbabel, Joshua,' Nehemiah, Seraiah, Reelaiah, Mordecai, Bilshan, Mispar,

---

*1.7 Nebuchadnezzar: Known as Nebuchadnezzar II, who ruled Babylonia from 605 to 562 BC. In 586 BC he destroyed Jerusalem and took many of its people to Babylonia.
*2.1 Nebuchadnezzar: See the note at 1.7.
See also: 1.2: Isa 44.28.

Bigvai, Rehum, and Baanah were in charge of the ones who were coming back. And here is a list of how many returned from each family group: 2,172 from the family of Parosh; 372 from the family of Shephatiah; 775 from the family of Arah; 2,812 descendants of Jeshua and Joab' from the family of Pahath Moab; 1,254 from the family of Elam; 945 from the family of Zattu; 760 from the family of Zaccai; 642 from the family of Bani; 623 from the family of Bebai; 1,222 from the family of Azgad; 666 from the family of Adonikam; 2,056 from the family of Bigvai; 454 from the family of Adin; 98 from the family of Ater, also known as Hezekiah; 323 from the family of Bezai; 112 from the family of Jorah; 223 from the family of Hashum; and 95 from the family of Gibbar.

²¹⁻³⁵ Here is how many people returned whose ancestors had come from the following towns: 123 from Bethlehem; 56 from Netophah; 128 from Anathoth; 42 from Azmaveth; 743 from Kiriatharim, Chephirah, and Beeroth; 621 from Ramah and Geba; 122 from Michmas; 223 from Bethel and Ai; 52 from Nebo; 156 from Magbish; 1,254 from Elam;' 320 from Harim; 725 from Lod, Hadid, and Ono; 345 from Jericho; and 3,630 from Senaah.

³⁶⁻³⁹ Here is a list of how many returned from each family of priests: 973 descendants of Jeshua from the family of Jedaiah; 1,052 from the family of Immer; 1,247 from the family of Pashhur; and 1,017 from the family of Harim.

⁴⁰⁻⁴² And here is a list of how many returned from the families of Levites: 74 descendants of Hodaviah from the families of Jeshua and Kadmiel; 128 descendants of Asaph from the temple musicians; and 139 descendants of Shallum, Ater, Talmon, Akkub, Hatita, and Shobai from the temple guards.

⁴³⁻⁵⁴ Here is a list of the families of temple workers whose descendants returned: Ziha, Hasupha, Tabbaoth, Keros, Siaha, Padon, Lebanah, Hagabah, Akkub, Hagab, Shamlai, Hanan, Giddel, Gahar, Reaiah, Rezin, Nekoda, Gazzam, Uzza, Paseah, Besai, Asnah, Meunim, Nephisim, Bakbuk, Hakupha, Harhur, Bazluth, Mehida, Harsha, Barkos, Sisera, Temah, Neziah, and Hatipha.

⁵⁵⁻⁵⁷ Here is a list of Solomon's servants whose descendants returned: Sotai, Hassophereth, Peruda, Jaalah, Darkon, Giddel, Shephatiah, Hattil, Pochereth Hazzebaim, and Ami.

⁵⁸ A total of 392 descendants of temple workers and of Solomon's servants returned.

⁵⁹⁻⁶⁰ There were 652 who returned from the families of Delaiah, Tobiah, and Nekoda, though they could not prove that they were Israelites. They had lived in the Babylonian towns of Tel-Melah, Tel-Harsha, Cherub, Addan, and Immer.

⁶¹⁻⁶² The families of Habaiah, Hakkoz, and Barzillai could not prove that they were priests. The ancestor of the family of Barzillai had married the daughter of Barzillai from Gilead and had taken his wife's family name. But the records of these three families could not be found, and none of them were allowed to serve as priests. ⁶³ In fact, the governor* told them, "You cannot eat the food offered to God until we find out if you really are priests."*

⁶⁴⁻⁶⁷ There were 42,360 who returned, in addition to 7,337 servants and 200 musicians, both women and men. They brought with them 736 horses, 245 mules, 435 camels, and 6,720 donkeys.

⁶⁸ When the people came to where the LORD's temple had been in Jerusalem, some of the family leaders gave gifts so it could be rebuilt in the same place. ⁶⁹ They gave all they could, and it came to a total of 500 kilogrammes of gold, 2,800 kilogrammes of silver, and 100 robes for the priests.

⁷⁰ Everyone returned to the towns from which their families had come, including the priests, the Levites, the musicians, the temple guards, and the workers.'

The altar is rebuilt, and work on the temple begins

CHAPTER 3

The first offering on the new altar

¹ During the seventh month* of the year, the Israelites who had settled in their towns went to Jerusalem. ² The priest Joshua son of

---

2.63 governor: In Nehemiah 8.9; 10.1, this same title is used of Nehemiah, though it is doubtful if he is the one referred to here.

2.63 until . . . priests: The Hebrew text has "until a priest comes with the urim and thummim", sacred objects which were used in some way to receive answers from God.

3.1 seventh month: Tishri (also called Ethanim), the seventh month of the Hebrew calendar, from about mid-September to mid-October.

See also: 2.63: Num 27.21. **2.70:** 1 Chron 9.2; Neh 11.3. **3.2:** Exod 27.1.

Jozadak, together with the other priests, and Zerubbabel son of Shealtiel and his relatives rebuilt the altar of Israel's God. Then they were able to offer sacrifices there by following the instructions God had given to Moses. ³ And they built the altar where it had stood before,' even though they were afraid of the people who were already living around there. Then every morning and evening they burnt sacrifices and offerings to the LORD.

⁴ The people followed the rules for celebrating the Festival of Shelters and offered the proper sacrifices each day. ⁵ They offered sacrifices to please the LORD,* sacrifices at each New Moon Festival, and sacrifices at the rest of the LORD's festivals. Every offering the people had brought was presented to the LORD.

⁶ Although work on the temple itself had not yet begun, the people started offering sacrifices on the LORD's altar on the first day of the seventh month of that year.

The rebuilding of the temple begins

⁷ King Cyrus of Persia had said the Israelites could have cedar trees brought from Lebanon to Joppa by sea. So they sent grain, wine, and olive oil to the cities of Tyre and Sidon as payment for these trees, and they gave money to the stoneworkers and carpenters.

⁸ During the second month* of the second year after the people had returned from Babylonia, they started rebuilding the LORD's temple. Zerubbabel son of Shealtiel, Joshua son of Jozadak, the priests, the Levites, and everyone else who had returned started working. Every Levite over twenty years of age was put in charge of some part of the work. ⁹ The Levites in charge of the whole project were Joshua and his sons and relatives and Kadmiel and his sons from the family of Hodaviah.' The family of Henadad worked along with them.

¹⁰ When the builders had finished laying the foundation of the temple, the priests put on their robes and blew trumpets in honour of the LORD, while the Levites from the family of Asaph praised God with cymbals. All of them followed the instructions

given years before by King David.*
¹¹ They praised the LORD and gave thanks as they took turns singing:

> "The LORD is good!
> His faithful love for Israel
>   will last for ever."

Everyone started shouting and praising the LORD because work on the foundation of the temple had begun. ¹² Many of the older priests and Levites and the heads of families cried aloud because they remembered seeing the first temple years before. But others were so happy that they celebrated with joyful shouts. ¹³ Their shouting and crying were so noisy that it all sounded alike and could be heard a long way off.

CHAPTER 4

Foreigners* want to help rebuild the temple

¹ The enemies of the tribes of Judah and Benjamin heard that the people had come back to rebuild the temple of the LORD God of Israel. ² So they went to Zerubbabel and to the family leaders and said, "Let us help! Ever since King Esarhaddon of Assyria* brought us here, we have worshipped your God and offered sacrifices to him."

³ But Zerubbabel, Joshua, and the family leaders answered, "You cannot take part in building a temple for the LORD our God! We will build it ourselves, just as King Cyrus of Persia commanded us."

⁴ Then the neighbouring people began to do everything possible to frighten the Jews* and to make them stop building. ⁵ During the time when Cyrus was king and even until Darius* became king, they kept bribing government officials to slow down the work.

3.10 King David: Ruled from about 1010 to 970 BC.
4.1 Foreigners: People from foreign countries who had been captured by Assyrian and Babylonian kings and forced to settle in Palestine.
4.2 King Esarhaddon of Assyria: Ruled from 681 to 669 BC. These people may have been brought to Palestine in 677 or 676 BC, when Esarhaddon invaded Syria.
4.4 Jews: This was the name given to those Israelites who settled in Judah after returning from Babylonia.
4.5 Cyrus . . . Darius: Cyrus ruled 539–530 BC (see the note at 1.1); Darius I, known as Darius the Great, ruled 522–486 BC.

See also: 3.11: 1 Chron 16.34; 2 Chron 5.13; 7.3; Psa 100.5; 106.1; 107.1; 118.1; 136.1; Jer 33.11.   4.2: 2 King 17.24–41.

3.5 sacrifices to please the LORD: In traditional translations these sacrifices are usually called "whole burnt offerings" (see Leviticus 1.1–16).
3.8 second month: Ziv, the second month of the Hebrew calendar, from about mid-April to mid-May.
See also: 3.3: Num 28.1–8.   3.4: Num 29.12–38.
3.5: Num 28.11–29.39.   3.10: 1 Chron 25.1.

Later trouble rebuilding Jerusalem

Trouble rebuilding Jerusalem*

6 In the first year that Xerxes was king,* the neighbouring people brought written charges against the people of Judah and Jerusalem.

7 Later, Bishlam, Mithredath, Tabeel, and their advisers got together and wrote a letter to Artaxerxes when he was king of Persia.* It was written in Aramaic and had to be translated.*

8-10 A letter was also written to Artaxerxes about Jerusalem by Governor Rehum, Secretary Shimshai, and their advisers, including the judges, the governors, the officials, and the local leaders. They were joined in writing this letter by people from Erech and Babylonia, the Elamites from Susa,ᵀ and people from other foreign nations that the great and famous Ashurbanipal* had forced to settle in Samaria and other parts of Western Province.*

11 This letter said:

Your Majesty King Artaxerxes, we are your servants from everywhere in Western Province, and we send you our greetings.

12 You should know that the Jews who left your country have moved back to Jerusalem and are now rebuilding that terrible city. In fact, they have almost finished rebuilding the walls and repairing the foundations. 13 You should also know that if the walls are completed and the city is rebuilt, the Jews won't pay any kind of taxes, and there will be less money in your treasury.

14 We are telling you this, because you have done so much for us, and we want everyone to respect you. 15 If you look up the official records of your ancestors, you will find that Jerusalem has constantly rebelled and has led others to rebel against kings and provinces. That's why the city was destroyed in the first place. 16 If Jerusalem is rebuilt and its walls completed, you will no longer have control over Western Province.

17 King Artaxerxes answered:

Greetings to Governor Rehum, Secretary Shimshai, and to your advisers in Samaria and other parts of Western Province.

18 After your letter was translated and read to me, 19 I had the old records checked. It is true that for years Jerusalem has rebelled and caused trouble for other kings and nations. 20 And powerful kings have ruled Western Province from Jerusalem and have collected all kinds of taxes.

21 I want you to command the people to stop rebuilding the city until I give further notice. 22 Do this straight away, so that no harm will come to the kingdom.

23 As soon as this letter was read, Governor Rehum, Secretary Shimshai, and their advisers went to Jerusalem and forced everyone to stop rebuilding the city.

The temple is rebuilt

Work on the temple starts again

24 The Jews were forced to stop work on the temple and were not able to do any more building until the year after Darius became king of Persia.*

CHAPTER 5

1 Then the LORD God of Israel told the prophets Haggai and Zechariahᵀ to speak in his name to the people of Judah and Jerusalem. And they did. 2 So Zerubbabel the governor and Joshua the priest urged the people to start working on the temple again, and God's prophets encouraged them.

3 Governor Tattenai of Western Province and his assistant Shethar Bozenai got together with some of their officials. Then they went to Jerusalem and said to the people, "Who told

---

*4.6 Jerusalem: Verses 6–23, which tell about the events of a later period, are placed here because they are also concerned with the problem of stopping or slowing down work on the temple.
*4.6 first year that Xerxes was king: Either the end of 486 or the beginning of 485 BC. The Hebrew has the king's Persian name "Ahasuerus", but he is better known as "Xerxes", the Greek form of the name.
*4.7 Artaxerxes . . . Persia: Artaxerxes I (465–425 BC).
*4.7 It was . . . translated: One possible meaning for the difficult Hebrew text. Ezra 4.8–6.18 is written in Aramaic, instead of in Hebrew like most of the Old Testament.
*4.8-10 Ashurbanipal: King of Assyria 669–633 (or possibly 627) BC. In Aramaic the king's name is "Osnapper", but he is better known as Ashurbanipal.
*4.8-10 Western Province: The land from the River Euphrates west to the Mediterranean Sea.
See also: 4.6: Esth 1.1.

*4.24 year after . . . king of Persia: 520 BC.
See also: 4.24: Hag 1.1; Zech 1.1. 5.1: Hag 1.1; Zech 1.1.
5.2: Hag 1.12; Zech 4.6–9.

you to rebuild this temple? ⁴ Give us the names of the workers!"

⁵ But God was looking after the Jewish leaders. So the governor and his group decided not to make the people stop working on the temple until they could report to Darius and get his advice.

⁶ Governor Tattenai, Shethar Bozenai, and their advisers sent a report to Darius, ⁷ which said:

King Darius, we wish you the best! ⁸ We went to Judah, where the temple of the great God is being built with huge stones and wooden beams set in the walls. Everyone is working hard, and the building is going up fast.

⁹ We asked those in charge to tell us who gave them permission to rebuild the temple. ¹⁰ We also asked for the names of their leaders, so that we could write them down for you.

¹¹ They claimed to be servants of the God who rules heaven and earth. And they said they were rebuilding the temple that was built many years ago by one of Israel's greatest kings.*

¹² We were told that their people had made God angry, and he let them be captured by Nebuchadnezzar,* the Babylonian king' who took them away as captives to Babylonia. Nebuchadnezzar tore down their temple, ¹³⁻¹⁵ took its gold and silver articles, and put them in the temple of his own god in Babylon.

They also said that during the first year Cyrus was king of Babylonia,* he gave orders for God's temple to be rebuilt in Jerusalem where it had stood before. So Cyrus appointed Sheshbazzar governor of Judah and sent these gold and silver articles for him to put in the temple. ¹⁶ Sheshbazzar then went to Jerusalem and laid the foundation for the temple, and the work is still going on.

¹⁷ Your Majesty, please order someone to look up the old records in Babylonia and find out if King Cyrus really did give orders to rebuild God's temple in Jerusalem. We will do whatever you think we should.

CHAPTER 6

King Cyrus' order is rediscovered

¹ King Darius ordered someone to go through the old records kept in Babylonia. ² Finally, a scroll* was found in Ecbatana, the capital of Media Province, and it said:

This official record will show ³ that in the first year Cyrus was king, he gave orders to rebuild God's temple in Jerusalem, so that sacrifices and offerings could be presented there.' It is to be built twenty-seven metres high and twenty-seven metres wide, ⁴ with one' row of wooden beams for each three rows of large stones. The royal treasury will pay for everything. ⁵ Then return to their proper places the gold and silver things that Nebuchadnezzar took from the temple and brought to Babylonia.

King Darius orders the work to continue

⁶ King Darius sent this message:

Governor Tattenai of Western Province and Shethar Bozenai, you and your advisers must stay away from the temple. ⁷ Let the Jewish governor and leaders rebuild it where it stood before. And stop slowing them down!

⁸ Starting at once, I am ordering you to help the leaders by paying their expenses from the tax money collected in Western Province. ⁹ And don't fail to let the priests in Jerusalem have whatever they need each day so they can offer sacrifices to the God of heaven. Give them young bulls, rams, sheep, as well as wheat, salt, wine, and olive oil. ¹⁰ I want them to be able to offer pleasing sacrifices to God and to pray for me and my family.

¹¹ If any of you don't obey this order, a wooden beam will be taken from your house and sharpened on one end. Then it will be driven through your body,* and your house will be torn down and turned into a rubbish dump. ¹² I ask the God who is worshipped in Jerusalem to destroy any king or nation who tries either to change what I have said or to tear down his temple. I, Darius, give these orders, and I expect them to be followed carefully.

---

*5.11 one of Israel's greatest kings: Solomon (ruled from about 970 to 931 BC).

*5.12 Nebuchadnezzar: See the note at 1.7.

*5.13–15 Cyrus was king of Babylonia: King Cyrus of Persia became king of Babylonia when the Persians conquered the city of Babylon in 539 BC.

See also: 5.12: 2 King 25.8–12; 2 Chron 36.17–20; Jer 52.12–15. 5.13: Ezra 1.2–11.

---

*6.2 scroll: A roll of paper or special leather used for writing on.

*6.11 driven through your body: A well-known punishment in the ancient Near East.

The temple is dedicated

13 Governor Tattenai, Shethar Bozenai, and their advisers carefully obeyed King Darius. 14 With great success the Jewish leaders continued working on the temple, while Haggai and Zechariah encouraged them by their preaching. And so, the temple was completed at the command of the God of Israel and by the orders of kings Cyrus, Darius, and Artaxerxes of Persia.* 15 On the third day of the month of Adar* in the sixth year of the rule of Darius,* the temple was finished.

16 The people of Israel, the priests, the Levites, and everyone else who had returned from exile were happy and celebrated as they dedicated God's temple. 17 One hundred bulls, two hundred rams, and four hundred lambs were offered as sacrifices at the dedication. Also twelve goats were sacrificed as sin offerings for the twelve tribes of Israel. 18 Then the priests and Levites were assigned their duties in God's temple in Jerusalem, according to the instructions Moses had written.

The Passover

19 Everyone who had returned from exile celebrated Passover on the fourteenth day of the first month.* 20 The priests and Levites had gone through a ceremony to make themselves acceptable to lead in worship. Then some of them killed Passover lambs for those who had returned, including the other priests and themselves.

21 The sacrifices were eaten by the Israelites who had returned and by the neighbouring people who had given up the sinful customs of other nations in order to worship the LORD God of Israel. 22 For seven days they celebrated the Festival of Thin Bread. Everyone was happy because the LORD God of Israel had made sure that the king of Assyria* would be kind to them and help them build the temple.

Ezra leads many Jews back to Jerusalem

CHAPTER 7

Ezra comes to Jerusalem

1-6 Much later, when Artaxerxes* was king of Persia, Ezra came to Jerusalem from Babylonia. Ezra was the son of Seraiah and the grandson of Azariah. His other ancestors were Hilkiah, Shallum, Zadok, Ahitub, Amariah, Azariah, Meraioth, Zerahiah, Uzzi, Bukki, Abishua, Phinehas, Eleazar, and Aaron, the high priest.

Ezra was an expert in the Law that the LORD God of Israel had given to Moses, and the LORD made sure that the king gave Ezra everything he asked for.

7 Other Jews, including priests, Levites, musicians, the temple guards, and servants, came to Jerusalem with Ezra. This happened during the seventh year that Artaxerxes* was king.

8-9 God helped Ezra, and he arrived in Jerusalem on the first day of the fifth month* of that seventh year, after leaving Babylonia on the first day of the first month.* 10 Ezra had spent his entire life studying and obeying the Law of the LORD and teaching it to others.

Artaxerxes gives a letter to Ezra

11 Ezra was a priest and an expert in the laws and commands that the LORD had given to Israel. One day King Artaxerxes gave Ezra a letter which said:

12 Greetings from the great King Artaxerxes to Ezra the priest and expert in the teachings of the God of heaven.

13-14 Any of the people of Israel or their priests or Levites in my kingdom may go with you to Jerusalem if they want to. My seven advisers and I agree that you may go to Jerusalem and Judah to find out if the laws of your God are being obeyed.

---

*6.14 Artaxerxes of Persia: See the note at 4.7.
*6.15 Adar: The twelfth month of the Hebrew calendar, from about mid-February to about mid-March.
*6.15 sixth year . . . Darius: 515 BC.
*6.19 the first month: Nisan or Abib, the first month of the Hebrew calendar, from about mid-March to mid-April.
*6.22 king of Assyria: Meaning the king of Persia, because Assyria was now part of the Persian Empire.
See also: 6.14: a Hag 1.1; b Zech 1.1.   6.19: Exod 12.1-20.

*7.1-6 Artaxerxes: Either Artaxerxes I (ruled from 465 to 425 BC) or Artaxerxes II (ruled from 405-358 BC).
*7.7 seventh year . . . Artaxerxes: 458 BC if this is Artaxerxes I; 398 BC, if this is Artaxerxes II (see the note at 7.1-6).
*7.8-9 fifth month: Ab, the fifth month of the Hebrew calendar, from about mid-July to mid-August.
*7.8-9 first month: See the note at 6.19.

15 When you go, take the silver and gold that I and my advisers are freely giving to the God of Israel, whose temple is in Jerusalem. 16 Take the silver and gold that you collect from everywhere in Babylonia. Also take the gifts that your own people and priests have so willingly contributed for the temple of your God in Jerusalem.

17 Use the money carefully to buy the best bulls, rams, lambs, grain, and wine. Then sacrifice them on the altar at God's temple in Jerusalem. 18 If any silver or gold is left, you and your people may use it for whatever pleases your God. 19 Give your God the other articles that have been contributed for use in his temple. 20 If you need to get anything else for the temple, you may have the money you need from the royal treasury.

21 Ezra, you are a priest and an expert in the laws of the God of heaven, and I order all treasurers in Western Province to do their very best to help you. 22 They will be allowed to give as much as 3,400 kilogrammes of silver, 10,000 kilogrammes of wheat, 2,000 litres of wine, 2,000 litres of olive oil, and all the salt you need.

23 They must provide whatever the God of heaven demands for his temple, so that he won't be angry with me and with the kings who rule after me. 24 We want you to know that no priests, Levites, musicians, guards, temple servants, or any other temple workers will have to pay any kind of taxes.

25 Ezra, use the wisdom God has given you and choose officials and leaders to govern the people of Western Province. These leaders should know God's laws and have them taught to anyone who doesn't know them. 26 Everyone who fails to obey God's Law or the king's law will be punished without pity. They will be executed or put in prison or forced to leave their country, or have all they own taken away.

Ezra praises God

27 Because King Artaxerxes was so kind, Ezra said:

Praise the LORD God of our ancestors! He made sure that the king honoured the LORD's temple in Jerusalem. 28 God has told the king, his advisers, and his powerful officials to treat me with kindness. The LORD God has helped me, and I have been able to bring many Jewish leaders back to Jerusalem.

CHAPTER 8

The families who came back with Ezra

1 Artaxerxes was king of Persia when I* led the following chiefs of the family groups from Babylonia to Jerusalem:

2-14 Gershom of the Phinehas family;
Daniel of the Ithamar family;
Hattush son of Shecaniah of the David family;
Zechariah and 150 other men of the Parosh family, who had family records;
Eliehoenai son of Zerahiah with 200 men of the Pahath Moab family;
Shecaniah son of Jahaziel with 300 men of the Zattu family;'
Ebed son of Jonathan with 50 men of the Adin family;
Jeshaiah son of Athaliah with 70 men of the Elam family;
Zebadiah son of Michael with 80 men of the Shephatiah family;
Obadiah son of Jehiel with 218 men of the Joab family;
Shelomith son of Josiphiah with 160 men of the Bani family;'
Zechariah son of Bebai with 28 men of the Bebai family;
Johanan son of Hakkatan with 110 men of the Azgad family;
Eliphelet, Jeuel, and Shemaiah who returned some time later with 60 men of the Adonikam family;
Uthai and Zaccur with 70 men of the Bigvai family.

Ezra finds Levites for the temple

15 I* brought everyone together by the river' that flows to the town of Ahava* where we camped for three days. Not one Levite could be found among the people and priests. 16 So I sent for the leaders Eliezer, Ariel, Shemaiah, Elnathan, Jarib, Elnathan, Nathan, Zechariah, and Meshullam. I also sent for Joiarib and Elnathan, who were very wise. 17 Then I sent them to Iddo, the leader at Casiphia,* and I told him to ask him and his temple workers to send people to serve in God's temple.

18 God was kind to us and made them send a skilful man named Sherebiah, who was a Levite from the family of Mahli. Eighteen of his relatives came with him. 19 We were also

---

*8.1,15 I: Ezra.
*8.15 town of Ahava: A town (or place) in Babylonia, but the exact location is unknown.
*8.17 Casiphia: The location is not known.

Life files

Ezra (a.k.a. Ezra the Scribe)

Background: son of Seraiah and the grandson of Azariah.

What's the story?

Ezra was an exiled Jew in Persia where he was a kind of 'Minister for Jewish Affairs'.

He was a 'priest and an expert in the laws and commands that the LORD had given to Israel'. He returned to Jerusalem around 458BC with orders from King Artaxerxes I to restore observance of the Jewish law.

He brought large number of fellow exiles as well as valuable gifts for the temple. He tried to deal with the problem of mixed marriages and led a revival in Jerusalem among those who had been living there. He may well have returned to Persia after this, since he was only sent on a temporary mission. But he returned later with Nehemiah and he led a public reading of the law of God which, again, led to revival among the hard-pressed residents of Jerusalem.

What's the point?

Ezra was a man in love with the law of God. That was his mission: to get people listening to God's word and obeying it. More than just an expert in the law, he was passionate about it; to him it wasn't an academic interest, it was life and death. That's why Ezra never did anything without prayer; he knew that without God nothing could be achieved.

Footsteps

A week with Ezra

Ezra: the brief version: Ezra 7.1–10
Ezra's job from the king: Ezra 7.11–28
Prayer before the journey: Ezra 8.15–23
Arrival: Ezra 8.31–36
Mixed marriages: Ezra 9.1–15
Ezra – it's up to you! Ezra 10.1–17
Ezra reads the law: Nehemiah 8.1–12

More...

Babylon p.437
Prayer p.1002

---

sent Hashabiah and Jeshaiah from the family of Merari along with twenty of their relatives. [20] In addition, 220 others came to help the Levites in the temple. The ancestors of these workers had been chosen years ago by King David* and his officials, and they were all listed by name.

Ezra asks the people to go without eating and to pray

[21] Beside the River﹐ Ahava, I* asked the people to go without eating* and to pray. We humbled ourselves and asked God to bring us and our children safely to Jerusalem with all our possessions. [22] I was ashamed to ask the king to send soldiers and cavalry to protect us against enemies along the way. After all, we had told the king that our God takes care of everyone who truly worships him, but that he gets very angry and punishes anyone who refuses to obey. [23] So we went without food and asked God himself to protect us, and he answered our prayers.

The gifts for the temple

[24] I* chose twelve of the leading priests — Sherebiah, Hashabiah and ten of their relatives. [25-27] Then I weighed the gifts that had been given for God's temple, and I divided them among the twelve priests I had chosen. There were gifts of silver and gold, as well as the articles that the king, his advisers and officials, and the people of Israel had contributed. In all there were: 22 tonnes of silver; 100 silver articles weighing 70 kilogrammes; 3,400 kilogrammes of gold; 20 gold bowls weighing over 8 kilogrammes; and 2 polished bronze articles as valuable as gold.

[28] I said to the priests:

> You belong to the LORD, the God of your ancestors, and these things also belong to him. The silver and gold were willingly given as gifts to the LORD. [29] Be sure to guard them and keep them safe until you reach Jerusalem. Then weigh them inside God's temple in the presence of the chief priests, the Levites, and the heads of the Israelite families.

---

*8.20 King David: See the note at 3.10.
*8.21,24 I: See the note at 8.1.
*8.21 to go without eating: The Jews often went without eating as a way of worshipping God. This is sometimes called "fasting".

30 The priests and Levites then took charge of the gifts that had been weighed, so they could take them to the temple of our God in Jerusalem.

The return to Jerusalem

31 On the twelfth day of the first month,* we left the River᾽ Ahava and started for Jerusalem. Our God watched over us, and as we travelled along, he kept our enemies from ambushing us.

32 After arriving in Jerusalem, we rested for three days. 33 Then on the fourth day we went to God's temple, where the silver, the gold, and the other things were weighed and given to the priest Meremoth son of Uriah. With him were Eleazar son of Phinehas and the two Levites, Jozabad son of Jeshua and Noadiah son of Binnui. 34 Everything was counted, weighed, and recorded.

35 Those who had returned from exile offered sacrifices on the altar to the God of Israel. Twelve bulls were offered for all Israel. Ninety-six rams and seventy-seven* lambs were offered on the altar. And twelve goats were sacrificed for the sins of the people. 36 Some of those who had returned took the king's orders to the governors and officials in Western Province. Then the officials did what they could for the people and for the temple of God.

Ezra forces men to divorce their Gentile wives

CHAPTER 9

Ezra condemns mixed marriages

1 Later the Jewish leaders came to me* and said:

Many Israelites, including priests and Levites, are living just like the people around them. They are even guilty of some of the horrible sins of the Canaanites, the Hittites, the Perizzites, the Jebusites, the Ammonites, the Moabites, the Egyptians, and the Amorites.

2 Some Israelite men have married foreign women and have let their sons do the same thing. Our own officials and leaders were the first to commit this disgusting sin, and now God's holy people are mixed with foreigners.

3 This news made me so angry that I ripped my clothes and tore hair from my head and beard. Then I just sat in shock 4 until time for the evening sacrifice. Many of our people were greatly concerned and gathered around me, because the God of Israel had warned us to stay away from foreigners.

Ezra's prayer

5 At the time of the evening sacrifice, I was still sitting there in sorrow with my clothes all torn. So I got down on my knees, then lifted my arms, 6 and prayed:

I am much too ashamed to face you, LORD God. Our sins and our guilt have swept over us like a flood that reaches up to the heavens. 7 Since the time of our ancestors, all of us have sinned. That's why we, our kings, and our priests have often been defeated by other kings. They have killed some of us and made slaves of others; they have taken our possessions and made us ashamed, just as we are today.

8 But for now, LORD God, you have shown great kindness to us. You made us truly happy by letting some of us settle in this sacred place and by helping us in our time of slavery. 9 We are slaves, but you have never turned your back on us. You love us, and because of you, the kings of Persia have helped us. It's as though you have given us new life! You let us rebuild your temple and live safely in Judah and Jerusalem.

10 Our God, what can we say now? Even after all this, we have disobeyed the commands 11 that were given to us by your servants the prophets. They said the land you are giving us is full of sinful and wicked people, who never stop doing disgusting things.* 12 And we were warned not to let our daughters and sons marry their sons and daughters.

Your prophets also told us never to help those foreigners or even let them live in peace. You wanted us to become strong and to enjoy the good things in the land, then some day to leave it to our children for ever.

13 You punished us because of our terrible sins. But you did not punish us nearly as much as we deserve, and you have brought some of us back home. 14 Why should we disobey your commands again by letting our sons and daughters marry these

---

*8.31 first month: See the note at 6.19.
*8.35 seventy-seven: Or "seventy-two".
*9.1 me: Ezra.

*9.11 doing disgusting things: Probably worshipping idols.
See also: 9.12: Exod 34.11–16; Deut 7.1–5.

foreigners who do such disgusting things? That would make you angry enough to destroy us all! [15] LORD God of Israel, you have been more than fair by letting a few of us survive. But once again, our sins have made us ashamed to face you.

CHAPTER 10

The plan for ending mixed marriages

[1] While Ezra was down on his knees in front of God's temple, praying with tears in his eyes, and confessing the sins of the people of Israel, a large number of men, women, and children gathered around him and cried bitterly.

[2] Shecaniah son of Jehiel from the family of Elam said:

Ezra, we have disobeyed God by marrying these foreign women. But there is still hope for the people of Israel, [3] if we follow your advice and the advice of others who truly respect the laws of God. We must promise God that we will divorce our foreign wives and send them away, together with their children.

[4] Ezra, it's up to you to do something! We will support whatever you do. So be brave!

[5] Ezra stood up and made the chief priests, the Levites, and everyone else in Israel swear that they would follow the advice of Shecaniah. [6] Then Ezra left God's temple and went to spend the night in the living quarters of Jehohanan son of Eliashib. He felt sorry for what the people had done, and he did not eat or drink a thing.

[7-8] The officials and leaders sent a message to all who had returned from Babylonia and were now living in Jerusalem and Judah. It told them to meet in Jerusalem within three days, or else they would lose everything they owned and would no longer be considered part of the people that had returned from Babylonia.

[9] Three days later, on the twentieth day of the ninth month,* everyone from Judah and Benjamin came to Jerusalem and sat in the temple courtyard. It was a serious meeting, and they sat there, trembling in the rain.

[10] Ezra the priest stood up and said:

You have broken God's Law by marrying foreign women, and you have made the whole nation guilty! [11] Now you must confess your sins to the LORD God of your ancestors and obey him. Divorce your foreign wives and don't have anything to do with the rest of the foreigners who live around here.

[12] Everyone in the crowd shouted:

You're right! We will do what you say. [13] But there are so many of us, and we can't just stay out here in this downpour. A lot of us have sinned by marrying foreign women, and the matter can't be settled in only a day or two.

[14] Why can't our officials stay on in Jerusalem and take care of this for us? Let everyone who has sinned in this way meet here at a certain time with leaders and judges from their own towns. If we take care of this problem, God will surely stop being so terribly angry with us.

[15] Jonathan son of Asahel and Jahzeiah son of Tikvah were the only ones who objected, except for the two Levites, Meshullam and Shabbethai.

[16] Everyone else who had returned from exile agreed with the plan. So Ezra the priest chose men' who were heads of the families, and he listed their names. They started looking into the matter on the first day of the tenth month,* [17] and they did not finish until the first day of the first month* of the next year.

The men who had foreign wives

[18-19] Here is a list of the priests who had agreed to divorce their foreign wives and to sacrifice a ram as a sin offering:

Maaseiah, Eliezer, Jarib, and Gedaliah from the family of Joshua son of Jozadak and his brothers; [20] Hanani and Zebadiah from the family of Immer; [21] Maaseiah, Elijah, Shemaiah, Jehiel, and Uzziah from the family of Harim; [22] Elioenai, Maaseiah, Ishmael, Nethanel, Jozabad, and Elasah from the family of Pashhur.

[23] Those Levites who had foreign wives were: Jozabad, Shimei, Kelaiah (also known as Kelita), Pethahiah, Judah, and Eliezer.

---

*10.9 ninth month: Chislev, the ninth month of the Hebrew calendar, from about mid-November to mid-December.

*10.16 tenth month: Tebeth, the tenth month of the Hebrew calendar, from about mid-December to mid-January.
*10.17 first month: See the note at 6.19.

²⁴ Eliashib, the musician, had a foreign wife.

These temple guards had foreign wives: Shallum, Telem, and Uri.

²⁵ Here is a list of the others from Israel who had foreign wives:

Ramiah, Izziah, Malchijah, Mijamin, Eleazar, Hashabiah,' and Benaiah from the family of Parosh;

²⁶ Mattaniah, Zechariah, Jehiel, Abdi, Jeremoth, and Elijah from the family of Elam;

²⁷ Elioenai, Eliashib, Mattaniah, Jeremoth, Zabad, and Aziza from the family of Zattu;

²⁸ Jehohanan, Hananiah, Zabbai, and Athlai from the family of Bebai;

²⁹ Meshullam, Malluch, Adaiah, Jashub, Sheal, and Jeremoth from the family of Bani;

³⁰ Adna, Chelal, Benaiah, Maaseiah, Mattaniah, Bezalel, Binnui, and Manasseh from the family of Pahath Moab;

³¹⁻³² Eliezer, Isshijah, Malchijah, Shemaiah, Shimeon, Benjamin, Malluch, and Shemariah from the family of Harim;

³³ Mattenai, Mattattah, Zabad, Eliphelet, Jeremai, Manasseh, and Shimei from the family of Hashum;

³⁴⁻³⁷ Maadai, Amram, Uel, Benaiah, Bedeiah, Cheluhi, Vaniah, Meremoth, Eliashib, Mattaniah, Mattenai, and Jaasu from the family of Bani;

³⁸⁻⁴² Shimei, Shelemiah, Nathan, Adaiah, Machnadebai, Shashai, Sharai, Azarel, Shelemiah, Shemariah, Shallum, Amariah, and Joseph from the family of Binnui;'

⁴³ Jeiel, Mattithiah, Zabad, Zebina, Jaddai, Joel, and Benaiah from the family of Nebo.

⁴⁴ These men divorced their foreign wives, then sent them and their children away.'

Additional notes

'**1.9–10 other dishes:** One possible meaning for the difficult Hebrew text.
'**2.2–20 Joshua:** Hebrew "Jeshua". In this translation the name "Joshua" is used of the descendant of Jozadak, the last chief priest before the exile; this same Joshua is often mentioned together with Zerubbabel (2.2–20; 3.2,8–9; 4.3; 5.2; 10.18–19). In other places the name "Jeshua" is used (2.2–20,36–39,40–42; 8.33).
'**2.2–20 Jeshua and Joab:** Hebrew "Jeshua Joab".
'**2.21–35 Elam:** Hebrew "the other Elam".
'**2.70 workers:** One possible meaning for the difficult Hebrew text of verse 70.

'**3.3 where it had stood before:** One possible meaning for the difficult Hebrew text.
'**3.9 Hodaviah:** Or "Yehudah" or "Hodiah".
'**4.8–10 the judges . . . Susa:** One possible translation for the names and titles.
'**5.1 Zechariah:** Aramaic "Zechariah son of Iddo".
'**5.12 the Babylonian king:** Aramaic "the Babylonian king from Chaldea", but Chaldea is another name for Babylonia.
'**6.3 so that . . . there:** One possible meaning for the difficult Aramaic text.
'**6.4 one:** One possible meaning for the difficult Aramaic text.
'**7.13–14 find out if:** Or "make sure that".
'**8.2–14 of the Zattu family:** One ancient translation; these words are not in the Hebrew text, but see 2.2–20, where Zattu is mentioned.
'**8.2–14 of the Bani family:** One ancient translation; these words are not in the Hebrew text, but see 2.2–20.
'**8.15 river:** Or "canal".
'**8.21 River:** See the note at 8.15.
'**8.31 River:** See the note at 8.15.
'**10.16 So . . . men:** One possible meaning for the difficult Hebrew text.
'**10.25 Hashabiah:** One ancient translation; Hebrew "Malchijah".
'**10.38–42 from the family of Binnui:** One possible meaning for the difficult Hebrew text.
'**10.44 away:** One possible meaning for the difficult Hebrew text of verse 44.

Nehemiah

The basics

What's the point? Nehemiah is about the need to obey God, take action and drench everything you do in prayer.

What happens? Nehemiah returns to Jerusalem and helps the Jews rebuild the city in the face of opposition.

What should I remember? 4.9 'But we kept on praying to our God, and we also stationed guards day and night.'

More details

Setting the scene It's twelve years after the end of the book of Ezra, and in the Persian city of Susa, a man called Nehemiah receives bad news...

What's it all about? The rebuilding of Jerusalem related in the book of Ezra has ground to a halt. In Susa a high-ranking Jewish official at the king's palace hears that the city's walls are broken and the defences are useless. The city is under threat.

So Nehemiah takes steps. He spends some time fasting and praying, asking God for the opportunity to put his case before the king. God answers his prayer; he notices that Nehemiah is depressed and asks him why. The result is that Artaxerxes gives Nehemiah permission to return and even gives him some building supplies to take with him.

Once at Jerusalem, Nehemiah has to overcome opposition from local enemies, but eventually the walls are finished and dedicated. Like Ezra, Nehemiah also calls the people to remain totally dedicated to God.

Nehemiah is about prayer and action. Nehemiah makes plans and puts those plans into action; but he also prays. The first thing he does when he hears the bad news about Jerusalem is to fast and pray. He prays before embarking on the journey and he prays when his life is threatened. Everything that Nehemiah does is grown out of prayer and dedication to God.

Footsteps

Nehemiah's tears: 1.1–11
Nehemiah's request: 2.1–10
Walking the walls: 2.11–20
Opposition: 4.1–23
Concern for the poor: 5.1–19
Finishing the walls: 6.1–19
Ezra reads the law: 8.1–18
Group confession: 9.1–37
The people agree: 9.38—10.39
Rededication: 13.1–31

King Artaxerxes sends Nehemiah to Jerusalem

CHAPTER 1

Nehemiah's prayer

1 I am Nehemiah son of Hacaliah, and in this book I tell what I have done.

During the month of Chislev* in the twentieth year that Artaxerxes* ruled Persia, I was in his fortress city of Susa,* 2 when my

---

*1.1 Chislev: The ninth month of the Hebrew calendar, from about mid-November to mid-December.

*1.1 Artaxerxes: Probably Artaxerxes I, who ruled Persia 465–425 BC.

*1.1 Susa: Capital of Elam Province, the winter home of Persian kings.

Life files

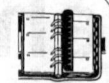

Nehemiah

Background: A Jew living in Persia and working for the king.

What's the story?

Nehemiah lives in the Persian city of Susa, where he works as the king's cup-bearer. When he hears of the situation in Jerusalem he is devastated. So he starts to pray and plan.

When the king asks why Nehemiah is depressed, Nehemiah asks for permission to go and repair the city's walls. The king not only allows him to go, he even sends some soldiers along to act as protection. In Jerusalem Nehemiah restarts the rebuilding programme, which, despite local opposition and plots against his life, takes 52 days. He encourages the people to recommit themselves to obeying God. After that he has to go back to Persia for a bit, as he promised the king.

While he is back in Persia, he hears that some of the abuses he had put down have reappeared so he returns to Jerusalem to sort things out.

What's the point?

Nehemiah really cares about his country. To him, Jerusalem was more than just a place, it was a symbol; a sign of the peoples' obedience to God. That they did not care about the city indicated that they had lost faith in God. So Nehemiah's work is about more than just putting up some walls again; it is about restoring the peoples' faith in God and helping them to live his way and not theirs.

Anorak corner

The cup-bearer was a kind of bodyguard for the King. He had to make certain that the wine was not poisoned. So Nehemiah had to be someone who was really trustworthy.

More...

Temples and shrines p.296
Persia p.510

brother Hanani came with some men from Judah. So I asked them about the Jews who had escaped' from being captives in Babylonia. I also asked them about the city of Jerusalem.

³ They told me, "Those captives who have come back are having all kinds of troubles. They are terribly disgraced, Jerusalem's walls are broken down, and its gates have been burnt."

⁴ When I heard this, I sat down and cried. Then for several days, I mourned; I went without eating to show my sorrow, and I prayed:

⁵ LORD God of heaven, you are great and fearsome. And you faithfully keep your promises to everyone who loves you and obeys your commands. ⁶ I am your servant, so please have mercy on me and answer the prayer that I make day and night for these people of Israel who serve you. I, my family, and the rest of your people have sinned ⁷ by choosing to disobey you and the laws and teachings you gave to your servant Moses.

⁸ Please remember the promise you made to Moses. You told him that if we were unfaithful, you would scatter us among foreign nations. ⁹ But you also said that no matter how far away we were, we could turn to you and start obeying your laws. Then you would bring us back to the place where you have chosen to be worshipped.

¹⁰ Our LORD, I am praying for your servants — those you rescued by your great strength and mighty power. ¹¹ Please answer my prayer and the prayer of your other servants who gladly honour your name. When I serve the king his wine today, make him pleased with me and let him do what I ask.

CHAPTER 2

Nehemiah goes to Jerusalem

¹ During the month of Nisan* in the twentieth year that Artaxerxes was king, I served him his wine, as I had done before. But this was the first time I had ever looked depressed. ² So the king said, "Why do you look so sad? You're not sick. Something must be bothering you."

---

*2.1 Nisan: Or Abib, the first month of the Hebrew calendar, from about mid-March to mid-April.
See also: 1.8: Lev 26.33. 1.9: Deut 30.1–5.

Even though I was frightened, ³ I answered, "Your Majesty, I hope you live for ever! I feel sad because the city where my ancestors are buried is in ruins, and its gates have been burnt down."

⁴ The king asked, "What do you want me to do?"

I prayed to the God who rules from heaven. ⁵ Then I told the king, "Sir, if it's all right with you, please send me back to Judah, so that I can rebuild the city where my ancestors are buried."

⁶ The queen was sitting beside the king when he asked me, "How long will it take, and when will you be back?" The king agreed to let me go, and I told him when I would return.

⁷ Then I asked, "Your Majesty, would you be willing to give me letters to the governors of the provinces west of the River Euphrates, so that I can travel safely to Judah? ⁸ I will need timber to rebuild the gates of the fortress near the temple and more timber to construct the city wall and to build a place for me to live. And so, I would appreciate a letter to Asaph, who is in charge of the royal forest." God was good to me, and the king did everything I asked.

⁹ The king sent some army officers and cavalry troops along with me, and as I travelled through the Western Provinces, I gave the letters to the governors. ¹⁰ But when Sanballat from Horon* and Tobiah the Ammonite official heard about what had happened, they became very angry, because they didn't want anyone to help the people of Israel.

Rebuilding the walls of Jerusalem

Nehemiah inspects the wall of Jerusalem

¹¹ Three days after arriving in Jerusalem, ¹² I got up during the night and left my house. I took some men with me, without telling anyone what I thought God wanted me to do for the city. The only animal I took was the donkey I rode on. ¹³ I went through Valley Gate on the west, then south past Dragon Spring, before coming to Rubbish Gate. As I rode along, I took a good look at the crumbled walls of the city and the gates that

had been torn down and burnt. ¹⁴ On the east side of the city, I headed north to Fountain Gate and King's Pool, but then the path became too narrow for my donkey. ¹⁵ So I went down to Kidron Valley and looked at the wall from there. Then before daylight I returned to the city through Valley Gate.

¹⁶ None of the city officials knew what I had in mind. And I had not even told any of the Jews — not the priests, the leaders, the officials, or any other Jews who would be helping in the work. ¹⁷ But when I got back, I said to them, "Jerusalem is truly in a mess! The gates have been torn down and burnt, and everything is in ruins. We must rebuild the city wall so that we can again take pride in our city."

¹⁸ Then I told them how kind God had been and what the king had said.

Immediately, they replied, "Let's start building now!" So they got everything ready.

¹⁹ When Sanballat, Tobiah, and Geshem the Arab heard about our plans, they started insulting us and saying, "Just look at you! Do you plan to rebuild the walls of the city and rebel against the king?"

²⁰ I answered, "We are servants of the God who rules from heaven, and he will make our work succeed. So we will start rebuilding Jerusalem, but you have no right to any of its property, because you have had no part in its history."

CHAPTER 3

Rebuilding the wall of Jerusalem

¹ These are the people who helped rebuild the wall and gates of Jerusalem:

The high priest Eliashib and the other priests rebuilt Sheep Gate and hung its doors. Then they dedicated Sheep Gate and the section of the wall as far as Hundred Tower and Hananel Tower.

² The people of Jericho rebuilt the next section of the wall, and Zaccur son of Imri rebuilt the section after that.

³ The family of Hassenaah built Fish Gate. They put the beams in place and hung the doors, then they added metal bolts and wooden beams as locks.

⁴ Meremoth, son of Uriah and grandson of Hakkoz, completed the next section of the wall.

Meshullam, son of Berechiah and grandson of Meshezabel, rebuilt the next section, and Zadok son of Baana rebuilt the section beside that.

---

*2.10 Horon: Possibly meaning that Sanballat was the official in charge of Beth-Horon, an important town on the road from Jerusalem to Lydda and the Mediterranean Sea.

See also: 2.3: 2 King 25.8–10; 2 Chron 36.19; Jer 52.12–14.

⁵ The next section was to be repaired by the men of Tekoa, but their town leaders refused to do the hard work they were assigned.'

⁶ Joiada son of Paseah and Meshullam son of Besodeiah restored Ancient Gate. They put the beams in place, hung the doors, and added metal bolts and wooden beams as locks. ⁷ Melatiah from Gibeon, Jadon from Meronoth, and the men from Gibeon and Mizpah rebuilt the next section of the wall. This section reached as far as the house of the governor of West Euphrates Province.'

⁸ Uzziel son of Harhaiah the goldsmith rebuilt the next section.

Hananiah the perfume maker rebuilt the section next after that, and it went as far as Broad Wall.

⁹ Rephaiah son of Hur ruled half of the Jerusalem District, and he rebuilt the next section of the wall.

¹⁰ The section after that was close to the home of Jedaiah son of Harumaph, and he rebuilt it.

Hattush son of Hashabneiah constructed the next section of the wall.

¹¹ Malchijah son of Harim and Hasshub son of Pahath Moab rebuilt the section after that, and they also built Oven Tower.

¹² Shallum son of Hallohesh ruled the other half of the Jerusalem District, and he rebuilt the next section of the wall. Shallum's daughters also worked with him.

¹³ Hanun and the people who lived in the town of Zanoah rebuilt Valley Gate. They hung the doors and added metal bolts and wooden beams as locks. They also rebuilt the wall for four hundred and forty metres, all the way to Rubbish Gate.

¹⁴ Malchijah son of Rechab ruled the district of Beth-Haccherem, and he rebuilt Rubbish Gate. He hung the doors and added metal bolts and wooden beams as locks.

¹⁵ Shallum' son of Colhozeh ruled the district of Mizpah, and he rebuilt Fountain Gate. He put a cover over the gateway, then hung the doors and added metal bolts and wooden beams as locks. He also rebuilt the wall at Shelah Pool. This section was next to the king's garden and went as far as the stairs leading down from David's City.

¹⁶ Nehemiah son of Azbuk ruled half of the district of Beth-Zur, and he rebuilt the next section of the wall. It went as far as the royal cemetery,' the artificial pool, and the army barracks.

Levites who worked on the wall

¹⁷ The Levites who worked on the next sections of the wall were Rehum son of Bani; Hashabiah, who ruled half of the district of Keilah and did this work for his district; ¹⁸ Binnui' son of Henadad, who ruled the other half of the district of Keilah; ¹⁹ Ezer son of Jeshua, who ruled Mizpah, rebuilt the section of the wall that was in front of the armoury and reached to the corner of the wall; ²⁰ Baruch son of Zabbai eagerly rebuilt the section of the wall that went all the way to the door of the house of Eliashib the high priest; ²¹ Meremoth, son of Uriah and grandson of Hakkoz, built up to the far end of Eliashib's house.

Priests who worked on the wall

²² Here is a list of the priests who worked on the wall:

Priests from the region around Jerusalem rebuilt the next section of the wall.

²³ Benjamin and Hasshub rebuilt the wall in front of their own houses.

Azariah, who was the son of Maaseiah and the grandson of Ananiah, rebuilt the section in front of his house.

²⁴ Binnui son of Henadad rebuilt the section of the wall from Azariah's house to the corner of the wall.

²⁵ Palal son of Uzai rebuilt the next section, which began at the corner of the wall and the tower of the upper palace near the court of the guard.

Pedaiah son of Parosh rebuilt the next section of the wall. ²⁶ He stopped at a place near the Water Gate on the east and the tower guarding the temple. This was close to a section in the city called Ophel, where the temple workers lived.'

Other builders who worked on the wall

²⁷ The men from Tekoa rebuilt the next section of the wall, and it was their second section.* It started at a place opposite the large tower that guarded the temple, and it went all the way to the wall near Ophel.

²⁸ Some priests rebuilt the next section of the wall. They began working north of Horse Gate, and each one worked on a section in front of his own house.

²⁹ Zadok son of Immer rebuilt the wall in front of his house.

---

*3.27 second section: See verse 5.

Shemaiah son of Shecaniah, who looked after the East Gate, rebuilt the section after that.

³⁰ Hananiah and Hanun' rebuilt the next section, which was the second section* for them.

Meshullam son of Berechiah rebuilt the next section, which happened to be in front of his house.

³¹ Malchijah, a goldsmith, rebuilt the next section, as far as the house used by the temple workers and merchants. This area was opposite Gathering Gate, near the room on top of the wall at the north-east corner.

³² The goldsmiths and merchants rebuilt the last section of the wall, which went from the corner room all the way to Sheep Gate.

CHAPTER 4

Nehemiah's enemies

¹ When Sanballat, the governor of Samaria, heard that we were rebuilding the walls of Jerusalem, he became angry and started insulting our people. ² In front of his friends and the Samaritan army he said, "What is this feeble bunch of Jews trying to do? Are they going to rebuild the wall and offer sacrifices all in one day? Do they think they can make something out of this pile of scorched stones?"

³ Tobiah from Ammon was standing beside Sanballat and said, "Look at the wall they are building! Why, even a fox could knock over this pile of stones."

⁴ But I prayed, "Our God, these people hate us and have wished horrible things for us. Please answer our prayers and make their insults fall on them! Let them be the ones to be dragged away as prisoners of war. ⁵ Don't forgive the mean and evil way they have insulted the builders."

⁶ The people worked hard, and we built the walls of Jerusalem halfway up again. ⁷ But Sanballat, Tobiah, the Arabs, the Ammonites, and the people from the city of Ashdod saw the walls going up and the holes being repaired. So they became angry ⁸ and decided to stir up trouble, and to fight against the people of Jerusalem. ⁹ But we kept on praying to our God, and we also stationed guards day and night.

¹⁰ Meanwhile, the people of Judah were singing a sorrowful song:

*3.30 second section: See verses 8,13.

Viewpoints

God will protect us – because he loves us!

Contributed by Anne-Marie P

'But we kept on praying to our God, and we also stationed guards day and night.'

This is an interesting verse because it can be interpreted in many different ways. Some would say that by posting a guard on duty the Jews did not fully trust God – but in fact it was a great leap of faith.

By having only one guard they showed that they trusted that God would provide. They prayed diligently and knew that all the people were needed to pray rather than guard the city.

They knew that with God on their side they were invincible and they prayed in faith until they received. That guard must have been a brave man. Even though he knew God was on their side he was one man against this huge threat of war. Yet he guarded knowing that his fellow men were praying for him and for protection from the LORD.

How many times have we shown this amount of faith? We can honestly step out knowing that God is backing us 100%. But it is one thing to say we will – when it's on the line it is very hard to be different. We can take hope from the great faith the Israelites had in their God, because that same God will protect us whatever we do because he loves us!

More...

Help! I'm scared! p.662

"So much rubble for us to haul!
  Worn out and weary,
will we ever finish this wall?"

[11] Our enemies were saying, "Before those Jews know what has happened, we will sneak up and kill them and put an end to their work."

[12] On at least ten different occasions, the Jews living near our enemies warned us against attacks from every side,' [13] and so I sent people to guard the wall at its lowest places and where there were still holes in it. I placed them according to families, and they stood guard with swords and spears and with bows and arrows. [14] Then I looked things over and told the leaders, the officials, and the rest of the people, "Don't be afraid of your enemies! The Lord is great and fearsome. So think of him and fight for your relatives and children, your wives and homes!"

[15] Our enemies found out that we knew about their plot against us, but God kept them from doing what they had planned. So we went back to work on the wall.

[16] From then on, I let half of the young men work while the other half stood guard. They wore armour and had spears and shields, as well as bows and arrows. The leaders helped the workers [17] who were rebuilding the wall. Everyone who hauled building materials kept one hand free to carry a weapon. [18] Even the workers who were rebuilding the wall strapped on a sword. The worker who was to blow the signal trumpet stayed with me.

[19] I told the people and their officials and leaders, "Our work is so spread out, that we are a long way from one another. [20] If you hear the sound of the trumpet, come quickly and gather around me. Our God will help us fight."

[21] Every day from dawn to dark, half of the workers rebuilt the walls, while the rest stood guard with their spears.

[22] I asked the men in charge and their workers to stay inside Jerusalem and stand guard at night. So they guarded the city at night and worked during the day. [23] I even slept in my work clothes at night; my children, the workers, and the guards slept in theirs as well. And we always kept our weapons close by.'

Nehemiah's concern for the poor

CHAPTER 5

[1] Some of the men and their wives complained about the Jews in power [2] and said, "We have large families, and it takes a lot of grain merely to keep them alive."

[3] Others said, "During the famine we even had to mortgage our fields, vineyards, and homes to them in order to buy grain."

[4] Then others said, "We had to borrow money from those in power to pay the government tax on our fields and vineyards. [5] We are Jews just as they are, and our children are as good as theirs. But we still have to sell our children as slaves, and some of our daughters have already been raped. We are completely helpless; our fields and vineyards have even been taken from us."

[6] When I heard their complaints and their charges, I became very angry. [7] So I thought it over and said to the leaders and officials, "How can you charge your own people interest?"

Then I called a public meeting and accused the leaders [8] by saying, "We have tried to buy back all of our people who were sold into exile. But here you are, selling more of them for us to buy back!" The officials and leaders did not say a word, because they knew this was true.

[9] I continued, "What you have done is wrong! We must honour our God by the way we live, so the Gentiles can't find fault with us. [10] My relatives, my friends, and I are also lending money and grain, but we must no longer demand payment in return. [11] Now give back the fields, vineyards, olive orchards, and houses you have taken and also the interest you have been paid."

[12] The leaders answered, "We will do whatever you say and return their property, without asking to be repaid."

So I made the leaders promise in front of the priests to give back the property. [13] Then I emptied my pockets and said, "If you don't keep your promise, that's what God will do to you. He will empty out everything you own, even taking away your houses."

The people answered, "We will keep our promise." Then they praised the LORD and did as they had promised.

See also: 5.7: Exod 22.25; Lev 25.35–37; Deut 23.19–20.

Nehemiah is generous

[14] I was governor of Judah from the twentieth year that Artaxerxes* was king until the thirty-second year. And during these entire twelve years, my relatives and I refused to accept the food that I was allowed. [15] Each governor before me had been a burden to the people by making them pay for his food and wine and by demanding forty silver coins a day. Even their officials had been a burden to the people. But I respected God, and I didn't think it was right to be so hard on them. [16] I spent all my time getting the wall rebuilt and did not buy any property. Everyone working for me did the same thing. [17] I usually fed a hundred and fifty of our own Jewish people and their leaders, as well as foreign visitors from surrounding lands. [18] Each day one ox, six of the best sheep, and lots of chickens were prepared. Then every ten days, a large supply of wine was brought in. I knew what a heavy burden this would have been for the people, and so I did not ask for my food allowance as governor. [19] I pray that God will bless me for everything I have done for my people.

The wall is finished, in spite of enemy plots

CHAPTER 6

Plots against Nehemiah

[1] Sanballat, Tobiah, Geshem, and our other enemies learnt that I had completely rebuilt the wall. All I lacked was hanging the doors in the gates. [2] Then Sanballat and Geshem sent a message, asking me to meet with them in one of the villages in Ono Valley. I knew they were planning to harm me in some way. [3] So I sent messengers to tell them, "My work is too important to stop now and go there. I can't afford to slow down the work just to visit you." [4] They invited me four times, but each time I refused to go.

[5] Finally, Sanballat sent an official to me with an unsealed letter, [6] which said:

> A rumour is going around among the nations that you and the other Jews are rebuilding the wall and planning to rebel, because you want to be their king. And Geshem᾽ says it's true! [7] You even have prophets in Jerusalem, claiming you are

now the king of Judah. You know the Persian king will hear about this, so let's get together and talk it over.

[8] I sent a message back to Sanballat, saying, "None of this is true! You are making it all up."

[9] Our enemies were trying to frighten us and to keep us from our work. But I asked God to give me strength.

[10] One day I went to visit Shemaiah.᾽ He was looking very worried, and᾽ he said, "Let's hurry to the holy place of the temple and hide there.* We will lock the temple doors, because your enemies are planning to kill you tonight."

[11] I answered, "Why should someone like me have to run and hide in the temple to save my life? I won't go!"

[12] Suddenly I realized that God had not given Shemaiah this message. But Tobiah and Sanballat had paid him to trick me [13] and to frighten me into doing something wrong, because they wanted to ruin my good name.

[14] Then I asked God to punish Tobiah and Sanballat for what they had done. I prayed that God would punish the prophet Noadiah and the other prophets who, together with her, had tried to frighten me.

The work is finished

[15] On the twenty-fifth day of the month Elul,* the wall was completely rebuilt. It had taken fifty-two days. [16] When our enemies in the surrounding nations learnt that the work was finished, they felt helpless, because they knew that our God had helped us rebuild the wall.

[17] All this time the Jewish leaders and Tobiah had been writing letters back and forth. [18] Many people in Judah were loyal to Tobiah for two reasons: Shecaniah son of Arah was his father-in-law, and Tobiah's son Jehohanan had married the daughter of Meshullam son of Berechiah.* [19] The people would always tell me about the good things Tobiah had done, and then they would tell Tobiah everything I had said. So Tobiah kept sending letters, trying to frighten me.

---

*6.10 holy place . . . hide there: Only priests were allowed to enter the holy place; anyone else could be put to death.

*6.15 Elul: The sixth month of the Hebrew calendar, from about mid-August to mid-September.

*6.18 Shecaniah . . . Berechiah: Jews who had helped rebuild the Jerusalem wall (see 3.4,29–30).

---

*5.14 Artaxerxes: See the note at 1.1.

Viewpoints 👁

Ever had those days when you just can't keep going?

Contributed by Rachel H

'But I asked God to give me strength.'

Have you ever had those days when you just can't keep going?

You didn't sleep last night. A friend needed to talk, which pushed the essay into the early hours of the morning. You didn't have time to clear your bed and sleep so you jumped in the shower to try and clear your head instead. Now the thought of staying awake for one more lesson, yet alone being God's presence at school, seems utterly impossible.

You're drained. You've dealt with confrontation, hopelessness, broken relationships – and now the printer won't work. You can hardly hold back the tears and know you won't be able to paste a smile on your face for one more hour, let alone love as Jesus loved.

You're confused. You've been faithful in sharing the good news with your friends, not giving up despite the ridicule. Now the hard questions are coming and doubt is challenging your passion. How can you remain faithful for even one more day?

I've only been at university for about two months now, and the number of times I just couldn't see how to keep going astounds me. In our own strength it's hard enough to survive on earth as humans, let alone to 'continue the work' as a follower of Christ.

I challenge you to pray. Even when the mess I've been in has been my own doing, in prayer I have found God to be gracious and completely faithful. He alone can give you strength to continue the work, and he will.

More...

Coping with suffering p.1391
Help! People are saying horrible things about me p.822
School p.64
Sharing with your friends p.1198
Sharing your faith p.1082

CHAPTER 7

1 After the wall had been rebuilt and the gates hung, then the temple guards, the singers, and the other Levites were assigned their work. 2 I put my brother Hanani in charge of Jerusalem, along with Hananiah, the commander of the fortress, because Hananiah could be trusted, and he respected God more than most people did. 3 I said to them, "Don't let the gates to the city be opened until the sun has been up for a while. And make sure that they are closed and barred before the guards go off duty at sunset. Choose people from Jerusalem to stand guard at different places around the wall and others to stand guard near their own houses."

Exiles who returned

A list of exiles who returned

This is also told in Ezra 2.1–70

4 Although Jerusalem covered a large area, not many people lived there, and no new houses had been built. 5-6 So God gave me the idea to bring together the people, their leaders, and officials and to check the family records of those who had returned from captivity in Babylonia, after having been taken there by King Nebuchadnezzar.* About this same time, I found records of those who had been the first to return to Jerusalem from Babylon Province.* By reading these records, I learnt that they settled in their own home towns, 7 and that they had come with Zerubbabel, Joshua, Nehemiah, Azariah, Raamiah, Nahamani, Mordecai, Bilshan, Mispereth, Bigvai, Nehum, and Baanah.

8-25 Here is how many had returned from each family group: 2,172 from Parosh; 372 from Shephatiah; 652 from Arah; 2,818 from Pahath Moab, who were all descendants of Jeshua and Joab; 1,254 from Elam; 845 from Zattu; 760 from Zaccai; 648 from Binnui; 628 from Bebai; 2,322 from Azgad; 667 from Adonikam; 2,067 from Bigvai; 655 from Adin; 98 from Ater, also known as Hezekiah; 328 from Hashum; 324 from Bezai; 112 from Hariph; and 95 from Gibeon.

---

*7.5–6 Nebuchadnezzar: Known as Nebuchadnezzar II, who ruled Babylonia from 605 to 562 BC. In 586 BC he destroyed Jerusalem and took many of its people to Babylonia.

*7.5–6 first to return . . . Province: Probably 539 BC, when Cyrus, the ruler of Persia, captured the city of Babylon.

26-38 Here is how many people returned whose ancestors had come from the following towns: 188 from Bethlehem and Netophah; 128 from Anathoth; 42 from Beth-Azmaveth; 743 from Kiriath-Jearim, Chephirah, and Beeroth; 621 from Ramah and Geba; 122 from Michmas; 123 from Bethel and Ai; 52 from Nebo;⸴ 1,254 from Elam;⸴ 320 from Harim; 345 from Jericho; 721 from Lod, Hadid, and Ono; and 3,930 from Senaah.

39-42 Here is how many returned from each family of priests: 973 descendants of Jeshua from Jedaiah; 1,052 from Immer; 1,247 from Pashhur; and 1,017 from Harim.

43-45 Here is how many returned from the families of Levites: 74 descendants of Hodevah from the families of Jeshua and Kadmiel; 148 descendants of Asaph from the temple musicians; and 138 descendants of Shallum, Ater, Talmon, Akkub, Hatita, and Shobai from the temple guards.

46-56 Here are the names of the families of temple workers whose descendants returned: Ziha, Hasupha, Tabbaoth, Keros, Sia, Padon, Lebana, Hagaba, Shalmai, Hanan, Giddel, Gahar, Reaiah, Rezin, Nekoda, Gazzam, Uzza, Paseah, Besai, Meunim, Nephushesim, Bakbuk, Hakupha, Harhur, Bazlith, Mehida, Harsha, Barkos, Sisera, Temah, Neziah, and Hatipha.

57-59 Here are the names of Solomon's servants whose descendants returned: Sotai, Sophereth, Perida, Jaala, Darkon, Giddel, Shephatiah, Hattil, Pochereth Hazzebaim, and Amon.

60 A total of 392 descendants of temple workers and of Solomon's servants returned.

61-62 There were 642 who returned from the families of Delaiah, Tobiah, and Nekoda, though they could not prove they were Israelites. They had lived in the Babylonian towns of Tel-Melah, Tel-Harsha, Cherub, Addon, and Immer.

63-64 The families of Hobaiah, Hakkoz, and Barzillai could not prove they were priests. The ancestor of the family of Barzillai had married the daughter of Barzillai from Gilead and had taken his wife's family name. But the records of these three families could not be found, and none of them were allowed to serve as priests.

65 In fact, the governor told them, "You cannot eat the food offered to God until he lets us know if you really are priests."*

---

*7.65 until . . . priests: The Hebrew text has "until a priest comes with the urim and thummim", sacred objects which were used in some way to receive answers from God.
See also: 7.65: Exod 28.30; Deut 33.8.

Holy history

Transport

For the most part, people walked.

Only the rich few had horses or vehicles drawn by animals. Chariots were generally military or government vehicles. Some people rode horses, but they were expensive to own and maintain.

Animals were used for transporting goods or equipment. It was always important to look after your animal, so, wherever possible, people walked alongside their donkey or mule, rather than rode on it.

Another reason why so many people walked was that the roads were not good. Even in Roman times, when the road network was pretty sophisticated, roads were still tracks. Road building consisted mainly of moving the big boulders out of the way and filling the holes.

The most common pack animals were asses and donkeys. Horses were more used for war than for transport. Camels, of course, were used by desert tribes and traders making long journeys. Returning to Jerusalem from exile in Babylon, the Jews used 435 camels (Nehemiah 7.69).

Mules were like turbo-charged donkeys. They were faster and hardier than donkeys or asses and were often used as steeds for a king to ride (1 Kings 1.44). Wagons were used mainly in the plains, where the going was easier. Again, most travellers walked alongside the wagon, rather than rode in it.

 Anorak corner

David had so many camels that he had to appoint an Arab expert – Ofil the Ishmaelite – to look after them. (1 Chronicles 27.30).

66-69 There were 42,360 who returned, in addition to 7,337 servants, and 245 musicians. Altogether, they brought with them 736 horses, 245 mules,' 435 camels, and 6,720 donkeys.

70-72 Many people gave gifts to help pay for the materials to rebuild the temple. The governor himself gave 8 kilogrammes of gold, 50 bowls to be used in the temple, and 530 robes for the priests. Family leaders gave 153 kilogrammes of gold and 1,458 kilogrammes of silver. The rest of the people gave 153 kilogrammes of gold, 1,325 kilogrammes of silver, and 67 robes for the priests.

73 And so, by the seventh month,* priests, Levites, temple guards, musicians, workers, and many of the ordinary people had settled in the towns of Judah.

Ezra reads God's Law to the people, and they celebrate the Festival of Shelters

CHAPTER 8

Ezra reads God's Law to the people

1-2 On the first day of the seventh month,* the people came together in the open area in front of the Water Gate. Then they asked Ezra, who was a teacher of the Law of Moses, to read to them from this Law that the LORD had given his people. Ezra the priest came with the Law and stood before the crowd of men, women, and the children who were old enough to understand. 3 From early morning till midday, he read the Law of Moses to them, and they listened carefully. 4 Ezra stood on a high wooden platform that had been built for this occasion. Mattithiah, Shema, Anaiah, Uriah, Hilkiah, and Maaseiah were standing to his right, while Pedaiah, Mishael, Malchijah, Hashum, Hash Baddanah, Zechariah, and Meshullam were standing to his left.

5 Ezra was up on the high platform, where he could be seen by everyone, and when he opened the book, they all stood up. 6 Ezra praised the great LORD God, and the people shouted, "Amen! Amen!" Then they bowed with their faces to the ground and worshipped the LORD.

7-8 After this, the Levites Jeshua, Bani, Sherebiah, Jamin, Akkub, Shabbethai, Hodiah, Maaseiah, Kelita, Azariah, Jozabad, Hanan, and Pelaiah went among the people, explaining the meaning of what Ezra had read.

9 The people started crying when God's Law was read to them. Then Nehemiah the governor, Ezra the priest and teacher, and the Levites who had been teaching the people all said, "This is a special day for the LORD your God. So don't be sad and don't cry!"

10 Nehemiah told the people, "Enjoy your good food and wine and share some with those who didn't have anything to bring. Don't be sad! This is a special day for the LORD, and he will make you happy and strong."

11 The Levites encouraged the people by saying, "This is a sacred day, so don't worry or mourn!" 12 When the people returned to their homes, they celebrated by eating and drinking and by sharing their food with those in need, because they had understood what had been read to them.

Celebrating the Festival of Shelters

13 On the second day of the seventh month,' the leaders of all the family groups came together with the priests and the Levites, so Ezra could teach them the Law 14 that the LORD had given to Moses. They learnt from the Law that the people of Israel were to live in shelters when they celebrated the festival in the seventh month of the year. 15 They also learnt that they were to go into the woods and gather branches of leafy trees such as olives, myrtles, and palms for making these shelters.

16 So the people gathered branches and made shelters on the flat roofs of their houses, in their yards, in the courtyard of the temple, and in the open areas around the Water Gate and Ephraim Gate. 17 Everyone who had returned from Babylonia built shelters. They lived in them and joyfully celebrated the Festival of Shelters for the first time since the days of Joshua son of Nun. 18 On each of the first seven days of the festival, Ezra read to the people from God's Law. Then on the eighth day, everyone gathered for worship, just as the Law had said they must.

---

*7.73 seventh month: Tishri (also called Ethanim), the seventh month of the Hebrew calendar, from about mid-September to mid-October.
*8.1-2 seventh month: See the note at 7.73.
See also: 7.73: 1 Chron 9.2; Neh 11.3.

See also: 8.14-15: Lev 23.33-36,39-43; Deut 16.13-15.

The people confess their sins

CHAPTER 9

[1] On the twenty-fourth day of the seventh month,' the people of Israel went without eating, and they dressed in sackcloth and threw dust on their heads to show their sorrow. [2] They refused to let foreigners join them, as they met to confess their sins and the sins of their ancestors. [3] For three hours they stood and listened to the Law of the LORD their God, and then for the next three hours they confessed their sins and worshipped the LORD.

[4] Jeshua, Bani, Kadmiel, Shebaniah, Bunni, Sherebiah, Bani, and Chenani stood on the special platform for the Levites and prayed aloud to the LORD their God. [5] Then the Levites Jeshua, Kadmiel, Bani, Hashabneiah, Sherebiah, Hodiah, Shebaniah, and Pethahiah said:

> "Stand and shout praises
> to your LORD,
>   the eternal God!'
> Praise his wonderful name,
> though he is greater
>   than words can express."

The people pray

[6] You alone are the LORD,
Creator of the heavens
   and all the stars,
Creator of the earth
   and those who live on it,
Creator of the ocean
   and all its creatures.
You are the source of life,
praised by the stars
   that fill the heavens.
[7] You are the LORD our God,
   the one who chose Abram —
you brought him from Ur
in Babylonia
   and named him Abraham.
[8] Because he was faithful,
   you made an agreement
to give his descendants
the land of the Canaanites
   and Hittites,
of the Amorites and Perizzites,
and of the Jebusites and Girgashites.

Now you have kept your promise,
   just as you always do.

[9] When our ancestors were in Egypt,
   you saw their suffering;
when they were at the Red Sea,*
   you heard their cry for help.
[10] You knew that the King of Egypt
   and his officials and his nation
   had ill-treated your people.
So you worked fearsome miracles
   against the Egyptians
and earned a reputation
   that still remains.
[11] You divided the deep sea,
and your people walked through
   on dry land.
But you tossed their enemies in,
and they sank down
   like a heavy stone.
[12] Each day you led your people
   with a thick cloud,
and at night you showed the way
   with a flaming fire.
[13] At Sinai you came down from heaven,
   and you gave your people
   good laws and teachings
   that are fair and honest.
[14] You commanded them to respect
   your holy Sabbath,
and you instructed
   your servant Moses
   to teach them your laws.
[15] When they were hungry,
   you sent bread from heaven,
and when they were thirsty,
   you let water flow from a rock.
Then you commanded them
   to capture the land
   that you had solemnly promised.

[16-17] Our stubborn ancestors
      refused to obey —
   they forgot about the miracles
      you had worked for them,
   and they were determined

9.9 Red Sea: Hebrew *yam suph* "Sea of Reeds", one of the marshes or fresh water lakes near the eastern part of the Nile Delta. This identification is based on Exodus 13.17—14.9, which lists the towns on the route of the Israelites before crossing the sea. In the Greek translation of the Scriptures made about 200 BC, the "Sea of Reeds" was named "Red Sea".

See also: 9.9: a Exod 3.7; b Exod 14.10–12.
9.10: Exod 7.8—12.32. 9.11: a Exod 14.21–29;
b Exod 15.4–5. 9.12: Exod 13.21–22.
9.13–14: Exod 19.18—23.33. 9.15: a Exod 16.4–15;
b Exod 17.1–7; c Deut 1.21. 9.16–17: Num 14.1–4;
Deut 1.26–33. 9.17: Exod 34.6; Num 14.18.

to return to Egypt
and become slaves again.
But, our God, you are merciful
and quick to forgive;
you are loving, kind,
and very patient.
So you never turned away from them —
18 not even when they made
an idol shaped like a calf
and insulted you by claiming,
"This is the god who rescued us
from Egypt."

19 Because of your great mercy,
you never abandoned them
in the desert.
And you always guided them
with a cloud by day and a fire at night.
20 Your gentle Spirit instructed them,'
and you gave them manna* to eat
and water to drink.
21 You took good care of them,
and for forty years
they never lacked a thing.
Their shoes didn't wear out,
and their feet were never swollen.

22 You let them conquer kings
and take their land,
including King Sihon of Heshbon
and King Og of Bashan.'
23 You brought them into the land
that you had promised their ancestors,
and you blessed their nation
with people who outnumbered
the stars in the sky.

24 Then their descendants
conquered the land.
You helped them defeat
the kings and nations
and treat their enemies
however they wished.
25 They captured strong cities
and rich farmland;
they took furnished houses,
as well as cisterns,*
vineyards, olive orchards,
and numerous fruit trees.
They ate till they were satisfied,
and they celebrated
your abundant blessings.

26 In spite of this, they rebelled
and disobeyed your laws.
They killed your prophets,
who warned them
to turn back to you,
and they cursed your name.
27 So you handed them over
to their enemies,
who treated them terribly.
But in their sufferings,
they begged you to help.
From heaven you listened
to their prayers
and because of your great mercy,
you sent leaders to rescue them.

28 But when they were at peace,
they would turn against you,
and you would hand them over
to their enemies.
Then they would beg for help,
and because you are merciful,
you rescued them
over and over again.
29 You warned them to turn back
and discover true life
by obeying your laws.
But they stubbornly refused
and continued to sin.
30 For years, you were patient,
and your Spirit' warned them
with messages spoken
by your prophets.
Still they refused to listen,
and you handed them over
to their enemies.
31 But you are merciful and kind,
and so you never forgot them
or let them be destroyed.

32 Our God, you are powerful,
fearsome, and faithful,
always true to your word.
So please keep in mind
the terrible sufferings
of our people, kings, leaders,
priests, and prophets,
from the time Assyria ruled
until this very day.
33 You have always been fair
when you punished us for our sins.

34 Our kings, leaders, and priests
have never obeyed your commands
or heeded your warnings.

---

*9.20 manna: This was something like a thin wafer (see Exodus 16.1–36).
*9.25 cisterns: Pits dug into the ground to hold water.
See also: 9.18: Exod 32.1–4. 9.19–21: Deut 8.2–4.
9.22: Num 21.21–35. 9.23: a Gen 15.5; 22.17;
b Josh 3.14–17. 9.24: Josh 11.23. 9.25: Deut 6.10–11.

See also: 9.26–28: Judg 2.11–16. 9.29: Lev 18.5.
9.30: 2 King 17.13–18; 2 Chron 36.15–16.
9.32: 2 King 15.19,29; 17.3–6; Ezra 4.2,10.

³⁵ You blessed them with a kingdom
and with an abundance
of rich, fertile land,
but they refused to worship you
or turn from their evil.
³⁶ Now we are slaves
in this fruitful land
you gave to our ancestors.
³⁷ Its plentiful harvest is taken
by kings you placed over us
because of our sins.
Our suffering is unbearable,
because they do as they wish
to us and our livestock.

The people sign an agreement to obey the Lord

³⁸ And so, a firm agreement was made that had the official approval of the leaders, the Levites, and priests.

CHAPTER 10

¹ As governor, I* signed the agreement together with Zedekiah and the following priests: ^{2–8} Seraiah, Azariah, Jeremiah, Pashhur, Amariah, Malchijah, Hattush, Shebaniah, Malluch, Harim, Meremoth, Obadiah, Daniel, Ginnethon, Baruch, Meshullam, Abijah, Mijamin, Maaziah, Bilgai, and Shemaiah.

⁹ The Levites who signed were: Jeshua son of Azaniah, Binnui from the clan of Henadad, Kadmiel, ¹⁰ Shebaniah, Hodiah, Kelita, Pelaiah, Hanan, ¹¹ Mica, Rehob, Hashabiah, ¹² Zaccur, Sherebiah, Shebaniah, ¹³ Hodiah, Bani, and Beninu.

¹⁴ The leaders who signed were: Parosh, Pahath Moab, Elam, Zattu, Bani, ¹⁵ Bunni, Azgad, Bebai, ¹⁶ Adonijah, Bigvai, Adin, ¹⁷ Ater, Hezekiah, Azzur, ¹⁸ Hodiah, Hashum, Bezai, ¹⁹ Hariph, Anathoth, Nebai, ²⁰ Magpiash, Meshullam, Hezir, ²¹ Meshezabel, Zadok, Jaddua, ²² Pelatiah, Hanan, Anaiah, ²³ Hoshea, Hananiah, Hasshub, ²⁴ Hallohesh, Pilha, Shobek, ²⁵ Rehum, Hashabnah, Maaseiah, ²⁶ Ahiah, Hanan, Anan, ²⁷ Malluch, Harim, and Baanah.

The agreement

^{28–29} All of us, including priests, Levites, temple guards, singers, temple workers and leaders, together with our wives and children, have separated ourselves from the foreigners in this land and now enter into an agreement with a complete understanding of what we are doing. And so, we now place ourselves under the curse of the LORD our God, if we fail to obey his laws and teachings that were given to us by his servant Moses.

³⁰ We won't let our sons and daughters marry foreigners.

³¹ We won't buy goods or grain on the Sabbath or on any other sacred day, not even from foreigners.

Every seven years we will let our fields rest, and we will cancel all debts.

³² Once a year we will each donate a small amount of silver to the temple of our God. ³³ This is to pay for the sacred bread, as well as for the daily sacrifices and special sacrifices such as those offered on the Sabbath and during the New Moon Festival and the other festivals. It will also pay for the sacrifices to forgive our sins and for all expenses connected with the worship of God in the temple.

³⁴ We have decided that the families' of priests, Levites, and ordinary people will supply firewood for the temple each year, so that sacrifices can be offered on the altar, just as the LORD our God has commanded.

³⁵ Each year we will bring to the temple the first part of our harvest of grain and fruit.

³⁶ We will bring our firstborn sons and the firstborn males of our herds and flocks and offer them to the priests who serve in the temple, because this is what is written in God's Law.*

³⁷ To the priests in the temple of our God, we will bring the bread dough from the first harvest, together with our best fruit, and an offering of new wine and olive oil.

We will bring ten per cent of our grain harvest to those Levites who are responsible for collecting it in our towns. ³⁸ A priest from the family of Aaron must be there when we give this to the Levites. Then the Levites will put one tenth of this part in the temple storeroom, ³⁹ which is also the place for the sacred objects used by

---

*10.1 I: Hebrew "Nehemiah son of Hacaliah".

*10.36 firstborn sons . . . God's Law: See Exodus 13.2, 12–15; 34.19–20.

See also: 10.30: Exod 34.16; Deut 7.3.
10.31: a Exod 23.10–11; Lev 25.1–7; b Deut 15.1–2.
10.32: Exod 30.11–16. 10.35: Exod 23.19; 34.26; Deut 26.2.
10.36: Exod 13.2. 10.37: Num 18.21. 10.38: Num 18.26.

the priests, the temple guards, and the singers.

Levites and everyone else must bring their gifts of grain, wine, and olive oil to this room.

We will not neglect the temple of our God.

The people who settled in Jerusalem and Judah

CHAPTER 11

People who settled in Jerusalem

¹ The nation's leaders and their families settled in Jerusalem. But there was room for only one out of every ten of the remaining families, and so they asked God to show them* who would live there. ² Then everyone else asked God to bless those who were willing to live in Jerusalem.

³ Some of the people of Israel, the priests, the Levites, the temple workers, and the descendants of Solomon's servants lived on their own property in the towns of Judah. But the leaders of the province lived in Jerusalem with their families.

The Judah tribe

⁴⁻⁶ From the Judah tribe, two leaders settled in Jerusalem with their relatives. One of them was Athaiah son of Uzziah. His ancestors were Zechariah, Amariah, Shephatiah, Mahalalel, and Perez, the son of Judah. From the descendants of Perez, four hundred and sixty-eight of the best men lived in Jerusalem.

The other leader from Judah was Maaseiah the son of Baruch. His ancestors were Colhozeh, Hazaiah, Adaiah, Joiarib, Zechariah, and Shelah, the son of Judah.

The Benjamin tribe

⁷⁻⁸ From the Benjamin tribe, three leaders settled in Jerusalem. The first was Sallu son of Meshullam, and the others were Gabbai and Sallai. Sallu's ancestors were Joed, Pedaiah, Kolaiah, Maaseiah, Ithiel, and Jeshaiah. Altogether, there were nine hundred and twenty-eight men of the Benjamin tribe living in Jerusalem. ⁹ Joel son of Zichri was

their leader, and Judah son of Hassenuah was second in command.

Priests

¹⁰ Four priests settled in Jerusalem. The first was Jedaiah; he was the son of Joiarib and the uncle of Jachin.*

¹¹ The second priest to settle there was Seraiah son of Hilkiah. His ancestors were Meshullam, Zadok, Meraioth, and Ahitub, who had been a high priest. ¹² Altogether, there were eight hundred and twenty-two from his clan who served in the temple.

The third priest to settle there was Adaiah son of Jeroham. His ancestors were Pelaliah, Amzi, Zechariah, Pashhur, and Malchijah. ¹³ Altogether, there were two hundred and forty-two clan leaders among his relatives.

The fourth priest to settle there was Amashsai son of Azarel. His ancestors were Ahzai, Meshillemoth, and Immer. ¹⁴ Altogether, there were one hundred and twenty-eight brave warriors from their clans, and their leader was Zabdiel son of Haggedolim.

Levites

¹⁵ Several Levites settled in Jerusalem. First, there was Shemaiah son of Hasshub. His ancestors were Azrikam, Hashabiah, and Bunni.

¹⁶ Next, there were Shabbethai and Jozabad, who were in charge of the work outside the temple.

¹⁷ Then there was Mattaniah son of Mica. His ancestors were Zabdi and Asaph. Mattaniah led the temple choir in the prayer of praise. Bakbukiah, who also settled in Jerusalem, was his assistant.

Finally, there was Abda son of Shammua; his grandfather was Galal, and his great-grandfather was Jeduthun.

¹⁸ Altogether, two hundred and eighty-four Levites settled in the holy city.

Temple guards and others

¹⁹ One hundred and seventy-two temple guards settled in Jerusalem; their leaders were Akkub and Talmon.

²⁰ The rest of the Israelites, including priests and Levites, lived on their own property in the other towns of Judah. ²¹ But

---

*11.1 asked God to show them: The Hebrew text has "cast lots". These were made of wood or stone and were thrown on the ground by a priest or official to find out how and when to do something.
See also: 11.3–6: Neh 7.73.

*11.10 son of Joiarib and the uncle of Jachin: See 1 Chronicles 9.10–12; the Hebrew text has "son of Joiarib, Jachin".

the temple workers lived in the section of Jerusalem known as Ophel, and the two men in charge of them were Ziha and Gishpa.

22 Uzzi son of Bani was the leader of the Levites in Jerusalem. His grandfather was Hashabiah, his great-grandfather was Mattaniah, and his great-great-grandfather was Mica. He belonged to the Asaph clan that was in charge of the music for the temple services, 23 though the daily choice of music and musicians was decided by royal decree of the Persian king.

24 The people of Israel were represented at the Persian court by Pethahiah son of Meshezabel from the Zerah clan of the Judah tribe.

The people in the other towns and villages

25 Some of the people of Judah lived in the following towns near their farms: Kiriath-Arba, Dibon, Jekabzeel, 26 Jeshua, Moladah, Beth-Pelet, 27 Hazar-Shual, Beersheba, 28 Ziklag, Meconah, 29 Enrimmon, Zorah, Jarmuth, 30 Zanoah, Adullam, Lachish, and Azekah. In fact, they settled the towns from Beersheba in the south to Hinnom Valley in the north.

31 The people of Benjamin lived in the towns of Geba, Michmash, Aija, Bethel with its nearby villages, 32 Anathoth, Nob, Ananiah, 33 Hazor, Ramah, Gittaim, 34 Hadid, Zeboim, Neballat, 35 Lod, and Ono, as well as in Craft Valley. 36 Several groups of Levites from the territory of Judah were sent to live among the people of Benjamin.

Priests and Levites who returned from exile

CHAPTER 12

A list of priests and Levites

1 Many priests and Levites had returned from Babylonia with Zerubbabel' and Joshua as their leaders. Those priests were Seraiah, Jeremiah, Ezra, 2 Amariah, Malluch, Hattush, 3 Shecaniah, Rehum, Meremoth, 4 Iddo, Ginnethoi, Abijah, 5 Mijamin, Maadiah, Bilgah, 6 Shemaiah, Joiarib, Jedaiah, 7 Sallu, Amok, Hilkiah, and another Jedaiah. These were the leading priests and their assistants during the time of Joshua.*

8 The Levites who returned were Jeshua, Binnui, Kadmiel, Sherebiah, Judah, and Mattaniah. They and their assistants were responsible for the songs of praise, 9 while Bakbukiah and Unno, together with their assistants, were responsible for the choral responses.

Descendants of Joshua the high priest

10 Joshua was the father of Joiakim, the grandfather of Eliashib, and the great-grandfather of Joiada. 11 Joiada was the father of Jonathan and the grandfather of Jaddua.

Leaders of the priestly clans

12 When Joiakim was high priest, the following priests were leaders of their clans: Meraiah of the Seraiah clan, Hananiah of Jeremiah, 13 Meshullam of Ezra, Jehohanan of Amariah, 14 Jonathan of Malluchi, Joseph of Shebaniah, 15 Adna of Harim, Helkai of Meraioth, 16 Zechariah of Iddo, Meshullam of Ginnethon, 17 Zichri of Abijah,' Piltai of Moadiah, 18 Shammua of Bilgah, Jehonathan of Shemaiah, 19 Mattenai of Joiarib, Uzzi of Jedaiah, 20 Kallai of Sallai, Eber of Amok, 21 Hashabiah of Hilkiah, and Nethanel of Jedaiah.

The priestly and Levite families

22 During the time of the high priests Eliashib, Joiada, Johanan, and Jaddua, and including the time that Darius was king of Persia, a record was kept of the heads of the Levite and priestly families. 23 However, no official record was kept of the heads of the Levite clans after the death of Johanan,* the grandson of Eliashib.

24 Hashabiah, Sherebiah, Jeshua son of Kadmiel,' and their assistants organized two choirs of Levites to offer praises to God, just as King David, the man of God, had commanded.

25 Mattaniah, Bakbukiah, Obadiah, Meshullam, Talmon, and Akkub were responsible for guarding the storerooms near the temple gates.

26 All these men lived during the time of Joiakim' and during the time that I was governor and Ezra, a teacher of the Law of Moses, was priest.

---

*12.7 Joshua: Joshua the high priest and friend of Zerubbabel (see verse 1 and Haggai 1.1; 2.2).

*12.23 death of Johanan: Probably between 408 and 405 BC, when Darius II died.

Nehemiah dedicates the city wall

27 When the city wall was dedicated, Levites from everywhere in Judah were invited to join in the celebration with songs of praise and with the music of cymbals, small harps, and other stringed instruments. 28-29 The Levite singers lived in villages around Jerusalem, and so they came from there, as well as from the villages around Netophah, Beth-Gilgal, Geba, and Azmaveth. 30 The priests and Levites held special ceremonies to make themselves holy, and then they did the same for the rest of the people and for the gates and walls of the city.

31 I brought the leaders of Judah to the top of the city wall and put them in charge of the two groups that were to march around on top of the wall, singing praises to God. One group marched to the right in the direction of Rubbish Gate. 32 Hoshaiah and half of the leaders followed them. 33 Then came the priests Azariah, Ezra, Meshullam, 34 Judah, Benjamin, Shemaiah, and Jeremiah, 35 all of them blowing trumpets. Next, there was Zechariah of the Asaph clan‚ 36 and his relatives, Shemaiah, Azarel, Milalai, Gilalai, Maai, Nethanel, Judah, and Hanani. They played musical instruments like those that had been played by David, the man of God. And they marched behind Ezra, the teacher of the Law. 37 When they reached Fountain Gate, they climbed the steps to David's City and went past his palace, before stopping at the Water Gate near the eastern wall of the city.

38 The second group of singers marched along the wall in the opposite direction, and I followed them, together with the other half of the leaders of Judah. We went past Oven Tower, Broad Wall, 39 Ephraim Gate, Old Gate, Fish Gate, Hananel Tower, Hundred Tower, and on to Sheep Gate. Finally, we stopped at Gate of the Guard, 40 where we stood in front of the temple with the other group, praising God. In the group with me were half of the leaders, 41 as well as the priests Eliakim, Maaseiah, Miniamin, Micaiah, Elioenai, Zechariah, and Hananiah, who were blowing trumpets. 42 Maaseiah, Shemaiah, Eleazar, Uzzi, Jehohanan, Malchijah, Elam, and Ezer also stood there, as Jezrahiah led the singers. 43 God had made the people very happy, and so on that day they celebrated and offered many sacrifices. The women and children joined in the

Viewpoints 👁

Praise the Lord – that means you!

Contributed by Sarah D

'The women and children joined in the festivities, and joyful shouts could be heard far from the city of Jerusalem.'

It may seem strange to see 'women and children' named specifically here – but this is because women and children did not usually attend assemblies during these times. Here in this passage, however, all of the people – including the women and children are gathered to dedicate the new wall they have built to protect Jerusalem. They are praising God because he has kept them safe and provided everything for them.

This verse makes it clear that everyone is to be involved in worship (see Ezra 3.13 also). No-one is to be excluded from worshipping God – and many often feel excluded from our churches or groups. We should never make anyone feel unwelcome or even forbid them to worship in a way we don't agree with (although within reason as worship must always bring glory to God!)

This should also challenge us – if no-one is to be excluded from worship, this means you also! How much praise have you been giving to God recently? You cannot excuse yourself on account of business, emotional problems, or just not 'feeling like it' – our praise to God should be continual! We have a multitude of reasons to praise him! In Philippians it says, 'Rejoice in the LORD always. I will say it again: Rejoice!' These people could be heard from 'far away' praising God – not that your worship to God should always be heard ten blocks down, but we should always be rejoicing in God and people around us should be able to see this.

More...

Worshipping God p.622

festivities, and joyful shouts could be heard far from the city of Jerusalem.

Preparation for worship

[44] On that same day, some leaders were appointed to be responsible for the safekeeping of gifts for the temple and to be in charge of receiving the first part of the harvest and the ten per cent of the crops and livestock that was offered to God. These same leaders also collected the part of crops that the Law of Moses taught was to be given to the Levites.

Everyone was pleased with the work of the priests and Levites, [45] when they performed the ceremonies to make people acceptable to worship God. And the singers and the temple guards did their jobs according to the instructions given by David and his son Solomon. [46] In fact, ever since the days of David and Asaph, there had been song leaders and songs of praise and worship. [47] During the time when Zerubbabel and I were in charge, everyone in Israel gave what they were supposed to give for the daily needs of the singers and temple guards from the Levi tribe. Then the Levites would give the priests their share from what they had received.

Changes Nehemiah made

CHAPTER 13

Foreigners are sent away

[1] On that day when the Law of Moses was read aloud to everyone, it was discovered that Ammonites and Moabites were forbidden to belong to the people of God. [2] This was because they had refused to give food and water to Israel and had hired Balaam* to call down a curse on them. However, our God turned the curse into a blessing. [3] Following the reading of the Law of Moses, the people of Israel started sending away anyone who had any foreign ancestors.

Nehemiah makes other changes

[4] The priest Eliashib was a relative of Tobiah and had earlier been put in charge of the temple storerooms. [5] So he let Tobiah live in one of these rooms, where all kinds of things had been stored — the grain offerings, incense, utensils for the temple, as well as the tenth of the grain, wine, and olive oil that had been given for the use of the Levites, singers, and temple guards, and the gifts for the priests.

[6] This happened in the thirty-second year that Artaxerxes* ruled Babylonia. I was away from Jerusalem at the time, because I was visiting him. Later I received permission from the king [7] to return to Jerusalem. Only then did I find out that Eliashib had done this terrible thing of letting Tobiah have a room in the temple. [8] It upset me so much that I threw out every bit of Tobiah's furniture. [9] Then I ordered the room to be cleaned and the temple utensils, the grain offerings, and the incense to be brought back into the room.

[10] I also found out that the temple singers and several other Levites had returned to work on their farms, because they had not been given their share of the harvest. [11] I called the leaders together and angrily asked them, "Why is the temple neglected?" Then I told them to start doing their jobs. [12] After this, everyone in Judah brought a tenth of their grain, wine, and olive oil to the temple storeroom. [13] Finally, I appointed three men with good reputations to be in charge of what was brought there and to distribute it to the others. They were Shelemiah the priest, Zadok the teacher of the Law, and Pedaiah the Levite. Their assistant was Hanan, the son of Zaccur and the grandson of Mattaniah.

[14] I pray that my God will remember these good things that I have done for his temple and for those who worship there.

The Sabbath

[15] I also noticed what the people of Judah were doing on the Sabbath. Not only were they trampling grapes to make wine, but they were harvesting their grain, grapes, figs, and other crops, and then loading these on donkeys to sell in Jerusalem. So I warned them not to sell food on the Sabbath. [16] People who had moved to Jerusalem from the city of Tyre were bringing in fish and other things to sell there on the Sabbath. [17] I got angry and said to the leaders of Judah, "This evil you are doing is an insult to the Sabbath! [18] Didn't God punish us and this city because our ancestors did these very same things? And here you are, about to make God furious again by disgracing the Sabbath!"

---

*13.2 Balaam: See Numbers 22.1–6.
See also: 12.45: a 1 Chron 25.1–8; b 1 Chron 26.12.
13.1–2: Deut 23.3–5. 13.2: Num 22.1–6.

*13.6 Artaxerxes: See the note at 1.1.
See also: 13.10: Deut 12.19. 13.12: Mal 3.10.
13.15: Exod 20.8–10; Deut 5.12–14; Jer 17.21–22.

537

¹⁹ I ordered the gates of Jerusalem to be closed on the eve of the Sabbath* and not to be opened until after the Sabbath had ended. Then I put some of my own men in charge of the gates to make certain that nothing was brought in on the Sabbath. ²⁰ Once or twice some merchants spent the night outside Jerusalem with their goods. ²¹ But I warned them, "If you do this again, I'll have you arrested." From then on, they did not come on the Sabbath. ²² I ordered the Levites to make themselves holy and to guard the gates on the Sabbath, so that it would be kept holy.

God is truly merciful, and I pray that he will treat me with kindness and bless me for doing this.

Mixed marriages

²³ I discovered that some Jewish men had married women from Ashdod, Ammon, and Moab. ²⁴ About half of their children could not speak Hebrew — they spoke only the language of Ashdod or some other foreign language. ²⁵ So in my anger, I called down curses on those men. I had them beaten and even pulled out the hair of some of them. Then I made them promise:

In the name of God we solemnly promise not to let our sons and daughters marry foreigners. ²⁶ God dearly loved King Solomon of Israel and made him the greatest king on earth, but Solomon's foreign wives led him into sin. ²⁷ So we will obey you and not rebel against our God by marrying foreign women.

²⁸ Jehoiada, the son of the high priest Eliashib, had a son who had married a daughter of Sanballat from Horon,* and I forced his son to leave.

²⁹ I pray that God will punish them for breaking their priestly vows and disgracing the Levi tribe.

³⁰ Then I made sure that the people were free from every foreign influence, and I assigned duties for the priests and Levites. ³¹ I also arranged for the people to bring firewood to the altar each day and for them to bring the first part of their harvest to the temple.

I pray that God will bless me for the good I have done.

Additional notes

›1.2 escaped: Or "returned".

›3.5 refused . . . assigned: One possible meaning for the difficult Hebrew text.

›3.7 as far as . . . Province: One possible meaning for the difficult Hebrew text.

›3.15 Shallum: A few Hebrew manuscripts and one ancient translation; most Hebrew manuscripts "Shallun"; one ancient translation "Solomon".

›3.16 royal cemetery: Hebrew "David's tombs".

›3.18 Binnui: Two ancient translations; Hebrew "Bavvai".

›3.26 This . . . lived: One possible meaning for the difficult Hebrew text.

›3.30 Hananiah and Hanun: Hebrew "Hananiah son of Shelemiah and Hanun, Zalaph's sixth son".

›4.12 against . . . side: One possible meaning for the difficult Hebrew text.

›4.23 And . . . by: One possible meaning for the difficult Hebrew text.

›6.6 Geshem: Hebrew "Gashmu" (see verse 1 and 2.19).

›6.10 Shemaiah: Hebrew "Shemaiah son of Delaiah son of Mehetabel."

›6.10 was . . . worried, and: Or "wasn't supposed to leave his house, but".

›7.26–38 Nebo: Hebrew "the other Nebo".

›7.26–38 Elam: Hebrew "the other Elam".

›7.66–69 736 horses, 245 mules: A few Hebrew manuscripts; this is not found in most Hebrew manuscripts of verse 68.

›8.13 seventh month: Hebrew "same month".

›9.1 seventh month: See the note at 8.13.

›9.5 shout . . . God: Or "shout eternal praises to the LORD your God."

›9.20 Your gentle Spirit instructed them: Or "You gently instructed them".

›9.22 Bashan: One possible meaning for the difficult Hebrew text of verse 22.

›9.30 your Spirit: Or "you".

›10.34 that the families: Or "which families".

›12.1 Zerubbabel: Hebrew "Zerubbabel son of Shealtiel".

›12.17 of Abijah: The Hebrew text adds " . . . of Miniamin".

›12.24 son of Kadmiel: Or possibly "Binnui, Kadmiel" (see 10.9; 12.8).

›12.26 Joiakim: Hebrew "Joiakim son of Joshua son of Jozadak".

›12.35 Zechariah of the Asaph clan: Hebrew "Zechariah son of Jonathan son of Shemaiah son of Mattaniah son of Micaiah son of Zaccur son of Asaph".

---

*13.19 eve of the Sabbath: The Jewish day began at sunset.

*13.28 Horon: See the note at 2.10.

See also: 13.23–25: Exod 34.11–16; Deut 7.1–5.
13.26: a 2 Sam 12.24–25; b 1 King 11.1–8. 13.28: Neh 4.1.

Esther

The basics

What's the point? God is in control. Even when we don't realise he's there.

What happens? Esther, a Jewish girl, becomes a queen in Persia and helps to save her people from being wiped out.

What should I remember? 4.14 "'If you don't speak up now, we will somehow get help, but you and your family will be killed. It could be that you were made queen for a time like this!'"

More detail

Setting the scene After the collapse of the Babylonian empire, some Jews stayed in Persia. When Emperor Xerxes stages a beauty contest for a replacement queen, a Jewish girl called Esther decides to enter...

What's it all about? Esther wins a contest to become one of Xerxes' wives. She keeps her Jewish nationality secret, because there is a lot of anti-semitism about. Particularly from Haman, one of the king's highest officials. Haman tricks the king into giving him permission to have all the Jews killed. The book tells how Queen Esther used her influence to save the Jews from this attack.

Esther is a book about liberation and rescue. It shows how God worked behind the scenes to rescue his people. This rescue is still celebrated today in the festival of Purim, which is described in the final chapter of the book.

And another thing

This is the only book of the Bible which doesn't mention God. However, God is in the background, arranging things so that his people will be protected.

Footsteps

Esther becomes queen: 2.1–18
Mordecai saves the king: 2.19–23
Haman's plot: 3.1–15
This is your moment! 4.1–17
The tables are turned: 6.1–7.10
The Jews' defence: 8.1–17
Purim: 9.20–32

Esther becomes queen

CHAPTER 1

Queen Vashti disobeys King Xerxes

1-2 King Xerxes* of Persia lived in his capital city of Susa* and ruled one hundred and twenty-seven provinces from India to Ethiopia.* ³ During the third year of his rule, Xerxes gave a big dinner for all his officials and officers. The governors and leaders of the provinces were also invited, and even the commanders of the Persian and Median armies came. ⁴ For one hundred and eighty days he showed off his wealth and spent a lot of money to impress his guests with the greatness of his kingdom.

---

*1.1–2 Xerxes: The Hebrew text has "Ahasuerus", who was better known as King Xerxes I (485–465 BC).
*1.1–2 in his capital city of Susa: Or "in his royal fortress in the city of Susa". Susa was a city east of Babylon and a winter home for Persian kings.
*1.1–2 Ethiopia: The Hebrew text has "Cush", which was a region south of Egypt that included parts of the present countries of Ethiopia and Sudan.
See also: 1.1–2: Ezra 4.6.

5 King Xerxes soon gave another dinner and invited everyone in the city of Susa, no matter who they were. The eating and drinking lasted seven days in the beautiful palace gardens.
6 The area was decorated with blue and white cotton curtains tied back with purple linen cords that ran through silver rings fastened to marble columns. Couches of gold and silver rested on pavement that had all kinds of designs made from costly bright-coloured stones and marble and mother-of-pearl.
7 The guests drank from gold cups, and each cup had a different design. The king was generous 8 and said to them, "Drink all you want!" Then he told his servants, "Keep their cups full."
9 While the men were enjoying themselves, Queen Vashti gave the women a big dinner inside the royal palace.
10 By the seventh day, King Xerxes was feeling happy because of so much wine. And he asked his seven personal servants, Mehuman, Biztha, Harbona, Bigtha, Abagtha, Zethar, and Carkas, 11 to bring Queen Vashti to him. The king wanted her to wear her crown and let his people and his officials see how beautiful she was. 12 The king's servants told Queen Vashti what he had said, but she refused to go to him, and this made him terribly angry.
13-14 The king called in the seven highest officials of Persia and Media. They were Carshena, Shethar, Admatha, Tarshish, Meres, Marsena, and Memucan. These men were very wise and understood all the laws and customs of the country, and the king always asked them what they thought about such matters.
15 The king said to them, "Queen Vashti refused to come to me when I sent my servants for her. What does the law say I should do about that?"
16 Then Memucan told the king and the officials:

Your Majesty, Queen Vashti has not only embarrassed you, but she has insulted your officials and everyone else in all the provinces.
17 The women in the kingdom will hear about this, and they will refuse to respect their husbands. They will say, "If Queen Vashti doesn't obey her husband, why should we?" 18 Before this day is over, the wives of the officials of Persia and Media will find out what Queen Vashti has done, and they will refuse to obey their husbands. They won't respect their husbands, and their husbands will be angry with them.

19 Your Majesty, if you agree, you should write for the Medes and Persians a law that can never be changed. This law would keep Queen Vashti from ever seeing you again. Then you could let someone who respects you be queen in her place.
20 When the women in your great kingdom hear about this new law, they will respect their husbands, no matter if they are rich or poor.

21 King Xerxes and his officials liked what Memucan had said, 22 and he sent letters to all his provinces. Each letter was written in the language of the province to which it was sent, and it said that husbands should have complete control over their wives and children.

CHAPTER 2

Esther becomes queen

1 After a while, King Xerxes got over being angry. But he kept thinking about what Vashti had done and the law that he had written because of her. 2 Then the king's personal servants said:

Your Majesty, a search must be made to find you some beautiful young women.
3 You can select officers in every province to bring them to the place where you keep your wives in the capital city of Susa. Put your servant Hegai in charge of them since that is his job. He can see to it that they are given the proper beauty treatments. 4 Then let the young woman who pleases you most take Vashti's place as queen.

King Xerxes liked these suggestions, and he followed them.
5 At this time a Jew named Mordecai was living in Susa. His father was Jair, and his grandfather Shimei was the son of Kish from the tribe of Benjamin. 6 Kish⸱ was one of the people whom Nebuchadnezzar had taken from Jerusalem, when he took King Jeconiah of Judah to Babylonia.
7 Mordecai had a very beautiful cousin named Esther, whose Hebrew name was Hadassah. He had raised her as his own daughter, after her father and mother died.
8 When the king ordered the search for beautiful women, many were taken to the king's palace in Susa, and Esther was one of them.

See also: 2.6: 2 King 24.10–16; 2 Chron 36.10.

Hegai was put in charge of all the women, [9] and from the first day, Esther was his favourite. He began her beauty treatments at once. He also gave her plenty of food and seven special maids from the king's palace, and they had the best rooms.

[10] Mordecai had warned Esther not to tell anyone that she was a Jew, and she obeyed him. [11] He was anxious to see how Esther was getting on and to learn what had happened to her. So each day he would walk back and forth in front of the court where the women lived.

[12] The young women were given beauty treatments for one whole year. The first six months their skin was rubbed with olive oil and myrrh, and the last six months it was treated with perfumes and cosmetics. Then each of them spent the night alone with King Xerxes. [13] When a young woman went to the king, she could wear whatever clothes or jewellery she chose from the women's living quarters. [14] In the evening she would go to the king, and the following morning she would go to the place where his wives stayed after being with him. There a man named Shaashgaz was in charge of the king's wives.* Only the ones the king wanted and asked for by name could go back to the king.

[15-16] Xerxes had been king for seven years when Esther's turn came to go to him during Tebeth,* the tenth month of the year. Everyone liked Esther. The king's personal servant Hegai was in charge of the women, and Esther trusted Hegai and asked him what she ought to take with her.⁑

[17] Xerxes liked Esther more than he did any of the other young women. None of them pleased him as much as she did, and straight away he fell in love with her and crowned her queen in place of Vashti. [18] In honour of Esther he gave a big dinner for his leaders and officials. Then he declared a holiday everywhere in his kingdom and gave expensive gifts.

Mordecai saves the king's life

[19] When the young women were brought together again, Esther's cousin Mordecai had become a palace official. [20] He had told Esther

---

*2.14 wives: This translates a Hebrew word for women who were legally bound to a man, but without the full privileges of a wife.

*2.15–16 Tebeth: The tenth month of the Hebrew calendar, from about mid-December to mid-January.

Life files

Esther (a.k.a. that's Queen Esther to you...)

Background: A Jewish girl living in the Persian city of Susa.

What's the story?

In the 5th century BC, Esther lived in exile with many other Jews in Persia (modern-day Iraq). The King of Persia banished his wife and held a beauty contest for a new queen – which Esther won.

Esther's cousin Mordecai worked in the palace and when he refused to bow down to a Persian official called Haman, Haman decided to take revenge on all Jews in Persia. He persuaded King Xerxes to issue a decree to that effect – a decree which could not be revoked.

Enter Esther. She threw a banquet for the king and persuaded him to overturn the ruling. But as the decree could not be overturned, the king ordered that all the Jews be armed. So, when Haman tried to attack, the Jews killed 500 soldiers. Haman was executed on the very gallows that he'd built to hang Mordecai.

What's the point?

Esther is a book about a people under oppression. For that reason it's always been a popular book with Jews living in conditions of oppression, such as they did in Nazi Germany. Esther was in the right place at the right time. God made her a queen so that she could rescue her people. She had the courage to act to save her people, when she could have kept her mouth shut.

Anorak corner

The book of Esther contains an account of the beauty treatments of the time (Esther 2.12–14). Six months rubbing with olive oil anyone?

More...

Guidance p.685
Racism p.1308
Feasts and festivals p.134
Suffering p.555

never to tell anyone that she was a Jew, and she obeyed him, just as she had always done.

²¹ Bigthana and Teresh were the two men who guarded King Xerxes' rooms, but they got angry with the king and decided to kill him. ²² Mordecai found out about their plans and asked Queen Esther to tell the king what he had found out. ²³ King Xerxes learnt that Mordecai's report was true, and he had the two men hanged. Then the king had all of this written down in his record book as he watched.

Haman plans to destroy the Jews

CHAPTER 3

¹ Later, King Xerxes promoted Haman the son of Hammedatha to the highest position in his kingdom. Haman was a descendant of Agag,* ² and the king had given orders for his officials at the royal gate to honour Haman by kneeling down to him. All of them obeyed except Mordecai. ³ When the other officials asked Mordecai why he disobeyed the king's command, ⁴ he said, "Because I am a Jew." They spoke to him for several days about kneeling down, but he still refused to obey. Finally, they reported this to Haman, to find out if he would let Mordecai get away with it.

⁵ Haman was furious to learn that Mordecai refused to kneel down and honour him. ⁶ And when he found out that Mordecai was a Jew, he knew that killing only Mordecai was not enough. Every Jew in the whole kingdom had to be killed.

⁷ It was now the twelfth year of the rule of King Xerxes. During Nisan,* the first month of the year, Haman said, "Find out the best time for me to do this."* The time chosen was Adar,* the twelfth month.

⁸ Then Haman went to the king and said:

Your Majesty, there are some people who live all over your kingdom and won't have a thing to do with anyone else. They have customs that are different from everyone else's, and they refuse to obey your laws. We would be better off to get rid of them! ⁹ Why not give orders for all of them to be killed? I can promise that you will get a great deal of silver for your treasury.

¹⁰ The king handed his official ring to Haman, who hated the Jews, and the king told him, ¹¹ "Do what you want with those people! You can keep their money."

¹² On the thirteenth day of Nisan, Haman called in the king's secretaries and ordered them to write letters in every language used in the kingdom. The letters were written in the name of the king and sealed by using the king's own ring.* At once they were sent to the king's highest officials, the governors of each province, and the leaders of the different nations in the kingdom of Xerxes.

¹³ The letters were taken by messengers to every part of the kingdom, and this is what was said in the letters:

On the thirteenth day of Adar, the twelfth month, all Jewish men, women, and children are to be killed. And their property is to be taken.

¹⁴⁻¹⁵ King Xerxes gave orders for these letters to be posted where they could be seen by everyone all over the kingdom. The king's command was obeyed, and one of the letters was read aloud to the people in the walled city of Susa. Then the king and Haman sat down to drink together, but no one in the city' could work out what was going on.

Mordecai asks for Esther's help

CHAPTER 4

¹ When Mordecai heard about the letter, he tore his clothes in sorrow and put on sackcloth. Then he covered his head with ashes and went through the city, crying and weeping. ² But he could go only as far as the palace gate, because no one wearing sackcloth was allowed inside the palace. ³ In every province where the king's orders were

---

*3.1 Agag: Agag was a king who had fought against the Jews long before the time of Esther (see 1 Samuel 15.1–33).
*3.7 Nisan: Or Abib, the first month of the Hebrew calendar, from about mid-March to mid-April.
*3.7 Find out . . . do this: The Hebrew text has "cast lots," which were pieces of wood or stone used to find out how and when to do something. For "lots" the Hebrew text uses the Babylonian word "purim".
*3.7 Adar: The twelfth month of the Hebrew calendar, from about mid-February to mid-March.

*3.12 king's own ring: Melted wax was used to seal a letter, and while the wax was still soft, the king's ring was pressed in the wax to show that the letter was official.

read, the Jews cried and mourned, and they went without eating.* Many of them even put on sackcloth and sat in ashes.

4 When Esther's servant girls and her other servants told her what Mordecai was doing, she became very upset and sent Mordecai some clothes to wear in place of the sackcloth. But he refused to take them.

5 Esther had a servant named Hathach, who had been given to her by the king. So she called him in and said, "Find out what's wrong with Mordecai and why he's acting this way."

6 Hathach went to Mordecai in the city square in front of the palace gate, 7 and Mordecai told him everything that had happened. He also told him how much money Haman had promised to add to the king's treasury, if all the Jews were killed.

8 Mordecai gave Hathach a copy of the orders for the murder of the Jews and told him that these had been read in Susa. He said, "Show this to Esther and explain what it means. Ask her to go to the king and beg him to have pity on her people, the Jews!"

9 Hathach went back to Esther and told her what Mordecai had said. 10 She answered, "Tell Mordecai 11 there is a law about going in to see the king, and all his officials and his people know about this law. Anyone who goes in to see the king without being invited by him will be put to death. The only way that anyone can be saved is for the king to hold out the gold sceptre to that person. And it's been thirty days since he has asked for me."

12 When Mordecai was told what Esther had said, 13 he sent back this reply, "Don't think that you will escape being killed with the rest of the Jews, just because you live in the king's palace. 14 If you don't speak up now, we will somehow get help, but you and your family will be killed. It could be that you were made queen for a time like this!"

15 Esther sent a message to Mordecai, saying, 16 "Bring together all the Jews in Susa and tell them to go without eating for my sake! Don't eat or drink for three days and nights. My servant girls and I will do the same. Then I will go in to see the king, even if it means I must die."

17 Mordecai did everything Esther told him to do.

---

*4.3 went without eating: The Israelites would sometimes go without eating (also called "fasting") in times of great sorrow or danger.

Mordecai is honoured, not killed

CHAPTER 5

Esther invites the king and Haman to a dinner

1 Three days later, Esther dressed in her royal robes and went to the inner court of the palace in front of the throne. The king was sitting there, facing the open doorway. 2 He was happy to see Esther, and he held out the gold sceptre to her.

When Esther came up and touched the tip of the sceptre, 3 the king said, "Esther, what brings you here? Just ask, and I will give you as much as half of my kingdom."

4 Esther answered, "Your Majesty, please come with Haman to a dinner I will prepare for you later today."

5 The king said to his servants, "Hurry and get Haman, so we can accept Esther's invitation."

The king and Haman went to Esther's dinner, 6 and while they were drinking wine, the king asked her, "What can I do for you? Just ask, and I will give you as much as half of my kingdom."

7-8 Esther replied, "Your Majesty, if you really care for me and are willing to do what I want, please come again tomorrow with Haman to the dinner I will prepare for you. At that time I will answer Your Majesty's question."

Haman plans to kill Mordecai

9 Haman was feeling great as he left. But when he saw Mordecai at the palace gate, he noticed that Mordecai did not stand up or show him any respect. This made Haman really angry, 10 but he did not say a thing.

When Haman got home, he called together his friends and his wife Zeresh 11 and started boasting about his great wealth and all his sons. He told them the many ways that the king had honoured him and how all the other officials and leaders had to respect him.

12 Haman added, "That's not all! Besides the king himself, I'm the only person Queen Esther invited for dinner. She has also invited the king and me to dinner tomorrow. 13 But none of this makes me happy, as long as I see that Jew Mordecai sitting at the palace gate."

14 Haman's wife and friends said to him, "Have a tower built about twenty-two metres high, and tomorrow morning ask the king to

hang Mordecai there. Then later, you can have dinner with the king and enjoy yourself."

This seemed like a good idea to Haman, and he had the tower built.

CHAPTER 6

The king honours Mordecai

¹ That night the king could not sleep, and he got a servant to read him the records of what had happened since he had been king. ² When the servant read how Mordecai had kept Bigthana and Teresh from killing the king, ³ the king asked, "What has been done to reward Mordecai for this?"

"Nothing, Your Majesty!" the king's servants replied.

⁴ About this time, Haman came in to ask the king to have Mordecai hanged on the tower he had built. The king saw him and asked, "Who is that man waiting in front of the throne room?"

⁵ The king's servants answered, "Your Majesty, it is Haman."

"Tell him to come in," the king commanded.

⁶ When Haman entered the room, the king asked him, "What should I do for a man I want to honour?"

Haman was sure that he was the one the king wanted to honour. ⁷ So he replied, "Your Majesty, if you wish to honour a man, ⁸ get someone to bring him one of your own robes and one of your own horses with a fancy head-dress. ⁹ Tell one of your highest officials to place your robe on this man and lead him through the streets on your horse, while someone shouts, 'This is how the king honours a man!' "

¹⁰ The king replied, "Hurry and do just what you have said! Don't forget a thing. Get the robe and the horse for Mordecai the Jew, who is on duty at the palace gate!"

¹¹ Haman got the king's robe and put it on Mordecai. He led him through the city on the horse and shouted as he went, "This is how the king honours a man!"

¹² Afterwards, Mordecai returned to his duties at the palace gate, and Haman hurried home, hiding his face in shame. ¹³ Haman told his wife and friends what had happened. Then his wife and his advisers said, "If Mordecai is a Jew, this is just the beginning of your troubles! You will end up a ruined man." ¹⁴ They were still talking, when the king's servants came and quickly took Haman to the dinner that Esther had prepared.

See also: 6.2: Esth 2.21–22.

544

Haman is put to death

CHAPTER 7

¹ The king and Haman were dining with Esther ² and drinking wine during the second dinner, when the king again said, "Esther, what can I do for you? Just ask, and I will give you as much as half of my kingdom!"

³ Esther answered, "Your Majesty, if you really care for me and are willing to help, you can save me and my people. That's what I really want, ⁴ because a reward has been promised to anyone who kills my people. Your Majesty, if we were merely going to be sold as slaves, I would not have bothered you."

⁵ "Who would dare to do such a thing?" the king asked.

⁶ Esther replied, "That evil Haman is the one out to get us!"

Haman was terrified, as he looked at the king and the queen.

⁷ The king was so angry that he got up, left his wine, and went out into the palace garden.

Haman realized that the king had already decided what to do with him, and he stayed and begged Esther to save his life.

⁸ Just as the king came back into the room, Haman got down on his knees beside Esther, who was lying on the couch. The king shouted, "Now you're even trying to rape my queen here in my own palace!"

As soon as the king said this, his servants covered Haman's head. ⁹ Then Harbona, one of the king's personal servants, said, "Your Majesty, Haman built a tower twenty-two metres high beside his house, so he could hang Mordecai on it. And Mordecai is the very one who spoke up and saved your life."

"Hang Haman from his own tower!" the king commanded. ¹⁰ Straight away, Haman was hanged on the tower he had built to hang Mordecai, and the king calmed down.

The Jews defend themselves and kill their enemies

CHAPTER 8

A happy ending for the Jews

¹ Before the end of the day, King Xerxes gave Esther everything that had belonged to Haman, the enemy of the Jews. Esther told the king that Mordecai was her cousin. So the king made Mordecai one of his highest

officials [2] and gave him the royal ring that Haman had worn. Then Esther put Mordecai in charge of Haman's property.

[3] Once again Esther went to speak to the king. This time she fell down at his feet, crying and begging, "Please stop Haman's evil plan to have the Jews killed!" [4] King Xerxes held out the golden sceptre to Esther, [5] and she got up and said, "Your Majesty, I know that you will do the right thing and that you really love me. Please stop what Haman has planned. He has already sent letters demanding that the Jews in all your provinces be killed, [6] and I can't bear to see my people and my own relatives destroyed."

[7] King Xerxes then said to Esther and Mordecai, "I have already ordered Haman to be hanged and his house given to Esther, because of his evil plans to kill the Jews. [8] I now give you permission to make a law that will save the lives of your people. You may use my ring to seal the law, so that it can never be changed."

[9] On the twenty-third day of Sivan,* the third month, the king's secretaries wrote the law. They obeyed Mordecai and wrote to the Jews, the rulers, the governors, and the officials of all one hundred and twenty-seven provinces from India to Ethiopia.* The letters were written in every language used in the kingdom, including the Jewish language. [10] They were written in the name of King Xerxes and sealed with his ring. Then they were taken by messengers who rode the king's finest and fastest horses.

[11-13] In these letters the king said:

On the thirteenth day of Adar,* the twelfth month, the Jews in every city and province will be allowed to get together and defend themselves. They may destroy any army that attacks them, and they may kill all their enemies, including women and children. They may also take everything that belongs to their enemies.

A copy of this law was to be posted in every province and read by everyone.

[14-15] Then the king ordered his messengers to take their fastest horses and deliver the law as quickly as possible to every province. When Mordecai left, he was wearing clothes fit for a king. He wore blue and white robes, a large gold crown, and a cape made of fine linen and purple cloth.

After the law was announced in Susa, everyone shouted and cheered, [16] and the Jews were no longer afraid. In fact, they were very happy and felt that they had won a victory.

[17] In every province and city where the law was sent, the Jews had parties and celebrated. Many of the people in the provinces accepted the Jewish religion, because they were now afraid of the Jews.

CHAPTER 9

The Jews destroy their enemies

[1] The first law that the king had made was to be followed on the thirteenth day of Adar,* the twelfth month. This was the very day that the enemies of the Jews had hoped to do away with them. But the Jews turned things around, [2] and in the cities of every province they came together to attack their enemies. Everyone was afraid of the Jews, and no one could do anything to oppose them.

[3] The leaders of the provinces, the rulers, the governors, and the court officials were afraid of Mordecai and took sides with the Jews. [4] Everyone in the provinces knew that the king had promoted him and had given him a lot of power.

[5] The Jews took their swords and did away with their enemies, without showing any mercy. [6-10] They killed five hundred people in Susa,' but they did not take anything that belonged to the ones they killed. Haman had been one of the worst enemies of the Jews, and ten of his sons were among those who were killed. Their names were Parshandatha, Dalphon, Aspatha, Poratha, Adalia, Aridatha, Parmashta, Arisai, Aridai, and Vaizatha.

[11] Later that day, someone told the king how many people had been killed in Susa.' [12] Then he told Esther, "Five hundred people, including Haman's ten sons, have been killed in Susa alone. If that many were killed here, what must have happened in the provinces? Is there anything else you want done? Just tell me, and it will be done."

[13] Esther answered, "Your Majesty, please let the Jews in Susa fight to defend themselves tomorrow, just as they did today. And order the bodies of Haman's ten sons to be hanged in public."

[14] King Xerxes did what Esther had requested, and the bodies of Haman's sons were hung in Susa. [15] Then on the fourteenth

---

*8.9 Sivan: The third month of the Hebrew calendar, from about mid-May to mid-June.
*8.9 Ethiopia: See the note at 1.1–2.
*8.11–13 Adar: See the note at 3.7.

*9.1 Adar: See the note at 3.7.

day of Adar the Jews of the city got together and killed three hundred more people. But they still did not take anything that belonged to their enemies.

16-17 On the thirteenth day of Adar, the Jews in the provinces had come together to defend themselves. They killed seventy-five thousand of their enemies, but the Jews did not take anything that belonged to the ones they killed. Then on the fourteenth day of the month the Jews celebrated with a feast.

18 On the fifteenth day of the month the Jews in Susa held a holiday and celebrated, after killing their enemies on the thirteenth and the fourteenth. 19 This is why the Jews in the villages now celebrate on the fourteenth day of the month. It is a joyful holiday that they celebrate by feasting and sending gifts of food to each other.

The Festival of Purim

20 Mordecai wrote down everything that had happened. Then he sent letters to the Jews everywhere in the provinces 21 and told them:

Each year you must celebrate on both the fourteenth and the fifteenth of Adar, 22 the days when we Jews defeated our enemies. Remember this month as a time when our sorrow was turned to joy, and celebration took the place of crying. Celebrate by having parties and by giving to the poor and by sharing gifts of food with each other.

23 They followed Mordecai's instructions and set aside these two days every year as a time of celebration.

The reason for the Festival of Purim

24 Haman was the son of Hammedatha and a descendant of Agag. He hated the Jews so much that he planned to destroy them, but he wanted to find out the best time to do it. So he cast lots.*

25 Esther went to King Xerxes and asked him to save her people. Then the king gave written orders for Haman and his sons to be punished in the same terrible way that Haman had in mind for the Jews. So they were hanged. 26 Mordecai's letter had said that the Jews must celebrate for two days because of what had happened to them. This

time of celebration is called Purim,* which is the Hebrew word for the lots that were cast. 27 Now every year the Jews set aside these two days for having parties and celebrating, just as they were told to do. 28 From now on, all Jewish families must remember to celebrate Purim on these two days each year.

29 Queen Esther, daughter of Abihail, wanted to give full authority to Mordecai's letter about the Festival of Purim, and with his help she wrote a letter about the feast. 30 Copies of this letter were sent to Jews in the one hundred and twenty-seven provinces of King Xerxes. In the letter they said:

We pray that all of you will live in peace and safety. 31 You and your descendants must always remember to celebrate Purim at the time and in the way that we have said. You must also follow the instructions that we have given you about mourning and going without eating.* 32 These laws about Purim are written by the authority of Queen Esther.

The greatness of Xerxes and Mordecai

CHAPTER 10

1 King Xerxes made everyone in his kingdom pay taxes, even those in lands across the sea. 2 All the great and famous things that King Xerxes did are written in the record books of the kings of Media and Persia. These records also tell about the honours that the king gave to Mordecai. 3 Next to the king himself, Mordecai was the highest official in the kingdom. He was a popular leader of the Jews, because he helped them in many ways and would even speak to the king for them.

*9.26 Purim: The Jewish Festival of Purim got its name from "purim", which is the Babylonian name for the lots that Haman used. Purim is celebrated each year on the 14th and 15th of Adar, which is about the first of March.
*9.31 going without eating: See the note at 4.3.

Additional notes

'2.6 Kish: Or "Mordecai". The Hebrew text has "He".
'2.15-16 her: The Hebrew text adds, "Esther was the daughter of Abihail and was the cousin of Mordecai, who had adopted her after her parents died" (see verse 7).

*9.24 cast lots: See the note at 3.7.
See also: 9.24: Esth 3.7.

›**3.14–15 walled city . . . city:** Or "royal fortress . . . rest of the city".
›**7.4 I would . . . bothered you:** One possible meaning for the difficult Hebrew text.
›**9.6–10 in Susa:** Or "in the royal fortress in Susa".
›**9.11 in Susa:** See the note at 9.6–10.

Holy history

Wisdom

The Hebrew word for 'wisdom' has a meaning similar to 'life skills'.

This is not some airy-fairy theory that we're talking about here, but practical advice to help you live your life.

Collecting wisdom, therefore, was very important to the people of ancient times. It was important to listen to people who were considered wise, to collect their observations and learn from their experiences.

Five books in the Bible – Psalms, Job, Proverbs, Ecclesiastes and the Song of Songs – are grouped together in a section called 'wisdom literature'. They're extremely varied in their subject matter. All human life is here. Pain, pleasure, love, hate, sex, anger, cynical boredom, wild jubilation – all the emotions and attitudes which fill our days can be found in these five books.

In many ways they are the most 'human' books of the Bible. They ask difficult questions and reflect bleak and often depressing moods, but just as they talk about the bad things, they also celebrate the good. There is often an almost awe-struck appreciation of the physical world and what it means to be human. However, these are not just pragmatic skills to get us through the day. They are focused on God, on his relationship with humanity and how all wisdom and knowledge is based on a proper respect for him and his works.

Job

A long examination of the problem of suffering. Job is a good man, but he ends up sitting on a rubbish heap and scratching himself with bits of pottery. How can that be right?

Psalms

A collection of 150 poems or songs, written by many different authors. Some are full of joy, some are full of despair – you get the complete range of human emotion in here. Psalms is a kind of spiritual journal, reflecting on all the ups and downs of a believer's life.

Proverbs

A collection of wise and insightful sayings to help you live your life right. It's a kind of mini-guide to human behaviour.

Ecclesiastes

One of the weirdest books in the Bible. A dark, almost depressive meditation on the futility of life. The book recognises God's greatness, but the mood is pretty sombre and bleak.

Song of Songs

A love poem, about how good it is to fall in love. It's about men and women and the joys of a physical relationship. Not to mention gazelles.

More...

Guidance p.685
Different types of psalm p.584

Job

The basics

What's the point? A look at one basic question: why do good men suffer?

What happens? Job is a good man who loses everything. His friends tell him he is suffering because of his sin. He knows this isn't true. He wants to find out the truth from God. In the end God confronts Job and all his questions disappear.

What should I remember? 19.25–26 'I know that my Saviour lives, and at the end he will stand on this earth. My flesh may be destroyed, yet from this body I will see God.'

More details

Setting the scene Job is a good man, a 'righteous' man. Then everything he has is taken away from him. Will he lose his faith as well? Now read on...

What's it all about? Suffering and faith.

Job is one of the most profound books of the Bible, because it deals with one of the most profound problems – why do good people suffer?

Job is a good man. He is described as a man of integrity. He's a bit like Abraham, rich in livestock, living to a great age and blessed with a big family. It's all going well.

Then he loses the lot. His family die, his riches are wiped out, he catches a horrible disease. He's reduced to sitting on a rubbish heap shouting out questions to God.

People used to talk about 'the patience of Job', to describe people who demonstrate a saintly endurance in the face of trial or disaster. But in fact, Job isn't patient. That's the point. Job shouts; he argues; he rants and raves. He is not prepared to wait until the ordeal is over; he wants an explanation. And he wants it now.

And yet he never loses his faith. Job firmly holds on to one fact: God exists. So he believes that there must be some kind of explanation. To find out what's going on, Job is 'helped' by a series of friends who argue and debate with him. They are certain that he must deserve this, he must have sinned. But Job remains resolute. He knows he hasn't sinned. He knows that he doesn't deserve this suffering. He doesn't lose faith in God, he just wants to know what's going on.

Job and his friends want a nice, neat solution to why suffering occurs, but they don't get one. Instead they come face to face with God; and in the light of that they accept that some questions just have to be put aside.

The book may be concerned with the problem of suffering, but in the end it doesn't actually answer the question. In the end, God sweeps in, washing away all the arguments and the shallow theories with the reality of his power and presence.

And another thing

Job lives in 'the land of Uz' which is 'somewhere in the East'. In other words, he's not an Israelite. This is an important point, because it shows that all people can worship God, and all people have to face the problem of suffering.

Footsteps

Job loses everything: 1.1–22
On the scrapheap: 2.1–13
I wish I'd never been born! 3.1–26
What have I done wrong? 6.1–30
Why do we suffer? 7.1–21
Sick of life: 10.1–22
You think you're so great: 12.1–25
Bildad accuses Job: 18.1–21

Job loses his wealth, family, and health

CHAPTER 1

Job and his family

¹ Many years ago, a man named Job lived in the land of Uz.* He was a truly good person, who respected God and refused to do evil.

² Job had seven sons and three daughters. ³ He owned seven thousand sheep, three thousand camels, five hundred pair of oxen, five hundred donkeys, and a large number of servants. He was the richest person in the East.

⁴ Job's sons took turns having feasts in their homes, and they always invited their three sisters to join in the eating and drinking. ⁵ After each feast, Job would send for his children and perform a ceremony, as a way of asking God to forgive them for any wrongs they might have done. He would get up early the next morning and offer a sacrifice for each of them, just in case they had sinned or silently cursed God.

Angels, the LORD, and Satan

⁶ One day, when the angels* had gathered around the LORD, and Satan⁹ was there with them, ⁷ the LORD asked, "Satan, where have you been?"

Satan replied, "I have been going all over the earth."

⁸ Then the LORD asked, "What do you think of my servant Job? No one on earth is like him — he is a truly good person, who respects me and refuses to do evil."

⁹ "Why shouldn't he respect you?" Satan remarked. ¹⁰ "You are like a wall protecting not only him, but his entire family and all

---

*1.1 Uz: The exact location of this place is unknown, though it was possibly somewhere in north-west Arabia.
*1.6 angels: See the note at 15.8.
See also: 1.6: Gen 6.2.   1.9–11: Rev 12.10.

Life files

Job

Background: A resident of Uz. Married with lots of children.

What's the story?

Job is a truly good man. But God allows him to be tested to the point of destruction, to see whether his faith is real. He loses most of his family, all his possessions and ends up sitting on a rubbish heap covered in sores. Various 'comforters' come along to try to get him to admit that he's done something wrong, but Job refuses to admit it.

They spend a lot of time arguing. In the end, God turns up in a storm and, faced with this majesty, Job humbles himself. God rewards Job by giving him more than before.

Job is portrayed as a kind of ancestor figure, similar to Abraham and Isaac. But, significantly, he is not a Hebrew. He doesn't figure in any of the family trees and he lived in Uz, a land east of the Jordan.

What's the point?

Job asks questions. Faced with suffering which he knows he has done little to deserve, he dares to ask difficult questions about suffering and existence. Yet he does not lose his faith. Even though he has to endure some appalling trials and conditions, he still believes in God.

The fact that Job is not a Hebrew is important, because the kind of questions that Job raises are universal. Everyone, struggles to understand the problem of suffering. And everyone, whatever their nationality, can have faith in God.

Anorak corner

Job is a patron saint of hospitals.

More...

Suffering p.555
Coping with suffering p.1391
Dealing with doubt p.554

his property. You make him successful in whatever he does, and his flocks and herds are everywhere. 11 Try taking away everything he owns, and he will curse you to your face."

12 The LORD replied, "All right, Satan, do what you want with anything that belongs to him, but don't harm Job."

Then Satan left.

Job loses everything

13 Job's sons and daughters were having a feast in the home of his eldest son, 14 when someone rushed up to Job and said, "While your servants were ploughing with your oxen, and your donkeys were nearby eating grass, 15 a gang of Sabeans* attacked and stole the oxen and donkeys! Your other servants were killed, and I was the only one who escaped to tell you."

16 That servant was still speaking, when a second one came running up and saying, "God sent down a fire that killed your sheep and your servants. I am the only one who escaped to tell you."

17 Before that servant finished speaking, a third one raced up and said, "Three gangs of Chaldeans* attacked and stole your camels! All your other servants were killed, and I am the only one who escaped to tell you."

18 That servant was still speaking, when a fourth one dashed up and said, "Your children were having a feast and drinking wine at the home of your eldest son, 19 when suddenly a storm from the desert blew the house down, crushing all your children. I am the only one who escaped to tell you."

20 When Job heard this, he tore his clothes and shaved his head because of his great sorrow. He knelt on the ground, then worshipped God 21 and said:

"We bring nothing at birth;
    we take nothing with us at death.
The LORD alone gives and takes.
    Praise the name of the LORD!"

22 In spite of everything, Job did not sin or accuse God of doing wrong.

CHAPTER 2

Job loses his health

1 When the angels* gathered around the LORD again, Satan' was there with them, 2 and the LORD asked, "Satan, where have you been?"

Satan replied, "I have been going all over the earth."

3 Then the LORD asked, "What do you think of my servant Job? No one on earth is like him — he is a truly good person, who respects me and refuses to do evil. And he hasn't changed, even though you persuaded me to destroy him for no reason."

4 Satan answered, "There's no pain like your own.' People will do anything to stay alive. 5 Try striking Job's own body with pain, and he will curse you to your face."

6 "All right!" the LORD replied. "Make Job suffer as much as you want, but just don't kill him." 7 Satan left and caused painful sores to break out all over Job's body — from head to toe.

8 Then Job sat on the ash-heap to show his sorrow. And while he was scraping his sores with a broken piece of pottery, 9 his wife asked, "Why do you still trust God? Why don't you curse him and die?"

10 Job replied, "Don't talk like a fool! If we accept blessings from God, we must accept trouble as well." In all that happened, Job never once said anything against God.

Job's three friends

11 Eliphaz from Teman, Bildad from Shuah, and Zophar from Naamah* were three of Job's friends, and they heard about his troubles. So they agreed to visit Job and comfort him. 12 When they came near enough to see Job, they could hardly recognize him. And in their great sorrow, they tore their clothes, then sprinkled dust on their heads and cried bitterly. 13 For seven days and nights, they sat silently on the ground beside him, because they realized what terrible pain he was in.

---

*2.1 **angels:** See the note at 15.8.
*2.11 **Teman . . . Shuah . . . Naamah:** Teman was a place in northern Edom; Shuah may have been a town on the River Euphrates or else further south, near the towns of Dedan and Sheba; Naamah may have been on the road between Beirut and Damascus, though its exact location is unknown.

*1.15 **Sabeans:** Perhaps the people of Sheba in what is now south-west Arabia (see Isaiah 60.6).
*1.17 **Chaldeans:** People from the region of Babylonia, north-east of Palestine.

Job curses the day of his birth

CHAPTER 3

Job's first speech

Blot out the day of my birth

¹ Finally, Job cursed the day of his birth ² by saying to God:

³ Blot out the day of my birth
and the night when my parents
created a son.
⁴ Forget about that day,
cover it with darkness,
⁵ and send thick, gloomy shadows
to fill it with dread.
⁶ Erase that night from the calendar
and conceal it with darkness.
⁷ Don't let children be created
or joyful shouts be heard ever again
in that night.
⁸ Let those with magic powers*
place a curse on that day.
⁹ Darken its morning stars
and remove all hope of light,
¹⁰ because it let me be born
into a world of trouble.

Why didn't I die at birth?

¹¹ Why didn't I die at birth?
¹²   Why was I accepted'
and allowed to nurse
at my mother's breast?
¹³ Now I would be at peace
in the silent world below
¹⁴ with kings and their advisers
whose palaces lie in ruins,
¹⁵   and with rulers once rich
with silver and gold.
¹⁶ I wish I had been born dead
and then buried,
never to see the light of day.
¹⁷ In the world of the dead,
the wicked and the weary rest
without a worry.

¹⁸⁻¹⁹ Everyone is there —
where captives and slaves
are free at last.

Why does God let me live?

²⁰ Why does God let me live
when life is miserable and so bitter?
²¹ I keep longing for death
more than I would seek
a valuable treasure.
²² Nothing could make me happier
than to be in the grave.
²³ Why do I go on living
when God has me surrounded,
and I can't see the road?
²⁴ Moaning and groaning
are my food and drink,
²⁵   and my worst fears
have all come true.
²⁶ I have no peace or rest —
only troubles and worries.

The first round of the debate

CHAPTER 4

Eliphaz's first speech

Please be patient and listen

¹ Eliphaz from Teman* said:

² Please be patient and listen
to what I have to say.
³⁻⁴ Remember how your words
have guided and encouraged
many in need.
⁵ But now you feel discouraged
when struck by trouble.
⁶ You respect God and live right,
so don't lose hope!
⁷ No truly innocent person
has ever died young.
⁸ In my experience, only those
who plant seeds of evil
harvest trouble,
⁹ and then they are swept away
by the angry breath of God.
¹⁰ They may roar and growl
like powerful lions.
But when God breaks their teeth,
¹¹   they starve,
and their children are scattered.

---

*3.8 those with magic powers: The Hebrew text has "those who can place a curse on the day and rouse up Leviathan", which was some kind of sea monster. God's victory over this monster sometimes stood for God's power over all creation and sometimes for his defeat of his enemies (see Isaiah 27.1). In Job 41.1, Leviathan is either a sea monster or a crocodile with almost supernatural powers.

See also: 3.1-19: Jer 20.14-18.

---

*4.1 Teman: See the note at 2.11.

See also: 3.21: Rev 9.6.

A secret was told to me

¹² A secret was told to me
in a faint whisper —
¹³ I was overcome by sleep,
but disturbed by dreams;
¹⁴ I trembled with fear,
¹⁵ and my hair stood on end,
as a wind blew past my face.
¹⁶ It stopped and stood still.
Then a form appeared —
a shapeless form.
And from the silence,
I heard a voice say,
¹⁷ "No humans are innocent
in the eyes of God their Creator.
¹⁸ He finds fault with his servants
and even with his angels.
¹⁹ Humans are formed from clay
and are fragile as moths,
so what chance do you have?
²⁰ Born after daybreak,
you die before nightfall
and disappear for ever.
²¹ Your tent pegs are pulled up,
and you leave this life,
having gained no wisdom."

CHAPTER 5

Eliphaz continues

Call out for help

¹ Job, call out for help
and see if an angel comes!

² Envy and jealousy
will kill a stupid fool.
³ I have seen fools take root.
But God sends a curse,
suddenly uprooting them
⁴ and leaving their children
helpless in court.
⁵ Then hungry and greedy people
gobble up their crops
and grab their wealth.'
⁶ Our suffering isn't caused
by the failure of crops;
⁷ it's all part of life,
like sparks shooting skyward.

⁸ Job, if I were you,
I would ask God for help.
⁹ His miracles are marvellous,
more than we can count.
¹⁰ God sends showers on earth
and waters the fields.
¹¹ He protects the sorrowful

and lifts up those
who have been disgraced.
¹²⁻¹³God swiftly traps the wicked
in their own evil schemes,
and their wisdom fails.
¹⁴ Darkness is their only companion,
hiding their path at midday.
¹⁵ God rescues the needy
from the words of the wicked
and the fist of the mighty.
¹⁶ The poor are filled with hope,
and injustice is silenced.

Consider yourself fortunate

¹⁷ Consider yourself fortunate
if God All-Powerful
chooses to correct you.
¹⁸ He may cause injury and pain,
but he will bandage and heal
your cuts and bruises.
¹⁹ God will protect you from harm,
no matter how often trouble may strike.

²⁰ In times of war and famine,
God will keep you safe.
²¹ You will be sheltered,
without fear of hurtful words
or any other weapon.
²² You will laugh at the threat
of destruction and famine.
And you won't be afraid
of wild animals —
²³ they will no longer be fierce,
and your rocky fields
will become friendly.
²⁴ Your home will be secure,
and your sheep will be safe.
²⁵ You will have more descendants
than there are blades of grass
on the face of the earth.
²⁶ You will live a long life,
and your body will be strong
until the day you die.
²⁷ Our experience has proved
these things to be true,
so listen and learn.

CHAPTER 6

Job's reply to Eliphaz

It's impossible

¹ Job said:

² It's impossible to weigh
my misery and grief!

See also: **5.13:** 1 Cor 3.19. **5.17:** Prov 3.11–12;
Heb 12.5–6. **5.18:** Hos 6.1.

Being christian ✝

Dealing with doubt

Job 6.1–13

Surely when you become a Christian all the questions and doubts disappear? You get perfect faith in God. No doubts. No questions. No problems.

No way.

That's not the way it happens. Even after we become Christians we will still have questions. Some bits of the Bible, for example, are difficult to understand and even the experts don't agree on them. Things happen to us in our lives that make us wonder what God is doing. There will always be questions. Paul says that in this world 'all we can see of God is like a cloudy picture in a mirror' (1 Corinthians 13.12). One day we'll see him face to face and then we'll understand things. For now, well, the questions persist.

God isn't afraid of questions; the Bible is full of people asking stuff, from Abraham in the Old Testament to Thomas in the New.

So it's not wrong to ask questions. But we shouldn't allow them to undermine our basic, fundamental relationship with God. The book of Job is one long question, but he never doubts that God loves him and that there are answers to be found.

Being Christian means dealing with the doubts we have. Not hiding them away and pretending they don't exist; but talking about them, praying about them, asking people to help us with answers.

Being Christian: Dealing with doubt

• Pray about your questions. Bring them honestly before God.
• Talk to others. Ask more experienced Christians what they think.
• Don't keep your questions to yourself. Don't try to pretend the doubts don't exist.
• Read the Bible. Read other Christian writers. Learn from people who have been there.
• Always, always, always remember: God loves you. Questions and all.

3 They outweigh the sand
  along the beach,
  and that's why I have spoken
  without thinking first.
4 The fearsome arrows of God All-Powerful
  have filled my soul with their poison.
5 Do oxen and wild donkeys
  cry out in distress
  unless they are hungry?
6 What is food without salt?
  What is more tasteless
  than the white of an egg?'
7   That's how my food tastes,
  and my appetite is gone.

8–9 How I wish that God
  would answer my prayer
  and do away with me.
10 Then I would be comforted,
  knowing that in all my pain
  I have never disobeyed God.
11 Why should I patiently hope
  when my strength is gone?
12 I am not strong as stone or bronze,
13   and I have finally reached
  the end of my rope.

My friends, I am desperate

14 My friends, I am desperate,
  and you should help me,
  even if I no longer respect
  God All-Powerful.'
15–16 But you are treacherous
  as streams that swell with
  melting snow,
17   then suddenly disappear
  in the summer heat.
18 I am like a caravan,
  lost in the desert
  while searching for water.
19 Caravans from Tema and Sheba*
20 thought they would find water.
  But they were disappointed,
21   just as I am with you.'
  Only one look at my suffering,
  and you run away scared.

What have I done wrong?

22 Have I ever asked any of you
  to give me a gift
23   or to purchase my freedom
  from brutal enemies?
24 What have I done wrong?

6.19 Tema and Sheba: Tema was a region in north-west Arabia, and Sheba was probably a region in south-west Arabia.

Big ideas

Suffering

Why does suffering happen? How can a God of love allow war, sickness, pain, and death? How can he allow innocent people to suffer?

These massive questions have no easy answers. They're not modern questions: people in the Bible asked them as well. Look at the Psalms, read Job. Even Jesus' disciples asked him the same question (John 9.1–3). In the end, only God really understands this problem. But there are some things we can say...

It wasn't supposed to be this way

The world is not the way it was supposed to be. Originally God made it good, but through sin, evil came into the world and the whole of creation was infected. And we're all sinful. This infection continues.

God understands suffering

In Jesus, God took on the form of a suffering human being. He was rejected, beaten and executed in the most horrific way. We have to recognise that God did not avoid suffering himself. Because he has suffered, he knows what it's like.

Much suffering is caused by deliberate choice

A lot of suffering is the result of people making wrong, evil or just plain dumb choices. Smoke forty cigarettes a day and you'll get lung cancer. Drink six pints of beer a day and your liver will rot. Drop a bomb on a city and you will kill people. God has given us responsibility for the way we live our lives. His way or our way: it's up to us.

This is true even when we consider things like floods, earthquakes, famine – things which are often called 'acts of God'. There is enough food in the world to feed everyone, it's just that most of it is eaten by the rich western world. If poor countries could afford to build better houses then earthquakes would be less devastating. If we stopped cutting down all the forests there would be less flooding. It's wrong to blame God for suffering, when our selfishness and stupidity is the cause.

Suffering is sometimes a pointer

Sometimes it is through suffering that people realise their need of God; sometimes by suffering, we develop more faith in and dependence on God. And when we suffer we're enabled to help those who are in the same position.

Whatever you think, do something

It's not bad to think about these issues, but we don't have the luxury of allowing ourselves to sit in a holy huddle and moan about how bad suffering is. We have to get our hands dirty and do something. That might mean supporting the work of Christian aid agencies, it might mean taking action ourselves.

It will be different

This life is not all there is. 'Whether we live therefore, or die, we are the LORD's writes Paul (Romans 14.8). One day, God will put all this right. He'll create a new heaven and a new earth, one that will be free from suffering, tears and pain.

Footsteps

Two weeks on suffering

Sin infects the world: Genesis 3.17
Why do we suffer? Job 7.1–21
Close to death: Psalms 13
So alone: Psalms 22
Intense suffering, intense faith: Psalms 102
The suffering servant: Isaiah 53.1–12
Isaiah sees the future: Isaiah 65.17–25
To show God's power: John 9.1–41
All creation waits: Romans 8.18–30
Suffering for Christ:
2 Corinthians 11.16–12.10
Suffering for the truth: Colossians 1.24—2.5
Being corrected: Hebrews 12.1–13
Suffering and leadership: 1 Peter 4.12—5.11
The new city: Rev 21.1—22.5

More...

Coping with suffering p.1391
Persecuted church p.1220
Persecution p.1215
Sin p.1261
How does God's love support us? p.219
We follow God – but doesn't he realise that it can be tough sometimes? p.596

Show me, and I will keep quiet.
25 The truth is always painful,
 but your arguments prove nothing.
26 Here I am desperate,
 and you consider my words
 as worthless as wind.
27 Why, you would sell an orphan
 or your own neighbour!
28 Look me straight in the eye;
 I won't lie to you.
29 Stop accusing me falsely;
 my reputation is at stake.
30 I know right from wrong,
 and I am not telling lies.

CHAPTER 7

Job continues

Why is life so hard?

1 Why is life so hard? Why do we suffer?
2 We are slaves in search of shade;
 we are labourers longing for our wages.
3 God has made my days drag on
 and my nights miserable.
4 I pray for night to end,
 but it stretches out
 while I toss and turn.
5 My parched skin is covered
 with worms, dirt, and sores,
6 and my days are running out
 quicker than the thread
 of a fast-moving needle.

Don't forget!

7 I beg you, God, don't forget!
 My life is just a breath,
 and trouble lies ahead.
8 I will vanish from sight,
 and no one, including you,
 will ever see me again.
9 I will disappear in the grave
 or vanish from sight like a passing cloud.
10 Never will I return home;
 soon I will be forgotten.

11 And so, I cry out to you
 in agony and distress.
12 Am I the sea or a sea monster?
 Is that why you imprison me?*
13 I go to bed, hoping for rest,

14 but you torture me with terrible dreams.
15-16 I'd rather choke to death
 than live in this body.
 Leave me alone and let me die;
 my life has no meaning.
17 What makes you so concerned
 about us humans?
18 Why do you test us
 from sunrise to sunset?
19 Won't you look away
 just long enough
 for me to swallow?
20 Why do you watch us so closely?
 What's it to you, if I sin?
 Why am I your target
 and such a heavy burden?
21 Why do you refuse to forgive?
 Soon you won't find me,
 because I'll be dead.

CHAPTER 8

Bildad's first speech

How long will you talk?

1 Bildad from Shuah* said:

2 How long will you talk
 and keep saying nothing?
3 Does God All-Powerful
 stand in the way of justice?
4 He made your children pay
 for their sins.
5 So why don't you turn to him
6 and start living right?
 Then he will decide
 to rescue and restore you
 to your place of honour.
7 Your future will be brighter
 by far than your past.

Our ancestors were wise

8 Our ancestors were wise,
 so learn from them.
9 Our own time has been short,
 like a fading shadow,
 and we know very little.
10 But they will instruct you
 with great understanding.

11 Papyrus reeds grow healthy
 only in a swamp,
12 and if the water dries up,
 they die sooner than grass.

---

*7.12 sea monster . . . imprison me: "Sea monster"
translates the Hebrew word "Tannin", which was
possibly a sea monster similar to Leviathan (3.8),
Rahab (9.13), and Behemoth (40.15). According to
38.8-11, God makes the sea his prisoner by setting its
boundaries.

*8.1 Shuah: See the note at 2.11.
See also: 7.17: Psa 8.4; 144.3.

¹³ Such is the hopeless future
 of all who turn from God
¹⁴ and trust in something as frail
 as a spider's web —
¹⁵ they take hold and fall
 because it's so flimsy.
¹⁶ Sinful people are like plants
 with spreading roots
 and plenty of sun and water.
¹⁷ They wrap their roots tightly
 around rocks.᾿
¹⁸ But once they are pulled up,
 they have no more place;
¹⁹ their life slips away,᾿
 and other plants grow there.

²⁰ We know God doesn't reject
 an innocent person
 or help a sinner.
²¹ And so, he will make you happy
 and give you something to smile about.
²² But your evil enemies
 will be put to shame
 and disappear for ever.

CHAPTER 9

Job's reply to Bildad

What you say is true

¹ Job said:

² What you say is true.
 No human is innocent
 in the sight of God.
³ Not once in a thousand times
 could we win our case
 if we took him to court.
⁴ God is wise and powerful —
 who could possibly
 oppose him and win?
⁵ When God becomes angry,
 he can move mountains
 before they even know it.
⁶ God can shake the earth loose
 from its foundations
⁷ or command the sun and stars
 to hold back their light.
⁸ God alone stretched out the sky,
 stepped on the sea,*
⁹ and set the stars in place —
 the Great Bear and Orion,
 the Pleiades and the stars
 in the southern sky.

¹⁰ Of all the miracles God works,
 we cannot understand a single one.
¹¹ God walks right past me,
 without making a sound.
¹² And if he grabs something,
 who can stop him
 or raise a question?

¹³ When God showed his anger,
 the servants of the sea monster*
 fell at his feet.
¹⁴ How, then, could I possibly
 argue my case with God?

Though I am innocent

¹⁵ Even though I am innocent,
 I can only beg for mercy.
¹⁶ And if God came into court
 when I called him,
 he would not hear my case.
¹⁷ He would strike me with a storm᾿
 and increase my injuries
 for no reason at all.
¹⁸ Before I could get my breath,
 my miseries would multiply.
¹⁹ God is much stronger than I am,
 and who would call me into court
 to give me justice?

²⁰ Even if I were innocent,
 God would prove me wrong.᾿
²¹ I am not guilty, but I no longer care
 what happens to me.
²² What difference does it make?
 God destroys the innocent
 along with the guilty.
²³ When a good person dies a sudden death,
 God sits back and laughs.
²⁴ And who else but God
 blindfolds the judges,
 then lets the wicked
 take over the earth?

My life is speeding by

²⁵ My life is speeding by,
 without a hope of happiness.
²⁶ Each day passes swifter
 than a sailing ship
 or an eagle swooping down.
²⁷ Sometimes I try to be cheerful
 and to stop complaining,
²⁸ but my sufferings frighten me,
 because I know that God
 still considers me guilty.

---

*9.8 sea: Or "sea monster" (see verse 13 and the note there).
See also: 9.2: Job 4.17. **9.9:** Job 38.31; Amos 5.8.

*9.13 the sea monster: The Hebrew text has "Rahab", which was some kind of sea monster with supernatural powers (see the notes at 3.8 and 26.12).

557

29 So what's the use of trying
to prove my innocence?
30   Even if I washed myself
with the strongest soap,
31 God would throw me into a pit
of stinking slime,
leaving me disgusting to my clothes.

32 God isn't a mere human like me.
I can't put him on trial.
33   Who could possibly judge
between the two of us?
34 Can someone snatch away the stick
God carries to frighten me?
35 Then I could speak up
without fear of him,
but for now, I cannot speak.'

CHAPTER 10

Job complains to God

I am sick of life!

1 I am sick of life!
And from my deep despair,
I complain to you, my God.
2 Don't just condemn me!
Point out my sin.
3 Why do you take such delight
in destroying those you created
and in smiling on sinners?
4 Do you look at things
the way we humans do?
5   Is your life as short as ours?
6 Is that why you are so quick
to find fault with me?
7 You know I am innocent,
but who can defend me against you?
8 Will you now destroy
someone you created?
9 Remember that you moulded me
like a piece of clay.
So don't turn me back
into dust once again.
10 As cheese is made from milk,
you created my body
from a tiny drop.
11 Then you tied my bones together
with muscles
and covered them with flesh
and skin.
12 You, the source of my life,
showered me with kindness
and watched over me.

You have not explained

13 You have not explained
all your mysteries,

14   but you catch and punish me
each time I sin.
15 Guilty or innocent,
I am condemned and ashamed
because of my troubles.
16 No matter how hard I try,
you keep hunting me down
like a powerful lion.'
17 You never stop accusing me;
you become furious and attack
over and over again.

18 Why did you let me be born?
I would rather have died before birth
19   and been carried to the grave
without ever breathing.
20 I have only a few days left.
Why don't you leave me alone?'
Let me find some relief,
21-22 before I travel to the land
of darkness and despair,
the place of no return.

CHAPTER 11

Zophar's first speech

So much foolish talk

1 Zophar from Naamah* said:

2 So much foolish talk
cannot go unanswered.
3 Your words have silenced others
and made them ashamed;
now it is only right for you
to be put to shame.
4 You claim to be innocent
and argue that your beliefs
are acceptable to God.
5 But I wish he would speak
6   and let you know
that wisdom has many different sides.
You would then discover
that God has punished you less
than you deserve.

7 Can you understand the mysteries
surrounding God All-Powerful?
8 They are higher than the heavens
and deeper than the grave.
So what can you do
when you know so little,
9   and these mysteries outreach
the earth and the sea?

10 If God puts you in prison
or drags you to court,
what can you do?

---

*11.1 Naamah: See the note at 2.11.

11 God has the wisdom to know
    when someone is worthless and sinful,
12 but it's easier to tame
    a wild donkey
    than to make a fool wise.'

Surrender your heart to God

13 Surrender your heart to God,
    turn to him in prayer,
14 and give up your sins —
    even those you do in secret.
15 Then you won't be ashamed;
    you will be confident and fearless.
16 Your troubles will go away
    like water beneath a bridge,
17 and your darkest night
    will be brighter than midday.
18 You will rest safe and secure,
    filled with hope and emptied of worry.
19 You will sleep without fear
    and be greatly respected.
20 But those who are evil
    will go blind and lose their way.
    Their only escape is death!

CHAPTER 12

Job's reply to Zophar

You think you are so great

1-2 Job said to his friends:

    You think you are so great,
       with all the answers.
3 But I know as much as you do,
    and so does everyone else.
4 I have always lived right,
    and God answered my prayers;
    now friends make fun of me.
5 It's easy to condemn
    those who are suffering,
    when you have no troubles.
6 Robbers and other godless people
    live safely at home
    and say, "God is in our hands!"'

If you want to learn

7 If you want to learn,
    then go and ask
    the wild animals and the birds,
8   the flowers and the fish.
9 Any of them can tell you
    what the LORD has done.'
10 Every living creature
    is in the hands of God.

11 We hear with our ears,
    taste with our tongues,

12 and gain some wisdom from those
    who have lived a long time.
13 But God is the real source
    of wisdom and strength.
14 No one can rebuild
    what he destroys,
    or release those he has imprisoned.
15 God can hold back the rain
    or send a flood,
16 just as he rules over liars
    and those they lie to.

17 God destroys counsellors,
    turns judges into fools,
18 and makes slaves of kings.
19 God removes priests and others
    who have great power —
20 he confuses wise,
    experienced advisers,
21 puts mighty kings to shame,
    and takes away their power.
22 God turns darkness to light;
23 he makes nations strong,
    then shatters their strength.
24 God strikes their rulers senseless,
    then leaves them to roam
    through barren deserts,
25 lost in the dark, staggering
    like someone drunk.

CHAPTER 13

Job continues

I know and understand

1 I know and understand
    every bit of this.
2 None of you are cleverer than I am;
    there's nothing you know that I don't.
3 But I prefer to argue my case
    with God All-Powerful —
4 you are merely useless doctors,
    who treat me with lies.
5 The wisest thing you can do
    is to keep quiet
6 and listen to my argument.
7 Are you telling lies for God
8 and not telling the whole truth
    when you argue his case?
9 If he took you to court,
    could you fool him,
    just as you fool others?
10 If you were secretly unfair,
    he would correct you,
11 and his glorious splendour
    would make you terrified.
12 Your wisdom and arguments
    are as delicate as dust.

Be quiet while I speak

¹³ Be quiet while I speak,
   then say what you will.
¹⁴ I will be responsible
   for what happens to me.
¹⁵ God may kill me, but still
   I will trust him'
   and offer my defence.
¹⁶ This may be what saves me,
   because no guilty person
   would come to his court.
¹⁷ Listen carefully to my words!
¹⁸ I have prepared my case well,
   and I am certain to win.
¹⁹ If you can prove me guilty,
   I will give up and die.

Job prays

I ask only two things

²⁰ I ask only two things
   of you, my God,
   and I will no longer hide from you —
²¹ stop punishing and terrifying me!
²² Then speak, and I will reply;
   or else let me speak,
   and you reply.
²³ Please point out my sins,
   so I will know them.
²⁴ Why have you turned your back
   and count me your enemy?
²⁵ Do you really enjoy
   frightening a fallen leaf?
²⁶ Why do you accuse me
   of horrible crimes
   and make me pay for sins
   I did in my youth?
²⁷ You have tied my feet down
   and keep me surrounded;
²⁸ I am rotting away like cloth
   eaten by worms.

CHAPTER 14

Job continues his prayer

Life is short and sorrowful

¹ Life is short and sorrowful
   for every living soul.
² We are flowers that fade
   and shadows that vanish.
³ And so, I ask you, God,
   why pick on me?
⁴ There's no way a human
   can be completely pure.

⁵ Our time on earth is brief;
   the number of our days
   is already decided by you.
⁶ Why don't you leave us alone
   and let us find some happiness
   while we toil and labour?

When a tree is chopped down

⁷ When a tree is chopped down,
   there is always the hope
   that it will sprout again.
⁸ Its roots and stump may rot,
⁹ but at the touch of water,
   fresh twigs shoot up.
¹⁰ Humans are different —
   we die, and that's the end.
¹¹ We are like streams and lakes
   after the water has gone;
¹² we fall into the sleep of death,
   never to rise again,
   until the sky disappears.
¹³ Please hide me, God,
   deep in the ground —
   and when you are angry no more,
   remember to rescue me.

Will we humans live again?

¹⁴ Will we humans live again?
   I would gladly suffer
   and wait for my time.
¹⁵ My Creator, you would want me;
   you would call out,
   and I would answer.
¹⁶ You would take care of me,
   but not count my sins —
¹⁷ you would put them in a bag,
   tie it tight,
   and toss them away.
¹⁸ But in the real world,
   mountains tumble,
   and rocks crumble;
¹⁹ streams wear away stones
   and wash away soil.
   And you destroy our hopes!
²⁰ You change the way we look,
   then send us away,
   wiped out for ever.
²¹ We never live to know
   if our children are praised
   or disgraced.
²² We feel no pain but our own,
   and when we mourn,
   it's only for ourselves.

See also: **13.27:** Job 33.11.

The second round of the debate

CHAPTER 15

Eliphaz's second speech

If you had any sense

¹ Eliphaz from Teman* said:

²⁻³ Job, if you had any sense,
you would stop spreading
all this hot air.
⁴ Your words are enough
to make others turn from God
and lead them to doubt.
⁵ And your sinful, scheming mind
is the source of all you say.
⁶ I am not here as your judge;
your own words are witnesses
against you.

⁷ Were you the first human?
Are you older than the hills?
⁸ Have you ever been present
when God's council* meets?
Do you alone have wisdom?
⁹ Do you know and understand
something we don't?
¹⁰ We have the benefit of wisdom
older than your father.
¹¹ And you have been offered
comforting words from God.
Isn't this enough?

¹² Your emotions are out of control,
making you look fierce;
¹³ that's why you attack God
with everything you say.
¹⁴ No human is pure and innocent,
¹⁵ and neither are angels —
not in the sight of God.
If God doesn't trust his angels,
¹⁶ what chance do humans have?
We are so terribly evil
that we thirst for sin.

Just listen to what I know

¹⁷ Just listen to what I know,
and you will learn
¹⁸ wisdom known by others
since ancient times.

¹⁹ Those who gained such insights
also gained the land,
and they were not influenced
by foreign teachings.
²⁰ But suffering is in store
each day for those who sin.
²¹ Even in times of success,
they constantly hear
the threat of doom.
²² Darkness, despair, and death
are their destiny.
²³ They scrounge around for food,
all the while dreading
the approaching darkness.
²⁴ They are overcome with despair,
like a terrified king
about to go into battle.
²⁵ This is because they rebelled
against God All-Powerful
²⁶ and have attacked him
with their weapons.

²⁷ They may be rich and fat,
²⁸ but they will live in the ruins
of deserted towns.
²⁹ Their property and wealth
will shrink and disappear.
³⁰ They won't escape the darkness,
and the blazing breath of God
will set their future aflame.
³¹⁻³² They have put their trust
in something worthless;
now they will become worthless
like a date palm tree without a leaf.›
³³ Or like vineyards or orchards
whose blossoms and unripe fruit
drop to the ground.
³⁴ Yes, the godless and the greedy
will have nothing but flames
feasting on their homes,
³⁵ because they are the parents
of trouble and vicious lies.

CHAPTER 16

Job's reply to Eliphaz

I have often heard this

¹ Job said:

² I have often heard this,
and it offers no comfort.
³ So why don't you keep quiet?
What's bothering you?
⁴ If I were in your place,
it would be easy to criticize
or to give advice.
⁵ But I would offer hope
and comfort instead.

---

*15.1 Teman: See the note at 2.11.
*15.8 God's council: The angels and others who
gather to discuss matters with God (see 1.6; 2.1).
See also: 15.14-16: Job 25.4-6.

⁶ If I speak, or if I don't,
  I suffer all the same.
  My torment continues.
⁷ God has worn me down
  and destroyed my family;
⁸ my shrivelled up skin proves
  that I am his prisoner.
⁹ God is my hateful enemy,
  glaring at me
  and attacking with his sharp teeth.
¹⁰ Everyone is against me;
  they sneer and slap my face.
¹¹ And God is the one
  who handed me over
  to this merciless mob.

Everything was going well

¹² Everything was going well,
  until God grabbed my neck
  and shook me to pieces.
  God set me up as the target
¹³ for his arrows,
  and without showing mercy,
  he slashed my stomach open,
  spilling out my insides.
¹⁴ God never stops attacking,
¹⁵ and so, in my sorrow
  I dress in sackcloth* and sit in the dust.
¹⁶ My face is red with tears,
  and dark shadows circle my eyes,
¹⁷ though I am not violent,
  and my prayers are sincere.

¹⁸ If I should die, I beg the earth
  not to cover my cry for justice.
¹⁹ Even now, God in heaven
  is both my witness
  and my protector.
²⁰ My friends have rejected me,
  but God is the one I beg'
²¹ to show that I am right,
  just as a friend should.
²² Because in only a few years,
  I will be dead and gone.

CHAPTER 17

Job complains to God

My hopes have died

¹ My hopes have died,
  my time is up,
  and the grave is ready.

---

*16.15 sackcloth:** A rough, dark-coloured cloth made
from goat or camel hair and used to make grain
sacks. It was worn in times of trouble or sorrow.
See also: 16.19: Job 19.25.

562

² All I can see are angry crowds,
  making fun of me.
³ If you, LORD, don't help,
  who will pay the price for my release?
⁴ My friends won't really listen,
  all because of you,
  and so you must be the one
  to prove them wrong.
⁵ They have condemned me,
  just to benefit themselves;
  now blind their children.

⁶ You, God, are the reason
  I am insulted and spat on.
⁷ I am almost blind with grief;
  my body is a mere shadow.

⁸ People who are truly good
  would feel so alarmed,
  that they would become angry
  with my worthless friends.
⁹ They would do the right thing
  and because they did,
  they would grow stronger.'
¹⁰ But none of my friends show any sense.

¹¹ My life is drawing to an end;
  hope has disappeared.
¹² But all my friends can do
  is offer empty hopes.'
¹³ I could tell the world below
  to prepare me a bed.
¹⁴ Then I could greet the grave as my father
  and say to the worms,
  "Hello, mother and sisters!"

¹⁵ But what kind of hope is that?
¹⁶ Will it keep me company
  in the world of the dead?

CHAPTER 18

Bildad's second speech

How long will you talk?

¹ Bildad from Shuah* said:

² How long will you talk?
  Be sensible! Let us speak.
³ Or do you think that we
  are dumb animals?
⁴ You cut yourself in anger.
  Will that shake the earth
  or even move the rocks?

⁵⁻⁶ The lamps of sinful people
  soon are snuffed out,
  leaving their tents dark.

---

*18.1 Shuah:** See the note at 2.11.
See also: 18.5-6: Job 21.17.

7 Their powerful legs become weak,
  and they stumble on schemes
  of their own doing.
8-10 Before they know it,
  they are trapped
  in a net, hidden along the path.
11 Terror strikes and pursues from every side.
12 Starving, they run, only to meet disaster,
13 then afterwards to be eaten alive
  by death itself.

14 Those sinners are dragged
  from the safety of their tents
  to die a gruesome death.
15 Then their tents and possessions
  are burnt to ashes,
16 and they are left like trees,
  dried up from the roots.
17 They are gone and forgotten,
18 thrown far from the light
  into a world of darkness,
19 without any children
  to carry on their name.
20 Everyone, from east to west,
  is overwhelmed with horror.
21 Such is the fate of sinners
  and their families
  who don't know God.

CHAPTER 19

Job's reply to Bildad

How long will you torture me?

1 Job said:

2 How long will you torture me
  with your words?
3 Isn't ten times enough
  for you to accuse me?
  Aren't you ashamed?
4 Even if I have sinned,
  you haven't been harmed.
5 You boast of your goodness,
  claiming I am suffering
  because I am guilty.
6 But God is the one at fault
  for finding fault with me.

7 Though I pray to be rescued
  from this torment,
  no whisper of justice answers me.
8 God has me trapped with a wall of darkness
9 and stripped of respect.
10 God rips me apart, uproots my hopes,
11 and attacks with fierce anger,
  as though I were his enemy.
12 His entire army advances,
  then surrounds my tent.

I am forgotten

13-14 God has turned relatives
  and friends against me,
  and I am forgotten.
15 My guests and my servants
  consider me a stranger,
16 and when I call my servants,
  they pay no attention.
17 My breath disgusts my wife;
  everyone in my family turns away.
18 Young children can't stand me,
  and when I come near, they make fun.
19 My best friends and loved ones
  have turned from me.
20 I am skin and bones — just barely alive.
21 My friends, I beg you for pity!
  God has made me his target.
22 Hasn't he already done enough?
  Why do you join the attack?

23 I wish that my words
  could be written down
24 or chiselled into rock.
25 I know that my Saviour▸ lives,
  and at the end
  he will stand on this earth.
26 My flesh may be destroyed,
  yet from this body I will see God.▸
27 Yes, I will see him for myself,
  and I long for that moment.

28 My friends, you think up ways
  to blame and torment me,
  saying I brought it on myself.
29 But watch out for the judgment,
  when God will punish you!

CHAPTER 20

Zophar's second speech

Your words are disturbing

1 Zophar from Naamah* said:

2 Your words are disturbing;
  now I must speak.
3 You have accused and insulted me,
  and reason requires a reply.
4 Since the time of creation,
  everyone has known
5 that sinful people are happy
  for only a while.
6 Though their pride and power
  may reach to the sky,
7 they will disappear like dust,
  and those who knew them
  will wonder what happened.

*20.1 Naamah: See the note at 2.11.

8 They will be forgotten like a dream
9 and vanish from the sight
of family and friends.
10 Their children will have to repay
what the parents took from the poor.
11 Indeed, the wicked will die
and go to their graves
in the prime of life.

Sinners love the taste of sin

12 Sinners love the taste of sin;
they relish every bite
13 and swallow it slowly.
14 But their food will turn sour
and poison their stomachs.
15 Then God will make them lose
the wealth they gobbled up.
16 They will die from the fangs
of poisonous snakes
17 and never enjoy rivers flowing
with milk and honey.
18 Their hard work will result
in nothing gained,
19 because they cheated the poor
and took their homes.

20 Greedy people want everything
and are never satisfied.ʼ
21 But when nothing remains
for them to grab,
they will be nothing.
22 Once they have everything,
distress and despair
will strike them down,
23 and God will make them swallow
his blazing anger.ʼ

24 While running from iron spears,
they will be killed
by arrows of bronze,
25 whose shining tips go straight
through their bodies.
They will be trapped by terror,
26 and what they treasure most
will be lost in the dark.
God will send flames
to destroy them in their tents
with all their property.
27 The heavens and the earth
will testify against them,
28 and all their possessions
will be dragged off
when God becomes angry.
29 This is what God has decided
for those who are evil.

CHAPTER 21

Job's reply to Zophar

If you want to offer comfort

1 Job said:

2 If you want to offer comfort,
then listen to me.
3 And when I have finished,
you can start your insults
all over again.
4 My complaint is against God;
that's why I am impatient.
5 Just looking at me is enough
to make you sick,
6 and the very thought of myself
fills me with disgust.

7 Why do evil people live so long
and gain such power?
8 Why are they allowed to see
their children grow up?ʼ
9 They have no worries at home,
and God never punishes them.
10 Their cattle have lots of calves
without ever losing one;
11 their children play and dance
safely by themselves.
12 These people sing and celebrate
to the sound of tambourines,
small harps, and flutes,
13 and they are successful,
without a worry,
until the day they die.

Leave us alone!

14 Those who are evil say
to God All-Powerful,
"Leave us alone! Don't bother us
with your teachings.
15 What do we gain from praying
and worshipping you?
16 We succeeded all on our own."
And so, I keep away from them
and their evil schemes.

17 How often does God become angry
and send disaster and darkness
to punish sinners?
18 How often does he strike them
like a storm that scatters straw?
19 You say, "God will punish
those sinners' children
in place of those sinners."
But I say, "Let him punish
those sinners themselves
until they really feel it.

20 Let God All-Powerful force them to drink
  their own destruction
  from the cup of his anger.
21 Because after they are dead,
  they won't care what happens
  to their children."

Who can tell God what to do?

22 Who can tell God what to do?
  He judges powerful rulers.
23-24 Some of us die prosperous,
  enjoying good health,
25 while others die in poverty,
  having known only pain.
26 But we all end up dead,
  beneath a blanket of worms.

27 My friends, I know that you
  are plotting against me.
28 You ask, "Where is the home
  of that important person
  who does so much evil?"

29 Everyone, near and far, agrees
30   that those who do wrong
  never suffer disaster,
  when God becomes angry.
31 No one points out their sin
  or punishes them.
32 Then at their funerals,
  they are highly praised;
33   the earth welcomes them home,
  while crowds mourn.

34 But empty, meaningless words
  are the comfort you offer me.

The third round of the debate

CHAPTER 22

Eliphaz's third speech
What use are we humans to God?

1 Eliphaz from Teman* said:

2 What use are we humans to God,
  even the wisest of us?
3 If you were completely sinless,
  that would still mean nothing
  to God All-Powerful.
4 Is he correcting you for worshipping him?
5   No! It's because
  of your terrible sins.

---

6 To guarantee payment of a debt,
  you have taken clothes
  from the poor.
7 And you refused bread and water
  to the hungry and thirsty,
8   although you were rich,
  respected, and powerful.
9 You have turned away widows
  and have broken the arms of orphans.
10 That's why you were suddenly
  trapped by terror,
11   blinded by darkness,
  and drowned in a flood.

God lives in the heavens

12 God lives in the heavens
  above the highest stars,
  where he sees everything.
13 Do you think the deep darkness
  hides you from God?
14 Do thick clouds cover his eyes,
  as he walks around heaven's dome
  high above the earth?
15 Give up those ancient ideas
  believed by sinners,
16   who were swept away
  without warning.
17 They rejected God All-Powerful,
  feeling he was helpless,
18 although he had been kind
  to their families.
  The beliefs of these sinners
  are truly disgusting.
19 When God's people see
  the godless swept away,
  they celebrate,
20   saying, "Our enemies are gone,
  and fire has destroyed
  their possessions."

Surrender to God All-Powerful

21 Surrender to God All-Powerful!
  You will find peace and prosperity.
22 Listen to his teachings
  and take them to heart.
23 If you return to God
  and turn from sin,
  all will go well for you.
24 So get rid of your finest gold,
  as though it were sand.
25 Let God All-Powerful
  be your silver and gold,
26   and you will find happiness
  by worshipping him.
27 God will answer your prayers,
  and you will keep the promises
  you made to him.

---

*22.1 Teman: See the note at 2.11.
See also: 22.2-3: Job 35.6-8.

28 He will do whatever you ask,
and life will be bright.
29 When others are disgraced,
God will clear their names
in answer to your prayers.
30 Even those who are guilty will be forgiven,
because you obey God.'

CHAPTER 23

Job's reply to Eliphaz

Today I complain bitterly

1 Job said:

2 Today I complain bitterly,
because God has been cruel
and made me suffer.
3 If I knew where to find God,
I would go there
4 and argue my case.
5 Then I would discover
what he wanted to say.
6 Would he overwhelm me
with his greatness?
No! He would listen
7 because I am innocent,
and he would say, "I now set you free!"

8 I cannot find God anywhere —
in front of or behind me,
9 to my left or my right.
God is always at work,
though I never see him.
10 But he knows what I am doing,
and when he tests me,
I will be pure as gold.
11–12 I have never refused to follow
any of his commands,
and I have always treasured
his teachings.'
13 But he alone is God,
and who can oppose him?
God does as he pleases,
14 and he will do exactly
what he intends with me.
15–16 Merely the thought of God All-Powerful
makes me tremble with fear.
17 God has covered me with darkness,
but I refuse to be silent.'

CHAPTER 24

Job continues

Why doesn't God set a time?

1 Why doesn't God set a time for court?
Why don't his people know
where he can be found?

2 Sinners remove boundary markers
and take care of sheep they have stolen.
3 They cheat orphans and widows
by taking their donkeys and oxen.
4 The poor are trampled
and forced to hide
5 in the desert,
where they and their children
must live like wild donkeys
and search for food.
6 If they want grain or grapes,*
they must go to the property
of these sinners.
7 They sleep naked in the cold,
because they have no cover,
8 and during a storm
their only shelters are caves
among the rocky cliffs.

9 Children whose fathers have died
are taken from their mothers
as payment for a debt.
10 Then they are forced to work
naked in the grain fields
because they have no clothes,
and they go hungry.
11 They crush olives to make oil
and grapes to make wine —
but still they go thirsty.
12 And along the city streets,
the wounded and dying cry out,
yet God does nothing.

Some reject the light

13 Some rebel and refuse
to follow the light.
14 Soon after sunset they murder
the poor and the needy,
and at night they steal.

15 Others wait for the dark,
thinking they won't be seen
if they sleep with the wife
or husband of someone else.
16 Robbers hide during the day,
then break in after dark
because they reject the light.
17 They prefer night to day,
since the terrors of the night
are their friends.

Sinners are filthy foam

18 Those sinners are filthy foam
on the surface of the water.

---

*24.6 *If they want grain or grapes:* Poor people
were allowed to gather what was left in the fields and
vineyards after the harvest.

Viewpoints 👁

God – he takes your breath away

Contributed by Bethan P

'To him, not even the light of the moon and stars can ever be pure.'

God is so glorious that even the moon and the stars scarcely shine compared to him.

Sometimes God's word is so succinct and beautiful that is almost impossible to do any expository writing on it. This is one of those verses, but I'm going to try my best to put down my thoughts.

This verse is so true, so real. And it makes perfect sense. Who created the moon? God. Who created the stars? God. So it almost goes without saying that he would be more glorious than them. And yet this verse goes even further than that. It tells us that the stars and moon scarcely shine compared to Him. Wow!

Let's think about the stars and moon. They act as guides and lights to us on earth, preventing us from being lost in the dark. And yet all this, amazing though it is, is practically nothing in comparison to the brilliance of God.

It is so important for us to try to grasp something of the glory of God and how that affects how we live. We can never in this life fully comprehend how glorious he is, but we should spend all our days searching the wide, deep, enormous mysteries of our God. And then our lives should in some way reflect that glory. We should live every day in a way that is pleasing to God. And the only way we can know what that lifestyle is is by studying his Word and getting to know him more through serious fellowship with his true followers.

More...

Creation p.3
Responding to God p.1052

And so, their fields and vineyards
    will fall under a curse
    and won't produce.
19 Just as the heat of summer
    swallows the snow,
    the world of the dead
    swallows those who sin.
20 Forgotten here on earth,
    and with their power broken,
    they taste sweet to worms.

21 Sinners take advantage of widows
    and other helpless women.'
22 But God's mighty strength
    destroys those in power.
    Even if they seem successful,
    they are doomed to fail.
23 God may let them feel secure,
    but they are never
    out of his sight.
24 Great for a while; gone for ever!
    Sinners are mowed down like weeds,
    then they wither and die.
25 If I haven't spoken the truth,
    then prove me wrong.

CHAPTER 25

Bildad's third speech

God is the one to fear

1 Bildad from Shuah* said:

2 God is the one to fear,
    because God is in control
    and rules the heavens.
3 Who can count his army of stars?
    Isn't God the source of light?
4 How can anyone be innocent
    in the sight of God?
5 To him, not even the light
    of the moon and stars
    can ever be pure.
6 So how can we humans,
    when we are merely worms?

CHAPTER 26

Job's reply to Bildad

You have really been helpful

1 Job said:

2 You have really been helpful
    to someone weak and weary.
3 You have given great advice
    and wonderful wisdom
    to someone truly in need.

*25.1 Shuah: See the note at 2.11.

4 How can anyone possibly speak
with such understanding?

5 Remember the terrible trembling
of those in the world of the dead
below the mighty ocean.
6 Nothing in that land
of death and destruction
is hidden from God,
7   who hung the northern sky
and suspended the earth
on empty space.
8 God stores water in clouds,
but they don't burst,
9   and he wraps them around
the face of the moon.
10 On the surface of the sea,
God has drawn a boundary line
between light and darkness.
11 And columns supporting the sky
tremble at his command.

12 By his power and wisdom,
God conquered the force
of the mighty ocean.ʼ
13 The heavens became bright
when he breathed,
and the escaping sea monster*
died at the hands of God.
14 These things are merely a whisper
of God's power at work.
How little we would understand
if this whisper
ever turned into thunder!

Job's closing statements

CHAPTER 27

Job continues

I am desperate

1 Job said:

2 I am desperate because
God All-Powerful
refuses to do what is right.
As surely as God lives,
3   and while he gives me breath,
4 I will tell only the truth.
5 Until the day I die,
I will refuse to do wrong
by saying you are right,
6 because each day my conscience
agrees that I am innocent.

7 I pray that my enemies
will suffer no less than the wicked.
8 Such people are hopeless,
and God All-Powerful
will cut them down,
9   without listening
when they beg for mercy.
10 And that is what God should do,
because they don't like him or ever pray.
11 Now I will explain in detail
what God All-Powerful does.
12 All of you have seen these things
for yourselves.
So you have no excuse.

How God treats the wicked

13 Here is how God All-Powerful
treats those who are wicked
and brutal.
14 They may have many children,
but most of them
will go hungry
or suffer a violent death.
15 Others will die of disease,
and their widows won't be able to weep.
16 The wicked may collect riches
and clothes in abundance
as easily as clay.
17 But God's people will wear
clothes taken from them
and divide up their riches.
18 No homes built by the wicked
will outlast a cocoon
or a shack.
19 Those sinners may go to bed rich,
but they will wake up poor.ʼ
20 Terror will strike at night
like a flood or a storm.
21 Then a scorching wind
will sweep them away
22   without showing mercy,
as they try to escape.
23 At last, the wind will celebrate
because they are gone.

CHAPTER 28

Job continues

Gold and silver are mined

1 Gold and silver are mined,
then purified;
2   the same is done with iron and copper.
3 Miners carry lanterns
deep into the darkness
to search for these metals.

---

*26.13 sea monster: The Hebrew text has "snake",
which probably stands for some kind of fearsome sea
monster, such as Leviathan (see Isaiah 27.1).

4 They dig tunnels
  in distant, unknown places,
  where they dangle by ropes.
5 Far beneath the grain fields,
  fires are built to break loose those rocks
6   that have jewels or gold.*

7 Miners go to places unseen
  by the eyes of hawks;
8   they walk on soil unknown
  to the proudest lions.
9 With their own hands
  they remove sharp rocks
  and uproot mountains.
10 They dig through the rocks
  in search of jewels
  and precious metals.
11 They also uncover the sources of* rivers
  and discover secret places.

Where is wisdom found?

12 But where is wisdom found?
13   No human knows the way.*
14   Nor can it be discovered
  in the deepest sea.
15-16 It is worth much more
  than silver or pure gold
  or precious stones.
17 Nothing is its equal —
  not gold or costly glass.*
18 Wisdom is worth much more than
  coral, jasper,* or rubies.
19 All the topaz* of Ethiopia*
  and the finest gold
  cannot compare with it.
20 Where then is wisdom?
21   It is hidden from human eyes
  and even from birds.
22 Death and destruction
  have merely heard rumours
  about where it is found.
23 God is the only one who knows
  the way to wisdom,
24   because he sees everything
  beneath the heavens.
25 When God divided out
  the wind and the water,
26 and when he decided the path
  for rain and lightning,

27   he also determined the truth
  and defined wisdom.
28 God told us, "Wisdom means
  that you respect me, the Lord,
  and turn from sin."

CHAPTER 29

Job continues

I long for the past

1 Job said:

2 I long for the past,
  when God took care of me,
3 and the light from his lamp
  showed me the way through the dark.
4 I was in the prime of life,
  God All-Powerful was my closest friend,
5   and all my children were nearby.
6 My herds gave enough milk
  to bathe my feet,
  and from my olive harvest
  flowed rivers of oil.
7-8 When I sat down at the meeting
  of the city council,
  the young leaders stepped aside,
  while the older ones stood
9-10   and remained silent.

Everyone was pleased

11 Everyone was pleased
  with what I said and did.
12 When poor people or orphans
  cried out for help,
  I came to their rescue.
13 And I was highly praised
  for my generosity to widows
  and others in poverty.
14 Kindness and justice
  were my coat and hat;
15   I was good to the blind and to the lame.
16 I was a father to the needy,
  and I defended them in court,
  even if they were strangers.
17 When criminals attacked,
  I broke their teeth
  and set their victims free.

18 I felt certain that I would live
  a long and happy life,
  then die in my own bed.
19 In those days I was strong
  like a tree with deep roots
  and with plenty of water,
20   or like an archer's new bow.

---

*28.17 **costly glass:** In the ancient world, objects
made of glass were costly.
*28.18 **jasper:** A valuable stone, usually green or clear.
*28.19 **topaz:** A valuable, yellow stone.
*28.19 **Ethiopia:** The Hebrew text has "Cush", which
was a region south of Egypt that included parts of the
present countries of Ethiopia and Sudan.

See also: 28.28: Psa 111.10; Prov 1.7; 9.10.

²¹ Everyone listened in silence
to my welcome advice,
²² and when I finished speaking,
nothing needed to be said.
²³ My words were eagerly accepted
like the showers of spring,
²⁴ and the smile on my face
renewed everyone's hopes.
²⁵ My advice was followed
as though I were a king leading my troops,
or someone comforting those in sorrow.

CHAPTER 30

Job continues

Young people now insult me

¹ Young people now insult me,
although their fathers
would have been a disgrace
to my sheep dogs.
² And those who insult me
are helpless themselves.
³ They must claw the desert sand
in the dark for something
to satisfy their hunger.'
⁴ They gather tasteless shrubs
for food and firewood,
⁵ and they are driven out of towns,
as though they were thieves.
⁶ Their only homes are ditches
or holes between rocks,
⁷ where they bray like donkeys
gathering around shrubs.
⁸ And like senseless donkeys
they are chased away.

Those worthless nobodies

⁹ Those worthless nobodies
make up jokes and songs
to disgrace me.
¹⁰ They are hateful
and keep their distance,
even while spitting in my direction.
¹¹ God has destroyed me,
and so they don't care what they do.'
¹² Their attacks never stop,
though I am defenceless,
and my feet are trapped.'
¹³ Without any help,
they prevent my escape,
destroying me completely'
¹⁴ and leaving me crushed.
¹⁵ Terror has me surrounded;
my reputation and my riches
have vanished like a cloud.

I am sick at heart

¹⁶ I am sick at heart!
Pain has taken its toll.
¹⁷ Night chews on my bones,
causing endless torment,
¹⁸ and God has shrunk my skin,
choking me to death.
¹⁹ I have been thrown in the dirt
and now am dirt myself.
²⁰ I beg God for help,
but there is no answer;
and when I stand up,
he simply stares.
²¹ God has turned brutal,
²² stirring up a storm to toss me about.
²³ Soon he will send me home
to the world of the dead,
where we all must go.

²⁴ No one refuses help to others,
when disaster strikes.'
²⁵ I mourned for the poor
and those who suffered.
²⁶ But when I beg for relief and light,
all I receive are disaster
and darkness.
²⁷ My stomach is tied in knots;
pain is my daily companion.
²⁸ Suffering has scorched my skin,
and in the city council
I stand and cry out,
²⁹ making mournful sounds
like jackals* and owls.
³⁰ My skin is so parched,
that it peels right off,
and my bones are burning.
³¹ My only songs are sorrow
and sadness.

Job swears that he is innocent

CHAPTER 31

Job continues

I promised myself

¹ I promised myself
never to stare with desire
at a young woman.
² God All-Powerful punishes
men who do that.

---

*30.29 jackals: Desert animals related to wolves, but smaller.

³ In fact, God sends disaster
on all who sin,
⁴ and he keeps a close watch
on everything I do.

⁵ I am not dishonest or deceitful,
⁶ and I beg God to prove my innocence.
⁷ If I have disobeyed him
or even wanted to,
⁸ then others can eat my harvest
and uproot my crops.
⁹ If I have desired someone's wife
and chased after her,
¹⁰ then let some stranger
steal my wife from me.
¹¹ If I took someone's wife,
it would be a horrible crime,
¹² sending me to destruction
and my crops to the flames.'

¹³ When my servants
complained against me,
I was fair to them.
¹⁴ Otherwise, what answer
would I give to God
when he judges me?
¹⁵ After all, God is the one
who gave life to each of us
before we were born.

I have never cheated anyone

¹⁶ I have never cheated widows
or others in need,
¹⁷ and I have always shared
my food with orphans.
¹⁸ Since the time I was young,
I have cared for orphans
and helped widows.'
¹⁹ I provided clothes for the poor,
²⁰ and I was praised
for supplying woollen garments
to keep them warm.
²¹ If I have ever raised my arm
to threaten an orphan
when the power was mine,
²² I hope that arm will fall
from its socket.
²³ I could not have been abusive;
I was terrified at the thought
that God might punish me.
²⁴ I have never trusted the power of wealth,
²⁵ or taken pride in owning
many possessions.
²⁶⁻²⁷ I have never openly or secretly
worshipped the sun or moon.
²⁸ Such horrible sins
would have deserved
punishment from God.

²⁹ I have never laughed
when my enemies
were struck by disaster.
³⁰ Neither have I sinned by asking God
to send down on them
the curse of death.
³¹ No one ever went hungry*
at my house,
³² and travellers were always welcome.
³³ Many have attempted to hide
their sins from others —
but I refused.
³⁴ And the fear of public disgrace
never forced me
to keep silent
about what I had done.

Why doesn't God listen?

³⁵ Why doesn't God All-Powerful
listen and answer?
If God has something against me,
let him speak up
or put it in writing!
³⁶ Then I would wear his charges
on my clothes and forehead.
³⁷ And with my head held high,
I would tell him everything
I have ever done.

³⁸ I have never ill-treated
the land I farmed
and made it mourn.*
³⁹ Nor have I cheated my workers
and caused them pain.'
⁴⁰ If I had, I would pray
for weeds instead of wheat
to grow in my fields.

After saying these things, Job was silent.

Elihu's speeches

CHAPTER 32

Elihu is upset with Job's friends

¹ Finally, these three men stopped arguing
with Job, because he refused to admit that he
was guilty.

---

*31.31 ever went hungry: Or "was ever sexually abused" (see Genesis 19.1–11; Judges 19.22–30). In ancient Israel, the lives of one's guests were sacred and had to be protected at any cost.
*31.38 mourn: In biblical times there were strict regulations for proper use of the land, and land that was abused was said to "mourn" and become no longer productive.

571

² Elihu from Buz* was there, and he had become upset with Job for blaming God instead of himself. ³ He was also angry with Job's three friends for not being able to prove that Job was wrong. ⁴ Elihu was younger than these three, and he let them speak first. ⁵ But he became irritated when they could not answer Job, ⁶ and he said to them:

> I am much younger than you,
>   so I have shown respect
>   by keeping silent.
> ⁷ I once believed age
>   was the source of wisdom;
> ⁸   now I truly realize
>   wisdom comes from God.
> ⁹ Age is no guarantee of wisdom
>   and understanding.
> ¹⁰   That's why I ask you
>   to listen to me.

I eagerly listened

> ¹¹⁻¹²I eagerly listened
>   to each of your arguments,
>   but not one of you proved
>   Job to be wrong.
> ¹³ You shouldn't say,
>   "We know what's right!
>   Let God punish him."
> ¹⁴ Job hasn't spoken against me,
>   and so I won't answer him
>   with your arguments.
>
> ¹⁵ All of you are shocked;
>   you don't know what to say.
> ¹⁶ But am I to remain silent,
>   just because you
>   have stopped speaking?
> ¹⁷ No! I will give my opinion,
> ¹⁸ because I have so much to say,
>   that I can't keep quiet.
> ¹⁹ I am like a swollen wineskin,
>   and I will burst*
> ²⁰   if I don't speak.
> ²¹⁻²²I don't know how to be unfair
>   or to flatter anyone —
>   if I did, my Creator
>   would quickly destroy me!

---

*32.2 Elihu from Buz: The Hebrew text has "Elihu son of Barachel from Buz of the family of Ram". Buz may have been somewhere in the territory of Edom; in Jeremiah 25.23 it is mentioned along with Dedan and Tema (see 6.19).

*32.19 swollen wineskin . . . burst: While the juice from grapes was becoming wine, it would swell and stretch the skins in which it had been stored; sometimes the swelling would burst the wineskins.

CHAPTER 33

Elihu speaks

Job, listen to me!

> ¹ Job, listen to me!
>   Pay close attention.
> ²⁻³   Everything I will say
>   is true and sincere,
> ⁴   just as surely as the Spirit
>   of God All-Powerful᾽
>   gave me the breath of life.
> ⁵ Now line up your arguments
>   and prepare to face me.
> ⁶ We were each made from clay,
>   and God has no favourites,
> ⁷   so don't be afraid of me
>   or what I might do.

I have heard you argue

> ⁸ I have heard you argue
> ⁹   that you are innocent,
>   guilty of nothing.
> ¹⁰ You claim that God
>   has made you his enemy,
> ¹¹   that he has bound your feet
>   and blocked your path.
> ¹² But, Job, you're wrong —
>   God is greater than any human.
> ¹³ So why do you challenge God
>   to answer you?᾽
> ¹⁴ God speaks in different ways,
>   and we don't always
>   recognize his voice.
> ¹⁵⁻¹⁶Sometimes in the night,
>   he uses terrifying dreams
>   to give us warnings.
> ¹⁷ God does this to make us turn
>   from sin and pride
> ¹⁸ and to protect us
>   from being swept away
>   to the world of the dead.
>
> ¹⁹ Sometimes we are punished
>   with a serious illness
>   and aching joints.
> ²⁰ Merely the thought
>   of our favourite food
>   makes our stomachs sick,
> ²¹ and we become so skinny
>   that our bones stick out.
> ²² We feel death and the grave
>   taking us in their grip.

See also: 33.11: Job 13.27.   33.15: Job 4.13.

23 One of a thousand angels
then comes to our rescue
by saying we are innocent.
24 The angel shows kindness,
commanding death to release us,
because the price was paid.
25 Our health is restored,
we feel young again,
26 and we ask God to accept us.
Then we joyfully worship God,
and we are rewarded
because we are innocent.
27 When that happens,
we tell everyone,
"I sinned and did wrong,
but God forgave me
28 and rescued me from death!
Now I will see the light."

29 God gives each of us
chance after chance
30 to be saved from death
and brought into the light
that gives life.
31 So, Job, pay attention
and don't interrupt,
32 though I would gladly listen
to anything you say
that proves you are right.
33 Otherwise, listen in silence
to my wisdom.

CHAPTER 34

Elihu continues

You men think you are wise

1 Elihu said:

2 You men think you are wise,
but just listen to me!
3 Think about my words,
as you would taste food.
4 Then we can decide the case
and give a just verdict.
5 Job claims he is innocent
and God is guilty
of ill-treating him.
6 Job also argues that God
considers him a liar
and that he is suffering severely
in spite of his innocence.
7 But to tell the truth,
Job is shameless!
8 He spends his time with sinners,
9 because he has said,
"It doesn't pay to please God."

If any of you are clever

10 If any of you are clever,
you will listen and learn
that God All-Powerful
does what is right.
11 God always treats everyone
the way they deserve,
12 and he is never unfair.
13 From the very beginning,
God has been in control
of all the world.
14 If God took back the breath
that he breathed into us,
15 we humans would die
and return to the soil.
16 So be wise and listen!
17 The mighty God is the one
who brings about justice,
and you are condemning him.
18 Indeed, God is the one
who condemns unfair rulers.
19 And God created us all;
he has no favourites,
whether rich or poor.
20 Even powerful rulers die
in the darkness of night
when they least expect it,
just like the rest of us.

God watches everything we do

21 God watches everything we do.
22 No evil person can hide
in the deepest darkness.
23 And so, God doesn't need
to set a time for judgment.
24 Without asking for advice,
God removes mighty leaders
and puts others in their place.
25 He knows what they are like,
and he wipes them out
in the middle of the night.
26 And while others look on,
he punishes them
because they were evil
27 and refused to obey him.
28 The persons they ill-treated
had prayed for help,
until God answered their prayers.
29 When God does nothing,
can any person or nation
find fault with him?
30 But still, he punishes rulers
who abuse their people.'

See also: 34.11: Psa 62.12.

31 Job, you should tell God
that you are guilty
and promise to do better.
32 Then ask him to point out
what you did wrong,
so you won't do it again.
33 Do you make the rules,
or does God?
You have to decide —
I can't do it for you;
now make up your mind.
34 Job, anyone with good sense
can easily see
35 that you are speaking nonsense
and lack good judgment.
36 So I pray for you to suffer
as much as possible
for talking like a sinner.
37 You have rebelled against God,
time after time,
and have even insulted us.

CHAPTER 35

Elihu continues

Are you really innocent?

1 Elihu said:

2 Job, are you really innocent
in the sight of God?᾽
3 Don't you honestly believe
it pays to obey him?
4 I will give the answers
to you and your friends.
5-6 Look up to the heavens and think!
Do your sins hurt God?
7 Is any good you may have done
at all helpful to him?
8 The evil or good you do
only affects other humans.

9 In times of trouble,
everyone begs the mighty God
to have mercy.
10 But after their Creator
helps them through hard times,
they forget about him,
11 though he makes us wiser
than animals or birds.
12 God won't listen to the prayers
of proud and evil people.
13 If God All-Powerful refuses
to answer their empty prayers,
14 he will surely deny your impatient request
to face him in court.

15 Job, you were wrong to say
God doesn't punish sin.
16 Everything you have said
adds up to nonsense.

CHAPTER 36

Elihu continues

Be patient a while longer

1 Elihu said:

2 Be patient a while longer;
I have something else to say
in God's defence.
3 God always does right —
and this knowledge
comes straight from God.*
4 You can rest assured
that what I say is true.
5 Although God is mighty,
he cares about everyone
and makes fair decisions.

6 The wicked are cut down,
and those who are wronged
receive justice.
7 God watches over good people
and places them
in positions of power and honour
for ever.
8 But when people are prisoners
of suffering and pain,
9-10 God points out their sin and their pride,
then he warns them to turn back to him.
11 And if they obey, they will be successful
and happy from then on.
12 But if they foolishly refuse,
they will be rewarded
with a violent death.

Godless people are too angry

13 Godless people are too angry
to ask God for help
when he punishes them.
14 So they die young
in shameful disgrace.
15 Hard times and trouble
are God's way of getting our attention!
16 And at this very moment,
God deeply desires
to lead you from trouble
and to spread your table
with your favourite food.

*36.3 comes straight from God: The Hebrew text
has "comes from a distant place", which refers to the
place where God lives; Elihu is claiming that he learnt
this from God.

17 Now that the judgment for your sins
has fallen upon you,
18 don't let your anger
and the pain you endured
make you sneer at God.
19 Your reputation and riches
cannot protect you from distress,
20 nor can you find safety
in the dark world below.'
21 Be on guard! Don't turn to evil
as a way of escape.
22 God's power is unlimited.
He needs no teachers
23 to guide or correct him.

Others have praised God

24 Others have praised God
for what he has done,
so join with them.
25 From down here on earth,
everyone has looked up and seen
26 how great God is —
God is more than we imagine;
no one can count the years
he has lived.
27-28 God gathers moisture into the clouds
and supplies us with rain.
29 Who can understand
how God scatters the clouds
and speaks from his home
in the thunderstorm?
30 And when God sends lightning,
it can be seen
at the bottom of the sea.
31 By producing such rainstorms,
God rules the world
and provides us with food.
32 Each flash of lightning
is one of his arrows
striking its target,
33 and the thunder tells
of his anger against sin.'

CHAPTER 37

Elihu continues

I am frightened

1 I am frightened and tremble all over,
2 when I hear the roaring voice
of God in the thunder,
3 and when I see his lightning
flash across the sky.
4 God's majestic voice
thunders his commands,'
5 creating miracles too marvellous
for us to understand.

6 Snow and heavy rainstorms
7 make us stop and think about
God's power,
8 and they force animals to seek shelter.
9 The storms of winter strike,
10 and the breath of God
freezes streams and rivers.
11 Rain clouds filled with lightning
appear at God's command,
12 travelling across the sky
13 to release their cargo —
sometimes as punishment for sin,
sometimes as kindness.

Consider carefully

14 Job, consider carefully
the many wonders of God.
15 Can you explain why lightning flashes
at the orders
16 of God who knows all things?
Or how he hangs the clouds
in empty space?
17 You almost melt in the heat
of fierce desert winds
when the sky is like brass.
18 God can spread out the clouds
to get relief from the heat,
but can you?

19 Tell us what to say to God!
Our minds are in the dark,
and we don't know how
to argue our case.
20 Should I risk my life by telling God
that I want to speak?
21 No one can stare at the sun
after a breeze has blown
the clouds from the sky.
22 Yet the glorious splendour
of God All-Powerful
is brighter by far.
23 God cannot be seen —
but his power is great,
and he is always fair.
24 And so we humans fear God,
because he shows no respect
for those who are proud
and think they know so much.

God's first speech

CHAPTER 38

The LORD speaks

From out of a storm

1 From out of a storm, the LORD said to Job:

² Why do you talk so much
  when you know so little?
³ Now get ready to face me!
  Can you answer the questions I ask?
⁴ How did I lay the foundation
  for the earth?
  Were you there?
⁵ Doubtless you know who decided
  its length and width.
⁶ What supports the foundation?
  Who placed the cornerstone,
⁷ while morning stars sang,
  and angels rejoiced?

⁸ When the ocean was born,
  I set its boundaries
⁹ and wrapped it in blankets of thickest fog.
¹⁰ Then I built a wall around it,
  locked the gates,
¹¹ and said,
  "Your powerful waves stop here!
  They can go no further."

Did you ever tell the sun to rise?

¹² Did you ever tell the sun to rise?
  And did it obey?
¹³ Did it take hold of the earth
  and shake out the wicked
  like dust from a rug?
¹⁴ Early dawn outlines the hills
  like stitches on clothing
  or sketches on clay.
¹⁵ But its light is too much
  for those who are evil,
  and their power is broken.

¹⁶ Job, have you ever walked
  on the ocean floor?
¹⁷ Have you seen the gate
  to the world of the dead?
¹⁸ And how large is the earth?
  Tell me, if you know!

¹⁹ Where is the home of light,
  and where does darkness live?
²⁰ Can you lead them home?
²¹ I'm certain you must be able to,
  since you were already born
  when I created everything.

²² Have you been to the places
  where I keep snow and hail,
²³ until I use them to punish
  and conquer nations?
²⁴ From where does lightning leap,
  or the east wind blow?

²⁵ Who carves out a path
  for thunderstorms?
  Who sends torrents of rain
²⁶ on empty deserts where no one lives?
²⁷ Rain that changes barren land
  to meadows green with grass.
²⁸ Who is the father of the dew
  and of the rain?
²⁹ Who gives birth to the sleet
  and the frost
³⁰ that fall in winter,
  when streams and lakes
  freeze solid as a rock?

Can you arrange stars?

³¹ Can you arrange stars in groups
  such as Orion and the Pleiades?
³² Do you control the stars
  or set in place the Great Bear
  and the Little Bear?
³³ Do you know the laws
  that govern the heavens,
  and can you make them rule the earth?
³⁴ Can you order the clouds
  to send a downpour,
³⁵ or will lightning flash at your command?
³⁶ Did you teach birds to know
  that rain or floods
  are on their way?
³⁷ Can you count the clouds
  or pour out their water
³⁸ on the dry, lumpy soil?

³⁹ When lions are hungry,
  do you help them hunt?
⁴⁰ Do you send an animal into their den?
⁴¹ And when starving young ravens
  cry out to me for food,
  do you satisfy their hunger?

CHAPTER 39

The LORD continues

When do mountain goats give birth?

¹ When do mountain goats
  and deer give birth?
  Have you been there
  when their young are born?
²⁻³ How long are they pregnant
  before they deliver?
⁴ Soon their young grow strong
  and then leave to be on their own.

⁵ Who set wild donkeys free?
⁶ I alone help them survive
  in salty desert sand.

See also: **38.8–11:** Jer 5.22.   See also: **38.31:** Job 9.9; Amos 5.8.

576

Real life

Genetic engineering

Contributed by Care

The term 'Genetic engineering' often conjures up fears of abuse, eugenics and 'playing God' but it is in fact a broad term, covering a range of genetic techniques and interventions, not all of which are negative. So, for instance, it includes gene therapies, the human genome project and adult stem cell research, as well as the more problematic prenatal genetic diagnosis, genetic screening and embryonic stem cell research.

These are all possible because we are able to manipulate the content of human cells. All our inherited characteristics are controlled by the action of genes, made up of DNA. DNA carries the codes for the function of cells, the 'building blocks' of our bodies. When errors occur in the copying of DNA this can cause disorders of the body, such as cancers. Some of these errors (mutations) are inheritable down the generations. Advances in genetics have made it possible to decode our human genes, to begin to identify genetic variations and to manipulate messages in the genes. Thus we have exciting prospects for diagnosing diseases and improving medicine and treatment. However, whilst some applications of genetics are desirable, others have potential for both good and ill.

One of the most widespread uses of genetic technology is in screening – the detection of genetic variants. Some screening is routine and beneficial (such as screening of babies for the disease PKU) but often it raises difficult ethical questions: Who should be tested? What privacy and confidentiality should be kept, particularly if others might be affected? What if there is no cure? Might there be discrimination in insurance or employment? How precise and predictive is the genetic test? The genetic testing of embryos (pre-implantation genetic diagnosis) raises further ethical issues in that it results in the disposal of embryos with particular 'disorders'.

Then there is gene therapy – the correction or replacement of defective genes – which has held out great potential for cures for years but has, as yet, produced few real successes, partly because of safety concerns. One type, germ line therapy, is more controversial and risky, as it alters genes in the reproductive tissues making any changes inheritable.

Whilst most people shun the idea that genetic engineering should be used to permanently enhance or alter individual characteristics, it can be difficult to clarify what is simply treatment (the alleviation of disease) and what is enhancement. It is often a small step between the two and one that will increasingly challenge us as genetic research advances.

Despite the central role our genes play in our lives, we are not simply the sum of our genes – we still have personal responsibility for our behaviour and actions. And we have a responsibility to ensure that this powerful tool of genetics is used to good, not ill, to harness its benefits and heed the biblical mandate to protect the weak and vulnerable.

Think

What biblical principles should a scientist involved in genetic engineering be familiar with?

Act

Keep an eye on stories about genetic engineering in the news.
For many more resources and papers on the issues surrounding genetics:
www.bioethics.ac.uk

Check

Job 10.9–12; 38.33—39.30; Psalms 22.9–10

More...

Abortion p.668
Creation p.3
Euthanasia p.641

⁷ They stay far from crowded cities
and refuse to be tamed.
⁸ Instead, they roam the hills,
searching for pasture land.

⁹ Would a wild ox agree to live in your barn
and labour for you?
¹⁰ Could you force him to plough
or to drag a heavy log
to smooth out the soil?
¹¹ Can you depend on him
to use his great strength
and do your heavy work?
¹² Can you trust him to harvest your grain
or take it to your barn
from the threshing place?

An ostrich proudly flaps her wings

¹³ An ostrich proudly flaps her wings,
but not because she loves her young.
¹⁴ She abandons her eggs
and lets the dusty ground
keep them warm.
¹⁵ And she doesn't seem to worry
that the feet of an animal
could crush them all.
¹⁶ She treats her eggs as though
they were not her own,
unconcerned that her work
might be for nothing.
¹⁷ I myself made her foolish
and without common sense.
¹⁸ But once she starts running,⸍
she laughs at a rider on the fastest horse.

Did you give horses their strength?

¹⁹ Did you give horses their strength
and the flowing hair along their necks?
²⁰ Did you make them able
to jump like grasshoppers
or to frighten people with their snorting?

²¹ Before horses are ridden into battle,
they paw at the ground,
proud of their strength.
²² Laughing at fear, they rush
towards the fighting,
²³ while the weapons of their riders
rattle and flash in the sun.
²⁴ Unable to stand still,
they gallop eagerly into battle
when trumpets blast.
²⁵ Stirred by the distant smells
and sounds of war,
they snort in reply to the trumpet.

²⁶ Did you teach hawks to fly south
for the winter?

²⁷⁻²⁸ Did you train eagles⸍ to build
their nests on rocky cliffs,
²⁹ where they can look down
to spot their next meal?
³⁰ Then their young gather to feast
wherever the victim lies.

God's second speech and Job's responses

CHAPTER 40

The LORD continues

I am the LORD All-Powerful

¹⁻² I am the LORD All-Powerful,
but you have argued that I am wrong.
Now you must answer me.

³ Job said to the LORD:

⁴ Who am I to answer you?
⁵ I did speak once or twice,
but never again.

⁶ Then out of the storm the LORD said to Job:

⁷ Face me and answer the questions I ask!
⁸ Are you trying to prove
that you are innocent
by accusing me of injustice?
⁹ Do you have a powerful arm
and a thundering voice
that compare with mine?
¹⁰ If so, then surround yourself
with glory and majesty.
¹¹⁻¹² Show your furious anger!
Throw down and crush
all who are proud and evil.
¹³ Wrap them in grave clothes
and bury them together
in the dusty soil.
¹⁴ Do this, and I will agree
that you have won this argument.

I created you

¹⁵ I created both you
and the hippopotamus.*
It eats only grass like an ox,
¹⁶ but look at the mighty muscles
in its body
¹⁷ and legs.

---

*40.15 the hippopotamus: The Hebrew text has
"Behemoth", which was sometimes understood to be
a sea monster like Rahab (9.13; 26.12), Leviathan
(3.8; 41.1), and Tannin (7.12).
See also: 39.30: Matt 24.28; Luke 17.37.

Its tail is like a cedar tree,
and its thighs are thick.
18 The bones in its legs
are like bronze or iron.

19 I made it more powerful
than any other creature,
yet I am stronger still.
20 Undisturbed, it eats grass
while the other animals play nearby.'
21-22 It rests in the shade of trees
along the river bank
or hides among reeds in the swamp.
23 It remains calm and unafraid
with the River Jordan rushing
and splashing in its face.
24 There is no way to capture
a hippopotamus —
not even by hooking its nose
or blinding its eyes.

CHAPTER 41

The LORD continues

Can you catch a sea monster?

1 Can you catch a sea monster*
by using a fish-hook?
Can you tie its mouth shut with a rope?
2 Can it be led around by a ring in its nose
or a hook in its jaw?
3 Will it beg for mercy?
4 Will it surrender as a slave for life?
5 Can it be tied by the leg
like a pet bird for little girls?
6 Is it ever chopped up
and its pieces bargained for
in the fish-market?
7 Can it be killed with harpoons or spears?
8 Wrestle with it just once —
that will be the end.
9 Merely a glimpse of this monster
makes all courage melt.
10 And if it is too fierce for anyone to attack,
who would dare oppose me?
11 I am in command of the world
and in debt to no one.

12 What powerful legs, what a stout body
this monster possesses!
13 Who could strip off its armour
or bring it under control with a harness?
14 Who would try to open its jaws,
full of fearsome teeth?

15-17 Its back' is covered
with shield after shield,
firmly bound and closer together
than breath to breath.

When this monster sneezes

18 When this monster sneezes,
lightning flashes,
and its eyes glow like the dawn.
19 Sparks and fiery flames
explode from its mouth.
20 And smoke spews from its nose
like steam from a boiling pot,
21 while its blazing breath
scorches everything in sight.

22 Its neck is so tremendous
that everyone trembles,
23 the weakest parts of its body
are harder than iron,
24 and its heart is stone.
25 When this noisy monster appears,
even the most powerful'
turn and run in fear.
26 No sword or spear can harm it,
27 and weapons of bronze
or iron are as useless
as straw or rotten wood.
28 Stones thrown from a sling
cause it no more harm
than husks of grain.
This monster fears no arrows,
29 it simply smiles at spears,
and striking it with a stick
is like slapping it with straw.

30 As it crawls through the mud,
its sharp and spiny hide
tears the ground apart.
31 And when it swims down deep,
the sea starts churning like boiling oil,
32 and it leaves behind a trail
of shining white foam.
33 No other creature on earth
is so fearless.
34 It is king of all proud creatures,
and it looks upon the others
as nothing.

CHAPTER 42

Job's reply to the LORD

No one can oppose you

1 Job said:

2 No one can oppose you,
because you have the power
to do what you want.

---

*41.1 sea monster: The Hebrew text has "Leviathan",
which may refer to a sea monster or possibly to a
crocodile in this verse (see the note at 3.8).
See also: 41.1: Psa 74.14; 104.26; Isa 27.1.

3 You asked why I talk so much
   when I know so little.
 I have talked about things
   that are far beyond my understanding.
4 You told me to listen
   and answer your questions.'
5 I heard about you from others;
   now I have seen you
   with my own eyes.
6 That's why I hate myself
   and sit here in dust and ashes
   to show my sorrow.

The Lord again blesses Job with health, wealth, and family

The LORD corrects Job's friends

7 The LORD said to Eliphaz:

What my servant Job has said about me is true, but I am angry with you and your two friends for not telling the truth. 8 So I want you to go over to Job and offer seven bulls and seven goats on an altar as a sacrifice to please me.* After this, Job will pray, and I will agree not to punish you for your foolishness.

9 Eliphaz, Bildad, and Zophar obeyed the LORD, and he answered Job's prayer.

A happy ending

10 After Job had prayed for his three friends, the LORD made Job twice as rich as he had been before. 11 Then Job gave a feast for his brothers and sisters and for his old friends. They expressed their sorrow for the suffering the LORD had brought on him, and they each gave Job some silver and a gold ring. 12 The LORD now blessed Job more than ever; he gave him fourteen thousand sheep, six thousand camels, a thousand pair of oxen, and a thousand donkeys. 13 In addition to seven sons, Job had three daughters, 14 whose names were Jemimah, Keziah, and Keren Happuch. 15 They were the most beautiful women in that part of the world, and Job gave them shares of his property, along with their brothers. 16 Job lived for another one hundred and forty years — long enough to see his great-grandchildren have children of their own — 17 and when he finally died, he was very old.

Additional notes

'1.6 Satan: Hebrew "the accuser".
'2.1 Satan: See the note at 1.6.
'2.4 There's no pain like your own: The Hebrew text has "Skin for skin", which was probably a popular saying.
'3.12 Why was I accepted: The Hebrew text has "Why were there knees to receive me", which may refer either to Job's mother or to his father, who would have placed Job on his knees to show that he had accepted him as his child.
'5.5 wealth: One possible meaning for the difficult Hebrew text of verse 5.
'6.6 What is more tasteless . . . egg: One possible meaning for the difficult Hebrew text.
'6.14 and you should help me . . . God All-Powerful: Or "and if you don't help me, you no longer respect God All-Powerful."
'6.21 just . . . you: One possible meaning for the difficult Hebrew text.
'8.17 rocks: One possible meaning for the difficult Hebrew text of verse 17.
'8.19 their . . . away: One possible meaning for the difficult Hebrew text.
'9.17 strike . . . storm: One possible meaning for the difficult Hebrew text.
'9.20 God . . . wrong: Or "my own words would prove me wrong."
'9.35 but . . . speak: One possible meaning for the difficult Hebrew text.
'10.16 lion: One possible meaning for the difficult Hebrew text of verse 16.
'10.20 I have only . . . alone: One possible meaning for the difficult Hebrew text.
'11.12 it's . . . wise: One possible meaning for the difficult Hebrew text.
'12.6 God is in our hands: One possible meaning for the difficult Hebrew text.
'12.9 Any . . . done: One possible meaning for the difficult Hebrew text.
'13.15 God . . . trust him: Or "God will surely kill me; I have lost all hope".
'15.31-32 leaf: One possible meaning for the difficult Hebrew text of verses 31-32.
'16.20 My friends . . . beg: Or "God is my friend, and he is the one I beg".

---

*42.8 sacrifice to please me: These sacrifices have traditionally been called "whole burnt offerings" because the whole animal was burnt on the altar. A main purpose of such sacrifices was to please the LORD with the smell of the sacrifice, and so in the CEV they are often called "sacrifices to please the LORD".
See also: 42.3: Job 38.2.   42.4: Job 38.3.   42.10: Job 1.1–3.

›**17.9 stronger:** One possible meaning for the difficult Hebrew text of verses 8,9.

›**17.12 hopes:** One possible meaning for the difficult Hebrew text of verse 12.

›**19.25 Saviour:** Or "Defender".

›**19.26 God:** One possible meaning for the difficult Hebrew text of verses 25–26.

›**20.20 are never satisfied:** One possible meaning for the difficult Hebrew text.

›**20.23 anger:** One possible meaning for the difficult Hebrew text of verse 23.

›**21.8 up:** One possible meaning for the difficult Hebrew text of verse 8.

›**22.30 God:** One possible meaning for the difficult Hebrew text of verses 29–30.

›**23.11–12 treasured his teachings:** One possible meaning for the difficult Hebrew text.

›**23.17 silent:** One possible meaning for the difficult Hebrew text of verse 17.

›**24.21 women:** One possible meaning for the difficult Hebrew text of verse 21.

›**26.12 the force of the mighty ocean:** The Hebrew text has "the ocean . . . Rahab". In this passage the sea monster Rahab stands for the fearsome power of the ocean (see the notes at 3.8 and 9.13).

›**27.19 poor:** Or "dead".

›**28.6 gold:** One possible meaning for the difficult Hebrew text of verses 5–6.

›**28.11 uncover the sources of:** Two ancient translations; Hebrew "dam up".

›**28.13 the way:** Or "its worth".

›**30.3 hunger:** One possible meaning for the difficult Hebrew text of verse 3.

›**30.11 God . . . do:** Or "They have destroyed me, and so they don't care what else they do."

›**30.12 trapped:** One possible meaning for the difficult Hebrew text of verse 12.

›**30.13 destroying . . . completely:** One possible meaning for the difficult Hebrew text.

›**30.24 strikes:** One possible meaning for the difficult Hebrew text of verse 24.

›**31.12 flames:** One possible meaning for the difficult Hebrew text of verse 12.

›**31.18 widows:** One possible meaning for the difficult Hebrew text of verse 18.

›**31.39 pain:** One possible meaning for the difficult Hebrew text of verse 39.

›**33.4 the Spirit of God All-Powerful:** Or "God All-Powerful".

›**33.13 answer you:** One possible meaning for the difficult Hebrew text of verse 13.

›**34.30 people:** One possible meaning for the difficult Hebrew text of verses 29–30.

›**35.2 are . . . God:** Or "is it right for you to accuse God?"

›**36.20 below:** One possible meaning for the difficult Hebrew text of verses 18–20.

›**36.33 sin:** One possible meaning for the difficult Hebrew text of verse 33.

›**37.4 commands:** One possible meaning for the difficult Hebrew text of verse 4.

›**38.36 way:** One possible meaning for the difficult Hebrew text of verse 36.

›**39.18 starts running:** One possible meaning for the difficult Hebrew text.

›**39.27–28 eagles:** Or "vultures".

›**40.20 nearby:** One possible meaning for the difficult Hebrew text of verse 20.

›**41.15–17 back:** Two ancient translations; Hebrew "pride".

›**41.25 most powerful:** Or "gods".

›**42.4 questions:** One possible meaning for the difficult Hebrew text of verse 4.

Psalms

The basics

Who wrote it? The Psalms are arranged in different collections according to authorship. Many are attributed to David, and link into certain events in his life. But there are other authors as well, including Moses.

What's the point? To reflect what it's like being a follower of God; good times and bad.

What should I remember? 27.1 'You, LORD are the light that keeps me safe. I am not afraid of anyone.

You protect me, and I have no fears.'

More details

Setting the scene Have you ever kept a diary? The Psalms are a bit like that. They're poems or songs which recount all the different moods of a believer's life. Highs and lows, ups and downs, good times and bad.

What's it all about? Psalms is a collection of poetry. Each 'chapter' of Psalms is a separate poem, composed at a different time for a different purpose, often by a different person.

The Hebrew title is 'Praises'. But actually, not all the Psalms praise God. The Book of Psalms is more like a diary or a spiritual journal, recording different feelings and circumstances, reflecting on how life is.

The psalms are not theological manuals; they're not neat little morality tales or lists of laws or nuggets of history – although they may contain all those things. The psalms are the emotional outpourings of real human beings. They are frequently quite emotionally raw. They can appear pleading, even shocking at times. More than perhaps any other part of the Bible, they record real feelings and raw emotion. Perhaps this is why Jesus, dying on the cross, screamed out a line from a psalm.

The Psalms are poetry, and like all great poetry, they're rich in imagery and metaphor. This is another reason why these psalms continue to speak to so many people today; we still find mountains as majestic and awe-inspiring as the ancient Hebrews did.

Above all, people still respond to the Psalms because they reflect a relationship with God, in all its different moods. Reading Psalms is like going on an emotional roller coaster ride: one minute you way up high, the next moment you're plunged into the deepest despair.

Enjoy the ride.

And another thing

'Psalms' is a Greek word which comes from the psalterion – a kind of ancient stringed instrument. (Nowadays it would be like calling the book 'Guitaros'.)

Footsteps

Praise the creator: Psalm 8
Close to death: Psalm 13
So alone: Psalm 22
The Lord is my shepherd: Psalm 23
Trust in God: Psalm 27
The hunted deer: Psalm 42
Forgiveness and mercy: Psalm 51
Saying thanks: Psalm 66
Joyful worship: Psalm 95
Intense suffering, intense faith: Psalm 102
The glory of creation: Psalm 104
The joy of the law: Psalm 119
Song of exile: Psalm 137
Praise God: Psalm 150

Holy history

Hebrew poetry

OK, if the Psalms are poetry, why don't they rhyme?

Well, they do. Just not in the way you expect. Hebrew poetry rhymes ideas rather than words. It uses 'thought' rhymes, rather than 'word' rhymes.

Rhyming by repeating ideas

Sometimes the rhyme consists of the same thought or idea, restated. The Psalmist makes two statements, very similar to each other.

> You judge the world fairly and treat all nations with justice. (Psalms 9.8)

Rhyming by contrasting ideas

Sometimes the rhyme is a contrast. The second half of the 'rhyme' contrasts with and strengthens the first half.

> The LORD protects everyone who follows him,
> but the wicked follow a road that leads to ruin. (Psalms 1.6)

Rhyming by developing ideas

Sometimes the second part of the rhyme develops the first part. The Psalmist makes several statements, adding or explaining a bit more each time. It's a bit like climbing stairs; each successive statement adds something to the whole idea, in a kind of progression.

> Who may climb the LORD's hill or stand in his holy temple?
> Only those who do right for the right reasons,
> and don't worship idols or tell lies under oath. (Psalms 24.3–4)

There are other kinds of 'rhyme' within the Psalms and other poetry, but those three are the main kind.

More...

Different types of psalm p.584
Wisdom p.548

BOOK 1

(Psalms 1–41)

Psalm 1

The way to happiness

1 God blesses those people
   who refuse evil advice
   and won't follow sinners
   or join in sneering at God.
2 Instead, the Law of the LORD
   makes them happy,
   and they think about it day and night.

3 They are like trees
   growing beside a stream,
   trees that produce fruit in season
   and always have leaves.
   Those people succeed
   in everything they do.

4 That isn't true of those who are evil,
   because they are like straw
   blown by the wind.
5 Sinners won't have an excuse
   on the day of judgment,
   and they won't have a place
   with the people of God.
6 The LORD protects everyone
   who follows him,
   but the wicked follow a road
   that leads to ruin.

Psalm 2

The LORD's chosen king

1 Why do the nations plot,′
   and why do their people
   make useless plans?′
2 The kings of this earth
   have all joined together
   to turn against the LORD
   and his chosen one.
3 They say, "Let's cut the ropes
   and set ourselves free!"

4 In heaven the LORD laughs
   as he sits on his throne,
   making fun of the nations.
5 The LORD becomes furious
   and threatens them.
   His anger terrifies them as he says,
6 "I've put my king on Zion,
   my sacred hill."

See also: 1.3: Jer 17.8. **2.1,2:** Acts 4.25–26.

Holy history

Different types of psalm

You can't squeeze the Psalms into neat little boxes, but there are some different types.

Cries for help

These are direct, passionate, emotional prayers. Bones break, bodies crumble, savage beasts pounce. From declarations of innocence (7,12,26) to complaints about God's apparent forgetfulness (9,10,22,44), still many end with renewed faith and confidence (6,22,69,140).

Thanks to God

These psalms thank God for answers to prayers; for a successful harvest, victory in battle, or God's goodness to the writer.

Praises

These psalms praise God generally for his greatness and power. Some celebrate God's reign over all (47,93,95–9), others compare God's rule with the rule of earthly kings (2,20–21,45,72,89,101,110,115,118,144).

Pilgrimage songs

Sometimes called 'songs of ascents', these were sung by people climbing the hill into Jerusalem, maybe pilgrims going to festivals.

Wise thoughts

These psalms are closer to proverbs, aiming to teach to the reader or listener.

Revenge psalms

For a Christian, these are tricky. The psalmist wants to wash his feet in his enemy's blood (58.10), or asks for blessing on anyone who smashes a Babylonian child's head against a rock (137.9). Outrageous – but they express the writer's passion for the rule of God. He wants to see evil-doing punished – now.

More...

Hebrew poetry p.583
Worshipping God p.622
Prayer p.1002

7 I will tell the promise
   that the LORD made to me:
   "You are my son, because today
   I have become your father.
8 Ask me for the nations,
   and every nation on earth
   will belong to you.
9 You will smash them with an iron rod
   and shatter them like dishes of clay."

10 Be wise, all you rulers,
   and pay close attention.
11   Serve and honour the LORD;
   be glad and tremble.
12 Show respect to his son
   because if you don't,
   the LORD might become furious
   and suddenly destroy you.'
   But he blesses and protects
   everyone who runs to him.

Psalm 3

*(Written by David when he was running
from his son Absalom.)*

An early morning prayer

1 I have a lot of enemies, LORD.
   Many fight against
2   me and say,
   "God won't rescue you!"

3 But you are my shield,
   and you give me victory
   and great honour.
4 I pray to you, and you answer
   from your sacred hill.
5 I sleep and wake up refreshed
   because you, LORD, protect me.
6 Ten thousand enemies attack
   from every side,
   but I am not afraid.

7 Come and save me, LORD God!
   Break my enemies' jaws
   and shatter their teeth,
8   because you protect
   and bless your people.

See also: 2.7: Acts 13.33; Heb 1.5; 5.5.   **2.9:** Rev 2.26–27;
12.5; 19.15.   **3 Title:** 2 Sam 15.13—17.22.

Psalm 4

(A psalm by David for the music leader.
Use stringed instruments.)

An evening prayer

1 You are my God and protector.
    Please answer my prayer.
  I was in terrible distress,
    but you set me free.
  Now have pity and listen as I pray.
2 How long will you people
    refuse to respect me?'
  You love foolish things,
    and you run after what is worthless.*

3 The LORD has chosen
    everyone who is faithful
  to be his very own,'
    and he answers my prayers.
4 But each of you had better tremble
    and turn from your sins.
  Silently search your heart
    as you lie in bed.
5   Offer the proper sacrifices
    and trust the LORD.

6 There are some who ask,
    "Who will be good to us?"
  Let your kindness, LORD,
    shine brightly on us.
7 You brought me more happiness
    than a rich harvest of grain and grapes.
8 I can lie down and sleep soundly
    because you, LORD,
    will keep me safe.

Psalm 5

(A psalm by David for the music leader.
Use flutes.)

A prayer for help

1 Listen, LORD, as I pray!
    Pay attention when I groan.'
2 You are my King and my God.
    Answer my cry for help
    because I pray to you.
3 Each morning you listen to my prayer,
    as I bring my requests' to you
    and wait for your reply.

4 You are not the kind of God
    who is pleased with evil.
  Sinners can't stay with you.

5 No one who boasts can stand
    in your presence, LORD,
    and you hate evil people.
6 You destroy every liar,
    and you despise violence and deceit.

7 Because of your great mercy,
    I come to your house, LORD,
  and I am filled with wonder
    as I bow down to worship
    at your holy temple.
8 You do what is right,
    and I ask you to guide me.
  Make your teaching clear
    because of my enemies.

9 Nothing they say is true!
    They just want to destroy.
  Their words are deceitful
    like a hidden pit,
    and their tongues are good
    only for telling lies.
10 Punish them, God,
    and let their own plans
    bring their downfall.
  Get rid of them!
    They keep committing crimes
    and turning against you.

11 Let all who run to you for protection
    always sing joyful songs.
  Provide shelter for those
    who truly love you
    and let them rejoice.
12 Our LORD, you bless those
    who live right,
    and you shield them
    with your kindness.

Psalm 6

(A psalm by David for the music leader.
*Use stringed instruments. *)*

A prayer in time of trouble

1 Don't punish me, LORD,
    or even correct me
    when you are angry!
2 Have pity on me and heal
    my feeble body.
  My bones tremble with fear,
3   and I am in deep distress.
  How long will it be?
4 Turn and come to my rescue.

---

*Psalm 6 instruments: The Hebrew text adds
"according to the sheminith", which may refer to a
musical instrument with eight strings.

4.2 foolish . . . worthless: This may refer to idols
and false gods.
See also: 4.4: Eph 4.26.

See also: 5.9: Rom 3.13. 6.1: Psa 38.1.

Show your wonderful love
and save me, LORD.
⁵ If I die, I cannot praise you
or even remember you.
⁶ My groaning has worn me out.
At night my bed and pillow
are soaked with tears.
⁷ Sorrow has made my eyes dim,
and my sight has failed
because of my enemies.

⁸ You, LORD, heard my crying,
and those hateful people
had better leave me alone.
⁹ You have answered my prayer
and my plea for mercy.
¹⁰ My enemies will be ashamed
and terrified,
as they quickly run away
in complete disgrace.

Psalm 7

(Written by David.* He sang this to the LORD because of Cush from the tribe of Benjamin.)

The LORD always does right

¹ You, LORD God, are my protector.
Rescue me and keep me safe
from all who chase me.
² Or else they will rip me apart
like lions attacking a victim,
and no one will save me.

³ I am innocent, LORD God!
⁴ I have not betrayed a friend
or had pity on an enemy›
who attacks for no reason.
⁵ If I have done any of this,
then let my enemies
chase and capture me.
Let them trample me to death
and leave me in the dirt.

⁶ Get angry, LORD God! Do something!
Attack my furious enemies.
See that justice is done.
⁷ Make the nations come to you,
as you sit on your throne›
above them all.

⁸ Our LORD, judge the nations!
Judge me and show that I
am honest and innocent.

⁹ You know every heart and mind,
and you always do right.
Now make violent people stop,
but protect all of us who obey you.

¹⁰ You, God, are my shield,
the protector of everyone
whose heart is right.
¹¹ You see that justice is done,
and each day you take revenge.
¹² Whenever your enemies refuse
to change their ways,
you sharpen your sword
and string your bow.
¹³ Your deadly arrows are ready
with flaming tips.

¹⁴ An evil person is like a woman
about to give birth
to a hateful, deceitful,
and rebellious child.
¹⁵ Such people dig a deep hole,
then fall in it themselves.
¹⁶ The trouble they cause
comes back on them,
and their heads are crushed
by their own evil deeds.

¹⁷ I will praise you, LORD!
You always do right.
I will sing about you,
the LORD Most High.

Psalm 8

(A psalm by David for the music leader.*)

The wonderful name of the LORD

¹ Our LORD and Ruler,
your name is wonderful
everywhere on earth!
You let your glory be seen›
in the heavens above.
² With praises from children
and from tiny infants,
you have built a fortress.
It makes your enemies silent,
and all who turn against you
are left speechless.

³ I often think of the heavens
your hands have made,
and of the moon and stars
you put in place.

***Psalm 7 Written by David:** The Hebrew text has "a shiggaion by David", which may refer to a psalm of mourning.
See also: 6.8: Matt 7.23; Luke 13.27.

***Psalm 8 leader:** The Hebrew text adds "according to the gittith", which may refer to either a musical instrument or a tune.
See also: 7.9: Rev 2.23. 8.2: Matt 21.16.

4 Then I ask, "Why do you care
about us humans?
Why are you concerned
for us weaklings?"
5 You made us a little lower
than you yourself,◆
and you have crowned us
with glory and honour.

6 You let us rule everything
your hands have made.
And you put all of it under our power —
7 the sheep and the cattle,
and every wild animal,
8 the birds in the sky,
the fish in the sea,
and all ocean creatures.

9 Our LORD and Ruler,
your name is wonderful
everywhere on earth!

Psalm 9

(A psalm by David for the music leader.
To the tune "The Death of the Son".)

Sing praises to the LORD

1 I will praise you, LORD,
with all my heart
and tell about the wonders
you have worked.
2 God Most High, I will rejoice;
I will celebrate and sing
because of you.

3 When my enemies face you,
they run away and stumble
and are destroyed.
4 You take your seat as judge,
and your fair decisions prove
that I was in the right.
5 You warn the nations
and destroy evil people;
you wipe out their names
for ever and ever.
6 Our enemies are destroyed
completely for all time.
Their cities are torn down,
and they will never
be remembered again.

7 You rule for ever, LORD,
and you are on your throne,
ready for judgment.
8 You judge the world fairly
and treat all nations with justice.

9 The poor can run to you
because you are a fortress
in times of trouble.
10 Everyone who honours your name
can trust you,
because you are faithful
to all who depend on you.

11 You rule from Zion, LORD,
and we sing about you
to let the nations know
everything you have done.
12 You did not forget
to punish the guilty
or listen to the cries
of those in need.

13 Please have mercy, LORD!
My enemies ill-treat me.
Keep me from the gates
that lead to death,
14 and I will sing about you
at the gate to Zion.
I will be happy there
because you rescued me.

15 Our LORD, the nations fell
into their own pits,
and their feet were caught
in their own traps.
16 You showed what you are like,
and you made certain
that justice is done,
but evil people are trapped
by their own evil deeds.
17 The wicked will go down
to the world of the dead
to be with those nations
that forgot about you.

18 The poor and the homeless
won't always be forgotten
and without hope.

19 Do something, LORD!
Don't let the nations win.
Make them stand trial
in your court of law.
20 Make the nations afraid
and let them all discover
just how weak they are.

Psalm 10

A prayer for help

1 Why are you far away, LORD?
Why do you hide yourself
when I am in trouble?

See also: **8.4:** Job 7.17–18; Psa 144.3; Heb 2.6–8.
8.6: 1 Cor 15.27; Eph 1.22; Heb 2.8.

² Proud and brutal people
  hunt down the poor.
  But let them get caught
  by their own evil plans!

³ The wicked boast about
  their deepest desires.
  Those greedy people hate
  and curse you, LORD.

⁴ The wicked are too proud
  to turn to you
  or even think about you.

⁵ They are always successful,
  though they can't understand
  your teachings,
  and they keep sneering
  at their enemies.

⁶ In their hearts they say,
  "Nothing can hurt us!
  We'll always be happy
  and free from trouble."

⁷ They curse and tell lies,
  and all they talk about
  is how to be cruel
  or how to do wrong.

⁸ They hide outside villages,
  waiting to strike and murder
  some innocent victim.

⁹ They are hungry lions
  hiding in the bushes,
  hoping to catch
  some helpless passer-by.
  They trap the poor in nets
  and drag them away.

¹⁰ They crouch down and wait
   to grab a victim.

¹¹ They say, "God can't see!
   He's got a blindfold on."

¹² Do something, LORD God,
   and use your powerful arm
   to help those in need.

¹³ The wicked don't respect you.
   In their hearts they say,
   "God won't punish us!"

¹⁴ But you see the trouble
   and the distress,
   and you will do something.
   The poor can count on you,
   and so can orphans.

¹⁵ Now break the arms
   of all merciless people.
   Punish them for doing wrong
   and make them stop.

¹⁶ Our LORD, you will always rule,
   but nations will vanish from the earth.

¹⁷ You listen to the longings
   of those who suffer.
   You offer them hope,
   and you pay attention
   to their cries for help.

¹⁸ You defend orphans
   and everyone else in need,
   so that no one on earth
   can terrify others again.

Psalm 11

(A psalm by David for the music leader.)

Trusting the LORD

¹ The LORD is my fortress!
  Don't say to me,
  "Escape like a bird
  to the mountains!"

² You tell me, "Watch out!
  Those evil people
  have put their arrows on their bows,
  and they are standing in the shadows,
  aiming at good people.

³ What can an honest person do
  when everything crumbles?"

⁴ The LORD is sitting in his sacred temple
  on his throne in heaven.
  He knows everything we do
  because he sees us all.

⁵ The LORD tests honest people,
  but despises those who are cruel
  and love violence.

⁶ He will send fiery coals'
  and flaming sulphur
  down on the wicked,
  and they will drink nothing
  but a scorching wind.

⁷ The LORD always does right
  and wants justice done.
  Everyone who does right
  will see his face.

Psalm 12

(A psalm by David for the music leader. *)*

A prayer for help

¹ Please help me, LORD!
  All who were faithful
  and all who were loyal
  have disappeared.

---

*Psalm 12 leader: See the note at Psalm 6.

2 Everyone tells lies,
    and no one is sincere.
3 Won't you chop off
    all flattering tongues
    that boast so loudly?
4 They say to themselves,
    "We are great speakers.
    No one else has a chance."

5 But you, LORD, tell them,
    "I will do something!
    The poor are ill-treated
    and helpless people moan.
    I'll rescue all who suffer."

6 Our LORD, you are true
    to your promises,
  and your word is like silver
    heated seven times in a fiery furnace.*

7 You will protect us
    and always keep us safe
    from those people.
8 But all who are wicked
    will keep on strutting,
    while everyone praises
    their shameless deeds.'

Psalm 13

(A psalm by David for the music leader.)

A prayer for the LORD's help

1 How much longer, LORD,
    will you forget about me?
    Will it be for ever?
    How long will you hide?
2 How long must I be confused
    and miserable all day?
    How long will my enemies
    keep beating me down?

3 Please listen, LORD God,
    and answer my prayers.
  Make my eyes sparkle again,
    or else I will fall
    into the sleep of death.
4 My enemies will say,
    "Now we've won!"
    They will be greatly pleased
    when I am defeated.

5 I trust your love,
    and I feel like celebrating
    because you rescued me.

---

*12.6 in a fiery furnace: The Hebrew text has "in a furnace to the ground", which may describe part of a process for refining silver in Old Testament times.

Helpline

Help! God seems to talk to everyone else but me

'God seems to talk to other people, but I struggle to hear from him. Is there something wrong with me?'

All around us in church, or in youth group, there are people lost in worship and praise – but nothing's happening for us. Our friends talk about God speaking to them and guiding them, but we can't hear him at all. Like David in Psalm 13, we want our eyes to sparkle again. But it's like we're in shadow.

Check your own walk with God. If you're not praying regularly, how is he going to speak to you? If you're not reading your Bible or going to church or making time for him, it's not surprising he can't get through.

But if that's not the case, then you need to feel reassured that these times just happen. God talks to different people in different ways. He loves each person equally, but distinctively. We're all individuals, so we all have a different relationship with God.

For some people, God speaks to them through the Bible. Sometimes he speaks to us through the words of friends. Often he speaks through prayer. Different people hear in different ways and at different times. Don't compare yourself with others. Concentrate on your own relationship with God. Maybe your eyes will sparkle sooner than you think.

Three things

Relax

Don't worry about other people. Concentrate on your relationship with God.

Listen

Check that you're actually listening to him. Are you praying, reading, worshipping?

List

List the ways in which God does speak. Is he speaking to you through the Bible? Through others? Or through things you see?

More...

Guidance p.685

⁶ You have been good to me, LORD,
    and I will sing about you.

Psalm 14

(A psalm by David for the music leader.)

No one can ignore the LORD

¹ Only a fool would say,
    "There is no God!"
People like that are worthless;
    they are heartless and cruel
    and never do right.

² From heaven the LORD
    looks down to see
if anyone is wise enough
    to search for him.

³ But all of them are corrupt;
    no one does right.

⁴ Won't you evil people learn?
    You refuse to pray,
and you gobble up
    the LORD's people.

⁵ But you will be frightened,
    because God is on the side
    of every good person.

⁶ You may spoil the plans
    of the poor,
but the LORD protects them.

⁷ I long for someone from Zion
    to come and save Israel!
Our LORD, when you bless
    your people again,
Jacob's family will be glad,
    and Israel will celebrate.

Psalm 15

(A psalm by David.)

Who may worship the LORD?

¹ Who may stay in God's temple
    or live on the holy mountain
    of the LORD?

² Only those who obey God
    and do as they should.
They speak the truth

³   and don't spread gossip;
    they treat others fairly
    and don't say cruel things.

⁴ They hate worthless people,
    but show respect for all
    who worship the LORD.

And they keep their promises,
    no matter what the cost.

⁵ They lend their money
    without charging interest,
and they don't take bribes
    to hurt the innocent.

Those who do these things
    will always stand firm.

Psalm 16

(A special psalm by David.)

The best choice

¹ Protect me, LORD God!
    I run to you for safety,

²   and I have said,
    "Only you are my Lord!
Every good thing I have
    is a gift from you."

³ Your people are wonderful,
    and they make me happy,ʼ

⁴   but worshippers of other gods
    will have much sorrow.ʼ
I refuse to offer sacrifices
    of blood to those gods
    or worship in their name.

⁵ You, LORD, are all I want!
    You are my choice,
    and you keep me safe.

⁶ You make my life pleasant,
    and my future is bright.

⁷ I praise you, LORD,
    for being my guide.
Even in the darkest night,
    your teachings fill my mind.

⁸ I will always look to you,
    as you stand beside me
    and protect me from fear.

⁹ With all my heart, I will celebrate,
    and I can safely rest.

¹⁰ I am your chosen one.
    You won't leave me in the grave
    or let my body decay.

¹¹ You have shown me the path to life,
    and you make me glad
    by being near to me.
Sitting at your right side,*
    I will always be joyful.

---

*16.11 **right side:** The place of power and honour.

See also: 14.1–3: Rom 3.10–12.

See also: 16.8–11: Acts 2.25–28.   16.10: Acts 13.35.

Helpline

Help! I don't want to go to college

'My parents keep on at me. My teachers keep pushing it. Even my friends expect it. But I'm really not sure I want to go.'

We get pressure from many directions in our life; from our friends, from our teachers, from our parents. Young people often feel this pressure with regard to the choice of a career or the choice of what they want to do after school.

Going to college is not obligatory. But you do need to be clear on your reasons for not going. Maybe they're just feelings of insecurity or fear. Maybe you know college will be best, but you're nervous.

If you're sure that you want to go a different route, talk to your parents. Be honest with them. (But make sure that you really think the whole thing through. Get your arguments sorted out.)

Have confidence that God is with you. Like Psalm 16 says, he is the best guide. Dedicate your future to him – wherever you end up.

Three things

Think

Make sure that you see the long-term picture. You might not miss college now, but will you regret it in years to come? Of course, it's not impossible to go to college or university when you're older. But it's more difficult.

Pause

Not sure? Then take a year out. Do something different. Do some travelling. Spend some time volunteering with a Christian agency or on short-term service – either in the UK or overseas. Time out can give you space to think.

Check

Pray. Listen to God. See what his plans are for your life. What do you think he wants you to do?

More...

Guidance p.685
Help! I can't cope with revision p.1011

Psalm 17

(A prayer by David.)

The prayer of an innocent person

¹ I am innocent, LORD!
   Won't you listen as I pray
      and beg for help?
   I am honest! Please hear my prayer.
² Only you can say
      that I am innocent,
   because only your eyes
      can see the truth.

³ You know my heart,
   and even during the night
      you have tested me
      and found me innocent.
   I have made up my mind
      never to tell a lie.
⁴ I don't do like others.
   I obey your teachings and am not cruel.
⁵ I have followed you,
      without ever stumbling.

⁶ I pray to you, God,
      because you will help me.
   Listen and answer my prayer!
⁷ Show your wonderful love.
   Your mighty arm protects those
      who run to you
      for safety from their enemies.
⁸ Protect me as you would
      your very own eyes;
   hide me in the shadow of your wings.

⁹ Don't let my brutal enemies
      attack from all sides and kill me.
¹⁰ They refuse to show mercy,
      and they keep boasting.
¹¹ They have caught up with me!
   My enemies are everywhere,
      eagerly hoping to pull me
      to the ground.
¹² They are like hungry lions
      hunting for food,
   or like young lions hiding in ambush.

¹³ Do something, LORD!
      Attack and defeat them.
   Take your sword and save me
      from those evil people.
¹⁴ Use your powerful arm and rescue me
   from the hands of mere humans
      whose world won't last.'

   You provide food for those you love.
   Their children have plenty,
      and their grandchildren
      will have more than enough.

15 I am innocent, LORD,
   and I will see your face!
   When I awake, all I want
   is to see you as you are.

Psalm 18

*(For the music leader. A psalm by David,
the LORD's servant. David sang this to the LORD
after the LORD had rescued him from his
enemies, but especially from Saul.)*

David's song of thanks

1 I love you, LORD God,
   and you make me strong.
2 You are my mighty rock,*
   my fortress, my protector,
   the rock where I am safe, my shield,
   my powerful weapon,*
   and my place of shelter.

3 I praise you, LORD!
   I prayed, and you rescued me
   from my enemies.
4 Death had wrapped its ropes around me,
   and I was almost swallowed
   by its flooding waters.

5 Ropes from the world of the dead
   had coiled around me,
   and death had set a trap in my path.
6 I was in terrible trouble
   when I called out to you,
   but from your temple you heard me
   and answered my prayer.

7 The earth shook and shivered,
   and the mountains trembled
   down to their roots.
   You were angry
8   and breathed out smoke.
   Scorching heat and fiery flames
   spewed from your mouth.

9 You opened the heavens like curtains,
   and you came down
   with storm clouds
   under your feet.
10 You rode on the backs
   of flying creatures
   and swooped down
   with the wind as wings.

---

*18.2 mighty rock: The Hebrew text has "rock",
which is sometimes used in poetry to compare the
Lord to a mountain where his people can run for
protection from their enemies.
*18.2 my powerful weapon: The Hebrew text has
"the horn", which refers to the horn of a bull, one of
the most powerful animals in ancient Palestine.

11 Darkness was your robe;
   thunderclouds filled the sky,
   hiding you from sight.
12 Hailstones and fiery coals
   lit up the sky in front of you.
13 LORD Most High, your voice
   thundered from the heavens,
   as hailstones and fiery coals
   poured down like rain.
14 You scattered your enemies
   with arrows of lightning.
15 You roared at the sea,
   and its deepest channels could be seen.
   You snorted, and the earth shook
   to its foundations.

16 You reached down from heaven,
   and you lifted me
   from deep in the ocean.
17 You rescued me from enemies,
   who were hateful
   and too powerful for me.
18 On the day disaster struck,
   they came and attacked,
   but you defended me.
19 When I was fenced in,
   you freed and rescued me
   because you love me.

20 You are good to me, LORD,
   because I do right,
   and you reward me
   because I am innocent.
21 I do what you want
   and never turn to do evil.
22 I keep your laws in mind
   and never look away
   from your teachings.
23 I obey you completely
   and guard against sin.
24 You have been good to me
   because I do right;
   you have rewarded me
   for being innocent
   by your standards.

25 You are always loyal
   to your loyal people,
   and you are faithful to the faithful.
26 With all who are sincere,
   you are sincere,
   but you treat the unfaithful
   as their deeds deserve.
27 You rescue the humble,
   but you put down all who are proud.

28 You, the LORD God,
   keep my lamp burning
   and turn darkness to light.

29 You help me defeat armies
  and capture cities.

30 Your way is perfect, LORD,
  and your word is correct.
  You are a shield for those
  who run to you for help.
31 You alone are God!
  Only you are a mighty rock.*
32 You give me strength
  and guide me right.
33 You make my feet run as fast
  as those of a deer,
  and you help me stand
  on the mountains.

34 You teach my hands to fight
  and my arms to use a bow of bronze.
35 You alone are my shield.
  Your right hand supports me,
  and by coming to help me,
  you have made me famous.
36 You clear the way for me,
  and now I won't stumble.

37 I kept chasing my enemies,
  until I caught them
  and destroyed them.
38 I stuck my sword through my enemies,
  and they were crushed under my feet.
39 You helped me win victories,
  and you forced my attackers
  to fall victim to me.

40 You made my enemies run,
  and I killed them.
41 They cried out for help,
  but no one saved them;
  they called out to you,
  but there was no answer.
42 I ground them to dust
  blown by the wind,
  and I poured them out
  like mud in the streets.

43 You rescued me from stubborn people,
  and you made me the leader
  of foreign nations,
  who are now my slaves.
44 They obey and come crawling.
45 They have lost all courage,
  and from their fortresses,
  they come trembling.

46 You are the living LORD!
  I will praise you.
  You are a mighty rock.*
  I will honour you for keeping me safe.

47 You took revenge for me,
  and you put nations in my power.
48 You protected me
  from violent enemies
  and made me much greater
  than all of them.

49 I will praise you, LORD,
  and I will honour you
  among the nations.
50 You give glorious victories
  to your chosen king.
  Your faithful love for David
  and for his descendants will never end.

Psalm 19

(A psalm by David for the music leader.)

The wonders of God and the goodness of his Law

1 The heavens keep telling
  the wonders of God,
  and the skies declare
  what he has done.
2 Each day informs the following day;
  each night announces to the next.
3 They don't speak a word,
  and there is never the sound of a voice.
4 Yet their message reaches all the earth,
  and it travels around the world.

  In the heavens a tent
  is set up for the sun.
5 It rises like a bridegroom
  and gets ready like a hero
  eager to run a race.
6 It travels all the way across the sky.
  Nothing hides from its heat.

7 The Law of the LORD is perfect;
  it gives us new life.
  His teachings last for ever,
  and they give wisdom
  to ordinary people.
8 The LORD's instruction is right;
  it makes our hearts glad.
  His commands shine brightly,
  and they give us light.

9 Worshipping the LORD is sacred;
  he will always be worshipped.
  All of his decisions are correct and fair.
10 They are worth more
  than the finest gold
  and are sweeter than honey
  from a honeycomb.

---

*18.31,46 mighty rock: See the note at 18.2.
See also: 18.33: Hab 3.19.

See also: 18.49: Rom 15.9. 19.4: Rom 10.18.

11 By your teachings, Lord,
    I am warned;
    by obeying them,
    I am greatly rewarded.
12 None of us know our faults.
    Forgive me when I sin
    without knowing it.
13 Don't let me do wrong
    on purpose, Lord,
    or let sin have control over my life.
    Then I will be innocent,
    and not guilty of some terrible fault.

14 Let my words and my thoughts
    be pleasing to you, LORD,
    because you are my mighty rock*
    and my protector.

Psalm 20

(A psalm by David for the music leader.)

A prayer for victory

1 I pray that the LORD will listen
    when you are in trouble,
    and that the God of Jacob
    will keep you safe.
2 May the LORD send help
    from his temple
    and come to your rescue
    from Mount Zion.
3 May he remember your gifts
    and be pleased with what you bring.

4 May God do what you want most
    and let all go well for you.
5 Then you will win victories,
    and we will celebrate,
    while raising our banners
    in the name of our God.
    May the LORD answer all of your prayers!

6 I am certain, LORD,
    that you will help your chosen king.
    You will answer my prayers
    from your holy place in heaven,
    and you will save me
    with your mighty arm.

7 Some people trust the power
    of chariots or horses,
    but we trust you, LORD God.
8 Others will stumble and fall,
    but we will be strong and stand firm.

9 Give the king victory, LORD,
    and answer our prayers.'

Psalm 21

(A psalm by David for the music leader.)

Thanking the LORD for victory

1 Our LORD, your mighty power
    makes the king glad,
    and he celebrates victories
    that you have given him.
2 You did what he wanted most
    and never told him "No."
3 You truly blessed the king,
    and you placed on him
    a crown of finest gold.
4 He asked to live a long time,
    and you promised him life
    that never ends.

5 The king is highly honoured.
    You have let him win victories
    that have made him famous.
6 You have given him blessings
    that will last for ever,
    and you have made him glad
    by being so near to him.
7 LORD Most High, the king trusts you,
    and your kindness
    keeps him from defeat.

8 With your mighty arm, LORD,
    you will strike down
    all of your hateful enemies.
9 They will be destroyed by fire
    once you are here,
    and because of your anger,
    flames will swallow them.
10 You will wipe their families
    from the earth,
    and they will disappear.
11 All their plans to harm you
    will come to nothing.
12 You will make them run away
    by shooting your arrows at their faces.

13 Show your strength, LORD,
    so that we may sing
    and praise your power.

Psalm 22

*(A psalm by David for the music leader.
To the tune "A Deer at Dawn".)*

Suffering and praise

1 My God, my God, why have you
    deserted me?
    Why are you so far away?

---

*19.14 mighty rock: See the note at 18.2.

See also: 22.1: Matt 27.46; Mark 15.34.

Won't you listen to my groans
and come to my rescue?
² I cry out day and night,
but you don't answer,
and I can never rest.

³ Yet you are the holy God,
ruling from your throne
and praised by Israel.
⁴ Our ancestors trusted you,
and you rescued them.
⁵ When they cried out for help,
you saved them,
and you did not let them down
when they depended on you.

⁶ But I am merely a worm,
far less than human,
and I am hated and rejected
by people everywhere.
⁷ Everyone who sees me
makes fun and sneers.
They shake their heads,
⁸ and say, "Trust the LORD!
If you are his favourite,
let him protect you and keep you safe."

⁹ You, LORD, brought me
safely through birth,
and you protected me
when I was a baby
at my mother's breast.
¹⁰ From the day I was born,
I have been in your care,
and from the time of my birth,
you have been my God.

¹¹ Don't stay far off when I am in trouble
with no one to help me.
¹² Enemies are all around
like a herd of wild bulls.
Powerful bulls from Bashan*
are everywhere.
¹³ My enemies are like lions
roaring and attacking
with jaws open wide.

¹⁴ I have no more strength
than a few drops of water.
All my bones are out of joint;
my heart is like melted wax.
¹⁵ My strength has dried up
like a broken clay pot,
and my tongue sticks
to the roof of my mouth.

You, God, have left me
to die in the dust.

¹⁶ Brutal enemies attack me
like a pack of dogs,
tearing at* my hands
and my feet.
¹⁷ I can count all my bones,
and my enemies just stare
and sneer at me.
¹⁸ They took my clothes
and gambled for them.

¹⁹ Don't stay far away, LORD!
My strength comes from you,
so hurry and help.
²⁰ Rescue me from enemy swords
and save me from those dogs.
²¹ Don't let lions eat me.
You rescued me from the horns
of wild bulls,
²² and when your people meet,
I will praise you, LORD.

²³ All who worship the LORD,
now praise him!
You belong to Jacob's family
and to the people of Israel,
so fear and honour the LORD!
²⁴ The LORD doesn't hate
or despise the helpless
in all their troubles.
When I cried out, he listened
and did not turn away.

²⁵ When your people meet,
you will fill my heart
with your praises, LORD,
and everyone will see me
keep my promises to you.
²⁶ The poor will eat and be full,
and all who worship you
will be thankful and live in hope.

²⁷ Everyone on this earth
will remember you, LORD.
People all over the world
will turn and worship you,
²⁸ because you are in control,
the ruler of all nations.

²⁹ All who are rich
and have more than enough
will bow down to you, Lord.
Even those who are dying
and almost in the grave
will come and bow down.

---

*22.12 Bashan:** A land east of the River Jordan, where there were pastures suitable for raising fine cattle.

See also: **22.7:** Matt 27.39; Mark 15.29; Luke 23.35. **22.8:** Matt 27.43.

See also: **22.18:** Matt 27.35; Mark 15.24; Luke 23.34; John 19.24. **22.22:** Heb 2.12.

³⁰ In the future, everyone will worship
    and learn about you, our Lord.
³¹ People not yet born will be told,
    "The Lord has saved us!"

Psalm 23

(A psalm by David.)

The good shepherd

¹ You, LORD, are my shepherd.
    I will never be in need.
² You let me rest in fields of green grass.
    You lead me to streams
        of peaceful water,
³   and you refresh my life.

You are true to your name,
    and you lead me
        along the right paths.
⁴ I may walk through valleys
    as dark as death,
        but I won't be afraid.
You are with me,
    and your shepherd's rod*
        makes me feel safe.

⁵ You treat me to a feast,
    while my enemies watch.
You honour me as your guest,
    and you fill my cup until it overflows.

⁶ Your kindness and love
    will always be with me
each day of my life,
    and I will live for ever
        in your house, LORD.

Psalm 24

(A psalm by David.)

Who can enter the LORD's temple?

¹ The earth and everything on it
    belong to the LORD.
    The world and its people belong to him.
² The LORD placed it all
    on the oceans and rivers.

³ Who may climb the LORD's hill*
    or stand in his holy temple?

---

*23.4 shepherd's rod: The Hebrew text mentions two objects carried by the shepherd: a club to defend against wild animals and a long pole to guide and control the sheep.
*24.3 the LORD's hill: The hill in Jerusalem where the temple was built.
See also: 23.2: Rev 7.17. 24.1: 1 Cor 10.26.

Viewpoints

We follow God – but doesn't he realise that it can be tough sometimes?

Contributed by Naomi H

'Your kindness and love will always be with me each day of my life...'

Sometimes we feel a long way from God. We had a bad day and made lots of mistakes and it seems impossible to worship him or pray properly. We feel like he is withholding his love from us because we've let him down so much.

But – surprise, surprise – this is not the biblical view of God's love for us. He sent his Son to die for us when we weren't even bothered about how much we let him down or hurt him. Why is he suddenly going to abandon us now?

Note that the verse does not say that God's love sits in heaven waiting for us to come and claim it. No – it follows us! How amazing is that? God's love is chasing me, trying to catch up and enable me to come back to a loving, thankful relationship with Him. Sinning is like running away from this love – which is pretty silly, really!

This should make us incredibly grateful to God. It should also motivate us to carry on walking with him even when things seem really dry. His love and goodness are still following us, and although at times we don't experience it as tangibly as at others, it is still there and he still rewards us when we are willing to make the effort to worship Him.

Let's tell others about this amazing love too. Once we really grasp the depth of how God feels toward us, we will never be able to stop praising him at all – although we'll never have the full picture here on earth, we can grow in our knowledge day by day and learn to love him more!

More...

Suffering p.555
Coping with suffering p.1391
Ever had those days when you just can't keep going? p.528
God's love p.958

4 Only those who do right
  for the right reasons,
  and don't worship idols
  or tell lies under oath.
5 The LORD God, who saves them,
  will bless and reward them,
6 because they worship and serve
  the God of Jacob.✦
7 Open the ancient gates,
  so that the glorious king may come in.

8 Who is this glorious king?
  He is our LORD, a strong
  and mighty warrior.
9 Open the ancient gates,
  so that the glorious king may come in.

10 Who is this glorious king?
   He is our LORD, the All-Powerful!

Psalm 25

(By David.)

A prayer for guidance and help

1 I offer you my heart, LORD God,
2   and I trust you.
   Don't make me ashamed
   or let enemies defeat me.
3 Don't disappoint any
   of your worshippers,
   but disappoint all deceitful liars.
4 Show me your paths
   and teach me to follow;
5   guide me by your truth
   and instruct me.
   You keep me safe,
   and I always trust you.

6 Please, LORD, remember,
   you have always been
   patient and kind.
7 Forget each wrong I did
   when I was young.
   Show how truly kind you are
   and remember me.
8 You are honest and merciful,
   and you teach sinners
   how to follow your path.

9 You lead humble people
   to do what is right
   and to stay on your path.
10 In everything you do,
   you are kind and faithful
   to everyone who keeps
   our agreement with you.

11 Be true to your name, LORD,
   by forgiving
   each one of my terrible sins.
12 You will show the right path
   to all who worship you.
13 They will have plenty,
   and then their children
   will receive the land.

14 Our LORD, you are the friend
   of your worshippers,
   and you make an agreement
   with all of us.
15 I always look to you,
   because you rescue me from every trap.
16 I am lonely and troubled.
   Show that you care
   and have pity on me.
17 My awful worries keep growing.
   Rescue me from sadness.
18 See my troubles and misery
   and forgive my sins.

19 Look at all my enemies!
   See how much they hate me.
20 I come to you for shelter.
   Protect me, keep me safe,
   and don't disappoint me.
21 I obey you with all my heart,
   and I trust you,
   knowing that you will save me.

22 Our God, please save Israel
   from all its troubles.

Psalm 26

(By David.)

The prayer of an innocent person

1 Show that I am right, LORD!
   I stay true to myself,
   and I have trusted you without doubting.
2 Test my thoughts and find out
   what I am like.
3 I never forget your kindness,
   and I am always faithful to you.✦
4 I don't spend my time
   with worthless liars
5   or go with evil crowds.

6 I wash my hands, LORD,
   to show my innocence,
   and I worship at your altar,
7   while gratefully singing
   about your wonders.
8 I love the temple where you live,
   and where your glory shines.

See also: 24.4: Matt 5.8.

9 Don't sweep me away,
   as you do sinners.
   Don't punish me with death
   as you do those people
   who are brutal
10 or full of meanness
   or who bribe others.
11 I stay true to myself.
   Be kind and rescue me.

12 Now I stand on solid ground!
   And when your people meet,
   I will praise you, LORD.

Psalm 27

(By David.)

A prayer of praise

1 You, LORD, are the light
   that keeps me safe.
   I am not afraid of anyone.
   You protect me, and I have no fears.
2 Brutal people may attack
   and try to kill me,
   but they will stumble.
   Fierce enemies may attack,
   but they will fall.
3 Armies may surround me,
   but I won't be afraid;
   war may break out, but I will trust you.

4 I ask only one thing, LORD:
   Let me live in your house
   every day of my life
   to see how wonderful you are
   and to pray in your temple.

5 In times of trouble,
   you will protect me.
   You will hide me in your tent
   and keep me safe
   on top of a mighty rock.*
6 You will let me defeat all of my enemies.
   Then I will celebrate,
   as I enter your tent
   with animal sacrifices
   and songs of praise.

7 Please listen when I pray!
   Have pity. Answer my prayer.
8 My heart tells me to pray.
   I am eager to see your face,
9   so don't hide from me.
   I am your servant,
   and you have helped me.
   Don't turn from me in anger.

---

*27.5 mighty rock: See the note at 18.2.

Helpline

Help! My parents are letting me down!

'My Dad's never around! My parents don't care about me! My Mum never listens...'

It's not easy being a parent.

There are many times we accuse our parents of bad parenting, when what we mean is that they're not letting us do what we want. It's not that they're not good parents – it's just we can't get our own way.

But there are parents who don't do the 'mum and dad' thing very well. Sometimes their jobs take all their time; sometimes they suffer from alcohol or other addictions; sometimes they're just not around. In such cases it's very easy to be bitter and angry. After all, these people have a responsibility! They should live up to it.

Three things

Forgiveness

We're called to forgive those who do wrong to us. You're angry, you're hurt, you feel like your parents are screwing up your life; but try not to give in to these feelings. Pray for them. Pray for opportunities to help them and to speak to them about your beliefs.

Help

Maybe your parents have some real, deep problems. They might be going through tough times of their own. Be understanding. Look at life from their point of view and see if that opens up some ways to get alongside them and give them help.

God

Remember, you have the perfect father in God. As David writes: 'Even if my father and mother should desert me, you will take care of me' (Psalms 27.10). He loves you and cherishes you. Draw near to him. He's the only perfect parent there has ever been.

More...

Help! My Dad's never around p.187
Families p.1224
Divorce p.1281

You alone keep me safe.
Don't reject or desert me.
¹⁰ Even if my father and mother
should desert me,
you will take care of me.

¹¹ Teach me to follow, LORD,
and lead me on the right path
because of my enemies.
¹² Don't let them do to me
what they want.
People tell lies about me
and make terrible threats,
¹³   but I know I will live
to see how kind you are.

¹⁴ Trust the LORD!
Be brave and strong
and trust the LORD.

Psalm 28

(By David.)

A prayer for help

¹ Only you, LORD,
are a mighty rock!*
Don't refuse to help me when I pray.
If you don't answer me,
I will soon be dead.
² Please listen to my prayer
and my cry for help,
as I lift my hands
towards your holy temple.

³ Don't drag me away, LORD,
with those cruel people,
who speak kind words,
while planning trouble.
⁴ Treat them as they deserve!
Punish them for their sins.
⁵ They don't pay any attention
to your wonderful deeds.
Now you will destroy them
and leave them in ruin.

⁶ I praise you, LORD,
for answering my prayers.
⁷   You are my strong shield,
and I trust you completely.
You have helped me,
and I will celebrate
and thank you in song.

⁸ You give strength to your people, LORD,
and you save and protect
your chosen ones.

⁹ Come, save us and bless us.
Be our shepherd and always
carry us in your arms.

Psalm 29

(A psalm by David.)

The voice of the LORD in a storm

¹ All you angels' in heaven,
honour the glory and power
of the LORD!
² Honour the wonderful name
of the LORD,
and worship the LORD
most holy and glorious.'

³ The voice of the LORD
echoes over the oceans.
The glorious LORD God thunders
above the roar of the raging sea,
⁴   and his voice is mighty
and marvellous.
⁵ The voice of the LORD
destroys the cedar trees;
the LORD shatters cedars
on Mount Lebanon.
⁶ God makes Mount Lebanon
skip like a calf
and Mount Hermon
jump like a wild ox.

⁷ The voice of the LORD
makes lightning flash
⁸   and the desert tremble.
And because of the LORD,
the desert near Kadesh
shivers and shakes.

⁹ The voice of the LORD
makes deer give birth
before their time.'
Forests are stripped of leaves,
and the temple is filled
with shouts of praise.

¹⁰ The LORD rules on his throne,
king of the flood* for ever.
¹¹ Pray that our LORD
will make us strong
and give us peace.

---

*28.1 mighty rock: See the note at 18.2.
See also: 28.4: Rev 22.12.

*29.10 king of the flood: In ancient times the people
of Israel believed that a mighty ocean surrounded all
of creation, and that God could release the water to
flood the earth.
See also: 29.1-2: Psa 96.7-9.

Psalm 30

(A psalm by David for the dedication of the temple.)

A prayer of thanks

¹ I will praise you, LORD!
  You saved me from the grave
    and kept my enemies
    from celebrating my death.
² I prayed to you, LORD God,
    and you healed me,
³   saving me from death and the grave.

⁴ Your faithful people, LORD,
    will praise you with songs
    and honour your holy name.
⁵ Your anger lasts a little while,
    but your kindness lasts for a lifetime.
  At night we may cry,
    but when morning comes
    we will celebrate.

⁶ I was carefree and thought,
    "I'll never be shaken!"
⁷ You, LORD, were my friend,
    and you made me strong
    as a mighty mountain.
  But when you hid your face,
    I was crushed.

⁸ I prayed to you, LORD,
    and in my prayer I said,
⁹   "What good will it do you
    if I am in the grave?
  Once I have turned to dust,
    how can I praise you
    or tell how loyal you are?
¹⁰ Have pity, LORD! Help!"

¹¹ You have turned my sorrow
    into joyful dancing.
  No longer am I sad
    and wearing sackcloth.*
¹² I thank you from my heart,
    and I will never stop
    singing your praises,
    my LORD and my God.

Psalm 31

(A psalm by David for the music leader.)

A prayer for protection

¹ I come to you, LORD, for protection.
    Don't let me be ashamed.

Do as you have promised
    and rescue me.
² Listen to my prayer
    and hurry to save me.
  Be my mighty rock*
    and the fortress where I am safe.

³ You, LORD God,
    are my mighty rock and my fortress.
  Lead me and guide me,
    so that your name will be honoured.
⁴ Protect me from hidden traps
    and keep me safe.
⁵ You are faithful,
    and I trust you
    because you rescued me.

⁶ I hate the worshippers
    of worthless idols,
    but I trust you, LORD.
⁷ I celebrate and shout
    because you are kind.
  You saw all my suffering,
    and you cared for me.
⁸ You kept me from the hands
    of my enemies,
    and you set me free.

⁹ Have pity, LORD!
  I am suffering and almost blind.
  My whole body aches.
¹⁰ I have known only sorrow
    all my life long,
  and I suffer year after year.
  I am weak from sin,
    and my bones are limp.

¹¹ My enemies insult me.
  Neighbours are even worse,
    and I disgust my friends.
  People meet me in the street,
    and they turn and run.
¹² I am completely forgotten
    like someone dead.
  I am merely a broken dish.
¹³ I hear the crowds whisper,
    "Everyone is afraid!"
  They are plotting and scheming
    to murder me.

¹⁴ But I trust you, LORD,
    and I claim you as my God.
¹⁵ My life is in your hands.
  Save me from enemies
    who hunt me down.
¹⁶ Smile on me, your servant.
  Have pity and rescue me.

---

*30.11 sackcloth: A rough, dark-coloured cloth made from goat or camel hair and used to make grain sacks. It was worn in times of trouble or sorrow.

*31.2 mighty rock: See the note at 18.2.
See also: 31.5: Luke 23.46.

17 I pray only to you.
  Don't disappoint me.
  Disappoint my cruel enemies
    until they lie silent in their graves.
18 Silence those proud liars!
  Make them stop boasting
    and insulting your people.

19 You are wonderful,
    and while everyone watches,
  you store up blessings for all
    who honour and trust you.
20 You are their shelter
    from harmful plots,
  and you are their protection
    from vicious gossip.

21 I will praise you, LORD,
    for showing great kindness
  when I was like a city under attack.
22 I was terrified and thought,
  "They've chased me
    far away from you!"
  But you answered my prayer
    when I shouted for help.

23 All who belong to the LORD,
    show how you love him.
  The LORD protects the faithful,
    but he severely punishes
      everyone who is proud.
24 All who trust the LORD,
    be cheerful and strong.

Psalm 32

(A special psalm by David.)

The joy of forgiveness

1 Our God, you bless everyone
    whose sins you forgive and wipe away.
2 You bless them by saying,
    "You told me your sins,
      without trying to hide them,
    and now I forgive you."

3 Before I confessed my sins,
    my bones felt limp,
  and I groaned all day long.
4 Night and day your hand
    weighed heavily on me,
  and my strength was gone
    as in the summer heat.

5 So I confessed my sins
    and told them all to you.
  I said, "I'll tell the LORD
    each one of my sins."

See also: **32.1–2:** Rom 4.7–8.

Viewpoints

What happens if we take a wrong turn?

Contributed by Marc W

'You said to me, "I will point out the road that you should follow. I will be your teacher and watch over you."'
  The LORD says, 'I will guide you along the best pathway for your life.'
  I was at a young people's housegroup the other night, and we were talking about Jonah. The guy that went completely the opposite way to the one God asked him to go, but then, with a little divine intervention, he turned round and ended up in Nineveh none the less.
  So his first lesson was that God always gets his way. But while I was looking at it, I couldn't help thinking that surely God knew that Jonah was going to run off anyway? He knows absolutely everything, after all. Then I realised that God used Jonah even when he went the wrong way, because the other people who were on the boat became believers because of what his God had done. So God saved Jonah, and he went where he was supposed to this time.
  Had he done what was asked of him in the first place, then Jonah would have saved a lot of time, money, effort, and wouldn't have got wet, but as it was, God was still with him, guided his path, and used him where he was, making him productive for God.
  So what's the best? Ask God. He knows best, and he knows where he can use you. And he knows the outcome of the choices before they are given to you. Whichever road you choose, listen to God before making up your mind, and walk it with him.

More...

Jonah p.982
The Bible is full of great heroes – what did they have that we don't? p.983
Our God is a God of second chances p.984

Then you forgave me
and took away my guilt.

⁶ We worship you, Lord,
and we should always pray
whenever we find out
that we have sinned.ʼ
Then we won't be swept away
by a raging flood.
⁷ You are my hiding place!
You protect me from trouble,
and you put songs in my heart
because you have saved me.

⁸ You said to me,
"I will point out the road
that you should follow.
I will be your teacher
and watch over you.
⁹ Don't be stupid like horses and mules
that must be led with ropes
to make them obey."

¹⁰ All kinds of troubles
will strike the wicked,
but your kindness shields those
who trust you, LORD.
¹¹ And so your good people
should celebrate and shout.

Psalm 33

Sing praises to the LORD

¹ You are the LORD's people.
Obey him and celebrate!
He deserves your praise.
² Praise the LORD with harps!
Use harps with ten strings
to make music for him.
³ Sing a new song. Shout!
Play beautiful music.

⁴ The LORD is truthful; he can be trusted.
⁵ He loves justice and fairness,
and he is kind to everyone
everywhere on earth.

⁶ The LORD made the heavens
and everything in them by his word.
⁷ He scooped up the ocean
and stored the water.
⁸ Everyone in this world
should worship
and honour the LORD!
⁹ As soon as he spoke
the world was created;
at his command, the earth was formed.

¹⁰ The LORD destroys the plans
and spoils the schemes of the nations.

¹¹ But what the LORD has planned
will stand for ever.
His thoughts never change.
¹² The LORD blesses each nation
that worships only him.
He blesses his chosen ones.
¹³ The LORD looks at the world
¹⁴ from his throne in heaven,
and he watches us all.
¹⁵ The LORD gave us each a mind,
and nothing we do
can be hidden from him.

¹⁶ Mighty armies alone
cannot win wars for a king;
great strength by itself
cannot keep a soldier safe.
¹⁷ In war the strength of a horse
cannot be trusted
to take you to safety.
¹⁸ But the LORD watches over all
who honour him
and trust his kindness.
¹⁹ He protects them from death
and starvation.

²⁰ We depend on you, LORD,
to help and protect us.
²¹ You make our hearts glad
because we trust you,
the only God.
²² Be kind and bless us!
We depend on you.

Psalm 34

*(Written by David when he pretended to be mad
in front of Abimelech, so that Abimelech would
send him away, and David could leave.)*

Honour the LORD

¹ I will always praise the LORD.
² With all my heart,
I will praise the LORD.
Let all who are helpless,
listen and be glad.
³ Honour the LORD with me!
Celebrate his great name.

⁴ I asked the LORD for help,
and he saved me from all my fears.
⁵ Keep your eyes on the LORD!
You will shine like the sun
and never blush with shame.
⁶ I was a nobody, but I prayed,
and the LORD saved me
from all my troubles.

See also: 34 Title: 1 Sam 21.13–15.

7 If you honour the LORD,
  his angel will protect you.
8 Discover for yourself
  that the LORD is kind.
  Come to him for protection,
  and you will be glad.

9 Honour the LORD!
  You are his special people.
  No one who honours the LORD
  will ever be in need.
10 Young lions* may go hungry
  or even starve,
  but if you trust the LORD,
  you will never miss out
  on anything good.

11 Come, my children, listen
  as I teach you to respect the LORD.
12 Do you want to live
  and enjoy a long life?
13 Then don't say cruel things
  and don't tell lies.
14 Do good instead of evil
  and try to live at peace.

15 If you obey the LORD,
  he will watch over you
  and answer your prayers.
16 But God despises evil people,
  and he will wipe them all
    from the earth,
  till they are forgotten.
17 When his people pray for help,
  he listens and rescues them
  from their troubles.
18 The LORD is there to rescue all
  who are discouraged
  and have given up hope.

19 The LORD's people may suffer a lot,
  but he will always
  bring them safely through.
20 Not one of his bones
  will ever be broken.

21 Wicked people are killed
  by their own evil deeds,
  and if you hate God's people
  you will be punished.
22 The LORD saves the lives
  of his servants.
  Run to him for protection,
  and you won't be punished.

---

*34.10 Young lions:** In the Psalms wild animals often
stand for God's enemies.

See also: 34.8: 1 Pet 2.3. **34.12–16:** 1 Pet 3.10–12.
34.20: John 19.36.

Helpline

Help! I'm being bullied

'They're picking on me and I can't do anything about it. I just feel so helpless.'

Throughout history – and generally in nature – the big guys have always picked on the little guys. Sometimes this is done through physical force; sometimes it's done in much more subtle ways: through emotional pressure or through verbal abuse. Doesn't change much, either way. It's still bullying and it's still wrong.

Being bullied is a horrible experience. It feels like there's nothing you can do; that whatever you do to get out of the situation won't work. Sometimes the people who are bullying us are supposed to be our friends. One minute they're friendly, the next...

But the situation doesn't have to be endured. You can do something about it. And you must do something about it. Tell someone about it. Don't suffer in silence.

Three things

Stop

If we're being bullied, sometimes we think that finding someone else to bully will make us feel better. It won't. Don't learn this kind of behaviour. Instead think how you feel and make sure you never make anyone else feel that way.

Tell

You have to tell someone. Talk to teachers, parents, youthleader. Find someone you trust and tell them about it.

Trust

Just think what God could do if he chose to be a bully! But he doesn't. Instead, he let himself be bullied and hurt for all of us. Try not to give into bitterness and revenge. Instead trust in God. He knows what you're going through: he went through it himself.

More...

Coping with suffering p.1391
Persecution p.1215
Help! I'm scared! p.662
Help! People are saying horrible things about me p.822

Psalm 35

(A psalm by David.)

A prayer for protection from enemies

1 Fight my enemies, LORD!
   Attack my attackers!
2 Shield me and help me.
3 Aim your spear at everyone
   who hunts me down,
   but promise to save me.

4 Let all who want to kill me
   be disappointed and disgraced.
   Chase away and confuse
   all who plan to harm me.
5 Send your angel after them
   and let them be like straw in the wind.
6 Make them run in the dark
   on a slippery road,
   as your angel chases them.
7 I did them no harm,
   but they hid a net to trap me,
   and they dug a deep pit
   to catch and kill me.
8 Surprise them with disaster!
   Trap them in their own nets
   and let them fall and rot
   in the pits they have dug.

9 I will celebrate and be joyful
   because you, LORD, have saved me.
10 Every bone in my body will shout:
   "No one is like the LORD!"
   You protect the helpless
   from those in power;
   you save the poor and needy
   from those who hurt them.

11 Liars accuse me of crimes
   I know nothing about.
12 They repay evil for good,
   and I feel all alone.
13 When they were sick,
   I wore sackcloth*
   and went without food.*
   I truly prayed for them,'
14 as I would for a friend
   or a relative.
   I was in sorrow and mourned,
   as I would for my mother.

15 I have stumbled,
   and worthless liars
   I don't even know
   surround me and sneer.

16 Worthless people make fun'
   and never stop laughing.
17 But all you do is watch!
   When will you do something?
   Save me from the attack
   of those vicious lions.
18 And when your people meet,
   I will praise you
   and thank you, Lord,
   in front of them all.

19 Don't let my brutal enemies
   be glad because of me.
   They hate me for no reason.
   Don't let them wink behind my back.
20 They say hurtful things,
   and they lie to people
   who want to live in peace.
21 They are quick to accuse me.
   They say, "You did it!
   We saw you ourselves."

22 You see everything, LORD!
   Please don't keep silent
   or stay so far away.
23 Fight to defend me, Lord God,
24 and prove that I am right
   by your standards.
   Don't let them laugh at me
25 or say to each other,
   "Now we've got what we want!
   We'll gobble him up!"

26 Disappoint and confuse
   all who are glad to see me in trouble,
   but disgrace and embarrass
   my proud enemies who say to me,
   "You are nothing!"

27 Let all who want me to win
   be happy and joyful.
   From now on let them say,
   "The LORD is wonderful!
   God is glad when all goes well
   for his servant."
28 Then I will shout all day,
   "Praise the LORD God!
   He did what was right."

Psalm 36

*(For the music leader by David,
the LORD's servant.)*

Human sin and God's goodness

1 Sinners don't respect God;
   sin is all they think about.

---

*35.13 sackcloth: See the note at 30.11.
*35.13 went without food: People sometimes went without food (called "fasting") to show sorrow.

See also: **35.19:** Psa 69.4; John 15.25. **36.1:** Rom 3.18.

2 They like themselves too much
    to hate their own sins
    or even to see them.
3 They tell deceitful lies,
    and they don't have the sense
    to live right.
4 Those people stay awake,
    thinking up mischief,
  and they follow the wrong road,
    refusing to turn from sin.

5 Your love is faithful, LORD,
    and even the clouds in the sky
    can depend on you.
6 Your decisions are always fair.
  They are firm like mountains,
    deep like the sea,
    and all people and animals
    are under your care.

7 Your love is a treasure,
    and everyone finds shelter
    in the shadow of your wings.
8 You give your guests a feast
    in your house,
    and you serve a tasty drink
    that flows like a river.
9 The life-giving fountain
    belongs to you,
    and your light gives light
    to each of us.

10 Our LORD, keep showing love
    to everyone who knows you,
  and use your power to save
    all whose thoughts please you.
11 Don't let those proud
    and merciless people
    kick me around or chase me away.

12 Look at those wicked people!
    They are knocked down,
    never to get up again.

Psalm 37

(By David.)

Trust the LORD

1 Don't be annoyed by anyone
    who does wrong,
    and don't envy them.
2 They will soon disappear
    like grass without rain.

3 Trust the LORD and live right!
    The land will be yours,
    and you will be safe.

4 Do what the LORD wants,
    and he will give you
    your heart's desire.

5 Let the LORD lead you
    and trust him to help.
6 Then it will be as clear
    as the noonday sun
    that you were right.

7 Be patient and trust the LORD.
    Don't let it bother you
    when all goes well for those
    who do sinful things.
8 Don't be angry or furious.
    Anger can lead to sin.
9 All sinners will disappear,
    but if you trust the LORD,
    the land will be yours.

10 Sinners will soon disappear,
    never to be found,
11 but the poor will take the land
    and enjoy a big harvest.

12 Merciless people make plots
    against good people
    and snarl like animals,
13 but the Lord laughs and knows
    their time is coming soon.
14 The wicked kill with swords
    and shoot arrows
  to murder the poor and the needy
    and all who do right.
15 But they will be killed
    by their own swords,
    and their arrows will be broken.

16 It is better to live right and be poor
    than to be sinful and rich.
17 The wicked will lose
    all of their power,
  but the LORD gives strength
    to everyone who is good.

18 Those who obey the LORD
    are daily in his care,
    and what he has given them
    will be theirs for ever.
19 They won't be in trouble
    when times are bad,
    and they will have plenty
    when food is scarce.

20 Wicked people are enemies
    of the LORD
    and will vanish like smoke
    from a field on fire.

See also: 37.11: Matt 5.5.

21 An evil person borrows
and never pays back;
a good person is generous
and never stops giving.
22 Everyone the LORD blesses
will receive the land;
everyone the LORD curses
will be destroyed.

23 If you do what the LORD wants,
he will make certain
each step you take is sure.
24 The LORD will hold your hand,
and if you stumble,
you still won't fall.

25 As long as I can remember,
good people have never
been left helpless,
and their children have never
gone begging for food.
26 They gladly give and lend,
and their children turn out good.

27 If you stop sinning
and start doing right,
you will keep living
and be secure for ever.
28 The LORD loves justice,
and he won't ever desert
his faithful people.
He always protects them,
but destroys the children of the wicked.
29 God's people will own the land
and live here for ever.

30 Words of wisdom come
when good people speak for justice.
31 They remember God's teachings,
and they never take a wrong step.
32 The wicked try to trap
and kill good people,
33 but the LORD is on their side,
and he will defend them
when they are on trial.

34 Trust the LORD and follow him.
He will give you the land,
and you will see the wicked destroyed.

35 I have seen brutal people abuse others
and grow strong like trees in rich soil.
36 Suddenly they disappeared!
I looked, but they were gone
and no longer there.

37 Think of the bright future waiting
for all the families of honest
and innocent and peace-loving people.

38 But not a trace will be left
of the wicked or their families.

39 The LORD protects his people,
and they can come to him
in times of trouble.
40 The LORD helps them
and saves them from the wicked
because they run to him.

Psalm 38

(A psalm by David to be used when an offering is made.)

A prayer in times of trouble

1 When you are angry, LORD,
please don't punish me
or even correct me.
2 You shot me with your arrows,
and you struck me with your hand.

3 My body hurts all over
because of your anger.
Even my bones are in pain,
and my sins
4 are so heavy that I am crushed.

5 Because of my foolishness,
I am covered with sores
that stink and spread.
6 My body is twisted and bent,
and I groan all day long.
7 Fever has my back in flames,
and I hurt all over.
8 I am worn out and weak,
moaning and in distress.

9 You, Lord, know every one
of my deepest desires,
and my noisy groans
are no secret to you.
10 My heart is beating fast.
I feel weak all over,
and my eyes are red.

11 Because of my sickness,
no friends or neighbours
will come near me.
12 All who want me dead
set traps to catch me,
and those who want
to harm and destroy me
plan and plot all day.

13 I am not able to hear or speak a word;
14 I am completely deaf
and can't make a sound.

15 I trust you, LORD God,
and you will do something.

16 I said, "Don't let them laugh
   or boast because I slip."

17 I am about to collapse
   from constant pain.
18 I told you my sins,
   and I am sorry for them.
19 Many deadly and powerful
   enemies hate me,
20 and they repay evil for good
   because I try to do right.

21 You are the LORD God!
   Stay nearby and don't desert me.
22 You are the one who saves me.
   Please hurry and help.

Psalm 39

*(A psalm by David for Jeduthun,
the music leader.)*

A prayer for forgiveness

1 I told myself, "I'll be careful
   not to sin by what I say,
   and I'll muzzle my mouth
   when evil people are near."
2 I kept completely silent,
   but it did no good,
   and I suffered even more.

3 I felt a fire burning inside,
   and the more I thought,
   the more it burnt,
   until at last I said:
4 "Please, LORD, show me my future.
   Will I soon be gone?
5 You made my life short,
   so brief that the time
   means nothing to you.

"Human life is but a breath,
6 and it disappears like a shadow.
Our struggles are senseless;
we store up more and more,
   without ever knowing
   who will get it all.

7 "What am I waiting for?
   I depend on you, Lord!
8 Save me from my sins.
   Don't let fools sneer at me.
9 You treated me like this,
   and I kept silent, not saying a word.

10 "Won't you stop punishing me?
   You have worn me down.
11 You punish us severely
   because of our sins.

Like a moth, you destroy
   what we treasure most.
   We are as frail as a breath.

12 "Listen, LORD, to my prayer!
   My eyes are flooded with tears,
   as I pray to you.
   I am merely a stranger
   visiting your home
   as my ancestors did.
13 Stop being angry with me
   and let me smile again
   before I am dead and gone."

Psalm 40

(A psalm by David for the music leader.)

A prayer for help

1 I patiently waited, LORD,
   for you to hear my prayer.
   You listened
2 and pulled me from a lonely pit
   full of mud and mire.
   You let me stand on a rock
   with my feet firm,
3 and you gave me a new song,
   a song of praise to you.
   Many will see this,
   and they will honour
   and trust you, the LORD God.

4 You bless all of those
   who trust you, LORD,
   and refuse to worship idols
   or follow false gods.
5 You, LORD God, have done
   many wonderful things,
   and you have planned
   marvellous things for us.
   No one is like you!
   I would never be able to tell
   all you have done.

6 Sacrifices and offerings
   are not what please you;
   gifts and payment for sin
   are not what you demand.
   But you made me willing
   to listen and obey.
7 And so, I said, "I am here
   to do what is written
   about me in the book,
   where it says,
8 'I enjoy pleasing you.
   Your Law is in my heart.'"

See also: 40.6–8: Heb 10.5–7.

607

9 When your people worshipped,
  you know I told them,
  "Our LORD always helps!"
10 When all your people met,
  I did not keep silent.
  I said, "Our LORD is kind.
  He is faithful and caring,
  and he saves us."
11 You, LORD, never fail
  to have pity on me;
  your love and faithfulness
  always keep me secure.

12 I have more troubles
  than I can count.
  My sins are all around me,
  and I can't find my way.
  My sins outnumber
  the hairs on my head,
  and I feel weak.
13 Please show that you care
  and come to my rescue.
  Hurry and help me!

14 Disappoint and confuse
  all who want me dead;
  turn away and disgrace
  all who want to hurt me.
15 Embarrass and shame
  all those who say,
  "Just look at you now!"

16 Our LORD, let your worshippers
  rejoice and be glad.
  They love you for saving them,
  so let them always say,
  "The LORD is wonderful!"

17 I am poor and needy,
  but, LORD God,
  you care about me,
  and you come to my rescue.
  Please hurry and help.

Psalm 41

(A psalm by David for the music leader.)

A prayer in time of sickness

1 You, LORD God, bless everyone
  who cares for the poor,
  and you rescue those people
  in times of trouble.
2 You protect them
  and keep them alive.
  You make them happy
  here in this land,
  and you don't hand them over
  to their enemies.

3 You always heal them
  and restore their strength
  when they are sick.
4 I prayed, "Have pity, LORD!
  Heal me,
  though I have sinned
  against you."

5 My vicious enemies ask me,
  "When will you die and be forgotten?"
6 When visitors come,
  all they ever bring are worthless words,
  and when they leave,
  they spread gossip.

7 My enemies whisper about me.
  They think the worst,
8   and they say,
  "You have some fatal disease!
  You'll never get well."
9 My most trusted friend
  has turned against me,
  though he ate at my table.

10 Have pity, LORD! Heal me,
  so I can pay them back.
11 Then my enemies won't defeat me,
  and I will know that you really care.
12 You have helped me
  because I am innocent,
  and you will always be close to my side.

13 You, the LORD God of Israel,
  will be praised for ever!
  Amen and amen.

BOOK 2

(Psalms 42–72)

Psalm 42

*(A special psalm for the people of Korah
and for the music leader.)*

Longing for God

1 As a deer gets thirsty
  for streams of water,
  I truly am thirsty for you, my God.
2 In my heart, I am thirsty
  for you, the living God.
  When will I see your face?
3 Day and night my tears
  are my only food,
  as everyone keeps asking,
  "Where is your God?"

See also: 41.9: Matt 26.23; Mark 14.18; Luke 22.21; John 13.18. 41.13: Psa 106.48.

4 Sorrow floods my heart,
    when I remember
leading the worshippers
    to your house.'
    I can still hear them shout
    their joyful praises.
5 Why am I discouraged?
    Why am I restless?
I trust you!
    And I will praise you again
    because you help me,
6   and you are my God.

I am deeply discouraged
    as I think about you
from where the Jordan begins
    at Mount Hermon
    and from Mount Mizar.*
7 Your vicious waves have swept over me
    like an angry ocean
    or a roaring waterfall.

8 Every day, you are kind,
    and at night you give me a song
    as my prayer to you,
    the living LORD God.
9 You are my mighty rock.*
    Why have you forgotten me?
    Why must enemies ill-treat me
    and make me sad?
10 Even my bones are in pain,
    while all day long
    my enemies sneer and ask,
    "Where is your God?"

11 Why am I discouraged?
    Why am I restless?
I trust you!
    And I will praise you again
    because you help me,
    and you are my God.

Psalm 43

A prayer in times of trouble

1 Show that I am right, God!
    Defend me against everyone
    who doesn't know you;
    rescue me from each
    of those deceitful liars.
2 I run to you for protection.
    Why have you turned me away?
    Why must enemies ill-treat me
    and make me sad?

3 Send your light and your truth
    to guide me.
    Let them lead me to your house
    on your sacred mountain.
4 Then I will worship at your altar
    because you make me joyful.
You are my God,
    and I will praise you.
    Yes, I will praise you as I play my harp.

5 Why am I discouraged?
    Why am I restless?
I trust you!
    And I will praise you again
    because you help me,
    and you are my God.

Psalm 44

*(A special psalm for the people of Korah
and for the music leader.)*

A prayer for help

1 Our God, our ancestors told us
    what wonders you worked
    and we listened carefully.
2 You chased off the nations
    by causing them trouble
    with your powerful arm.
Then you let our ancestors
    take over their land.
3 Their strength and weapons were not
    what won the land
    and gave them victory!
You loved them and fought
    with your powerful arm
    and your shining glory.

4 You are my God and King,
    and you give victory'
    to the people of Jacob.
5 By your great power,
    we knocked our enemies down
    and trampled on them.
6 I don't depend on my arrows
    or my sword to save me.
7 But you saved us
    from our hateful enemies,
    and you put them to shame.
8 We boast about you, our God,
    and we are always grateful.

9 But now you have rejected us;
    you don't lead us into battle,
    and we look foolish.
10 You made us retreat,
    and our enemies have taken
    everything we own.

---

*42.6 **Mount Mizar:** The location is not known.
*42.9 **mighty rock:** See the note at 18.2.

11 You let us be slaughtered like sheep,
   and you scattered us
   among the nations.
12 You sold your people
   for little or nothing,
   and you earned no profit.

13 You made us look foolish
   to our neighbours,
   and people who live nearby
   insult us and sneer.
14 Foreigners joke about us
   and shake their heads.
15 I am embarrassed every day,
   and I blush with shame.
16 But others mock and sneer,
   as they watch my enemies
   take revenge on me.

17 All of this has happened to us,
   though we didn't forget you
   or break our agreement.
18 We always kept you in mind
   and followed your teaching.
19 But you crushed us,
   and you covered us
   with deepest darkness
   where wild animals live.

20 We did not forget you
   or lift our hands in prayer
   to foreign gods.
21 You would have known it
   because you discover
   every secret thought.
22 We face death all day for you.
   We are like sheep on their way
   to be slaughtered.

23 Wake up! Do something, Lord!
   Why are you sleeping?
   Don't desert us for ever.
24 Why do you keep looking away?
   Don't forget our sufferings
   and all our troubles.
25 We are flat on the ground,
   holding on to the dust.
26 Do something! Help us!
   Show how kind you are
   and come to our rescue.

Psalm 45

(A special psalm for the people of Korah and for the music leader. To the tune "Lilies". A love song.)

For a royal wedding

1 My thoughts are filled
   with beautiful words
   for the king,
   and I will use my voice
   as a writer would use pen and ink.

2 No one is as handsome as you!
   Your words are always kind.
   That is why God will always bless you.
3 Mighty king, glorious ruler,
   strap on your sword
4   and ride out in splendour!
   Win victories for truth
   and mercy and justice.
   Do fearsome things
   with your powerful arm.
5 Send your sharp arrows
   through enemy hearts
   and make all nations fall at your feet.

6 You are God, and you will rule
   for ever as king.›
   Your royal power brings about justice.
7 You love justice and hate evil.
   And so, your God chose you
   and made you happier
   than any of your friends.
8 The sweet aroma of the spices
   myrrh, aloes, and cassia,
   covers your royal robes.
   You enjoy the music of harps
   in palaces decorated with ivory.
9 Daughters of kings are here,
   and your bride stands at your right side,
   wearing a wedding gown
   trimmed with pure gold.*

10 Bride of the king,
   listen carefully to me.
   Forget your own people
   and your father's family.
11 The king is your husband,
   so do what he desires.
12 All the richest people
   from the city of Tyre
   will try to influence you
13 with precious treasures.

---

*45.9 trimmed with pure gold: Hebrew has "with gold from Ophir", which may have been in Africa or India. Gold from there was considered the very best.

See also: 44.22: Rom 8.36.
See also: 45.6–7: Heb 1.8–9.

Your bride, my king,
 has inward beauty,'
and her wedding gown is woven
 with threads of gold.
¹⁴ Wearing the finest garments,
 she is brought to you,
followed by her young friends,
 the bridesmaids.
¹⁵ Everyone is excited,
 as they follow you to the royal palace.

¹⁶ Your sons and your grandsons
 will also be kings
 as your ancestors were.
You will make them the rulers
 everywhere on earth.

¹⁷ I will make your name famous
 from now on,
and you will be praised
 for ever and ever.

Psalm 46

(A special song for the people of Korah and for the music leader.)

God is our mighty fortress

¹ God is our mighty fortress,
 always ready to help
 in times of trouble.
² And so, we won't be afraid!
Let the earth tremble
 and the mountains tumble
 into the deepest sea.
³ Let the ocean roar and foam,
 and its raging waves
 shake the mountains.

⁴ A river and its streams
 bring joy to the city,
which is the sacred home
 of God Most High.
⁵ God is in that city,
 and it won't be shaken.
He will help it at dawn.

⁶ Nations rage! Kingdoms fall!
 But at the voice of God
 the earth itself melts.
⁷ The LORD All-Powerful is with us.
 The God of Jacob is our fortress.

⁸ Come! See the fearsome things
 the LORD has done on earth.
⁹ God brings wars to an end
 all over the world.
He breaks the arrows,
 shatters the spears,
 and burns the shields.'

¹⁰ Our God says, "Calm down,
 and learn that I am God!
All nations on earth will honour me."

¹¹ The LORD All-Powerful is with us.
 The God of Jacob is our fortress.

Psalm 47

(A psalm for the people of Korah and for the music leader.)

God rules the nations

¹ All you nations, clap your hands
 and shout joyful praises to God.
² The LORD Most High is fearsome,
 the ruler of all the earth.
³ God has put every nation
 under our power,
⁴ and he chose for us the land
 that was the pride of Jacob,
 his favourite.

⁵ God goes up to his throne,
 as people shout and trumpets blast.
⁶ Sing praises to God our King,
⁷ the ruler of all the earth!
Praise God with songs.

⁸ God rules the nations
 from his sacred throne.
⁹ Their leaders come together
 and are now the people
 of Abraham's God.
All rulers on earth
 surrender their weapons,
 and God is greatly praised!

Psalm 48

(A song and a psalm for the people of Korah.)

The city of God

¹ The LORD God is wonderful!
 He deserves all praise
 in the city where he lives.
His holy mountain,
² beautiful and majestic,
 brings joy to all on earth.
Mount Zion, truly sacred,
 is home for the Great King.
³ God is there to defend it
 and has proved to be its protector.

⁴ Kings joined forces to attack the city,
⁵ but when they saw it,
 they were terrified and ran away.

See also: 48.2: Matt 5.35.

⁶ They trembled all over
  like women giving birth
⁷ or like seagoing ships*
  wrecked by eastern winds.
⁸ We had heard about it,
  and now we have seen it
  in the city of our God,
  the LORD All-Powerful.
  This is the city that God
  will let stand for ever.

⁹ Our God, here in your temple
  we think about your love.
¹⁰ You are famous and praised
  everywhere on earth,
  as you win victories
  with your powerful arm.
¹¹ Mount Zion will celebrate,
  and all Judah will be glad,
  because you bring justice.

¹² Let's walk around Zion
  and count its towers.
¹³ We will see its strong walls
  and visit each fortress.
  Then you can say
  to future generations,
¹⁴ "Our God is like this for ever
  and will always' guide us."

Psalm 49

*(A psalm for the people of Korah
and for the music leader.)*

Don't depend on wealth

¹ Everyone on this earth,
  now listen to what I say!
² Listen, no matter who you are,
  rich or poor.
³ I speak words of wisdom,
  and my thoughts make sense.
⁴ I have in mind a mystery
  that I will explain
  while playing my harp.

⁵ Why should I be afraid
  in times of trouble,
  when I am surrounded
  by vicious enemies?
⁶ They trust in their riches
  and boast about all their wealth.
⁷ You cannot buy back your life
  or pay off God!

⁸ It costs far too much
  to buy back your life.
  You can never pay God enough
⁹ to stay alive for ever
  and safe from death.

¹⁰ We see that wise people die,
  and so do stupid fools.
  Then their money is left
  for someone else.
¹¹ The grave' will be their home
  for ever and ever,
  although they once had land
  of their own.
¹² Our human glory disappears,
  and, like animals, we die.

¹³ Here is what happens to fools
  and to those who trust
  the words of fools:
¹⁴ They are like sheep
  with death as their shepherd,
  leading them to the grave.'
  In the morning God's people
  will walk all over them,
  as their bodies lie rotting
  in their home, the grave.
¹⁵ But God will rescue me
  from the power of death.

¹⁶ Don't let it bother you
  when others get rich and live in luxury.
¹⁷ Soon they will die
  and all their wealth will be left behind.

¹⁸ We humans are praised
  when we do well,
  and all of us are glad to be alive.
¹⁹ But we will each go down
  to our ancestors,
  never again to see the light of day.
²⁰ Our human glory disappears,
  and, like animals, we die.

Psalm 50

(A psalm by Asaph.)

What pleases God

¹ From east to west,
  the powerful LORD God
  has been calling together
  everyone on earth.
² God shines brightly from Zion,
  the most beautiful city.

³ Our God approaches, but not silently;
  a flaming fire comes first,
  and a storm surrounds him.

---

*48.7 seagoing ships: The Hebrew text has "ships of
Tarshish", which probably means large, seagoing
ships.

⁴ God comes to judge his people.
  He shouts to the heavens
  and to the earth,
⁵ "Call my followers together!
  They offered me a sacrifice,
  and we made an agreement."

⁶ The heavens announce,
  "God is the judge,
  and he is always honest."

⁷ My people, I am God!
  Israel, I am your God.
  Listen to my charges against you.
⁸ Although you offer sacrifices
  and always bring gifts,
⁹ I won't accept your offerings
  of bulls and goats.

¹⁰ Every animal in the forest belongs to me,
  and so do the cattle on a thousand hills.
¹¹ I know all the birds
  in the mountains,
  and every wild creature is in my care.

¹² If I were hungry, I wouldn't tell you,
  because I own the world
  and everything in it.
¹³ I don't eat the meat of bulls
  or drink the blood of goats.
¹⁴ I am God Most High!
  The only sacrifice I want
  is for you to be thankful
  and to keep your word.
¹⁵ Pray to me in time of trouble.
  I will rescue you,
  and you will honour me.

¹⁶ But to the wicked I say:
  "You don't have the right
  to mention my laws
  or claim to keep our agreement!
¹⁷ You refused correction
  and rejected my commands.
¹⁸ You made friends
  with every criminal you met,
  and you liked people who break
  their wedding vows.
¹⁹ You talked only about violence
  and told nothing but lies;
²⁰ you sat around gossiping,
  ruining the reputation
  of your own relatives."

²¹ When you did all this,
  I didn't say a word,
  and you thought, "God is just like us!"
  But now I will accuse you.
²² You have ignored me!
  So pay close attention

or I will tear you apart,
  and no one can help you.

²³ The sacrifice that honours me
  is a thankful heart.
  Obey me,' and I, your God,
  will show my power to save.

Psalm 51

*(For the music leader. A psalm by David when
the prophet Nathan came to him after David
had been with Bathsheba.)*

A prayer for forgiveness

¹ You are kind, God!
  Please have pity on me.
  You are always merciful!
  Please wipe away my sins.
² Wash me clean from all
  of my sin and guilt.
³ I know about my sins,
  and I cannot forget my terrible guilt.
⁴ You are really the one
  I have sinned against;
  I have disobeyed you
  and have done wrong.
  So it is right and fair for you
  to correct and punish me.

⁵ I have sinned and done wrong
  since the day I was born.
⁶ But you want complete honesty,
  so teach me true wisdom.
⁷ Wash me with hyssop*
  until I am clean and whiter than snow.
⁸ Let me be happy and joyful!
  You crushed my bones,
  now let them celebrate.
⁹ Turn your eyes from my sin
  and cover my guilt.
¹⁰ Create pure thoughts in me
  and make me faithful again.
¹¹ Don't chase me away from you
  or take your Holy Spirit away from me.

¹² Make me as happy as you did
  when you saved me;
  make me want to obey!
¹³ I will teach sinners your Law,
  and they will return to you.
¹⁴ Keep me from any deadly sin.
  Only you can save me!

---

*51.7 hyssop: A small bush with bunches of small,
white flowers. It was sometimes used as a symbol for
making a person clean from sin.
See also: 51 Title: 2 Sam 12.1–15. **51.4:** Rom 3.4.

Big ideas

Forgiveness

The Bible is full of people making a mess of things. It's full of the bad things in life: violence, betrayal, deceit, despair. But there is also forgiveness. And God wants to forgive us for the bad things we do.

And all of us do bad things or dumb things or things that just go wrong. We all need to say 'sorry'.

First, we need to say sorry to God. God's grace means that, once we turn to him, we can always receive forgiveness. When sin happens, we can turn again to God.

Secondly, we need to forgive others. Christianity means nothing if it isn't lived out in our lives. Jesus gives us several stories warning that, if God forgives us, we should forgive others.

Forgiveness is one of the most powerful witnesses to the truth of Christianity. The world doesn't forgive people. The media, the press, the people, they'd rather punish; an eye for an eye and a tooth for a tooth and all that. But Christianity knows that people need to be forgiven. Otherwise we'll all end up blind and toothless.

So understand this: God has forgiven us. Now we need to forgive others. If we don't do that it would be, well, unforgivable.

 Footsteps

Ten days on Forgiveness

Confessed – forgiven: Psalms 32.1–11
God washes us clean: Psalms 51.1–19
Turn to the Lord: Isaiah 55.7–13
Forgive and forget: Jeremiah 31.31–37
Love your enemies: Matthew 5.38–48
Forgiveness = forgiveness: Matthew 6.9–15
Seventy times seven: Matthew 18.21–35
Something in your eye? Luke 6.37–42
Stop being so stupid! Ephesians 4.17–32
Living in light: 1 John 1.1—2.2

More...

God's love p.958
Redemption p.1203
Saying sorry p.1258
Forgiving others p.1162

Then I will shout and sing
about your power to save.
15 Help me to speak,
and I will praise you, Lord.
16 Offerings and sacrifices
are not what you want.
17 The way to please you
is to feel sorrow deep in our hearts.
This is the kind of sacrifice
you won't refuse.

18 Please be willing, Lord,
to help the city of Zion
and to rebuild its walls.
19 Then you will be pleased
with the proper sacrifices,
and we will offer bulls
on your altar once again.

Psalm 52

(A special psalm by David for the music leader. He wrote this when Doeg from Edom went to Saul and said, "David has gone to Ahimelech's house.")

God is in control

1 You people may be strong
and boast about your sins,
but God can be trusted day after day.
2 You plan brutal crimes,
and your lying words cut
like a sharp razor.
3 You would rather do evil than good,
and tell lies than speak the truth.
4 You love to say cruel things,
and your words are a trap.

5 God will destroy you for ever!
He will grab you and drag you
from your homes.
You will be uprooted
and left to die.
6 When good people see
this fearsome sight,
they will laugh and say,
7 "Just look at them now!
Instead of trusting God,
they trusted their wealth
and their cruelty."

8 But I am like an olive tree
growing in God's house,
and I can count on his love
for ever and ever.

See also: 52 Title: 1 Sam 22.9–10.

9 I will always thank God
   for what he has done;
I will praise his good name
   when his people meet.

Psalm 53

*(A special psalm by David for the music
leader. To the tune "Mahalath".)*

No one can ignore God

1 Only a fool would say,
   "There is no God!"
People like that are worthless!
   They are heartless and cruel
   and never do right.

2 From heaven God looks down to see
   if anyone is wise enough
   to search for him.
3 But all of them are crooked and corrupt.
   Not one of them does right.

4 Won't you lawbreakers learn?
   You refuse to pray,
   and you gobble up the people of God.
5 But you will be more terrified
   than ever before.
God will scatter the bones
   of his enemies,
   and you will be ashamed
   when God rejects you.

6 I long for someone from Zion
   to come and save Israel!
Our God, when you bless
   your people again,
Jacob's family will be glad,
   and Israel will celebrate.

Psalm 54

*(For the music leader. Use with stringed
instruments. A special psalm that David wrote
when the people of Ziph went to Saul and said,
"David is hiding here with us.")*

Trusting God in times of trouble

1 Save me, God, by your power
   and prove that I am right.
2 Listen to my prayer
   and hear what I say.
3 Cruel strangers have attacked
   and want me dead.
Not one of them cares about you.

4 You will help me, Lord God,
   and keep me from falling;
5 you will punish my enemies
   for their evil deeds.
Be my faithful friend and destroy them.

6 I will bring a gift
   and offer a sacrifice to you, LORD.
I will praise your name
   because you are good.
7 You have rescued me
   from all my troubles,
   and my own eyes have seen
   my enemies fall.

Psalm 55

*(A special psalm by David for the music
leader. Use with stringed instruments.)*

Betrayed by a friend

1 Listen, God, to my prayer!
   Don't reject my request.
2 Please listen and help me.
   My thoughts are troubled,
   and I keep groaning
3 because my loud enemies
   shout and attack.
They treat me terribly
   and hold angry grudges.
4 My heart is racing fast,
   and I am afraid of dying.
5 I am trembling with fear,
   completely terrified.

6 I wish I had wings like a dove,
   so I could fly far away
   and be at peace.
7 I would go and live
   in some distant desert.
8 I would quickly find shelter
   from howling winds
   and raging storms.

9 Confuse my enemies, Lord!
   Upset their plans.
Cruelty and violence
   are all I see in the city,
10 and they are like guards
   on patrol day and night.
The city is full of trouble, evil,
11 and corruption.
Troublemakers and liars
   freely roam the streets.

12 My enemies are not the ones
   who sneer and make fun.
I could put up with that
   or even hide from them.

Helpline

Help! My best friends don't want to know me any more

'I thought they were my mates. Best friends. But now they've gone off with someone else...'

Friends are great. Friends are important. Friends move on. It's hard to accept this, but maybe you could start by thinking back to when you were very young. How many of your friends do you still see? How many are you still close to? Not many people have the same best friend now they did back then.

People change. Maybe school friends go to university or college and make new friends. Life moves on and sometimes it leaves you behind.

That's hard to accept. We end up feeling unwanted or rejected. But we also need to accept that friendships do change over time. It's happening now and it will continue to happen throughout your life. In fact, even the closest friendships go through peaks and troughs; sometimes years may go by before old friendships are resumed.

It's not wrong to feel sad at this. It's not wrong to 'grieve' for what has been lost. Maybe the friendship will resume in time. But maybe we just need to move on.

Three things

Forgive

Don't take revenge on your friend. Don't gossip or slag them off. Don't leave nasty messages on their answerphone or send texts that you may later regret.

Pray

Pray for your friend and keep praying for them. Ask God to heal the hurt that you feel and to give you new friendships

New

Recognise that God has new things in store for you. There are new people to meet, new friends to discover, new relationships ahead.

More...

Help! I can't make friends p.714
Going against the crowd p.1045

---

¹³ But it was my closest friend,
   the one I trusted most.
¹⁴ We enjoyed being together,
   and we went with others
   to your house, our God.

¹⁵ All who hate me are controlled
   by the power of evil.
   Sentence them to death
   and send them down alive
   to the world of the dead.
¹⁶ I ask for your help, LORD God,
   and you will keep me safe.
¹⁷ Morning, noon, and night
   you hear my concerns
   and my complaints.
¹⁸ I am attacked from all sides,
   but you will rescue me
   unharmed by the battle.
¹⁹ You have always ruled,
   and you will hear me.
   You will defeat my enemies
   because they won't turn
   and worship you.

²⁰ My friend turned against me
   and broke his promise.
²¹ His words were smoother than butter,
   and softer than olive oil.
   But hatred filled his heart,
   and he was ready to attack
   with a sword.

²² Our LORD, we belong to you.
   We tell you what worries us,
   and you won't let us fall.
²³ But what about those people
   who are cruel and brutal?
   You will throw them down
   into the deepest pit
   long before their time.
   I trust you, LORD!

Psalm 56

(For the music leader. To the tune "A Silent Dove in the Distance".ᵇ A special psalm by David when the Philistines captured him in Gath.)

A prayer of trust in God

¹ Have pity, God Most High!
   My enemies chase me all day.
² Many of them are pursuing
   and attacking me,
³ but even when I am afraid,
   I keep on trusting you.

See also: 56 Title: 1 Sam 21.13–15.

4 I praise your promises!
I trust you and am not afraid.
No one can harm me.

5 Enemies spend the whole day
finding fault with me;
all they think about
is how to do me harm.

6 They attack from ambush,
watching my every step
and hoping to kill me.

7 They won't get away'
with these crimes, God,
because when you get angry,
you destroy people.

8 You have kept record
of my days of wandering.
You have stored my tears in your bottle
and counted each of them.

9 When I pray, LORD God,
my enemies will retreat,
because I know for certain
that you are with me.

10 I praise your promises!

11 I trust you and am not afraid.
No one can harm me.

12 I will keep my promises
to you, my God,
and bring you gifts.

13 You protected me from death
and kept me from stumbling,
so that I would please you
and follow the light that leads to life.

Psalm 57

(For the music leader. To the tune "Don't Destroy".' A special psalm by David when he was in the cave while running from Saul.)

Praise and trust in times of trouble

1 God Most High, have pity on me!
Have mercy.
I run to you for safety.
In the shadow of your wings,
I seek protection till danger dies down.

2 I pray to you, my protector.

3 You will send help from heaven
and save me,
but you will bring trouble
on my attackers.
You are faithful,
and you can be trusted.

4 I live among lions,
who gobble up people!
They have spears and arrows
instead of teeth,
and they have sharp swords
instead of tongues.

5 May you, my God, be honoured
above the heavens;
may your glory be seen
everywhere on earth.

6 Enemies set traps for my feet
and struck me down.
They dug a pit in my path,
but fell in it themselves.

7 I am faithful to you,
and you can trust me.
I will sing and play music
for you, my God.

8 I feel wide awake!
I will wake up my harp
and wake up the sun.

9 I will praise you, Lord,
for everyone to hear,
and I will sing hymns to you
in every nation.

10 Your love reaches higher
than the heavens;
your loyalty extends
beyond the clouds.

11 May you, my God, be honoured
above the heavens;
may your glory be seen
everywhere on earth.

Psalm 58

(A special psalm by David for the music leader. To the tune "Don't Destroy".')

A prayer when all goes wrong

1 Do you mighty people' talk
only to oppose justice?'
Don't you ever judge fairly?

2 You are always planning evil,
and you are brutal.

3 You have done wrong and lied
from the day you were born.

4 Your words spread poison
like the bite of a cobra

5 that refuses to listen
to the snake charmer.

6 My enemies are fierce
as lions, LORD God!
Shatter their teeth.
Snatch out their fangs.

See also: 57 Title: 1 Sam 22.1; 24.3.

7 Make them disappear like leaking water,
   and make their arrows miss.
8 Let them dry up like snails
   or be like a child that dies
   before seeing the sun.
9 Wipe them out quicker
   than a pot can be heated
   by setting thorns on fire.◗

10 Good people will be glad
    when they see the wicked
    getting what they deserve,
    and they will wash their feet
    in their enemies' blood.
11 Everyone will say, "It's true!
    Good people are rewarded.
    God does rule the earth with justice."

Psalm 59

*(For the music leader. To the tune "Don't
Destroy".◗ A special psalm by David
when Saul had David's house watched
so that he could kill him.)*

A prayer for protection

1 Save me, God! Protect me
   from enemy attacks!
2 Keep me safe from brutal people
   who want to kill me.

3 Merciless enemies, LORD,
   are hiding and plotting,
   hoping to kill me.
   I have not hurt them in any way at all.
4 But they are ready to attack.
   Do something! Help me!
   Look at what's happening.
5 LORD God All-Powerful,
   you are the God of Israel.
   Punish the other nations
   and don't pity those terrible
   and rebellious people.

6 My enemies return at evening,
   growling like dogs roaming the city.
7 They curse and their words
   cut like swords,
   as they say to themselves,
   "No one can hear us!"

8 You, LORD, laugh at them
   and sneer at the nations.
9 You are my mighty fortress,
   and I depend on you.
10 You love me and will let me
    see my enemies defeated.

11 Don't kill them,
    or everyone may forget!
   Just use your mighty power
   to make them tremble and fall.

   You are a shield for your people.
12 My enemies are liars!
   So let them be trapped
   by their boastful lies.
13 Get angry and destroy them.
    Leave them in ruin.
   Then all the nations will know
   that you rule in Israel.

14 Those liars return at evening,
    growling like dogs roaming the city.
15 They search for scraps of food,
    and they snarl until they are full.

16 But I will sing about
    your strength, my God,
    and I will celebrate
    because of your love.
   You are my fortress,
   my place of protection
   in times of trouble.
17 I will sing your praises!
    You are my mighty fortress,
    and you love me.

Psalm 60

*(For the music leader. To the tune "Lily of the
Promise". A special psalm by David for teaching.
He wrote it during his wars with the Arameans of
northern Syria,* when Joab came back and killed
twelve thousand Edomites* in Salt Valley.)*

You can depend on God

1 You, God, are angry with us!
   We are rejected and crushed.
   Make us strong again!
2 You made the earth shake
   and split wide open;
   now heal its wounds
   and stop its trembling.
3 You brought hard times
   on your people,
   and you gave us wine
   that made us stagger.

4 You gave a signal to those
   who worship you,

---

*Psalm 60 wars . . . Syria: See 2 Samuel 8.3–8;
10.16–18; 1 Chronicles 18.3–11; 19.6–19.
*Psalm 60 killed . . . Edomites: See 2 Samuel 8.13;
1 Chronicles 18.12.

See also: 60 Title: 2 Sam 8.13; 1 Chron 18.12.

See also: 59 Title: 1 Sam 19.11.

so they could escape
from enemy arrows.'
5 Answer our prayers!
Use your powerful arm
and give us victory.
Then the people you love will be safe.

6 Our God, you solemnly promised,
"I would gladly divide up
the city of Shechem
and give away Succoth Valley
piece by piece.
7 The lands of Gilead
and Manasseh are mine.
Ephraim is my war helmet,
and Judah is the symbol
of my royal power.
8 Moab is merely my washbasin.
Edom belongs to me,
and I shout in triumph
over the Philistines."

9 Our God, who will bring me
to the fortress,
or lead me to Edom?
10 Have you rejected us
and deserted our armies?
11 Help us defeat our enemies!
No one else can rescue us.
12 You will give us victory
and crush our enemies.

Psalm 61

*(A psalm by David for the music leader.
Use with stringed instruments.)*

Under the protection of God

1 Please listen, God,
and answer my prayer!
2 I feel hopeless,
and I cry out to you
from a faraway land.

Lead me to the mighty rock*
high above me.
3 You are a strong tower,
where I am safe
from my enemies.

4 Let me live with you for ever
and find protection
under your wings, my God.
5 You heard my promises,
and you have blessed me,
just as you bless everyone
who worships you.

*61.2 mighty rock: See the note at 18.2.

Helpline

Help! I'm praying but God isn't doing anything!

'The Bible says that if we ask for something then we'll get it. So why aren't my prayers answered?'

The Bible tells us to have faith that our prayers will be answered. Many Christians have seen remarkable answers to prayer. But there are times when we don't receive the answers to prayer that we wanted. Sometimes this is very painful. Sometimes it's hard to deal with. But remember that God loves you. If he doesn't answer your prayers the way you want, it's not because he doesn't love you and care for you.

One consolation is that we're not alone. The Psalms are stuffed with complaints to God, and urgent requests for him to answer prayers. Paul didn't get all his prayers answered. So if it didn't work for them...

Three things

Motives

I might believe that if God makes me a millionaire it will bring glory to his name, he might have a another view of it entirely. So check out the motives behind your prayers. Is it what God wants, or what you want?

Trust

The Bible tells us to trust God. He sees everything and knows everything. He sees the big picture, we only see our small part of it. Perhaps our prayers aren't answered because of other reasons and factors which we can't see or understand.

Freedom

People have free will. God's plan overall will be achieved and nothing is going to stop that, but, at an individual level, people make their own decisions and choices. We're not robots. So perhaps sometimes our prayers aren't answered because, well, people make choices that God doesn't want.

More...

Coping with suffering p.1391
Prayer p.1002
Help! I feel stuck p.762

⁶ Let the king have a long and healthy life.
⁷ May he always rule
   with you, God, at his side;
   may your love and loyalty
   watch over him.

⁸ I will sing your praises for ever
   and will always keep my promises.

Psalm 62

(A psalm by David for Jeduthun, the music leader.)

God is powerful and kind

¹ Only God can save me,
   and I calmly wait for⁎ him.
² God alone is the mighty rock*
   that keeps me safe
   and the fortress where I am secure.

³ I feel like a shaky fence or a sagging wall.
   How long will all of you
   attack and assault me?
⁴ You want to bring me down
   from my place of honour.
   You love to tell lies,
   and when your words are kind,
   hatred hides in your heart.

⁵ Only God gives inward peace,
   and I depend on him.
⁶ God alone is the mighty rock
   that keeps me safe,
   and he is the fortress where I feel secure.
⁷ God saves me and honours me.
   He is that mighty rock
   where I find safety.
⁸ Trust God, my friends,
   and always tell him
   each one of your concerns.
   God is our place of safety.

⁹ We humans are only a breath;
   none of us are truly great.
   All of us together weigh less
   than a puff of air.
¹⁰ Don't trust in violence
   or depend on dishonesty
   or rely on great wealth.
¹¹ I heard God say two things:
   "I am powerful,
¹² and I am very kind."
   The Lord rewards each of us
   according to what we do.

Psalm 63

*(A psalm by David when he was in
the desert of Judah.)*

God's love means more than life

¹ You are my God. I worship you.
   In my heart, I long for you,
   as I would long for a stream
   in a scorching desert.

² I have seen your power
   and your glory
   in the place of worship.
³ Your love means more than life to me,
   and I praise you.
⁴ As long as I live,
   I will pray to you.
⁵ I will sing joyful praises
   and be filled with excitement
   like a guest at a banquet.

⁶ I think about you before I go to sleep,
   and my thoughts turn to you
   during the night.
⁷ You have helped me,
   and I sing happy songs
   in the shadow of your wings.
⁸ I stay close to you,
   and your powerful arm supports me.

⁹ All who want to kill me
   will end up in the ground.
¹⁰ Swords will run them through,
   and wild dogs will eat them.

¹¹ Because of you, our God,
   the king will celebrate
   with your faithful followers,
   but liars will be silent.

Psalm 64

(A psalm by David for the music leader.)

Celebrate because of the LORD

¹ Listen to my concerns, God,
   and protect me
   from my terrible enemies.
² Keep me safe from secret plots
   of corrupt and evil gangs.
³ Their words cut like swords,
   and their cruel remarks
   sting like sharp arrows.
⁴ They fearlessly ambush
   and shoot innocent people.

---

*62.2 mighty rock: See the note at 18.2.
See also: 62.12: Job 34.11; Jer 17.10; Matt 16.27; Rom 2.6;
Rev 2.23.

See also: 63 Title: 1 Sam 23.14.

5 They are determined to do evil,
   and they tell themselves,
   "Let's set traps! No one can see us."*
6 They make evil plans and say,
   "We'll commit a perfect crime.
   No one knows our thoughts."*

7 But God will shoot his arrows
   and quickly wound them.
8 They will be destroyed
   by their own words,
   and everyone who sees them
   will tremble with fear.*
9 They will be afraid and say,
   "Look at what God has done
   and keep it all in mind."

10 May the LORD bless his people
   with peace and happiness
   and let them celebrate.

Psalm 65

*(A psalm by David and a song
for the music leader.)*

God answers prayer

1 Our God, you deserve* praise in Zion,
   where we keep our promises to you.
2 Everyone will come to you
   because you answer prayer.
3 Our terrible sins get us down,
   but you forgive us.
4 You bless your chosen ones,
   and you invite them
   to live near you in your temple.
   We will enjoy your house,
   the sacred temple.

5 Our God, you save us,
   and your fearsome deeds
   answer our prayers for justice!
   You give hope to people
   everywhere on earth,
   even those across the sea.
6 You are strong,
   and your mighty power
   put the mountains in place.
7 You silence the roaring waves
   and the noisy shouts of the nations.
8 People far away marvel
   at your fearsome deeds,
   and all who live under the sun
   celebrate and sing because of you.

9 You take care of the earth
   and send rain
   to help the soil
   grow all kinds of crops.

Your rivers never run dry,
   and you prepare the earth
   to produce much grain.
10 You water all its fields
   and level the lumpy ground.
   You send showers of rain
   to soften the soil
   and help the plants sprout.
11 Wherever your footsteps
   touch the earth,
   a rich harvest is gathered.
12 Desert pastures blossom,
   and mountains celebrate.
13 Meadows are filled
   with sheep and goats;
   valleys overflow with grain
   and echo with joyful songs.

Psalm 66

(A song and a psalm for the music leader.)

Shout praises to God

1 Tell everyone on this earth
   to shout praises to God!
2 Sing about his glorious name.
   Honour him with praises.
3 Say to God, "Everything you do
   is fearsome,
   and your mighty power makes
   your enemies come crawling.
4 You are worshipped by everyone!
   We all sing praises to you."

5 Come and see the fearsome things
   our God has done!
6 When God made the sea dry up,
   our people walked across,
   and because of him,
   we celebrated there.
7 His mighty power rules for ever,
   and nothing the nations do
   can be hidden from him.
   So don't turn against God.

8 All you people, come, praise our God!
   Let his praises be heard.
9 God protects us from death
   and keeps us steady.

10 Our God, you tested us,
   just as silver is tested.
11 You trapped us in a net
   and gave us heavy burdens.
12 You sent war chariots
   to crush our skulls.

See also: 66.6: a Exod 14.21; **b** Josh 3.14–17.

Being christian

Worshipping God

Psalms 66.1–4

What does it mean to worship God?

When we think about worship, we probably think of singing; of taking part in 'times of worship' in church or at Christian events.

But worship is more than singing. The word 'worship' comes from old English meaning 'worth ship'; that is, recognising what something is worth. When we worship God, what we're doing is recognising what we owe to God, who he is, what he's worth to us.

So worship is much more than singing a few songs! You can worship God in your prayers. You can worship God through art or poetry or writing. You can worship God through your actions. The fact is, whenever you tell God what he means to you, whenever you recognise what he has done for you, you're worshipping him.

Christians, of course, have many reasons to recognise God's worth; not least the fact that he has wiped away our sins and given us new life. That's something that should be celebrated.

So however you choose to worship doesn't matter. What is important is that you tell God how you feel about him and all he's done. When you recognise how great God is, then that's worship. However you choose to express it.

Being Christian: Worshipping God

• Don't just sing the songs; think about the words. Sing what you feel.

• In fact, don't just sing. Like painting? Then paint a picture which expresses how you feel about God. Write a poem. Do a dance. It doesn't matter.

• What do you think God is worth? How can you express that?

We travelled through fire
    and through floods,
    but you brought us
    to a land of plenty.
13 I will bring sacrifices
    into your house, my God,
    and I will do what I promised
14   when I was in trouble.
15 I will sacrifice my best sheep
    and offer bulls and goats on your altar.

16 All who worship God,
    come here and listen;
    I will tell you everything
    God has done for me.
17 I prayed to the Lord,
    and I praised him.
18 If my thoughts had been sinful,
    he would have refused to hear me.
19 But God did listen
    and answered my prayer.
20 Let's praise God!
    He listened when I prayed,
    and he is always kind.

Psalm 67

(A psalm and a song for the music leader. Use with stringed instruments.)

Tell the nations to praise God

1 Our God, be kind and bless us!
    Be pleased and smile.
2 Then everyone on earth
    will learn to follow you,
    and all nations will see
    your power to save us.

3 Make everyone praise you
    and shout your praises.
4 Let the nations celebrate
    with joyful songs,
    because you judge fairly
    and guide all nations.
5 Make everyone praise you
    and shout your praises.

6 Our God has blessed the earth
    with a wonderful harvest!
7 Pray for his blessings to continue
    and for everyone on earth
    to worship our God.

Psalm 68

*(A psalm and a song by David
for the music leader.)*

God will win the battle

¹ Do something, God!
   Scatter your hateful enemies.
   Make them turn and run.
² Scatter them like smoke!
   When you come near,
   make them melt like wax in a fire.
³ But let your people be happy
   and celebrate because of you.

⁴ Our God, you are the one
   who rides on the clouds,
   and we praise you.
   Your name is the LORD,
   and we celebrate as we worship you.

⁵ Our God, from your sacred home
   you take care of orphans
   and protect widows.
⁶ You find families
   for those who are lonely.
   You set prisoners free
   and let them prosper,'
   but all who rebel will live
   in a scorching desert.

⁷ You set your people free,
   and you led them
   through the desert.
⁸ God of Israel,
   the earth trembled,
   and rain poured down.
   You alone are the God
   who rules from Mount Sinai.
⁹ When your land was thirsty,
   you sent showers to refresh it.
¹⁰ Your people settled there,
   and you were generous
   to everyone in need.

¹¹ You gave the command,
   and a chorus of women told
   what had happened:
¹² "Kings and their armies
   retreated and ran,
   and everything they left
   is now being divided.
¹³ And for those who stayed back
   to guard the sheep,
   there are metal doves
   with silver-coated wings
   and shiny gold feathers."

¹⁴ God All-Powerful, you scattered the kings
   like snow falling
   on Mount Zalmon.*

¹⁵ Our LORD and our God,
   Bashan is a mighty mountain
   covered with peaks.
¹⁶ Why is it jealous of Zion,
   the mountain you chose
   as your home for ever?

¹⁷ When you, LORD God, appeared
   to your people' at Sinai,
   you came with thousands
   of mighty chariots.
¹⁸ When you climbed
   the high mountain,
   you took prisoners with you
   and were given gifts.
   Your enemies didn't want you
   to live there,
   but they gave you gifts.

¹⁹ We praise you, Lord God!
   You treat us with kindness
   day after day,
   and you rescue us.
²⁰ You always protect us
   and save us from death.

²¹ Our Lord and our God,
   your terrible enemies
   are ready for war,'
   but you will crush their skulls.
²² You promised to bring them
   from Bashan
   and from the deepest sea.
²³ Then we could stamp
   on their blood,
   and our dogs could chew
   on their bones.

²⁴ We have seen crowds marching
   to your place of worship,
   our God and King.
²⁵ The singers come first,
   and then the musicians,
   surrounded by young women
   playing tambourines.
²⁶ They come shouting,
   "People of Israel,
   praise the LORD God!"
²⁷ The small tribe of Benjamin
   leads the way,
   followed by the leaders from Judah.

*68.14 Mount Zalmon: The location of this mountain
is not known.

See also: 68.8: Exod 19.18. See also: 68.18: Eph 4.8.

Then come the leaders
  from Zebulun and Naphtali.

28 Our God, show your strength!
  Show us once again.
29 Then kings will bring gifts
  to your temple in Jerusalem.›

30 Punish that animal
  that lives in the swamp!*
Punish that nation
  whose leaders and people
  are like wild bulls.
Make them come crawling
  with gifts of silver.
Scatter those nations
  that enjoy making war.›
31 Force the Egyptians to bring
  gifts of bronze;
  make the Ethiopians* hurry
  to offer presents.›

32 Now sing praises to God!
  Every kingdom on earth,
  sing to the Lord!
33 Praise the one who rides
  across the ancient skies;
  listen as he speaks
  with a mighty voice.
34 Tell about God's power!
  He is honoured in Israel,
  and he rules the skies.
35 The God of Israel is fearsome
  in his temple,
  and he makes us strong.
  Let's praise our God!

Psalm 69

*(By David for the music leader.
To the tune "Lilies".)*

God can be trusted

1 Save me, God!
  I am about to drown.
2 I am sinking deep in the mud,
  and my feet are slipping.
I am about to be swept under
  by a mighty flood.
3 I am worn out from crying,
  and my throat is dry.

I have waited for you
  till my eyes are blurred.
4 There are more people
  who hate me for no reason
  than there are hairs on my head.
Many terrible enemies
  want to destroy me, God.
Am I supposed to give back
  something I didn't steal?
5 You know my foolish sins.
  Not one is hidden from you.

6 LORD God All-Powerful, ruler of Israel,
  don't let me embarrass anyone
  who trusts and worships you.
7 It is for your sake alone
  that I am insulted
  and blush with shame.
8 I am like a stranger to my relatives
  and like a foreigner to my own family.

9 My love for your house
  burns in me like a fire,
and when others insulted you,
  they insulted me as well.
10 I cried and went without food,*
  but they still insulted me.
11 They sneered at me
  for wearing sackcloth*
  to show my sorrow.
12 Rulers and judges gossip about me,
  and drunkards make up songs
  to mock me.

13 But I pray to you, LORD.
So when the time is right, answer me
  and help me
  with your wonderful love.
14 Don't let me sink in the mud,
  but save me from my enemies
  and from the deep water.
15 Don't let me be swept away by a flood
  or drowned in the ocean
  or swallowed by death.

16 Answer me, LORD!
  You are kind and good.
Pay attention to me!
  You are truly merciful.
17 Don't turn away from me.
  I am your servant,
  and I am in trouble.
Please hurry and help!
18   Come and save me from my enemies.

68.30 animal . . . swamp: Probably Egypt.
68.31 the Ethiopians: The Hebrew text has "the
people of Cush", which was a region south of Egypt
that included parts of the present countries of
Ethiopia and Sudan.

69.10 went without food: See the note at 35.13.
69.11 sackcloth: See the note at 30.11.
See also: 69.4: Psa 35.19; John 15.25. 69.9: John 2.17;
Rom 15.3.

¹⁹ You know how I am insulted,
   mocked, and disgraced;
   you know every one of my enemies.
²⁰ I am crushed by insults, and I feel sick.
   I had hoped for mercy and pity,
   but there was none.
²¹ Enemies poisoned my food,
   and when I was thirsty,
   they gave me vinegar.

²² Make their table a trap
   for them and their friends.
²³ Blind them with darkness
   and make them tremble.
²⁴ Show them how angry you are!
   Be furious and catch them.
²⁵ Destroy their camp
   and don't let anyone live in their tents.

²⁶ They cause trouble for people
   you have already punished;
   their gossip hurts those
   you have wounded.
²⁷ Make them guiltier than ever
   and don't forgive them.
²⁸ Wipe their names from the book
   of the living;
   remove them from the list
   of the innocent.
²⁹ I am ill-treated and in pain.
   Protect me, God,
   and keep me safe!

³⁰ I will praise the LORD God
   with a song and a thankful heart.
³¹ This will please the LORD
   better than offering an ox
   or a full-grown bull.
³² When those in need see this,
   they will be happy,
   and the LORD's worshippers
   will be encouraged.
³³ The LORD will listen
   when the homeless cry out,
   and he will never forget
   his people in prison.

³⁴ Heaven and earth will praise our God,
   and so will the oceans
   and everything in them.
³⁵ God will rescue Jerusalem,
   and he will rebuild the towns of Judah.
   His people will live there
   on their own land,
³⁶ and when the time comes,
   their children will inherit the land.

Then everyone who loves God
   will also settle there.

Psalm 70

*(By David for the music leader.
To be used when an offering is made.)*

God is wonderful

¹ Save me, LORD God!
   Hurry and help.
² Disappoint and confuse
   all who want to kill me.
Turn away and disgrace
   all who want to hurt me.
³ Embarrass and shame those
   who say, "We told you so!"

⁴ Let your worshippers celebrate
   and be glad because of you.
They love your saving power,
   so let them always say,
   "God is wonderful!"
⁵ I am poor and needy,
   but you, the LORD God,
   care about me.
You are the one who saves me.
   Please hurry and help!

Psalm 71

A prayer for God's protection

¹ I run to you, LORD, for protection.
   Don't disappoint me.
² You do what is right,
   so come to my rescue.
   Listen to my prayer and keep me safe.
³ Be my mighty rock,*
   the place where I can always run
   for protection.
Save me by your command!
   You are my mighty rock and my fortress.

⁴ Come and save me, LORD God,
   from vicious and cruel
   and brutal enemies!
⁵ I depend on you,
   and I have trusted you
   since I was young.
⁶ I have relied on you
   from the day I was born.
You brought me safely through birth,
   and I always praise you.

⁷ Many people think of me
   as something evil.

See also: **69.21:** Matt 27.48; Mark 15.36; Luke 23.26;
John 19.28–29.   **69.22–23:** Rom 11.9–10.   **69.25:** Acts 1.20.
69.28: Exod 32.32; Rev 3.5; 13.8; 17.8.

*71.3 mighty rock: See the note at 18.2.

Viewpoints

What can we learn from David's life?

Contributed by Naomi H

'Many people think of me as something evil. But you are my mighty protector'

This Psalm is written toward the end of a long life spent walking closely with God. It had not all been easy: David had made some vicious enemies – but as he looks back over the years he realises that God never once left him.

It's fine to say this when you've got a whole lifetime to look back on – but what about when we're young and we haven't got years of victories behind us?

We need to realise that although something may be new and scary to us, God has placed it into our life in order to teach us something specific from it. He wants to help us through! It's easy to feel sometimes that God's faithfulness starts when we're old and wise – but we'd never get old or wise if he wasn't faithful all the way through!

And notice the result of this faith and protection. Everyone else saw how David had come unharmed through so much, and they were able to discern God at work.

You've probably heard or read stuff like this a good few hundred times before in your life so just take a minute now to think about what it really means, that God is our strength and our protection, our whole life long, and pray that he will help us to trust him so much more, for our help, for others' encouragement and for his glory.

More...

David p.314
Help! I've messed up really badly p.347
Forgiveness p.614
Suffering p.555

But you are my mighty protector,
8 and I praise and honour you
    all day long.
9 Don't throw me aside when I am old;
    don't desert me
    when my strength is gone.
10 My enemies are plotting
    because they want me dead.
11 They say, "Now we'll catch you!
    God has deserted you,
    and no one can save you."
12 Come closer, God!
    Please hurry and help.
13 Embarrass and destroy
    all who want me dead;
    disgrace and confuse
    all who want to hurt me.
14 I will never give up hope
    or stop praising you.
15 All day long I will tell
    the wonderful things you do
    to save your people.
    But you have done much more
    than I could possibly know.
16 I will praise you, LORD God,
    for your mighty deeds
    and your power to save.

17 You have taught me since I was a child,
    and I never stop telling about
    your marvellous deeds.
18 Don't leave me when I am old
    and my hair turns grey.
    Let me tell future generations
    about your mighty power.
19 Your deeds of kindness
    are known in the heavens.
    No one is like you!

20 You made me suffer a lot,
    but you will bring me
    back from this deep pit
    and give me new life.
21 You will make me truly great
    and take my sorrow away.

22 I will praise you, God,
    the Holy One of Israel.
    You are faithful.
    I will play the harp
    and sing your praises.
23 You have rescued me!
    I will celebrate and shout,
    singing praises to you with all my heart.
24 All day long I will announce
    your power to save.
    I will tell how you disgraced
    and disappointed
    those who wanted to hurt me.

Psalm 72

(By Solomon.)

A prayer for God to guide and help the king

1 Please help the king
   to be honest and fair
   just like you, our God.
2 Let him be honest and fair
   with all your people,
   especially the poor.
3 Let peace and justice rule
   every mountain and hill.
4 Let the king defend the poor,
   rescue the homeless,
   and crush everyone who hurts them.
5 Let the king live* for ever
   like the sun and the moon.
6 Let him be as helpful as rain
   that refreshes the meadows
   and the ground.
7 Let the king be fair with everyone,
   and let there be peace
   until the moon
   falls from the sky.

8 Let his kingdom reach from sea to sea,
   from the River Euphrates
   across all the earth.
9 Force the desert tribes
   to accept his rule,
   and make his enemies
   crawl in the dust.
10 Force the rulers of Tarshish*
   and of the islands
   to pay taxes to him.
   Make the kings of Sheba
   and of Seba* bring gifts.
11 Make other rulers bow down
   and all nations serve him.

12 Do this because the king
   rescues the homeless
   when they cry out,
   and he helps everyone
   who is poor and in need.
13 The king has pity
   on the weak and the helpless
   and protects those in need.
14 He cares when they suffer,
   and he saves them from cruel
   and violent deaths.

15 Long live the king!
   Give him gold from Sheba.
   Always pray for the king
   and praise him each day.
16 Let cities overflow with food
   and hills be covered with grain,
   just like Mount Lebanon.
   Let the people in the cities
   prosper like wild flowers.
17 May the glory of the king
   shine brightly for ever
   like the sun in the sky.
   Let him make nations prosper
   and learn to praise him.

18 LORD God of Israel, we praise you.
   Only you can work miracles.
19 We will always praise
   your glorious name.
   Let your glory be seen
   everywhere on earth.
   Amen and amen.

20 This ends the prayers
   of David, the son of Jesse.

BOOK 3

(Psalms 73–89)

Psalm 73

(A psalm by Asaph.)

God is good

1 God is truly good to Israel,*
   especially to everyone
   with a pure heart.
2 But I almost stumbled and fell,
3 because it made me jealous
   to see proud and evil people
   and to watch them prosper.
4 They never have to suffer,*
   they stay healthy,
5 and they don't have troubles
   like everyone else.

6 Their pride is like a necklace,
   and they commit sin
   more often than they dress themselves.
7 Their eyes bulge with fat,
   and their minds are flooded
   with foolish thoughts.
8 They sneer and say cruel things,
   and because of their pride,
   they make violent threats.
9 They dare to speak against God
   and to order others around.

---

*72.10 Tarshish: Possibly a city in Spain.
*72.10 Sheba . . . Seba: Sheba may have been a place in what is now south-west Arabia, and Seba may have been in southern Arabia.
See also: 72.8: Zech 9.10.

¹⁰ God will bring his people back,
  and they will drink the water
  he so freely gives.'

¹¹ Only evil people would say,
  "God Most High cannot
  know everything!"

¹² Yet all goes well for them,
  and they live in peace.

¹³ What good did it do me
  to keep my thoughts pure
  and refuse to do wrong?

¹⁴ I am sick all day,
  and I am punished each morning.

¹⁵ If I had said evil things,
  I would not have been loyal
  to your people.

¹⁶ It was hard for me
  to understand all this!

¹⁷ Then I went to your temple,
  and there I understood
  what will happen to my enemies.

¹⁸ You will make them stumble,
  never to get up again.

¹⁹ They will be terrified,
  suddenly swept away
  and no longer there.

²⁰ They will disappear, Lord,
  despised like a bad dream
  the morning after.

²¹ Once I was bitter
  and brokenhearted.

²² I was stupid and ignorant,
  and I treated you
  as a wild animal would.

²³ But I never really left you,
  and you hold my right hand.

²⁴ Your advice has been my guide,
  and later you will welcome me
  in glory.'

²⁵ In heaven I have only you,
  and on this earth you are all I want.

²⁶ My body and mind may fail,
  but you are my strength
  and my choice for ever.

²⁷ Powerful LORD God,
  all who stay far from you will be lost,
  and you will destroy those
  who are unfaithful.

²⁸ It is good for me to be near you.
  I choose you as my protector,
  and I will tell about
  your wonderful deeds.

Psalm 74

(A special psalm by Asaph.)

A prayer for the nation in times of trouble

¹ Our God, why have you
  completely rejected us?
  Why are you so angry
  with the ones you care for?

² Remember the people
  you rescued long ago,
  the tribe you chose to be your very own.

Think of Mount Zion, your home;

³ walk over to the temple
  left in ruins for ever
  by those who hate us.

⁴ Your enemies roared like lions
  in your holy temple,
  and they have placed their banners there.

⁵ It looks like a forest chopped to pieces.'

⁶ They used axes and hatchets
  to smash the carvings.

⁷ They burnt down your temple
  and badly disgraced it.

⁸ They said to themselves,
  "We'll crush them!"
  Then they burnt every one
  of your meeting places
  all over the country.

⁹ There are no more miracles
  and no more prophets.
  Who knows how long it will be like this?

¹⁰ Our God, how much longer
  will our enemies sneer?
  Won't they ever stop insulting you?

¹¹ Why don't you punish them?
  Why are you holding back?

¹² Our God and King, you have ruled
  since ancient times;
  you have won victories
  everywhere on this earth.

¹³ By your power you made a path
  through the sea,
  and you smashed the heads
  of sea monsters.

¹⁴ You crushed the heads
  of the monster Leviathan,*
  then fed him to wild creatures
  in the desert.

---

*74.14 Leviathan: God's victory over this monster sometimes stands for his power over all creation and sometimes for his defeat of Egypt.

See also: **74.13:** Exod 14.21. **74.14:** Job 41.1; Psa 104.26; Isa 27.1.

¹⁵ You opened the ground
    for streams and springs
    and dried up mighty rivers.
¹⁶ You rule the day and the night,
    and you put the moon
    and the sun in place.
¹⁷ You made summer and winter
    and gave them to the earth.ᐟ

¹⁸ Remember your enemies, LORD!
    They foolishly sneer
    and won't respect you.
¹⁹ You treat us like pet doves,
    but they ill-treat us.
    Don't keep forgetting us
    and letting us be fed
    to those wild animals.
²⁰ Remember the agreement
    you made with us.
    Violent enemies are hiding
    in every dark corner of the earth.
²¹ Don't disappoint those in need
    or make them turn from you,
    but help the poor and homeless
    to shout your praises.
²² Do something, God! Defend yourself.
    Remember how those fools
    sneer at you all day long.
²³ Don't forget the loud shouts
    of your enemies.

Psalm 75

(A psalm and a song by Asaph for the music leader. To the tune "Don't Destroy".ᐟ)

Praise God for all he has done

¹ Our God, we thank you
    for being so near to us!
    Everyone celebrates
    your wonderful deeds.

² You have set a time
    to judge with fairness.
³ The earth trembles,
    and its people shake;
    you alone keep its foundations firm.
⁴ You tell every boaster,
    "Stop boasting!"
    And to the wicked you say,
    "Don't boast of your power!
⁵ Stop boasting! Stop telling me
    how great you are."

⁶ Our LORD and our God,
    victory doesn't come
    from the east or the west
    or from the desert.

⁷ You are the one who judges.
    You can take away power
    and give it to others.
⁸ You hold in your hand
    a cup filled with wine,*
    strong and foaming.
    You will pour out some
    for every sinful person on this earth,
    and they will have to drink
    until it is gone.
⁹ But I will always tell about you,
    the God of Jacob,
    and I will sing your praise.

¹⁰ Our Lord, you will destroy
    the power of evil people,
    but you will give strength
    to those who are good.

Psalm 76

(A song and a psalm for the music leader. Use stringed instruments.)

God always wins

¹ You, our God, are famous in Judah
    and honoured in Israel.
² Your home is on Mount Zion
    in the city of peace.
³ There you destroyed
    fiery arrows, shields, swords,
    and all the other weapons.

⁴ You are more glorious than
    the eternal mountains.ᐟ
⁵ Brave warriors were robbed
    of what they had taken,
    and now they lie dead,
    unable to lift an arm.
⁶ God of Jacob, when you roar,
    enemy chariots and horses
    drop dead in their tracks.

⁷ Our God, you are fearsome,
    and no one can oppose you
    when you are angry.
⁸ From heaven you announced
    your decisions as judge!
    And all who live on this earth
    were terrified and silent
⁹ when you took over as judge,
    ready to rescue everyone in need.
¹⁰ Even the most angry people
    will praise you
    when you are furious.ᐟ

---

*75.8 a cup . . . wine: In the Old Testament "a cup filled with wine" sometimes stands for God's anger.

11 Everyone, make your promises
   to the LORD your God
   and do what you promise.
The LORD is fearsome,
   and all his servants
   should bring him gifts.
12 God destroys the courage
   of rulers and kings
   and makes cowards of them.

Psalm 77

*(A psalm by Asaph for Jeduthun,
the music leader.)*

In times of trouble
God is with his people

1 I pray to you, Lord God,
   and I beg you to listen.
2   In days filled with trouble,
   I search for you.
And at night I tirelessly
   lift my hands in prayer,
   refusing comfort.
3 When I think of you,
   I feel restless and weak.

4 Because of you, Lord God,
   I can't sleep.
I am restless and can't even talk.
5   I think of times gone by,
   of those years long ago.
6 Each night my mind
   is flooded with questions:'
7 "Have you rejected me for ever?
   Won't you be kind again?
8 Is this the end of your love
   and your promises?
9 Have you forgotten how to have pity?
   Do you refuse to show mercy
   because of your anger?"
10 Then I said, "God Most High,
   what hurts me most
   is that you no longer help us
   with your mighty arm."

11 Our LORD, I will remember
   the things you have done,
   your miracles of long ago.
12 I will think about each one
   of your mighty deeds.
13 Everything you do is right,
   and no other god compares with you.
14 You alone work miracles,
   and you have let nations
   see your mighty power.

15 With your own arm you rescued
   your people,
   the descendants of Jacob and Joseph.

16 The ocean looked at you, God,
   and it trembled deep down with fear.
17 Water flowed from the clouds.
   Thunder was heard above
   as your arrows of lightning flashed about.
18 Your thunder roared like chariot wheels.
   The world was made bright by lightning,
   and all the earth trembled.

19 You walked through the water
   of the mighty sea,
   but your footprints were never seen.
20 You guided your people
   like a flock of sheep,
   and you chose Moses and Aaron
   to be their leaders.

Psalm 78

(A special psalm by Asaph.)

What God has done for his people

1 My friends, I beg you
   to listen as I teach.
2 I will give instruction
   and explain the mystery
   of what happened long ago.
3 These are things we learnt
   from our ancestors,
4   and we will tell them
   to the next generation.
We won't keep secret the glorious deeds
   and the mighty miracles of the LORD.

5 God gave his Law
   to Jacob's descendants,
   the people of Israel.
And he told our ancestors
   to teach their children,
6 so that each new generation
   would know his Law
   and tell it to the next.
7 Then they would trust God
   and obey his teachings,
   without forgetting anything
   God had done.
8 They would be different
   from their ancestors,
   who were stubborn, rebellious,
   and unfaithful to God.

9 The warriors from Ephraim
   were armed with arrows,

See also: 78.2: Matt 13.35.

but they ran away when the battle began.
10 They broke their agreement with God,
   and they turned their backs
   on his teaching.
11 They forgot all he had done,
   even the mighty miracles
12 he did for their ancestors
   near Zoan* in Egypt.

13 God made a path in the sea
   and piled up the water
   as he led them across.
14 He guided them during the day
   with a cloud,
   and each night he led them
   with a flaming fire.
15 God made water flow from rocks
   he split open in the desert,
   and his people drank freely,
   as though from a lake.
16 He made streams gush out
   like rivers from rocks.

17 But in the desert,
   the people of God Most High
   kept sinning and rebelling.
18 They stubbornly tested God
   and demanded from him
   what they wanted to eat.
19 They challenged God by saying,
   "Can God provide food
   out here in the desert?
20 It's true God struck the rock
   and water gushed out like a river,
   but can he give his people
   bread and meat?"

21 When the LORD heard this,
   he was angry and furious
   with Jacob's descendants,
   the people of Israel.
22 They had refused to trust him,
   and they had doubted his saving power.

23 But God gave a command to the clouds,
   and he opened the doors in the skies.
24 From heaven he sent grain
   that they called manna.*

25 He gave them more than enough,
   and each one of them ate
   this special food.

26 God's mighty power
   brought a strong wind
   from the south-east,
27 and it brought birds
   that covered the ground,
   like sand on the beach.
28 Then God made the birds fall
   in the camp of his people
   near their tents.

29 God gave his people all they wanted,
   and each of them ate
   until they were full.
30 But before they had swallowed the last bite,
31 God became angry and killed the strongest
   and best from the families of Israel.

32 But the rest kept on sinning
   and would not trust God's miracles.
33 So he cut their lives short
   and made them terrified.
34 After he killed some of them,
   the others turned to him
   with all their hearts.
35 They remembered God Most High,
   the mighty rock* that kept them safe.
36 But they tried to flatter God,
   and they told him lies;
37 they were unfaithful
   and broke their promises.

38 Yet God was kind.
   He kept forgiving their sins
   and didn't destroy them.
   He often became angry,
   but never lost his temper.
39 God remembered that they
   were made of flesh
   and were like a wind that blows once
   and then dies down.

40 While they were in the desert,
   they often rebelled and made God sad.
41 They kept testing him
   and caused terrible pain
   for the Holy One of Israel.
42 They forgot about his power
   and how he had rescued them
   from their enemies.

43 God showed them all kinds
   of wonderful miracles
   near Zoan* in Egypt.

---

*78.12 Zoan: A city in the eastern part of the Nile Delta.
*78.24 manna: When the people of Israel were wandering through the desert, the Lord gave them a special kind of food to eat. It tasted like a wafer and was called "manna", which in Hebrew means, "What is this?"

See also: 78.12: Exod 7.8–12.32. 78.13: Exod 14.21–22. 78.14: Exod 13.21–22. 78.15,16: Exod 17.1–7; Num 20.2–13. 78.18–31: Exod 16.2–15; Num 11.4–23,31–35. 78.24: John 6.31.

---

*78.35 mighty rock: See the note at 18.2.
*78.43 Zoan: See the note at 78.12.
See also: 78.37: Acts 8.21.

44 He turned the rivers
  of Egypt into blood,
  and no one could drink
    from the streams.
45 He sent swarms of flies
  to pester the Egyptians,
  and he sent frogs
    to cause them trouble.

46 God let worms and grasshoppers
  eat their crops.
47 He destroyed their grapevines
  and their fig trees
  with hail and floods.'
48 Then he killed their cattle with hail
  and their other animals
  with lightning.

49 God was so angry and furious
  that he went into a rage
  and caused them great trouble
  by sending swarms
  of destroying angels.
50 God gave in to his anger
  and slaughtered them
  in a terrible way.
51 He killed the firstborn son
  of each Egyptian family.

52 Then God led his people out of Egypt
  and guided them in the desert
  like a flock of sheep.
53 He led them safely along,
  and they were not afraid,
  but their enemies drowned in the sea.

54 God brought his people
  to the sacred mountain
  that he had taken by his own power.
55 He made nations run
  from the tribes of Israel,
  and he let the tribes
  take over their land.

56 But the people tested God Most High,
  and they refused to obey his laws.
57 They were as unfaithful
  as their ancestors,
  and they were as crooked
  as a twisted arrow.
58 God demanded all their love,
  but they made him angry
  by worshipping idols.

59 So God became furious
  and completely rejected
  the people of Israel.
60 Then he deserted his home at Shiloh,
  where he lived here on earth.
61 He let enemies capture
  the sacred chest*
  and let them dishonour him.

62 God took out his anger
  on his chosen ones
  and let them be killed by enemy swords.
63 Fire destroyed the young men,
  and the young women were left
  with no one to marry.
64 Priests died violent deaths,
  but their widows
  were not allowed to mourn.

65 Finally the Lord woke up,
  and he shouted like a drunken soldier.
66 God scattered his enemies
  and made them ashamed for ever.

67 Then the Lord decided
  not to make his home
  with Joseph's descendants in Ephraim.*
68 Instead he chose the tribe of Judah,
  and he chose Mount Zion,
  the place he loves.
69 There he built his temple
  as lofty as the mountains
  and as solid as the earth
  that he had made to last for ever.

70 The Lord God chose David
  to be his servant
  and took him from tending sheep
71   and from caring for lambs.
  Then God made him the leader
  of Israel, his own nation.
72 David treated the people fairly
  and guided them with wisdom.

---

*78.61 sacred chest: The Hebrew text has "his power", which refers to the sacred chest. In Psalm 132.8 it is called "powerful".

*78.67 with . . . Ephraim: Ephraim was Joseph's youngest son. One of the twelve tribes was named after him, and sometimes the northern kingdom of Israel was also known as Ephraim. The town of Shiloh was in the territory of Ephraim, but the place where God was worshipped was moved from there to Zion (Jerusalem) in the territory of Judah.

See also: **78.60**: Josh 18.1; Jer 7.12–14; 26.6. **78.61**: 1 Sam 4.4–22. **78.70–71**: 1 Sam 16.11–12; 2 Sam 7.8; 1 Chron 17.7.

See also: **78.44**: Exod 7.17–21. **78.45**: a Exod 8.20–24; b Exod 8.1–6. **78.46**: Exod 10.12–15. **78.47–48**: Exod 9.22–25. **78.51**: Exod 12.29. **78.52**: Exod 13.17–22. **78.53**: Exod 14.26–28. **78.54**: Exod 15.17; Josh 3.14–17. **78.55**: Josh 11.16–23. **78.56**: Judg 2.11–15.

Psalm 79

(A psalm by Asaph.)

Have pity on Jerusalem

¹ Our God, foreign nations
    have taken your land,
    disgraced your temple,
    and left Jerusalem in ruins.
² They have fed the bodies
    of your servants
  to flesh-eating birds;
    your loyal people are food
    for savage animals.
³ All Jerusalem is covered
    with their blood,
    and there is no one left to bury them.
⁴ Every nation around us
    sneers and makes fun.

⁵ Our LORD,
    will you keep on being angry?
    Will your angry feelings
    keep flaming up like fire?
⁶ Get angry with those nations
    that don't know you
    and won't worship you!
⁷ They have gobbled up
    Jacob's descendants
    and left the land in ruins.

⁸ Don't make us pay for the sins
    of our ancestors.
    Have pity and come quickly!
    We are completely helpless.
⁹ Our God, you keep us safe.
    Now help us! Rescue us.
    Forgive our sins
    and bring honour to yourself.

¹⁰ Why should nations ask us,
    "Where is your God?"
  Let us and the other nations
    see you take revenge
    for your servants who died
    a violent death.

¹¹ Listen to the prisoners groan!
    Let your mighty power save all
    who are sentenced to die.
¹² Each of those nations sneered
    at you, our Lord.
  Now let others sneer at them,
    seven times as much.
¹³ Then we, your people,
    will always thank you.

See also: 79.1: 2 King 25.8–10; 2 Chron 36.17–19; Jer 52.12–14.

We are like sheep
    with you as our shepherd,
    and all generations
    will hear us praise you.

Psalm 80

(A psalm by Asaph for the music leader. To the tune "Lilies of the Agreement".)

Help our nation

¹ Shepherd of Israel, you lead
    the descendants of Joseph,
  and you sit on your throne
    above the winged creatures.*
  Listen to our prayer
    and let your light shine
² for the tribes of Ephraim,
    Benjamin, and Manasseh.
  Save us by your power.

³ Our God, make us strong again!
    Smile on us and save us.

⁴ LORD God All-Powerful,
    how much longer
    will the prayers of your people
    make you angry?
⁵ You gave us tears for food,
    and you made us drink them
    by the bowlful.
⁶ Because of you,
    our enemies who live nearby
    laugh and joke about us.
⁷ But if you smile on us, we will be saved.

⁸ We were like a grapevine
    you brought out of Egypt.
    You chased other nations away
    and planted us here.
⁹ Then you cleared the ground,
    and we put our roots deep,
    spreading over the land.
¹⁰ Shade from this vine
    covered the mountains.
    Its branches climbed the mighty cedars
¹¹ and stretched to the sea;
    its new growth reached to the river.*

80.1 winged creatures: Two winged creatures
made of gold were on the top of the sacred chest
and were symbols of the LORD's throne on earth
(see Exodus 25.18).
80.11 the sea . . . the river: The Mediterranean Sea
and the River Euphrates were part of the ideal
boundaries for Israel.
See also: 80.1: Exod 25.22.

12 Our Lord, why have you
  torn down the wall
  from around the vineyard?
  You let everyone who walks by
  pick the grapes.
13 Now the vine is gobbled up
  by pigs from the forest
  and other wild animals.

14 God All-Powerful,
  please do something!
  Look down from heaven
  and see what's happening
  to this vine.
15 With your own hands
  you planted its roots,
  and you raised it as your very own.

16 Enemies chopped the vine down
  and set it on fire.
  Now show your anger and destroy them.
17 But help the one who sits
  at your right side,*
  the one you raised to be your own.
18 Then we will never turn away.
  Put new life into us,
  and we will worship you.

19 LORD God All-Powerful,
  make us strong again!
  Smile on us and save us.

Psalm 81

(By Asaph for the music leader.)*

God makes us strong

1 Be happy and shout to God
  who makes us strong!
  Shout praises to the God of Jacob.
2 Sing as you play tambourines
  and the lovely sounding
  stringed instruments.
3 Sound the trumpets and start
  the New Moon Festival.*
  We must also celebrate
  when the moon is full.
4 This is the law in Israel,
  and it was given to us
  by the God of Jacob.

5 The descendants of Joseph
  were told to obey it,
  when God led them out
  from the land of Egypt.

In a language unknown to me,
  I heard someone say:
6 "I lifted the burden from your shoulder
  and took the heavy basket
  from your hands.
7 When you were in trouble,
  I rescued you,
  and from the thunderclouds,
  I answered your prayers.
  Later I tested you at Meribah Spring.*

8 "Listen, my people,
  while I, the Lord, correct you!
  Israel, if you would only
  pay attention to me!
9 Don't worship foreign gods
  or bow down to gods
  you know nothing about.
10 I am the LORD your God.
  I rescued you from Egypt.
  Just ask, and I will give you
  whatever you need.

11 "But, my people, Israel,
  you refused to listen,
  and you would have nothing
  to do with me!
12 So I let you be stubborn
  and keep on following
  your own advice.

13 "My people, Israel,
  if only you would listen
  and do as I say!
14 I, the LORD, would quickly
  defeat your enemies
  with my mighty power.
15 Everyone who hates me
  would come crawling,
  and that would be the end of them.
16 But I would feed you
  with the finest bread
  and with the best honey‣
  until you were full."

---

*80.17 right side: See the note at 16.11.
*Psalm 81 leader: See the note at Psalm 8.
*81.3 New Moon Festival: Celebrated on the first
day of each new moon, which was the beginning of
the month. But this may refer to either the New Year
celebration or the Harvest Festival. "The moon is full"
suggests a festival in the middle of the month.
See also: 81.3: Num 10.10.

*81.7 Meribah Spring: When the people of Israel
complained to Moses about the need for water, God
commanded Moses to strike a rock with his walking
stick, and water came out. The place was then named
Massah ("test") and Meribah ("complaining").
See also: 81.7: Exod 17.7; Num 20.13.   81.9: Exod 20.2–3;
Deut 5.6–7.

Psalm 82

(A psalm by Asaph.)

Please do something, God!

1 When all the other gods*
   have come together,
   the Lord God judges them and says:
2 "How long will you keep judging unfairly
   and favouring evil people?
3 Be fair to the poor and to orphans.
   Defend the helpless
   and everyone in need.
4 Rescue the weak and homeless
   from the powerful hands
   of heartless people.

5 "None of you know
   or understand a thing.
   You live in darkness,
   while the foundations
   of the earth tremble.*

6 "I, the Most High God, say
   that all of you are gods*
   and also my own children.
7 But you will die,
   just like everyone else,
   including powerful rulers."

8 Do something, God!
   Judge the nations of the earth;
   they belong to you.

Psalm 83

(A song and a psalm by Asaph.)

God rules all the earth

1 Our God, don't just sit there,
   silently doing nothing!
2 Your hateful enemies
   are turning against you and rebelling.
3 They are sly, and they plot
   against those you treasure.
4 They say, "Let's wipe out
   the nation of Israel
   and make sure that no one
   remembers its name!"

5 All of them fully agree
   in their plans against you,
   and among them are
6 Edom and the Ishmaelites;
   Moab and the Hagrites;
7 Gebal, Ammon, and Amalek;
   Philistia and Phoenicia.ᵇ
8 Even Assyria has joined forces
   with Moab and Ammon.*

9 Our Lord, punish all of them
   as you punished Midian.
   Destroy them, as you destroyed
   Sisera and Jabin
   at Kishon Creek
10   near Endor,
   and let their bodies rot.
11 Treat their leaders as you did
   Oreb and Zeeb,
   Zebah and Zalmunna.
12 All of them said, "We'll take
   God's valuable land!"

13 Our God, scatter them around
   like dust in a whirlwind.
14 Just as flames destroy forests
   on the mountains,
15   pursue and terrify them
   with storms of your own.
16 Make them blush with shame,
   until they turn and worship
   you, our LORD.
17 Let them be for ever ashamed
   and confused.
   Let them die in disgrace.
18 Make them realize that you
   are the LORD Most High,
   the only ruler of earth!

Psalm 84

(For the music leader. A psalm for
the people of Korah.)*

The joy of worship

1 LORD God All-Powerful,
   your temple is so lovely!
2 Deep in my heart I long for your temple,
   and with all that I am
   I sing joyful songs to you.

---

*82.1 the other gods:** This probably refers to the
gods of the nations that God defeated, but it could
refer to God's servants (angels) in heaven or even to
human rulers.
*82.5 foundations . . . tremble:** In ancient times it
was believed that the earth was flat and supported by
columns.
*82.6 all of you are gods:** See the note at 82.1.
See also: 82.6: John 10.34.

*83.8 Moab and Ammon:** The Hebrew text has "the
descendants of Lot", whose elder daughter was the
mother of the Moabites and whose younger
daughter was the mother of the Ammonites (see
Genesis 19.30–38).
*Psalm 84 leader:** See the note at Psalm 8.
See also: 83.9: a Judg 7.1–23; **b** Judg 4.6–22.
83.11: a Judg 7.25; **b** Judg 8.12.

³ LORD God All-Powerful,
  my King and my God,
sparrows find a home near your altars;
  swallows build nests there
  to raise their young.

⁴ You bless everyone
  who lives in your house,
  and they sing your praises.
⁵ You bless all who depend
  on you for their strength
  and all who deeply desire
  to visit your temple.
⁶ When they reach Dry Valley,'
  springs start flowing,
  and the autumn rain fills it
  with pools of water.'
⁷ Your people grow stronger,
  and you, the God of gods,
  will be seen in Zion.

⁸ LORD God All-Powerful,
  the God of Jacob,
  please answer my prayer!
⁹ You are the shield
  that protects your people,
  and I am your chosen one.
  Won't you smile on me?

¹⁰ One day in your temple is better
  than a thousand anywhere else.
  I would rather serve in your house,
  than live in the homes of the wicked.

¹¹ Our LORD and our God,
  you are like the sun
  and also like a shield.
  You treat us with kindness
  and with honour,
  never denying any good thing
  to those who live right.

¹² LORD God All-Powerful,
  you bless everyone who trusts you.

Psalm 85

*(A psalm by the people of Korah
for the music leader.)*

A prayer for peace

¹ Our LORD, you have blessed your land
  and made all go well
  for Jacob's descendants.
² You have forgiven the sin
  and taken away the guilt
  of your people.
³ Your fierce anger is no longer
  aimed at us.

⁴ Our LORD and our God, you save us!
  Please bring us back home
  and don't be angry.
⁵ Will you always be angry
  with us and our families?
⁶ Won't you give us fresh life
  and let your people be glad
  because of you?
⁷ Show us your love and save us!

⁸ I will listen to you, LORD God,
  because you promise peace to those
  who are faithful and no longer foolish.
⁹ You are ready to rescue
  everyone who worships you,
  so that you will live with us
  in all your glory.

¹⁰ Love and loyalty will come together;
  goodness and peace will unite.
¹¹ Loyalty will sprout from the ground;
  justice will look down
  from the sky above.

¹² Our LORD, you will bless us;
  our land will produce wonderful crops.
¹³ Justice will march in front,
  making a path for you to follow.

Psalm 86

(A prayer by David.)

A prayer for help

¹ Please listen, LORD,
  and answer my prayer!
  I am poor and helpless.
² Protect me and save me
  because you are my God.
  I am your faithful servant,
  and I trust you.
³ Be kind to me! I pray to you all day.
⁴ Make my heart glad!
  I serve you, and my prayer is sincere.
⁵ You willingly forgive,
  and your love is always there
  for those who pray to you.
⁶ Please listen, LORD!
  Answer my prayer for help.
⁷ When I am in trouble, I pray,
  knowing you will listen.

⁸ No other gods are like you;
  only you work miracles.
⁹ You created each nation,
  and they will all bow down
  to worship and honour you.

See also: **86.9:** Rev 15.4.

¹⁰ You perform great wonders
because you alone are God.

¹¹ Teach me to follow you,
and I will obey your truth.
Always keep me faithful.
¹² With all my heart I thank you.
I praise you, LORD God.
¹³ Your love for me is so great
that you protected me
from death and the grave.

¹⁴ Proud and violent enemies,
who don't care about you,
have ganged up to attack and kill me.
¹⁵ But you, the Lord God,
are kind and merciful.
You don't easily get angry,
and your love can always be trusted.
¹⁶ I serve you, LORD,
and I am the child of one of your servants.
Look on me with kindness.
Make me strong and save me.
¹⁷ Show that you approve of me!
Then my hateful enemies
will feel like fools,
because you have helped
and comforted me.

Psalm 87

(A psalm and a song by the people of Korah.)

The glory of Mount Zion

¹ Zion was built by the LORD
on the holy mountain,
² and he loves that city
more than any other place in all of Israel.
³ Zion, you are the city of God,
and wonderful things are told about you.

⁴ Egypt,* Babylonia, Philistia,
Phoenicia,* and Ethiopia*
are some of those nations that know you,
and their people all say,
"I was born in Zion."

⁵ God Most High will strengthen
the city of Zion.
Then everyone will say,
"We were born here too."
⁶ The LORD will make a list of his people,
and all who were born here
will be included.

⁷ All who sing or dance will say,
"I too am from Zion."

---

*87.4 Phoenicia: See the note at 83.7.
*87.4 Ethiopia: See the note at 68.31.

Psalm 88

*(A song and a psalm by the people of Korah
for the music leader. To the tune "Mahalath
Leannoth".* A special psalm by Heman the
Ezrahite.)*

A prayer when you can't find the way

¹ You keep me safe, LORD God.
So when I pray at night,
² please listen carefully
to each of my concerns.

³ I am deeply troubled
and close to death;
⁴ I am as good as dead
and completely helpless.
⁵ I am no better off
than those in the grave,
those you have forgotten
and no longer help.

⁶ You have put me in the deepest
and darkest grave;
⁷ your anger rolls over me
like ocean waves.
⁸ You have made my friends turn
in horror from me.
I am a prisoner who cannot escape,
⁹ and I am almost blind
because of my sorrow.

Each day I lift my hands
in prayer to you, LORD.
¹⁰ Do you work miracles for the dead?
Do they stand up and praise you?
¹¹ Are your love and loyalty announced
in the world of the dead?
¹² Do they know of your miracles
or your saving power
in the dark world below
where all is forgotten?

¹³ Each morning I pray to you, LORD.
¹⁴ Why do you reject me?
Why do you turn from me?
¹⁵ Ever since I was a child,
I have been sick and close to death.
You have terrified me
and made me helpless.*

¹⁶ Your anger is like a flood!
And I am shattered by your furious attacks
¹⁷ that strike each day
and from every side.
¹⁸ My friends and neighbours
have turned against me because of you,
and now darkness
is my only companion.

Psalm 89

(A special psalm by Ethan the Ezrahite.)

The LORD's agreement with David

¹ Our LORD, I will sing
  of your love for ever.
  Everyone yet to be born
  will hear me praise your faithfulness.
² I will tell them,
  "God's love can always be trusted,
  and his faithfulness lasts
  as long as the heavens."

³ You said, "David, my servant,
  is my chosen one,
  and this is the agreement
  I made with him:
⁴ David, one of your descendants
  will always be king."

⁵ Our LORD, let the heavens
  now praise your miracles,
  and let all your angels
  praise your faithfulness.

⁶ None who live in the heavens
  can compare with you.
⁷ You are the most fearsome
  of all who live in heaven;
  all the others fear
  and greatly honour you.
⁸ You are LORD God All-Powerful!
  No one is as loving
  and faithful as you are.
⁹ You rule the roaring sea
  and calm its waves.
¹⁰ You crushed the monster Rahab,*
  and with your powerful arm
  you scattered your enemies.
¹¹ The heavens and the earth belong to you.
  And so does the world
  with all its people,
  because you created them
¹² and everything else.'

  Mount Tabor and Mount Hermon
  gladly praise you.
¹³ You are strong and mighty!
¹⁴ Your kingdom is ruled
  by justice and fairness,
  with love and faithfulness
  leading the way.

¹⁵ Our LORD, you bless those
  who join in the festival
  and walk in the brightness
  of your presence.
¹⁶ We are happy all day because of you,
  and your saving power
  brings honour to us.
¹⁷ Your own glorious power
  makes us strong,
  and because of your kindness,
  our strength increases.
¹⁸ Our LORD and our King,
  the Holy One of Israel,
  you are truly our shield.

¹⁹ In a vision, you once said
  to your faithful followers:
  "I have helped a mighty hero.
  I chose him from my people
  and made him famous.
²⁰ David, my servant, is the one
  I chose to be king,
²¹ and I will always be there
  to help and strengthen him.

²² "No enemy will outsmart David,
  and he won't be defeated
  by any hateful people.
²³ I will strike down and crush
  his troublesome enemies.
²⁴ He will always be able
  to depend on my love,
  and I will make him strong
  with my own power.
²⁵ I will let him rule the lands
  across the rivers and seas.
²⁶ He will say to me,
  'You are my Father and my God,
  as well as the mighty rock*
  where I am safe.'

²⁷ "I have chosen David
  as my firstborn son,
  and he will be the ruler
  of all kings on earth.
²⁸ My love for him will last,
  and my agreement with him
  will never be broken.

²⁹ "One of David's descendants
  will always be king,
  and his family will rule
  until the sky disappears.
³⁰ Suppose some of his children
  should reject my Law
  and refuse my instructions.

---

*89.10 Rahab: Many people in the ancient world thought that the world was controlled by this sea monster that the Lord destroyed at the time of creation (see Isaiah 51.9).

See also: 89 Title: 1 King 4.31. 89.4: 2 Sam 7.12–16; 1 Chron 17.11–14; Psa 132.11; Acts 2.30.

---

*89.26 mighty rock: See the note at 18.2.

See also: 89.20: a 1 Sam 13.14; Acts 13.22; b 1 Sam 16.12. 89.27: Rev 1.5.

31 Or suppose they should disobey
all of my teachings.
32 Then I will correct
and punish them
because of their sins.
33 But I will always love David
and faithfully keep all
of my promises to him.

34 "I won't break my agreement
or go back on my word.
35 I have sworn once and for all
by my own holy name,
and I won't lie to David.
36 His family will always rule.
I will let his kingdom last
as long as the sun
37 and moon appear in the sky."

38 You are now angry, God,
and you have turned your back
on your chosen king.
39 You broke off your agreement
with your servant, the king,
and you completely destroyed
his kingdom.
40 The walls of his city
have been broken through,
and every fortress now lies in ruin.
41 All who pass by take what they want,
and nations everywhere
joke about the king.

42 You made his enemies powerful
and let them celebrate.
43 But you forced him to retreat
because you did not
fight on his side.
44 You took his crown'
and threw his throne to the ground.
45 You made an old man of him
and put him to shame.

46 How much longer, LORD?
Will you hide for ever?
How long will your anger
keep burning like fire?
47 Remember, life is short!'
Why did you empty our lives
of all meaning?
48 No one can escape the power
of death and the grave.

49 Our Lord, where is the love
you have always shown
and that you promised
so faithfully to David?
50 Remember your servant, Lord!
People make jokes about me,
and I suffer many insults.

51 I am your chosen one,
but your enemies chase
and make fun of me.
52 Our LORD, we praise you
for ever. Amen and amen.

BOOK 4

(Psalms 90–106)

Psalm 90

(A prayer by Moses, the man of God.)

God is eternal

1 Our Lord, in all generations
you have been our home.
2 You have always been God —
long before the birth
of the mountains,
even before you created
the earth and the world.

3 At your command we die
and turn back to dust,
4 but a thousand years
mean nothing to you!
They are merely a day gone by
or a few hours in the night.

5 You bring our lives to an end
just like a dream.
We are merely tender grass
6 that sprouts and grows
in the morning,
but dries up by evening.
7 Your furious anger frightens
and destroys us,
8 and you know all our sins,
even those we do in secret.

9 Your anger is a burden
each day we live,
then life ends like a sigh.
10 We can expect seventy years,
or perhaps eighty,
if we are healthy,
but even our best years
bring trouble and sorrow.
Suddenly our time is up,
and we disappear.
11 No one knows the full power
of your furious anger,
but it is as great as the fear
that we owe to you.

See also: 90.4: 2 Pet 3.8.

12 Teach us to use wisely
all the time we have.

13 Help us, LORD! Don't wait!
Pity your servants.

14 When morning comes,
let your love satisfy all our needs.
Then we can celebrate
and be glad for what time we have left.

15 Make us happy for as long
as you caused us trouble and sorrow.

16 Do wonderful things for us,
your servants,
and show your mighty power
to our children.

17 Our Lord and our God,
treat us with kindness
and let all go well for us.
Please let all go well!

Psalm 91

The LORD is my fortress

1 Live under the protection
of God Most High
and stay in the shadow
of God All-Powerful.

2 Then you will say to the LORD,
"You are my fortress,
my place of safety;
you are my God,
and I trust you."

3 The Lord will keep you safe
from secret traps and deadly diseases.

4 He will spread his wings over you
and keep you secure.
His faithfulness is like
a shield or a city wall.'

5 You won't need to worry
about dangers at night
or arrows during the day.

6 And you won't fear diseases
that strike in the dark
or sudden disaster at midday.

7 You will not be harmed,
though thousands fall all around you.

8 And with your own eyes you will see
the punishment of the wicked.

9 The LORD Most High is your fortress.
Run to him for safety,

10 and no terrible disasters
will strike you or your home.

11 God will command his angels
to protect you wherever you go.

12 They will carry you in their arms,
and you won't hurt your feet
on the stones.

13 You will overpower the strongest lions
and the most deadly snakes.

14 The Lord says,
"If you love me
and truly know who I am,
I will rescue you and keep you safe.

15 When you are in trouble,
call out to me.
I will answer and be there
to protect and honour you.

16 You will live a long life
and see my saving power."

Psalm 92

(A psalm and a song for the Sabbath.)

Sing praises to the LORD

1 It is wonderful to be grateful
and to sing your praises,
LORD Most High!

2 It is wonderful each morning
to tell about your love
and at night to announce
how faithful you are.

3 I enjoy praising your name
to the music of harps,

4 because everything you do
makes me happy,
and I sing joyful songs.

5 You do great things, LORD.
Your thoughts are too deep

6 for an ignorant fool
to know or understand.

7 Though the wicked sprout
and spread like grass,
they will be pulled up by their roots.

8 But you will rule over all of us for ever,

9 and your hateful enemies
will be scattered
and then destroyed.

10 You have given me
the strength of a wild ox,
and you have chosen me
to be your very own.

11 My eyes have seen,
and my ears have heard
the doom and destruction
of my terrible enemies.

See also: 91.11: Matt 4.6; Luke 4.10.

See also: 91.12: Matt 4.6; Luke 4.11. **91.13:** Luke 10.19.

Real life

Euthanasia

Contributed by Care

What is it?

In legal terms euthanasia is the intentional killing of a patient as part of his/her medical treatment. It is sometimes referred to as 'mercy killing'. The key factor is the intention behind the act. Euthanasia occurs when a doctor, friend or relative intentionally ends a person's life, to 'put them out of their misery', i.e. kill them. In contrast, the intention of good medical practice is to maximise the patient's quality of life, but never to end life intentionally.

Voluntary euthanasia is euthanasia requested by the patient (i.e. they know what they are asking for) and the doctor, say, gives a lethal injection. Involuntary euthanasia occurs when a patient may be competent to request or consent to treatment but is not consulted and is intentionally killed. Non-voluntary euthanasia occurs when a patient is not in a position to understand their circumstances; they may be mentally incapacitated, and therefore cannot exercise their judgement.

What about assisted suicide – isn't that different?

Over the last few years, some patients have asked their doctors to end their life if they feel they no longer want to live. This is often referred to as doctor-assisted dying or physician-assisted suicide rather than euthanasia, but they are essentially the same. In assisted suicide, a doctor provides lethal medication that the patient then administers. Both the Disability Rights Commission and the British Medical Association are opposed to changing the law to allow doctors to help people take their own lives.

Aren't doctors already helping people to die?

The end of life and suffering inevitably raises many fears. Some feel they will not be able to cope and do not want to lose their 'quality of life'. Others do not want to see their loved ones suffer. All of these feelings are entirely understandable.

The current law allows doctors to increase pain relief for patients even if it may cause a shortening of the patient's life. This principle is known as 'double effect' and has been upheld by the courts. Everything depends on the doctor's intention. In giving pain relief, the doctor intends to relieve pain, not to kill the patient. In other words – 'You don't have to kill the patient to kill the pain'.

Euthanasia is morally, legally and medically unacceptable.

• Morally: As a society we have a moral obligation and social responsibility to care for those who are elderly, dying or disabled.
• Legally: The prohibition of intentional killing protects us all, and any change, as has been found in the Netherlands, would be impossible to police, not least because the key witness is dead.
• Medically: Doctors should seek to cure and care but not to to kill their patients. The legalisation of euthanasia would fundamentally change the role of the doctor and the relationship of trust between the doctor and the patient.

Think

What does the Bible say about death? And murder?
What does it say about caring for the vulnerable?

Act

Find out about your nearest local hospice. Consider getting involved with or praying for them.
Think through what principles you would like doctors to adhere to, if they were treating you for a serious illness. What kind of care would you want from family or friends?

Check

Deuteronomy 5.17; Psalms 71.7–9; 92.12–15; Proverbs 16.31; Romans 3.5–8

More...

Abortion p.668

12 Good people will prosper
    like palm trees,
    and they will grow strong
    like the cedars of Lebanon.
13 They will take root
    in your house, LORD God,
    and they will do well.
14 They will be like trees
    that stay healthy and fruitful,
    even when they are old.
15 And they will say about you,
    "The LORD always does right!
    God is our mighty rock."*

Psalm 93

The LORD is king

1 Our LORD, you are King!
    Majesty and power are your royal robes.
    You put the world in place,
    and it will never be moved.
2   You have always ruled,
    and you are eternal.

3 The ocean is roaring, LORD!
    The sea is pounding hard.
4 Its mighty waves are majestic,
    but you are more majestic,
    and you rule over all.
5 Your decisions are firm,
    and your temple will always
    be beautiful and holy.

Psalm 94

The LORD punishes the guilty

1 LORD God, you punish the guilty.
    Show what you are like
    and punish them now.
2 You judge the earth.
    Come and help us!
    Pay back those proud people
    for what they have done.
3   How long will the wicked
    celebrate and be glad?

4 All those cruel people strut and boast,
5   and they crush and wound
    your chosen nation, LORD.
6 They murder widows,
    foreigners, and orphans.
7 Then they say,
    "The LORD God of Jacob
    doesn't see or know."

8 Can't you fools see?
    Won't you ever learn?
9   God gave us ears and eyes!
    Can't he hear and see?
10 God instructs the nations
    and gives knowledge to us all.
    Won't he also correct us?
11 The LORD knows how useless
    our plans really are.
12 Our LORD, you bless everyone
    whom you instruct and teach
    by using your Law.
13 You give them rest from their troubles,
    until a pit can be dug for the wicked.
14 You won't turn your back
    on your chosen nation.
15 Justice and fairness will go hand in hand,
    and all who do right will follow along.

16 Who will stand up for me
    against those cruel people?
17 If you had not helped me, LORD,
    I would soon have gone
    to the land of silence.*
18 When I felt my feet slipping,
    you came with your love
    and kept me steady.
19 And when I was burdened with worries,
    you comforted me
    and made me feel secure.
20 But you are opposed
    to dishonest lawmakers
21   who gang up to murder
    innocent victims.
22 You, LORD God, are my fortress,
    that mighty rock* where I am safe.
23 You will pay back my enemies,
    and you will wipe them out
    for the evil they did.

Psalm 95

Worship and obey the LORD

1 Sing joyful songs to the LORD!
    Praise the mighty rock*
    where we are safe.
2 Come to worship him
    with thankful hearts
    and songs of praise.

3 The LORD is the greatest God,
    king over all other gods.

---

*94.17 land of silence: The grave or the world of the dead.
*94.22; 95.1 mighty rock: See the note at 18.2.
See also: 94.11: 1 Cor 3.20.

---

*92.15 mighty rock: See the note at 18.2.

4 He holds the deepest part
of the earth in his hands,
and the mountain peaks
belong to him.
5 The ocean is the Lord's
because he made it,
and with his own hands
he formed the dry land.

6 Bow down and worship
the LORD our Creator!
7 The LORD is our God,
and we are his people,
the sheep he takes care of
in his own pasture.

Listen to God's voice today!
8 Don't be stubborn and rebel
as your ancestors did
at Meribah and Massah*
out in the desert.
9 For forty years they tested God
and saw the things he did.
10 Then God got tired of them and said,
"You never show good sense,
and you don't understand
what I want you to do."
11 In his anger, God told them,
"You people will never enter
my place of rest."

Psalm 96

Sing a new song to the LORD

1 Sing a new song to the LORD!
Everyone on this earth,
sing praises to the LORD,
2 sing and praise his name.

Day after day announce,
"The LORD has saved us!"
3 Tell every nation on earth,
"The LORD is wonderful
and does marvellous things!
4 The LORD is great and deserves
our greatest praise!
He is the only God
worthy of our worship.
5 Other nations worship idols,
but the LORD created the heavens.
6 Give honour and praise to the LORD,
whose power and beauty
fill his holy temple."

7 Tell everyone of every nation,
"Praise the glorious power of the LORD.
8 He is wonderful! Praise him
and bring an offering into his temple.
9 Everyone on earth, now tremble
and worship the LORD,
majestic and holy."

10 Announce to the nations,
"The LORD is King!
The world stands firm,
never to be shaken,
and he will judge its people with fairness."

11 Tell the heavens and the earth
to be glad and celebrate!
Command the ocean to roar
with all its creatures,
12 and the fields to rejoice
with all their crops.
Then every tree in the forest
will sing joyful songs
13 to the LORD.
He is coming to judge
all people on earth
with fairness and truth.

Psalm 97

The LORD brings justice

1 The LORD is King!
Tell the earth to celebrate
and all islands to shout.
2 Dark clouds surround him,
and his throne is supported
by justice and fairness.
3 Fire leaps from his throne,
destroying his enemies,
4 and his lightning is so bright
that the earth sees it and trembles.
5 Mountains melt away like wax
in the presence of the LORD
of all the earth.

6 The heavens announce,
"The LORD brings justice!"
Everyone sees God's glory.
7 Those who boast about
the useless idols they worship
are terribly ashamed,
and all the false gods
bow down to the LORD.

8 When the people of Zion
and of the towns of Judah
hear that God brings justice,
they will celebrate.

---

*95.8 Meribah and Massah: See the note at 81.7.
See also: 95.7-11: Heb 3.7-11. 95.7,8: Heb 3.15; 4.7.
95.8-9: Exod 17.1-7; Num 20.2-13. 95.11: a Num 14.20-23;
Deut 1.34-36; Heb 4.3,5; b Deut 12.9-10.

See also: 96.7-9: Psa 29.1-2.

Holy history

Musical instruments

Music plays a huge role in the Bible – as it continues to do in the church today. The Bible lists a lot of musical instruments.

Ram's horn

This was mainly used for signalling – to announce events or call people together. It could only do two or three notes, so it wasn't particularly good for tunes.

Trumpet

A tube of straight metal (bronze or silver) which was higher pitched than the ram's horn, but still only had a couple of notes.

Pipes or flutes

Wood or bone with drilled holes. Probably more like oboes, with a mouthpiece of one or two reeds. They were sometimes used for sad music, during times of mourning.

Harps

These came in different shapes and sizes, with strings made of stretched sheepgut. The Psaltery was a larger harp usually with 10 or more strings. The lyre had a soundbox, so was a cross between a harp and a guitar.

Percussion instruments

Tambourines were either beaten with the bare hand or with sticks. Often they were used by dancers. Cymbals were made of copper. There was also the sistrum – a kind of rattle, either with metal plates attached to rods, or with beads in an empty gourd.

Footsteps

Five days on Musical instruments

Jubal, the first musician: Genesis 4.19–22
A prophetic band: 1 Samuel 10.1–8
David's chill-out music: 1 Samuel 16.14–23
Sing a new song: Psalms 98.1–9
The temple orchestra: 2 Chronicles 5.11–14

More...

Worshipping God p.622

⁹ The LORD rules the whole earth,
  and he is more glorious
  than all the false gods.

¹⁰ Love the LORD and hate evil!
  God protects his loyal people
  and rescues them from violence.
¹¹ If you obey and do right,
  a light will show you the way
  and fill you with happiness.
¹² You are the LORD's people!
  So celebrate and praise the only God.

Psalm 98

The LORD works miracles

¹ Sing a new song to the LORD!
  He has worked miracles,
  and with his own powerful arm,
  he has won the victory.
² The LORD has shown the nations
  that he has the power to save
  and to bring justice.
³ God has been faithful
  in his love for Israel,
  and his saving power is seen
  everywhere on earth.

⁴ Tell everyone on this earth
  to sing happy songs
  in praise of the LORD.
⁵ Make music for him on harps.
  Play beautiful melodies!
⁶ Sound the trumpets and horns
  and celebrate with joyful songs
  for our LORD and King!

⁷ Command the ocean to roar
  with all its creatures,
  and the earth to shout with all its people.
⁸ Order the rivers to clap their hands,
  and all the hills to sing together.
⁹ Let them worship the LORD!
  He is coming to judge
  everyone on the earth,
  and he will be honest and fair.

Psalm 99

Our LORD is King

¹ Our LORD, you are King!
  You rule from your throne
  above the winged creatures,*
  as people tremble
  and the earth shakes.

*99.1 winged creatures: See the note at 80.1.
See also: 99.1: Exod 25.22.

² You are praised in Zion,
   and you control all nations.
³ Only you are God!
   And your power alone,
   so great and fearsome,
   is worthy of praise.
⁴ You are our mighty King,◆
   a lover of fairness,
   who sees that justice is done
   everywhere in Israel.
⁵ Our LORD and our God,
   we praise you
   and kneel down to worship you,
   the God of holiness!

⁶ Moses and Aaron were two
   of your priests.
   Samuel was also one of those
   who prayed in your name,
   and you, our LORD,
   answered their prayers.
⁷ You spoke to them from a thick cloud,
   and they obeyed your laws.

⁸ Our LORD and our God,
   you answered their prayers
   and forgave their sins,
   but when they did wrong,
   you punished them.
⁹ We praise you, LORD God,
   and we worship you
   at your sacred mountain.
   Only you are God!

Psalm 100

(A psalm of praise.)

The LORD is God

¹ Shout praises to the LORD,
   everyone on this earth.
² Be joyful and sing
   as you come in to worship the LORD!

³ You know the LORD is God!
   He created us,
   and we belong to him;
   we are his people,
   the sheep in his pasture.

⁴ Be thankful and praise the LORD
   as you enter his temple.
⁵ The LORD is good!
   His love and faithfulness
   will last for ever.

See also: 99.7: Exod 33.9. **100.5:** 1 Chron 16.34;
2 Chron 5.13; 7.3; Ezra 3.11; Psa 106.1; 107.1; 118.1; 136.1;
Jer 33.11.

Psalm 101

(A psalm by David.)

A king and his promises

¹ I will sing to you, LORD!
   I will celebrate your kindness
   and your justice.
² Please help me learn
   to do the right thing,
   and I will be honest and fair
   in my own kingdom.

³ I refuse to be corrupt
   or to take part in anything crooked,
⁴ and I won't be dishonest or deceitful.

⁵ Anyone who spreads gossip
   will be silenced,
   and no one who is conceited
   will be my friend.

⁶ I will find trustworthy people
   to serve as my advisers,
   and only an honest person
   will serve as an official.

⁷ No one who cheats or lies
   will have a position in my royal court.
⁸ Each morning I will silence
   any lawbreakers I find
   in the countryside
   or in the city of the LORD.

Psalm 102

*(A prayer for someone who suffers
and needs to ask the LORD for help.)*

A prayer in time of trouble

¹ I pray to you, LORD! Please listen.
²   Don't hide from me
   in my time of trouble.
   Pay attention to my prayer
   and quickly give an answer.

³ My days disappear like smoke,
   and my bones are burning
   as though in a furnace.
⁴ I am wasting away like grass,
   and my appetite is gone.
⁵ My groaning never stops,
   and my bones can be seen
   through my skin.
⁶ I am like a lonely owl in the desert
⁷   or a restless sparrow
   alone on a roof.
⁸ My enemies insult me all day,
   and they use my name
   for a curse word.

9 Instead of food,
  I have ashes to eat and tears to drink,
10 because you are furious
  and have thrown me aside.
11 My life fades like a shadow
  at the end of day
  and withers like grass.

12 Our LORD, you are King for ever
  and will always be famous.
13 You will show pity to Zion
  because the time has come.
14 We, your servants,
  love each stone in the city,
  and we are sad to see them
  lying in the dust.

15 Our LORD, the nations
  will honour you,
  and all kings on earth
  will praise your glory.
16 You will rebuild the city of Zion.
  Your glory will be seen,
17 and the prayers of the homeless
  will be answered.

18 Future generations must also
  praise the LORD,
  so write this for them:
19 "From his holy temple,
  the LORD looked down at the earth.
20 He listened to the groans of prisoners,
  and he rescued everyone
  who was doomed to die."

21 All Jerusalem should praise you, our LORD,
22 when people from every nation
  meet to worship you.

23 I should still be strong,
  but you, LORD, have made
  an old person of me.
24 You will live for ever!
  Years mean nothing to you.
  Don't cut my life in half!

25 In the beginning, LORD,
  you laid the earth's foundation
  and created the heavens.
26 They will all disappear
  and wear out like clothes.
  You change them,
  as you would a coat,
  but you last for ever.
27 You are always the same.
  Years cannot change you.
28 Every generation of those
  who serve you will
  live in your presence.

See also: 102.25–27: Heb 1.10–12.

Psalm 103

(By David.)

The LORD's wonderful love

1 With all my heart I praise the LORD,
  and with all that I am
  I praise his holy name!
2 With all my heart I praise the LORD!
  I will never forget how kind he has been.

3 The LORD forgives our sins,
  heals us when we are sick,
4 and protects us from death.
  His kindness and love
  are a crown on our heads.
5 Each day that we live,⟩
  he provides for our needs
  and gives us the strength
  of a young eagle.

6 For all who are ill-treated,
  the LORD brings justice.
7 He taught his Law to Moses
  and showed all Israel
  what he could do.

8 The LORD is merciful!
  He is kind and patient,
  and his love never fails.
9 The LORD won't always be angry
  and point out our sins;
10 he doesn't punish us
  as our sins deserve.

11 How great is God's love for all
  who worship him?
  Greater than the distance
  between heaven and earth!
12 How far has the LORD taken
  our sins from us?
  Further than the distance
  from east to west!

13 Just as parents are kind to their children,
  the LORD is kind to all who worship him,
14 because he knows
  we are made of dust.
15 We humans are like grass
  or wild flowers that quickly bloom.
16 But a scorching wind blows,
  and they quickly wither
  to be for ever forgotten.

17 The LORD is always kind
  to those who worship him,
  and he keeps his promises
  to their descendants
18 who faithfully obey him.

See also: 103.8: Jam 5.11.

¹⁹ God has set up his kingdom in heaven,
    and he rules the whole creation.
²⁰ All you mighty angels,
    who obey God's commands,
    come and praise your LORD!
²¹ All you thousands
    who serve and obey God,
    come and praise your LORD!
²² All God's creation
    and all that he rules,
    come and praise your LORD!
    With all my heart I praise the LORD!

Psalm 104

The LORD takes care of his creation

¹ I praise you, LORD God,
    with all my heart.
    You are glorious and majestic,
    dressed in royal robes
²   and surrounded by light.
    You spread out the sky like a tent,
³   and you built your home
    over the mighty ocean.
    The clouds are your chariot
    with the wind as its wings.
⁴ The winds are your messengers,
    and flames of fire are your servants.
⁵ You built foundations for the earth,
    and it will never be shaken.
⁶ You covered the earth with the ocean
    that rose above the mountains.
⁷ Then your voice thundered!
    And the water flowed
⁸   down the mountains
    and through the valleys
    to the place you prepared.
⁹ Now you have set boundaries,
    so that the water will never
    flood the earth again.

¹⁰ You provide streams of water
    in the hills and valleys,
¹¹ so that the donkeys
    and other wild animals
    can satisfy their thirst.
¹² Birds build their nests nearby
    and sing in the trees.
¹³ From your home above
    you send rain on the hills
    and water the earth.
¹⁴ You let the earth produce
    grass for cattle,
    plants for our food,
¹⁵   wine to cheer us up,

olive oil for our skin,
    and grain for our health.
¹⁶ Our LORD, your trees always have water,
    and so do the cedars
    you planted in Lebanon.
¹⁷ Birds nest in those trees,
    and storks make their home
    in the fir trees.
¹⁸ Wild goats find a home
    in the tall mountains,
    and small animals can hide
    between the rocks.

¹⁹ You created the moon
    to tell us the seasons.
    The sun knows when to set,
²⁰   and you made the darkness,
    so the animals in the forest
    could come out at night.
²¹ Lions roar as they hunt
    for the food you provide.
²² But when morning comes,
    they return to their dens,
²³   then we go out to work
    until the end of day.

²⁴ Our LORD, by your wisdom
    you made so many things;
    the whole earth is covered
    with your living creatures.
²⁵ But what about the ocean
    so big and wide?
    It is alive with creatures,
    large and small.
²⁶ And there are the ships,
    as well as Leviathan,*
    the monster you created
    to splash in the sea.

²⁷ All of these depend on you
    to provide them with food,
²⁸ and you feed each one
    with your own hand,
    until they are full.
²⁹ But when you turn away,
    they are terrified;
    when you end their life,
    they die and rot.
³⁰ You created all of them by your Spirit,
    and you give new life to the earth.

³¹ Our LORD, we pray that your glory
    will last for ever
    and that you will be pleased
    with what you have done.

See also: 104.4: Heb 1.7.

*104.26 **Leviathan:** See the note at 74.14.
See also: 104.26: Job 41.1; Psa 74.14; Isa 27.1.

³² You look at the earth, and it trembles.
  You touch the mountains,
  and smoke goes up.
³³ As long as I live,
  I will sing and praise you,
  the LORD God.
³⁴ I hope my thoughts will please you,
  because you are the one
  who makes me glad.

³⁵ Destroy all wicked sinners
  from the earth once and for all.
  With all my heart I praise you, LORD!
  I praise you!

Psalm 105

The LORD can be trusted

¹ Praise the LORD and pray in his name!
  Tell everyone what he has done.
² Sing praises to the LORD!
  Tell about his miracles.
³ Celebrate and worship
  his holy name with all your heart.

⁴ Trust the LORD and his mighty power.
⁵ Remember his miracles
  and all his wonders
  and his fair decisions.
⁶ You belong to the family
  of Abraham, his servant;
  you are his chosen ones,
  the descendants of Jacob.

⁷ The LORD is our God,
  bringing justice everywhere on earth.
⁸ He will never forget
  his agreement or his promises,
  not in thousands of years.
⁹⁻¹⁰ God made an eternal promise
  to Abraham, Isaac, and Jacob,
¹¹ when he said, "I'll give you
  the land of Canaan."

¹² At the time there were only a few of us,
  and we were homeless.
¹³ We wandered from nation to nation,
  from one country to another.
¹⁴ God did not let anyone
  ill-treat our people.
  Instead he protected us
  by punishing rulers
¹⁵ and telling them,
  "Don't touch my chosen leaders
  or harm my prophets!"

¹⁶ God kept crops from growing
  until food was scarce
  everywhere in the land.
¹⁷ But he had already sent Joseph,
  sold as a slave into Egypt,
¹⁸ with chains of iron
  around his legs and neck.

¹⁹ Joseph remained a slave
  until his own words had come true,
  and the LORD had finished testing him.
²⁰ Then the king of Egypt set Joseph free
²¹ and put him in charge
  of everything he owned.
²² Joseph was in command of the officials,
  and he taught the leaders
  how to use wisdom.

²³ Jacob and his family came
  and settled in Egypt as foreigners.
²⁴ They were the LORD's people,
  so he let them grow stronger
  than their enemies.
²⁵ They served the LORD,
  and he made the Egyptians plan
  hateful things against them.
²⁶ God sent his servant Moses.
  He also chose and sent Aaron
²⁷ to his people in Egypt,
  and they worked miracles
  and wonders there.
²⁸ Moses and Aaron obeyed God,
  and he sent darkness to cover Egypt.
²⁹ God turned their rivers
  into streams of blood,
  and the fish all died.
³⁰ Frogs were everywhere,
  even in the royal palace.
³¹ When God gave the command,
  flies and gnats swarmed all around.

³² In place of rain,
  God sent hailstones
  and flashes of lightning.
³³ He destroyed their grapevines
  and their fig trees,
  and he made splinters
  of all the other trees.
³⁴ God gave the command,
  and more grasshoppers came
  than could be counted.

See also: 105.16: Gen 41.53–57. 105.17: Gen 37.28; 45.5.
105.18–19: Gen 39.20—40.23. 105.20: Gen 41.14.
105.21: Gen 41.39–41. 105.23: a Gen 46.6; b Gen 47.11.
105.24–25: Exod 1.7–14. 105.26: Exod 3.1—4.17.
105.28: Exod 10.21–23. 105.29: Exod 7.17–21.
105.30: Exod 8.1–6. 105.31: a Exod 8.20–24;
b Exod 8.16–17. 105.32–33: Exod 9.22–25.
105.34–35: Exod 10.12–15.

See also: 105.9: a Gen 12.7; 17.8; b Gen 26.3.
105.10–11: Gen 28.13. 105.14–15: Gen 20.3–7.

35 They ate every green plant
    and all the crops that grew
    in the land of Egypt.
36 Then God took the life
    of every firstborn son.

37 When God led Israel from Egypt,
    they took silver and gold,
    and no one was left behind.
38 The Egyptians were afraid
    and gladly let them go.
39 God hid them under a cloud
    and guided them by fire
    during the night.

40 When they asked for food,
    he sent more birds than they could eat.
41 God even split open a rock,
    and streams of water
    gushed into the desert.
42 God never forgot his sacred promise
    to his servant Abraham.

43 When the Lord rescued
    his chosen people from Egypt,
    they celebrated with songs.
44 The Lord gave them the land
    and everything else
    the nations had worked for.
45 He did this so that his people
    would obey all his laws.
    Shout praises to the LORD!

Psalm 106

A nation asks for forgiveness

1 We will celebrate
    and praise you, LORD!
    You are good to us,
    and your love never fails.
2 No one can praise you enough
    for all the mighty things you have done.
3 You bless those people
    who are honest and fair
    in everything they do.

4 Remember me, LORD,
    when you show kindness
    by saving your people.
5 Let me prosper with the rest
    of your chosen ones,
    as they celebrate with pride
    because they belong to you.

6 We and our ancestors
    have sinned terribly.
7 When they were in Egypt,
    they paid no attention
    to your marvellous deeds
    or your wonderful love.
    And they turned against you
    at the Red Sea.*

8 But you were true to your name,
    and you rescued them to prove
    how mighty you are.
9 You said to the Red Sea,*
    "Dry up!"
    Then you led your people across
    on land as dry as a desert.
10 You saved all of them
11 and drowned every one
    of their enemies.
12 Then your people trusted you
    and sang your praises.

13 But they soon forgot
    what you had done
    and rejected your advice.
14 They became greedy for food
    and tested you there in the desert.
15 So you gave them what they wanted,
    but later you destroyed them
    with a horrible disease.

16 Everyone in camp was jealous
    of Moses and of Aaron,
    your chosen priest.
17 Dathan and Abiram rebelled,
    and the earth opened up
    and swallowed them.
18 Then fire broke out
    and destroyed all of their followers.

19 At Horeb your people
    made and worshipped the statue
20 of a bull, instead of you,
    their glorious God.
21 You worked powerful miracles
    to save them from Egypt,
    but they forgot about you
22 and the fearsome things
    you did at the Red Sea.*

*106.7,9,22 Red Sea: Hebrew *yam suph* "Sea of Reeds", one of the marshes or fresh water lakes near the eastern part of the Nile Delta. This identification is based on Exodus 13.17—14.9, which lists the towns on the route of the Israelites before crossing the sea. In the Greek translation of the Scriptures made about 200 BC, the "Sea of Reeds" was named "Red Sea".

See also: 106.7: Exod 14.10-12. 106.9-12: Exod 14.21-31. 106.12: Exod 15.1-21. 106.14-15: Num 11.4-34. 106.16-18: Num 16.1-35. 106.19-23: Exod 32.1-14.

See also: 105.36: Exod 12.29. 105.37-38: Exod 12.33-36. 105.39: Exod 13.21-22. 105.40: Exod 16.2-15. 105.41: Exod 17.1-7; Num 20.2-13. 105.44: Josh 11.16-23. 106.1: 1 Chron 16.34; 2 Chron 5.13; 7.3; Ezra 3.11; Psa 100.5; 107.1; 118.1; 136.1; Jer 33.11.

23 You were angry and started
   to destroy them,
   but Moses, your chosen leader,
   begged you not to do it.

24 They would not trust you, LORD,
   and they did not like
   the promised land.

25 They would not obey you,
   and they grumbled in their tents.

26 So you threatened them by saying,
   "I'll kill you out here in the desert!

27 I'll scatter your children
   everywhere in the world."

28 Your people became followers
   of a god named Baal Peor,
   and they ate sacrifices
   offered to the dead.'

29 They did such terrible things
   that you punished them
   with a deadly disease.

30 But Phinehas* helped them,
   and the sickness stopped.

31 Now he will always be highly honoured.

32 At Meribah Spring*
   they turned against you
   and made you furious.

33 Then Moses got into trouble
   for speaking in anger.

34 Our LORD, they disobeyed you
   by refusing to destroy the nations.

35 Instead they were friendly
   with those foreigners
   and followed their customs.

36 Then they fell into the trap
   of worshipping idols.

37 They sacrificed their sons
   and their daughters to demons

38 and to the gods of Canaan.
   Then they poured out the blood
   of these innocent children
   and made the land filthy.

39 By doing such gruesome things,
   they also became filthy.

40 Finally, LORD, you were angry
   and terribly disgusted with your people.

41 So you put them in the power

of nations that hated them.

42 They were ill-treated and abused
   by their enemies,

43 but you saved them time after time.
   They were determined to rebel,
   and their sins caused their downfall.

44 You answered their prayers
   when they were in trouble.

45 You kept your agreement
   and were so merciful

46 that their enemies had pity on them.

47 Save us, LORD God!
   Bring us back from among the nations.
   Let us celebrate and shout
   in praise of your holy name.

48 LORD God of Israel,
   you deserve to be praised
   for ever and ever.
   Let everyone say, "Amen!
   Shout praises to the LORD!"

BOOK 5

(Psalms 107–150)

Psalm 107

The LORD is good to his people

1 Shout praises to the LORD!
   He is good to us,
   and his love never fails.

2 Everyone the LORD has rescued
   from trouble should praise him,

3 everyone he has brought
   from the east and the west,
   the north and the south.'

4 Some of you were lost
   in the scorching desert,
   far from a town.

5 You were hungry and thirsty
   and about to give up.

6 You were in serious trouble,
   but you prayed to the LORD,
   and he rescued you.

7 Straight away he brought you
   to a town.

8 You should praise the LORD for his love
   and for the wonderful things
   he does for all of us.

9 To everyone who is thirsty,
   he gives something to drink;

106.30 Phinehas: The grandson of Aaron, who
put two people to death and kept the Lord from
being angry with the rest of his people (see
Numbers 25.1–13).
106.32 Meribah Spring: See the note at 81.7.
See also: **106.24–26:** Num 14.1–35. **106.27:** Lev 26.33.
106.28–31: Num 25.1–13. **106.32–33:** Num 20.2–13.
106.34–36: Judg 2.1–3; 3.5–6. **106.37:** 2 King 17.17.
106.38: Num 35.33. **106.40–46:** Judg 2.14–18.

See also: **106.47–48:** 1 Chron 16.35–36.
107.1: 1 Chron 16.34; 2 Chron 5.13; 7.3; Ezra 3.11; Psa 100.5;
106.1; 118.1; 136.1; Jer 33.11.

to everyone who is hungry,
 he gives good things to eat.

¹⁰ Some of you were prisoners
 suffering in deepest darkness
 and bound by chains,
¹¹ because you had rebelled
 against God Most High
 and refused his advice.
¹² You were worn out
 from working like slaves,
 and no one came to help.
¹³ You were in serious trouble,
 but you prayed to the LORD,
 and he rescued you.
¹⁴ He brought you out
 of the deepest darkness
 and broke your chains.

¹⁵ You should praise the LORD
 for his love
 and for the wonderful things
 he does for all of us.
¹⁶ He breaks down bronze gates
 and shatters iron locks.

¹⁷ Some of you had foolishly
 committed a lot of sins
 and were in terrible pain.
¹⁸ The very thought of food
 was disgusting to you,
 and you were almost dead.
¹⁹ You were in serious trouble,
 but you prayed to the LORD,
 and he rescued you.
²⁰ By the power of his own word,
 he healed you and saved you
 from destruction.

²¹ You should praise the LORD
 for his love
 and for the wonderful things
 he does for all of us.
²² You should celebrate
 by offering sacrifices
 and singing joyful songs
 to tell what he has done.

²³ Some of you made a living
 by sailing the mighty sea,
²⁴ and you saw the miracles
 the LORD performed there.
²⁵ At his command a storm arose,
 and waves covered the sea.
²⁶ You were tossed to the sky
 and to the ocean depths,
 until things looked so bad
 that you lost your courage.
²⁷ You staggered like drunkards
 and gave up all hope.

²⁸ You were in serious trouble,
 but you prayed to the LORD,
 and he rescued you.
²⁹ He made the storm stop
 and the sea be quiet.
³⁰ You were happy because of this,
 and he brought you to the port
 where you wanted to go.

³¹ You should praise the LORD
 for his love
 and for the wonderful things
 he does for all of us.
³² Honour the LORD
 when you and your leaders
 meet to worship.

³³ If you start doing wrong,
 the LORD will turn rivers into deserts,
³⁴ flowing streams into scorched land,
 and fruitful fields into beds of salt.

³⁵ But the LORD can also turn
 deserts into lakes
 and scorched land
 into flowing streams.
³⁶ If you are hungry,
 you can settle there
 and build a town.
³⁷ You can plant fields
 and vineyards that produce
 a good harvest.
³⁸ The LORD will bless you
 with many children
 and with herds of cattle.

³⁹ Sometimes you may be crushed
 by troubles and sorrows,
 until only a few of you
 are left to survive.
⁴⁰ But the LORD will take revenge
 on those who conquer you,
 and he will make them wander
 across desert sands.
⁴¹ When you are suffering and in need,
 he will come to your rescue,
 and your families will grow
 as fast as a herd of sheep.
⁴² You will see this because
 you obey the LORD,
 but everyone who is wicked
 will be silenced.

⁴³ Be wise! Remember this
 and think about the kindness
 of the LORD.

Psalm 108

(A song and a psalm by David.)

With God on our side

¹ Our God, I am faithful to you
     with all my heart,
     and you can trust me.
   I will sing and play music for you
     with all that I am.
² I will start playing my harps
     before the sun rises.
³ I will praise you, LORD,
     for everyone to hear;
   I will sing hymns to you
     in every nation.
⁴ Your love reaches higher
     than the heavens,
     and your loyalty extends
     beyond the clouds.

⁵ Our God, may you be honoured
     above the heavens;
     may your glory be seen
     everywhere on earth.
⁶ Answer my prayers
     and use your powerful arm
     to give us victory.
   Then the people you love
     will be safe.

⁷ Our God, from your holy place
     you made this promise:
   "I will gladly divide up
     the city of Shechem
     and give away Succoth Valley
     piece by piece.
⁸ The lands of Gilead
     and Manasseh are mine.
   Ephraim is my war helmet,
     and Judah is my symbol
     of royal power.
⁹ Moab is merely my washbasin,
     and Edom belongs to me.
   I shout with victory
     over the Philistines."

¹⁰ Our God, who will bring me
     to the fortress
     or lead me to Edom?
¹¹ Have you rejected us?
     You don't lead our armies.
¹² Help us defeat our enemies!
     No one else can rescue us.
¹³ You are the one
     who gives us victory
     and crushes our enemies.

Helpline

Help! It wasn't my fault!

'I feel so awful, but it wasn't my fault! People are blaming me, but I've done nothing wrong!'

Sometimes we've done nothing wrong, but we're the ones who suffer.

Your parents broke up and it causes you pain. Your brother or sister did something and your parents are taking it out on you. Someone put words in your mouth. You're suffering for something you didn't do...

We live in a fallen world, where one person's sin can affect another. And the bad news is that there's often not a lot we can do. You can try to patch things up, but sometimes the damage is done and the consequences must be endured.

So turn to God. 'You help everyone in need, and you defend them when they are on trial' wrote David (Psalms 109.31). If you are tired from carrying heavy burdens, says Jesus, 'come to me and I will give you rest.' (Matthew 11.28) God will help you to forgive and comfort you in your pain. No-one knows more about innocent suffering than Jesus.

Three things

Reconcile

Do what you can to bring reconciliation. Be prepared to forgive. Be prepared to talk to people. Show God's love in action.

Hope

Even out of the darkest, most stormiest times of our lives, God can bring good. So don't give up hope. Keep praying, keep loving, keep moving forward.

Trust

Though others have hurt you, God loves you. And he will go on loving you. Whatever others have done or said, God knows the truth and he will always be with you.

More...

Suffering p.555
Coping with suffering p.1391

Psalm 109

(A psalm by David for the music leader.)

A prayer for the LORD's help

¹ I praise you, God! Don't keep silent.
² Destructive and deceitful lies
are told about me,
³ and hateful things are said
for no reason.
⁴ I had pity and prayed'
for my enemies,
but their words to me
were harsh and cruel.
⁵ For being friendly and kind,
they paid me back
with meanness and hatred.

⁶ My enemies said,
"Find some worthless fools
to accuse him of a crime.
⁷ Try him and find him guilty!
Consider his prayers a lie.
⁸ Cut his life short
and let someone else have his job.
⁹ Make orphans of his children
and a widow of his wife;
¹⁰ make his children beg for food
and live in the slums.
¹¹ "Let the people he owes
take everything he owns.
Give it all to strangers.
¹² Don't let anyone be kind to him
or have pity on the children
he leaves behind.
¹³ Bring an end to his family,
and from now on let him be
a forgotten man.
¹⁴ "Don't let the LORD forgive
the sins of his parents
and his ancestors.
¹⁵ Don't let the LORD forget
the sins of his family,
or let anyone remember
his family ever lived.
¹⁶ He was so cruel to the poor,
homeless, and discouraged
that they died young.
¹⁷ "He cursed others.
Now place a curse on him!
He never wished others well.
Wish only trouble for him!
¹⁸ He cursed others more often
than he dressed himself.
Let his curses strike him deep,

just as water and olive oil
soak through to our bones.
¹⁹ Let his curses surround him,
just like the clothes he wears each day."

²⁰ Those are the cruel things
my enemies wish for me.
Let it all happen to them!
²¹ Be true to your name, LORD God!
Show your great kindness and rescue me.

²² I am poor and helpless,
and I have lost all hope.
²³ I am fading away
like an evening shadow;
I am tossed aside like a crawling insect.
²⁴ I have gone without eating,*
until my knees are weak,
and my body is bony.
²⁵ When my enemies see me,
they say cruel things
and shake their heads.

²⁶ Please help me, LORD God!
Come and save me
because of your love.
²⁷ Let others know that you alone
have saved me.
²⁸ I don't care if they curse me,
as long as you bless me.
You will make my enemies fail
when they attack,
and you will make me glad
to be your servant.
²⁹ You will cover them with shame,
just as their bodies
are covered with clothes.

³⁰ I will sing your praises
and thank you, LORD,
when your people meet.
³¹ You help everyone in need,
and you defend them
when they are on trial.

Psalm 110

(A psalm by David.)

The LORD gives victory

¹ The LORD said to my Lord,
"Sit at my right side,*
until I make your enemies
into a footstool for you."

---

*109.24 without eating: See the note at 35.13.
*110.1 right side: See the note at 16.11.
See also: 109.25: Matt 27.39; Mark 15.29.
110.1: Matt 22.44; Mark 12.36; Luke 20.42–43; Acts 2.34–35;
1 Cor 15.25; Eph 1.20–22; Col 3.1; Heb 1.13; 8.1; 10.12–13.

See also: 109.8: Acts 1.20.

2 The LORD will let your power
reach out from Zion,
and you will rule over your enemies.
3 Your glorious power will be seen
on the day you begin to rule.
You will wear the sacred robes
and shine like the morning sun
in all your strength.ʾ
4 The LORD has made a promise
that will never be broken:
"You will be a priest for ever,
just like Melchizedek."

5 My Lord is at your right side,
and when he gets angry he will crush
the other kings.
6 He will judge the nations
and crack their skulls,
leaving piles of dead bodies
all over the earth.
7 He will drink from any stream
that he chooses,
while winning victory after victory.ʾ

Psalm 111

Praise the LORD for all he has done

1 Shout praises to the LORD!
With all my heart
I will thank the LORD
when his people meet.
2 The LORD has done
many wonderful things!
Everyone who is pleased
with God's marvellous deeds
will keep them in mind.
3 Everything the LORD does
is glorious and majestic,
and his power to bring justice
will never end.

4 The LORD God is famous
for his wonderful deeds,
and he is kind and merciful.
5 He gives food to his worshippers
and always keeps his agreement
with them.
6 He has shown his mighty power
to his people
and has given them the lands
of other nations.

7 God is always honest and fair,
and his laws can be trusted.
8 They are true and right
and will stand for ever.

9 God rescued his people,
and he will never break
his agreement with them.
He is fearsome and holy.

10 Respect and obey the LORD!
This is the first step
to wisdom and good sense.ʾ
God will always be respected.

Psalm 112

God blesses his worshippers

1 Shout praises to the LORD!
The LORD blesses everyone
who worships him and gladly
obeys his teachings.
2 Their descendants will have
great power in the land,
because the LORD blesses
all who do right.
3 They will get rich and prosper
and will always be remembered
for their fairness.
4 They will be so kind and merciful and good,
that they will be a light
in the dark for others
who do the right thing.

5 Life will go well for those who freely lend
and are honest in business.
6 They won't ever be troubled,
and the kind things they do
will never be forgotten.
7 Bad news won't bother them;
they have decided to trust the LORD.
8 They are dependable and not afraid,
and they will live to see
their enemies defeated.
9 They will always be remembered
and greatly praised,
because they were kind
and freely gave to the poor.
10 When evil people see this,
they angrily bite their tongues
and disappear.
They will never get what they really want.

Psalm 113

The LORD helps people in need

1 Shout praises to the LORD!
Everyone who serves him,
come and praise his name.

See also: 110.4: Heb 5.6; 6.20; 7.17,21.

See also: 111.10: Job 28.28; Prov 1.7; 9.10.
112.9: 2 Cor 9.9.

² Let the name of the LORD
   be praised now and for ever.
³ From dawn until sunset
   the name of the LORD
   deserves to be praised.
⁴ The LORD is far above all the nations;
   he is more glorious than the heavens.

⁵ No one can compare
   with the LORD our God.
   His throne is high above,
⁶   and he looks down to see
   the heavens and the earth.
⁷ God lifts the poor and needy
   from dust and ashes,
⁸   and he lets them take part
   in ruling his people.
⁹ When a wife has no children,
   he blesses her with some,
   and she is happy.
   Shout praises to the LORD!

Psalm 114

The LORD works wonders

¹ God brought his people out of Egypt,
   that land with a strange language.
² He made Judah his holy place
   and ruled over Israel.

³ When the sea looked at God,
   it ran away,
   and the River Jordan flowed
   upstream.
⁴ The mountains and the hills
   skipped around like goats.

⁵ Ask the sea why it ran away
   or ask the Jordan
   why it flowed upstream.
⁶ Ask the mountains and the hills
   why they skipped like goats!

⁷ Earth, you will tremble,
   when the Lord God of Jacob
   comes near,
⁸ because he turns solid rock
   into flowing streams
   and pools of water.

Psalm 115

The LORD deserves to be praised

¹ We don't deserve praise!
   The LORD alone deserves all the praise,
   because of his love and faithfulness.

² Why should the nations ask,
   "Where is your God?"

³ Our God is in the heavens,
   doing as he chooses.
⁴   The idols of the nations
   are made of silver and gold.
⁵ They have a mouth and eyes,
   but they can't speak or see.
⁶ Their ears can't hear,
   and their noses can't smell.
⁷ Their hands have no feeling,
   their legs don't move,
   and they can't make a sound.
⁸ Everyone who made the idols
   and all who trust them
   are just as helpless as those useless gods.

⁹ People of Israel, you must trust the LORD
   to help and protect you.
¹⁰ Family of Aaron the priest,
   you must trust the LORD
   to help and protect you.
¹¹ All of you worship the LORD,
   so you must trust him
   to help and protect you.

¹² The LORD will not forget
   to give us his blessing;
   he will bless all Israel
   and the family of Aaron.
¹³ All who worship the LORD,
   no matter who they are,
   will receive his blessing.

¹⁴ I pray that the LORD
   will let your family
   and your descendants
   always grow strong.
¹⁵ May the LORD who created
   the heavens and the earth
   give you his blessing.

¹⁶ The LORD has kept the heavens
   for himself, but he has given the earth
   to us humans.
¹⁷ The dead are silent
   and cannot praise the LORD,
¹⁸   but we will praise him
   now and for evermore.
   Shout praises to the LORD!

Psalm 116

When the LORD saves you from death

¹ I love you, LORD!
   You answered my prayers.

See also: 114.1: Exod 12.51. 114.3: a Exod 14.21;
b Josh 3.16. 114.8: Exod 17.1–7; Num 20.2–13.

See also: 115.4–8: Psa 135.15–18; Rev 9.20.
115.13: Rev 11.18; 19.5.

2 You paid attention to me,
and so I will pray to you
as long as I live.
3 Death attacked from all sides,
and I was captured
by its painful chains.
But when I was really suffering,
4 I prayed and said,
"LORD, please don't let me die!"

5 You are kind, LORD,
so good and merciful.
6 You protect ordinary people,
and when I was helpless,
you saved me
7 and treated me so kindly
that I don't need
to worry any more.

8 You, LORD, have saved
my life from death,
my eyes from tears,
my feet from stumbling.
9 Now I will walk at your side
in this land of the living.
10 I was faithful to you
when I was suffering,
11 though in my confusion I said,
"I can't trust anyone!"

12 What must I give you, LORD,
for being so good to me?
13 I will pour out an offering
of wine to you,
and I will pray in your name
because you have saved me.
14 I will keep my promise to you
when your people meet.
15 You are deeply concerned
when one of your loyal people
faces death.

16 I worship you, LORD,
just as my mother did,
and you have rescued me
from the chains of death.
17 I will offer you a sacrifice
to show how grateful I am,
and I will pray.
18 I will keep my promise to you
when your people
19 gather at your temple in Jerusalem.
Shout praises to the LORD!

Psalm 117

Come, praise the LORD

1 All you nations,
come, praise the LORD!
Let everyone praise him.
2 His love for us is wonderful;
his faithfulness never ends.
Shout praises to the LORD!

Psalm 118

The LORD is always merciful

1 Tell the LORD how thankful you are,
because he is kind and always merciful.

2 Let Israel shout,
"God is always merciful!"
3 Let the family of Aaron
the priest shout,
"God is always merciful!"
4 Let every true worshipper
of the LORD shout,
"God is always merciful!"

5 When I was really suffering,
I prayed to the LORD.
He answered my prayer,
and took my worries away.
6 The LORD is on my side,
and I am not afraid
of what others can do to me.
7 With the LORD on my side,
I will defeat all of my hateful enemies.
8 It is better to trust the LORD
for protection
than to trust anyone else,
9 including strong leaders.

10 Nations surrounded me,
but I got rid of them
by the power of the LORD.
11 They attacked from all sides,
but I got rid of them
by the power of the LORD.
12 They swarmed around like bees,
but by the power of the LORD,
I got rid of them and their fiery sting.
13 Their attacks were so fierce
that I nearly fell,
but the LORD helped me.
14 My power and my strength
come from the LORD,
and he has saved me.

See also: 117.1: Rom 15.11. 118.1: 1 Chron 16.34;
2 Chron 5.13; 7.3; Ezra 3.11; Psa 100.5; 106.1; 107.1; 136.1;
Jer 33.11. 118.6: Heb 13.6. 118.14: Exod 15.2; Isa 12.2.

See also: 116.10: 2 Cor 4.13.

¹⁵ From the tents of God's people
   come shouts of victory:
   "The LORD is powerful!
¹⁶ With his mighty arm
   the LORD wins victories!
   The LORD is powerful!"

¹⁷ And so my life is safe,
   and I will live to tell
   what the LORD has done.
¹⁸ He punished me terribly,
   but he did not let death
   lay its hands on me.

¹⁹ Open the gates of justice!
   I will enter and tell the LORD
   how thankful I am.

²⁰ Here is the gate of the LORD!
   Everyone who does right
   may enter this gate.

²¹ I praise the LORD
   for answering my prayers
   and saving me.
²² The stone that the builders
   tossed aside has now become
   the most important stone.

²³ The LORD has done this,
   and it is amazing to us.
²⁴ This day belongs to the LORD!
   Let's celebrate and be glad today.
²⁵ We'll ask the LORD to save us!
   We'll sincerely ask the LORD
   to let us win.

²⁶ God bless the one who comes
   in the name of the LORD!
   We praise you from here
   in the house of the LORD.

²⁷ The LORD is our God,
   and he has given us light!
   Start the celebration!
   March with palm branches
   all the way to the altar.'

²⁸ The LORD is my God!
   I will praise him and tell him
   how thankful I am.

²⁹ Tell the LORD
   how thankful you are,
   because he is kind
   and always merciful.

Psalm 119

In praise of the Law of the LORD

¹ Our LORD, you bless everyone
   who lives right
   and obeys your Law.
² You bless all those
   who follow your commands
   from deep in their hearts
³ and who never do wrong
   or turn from you.
⁴ You have ordered us always
   to obey your teachings;
⁵ I don't ever want to stray
   from your laws.
⁶ Thinking about your commands
   will keep me from doing
   some foolish thing.
⁷ I will do right and praise you
   by learning to respect
   your perfect laws.
⁸ I will obey all of them!
   Don't turn your back on me.

⁹ Young people can live a clean life
   by obeying your word.
¹⁰ I worship you with all my heart.
   Don't let me walk away
   from your commands.
¹¹ I treasure your word above all else;
   it keeps me from sinning against you.
¹² I praise you, LORD!
   Teach me your laws.
¹³ With my own mouth,
   I tell others the laws
   that you have spoken.
¹⁴ Obeying your instructions
   brings as much happiness
   as being rich.
¹⁵ I will study your teachings
   and follow your footsteps.
¹⁶ I will take pleasure in your laws
   and remember your words.

¹⁷ Treat me with kindness, LORD,
   so that I may live
   and do what you say.
¹⁸ Open my mind and let me discover
   the wonders of your Law.
¹⁹ I live here as a stranger.
   Don't keep me from knowing
   your commands.
²⁰ What I want most of all
   and at all times
   is to honour your laws.
²¹ You punish those boastful,
   worthless nobodies who turn
   from your commands.

See also: 118.22: Luke 20.17; Acts 4.11; 1 Pet 2.7.
118.22–23: Matt 21.42; Mark 12.10–11.   **118.25:** Matt 21.9;
Mark 11.9; John 12.13.   **118.26:** Matt 21.9; 23.39; Mark 11.9;
Luke 13.35; 19.38; John 12.13.

22 Don't let them sneer and insult me
    for following you.
23 I keep thinking about
    your teachings, LORD,
    even if rulers plot against me.
24 Your laws are my greatest joy!
    I follow their advice.

25 I am at the point of death.
    Let your teachings
    breathe new life into me.
26 When I told you my troubles,
    you answered my prayers.
    Now teach me your laws.
27 Help me to understand your teachings,
    and I will think about
    your marvellous deeds.
28 I am overcome with sorrow.
    Encourage me,
    as you have promised to do.
29 Keep me from being deceitful,
    and be kind enough
    to teach me your Law.
30 I am determined to be faithful
    and to respect your laws.
31 I follow your rules, LORD.
    Don't let me be ashamed.
32 I am eager to learn all
    that you want me to do;
    help me to understand
    more and more.

33 Point out your rules to me,
    and I won't disobey even one of them.
34 Help me to understand your Law;
    I promise to obey it with all my heart.
35 Direct me by your commands!
    I love to do what you say.
36 Make me want to obey you,
    rather than to be rich.
37 Take away my foolish desires,
    and let me find life
    by walking with you.
38 I am your servant!
    Do for me what you promised
    to those who worship you.
39 Your wonderful teachings
    protect me from the insults
    that I hate so much.
40 I long for your teachings.
    Be true to yourself and let me live.

41 Show me your love
    and save me, LORD,
    as you have promised.
42 Then I will have an answer
    for everyone who insults me
    for trusting your word.

43 I rely on your laws!
    Don't take away my chance
    to speak your truth.
44 I will keep obeying your Law
    for ever and ever.
45 I have gained perfect freedom
    by following your teachings,
46 and I trust them so much
    that I tell them to kings.
47 I love your commands!
    They bring me happiness.
48 I love and respect them
    and will keep them in mind.

49 Don't forget your promise
    to me, your servant.
    I depend on it.
50 When I am suffering,
    I find comfort in your promise
    that leads to life.
51 Conceited people sneer at me,
    but I obey your Law.
52 I find true comfort, LORD,
    because your laws have stood
    the test of time.
53 I get furious when evil people
    turn against your Law.
54 No matter where I am,
    your teachings fill me with songs.
55 Even in the night
    I think about you, LORD,
    and I obey your Law.
56 You have blessed me
    because I have always followed
    your teachings.

57 You, LORD, are my choice,
    and I will obey you.
58 With all my heart
    I beg you to be kind to me,
    just as you have promised.
59 I pay careful attention as you lead me,
    and I follow closely.
60 As soon as you command,
    I do what you say.
61 Evil people may set a trap,
    but I obey your Law.
62 Your laws are so fair that I wake up
    and praise you
    in the middle of the night.
63 I choose as my friends
    everyone who worships you
    and follows your teachings.
64 Our LORD, your love is seen
    all over the world.
    Teach me your laws.

65 I am your servant, LORD,
  and you have kept your promise
  to treat me with kindness.
66 Give me wisdom and good sense.
  I trust your commands.
67 Once you corrected me
  for not obeying you,
  but now I obey.
68 You are kindhearted,
  and you do good things,
  so teach me your laws.
69 My reputation is being ruined
  by conceited liars,
  but with all my heart
  I follow your teachings.
70 Those liars have no sense,
  but I find happiness in your Law.
71 When you corrected me,
  it did me good because it taught me
  to study your laws.
72 I would rather obey you
  than have a thousand pieces
  of silver and gold.

73 You created me and put me together.
  Make me wise enough to learn
  what you have commanded.
74 Your worshippers will see me,
  and they will be glad
  that I trust your word.
75 Your decisions are correct,
  and you were right to punish me.
76 I serve you, LORD.
  Comfort me with your love,
  just as you have promised.
77 I love to obey your Law!
  Have mercy and let me live.
78 Put down those proud people
  who hurt me with their lies,
  because I have chosen
  to study your teachings.
79 Let your worshippers come to me,
  so they will learn to obey your rules.
80 Let me truly respect your laws,
  so I won't be ashamed.

81 I long for you to rescue me!
  Your word is my only hope.
82 I am worn out from waiting
  for you to keep your word.
  When will you have mercy?
83 My life is wasting away
  like a dried-up wineskin,*
  but I have not forgotten your teachings.

84 I am your servant!
  How long must I suffer?
  When will you punish
  those troublemakers?
85 Those proud people reject
  your teachings,
  and they dig pits for me to fall in.
86 Your laws can be trusted!
  Protect me from cruel liars.
87 They have almost killed me,
  but I have been faithful
  to your teachings.
88 Show that you love me
  and let me live,
  so that I may obey
  all of your commands.

89 Our LORD, you are eternal!
  Your word will last as long
  as the heavens.
90 You remain faithful
  in every generation,
  and the earth you created
  will keep standing firm.
91 All things are your servants,
  and the laws you made
  are still in effect today.
92 If I had not found happiness
  in obeying your Law,
  I would have died in misery.
93 I won't ever forget your teachings,
  because you give me new life
  by following them.
94 I belong to you,
  and I have respected your laws,
  so keep me safe.
95 Brutal enemies are waiting
  to ambush and destroy me,
  but I obey your rules.
96 Nothing is completely perfect,
  except your teachings.

97 I deeply love your Law!
  I think about it all day.
98 Your laws never leave my mind,
  and they make me much wiser
  than my enemies.
99 Thinking about your teachings
  gives me better understanding
  than my teachers,
100 and obeying your laws
  makes me wiser than those
  who have lived a long time.
101 I obey your word
  instead of following a way
  that leads to trouble.
102 You have been my teacher,
  and I won't reject your instructions.

*119.83 a dried-up wineskin: The Hebrew text has "a wineskin in the smoke". In ancient times bags were made from animal skins to hold wine, but when the bags dried up they cracked and could no longer be used.

103 Your teachings are sweeter
than honey.
104 They give me understanding
and make me hate all lies.

105 Your word is a lamp
that gives light wherever I walk.
106 Your laws are fair,
and I have given my word
to respect them all.
107 I am in terrible pain!
Save me, LORD,
as you said you would.
108 Accept my offerings of praise
and teach me your laws.
109 I never forget your teachings,
although my life is always in danger.
110 Some merciless people
are trying to trap me,
but I never turn my back
on your teachings.
111 They will always be
my most prized possession
and my source of joy.
112 I have made up my mind
to obey your laws for ever,
no matter what.

113 I hate anyone
whose loyalty is divided,
but I love your Law.
114 You are my place of safety
and my shield.
Your word is my only hope.
115 All you worthless people,
get away from me!
I am determined to obey
the commands of my God.
116 Be true to your word, LORD.
Keep me alive and strong;
don't let me be ashamed
because of my hope.
117 Keep me safe and secure,
so that I will always respect your laws.
118 You reject all deceitful liars
because they refuse your teachings.
119 As far as you are concerned,
all evil people are' rubbish,
and so I follow your rules.
120 I tremble all over when I think of you
and the way you judge.

121 I did what was fair and right!
Don't hand me over to those
who want to ill-treat me.
122 Take good care of me, your servant,
and don't let me be harmed
by those conceited people.

Being christian

Finding God every day
Psalms 119.130

God is an everyday God. He's not a God
who only appears on Sundays; he wants to
be part of our life Monday through Sunday,
24/7!

Psalm 119 is the longest Psalm in the Bible
and it's all about God's law. More than that,
it's about putting the law to work day and
night. The writer thinks about God's
promises at night and before sunrise
(119.141–8). 'Understanding your word,' he
says, 'brings light to the minds of ordinary
people' (119.130).

God is interested in ordinary people.
When Jesus walked on earth, his special
friends weren't experts in the scriptures,
they weren't priests; they were fishermen
and tax collectors.

Similarly, when Jesus talked about God,
he used images from the ordinary world
around him. He talked about sheep and
vineyards and oil lamps and servants. He
likened himself to bread and wine; ordinary,
everyday things that everyone knew about.

So, we shouldn't reserve God for special
occasions. God should be a part of all our
lives. Our work, our college, our school.
There is no part of our life that is out of
bounds to God. He wants to be part of all of
it.

Being Christian: Finding God every day
• Pray whenever you can and no matter
where you are.
• Make a special time for God every day.
• Bring all areas of your life before God;
there's nothing too ordinary for him.
• Speak in ordinary ways about God. Don't
use 'religious' language if you can avoid it.
• Try to spot God at work in all areas of your
life. He's there!

123 My eyes are weary from waiting
   to see you keep your promise
   to come and save me.
124 Show your love for me, your servant,
   and teach me your laws.
125 I serve you,
   so let me understand your teachings.
126 Do something, LORD!
   They have broken your Law.
127 Your laws mean more to me
   than the finest gold.
128 I follow all your commands,'
   but I hate anyone who leads me astray.

129 Your teachings are wonderful,
   and I respect them all.
130 Understanding your word
   brings light to the minds
   of ordinary people.
131 I honestly want to know
   everything you teach.
132 Think about me and be kind,
   just as you are to everyone
   who loves your name.
133 Keep your promise
   and don't let me stumble
   or let sin control my life.
134 Protect me from abuse,
   so I can obey your laws.
135 Smile on me, your servant,
   and teach me your laws.
136 When anyone disobeys you,
   my eyes overflow with tears.

137 Our LORD, you always do right,
   and your decisions are fair.
138 All your teachings are true
   and trustworthy.
139 It upsets me greatly
   when my enemies neglect
   your teachings.
140 Your word to me, your servant,
   is like pure gold;
   I treasure what you say.
141 Everyone calls me a nobody,
   but I remember your laws.
142 You will always do right,
   and your teachings are true.
143 I am in deep distress,
   but I love your teachings.
144 Your rules are always fair.
   Help me to understand them
   and live.

145 I pray to you, LORD!
   Please answer me.
   I promise to obey your laws.
146 I beg you to save me,
   so I can follow your rules.

147 Even before sunrise,
   I pray for your help,
   and I put my hope
   in what you have said.
148 I lie awake at night,
   thinking of your promises.
149 Show that you love me, LORD,
   and answer my prayer.
   Please do the right thing
   and save my life.
150 People who disobey your Law
   have made evil plans
   and want to hurt me,
151 but you are with me,
   and all your commands can be trusted.
152 From studying your laws,
   I found out long ago
   that you made them to last for ever.

153 I have not forgotten your Law!
   Look at the trouble I am in,
   and rescue me.
154 Be my defender and protector!
   Keep your promise and save my life.
155 Evil people won't obey you,
   and so they have no hope of being saved.
156 You are merciful, LORD!
   Please do the right thing
   and save my life.
157 I have a lot of brutal enemies,
   but still I never turn from your laws.
158 All those unfaithful people
   who refuse to obey you
   are disgusting to me.
159 Remember how I love your laws,
   and show your love for me
   by keeping me safe.
160 All you say can be trusted;
   your teachings are true
   and will last for ever.

161 Rulers are cruel to me for no reason.
   But with all my heart
   I respect your words,
162 because they bring happiness
   like treasures taken in war.
163 I can't stand liars,
   but I love your Law.
164 I praise you seven times a day
   because your laws are fair.
165 You give peace of mind
   to all who love your Law.
   Nothing can make them fall.
166 You are my only hope
   for being saved, LORD,
   and I do all you command.
167 I love and obey your laws
   with all my heart.

168 You know everything I do.
   You know I respect every law
   you have given.

169 Please, LORD, hear my prayer
   and give me the understanding
   that comes from your word.
170 Listen to my concerns
   and keep me safe,
   just as you have promised.
171 If you will teach me your laws,
   I will praise you
172 and sing about your promise,
   because all your teachings
   are what they ought to be.
173 Be ready to protect me
   because I have chosen
   to obey your laws.
174 I am waiting for you
   to save me, LORD.
   Your Law makes me happy.
175 Keep me alive, so I can praise you,
   and let me find help in your teachings.
176 I am your servant,
   but I have wandered away
   like a lost sheep.
   Please come after me,
   because I have not forgotten
   your teachings.

Psalm 120

(A song for worship.)

A prayer for the LORD's help

1 When I am in trouble, I pray,
2 "Come and save me, LORD,
   from deceitful liars!"

3 What punishment is fitting
   for you deceitful liars?
4 Your reward should be
   sharp and flaming arrows!

5 But I must live as a foreigner
   among the people of Meshech
   and in the tents of Kedar.*
6 I have spent too much time
   living among people who hate peace.
7 I am in favour of peace,
   but when I speak of it,
   all they want is war.

---

*120.5 Meshech . . . Kedar: Meshech was a country near the Black Sea, and Kedar was a tribe of the Syrian desert.

Helpline

Help! I'm scared!

'I'm scared of heights! I worried about the future! I'm scared I'm going to fail!'

Whether it's facing the future, coping with exams or dealing with difficult situations, everyone gets scared sometimes. So what do you do? Where can we turn during those times when the world is a big, scary place?

The first, most important thing to remember is that God loves you. He cares for you. So put your trust in him. The Bible says 'God cares for you, so turn all your worries over to him.' (1 Peter 5.7). The Psalmist learnt that the Lord will protect us 'now and always wherever you go' (Psalms 121.8)

But sometimes that's difficult to do. We know it's right in theory, we pray about it, but still the worries persist. So talk to others. Share this promise with them. They'll reassure you, give you wisdom and help you to cope with your fears.

Three things

Confront

Hiding or running away from the things that scare us is not the best thing to do. Try to work out what it is you're scared of. Write it down. Pray about it. When you confront it head on, you might find that there's not much to be frightened of after all.

Share

Talk to others. Explain how you're feeling. They'll help you confront your fears or plan what to do. They'll pray with you and reassure you of the truth of God's love.

Trust

Understand that God loves you. His protection is bigger than our problems. He can give you true peace.

More...

God is more than a friend – he's a best friend p.468
God will protect us – because he loves us! p.525
God's love p.958

Psalm 121

(A song for worship.)

The LORD will protect his people

¹ I look to the hills!
  Where will I find help?
² It will come from the LORD,
  who created the heavens
  and the earth.

³ The LORD is your protector,
  and he won't go to sleep
  or let you stumble.
⁴ The protector of Israel doesn't doze
  or ever get drowsy.

⁵ The LORD is your protector,
  there at your right side
  to shade you from the sun.
⁶ You won't be harmed
  by the sun during the day
  or by the moon* at night.

⁷ The LORD will protect you
  and keep you safe from all dangers.
⁸ The LORD will protect you
  now and always wherever you go.

Psalm 122

(A song by David for worship.)

A song of praise

¹ It made me glad to hear them say,
  "Let's go to the house of the LORD!"
² Jerusalem, we are standing
  inside your gates.

³ Jerusalem, what a strong
  and beautiful city you are!
⁴ Every tribe of the LORD obeys him
  and comes to you to praise his name.
⁵ David's royal throne is here
  where justice rules.

⁶ Jerusalem, we pray
  that you will have peace,
  and that all will go well
  for those who love you.
⁷ May there be peace
  inside your city walls
  and in your palaces.

⁸ Because of my friends
  and my relatives,
  I will pray for peace.
⁹ And because of the house
  of the LORD our God,
  I will work for your good.

Psalm 123

(A song for worship.)

A prayer for mercy

¹ Our LORD and our God,
  I turn my eyes to you,
  on your throne in heaven.
² Servants look to their master,
  but we will look to you,
  until you have mercy on us.

³ Please have mercy, LORD!
  We have been insulted
  more than we can stand,
⁴ and we can't take more abuse
  from those proud, conceited people.

Psalm 124

(A song by David for worship.)

Thanking the LORD for victory

¹ The LORD was on our side!
  Let everyone in Israel say:
² "The LORD was on our side!
  Otherwise, the enemy attack
³ would have killed us all,
  because it was furious.
⁴ We would have been swept away
  in a violent flood
⁵ of high and roaring waves."

⁶ Let's praise the LORD!
  He protected us from enemies
  who were like wild animals,
⁷ and we escaped like birds
  from a hunter's torn net.

⁸ The LORD made heaven and earth,
  and he is the one who sends us help.

Psalm 125

(A song for worship.)

The LORD's people are safe

¹ Everyone who trusts the LORD
  is like Mount Zion
  that cannot be shaken
  and will stand for ever.

---

*121.6 harmed . . . sun . . . moon: In ancient times
people saw the harmful effects of the rays of the sun,
and they thought that certain illnesses (especially
mental disorders) were also caused by the rays of the
moon.

2 Just as Jerusalem is protected
   by mountains on every side,
   the LORD protects his people
   by holding them in his arms
   now and for ever.
3 He won't let the wicked rule his people
   or lead them to do wrong.
4 Let's ask the LORD to be kind
   to everyone who is good
   and completely obeys him.

5 When the LORD punishes the wicked,
   he will punish everyone else
   who lives a crooked life.
   Pray for peace in Israel!

Psalm 126

(A song for worship.)

Celebrating the harvest

1 It seemed like a dream
   when the LORD brought us back
   to the city of Zion.ᛉ
2 We celebrated with laughter
   and joyful songs.
   In foreign nations it was said,
   "The LORD has worked miracles
   for his people."
3 And so we celebrated
   because the LORD had indeed
   worked miracles for us.

4 Our LORD, we ask you to bless
   our people again,
   and let us be like streams
   in the Southern Desert.
5 We cried as we went out
   to plant our seeds.
   Now let us celebrate
   as we bring in the crops.
6 We cried on the way to plant our seeds,
   but we will celebrate and shout
   as we bring in the crops.

Psalm 127

(A song by Solomon for worship.)

Only the LORD can bless a home

1 Without the help of the LORD
   it is useless to build a home
   or to guard a city.
2 It is useless to get up early
   and stay up late
   in order to earn a living.
   God takes care of his own,
   even while they sleep.ᛉ

3 Children are a blessing
   and a gift from the LORD.
4 Having a lot of children
   to take care of you in your old age
   is like a warrior with a lot of arrows.
5 The more you have,
   the better off you will be,
   because they will protect you
   when your enemies attack
   with arguments.

Psalm 128

(A song for worship.)

The LORD rewards his faithful people

1 The LORD will bless you
   if you respect him
   and obey his laws.
2 Your fields will produce,
   and you will be happy
   and all will go well.
3 Your wife will be as fruitful
   as a grapevine,
   and just as an olive tree
   is rich with olives,
   your home will be rich
   with healthy children.
4 That is how the LORD will bless
   everyone who respects him.

5 I pray that the LORD
   will bless you from Zion
   and let Jerusalem prosper
   as long as you live.
6 May you live long enough
   to see your grandchildren.
   Let's pray for peace in Israel!

Psalm 129

(A song for worship.)

A prayer for protection

1 Since the time I was young,
   enemies have often attacked!
   Let everyone in Israel say:
2 "Since the time I was young,
   enemies have often attacked!
   But they have not defeated me,
3 though my back is like a field
   that has just been ploughed."

4 The LORD always does right,
   and he has set me free
   from the ropes
   of those cruel people.

5 I pray that all who hate the city of Zion
   will be made ashamed
   and forced to turn and run.
6 May they be like grass
   on the flat roof of a house,
   grass that dries up as soon as it sprouts.
7 Don't let them be like wheat
   gathered in bundles.
8 And don't let anyone
   who passes by say to them,
   "The LORD bless you!
   I give you my blessing
   in the name of the LORD."

Psalm 130

(A song for worship.)

Trusting the LORD in times of trouble

1 From a sea of troubles
   I call out to you, LORD.
2 Won't you please listen
   as I beg for mercy?

3 If you kept record of our sins,
   no one could last long.
4 But you forgive us,
   and so we will worship you.

5 With all my heart,
   I am waiting, LORD, for you!
   I trust your promises.
6 I wait for you more eagerly
   than a soldier on guard duty
   waits for the dawn.
   Yes, I wait more eagerly
   than a soldier on guard duty
   waits for the dawn.

7 Israel, trust the LORD!
   He is always merciful,
   and he has the power to save you.
8 Israel, the LORD will save you
   from all your sins.

Psalm 131

(A song by David for worship.)

Trust the LORD!

1 I am not conceited, LORD,
   and I don't waste my time
   on impossible schemes.
2 But I have learnt to feel safe
   and satisfied,

just like a young child
   on its mother's lap.

3 People of Israel,
   you must trust the LORD
   now and for ever.

Psalm 132

(A song for worship.)

The LORD is always with his people

1 Our LORD, don't forget David
   and how he suffered.
2 Mighty God of Jacob,
   remember how he promised:
3 "I won't go home or crawl into bed
4 or close my eyelids,
5 until I find a home for you,
   the mighty LORD God of Jacob."

6 When we were in Ephrath,
   we heard that the sacred chest
   was somewhere near Jaar.
7 Then we said, "Let's go
   to the throne of the LORD
   and worship at his feet."

8 Come to your new home, LORD,
   you and the sacred chest
   with all its power.
9 Let victory be like robes for the priests;
   let your faithful people
   celebrate and shout.
10 David is your chosen one,
   so don't reject him.
11 You made a solemn promise
   to David, when you said,
   "I, the LORD, promise
   that someone in your family
   will always be king.
12 If they keep our agreement
   and follow my teachings,
   then someone in your family
   will rule for ever."

13 You have gladly chosen Zion
   as your home, our LORD.
14 You said, "This is my home!
   I will live here for ever.
15 I will bless Zion with food,
   and even the poor will eat
   until they are full.
16 Victory will be like robes for the priests,
   and its faithful people
   will celebrate and shout.

See also: **132.6–10:** 2 Chron 6.41–42.
132.11: 2 Sam 7.12–16; 1 Chron 17.11–14; Psa 89.3–4;
Acts 2.30.

See also: **130.8:** Matt 1.21; Titus 2.14.

17 I will give mighty power
  to the kingdom of David.
Each one of my chosen kings
  will shine like a lamp
18 and wear a sparkling crown.
  But I will disgrace their enemies."

Psalm 133

(A song for worship.)

Living together in peace

1 It is truly wonderful
  when relatives live together in peace.
2 It is as beautiful as olive oil
  poured on Aaron's head*
  and running down his beard
  and the collar of his robe.
3 It is like the dew from Mount Hermon,
  falling on Zion's mountains,
  where the LORD has promised
  to bless his people
  with life for evermore.

Psalm 134

(A song for worship.)

Praising the LORD at night

1 Everyone who serves the LORD,
  come and offer praises.
Everyone who has gathered
  in his temple tonight,
2 lift your hands in prayer
  towards his holy place
  and praise the LORD.

3 The LORD is the Creator
  of heaven and earth,
  and I pray that the LORD
  will bless you from Zion.

Psalm 135

In praise of the LORD's kindness

1 Shout praises to the LORD!
  You are his servants,
  so praise his name.
2 All who serve in the temple
  of the LORD our God,
3 come and shout praises.
  Praise the name of the LORD!
  He is kind and good.

4 He chose the family of Jacob
  and the people of Israel
  for his very own.
5 The LORD is much greater
  than any other god.
6 He does as he chooses
  in heaven and on earth
  and deep in the sea.
7 The LORD makes the clouds rise
  from far across the earth,
  and he makes lightning
  to go with the rain.
Then from his secret place
  he sends out the wind.

8 The LORD killed the firstborn
  of people and animals
  in the land of Egypt.
9 God used miracles and wonders
  to fight the king of Egypt
  and all his officials.
10 He destroyed many nations
  and killed powerful kings,
11 including King Sihon of the Amorites
  and King Og of Bashan.
He conquered every kingdom
  in the land of Canaan
12 and gave their property
  to his people Israel.

13 The name of the LORD
  will be remembered for ever,
  and he will be famous
  for all time to come.
14 The LORD will bring justice
  and show mercy
  to all who serve him.

15 Idols of silver and gold are made
  and worshipped in other nations.
16 They have a mouth and eyes,
  but they can't speak or see.
17 They are completely deaf,
  and they can't breathe.
18 Everyone who makes idols
  and all who trust them
  will end up as helpless as their idols.

19 Everyone in Israel,
  come, praise the LORD!
All the family of Aaron
20 and all the tribe of Levi,*
  come, praise the LORD!

---

*133.2 head:** Olive oil was poured on Aaron's head to
show that God had chosen him to be the high priest.
See also: 132.17: 1 King 11.36.

*135.19–20 Aaron . . . Levi:** Aaron was from the tribe
of Levi, and all priests were from his family. The
temple helpers, singers, and musicians were also from
the tribe of Levi.
See also: 135.15–18: Psa 115.4–8; Rev 9.20.

All of his worshippers,
come, praise the LORD.
²¹ Praise the LORD from Zion!
He lives here in Jerusalem.
Shout praises to the LORD!

Psalm 136

God's love never fails

¹ Praise the LORD! He is good.
God's love never fails.
² Praise the God of all gods.
God's love never fails.
³ Praise the Lord of lords.
God's love never fails.

⁴ Only God works great miracles.
God's love never fails.
⁵ With wisdom he made the sky.
God's love never fails.
⁶ The Lord stretched the earth over the ocean.
God's love never fails.
⁷ He made the bright lights in the sky.
God's love never fails.
⁸ He lets the sun rule each day.
God's love never fails.
⁹ He lets the moon and the stars
rule each night.
God's love never fails.

¹⁰ God struck down the firstborn
in every Egyptian family.
God's love never fails.
¹¹ He rescued Israel from Egypt.
God's love never fails.
¹² God used his great strength
and his powerful arm.
God's love never fails.
¹³ He split the Red Sea* apart.
God's love never fails.

¹⁴ The Lord brought Israel safely
through the sea.
God's love never fails.
¹⁵ He destroyed the Egyptian king
and his army there.
God's love never fails.
¹⁶ The Lord led his people
through the desert.
God's love never fails.

¹⁷ Our God defeated mighty kings.
God's love never fails.

¹⁸ And he killed famous kings.
God's love never fails.
¹⁹ One of them was Sihon,
king of the Amorites.
God's love never fails.
²⁰ Another was King Og of Bashan.
God's love never fails.
²¹ God took away their land.
God's love never fails.
²² He gave their land to Israel,
the people who serve him.
God's love never fails.

²³ God saw the trouble we were in.
God's love never fails.
²⁴ He rescued us from our enemies.
God's love never fails.
²⁵ He gives food to all who live.
God's love never fails.

²⁶ Praise God in heaven!
God's love never fails.

Psalm 137

A prayer for revenge

¹ Beside the rivers of Babylon
we thought about Jerusalem,
and we sat down and cried.
² We hung our small harps
on the willow* trees.
³ Our enemies had brought us here
as their prisoners,
and now they wanted us to sing
and entertain them.
They insulted us and shouted,
"Sing about Zion!"

⁴ Here in a foreign land,
how can we sing about the LORD?
⁵ Jerusalem, if I forget you,
let my right hand go limp.
⁶ Let my tongue stick
to the roof of my mouth,
if I don't think about you
above all else.

⁷ Our LORD, punish the Edomites!
Because the day Jerusalem fell,
they shouted,
"Completely destroy the city!
Tear down every building!"

⁸ Babylon, you are doomed!
I pray the Lord's blessings
on anyone who punishes you
for what you did to us.

*136.13 **Red Sea:** See the note at 106.7.
See also: 136.1: 1 Chron 16.34; 2 Chron 5.13; 7.3; Ezra 3.11;
Psa 100.5; 106.1; 107.1; 118.1; Jer 33.11. **136.5:** Gen 1.1.
136.6: Gen 1.2. **136.7-9:** Gen 1.16. **136.10:** Exod 12.29.
136.11: Exod 12.51. **136.13-15:** Exod 14.21-29.

See also: 136.19: Num 21.21-30. **136.20:** Num 21.31-35.
137.8: Rev 18.6.

Real life

Abortion

Contributed by Care

Towards the end of the twentieth century, an estimated 50 million abortions were taking place annually worldwide. That's more than one abortion every second. The UK has some of the most liberal laws regarding this issue, allowing for abortion right up until 24 weeks into pregnancy. In cases of serious physical or mental handicap a mother can abort at any time before birth.

What does God think?

A child is created in the image of God (Genesis 1.27) and is to be protected. Why? Because from the moment of conception, every child has its own unique genetic make-up with everything there to provide life. God counts them as a valuable individual in their own right. In Psalm 139, David states that he was as valuable in the womb as he was outside of it. Even while his body was 'being formed', God's eyes were on him and God was deeply concerned about him. God had specific plans for David before he was fully formed and he have plans for every baby ever conceived.

So why do women choose abortion? And how do they feel?

Women don't make this decision lightly. They don't grow up thinking that abortion will be part of their lives. For many women, keeping the child could mean losing a current boyfriend or career, disappointing parents, having to raise it alone or adding pressure to an already strained family.

Although many women are told that abortion is a normal, minor surgical procedure, not every woman experiences this. Women are suffering more and more emotional and physical consequences of their decision to abort, including depression, grief, overwhelming guilt or anger, recurrent memories or dreams, emotional numbing, a sense of detachment from others and eating disorders.

What should our response be?

Christians have a responsibility to defend the weak and to stand for justice. But we also have a responsibility to respond in mercy. If we say that abortion is not found in the heart of God then there will be a cost involved as we support women in crisis pregnancy – who will care for these children brought into the world? Jesus rebuked the Pharisees saying 'you load people down with burdens they can hardly carry, and you yourselves will not lift one finger to help them' (Luke 11.46). An inevitable result of fewer abortions will be a greater need for child-care and adoption. In what ways can you and your church respond with compassion?

Think

What are the reasons that might cause someone to choose abortion?
How could churches respond in positive ways?
Is it enough for Christians to say 'abortion's wrong?' What else should we be doing?

Act

Let your friends know what you've discovered about this issue.
Find out more information by visiting the website www.care.org.uk.

Check

Job 10.8–11; 31.15; Psalm 22.9–10; 51.5; 71.6; 119.73; Jeremiah 1.5; Luke 1.5–56; Ephesians 1.4; 2 Timothy 1.9

More...

Euthanasia p.641
Fostering and adoption p.63
Families p.1224
Help! I've messed up really badly p.347

9 May the Lord bless everyone
   who beats your children
   against the rocks!

Psalm 138

(By David.)

Praise the Lord with all your heart

1 With all my heart I praise you, Lord.
   In the presence of angels⸰
   I sing your praises.
2 I worship at your holy temple
   and praise you for your love
   and your faithfulness.
   You were true to your word
   and made yourself more famous
   than ever before.⸰
3 When I asked for your help,
   you answered my prayer
   and gave me courage.⸰

4 All kings on this earth
   have heard your promises, Lord,
   and they will praise you.
5 You are so famous
   that they will sing
   about the things you have done.
6 Though you are above us all,
   you care for humble people,
   and you keep a close watch
   on everyone who is proud.

7 I am surrounded by trouble,
   but you protect me
   against my angry enemies.
   With your own powerful arm
   you keep me safe.

8 You, Lord, will always
   treat me with kindness.
   Your love never fails.
   You have made us what we are.
   Don't give up on us now!⸰

Psalm 139

(A psalm by David for the music leader.)

The Lord is always near

1 You have looked deep
   into my heart, Lord,
   and you know all about me.
2 You know when I am resting
   or when I am working,
   and from heaven
   you discover my thoughts.

3 You notice everything I do
   and everywhere I go.
4 Before I even speak a word,
   you know what I will say,
5 and with your powerful arm
   you protect me from every side.
6 I can't understand all this!
   Such wonderful knowledge
   is far above me.

7 Where could I go to escape
   from your Spirit
   or from your sight?
8 If I were to climb up
   to the highest heavens,
   you would be there.
   If I were to dig down
   to the world of the dead
   you would also be there.

9 Suppose I had wings
   like the dawning day
   and flew across the ocean.
10 Even then your powerful arm
   would guide and protect me.
11 Or suppose I said, "I'll hide
   in the dark until night comes
   to cover me over."
12 But you see in the dark
   because daylight and dark
   are all the same to you.

13 You are the one who put me together
   inside my mother's body,
14 and I praise you
   because of the wonderful way
   you created me.
   Everything you do is marvellous!
   Of this I have no doubt.

15 Nothing about me
   is hidden from you!
   I was secretly woven together
   deep in the earth below,
16 but with your own eyes
   you saw my body being formed.
   Even before I was born,
   you had written in your book
   everything I would do.

17 Your thoughts are far beyond
   my understanding,
   much more than
   I could ever imagine.
18 I try to count your thoughts,
   but they outnumber the grains
   of sand on the beach.
   And when I awake,
   I will find you nearby.

19 How I wish that you would kill
   all cruel and heartless people
   and protect me from them!
20 They are always rebelling
   and speaking evil of you.›
21 You know I hate anyone
   who hates you, LORD,
   and refuses to obey.
22 They are my enemies too,
   and I truly hate them.

23 Look deep into my heart, God,
   and find out everything
   I am thinking.
24 Don't let me follow evil ways,
   but lead me in the way
   that time has proved true.

Psalm 140

(A psalm by David for the music leader.)

A prayer for the LORD's help

1 Rescue me from cruel
   and violent enemies, LORD!
2 They think up evil plans
   and always cause trouble.
3 Their words bite deep
   like the poisonous fangs of a snake.

4 Protect me, LORD, from cruel
   and brutal enemies,
   who want to destroy me.
5 Those proud people have hidden
   traps and nets to catch me as I walk.

6 You, LORD, are my God!
   Please listen to my prayer.
7 You have the power to save me,
   and you keep me safe in every battle.

8 Don't let the wicked succeed
   in doing what they want,
   or else they might never
   stop planning evil.
9 They have me surrounded,
   but make them the victims
   of their own vicious lies.›
10 Tip flaming coals on them
    and throw them into pits
    where they can't climb out.
11 Chase those cruel liars away!
    Let trouble hunt them down.

12 Our LORD, I know that you
    defend the homeless
    and see that the poor
    are given justice.

13 Your people will praise you
   and will live with you
   because they do right.

Psalm 141

(A psalm by David.)

A prayer for the LORD's protection

1 I pray to you, LORD!
   Please listen when I pray
   and hurry to help me.
2 Think of my prayer
   as sweet-smelling incense,
   and think of my lifted hands
   as an evening sacrifice.

3 Help me to guard my words
   whenever I say something.
4 Don't let me want to do evil
   or waste my time doing wrong
   with wicked people.
   Don't let me even taste
   the good things they offer.

5 Let your faithful people
   correct and punish me.
   My prayers condemn the deeds
   of those who do wrong,
   so don't let me be friends
   with any of them.
6 Everyone will admit that I was right
   when their rulers are thrown
   down a rocky cliff,
7 and their bones lie scattered
   like broken rocks on top of a grave.›

8 You are my LORD and God,
   and I look to you for safety.
   Don't let me be harmed.
9 Protect me from the traps
   of those violent people,
10 and make them fall
    into their own traps
    while you help me escape.

Psalm 142

*(A special psalm and a prayer by David
when he was in the cave.)*

A prayer for help

1 I pray to you, LORD. I beg for mercy.
2 I tell you all my worries and my troubles,
3 and whenever I feel low,
   you are there to guide me.

See also: 140.3: Rom 3.13.

See also: 141.2: Rev 5.8.   **142 Title:** 1 Sam 22.1; 24.3.

A trap has been hidden
along my pathway.
⁴ Even if you look,
you won't see anyone
who cares enough to walk beside me.
There is no place to hide,
and no one who really cares.

⁵ I pray to you, LORD!
You are my place of safety,
and you are my choice
in the land of the living.
Please answer my prayer.
I am completely helpless.

⁶ Help! They are chasing me,
and they are too strong.
⁷ Rescue me from this prison,
so I can praise your name.
And when your people notice
your wonderful kindness to me,
they will rush to my side.

Psalm 143

(A psalm by David.)

A prayer in time of danger

¹ Listen, LORD, as I pray!
You are faithful and honest
and will answer my prayer.
² I am your servant.
Don't try me in your court,
because no one is innocent
by your standards.
³ My enemies are chasing me,
crushing me in the ground.
I am in total darkness,
like someone long dead.
⁴ I have given up all hope,
and I feel numb all over.
⁵ I remember to think about
the many things you did
in years gone by.
⁶ Then I lift my hands in prayer,
because my soul is a desert,
thirsty for water from you.

⁷ Please hurry, LORD,
and answer my prayer.
I feel hopeless.
Don't turn away
and leave me here to die.
⁸ Each morning let me learn
more about your love
because I trust you.

I come to you in prayer,
asking for your guidance.
⁹ Please rescue me from my enemies, LORD!
I come to you for safety.⁰
¹⁰ You are my God. Show me
what you want me to do,
and let your gentle Spirit
lead me in the right path.

¹¹ Be true to your name, LORD,
and keep my life safe.
Use your saving power
to protect me from trouble.
¹² I am your servant.
Show how much you love me
by destroying my enemies.

Psalm 144

(By David.)

A prayer for the nation

¹ I praise you, LORD!
You are my mighty rock,*
and you teach me
how to fight my battles.
² You are my friend,
and you are my fortress where I am safe.
You are my shield,
and you made me the ruler
of our people.⁰

³ Why do we humans mean anything
to you, our LORD?
Why do you care about us?
⁴ We disappear like a breath;
we last no longer than a faint shadow.

⁵ Open the heavens like a curtain
and come down, LORD.
Touch the mountains
and make them send up smoke.
⁶ Use your lightning as arrows
to scatter my enemies
and make them run away.
⁷ Reach down from heaven and set me free.
Save me from the mighty flood
⁸ of those lying foreigners
who can't tell the truth.

⁹ In praise of you, our God,
I will sing a new song,
while playing my harp.
¹⁰ By your power, kings win wars,
and your servant David is saved
from deadly swords.

---

*144.1 mighty rock: See the note at 18.2.
See also: 144.3: Job 7.17–18; Psa 8.4.

See also: 143.2: Rom 3.20; Gal 2.16.

11 Won't you keep me safe
     from those lying foreigners
     who can't tell the truth?

12 Let's pray that our young sons
     will grow like strong plants
   and that our daughters
     will be as lovely as columns
     in the corner of a palace.
13 May our barns be filled
     with all kinds of crops.
   May our fields be covered
     with sheep by the thousands,
14 and every cow have calves.'
   Don't let our city be captured
     or any of us be taken away,
     and don't let cries of sorrow
     be heard in our streets.

15 Our LORD and our God,
     you give these blessings
     to all who worship you.

Psalm 145

(By David for praise.)

The LORD is kind and merciful

1 I will praise you, my God and King,
     and always honour your name.
2 I will praise you each day
     and always honour your name.
3 You are wonderful, LORD,
     and you deserve all praise,
   because you are much greater
     than anyone can understand.

4 Each generation will announce
     to the next your wonderful
     and powerful deeds.
5 I will keep thinking about
     your marvellous glory
     and your mighty miracles.'
6 Everyone will talk about
     your fearsome deeds,
   and I will tell all nations
     how great you are.
7 They will celebrate and sing
     about your matchless mercy
     and your power to save.

8 You are merciful, LORD!
     You are kind and patient
     and always loving.
9 You are good to everyone,
     and you take care of all your creation.

10 All creation will thank you,
     and your loyal people
     will praise you.

11 They will tell about
     your marvellous kingdom
     and your power.
12 Then everyone will know about
     the mighty things you do
     and your glorious kingdom.
13 Your kingdom will never end,
     and you will rule for ever.

   Our LORD, you keep your word
     and do everything you say.'
14 When someone stumbles or falls,
     you give a helping hand.
15 Everyone depends on you,
     and when the time is right,
     you provide them with food.
16 By your own hand you satisfy
     the desires of all who live.

17 Our LORD, everything you do
     is kind and thoughtful,
18 and you are near to everyone
     whose prayers are sincere.
19 You satisfy the desires
     of all your worshippers,
   and you come to save them
     when they ask for help.
20 You take care of everyone
     who loves you,
   but you destroy the wicked.

21 I will praise you, LORD,
     and everyone will respect
     your holy name for ever.

Psalm 146

Shout praises to the LORD

1 Shout praises to the LORD!
     With all that I am,
     I will shout his praises.
2 I will sing and praise
     the LORD God for as long as I live.

3 You can't depend on anyone,
     not even a great leader.
4 Once they die and are buried,
     that will be the end of all their plans.

5 The LORD God of Jacob blesses
     everyone who trusts him
     and depends on him.
6 God made heaven and earth;
     he created the sea and everything else.
   God always keeps his word.
7 He gives justice to the poor
     and food to the hungry.

See also: 146.6: Acts 4.24; 14.15.

The LORD sets prisoners free
8 and heals blind eyes.
He gives a helping hand
to everyone who falls.
The LORD loves good people
9 and looks after strangers.
He defends the rights
of orphans and widows,
but destroys the wicked.

10 The LORD God of Zion
will rule for ever!
Shout praises to the LORD!

Psalm 147

Sing and praise the LORD

1 Shout praises to the LORD!
Our God is kind,
and it is right and good
to sing praises to him.
2 The LORD rebuilds Jerusalem
and brings the people of Israel
back home again.
3 He renews our hopes
and heals our bodies.
4 He decided how many stars
there would be in the sky
and gave each one a name.
5 Our LORD is great and powerful!
He understands everything.
6 The LORD helps the poor,
but he pulls the wicked to the ground.

7 Celebrate and sing!
Play your harps for the LORD our God.
8 He fills the sky with clouds
and sends rain to the earth,
so that the hills will be green with grass.
9 He provides food for cattle
and for the young ravens,
when they cry out.
10 The LORD doesn't care about
the strength of horses
or powerful armies.
11 The LORD is pleased only
with those who worship him
and trust his love.

12 Everyone in Jerusalem,
come and praise the LORD your God!
13 He makes your city gates strong
and blesses your people
by giving them children.
14 God lets you live in peace,
and he gives you the very best wheat.

15 As soon as God speaks,
the earth obeys.

16 He covers the ground with snow
like a blanket of wool,
and he scatters frost
like ashes on the ground.
17 God sends down hailstones
like chips of rocks.
Who can stand the cold?
18 At his command the ice melts,
the wind blows,
and streams begin to flow.

19 God gave his laws and teachings
to the descendants of Jacob,
the nation of Israel.
20 But he has not given his laws
to any other nation.
Shout praises to the LORD!

Psalm 148

Come, praise the LORD

1 Shout praises to the LORD!
Shout the LORD's praises
in the highest heavens.
2 All you angels,
and all who serve him above,
come and offer praise.

3 Sun and moon,
and all you bright stars,
come and offer praise.

4 Highest heavens, and the water
above the highest heavens,*
come and offer praise.

5 Let all things praise the name of the LORD,
because they were created
at his command.
6 He made them to last for ever,
and nothing can change
what he has done.'

7 All creatures on earth,
you obey his commands,
so come, praise the LORD!

8 Sea monsters and the deep sea,
fire and hail,
snow and frost,
and every stormy wind,
come, praise the LORD!

9 All mountains and hills,
fruit trees and cedars,
10 every wild and tame animal,
all reptiles and birds,
come, praise the LORD!

---

*148.4 the water . . . heavens: It was believed that
the earth and the heavens were surrounded by water.

¹¹ Every king and every ruler,
   all nations on earth,
¹² every man and every woman,
   young people and old,
   come, praise the LORD!

¹³ All creation, come and praise
   the name of the LORD.
   Praise his name alone.
   The glory of God is greater
   than heaven and earth.

¹⁴ Like a bull with mighty horns,
   the LORD protects his faithful nation Israel,
   because they belong to him.
   Shout praises to the LORD!

Psalm 149

A new song of praise

¹ Shout praises to the LORD!
   Sing him a new song of praise
   when his loyal people meet.
² People of Israel, rejoice
   because of your Creator.
   People of Zion, celebrate
   because of your King.
³ Praise his name by dancing
   and playing music on harps
   and tambourines.
⁴ The LORD is pleased
   with his people,
   and he gives victory
   to those who are humble.
⁵ All you faithful people,
   praise our glorious LORD!
   Celebrate and worship.
⁶ Praise God with songs on your lips
   and a sword in your hand.
⁷ Take revenge and punish the nations.
⁸ Put chains of iron
   on their kings and rulers.
⁹ Punish them as they deserve;
   this is the privilege
   of God's faithful people.
   Shout praises to the LORD!

Psalm 150

The LORD is good to his people

¹ Shout praises to the LORD!
   Praise God in his temple.
   Praise him in heaven,
   his mighty fortress.
² Praise our God!
   His deeds are wonderful,
   too marvellous to describe.

³ Praise God with trumpets
   and all kinds of harps.
⁴ Praise him with tambourines
   and dancing,
   with stringed instruments
   and woodwinds.
⁵ Praise God with cymbals,
   with clashing cymbals.
⁶ Let every living creature
   praise the LORD.
   Shout praises to the LORD!

Additional notes

'2.1 Why . . . plot?: Or "Why are the nations restless?"
'2.1 make useless plans: Or "grumble uselessly".
'2.11–12 Serve . . . you: One possible meaning for the difficult Hebrew text of verses 11–12.
'4.2 me: Or "my God".
'4.3 has chosen . . . very own: Some Hebrew manuscripts have "work miracles for his faithful people".
'5.1 when I groan: Or "to my thoughts" or "to my words".
'5.3 requests: Or "sacrifices".
'7.4 had pity on an enemy: Or "failed to have pity on an enemy".
'7.7 sit . . . throne: Or "return to your place".
'8.1 You . . . seen: Or "I will worship your glory".
'8.5 you yourself: Or "the angels" or "the beings in heaven".
'11.6 fiery coals: Or "trouble, fire".
'12.8 while . . . deeds: One possible meaning for the difficult Hebrew text.
'16.3 Your people . . . happy: Or "I was happy worshipping gods I thought were powerful."
'16.4 but . . . sorrow: One possible meaning for the difficult Hebrew text.
'17.14 last: One possible meaning for the difficult Hebrew text of verse 14.
'20.9 victory . . . prayers: Or "victory. He (God or the king) answers us."
'22.16 tearing at: One possible meaning for the difficult Hebrew text.
'24.6 worship . . . Jacob: Two ancient translations; Hebrew "worship God and serve the descendants of Jacob".
'26.3 I am . . . to you: Or "I trust your faithfulness."
'29.1 angels: Or "supernatural beings" or "gods".
'29.2 most . . . glorious: Or "in his holy place" or "and wear your glorious clothes".
'29.9 makes . . . time: Or "twists the oak trees around".
'32.6 whenever . . . sinned: Hebrew "at a time of finding only".
'35.13 I . . . them: Or "My prayer wasn't answered, but I prayed".

ʾ35.16 Worthless . . . fun: One possible meaning for the difficult Hebrew text.

ʾ37.35 like . . . soil: One possible meaning for the difficult Hebrew text.

ʾ39.2 but . . . good: One possible meaning for the difficult Hebrew text.

ʾ42.4 leading . . . house: One possible meaning for the difficult Hebrew text.

ʾ44.4 and . . . victory: One ancient translation; Hebrew "please give victory".

ʾ45.6 You . . . king: Or "God has made you king, and you will rule for ever."

ʾ45.13 has inward beauty: Or "is dressed in her room".

ʾ46.9 shields: Or "chariots".

ʾ48.14 always: One possible meaning for the difficult Hebrew text.

ʾ49.11 The grave: Some ancient translations; Hebrew "Their inward thoughts".

ʾ49.14 as their . . . grave: One possible meaning for the difficult Hebrew text.

ʾ50.23 Obey me: One possible meaning for the difficult Hebrew text.

ʾPsalm 53 Mahalath: Or "For flutes", one possible meaning for the difficult Hebrew text.

ʾPsalm 56 A Silent . . . Distance: One possible meaning for the difficult Hebrew text.

ʾ56.7 They . . . away: One possible meaning for the difficult Hebrew text.

ʾPsalm 57 Don't Destroy: One possible meaning for the difficult Hebrew text.

ʾPsalm 58 Don't Destroy: See the note at Psalm 57.

ʾ58.1 mighty people: Or "mighty rulers" or "mighty gods".

ʾ58.1 Do . . . justice: One possible meaning for the difficult Hebrew text.

ʾ58.9 Wipe . . . fire: One possible meaning for the difficult Hebrew text..

ʾPsalm 59 Don't Destroy: See the note at Psalm 57.

ʾ60.4 so . . . arrows: Some ancient translations and one possible meaning for the difficult Hebrew text.

ʾ62.1 calmly wait for: Or "am at peace with".

ʾ64.5 us: One ancient translation; Hebrew "them".

ʾ64.6 thoughts: One possible meaning for the difficult Hebrew text of verse 6.

ʾ64.8 tremble with fear: Or "turn and run".

ʾ65.1 deserve: One possible meaning for the difficult Hebrew text.

ʾ68.6 and let them prosper: Or "and give them a song".

ʾ68.17 to your people: Or "in all your holiness" or "in your holy place".

ʾ68.21 are ready for war: The Hebrew text has "have long hair", which probably refers to the ancient custom of wearing long hair on special occasions, such as a "holy war".

ʾ68.28–29 Our God . . . Jerusalem: One possible meaning for the difficult Hebrew text of verses 28–29.

ʾ68.30 war: One possible meaning for the difficult Hebrew text of verse 30.

ʾ68.31 presents: One possible meaning for the difficult Hebrew text of verse 31.

ʾ71.6 I . . . you: One possible meaning for the difficult Hebrew text.

ʾ72.5 Let the king live: One ancient translation; Hebrew "Let them worship you".

ʾ73.1 to Israel: Or "to those who do right".

ʾ73.4 They . . . suffer: Or "They die a painless death".

ʾ73.10 gives: One possible meaning for the difficult Hebrew text of verse 10.

ʾ73.24 in glory: Or "with honour".

ʾ74.5 pieces: One meaning for the difficult Hebrew text of verse 5.

ʾ74.17 gave . . . earth: Or "made boundaries for the earth".

ʾPsalm 75 Don't Destroy: See the note at Psalm 57.

ʾ76.4 the eternal mountains: One ancient translation; Hebrew "the mountains of victims (of wild animals)".

ʾ76.10 furious: One possible meaning for the difficult Hebrew text of verse 10.

ʾ77.6 my mind . . . questions: One ancient translation; Hebrew "I remember my music".

ʾ78.47 floods: Or "frost".

ʾ81.16 the best honey: The Hebrew text has "honey from rocks", referring to honey taken from beehives in holes or cracks in large rocks.

ʾ83.7 Phoenicia: The Hebrew text has "Tyre", the main city in Phoenicia.

ʾ84.6 Dry Valley: Or "Balsam Tree Valley". The exact location is not known.

ʾ84.6 and . . . water: One possible meaning for the difficult Hebrew text.

ʾ87.4 Egypt: The Hebrew text has "Rahab", the name of a monster that stands for Egypt (see Isaiah 30.7).

ʾPsalm 88 To . . . Leannoth: Or "For the flutes", one possible meaning for the difficult Hebrew text.

ʾ88.15 and made me helpless: One possible meaning for the difficult Hebrew text.

ʾ89.12 and everything else: The Hebrew text has "Zaphon and Yamin", which may either be the names of mountains or refer to the directions "north and south", with the meaning "everything from north to south".

ʾ89.44 You took . . . crown: One possible meaning for the difficult Hebrew text.

ʾ89.47 Remember . . . short: One possible meaning for the difficult Hebrew text.

ʾ91.4 city wall: One possible meaning for a difficult Hebrew word; it may possibly mean some kind of shield or weapon.

ʾ99.4 You . . . King: One possible meaning for the difficult Hebrew text.

ʾ103.5 Each . . . live: One possible meaning for the difficult Hebrew text.

ʾ106.28 the dead: Or "lifeless idols".

ʾ107.3 south: The Hebrew text has "sea", probably referring to the Mediterranean Sea.

ʾ109.4 and prayed: One possible meaning for the difficult Hebrew text.

ʾ110.3 You will . . . strength: One possible meaning for the difficult Hebrew text.

›**110.7 while . . . victory:** Or "God will give him victory after victory."

›**111.10 This . . . sense:** Or "This is what wisdom and good sense are all about."

›**118.27 Start . . . altar:** One possible meaning for the difficult Hebrew text.

›**119.89 Our . . . heavens:** Or "Our LORD, your word is eternal. It will last as long as the heavens."

›**119.119 As far as . . . are:** A few Hebrew manuscripts and ancient translations. Most Hebrew manuscripts have "You get rid of evil people as if they were".

›**119.128 I . . . commands:** One possible meaning for the difficult Hebrew text.

›**126.1 brought . . . Zion:** Or "made the city of Zion prosperous again."

›**127.2 God . . . sleep:** One possible meaning for the difficult Hebrew text.

›**136.4 great miracles:** One Hebrew manuscript and one ancient translation have "miracles".

›**137.2 willow:** Or "poplar".

›**138.1 angels:** Or "gods" or "supernatural beings" who worship and serve God in heaven or "rulers" or "leaders".

›**138.2 You were . . . before:** One possible meaning for the difficult Hebrew text.

›**138.3 and gave me courage:** One possible meaning for the difficult Hebrew text.

›**138.8 You have . . . now:** Or "Please don't desert your people."

›**139.20 you:** One possible meaning for the difficult Hebrew text of verse 20.

›**140.8-9 or else . . . lies:** One possible meaning for the difficult Hebrew text.

›**141.5-7 Let . . . grave:** One possible meaning for the difficult Hebrew text of verses 5-7.

›**143.9 I . . . safety:** Or "You are my hiding place."

›**144.2 of our people:** Some Hebrew manuscripts and ancient translations have "of the nations".

›**144.14 have calves:** Or "grow fat".

›**145.5 and . . . miracles:** One Hebrew manuscript and two ancient translations have "as others tell about your mighty miracles".

›**145.13 Our . . . say:** These words are found in one Hebrew manuscript and two ancient translations.

›**148.6 nothing . . . done:** Or "his laws will never change".

Proverbs

The basics

What's the point? It's a collection of wisdom. Things to do, things to avoid, stuff to think about. It's about how God wants you to live.

What happens? Various authors give advice that they've found helpful in their lives.

What should I remember? 1.7 'Respect and obey the LORD! This is the beginning of knowledge. Only a fool rejects wisdom and good advice.'

More details

Setting the scene How do you live your life? What are the rules? Wouldn't it be cool if we could have the advice of some of the wisest people who ever lived.

What's it all about? Proverbs is a collection of practical advice. 'Proverb' doesn't quite capture what this book is about. The Hebrew word can also be translated 'taunt'. They're provocations; nuggets of wisdom for us to chew over. Stuff to make you think.

Sometimes the verses run together, other times each verse seems a one-off. Don't worry about that; just take each proverb and study it. Add it to your store of wisdom.

But there are some recurring themes:

Collect wisdom Proverbs urges us to treasure wisdom when we find it.

Avoid bad influences Don't hang around with bad people. Choose real, wise friends.

Help the poor Proverbs, like so much of the Bible, stresses the need for social responsibility.

Watch your words Give up gossip, lies and foolish talk. Say the right things instead.

Get out of bed Don't just slob around – get out of bed and work.

Don't get *into* bed Don't sleep around. Avoid adultery, prostitutes or people who don't see anything wrong with their actions (30.20).

Footsteps

Instructions for use: 1.1–7
Look for good friends: 1.8–33
The value of wisdom: 3.13–35
The words of wisdom: 8.12–36
Watch your language: 26.17—27.7
True friendship: 27.17–27
The poor: 28.1–28
Lemuel's mum: 31.1–31

Introduction: how proverbs can be used

CHAPTER 1

¹ These are the proverbs
   of King Solomon of Israel,
   the son of David.
² Proverbs will teach you
   wisdom and self-control
   and how to understand
   sayings with deep meanings.
³ You will learn what is right
   and honest and fair.
⁴ From these, an ordinary person
   can learn to be clever,
   and young people can gain
   knowledge and good sense.

⁵ If you are already wise,
   you will become even wiser.
   And if you are clever,
   you will learn to understand

See also: 1.1: 1 King 4.32.

6 proverbs and sayings,
    as well as words of wisdom
    and all kinds of riddles.
7 Respect and obey the LORD!
    This is the beginning of knowledge.'
    Only a fool rejects wisdom
    and good advice.

Parental advice on the importance of seeking wisdom and not being foolish

Warnings against bad friends

8 My child, obey the teachings
    of your parents,
9 and wear their teachings
    as you would a lovely hat
    or a pretty necklace.
10 Don't be tempted by sinners
    or listen
11   when they say,
    "Come on! Let's gang up
    and kill somebody,
    just for the fun of it!
12 They're well and healthy now,
    but we'll finish them off
    once and for all.
13 We'll take their valuables
    and fill our homes
    with stolen goods.
14 If you join our gang,
    you'll get your share."

15 Don't follow anyone like that
    or do what they do.
16 They are in a big hurry
    to commit some crime,
    perhaps even murder.
17 They are like a bird that sees the bait,
    but ignores the trap.'
18 They gang up to murder someone,
    but they are the victims.
19 The wealth you get from crime
    robs you of your life.

Wisdom speaks

20 Wisdom* shouts in the streets
    wherever crowds gather.

---

*1.20 Wisdom: In the book of Proverbs the word
"wisdom" is sometimes used as though wisdom were
a supernatural being who was with God at the time
of creation.

See also: 1.7: Job 28.28; Psa 111.10; Prov 9.10.
1.20–21: Prov 8.1–3.

21 She shouts in the market places
    and near the city gates
    as she says to the people,
22 "How much longer will you enjoy
    being stupid fools?
    Won't you ever stop sneering
    and laughing at knowledge?
23   Listen as I correct you
    and tell you what I think.
24 You completely ignored me
    and refused to listen;
25 you rejected my advice
    and paid no attention
    when I warned you.

26 "So when you are struck
    by some terrible disaster,
27 or when trouble and distress
    surround you like a whirlwind,
    I will laugh and make fun of you.
28 You will ask for my help,
    but I won't listen;
    you will search,
    but you won't find me.
29 No, you would not learn,
    and you refused to respect the LORD.
30 You rejected my advice
    and paid no attention
    when I warned you.

31 "Now you will eat the fruit
    of what you have done,
    until you are stuffed full
    with your own schemes.
32 Sin and self-satisfaction
    bring destruction and death
    to stupid fools.
33 But if you listen to me,
    you will be safe and secure
    without fear of disaster."

CHAPTER 2

Wisdom and bad friends

1 My child, you must follow and treasure
    my teachings and my instructions.
2 Keep in tune with wisdom
    and think what it means
    to have common sense.
3 Beg as loud as you can
    for good common sense.
4 Search for wisdom
    as you would search for silver
    or hidden treasure.
5 Then you will understand
    what it means to respect
    and to know the LORD God.

⁶ All wisdom comes from the LORD,
  and so do common sense
  and understanding.
⁷ God gives helpful advice⁾
  to everyone who obeys him
  and protects all those
  who live as they should.
⁸ God sees that justice is done,
  and he watches over everyone
  who is faithful to him.
⁹ With wisdom you will learn
  what is right
  and honest and fair.

¹⁰ Wisdom will control your mind,
  and you will be pleased
  with knowledge.
¹¹ Sound judgment and good sense
  will watch over you.
¹² Wisdom will protect you
  from evil schemes
  and from those liars
¹³ who turned from doing good
  to live in the darkness.
¹⁴ Most of all they enjoy
  being mean and deceitful.
¹⁵ They are dishonest themselves,
  and all they do is crooked.

Wisdom and sexual purity

¹⁶ Wisdom will protect you
  from the smooth talk
  of a sinful woman,
¹⁷ who breaks her wedding vows
  and leaves the man she married
  when she was young.
¹⁸ The road to her house leads down
  to the dark world of the dead.
¹⁹ Visit her, and you will never
  find the road to life again.

²⁰ Follow the example of good people
  and live an honest life.
²¹ If you are honest and innocent,
  you will keep your land;
²² if you do wrong
  and can never be trusted,
  you will be rooted out.

CHAPTER 3

Trust God

¹ My child, remember
  my teachings and instructions
  and obey them completely.
² They will help you live
  a long and prosperous life.

³ Let love and loyalty
  always show like a necklace,
  and write them in your mind.
⁴ God and people will like you
  and consider you a success.

⁵ With all your heart
  you must trust the LORD
  and not your own judgment.
⁶ Always let him lead you,
  and he will clear the road
  for you to follow.
⁷ Don't ever think that you
  are wise enough,
  but respect the LORD
  and stay away from evil.
⁸ This will make you healthy,
  and you will feel strong.
⁹ Honour the LORD
  by giving him your money
  and the first part of all your crops.
¹⁰ Then you will have
  more grain and grapes
  than you will ever need.

¹¹ My child, don't turn away
  or become bitter
  when the LORD corrects you.
¹² The LORD corrects everyone he loves,
  just as parents correct
  their favourite child.

The value of wisdom

¹³ God blesses everyone who has wisdom
  and common sense.
¹⁴ Wisdom is worth more than silver;
  it makes you much richer than gold.
¹⁵ Wisdom is more valuable
  than precious jewels;
  nothing you want compares with her.

¹⁶ In her right hand
  Wisdom holds a long life,
  and in her left hand
  are wealth and honour.
¹⁷ Wisdom makes life pleasant
  and leads us safely along.
¹⁸ Wisdom is a life-giving tree,
  the source of happiness
  for all who hold on to her.

¹⁹ By his wisdom and knowledge
  the LORD created heaven and earth.
²⁰ By his understanding
  he let the ocean break loose
  and clouds release the rain.

See also: **3.4:** Luke 2.52.   **3.7:** Rom 12.16.   **3.11:** Job 5.17.
3.11–12: Heb 12.5–6.   **3.12:** Rev 3.19.

Viewpoints

Make God's will your first choice

Contributed by Dave R

'Always let him lead you, and he will clear the road for you to follow.'

Firstly, do we really want God to direct our paths, or are we content making our own choices? So often we ask God for 'guidance' when what we really want is for him to confirm the decision we've already made. Yet when we go our own way, it often ends in disaster. Jesus came so that we could live life to the max, but we need to let him have control. Our own way will never satisfy – it may well bring temporary happiness, but true joy comes when we know we're where God wants us to be, whatever the situation is like.

In order to get into that position, we need to seek God's will. And that means total surrender of our own ideas.

We need to be willing to let God have his will, even if it isn't our first choice – he knows best. When we do put God first in our decisions, he will help us to know what is right. But the seeking-his-will bit comes first, then he'll direct our paths. Solomon's (the guy who wrote this verse) advice is simple, but sometimes it's so hard to surrender to God's will. Yet in a world with so many options and decisions to make, it's well worthwhile. So many people refuse to go God's way and make a mess of life. God is powerful and he knows everything – his way is best, and we should be looking to find out what that way is for our lives. When we do that, he will take the reins of our life and lead us in his ways.

More...

Choices p.210
Guidance p.685
Help! I don't know what to do in my gap year p.692

---

21 My child, use common sense
    and sound judgment!
    Always keep them in mind.
22 They will help you to live
    a long and beautiful life.
23 You will walk safely and never stumble;
24 you will rest without a worry
    and sleep soundly.
25 So don't be afraid of sudden disasters
    or storms that strike those who are evil.
26 You can be sure that the LORD
    will protect you from harm.

27 Do all you can for everyone
    who deserves your help.
28 Don't tell your neighbour
    to come back tomorrow,
    if you can help today.
29 Don't try to be mean
    to neighbours who trust you.
30 Don't argue just to be arguing,
    when you haven't been hurt.
31 Don't be jealous of cruel people
    or follow their example.

32 The LORD doesn't like
    anyone who is dishonest,
    but he lets good people be his friends.
33 He places a curse on the home
    of everyone who is evil,
    but he blesses the home
    of every good person.
34 The LORD sneers at those
    who sneer at him,
    but he is kind to everyone
    who is humble.
35 You will be praised if you are wise,
    but you will be disgraced
    if you are a stubborn fool.

CHAPTER 4

Advice to young people

1 My child, listen closely
    to my teachings
    and learn common sense.
2 My advice is useful,
    so don't turn away.
3 When I was still very young
    and my mother's favourite child,
    my father
4   said to me:
    "If you follow my teachings
    and keep them in mind,
    you will live.
5 Be wise and learn good sense;
    remember my teachings

See also: 3.34: Jam 4.6; 1 Pet 5.5.

and do what I say.
⁶ If you love Wisdom and don't reject her,
    she will watch over you.
⁷ The best thing about Wisdom
    is Wisdom herself;
    good sense is more important
    than anything else.
⁸ If you value Wisdom
    and hold tightly to her,
    great honours will be yours.
⁹ It will be like wearing
    a glorious crown
    of beautiful flowers.

The right way and the wrong way

¹⁰ My child, if you listen
    and obey my teachings,
    you will live a long time.
¹¹ I have shown you the way
    that makes sense;
    I have guided you along the right path.
¹² Your road won't be blocked,
    and you won't stumble when you run.
¹³ Hold firmly to my teaching
    and never let go.
    It will mean life for you.
¹⁴ Don't follow the bad example
    of cruel and evil people.
¹⁵ Turn aside and keep going.
    Stay away from them.
¹⁶ They can't sleep or rest
    until they do wrong
    or harm some innocent victim.
¹⁷ Their food and drink
    are violence and cruelty.

¹⁸ The lifestyle of good people
    is like sunlight at dawn
    that keeps getting brighter
    until broad daylight.
¹⁹ The lifestyle of the wicked
    is like total darkness,
    and they will never know
    what makes them stumble.

²⁰ My child, listen carefully
    to everything I say.
²¹ Don't forget a single word,
    but think about it all.
²² Knowing these teachings
    will mean true life
    and good health for you.
²³ Carefully guard your thoughts
    because they are the source of true life.
²⁴ Never tell lies or be deceitful
    in what you say.
²⁵ Keep looking straight ahead,
    without turning aside.

²⁶ Know where you are headed,
    and you will stay on solid ground.
²⁷ Don't make a mistake by turning
    to the right or the left.

CHAPTER 5

Be faithful to your wife

¹ My son, if you listen closely
    to my wisdom and good sense,
² you will have sound judgment,
    and you will always know
    the right thing to say.
³ The words of an immoral woman
    may be as sweet as honey
    and as smooth as olive oil.
⁴ But all that you really get
    from being with her
    is bitter poison and pain.
⁵ If you follow her,
    she will lead you down
    to the world of the dead.
⁶ She has missed the path that leads to life
    and doesn't even know it.

⁷ My son, listen to me
    and do everything I say.
⁸ Stay away from a bad woman!
    Don't even go near the door
    of her house.
⁹ You will lose your self-respect
    and end up in debt
    to some cruel person
    for the rest of your life.
¹⁰ Strangers will get your money
    and everything else you have worked for.
¹¹ When it's all over,
    your body will waste away,
    as you groan
¹² and shout,
    "I hated advice and correction!
¹³ I paid no attention to my teachers,
¹⁴ and now I am disgraced
    in front of everyone."

¹⁵ You should be faithful to your wife,
    just as you take water
    from your own well.*
¹⁶ And don't be like a stream
    from which just any woman
    may take a drink.
¹⁷ Save yourself for your wife
    and don't have sex with other women.
¹⁸ Be happy with the wife you married
    when you were young.

---

*5.15 own well: In biblical times water was scarce
and wells were carefully guarded.
See also: 4.26: Heb 12.13.

19 She is beautiful and graceful,
      just like a deer;
   you should be attracted to her
      and stay deeply in love.

20 Don't go mad over a woman
      who is unfaithful to her own husband!
21 The LORD sees everything,
      and he watches us closely.
22 Sinners are trapped and caught
      by their own evil deeds.
23 They get lost and die
      because of their foolishness
      and lack of self-control.

CHAPTER 6

Don't be foolish

1 My child, suppose you agree
      to pay the debt of someone,
      who cannot repay a loan.
2 Then you are trapped
      by your own words,
3   and you are now in the power
      of someone else.
   Here is what you should do:
      go and beg for permission
      to call off the agreement.
4 Do this before you fall asleep
      or even get sleepy.
5 Save yourself, just as a deer or a bird
      tries to escape from a hunter.

6 You lazy people can learn
      by watching an anthill.
7 Ants don't have leaders,
8   but they store up food
      during harvest season.
9 How long will you lie there
      doing nothing at all?
   When are you going to get up
      and stop sleeping?
10 Sleep a little. Doze a little.
      Fold your hands
      and twiddle your thumbs.
11 Suddenly, everything is gone,
      as though it had been taken
      by an armed robber.

12 Worthless liars go around
13   winking and giving signals
      to deceive others.
14 They are always thinking up
      something cruel and evil,
      and they stir up trouble.
15 But they will be struck by sudden disaster
      and left without a hope.

16 There are six or seven kinds of people
      the LORD doesn't like:
17 Those who are too proud
      or tell lies or murder,
18   those who make evil plans
      or are quick to do wrong,
19 those who tell lies in court
      or stir up trouble in a family.

20 Obey the teaching of your parents —
21   always keep it in mind
      and never forget it.
22 Their teaching will guide you
      when you walk,
   protect you when you sleep,
      and talk to you when you are awake.

23 The Law of the Lord is a lamp,
      and its teachings shine brightly.
   Correction and self-control
      will lead you through life.
24 They will protect you
      from the flattering words
      of someone else's wife.'
25 Don't let yourself be attracted
      by the charm
      and lovely eyes of someone like that.
26 A woman who sells her love
      can be bought for as little
      as the price of a meal.
   But making love
      to another man's wife
      will cost you everything.
27 If you carry burning coals,
      you burn your clothes;
28   if you step on hot coals,
      you burn your feet.
29 And if you go to bed
      with another man's wife,
      you pay the price.

30 We don't put up with thieves,
      not even' with one who steals
      for something to eat.
31 And thieves who get caught must pay back
      seven times what was stolen
      and lose everything.
32 But if you go to bed
      with another man's wife,
      you will destroy yourself
      by your own stupidity.
33 You will be beaten
      and for ever disgraced,
34 because a jealous husband
      can be furious and merciless
      when he takes revenge.
35 He won't let you pay him off,
      no matter what you offer.

See also: 6.10–11: Prov 24.33–34.

Helpline

Help! My parents won't give me any freedom

'My life is full of rules. I have to go to bed when they say. I'm not allowed to do what I want. They won't treat me like an adult.'

What we need to understand is that our parents are – in most cases – looking out for our best interests. Their teaching is for our guidance and protection (Proverbs 6.20–22). They know you want independence, but they're concerned for you. They don't want you to get into bad habits, or to put yourself in risky situations.

Sometimes that makes them over-cautious or worried. But it explains why they put the rules there in the first place.

When you want to change the rules it's always good to think about them first, to understand why they're there, to get your arguments together and state them simply and without losing your temper.

Three things

Communicate

Talk to them about the situation. Where there are rules that you think are restrictive, The key thing is to talk – calmly and honestly – about the situation. Don't nag them, don't shout at them, try not to get into any arguments. Let them know how you feel and why you want more freedom.

Prove

If you want more freedom, you're going to have to prove you can act responsibly. Do some errands, take on some extra tasks. Show you deserve it.

Obey

If they do give you more freedom, don't abuse it. If you're allowed to stay out an hour longer, then make sure that it's only an hour. If you stay out two hours, you'll lose all the advantages you've gained, and you've shown that you can't be trusted.

More...
Families p.1224
Help! I want to leave home p.395
Help! My parents have favourites p.42

CHAPTER 7

The foolishness of unfaithfulness

¹ My son, pay close attention
  and don't forget what I tell you to do.
² Obey me, and you will live!
  Let my instructions be
  your greatest treasure.
³ Keep them at your fingertips
  and write them in your mind.
⁴ Let wisdom be your sister
  and make common sense
  your closest friend.
⁵ They will protect you
  from the flattering words
  of someone else's wife.

⁶ From the window of my house,
  I once happened to see
⁷ some foolish young men.
⁸ It was late in the evening,
  some time after dark.
⁹ One of these young men
  turned the corner
  and was walking by the house
  of an unfaithful wife.
¹⁰ She was dressed up
  like a woman of the street
  with only one thing in mind.
¹¹ She was one of those women
  who are loud and restless
  and never stay at home,
¹² who walk street after street,
  waiting to trap a man.

¹³ She grabbed him and kissed him,
  and with no sense of shame, she said:
¹⁴ "I had to offer a sacrifice,
  and there is enough meat
  left over for a feast.
¹⁵ So I came looking for you,
  and here you are!
¹⁶ The sheets on my bed
  are bright-coloured cloth from Egypt.
¹⁷ And I have covered it with perfume
  made of myrrh, aloes, and cinnamon.

¹⁸ "Let's go there and make love all night.
¹⁹ My husband is travelling,
  and he's far away.
²⁰ He took a lot of money along,
  and he won't be back home
  before the middle of the month."

²¹ And so, she tricked him
  with all her sweet talk and her flattery.
²² Straight away he followed her
  like an ox on the way to be slaughtered,
  or like a fool on the way to be punished▸

23 and killed with arrows.
   He was no more than a bird
     rushing into a trap,
       without knowing
         it would cost him his life.

24 My son, pay close attention
     to what I have said.
25 Don't even think about
     that kind of woman
       or let yourself be misled
         by someone like her.
26 Such a woman has caused the downfall
     and destruction of a lot of men.
27 Her house is a one-way street
     leading straight down
       to the world of the dead.

In praise of wisdom

CHAPTER 8

1 With great understanding,
   Wisdom* is calling out
2   as she stands at the crossroads
     and on every hill.
3 She stands by the city gate
     where everyone enters the city,
       and she shouts:
4 "I am calling out to each one of you!
5 Good sense and sound judgment
     can be yours.
6   Listen, because what I say
     is worthwhile and right.
7 I always speak the truth
     and refuse to tell a lie.
8 Every word I speak is honest,
     not one is misleading or deceptive.

9 "If you have understanding,
     you will see that my words
       are just what you need.
10 Let instruction and knowledge
     mean more to you
       than silver or the finest gold.
11 Wisdom is worth much more
     than precious jewels
       or anything else you desire."

Wisdom speaks

12 I am Wisdom* — Common Sense
     is my closest friend;
       I possess knowledge
         and sound judgment.

13 If you respect the LORD,
     you will hate evil.
   I hate pride and conceit
     and deceitful lies.
14 I am strong,
     and I offer sensible advice
       and sound judgment.
15 By my power kings govern,
     and rulers make laws that are fair.
16 Every honest leader rules
     with help from me.

17 I love everyone who loves me,
     and I will be found by all
       who honestly search.
18 I can make you rich and famous,
     important and successful.
19 What you receive from me
     is more valuable
       than even the finest gold
         or the purest silver.
20 I always do what is right,
21   and I give great riches
     to everyone who loves me.

22 From the beginning,
     I was with the LORD.◗
   I was there before he began
23   to create the earth.
   At the very first,
     the LORD gave life to◗ me.
24 When I was born,
     there were no oceans
       or springs of water.
25 My birth was before
     mountains were formed
       or hills were put in place.
26 It happened long before God
     had made the earth
       or any of its fields or even the dust.

27 I was there when the LORD
     put the heavens in place
       and stretched the sky
         over the surface of the sea.
28 I was with him when he placed
     the clouds in the sky
       and created the springs
         that fill the ocean.
29 I was there when he set
     boundaries for the sea
   to make it obey him,
     and when he laid foundations
       to support the earth.

30 I was right beside the LORD,
     helping him plan and build.◗

---

*8.1,12 Wisdom: See the note at 1.20.
See also: 8.1–3: Prov 1.20–21.

See also: 8.22: Rev 3.14.

Big ideas

Guidance

You're facing choices. You've got things you want to do, you've got plans. You want to hear from God, to get some guidance.

But how does that happen?

Not many people experience God's voice telling them directly to do something. It would be nice if God sent an angel to tell us what to do, but it doesn't happen very often! No, mainly we have to rely on what that God has given us. Which means praying, using our common sense, talking to trusted friends and family, listening to experts.

And reading the Bible. Because the Bible is the basis for understanding who God is, what he's like and how he wants us to live our lives. We know, for example, that we're not supposed to lie; we're not supposed to cheat or steal, etc. We know the kinds of things we're supposed to do as Christians.

But what about all those grey areas? What about which school to go to, which college to choose, which packet of biscuits to open next? Doesn't he care about these? (Actually he really doesn't much care about the biscuits...)

The Bible talks a lot about the importance of wisdom. Wisdom will give us the resources we need to weigh up the different options, to think things through, to come to a decision. 'Let understanding guide your steps,' it says in Proverbs 9.6.

God might speak to you direct; he might speak to you through the advice and wisdom of others; he might just leave it up to you. Whatever the case, take it to him and then trust in him that, whatever the decision, he will be with you on the way.

More...

What mountains are there in your life at the moment? Meet the God who can lift you up p.1003

I made him happy each day,
and I was happy at his side.
31 I was pleased with his world
and pleased with its people.

32 Pay attention, my children!
Follow my advice,
and you will be happy.
33 Listen carefully to my instructions,
and you will be wise.

34 Come to my home each day
and listen to me.
You will find happiness.
35 By finding me, you find life,
and the LORD will be pleased with you.
36 But if you don't find me,
you hurt only yourself,
and if you hate me,
you are in love with death.

Wisdom's feast

CHAPTER 9

1 Wisdom has built her house
with its seven columns.
2 She has prepared the meat
and set out the wine.
Her feast is ready.

3 She has sent her servant women
to announce her invitation
from the highest hills:
4 "Everyone who is ignorant
or foolish is invited!
5 All of you are welcome
to my meat and wine.
6 If you want to live,
give up your foolishness
and let understanding
guide your steps."

True wisdom

7 Correct a worthless boaster,
and all you will get
are insults and injuries.
8 Any boaster you correct
will only hate you.
But if you correct someone
who has common sense,
you will be loved.
9 If you have good sense,
instruction will help you
to have even better sense.
And if you live right,
education will help you
to know even more.

10 Respect and obey the LORD!
   This is the beginning of wisdom.*
To have understanding,
   you must know the Holy God.
11 I am Wisdom.
   If you follow me,
   you will live a long time.
12 Good sense is good for you,
   but if you boast,
   you hurt yourself.

A foolish invitation

13 Stupidity* is reckless,
   senseless, and foolish.
14 She sits in front of her house
   and on the highest hills in the town.
15 She shouts to everyone who passes by,
16   "If you are stupid, come on inside!"
   And to every fool she says,
17   "Stolen water tastes best,
   and the food you eat in secret
   tastes best of all."
18 None who listen to Stupidity understand
   that her guests are as good as dead.

Solomon's wise sayings

CHAPTER 10

1 Here are some proverbs of Solomon:
   Children with good sense
   make their parents happy,
   but foolish children make them sad.
2 What you gain by doing evil
   won't help you at all,
   but being good*
   can save you from death.
3 If you obey the LORD,
   you won't go hungry;
   if you are wicked,
   God won't let you have what you want.
4 Laziness leads to poverty;
   hard work makes you rich.
5 At harvest season
   it's clever to work hard,
   but stupid to sleep.
6 Everyone praises good people,
   but evil hides behind
   the words of the wicked.
7 Good people are remembered
   long after they are gone,
   but the wicked are soon forgotten.

8 If you have good sense,
   you will listen and obey;
   if all you do is talk,
   you will destroy yourself.
9 You will be safe,
   if you always do right,
   but you will get caught,
   if you are dishonest.
10 Deceit causes trouble,
   and foolish talk will bring you to ruin.*
11 The words of good people
   are a source of life,
   but evil hides behind
   the words of the wicked.
12 Hatred stirs up trouble;
   love overlooks the wrongs
   that others do.
13 If you have good sense,
   it will show when you speak.
   But if you are stupid,
   you will be beaten with a stick.
14 If you have good sense,
   you will learn all you can,
   but foolish talk will soon destroy you.
15 Great wealth can be a fortress,
   but poverty is no protection at all.
16 If you live right,
   the reward is a good life;
   if you are evil, all you have is sin.
17 Accept correction,
   and you will find life;
   reject correction,
   and you will miss the road.
18 You can hide your hatred by telling lies,
   but you are a fool to spread lies.
19 You will say the wrong thing
   if you talk too much —
   so be sensible and watch what you say.
20 The words of a good person
   are like pure silver,
   but the thoughts of an evil person
   are almost worthless.
21 Many are helped by useful instruction,
   but fools are killed
   by their own stupidity.
22 When the LORD blesses you with riches,
   you have nothing to regret.*
23 Fools enjoy doing wrong,
   but anyone with good sense
   enjoys acting wisely.
24 What evil people dread most
   will happen to them,
   but good people will get
   what they want most.

See also: 9.10: Job 28.28; Psa 111.10; Prov 1.7.
See also: 10.12: Jam 5.20; 1 Pet 4.8.

25 Those crooks will disappear
when a storm strikes,
but God will keep safe
all who obey him.
26 Having a lazy person on the job
is like a mouth full of vinegar
or smoke in your eyes.

27 If you respect the LORD,
you will live longer;
if you keep doing wrong,
your life will be cut short.
28 If you obey the Lord,
you will be happy,
but there is no future for the wicked.
29 The LORD protects everyone
who lives right,
but he destroys anyone who does wrong.
30 Good people will stand firm,
but the wicked will lose their land.
31 Honest people speak sensibly,
but deceitful liars will be silenced.
32 If you obey the Lord,
you will always know
the right thing to say.
But no one will trust you if you tell lies.

CHAPTER 11

Watch what you say and do

1 The LORD hates anyone who cheats,
but he likes everyone who is honest.
2 Too much pride can put you to shame.
It's wiser to be humble.
3 If you do the right thing,
honesty will be your guide.
But if you are crooked,
you will be trapped
by your own dishonesty.

4 When God is angry,
money won't help you.
Obeying God is the only way
to be saved from death.
5 If you are truly good, you will do right;
if you are wicked,
you will be destroyed by your own sin.
6 Honesty can keep you safe,
but if you can't be trusted,
you trap yourself.
7 When the wicked die,
their hopes die with them.
8 Trouble goes right past the LORD's people
and strikes the wicked.

9 Dishonest people use gossip
to destroy their neighbours;
good people are protected
by their own good sense.

10 When honest people prosper
and the wicked disappear,
the whole city celebrates.
11 When God blesses his people,
their city prospers,
but deceitful liars can destroy a city.

12 It's stupid to say bad things
about your neighbours.
If you are sensible,
you will keep quiet.
13 A gossip tells everything,
but a true friend will keep a secret.
14 A city without wise leaders
will end up in ruin;
a city with many wise leaders
will be kept safe.

15 It's a dangerous thing
to guarantee payment
for someone's debts.
Don't do it!
16 A gracious woman will be respected,
but a man must work hard to get rich.▸
17 Kindness is rewarded —
but if you are cruel,
you hurt yourself.
18 Meanness gets you nowhere,
but goodness is rewarded.
19 Always do the right thing,
and you will live;
keep on doing wrong, and you will die.

20 The LORD hates cunning people,
but he likes everyone who lives right.
21 You can be sure of this:
all crooks will be punished,
but God's people won't.
22 A beautiful woman who acts foolishly
is like a gold ring on the snout of a pig.
23 Good people want what is best,
but troublemakers
hope to stir up trouble.▸

24 Sometimes you can become rich
by being generous
or poor by being greedy.
25 Generosity will be rewarded:
give a cup of water,
and you will receive
a cup of water in return.
26 Charge too much for grain,
and you will be cursed;
sell it at a fair price,
and you will be praised.
27 Try hard to do right,
and you will win friends;
go looking for trouble,
and you will find it.

28 Trust in your wealth,
    and you will be a failure,
    but God's people will prosper
    like healthy plants.

29 Fools who cause trouble
    in the family won't inherit a thing.
    They will end up as slaves
    of someone with good sense.

30 Live right, and you will eat
    from the life-giving tree.
    And if you act wisely,
    others will follow.'

31 If good people are rewarded'
    here on this earth,
    all who are cruel and mean
    will surely be punished.

CHAPTER 12

You can't hide behind evil

1 To accept correction is wise,
    to reject it is stupid.

2 The LORD likes everyone who lives right,
    but he punishes everyone
    who makes evil plans.

3 Sin cannot offer security!
    But if you live right,
    you will be as secure
    as a tree with deep roots.

4 A helpful wife is a jewel
    for her husband,
    but a shameless wife
    will make his bones rot.

5 Good people have kind thoughts,
    but you should never trust
    the advice of someone evil.

6 Bad advice is a deadly trap,
    but good advice is like a shield.

7 Once the wicked are defeated,
    they are gone for ever,
    but no one who obeys God
    will ever be thrown down.

8 Good sense is worthy of praise,
    but stupidity is a curse.

9 It's better to be ordinary
    and have only one servant'
    than to think you are somebody
    and starve to death.

10 Good people are kind to their animals,
    but a mean person is cruel.

11 Hard working farmers have more
    than enough food;
    daydreamers are nothing more
    than stupid fools.

12 An evil person tries to hide behind evil;'
    good people are like trees
    with deep roots.

13 We trap ourselves by telling lies,
    but we stay out of trouble
    by living right.

14 We are rewarded or punished
    for what we say and do.

15 Fools think they know what is best,
    but a sensible person listens to advice.

16 Losing your temper is foolish;
    ignoring an insult is sensible.

17 An honest person
    tells the truth in court,
    but a dishonest person
    tells nothing but lies.

18 Sharp words cut like a sword,
    but words of wisdom heal.

19 Truth will last for ever;
    lies are soon found out.

20 An evil mind is deceitful,
    but gentle thoughts bring happiness.

21 Good people never have trouble,
    but troublemakers
    have more than enough.

22 The LORD hates every liar,
    but he is the friend of all
    who can be trusted.

23 Be sensible and don't tell
    everything you know —
    only fools spread
    foolishness everywhere.

24 Work hard, and you will be a leader;
    be lazy, and you will end up a slave.

25 Worry is a heavy burden,
    but a kind word always brings cheer.

26 You are better off doing right,
    than losing your way
    by doing wrong.'

27 Anyone too lazy to cook will starve,
    but a hard worker
    is a valuable treasure.'

28 Follow the road to life,
    and you won't be bothered by death.

CHAPTER 13

Wise friends make you wise

1 Children with good sense
    accept correction from their parents,
    but stubborn children
    ignore it completely.

2 You will be well rewarded
    for saying something kind,
    but all some people think about
    is how to be cruel and mean.

See also: 11.31: 1 Pet 4.18.

3 Keep what you know to yourself,
  and you will be safe;
  talk too much, and you are done for.
4 No matter how much you want,
  laziness won't help a bit,
  but hard work will reward you
  with more than enough.
5 A good person hates deceit,
  but those who are evil
  cause shame and disgrace.
6 Live right, and you are safe!
  But sin will destroy you.

7 Some who have nothing
  may pretend to be rich,
  and some who have everything
  may pretend to be poor.
8 The rich may have to pay a ransom,
  but the poor don't have that problem.
9 The lamp of a good person
  keeps on shining;
  the lamp of an evil person
  soon goes out.
10 Too much pride causes trouble.
  Be sensible and take advice.

11 Money wrongly got
  will disappear bit by bit;
  money earned little by little
  will grow and grow.
12 Not getting what you want
  can make you feel sick,
  but a wish that comes true
  is a life-giving tree.
13 If you reject God's teaching,
  you will pay the price;
  if you obey his commands,
  you will be rewarded.

14 Sensible instruction
  is a life-giving fountain
  that helps you escape all deadly traps.
15 Sound judgment is praised,
  but people without good sense
  are on the way to disaster.'
16 If you have good sense,
  you will act sensibly,
  but fools act like fools.
17 Whoever delivers your message
  can make things better
  or worse for you.

18 All who refuse correction
  will be poor and disgraced;
  all who accept correction will be praised.
19 It's a good feeling
  to get what you want,
  but only a stupid fool
  hates to turn from evil.

20 Wise friends make you wise,
  but you hurt yourself
  by going around with fools.
21 You are in for trouble if you sin,
  but you will be rewarded if you live right.
22 If you obey God,
  you will have something
  to leave your grandchildren.
  If you don't obey God,
  those who live right
  will get what you leave.

23 Even when the land of the poor
  produces good crops,
  they get cheated out of what they grow.'
24 If you love your children,
  you will correct them;
  if you don't love them,
  you won't correct them.
25 If you live right,
  you will have plenty to eat;
  if you don't live right,
  you will go away empty.

CHAPTER 14

Wisdom makes good sense

1 A woman's family is held together
  by her wisdom,
  but it can be destroyed
  by her foolishness.
2 By living right, you show
  that you respect the LORD;
  by being deceitful, you show
  that you despise him.
3 Proud fools are punished
  for their stupid talk,
  but sensible talk can save your life.
4 Without the help of an ox
  there can be no crop,
  but with a strong ox
  a big crop is possible.
5 An honest witness tells the truth;
  a dishonest witness
  tells nothing but lies.

6 Make fun of wisdom,
  and you will never find it.
  But if you have understanding,
  knowledge comes easily.
7 Stay away from fools,
  or you won't learn a thing.
8 Wise people have enough sense
  to find their way,
  but stupid fools get lost.
9 Fools don't care if they are wrong,'
  but God is pleased
  when people do right.

¹⁰ No one else can really know
how sad or happy you are.
¹¹ The tent of a good person stands longer
than the house of someone evil.
¹² You may think you are
on the right road
and still end up dead.
¹³ Sorrow may hide behind laughter,
and happiness may end in sorrow.
¹⁴ You harvest what you plant,
whether good or bad.

¹⁵ Don't be stupid and believe all you hear;
be clever and know
where you are headed.
¹⁶ Only a stupid fool is never cautious —
so be extra careful
and stay out of trouble.
¹⁷ Fools have quick tempers,
and no one likes you
if you can't be trusted.
¹⁸ Stupidity leads to foolishness;
be clever and learn.

¹⁹ The wicked will come crawling
to those who obey God.
²⁰ You have no friends if you are poor,
but you have lots of friends
if you are rich.
²¹ It's wrong to hate others,
but God blesses everyone
who is kind to the poor.
²² It's a mistake to make evil plans,
but you will have loyal friends
if you want to do right.
²³ Hard work is worthwhile,
but empty talk will make you poor.
²⁴ Wisdom can make you rich,
but foolishness leads
to more foolishness.
²⁵ An honest witness can save your life,
but liars can't be trusted.

²⁶ If you respect the LORD,
you and your children have
a strong fortress
²⁷ and a life-giving fountain
that keeps you safe from deadly traps.

²⁸ Rulers of powerful nations
are held in honour;
rulers of weak nations are nothing at all.
²⁹ It's clever to be patient,
but it's stupid to lose your temper.
³⁰ It's healthy to be content,
but envy can eat you up.
³¹ If you ill-treat the poor,
you insult your Creator;

if you are kind to them,
you show him respect.
³² In times of trouble
the wicked are destroyed,
but even at death
the innocent have faith.'
³³ Wisdom is found in the minds
of people with good sense,
but fools don't know it.'
³⁴ Doing right brings honour to a nation,
but sin brings disgrace.
³⁵ Kings reward servants who act wisely,
but they punish those
who act foolishly.

CHAPTER 15

The LORD sees everything

¹ A kind answer soothes angry feelings,
but harsh words stir them up.
² Words of wisdom come from the wise,
but fools speak foolishness.

³ The LORD sees everything,
whether good or bad.
⁴ Kind words are good medicine,
but deceitful words can really hurt.
⁵ Don't be a fool
and disobey your parents.
Be clever! Accept correction.
⁶ Good people become wealthy,
but those who are evil
will lose what they have.
⁷ Words of wisdom make good sense;
the thoughts of a fool
make no sense at all.

⁸ The LORD is disgusted
by gifts from the wicked,
but it makes him happy
when his people pray.
⁹ The LORD is disgusted
with all who do wrong,
but he loves everyone who does right.
¹⁰ If you turn from the right way,
you will be punished;
if you refuse correction,
you will die.

¹¹ If the LORD can see everything
in the world of the dead,
he can see in our hearts.
¹² Those who sneer at others
don't like to be corrected,
and they won't ask help
from someone with sense.
¹³ Happiness makes you smile;
sorrow can crush you.

See also: 14.12: Prov 16.25.

¹⁴ Anyone with good sense
is eager to learn more,
but fools are hungry for foolishness.

¹⁵ The poor have a hard life,
but being content is as good
as an endless feast.

¹⁶ It's better to obey the LORD
and have only a little,
than to be very rich
and terribly confused.

¹⁷ A simple meal with love
is better than a feast
where there is hatred.

¹⁸ Losing your temper
causes a lot of trouble,
but staying calm settles arguments.

¹⁹ Being lazy is like walking
in a thorn patch,
but everyone who does right
walks on a smooth road.

²⁰ Children with good sense
make their parents happy,
but foolish children
are hateful to them.

²¹ Stupidity brings happiness
to senseless fools,
but everyone with good sense
follows the straight path.

²² Without good advice
everything goes wrong —
it takes careful planning
for things to go right.

²³ Giving the right answer at the right time
makes everyone happy.

²⁴ All who are wise follow a road
that leads upward to life
and away from death.

²⁵ The LORD destroys the homes
of those who are proud,
but he protects the property of widows.

²⁶ The LORD hates evil thoughts,
but kind words please him.

²⁷ Being greedy causes trouble
for your family,
but you protect yourself
by refusing bribes.

²⁸ Good people think before they answer,
but the wicked speak evil
without ever thinking.

²⁹ The LORD never even hears
the prayers of the wicked,
but he answers the prayers
of all who obey him.

³⁰ A friendly smile makes you happy,
and good news makes you feel strong.

³¹ Healthy correction is good,
and if you accept it,
you will be wise.

³² You hurt only yourself
by rejecting instruction,
but it makes good sense to accept it.

³³ Showing respect to the LORD
will make you wise,
and being humble
will bring honour to you.

CHAPTER 16

The LORD has the final word

¹ We humans make plans,
but the LORD has the final word.

² We may think we know what is right,
but the LORD is the judge of our motives.

³ Share your plans with the LORD,
and you will succeed.

⁴ The LORD has a reason
for everything he does,
and he lets evil people live
only to be punished.

⁵ The LORD doesn't like
anyone who is conceited —
you can be sure they will be punished.

⁶ If we truly love God,
our sins will be forgiven;
if we show him respect,
we will keep away from sin.

⁷ When we please the LORD,
even our enemies make friends with us.

⁸ It's better to be honest and poor
than to be dishonest and rich.

⁹ We make our own plans,
but the LORD decides where we will go.

¹⁰ Rulers speak with authority
and are never wrong.

¹¹ The LORD doesn't like it
when we cheat in business.

¹² Justice makes rulers powerful.
They should hate evil

¹³ and like honesty and truth.

¹⁴ An angry ruler can put you to death.
So be wise!
Don't make one angry.

¹⁵ When a ruler is happy
and pleased with you,
it's like refreshing rain,
and you will live.

¹⁶ It's much better to be wise
and sensible than to be rich.

¹⁷ God's people avoid evil ways,
and they protect themselves
by watching where they go.

¹⁸ Too much pride will destroy you.
¹⁹ You are better off being humble and poor
    than getting rich
    from what you take by force.
²⁰ If you know what you're doing,'
    you will prosper.
    God blesses everyone who trusts him.
²¹ Good judgment proves
    that you are wise,
    and if you speak kindly,
    you can teach others.
²² Good sense is a fountain that gives life,
    but fools are punished
    by their foolishness.
²³ You can persuade others
    if you are wise
    and speak sensibly.

²⁴ Kind words are like honey —
    they cheer you up
    and make you feel strong.
²⁵ Sometimes what seems right
    is really a road to death.
²⁶ The hungrier you are,
    the harder you work.
²⁷ Worthless people plan trouble.
    Even their words burn
    like a flaming fire.
²⁸ Gossip is no good!
    It causes hard feelings
    and comes between friends.

²⁹ Don't trust violent people.
    They will mislead you
    to do the wrong thing.
³⁰ When someone winks
    or grins behind your back,
    trouble is on the way.
³¹ Grey hair is a glorious crown
    worn by those who have lived right.
³² Controlling your temper
    is better than being a hero
    who captures a city.
³³ We make our own decisions,
    but the LORD alone
    determines what happens.

CHAPTER 17

Our thoughts are tested by the LORD

¹ A dry crust of bread eaten
    in peace and quiet
    is better than a feast eaten
    where everyone argues.
² A hard-working slave
    will be placed in charge
    of a no-good child,

See also: 16.25: Prov 14.12.

Helpline

Help! I don't know what to do in my gap year

'I want to take some time out before University, but what should I do? Where should I go?'

Gap years offer a lot of opportunities. A chance to go somewhere special and do something different. So how do you choose?

Listen to your heart. What do you want to do? God doesn't ignore our interests and passions; he wants us to feel passionate and involved. So don't ignore your own feelings.

Check out Proverbs 16.3 and share your plans with God. Ask him to give you wisdom and help you make them real.

You'll have to earn some money. Your parents or church might support you, but you can make their task easier by earning some money yourself. Show your commitment by doing some jobs or maybe doing some fund-raising yourself.

Commit yourself to learn. It's not a holiday. Go into it with the right frame of mind. You're going to serve, not be served.

Three things

Heart

What does your heart say? What are the issues and interests that drive you? Is there a country or a city that has always been of interest to you? Is there a topic that you feel strongly about? Are there issues you really want to understand better?

Research

Talk your options over with your parents/friends/youthleaders/church. There are Christian agencies to advise and help.

Plan

What can you do? Plan and prepare. Raise funds. Organise some prayer support. Make sure that you're going in to serve.

More...

Guidance p.685
What happens if we take a wrong turn? p.601
Our ideas are often radically different from God's. So who's right? p.786

and that slave will be given
the same inheritance
that each child receives.

3 Silver and gold are tested by flames of fire;
our thoughts are tested by the LORD.

4 Troublemakers listen to troublemakers,
and liars listen to liars.

5 By insulting the poor,
you insult your Creator.
You will be punished
if you make fun
of someone in trouble.

6 Grandparents are proud
of their grandchildren,
and children should be proud
of their parents.

7 It sounds strange for a fool
to talk sensibly,
but it's even worse for a ruler to tell lies.

8 A bribe works miracles like a magic charm
that brings good luck.

9 You will keep your friends
if you forgive them,
but you will lose your friends
if you keep talking about
what they did wrong.

10 A sensible person accepts correction,
but you can't beat sense into a fool.

11 Cruel people want to rebel,
and so vicious attackers
will be sent against them.

12 A bear robbed of her cubs
is far less dangerous
than a stubborn fool.

13 You will always have trouble
if you are mean to those
who are good to you.

14 The start of an argument
is like a water leak —
so stop it before real trouble breaks out.

15 The LORD doesn't like those
who defend the guilty
or condemn the innocent.

16 Why should fools have money
for an education
when they refuse to learn?

17 A friend is always a friend,
and relatives are born
to share our troubles.

18 It's stupid to guarantee
someone else's loan.

19 The wicked and the proud love trouble
and keep begging to be hurt.

20 Dishonesty does you no good,
and telling lies will get you in trouble.

21 It's never pleasant
to be the parent of a fool
and have nothing but pain.

22 If you are cheerful, you feel good;
if you are sad, you hurt all over.

23 Crooks accept secret bribes
to keep justice from being done.

24 Anyone with wisdom knows
what makes good sense,
but fools can never
make up their minds.

25 Foolish children bring sorrow
to their father
and pain to their mother.

26 It isn't fair to punish the innocent
and those who do right.

27 It makes a lot of sense
to be a person of few words
and to stay calm.

28 Even fools seem clever
when they are quiet.

CHAPTER 18

It's wrong to favour the guilty

1 It's selfish and stupid
to think only of yourself
and to sneer at people
who have sense.'

2 Fools have no desire to learn;
they would much rather
give their own opinion.

3 Wrongdoing leads to shame and disgrace.

4 Words of wisdom are a stream
that flows from a deep fountain.

5 It's wrong to favour the guilty
and keep the innocent
from getting justice.

6 Foolish talk will get you
into a lot of trouble.

7 Saying foolish things
is like setting a trap
to destroy yourself.

8 There's nothing so delicious
as the taste of gossip!
It melts in your mouth.

9 Being lazy is no different
from being a troublemaker.

10 The LORD is a mighty tower
where his people can run for safety —

11 the rich think their money
is a wall of protection.

12 Pride leads to destruction;
humility leads to honour.

13 It's stupid and embarrassing
to give an answer before you listen.

¹⁴ Being cheerful helps when we are sick,
but nothing helps when we give up.
¹⁵ Everyone with good sense wants to learn.
¹⁶ A gift will get you in to see anyone.
¹⁷ You may think you have won
your case in court,
until your opponent speaks.
¹⁸ Drawing straws is one way
to settle a difficult case.
¹⁹ Making up with a friend
you have offended⁑
is harder than breaking
through a city wall.

²⁰ Make your words good —
you will be glad you did.
²¹ Words can bring death or life!
Talk too much, and you will eat
everything you say.
²² A man's greatest treasure is his wife —
she is a gift from the LORD.
²³ The poor must beg for help,
but the rich can give a harsh reply.
²⁴ Some friends don't help,⁑
but a true friend is closer
than your own family.

CHAPTER 19

It's wise to be patient

¹ It's better to be poor
and live right
than to be a stupid liar.
² Willingness and stupidity
don't go well together.
If you are too eager,
you will miss the road.
³ We are ruined by our own stupidity,
though we blame the LORD.

⁴ The rich have many friends;
the poor have none.
⁵ Dishonest witnesses and liars
won't escape punishment.
⁶ Everyone tries to be friends
of those who can help them.
⁷ If you are poor,
your own relatives reject you,
and your friends are worse.
When you really need them,
they are not there.⁑

⁸ Do yourself a favour
by having good sense —
you will be glad you did.
⁹ Dishonest witnesses and liars
will be destroyed.

Helpline

Help! My friends slag off other people

'My friends slag off other people. I know I shouldn't join in, but what can I do?'

Even though they're your friends, if they're not Christians, they don't have the same set of values that you do. So when they do things that you know God wouldn't want you to do, you're faced with a choice; go with the crowd or go with God.

They might be your friends, but you have to think for yourself. Work out what God wants you to do. Just because they do something doesn't mean you have to do it.

Trust God. He knows what the outcome of this situation will be. Maybe your friends will respect you more for your stance; maybe they'll turn away from you (in which case they probably weren't great friends in the first place). Whatever the outcome God intends us to stand up for what is right. And we can't change that, not even for our friends.

Three things

Live

It probably won't help to lecture your friends about their behaviour. Just live your life the way God intends you to live it. If they ask you about it, explain simply why you do the things you do.

Quiet

If you can't agree with what they say, but you don't feel you can confront them, then just keep quiet. Say nothing. You'll be surprised at how eloquent silence can be.

Cost

Ultimately, you can't compromise. They might be angry at you, but you have to do what God wants. Being a Christian is costly sometimes, but we have to obey what we know are God's commands.

More...

Help! How do I stop my friends doing wrong? p.1312
Living truthfully p.1070
Forgiving others p.1162

¹⁰ It isn't right for a fool
    to live in luxury
    or for a slave to rule in place of a king.
¹¹ It's wise to be patient
    and show what you are like
    by forgiving others.
¹² An angry king roars like a lion,
    but when a king is pleased,
    it's like dew on the crops.

¹³ A foolish son brings disgrace
    to his father.
    A nagging wife goes on and on
    like the drip, drip, drip of the rain.
¹⁴ You may inherit all you own
    from your parents,
    but a sensible wife
    is a gift from the LORD.
¹⁵ If you are lazy and sleep your time away,
    you will starve.

¹⁶ Obey the Lord's teachings
    and you will live —
    disobey and you will die.
¹⁷ Caring for the poor
    is lending to the LORD,
    and you will be well repaid.
¹⁸ Correct your children
    before it's too late;
    if you don't punish them,
    you are destroying them.
¹⁹ People with bad tempers
    are always in trouble,
    and they need help over and over again.'

²⁰ Pay attention to advice
    and accept correction,
    so you can live sensibly.
²¹ We may make a lot of plans,
    but the LORD will do
    what he has decided.
²² What matters most is loyalty.
    It's better to be poor than to be a liar.
²³ Showing respect to the LORD
    brings true life —
    if you do it, you can relax
    without fear of danger.

²⁴ Some people are too lazy
    to lift a hand to feed themselves.
²⁵ Stupid fools learn good sense
    by seeing others punished;
    a sensible person learns
    by being corrected.
²⁶ Children who bring disgrace
    rob their father
    and chase their mother away.
²⁷ If you stop learning, you will forget
    what you already know.

²⁸ A lying witness makes fun
    of the court system,
    and criminals think crime
    is really delicious.
²⁹ Every stupid fool is just waiting
    to be punished.

CHAPTER 20

Words of wisdom are better than gold

¹ It isn't clever to get drunk!
    Drinking makes a fool of you
    and leads to fights.
² An angry ruler is like a roaring lion —
    make either one angry,
    and you are dead.
³ It makes you look good
    when you avoid a fight —
    only fools love to quarrel.
⁴ If you are too lazy to plough,
    don't expect a harvest.
⁵ Someone's thoughts may be
    as deep as the ocean,
    but if you are clever,
    you will discover them.

⁶ There are many who say,
    "You can trust me!"
    But can they be trusted?
⁷ Good people live right,
    and God blesses the children
    who follow their example.
⁸ When rulers decide cases,
    they weigh the evidence.
⁹ Can any of us really say,
    "My thoughts are pure,
    and my sins are gone"?

¹⁰ Two things the LORD hates
    are dishonest scales
    and dishonest measures.
¹¹ The good or bad that children do
    shows what they are like.
¹² Hearing and seeing
    are gifts from the LORD.
¹³ If you sleep all the time,
    you will starve;
    if you get up and work,
    you will have enough food.
¹⁴ Everyone likes to boast
    about getting a bargain.
¹⁵ Sensible words are better
    than gold or jewels.

¹⁶ You deserve to lose your coat
    if you loan it to someone
    to guarantee payment
    for the debt of a stranger.

17 The food you get by cheating
   may taste delicious,
   but it turns to gravel.
18 Be sure you have sound advice
   before making plans
   or starting a war.
19 Stay away from gossips —
   they tell everything.
20 Children who curse their parents
   will go to the land of darkness
   long before their time.
21 Getting rich quick'
   may turn out to be a curse.
22 Don't try to get even.
   Trust the LORD,
   and he will help you.

23 The LORD hates dishonest scales
   and dishonest weights.
   So don't cheat!
24 How can we know
   what will happen to us
   when the LORD alone decides?
25 Don't fall into the trap
   of making promises to God
   before you think!
26 A wise ruler severely punishes
   every criminal.
27 Our inner thoughts are a lamp
   from the LORD,
   and they search our hearts.
28 Rulers are protected
   by God's mercy and loyalty,
   but' they must be merciful
   for their kingdoms to last.
29 Young people take pride
   in their strength,
   but the grey hairs of wisdom
   are even more beautiful.
30 A severe beating can knock all
   of the evil out of you!

CHAPTER 21

The LORD is in charge

1 The LORD controls rulers,
   just as he determines
   the course of rivers.
2 We may think we are doing
   the right thing,
   but the LORD always knows
   what is in our hearts.
3 Doing what is right and fair
   pleases the LORD
   more than an offering.
4 Evil people are proud and arrogant,
   but sin is the only crop they produce.'

5 If you plan and work hard,
   you will have plenty;
   if you get in a hurry,
   you will end up poor.
6 Cheating to get rich is a foolish dream
   and no less than suicide.'
7 You destroy yourself
   by being cruel and violent
   and refusing to live right.
8 All crooks are liars,
   but anyone who is innocent
   will do right.
9 It's better to stay outside
   on the roof of your house
   than to live inside with a nagging wife.
10 Evil people want to do wrong,
   even to their friends.
11 An ignorant fool learns
   by seeing others punished;
   a sensible person learns
   by being instructed.

12 God is always fair!
   He knows what the wicked do
   and will punish them.
13 If you won't help the poor,
   don't expect to be heard
   when you cry out for help.
14 A secret bribe will save you
   from someone's fierce anger.
15 When justice is done,
   good citizens are glad
   and crooks are terrified.
16 If you stop using good sense,
   you will find yourself in the grave.
17 Heavy drinkers and others
   who live only for pleasure
   will lose all they have.
18 God's people will escape,
   but all who are wicked
   will pay the price.
19 It's better out in the desert
   than at home with a nagging,
   complaining wife.
20 Be sensible and store up
   precious treasures —
   don't waste them like a fool.
21 If you try to be kind and good,
   you will be blessed with life
   and goodness and honour.
22 One wise person can defeat
   a city full of soldiers
   and capture their fortress.
23 Watching what you say
   can save you a lot of trouble.
24 If you are proud and conceited,
   everyone will say, "You're a snob!"

Real life

Debt

Contributed by Credit Action

Are you worried about debt? If not, you should be. Some of you will already be facing up to huge student loans and may have other debts that are dragging you down as well. Proverbs 22.7 tells us that 'those who borrow are slaves of moneylenders.' This means, in fact, that the people from whom you borrow begin to dictate your future – they lay claim to both your money and your life. This is a bit rich given that everything belongs to God. So, is this how you are living? Or do you try to glorify Jesus in your handling of money?

Debt is sometimes literally a killer. It is the main cause of family breakdown, arguments and visits to the GP. When we borrow, we are told in Romans 13.8 that we need to repay all that we owe. But for many people who get in too far, this seems impossible. They thus get increasingly more guilty, frightened and lonely. You will certainly know someone in debt. Millions of people in Britain are struggling with it.

Calls to our helpline show many young adults getting into debt. As soon as you turn eighteen you are bombarded with offers of credit and the temptations are overwhelming. A child born today will see more than one million advertisements before they are twenty-one. Little wonder then that we succumb to all this buying pressure. Credit agencies make things that would otherwise be unaffordable for years, suddenly available. But it is very easy to spend on the whims of today and then be in such a mess that you don't have enough to meet the needs of tomorrow. If you get into too much debt, and you can't pay back what you should, you may end up with a County Court Judgement stopping you getting any more credit for six years. So you can't borrow when you most need to.

Think

How concerned are you about what you wear, eat or drive?

Have you prayed through what your priorities should be, and what your goals are for the rest of your life?

Do you think people get into debt because they are too absorbed with themselves?

Are you thinking of buying something on credit? Why? Is it a need or a want?

Act

To avoid debt, try and budget and stick to what you can afford.

Look at James 4.13–15 and determine your priorities.

Establish both long term and short term spending goals – and stick to them.

Don't borrow for anything other than essentials.

Try and repay what you owe as quickly as you can.

At the first sign of trouble seek free advice from our helpline.

Check

Proverbs 22.7; Romans 13.8; James 4.13–15

More...

Money p.1043
Materialism p.1141
Shopping p.973

25 If you want too much
and are too lazy to work,
it could be fatal.
26 But people who obey God
are always generous.

27 The Lord despises the offerings
of wicked people
with evil motives.
28 If you tell lies in court, you are done for;
only a reliable witness can do the job.
29 Wicked people bluff their way,
but God's people think
before they take a step.

30 No matter how much you know
or what plans you make,
you can't defeat the LORD.
31 Even if your army has horses
ready for battle,
the LORD will always win.

CHAPTER 22

The value of a good reputation

1 A good reputation and respect
are worth much more
than silver and gold.
2 The rich and the poor
are all created by the LORD.
3 When you see trouble coming,
don't be stupid
and walk right into it —
be clever and hide.

4 Respect and serve the LORD!
Your reward will be wealth,
a long life, and honour.
5 Crooks walk down a road
full of thorny traps.
Stay away from there!
6 Teach your children right from wrong,
and when they are grown
they will still do right.
7 The poor are ruled by the rich,
and those who borrow
are slaves of moneylenders.
8 Troublemakers get in trouble,
and their terrible anger
will get them nowhere.
9 The LORD blesses everyone
who freely gives food to the poor.
10 Arguments and fights will come to an end,
if you chase away those
who insult others.
11 The king is the friend of all
who are sincere
and speak with kindness.

12 The LORD watches over everyone
who shows good sense,
but he frustrates the plans
of deceitful liars.
13 Don't be so lazy that you say,
"If I go to work, a lion will eat me!"
14 The words of a bad woman
are like a deep pit;
if you make the LORD angry,
you will fall right in.
15 All children are foolish,
but firm correction
will make them change.
16 Cheat the poor to make profit
or give gifts to the rich —
either way you lose.

Thirty wise sayings

17 Here are some sayings
of people with wisdom,
so listen carefully as I teach.
18 You will be glad
that you know these sayings
and can recite them.
19 I am teaching them today,
so that you may trust the LORD.
20 I have written thirty sayings
filled with sound advice.
21 You can trust them completely
to give you the right words
for those in charge of you.

First saying

22 Don't take advantage of the poor
or cheat them in court.
23 The LORD is their defender,
and what you do to them,
he will do to you.

Second saying

24 Don't make friends with anyone
who has a bad temper.
25 You might turn out like them
and get caught in a trap.

Third saying

26 Don't guarantee to pay
someone else's debt.
27 If you don't have the money,
you might lose your bed.

Fourth saying

28 Don't move a boundary marker*
set up by your ancestors.

---

*22.28 marker: In ancient Israel boundary lines were
sacred because all property was a gift from the Lord
(see Deuteronomy 19.14).

Fifth saying

²⁹ If you do your job well,
   you will work for a ruler
   and never be a slave.

CHAPTER 23

Sixth saying

¹ When you are invited to eat with a king,
   use your best manners.
² Don't go and stuff yourself!
   That would be just the same
   as cutting your throat.
³ Don't be greedy for all that fancy food!
   It may not be so tasty.

Seventh saying

⁴ Give up trying so hard to get rich.
⁵ Your money flies away before you know it,
   just like an eagle suddenly taking off.

Eighth saying

⁶ Don't accept an invitation
   to eat a selfish person's food,
   no matter how good it is.
⁷ People like that take note
   of how much you eat.'
   They say, "Take all you want!"
   But they don't mean it.
⁸ Each bite will come back up,
   and all your kind words will be wasted.

Ninth saying

⁹ Don't talk to fools —
   they will just make fun of you.

Tenth saying

¹⁰ Don't move a boundary marker*
   or take the land that belongs to orphans.
¹¹ God All-Powerful is there
   to defend them against you.

Eleventh saying

¹² Listen to instruction
   and do your best to learn.

Twelfth saying

¹³ Don't fail to correct your children.
   You won't kill them by being firm,
¹⁴ and it may even save their lives.

Thirteenth saying

¹⁵ My children, if you show good sense,
   I will be happy,
¹⁶ and if you are truthful, I will really be glad.

Fourteenth saying

¹⁷ Don't be jealous of sinners,
   but always honour the LORD.
¹⁸ Then you will truly have hope
   for the future.

Fifteenth saying

¹⁹ Listen to me, my children!
   Be wise and have enough sense
   to follow the right path.
²⁰ Don't be a heavy drinker
   or stuff yourself with food.
²¹ It will make you feel drowsy,
   and you will end up poor
   with only rags to wear.

Sixteenth saying

²² Pay attention to your father,
   and don't neglect your mother
   when she grows old.
²³ Invest in truth and wisdom,
   discipline and good sense,
   and don't part with them.
²⁴ Make your father truly happy
   by living right
   and showing sound judgment.
²⁵ Make your parents proud,
   especially your mother.

Seventeenth saying

²⁶ My son, pay close attention,
   and gladly follow my example.
²⁷ Bad women and unfaithful wives
   are like a deep pit —
²⁸ they are waiting to attack you
   like a gang of robbers
   with victim after victim.

Eighteenth saying

²⁹ Who is always in trouble?
   Who argues and fights?
   Who has cuts and bruises?
   Whose eyes are red?
³⁰ Everyone who stays up late,
   having just one more drink.
³¹ Don't even look
   at that colourful stuff
   bubbling up in the glass!
   It goes down so easily,
³² but later it bites
   like a poisonous snake.
³³ You will see weird things,
   and your mind will play tricks on you.
³⁴ You will feel tossed about
   like someone trying to sleep
   on a ship in a storm.

---

*23.10 marker: See the note at 22.28.

Real life

Alcohol

Contributed by HopeUK

Drinking alcohol is one of those issues which is and will continue to be controversial. Six hundred or more biblical references and two thousand years of Christian tradition have not yet provided a clear answer. As a body the Christian church appears to send out mixed messages about alcohol.

The Bible tells us that Jesus wined and dined with sinners (Matthew 11.19); Paul advised Timothy to drink a little wine (1 Timothy 5.23) and Jesus turned water into wine (John 2.1–11); while Psalm 104.15 mentions 'wine that gladdens the heart of man'. However, there are strong statements about not getting drunk (Proverbs 20.1; 23.29–35; Ephesians 5.18; 1 Peter 4). And in Proverbs 31.1–9 a king is advised to stay away from drink if he wants to make wise decisions. So although there is no 11th Commandment saying 'Thou shalt not drink alcohol', to drink without thinking of the consequences is to act without exercising responsibility.

Let's look at the context in which all this was written. The chances are that first century Palestine didn't have the huge amount of drink problems we have today. 'Alcopops' and spirits, as well as persuasion by advertising, did not exist. And riding a donkey after a drink was less dangerous than drinking and driving today! Sanitation, was non-existent by our standards so there is no doubt that Paul was offering Timothy sound medical advice about avoiding the local water! But Jewish culture was strict about its use of alcohol: drunkenness was condemned.

Today alcohol may be legally available, under certain conditions, but the Bible says that not everything that's permissible is beneficial (1 Corinthians 10.23). A drug does not have to be illegal to be dangerous. And whilst some people consume alcohol without any apparent problems, millions of people are harmed as a result of drinking.

Members of the International Blue Cross Federation (a Christian organisation with member societies in over 50 countries) choose to help by adopting an alcohol-free lifestyle. Their personal sacrifice encourages alcoholics to stay 'dry' and helps people to be confident about choosing to live without drink.

Think

Jesus made up to 160 gallons of wine at Cana, but would he have made anything that would intoxicate or bring harm to anyone? Would he have done this today? If alcohol, cannabis, tobacco had all been discovered recently and only one could be made available legally, which one should it be?
Would you consider adopting an alcohol-free lifestyle?

Act

Find out more about the International Blue Cross Federation and Hope UK

Check

Psalm 104.15; Proverbs 20.1; 23.29–35; 31.1–9; Matthew 11.19; John 2.1–11; 1 Corinthians 10.23; Ephesians 5.18; 1 Timothy 5.23; 1 Peter 4.

More...

Addiction p.1182
Drugs p.1318
Help! I'm in trouble with the police p.378
Food and drink p.355

35 You will be bruised all over,
without even remembering
how it all happened.
And you will lie awake asking,
"When will morning come,
so I can drink some more?"

CHAPTER 24

Nineteenth saying

1 Don't be jealous of crooks
or want to be their friends.
2 All they think about
and talk about is violence and cruelty.

Twentieth saying

3 Use wisdom and understanding
to establish your home;
4 let good sense fill the rooms
with priceless treasures.

Twenty-first saying

5 Wisdom brings strength,
and knowledge gives power.
6 Battles are won by listening to advice
and making a lot of plans.

Twenty-second saying

7 Wisdom is too much for fools!
Their advice is no good.

Twenty-third saying

8 No one but troublemakers
think up trouble.
9 Everyone hates senseless fools
who think up ways to sin.

Twenty-fourth saying

10 Don't give up and be helpless
in times of trouble.

Twenty-fifth saying

11 Don't fail to rescue those
who are doomed to die.
12 Don't say, "I didn't know it!"
God can read your mind.
He watches each of us
and knows our thoughts.
And God will pay us back
for what we do.

Twenty-sixth saying

13 Honey is good for you, my children,
and it tastes sweet.
14 Wisdom is like honey for your life —
if you find it, your future is bright.

Twenty-seventh saying

15 Don't be a cruel person
who attacks good people
and hurts their families.
16 Even if good people fall seven times,
they will get back up.
But when trouble strikes the wicked,
that's the end of them.

Twenty-eighth saying

17 Don't be happy to see your enemies trip
and fall down.
18 The LORD will find out and be unhappy.
Then he will stop
being angry with them.

Twenty-ninth saying

19 Don't let evil people worry you
or make you jealous.
20 They will soon be gone
like the flame of a lamp that burns out.

Thirtieth saying

21 My children, you must respect
the LORD and the king,
and you must not make friends
with anyone
who rebels against either of them.
22 Who knows what sudden disaster
the LORD or a ruler might bring?

More sayings that make good sense

23 Here are some more sayings
that make good sense:
When you judge,
you must be fair.
24 If you let the guilty go free,
people of all nations
will hate and curse you.
25 But if you punish the guilty,
things will go well for you,
and you will prosper.
26 Giving an honest answer
is a sign of true friendship.
27 Get your fields ready
and plant your crops
before setting up home.
28 Don't accuse anyone who isn't guilty.
Don't ever tell a lie
29 or say to someone,
"I'll get even with you!"
30 I once walked by the field
and the vineyard of a lazy fool.
31 Thorns and weeds were everywhere,
and the stone wall had fallen down.
32 When I saw this,

it taught me a lesson:
³³ Sleep a little. Doze a little.
Fold your hands
and twiddle your thumbs.
³⁴ Suddenly poverty hits you
and everything is gone!

More of Solomon's wise sayings

CHAPTER 25

¹ Here are more of Solomon's proverbs.
They were copied by the officials
of King Hezekiah of Judah.
² God is praised for being mysterious;
rulers are praised for explaining mysteries.
³ Who can fully understand
the thoughts of a ruler?
They reach beyond the sky
and go deep in the earth.

⁴ Silver must be purified
before it can be used
to make something of value.
⁵ Evil people must be removed
before anyone can rule with justice.

⁶ Don't try to seem important
in the court of a ruler.
⁷ It's better for the ruler
to give you a high position
than for you to be embarrassed
in front of royal officials.
Be sure you are right
⁸ before you sue someone,
or you might lose your case
and be embarrassed.

⁹ When you and someone else
can't get along,
don't gossip about it.'
¹⁰ Others will find out,
and your reputation will then be ruined.

¹¹ The right word at the right time
is like precious gold set in silver.
¹² Listening to good advice
is worth much more
than jewellery made of gold.
¹³ A messenger you can trust
is just as refreshing
as cool water in summer.
¹⁴ Broken promises
are worse than rain clouds
that don't bring rain.

¹⁵ Patience and gentle talk
can convince a ruler
and overcome any problem.
¹⁶ Eating too much honey
can make you sick.
¹⁷ Don't visit friends too often,
or they will get tired of it
and start hating you.
¹⁸ Telling lies about friends
is like attacking them
with clubs and swords
and sharp arrows.
¹⁹ A friend you can't trust in times of trouble
is like having a toothache
or a sore foot.
²⁰ Singing to someone in deep sorrow
is like pouring vinegar in an open cut.'

²¹ If your enemies are hungry,
give them something to eat.
And if they are thirsty,
give them something to drink.
²² This will be the same
as piling burning coals on their heads.
And the LORD will reward you.
²³ As surely as rain blows in from the north,
anger is caused by cruel words.
²⁴ It's better to stay outside
on the roof of your house
than to live inside with a nagging wife.

²⁵ Good news from far away
refreshes like cold water
when you are thirsty.
²⁶ When a good person gives in
to the wicked,
it's like dumping rubbish
in a stream of clear water.
²⁷ Don't eat too much honey
or always want praise.'
²⁸ Losing self-control
leaves you as helpless
as a city without a wall.

CHAPTER 26

Don't be a fool

¹ Expecting snow in summer
and rain in the dry season
makes more sense
than honouring a fool.
² A curse you don't deserve will take wings
and fly away like a sparrow or a swallow.
³ Horses and donkeys
must be beaten and bridled —
and so must fools.

See also: 24.33–34: Prov 6.10–11.   25.6–7: Luke 14.8–10.

See also: 25.21–22: Rom 12.20.

4 Don't make a fool of yourself
   by answering a fool.
5 But if you answer any fools,
   show how foolish they are,
   so they won't feel clever.

6 Sending a message by a fool
   is like chopping off your foot
   and drinking poison.
7 A fool with words of wisdom
   is like an athlete
   with legs that can't move.ᵇ
8 Are you going to honour a fool?
   Why not shoot a slingshot
   with the stone tied tight?
9 A thorn bush waved around
   in the hand of a drunkard
   is no worse than a proverb
   in the mouth of a fool.

10 It's no cleverer to shoot arrows
    at every passer-by
    than it is to hire a bunch
    of worthless nobodies.ᵇ
11 Dogs return to eat their vomit,
    just as fools repeat their foolishness.
12 There is more hope for a fool
    than for someone who says,
    "I'm really clever!"

13 Don't be lazy and keep saying,
    "There's a lion outside!"
14 A door turns on its hinges,
    but a lazy person just turns over in bed.
15 Some of us are so lazy
    that we won't lift a hand
    to feed ourselves.
16 A lazy person says,
    "I am cleverer than everyone else."

17 It's better to take hold
    of a mad dog by the ears
    than to take part
    in someone else's argument.
18 It's no crazier to shoot
    sharp and flaming arrows
19 than to cheat someone and say,
    "I was only fooling!"

20 Where there is no fuel a fire goes out;
    where there is no gossip
    arguments come to an end.
21 Troublemakers start trouble,
    just as sparks and fuel start a fire.
22 There is nothing so delicious
    as the taste of gossip!
    It melts in your mouth.

23 Hiding hateful thoughts
    behind smoothᵇ talk
    is like coating a clay pot
    with a cheap glaze.
24 The pleasant talk of an enemy
    hides more evil plans
25 than can be counted —
    so don't believe a word!
26 Everyone will see through
    those evil plans.
27 If you dig a pit, you will fall in;
    if you start a stone rolling,
    it will roll back on you.
28 Watch out for anyone
    who tells lies and flatters —
    they are out to get you.

CHAPTER 27
Don't boast about tomorrow

1 Don't boast about tomorrow!
   Each day brings its own surprises.
2 Don't boast about yourself —
   let others praise you.
3 Stones and sand are heavy,
   but trouble caused by a fool
   is a much heavier load.
4 An angry person is dangerous,
   but a jealous person is even worse.

5 A truly good friend
   will openly correct you.
6 You can trust a friend who corrects you,
   but kisses from an enemy
   are nothing but lies.
7 If you have had enough to eat,
   honey doesn't taste good,
   but if you are really hungry,
   you will eat anything.

8 When you are far from home,
   you feel like a bird without a nest.
9 The sweet smell of incense
   can make you feel good,
   but true friendship is better still.ᵇ
10 Don't desert an old friend of your family
    or visit your relatives
    when you are in trouble.
   A friend nearby is better
   than relatives far away.

11 My child, show good sense!
    Then I will be happy
    and able to answer anyone
    who criticizes me.

See also: 26.11: 2 Pet 2.22.
See also: 27.1: Jam 4.13–16.

Being christian

Being accountable

Proverbs 27.1–6, 17

One of the reasons that we meet together as Christians is so that we can keep an eye on each other.

It's like when you're keeping fit, or losing weight, or even revising for exams: it's always good if you've got someone to keep tabs on you. They keep you going; they keep your eye on the target. As Proverbs puts it, we make each other sharper for the battle.

Christians should be accountable to each other. It's not a question of someone rapping you over the knuckles or telling you off; it's a question of someone helping you with your walk.

If you see a fellow Christian going the wrong way, it's your job to bring them back. Not in a rough way; not in a way which embarrasses or condemns them. But gently – steering them back on the right course.

Are you accountable to others? Are there people who will ask you the tough questions in your life? It's important to have people who will check up on us. That way, if we do fall, there will always be someone there to help lift us up.

Being Christian: Being accountable

• Share your life with others. Ask them to pray with you and help you in your walk.
• Make sure you take the lump of timber out of your own eye before you criticise the speck in someone else's.
• Be sensitive to others who are drifting off course. Don't barge in, but get alongside.
• Meet regularly with friends you trust; people with whom you can share all the details of your life.

12 Be cautious and hide
    when you see danger —
    don't be stupid and walk
    right into trouble.
13 Don't loan money to a stranger
    unless you are given something
    to guarantee payment.
14 A loud greeting
    early in the morning
    is the same as a curse.
15 The steady dripping of rain
    and the nagging of a wife
    are one and the same.
16 It's easier to catch the wind
    or hold olive oil in your hand
    than to stop a nagging wife.

17 Just as iron sharpens iron,
    friends sharpen the minds of each other.
18 Take care of a tree,
    and you will eat its fruit;
    look after your master,
    and you will be praised.
19 You see your face in a mirror
    and your thoughts
    in the minds of others.
20 Death and the grave are never satisfied,
    and neither are we.
21 Gold and silver are tested
    in a red-hot furnace,
    but we are tested by praise.
22 No matter how hard you beat a fool,
    you can't pound out the foolishness.

23 You should take good care
    of your sheep and goats,
24 because wealth and honour
    don't last for ever.
25 After the hay is cut
    and the new growth appears
    and the harvest is over,
26 you can sell lambs and goats
    to buy clothes and land.
27 From the milk of the goats,
    you can make enough cheese
    to feed your family and all your servants.

CHAPTER 28

The Law of God makes sense

1 Wicked people run away
    when no one chases them,
    but those who live right
    are as brave as lions.
2 In time of civil war
    there are many leaders,
    but a sensible leader
    restores law and order.'

3 When someone poor takes over
    and ill-treats the poor,
    it's like a heavy rain
    destroying the crops.

4 Lawbreakers praise criminals,
    but law-abiding citizens
    always oppose them.

5 Criminals don't know what justice means,
    but all who respect the LORD
    understand it completely.

6 It's better to be poor and live right,
    than to be rich and dishonest.

7 It makes good sense
    to obey the Law of God,
    but you disgrace your parents
    if you make friends
    with worthless nobodies.

8 If you make money by charging
    high interest rates,
    you will lose it all to someone
    who cares for the poor.

9 God cannot stand the prayers
    of anyone who disobeys his Law.

10 By leading good people to sin,
    you dig a pit for yourself,
    but all who live right
    will have a bright future.

11 The rich think highly of themselves,
    but anyone poor and sensible
    sees right through them.

12 When an honest person wins,
    it's time to celebrate;
    when crooks are in control,
    it's best to hide.

13 If you don't confess your sins,
    you will be a failure.
    But God will be merciful
    if you confess your sins and give them up.

14 The LORD blesses everyone
    who is afraid to do evil,
    but if you are cruel,
    you will end up in trouble.

15 A ruler who ill-treats the poor
    is like a roaring lion
    or a bear hunting for food.

16 A heartless leader is a fool,
    but anyone who refuses
    to get rich by cheating others
    will live a long time.

17 Don't give help to murderers!
    Make them stay on the run
    for as long as they live.◆

18 Honesty will keep you safe,
    but everyone who is crooked
    will suddenly fall.

19 Work hard, and you will have
    a lot of food;
    waste time, and you will have
    a lot of trouble.

20 God blesses his loyal people,
    but punishes all who want
    to get rich quick.

21 It isn't right to be unfair,
    but some people can be bribed
    with only a piece of bread.

22 Don't be selfish and eager to get rich —
    you will end up worse off
    than you can imagine.

23 Honest correction is appreciated
    more than flattery.

24 If you cheat your parents
    and don't think it's wrong,
    you are a common thief.

25 Selfish people cause trouble,
    but you will live a full life
    if you trust the LORD.

26 Only fools would trust
    what they alone think,
    but if you live by wisdom,
    you will do all right.

27 Giving to the poor
    will keep you from poverty,
    but if you close your eyes to their needs,
    everyone will curse you.

28 When crooks are in control,
    everyone tries to hide,
    but when they lose power,
    good people are everywhere.

CHAPTER 29

Use good sense

1 If you keep being stubborn
    after many warnings,
    you will suddenly discover
    you have gone too far.

2 When justice rules a nation,
    everyone is glad;
    when injustice rules,
    everyone groans.

3 If you love wisdom,
    your parents will be glad,
    but chasing after bad women
    will cost you everything.

4 An honest ruler
    makes the nation strong;
    a ruler who takes bribes
    will bring it to ruin.

5 Flattery is nothing less
    than setting a trap.

6 Your sins will catch you,
   but everyone who lives right
   will sing and celebrate.
7 The wicked don't care
   about the rights of the poor,
   but good people do.
8 Sneering at others is a spark
   that sets a city on fire;
   using good sense can put out
   the flames of anger.

9 Be wise and don't sue a fool.
   You won't get satisfaction,
   because all the fool will do
   is sneer and shout.
10 A murderer hates everyone
   who is honest and lives right.›
11 Don't be a fool
   and quickly lose your temper —
   be sensible and patient.

12 A ruler who listens to lies
   will have corrupt officials.
13 The poor and all who misuse them
   must each depend on God for light.
14 Kings who are fair to the poor
   will rule for ever.

15 Correct your children,
   and they will be wise;
   children out of control
   disgrace their mothers.
16 Crime increases
   when crooks are in power,
   but law-abiding citizens
   will see them fall.
17 If you correct your children,
   they will bring you peace and happiness.

18 Without guidance from God,
   law and order disappear,
   but God blesses everyone
   who obeys his Law.
19 Even when servants are clever,
   it takes more than words
   to make them obey.
20 There is more hope for a fool
   than for someone who speaks
   without thinking.
21 Slaves you treat kindly
   from their childhood
   will cause you sorrow.›
22 A person with a quick temper
   stirs up arguments
   and commits a lot of sins.

23 Too much pride brings disgrace;
   humility leads to honour.
24 If you take part in a crime,
   you are your worst enemy,
   because even under oath
   you can't tell the truth.
25 Don't fall into the trap
   of being a coward —
   trust the LORD, and you will be safe.
26 Many try to make friends with a ruler,
   but justice comes from the LORD.
27 Good people and criminals
   can't stand each other.

The sayings of Agur

CHAPTER 30

1 These are the sayings
   and the message of Agur son of Jakeh.
   Someone cries out to God,
   "I am completely worn out!
   How can I last?›
2 I am far too stupid
   to be considered human.
3 I never was wise,
   and I don't understand what God is like."

4 Has anyone gone up to heaven
   and come back down?
   Has anyone grabbed hold of the wind?
   Has anyone wrapped up the sea
   or marked out boundaries
   for the earth?
   If you know of any
   who have done such things,
   then tell me their names
   and their children's names.

5 Everything God says is true —
   and it's a shield for all
   who come to him for safety.
6 Don't change what God has said!
   He will correct you and show
   that you are a liar.

7 There are two things, Lord,
   I want you to do for me before I die:
8 make me absolutely honest,
   and don't let me be too poor or too rich.
   Give me just what I need.
9 If I have too much to eat,
   I might forget about you;
   if I don't have enough,
   I might steal and disgrace your name.

10 Don't tell a slave owner something bad
   about one of the slaves.
   That slave will curse you,
   and you will be in trouble.

11 Some people curse their father
   and even their mother;

Real life

Human rights

Christian Solidarity

How would you feel if someone stole your lunch money? Upset? Angry? Helpless? Hungry? What if someone stole your little sister's lunch money? Would you be equally upset? What if someone stole someone else's little sister's lunch money? What would you do about that?

The God of the Bible is very strong on human rights and is really angry when those rights are abused. He hates it when poor people are trampled on, and actively intervenes when he sees injustice. Those who follow this God are called to live out his values as a sign that we are truly one of his family.

In Proverbs 31.8–9 we read: 'Speak up for those who cannot speak for themselves, for the rights of all who are suffering hardship. Speak up and judge fairly, defend the rights of the poor and needy.'

If we see people in the developing world being deprived of the freedom to trade fairly or unable to get water or unable to spend on schooling for their children because they are still paying the interest on a long-term debt, we have to speak out.

Basic human rights are set out in the Universal Declaration of Human Rights, adopted in 1948 by the United Nations. It covers all sorts of things from the right to bring up a family, the right to education, health, treatment before the law, rights to work and rest and the right to live out your religious beliefs.

As Christians, we are to be change makers in our society. We cannot afford to live comfortable lives in the West and ignore those who are despised by everybody else. Getting involved with campaigning for human rights is immensely rewarding as well as the right thing to do. How are you going to make a difference?

Think

Can you recite any of the Universal Declaration of Human Rights?
Have you ever come across an unfair situation that made you really cross? Who was being unfairly treated? Why did it make you cross? What did you do about it?
Have you ever taken part in any kind of campaign for human rights? What were you required to do?

Act

Find out which organisations are working to create positive changes in the field of human rights.
Read more about the area which concerns you most: for instance work, children, imprisonment, torture, education, the status of women.
Write letters on behalf of persecuted Christians.
Get active in your school or church, letting others know about trade and justice issues.
Buy fairly traded chocolate and clothes; make sure your household drinks fairly traded coffee and tea.

Check

Isaiah 58.1–14; Matthew 25.35–36; Luke 10.33–37

More...

Persecuted church p.1220
Persecution p.1215
Civil disobedience p.1247
Politics p.1358

¹² others think they are perfect,
   but they are stained by sin.
¹³ Some people are stuck-up
   and act like snobs;
¹⁴ others are so greedy
   that they gobble up
   the poor and homeless.

¹⁵ Greed⸀ has twins,
   each named "Give me!"
There are three or four things
   that are never satisfied:
¹⁶   the world of the dead
   and a childless wife,
   the thirsty earth and a flaming fire.

¹⁷ Don't make fun of your father
   or disobey your mother —
crows will peck out your eyes,
   and vultures will eat the rest of you.

¹⁸ There are three or four things
   I cannot understand:
¹⁹ how eagles fly so high
   or snakes crawl on rocks,
   how ships sail the ocean
   or people fall in love.

²⁰ An unfaithful wife says,
   "Sleeping with another man
   is as natural as eating."

²¹ There are three or four things
   that make the earth tremble
   and are unbearable:
²² a slave who becomes king,
   a fool who eats too much,
²³ a hateful woman
   who finds a husband, and a slave
   who takes the place
   of the woman who owns her.

²⁴ On this earth four things
   are small but very wise:
²⁵ ants, who seem to be feeble,
   but store up food all summer long;
²⁶ badgers, who seem to be weak,
   but live among the rocks;
²⁷ locusts, who have no king,
   but march like an army;
²⁸ lizards,⸀ which can be caught
   in your hand,
   but sneak into palaces.

²⁹ Three or four creatures
   really strut around:
³⁰ those fearless lions
   who rule the jungle,
³¹ those proud cocks,
   those mountain goats,
   and those rulers who have no enemies.⸀

³² If you are foolishly boasting
   or planning something evil,
   then stop it now!
³³ If you churn milk you get butter;
   if you hit your nose,
   you get blood —
   and if you stay angry,
   you get in trouble.

What King Lemuel's mother taught him

CHAPTER 31

¹ These are the sayings
   that King Lemuel of Massa
   was taught by his mother.
² My son Lemuel, you were born
   in answer to my prayers,
   so listen carefully.
³ Don't waste your life
   chasing after women!
   This has ruined many kings.

⁴ Kings and leaders should not get drunk
   or even want to drink.
⁵ Drinking makes you forget
   your responsibilities,
   and you ill-treat the poor.
⁶ Beer and wine are only for the dying
   or for those who have lost all hope.
⁷ Let them drink and forget
   how poor and miserable they feel.
⁸ But you must defend
   those who are helpless
   and have no hope.
⁹ Be fair and give justice
   to the poor and homeless.

In praise of a good wife

¹⁰ A truly good wife
   is the most precious treasure
   a man can find!
¹¹ Her husband depends on her,
   and she never lets him down.
¹² She is good to him every day of her life,
¹³   and with her own hands
   she gladly makes clothes.
¹⁴ She is like a sailing ship
   that brings food from across the sea.
¹⁵ She gets up before daylight
   to prepare food for her family
   and for her servants.⸀
¹⁶ She knows how to buy land
   and how to plant a vineyard,
¹⁷   and she always works hard.

¹⁸ She knows when to buy or sell,
and she stays busy until late at night.
¹⁹ She spins her own cloth,
²⁰ and she helps the poor and the needy.
²¹ Her family has warm clothing,
and so she doesn't worry when it snows.
²² She does her own sewing,
and everything she wears is beautiful.

²³ Her husband is a well-known
and respected leader
in the city.
²⁴ She makes clothes to sell
to the shop owners.
²⁵ She is strong and graceful,›
as well as cheerful about the future.
²⁶ Her words are sensible,
and her advice is thoughtful.
²⁷ She takes good care
of her family and is never lazy.
²⁸ Her children praise her,
and with great pride her husband says,
²⁹ "There are many good women,
but you are the best!"

³⁰ Charm can be deceiving,
and beauty fades away,
but a woman who honours the LORD
deserves to be praised.
³¹ Show her respect —
praise her in public
for what she has done.

Additional notes

›**1.7 the beginning of knowledge:** Or "what knowledge is all about".
›**1.17 They are . . . trap:** Or "Be like a bird that won't go for the bait, if it sees the trap."
›**2.7 helpful advice:** Or "wisdom".
›**6.24 someone else's wife:** Or "an evil woman".
›**6.30 not even:** Or "except".
›**7.22 a fool . . . punished:** One possible meaning for the difficult Hebrew text.
›**8.22 From the beginning . . . with the LORD:** Or "In the very beginning, the LORD created me."
›**8.23 gave life to:** Or "formed".
›**8.30 helping . . . build:** Or "like his own child".
›**9.10 the beginning of wisdom:** Or "what wisdom is all about".
›**9.13 Stupidity:** Or "A foolish woman".
›**10.2 good:** Or "generous".
›**10.10 and foolish . . . ruin:** One ancient translation "but you can help people by correcting them."
›**10.22 When . . . regret:** Or "No matter how hard you work, your riches really come from the Lord."

›**11.16 but . . . rich:** Or "a ruthless man will only get rich".
›**11.23 Good people . . . trouble:** Or "Good people do what is best, but troublemakers just stir up trouble."
›**11.30 act . . . follow:** Hebrew; one ancient translation "but violence leads to death."
›**11.31 rewarded:** Or "punished".
›**12.9 It's . . . servant:** Or "It is better just to have an ordinary job."
›**12.12 An evil . . . evil:** Or "Evil people love what they get from being evil".
›**12.26 wrong:** One possible meaning for the difficult Hebrew text of verse 26.
›**12.27 but . . . treasure:** One possible meaning for the difficult Hebrew text.
›**13.15 people . . . disaster:** One possible meaning for the difficult Hebrew text.
›**13.23 grow:** One possible meaning for the difficult Hebrew text of verse 23.
›**14.9 Fools . . . wrong:** One possible meaning for the difficult Hebrew text.
›**14.32 but even . . . faith:** One possible meaning for the difficult Hebrew text. Some ancient translations "but good people trust their innocence".
›**14.33 but . . . it:** One possible meaning for the difficult Hebrew text. Some ancient translations "but not in the mind of a fool".
›**16.20 know what . . . doing:** Or "do what you're taught".
›**18.1 sense:** One possible meaning for the difficult Hebrew text of verse 1.
›**18.19 Making . . . offended:** One possible meaning for the difficult Hebrew text.
›**18.24 Some . . . help:** One possible meaning for the difficult Hebrew text.
›**19.7 When . . . there:** One possible meaning for the difficult Hebrew text.
›**19.19 and they . . . again:** One possible meaning for the difficult Hebrew text.
›**20.21 quick:** Or "the wrong way".
›**20.28 by God's mercy . . . but:** Or "by their mercy . . . and".
›**21.4 but sin . . . produce:** Or "but sin is the only light they ever follow."
›**21.6 and . . . suicide:** One possible meaning for the difficult Hebrew text.
›**23.7 People . . . eat:** One possible meaning for the difficult Hebrew text.
›**25.9 When . . . it:** Or "Settle a problem privately between you and your neighbour and don't involve others."
›**25.20 cut:** One possible meaning for the difficult Hebrew text of verse 20.
›**25.27 or . . . praise:** One possible meaning for the difficult Hebrew text.
›**26.7 with . . . move:** One possible meaning for the difficult Hebrew text.
›**26.10 nobodies:** One possible meaning for the difficult Hebrew text of verse 10.
›**26.23 smooth:** One ancient translation; Hebrew "hateful".

'27.9 still: One possible meaning for the difficult Hebrew text of verse 9.

'28.2 but . . . order: One possible meaning for the difficult Hebrew text.

'28.17 live: One possible meaning for the difficult Hebrew text of verse 17.

'29.10 and lives right: Or "and those who live right are friends of honest people."

'29.21 will . . . sorrow: One possible meaning for the difficult Hebrew text.

'30.1 last: One possible meaning for the difficult Hebrew text of verse 1.

'30.15 Greed: Or "A leech".

'30.28 lizards: Or "spiders".

'30.31 enemies: One possible meaning for the difficult Hebrew text of verse 31.

'31.15 and . . . servants: Or "and to tell her servants what to do."

'31.25 She . . . graceful: Or "The clothes she makes are attractive and of good quality."

Ecclesiastes

The basics

What's the point? A picture of someone desperately searching for meaning.

What happens? An old bloke looks at life and can't see much to excite him. He praises God, but it's not exactly full-on worship.

What should I remember? 1.2 'Nothing makes sense! Everything is nonsense. I have seen it all – nothing makes sense!'

More details

Setting the scene An old man looks about him and reflects on life. It all seems pointless...

What's it all about? Ecclesiastes is one of the most surprising books of the Bible; a cynical, weary dismissal of life from one who says 'everything is meaningless'. This bloke is emotionally and spiritually knackered.

It's the flip-side of the Bible. It's a wake-up call, because there are people who feel this way, who see no purpose in life. We pass them every day in our schools, colleges or places of work. (Maybe we even see them in the mirror, first thing on Monday morning.)

We have to face this attitude. Life is not meaningless, life is purposeful. We should do all we can to help those who are trapped in the attitudes depicted in Ecclesiastes.

Footsteps

The search for meaning in life

CHAPTER 1

Nothing makes sense

¹ When the son of David was king in Jerusalem, he was known to be very wise,* and he said:

² Nothing makes sense!
Everything is nonsense.
I have seen it all –
nothing makes sense!
³ What is there to show
for all our hard work
here on this earth?
⁴ People come, and people go,
but still the world never changes.

⁵ The sun comes up, the sun goes down;
it hurries right back
to where it started from.
⁶ The wind blows south,
the wind blows north;
round and round it blows
over and over again.
⁷ All rivers empty into the sea,
but it never spills over;
one by one the rivers return
to their source.▸

⁸ All of life is far more boring
than words could ever say.

---

*1.1 known to be very wise: This stands for the Hebrew word often translated "preacher" or "teacher". The word may refer to someone who was a very wise leader or to someone who had become wise from collecting sayings about wisdom.

Viewpoints

Do we centre our dreams on God?

Contributed by Bug P

'The more you know, the more you hurt; the more you understand, the more you suffer.'

Where do you want to be in 30 years? The ambitious might say, 'rich and famous' – wouldn't that be nice? The pessimistic might say, 'just living out my life, bored probably.'

Why do we give the evil one such grounds to be able to catch us out? Think about it: if you think, 'where will I be in ...,' and imagine a situation that you think you're going to be in, nine times out of ten, you don't include God.

A life without God is like chasing after the wind. If your ideal situation does not include God as the centrepiece, you are going to be very disappointed. The verse spells it out: knowing things, being wise, achieving things will only lead you to contemplate the futility of what you have done. A relationship with God however – wow! What more could we possibly want?

So then, re-imagine yourself, ignore all the material things, all the achievements you may or may not go on to experience – here it is in black and white. There is simply no use in living if you don't live with God. Let's get on good terms with him. Think of all the little things in life that seem to get in the way of our relationship with God: I'm studying A-levels, with all the pressures. Imagine all the different people who read this – all the pressures of so many different lives. Let us focus our spiritual eyes on God, and make him the most important part of our lives. Doing anything else is futile and will make you miserable.

More...

Dreams and visions p.1410
Guidance p.685
Help! I don't know what to do in my gap year p.692
Help! I don't want to go to college p.591
Work p.1343

Our eyes and our ears are never satisfied
  with what we see and hear.
9 Everything that happens
  has happened before;
  nothing is new, nothing under the sun.
10 Someone might say,
  "Here is something new!"
  But it happened before,
  long before we were born.
11 No one who lived in the past
  is remembered any more,
  and everyone yet to be born
  will be forgotten too.

It is senseless to be wise

12 I said these things when I lived in Jerusalem as king of Israel. 13 With all my wisdom I tried to understand everything that happens here on earth. And God has made this so hard for us humans to do. 14 I have seen it all, and everything is just as senseless as chasing the wind.'

15 If something is crooked,
  it can't be made straight;
  if something isn't there,
  it can't be counted.

16 I said to myself, "You are by far the wisest person who has ever lived in Jerusalem. You are eager to learn, and you have learnt a lot." 17 Then I decided to find out all I could about wisdom and foolishness. Soon I realized that this too was as senseless as chasing the wind.'

18 The more you know,
  the more it hurts;
  the more you understand,
  the more you suffer.

CHAPTER 2

It is senseless to be selfish

1 I said to myself, "Have fun and enjoy yourself!" But this didn't make sense.
2 Laughing and having fun is mad. What good does it do? 3 I wanted to find out what was best for us during the short time we have on this earth. So I decided to make myself happy with wine and find out what it means to be foolish, without really being foolish myself.

4 I did some great things. I built houses and planted vineyards. 5 I had flower gardens and orchards full of fruit trees. 6 And I had pools where I could get water for the trees.

See also: 1.16: 1 King 4.29–31.   **2.4–8:** 1 King 10.23–27; 2 Chron 9.22–27.

7 I owned slaves, and their sons and daughters became my slaves. I had more sheep and goats than anyone who had ever lived in Jerusalem. 8 Foreign rulers brought me silver, gold, and precious treasures. Men and women sang for me, and I had many wives' who gave me great pleasure.

9 I was the most famous person who had ever lived in Jerusalem, and I was very wise. 10 I got whatever I wanted and did whatever made me happy. But most of all, I enjoyed my work. 11 Then I thought about everything I had done, including the hard work, and it was simply chasing the wind.' Nothing on earth is worth the trouble.

Wisdom makes sense

12 I asked myself, "What can the next king do that I haven't done?" Then I decided to compare wisdom with foolishness and stupidity. 13 And I discovered that wisdom is better than foolishness, just as light is better than darkness. 14 Wisdom is like having two good eyes; foolishness leaves you in the dark. But wise or foolish, we all end up the same. 15 Finally, I said to myself, "Being wise got me nowhere! The same thing will happen to me that happens to fools. Nothing makes sense. 16 Wise or foolish, we all die and are soon forgotten." 17 This made me hate life. Everything we do is painful; it's just as senseless as chasing the wind.'

18 Suddenly I realized that others would some day get everything I had worked so hard for, then I started hating it all. 19 Who knows if those people will be sensible or stupid? Either way, they will own everything I have earned by hard work and wisdom. It doesn't make sense.

20 I thought about all my hard work, and I felt depressed. 21 When we use our wisdom, knowledge, and skill to get what we own, why do we have to leave it to someone who didn't work for it? This is senseless and wrong. 22 What do we really gain from all our hard work? 23 Our bodies ache during the day, and work is torture. Then at night our thoughts are troubled. It just doesn't make sense.

24 The best thing we can do is to enjoy eating, drinking, and working.' I believe these are God's gifts to us, 25 and no one enjoys eating and living more than I do. 26 If we please God, he will make us wise, understanding, and happy. But if we sin, God will make us struggle for a living, then he will give all we own to someone who pleases him. This makes no more sense than chasing the wind.'

Everything has its time

CHAPTER 3

1 Everything on earth has its own time
and its own season.
2 There is a time for birth and death,
planting and reaping,
3 for killing and healing,
destroying and building,
4 for crying and laughing,
weeping and dancing,
5 for throwing stones
and gathering stones,
embracing and parting.
6 There is a time for finding and losing,
keeping and giving,
7 for tearing and sewing,
listening and speaking,
8 There is also a time for love and hate,
for war and peace.

Life isn't always fair, so live wisely

What God has given us to do

9 What do we gain by all our hard work? 10 I have seen what difficult things God demands of us. 11 God makes everything happen at the right time. Yet none of us can ever fully understand all he has done, and he puts questions in our minds about the past and the future. 12 I know the best thing we can do is always to enjoy life, 13 because God's gift to us is the happiness we get from our food and drink and from the work we do. 14 Everything God has done will last for ever; nothing he does can ever be changed. God has done all this, so that we will worship him.

15 Everything that happens
has happened before,
and all that will be has already been —
God does everything
over and over again.'

The future is known only to God

16 Everywhere on earth I saw violence and injustice instead of fairness and justice. 17 So I told myself that God has set a time and

See also: 2.7: 1 King 4.23. **2.8:** 1 King 10.10,14–22. **2.9:** 1 Chron 29.25. **2.23:** Job 5.7; 14.1. **2.24:** Ecc 3.13; 5.18; 9.7; Isa 56.12; Luke 12.19; 1 Cor 15.32. **2.26:** Job 32.8; Prov 2.6.

a place for everything. He will judge everyone, both the wicked and the good. ¹⁸ I know that God is testing us to show us that we are merely animals. ¹⁹ Like animals we breathe and die, and we are no better off than they are. It just doesn't make sense. ²⁰ All living creatures go to the same place. We are made from earth, and we return to the earth. ²¹ Who really knows if our spirits go up and the spirits of animals go down into the earth? ²² We were meant to enjoy our work, and that's the best thing we can do. We can never know the future.

CHAPTER 4

¹ I looked again and saw people being ill-treated everywhere on earth. They were crying, but no one was there to offer comfort, and those who ill-treated them were powerful. ² I said to myself, "The dead are better off than the living. ³ But those who have never been born are better off than anyone else, because they have never seen the terrible things that happen on this earth."

⁴ Then I realized that we work and do wonderful things just because we are jealous of others. This makes no more sense than chasing the wind.'

⁵ Fools will fold their hands
   and starve to death.
⁶ Yet a very little food eaten in peace
is better than twice as much
   earned from overwork
   and chasing the wind.'

⁷ Once again I saw that nothing on earth makes sense. ⁸ For example, some people don't have friends or family. But they are never satisfied with what they own, and they never stop working to get more. They should ask themselves, "Why am I always working to have more? Who will get what I leave behind?" What a senseless and miserable life!

It is better to have a friend

⁹ You are better off having a friend than being all alone, because then you will get more enjoyment out of what you earn. ¹⁰ If you fall, your friend can help you up. But if you fall without having a friend nearby, you are really in trouble. ¹¹ If you sleep alone, you won't have anyone to keep you warm on a cold night. ¹² Someone might be able to beat up one of you, but not both of you. As the saying goes, "A rope made from three strands of cord is hard to break."

Helpline

Help! I can't make friends

'I just can't make friends. No-one seems to want to be real friends with me; they're all in their own groups. Maybe there's something wrong with me?'

The Bible is full of passages about the importance of friendship, such as Ecclesiastes 4.9–12. But often we have difficulty in making friends. We're in a new place where we don't know anyone; or we're in a new job or new at school. Or, simply, we don't make friends easily.

Friendships change over time. You'll make friends at school, at college, at work, but you won't necessarily have those friends forever. Some friendships last all our lives. But other friends join us on the road for a while, then go off in a different direction.

Whatever happens, remember Jesus is our friend. We can always rely on his friendship.

Three things

Give

You can't just go into a friendship for what you're going to get out of it. Give your time and your attention. Be hospitable.

Look

Sometimes, when we say we want to be friends, we mean we want to be friends with a certain group of people; the 'in-crowd'. Stop worrying about that. Look for others who need friends as well.

Relax

When you are friends with someone, don't overload them with expectations, or overwhelm them with demands (Proverbs 25.17). People want to be friends with you, not your therapist. It doesn't mean you always have to do everything together. Just be relaxed about things.

More...

Help! How do I stop my friends doing wrong? p.1312
Help! I haven't got a boyfriend or girlfriend p.722

¹³ You may be poor and young. But if you are wise, you are better off than a foolish old king who won't listen to advice. ¹⁴ Even if you were not born into the royal family and have been a prisoner and poor, you can still be king. ¹⁵ I once saw everyone in the world follow a young leader who came to power after the king was gone. ¹⁶ His followers could not even be counted. But years from now, no one will praise him — this makes no more sense than chasing the wind.'

CHAPTER 5

Be careful how you worship

¹ Be careful what you do when you enter the house of God. Some fools go there to offer sacrifices, even though they haven't sinned.' But it's best just to listen when you go to worship. ² Don't talk before you think or make promises to God without thinking them through. God is in heaven, and you are on earth, so don't talk too much. ³ If you keep thinking about something, you will dream about it. If you talk too much, you will say the wrong thing.

⁴ God doesn't like fools. So don't be slow to keep your promises to God. ⁵ It's better not to make a promise at all than to make one and not keep it. ⁶ Don't let your mouth get you in trouble! And don't say to the worship leader,' "I didn't mean what I said." God can destroy everything you have worked for, so don't say something that makes God angry.

⁷ Respect and obey God! Daydreaming leads to a lot of senseless talk.'

⁸ Don't be surprised if the poor of your country are abused, and injustice takes the place of justice. After all, the lower officials must do what the higher ones order them to do. ⁹ And since the king is the highest official, he benefits most from the taxes paid on the land.'

¹⁰ If you love money and wealth, you will never be satisfied with what you have. This doesn't make sense either. ¹¹ The more you have, the more everyone expects from you. Your money won't do you any good — others will just spend it for you. ¹² If you have to work hard for a living, you can rest well at night, even if you don't have much to eat. But if you are rich, you can't even sleep.

¹³ I have seen something terribly unfair. People get rich, but it does them no good. ¹⁴ Suddenly they lose everything in a bad business deal, then have nothing to leave for

See also: 5.4: Psa 66.13–14.

Helpline

Help! I'm bored with my church

'I know I should go, but it's boring me to death. Do I really have to?'

Christianity should be exciting, thrilling, alive. But sometimes we think that's not being reflected in our churches.

However, before you rush to judgment, don't assume just because you're bored other people are too. Some like the beauty and quietness of a very traditional service; others like guitars, drums and a lot of leaping about. Neither is wrong – they're just different. Try and work out what others appreciate in what you don't like.

If you really don't feel at home, if you really can't cope, maybe you do need to find a different kind of worship. In which case, pray about it, and try some different churches. Don't give up church completely, you'll never get anywhere that way. But it's OK to try a different church.

Remember, we're all one body. We're all in this together.

Three things

Attitude

We come from a society that wants to be entertained. So check your attitudes. Read Ecclesiastes 5.1–3. Are you going to church to hear from God? Are you really going to try to enter into things? Are you prepared to give it your best shot?

Different

Try different kinds of churches. Go into them asking God to speak to you. You might be surprised at what you discover.

Love

Whatever you do, do it with love. Don't just up and leave. If it's your parents' church, talk to them about it. And if you do move churches, don't slag off your old one.

More...

Church p.1315
Meeting together p.1371
Does church seem routine? Is this what God intends? p.1276

their children. ¹⁵ They came into this world naked, and when they die, they will be just as naked. They can't take anything with them, and they won't have anything to show for all their work. ¹⁶ That's terribly unfair. They leave the world just as they came into it. They gained nothing from running after the wind. ¹⁷ Besides all this, they are always gloomy at mealtimes, and they are troubled, sick, and bitter.'

¹⁸ What is the best thing to do in the short life that God has given us? I think we should enjoy eating, drinking, and working hard. This is what God intends us to do. ¹⁹ Suppose you are very rich and able to enjoy everything you own. Then go ahead and enjoy working hard — this is God's gift to you. ²⁰ God will keep you so happy that you won't have time to worry about each day.

CHAPTER 6

Don't depend on wealth

¹ There is something else terribly unfair, and it troubles everyone on earth. ² God may give you everything you want — money, property, and wealth. Then God doesn't let you enjoy it, and someone you don't even know gets it all. That's senseless and terribly unfair!

³ You may live a long time and have a hundred children. But a child born dead is better off than you, unless you enjoy life and have a decent burial. ⁴⁻⁵ That child will never live to see the sun or to have a name, and it will go straight to the world of darkness. But it will still find more rest than you, ⁶ even if you live two thousand years and don't enjoy life. As you know, we all end up in the same place.

⁷ We struggle just to have enough to eat, but we are never satisfied. ⁸ We may be sensible, yet we are no better off than a fool. And if we are poor, it still doesn't do us any good to try to live right. ⁹ It's better to enjoy what we have than always to want something else, because that makes no more sense than chasing the wind.'

¹⁰ Everything that happens was decided long ago. We humans know what we are like, and we can't argue with God, because he is' too strong for us. ¹¹ The more we talk, the less sense we make, so what good does it do to talk? ¹² Life is short and meaningless, and it fades away like a shadow. Who knows what is best for us? Who knows what will happen after we are gone?

No one knows what the future will bring

CHAPTER 7

The best in life

¹ A good reputation
at the time of death
is better than loving care
at the time of birth.'

² It's better to go to a funeral
than to attend a feast;
funerals remind us
that we all must die.

³ Choose sorrow over laughter
because a sad face
may hide a happy heart.

⁴ A sensible person mourns,
but fools always laugh.

⁵ Harsh correction is better
than the songs of a fool.

⁶ Foolish laughter is stupid.
It sounds like thorns crackling in a fire.

⁷ Corruption' makes fools
of sensible people,
and bribes can ruin you.

⁸ Something completed is better
than something just begun;
patience is better than too much pride.

⁹ Only fools get angry quickly
and hold a grudge.

¹⁰ It isn't wise to ask,
"Why is everything worse
than it used to be?"

¹¹ Having wisdom is better
than an inheritance.

¹² Wisdom will protect you just like money;
knowledge with good sense
will lead you to life.

¹³ Think of what God has done!
If God makes something crooked,
can you make it straight?

¹⁴ When times are good,
you should be cheerful;
when times are bad,
think what it means.
God makes them both
to keep us from knowing
what will happen next.

Some of life's questions

¹⁵ I have seen everything during this senseless life of mine. I have seen good citizens die for doing the right thing, and I have seen

criminals live to a ripe old age. ¹⁶ So don't destroy yourself by being too good or acting too clever! ¹⁷ Don't die before your time by being too evil or acting like a fool. ¹⁸ Keep to the middle of the road. You can do this if you truly respect God.

¹⁹ Wisdom will make you stronger than the ten most powerful leaders in your city.

²⁰ No one in this world always does right.

²¹ Don't listen to everything that everyone says, or you might hear your servant cursing you. ²² Haven't you cursed many others?

²³ I told myself that I would be clever and try to understand all of this, but it was too much for me. ²⁴ The truth is beyond us. It's far too deep. ²⁵ So I decided to learn everything I could and become wise enough to discover what life is all about. At the same time, I wanted to understand why it's stupid and senseless to be an evil fool.

²⁶ Here is what I discovered: a bad woman is worse than death. She is a trap, reaching out with body and soul to catch you. But if you obey God, you can escape. If you don't obey, you are done for. ²⁷ With all my wisdom I have tried to find out how everything fits together, ²⁸ but so far I have not been able to. I do know there is one good man in a thousand, but never have I found a good woman. ²⁹ I did learn one thing: we were completely honest when God created us, but now we have twisted minds.

CHAPTER 8

¹ Who is clever enough
to explain everything?
Wisdom makes you cheerful
and gives you a smile.

Obey the king

² If you promised God that you would be loyal to the king, I advise you to keep that promise. ³ Don't quickly oppose the king or argue when he has already made up his mind. ⁴ The king's word is law. No one can ask him, "Why are you doing this?" ⁵ If you obey the king, you will stay out of trouble. So be clever and learn what to do and when to do it. ⁶ Life is hard, but there is a time and a place for everything, ⁷ though no one can tell the future. ⁸ We cannot control the wind' or determine the day of our death. There is no escape in time of war, and no one can hide behind evil.

⁹ I noticed all this and thought seriously about what goes on in the world. Why does one person have the power to hurt another?

Who can understand the ways of God?

¹⁰ I saw the wicked buried with honour, but God's people had to leave the holy city and were forgotten.' None of this makes sense. ¹¹ When we see criminals commit crime after crime without being punished, it makes us want to start a life of crime. ¹² They commit hundreds of crimes and live to a ripe old age, in spite of the saying:

Everyone who lives right
and respects God will prosper,
¹³ but no one who sins
and rejects God
will prosper or live very long.

¹⁴ There is something else that doesn't make sense to me. Good citizens are treated as criminals, while criminals are honoured as though they were good citizens. ¹⁵ So I think we should get as much out of life as we possibly can. There is nothing better than to enjoy our food and drink and to have a good time. Then we can make it through this troublesome life that God has given us here on earth.

¹⁶ Day and night I went without sleep, trying to understand what goes on in this world. ¹⁷ I saw everything God does, and I realized that no one can really understand what happens. We may be very wise, but no matter how much we try or how much we claim to know, we cannot understand it all.

CHAPTER 9

One day at a time

¹ I thought about these things. Then I understood that God has power over everyone, even those of us who are wise and live right. Anything can happen to any of us, and so we never know if life will be good or bad.' ² But exactly' the same thing will finally happen to all of us, whether we live right and respect God or sin and don't respect God. Yes, the same thing will happen if we offer sacrifices to God or if we don't, if we keep our promises or break them.

³ It's terribly unfair for the same thing to happen to each of us. We are mean and foolish while we live, and then we die. ⁴ As long as we are alive, we still have hope, just as a live dog is better off than a dead lion. ⁵ We know that we will die, but the dead don't know a thing. Nothing good will happen to them — they are gone and forgotten. ⁶ Their loves, their hates, and their jealous feelings have all disappeared with

them. They will never again take part in anything that happens on this earth.

7 Be happy and enjoy eating and drinking! God decided long ago that this is what you should do. 8 Dress up, comb your hair, and look your best. 9 Life is short, and you love your wife, so enjoy being with her. This is what you are supposed to do as you struggle through life on this earth. 10 Work hard at whatever you do. You will soon go to the world of the dead, where no one works or thinks or reasons or knows anything.

11 Here is something else I have learnt:

> The fastest runners
>   and the greatest heroes
>   don't always win races and battles.
> Wisdom, intelligence, and skill
>   don't always make you healthy,
>   rich, or popular.
>   We each have our share of bad luck.

12 None of us know when we might fall victim to a sudden disaster and find ourselves like fish in a net or birds in a trap.

Better to be wise than foolish

13 Once I saw what people really think of wisdom. 14 It happened when a powerful ruler surrounded and attacked a small city where only a few people lived. The enemy army was getting ready to break through the city walls. 15 But the city was saved by the wisdom of a poor person who was soon forgotten. 16 So I decided that wisdom is better than strength. Yet if you are poor, no one pays any attention to you, no matter how clever you are.

> 17 Words of wisdom spoken softly
>   make much more sense
>   than the shouts of a ruler
>   to a crowd of fools.
> 18 Wisdom is more powerful than weapons,
>   yet one mistake can destroy
>   all the good you have done.

CHAPTER 10

> 1 A few dead flies in perfume
>   make all of it stink,
>   and a little foolishness
>   outweighs a lot of wisdom.
> 2 Sensible thoughts lead you to do right;
>   foolish thoughts lead you to do wrong.
> 3 Fools show their stupidity
>   by the way they live;
>   it's easy to see they have no sense.

> 4 Don't give up your job
>   when your boss gets angry.
>   If you stay calm, you'll be forgiven.

5 Some things rulers do are terribly unfair:
6 they honour fools, but dishonour the rich;
7 they let slaves ride on horses, but force slave owners to walk.

> 8 If you dig a pit,
>   you might fall in;
>   if you break down a wall,
>   a snake might bite you.*
> 9 You could even get hurt
>   by chiselling a stone
>   or chopping a log.
> 10 If you don't sharpen your axe,
>   it will be harder to use;
>   if you are clever,
>   you'll know what to do.'
> 11 The power to charm a snake does you
>   no good if it bites you anyway.

> 12 If you talk sensibly,
>   you will have friends;
>   if you talk foolishly,
>   you will destroy yourself.
> 13 Fools begin with nonsense,
>   and their stupid chatter
>   ends with disaster.
> 14 They never tire of talking,
>   but none of us really know
>   what the future will bring.
> 15 Fools wear themselves out —
>   they don't know enough
>   to find their way home.'

> 16 A country is in for trouble
>   when its ruler is childish,
>   and its leaders feast all day long.
> 17 But a nation will prosper
>   when its ruler is mature,
>   and its leaders don't feast too much.
> 18 Some people are too lazy
>   to fix a leaky roof —
>   then the house falls in.
> 19 Eating and drinking
>   make you feel happy,
>   and bribes can buy
>   everything you need.

---

*10.8 a snake might bite you: Walls of houses were often made of stones with mud to fill in the cracks between them. If some of the mud washed out, a snake could be living inside the wall.
See also: 10.8: Psa 7.15; Prov 26.27.

²⁰ Don't even think about cursing the king;
don't curse the rich,
not even in secret.
A little bird might hear
and tell everything.

CHAPTER 11

It pays to work hard

¹ Be generous, and some day
you will be rewarded.ᵇ
² Share what you have
with seven or eight others,
because you never know
when disaster may strike.
³ Rain clouds always bring rain;
trees always stay wherever they fall.
⁴ If you worry about the weather
and don't plant seeds,
you won't harvest a crop.

⁵ No one can explain how a baby breathes
before it is born.ᵇ So how can anyone explain
what God does? After all, he created
everything.

⁶ Plant your seeds early in the morning and
keep working in the field until dark. Who
knows? Your work might pay off, and your
seeds might produce.

Respect and obey God

Youth and old age

⁷ Nothing on earth is more beautiful than the
morning sun. ⁸ Even if you live to a ripe old
age, you should try to enjoy each day,
because darkness will come and will last a
long time. Nothing makes sense.ᵇ

⁹ Be cheerful and enjoy life while you are
young! Do what you want and find pleasure
in what you see. But don't forget that God
will judge you for everything you do.

¹⁰ Rid yourself of all worry and pain,
because the wonderful moments of youth
quickly disappear.

CHAPTER 12

¹ Keep your Creator in mind while you are
young! In years to come, you will be
burdened down with troubles and say,
"I don't enjoy life any more."

² Some day the light of the sun
and the moon and the stars
will all seem dim to you.
Rain clouds will remain over your head.

Helpline

Help! I can't be bothered with homework

'I can't stand it! Every night I've got loads to
do. I just want to chuck it into a corner.'

Homework has always been a bit of a
chore. But there are some good reasons
why, as Christians, we shouldn't just chuck
it into a corner and ignore it.

Whether we like it or not, God wants us to
obey those in authority over us and whether
we like it or not, while we're at school, that
means the teachers and staff. This doesn't
mean blindly obeying everything we are
ordered to do. But it does mean trying to be
conscientious about schoolwork.

Maybe we could change the way we view
things. When you hand your homework in
on time, when you've done it to the best of
your abilities, that's a witness to God.

Three things

Honest

If you're having problems understanding
the work, talk to your teacher. (Most)
teachers are normal human beings. They're
there to help; that's their job. Ask them, or
your friends. Don't be ashamed to ask
questions.

Future

School is a building block for your life. What
you're doing now has a huge effect on what
you'll do in the future. It may well be that
God is giving you certain subjects to study
and things to do in order to prepare you for
some task in the future.

Discipline

Being a Christian means being
self-disciplined. The chores that bore, the
jobs we hate, are all part of learning how to
be self-disciplined. When we achieve those
tasks, it will give us training for other tasks
we have to do in the future.

More...

Work p.1343
Help! I can't cope with revision p.1011
School p.64
Resisting temptation p.1124

3 Your body will grow feeble,
    your teeth will decay,
    and your eyesight fail.
4 The noisy grinding of grain
  will be shut out by your deaf ears,
    but even the song of a bird
    will keep you awake.

5 You will be afraid to climb up a hill
  or walk down a road.
    Your hair will turn as white
    as almond blossoms.
  You will feel lifeless and drag along
    like an old grasshopper.

We each go to our eternal home,
  and the streets are filled
    with those who mourn.
6 The silver cord snaps,
  the golden bowl breaks;
  the water pitcher is smashed,
    and the pulley at the well is shattered.
7 So our bodies return to the earth,
  and the life-giving breath›
    returns to God.
8 Nothing makes sense.
  I have seen it all —
    nothing makes sense.

Respect and obey God

9 I was a wise teacher with much understanding, and I collected a number of proverbs that I had carefully studied. 10 Then I tried to explain these things in the best and most accurate way.
11 Words of wisdom are like the stick a farmer uses to make animals move. These sayings come from God, our only shepherd, and they are like nails that fasten things together.› 12 My child, I warn you to stay away from any teachings except these.

There is no end to books,
  and too much study will wear you out.

13 Everything you were taught can be put into a few words:

Respect and obey God!
  This is what life is all about.
14 God will judge everything we do,
  even what is done in secret,
    whether good or bad.

Additional notes

›**1.7 return to their source:** Or "flow into the sea".
›**1.14 chasing the wind:** Or "eating the wind."
›**1.17 chasing the wind:** See the note at 1.14.
›**2.8 many wives:** One possible meaning for the difficult Hebrew text.
›**2.11 chasing the wind:** See the note at 1.14.
›**2.17 chasing the wind:** See the note at 1.14.
›**2.24 The best . . . working:** One possible meaning for the difficult Hebrew text.
›**2.26 chasing the wind:** See the note at 1.14.
›**3.15 God does . . . again:** One possible meaning for the difficult Hebrew text.
›**4.4 chasing the wind:** See the note at 1.14.
›**4.6 chasing the wind:** See the note at 1.14.
›**4.16 chasing the wind:** See the note at 1.14.
›**5.1 even . . . sinned:** One possible meaning for the difficult Hebrew text.
›**5.6 worship leader:** Or "messenger".
›**5.7 Daydreaming . . . talk:** One possible meaning for the difficult Hebrew text.
›**5.9 land:** One possible meaning for the difficult Hebrew text of verse 9.
›**5.17 bitter:** One possible meaning for the difficult Hebrew text of verse 17.
›**6.9 chasing the wind:** See the note at 1.14.
›**6.10 with God, because he is:** Or "with anyone who is".
›**7.1 birth:** One possible meaning for the difficult Hebrew text of verse 1.
›**7.7 Corruption:** Or "Oppression".
›**8.8 control the wind:** Or "escape from death".
›**8.10 but . . . forgotten:** One possible meaning for the difficult Hebrew text.
›**9.1 or bad:** Three ancient translations; the Hebrew text does not have these words.
›**9.2 exactly:** One possible meaning for the difficult Hebrew text.
›**10.10 do:** One possible meaning for the difficult Hebrew text of verse 10.
›**10.15 home:** One possible meaning for the difficult Hebrew text of verse 15.
›**11.1 Be generous . . . rewarded:** Or "Don't be afraid to invest. Some day it will pay off."
›**11.5 how . . . born:** Or "what makes the wind blow or how a baby grows inside its mother".
›**11.8 Nothing makes sense:** Or "There's nothing to look forward to!"
›**12.7 life-giving breath:** Or "spirit".
›**12.11 These sayings . . . together:** One possible meaning for the difficult Hebrew text.

Song of Songs

The basics

What's the point?   A celebration of the love between a man and a woman.

What happens?   They meet. They snog. They tell each other how they feel. Sometimes they speak to friends, sometimes to each other, sometimes to themselves. Sometimes they remember earlier times, aometimes they're in the here and now. But it's all about love.

What should I remember?   8.6–7 'Always keep me in your heart and wear this bracelet to remember me by.

The passion of love bursting into flame is more powerful than death, stronger than the grave.

Love cannot be drowned by oceans or floods; it cannot be bought, no matter what is offered.'

More details

Setting the scene   A man and a woman in love, and all that follows...

What's it all about?   Sex. Love. Romance. Everything that makes the relationship between women and men special.

It's a love poem, one of the most startling things in the Bible – eight chapters celebrating erotic, physical love. A lot of people have problems with this.

Maybe the problem is not with the poem, but with the readers. The Bible is not coy about sex. It has a lot to say about the bad side of love, about adultery, lust, perversion, rape. What Song of Songs does is celebrate the good side; its spontaneity, power and mystery. If you're uncomfortable with that, then you'll be uncomfortable with this book.

And another thing

Traditionally this has been ascribed to King Solomon. Given he married over 1000 women, tracking down the woman's identity is a bit more tricky.

Footsteps

Love is better than wine: 1.1–2.7
The wedding: 3.6–5.1
Dream lover: 5.2–16
Wedding dance: 7.1–13
If only... 8.1–14

Love is better than wine

CHAPTER 1

¹ This is Solomon's
  most beautiful song.

She speaks:

² Kiss me tenderly!
  Your love is better than wine,
³   and you smell so sweet.
  All the young women adore you;
  the very mention of your name
  is like spreading perfume.
⁴⁻⁵ Hurry, my king! Let's hurry.
  Take me to your home.

The young women speak:

  We are happy for you!
  And we praise your love
  even more than wine.

See also   1.1: 1 King 4.32.

She speaks:

> Young women of Jerusalem,
>   it is only right
>   that you should adore him.
> My skin is dark and beautiful,
>   like a tent in the desert
>   or like Solomon's curtains.
> ⁶ Don't stare at me just because the sun
>   has darkened my skin.
> My brothers were angry with me;
>   they made me work in the vineyard,
>   and so I neglected my complexion.
>
> Don't let the other shepherds
>   think badly of me.›
> ⁷ I'm not one of those women
>   who shamelessly follow
>   after shepherds.›
> My darling, I love you!
>   Where do you feed your sheep
>   and let them rest at midday?

He speaks:

> ⁸ My dearest, if you don't know,
>   just follow the path of the sheep.
> Then feed your young goats
>   near the shepherds' tents.
> ⁹ You move as gracefully as the pony
>   that leads the chariot of the king.
> ¹⁰ Earrings add to your beauty,
>   and you wear a necklace
>   of precious stones.
> ¹¹ Let's make you some jewellery
>   of gold, woven with silver.

She speaks:

> ¹² My king, while you
>   were on your couch,
>   my love was a magic charm.›
> ¹³ My darling, you are perfume
>   between my breasts;
> ¹⁴ you are flower blossoms
>   from the gardens of En-Gedi.*

He speaks:

> ¹⁵ My darling, you are lovely,
>   so very lovely —
>   your eyes are those of a dove.

She speaks:

> ¹⁶ My love, you are handsome,
>   truly handsome —
>   the fresh green grass
>   will be our wedding bed
> ¹⁷ in the shade of cedar
>   and cypress trees.

---

*1.14 En-Gedi: An oasis west of the Dead Sea.

Helpline

Help! I haven't got a boyfriend or girlfriend

'Is there something wrong with me? Why does everyone else seem to have a partner except for me?'

Yes, yes, it's all very well all this love poetry. It's all very well for these two to go on and on about gazelles and all that – but what about me? Why don't I have anyone?

Sometimes being single can seem like the loneliest place in the world. It's easy to think that something's wrong with you. You start comparing yourself with other people. You start to wish you were a different shape, better looking, or had better clothes. But here's the important point: God has made you unique. So concentrate on developing the gifts he has given you, instead of wishing that you were like everyone else.

Relax. Don't be so desperate to tick the box marked 'partner'. Try concentrating more on your friends and forget about the boyfriend/girlfriend bit for a while.

In fact, if you look at 1.6 in this book, you'll find that the woman in the story wasn't conventionally attractive. She's sun-tanned from working in the vineyards – in those days not what women should do. She is loved for herself.

Three things

Relax

Don't get anxious, don't compare yourself to others. Many people don't start to go out with others until they are older. There are many years ahead of you yet.

Prioritise

Put God first. Do what God wants you to do. He doesn't think any less of you if you haven't got a partner. And you can still find fulfilment in following him and serving him.

Friends

Concentrate on your friends. Share with them and spend time with them.

More...

Sex p.727
Help! I hate myself! p.1332

Love makes everything beautiful

CHAPTER 2

She speaks:

¹ I am merely a rose*
from the land of Sharon,
a lily from the valley.

He speaks:

² My darling, when compared
with other young women,
you are a lily among thorns.

She speaks:

³ And you, my love,
are an apple tree
among trees of the forest.
Your shade brought me pleasure;
your fruit was sweet.
⁴ You led me to your banquet room
and showered me with love.
⁵ Refresh and strengthen me
with raisins and apples.
I am hungry for love!
⁶ Put your left hand under my head
and embrace me with your right arm.

⁷ Young women of Jerusalem,
promise me by the power
of deer and gazelles*
never to awaken love before it is ready.

Winter is past

She speaks:

⁸ I hear the voice of the one I love,
as he comes leaping
over mountains and hills
⁹ like a deer or a gazelle.
Now he stands outside our wall,
looking through the window
¹⁰ and speaking to me.

He speaks:

My darling, I love you!
Let's go away together.
¹¹ Winter is past,
the rain has stopped;

¹² flowers cover the earth,
it's time to sing.▸
The cooing of doves
is heard in our land.
¹³ Fig trees are bearing fruit,
while blossoms on grapevines
fill the air with perfume.
My darling, I love you!
Let's go away together.
¹⁴ You are my dove
hiding among the rocks
on the side of a cliff.
Let me see how lovely you are!
Let me hear the sound
of your melodious voice.
¹⁵ Our vineyards are in blossom;
we must catch the little foxes
that destroy the vineyards.▸

She speaks:

¹⁶ My darling, I am yours,
and you are mine,
as you feed your sheep
among the lilies.
¹⁷ Pretend to be a young deer
dancing on mountain slopes▸
until daylight comes
and shadows fade away.

CHAPTER 3

Beautiful dreams

She speaks:

¹ While in bed at night,
I reached for the one I love
with heart and soul.
I looked for him,
but he wasn't there.
² So I searched through the town
for the one I love.
I looked in every street,
but he wasn't there.
³ I even asked the guards
patrolling the town,
"Have you seen the one
I love so much?"
⁴ Straight after that, I found him.
I held him and would not let go
until I had taken him
to the home of my mother.
⁵ Young women of Jerusalem,
promise me by the power
of deer and gazelles,*
never to awaken love
before it is ready.

---

*2.1 **rose:** The traditional translation. The exact variety of the flower is not known, though it may have been a crocus.

*2.7 **deer and gazelles:** Deer and gazelles were sacred animals in some religions of Old Testament times, and they were thought to have special powers.

*3.5 **deer and gazelles:** See the note at 2.7.

The wedding

The groom and the wedding party

Their friends speak:

6 What do we see approaching
from the desert
like a cloud of smoke?
With it comes the sweet smell of spices,
including myrrh and frankincense.

7 It is King Solomon carried on a throne,
surrounded by sixty
of Israel's best soldiers.

8 Each of them wears a sword.
They are experts at fighting,
even in the dark.

9 The throne is made of trees
from Lebanon.

10 Its posts are silver, the back is gold,
and the seat is covered
with purple cloth.
You women of Jerusalem
have taken great care
to furnish the inside.'

11 Now come and see the crown
given to Solomon by his mother
on his happy wedding day.

CHAPTER 4

What a beautiful bride

He speaks:

1 My darling, you are lovely,
so very lovely —
as you look through your veil,
your eyes are those of a dove.
Your hair tosses about
as gracefully as goats
coming down from Gilead.

2 Your teeth are whiter
than sheep freshly washed;
they match perfectly,
not one is missing.

3 Your lips are crimson cords,
your mouth is shapely;
behind your veil are hidden
beautiful rosy cheeks.'

4 Your neck is more graceful
than the tower of David,
decorated with thousands
of warriors' shields.

5 Your breasts are perfect;
they are twin deer
feeding among lilies.

6 I will hasten to those hills
sprinkled with sweet perfume
and stay there till sunrise.

7 My darling, you are lovely in every way.

8 My bride, together
we will leave Lebanon!
We will say goodbye to the peaks
of Mount Amana, Senir, and Hermon,
where lions and leopards
live in the caves.

9 My bride, my very own,
you have stolen my heart!
With one glance from your eyes
and the glow of your necklace,
you have stolen my heart.

10 Your love is sweeter than wine;
the smell of your perfume
is more fragrant than spices.

11 Your lips are a honeycomb;
milk and honey flow from your tongue.
Your dress has the aroma
of cedar trees from Lebanon.

12 My bride, my very own,
you are a garden,
a fountain closed off to all others.

13 Your arms' are vines,
covered with delicious fruits
and all sorts of spices —
henna, nard,

14 saffron, calamus, cinnamon,
frankincense, myrrh, and aloes —
all the finest spices.

15 You are a spring in the garden,
a fountain of pure water,
and a refreshing stream
from Mount Lebanon.

She speaks:

16 Let the north wind blow,
the south wind too!
Let them spread the aroma of my garden,
so the one I love may enter
and taste its delicious fruits.

CHAPTER 5

He speaks:

1 My bride, my very own,
I come to my garden
and enjoy its spices.
I eat my honeycomb and honey;
I drink my wine and milk.

Their friends speak:

Eat and drink
until you are drunk with love.

Why is the one you love more special than others?

Another dream

She speaks:

² I was asleep, but dreaming:
the one I love was at the door,
knocking and saying,
"My darling, my very own,
my flawless dove,
open the door for me!
My head is drenched with evening dew."

³ But I had already undressed
and bathed my feet.
Should I dress again
and get my feet dirty?
⁴ Then my darling's hand
reached to open the latch,
and my heart stood still.
⁵ When I rose to open the door,
my hands and my fingers
dripped with perfume.

⁶ My heart stood still
while he spoke to me,
but when I opened the door,
my darling had disappeared.
I searched and shouted,
but I could not find him —
there was no answer.
⁷ Then I was found by the guards
patrolling the town
and guarding the wall.
They beat me up
and stripped off my robe.

⁸ Young women of Jerusalem,
if you find the one I love,
please say to him,
"She is weak with desire."

Their friends speak:

⁹ Most beautiful of women,
why is the one you love
more special than others?
Why do you ask us
to tell him how you feel?

She speaks:

¹⁰ He is handsome and healthy,
the most outstanding
among ten thousand.
¹¹ His head is purest gold;
his hair is wavy,
black as a raven.

¹² His eyes are a pair of doves
bathing in a stream
flowing with milk.◆
¹³ His face is a garden
of sweet-smelling spices;
his lips are lilies
dripping with perfume.

¹⁴ His arms are branches of gold
covered with jewels;
his body is ivory◆
decorated with sapphires.
¹⁵ His legs are columns of marble
on feet of gold.
He stands there majestic
like Mount Lebanon
and its choice cedar trees.
¹⁶ His kisses are sweet.
I desire him so much!
Young women of Jerusalem,
he is my lover and friend.

CHAPTER 6

Their friends speak:

¹ Most beautiful of women,
tell us where he has gone.
Let us help you find him.

She speaks:

² My darling has gone down
to his garden of spices,
where he will feed his sheep
and gather lilies.
³ I am his, and he is mine,
as he feeds his sheep among the lilies.

He speaks:

⁴ My dearest, the cities of Tirzah
and Jerusalem
are not as lovely as you.
Your charms are more powerful
than all the stars in the heavens.◆
⁵ Turn away your eyes —
they make me melt.
Your hair tosses about
as gracefully as goats
coming down from Gilead.
⁶ Your teeth are whiter
than sheep freshly washed;
they match perfectly,
not one is missing.
⁷ Behind your veil are hidden
beautiful rosy cheeks.◆

⁸ What if I could have
sixty queens, eighty wives,
and thousands of others!

⁹ You would be my only choice,
my flawless dove,
the favourite child of your mother.
The young women, the queens,
and all the others
tell how excited you are
as they sing your praises:
¹⁰ "You are as majestic
as the morning sky —
glorious as the moon —
blinding as the sun!
Your charms are more powerful
than all the stars above."▸

She speaks:

¹¹ I went down to see if blossoms
were on the walnut trees,
grapevines, and fruit trees.
¹² But in my imagination
I was suddenly riding
on a glorious chariot.▸

Their friends speak:

¹³ Dance! Dance!
Beautiful woman from Shulam,
let us see you dance!

She speaks:

Why do you want to see
this woman from Shulam
dancing with the others?▸

CHAPTER 7

The wedding dance

He speaks:

¹ You are a princess,
and your feet are graceful
in their sandals.
Your thighs are works of art,
each one a jewel;
² your navel is a wine glass
filled to overflowing.
Your body is full and slender
like a bundle of wheat
bound together by lilies.
³ Your breasts are like twins of a deer.
⁴ Your neck is like ivory,
and your eyes sparkle
like the pools of Heshbon
by the gate of Bath-Rabbim.
Your nose is beautiful
like Mount Lebanon
above the city of Damascus.

⁵ Your head is held high
like Mount Carmel;
your hair is so lovely
it holds a king prisoner.▸
⁶ You are beautiful, so very desirable!
⁷ You are tall and slender
like a palm tree,
and your breasts are full.
⁸ I will climb that tree
and cling to its branches.
I will discover that your breasts
are clusters of grapes,
and that your breath
is the aroma of apples.
⁹ Kissing you is more delicious
than drinking the finest wine.
How wonderful and tasty!▸

She speaks:

¹⁰ My darling, I am yours,
and you desire me.
¹¹ Let's stroll through the fields
and sleep in the villages.
¹² At dawn let's slip out and see
if grapevines and fruit trees
are covered with blossoms.
When we are there,
I will give you my love.
¹³ Perfume from the magic flower*
fills the air, my darling.
Right at our doorstep
I have stored up for you
all kinds of tasty fruits.

If only you and I . . .

CHAPTER 8

She speaks:

¹ If you were my brother,
I could kiss you
whenever we happen to meet,
and no one would say I did wrong.
² I could take you to the home
of my mother,
who taught me all I know.▸
I would give you delicious wine
and fruit juice as well.
³ Put your left hand under my head
and embrace me with your right arm.

⁴ Young women of Jerusalem,
promise me by the power

---

*7.13 magic flower: The Hebrew text has "mandrake", a plant that was thought to give sexual powers.

Real life

Sex

Think about fire for a moment. It can be a good thing or a bad thing, depending on how you use it. Put it in a fireplace and it provides warmth; set fire to your curtains and the house will burn down. It's the same with sex. Passion can easily 'burst into flames' (Song of Songs 8.6). Use it right and it's great, get it wrong and it can do enormous damage.

This is not a popular view. We have a sex-obsessed society. (One reason why we also have the highest teenage pregnancy rate in Europe and a growing rate of HIV and sexually-transmitted diseases.)

So what's the safe way to do sex? In Genesis 2.24 God outlines his plan: 'That's why a man will leave his own father and mother. He marries a woman, and the two of them become like one person.'

Sex is more than a physical function. It's about becoming one with another person. It's more than a physical act; it's a union of two spirits; part of a lifetime commitment between a man and a woman. God is not anti-sex – he invented it! He wants people to enjoy a full and fulfilling sex life. Song of Songs is a poem all about physical love. But the place for sex is marriage. It's a way for people in a committed, permanent relationship to say 'I love you'. Which is why the Bible also says we should not sleep around or sleep with another person's wife or husband.

But what if you're not married? How far should you go? The Bible doesn't give detailed instructions. We have to use our God-given wisdom.

After all, sex doesn't happen by accident. Relationships are progressive; one act leads to another. Be realistic; people in love do get carried away with things. But set your boundaries far enough back from full sex and you won't be tempted to go just that one step further.

And make sure that you do set boundaries. Think through your own limits. Pray them through with God. Talk them through with your partner. Ask the Holy Spirit to give you self-control.

Of course things go wrong. People get carried away; they make decisions that they later regret; relationships break down and people find other partners. Whatever may have happened, God offers forgiveness. You can't wipe out the past, but you can make a new start. Pray to God and start again. Talk to your church leaders or trusted friends and they'll help you.

Think

Why do you think sex is special? Why is it more than just a physical activity?
Do you think our society is obsessed with sex? Why is that?
How can we protect ourselves from the sexually-charged culture around us?

Act

Set your boundaries. Talk to your partner about them.
Try not to put yourself into situations where things could get out of control.
Don't pressurise your partner into going further than they want to.

Check

Genesis 2.24–25; Song of Songs 8.5–7;
Hosea 4.17–19; John 8.3–11;
1 Corinthians 7.1–6; Colossians 3.5–9;
1 Thessalonians 4.1–8

More...

Pornography p.952
Abortion p.668
Help! I can't stop masturbating p.1339
Help! I'm struggling with lust p.954
Marriage p.205

of deer and gazelles*
never to awaken love before it is ready.

Their friends speak:

5 Who is this young woman
coming in from the desert
and leaning on the shoulder
of the one she loves?

She speaks:

I stirred up your passions
under the apple tree
where you were born.
6 Always keep me in your heart
and wear this bracelet
to remember me by.
The passion of love bursting into flame
is more powerful than death,
stronger than the grave.
7 Love cannot be drowned
by oceans or floods;
it cannot be bought,
no matter what is offered.

Their friends speak:

8 We have a little sister whose breasts
are not yet formed.
If someone asks to marry her,
what should we do?
9 She isn't a wall that we can defend
behind a silver shield.
Neither is she a room that we can protect
behind a wooden door.

She speaks:

10 I am a wall around a city,
my breasts are towers,
and just looking at me
brings him great pleasure.
11 Solomon has a vineyard
at Baal-Hamon,
which he rents to others
for a thousand pieces of silver each.
12 My vineyard is mine alone!
Solomon can keep his silver
and the others can keep
their share of the profits.

He speaks:

13 You are in the garden
with friends all around.
Let me hear your voice!

She speaks:

14 Hurry to me, my darling!
Run faster than a deer
to mountains of spices.

Additional notes

›**1.6 Don't . . . me:** One possible meaning for the difficult Hebrew text.
›**1.7 I'm . . . shepherds:** One possible meaning for the difficult Hebrew text.
›**1.12 magic charm:** The Hebrew text has "spikenard" (or "nard"), a sweet-smelling ointment made from a plant that comes from India. The ointment was sometimes used as a love charm.
›**2.12 sing:** Or "trim the vines".
›**2.15 vineyards:** One possible meaning for the difficult Hebrew text of verse 15.
›**2.17 mountain slopes:** One possible meaning for the difficult Hebrew text.
›**3.10 inside:** One possible meaning for the difficult Hebrew text.
›**4.3 beautiful rosy cheeks:** One possible meaning for the difficult Hebrew text.
›**4.13 Your arms:** One possible meaning for the difficult Hebrew text.
›**5.12 milk:** One possible meaning for the difficult Hebrew text of verse 12.
›**5.14 his . . . ivory:** One possible meaning for the difficult Hebrew text.
›**6.4 all . . . heavens:** Or "a mighty army ready for war."
›**6.7 cheeks:** One possible meaning for the difficult Hebrew text of verse 7.
›**6.10 all . . . above:** Or "a mighty army ready for war."
›**6.12 chariot:** One possible meaning for the difficult Hebrew text of verse 12.
›**6.13 dancing . . . others:** One possible meaning for the difficult Hebrew text.
›**7.5 it . . . prisoner:** One possible meaning for the difficult Hebrew text.
›**7.9 How . . . tasty:** One possible meaning for the difficult Hebrew text.
›**8.2 who . . . know:** One possible meaning for the difficult Hebrew text.

---

*8.4 deer and gazelles: See the note at 2.7.

Isaiah

The basics

What's the point? Doom is coming for Judah. But beyond that there will come a Messiah and eventually a new heaven and new earth.

What happens? Isaiah calls the people to renew their commitment to God; he warns them of imminent punishment and he paints a picture of a glorious future, when God will be with his people.

What should I remember? 65.17–19 'I am creating new heavens and a new earth; everything of the past will be forgotten. Celebrate and be glad for ever! I am creating a Jerusalem, full of happy people. I will celebrate with Jerusalem and all its people; there will be no more crying or sorrow in that city.'

More details

Setting the scene Judah. The southern kingdom. Over a period of forty years, and through the reigns of four kings, the prophet Isaiah gives his message of doom and hope.

What's it all about? Judgement and redemption. Isaiah's core message is that God will punish his people, but he will also rescue them.

Reading Isaiah can be hard work. It's not really chronologically arranged, so we're thrown about from one point in time to another. The prophet mixes visions of the future with accounts of the goings-on in the court of his day. He mixes passages of wonderful power and beauty with attacks on Israel's enemies and even put-downs of palace officials. He talks about events which are imminent and events which are far off, and untangling these things is tricky.

But there are major themes we can hold on to. Perhaps the main one is summed up in Isaiah's name. Isaiah's name means 'the Lord saves' and that sums up his prophecy. Faced with the expanding threat of the terrifying Assyrians, the rulers and people of Judah carried on as before; corrupt officials, violence and injustice on the streets, unfaithful kings. They didn't seem to be worried.

Isaiah tries to tell them what will happen. God is a powerful, mighty fire that will scorch the earth. His judgment is coming. The Israelites will be in exile. Isaiah calls for the people to truly turn back to God; to offer to him things that really matter; to once again take seriously the job of being God's people.

But God also offers a road back.

Exile will come, but Isaiah also points to a wonderful new age, an age of peace and wholeness when the Messiah will reign. Isaiah contains some of the most inspiring, moving and powerful pictures of God's reign in all its glory, when the exiles are brought back home. We're given peeps through a window into the future, when the Lord will create a new world, free of suffering, sadness and pain.

And another thing

Isaiah wrote a biography of King Uzziah (2 Chronicles 26.22) and, according to Jewish tradition, died a particularly gruesome death: he was sawn in half (Hebrews 11.37 makes reference to this).

Footsteps

Introduction

CHAPTER 1

¹ I am Isaiah, the son of Amoz.

And this is the message that I was given about Judah and Jerusalem when Uzziah, Jotham, Ahaz, and Hezekiah were the kings of Judah:*

A guilty nation

² The LORD has said,
   "Listen, heaven and earth!
   The children I raised
      have turned against me.
³ Oxen and donkeys know
      who owns and feeds them,
   but my people won't ever learn."

⁴ Israel, you are a sinful nation
      loaded down with guilt.
   You are wicked and corrupt
   and have turned from the LORD,
      the holy God of Israel.
⁵ Why be punished more?
   Why not give up your sin?
   Your head is badly bruised,
      and you are weak all over.
⁶ From your head to your toes
      there isn't a healthy spot.
   Bruises, cuts, and open sores
   go without care
      or oil to ease the pain.

---

*1.1 kings of Judah: Uzziah (783–742 BC); Jotham (742–735 BC); Ahaz (735–715 BC); Hezekiah (715–687 BC).

See also: 1.1: a 2 King 15.1–7; 2 Chron 26.1–23; b 2 King 15.32–38; 2 Chron 27.1–9; c 2 King 16.1–20; 2 Chron 28.1–27; d 2 King 18.1–20.21; 2 Chron 29.1–32.33.

Big ideas

Prophecy

Prophecy in the Bible is about more than seeing into the future; it's about speaking the truth. Prophets were given messages by God, not only about the future, but also about the society around them. This made being a prophet a risky business. After all, the last thing any great and powerful king wanted was for some hairy bloke to come and tell them that God was angry with the way they were behaving.

And what if you got it wrong? The punishment for false prophecy was severe. If a prophet's words were proved not to be true they could be taken and stoned to death. So being a prophet was not a career move that everyone wanted. You didn't choose to be a prophet; you were chosen. The prophets couldn't help themselves. They shake; the message burns inside their bones; they have to speak out.

Perhaps this is one of the reasons why the prophets seem so outspoken. They were not diplomatic in their language; they were outrageous and outspoken. They shocked their listeners. But then again, God is a passionate God and his prophets simply reflected his anger and passion. Prophets had several roles:

Calling for repentance

Time and again the leaders of Israel and Judah turned to false religions. In such times it was the prophets who called the people back to God.

Showing God's power

Prophets demonstrated God's power, both through miraculous acts and showing that God was really in charge, by appointing kings and leaders.

Calling for justice

The prophets were powerful critics of corrupt, unjust regimes. They called for social justice, reminding the rich and powerful of God's concern for the poor.

Warning of judgment

The prophets warned Israel and Judah about the destruction that would come if they didn't change their ways. And not just Israel and Judah; the prophets also warned other nations of God's anger against them.

Living symbols

Prophets didn't just talk about God's truth: they lived it. Prophets often acted out their messages, visibly demonstrating the truth of God's love, judgment and mercy.

Pointing to the future

The prophets saw the destruction that was coming, but they also saw beyond that, to a time of mercy and rescue. Most of all, they pointed to Jesus, the Messiah, who would usher in God's reign of peace, justice, mercy, compassion, safety, shelter and love.

 footsteps

Ten days with the Prophets

Elijah – a prophet confronts evil:
1 Kings 18.1–40
Elisha – a prophet shows God's power:
2 Kings 6.8–23
Jeremiah – a prophet is called by God:
Jeremiah 1.1–19
Amos – a prophet calls for justice:
Amos 5.1–27
Jeremiah – a prophet warns of punishment:
Jeremiah
Ezekiel – a prophet acts out a message:
Ezekiel
Haggai – a prophet encourages the people:
Haggai 1.1–15
Isaiah – a prophet tells of the future:
Isaiah 65.17–25
Hosea – a prophet demonstrates God's love:
Hosea 3.1–5
Micah – a prophet talks of the Messiah:
Micah 5.1–5

More...

A country in ruins

⁷ Your country lies in ruins;
    your towns are in ashes.
Foreigners and strangers
take and destroy your land
    while you watch.
⁸ Enemies surround Jerusalem,
    alone like a hut in a vineyard*
    or in a cucumber field.
⁹ Zion would have disappeared
    like Sodom and Gomorrah,*
    if the LORD All-Powerful
had not let a few of its people survive.

Justice, not sacrifices

¹⁰ You are no better
    than the leaders and people
of Sodom and Gomorrah!
    So listen to the LORD God:
¹¹ "Your sacrifices
    mean nothing to me.
I am sick of your offerings
    of rams and choice cattle;
I don't like the blood
    of bulls or lambs or goats.

¹² "Who asked you to bring all this
    when you come to worship me?
    Stay out of my temple!
¹³ Your sacrifices are worthless,
    and incense is disgusting.
I can't stand the evil you do
    on your New Moon Festivals
or on your Sabbaths
    and other times of worship.
¹⁴ I hate your New Moon Festivals
    and all others as well.
They are a heavy burden
    I am tired of carrying.

¹⁵ "No matter how much you pray,
    I won't listen.
    You are too violent.
¹⁶ Wash yourselves clean!
    I am disgusted
    with your filthy deeds.

---

*1.8 a hut in a vineyard: When it was almost time for grapes to ripen, farmers would put up a temporary shelter or hut in the field or vineyard and stay there to keep thieves and wild animals away.
*1.9 Sodom and Gomorrah: Two ancient cities of Palestine that God destroyed because the people were so wicked (see Genesis 19.1–29).
See also: 1.9: Gen 19.24; Rom 9.29.
1.11–14: Amos 5.21–22.

Stop doing wrong
17   and learn to live right.
See that justice is done.
Defend widows and orphans
and help those in need."'

An invitation from the LORD

18 I, the LORD, invite you
to come and talk it over.
Your sins are scarlet red,
but they will be whiter
than snow or wool.
19 If you willingly obey me,
the best crops in the land
will be yours.
20 But if you turn against me,
your enemies will kill you.
I, the LORD, have spoken.

The LORD condemns Jerusalem

21 Jerusalem, you are like
an unfaithful wife.
Once your judges were honest
and your people lived right;
now you are a city
full of murderers.
22 Your silver is fake,
and your wine is watered down.
23 Your leaders have rejected me
to become friends of crooks;
your rulers are looking
for gifts and bribes.
Widows and orphans
never get a fair trial.

24 I am the LORD All-Powerful,
the mighty ruler of Israel,
and I make you a promise:
you are now my enemy,
and I will show my anger
by taking revenge on you.
25 I will punish you terribly
and burn away everything
that makes you unfit
to worship me.
26 Jerusalem, I will choose
judges and advisers
like those you had before.
Your new name will be
"Justice and Faithfulness".

The LORD will save Jerusalem

27 Jerusalem, you will be saved
by showing justice;'
Zion's people who turn to me
will be saved by doing right.
28 But those rebellious sinners

Life files

Isaiah

Background: Son of Amos... whoever he
was.

What's the story?

Isaiah lived during a time of turmoil and
decline. Kings like Uzziah brought prosperity
to the country, but also tolerated idolatry,
injustice, oppression and corruption. Even
when worshipping God , many people were
just going through the motions.

The Assyrians were threatening invasion
and there were different factions within the
court. Some wanted to make an alliance
with Assyria, others wanted to ally
themselves to Egypt.

Isaiah argued that to rely on human
solutions was pointless: what really
mattered was to seek forgiveness, stop
sinning and trust in God.

What's the point?

Isaiah was one of the greatest of Hebrew
prophets. He was a brave, courageous man
who spoke out for God even when his life
was at stake. He challenged the sins of the
people, called on the kings to mend their
ways and even accused the priests.

More than that, Isaiah pointed to the
enduring love of God. Many of his
prophecies contain beautiful pictures of a
future, restored world, where people will
live in peace and where the love of God will
be evident. He also spoke of a Messiah, a
suffering servant who would bring salvation
to the world. In a society that was
desperately trying to find human solutions
for its problems, Isaiah reminded them that
the only true salvation is to be found in God.

Anorak corner

Along with the book of Isaiah, Isaiah also
wrote a history of the reigns of Uzziah and
Hezekiah (2 Chronicles 26.22; 32.32).

More...

Prophecy p.730
Messiah p.770
Assyria p.500

who turn against me, the LORD,
will all disappear.

²⁹ You will be made ashamed
of those groves of trees
where you worshipped idols.

³⁰ You will be like a grove of trees
dying in a drought.

³¹ Your strongest leaders
will be like dry wood
set on fire by their idols.'
No one will be able to help,
as they all go up in flames.

Messages about Judah and Israel

CHAPTER 2

Peace that lasts for ever

¹ This is the message' that I was given about Judah and Jerusalem:

² In the future, the mountain
with the LORD's temple
will be the highest of all.
It will reach above the hills;
every nation will rush to it.

³ Many people will come and say,
"Let's go to the mountain
of the LORD God of Jacob
and worship in his temple."

The LORD will teach us his Law
from Jerusalem,
and we will obey him.

⁴ He will settle arguments
between nations.
They will beat their swords
and their spears
into rakes and shovels;
they will never make war
or attack one another.

⁵ People of Israel, let's live
by the light of the LORD.

Following sinful customs

⁶ Our LORD, you have deserted
your people, Israel,
because they follow customs
of nations from the east.
They worship Philistine gods
and are close friends
of foreigners.'

⁷ They have endless treasures
of silver and gold;

they have countless horses
and war chariots.

⁸ Everywhere in the country
they worship the idols
they have made.

⁹ And so, all of them
will be ashamed and disgraced.
Don't help them!

A day of judgment

¹⁰ Every one of you,
hide among the rocks
and in the ground,
because the LORD is fearsome,
marvellous, and glorious.

¹¹ When the LORD comes,
everyone who is proud
will be made humble,
and the LORD alone
will be honoured.

¹² The LORD All-Powerful
has chosen a day
when those who are proud and conceited
will be put down.

¹³ The tall and towering
cedars of Lebanon will be destroyed.
So will the oak trees of Bashan,

¹⁴ all high mountains and hills,

¹⁵ every strong fortress,

¹⁶ all the seagoing ships,*
and every beautiful boat.

¹⁷ When that day comes,
everyone who is proud
will be put down.
Only the LORD will be honoured.

¹⁸ Idols will be gone for good.

¹⁹ You had better hide
in caves and holes —
the LORD will be fearsome,
marvellous, and glorious
when he comes to terrify
people on earth.

²⁰ On that day everyone will throw
to the rats and bats
their idols of silver and gold
they made to worship.

²¹ The LORD will be fearsome,
marvellous, and glorious
when he comes to terrify
people on earth —

---

*2.16 seagoing ships: The Hebrew text has "ships of Tarshish", which may have been a Phoenician city in Spain. "Ships of Tarshish" probably means large, seagoing ships.

See also: 2.10: Rev 6.15; 2 Thes 1.9.

See also: 2.4: Joel 3.10; Mic 4.3.

they will hide in caves
    and in the hills.
22 Stop trusting the power
        of humans.
They are all going to die,
    so how can they help?3

CHAPTER 3

Judgment on Jerusalem and Judah

1 The mighty LORD All-Powerful
    is going to take away
        from Jerusalem and Judah
everything you need —
    your bread and water,
2-3 soldiers and heroes,
    judges and prophets,
        leaders and army officers,
officials and advisers,
    fortune-tellers and others
        who tell the future.
4 He will let children and babies·
    become your rulers.
5 You will each be cruel
    to friends and neighbours.
Young people will insult
    their elders;
no one will show respect
    to those who deserve it.

6 Some of you will grab hold
    of a relative and say,
"You still have a coat.
Be our leader and rule
    this pile of ruins."
7 But the answer will be,
"I can't do you any good.
    Don't make me your leader.
There's no food or clothing
    left in my house."

8 Jerusalem and Judah,
    you rebelled against
        your glorious LORD —
your words and your actions,
    made you stumble and fall.
9 The look on your faces shows
    that you are sinful as Sodom,
        and you don't try to hide it.
You are in for trouble,
    and you have brought it all
        on yourselves.

The wrong kind of leaders

10 Tell those who obey God,
    "You're very fortunate —
        you will be rewarded
            for what you have done."

11 Tell those who disobey,
    "You're in big trouble —
        what you did to others
            will come back to you."
12 Though you are God's people,
    you are ruled and abused
        by women and children.
You are confused by leaders
    who guide you
        down the wrong path.

13 The LORD is ready to accuse
    and judge all nations.
14 He will even judge
    you rulers and leaders
        of his own nation.
You destroyed his vineyard*
    and filled your houses
        by robbing the poor.
15 The LORD All-Powerful says,
    "You have crushed my people
        and rubbed in the dust
            the faces of the poor."

The women of Jerusalem

16 The LORD says:

The women of Jerusalem
    are proud and strut around,
        winking shamelessly.
They wear anklets that jingle
    and call attention
        to the way they walk.
17 But I, the LORD, will cover
    their heads with sores,
and I will uncover
    their private parts.

18-23 When that day comes, I will take away
from those women all the fine jewellery they
wear on their ankles, heads, necks, ears,
arms, noses, fingers, and on their clothes.
I will remove their veils, their belts, their
perfume, their magic charms, their royal
robes, and all their fine dresses, hats, and
purses.

24 In place of perfume,
    there will be a stink;
in place of belts,
    there will be ropes;
in place of fancy hair styles,
    they will have bald heads.
Instead of expensive clothes,
    they will wear sackcloth;
instead of beauty,
    they will have ugly scars.

---

*3.14 his vineyard: The nation Israel (see 5.1–7).

25 The fighting men of Jerusalem
  will be killed in battle.
26 The city will mourn
  and sit in the dust,
  emptied of its people.

CHAPTER 4

1 When this happens, seven women will grab the same man, and each of them will say, "I'll buy my own food and clothes! Just marry me and take away my disgrace."*

The LORD will bless
his people who survive

2 The time is coming when the LORD will make his land fruitful and glorious again, and the people of Israel who survive will take great pride in what the land produces. 3 Everyone who is left alive in Jerusalem will be called special, 4 after the LORD sends a fiery judgment to clean the city and its people of their violent deeds.

5 Then the LORD will cover the whole city and its meeting places with a thick cloud each day and with a flaming fire* each night. God's own glory will be like a huge tent that covers everything. 6 It will provide shade from the heat of the sun and a place of shelter and protection from storms and rain.

CHAPTER 5

A song about a vineyard

The LORD said:

1 I will sing a song
  about my friend's vineyard
  that was on the side
  of a fertile hill.
2 My friend dug the ground,
  removed the stones,
  and planted the best vines.
  He built a watchtower
  and dug a pit in rocky ground
  for pressing the grapes.
  He hoped they would be sweet,
  but bitter grapes
  were all it produced.

3 Listen, people of Jerusalem
  and of Judah!
  You be the judge of me
  and my vineyard.
4 What more could I have done
  for my vineyard?
  I hoped for sweet grapes,
  but bitter grapes
  were all that grew.
5 Now I will let you know
  what I am going to do.
  I will cut down the hedge
  and tear down the wall.
  My vineyard will be trampled
  and left in ruins.
6 It will turn into a desert,
  neither pruned nor hoed;
  it will be covered
  with thorns and briars.
  I will command the clouds
  not to send rain.
7 I am the LORD All-Powerful!
  Israel is the vineyard,
  and Judah is the garden
  I tended with care.
  I had hoped for honesty
  and for justice,
  but dishonesty
  and cries for mercy
  were all I found.

Isaiah condemns social injustice

8 You are in for trouble! You take over house after house and field after field, until there is no room left for anyone else in all the land. 9 But the LORD All-Powerful has made this promise to me:

Those large and beautiful homes will be left empty, with no one to take care of them. 10 Four hectares of grapevines will produce only twenty-seven litres of juice, and a hundred and eighty litres of seed will produce merely eighteen litres of grain.

11 You are in for trouble! You get up early to start drinking, and you keep it up late into the night. 12 At your drinking parties you have the music of stringed instruments, tambourines, and flutes. But you never even think about all the LORD has done, 13 and so his people know nothing about him. That's why many of you will be dragged off to foreign lands. Your leaders will starve to death, and everyone else will suffer from thirst.

---

*4.1 take away my disgrace: If a woman did not have a husband or children, it was thought that God was punishing her.
*4.5 thick . . . fire: This is how the LORD led the people of Israel during the forty years they were in the desert (see Exodus 13.20–22; 40.36–38).
See also: 4.5: Exod 13.21; 24.16. 5.1–2: Matt 21.33; Mark 12.1; Luke 20.9.

14 The world of the dead has opened its mouth wide and is eagerly waiting for the leaders of Jerusalem and for its noisy crowds, especially for those who take pride in that city. 15 Its citizens have been put down, and its proud people have been brought to shame. 16 But the holy LORD God All-Powerful is praised, because he has shown who he is by bringing justice. 17 His people will be like sheep grazing in their own pasture, and they will take off what was left by others.'

18 You are in for trouble! The lies you tell are like ropes by which you drag along sin and evil. 19 And you say, "Let the holy God of Israel hurry up and do what he has promised, so we can see it for ourselves." 20 You are headed for trouble! You say wrong is right, darkness is light, and bitter is sweet.

21 You think you are clever and wise. 22 And you are great at drinking and mixing drinks. But you are in for trouble. 23 You accept bribes to let the guilty go free, and you cheat the innocent out of a fair trial.

24 You will go up in flames like straw and hay! You have rejected the teaching of the holy LORD God All-Powerful of Israel. Now your roots will rot, and your blossoms will turn to dust.

25 You are the LORD's people, but you made him terribly angry, and he struck you with his mighty arm. Mountains shook, and dead bodies covered the streets like rubbish. The LORD is still angry, and he is ready to strike you again.'

Foreign nations will attack

26 The LORD has signalled for the foreign nations to come and attack you. He has already whistled, and they are coming as fast as they can. 27 None of them are tired. They don't sleep or get drowsy, and they run without stumbling. Their belts don't come loose; their sandal straps don't break. 28 Their arrows are sharp, and their bows are ready. The hoofs of their horses are hard as flint; the wheels of their war chariots turn as fast as a whirlwind.

29 They roar and growl like fierce young lions as they grab their victims and drag them off where no one can rescue them. 30 On the day they attack, they will roar like the sea. And across the land you will see nothing but darkness and trouble, because the light of day will be covered by thick clouds.

Events from Isaiah's ministry

CHAPTER 6

A vision of the LORD in the temple

1 In the year that King Uzziah died,* I had a vision of the LORD. He was on his throne high above, and his robe filled the temple. 2 Flaming creatures with six wings each were flying over him. They covered their faces with two of their wings and their bodies with two more. They used the other two wings for flying, 3 as they shouted,

> "Holy, holy, holy,
>   LORD All-Powerful!
> The earth is filled
>   with your glory."

4 As they shouted, the doorposts of the temple shook, and the temple was filled with smoke. 5 Then I cried out, "I'm doomed! Everything I say is sinful, and so are the words of everyone around me. Yet I have seen the King, the LORD All-Powerful."

6 One of the flaming creatures flew over to me with a burning coal that it had taken from the altar with a pair of metal tongs. 7 It touched my lips with the hot coal and said, "This has touched your lips. Your sins are forgiven, and you are no longer guilty."

8 After this, I heard the LORD ask, "Is there anyone I can send? Will someone go for us?"

"I'll go," I answered. "Send me!"

9 Then the LORD told me to go and speak this message to the people:

> "You will listen and listen,
>   but never understand.
> You will look and look,
>   but never see."

The LORD also said,

> 10 "Make these people stubborn!
> Make them stop up their ears,
>   cover their eyes,
>   and fail to understand.
> Don't let them turn to me
>   and be healed."

11 Then I asked the LORD, "How long will this last?"

---

*6.1 the year that King Uzziah died: Probably 742 BC.

See also: 6.1: 2 King 15.7; 2 Chron 26.23. 6.3: Rev 4.8.
6.4: Rev 15.8. 6.9,10: Matt 13.14–15; Mark 4.12; Luke 8.10; John 12.40; Acts 28.26–27.

Viewpoints

Are your spiritual bags packed?

Contributed by Dave H

'After this, I heard the LORD ask, "Is there anyone I can send? Will someone go for us?" "I'll go," I answered. "Send me!"'

'Are you ready to go?' enquires Mum. 'I'm coming,' she responds. 'We need to go!' 'I'm coming!' 'We're in the car!' 'Just a minute!' Five minutes later everyone's in the car and reversing out of the drive.

'Ahhhrrrr!! I need to get something – it's really important!' Ten minutes later everyone's back where they were ten minutes ago, plus a little extra make-up.

God has a plan for the Gospel to go to the ends of earth, to every nation, tribe and language. And every Christian in the world is a part of this plan. Some Christians don't accept this and will always stay in their world where they know they're completely safe. Others jump up and down shouting, 'I'll go! Pick me! Send me, send me NOW!' Then there's the third category, who accept there's a need accept, they're a part of the answer, but are never quite ready to go.

God has a plan for every Christian – a plan to use them to bring his Kingdom on earth. But how can he use someone who isn't ready to go? How can he use someone who has a list of excuses of why they can't go, right now? If you heard a big booming voice say 'Go to the cannibal tribe: Nicejuicyleg in the Arctic' would you be ready? Are you ready? Or are you too attached to the things in your life to let go?

Start living with your spiritual bags packed, with no worldly goods in your baggage, a passport from Heaven, and a visa for the world.

More...

Are you ready to move in faith? Really ready? p.485
Serving others p.1190
Sharing your faith p.1082

The LORD answered:

Until their towns are destroyed and their houses are deserted, until their fields are empty, [12] and I have sent them far away, leaving their land in ruins. [13] If only a tenth of the people are left, even they will be destroyed. But just as stumps remain after trees have been cut down,' some of my chosen ones will be left.

CHAPTER 7

Isaiah offers hope to King Ahaz

[1] Ahaz, the son of Jotham and the grandson of Uzziah, was king of Judah when King Rezin of Syria and King Pekah son of Remaliah of Israel went to attack Jerusalem. But they were not able to do what they had planned.' [2] When news reached the royal palace that Syria had joined forces with Israel, King Ahaz and everyone in Judah were so terrified that they shook like trees in a storm.

[3] Then the LORD said to me:

Take your son Shearjashub* and go and see King Ahaz. You will find him on the road near the cloth makers' shops at the end of the canal that brings water from the upper pool. [4] Tell Ahaz to stop worrying. There's no need for him to be afraid of King Rezin and King Pekah. They are very angry, but they are nothing more than a dying fire. Ahaz doesn't need to fear [5] their evil threats [6] to invade and defeat Judah and Jerusalem and to let the son of Tabeel be king in his place.

[7] I, the LORD, promise that this will never happen. [8-9] Damascus is just the capital of Syria, and King Rezin rules only in Damascus. Samaria is just the capital of Israel, and King Pekah rules only in Samaria. But in less than sixty-five years, Israel will be destroyed. And if Ahaz and his officials don't trust me, they will be defeated.

A son named Immanuel

[10] Once again the LORD God spoke to King Ahaz. This time he said, [11] "Ask me for proof that my promise will come true. Ask for something to happen deep in the world of the dead or high in the heavens above."

*7.3 Shearjashub: In Hebrew "Shearjashub" means "a few will return".
See also: 7.1: 2 King 16.5; 2 Chron 28.5–6.

¹² "No, LORD," Ahaz answered. "I won't test you!"

¹³ Then I said:

Listen, every one of you in the royal family of David. You have already tried my patience. Now you are trying God's patience by refusing to ask for proof. ¹⁴ But the LORD will still give you proof. A virgin* is pregnant; she will have a son and will name him Immanuel.* ¹⁵⁻¹⁶ Even before the boy is old enough to know how to choose between right and wrong, he will eat yoghurt and honey,* and the countries of the two kings you fear will be destroyed. ¹⁷ But the LORD will make more trouble for your people and your kingdom than any of you have known since Israel broke away from Judah. He will even bring the king of Assyria to attack you.

The threat of an invasion

¹⁸ When that time comes, the LORD will whistle, and armies will come from Egypt like flies and from Assyria like bees. ¹⁹ They will settle everywhere — in the deep valleys and between the rocks, on every bush and all over the pasture land.

²⁰ The Lord will pay the king of Assyria to bring a razor from across the River Euphrates and shave your head and every hair on your body, including your beard.*

²¹ No one will have more than one young cow and two sheep, ²² but those who do will have enough milk to make yoghurt. In fact, everyone left in the land will eat yoghurt and honey.*

²³ Vineyards that had a thousand vines and were worth a thousand pieces of silver will turn into thorn patches. ²⁴ You will go there to hunt with your bow and arrows, because the whole country will be covered with thorn bushes. ²⁵ The hills where you once planted crops will be overgrown with thorns and thistles. You will be afraid to go there, and your cattle, sheep, and goats will be turned loose on those hills.

CHAPTER 8

A warning and a hope

¹ The LORD said, "Isaiah, get something to write on. Then write in big clear letters' the name, MAHER-SHALAL-HASH-BAZ.* ² I will tell Uriah the priest and Zechariah son of Jeberechiah to serve as witnesses to this."

³ Some time later, my wife and I had a son, and the LORD said, "Name him Maher-Shalal-Hash-Baz. ⁴ Because before he can say 'Mummy' or 'Daddy', the king of Assyria will attack and take everything of value from Damascus and Samaria."

⁵ The LORD spoke to me again and said:

⁶ These people have refused the gentle waters of Shiloah* and have gladly gone over to the side of King Rezin and King Pekah. ⁷ Now I will send the king of Assyria against them with his powerful army, which will attack like the mighty River Euphrates overflowing its banks. ⁸ Enemy soldiers will cover Judah like a flood reaching up to your neck.

But God is with us.*
He will spread his wings
    and protect our land.'
⁹ All you foreign nations,
go ahead and prepare for war,
    but you will be crushed.
¹⁰ Get together and make plans,
    but you will fail
because God is with us.

¹¹ The LORD took hold of me with his powerful hand and said:

I'm warning you! Don't act like these people. ¹² Don't call something a rebellious plot, just because they do, and don't be

---

*7.14 virgin: Or "young woman". In this context the difficult Hebrew word did not imply a virgin birth. However, in the Greek translation made about 200 BC and used by the early Christians, the word *parthenos* had a double meaning. While the translator took it to mean "young woman", Matthew understood it to mean "virgin" and quoted the passage (Matthew 1.23) because it was the appropriate description of Mary, the mother of Jesus.

*7.14 Immanuel: In Hebrew "Immanuel" means "God is with us".

*7.15–16,22 yoghurt and honey: This may refer either to expensive foods eaten in a time of plenty or to a limited diet eaten in times of a food shortage.

*7.20 shave . . . head . . . body . . . beard: This would mean be a terrible insult.

See also: 7.14: Matt 1.23.

---

*8.1 MAHER-SHALAL-HASH-BAZ: In Hebrew "Maher-Shalal-Hash-Baz" means "suddenly attacked, quickly taken".

*8.6 Shiloah: The canal that brought water from Gihon Spring to Jerusalem.

*8.8 God is with us: Here and in verse 10 this translates the Hebrew word "Immanuel" (see 7.14).

See also: 8.12–13: 1 Pet 3.14–15.

afraid of something, just because they are.
¹³ I am the one you should fear and respect. I am the holy God, the LORD All-Powerful!
¹⁴⁻¹⁵ Run to me for protection. I am a rock that will make both Judah and Israel stumble and break their bones. I am a trap that will catch the people of Jerusalem — they will be captured and dragged away.

Isaiah and his followers

¹⁶ My message and my teachings are to be sealed and given to my followers.
¹⁷ Meanwhile, I patiently trust the LORD, even though he is no longer pleased with Israel.
¹⁸ My children and I are warning signs to Israel from the LORD All-Powerful, who lives on Mount Zion.
¹⁹ Someone may say to you, "Go to the fortune-tellers who make soft chirping sounds or ask the spirits of the dead. After all, a nation ought to be able to ask its own gods
²⁰ what it should do."

None of those who talk like that will live to see the light of day! ²¹ They will go around in great pain and will become so hungry that they will angrily curse their king and their gods. And when they try to find help in heaven ²² and on earth, they will find only trouble and darkness, terrible trouble and deepest darkness.

CHAPTER 9

¹ But those who have suffered will no longer be in pain.⸴ The territories of Zebulun and Naphtali in Galilee were once hated. But this land of the Gentiles across the River Jordan and along the Mediterranean Sea will be greatly respected.

War is over

² Those who walked in the dark
    have seen a bright light.
  And it shines upon everyone
    who lives in the land
    of darkest shadows.
³ Our LORD, you have made
    your nation stronger.⸴
  Because of you, its people
    are glad and celebrate
  like workers at harvest time
    or like soldiers dividing up
    what they have taken.

⁴ You have broken the power
  of those who abused
    and enslaved your people.
  You have rescued them
  just as you saved your people
    from Midian.*
⁵ The boots of marching warriors
    and the blood-stained uniforms
  have been fed to flames
    and eaten by fire.

A child has been born

⁶ A child has been born for us.
  We have been given a son
    who will be our ruler.
  His names will be
  Wonderful Adviser and Mighty God,
  Eternal Father and Prince of Peace.
⁷ His power will never end;
    peace will last for ever.
  He will rule David's kingdom
    and make it grow strong.
  He will always rule
    with honesty and justice.
  The LORD All-Powerful
  will make certain that all of this is done.

More messages about Judah and Israel

God will punish Israel

⁸ The Lord had warned the people of Israel, ⁹ and all of them knew it, including everyone in the capital city of Samaria. But they were proud and stubborn and said,

¹⁰ "Houses of brick and sycamore
    have fallen to the ground,
  but we will build houses
    with stones and cedar."

¹¹ The LORD made their enemies⸴ attack them. ¹² He sent the Arameans from the east and the Philistines from the west, and they swallowed up Israel. But even this did not stop him from being angry, so he kept on punishing them.⸴ ¹³ The people of Israel still did not turn back to the LORD All-Powerful and worship him.

¹⁴ In one day he cut off their head and tail, their leaves and branches. ¹⁵ Their rulers and leaders were the head, and the lying prophets

*9.4 rescued . . . from Midian: The time when Gideon defeated the people of Midian in Jezreel Valley (see Judges 6—8).
See also: 9.7: Luke 1.32–33.

See also: 8.14–15: 1 Pet 2.8.   8.17: Heb 2.13.
8.18: Heb 2.13.   9.1: Matt 4.15.   9.2: Matt 4.16; Luke 1.79.

739

were the tail. [16] They had led the nation down the wrong path, and the people were confused. [17] The Lord was angry with his people and kept punishing them, because they had turned against him.' They were evil and spoke foolishly. That's why he did not have pity on their young people or on their widows and orphans.

[18] Evil had spread like a raging forest fire sending thorn bushes up in smoke. [19] The LORD All-Powerful was angry and used the people as fuel for a fire that scorched the land. They turned against each other [20] like wild animals attacking and eating everyone around them, even their own relatives.' But still they were not satisfied. [21] The tribes of Ephraim and Manasseh turned against each other, then joined forces to attack Judah. But the LORD was still angry and ready to punish the nation even more.

CHAPTER 10

[1] You people are in for trouble! You have made cruel and unfair laws [2] that let you cheat the poor and needy and rob widows and orphans. [3] But what will you do when you are fiercely attacked and punished by foreigners? Where will you run for help? Where will you hide your valuables? [4] How will you escape being captured' or killed? The Lord is still angry, and he isn't through with you yet!'

The Lord's purpose and the king of Assyria

[5] The Lord says:

I am furious! And I will use the king of Assyria* as a club [6] to beat down you godless people. I am angry with you, and I will send him to attack you. He will take what he wants and walk on you like mud in the streets. [7] He has even bigger plans in mind, because he wants to destroy many nations.

[8] The king of Assyria says:

My army commanders are kings! [9] They have already captured* the cities of Calno, Carchemish, Hamath, Arpad, Samaria, and

Damascus. [10-11] The gods of Jerusalem and Samaria are weaker than the gods of those powerful nations. And I will destroy Jerusalem, together with its gods and idols, just as I did Samaria.

[12] The Lord will do what he has planned against Jerusalem and Mount Zion. Then he will punish the proud and boastful king of Assyria, [13] who says:

I did these things by my own power because I am clever and wise. I attacked kings like a wild bull, and I took the land and the treasures of their nations. [14] I have conquered the whole world! And it was easier than taking eggs from an unguarded nest. No one even flapped a wing or made a cheep.

[15] King of Assyria, can an axe or a saw overpower the one who uses it? Can a wooden pole lift whoever holds it? [16] The mighty LORD All-Powerful will send a terrible disease to strike down your army, and you will burn with fever under your royal robes. [17] The holy God, who is the light of Israel, will turn into a fire, and in one day you will go up in flames, just like a thorn bush. [18] The Lord will make your beautiful forests and fertile fields slowly rot. [19] There will be so few trees that even a young child can count them.

Only a few will come back

[20] A time is coming when the survivors from Israel and Judah will completely depend on the holy LORD of Israel, instead of the nation* that defeated them. [21-22] There were as many people as there are grains of sand along the seashore, but only a few will survive to come back to Israel's mighty God. This is because he has threatened to destroy their nation, just as they deserve. [23] The LORD All-Powerful has promised that everyone on this earth' will be punished.

[24] Now the LORD God All-Powerful says to his people in Jerusalem:

The Assyrians will beat you with sticks and abuse you, just as the Egyptians did. But don't be afraid of them. [25] Soon I will stop being angry with you, and I will punish them for their crimes.' [26] I will beat the Assyrians with a whip, as I did the people of Midian near the rock at Oreb. And I will show the same mighty power that I used

---

*10.5 king of Assyria: Probably King Sennacherib who invaded Israel in 701 BC.
*10.9 already captured: Calno (in northern Syria), Carchemish (on the River Euphrates), Hamath (on the River Orontes), Arpad (near Aleppo in northern Syria), Samaria, and Damascus had already been captured by Assyrian kings (738–717 BC).
See also: 10.5–34: Isa 14.24–27; Nah 1.1–3.19; Zeph 2.13–15.

*10.20 nation: That is, Assyria.
See also: 10.22–23: Rom 9.27.

when I made a path through the sea in Egypt. ²⁷ Then they will no longer rule your nation. All will go well for you,' and your burden will be lifted.

²⁸ Enemy troops have reached the town of Aiath.* They have gone through Migron, and they stored their supplies at Michmash, ²⁹ before crossing the valley and spending the night at Geba.* The people of Ramah are terrified; everyone in Gibeah, the home town of Saul, has run away. ³⁰ Loud crying can be heard in the towns of Gallim, Laishah, and sorrowful Anathoth. ³¹ No one is left in Madmenah or Gebim. ³² Today the enemy will camp at Nob* and shake a threatening fist at Mount Zion in Jerusalem.

³³ But the LORD All-Powerful
  will use his fearsome might
to bring down the tallest trees
  and chop off every branch.
³⁴ With an axe, the glorious Lord
  will destroy every tree
  in the forests of Lebanon.'

CHAPTER 11

Peace at last

¹ Like a branch that sprouts
    from a stump,
  someone from David's family*
    will some day be king.
² The Spirit of the LORD
    will be with him
  to give him understanding,
    wisdom, and insight.
  He will be powerful,
    and he will know
    and honour the LORD.
³ His greatest joy will be
    to obey the LORD.

  This king won't judge
  by appearances
    or listen to rumours.
⁴ The poor and the needy
  will be treated with fairness
    and with justice.

His word will be law
  everywhere in the land,
and criminals
  will be put to death.
⁵ Honesty and fairness
  will be his royal robes.

⁶ Leopards will lie down
    with young goats,
  and wolves will rest
    with lambs.
  Calves and lions
    will eat together
  and be cared for
    by little children.
⁷ Cows and bears will share
    the same pasture;
  their young will rest
    side by side.
  Lions and oxen
    will both eat straw.

⁸ Little children will play
    near snake holes.
  They will stick their hands
  into dens of poisonous snakes
    and never be hurt.

⁹ Nothing harmful will take place
    on the LORD's holy mountain.
  Just as water fills the sea,
    the land will be filled
  with people who know
    and honour the LORD.

God's people will come back home

¹⁰ The time is coming when one of David's descendants* will be the signal for the people of all nations to come together. They will follow his advice, and his own nation will become famous.
¹¹ When that day comes, the Lord will again reach out his mighty arm and bring home his people who have survived in Assyria, Egypt, Pathros, Ethiopia,* Elam, Shinar, Hamath, and the land along the coast.' ¹² He will give a signal to the nations, and he will bring together the refugees from Judah and Israel, who have been scattered all over the earth. ¹³ Israel will stop being jealous of Judah, and Judah will no longer be the enemy of Israel. ¹⁴ Instead, they

---

*10.28 Aiath: Probably Ai (Joshua 7.2).
*10.29 Geba: Only nine kilometres from Jerusalem.
*10.32 Nob: Perhaps within three kilometres of Jerusalem.
*11.1 David's family: Hebrew "Jesse's family". Jesse was the father of King David.
See also: 11.1: Rev 5.5; 22.16. 11.4: 2 Thes 2.8.

*11.10 David's descendants: Hebrew "Jesse's descendants" (see the note at 11.1).
*11.11 Ethiopia: The Hebrew text has "Cush", which was a region south of Egypt that included parts of the present countries of Ethiopia and Sudan.
See also: 11.5: Eph 6.14. 11.6–9: Isa 65.25.
11.9: Hab 2.14. 11.10: Rom 15.12.

will get together and attack the Philistines in the west. Then they will defeat the Edomites, the Moabites, and the Ammonites in the east. They will rule those people and take from them whatever they want.

¹⁵ The Lord will dry up the arm of the Red Sea near Egypt,* and he will send a scorching wind to divide the River Euphrates into seven streams that anyone can step across. ¹⁶ Then for his people who survive, there will be a good road from Assyria, just as there was a good road for their ancestors when they left Egypt.

CHAPTER 12

A song of praise

¹ At that time you will say,
"I thank you, LORD!
You were angry with me,
but you stopped being angry
and gave me comfort.
² I trust you to save me, LORD God,
and I won't be afraid.
My power and my strength'
come from you,
and you have saved me."

³ With great joy, you people
will get water
from the well of victory.
⁴ At that time you will say,
"Our LORD, we are thankful,
and we worship only you.
We will tell the nations
how glorious you are
and what you have done.
⁵ Because of your wonderful deeds
we will sing your praises
everywhere on earth."

⁶ Sing, people of Zion!
Celebrate the greatness
of the holy LORD of Israel.
God is here to help you.

God will punish other nations

CHAPTER 13

Babylon will be punished

¹ This is the message' that I was given about Babylon:

---

*11.15 arm of the Red Sea near Egypt: Gulf of Suez.
See also: 11.15: Rev 16.12. 12.2: Exod 15.2; Psa 118.14.
13.1—14.23: Isa 47.1–15; Jer 50.1—51.64.

742

Helpline

Help! I know I have been saved, but somehow I don't feel that way

'I know that Jesus has saved me, but I don't feel it. I wish I believed it more...'

Salvation is not a theory, it's a fact. If you've asked Jesus for forgiveness and promised to follow him, then that's it. It's not a matter of feeling it; you don't say, 'Well, two plus two might be four, but I can't help feeling it's really three'.

'I trust you to save me, LORD God, and I won't be afraid. My power and my strength come from you, and you have saved me.' says Isaiah (12.2). He doesn't say 'I feel like you've saved me.' He doesn't say 'you might have saved me.' He knows.

Perhaps you're feeling you don't deserve it, but who does? God, in his grace, gave it to us. All we have to do is accept it.

Still don't feel it? Talk to others. Read the Bible. The Bible is full of reassurances about God's saving love. Keep reading – you'll find it adds up.

Three things

Fact

Concentrate on the facts. If you've asked Jesus to be your saviour then he is. It's not a nice idea, it's a great, life-changing reality.

Talk

Talk to others. Sometimes it helps to hear the truth from someone else. It's not that the truth is any more or less true, it's just somehow more reassuring.

Promise

God has promised that anyone who believes in him is saved. That's what he says. And God always keeps his promises. So try to remind yourself of that each day. God keeps his promises. And he's promised to save all who believe in him. 2+2=4.

More...

Starting again p.1172
Trusting in Jesus p.1164
It's a simple choice: true or not? p.1294

2 From high on a barren hill
give a signal, shout the orders,
   and point the way
to enter the gates
   of Babylon's proud rulers.
3 The LORD has commanded
his very best warriors
and his proud heroes
to show how angry he is.

4 Listen to the noisy crowds
on the mountains!
Kingdoms and nations
are joining forces.
The LORD All-Powerful
is bringing together
   an army for battle.
5 From a distant land
the LORD is coming
   fierce and furious —
he brings his weapons
   to destroy the earth.

6 Cry and weep!
   The day is coming
when the mighty LORD
   will bring destruction.
7-8 All people will be terrified.
Hands will grow limp;
   courage will melt away.
Everyone will tremble with pain
   like a woman giving birth;
they will stare at each other
   with horror on their faces.

There will be no mercy

9 I, the LORD,
will show no mercy or pity
   when that time comes.
In my anger I will destroy
the earth and every sinner
   who lives on it.
10 Light will disappear
   from the stars in the sky;
the dawning sun will turn dark,
   and the moon
   will lose its glow.

11 I will punish this evil world
and its people
   because of their sins.
I will crush the horrible pride
   of those who are cruel.
12 Survivors will be harder to find
   than the purest gold.

13 I, the LORD All-Powerful,
   am terribly angry —
I will make the sky tremble
   and the earth shake loose.

14 Everyone will run
   to their homelands,
just as hunted deer run,
   and sheep scatter
   when they have no shepherd.
15 Those who are captured
   will be killed by a sword.
16 They will see their children
   beaten against rocks,
their homes robbed,
   and their wives abused.

17 The Medes* can't be bought off
   with silver or gold,
and I'm sending them
   to attack Babylonia.
18 Their arrows will slaughter
   the young men;
no pity will be shown
   to babies and children.

The LORD will destroy Babylon

19 The city of Babylon
is glorious and powerful,
   the pride of the nation.
But it will be like the cities
   of Sodom and Gomorrah
after I, the Lord,
   destroyed them.
20 No one will live in Babylon.
Even nomads won't camp nearby,
   and shepherds won't let
   their sheep rest there.
21 Only desert creatures,
owls, and ostriches
   will live in its ruins,
   and goats' will leap about.
22 Hyenas and wolves will howl
from Babylon's fortresses
   and beautiful palaces.
   Its time is almost up!

CHAPTER 14

The LORD's people will come home

1 The LORD will have mercy on Israel and will let them be his chosen people once again. He will bring them back to their own land, and

---

*13.17 Medes:** People of a nation north-east of Babylonia, which became part of the Persian Empire.

See also: **13.19:** Gen 19.24. **13.21:** Isa 34.14; Zeph 2.14; Rev 18.2.

See also: **13.6:** Joel 1.15. **13.10:** Ezek 32.7; Matt 24.29; Mark 13.24–25; Luke 21.25; Rev 6.12–13; 8.12.

foreigners will join them as part of Israel.
² Other nations will lead them home, and Israel will make slaves of them in the land that belongs to the Lord. Israel will rule over those who once governed and ill-treated them.

Death to the king of Babylonia!

³ The LORD will set you free from your sorrow, suffering, and slavery. ⁴ Then you will make fun of the king of Babylonia by singing this song:

> That cruel monster is done for!
>   He won't attack us again.'
⁵ The LORD has crushed the power
>   of those evil kings,
⁶ who were furious
> and never stopped abusing
>   the people of other nations.

⁷ Now all the world is at peace;
>   its people are celebrating
>   with joyful songs.
⁸ King of Babylonia,
>   even the cypress trees
> and the cedars of Lebanon
>   celebrate and say,
> "Since you were put down,
> no one comes along
>   to chop us down."

⁹ The world of the dead
>   eagerly waits for you.
> With great excitement,
>   the spirits of ancient rulers
>   hear about your coming.
¹⁰ Each one of them will say,
>   "Now you are just as weak as any of us!
¹¹ Your pride and your music
> have ended here
>   in the world of the dead.
> Worms are your blanket,
>   maggots are your bed."

¹² You, the bright morning star,
>   have fallen from the sky!
> You brought down other nations;
>   now you are brought down.
¹³ You said to yourself,
>   "I'll climb to heaven
> and place my throne
>   above the highest stars.
> I'll sit there with the gods
>   far away in the north.
¹⁴ I'll be above the clouds,
>   just like God Most High."

¹⁵ But now you are deep
>   in the world of the dead.
¹⁶ Those who see you will stare
> and wonder, "Is this the man
> who made the world tremble
>   and shook up kingdoms?
¹⁷ Did he capture every city
>   and make earth a desert?
> Is he the one who refused
>   to let prisoners go home?"

¹⁸ When kings die, they are buried
>   in glorious tombs.
¹⁹ But you will be left unburied,
>   just another dead body
> lying underfoot like a broken branch.
> You will be one of many
> killed in battle and gone down
>   to the deep rocky pit.*
²⁰ You won't be buried with kings;
>   you ruined your country
>   and murdered your people.

> You evil monster!
> We hope that your family
>   will be forgotten for ever.
²¹ We will slaughter your sons
> to make them pay for the crimes
>   of their ancestors.
> They won't take over the world
> or build cities
>   anywhere on this earth.

²² The LORD All-Powerful has promised to attack Babylonia and destroy everyone there, so that none of them will ever be remembered again. ²³ The LORD will sweep out the people, and the land will become a swamp for wild animals.

Assyria will be punished

²⁴ The LORD All-Powerful has made this promise:

> Everything I have planned
>   will happen just as I said.
²⁵ I will wipe out every Assyrian
>   in my country,
> and I will crush those
>   on my mountains.
> I will free my people from slavery
>   to the Assyrians.
²⁶ I have planned this for the whole world,
>   and my mighty arm
>   controls every nation.

---

*14.19 deep rocky pit: The world of the dead.

See also: 14.12: Rev 8.10; 9.1. 14.13-15: Matt 11.23; Luke 10.15.

See also: 14.24-27: Isa 10.5-34; Nah 1.1–3.19; Zeph 2.13-15.

27 I, the LORD All-Powerful,
   have made these plans.
      No one can stop me now!

The Philistines will be punished

28 This message came from the LORD in the year King Ahaz died:*

29 Philistines, don't be happy
   just because the rod
   that punished you is broken.
   That rod will become
   a poisonous snake, and then
   a flying fiery dragon.

30 The poor and needy will find
   pastures for their sheep
   and will live in safety.
   But I will starve some of you,
   and others will be killed.

31 Cry and weep in the gates of your towns,
   you Philistines!
   Smoke blows in from the north,*
   and every soldier is ready.

32 If a messenger comes
   from a distant nation, you must say:
   "The LORD built Zion.
   Even the poorest of his people
   will find safety there."

CHAPTER 15

Moab will be punished

1This is a message about Moab:

   The towns of Ar and Kir
   were destroyed in a night.
   Moab is left in ruins!

2 Everyone in Dibon has gone up
   to the temple' and the shrines
   to cry and weep.
   All of Moab is crying.
   Heads and beards are shaved*
   because of what happened
   at Nebo and Medeba.

3 In the towns and at home,
   everyone wears sackcloth
   and cries loud and long.

4 From Heshbon and Elealeh,
   weeping is heard in Jahaz;
   Moab's warriors scream
   while trembling with fear.

Pity Moab

5 I pity Moab!
   Its people are running to Zoar
   and to Eglath-Shelishiyah.
   They cry on their way up
   to the town of Luhith;
   on the road to Horonaim
   they tell of disasters.

6 The streams of Nimrim
   and the grasslands
   have dried up.
   Every plant is parched.

7 The people of Moab are leaving,
   crossing over Willow Brook,
   taking everything they own
   and have worked for.

8 In the towns of Eglaim
   and of Beerelim
   and everywhere else in Moab
   mournful cries are heard.

9 The streams near Dimon
   are flowing with blood.
   But the Lord will bring
   even worse trouble to Dimon,'
   because all in Moab who escape
   will be attacked by lions.

CHAPTER 16

More troubles for Moab

1 Send lambs* as gifts
   to the ruler of the land.
   Send them across the desert
   from Sela* to Mount Zion.

2 The women of Moab
   crossing the River Arnon
   are like a flock of birds
   scattered from their nests.

3 Moab's messengers say
   to the people of Judah,
   "Be kind and help us!
   Shade us from the heat
   of the noonday sun.
   Hide our refugees!
   Don't turn them away.

4 Let our people live
   in your country
   and find safety here."

---

*14.28 King Ahaz died: 715 BC.
*14.31 north: The Assyrian and Babylonian attacks came from the north.
*15.2 Heads . . . shaved: As a sign of sorrow and mourning.
See also: 14.28: 2 King 16.20; 2 Chron 28.27.
14.29–31: Jer 47.1–7; Ezek 25.15–17; Joel 3.4–8; Amos 1.6–8; Zeph 2.4–7; Zech 9.5–7. 15.1–16.14: Isa 25.10–12; Jer 48.1–47; Ezek 25.8–11; Amos 2.1–3; Zeph 2.8–11.

*16.1 lambs: The main product of Moab.
*16.1 Sela: A town in Edom.

Moab, your cruel enemies will disappear;
they will no longer attack
and destroy your land.
⁵ Then a kingdom of love
will be set up,
and someone from David's family
will rule with fairness.
He will do what is right
and quickly bring justice.

Moab's pride is destroyed

⁶ We have heard of Moab's pride.
Its people strut and boast,
but without reason.
⁷ Tell everyone in Moab
to mourn for their nation.
Tell them to cry and weep
for those fine raisins*
of Kir-Hareseth.

⁸ Vineyards near Heshbon and Sibmah
have turned brown.
The rulers of nations used to get drunk
on wine from those vineyards›
that spread to Jazer,
then across the desert
and beyond the sea.

⁹ Now I mourn like Jazer
for the vineyards of Sibmah.
I shed tears for Heshbon
and for Elealeh.
There will be no more
harvest celebrations
¹⁰ or joyful and happy times,
while bringing in the crops.
Singing and shouting are gone
from the vineyards.
There are no joyful shouts
where grapes were pressed.
God has silenced them all.

¹¹ Deep in my heart I suffer
for Moab and Kir-Heres.
¹² It's useless for Moab's people
to wear themselves out
by going to their altars
to worship and pray.

¹³ The LORD has already said all this about Moab. ¹⁴ Now he says, "The contract of a hired worker is good for three years, but Moab's glory and greatness won't last any longer than that. Only a few of its people will survive, and they will be left helpless."

---

*16.7 fine raisins: The Hebrew text has "raisin-cakes", which could mean either the rich produce or the prosperous farmers.

CHAPTER 17

Damascus will be punished

¹ This is a message about Damascus:

Damascus is doomed!
It will end up in ruins.
² The villages around Aroer*
will be deserted,
with only sheep living there
and no one to bother them.
³ Israel› will lose its fortresses.
The kingdom of Damascus
will be destroyed;
its survivors will suffer
the same fate as Israel.
The LORD All-Powerful
has promised this.

Sin and suffering

⁴ When that time comes,
the glorious nation of Israel
will be brought down;
its prosperous people
will be skin and bones.
⁵ Israel will be like wheat fields
in Rephaim Valley
picked clean of grain.
⁶ It will be like an olive tree
beaten with a stick,
leaving two or three olives
or perhaps four or five
on the highest
or most fruitful branches.
The LORD God of Israel
has promised this.

⁷ At that time the people will turn and trust their Creator, the holy God of Israel. ⁸ They have built altars and places for burning incense to their goddess Asherah, and they have set up sacred poles* for her. But they will stop worshipping at these places.

⁹ Israel captured powerful cities and chased out the people who lived there. But these cities will lie in ruins, covered over with weeds and undergrowth.›

---

*17.2 Aroer: Either a city near Damascus with the same name as the Moabite city or the Moabite city itself, here used as an example of what will happen to Damascus.

*17.8 sacred poles: Or "trees", used as symbols of Asherah, the goddess of fertility.

See also: 17.1–3: Jer 49.23–27; Amos 1.3–5; Zech 9.1.

¹⁰ Israel, you have forgotten
    the God who saves you,
  the one who is the mighty rock*
    where you find protection.
  You plant the finest flowers
    to honour a foreign god.
¹¹ The plants may sprout and blossom
    that very same morning,
  but it will do you no good,
  because you will suffer
    endless agony.

God defends his people

¹² The nations are a noisy,
    thunderous sea.
¹³ But even if they roar
    like a fearsome flood,
  God will give the command
    to turn them back.
  They will be like dust,
    or like straw
  blowing across the hills
    in a storm.
¹⁴ In the evening
    their attack is fierce,
  but by morning
    they are destroyed.
  This is what happens to those
    who raid and rob us.

CHAPTER 18

Ethiopia will be punished

¹ Downstream from Ethiopia*
    lies the country of Egypt,
    swarming with insects.▸
² Egypt sends messengers
    up the River Nile
  on ships made of reeds.*
  Send them fast to Ethiopia,
    whose people are tall
    and have smooth skin.
  Their land is divided by rivers;
  they are strong and brutal,
    feared all over the world.▸

³ Everyone on this earth,
    listen with care!

A signal will be given
  on the mountains,
    and you will hear a trumpet.
⁴ The LORD said to me,
  "I will calmly look down
    from my home above —
  as calmly as the sun at midday
  or clouds in the heat
    of harvest season."

⁵ Before the blossoms
    can turn into grapes,
  God will cut off the shoots
    and hack off the branches.
⁶ Ethiopians will be food
    for mountain eagles
    during the summer
  and for wild animals
    during the winter.

⁷ Those Ethiopians are tall and their skin is
smooth. They are feared all over the world,
because they are strong and brutal. But at that
time they will come from their land divided
by rivers, and they will bring gifts to the
LORD All-Powerful, who is worshipped on
Mount Zion.

CHAPTER 19

Egypt will be punished

¹ This is a message about Egypt:

  The LORD comes to Egypt,
    riding swiftly on a cloud.
  The people are weak from fear.
  Their idols tremble
    as he approaches and says,
² "I will punish Egypt with civil war —
  neighbours, cities, and kingdoms
    will fight each other.

³ "Egypt will be discouraged
    when I confuse their plans.
  They will try to get advice
    from their idols,
  from the spirits of the dead,
    and from fortune-tellers.
⁴ I will put the Egyptians
  under the power of a cruel,
    heartless king.
  I, the LORD All-Powerful,
    have promised this."

Trouble along the Nile

⁵ The River Nile will dry up
    and become parched land.

---

*17.10 mighty rock: The Hebrew text has "rock",
which is sometimes used in poetry to compare the
Lord to a mountain where his people can run for
protection from their enemies.
*18.1 Ethiopia: See the note at 11.11.
*18.2 reeds: Ancient Egypt was famous for the
papyrus reeds that grew in the Nile Delta.
See also: 18.1–7: Zeph 2.12.

See also: 19.1–25: Jer 46.2–26; Ezek 29.1–32.32.

⁶ Its streams will stink,
  Egypt will have no water,
  and the reeds and tall grass
  will dry up.
⁷ Fields along the Nile
  will be completely barren;
  every plant will disappear.

⁸ Those who fish in the Nile
  will be discouraged
  and mourn.
⁹ None of the cloth makers*
  will know what to do,
  and they will turn pale.'
¹⁰ Weavers will be confused;
  paid workers will cry and mourn.

Egypt's helpless leaders

¹¹ The king's officials in Zoan*
  are foolish themselves
  and give stupid advice.
  How can they say to him,
  "We are very wise,
  and our families go back
  to kings of long ago"?
¹² Where are those wise men now?
  If they can, let them say
  what the LORD All-Powerful
  intends for Egypt.

¹³ The royal officials in Zoan
  and in Memphis
  are foolish and deceived.
  The leaders in every state
  have given bad advice
  to the nation.
¹⁴ The LORD has confused Egypt;
  its leaders have made it stagger
  and vomit like a drunkard.
¹⁵ No one in Egypt can do a thing,
  no matter who they are.

¹⁶ When the LORD All-Powerful punishes Egypt with his mighty arm, the Egyptians will become terribly weak and will tremble with fear. ¹⁷ They will be so terrified of Judah that they will be frightened by the very mention of its name. This will happen because of what the LORD All-Powerful is planning against Egypt.

The LORD will bless Egypt, Assyria, and Israel

¹⁸ The time is coming when Hebrew will be spoken in five Egyptian cities, and their people will become followers of the LORD. One of these cities will be called City of the Sun.'

¹⁹ In the heart of Egypt an altar will be set up for the LORD; at its border a shrine will be built to honour him. ²⁰ These will remind the Egyptians that the LORD All-Powerful is with them. And when they are in trouble and ask for help, he will send someone to rescue them from their enemies. ²¹ The LORD will show the Egyptians who he is, and they will know and worship the LORD. They will bring him sacrifices and offerings, and they will keep their promises to him. ²² After the LORD has punished Egypt, the people will turn to him. Then he will answer their prayers, and the Egyptians will be healed.

²³ At that time a good road will run from Egypt to Assyria. The Egyptians and the Assyrians will travel back and forth from Egypt to Assyria, and they will worship together. ²⁴ Israel will join with these two countries. They will be a blessing to everyone on earth, ²⁵ then the LORD All-Powerful will bless them by saying,

  "The Egyptians are my people.
  I created the Assyrians
  and chose the Israelites."

CHAPTER 20

Isaiah acts out the defeat of Egypt and Ethiopia

¹ King Sargon of Assyria gave orders for his army commander to capture the city of Ashdod.* ² About this same time the LORD had told me, "Isaiah, take off everything, including your sandals!" I did this and went around naked and barefoot ³ for three years.

Then the LORD said:

What Isaiah has done is a warning to Egypt and Ethiopia.* ⁴ Everyone in these two countries will be led away naked and barefoot by the king of Assyria. Young or old, they will be taken prisoner, and Egypt will be disgraced. ⁵ They will be confused and frustrated, because they depended on Ethiopia and boasted about Egypt. ⁶ When this happens, the people who live along the coast* will say, "Look what happened

---

*19.9 cloth makers: Cloth was made from several kinds of plants that grew in the fields along the Nile.
*19.11 Zoan: The city of Tanis in the Nile delta.

*20.1 Ashdod: King Sargon II of Assyria captured this Philistine city in 711 BC.
*20.3 Ethiopia: See the note at 11.11.
*20.6 people . . . coast: Probably the Philistines.

to them! We ran to them for safety, hoping
they would protect us from the king of
Assyria. But now, there is no escape for us."

CHAPTER 21

The fall of Babylonia*

¹ This is a message about a desert beside the
sea:*

> Enemies from a hostile nation
> attack like a whirlwind
>   from the Southern Desert.
² What a horrible vision
>   was shown to me —
> a vision of betrayal and destruction.
> Tell Elam and Media*
> to surround and attack
>   the Babylonians.
> The Lord has sworn to end
>   the suffering they caused.

³ I'm in terrible pain
>   like a woman giving birth.
> I'm shocked and hurt so much
>   that I can't hear or see.
⁴ My head spins; I'm horrified!
> Early evening, my favourite time,
>   has become a nightmare.

⁵ In Babylon the high officials
>   were having a feast.
> They were eating and drinking,
>   when someone shouted,
> "Officers, take your places!
>   Grab your shields."

⁶ The Lord said to me,
>   "Send guards to find out
>   what's going on.
⁷ When they see cavalry troops
>   and columns of soldiers
> on donkeys and camels,
>   tell them to be ready!"

⁸ Then a guard⁰ said,
> "I have stood day and night
>   on this watchtower, Lord.

⁹ Now I see column after column
>   of cavalry troops."
> Straight away someone shouted,
>   "Babylon has fallen!
> Every idol in the city
>   lies broken on the ground."

¹⁰ Then I said, "My people,
>   you have suffered terribly,
> but I have a message for you
> from the Lord All-Powerful,
>   the God of Israel."

How much longer?

¹¹ This is a message about Dumah:

> From the country of Seir,*
>   someone shouts to me,
> "Guard, how much longer
>   before daylight?"

¹² From my guard post, I answered,
>   "Morning will soon be here,
>   but night will return.
> If you want to know more,
>   come back later."

¹³ This is a message for Arabs who live in the
barren desert in the region of Dedan:*

> You must order your caravans
¹⁴ to bring water for those
>   who are thirsty.
> You people of Tema*
> must bring food
>   for the hungry refugees.
¹⁵ They are worn out and weary
> from being chased by enemies
>   with swords and arrows.

¹⁶ The Lord said to me:

A year from now the glory of the people of
Kedar* will all come to an end, just as a
worker's contract ends after a year. ¹⁷ Only
a few of their warriors will be left with
bows and arrows. This is a promise that I,
the Lord God of Israel, have made.

---

*21.1 **Babylonia:** King Cyrus and his army of Medes
and Persians captured the city of Babylon in 539 BC.
*21.1 **This . . . sea:** One possible meaning for the
difficult Hebrew text. The prophet may be speaking
of Babylonia as a desert, because of the terrible
punishment God will bring on it. The southern part of
Babylonia on the Persian Gulf was sometimes called
"the land beside the sea".
*21.2 **Elam and Media:** People from the Iranian
highlands; the capital of Elam was Susa, in the hill
country east of Babylon.

*21.11 **Dumah . . . Seir:** Dumah was an oasis in the
Arabian desert. One ancient translation has "Edom",
which may be what is meant. Seir is a mountainous
region of Edom south-west of the Dead Sea.
*21.13 **Dedan:** A region in north-west Arabia.
*21.14 **Tema:** A region in north Arabia.
*21.16 **Kedar:** A region in the Arabian desert.
See also: 21.9: Rev 14.8; 18.2.

CHAPTER 22

Trouble in Vision Valley

¹ This is a message about Vision Valley:*

> Why are you celebrating
> on the flat roofs*
> of your houses?
> ² Your city is filled
> with noisy shouts.
> Those who lie drunk
> in your streets
> were not killed in battle.
> ³ Your leaders ran away,
> but they were captured
> without a fight.
> No matter how far they ran,
> they were found and caught.'
>
> ⁴ Then I said, "Leave me alone!
> Let me cry bitter tears.
> My people have been destroyed,
> so don't try to comfort me."
>
> ⁵ The LORD All-Powerful
> had chosen a time
> for noisy shouts and confusion
> to fill Vision Valley,
> and for everyone to beg
> the mountains for help.'
> ⁶ The people of Elam and Kir*
> attacked with chariots'
> and carried shields.
> ⁷ Your most beautiful valleys
> were covered with chariots;
> your cities were surrounded
> by cavalry troops.
> ⁸ Judah was left defenceless.

At that time you trusted in the weapons you had stored in Forest Palace.* ⁹ You saw the holes in the outer wall of Jerusalem, and you brought water from the lower pool.* ¹⁰ You counted the houses in Jerusalem and tore down some of them, so you could get stones to repair the city wall. ¹¹ Then you built a large tank between the walls* to store the water. But you refused to trust the God who planned this long ago and made it happen.

A time to weep

> ¹² When all this happened,
> the LORD All-Powerful told you
> to weep and mourn,
> to shave your heads,
> and wear sackcloth.
> ¹³ But instead, you celebrated
> by feasting on beef and lamb
> and by drinking wine,
> because you said,
> "Let's eat and drink!
> Tomorrow we may die."
>
> ¹⁴ The LORD All-Powerful
> has spoken to me
> this solemn promise:
> "I won't forgive them for this,
> not as long as they live."

Selfish officials are doomed

¹⁵ The LORD All-Powerful is sending you with this message for Shebna, the prime minister:

¹⁶ Shebna, what gives you the right to have a tomb carved out of rock in this burial place of royalty? None of your relatives are buried here. ¹⁷ You may be powerful, but the LORD is about to snatch you up and throw you away. ¹⁸ He will roll you into a ball and throw you into a wide open country, where you will die and your chariots will be destroyed. You're a disgrace to those you serve.

¹⁹ The LORD is going to take away your job! ²⁰⁻²¹ He will give your official robes and your authority to his servant Eliakim son of Hilkiah.

Eliakim will be like a father to the people of Jerusalem and to the royal family of Judah. ²² The LORD will put him in charge of the key that belongs to King David's family. No one will be able to unlock what he locks, and no one will be able to lock what he unlocks. ²³ The LORD will make

---

22.1 Vision Valley: The exact location is not known. In Hebrew the name sounds something like "Hinnom Valley", where the people of Jerusalem sometimes offered human sacrifices to the gods of Canaan.

22.1 flat roofs: In Palestine the houses usually had a flat roof. Stairs on the outside led up to the roof, which was made of beams and boards covered with packed earth.

22.6 Elam and Kir: Regions in the Iranian highlands.

22.8 Forest Palace: Built by Solomon (1 Kings 7.2) and used as a place for storing weapons.

22.9 the lower pool: Mentioned only here; probably in the southern part of the Central Valley (Tyropoean Valley) of Jerusalem.

22.11 between the walls: Some cities had two walls with a space between them. If the enemy broke through the outer wall, the city was still protected by the inner wall. The houses that were torn down to repair the outer wall were probably squatters' huts that had been built between the two walls.

See also: 22.13: 1 Cor 15.32. 22.22: Rev 3.7.

him as firm in his position as a tent peg hammered in the ground, and Eliakim will bring honour to his family.

²⁴ His children and relatives will be supported by him, like pans hanging from a peg on the wall. ²⁵ That peg is fastened firmly now, but some day it will be shaken loose and fall down. Then everything that was hanging on it will be destroyed. This is what the LORD All-Powerful has promised.

CHAPTER 23

The city of Tyre will be punished

¹ This is a message from distant islands about the city of Tyre:*

Cry, you seagoing ships!*
Tyre and its houses lie in ruins.'
² Mourn in silence,
you shop owners of Sidon,*
you people on the coast.
Your sailors crossed oceans,
making your city rich.
³ Your merchants sailed the seas,
making you wealthy by trading
with nation after nation.
They brought back grain
that grew along the Nile.'
⁴ Sidon, you are a mighty fortress
built along the sea.
But you will be disgraced
like a married woman
who never had children.'

⁵ When Egypt hears about Tyre,
it will tremble.
⁶ All of you along the coast
had better cry and sail
far across the ocean.'
⁷ Can this be the happy city
that has stood for centuries?
Its people have spread to distant lands;
⁸ its merchants were kings
honoured all over the world.
Who planned to destroy Tyre?
⁹ The LORD All-Powerful planned it
to bring shame and disgrace
to those who are honoured
by everyone on earth.

¹⁰ People of Tyre,'
your harbour is destroyed!
You will have to become farmers
just like the Egyptians.'

Tyre will be forgotten

¹¹ The LORD's hand has reached
across the sea,
upsetting the nations.
He has given a command
to destroy fortresses
in the land of Canaan.
¹² The LORD has said
to the people of Sidon,
"Your celebrating is over —
you are crushed.
Even if you escape to Cyprus,
you won't find peace."

¹³ Look what the Assyrians have done to Babylonia! They have attacked, destroying every palace in the land. Now wild animals live among the ruins.' ¹⁴ Not a fortress will be left standing, so tell all the seagoing ships* to mourn.

¹⁵ The city of Tyre will be forgotten for seventy years, which is the lifetime of a king. Then Tyre will be like that evil woman in the song:

¹⁶ You're gone and forgotten,
you evil woman!
So strut through the town,
singing and playing
your favourite tune
to be remembered again.

¹⁷ At the end of those seventy years, the LORD will let Tyre get back into business. The city will be like a woman who sells her body to everyone of every nation on earth, ¹⁸ but none of what is earned will be kept in the city. That money will belong to the LORD, and it will be used to buy more than enough food and good clothes for those who worship the LORD.

Messages of hope for the Lord's people who are suffering

CHAPTER 24

The earth will be punished

¹ The LORD is going to twist the earth out of shape and turn it into a desert. Everyone will

---

*23.1 Tyre: A fortress city built on an island in the Mediterranean Sea off the coast of what is now Lebanon.
*23.1 seagoing ships: See the note at 2.16.
*23.2 Sidon: A coastal city just north of Tyre.
See also: 23.1–18: Ezek 26.1–28.19; Joel 3.4–8; Amos 1.9–10; Zech 9.1–4; Matt 11.21–22; Luke 10.13–14.

*23.14 seagoing ships: See the note at 2.16.

be scattered, ² including ordinary people and priests, slaves and slave owners, buyers and sellers, lenders and borrowers, the rich and the poor. ³ The earth will be stripped bare and left that way. This is what the LORD has promised.

⁴ The earth wilts away;
   its mighty leaders melt
   to nothing.'
⁵ The earth is polluted
   because its people
disobeyed the laws of God,
   breaking their agreement
   that was to last for ever.

⁶ The earth is under a curse;
   its people are dying out
   because of their sins.
⁷ Grapevines have dried up:
   wine is almost gone —
mournful sounds are heard
   instead of joyful shouts.

⁸ No one plays tambourines
   or stringed instruments;
all noisy celebrating
   has come to an end.
⁹ They no longer sing
   as they drink their wine,
   and it tastes sour.

¹⁰ Towns are crushed and in chaos;
   houses are locked tight.
¹¹ Happy times have disappeared
   from the earth,
and people shout in the streets,
   "We're out of wine!"
¹² Cities are destroyed;
   their gates are torn down.
¹³ Nations will be stripped bare,
   like olive trees or vineyards
   after the harvest season.

Praise the God of justice

¹⁴ People in the west shout;
   they joyfully praise
   the majesty of the LORD.
¹⁵ And so, everyone in the east
   and those on the islands
should praise the LORD,
   the God of Israel.
¹⁶ From all over the world
   songs of praise are heard
   for the God of justice.'
But I feel awful,
   terribly miserable.
Can anyone be trusted?
   So many are treacherous!

There's no escape

¹⁷ Terror, traps, and pits
   are waiting for everyone.
¹⁸ If you are terrified and run,
   you will fall into a pit;
   if you crawl out of the pit,
   you will get caught in a trap.

The sky has split apart
   like a window thrown open.
The foundations of the earth
   have been shaken;
¹⁹ the earth is shattered,
   ripped to pieces.
²⁰ It staggers and shakes like a drunkard
   or a hut in a storm.
It is burdened down with sin;
   the earth will fall,
   never again to get up.

²¹ On that day the LORD
   will punish the powers
in the heavens*
   and the kings of the earth.
²² He will put them in a pit
   and keep them prisoner.
Then later on,
   he will punish them.
²³ The moon and sun will both
   be embarrassed and ashamed.
The LORD All-Powerful will rule
   on Mount Zion in Jerusalem,
where he will show its rulers
   his wonderful glory.

CHAPTER 25

A prayer of thanks to God

¹ You, LORD, are my God!
   I will praise you
for doing the wonderful things
   you had planned and promised
   since ancient times.
² You have destroyed the fortress
   of our enemies,
leaving their city in ruins.
Nothing in that foreign city
   will ever be rebuilt.
³ Now strong and cruel nations
   will fear and honour you.

⁴ You have been a place of safety
   for the poor and needy
   in times of trouble.
Brutal enemies pounded us

---

*24.21 the powers in the heavens: In ancient times the stars were thought of as powerful spiritual beings, and sometimes they stood for pagan gods.

like a heavy rain
or the heat of the sun at midday,
but you were our shelter.
5 Those wild foreigners struck
like scorching desert heat.
But you were like a cloud,
protecting us from the sun.
You kept our enemies from singing
songs of victory.

The LORD has saved us

6 On this mountain
the LORD All-Powerful
will prepare for all nations
a feast of the finest foods.
Choice wines and the best meats
will be served.
7 Here the LORD will strip away
the burial clothes
that cover the nations.
8 The LORD All-Powerful
will destroy the power of death
and wipe away all tears.
No longer will his people
be insulted everywhere.
The LORD has spoken!

9 At that time, people will say,
"The LORD has saved us!
Let's celebrate.
We waited and hoped —
now our God is here."
10 The powerful arm of the LORD
will protect this mountain.

The Moabites will be put down
and trampled on like straw
in a pit of manure.
11 They will struggle to get out,
but God will humiliate them
no matter how hard they try.◆
12 The walls of their fortresses
will be knocked down
and scattered in the dust.

CHAPTER 26

A song of victory

1 The time is coming
when the people of Judah
will sing this song:
"Our city* is protected.

The LORD is our fortress,
and he gives us victory.
2 Open the city gates
for a law-abiding nation
that is faithful to God.
3 The LORD gives perfect peace
to those whose faith is firm.
4 So always trust the LORD
because he is for ever
our mighty rock.*
5 God has put down our enemies
in their mountain city◆
and rubbed it in the dust.
6 Now the poor and abused
trample all over that city."

The LORD can be trusted

7 Our LORD, you always do right,
and you make the path smooth
for those who obey you.
8 You are the one we trust
to bring about justice;
above all else we want
your name to be honoured.
9 Throughout the night,
my heart searches for you,
because your decisions
show everyone on this earth
how to live right.

10 Even when the wicked
are treated with mercy
in this land of justice,
they do wrong and are blind
to your glory, our LORD.
11 Your hand is raised and ready
to punish them,
but they don't see it.
Put them to shame!
Show how much you care for us
and throw them into the fire
intended for your enemies.

12 You will give us peace, LORD,
because everything we have done
was by your power.
13 Others have ruled over us
besides you, our LORD God,
but we obey only you.
14 Those enemies are now dead
and can never live again.
You have punished them —
they are destroyed,
completely forgotten.

---

*26.1 city: Probably Jerusalem.
See also: 25.8: a 1 Cor 15.54; b Rev 7.17; 21.4.
25.10–12: Isa 15.1—16.14; Jer 48.1–47; Ezek 25.8–11;
Amos 2.1–3; Zeph 2.8–11.

*26.4 mighty rock: See the note at 17.10.
See also: 26.11: Heb 10.27.

¹⁵ Our nation has grown
   because of you, our LORD.
We have more land than before,
   and you are honoured.

The LORD gives life to the dead

¹⁶ When you punished our people,
   they turned and prayed
      to you, our LORD.'
¹⁷ Because of what you did to us,
   we suffered like a woman
      about to give birth.
¹⁸ But instead of having a child,
   our terrible pain
      produced only wind.
We have won no victories,
   and we have no descendants
      to take over the earth.

¹⁹ Your people will rise to life!
Tell them to leave their graves
   and celebrate with shouts.
You refresh the earth
   like morning dew;
      you give life to the dead.

²⁰ Go inside and lock the doors,
   my people.
Hide there for a little while,
   until the LORD is no longer angry.

The earth and the sea will be punished

²¹ The LORD will come out
   to punish everyone on earth
      for their sins.
And when he does,
   those who did violent crimes
      will be known and punished.

CHAPTER 27

¹ On that day, Leviathan,*
   the sea monster,
will squirm and try to escape,
but the LORD will kill him
   with a cruel, sharp sword.

Protection and forgiveness

The LORD said:

² At that time you must sing
   about a fruitful' vineyard.

---

*27.1 **Leviathan:** God's victory over this monster
sometimes stands for God's power over all creation
and sometimes for his defeat of his enemies,
especially Egypt.
See also: 27.1: Job 41.1; Psa 74.14; 104.26.

754

³ I, the LORD, will protect it
   and always keep it watered.
I will guard it day and night
   to keep it from harm.
⁴ I am no longer angry.
   But if it produces thorns,
I will go to war against it
   and burn it to the ground.
⁵ Yet if the vineyard depends
   on me for protection,
it will become my friend
   and be at peace with me.

⁶ Some day Israel will take root
   like a vine.
It will blossom and bear fruit
   that covers the earth.

⁷ I, the LORD, didn't punish and kill
   the people of Israel
as fiercely as I punished
   and killed their enemies.
⁸ I carefully measured out
   Israel's punishment'
and sent the scorching heat
   to chase them far away.

⁹ There's only one way
   that Israel's sin and guilt
      can be completely forgiven:
they must crush the stones
   of every pagan altar
      and place of worship.

The LORD will bring his people together

¹⁰ Fortress cities are left
   like a desert
      where no one lives.
Cattle walk through the ruins,
   stripping the trees bare.
¹¹ When broken branches
   fall to the ground,
women pick them up
   to feed the fire.
But these people are so stupid
   that the God who created them
      will show them no mercy.

¹² The time is coming when the LORD will shake the land between the River Euphrates and the border of Egypt, and one by one he will bring all his people together. ¹³ A loud trumpet will be heard. Then the people of Israel who were dragged away to Assyria and Egypt will return to worship the LORD on his holy mountain in Jerusalem.

The Lord will punish his rebellious people

CHAPTER 28

Samaria will be punished

¹ The city of Samaria
above a fertile valley
is in for trouble!
Its leaders are drunkards,
who stuff themselves
with food and wine.
But they will be like flowers
that dry up and wilt.
² Only the Lord is strong and powerful!
His mighty hand
will strike them down
with the force of a hailstorm
or a mighty whirlwind
or an overwhelming flood.

³ Every drunkard in Ephraim*
takes pride in Samaria,
but it will be crushed.
⁴ Samaria above a fertile valley
will quickly lose its glory.
It will be gobbled up
like the first ripe fig
at harvest season.
⁵ When this time comes,
the LORD All-Powerful
will be a glorious crown
for his people who survive.
⁶ He will see that justice rules
and that his people are able
to defend their cities.

Corrupt leaders will be punished

⁷ Priests and prophets stumble
because they are drunk.
Their minds are too confused
to receive God's messages
or give honest decisions.
⁸ Their tables are covered,
completely covered,
with their stinking vomit.

⁹ You drunken leaders are like babies!
How can you possibly understand
or teach the LORD's message?
¹⁰ You don't even listen —
all you hear is senseless sound
after senseless sound.'

¹¹ So, the Lord will speak
to his people in strange sounds
and foreign languages.*
¹² He promised you
perfect peace and rest,
but you refused to listen.
¹³ Now his message to you
will be senseless sound
after senseless sound.'
Then you will fall backwards,
injured and trapped.

False security is fatal

¹⁴ You rulers of Jerusalem
do nothing but sneer;
now you must listen
to what the LORD says.
¹⁵ Do you think you have
an agreement with death
and the world of the dead?
Why do you trust in your lies
to keep you safe from danger
and the mighty flood?

¹⁶ And so the LORD says,
"I'm laying a firm foundation
for the city of Zion.
It's a valuable cornerstone
proved to be trustworthy;
no one who trusts in it
will ever be disappointed.
¹⁷ Justice and fairness
will be the measuring lines
that help me build."

Hailstones and floods
will destroy and wash away
your shelter of lies.
¹⁸ Your agreement with death
and the world of the dead
will be broken.
Then angry, roaring waves
will sweep over you.
¹⁹ Morning, noon, and night
an overwhelming flood
will wash you away.
The terrible things that happen
will teach you this lesson:
²⁰ your bed is too short,
your blanket too skimpy.*

---

*28.11 in . . . foreign languages: This probably refers to the language of the Assyrians.

*28.20 your bed . . . skimpy: Isaiah quotes a popular saying to teach that the treaty made with Egypt (verse 18) cannot give the nation security from its enemies.

See also: 28.11–12: 1 Cor 14.21. 28.16: Psa 118.22–23; Rom 9.33; 10.11; 1 Pet 2.6.

*28.3 Ephraim: The northern kingdom of Israel; Samaria was its capital.

21 The LORD will fiercely attack
   as he did at Mount Perazim*
   and in Gibeon Valley.*
   But this time the LORD
   will do something surprising,
   not what you expect.
22 So you had better stop sneering
   or you will be in worse shape
   than ever before.
   I heard the LORD All-Powerful
   threaten the whole country
   with destruction.

All wisdom comes from the LORD

23 Pay close attention
   to what I am saying.
24 Farmers don't just plough
   and break up the ground.
25 When a field is ready,
   they scatter the seeds
   of dill and cumin;
   they plant the seeds
   of wheat and barley
   in the proper places.
26 They learn this from their God.

27 After dill and cumin
   have been harvested,
   the stalks are beaten,
   not run over with a wagon.
28 Wheat and barley are pounded,
   but not beaten to pulp;
   they are run over with a wagon,
   but not ground to dust.
29 This wonderful knowledge comes
   from the LORD All-Powerful,
   who has such great wisdom.

CHAPTER 29

Jerusalem will suffer

The LORD said:

1 Jerusalem, city of David,
   the place of my altar,'
   you are in for trouble!
   Celebrate your festivals year after year.
2 I will still make you suffer,
   and your people will cry
   when I make an altar of you.'

3 I will surround you and prepare
   to attack from all sides.'
4 From deep in the earth,
   you will call out for help
   with only a faint whisper.

5 Then your cruel enemies
   will suddenly be swept away
   like dust in a storm.
6 I, the LORD All-Powerful,
   will come to your rescue
   with a thundering earthquake
   and a fiery whirlwind.

7 Every brutal nation
   that attacks Jerusalem
   and makes it suffer
   will disappear like a dream
   when night is over.
8 Those nations that attack
   Mount Zion
   will suffer from hunger and thirst.
   They will dream of food and drink
   but wake up weary and hungry
   and thirsty as ever.

Prophets who fool themselves

9 Be shocked and stunned,
   you prophets!
   Refuse to see.
   Get drunk and stagger,
   but not from wine.
10 The LORD has made you drowsy;
   he put you into a deep sleep
   and covered your head.

11 Now his message is like a sealed letter to
you. Some of you say, "We can't read it,
because it's sealed." 12 Others say, "We can't
read it, because we don't know how to read."
13 The Lord has said:

"These people praise me
   with their words,
but they never really
   think about me.
They worship me by repeating
   rules made up by humans.
14 So once again I will do things
   that shock and amaze them,
   and I will destroy the wisdom
of those who claim to know
   and understand."

15 You are in for trouble,
   if you try to hide your plans
   from the LORD!

---

*28.21 Mount Perazim: This may refer to
David's defeat of the Philistines at Baal Perazim
(2 Samuel 5.17–21).
*28.21 Gibeon Valley: This refers to Joshua's
victory at Gibeon (Joshua 10.1–11).
See also: 28.21: a 2 Sam 5.20; 1 Chron 14.11;
b Josh 10.10–12.

See also: 29.10: Rom 11.8.   29.13: Matt 15.8–9;
Mark 7.6–7.   29.14: 1 Cor 1.19.

Or if you think what you do
   in the dark can't be seen.
16 You have it all backwards.
   A clay dish doesn't say to the potter,
   "You didn't make me.
   You don't even know how."

Hope for the future

17 Soon the forest of Lebanon
   will become a field with crops,
      thick as a forest.ʼ
18 The deaf will be able to hear
   whatever is read to them;
   the blind will be freed
      from a life of darkness.
19 The poor and the needy
   will celebrate and shout
   because of the LORD,
      the holy God of Israel.

20 All who are cruel and arrogant
   will be gone for ever.
   Those who live by crime will disappear,
21 together with everyone
   who tells lies in court
   and keeps innocent people
      from getting a fair trial.

22 The LORD who rescued Abraham
   has this to say
      about Jacob's descendants:
   "They will no longer
      be ashamed and disgraced.
23 When they see how great
      I have made their nation,
   they will praise and honour me,
      the holy God of Israel.
24 Everyone who is confused
      will understand,
   and all who have complained
      will obey my teaching."

CHAPTER 30

Don't expect help from Egypt

1 This is the LORD's message for his rebellious
people:

   "You follow your own plans
      instead of mine;
   you make treaties
   without asking me,
      and you keep on sinning.
2 You trust Egypt for protection.
   So you refuse my advice
   and send messengers to Egypt
      to beg their king for help.

See also: 29.16: Isa 45.9; Rom 9.20.

3 You will be disappointed,
   completely disgraced
      for trusting Egypt.
4 The king's power reaches
   from the city of Zoan
      as far south as Hanes.*
5 But Egypt can't protect you,
   and to trust that nation
      is useless and foolish."

6 This is a message about the animals of the
Southern Desert:

   "You people carry treasures
      on donkeys and camels.
   You travel to a feeble nation
   through a troublesome desert
      filled with lions
      and flying fiery dragons.
7 Egypt can't help you!
   That's why I call that nation
      a helpless monster."ʼ

Israel refuses to listen

8 The LORD told me to write down his
message for his people, so that it would be
there for ever. 9 They have turned against the
LORD and can't be trusted. They have refused
his teaching 10 and have said to his
messengers and prophets:

   Don't tell us what God has shown you and
   don't preach the truth. Just say what we
   want to hear, even if it's false. 11 Stop telling
   us what God has said! We don't want to
   hear any more about the holy God of Israel.

12 Now this is the answer
      of the holy God of Israel:
   "You rejected my message,
      and you trust in violence and lies.
13 This sin is like a crack
      that makes a high wall
   quickly crumble
14 and shatter like a crushed bowl.
   There's not a piece left
   big enough to carry hot coals
      or to scoop up water."

Trust the LORD

15 The holy LORD God of Israel
      had told all of you,
   "I will keep you safe
   if you turn back to me
      and calm down.

---

*30.4 Zoan . . . Hanes: Or "Your messengers have
reached the city of Zoan and gone as far as Hanes."
Zoan was in north-east Egypt; Hanes was to the south.

I will make you strong
  if you quietly trust me."

Then you stubbornly
16 said, "No! We will safely escape
  on speedy horses."

But those who chase you
  will be even faster.
17 As few as five of them,
  or even one, will be enough
  to chase a thousand of you.
Finally, all that will be left
  will be a few survivors
as lonely as a flag pole
  on a barren hill.

The LORD will show mercy

18 The LORD God is waiting
  to show how kind he is
  and to have pity on you.
The LORD always does right;
  he blesses those who trust him.

19 People of Jerusalem, you don't need to cry
any more. The Lord is kind, and as soon as
he hears your cries for help, he will come.
20 The Lord has given you trouble and sorrow
as your food and drink. But now you will
again see the Lord, your teacher, and he will
guide you. 21 Whether you turn to the right
or to the left, you will hear a voice saying,
"This is the road! Now follow it." 22 Then
you will treat your idols of silver and gold
like rubbish; you will throw them away like
filthy rags.
23 The Lord will send rain to water the seeds
you have planted — your fields will produce
more crops than you need, and your cattle
will graze in open pastures. 24 Even the oxen
and donkeys that plough your fields will be
fed the finest grain.*
25 On that day people will be slaughtered
and towers destroyed, but streams of water
will flow from high hills and towering
mountains. 26 Then the Lord will bandage
his people's injuries and heal the wounds he
has caused. The moon will shine as bright as
the sun, and the sun will shine seven times
brighter than usual. It will be like the light of
seven days all at once.

Assyria will be punished

27 The LORD is coming from far away
  with his fiery anger

and thick clouds of smoke.'
His angry words flame up
  like a destructive fire;
28 he breathes out a flood
  that comes up to the neck.
He sifts the nations
  and destroys them.
Then he puts a bridle
  in every foreigner's mouth
  and leads them to doom.

29 The LORD's people will sing as they do
when they celebrate a religious festival* at
night. The LORD is Israel's mighty rock,* and
his people will be as happy as they are when
they follow the sound of flutes to the
mountain where he is worshipped.
30 The LORD will get furious. His fearsome
voice will be heard, his arm will be seen
ready to strike, and his anger will be like a
destructive fire, followed by thunderstorms
and hailstones. 31 When the Assyrians hear
the LORD's voice and see him striking with
his iron rod, they will be terrified. 32 He will
attack them in battle, and each time he
strikes them, it will be to the music of
tambourines and harps.
33 Long ago the LORD got a place ready for
burning the body of the dead king.* The
place for the fire is deep and wide, the wood
is piled high, and the LORD will start the fire
by breathing out flaming sulphur.

CHAPTER 31

Don't trust the power of Egypt

1 You are in for trouble
  if you go to Egypt for help,
or if you depend on
  an army of chariots
  or a powerful cavalry.
Instead you should depend on
  and trust the holy LORD God
  of Israel.
2 The LORD isn't stupid!
He does what he promises,
  and he can bring doom.
If you are cruel yourself,
  or help those who are evil,
  you will be destroyed.

---

*30.29 a religious festival: Probably Passover.
*30.29 mighty rock: See the note at 17.10.
*30.33 burning . . . king: Or "sacrificing the king" or
"sacrificing to Molech". Human sacrifices were
sometimes offered to Molech, a god whose name
sounds like the Hebrew word for "king" (see
2 Kings 23.10; Jeremiah 32.35).

---

*30.24 the finest grain: The Hebrew text refers to
grain with the husks removed.

3 The Egyptians are mere humans.
   They aren't God.
Their horses are made of flesh;
   they can't live for ever.
When the LORD shows his power,
he will destroy the Egyptians
   and all who depend on them.
Together they will fall.

4 The LORD All-Powerful
   said to me,
"I will roar and attack
   like a fearless lion
not frightened by the shouts
of shepherds trying to protect
   their sheep.
That's how I will come down
   and fight on Mount Zion.
5 I, the LORD All-Powerful,
   will protect Jerusalem
like a mother bird circling
   over her nest."

Come back to the LORD

6 People of Israel, come back!
You have completely turned
   from the LORD.
7 The time is coming
   when you will throw away
your idols of silver and gold,
   made by your sinful hands.

8 The Assyrians will be killed,
   but not by the swords
   of humans.
Their young men will try
   to escape,
but they will be captured
   and forced into slavery.
9 Their fortress' will fall
   when terror strikes;
their army officers
will be frightened
   and run from the battle.
This is what the LORD has said,
the LORD whose fiery furnace
   is built on Mount Zion.

The Lord will punish Edom and bless Jerusalem

CHAPTER 32

Justice will rule

1 A king and his leaders
   will rule with justice.

2 They will be a place of safety
   from stormy winds,
a stream in the desert,
and a rock that gives shade
   from the heat of the sun.
3 Then everyone who has eyes
   will open them and see,
and those who have ears
   will pay attention.
4 All who are impatient
   will take time to think;
everyone who stutters
   will talk clearly.

5 Fools will no longer
   be highly respected,
and crooks won't be given
   positions of honour.
6 Fools talk foolishness.
They always make plans
   to do sinful things,
to lie about the LORD,
to let the hungry starve,
and to keep water from those
   who are thirsty.
7 Cruel people tell lies —
   they do evil things,
   and make cruel plans
to destroy the poor and needy,
even when they beg
   for justice.
8 But helpful people
   can always be trusted
   to make helpful plans.

Punishment for the women of Jerusalem

9 Listen to what I say,
   you women who are carefree
   and careless!
10 You may not have worries now,
   but in about a year,
the grape harvest will fail,
   and you will tremble.

11 Shake and shudder,
   you women without a care!
Strip off your clothes —
   put on sackcloth.
12 Slap your breasts in sorrow
   because of what happened
to the fruitful fields
   and vineyards,
13 and to the happy homes
   in Jerusalem.
The land of my people
   is covered with thorns.

¹⁴ The palace will be deserted,
   the crowded city empty.
Fortresses and towers
   will for ever become
playgrounds for wild donkeys
   and pastures for sheep.

God's Spirit makes the difference

¹⁵ When the Spirit is given to us
      from heaven,
   deserts will become orchards
      thick as fertile forests.
¹⁶ Honesty and justice will prosper there,
¹⁷ and justice will produce
      lasting peace and security.

¹⁸ You, the LORD's people,
   will live in peace,
   calm and secure,
¹⁹ even if hailstones flatten
   forests and cities.
²⁰ You will have God's blessing,
   as you plant your crops
      beside streams,
   while your donkeys and cattle
      roam freely about.

CHAPTER 33

Jerusalem will be safe

¹ You defeated my people.
   Now you're in for trouble!
You've never been destroyed,
   but you will be destroyed;
you've never been betrayed,
   but you will be betrayed.
When you have finished
   destroying and betraying,
you will be destroyed
   and betrayed in return.

² Please, LORD, be kind to us!
   We depend on you.
Make us strong each morning,
   and come to save us
      when we are in trouble.
³ Nations scatter when you roar
   and show your greatness.'
⁴ We attack our enemies
   like swarms of locusts;*
we take everything
   that belongs to them.'

⁵ You, LORD, are above all others,
   and you live in the heavens.

You have brought justice
   and fairness to Jerusalem;
⁶ you are the foundation
   on which we stand today.
You always save us and give
   true wisdom and knowledge.
Nothing means more to us'
   than obeying you.

The LORD will do something

⁷ Listen! Our bravest soldiers
   are running through the streets,
      screaming for help.'
Our messengers hoped for peace,
   but came home crying.
⁸ No one travels any more;
   every road is empty.
Treaties are broken,
   and no respect is shown
      to any who keep promises.'
⁹ Fields are dry and barren;
   Mount Lebanon wilts with shame.
Sharon Valley is a desert;
   the forests of Bashan and Carmel
      have lost their leaves.

¹⁰ But the LORD says,
   "Now I will do something
      and be greatly praised.
¹¹ Your deeds are straw
   that will be set on fire
      by your very own breath.
¹² You will be burnt to ashes
   like thorns in a fire.
¹³ Everyone, both far and near,
   come, look at what I have done.
      See my mighty power!"

Punishment and rewards

¹⁴ Those terrible sinners
   on Mount Zion tremble
      as they ask in fear,
"How can we possibly live
   where a raging fire
      never stops burning?"

¹⁵ But there will be rewards
   for those who live right
      and tell the truth,
   for those who refuse
      to take money by force
      or accept bribes,
   for all who hate murder
      and violent crimes.
¹⁶ They will live in a fortress
   high on a rocky cliff,
      where they will have food
      and plenty of water.

---

*33.4 locusts: Insects like grasshoppers that travel in
swarms and cause great damage to crops.

The LORD is our King

17 With your own eyes
you will see the glorious King;
you will see his kingdom
reaching far and wide.
18 Then you will ask yourself,
"Where are those officials
who terrified us and forced us
to pay such heavy taxes?"
19 You will never again have to see
the proud people who spoke
a strange and foreign language
you could not understand.

20 Look to Mount Zion
where we celebrate
our religious festivals.
You will see Jerusalem,
secure as a tent with pegs
that cannot be pulled up
and fastened with ropes
that can never be broken.
21 Our wonderful LORD
will be with us!
There will be deep rivers
and wide streams
safe from enemy ships.*

The LORD is our judge

22 The LORD is our judge
and our ruler;
the LORD is our king
and will keep us safe.
23 But your nation* is a ship
with its rigging loose,
its mast shaky,
and its sail not spread.

Some day even you who are lame
will take everything you want
from your enemies.
24 The LORD will forgive your sins,
and none of you will say, "I feel ill."

CHAPTER 34

The nations will be judged

1 Everyone of every nation,
the entire earth,
and all its creatures,
come here and listen!
2 The LORD is terribly angry
with the nations;

he has condemned them
to be slaughtered.
3 Their dead bodies will be left
to rot and stink;
their blood will flow
down the mountains.
4 Each star* will disappear —
the sky will roll up
like a scroll.*
Everything in the sky
will dry up and wilt
like leaves on a vine
or fruit on a tree.

Trouble for Edom

5 After the sword of the LORD
has done what it wants
to the skies above,↑
it will come down on Edom,
the nation that the LORD
has doomed for destruction.

6 The sword of the LORD
is covered with blood
from lambs and goats,
together with fat
from kidneys of rams.
This is because the LORD
will slaughter many people
and make a sacrifice of them
in the city of Bozrah
and everywhere else
in Edom.
7 Edom's leaders are wild oxen.
They are powerful bulls,
but they will die
with the others.
Their country will be soaked
with their blood,
and its soil made fertile
with their fat.

8 The LORD has chosen
the year and the day,
when he will take revenge
and come to Zion's defence.
9 Edom's streams will turn into tar
and its soil into sulphur —
then the whole country
will go up in flames.

---

*33.21 safe . . . ships:** This probably means that
Jerusalem will have a lot of water, without the danger
of attacks from enemy ships.
*33.23 your nation:** Possibly Judah or Assyria.

*34.4 star:** Stars were worshipped as gods.
*34.4 scroll:** A roll of paper or specially prepared
leather used for writing on.
See also: 34.4: Matt 24.29; Mark 13.25; Luke 21.26;
Rev 6.13–14. **34.5–17:** Isa 63.1–6; Jer 49.7–22;
Ezek 25.12–14; 35.1–15; Amos 1.11–12; Obad 1–14;
Mal 1.2–5.

¹⁰ It will burn night and day
  and never stop smoking.
  Edom will be a desert,
  generation after generation;
  no one will ever travel
  through that land.
¹¹ Owls, hawks, and wild animals▸
  will make it their home.
  God will leave it in ruins,
  merely a pile of rocks.

The end of Edom

¹² Edom will be called
  "Kingdom of Nothing".
  Its rulers will also be nothing.
¹³ Its palaces and fortresses
  will be covered with thorns;
  only wolves and ostriches
  will make their home there.
¹⁴ Wildcats and hyenas
  will hunt together,
  demons will scream to demons,
  and creatures of the night
  will live among the ruins.
¹⁵ Owls will nest there
  to raise their young
  among its shadows,▸
  while families of vultures
  circle around.

¹⁶ In *The Book of the* LORD*
  you can search and find
  where it is written,
  "The LORD brought together
  all his creatures
  by the power of his Spirit.
  Not one is missing."
¹⁷ The LORD has decided
  where they each should live;
  they will be there for ever,
  generation after generation.

CHAPTER 35

God's splendour will be seen

¹ Thirsty deserts will be glad;
  barren lands will celebrate
  and blossom with flowers.
² Deserts will bloom everywhere
  and sing joyful songs.
  They will be as majestic
  as Mount Lebanon,
  as glorious as Mount Carmel
  or Sharon Valley.

---

*34.16 *The Book of the LORD*: The book that Isaiah
refers to is unknown.
See also: 34.10: Rev 14.11; 19.3.

Helpline

Help! I feel stuck

'I want to move forward in my Christian life
and in my relationship with God. But at the
moment I just feel stuck.'

Sometimes it just seems like we're caught.
We know that our Christian life should feel
full of energy and vitality and be filled with
discoveries about God, but it's just, well,
dull. We should be running the race, but
instead it feels more like trudging through a
desert (Isaiah 35.3–10)!

In times like these, what we have to
concentrate on are the basics. Remember
that God loves you and has a plan for you.
Keep praying to him and reading the Bible.
We have to keep going to church and
sharing with our Christian friends. Keep
looking and listening for God and he will
answer you.

It's not about being stuck; it's about your
'stickability'. Every Christian has times when
following Jesus seems hard. We don't hear
from God, we don't seem to be as 'fired up'
as once we were.

But that's why it's important to keep
going. Because those times will return. God
hasn't gone away.

Three things

Explain

Get together with Christian friends or your
youth group. Explain how you feel.

Persevere

Keep on going! Don't give up on church or
youth group.

Listen

Keep praying. You might be feeling that
God isn't listening, but he is. So we need to
keep the lines of communication open.

More...

What mountains are there in your life at the
moment? p.1003
Wherever you are, run towards God p.960

Everyone will see
the wonderful splendour
of the LORD our God.

God changes everything

3-4 Here is a message for all who are weak,
trembling, and worried:

> "Cheer up! Don't be afraid.
> Your God is coming
> to punish your enemies.
> God will take revenge on them
> and rescue you."

5 The blind will see,
and the ears of the deaf
will be healed.
6 Those who were lame
will leap around like deer;
tongues once silent
will begin to shout.
Water will rush
through the desert.
7 Scorching sand
will turn into a lake,
and thirsty ground
will flow with fountains.
Grass will grow in wetlands,
where packs of wild dogs
once made their home.'

God's sacred highway

8 A good road will be there,
and it will be named
"God's Sacred Highway".
It will be for God's people;
no one unfit to worship God
will walk on that road.
And no fools can travel
on that highway.'
9 No lions or other wild animals
will come near that road;
only those the LORD has saved
will travel there.

10 The people the LORD has rescued
will come back singing
as they enter Zion.
Happiness will be a crown
they will always wear.
They will celebrate and shout
because all sorrows and worries
will be gone far away.

Assyria, Babylonia, King Hezekiah, and Isaiah

CHAPTER 36

The Assyrians surround Jerusalem

This is also told in 2 Kings 18.13–27;
2 Chronicles 32.1–19

1 Hezekiah had been king of Judah for
fourteen years when King Sennacherib of
Assyria invaded the country and captured
every walled city 2 except Jerusalem. The
Assyrian king ordered his army commander
to leave the city of Lachish and to take a large
army to Jerusalem.

The commander went there and stood on
the road near the cloth makers' shops along
the canal from the upper pool. 3 Three of the
king's highest officials came out of Jerusalem
to meet him. One of them was Hilkiah's son
Eliakim, who was the prime minister. The
other two were Shebna, assistant to the prime
minister, and Joah son of Asaph, keeper of
the government records.

4 The Assyrian commander told them:

I have a message for Hezekiah from the
great king of Assyria. Ask Hezekiah why he
feels so sure of himself. 5 Does he think he
can plan and win a war with nothing but
words? Who is going to help him, now
that he has turned against the king of
Assyria? 6 Is he depending on Egypt and its
king? That's the same as leaning on a
broken stick, and it will go right through
his hand.

7 Is Hezekiah now depending on the
LORD, your God? Didn't Hezekiah tear
down all except one of the LORD's altars
and places of worship?* Didn't he tell the
people of Jerusalem and Judah to worship
at that one place?

8 The king of Assyria wants to make a bet
with you people! He will give you two
thousand horses, if you have enough
troops to ride them. 9 How could you
defeat even our lowest ranking officer,
when you have to depend on Egypt for
chariots and cavalry? 10 Don't forget that it

---

*36.7 worship: Hezekiah actually had torn down the
places where idols were worshipped, and he had told
the people to worship the LORD at the one place of
worship in Jerusalem. But the Assyrian leader was
confused and thought these were also places where
the LORD was supposed to be worshipped.

See also: 35.3: Heb 12.12. 35.5–6: Matt 11.5; Luke 7.22. See also: 36.6: Ezek 29.6–7.

was the LORD who sent me here with orders to destroy your nation!

[11] Eliakim, Shebna, and Joah said, "Sir, we don't want the people listening from the city wall to understand what you are saying. So please speak to us in Aramaic instead of Hebrew."

[12] The Assyrian army commander answered, "My king sent me to speak to everyone, not just to you leaders. These people will soon have to eat their own body waste and drink their own urine! And so will the three of you!"

[13] Then, in a voice loud enough for everyone to hear, he shouted out in Hebrew:

Listen to what the great king of Assyria says! [14] Don't be fooled by Hezekiah. He can't save you. [15] Don't trust him when he tells you that the LORD will protect you from the king of Assyria. [16] Stop listening to Hezekiah. Pay attention to my king. Surrender to him. He will let you keep your own vineyards, fig trees, and cisterns [17] for a while. Then he will come and take you away to a country just like yours, where you can plant vineyards and raise your own grain.

[18] Hezekiah claims the LORD will save you. But don't be fooled by him. Were any other gods able to defend their land against the king of Assyria? [19] What happened to the gods of Hamath, Arpad, and Sepharvaim? Were the gods of Samaria able to protect their land against the Assyrian forces? [20] None of these gods kept their people safe from the king of Assyria. Do you think the LORD, your God, can do any better?

[21-22] Eliakim, Shebna, and Joah had been warned by King Hezekiah not to answer the Assyrian commander. So they tore their clothes in sorrow and reported to Hezekiah everything the commander had said.

CHAPTER 37

Hezekiah asks Isaiah for advice

This is also told in 2 Kings 19.1–13

[1] As soon as Hezekiah heard the news, he tore off his clothes in sorrow and put on sackcloth. Then he went into the temple of the LORD. [2] He told Prime Minister Eliakim, Assistant Prime Minister Shebna, and the senior priests to dress in sackcloth and tell me:

[3] Isaiah, these are difficult and disgraceful times. Our nation is like a woman too weak to give birth, when it's time for her baby to be born. [4] Please pray for those of us who are left alive. The king of Assyria sent his army commander to insult the living God. Perhaps the LORD heard what he said and will do something, if you will pray.

[5] When these leaders came to me, [6] I told them that the LORD had this message for Hezekiah:

I am the LORD. Don't worry about the insulting things that have been said about me by these messengers from the king of Assyria. [7] I will upset him with rumours about what's happening in his own country. He will go back, and there I will make him die a violent death.

[8] Meanwhile the commander of the Assyrian forces heard that his king had left the town of Lachish and was now attacking Libnah. So he went there.

[9] About this same time, the king of Assyria learnt that King Tirhakah of Ethiopia* was on his way to attack him. Then the king of Assyria sent some messengers with this note for Hezekiah:

[10] Don't trust your God or be fooled by his promise to defend Jerusalem against me. [11] You have heard how we Assyrian kings have completely wiped out other nations. What makes you feel so safe? [12] The Assyrian kings before me destroyed the towns of Gozan, Haran, Rezeph, and everyone from Eden who lived in Telassar. What good did their gods do them? [13] The kings of Hamath, Arpad, Sepharvaim, Hena, and Ivvah have all disappeared.

Hezekiah prays

This is also told in 2 Kings 19.14–19

[14] After Hezekiah had read the note from the king of Assyria, he took it to the temple and spread it out for the LORD to see. [15] Then he prayed:

[16] LORD God All-Powerful of Israel, your throne is above the winged creatures.* You

---

*37.9 Ethiopia: See the note at 11.11.

*37.16 winged creatures: Two winged creatures made of gold were on the top of the sacred chest and were symbols of the LORD's throne on earth (see Exodus 25.18; 2 Samuel 6.2).

See also: 37.16: Exod 25.22.

created the heavens and the earth, and you alone rule the kingdoms of this world. [17] Just look and see how Sennacherib has insulted you, the living God.

[18] It is true, our LORD, that Assyrian kings have turned nations into deserts. [19] They destroyed the idols of wood and stone that the people of those nations had made and worshipped. [20] But you are our LORD and our God! We ask you to keep us safe from the Assyrian king. Then everyone in every kingdom on earth will know that you are the only LORD.

Isaiah gives the LORD's answer to Hezekiah

This is also told in 2 Kings 19.20–34

[21-22] I went to Hezekiah and told him that the LORD God of Israel had said:

Hezekiah, you prayed to me about King Sennacherib of Assyria.' Now this is what I say to that king:

The people of Jerusalem
hate and make fun of you;
    they laugh behind your back.

[23] Sennacherib, you cursed,
    shouted, and sneered at me,
        the holy God of Israel.
[24] You let your officials
    insult me, the Lord.
And here is what you
    have said about yourself,
"I led my chariots
to the highest heights
    of Lebanon's mountains.
I went deep into its forest,
cutting down the best cedar
    and cypress trees.
[25] I dried up every stream
    in the land of Egypt,
and I drank water
    from wells I had dug."

[26] Sennacherib, now listen
    to me, the LORD.
I planned all this long ago.
And you don't even know
    that I alone am the one
who decided that you
    would do these things.
I let you make ruins
    of fortified cities.
[27] Their people became weak,
    terribly confused.

They were like wild flowers
or like tender young grass
    growing on a flat roof
or like a field of grain
    before it matures.*

[28] I know all about you,
    even how fiercely angry
        you are with me.
[29] I have seen your pride
    and the tremendous hatred
        you have for me.
Now I will put a hook in your nose,
    a bit in your mouth,*
then I will send you back
    to where you came from.

[30] Hezekiah, I will tell you what's going to happen. This year you will eat crops that grow on their own, and the next year you will eat whatever springs up where those crops grew. But the third year, you will plant grain and vineyards, and you will eat what you harvest. [31] Those who survive in Judah will be like a vine that puts down deep roots and bears fruit. [32] I, the LORD All-Powerful, will see to it that some who live in Jerusalem will survive.

[33] I promise that the king of Assyria won't get into Jerusalem, or shoot an arrow into the city, or even surround it and prepare to attack. [34] As surely as I am the LORD, he will return by the way he came and will never enter Jerusalem. [35] I will protect it for the sake of my own honour and because of the promise I made to my servant David.

The death of King Sennacherib

This is also told in 2 Kings 19.35–37

[36] The LORD sent an angel to the camp of the Assyrians, and he killed one hundred and eighty-five thousand of them all in one night. The next morning, the camp was full of dead bodies. [37] After this, King Sennacherib went back to Assyria and lived in the city of Nineveh. [38] One day he was

---

*37.27 tender young grass . . . matures: The Standard Hebrew Text; the Dead Sea Scrolls and some Hebrew manuscripts "tender young grass, growing on a flat roof and scorched by the heat". Many of the houses had roofs made of packed earth. Grass would sometimes grow on the roof, but would die quickly because of the sun and hot winds.
*37.29 I will put . . . your mouth: This is how the Assyrians treated their prisoners, and now the LORD will treat Sennacherib the same way.

worshipping in the temple of his god
Nisroch, when his sons, Adrammelech and
Sharezer, killed him with their swords. They
escaped to the land of Ararat, and his son
Esarhaddon became king.*

CHAPTER 38

Hezekiah gets sick and almost dies

This is also told in 2 Kings 20.1–11;
2 Chronicles 32.24–26

¹ About this time, Hezekiah got sick and was
almost dead. So I went in and told him, "The
LORD says you won't ever get well. You are
going to die, and so you had better start
doing what needs to be done."

² Hezekiah turned towards the wall and
prayed, ³ "Don't forget that I have been
faithful to you, LORD. I have obeyed you with
all my heart, and I do whatever you say is
right." After this, he cried hard.

⁴ Then the LORD sent me ⁵ with this
message for Hezekiah:

I am the LORD God, who was worshipped
by your ancestor David. I heard you pray,
and I saw you cry. I will let you live fifteen
years more, ⁶ while I protect you and your
city from the king of Assyria. ⁷ Now I will
prove to you that I will keep my promise.
⁸ Do you see the shadow made by the
setting sun on the stairway built for King
Ahaz? I will make the shadow go back
ten steps.

Then the shadow went back ten steps.'

King Hezekiah's song of praise

⁹ This is what Hezekiah wrote after he got
well:

¹⁰ I thought I would die
    during my best years
and stay as a prisoner for ever
    in the world of the dead.
¹¹ I thought I would never again
    see you, my LORD,
or any of the people
    who live on this earth.
¹² My life was taken from me
    like the tent that a shepherd
    pulls up and moves.
You cut me off like thread
    from a weaver's loom;

you make a wreck of me
    day and night.
¹³ Until morning came, I thought
you would crush my bones
    just like a hungry lion;
both night and day
    you make a wreck of me.'
¹⁴ I cry like a swallow;
    I mourn like a dove.
My eyes are red
    from looking to you, LORD.
I am terribly abused.
    Please come and help me.'
¹⁵ There's nothing I can say
    in answer to you,
since you are the one
    who has done this to me.'
My life has turned sour;
    I will limp until I die.

¹⁶ Your words and your deeds
    bring life to everyone,
        including me.'
Please make me healthy
    and strong again.
¹⁷ It was for my own good
    that I had such hard times.
But your love protected me
    from doom in the deep pit,*
and you turned your eyes
    away from my sins.

¹⁸ No one in the world of the dead
    can thank you or praise you;
none of those in the deep pit
    can hope for you to show them
        how faithful you are.
¹⁹ Only the living can thank you,
    as I am doing today.
Each generation tells the next
    about your faithfulness.'

²⁰ You, LORD, will save me,
    and every day that we live
we will sing in your temple
    to the music
        of stringed instruments.

Isaiah's advice to Hezekiah

²¹ I had told King Hezekiah's servants to put
some mashed figs on the king's open sore,
and he would get well. ²² Then Hezekiah
asked for proof that he would again worship
in the LORD's temple.

---

*37.38 Esarhaddon became king: He ruled Assyria
681–669 BC.

*38.17 deep pit: The world of the dead, as in
verse 18.

CHAPTER 39

Isaiah speaks the LORD's message to Hezekiah

This is also told in 2 Kings 20.12–19

1 Merodach Baladan, the son of Baladan, was now king of Babylonia. And when he learnt that Hezekiah was well, he sent messengers with letters and a gift for him. 2 Hezekiah welcomed the messengers and showed them all the silver, the gold, the spices, and the fine oils that were in his storehouse. He even showed them where he kept his weapons. Nothing in his palace or in his entire kingdom was kept hidden from them.

3 I asked Hezekiah, "Where did these men come from? What did they want?"

"They came all the way from Babylonia," Hezekiah answered.

4 "What did you show them?" I asked.

Hezekiah answered, "I showed them everything in my kingdom."

5 Then I told Hezekiah:

I have a message for you from the LORD All-Powerful. 6 One day everything you and your ancestors have stored up will be taken to Babylonia. The LORD has promised that nothing will be left. 7 Some of your own sons will be taken to Babylonia, where they will be disgraced and made to serve in the king's palace.

8 Hezekiah thought, "At least our nation will be at peace for a while." So he told me, "The message you brought from the LORD is good."

The Lord will rescue his people

CHAPTER 40

Encourage God's people

1 Our God has said:

"Encourage my people!
    Give them comfort.
2 Speak kindly to Jerusalem
    and announce:
Your slavery is past;
    your punishment is over.
I, the LORD, made you pay
    double for your sins."

3 Someone is shouting:
"Clear a path in the desert!
    Make a straight road
    for the LORD our God.
4 Fill in the valleys;
    flatten every hill
        and mountain.
Level the rough
    and rugged ground.
5 Then the glory of the LORD
    will appear for all to see.
The LORD has promised this!"

6 Someone told me to shout,
    and I asked,
    "What should I shout?"
We humans are merely grass,
    and we last no longer
        than wild flowers.
7 At the LORD's command,
    flowers and grass disappear,
        and so do we.
8 Flowers and grass fade away,
    but what our God has said
        will never change.

Your God is here!

9 There is good news
    for the city of Zion.
Shout it as loud as you can'
    from the highest mountain.
Don't be afraid to shout
    to the towns of Judah,
    "Your God is here!"
10 Look! The powerful LORD God
    is coming to rule
        with his mighty arm.
He brings with him
    what he has taken in war,
        and he rewards his people.
11 The LORD cares for his nation,
    just as shepherds care
        for their flocks.
He carries the lambs
    in his arms,
while gently leading
    the mother sheep.

Who compares with God?

12 Did any of you measure
    the ocean by yourself
    or stretch out the sky
    with your own hands?

See also: 39.7: Dan 1.1–7; 2 King 24.10–16; 2 Chron 36.10.

See also: 40.3: Matt 3.3; Mark 1.3; John 1.23.
40.3–5: Luke 3.4–6.   40.6–8: Jam 1.10–11; 1 Pet 1.24–25.
40.10: Isa 61.11; Rev 22.12.   40.11: Ezek 34.15; John 10.11.

Did you put the soil
   of the earth in a bucket
or weigh the hills and mountains
   on balance scales?

13 Has anyone told the LORD'
   what he must do
   or given him advice?
14 Did the LORD ask anyone
   to teach him wisdom
   and justice?
Who gave him knowledge
   and understanding?
15 To the LORD, all nations
are merely a drop in a bucket
   or dust on balance scales;
all the islands
   are but a handful of sand.
16 The cattle on Lebanon's mountains
   would not be enough to offer
   as a sacrifice to God,
and the trees would not
   be enough for the fire.
17 God thinks of the nations
   as far less than nothing.

18 Who compares with God?
   Is anything like him?
19 Is an idol at all like God?
It is made of bronze
   with a thin layer of gold,
   and decorated with silver.
20 Or special wood may be chosen*
   because it doesn't rot —
then skilled hands
   take care to make an idol
   that won't fall on its face.

God rules the whole earth

21 Don't you know?
   Haven't you heard?
Isn't it clear that God
   created the world?'
22 God is the one who rules
   the whole earth,
and we who live here
   are merely insects.
He spread out the heavens
   like a curtain or an open tent.
23 God brings down rulers
   and turns them into nothing.

24 They are like flowers
   freshly sprung up
   and starting to grow.
But when God blows on them,
   they wilt and are carried off
   like straw in a storm.

25 The holy God asks,
   "Who compares with me?
   Is anyone my equal?"

26 Look at the evening sky!
   Who created the stars?
   Who gave them each a name?
   Who leads them like an army?
The LORD is so powerful
   that none of the stars
   are ever missing.

The LORD gives strength

27 You people of Israel, say,
   "God pays no attention to us!
   He doesn't care if we
   are treated unjustly."

But how can you say that?
28 Don't you know?
   Haven't you heard?
The LORD is the eternal God,
   Creator of the earth.
He never gets weary or tired;
   his wisdom cannot be measured.

29 The LORD gives strength
   to those who are weary.
30 Even young people get tired,
   then stumble and fall.
31 But those who trust the LORD
   will find new strength.
They will be strong like eagles
   soaring upward on wings;
they will walk and run
   without getting tired.

CHAPTER 41

The LORD controls human events

1 Be silent and listen,
   every island in the sea.
Have courage and come near,
   every one of you nations.
Let's settle this matter!
2 Who appointed this ruler
   from the east?*

---

*40.20 Or . . . chosen: One possible meaning for the
difficult Hebrew text. Two kinds of idols seem to be
described: bronze idols covered with gold (verse 19)
and wooden idols (verse 20).

See also: 40.13: Rom 11.34; 1 Cor 2.16.
40.18-19: Acts 17.29.

*41.2 ruler from the east: Probably Cyrus (see 44.28;
45.1; 48.14).

Who puts nations and kings
   in his power?'
His sword and his arrows
   turn them to dust
     blown by the wind.
3 He goes after them so quickly
   that his feet barely touch the ground —
   he doesn't even get hurt.

4 Who makes these things happen?
   Who controls human events?
     I do! I am the LORD.
   I was there at the beginning;
   I will be there at the end.
5 Islands and foreign nations
   saw what I did and trembled
     as they came near.

What can idols do?

6 Worshippers of idols comfort each other,
   saying, "Don't worry!"
7 Woodcarvers, goldsmiths,
   and other workers'
encourage one another and say,
   "We've done a great job!"
Then they nail the idol down,
   so it won't fall over.

The LORD's chosen servant

8 Israel, you are my servant.
   I chose you, the family
     of my friend Abraham.
9 From far across the earth
   I brought you here and said,
   "You are my chosen servant.
   I haven't forgotten you."

10 Don't be afraid. I am with you.
   Don't tremble with fear.
     I am your God.
   I will make you strong,
   as I protect you with my arm
     and give you victories.
11 Everyone who hates you
   will be terribly disgraced;
   those who attack
     will vanish into thin air.
12 You will look around
   for those brutal enemies,
   but you won't find them
     because they will be gone.

13 I am the LORD your God.
   I am holding your hand,
   so don't be afraid.
   I am here to help you.

14 People of Israel, don't worry,
   though others may say,
   "Israel is only a worm!"
   I am the holy God of Israel,
   who saves and protects you.
15 I will let you be like a log
   covered with sharp spikes.*
You will grind and crush
   every mountain and hill*
     until they turn to dust.
16 A strong wind will scatter them
   in all directions.
Then you will celebrate
and praise me, your LORD,
   the holy God of Israel.

The LORD helps the poor

17 When the poor and needy
   are dying of thirst
     and cannot find water,
I, the LORD God of Israel,
will come to their rescue.
   I won't forget them.
18 I will make rivers flow
   on mountain peaks.
I will send streams
   to fill the valleys.
Dry and barren land
will flow with springs
   and become a lake.
19 I will fill the desert
   with all kinds of trees —
cedars, acacias, and myrtles;
olive and cypress trees;
   fir trees and pines.
20 Everyone will see this
   and know that I,
the holy LORD God of Israel,
   created it all.

Idols are useless

21 I am the LORD,
   the King of Israel!
Come, argue your case with me.
   Present your evidence.
22 Come near me, you idols.'
   Tell us about the past,
   and we will think about it.

---

*41.15 I will let . . . sharp spikes: In ancient times a heavy object was sometimes dragged over wheat or barley to separate the grain from the husk. This was called threshing.

*41.15 mountain and hill: These stand for the power and pride of Israel's enemies.

See also: 41.8: 2 Chron 20.7; Jam 2.23.

Tell us about the future,
so we will know
what is going to happen.
²³ Prove that you are gods
by making your predictions come true.
Do something good or evil,
so we can be amazed
and terrified.'
²⁴ You idols are nothing,
and you are powerless.'
To worship you
would be disgusting.

²⁵ I, the LORD, appointed a ruler
in the north;
now he comes from the east
to honour my name.
He tramples' kings like mud,
as potters trample clay.*
²⁶ Did any of you idols predict
what would happen?
Did any of you get it right?
None of you told about this
or even spoke a word.
²⁷ I was the first to tell
the people of Jerusalem,
"Look, it's happening!"'
I was the one who announced
this good news to Zion.

²⁸ None of these idols
are able to give advice
or answer questions.
²⁹ They are nothing,'
and they can do nothing —
they are less than a passing breeze.

CHAPTER 42

The LORD's servant

¹ Here is my servant!
I have made him strong.
He is my chosen one;
I am pleased with him.
I have given him my Spirit,
and he will bring justice
to the nations.
² He won't shout or yell
or call out in the streets.
³ He won't break off a bent reed
or put out a dying flame,
but he will make sure
that justice is done.

---

*41.25 trample clay:** This was done to soften the clay
and make it easier to shape.

See also: 42.1: Matt 3.17; 17.5; Mark 1.11; Luke 3.22; 9.35.
42.1–4: Matt 12.18–21.

Big ideas

Messiah

Messiah is a Hebrew word which means
'anointed'. For centuries, Israel waited for
someone to rescue them from their enemies.
Old Testament prophets predicted a
Messiah, a saviour from God to drive out the
oppressors.

They were looking for a warrior, a mighty
military hero in the mould of King David,
and when the Romans took over, their
desperation increased. Before Jesus there
were others who claimed the title. All of
them failed and were brutally punished.

Then came Jesus. His followers believed he
was the Messiah, but he didn't look much
like one. He wasn't a military leader; he
wasn't leading an armed uprising. And Jesus
himself didn't like to be called Messiah. Not
because he wasn't the Messiah, but to
distance himself from the stereotypes. He
was preaching a revolutionary message and
he was setting up a new kingdom, but not
in the way that the Jews were expecting.

After his death and resurrection, the secret
was out. Christians saw how the many Old
Testament prophecies of the Messiah had
been fulfilled in Jesus. Jesus really was the
anointed one, the Messiah. He defeated, not
the Romans, but death.

 Anorak corner

The Greek word for 'anointed' is christos,
from which we get Christ.

 Footsteps

A week with the Messiah

The Messiah will suffer: Isaiah 53.1–12
The Messiah from Bethlehem: Micah 5.2–5
Entering Jerusalem: Zechariah 9.9–10
Jesus identifies himself: Luke 4.16–30
Peter's recognition: Matthew 16.13–20
Jesus explains: Luke 24.13–35
Andrew finds the Messiah: John 1.35–41

More...

Prophecy p.730
David p.314
Isaiah p.732

⁴ He won't stop or give up
  until he brings justice
    everywhere on earth,
  and people in foreign nations
    long for his teaching.

⁵ I am the LORD God.
  I created the heavens
    like an open tent above.
  I made the earth and everything
    that grows on it.
  I am the source of life
  for all who live on this earth,
    so listen to what I say.
⁶ I chose you to bring justice,
    and I am here at your side.
  I selected and sent you'
    to bring light
  and my promise of hope
    to the nations.
⁷ You will give sight
    to the blind;
  you will set prisoners free
    from dark dungeons.

⁸ My name is the LORD!
  I won't let idols or humans
    share my glory and praise.
⁹ Everything has happened
    just as I said it would;
  now I will announce
    what will happen next.

Sing praises to the LORD

¹⁰ Tell the whole world to sing
    a new song to the LORD!
  Tell those who sail the ocean
  and those who live far away
    to join in the praise.
¹¹ Tell the tribes of the desert
  and everyone in the mountains'
    to celebrate and sing.
¹² Let them announce
    his praises everywhere.
¹³ The LORD is marching out
    like an angry soldier,
  shouting with all his might
    while attacking his enemies.

The LORD will help his people

¹⁴ For a long time, I, the LORD,
    have held my temper;
  now I will scream and groan
    like a woman giving birth.

¹⁵ I will destroy the mountains
    and what grows on them;
  I will dry up rivers and ponds.

¹⁶ I will lead the blind on roads
    they have never known;
  I will guide them on paths
    they have never travelled.
  Their road is dark and rough,
    but I will give light
  to keep them from stumbling.
    This is my solemn promise.

¹⁷ Everyone who worships idols
    as though they were gods
    will be terribly ashamed.

God's people won't obey

¹⁸ You people are deaf and blind,
    but the LORD commands you
    to listen and to see.
¹⁹ No one is as blind or deaf
    as his messenger,
    his chosen servant,
²⁰ who sees and hears so much,
    but pays no attention.

²¹ The LORD always does right,
    and so he wanted his Law
    to be greatly praised.'
²² But his people were trapped
  and imprisoned in holes
    with no one to rescue them.
  All they owned had been taken,
  and no one was willing
    to give it back.
²³ Why won't his people
    ever learn to listen?

²⁴ Israel sinned and refused
    to obey the LORD
    or follow his instructions.
  So the LORD let them be robbed
    of everything they owned.
²⁵ He was furious with them
  and punished their nation
    with the fires of war.
  Still they paid no attention.
    They didn't even care
  when they were surrounded
    and scorched by flames.

CHAPTER 43

The LORD has rescued his people

¹ Descendants of Jacob,
  I, the LORD, created you
    and formed your nation.

See also: 42.5: Acts 17.24–25.   **42.6:** Isa 49.6; Luke 2.32; Acts 13.47; 26.23.

Israel, don't be afraid.
   I have rescued you.
I have called you by name;
   now you belong to me.
2 When you cross deep rivers,
   I will be with you,
      and you won't drown.
When you walk through fire,
you won't be burnt
   or scorched by the flames.

3 I am the LORD, your God,
   the Holy One of Israel,
      the God who saves you.
I gave up Egypt, Ethiopia,*
   and the region of Seba*
      in exchange for you.
4 To me, you are very dear,
   and I love you.
That's why I gave up nations
   and people to rescue you.

5 Don't be afraid! I am with you.
From both east and west
   I will bring you together.
6 I will say to the north
   and to the south,
"Free my sons and daughters!
Let them return
   from distant lands.
7 They are my people —
   I created each of them
      to bring honour to me."

The LORD alone is God

The LORD said:

8 Bring my people together.
They have eyes and ears,
   but they can't see or hear.
9 Tell everyone of every nation
   to gather around.
None of them can honestly say,
   "We told you so!"
If someone heard them say this,
   then tell us about it now.

10 My people, you are my witnesses
   and my chosen servant.
I want you to know me,
to trust me, and understand
   that I alone am God.
I have always been God;
   there can be no others.

11 I alone am the LORD;
   only I can rescue you.
12 I promised to save you,
   and I kept my promise.
You are my witnesses
   that no other god did this.
   I, the LORD, have spoken.
13 I am God now and for ever.
No one can snatch you from me
   or stand in my way.

The LORD will prepare the way

14 I, the LORD, will rescue you!
I am Israel's holy God,
   and this is my promise:
For your sake, I will send
   an army against Babylon
to drag its people away,
   crying as they go.'

15 I am the LORD, your holy God,
   Israel's Creator and King.
16 I am the one who cut a path
   through the mighty ocean.
17 I sent an army to chase you
   with chariots and horses;
now they lie dead,
   unable to move.
They are like an oil lamp
   with the flame snuffed out.

Forget the past

The LORD said:

18 Forget what happened long ago!
   Don't think about the past.
19 I am creating something new.
   There it is! Do you see it?
I have put roads in deserts,
   streams' in thirsty lands.
20 Every wild animal honours me,
   even jackals* and owls.
I provide water in deserts —
streams in thirsty lands
   for my chosen people.
21 I made them my own nation,
   so they would praise me.

22 I, the LORD, said to Israel:
You have become weary,
   but not from worshipping me.
23 You have not honoured me
   by sacrificing sheep
      or other animals.

---

*43.3 **Ethiopia:** See the note at 11.11.
*43.3 **Seba:** A region in south-west Arabia. Egypt, Ethiopia, and Seba probably stood for all that was known of Africa in biblical times.

*43.20 **jackals:** Desert animals related to wolves, but smaller.

And I have not burdened you
with demands for sacrifices
or sweet-smelling incense.
24 You have not brought
delicious spices for me
or given me the best part
of your sacrificed animals.
Instead, you burden me down
with your terrible sins.
25 But I wipe away your sins
because of who I am.
And so, I will forget
the wrongs you have done.

26 Meet me in court!
State your case and prove
that you are right.
27 Your earliest ancestor*
and all your leaders*
rebelled against me.
28 That's why I don't allow
your priests to serve me;
I let Israel be destroyed
and your people disgraced.

CHAPTER 44

The LORD's promise to Israel

1 People of Israel,
I have chosen you as my servant.
2 I am your Creator.
You were in my care
even before you were born.
Israel, don't be terrified!
You are my chosen servant,
my very favourite.'

3 I will bless the thirsty land
by sending streams of water;
I will bless your descendants
by giving them my Spirit.
4 They will spring up like grass'
or like willow trees
near flowing streams.
5 They will worship me
and become my people.
They will write my name
on the back of their hands.*

6 I am the LORD All-Powerful,
the first and the last,
the one and only God.

Israel, I have rescued you!
I am your King.
7 Can anyone compare with me?
If so, let them speak up
and tell me now.
Let them say what has happened
since I made my nation long ago,
and let them tell
what is going to happen.'
8 Don't tremble with fear!
Didn't I tell you long ago?
Didn't you hear me?
I alone am God —
no one else is a mighty rock.*

Idols can't do a thing

The LORD said:

9 Those people who make idols
are nothing themselves,
and the idols they treasure
are just as worthless.
Worshippers of idols are blind,
stupid, and foolish.
10 Why make an idol or an image
that can't do a thing?
11 Everyone who makes idols
and all who worship them
are mere humans,
who will end up
sadly disappointed.
Let them face me in court
and be terrified.

Idols and firewood

12 A metalworker shapes an idol
by using a hammer'
and heat from the fire.
In his powerful hand
he holds a hammer,
as he pounds the metal
into the proper shape.
But he gets hungry and thirsty
and loses his strength.

13 Some woodcarver measures
a piece of wood,
then draws an outline.
The idol is carefully carved
with each detail exact.
At last it looks like a person
and is placed in a temple.
14 Cedar, cypress, oak,
or any tree from the forest
may be chosen.

---

*43.27 earliest ancestor: Jacob, also known as Israel.
*43.27 leaders: Probably prophets, but perhaps also priests and kings.
*44.5 write . . . hands: To show that they belong to the LORD and to Israel.
See also: 44.6: Isa 48.12; Rev 1.17; 2.8; 22.13.

*44.8 mighty rock: See the note at 17.10.

Or even a pine tree planted
by the woodcarver
and watered by the rain.

¹⁵ Some of the wood is used
to make a fire for heating
or for cooking.
One piece is made into an idol,
then the woodcarver bows down
and worships it.
¹⁶ He enjoys the warm fire
and the meat that was roasted
over the burning coals.
¹⁷ Afterwards, he bows down
to worship the wooden idol.
"Protect me!" he says.
"You are my god."

¹⁸ Those who worship idols are stupid and
blind! ¹⁹ They don't have enough sense to
say to themselves, "I made a fire with half of
the wood and cooked my bread and meat
on it. Then I made something worthless
with the other half. Why worship a block of
wood?"

²⁰ How can anyone be stupid enough to
trust something that can be burnt to ashes?
No one can save themselves like that. Don't
they realize that the idols they hold in their
hands are not really gods?

The LORD won't forget his people

²¹ People of Israel,
you are my servant,
so remember all of this.
Israel, I created you,
and you are my servant.
I won't forget you.
²² Turn back to me!
I have rescued you
and swept away your sins
as though they were clouds.

Sing praises to the LORD

²³ Tell the heavens and the earth
to start singing!
Tell the mountains
and every tree in the forest
to join in the song!

The LORD has rescued his people;
now they will worship him.

The LORD created everything

²⁴ Israel, I am your LORD.
I am your source of life,
and I have rescued you.

I created everything
from the sky above
to the earth below.

²⁵ I make liars of false prophets
and fools of fortune-tellers.
I take human wisdom
and turn it into nonsense.
²⁶ I will make the message
of my prophets come true.
They are saying, "Jerusalem
will be filled with people,
and the LORD will rebuild
the towns of Judah."

²⁷ I am the one who commands
the sea and its streams to run dry.
²⁸ I am also the one who says,
"Cyrus will lead my people
and obey my orders.
Jerusalem and the temple
will be rebuilt."

CHAPTER 45

Cyrus obeys the LORD's commands

¹ The LORD said to Cyrus, his chosen one:

I have taken hold
of your right hand
to help you capture nations
and remove kings from power.
City gates will open for you;
not one will stay closed.
² As I lead you,
I will level mountains
and break the iron bars
on bronze gates of cities.

³ I will give you treasures
hidden in dark
and secret places.
Then you will know that I,
the LORD God of Israel,
have called you by name.
⁴ Cyrus, you don't even know me!
But I have called you by name
and highly honoured you
because of Israel,
my chosen servant.

⁵ Only I am the LORD!
There are no other gods.
I have made you strong,
though you don't know me.
⁶ Now everyone from east to west
will learn that I am the LORD.

See also: 44.25: 1 Cor 1.20. **44.28:** 2 Chron 36.23; Ezra 1.2.

No other gods are real.
⁷ I create light and darkness,
happiness and sorrow.
I, the LORD, do all of this.

⁸ Tell the heavens
to send down justice
like showers of rain.
Prepare the earth
for my saving power
to sprout and produce justice
that I, the LORD, create.'

The LORD's mighty power

The LORD said:

⁹ Israel, you have no right
to argue with your Creator.
You are merely a clay pot
shaped by a potter.
The clay doesn't ask,
"Why did you make me this way?
Where are the handles?"
¹⁰ Children don't have the right
to demand of their parents,
"What have you done
to make us what we are?"

¹¹ I am the LORD, the Creator,
the holy God of Israel.
Do you dare question me
about my own nation
or about what I have done?
¹² I created the world
and covered it with people;
I stretched out the sky
and filled it with stars.
¹³ I have done the right thing
by placing Cyrus in power,
and I will make the roads easy
for him to follow.
I am the LORD All-Powerful!
Cyrus will rebuild my city
and set my people free
without being paid a thing.
I, the LORD, have spoken.

The LORD alone can save

¹⁴ My people, I, the LORD, promise
that the riches of Egypt
and the treasures of Ethiopia*
will belong to you.
You will force into slavery
those tall people of Seba.*

They will bow down and say,
"The only true God is with you;
there are no other gods."
¹⁵ People of Israel,
your God is a mystery,
though he alone can save.
¹⁶ Anyone who makes idols
will be confused
and terribly disgraced.
¹⁷ But Israel, I, the LORD,
will always keep you safe
and free from shame.

Everyone is invited

¹⁸ The LORD alone is God!
He created the heavens
and made a world
where people can live,
instead of creating an empty desert.
The LORD alone is God;
there are no others.
¹⁹ The LORD did not speak
in a dark secret place
or command Jacob's descendants
to search for him in vain.

The LORD speaks the truth,
and this is what he says
²⁰ to every survivor
from every nation:
"Gather around me!
Learn how senseless it is
to worship wooden idols
or pray to helpless gods.

²¹ "Why don't you get together
and meet me in court?
Didn't I tell you long ago
what would happen?
I am the only God!
There are no others.
I bring about justice,
and have the power to save.

²² "I invite the whole world
to turn to me and be saved.
I alone am God!
No others are real.
²³ I have made a solemn promise,
one that won't be broken:
everyone will bow down
and worship me.
²⁴ They will admit that I alone
can bring about justice.
Everyone who is angry with me
will be terribly ashamed
and will turn to me.

---

*45.14 **Ethiopia:** See the note at 11.11.
*45.14 **Seba:** See the note at 43.3.
See also: 45.9: Isa 29.16; Rom 9.20.

See also: 45.23: Rom 14.11; Phil 2.10–11.

²⁵ I, the LORD, will give
  victory and great honour
  to the people of Israel."

CHAPTER 46

Babylonia's gods are helpless

The LORD said:

¹ The gods Bel and Nebo*
  are down on their knees,
  as wooden images of them
  are carried away
  on weary animals.'
² They are down on their knees
  to rescue the heavy load,
  but the images are still taken
  to a foreign country.

³ You survivors in Israel,
  listen to me, the LORD.
  Since the day you were born,
  I have carried you along.
⁴ I will still be the same
  when you are old and grey,
  and I will take care of you.
  I created you. I will carry you
  and always keep you safe.

⁵ Can anyone compare with me?
  Is anyone my equal?
⁶ Some people hire a goldsmith
  and give silver and gold
  to be formed into an idol
  for them to worship.
⁷ They carry the idol
  on their shoulders,
  then put it on a stand,
  but it cannot move.

  They call out to the idol
  when they are in trouble,
  but it doesn't answer,
  and it cannot help.
⁸ Now keep this in mind,'
  you sinful people.
  And don't ever forget it.

The LORD alone is God

⁹ I alone am God!
  There are no other gods;
  no one is like me.
  Think about what happened
  many years ago.

¹⁰ From the very beginning,
  I told what would happen
  long before it took place.

  I kept my word
¹¹ and brought someone from a distant land
  to do what I wanted.
  He attacked from the east,
  like a hawk swooping down.
  Now I will keep my promise
  and do what I planned.

¹² You people are stubborn
  and far from being safe,
  so listen to me.
¹³ I will soon come to save you.
  I am not far away
  and will waste no time;
  I take pride in Israel
  and will save Jerusalem.

CHAPTER 47

Babylon will fall

The LORD said:

¹ City of Babylon,
  you are delicate and untouched,
  but that will change.
  Surrender your royal power
  and sit in the dust.
² Start grinding grain!
  Take off your veil.
  Strip off your fine clothes
  and cross over rivers.*
³ You will suffer the shame
  of going naked,
  because I will take revenge,
  and no one can escape.'
⁴ I am the LORD All-Powerful,
  the holy God of Israel.
  I am their Saviour.

⁵ Babylon, be silent!
  Sit in the dark.
  No longer will nations
  accept you as their queen.
⁶ I was angry with my people.
  So I let you take their land
  and bring disgrace on them.
  You showed them no mercy,
  but were especially cruel
  to those who were old.

*47.2 Strip . . . rivers: This may be a command to get
ready for work that requires wading in the river, or it
may be a warning that they are going to be taken
away as slaves.

See also: 47.1–15: Isa 13.1–14.23; Jer 50.1–51.64.

---

*46.1 Bel and Nebo: Bel was another name for
Marduk, the chief god of the Babylonians. Nebo was
the son of Marduk and also an important god.

7 You thought that you
would be queen for ever.
You didn't care what you did;
it never entered your mind
that you might get caught.

8 You think that you alone
are all-powerful,
that you won't be a widow
or lose your children.
All you care about is pleasure,
but listen to what I say.

9 Your magic powers and charms
will suddenly fail,
then you will be a widow
and lose your children.

10 You hid behind evil
like a shield and said,
"No one can see me!"
You were fooled by your wisdom
and your knowledge;
you felt sure that you alone
were in full control.

11 But without warning,
disaster will strike —
and your magic charms
won't help at all.

12 Keep using your magic powers
and your charms
as you have always done.
Perhaps — just perhaps —
you will frighten somebody!

13 You have worn yourself out,
asking for advice
from those who study the stars
and tell the future
month after month.
Go and ask them how to be saved
from what will happen.

14 People who trust the stars
are as helpless as straw
in a flaming fire.
No one can even keep warm,'
sitting by a fire
that feeds only on straw.

15 These are the fortune-tellers
you have done business with
all your life.
But they don't know
where they are going,
and they can't save you.

CHAPTER 48

The LORD corrects his people

1 People of Israel,
you come from Jacob's family
and the tribe' of Judah.
You claim to worship me,
the LORD God of Israel,
but you are lying.

2 You call Jerusalem your home
and say you depend on me,
the LORD All-Powerful,
the God of Israel.

3 Long ago I announced
what was going to be,
then without warning,
I made it happen.

4 I knew you were stubborn
and hard-headed.

5 And I told you these things,
so that when they happened
you would not say,
"The idols we worship did this."

6 You heard what I said,
and you have seen it happen.
Now admit that it's true!
I will show you secrets
you have never known.

7 Today I am doing something new,
something you cannot say
you have heard before.

8 You have never been willing
to listen to what I say;
from the moment of your birth,
I knew you would rebel.

The LORD warns Israel

9 I, the LORD, am true to myself;
I will be praised for not punishing
and destroying you.

10 I tested you in hard times
just as silver is refined
in a heated furnace.'

11 I did this because of who I am.
I refuse to be dishonoured'
or share my praise
with any other god.

12 Israel, my chosen people,
listen to me.
I alone am the LORD,
the first and the last.

13 With my own hand
I created the earth

---

and stretched out the sky.
They obey my every command.

The LORD speaks to the nations

¹⁴ Gather around me, all of you!
  Listen to what I say.
Did any of your idols
  predict this would happen?
Did they say that my friend*
  would do what I want done
  to Babylonia?◦
¹⁵ I was the one who chose him.
I have brought him this far,
  and he will be successful.
¹⁶ Come closer and listen!
I have never kept secret
  the things I have said,
and I was here before time began.

It is best to obey the LORD

By the power of his Spirit the LORD God has
sent me ¹⁷ with this message:

People of Israel,
I am the holy LORD God,
  the one who rescues you.
For your own good,
I teach you, and I lead you
  along the right path.
¹⁸ How I wish that you
  had obeyed my commands!
Your success and good fortune
  would then have overflowed
  like a flooding river.
¹⁹ Your nation would be blessed
  with more people
than there are grains of sand
  along the seashore.
And I would never have let
  your country be destroyed.

²⁰ Now leave Babylon!
  Celebrate as you go.
Be happy and shout
  for everyone to hear,
"The LORD has rescued
  his servant Israel!
²¹ He led us through the desert
and made water flow from a rock
  to satisfy our thirst.
²² But the LORD has promised
  that none who are evil
  will live in peace."

The Lord's servant

CHAPTER 49

The work of the LORD's servant

¹ Everyone, listen,
  even you foreign nations across the sea.
The LORD chose me
  and gave me a name
  before I was born.
² He made my words pierce
  like a sharp sword
  or a pointed arrow;
he kept me safely hidden
  in the palm of his hand.
³ The LORD said to me,
  "Israel, you are my servant;
and because of you
  I will be highly honoured."

⁴ I said to myself,
  "I'm completely worn out;
  my time has been wasted.
But I did it for the LORD God,
  and he will reward me."

⁵ Even before I was born,
  the LORD God chose me
to serve him and to lead back
  the people of Israel.
So the LORD has honoured me
  and made me strong.

⁶ Now the LORD says to me,
  "It isn't enough for you
  to be merely my servant.
You must do more than lead back
  survivors from the tribes of Israel.
I have placed you here as a light
  for other nations;
you must take my saving power
  to everyone on earth."

The LORD will rescue his people

⁷ Israel, I am the holy LORD God,
  the one who rescues you.
You are slaves of rulers
  and of a nation
  who despises you.◦
Now this is what I promise:
  kings and rulers will honour you
  by kneeling at your feet.
You can trust me! I am your LORD,
  the holy God of Israel,
  and you are my chosen ones.

---

*48.14 my friend: Probably Cyrus (see 44.28; 45.1).
See also: 48.20: Rev 18.4. 48.22: Isa 57.21.

See also: 49.1: Jer 1.5. 49.2: Heb 4.12; Rev 1.16.
49.6: a Isa 42.6; Luke 2.32; Acts 26.23; b Acts 13.47.

Real life

Culture

Contributed by Wycliffe

'Everyone listen, even you foreign nations across the sea...'

This passage is talking about the role of Israel. But it's the ideal Israel – Israel as it should have been, a light for other nations, a group of God-followers who would take God's saving power into other nations and other cultures.

Culture is important; not in the sense of 'being cultured', of whether or not we go to the theatre, but the entirety of how we live – our habits, customs, language, etc. Sociologists and psychologists agree that the culture, the nation and society into which we are born, helps to define who we are as individuals. It affects what we believe and how we behave.

The Bible, however, says that we are just strangers in this land. We don't really belong here. So where are we from? What is our culture? If we've been born again of the Spirit, we're citizens of heaven and our lives should reflect that. Maybe we get too caught up in the culture of earth: 'white' lies, petty theft, disobedience to parents, drunkenness, sleeping around.

Paul says in Ephesians that when we become Christians, we need to put off the 'old self' (Ephesians 4.22), the way we used to live before we knew Christ. We need to give up the bad habits that come from our culture and put on the new self that longs for God and his ways. And we need to keep working at that.

At the same time, we need to use the culture. In Acts 17, Paul used the religious culture around him to talk about God. Today, in Islamic countries, many churches meet in buildings looking like mosques. That might seem to shocking to us, but what is the most important thing? Surely it's the people. It doesn't matter if we wear tattoos and earrings or have the perfect haircut to go with our desk job. What God looks at is the inside and so should we. God created diversity and so there are loads of different, equally valid, ways to meet with him and have a relationship with him.

Culture should neither be decried nor embraced without reservation. Instead 'Let the Spirit change your way of thinking and make you into a new person' Ephesians 4.23.

Think

Imagine you have met a Martian on a mission. Try describing the culture you live in – its habits and customs, aspirations and achievements – to him.

What messages does the media give about our culture? Pick up a handful of magazines. What impression would they give to an alien?

Act

Look at the clash of cultures in the New Testament. Explore Paul's background. Why was it so significant that he became a Christian?

Get involved in WYnet; find out how God is using the diversity in the cultures today to make his Word available to all nations in a language that they can understand.

Check

Psalms 96.7–10; Isaiah 42.1–4; 49.1–6; Matthew 28.18–20; Acts 17.16–34; Romans 15.7–13; Revelation 21.22–27

More...

Language p.1208
Living truthfully p.1070
Media p.1235
Movies p.1297

The LORD will lead his people home

⁸ This is what the LORD says:

I will answer your prayers
  because I have set a time
  when I will help
  by coming to save you.
I have chosen you
  to take my promise of hope
  to other nations.'
You will rebuild the country
  from its ruins,
then people will come
  and settle there.
⁹ You will set prisoners free
from dark dungeons
  to see the light of day.

On their way home,
  they will find plenty to eat,
  even on barren hills.
¹⁰ They won't go hungry
  or get thirsty;
  they won't be bothered
  by the scorching sun
  or hot desert winds.
I will be merciful
  while leading them along
  to streams of water.
¹¹ I will level the mountains
  and make roads.
¹² Then my people will return
  from distant lands
  in the north and the west
  and from the city of Syene.*

The LORD's mercy

¹³ Tell the heavens and the earth
  to celebrate and sing;
command every mountain
  to join in the song.
The LORD's people have suffered,
  but he has shown mercy
  and given them comfort.

¹⁴ The people of Zion said,
  "The LORD has turned away
  and forgotten us."

¹⁵ The LORD answered,
  "Could a mother forget a child
  who nurses at her breast?
Could she fail to love an infant
  who came from her own body?

Even if a mother could forget,
  I will never forget you.
¹⁶ A picture of your city
  is drawn on my hand.
You are always in my thoughts!

¹⁷ "Your city will be built faster
  than it was destroyed' —
  those who attacked it
  will retreat and leave.
¹⁸ Look around! You will see
  your people coming home.
As surely as I live,
  I, the LORD, promise
that your city with its people
  will be as lovely as a bride
  wearing her jewellery."

Jerusalem's bright future

¹⁹ Jerusalem is now in ruins!
  Nothing is left of the city.
But it will be rebuilt
  and soon overcrowded;
its cruel enemies
  will be gone far away.

²⁰ Jerusalem is a woman
  whose children were born
while she was in deep sorrow*
  over the loss of her husband.
Now those children
  will come and seek room
  in the crowded city,
²¹ and Jerusalem will ask,
  "Am I really their mother?
How could I have given birth
  when I was still mourning
  in a foreign land?
Who raised these children?
  Where have they come from?"

²² The LORD God says:
  "I will soon give a signal
  for the nations
to return your sons
  and your daughters
  to the arms of Jerusalem.
²³ The kings and queens
  of those nations
where they were raised
  will come and bow down.
They will take care of you
  just like a slave

---

*49.12 Syene: The Dead Sea Scrolls; the Standard
Hebrew Text "Sinim". The reference may be to
modern Aswan, a city in southern Egypt.
See also: 49.8: 2 Cor 6.2.   49.10: Rev 7.16–17.

*49.20 whose children . . . sorrow: These "children"
are Jews who were born in foreign countries during
the time that Jerusalem was in ruins. Jerusalem
probably stands for all the cities in Judah that were
destroyed by the Babylonians.

taking care of a child.
Then you will know
  that I am the LORD.
You won't be disappointed
  if you trust me."

The LORD is on our side

24 Is it possible to rescue victims
  from someone strong
    and cruel?'
25 But the LORD has promised
  to fight on our side
  and to rescue our children
  from those strong
    and violent enemies.
26 He will make those cruel people
    dine on their own flesh
  and get drunk from drinking
    their own blood.
  Then everyone will know
    that the LORD is our Saviour;
  the powerful God of Israel
    has rescued his people.

CHAPTER 50

The LORD's power to punish

1 The LORD says, "Children,
  I didn't divorce your mother
    or sell you to pay debts;
  I divorced her and sold you
    because of your sins.
2 I came and called out,
    but you didn't answer.
  Have I lost my power
    to rescue and save?
  At my command oceans and rivers
    turn into deserts;
  fish rot and stink
    for lack of water.
3 I make the sky turn dark
  like the sackcloth
    you wear at funerals."

God's servant must suffer

4 The LORD God gives me
  the right words
    to encourage the weary.
  Each morning he awakens me
    eager to learn his teaching.
5 he made me willing to listen
    and not rebel or run away.

6 I let them beat my back
    and pull out my beard.

Viewpoints

God's perfect judgement. Are you scared or reassured?

Contributed by Austin A

'My protector is nearby; no one can stand here to accuse me of wrong.'

This verse is saying that God has declared us (Christians) innocent, as in a court of law. The rest then makes sense: it is saying that no matter who says otherwise, no-one can change God's decision. Ever. Satan and his followers are constantly trying to stop us from being in a good relationship with God, and if they can convince us the things we've done are too bad for him to forgive, that keeps us away from God pretty effectively.

But this verse is saying that nothing can change God's judgement; no-one can stand up to God and make him change. That means that no matter what we do, or have done, God still loves us, and wants to be in a relationship with us. The same applies for anyone becoming a Christian – nothing is too much for God to forgive, and once the forgiveness has happened, it cannot be reversed. This is what allows us to stand up to Satan and say that God loves us, that we are valued, and that we don't need him or the things he is trying to get us to do. This is our strength.

More...

Forgiveness p.614
Help! I know I have been saved, but somehow I don't feel that way p.742
God's love p.958

See also: **50.6:** Matt 26.67; Mark 14.65.

I didn't turn aside
when they insulted me
    and spat in my face.
⁷ But the LORD God keeps me
    from being disgraced.
So I refuse to give up,
because I know
    God will never let me down.

⁸ My protector is nearby;
no one can stand here
    to accuse me of wrong.
⁹ The LORD God will help me
    and prove I am innocent.
My accusers will wear out
    like moth-eaten clothes.

¹⁰ None of you respect the LORD
    or obey his servant.
You walk in the dark
    instead of the light;
you don't trust the name
    of the LORD your God.'
¹¹ Go ahead and walk in the light
    of the fires you have lit.'
But with his own hand,
    the LORD will punish you
    and make you suffer.

CHAPTER 51

The LORD will bring comfort

¹ If you want to do right
and obey the LORD,
    follow Abraham's example.
He was the rock from which
    you were chipped.
² God chose Abraham and Sarah
    to be your ancestors.
The LORD blessed Abraham,
and from that one man
    came many descendants.

³ Though Zion is in ruins,
    the LORD will bring comfort,
and the city will be as lovely
    as the garden of Eden
    that he provided.
Then Zion will celebrate;
it will be thankful
    and sing joyful songs.

The LORD's victory will last

⁴ The LORD says:

You are my people and nation!
    So pay attention to me.

My teaching will cause justice
to shine like a light
    for every nation.
⁵ Those who live across the sea
are eagerly waiting
    for me to rescue them.
I am strong and ready;
soon I will come to save
    and to rule all nations.

⁶ Look closely at the sky!
    Stare at the earth.
The sky will vanish like smoke;
the earth will wear out like clothes.
Everyone on this earth
    will die like flies.
But my victory will last;
my saving power never ends.

⁷ If you want to do right
    and to obey my teaching
with all your heart,
    then pay close attention.
Don't be discouraged
    when others insult you
    and say hurtful things.
⁸ They will be eaten away
    like a moth-eaten coat.
But my victory will last;
my saving power will never end.

A prayer for the LORD's help

⁹ Wake up! Do something, LORD.
    Be strong and ready.
Wake up! Do what you did
    for our people long ago.
Didn't you chop up
    Rahab* the monster?
¹⁰ Didn't you dry up the deep sea
    and make a road for your people
    to follow safely across?
¹¹ Now those you have rescued
    will return to Jerusalem,
    singing on their way.
They will be crowned
    with great happiness,
never again to be burdened
    with sadness and sorrow.

The LORD gives hope

¹² I am the LORD, the one
    who encourages you.
Why are you afraid
    of mere humans?
They dry up and die like grass.

See also: 50.8–9: Rom 8.33–34.

*51.9 Rahab: This may refer to Egypt at the time of the exodus.

¹³ I spread out the heavens
and laid foundations
for the earth.
But you have forgotten me,
your LORD and Creator.
All day long you were afraid
of those who were angry
and hoped to abuse you.
Where are they now?

¹⁴ Everyone crying out in pain
will be quickly set free;
they will be rescued
from the power of death
and never go hungry.
¹⁵ I will help them
because I am your God,
the LORD All-Powerful,
who makes the ocean roar.

¹⁶ I have told you what to say,
and I will keep you safe
in the palm of my hand.
I spread out the heavens
and laid foundations
for the earth.
Now I say, "Jerusalem,
your people are mine."

A warning to Jerusalem

¹⁷ Jerusalem, wake up! Stand up!
You've drunk too much
from the cup filled
with the LORD's anger.
You have swallowed every drop,
and you can't walk straight.
¹⁸ Not one of your many children
is there to guide you
or to offer a helping hand.
¹⁹ You have been destroyed
by war and by famine;
I cannot comfort you.›
²⁰ The LORD your God is angry,
and on every street corner
your children lie helpless,
like deer trapped in nets.

²¹ You are in trouble and drunk,
but not from wine.
So pay close attention
²² to the LORD your God,
who defends you and says,
"I have taken from your hands
the cup filled with my anger
that made you drunk.
You will never be forced
to drink it again.

²³ Instead I will give it
to your brutal enemies,
who treated you like dirt
and walked all over you."

CHAPTER 52

Jerusalem can celebrate

¹ Jerusalem, wake up!
Stand up and be strong.
Holy city of Zion,
dress in your best clothes.
Those foreigners who ruined
your sacred city
won't bother you again.
² Zion, rise from the dust!
Free yourself from the rope
around your neck.

Suffering will end

³ The LORD says:

My people, you were sold,
but not for money;
now you will be set free,
but not for a payment.
⁴ Long ago you went to Egypt
where you lived as foreigners.
Then Assyria was cruel to you,
⁵   and now another nation*
has taken you prisoner
for no reason at all.
Your leaders groan with pain,›
and day after day
my own name is cursed.
⁶ My people, you will learn
who I am and who is speaking
because I am here.

A message of hope for Jerusalem

⁷ What a beautiful sight!
On the mountains a messenger
announces to Jerusalem,
"Good news! You're saved.
There will be peace.
Your God is now King."
⁸ Everyone on guard duty,
sing and celebrate!
Look! You can see the LORD
returning to Zion.
⁹ Jerusalem, rise from the ruins!
Join in the singing.

---

*52.5 another nation: Babylonia.
See also: 52.1: Rev 21.2,27. 52.5: Rom 2.24.
52.7: Nah 1.15; Rom 10.15; Eph 6.15.

See also: 51.17: Rev 14.10; 16.19.

The LORD has given comfort
to his people;
    he comes to your rescue.
[10] The LORD has shown all nations
    his mighty strength;
now everyone will see
    the saving power of our God.

A command to leave Babylon

[11] Leave the city of Babylon!
    Don't touch anything filthy.
Wash yourselves. Be ready
to carry back everything sacred
    that belongs to the LORD.
[12] You won't need to run.
    No one is chasing you.
The LORD God of Israel
will lead and protect you
    from enemy attacks.

The suffering servant

[13] The LORD says:

My servant will succeed!
He will be given great praise
    and the highest honours.
[14] Many were horrified
    at what happened to him.ʼ
But everyone who saw him
    was even more horrified
because he suffered until
    he no longer looked human.ʼ
[15] My servant will make
nations worthy to worship me;ʼ
    kings will be silent
    as they bow in wonder.ʼ
They will see and think about
things they have never seen
    or thought about before.

CHAPTER 53

What God's servant did for us

[1] Has anyone believed us
or seen the mighty power
    of the LORD in action?
[2] Like a young plant or a root
    that sprouts in dry ground,
the servant grew up
    obeying the LORD.
He wasn't some handsome king.
Nothing about the way he looked
made him attractive to us.

[3] He was hated and rejected;
his life was filled with sorrow
    and terrible suffering.
No one wanted to look at him.
We despised him and said,
    "He is a nobody!"

[4] He suffered and endured
    great pain for us,
but we thought his suffering
    was punishment from God.
[5] He was wounded and crushed
    because of our sins;
by taking our punishment,
    he made us completely well.
[6] All of us were like sheep
    that had wandered off.
We had each gone our own way,
but the LORD gave him
    the punishment we deserved.

[7] He was painfully abused,
    but he did not complain.
He was silent like a lamb
    being led to the butcher,
as quiet as a sheep
    having its wool cut off.

[8] He was condemned to death
    without a fair trial.
Who could have imagined
    what would happen to him?
His life was taken away
because of the sinful things
    my peopleʼ had done.
[9] He wasn't dishonest or violent,
but he was buried in a tomb
    of cruel and rich people.ʼ

[10] The LORD decided his servant
    would suffer as a sacrifice
to take away the sin
    and guilt of others.
Now the servant will live
    to see his own descendants.ʼ
He did everything
    the LORD had planned.

[11] By suffering, the servant
will learn the true meaning
    of obeying the LORD.
Although he is innocent,
he will take the punishment
    for the sins of others,
so that many of them
    will no longer be guilty.

See also: 52.11: 2 Cor 6.17. **52.15:** Rom 15.21.
53.1: Rom 10.16; John 12.38.
See also: 53.4: Matt 8.17. **53.5:** 1 Pet 2.24.
53.6: 1 Pet 2.25. **53.7:** Rev 5.6. **53.7,8:** Acts 8.32–33.
53.9: 1 Pet 2.22.

¹² The Lord will reward him
with honour and power
for sacrificing his life.
Others thought he was a sinner,
but he suffered for our sins
and asked God to forgive us.

The Lord will keep all his promises

CHAPTER 54

A promise of the Lord's protection

¹ Sing and shout,
even though you have never
had children!
The Lord has promised that you
will have more children
than someone married
for a long time.
² Make your tents larger!
Spread out the tent pegs;
fasten them firmly.
³ You and your descendants
will take over the land
of other nations.
You will settle in towns
that are now in ruins.

⁴ Don't be afraid or ashamed
and don't be discouraged.
You won't be disappointed.
Forget how sinful you were
when you were young;
stop feeling ashamed
for being left a widow.
⁵ The Lord All-Powerful,
the Holy God of Israel,
rules all the earth.
He is your Creator and husband,
and he will rescue you.
⁶ You were like a young wife,
brokenhearted and crying
because her husband
had divorced her.

But the Lord your God says,
"I am taking you back!
⁷ I rejected you for a while,
but with love and tenderness
I will embrace you again.
⁸ For a while, I turned away
in furious anger.

Now I will have mercy
and love you for ever!
I, your protector and Lord,
make this promise."

The Lord promises lasting peace

⁹ I once promised Noah that I
would never again destroy
the earth by a flood.
Now I have promised that I
will never again get angry
and punish you.
¹⁰ Every mountain and hill
may disappear.
But I will always be kind
and merciful to you;
I won't break my agreement
to give your nation peace.

The new Jerusalem

¹¹ Jerusalem, you are sad
and discouraged,
tossed around in a storm.
But I, the Lord,
will rebuild your city
with precious stones;*
for your foundation
I will use blue sapphires.
¹² Your fortresses* will be built of rubies,
your gates of jewels,
and your walls of gems.
¹³ I will teach your children
and make them successful.

¹⁴ You will be built on fairness
with no fears of injustice;
every one of your worries
will be taken far from you.
¹⁵ I will never send anyone
to attack your city,
and you will make prisoners
of those who do attack.
¹⁶ Don't forget that I created
metalworkers who make weapons
over burning coals.
I also created armies
that can bring destruction.
¹⁷ Weapons made to attack you
won't be successful;
words spoken against you
won't hurt at all.

My servants, Jerusalem is yours!
I, the Lord, promise
to bless you with victory.

See also: 53.12: Mark 15.28; Luke 22.37.   **54.1:** Gal 4.27.

See also: **54.9:** Gen 9.8–17.   **54.11–12:** Rev 21.18–21.
54.13: John 6.45.

CHAPTER 55

The Lord's invitation

¹ If you are thirsty,
  come and drink water!
If you don't have any money,
  come, eat what you want!
Drink wine and milk
  without paying a penny.
² Why waste your money
  on what isn't really food?
Why work hard for something
  that doesn't satisfy?
Listen carefully to me,
  and you will enjoy the very best foods.

³ Pay close attention!
  Come to me and live.
I will promise you
  the eternal love and loyalty
  that I promised David.
⁴ I made him the leader and ruler
  of the nations;
  he was my witness to them.
⁵ You will call out to nations
  you have never known.
And they have never known you,
  but they will come running
  because I am the Lord,
  the holy God of Israel,
  and I have honoured you.

God's words are powerful

⁶ Turn to the Lord!
  He can still be found.
  Call out to God! He is near.
⁷ Give up your crooked ways
  and your evil thoughts.
Return to the Lord our God.
  He will be merciful
  and forgive your sins.

⁸ The Lord says:
  "My thoughts and my ways
  are not like yours.
⁹ Just as the heavens
  are higher than the earth,
  my thoughts and my ways
  are higher than yours.

¹⁰ "Rain and snow fall from the sky.
  But they don't return
  without watering the earth
  that produces seeds to plant
  and grain to eat.

Viewpoints

Our ideas are often radically different from God's. So who's right?

Contributed by Naomi C

'The Lord says, "My thoughts and my ways are not like yours."'

A friend of mine volunteered to be a catering assistant at a Christian summer camp. She'd had some experience with cooking in a small residential home for the elderly, but wasn't particularly confident about her cooking abilities. So when the leader of the camp rang her up and asked her if she would be the head cook, she was sure that she couldn't and wouldn't do the job. However, the camp leader was desperate for someone to oversee the catering, so she promised to pray about it.

My friend prayed hard that God would send someone else to come along and cook for all the campers. However, no news of such a person came, and when the camp leader rang back, she very reluctantly agreed to be head cook.

At that moment, she was filled with peace and she knew that with God's help, she could do this job – even though three years previously, she could not cook anything. Sure enough, God provided amazingly for her and the other people helping her with the catering. The food tasted lovely and the kitchen had a great atmosphere. My friend was taken aback by God's goodness!

Putting someone with no experience into a position that usually requires a fair amount of skill is not the kind of idea a human would come up with. But as this verse says, the thoughts of the Lord are totally different from our ideas – they're much, much better.

More...

Serving others p.1190
Help! I'm scared! p.662

See also: 55.1: Rev 21.6; 22.17. 55.3: Acts 13.34.
55.10: 2 Cor 9.10.

11 That's how it is with my words.
They don't return to me
without doing everything
I send them to do."

God's people will celebrate

12 When you are set free,
you will celebrate
and travel home in peace.
Mountains and hills will sing
as you pass by,
and trees will clap.
13 Cypress and myrtle trees
will grow in fields
once covered by thorns.
And then those trees will stand
as a lasting witness
to the glory of the LORD.

All nations will be part of God's people

CHAPTER 56

1 The LORD said:

Be honest and fair!
Soon I will come to save you;
my saving power will be seen
everywhere on earth.

2 I will bless everyone
who respects the Sabbath
and refuses to do wrong.

3 Foreigners who worship me
must not say,
"The LORD won't let us
be part of his people."
Men who are unable
to become fathers
must no longer say,
"We are dried-up trees."

4 To them, I, the LORD, say:
Respect the Sabbath,
obey me completely,
and keep our agreement.

5 Then I will set up monuments
in my temple with your names
written on them.
This will be much better
than having children,
because these monuments
will stand there for ever.

6 Foreigners will follow me.
They will love me and worship
in my name;

they will respect the Sabbath
and keep our agreement.

7 I will bring them
to my holy mountain,
where they will celebrate
in my house of worship.
Their sacrifices and offerings
will always be welcome
on my altar.
Then my house will be known
as a house of worship
for all nations.

8 I, the LORD, promise
to bring together my people
who were taken away,
and let them join the others.

Leaders unfaithful to God will be punished

God promises to punish Israel's leaders

9 Come from the forest,
you wild animals!
Attack and gobble up
your victims.

10 You leaders of Israel
should be watchdogs,
protecting my people.
But you can't see a thing,
and you never warn them.
Dozing and daydreaming
are all you ever do.

11 You stupid leaders are a pack
of hungry and greedy dogs
that never get enough.
You are shepherds
who ill-treat your own sheep
for selfish gain.

12 You say to each other,
"Let's drink till we're drunk!
Tomorrow we'll do it again.
We'll really enjoy ourselves."

CHAPTER 57

God's faithful people suffer

1 God's faithful people
are dragged off and killed,
and no one even cares.
Evil sweeps them away,
2 but in death they find peace
for obeying God.'

See also: 56.7: Matt 21.13; Mark 11.17; Luke 19.46.

The LORD condemns idolatry

3 You people are unfaithful!
You go to fortune-tellers,
  and you worship idols.
Now pay close attention!
4 Who are you making fun of?
  Who are you sneering at?
Look how your sins
  have made fools of you.

5 All you think about is sex
under those green trees
  where idols are worshipped.
You sacrifice your children
on altars built in valleys
  under rocky slopes.
6 You have chosen to worship
  idols made of stone;'
you have given them offerings
of wine and grain.
  Should I be pleased?

7 You have spread out your beds
on the tops of high mountains,
  where you sacrifice to idols.
8 Even in your homes
you have placed pagan symbols
all around your huge beds.
Yes, you have rejected me,
sold yourselves to your lovers,
  and gone to bed with them.'

9 You smear on olive oil
and all kinds of perfume
  to worship the god Molech.'
You even seek advice
  from spirits of the dead.
10 Though you tired yourself out
by running after idols,
  you refused to stop.
Your desires were so strong
  that they kept you going.

11 Did you forget about me
  and become unfaithful
because you were more afraid
  of someone else?
Have I been silent so long'
  that you no longer fear me?
12 You think you're so good,
  but I'll point out the truth.
13 Ask your idols to save you
  when you are in trouble.
Be careful though —
it takes only a faint breath
  to blow them over.
But if you come to me for protection,
this land and my holy mountain
  will always belong to you.

The LORD helps the helpless

14 The LORD says,
 "Clear the road!
  Get it ready for my people."

15 Our holy God lives for ever in the highest
heavens, and this is what he says:

Though I live high above
  in the holy place,
I am here to help those
who are humble
  and depend only on me.

16 My people, I won't stay angry
  and keep on accusing you.
After all, I am your Creator.
I don't want you to give up
  in complete despair.
17 Your greed made me furious.
That's why I punished you
  and refused to be found,
while you kept returning
  to your old sinful ways.

18 I know what you are like!
But I will heal you, lead you,
  and give you comfort,
until those who are mourning
19   start singing my praises.'
No matter where you are,
I, the LORD, will heal you'
  and give you peace.

20 The wicked are a restless sea
  tossing up mud.
21 But I, the LORD, have promised
that none who are evil
  will live in peace.

CHAPTER 58

True religion

1 Shout the message!
  Don't hold back.
Say to my people Israel:
You've sinned! You've turned
  against the LORD.
2 Day after day, you worship him
and seem eager to learn
  his teachings.
You act like a nation
that wants to do right
  by obeying his laws.
You ask him about justice,
and say you enjoy
  worshipping the LORD.

See also: 57.19: Eph 2.17. 57.21: Isa 48.22.

³ You wonder why the LORD
    pays no attention
when you go without eating
    and act humble.
But on those same days
    that you give up eating,
you think only of yourselves▸
    and abuse your workers.
⁴ You even get angry
    and ready to fight.
No wonder God won't listen
    to your prayers!

⁵ Do you think the LORD
    wants you to give up eating
and to act as humble
    as a bent-over bush?
Or to dress in sackcloth
    and sit in ashes?
Is this really what he wants
    on a day of worship?

⁶ I'll tell you
    what it really means
    to worship the LORD.
Remove the chains of prisoners
    who are chained unjustly.
Free those who are abused!
⁷ Share your food with everyone
    who is hungry;
share your home
    with the poor and homeless.
Give clothes to those in need;
    don't turn away your relatives.

⁸ Then your light will shine
    like the dawning sun, and you
    will quickly be healed.
Your honesty▸ will protect you
    as you advance,
and the glory of the LORD
    will defend you from behind.
⁹ When you beg the LORD for help,
    he will answer, "Here I am!"

Don't ill-treat others
    or falsely accuse them
    or say something cruel.
¹⁰ Give your food to the hungry
    and care for the homeless.
Then your light will shine
    in the dark;
your darkest hour will be
    like the noonday sun.

¹¹ The LORD will always guide you
    and provide good things to eat
    when you are in the desert.

See also: 58.7: Matt 25.34.

Real life

Homelessness

When Isaiah talks about what true worship is, he writes, 'I'll tell you what it really means to worship the LORD. Remove the chains of prisoners who are chained unjustly. Free those who are abused! Share your food with everyone who is hungry; share your home with the poor and homeless...' (Isaiah 58.6–7)

To the Israelites a home meant security, peace, safety. A home was God's blessing.

Many people in this world are not secure, safe or blessed. They sleep on the streets. Many are trapped in addiction or mental illness, trying to escape from their problems. They cannot get health care or benefits.

Isaiah says that helping the homeless is part of our worship. Some people give money to beggars on the streets; others argue that the best way is to give to agencies who are working with the homeless. Many cities and towns have organisations that give food and shelter to those on the streets.

Whatever we do, we can't just walk on by. What kind of worship is that?

Think

Why are people homeless? What causes them to sleep rough?
Imagine you are homeless. What would you miss the most?
Why is helping the homeless an act of worship?

Act

Find out about work being done with the homeless in your town, and get involved.
Organise some fundraising for the homeless with your youth group or church.
Contact a shelter or hostel to see if there's anything you can do.

Check

Deuteronomy 8.10–13; Psalms 69.30–33; Proverbs 31.8–9; Isaiah 58.6–14; 65.17–24

More...

Refugees p.129
The poor p.991

He will make you healthy.
You will be like a garden
  that has plenty of water
or like a stream that never runs dry.
¹² You will rebuild those houses
  left in ruins for years;
you will be known
  as a builder and repairer
  of city walls and streets.

¹³ But first, you must start
respecting the Sabbath
  as a joyful day of worship.
You must stop doing and saying
whatever you please
  on this special day.
¹⁴ Then you will truly enjoy
  knowing the LORD.
He will let you rule
  from the highest mountains
and bless you with the land
  of your ancestor Jacob.
  The LORD has spoken!

CHAPTER 59

Social injustice is condemned

¹ The LORD hasn't lost
  his powerful strength;
he can still hear
  and answer prayers.
² Your sins are the roadblock
  between you and your God.
That's why he doesn't answer
your prayers or let you see his face.

³ Your talk is filled with lies
  and plans for violence;
every finger on your hands
  is covered with blood.
⁴ You falsely accuse others
  and tell lies in court;
sin and trouble are the names
  of your children.
⁵ You eat the deadly eggs
  of poisonous snakes,
and more snakes crawl out
  from the eggs left to hatch.
You weave spider's webs,
⁶ but you can't make clothes
  with those webs
  or hide behind them.

You're sinful and brutal.
⁷ You hurry off to do wrong
  or murder innocent victims.

All you think about is sin;
you leave ruin and destruction
  wherever you go.
⁸ You don't know how to live in peace
  or to be fair with others.
The roads you make are crooked;
your followers cannot find peace.

The people confess their sins

⁹ No one has come to defend us
  or to bring about justice.
We hoped for a day of sunshine,
but all we found
  was a dark, gloomy night.
¹⁰ We feel our way along,
  as if we were blind;
we stumble at midday,
  as if it were night.
We can see no better
  than someone dead.'

¹¹ We growl like bears
  and mourn like doves.
We hope for justice and victory,
  but they escape us.
¹² How often have we sinned
  and turned against you,
  the LORD God?
Our sins condemn us!
  We have done wrong.
¹³ We have rebelled and refused
  to follow you.
Our hearts were deceitful,
  and so we lied;
we planned to abuse others
  and turn our backs on you.

¹⁴ Injustice is everywhere;
  justice seems far away.
Truth is chased out of court;
  honesty is shoved aside.
¹⁵ Everyone tells lies;
  those who turn from crime
  end up ruined.

The LORD will rescue his people

When the LORD noticed
  that justice had disappeared,
  he became very displeased.
¹⁶ It disgusted him even more
  to learn that no one
  would do a thing about it.
So with his own powerful arm,
  he won victories for truth.
¹⁷ Justice was the LORD's armour;
  saving power was his helmet;

anger and revenge
were his clothes.

¹⁸ Now the LORD will get furious
and do to his enemies,
both near and far,
what they did to his people.
¹⁹ He will attack like a flood
in a mighty storm.
Nations in the west and the east
will then honour and praise
his wonderful name.
²⁰ The LORD has promised to rescue
the city of Zion
and Jacob's descendants
who turn from sin.

²¹ The LORD says: "My people,
I promise to give you my Spirit
and my message.
These will be my gifts to you
and your families for ever.
I, the LORD, have spoken."

The future glory of Jerusalem

CHAPTER 60

A new day for Jerusalem

¹ Jerusalem, stand up! Shine!
Your new day is dawning.
The glory of the LORD
shines brightly on you.
² The earth and its people
are covered with darkness,
but the glory of the LORD
is shining upon you.
³ Nations and kings
will come to the light
of your dawning day.

Crowds are coming to Jerusalem

The LORD said:

⁴ Open your eyes! Look around!
Crowds are coming.
Your sons are on their way
from distant lands;
your daughters are being carried
like little children.
⁵ When you see this,
your faces will glow;
your hearts will pound
and swell with pride.›

Treasures from across the sea
and the wealth of nations
will be brought to you.
⁶ Your country will be covered
with caravans of young camels
from Midian and Ephah.*
The people of Sheba*
will bring gold and spices
in praise of me, the LORD.
⁷ Every sheep of Kedar
will come to you;
rams from Nebaioth*
will be yours as well.
I will accept them as offerings
and bring honour to my temple.

⁸ What is that sailing by
like clouds
or like doves flying home?
⁹ On those distant islands
your people are waiting
for me, the LORD.›
Seagoing ships* lead the way
to bring them home
with their silver and gold.
I, the holy LORD God of Israel,
do this to honour your people,
so they will honour me.

Jerusalem will be rebuilt

The LORD said:

¹⁰ Jerusalem, your city walls
will be rebuilt by foreigners;
their rulers will become
your slaves.
I punished you in my anger;
now I will be kind
and treat you with mercy.

¹¹ Your gates will be open day and night
to let the rulers of nations
lead their people to you
with all their treasures.
¹² Any nation or kingdom
that refuses to serve you
will be wiped out.

---

*60.6 Midian . . . Ephah:** Midian was the ancestor of
a nomadic tribe of the Arabian desert, east of the Gulf
of Aqaba. Ephah was a clan within the tribe of
Midian.
*60.6 Sheba:** Perhaps a place in what is now
south-west Arabia. The Queen of Sheba brought gifts
to Solomon (1 Kings 10.1–13).
*60.7 Kedar . . . Nebaioth:** Regions in northern
Arabia.
*60.9 Seagoing ships:** See the note at 2.16.

See also: 59.20: Rom 11.26.   **See also:** 60.11: Rev 21.25–26.

¹³ Wood from Lebanon's best trees
will be brought to you —
    the pines, the firs,
    and the cypress trees.
It will be used in my temple
to make beautiful the place
    where I rest my feet.

¹⁴ The descendants of enemies
who hated and ill-treated you
    will kneel at your feet.
They will say, "You are Zion,
the city of the LORD,
    the holy God of Israel."

¹⁵ You were hated and deserted,
    rejected by everyone.
But I will make you beautiful,
a city to be proud of for all time to come.
¹⁶ You will drain the wealth
    of kings and foreign nations.
You will know that I,
the mighty LORD God of Israel,
    have saved and rescued you.

¹⁷ I will bring bronze and iron
    in place of wood and stone;
in place of bronze and iron,
    I will bring gold and silver.
I will appoint peace and justice
    as your rulers and leaders.
¹⁸ Violence, destruction, and ruin
will never again be heard of
    within your borders.
"Victory" will be the name
    you give to your walls;
"Praise" will be the name
    you give to your gates.

¹⁹ You won't need the light
    of the sun or the moon.
I, the LORD your God,
will be your eternal light
    and bring you honour.
²⁰ Your sun will never set
    or your moon go down.
I, the LORD, will be your everlasting light,
and your days of sorrow
    will come to an end.
²¹ Your people will live right
    and always own the land;
they are the trees I planted
    to bring praise to me.
²² Even the smallest family
    will be a powerful nation.
I am the LORD,
and when the time comes,
    I will quickly do all this.

CHAPTER 61

The good news of victory

¹ The Spirit of the LORD God
    has taken control of me!
The LORD has chosen and sent me
to tell the oppressed
    the good news,
to heal the brokenhearted,
and to announce freedom
    for prisoners and captives.
² This is the year
    when the LORD God
will show kindness to us
    and punish our enemies.

The LORD has sent me
to comfort those who mourn,
³   especially in Jerusalem.
He sent me to give them flowers
    in place of their sorrow,
olive oil in place of tears,
and joyous praise
    in place of broken hearts.
They will be called
    "Trees of Justice",
planted by the LORD
    to honour his name.
⁴ Then they will rebuild cities
that have been in ruins
    for many generations.

⁵ They will hire foreigners
to take care of their sheep
    and their vineyards.
⁶ But they themselves will be
priests and servants
    of the LORD our God.
The treasures of the nations
will belong to them,
    and they will be famous.'
⁷ They were terribly insulted
    and horribly ill-treated;
now they will be greatly blessed
    and joyful for ever.

The LORD loves justice

⁸ I, the LORD, love justice!
But I hate robbery
    and injustice.'
My people, I solemnly promise
to reward you
    with an eternal agreement.
⁹ Your descendants will be known
    in every nation.

See also: 60.14: Rev 3.9.   60.19: Rev 21.23; 22.5.

See also: **61.1:** Matt 11.5; Luke 7.22.
61.1–2: Luke 4.18–19.   **61.2:** Matt 5.4.

All who see them will realize
that they have been blessed,
by me, the LORD.

Celebrate and shout

¹⁰ I celebrate and shout
because of my LORD God.
His saving power and justice
are the very clothes I wear.
They are more beautiful
than the jewellery worn
by a bride or a groom.
¹¹ The LORD will bring about
justice and praise
in every nation on earth,
like flowers blooming in a garden.

CHAPTER 62

Jerusalem will be saved

¹ Jerusalem, I will speak up
for your good.
I will never be silent
till you are safe and secure,
sparkling like a flame.
² Your great victory will be seen
by every nation and king;
the LORD will even give you
a new name.
³ You will be a glorious crown,
a royal headband,
for the LORD your God.

⁴ Your name will no longer be
"Deserted and Childless",
but "Happily Married".
You will please the LORD;
your country
will be his bride.
⁵ Your people will take the land,'
just as a young man
takes a bride.
The LORD will be pleased
because of you,
just as a husband is pleased
with his bride.

⁶ Jerusalem, on your walls
I have stationed guards,
whose duty it is
to speak out day and night,
without resting.
They must remind the LORD
⁷ and not let him rest
till he makes Jerusalem strong
and famous everywhere.

⁸ The LORD has given his word
and made this promise:
"Never again will I give
to your enemies
the grain and grapes
for which you struggled.
⁹ As surely as you harvest
your grain and grapes,
you will eat your bread
with thankful hearts,
and you will drink your wine
in my temple."

¹⁰ People of Jerusalem,
open your gates!
Repair the road to the city
and clear it of stones;
raise a banner to help
the nations find their way.
¹¹ Here is what the LORD has said
for all the earth to hear:
"Soon I will come to save
the city of Zion,
and to reward you.
¹² Then you will be called,
The LORD's Own People,
The Ones He Rescued!
Your city will be known
as a good place to live
and a city full of people."

God's wonderful new creation

CHAPTER 63

The LORD's victory over the nations

¹ Who is this coming
from Bozrah* in Edom
with clothes stained red?
Who is this hero marching
in his glorious uniform?

"It's me, the LORD!
I have won the battle,
and I can save you!"

² What are those red spots?
Your clothes look stained
from trampling on grapes.*

---

*63.1 Bozrah: The main city of Edom.
*63.2 trampling on grapes: This is one way that
grapes were crushed to make them into juice.
See also: 62.11: Isa 40.10; Rev 22.12. 63.1–6: Isa 34.5–17;
Jer 49.7–22; Ezek 25.12–14; 35.1–15; Amos 1.11–12;
Obad 1–14; Mal 1.2–5.

See also: 61.10: Rev 21.2.

3 "I alone trampled the grapes!
    None of the nations helped.
 I trampled nations in my anger
    and stained my clothes
        with their blood.
4 I did this because I wanted
    to take revenge —
 the time had come to rescue my people.
5 No one was there to help me
    or to give support;
 my mighty arm won the battle,
    strengthened by my anger.
6 In my fury I trampled on nations
    and made them drunk;
 their blood poured out
    everywhere on earth."

The LORD's goodness to his people

7 I will tell about the kind deeds
    the LORD has done.
    They deserve praise!
 The LORD has shown mercy
    to the people of Israel;
 he has been kind and good.

8 The LORD rescued his people,
    and said, "They are mine.
    They won't betray me."
9 It troubled the LORD
    to see them in trouble,
        and his angel saved them.⁕
 The LORD was truly merciful,
    so he rescued his people.
 He took them in his arms
    and carried them all those years.

10 Then the LORD's people
    turned against him and made
        his Holy Spirit sad.
 So he became their enemy
    and attacked them.
11 But his people remembered
    what had happened
        during the time of Moses.⁕
 Didn't the LORD⁕ bring them
    and their leaders
        safely through the sea?
 Didn't he⁕ give them his Holy Spirit?
12 The glorious power of the LORD
    marched beside Moses.
 The LORD will be praised for ever
    for dividing the sea.
13 He led his people across
    like horses running wild
        without stumbling.

14 His Spirit gave them rest,
    just as cattle find rest
        when led into a valley.⁕
 The name of the LORD was praised
    for doing these things.

A prayer for mercy and help

15 Please, LORD, look down
    from your holy and glorious
 home in the heavens
    and see what's going on.
 Have you lost interest?
    Where is your power?
 Show that you care about us⁕
    and have mercy!
16 Our ancestors Abraham and Jacob
    have both rejected us.
 But you are still our Father;
 you have been our protector
    since ancient times.

17 Why did you make us turn away
    from you, our LORD?
 Why did you make us want
    to disobey you?
 Please change your mind!
 We are your servants,
    your very own people.
18 For a little while,
    your temple belonged to us;⁕
 and now our enemies
    have torn it down.
19 We act as though you
    had never ruled us
 or called us your people.

CHAPTER 64

1 Rip the heavens apart!
 Come down, LORD;
    make the mountains tremble.
2 Be a spark that starts a fire
    causing water to boil.⁕
 Then your enemies will know
    who you are;
 all nations will tremble
    because you are nearby.

3 Your fearsome deeds
    have completely amazed us;
 even the mountains shake
    when you come down.
4 You are the only God
    ever seen or heard of
 who works miracles
    for his followers.

See also: 63.3: a Rev 14.20; 19.15; **b** Rev 19.13.
63.5: Isa 59.16. **63.12:** Exod 14.21.

See also: 64.4: 1 Cor 2.9.

⁵ You help all who gladly obey
   and do what you want,
      but sin makes you angry.
   Only by your help
      can we ever be saved.›
⁶ We are unfit to worship you;
   each of our good deeds
      is merely a filthy rag.
   We dry up like leaves;
      our sins are storm winds
         sweeping us away.
⁷ No one worships in your name
      or remains faithful.
   You have turned your back on us
      and let our sins melt us away.›

⁸ You, LORD, are our Father.
      We are nothing but clay,
   but you are the potter
      who moulded us.
⁹ Don't be so furious
   or keep our sins
      in your thoughts for ever!
   Remember that all of us are your people.
¹⁰ Every one of your towns
      has turned into a desert,
         especially Jerusalem.
¹¹ Zion's glorious and holy temple
      where our ancestors praised you
   has been destroyed by fire.
   Our beautiful buildings
      are now a pile of ruins.
¹² When you see these things,
      how can you just sit there
         and make us suffer more?

CHAPTER 65

The LORD will punish the guilty

¹ I, the LORD, was ready
   to answer even those
      who were not asking
   and to be found by those
      who were not searching.
   To a nation that refused to worship me,›
      I said, "Here I am!"

² All day long I have reached out
   to stubborn and sinful people
      going their own way.
³ They keep making me angry
      by sneering at me,
   while offering sacrifices
      to idols in gardens
   and burning incense
      to them on bricks.

⁴ They spend their nights
      hiding in burial caves;
   they eat the meat of pigs,*
      cooked in sauces
         made of stuff unfit to eat.
⁵ And then they say to others,
   "Don't come near us!
      We're dedicated to God."
   Such people are like smoke,
      irritating my nose all day.
⁶ I have written this down;
      I won't keep silent.
   I'll pay them back
      just as their sins deserve.
⁷ I, the LORD, will make them pay
   for their sins and for those
      of their ancestors —
   they have disgraced me
   by burning incense
      on mountains.

⁸ Here is what the LORD says:
   A cluster of grapes
      that produces wine
         is worth keeping!
   So, because of my servants,
      I won't destroy everyone.
⁹ I have chosen the people
      of Israel and Judah,
   and I will bless them
      with many descendants.
   They will settle here
      in this land of mountains,
         and it will be theirs.
¹⁰ My people will worship me.
   Then the coastlands of Sharon
      and the land as far
         as Achor Valley*
   will turn into pasture land
      where cattle and sheep
         will feed and rest.

¹¹ What will I, the LORD, do
      if any of you reject me
         and my holy mountain?
   What will happen to you
      for offering food and wine
   to the gods you call
      "Good Luck" and "Fate"?

---

*65.4 burial . . . pigs: Coming in contact with the
dead or eating the meat of pigs made a person
unacceptable to God.
*65.10 coastlands of Sharon . . . Achor Valley:
Sharon is the coastal plain on the west, and Achor
Valley is in the east near Jericho. These two places
stand for the whole country.

See also: 65.1: Rom 10.20.   65.2: Rom 10.21.   See also: 65.10: Josh 7.24–26.

¹² Your luck will end!
I will see to it that you
are slaughtered with swords.
You refused to answer
when I called out;
you paid no attention
to my instructions.
Instead, you did what I hated,
knowing it was wrong.

¹³ I, the LORD God, will give
food and drink to my servants,
and they will celebrate.
But all of you sinners
will go hungry and thirsty,
overcome with disgrace.

¹⁴ My servants will laugh and sing,
but you will be sad
and cry out in pain.

¹⁵ I, the LORD God, promise
to see that you are killed
and that my chosen servants use
your names as curse words.
But I will give new names*
to my servants.'

¹⁶ I am God! I can be trusted.
Your past troubles are gone;
I no longer think of them.
When you pray for someone
to receive a blessing,
or when you make a promise,
you must do it in my name.
I alone am the God
who can be trusted.

The LORD's new creation

¹⁷ I am creating new heavens
and a new earth;
everything of the past
will be forgotten.

¹⁸ Celebrate and be glad for ever!
I am creating a Jerusalem,
full of happy people.

¹⁹ I will celebrate with Jerusalem
and all its people;
there will be no more crying
or sorrow in that city.

²⁰ No child will die in infancy;
everyone will live
to a ripe old age.
Anyone a hundred years old
will be considered young,

65.15 new names: The giving of a new name
suggests the beginning of a new life.
See also: 65.17: Isa 66.22; 2 Pet 3.13; Rev 21.1.
65.19: Rev 21.4.

Viewpoints 👁

Heaven will be great – but it just seems so far away...

Contributed by Dave H

'I am creating new heavens and a new earth; everything of the past will be forgotten.'

Marshmallow clouds, harp-playing angels, and all the Lego in the world! And then of course you wake up, and none of it's real. I could never quite get my head around 'The bestest, most fun place in all the world, and it lasts forever?!' Heaven seemed to be this thing that was almost impossible, unreal. It's miles away from us, isn't it?

This prophecy in Isaiah will be perfectly fulfilled after Jesus has returned, and all have been judged according to the Book of Life (Revelation 21). God will create a new world for us, a world that is perfect in every way. A place where we can worship God 24/7, for the rest of our lives.

Our purpose in this world was to worship God, but sin gets in the way, we daily fall short of our task to give complete glory. Heaven can seem to be miles away.

When you give your life to Jesus, you've got your spot in heaven booked. There's absolutely nothing in this world that can take that away from you. There's also nothing you can do to increase your chances of staying in heaven – you're already there, full stop. 'Anyone who belongs to Christ is a new person. The past is forgotten, and everything is new' (2 Corinthians 5.17). A new life, that has no reason to be sad, depressed or lonely. But has every reason and opportunity to give praise and glory to the saving God, 24/7, which is the bestest, most fun thing to do in all the world.

Heaven's not far away, eternal life starts right here, right now.

More...

Heaven p.1412
Why can't we just go to heaven as soon as we become Christians? p.497
New heaven & new earth p.1427

and to die younger than that
will be considered a curse.

21 My people will live
in the houses they build;
they will enjoy grapes
from their own vineyards.
22 No one will take away
their homes or vineyards.
My chosen people will live
to be as old as trees,
and they will enjoy
what they have earned.
23 Their work won't be wasted,
and their children won't die
of dreadful diseases.[']
I will bless their children
and their grandchildren.
24 I will answer their prayers
before they finish praying.

25 Wolves and lambs
will graze together;
lions and oxen
will feed on straw.
Snakes will eat only dust!
They won't bite or harm anyone
on my holy mountain.
I, the LORD, have spoken!

CHAPTER 66

True worship

1 The LORD said:

Heaven is my throne;
the earth is my footstool.
What kind of house
could you build for me?
In what place will I rest?
2   I have made everything;
that's how it all came to be.[']
I, the LORD, have spoken.

The people I treasure most
are the humble —
they depend only on me
and tremble when I speak.

3 You sacrifice oxen to me,
and you commit murder;
you sacrifice lambs to me
and dogs to other gods;
you offer grain to me
and pigs' blood to idols;
you burn incense to me
and praise your idols.[']

You have made your own choice
to do these disgusting things
that you enjoy so much.
4 You refused to answer
when I called out;
you paid no attention
to my instructions.
Instead, you did what I hated,
knowing it was wrong.
Now I will punish[']you
in a way you dread the most.

The LORD will help Jerusalem

5 If you tremble
when the LORD speaks,
listen to what he says:
"Some of your own people hate
and reject you because of me.
They make fun and say,
'Let the LORD show his power!
Let us see him
make you truly happy.[']
But those who say these things
will be terribly ashamed."

6 Do you hear that noise
in the city and those shouts
coming from the temple?
It is the LORD shouting
as he punishes his enemies.

7 Have you ever heard of a woman
who gave birth to a child
before having labour pains?
8 Who ever heard of such a thing
or imagined it could happen?
Can a nation be born in a day
or come to life in a second?
Jerusalem is like a mother
who gave birth to her children
as soon as she was in labour.
9 The LORD is the one
who makes birth possible.
And he will see that Zion
has many more children.
The LORD has spoken.

10 If you love Jerusalem,
celebrate and shout!
If you were in sorrow
because of the city,
you can now be glad.
11 She will nurse and comfort you,
just like your own mother,
until you are satisfied.
You will fully enjoy
her wonderful glory.

See also: 65.25: Isa 11.6–9. 66.1: a Matt 5.34; 23.22;
b Matt 5.35. 66.1–2a: Acts 7.49–50.

See also: 66.7: Rev 12.5.

¹² The LORD has promised:
"I will flood Jerusalem
  with the wealth of nations
    and make the city prosper.
Zion will nurse you at her breast,
  carry you in her arms,
    and hold you in her lap.
¹³ I will comfort you there
  like a mother
    comforting her child."

¹⁴ When you see this happen,
  you will celebrate;
your strength will return
  faster than grass can sprout.
Then everyone will know
  that the LORD is present
    with his servants,
but he is angry
  with his enemies.
¹⁵ The LORD will come down
  like a whirlwind
    with his flaming chariots.
He will be terribly furious
  and punish his enemies
    with fire.
¹⁶ The LORD's fiery sword
  will bring justice
everywhere on this earth
  and execute many people.

A threat and a promise

¹⁷ Some of you get yourselves ready and go to a garden to worship a foreign goddess.' You eat the meat of pigs, lizards, and mice. But I, the LORD, will destroy you for this.

¹⁸ I know everything you do and think! The time has now come' to bring together the people of every language and nation and to show them my glory ¹⁹ by proving what I can do.' I will send the survivors to Tarshish, Pul,* Lud, Meshech,' Tubal, Javan,* and to the distant islands. I will send them to announce my wonderful glory to nations that have never heard about me.

²⁰ They will bring your relatives from the nations as an offering to me, the LORD. They will come on horses, chariots, wagons, mules, and camels' to Jerusalem, my holy mountain. It will be like the people of Israel bringing the right offering to my temple. ²¹ I promise that some of them will be priests and others will be helpers in my temple. I, the LORD, have spoken.

²² I also promise that you will always have descendants and will never be forgotten, just as the new heavens and the new earth that I create will last for ever. ²³ On the first day of each month and on each Sabbath, everyone will worship me. I, the LORD, have spoken.

²⁴ My people will go out and look at the dead bodies of those who turned against me. The worms there never die, the fire never stops burning, and the sight of those bodies will be disgusting to everyone.

See also: **66.22:** Isa 65.17; 2 Pet 3.13; Rev 21.1.
66.24: Mark 9.48.

Additional notes

'**1.1 message:** Or "vision".
'**1.17 and help those in need:** Or "and punish cruel people".
'**1.27 by showing justice:** Or "by my saving power".
'**1.31 Your . . . idols:** Or "Your wealth will be like dry wood, set on fire by its owners."
'**2.1 message:** See the note at 1.1.
'**2.6 because . . . foreigners:** One possible meaning for the difficult Hebrew text.
'**3.4 babies:** Or "worthless nobodies".
'**5.17 and they . . . others:** One possible meaning for the difficult Hebrew text.
'**5.25 is ready . . . again:** Or "hasn't given up on you yet".
'**6.13 But just . . . down:** One possible meaning for the difficult Hebrew text.
'**7.1 went . . . had planned:** Or "attacked Jerusalem, but could not capture it".
'**8.1 in big clear letters:** One possible meaning for the difficult Hebrew text.
'**8.8 But . . . land:** One possible meaning for the difficult Hebrew text.
'**9.1 will . . . pain:** One possible meaning for the difficult Hebrew text.
'**9.3 stronger:** Or "happy" or "larger".
'**9.11 their enemies:** Hebrew "the enemies of Rezin".
'**9.12 so . . . them:** Or "but he hasn't given up on them yet".
'**9.17 and kept . . . against him:** Or "but even though they had turned against him, he still had not given up on them."
'**9.20 their own relatives:** One possible meaning for the difficult Hebrew text.
'**10.4 escape being captured:** One possible meaning for the difficult Hebrew text.
'**10.4 and he . . . yet:** Or "but he hasn't given up on you yet!"

---

*66.19 Pul:** Hebrew; one ancient translation "Put", a country in Africa, but the location of neither Pul nor Put is known for certain.
*66.19 Tarshish . . . Javan:** Tarshish may have been a Phoenician city in Spain; Put (see note on Pul) and Lud were African people; Meshech and Tubal were regions south or south-east of the Black Sea; the Javan were people of Asia Minor and the Greek islands.

›10.23 on this earth: Or "in this land".

›10.25 punish . . . crimes: Or "completely destroy them".

›10.27 All . . . you: One possible meaning for the difficult Hebrew text.

›10.34 Lebanon: One possible meaning for the difficult Hebrew text of verse 34.

›11.11 land along the coast: Or "islands".

›12.2 strength: Or "song".

›13.1 message: See the note at 1.1.

›13.21 goats: Or "demons".

›14.4 He . . . again: One possible meaning for the difficult Hebrew text.

›15.2 Everyone . . . temple: One possible meaning for the difficult Hebrew text.

›15.9 Dimon . . . Dimon: The Standard Hebrew Text; the Dead Sea Scrolls and one ancient translation have *Dibon . . . Dibon.*

›16.8 The rulers . . . vineyards: Or "The rulers of nations have destroyed those vineyards."

›17.3 Israel: The Hebrew text has "Ephraim", another name for the northern kingdom.

›17.9 covered . . . undergrowth: Hebrew; one ancient translation "like the cities of the Hivites and the Amorites".

›18.1 insects: Or "sailing ships".

›18.2 world: One possible meaning for the difficult Hebrew text of verse 2.

›19.9 turn pale: One possible meaning for the difficult Hebrew text.

›19.18 City of the Sun: Some manuscripts of the Standard Hebrew Text, the Dead Sea Scrolls, and one ancient translation; most manuscripts of the Standard Hebrew Text have "City of Destruction". This probably refers to Heliopolis which means "City of the Sun" (see Jeremiah 43.13).

›21.8 guard: The Dead Sea Scrolls and one ancient translation; the Standard Hebrew Text has "lion".

›22.3 No matter . . . caught: One possible meaning for the difficult Hebrew text.

›22.5 and for . . . help: One possible meaning for the difficult Hebrew text.

›22.6 chariots: One possible meaning for the difficult Hebrew text.

›23.1 Tyre . . . ruins: One possible meaning for the difficult Hebrew text.

›23.3 along the Nile: The Hebrew text has "grain of Shihor, the harvest of the Nile", but Shihor is probably a name for a region near the lower part of the Nile.

›23.4 children: One possible meaning for the difficult Hebrew text.

›23.6 far across the ocean: The Hebrew text has "to Tarshish", probably meaning a long distance.

›23.10 People of Tyre: The Hebrew text has "the people of Tarshish", which stands for the colonies of Tyre.

›23.10 Egyptians: One possible meaning for the difficult Hebrew text of verse 10.

›23.13 ruins: One possible meaning for the difficult Hebrew text of verse 13.

›24.4 its . . . to nothing: One possible meaning for the difficult Hebrew text.

›24.16 God of justice: Or "people who do right".

›25.11 no matter . . . try: One possible meaning for the difficult Hebrew text.

›26.5 our enemies . . . city: One possible meaning for the difficult Hebrew text.

›26.16 LORD: One possible meaning for the difficult Hebrew text of verse 16.

›27.2 fruitful: Some Hebrew manuscripts have "lovely".

›27.8 I . . . punishment: One possible meaning for the difficult Hebrew text.

›28.10 sound: One possible meaning for the difficult Hebrew text of verses 9,10.

›28.13 Now . . . sound: One possible meaning for the difficult Hebrew text.

›29.1 the place of my altar: One possible meaning for "ariel, ariel" of the Hebrew text. In Hebrew "ariel" can mean "God's hero" or "God's lion" or "God's altar".

›29.2 when . . . you: One possible meaning for the difficult Hebrew text.

›29.3 from all sides: One possible meaning for the difficult Hebrew text. One ancient translation has "like David".

›29.17 with . . . forest: Or "and Mount Carmel will be covered with forests".

›30.7 a helpless monster: One possible meaning for the difficult Hebrew text.

›30.27 with . . . smoke: One possible meaning for the difficult Hebrew text.

›31.9 fortress: The Hebrew text has "rock", which may refer to the Assyrian god or king, or to their army.

›33.3 greatness: One possible meaning for the difficult Hebrew text of verse 3.

›33.4 them: One possible meaning for the difficult Hebrew text of verse 4.

›33.6 Nothing . . . us: One possible meaning for the difficult Hebrew text.

›33.7 Listen . . . help: Or "The LORD heard our shouts and will come to help us."

›33.8 to any . . . promises: The Dead Sea Scrolls; the Standard Hebrew Text "to those in the cities".

›34.5 has done . . . above: The Standard Hebrew Text; the Dead Sea Scrolls "appears in the skies above".

›34.11 Owls . . . animals: One possible meaning for the difficult Hebrew text.

›34.15 Owls . . . shadows: One possible meaning for the difficult Hebrew text.

›35.7 where . . . home: One possible meaning for the difficult Hebrew text.

›35.8 And . . . highway: Or "And not even a fool can miss that highway."

›37.21–22 Hezekiah, you prayed . . . Assyria: One possible meaning for the difficult Hebrew text.

›38.8 steps: One possible meaning for the difficult Hebrew text of verse 8.

›38.13 of me: One possible meaning for the difficult Hebrew text of verse 13.

›38.14 help me: One possible meaning for the difficult Hebrew text of verse 14.

᾿38.15 There's . . . me: One possible meaning for the difficult Hebrew text.

᾿38.16 Your . . . me: One possible meaning for the difficult Hebrew text.

᾿38.19 about your faithfulness: One possible meaning for the difficult Hebrew text.

᾿40.9 There . . . can: Or "City of Jerusalem, you have good news. Shout it as loud as you can."

᾿40.13 the LORD: Or "the LORD's Spirit".

᾿40.21 Isn't . . . world: Or "Hasn't it been clear since the time of creation?"

᾿41.2 Who puts . . . power: One possible meaning for the difficult Hebrew text.

᾿41.7 and other workers: One possible meaning for the difficult Hebrew text.

᾿41.22 Come near . . . idols: One possible meaning for the difficult Hebrew text.

᾿41.23 and terrified: Or "when we see it".

᾿41.24 powerless: One possible meaning for the difficult Hebrew text.

᾿41.25 tramples: One possible meaning for the difficult Hebrew text.

᾿41.27 Look . . . happening: One possible meaning for the difficult Hebrew text.

᾿41.29 nothing: One possible meaning for the difficult Hebrew text.

᾿42.6 I selected . . . you: One possible meaning for the difficult Hebrew text.

᾿42.11 desert . . . mountains: The Hebrew text includes the place names of Kedar in the desert and Sela in the mountains.

᾿42.21 greatly praised: One possible meaning for the difficult Hebrew text of verse 21.

᾿43.14 crying as they go: Or "in their glorious ships".

᾿43.19 streams: The Standard Hebrew Text; the Dead Sea Scrolls "paths".

᾿44.2 my very favourite: Or "Jeshurun".

᾿44.4 like grass: One possible meaning for the difficult Hebrew text.

᾿44.7 Let them say . . . happen: One possible meaning for the difficult Hebrew text.

᾿44.12 by using a hammer: One possible meaning for the difficult Hebrew text.

᾿44.20 How . . . ashes: One possible meaning for the difficult Hebrew text.

᾿44.21 I won't forget you: One possible meaning for the difficult Hebrew text.

᾿45.2 mountains: The Dead Sea Scrolls and one ancient translation; the Standard Hebrew Text "rising waves".

᾿45.4 But . . . you: One possible meaning for the difficult Hebrew text.

᾿45.8 Prepare . . . create: One possible meaning for the difficult Hebrew text.

᾿46.1 as . . . animals: One possible meaning for the difficult Hebrew text.

᾿46.8 Now . . . mind: One possible meaning for the difficult Hebrew text.

᾿47.3 escape: Or "oppose me".

᾿47.14 keep warm: Or "cook food".

᾿48.1 tribe: Hebrew "waters".

᾿48.10 furnace: One possible meaning for the difficult Hebrew text of verse 10.

᾿48.11 I refuse to be dishonoured: One possible meaning for the difficult Hebrew text.

᾿48.14 Babylonia: One possible meaning for the difficult Hebrew text of verse 14.

᾿49.7 You . . . you: One possible meaning for the difficult Hebrew text.

᾿49.8 my . . . nations: One possible meaning for the difficult Hebrew text.

᾿49.17 Your city . . . destroyed: One possible meaning for the difficult Hebrew text.

᾿49.24 cruel: The Dead Sea Scrolls and two ancient translations; the Standard Hebrew Text "good".

᾿50.10 God: One possible meaning for the difficult Hebrew text of verse 10.

᾿50.11 Go . . . lit: One possible meaning for the difficult Hebrew text.

᾿51.1 I . . . you: One possible meaning for the difficult Hebrew text.

᾿52.5 groan with pain: One possible meaning for the difficult Hebrew text.

᾿52.14 him: One ancient translation; Hebrew "you".

᾿52.14 human: One possible meaning for the difficult Hebrew text of verse 14.

᾿52.15 My . . . me: Hebrew; one ancient translation "The nations will be amazed at him."

᾿52.15 kings . . . wonder: One possible meaning for the difficult Hebrew text.

᾿53.8 my people: Or "his people".

᾿53.9 but he . . . people: One possible meaning for the difficult Hebrew text.

᾿53.10 The LORD . . . descendants: One possible meaning for the difficult Hebrew text.

᾿54.11 with precious stones: One possible meaning for the difficult Hebrew text.

᾿54.12 fortresses: One possible meaning for the difficult Hebrew text.

᾿57.1–2 Evil . . . God: One possible meaning for the difficult Hebrew text.

᾿57.6 You have . . . stone: One possible meaning for the difficult Hebrew text.

᾿57.8 them: One possible meaning for the difficult Hebrew text of verse 8.

᾿57.9 the god Molech: Or "the king". In Hebrew "Molech" and "king" sound alike.

᾿57.11 so long: One possible meaning for the difficult Hebrew text.

᾿57.18–19 until . . . praises: One possible meaning for the difficult Hebrew text.

᾿57.19 heal you: One possible meaning for the difficult Hebrew text.

᾿58.3 you think . . . yourselves: One possible meaning for the difficult Hebrew text.

᾿58.8 honesty: Or "honest leader".

᾿59.10 We can . . . dead: One possible meaning for the difficult Hebrew text.

᾿60.5 swell with pride: One possible meaning for the difficult Hebrew text.

᾿60.9 On . . . LORD: One possible meaning for the difficult Hebrew text.

˒**61.6 and . . . famous:** One possible meaning for the difficult Hebrew text.

˒**61.8 But . . . injustice:** One possible meaning for the difficult Hebrew text.

˒**62.5 Your . . . land:** One possible meaning for the difficult Hebrew text.

˒**63.9 It . . . them:** One possible meaning for the difficult Hebrew text.

˒**63.11 But . . . Moses:** One possible meaning for the difficult Hebrew text.

˒**63.11 the LORD:** Or "Moses".

˒**63.11 he:** Or "Moses".

˒**63.14 His . . . valley:** One possible meaning for the difficult Hebrew text.

˒**63.15 us:** Hebrew "me".

˒**63.18 For . . . us:** One possible meaning for the difficult Hebrew text.

˒**64.2 Be . . . boil:** One possible meaning for the difficult Hebrew text.

˒**64.5 saved:** One possible meaning for the difficult Hebrew text of verse 5.

˒**64.7 and let . . . away:** One possible meaning for the difficult Hebrew text.

˒**65.1 refused . . . me:** One possible meaning for the difficult Hebrew text.

˒**65.15 But I . . . servants:** One possible meaning for the difficult Hebrew text.

˒**65.23 their children . . . diseases:** One possible meaning for the difficult Hebrew text.

˒**66.2 that's . . . be:** One possible meaning for the difficult Hebrew text.

˒**66.3 You sacrifice oxen . . . idols:** Or "Sacrificing oxen to me is the same as murder; sacrificing lambs to me is the same as sacrificing dogs to other gods; offering grain to me is the same as offering pigs' blood to idols; and burning incense to me is the same as praising idols."

˒**66.4 punish:** One possible meaning for the difficult Hebrew text.

˒**66.5 Some . . . happy:** One possible meaning for the difficult Hebrew text.

˒**66.17 Some . . . goddess:** One possible meaning for the difficult Hebrew text.

˒**66.18 I . . . come:** One possible meaning for the difficult Hebrew text.

˒**66.19 by . . . do:** One possible meaning for the difficult Hebrew text.

˒**66.19 Meshech:** One ancient translation; Hebrew "those who use bows and arrows".

˒**66.20 camels:** One possible meaning for the difficult Hebrew text.

Jeremiah

The basics

What's the point? Warnings of judgment. The LORD is going to punish Judah for their unfaithful behaviour. The Babylonians are coming.

What happens? Jeremiah starts prophesying as a young man and continues for many years. He warns the people of what will happen if they don't repent, but no-one listens to him. In the end, the Babylonians capture Judah, dismantle the country and take the people away. All that Jeremiah has foreseen comes true.

What should I remember? 31.33 'Here is the new agreement that I, the LORD, will make with the people of Israel: "I will write my laws on their hearts and minds. I will be their God, and they will be my people."'

More details

Setting the scene Jeremiah is a priest from Anathoth, about three miles north of Jerusalem. As a young man, he is chosen by the LORD to take a message to the people of Judah. A message that, on the whole, they really don't want to hear...

What's it all about? God is going to punish Judah for their evil. And Jeremiah has the job of telling them about it.

Jeremiah lived through the reigns of a succession of increasingly ineffective and appalling monarchs. He tried to call the leaders and the people to repent and change their ways; he tried to warn them that God would use the powerful Babylonian empire to punish the nation, but the people and leaders were so wrapped up in their own evil that they didn't want to listen to him.

Few people in the Bible have suffered so much for passing on God's words. Jeremiah was thrown into jail, put on trial for his life, forced to flee, publicly humiliated by false prophets and even thrown down a sewer.

The reason for this harsh treatment is simple: the powers that be simply did not want to hear his message. Jeremiah was a political and social revolutionary, who warned the powers that, unless they turned around, the kingdom would fall. If you're living in – or if you're running – a prosperous, apparently safe country, it's not the kind of thing you like to hear. So you try to shut the speaker up. You try to find your own 'tame' prophets who will only give you the good news.

Not surprisingly, Jeremiah frequently feels like giving up. He often calls for vengeance on his enemies and he often breaks down in tears. Yet he does remain strong. He keeps the memory of his first calling close to his heart and he keeps going.

Even at the end, when all that he has prophesied has come true and when he stands in the rubble of what had been his country, Jeremiah's foundations remain firm. The country might have been destroyed, but the relationship with God would go on.

And another thing

Jeremiah gives us a unique look at how a prophet actually composed his prophecies. He worked using a scribe, called Baruch and wrote his prophecies on a scroll. In fact, when the king, in a fit of anger, burns the scroll, Jeremiah dictates the whole thing to Baruch again – and even adds a lot more (Jeremiah 36)!

Footsteps

God chooses Jeremiah to speak for him

CHAPTER 1

¹ My name is Jeremiah. I am a priest, and my father Hilkiah and everyone else in my family are from Anathoth in the territory of the Benjamin tribe. This book contains the things that the LORD told me to say. ² The LORD first spoke to me in the thirteenth year that Josiah* was king of Judah, ³ and he continued to speak to me during the rule of Josiah's son Jehoiakim.* The last time the LORD spoke to me was in the fifth month* of the eleventh year that Josiah's son Zedekiah* was king. That was also when the people of Jerusalem were taken away as prisoners.

The LORD chooses Jeremiah

⁴ The LORD said:

⁵ "Jeremiah, I am your Creator,
    and before you were born,
  I chose you to speak for me
    to the nations."

⁶ I replied, "I'm not a good speaker, LORD, and I'm too young."

⁷ "Don't say you're too young," the LORD answered. "If I tell you to go and speak to someone, then go! And when I tell you what to say, don't leave out a word! ⁸ I promise to be with you and keep you safe, so don't be afraid."

---

*1.2 Josiah: Ruled 640–609 BC.
*1.3 Jehoiakim: Ruled 609–598 BC.
*1.3 fifth month: Ab, the fifth month of the Hebrew calendar, from about mid-July to mid-August.
*1.3 Zedekiah: Ruled 598–586 BC.

See also: 1.2: 2 King 22.3–23.27; 2 Chron 34.8–35.19.
1.3: a 2 King 23.36–24.7; 2 Chron 36.5–8;
b 2 King 24.18–25.21; 2 Chron 36.11–21.

Life files

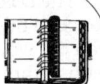

Jeremiah

Background: Son of Hilkiah, from Anathoth

What's the story?

Jeremiah lived in turbulent times.

He was called to be a prophet when he was very young and he continued in this role for around 50 years.

His prophecies about the imminent destruction of Jerusalem made him many enemies among the authorities of his day. They frequently beat, abused and humiliated him. But he never gave up. When Jeremiah sent a scroll of prophecies to King Joakim, the king cut it into pieces and burnt every bit. Jeremiah responded by dictating the whole thing again to the faithful Baruch – and adding a lot of new stuff (36.27–32).

He never married and had few friends he could trust. Perhaps his closest friend was Baruch, his P.A., who copied down his prophecies and read them publicly before the people. After the destruction of Jerusalem, Jeremiah was not taken into exile. He remained behind in what remained of the country.

What's the point?

Jeremiah's life is an example of the cost of following God. Few prophets have suffered as much for their job as Jeremiah. He was always being punished for his prophecies; he was always being hit, or abused, or ridiculed or thrown into jail. Several times he cries to God about his life. He wants to hide (Jeremiah 9.2); he wishes he had never been born (Jeremiah 20.14–18).

But he could not stop speaking out. God's message burned in his bones (Jeremiah 20.9). And while he spoke out against the evil kings of Judah, he also gave many words of hope and encouragement, including messages which pointed to the eventual Messiah (Jeremiah 30–31).

More...

Babylon p.437
Prophecy p.730
Suffering p.555

9 The LORD reached out his hand, then he touched my mouth and said, "I am giving you the words to say, 10 and I am sending you with authority to speak to the nations for me. You will tell them of doom and destruction, and of rising and rebuilding again."

11 The LORD showed me something in a vision. Then he asked, "What do you see, Jeremiah?"

I answered, "A branch of almonds that ripen early."

12 "That's right," the LORD replied, "and I always rise early* to keep a promise."

13 Then the LORD showed me something else and asked, "What do you see now?"

I answered, "I see a pot of boiling water in the north, and it's about to spill out towards us."

14 The LORD said:

I will pour out destruction
    all over the land.
15 Just watch while I send
    for the kings of the north.
They will attack and capture
    Jerusalem and other towns,
then set up their thrones
    at the gates of Jerusalem.

16 I will punish my people,
    because they are guilty
of turning from me
    to worship idols.

17 Jeremiah, get ready!
Go and tell the people
    what I command you to say.
Don't be frightened by them,
or I will make you terrified
    while they watch.

18 My power will make you strong
    like a fortress
    or a column of iron
    or a wall of bronze.
You will oppose all of Judah,
    including its kings and leaders,
    its priests and people.
19 They will fight back,
    but they won't win.
I, the LORD, give my word —
    I won't let them harm you.

God will punish the people of Judah and Jerusalem

CHAPTER 2

Israel's unfaithfulness

1 The LORD told me 2 to go to Jerusalem and tell everyone that he had said:

When you were my young bride,
    you loved me
    and followed me
        through the barren desert.
3 You belonged to me alone,
    like the first part of the harvest,
    and I severely punished
        those who ill-treated you.

4 Listen, people of Israel,*
5   and I, the LORD, will speak.
I was never unfair
    to your ancestors,
but they left me
and became worthless
    by following worthless idols.
6 Your ancestors refused
    to ask for my help,
though I had rescued them from Egypt
and led them through
a treacherous, barren desert,
    where no one lives
    or dares to travel.

7 I brought you here to my land,
    where food is abundant,
but you made my land filthy
    with your sins.
8 The priests who teach my laws
    don't care to know me.
Your leaders rebel against me;
    your prophets
    give messages from Baal
    and worship false gods.

The LORD accuses his people

The LORD said:

9 I will take you to court and accuse you
        and your descendants
10-11 of a crime that no nation
        has ever committed before.

1.11–12 almonds . . . rise early: In Hebrew "almonds that ripen early" sounds like "always rise early".

2.4 Israel: After the nation was divided, the northern kingdom was called "Israel", and the southern kingdom was called "Judah" (see 1 Kings 12.1–20). In 722 BC the Assyrians conquered the northern kingdom, and Judah was all that was left. And so in the book of Jeremiah the name "Israel" is most often used of the southern kingdom.

Just ask anyone, anywhere,
from the eastern deserts
to the islands in the west.
You will find that no nation
has ever abandoned its gods
even though they were false.
I am the true and glorious God,
but you have rejected me
to worship idols.
¹² Tell the heavens
to tremble with fear!
¹³ You, my people, have sinned
in two ways —
you have rejected me, the source
of life-giving water,
and you've tried to collect water
in cracked and leaking pits
dug in the ground.

¹⁴ People of Israel,
you weren't born slaves;
you were captured in war.
¹⁵ Enemies roared like lions
and destroyed your land;
towns lie burnt and empty.
¹⁶ Soldiers from the Egyptian towns
of Memphis and Tahpanhes
have cracked your skulls.
¹⁷ It's all your own fault!
You stopped following me,
the LORD your God,
¹⁸ and you trusted the power
of Egypt and Assyria.'
¹⁹ Your own sins will punish you,
because it was a bitter mistake
for you to reject me
without fear of punishment.
I, the LORD All-Powerful,
have spoken.

²⁰ Long ago you left me
and broke all ties between us,
refusing to be my servant.
Now you worship other gods
by having sex
on hilltops or in the shade
of large trees.*
²¹ You were a choice grapevine,
but now you produce nothing
but small, rotten grapes.

---

*2.20 having sex . . . trees: In some Canaanite
religions, worshippers had sex with temple
prostitutes, who represented their gods; many of the
Canaanite places of worship were on hilltops or
under large trees.

Viewpoints

It was Baal in the days of Jeremiah but what are the false gods today?

Contributed by Emma L

'I am the true and glorious God, but you have rejected me to worship idols.'

Fools! Only fools would do such a thing as to abandon their most worthy God for something mediocre and useless and certainly of this world. Surely? But this is the temptation that all Christians face. It was Baal in the days of Jeremiah but today we can substitute God with religion, possessions, relationships and any other self-gratifying behaviour. It's easy to do this, to lose sight of Jesus and to let our faith get bogged down by the things of the world. Jesus warns against this in his story about the farmer planting grain; 'The seeds that fell among the thorn bushes are also people who hear the message. But they start worrying about the needs of this life and are fooled by the desire to get rich.' (Matthew 13.22)

But don't let this be you. Dedicate your life to God daily, pray and worship God through everything you do. Try to put into practise what you learn in church. Live your Christian life – and not just on a Sunday! By doing these things we grow closer to God and see him for who he really is. We might get glimpses of his gGlory and his amazing love for us. When we fully realise how he loves us and what he's done for us, it should be our highest goal to worship and please him. Naturally, our response to his love is praise. God demands it and nothing less of us, and being the worthiest of all, why shouldn't he ask everything of us? Take up your cross, says Jesus, and follow him. Only him.

More...

Foreign gods p.262
Finding God every day p.660

Israel is stained with guilt

22 The LORD said:

> People of Israel,
>   you are stained with guilt,
> and no soap or bleach
>   can wash it away.

23 You deny your sins
    and say, "We aren't unclean.
    We haven't worshipped Baal."'
But think about what you do
    in Hinnom Valley.*
And you run back and forth
    like young camels,
as you rush to worship one idol
    after another.

24 You are a female donkey
    sniffing the desert air,
wanting to mate with just anyone.
    You are an easy catch!

25 Your shoes are worn out,
    and your throat is parched
from running here and there
    to worship foreign gods.
"Stop!" I shouted, but you replied, "No!
    I love those gods too much."

26 You and your leaders
    are more disgraceful
       than thieves —
you and your kings,
    your priests and prophets
27 worship stone idols
    and sacred poles
as if they had created you
    and had given you life.
You have rejected me,
    but when you're in trouble,
    you cry to me for help.
28 Go and cry to the gods you made!
    There should be enough of them
       to save you,
because Judah has as many gods
    as it has towns.

Israel rebels against the LORD

29 The LORD said to Israel:

> You accuse me of not saving you,
>   but I say you have rebelled.
> 30 I tried punishing you,
>   but you refused
>   to come back to me,
> and like fierce lions
>   you killed my prophets.

31 Now listen to what I say!
    Did I abandon you in the desert
       or surround you with darkness?
You are my people,
    yet you have told me,
"We'll do what we want,
    and we refuse
       to worship you!"
32 A bride could not forget
    to wear her jewellery
       to her wedding,
but you have forgotten me
    day after day.
33 You are so clever
    at finding lovers
that you could give lessons
    to a prostitute.
34 You killed innocent people
    for no reason at all.
And even though their blood
    can be seen on your clothes,
35 you claim to be innocent,
    and you want me to stop
       being angry with me.
So I'll take you to court,
    and we'll see who is right.

36 When Assyria let you down,
    you ran to Egypt,
but you'll find no help there,
37 and you will leave
    in great sadness.'
I won't let you find help
    from those you trust.

CHAPTER 3

Sin and shame

1 The LORD said to the people of Israel:

> If a divorced woman marries,
>   can her first husband
>   ever marry her again?
> No, because this
>   would pollute the land.
> But you have more gods
>   than a prostitute has lovers.
>   Why should I take you back?
> 2 Just try to find one hilltop
>   where you haven't gone
> to worship other gods
>   by having sex.*
> You sat beside the road
>   like a robber in ambush,
> except you offered yourself
>   to every passer-by.

---

*2.23 Hinnom Valley: Hebrew "the valley" (see 7.31–32; 19.1–6).

*3.2 hilltop . . . sex: See the note at 2.20.

Your sins of unfaithfulness
have polluted the land.
3 So I, the LORD, refused
to let the spring rains fall.
But just like a prostitute,
you still have no shame
for what you have done.
4 You call me your father
or your long-lost friend;
5 you beg me to stop being angry,
but you won't stop sinning.

The LORD asks Israel to come back to him

6 When Josiah* was king, the LORD said:

Jeremiah, the kingdom of Israel* was like an unfaithful wife who became a prostitute on the hilltops and in the shade of large trees.*
7-8 I knew that the kingdom of Israel had been unfaithful and committed many sins, yet I still hoped she might come back to me. But she didn't, so I divorced her and sent her away.

Her sister, the kingdom of Judah, saw what happened, but she wasn't worried in the least, and I watched her become unfaithful like her sister. 9 The kingdom of Judah wasn't sorry for being a prostitute, and she didn't care that she had made both herself and the land unclean by worshipping idols of stone and wood. 10 And worst of all, the people of Judah pretended to come back to me. 11 Even the people of Israel were honest enough not to pretend.

12 Jeremiah, shout towards the north:

Israel, I am your LORD —
come back to me!
You were unfaithful
and made me furious,
but I am merciful,
and so I will forgive you.
13 Just admit that you rebelled
and worshipped foreign gods
under large trees everywhere.
14 You are unfaithful children,
but you belong to me.
Come home!
I'll take one or two of you
from each town and clan
and bring you to Zion.

15 Then I'll appoint wise rulers
who will obey me,
and they will care for you
like shepherds.
16 You will increase in numbers,
and there will be no need
to remember the sacred chest
or to make a new one.*
17 The whole city of Jerusalem
will be my throne.*
All nations will come here
to worship me,
and they will no longer follow
their stubborn, evil hearts.
18 Then, in countries to the north,
you people of Judah and Israel
will be reunited,
and you will return to the land
I gave your ancestors.
19 I have always wanted
to treat you as my children
and give you the best land,
the most beautiful on earth.
I wanted you to call me "Father"
and not turn from me.
20 But instead, you are like a wife
who broke her wedding vows.
You have been unfaithful to me.
I, the LORD, have spoken.

The people confess their sins

The LORD said:

21 Listen to the noise
on the hilltops!
It's the people of Israel,
weeping and begging me
to answer their prayers.
They forgot about me
and chose the wrong path.
22 I will tell them, "Come back,
and I will cure you
of your unfaithfulness."

They will answer,
"We will come back, because you
are the LORD our God.
23 On hilltops, we worshipped idols
and made loud noises,
but it was all for nothing —
only you can save us.

*3.6 Josiah: See the note at 1.2.
*3.6 Israel: The northern kingdom (see the note at 2.4).
*3.6 prostitute . . . trees: See the note at 2.20.
See also: 3.6: 2 King 22.1–23.30; 2 Chron 34.1–35.27.

*3.16 make a new one: The sacred chest was probably destroyed or taken away by the Babylonians when they captured Jerusalem in 586 BC.
*3.16-17 sacred chest . . . throne: The sacred chest was thought to be God's throne on earth.

24 Since the days of our ancestors
  when our nation was young,
  that shameful god Baal* has taken
  our crops and livestock,
  our sons and daughters.
25 We have rebelled against you
  just like our ancestors,
  and we are ashamed of our sins."

CHAPTER 4

How Israel can return to the LORD

1 The LORD said:

  Israel, if you really want
  to come back to me, get rid
  of those disgusting idols.
2 Make promises only in my name,
  and do what you promise!
  Then all nations will praise me,
  and I will bless them.
3 People of Jerusalem and Judah,
  don't be so stubborn!
  Your hearts have become hard,
  like unploughed ground
  where thorn bushes grow.
4 With all your hearts,
  keep the agreement
  I made with you.
  But if you are stubborn
  and keep on sinning,
  my anger will burn like a fire
  that cannot be put out.

Disaster is coming

The LORD said:

5-6 "Sound the trumpets, my people.
  Warn the people of Judah,*
    'Run for your lives!
  Head for Jerusalem
    or another walled town!'

  "Jeremiah, tell them I'm sending
  disaster from the north.
7 An army will come out,
  like a lion from its den.
  It will destroy nations
  and leave your towns empty
  and in ruins."

8 Then I said
  to the people of Israel,
  "Put on sackcloth!*

  Mourn and cry out,
  'The LORD is still angry
    with us'."

9 The LORD said,

  "When all this happens,
  the king and his officials,
  the prophets and the priests
  will be shocked and terrified."

10 I said, "You are the LORD God. So why have you fooled everyone, especially the people of Jerusalem? Why did you promise peace, when a knife is at our throats?"

The coming disaster

11-12 When disaster comes, the LORD will tell you people of Jerusalem,

  "I am sending a storm
  from the desert —
    not a welcome breeze.*
  And it will sweep you away
    as punishment for your sins.
13 Look! The enemy army
  swoops down like an eagle;
  their cavalry and chariots
  race faster than storm clouds
    blown by the wind."

  Then you will answer,
  "We are doomed!"

14 But Jerusalem, there is still time
  for you to be saved.
  Wash the evil from your hearts
  and stop making sinful plans,
15 before a message of disaster
  arrives from the hills of Ephraim
  and the town of Dan.*

16-17 The LORD said,

  "Tell the nations that my people
  have rebelled against me.
  And so an army will come
    from far away
  to surround Jerusalem
  and the towns of Judah.
  I, the LORD, have spoken.

---

*4.8 sackcloth: A rough, dark-coloured cloth made from goat or camel hair and used to make grain sacks. It was worn in times of trouble or sorrow.
See also: 4.3: Hos 10.12.

*4.11–12 a welcome breeze: Hebrew "a wind to blow away the husks". Farmers used a special shovel to pitch grain and husks into the air. Wind would blow away the light husks, and the grain would fall back to the ground, where it could be gathered up.
*4.15 Ephraim . . . Dan: The hills of Ephraim were to the north of Jerusalem, and Dan was even further north. They would be reached by the invading army first.

18 "People of Judah,
   your hearts will be in pain,
but it's your own fault
   that you will be punished."

Jeremiah's vision of the coming punishment

19 I can't stand the pain!
My heart pounds,
   as I twist and turn in agony.
I hear the signal trumpet
and the battle cry of the enemy,
   and I cannot be silent.
20 I see the enemy defeating us
   time after time,
      leaving everything in ruins.
Even my own home
   is destroyed in a moment.
21 How long will I see enemy flags
   and hear their trumpets?

22 I heard the LORD say,
   "My people ignore me.
They are foolish children
   who do not understand
      that they will be punished.
All they know is how to sin."

23 After this, I looked around.
The earth was barren,
   with no form of life.
The sun, moon, and stars
   had disappeared.
24 The mountains were shaking;
25 no people could be seen,
   and all the birds
      had flown away.
26 Farmland had become a desert,
   and towns were in ruins.
The LORD's fierce anger
   had done all of this.

The death of Jerusalem

27-28 The LORD said:

I have made my decision,
   and I won't change my mind.
This land will be destroyed,
   although not completely.
The sky will turn dark,
   and the earth will mourn.

29 Enemy cavalry and archers
   shout their battle cry.
People run for their lives
and try to find safety
   among trees and rocks.
Every town is empty.

30 Jerusalem, your land
   has been wiped out.
But you act like a prostitute
and try to win back your lovers,
   who now hate you.
You can put on a red dress,
gold jewellery, and eye shadow,
   but it's no use —
your lovers are out to kill you!

31 I heard groaning and crying.
Was it a woman giving birth
   to her first child?
No, it was Jerusalem.
She was gasping for breath
   and begging for help.
"I'm dying!" she said.
   "They have murdered me."

CHAPTER 5

Is anyone honest and faithful?

The LORD said to me:

1 "Search Jerusalem
for honest people
   who try to be faithful.
If you can find even one,
   I'll forgive the whole city.
2 Everyone breaks promises
   made in my name."

3 I answered, "I know
   that you look for truth.
You punished your people
   for their lies,
but in spite of the pain,
   they became more stubborn
and refused to turn back
   to you."

4 Then I thought to myself,
"These common people
   act like fools,
and they have never learnt
what the LORD their God
   demands of them.
5 I'll go and talk to the leaders.
They know what God demands."
But even they had decided
   not to obey the LORD.

6 The people have rebelled
and rejected the LORD
   too many times.
So enemies will attack
like lions from the forest
   or wolves from the desert.
Those enemies will watch
   the towns of Judah,

and like leopards
they will tear to pieces
whoever goes outside.

Enemies will punish Judah

The LORD said:

⁷ People of Judah,
how can I forgive you?
I gave you everything,
but you abandoned me
and worshipped idols.
You men go to prostitutes
and are unfaithful
to your wives.
⁸ You are no better than animals,
and you always want sex
with someone else's wife.

⁹ Why shouldn't I punish
the people of Judah?
¹⁰ I will tell their enemies,
"Go through my vineyard.
Don't destroy the vines,
but cut off the branches,
because they are the people
who don't belong to me."

¹¹ In every way, Judah and Israel
have been unfaithful to me.
¹²⁻¹³Their prophets lie and say,
"The LORD won't punish us.
We will have peace
and plenty of food."
They tell these lies in my name,
so now they will be killed in war
or starve to death.

¹⁴ I am the LORD God All-Powerful.
Jeremiah, I will tell you
exactly what to say.
Your words will be a fire;
Israel and Judah
will be the fuel.

¹⁵ People of Israel,
I have made my decision.
An army from a distant country
will attack you.
I've chosen an ancient nation,
and you won't understand
their language.
¹⁶ All of them are warriors,
and their arrows bring death.
¹⁷ This nation will eat your crops
and livestock;
they will leave no fruit
on your vines or trees.
And although you feel safe
behind thick walls,

your towns will be destroyed
and your children killed.

Israel refused to worship the LORD

¹⁸ The LORD said:

Jeremiah, the enemy army won't kill
everyone in Judah. ¹⁹ And the people who
survive will ask, "Why did the LORD our
God do such terrible things to us?" Then
tell them:

I am the LORD,
but you abandoned me
and worshipped other gods
in your own land.
Now you will be slaves
in a foreign country.
²⁰ Tell these things to each other,
you people of Judah,
you descendants of Jacob.

²¹ You fools! Why don't you listen
when I speak?
Why can't you understand
²² that you should worship me
with fear and trembling?
I'm the one who made the shore
to hold back the ocean.
Waves may crash on the beach,
but they can come no further.
²³ You stubborn people have rebelled
and turned your backs on me.
²⁴ You refuse to say,
"Let's worship the LORD!
He's the one who sends rain
in spring and autumn
and gives us a good harvest."
²⁵ That's why I cannot bless you!

²⁶⁻²⁷A hunter traps birds
and puts them in a cage,
but some of you trap humans
and make them your slaves.
You are evil, and you lie and cheat
to make yourselves rich.
You are powerful
²⁸ and prosperous,
but you refuse to help the poor
get the justice they deserve.
²⁹ You need to be punished,
and so I will take revenge.
³⁰ Look at the terrible things
going on in this country.
I am shocked!

See also: **5.21:** Isa 6.9–10; Ezek 12.2; Mark 8.18.
5.22: Job 38.8–11.

³¹ Prophets give their messages
in the name of a false god,'
my priests don't want to serve me,'
and you — my own people —
like it this way!
But on the day of disaster,
where will you turn for help?

CHAPTER 6

A warning for the people of Jerusalem

The LORD said:

¹ Run for your lives,
people of Benjamin.
Get out of Jerusalem.
Sound a trumpet in Tekoa
and light a signal fire
in Beth-Haccherem.
Soon you will be struck
by disaster from the north.

²⁻³ Jerusalem is a lovely pasture,
but shepherds will surround it
and divide it up,
then let their flocks
eat all the grass.'

⁴ Kings will tell their troops,
"If we reach Jerusalem
in the morning,
we'll attack at midday.
But if we arrive later,

⁵ we'll attack after dark
and destroy its fortresses."

⁶ I am the LORD All-Powerful,
and I will command these armies
to chop down trees
and build a ramp up to the walls
of Jerusalem.

People of Jerusalem,
I must punish you
for your injustice.

⁷ Evil pours from your city
like water from a spring.
Sounds of violent crimes
echo within your walls;
victims are everywhere,
wounded and dying.

⁸ Listen to me,
you people of Jerusalem and Judah.
I will abandon you,
and your land will become
an empty desert.

⁹ I will tell your enemies
to leave your nation bare
like a vine stripped of grapes.
I, the LORD All-Powerful,
have spoken.

Jeremiah's anger

¹⁰ I have told the people
that you, LORD,
will punish them,
but they just laugh
and refuse to listen.

¹¹ Your anger against Judah
flames up inside me,
and I can't hold it in
much longer.

The LORD's anger will sweep everyone away

The LORD answered:

Don't hold back my anger!
Let it sweep away everyone —
the children at play and all adults,
young and old alike.

¹² I'll punish the people of Judah
and give to others
their houses and fields,
as well as their wives.
I, the LORD, have spoken.

¹³ Everyone is greedy and dishonest,
whether poor or rich.
Even the prophets and priests
cannot be trusted.

¹⁴ All they ever offer
to my deeply wounded people
are empty hopes for peace.

¹⁵ They should be ashamed
of their disgusting sins,
but they don't even blush.
And so, when I punish Judah,
they will end up on the ground,
dead like everyone else.
I, the LORD, have spoken.

The people of Judah rejected God's way of life

¹⁶ The LORD said:

My people, when you stood
at the crossroads,
I told you, "Follow the road
your ancestors took,
and you will find peace."
But you refused.

¹⁷ I also sent prophets
to warn you of danger,
but when they sounded the alarm,
you paid no attention.

¹⁸⁻¹⁹ So I tell all nations on earth,
"Watch what I will do!

See also: 6.12–15: Jer 8.10–12. **6.14:** Ezek 13.10.

My people ignored me
    and rejected my laws.
They planned to do evil,
    and now the evil they planned
      will happen to them."

20 People of Judah,
    you bring me incense from Sheba
      and spices from distant lands.
    You offer sacrifices of all kinds.
But why bother?
    I hate these gifts of yours!
21 So I will put stumbling blocks
    in your path,
and everyone will die,
    including parents and children,
    neighbours and friends.

An army from the north

22 The LORD said,

"Look towards the north,
    where a powerful nation
    has prepared for war.
23 Its well-armed troops are cruel
    and never show mercy.
Their galloping horses sound
    like ocean waves
      pounding on the shore.
This army will attack you,
    lovely Jerusalem."

24 Then the people said,

"Just hearing about them
    makes us tremble with fear,
and we twist and turn in pain
    like a woman giving birth."

25 The LORD said,

"Don't work in your fields
    or walk along the roads.
It's too dangerous.
    The enemy is well armed
26   and attacks without warning.
So mourn, my people, as though
    your only child had died.
Wear clothes made of sackcloth*
    and roll in the ash heap."

The LORD's people must be tested

The LORD said:

27 Jeremiah, test my people
    as though they were metal.
28 And you'll find they are hard
    like bronze and iron.

They are stubborn rebels,
    always spreading lies.
29-30 Silver can be purified
    in a fiery furnace,
but my people are too wicked
    to be made pure,
    and so I have rejected them.

CHAPTER 7

Jeremiah speaks in the temple

This is also told in Jeremiah 26.1–6

1-3 The LORD told me to stand by the gate of the temple⟩ and to tell the people who were going in that the LORD All-Powerful, the God of Israel, had said:

Pay attention, people of Judah! Change your ways and start living right, then I will let you keep on living in your own country.⟩ 4 Don't fool yourselves! My temple is here in Jerusalem, but that doesn't mean I will protect you. 5 I will keep you safe only if you change your ways. Be fair and honest with each other. 6 Stop taking advantage of foreigners, orphans, and widows. Don't kill innocent people. And stop worshipping other gods. 7 Then I will let you enjoy a long life in this land I gave your ancestors.

8 But just look at what is happening! You put your trust in worthless lies. 9 You steal and murder; you lie in court and are unfaithful in marriage. You worship idols and offer incense to Baal, when these gods have never done anything for you. 10 And then you come into my temple and worship me! Do you think I will protect you so that you can go on sinning? 11 You are thieves, and you have made my temple your hideout. But I've seen everything you have done.

12 Go to Shiloh, where my sacred tent once stood. Take a look at what I did there. My people Israel sinned, and so I destroyed Shiloh!

13 While you have been sinning, I have been trying to talk to you, but you refuse to listen. 14 Don't think this temple will protect you. Long ago I told your ancestors to build it and worship me here, but now I have decided to tear it down, just as I destroyed Shiloh. 15 And as for you, people of Judah, I'm going to send you away from my land, just as I sent away the people of Ephraim and the other northern tribes.

---

*6.26 sackcloth: See the note at 4.8.

See also: 7.11: Matt 21.13; Mark 11.17; Luke 19.46.
7.12–14: Josh 18.1; Psa 78.60; Jer 26.6.

Punishment for worshipping other gods

The LORD said:

16 Jeremiah, don't pray for these people! I, the LORD, would refuse to listen. 17 Do you see what the people of Judah are doing in their towns and in the streets of Jerusalem? 18 Children gather firewood, their fathers build fires, and their mothers mix dough to bake bread for the goddess they call the Queen of Heaven.* They even offer wine sacrifices to other gods, just to insult me. 19 But they are not only insulting me; they are also insulting themselves by doing these shameful things.

20 And now, I, the LORD All-Powerful, will flood Judah with my fiery anger until nothing is left — no people or animals, no trees or crops.

It is useless to offer sacrifices

21 The LORD told me to say to the people of Judah:

I am the LORD All-Powerful, the God of Israel, but I won't accept sacrifices from you. So don't even bother bringing them to me. You might as well just cook the meat for yourselves.

22 At the time I brought your ancestors out of Egypt, I didn't command them to offer sacrifices to me. 23 Instead, I told them, "If you listen to me and do what I tell you, I will be your God, you will be my people, and all will go well for you." 24 But your ancestors refused to listen. They were stubborn, and whenever I wanted them to go one way, they always went the other. 25 Ever since your ancestors left Egypt, I have been sending my servants the prophets to speak for me. 26 But you have ignored me and become even more stubborn and sinful than your ancestors ever were!

Slaughter Valley

The LORD said:

27 Jeremiah, no matter what you do, the people won't listen. 28 So you must say to them:

People of Judah, I am the LORD your God, but you have refused to obey me, and you didn't change when I punished you. And now, you no longer even pretend to be faithful to me.

29 Shave your head bald
  and throw away the hair.
Sing a funeral song
  on top of a barren hill.
You people have made me angry,
  and I have abandoned you.

30 You have disobeyed me by putting your disgusting idols in my temple, and now the temple itself is disgusting to me. 31 At Topheth in Hinnom Valley you have built altars where you kill your children and burn them as sacrifices to other gods. I would never think of telling you to do this. 32 So watch out! Some day that place will no longer be called Topheth or Hinnom Valley. It will be called Slaughter Valley, because you will bury your dead there until you run out of room, 33 and then bodies will lie scattered on the ground. Birds and wild animals will come and eat, and no one will be around to scare them off. 34 When I have finished with your land, there will be deathly silence in the empty ruins of Jerusalem and the towns of Judah — no happy voices, no sounds of parties or wedding celebrations.

CHAPTER 8

The LORD said:

1 Then the bones of the dead kings of Judah and their officials will be dug up, along with the bones of the priests, the prophets, and everyone else in Jerusalem 2 who loved and worshipped the sun, moon, and stars. These bones will be scattered and left lying on the ground like rubbish, where the sun and moon and stars can shine on them.

3 Some of you people of Judah will be left alive, but I will force you to go to foreign countries, and you will wish you were dead. I, the LORD God All-Powerful, have spoken.

The people took the wrong road

4 The LORD said:

People of Jerusalem,
when you stumble and fall,
  you get back up,
and if you take a wrong road,
  you turn round and go back.'

***7.18 Queen of Heaven:** Probably another name for the goddess Astarte.*

See also: 7.18: Jer 44.17–19.

See also: 7.31: a 2 King 23.10; Jer 32.35; b Lev 18.21. 7.34: Jer 16.9; 25.10; Rev 18.23.

5 So why do you refuse
   to come back to me?
Why do you hold so tightly
   to your false gods?

6 I listen carefully,
   but none of you admit
      that you've done wrong.
Without a second thought,
   you run down the wrong road'
      like cavalry troops
      charging into battle.

7 Storks, doves, swallows,
   and thrushes
      all know when it's time
to fly away for the winter
   and when to come back.
But you, my people,
   don't know what I demand.

8 You say, "We are wise
because we have the teachings
   and laws of the LORD."
But I say that your teachers
   have turned my words into lies!

9 Your wise men have rejected what I say,
   and so they have no wisdom.
Now they will be trapped
   and put to shame;
      they won't know what to do.

10 I'll give their wives and fields
   to strangers.

Everyone is greedy and dishonest,
   whether poor or rich.
Even the prophets and priests
   cannot be trusted.

11 All they ever offer
   to my deeply wounded people
      are empty hopes for peace.

12 They should be ashamed
   of their disgusting sins,
      but they don't even blush.
And so, when I punish Judah,
   they will end up on the ground,
      dead like everyone else.

13 I will wipe them out.'
They are vines without grapes;
   fig trees without figs or leaves.
They have not done a thing
   that I told them!'
I, the LORD, have spoken.

The people and their punishment

14 The people of Judah
   say to each other,
      "What are we waiting for?

Let's run to a town with walls
   and die there.
We rebelled against the LORD,
   and we were sentenced to die
      by drinking poison.

15 We had hoped for peace
   and a time of healing,
      but all we got was terror.

16 Our enemies have reached
   the town of Dan in the north,
and the snorting of their horses
   makes us tremble with fear.
The enemy will destroy Jerusalem
   and our entire nation.
      No one will survive."

17 "Watch out!" the LORD says.
"I'm sending poisonous snakes
   to attack you,
      and no one can stop them."

Jeremiah mourns for his people

18 I'm burdened with sorrow
   and feel like giving up.

19 In a foreign land
   my people are crying.
Listen! You'll hear them say,
   "Has the LORD deserted Zion?
      Is he no longer its king?"

I hear the LORD reply,
   "Why did you make me angry
      by worshipping useless idols?"

20 The people complain,
   "Spring and summer
      have come and gone,
but still the LORD
   hasn't rescued us."

21 My people are crushed,
   and so is my heart.
I am horrified and mourn.

22 If medicine and doctors
   may be found in Gilead,
      why aren't my people healed?

CHAPTER 9

1 I wish that my eyes
   were fountains of tears,
so I could cry day and night
   for my people who were killed.

2 I wish I could go into the desert
   and find a hiding place
from all who are treacherous
   and unfaithful to God.

See also: **8.10-12:** Jer 6.12-15.   **8.11:** Ezek 13.10.

The LORD answers Jeremiah

³ The LORD replied:

> Lies come from the mouths
>   of my people,
>   like arrows from a bow.
> With each dishonest deed
>   their power increases,
> and not one of them will admit
>   that I am God.

⁴ Jeremiah, all your friends
   and relatives
      tell lies about you,
         so don't trust them.
⁵ They wear themselves out,
   always looking for a new way
      to cheat their friends.
⁶ Everyone takes advantage
   of everyone else,
and no one will admit
   that I am God.

⁷ And so I will purify
   the hearts of my people
just as gold is purified in a furnace.
   I have no other choice.
⁸ They say they want peace,
   but this lie is deadly,
like an arrow that strikes
   when you least expect it.
⁹ Give me one good reason
   not to punish them
      as they deserve.
I, the LORD All-Powerful, have spoken.

Jeremiah weeps for his people

¹⁰ I weep for the pasture land
   in the hill country.
It's so barren and scorched
   that no one travels there.
No cattle can be found there,
   and birds and wild animals
      have all disappeared.

¹¹ I heard the LORD reply,
   "When I have finished,
Jerusalem and the towns of Judah
   will be piles of ruins
      where only jackals* live."

Why the land was destroyed

¹² I said to the LORD, "None of us can
understand why the land has become like an
uncrossable desert. Won't you explain why?"

¹³ The LORD said:

I destroyed the land because the people
disobeyed me and rejected my laws and
teachings. ¹⁴ They were stubborn and
worshipped Baal,⸸ just as their ancestors
did. ¹⁵ So I, the LORD All-Powerful, the God
of Israel, promise them poison to eat and
drink.⸸ ¹⁶ I'll scatter them in foreign
countries that they and their ancestors
have never even heard of. Finally, I will
send enemy soldiers to kill every last one
of them.

The women who are paid to weep

¹⁷ The LORD All-Powerful said,
   "Send for the women
      who are paid to weep
         at funerals,*
especially the women
   who can cry the loudest."

¹⁸ The people answered,
   "Let them come quickly
      and cry for us,
until our own eyes
   are flooded with tears.
¹⁹ Now those of us on Zion cry,
   'We are ruined!
   We can't stand the shame.
Our homes have been destroyed,
   and we must leave our land.'

²⁰ "We ask you women
   to pay attention
      to what the LORD says.
We will teach you a funeral song
   that you can teach
      your daughters and friends:
²¹ 'We were in our fortress,
   but death sneaked in
      through our windows.
It even struck down
   children at play
      and our strongest young men.'

²² "The LORD has told us
   the ground will be covered
      with dead bodies,
like stalks of ungathered grain
   or like manure."

---

*9.11 jackals: Desert animals related to wolves, but
smaller.

*9.17 women . . . weep at funerals: Or "the women
who weep for Baal"; the god Baal was believed to
have died and come back to life, and some women
would go to places of worship and weep over the
death of Baal.

What the LORD likes best

23 The LORD says:

> Don't boast about your wisdom
>   or strength or wealth.
> 24 If you feel you must boast,
>   then have enough sense
> to boast about worshipping me,
>   the LORD.
> What I like best
>   is showing kindness,
> justice, and mercy
>   to everyone on earth.

25-26 Some day I will punish the nations of Egypt, Edom, Ammon, and Moab, and the tribes of the desert.' The men of these nations are circumcised, but they don't worship me. And it's the same with you people of Judah. Your bodies are circumcised, but your hearts are unchanged.

CHAPTER 10

The LORD talks about idols

1-2 The LORD said:

> Listen to me,
>   you people of Israel.
> Don't follow the customs
>   of those nations
> who become frightened
> when they see something strange
>   happen in the sky.
> 3 Their religion is worthless!
> They chop down a tree,
>   carve the wood into an idol,
> 4 cover it with silver and gold,
>   and then nail it down
>   so it won't fall over.

> 5 An idol is no better
>   than a scarecrow.
> It can't speak,
> and it has to be carried,
>   because it can't walk.
> Why worship an idol
>   that can't help or harm you?

Jeremiah praises the LORD

> 6 Our LORD, great and powerful,
>   you alone are God.
> 7 You are King of the nations.
>   Everyone should worship you.
> No human anywhere on earth
>   is wiser than you.

> 8 Idols are worthless,
> and anyone who worships them
>   is a fool!
> 9 Idols are made by humans.
> A carver shapes the wood.
> A metalworker hammers out
> a covering of gold from Uphaz
>   or of silver from Tarshish.
> Then the idol is dressed
>   in blue and purple clothes.

> 10 You, LORD, are the only true
>   and living God.
>   You will rule for all time.
> When you are angry
>   the earth shakes,
>   and nations are destroyed.

> 11 You told me to say
> that idols did not create
>   the heavens and the earth,
> and that you, the LORD,
>   will destroy every idol.

> 12 With your wisdom and power
>   you created the earth
>   and spread out the heavens.
> 13 The waters in the heavens roar
>   at your command.
> You make clouds appear —
> you send the winds
>   from your storehouse
> and make lightning flash
>   in the rain.

> 14 People who make idols
>   are so stupid!
> They will be disappointed,
>   because their false gods
>   are not alive.
> 15 Idols are merely a joke,
> and when the time is right,
>   they will be destroyed.

> 16 But you, Israel's God,
>   created all things,
> and you chose Israel
>   to be your very own.
> Your name is the LORD
>   All-Powerful.

Judah will be thrown from its land

> 17 I said to the people of Judah,
>   "Gather your things;
>   you are surrounded.
> 18 The LORD said these troubles
>   will lead to your capture,
> and he will throw you from this land
>   like a stone from a sling."'

See also: 9.24: 1 Cor 1.31; 2 Cor 10.17. 10.7: Rev 15.4.

19 The people answered,
   "We are wounded
      and doomed to die.
   Why did we say
      we could stand the pain?
20 Our homes are destroyed;
      our children are dead.
   No one is left
      to help us find shelter."

21 But I told them,
   "Our leaders were stupid failures,
      because they refused
      to listen to the LORD.
   And so we've been scattered
      like sheep.

22 "Sounds of destruction
      rumble from the north
      like distant thunder.
   Soon our towns will be ruins
      where jackals* live."

Jeremiah prays

23 I know, LORD, that we humans
      are not in control
      of our own lives.
24 Correct me, as I deserve,
      but not in your anger,
      or I will be dead.
25 Our enemies refuse
      to admit that you are God
      or to worship you.
   They have wiped out our people
      and left our nation
      lying in ruins.
   So get angry
      and sweep them away!

CHAPTER 11

Judah has broken the LORD's agreement

1-3 The LORD God told me to say to the people of Judah and Jerusalem:

I, the LORD, am warning you that I will put a curse on anyone who doesn't keep the agreement I made with Israel. So pay attention to what it says. 4 My commands haven't changed since I brought your ancestors out of Egypt, a nation that seemed like a blazing furnace where iron ore is melted. I told your ancestors that if they obeyed my commands, I would be their God, and they would be my people.

5 Then I did what I had promised and gave them this wonderful land, where you now live.

"Yes, LORD," I replied, "that's true."
6 Then the LORD told me to say to everyone in the streets of Jerusalem and in the towns of Judah:

Pay attention to the commands in my agreement with you. 7 Ever since I brought your ancestors out of Egypt, I have been telling your people to obey me. But you and your ancestors 8 have always been stubborn. You have refused to listen, and instead you have done whatever your sinful hearts have desired.

You have not kept the agreement we made, so I will make you suffer every curse that goes with it.

9 The LORD said to me:

Jeremiah, the people of Judah and Jerusalem are plotting against me. 10 They have sinned in the same way their ancestors did, by turning from me and worshipping other gods. The northern kingdom of Israel broke the agreement I made with your ancestors, and now the southern kingdom of Judah* has done the same.

11 Here is what I've decided to do. I will bring suffering on the people of Judah and Jerusalem, and no one will escape. They will beg me to help, but I won't listen to their prayers. 12-13 Then they will offer sacrifices to their other gods and ask them for help. After all, the people of Judah have more gods than towns, and more altars for Baal than there are streets in Jerusalem. But those gods won't be able to rescue the people of Judah from disaster.

14 Jeremiah, don't pray for these people or beg me to rescue them. If you do, I won't listen, and I certainly won't listen if they pray!

15 Then the LORD told me to say to the people of Judah:

You are my chosen people,
   but you have no right
to be here in my temple,
   doing such terrible things.
The sacrifices you offer me
won't protect you from disaster,
   so stop celebrating.'

---

*10.22 jackals: See the note at 9.11.

*11.10 Israel . . . Judah: See the note at 2.4.

16 Once you were like an olive tree
        covered with fruit.
    But soon I will send a noisy mob
    to break off your branches
        and set you on fire.

17 I am the LORD All-Powerful. You people of Judah were like a tree that I had planted, but you have made me angry by offering sacrifices to Baal, just as the northern kingdom did. And now I'm going to pull you up by the roots.

The plot to kill Jeremiah

18-19Some people plotted to kill me.
    And like a lamb
        being led to the butcher,
    I knew nothing about their plans.
    But then the LORD told me
        that they had planned
    to chop me down like a tree —
        fruit and all —
    so that no one would ever
        remember me again.
20 I prayed, "LORD All-Powerful,
    you always do what is right,
        and you know every thought.
    So I trust you to help me
        and to take revenge."

21 Then the LORD said:

Jeremiah, some men from Anathoth* say they will kill you, if you keep on speaking for me. 22 But I will punish them. Their young men will die in battle, and their children will starve to death. 23 And when I have finished, no one from their families will be left alive.

CHAPTER 12

Jeremiah complains to the LORD

1 Whenever I complain to you, LORD,
    you are always fair.
    But now I have questions
        about your justice.
    Why is life easy for sinners?
        Why are they successful?
2 You plant them like trees;
    you let them prosper and produce fruit.
    Yet even when they praise you,
        they don't mean it.

3 But you know, LORD,
    how faithful I've always been,
        even in my thoughts.

So drag my enemies away
    and butcher them like sheep!
4 How long will the ground be dry
    and the pasture lands parched?
    The birds and animals
        are dead and gone.
    And all this happened because
        the people are so sinful.
    They even boast, "God can't see
        the sins we commit."

The LORD answers Jeremiah

The LORD said:

5 Jeremiah, if you get tired
        in a race against people,
    how can you possibly run
        against horses?
    If you fall in open fields,
    what will happen in the forest
        along the River Jordan?
6 Even your own family
        has turned against you.
    They act friendly,
        but don't trust them.
    They're out to get you,
        and so is everyone else.

The LORD is furious with his people

The LORD said:

7 I loved my people and chose them
        as my very own.
    But now I will reject them
    and hand them over
        to their enemies.
8 My people have turned against me
    and roar at me like lions.
        That's why I hate them.

9 My people are like a hawk
    surrounded and attacked
        by other hawks.
    Tell the wild animals
        to come and eat their fill.
10 My beautiful land is ruined
        like a field or a vineyard
    trampled by shepherds
        and stripped bare
        by their flocks.
11 Every field I see lies barren,
        and no one cares.

12 A destroying army
    marches along desert roads
        and attacks everywhere.
    They are my deadly sword;
        no one is safe from them.

*11.21 Anathoth: Jeremiah's home town (see 1.1).

¹³ My people, you planted wheat,
    but because I was furious,
        I let only weeds grow.
    You wore yourselves out for nothing!

The LORD will have pity on other nations

¹⁴ The LORD said:

I gave this land to my people Israel, but enemies around it have attacked and robbed it. So I will uproot them from their own countries just as I will uproot Judah from its land. ¹⁵ But later, I will have pity on these nations and bring them back to their own lands. ¹⁶ They once taught my people to worship Baal. But if they admit I am the only true God, and if they let my people teach them how to worship me, these nations will also become my people. ¹⁷ However, if they don't listen to me, I will uproot them from their lands and completely destroy them. I, the LORD, have spoken.

CHAPTER 13

Jeremiah's linen shorts

¹ The LORD told me, "Go and buy a pair of linen shorts. Wear them for a while, but don't wash them." ² So I bought a pair of shorts and put them on.

³ Then the LORD said, ⁴ "Take off the shorts. Go to Parah* and hide the shorts in a crack between some large rocks." ⁵ And that's what I did.

⁶ Some time later the LORD said, "Go back and get the shorts." ⁷ I went back and dug the shorts out of their hiding place, but the cloth had rotted, and the shorts were ruined.

⁸ Then the LORD said:

⁹ Jeremiah, I will use Babylonia to' destroy the pride of the people of Judah and Jerusalem. ¹⁰ The people of Judah are evil and stubborn. So instead of listening to me, they do whatever they want and even worship other gods. When I have finished with these people, they will be good for nothing, just like this pair of shorts. ¹¹ These shorts were tight around your waist, and that's how tightly I held on to the kingdoms of Israel and Judah. I wanted them to be my people. I wanted to make them famous, so that other nations would praise and honour me, but they refused to obey me.

Wine jars

The LORD said:

¹² Jeremiah, tell the people of Judah, "The LORD God of Israel orders you to fill your wine jars with wine."

They will answer, "Of course we fill our wine jars with wine! Why are you telling us something we already know?"

¹³ Then say to them:

I am the LORD, and what I'm going to do will make everyone in Judah and Jerusalem appear to be full of wine. And the worst ones will be the kings of David's family and the priests and the prophets. ¹⁴ Then I will smash them against each other like jars. I will have no pity on the young or the old, and they will all be destroyed. I, the LORD, have spoken.

The people of Judah will be taken away

¹⁵ People of Judah,
    don't be too proud to listen
        to what the LORD has said.
¹⁶ You hope for light,
    but God is sending darkness.
    Evening shadows already deepen
        in the hills.
    So return to God
    and confess your sins to him
        before you trip and fall.
¹⁷ If you are too proud to listen,
        I will weep alone.
    Tears will stream from my eyes
    when the LORD's people
        are taken away as prisoners.

¹⁸ The LORD told me to tell you
    that your king and his mother*
    must surrender their thrones
        and remove their crowns.'
¹⁹ The cities in the Southern Desert
    are surrounded;
        no one can get in or out.
    Everyone in Judah will be taken away.
²⁰ Jerusalem, you were so proud
    of ruling the people of Judah.
        But where are they now?

    Look north, and you will see
        your enemies approaching.
²¹ You once trusted them to help,
    but now I'll let them rule you.'

---

*13.4 Parah: Or "the River Euphrates". Parah was a village about nine kilometres north-east of Jerusalem.

*13.18 mother: The king's mother usually had an important position in the royal court.

What do you say about that?
You will be in pain
    like a woman giving birth.

22 Do you know why
    your clothes were torn off
    and you were abused?
It was because of your terrible sins.
23 Can you ever change
    and do what's right?
Can people change the colour
    of their skin,
or can a leopard remove its spots?
If so, then perhaps you can change
    and learn to do right.

24 I will scatter you,
    just as the desert wind
blows husks from grain
    tossed in the air.
25 I won't change my mind.
    I, the LORD, have spoken.

You rejected me
    and worshipped false gods.
26-27You were married to me,
    but you were unfaithful.
You even became a prostitute*
by worshipping disgusting gods
    on hilltops and in fields.
So I'll rip off your clothes
and leave you naked and ashamed
    for everyone to see.
You are doomed!
Will you ever be worthy
    to worship me again?

CHAPTER 14

The land dries up

1 When there had been no rain for a long
time, the LORD told me to say to the people:

2 Judah and Jerusalem weep
    as the land dries up.
3 Rulers send their servants
    to the storage pits for water.*
But there's none to be found;
they return in despair
    with their jars still empty.

4 There has been no rain,
    and farmers feel sick
as they watch cracks appear
    in the dry ground.‚

5 A deer gives birth in a field,
    then abandons her newborn fawn
    and leaves in search of grass.
6 Wild donkeys go blind from starvation.
    So they stand on barren hilltops
    and sniff the air,‚
    hoping to smell green grass.

The LORD's people pray

7 Our terrible sins may demand
    that we be punished.
But if you rescue us, LORD,
everyone will see how great you are.
8 You're our only hope;
    you alone can save us now.
You help us one day,
    but you're gone the next.
9 Did this disaster take you by surprise?
Are you a warrior
    with your hands tied?
You have chosen us,
and your temple is here.
    Don't abandon us!

The LORD's answer

The LORD said:

10 My people,
    you love to wander away;
you don't even try
    to stay close to me.
So now I will reject you
and punish you for your sins.
    I, the LORD, have spoken.

Lying prophets

11 The LORD said, "Jeremiah, don't ask me to
help these people. 12 They may even go
without eating* and offer sacrifices to please
me* and to give thanks.* But when they cry
out for my help, I won't listen, and I won't
accept their sacrifices. Instead, I'll send war,
starvation, and disease to wipe them out."

---

*14.12 go without eating: The people of Israel
sometimes went without eating to show sorrow for
their sins.
*14.12 sacrifices to please me: These sacrifices have
traditionally been called "whole burnt offerings"
because the whole animal was burnt on the altar.
A main purpose of such sacrifices was to please the LORD
with the smell of the sacrifice, and so in the CEV they are
sometimes called "sacrifices to please the LORD".
*14.12 sacrifices . . . to give thanks: These sacrifices
have traditionally been called "grain offerings". A main
purpose of such sacrifices was to thank the LORD with a
gift of grain, and so in the CEV they are sometimes
called "sacrifices to give thanks to the LORD".

---

*13.26–27 prostitute: See the note at 2.20.
*14.3 storage pits for water: Since water was scarce,
pits were dug into solid rock for collecting and storing
rainwater. These pits were called "cisterns".

13 I replied, "The other prophets keep telling everyone that you won't send starvation or war, and that you're going to give us peace."

14 The LORD answered:

They claim to speak for me, but they're lying! I didn't even speak to them, much less choose them to be my prophets. Their messages come from worthless dreams, useless fortune-telling, and their own imaginations.

15 Those lying prophets say there will be peace and plenty of food. But I say that those same prophets will die from war and hunger. 16 And everyone who listens to them will be killed, just as they deserve. Their dead bodies will be thrown out into the streets of Jerusalem, because their families will also be dead, and no one will be left to bury them.*

17 Jeremiah, go and tell the people how you feel about all this.

So I told them:

"Tears will flood my eyes
   both day and night,
because my nation suffers
   from a deadly wound.
18 In the fields I see the bodies
   of those killed in battle.
And in the towns I see crowds
   dying of hunger.
But the prophets and priests
   go about their business,
without understanding
   what has happened.'"

Jeremiah prays to the LORD

19 Have you rejected Judah, LORD?
   Do you hate Jerusalem?
Why did you strike down Judah
   with a fatal wound?
We had hoped for peace
   and a time of healing,
but all we got was terror.
20 We and our ancestors are guilty
   of rebelling against you.
21 If you save us, it will show
   how great you are.
Don't let our enemies
   disgrace your temple,
   your beautiful throne.
Don't forget that you promised
   to rescue us.

22 Idols can't send rain,
   and showers don't fall
      by themselves.
Only you control the rain,
   so we put our trust in you,
      the LORD our God.

CHAPTER 15

The people of Judah will die

1 The LORD said to me:

Even if Moses and Samuel were here,
praying with you, I wouldn't change my
mind. So send the people of Judah away.
2 And when they ask where they are going,
tell them that I, the LORD, have said:

Some of you are going to die
   of horrible diseases.
Others are going to die in war
   or from starvation.
The rest will be led away
   to a foreign country.
3 I will punish you
   in four different ways:
You will be killed in war
   and your bodies dragged off by dogs,
your flesh will be eaten by birds,
   and your bones will be chewed on
      by wild animals.
4 This punishment will happen
because of the horrible things*
   your King Manasseh* did.
And you will be disgusting
   to all nations on earth.
5 People of Jerusalem,
   who will feel sorry for you?
Will anyone bother
   to ask if you are well?

6 My people, you abandoned me
   and walked away.
I am tired of showing mercy;
   that's why I'll destroy you
7 by scattering you like straw
   blown by the wind.
I will punish you with sorrow and death,
because you refuse
   to change your ways.
8 There will be more widows in Judah
   than grains of sand on a beach.

---

*15.4 the horrible things: See 2 Kings 21.1-16.
*15.4 Manasseh: Hebrew "Manasseh son of Hezekiah"; he ruled 687-642 BC.

See also: 15.1: a Exod 32.11-14; Num 14.13-19;
b 1 Sam 7.5-9. 15.2: Rev 13.10. 15.4: 2 King 21.1-16;
2 Chron 33.1-9.

---

*14.16 dead bodies . . . bury them: A proper burial was considered very important.

Helpline

Help! People are saying horrible things about me

'I don't know what I've done, but people are really slagging me off. Why are they being so nasty?'

Being insulted is something that Christians should expect.

Being Christian puts you at odds with the world around you; you have different values, different goals in life. And what the world doesn't understand, it ridicules. That's why Jesus said 'God will bless you when people insult you, mistreat you, and tell all kinds of evil lies about you because of me' (Matthew 5.11). Sometimes, insults are a sign that we're doing something right.

But not always. Sometimes it's nothing to do with our faith, it's just that people are nasty. People get spiteful and mean.

The test of your faith is how you respond. Bad experiences will come our way, but it's how you react to them that counts. Are you going to love your enemies? Or are you going to have a go back?

Three things

Love

Jesus told us to love our enemies. That means no matter what people say about us we should try to love them. It's very hard thing to do, but it's what Jesus did.

Follow

God goes through this every day. Every day people abuse God, blame him, ignore him, use his name as a swearword. But he forgives and he loves. So we've got to do the same.

Resist

It's tempting to snipe back, isn't it? It's tempting to think up a really good reply and then just let rip. Don't give into the urge to get your own back. Speak words of peace.

More...

Suffering p.555
Persecution p.1215
Coping with suffering p.1391
Going against the crowd p.1045

A surprise attack at midday!
And the mothers in Jerusalem
mourn for their children.
⁹ A mother is in deep despair
and struggles for breath.
Her daylight has turned
to darkness —
she has suffered the loss
of her seven sons.

I will kill anyone who survives.
I, the LORD, have spoken.

Jeremiah complains

¹⁰ I wish I had never been born!
I'm always in trouble
with everyone in Judah.
I never lend or borrow money,
but everyone curses me
just the same.

¹¹ Then the LORD replied,
"I promise to protect you,
and when disaster comes,
even your enemies
will beg you for help."

The enemy cannot be defeated

The LORD told me to say:

¹² People of Judah,
just as you can't break iron
mixed with bronze,
you can't defeat the enemies
who will attack from the north.
¹³ I will give them
everything you own,
because you have sinned
everywhere in your country.
¹⁴ My anger is a fire
that cannot be put out,
so I will make you slaves
of your enemies
in a foreign land.

Jeremiah complains again

¹⁵ You can see how I suffer
insult after insult,
all because of you, LORD.
Don't be so patient
with my enemies;
take revenge on them
before they kill me.

¹⁶ When you spoke to me,
I was glad to obey,
because I belong to you,
the LORD All-Powerful.

¹⁷ I don't go to parties
    and have a good time.
Instead, I keep to myself,
    because you have filled me
    with your anger.

¹⁸ I am badly injured
    and in constant pain.
Are you going to disappoint me,
    like a stream that goes dry
    in the heat of summer?

The LORD replies

¹⁹ Then the LORD told me:

Stop talking like a fool!
If you turn back to me
    and speak my message,
I will let you be my prophet
    once again.
I hope the people of Judah
    will accept what you say.
But you can ignore their threats,
²⁰⁻²¹ because I am making you strong,
    like a bronze wall.
They are evil and violent,
    but when they attack,
I will be there to rescue you.
I, the LORD, have spoken.

CHAPTER 16

Jeremiah must live his message

¹ The LORD said to me:

² Jeremiah, don't get married and have
children — Judah is no place to raise a
family. ³ I'll tell you what's going to happen
to children and their parents here. ⁴ They
will die of horrible diseases and of war and
starvation. No one will give them a funeral
or bury them,* and their bodies will be
food for the birds and wild animals. And
what's left will lie on the ground like
manure.
⁵ When someone dies, don't visit the
family or show any sorrow. I will no
longer love or bless or have any pity on
the people of Judah. ⁶ Rich and poor
alike will die and be left unburied. No
one will mourn and show their sorrow by
cutting themselves or shaving their heads.*
⁷ No one will bring food and wine to help

comfort those who are mourning the death
of their father or mother.
⁸ Don't even set foot in a house where
there is eating and drinking and
celebrating. ⁹ Warn the people of Judah that
I, the LORD All-Powerful, will put an end to
all their parties and wedding celebrations.
¹⁰ They will ask, "Why has the LORD our
God threatened us with so many disasters?
Have we done something wrong or sinned
against him?"
¹¹ Then tell them I have said:

People of Judah, your ancestors turned
away from me; they rejected my laws and
teachings and started worshipping other
gods. ¹² And you have done even worse!
You are stubborn, and instead of obeying
me, you do whatever evil comes to your
mind. ¹³ So I will throw you into a land
that you and your ancestors know nothing
about, a place where you will have to
worship other gods both day and night.
And I won't feel the least bit sorry for you.
¹⁴ A time will come when you will again
worship me. But you will no longer call me
the Living God who rescued Israel from
Egypt. ¹⁵ Instead, you will call me the
Living God who rescued you from that
country in the north and from the other
countries where I had forced you to go.
Some day I will bring you back to this
land that I gave your ancestors. ¹⁶ But for
now, I am sending enemies who will catch
you like fish and hunt you down like wild
animals in the hills and the caves.
¹⁷ I can see everything you are doing,
even if you try to hide your sins from me.
¹⁸ I will punish you double for your sins,
because you have made my own land
disgusting. You have filled it with lifeless
idols that remind me of dead bodies.

The LORD gives strength

I prayed to the LORD:

¹⁹ Our LORD, you are the one
    who gives me strength
    and protects me like a fortress
    when I am in trouble.
People will come to you
    from distant nations and say,
"Our ancestors worshipped
    false and useless gods,
²⁰ worthless idols
    made by human hands."

---

*16.4 bury them: See the note at 14.16.
*16.6 mourn and show their sorrow by cutting
themselves or shaving their heads: A custom in
some Canaanite religions.

See also: 16.9: Jer 7.34; 25.10; Rev 18.23.

21 Then the LORD replied,
  "That's why I will teach them
    about my power,
  and they will know
    that I am the true God."

CHAPTER 17

The LORD will punish Judah

The LORD said:

1 People of Judah,
    your sins cannot be erased.
  They are written on your hearts
    like words chiselled in stone
  or carved on the corners
    of your altars.*
2-3 One generation after another
    has set up pagan altars
  and worshipped the goddess Asherah
    everywhere in your country —
    on hills and mountains,
    and under large trees.
  So I'll take everything you own,
    including your altars,
    and give it all to your enemies.▸
4 You will lose▸ the land
    that I gave you,
  and I will make you slaves
    in a foreign country,
  because you have made my anger
    blaze up like a fire
    that won't stop burning.

Trust the LORD

The LORD said:

5 I, the LORD, have put a curse
    on those who turn from me
    and trust in human strength.
6 They will dry up like a bush
    in salty desert soil,
    where nothing can grow.

7 But I will bless those who trust me.
8 They will be like trees
    growing beside a stream —
  trees with roots that reach
    down to the water,
  and with leaves
    that are always green.

They bear fruit every year
  and are never worried
    by a lack of rain.
9 You people of Judah
    are so deceitful
  that you even fool yourselves,
    and you can't change.
10 But I know your deeds
    and your thoughts,
  and I will make sure
    you get what you deserve.
11 You cheated others,
    but everything you gained
  will fly away, like birds
    hatched from stolen eggs.
  Then you will discover
    what fools you are.

Jeremiah prays to the LORD

12 Our LORD, your temple
    is a glorious throne
  that has stood on a mountain
    from the beginning.
13 You are a spring of water
    giving Israel life and hope.
  But if the people reject
    what you have told me,
  they will be swept away
    like words written in dust.▸
14 You, LORD, are the one I praise.
    So heal me and rescue me!
  Then I will be completely well
    and perfectly safe.

15 The people of Judah say to me,
    "Jeremiah, you claimed to tell us
  what the LORD has said.
  So why hasn't it come true?"

16 Our LORD, you chose me
    to care for your people,
    and that's what I have done.
  You know everything I have said,
    and I have never once
    asked you to punish them.▸
17 I trust you for protection
    in times of trouble,
    so don't frighten me.
18 Keep me from failure
    and disgrace,
  but make my enemies fail
    and be disgraced.
  Send destruction to make
    their worst fears come true.

---

*17.1 carved on the corners of your altars:** When
sacrifices were offered to the LORD to ask him to forgive
sins, some of the blood was smeared on the corners of
the altar (see Leviticus 4.7,16–35; 16.18). But now the
LORD refuses to accept these sacrifices.
See also: 17.8: Psa 1.3.

See also: 17.10: a Rev 2.23; b Psa 62.12.

Resting on the Sabbath

¹⁹⁻²⁰ The LORD said:

Jeremiah, stand at each city gate in Jerusalem, including the one the king uses, and speak to him and everyone else. Tell them I have said:

I am the LORD, so pay attention. ²¹⁻²⁴ If you value your lives, don't do any work on the Sabbath. Don't carry anything through the city gates or through the door of your house, or anywhere else. Keep the Sabbath day sacred!

I gave this command to your ancestors, but they were stubborn and refused to obey or to be corrected. But if you obey, ²⁵ then Judah and Jerusalem will always be ruled by kings from David's family. The king and his officials will ride through these gates on horses or in chariots, and the people of Judah and Jerusalem will be with them. There will always be people living in Jerusalem, ²⁶ and others will come here from the nearby villages, from the towns of Judah and Benjamin,* from the hill country and the foothills to the west, and from the Southern Desert. They will bring sacrifices to please me and to give me thanks,* as well as offerings of grain and incense.

²⁷ But if you keep on carrying things through the city gates on the Sabbath and keep treating it as any other day, I will set fire to these gates and burn down the whole city, including the fortresses.

CHAPTER 18

Jeremiah goes to the pottery shop

¹ The LORD told me, ² "Go to the pottery shop, and when you get there, I will tell you what to say to the people."

³ I went there and saw the potter making clay pots on his pottery wheel. ⁴ And whenever the clay would not take the shape he wanted, he would change his mind and form it into some other shape.

⁵ Then the LORD told me to say:

⁶ People of Israel, I, the LORD, have power over you, just as a potter has power over clay. ⁷ If I threaten to uproot and shatter an evil nation ⁸ and that nation turns from its evil, I will change my mind.

⁹ If I promise to make a nation strong, ¹⁰ but its people start disobeying me and doing evil, then I will change my mind and not help them at all.

¹¹ So listen to me, people of Judah and Jerusalem! I have decided to strike you with disaster, and I won't change my mind unless you stop sinning and start living right.

¹² But I know you won't listen. You might as well answer, "We don't care what you say. We have made plans to sin, and we are going to be stubborn and do what we want!"

¹³ So I, the LORD, command you to ask the nations, and find out if they have ever heard of such a horrible sin as what you have done.

¹⁴ The snow on Lebanon's mountains
    never melts away,
and the streams there
    never run dry.*
¹⁵ But you, my people,
    have turned from me
to burn incense to worthless idols.
You have left the ancient road
    to follow an unknown path
    where you stumble over idols.

¹⁶ Your land will be ruined,
    and every passer-by
will look at it with horror
    and make insulting remarks.
¹⁷ When your enemies attack,
    I will scatter you like dust
    blown by an eastern wind.
Then, on that day of disaster,
    I will turn my back on you.

The plot against Jeremiah

¹⁸ Some of the people said, "Let's get rid of Jeremiah! We will always have priests to teach us God's laws, as well as wise people to give us advice, and prophets to speak the LORD's messages. So, instead of listening to Jeremiah any longer, let's accuse him of a crime."

Jeremiah prays about his enemies

¹⁹ Please, LORD, answer my prayer.
    Make my enemies stop
        accusing me of evil.
²⁰ I tried to help them,
    but they are paying me back
        by digging a pit to trap me.
    I even begged you
        not to punish them.

---

*17.26 Judah and Benjamin: These two tribes made up the southern kingdom of Judah.
*17.26 sacrifices to please me and to give me thanks: See the notes at 14.12.
See also: 17.21: Neh 13.15–22. 17.22: Exod 20.8–10; Deut 5.12–14.

21 But now I am asking you
  to let their children starve
    or be killed in war.
  Let women lose
  their husbands and sons
    to disease and violence.
22 These people have dug pits
    and set traps for me, LORD.
  Make them scream in fear
  when you send enemy troops
    to attack their homes.
23 You know they plan to kill me.
  So get angry and punish them!
  Don't ever forgive
    their terrible crimes.

CHAPTER 19

Jeremiah and the clay jar

1 The LORD said:

Jeremiah, go to the pottery shop and buy a clay jar. Then take along some of the city officials and leading priests 2 and go to Hinnom Valley, just outside Potsherd* Gate. Tell the people that I have said:

3 I am the LORD All-Powerful, the God of Israel, and you kings of Judah and you people of Jerusalem had better pay attention. I am going to bring so much trouble on this valley that everyone who hears about it will be shocked. 4-5 The people of Judah stopped worshipping me and made this valley into a place of worship for Baal and other gods that have never helped them or their ancestors or their kings. And they have committed murder here, burning their young, innocent children as sacrifices to Baal. I have never even thought of telling you to do that. 6 So watch out! Some day this place will no longer be called Topheth or Hinnom Valley. It will be called Slaughter Valley!

7 You people of Judah and Jerusalem may have big plans, but here in this valley I'll ruin* those plans. I'll let your enemies kill you, and I'll tell the birds and wild animals to eat your dead bodies. 8 I will turn Jerusalem into a pile of rubble, and every passer-by will be shocked and horrified and will make insulting remarks. 9 And while your enemies are trying to break through

your city walls to kill you, the food supply will run out. You will become so hungry that you will eat the flesh of your friends and even of your own children.

10 Jeremiah, as soon as you have said this, smash the jar while the people are watching. 11 Then tell them that I have also said:

I am the LORD All-Powerful, and I warn you that I will shatter Judah and Jerusalem just like this jar that is broken beyond repair. You will bury your dead here in Topheth, but so many of you will die that there won't be enough room.

12-13 I will make Jerusalem as unclean as Topheth, by filling the city with your dead bodies. I will do this because you and your kings have gone up to the roofs of your houses and burnt incense to the stars in the sky, as though they were gods. And you have given sacrifices of wine to foreign gods.

Jeremiah speaks in the temple courtyard

14 I went to Topheth, where I told the people what the LORD had said. Then I went to the temple courtyard and shouted to the people, 15 "Listen, everyone! Some time ago, the LORD All-Powerful, the God of Israel, warned you that he would bring disaster on Jerusalem and all nearby villages. But you were stubborn and refused to listen. Now the LORD is going to bring the disaster he promised."

CHAPTER 20

Pashhur arrests Jeremiah

1 Pashhur son of Immer was a priest and the chief of temple security. He heard what I had said, 2 and so he hit me.‣ Then he had me arrested and put in chains‣ at the Benjamin Gate in the LORD's temple.* 3 The next day, when Pashhur let me go free, I told him that the LORD had said:

No longer will I call you Pashhur. Instead, I will call you Afraid-of-Everything.‣ 4 You will be afraid, and you will bring fear to your friends as well. You will see enemies kill them in battle. Then I will make the king of Babylonia take everyone in Judah prisoner, killing some and dragging the rest away to Babylonia. 5 He will clean out

---

*19.2 Potsherd: A piece of broken pottery.
*19.7 ruin: In Hebrew "ruin" sounds like "jar" (see verse 1).
See also: 19.2: 2 King 23.10; Jer 7.30–32; 32.34–35.
19.5: Lev 18.21.

*20.2 the Benjamin Gate in the LORD's temple: The Hebrew text has "the upper Benjamin Gate in the temple"; the lower Benjamin Gate may have been the city gate of that name.

the royal treasury and take everything else of value from Jerusalem.

⁶ Pashhur, you are guilty of telling lies and claiming they were messages from me. That's why I will make the Babylonians take you, your family, and your friends as prisoners to Babylonia, where you will all die and be buried.

Jeremiah complains to the LORD

⁷ You tricked me, LORD,
   and I was really fooled.
You are stronger than I am,
   and you have defeated me.
People never stop sneering
   and insulting me.
⁸ You have let me announce
   only destruction and death.
Your message has brought me
   nothing but insults
   and trouble.
⁹ Sometimes I tell myself
   not to think about you, LORD,
   or even mention your name.
But your message burns
   in my heart and bones,
   and I cannot keep silent.

¹⁰ I heard the crowds whisper,
   "Everyone is afraid.
Now's our chance
   to accuse Jeremiah!"
All of my so-called friends
   are just waiting
   for me to make a mistake.
They say, "Perhaps Jeremiah
   can be tricked.
Then we can overpower him
   and get even at last."

¹¹ But you, LORD,
   are a mighty soldier,
   standing at my side.
Those troublemakers
   will fall down and fail —
   terribly embarrassed,
   for ever ashamed.

¹² LORD All-Powerful,
   you test those who do right,
   and you know every heart
   and mind.
I have told you my complaints,
   so let me watch you
   take revenge on my enemies.

¹³ I sing praises to you, LORD.
   You rescue the oppressed
   from the wicked.

¹⁴ Put a curse on the day I was born!
   Don't bless my mother.
¹⁵ Put a curse on the man
   who told my father, "Good news!
   You have a son."
¹⁶ May that man be like the towns
   you destroyed without pity.
Let him hear shouts of alarm
   in the morning
   and battle cries at midday.
¹⁷ He deserves to die
   for not killing me
   before I was born.
Then my mother's body
   would have been my grave.
¹⁸ Why did I have to be born?
   Was it just to suffer
   and die in shame?

CHAPTER 21

The LORD will fight against Jerusalem

¹ King Zedekiah* of Judah sent for Pashhur son of Malchiah and for a priest named Zephaniah son of Maaseiah. Then he told them, "Talk with Jeremiah for me."

So they came to me and said, ² "King Nebuchadnezzar* of Babylonia has attacked Judah. Please ask the LORD to work miracles for our people, as he has done in the past, so that Nebuchadnezzar will leave us alone."

³⁻⁷ I told them that the LORD God of Israel had told me to say to King Zedekiah:

The Babylonians have surrounded Jerusalem and want to kill you and your people. You are asking me to save you, but you have made me furious. So I will stretch out my mighty arm and fight against you myself. Your army is using spears and swords to fight the Babylonians, but I will make your own weapons turn and attack you. I will send a horrible disease to kill many of the people and animals in Jerusalem, and there will be nothing left to eat. Finally, I will let King Nebuchadnezzar and his army fight their way to the centre of Jerusalem and capture everyone who is left alive, including you and your officials. But Nebuchadnezzar won't be kind or show any mercy — he will have you killed! I, the LORD, have spoken.

---

*21.1 Zedekiah: See the note at 1.3.
*21.2 Nebuchadnezzar: Ruled 605–562 BC.
See also: 20.14–18: Job 3.1–19. 21.2: 2 King 25.1–11; 2 Chron 36.17–21.

8 Then I told them that the LORD had said:

People of Jerusalem, I, the LORD, give you the choice of life or death. 9 The Babylonian army has surrounded Jerusalem, so if you want to live, you must go out and surrender to them. But if you want to die because of hunger, disease, or war, then stay here in the city. 10 I have decided not to rescue Jerusalem. Instead, I am going to let the king of Babylonia burn it to the ground. I, the LORD, have spoken.

The LORD warns the king of Judah

The LORD said:

11-12 Pay attention, you who belong
    to the royal family.
Each new day, make sure
    that justice is done,
and rescue those
    who are being robbed.
Or else my anger will flame up
    like a fire that never goes out.

13 Jerusalem,
    from your mountaintop
you look out over the valleys>
    and think you are safe.
But I, the LORD, am angry,
14 and I will punish you
    as you deserve.
I'll set your palace* on fire,
and everything around you
    will go up in smoke.

CHAPTER 22

The LORD will punish
the king of Judah

1-3 The LORD sent me to the palace of the king of Judah to speak to the king, his officials, and everyone else who was there. The LORD told me to say:

I am the LORD, so pay attention! You have been allowing people to cheat, rob, and take advantage of widows, orphans, and foreigners who live here. Innocent people have become victims of violence, and some of them have even been killed. But now I command you to do what is right and see that justice is done. Rescue everyone who has suffered from injustice.

4 If you obey me, the kings from David's family will continue to rule Judah from this palace. They and their officials will ride in and out on their horses or in their chariots. 5 But if you ignore me, I promise in my own name that this palace will lie in ruins. 6 Listen to what I think about it:

the palace of Judah's king
    is as glorious as Gilead
    or Lebanon's highest peaks.
But it will be as empty
    as a ghost town
    when I'm through with it.
7 I'll send troops to tear it apart,
and its beautiful cedar beams
    will be used for firewood.

8 People from different nations will pass by and ask, "Why did the LORD do this to such a great city as Jerusalem?" 9 Others will answer, "It's because the people worshipped foreign gods and broke the agreement that the LORD their God had made with them."

King Jehoahaz

The LORD said:

10 King Josiah is dead,
    so don't cry for him.*
Instead, cry for his son
    King Jehoahaz,
dragged off to another country,*
    never to return.

11-12 Jehoahaz> became king of Judah after his father King Josiah died. But Jehoahaz was taken as a prisoner to a foreign country. Now I, the LORD, promise that he will die there without ever seeing his own land again.

King Jehoiakim

The LORD told me to say:

13-14 King Jehoiakim,* you are doomed!
    You built a palace
    with large rooms upstairs.

---

*21.14 your palace: The Hebrew text has "the forest"; the largest room in the king's palace was known as Forest Hall (see 1 Kings 7.2-3).

*22.10 King Josiah . . . him: The Hebrew text has "don't cry for the dead one", meaning King Josiah, who ruled 640–609 BC.
*22.10 his son, King Jehoahaz . . . country: The Hebrew text has "the one who was dragged off to another country", meaning King Jehoahaz, who ruled for three months in 609 BC.
*22.13-14 Jehoiakim: See the note at 1.3.
See also: 22.5: Matt 23.28; Luke 13.35.
22.11: 2 King 23.31–34; 2 Chron 36.1–4.

You put in big windows
and used cedar panelling
and red paint.
But you were unfair
and forced the builders to work
without pay.

15-16More cedar in your palace
doesn't make you a better king
than your father Josiah.
He always did right —
he gave justice to the poor
and was honest.
That's what it means
to truly know me.
So he lived a comfortable life
and always had enough
to eat and drink.

17 But all you think about
is how to cheat
or abuse or murder
some innocent victim.
18 Jehoiakim, no one will cry
at your funeral.
They won't turn to each other
and ask,
"Why did our great king have to die?"
19 You will be given a burial
fit for a donkey;
your body will be dragged
outside the city gates
and tossed in the dust.
I, the LORD, have spoken.

King Jehoiachin and the people of Jerusalem

The LORD told me to say:

20 People of Jerusalem,
the nations' you trusted
have been crushed.
Go to Lebanon and weep;
cry in the land of Bashan
and in Moab.
21 When times were good,
I warned you.
But you ignored me,
just as you have done
since Israel was young.
22 Now you will be disgraced
because of your sins.
Your leaders will be swept away
by the wind,
and the nations you trusted
will be captured and dragged
to a foreign country.

23 Those who live in the palace
panelled with cedar*
will groan with pain
like women giving birth.

24 King Jehoiachin,* son of Jehoiakim,*
even if you were the ring I wear as the sign
of my royal power, I would still pull you
from my finger. 25 I would hand you over
to the enemy you fear, to King
Nebuchadnezzar* and his army, who want
to kill you. 26 You and your mother* were
born in Judah, but I will throw both of you
into a foreign country, where you will die,
27 longing to return home.

28 Jehoiachin, you are unwanted
like a broken clay pot.
So you and your children
will be thrown into a country
you know nothing about.

29 Land of Judah, I am the LORD.
Now listen to what I say!
30 Erase the names
of Jehoiachin's children
from the royal records.
He is a complete failure,
and so none of them
will ever be king.
I, the LORD, have spoken.

CHAPTER 23

A message of hope

The LORD said:

1 You leaders of my people are like
shepherds that kill and scatter the sheep.
2 You were supposed to take care of my
people, but instead you chased them away.
So now I'll really take care of you, and
believe me, you will pay for your crimes!
3 I will bring the rest of my people home
from the lands where I have scattered them,
and they will grow into a mighty nation.

22.23 who live in the palace panelled with cedar:
The Hebrew text has "who live in Lebanon and who
nest among the cedars", which probably means
Forest Hall in the royal palace at Jerusalem, which
was panelled with cedar and had cedar columns and
a cedar ceiling, all from Lebanon (see 1 Kings 7.2–3).
22.24 Jehoiachin: The Hebrew text has "Coniah",
another form of Jehoiachin's name; he ruled for three
months in 598 BC.
22.24 Jehoiakim: See the note at 1.3.
22.25 Nebuchadnezzar: See the note at 21.2.
22.26 mother: See the note at 13.18.
See also: 22.24: 2 King 24.8–15; 2 Chron 36.9–10.

See also: 22.18: 2 King 23.36—24.6; 2 Chron 36.5–7.

⁴ I promise to choose leaders who will care for them like real shepherds. All my people will be there, and they will never again be frightened.

⁵ Some day I will appoint
an honest king
from the family of David,
a king who will be wise
and rule with justice.
⁶ As long as he is king,
Israel will have peace,
and Judah will be safe.
The name of this king will be
"The LORD Gives Justice".

⁷ A time will come when you will again worship me. But you will no longer call me the Living God who rescued Israel from Egypt. ⁸ Instead, you will call me the Living God who rescued you from the land in the north and from all the other countries where I had forced you to go. And you will once again live in your own land.

Jeremiah thinks about unfaithful prophets

⁹ When I think of the prophets,
I am shocked, and I tremble⁾
like someone drunk,
because of the LORD
and his sacred words.
¹⁰ Those unfaithful prophets
misuse their power
all over the country.
So God turned the pasture lands
into scorching deserts.⁾

The LORD will punish unfaithful prophets

¹¹ The LORD told me to say:

You prophets and priests
think so little of me, the LORD,
that you even sin
in my own temple!
¹² Now I will punish you with disaster,
and you will slip and fall
in the darkness.
I, the LORD, have spoken.

¹³ The prophets in Samaria
were disgusting to me,
because they preached
in the name of Baal
and led my people astray.

¹⁴ And you prophets in Jerusalem
are even worse.
You're unfaithful in marriage⁾
and never tell the truth.⁾
You even lead others to sin
instead of helping them
turn back to me.
You and the people of Jerusalem
are evil like Sodom and Gomorrah.*
¹⁵ You prophets in Jerusalem
have spread evil everywhere.
That's why I, the LORD, promise
to give you bitter poison
to eat and drink.

The LORD gives a warning

The LORD said:

¹⁶ Don't listen to the lies
of these false prophets,
you people of Judah!
The message they preach
is something they imagined;
it did not come from me,
the LORD All-Powerful.
¹⁷ These prophets go to people
who refuse to respect me
and who are stubborn
and do whatever they want.
The prophets tell them,
"The LORD has promised
everything will be fine."

¹⁸ But I, the LORD, tell you
that these prophets
have never attended a meeting
of my council in heaven*
or heard me speak.
¹⁹ They are evil! So in my anger
I will strike them
like a violent storm.
²⁰ I won't calm down,
until I have finished
what I have decided to do.
Some day you will understand
exactly what I mean.
²¹ I did not send these prophets
or speak to them,
but they ran to find you
and to preach their message.

---

*23.14 Sodom and Gomorrah:** Two cities that the LORD destroyed because their people were so evil (see Genesis 18.16—19.29).
*23.18 a meeting of my council in heaven:** Sometimes, prophets had visions of the LORD meeting with his angels (see 1 Kings 22.19–23).

See also: 23.14: Gen 18.20; Ezek 16.49.

See also: 23.5–6: Jer 33.14–16.

22 If they had been in a meeting
of my council in heaven,
they would have told
you people of Judah
to give up your sins
and come back to me.

23 I am everywhere —
both near and far,
24 in heaven and on earth.
There are no secret places
where you can hide from me.

25 These unfaithful prophets claim that I have given them a dream or a vision, and then they tell lies in my name. 26 But everything they say comes from their own twisted minds. How long can this go on? 27 They tell each other their dreams and try to get my people to reject me, just as their ancestors left me and worshipped Baal. 28 Their dreams and my truth are as different as straw and wheat. But when prophets speak for me, they must say only what I have told them. 29 My words are a powerful fire; they are a hammer that shatters rocks.

30-32 These unfaithful prophets claim I give them their dreams, but it isn't true. I didn't choose them to be my prophets, and yet they babble on and on, speaking in my name, while stealing words from each other. And when my people hear these liars, they are led astray instead of being helped. So I warn you that I am now the enemy of these prophets. I, the LORD, have spoken.

News and nuisance

The LORD said to me:

33 Jeremiah, when a prophet or a priest or anyone else comes to you and asks, "Does the LORD have news for us?" tell them, "You people are a nuisance* to the LORD, and he' will get rid of you." 34 If any of you say, "Here is news from the LORD," I will punish you and your families, even if you are a prophet or a priest. 35 Instead, you must ask your friends and relatives, "What answer did the LORD give?" or "What has the LORD said?" 36 It seems that you each have your own news! So if you say, "Here is news from the LORD," you are twisting my words into a lie. Remember that I am your God, the LORD All-Powerful.

37 If you go to a prophet, it's all right to ask, "What answer did the LORD give to my question?" or "What has the LORD said?" 38 But if you disobey me and say, "Here is news from the LORD," 39 I will pick you up' and throw you far away. And I will abandon this city of Jerusalem that I gave to your ancestors. 40 You will never be free from your shame and disgrace.

CHAPTER 24

Jeremiah has a vision of two baskets of figs

1 The LORD spoke to me in a vision after King Nebuchadnezzar* of Babylonia had come to Judah and taken King Jehoiachin,* his officials, and all the skilled workers back to Babylonia. In this vision I saw two baskets of figs in front of the LORD's temple. 2 One basket was full of very good figs that ripened early, and the other was full of rotten figs that were not fit to eat.

3 "Jeremiah," the LORD asked, "what do you see?"

"Figs," I said. "Some are very good, but the others are too rotten to eat."

4 Then the LORD told me to say:

5 People of Judah, the good figs stand for those of you I sent away as exiles to Babylonia, 6 where I am watching over them. Then some day I will bring them back to this land. I will plant them, instead of uprooting them, and I will build them up, rather than tearing them down. 7 I will give them a desire to know me and to be my people. They will want me to be their God, and they will turn back to me with all their heart.

8 The rotten figs stand for King Zedekiah* of Judah, his officials, and all the others who were not taken away to Babylonia, whether they stayed here in Judah or went to live in Egypt. 9 I will punish them with a terrible disaster, and everyone on earth will tremble when they hear about it. I will force the people of Judah to go to foreign countries, where they will be cursed and insulted. 10 War and hunger and disease will strike them,

---

23.33 news . . . nuisance: The Hebrew word for "news" in verses 33–38 is the same as "nuisance" and is related to "pick up" in verse 39.

24.1 Nebuchadnezzar: See the note at 21.2.
24.1 Jehoiachin: The Hebrew text has "Jeconiah", another form of Jehoiachin's name; he ruled for three months in 598 BC.
24.8 Zedekiah: See the note at 1.3.
See also: 24.1: 2 King 24.12–16; 2 Chron 36.10.

until they finally disappear from the land that I gave them and their ancestors.

CHAPTER 25

Seventy years of exile

1-2 In the fourth year that Jehoiakim was king of Judah,* which was the first year that Nebuchadnezzar* was king of Babylonia, the LORD told me to speak to the people of Judah and Jerusalem. So I told them:

3 For twenty-three years now, ever since the thirteenth year that Josiah* was king, I have been telling you what the LORD has told me. But you have not listened.

4 The LORD has sent prophets to you time after time, but you refused to listen. 5 They told you that the LORD had said:

Change your ways! If you stop doing evil, I will let you stay for ever in this land that I gave your ancestors. 6 I don't want to harm you. So don't make me angry by worshipping idols and other gods.

7 But you refused to listen to my prophets. So I, the LORD, say that you have made me angry by worshipping idols, and you are the ones who were hurt by what you did. 8 You refused to listen to me, 9 and now I will let you be attacked by nations from the north, and especially by my servant, King Nebuchadnezzar of Babylonia. You and other nearby nations will be destroyed and left in ruins for ever. Everyone who sees what has happened will be shocked, but they will still make fun of you. 10 I will put an end to your parties and wedding celebrations; no one will grind grain or be here to light the lamps at night. 11 This country will be as empty as a desert, because I will make all of you the slaves of the king of Babylonia for seventy years.

12 When that time is up, I will punish the king of Babylonia and his people for everything they have done wrong, and I will turn that country into a wasteland for ever. 13 My servant Jeremiah has told you what I said I will do to Babylonia and to the other nations, and he wrote it all down in this book. I will do everything I

threatened. 14 I will pay back the Babylonians for every wrong they have done. Great kings from many other nations will conquer the Babylonians and force them to be slaves.

The cup full of God's anger

15 The LORD God of Israel showed me a vision in which he said, "Jeremiah, here is a cup filled with the wine of my anger. Take it and make every nation drink some. 16 They will vomit and act mad, because of the war this cup of anger will bring to them."

17 I took the cup from the LORD's hand, and I went to the kings of the nations and made each of them drink some. 18 I started with Jerusalem and the towns of Judah, and the king and his officials were removed from power in disgrace. Everyone still makes insulting jokes about them and uses their names as curse words. 19 The second place I went was Egypt, where everyone had to drink from the cup, including the king and his officials, the other government workers, the rest of the Egyptians, 20 and all the foreigners who lived in the country.

Next I went to the king of Uz, and then to the four kings of Philistia, who ruled from Ashkelon, Gaza, Ekron, and what was left of Ashdod.* 21 Then I went to the kings of Edom, Moab, Ammon, 22 and to the kings of Tyre, Sidon, and their colonies across the sea. 23-24 After this, I went to the kings of Dedan, Tema, Buz, the tribes of the Arabian Desert,⟩ 25 Zimri, Elam, Media, 26 and the countries in the north, both near and far.

I went to all the countries on earth, one after another, and finally to Babylonia.⟩

27 The LORD had said I must tell each king, "The LORD All-Powerful, the God of Israel, commands you to drink from this cup that is full of the wine of his anger. It will make you so drunk that you will vomit. And when the LORD sends war against the nations, you will be completely defeated."

28 The LORD told me that if any of them refused to drink from the cup, I must tell them that he had said, "I, the LORD All-Powerful, command you to drink. 29 Starting with my own city of Jerusalem, everyone on earth will suffer from war. So there is no way I will let you escape unharmed."

30 The LORD told me to say:

---

*25.1–2 Jehoiakim . . . Judah: See the note at 1.3.
*25.1–2 Nebuchadnezzar: See the note at 21.2.
*25.3 Josiah: Hebrew "Josiah son of Amon"; see also the note at 1.2.

See also: 25.1: 2 King 24.1; 2 Chron 36.5–7; Dan 1.–,2.
25.10: a Jer 7.34; 16.9; b Rev 18.22–23.
25.11: 2 Chron 36.21; Jer 29.10; Dan 9.2.

*25.20 what was left of Ashdod: It was defeated by the king of Egypt after being surrounded for twenty-nine years.

From my sacred temple
I will roar like thunder,
while I trample my people
and everyone else
as though they were grapes.
31 My voice will be heard
everywhere on earth,
accusing nations of their crimes
and sentencing the guilty
to death.

Disaster is coming

32 The LORD All-Powerful says:

You can see disaster spreading
from far across the earth,
from nation to nation
like a horrible storm.

33 When it strikes, I will kill so many people
that their bodies will cover the ground like
manure. No one will be left to bury them*
or to mourn.

The leaders of Judah will be punished

34 The LORD's people are his flock,
and you leaders
were the shepherds.
But now it's your turn
to be butchered like sheep.
You'll shatter like fine pottery
dropped on the floor.'
So roll on the ground,
crying and mourning.
35 You have nowhere to run,
nowhere to hide.

36-38Listen to the cries
of the shepherds,
as the LORD's burning anger
turns' peaceful meadows
into barren deserts.
The LORD has abandoned
his people'
like a lion leaving its den.

CHAPTER 26

Jeremiah's message in the temple

This is also told in Jeremiah 7.1–15.

1 Soon after Jehoiakim* became king of
Judah, the LORD said:

2 Jeremiah, I have a message for everyone
who comes from the towns of Judah to
worship in my temple. Go to the temple
courtyard and speak every word that I tell
you. 3 Perhaps the people will listen this
time. And if they stop doing wrong, I will
change my mind and not punish them for
their sins. 4 Tell them that I have said:

You have refused to listen to me and to
obey my laws and teachings. 5 Again and
again I have sent my servants the prophets
to preach to you, but you ignored them as
well. Now I am warning you that if you
don't start obeying me straight away,
6 I will destroy this temple, just as I
destroyed the town of Shiloh.* Then
everyone on earth will use the name
"Jerusalem" as a curse word.

Jeremiah on trial

7 The prophets, the priests, and everyone else
in the temple heard what I said, 8-9 and as
soon as I finished, they all crowded around
me and started shouting, "Why did you
preach that the LORD will destroy this temple,
just as he destroyed Shiloh*? Why did you
say that Jerusalem will be empty and lie in
ruins? You ought to be put to death for
saying such things in the LORD's name!"
Then they had me arrested.
10 The royal officers heard what had
happened, and they came from the palace to
the new gate of the temple to be the judges at
my trial.* 11 While they listened, the priests
and the prophets said to the crowd, "All of
you have heard Jeremiah prophesy that
Jerusalem will be destroyed. He deserves the
death penalty."
12-13 Then I told the judges and everyone
else:

The LORD himself sent me to tell you about
the terrible things he will do to you, to
Jerusalem, and to the temple. But if you
change your ways and start obeying the
LORD, he will change his mind.
14 You must decide what to do with me.
Just do whatever you think is right. 15 But if
you put me to death, you and everyone
else in Jerusalem will be guilty of

*26.6,8–9 Shiloh: The sacred tent had once stood at
Shiloh.
*26.10 new gate . . . trial: Public trials were often
held in an open area at a gate of a city, palace, or
temple.
See also: 26.6: Josh 18.1; Psa 78.60; Jer 7.12–14.

*25.33 bury them: See the note at 14.16.
*26.1 Jehoiakim: See the note at 1.3.
See also: 26.1: 2 King 23.36—24.6; 2 Chron 36.5–7.

murdering an innocent man, because everything I preached came from the LORD."

¹⁶ The judges and the other people told the priests and prophets, "Since Jeremiah only told us what the LORD our God had said, we don't think he deserves to die."

¹⁷ Then some of the leaders from other towns stepped forward. They told the crowd that ¹⁸ years ago when Hezekiah* was king of Judah, a prophet named Micah from the town of Moresheth had said:

"I, the LORD All-Powerful, say
Jerusalem will be ploughed under
   and left in ruins.
Thorns will cover the mountain
   where the temple
   now stands."*

¹⁹ Then the leaders continued:

No one put Micah to death for saying that. Instead, King Hezekiah prayed to the LORD with fear and trembling and asked him to have mercy. Then the LORD decided not to destroy Jerusalem, even though he had already said he would.

People of Judah, if Jeremiah is killed, we will bring a terrible disaster on ourselves.

²⁰⁻²⁴ After these leaders finished speaking, an important man named Ahikam son of Shaphan spoke up for me as well. And so, I wasn't handed over to the crowd to be killed.

Uriah the prophet

While Jehoiakim* was still king of Judah, a man named Uriah son of Shemaiah left his home town of Kiriath-Jearim and came to Jerusalem. Uriah was one of the LORD's prophets, and he was saying the same things about Judah and Jerusalem that I had been saying. And when Jehoiakim and his officials and military officers heard what Uriah said, they tried to arrest him, but he escaped to Egypt. So Jehoiakim sent Elnathan son of Achbor and some other men after Uriah, and they brought him back. Then Jehoiakim had Uriah killed and his body dumped in a common burial pit.

Jeremiah against the lying prophets

CHAPTER 27

Slaves of Nebuchadnezzar

¹⁻² Not long after Zedekiah became king of Judah,' the LORD told me:

Jeremiah, make a wooden yoke* with leather straps, and place it on your neck. ³ Then send a message to the kings of Edom, Moab, Ammon, Tyre, and Sidon. Some officials from these countries are in Jerusalem, meeting with Zedekiah. ⁴ So order them to tell their kings that I have said:

I am the All-Powerful LORD God of Israel, ⁵ and with my power I created the earth, its people, and all animals. I decide who will rule the earth, ⁶⁻⁷ and I have chosen my servant King Nebuchadnezzar* of Babylonia to rule all nations, including yours. I will even let him rule the wild animals. All nations will be slaves of Nebuchadnezzar, his son, and his grandson. Then many nations will join together, and their kings will be powerful enough to make slaves of the Babylonians.

⁸ This yoke stands for the power of King Nebuchadnezzar, and I will destroy any nation that refuses to obey him. Nebuchadnezzar will attack, and many will die in battle or from hunger and disease. ⁹ You might have people in your kingdom who claim they can tell the future by magic or by talking with the dead or by dreams or messages from a god. But don't pay attention if any of them tell you not to obey Nebuchadnezzar. ¹⁰ If you listen to such lies, I will have you dragged far from your country and killed. ¹¹ But if you and your nation are willing to obey Nebuchadnezzar, I will let you stay in your country, and your people will continue to live and work on their farms.

¹² After I had spoken to the officials from the nearby kingdoms, I went to King Zedekiah and told him the same thing. Then I said:

Zedekiah, if you and the people of Judah want to stay alive, you must obey

---

*26.18 Hezekiah:** Ruled 716–687 BC.
*26.18 Jerusalem . . . stands:** See Micah 3.12.
*26.20–24 Jehoiakim:** See the note at 1.3.
See also: 26.18: Mic 3.12.

*27.1–2 yoke:** A wooden collar that fits around the neck of an ox, so the ox can be made to pull a plough or a cart.
*27.6–7 Nebuchadnezzar:** See the note at 21.2.
See also: 27.1: 2 King 24.18–20; 2 Chron 36.11–13.

Nebuchadnezzar and the Babylonians.
[13] But if you refuse, then you and your people will die from war, hunger, and disease, just as the LORD has warned. [14] Your prophets have told you that you don't need to obey Nebuchadnezzar, but don't listen to their lies. [15] Those prophets claim to be speaking for the LORD, but he didn't send them. They are lying! If you do what they say, he will have both you and them dragged off to another country and killed. The LORD has spoken.

[16] When I finished talking to the king, I went to the priests and told them that the LORD had said:

Don't listen to the prophets when they say that very soon the Babylonians will return the things they took from my temple. Those prophets are lying! [17] If you choose to obey the king of Babylonia, you will live. But if you listen to those prophets, this whole city will be nothing but a pile of rubble.

[18] If I really had spoken to those prophets, they would know what I am going to do. Then they would be begging me not to let everything else be taken from the temple and the king's palace and the rest of Jerusalem. [19-21] After all, when Nebuchadnezzar took King Jehoiachin* to Babylonia as a prisoner, he didn't take everything of value from Jerusalem. He left the bronze pillars, the huge bronze bowl called the Sea, and the moveable bronze stands in the temple, and he left a lot of other valuable things in the palace and in the rest of Jerusalem.

But now I, the LORD All-Powerful, the God of Israel, say that all these things [22] will be taken to Babylonia, where they will remain until I decide to bring them back to Jerusalem. I, the LORD, have spoken.

CHAPTER 28

Jeremiah accuses Hananiah of being a false prophet

[1] Later that same year, in the fifth month of the fourth year that Zedekiah* was king,' the prophet Hananiah son of Azzur from Gibeon came up to me in the temple. And while the priests and others in the temple were listening, [2] he told me that the LORD had said:

I am the LORD All-Powerful, the God of Israel, and I will smash the yoke* that Nebuchadnezzar* put on the necks of the nations to make them his slaves. [3] And within two years, I will bring back to Jerusalem everything that he took from my temple and carried off to Babylonia. [4] King Jehoiachin* and the other people who were taken from Judah to Babylonia will be allowed to come back here as well. All this will happen because I will smash the power of the king of Babylonia!

[5] The priests and the others were still standing there, so I said:

[6] Hananiah, I hope the LORD will do exactly what you said. I hope he does bring back everything the Babylonians took from the temple, and that our people who were taken to Babylonia will be allowed to return home. [7] But let me remind you and everyone else [8] that long before we were born, prophets were saying powerful kingdoms would be struck by war, disaster, and disease. [9] Now you are saying we will have peace. We will just have to wait and see if that is really what the LORD has said.*

[10] Hananiah grabbed the wooden yoke from my neck and smashed it. [11] Then he said, "The LORD says this is the way he will smash the power Nebuchadnezzar has over the nations, and it will happen in less than two years."

I left the temple, [12] and a little while later, the LORD told me [13-14] to go back and say to Hananiah:

I am the LORD All-Powerful, the God of Israel. You smashed a wooden yoke, but I will replace it with one made of iron. I will put iron yokes on all the nations, and they will have to do what King Nebuchadnezzar commands. I will even let him rule the wild animals.

[15-16] Hananiah, I have never sent you to speak for me. And yet you have talked my people into believing your lies and rebelling against me. So now I will send

---

*27.19-21 Jehoiachin: Hebrew "Jeconiah" (see the note at 24.1).
*28.1 Zedekiah: See the note at 1.3.
See also: 28.1: 2 King 24.18-20; 2 Chron 36.11-13.

*28.2 yoke: See the note at 27.1-2.
*28.2 Nebuchadnezzar: See the note at 21.2.
*28.4 Jehoiachin: Hebrew "Jeconiah" (see the note at 24.1).
*28.9 We will . . . said: See Deuteronomy 18.21-22.

835

you — I'll send you right off the face of the earth! You will die before this year is over.

[17] Two months later, Hananiah died.

CHAPTER 29

Jeremiah's letter to the people of Judah in Babylonia

[1-2] I had been left in Jerusalem when King Nebuchadnezzar* took many of the people of Jerusalem and Judah to Babylonia as prisoners, including King Jehoiachin,* his mother, his officials, and the metal workers and others in Jerusalem who were skilled in making things. So I wrote a letter to the prophets, the priests, the leaders, and the rest of our people in Babylonia. [3] I gave the letter to Elasah and Gemariah,ᵇ two men that King Zedekiah* of Judah was sending to Babylon to talk with Nebuchadnezzar. In the letter, I wrote [4] that the LORD All-Powerful, the God of Israel, had said:

> I had you taken from Jerusalem to Babylonia. Now I tell you [5] to settle there and build houses. Plant gardens and eat what you grow in them. [6] Get married and have children, then help your sons find wives and help your daughters find husbands, so they can have children as well. I want your numbers to grow, not to get smaller.
>
> [7] Pray for peace in Babylonia and work hard to make it prosperous. The more successful that nation is, the better off you will be.
>
> [8-9] Some of your people there in Babylonia are fortune-tellers, and you have asked them to tell you what will happen in the future. But they will only lead you astray. And don't let the prophets fool you, either. They speak in my name, but they are liars. I have not spoken to them.
>
> [10] After Babylonia has been the strongest nation for seventy years, I will be kind and bring you back to Jerusalem, just as I have promised. [11] I will bless you with a future filled with hope — a future of success, not of suffering. [12] You will turn back to me and ask for help, and I will answer your prayers. [13] You will worship me with all your heart,

and I will be with you [14] and accept your worship. Then I will gather you from all the nations where I scattered you, and you will return to Jerusalem.

> [15] You feel secure, because you think I have sent prophets to speak for me in Babylonia.
>
> [16-19] But I have been sending prophets to the people of Judah for a long time, and the king from David's family and the people who are left in Jerusalem and Judah still don't obey me. So I, the LORD All-Powerful, will keep attacking them with war and hunger and disease, until they are as useless as rotten figs. I will force them to leave the land, and all nations will be disgusted and shocked at what happens to them. The nations will sneer and make fun of them and use the names "Judah" and "Jerusalem" as curse words.
>
> And you have not obeyed me, even though [20] I had you taken from Jerusalem to Babylonia. But you had better listen to me now. [21-23] You think Ahab son of Kolaiah and Zedekiah son of Maaseiah are prophets because they claim to speak for me. But they are lying! I haven't told them anything. They are also committing other horrible sins in your community, such as sleeping with the wives of their friends. So I will hand them over to King Nebuchadnezzar, who will put them to death while the rest of you watch. And in the future, when you want to put a curse on someone, you will say, "I pray that the LORD will kill you in the same way the king of Babylonia burnt Zedekiah and Ahab to death!"

A message for Shemaiah

[24-25] The LORD All-Powerful, the God of Israel, told me what would happen to Shemaiah,ᵇ who was one of our people in Babylonia. After my letter reached Babylonia, Shemaiah wrote letters to the people of Jerusalem, including the priest Zephaniah son of Maaseiah, and the other priests. The letter to Zephaniah said:

> [26] After the death of Jehoiada the priest, the LORD chose you to be the priest in charge of the temple security force. You know that anyone who acts mad and pretends to be a prophet should be arrested and put in chainsᵇ and iron collars. [27] Jeremiah from the town of Anathoth is pretending to be a prophet there in Jerusalem, so why haven't you punished him? [28] He even wrote a letter to the people here in Babylonia, saying we

---

*29.1-2 **Nebuchadnezzar:** See the note at 21.2.
*29.1-2 **Jehoiachin:** Hebrew "Jeconiah" (see the note at 24.1).
*29.3 **Zedekiah:** See the note at 1.3.
See also: 29.1-2: 2 King 24.12-16; 2 Chron 36.10.
29.10: 2 Chron 36.21; Jer 25.11; Dan 9.2.   29.13: Deut 4.29.

would be here a long time. He told us to build homes and to plant gardens and grow our own food.

29 When Zephaniah received Shemaiah's letter, he read it to me. 30 Then the LORD told me what to write in a second letter 31 to the people of Judah who had been taken to Babylonia. In this letter, I wrote that the LORD had said:

I, the LORD, have not chosen Shemaiah to be one of my prophets, and he has misled you by telling lies in my name. 32 He has even talked you into disobeying me. So I will punish Shemaiah. He and his descendants won't live to see the good things I will do for my people. I, the LORD, have spoken.

God will some day bring his people back to their land

CHAPTER 30

The LORD will rescue Israel and Judah

1-2 The LORD God of Israel said, "Jeremiah, get a scroll* and write down everything I have told you. 3 Some day I will let my people from both Israel* and Judah return to the land I gave their ancestors."

4-5 Then the LORD told me to say to Israel and Judah:

I, the LORD, hear screams
of terror,
    and there is no peace.
6 Can men give birth?
Then why do I see them
    looking so pale
and clutching their stomachs
    like women in labour?
7 My people, soon you will suffer
worse than ever before,
    but I will save you.

8 Now you are slaves of other nations,
but I will break the chains
and smash the yokes*
    that keep you in slavery.
9 Then you will be my servants,
and I will choose a king for you
    from the family of David.

---

*30.1–2 scroll: A roll of paper or special leather used for writing on.
*30.3 Israel: The northern kingdom.
*30.8 yokes: See the note at 27.1–2.

Helpline

Help! I feel like I've failed

'I didn't get the grades. I broke up with someone I really liked. I tried to give up smoking. I keep doing that same old sin...'

The question is not, 'will I fail?' Of course you will. The question is 'how will you deal with it?' We can let failure cripple us. We can let it fester within us, gnaw away at our confidence, stop us from ever trying again. Or we can pick ourselves up and start again.

The Bible is full of failures. David slept with another woman and had her husband killed. Peter denied ever knowing Jesus. The entire nation of Israel failed God and saw their city destroyed (Jeremiah 30.18). But they all found they could restore their relationship with God. Because God is a God of second chances (and third chances. And fourth chances. And fifth and sixth and... well, you get the idea). Bring your failures to him. Let him rebuild you. As Jeremiah wrote, 'It will be just like old times' (Jeremiah 30.20–22).

Three things

Admit

Be honest and humble about your failure – don't try to pretend it never happened. Instead, own up to it. Apologise if necessary. Show the people involved what you're doing to make the situation right. Use it as a springboard to a new relationship with God.

Learn

Look at the failure honestly and openly. Talk it through with others. What can you learn from it? Is God speaking through it? How can you avoid making the same mistake in the future?

Trust

Believe that God loves you. Confess to him. Give over your failures to him. Let him comfort you.

More...

Forgiveness p.614
David p.314
Saying sorry p.1258

10-11 Israel,* you belong to me,
    so don't be afraid.
You deserved to be punished;
    that's why I scattered you
    in distant nations.
But I am with you,
    and some day I will destroy
    those nations.
Then I will bring you
    and your descendants
    back to your land,
    where I will protect you
    and give you peace.
Then your fears will be gone.
    I, the LORD, have spoken.

The LORD will heal Israel and Judah

12 The LORD said:

My people, you are wounded
    and near death.
13 You are accused of a crime
    with no one to defend you,
    and you are covered with sores
    that no medicine can cure.
14-15 Your friends have forgotten you;
    they don't care any more.
Even I have acted like an enemy.
    And because your sins
    are horrible and countless,
I will be cruel
    as I punish you.
So don't bother to cry out
    for relief from your pain.

16 But if your enemies try to rob
    or destroy you,
I will rob and destroy them,
    and they will be led as captives
    to foreign lands.
17 No one wants you as a friend
    or cares what happens to you.
But I will heal your injuries,
    and you will get well.

The LORD will rescue Israel and Judah

18 The LORD said:

Israel, I will be kind to you
    and let you come home.
Jerusalem now lies in ruins,
    but you will rebuild it,
    complete with a new palace.›

19 Other nations will respect
    and honour you.
Your homes will be filled
    with children,
    and you will celebrate,
    singing praises to me.
20 It will be just like old times.
Your nation will worship me,
    and I will punish anyone
    who abuses you.
21 One of your own people
    will become your ruler.
And when I invite him
    to come near me
    at the place of worship,
    he will do so.
No one would dare to come near
    without being invited.
22 You will be my people,
    and I will be your God.
    I, the LORD, have spoken.

23 I am furious!
And like a violent storm
    I will strike those
    who do wrong.
24 I won't calm down
    until I have finished
    what I have decided to do.
Some day, you will understand
    what I mean.

CHAPTER 31

Israel will return to God

1 The LORD said:

Israel, I promise
    that some day all your tribes
    will again be my people,
    and I will be your God.
2 In the desert I was kind
    to those who escaped death.
I gave them peace,
    and when the time is right,
    I'll do the same for you.›
    I, the LORD, have spoken.

The LORD will rebuild Israel

3 Some time ago, the LORD appeared to me›
and told me to say:

Israel, I will always love you;
    that's why I've been so patient and kind.
4 You are precious to me,
    and so I will rebuild your nation.
Once again you will dance for joy
    and play your tambourines.

---

*30.10–11 Israel: The people of the northern and
southern kingdoms.
See also: 30.10–11: Jer 46.27–28.

⁵ You will plant vineyards
   on the hills of Samaria
   and enjoy the grapes.
⁶ Some day those who guard
   the hill country of Ephraim
   will shout, "Let's go to Zion
   and worship the LORD our God."

Israel will return to its own land

⁷ The LORD says:

Celebrate and sing for Israel,
   the greatest of nations.
Offer praises and shout,
   "Come and rescue
   your people, LORD!
Save what's left of Israel."

⁸ I, the LORD, will bring
   my people back from Babylonia▸
   and everywhere else on earth.
The blind and the lame
   will be there.
Expectant mothers
   and women about to give birth
   will come and be part
   of that great crowd.
⁹ They will weep and pray
   as I bring them home.
I will lead them
   to streams of water.
They will walk on a level▸ road
   and not stumble.
I am a father to Israel,▸
   my favourite children.

¹⁰ Listen to me, you nations
   nearby or across the sea.
I scattered the people of Israel,
   but I will gather them again.
I will protect them like a shepherd
   guarding a flock;
¹¹ I will rescue them from enemies
   who could overpower them.
¹² My people will come
   to Mount Zion and celebrate;
   their faces will glow
   because of my blessings.
I'll give them grain, grapes,
   and olive oil,
   as well as sheep and cattle.
Israel will be prosperous
   and grow like a garden
   with plenty of water.
¹³ Young women and young men,
   together with the elderly,
   will celebrate and dance,
   because I will comfort them

and turn their sorrow
   into happiness.
¹⁴ I will bless my people
   with more food
   than they need,
   and the priests will enjoy
   the choice cuts of meat.
I, the LORD, have spoken.

The LORD offers hope

The LORD said:

¹⁵ In Ramah▸ a voice is heard,
   crying and weeping loudly.
Rachel mourns for her children*
   and refuses to be comforted,
   because they are dead.
¹⁶⁻¹⁷ But I, the LORD, tell you
   to dry your tears.
Some day your children
   will come home
   from the enemy's land.
Then all you have done for them
   will be greatly rewarded.
So don't lose hope.
   I, the LORD, have spoken.

¹⁸ The people of Israel▸ moan
   and say to me,
"We were like wild bulls,
   but you, LORD, broke us,
   and we learnt to obey.
You are our God —
   please let us come home.
¹⁹ When we were young,
   we strayed and sinned,
   but then we realized
   what we had done.
We are ashamed and disgraced
   and want to return to you."

²⁰ People of Israel,
   you are my own dear children.
   Don't I love you best of all?
Though I often make threats,
   I want you to be near me,
   so I will have mercy on you.
I, the LORD, have spoken.

²¹ With rock piles and signposts,
   mark the way home,
   my dear people.

31.15 Rachel . . . children: Rachel was one of the wives of Jacob, the ancestor of the nation of Israel. She was the mother of Joseph and Benjamin. Joseph's two sons Ephraim and Manasseh were the ancestors of the leading tribes of the northern kingdom of Israel.
See also: **31.15: a** Gen 35.16–19; **b** Matt 2.18.

It is the same road
by which you left.
22 Will you ever decide
to be faithful?
I will make sure that some day
things will be different,
as different as a woman
protecting a man.'

The Lord will bring Judah home

23 The Lord All-Powerful, the God of Israel,
said:

I promise to set the people of Judah free
and to lead them back to their home
towns. And when I do, they will once again
say,

"We pray that the Lord
will bless his home,
the sacred hill in Jerusalem
where his temple stands."

24 The people will live in Jerusalem and in
the towns of Judah. Some will be farmers,
and others will be shepherds. 25 Those who
feel tired and worn out will find new life
and energy, 26 and when they sleep, they
will wake up refreshed.'
27 Some day, Israel and Judah will be my
field where my people and their livestock
will grow. 28 In the past, I took care to
uproot them, to tear them down, and to
destroy them. But when that day comes,
I will take care to plant them and help
them grow. 29 No longer will anyone go
around saying,

"Sour grapes eaten by parents
leave a sour taste in the mouths
of their children."

30 When that day comes, only those who
eat sour grapes will get the sour taste, and
only those who sin will be put to death.

The new agreement with Israel and Judah

31 The Lord said:

The time will surely come when I will make
a new agreement with the people of Israel
and Judah. 32 It will be different from the
agreement I made with their ancestors
when I led them out of Egypt. Although I
was their God, they broke that agreement.

33 Here is the new agreement that I, the
Lord, will make with the people of Israel:

"I will write my laws
on their hearts and minds.
I will be their God,
and they will be my people.

34 "No longer will they have to teach one
another to obey me. I, the Lord, promise
that all of them will obey me, ordinary
people and rulers alike. I will forgive their
sins and forget the evil things they have
done."

35 I am the Lord All-Powerful.
I command the sun
to give light each day,
the moon and stars
to shine at night,
and ocean waves to roar.
36 I will never forget
to give those commands,
and I will never let Israel
stop being a nation.
I, the Lord, have spoken.

37 Can you measure the heavens?
Can you explore
the depths of the earth?
That's how hard it would be
for me to reject Israel for ever,
even though they have sinned.
I, the Lord, have spoken.

Jerusalem will be rebuilt

38 The Lord said:

Some day, Jerusalem will truly belong to
me. It will be rebuilt with a boundary line
running from Hananel Tower to Corner
Gate. 39 From there, the boundary will go
in a straight line to Gareb Hill, then turn
towards Goah. 40 Even that disgusting
Hinnom Valley* will be sacred to me,
and so will the eastern slopes that go
down from Horse Gate into Kidron
Valley. Jerusalem will never again be
destroyed.

---

*31.40 that disgusting Hinnom Valley: The Hebrew
text has "the whole valley of the dead bodies and of
the fatty ashes", which probably refers to Hinnom
Valley, just south-west of Jerusalem, where human
sacrifices had been offered to foreign gods.
See also: 31.33: Heb 10.16. 31.34: Heb 10.17.

See also: 31.29: Ezek 18.2. 31.31: Matt 26.28; Mark 14.24;
Luke 22.20; 1 Cor 11.25; 2 Cor 3.6. 31.31–34: Heb 8.8–12.

Viewpoints 👁

Get closer to God through his written Word

Contributed by Naomi C

'Here is the new agreement that I, the LORD, will make with the people of Israel. "I will write my laws on their hearts and minds. I will be their God, and they will be my people."'

This verse was part of a big prophecy from Jeremiah to God's chosen people, given thousands of years ago. God promised that times would change – there would be a new covenant, or a new agreement – between him and his people.

Part of that change would be the way that God interacted with his people. Rather than communicating mostly through priests and prophets, God would have a more personal relationship with individuals. Laws would be put into minds, God's word would be etched into people's hearts.

This new covenant was put into place through Jesus, about two thousand years ago. He promises that those who believe in him can become children of God. That's the opportunity to have a really close relationship with the Almighty God! It's a relationship that should change the way we think and the things we place as our top priorities.

So if you're a Christian, God has written his law on our heart. Do you feel like you take God's word around with you? Is the Bible on your mind; do you think about it much? Jesus tells us that the stuff that is on our heart will shape our actions. This verse should encourage us to get into reading the Bible more and to think about what we read. These are the words of the God of the universe in our hearts!

More...

Covenant p.17

CHAPTER 32

Jeremiah buys a field

[1] The LORD spoke to me in the tenth year that Zedekiah* was king of Judah, which was the eighteenth year that Nebuchadnezzar* was king of Babylonia. [2] At that time, the Babylonian army had surrounded Jerusalem, and I was in the prison at the courtyard of the palace guards. [3] Zedekiah had ordered me to be held there because I told everyone that the LORD had said:

I am the LORD, and I am about to let the king of Babylonia conquer Jerusalem.
[4] King Zedekiah will be captured and taken to King Nebuchadnezzar, who will speak with him face to face. [5] Then Zedekiah will be led away to Babylonia, where he will stay until I have finished with him. So, if you people of Judah fight against the Babylonians, you will lose. I, the LORD, have spoken.

[6] Later, when I was in prison, the LORD said:

[7] Jeremiah, your cousin Hanamel, the son of your uncle Shallum, will visit you. He must sell his field near the town of Anathoth, and because you are his nearest relative, you have the right and the responsibility to buy it and keep it in the family.*

[8] Hanamel came, just as the LORD had promised. And he said, "Please buy my field near Anathoth in the territory of the Benjamin tribe. You have the right to buy it, and if you do, it will stay in our family."

The LORD had told me to buy it [9] from Hanamel, and so I did. The price was seventeen pieces of silver, and I weighed out the full amount on a scale. [10-11] I had two copies of the bill of sale written out, each containing all the details of our agreement. Some witnesses and I signed the official copy, which was folded and tied, before being sealed shut with hot wax.* Then I gave Hanamel the silver. [12] And while he, the witnesses, and all the other Jews sitting in the

---

*32.1 Zedekiah: See the note at 1.3.
*32.1 Nebuchadnezzar: See the note at 21.2.
*32.7 you have the right . . . in the family: See Leviticus 25.25–32.
*32.10–11 signed the official copy, which was folded and tied, before being sealed shut with hot wax: The signing was actually done by pressing a carved clay stamp (called a "seal") into the hot wax, leaving the design in the wax.
See also: 32.1: 2 King 25.1–7.

courtyard were still watching, I gave both copies to Baruch son of Neriah.'

¹³⁻¹⁴ I told Baruch that the LORD had said:

Take both copies of this bill of sale, one sealed shut and the other open, and put them in a clay jar so they will last a long time. ¹⁵ I am the LORD All-Powerful, the God of Israel, and I promise you that people will once again buy and sell houses, farms, and vineyards in this country.

Jeremiah questions the LORD

¹⁶ Then I prayed:

¹⁷ LORD God, you stretched out your mighty arm and made the sky and the earth. You can do anything. ¹⁸ You show kindness for a thousand generations,' but you also punish people for the sins of their parents. You are the LORD All-Powerful. ¹⁹ With great wisdom you make plans, and with your great power you do all the mighty things you planned. Nothing we do is hidden from your eyes, and you reward or punish us as we deserve.

²⁰ You are famous because you worked miracles in Egypt, and you are still working them in Israel and in the rest of the world as well. ²¹ You terrified the Egyptians with your miracles, and you reached out your mighty arm and rescued your people Israel from Egypt. ²² Then you gave Israel this land rich with milk and honey, just as you had promised our ancestors.

²³ But when our ancestors took over the land, they did not obey you. And now you have punished Israel with disaster.

²⁴ Jerusalem is under attack, and we suffer from hunger and disease. The Babylonians have already built earth ramps up to the city walls, and you can see that Jerusalem will be captured just as you said.

²⁵ So why did you tell me to get some witnesses and buy a field with my silver, when Jerusalem is about to be captured by the Babylonians?

The LORD explains about the field

²⁶ The LORD explained:

²⁷ Jeremiah, I am the LORD God. I rule the world, and I can do anything!

²⁸ It is true that I am going to let King Nebuchadnezzar* of Babylonia capture

Jerusalem. ²⁹ The Babylonian army is already attacking, and they will capture the city and set it on fire. The people of Jerusalem have made me angry by going up to the flat roofs of their houses and burning incense to Baal and offering wine sacrifices to other gods. Now these houses will be burnt to the ground!

³⁰⁻³³ The kings and the officials, the priests and the prophets, and everyone else in Israel and Judah have turned from me and made me angry by worshipping idols. Again and again I have tried to teach my people to obey me, but they refuse to be corrected.

I am going to get rid of Jerusalem, because its people have done nothing but evil. ³⁴ They have set up disgusting idols in my temple, and now it isn't a fit place to worship me. ³⁵ And they led Judah into sin by building places to worship Baal in Hinnom Valley, where they also sacrificed their sons and daughters to the god Molech. I have never even thought of telling them to commit such disgusting sins.

³⁶ Jeremiah, what you said is true. The people of Jerusalem are suffering from hunger and disease, and so the king of Babylonia will be able to capture Jerusalem.

³⁷ I am angry with the people of Jerusalem, and I will scatter them in foreign countries. But some day I will bring them back here and let them live in safety. ³⁸ They will be my people, and I will be their God. ³⁹⁻⁴¹ I will make their thoughts and desires pure. Then they will realize that, for their own good and the good of their children, they must worship only me. They will even be afraid to turn away from me. I will make an agreement with them that will never end, and I won't ever stop doing good things for them. With all my heart I promise that they will be planted in this land once again. ⁴² Even though I have brought disaster on the people, I will some day do all these good things for them.

⁴³ Jeremiah, when you bought the field, you showed that fields will some day be bought and sold again. You say that this land has been conquered by the Babylonians and has become a desert, emptied of people and animals. ⁴⁴ But some day, people will again spend their silver to buy fields everywhere — in the territory of Benjamin, the region around Jerusalem and the towns

---

*32.28 Nebuchadnezzar: See the note at 21.2.
See also: 32.28: 2 King 25.1–11; 2 Chron 36.17–21.

See also: 32.34: 2 King 23.10; Jer 7.30–31; 19.1–6.
32.35: a 2 King 23.10; Jer 7.31; b Lev 18.21.

842

Holy history

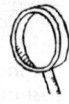

Weights, measures and currency

Weight

Old Testament: The shekel weighed 11.4g. Fifty shekels made one mina and 60 minas made one talent. So a talent was 3,000 shekels.

New Testament: By the time of Jesus, Roman measures had taken over and the standard measure was the Roman 'pound', which weighed 325g or 3/4lb.

Currency

Old Testament: In early times nobody used coins. At first people paid for goods by bartering or exchanging them for other goods such as livestock, timber, wine, or honey. This was eventually replace by precious metal, mainly in the form of silver, which was weighed out. So, for example, Solomon purchased chariots at 600 shekels of silver – that is, 6.84kg of silver. Thus, the shekel, the mina, etc. became the unit of currency.

For example, Jeremiah's field cost him 17 shekels of silver (Jeremiah 32.9) and Omri bought the hill and city of Samaria for two talents of silver (around 68kg).

(We have a development of exactly the same system here, when you think about it. We pay in 'pounds', which originally were weights of gold or silver.)

New Testament: Coins came in around the seventh and eighth centuries BC, but they spread slowly to Israel and Judah – perhaps because the coins had images on them and the Jews were opposed to anything with an image on it, because of the ten commandments.

By Jesus' time there were three major currencies available: Jewish, Greek and Roman.

The Jews still had the shekel – which was now an 11.4g coin. The Greek currency was the drachma, and the Roman, the denarius.

The denarius was roughly one day's pay for a working man. The Jews also had smaller currency, notably the lepton – a bronze coin which represented the smallest coin imaginable. It is this coin that Jesus talks about when he sees the poor widow giving it in Luke 21.2.

Linear measures

The standard unit of length in the Bible was the cubit – roughly the length of an arm, from elbow to fingertips. Accordingly, the value of the cubit varied between 44 and 53cm.

The Old Testament cubit was around 45cm, the New Testament cubit 55cm. In the New Testament, the Roman system of measurements is more apparent; ships measured depths in fathoms (1.8m), and longer distances included the stadion (furlong) at 185m and the milion (mile) at 1478m.

Anorak corner

Big stuff

1. Where would you find twelve gates carved out of giant pearls?
2. Whose coffin was 13ft long and 6ft wide
3. How tall was Goliath?
4. Who said that the Canaanites were like giants?
5. Who is Leviathan?
   (Answers on p.1431)

of Judah, and in the hill country, the foothills to the west, and the Southern Desert. Buyers and sellers and witnesses will sign and seal the bills of sale for the fields. It will happen, because I will give this land back to my people. I, the LORD, have spoken.

CHAPTER 33

The LORD promises to give the land back to his people

1-2 I was still being held prisoner in the courtyard of the palace guards when the LORD told me:

I am the LORD, and I created the whole world.' 3 Ask me, and I will tell you things that you don't know and can't find out.

4-5 Many of the houses in Jerusalem and some of the buildings at the royal palace have been torn down to be used in repairing the walls to keep out the Babylonian attackers.' Now there are empty spaces where the buildings once stood. But I am furious, and these spaces will be filled with the bodies of the people I kill. The people of Jerusalem will cry out to me for help, but they are evil, and I will ignore their prayers.

6 Then some day, I will heal this place and my people as well, and let them enjoy unending peace.' 7 I will give this land to Israel and Judah once again, and I will make them as strong as they were before. 8 They sinned and rebelled against me, but I will forgive them and take away their guilt. 9 When that happens, all nations on earth will see the good things I have done for Jerusalem, and how I have given it complete peace. The nations will celebrate and praise and honour me, but they will also tremble with fear.

10 Jeremiah, you say that this land is a desert without people or animals, and for now, you are right. The towns of Judah and the streets of Jerusalem are deserted, and people and animals are nowhere to be seen. But some day you will hear 11 happy voices and the sounds of parties and wedding celebrations. And when people come to my temple to offer sacrifices to thank me, you will hear them say:

"We praise you,
   LORD All-Powerful!
You are good to us,
   and your love never fails."

The land will once again be productive. 12-13 Now it is empty, without people or animals. But when that time comes, shepherds will take care of their flocks in pastures near every town in the hill country, in the foothills to the west, in the Southern Desert, in the land of the Benjamin tribe, and around Jerusalem and the towns of Judah.

I, the LORD, have spoken.

The LORD's wonderful promise

14 The LORD said:

I made a wonderful promise to Israel and Judah,* and the days are coming when I will keep it.

15 I promise that the time will come
      when I will appoint a king
         from the family of David,
      a king who will be honest
         and rule with justice.
16 In those days, Judah will be safe;
      Jerusalem will have peace
      and will be named,
   "The LORD Gives Justice".

17 The king of Israel will be one of David's descendants, 18 and there will always be priests from the Levi tribe serving at my altar and offering sacrifices to please me and to give thanks.*

19 Then the LORD told me:

20 I, the LORD, have an agreement with day and night, so they always come at the right time. You can't break the agreement I made with them, 21 and you can't break the agreements I have made with David's family and with the priests from the Levi tribe who serve at my altar. A descendant of David will always rule as king of Israel, 22 and there will be more descendants of David and of the priests from the Levi tribe than stars in the sky or grains of sand on the beach.

23 The LORD also said:

24 You've heard foreigners insult my people by saying, "The LORD chose Israel and Judah, but now he has rejected them, and they are no longer a nation."

25 Jeremiah, I will never break my agreement with the day and the night or let

---

33.14 Israel and Judah: See the note at 2.4.
33.18 sacrifices to please me and to give thanks: See the notes at 14.12.

See also: 33.11: 1 Chron 16.34; 2 Chron 5.13; 7.3; Ezra 3.11; Psa 100.5; 106.1; 107.1; 118.1; 136.1.

See also: 33.14–16: Jer 23.5–6. 33.17: 2 Sam 7.12–16; 1 King 2.4; 1 Chron 17.11–14. 33.18: Num 3.5–10.

the sky and the earth stop obeying my commands. 26 In the same way, I will never reject the descendants of Abraham, Isaac, and Jacob or break my promise that they will always have a descendant of David as their king. I will be kind to my people Israel, and they will be successful again.

Scenes from Jeremiah's ministry

CHAPTER 34

Jeremiah warns Zedekiah

1 King Nebuchadnezzar* had a large army made up of people from every kingdom in his empire. He and his army were attacking Jerusalem and all the nearby towns, when the LORD told me 2 to say to King Zedekiah:*

I am the LORD, and I am going to let Nebuchadnezzar capture this city and burn it down. 3 You will be taken prisoner and brought to Nebuchadnezzar, and he will speak with you face to face. Then you will be led away to Babylonia.

4 Zedekiah, I promise that you won't die in battle. 5 You will die a peaceful death. People will mourn when you die, and they will light bonfires in your honour, just as they did for your ancestors, the kings who ruled before you.

6 I went to Zedekiah and told him what the LORD had said. 7 Meanwhile, the king of Babylonia was trying to break through the walls of Lachish, Azekah, and Jerusalem, the only three towns of Judah that had not been captured.

The people break a promise

8-10 King Zedekiah,* his officials, and everyone else in Jerusalem made an agreement to free all Hebrew* men and women who were slaves. No Jew would keep another as a slave. And so, all the Jewish slaves were given their freedom. 11 But those slave owners changed their minds and forced their former slaves back into slavery. 12 That's when the LORD told me to say to the people:

13 I am the LORD God of Israel, and I made an agreement with your ancestors when I brought them out of Egypt, where they had been slaves. 14 As part of this agreement, you must let a Hebrew slave go free after six years of service.

Your ancestors did not obey me, 15-16 but you decided to obey me and do the right thing by setting your Hebrew slaves completely free. You even went to my temple, and in my name you made an agreement to set them free. But you have abused my name, because you broke your agreement and forced your former slaves back into slavery.

17 You have disobeyed me by not giving your slaves their freedom. So I will give you freedom — the freedom to die in battle or from disease or hunger. I will make you disgusting to all other nations on earth.

18 You asked me to be a witness when you made the agreement to set your slaves free. And as part of the ceremony you cut a calf into two parts, then walked between the parts. But you people of Jerusalem have broken that agreement as well as my agreement with Israel. So I will do to you what you did to that calf. 19-20 I will let your enemies take all of you prisoner, including the leaders of Judah and Jerusalem, the royal officials, the priests, and everyone else who walked between the two parts of the calf. These enemies will kill you and leave your bodies lying on the ground as food for birds and wild animals.

21-22 These enemies are King Nebuchadnezzar* of Babylonia and his army. They have stopped attacking Jerusalem, but they want to kill King Zedekiah and his high officials. So I will command them to return and attack again. This time they will conquer the city and burn it down, and they will capture Zedekiah and his officials. I will also let them destroy the towns of Judah, so that no one can live there any longer.

CHAPTER 35

Learn a lesson from the Rechabites

1 When Jehoiakim* was king of Judah, the LORD told me, 2 "Go to the Rechabite clan and invite them to meet you in one of the

---

*34.1 Nebuchadnezzar: See the note at 21.2.
*34.2,8-10 Zedekiah: See the note at 1.3.
*34.8-10 Hebrew: An earlier term for "Israelite" and "Jewish".
See also: 34.1: 2 King 25.1-11; 2 Chron 36.17-21.

---

*34.21-22 Nebuchadnezzar: See the note at 21.2.
*35.1 Jehoiakim: See the note at 1.3.
See also: 34.14: Exod 21.2; Deut 15.12.
35.1: 2 King 23.36—24.6; 2 Chron 36.5-7.

side rooms* of the temple. When they arrive, offer them a drink of wine."

3 So I went to Jaazaniah,ᵇ the leader of the clan, and I invited him and all the men of his clan. 4 I brought them into the temple courtyard and took them upstairs to a room belonging to the prophets who were followers of Hanan son of Igdaliah. It was next to a room belonging to some of the officials, and that room was over the one belonging to Maaseiah, a priest who was one of the high officials in the temple.ᵇ

5 I set out some large bowls full of wine together with some cups, and then I said to the Rechabites, "Have some wine!"

6 But they answered:

No! The ancestor of our clan, Jonadab son of Rechab,* made a rule that we must obey. He said, "Don't ever drink wine 7 or build houses or plant crops and vineyards. Instead, you must always live in tents and move from place to place. If you obey this command, you will live a long time."

8-10 Our clan has always obeyed Jonadab's command. To this very day, we and our wives and sons and daughters don't drink wine or build houses or plant vineyards or crops. And we have lived in tents, 11 except now we have to live inside Jerusalem because Nebuchadnezzar* has taken over the countryside with his army from Babylonia and Syria.

12-13 Then the LORD told me to say to the people of Judah and Jerusalem:

I, the LORD All-Powerful, the God of Israel, want you to learn a lesson 14 from the Rechabite clan. Their ancestor Jonadab told his descendants never to drink wine, and to this very day they have obeyed him. But I have spoken to you over and over, and you haven't obeyed me! 15 You refused to listen to my prophets, who kept telling you, "Stop doing evil and worshipping other gods! Start obeying the LORD, and he will let you live in this land he gave your ancestors."

16 The Rechabites have obeyed the command of their ancestor Jonadab, but

you have not obeyed me, 17 your God. I am the LORD All-Powerful, and I warned you about the terrible things that would happen to you if you did not listen to me. You have ignored me, so now disaster will strike you. I, the LORD, have spoken.

The LORD makes a promise to the Rechabites

18 Then the LORD told me to say to the Rechabite clan:

I am the LORD All-Powerful, the God of Israel. You have obeyed your ancestor Jonadab, 19 so I promise that your clan will be my servants and will never die out.

CHAPTER 36

King Jehoiakim burns Jeremiah's first scroll

1 During the fourth year that Jehoiakim* son of Josiah* was king of Judah, the LORD said to me, "Jeremiah, 2 since the time Josiah was king, I have been speaking to you about Israel, Judah, and the other nations. Now, get a scroll* and write down everything I have told you, 3 then read it to the people of Judah. Perhaps they will stop sinning when they hear what terrible things I plan for them. And if they turn to me, I will forgive them."

4 I sent for Baruch son of Neriah and asked him to help me. I repeated everything the LORD had told me, and Baruch wrote it all down on a scroll. 5 Then I said,

Baruch, the officials refuse to let me go into the LORD's temple, 6 so you must go instead. Wait for the next holy day when the people of Judah come to the temple to pray and to go without eating.* Then take this scroll to the temple and read it aloud. 7 The LORD is furious, and if the people hear how he is going to punish them, perhaps they will ask to be forgiven.

8-10 In the ninth month* of the fifth year that Jehoiakim was king, the leaders set a day

---

35.2 side rooms: Probably a room with walls on three sides, and open to the courtyard on the fourth side.
35.6 Jonadab son of Rechab: See 2 Kings 10.15–23. In the Hebrew of this chapter, "Jonadab" is sometimes spelt "Jehonadab".
35.11 Nebuchadnezzar: See the note at 21.2.

36.1 Jehoiakim: See the note at 1.3.
36.1 Josiah: See the note at 1.2.
36.2 scroll: See the note at 30.1–2.
36.6 to go without eating: As a way of asking for God's help.
36.8–10 ninth month: Chislev, the ninth month of the Hebrew calendar, from about mid-November to mid-December.

See also: 36.1: 2 King 24.1; 2 Chron 36.5–7; Dan 1.1–2.

when everyone who lived in Jerusalem or who was visiting here had to pray and go without eating. So Baruch took the scroll to the upper courtyard of the temple. He went over to the side of the courtyard and stood in a covered area near New Gate, where he read the scroll aloud.

This covered area belonged to Gemariah,* one of the king's highest officials. ¹¹ Gemariah's son Micaiah was there and heard Baruch read what the LORD had said. ¹² When Baruch finished reading, Micaiah went down to the palace. His father Gemariah was in the officials' room, meeting with the rest of the king's officials, including Elishama, Delaiah, Elnathan, and Zedekiah.ʼ ¹³ Micaiah told them what he had heard Baruch reading to the people. ¹⁴ Then the officials sent Jehudi and Shelemiahʼ to tell Baruch, "Bring us that scroll."

When Baruch arrived with the scroll, ¹⁵ the officials said, "Please sit down and read it to us," which he did. ¹⁶ After they heard what was written on the scroll, they were worried and said to each other, "The king needs to hear this!" Turning to Baruch, they asked, ¹⁷ "Did someone tell you what to write on this scroll?"

¹⁸ "Yes, Jeremiah did," Baruch replied. "I wrote down just what he told me."

¹⁹ The officials said, "You and Jeremiah must go into hiding, and don't tell anyone where you are."

²⁰⁻²² The officials put the scroll in Elishama's room and went to see the king, who was in one of the rooms where he lived and worked during the winter. It was the ninth month* of the year, so there was a fire burning in the fireplace,* and the king was sitting nearby. After the officials told the king about the scroll, he sent Jehudi to get it. Then Jehudi started reading the scroll to the king and his officials. ²³⁻²⁵ But every time Jehudi finished reading three or four columns, the king would tell him to cut them off with his penknife and throw them in the fire. Elnathan, Delaiah, and Gemariah begged the king not to burn the scroll, but he ignored them, and soon there was nothing left of it.

The king and his servants listened to what was written on the scroll, but they were not afraid, and they did not tear their clothes in sorrow.*

²⁶ The king told his son Jerahmeel to take Seraiah and Shelemiahʼ and to go and arrest Baruch and me.* But the LORD kept them from finding us.

Jeremiah's second scroll

²⁷ I had told Baruch what to write on that first scroll,* but King Jehoiakim* had burnt it. So the LORD told me ²⁸ to get another scroll and write down everything that had been on the first one. ²⁹ Then he told me to say to King Jehoiakim:

Not only did you burn Jeremiah's scroll, you had the nerve to ask why he had written that the king of Babylonia would attack and ruin the land, killing all the people and even the animals. ³⁰ So I, the LORD, promise that you will be killed and your body thrown out on the ground. The sun will beat down on it during the day, and the frost will settle on it at night. And none of your descendants will ever be king of Judah. ³¹ You, your children, and your servants are evil, and I will punish all of you. I warned you and the people of Judah and Jerusalem that I would bring disaster, but none of you have listened. So now you are doomed!

³² After the LORD finished speaking to me, I got another scroll and gave it to Baruch. Then I told him what to write, so this second scroll would contain even more than was on the scroll Jehoiakim had burnt.

CHAPTER 37

King Zedekiah asks Jeremiah to pray

¹ King Nebuchadnezzar* of Babylonia had removed Jehoiachin* son of Jehoiakim* from being the king of Judah and had made

---

*36.23–25 they did not tear their clothes in sorrow: Such actions would have shown that they were sorry for disobeying the LORD and were turning back to him.
*36.26 me: Jeremiah.
*36.27 scroll: See the note at 30.1–2.
*36.27; 37.1 Jehoiakim: See the note at 1.3.
*37.1 Nebuchadnezzar: See the note at 21.2.
*37.1 Jehoiachin: Hebrew "Coniah" (see the note at 1.2).
See also: 37.1: 2 King 24.17; 2 Chron 36.10.

*36.8–10 Gemariah: Hebrew "Gemariah son of Shaphan"; Gemariah's brother Ahikam had earlier protected Jeremiah (see 26.20–24).
*36.20–22 ninth month: See the note at 36.8–10.
*36.20–22 fireplace: Probably a large metal or clay pot on a moveable stand, with the fire burning inside.

Josiah's* son Zedekiah* king instead.* [2] But Zedekiah, his officials, and everyone else in Judah ignored everything the LORD had told me.

[3-5] Later, the Babylonian army attacked Jerusalem, but they left after learning that the Egyptian army᾿ was headed in this direction.

One day, Zedekiah sent Jehucal and the priest Zephaniah᾿ to talk with me. At that time, I was free to go wherever I wanted, because I had not yet been put in prison. Jehucal and Zephaniah said, "Jeremiah, please pray to the LORD our God for us."

[6-7] Then the LORD told me to send them back to Zedekiah with this message:

Zedekiah, you wanted Jeremiah to ask me, the LORD God of Israel, what is going to happen. So I will tell you. The king of Egypt and his army came to your rescue, but soon they will go back to Egypt. [8] Then the Babylonians will return and attack Jerusalem, and this time they will capture the city and set it on fire. [9] Don't fool yourselves into thinking that the Babylonians will leave as they did before. [10] Even if you could defeat their entire army, their wounded survivors would still be able to leave their tents and set Jerusalem on fire.

Jeremiah is put in prison

[11] The Babylonian army had left because the Egyptian army was on its way to help us. [12] So I decided to leave Jerusalem and go to the territory of the Benjamin tribe to claim my share of my family's land. [13] I was leaving Jerusalem through Benjamin Gate, when I was stopped by Irijah,᾿ the officer in charge of the soldiers at the gate. He said, "Jeremiah, you're under arrest for trying to join the Babylonians."

[14] "I'm not trying to join them!" I answered. But Irijah wouldn't listen, and he took me to the king's officials. [15-16] They were angry and ordered the soldiers to beat me. Then I was taken to the house that belonged to Jonathan, one of the king's officials. It had been turned into a prison, and I was kept in a basement room.

After I had spent a long time there, [17] King Zedekiah secretly had me brought to his palace, where he asked, "Is there any message for us from the LORD?"

"Yes, there is, Your Majesty," I replied. "The LORD is going to let the king of Babylonia capture you."

[18] Then I continued, "Your Majesty, why have you put me in prison? Have I committed a crime against you or your officials or the nation? [19] Have you locked up the prophets who lied to you and said that the king of Babylonia would never attack Jerusalem? [20] Please, don't send me back to that prison at Jonathan's house. If you do, I will die."

[21] King Zedekiah had me taken to the prison cells in the courtyard of the palace guards. He told the soldiers to give me a loaf of bread* from one of the bakeries every day until the city ran out of grain.

CHAPTER 38

Jeremiah is held prisoner in a dry well

[1] One day, Shephatiah, Gedaliah, Jehucal,᾿ and Pashhur᾿ heard me tell the people of Judah [2-3] that the LORD had said, "If you stay here in Jerusalem, you will die in battle or from disease or hunger, and the Babylonian army will capture the city anyway. But if you surrender to the Babylonians, they will let you live."

[4] So the four of them went to the king and said, "You should put Jeremiah to death, because he is making the soldiers and everyone else lose hope. He isn't trying to help our people; he's trying to harm them."

[5] Zedekiah replied, "Do what you want with him. I can't stop you."

[6] Then they took me back to the courtyard of the palace guards and let me down with ropes into the well that belonged to Malchiah, the king's son. There was no water in the well, and I sank down in the mud.

[7-8] Ebedmelech from Ethiopia* was an official at the palace, and he heard what they had done to me. So he went to speak with King Zedekiah, who was holding court at Benjamin Gate. [9] Ebedmelech said, "Your Majesty, Jeremiah is a prophet, and those men were wrong to throw him into a well.

---

*37.1 Josiah's: Josiah was the father of both Jehoiakim and Zedekiah. Josiah ruled 640–609 BC.
*37.1 Zedekiah: See the note at 1.3.
*37.1 King Nebuchadnezzar . . . instead: See 2 Kings 24.10–17.

*37.21 a loaf of bread: Bread was the main food of the Israelites. During this time of emergency in Jerusalem, everyone probably received the same amount each day.
*38.7–8 Ethiopia: The Hebrew text has "Cush", a region south of Egypt that included parts of the present countries of Ethiopia and Sudan.

And when Jerusalem runs out of food,
Jeremiah will starve to death down there."

¹⁰ Zedekiah answered, "Take thirty⁾ of my
soldiers and pull Jeremiah out before he
dies."

¹¹ Ebedmelech and the soldiers went to the
palace and got some rags from the room
under the treasury. He used ropes to lower
them into the well. ¹² Then he said, "Put
these rags under your arms so the ropes
won't hurt you." After I had done that, ¹³ the
men pulled me out. And from then on, I was
kept in the courtyard of the palace guards.

King Zedekiah questions Jeremiah

¹⁴ King Zedekiah* had me brought to his
private entrance⁾ to the temple, and he said,
"I'm going to ask you something, and I want
to know the truth."

¹⁵ "Why?" I replied. "You won't listen, and
you might even have me killed!"

¹⁶ He said, "I swear in the name of the
living LORD our Creator that I won't have you
killed. No one else can hear what we say, and
I won't let anyone kill you."

¹⁷ Then I told him that the LORD had said:
"Zedekiah, I am the LORD God All-Powerful,
the God of Israel. I promise that if you
surrender to King Nebuchadnezzar's*
officers, you and your family won't be killed,
and Jerusalem won't be burnt down. ¹⁸ But if
you don't surrender, I will let the Babylonian
army capture Jerusalem and burn it down,
and you will be taken prisoner."

¹⁹ Zedekiah answered, "I can't surrender to
the Babylonians. I'm too afraid of the Jews
who have already joined them. The
Babylonians might hand me over to those
Jews, and they would torture me."

²⁰ I said, "If you will just obey the LORD,
the Babylonians won't hand you over to
those Jews. You will be allowed to live, and
all will go well for you. ²¹ But the LORD has
shown me that if you refuse to obey, ²² then
the women of your palace will be taken
prisoner by Nebuchadnezzar's officials. And
those women will say to you:

Friends you trusted led you astray.
Now you're trapped in mud,
and those friends you trusted
have all turned away.

²³ The Babylonian army will take your wives
and children captive, you will be taken as a

prisoner to the King of Babylonia, and
Jerusalem will be burnt down."⁾

²⁴ Zedekiah said, "Jeremiah, if you tell
anyone what we have talked about, you
might lose your life. ²⁵ And I'm sure that if
my officials hear about our meeting, they
will ask you what we said to each other. They
might even threaten to kill you if you don't
tell them. ²⁶ So if they question you, tell them
you were begging me not to send you back to
the prison at Jonathan's house, because
going back there would kill you."

²⁷ The officials did come and question me
about my meeting with the king, and I told
them exactly what he had ordered me to say.
They never spoke to me about the meeting
again, since no one had heard us talking.

²⁸ I was held in the courtyard of the palace
guards until the day Jerusalem was captured.

The fall of Jerusalem and later events in Judah

CHAPTER 39

Jerusalem is captured by the Babylonians
This is also told in Jeremiah 52.4–16; 2 Kings 25.1–12

¹⁻³ In the tenth month* of the ninth year that
Zedekiah* was king of Judah, King
Nebuchadnezzar* and the Babylonian army
began their attack on Jerusalem. They kept
the city surrounded for a year and a half.
Then, on the ninth day of the fourth month*
of the eleventh year that Zedekiah was king,
they broke through the city walls.

After Jerusalem was captured,*
Nebuchadnezzar's highest officials,⁾
including Nebo Sarsechim⁾ and Nergal
Sharezer from Simmagir,⁾ took their places at
Middle Gate to show they were in control of
the city.*

---

*39.1–3 the tenth month: Tebeth, the tenth month
of the Hebrew calendar, from about mid-December
to mid-January.
*39.1–3 Zedekiah: See the note at 1.3.
*39.1–3 Nebuchadnezzar: See the note at 21.2.
*39.1–3 fourth month: Tammuz, the fourth month of
the Hebrew calendar, from about mid-June to mid-July.
*39.1–3 After Jerusalem was captured: This phrase
is from 38.28.
*39.1–3 took their places . . . control of the city: The
rulers and leaders often sat in the broad open area at
the gate of a city to take care of official business and
hold trials.
See also: 38.28: Ezek 33.21.

---

*38.14 Zedekiah: See the note at 1.3.
*38.17 Nebuchadnezzar's: See the note at 21.2.

4 When King Zedekiah and his troops saw that Jerusalem had been captured, they tried to escape from the city that same night. They went to the king's garden, where they slipped through the gate between the two city walls* and headed towards the valley of the River Jordan. 5 But the Babylonian troops caught up with them near Jericho. They arrested Zedekiah and took him to the town of Riblah in the land of Hamath, where Nebuchadnezzar put him on trial, then found him guilty 6 and gave orders for him to be punished. Zedekiah's sons were killed there in front of him, and so were the leaders of Judah's ruling families. 7 His eyes were put out, and he was put in chains, so he could be dragged off to Babylonia.

8 Meanwhile, the Babylonian army had burnt the houses in Jerusalem, including' the royal palace, and they had broken down the city walls. 9 Nebuzaradan, the Babylonian officer in charge of the guards, led away everyone from the city as prisoners, even those who had deserted to Nebuchadnezzar. 10 Only the poorest people who owned no land were left behind in Judah, and Nebuzaradan gave them fields and vineyards.

11 Nebuchadnezzar had given the following orders to Nebuzaradan: 12 "Find Jeremiah and keep him safe. Take good care of him and do whatever he asks."

13 Nebuzaradan, Nebushazban, Nergal Sharezer, and the other officers of King Nebuchadnezzar 14 sent some of their troops to bring me from the courtyard of the royal palace guards. They put me in the care of Gedaliah son of Ahikam' and told him to take me to my home. And so I was allowed to stay with the people who remained in Judah.

The LORD promises to protect Ebedmelech

15 While I was a prisoner in the courtyard of the palace guard, the LORD told me to say 16 to Ebedmelech from Ethiopia:*

I am the LORD All-Powerful, the God of Israel. I warned everyone that I would bring disaster, not prosperity, to this city. Now very soon I will do what I said, and you will see it happen. 17-18 But because you trusted me,* I will protect you from

the officials of Judah, and when Judah is struck by disaster, I will rescue you and keep you alive. I, the LORD, have spoken.

CHAPTER 40
Jeremiah is set free

1 I was led away in chains along with the people of Judah and Jerusalem who were being taken to Babylonia. Nebuzaradan was the officer in charge of the guard, and when we stopped at Ramah, the LORD made him set me free. 2 Nebuzaradan said:

Jeremiah, the LORD your God warned your people that he would bring disaster on this land. 3 But they continued to rebel against him, and now he has punished them just as he threatened.

4 Today I am taking the chains off your wrists and setting you free! If you want to, you can come with me to Babylonia, and I will see that you are taken care of. Or if you decide to stay here, you can go wherever you wish. 5 King Nebuchadnezzar* has chosen Gedaliah to rule Judah. You can live near Gedaliah, and he will provide for you, or you can live anywhere else you want.

Nebuzaradan gave me a supply of food, then let me leave. 6 I decided to stay with the people of Judah, and I went to live near Gedaliah in Mizpah.

The harvest is brought in

7-8 Ishmael the son of Nethaniah, together with Johanan and Jonathan, the two sons of Kareah, had been officers in Judah's army. And so had Seraiah the son of Tanhumeth, the sons of Ephai the Netophathite, and Jezaniah from Maacah. They and their troops had been stationed outside Jerusalem and had not been captured. They heard that Gedaliah had been chosen to rule Judah, and that the poorest men, women, and children had not been taken away to Babylonia. So they went to Mizpah and met with their new ruler.

9 Gedaliah told them, "There's no need to be afraid of the Babylonians. Everything will be fine, if we live peacefully and obey King Nebuchadnezzar.* 10 I will stay here at Mizpah and meet with the Babylonian officials on each of their visits. But you must

*39.4 the gate between the two city walls: The construction of the city walls at this point is not known.
*39.16 Ethiopia: See the note at 38.7-8.
*39.17-18 you trusted me: See 38.7-13, where Ebedmelech helped Jeremiah.

*40.5,9 Nebuchadnezzar: See the note at 21.2.
See also: 40.7-9: 2 King 25.22-24.

Exile

The inhabitants of Judah were to spend many years in captivity in Babylon, before the collapse of the Babylonian empire led to their release.

The first group of Jews were deported in 605BC; their group included Ezekiel and Daniel (Daniel 1.1). Another group were taken away in 597BC (2 Kings 24.8–14) and Jerusalem was finally destroyed in 586BC (2 Kings 25.1–12; Jeremiah 39.1–10; 52.4–16).

They stayed in exile until the fall of Babylon in 539BC. Then the Persians invaded, led by Cyrus the Great. One of the first things he did was to allow the Jews to return home. The first group went back in 537BC, led by King Zerubbabel (Ezra 1–2). For the next eighty years or so, different groups of Jews returned to Israel. In 458BC Ezra (Ezra 7–10) led a group, followed by Nehemiah in 445BC (Nehemiah 1).

Jeremiah escaped captivity in Babylon, but after a group of Israelites assassinated the Governor of Jerusalem, he was kidnapped, and taken to Egypt, where he spent the rest of his life.

Daniel was among the first captives taken. He was chosen to be an official in the king's palace where he faced the challenge of staying true to his faith in the face of pressure to worship the Babylonian gods.

Ezekiel was taken into captivity with the first captives. He prophesied the final fall of Judah, often through strange, dramatic acts. He also left a detailed prophecy of a rebuilt, ideal temple.

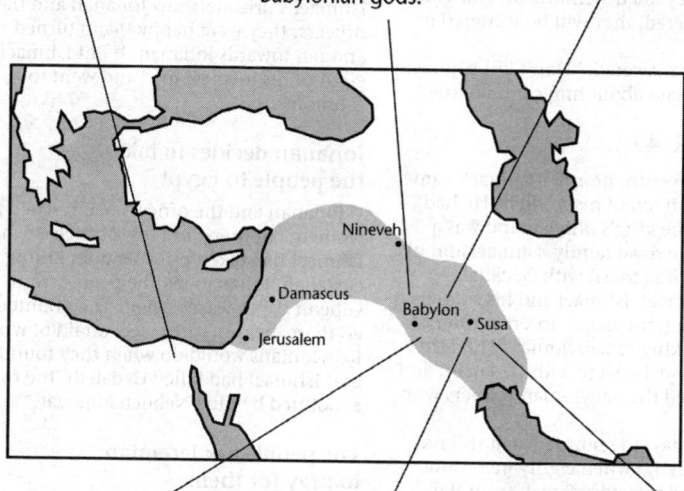

Ezra was a senior official in the Persian empire – the empire that took over from the Babylonians. He was sent back from Persia to reform Jerusalem and restore the worship in the temple.

Nehemiah was a bodyguard to Artaxerxes I, the king of Persia. When he heard that the walls of Jerusalem were still in disrepair, he asked permission from the king to go and finish the work.

Not all the exiles returned. Esther became queen to King Xerxes of Persia, and with her cousin Mordecai she managed to foil a massacre of the Jews in the Persian empire.

go back to your towns and bring in the harvest, then store the wine, olive oil, and dried fruit."

¹¹⁻¹² Earlier, when the Babylonians had invaded Judah, many of the Jews escaped to Moab, Ammon, Edom, and several other countries. But these Jews heard that the king of Babylonia had appointed Gedaliah as ruler of Judah, and that only a few people were left there. So the Jews in these other countries came back to Judah and helped with the grape and fruit harvest, which was especially large that year.

Gedaliah is murdered

¹³ One day, Johanan got together with some of the other men who had been army officers, and they came to Mizpah and met with Gedaliah. ¹⁴ They said, "Gedaliah, we came to warn you that King Baalis of Ammon hired Ishmael to murder you!"

Gedaliah refused to believe them, ¹⁵ so Johanan went to Gedaliah privately and said, "Let me kill Ishmael. No one will find out who did it. There are only a few people left in Judah, but they are depending on you. And if you are murdered, they will be scattered or killed."

¹⁶ Gedaliah answered, "Don't kill Ishmael! What you've said about him can't be true."

CHAPTER 41

¹ But in the seventh month,* Ishmael came to Mizpah with ten of his soldiers. He had been one of the king's officials and was a member of the royal family. Ishmael and his men were invited to eat with Gedaliah. ² During the meal, Ishmael and his soldiers killed Gedaliah, the man chosen as ruler of Judah by the king of Babylonia. ³ Then they killed the Jews who were with Gedaliah, and they also killed the Babylonian soldiers who were there.

⁴ The next day, the murders had still not been discovered, ⁵ when eighty men came down the road towards Mizpah from the towns of Shechem, Shiloh, and Samaria. They were on their way to the temple to offer gifts of grain and incense to the LORD. They had shaved off their beards, torn their clothes, and cut themselves, because they were mourning.

⁶ Ishmael went out of the town gate to meet them. He pretended to be weeping, and he asked them to come into Mizpah to meet with Gedaliah, the ruler of Judah. ⁷ But after they were inside the town, Ishmael ordered his soldiers to kill them and throw their bodies into a well. ⁸ He let ten of the men live, because they offered to give him supplies of wheat, barley, olive oil, and honey they had hidden in a field. ⁹ The well that he filled with bodies had been dug by King Asa* of Judah to store rainwater, because he was afraid that King Baasha* of Israel might surround Mizpah and keep the people from getting to their water supply.

¹⁰ Nebuzaradan, King Nebuchadnezzar's* officer in charge of the guard, had left King Zedekiah's* daughters and many other people at Mizpah, and he had put Gedaliah in charge of them. But now Ishmael took them all prisoner and led them towards Ammon, on the other side of the River Jordan.

¹¹ Johanan and the other army officers heard what Ishmael had done. ¹² So they and their troops chased Ishmael and caught up with him at the large pit at Gibeon. ¹³ When Ishmael's prisoners saw Johanan and the officers, they were happy ¹⁴ and turned round and ran towards Johanan. ¹⁵ But Ishmael and eight of his men escaped and went to Ammon.

Johanan decides to take the people to Egypt

¹⁶ Johanan and the officers had rescued the women, children, and royal officials whom Ishmael had taken prisoner after killing Gedaliah. Johanan led the people from Gibeon ¹⁷⁻¹⁸ towards Egypt. They wanted to go there, because they were afraid of what the Babylonians would do when they found out that Ishmael had killed Gedaliah, the ruler appointed by King Nebuchadnezzar.*

The people ask Jeremiah to pray for them

On the way to Egypt, we* stopped at the town of Geruth Chimham near Bethlehem.

---

*41.9 Asa: Ruled 911–870 BC.
*41.9 Baasha: Ruled 909–886 BC.
*41.10,17-18 Nebuchadnezzar's: See the note at 21.2.
*41.10 Zedekiah's: See the note at 1.3.
*41.17-18 we: The group of people included Jeremiah, since he had been staying with Gedaliah near Mizpah (see 40.6).

---

*41.1 seventh month: Tishri, also called Ethanim, the seventh month of the Hebrew calendar, from about mid-September to mid-October.
See also: 41.1-3: 2 King 25.25.

CHAPTER 42

[1] Johanan, Jezaniah,' the other army officers, and everyone else in the group, came to me [2] and said, "Please pray to the LORD your God for us. Judah used to have many people, but as you can see, only a few of us are left. [3] Ask the LORD to tell us where he wants us to go and what he wants us to do."

[4] "All right," I answered, "I will pray to the LORD your God, and I will tell you everything he says."

[5] They answered, "The LORD himself will be our witness that we promise to do whatever he says, [6] even if it isn't what we want to do. We will obey the LORD so that all will go well for us."

[7] Ten days later, the LORD gave me an answer for [8] Johanan, the officers, and the other people. So I called them together [9] and told them that the LORD God of Israel had said:

You asked Jeremiah to pray and find out what you should do. [10] I am sorry that I had to punish you, and so I now tell you to stay here in Judah, where I will plant you and build you up, instead of tearing you down and uprooting you. [11] Don't be afraid of the King of Babylonia. I will protect you from him, [12] and I will even force him to have mercy on you and give back your farms.

[13] But you might keep on saying, "We won't stay here in Judah, and we won't obey the LORD our God. [14] We are going to Egypt, where there is plenty of food and no danger of war."

[15] People of Judah, you survived when the Babylonian army attacked. Now you are planning to move to Egypt, and if you do go, this is what will happen. [16-17] You are afraid of war, starvation, and disease here in Judah, but they will follow you to Egypt and kill you there. None of you will survive the disasters I will send.

[18] I, the LORD, was angry with the people of Jerusalem and punished them. And if you go to Egypt, I will be angry and punish you the same way. You will never again see your homeland. People will be horrified at what I do to you, and they will use the name of your city as a curse word.

Jeremiah gives a warning

[19] I told the people:

You escaped the disaster that struck Judah, but now the LORD warns you to stay away from Egypt. [20] You asked me to pray and find out what the LORD our God wants you to do, and you promised to obey him. But that was a terrible mistake, [21] because now that I have given you the LORD's answer, you refuse to obey him. [22] And so, you will die in Egypt from war, hunger, and disease.

Jeremiah in Egypt

CHAPTER 43

The people go to Egypt

[1] I told the people everything the LORD had told me. [2] But Azariah, Johanan' and some other arrogant men said to me, "You're lying! The LORD didn't tell you to say that we shouldn't go to Egypt. [3] Baruch son of Neriah must have told you to say that. He wants the Babylonians to capture us, so they can take us away to Babylonia or even kill us."

[4] Johanan, the other army officers, and everyone else refused to stay in Judah in spite of the LORD's command. [5] So Johanan and the officers led us away towards Egypt. The group that left Judah included those who had been scattered in other countries and who had then come back to live in Judah. [6] Baruch and I and others in the group had been staying with Gedaliah, because Nebuzaradan, the Babylonian officer in charge of the guard, had ordered him to take care of the king's daughters and quite a few men, women, and children.

[7] The people disobeyed the LORD and went to Egypt. The group had settled in Tahpanhes, [8] when the LORD told me:

[9] Jeremiah, carry some large stones to the entrance of the government building in Tahpanhes. Bury the stones underneath the brick pavement' and be sure the Jews are watching.

[10] Then tell them that I, the LORD All-Powerful, the God of Israel, have sent for my servant, Nebuchadnezzar* of Babylonia. I will bring him here and make him set up his throne and his royal tent over these stones that I told you to bury. [11] He will attack Egypt and kill many of its people; others will die of disease or be dragged away as prisoners. [12-13] I will let him set Egypt's temples on fire, and he will either burn or carry off their idols. He will

---

*43.10 Nebuchadnezzar: See the note at 21.2.
See also: 43.5–7: 2 King 25.26.

destroy the sacred monuments at the temple of the sun-god.' Then Nebuchadnezzar will pick the land clean, just like a shepherd picking the lice off his clothes. And he will return safely home.

CHAPTER 44

The LORD will destroy the people of Judah

¹ The LORD told me to speak with the Jews who were living in the towns of Migdol, Tahpanhes, and Memphis in northern Egypt, and also to those living in southern Egypt. He told me to tell them:

² I am the LORD All-Powerful, the God of Israel. You saw how I destroyed Jerusalem and the towns of Judah. They lie empty and in ruins today, ³ because the people of Judah made me angry by worshipping gods that had never helped them or their ancestors.

⁴ Time after time I sent my servants the prophets to tell the people of Judah how much I hated their disgusting sins. The prophets warned them to stop sinning, ⁵ but they refused to listen and would not stop worshipping other gods. ⁶ Finally, my anger struck like a raging flood, and today Jerusalem and the towns of Judah are nothing but empty ruins.

⁷ Why do you now insist on heading for another disaster? A disaster that will destroy not only you, but also your children and babies. ⁸ You have made me angry by worshipping idols and burning incense to other gods after you came here to Egypt. You will die such a disgusting death, that other nations will use the name of Judah as a curse word. ⁹ When you were living in Jerusalem and Judah, you followed the example of your ancestors in doing evil things, just like your kings and queens. ¹⁰ Even now, your pride keeps you from respecting me and obeying the laws and teachings I gave you and your ancestors.

¹¹ I, the LORD All-Powerful, have decided to wipe you out with disasters. ¹² There were only a few of you left in Judah, and you decided to go to Egypt. But you will die such horrible deaths in war or from starvation, that people of other countries will use the name of Judah as a curse word. ¹³ I punished Jerusalem with war, hunger, and disease, and that's how I will punish you. ¹⁴ None of you will survive. You may

hope to return to Judah some day, but only a very few of you will escape death and be able to go back.

The people refuse to worship the LORD

¹⁵ A large number of Jews from both northern and southern Egypt listened to me as I told them what the LORD had said. Most of the men in the crowd knew that their wives often burnt incense to other gods. So they and their wives shouted:

¹⁶ Jeremiah, what do we care if you speak in the LORD's name? We refuse to listen! ¹⁷ We have promised to worship the goddess Astarte, the Queen of Heaven,' and that is exactly what we are going to do. We will burn incense and offer sacrifices of wine to her, just as we, our ancestors, our kings, and our leaders did when we lived in Jerusalem and the other towns of Judah. We had plenty of food back then. We were well off, and nothing bad ever happened to us. ¹⁸ But since the time we stopped burning incense and offering wine sacrifices to her, we have been dying from war and hunger.

¹⁹ Then the women said, "When we lived in Judah, we worshipped the Queen of Heaven and offered sacrifices of wine and special loaves of bread shaped like her. Our husbands knew what we were doing, and they approved of it."

²⁰ Then I told the crowd:

²¹ Don't you think the LORD knew that you and your ancestors, your leaders and kings, and the rest of the people were burning incense to other gods in Jerusalem and everywhere else in Judah? ²² And when he could no longer put up with your disgusting sins, he placed a curse on your land and turned it into a desert, as it is today. ²³ This disaster happened because you worshipped other gods and rebelled against the LORD by refusing to obey him or follow his laws and teachings.

²⁴⁻²⁵ Then I told the men and their wives, that the LORD All-Powerful, the God of Israel, had said:

Here in Egypt you still keep your promises to burn incense and offer sacrifices of wine to the so-called Queen of Heaven. ²⁶ Keep these promises! But let me tell you what will happen. As surely as I am the LORD God, I swear that I will never again accept any promises you make in my name.

27 Instead of watching over you, I will watch for chances to harm you. Some of you will die in war, and others will starve to death. 28 Only a few will escape and return to Judah. Then everyone who went to live in Egypt will know that when I say something will happen, it will — no matter what you say.

29 And here is how you will know that I will keep my threats to punish you in Egypt. 30 I will hand over King Hophra of Egypt to those who want to kill him,* just as I handed Zedekiah* over to Nebuchadnezzar,* who wanted to kill him.

A message for Baruch

CHAPTER 45

The LORD will not let Baruch be killed

1 In the fourth year that Jehoiakim* was king of Judah, Baruch wrote down everything I had told him.* 2 Then later, the LORD God of Israel told me to say to Baruch:

3 You are moaning and blaming me, the LORD, for your troubles and sorrow, and for being so tired that you can't even rest. 4 But all over the earth I am tearing down what I built and pulling up what I planted. 5 I am bringing disaster everywhere, so don't even think about making any big plans for yourself. However, I promise that wherever you go, I will at least protect you from death. I, the LORD, have spoken.

The Lord speaks about the nations

CHAPTER 46

1 The LORD often told me what to say about the different nations of the world.

What the LORD says about Egypt

2 In the fourth year that Jehoiakim* was king of Judah, King Nebuchadnezzar* of Babylonia defeated King Neco of Egypt* in a battle at the city of Carchemish near the River Euphrates. And here is what the LORD told me to say about the Egyptian army:

3 It's time to go into battle!
   So grab your shields,
4   saddle your horses,
   and polish your spears.
Put on your helmets and armour,
   then take your positions.

5 I can see the battle now —
   you are defeated
and running away,
   never once looking back.
Terror is all around.
6 You are strong and run fast,
   but you can't escape.
You fall in battle
   near the River Euphrates.

7 What nation is this,
   that rises like the River Nile
   overflowing its banks?
8 It is Egypt, rising with a roar
   like a raging river
   and saying,
"I'll flood the earth,
destroying cities, and killing
   everyone in them."

9 Go ahead, Egypt.
Tell your chariots and cavalry
   to attack and fight hard.
Order your troops to march out,
   with Ethiopians* and Libyans
   carrying shields,
and the Lydians* armed with bows
   and arrows.

10 But the LORD All-Powerful
   will win this battle
and take revenge
   on his enemies.

---

*44.30 King Hophra . . . kill him: Hophra, also known as Apries, ruled Egypt from 589 to 570 BC, when he was killed by Ahmosis II, who then became king of Egypt and ruled until 526 BC.
*44.30 Zedekiah: See the note at 1.3.
*44.30 Nebuchadnezzar: See the note at 21.2.
*45.1 Jehoiakim: See the note at 1.3.
*45.1 Baruch wrote down everything I had told him: See 36.1–32.

See also: 44.30: 2 King 25.1-7. 45.1: 2 King 24.1; 2 Chron 36.5-7; Dan 1.1-2.

*46.2 Jehoiakim: See the note at 1.3.
*46.2 King Nebuchadnezzar: Ruled 605-562 BC. At the time of the battle in 605 BC, he was crown prince, but his father died a few months later, and he became king.
*46.2 King Neco of Egypt: Neco II, ruled 609-594 BC.
*46.9 Ethiopians: See the note at 38.7-8.
*46.9 Lydians: Probably hired soldiers from Lydia, an area in west-central Asia Minor.
See also: 46.2-26: Isa 19.1-25; Ezek 29.1–32.32.

His sword will eat them
and drink their blood
    until it is full.
They will be killed in the north
near the River Euphrates,
    as a sacrifice to the LORD.

11 Egypt, no medicine can heal you,
not even the soothing lotion
    from Gilead.
12 All nations have heard you weep;
you are disgraced,
    and they know it.
Your troops fall to the ground,
    stumbling over each other.

A warning for Egypt

13-14 When King Nebuchadnezzar* of
Babylonia was on his way to attack Egypt,
the LORD sent me with a warning for every
Egyptian town, but especially for Migdol,
Memphis, and Tahpanhes. He said I must tell
them:

Prepare to defend yourselves!
Everywhere in your nation,
    people are dying in war.
15 I have struck down
your mighty god Apis*
    and chased him away.'
16 Your soldiers stumble
over each other
and say, "Get up!
    The enemy will kill us,
unless we can escape
    to our own land."

17 Give the king of Egypt
this new name,
    "Talks-Big-Does-Nothing".

18 Egypt, I am the true king,
the LORD All-Powerful,
and as surely as I live,
those enemies who attack
    will tower over you
like Mount Tabor among the hills
    or Mount Carmel by the sea.
19 You will be led away captive,
so pack a few things
    to bring with you.
Your capital, Memphis,
    will lie empty and in ruins.

20 An enemy from the north
will attack you, beautiful Egypt,
    like a fly biting a cow.
21 The foreign soldiers you hired
    will turn and run.
But they are doomed,
like well-fed calves
    being led to the butcher.

22-23 The enemy army will go forward
like a swarm of locusts.*
Your troops will feel helpless,
like a snake in a forest
when men with axes
    start chopping down trees.
It can only hiss
    and try to escape.
24 Your people will be disgraced
and captured by the enemy
    from the north.

25 I am the LORD All-Powerful, the God of
Israel. Soon I will punish the god Amon of
Thebes* and the other Egyptian gods, the
Egyptian kings, the people of Egypt, and
everyone who trusts in the Egyptian power.
26 I will hand them over to King
Nebuchadnezzar and his army. But I also
promise that Egypt will some day have
people living here again, just as it had
before. I, the LORD, have spoken.

The LORD will bring Israel home

The LORD said:

27 Israel,* don't be afraid.
Some day I will bring you home
    from foreign lands.
You and your descendants
will live in peace and safety,
    with nothing to fear.
28 So don't be afraid,
even though now
    you deserve to be punished
and have been scattered
    among other nations.
But when I destroy them,
    I will protect you.
I, the LORD, have spoken.

---

*46.13-14 Nebuchadnezzar: See the note at 21.2.
*46.15 Apis: A sacred bull, kept in a temple at
Memphis, Egypt, and worshipped as a god.
See also: 46.13: Jer 43.10-13.

*46.22-23 locusts: A type of grasshopper that comes
in swarms and causes great damage to plant life.
*46.25 the god Amon of Thebes: Amon was the king
of the Egyptian gods and was the special god of the
Egyptian kings.
*46.27 Israel: See the note at 30.10-11.
See also: 46.27-28: Jer 30.10-11.

CHAPTER 47

What the LORD says about the Philistines

¹ Before the king of Egypt attacked the town of Gaza,* the LORD told me to say to the Philistines:

² I, the LORD, tell you
that your land will be flooded
    with an army from the north.
It will destroy your towns
and sweep you away,
    moaning and screaming.
³ When you hear the thunder
of horses and chariots,
    your courage will vanish,
and parents will abandon
    their own children.

⁴ You refugees from Crete,ᐟ
your time has now come,
    and I will destroy you.
None of you will be left
to help the cities
    of Tyre and Sidon.
⁵⁻⁶ The Anakim who survive*
    in Gaza and Ashkelon
will mourn for you
by shaving their heads
    and sitting in silence.
You ask how long will I continue
    to attack you with my sword,
then you tell me to put it away
    and leave you alone.
⁷ But how can my sword rest,
when I have commanded it
    to attack Ashkelon
    and the coast?

CHAPTER 48

What the LORD says about Moab

¹ The LORD All-Powerful, the God of Israel, told me to say to the nation of Moab:

---

*47.1 attacked the town of Gaza: One of the major Philistine towns; nothing is known about this attack.
*47.5–6 Anakim who survive: One ancient translation; Hebrew "people in the valley who survive". The Anakim may have been a group of people of great stature that lived in Palestine before the Israelites (see Numbers 13.33; Deuteronomy 2.10–11,20–21; and Joshua 11.21–22).
See also: 47.1–7: Isa 14.29–31; Ezek 25.15–17; Joel 3.4–8; Amos 1.6–8; Zeph 2.4–7; Zech 9.5–7. 48.1–47: Isa 15.1–16.14; 25.10–12; Ezek 25.8–11; Amos 2.1–3; Zeph 2.8–11.

The town of Nebo is doomed;
Kiriathaim will be captured
    and disgraced,
and even its fortress
    will be left in ruins.
² No one honours you, Moab.
In Heshbon, enemies make plans
    to end your life.
My sword will leave only silence
    in your town named "Quiet".*
³ The people of Horonaim
    will cry for help,
as their town is attacked
    and destroyed.

⁴ Moab will be shattered!
Your children will sob
⁵ and cry on their way up
    to the town of Luhith;
on the road to Horonaim
    they will tell of disasters.

⁶ Run for your lives!
Head into the desert
    like a wild donkey.ᐟ
⁷ You thought you could be saved
    by your power and wealth,
but you will be captured
along with your god Chemosh,
    his priests, and officials.
⁸ Not one of your towns
    will escape destruction.

I have told your enemies,
"Wipe out the valley
    and the flat lands of Moab.
⁹ Spread salt on the ground
    to kill the crops.ᐟ
Leave its towns in ruins,
    with no one living there.
¹⁰ I want you to kill the Moabites,
and if you let them escape,
    I will put a curse on you."

¹¹ Moab, you are like wine
left to settle undisturbed,
    never poured from jar to jar.
And so, your nation continues
    to prosper and improve.ᐟ
¹² But now, I will send enemies
to pour out the wine
    and smash the jars!
¹³ Then you will be ashamed,
because your god Chemosh
    cannot save you,

---

*48.2 silence . . . Quiet: In Hebrew the name of the town was "Madmen", which sounds like the word for "silence".

just as Bethel* could not help
the Israelites.

¹⁴ You claim that your soldiers
are strong and brave.
¹⁵ But I am the LORD,
the all-powerful King,
and I promise that enemies
will overpower your towns.
Even your best warriors
will die in the battle.
¹⁶ It won't be long now —
disaster will hit Moab!

¹⁷ I will order the nearby nations
to mourn for you and say,
"Isn't it sad? Moab ruled others,
but now its glorious power
has been shattered."

¹⁸ People in the town of Dibon,*
you will be honoured no more,
so have a seat in the dust.
Your walls will be torn down
when the enemies attack.

¹⁹ You people of Aroer,*
wait beside the road,
and when refugees run by,
ask them, "What happened?"
²⁰ They will answer,
"Moab has been defeated!
Weep with us in shame.
Tell everyone at the River Arnon
that Moab is destroyed."

²¹⁻²⁴I will punish every town
that belongs to Moab,
but especially Holon,
Jahzah, Mephaath,
Dibon, Nebo,
Beth-Diblathaim, Kiriathaim,
Beth-Gamul, Beth-Meon,
Kerioth, and Bozrah.›
²⁵ My decision is final —
your army will be crushed,
and your power broken.

²⁶ People of Moab, you claim
to be stronger than I am.
Now I will tell other nations
to make you drunk

and to laugh while you collapse
in your own vomit.
²⁷ You made fun of my people
and treated them like criminals
caught in the act.
²⁸ Now you must leave your towns
and live like doves
in the shelter of cliffs
and canyons.

²⁹ I know about your pride,
and how you strut and boast.
³⁰ But I also know boasting
will never save you.
³¹ So I will cry and mourn
for Moab
and its town of Kir-Heres.

³² People of Sibmah,
you were like a vineyard
heavy with grapes,
and with branches reaching
north to the town of Jazer
and west to the Dead Sea.›
But you have been destroyed,
and so I will weep for you,
as the people of Jazer weep
for the vineyards.

³³ Harvest celebrations are gone
from the orchards and farms
of Moab.
There are no happy shouts
from people making wine.
³⁴ Weeping from Heshbon
can be heard as far
as Elealeh and Jahaz;
cries from Zoar are heard
in Horonaim
and Eglath-Shelishiyah.
And Nimrim Brook has run dry.

³⁵ I will get rid of anyone
who burns incense
to the gods of Moab
or offers sacrifices
at their shrines.
I, the LORD, have spoken.

³⁶ In my heart I moan for Moab,
like a funeral song
played on a flute.
I mourn for the people
of the town of Kir-Heres,
because their wealth is gone.

³⁷⁻³⁸The people of Moab
mourn on the rooftops
and in the streets.

---

*48.13 Bethel: It may refer to the Phoenician or
Canaanite god of that name; or it may refer to the
town where people of the northern kingdom
worshipped at a local shrine (see 1 Kings 12.26–30).
*48.18 Dibon: The capital city of Moab.
*48.19 Aroer: A Moabite town just north of the River
Arnon.

Men cut off their beards,
    people shave their heads;
they make cuts on their hands
    and wear sackcloth.*
And it's all because I, the LORD,
have shattered Moab like a jar
    that no one wants.
39 Moab lies broken!
Listen to its people cry
    as they turn away in shame.
Other nations are horrified
at what happened,
    but still they laugh.

40 Moab, an enemy swoops down
like an eagle spreading its wings
    over your land.
41 Your cities' and fortresses
    will be captured,
and your warriors gripped by fear.'
42 You are finished as a nation,
    because you dared oppose me,
    the LORD.
43 Terror, pits, and traps
    are waiting for you.
44 If you are terrified and run,
    you will fall into a pit;
and if you crawl out of the pit,
    you'll get caught in a trap.
The time has come
    for you to be punished.

45 Near the city of Heshbon,
    where Sihon once ruled,
tired refugees stand in shadows
cast by the flames
    of their burning city.
Soon, the towns on other hilltops,
where those warlike people live,
    will also go up in smoke.

46 People of Moab, you worshipped
Chemosh, your god,
    but now you are done for,
and your children are prisoners
    in a foreign country.
47 Yet some day, I will bring
    your people back home.
I, the LORD, have spoken.

CHAPTER 49

What the LORD says about Ammon

1 The LORD has this to say about the nation of Ammon:

The people of Israel
have plenty of children
    to inherit their lands.
So why have you worshippers
    of the god Milcom*
taken over towns and land
    belonging to the Gad tribe?
2 Some day I will send an army
to attack you in Rabbah,
    your capital city.
It will be left in ruins,
and the surrounding villages
    will lie in ashes.
You took some of Israel's land,
but on that day
    Israel will take yours!

3 Cry, people of Heshbon;*
your town will become
    a pile of rubble.'
You will turn here and there,
    but your path will be blocked.'

Put on sackcloth* and mourn,
    you citizens of Rabbah,
because the idol you worship*
will be taken
    to a foreign country,
along with its priests
    and temple officials.
4 You rebellious Ammonites
trust your wealth and ask,
    "Who could attack us?"
But I warn you not to boast
    when your strength is fading.'
5 I, the LORD All-Powerful,
will send neighbouring nations
    to strike you with terror.
You will be scattered,
with no one to care
    for your refugees.
6 Yet some day, I will bring
    your people back home.
I, the LORD, have spoken.

What the LORD says about Edom

7-8 The LORD All-Powerful says about Edom:

49.1 Milcom: The national god of Ammon, probably the same as the god Molech in 32.35.
49.3 Heshbon: See also 48.45; since Heshbon was near the border of Moab and Ammon, it was probably ruled by the country that was stronger at the time.
49.3 sackcloth: See the note at 4.8.
49.3 the idol you worship: Hebrew "Milcom" (see verse 1 and the note there).

See also: 49.7-22: Isa 34.5-17; 63.1-6; Ezek 25.12-14; 35.1-15; Amos 1.11-12; Obad 1-14; Mal 1.2-5.

48.37-38 sackcloth: See the note at 4.8.
See also: 49.1-6: Ezek 21.28-32; 25.1-7; Amos 1.13-15; Zeph 2.8-11.

Wisdom and common sense
have vanished from Teman.*
I will send disaster to punish
you descendants of Esau,*
so anyone from Dedan*
had better turn round
and run back home.'
⁹ People who harvest grapes
leave some for the poor.
Thieves who break in at night
take only what they want.
¹⁰ But I will take everything
that belongs to you,
people of Edom,
and I will uncover every place
where you try to hide.
Then you will die,
and so will your children,
relatives, and neighbours.
¹¹ But I can be trusted
to care for your orphans
and widows.

¹² Even those nations that don't deserve to
be punished will have to drink from the
cup of my anger. So how can you possibly
hope to escape? ¹³ I, the LORD, swear in my
own name that your city of Bozrah* and all
your towns will suffer a horrible fate. They
will lie in ruins for ever, and people will use
the name "Bozrah" as a curse word.

¹⁴ I have sent a messenger
to command the nations
to prepare for war
against you people of Edom.
¹⁵ Your nation will be small,
yet hated by other nations.
¹⁶ Pride tricks you into thinking
that other nations
look at you with fear.'
You live along the cliffs
and high in the mountains
like the eagles,
but I am the LORD,
and I will bring you down.
¹⁷ People passing by your country
will be shocked and horrified
to see a disaster

¹⁸ as bad as the destruction
of Sodom and Gomorrah
and towns nearby.
The towns of Edom will be empty.

¹⁹ I will attack you
like a lion from the forest,
attacking sheep in a meadow
along the Jordan.
In a moment the flock runs,
and the land is empty.
Who will I choose to attack you?
I will do it myself!
No one can force me to fight
or chase me away.
²⁰ Listen to my plans for you,
people of Edom.'
Your children will be dragged off
and your country destroyed.
²¹ The sounds of your destruction
will reach the Red Sea*
and cause the earth to shake.
²² An enemy will swoop down
to attack you,
like an eagle spreading its wings
and circling over Bozrah.
Your warriors will be gripped
by fear.'

What the LORD says about Damascus

²³ The LORD says about Damascus:

The towns of Hamath and Arpad*
have heard your bad news.
They have lost hope,
and worries roll over them
like ocean waves.'
²⁴ You people of Damascus
have lost your courage,
and in panic you turn to run,
gripped by fear and pain.'

²⁵ I once was pleased
with your famous city.
But now I warn you, "Escape
while you still can!"'
²⁶ Soon, even your best soldiers
will lie dead in your streets.

---

*49.7-8 Teman: The name of a town in Edom,
sometimes used as the name of the northern half of
the nation of Edom; here it probably stands for the
whole nation.
*49.7-8 Esau: The ancestor of the nation of Edom.
*49.7-8 Dedan: The name of a town in north-west
Arabia, also used of the north-west region of Arabia
along the Red Sea.
*49.13 Bozrah: The main city and capital of Edom.

*49.21 Red Sea: Hebrew *yam suph*, here referring to
the Gulf of Aqaba, since the term is extended to
include the north-eastern arm of the Red Sea (see also
the note at Exodus 13.18).
*49.23 Hamath and Arpad: Two towns in Syria that
had been the capitals of small kingdoms allied with
the more powerful kingdom whose capital was
Damascus.
See also: 49.18: Gen 19.24-25. 49.23-27: Isa 17.1-3;
Amos 1.3-5; Zech 9.1.

I, the LORD All-Powerful,
have spoken.

27 I will set fire to your city walls
and burn down the fortresses
King Benhadad built.

Nebuchadnezzar and the people of the desert

28 Here is what the LORD says about the Kedar tribe and the desert villages' that were conquered by King Nebuchadnezzar* of Babylonia:

Listen, you people of Kedar
and the other tribes
of the eastern desert.
I have told Nebuchadnezzar
to attack and destroy you.
29 His fearsome army
will surround you,
taking your tents and possessions,
your sheep and camels.

30 Run and hide,
you people of the desert
who live in villages!'
Nebuchadnezzar has big plans
for you.
31 You have no city walls
and no neighbours to help,
yet you think you're safe —
so I told him to attack.
32 Then your camels and large herds
will be yours no longer.

People of the Arabian Desert,'
disaster will strike you
from every side,
and you will be scattered
everywhere on earth.
33 Only jackals* will live
where your villages' once stood.
I, the LORD, have spoken.

What the LORD says about Elam

34-35 Not long after Zedekiah* became king of Judah, the LORD told me to say:

People of Elam,*
I, the LORD All-Powerful,
will kill the archers
who make your army strong.

36 Enemies will attack
from all directions,
and you will be led captive
to every nation on earth.
37 Their armies will crush
and kill you,
and you will face the disaster
that my anger brings.
38 Your king and his officials
will die, and I will rule
in their place.
I, the LORD, have spoken.

39 But I promise that some day
I will bring your people
back to their land.

CHAPTER 50

Babylon will be captured

1-2 The LORD told me to say:

Announce what will happen
and don't leave anything out.
Raise the signal flags;
shout so all nations can hear —
Babylon will be captured!

Marduk,' Babylon's god,
will be ashamed and terrified,
and his idols broken.
3 The attack on the Babylonians
will come from the north;
they and their animals will run,
leaving the land empty.

Israel and Judah will return to their land

4 The LORD said:

People of Israel and Judah,
when these things happen
you will weep, and together
you will return to your land
and worship me,
the LORD your God.
5 You will ask the way to Zion
and then come and join with me
in making an agreement
you won't break or forget.

6 My people, you are lost sheep
abandoned by their shepherds
in the mountains.
You don't even remember
your resting place.

---

*49.28 Nebuchadnezzar: See the note at 21.2.
*49.33 jackals: See the note at 9.11.
*49.34–35 Zedekiah: See the note at 1.3.
*49.34–35 Elam: A nation east of Babylonia, attacked by Nebuchadnezzar about 596 BC.

See also: 50.1—51.64: Isa 13.1—14.23; 47.1–15.

7 I am your true pasture land,
   the one who gave hope
      to your ancestors.
   But you abandoned me,
   so when your enemies found you,
      they felt no guilt
         as they gobbled you up.

8 Escape from Babylonia,
   my people.
   Get out of that country!
      Don't wait for anyone else.
9 In the north I am bringing
      great nations together.
   They will attack Babylon
      and capture it.
   The arrows they shoot
   are like the best soldiers,'
      always finding their target.
10 Babylonia will be conquered,
   and its enemies will carry off
      everything they want.

Babylon will be disgraced

The LORD said:

11 People of Babylonia,
   you were glad
      to rob my people.
   You had a good time,
   making more noise
      than horses
   and jumping around
      like calves threshing grain.'
12 The city of Babylon
      was like a mother to you.
   But it will be disgraced
   and become nothing
      but a barren desert.
13 My anger will destroy Babylon,
      and no one will live there.
   Everyone who passes by
   will be shocked to see
      what has happened.

14 Babylon has rebelled against me.
      Archers, take your places.
   Shoot all your arrows at Babylon.
15   Attack from every side!

   Babylon surrenders!
   The enemy tears down
      its walls and towers.
   I am taking my revenge
   by doing to Babylon what it did
      to other cities.

16 There is no one in Babylonia
      to plant or harvest crops.
   Even foreigners who lived there
   have left for their homelands,
      afraid of the enemy armies.

17 Israel is a flock of sheep
      scattered by hungry lions.
   The king of Assyria*
      first gobbled Israel up.
   Then Nebuchadnezzar,*
      king of Babylonia,
   crunched on Israel's bones.
18 I, the LORD All-Powerful,
   the God of Israel,
      punished the king of Assyria,
   and I will also punish
      the king of Babylonia.
19 But I will bring Israel
      back to its own land.
   The people will be like sheep
      eating their fill
   on Mount Carmel
      and in Bashan,
   in the hill country of Ephraim
      and in Gilead.
20 I will rescue a few people
      from Israel and Judah.
   I will forgive them so completely
   that their sin and guilt
      will disappear,
      never to be found.

The LORD's commands to the enemies of Babylonia

21 The LORD said:

   I have told
      the enemies of Babylonia,
   "Attack the people of Merathaim
      and Pekod.'
   Kill them all!
      Destroy their possessions!"

22 Sounds of war
   and the noise of destruction
      can be heard.
23 Babylonia was a hammer
   pounding every country,
      but now it lies broken.
   What a shock to the nations
      of the world!

---

*50.17 king of Assyria:** Either Shalmaneser V, who
ruled 726–722 BC, conquered most of the northern
kingdom, and surrounded its capital city Samaria; or
Sargon II, who ruled 721–705 BC and took thousands
of prisoners back to Assyria.
*50.17 Nebuchadnezzar:** See the note at 21.2.

See also: 50.8: Rev 18.4.

24 Babylonia challenged me,
  the LORD God All-Powerful,
but that nation doesn't know
  it is caught in a trap that I set.
25 I've brought out my weapons,
  and with them
  I will put a curse on Babylonia.

26 Come from far away,
  you enemies of Babylon!
Pile up the grain from its storehouses,
  and destroy it completely,
  along with everything else.
27 Kill the soldiers of Babylonia,
  because the time has come
  for them to be punished.

28 The Babylonian army
  destroyed my temple,
  but soon I will take revenge.
Then refugees from Babylon
  will tell about it in Zion.

29 Attack Babylon, enemy archers;
set up camp around the city,
  and don't let anyone escape.
It challenged me, the holy God,
  so do to it
  what it did to other cities.

Proud Babylon will fall

The LORD said:

30 People of Babylon,
  I, the LORD, promise
that even your best soldiers
  will lie dead in the streets.

31 Babylon, you should be named,
  "The Proud One".
But the time has come when I,
  the LORD All-Powerful,
  will punish you.
32 You are proud,
  but you will stumble and fall,
  and no one will help you up.
I will set your villages on fire,
  and everything around you
  will go up in flames.

33 You Babylonians were cruel
  to Israel and Judah.
You took them captive, and now
  you refuse to let them go.
34 But I, the LORD All-Powerful,
  will rescue and protect them.
I will bring peace to their land
  and trouble to yours.

35 I have declared war on you,
  your officials, and advisers.
36 This war will prove
  that your prophets
  are liars and fools.
And it will frighten
  your warriors.
37 Then your chariot horses
  and the foreigners in your army
  will refuse to go into battle,
  and the enemy will carry away
  everything you treasure.
38 Your rivers and canals
  will dry up.

All this will happen,
  because your land
  is full of idols,
and they have made fools
  of you.
39 Never again will people live
  in your land —
only desert animals, jackals,*
  and unclean birds.
40 I destroyed Sodom and Gomorrah
  and the nearby towns,
  and I will destroy Babylon
  just as completely.
No one will live there again.

Babylonia is invaded

The LORD said:

41 Far to the north,
  a nation and its allies
  have been awakened.
They are powerful
  and ready for war.
42 Bows and arrows and swords
  are in their hands.
The soldiers are cruel
  and show no pity.
The hoofbeats of their horses
  echo like ocean waves
  crashing against the shore.
The army has lined up for battle
  and is coming to attack you,
  people of Babylonia!

43 Ever since your king heard
  about this army,
he has been weak with fear;
he twists and turns in pain
  like a woman giving birth.
44 Babylonia, I will attack you
  like a lion from the forest,

*50.39 jackals: See the note at 9.11.

See also: 50.39: Rev 18.2. 50.40: Gen 19.24–25.

See also: 50.29: Rev 18.6.

attacking sheep in a meadow
along the Jordan.
In a moment the flock runs,
and the land is empty.
Who will I choose to attack you?
I will do it myself!
No one can force me to fight
or chase me away.

⁴⁵ Listen to my plans for you,
people of Babylonia.
Your children will be dragged off,
and your country destroyed.

⁴⁶ The sounds of your destruction
will be heard among the nations,
and the earth will shake.

CHAPTER 51

Babylon will be destroyed

The LORD said:

¹ I, the LORD, am sending
a wind᾿ to destroy
the people of Babylonia᾿
and Babylon, its capital.

² Foreign soldiers will come
from every direction,
and when the disaster is over,
Babylonia will be empty
and worthless.

³ I will tell these soldiers,
"Attack quickly,
before the Babylonians
can string their bows
or put on their armour.᾿
Kill their best soldiers
and destroy their army!"

⁴ Their troops will fall wounded
in the streets of Babylon.

⁵ Everyone in Israel and Judah
is guilty.
But I, the LORD All-Powerful,
their holy God,
have not abandoned them.

⁶ Get out of Babylon!
Run for your lives!
If you stay, you will be killed
when I take revenge on the city
and punish it for its sins.

⁷ Babylon was my golden cup,
filled with the wine
of my anger.
The nations of the world
got drunk on this wine
and went insane.

⁸ But suddenly, Babylon will fall
and be destroyed.

I, the LORD, told the foreigners᾿
who lived there,
"Weep for the city!
Get medicine for its wounds;
perhaps they will heal."

⁹ The foreigners answered,
"We have already tried
to treat Babylon's wounds,
but they would not heal.
Come on, let's all go home
to our own countries.
Nothing is left in Babylonia;
everything is destroyed."

¹⁰ The people of Israel said,
"Tell everyone in Zion!
The LORD has taken revenge
for what Babylon did to us."

The LORD wants Babylon destroyed

The LORD said:

¹¹ I, the LORD,
want Babylon destroyed,
because its army
destroyed my temple.
So, you kings of Media,*
sharpen your arrows
and pick up your shields.

¹² Raise the signal flag
and attack the city walls.
Post more guards.
Command soldiers to watch the city
and set up ambushes.
I have made plans to destroy Babylon,
and nothing will stop me.

¹³ People of Babylon, you live
along the River Euphrates
and are surrounded by canals.
You are rich,
but now the time has come
for you to die.᾿

¹⁴ I, the LORD All-Powerful,
swear by my own life
that enemy soldiers
will fill your streets
like a swarm of locusts.*
They will shout
and celebrate their victory.

---

*51.11 kings of Media: Probably kings of smaller
kingdoms that were part of the Median empire (see
also verse 27 and the note there).
*51.14 locusts: See the note at 46.22–23.
See also: 51.9: Rev 18.5.   51.13: Rev 17.1.

A hymn of praise

This is also told in Jeremiah 10.12–16

15 God used his wisdom and power
    to create the earth
    and spread out the heavens.
16 The waters in the heavens roar
    at his command.
He makes clouds appear;
he sends the wind
    from his storehouse
and makes lightning flash
    in the rain.

17 People who make idols
    are stupid!
They will be disappointed,
because their false gods
    cannot breathe.
18 Idols are merely a joke,
    and when the time is right,
    they will be destroyed.
19 But the LORD, Israel's God,
    is all-powerful.
He created everything,
    and he chose Israel
    to be his very own.

God's hammer

The LORD said:

20 Babylonia, you were my hammer;
    I used you to pound nations
    and break kingdoms,
21 to shatter cavalry and chariots,
22 as well as men and women,
    young and old,
23 shepherds and their flocks,
    farmers and their oxen,
    and governors and leaders.

24 But now, my people will watch,
    while I repay you
    for what you did to Zion.

25 You destroyed the nations
    and seem strong as a mountain,
    but I am your enemy.
I might even grab you
    and roll you off a cliff.
When I have finished,
    you'll only be a pile
    of scorched bricks.
26 Your stone blocks won't be reused
    for cornerstones
    or foundations,
    and I promise that for ever
    you will be a desert.
I, the LORD, have spoken.

The nations will attack Babylon

The LORD said:

27 Signal the nations
    to get ready to attack.
Raise a flag and blow a trumpet.
Send for the armies of Ararat,
    Minni, and Ashkenaz.*
Choose a commander;
let the cavalry attack
    like a swarm of locusts.
28 Tell the kings and governors,
    the leaders and the people
of the kingdoms of the Medes
    to prepare for war!

29 The earth twists and turns
    in torment,
because I have decided
to make Babylonia a desert
    where no one can live,
and I won't change my mind.

30 The Babylonian soldiers
have lost their strength
    and courage.'
They stay in their fortresses,
    unable to fight,
while the enemy breaks through
    the city gates,
    then sets their homes on fire.
31 One messenger after another
    announces to the king,
    "Babylon has been captured!"
32 The enemy now controls
    the river crossings!
The marshes* are on fire!
    Your army has panicked!"

33 I am the LORD All-Powerful,
    the God of Israel,
    and I make this promise —
    "Soon Babylon will be levelled
    and packed down
    like a threshing place
    at harvest time."*

---

*51.27 Ararat, Minni, and Ashkenaz: Kingdoms to the north of Babylonia that were part of the Median empire (see also verse 28).
*51.32 marshes: The tall grass in the marshes could have provided hiding places for people trying to escape from Babylon.
*51.33 levelled . . . harvest time: A threshing place with an earth surface had to be levelled and packed down before it could be used.

Babylonia will pay!

34 The people of Jerusalem say,
   "King Nebuchadnezzar*
   made us panic.
That monster stuffed himself
   with us and our treasures,
      leaving us empty —
he gobbled up
   what he wanted
      and spat out the rest.
35 The people of Babylonia
   harmed some of us'
      and killed others.
Now, LORD, make them pay!"

The LORD will take revenge on Babylon

The LORD said:

36 My people, I am on your side,
   and I will take revenge on Babylon.
I will cut off its water supply,
   and its stream* will dry up.
37 Babylon will be a pile of rubble
   where only jackals* live.
People will laugh,
   but they will be afraid
      to walk among the ruins.
38 The Babylonians roar and growl
   like young lions.
39 And since they are hungry,
   I will give them a banquet.
They will celebrate, get drunk,
   then fall asleep,
      never to wake up!
40 I will lead them away to die,
   like sheep, lambs, and goats
      being led to the butcher.
41 All nations now praise Babylon,'
   but when it is captured,
      those same nations will be horrified.
42 Babylon's enemies will rise
   like ocean waves
      and flood the city.
43 Horrible destruction will strike
   the nearby towns.
The land will become
   a barren desert,
where no one can live
   or even travel.
44 I will punish Marduk,'
   the god of Babylon,
and make him vomit
   everything he gobbled up.

Then nations will no longer
   bring him gifts,
and Babylon's walls will crumble.

The LORD offers hope to his people

The LORD said:

45 Get out of Babylon, my people,
   and run for your lives,
before I strike the city
   in my anger!
46 Don't be afraid or lose hope,
   though year after year
      there are rumours
of leaders fighting for control
   in the city of Babylon.
47 The time will come
   when I will punish
      Babylon's false gods.
Everyone there will die,
   and the whole nation
      will be disgraced,
48 when an army attacks
   from the north
      and brings destruction.
Then the earth and the heavens
   and everything in them will celebrate.
49 Babylon must be overthrown,
   because it slaughtered
      the people of Israel
      and of many other nations.

50 My people, you escaped death
   when Jerusalem fell.
Now you live far from home,
   but you should trust me
      and think about Jerusalem.
Leave Babylon! Don't stay!

51 You feel ashamed and disgraced,
   because foreigners have entered
      my sacred temple.
52 Soon I will send a war
   to punish Babylon's idols
and leave its wounded people
   moaning everywhere.
53 Although Babylon's walls
   reach to the sky,
the army I send
   will destroy that city.
I, the LORD, have spoken.

Babylon will be destroyed

The LORD said:

54 Listen to the cries for help
   coming from Babylon.

---

*51.34 Nebuchadnezzar: See the note at 21.2.
*51.36 stream: Probably the River Euphrates.
*51.37 jackals: See the note at 9.11.

See also: 51.48: Rev 18.20.   51.49: Rev 18.24.

Everywhere in the country
the sounds of destruction
can be heard.
⁵⁵ The shouts of the enemy,
like crashing ocean waves,
will drown out Babylon's cries
as I level the city.

⁵⁶ An enemy will attack
and destroy Babylon.
Its soldiers will be captured
and their weapons broken,
because I am a God
who takes revenge against nations
for what they do.
⁵⁷ I, the LORD All-Powerful,
the true King, promise
that the officials and advisers,
the governors and leaders
and the soldiers of Babylon
will get drunk, fall asleep,
and never wake up.
⁵⁸ The thick walls of that city
will be torn down,
and its huge gates burnt.
Everything that nation
worked so hard to gain
will go up in smoke.

Jeremiah gives Seraiah a scroll

⁵⁹ During Zedekiah's* fourth year as king of
Judah, he went to Babylon. And Baruch's
brother Seraiah* went along as the officer in
charge of arranging for places to stay
overnight.'
⁶⁰ Before they left, I wrote on a scroll* all the
terrible things that would happen to Babylon.
⁶¹ I gave the scroll to Seraiah and said:

When you get to Babylon, read this scroll
aloud, ⁶² then pray, "Our LORD, you
promised to destroy this place and make it
into a desert where no people or animals
will ever live."

⁶³ When you finish praying, tie the scroll
to a rock and throw it in the River
Euphrates. Then say, ⁶⁴ "This is how
Babylon will sink when the LORD destroys
it. Everyone in the city will die, and it
won't have the strength to rise again."

The end of Jeremiah's writing

Jeremiah's writing ends here.

Another account of the fall of Jerusalem

CHAPTER 52

Jerusalem is captured

This is also told in 2 Kings 24.18—25.30;
2 Chronicles 36.11–21

¹ Zedekiah was twenty-one years old when he
was appointed king of Judah,* and he ruled
from Jerusalem for eleven years.* His mother
Hamutal was the daughter of Jeremiah from
the town of Libnah.* ² Zedekiah disobeyed
the LORD, just as Jehoiakim had done, ³ and it
was Zedekiah who finally rebelled against
Nebuchadnezzar.*

The people of Judah and Jerusalem had
made the LORD so angry that he finally
turned his back on them. That's why horrible
things were happening.

⁴ In Zedekiah's ninth year as king, on the
tenth day of the tenth month,* King
Nebuchadnezzar of Babylonia led his entire
army to attack Jerusalem. The troops set up
camp outside the city and built ramps up to
the city walls.

⁵⁻⁶ After a year and a half,* all the food in
Jerusalem was gone. Then on the ninth day of
the fourth month,* ⁷ the Babylonian troops
broke through the city wall. That same night,
Zedekiah and his soldiers tried to escape
through the gate near the royal garden, even
though they knew the enemy had the city
surrounded. They headed towards the Jordan
valley, ⁸ but the Babylonian troops caught up
with them near Jericho. The Babylonians
arrested Zedekiah, but his soldiers scattered in
every direction. ⁹ Zedekiah was taken to
Riblah in the land of Hamath, where
Nebuchadnezzar put him on trial and found
him guilty. ¹⁰ Zedekiah's sons and the officials

---

*51.59 **Zedekiah's:** See the note at 1.3.
*51.59 **Baruch's brother Seraiah:** Hebrew "Seraiah
son of Neriah and grandson of Mahseiah"; Baruch
helped Jeremiah write down his messages (see 32.12;
36.4–10).
*51.60 **scroll:** See the note at 30.1–2.
See also: 51.63–64: Rev 18.21.

*52.1 **appointed king of Judah:** By Nebuchadnezzar
(see 37.1).
*52.1 **he ruled . . . years:** Ruled 598–586 BC.
*52.1 **Jeremiah from the town of Libnah:** Not the
same Jeremiah as the author of this book (see 1.1).
*52.3 **Nebuchadnezzar:** See the note at 21.2.
*52.4 **tenth month:** See the note at 39.1–3.
*52.5–6 **After a year and a half:** Jerusalem was
captured in 586 BC.
*52.5–6 **fourth month:** See the note at 39.1–3.
See also: 52.4: Ezek 24.2. **52.7:** Ezek 33.21.

of Judah were killed while he watched, 11 then his eyes were put out. He was put in chains, then dragged off to Babylon and kept in prison until he died.

12 Jerusalem was captured during Nebuchadnezzar's nineteenth year as king of Babylonia.

About a month later,◗ Nebuchadnezzar's officer in charge of the guards arrived in Jerusalem. His name was Nebuzaradan, 13 and he burnt down the LORD's temple, the king's palace, and every important building in the city, as well as all the houses. 14 Then he ordered the Babylonian soldiers to break down the walls around Jerusalem. 15 He led away the people left in the city, including everyone who had become loyal to Nebuchadnezzar, the rest of the skilled workers,* and even some of the poor people of Judah. 16 Only the very poorest were left behind to work the vineyards and the fields.

17-20 Nebuzaradan ordered his soldiers to go to the temple and take everything made of gold or silver, including bowls, fire pans, sprinkling bowls, pans, lampstands, dishes for incense, and the cups for wine offerings. The Babylonian soldiers took all the bronze things used for worship at the temple, including the pans for hot ashes, and the shovels, lamp snuffers, sprinkling bowls, and dishes for incense. The soldiers also took everything else made of bronze, including the two columns that stood in front of the temple, the large bowl called the Sea, the twelve bulls that held it up, and the moveable stands.◗ The soldiers broke these things into pieces so they could take them to Babylonia. There was so much bronze that it could not be weighed. 21 For example, the columns were about eight metres high and five metres around. They were hollow, but the bronze was about seventy-five millimetres thick. 22 Each column had a bronze cap over two metres high that was decorated with bronze designs. Some of these designs were like chains and others were like pomegranates.* 23 There were ninety-six pomegranates evenly spaced◗ around each column, and a total of one hundred pomegranates were above the chains.

24 Next, Nebuzaradan arrested Seraiah the chief priest, Zephaniah his assistant, and three temple officials. 25 Then he arrested one of the army commanders, seven of King Zedekiah's personal advisers, and the officer in charge of gathering the troops for battle. He also found sixty more soldiers who were still in Jerusalem. 26-27 Nebuzaradan led them to Riblah in the land of Hamath, where Nebuchadnezzar had them killed.

The people of Judah no longer lived in their own country.

People of Judah taken prisoner

28-30 Here is a list of the number of the people of Judah that Nebuchadnezzar* took to Babylonia as prisoners:

> In his seventh year as king, he took
> 3,023 people.
> In his eighteenth year as king, he took
> 832 from Jerusalem.
> In his twenty-third year as king, his
> officer Nebuzaradan took 745 people.

So, Nebuchadnezzar took a total of 4,600 people from Judah to Babylonia.

Jehoiachin is set free

This is also told in 2 Kings 25.27-30

31 Jehoiachin* was a prisoner in Babylon for thirty-seven years. Then Evil Merodach* became king of Babylonia, and in the first year of his rule, on the twenty-fifth day of the twelfth month,* he let Jehoiachin out of prison. 32 Evil Merodach was kind to Jehoiachin and honoured him more than any of the other kings held prisoner there. 33 Jehoiachin was allowed to wear ordinary clothes instead of a prison uniform, and he even ate at the king's table every day. 34 As long as Jehoiachin lived, he was paid a daily allowance to buy whatever he needed.

---

*52.28-30 Nebuchadnezzar: See the note at 21.2.
*51.31 Jehoiachin: See the note at 24.1.
*52.31 Evil Merodach: The son of Nebuchadnezzar who ruled Babylonia from 562–560 BC.
*52.31 twelfth month: Adar, the twelfth month of the Hebrew calendar, from about mid-February to mid-March.

Additional notes

◗2.18 trusted . . . Assyria: Hebrew "went to Egypt and drank from the River Shihor, and you went to Assyria and drank from the River Euphrates."

---

*52.15 the rest of the skilled workers:
Nebuchadnezzar had taken away some of the skilled workers eleven years before (see 2 Kings 24.14–16).
*2.22 pomegranates: A small red fruit that looks like an apple.
See also: 52.11: Ezek 12.13.   52.13: 1 King 9.8.
52.17-23: 1 King 7.15-47.

›**2.23 Baal:** The Hebrew text has "the Baals", probably because the god Baal was believed to be present in different forms at different places of worship.

›**2.37 in great sadness:** Or "as prisoners".

›**3.24 that shameful god Baal:** The Hebrew text has "The Shame", which was sometimes used as a way of making fun of the Canaanite god Baal.

›**4.5–6 Judah:** Hebrew "Judah and Jerusalem".

›**5.28 refuse to help:** One possible meaning for the difficult Hebrew text.

›**5.31 give . . . god:** Or "tell lies".

›**5.31 don't . . . me:** Or "don't care what I want".

›**6.2–3 Jerusalem . . . grass:** One possible meaning for the difficult Hebrew text.

›**7.1–3 temple:** The Hebrew text has "house of the LORD", another name for the temple.

›**7.1–3 let you . . . own country:** Or "live here with you".

›**8.4 if you take . . . go back:** One possible meaning for the difficult Hebrew text.

›**8.6 you run down the wrong road:** One possible meaning for the difficult Hebrew text.

›**8.13 I will wipe them out:** One possible meaning for the difficult Hebrew text.

›**8.13 They have not . . . them:** One possible meaning for the difficult Hebrew text.

›**9.14 Baal:** See the note at 2.23.

›**9.15 poison to eat and drink:** Or "bitter disappointment to eat, and tears to drink".

›**9.25–26 the tribes of the desert:** One possible meaning for the difficult Hebrew text.

›**10.18 like a stone from a sling:** One possible meaning for the difficult Hebrew text.

›**11.15 celebrating:** One possible meaning for the difficult Hebrew text of verse 15.

›**12.4 God can't see the sins we commit:** Or "Jeremiah won't live to see what happens to us."

›**12.9 My people . . . other hawks:** Or "My land has become a hyena's den with vultures circling above."

›**13.9 I will use Babylonia to:** Or "that's how I'm going to".

›**13.18 and remove their crowns:** One possible meaning for the difficult Hebrew text.

›**13.21 You once . . . rule you:** One possible meaning for the difficult Hebrew text.

›**14.4 cracks . . . ground:** One possible meaning for the difficult Hebrew text.

›**14.6 sniff the air:** The Hebrew text has "sniff the air, like jackals" (see the footnote at 9.11).

›**14.18 go about . . . has happened:** One possible meaning for the difficult Hebrew text.

›**15.11 help:** One possible meaning for the difficult Hebrew text of verse 11.

›**15.14 that cannot be put out:** Some Hebrew manuscripts; most Hebrew manuscripts "against you".

›**15.14 I will make . . . land:** Many Hebrew manuscripts; most Hebrew manuscripts "I will make your enemies go through to a land you don't know about."

›**17.2–3 enemies:** One possible meaning for the difficult Hebrew text of verses 2,3.

›**17.4 You will lose:** One possible meaning for the difficult Hebrew text.

›**17.13 reject . . . dust:** One possible meaning for the difficult Hebrew text.

›**17.16 you chose . . . punish them:** One possible meaning for the difficult Hebrew text.

›**18.14 dry:** One possible meaning for the difficult Hebrew text of verse 14.

›**20.2 hit me:** Or "beat me up" or "had me beaten up".

›**20.2 in chains:** Or "in the stocks" (a wooden frame with holes for the hands, neck, or feet of a prisoner) or "in a prison cell".

›**20.3 Afraid-of-Everything:** Hebrew "Magor-Missabib".

›**21.13 Jerusalem . . . valleys:** One possible meaning for the difficult Hebrew text.

›**22.11–12 Jehoahaz:** The Hebrew text has "Shallum", another name for Jehoahaz.

›**22.20 nations:** Or "gods".

›**23.9 tremble:** Or "become weak".

›**23.10 deserts:** One possible meaning for the difficult Hebrew text of verse 10.

›**23.14 in marriage:** Or "to me".

›**23.14 never tell the truth:** Or "worship other gods".

›**23.33 You people are a nuisance to the LORD, and he:** Two ancient translations; Hebrew "Does the LORD have news for us? He".

›**23.39 pick you up:** A few Hebrew manuscripts and three ancient translations; most Hebrew manuscripts "forget you completely".

›**25.23–24 the tribes of the Arabian Desert:** One possible meaning for the difficult Hebrew text.

›**25.26 Babylonia:** The Hebrew text has "Sheshach", a secret way of writing "Babylonia".

›**25.34 You'll shatter . . . floor:** One possible meaning for the difficult Hebrew text.

›**25.36–38 anger turns:** Or "anger and enemy armies turn".

›**25.36–38 The LORD has . . . people:** Or "And his people leave their homes".

›**27.1–2 Not long after Zedekiah became king of Judah:** A few manuscripts and one ancient translation; most Hebrew manuscripts "Not long after Jehoiakim became king of Judah"; most manuscripts of another ancient translation do not have these words. Jehoiakim ruled 609–598 BC, and Zedekiah ruled 598–586 BC.

›**28.1 Later . . . king:** One possible meaning for the difficult Hebrew text.

›**29.3 Elasah and Gemariah:** Hebrew "Elasah son of Shaphan and Gemariah son of Hilkiah".

›**29.24–25 Shemaiah:** Hebrew "Shemaiah, who came from the town of Nehelam".

›**29.26 in chains:** See the note at 20.2.

›**30.18 Jerusalem . . . palace:** Or "Your towns lie in ruins, but you will rebuild them, and your homes will be where they were before".

›**31.2 In the desert . . . same for you:** One possible meaning for the difficult Hebrew text.

'31.3 Some time . . . me: Or "The LORD appeared to me from far away".

'31.8 Babylonia: The Hebrew text has "that country in the north", referring to Babylonia.

'31.9 level: Or "straight".

'31.9 Israel: The Hebrew text also has "Ephraim", the leading tribe of the northern kingdom of Israel, which sometimes stands for the whole northern kingdom.

'31.15 In Ramah: Or "In the hills".

'31.18 Israel: Hebrew "Ephraim" (see the note at 31.9).

'31.22 I will make sure . . . a woman protecting a man: One possible meaning for the difficult Hebrew text.

'31.26 and when they sleep . . . refreshed: One possible meaning for the difficult Hebrew text.

'32.12 Baruch son of Neriah: Hebrew "Baruch son of Neriah and grandson of Mahseiah".

'32.18 for a thousand generations: Or "to thousands of people".

'33.1-2 the whole world: One ancient translation; Hebrew "it".

'33.4,5 have been torn down . . . Babylonian attackers: One possible meaning for the difficult Hebrew text.

'33.6 let them enjoy unending peace: One possible meaning for the difficult Hebrew text.

'35.3 Jaazaniah: The Hebrew text has "Jaazaniah son of Jeremiah son of Habazziniah"; this is a different Jeremiah from the author of the book.

'35.4 Maaseiah . . . temple: Hebrew "Maaseiah son of Shallum, the keeper of the temple door".

'36.12 Delaiah, Elnathan, and Zedekiah: Hebrew "Delaiah son of Shemaiah, Elnathan son of Achbor, and Zedekiah son of Hananiah".

'36.14 Jehudi and Shelemiah: Hebrew "Jehudi son of Nethaniah and Shelemiah son of Cushi".

'36.26 Seraiah and Shelemiah: Hebrew "Seraiah son of Azriel and Shelemiah son of Abdeel".

'37.3-5 Egyptian army: Led by King Apries, also known as Hophra.

'37.3-5 Jehucal and the priest Zephaniah: Hebrew "Jehucal son of Shelemiah, and the priest Zephaniah son of Maaseiah".

'37.13 Irijah: Hebrew "Irijah son of Shelemiah and grandson of Hananiah".

'38.1 Jehucal: The Hebrew text has "Jucal", another form of the name.

'38.1 Shephatiah, Gedaliah, Jehucal, and Pashhur: Hebrew "Shephatiah son of Mattan, Gedaliah son of Pashhur, Jucal son of Shelemiah, and Pashhur son of Malchiah".

'38.10 thirty: Most Hebrew manuscripts; one Hebrew manuscript "three".

'38.14 his private entrance: One possible meaning for the difficult Hebrew text.

'38.23 Jerusalem will be burnt down: A few Hebrew manuscripts and three ancient translations; most Hebrew manuscripts "you will burn Jerusalem down"; one ancient translation "he will burn Jerusalem down".

'39.1-3 highest officials: The Hebrew text gives Nergal Sharezer's title as "the Rabmag", and Nebo Sarsechim's title as "the Rabsaris", but the exact meaning of the titles and the duties of these offices are not known.

'39.1-3 Nebo Sarsechim: Probably another form of the name Nebushazban (see verse 13).

'39.1-3 Nergal Sharezer from Simmagir: One possible meaning for the difficult Hebrew text. Probably Nebuchadnezzar's son-in-law, who was king of Babylonia 560-556 BC. It is also possible that the Hebrew text mentions a second official named Nergal Sharezer.

'39.8 the houses in Jerusalem, including: Or "the temple and".

'39.14 son of Ahikam: Hebrew "son of Ahikam and grandson of Shaphan".

'41.1 Ishmael: Hebrew "Ishmael son of Nethaniah and grandson of Elishama".

'42.1 Jezaniah: Hebrew "Jezaniah son of Hoshaiah"; one ancient translation "Azariah son of Hoshaiah" (see also 43.2 and the note there).

'43.2 Azariah, Johanan: Hebrew "Azariah son of Hoshaiah, Johanan son of Kareah".

'43.9 underneath the brick pavement: One possible meaning for the difficult Hebrew text.

'43.12-13 at the temple of the sun-god: Or "in the city of Heliopolis".

'44.17 the goddess Astarte, the Queen of Heaven: The Hebrew text has "the queen of heaven", which probably refers to the goddess Astarte.

'46.15 I have . . . him away: One possible meaning for the difficult Hebrew text.

'47.4 Crete: Hebrew "Caphtor", another name for Crete, the original homeland of the ancestor of the Philistines.

'48.6 like a wild donkey: One ancient translation; Hebrew "like (the town of) Aroer" (see verse 19).

'48.9 Spread salt . . . crops: One possible meaning for the difficult Hebrew text.

'48.11 continues . . . improve: Or "remains as evil as ever".

'48.21-24 Bozrah: Not the same Bozrah as in 49.13.

'48.32 reaching north . . . Dead Sea: One possible meaning for the difficult Hebrew text.

'48.41 Your cities: Or "Kerioth".

'48.41 gripped by fear: One possible meaning for the difficult Hebrew text.

'49.3 your town will become a pile of rubble: Or "because the town of Ai has been destroyed"; referring to an Ammonite town named Ai, not the town of that name near Bethel in the land of Israel.

'49.3 You will turn . . . blocked: One possible meaning for the difficult Hebrew text.

'49.4 when . . . fading: One possible meaning for the difficult Hebrew text.

'49.7-8 anyone . . . home: One possible meaning for the difficult Hebrew text.

'49.16 Pride . . . fear: One possible meaning for the difficult Hebrew text.

›**49.20 Edom:** The Hebrew text also uses the name "Teman" (see the note at verses 7–8).

›**49.22 will be gripped by fear:** One possible meaning for the difficult Hebrew text.

›**49.23 worries . . . waves:** One possible meaning for the difficult Hebrew text.

›**49.24 gripped by fear and pain:** One possible meaning for the difficult Hebrew text.

›**49.25 can:** One possible meaning for the difficult Hebrew text of verse 25.

›**49.28 desert villages:** The Hebrew text has "kingdoms of Hazor", which probably refers to several kingdoms of desert peoples who were not nomads, but who lived in small villages.

›**49.30 villages:** See the note at 49.28.

›**49.32 People of the Arabian Desert:** One possible meaning for the difficult Hebrew text.

›**49.33 villages:** See the note at 49.28.

›**50.1–2 Marduk:** The Hebrew text has "Bel" and "Marduk", two names for the same god.

›**50.9 the best soldiers:** Some Hebrew manuscripts and two ancient translations; most Hebrew manuscripts "soldiers who kill children".

›**50.11 threshing grain:** Hebrew; two ancient translations "in a pasture".

›**50.21 Merathaim . . . Pekod:** Hebrew forms of two Babylonian names that refer to the land of Babylonia. Merathaim probably referred to lagoons near the mouth of the Rivers Tigris and Euphrates or to the Persian Gulf, but in Hebrew it means "Twice as Rebellious". Pekod referred to a tribe of south-eastern Babylonia, but in Hebrew it means "Punishment".

›**51.1 wind:** Or "spirit".

›**51.1 Babylonia:** The Hebrew text has "Leb-Qamai", a secret way of writing "Babylonia".

›**51.3 I will tell . . . armour:** Or "Attack quickly! String your bows and put on your armour."

›**51.8 the foreigners:** Or "my people".

›**51.13 for you to die:** One possible meaning for the difficult Hebrew text.

›**51.30 have lost their strength and courage:** Hebrew "have lost their strength and have become like women".

›**51.35 harmed some of us:** One possible meaning for the difficult Hebrew text.

›**51.41 Babylon:** The Hebrew text has "Sheshach", a secret way of writing the name "Babylon".

›**51.44 Marduk:** Hebrew "Bel" (see the note at 50.2).

›**51.59 arranging for places to stay overnight:** Hebrew and one ancient translation; two ancient translations, "the tax money".

›**52.12 About a month later:** Hebrew "On the seventh day of the fifth month".

›**52.17–20 the large bowl called the Sea, the twelve bulls that held it up, and the moveable stands:** One ancient translation; Hebrew "the large bowl called the Sea, and the twelve bulls under the moveable stands".

›**52.23 evenly spaced:** One possible meaning for the difficult Hebrew text.

Lamentations

The basics

What's the point? Lamenting the destruction of Jerusalem

What happens? Five poems, reflecting on what happened and trying to find hope.

What should I remember? 3.22–3 'The LORD's kindness never fails! If he had not been merciful, we would have been destroyed. The Lord can always be trusted to show mercy each morning.'

More details

Setting the scene Jerusalem has been destroyed by the Babylonians. Looking out over the ruins, the prophet begins to lament...

What's it all about? Jerusalem fell in 588BC. This book consists of five short poems, about what has happened. The writer – possibly Jeremiah – knows that Jerusalem's suffering is deserved, but he also knows this will not last. In one passage he dares to hope that the LORD will build up his city and his people again.

And another thing

The first four chapters of Lamentations are written as acrostics with each verse of each chapter beginning with successive letters of the Hebrew alphabet. It's as if you wrote a poem in which the first sentence begins with 'A', the second with 'B', the third with 'C' and so on. Perhaps the prophet is indicating that the suffering of the people has gone from A–Z – across the complete range of experience.

Footsteps

The lonely city: 1.1–22
The angry God: 2.1–22
Hope in the ruins: 3.1–66

First lament

CHAPTER 1

Lonely Jerusalem

The prophet speaks:

¹ Jerusalem, once so crowded,
    lies deserted and lonely.
This city that was known
    all over the world
is now like a widow.
This queen of the nations
    has been made a slave.
² Each night, bitter tears
    flood her cheeks.
None of her former lovers
    are there to offer comfort;
her friends* have betrayed her
    and are now her enemies.

³ The people of Judah are slaves,
    suffering in a foreign land,
    with no rest from sorrow.
Their enemies captured them
    and were terribly cruel.▸
⁴ The roads to Zion mourn
    because no one travels there
    to celebrate the festivals.
The city gates are deserted;
    priests are weeping.
Young women are raped;▸
    Zion is in sorrow!
⁵ Enemies now rule the city
    and live as they please.
The LORD has punished Jerusalem
because of her awful sins;
    he has let her people
    be dragged away.

---

*1.2 lovers . . . friends: Israel's former allies.

⁶ Zion's glory has disappeared.
Her leaders are like deer
  that cannot find pasture;
  they are hunted down
  till their strength is gone.
⁷ Her people recall the good life
  that once was theirs;
  now they suffer and are scattered.
No one was there to protect them
  from their enemies
  who sneered when their city was taken.

⁸ Jerusalem's horrible sins
  have made the city a joke.
Those who once admired her
  now hate her instead —
  she has been disgraced;
  she groans and turns away.

⁹ Her sins had made her filthy,
  but she wasn't worried
  about what could happen.
And when Jerusalem fell,
  it was so tragic.
No one gave her comfort
  when she cried out,
  "Help! I'm in trouble, LORD!
  The enemy has won."

¹⁰ Zion's treasures were stolen.
Jerusalem saw foreigners
  enter her place of worship,
  though the LORD
  had forbidden them
  to belong to his people.ʼ
¹¹ Everyone in the city groans
  while searching for food;
  they trade their valuables
  for barely enough scraps to stay alive.

Jerusalem speaks:

Jerusalem shouts to the LORD,
  "Please look and see
  how miserable I am!"
¹² No passer-by even cares.ʼ
  Why doesn't someone notice
  my terrible sufferings?
You were fiercely angry, LORD,
  and you punished me worst of all.
¹³ From heaven you sent a fire
  that burnt in my bones;
  you set a trap for my feet
  and made me turn back.
All day long you leave me
  in shock from constant pain.
¹⁴ You have tied my sins
  around my neck,ʼ
  and they weigh so heavily
  that my strength is gone.

You have put me in the power of enemies
  too strong for me.

¹⁵ You, LORD, have turned back my warriors
  and crushed my young heroes.
Judah was a woman untouched,
  but you let her be trampled
  like grapes in a wine-pit.
¹⁶ Because of this, I mourn,
  and tears flood my eyes.
No one is here to comfort
  or to encourage me;
  we have lost the war —
  my people are suffering.

The prophet speaks:

¹⁷ Zion reaches out her hands,
  but no one offers comfort.
The LORD has turned
  the neighbouring nations
  against Jacob's descendants.
Jerusalem is merely a filthy rag
  to her neighbours.

Jerusalem speaks:

¹⁸ The LORD was right,
  but I refused to obey him.
Now I ask all of you to look
  at my sufferings —
  even my young people
  have been dragged away.
¹⁹ I called out to my lovers,
  but they betrayed me.
My priests and my leaders died
  while searching the city
  for scraps of food.

²⁰ Won't you look and see
  how upset I am, our LORD?
My stomach is in knots,
  and my heart is broken
  because I betrayed you.
In the streets and at home,
  my people are slaughtered.

²¹ Everyone heard my groaning,
  but no one offered comfort.
My enemies know of the trouble
  that you have brought on me,
  and it makes them glad.
Hurry and punish them,
  as you have promised.
²² Don't let their evil deeds
  escape your sight.
Punish them as much
  as you have punished me
  because of my sins.
I never stop groaning —
  I've lost all hope!

Second lament

CHAPTER 2

The LORD was like an enemy

The prophet speaks:

¹ The Lord was angry!
  So he disgraced⸣ Zion
  though it was Israel's pride
  and his own place of rest.
In his anger he threw Zion down
  from heaven to earth.
² The LORD had no mercy!
  He destroyed the homes
  of Jacob's descendants.
In his anger he tore down
  every walled city in Judah;
he toppled the nation
  together with its leaders,
  leaving them in shame.

³ The Lord was so furiously angry
that he wiped out
  the whole army⸣ of Israel
  by not supporting them
  when the enemy attacked.
He was like a raging fire
  that swallowed up
  the descendants of Jacob.
⁴ He attacked like an enemy
  with a bow and arrows,
  killing our loved ones.
He has burnt to the ground
  the homes on Mount Zion.⸣

⁵ The Lord was like an enemy!
  He left Israel in ruins
with its palaces
  and fortresses destroyed,
  and with everyone in Judah
  moaning and weeping.
⁶ He shattered his temple
  like a hut in a garden;⸣
  he completely wiped out
  his meeting place,
and did away with festivals and Sabbaths
  in the city of Zion.
In his fierce anger he rejected
  our king and priests.

⁷ The Lord abandoned his altar
  and his temple;
  he let Zion's enemies
  capture her fortresses.
Noisy shouts were heard
  from the temple,
  as if it were a time of celebration.

⁸ The LORD had decided
  to tear down the walls of Zion
  stone by stone.
So he started destroying
  and did not stop
  until walls and fortresses
  mourned and trembled.
⁹ Zion's gates have fallen
  face down on the ground;
  the bars that locked the gates
  are smashed to pieces.
Her king and royal family
  are prisoners in foreign lands.
Her priests don't teach,
  and her prophets don't have
  a message from the LORD.

¹⁰ Zion's leaders are silent.
  They just sit on the ground,
tossing dust on their heads
  and wearing sackcloth.
Her young women can do nothing
  but stare at the ground.
¹¹ My eyes are red from crying,
  my stomach is in knots,
  and I feel sick all over.
My people are being wiped out,
  and children lie helpless
  in the streets of the city.
¹² A child begs its mother
  for food and drink,
then blacks out like a wounded soldier
  lying in the street.
  The child slowly dies
  in its mother's arms.

¹³ Zion, how can I comfort you?
  How great is your pain?⸣
Lovely city of Jerusalem,
  how can I heal your wounds,
  gaping as wide as the sea?
¹⁴ Your prophets deceived you
  with false visions and lying messages —
they should have warned you
  to leave your sins
  and be saved from disaster.
¹⁵ Those who pass by
  shake their heads and sneer
  as they make fun and shout,
"What a lovely city you were,
  the happiest on earth,
  but look at you now!"

¹⁶ Zion, your enemies curse you
  and snarl like wild animals,
  while shouting,
"This is the day we've waited for!
  At last, we've got you!"

¹⁷ The LORD has done everything
that he had planned
and threatened long ago.
He destroyed you without mercy
and let your enemies boast
about their powerful forces.'

¹⁸ Zion, deep in your heart
you cried out to the Lord.
Now let your tears overflow
your walls day and night.
Don't ever lose hope
or let your tears stop.

¹⁹ Get up and pray for help
all through the night.
Pour out your feelings
to the Lord,
as you would pour water
out of a jug.
Beg him to save your people,
who are starving to death
at every street crossing.

Jerusalem speaks:

²⁰ Think about it, LORD!
Have you ever been this cruel
to anyone before?
Is it right for mothers
to eat their children,
or for priests and prophets
to be killed in your temple?

²¹ My people, both young and old,
lie dead in the streets.
Because you were angry,
my young men and women
were brutally slaughtered.

²² When you were angry, LORD,
you invited my enemies
like guests for a party.
No one survived that day;
enemies killed my children,
my own little ones.

Third lament

CHAPTER 3

There is still hope

The prophet speaks:

¹ I have suffered much
because God was angry.

² He chased me into a dark place,
where no light could enter.

³ I am the only one he punishes
over and over again,
without ever stopping.

⁴ God caused my skin and flesh
to waste away,
and he crushed my bones.

⁵ He attacked and surrounded me
with hardships and trouble;

⁶ he forced me to sit in the dark
like someone long dead.

⁷ God built a fence around me
that I cannot climb over,
and he chained me down.

⁸ Even when I shouted
and prayed for help,
he refused to listen.

⁹ God put big rocks in my way
and made me follow a crooked path.

¹⁰ God was like a bear or a lion
waiting in ambush for me;

¹¹ he dragged me from the road,
then tore me to shreds.'

¹² God took careful aim and shot his arrows
¹³ straight through my heart.

¹⁴ I am a joke to everyone —
no one ever stops
making fun of me.

¹⁵ God has turned my life sour.

¹⁶ He made me eat gravel
and rubbed me in the earth.

¹⁷ I cannot find peace
or remember happiness.

¹⁸ I tell myself, "I am finished!
I can't count on the LORD
to do anything for me."

¹⁹ Just thinking of my troubles
and my lonely wandering
makes me miserable.

²⁰ That's all I ever think about,
and I am depressed.'

²¹ Then I remember something
that fills me with hope.

²² The LORD's kindness never fails!
If he had not been merciful,
we would have been destroyed.'

²³ The LORD can always be trusted
to show mercy each morning.

²⁴ Deep in my heart I say,
"The LORD is all I need;
I can depend on him!"

²⁵ The LORD is kind to everyone
who trusts and obeys him.

²⁶ It is good to wait patiently
for the LORD to save us.

²⁷ When we are young,
it is good to struggle hard

²⁸ and to sit silently alone,
if this is what the LORD intends.

Real life

Prisons and criminal justice

Contributed by Churches' Criminal Justice Forum

God loves prisoners.

It's a shocking fact, but he loves the prostitute and the paedophile, the murderer and the mugger. He loves the con-man, the drunk driver, the burglar, the wife-beater.

Of course, he hates what they've done, but, whatever their sin, there is no-one who is beyond the love of God, or who cannot receive forgiveness and turn their life around. God condemns wrong-doing but not wrong-doers. The Bible teaches that all human beings are made in the image of God. We're all precious to him.

Jesus went out of his way to get involved with those on the margins of society, who included both victims and wrongdoers. He not only preached, he also lived compassion, respect for human life and – crucially – repentance, forgiveness, reconciliation and restoration.

In the New Testament, some men bring to Christ a woman who has been sleeping with someone she's not married to. They want to stone her to death. Jesus doesn't reply to them straight away; then he simply says 'If any of you have never sinned, then go ahead and throw the first stone at her!' Stoning suddenly doesn't seem such a good idea and, one by one, the accusers drift away.

Having saved her from losing her life; Jesus now wants her to change the way she lives. 'Don't sin any more,' he tells her. He doesn't pretend that she's done nothing wrong, he gives her the chance to change.

God never gives up on people, and neither should we. We should remember those in prison and those caught up in the criminal justice system. We should seek to help them find the best ways to turn their lives around. We should examine alternatives to prison, such as restorative justice, which seeks to involve both victim and offender in finding the best solution to the crime.

We should do all we can to address problems which lead to offending. Poor education and employment prospects, mental ill-health, lack of life skills and the absence of supportive families are crucial factors which lead to offending. Eighty per cent of prisoners, for example, have writing skills no better than those of a child aged eleven. And compared with the general population, prisoners are thirteen times as likely to have been in care as a child.

Criminal justice is not only about broken laws, it is also about broken lives. God is a God of justice; but he is also a God of forgiveness and new life.

Questions

Read Lamentations 3.34–6 and Hebrews 13.3. How can we remember those who are in jail?
Have you ever broken the law? What punishment do you think you deserved? Which is more important: making sure that offenders are heavily punished, or making sure that they don't offend again?

Ask an expert

Invite someone involved in criminal justice to a prayer meeting or house group to talk about their work. You could invite the chaplain from your nearest prison. Or maybe there's a probation officer in your church. Organisations like the Churches' Criminal Justice Forum can also help to provide speakers.

Get involved

Contact your local prison chaplain to see if you can help out in any way. Ring the prison and ask to be put through to the chaplaincy department. (Some age restrictions may apply).

Prisoners Sunday

Prisoners Sunday is the third Sunday in November. Ask your church leader to focus church services on prisoners and their families. (To help with ideas there are Prisoners Sunday Packs available.)

More...

Forgiveness p.614
God's love p.958

²⁹ Being rubbed in the earth
    can teach us a lesson;ᵖ
³⁰   we can also learn from insults
    and hard knocks.

³¹ The Lord won't always reject us!
³² He causes a lot of suffering,
    but he also has pity
    because of his great love.
³³ The Lord doesn't enjoy
    sending grief or pain.

³⁴ Don't trample prisoners
    under your feet
³⁵   or cheat anyone out of
    what is rightfully theirs.
    God Most High sees everything,
³⁶   and he knows
    when you refuse
    to give someone a fair trial.
³⁷ No one can do anything
    without the Lord's approval.
³⁸ Good and bad each happen
    at the command
    of God Most High.
³⁹ We're still alive!
    We shouldn't complain
    when we are being punished
    for our sins.
⁴⁰ Instead, we should think
    about the way we are living,
    and turn back to the LORD.

⁴¹ When we lift our hands
    in prayer to God in heaven,
    we should offer him our hearts and say,
⁴² "We've sinned!
    We've rebelled against you,
    and you haven't forgiven us!
⁴³ Anger is written all over you,
    as you pursue and slaughter us
    without showing pity.
⁴⁴ You are behind a wall of clouds
    that blocks out our prayers.
⁴⁵ You allowed nations
    to treat us like rubbish;
⁴⁶   our enemies curse us.
⁴⁷ We are terrified and trapped,
    caught and crushed."

⁴⁸ My people are destroyed!
    Tears flood my eyes,
⁴⁹   and they won't stop
⁵⁰   until the LORD looks down
    from heaven and helps.
⁵¹ I am horrified when I see
    what enemies have done
    to the young women of our city.

⁵² No one had reason to hate me,
    but I was hunted down like a bird.
⁵³ Then they tried to kill me
    by tossing me into a pit
    and throwing stones at me.
⁵⁴ Water covered my head —
    I thought I was gone.
⁵⁵ From the bottom of the pit,
    I prayed to you, LORD.
⁵⁶ I begged you to listen.
    "Help!" I shouted. "Save me!"
    You answered my prayer
⁵⁷   and came when I was in need.
    You told me, "Don't worry!"
⁵⁸   You rescued me and saved my life.
⁵⁹ You saw them abuse me, LORD,
    so make things right.
⁶⁰ You know every plot
    they have made against me.
⁶¹   Yes, you know their insults
    and their evil plans.
⁶² All day long they attack
    with words and whispers.
⁶³ No matter what they are doing,
    they keep on mocking me.

⁶⁴ Pay them back for everything
    they have done, LORD!
⁶⁵   Put your curse on them
    and make them suffer.ᵖ
⁶⁶ Get angry and go after them
    until not a trace is left
    under the heavens.

Fourth lament

CHAPTER 4

The punishment of Jerusalem

The prophet speaks:

¹ The purest gold is ruined
    and has lost its shine;
    jewels from the temple
    lie scattered in the streets.

² These are Zion's people,
    worth more than purest gold;
    yet they are counted worthless
    like dishes of clay.

³ Even jackals* nurse their young,
    but my people are like ostriches
    that abandon their own.

⁴ Babies are so thirsty that their tongues
    are stuck to the roof of the mouth.

---

*4.3 jackals: Desert animals related to wolves, but smaller.

Children go begging for food,
   but no one gives them any.
5 All who ate expensive foods
   lie starving in the streets;
   those who grew up in luxury
   now sit on rubbish heaps.

6 My nation was punished worse
   than the people of Sodom,
   whose city was destroyed in a flash
   without the help of human hands.⁕

7 The leaders of Jerusalem
   were purer than snow
   and whiter than milk;
   their bodies were healthy
   and glowed like jewels.⁕

8 Now they are blacker than tar,
   and no one recognizes them;
   their skin clings to their bones
   and is drier than firewood.

9 Being killed with a sword is better
   than slowly starving to death.

10 Life in the city is so bad
   that loving mothers
   have boiled and eaten
   their own children.

11 The LORD was so fiercely angry
   that he burnt the city of Zion
   to the ground.

12 Not a king on this earth
   or the people of any nation
   believed enemies could break
   through her gates.

13 Jerusalem was punished because
   her prophets and her priests
   had sinned and caused the death
   of innocent victims.

14 Yes, her prophets and priests
   were covered with blood;
   no one would come near them,
   as they wandered
   from street to street.

15 Instead, everyone shouted,
   "Go away! Don't touch us!
   You're filthy and unfit
   to belong to God's people!"

So they had to leave
   and become refugees.
   But foreign nations told them,
   "You can't stay here!"⁕

16 The LORD is the one
   who sent them scattering,
   and he has forgotten them.
   No respect or kindness will be shown
   to the priests or leaders.

17 Our eyes became weary,
   hopelessly looking for help
   from a nation⁕ that could not save us.

18 Enemies hunted us down
   on every public street.
   Our time was up;
   our doom was near.

19 They swooped down faster
   than eagles from the sky.
   They hunted for us in the hills
   and set traps to catch us
   out in the desert.

20 The LORD's chosen leader⁕
   was our hope for survival!
   We thought he would keep us safe
   somewhere among the nations,
   but even he was caught
   in one of their traps.

21 You people of Edom
   can celebrate now!
   But your time will come to suffer
   and stagger around naked.

22 The people of Zion
   have paid for their sins,
   and the Lord will soon
   let them return home.
   But, people of Edom,
   you will be punished,
   and your sins exposed.

Fifth lament

CHAPTER 5

A prayer for mercy

The people of Jerusalem pray:⁕

1 Our LORD, don't forget
   how we have suffered
   and been disgraced.

2 Foreigners and strangers
   have taken our land
   and our homes.

3 We are like children
   whose mothers are widows.

4 The water we drink
   and the wood we burn
   cost far too much.

5 We are terribly ill-treated;⁕
   we are worn out and can find no rest.

6 We had to surrender
   to⁕ Egypt and Assyria
   because we were hungry.

⁕**4.17 nation:** Egypt, a former ally of Judah.
⁕**4.20 chosen leader:** Probably Zedekiah, the last
king of Judah, taken away to Babylonia in 586 BC.

See also: 4.6: Gen 19.24.   4.10: Deut 28.57; Ezek 5.10.

Footsteps

Ezekiel sees the Lord's glory and is chosen to be his prophet

CHAPTER 1

1-3 I am Ezekiel — a priest and the son of Buzi.⸆

Five years after King Jehoiachin of Judah had been led away as a prisoner to Babylonia, I was living near the River Chebar among those who had been taken there with him. Then on the fifth day of the fourth month* of the thirtieth year,* the heavens suddenly opened. The LORD placed his hand upon me* and showed me some visions.

4 I saw a storm blowing in from the north. Lightning flashed from a huge cloud and lit up the whole sky with a dazzling brightness. The fiery centre of the cloud was as shiny as polished metal, 5 and in that centre I saw what looked like four living creatures. They were somewhat like humans, 6 except that each one had four faces and four wings. 7 Their legs were straight, but their feet looked like the hoofs of calves and sparkled like bronze. 8 Under each of their wings, these creatures had a human hand. 9 The four creatures were standing back-to-back with the tips of their wings touching. They moved together in every direction, without turning their bodies.

---

*1.1–3 Five years . . . prisoner . . . fourth month: Jehoiachin ruled for three months in 598 BC. The fourth month was probably July of 593 BC.
*1.1–3 thirtieth year: The event from which this date is worked out is unknown.
*1.1–3 The LORD placed his hand upon me: This was a sign that the LORD had chosen Ezekiel to be his prophet.

See also: 1.1: Rev 19.11. 1.2: 2 King 24.10–16; 2 Chron 36.9–10. 1.5: Rev 4.6.

Life files

Ezekiel

Background: Son of Buzi. One of the four great Prophets.

What's the story?

Ezekiel was in his mid-twenties and training to be a priest when, in 598BC, the Babylonians invaded Judah for a second time and took him away to captivity – along with around 10,000 of the most prominent leaders, soldiers, and craftsmen (2 Kings 24.14). Ezekiel settled in his own house in a village near the Chebar river in Babylonia (Ezekiel 3.15,24).

He prophesied for at least 22 years, probably receiving the call to be a prophet when he was about 30. Through his sometimes extreme prophecies, God explained to his people why he had allowed the captivity to happen, and also how one day the land of Israel would be restored.

What's the point?

Few prophets saw their visions, or lived their lives, with such intensity as Ezekiel. He didn't only tell people his prophecies, he lived out the message to the people around him. This meant more than putting on a little bit of drama, he had to do things like lie on his side for 390 days or break a hole in the wall of his house and creep out. The words he spoke were passionate, even outrageous (see for example Ezekiel 16. Now that's being rude.) But God is not a reserved gentleman, he's a being who feels passionately about people and Ezekiel, more than any other prophet, reflected that passion.

🐚 Anorak corner

Ezekiel was in Babylon at the same time as Daniel. Don't know if they ever met, but the conversation would have been interesting.

More...
Prophecy p.730
Dreams and visions p.1131
Heaven p.1412
Babylon p.437

¹⁰ Each creature had the face of a human in front, the face of a lion on the right side, the face of a bull on the left, and the face of an eagle at the back. ¹¹ Two wings⁰ of each creature were spread out and touched the wings of the creatures on either side. The other two wings of each creature were folded against its body.

¹² Wherever the four living creatures went, they moved together without turning their bodies, because each creature faced straight ahead. ¹³ The creatures were glowing like hot coals, and I saw something like a flaming torch moving back and forth among them. Lightning flashed from the torch every time its flame blazed up.⁰ ¹⁴ The creatures themselves moved as quickly as sparks jumping from a fire.⁰

¹⁵ I then noticed that on the ground beside each of the four living creatures was a wheel,⁰ ¹⁶ shining like chrysolite.* Each wheel was exactly the same and had a second wheel that cut through the middle of it,⁰ ¹⁷ so that they could move in any direction without turning. ¹⁸ The rims of the wheels were large and had eyes all the way around them.⁰ ¹⁹⁻²¹ The creatures controlled when and where the wheels moved — the wheels went wherever the four creatures went and stopped whenever they stopped. Even when the creatures flew in the air, the wheels were beside them.

²²⁻²³ Above the living creatures, I saw something that was sparkling like ice, and it reminded me of a dome. Each creature had two of its wings stretched out towards the creatures on either side, with the other two wings folded against its body. ²⁴ Whenever the creatures flew, their wings roared like an ocean or a large army or even the voice of God All-Powerful. And whenever the creatures stopped, they folded their wings against their bodies.

²⁵ When the creatures stopped flapping their wings, I heard a sound coming from above the dome. ²⁶ I then saw what looked like a throne made of sapphire,* and sitting on the throne was a figure in the shape of a human. ²⁷ From the waist up, it was glowing like metal in a hot furnace, and from the waist down it looked like the flames of a fire. The figure was surrounded by a bright light, ²⁸ as colourful as a rainbow that appears after a storm.

I realized I was seeing the brightness of the LORD's glory! So I bowed with my face to the ground, and just then I heard a voice speaking to me.

CHAPTER 2

The LORD chooses Ezekiel

¹ The LORD⁰ said, "Ezekiel, son of man,* I want you to stand up and listen." ² After he said this, his Spirit took control of me and lifted me to my feet. Then the LORD said:

³ Ezekiel, I am sending you to the people of Israel. They are just like their ancestors who rebelled against me and refused to stop. ⁴ They are stubborn and hard-headed. But I, the LORD God, have chosen you to tell them what I say. ⁵ Those rebels may not even listen, but at least they will know that a prophet has come to them.

⁶ Don't be afraid of them or of anything they say. You may think you're in the middle of thorn bushes or scorpions. But be brave ⁷ and preach my message to them, whether they choose to listen or not. ⁸ Ezekiel, don't rebel against me, as they have done. Instead, listen to everything I tell you.

And now, Ezekiel, open your mouth and eat what I am going to give you.

⁹ Just then, I saw a hand stretched out towards me. And in it was a scroll.* ¹⁰ The hand opened the scroll, and both sides of it were filled with words of sadness, mourning, and grief.

CHAPTER 3

¹ The LORD said, "Ezekiel, son of man, after you eat this scroll, go and speak to the people of Israel."

---

*1.16 chrysolite: A precious stone that has an olive green colour.
*1.26 sapphire: A precious stone that has a blue colour.
See also: 1.10: Ezek 10.14; Rev 4.7. 1.13: Rev 4.5.
1.15–21: Ezek 10.9–13. 1.18: Rev 4.8. 1.22: Rev 4.6.
1.24: Rev 1.4–15; 19.6. 1.26: Ezek 10.1; Rev 4.2–3.
1.27: Ezek 8.2.

*2.1 Ezekiel, son of man: The Hebrew text has "Son of man", which is often used in this book when the LORD speaks directly to Ezekiel. It means that Ezekiel is a mere human, yet he is the one the LORD has chosen to be his prophet who speaks for him to the people of Israel.
*2.9 scroll: A roll of paper or special leather used for writing on.
See also: 2.9–10: Rev 5.1. 3.1–3: Rev 10.9–10.

2-3 He handed me the scroll and said, "Eat this and fill your stomach with it." So I ate the scroll, and it tasted sweet as honey.

4 The LORD said:

Ezekiel, I am sending you to your own people. 5-6 They are Israelites, not strangers who speak a foreign language you can't understand. If I were to send you to foreign nations, they would listen to you. 7 But the people of Israel will refuse to listen, because they have refused to listen to me. All of them are stubborn and hard-headed, 8 so I will make you as stubborn as they are. 9 You will be so determined to speak my message that nothing will stop you. I will make you hard like a diamond, and you'll have no reason to be afraid of those arrogant rebels.

10 Listen carefully to everything I say and then think about it. 11 Then go to the people who were brought here to Babylonia with you and tell them you have a message from me, the LORD God. Do this, whether they listen to you or not.

12 The Spirit' lifted me up, and as the glory of the LORD started to leave,' I heard a loud, thundering noise behind me. 13 It was the sound made by the creatures' wings as they brushed against each other, and by the rumble of the wheels beside them. 14 Then the Spirit carried me away.

The LORD's power had taken complete control of me, and I was both annoyed and angry.

15 When I was back with the others living at Abib Hill near the River Chebar, I sat among them for seven days, shocked at what had happened to me.

The LORD appoints Ezekiel to stand watch

This is also told in Ezekiel 33.1–9

16 Seven days after I had seen the brightness of the LORD's glory, the LORD said:

17 Ezekiel, son of man, I have appointed you to stand watch for the people of Israel. So listen to what I say, then warn them for me. 18 When I tell wicked people they will die because of their sins, you must warn them to turn from their sinful ways so they won't be punished. If you refuse, you are responsible for their death. 19 However, if you do warn them, and they keep on sinning, they will die because of their sins, and you will be innocent.

20 Now suppose faithful people start sinning, and I decide to put stumbling blocks in their paths to make them fall. They deserve to die because of their sins. So if you refuse to warn them, I will forget about the times they were faithful, and I will hold you responsible for their death. 21 But if you do warn them, and they listen to you and stop sinning, I will let them live. And you will be innocent.

Ezekiel cannot talk

22 The LORD took control of me and said, "Stand up! Go into the valley, and I will talk with you there."

23 I immediately went to the valley, where I saw the brightness of the LORD's glory, just as I had seen near the River Chebar, and I bowed with my face to the ground. 24 His Spirit took control of me and lifted me to my feet. Then the LORD said:

Go back and lock yourself in your house! 25 You will be tied up to keep you inside, 26 and I will make you unable to talk or to warn those who have rebelled against me. 27 But the time will come, when I will tell you what to say, and you will again be able to speak my message.* Some of them will listen; others will be stubborn and refuse to listen.

Ezekiel acts out the coming destruction of Judah and Jerusalem

CHAPTER 4

The LORD said:

1 Ezekiel, son of man, find a brick and sketch a picture of Jerusalem on it. 2 Then prepare to attack the brick as if it were a real city. Build an earth mound and a ramp up to the top and surround the brick with enemy camps. On every side put large wooden poles as though you were going to break down the gate to the city. 3 Set up an iron pan like a wall between you and the brick. All this will be a warning for the people of Israel.

4-5 After that, lie down on your left side and stay there for three hundred and ninety days as a sign of Israel's punishment* —

---

*3.27 again . . . speak my message: See 33.21–22.
*4.4–5 Israel's punishment: Israel here refers to the northern kingdom that was destroyed in 722 BC.

one day for each year of its suffering. ⁶ Then turn over and lie on your right side forty more days. That will be a sign of Judah's punishment — one day for each year of its suffering.

⁷ The brick stands for Jerusalem, so attack it! Stare at it and shout angry warnings. ⁸ I will tie you up, so you can't leave until your attack has ended.

⁹ Get a large bowl. Then mix together wheat, barley, beans, lentils, and millet, and make some bread. This is what you will eat for the three hundred and ninety days you are lying down. ¹⁰ Eat only a small loaf of bread each day ¹¹ and drink only two large cups of water. ¹² Use dried human waste to start a fire, then bake the bread on the coals where everyone can watch you. ¹³ When I scatter the people of Israel among the nations, they will also have to eat food that is unclean, just as you must do.*

¹⁴ I said, "LORD God, please don't make me do that! Never in my life have I eaten food that would make me unacceptable to you. I've never eaten anything that died a natural death or was killed by a wild animal or that you said was unclean."

¹⁵ The LORD replied, "Instead of human waste, I will let you bake your bread on a fire made from cow manure. ¹⁶ Ezekiel, the people of Jerusalem will starve. They will have so little food and water that they will be afraid and hopeless. ¹⁷ Everyone will be shocked at what is happening, and, because of their sins, they will die a slow death."

CHAPTER 5

Jerusalem's coming destruction

The LORD said:

¹ Ezekiel, son of man, get a sharp sword and use it to cut off your hair and beard. Weigh the hair and divide it into three equal piles. ² After you attack the brick that stands for Jerusalem, burn one pile of your hair on the brick. Chop up the second pile and let the small pieces of hair fall around the brick. Throw the third pile into the wind, and I will strike it with my own sword.

³ Keep a few of the hairs and wrap them in the hem of your clothes. ⁴ Then pull out a few of those hairs and throw them in the fire, so they will also burn. This fire will spread, destroying everyone in Israel.

⁵ I am the LORD God, and I have made Jerusalem the most important place in the world, and all other nations admire it. ⁶ But the people of Jerusalem rebelled and refuse to obey me. They ignored my laws and have become even more sinful than the nations around them.

⁷ So tell the people of Jerusalem:

I am the LORD God! You have refused to obey my laws and teachings, and instead you have obeyed the laws of the surrounding nations. You have become more rebellious than any of them! ⁸ Now all those nations will watch as I turn against you and punish you ⁹ for your sins. Your punishment will be more horrible than anything I've ever done or will ever do again. ¹⁰ Parents will be so desperate for food that they will eat their own children, and children will eat their parents. Those who survive this horror will be scattered in every direction.

¹¹ Your disgusting sins have made my temple unfit as a place to worship me. So I swear by my own life that I will turn my back on you and show you no pity. ¹² A third of you will die here in Jerusalem from disease or starvation. Another third will be killed in war. And I will scatter the last third of you in every direction, then track you down and kill you.

¹³ You will feel my fierce anger until I have finished taking revenge. Then you will know that I, the LORD, was furious because of your disobedience. ¹⁴ Every passer-by will laugh at your destruction. Foreign nations ¹⁵ will insult you and make fun of you, but they will also be shocked and terrified at what I did in my anger. ¹⁶ I will destroy your crops until you starve to death, and disasters will strike you like arrows. ¹⁷ Starvation and wild animals will kill your children. I'll punish you with horrible diseases, and your enemies will strike you down with their swords. I, the LORD, have spoken.

---

*4.13 have to eat food that is unclean, just as you must do: The LORD had forbidden the people of Israel to mix certain things (see Deuteronomy 22.9–11), and so the people would not have been allowed to eat this bread under normal conditions. It is used here to show that when a city is under attack, people eat whatever food is left, even if the LORD had said it was unclean.

See also: 5.10: Lam 4.10.   5.17: Rev 6.8.

Disaster is near

CHAPTER 6

Israel is doomed

¹ The LORD God said:

² Ezekiel, son of man, face the hills of Israel and tell them:

³ Listen, you mountains and hills, and every valley and gorge! I, the LORD, am about to turn against you and crush all the places where foreign gods are worshipped. ⁴ Every altar will be smashed, and in front of the idols I will put to death the people who worship them. ⁵ Dead bodies and bones will be lying around the idols and the altars. ⁶ Every town in Israel will be destroyed to make sure that each shrine, idol, and altar is smashed — everything the Israelites made will be a pile of ruins. ⁷ All over the country, your people will die. And those who survive will know that I, the LORD, did these things. ⁸ I will let some of the people live through this punishment, but I will scatter them among the nations, ⁹ where they will be prisoners. And when they think of me, they will realize that they disgraced me by rebelling and by worshipping idols. They will hate themselves for the evil things they did, ¹⁰ and they will know that I am the LORD and that my warnings must be taken seriously.

¹¹ The LORD God then said:

Ezekiel, beat your fists together and stamp your feet in despair! Moan in sorrow, because the people of Israel have done disgusting things and now will be killed by enemy troops, or they will die from starvation and disease. ¹² Those who live far away will be struck with deadly diseases. Those who live nearby will be killed in war. And the ones who are left will starve to death. I will let loose my anger on them! ¹³ These people used to offer incense to idols at altars built on hills and mountaintops and in the shade of large oak trees. But when they see dead bodies lying around those altars, they will know that I am the LORD. ¹⁴ I will make their country a barren wasteland, from the Southern Desert to the town of Diblah in the north. Then they will know that I, the LORD, have done these things.

CHAPTER 7

Disaster is near

¹ The LORD God said:

² Ezekiel, son of man, tell the people of Israel that I am saying:

Israel will soon come to an end! Your whole country is about to be destroyed ³ as punishment for your disgusting sins. I, the LORD, am so angry ⁴ that I will show no pity. I will punish you for the evil you've done, and you will know that I am the LORD.

⁵ There's never been anything like the coming disaster.‣ ⁶ And when it comes, your life will be over. ⁷ You people of Israel are doomed! Soon there will be panic on the mountaintops instead of celebration.‣ ⁸ I will let loose my anger and punish you for the evil things you've done. You'll get what you deserve. ⁹ Your sins are so terrible, that you'll get no mercy from me. Then you will know that I, the LORD, have punished you.

¹⁰ Disaster is near! Injustice and arrogance are everywhere, ¹¹ and violent criminals run free. None of you will survive the disaster, and everything you own and value will be shattered.‣ ¹² The time is coming when everyone will be ruined. Buying and selling will stop, ¹³ and people who sell property will never get it back, because all of you must be punished for your sins. And I won't change my mind!‣

¹⁴ A signal has been blown on the trumpet, and weapons are prepared for battle. But no one goes to war, because in my anger I will strike down everyone in Israel.

Israel is surrounded

The LORD said to the people of Israel:

¹⁵ War, disease, and starvation are everywhere! People who live in the countryside will be killed in battle, and those who live in towns will die from starvation or deadly diseases. ¹⁶ Anyone who survives will escape into the hills, like doves who leave the valleys to find safety.

All of you will moan‣ because of your sins. ¹⁷ Your hands will tremble, and your knees will go limp. ¹⁸ You will put on sackcloth* to show your sorrow, but terror

---

*7.18 sackcloth: A rough, dark-coloured cloth made from goat or camel hair and used to make grain sacks. It was worn in times of trouble or sorrow.

will overpower you. Shame will be written all over your faces, and you will shave your heads in despair. [19] Your silver and gold will be thrown into the streets like rubbish, because those are the two things that led you into sin, and now they cannot save you from my anger. They are not even worth enough to buy food. [20] You took great pride in using your beautiful jewellery to make disgusting idols of foreign gods. So I will make your jewellery worthless.

[21] Wicked foreigners will rob and disgrace you. [22] They will break into my temple' and leave it unfit as a place to worship me, but I will look away and let it happen.

[23] Your whole country is in confusion!' Murder and violence are everywhere in Israel, [24] so I will tell the most wicked nations to come and take over your homes. They will put an end to the pride you have in your strong army, and they will make your places of worship unfit to use. [25] You will be terrified and will desperately look for peace — but there will be no peace. [26] One tragedy will follow another, and you'll hear only bad news. People will beg prophets to give them a message from me. Priests will stop teaching my Law, and wise leaders won't be able to give advice. [27] Even your king and his officials will lose hope and cry in despair. Your hands will tremble with fear.

I will punish you for your sins and treat you the same way you have treated others. Then you will know that I am the LORD.

The Lord's glory leaves sinful Jerusalem

CHAPTER 8

Ezekiel sees the terrible sins of Jerusalem

[1] Six years after King Jehoiachin and the rest of us had been led away as prisoners to Babylonia, the leaders of Judah were meeting with me in my house. On the fifth day of the sixth month,* the LORD God suddenly took control of me, [2] and I saw something in the shape of a human.' This figure was like fire from the waist down, and it was bright as polished metal from the waist up. [3] It reached

out what seemed to be a hand and grabbed my hair. Then in my vision the LORD's Spirit lifted me into the sky and carried me to Jerusalem.

The Spirit took me to the north gate of the temple's inner courtyard, where there was an idol that disgusted the LORD and made him furious. [4] Then I saw the brightness of the glory of the God of Israel, just as I had seen it near the River Chebar.

[5] God said to me, "Ezekiel, son of man, look north." And when I did, I saw that disgusting idol by the altar near the gate.

[6] God then said, "Do you see the terrible sins of the people of Israel? Their sins are making my holy temple unfit as a place to worship me. Yet you will see even worse things than this."

[7] Next, I was taken to the entrance of the courtyard, where I saw a hole in the wall.

[8] God said, "Make this hole bigger." And when I did, I realized it was a doorway. [9] "Go in," God said, "and see what horrible and evil things the people are doing."

[10] Inside, I saw that the walls were covered with pictures of reptiles and disgusting, unclean animals,* as well as with idols that the Israelites were worshipping. [11] Seventy Israelite leaders were standing there, including Jaazaniah son of Shaphan. Each of these leaders was holding an incense burner, and the smell of incense filled the room.

[12] God said, "Ezekiel, do you see what horrible things Israel's leaders are doing in secret? They have filled their rooms with idols. And they say I can't see them, because they think I have already deserted Israel. [13] But I will show you something even worse than this."

[14] He took me to the north gate of the temple, where I saw women mourning for the god Tammuz.* [15] God asked me, "Can you believe what these women are doing? But now I want to show you something worse."

[16] I was then led into the temple's inner courtyard, where I saw about twenty-five men standing near the entrance, between the porch and the altar. Their backs were to the LORD's temple, and they were bowing down to the rising sun.

---

*8.1 Six years . . . sixth month: Probably September of 592 BC.
See also: 8.2: Ezek 1.27.

*8.10 disgusting, unclean animals: See, for example, Leviticus 11.9–19.
*8.14 the god Tammuz: A god of vegetation who was thought to die in the dry season. During the Hebrew month of Tammuz (from about mid-June to mid-July), women mourned the death of this god, hoping to bring him back to life.
See also: 8.4: Ezek 1.28.

¹⁷ God said, "Ezekiel, it's bad enough that the people of Judah are doing these disgusting things. But they have also spread violence and injustice everywhere in Israel and have made me very angry. They have disgraced and insulted me in the worst possible way.' ¹⁸ So in my fierce anger, I will punish them without mercy and refuse to help them when they cry out to me."

CHAPTER 9

The LORD gives the command to punish Jerusalem

¹ After that, I heard the LORD shout, "Come to Jerusalem, you men chosen to destroy the city. And bring your weapons!"
² I saw six men come through the north gate of the temple, each one holding a deadly weapon. A seventh man dressed in a linen robe was with them, and he was carrying things to write with. The men went into the temple and stood by the bronze altar.
³ The brightness of God's glory then left its place above the statues of the winged creatures* inside the temple and moved to the entrance. The LORD said to the man in the linen robe, ⁴ "Walk through the city of Jerusalem and mark the forehead of anyone who is truly upset and sad about the disgusting things that are being done here."
⁵⁻⁶ He turned to the other six men and said, "Follow him and put to death everyone who doesn't have a mark on their forehead. Show no mercy or pity! Kill men and women, parents and children. Begin here at my temple and be sure not to harm those who are marked."
The men immediately killed the leaders who were standing there.
⁷ Then the LORD said, "Pollute the temple by piling the dead bodies in the courtyards. Now get busy!" They left and started killing the people of Jerusalem.
⁸ I was then alone, so I bowed down and cried out to the LORD, "Why are you doing this? Are you so angry at the people of Jerusalem that everyone must die?"
⁹ The LORD answered, "The people of Israel and Judah have done horrible things. Their country is filled with murderers, and Jerusalem itself is filled with violence. They think that I have deserted them, and that I can't see what they are doing. ¹⁰ And so I will not have pity on them or forgive them. They will be punished for what they have done."
¹¹ Just then, the man in the linen robe returned and said, "I have done what you commanded."

CHAPTER 10

The LORD's glory leaves the temple

¹ I saw the dome that was above the four winged creatures,* and on it was the sapphire* throne.* ² The LORD said to the man in the linen robe, "Walk among the four wheels beside the creatures and pick up as many hot coals as you can carry. Then scatter them over the city of Jerusalem." I watched him as he followed the LORD's instructions.
³ The winged creatures were standing south of the temple when the man walked among them. A cloud filled the inner courtyard, ⁴ and the brightness of the LORD's glory moved from above the creatures and stopped at the entrance of the temple. The entire temple was filled with his glory, and the courtyard was dazzling bright. ⁵ The sound of the creatures' wings was as loud as the voice of God All-Powerful and could even be heard in the outer courtyard.
⁶ The man in the robe was now standing beside a wheel. ⁷ One of the four creatures reached its hand into the fire among them and gave him some of the hot coals. The man took the coals and left.
⁸ I noticed again that each of the four winged creatures had what looked like human hands under their wings, ⁹ and I saw the four wheels near the creatures. These wheels were shining like chrysolite.* ¹⁰ Each wheel was exactly the same and had a second wheel that cut through the middle of it,' ¹¹ so that they could move in any direction without turning. The wheels moved together whenever the creatures moved. ¹² I also noticed that the wheels and the creatures' bodies, including their backs, their hands, and their wings, were covered with eyes. ¹³ And I heard a voice calling these "the wheels that spin".

---

*9.3 the statues of the winged creatures:** These were symbols of the LORD's throne on earth (see Exodus 25.18–22; 1 Kings 6.23–28).
See also: 9.4: Rev 7.3; 9.4; 14.1.

*10.1 winged creatures:** See the note at 9.3.
*10.1 sapphire:** See the note at 1.26.
*10.1 dome . . . creatures . . . throne:** See 1.22–26.
*10.9 chrysolite:** See the note at 1.16.
See also: 10.1: Ezek 1.26; Rev 4.2. 10.2: Rev 8.5. 10.9–13: Ezek 1.15–21. 10.12: Rev 4.8.

14 Each of the winged creatures had four faces: the face of a bull,* the face of a human, the face of a lion, and the face of an eagle. 15-17 These were the same creatures I had seen near the River Chebar. They controlled when and where the wheels moved — the wheels went wherever the creatures went and stopped whenever they stopped. Even when the creatures flew in the air, the wheels stayed beside them.

18 Then I watched the brightness of the LORD's glory move from the entrance of the temple and stop above the winged creatures. 19 They spread their wings and flew into the air with the wheels at their side. They stopped at the east gate of the temple, and the LORD's glory was above them.

20 I knew for certain that these were the same creatures I had seen beneath the LORD's glory near the River Chebar. 21-22 They had four wings with hands beneath them, and they had the same four faces as those near the River. Each creature moved straight ahead without turning.

CHAPTER 11

Ezekiel condemns Jerusalem's wicked leaders

1 The LORD's Spirit⸀ lifted me up and took me to the east gate of the temple, where I saw twenty-five men, including the two leaders, Jaazaniah son of Azzur and Pelatiah son of Benaiah. 2 The LORD said, "Ezekiel, son of man, these men are making evil plans and giving dangerous advice to the people of Jerusalem. 3 They say things like, 'Let's build more houses.⸀' This city is like a cooking pot over a fire, and we are the meat, but at least the pot keeps us from being burnt in the fire.'* 4 So, Ezekiel, condemn them!"

5 The LORD's Spirit took control of me and told me to tell these leaders:

I, the LORD God, know what you leaders are saying. 6 You have murdered so many people that the city is filled with dead bodies! 7 This city is indeed a cooking pot, but the bodies of those you killed are the meat. And so I will force you to leave Jerusalem, 8 and I'll

send armies to attack you, just as you fear. 9 Then you will be captured and punished by foreign enemies.* 10 You will be killed in your own country, but not before you realize that I, the LORD, have done these things.

11 You leaders claim to be meat in a cooking pot, but you won't be protected by this city. No, you will die at the border of Israel. 12 You will realize that while you were following the laws of nearby nations, you were disobeying my laws and teachings. And I am the LORD!

13 Before I finished speaking, Pelatiah dropped dead. I bowed down and cried out, "Please, LORD God, don't kill everyone left in Israel."

A promise of hope

14 The LORD replied:

15 Ezekiel, son of man, the people living in Jerusalem claim that you and the other Israelites who were taken to Babylonia are too far away to worship me. They also claim that the land of Israel now belongs only to them. 16 But here is what I want you to tell the Israelites in Babylonia:

It's true that I, the LORD God, have forced you out of your own country and made you live among foreign nations. But for now, I will be with you wherever you are, so that you can worship me. 17 And some day, I will gather you from the nations where you are scattered and let you live in Israel again. 18 When that happens, I want you to clear the land of all disgusting idols. 19 Then I will take away your stubbornness and make you eager to be completely faithful to me. You will want to obey me 20 and all my laws and teachings. You will be my people, and I will be your God. 21 But those who worship idols will be punished and get what they deserve. I, the LORD God, have spoken.

The LORD's glory leaves Jerusalem

22 After the LORD had finished speaking, the winged creatures spread their wings and flew into the air, and the wheels were beside them. The brightness of the LORD's glory above them 23 left Jerusalem and stopped at a hill east of the city.

24 Then in my vision, the LORD's Spirit⸀ lifted me up and carried me back to the other

---

*10.14 a bull: The Hebrew text has "a winged creature", but see 1.10.

*11.3 the pot keeps us from being burnt in the fire: These leaders were trying to convince the people of Jerusalem that they were secure, and that their future was bright.

See also: 10.14: Ezek 1.10; Rev 4.7.

---

*11.9 foreign enemies: That is, the Babylonians.

See also: 11.19-20: Ezek 36.26-28. 11.22-23: Ezek 43.2-5.

exiles in Babylonia. The vision faded away, 25 and I told them everything the LORD had shown me.

Messages of doom for Judah and Jerusalem

CHAPTER 12
Ezekiel acts out Israel's captivity

1 The LORD said:

2 Ezekiel, son of man, you are living among rebellious people. They have eyes, but refuse to see; they have ears, but refuse to listen. 3 So before it gets dark, here is what I want you to do. Pack a few things as though you were going to be taken away as a prisoner. Then go outside where everyone can see you and walk around from place to place. Perhaps as they watch, they will realize what rebels they are. 4 After you have done this, return to your house.

Later that evening leave your house as if you were going into exile. 5 Dig through the wall of your house* and crawl out, carrying the bag with you. Make sure everyone is watching. 6 Lift the bag to your shoulders, and with your face covered, take it into the darkness, so that you cannot see the land you are leaving. All this will be a warning for the people of Israel.

7 I did everything the LORD had said. I packed a few things. Then as the sun was going down, and while everyone was watching, I dug a hole through one of the walls of my house. I pulled out my bag, then lifted it to my shoulders and left in the darkness.

8 The next morning, the LORD 9 reminded me that those rebellious people didn't even ask what I was doing. 10 So he sent me back to tell them:

The LORD God has a message for the leader of Jerusalem and everyone living there! 11 I have done these things to show them what will happen when they are taken away as prisoners.

12 The leader of Jerusalem will lift his own bag to his shoulders at sunset and leave through a hole that the others have dug in the wall of his house. He will cover his face, so he can't see the land he is leaving. 13 The LORD will spread out a net and trap him as he leaves Jerusalem. He will then be led away to the city of Babylon, but will never see that place,* even though he will die there. 14 His own officials and troops will scatter in every direction, and the LORD will track them down and put them to death.

15 The LORD will force the rest of the people in Jerusalem to live in foreign nations, where they will realize that he has done all these things. 16 Some of them will survive the war, the starvation, and the deadly diseases. That way, they will be able to tell foreigners how disgusting their sins were, and that it was the LORD who punished them in this way.

A sign of fear

17 The LORD said:

18 Ezekiel, son of man, shake with fear when you eat, and tremble when you drink. 19 Tell the people of Israel that I, the LORD, say that some day everyone in Jerusalem will shake when they eat and tremble when they drink. Their country will be destroyed and left empty, because they have been cruel and violent. 20 Every town will lie in ruins, and the land will be a barren desert. Then they will know that I am the LORD.

The words of the LORD will come true

21 The LORD said:

22 Ezekiel, son of man, you've heard people in Israel use the saying, "Time passes, and prophets are proved wrong." 23 Now tell the people that I, the LORD, am going to prove that saying wrong. No one will ever be able to use it again in Israel, because very soon everything I have said will come true! 24 The people will hear no more useless warnings and false messages. 25 I will give them my message, and what I say will certainly happen. Warn those rebels that the time has come for them to be punished. I, the LORD, make this promise.

26-27 Ezekiel, the people of Israel are also saying that your visions and messages are only about things in the future. 28 So tell

---

*12.5 Dig through the wall of your house: The walls of most houses in Babylonia were made of mud bricks that had been dried in the sun. A hole could easily have been dug through these bricks.
See also: 12.2: Isa 6.9–10; Jer 5.21; Mark 8.18.

*12.13 He will then be led away . . . that place: According to 2 Kings 25.6–7, King Zedekiah of Judah was blinded before he was taken to Babylon.
See also: 12.13: 2 Kings 25.7; Jer 52.11.

them that my words will soon come true, just as I have warned. I, the LORD, have spoken.

CHAPTER 13

Lying prophets

¹ The LORD said:

² Ezekiel, son of man, condemn the prophets of Israel who say they speak in my name, but who preach messages that come from their own imagination. Tell them it's time to hear my message.

³ I, the LORD God, say those lying prophets are doomed! They don't see visions — they make up their own messages! ⁴ Israel's prophets are no better than jackals* that hunt for food among the ruins of a city. ⁵ They don't warn the people about coming trouble or tell them how dangerous it is to sin against me. ⁶ Those prophets lie by claiming they speak for me, but I have not even chosen them to be my prophets. And they still think their words will come true. ⁷ They say they're preaching my messages, but they are full of lies — I did not speak to them!

⁸ So I am going to punish those lying prophets for deceiving the people of Israel with false messages. ⁹ I will turn against them and no longer let them belong to my people. They will not be allowed to call themselves Israelites or even to set foot in Israel. Then they will realize that I am the LORD God.

¹⁰ Those prophets refuse to be honest. They tell my people there will be peace, even though there's no peace to be found. They are like workers who think they can fix a shaky wall by covering it with paint. ¹¹ But when I send rainstorms, hailstones, and strong winds, the wall will surely collapse. ¹² People will then ask the workers why the paint didn't hold it up.

¹³ That wall is the city of Jerusalem. And I, the LORD God, am so angry that I will send strong winds, rainstorms, and hailstones to destroy it. ¹⁴ The lying prophets have tried to cover up the evil in Jerusalem, but I will tear down the city, all the way to its foundations. And when it collapses, those prophets will be killed, and everyone will know that I have done these things.

¹⁵ The city of Jerusalem and its lying prophets will feel my fierce anger. Then I will announce that the city has fallen and that the lying prophets are dead, ¹⁶ because they promised my people peace, when there was no peace. I, the LORD God, have spoken.

Women who wear magic charms

The LORD said:

¹⁷ Ezekiel, son of man, now condemn the women of Israel who preach messages that come from their own imagination. ¹⁸ Tell them they're doomed! They wear magic charms on their wrists and scarves on their heads, then trick others into believing they can predict the future.ᵗ They won't get away with telling those lies. ¹⁹ They charge my people a few handfuls of barley and a couple of pieces of bread, and then give messages that are insulting to me. They use lies to sentence the innocent to death and to help the guilty go free. And my people believe them!

²⁰ I hate the magic charms they use to trick people into believing their lies. I will rip those charms from their wrists and set free the people they have trapped like birds.ᵗ ²¹ I will tear the scarves from their heads and rescue my people from their power once and for all. Then they will know that I am the LORD God.

²² They do things I would never do. They lie to good people and encourage them to do wrong, and they convince the wicked to keep sinning and ruin their lives. ²³ I will no longer let these women give false messages and use magic, and I will free my people from their control. Then they will know that I, the LORD, have done these things.

CHAPTER 14

Ezekiel encourages the people to turn back to the LORD

¹ One day, some of Israel's leaders came to me and asked for a message from the LORD. ² While they were there, the LORD said:

³ Ezekiel, son of man, these men have started worshipping idols, though they know it will cause them to sin even more. So I refuse to give them a message!

⁴ Tell the people of Israel that if they sin by worshipping idols and then go to a prophet to find out what I say, I will give them the answer their sins deserve. ⁵ When they hear my message, perhaps they will see that they need to turn back to me and stop worshipping those idols.

---

*13.4 jackals: Desert animals related to wolves, but smaller.

See also: 13.10: Jer 6.14; 8.11.

⁶ Now, Ezekiel, tell everyone in Israel:

I am the Lord God. Stop worshipping your disgusting idols and come back to me.

⁷ Suppose one of you Israelites or a foreigner living in Israel rejects me and starts worshipping idols. If you then go to a prophet to find out what I say, I will answer ⁸ by turning against you. I will make you a warning to anyone who might think of doing the same thing, and you will no longer belong to my people. Then you will know that I am the Lord and that you have sinned against me.

⁹ If a prophet gives a false message, I am the one who caused that prophet to lie. But I will still reject him and cut him off from my people, ¹⁰ and anyone who goes to that prophet for a message will be punished in the same way. ¹¹ I will do this, so that you will come back to me and stop destroying yourselves with these disgusting sins. So turn back to me! Then I will be your God, and you will be my people. I, the Lord God, make this promise.

Judgment on a sinful nation

¹² The Lord God said:

¹³ Ezekiel, son of man, suppose an entire nation sins against me, and I punish it by destroying the crops and letting its people and livestock starve to death. ¹⁴ Even if Noah, Daniel,* and Job were living in that nation, their faithfulness would not save anyone but themselves.

¹⁵ Or suppose I punish a nation by sending wild animals to eat people and scare away every passer-by, so that the land becomes a barren desert. ¹⁶ As surely as I live, I promise that even if these three men lived in that nation, their own children would not be spared. The three men would live, but the land would be an empty desert.

¹⁷ Or suppose I send an enemy to attack a sinful nation and kill its people and livestock. ¹⁸ If these three men were in that nation when I punished it, not even their children would be spared. Only the three men would live.

¹⁹ And suppose I am so angry that I send a deadly disease to wipe out the people and livestock of a sinful nation. ²⁰ Again, even if Noah, Daniel, and Job were living

there, I, the Lord, promise that the children of these faithful men would also die. Only the three of them would be spared.

²¹ I am the Lord God, and I promise to punish Jerusalem severely. I will send war, starvation, wild animals, and deadly disease to slaughter its people and livestock. ²² And those who survive will be taken from their country and led here to Babylonia. Ezekiel, when you see how sinful they are, you will know why I did all these things to Jerusalem. ²³ You will be convinced that I, the Lord God, was right in doing what I did.

CHAPTER 15

Jerusalem is a useless vine

¹ Some time later, the Lord said:

² Ezekiel, son of man, what happens to the wood of a grapevine after the grapes have been picked? It isn't like other trees in the forest, ³ because the wood of a grapevine can't be used to make anything, not even a small peg to hang things on. ⁴ It can only be used as firewood. But after its ends are burnt and its middle is charred, it can't be used for anything. ⁵ The wood is useless before it is burnt, and afterwards, it is completely worthless.

⁶ I, the Lord God, promise that just as the wood of a grapevine is burnt as firewood, ⁷ I will punish the people of Jerusalem with fire. Some of them have escaped one destruction, but soon they will be completely burnt. And when that happens, you, Ezekiel, will know that I am the Lord. ⁸ I will make their country an empty wasteland, because they have not been loyal to me. I, the Lord God, have spoken.

CHAPTER 16

Jerusalem is unfaithful

¹ The Lord said:

² Ezekiel, son of man, remind the people of Jerusalem of their disgusting sins ³ and tell them that I, the Lord God, am saying:

Jerusalem, you were born in the country where Canaanites lived. Your father was an Amorite, and your mother was a Hittite.*

---

*14.14 Daniel: Or "Danel", possibly a well-known hero or wise man.

*16.3 Amorite . . . Hittite: People who lived in Canaan before the Israelites and who worshipped idols. See also: 14.21: Rev 6.8.

4 When you were born, no one cut you loose from your mother or washed your body. No one rubbed your skin with salt and olive oil,* and wrapped you in warm blankets. 5 Not one person loved you enough to do any of these things, and no one even felt sorry for you. You were despised, thrown into a field, and forgotten.

6 I saw you lying there, rolling around in your own blood, and I couldn't let you die. 7 I took care of you, like someone caring for a tender, young plant. You grew up to be a beautiful young woman with perfect breasts and long hair, but you were still naked.

8 When I saw you again, you were old enough to have sex. So I covered your naked body with my own robe.* Then I solemnly promised that you would belong to me and that I, the LORD God, would take care of you.

9 I washed the blood off you and rubbed your skin with olive oil. 10 I gave you the finest clothes and the most expensive robes,' as well as sandals made from the best leather. 11 I gave you bracelets, a necklace, 12 a ring for your nose, some earrings, and a beautiful crown. 13 Your jewellery was gold and silver, and your clothes were made of only the finest material and embroidered linen. Your bread was baked from fine flour, and you ate honey and olive oil. You were as beautiful as a queen, 14 and everyone on earth knew it. I, the LORD God, had helped you become a lovely young woman.

15 You learnt that you were attractive enough to have any man you wanted, so you offered yourself to every passer-by.' 16 You made shrines for yourself and decorated them with some of your clothes. That's where you took your visitors to have sex with them. These things should never have happened!' 17 You made idols out of the gold and silver jewellery I gave you, then you sinned by worshipping those idols. 18 You dressed them in the clothes you got from me, and you offered them the olive oil and incense I gave you. 19 I supplied you with fine flour, olive oil, and honey, but you sacrificed it all as offerings to please those idols. I, the LORD God, watched this happen.

20 But you did something even worse than that — you sacrificed your own children to those idols! 21 You slaughtered my children, so you could offer them as sacrifices. 22 You were so busy sinning and being a prostitute that you refused to think about the days when you were young and were rolling around naked in your own blood.

23 Now I, the LORD God, say you are doomed! Not only did you do these evil things, 24 but you also built places on every street corner 25 where you disgraced yourself by having sex with anyone who walked by. And you did that more and more every day! 26 To make me angry, you even offered yourself to Egyptians, who were always ready to sleep with you.

27 So I punished you by letting those greedy Philistine enemies take over some of your territory. But even they were offended by your disgusting behaviour.

28 You couldn't get enough sex, so you chased after Assyrians and slept with them. You still weren't satisfied, 29 so you went after Babylonians. But those merchants could not satisfy you either.

30 I, the LORD God, say that you were so disgusting that you would have done anything to get what you wanted.' 31 You had sex on every street corner, and when you finished, you refused to accept money. That's worse than being a prostitute! 32 You are nothing but an unfaithful wife who would rather have sex with strangers than with your own husband. 33 Prostitutes accept money for having sex, but you bribe men from everywhere to have sex with you. 34 You're not like other prostitutes. Men don't ask you for sex — you offer to pay them!

Jerusalem must be punished

The LORD said:

35 Jerusalem, you prostitute, listen to me. 36 You chased after lovers, then took off your clothes and had sex. You even worshipped disgusting idols and sacrificed your own children as offerings to them. 37 So I, the LORD God, will gather every one of your lovers, those you liked and those you hated. They will stand around you, and I will rip off your clothes and let all those lovers stare at your nakedness. 38 I will find you guilty of being an unfaithful wife and a murderer, and in my fierce anger I will sentence you to death! 39 Then I will hand you over to your lovers, who will tear down the places where you had sex. They will take

---

*16.4 rubbed your skin with salt and olive oil:
People believed this toughened the skin of the babies.
*16.8 I covered your naked body with my own robe:
To show that he would protect and take care of her.

your clothes and jewellery, leaving you naked and empty-handed.

⁴⁰ Your lovers and an angry mob will stone you to death; they will cut your dead body into pieces ⁴¹ and burn down your houses. Other women will watch these terrible things happen to you. I promise to stop you from being a prostitute and paying your lovers for sex.

⁴² Only then will I calm down and stop being angry and jealous. ⁴³ You made me furious by doing all these disgusting things and by forgetting how I took care of you when you were young. Then you made things worse by acting like a prostitute. You must be punished! I, the LORD God, have spoken.

Jerusalem's two sisters

The LORD said:

⁴⁴ People will use this saying about you, Jerusalem: "If the mother is bad, so is her daughter." ⁴⁵ You are just like your mother, who hated her husband and her own children. You are also like your sisters, who hated their husbands and children. Your father was an Amorite, and your mother was a Hittite.* ⁴⁶ Your elder sister was Samaria, that city to your north with her nearby villages. Your younger sister was Sodom, that city to your south with her nearby villages. ⁴⁷ You followed their way of life and their wicked customs, and soon you were more disgusting than they were.

⁴⁸ As surely as I am the living LORD God, the people of Sodom and its nearby villages were never as sinful as you. ⁴⁹ They were arrogant and spoilt; they had everything they needed and still refused to help the poor and needy. ⁵⁰ They thought they were better than everyone else, and they did things I hate. And so I destroyed them.

⁵¹ You people of Jerusalem have sinned twice as much as the people of Samaria. In fact, your evil ways have made both Sodom and Samaria look innocent. ⁵² So their punishment will seem light compared to yours. You will be disgraced and put to shame because of your disgusting sins.

Jerusalem will be ashamed

The LORD said to Jerusalem:

⁵³ Some day I will bless Sodom and Samaria and their nearby villages. I will also bless

you, Jerusalem. ⁵⁴ Then you will be ashamed of how you've acted, and Sodom and Samaria will be relieved that they weren't as sinful as you. ⁵⁵ When that day comes, you and Sodom and Samaria will once again be well off, and all nearby villages will be restored.

⁵⁶ Jerusalem, you were so arrogant that you sneered at Sodom. ⁵⁷ But now everyone has learnt how wicked you really are. The countries of Syria and Philistia, as well as your other neighbours, hate you and make insulting remarks. ⁵⁸ You must pay for all the vulgar and disgusting things you have done. I, the LORD, have spoken.

The LORD makes a promise to Jerusalem

The LORD said:

⁵⁹ Jerusalem, you deserve to be punished, because you broke your promises and ignored our agreement. ⁶⁰ But I remember the agreement I made with you when you were young,* and so I will make you a promise that will last for ever. ⁶¹ When you think about how you acted, you will be ashamed, especially when I return your sisters* to you as daughters, even though this was not part of our agreement.› ⁶² I will keep this solemn promise, and you will know that I am the LORD. ⁶³ I will forgive you, but you will think about your sins and be too ashamed to say a word. I, the LORD God, have spoken.

CHAPTER 17

A story about two eagles and a vine

¹ The LORD said:

² Ezekiel, son of man, tell the people of Israel the following story, ³ so they will understand what I am saying to them:

A large eagle with strong wings and beautiful feathers once flew to Lebanon. It broke the top branch off a cedar tree, ⁴ then carried it to a nation of merchants and left it in one of their cities. ⁵ The eagle also took seed from Israel and planted it in a fertile field with plenty of water, like a willow tree beside a stream.› ⁶ The seed sprouted and grew into a grapevine that spread over the ground. It had lots of leaves

*16.45 Amorite . . . Hittite: See the note at 16.3.

*16.60 the agreement . . . when you were young: See verse 8.
*16.61 sisters: Sodom and Samaria (see verses 44–52).

and strong, deep roots, and its branches grew upward towards the eagle.

⁷ There was another eagle with strong wings and thick feathers. The roots and branches of the grapevine soon turned towards this eagle, hoping it would bring water for the soil. ⁸ But the vine was already growing in fertile soil, where there was plenty of water to produce healthy leaves and large grapes.

⁹ Now tell me, Ezekiel, do you think this grapevine will live? Or will the first eagle pull it up by its roots and pluck off the grapes and let its new leaves die? The eagle could easily kill it without the help of a large and powerful army. ¹⁰ The grapevine is strong and healthy, but as soon as the scorching desert wind blows, it will quickly wither.

The LORD explains the story

¹¹ The LORD said:

¹² Ezekiel, ask the rebellious people of Israel if they know what this story means.

Tell them that the king of Babylonia came to Jerusalem, then he captured the king of Judah* and his officials, and took them back to Babylon as prisoners. ¹³ He chose someone from the family of Judah's king* and signed a treaty with him, then made him swear to be loyal. He also led away other important citizens, ¹⁴ so that the rest of the people of Judah would obey only him and never gain control of their own country again.

¹⁵ But this new king of Judah later rebelled against Babylonia and sent officials to Egypt to get horses and troops. Will this king be successful in breaking the treaty with Babylonia? Or will he be punished for what he's done?

¹⁶ As surely as I am the living LORD God, I swear that the king of Judah will die in Babylon, because he broke the treaty with the king of Babylonia, who appointed him king. ¹⁷ Even the king of Egypt and his powerful army will be useless to Judah when the Babylonians attack and build earth ramps to invade the cities of Judah and kill its people. ¹⁸ The king of Judah broke his own promises and ignored the treaty with Babylonia. And so he will be punished!

¹⁹ He made a promise in my name and swore to honour the treaty. And now that he has broken that promise, my name is disgraced. He must pay for what he's done. ²⁰ I will spread out a net to trap him. Then I will drag him to Babylon and see that he is punished for his unfaithfulness to me. ²¹ His best troops' will be killed in battle, and the survivors will be scattered in every direction. I, the LORD, have spoken.

²²⁻²³Some day, I, the LORD,
   will cut a tender twig
      from the top of a cedar tree,
   then plant it on the peak
      of Israel's tallest mountain,
   where it will grow
   strong branches
      and produce large fruit.
All kinds of birds will find
      shelter under the tree,
   and they will rest in the shade
      of its branches.
²⁴ Every tree in the forest
   will know that I, the LORD,
can bring down tall trees
   and help short ones grow.
I dry up green trees
   and make dry ones green.
I, the LORD, have spoken,
   and I will keep my word.

CHAPTER 18

Those who sin will die

¹ The LORD said:

² Ezekiel, I hear the people of Israel using the old saying,

"Sour grapes eaten by parents
leave a sour taste in the mouths
   of their children."

³ Now tell them that I am the LORD God, and as surely as I live, that saying will no longer be used in Israel. ⁴ The lives of all people belong to me — parents as well as children. Only those who sin will be put to death.

⁵ Suppose there is a truly good man who always does what is fair and right. ⁶ He refuses to eat meat sacrificed to foreign gods at local shrines or to worship Israel's idols. He doesn't have sex with someone else's wife or with a woman having her monthly period. ⁷ He never cheats or robs anyone and always returns anything taken as

*17.12 king of Judah: Probably King Jehoiachin (see 2 Kings 24.10–12,15–16).
*17.13 someone from the family of Judah's king: Probably King Zedekiah (see 2 Kings 24.17).
See also: 17.12–15: 2 King 24.15–20; 2 Chron 36.10–13.

See also: 18.2: Jer 31.29.

security for a loan; he gives food and clothes to the poor [8] and doesn't charge interest when lending money. He refuses to do anything evil; he is fair to everyone [9] and faithfully obeys my laws and teachings. This man is good, and I promise he will live.

[10] But suppose this good man has an evil son who is violent and commits sins [11] his father never did. He eats meat at local shrines, has sex with someone else's wife, [12] cheats the poor, and robs people. He keeps what is given to him as security for a loan. He worships idols, does disgusting things, [13] and charges high interest when lending money. An evil man like that will certainly not live. He is the one who has done these horrible sins, so it's his own fault that he will be put to death.

[14] But suppose this evil man has a son who sees his father do these things and refuses to act like him. [15] He doesn't eat meat at local shrines or worship Israel's idols, and he doesn't have sex with someone else's wife. [16] He never cheats or robs anyone and doesn't even demand security for a loan. He gives food and clothes to the poor [17] and refuses to do anything evil' or to charge interest. And he obeys all my laws and teachings. Such a man will live. His own father sinned, but this good man will not be put to death for the sins of his father. [18] It is his father who will die for cheating and robbing and doing evil.

[19] You may wonder why a son isn't punished for the sins of his father. It is because the son does what is right and obeys my laws. [20] Only those who sin will be put to death. Children won't suffer for the sins of their parents, and parents won't suffer for the sins of their children. Good people will be rewarded for what they do, and evil people will be punished for what they do.

[21] Suppose wicked people stop sinning and start obeying my laws and doing right. They won't be put to death. [22] All their sins will be forgiven, and they will live because they did right. [23] I, the LORD God, don't like to see wicked people die. I enjoy seeing them turn from their sins and live.

[24] But when good people start sinning and doing disgusting things, will they live? No! All their good deeds will be forgotten, and they will be put to death because of their sins.

[25] You people of Israel accuse me of being unfair! But listen — I'm not unfair; you are!

[26] If good people start doing evil, they must be put to death, because they have sinned. [27] And if wicked people start doing right, they will save themselves from punishment. [28] They will think about what they've done and stop sinning, and so they won't be put to death. [29] But you still say that I am unfair. You are the ones who have done wrong and are unfair!

[30] I will judge each of you for what you've done. So stop sinning, or else you will certainly be punished. [31] Give up your evil ways and start thinking pure thoughts. And be faithful to me! Do you really want to be put to death for your sins? [32] I, the LORD God, don't want to see that happen to anyone. So stop sinning and live!

CHAPTER 19

A funeral song for Israel's leaders

The LORD said:

[1] Ezekiel, sing a funeral song for two of Israel's leaders:*

[2] Your mother was a brave lioness
  who raised her cubs
    among lions.
[3] She taught one of them to hunt,
    and he learnt to eat people.
[4] When the nations heard of him,
    they trapped him in a pit,
  then they used hooks
    to drag him to Egypt.

[5] His mother waited
    for him to return.
  But soon she lost all hope
  and raised another cub,
    who also became fierce.
[6] He hunted with other lions
    and learnt to eat people.
[7] He destroyed fortresses'
    and ruined towns;
  his mighty roar
    terrified everyone.
[8] Nations plotted to kill him,
  and people came from everywhere
    to spread out a net
    and catch him in a trap.
[9] They put him in a cage
    and took him to Babylonia.
  The lion was locked away,
    so that his mighty roar

*19.1 two of Israel's leaders:** Probably Jehoahaz (ruled three months in 609 BC) and Jehoiachin (ruled three months in 598 BC) or Zedekiah (598–586 BC).

would never again be heard
  on Israel's hills.

¹⁰ Your mother was a vine⁾
    growing near a stream.
  There was plenty of water,
    so she was filled with branches
    and with lots of fruit.
¹¹ Her strong branches
    became symbols of authority,
  and she was taller
    than all other trees —
  everyone could see how strong
    and healthy she was.
¹² But in anger, I pulled her up
    by the roots
  and threw her to the ground,
    where the scorching desert wind
    dried out her fruit.
  Her strong branches wilted
    and burnt up.
¹³ Then she was planted
    in a hot, dry desert,
¹⁴ where her stem caught fire,
    and flames burnt
    her branches and fruit.
  Not one strong branch is left;
    she is stripped bare.

This funeral song must be sung with sorrow.

CHAPTER 20

Israel keeps on rebelling

¹ Seven years after King Jehoiachin and the rest of us had been led away as prisoners to Babylonia, some of Israel's leaders came to me on the tenth day of the fifth month.* They sat down and asked for a message from the LORD. ² Just then, the LORD God said:

³ Ezekiel, son of man, these leaders have come to find out what I want them to do. As surely as I live, I will not give them an answer of any kind.

⁴ Are you willing to warn them, Ezekiel? Then remind them of the disgusting sins of their ancestors.

⁵ Tell them that long ago I, the LORD God, chose Israel to be my own. I appeared to their ancestors in Egypt and made a solemn promise that I would be their God and the God of their descendants. ⁶ I swore that I would rescue them from Egypt and lead them to a land I had already chosen. This

land was rich with milk and honey and was the most splendid land of all. ⁷ I told them to get rid of their disgusting idols and not to sin by worshipping the gods of Egypt. I reminded them that I was the LORD their God, ⁸ but they still rebelled against me. They refused to listen and kept on worshipping their idols and foreign gods.

In my anger, I decided to punish the Israelites in Egypt. ⁹ But that would have made me look like a liar, because I had already promised in front of everyone that I would lead them out of Egypt. ¹⁰ So I brought them out and led them into the desert. ¹¹ I gave them my laws and teachings, so they would know how to live right. ¹² And I commanded them to respect the Sabbath as a way of showing that they were holy and belonged to me. ¹³ But the Israelites rebelled against me in the desert. They refused to obey my laws and teachings, and they treated the Sabbath like any other day.

Then in my anger, I decided to destroy the Israelites in the desert once and for all. ¹⁴ But that would have disgraced me, because many other nations had seen me bring the Israelites out of Egypt. ¹⁵ Instead, I told them in the desert that I would not lead them into the beautiful, fertile land I had promised. ¹⁶ I said this because they had not only ignored my laws and teachings, but had disgraced my Sabbath and worshipped idols.

¹⁷ Yet, I felt sorry for them and could not let them die in the desert. ¹⁸ So I warned the children not to act like their parents or follow their evil ways or worship their idols. ¹⁹ I reminded them that I was the LORD their God and that they should obey my laws and teachings. ²⁰ I told them to respect my Sabbath to show that they were my people and that I was the LORD their God. ²¹ But the children also rebelled against me. They refused to obey my laws and teachings, and they treated the Sabbath as any other day.

I became angry and decided to punish them in the desert. ²² But I did not. That would have disgraced me in front of the nations that had seen me bring the Israelites out of Egypt. ²³ So I solemnly swore that I would scatter the people of Israel across the nations, ²⁴ because they had disobeyed my laws and ignored my teachings; they had disgraced my Sabbath and worshipped the idols their ancestors had made. ²⁵ I gave them laws that bring punishment instead of life,

*20.1 Seven years . . . fifth month: Probably August of 591 BC.
See also: 20.5–6: Exod 6.2–8.
896

See also: 20.11,13: Lev 18.5. 20.12: Exod 31.13–17. 20.15: Num 14.26–35. 20.23: Lev 26.33.

26 and I let them offer me unacceptable sacrifices, including their firstborn sons. I did this to horrify them and to let them know that I, the LORD, was punishing them.

27 Ezekiel, tell the people of Israel that their ancestors also rejected and insulted me 28 by offering sacrifices, incense, and wine to gods on every hill and under every large tree. I was very angry, because they did these things in the land I had given them! 29 I asked them where they went to worship those gods, and they answered, "At the local shrines."* And those places of worship are still called shrines.

30 Then ask the Israelites why they are following the example of their wicked ancestors 31 by worshipping idols and by sacrificing their own children as offerings. They commit these sins and still think they can ask me for a message. As surely as I am the living LORD God, I will give them no answer. 32 They may think they can be like other nations and get away with worshipping idols made of wood and stone. But that will never happen!

The LORD promises to restore Israel

The LORD said to the people of Israel:

33 As surely as I am the living LORD God, I will rule over you with my powerful arm. You will feel my fierce anger 34 and my power, when I gather you from the places where you are scattered 35 and lead you into a desert surrounded by nations. I will meet you there face to face. Then I will pass judgment on you 36 and punish you, just as I punished your ancestors in the desert near Egypt.* 37 I will force each of you to obey the regulations of our solemn agreement. 38 I will separate the sinful rebels from the rest of you, and even though I will bring them from the nations where they live in exile, they won't be allowed to return to Israel. Then you will know that I am the LORD.

39 Go ahead and worship your idols for now, you Israelites, because soon I will no longer let you dishonour me by offering gifts to them. You will have no choice but to obey me!▸ 40 When that day comes, everyone in Israel will worship me on Mount Zion, my holy mountain in Jerusalem. I will once

again call you my own, and I will accept your sacred offerings and sacrifices. 41 When I bring you home from the places where you are now scattered, I will be pleased with you, just as I am pleased with the smell of the smoke from your sacrifices. Every nation on earth will see that I am holy, 42 and you will know that I, the LORD, am the one who brought you back to Israel, the land I promised your ancestors. 43 Then you will remember your wicked sins, and you will hate yourselves for doing such horrible things. They have made you unacceptable to me, 44 so you deserve to be punished. But I will treat you in a way that will bring honour to my name, and you will know that I am the LORD God.

Fire from the south

45 The LORD said, 46 "Ezekiel, son of man, turn towards the south and warn the forests 47 that I, the LORD God, will start a fire that will burn up every tree, whether green or dry. Nothing will be able to put out the blaze of that fire as it spreads to the north and burns everything in its path. 48 Everyone will know that I started it, and that it cannot be stopped."

49 But I complained, "LORD God, I don't want to do that! People already say I confuse them with my messages."

CHAPTER 21
The LORD will punish Jerusalem

1 The LORD said:

2 Ezekiel, son of man, condemn the places in Jerusalem where people worship. Warn everyone in Israel 3 that I am about to punish them. I will pull out my sword and have it ready to kill everyone, whether good or evil. 4 From south to north, people will die, 5 knowing that my sword will never be put away.

6 Ezekiel, groan in sorrow and despair so that everyone can hear you. 7 When they ask why you are groaning, tell them you have terrifying news that will make them faint and tremble in fear and lose all courage. These things will happen soon. I, the LORD God, make this promise!

A sword is ready to attack Israel

8 The LORD said:

9-10 Ezekiel, son of man, tell the people of Jerusalem:

---

*20.29 where they went to worship those gods . . . local shrines: In Hebrew "where they went" sounds like "local shrines". These were places to worship foreign gods.

*20.36 the desert near Egypt: The Sinai Desert.

I have sharpened my sword
  to slaughter you;
it is shiny and will flash
  like lightning!
Don't celebrate —
  punishment is coming,
because everyone has ignored
  my warnings.'
¹¹ My sword has been polished;
  it's sharp and ready to kill.

¹² Groan in sorrow, Ezekiel;
  the sword is drawn against
    my people
  and their leaders.
They will die!
  So give up all hope.
¹³ I am testing my people,
  and they can do nothing
    to stop me.'
I, the Lord, have spoken.

¹⁴ Ezekiel, warn my people,
  then celebrate my victory
    by clapping your hands.
My vicious sword will attack
  again and again,
killing my people
  with every stroke.
¹⁵ They will lose all courage
  and stumble with fear.
My slaughtering sword
  is waiting at every gate,
flashing and ready to kill.'
¹⁶ It will slash right and left,
  wherever the blade is pointed.
¹⁷ Then I will stop being angry,
  and I will clap my hands
    in victory.
I, the Lord, have spoken.

The king of Babylonia and his sword

¹⁸ The Lord said:

¹⁹ Ezekiel, son of man, mark two roads
for the king of Babylonia to follow when
he comes with his sword. The roads will
begin at the same place, but be sure to
put up a signpost where the two roads
separate and go in different directions.
²⁰ Clearly mark where the two roads lead.
One goes to Rabbah, the capital of
Ammon, and the other goes to Jerusalem,
the fortified capital of Judah. ²¹ When the
Babylonian king stands at that signpost,
he will decide which way to go by shaking
his arrows, by asking his idols, and by
carefully looking at the liver of a sacrificed

animal.* ²² His right hand will pull out the
arrow marked "Jerusalem". Then he will
immediately give the signal to shout the
battle cry, to build earth ramps to the top
of the city walls, to break down its walls
and gates with large wooden poles, and to
kill the people. ²³ Everyone in Jerusalem
had promised to be loyal to Babylonia, and
so none of them will believe that this could
happen to them. But Babylonia's king will
remind them of their sinful ways and warn
them of their coming captivity.

²⁴ Ezekiel, tell the people of Jerusalem and
their ruler that I, the Lord God, am saying:

Everything you do is wicked and shows
how sinful you are. You are guilty and will
be taken away as prisoners.

²⁵ And now, you evil and wicked ruler of
Israel, your day of final punishment is
almost here. ²⁶ I, the Lord God, command
you to take off your royal turban and your
crown, because everything will be different.
Those who had no power will be put in
charge, and those who now rule will
become nobodies. ²⁷ I will leave Jerusalem
in ruins when my chosen one comes to
punish this city.

Judgment against Ammon

²⁸ The Lord God said:

Ezekiel, son of man, the Ammonites have
insulted Israel, so condemn them and tell
them I am saying:

  A sword is drawn,
    ready to slaughter;
  it is polished and prepared
    to kill as fast as lightning.

²⁹ You wicked Ammonites see false visions
and believe untrue messages. But your day
of punishment is coming soon, and my
sword will slaughter you!

³⁰ Your days of punishing others are over,
so put your swords away.' You will be
punished in the land of your birth. ³¹ My
furious anger will scorch you like fire, and I
will hand you over to cruel men who are
experts in killing. ³² You will be burnt and
will die in your own land. Then you will be
forgotten for ever. I, the Lord, have spoken.

---

*21.21 shaking . . . animal: These were ways the
Babylonians found out what their gods wanted them
to do.
See also: 21.28–32: Jer 49.1–6; Ezek 25.1–7; Amos 1.3–15;
Zeph 2.8–11.

CHAPTER 22

Jerusalem is condemned

1 Some time later, the LORD said:

2 Ezekiel, son of man, are you ready to condemn Jerusalem? That city is filled with murderers, so remind the people of their sins 3 and tell them I am saying:

Jerusalem, you have murdered many of your own people and have worshipped idols. You will soon be punished! 4 Those crimes have made you guilty, and the idols have made you unacceptable to me. So your final punishment is near. Other nations will laugh at you and make insulting remarks, 5 and people far and near will make fun of your misery.

6 Your own leaders use their power to murder. 7 None of you honour your parents, and you cheat foreigners, orphans, and widows. 8 You show no respect for my sacred places and treat the Sabbath just like any other day. 9 Some of your own people tell lies, so that others will be put to death. Some of you eat meat sacrificed to idols at local shrines, and others never stop doing vulgar things. 10 Men have sex with their father's wife or with women who are having their monthly period 11 or with someone else's wife. Some men even sleep with their own daughter-in-law or half-sister. 12 Others of you accept money to murder someone. Your own people charge high interest when making a loan to other Israelites, and they get rich by cheating. Worst of all, you have forgotten me, the LORD God.

13 I will shake my fist in anger at your violent crimes. 14 When I've finished with you, your courage will disappear, and you will be so weak that you won't be able to lift your hands. I, the LORD, have spoken and will not change my mind. 15 I will scatter you throughout every nation on earth and put a stop to your sinful ways. 16 You᾽ will be humiliated in the eyes of other nations. Then you will know that I, the LORD God, have done these things.

Jerusalem must be purified

17 The LORD said:

18 Ezekiel, son of man, I consider the people of Israel as worthless as the leftover metal in a furnace after silver has been purified. 19 So I am going to bring them together in Jerusalem. 20-21 I will be like a metalworker who collects that metal from the furnace and melts it down. I will collect the Israelites and blow on them with my fiery anger. They will melt inside the city of Jerusalem 22 like silver in a furnace. Then they will know that I, the LORD, have punished them in my anger.

Everyone in Jerusalem is guilty

23 The LORD said:

24 Ezekiel, son of man, tell the people of Israel that their country is full of sin, and that I, the LORD, am furious! 25 Their leaders are like᾽ roaring lions, tearing apart their victims. They put people to death, then steal everything of value. Husbands are killed, and many women are left as widows.

26 The priests of Israel ignore my Law! Not only do they refuse to respect any of my sacred things, but they don't even teach the difference between what is sacred and what is ordinary, or between what is clean and what is unclean. They treat my Sabbath like any other day, and so my own people no longer honour me.

27 Israel's officials are like ferocious wolves, ripping their victims apart. They make a dishonest living by injuring and killing people.

28 And then the prophets in Israel cover up these sins by giving false visions. I have never spoken to them, but they lie and say they have a message from me. 29 The people themselves cheat and rob; they abuse the poor and take advantage of foreigners.

30 I looked for someone to defend the city and to protect it from my anger, as well as to stop me from destroying it. But I found no one. 31 So in my fierce anger, I will punish the Israelites for what they have done, and they will know that I am furious. I, the LORD, have spoken.

CHAPTER 23

Two sinful sisters

1 The LORD said:

2 Ezekiel, son of man, listen to this story about two sisters. 3 While they were young

See also: **22.7:** a Exod 20.12; Deut 5.16; b Exod 22.21–22; Deut 24.17.   **22.8:** Lev 19.30; 26.2.   **22.10,11:** Lev 18.7–20. **22.12:** Exod 23.8; Deut 16.19; Exod 22.25; Lev 25.36–37; Deut 23.19.

See also: **22.26:** Lev 10.10.

and living in Egypt, they became prostitutes.
4 The elder one was named Oholah, which stands for Samaria; the younger one was Oholibah, which stands for Jerusalem.* They became my wives and gave birth to my children.

5 Even though Oholah was my wife, she continued to be a prostitute and chased after Assyrian lovers. 6 She offered herself to soldiers in purple uniforms, to every handsome, high-ranking officer, and to cavalry troops. 7 She had sex with all the important Assyrian officials and even worshipped their disgusting idols. 8 Once she started doing these things in Egypt, she never stopped. Men slept with her, and she was always ready for sex.

9 So I gave Oholah to the Assyrian lovers she wanted so badly. 10 They ripped off her clothes, then captured her children and killed her. Women everywhere talked about what had happened to Oholah.

11 Oholibah saw all this, but she was more sinful and wanted sex more than her sister Oholah ever did. 12 Oholibah also chased after good-looking Assyrian officers, uniformed soldiers, and cavalry troops. 13 Just like her sister, she did vulgar things.

14 But Oholibah behaved worse than her sister. Oholibah saw images of Babylonian men carved into walls and painted red. 15 They had belts around their waists and large turbans on their heads, and they reminded her of Babylonian cavalry officers. 16 As soon as she looked at them, she wanted to have sex with them. And so, she sent messengers to bring them to her. 17 Men from Babylonia came and had sex with her so many times that she got disgusted with them. 18 She let everyone see her naked body and didn't care if they knew she was a prostitute. That's why I turned my back on her, just as I had done with her elder sister.

19 Oholibah didn't stop there, but became even more immoral and acted as she had back in Egypt. 20 She eagerly wanted to go to bed with Egyptian men, who were famous for their sexual powers. 21 And she longed for the days when she was a young prostitute, when men enjoyed having sex with her.

The LORD will punish Oholibah

22 The LORD God said:

Oholibah,* though you no longer want to be with your lovers, they will surround you like enemies, when I turn them against you. 23 I will gather all the handsome young officials and the high-ranking cavalry officers from Babylonia and Assyria, as well as from the Chaldean tribes of Pekod, Shoa, and Koa. 24 Their large armies will come from the north' with chariots and wagons carrying weapons. They will wear shields and helmets and will surround you, and I will let them judge and sentence you according to their own laws. 25 I am angry with you, so I will let them be very cruel. They will cut off your nose and ears; they will kill your children and put to death anyone in your family who is still alive. 26 Your clothes and jewellery will be torn off. 27 I will stop your wickedness and the prostitution you started back in Egypt. You will never want to think about those days again.

28 I, the LORD God, am ready to hand you over to those hateful enemies that you find so disgusting. 29 They will cruelly take away everything you have worked for and strip you naked. Then everyone will see you for the prostitute you really are. Your own vulgar sins 30 have led to this. You were the one determined to have sex with men from other nations and to worship their idols. 31 You have turned out no better than your elder sister, and now you must drink from the cup filled with my anger.

32 I, the LORD God, gave your sister a large, deep cup filled with my anger. And when you drink from that cup, you will be mocked and insulted. 33 You will end up drunk and devastated, because that cup is filled with horror and ruin. 34 But you must drink every drop! Then smash the cup to pieces and use them to cut your breasts in sorrow. I, the LORD God, have spoken.

35 You have completely rejected me, and so I promise that you will be punished for the disgusting things you did as a prostitute.

The two sisters are condemned

36 The LORD said:

Ezekiel, son of man, it's time for you to tell Oholah and Oholibah* that they are guilty.

---

*23.4 Samaria . . . Jerusalem: After the nation of Israel was divided, the northern kingdom was called "Israel", and the southern kingdom was called "Judah". Samaria was the capital of the northern kingdom, and Jerusalem was the capital of the southern kingdom.

*23.22 Oholibah: That is, Jerusalem (see verse 4).
*23.36 Oholah and Oholibah: That is, Samaria and Jerusalem (see verse 4).

Remind them of their evil ways! ³⁷ They have been unfaithful by worshipping idols, and they have committed murder by sacrificing my own children as offerings to idols. ³⁸⁻³⁹ They came into my temple that same day, and that made it unfit as a place to worship me. They have even stopped respecting the Sabbath.

⁴⁰ They sent messengers to attract men from far away. When those men arrived, the two sisters took baths and put on eye shadow and jewellery. ⁴¹ They sat on a fine couch, and in front of them was a table for the olive oil and incense that had belonged to me. ⁴² Their room was always filled with a noisy crowd of drunkards brought in from the desert. These men gave the women bracelets and beautiful crowns, ⁴³ and I noticed that the men were eager to have sex with these women, though they were exhausted from being prostitutes.ᵖ ⁴⁴ In fact, the men had sex over and over with Oholah and Oholibah, the two sinful sisters. ⁴⁵ But good men will some day accuse those two of murder and of being unfaithful, because they are certainly guilty.

⁴⁶ So I, the LORD God, now say to these sisters:

I will call together an angry mob that will abuse and rob you. ⁴⁷ They will stone you to death and cut you to pieces; they will kill your children and burn down your houses. ⁴⁸ I will get rid of sinful prostitution in this country, so that women everywhere will be warned not to act as you have. ⁴⁹ You will be punished for becoming prostitutes and for worshipping idols, and you will know that I am the LORD God.

CHAPTER 24

A cooking pot

¹ Nine years after King Jehoiachin and the rest of us had been led away as prisoners to Babylonia, the LORD spoke to me on the tenth day of the tenth month.* He said:

² Ezekiel, son of man, write down today's date, because the king of Babylonia has just begun attacking the city of Jerusalem. ³ Then tell my rebellious people:

"Pour water in a cooking pot
  and set it over a fire.

⁴⁻⁵ Throw in the legs and shoulders
  of your finest sheep
  and put in the juicy bones.
Pile woodᵖ underneath the pot,
  and let the meat and bones
  boil until they are done."

⁶ These words mean that Jerusalem is doomed! The city is filled with murderers and is like an old, rusty pot. The meat is taken out piece by piece, and no one cares what happens to it.ᵖ ⁷ The people of Jerusalem murdered innocent people in the city and didn't even try to cover up the blood that flowed out on the hard ground. ⁸ But I have seen that blood, and it cries out for me to take revenge.

⁹ I, the LORD God, will punish that city of violence! I will make a huge pile of firewood, ¹⁰ so bring more wood and light it. Cook the meat and boil away the brothᵖ to let the bones scorch. ¹¹ Then set the empty pot over the hot coals until it is red-hot. That will clean the pot and burn off the rust. ¹² I've tried everything else. Now the rust must be burnt away.ᵖ

¹³ Jerusalem is so full of sin and evil that I can't get it clean, even though I have tried. It will stay filthy until I let loose my fierce anger against it. ¹⁴ That time will certainly come! And when it does, I won't show the people of Jerusalem any pity or change my mind. They must be punished for the evil they have done. I, the LORD God, have spoken.

Ezekiel's wife dies

¹⁵ The LORD said, ¹⁶ "Ezekiel, son of man, I will suddenly take the life of the person you love most. But I don't want you to complain or cry. ¹⁷ Mourn in silence and don't show that you are grieving. Don't remove your turban or take off your sandals; don't cover your face to show your sorrow, or eat the food that mourners eat."*

¹⁸ One morning, I was talking with the people as usual, and by sunset my wife was dead. The next day I did what the LORD told me, ¹⁹ and when people saw me, they asked, "Why aren't you mourning for your wife?"

²⁰ I answered:

---

*24.1 Nine years . . . tenth month: Probably January of 588 BC.

See also: 24.2: 2 King 25.1; Jer 52.4.

*24.17 Don't remove your turban . . . take off your sandals . . . cover your face . . . eat the food that mourners eat: The usual way people mourned was to remove anything worn on the head, to go barefoot, to cover their faces, and to eat special food to show they were grieving.

The LORD God says ²¹ he is ready to destroy the temple in which you take such pride and which makes you feel so safe. Your children who now live in Jerusalem will be killed. ²² Then you will do the same things I have done. You will leave your face uncovered and refuse to eat the food that mourners usually eat. ²³ You won't take off your turbans and your sandals.* You won't cry or mourn, but all day long you will go around groaning because of your sins.

²⁴ I am a warning sign — everything I have done, you will also do. And then you will know the LORD God has made these things happen.

²⁵ The LORD said, "Ezekiel, I will soon destroy the temple that makes everyone feel proud and safe, and I will take away their children as well. ²⁶ On that same day, someone will escape from the city and come to tell you what has happened. ²⁷ Then you will be able to speak again,* and the two of you will talk. You will be a warning sign to the people, and they will know that I am the LORD."

Judgment on foreign nations

CHAPTER 25

Judgment on Ammon

¹ The LORD God said:

² Ezekiel, son of man, condemn the people of Ammon ³ and tell them:

You celebrated when my temple was destroyed, when Israel was defeated, and when my people were taken away as prisoners. ⁴ Now I am going to let you be conquered by tribes from the eastern desert. They will set up their camps in your land and eat your fruit and drink your milk. ⁵ Your capital city of Rabbah will be nothing but pasture land for camels, and the rest of the country will be pastures for sheep. Then you will know that I am the LORD God.

⁶ You hated Israel so much that you clapped and shouted and celebrated. ⁷ And so I will hand you over to enemies who will rob you. I will completely destroy you. There won't be enough of your people left to be a nation ever again, and you will know that I, the LORD, have done these things.

Judgment on Moab

⁸ The LORD God said, "The people of Moab thought Judah was no different from any other nation. ⁹ So I will let Moab's fortress towns along its border be attacked, including Beth-Jeshimoth, Baal-Meon, and Kiriathaim. ¹⁰ The same eastern desert tribes that invade Ammon will invade Moab, and just as Ammon will be forgotten for ever, ¹¹ Moab will be punished. Then the people there will know that I am the LORD."

Judgment on Edom

¹² The LORD God then said, "The people of Edom are guilty of taking revenge on Judah. ¹³ So I will punish Edom by killing all its people and livestock. It will be an empty wasteland all the way from Teman to Dedan. ¹⁴ I will send my own people to take revenge on the Edomites by making them feel my fierce anger. And when I punish them, they will know that I am the LORD God."

Judgment on Philistia

¹⁵ The LORD God said, "The cruel Philistines have taken revenge on their enemies over and over and have tried to destroy them. ¹⁶ Now it's my turn to treat the Philistines as my enemies and to kill everyone living in their towns along the coast. ¹⁷ In my fierce anger, I will take revenge on them. And when I punish them, they will know that I am the LORD."

CHAPTER 26

Judgment on the city of Tyre

¹ Eleven years* after King Jehoiachin and the rest of us had been led away as prisoners to Babylonia, the LORD spoke to me on the first day of the month. He said:

*24.22–23 You will leave your face uncovered . . . refuse to eat the food . . . won't take off your turbans and your sandals: See the note at 24.17.
*24.27 you will be able to speak again: See 3.25–27; 33.21–22.
See also: 25.1–7: Jer 49.1–6; Ezek 21.28–32; Amos 1.13–15; Zeph 2.8–11.

*26.1 Eleven years: Probably late in 587 BC.
See also: 25.8–11: Isa 15.1–16.14; 25.10–12; Jer 48.1–47; Amos 2.1–3; Zeph 2.8–11. 25.12–14: Isa 34.5–17; 63.1–6; Jer 49.7–22; Ezek 35.1–15; Amos 1.11,12; Obad 1–14; Mal 1.2–5. 25.15–17: Isa 14.29–31; Jer 47.1–7; Joel 3.4–8; Amos 1.6–8; Zeph 2.4–7; Zech 9.5–7.
26.1–28.19: Isa 23.1–18; Joel 3.4–8; Amos 1.9,10; Zech 9.1–4; Matt 11.21–22; Luke 10.13,14.

2 Ezekiel, son of man, the people of the city of Tyre* have celebrated Jerusalem's defeat by singing,

> "Jerusalem has fallen!
> It used to be powerful,
>   a centre of trade.
> Now the city is shattered,
>   and we will take its place."

3 Because the people of Tyre have sung that song, I have the following warning for them: I am the LORD God, and I am now your enemy! I will send nations to attack you, like waves crashing against the shore. 4 They will tear down your city walls and defence towers. I will sweep away the ruins until all that's left of you is a bare rock, 5 where fishermen can dry their nets along the coast. I promise that you will be robbed 6 and that the people who live in your towns along the coast will be killed. Then you will know that I am the LORD.

7 King Nebuchadnezzar of Babylonia is the world's most powerful king, and I will send him to attack you. He will march from the north with a powerful army, including horses and chariots and cavalry troops. 8 First, he will attack your towns along the coast and kill the people who live there. Then he will build earth ramps up to the top of your city walls and set up rows of shields around you. 9 He will command some of his troops to use large wooden poles to beat down your walls, while others use iron rods to knock down your watchtowers. 10 He will have so many horses that the dust they stir up will seem like a thick fog. And as his chariots and cavalry approach, even the walls will shake, especially when he proudly enters your ruined city. 11 His troops will ride through your streets, killing people left and right, and your strong columns will crumble to the ground. 12 The troops will steal your valuable possessions; they will break down your walls, and crush your expensive houses. Then the stones and wood and all the remains will be dumped into the sea. 13 You will have no reason to sing or play music on harps, 14 because I will turn you into a bare rock where fishermen can dry their nets. And you will never rebuild your city. I, the LORD God, make this promise.

15 The people of the nations up and down the coast will shudder when they hear your screams and moans of death. 16 The kings will step down from their thrones, then take off their royal robes and fine clothes, and sit on the ground, trembling. They will be so shocked at the news of your defeat that they will shake in fear 17 and sing this funeral song:

> "The great city beside the sea
>   is destroyed!›
> Its people once ruled the coast
>   and terrified everyone there.
> 18 But now Tyre is in ruins,
>   and the people on the coast
>   stare at it in horror
>   and tremble in fear."

19 I, the LORD God, will turn you into a ghost town. The ocean depths will rise over you 20 and carry you down to the world of the dead, where you will join people of ancient times and towns ruined long ago. You will stay there and never again be a city filled with people.› 21 You will die a horrible death! People will come looking for your city, but it will never be found. I, the LORD, have spoken.

CHAPTER 27

A funeral song for Tyre

1 The LORD said:

2 Ezekiel, son of man, sing a funeral song for Tyre,* 3 the city that is built along the sea and that trades with nations along the coast. Tell the people of Tyre that the following message is from me:

> Tyre, you boast about
>   your perfect beauty,
> 4   and your control of the sea.›
>
> You are a ship
>   built to perfection.
> 5 Builders used cypress trees
>   from Mount Hermon
>   to make your planks
>   and a cedar tree from Lebanon
>   for your tall mast.
> 6 Oak trees from Bashan
>   were shaped into oars;
>   pine trees from Cyprus›
>   were cut for your deck,
>   which was then decorated

---

*26.2 Tyre: One of the two major cities of Phoenicia; Sidon was the other.
See also: 26.13: Rev 18.22.

*27.2 Tyre: See the note at 26.2.
See also: 26.16–18: Rev 18.9–10.   26.21: Rev 18.21.

with strips of ivory.
⁷ The builders used fine linen
   from Egypt for your sails,
      so everyone could see you.
   Blue and purple cloth
   from Cyprus was used
      to shade your deck.
⁸ Men from Sidon and Arvad
   did the rowing,
   and your own skilled workers
      were the captains.
⁹ Experienced men from Byblos
   repaired any damages.
   Sailors from all over
   shopped at the stores
      in your port.

¹⁰ Brave soldiers from Persia,
   Lydia, and Libya
      served in your navy,
   protecting you with shields
   and helmets,
      and making you famous.
¹¹ Your guards came from
   Arvad and Cilicia,
   and men from Gamad
      stood watch in your towers.
   With their weapons
   hung on your walls,
      your beauty was complete.

¹² Merchants from southern Spain⟩ traded silver, iron, tin, and lead for your products. ¹³ The people of Greece, Tubal, and Meshech traded slaves and things made of bronze, ¹⁴ and those from Beth-Togarmah traded work horses, war horses, and mules. ¹⁵ You also did business with people from Rhodes,⟩ and people from nations along the coast gave you ivory and ebony* in exchange for your goods. ¹⁶ Edom⟩ traded emeralds, purple cloth, embroidery, fine linen, coral, and rubies. ¹⁷ Judah and Israel gave you their finest wheat, best figs,⟩ honey, olive oil, and spices in exchange for your merchandise. ¹⁸ The people of Damascus saw what you had to offer and brought you wine from Helbon and wool from Zahar. ¹⁹ Vedan and Javan near Uzal⟩ traded you iron and spices. ²⁰ The people of Dedan supplied you with saddle blankets, ²¹ while people from Arabia and the rulers of Kedar traded lambs, sheep, and goats. ²² Merchants from Sheba and Raamah gave you excellent spices, precious stones, and gold in exchange for your products. ²³ You

also did business with merchants from the cities of Haran, Canneh, Eden, Sheba, Asshur, and Chilmad, ²⁴ and they gave you expensive clothing, purple and embroidered cloth, brightly-coloured rugs, and strong rope. ²⁵ Large, seagoing ships* carried your goods wherever they needed to go.

   You were like a ship
   loaded with heavy cargo
²⁶   and sailing across the sea,
   but you were wrecked
      by strong eastern winds.
²⁷ Everything on board was lost —
   your valuable cargo,
   your sailors and carpenters,
      merchants and soldiers.
²⁸ The shouts of your drowning crew
      were heard on the shore.

²⁹ Every ship is deserted;
   rowers and sailors and captains
      all stand on shore,
³⁰   mourning for you.
   They show their sorrow
   by putting dust on their heads
      and rolling in ashes;
³¹ they shave their heads
   and dress in sackcloth*
      as they cry in despair.
³² In their grief they sing
   a funeral song for you:
   "Tyre, you were greater
      than all other cities.
   But now you lie in silence
      at the bottom of the sea.⟩

³³ "Nations that received
   your merchandise
      were always pleased;
   kings everywhere got rich
      from your costly goods.
³⁴ But now you are wrecked
   in the deep sea,
   with your cargo and crew
      scattered everywhere.
³⁵ People living along the coast
   are shocked at the news.
   Their rulers are horrified,
   and terror is written
      across their faces.
³⁶ The merchants of the world

---

*27.25 **Large, seagoing ships:** The Hebrew text has "Ships of Tarshish", which may have been a Phoenician city in Spain. "Ships of Tarshish" probably means large, seagoing ships.
*27.31 **sackcloth:** See the note at 7.18.
See also: 27.25-36: Rev 18.11-19.

---

*27.15 **ebony:** A valuable black wood.

can't believe what happened.
Your death was gruesome,
   and you are gone for ever."

CHAPTER 28

Judgment on the king of Tyre

[1] The LORD God said:

[2] Ezekiel, son of man, tell the king of Tyre*
that I am saying:

You are so arrogant that you think you're a
god and that the city of Tyre is your throne.
You may claim to be a god, though you're
nothing but a mere human. [3] You think
you're wiser than Daniel* and know
everything.'

[4] Your wisdom has certainly made you
rich, because you have storehouses filled
with gold and silver. [5] You're a clever
businessman and are extremely wealthy,
but your wealth has led to arrogance!

[6] You compared yourself to a god, so
now I, the LORD God, [7] will make you the
victim of cruel enemies. They will destroy
all the possessions you've worked so hard
to get. [8] Your enemies will brutally kill you,
and the sea will be your only grave.

[9] When you face your enemies, will you
still claim to be a god? They will attack,
and you will suffer like any other human.
[10] Foreigners will kill you, and you will die
the death of those who don't worship me.
I, the LORD, have spoken.

A funeral song for the king of Tyre

[11] The LORD said:

[12] Ezekiel, son of man, sing a funeral song
for the king of Tyre* and tell him I am
saying:

At one time, you were perfect,' intelligent,
and good-looking. [13] You lived in the garden
of Eden and wore jewellery made of
brightly-coloured gems and precious stones.
They were all set in gold' and were ready for
you on the day you were born. [14] I appointed
a winged creature to guard your home' on
my holy mountain, where you walked
among gems that dazzled like fire.

[15] You were truly good from the time of
your birth, but later you started doing
wicked things. [16] You traded with other
nations and became more and more cruel

and evil. So I forced you to leave my
mountain, and the creature that had been
your protector now chased you away from
the gems.

[17] It was your good looks that made you
arrogant, and you were so famous that you
started acting like a fool. That's why I
threw you to the ground and let other
kings sneer at you. [18] You have cheated so
many other merchants that your places of
worship are corrupt. So I set your city on
fire and burnt it down. Now everyone sees
only ashes where your city once stood,
[19] and the people of other nations are
shocked. Your punishment was horrible,
and you are gone for ever.

Judgment on Sidon and peace for Israel

[20] The LORD said:

[21] Ezekiel, son of man, condemn the city of
Sidon* [22] and tell its people:

I, the LORD God, am your enemy! People
will praise me when I punish you, and they
will see that I am holy. [23] I will send deadly
diseases to wipe you out, and I will send
enemies to invade and surround you. Your
people will be killed, and you will know
that I am the LORD.

[24] When that happens, the people of
Israel will no longer have cruel
neighbours that abuse them and make
them feel as though they are in a field of
thorns and briers. And the Israelites will
know that I, the LORD God, have done
these things.

A blessing for Israel

[25] The LORD God said:

Some day I will gather the people of Israel
from the nations where they are now
scattered, and every nation will see that I
am holy. The Israelites will once again live
in the land I gave to my servant Jacob.
[26] They will be safe and will build houses
and plant vineyards. They will no longer be
in danger, because I will punish their
hateful neighbours. Israel will know that
I am the LORD their God.

---

*28.2,12 **Tyre:** See the note at 26.2.
*28.3 **Daniel:** See the note at 14.14.

*28.21 **Sidon:** See the note at 26.2.
See also: 28.20–26: Joel 3.4–8; Zech 9.1–2; Matt 11.21–22;
Luke 10.13–14.

CHAPTER 29

Judgment on the king of Egypt

¹ Ten years after King Jehoiachin and the rest of us had been led away as prisoners to Babylonia, the LORD spoke to me on the twelfth day of the tenth month.* He said:

² Ezekiel, son of man, condemn the king of Egypt. Tell him and his people ³ that I am saying:

King of Egypt, you were like a giant crocodile lying in a river. You acted as though you owned the Nile and made it for yourself. But now I, the LORD God, am your enemy! ⁴ I will put a hook in your jaw and pull you out of the water, and all the fish in your river will stick to your scaly body.* ⁵ I'll throw you and the fish into the desert, and your body will fall on the hard ground. You will be left unburied,* and wild animals and birds will eat your flesh. ⁶ Then everyone in Egypt will know that I am the LORD.

You and your nation refused to help the people of Israel and were nothing more than a broken stick. ⁷ When they reached out to you for support, you broke in half, cutting their arms and making them fall.ᵇ

⁸ So I, the LORD God, will send troops to attack you, king of Egypt. They will kill your people and livestock, ⁹ until your land is a barren desert. Then you will know that I have done these things.

You claimed that you made the River Nile and control it. ¹⁰ Now I am turning against you and your river. Your nation will be nothing but an empty wasteland all the way from the town of Migdol in the north to Aswan in the south, and as far as the border of Ethiopia.* ¹¹ No human or animal will even dare travel through Egypt, because no sign of life will be found there for forty years.

¹² It will be the most barren place on earth. Every city in Egypt will lie in ruins during those forty years, and I will scatter your people throughout the nations of the world.

¹³ Then after those forty years have passed, I will bring your people back from the places where I scattered them. ¹⁴ They will once again live in their homeland in southern Egypt. But they will be a weak kingdom ¹⁵ and won't ever be strong enough to rule nations, as they did in the past. ¹⁶ My own people Israel will never again depend on your nation. In fact, when the Israelites remember what happened to you Egyptians, they will realize how wrong they were to turn to you for help. Then the Israelites will know that I, the LORD God, did these things.

King Nebuchadnezzar of Babylonia will conquer Egypt

¹⁷ Twenty-seven years after King Jehoiachin and the rest of us had been led away as prisoners to Babylonia, the LORD spoke to me on the first day of the first month.* He said:

¹⁸ King Nebuchadnezzar of Babylonia has attacked the city of Tyre. He forced his soldiers to carry so many heavy loads that their heads were rubbed bald, and their shoulders were red and sore. Nebuchadnezzar and his army still could not capture the city. ¹⁹ So now I will hand over the nation of Egypt to him. He will take Egypt's valuable treasures and give them to his own troops. ²⁰ Egypt will be his reward, because he and his army have been following my orders. I, the LORD God, have spoken.

²¹ Ezekiel, when Egypt is defeated, I will make the people of Israel strong, and I will give you the power to speak to them. Then they will know that I, the LORD, have done these things.

CHAPTER 30

Egypt will be a barren desert

¹ The LORD said:

² Ezekiel, son of man, tell the people of Egypt that I am saying:

Cry out in despair,
³ because you will soon be punished!

---

*29.1 Ten years . . . tenth month: Probably January of 587 BC.
*29.4 all the fish in your river will stick to your scaly body: All the king's officials will be removed from power and destroyed along with the king himself.
*29.5 You will be left unburied: A proper burial in a royal tomb was extremely important to Egyptian kings, because they often thought of themselves as gods.
*29.10 Ethiopia: The Hebrew text has "Cush", which was a region south of Egypt that included parts of the present countries of Ethiopia and Sudan.
See also: 29.1–32.32: Isa 19.1–25; Jer 46.2–26. 29.6: Isa 36.6.

*29.17 Twenty-seven . . . first month: Probably March of 571 BC.

That will be a time
of darkness and doom
for all nations.
⁴ Your own nation of Egypt
will be attacked,
and Ethiopia* will suffer.
You will be killed in battle,
and your land will be robbed
and left in ruins.

⁵ Soldiers hired from Ethiopia, Libya, Lydia, Arabia, Kub, as well as from Israel,' will die in that battle. ⁶ All your allies will be killed, and your proud strength will crumble. People will die from Migdol in the north to Aswan in the south. I, the LORD, have spoken.

⁷ Your nation of Egypt will be the most deserted place on earth, and its cities will lie in complete ruin. ⁸ I will set fire to your land, and anyone who defended your proud nation will die. Then you will know that I am the LORD.

⁹ On the same day I destroy Egypt, I will send messengers to the Ethiopians to announce their coming destruction. They think they are safe, but they will be terrified.

¹⁰ Your Egyptian army is very strong, but I will send King Nebuchadnezzar of Babylonia to completely defeat that army. ¹¹ He and his cruel troops will invade and destroy your land and leave your dead bodies piled everywhere.

¹² I will dry up the River Nile, then sell the land to evil buyers. I will send foreigners to turn your entire nation into a barren desert. I, the LORD, have spoken.

Egypt's proud cities will lie in ruins

The LORD said to the people of Egypt:

¹³ All the idols and images you Egyptians worship in the city of Memphis' will be smashed. No one will be left to rule your nation, and terror will fill the land. ¹⁴ The city of Pathros will be left in ruins, and Zoan will be burnt to the ground. Thebes,' your capital city, will also be destroyed! ¹⁵ The fortress city of Pelusium will feel my fierce anger, and all the troops stationed at Thebes will be slaughtered.

¹⁶ I will set fire to your nation of Egypt! The city of Pelusium will be in anguish. Thebes will fall, and the people of Memphis will live in constant fear.' ¹⁷ The young soldiers in the cities of Heliopolis and Bubastis' will die in battle, and the rest of the people will be taken prisoner. ¹⁸ You were so proud of your nation's power, but when I crush that power and kill that pride, darkness will fall over the city of Tahpanhes. A dark, gloomy cloud will cover the land as you are being led away into captivity. ¹⁹ When I've finished punishing Egypt, you will know that I am the LORD.

Egypt's king is powerless

²⁰ Eleven years after King Jehoiachin and the rest of us had been led away as prisoners to Babylonia, the LORD spoke to me on the seventh day of the first month.* He said:

²¹ Ezekiel, son of man, I, the LORD, have defeated the king of Egypt! I broke his arm, and no one has wrapped it or put it in a sling, so that it could heal and get strong enough to hold a sword. ²² So tell him that I am now his worst enemy. I will break both his arms — the good one and the broken one! His sword will drop from his hand for ever, ²³ and I will scatter the Egyptians all over the world.

²⁴⁻²⁵ I will strengthen the power of Babylonia's king and give him my sword to use against Egypt. I will also make the wounded king of Egypt powerless, and he will moan in pain and die in front of the Babylonian king. Then everyone on earth will know that I am the LORD. ²⁶ I will force the Egyptians to live as prisoners in foreign nations, and they will know that I, the LORD, have punished them.

CHAPTER 31

Egypt's king will be chopped down like a cedar tree

¹ Eleven years after King Jehoiachin and the rest of us had been led away as prisoners to Babylonia, the LORD spoke to me on the first day of the third month.* He said:

² Ezekiel, son of man, tell the king of Egypt and his people that I am saying:

You are more powerful
than anyone on earth.
Now listen to this.
³ There was once a cedar tree
in Lebanon

---

*30.4 Ethiopia: See the note at 29.10.

*30.20 Eleven years . . . first month: Probably March of 587 BC.

*31.1 Eleven years . . . third month: Probably May of 587 BC.

with large, strong branches
    reaching to the sky.'
⁴ This tree had plenty of water
    to help it grow tall,
and nearby streams watered
    the other trees
    in the forest.
⁵ But this tree towered over
    those other trees,
and its branches
    grew long and thick.
⁶ Birds built nests
    in its branches,
and animals were born
    beneath it.
People from all nations
    lived in the shade
    of this strong tree.

⁷ It had beautiful,
    long branches,
and its roots found water
    deep in the soil.
⁸ None of the cedar trees
    in my garden of Eden
were as beautiful
    as this tree;
no tree of any kind
    had such long branches.
⁹ I, the LORD, gave this tree
    its beauty,
and I helped the branches
    grow strong.
All other trees in Eden
    wanted to be just like it.

¹⁰ King of Egypt, now listen to what I, the
LORD God, am saying about that tree:

The tree grew so tall that it reached the sky'
and became very proud and arrogant. ¹¹ So I,
the LORD God, will reject the tree and hand
it over to a foreign ruler, who will punish it
for its wickedness. ¹² Cruel foreigners will
chop it down and leave it wherever it falls.
Branches and broken limbs will be scattered
over the mountains and in the valleys. The
people living in the shade of those branches
will go somewhere else. ¹³ Birds will then
nest on the stump of the fallen tree, and wild
animals will trample its branches.

¹⁴ Never again will any tree dare to grow as
tall as this tree, no matter how much water it
has. Every tree must die, just as humans die
and go down to the world of the dead.

¹⁵ On the day this tree dies and goes to the
world below, I, the LORD God, will

command rivers and streams to mourn its
death. Every underground spring of water
and every river will stop flowing.' The
mountains in Lebanon will be covered with
darkness as a sign of their sorrow, and all the
trees in the forest will wither. ¹⁶ This tree will
crash to the ground, and I will send it to the
world below. Then the nations of the earth
will tremble.

The trees from Eden and the choice trees
from Lebanon are now in the world of the
dead, and they will be comforted when this
tree falls. ¹⁷ Those people who found
protection in its shade will also be sent to the
world below, where they will join the dead.'

¹⁸ King of Egypt, all these things will
happen to you and your people! You were
like this tree at one time — taller and stronger
than anyone on earth. But now you will be
chopped down, just as every tree in the
garden of Eden must die. You will be sent
down to the world of the dead, where you
will join the godless and the other victims of
violent death. I, the LORD God, have spoken.

CHAPTER 32

A funeral song for the king of Egypt

¹ Twelve years after King Jehoiachin and the
rest of us had been led away as prisoners to
Babylonia, the LORD spoke to me on the first
day of the twelfth month.* He said:

² Ezekiel, son of man, condemn the king of
Egypt and tell him I am saying:

You act like a lion
    roaming the earth;
but you are nothing more than
    a crocodile in a river,
churning up muddy water
    with your feet.

³ King of Egypt, listen to me. I, the LORD
God, will catch you in my net and let a
crowd of foreigners drag you to shore. ⁴ I will
throw you into an open field, where birds
and animals will come to feed on your body.
⁵ I will spread your rotting flesh' over the
mountains and in the valleys, ⁶ and your
blood will flow throughout the land and fill
up the streams. ⁷ I will cover the whole sky
and every star with thick clouds, so that the
sun and moon will stop shining. ⁸ The

---

*32.1 Twelve years . . . twelfth month: Probably
February of 585 BC.

See also: 32.7: Isa 13.10; Matt 24.29; Mark 13.24–25;
Luke 21.25; Rev 6.12–13; 8.12.

heavens will become black, leaving your country in total darkness. I, the LORD, have spoken.

⁹ Foreign nations you have never heard of will be shocked when I tell them how I destroyed you.' ¹⁰ They will be horrified, and when I flash my sword in victory on the day of your death, their kings will tremble in the fear of what could happen to them.

¹¹ The king of Babylonia is coming to attack you, king of Egypt! ¹² Your soldiers will be killed by the cruellest army in the world, and everything you take pride in will be crushed. ¹³ I will slaughter your cattle that graze by the river,* and no people or livestock will be left to muddy its water. ¹⁴ The water will be clear, and streams will be calm. I, the LORD God, have spoken.

¹⁵ Egypt will become a barren wasteland, and no living thing will ever survive there. Then you and your people will know that I am the LORD.

¹⁶ This is your warning, and it will be used as a funeral song by foreign women to mourn the death of your people. I, the LORD God, have spoken.

A sad ending for Egypt

¹⁷ On the fifteenth day of that same month,* the LORD said:

¹⁸ Ezekiel, son of man, mourn for the Egyptians and condemn them to the world of the dead, where they will be buried beside the people of other powerful nations.' ¹⁹ Say to them:

You may be more beautiful
than the people
   of other nations,
but you will also die
and join the godless
   in the world below.

²⁰ You cannot escape! The enemy's sword is ready to slaughter every one of you.' ²¹ Brave military leaders killed in battle will gladly welcome you and your allies into the world of the dead.

²²⁻²³ The graves of soldiers from Assyria are there. They once terrified people, but they were killed in battle and now lie deep in the world of the dead.*

²⁴⁻²⁵ The graves of soldiers from Elam are there. The very sight of those godless soldiers once terrified their enemies and made them panic. But now they are disgraced and ashamed as they lie in the world of the dead, beside others who were killed in battle.

²⁶ The graves of soldiers from Meshech and Tubal are there. These godless soldiers who terrified people were all killed in battle. ²⁷ They were not given a proper burial like the heroes of long ago,' who were buried with their swords under their heads and with their shields' over their bodies. These were the heroes who made their enemies panic.

²⁸ You Egyptians will be cruelly defeated, and you will be buried beside these other godless soldiers who died in battle.

²⁹ The graves of kings and leaders from Edom are there. They were powerful at one time. Now they are buried in the world of the dead with other godless soldiers killed in battle.

³⁰ The graves of the rulers of the north* are there, as well as those of the Sidonians. Their powerful armies once terrified enemies. Now they lie buried in the world of the dead, where they are disgraced like other soldiers killed in battle.

³¹ The LORD God says:

When your king of Egypt sees all these graves, he and his soldiers will be glad they are not the only ones suffering. ³² I sent him to terrify people all over the earth. But he and his army will be killed and buried beside other godless soldiers in the world of the dead. I, the LORD God, have spoken.

Ezekiel must warn the people to turn from their sinful ways

CHAPTER 33

The LORD appoints Ezekiel to stand watch

This is also told in Ezekiel 3.16–21

¹ The LORD said:

² Ezekiel, son of man, warn your people by saying:

Some day, I, the LORD, may send an enemy to invade a country. And suppose its people

---

*32.13 the river: This possibly refers to the River Nile.
*32.17 that same month: See verse 1.
*32.22–23 deep in the world of the dead: The place of greatest dishonour.

*32.30 the rulers of the north: Probably the Phoenicians.

choose someone to stand watch ³ and to sound a warning signal when the enemy is seen coming. ⁴⁻⁵ If any of these people hear the signal and ignore it, they will be killed in battle. But it will be their own fault, because they could have escaped if they had paid attention.

⁶ But suppose the person watching fails to sound the warning signal. The enemy will attack and kill some of the sinful people in that country, and I, the LORD, will hold that person responsible for their death.

⁷ Ezekiel, I have appointed you to stand watch for the people of Israel. So listen to what I say, then warn them for me. ⁸ When I tell wicked people they will die because of their sins, you must warn them to turn from their sinful ways. But if you refuse to warn them, you are responsible for their death. ⁹ If you do warn them, and they keep sinning, they will die because of their sins, and you will be innocent.

The LORD is always fair

This is also told in Ezekiel 18.21–30

¹⁰ The LORD said:

Ezekiel, son of man, the people of Israel are complaining that the punishment for their sins is more than they can stand. They have lost all hope for survival, and they blame me. ¹¹ Tell them that as surely as I am the living LORD God, I don't like to see wicked people die. I enjoy seeing them turn from their sins and live. So if the Israelites want to live, they must stop sinning and turn back to me.

¹² Tell them that when good people start sinning, all the good they did in the past cannot save them from being punished. And remind them that when wicked people stop sinning, their past sins will be completely forgiven, and they won't be punished. ¹³ Suppose I promise good people that they will live, then later they start sinning and believe they will be saved by the good they did in the past. These people will certainly be put to death because of their sins. Their good deeds will be forgotten. ¹⁴ Suppose I warn wicked people that they will die because of their sins, and they stop sinning and start doing right. ¹⁵ For example, they need to return anything they have taken as security for a loan and anything they have stolen. Then if they stop doing evil and start obeying my Law, they will live.

¹⁶ Their past sins will be forgiven, and they will live because they have done right.

¹⁷ Ezekiel, your people accuse me of being unfair. But they are the ones who are unfair. ¹⁸ If good people start doing evil, they will be put to death, because they have sinned. ¹⁹ And if wicked people stop sinning and start doing right, they will save themselves from punishment. ²⁰ But the Israelites still think I am unfair. So warn them that they will be punished for what they have done.

The news of Jerusalem's fall

²¹ Twelve years after King Jehoiachin and the rest of us had been led away as prisoners to Babylonia, a refugee who had escaped from Jerusalem came to me on the fifth day of the tenth month.* He told me that the city had fallen.

²² The evening before this man arrived at my house, the LORD had taken control of me. So when the man came to me the next morning, I could once again speak.*

What will happen to those left in Israel?

²³ Then the LORD said:

²⁴ Ezekiel, son of man, the people living in the ruined cities of Israel are saying, "Abraham was just one man, and the LORD gave him this whole land of Israel. There are many of us, and so this land must be ours."

²⁵ So, Ezekiel, tell them I am saying:

How can you think the land is still yours? You eat meat with blood in it and worship idols. You commit murder ²⁶ and spread violence throughout the land. Everything you do is wicked; you are even unfaithful in marriage. And you claim the land is yours!

²⁷ As surely as I am the living LORD God, you people in the ruined cities will be killed in battle. Those of you living in the countryside will be eaten by wild animals, and those hiding in caves and on rocky cliffs will die from deadly diseases. ²⁸ I will make the whole country an empty wasteland and crush the power in which you take such pride. Even the mountains will be bare, and no one will try to cross them. ²⁹ I will punish you because of your

---

*33.21 Twelve years . . . tenth month: Probably December of 586 BC.
*33.22 I could once again speak: See 3.27.
See also: 33.21: 2 King 25.3–10; Jer 39.2–8; 52.4–14.

sins, and I will turn your nation into a barren desert. Then you will know that I am the LORD.

The people listen, but don't change

The LORD said:

[30] Ezekiel, son of man, the people with you in Babylonia talk about you when they meet by the city walls or in the doorways of their houses. They say, "Let's ask Ezekiel what the LORD has said today." [31] So they all come and listen to you, but they refuse to do what you tell them. They claim to be faithful, but they are for ever trying to cheat others out of their money. [32] They treat you as though you were merely singing love songs or playing music. They listen, but don't do anything you say.

[33] Soon they will be punished, just as you warned, and they will know that a prophet has been among them.

The Lord promises to bring the people home and to restore Judah

CHAPTER 34

Israel's leaders are worthless shepherds

[1] The LORD God said:

[2] Ezekiel, son of man, Israel's leaders are like shepherds taking care of my sheep, the people of Israel. But I want you to condemn these leaders and tell them:

I, the LORD God, say you shepherds of Israel are doomed! You take care of yourselves while ignoring my sheep. [3] You drink their milk and use their wool to make your clothes. Then you butcher the best ones for food. But you don't take care of the flock! [4] You have never protected the weak ones or healed the sick ones or bandaged those that get hurt. You let them wander off and never look for those that get lost. You are cruel and mean to my sheep. [5] They strayed in every direction, and because there was no shepherd to watch them, they were attacked and eaten by wild animals. [6] So my sheep were scattered across the earth. They roamed on hills and mountains, without anyone even bothering to look for them.

[7-8] Now listen to what I, the living LORD God, am saying to you shepherds. My sheep have been attacked and eaten by wild animals, because you refused to watch them. You never went looking for the lost ones, and you fed yourselves without feeding my sheep. [9-10] So I, the LORD, will punish you! I will rescue my sheep from you and never let you be their shepherd again or butcher them for food. I, the LORD, have spoken.

The LORD is the good shepherd

[11] The LORD God then said:

I will look for my sheep and take care of them myself, [12] just as a shepherd looks for lost sheep. My sheep have been lost since that dark and miserable day when they were scattered throughout the nations.* But I will rescue them [13] and bring them back from the foreign nations where they now live. I will be their shepherd and will let them graze on Israel's mountains and in the valleys and fertile fields. [14] They will be safe as they feed on grassy meadows and green hills. [15] I promise to take care of them and keep them safe, [16] to look for those that are lost and bring back the ones that wander off, to bandage those that are hurt and protect the ones that are weak. I will also slaughter' those that are fat and strong, because I always do right.

Judgment on the strong sheep

[17] The LORD God said to his sheep, the people of Israel:

I will carefully watch each one of you to decide which ones are the strong sheep and which ones are weak. [18] Some of you eat the greenest grass, then trample down what's left when you finish. Others drink clean water, then step in the water to make the rest of it muddy. [19] That means my other sheep have nothing fit to eat or drink.

[20] So I, the LORD God, will separate you strong sheep from the weak. [21] You strong ones have used your powerful horns to chase off those that are weak, [22] but I will rescue them and no longer let them be ill-treated. I will separate the good from the bad.

---

*34.12 **dark and miserable day . . . nations:** That is, the day the Babylonians defeated Jerusalem and led its people away as prisoners.

See also: **34.5:** Num 27.17; 1 King 22.17; Matt 9.36; Mark 6.34.

911

Being christian

Demonstrating hope

Christians are people of hope.

When we become a Christian we become certain of our place in God's plan. The fact that there is a heaven, and that we're going to go there one day, brings us enormous hope. Jesus has saved us and we're going to meet him face to face. Whatever happens here on earth.

Never give up on people. The Bible likens Jesus to a good shepherd; when one of his sheep goes missing, he doesn't just shrug his shoulders and write it off as a loss, he goes out and searches and searches until he finds that sheep. The same shepherd occurs in Ezekiel (Ezekiel 34.23). God never writes anyone off. He wants all people to be saved. We should always hope that the people we pray for, the people we meet every day, will one day acknowledge God.

And, in the best possible way, we should also hope for the best. We live in a cynical, disbelieving society, where people are always assumed to be lying or looking out for themselves. Many people we meet will be like the writer of Ecclesiastes – cynical and disillusioned and convinced that 'everything is meaningless'. We shouldn't be like that. Don't get into that cynical mind-set, don't be disillusioned by the world, but never give up trying to make things better. We've been rescued by the good shepherd, we're going to be with him. We're people of hope.

Being Christian: Demonstrating hope

• Remember you're going to heaven. Whatever happens down here.

• Believe in people. Look for the best in them. After all, God thought you worth rescuing!

• Never give up praying for others and helping them all you can. Everyone can change. There is always hope.

---

23 After that, I will give you a shepherd from the family of my servant King David. All of you, both strong and weak, will have the same shepherd, and he will take good care of you. 24 He will be your leader, and I will be your God. I, the LORD, have spoken.

A bright future for the LORD's sheep

The LORD God said:

25 The people of Israel are my sheep, and I solemnly promise that they will live in peace. I will chase away every wild animal from the desert and the forest, so my sheep will not be afraid. 26 They will live around my holy mountain,* and I will bless them by sending more than enough rain 27 to make their trees produce fruit and their crops grow. I will set them free from slavery and let them live safely in their own land. Then they will know that I am the LORD. 28 Foreign nations will never again rob them, and wild animals will no longer kill and eat them. They will have nothing to fear. 29 I will make their fields produce large amounts of crops, so they will never again go hungry or be laughed at by foreigners. 30 Then everyone will know that I protect my people Israel. I, the LORD, make this promise. 31 They are my sheep; I am their God, and I take care of them.

CHAPTER 35

Edom will be a wasteland

1 The LORD said:

2 Ezekiel, son of man, condemn the people of Edom, 3 and say to them:

I, the LORD God,
  am now your enemy!
And I will turn your nation
  into an empty wasteland,
4   leaving your towns in ruins.
Your land will be a desert,
  and then you will know
    that I am the LORD.

5 People of Edom, not only have you been Israel's longtime enemy, you simply watched when disaster wiped out its people as punishment for their sins. 6 And so, as

---

*34.26 my holy mountain: That is, Mount Zion in Jerusalem.

See also: 34.23: Rev 7.17.   34.24: Ezek 37.24.
35.1–15: Isa 34.5–17; 63.1–6; Jer 49.7–22; Ezek 25.12–14; Amos 1.11–12; Obad 1–14; Mal 1.2–5.

surely as I am the living LORD God, you are guilty of murder and must be put to death. [7] I will destroy your nation and kill anyone who travels through it. [8] Dead bodies will cover your mountains and fill up your valleys, [9] and your land will lie in ruins for ever. No one will live in your towns ever again. You will know that I am the LORD.

[10] You thought the nations of Judah and Israel belonged to you, and that you could take over their territory. But I am their God, [11] and as surely as I live, I will punish you for treating my people with anger and hatred. Then they will know that I, the LORD, am punishing you! [12] And you will finally realize that I heard you laugh at their destruction and say their land was yours to take. [13] You even insulted me, but I heard it all.

[14] Everyone on earth will celebrate when I destroy you, [15] just as you celebrated when Israel was destroyed. Your nation of Edom will be nothing but a wasteland. Then everyone will know that I am the LORD.

CHAPTER 36

A message for Israel's mountains

[1] The LORD said:

Ezekiel, son of man, tell the mountains of Israel [2] that I, the LORD God, am saying:

Your enemies sneered and said that you mountains belonged to them. [3] They ruined and crushed you from every side, and foreign nations captured and made fun of you. [4] So all you mountains and hills, streams and valleys, listen to what I will do. Your towns may now lie in ruins, and foreign nations may laugh and insult you. [5] But in my fierce anger, I will turn against those nations, and especially the Edomites, because they laughed at you the loudest and took over your pasture lands. [6] You have suffered long enough, and, I, the LORD God, am very angry! Nations have insulted you, [7] so I will now insult and disgrace them. That is my solemn promise.

[8] Trees will grow on you mountains of Israel and produce fruit for my people, because they will soon come home. [9] I will take care of you by ploughing your soil and planting crops on your fertile slopes. [10] The people of Israel will return and rebuild your ruined towns and live in them. [11] Children will be born, and animals will give birth to their young. You will no longer be deserted as you are now, but you will be covered

with people and treated better than ever. Then you will know that I am the LORD.

[12] I will bring my people Israel home, and they will live on you mountains, because you belong to them, and your fertile slopes will never again let them starve. [13] It's true that you have been accused of not producing enough food and of letting your people starve. [14-15] But I, the LORD, promise that you won't hear other nations laugh and sneer at you ever again. From now on, you will always produce plenty of food for your people. I, the LORD God, have spoken.

The LORD will be honoured

[16] The LORD said:

[17] Ezekiel, son of man, when the people of Israel were living in their own country, they made the land unclean by the way they behaved, just as a woman's monthly period makes her unclean. [18] They committed murders and worshipped idols, which made the land even worse. So in my anger, I punished my people [19] and scattered them throughout the nations, just as they deserved. [20] Wherever they went, my name was disgraced, because foreigners insulted my people by saying I had forced them out of their own land.

[21] I care what those foreigners think of me, [22] so tell the Israelites that I am saying:

You have disgraced my holy name among the nations where you now live. So you don't deserve what I'm going to do for you. I will lead you home to bring honour to my name [23] and to show foreign nations that I am holy. Then they will know that I am the LORD God. I have spoken.

[24] I will gather you from the foreign nations and bring you home. [25] I will sprinkle you with clean water, and you will be clean and acceptable to me. I will wash away everything that makes you unclean, and I will remove your disgusting idols. [26] I will take away your stubborn heart and give you a new heart and a desire to be faithful. You will have only pure thoughts, [27] because I will put my Spirit in you and make you eager to obey my laws and teachings. [28] You will once again live in the land I gave your ancestors; you will be my people, and I will be your God.

[29] I will protect you from anything that makes you unclean. Your fields will

---

See also: **36.26-28:** Ezek 11.19-20.

overflow with grain, and no one will starve.
³⁰ Your trees will be filled with fruit, and
crops will grow in your fields, so that you
will never again feel ashamed for not
having enough food. ³¹ You will remember
your evil ways and hate yourselves for what
you've done. ³² People of Israel, I'm not
doing these things for your sake. You
sinned against me, and you must suffer
shame and disgrace for what you have
done. I, the LORD God, have spoken.

³³ After I have made you clean, I will let
you rebuild your ruined towns and let you
live in them. ³⁴ Your land will be ploughed
again, and nobody will be able to see that it
was once barren. ³⁵ Instead, they will say that
it looks as beautiful as the garden of Eden.
They won't see towns lying in ruins, but
they will see your strong cities filled with
people. ³⁶ Then the nearby nations that
survive will know that I am the one who
rebuilt the ruined places and replanted the
barren fields. I, the LORD, make this promise.

³⁷ I will once again answer your prayers,
and I will let your nation grow until you are
like a large flock of sheep. ³⁸ The towns that
now lie in ruins will be filled with people,
just as Jerusalem was once filled with sheep
to be offered as sacrifices during a festival.
Then you will know that I am the LORD.

CHAPTER 37

Dry bones live again

¹ Some time later, I felt the LORD's power take
control of me, and his Spirit carried me to a
valley full of bones. ² The LORD showed me all
around, and everywhere I looked I saw bones
that were dried out. ³ He said, "Ezekiel, son of
man, can these bones come back to life?"

I replied, "LORD God, only you can answer
that."

⁴ He then told me to say:

Dry bones, listen to what the LORD is
saying to you, ⁵ "I, the LORD God, will put
breath in you, and once again you will live.
⁶ I will wrap you with muscles and skin and
breathe life into you. Then you will know
that I am the LORD."

⁷ I did what the LORD said, but before I finished
speaking, I heard a rattling noise. The bones
were coming together! ⁸ I saw muscles and skin
cover the bones, but they had no life in them.

⁹ The LORD said:

Ezekiel, now say to the wind,[*] "The LORD
God commands you to blow from every

direction and to breathe life into these
dead bodies, so they can live again."

¹⁰ As soon as I said this, the wind blew among
the bodies, and they came back to life! They
all stood up, and there were enough to make
a large army.

¹¹ The LORD said:

Ezekiel, the people of Israel are like dead
bones. They complain that they are dried up
and that they have no hope for the future.
¹² So tell them, "I, the LORD God, promise to
open your graves and set you free. I will
bring you back to Israel, ¹³ and when that
happens, you will realize that I am the
LORD. ¹⁴ My Spirit will give you breath, and
you will live again. I will bring you home,
and you will know that I have kept my
promise. I, the LORD, have spoken."

Judah and Israel together again

¹⁵ The LORD said:

¹⁶ Ezekiel, son of man, get a stick and write
on it, "The kingdom of Judah". Then get
another stick and write on it, "The kingdom
of Israel".[*] ¹⁷ Hold these two sticks end to
end, so they look like one stick. ¹⁸ And when
your people ask you what this means, ¹⁹ tell
them that I, the LORD, will join together the
stick of Israel and the stick of Judah. I will
hold them in my hand, and they will
become one.

²⁰ Hold these two sticks where they can be
seen by everyone ²¹ and then say:

I, the LORD God, will gather the people of
Israel and bring them home from the
foreign nations where they now live.
²² I will make them into one nation and let
them once again live in the land of Israel.
Only one king will rule them, and they will
never again be divided into two nations.
²³ They will no longer worship idols and do
things that make them unacceptable to me.
I will wash away their sin and make them
clean, and I will protect them from
everything that makes them unclean. They
will be my people, and I will be their God.

²⁴⁻²⁵ Their king will always come from the
family of my servant King David and will
care for them like a shepherd. The people of
Israel will faithfully obey my laws. They and
their descendants will live in the land I gave
my servant Jacob, just as their ancestors did.
²⁶ I solemnly promise to bless the people of

See also: 37.10: Rev 11.11. 37.24: Ezek 34.24.

Israel with unending peace. I will protect them and let them become a powerful nation. My temple will stand in Israel for all time, ²⁷ and I will live among my people and be their God. ²⁸ Every nation on earth will know that my temple is in Israel and that I have chosen the Israelites to be my people.

Gog will be defeated and Israel will be restored

CHAPTER 38

Gog invades Israel

¹ The LORD said:

² Ezekiel, son of man, condemn Gog, that wicked ruler of the kingdoms of Meshech and Tubal in the land of Magog. Tell him:

³ I, the LORD God, am your enemy, ⁴ and I will make you powerless! I will put a hook in your jaw and drag away both you and your large army. You command cavalry troops that wear heavy armour and carry shields and swords. ⁵ Your army includes soldiers from Persia, Ethiopia,* and Libya, ⁶ as well as from Gomer and Beth-Togarmah in the north. Your army is enormous!

⁷ So keep your troops prepared to fight, ⁸ because in a few years, I will command you to invade Israel, a country that was ruined by war. It was deserted for a long time, but its people have returned from the foreign nations where they once lived. The Israelites now live in peace in the mountains of their own land. ⁹ But you and your army will attack them like a fierce thunderstorm and surround them like a cloud.

¹⁰ When that day comes, I know that you will have an evil plan ¹¹ to take advantage of Israel, that weak and peaceful country where people live safely inside towns that have no walls or gates or locks. ¹² You will rob the people in towns that were once a pile of rubble. These people lived as prisoners in foreign nations, but they have returned to Israel, the most important place in the world, and they own livestock and property. ¹³ The people of Sheba and Dedan, along with merchants from villages in' southern Spain,' will be your allies. They will want some of the silver and gold, as

well as the livestock and property that your army takes from Israel.

¹⁴ I, the LORD God, know that when you see' my people Israel living in peace, ¹⁵ you will lead your powerful cavalry from your kingdom in the north. ¹⁶ You will attack my people like a storm-cloud that covers their land. I will let you invade my country Israel, so that every nation on earth will know that I, the LORD, am holy.

Judgment on Gog

¹⁷ The LORD said to Gog:

Long ago, I made my prophets warn the people of Israel that some day I would send an enemy to attack them. You, Gog, are that enemy, and that day is coming. ¹⁸ When you invade Israel, I will become furious, ¹⁹ and in my anger I will send a terrible earthquake to shake Israel. ²⁰ Every living thing on earth will tremble in fear of me — every fish and bird, every wild animal and reptile, and every human. Mountains will crumble, cliffs will fall, and cities will collapse. ²¹ I, the LORD, will make the mountains of Israel turn against you.' Your troops will be so terrified that they will attack each other. ²² I will strike you with diseases and punish you with death. You and your army will be pounded with rainstorms, hailstones, and burning sulphur. ²³ I will do these things to show the world that I, the LORD, am holy.

CHAPTER 39

Gog is defeated

The LORD said:

¹ Ezekiel, son of man, condemn Gog and tell him:

You are the ruler of Meshech and Tubal, but I, the LORD, am your enemy! ² I will turn you around and drag you from the north until you reach the mountains of Israel. ³ I will knock the bow out of your left hand and the arrows out of your right hand, ⁴ and you and your army will die on those mountains. Then birds and wild animals will eat the flesh ⁵ of your dead bodies left lying in open fields. I, the LORD, have spoken.

⁶ I will set fire to the land of Magog and to those nations along the coast that think they are so secure, and they will know that I am the LORD.

⁷ My people Israel will know me, and they will no longer disgrace my holy name.

*38.5 Ethiopia: See the note at 29.10.
See also: 37.27: 2 Cor 6.16; Rev 21.3.   38.2: Rev 20.8.

Everyone on earth will know that I am the holy LORD God of Israel. ⁸ The day is coming when these things will happen, just as I have promised.

⁹ When that day comes, the people in the towns of Israel will collect the weapons of their dead enemies. They will use these shields, bows and arrows, spears, and clubs as firewood, and there will be enough to last for seven years. ¹⁰ They will burn these weapons instead of gathering sticks or chopping down trees. That's how the Israelites will take revenge on those who robbed and abused them. I, the LORD, have spoken.

The burial of Gog

The LORD said:

¹¹ After Gog has been destroyed, I will bury him and his army in Israel, in Travellers'⟩ Valley, east of the Dead Sea. That graveyard will be so large that it will block the way of anyone who tries to walk through the valley,⟩ which will then be known as "The Valley of Gog's Army".⟩ ¹² The Israelites will spend seven months burying dead bodies and cleaning up their land. ¹³ Everyone will help with the burial, and they will be honoured for this on the day the brightness of my glory is seen. ¹⁴ After those seven months, the people will appoint a group of men to look for any dead bodies left unburied. This must be done for seven months to make sure that the land is no longer unclean. ¹⁵ Whenever they find a human bone, they will set up a marker next to it. Then the gravediggers will bury it in "The Valley of Gog's Army" ¹⁶ near the town of "Gog's Army". After that, the land will be pure again.

¹⁷ Ezekiel, son of man, I am going to hold a feast on Israel's mountains and offer sacrifices there. So invite all the birds and wild animals to come from every direction and eat the meat of sacrifices and drink the blood. The birds and animals ¹⁸ will feast on the bodies of warriors and foreign rulers that I will sacrifice like sheep, goats, and bulls. ¹⁹ I want the birds and animals to eat until they are full and drink until they are drunk. ²⁰ They will come to my table and stuff themselves with the flesh of horses and warriors of every kind. I, the LORD God, have spoken.

Israel will be restored

The LORD said:

²¹ When I punish the nations of the earth, they will see the brightness of my glory. ²² The people of Israel will know from then on that I am the LORD their God. ²³ Foreign nations will realize that the Israelites were forced to leave their own land because they sinned against me. I turned my back on my people and let enemies attack and kill them. ²⁴ Their lives were wicked and corrupt, and they deserved to be punished.

²⁵ Now I will show mercy to the people of Israel and bring them back from the nations where they are living. They are Jacob's descendants, so I will bless them and show that I am holy. ²⁶ They will live safely in their own land, but will be ashamed when they remember their evil ways and how they disgraced me.⟩ ²⁷ Foreign nations will watch as I take the Israelites from enemy lands and bring them back home, and those nations will see that I am holy.

²⁸ My people will realize that I, the LORD their God, sent them away as prisoners and now will bring them back to their own land. ²⁹ Never again will I turn my back on the people of Israel, and my Spirit will live in them. I, the LORD, have spoken.

Ezekiel sees the future temple in Jerusalem

CHAPTER 40

¹⁻² Twenty-five years after King Jehoiachin and the rest of us had been led away as prisoners to Babylonia, and fourteen years after the Babylonians had captured Jerusalem, the LORD's power took control of me on the tenth day of the first month.* The LORD showed me some visions in which I was carried to the top of a high mountain in Jerusalem. I looked to the south and saw what looked like a city full of buildings. ³ In my vision the LORD took me closer, and I saw a man who was sparkling like polished bronze. He was standing near one of the gates and was holding a tape measure in one hand and a measuring stick in the other. ⁴ The man said, "Ezekiel, son of man, pay close attention to everything I'm going to show you — that's why you've been brought here.

40.1–2 Twenty-five years . . . first month: Probably March of 573 BC.

See also: 39.17–20: Rev 19.17–18.   40.2: Rev 21.10.   40.3: Rev 11.1; 21.15.

Listen carefully, because you must tell the people of Israel what you see."

The east gate

⁵ The first thing I saw was an outer wall that completely surrounded the temple area. The man took his measuring stick, which was three metres long, and measured the wall; it was three metres high and three metres thick. ⁶⁻⁷ Then he went to the east gate, where he walked up steps that led to a long passageway. On each side of this passageway were three guardrooms, which were three metres square, and they were separated by walls two and a half metres thick. The man measured the distance between the opening of the gate and the first guardroom, and it was three metres, the thickness of the outer wall.

At the far end of this passageway, I saw an entrance room that faced the courtyard of the temple itself. There was also a distance of three metres between the last guardroom and the entrance room ⁸⁻⁹ at the end of the passageway. The man measured this room: it was four metres from the doorway to the opposite wall, and the distance from the doorway to the wall on either side was one metre. ¹⁰ The three guardrooms on each side of the passageway were the same size, and the walls that separated them were the same thickness.

¹¹ Next, the man measured the width of the passageway, and it was six and a half metres, but the two doors of the gate were only five metres wide.* ¹² In front of the guardrooms, which were three metres square, was a railing about fifty centimetres high and fifty centimetres thick. ¹³ The man measured the distance from the back wall♦ of one of these rooms to the same spot in the room directly across the passageway, and it was twelve and a half metres. ¹⁴ He measured the entrance room at the far end of the passageway, and it was ten metres wide.♦ ¹⁵ Finally, he measured the total length of the passageway, from the outer wall to the entrance room, and it was twenty-five metres. ¹⁶ The three walls in the guardrooms had small windows in them, just like the ones in the entrance room.♦ The

walls along the passageway were decorated with carvings of palm trees.

The outer courtyard

¹⁷ The man then led me through the passageway and into the outer courtyard of the temple, where I saw thirty rooms built around the outside of the courtyard.* These side rooms were built against the outer wall, and in front of them was a pavement that circled the courtyard. ¹⁸ This was known as the lower pavement, and it was twenty-five metres wide.

¹⁹ I saw the gates that led to the inner courtyard of the temple and noticed that they were higher than those leading to the outer courtyard. The man measured the distance between the outer and inner gates, and it was fifty metres.♦

The north gate

²⁰ Next, the man measured the north gate that led to the outer courtyard. ²¹ This gate also had three guardrooms on each side of a passageway. The measurements of these rooms, the walls between them, and the entrance room at the far end of the passageway were exactly the same as those of the east gate. The north gate was also twenty-five metres long and twelve and a half metres wide, ²² and the windows, the entrance room, and the carvings of palm trees were just like those in the east gate. The entrance room also faced the courtyard of the temple and had seven steps leading up to it. ²³ Directly across the outer courtyard was a gate that led to the inner courtyard, just as there was for the east gate. The man measured the distance between the outer and inner gate, and it was fifty metres.

The south gate

²⁴ The man then took me to the south gate. He measured the walls and the entrance room of this gate, and the measurements were exactly the same as those of the other two gates. ²⁵ There were windows in the guardrooms of this gate and in the entrance room, just like the others, and this gate was also twenty-five metres long and twelve and a half metres wide. ²⁶ Seven steps led up to the gate; the entrance room was at the far end of the passageway and faced the

*40.11 the width of the passageway . . . six and a half metres . . . the two doors of the gate . . . five metres wide: The doors themselves probably were hung on stone sockets, which could explain the one-and-a-half-metre difference in width between the passageway and the doors.
See also: 40.5—42.20: 1 King 6.1–38; 2 Chron 3.1–9.

*40.17 thirty rooms built around the outside of the courtyard: These were probably used by worshippers as places to meet and share sacrificial meals (see, for example, Jeremiah 35.2).

courtyard of the temple. Carvings of palm trees decorated the walls along the passageway. [27] And directly across the outer courtyard was a gate on the south side of the inner courtyard. The man measured the distance between the outer and inner gate, and it was also fifty metres.

The gates leading to the inner courtyard

[28] We then went into the inner courtyard, through the gate on the south side of the temple. The man measured the gate, and it was the same size as the gates in the outer wall. [29-30] In fact, everything along the passageway was also the same size, including the guardrooms, the walls separating them, the entrance room at the far end, and the windows. This gate, like the others, was twenty-five metres long and twelve and a half metres wide. [31] The entrance room of this gate faced the outer courtyard, and carvings of palm trees decorated the walls of the passageway. Eight steps led up to this gate.

[32] Next, we went through the east gate to the inner courtyard. The man measured this gate, and it was the same size as the others. [33] The guardrooms, the walls separating them, and its entrance room had the same measurements as the other gates. The guardrooms and the entrance room had windows, and the gate was twenty-five metres long and twelve and a half metres wide. [34] The entrance room faced the outer courtyard, and the walls in the passageway were decorated with carvings of palm trees. Eight steps also led up to this gate.

[35] Then the man took me to the north gate. He measured it, and it was the same size as the others, [36] including the guardrooms, the walls separating them, and the entrance room. There were also windows in this gate. It was twenty-five metres long and twelve and a half metres wide, [37] and like the other inner gates, its entrance room faced the outer courtyard, and its walls were decorated with carvings of palm trees. Eight steps also led up to this gate.

The rooms for sacrificing animals

[38-39] Inside the entrance room of the north gate, I saw four tables, two on each side of the room, where the animals to be sacrificed were killed. Just outside⁺ this room was a small building used for washing the animals

before they were offered as sacrifices to please the LORD* or sacrifices for sin* or sacrifices to make things right.* [40] Four more tables were in the outer courtyard, two on each side of the steps leading into the entrance room. [41] So there was a total of eight tables, four inside and four outside, where the animals were killed, [42-43] and where the meat was placed until it was sacrificed on the altar.⁺

Next to the tables in the entrance room were four stone tables fifty centimetres high and seventy-five centimetres square; the equipment used for killing the animals was kept on top of these tables. All around the walls of this room was a seventy-five-millimetre shelf.⁺

The rooms belonging to the priests

[44] The man then took me to the inner courtyard, where I saw two buildings, one beside the inner gate on the north and the other beside the inner gate on the south.⁺ [45] He said, "The building beside the north gate belongs to the priests who serve in the temple, [46] and the building beside the south gate belongs to those who serve at the altar. All of them are descendants of Zadok and are the only Levites allowed to serve as the LORD's priests."

The inner courtyard and the temple

[47] Now the man measured the inner courtyard; it was fifty metres square. I also saw an altar in front of the temple.

[48] We walked to the porch of the temple, and the man measured the doorway of the porch: it was seven metres long,⁺ two and a half metres wide, and the distance from the doorway to the wall on either side was one and a half metres. [49] The porch itself was ten metres by six⁺ metres, with steps⁺ leading up to it. There was a column on each side of these steps.

---

*40.38-39 sacrifices to please the LORD: These sacrifices have traditionally been called "whole burnt offerings" because the whole animal was burnt on the altar. A main purpose of such sacrifices was to please the LORD with the smell of the sacrifice, and so in the CEV they are often called "sacrifices to please the LORD".
*40.38-39 sacrifices for sin: See Leviticus 4.1-2; 6.24-30.
*40.38-39 sacrifices to make things right: See Leviticus 5.14-19; 7.1-10.

CHAPTER 41

¹ Next we went into the main room of the temple. The man measured the doorway of this room: it was three metres wide,' ² five metres long, and the distance from the doorway to the wall on either side was two and a half metres. The main room itself was twenty metres by ten metres.

³⁻⁴ Then the man walked to the far end of the temple's main room and said, "Beyond this doorway is the most holy place." He first measured the doorway: it was one metre wide, three metres long, and the distance from the doorway to the wall on either side was three and a half metres. Then he measured the most holy place, and it was ten metres square.

The storage rooms of the temple

⁵ The man measured the wall of the temple, and it was three metres thick. Storage rooms two metres wide were built against the outside of the wall. ⁶ There were three levels of rooms, with thirty rooms on each level, and they rested on ledges that were attached to the temple walls, so that nothing was built into the walls. ⁷ The walls of the temple were thicker at the bottom than at the top, which meant that the storage rooms on the top level were wider than those on the bottom level.' Steps led from the bottom level, through the middle level, and into the top level.

⁸ The temple rested on a stone base three metres high, which also served as the foundation for the storage rooms. ⁹ The outside walls of the storage rooms were two and a half metres thick; there was nothing between these walls ¹⁰ and the nearest buildings ten metres away. ¹¹ One door led into the storage rooms on the north side of the temple, and another door led to those on the south side. The stone base extended two and a half metres beyond the outside wall of the storage rooms.

The west building and the measurements of the temple

¹² I noticed another building: it faced the west end of the temple and was thirty-five metres wide, forty-five metres long, and had walls over two and a half metres thick.

¹³ The man measured the length of the temple, and it was fifty metres. He then measured from the back wall of the temple, across the open space behind the temple, to the back wall of the west building; it was fifty metres. ¹⁴ The distance across the front of the temple, including the open space on either side, was also fifty metres.

¹⁵ Finally, the man measured the length of the west building, including the side rooms on each end, and it was also fifty metres.

The inside of the temple

The inside walls of the temple's porch and main room' ¹⁶ were panelled with wood all the way from the floor to the windows, while the doorways, the small windows, and the three side rooms were trimmed in wood.' ¹⁷ The panelling stopped just above the doorway. These walls were decorated' ¹⁸⁻²⁰ with carvings of winged creatures and had a carving of a palm tree between the creatures. Each winged creature had two faces: a human face looking at the palm tree on one side, and a lion's face looking at the palm tree on the other side. These designs were carved into the panelling all the way around the two rooms.

²¹ The doorframe to the temple's main room was in the shape of a rectangle.

The wooden altar

In front of the doorway to the most holy place was something that looked like ²² a wooden altar. It was one and a half metres high and one metre square,' and its corners, its base,' and its sides were made of wood. The man said, "This is a reminder that the LORD is constantly watching over his temple."

The doors in the temple

²³ Both the doorway to the main room of the temple and the doorway to the most holy place had two doors, ²⁴ and each door had two sections that could fold open. ²⁵ The doors to the main room were decorated with carvings of winged creatures and palm trees just like those on the walls, and there was a wooden covering over the porch just outside these doors. ²⁶ The walls on each side of this porch had small windows and were also decorated with carvings of palm trees.

CHAPTER 42

The sacred rooms for the priests

¹⁻² After the man and I left the temple and walked back to the outer courtyard, he showed me a set of rooms on the north side of the west building.' This set of rooms was fifty metres long and twenty-five metres wide. ³ On one side of them was the ten metres of open space that

ran beside the temple,* and on the other side was the pavement that circled the outer courtyard.* The rooms were arranged in three levels [4] with doors that opened towards the north, and in front of them was a passage five metres wide and fifty metres long.' [5] The rooms on the top level were narrower than those on the middle level, and the rooms on the middle level were narrower than those on the bottom level. [6] The rooms on the bottom level supported those on the two upper levels, and so these rooms did not have columns like other buildings in the courtyard. [7-8] To the north was a screening wall twenty-five metres long,' [9-10] and at the east end of this wall was the door leading from the courtyard to these rooms.

There was also a set of rooms on the south' side of the west building. [11] These rooms were exactly like those on the north side, and they also had a passage in front of them. [12] The door to these rooms was at the east end of the wall that stood in front of them.

[13] The man then said to me:

These rooms on the north and south sides of the temple are the sacred rooms where the LORD's priests will eat the most holy offerings. These offerings include the grain sacrifices,* the sacrifices for sin,* and the sacrifices to make things right.* [14] When the priests are ready to leave the temple, they must go through these rooms before they return to the outer courtyard. They must leave their sacred clothes in these rooms and put on ordinary clothes before going anywhere near other people.

The size of the temple area

[15] After the man had finished measuring the buildings inside the temple area, he took me back through the east gate and measured the wall around this area. [16] He used his measuring stick to measure the east side of this wall; it was two hundred and fifty metres long. [17-19] Then he measured the north side, the south side, and the west side of the wall, and they were each two hundred and fifty metres long, [20] and so the temple area was a perfect square. The wall

around this area separated what was sacred from what was ordinary.

CHAPTER 43

The LORD's glory returns to the temple

[1] The man took me back to the east gate of the temple, [2] where I saw the brightness of the glory of Israel's God coming from the east. The sound I heard was as loud as ocean waves, and everything around was shining with the dazzling brightness of his glory. [3] This vision was like the one I had seen when God came to destroy Jerusalem and like the one I had seen near the River Chebar.

I immediately bowed with my face to the ground, [4] and the LORD's glory came through the east gate and into the temple.* [5] The LORD's Spirit lifted me to my feet and carried me to the inner courtyard, where I saw that the LORD's glory had filled the temple.

[6] The man was standing beside me, and I heard the LORD' say from inside the temple:

[7] Ezekiel, son of man, this temple is my throne on earth. I will live here among the people of Israel for ever. They and their kings will never again disgrace me by worshipping idols at local shrines or by setting up memorials to their dead kings.' [8] Israel's kings built their palaces so close to my holy temple that only a wall separated them from me. Then these kings disgraced me with their evil ways, and in my fierce anger I destroyed them. [9] But if the people and their kings stop worshipping other gods and tear down those memorials, I will live among them for ever.

[10] The people of Israel must suffer shame for sinning against me, so tell them about my holy temple. Let them think about it, [11] then if they are truly sorry, describe for them the design and shape of the temple, the gates, the measurements, and how the buildings are arranged. Explain the regulations about worshipping there, then write down these things, so they can study and obey them.

[12] The temple area on my holy mountain must be kept sacred! This is the most important law about the temple.

---

*42.3 the ten metres of open space . . . the temple: See 41.10.

*42.3 the pavement that circled the outer courtyard: See 40.17.

*42.13 grain sacrifices: See Leviticus 2.1.

*42.13 sacrifices for sin: See the note at 40.38–39.

*42.13 sacrifices to make things right: See the note at 40.38–39.

*43.4 the LORD's glory . . . temple: This was the same gate the LORD's glory went through when it left Jerusalem (see 10.19 and 11.22–23).

See also: 43.2: Ezek 10.3–4,18–19; 11.22–23; Rev 1.15.

The altar

13 According to the official standards, the altar in the temple had the following measurements: around the bottom of the altar was a gutter fifty centimetres wide and fifty centimetres deep, with a twenty-five-centimetre ledge on the outer rim. 14–17 The altar rested on a base and had three sections, each one of them square. The bottom section was eight metres on each side and one metre high. The middle section was seven metres on each side and two metres high, and it had a twenty-five-centimetre rim around its outer edge. The top section, which was six metres on each side and two metres high, was the place where sacrifices were burnt, and the four corners of the top section looked like the horns of a bull. The steps leading up to the altar were on the east side.

The dedication of the altar

18 The LORD God said:

Ezekiel, son of man, after the altar is built, it must be dedicated by offering sacrifices on it and by splattering it with blood. Here is what you must do: 19 the priests of the Levi tribe from the family of Zadok the priest are the only ones who may serve in my temple — this is my law. So give them a young bull to slaughter as a sacrifice for sin. 20 Take some of the animal's blood and smear it on the four corners of the altar, some on the corners of the middle section, and some more on the rim around its edge. That will purify the altar and make it fit for offering sacrifices to me. 21 Then take the body of the bull outside the temple area and burn it at the special place.

22 The next day, a goat* that has nothing wrong with it must be offered as a sacrifice for sin. Purify the altar with its blood, just as you did with the blood of the bull. 23 Then choose a young bull and a young ram that have nothing wrong with them, 24 and bring them to my temple. The priests will sprinkle salt on them* and offer them as sacrifices to please me.*

25 Each day for the next seven days, you must offer a goat and a bull and a ram as sacrifices for sin. These animals must have

nothing wrong with them. 26 The priests will purify the altar during those days, so that it will be acceptable to me and ready to use. 27 From then on, the priests will use this altar to offer sacrifices to please me and sacrifices to ask my blessing.* Then I will be pleased with the people of Israel. I, the LORD God, have spoken.

CHAPTER 44

The east gate must remain closed

1 The man took me back to the outer courtyard, near the east gate of the temple area. I saw that the doors to this gate were closed. 2 The LORD said:

I, the LORD God of Israel, came through this gate, so it must remain closed for ever! No one must ever use it. 3 The ruler of Israel may come here to eat a sacrificial meal that has been offered to me, but he must use only the entrance room of this gate.

People who are not allowed in the temple

4 Then the man took me through the north gate to the front of the temple. I saw that the brightness of the LORD's glory had filled the temple, and I immediately bowed with my face to the ground.
5 The LORD said:

Ezekiel, son of man, I am going to give you the laws for my temple. So pay attention and listen carefully to what kind of people are allowed to come in the temple, and what kind are not. 6 Tell those rebellious people of Israel:

I, the LORD God, command you to stop your evil ways! 7 My temple has been disgraced, because you have let godless, stubborn foreigners come here when sacrifices are being offered to me. You have sinned and have broken our solemn agreement. 8 Instead of following the proper ways to worship me, you have put foreigners in charge of worship at my temple.

9 And so I, the LORD God, say that no godless foreigner who disobeys me will be allowed in my temple. This includes any foreigner living in Israel.

---

*43.24 **The priests will sprinkle salt on them:** See Leviticus 2.13.
*43.24 **sacrifices to please me:** See the note at 40.38–39.
See also: 43.13–17: Exod 27.1–2; 2 Chron 4.1.
43.18–27: Exod 29.35–37.

*43.27 **sacrifices to ask my blessing:** These sacrifices have traditionally been called "peace offerings" or "offerings of well-being". A main purpose was to ask for the LORD's blessing, and so in the CEV they are sometimes called "sacrifices to ask the LORD's blessing".

The Levites are punished

The LORD said:

[10] Some of the Levites turned their backs on me and joined the other people of Israel in worshipping idols. So these Levites must be punished! [11] They will still be allowed to serve me as temple workers by guarding the gates and by killing the animals to be sacrificed and by helping the worshippers. [12] But because these Levites served the people of Israel when they worshipped idols, I, the LORD God, promise that the Levites will be punished. They did not stop the Israelites from sinning, [13] and now I will no longer let the Levites serve as my priests or come near anything sacred to me. They must suffer shame and disgrace for their disgusting sins. [14] They will be responsible for all the hard work that must be done in the temple.

Rules for priests

The LORD said:

[15] The priests of the Levi tribe who are descendants of Zadok the priest were faithful to me, even when the rest of the Israelites turned away. And so, these priests will continue to serve as my priests and to offer the fat and the blood of sacrifices. [16] They will come into my temple, where they will offer sacrifices at my altar and lead others in worship.

[17] When they come to the inner courtyard, they must wear their linen priestly clothes. My priests must never wear anything made of wool when they are on duty in this courtyard or in the temple. [18] Even their turbans and underwear must be made of linen to keep my priests from sweating when they work. [19] And before they leave to join the other people in the outer courtyard, they must take off their priestly clothes, then place them in the sacred rooms and put on their ordinary clothes.* That way, no one will touch their sacred clothes and be harmed.*

[20] Priests must never shave their heads when they are mourning. But they must keep their hair properly trimmed and not let it grow too long. [21] They must not drink wine before going to the inner courtyard.

[22] A priest must not marry a divorced woman; he can marry only a virgin from Israel or the widow of another priest.

[23] Priests must teach my people the difference between what is sacred and what is ordinary, and between what is clean and what is unclean. [24] They will make decisions in difficult legal cases, according to my own laws. They must also observe the religious festivals my Law requires and must always respect the Sabbath.

[25] Touching a dead body will make a person unclean. So a priest must not go near a dead body, unless it is one of his parents or children, or his brother or unmarried sister. [26] If a priest touches a dead body, he is unclean and must go through a ceremony to make himself clean. Then seven days later, [27] he must go to the inner courtyard of the temple and offer a sacrifice for sin.* After that, he may once again serve as my priest. I, the LORD God, have spoken.

[28] I myself will provide for my priests, and so they won't receive any land of their own. [29] Instead, they will receive part of the grain sacrifices,* as well as part of the sacrifices for sin* and sacrifices to make things right.* They will also be given everything in Israel that has been completely dedicated to me.* [30] The first part of every harvest will belong to the priests. They will also receive part of all special gifts and offerings the Israelites bring to me. And whenever any of my people bake bread, they will give their first loaf as an offering to the priests, and I will bless the homes of the people when they do this.

[31] Priests must not eat any bird or animal that dies a natural death or that has been killed by a wild animal.

44.27,29 sacrifice(s) for sin: See the note at 40.38–39.

44.29 grain sacrifices: See the note at 42.13.

44.29 sacrifices to make things right: See the note at 40.38–39.

44.29 that has been completely dedicated to me: This translates a Hebrew word that describes property and things that were taken away from humans and given to God. In the early history of Israel, such things often had to be destroyed (see Joshua 6.15–19).

See also: 44.21: Lev 10.9. 44.22: Lev 21.7,13–14.
44.23: Lev 10.10. 44.25: Lev 21.1–4. 44.28: Num 18.20.
44.29-30: Num 18.8-19. 44.31: Lev 22.8.

44.19 take off their priestly clothes . . . put on their ordinary clothes: See 42.14.

44.19 no one will touch . . . and be harmed: Ordinary people were forbidden to touch anything that was sacred. If they did, it was believed they would somehow be harmed.

See also: 44.17–18: Exod 28.39–43; Lev 16.4.
44.19: Lev 16.23. 44.20: Lev 21.5.

Real life

Fair trade

Contributed by Tearfund

The scales of international trade are tipped towards the powerful multi-national companies, who influence the global price of cash crops, such as coffee and cocoa. This can mean that Third World Producers get paid less per kilo of coffee or cocoa, than it cost to produce it. We think it's time to put people before profits and ensuring we buy Fairtrade products is a sure way of doing this.

Why is Fairtrade needed?

International trade affects the lives of millions of the world's poorest people every day. When commodity prices fall it can have a catastrophic effect on millions of small scale producers, forcing many of them into crippling debt so they lose their land and their homes. God's word has a lot to say about the need for justice in trade, the need to pay workers fairly and not exploit them to make money. All over our world these biblical values are being ignored – as many people who make the food and clothes we buy are not paid a fair living wage or treated with dignity and respect.

Victor is 18 and lives in Mim, in Central Ghana. He is the son of a cocoa farmer, who is a member of Kuapa Kokoo – a co-operative in Ghana which sells as much of its cocoa as possible to the Fairtrade market.

Victor says, 'This Fairtrade way of trading helps us farmers to earn our way out of poverty and allows us to plan for a better future. We need fair prices so that we can invest in the things we really need – like tools, clean water wells and education. I am hoping that soon my father will be able to send me to train as a mechanic thanks to the extra money earned from Fairtrade.'

Fairtrade works by paying small scale producers like Victor's dad a secure, guaranteed price for their crops and givingthe security of knowing that they can plan for their future.

Is Fairtrade working?

UK consumers already spend around £59 million a year on Fairtrade products, which means that over half a million people in poor countries are now benefiting.

Which Fairtrade food is available?

Fairtrade products include many different foods such as cocoa, chocolate, coffee, tea, sugar, bananas, orange and tropical juice, and honey. The world's first Fairtrade pineapples went on sale in December 2002, as did the first Fairtrade cola. Fairtrade mangoes were launched in January this year.

Think

Why is Fairtrade a good thing?
Why should Christians support Fairtrade?
What do you buy that you could buy fairly traded?

Act

Look for Fairtrade products are labelled with the Fairtrade mark
Make sure your church or youth group is using fairly traded goods whenever possible

Check

Genesis 18.17–19; Deuteronomy 1.14–17; 10.16–19; Psalms 106.1–3; Isaiah 59.3–8; Ezekiel 45.9–10; Luke 11.42–48; Titus 1.7–9

More...

Materialism p.1141
Shopping p.973
Fighting evil p.201
Civil disobedience p.1247

CHAPTER 45

The LORD's sacred land

The LORD said:

¹ When the land of Israel is divided among the twelve tribes, you must set aside an area that will belong to me. This sacred area will be twelve and a half kilometres long and ten' kilometres wide. ² The temple will be on a piece of land two hundred and fifty-five metres square, and the temple will be completely surrounded by an open space twenty-five metres wide.

³⁻⁴ I will give half of my sacred land, a section twelve and a half kilometres long and five kilometres wide, to the priests who serve in the temple. Their houses will be in this half, as well as my temple, which is the most sacred place of all.

⁵ I will give the other half of my land to the Levites who work in my temple, and the towns' where they will live will be there.

⁶ Next to my sacred land will be an area twelve and a half kilometres long and three kilometres wide. This will belong to the people of Israel and will include the city of Jerusalem.

Land for Israel's ruler

The LORD said:

⁷⁻⁸ The regions west and east of my sacred land and the city of Jerusalem will belong to the ruler of Israel. He will be given the region between the western edge of my land and the Mediterranean Sea, and between the eastern edge of my land and the River Jordan. This will mean that the length of his property will be the same as the sections of land given to the tribes.

This property will belong to every ruler of Israel, so they will always be fair to my people and will let them live peacefully in the land given to their tribes.

Israel's rulers must be honest

⁹ The LORD God said:

You leaders of Israel have robbed and cheated my people long enough! I want you to stop sinning and start doing what is right and fair. You must never again force my people off their own land. I, the LORD, have spoken.

¹⁰ So from now on, you must use honest weights and measures. ¹¹ The *ephah* will be

See also: 45.10: Lev 19.36.

the standard dry measure, and the *bath* will be the standard liquid measure. Their size will be based on the *homer*, which will equal ten *ephahs* or ten *baths*.*

¹² The standard unit of weight will be the *shekel*.* One *shekel* will equal twenty *gerahs*, and sixty *shekels* will equal one *mina*.

¹³ Leaders of Israel, the people must bring you one sixtieth of their grain harvests as offerings to me. ¹⁴ They will also bring one per cent of their olive oil. These things will be measured according to the *bath*, and ten *baths* is the same as one *homer* or one *cor*.

¹⁵ Finally, they must bring one sheep out of every two hundred from their flocks.

These offerings will be used as grain sacrifices, as well as sacrifices to please me* and those to ask my blessing.* I, the LORD, will be pleased with these sacrifices and will forgive the sins of my people.

¹⁶ The people of Israel will bring you these offerings. ¹⁷ But during New Moon Festivals, Sabbath celebrations, and other religious feasts, you leaders will be responsible for providing animals for the sacrifices, as well as the grain and wine. All these will be used for the sacrifices for sin,* the grain sacrifices,* the sacrifices to please me,* and those to ask my blessing.* I will be pleased and will forgive the sins of my people.

The festivals

This is also told in Exodus 12.1–20; Leviticus 23.33–43

¹⁸ The LORD God said:

On the first day of the first month,* a young bull that has nothing wrong with it must be offered as a sacrifice to purify the temple. ¹⁹ The priest will take some blood from this sacrifice and smear it on the doorposts of

---

*45.11 the *homer* . . . ten *ephahs* . . . ten *baths*: A *homer* was either a dry or a liquid measure and equalled about one hundred and seventy-five litres; an *ephah* would be about nine kilogrammes, and a *bath* would be about seventeen and a half litres.
*45.12 the *shekel*: The *shekel* was about eleven grammes.
*45.15,17 sacrifices to please me: See the note at 40.38–39.
*45.15,17 sacrifices . . . to ask my blessing: See the note at 43.27.
*45.17 sacrifices for sin: See the note at 40.38–39.
*45.17 grain sacrifices: See the note at 42.13.
*45.18 the first month: Abib (also called Nisan), the first month of the Hebrew calendar, from about mid-March to mid-April.

the temple, as well as on the four corners of the altar and on the doorposts of the gates that lead into the inner courtyard.

20 The same ceremony must also be done on the seventh day of the month, so that anyone who sins accidentally or without knowing it will be forgiven, and so that my temple will remain holy.

21 Beginning on the fourteenth day of the first month, and continuing for seven days, everyone will celebrate Passover and eat bread made without yeast. 22 On the first day, the ruler will bring a bull to offer as a sacrifice for his sins and for the sins of the people. 23 Each day of the festival he is to bring seven bulls and seven rams as sacrifices to please me,* and he must bring a goat' as a sacrifice for sin. These animals must have nothing wrong with them. 24 He will also provide nine kilogrammes of grain and three litres of olive oil to be offered with each bull and each ram.

25 The Festival of Shelters will begin on the fifteenth day of the seventh month* and will continue for seven days. On each day of this festival, the ruler will provide the same number of animals that he did each day during Passover, as well as the same amount of grain and olive oil for the sacrifices.

CHAPTER 46

Various laws for the ruler and the people

1 The LORD said:

The east gate of the inner courtyard must remain closed during the six working days of each week. But on the Sabbath and on the first day of the month, this gate will be opened. 2 Israel's ruler will go from the outer courtyard into the entrance room of this gate and stand in the doorway while the priest offers sacrifices to ask my blessing* and sacrifices to please me.* The ruler will bow with his face to the ground to show that he has worshipped me. Then he will leave, and the gate will remain open until evening.

3 Each Sabbath and on the first day of each month, the people of Israel must also come to the east gate and worship me. 4 On the Sabbath, the ruler will bring six lambs and one ram to be offered as sacrifices to please me. There must be nothing wrong with any of these animals. 5 With the ram, he is to offer nine kilogrammes of grain, and with each of the lambs, he can offer as much as he wants. He must also offer three litres of olive oil with every nine kilogrammes of grain.

6 The ruler is to bring six lambs, a bull, and a ram to be offered as sacrifices at the New Moon Festival. There must be nothing wrong with any of these animals. 7 With the bull and the ram, he is to offer nine kilogrammes of grain, and with each of the lambs, he can offer as much as he wants. He must also offer three litres of olive oil with every nine kilogrammes of grain. 8 The ruler must come through the entrance room of the east gate and leave the same way.

9 When my people come to worship me during any festival, they must always leave by the opposite gate from which they came: those who come in the north gate must leave by the south gate, and those who come in the south gate must leave by the north gate. 10 Their ruler will come in at the same time they do and leave at the same time they leave.

11 At all other festivals and celebrations, nine kilogrammes of grain will be offered with a bull, and nine kilogrammes will be offered with a ram. The worshippers can offer as much grain as they want with each lamb. Three litres of olive oil must be offered with every nine kilogrammes of grain.

12 If the ruler voluntarily offers a sacrifice to please me or to ask my blessing, the east gate of the inner courtyard will be opened for him. He will offer his sacrifices just as he does on each Sabbath; then he will leave, and the gate will be closed.

13 Each morning a year-old lamb that has nothing wrong with it must be offered as a sacrifice to please me. 14 Along with it, two kilogrammes of fine flour mixed with a litre of olive oil must be offered as a grain sacrifice. This law will never change — 15 the lamb, the flour, and the olive oil will be offered to me every morning for all time.

---

*45.23; 46.2 sacrifices to please me: See the note at 40.38–39.

*45.25 seventh month: Tishri (also called Ethanim), the seventh month of the Hebrew calendar, from about mid-September to mid-October.

*46.2 sacrifices to ask my blessing: See the note at 43.27.

See also: 45.21: Exod 12.1–20; Num 28.16–25.
45.25: Lev 23.33–36; Num 29.12–38.

Laws about the ruler's land

¹⁶ The LORD God said:

If the ruler of Israel gives some of his land to one of his children, it will belong to the ruler's child as part of the family property. ¹⁷ But if the ruler gives some of his land to one of his servants, the land will belong to the servant until the Year of Celebration, when it will be returned to the ruler.* Only the ruler's children can keep what is given to them.

¹⁸ The ruler must never abuse my people by taking land from them. Any land he gives his children must already belong to him.

The sacred kitchens

¹⁹ The man who was showing me the temple* then took me back to the inner courtyard. We walked to the south side of the courtyard and stopped at the door to the sacred rooms that belonged to the priests. He showed me more rooms at the western edge of the courtyard ²⁰ and said, "These are the kitchens where the priests must boil the meat to be offered as sacrifices to make things right* and as sacrifices for sin.* They will also bake the grain for sacrifices in these kitchens. That way, these sacred offerings won't have to be carried through the outer courtyard, where someone could accidentally touch them and be harmed."*

²¹ We went back to the outer courtyard and walked past the four corners. ²² At each corner I saw a smaller courtyard, twenty metres long and fifteen metres wide. ²³ Around the inside of these smaller courtyards was a low wall of stones, and against the wall were places to build fires.' ²⁴ The man said, "These are the kitchens where the temple workers will boil the meat that worshippers offer as sacrifices."

The stream flowing from the temple

CHAPTER 47

¹ The man took me back to the temple, where I saw a stream flowing from under the entrance. It began in the south part of the temple, where it ran past the altar and continued east through the courtyard.

² We walked out of the temple area through the north gate and went around to the east gate. I saw the small stream of water flowing east from the south side of the gate.

³ The man walked east, then took out his measuring stick and measured five hundred metres downstream. He told me to wade through the stream there, and the water came up to my ankles. ⁴ Then he measured another five hundred metres downstream, and told me to wade through it there. The water came up to my knees. Another five hundred metres downstream the water came up to my waist. ⁵ Another five hundred metres downstream, the stream had become a river that could be crossed only by swimming. ⁶ The man said, "Ezekiel, son of man, pay attention to what you've seen."

We walked to the river bank, ⁷ where I saw dozens of trees on each side. ⁸ The man said:

This water flows eastwards to the valley of the River Jordan and empties into the Dead Sea, where it turns the salt water into fresh water. ⁹ Wherever this water flows, there will be all kinds of animals and fish, because it will bring life and fresh water to the Dead Sea. ¹⁰ From En-Gedi to Eneglaim, people will fish in the sea and dry their nets along the coast. There will be as many kinds of fish in the Dead Sea as there are in the Mediterranean Sea. ¹¹ But the marshes along the shore will remain salty, so that people can use the salt from them. ¹² Fruit trees will grow all along this river and produce fresh fruit every month. The leaves will never dry out, because they will always have water from the stream that flows from the temple, and they will be used for healing people.

---

*46.17 the Year of Celebration . . . to the ruler: This was a sacred year for Israel, traditionally called the "Year of Jubilee". During this year, all property had to go back to its original owner (see Leviticus 25.8–34).
*46.19 The man . . . temple: See 40.3.
*46.20 sacrifices to make things right: See the note at 40.38–39.
*46.20 sacrifices for sin: See the note at 40.38–39.
*46.20 someone . . . touch them and be harmed: See the note at 44.19.
See also: 46.17: Lev 25.10.

See also: 47.1: Zech 14.8; John 7.38; Rev 22.1.
47.12: Rev 22.2.

The borders of the restored land and its division among the tribes

The borders of the land

13-14 The LORD God said to the people of Israel:

When the land is divided among the twelve tribes of Israel, the Joseph tribe* will receive two shares. Divide the land equally, because I promised your ancestors that this land would some day belong to their descendants. These are the borders of the land:

15 The northern border will begin at the Mediterranean Sea, then continue eastward to Hethlon, to Lebo-Hamath, then across to Zedad, 16 Berothah,' and Sibraim, which is on the border between the two kingdoms of Damascus and Hamath. The border will end at Hazar-Hatticon, which is on the border of Hauran. 17 So the northern border will run between the Mediterranean Sea and Hazar-Enon, which is on the border between Damascus and Hamath.'

18 The eastern border will begin on the border between the two kingdoms of Hauran and Damascus. It will run south along the River Jordan, which separates the territories of Gilead and Israel, and it will end at the Dead Sea near the town of Tamar.'

19 The southern border will begin at Tamar, then run south-west to the springs near Meribath-Kadesh. It will continue along the Egyptian Gorge and will end at the Mediterranean Sea.

20 The western border will run north along the Mediterranean Sea to a point just west of Lebo-Hamath.

21 That is the land to be divided among the tribes of Israel. 22 It will belong to the Israelites and to any foreigners living among them whose children were born in Israel. These foreigners must be treated like any other Israelite citizen, and they will receive 23 a share of the land given to the tribe where they live. I, the LORD God, have spoken.

CHAPTER 48

The division of land among tribes in the north

The LORD said:

1-7 Each tribe will receive a section of land that runs from the eastern border of Israel west to the Mediterranean Sea. The northern border of Israel will run along the towns of Hethlon and Lebo-Hamath, and will end at Hazar-Enon, which is on the border between the kingdoms of Damascus and Hamath. The tribes will receive their share of land in the following order, from north to south: Dan, Asher, Naphtali, Manasseh, Ephraim, Reuben, and Judah.

The special section of land

The LORD said:

8 South of Judah's territory will be a special section of land. Its length will be twelve and a half kilometres, and its width will run from the eastern border of Israel west to the Mediterranean Sea. My temple will be in this section of land.

9 An area in the centre of this land will belong to me. It will be twelve and a half kilometres long and ten' kilometres wide.

10 I, the LORD, will give half of my sacred land to the priests. Their share will be twelve and a half kilometres long and five kilometres wide, and my temple will be right in the middle. 11 Only priests who are descendants of Zadok will receive a share of this sacred land, because they remained faithful to me when the Levites and the rest of the Israelites started sinning. 12 The land belonging to the priests will be the most sacred area and will lie south of the area that belongs to the Levites.

13 I will give the other half of my sacred land to the Levites. Their share will also be twelve and a half kilometres long and five kilometres wide, 14 and they must never sell or trade any of this land — it is the best land and belongs to me.

15 South of my sacred land will be a section twelve and a half kilometres long and three kilometres wide. It will not be sacred, but will belong to the people of Israel and will include the city of Jerusalem, together with its houses and pasture land. 16 The city will be a square: each side will be two kilometres long, 17 and an open area one hundred and twenty-five metres wide will surround the city. 18 The land on the

---

*47.13-14 the Joseph tribe: That is, the two tribes of Manasseh and Ephraim, Joseph's sons.

east and west sides of the city boundaries will be farmland for the people of Jerusalem; both sections will be five kilometres long and three kilometres wide. ¹⁹ People from the city will farm the land, no matter which tribe they belong to.

²⁰ And so the centre of this special section of land will be for my sacred land, as well as for the city and its property. The land will be a square, twelve and a half kilometres on each side.

²¹ The regions east and west of this square of land will belong to the ruler of Israel. His property will run east to the River Jordan and west to the Mediterranean Sea. In the very centre of his property will be my sacred land, as well as the temple, ²² together with the share belonging to the Levites and the city of Jerusalem. The northern border of the ruler's property will be the land that belongs to Judah, and the southern border will be the land that belongs to Benjamin.

The division of land among tribes in the south

The LORD God said:

²³⁻²⁷ South of this special section will be the land that belongs to the rest of Israel's tribes. Each tribe will receive a section of land that runs from the eastern border of Israel west to the Mediterranean Sea. The tribes will receive their share of land in the following order, from north to south: Benjamin, Simeon, Issachar, Zebulun, and Gad.

²⁸ Gad's southern border is also the southern border of Israel. It will begin at the town of Tamar, then run south-west to the springs near Meribath-Kadesh. It will continue along the Egyptian Gorge and end at the Mediterranean Sea.

²⁹ That's how the land of Israel will be divided among the twelve tribes. I, the LORD God, have spoken.

The gates of Jerusalem

The LORD said:

³⁰⁻³⁴ The city of Jerusalem will have twelve gates, three on each of the four sides of the city wall. These gates will be named after the twelve tribes of Israel. The gates of Reuben, Judah, and Levi will be in the north; Joseph, Benjamin, and Dan will be in the east; Simeon, Issachar, and Zebulun will be in the south; Gad, Asher, and Naphtali will be in

See also: 48.30–34: Rev 21.12–13.

the west. Each side of the city wall will be two kilometres long, ³⁵ and so the total length of the wall will be ten kilometres. The new name of the city will be "The-LORD-Is-Here!"

Additional notes

›1.1–3 a priest and the son of Buzi: Or "the son of Buzi the priest".
›1.11 Two wings: One possible meaning for the difficult Hebrew text.
›1.13 up: One possible meaning for the difficult Hebrew text of verse 13.
›1.14 as sparks jumping from a fire: Or "as flashes of lightning".
›1.15 wheel: One possible meaning for the difficult Hebrew text of verse 15.
›1.16 a second wheel that cut through the middle of it: Or "a smaller wheel inside it".
›1.18 them: One possible meaning for the difficult Hebrew text of verse 18.
›2.1 The LORD: Hebrew "The voice".
›3.12 The Spirit: Or "A wind".
›3.12 as the glory of the LORD started to leave: One possible meaning for the difficult Hebrew text.
›7.5 disaster: One possible meaning for the difficult Hebrew text of verse 5.
›7.7 celebration: One possible meaning for the difficult Hebrew text of verse 7.
›7.11 shattered: One possible meaning for the difficult Hebrew text of verses 10–11.
›7.13 mind: One possible meaning for the difficult Hebrew text of verse 13.
›7.16 will moan: Hebrew; two ancient translations "will die".
›7.22 my temple: The Hebrew text has "my treasure", which may refer to the temple, to Jerusalem, or to Israel itself.
›7.23 Your whole country is in confusion: One ancient translation; Hebrew "Get chains ready to drag away the dead bodies of your people."
›8.2 a human: One ancient translation; Hebrew "a fiery figure".
›8.17 disgraced and insulted me . . . way: One possible meaning for the difficult Hebrew text.
›10.10 a second wheel that cut through the middle of it: See the note at 1.16.
›11.1 The LORD's Spirit: See the note at 3.12.
›11.3 Let's . . . houses: One possible meaning for the difficult Hebrew text.
›11.24 the LORD's Spirit: See the note at 3.12.
›13.18 They wear . . . the future: One possible meaning for the difficult Hebrew text.
›13.20 like birds: One possible meaning for the difficult Hebrew text.
›16.10 most expensive robes: One possible meaning for the difficult Hebrew text.

›**16.15 so you offered yourself to every passer-by:** One possible meaning for the difficult Hebrew text.

›**16.16 These things should never have happened:** One possible meaning for the difficult Hebrew text.

›**16.30 wanted:** One possible meaning for the difficult Hebrew text of verse 30.

›**16.61 even though this was not part of our agreement:** One possible meaning for the difficult Hebrew text.

›**17.5 like a willow tree beside a stream:** One possible meaning for the difficult Hebrew text.

›**17.21 best troops:** Two ancient translations; Hebrew "troops that ran away".

›**18.17 evil:** One ancient translation; Hebrew "for the poor".

›**19.7 He destroyed fortresses:** One possible meaning for the difficult Hebrew text.

›**19.10 Your mother was a vine:** One possible meaning for the difficult Hebrew text.

›**20.39 me:** One possible meaning for the difficult Hebrew text of verse 39.

›**21.9,10 Don't celebrate . . . my warnings:** One possible meaning for the difficult Hebrew text.

›**21.13 I am testing . . . me:** One possible meaning for the difficult Hebrew text.

›**21.15 My slaughtering sword . . . ready to kill:** One possible meaning for the difficult Hebrew text.

›**21.30 Your days . . . put your swords away:** One possible meaning for the difficult Hebrew text.

›**22.16 You:** Hebrew; two ancient translations "Because of you, I".

›**22.25 Their leaders are like:** One ancient translation; Hebrew "Their prophets are like herds of".

›**23.24 from the north:** One ancient translation; Hebrew "with weapons".

›**23.43 prostitutes:** One possible meaning for the difficult Hebrew text of verse 43.

›**24.4,5 Pile wood:** Or "Stack the bones".

›**24.6 and no one cares what happens to it:** One possible meaning for the difficult Hebrew text.

›**24.10 boil away the broth:** One ancient translation; Hebrew "mix the spices".

›**24.12 away:** One possible meaning for the difficult Hebrew text of verse 12.

›**25.8 Moab:** One ancient translation; Hebrew "Moab and Edom".

›**25.16 kill everyone:** The Hebrew text also has the name "Cherethites", which was a group of people that lived just south-east of Philistia, and was often identified with the Philistines.

›**26.17 The great city . . . is destroyed:** One possible meaning for the difficult Hebrew text.

›**26.20 You will stay there . . . with people:** One possible meaning for the difficult Hebrew text.

›**27.4 and your control of the sea:** One possible meaning for the difficult Hebrew text.

›**27.6 pine trees from Cyprus:** One possible meaning for the difficult Hebrew text.

›**27.12 southern Spain:** The Hebrew text has "Tarshish", which may have been a Phoenician city in southern Spain.

›**27.15 Rhodes:** One ancient translation; Hebrew "Dedan".

›**27.16 Edom:** Some Hebrew manuscripts and one ancient translation; most Hebrew manuscripts "Syria".

›**27.17 their finest wheat, best figs:** One possible meaning for the difficult Hebrew text.

›**27.19 Vedan and Javan near Uzal:** One possible meaning for the difficult Hebrew text.

›**27.32 Tyre, you were greater . . . the bottom of the sea:** One possible meaning for the difficult Hebrew text.

›**28.3 and know everything:** One possible meaning for the difficult Hebrew text.

›**28.12 you were perfect:** One possible meaning for the difficult Hebrew text.

›**28.13 They were all set in gold:** One possible meaning for the difficult Hebrew text.

›**28.14 I appointed a winged creature to guard your home:** One possible meaning for the difficult Hebrew text.

›**29.7 making them fall:** One possible meaning for the difficult Hebrew text.

›**30.5 as well as from Israel:** One possible meaning for the difficult Hebrew text.

›**30.13 Memphis:** Hebrew "Noph".

›**30.14 Thebes:** Hebrew "No".

›**30.16 the people of Memphis . . . constant fear:** One possible meaning for the difficult Hebrew text.

›**30.17 Heliopolis and Bubastis:** Hebrew "On and Pi-Beseth".

›**31.3 sky:** One possible meaning for the difficult Hebrew text of verse 3.

›**31.10 the sky:** One ancient translation; Hebrew "over the thick branches".

›**31.15 rivers and streams . . . stop flowing:** One possible meaning for the difficult Hebrew text.

›**31.17 dead:** One possible meaning for the difficult Hebrew text of verse 17.

›**32.5 rotting flesh:** One possible meaning for the difficult Hebrew text.

›**32.9 when I tell them how I destroyed you:** Hebrew; one ancient translation "when I scatter you like prisoners among them."

›**32.18 where they will be buried . . . powerful nations:** One possible meaning for the difficult Hebrew text.

›**32.20 The enemy's sword . . . you:** One possible meaning for the difficult Hebrew text.

›**32.27 heroes of long ago:** One ancient translation; Hebrew "godless heroes".

›**32.27 shields:** One possible meaning for the difficult Hebrew text.

›**34.16 slaughter:** Hebrew; three ancient translations "take care of".

›**35.2 Edom:** The Hebrew text has "Mount Seir", another name for Edom.

›**37.9 wind:** Or "breath". The Hebrew word may mean either.

›**37.16 Israel:** The Hebrew text has "Joseph, that is, Ephraim", the leading tribe in the northern kingdom.

'38.13 from villages in: One ancient translation; Hebrew "and soldiers from".

'38.13 southern Spain: See the note at 27.12.

'38.14 when you see: One possible meaning for the difficult Hebrew text.

'38.21 I, the LORD . . . against you: One possible meaning for the difficult Hebrew text.

'39.11 Travellers': Hebrew "Abarim".

'39.11 That graveyard . . . the valley: One possible meaning for the difficult Hebrew text.

'39.11 Gog's Army: Hebrew "Hamon-Gog".

'39.26 me: One possible meaning for the difficult Hebrew text of verse 26.

'40.13 back wall: One ancient translation; Hebrew "roof".

'40.14 wide: One possible meaning for the difficult Hebrew text of verse 14.

'40.16 just like the ones in the entrance room: One possible meaning for the difficult Hebrew text.

'40.19 metres: The Hebrew text adds "the east and the north".

'40.38–39 Just outside: Or "Inside".

'40.42–43 where the meat . . . altar: One possible meaning for the difficult Hebrew text.

'40.42–43 was a seventy-five-millimetre shelf: Or "were seventy-five-millimetre pegs".

'40.44 south: One possible meaning for the difficult Hebrew text of verse 44.

'40.48 seven metres long: One ancient translation; these words are not in the Hebrew text of this verse.

'40.49 six: One ancient translation; Hebrew "five and a half".

'40.49 steps: Hebrew; one ancient translation "ten steps".

'41.1 it was three metres wide: One possible meaning for the difficult Hebrew text.

'41.7 which meant that . . . on the bottom level: One possible meaning for the difficult Hebrew text.

'41.15 The inside walls of the temple's porch and main room: One possible meaning for the difficult Hebrew text.

'41.16 were trimmed in wood: One possible meaning for the difficult Hebrew text.

'41.17 decorated: One possible meaning for the difficult Hebrew text of verse 17.

'41.22 one metre square: One ancient translation; Hebrew "one metre wide".

'41.22 base: One ancient translation; Hebrew "length".

'42.1–2 he showed me . . . the west building: One possible meaning for the difficult Hebrew text.

'42.4 fifty metres long: Two ancient translations; Hebrew "fifty centimetres long".

'42.7–8 long: One possible meaning for the difficult Hebrew text of verses 5–8.

'42.9–10 south: One ancient translation; Hebrew "east".

'43.6 the LORD: Hebrew "a voice".

'43.7 by setting up memorials to their dead kings: One possible meaning for the difficult Hebrew text.

'43.22 goat: Hebrew "male goat".

'45.1 ten: One ancient translation; Hebrew "five".

'45.5 the towns: One ancient translation; Hebrew "the twenty rooms".

'45.23 goat: See the note at 43.22.

'46.23 fires: One possible meaning for the difficult Hebrew text of verse 23.

'47.15–16 to Lebo-Hamath, then across to Zedad, ¹⁶ Berothah: One ancient translation; Hebrew "to Lebo-Zedad, ¹⁶ then across to Hamath, Berothah".

'47.17 which is on the border between Damascus and Hamath: One possible meaning for the difficult Hebrew text.

'47.18 near the town of Tamar: One possible meaning for the difficult Hebrew text.

'48.9 ten: The Hebrew text has "five" (but see 45.1 and the note there).

Daniel

The basics

What's the point? To show that God is in control of this world, and to demonstrate the importance of not compromising the faith.

What happens? Daniel and his companions are under pressure to worship other gods. They refuse, and God protects them from punishment.

What should I remember? 7.13–14 'As I continued to watch the vision that night, I saw what looked like a son of man coming with the clouds of heaven, and he was presented to the Eternal God. He was crowned king and given power and glory, so that all people of every nation and race would serve him. He will rule forever, and his kingdom is eternal, never to be destroyed.'

More details

Setting the scene Daniel is a young Jew, taken into captivity in Babylon when Jerusalem was captured. There, he gets a choice: compromise his faith, or lose his life...

What's it all about? Daniel, to adapt a footballing cliché, is a book of two halves.

The first half is about integrity. Daniel and his companions become members of the Babylonian government, but they have to make a choice; do they worship the ruler of Babylon or the God of Israel?

Babylon was a 'multicultural' empire which had absorbed knowledge and customs from those it had conquered. Daniel, however, remained true to his God and refused to water down his faith. Daniel reminds us that we should not bow down to the gods of this world; we should stay faithful and God will support us in that struggle.

This is a theme which is especially relevant to us today, in a world which constantly pressurises us to conform to its values. It was also immensely relevant to the original audience who, from the time of the exile onwards, had to live under a succession of invading empires, including Greeks and Romans – all of whom wanted to impose their own worship and values on the people of Israel.

The second half of the book is full of dreams and prophecies of empires in the future. There are beasts and rams and goats, and angels – who explain the meaning of the visions to Daniel. Some of them are hard to understand, but the overall theme is that God is in control of human events. He builds empires up; and he will pull them down.

Footsteps

A vegetarian diet: 1.1–21
Nebuchadnezzar's dream: 2.1–49
The fiery furnace: 3.1–30
The writing on the wall: 5.1–31
The lion's den: 6.1–28
The four beasts: 7.1–28
Seventy years: 9.1–19

Daniel and his three friends

CHAPTER 1

¹ In the third year that Jehoiakim was king of Judah,* King Nebuchadnezzar of Babylonia

---

*1.1 Jehoiakim . . . king of Judah: Ruled 609–598 BC.
See also: 1.1: 2 King 24.1; 2 Chron 36.5–7.

Life files

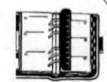

Daniel a.k.a. Belteshazzar (Daniel 1.7)

Background: A Jew who was captured by the Babylonians

What's the story?

Daniel was probably only about 14 when he was taken captive to Babylon. Possibly he came from the royal family, which is why he was taken to serve in the Babylonian royal palace. There, with his friends, he decided to live according to God's law. He ate a vegetarian diet and despite the anxieties of his teachers, he looked good on it. His God-given wisdom helped him to interpret the King's dreams, and understand some mystical writing on the wall of a banquet house. But his faith brought him into conflict with another king when he refused to pray to the new Emperor, Darius. He was thrown into the lion's den, but survived because God protected him. Oh, and he had a succession of visions to do with the future.

What's the point?

Daniel is a story about integrity. No matter what laws were passed by the powers in Babylon, Daniel put God's laws first. Think about the pressures on him: there he was in a foreign court, given a foreign name and surrounded by luxury and wealth. He could so easily have 'gone native'; he could have compromised his faith. But he didn't, he carried on as he had always done; he prayed to his God and lived by God's rules. Even though his life was at stake, he kept to his principles – and God rewarded him.

More...

Babylon p.437
Dreams and visions p.1410
Living truthfully p.1070

attacked Jerusalem. ² The Lord let Nebuchadnezzar capture Jehoiakim and take away some of the things used in God's temple. And when the king returned to Babylonia,ᵇ he put these things in the temple of his own god.

³ One day the king ordered Ashpenaz, his highest palace official, to choose some young men from the royal family of Judah and from other leading Jewish families. ⁴ The king said, "They must be healthy, handsome, clever, wise, educated, and fit to serve in the royal palace. Teach them how to speak and write our language ⁵ and give them the same food and wine that I am served. Train them for three years, and then they can become court officials."

⁶ Four of the young Jews chosen were Daniel, Hananiah, Mishael, and Azariah, all from the tribe of Judah. ⁷ But the king's chief official gave them Babylonian names: Daniel became Belteshazzar, Hananiah became Shadrach, Mishael became Meshach, and Azariah became Abednego.

⁸ Daniel made up his mind to eat and drink only what God had approved for his people to eat. And he asked the king's chief official for permission not to eat the food and wine served in the royal palace. ⁹ God had made the official friendly and kind to Daniel. ¹⁰ But the man still told him, "The king has decided what you must eat and drink. And I am afraid he will kill me, if you eat something else and end up looking worse than the other young men."

¹¹ The king's official had put a guard in charge of Daniel and his three friends. So Daniel said to the guard, ¹² "For the next ten days, let us have only vegetables and water at mealtimes. ¹³ When the ten days are up, compare how we look with the other young men, and decide what to do with us." ¹⁴ The guard agreed to do what Daniel had asked.

¹⁵ Ten days later, Daniel and his friends looked healthier and better than the young men who had been served food from the royal palace. ¹⁶ After this, the guard let them eat vegetables instead of the rich food and wine.

¹⁷ God made the four young men clever and wise. They read a lot of books and became well educated. Daniel could also tell the meaning of dreams and visions.

¹⁸ At the end of the three-year period set by King Nebuchadnezzar, his chief palace

See also: 1.2–4: 2 King 20.17–18; 24.10–16; 2 Chron 36.10; Isa 39.7–8.

Real life

Peer pressure

Contributed by Discovery

Pete was no 'ordinary' teenager. Having been born and largely brought up in Kenya, he moved to England to attend boarding school and continue his education. Pete made some good friends there, joined in with the usual practical jokes and made a life for himself in the cold climates of England.

But there were a few things that made Pete stand out from the rest of his friends. He lifted the atmosphere of a room simply by walking into it... he accepted everybody, no matter where they were from... and most of all, he was totally sold out for God and wasn't afraid to show that to the people around him.

Some people thought he was a bit of a freak because of his faith. He didn't always fit in, and that often left him feeling lonely and isolated. But all Pete ever wanted to do with his life was serve God. He became an ambassador for Christ in that school by being true to himself, not pretending to be anything different, getting stuck into all the things he enjoyed with his friends, but totally allowing God to use him to show Jesus to his friends and teachers.

Everybody knew that Pete was a Christian... it was who and what he was. After his A-levels, Pete decided to return to his beloved Africa as a missionary for a year. He spent that time living out who he was as a Christian in that place, having a massive impact on the people there. Sadly Pete never came back home. At the age of 19, he was caught up in a cattle raid and was shot dead. In his 19 short years, Pete had stood firm in his faith even though that made him different, helped friends get to know Jesus, impacted the lives of so many people for God, and died doing the one thing he had given his life to... serving God with his whole heart, no matter what the cost. How many could boast of such a life and such strength, whatever their age?

Think

Read Romans 12.1–2, 9–11. What are these verses telling us to do?
Where do you think strength for 'being different' comes from?
What do you think the consequences would have been if Pete had given in to peer pressure and denied his faith?
Are you like Pete in any way? Why/why not?
What would it look like for you to not 'be like the people of this world, but let God change the way you think'?

Act

Write a letter, as if to your granddaughter or son, giving advice on how to live as a teenager and a Christian in the 21st century. If you've been baptised in church as a child, remind yourself of the vows your parents and godparents made on your behalf (you may be able to find them in the prayerbook).
Make a card for a friend who needs encouraging to stand out from the crowd.

Check

Daniel 1.1–21; Hebrews 2.18;
Proverbs 18.24; Hebrews 13.5b; Psalm 1;
Mark 15.1–20

More...

Help! I'm being bullied p.603
Help! My friends slag off other people p.694
School p.64

official brought all the young men to him. ¹⁹ The king interviewed them and discovered that none of the others were as outstanding as Daniel, Hananiah, Mishael, and Azariah. So they were given positions in the royal court. ²⁰ From then on, whenever the king asked for advice, he found their wisdom was ten times better than that of any of his other advisers and magicians. ²¹ Daniel served there until the first year of King Cyrus.*

King Nebuchadnezzar's dream

CHAPTER 2

¹ During the second year that Nebuchadnezzar was king, he had such horrible nightmares that he could not sleep. ² So he called in his counsellors, advisers, magicians, and wise men, ³ and said, "I am disturbed by a dream that I don't understand, and I want you to explain it."

⁴ They answered in Aramaic,* "Your Majesty, we hope you live for ever! We are your servants. Please tell us your dream, and we will explain what it means."

⁵ But the king replied, "No! I have made up my mind. If you don't tell me both the dream and its meaning, you will be chopped to pieces and your houses will be torn down. ⁶ However, if you do tell me both the dream and its meaning, you will be greatly rewarded and highly honoured. Now tell me the dream and explain what it means."

⁷ "Your Majesty," they said, "if you will only tell us your dream, we will interpret it for you."

⁸ The king replied, "You're just stalling for time, ⁹ because you know what's going to happen if you don't come up with the answer. You've decided to make up a pack of lies, hoping I might change my mind. Now tell me the dream, and that will prove that you can interpret it."

¹⁰ His advisers explained, "Your Majesty, you are demanding the impossible! No king, not even the most famous and powerful, has ever ordered his advisers, magicians, or wise men to do such a thing. ¹¹ It can't be done, except by the gods, and they don't live here on earth."

¹²⁻¹³ This made the king so angry that he gave orders for every wise man in Babylonia to be put to death, including Daniel and his three friends.

God tells Nebuchadnezzar's dream to Daniel

¹⁴ Arioch was the king's official in charge of putting the wise men to death. He was on his way to have it done, when Daniel very wisely went to him ¹⁵ and asked, "Why did the king give such cruel⁰ orders?" After Arioch explained what had happened, ¹⁶ Daniel rushed off and said to the king, "If you will just give me some time, I'll explain your dream."

¹⁷ Daniel returned home and told his three friends. ¹⁸ Then he said, "Pray that the God who rules from heaven will be merciful and explain this mystery, so that we and the others won't be put to death." ¹⁹ In a vision one night, Daniel was shown the dream and its meaning. Then he praised the God who rules from heaven:

> ²⁰ "Our God, your name
>   will be praised
>   for ever and for ever.
> You are all-powerful,
>   and you know everything.
> ²¹ You control human events —
>   you give rulers their power
>   and take it away,
>   and you are the source
>   of wisdom and knowledge.
> ²² "You explain deep mysteries,
>   because even the dark
>   is light to you.
> ²³ You are the God
>   who was worshipped
>   by my ancestors.
>   Now I thank you and praise you
>   for making me wise
>   and telling me the king's dream,
>   together with its meaning."

Daniel interprets the dream

²⁴ Daniel went back to Arioch, the official in charge of executing the wise men. Daniel said, "Don't kill those men! Take me to the king, and I will explain the meaning of his dream."

²⁵ Arioch rushed Daniel to the king and announced, "Your Majesty, I have found out that one of the men brought here from Judah can explain your dream."

²⁶ The king asked Daniel,⁰ "Can you tell me my dream and what it means?"

---

*1.21 first year of King Cyrus: 539 BC.
*2.4 Aramaic: Chapters 2.4—7.28 are written in Aramaic, a language closely related to Hebrew.

27 Daniel answered:

Your Majesty, not even the cleverest person in all the world can do what you are demanding. 28-29 But the God who rules from heaven can explain mysteries. And while you were sleeping, he showed you what will happen in the future. 30 However, you must realize that these mysteries weren't explained to me because I am cleverer than everyone else. Instead, it was done so that you would understand what you have seen.

31 Your Majesty, what you saw standing in front of you was a huge and terrifying statue, shining brightly. 32 Its head was made of gold, its chest and arms were silver, and from its waist down to its knees, it was bronze. 33 From there to its ankles it was iron, and its feet were a mixture of iron and clay.

34 As you watched, a stone was cut from a mountain — but not by human hands. The stone struck the feet, completely shattering the iron and clay. 35 Then the iron, the clay, the bronze, the silver, and the gold were crushed and blown away without a trace, like husks of wheat at threshing time. But the stone became a tremendous mountain that covered the entire earth.

36 That was the dream, and now I'll tell you what it means. 37 Your Majesty, you are the greatest of kings, and God has highly honoured you with power 38 over all humans, animals, and birds. You are the head of gold. 39 After you are gone, another kingdom will rule, but it won't be as strong. Then it will be followed by a kingdom of bronze that will rule the whole world. 40 Next, a kingdom of iron will come to power, crushing and shattering everything.'

41-42 This fourth kingdom will be divided — it will be both strong and brittle, just as you saw that the feet and toes were a mixture of iron and clay. 43 This kingdom will be the result of a marriage between kingdoms, but it will crumble, just as iron and clay don't stick together.

44-45 During the time of those kings, the God who rules from heaven will set up an eternal kingdom that will never fall. It will be like the stone that was cut from the mountain, but not by human hands — the stone that crushed the iron, bronze, clay, silver, and gold. Your Majesty, in your dream the great God has told you what is going to happen, and you can trust this interpretation.

Daniel is promoted

46 King Nebuchadnezzar bowed low to the ground and worshipped Daniel. Then he gave orders for incense to be burnt and a sacrifice of grain to be offered in honour of Daniel. 47 The king said, "Now I know that your God is above all other gods and kings, because he gave you the power to explain this mystery." 48 The king then presented Daniel with a lot of gifts; he promoted him to governor of Babylon Province and put him in charge of the other wise men. 49 At Daniel's request, the king appointed Shadrach, Meshach, and Abednego to high positions in Babylon Province, and he let Daniel stay on as a palace official.

God rescues Shadrach, Meshach, and Abednego

CHAPTER 3

King Nebuchadnezzar's gold statue

1 King Nebuchadnezzar ordered a gold statue to be built twenty-seven metres high and nearly three metres wide. He had it set up in Dura Valley near the city of Babylon, 2 and he commanded his governors, advisers, treasurers, judges, and his other officials to come from everywhere in his kingdom to the dedication of the statue. 3 So all of them came and stood in front of it.

4 Then an official stood up and announced:

People of every nation and race, now listen to the king's command! 5 Trumpets, flutes, harps, and all other kinds of musical instruments will soon start playing. When you hear the music, you must bow down and worship the statue that King Nebuchadnezzar has set up. 6 Anyone who refuses will at once be thrown into a flaming furnace.

7 As soon as the people heard the music, they bowed down and worshipped the gold statue that the king had set up.

8 Some Babylonians used this as a chance to accuse the Jews to King Nebuchadnezzar. 9 They said, "Your Majesty, we hope you live for ever! 10 You commanded everyone to bow down and worship the gold statue when the music played. 11 And you said that anyone who did not bow down and worship it would be thrown into a flaming furnace. 12 Sir, you appointed three men to high positions in Babylon Province, but they have disobeyed

you. Those Jews, Shadrach, Meshach, and Abednego, refuse to worship your gods and the statue you have set up."

¹³ King Nebuchadnezzar was furious. So he sent for the three young men and said, ¹⁴ "I hear that you refuse to worship my gods and the gold statue I have set up. ¹⁵ Now I am going to give you one more chance. If you bow down and worship the statue when you hear the music, everything will be all right. But if you don't, you will at once be thrown into a flaming furnace. No god can save you from me."

¹⁶ The three men replied, "Your Majesty, we don't need to defend ourselves. ¹⁷ The God we worship can save us from you and your flaming furnace. ¹⁸ But even if he doesn't, we still won't worship your gods and the gold statue you have set up."

¹⁹ Nebuchadnezzar's face twisted with anger at the three men. And he ordered the furnace to be heated seven times hotter than usual. ²⁰ Next, he commanded some of his strongest soldiers to tie up the men and throw them into the flaming furnace. ²¹⁻²³ The king wanted it done at that very moment. So the soldiers tied up Shadrach, Meshach, and Abednego and threw them into the flaming furnace with all their clothes still on, including their turbans. The fire was so hot that flames leaped out and killed the soldiers.

²⁴ Suddenly the king jumped up and shouted, "Weren't only three men tied up and thrown into the fire?"

"Yes, Your Majesty," the people answered.

²⁵ "But I see four men walking around in the fire," the king replied. "None of them is tied up or harmed, and the fourth one looks like a god."›

²⁶ Nebuchadnezzar went closer to the flaming furnace and said to the three young men, "You servants of the Most High God, come out at once!"

They came out, ²⁷ and the king's high officials, governors, and advisers all crowded around them. The men were not burnt, their hair wasn't scorched, and their clothes didn't even smell of smoke. ²⁸ King Nebuchadnezzar said:

Praise their God for sending an angel to rescue his servants! They trusted their God and refused to obey my commands. Yes, they chose to die rather than to worship or serve any god except their own. ²⁹ And I won't allow people of any nation or race to say anything against their God. Anyone who does will be chopped up and their houses will be torn down, because no other god has such great power to save.

³⁰ After this happened, the king appointed Shadrach, Meshach, and Abednego to even higher positions in Babylon Province.

Nebuchadnezzar loses his kingdom for seven years

CHAPTER 4

King Nebuchadnezzar's letter about his second dream

¹ King Nebuchadnezzar sent the following letter to the people of all nations and races on the earth:

Greetings to all of you!
² I am glad to tell about
    the wonderful miracles
    God Most High
    has done for me.
³ His miracles are mighty
    and marvellous.
He will rule for ever,
    and his kingdom
    will never end.

⁴ I was enjoying a time of peace and prosperity, ⁵ when suddenly I had some horrifying dreams and visions. ⁶ Then I commanded every wise man in Babylonia to appear in my court, so they could explain the meaning of my dream. ⁷ After they arrived, I told them my dream, but they were not able to say what it meant. ⁸ Finally, a young man named Daniel came in, and I told him the dream. The holy gods had given him special powers, and I had renamed him Belteshazzar after my own god.

⁹ I said, "Belteshazzar, not only are you the wisest of all advisers and counsellors, but the holy gods have given you special powers to solve the most difficult mysteries. So listen to what I dreamed and tell me what it means:

¹⁰ In my sleep I saw
    a very tall tree
    in the centre of the world.
¹¹ It grew stronger and higher,
    until it reached to heaven
and could be seen
    from anywhere on earth.

¹² It was covered with leaves
 and heavy with fruit —
   enough for all nations.
 Wild animals enjoyed its shade,
   birds nested in its branches,
 and all creatures on earth
   lived on its fruit.

¹³ "While I was in bed, having this vision,
a holy angel' came down from heaven
¹⁴ and shouted:

 'Chop down the tree
   and cut off its branches;
 strip off its leaves
   and scatter its fruit.
 Make the animals leave its shade
 and send the birds flying
   from its branches.
¹⁵ But leave its stump and roots
   in the ground,
 surrounded by grass
 and held by chains
   of iron and bronze.

 'Make sure that this ruler
   lives like the animals
 out in the open fields,
   unprotected from the dew.
¹⁶ Give him the mind
 of a wild animal
   for seven long years.'
¹⁷ This punishment is given
   at the command
   of the holy angels.'
 It will show to all who live
   that God Most High
     controls all kingdoms
 and chooses for their rulers
   persons of humble birth.'

¹⁸ "Daniel,' that was the dream that none of
the wise men in my kingdom were able to
understand. But I am sure that you will
understand what it means, because the holy
gods have given you some special powers."

¹⁹ For a while, Daniel' was terribly
confused and worried by what he was
thinking. But I said, "Don't be bothered
either by the dream or by what it means."
Daniel replied:

Your Majesty, I wish the dream had been
against your enemies. ²⁰ You saw a tree that
grew so big and strong that it reached up to
heaven and could be seen from anywhere
on earth. ²¹ Its leaves were beautiful, and it
produced enough fruit for all living
creatures; animals lived in its shade, and
birds nested in its branches. ²² Your

Majesty, that tree is you. Your glorious
reputation has reached heaven, and your
kingdom covers the earth.

²³ Then you saw a holy angel' come
down from heaven and say, "Chop down
the tree and destroy it! But leave its stump
and roots in the ground, fastened there by
a chain of iron and bronze. Let it stay for
seven years' out in the field with the wild
animals, unprotected from the dew."

²⁴ Your Majesty, God Most High has sent
you this message, and it means ²⁵ that you
will be forced to live with the wild animals,
far away from humans. You will eat grass
like a wild animal and live outdoors for
seven years,' until you learn that God Most
High controls all earthly kingdoms and
chooses their rulers. ²⁶ But he gave orders
not to disturb the stump and roots. This is
to show that you will be king once again,
after you learn that the God who rules
from heaven is in control. ²⁷ Your
Majesty, please be willing to do what I say.
Turn from your sins and start living right;
have mercy on those who are ill-treated.
Then all will go well with you for a long
time.

The rest of Nebuchadnezzar's letter about his second dream

²⁸⁻³⁰ About twelve months later, I was
walking on the flat roof of my royal palace
and admiring the beautiful city of Babylon,
when these things started happening to me.
I was saying to myself, "Just look at this
wonderful capital city that I have built by
my own power and for my own glory!"

³¹ But before I could finish speaking,
a voice from heaven interrupted:

King Nebuchadnezzar, this kingdom is no
longer yours. ³² You will be forced to live
with the wild animals, away from people.
For seven years' you will eat grass, as
though you were an ox, until you learn
that God Most High is in control of all
earthly kingdoms and that he is the one
who chooses their rulers.

³³ This was no sooner said than done — I
was forced to live like a wild animal; I ate
grass and was unprotected from the dew. As
time went by, my hair grew longer than
eagle feathers, and my fingernails looked
like the claws of a bird.

³⁴ Finally, I prayed to God in heaven, and
my mind was healed. Then I said:

"I praise and honour
  God Most High.
He lives for ever,
  and his kingdom
  will never end.
35 To him the nations
  are far less than nothing;
God controls the stars in the sky
  and everyone on this earth.
When God does something,
  we cannot change it
  or even ask why."

36 At that time my mind was healed, and once again I became the ruler of my glorious kingdom. My advisers and officials returned to me, and I had greater power than ever before. 37 That's why I say:

"Praise and honour the King
  who rules from heaven!
Everything he does
  is honest and fair,
and he can shatter the power
  of those who are proud."

King Belshazzar and the writing on the wall

CHAPTER 5

King Belshazzar's banquet

1 One evening, King Belshazzar gave a great banquet for a thousand of his highest officials, and he drank wine with them. 2 He got drunk and ordered his servants to bring in the gold and silver cups his father Nebuchadnezzar* had taken from the temple in Jerusalem. Belshazzar wanted the cups, so that he and all his wives and officials could drink from them.

3-4 When the gold cups were brought in, everyone at the banquet drank from them and praised their idols made of gold, silver, bronze, iron, wood, and stone.

5 Suddenly a human hand was seen writing on the plaster wall of the palace. The hand was just behind the lampstand, and the king could see it writing. 6 He was so frightened that his face turned pale, his knees started shaking, and his legs became weak.

---

*5.2 his father Nebuchadnezzar: Belshazzar was actually the son of King Nabonidus, who was from another family. But in ancient times, it was possible to refer to a previous king as the "father" of the present king.

7 The king called in his advisers, who claimed they could talk with the spirits of the dead and understand the meanings found in the stars. He told them, "The man who can read this writing and tell me what it means will become the third most powerful man in my kingdom. He will wear robes of royal purple and a gold chain around his neck."

8 All of King Belshazzar's highest officials came in, but not one of them could read the writing or tell what it meant, 9 and they were completely puzzled. Now the king was more afraid than ever before, and his face turned white as a ghost.

10 When the queen heard the king and his officials talking, she came in and said:

Your Majesty, I hope you live for ever! Don't be afraid or look so pale. 11 In your kingdom there is a man who has been given special powers by the holy gods. When your father Nebuchadnezzar was king, this man was known to be as clever, intelligent, and wise as the gods themselves. Your father put him in charge of all who claimed they could talk with the spirits or understand the meanings in the stars or tell about the future. 12 He also changed the man's name from Daniel to Belteshazzar. Not only is he wise and intelligent, but he can explain dreams and riddles and solve difficult problems. Send for Daniel, and he will tell you what the writing means.

13 When Daniel was brought in, the king said:

So you are Daniel, one of the captives my father brought back from Judah! 14 I was told that the gods have given you special powers and that you are intelligent and very wise. 15 Neither my advisers nor the men who talk with the spirits of the dead could read this writing or tell me what it means. 16 But I have been told that you understand everything and that you can solve difficult problems. Now then, if you can read this writing and tell me what it means, you will become the third most powerful man in my kingdom. You will wear royal purple robes and have a gold chain around your neck.

17 Daniel answered:

Your Majesty, I will read the writing and tell you what it means. But you may keep your gifts or give them to someone else. 18 Sir, the Most High God made your father a great and powerful man and brought him much honour and glory. ¹⁹ God did such great things for him that people of all nations and races shook with fear.

Your father had the power of life or death over everyone, and he could honour or ruin anyone he chose. ²⁰ But when he became proud and stubborn, his glorious kingdom was taken from him. ²¹ His mind became like that of an animal, and he was forced to stay away from people and live with wild donkeys. Your father ate grass like an ox, and he slept outside where his body was soaked with dew. He was forced to do this until he learnt that the Most High God rules all kingdoms on earth and chooses their kings.

²² King Belshazzar, you knew all this, but you still refused to honour the Lord who rules from heaven. ²³ Instead, you turned against him and ordered the cups from his temple to be brought here, so that you and your wives and officials could drink wine from them. You praised idols made of silver, gold, bronze, iron, wood, and stone, even though they cannot see or hear or think. You refused to worship the God who gives you breath and controls everything you do. ²⁴ That's why he sent the hand to write this message on the wall.

²⁵⁻²⁸ The words written there are *mene*, which means "numbered", *tekel*, which means "weighed", and *parsin*, which means "divided". God has numbered the days of your kingdom and has brought it to an end. He has weighed you on his balance scales, and you fall short of what it takes to be king. So God has divided your kingdom between the Medes and the Persians.

²⁹ Belshazzar gave a command for Daniel to be made the third most powerful man in his kingdom and to be given a purple robe and a gold chain.

³⁰ That same night, the king was killed. ³¹ Then Darius the Mede, who was sixty-two years old, took over his kingdom.

God rescues Daniel from the pit of lions

CHAPTER 6

¹ Darius divided his kingdom into a hundred and twenty states and placed a governor in charge of each one. ² In order to make sure that his government was run properly, Darius put three other officials in charge of the governors. One of these officials was Daniel. ³ And he did his work so much better than the other governors and officials that the king decided to let him govern the whole kingdom.

⁴ The other men tried to find something wrong with the way Daniel did his work for the king. But they could not accuse him of anything wrong, because he was honest and faithful and did everything he was supposed to do. ⁵ Finally, they said to one another, "We will never be able to bring any charge against Daniel, unless it has to do with his religion."

⁶ They all went to the king and said:

Your Majesty, we hope you live for ever! ⁷ All of your officials, leaders, advisers, and governors agree that you should make a law forbidding anyone to pray to any god or human except you for the next thirty days. Everyone who disobeys this law must be thrown into a pit of lions. ⁸ Order this to be written and then sign it, so it cannot be changed, just as no written law of the Medes and Persians can be changed."

⁹ So King Darius made the law and had it written down.

¹⁰ Daniel heard about the law, but when he returned home, he went upstairs and prayed in front of the window that faced Jerusalem. In the same way that he had always done, he knelt down in prayer three times a day, giving thanks to God.

¹¹ The men who had spoken to the king watched Daniel and saw him praying to his God for help. ¹² They went back to the king and said, "Didn't you make a law that forbids anyone to pray to any god or human except you for the next thirty days? And doesn't the law say that everyone who disobeys it will be thrown into a pit of lions?"

"Yes, that's the law I made," the king agreed. "And just like all written laws of the Medes and Persians, it cannot be changed."

¹³ The men then told the king, "That Jew named Daniel, who was brought here as a captive, refuses to obey you or the law that you ordered to be written. And he still prays to his god three times a day." ¹⁴ The king was really upset to hear about this, and for the rest of the day he tried to think how he could save Daniel.

¹⁵ At sunset the men returned and said, "Your Majesty, remember that no written law

of the Medes and Persians can be changed, not even by the king."

¹⁶ So Darius ordered Daniel to be brought out and thrown into a pit of lions. But he said to Daniel, "You have been faithful to your God, and I pray that he will rescue you."

¹⁷ A stone was rolled over the pit, and it was sealed. Then Darius and his officials stamped the seal to show that no one should let Daniel out. ¹⁸ All night long the king could not sleep. He did not eat anything, and he would not let anyone come in to entertain him.

¹⁹ At daybreak the king got up and ran to the pit. ²⁰ He was anxious and shouted, "Daniel, you were faithful and served your God. Was he able to save you from the lions?"

²¹ Daniel answered, "Your Majesty, I hope you live for ever! ²² My God knew that I was innocent, and he sent an angel to keep the lions from eating me. Your Majesty, I have never done anything to hurt you."

²³ The king was relieved to hear Daniel's voice, and he gave orders for him to be taken out of the pit. Daniel's faith in his God had kept him from being harmed. ²⁴ And the king ordered the men who had brought charges against Daniel to be thrown into the pit, together with their wives and children. But before they even reached the bottom, the lions ripped them to pieces.

²⁵ King Darius then sent this message to all people of every nation and race in the world:

"Greetings to all of you!
²⁶ I command everyone
    in my kingdom
to worship and honour
    the God of Daniel.
He is the living God,
    the one who lives for ever.
His power and his kingdom
    will never end.
²⁷ He rescues people
    and sets them free
    by working great miracles.
Daniel's God has rescued him
    from the power of the lions."

²⁸ All went well for Daniel while Darius was king, and even when Cyrus the Persian ruled.*

Daniel's vision of four beasts

CHAPTER 7

¹⁻² Daniel wrote:

In the first year of King Belshazzar* of Babylonia, I had some dreams and visions while I was asleep one night, and I wrote them down.

The four winds were stirring up the mighty sea, ³ when suddenly four powerful beasts came out of the sea. Each beast was different. ⁴ The first was like a lion with the wings of an eagle. As I watched, its wings were pulled off. Then it was lifted to an upright position and made to stand on two feet, just like a human, and it was given a human mind.

⁵ The second beast looked like a bear standing on its hind legs.ᵇ It held three ribs in its teeth, and it was told, "Attack! Eat all the flesh you want."

⁶ The third beast was like a leopard — except that it had four wings and four heads. It was given authority to rule.

⁷ The fourth beast was stronger and more terrifying than the others. Its huge teeth were made of iron, and what it didn't grind with its teeth, it smashed with its feet. It was different from the others, and it had horns on its head — ten of them. ⁸ Just as I was thinking about these horns, a smaller horn appeared, and three of the other horns were pulled up by the roots to make room for it. This horn had the eyes of a human and a mouth that spoke with great pride.

Judgment

Daniel wrote:

⁹ Thrones were set up
    while I was watching,
and the Eternal Godᵇ
    took his place.
His clothing and his hair
    were white as snow.
His throne was a blazing fire
    with fiery wheels,
¹⁰ and flames were dashing out
    from all around him.
Countless thousands

---

*7.1-2 first year of King Belshazzar: 554 BC.

See also: 7.3: Rev 13.1; 17.8.   7.4-6: Rev 13.2.
7.7: Rev 12.3; 13.1.   7.8: Rev 13.5-6.   7.9: a Rev 20.4;
b Rev 1.14.   7.10: a Rev 5.11; b Rev 20.12.

---

*6.28 Cyrus the Persian ruled: 539–530 BC.

were standing there
to serve him.
The time of judgment began,
and the books* were opened.

[11] I watched closely to see what would happen to this smaller horn because of the arrogant things it was saying. Then before my very eyes, the fourth beast was killed and its body destroyed by fire. [12] The other three beasts had their authority taken from them, but they were allowed to live a while longer.' [13] As I continued to watch the vision that night,

I saw what looked like
a son of man'
coming with the clouds of heaven,
and he was presented
to the Eternal God.'
[14] He was crowned king
and given power and glory,
so that all people
of every nation and race
would serve him.
He will rule for ever,
and his kingdom is eternal,
never to be destroyed.

The meaning of Daniel's vision

[15] Daniel wrote:

I was terrified by these visions, and I didn't know what to think. [16] So I asked one of those standing there,* and he explained, [17] "The four beasts are four earthly kingdoms. [18] But God Most High will give his kingdom to his chosen ones, and it will be theirs for ever and ever."

[19] I wanted to know more about the fourth beast,* because it was so different and much more terrifying than the others. What was the meaning of its iron teeth and bronze claws and of its feet that smashed what the teeth and claws had not ground and crushed? [20] I also wanted to know more about all ten of those horns on its head. I especially wanted to know more about the one that took the place of three of the

others — the horn that had eyes and spoke with arrogance and seemed greater than the others. [21] While I was looking, this horn attacked God's chosen ones and was winning the battle. [22] Then God Most High, the Eternal God,' came and judged in favour of his chosen ones, because the time had arrived for them to be given the kingdom.

[23] Then I was told
by the one standing there:
"The fourth beast
will be a fourth kingdom
to appear on earth.
It will be different
from all the others —
it will trample the earth
and crush it to pieces.
[24] All ten of those horns are kings
who will come from this kingdom,
and one more will follow.
This horn will be different
from the others,
and it will conquer
three other kings.

[25] "This king will speak evil
of God Most High,
and he will be cruel
to God's chosen ones.
He will try to change God's Law
and the sacred seasons.
And he will be able to do this
for a time, two times,
and half a time.'
[26] But he will finally be judged,
and his kingdom
completely destroyed.

[27] "Then the greatest kingdom of all
will be given
to the chosen ones
of God Most High.
His kingdom will be eternal,
and all others will serve
and obey him."

[28] That was what I saw and heard. I turned pale with fear and kept it all to myself.

---

*7.10 **books:** Containing the record of the good and evil that each person has done.
*7.16 **one of those standing there:** Possibly an angel sent to interpret the visions or one of those thousands mentioned in verse 10.
*7.19 **fourth beast:** See verses 7–8.

See also: **7.13:** Matt 24.30; 26.64; Mark 13.26; 14.62; Luke 21.27; Rev 1.7,13; 14.14. **7.14:** Rev 11.15. **7.18:** Rev 22.5.

See also: **7.21:** Rev 13.7.   **7.22:** Rev 20.4.   **7.24:** Rev 17.12. **7.25:** Rev 12.14; 13.5–6.   **7.27: a** Rev 20.4; **b** Rev 22.5.

Daniel's vision of a ram and a goat

CHAPTER 8

[1] Daniel wrote:

In the third year of King Belshazzar of Babylonia,* I had a second vision [2] in which I was in Susa, the chief city of Babylonia's Elam Province. I was beside the River⸗ Ulai, [3] when I looked up and saw a ram standing there with two horns on its head — both of them were long, but the second one was longer than the first. [4] The ram went charging towards the west, the north, and the south. No other animals were strong enough to oppose him, and nothing could save them from his power. So he did as he pleased and became even more powerful.

[5] I kept on watching and saw a goat come from the west and charge across the entire earth, without even touching the ground. Between his eyes was a powerful horn,⸗ [6] and with tremendous anger the goat started towards the ram that I had seen beside the river.⸗ [7] The goat was so fierce that its attack broke both horns of the ram, leaving him powerless. Then the goat trampled on the ram, and no one could do anything to help. [8] After this, the goat became even more powerful. But at the peak of his power, his mighty horn was broken, and four other mighty horns took its place — one pointing to the north and one to the east, one to the south and one to the west.

[9] A little horn came from one of these, and its power reached to the south, the east, and even to the holy land.⸗ [10] It became so strong that it attacked the stars in the sky, which were heaven's army.* Then it threw some of them down to the earth and trampled on them. [11-12] It humiliated heaven's army and dishonoured its leader⸗ by keeping him from offering the daily sacrifices. In fact, it was so terrible that it even disgraced the temple and wiped out true worship. It also did everything else it wanted to do.

[13] Then one of the holy angels asked another, "When will the daily sacrifices be offered again? What about this horrible rebellion? When will the temple and heaven's army no longer be trampled in the dust?"

[14] The other answered, "It will be two thousand three hundred evenings and mornings before the temple is dedicated and in use again."

Gabriel interprets the vision

[15] Daniel wrote:

I was trying to understand the meaning of the vision, when someone suddenly appeared there beside me. [16] And from beside the River⸗ Ulai, a voice like that of a human said, "Gabriel, help him understand the vision."

[17] Gabriel came over, and I fell to the ground in fear. Then he said, "You are merely a human, but you need to understand that this vision is about the end of time."

[18] While he was speaking, I fell face down in a deep sleep. But he lifted me to my feet [19] and said:

Listen, and I will tell you what will happen at the end of time, when God has chosen to show his anger. [20] The two horns of the ram are the kings of Media and Persia, [21] the goat is the kingdom of Greece, and the powerful horn between his eyes is the first of its kings. [22] After this horn is broken, four other kingdoms will appear, but they won't be as strong.

[23] When these rulers have become as evil as possible, their power will end, and then a king who is dangerous and cannot be trusted will appear. [24] He will gain strength, but not on his own, and he will cause terrible destruction. He will wipe out powerful leaders and God's people as well. [25] His deceitful lies will make him so successful, that he will think he is really great. Suddenly he will kill many people, and he will even attack God, the Supreme Ruler. But God will crush him!

[26] This vision about the evenings and mornings is true, but these things won't happen for a long time, so don't tell it to others.

[27] After this, I was so worn out and weak that it was several days before I could get out of bed and go about my duties for the king. I was disturbed by this vision that made no sense to me.

---

*8.1 third year . . . Babylonia: 552 BC, two years after the first vision (see 7.1–2).
*8.10 heaven's army: In verses 10–13 the Hebrew word translated "heaven's army" may also mean "God's people".
See also: 8.10: Rev 12.4.

See also: 8.16: Luke 1.19,26.

Daniel prays for his people

CHAPTER 9

1-2 Daniel wrote:

Some years later, Darius the Mede,* who was the son of Xerxes,' had become king of Babylonia. And during his first year as king, I found out from studying the writings of the prophets that the LORD had said to Jeremiah, "Jerusalem will lie in ruins for seventy years."* 3-4 Then, to show my sorrow, I went without eating and dressed in sackcloth* and sat in ashes. I confessed my sins and earnestly prayed to the LORD my God:

Our Lord, you are a great and fearsome God, and you faithfully keep your agreement with those who love and obey you. 5 But we have sinned terribly by rebelling against you and rejecting your laws and teachings. 6 We have ignored the message your servants the prophets spoke to our kings, our leaders, our ancestors, and everyone else.

7 Everything you do is right, our Lord. But still we suffer public disgrace because we have been unfaithful and have sinned against you. This includes all of us, both far and near — the people of Judah, Jerusalem, and Israel, as well as those you dragged away to foreign lands, 8 and even our kings, our officials, and our ancestors. 9 LORD God, you are merciful and forgiving, even though we have rebelled against you 10 and rejected your teachings that came to us from your servants the prophets.

11 Everyone in Israel has stubbornly refused to obey your laws, and so those curses written by your servant Moses have fallen upon us. 12 You warned us and our leaders that Jerusalem would suffer the worst disaster in human history, and you did exactly as you had threatened. 13 We have not escaped any of the terrible curses written by Moses, and yet we have refused to beg you for mercy and to remind ourselves of how faithful you have always been. 14 And when you finally punished us with this horrible disaster, that was also the right thing to do, because we deserved it so much.

15 Our Lord God, with your own mighty arm you rescued us from Egypt and made yourself famous to this very day, but we have sinned terribly. 16 In the past, you treated us with such kindness, that we now beg you to stop being so terribly angry with Jerusalem. After all, it is your chosen city built on your holy mountain, even though it has suffered public disgrace because of our sins and those of our ancestors.

17 I am your servant, Lord God, and I beg you to answer my prayers and bring honour to yourself by having pity on your temple that lies in ruins. 18 Please show mercy to your chosen city, not because we deserve it, but because of your great kindness. 19 Forgive us! Hurry and do something, not only for your city and your chosen people, but to bring honour to yourself.

The seventy weeks

Daniel wrote:

20 I was still confessing my sins and those of all Israel to the LORD my God, and I was praying for the good of his holy mountain,* 21 when Gabriel suddenly came flying in at the time of the evening sacrifice. This was the same Gabriel I had seen in my vision, 22 and he explained:

Daniel, I am here to help you understand the vision. 23 God thinks highly of you, and at the very moment you started praying, I was sent to give you the answer. 24 God has decided that for seventy weeks,' your people and your holy city must suffer as the price of their sins. Then evil will disappear, and justice will rule for ever; the visions and words of the prophets will come true, and a most holy place will be dedicated.'

25 You need to realize that from the command to rebuild Jerusalem until the coming of the Chosen Leader,' it will be seven weeks and another sixty-two weeks.' Streets will be built in Jerusalem, and a trench will be dug around the city for protection, but these will be difficult times.' 26 At the end of the sixty-two weeks,' the Chosen Leader' will be killed and left with nothing.'

A foreign ruler and his army will sweep down like a mighty flood, leaving both the city and the temple in ruins, and war and

---

*9.1-2 Darius the Mede: See 5.31.
*9.1-2 seventy years: See Jeremiah 25.11-13; 29.10.
*9.3-4 sackcloth: A rough, dark-coloured cloth made from goat or camel hair and used to make grain sacks. It was worn in times of trouble or sorrow.
See also: 9.2: Jer 25.11; 29.10.

---

*9.20 holy mountain: Jerusalem (see verse 16) or the temple.
See also: 9.21: Luke 1.19,26.

destruction will continue until the end, just as God has decided. 27 For one week⟩ this foreigner⟩ will make a firm agreement with many people, and halfway through this week,⟩ he will end all sacrifices and offerings. Then the "Horrible Thing" that causes destruction will be put there. And it will stay there until the time God has decided to destroy this one who destroys.

Daniel has a vision beside the River Tigris

CHAPTER 10

1 In the third year* of Cyrus the king of Persia, a message came to Daniel⟩ from God, and it was explained in a vision. The message was about a horrible war, and it was true. 2 Daniel wrote:

For three weeks I was in sorrow. 3 I ate no fine food or meat, I drank no wine, and I put no olive oil on my face or hair.* 4 Then, on the twenty-fourth day of the first month,* I was standing on the banks of the great River Tigris, 5 when I looked up and saw someone dressed in linen and wearing a solid gold belt.⟩ 6 His body was like a precious stone,⟩ his face like lightning, his eyes like flaming fires, his arms and legs like polished bronze, and his voice like the roar of a crowd. 7 Although the people who were with me did not see the vision, they became so frightened that they scattered and hid. 8 Only I saw this great vision. I became weak and pale, 9 and at the sound of his voice, I fell face down in a deep sleep.

10 He raised me to my hands and knees 11 and then said, "Daniel, your God thinks highly of you, and he has sent me. So stand up and pay close attention." I stood trembling, while the angel said:

12 Daniel, don't be afraid! God has listened to your prayers since the first day you humbly asked for understanding, and he has sent me here. 13 But the guardian angel⟩ of Persia opposed me for twenty-one days.

Then Michael, who is one of the strongest guardian angels,⟩ came to rescue me from the kings of Persia.⟩ 14 Now I have come here to give you another vision about what will happen to your people in the future.

15 While this angel was speaking to me, I stared at the ground, speechless. 16 Then he appeared in human form and touched my lips. I said, "Sir, this vision has brought me great pain and has drained my strength. 17 I am merely your servant. How can I possibly speak with someone so powerful, when I am almost too weak to get my breath?"

18-19 The angel touched me a second time and said, "Don't be frightened! God thinks highly of you, and he intends this for your good, so be brave and strong."

At this, I regained my strength and replied, "Please speak! You have already made me feel much better." 20 Then the angel said:

Now do you understand why I have come? Soon I must leave to fight against the guardian angel of Persia. Then after I have defeated him, the guardian angel of Greece will attack me. 21 I will tell you what is written in *The Book of Truth.* But first, you must realize that no one except Michael, the guardian angel of Israel, is on my side.

CHAPTER 11

1 You also need to know that I protected and helped Darius the Mede* in his first year as king.

The angel's message to Daniel

Part one: the four kings and their successors

2 What I am going to tell you is certain to happen. Four kings will rule Persia, one after the other, but the fourth one will become much richer than the others. In fact, his wealth will make him so powerful that he will turn everyone against the kingdom of Greece. 3 Then a mighty king will come to power and will be able to do whatever he pleases. 4 But suddenly his kingdom will be crushed and scattered to the four corners of the earth, where four more kingdoms will rise. But these won't be ruled by his descendants or be as powerful as his kingdom.

---

*10.1 **third year:** 536 BC.
*10.3 **olive oil . . . hair:** On special occasions, it was the custom to put olive oil on one's face and hair.
*10.4 **first month:** Nisan (also known as Abib), the first month of the Hebrew calendar, from about mid-March to mid-April.
See also: 9.27: Dan 11.31; 12.11; Matt 24.15; Mark 13.14. 10.5–6: Rev 1.13–15; 2.18; 19.12. 10.13: Rev 12.7.

*11.1 **Darius the Mede:** See 5.31.
See also: 10.21: Rev 12.7.

⁵ The king of the south will grow powerful. Then one of his generals will rebel and take over most of the kingdom. ⁶ Years later the southern kingdom and the northern kingdom will make a treaty, and the daughter of the king of the south will marry the king of the north. But she will lose her power. Then she, her husband, their child,ᶦ and the servants who came with her will all be killed.

After this, ⁷ one of her relatives will become the ruler of the southern kingdom. He will attack the army of the northern kingdom and capture its fortresses. ⁸ Then he will carry their idols to Egypt, together with their precious treasures of silver and gold, but it will be a long time before he attacks the northern kingdom again. Some years later ⁹ the king of the north will invade the southern kingdom, but he will be forced back to his own country.

¹⁰ The sons of the king of the north will gather a huge army that will sweep down like a roaring flood, reaching all the way to the fortress of the southern kingdom. ¹¹ But this will make the king of the south angry, and he will defeat this large army from the north. ¹² The king of the south will feel proud because of the many thousands he has killed. But his victories won't last long, ¹³ because the king of the north will gather a larger and more powerful army than ever before. Then in a few years, he will start invading other countries.

¹⁴ At this time many of your own people will try to make this vision come true by rebelling against the king of the south, but their rebellion will fail. ¹⁵ Then the army from the north will surround and capture a fortress in the south, and not even the most experienced troops of the southern kingdom will be able to make them retreat. ¹⁶ The king who invaded from the north will do as he pleases, and he will even capture and destroy the holy land.ᶦ ¹⁷ In fact, he will decide to invade the south with his entire army. Then he will attempt to make peace by giving the king of the south a bride from the northern kingdom, but this won't be successful.

¹⁸ Afterwards, this proud king of the north will invade and conquer many of the nations along the coast, but a military leader will defeat him and make him lose his pride. ¹⁹ He will retreat to his fortresses in his own country, but on the way he will be defeated and never again be seen.

²⁰ The next king of the north will try to collect taxes for the glory of his kingdom. However, he will come to a sudden end in some mysterious way, instead of in battle or because of someone's anger.

Part two: the evil king from the north

²¹ The successor of this king of the north will be a worthless nobody, who doesn't come from a royal family. He will suddenly appear and gain control of the kingdom by treachery. ²² Then he will destroy armies and remove God's chosen high priest. ²³ He will make a treaty, but he will be deceitful and break it, even though he has only a few followers. ²⁴ Without warning, he will successfully invade a wealthy province, which is something his ancestors never did. Then he will divide among his followers all of its treasures and property. But none of this will last very long.

²⁵ He will gather a large and powerful army, and with great courage he will attack the king of the south. The king of the south will meet him with a much stronger army, but he will lose the battle, because he will be betrayed ²⁶ by members of the royal court. He will be ruined, and most of his army will be slaughtered.

²⁷ The two kings will meet around a table and tell evil lies to each other. But their plans will fail, because God has already decided what will happen. ²⁸ Then the king of the north will return to his country with great treasures. But on the way, he will attack the religion of God's people and do whatever else he pleases.

²⁹ At the time God has decided, the king of the north will invade the southern kingdom again, but this time, things will be different. ³⁰ Ships from the west will come to attack him, and he will be discouraged. Then he will start back to his own country and take out his anger on the religion of God's faithful people, while showing kindness to those who are unfaithful. ³¹ He will send troops to pollute the temple and the fortress, and he will stop the daily sacrifices. Then he will set up that "Horrible Thing" that causes destruction. ³² The king will use deceit to win followers from those who are unfaithful to God, but those who remain faithful will do everything possible to oppose him.

See also: **11.31:** Dan 9.27; 12.11; Matt 24.15; Mark 13.14.

³³ Wise leaders will instruct many of the people. But for a while, some of these leaders will either be killed with swords or burnt alive, or else robbed of their possessions and thrown into prison. ³⁴ They will receive only a little help in their time of trouble, and many of their followers will be treacherous. ³⁵ Some of those who are wise will suffer, so that God will make them pure and acceptable until the end, which will still come at the time he has decided.

³⁶ This king will do as he pleases. He will proudly claim to be greater than any god and will insult the only true God. Indeed, he will be successful until God is no longer angry with his people. ³⁷ This king will reject the gods his ancestors worshipped and the god preferred by women.* In fact, he will put himself above all gods ³⁸ and worship only the so-called god of fortresses, who was unknown to his ancestors. And he will honour it with gold, silver, precious stones, and other costly gifts. ³⁹ With the help of this foreign god, he will capture the strongest fortresses. Everyone who worships this god will be put in a position of power and rewarded with wealth and land.

Part three: the time of the end

⁴⁰ At the time of the end, the king of the south will attack the kingdom of the north. But its king will rush out like a storm with war chariots, cavalry, and many ships. Indeed, his forces will flood one country after another, ⁴¹ and when they reach the holy land,' tens of thousands will be killed. But the countries of Edom and Moab and the ruler of Ammon' will escape.

⁴² The king of the north will invade many countries, including Egypt, ⁴³ and he will take its rich treasures of gold and silver. He will also conquer Libya and Ethiopia.* ⁴⁴ But he will be alarmed by news from the east and the north, and he will become furious and cause great destruction. ⁴⁵ After this, he will set up camp between the Mediterranean Sea and Mount Zion. Then he will be destroyed, and no one will be able to save him.

CHAPTER 12

Part four: the dead will rise to life

¹ Michael, the chief of the angels, is the protector of your people, and he will come at a time of terrible suffering, the worst in all of history. And your people who have their names written in *The Book** will be protected. ² Many of those who lie dead in the ground will rise from death. Some of them will be given eternal life, and others will receive nothing but eternal shame and disgrace. ³ Everyone who has been wise will shine as bright as the sky above, and everyone who has led others to please God will shine like the stars.

⁴ Daniel, I now command you to keep the message of this book secret until the end of time, even though many people will go everywhere, searching for the knowledge to be found in it.'

The end of time

⁵ Daniel wrote:

I looked around and saw two other people — one on this side of the river and one on the other side. ⁶ The angel who had spoken to me was dressed in linen and was standing upstream from them.* So one of the two beside the river asked him, "How long before these amazing things happen?"

⁷ The angel then raised both hands towards heaven and said, "In the name of the God who lives for ever, I solemnly promise that it will be a time, two times, and half a time.* Everything will be over, when the suffering of God's holy people comes to an end."

⁸ I heard what the angel said, but I didn't understand. So I asked, "Sir, how will it all end?"

The angel in my vision then replied:

⁹ Daniel, go about your business, because the meaning of this message will remain secret until the end of time. ¹⁰ Many people will have their hearts and lives made pure

---

*11.37 god preferred by women: Perhaps Tammuz or Adonis, which were popular among the women of that time.
*11.43 Ethiopia: The Hebrew text has "Cush", which was a region south of Egypt that included parts of the present countries of Ethiopia and Sudan.
See also: 11.36: a 2 Thes 2.3–4; b Rev 13.5–6.

*12.1 The Book: Either the book with the names of God's people in it or the book with the record of the good and evil that people have done.
*12.6 angel . . . upstream from them: See 10.4–6.
*12.7 a time, two times, and half a time: Or "a year, two years, and half a year", that is, about 1260 days.
See also: 12.1: a Rev 12.7; b Matt 24.21; Mark 13.19; Rev 7.14; 12.7. 12.2: a Isa 26.19; Matt 25.46; John 5.29. 12.4: Rev 22.10. 12.7: a Rev 10.5; b Rev 12.14. 12.10: Rev 22.11.

and clean, but those who are evil will keep on being evil and never understand. Only the wise will understand. ¹¹ There will be one thousand two hundred and ninety days from the time that the daily sacrifices are stopped, until someone sets up the "Horrible Thing" that causes destruction. ¹² God will bless everyone who patiently waits until one thousand three hundred and thirty-five days have gone by.

¹³ So, Daniel, be faithful until the end! You will rest, and at the end of time, you will rise from death to receive your reward.

See also: 12.11: Dan 9.27; 11.31; Matt 24.15; Mark 13.14.

Additional notes

›**1.2 Babylonia:** The Hebrew text has "Shinar", another name for Babylonia.

›**2.15 cruel:** Or "urgent".

›**2.26 Daniel:** Aramaic "Daniel whose name was Belteshazzar" (see 1.7).

›**2.40 crushing . . . everything:** Three ancient translations; Aramaic adds "and like iron crushing".

›**3.25 a god:** Aramaic, "a son of the gods".

›**4.13 angel:** The Aramaic text has "watcher", which may be some special class of angel.

›**4.16 long years:** Aramaic "times".

›**4.17 angel:** See the note at 4.13.

›**4.18 Daniel:** See the note at 2.26.

›**4.19 Daniel:** See the note at 2.26.

›**4.23 angel:** See the note at 4.13.

›**4.23 years:** See the note at 4.16.

›**4.25 years:** See the note at 4.16.

›**4.32 years:** See the note at 4.16.

›**5.25–28 mene . . . tekel . . . parsin:** In the Aramaic text of verse 25, the words "mene, tekel, parsin," are used, and in verses 26–28 the words "mene, tekel, peres" (the singular of "parsin") are used. "Parsin" means "divided", but "peres" can mean either "divided" or "Persia".

›**7.5 standing on its hind legs:** Or "higher on one side than the other" or "with a paw lifted up".

›**7.9 Eternal God:** Aramaic "Ancient of Days".

›**7.12 a while longer:** Aramaic "for a time and a season".

›**7.13 son of man:** Or "human". In Aramaic "son of man" may mean a human or even "oneself" ("I" or "me"). Jesus often used the phrase "the Son of Man" when referring to himself.

›**7.13 Eternal God:** See the note at 7.9.

›**7.22 Eternal God:** See the note at 7.9.

›**7.25 for . . . time:** Or "for a year, two years, and half a year".

›**8.2 River:** Or "Gate".

›**8.5 powerful horn:** Hebrew "horn of vision".

›**8.6 river:** See the note at 8.2.

›**8.9 holy land:** Hebrew "the lovely land".

›**8.11–12 leader:** Hebrew "prince".

›**8.16 River:** See the note at 8.2.

›**9.1–2 Xerxes:** Hebrew "Ahasuerus".

›**9.24 seventy weeks:** Or "seventy times seven years".

›**9.24 a most holy place will be dedicated:** Or "God's Holy One will appear".

›**9.25 the Chosen Leader:** Or "a chosen leader". In Hebrew the word "chosen" means "to pour oil (on someone's head)". In Old Testament times it was the custom to pour oil on a person's head when that person was chosen to be a priest or a king.

›**9.25 seven weeks and another sixty-two weeks:** Or "seven times seven years and another sixty-two times seven years".

›**9.25 it will be seven . . . difficult times:** Or "it will be seven weeks. Then streets will be built in Jerusalem, and a trench will be dug around the city for protection. But Jerusalem will have difficult times for sixty-two weeks."

›**9.26 sixty-two weeks:** Or "sixty-two times seven years".

›**9.26 the Chosen Leader:** See the note at 9.25.

›**9.26 left with nothing:** Or "no one will take his place".

›**9.27 one week:** Or "seven years".

›**9.27 this foreigner:** Or "the Chosen Leader".

›**9.27 halfway through this week:** Or "for half of this week of seven years."

›**10.1 Daniel:** See the note at 2.26.

›**10.5 solid gold belt:** Hebrew "belt of gold from Uphaz".

›**10.6 a precious stone:** The Hebrew text has "beryl", which is green or bluish-green.

›**10.13 guardian angel:** Hebrew "prince".

›**10.13 one of the strongest guardian angels:** Hebrew "chief prince".

›**10.13 came . . . Persia:** One possible meaning for the difficult Hebrew text.

›**11.6 their child:** One Hebrew manuscript and two ancient translations; most Hebrew manuscripts "her father".

›**11.16 the holy land:** See the note at 8.9.

›**11.41 the holy land:** See the note at 8.9.

›**11.41 the ruler of Ammon:** Or "what is left of Ammon".

›**12.4 even though . . . in it:** One possible meaning for the difficult Hebrew text.

Hosea

The basics

What's the point? To show how God loves his people – despite their unfaithfulness.

What happens? The prophet Hosea marries a prostitute, to demonstrate how much God loves his people, despite their unfaithfulness.

What should I remember? 6.6 'I'd rather you were faithful and knew me than offered sacrifices.'

More details

Setting the scene Hosea is a prophet in the northern kingdom of Israel, during its final years. God tells him to get married. But there's a catch; the woman who he is to marry is a prostitute...

What's it all about? Hosea is a dramatic tale of one man's love for his unfaithful wife. It's a picture of how God loves his unfaithful people. Hosea's love for his wife mirrors the merciful, forgiving love of God.

And the message was this: despite their faithlessness, God still loves his people. He doesn't want to punish them, but the way they have 'slept' with other gods gives him little choice.

This is a violent and unsettled society. The people are dishonest; the priests are idol worshippers; the kings are corrupt. Like Amos, Hosea condemns social injustice and the false gods and fake worship which bring it forth.

It was a message which was to consume his entire life. He had to marry a woman who would be unfaithful to him. He even named his children to show how God is feeling. He was a living prophecy, a 3-D message from God.

The heart of his message is found in chapter 6. God doesn't want a load of meaningless sacrifices, he wants real faith. He wants his people to be like Hosea, to live for their God, to be living examples of what the living God can do. What would our society say, I wonder, if we lived out the truth of God as completely and compellingly as Hosea did?

But they choose their own path. And they will have to bear their own punishment. Still the book ends with a vision of a final reconcilaition. There will be punishment, but there will also be forgiveness. There will be unfaithfulness but there will always be love.

Footsteps

Hosea's family: 1.1—2.1
Punishment and hope: 2.2—3.5
False priests, false people: 4.4–19
Pretend worship: 6.1–11
My child: 11.1–11
Terrible fate: 13.1–16
Future forgiveness: 14.1–9

Hosea's family is a picture of the Lord's unfaithful people

CHAPTER 1

[1] I am Hosea son of Beeri. When Uzziah, Jotham, Ahaz, and Hezekiah were the kings

---

See also: 1.1: a 2 King 15.1–7; 2 Chron 26.1–23;
b 2 King 15.32–38; 2 Chron 27.1–8; **c** 2 King 16.1–20;
2 Chron 28.1–27; **d** 2 King 18.1–20.21; 2 Chron 29.1–32.33;
e 2 King 14.23–29.

Holy history

Performing prophets

Being a prophet was not just about speaking your message, or even writing it down.

Being a prophet was about living out your message.

Prophets like Hosea and Ezekiel had to 'act out' their prophecies, performing dramatic acts to make a point to the people. Ezekiel had to cook over dung (Ezekiel 4.1–17), weigh his hair (Ezekiel 5.1–6), knock a hole in his wall (Ezekiel 12.1–16) and, perhaps most painfully, he was ordered not to mourn the death of his wife (Ezekiel 24.15–27). Jeremiah wore a yoke (Jeremiah 27.1–11), smashed some jars (Jeremiah 19.1–13) and threw away his underwear (Jeremiah 12.1–11).

Hosea's entire life was a prophetic act: he married a prostitute who slept around, he named his children 'Not pitied' and 'Not my people': he was a living metaphor.

 Anorak corner

10 of the worst meals in the Bible

Donkey head and pigeon droppings
(2 Kings 6.25)
Your own son (2 Kings 6.28)
Your own bodily waste and urine
(Isaiah 36.12)
Pigs, lizards, and mice. (Isaiah 66.17)
Your friends (Jeremiah 19.9)
Gravel (Lamentations 3.16)
A scroll (Ezekiel 3.1–3)
Your own parents (Ezekiel 5.10)
Grass (Daniel 4.25)
Grasshoppers (Matthew 3.4)

of Judah, and when Jeroboam son of Jehoash⁾ was king of Israel,* the LORD spoke this message to me.

Hosea's family

2 The LORD said, "Hosea, Israel has betrayed me like an unfaithful wife.* Marry such a woman and have children by her." 3 So I married Gomer the daughter of Diblaim, and we had a son.

4 Then the LORD said, "Hosea, name your son Jezreel,* because I will soon punish the descendants of King Jehu of Israel for the murders he committed in Jezreel Valley.* I will destroy his kingdom, 5 and in Jezreel Valley I will break the power of Israel."

6 Later, Gomer had a daughter, and the LORD said, "Name her Lo-Ruhamah,* because I will no longer have mercy and forgive Israel. 7 But I am the LORD God of Judah, and I will have mercy and save Judah by my own power — not by wars and arrows or swords and cavalry."

8 After Gomer had stopped nursing Lo-Ruhamah, she had another son. 9 Then the LORD said, "Name him Lo-Ammi,* because these people are not mine, and I am not their God."

Hope for Israel

The LORD said:

10 Some day it will be impossible to count
the people of Israel, because there will be as

---

*1.1 kings of Judah . . . king of Israel: Uzziah (781–740 BC), Jotham (740–736), Ahaz (736–716), Hezekiah (716–687), and Jeroboam II (783–743).
*1.2 unfaithful wife: In some Canaanite religions of Old Testament times, young women were expected to have sex with the worshippers of their god before marriage. Such women were called "temple prostitutes". Many of the Israelite women did this same thing, and Hosea is told to marry one of them to show that the nation has turned from the LORD to worship idols.
*1.4 Jezreel: In Hebrew "Jezreel" means "God scatters (seed)". Here the name is used as a threat (meaning the LORD will punish Israel by scattering its people), while in verse 11 it is used as a promise (meaning the LORD will bless Israel by giving their nation many people, just as a big harvest comes when many seeds are scattered in a field).
*1.4 murders . . . Valley: Jehu murdered the wife and relatives of King Ahab (see 2 Kings 9.15—10.14).
*1.6 Lo-Ruhamah: In Hebrew "Lo-Ruhamah" means "No Mercy".
*1.9 Lo-Ammi: In Hebrew "Lo-Ammi" means "Not My People".
See also: 1.4: 2 King 10.11. **1.10:** Rom 9.26.

many of them as there are grains of sand along the seashore. They are now called "Not My People", but in the future they will be called "Children of the Living God".
¹¹ Israel and Judah will unite and choose one leader. Then they will take back their land, and this will be a great day for Jezreel.*

CHAPTER 2

¹ So let your brothers be called "My People" and your sisters be called "Shown Mercy".*

The LORD promises to punish Israel

² Accuse! Accuse your mother!
  She is no longer my wife,
  and now I, the LORD,
  am not her husband.
Beg her to give up prostitution
  and stop being unfaithful,*
³ or I will strip her naked
  like the day she was born.
I will make her barren like a desert,
  and she will die of thirst.
⁴ You children are the result
  of her unfaithfulness,
  and I'll show you no pity.
⁵ Your mother was unfaithful.
  She was disgraceful and said,
  "I'll run after my lovers.
Everything comes from them —
  my food and drink,
  my linen and wool,
  my olive oil and wine."

⁶ I, the LORD, will build
  a fence of thorns
  to block her path.
⁷ She will run after her lovers,
  but not catch them;
  she will search,
  but not find them.
Then she will say, "I'll return
  to my first husband.
  Life was better then."
⁸ She didn't know that her grain,
  wine, and olive oil
  were gifts from me,
as were the gold and silver
  she used in worshipping Baal.*

⁹ So I'll hold back the harvest
  of grain and grapes.
I'll take back
  my wool and my linen
  that cover her body.
¹⁰ Then I'll strip her naked
  in the sight of her lovers.
  No one can rescue her.

¹¹ I'll stop Israel's celebrations —
  no more New Moon Festivals,
  Sabbaths, or other feasts.
¹² She said, "My lovers gave me
  vineyards and fig trees
  as payment for sex."

Now I, the LORD, will ruin
  her vineyards and fig trees;
they will become clumps of weeds
  eaten by wild animals.

¹³ I'll punish her for the days
  she worshipped Baal
  and burnt incense to him.
I'll punish her for the times
  she forgot about me
and wore jewellery and rings
  to attract her lovers.
  I, the LORD, have spoken!

The LORD will help Israel

¹⁴ Israel, I, the LORD,
  will lure you into the desert
  and speak gently to you.
¹⁵ I will return your vineyards,
  and then Trouble Valley*
  will become Hopeful Valley.
You will say "Yes" to me
  as you did in your youth,
  when leaving Egypt.

¹⁶ I promise that from that day on, you will call me your husband instead of your master.* ¹⁷ I will no longer even let you mention the names of those pagan gods that you called "Master". ¹⁸ And I will agree to let you live in peace — you will no longer be

---

*1.11 Jezreel: See the note at verse 4.
*2.1 My People . . . Shown Mercy: In Hebrew "My People" is "Ammi" and "Shown Mercy" is "Ruhamah" (see Lo-Ruhamah in 1.6 and Lo-Ammi in 1.9).
*2.2 prostitution . . . unfaithful: See the note at 1.2.
*2.8 Baal: A Canaanite god of fertility.

*2.15 Trouble Valley: Or "Achor Valley". The exact location of the valley is unknown, but in Hebrew "Achor" sounds like "Achan", who brought trouble on Israel by disobeying the LORD (see Joshua 7.24–26).
*2.16 husband . . . master: In Hebrew the word "master" is the same as the name of the god Baal. But the LORD promises that his people will have a deep personal relationship with him (like a devoted wife and husband) rather than merely a legal tie (like a wife and her "master").
See also: 2.15: Josh 7.24–26.

attacked by wild animals and birds or by weapons of war. ¹⁹ I will accept you as my wife for ever, and instead of a bride price* I will give you justice, fairness, love, kindness, ²⁰ and faithfulness. Then you will truly know who I am.

²¹ I will command the sky to send rain on the earth, ²² and it will produce grain, grapes, and olives in Jezreel Valley. ²³ I will scatter the seeds and show mercy to Lo-Ruhamah.* I will say to Lo-Ammi,* "You are my people," and they will answer, "You are our God."

CHAPTER 3
God's love offers hope

¹ Once again the LORD spoke to me. And this time he said, "Hosea, fall in love with an unfaithful woman* who has a lover. Do this to show that I love the people of Israel, even though they worship idols and enjoy the offering cakes made with fruit."

² So I paid fifteen pieces of silver and about a hundred and fifty kilogrammes of grain for such a woman. ³ Then I said, "Now you are mine! You will have to remain faithful to me, though it will be a long time before we sleep together."

⁴ It will also be a long time before Israel has a king or before sacrifices are offered at the temple or before there is any way to get guidance from God. ⁵ But later, Israel will turn back to the LORD their God and to David their king. At that time they will come to the LORD with fear and trembling, and he will be good to them.

The Lord accuses Israel, Judah, and their leaders

CHAPTER 4
Israel is unfaithful

¹ Israel, listen
as the LORD accuses
everyone in the land!

---

*2.19 bride price: It was the custom for the husband to pay his wife's parents a bride price. Instead of money, the LORD will give much better benefits to Israel.
*2.23 Lo-Ruhamah: See the note at 1.6.
*2.23 Lo-Ammi: See the note at 1.9.
*3.1 unfaithful woman: This may refer to Gomer, the woman Hosea married (see 1.3), or it may refer to another woman.
See also: 2.23: Rom 9.25; 1 Pet 2.10.

No one is faithful or loyal
or truly cares about God.
² Cursing, dishonesty, murder,
robbery, unfaithfulness —
these happen all the time.
Violence is everywhere.
³ And so your land is a desert.
Every living creature is dying —
people and wild animals,
birds and fish.

The LORD warns the priests

⁴ Don't accuse just anyone!
Not everyone is at fault.
My case is against you,
the priests.›
⁵ You and the prophets
will stumble day and night;
I'll silence your mothers.
⁶ You priests have rejected me,
and my people are destroyed
by refusing to obey.
Now I'll reject you and forget
your children, because you
have forgotten my Law.

⁷ By adding more of you priests,
you multiply the number
of people who sin.
Now I'll change your pride
into shame.
⁸ You encourage others to sin,
so you can stuff yourselves
on their sin offerings.

⁹ That's why I will punish
the people for their deeds,
just as I will punish
you priests.
¹⁰ Their food won't satisfy,
and having sex at pagan shrines
won't produce children.
My people have rebelled
¹¹ and have been unfaithful
to me, their LORD.

God condemns Israel's idolatry

My people, you are foolish
because of too much pleasure
and too much wine.
¹² You expect wooden idols
and other objects of wood
to give you advice.
Lusting for sex at pagan shrines
has made you unfaithful
to me, your God.
¹³ You offer sacrifices
on mountaintops and hills,

Real life

Pornography

Lots of people seem to think that pornography is acceptable these days. 'After all,' they say, 'no-one gets hurt, do they?'

Depends what you mean by 'hurt'. For one thing, pornography is addictive. You can get hooked. Start with the softcore and you'll soon be moving to more and more extreme forms of porn. The desire for sex, as people in the Bible found, pulls you away from faith in God (Hosea 4.12).

Pornography turns people – women mainly – into objects, lumps of flesh to be used how we please. And many women have been badly abused and damaged through involvement in the porn business.

Pornography hurts us. Jesus, particularly, had strong words to say about lust and the way it infects our brains. He made no distinction between lusting after someone in our head, and taking someone else to bed.

The Bible is not ashamed of sex; it doesn't shy away from talking about it. But it recognises that the desire for sex can take control of out whole life. God views sex as part of a relationship. Man and woman, committed together, loving one another and expressing that love. Pornography is not about love, but lust.

Think

Why was Jesus so strict about lust?
Why is our society so obsessed with sex?

Act

Keep away from temptation. Avoid the top shelf of the newsagents.
Try to avoid internet sites that have pornographic content. Pray as you surf.

Check

Proverbs 5.15–23; Hosea 4.9–14; Matthew 5.27–30; Romans 1.18–32; Colossians 3.5–11; 2 Peter 2.12–14

More...

Internet p.1269
Help! I can't stop masturbating p.1339
Help! I'm struggling with lust p.954
Sex p.727

under oak trees, and wherever
  good shade is found.

Your own daughters
  and daughters-in-law
    sell themselves for sex.
14 But I won't punish them.
  You men are to blame,
because you go to prostitutes
  and offer sacrifices with them
    at pagan shrines.
  Your own foolishness
    will lead to your ruin.
15 Israel, you are unfaithful,
  but don't lead Judah to sin.
Stop worshipping at Gilgal
  or at sinful Bethel.*
And stop making promises
  in my name — the name
    of the living LORD.
16 You are nothing more
  than a stubborn cow —
so stubborn that I, the LORD,
  cannot feed you like lambs
    in an open pasture.

17 You people of Israelʼ
  are charmed byʼ idols.
  Leave them alone!
18 You get drunk, then sleep
  with prostitutes;
you would rather be vulgar
  than lead a decent life.ʼ
19 And so you will be swept away
  in a whirlwind
    for sacrificing to idols.

CHAPTER 5

Israel and Judah will be judged

The LORD said:

1 Listen, you priests!
  Pay attention, Israel!*
Listen, you members
  of the royal family.
Justice was your duty.
  Butʼ at Mizpah and Mount Tabor
    you trapped the people.
2 At the place of worship
  you were a treacherous pit,ʼ
    and I will punish you.

---

*4.15 sinful Bethel: The Hebrew text has "Beth-Aven", which means "house of sin" or "house of nothing", referring to "Bethel", which means "house of God".
*5.1 Israel: Probably meaning the tribal leaders of Israel.

³ Israel, I know all about you,
and because of your unfaithfulness,
I find you unacceptable.
⁴ Your evil deeds are the reason
you won't return to me,
your LORD God.
And your constant craving for sex
keeps you from knowing me.

⁵ Israel, your pride
testifies to your guilt;
it makes you stumble,
and Judah stumbles too.
⁶ You offer sheep and cattle
as sacrifices to me,
but I have turned away
and refuse to be found.
⁷ You have been unfaithful
to me, your LORD;
you have had children
by prostitutes.*
So at the New Moon Festival,
you and your crops
will be destroyed.›

The LORD warns Israel and Judah

⁸ Give a warning on the trumpet!
Let it be heard in Gibeah,
Ramah, and sinful Bethel.*
Benjamin, watch out!›
⁹ I, the LORD, will punish
and wipe out Israel.
This is my solemn promise
to every tribe of Israel.
¹⁰ Judah's leaders are like crooks
who move boundary markers;
that's why I will flood them
with my anger.

¹¹ Israel was brutally crushed.
They got what they deserved
for worshipping useless idols.›
¹² Now I, the LORD,
will fill Israel with maggots
and make Judah rot.
¹³ When Israel and Judah saw
their sickness and wounds,
Israel asked help from Assyria
and its mighty king.›

*5.7 prostitutes: See 4.14, and the note at 1.2.
*5.8 sinful Bethel: See the note at 4.15. Gibeah is
about five kilometres north of Jerusalem, Ramah is
eight kilometres north, and Bethel is seventeen and a
half kilometres north. The attack comes from the
south, and all the land of Benjamin (belonging to
Israel) is in danger.

But the king cannot cure them
or heal their wounds.
¹⁴ So I'll become a fierce lion
attacking Israel and Judah.
I'll snatch and carry off
what I want,
and no one can stop me.
¹⁵ Then I'll return to my temple
until they confess their guilt
and worship me,
until they are desperate
and beg for my help.

The people pretend to turn to the Lord

CHAPTER 6

The LORD's people speak

¹ Let's return to the LORD.
He has torn us to shreds,
but he will bandage our wounds
and make us well.
² In two or three days
he will heal us
and restore our strength
that we may live with him.
³ Let's do our best
to know the LORD.
His coming is as certain
as the morning sun;
he will refresh us like rain
renewing the earth
in the springtime.

The LORD speaks to Israel and Judah

⁴ People of Israel and Judah,
what can I do with you?
Your love for me disappears
more quickly than mist
or dew at sunrise.
⁵ That's why I slaughtered you
with the words
of my prophets.
That's why my judgments blazed
like the dawning sun.›
⁶ I'd rather you were faithful
and knew me
than offered sacrifices.

⁷ At a place named Adam,
you› betrayed me
by breaking our agreement.

See also: 6.6: Matt 9.13; 12.7.

⁸ Everyone in Gilead is evil;
  your hands are stained
    with the blood of victims.*
⁹ You priests are like a gang
    of robbers in ambush.⸌
  On the road to Shechem*
    you murder and commit
      other horrible crimes.
¹⁰ I have seen a terrible thing
    in Israel —
  you are unfaithful
    and unfit to worship me.
¹¹ People of Judah,
    your time is coming too.

The LORD wants to help Israel

I, the LORD, would like to make
  my nation prosper again

CHAPTER 7

¹ and to heal its wounds.
  But then I see the crimes
    in Israel⸌ and Samaria.
  Everyone is deceitful;
    robbers roam the streets.
² No one realizes
    that I have seen their sins
  surround them like a flood.

³ The king and his officials
    take great pleasure
  in their sin and deceit.
⁴ Everyone burns with desire —
  they are like coals in an oven,
    ready to burst into flames.
⁵ On the day their king
    was crowned,
  his officials got him drunk,
    and he joined
      in their foolishness.⸌

⁶ Their anger is a fire
    that smoulders all night,
  then flares up at dawn.
⁷ They are flames
    destroying their leaders.
  And their kings are powerless;
    none of them trust me.

⁸ The people of Israel⸌
  have mixed with foreigners;

Helpline

Help! I'm struggling with lust

'I can't seem to help myself. I know it's wrong to think this way, but I just keep thinking about it...'

Yeah, right. And you think nobody else does? Throughout the Bible there are people who struggled with this issue. We know it was an issue for people like David, Samson and Solomon, and I doubt that any of us would claim to be more godly than them. Hosea describes a society which burns with lust, like a load of over-heating ovens (7.3–5).

And in our world – a world full of erotic imagery – it becomes even tougher to control. You walk down the street, there's a lingerie advert; you cross the road and there's a good looking bloke or girl coming in the opposite direction. So, in this world it's pretty unlikely that you'll go through life without experiencing this temptation.

The issue is, how far do you indulge in it? Don't indulge in sexual fantasies about the people who you find attractive. When you do get these thoughts, don't dwell on them. Instead, try to focus on God.

Three things

Admit

Recognise you have this problem. Be honest. Don't pretend it's not an issue.

Control

Try to pray about it. Try to master your mind. It's difficult to stop the thoughts entering your mind, but you don't have to encourage them to take up residence there.

Focus

The more you think about God, the less room there is for unhealthy thoughts.

More...

Help! I can't stop masturbating p.1339
Resisting temptation p.1124
Being accountable p.704
Help! I feel like I've failed p837
Internet p.1269
Pornography p.952

---

*6.8 your hands . . . victims: This may refer to child sacrifice.
*6.9 Shechem: This was one of the towns where people could run for safety, if they had accidentally killed someone (see Joshua 20.1–9).

they are a thin piece of bread
   scorched on one side.
⁹ They don't seem to realize
   how weak and feeble they are;
   their hair has turned grey,
   while foreigners rule.
¹⁰ I am the LORD, their God,
   but in all their troubles
   their pride keeps them
   from returning to me.

Israel refused to trust the Lord

No help from foreign nations

The LORD said:

¹¹ Israel' is a senseless bird,
   fluttering back and forth
   between Egypt and Assyria.
¹² But I will catch them in a net
   as hunters trap birds;
   I threatened to punish them,
   and indeed I will.'
¹³ Trouble and destruction
   will be their reward
   for rejecting me.
   I would have rescued them,
   but they told me lies.

¹⁴ They don't really pray to me;
   they just howl in their beds.
   They have rejected me for Baal
   and slashed themselves,'
   in the hope that Baal
   will bless their crops.
¹⁵ I taught them what they know,
   and I made them strong.
   Now they plot against me
¹⁶ and refuse to obey.'
   They are more useless
   than a crooked arrow.
   Their leaders will die in war
   for saying foolish things.
   Egyptians will laugh at them.

CHAPTER 8

Israel rejects the LORD

The LORD said:

¹ Sound a warning!
   Israel, you broke our agreement
   and ignored my teaching.
   Now an eagle is swooping down
   to attack my land.
² Israel, you say, "We claim you,
   the LORD, as our God."

³ But your enemies
   will chase you for rejecting
   our good agreement.'
⁴ You chose kings and leaders
   without consulting me;
   you made silver and gold idols
   that led to your downfall.
⁵ City of Samaria, I'm angry
   because of your idol
   in the shape of a calf.
   When will you ever
   be innocent again?
⁶ Someone from Israel built
   that idol for you,
   but only I am God.
   And so it will be smashed
   to pieces.'

⁷ If you scatter wind
   instead of wheat,
   you will harvest a whirlwind
   and have no wheat.
   Even if you harvest grain,
   enemies will steal it all.

⁸ Israel, you are ruined,
   and now the nations
   consider you worthless.
⁹ You are like a wild donkey
   that goes its own way.
   You've run off to Assyria
   and hired them as allies.
¹⁰ You can bargain with nations,
   but I'll catch you anyway.
   Soon you will suffer abuse
   by kings and rulers.

¹¹ Israel, you have built
   many altars where you offer
   sacrifices for sin.
   But these altars have become
   places for sin.
¹² My instructions for sacrifices
   were written in detail,
   but you ignored them.
¹³ You sacrifice your best animals
   and eat the sacrificial meals,*
   but I, the LORD,
   refuse your offerings.

8.13 sacrifice . . . sacrificial meals: One possible
meaning for the difficult Hebrew text. Two kinds of
sacrifices are referred to: those in which the whole
animal is burnt on the altar ("whole burnt offerings"
in traditional translations) and those in which part is
eaten by the worshippers ("fellowship offerings" in
traditional translations).

I will remember your sins
  and punish you.
Then you will return to Egypt.*

14 Israel, I created you,
  but you forgot me.
You and Judah built palaces
  and many strong cities.*
Now I will send fire to destroy
  your towns and fortresses.

Israel will get the punishment it deserves

CHAPTER 9

1 Israel, don't celebrate
  or make noisy shouts'
  like other nations.
You have been unfaithful
  to your God.
Wherever grain is threshed,
  you behave like prostitutes
because you enjoy
  the money you receive.*
2 But you will run short
  of grain and wine,
3 and you will have to leave
  the land of the LORD.
Some of you will go to Egypt;
  others will go to Assyria
  and eat unclean food.

4 You won't be able to offer
  sacrifices of wine
  to the LORD.
None of your sacrifices
  will please him —
they will be unclean
  like food offered to the dead.
Your food will only be used
  to satisfy your hunger;
none of it will be brought
  to the LORD's temple.

5 You will no longer be able
  to celebrate the festival
  of the LORD.*
6 Even if you escape alive,
  you will end up in Egypt
  and be buried in Memphis.*
Your silver treasures
  will be lost among weeds;'
thorns will sprout in your tents.

7 Israel, the time has come.
You will get what you deserve,
  and you will know it.
"Prophets are fools," you say.
"And God's messengers are mad."
Your terrible guilt
  has filled you with hatred.

8 Israel, the LORD sent me
  to look after you.'
But you trap his prophets
  and flood his temple
  with your hatred.
9 You are brutal and corrupt,
  as were the men of Gibeah.*
But God remembers your sin,
  and you will be punished.

Sin's terrible results

The LORD said:

10 Israel, when I, the LORD,
  found you long ago
it was like finding
  grapes in a barren desert
  or tender young figs.
Then you worshipped Baal Peor,
  that disgusting idol,
and you became as disgusting
  as the idol you loved.

11 And so, Israel, your glory
  will fly away like birds —
your women will no longer
  be able to give birth.
12 Even if you do have children,
  I will take them all
  and leave you to mourn.
I will turn away,
  and you will sink down
  in deep trouble.

---

*8.13 return to Egypt: Either as slaves or to find help against Assyria.
*8.14 built palaces . . . cities: They did this because they no longer trusted the LORD to protect them. "Palaces" may also mean "temples".
*9.1 Wherever . . . receive: Grain was threshed on hills or other places where the wind could blow away the husks. People also met at these places to worship Baal, the god they thought had given them the grain harvest.

*9.5 festival of the LORD: Probably the Festival of Shelters.
*9.6 Memphis: An Egyptian city with a famous cemetery.
*9.9 the men of Gibeah: They raped and murdered a woman (see Judges 19).
See also: 9.7: Luke 21.22. 9.9: Judg 19.1–30.
9.10: Num 25.1–5.

¹³ Israel, when I first met you,
  I thought of you as palm trees
    growing in fertile ground.'
  Now you lead your people out,
    only to be slaughtered.

Hosea's advice

¹⁴ Our LORD, do just one thing
    for your people —
  make their women unable
  to have children
    or to nurse their babies.

The LORD's judgment on Israel

¹⁵ Israel, I first began
  to hate you because
    you did evil at Gilgal.*
  Now I will chase you
    out of my house.
  No longer will I love you;
    your leaders betrayed me.
¹⁶ Israel, you are a vine
    with dried-up roots
    and fruitless branches.
  Even if you had more children
  and loved them dearly,
    I would slaughter them all.

Warnings for Israel

¹⁷ Israel, you disobeyed my God.
  Now he will force you to roam
    from nation to nation.

CHAPTER 10

¹ You were a healthy vine
    covered with grapes.
  But the more grapes you grew,
    the more altars you built;
  the better off you became,
  the better shrines you set up
    for pagan gods.
² You are deceitful and disloyal.
  So you will pay
    for your sins,
  because the LORD will destroy
    your altars and images.
³ "We don't have a king,"
    you will say.
  "We don't fear the LORD.
  And what good are kings?"
⁴ Israel, you break treaties
    and don't keep promises;

you turn justice
    into poisonous weeds
  where healthy plants should grow.'

⁵ All who live in Samaria tremble
  with concern for the idols'
    at sinful Bethel.*
  The idol there was the pride
    of the priests,
  but it has been put to shame;
    now everyone will cry.
⁶ It will be taken to Assyria
    and given to the great king.
  Then Israel will be disgraced
    for worshipping that idol.

⁷ Like a twig in a stream,
  the king of Samaria
    will be swept away.
⁸ The altars at sinful Bethel
  will be destroyed
    for causing Israel to sin;
  they will be overgrown
    with thorns and thistles.
  Then everyone will beg
  the mountains and hills
    to cover and protect them.

The LORD promises to punish Israel

⁹ Israel, you have never
  stopped sinning'
    since that time at Gibeah.*
  That's why you
    will be attacked at Gibeah.'
¹⁰ Your sins have doubled,
    and you are rebellious.
  Now I have decided
  to send nations to attack
    and put you in chains.

¹¹ Once you were obedient
  like a calf
    that loved to thresh grain.
  But I will put a harness
    on your powerful neck;
  you and Judah must plough
    and cultivate the ground.
¹² Plough your fields,
    scatter seeds of justice,
    and harvest faithfulness.
  Worship me, the LORD,
  and I will send my saving power
    down like rain.

---

*9.15 Gilgal: See 4.15.

*10.5 sinful Bethel: See the note at 4.15.
*10.9 Gibeah: See the note at 9.9.
See also: 10.8: Luke 23.30; Rev 6.16. 10.9: Judg 19.1–30.
10.12: Jer 4.3.

¹³ You have planted evil,
   harvested injustice, and eaten
      the fruit of your lies.
   You trusted your own strength
      and your powerful forces.
¹⁴ So war will break out,
      and your fortresses
         will be destroyed.
   Your enemies will do to you
      what Shalman* did to the people
         of Beth-Arbel —
   mothers and their children
      will be beaten to death
         against rocks.
¹⁵ Bethel, this will be your fate
      because of your evil.
   Israel, at dawn your king
      will be killed.

God's love for his people

CHAPTER 11

¹ When Israel was a child,
   I loved him, and I called
      my son out of Egypt.
² But as the saying goes,
   "The more they were called,
      the more they rebelled."›
   They never stopped offering
   incense and sacrifices
      to the idols of Baal.

³ I took Israel by the arm
      and taught them to walk.
   But they would not admit
   that I was the one
      who had healed them.
⁴ I led them with kindness
   and with love,
      not with ropes.
   I held them close to me;›
   I bent down to feed them.

⁵ But they trusted Egypt
   instead of returning to me;
      now Assyria will rule them.
⁶ War will visit their cities,
      and their plans will fail.›
⁷ My people are determined
   to reject me for a god
   they think is stronger,
      but he can't help.›

---

*10.14 Shalman: Perhaps a Moabite king, also known as Salamanu.
See also: 11.1: Exod 4.22; Matt 2.15.

Big ideas

God's love

The Bible begins and ends with love. It begins with a God in love with his new creation and ends with a new creation filled with God's love.

God's love floods the pages of the Bible. Time and again he decides not to wipe out his people – even though they deserve it – because he loves them. In the end, because he loves them so much, he sends his only son, Jesus Christ, to die for them.

This is the most important thing to understand about God: God is love. But what does that mean? After all, some people say love is blind, so does that mean that God should be 'blind' to our faults?

Hardly. If we love people, we will also want to protect and even correct them. It's not love to let someone walk over the edge of a cliff. It's not loving your creation to allow evil to ruin it.

Love can be tough. God's love is not a weak thing. It's the love of a perfect father, strong, passionate, demanding something of its beloved; a love that is not blind, but which will forgive us when we ask and which wants the very best for his children.

And the more we allow God to love us, the more we will be able to love others. Because that's the other thing about God's love. It's not limited. There's enough for everyone. All we have to do is tell them about it.

 Footsteps

A week on God's love

Love the Lord: Deuteronomy 6.1–18
A love you can trust: Psalms 86.1–17
God's love for Israel: Hosea 11.1–11
Stories of God's love: Luke 15
The extent of God's love: John 3.16–21
God is love: 1 John 3.7–21
God's city of love: Revelation 21.1–4

More...

Forgiveness p.614
Saying sorry p.1258
Worshipping God p.622
Incarnation p.1168
Redemption p.292

8 Israel, I can't let you go.
  I can't give you up.
  How could I possibly destroy you
  as I did the towns of Admah
  and Zeboiim?*
  I just can't do it.
  My feelings for you
  are much too strong.
9 Israel, I won't lose my temper
  and destroy you again.
  I am the Holy God —
  not merely a human being,
  and I won't stay angry.
10 I, the LORD, will roar like a lion,
   and my children will return,
   trembling from the west.
11 They will come back,
   fluttering like birds from Egypt
   or like doves from Assyria.
   Then I will bring them
   back to their homes.
   I, the LORD, have spoken!

Israel and Judah are doomed

Israel and Judah compared

12 Israel is deceitful to me,
   their loyal and holy God;
   they surround me with lies,
   and Judah worships
   other gods.'

CHAPTER 12

1 All day long Israel chases
  wind from the desert;
  deceit and violence
  are found everywhere.
  Treaties are made with Assyria;
  olive oil is taken to Egypt.

Israel and Judah condemned

2 The LORD also brings charges
  against the people of Judah,
  the descendants of Jacob.
  He will punish them
  for what they have done.

3 Even before Jacob was born,
  he cheated his brother,*
  and when he grew up,
  he fought against God.*
4 At Bethel, Jacob wrestled
  with an angel and won;
  then with tears in his eyes,
  he asked for a blessing,
  and God spoke to us' there.
5 God's name is the LORD,
  the LORD God All-Powerful.
6 So return to your God.
  Patiently trust him,
  and show love and justice.
7 Israel, you enjoy cheating
  and taking advantage
  of others.
8 You say to yourself, "I'm rich!
  I earned it all on my own,
  without committing a sin."'

The LORD is still the God of Israel

9 Israel, I, the LORD,
  am still your God,
  just as I have been
  since the time
  you were in Egypt.
  Now I will force you
  to live in tents once again,
  as you did in the desert.*
10 I spoke to the prophets —
   often I spoke in visions.
   And so, I will send my prophets
   with messages of doom.
11 Gilead is terribly sinful
   and will end up ruined.
   Bulls are sacrificed in Gilgal
   on altars made of stones,
   but those stones will be scattered
   in every field.

---

*12.3 Jacob . . . cheated . . . brother: In Hebrew "Jacob" sounds like "cheat" and also like "heel". Jacob grabbed his twin brother Esau by the heel at the time of their birth (see Genesis 25.26). Later he cheated him out of his rights and blessings as the firstborn son (see Genesis 25.29–34; 27.1–40).
*12.3 fought against God: See Genesis 32.22–32.
*12.9 as . . . desert: One possible meaning for the difficult Hebrew text. This probably refers to the forty years of wandering through the desert after leaving Egypt, though it could refer to the "tents" (or "shelters") in which the Israelites lived during the Festival of Shelters (see 9.5–6).

See also: 12.3: Gen 25.26. 12.3,4: Gen 32.24–26. 12.4: Gen 28.10–22. 12.9: Lev 23.42–43.

---

*11.8 Admah and Zeboiim: When the LORD destroyed Sodom and Gomorrah, he also destroyed these two towns (see Deuteronomy 29.23).
See also: 11.8: Deut 29.23.

Viewpoints 👁

Wherever you are, run towards God

Contributed by Rachel H

'So return to your God. Patiently trust him, and show love and justice.'

You are not citizens of this world. Come back to your God. We wander, often walking in the woods between the popular road and 'the road less travelled.' Not quite living without God; certainly not living in abandoned surrender to God.

Come back to your God. He stands, waiting, with welcoming arms, longing to teach you his ways. Those who travel the popular road – the way of our society – act on the principles of self, of gain, of casual compromise. Those who travel the way of joy (though it may be through many obstacles) act on the principles of love and justice. This is the heart of God.

The paradox, the mysterious marriage of justice and love: this is the heart of God. For God is a just God, and cannot let injustice reign. Yet he is, in his very essence, love. His love is highlighted by his sacrificial mercy; and the greatest act of mercy ever shown was the fulfilment of perfect justice.

So what's our response? Do we follow the heart of God? Will we reject the ideals of this world that is not our home, and act instead on the principles of love and justice? Will we tune our spirits to his Spirit and take the consequential ridicule on earth, depending on our God? When we take steps of faith believing that God is who he says he is, depending on his ways, depending on him to come through, we'll find God to be Most Beautiful, Most Powerful, Most Faithful.

So let's choose the road less travelled – and when it hurts, let's live in confident dependence on our God.

More...

Going against the crowd p.1045

12 Jacob* escaped to Syria'
  where he tended sheep
    to earn himself a wife.
13 I sent the prophet Moses
  to lead Israel from Egypt
    and to keep them safe.
14 Israel, I will make you pay
  for your terrible sins
    and for insulting me.

CHAPTER 13

Israel is doomed

The LORD said:

1 When your leaders' spoke,
  everyone in Israel trembled
    and showed great respect.
  But you sinned by worshipping Baal,
    and you were destroyed.
2 Now you continue to sin
  by designing and making
    idols of silver
  in the shape of calves.
  You are told to sacrifice
    to these idols' —
  yes, even to kiss them.
3 And so, all of you will vanish
  like the mist or the dew
    of early morning,
  or husks of grain in the wind
    or smoke from a chimney.

4 I, the LORD, have been your God
  since the time
    you were in Egypt.
  I am the only God you know,
    the only one who can save.
5 I took care of you
    in a thirsty desert.*
6 I fed you till you were satisfied,
  then you became proud
    and forgot about me.
7 Now I will attack like a lion,
  ambush you like a leopard,
8 and rip you apart like a bear
  robbed of her cubs.
  I will gnaw on your bones,
  as though I were a lion
    or some other wild animal.
9 Israel, you are done for.

---

*12.12 Jacob: His name was later changed to Israel (see Genesis 32.28), and he became the ancestor of the nation by that name.
*13.5 thirsty desert: The forty years that Israel wandered through the desert, after leaving Egypt.
See also: 12.12: Gen 29.1–20. **12.13:** Exod 12.50–51. **13.5–6:** Deut 8.11–17.

Don't expect help from me.'
¹⁰ You wanted a king and rulers.
    Where is your king now?
    What cities have rulers?
¹¹ In my anger, I gave you a king;
    in my fury, I took him away.

Israel's terrible fate

The LORD said:

¹² Israel, your terrible sins
    are written down
    and stored away.
¹³ You are like a senseless child
    who refuses to be born
    at the proper time.
¹⁴ Should I, the LORD, rescue you
    from death and the grave?
    No! I call death and the grave
    to strike you like a plague.
    I refuse to show mercy.

¹⁵ No matter how much you prosper
    more than the other tribes,'
    I, the LORD, will wipe you out,
    just as a scorching desert wind
    dries up streams of water.
    I will take away
    your precious treasures.
¹⁶ Samaria* will be punished
    for turning against me.
    It will be destroyed in war —
    children will be beaten
    against rocks,
    and pregnant women
    will be ripped open.

Future forgiveness and blessings

CHAPTER 14

Turn back to the LORD

¹ Israel, return! Come back
    to the LORD, your God.
    Sin has made you fall.
² Return to the LORD and say,
    "Please forgive our sins.
    Accept our good sacrifices
    of praise instead of bulls.'

³ Assyria can't save us,
    and chariots can't help.
    So we will no longer worship
    the idols we have made.
    Our LORD, you show mercy
    to orphans."

The LORD promises to forgive

⁴ Israel, you have rejected me,
    but my anger is gone;
    I will heal you and love you
    without limit.
⁵ I will be like the dew —
    then you will blossom like lilies
    and have roots like a tree.'
⁶ Your branches will spread
    with the beauty
    of an olive tree
    and with the aroma
    of Lebanon Forest.
⁷ You will rest in my shade,
    and your grain will grow.
    You will blossom
    like a vineyard
    and be famous as the wine
    from Lebanon.

⁸ Israel, give up your idols!
    I will answer your prayers
    and take care of you.'
    I am that glorious tree,
    the source of your fruit.*

⁹ If you are wise, you will know
    and understand what I mean.
    I am the LORD, and I lead you
    along the right path.
    If you obey me,
    we will walk together,
    but if you are wicked,
    you will stumble.

---

*14.8 I am . . . fruit: This is the only place in the Old Testament where the LORD is compared to a tree. Hosea reminds the people that it is the LORD who is the source of life, rather than the Canaanite gods and goddesses that are worshipped under trees at the local shrines.

Additional notes

'1.1 Jehoash: The Hebrew text has "Joash", another spelling of the name.
'2.10 I'll strip . . . lovers: Or "I'll show her lovers how disgusting she is."
'2.12 fig trees . . . payment: Hosea uses an unusual word for "fig tree", which is spelt something like the word for "payment".

---

*13.16 Samaria: The capital of the northern kingdom of Israel.

See also: 13.10: 1 Sam 8.5–6. 13.11: a 1 Sam 10.17–24;
b 1 Sam 15.26. 13.14: 1 Cor 15.55.

›**4.4 priests:** One possible meaning for the difficult Hebrew text of verse 4. Hosea may have had in mind only one priest, possibly the chief priest.

›**4.17 Israel:** The Hebrew text has "Ephraim", the leading tribe of the northern kingdom of Israel, which sometimes stands for the whole kingdom.

›**4.17 charmed by:** Or "joined to".

›**4.18 life:** One possible meaning for the difficult Hebrew text of verse 18.

›**5.1 Justice . . . duty. But:** Or "You are doomed, because".

›**5.2 At . . . pit:** One possible meaning for the difficult Hebrew text.

›**5.7 So . . . destroyed:** One possible meaning for the difficult Hebrew text.

›**5.8 watch out:** Or "lead the way".

›**5.11 for . . . idols:** One possible meaning for the difficult Hebrew text.

›**5.13 and . . . king:** One possible meaning for the difficult Hebrew text.

›**6.5 That's why my . . . sun:** One possible meaning for the difficult Hebrew text.

›**6.7 At . . . you:** Or "Like Adam, you" or "Each one of you".

›**6.9 You . . . ambush:** One possible meaning for the difficult Hebrew text.

›**7.1 Israel:** See the note at 4.17. Samaria was the capital city of Israel.

›**7.5 foolishness:** One possible meaning for the difficult Hebrew text of verse 5.

›**7.8 Israel:** See the note at 4.17.

›**7.11 Israel:** See the note at 4.17.

›**7.12 I threatened . . . will:** One possible meaning for the difficult Hebrew text.

›**7.14 slashed themselves:** One ancient translation and some Hebrew manuscripts; other Hebrew manuscripts "gather together". Slashing themselves was one way of worshipping Baal (see 1 Kings 18.28).

›**7.16 and . . . obey:** One possible meaning for the difficult Hebrew text.

›**8.3 our good agreement:** Or "me, the Good One" (referring to God).

›**8.6 smashed to pieces:** Or "destroyed by fire".

›**9.1 or . . . shouts:** One possible meaning for the difficult Hebrew text.

›**9.6 Your silver . . . weeds:** One possible meaning for the difficult Hebrew text.

›**9.8 Israel . . . you:** One possible meaning for the difficult Hebrew text.

›**9.13 Israel, when . . . ground:** One possible meaning for the difficult Hebrew text.

›**10.4 you turn . . . grow:** One possible meaning for the difficult Hebrew text.

›**10.5 idols:** The Hebrew text has "calves", referring to the idols made in the shape of calves.

›**10.9 never stopped sinning:** One possible meaning for the difficult Hebrew text.

›**10.9 That's why . . . Gibeah:** One possible meaning for the difficult Hebrew text.

›**11.2 But . . . rebelled:** One possible meaning for the difficult Hebrew text.

›**11.4 I held . . . to me:** One possible meaning for the difficult Hebrew text.

›**11.6 fail:** One possible meaning for the difficult Hebrew text of verse 6.

›**11.7 help:** One possible meaning for the difficult Hebrew text of verse 7.

›**11.12 and Judah worships other gods:** Or "but Judah remains faithful".

›**12.4 us:** Hebrew; two ancient translations "him".

›**12.8 without . . . sin:** One possible meaning for the difficult Hebrew text.

›**12.12 Syria:** The Hebrew text has "Aram", probably referring to northern Syria in the region of Haran.

›**13.1 your leaders:** The Hebrew text has "Ephraim", here meaning Mount Ephraim, where the royal palace of Samaria (capital of the northern kingdom of Israel) was situated.

›**13.2 You are told . . . idols:** One possible meaning for the difficult Hebrew text.

›**13.9 Don't . . . me:** Or "You are against me, the one who helps you."

›**13.15 more . . . tribes:** One possible meaning for the difficult Hebrew text.

›**14.2 Accept . . . bulls:** One possible meaning for the difficult Hebrew text.

›**14.5 like a tree:** The Hebrew text has "like Lebanon", probably referring to the famous cedar trees on Mount Lebanon.

›**14.8 Israel . . . you:** One possible meaning for the difficult Hebrew text.

Joel

The basics

What's the point? Judgment is coming like a swarm of locusts; the people must repent.

What happens? Joel likens the devastation caused by a swarm of locusts to the punishment that will be handed out by the Lord.

What should I remember? 2.13 'Don't rip your clothes to show your sorrow. Instead, turn back to me with broken hearts. I am merciful, kind, and caring. I don't easily lose my temper, and I don't like to punish.'

More details

Setting the scene A swarm of locusts has devastated Judah. Joel explains why...

What's it all about? Locusts were an unfortunate feature of life in the ancient middle east. One such swarm sweeps through Judah, devastating Jerusalem.

But this book isn't really about locusts as such. It uses them as an image, a picture of the LORD's judgment. A day is coming when the people are going to have to pay for their sins.

Joel uses the locusts as a picture of a real army; an army that would be far more devastating. And the only insect repellent that will work against this army is for the people to turn back to their God.

Footsteps

Locusts and an enemy army

CHAPTER 1

¹ I am Joel the son of Pethuel.
  And this is the message
    the LORD gave to me.

Locusts cover the land

² Listen, you leaders
  and everyone else
    in the land.
  Has anything like this
    ever happened before?
³ Tell our children!
  Let it be told
    to our grandchildren
    and their children too.

⁴ Swarm after swarm of locusts*
  has attacked our crops,
    eating everything in sight.
⁵ Sober up, you drunkards!
  Cry long and loud;
    your wine supply is gone.
⁶ A powerful nation*
  with countless troops
    has invaded our land.
  They have the teeth and jaws
    of powerful lions.
⁷ Our grapevines and fig trees
  are stripped bare;
    only naked branches remain.

---

*1.4 Swarm . . . locusts: The Hebrew text lists either four kinds of locusts or locusts in four stages of their development. Locusts are a type of grasshopper that comes in swarms and causes great damage to plant life.

*1.6 A powerful nation: The swarms of locusts.

See also: 1.6: Rev 9.8.

8 Grieve like a young woman
    mourning for the man
      she was to marry.
9 Offerings of grain and wine
    are no longer brought
      to the LORD's temple.
    His servants, the priests,
      are deep in sorrow.
10 Barren fields mourn;
    grain, grapes, and olives
      are scorched and shrivelled.

11 Mourn for our farms
    and our vineyards!
    There's no wheat or barley
      growing in our fields.
12 Grapevines have dried up
    and so has every tree —
    figs and pomegranates,*
      date palms and apples.
    All happiness has faded away.

Return to God

13 Mourn, you priests who serve
    at the altar of my God.
    Spend your days and nights
      wearing sackcloth.*
    Offerings of grain and wine
    are no longer brought
      to the LORD's temple.

14 Tell the leaders and people
    to come together
      at the temple.
    Order them to go without eating*
      and to pray sincerely.
15 We are in for trouble!
    Soon the LORD All-Powerful
      will bring disaster.
16 Our food is already gone;
    there's no more celebrating
      at the temple of our God.

17 Seeds dry up in the ground;'
      no harvest is possible.
    Our barns are in bad shape,
      with no grain
        to store in them.

18 Our cattle wander aimlessly,
    moaning for lack of pasture,
      and sheep are suffering.'
19 I cry out to you, LORD.
    Grasslands and forests are eaten
      by the scorching heat.
20 Wild animals have no water
      because of you;
    rivers and streams are dry,
      and pastures are parched.

CHAPTER 2

Locusts and an enemy army

1 Sound the trumpet on Zion,
    the LORD's sacred hill.
    Warn everyone to tremble!
    The judgment day of the LORD
      is coming soon.
2 It will be dark and gloomy
    with storm clouds overhead.
    Troops will cover the mountains
      like thunderclouds.
    No army this powerful
    has ever been gathered before
      or will ever be again.
3 Fiery flames surround them;
      no one escapes.
    Before they invaded,
    the land was like Eden;
      now only a desert remains.

4 They look like horses
    and charge like cavalry.
5 They roar over mountains
    like noisy chariots,
    or a mighty army
      ready for battle.
    They are a forest fire
      that feasts on straw.
6 The very sight of them
    is frightening.'
7 They climb over walls
    like warriors;
    they march in columns
      and never turn aside.
8 They charge straight ahead,
      without pushing each other;
    even arrows and spears
      cannot make them retreat.
9 They swarm over city walls
    and enter our homes;
    they crawl in through windows,
      just like thieves.

---

*1.12 pomegranates: A bright red fruit that looks like
an apple.
*1.13 sackcloth: A rough, dark-coloured cloth made
from goat or camel hair and used to make grain
sacks. It was worn in times of trouble or sorrow.
*1.14 go without eating: As a way of showing
sorrow for their sins.
See also: 1.15: Isa 13.6.

See also: 2.4–5: Rev 9.7–9.

10 They make the earth tremble
   and the heavens shake;
   the sun and moon turn dark,
   and stars stop shining.
11 The LORD God leads this army
   of countless troops,
   and they obey his commands.
   The day of his judgment is so terrible
   that no one can stand it.

The LORD's invitation

12 The LORD said:

It isn't too late.
You can still return to me
   with all your heart.
Start crying and mourning!
Go without eating.
13 Don't rip your clothes
   to show your sorrow.
Instead, turn back to me
   with broken hearts.
I am merciful, kind, and caring.
I don't easily lose my temper,
   and I don't like to punish.

14 I am the LORD your God.
Perhaps I will change my mind
   and treat you with mercy.
Then you will be blessed
with enough grain and wine
   for offering sacrifices to me.

15 Sound the trumpet on Zion!
   Call the people together.
Show your sorrow
   by going without food.
16 Make sure that everyone
   is fit to worship me.*
Bring adults, children, babies,
   and even bring newlyweds
   from their festivities.

17 Tell my servants, the priests,
   to cry inside the temple
and to offer this prayer
   near the altar:◊
"Save your people, LORD God!
Don't let foreign nations
   make jokes about us.
Don't let them laugh and ask,
   'Where is your God?' "

The Lord will bless his people

The LORD will bless the land

18 The LORD was deeply concerned
   about his land
   and had pity on his people.
19 In answer to their prayers
   he said,
   "I will give you enough grain,
   wine, and olive oil
   to satisfy your needs.
No longer will I let you
   be insulted by the nations.
20 An army attacked from the north,
   but I will chase it
   into a scorching desert.
There it will rot and stink
from the Dead Sea
   to the Mediterranean."

The LORD works wonders
21   and does great things.
So tell the soil to celebrate
22 and wild animals
   to stop being afraid.
Grasslands are green again;
fruit trees and fig trees
   are loaded with fruit.
Grapevines are covered
   with grapes.

23 People of Zion,*
celebrate in honour
   of the LORD your God!
He is generous and has sent
the autumn and spring rains
   in the proper seasons.◊
24 Grain will cover
   your threshing places;
jars will overflow
   with wine and olive oil.

The LORD will rescue his people

25 I, the LORD your God,
   will make up for the losses
   caused by those swarms
   and swarms of locusts*
   I sent to attack you.
26 My people, you will eat
   until you are satisfied.
Then you will praise me
for the wonderful things
   I have done.

Viewpoints 👁

Time is running out on Earth – but are we ready for Heaven?

Contributed by Rachel H

'Later, I will give my Spirit to everyone. Your sons and daughters will prophesy. Your old men will have dreams, and your young men will see visions.' Joel looked ahead to a time when God would pour out his Spirit not just on prophets, but 'upon all people'. We live in that time now... but more is coming. I can't even promise you that this comment will get through grammar checking before Jesus comes back – and that's not just because of my awful grammar!

Seriously, 'the day of the Lord' is nearly upon us. 'The storage vats are overflowing with the wickedness of these people' (3.13); the world is dying, society is deteriorating. When the levels of wickedness get too much, Jesus will not hold back. He's coming soon.

But.

He's holding out, waiting, longing for more to know him... we have time NOW. He won't hold out forever; he's coming. He's given us his Spirit, time is ticking – why do we sit in utter complacency? Guys – this is URGENT. 'The day of the Lord is an awesome, terrible thing. Who can endure it?' Who could dream of standing up before the judgement of our awesome God... except those covered by the blood of his perfect Son Jesus. 'That is why the LORD says, 'Turn to me now while there is still time! Give me your hearts.'

I implore you, 'Return to the LORD your God, for he is gracious and merciful. He is not easily angered. He is filled with kindness and is eager not to punish you' (Joel 2.13).

Be His.

More...

Dreams and visions p.1410
New heaven & new earth p.1427

Never again will you
be put to shame.
²⁷ Israel, you will know
that I stand at your side.
I am the LORD your God —
there are no other gods.
Never again will you
be put to shame.

The LORD will work wonders

The LORD said:

²⁸ Later, I will give my Spirit to everyone.
Your sons and daughters will prophesy.
Your old men will have dreams,
and your young men
will see visions.
²⁹ In those days I will even give
my Spirit to my servants,
both men and women.

³⁰ I will work wonders
in the sky above
and on the earth below.
There will be blood and fire
and clouds of smoke.
³¹ The sun will turn dark,
and the moon
will be as red as blood
before that great
and terrible day
when I appear.

³² Then the LORD will save everyone who faithfully worships him. He has promised there will be survivors on Mount Zion and in Jerusalem, and among them will be his chosen ones.

The Lord will punish the nations

CHAPTER 3

The LORD said:

¹ At that time I, the LORD, will make Judah and Jerusalem prosperous again. ² Then in Judgment Valley⁹ I will bring together the nations that scattered my people Israel everywhere in the world, and I will bring charges against those nations. They divided up my land ³ and gambled to see who would get my people; they sold boys and girls to pay for prostitutes and wine.

See also: **2.28-32:** Acts 2.17-21.   **2.31:** Matt 24.29; Mark 13.24-25; Luke 21.25; Rev 6.12-13.   **2.32:** Rom 10.13.

⁴ You people of Tyre and Sidon* and you Philistines, why are you doing this? Are you trying to get even with me? I'll strike back before you know what's happened. ⁵ You've taken my prized possessions, including my silver and gold, and carried them off to your temples.' ⁶ You have dragged the people of Judah and Jerusalem from their land and sold them to the Greeks.

⁷ But I'll make the people of Judah determined to come home, and what happened to them will happen to you. ⁸ I'll hand over your sons and daughters to the people of Judah, and they will sell them to the Sabeans,* who live far away. I, the LORD, have spoken!

Judgment in Judgment Valley

The LORD said:

⁹ Say to the nations:

"Get ready for war!
  Be eager to fight.
Line up for battle and prepare to attack.
¹⁰ Make swords out of ploughs
  and spears out of garden tools.
  Strengthen every weakling."

¹¹ Hurry, all you nations!
  Come quickly.
Ask the LORD to bring
  his warriors along.'
¹² You must come now
  to Judgment Valley,'
where the LORD will judge
  the surrounding nations.

¹³ They are a field of ripe crops.
  Bring in the harvest!
They are grapes piled high.
  Start trampling them now!*
If our enemy's sins were wine,
  every jar would overflow.
¹⁴ Crowds fill Decision Valley.
The judgment day of the LORD
  will soon be here —
¹⁵ no light from the sun or moon,
  and stars no longer shine.

¹⁶ From the heart of Jerusalem
  the LORD roars like a lion,
  shaking the earth and sky.
But the LORD is a fortress,
  a place of safety for his people Israel.

God will bless his people

¹⁷ I am the LORD your God.
  And you will know I live on Zion,
  my sacred hill,
  because Jerusalem will be sacred,
  untouched by foreign troops.
¹⁸ On that day, fruitful vineyards
  will cover the mountains.
And your cattle and goats
  that graze on the hills
  will produce a lot of milk.
Streams in Judah will never run dry;
  a stream from my house
  will flow in Acacia Valley.*

¹⁹ Egypt and Edom were cruel
  and brutal to Judah,
  without a reason.
Now their countries will become
  a barren desert,
²⁰ but Judah and Jerusalem
  will always have people.
²¹ I, the LORD, live on Mount Zion.
I will punish the guilty
  and defend the innocent.'

---

*3.18 **Acacia Valley:** In the plains of Moab, north-east of the Dead Sea.
See also: 3.16: Amos 1.2.

Additional notes

'1.17 **Seeds . . . ground:** One possible meaning for the difficult Hebrew text.
'1.18 **sheep are suffering:** One possible meaning for the difficult Hebrew text.
'2.6 **The very . . . frightening:** One possible meaning for the difficult Hebrew text.
'2.17 **inside . . . altar:** The Hebrew text has "between the porch and the altar", which is the place where the priests usually prayed for the people.
'2.23 **in . . . seasons:** Or "as he used to do".
'3.2 **Judgment Valley:** The Hebrew text has "Jehoshaphat Valley", which means "Valley of the LORD's Judgment". This valley is mentioned here and in verse 12, but nowhere else in the Bible.
'3.5 **temples:** Or "palaces".
'3.11 **Ask . . . along:** One possible meaning for the difficult Hebrew text.
'3.12 **Judgment Valley:** See the note at 3.2.
'3.21 **I will . . . innocent:** One possible meaning for the difficult Hebrew text.

---

*3.4 **Tyre and Sidon:** Two Phoenician coastal cities.
*3.8 **Sabeans:** The people of Seba, a region in south-west Arabia.
*3.13 **grapes . . . now:** People trampled grapes with their bare feet to squeeze out the juice.

See also: 3.4–8: Isa 23.1–18; Ezek 26.1—28.26; Amos 1.9–10; Zech 9.1–4; Matt 11.21–22; Luke 10.13–14.
3.4–8: Isa 14.29–31; Jer 47.1–7; Ezek 25.15–17; Amos 1.6–8; Zeph 2.4–7; Zech 9.5–7. **3.10:** Isa 2.4; Mic 4.3.
3.13: a Rev 14.14–16; **b** Rev 14.19–20; 19.15.

Amos

The basics

What's the point? God hates pretend religion.

What happens? Amos the shepherd goes north to Israel and gives them a message from God: pay attention to the needs of the poor and to act with justice.

What should I remember? 5.23–4 'No more of your noisy songs! I won't listen when you play your harps. But let justice and fairness flow like a river that never runs dry.'

More details

Setting the scene Amos is a shepherd from Tekoa in Judah. He crosses into the northern kingdom of Israel. There, he starts to condemn Israel's smug, self-satisfied hypocrisy...

What's it all about? Amos was a blunt, straightforward small-businessman. He bred sheep and tended fig trees. But when the word of the Lord came on him he had to speak out.

He travels north to Israel to deliver his message. First he attacks other nations, which must have made his listeners happy. But then he delivers a stinging attack on Israel's skin-deep religion. They pretended to be holy, but their society was full of idolatry, corruption and injustice. The Lord wants true faith; not nice words and no actions.

Footsteps

Crimes of the nations will be punished

CHAPTER 1

¹ I am Amos. And I raised sheep near the town of Tekoa* when Uzziah was king of Judah and Jeroboam* son of Jehoash' was king of Israel.

Two years before the earthquake,* the LORD gave me several messages' about Israel, ² and I said:

> When the LORD roars
> from Jerusalem,
> pasture lands and Mount Carmel
> dry up and turn brown.

Judgment on Syria

³ The LORD said:

> I will punish Syria'
> for countless crimes,
> and I won't change my mind.
> They dragged logs with spikes*
> over the people of Gilead.

---

*1.1 Tekoa: In the hill country of Judah about eight kilometres south of Bethlehem.

*1.1 Uzziah . . . Jeroboam: Uzziah was king of Judah 781–740 BC, and Jeroboam II was king of Israel 783–743 BC.

*1.1 Two years . . . earthquake: Possibly the earthquake of 760 BC, which seems to have been especially violent.

*1.3 logs with spikes: These were dragged over grain to thresh it.

See also: 1.1: a 2 King 15.1–7; 2 Chron 26.1–23; b 2 King 14.23–29. 1.2: Joel 3.16. 1.3–5: Isa 17.1–3; Jer 49.23–27; Zech 9.1.

⁴ Now I will burn down the palaces
and fortresses
  of King Hazael
  and of King Benhadad.*
⁵ I will break through
  the gates of Damascus.
I will destroy the people›
of Wicked Valley›
and the ruler of Beth-Eden.›
Then the Syrians will be dragged
as prisoners to Kir.*
I, the LORD, have spoken!

Judgment on Philistia

⁶ The LORD said:

I will punish Philistia›
for countless crimes,
  and I won't change my mind.
They dragged off my people*
  from town after town
to sell them as slaves
  to the Edomites.

⁷ That's why I will burn down
the walls and fortresses
of the city of Gaza.
⁸ I will destroy the king› of Ashdod
and the ruler of Ashkelon.
I will strike down Ekron,*
and that will be the end
of the Philistines.
I, the LORD, have spoken!

Judgment on Phoenicia

⁹ The LORD said:

I will punish Phoenicia›
for countless crimes,
  and I won't change my mind.
They broke their treaty
and dragged off my people*
  from town after town
to sell them as slaves
  to the Edomites.

¹⁰ That's why I will send flames
to burn down the city of Tyre
along with its fortresses.

Judgment on Edom

¹¹ The LORD said:

I will punish Edom
for countless crimes,
  and I won't change my mind.
They killed their own relatives*
and were so terribly furious
  that they showed no mercy.
¹² Now I will send fire to wipe out
the fortresses of Teman
and Bozrah.*

Judgment on Ammon

¹³ The LORD said:

I will punish Ammon
for countless crimes,
  and I won't change my mind.
In Gilead they ripped open
pregnant women,
  just to take the land.

¹⁴ Now I will send fire to destroy
the walls and fortresses
of Rabbah.*
Enemies will shout and attack
like a whirlwind.
¹⁵ Ammon's king and leaders
will be dragged away.
I, the LORD, have spoken!

CHAPTER 2

Judgment on Moab

¹ The LORD said:

I will punish Moab
for countless crimes,
  and I won't change my mind.

---

*1.4 Hazael . . . Benhadad:** Two Syrian kings.
*1.5 Kir:** The exact location of this country is not
known; in 9.7 Amos refers to Kir as the original home
of the Syrians, and so the verse probably means that
the Syrians will lose everything they have gained as a
people.
*1.6 my people:** The people of Israel.
*1.8 Ashdod . . . Ashkelon . . . Ekron:** Philistine cities.
*1.9 my people:** See the note at 1.6.
See also: 1.6-8: Isa 14.29-31; Jer 47.1-7; Ezek 25.15-17;
Joel 3.4-8; Zeph 2.4-7; Zech 9.5-7. 1.9-10: Isa 23.1-18;
Ezek 26.1—28.19; Joel 3.4-8; Zech 9.1-4; Matt 11.21-22;
Luke 10.13-14.

*1.11 their own relatives:** The Edomites were
descendants of Esau, the brother of Jacob, the
ancestor of the Israelites.
*1.12 Teman and Bozrah:** These stand for all of
Edom; Teman may have been a city or a district.
Bozrah, the chief city of northern Edom, was
forty-eight kilometres south-east of the Dead Sea.
*1.14 Rabbah:** The capital city of Ammon.
See also: 1.11-12: Isa 34.5-17; 63.1-6; Jer 49.7-22;
Ezek 25.12-14; 35.1-15; Obad 1-14; Mal 1.2-5.
1.13-15: Jer 49.1-6; Ezek 21.28-32; 25.1-7; Zeph 2.8-11.
2.1-3: Isa 15.1—16.14; 25.10-12; Jer 48.1-47; Ezek 25.8-11;
Zeph 2.8-11.

They made lime from the bones*
    of the king of Edom.
2 Now I will send fire to destroy
    the fortresses of Kerioth.*
Battle shouts and trumpet blasts
will be heard
    as I destroy Moab
3   with its king and leaders.
I, the LORD, have spoken!

Judgment on Judah

4 The LORD said:

I will punish Judah for countless crimes,
    and I won't change my mind.
They have rejected my teachings
    and refused to obey me.
They were led astray
by the same false gods
    their ancestors worshipped.
5 Now I will send fire on Judah
and destroy the fortresses
    of Jerusalem.

Judgment on Israel

6 The LORD said:

I will punish Israel
for countless crimes,
    and I won't change my mind.
They sell honest people for money,
and the needy are sold
    for the price of sandals.
7 They throw the poor to the ground
and push aside
    those who are helpless.

My holy name is dishonoured,
because fathers and sons sleep
    with the same young women.
8 They lie down beside altars
on clothes taken
    as security for loans.
And they drink wine in my temple,
wine bought with the money
    they received from fines.

9 Israel, the Amorites* were there
    when you entered Canaan.

They were tall as cedars
    and strong as oaks.
But I wiped them out —
I destroyed their branches
    and their roots.
10 I had rescued you from Egypt,
    and for forty years I had led you
        through the desert.
Then I gave you the land
    of the Amorites.

11 I chose some of you
    to be prophets
        and others to be Nazirites.*
People of Israel,
    you know this is true.
    I, the LORD, have spoken!
12 But you commanded the prophets
    not to speak their message,
    and you pressured the Nazirites
        into drinking wine.

13 And so I will crush you,
    just as a wagon full of grain
        crushes the ground.'
14 No matter how fast you run,
    you won't escape.
No matter how strong you are,
    you will lose your strength
        and your life.
15 Even if you are an expert
    with a bow and arrow,
        you will retreat.
And you won't get away alive,
    not even if you run fast
        or ride a horse.
16 You may be brave and strong,
    but you will run away,
        stripped naked.
I, the LORD, have spoken!

CHAPTER 3

1 People of Israel,
    I rescued you from Egypt.
Now listen to my judgment
    against you.
2 Of all nations on earth,
    you are the only one
        I have chosen.
That's why I will punish you
    because of your sins.

---

*2.1 They . . . bones: They dug up the bodies of
kings and made lime out of them to use as whitewash
on their houses and walls.
*2.2 Kerioth: A leading city of Moab and a centre for
the worship of Chemosh, the chief god of Moab.
*2.9 Amorites: This word is used for all the people
who lived in Canaan at the time Israel took over the
land.
See also: 2.9: Deut 3.8–11.

*2.11 Nazirites: People who promised the LORD that
they would never drink wine or cut their hair or come
in contact with a dead body.
See also: 2.11: Num 6.1–8.

Israel and Samaria will be destroyed

The work of a prophet

3 Can two people walk together
   without agreeing to meet?
4 Does a lion roar in the forest
   unless it has caught
   a victim?
   Does it growl in its den
   unless it is eating?
5 How can anyone catch a bird
   without using a net?
   Does a trap spring shut
   unless something is caught?

6 Isn't the whole city frightened
   when the trumpet
   signals an attack?
   Isn't it the LORD who brings
   disaster on a city?
7 Whatever the LORD God
   plans to do,
   he tells his servants,
   the prophets.
8 Everyone is terrified
   when a lion roars —
   and ordinary people
   become prophets
   when the LORD God speaks.

Samaria is doomed

9 Here is a message
   for the leaders
   of Philistia⟩ and Egypt —
   tell everyone to come together
   on the hills of Samaria.
   Let them see the injustice
   and the lawlessness
   in that city.
10 The LORD has said
   that they don't even know how
   to do right.
   They have become rich
   from violence and robbery.
11 And so the LORD God has sworn
   that they will be surrounded.
   Enemies will break through
   their defences
   and steal their treasures.

12 The LORD has promised
   that only a few from Samaria
   will escape with their lives
   and with some broken pieces
   of their beds and couches.⟩

It will be like when a shepherd
   rescues two leg bones
   and part of a sheep's ear
   from the jaws of a lion.*

The altars at Bethel

13 The LORD God All-Powerful
   told me to speak this message
   against Jacob's descendants:

14 When I, the LORD, punish Israel
   for their sins,
   I will destroy the altars
   at Bethel.
   Even the corners of the altar*
   will be left in the dust.
15 I will tear down winter homes
   and summer homes.
   Houses decorated with ivory
   and all other mansions
   will be gone for ever.
   I, the LORD, have spoken!

CHAPTER 4

The women of Samaria

The LORD said:

1 You women of Samaria
   are fat cows!⟩
   You ill-treat and abuse
   the poor and needy,
   then you say to your husbands,
   "Bring us more drinks!"
2 I, the LORD God, have sworn
   by my own name
   that your time is coming.
   Not one of you will be left —
   you will be taken away
   by sharp hooks.⟩
3 You will be dragged through holes
   in your city walls,
   and you will be thrown
   towards Harmon.⟩
   I, the LORD, have spoken!

---

*3.12 lion: When a wild animal attacked and killed a sheep, the shepherd had to rescue part of the sheep and take it to the owner as proof that it had been killed by an animal. Otherwise, the shepherd had to pay the owner the cost of the sheep.

*3.14 altar: Altars were places of worship but also places of protection. People whose lives were in danger could grab hold of the corners of an altar, and no one was allowed to kill them.

See also: 3.14: 2 King 23.15.

Israel refuses to obey

The LORD said:

4 Come to Bethel and Gilgal.*
    Sin all you want!
Offer sacrifices the next morning
and bring a tenth of your crops
    on the third day.*
5 Bring offerings to show me
    how thankful you are.
Gladly bring more offerings
than I have demanded.
    You really love to do this.
I, the LORD God, have spoken!

How the LORD warned Israel

6 I, the LORD, took away the food
    from every town and village,
    but still you rejected me.
7 Three months before harvest,
    I kept back the rain.
Sometimes I would let it fall
    on one town or field
but not on another,
    and pastures dried up.
8 People from two or three towns
    would go to a town
    that still had water,
    but it wasn't enough.
Even then you rejected me.
    I, the LORD, have spoken!

9 I dried up your grain fields;
your gardens and vineyards
    turned brown.
Locusts* ate your fig trees
    and olive orchards,
but even then you rejected me.
    I, the LORD, have spoken!

10 I did terrible things to you,
    just as I did to Egypt —
I killed your young men in war;
    I let your horses be stolen,
and I made your camp stink
    with dead bodies.
Even then you rejected me.
    I, the LORD, have spoken!

11 I destroyed many of you,
    just as I did the cities
        of Sodom and Gomorrah.
You were a burning stick
    I rescued from the fire.
Even then you rejected me.
    I, the LORD, have spoken!

12 Now, Israel, I myself
    will deal with you.
    Get ready to face your God!

13 I created the mountains
    and the wind.
I let humans know
    what I am thinking.›
I bring darkness at dawn
    and step over hills.
I am the LORD God All-Powerful!

CHAPTER 5

Turn back to the LORD

1 Listen, nation of Israel,
    to my mournful message:
2 you, dearest Israel, have fallen,
    never to rise again —
you lie deserted in your own land,
    with no one to help you up.

3 The LORD God has warned,
    "From every ten soldiers
        only one will be left;
    from a thousand troops,
        only a hundred will survive."

4 The LORD keeps saying,
    "Israel, turn back to me
        and you will live!
5 Don't go to Gilgal or Bethel
    or even to Beersheba.*
Gilgal will be dragged away,
    and Bethel will end up
        as nothing."›

6 Turn back to the LORD,
    you descendants of Joseph,*
        and you will live.
If you don't, the LORD
    will attack like fire.
Bethel will burn to the ground,
    and no one can save it.

4.4 Bethel and Gilgal: These were two of the most important centres of worship in northern Israel. Amos mentions these together again in 5.5.
4.4 Offer . . . day: Or "Offer sacrifices each morning and bring a tenth of your crops every three days." In verses 4–5 God is condemning the people for meaningless acts of worship.
4.9 Locusts: A type of grasshopper that comes in swarms and causes great damage to plant life.

5.5 Gilgal . . . Bethel . . . Beersheba: These were ancient places of worship, but the LORD had warned his people to stay away from them.
5.6 descendants of Joseph: Another name for the people of the northern kingdom of Israel.
See also: 4.11: Gen 19.24.

⁷ You people are doomed!
  You twist the truth
    and trample on justice.

⁸ But the LORD created the stars
    and put them in place.*
  He turns darkness to dawn
    and daylight to darkness;
  he scoops up the ocean
    and empties it on the earth.
⁹ God destroys mighty soldiers
    and strong fortresses.

Choose good instead of evil!

The LORD said:

¹⁰ You people hate judges
    and honest witnesses;
¹¹ you abuse the poor and demand
    heavy taxes from them.
  You have built expensive homes,
    but you won't enjoy them;
  you have planted vineyards,
    but you will get no wine.
¹² I am the LORD, and I know
    your terrible sins.
  You cheat honest people and take bribes;
    you rob the poor of justice.
¹³ Times are so evil
    that anyone with good sense
      will keep quiet.

¹⁴ If you really want to live,
    you must stop doing wrong
      and start doing right.
  I, the LORD God All-Powerful,
    will then be on your side,
      just as you claim I am.
¹⁵ Choose good instead of evil!
    See that justice is done.
  Perhaps I, the LORD All-Powerful,
    will be kind to what's left
      of your people.*

Judgment is coming

¹⁶ This is what the LORD has sworn:

  Noisy crying will be heard
    in every town and street.

---

*5.8 the stars . . . place: The Hebrew text mentions
two groups of stars, Pleiades and Orion. Since the
LORD is the Creator of the stars, he controls the
seasons that are signalled by the different positions of
the stars. Moreover, the stars are created objects and
should not be worshipped.
*5.15 your people: Hebrew "Joseph's descendants"
(see the note at verse 6).
See also: 5.8: Job 9.9; 38.31.

Real life

Shopping

Contributed by Tearfund

'It was a hot, quiet day in the old streets of
Jerusalem. A few traders were about, selling
their distinctive crockery from blankets laid
out on the cobbled streets. A tourist was
haggling over a mug, driving the price lower
and lower. Eventually, satisfied, he handed
over a couple of small coins. When I
approached the stallholder, he looked up
with tears in his eyes. A blockade on the city
meant supplies were scarce, he explained.
He'd barely enough money to cover his
family's meals. The tears weren't a ploy. The
tourist could easily have afforded more.
Here were people suffering because of the
way someone else had chosen to do their
shopping.'

Most of the time, our shopping isn't this
intimate: we select our stuff from shelves
and the first contact we have with another
human being is at the till. Yet the truth is
that from mugs to mobiles, satsumas to
sandals, your hands are not the first to touch
what you buy. Workers as far as India may
have stitched your favourite top or farmers
in Africa harvested the cocoa that makes
your hot chocolate taste so good.

Global business is the norm. Sourcing raw
material and labour as cheaply as possible is
what most big businesses consider good
sense, which is why your stuff often comes
from so far away. But when our shopping
exploits people, as Christians, shouldn't we
be asking why?

The way trade is carried out often favours
the powerful and wealthy. Businesses try to
keep production costs low so they can keep
profits high, profits which usually only
benefit the business itself and its
shareholders. Concerns for the actual
producers of the goods – for their pay and
safety for example – are often ignored. The
producers of your £100 trainers may actually
be very poor.

Companies often say that they have little
influence over the local firms who handle
the work, or that people in different
countries have different expectations about

work. But does anyone, anywhere, expect to be locked in a dirty, dangerous factory? They may say their customers' only concern is value for money, but at what price?

God maps out real values in the Bible where trade and concern do go together. One of the complaints of Jeremiah was that the rich were building big posh houses with profits from exploited labour (Jeremiah 22.13–17). Elsewhere the Bible describes rich businessmen who live only to make money (Amos 5.8); dishonesty in trading (Leviticus 19.35–36 and Proverbs 16.11); getting unfair profits (Amos 5.5); and treating the poor like things rather than people (Amos 5.6). Doesn't sound too different from some of today's businesses. In contrast, the early church shared possessions: the New Testament stresses that it isn't how wealthy you are that counts, but your attitude to wealth and how you use it.

Think

How important to you is it to 'get a bargain'? Do you need to change your shopping habits out of consideration for the producers?
Are you involved in producing or selling goods yourself? How does your experience compare with workers in other countries?

Act

Create a Sharing Directory for your church, listing what's available and who owns it. Try to find out where goods come from before you buy them. Do you really know what you're buying?

Check

Leviticus 19.35–36; Proverbs 16.11; Jeremiah 22.13–17; Amos 5.6–8

More...

Fair trade p.923
Materialism p.1141
Money p.1043
Debt p.697
Giving your money p.1300

Even farmers will be told
   to mourn for the dead,
together with those
   who are paid to mourn.*
17 Your vineyards will be filled
   with crying and weeping,*
   because I will punish you.
   I, the LORD, have spoken!

When the LORD judges

18 You look forward to the day
   when the LORD comes to judge.
   But you are in for trouble!
   It won't be a time of sunshine;
   all will be darkness.
19 You will run from a lion,
   only to meet a bear.
   You will escape to your house,
   rest your hand on the wall,
   and be bitten by a snake.
20 The day when the LORD judges
   will be dark, very dark,
   without a ray of light.

What the LORD demands

The LORD said:

21 I, the LORD, hate and despise
   your religious celebrations
   and your times of worship.
22 I won't accept your offerings
   or animal sacrifices —
   not even your very best.
23 No more of your noisy songs!
   I won't listen when you play your harps.
24 But let justice and fairness
   flow like a river
   that never runs dry.

25 Israel, for forty years
   you wandered in the desert,
   without bringing offerings
   or sacrifices to me.
26 Now you will have to carry
   the two idols you made —
   Sakkuth, the one you call king,
   and Kaiwan,
   the one you built
   in the shape of a star.'
27 I will force you to march
   as captives beyond Damascus.

5.16 paid to mourn: In ancient times some people were paid to mourn and make loud cries at funerals.
5.17 Your vineyards . . . weeping: Instead of happy celebrations that were often held in vineyards after the harvest.
See also: 5.21–22: Isa 1.11–14. 5.25–27: Acts 7.42–43.

I, the LORD God All-Powerful,
have spoken!*

CHAPTER 6

Israel will be punished

¹ Do you rulers in Jerusalem
and in the city of Samaria
feel safe and at ease?
Everyone bows down to you,
and you think you are better
than any other nation.
But you are in for trouble!
² Look what happened
to the cities of Calneh,
powerful Hamath,
and Gath⁕ in Philistia.
Are you greater than any
of those kingdoms?
³ You are cruel, and you forget
the coming day of judgment.

⁴ You rich people lounge around
on beds with ivory posts,
while dining on the meat
of your lambs and calves.
⁵ You sing foolish songs
to the music of harps,
and you make up new tunes,
just as David used to do.
⁶ You drink all the wine you want
and wear expensive perfume,
but you don't care about
the ruin of your nation.*

⁷ So you will be the first
to be dragged off as captives;
your good times will end.

⁸ The LORD God All-Powerful
has sworn by his own name:
"You descendants of Jacob
make me angry by your pride,
and I hate your fortresses.
And so I will surrender your city
and possessions
to your enemies."

⁹ If only ten of you survive
by hiding in a house you will still die.
¹⁰ As you carry out a corpse
to prepare it for burial,⁕
your relative in the house
will ask, "Are there others?"
You will answer, "No!"
Then your relative will reply,
"Be quiet!
Don't dare mention
the name of the LORD."*
¹¹ At the LORD's command,
houses great and small
will be smashed to pieces.

¹² Horses can't gallop on rocks;
oceans⁕ can't be ploughed.
But you have turned justice and fairness
into bitter poison.
¹³ You celebrate the defeat
of Lo-Debar and Karnaim,*
and you boast by saying,
"We did it on our own."

¹⁴ But the LORD God All-Powerful
will send a nation to attack
you people of Israel.
They will capture Lebo-Hamath
in the north,
Arabah Brook* in the south,
and everything in between.

Five visions of Israel's punishment

CHAPTER 7

A vision of locusts

¹ The LORD God showed me that he is going to send locusts* to attack your crops. It will happen after the king has already been given

---

*5.27 I, the LORD . . . spoken: Israel did not offer sacrifices and gifts to the LORD during the time they wandered through the desert. But now they have made idols to carry during their ceremonies. So the LORD warns that he will make them "march" away as captives beyond Damascus, where Israel had extended its borders by victories in war (see 2 Kings 14.28).
*6.6 your nation: Hebrew "Joseph's descendants" (see the note at 5.6).

*6.10 the name of the LORD: Two relatives seem to be carrying out corpses for burial. One of them warns the other to be careful not even to say "Thank the LORD!" for fear that the mention of his name may cause something worse to happen.
*6.13 Lo-Debar and Karnaim: Two cities east of the River Jordan that were captured by Jeroboam II (see 2 Kings 14.25). In Hebrew "Lo-Debar" can mean "nothing", and "Karnaim" means "two horns (of a bull)". Horns were symbols of strength, and so the people are boasting about their military power (defeat of "two horns"), which Amos says is "nothing" (Lo-Debar).
*6.14 Lebo-Hamath . . . Arabah Brook: The northern and southern boundaries of the northern kingdom.
*7.1 locusts: See the note at 4.9.

his share of the grain and before the rest of the grain has been harvested.* ² In my vision the locusts ate every crop in the land, and I said to the LORD, "Forgive me for asking, but how can the nation survive? It's so weak."

³ Then the LORD felt sorry and answered, "I won't let it be destroyed."

A vision of fire

⁴ The LORD showed me that he is going to send a ball of fire to burn up everything on earth, including the sea. ⁵ Then I said, "Won't you please stop? How can our weak nation survive?"

⁶ Again the LORD felt sorry and answered, "I won't let it be destroyed."

A vision of a measuring line

⁷ The LORD showed me a vision of himself standing beside a wall and holding a string with a weight tied to the end of it. The string and weight had been used to measure the straightness of the wall. ⁸ Then he asked, "Amos, what do you see?"

"A measuring line," I answered.

The LORD said, "I'm using this measuring line to show that my people Israel don't measure up, and I won't forgive them any more. ⁹ Their sacred places will be destroyed, and I will send war against the nation of King Jeroboam."*

Amos and Amaziah

¹⁰ Amaziah the priest at Bethel sent this message to King Jeroboam of Israel, "Amos is plotting against you in the very heart of Israel. Our nation cannot put up with his message for very long. ¹¹ Here is what he is saying:

'Jeroboam will be put to death,
and the people will be taken
to a foreign country.' "

¹² Then Amaziah told me, "Amos, take your visions and get out! Go back to Judah and earn your living there as a prophet. ¹³ Don't do any more preaching at Bethel. The king worships here at our national temple."

¹⁴ I answered:

I'm not a prophet! And I wasn't trained to be a prophet. I am a shepherd, and I take care of fig trees. ¹⁵ But the LORD told me to leave my herds and preach to the people of Israel. ¹⁶ And here you are, telling me not to preach! ¹⁷ Now, listen to what the LORD says about you:

Your wife will become
a prostitute in the city,
your sons and daughters
will be killed in war,
and your land will be divided
among others.
You will die in a country
of foreigners,
and the people of Israel
will be dragged
from their homeland.

CHAPTER 8

A basket of fruit

¹ The LORD God showed me a basket of ripe fruit ² and asked, "Amos, what do you see?"

"A basket of ripe fruit," I replied.

Then he said,

"This is the end*
for my people Israel.
I won't forgive them again.
³ Instead of singing
in the temple,
they will cry and weep.
Dead bodies will be everywhere.
So keep silent!
I, the LORD, have spoken!"

Israel is doomed

The LORD said:

⁴ You people crush those in need
and wipe out the poor.
⁵ You say to yourselves,
"How much longer before the end
of the New Moon Festival?
When will the Sabbath* be over?
Our wheat is ready,
and we want to sell it now.
We can't wait to cheat
and charge high prices
for the grain we sell.

---

*7.1 harvested: This would have been an especially bad time for a locust attack. The non-grain crops such as vegetables and onions were just beginning to sprout, and the grain crops were almost ready to be harvested.

*7.9 Jeroboam: Jeroboam II, who ruled Israel 783–743 BC.

*8.2 end: In Hebrew "ripe fruit" and "end" sound alike.

*8.5 New Moon Festival . . . Sabbath: Selling grain at these times was forbidden by the Law of Moses.

We will use dishonest scales
6   and mix dust in the grain.
Those who are needy and poor
    don't have any money.
We will make them our slaves
for the price
    of a pair of sandals."

7 I, the LORD, won't forget any of this,
though you take great pride
    in your ancestor Jacob.'
8 Your country will tremble,
    and you will mourn.
It will be like the River Nile
that rises and overflows,
    then sinks back down.

9 On that day, I, the LORD God,
will make the sun
    go down at midday,
and I will turn daylight into darkness.
10 Your festivals and joyful singing
    will turn into sorrow.
You will wear sackcloth*
    and shave your heads,
as you would at the death
    of your only son.
    It will be a horrible day.

11 I, the LORD, also promise you
a terrible shortage,
    but not of food and water.
You will hunger and thirst
    to hear my message.
12 You will search everywhere —
from north to south,
    from east to west.
You will go all over the earth,
    seeking a message
from me, the LORD.
    But you won't find one.

13 Your beautiful young women
and your young men
    will faint from thirst.
14 You made promises
in the name of Ashimah,
    the goddess of Samaria.
And you made vows in my name
at the shrines
    of Dan and Beersheba.'
But you will fall
    and never get up.

CHAPTER 9

Judgment on Israel

1 I saw a vision of the LORD
standing by the temple altar,*
    and he said,
"Shake the columns
until the tops fall loose,
    and the doorposts crumble.
Then make the pieces fall
    on the people below.
I will take a sword and kill
    anyone who escapes.

2 "If they dig deep into the earth
or climb to the sky,
    I'll reach out and get them.
3 If they escape to the peaks
of Mount Carmel,
    I'll search and find them.
And if they hide from me
    at the bottom of the ocean,
I'll command a sea monster
    to bite them.
4 I'll send a sword to kill them,
wherever their enemies
    drag them off as captives.
I'm determined to hurt them,
    not to help them."

His name is the LORD

5 When the LORD God All-Powerful
touches the earth, it melts,
    and its people mourn.
God makes the earth rise
and then fall,
    just like the River Nile.
6 He built his palace in the heavens
and let its foundations
    rest on the earth.'
He scoops up the ocean
and empties it on the earth.
    His name is the LORD.

The LORD is God

7 Israel, I am the LORD God,
    and the Ethiopians*
are no less important to me
    than you are.
I brought you out of Egypt,
    but I also brought

---

*8.10 sackcloth: A rough, dark-coloured cloth made
from goat or camel hair and used to make grain
sacks. It was worn in times of trouble or sorrow.

*9.1 the temple altar: The one at Bethel.
*9.7 Ethiopians: The Hebrew text has "people of
Cush", which was a region south of Egypt that
included parts of the present countries of Ethiopia
and Sudan.

the Philistines from Crete'
and the Arameans from Kir.*

8 My eyes have seen
what a sinful nation you are,
and I'll wipe you out.
But I will leave a few
of Jacob's descendants.
I, the LORD, have spoken!

9 At my command, all of you
will be sifted like grain.
Israelites who remain faithful
will be scattered among the nations.
And the others will be trapped
like rubbish in a sieve.
10 Some of you are evil,
and you deny
that you will ever get caught.
But you will be killed.

Israel's bright future

The LORD's promise to Israel

11 In the future, I will rebuild
David's fallen kingdom.
I will build it from its ruins
and set it up again,
just as it used to be.
12 Then you will capture Edom
and the other nations that are mine.
I, the LORD, have spoken,
and my words will come true.

13 You will have such a harvest
that you won't be able
to bring in all your wheat
before ploughing time.
You will have grapes left over
from season to season;
your fruitful vineyards
will cover the mountains.
14 I'll make Israel prosper again.
You will rebuild your towns
and live in them.
You will drink wine
from your own vineyards
and eat the fruit you grow.
15 I'll plant your roots deep
in the land I have given you,
and you won't ever be uprooted again.
I, the LORD God, have spoken!

Additional notes

'1.1 Jehoash: The Hebrew text has "Joash", another spelling of the name.
'1.1 messages: Or "visions".
'1.3 Syria: The Hebrew text has "Damascus", the leading city of Syria.
'1.5 people: Or "king".
'1.5 Wicked Valley: The Hebrew text has "Aven Valley", probably the fertile valley between the Lebanon and the anti-Lebanon mountains.
'1.5 I will . . . Beth-Eden: Or "I will destroy the people of Wicked Valley and the king who rules from Beth-Eden." Beth-Eden was a city-state on the banks of the River Euphrates.
'1.6 Philistia: The Hebrew text has "Gaza", one of the main Philistine cities.
'1.8 king: Or "people".
'1.9 Phoenicia: The Hebrew text has "Tyre", which was one of the two Phoenician cities; the other was Sidon, which is not mentioned by Amos.
'2.13 ground: One possible meaning for the difficult Hebrew text of verse 13.
'3.9 Philistia: The Hebrew text has "Ashdod", one of the leading cities of Philistia.
'3.12 some . . . couches: One possible meaning for the difficult Hebrew text.
'4.1 fat cows: The Hebrew text has "cows of Bashan", a fertile plain famous for its rich pastures and well-fed cattle.
'4.2 taken . . . hooks: One possible meaning for the difficult Hebrew text.
'4.3 Harmon: Hebrew; some manuscripts of one ancient translation "Mount Hermon", a mountain in the north of Palestine, on the way to Assyria.
'4.13 I let . . . thinking: Or "No one's secret thoughts are hidden from me."
'5.5 Gilgal . . . nothing: In Hebrew "Gilgal" and "dragged away" sound something alike. Bethel (meaning "house of God") is sometimes called "house of nothing" or "house of sin" by the prophets (see Hosea 4.15; 5.8; 10.5–8).
'5.26 star: One possible meaning for the difficult Hebrew text of verse 26.
'6.2 Calneh . . . Hamath . . . Gath: City-states captured by the Assyrians: Calneh in 738 BC, Hamath in 720, and Gath in 711.
'6.10 prepare . . . burial: Or "burn it" or "burn incense for it".
'6.12 oceans: Or "rocks".
'8.7 though . . . Jacob: Or "though I am the God that Jacob proudly worshipped."
'8.14 You made . . . Beersheba: Or "You made promises to the goddess Ashimah at Samaria, and you made vows in the names of other gods at the shrines of Dan and Beersheba."
'9.6 He built . . . earth: One possible meaning for the difficult Hebrew text.
'9.7 Crete: Hebrew "Caphtor".

---

*9.7 Philistines . . . Arameans from Kir: The Philistines were Israel's enemies to the west, and the Arameans were enemies to the north-east. For Kir, see the note at 1.5.

See also: 9.11–12: Acts 15.16–18.

Obadiah

The basics

What's the point? You cannot escape the judgment of God

What happens? Obadiah prophesies that God will destroy Edom.

What should I remember? 15 'The day is coming when I, the LORD, will judge the nations. And, Edom, you will pay in full for what you have done.'

More details

Setting the scene The Edomites had been cruel to Israel. Now they'll be punished...

What's it all about? A prediction of the destruction of Edom. They have attacked his people, now he will attack them. It's short, but to the point.

Footsteps

Edom's pride: 1.1–14
Israel's victory: 1.15–21

Edom's pride and punishment

¹ The LORD God gave Obadiah
a message▸ about Edom,
  and this is what we heard:
"I, the LORD, have sent a messenger
with orders for the nations
  to attack Edom."

² The LORD said to Edom:
  I will make you the weakest
  and most despised nation.
³ You live in a mountain fortress,▸

because your pride
makes you feel safe from attack,
  but you are mistaken.
⁴ I will still bring you down,
even if you fly higher
  than an eagle
or nest among the stars.
  I, the LORD, have spoken!

⁵ If thieves break in at night, they steal
  only what they want.
And people who harvest grapes
  always leave some unpicked.
But, Edom, you are doomed!
⁶ Everything you treasure most
  will be taken from you.
⁷ Your allies can't be trusted.
They will force you out
  of your own country.
Your best friends
will trick and trap you,
  even before you know it.

⁸ Edom, when this happens,
I, the LORD, will destroy
  all your marvellous wisdom.
⁹ Warriors from the city of Teman*
  will be terrified,
and you descendants of Esau*
  will be wiped out.

Edom's cruelty

The LORD condemns Edom's cruelty

¹⁰ You were cruel to your relatives,
  the descendants of Jacob.*

---

*v9 **Teman:** A famous city in Edom.
*v9 **descendants of Esau:** The people of Edom were descendants of Esau, the brother of Jacob (Israel).
*v10 **descendants of Jacob:** Jacob and Esau were brothers (see the note on Esau at verse 9).

See also: **v1–14:** Isa 34.5–17; 63.1–6; Jer 49.7–22; Ezek 25.12–14; 35.1–15; Amos 1.11–12; Mal 1.2–5.

Now you will be destroyed,
disgraced for ever.
[11] You stood there and watched
as foreigners entered Jerusalem
and took what they wanted.
In fact, you were no better
than those foreigners.

[12] Why did you celebrate
when such a dreadful disaster
struck your relatives?
Why were you so pleased
when everyone in Judah
was suffering?
[13] They are my people,
and you were cruel to them.
You went through their towns,
sneering and stealing
whatever was left.
[14] In their time of torment,
you ambushed refugees
and handed them over
to their attackers.

Victory for Israel

The LORD will judge the nations

[15] The day is coming
when I, the LORD,
will judge the nations.
And, Edom, you will pay in full
for what you have done.

[16] I forced the people of Judah▸
to drink the wine of my anger
on my sacred mountain.
Soon the neighbouring nations
must drink their fill —
then vanish without a trace.

Victory for Israel

[17] The LORD's people who escape
will go to Mount Zion,
and it will be holy.
Then Jacob's descendants
will capture the land of those
who took their land.
[18] Israel▸ will be a fire,
and Edom will be straw
going up in flames.
The LORD has spoken!

[19] The people of Israel
who live in the Southern Desert
will take the land of Edom.
Those who live in the hills
will capture Philistia,
Ephraim, and Samaria.

And the tribe of Benjamin
will conquer Gilead.

[20] Those who return from captivity
will control Phoenicia
as far as Zarephath.▸
Captives from Jerusalem
who were taken to Sepharad*
will capture the towns
of the Southern Desert.
[21] Those the LORD has saved
will live on Mount Zion
and rule over Edom.▸
Then the kingdom will belong
to the LORD.

---

*v20 Sepharad: Possibly the city of Sardis, the capital of Lydia, a country north and west of Media. This would refer to those captives from Judah who had been taken beyond the kingdom of Babylonia.

Additional notes

▸v1 message: Or "vision".
▸v3 mountain fortress: The Hebrew text has "rocky cliff", which sounds like "Sela", the capital of Edom, a fortress city built on a mountain.
▸v16 I forced . . . Judah: Or "I will force the people of Edom".
▸v18 Israel: Hebrew "The descendants of Jacob and of Joseph".
▸v20 Those who return . . . Zarephath: One possible meaning for the difficult Hebrew text.
▸v21 Those the LORD . . . Edom: Or "Leaders on (from) Mount Zion will save the people and rule over Edom."

Jonah

The basics

What's the point? God is always ready to forgive anyone.

What happens? Jonah is told to tell the Assyrians to repent. He runs away. God brings him back. Using a fish. The Assyrians repent. Jonah is grumpy.

What should I remember? 4.2 'You are a kind and merciful God, and you are very patient. You always show love, and you don't like to punish anyone, not even foreigners.'

More details

Setting the scene Jonah is a prophet in Israel. Then God tells him to go and prophesy to the most frightening people on earth...

What's it all about? Jonah is much more than an entertaining story about a disobedient bloke and a very big fish. It's a story about how even your worst enemies can receive God's forgiveness.

Who wouldn't run from the Assyrians? They were the Nazis of their day; a frightening, brutal people. 'See?' God is saying. 'They are my children too. Even they can repent.'

And another thing

Although it's in the 'Prophets' section, Jonah only contains one line of prophecy: 'Forty days from now, Nineveh will be destroyed!'

Footsteps

Jonah prophesies for Jeroboam: 2 Kings 14.25
Jonah runs away: 1.1–17
In the belly of the fish: 2.1–10
The Assyrians repent: 3.1–10
All people matter: 4.1–11

Jonah runs from the Lord

CHAPTER 1

¹ One day the LORD told Jonah, the son of Amittai, ² to go to the great city of Nineveh* and say to the people, "The LORD has seen your terrible sins. You are doomed!"

³ Instead, Jonah ran from the LORD. He went to the seaport of Joppa and bought a ticket on a ship that was going to Spain. Then he got on the ship and sailed away to escape.

⁴ But the LORD made a strong wind blow, and such a bad storm came up that the ship was about to be broken to pieces. ⁵ The sailors were frightened, and they all started praying to their gods. They even threw the ship's cargo overboard to make the ship lighter.

All this time, Jonah was down below deck, sound asleep. ⁶ The ship's captain went to him and said, "How can you sleep at a time like this? Get up and pray to your God! Perhaps he will have pity on us and keep us from drowning."

⁷ Finally, the sailors got together and said, "Let's ask our gods to show us* who caused all this trouble." It turned out to be Jonah.

⁸ They started asking him, "Are you the one who brought all this trouble on us? What business are you in? Where do you come from? What is your country? Who are your people?"

---

*1.2 Nineveh: Capital city of Assyria, a hated enemy of Israel.
*1.7 ask . . . show us: The Hebrew text has "cast lots", which were pieces of wood or stone used to find out how and when to do something. In this case, the lots would show who was the guilty person.
See also: 1.1: 2 King 14.25.

Life files

Jonah

Background: Son of Ammitai

What's the story?

Jonah is a successful prophet in Israel (2 Kings 14.25) but one day God commands him to do a different task: he is to go to Nineveh and call on the Assyrians to repent. Jonah, not unreasonably, looks on this as a suicide mission and promptly zooms off in the opposite direction. However, a storm blows up, and Jonah is thrown overboard. He is swallowed by an enormous sea creature and, after three days and three nights the fish spews him up onto dry land. Jonah agrees to go to Nineveh.

When he gets there he preaches his simple message... and the city repents. This centre of wickedness and cruelty hears Jonah's words and changes its ways. Wholesale repentance breaks out. At which Jonah is very annoyed, mainly because he feels the whole thing was going to happen anyway. If God was going to do this anyway, then why did he have to go through all that stuff with the fish?

What's the point?

Jonah's journey was not just about giving a message to the worst city on earth. It was also about giving a message to Jonah. Jonah wanted to keep God's grace for himself and for his people. He didn't want it extended to other people – certainly not those in such an evil place as Nineveh. But God is concerned for all people. As Jonah says of him, 'you don't like to punish anyone; not even foreigners.'

More...

Assyria p.500
Our God is a God of second chances p.984
Racism p.1308
What happens if we take a wrong turn? p.601

---

[9] Jonah answered, "I'm a Hebrew, and I worship the LORD God of heaven, who made the sea and the dry land."

[10] When the sailors heard this, they were frightened, because Jonah had already told them he was running from the LORD. Then they said, "Do you know what you have done?"

[11] The storm kept getting worse, until finally the sailors asked him, "What should we do with you to make the sea calm down?"

[12] Jonah told them, "Throw me into the sea, and it will calm down. I'm the cause of this terrible storm."

[13] The sailors tried their best to row to the shore. But they could not do it, and the storm kept getting worse every minute. [14] So they prayed to the LORD, "Please don't let us drown for taking this man's life. Don't hold us guilty for killing an innocent man. All this happened because you wanted it to." [15] Then they threw Jonah overboard, and the sea calmed down. [16] The sailors were so terrified that they offered a sacrifice to the LORD and made all kinds of promises.

[17] The LORD sent a big fish to swallow Jonah, and Jonah was inside the fish for three days and three nights.

Jonah prays to the Lord

CHAPTER 2

[1] From inside the fish, Jonah prayed to the LORD his God:

[2] When I was in trouble, LORD,
    I prayed to you,
        and you listened to me.
    From deep in the world
        of the dead,
    I begged for your help,
        and you answered my prayer.

[3] You threw me down
        to the bottom of the sea.
    The water was churning all around;
    I was completely covered
        by your mighty waves.
[4] I thought I was swept away
        from your sight,
    never again to see
        your holy temple.

[5] I was almost drowned
    by the swirling waters
        that surrounded me.

See also: 1.17: Matt 12.40.

Seaweed had wrapped
  around my head.
6 I had sunk down below
    the underwater mountains;
  I knew that for ever,
    I would be a prisoner there.

But, you, LORD God,
  rescued me from that pit.
7 When my life was slipping away,
  I remembered you —
and in your holy temple
  you heard my prayer.

8 All who worship worthless idols
  turn from the God
    who offers them mercy.
9 But with shouts of praise,
  I will offer a sacrifice
    to you, my LORD.
  I will keep my promise,
  because you are the one
    with power to save.

10 The LORD commanded the fish to vomit up
Jonah on the shore. And it did.

Jonah goes to Nineveh, and its people believe God's message

CHAPTER 3

1 Once again the LORD told Jonah 2 to go to
that great city of Nineveh and preach his
message of doom.

3 Jonah obeyed the LORD and went to
Nineveh. The city was so big that it took
three days just to walk through it. 4 After
walking for a day, Jonah warned the people,
"Forty days from now, Nineveh will be
destroyed!"

5 They believed God's message and set a
time when they would go without eating to
show their sorrow. Then everyone in the city,
no matter who they were, dressed in
sackcloth.

6 When the king of Nineveh heard what
was happening, he also dressed in sackcloth;
he left the royal palace and sat in dust.*

---

*3.5–6 dressed in sackcloth . . . sat in dust:
Sackcloth was a rough, dark-coloured cloth made
from goat or camel hair and used to make grain
sacks. Sometimes people wore sackcloth and sat in
dust to show how sorry they were for their sins.
See also: 3.4–5: Matt 12.41; Luke 11.32.

Viewpoints

The Bible is full of great heroes – what did they have that we don't?

Contributed by Austin A

'Once again the LORD told Jonah to go to
that great city of Nineveh and preach his
message of doom. Jonah obeyed the LORD
and went to Nineveh.'

I expect you know the story of Jonah – he
heard God's instructions, tried to run away
from God, got swallowed by a fish, God
saved him, and Jonah finally did what he
was told. At this point he has just been
rescued from the fish, and God calls him to
go to Nineveh and deliver his message.

I think this passage really shows God's
character. So many times we run away from
what God tells us to do. If you have become
a Christian, then you have given your life to
God. All of it. No ifs, buts or maybes: all of it.
Even if we try to run away, God still has
plans for us, and still wants to work through
us. It doesn't matter what we've done or
how far we've strayed, if we turn around
God will return to us and keep working. God
will not only keep working, but if we follow
his commands he will do amazing things
through us.

Jonah, when he finally obeyed, was able to
bring God's message to a city of 120,000
people who, most of them, decided to go
back to God too. God will work in us, no
matter who we are or what we've done.
God loves us.

'God does not choose the equipped, he
equips the chosen.'

More...

Jonah p.982
Our God is a God of second chances p.984
Assyria p.500

7-9 Then he and his officials sent out an order for everyone in the city to obey. It said:

> None of you or your animals may eat or drink a thing. Each of you must wear sackcloth, and you must even put sackcloth on your animals.
>
> You must also pray to the LORD God with all your heart and stop being sinful and cruel. Perhaps God will change his mind and have mercy on us, so we won't be destroyed.

10 When God saw that the people had stopped doing evil things, he had pity and did not destroy them as he had planned.

Jonah is angry because the Lord showed mercy

CHAPTER 4

1 Jonah was really upset and angry. 2 So he prayed:

> Our LORD, I knew from the very beginning that you wouldn't destroy Nineveh. That's why I left my own country and headed for Spain. You are a kind and merciful God, and you are very patient. You always show love, and you don't like to punish anyone, not even foreigners.
>
> 3 Now let me die! I'd be better off dead.

4 The LORD replied, "What right do you have to be angry?"

5 Jonah then left through the east gate of the city and made a shelter to protect himself from the sun. He sat under the shelter, waiting to see what would happen to Nineveh.

6 The LORD made a vine grow up to shade Jonah's head and protect him from the sun. Jonah was very happy to have the vine, 7 but early the next morning the LORD sent a worm to chew on the vine, and the vine dried up. 8 During the day the LORD sent a scorching wind, and the sun beat down on Jonah's head, making him feel faint. Jonah was ready to die, and he shouted, "I wish I were dead!"

9 But the LORD asked, "Jonah, do you have the right to be angry about the vine?"

"Yes, I do," he answered, "and I'm angry enough to die."

10 But the LORD said:

Viewpoints

Our God is a God of second chances

Contributed by Lucy S

'Don't you think I should be concerned about that big city?'

Jonah was a bit of a complainer. Not only did he run away from God's calling, but when he finally got to Nineveh, by a very, very long way around, he kept on complaining! Not because the people didn't listen to him, but because they did!

What was up with this man? Well, he was angry with God. This was because when God saw that the people of Nineveh had repented, he could no longer destroy them but instead had mercy on them.

God tried to explain this to an angry Jonah. He sent a plant that protected Jonah from the sun, and then destroyed it the next day, and guess what? Jonah started complaining! But God told him that he had no right to be angry: Jonah had not created the plant or cared for it. But God had, just like he created and loved the people of Nineveh.

Even though many people are living in 'spiritual darkness', God still cares for them immensely. He is the fairest judge and treats everyone with mercy. Not only does he give second chances but third, sixth and tenth – as many as we need. When people think of Jonah they think of a big fish. But Jonah's message is about how the Lord wants to have mercy on EVERYONE, no matter what they've done; God still loves them and wants to forgive them!

Who do you know who needs to be told this today? Don't be a Jonah and run the other way, instead take that step of faith and tell people about the heart of God and how it's full of love for them no matter what they've done in the past.

More...

Jonah p.982
Assyria p.500

See also: 4.2: Exod 34.6. 4.3: 1 King 19.4.

You are concerned about a vine that you
did not plant or take care of, a vine that
grew up in one night and died the next.
[11] In that city of Nineveh there are more
than a hundred and twenty thousand
people who cannot tell right from wrong,
and many cattle are also there. Don't you
think I should be concerned about that
big city?

Micah

The basics

What's the point? God will punish. But one day a chosen king will bring peace.

What happens? Micah delivers a series of prophecies against Israel and Judah, condemning their behaviour.

What should I remember? 6.8 'The LORD God has told us what is right and what he demands: "See that justice is done, let mercy be your first concern, and humbly obey your God."'

More details

Setting the scene Israel and Judah are under threat. Micah is told to speak out...

What's it all about? Micah is a resident of Moresheth, a small town in southern Judah.

He brings a message to Jerusalem, the capital of Judah, and Samaria, the capital of Israel. Instead of worshipping God the nations have been worshipping false idols; instead of obeying God's laws, they have been dealing in injustice and cheating the poor. Now God is going to punish them.

Micah also looks beyond the impending punishment. It won't end there. Micah also points ahead to a chosen king, a figure in the future who will take care of all his people, just like a shepherd taking care of his sheep. And he'll be born in Bethlehem.

Now, I wonder who that could be...

And another thing

Micah talks about temple prostitutes. At many pagan temples men were encouraged to pay to have sex with temple prostitutes. This was supposed to be a way of worshipping the local

god, but it was also a way for the temple to make a profit. God sees sex as something pure between husband and wife; these religions had turned it a shameful, profit-making activity.

Footsteps

Judgment: 1.1–16
Evil rulers: 3.1–12
Out of Bethlehem: 5.1–5
Empty inside: 7.1–7
Come and lead us! 7.14–20

The Lord will punish his people

CHAPTER 1

¹ I am Micah from Moresheth.* And this is the message about Samaria and Jerusalem* that the LORD gave to me when Jotham, Ahaz, and Hezekiah* were the kings of Judah.

---

*1.1 Moresheth: A town in southern Judah not far from Gath. In verse 14 it is called Moresheth-Gath.

*1.1 Samaria and Jerusalem: Samaria was the capital of the northern kingdom (Israel), and Jerusalem was the capital of the southern kingdom (Judah).

*1.1 Jotham, Ahaz, and Hezekiah: Jotham, the son of Uzziah, ruled Judah 740–736 BC; Ahaz, the son of Jotham, ruled 736–716 BC; Hezekiah, the son of Ahaz, ruled 716–687 BC.

See also: 1.1: a 2 King 15.32–38; 2 Chron 27.1–7; b 2 King 16.1–20; 2 Chron 28.1–27; c 2 King 16.1–20.21; 2 Chron 29.1–32.33.

Judgment on Samaria

2 Listen, all of you!
Earth and everything on it,
pay close attention.
The LORD God accuses you
from his holy temple.*

3 And he will come down
to crush underfoot
every pagan altar.

4 Mountains will melt
beneath his feet
like wax beside a fire.
Valleys will vanish like water
rushing down a ravine.

5 This will happen because of
the terrible sins of Israel,
the descendants of Jacob.
Samaria has led Israel to sin,
and pagan altars at Jerusalem
have made Judah sin.

6 So the LORD will leave Samaria
in ruins —
merely an empty field
where vineyards are planted.
He will scatter its stones
and destroy its foundations.

7 Samaria's idols will be smashed,
and the wages
of temple prostitutes*
will be destroyed by fire.
Silver and gold from those idols
will then be used
by foreigners
as payment for prostitutes.

Judah is doomed

8 Because of this tragedy,*
I go barefoot and naked.
My crying and weeping
sound like howling wolves
or ostriches.

9 The nation is fatally wounded.
Judah is doomed.
Jerusalem will fall.

10 Don't tell it in Gath!
Don't even cry.

Instead, roll in the dust
at Beth-Leaphrah.*

11 Depart naked and ashamed,
you people of Shaphir.'
The town of Bethezel' mourns
because no one from Zaanan'
went out to help.'

12 Everyone in Maroth'
hoped for the best,
but the LORD sent disaster
down on Jerusalem.

13 Get the war chariots ready,
you people of Lachish.*
You led Jerusalem into sin,
just as Israel did.*

14 Now you will have to give
a going-away gift*
to Moresheth.*
Israel's kings will discover
that they cannot trust
the town of Achzib.*

15 People of Mareshah,*
the LORD will send someone
to capture your town.
Then Israel's glorious king
will be forced to hide
in Adullam Cave.*

---

*1.2 holy temple: Possibly the one in heaven, though it may be the Jerusalem temple.
*1.7 wages of temple prostitutes: At pagan temples, people had sex with prostitutes as a way of worshipping the idols, and the money earned in this way was used to support the pagan religion.
*1.8 this tragedy: Either the destruction of Samaria (verses 6-7) or the coming destruction of Judah and Jerusalem.
*1.10 Gath . . . Beth-Leaphrah: Gath was a Philistine city; Beth-Leaphrah is unknown, but in Hebrew it sounds like "House of Dust."
*1.13 Lachish: The chief city of south-west Judah, about forty-eight kilometres from Jerusalem.
*1.13 led . . . sin . . . did: Or "You led Jerusalem and Israel into sin." In Hebrew "Lachish" sounds like "a team of horses (that pulls a war chariot)". And the sin may be that Lachish led the nation to trust the power of war chariots instead of the LORD. But the sin could be idolatry or some false teachings that were brought in from Egypt by way of Lachish.
*1.14 going-away gift: The gift (dowry) that a bride's father gave her when she left the home of her parents to live with the family of her husband. In Hebrew the word for "bride" or "fiancee" sounds like "Moresheth".
*1.14 Moresheth: Hebrew "Moresheth-Gath"; the home of Micah (see verse 1).
*1.14 Achzib: Meaning "lie" or "deception" was near Adullam Cave (verse 15), where David hid from King Saul (see 1 Samuel 22.1-2). Micah probably means that the people of Israel (including their king) will have to run for their lives, but will find that all hope for escape is merely a "lie" (see verse 15).
*1.15 Mareshah: Sounds something like the Hebrew word for "conqueror" and was only a few kilometres north-east of Lachish.
*1.15 Adullam Cave: See the note at 1.14.

¹⁶ Judah, shave your head
  as bald as a vulture
    and start mourning.
  Your precious children*
  will be dragged off
    to a foreign country.

CHAPTER 2

Punishment for those who abuse their power

¹ Doomed! You're doomed!
  At night you lie in bed,
    making evil plans.
  And when morning comes,
  you do what you've planned
    because you have the power.
² You grab any field or house
    that you want;
  you cheat families
    out of homes and land.

³ But here is what the LORD says:
  "I am planning trouble for you.
  Your necks will be caught
    in a noose,
  and you will be disgraced
    in this time of disaster."

⁴ When that happens,
  this sorrowful song
    will be sung about you:
  "Ruined! Completely ruined!
  The LORD has taken our land
    and given it to traitors."
⁵ And so you will never again
  own property
    among the LORD's people.

⁶ "Enough of your preaching!"
    That's what you tell me.
  "We won't be disgraced,
    so stop preaching!"

⁷ Descendants of Jacob,
    is it right for you to claim
  that the LORD did what he did
    because he was angry?
  Doesn't he always bless
    those who do right?
⁸ My people, you have even stolen
    clothes right off the backs
  of your unsuspecting soldiers
    returning home from battle.

⁹ You take over lovely homes
  that belong to the women
    of my nation.
  Then you cheat their children
  out of the inheritance
    that comes from the LORD.

¹⁰ Get out of here, you crooks!
  You'll find no rest here.
  You're not fit to belong
    to the LORD's people,
    and you will be destroyed.
¹¹ The only prophet you want
  is a liar who will say,
  "Drink and get drunk!"

A promise of hope

The LORD said:

¹² I, the LORD, promise
    to bring together
  the people of Israel
    who have survived.
  I will gather them,
    just as a shepherd
  brings sheep together,
    and there will be many.
¹³ I will break down the gate
  and lead them out —
    then I will be their king.

The Lord will punish evil rulers and lying prophets

CHAPTER 3

¹ Listen to me,
    you rulers of Israel!
  You know right from wrong,
² but you prefer to do evil
    instead of what is right.
  You skin my people alive.
  You strip off their flesh,
³   break their bones,
    cook it all in a pot,
  and gulp it down.

⁴ Some day you will beg the LORD
    to help you,
  but he will turn away
    because of your sins.

⁵ You lying prophets promise
  security for anyone
    who gives you food,
  but disaster for anyone
    who refuses to feed you.

---

*1.16 **precious children:** The towns mentioned in verses 10–15.

Here is what the LORD says to you prophets:

6 "You will live in the dark,
    far from the sight of the sun,
        with no message from me.
7 You prophets and fortune-tellers
    will all be disgraced,
        with no message from me."

8 But the LORD has filled me
    with power and his Spirit.
I have been given the courage
    to speak about justice
and to tell you people of Israel
    that you have sinned.
9 So listen to my message,
    you rulers of Israel!
You hate justice
    and twist the truth.
10 You make cruelty and murder
    a way of life in Jerusalem.
11 You leaders accept bribes
    for dishonest decisions.
You priests and prophets
    teach and preach,
        but only for money.

Then you say,
"The LORD is on our side.
    No harm will come to us."
12 And so, because of you,
    Jerusalem will be ploughed under
    and left in ruins.
Thorns will cover the mountain
    where the temple now stands.

A new temple in a new Israel

CHAPTER 4

Peace and prosperity

1 In the future, the mountain
    with the LORD's temple
        will be the highest of all.
It will reach above the hills,
    and every nation will rush to it.
2 People of many nations
    will come and say,
"Let's go up to the mountain
    of the LORD God of Jacob
        and worship in his temple."

The LORD will teach us his Law
    from Jerusalem,
        and we will obey him.

3 He will settle arguments
    between distant
        and powerful nations.
They will beat their swords
    and their spears
        into rakes and shovels;
they will never again make war
    or attack one another.
4 Everyone will find rest
    beneath their own fig trees
        or grape vines,
and they will live in peace.
This is a solemn promise
    of the LORD All-Powerful.

5 Others may follow their gods,
    but we will always follow
        the LORD our God.

The LORD will lead his people home

6 The LORD said:

At that time
    I will gather my people —
the lame and the outcasts,
    and all into whose lives
        I have brought sorrow.
7 Then the lame and the outcasts
    will belong to my people
        and become a strong nation.
I, the LORD, will rule them
    from Mount Zion for ever.
8 Mount Zion in Jerusalem,
    guardian of my people,
        you will rule again.

9 Jerusalem, why are you crying?
    Don't you have a king?
        Have your advisers gone?
Are you suffering
    like a woman in childbirth?
10 Keep on groaning with pain,
    you people of Jerusalem!
If you escape from your city
    to the countryside,
you will still be taken
    as prisoners to Babylonia.
But later I will rescue you
    from your enemies.

11 Zion, because of your sins
    you are surrounded
        by many nations who say,
"We can hardly wait
    to see you disgraced."
12 But they don't know
    that I, the LORD,

See also: 3.12: Jer 26.18.   See also: 4.3: Isa 2.4; Joel 3.10. 4.4: Zech 3.10.

989

have gathered them here
  to grind them like grain.
¹³ Smash them to pieces, Zion!
  I'll let you be like a bull
  with iron horns and bronze hoofs.
  Crush those nations
  and bring their wealth to me,
  the LORD of the earth.

CHAPTER 5

A promised ruler

¹ Jerusalem, enemy troops
  have surrounded you;ᵇ
  they have struck Israel's ruler
  in the face with a stick.

² Bethlehem Ephrath,
  you are one of the smallest towns
  in the nation of Judah.
  But the LORD will choose
  one of your people
  to rule the nation —
  someone whose family
  goes back to ancient times.ᵇ
³ The LORD will abandon Israel
  only until this ruler is born,
  and the rest of his family
  returns to Israel.
⁴ Like a shepherd
  taking care of his sheep,
  this ruler will lead
  and care for his people
  by the power and glorious name
  of the LORD his God.
  His people will live securely,
  and the whole earth will know
  his true greatness,
⁵ because he will bring peace.

Assyria will be defeated

Let Assyria attack our country
  and our palaces.
  We will counter-attack,
  led by a number of rulers
⁶ whose strong army will defeat
  the nation of Assyria.ᵇ
  Yes, our leaders will rescue us,
  if those Assyrians
  dare to invade our land.

The survivors will be safe

⁷ A few of Jacob's descendants
  survived and are scattered
  among the nations.

But the LORD will let them
  cover the earth
  like dew and rain
  that refreshes the soil.
⁸ At present they are scattered,
  but later they will attack,
  as though they were fierce lions
  pouncing on sheep.
  Their enemies will be torn to shreds,
  with no one to save them;
⁹ they will be helpless,
  completely destroyed.

Idols will be destroyed in Israel

¹⁰ The LORD said:

At that time I will wipe out
  your cavalry and chariots,
¹¹ as well as your cities
  and your fortresses.
¹² I will stop you
  from telling fortunes
  and practising witchcraft.
¹³ You will no longer worship
  the idols or stone images
  you have made —
  I will destroy them,
¹⁴ together with the sacred poles*
  and even your towns.
¹⁵ I will become furious
  and take revenge
  on the nations
  that refuse to obey me.

Israel is declared guilty

CHAPTER 6

The LORD's challenge to his people

¹ The LORD said to his people:

Come and present your case
  to the hills and mountains.
² Israel, I am bringing charges
  against you —
  I call upon the mountains
  and the earth's firm foundation
  to be my witnesses.

³ My people, have I wronged you
  in any way at all?
  Please tell me.
⁴ I rescued you from Egypt,
  where you were slaves.

---

*5.14 **sacred poles:** Used in the worship of Asherah,
the fertility goddess.

See also: **5.2:** Matt 2.6; John 7.42.   **5.6:** Gen 10.8–11.

See also: **6.4: a** Exod 12.50–51; **b** Exod 4.10–16; **c** Exod 15.20.

Real life

The poor

Contributed by Tearfund

The Bible is full of God's demands on behalf of the poor. Isaiah 58 talks about loosing chains of injustice, freeing the oppressed, sharing food with the hungry, sheltering the homeless and clothing the naked. Micah 6.8 calls for a just and merciful life.

A concern for the poor is at the very centre of who God is; you could say it is at the very heart of God. Not simply in terms of his love, as we often refer to the heart, but also in his actions – the heart is a 'doing' organ after all! Someone whose feelings lack consequences is often referred to as half-hearted. God's heart simply overflows with love in action in the Old Testament, and doesn't stop in the New...

Colossians 1.15 describes Jesus as the visible likeness of an invisible God. In which case you'd expect him to have his father's heart for his people. Jesus was the ultimate demonstration of feelings in action. From the beginning of his ministry, Jesus makes it clear that he is the Messiah and the evidence of this will be seen in the transformation of the lives of the poor, outcasts and marginalised.

'The Spirit of the LORD is on me, because he has anointed me to preach good news to the poor. He has sent me to proclaim freedom for the prisoners and recovery of sight for the blind, to release the oppressed, to proclaim the year of the LORD's favour.' (Luke 4.18–19)

That's all great, but what about us? Well the scary thing is that Jesus's departure left us with this challenge.

'I tell you the truth, anyone who has faith in me will do what I have been doing. He will do even greater things than these.' (John 14.12)

So it's clear then – God has a heart for the poor, Jesus expresses this through his life of action and we are called to do even more on his behalf. Tearfund exists as just one way to help you to take part in God's mission to his world.

Think

Who do we mean by 'the poor'?
Look at the passages in Psalms and the prophets again. Could you truthfully substitute your own name for God's in these verses?

Act

Pray for projects run by Tearfund and other agencies.
Spot news stories about global poverty and find out what you can do.
Become a volunteer advocate in your locality, speaking up for people who can't speak for themselves.

Check

In the Psalms, God uses many words in connection with the poor that suggest they are high on his agenda.
    DEFEND Psalm 10.18;
    GIVE Psalm 146.7;
    FILL Psalm 107.9;
    STAND Psalm 109.31;
    RAISE Psalm 113.7;
    LIFT Psalm 113.7;
    PROVIDE JUSTICE Psalm 140.12

More...

Fair trade p.923
Giving your money p.1300
Shopping p.973
Civil disobedience p.1247

I sent Moses, Aaron, and Miriam
   to be your leaders.
⁵ Don't forget the evil plans
   of King Balak of Moab
or what Balaam son of Beor*
   said to him.
Remember how I, the LORD,
   saved you many times
on your way from Acacia
   to Gilgal.*

True obedience

⁶ What offering should I bring
when I bow down to worship
   the LORD God Most High?
Should I try to please him*
by sacrificing
   calves a year old?
⁷ Will thousands of sheep
or rivers of olive oil
   make God satisfied with me?
Should I sacrifice to the LORD
my firstborn child as payment
   for my terrible sins?
⁸ The LORD God has told us
what is right
   and what he demands:
"See that justice is done,
let mercy be your first concern,
   and humbly obey your God."

Cheating and violence

The LORD said:

⁹ I am the LORD,
and it makes sense to respect
   my power to punish.
So listen to my message
   for the city of Jerusalem:ᵇ
¹⁰ You store up stolen treasures
   and use dishonest scales.ᵇ
¹¹ But I, the LORD, will punish you
for cheating with weights
   and with measures.
¹² You rich people are violent,
   and everyone tells lies.

¹³ Because of your sins,
   I will wound you and leave you
      ruined and defenceless.
¹⁴ You will eat,
      but still be hungry;
   you will store up goods,
      but lose everything —
   I, the LORD, will let it all
      be captured in war.
¹⁵ You won't harvest what you plant
   or use the oil
      from your olive trees
   or drink the wine
      from grapes you grow.

¹⁶ Jerusalem, this will happen
      because you followed
   the sinful example
      of kings Omri and Ahab.*
   Now I will destroy you
      and your property.
   Then the people of every nation
      will make fun and insult you.

CHAPTER 7

Israel is corrupt

¹ I feel so empty inside —
   like someone starving
      for grapes or figs,
   after the vines and trees
      have all been picked clean.
² No one is loyal to God;
   no one does right.
Everyone is brutal
and eager to deceive
   everyone else.
³ People co-operate to commit crime.
Judges and leaders demand bribes,
   and rulers cheat in court.ᵇ
⁴ The most honest of them
   is worse than a thorn patch.

Your doom has come!
Lookouts sound the warning,
   and everyone panics.
⁵ Don't trust anyone,
   not even your best friend,
and be careful what you say
   to the one you love.

---

*6.5 **Balak . . . Beor:** See Numbers 22—24.
*6.5 **Acacia to Gilgal:** Acacia was where the Israelites camped after the experience with Balaam (see Numbers 25.1; Joshua 2.1; 3.1); Gilgal was where they camped while waiting to attack Jericho (see Joshua 4.19—5.12).
*6.6 **try to please him:** This refers to what are traditionally called "burnt sacrifices", which were offered as a way of pleasing the LORD.
See also: 6.5: a Num 22.2—24.25; **b** Josh 3.1—4.19.

*6.16 **Omri and Ahab:** King Ahab was the son of Omri and the husband of the evil Jezebel. Almost two centuries before Micah, the prophet Elijah had spoken against the idolatry and the other sinful practices that Ahab had encouraged in Israel (see 1 Kings 16.21—34; 18.1—18; 21.1—26).
See also: 6.16: a 1 King 16.23—28; **b** 1 King 16.29—34; 21.25—26.

⁶ Sons refuse to respect
　　their own fathers,
　daughters rebel against
　　their own mothers,
　and daughters-in-law despise
　　their mothers-in-law.
　Your family is now your enemy.
⁷ But I trust the LORD God
　　to save me,
　and I will wait for him
　　to answer my prayer.

The nation turns to God

⁸ My enemies, don't be glad
　　because of my troubles!
　I may have fallen,
　　but I will get up;
　I may be sitting in the dark,
　　but the LORD is my light.
⁹ I have sinned against the LORD.
　And so I must endure his anger,
　　until he comes to my defence.
　But I know that I will see him
　　making things right for me
　　and leading me to the light.

¹⁰ You, my enemies, said,
　　"The LORD God is helpless."
　Now each of you
　will be disgraced
　　and put to shame.
　I will see you trampled
　　like mud in the street.

A bright future

¹¹ Towns of Judah, the day is coming
　　when your walls will be rebuilt,
　　and your boundaries enlarged.
¹² People will flock to you
　　from Assyria and Egypt,
　from Babylonia'
　　and everywhere else.
¹³ Those nations will suffer disaster
　　because of what they did.

Micah's prayer and the LORD's answer

¹⁴ Lead your people, LORD!
　　Come and be our shepherd.
　Grasslands surround us,
　　but we live in a forest.
　So lead us to Bashan and Gilead,*

---

*7.14 **Bashan and Gilead:** Two regions east of the
River Jordan, known for their fertile pasture lands.
See also: 7.6: Matt 10.35–36; Luke 12.53.

Helpline

Help! I can't stop feeling guilty!

'I feel so guilty. I've prayed for forgiveness, but I can't stop feeling this way.'

The first step in becoming a Christian is to understand that we're all guilty; that all of us have sinned. The next step is to understand that, as soon as we ask, God can take away that guilt.

But sometimes, even after confessing a particular sin and putting things right, we just don't feel as though God has truly forgiven us. As Micah says, God will 'freely forgive our sin and guilt' (Micah 7.18).

Sometimes we just can't believe it's that simple. Sometimes, the problem is that Satan doesn't want you to feel forgiven. Satan is described in Revelation as an 'accuser', so he's happy to remind you of your sin. But, God has thrown our sin away. Micah says God has trampled on all our sins and thrown them into the ocean!

Don't go deep sea diving for your sins. Don't bring them back from the depths. God has taken your guilt and destroyed it: your sins have been trampled to death and buried at sea!

Three things

Confess

Confess your sins to God. Ask for his forgiveness. You're forgiven.

Understand

Understand that Jesus died for you. He's dealt with your guilt. Try to let it go.

Reassure

If it helps, talk things through with someone you trust. Often it helps to have someone else remind us and reassure us of God's forgiveness. Only God can forgive our sins, but sometimes it's really good to have someone else reassure us of that fact.

More...

Forgiveness p.614
Redemption p.292

and let us find pasture
as we did long ago.

The LORD said:

15 I, the LORD, will work miracles
just as I did when I led you
out of Egypt.

16 Nations will see this
and be ashamed because
of their helpless armies.
They will be in shock,
unable to speak or hear,

17 because of their fear of me,
your LORD and God.
Then they will come trembling,
crawling out of their fortresses
like insects or snakes,
lapping up the dust.

No one is like God

The people said:

18 Our God, no one is like you.
We are all that is left
of your chosen people,
and you freely forgive
our sin and guilt.
You don't stay angry for ever;
you're glad to have pity

19 and pleased to be merciful.
You will trample on our sins
and throw them in the sea.

20 You will keep your word
and be faithful to Jacob
and to Abraham,
as you promised our ancestors
many years ago.

'2.9 inheritance . . . LORD: The Hebrew text has "my glory", which refers to the inheritance of land that the LORD had promised his people.

'2.10 destroyed: One possible meaning for the difficult Hebrew text.

'4.11 We . . . disgraced: Or "We'll pull up your skirt and expose your nakedness!"

'5.1 Jerusalem . . . you: Or "Jerusalem, you are slashing yourself in sorrow, because of the enemy troops".

'5.2 family . . . times: Or "kingdom is eternal".

'5.6 the nation of Assyria: The Hebrew text uses both "land of Assyria" and "land of Nimrod", which was a poetic name for Assyria.

'6.9 Jerusalem: One possible meaning for the difficult Hebrew text of verse 9.

'6.10 scales: One possible meaning for the difficult Hebrew text of verse 10.

'7.3 court: One possible meaning for the difficult Hebrew text of verse 3.

'7.12 Babylonia: The Hebrew text has "the river", meaning the River Euphrates, which stood for Babylonia.

Additional notes

'1.11 Shaphir: Mentioned only here in the Old Testament; in Hebrew "Shaphir" means "beautiful".

'1.11 Bethezel: Mentioned only here in the Old Testament; in Hebrew "Bethezel" means "house next door".

'1.11 Zaanan: Mentioned only here in the Old Testament; in Hebrew "Zaanan" means "one who goes out".

'1.11 The town . . . help: Or "No one from Zaanan refused to desert their town, and Bethezel mourns because it is left undefended."

'1.12 Maroth: Mentioned only here in the Old Testament; in Hebrew "Maroth" means "bitter".

'2.4 The LORD . . . traitors: One possible meaning for the difficult Hebrew text.

Nahum

The basics

What's the point? To show how God would punish the evil Assyrians.

What happens? Nahum tells them that the Lord is angry. Only those who turn to the Lord will be saved. Which means that the time is up for the Assyrians.

What should I remember? 1.3 'The LORD is powerful, yet patient; he makes sure that the guilty are always punished. He can be seen in storms and in whirlwinds; clouds are the dust from his feet.'

More details

Setting the scene Assyria is the mightiest and cruellest power on earth. But its time is running out...

What's it all about? Nahum's name means 'comforter', although, since he prophesied the complete destruction of Nineveh, he wasn't much of a comfort to the Assyrians. His message is simple: the Assyrians are doomed. Nahum talks about the destruction of Nineveh, the capital city of Assyria. It's payback time. God may be 'slow to anger', but he's not going to leave evil unpunished.

Footsteps

When God gets angry: 1.1–6
The messenger is coming: 1.7–15
Doom to the crime capital! 3.1–19

The fierce anger of the Lord

CHAPTER 1

¹ I am Nahum from Elkosh.* And this is the message⁴ that I wrote down about Nineveh.*

The fierce anger of the LORD

² The LORD God demands loyalty.
In his anger, he takes revenge
on his enemies.
³ The LORD is powerful,
yet patient;
he makes sure that the guilty
are always punished.
He can be seen in storms
and in whirlwinds;
clouds are the dust from his feet.

⁴ At the LORD's command,
oceans and rivers dry up.
Bashan, Mount Carmel,
and Lebanon* wither,
and their flowers fade.
⁵ At the sight of the LORD,
mountains and hills
tremble and melt;
the earth and its people
shudder and shake.
⁶ Who can stand the heat
of his furious anger?
It flashes out like fire
and shatters stones.

---

*1.1 **Elkosh:** The location of Elkosh is not known.
*1.1 **Nineveh:** The capital of Assyria, the hated enemy of Israel.
*1.4 **Bashan, Mount Carmel, and Lebanon:** Three regions noted for their trees and flowers.
See also: 1.1–3.19: Isa 10.5–34; 14.24–27; Zeph 2.13–15.

Assyria's doom brings hope for the Lord's people

The power of Assyria will be broken

7 The LORD is good.
  He protects those who trust him
    in times of trouble.
8 But like a roaring flood,
  the LORD chases his enemies
    into dark places and destroys them.
9 So don't plot against the LORD!
  He wipes out his enemies,
    and they never revive.
10 They are like drunkards
    overcome by wine,
  or like dry thorn bushes
    burning in a fire.'
11 Assyria, one of your rulers
  has made evil plans
    against the LORD.

12 But the LORD says, "Assyria,
  no matter how strong you are,
    you are doomed!
  My people Judah,
  I have troubled you before,
    but I won't do it again.
13 I'll snap your chains and set you free
    from the Assyrians."

14 Assyria, this is what else
    the LORD says to you:
  "Your name will be forgotten.
  I will destroy every idol
    in your temple,
  and I will send you to the grave,
    because you are worthless."

15 Look towards the mountains,
    people of Judah!
  Here comes a messenger
    with good news of peace.
  Celebrate your festivals.
    Keep your promises to God.
  Your evil enemies are destroyed
  and will never again
    invade your country.

Nineveh, the capital of Assyria, will be destroyed

CHAPTER 2

1 Nineveh, someone is coming
  to attack and scatter you.

See also: 1.15: Isa 52.7.

Guard your fortresses!
Watch the road!
  Be brave!
  Prepare for battle!
2 Judah and Israel are like trees
  with branches broken
    by their enemies.
  But the LORD is going to restore
    their power and glory.

3-4 Nineveh, on this day of attack,
  your enemies' shields are red;
    their uniforms are crimson.
  Their horses' prance,
    and their armoured' chariots
  dart around like lightning
    or flaming torches.
5 An officer gives a command.
  But his soldiers stumble,
    as they hasten to build
  a shelter to protect themselves
  against rocks thrown down
    from the city wall.

6 The river gates* fly open,
  and panic floods the palace.
7 Nineveh is disgraced.
  The queen is dragged off.
  Her servant women mourn;
  they sound like doves,
  and they beat their breasts
    in sorrow.'
8 Nineveh is like a pond
  with leaking water.
  Shouts of "Stop! Don't go!"
    can be heard everywhere.
  But everyone is leaving.

9 Enemy soldiers shout,
  "The city is full of treasure
    and all kinds of wealth.
  Steal her silver! Grab her gold!"

10 Nineveh is doomed! Destroyed!
  Her people tremble with fear;
    their faces turn pale.'
11 What happened to this city?
  They were safer there
  than powerful lions in a den,
    with no one to disturb them.
12 These are the same lions
  that ferociously attacked
    their victims,
  then dragged away the flesh
    to feed their young.

*2.6 river gates: Nineveh was protected by a moat filled with water from the nearby River Tigris.

13 The LORD All-Powerful,
    is against you, Nineveh.
God will burn your chariots
and send an army to kill
    those young lions of yours.
You will never again
    make victims of others
or send messengers to threaten
    everyone on this earth.

CHAPTER 3

Punishment for Nineveh

The LORD said:

1 Doom to the crime capital!
Nineveh, city of murder
    and treachery,
2 here is your fate —
cracking whips,
    churning wheels;
galloping horses,
    roaring chariots;
3 cavalry attacking,
    swords and spears flashing;
soldiers stumbling
    over piles of dead bodies.
4 You were nothing more
    than a prostitute
using your magical charms
and witchcraft
    to attract and trap nations.

5 But I, the LORD All-Powerful,
    am now your enemy.
I will pull up your skirt
and let nations and kingdoms
    stare at your nakedness.
6 I will cover you with rubbish,
    treat you like trash,
    and rub you in the dirt.
7 Everyone who sees you
    will turn away and shout,
"Nineveh is done for!
Is anyone willing to mourn
    or to give her comfort?"

Nineveh's fate is sealed

8 Nineveh, do you feel safer
    than the city of Thebes?*
The River Nile
    was its wall of defence.'

9 Thebes trusted the mighty power
    of Ethiopia* and Egypt;
the nations of Put* and Libya
    were her allies.
10 But she was captured and taken
    to a foreign country.
Her children were murdered
    at every street corner.
The members of her royal family
    were auctioned off,
and her high officials
    were bound in chains.

11 Nineveh, now it's your turn!
You will get drunk and try to hide
    from your enemy.
12 Your fortresses are fig trees
    with ripe figs.
Merely shake the trees,
    and fruit will fall
    into every open mouth.
13 Your army is weak.
Fire has destroyed the crossbars
    on your city gates;
now they stand wide open
    to your enemy.

14 Your city is under attack.
Haul in extra water!
    Strengthen your defences!
Start making bricks!
Stir the mortar!
15 You will still go up in flames
    and be cut down by swords
that will wipe you out like wheat
    attacked by grasshoppers.
So, go ahead and increase
    like a swarm of locusts!*

16 More merchants are in your city
    than there are stars
    in the sky —
but they are like locusts
    that eat everything,
    then fly away.
17 Your guards and your officials
    are swarms of locusts.
On a chilly day
    they settle on a fence,

---

*3.9 Ethiopia: The Hebrew text has "Cush", which
was a region south of Egypt that included parts of the
present countries of Ethiopia and Sudan.
*3.9 Put: A region in Africa, possibly part of the
present country of Libya.
*3.15 locusts: A type of grasshopper that comes in
swarms and causes great damage to plant life.

---

*3.8 Thebes: In 663 BC, the Assyrian King
Ashurbanipal captured this Egyptian city, which
seems to have been built with protection similar to
that of Nineveh.

but when the sun comes out,
    they take off
        to who-knows-where.

18 King of Assyria,
    your officials and leaders
        sleep the eternal sleep,
    while your people are scattered
        in the mountains.
    Yes, your people are sheep
        without a shepherd.
19 You're fatally wounded.
        There's no hope for you.
    But everyone claps
        when they hear this news,
    because your constant cruelty
        has caused them pain.

Additional notes

›**1.1 message:** Or "vision".
›**1.10 fire:** One possible meaning for the difficult
Hebrew text of verse 10.
›**2.3–4 horses:** Two ancient translations; Hebrew
"spears".
›**2.3–4 armoured:** One possible meaning for the
difficult Hebrew text.
›**2.7 sorrow:** One possible meaning for the difficult
Hebrew text of verse 7.
›**2.10 faces turn pale:** Or "ashes cover their faces".
›**3.8 was its . . . defence:** One possible meaning for
the difficult Hebrew text.

Habakkuk

The basics

What's the point? Why is God allowing bad things to happen to his people?

What happens? Habbakuk asks God questions. And God replies.

What should I remember? 3.19 'The LORD gives me strength. He makes my feet as sure as those of a deer, and he helps me stand on the mountains.'

More details

Setting the scene Judah is a violent, unjust country. Invasion is imminent.

What's it all about? Habbakuk lived in troubled times. Everything was falling apart. So Habakkuk argues with God. He asks questions and God replies. And in the end, Habakkuk responds with a moving song of faith.

Footsteps

The first conversation: 1.1–11
The second conversation: 1.12–2.20
Praise the LORD: 3.1–19

Habakkuk complains, and the Lord answers

CHAPTER 1

¹ I am Habakkuk the prophet. And this is the message᾽ that the LORD gave me.

Habakkuk complains to the LORD

² Our LORD, how long must I beg
for your help
before you listen?
How long before you save us
from all this violence?
³ Why do you make me watch
such terrible injustice?
Why do you allow violence,
lawlessness, crime, and cruelty
to spread everywhere?
⁴ Laws cannot be enforced;
justice is always the loser;
criminals crowd out honest people
and twist the laws around.

The LORD answers Habakkuk

⁵ Look and be amazed
at what's happening
among the nations!
Even if you were told,
you would never believe
what's taking place now.
⁶ I am sending the Babylonians.
They are fierce and cruel —
marching across the land,
conquering cities and towns.

⁷ How fearsome and frightening.
Their only laws and rules
are the ones they make up.
⁸ Their cavalry troops are faster
than leopards,
more ferocious than wolves
hunting at sunset,
and swifter than hungry eagles
suddenly swooping down.

⁹ They are eager to destroy,᾽
and they gather captives
like handfuls of sand.
¹⁰ They make fun of rulers
and laugh at fortresses,

See also: 1.5: Acts 13.41. 1.6: 2 King 24.2.

while building earth mounds
so they can capture cities.*
¹¹ Then suddenly they disappear
like a gust of wind —
those sinful people who worship
their own strength.

Habakkuk complains again

¹² Holy LORD God, mighty rock,*
you are eternal,
and we᾽ are safe from death.
You are using those Babylonians
to judge and punish others.᾽
¹³ But you can't stand sin or wrong.
So don't sit by in silence
while they gobble up people
who are better than they are.

¹⁴ The people you put on this earth
are like fish or reptiles
without a leader.
¹⁵ Then an enemy comes along
and takes them captive
with hooks and nets.
It makes him so happy
¹⁶ that he offers sacrifices
to his fishing nets,
because they make him rich
and provide choice foods.
¹⁷ Will he keep hauling in his nets
and destroying nations
without showing mercy?

CHAPTER 2

The LORD answers Habakkuk again

¹ While standing guard
on the watchtower,
I waited for the LORD's answer,
before explaining the reason
for my complaint.᾽
² Then the LORD told me:
"I will give you my message
in the form of a vision.
Write it clearly enough
to be read at a glance.
³ At the time I have decided,
my words will come true.

You can trust what I say
about the future.
It may take a long time,
but keep on waiting —
it will happen!

⁴ "I, the LORD, refuse to accept
anyone who is proud.
Only those who live by faith
are acceptable to me."᾽

Trouble for evil people

⁵ Wine᾽ is treacherous,
and arrogant people
are never satisfied.
They are no less greedy
than death itself —
they open their mouths as wide
as the world of the dead
and swallow everyone.

⁶ But they will be mocked
with these words:
You're doomed!
You stored up stolen goods
and cheated others
of what belonged to them.
⁷ But without warning,
those you owe
will demand payment.
Then you will become
a frightened victim.
⁸ You robbed cities and nations
everywhere on earth
and murdered their people.
Now those who survived
will be as cruel to you.

⁹ You're doomed!
You made your family rich
at the expense of others.
You even said to yourself,
"I'm above the law."
¹⁰ But you will bring shame
on your family
and ruin to yourself
for what you did to others.
¹¹ The very stones and wood
in your home
will testify against you.

¹² You're doomed! You built a city
on crime and violence.
¹³ But the LORD All-Powerful
sends up in flames
what nations and people
work so hard to gain.

---

*1.10 earth mounds . . . cities:** Attacking armies
often built earth mounds against city walls to make it
easier for them to climb the wall and capture the city.
*1.12 mighty rock:** The Hebrew text has "rock",
which is sometimes used in poetry to compare the
LORD to a mountain where his people can run for
protection from their enemies.
See also: 2.3: Heb 10.37.

See also: 2.4: Rom 1.17; Gal 3.11; Heb 10.38.

Viewpoints

What is God's glory? And where is it?

Contributed by Esther S

'Just as water fills the sea, the land will be filled with people who know and honour the LORD.'

The part of this verse, which stood out to me first, and is incredibly exciting, was the word 'know'. The earth is already filled with God's glory – you can see him in every part of his creation. But there will be a day when every person on earth will KNOW of that glory – they'll all see the awesome God we serve reflected in everything around them.

So what is God's 'glory'? I found a very cool dictionary definition of the word: 'Radiant beauty, brightness, magnificence, splendour'. When we recognise the incredible beauty and awesomeness of our Creator, the only possible way to respond is with worship! Even when I know that though, it's so easy to become dulled to God by routine, tiredness, circumstances, which I allow to dictate the way I look at him – but that's when we've lost sight of his glory. In those 'dulled' times, refuse to be led by your feelings and ask God for an awareness of his radiant beauty, brightness, magnificence and splendour – and remember that one day the earth will be FILLED with people who are aware of it!

More...

Creation p.3

✿ Anorak corner

Firsts

1. Who was the first person in the Bible to get drunk?
2. Who was the first blacksmith in the Bible?
3. Where were the followers of Jesus first called Christians?
4. Who was the first person to see the risen Jesus?
5. David was the first king of Israel – true or false?
(Answers on p.1431)

14 Just as water fills the sea,
     the land will be filled
with people who know
     and honour the LORD.

15 You're doomed!
     You get your friends drunk,
just to see them naked.
16 Now you will be disgraced
     instead of praised.
The LORD will make you drunk,
     and when others see you naked,
you will lose their respect.
17 You destroyed trees and animals
     on Mount Lebanon;
you were ruthless to towns
     and people everywhere.
Now you will be terrorized.

Idolatry is foolish

18 What is an idol worth?
     It's merely a false god.
Why trust a speechless image
     made from wood or metal
by human hands?
19 What can you learn from idols
     covered with silver or gold?
They can't even breathe.
Pity anyone who says to an idol
     of wood or stone,
     "Get up and do something!"

20 Let all the world be silent —
     the LORD is present
in his holy temple.

Habakkuk gives praise to the Lord

CHAPTER 3

Habakkuk's prayer

1 This is my prayer:▸
2 I know your reputation, LORD,
     and I am amazed
at what you have done.
Please turn from your anger
     and be merciful;
do for us what you did
     for our ancestors.

See also: 2.14: Isa 11.9.

Big ideas

Prayer

Often we think of prayer as asking God for something. But prayer is more than just asking; it's also worshipping God, confessing to God, thanking God... it's really being in a relationship with God.

Prayer is relating to the Father, and, as any good father will tell you, sometimes your children will ask you for things, sometimes they'll tell you things, sometimes they'll just sit on your knee.

So prayer is about more than asking. It's about spending time in God's presence. You might have things you want to talk about with God, you might have requests you want to make for other people.

You might want to think about a particular verse or passage of the Bible, or pray about something that someone has said to you. All these things are aspects of prayer. (If you want to see prayer in all its variety, dip into Psalms. Psalms is 'prayer unlimited'.)

So we should not limit prayer. The Bible is full of people praying. They pray as individuals, as small groups and as nations. They pray in times of panic and distress, and in times of goodness and thankfulness. Sometimes they cry aloud at God, sometimes they sit and listen.

The important thing is to pray. Prayer is coming into the presence of God. So what's stopping you?

Footsteps

A week with Prayer

A cry for help: Psalms 5.1–12
A nation confesses: Ezra 9.5–15
Job begs God: Job 7.7–21
A prayer of trust: Psalms 11.1–7
The prayer of faith: Matthew 21.18–22
Jesus tells us how to pray: Matthew 6.5–18
Prayer in good times or bad: James 5.13–18

More...

God's love p.958
Praying to God p.1334

3 You are the same Holy God
  who came from Teman
    and Paran* to help us.
The brightness of your glory
    covered the heavens,
  and your praises were heard
    everywhere on earth.
4 Your glory shone like the sun,
    and light flashed from your hands,
      hiding your mighty power.
5 Dreadful diseases and plagues
    marched in front
      and followed behind.
6 When you stopped,
    the earth shook;
  when you stared,
    nations trembled;
  when you walked
    along your ancient paths,
  eternal mountains and hills
    crumbled and collapsed.
7 The tents of desert tribes
  in Cushan and Midian*
    were ripped apart.

8 Our LORD, were you angry
    with the monsters of the deep?*
  You attacked in your chariot
    and wiped them out.
9 Your arrows were ready
    and obeyed your commands.*

You split the earth apart
    with rivers and streams;
10 mountains trembled
    at the sight of you;
  rain poured from the clouds;
    ocean waves roared and rose.
11 The sun and moon stood still,
    while your arrows and spears
      flashed like lightning.

12 In your furious anger,
    you trampled on nations
13 to rescue your people
    and save your chosen one.*
  You crushed a nation's ruler
    and stripped his evil kingdom
      of its power.*

*3.3 Teman . . . Paran: Teman is a district in Edom, but the name is sometimes used of the whole country of Edom; Paran is the hill country along the western border of the Gulf of Aqaba. In Judges 5.4, the LORD is said to have marched from Edom to help his people; in Deuteronomy 33.2, Paran is mentioned in connection with the LORD's appearance at Sinai.
*3.7 Cushan and Midian: Tribes of the Arabian desert who were enemies of Israel.

Viewpoints

What mountains are there in your life at the moment? Meet the God who can lift you up

Contributed by Anne-Marie P

'The LORD gives me strength. He makes my feet as sure as those of a deer, and he helps me stand on the mountains.'

This verse is the concluding verse of a prayer in the form of song. It is also the last verse of the book of Habakkuk. So it must have some importance! It is a verse that gives hope and shows the almighty grace and power of the Lord! The rest of the prayer talks of Habakkuk standing in awe of God, and then it describes how he will praise God even through trials.

But he concludes with this amazing hope!

The verse sounds very beautiful and poetic – but what does it mean? Well, it basically means that God strengthens us and enables us to be light-footed and climb mountains. So what is the relationship between climbing mountains and us in 21st century non-mountainous Britain?

Think about the most taxing and traumatic problem in your life. It could be fitting into new schools, jobs, colleges or universities. Or you didn't get the exam results you needed. In these hard times God can seem the furthest person from you. But in fact you're actually sitting in his hands. When you feel like everything is over and that there is no hope, God fills that place that needs hope and strength. He gives you the strength to overcome those mountains and be set free! As one door closes another is opened – as cliched as it sounds, it's true! God opens those doors.

He will always remain with you. And he has the perfect plan for you!

More...

Prayer p.1002
Praying to God p.1334
Guidance p.685
Coping with suffering p.1391

¹⁴ His troops had come like a storm,
    hoping to scatter us
      and glad to gobble us up.
  To them we were refugees
    in hiding —
  but you smashed their heads
    with their own weapons.'
¹⁵ Then your chariots churned
    the waters of the sea.

Habakkuk's response to God's message

¹⁶ When I heard this message,'
  I felt weak from fear,
    and my lips quivered.
  My bones seemed to melt,
    and I stumbled around.
  But I will patiently wait.
  Some day those vicious enemies
    will be struck by disaster.'

Trust in a time of trouble

¹⁷ Fig trees may no longer bloom,
    or vineyards produce grapes;
  olive trees may be fruitless,
    and harvest time a failure;
  sheep pens may be empty,
    and cattle stalls vacant —
¹⁸ but I will still celebrate
  because the LORD God
    saves me.
¹⁹ The LORD gives me strength.
  He makes my feet as sure
    as those of a deer,
  and he helps me stand
    on the mountains.'

  To the music director:
  Use stringed instruments.

See also: 3.19: 2 Sam 22.34; Psa 18.33.

Additional notes

'**1.1 message:** Or "vision".
'**1.9 eager to destroy:** One possible meaning for the difficult Hebrew text.
'**1.12 we:** Hebrew; one ancient Jewish tradition "you".
'**1.12 You . . . others:** Or "You will judge and punish those Babylonians."
'**2.1 I . . . complaint:** One possible meaning for the difficult Hebrew text.
'**2.4 Only . . . me:** Or "But those who are acceptable to me will live because of their faithfulness."
'**2.5 Wine:** The Standard Hebrew Text; the Dead Sea Scrolls "Wealth".

›**3.1 prayer:** The Hebrew text adds "according to the shigionoth", which may mean a prayer of request or a prayer to be accompanied by a special musical instrument.

›**3.8 monsters of the deep:** The Hebrew text has "rivers and oceans", which may stand for the powerful monsters that were thought to have lived there before the LORD defeated them.

›**3.9 obeyed your commands:** One possible meaning for the difficult Hebrew text.

›**3.13 chosen one:** Or "chosen ones".

›**3.13 You crushed . . . power:** One possible meaning for the difficult Hebrew text.

›**3.14 but you . . . weapons:** One possible meaning for the difficult Hebrew text.

›**3.16 heard this message:** Or "saw this vision".

›**3.16 I will . . . disaster:** One possible meaning for the difficult Hebrew text.

›**3.19 stand on the mountains:** One possible meaning for the difficult Hebrew text.

Zephaniah

The basics

What's the point? The judgment of the LORD is on its way.

What happens? Zephaniah reveals that, on the day of the LORD, Judah will also be punished.

What should I remember? 2.3 'If you humbly obey the LORD, then come and worship him. If you do right and are humble, perhaps you will be safe on that day when the LORD turns loose his anger.'

More details

Setting the scene The people of Judah are looking forward to the day of the LORD, a wonderful time when God would come and punish their enemies. But Zephaniah tells them that it may not be as wonderful as they hoped.

What's it all about? Zephaniah talks about 'the day of the LORD'. The people of Judah believed that this would be the time when the LORD would zoom in and wipe out all their enemies. But Zephaniah tells them that they too will be judged. It was not only the other nations who had disobeyed God; Judah too would get what it deserved.

And another thing

Zephaniah prophesied during the reign of King Josiah (640–609BC), who was that rare thing, a good king (2 Kings 22.1–23.30; 2 Chronicles 34–5). Which means that Zephaniah himself might have been that even rarer thing: a prophet who was listened to.

Footsteps

Judgment on Judah: 1.1—2.3
Judgment on other nations: 2.4–15
Turn to the LORD: 3.1–20

Judah and Jerusalem will be punished on the day of the Lord

CHAPTER 1

¹ I am Zephaniah, the son of Cushi, the grandson of Gedaliah, the great-grandson of Amariah, and the great-great-grandson of Hezekiah.*

When Josiah son of Amon was king of Judah,* the LORD gave me this message.

Judgment on Judah

² I, the LORD, now promise
  to destroy everything
    on this earth —
³ people and animals,
    birds and fish.
  Everyone who is evil
    will crash to the ground,
  and I will wipe out
    the entire human race.
⁴ I will reach out to punish
    Judah and Jerusalem —
  nothing will remain of the god Baal;*
  nothing will be remembered
    of his pagan priests.
⁵ Not a trace will be found
  of those who worship stars
    from their rooftops,
  or bow down to the god Milcom,*
  while claiming loyalty
    to me, the LORD.

---

*1.1 **Hezekiah:** Ruled 716–687 BC.
*1.1 **Josiah . . . king of Judah:** Ruled 640–609 BC.
*1.4 **Baal:** A Canaanite fertility god.
*1.5 **Milcom:** An Ammonite fertility god.
See also: 1.1: 2 King 22.1–23.30; 2 Chron 34.1–35.27.

6 Nothing will remain of anyone
   who has turned away
   and rejected me.

7 Be silent! I am the LORD God,
   and the time is near.
   I am preparing
   to sacrifice my people
   and to invite my guests.

8 On that day I will punish
   national leaders
   and sons of the king,
   along with all who follow
   foreign customs.'

9 I will punish worshippers
   of pagan gods'
   and cruel palace officials
   who abuse their power.

10 I, the LORD, promise
   that on that day
   noisy crying will be heard
   from Fish Gate, New Town,
   and Upper Hills.

11 Everyone in Lower Hollow*
   will mourn loudly,
   because merchants
   and money changers
   will be wiped out.

12 I'll search Jerusalem with lamps
   and punish those people
   who sit there unworried
   while thinking,
   "The LORD won't do anything,
   good or bad."

13 Their possessions will be taken,
   their homes left in ruins.
   They won't get to live
   in the houses they build,
   or drink wine from the grapes
   in their own vineyards.

A terrible day

14 The great day of the LORD
   is coming soon, very soon.
   On that terrible day,
   fearsome shouts of warriors
   will be heard everywhere.

15 It will be a time of anger —
   of trouble and torment,

of disaster and destruction,
   of darkness and despair,
   of storm clouds and shadows,

16 of trumpet calls
   and battle cries
   against fortified cities
   and mighty fortresses.

17 The LORD warns everyone
   who has sinned against him,
   "I'll strike you blind!
   Then your blood and your insides
   will gush out like vomit.

18 Not even your silver or gold
   can save you on that day
   when I, the LORD, am angry.
   My anger will flare up
   like a furious fire
   scorching the earth
   and everyone on it."

Turn to the Lord

CHAPTER 2

1 You disgraceful nation,
   gather around,
2   before it's too late.
   The LORD has set a time
   when his fierce anger
   will strike like a storm
   and sweep you away.

3 If you humbly obey the LORD,
   then come and worship him.
   If you do right and are humble,
   perhaps you will be safe
   on that day when the LORD
   turns loose his anger.

The nations will be punished

Judgment on Philistia

4 Gaza and Ashkelon
   will be deserted
   and left in ruins.
   Ashdod will be emptied
   in broad daylight,
   and Ekron* uprooted.

---

*1.10–11 Fish Gate, New Town, and Upper Hills . . .
Lower Hollow: Names for different sections of
Jerusalem: Fish Gate was probably the main gate on
the north side of the city; New Town was a newer
section; Upper Hills may have been a suburb north of
the city; Lower Hollow was probably on the southern
edge of town.

*2.4 Gaza . . . Ekron: Gaza, Ashkelon, Ashdod, Ekron,
and Gath (not mentioned because it was already
destroyed) were the five major Philistine towns.
See also: 2.4–7: Isa 14.29–31; Jer 47.1–7; Ezek 25.15–17;
Joel 3.4–8; Amos 1.6–8; Zech 9.5–7.

⁵ To you people of Philistia⁾
who live along the coast,
the LORD has this to say:
"I am now your enemy,
and I'll wipe you out!"

⁶ Your coast will be changed
into pasture land
and sheep pens.⁾
⁷ The LORD God hasn't forgotten
those survivors in Judah,
and he will help them —
his people will take your land
to use for pasture.
And when evening comes,
they will rest
in houses at Ashkelon.*

Judgment on Moab and Ammon

⁸⁻⁹ The LORD All-Powerful,
the God of Israel, said:
I've heard Moab and Ammon
insult my people
and threaten their nation.⁾
And so, I swear by my very life
that Moab and Ammon will end up
like Sodom and Gomorrah —
covered with thorn bushes
and salt pits for ever.
Then my people who survive
will take their land.
¹⁰ This is how Moab and Ammon
will at last be repaid
for their pride —
and for sneering at the nation
that belongs to me,
the LORD All-Powerful.
¹¹ I will fiercely attack.
Then every god on this earth
will shrink to nothing,
and everyone of every nation
will bow down to me,
right where they are.

Judgment on Ethiopia

¹² People of Ethiopia,*
the sword of the LORD
will slaughter you!

Judgment on Assyria

¹³ The LORD will reach to the north
to crush Assyria
and overthrow Nineveh.*
¹⁴ Herds of wild animals
will live in its rubble;
all kinds of desert owls
will perch on its stones
and hoot in the windows.
Noisy ravens will be heard
inside its buildings,
stripped bare of cedar.⁾
¹⁵ This is the glorious city
that felt secure and said,
"I am the only one!"
Now it's merely ruins,
a home for wild animals.
Every passer-by simply sneers
and makes vulgar signs.

Judah and other nations will turn to the Lord

CHAPTER 3

Sinful Jerusalem

¹ Too bad for that disgusting,
corrupt, and lawless city!
² For ever rebellious
and rejecting correction,
Jerusalem refuses to trust
or obey the LORD God.
³ Its officials are roaring lions,
its judges are wolves;
in the evening they attack,
by morning nothing is left.
⁴ Jerusalem's prophets are proud
and not to be trusted.
The priests have disgraced
the place of worship
and abused God's Law.
⁵ All who do evil are shameless,
but the LORD does right
and is always fair.
With the dawn of each day,
God brings about justice.

⁶ The LORD wiped out nations
and left fortresses
crumbling in the dust.

---

*2.7 Ashkelon: A Philistine town; see the note at 2.4.
*2.12 Ethiopia: The Hebrew text has "Cush", which was a region south of Egypt that included parts of the present countries of Ethiopia and Sudan.
See also: 2.8–11: a Isa 15.1–16.14; 25.10–12; Jer 48.1–47; Ezek 25.8–11; Amos 1.13–15; **b** Jer 49.1–6; Ezek 21.28–32; 25.1–7; Amos 1.13–15. **2.9:** Gen 19.24. **2.12:** Isa 18.1–7.

*2.13 Nineveh: The capital of Assyria; Nineveh was protected by a moat filled with water from the nearby River Tigris.
See also: 2.13–15: Isa 10.5–34; 14.24–27; Nah 1.1–3.19.

Their streets and towns
were reduced to ruins
and emptied of people.
7 God felt certain that Jerusalem
would learn to respect
and obey him.
Then he would hold back
from punishing the city
and not wipe it out.
But everyone there was eager
to start sinning again.

Nations will turn to the LORD

8 The LORD said:
Just wait for the day
when I accuse you nations.
I have decided on a day,
when I will bring together
every nation and kingdom
and punish them all
in my fiery anger.
I will become furious
and destroy the earth.

9 I will purify each language
and make those languages
acceptable for praising me.'
Then, with hearts united,
everyone will serve
only me, the LORD.
10 From across the rivers of Ethiopia,*
my scattered people,
my true worshippers,
will bring offerings to me.

11 When that time comes,
you won't rebel against me
and be put to shame.
I'll do away with those
who are proud and arrogant.
Never will any of them strut around
on my holy mountain.
12 But I, the LORD, won't destroy
any of your people
who are truly humble
and turn to me for safety.
13 The people of Israel who survive
will live right and refuse to tell lies.
They will eat and rest
with nothing to fear.

A song of celebration

14 Everyone in Jerusalem and Judah,
celebrate and shout
with all your heart!

*3.10 Ethiopia: See the note at 2.12.
See also: 3.13: Rev 14.5.

Viewpoints 👁

People talk about God – but what are they really saying?

Contributed by Naomi C

'I will purify each language and make those languages acceptable for praising me.

Then, with hearts united, everyone will serve only me, the LORD.'

I hear people saying God's name many times a day – they say 'God' when something happens which they don't like, or if they're shocked. I guess a lot of the times people don't really think about what they're saying. Most people don't actually believe in God, and if they do then they often don't think he's relevant.

This verse of the Bible, along with quite a few others, tells us that one day, all the people of the earth will worship God with their words. Everyone will be so gobsmacked by the presence of God that they'll have to bow down and give him his worth – which is what 'worship' means.

This particular verse of the Bible is from the book of Zephaniah. In this section of the book, judgement is promised for the city of Jerusalem, which would not listen to God. But God also promises that there will be judgement for all the nations of the world, one day. We reckon this is talking about the day when Jesus comes back.

I know that what is written in this verse will actually happen, because it's a part of the Bible, completely trustworthy and true. But what I'd really like to see is everyone worshipping God together now; and if we believe that Jesus is coming soon, that's a pretty good incentive to start sharing the good news. And if people are talking about God already, even if it's not respectfully, maybe that's a good starting point?

More...

Help! How do I stop my friends doing wrong? p.1312
Worshipping God p.622

¹⁵ Zion, your punishment is over.
  The LORD has forced your enemies
    to turn and retreat.
  Your LORD is King of Israel
    and stands at your side;
  you don't have to worry
    about any more troubles.

¹⁶ Jerusalem, the time is coming,
    when it will be said to you:
  "Don't be discouraged
    or grow weak from fear!
¹⁷ The LORD your God
    wins victory after victory
    and is always with you.
  He celebrates and sings
    because of you,
  and he will refresh your life
    with his love."▸

The LORD's promise to his people

¹⁸ The LORD has promised:
  Your sorrow has ended,
    and you can celebrate.▸
¹⁹ I will punish those who ill-treat you.
  I will bring together the lame
    and the outcasts,
  then they will be praised,
    instead of despised,
  in every country on earth.
²⁰ I will lead you home,
    and with your own eyes
  you will see me bless you
    with all you once owned.
  Then you will be famous
    everywhere on this earth.
  I, the LORD, have spoken!

Additional notes

▸**1.3 Everyone . . . ground:** One possible meaning for the difficult Hebrew text.
▸**1.8 follow foreign customs:** Hebrew "wear foreign clothes".
▸**1.9 worshippers . . . gods:** The Hebrew text has "all who jump over the threshold", which was a Philistine religious practice (see 1 Samuel 5.5).
▸**2.5 people of Philistia:** The Hebrew text also mentions "Canaan" and "Cherethites", which are other ways of referring to the Philistines.
▸**2.6 pens:** One possible meaning for the difficult Hebrew text of verse 6.
▸**2.8–9 threaten their nation:** Or "boast about their own nation".
▸**2.14 stripped . . . cedar:** One possible meaning for the difficult Hebrew text.

▸**3.9 I will . . . praising me:** Or "I will change the hearts of all people and make them fit for praising me."
▸**3.17 refresh . . . love:** Two ancient translations; Hebrew "silently show you his love".
▸**3.18 celebrate:** One possible meaning for the difficult Hebrew text of verse 18.

Haggai

The basics

What's the point? What you spend your time and energy on reflects your real priorities.

What happens? Haggai inspires the weary people to rebuild the temple.

What should I remember? 2.5 'Don't worry. My Spirit is right here with you.'

More details

Setting the scene It's 520BC. The Jews who had been in exile have returned. But life is hard, and the temple is still in ruins...

What's it all about? The first Jews thought it was going to be a glorious return, but it's a major challenge just to stay alive. Haggai tells them to rethink their priorities. Get cracking on the temple: it's a sign that their lives and their land are dedicated to God.

Footsteps

Rebuild the temple: 1.1–15
I'll be here: 2.1–23

The Lord says the temple must be rebuilt

CHAPTER 1

¹ On the first day of the sixth month of the second year that Darius was king of Persia,* the LORD told Haggai the prophet to speak

*1.1 sixth month . . . king of Persia: Elul, the sixth month of the Hebrew calendar, from about mid-August to mid-September; the second year of the rule of Darius was 520 BC.

See also: 1.1: Ezra 4.24—5.2; 6.14.

his message to the governor of Judah and to the high priest.

So Haggai told Governor Zerubbabel and High Priest Joshua₂ ²⁻⁵ that the LORD All-Powerful had said to them and to the people:

You say this isn't the right time to build a temple for me. But is it right for you to live in expensive houses,* while my temple is a pile of ruins? Just look at what's happening. ⁶ You harvest less than you plant, you never have enough to eat or drink, your clothes don't keep you warm, and your wages are stored in bags full of holes.

⁷ Think about what I have said! ⁸ But first, go to the hills and get wood for my temple, so I can take pride in it and be worshipped there. ⁹ You expected much, but received only a little. And when you brought it home, I made that little disappear. Why have I done this? It's because you hurry off to build your own houses, while my temple is still in ruins. ¹⁰ That's also why the dew doesn't fall and your harvest fails. ¹¹ And so, at my command everything will become barren — your farmland and pastures, your vineyards and olive trees, your animals and you yourselves. All your hard work will be for nothing.

¹² Zerubbabel and Joshua, together with the others who had returned from exile in Babylonia, obeyed the LORD's message spoken by his prophet Haggai, and they started showing proper respect for the LORD. ¹³ Haggai then told them that the LORD had

*1.2–5 expensive houses: Either houses with panelled interiors or with roofs; the temple was not yet completely rebuilt at this time.

promised to be with them. ¹⁴ So the LORD God All-Powerful made everyone eager to work on his temple, especially Zerubbabel and Joshua. ¹⁵ And the work began on the twenty-fourth day of that same month.

The Lord promises to bless his people

CHAPTER 2

The glorious new temple

¹⁻² On the twenty-first day of the next month,* the LORD told Haggai the prophet to speak this message to Governor Zerubbabel, High Priest Joshua, and everyone else:

> ³ Does anyone remember how glorious this temple used to be? Now it looks like nothing. ⁴ But cheer up! Because I, the LORD All-Powerful, will be here to help you with the work, ⁵ just as I promised your ancestors when I brought them out of Egypt. Don't worry. My Spirit is⁾ here with you.
>
> ⁶ Soon I will again shake the heavens and the earth, the sea and the dry land. ⁷ I will shake the nations, and their treasures⁾ will be brought here. Then the brightness of my glory will fill this temple. ⁸ All silver and gold belong to me, ⁹ and I promise that this new temple will be more glorious than the first one. I will also bless this city⁾ with peace.

The past and the future

¹⁰ On the twenty-fourth day of the ninth month,* the LORD God All-Powerful told the prophet Haggai ¹¹ to ask the priests for their opinion on the following matter:

> ¹² Suppose meat ready to be sacrificed to God is being carried in the folds of someone's clothing, and the clothing rubs against some bread or stew or wine or olive oil or any other food. Would those foods that were touched then become acceptable for sacrifice?

*2.1–2 the next month: Tishri (also called Ethanim), the seventh month of the Hebrew calendar, from about mid-September to mid-October (see the note at 1.1).

*2.10 ninth month: Chislev, the ninth month of the Hebrew calendar, from about mid-November to mid-December.

See also: 2.3: Ezra 3.12. 2.5: Exod 29.45–46. 2.6: Heb 12.26.

Helpline

Help! I can't cope with revision

'I can't cope with this. The pressure, the expectations, all the work! I want to have fun again!'

There are times when there is nothing to do but get our heads down and go for it. When the Jews returned to Jerusalem they faced the daunting task of rebuilding the temple – it seemed like they would never finish. 'Don't worry, God tells them, "My Spirit is right here with you"' (Haggai 2.5).

You need self-discipline and perseverance when revising for exams. You've got to be organised and maybe a bit hard on yourself.

Talk to God. Get together with others who are facing similar pressures and pray together. Just before you enter the exam pray for a bit of calm and a good memory!

Exams are important, but don't cripple yourself with anxiety. Take revision seriously and do the best you can, but don't heap more pressure on yourself by imagining that absolutely everything hinges on them.

Three things

Concentrate

Get rid of distractions. Turn off the mobile, stop surfing the internet. Shut the door.

Organise

Write a revision plan. Schedule your study in. And then stick to it. Don't ignore the basic, practical stuff that will help you through the time. God will help you, but he expects you to do the work as well!

Support

Enlist the help of your parents, if possible. They'll help you to stick at it. Get together with friends to revise – make sure you do revise, don't just spend the time chatting! Many people have been through similar pressures before. They can understand and help and just give you someone so it doesn't feel like you're out there fighting on your own.

"Of course not," the priests answered.

¹³ Then Haggai said, "Suppose someone has touched a dead body and is considered unacceptable to worship God. If that person touches these foods, would they become unclean?"

"Of course they would," the priests answered.

¹⁴ So the LORD told Haggai to say:

That's how it is with this entire nation. Everything you do and every sacrifice you offer is unacceptable to me. ¹⁵ But from now on, things will get better. Before you started laying the foundation for the temple, ¹⁶ you recalled what life was like in the past.⁾ When you wanted two hundred kilogrammes of wheat, there were only a hundred, and when you wanted fifty jars of wine, there were only twenty. ¹⁷ I made all your hard work useless by sending mildew, mould, and hail — but you still did not return to me, your LORD.

¹⁸ Today you have completed the foundation for my temple, so listen to what your future will be like. ¹⁹ Although you have not yet harvested any grain, grapes, figs, pomegranates,* or olives, I will richly bless you in the days ahead.

The Lord promises to be with Zerubbabel

²⁰ That same day the LORD spoke to Haggai again and said:

²¹ Tell Governor Zerubbabel of Judah that I am going to shake the heavens and the earth ²² and wipe out kings and their kingdoms. I will overturn war chariots, and then cavalry troops will start slaughtering each other. ²³ But tell my servant Zerubbabel that I, the LORD All-Powerful, have chosen him, and he will rule in my name.⁾

---

*2.19 pomegranates:** A bright red fruit that looks like an apple.

See also: 2.13: Num 19.11–22.

Additional notes

›1.1 Governor . . . Joshua:** Hebrew "Governor Zerubbabel son of Shealtiel and High Priest Joshua son of Jehozadak".

›2.5 My Spirit is:** Or "I am".

›2.7 their treasures:** Hebrew "what they most desire".

›2.9 city:** Or "temple".

›2.16 you recalled . . . past:** One possible meaning for the difficult Hebrew text.

›2.23 rule in my name:** The Hebrew text has "be my signet ring", which signified authority.

Zechariah

The basics

What's the point? The future is in God's hands – and he knows what is going to happen.

What happens? Zechariah gives a series of messages to help the people. Enemy nations and unfaithful leaders will be punished. And, in the far future the glory will return. One day, the king will be back in Jerusalem.

What should I remember? 7.8–9 'So once again, I, the LORD All-Powerful, tell you, "See that justice is done and be kind and merciful to one another!"'

More details

Setting the scene Zechariah is living in Jerusalem, after the exiles have returned from Babylon. The city is demoralised and damaged. But Zechariah is given a fantastic glimpse into the future...

What's it all about? Good question. The book falls into three main sections. The first part contains a series of eight visions which are designed to encourage the people to keep going. The second part talks about the punishment that the LORD is going to inflict on nearby nations and unfaithful leaders.

The third part is about a time in the far future, where the LORD will return and rescue his people, where life-giving streams will flow out from Jerusalem to the rest of the earth.

Some of these visions, however, are very complicated and difficult to understand. The fact is that few books of the Bible are as difficult to understand as Zechariah. There are bits that baffle even the experts.

The good news, however, is that there are loads of bits we can understand. In particular,

there is a lot of good stuff about the Messiah – no Old Testament book of prophecy points more clearly to Jesus.

Zechariah pictures a time far in the future when the people will turn back to the Lord and be forgiven, when Jerusalem will be the centre of a great event, an event which will change the world.

Zechariah saw a great king coming, a shepherd, someone all creation was waiting for. No wonder you can feel his excitement on virtually every line.

And he wasn't exactly living in exciting times. Like Haggai, his contemporary, Zechariah was living in a demoralised city. In Jerusalem, the foundations of the temple had been laid, but nothing more. There were no priests worthy to make sacrifices, and the glory days seemed a long, long time ago.

But Zechariah inspires the people. They might be living in tough times, but one day the glory will return.

One day, the king will be back in Jerusalem. And this time it will be for good.

Footsteps

Get back to God: 1.1–17
The measuring line: 2.1–13
The ruling branch: 6.9–15
Did you really do it for me? 7.1–14
Punishment on the enemies: 8.1–23
The wounded shepherd: 13.7–9
Streams of life: 14.1–21

CHAPTER 1

Turn to the LORD

¹ I am the prophet Zechariah, the son of Berechiah and the grandson of Iddo.

In the eighth month of the second year that Darius was king of Persia,* the LORD told me to say:

2-3 Israel, I, the LORD All-Powerful, was very angry with your ancestors. But if you people will return to me, I will turn and help you. ⁴ Don't be stubborn like your ancestors. They were warned by the earlier prophets* to give up their evil and turn back to me, but they paid no attention.

⁵ Where are your ancestors now? Not even prophets live for ever. ⁶ But my warnings and my words spoken by the prophets caught up with your ancestors. So they turned back to me and said, "LORD All-Powerful, you have punished us for our sins, just as you had planned."

First vision: horses and riders

7-8 On the twenty-fourth day of Shebat,* which was the eleventh month of that same year,* the LORD spoke to me in a vision during the night: in a valley among myrtle trees,* I saw someone on a red horse, with riders on red, brown, and white horses behind him. ⁹ An angel was there to explain things to me, and I asked, "Sir, who are these riders?"

"I'll tell you," the angel answered.

¹⁰ Straight away, the man standing among the myrtle trees said, "These are the ones the LORD has sent to find out what's happening on earth."

¹¹ Then the riders spoke to the LORD's angel, who was standing among the myrtle trees, and they said, "We have gone everywhere and have discovered that the whole world is at peace."

¹² At this, the angel said, "LORD All-Powerful, for seventy years you have been angry with Jerusalem and the towns of Judah. When are you ever going to have mercy on them?"

¹³ The LORD's answer was kind and comforting. ¹⁴ So the angel told me to announce:

I, the LORD All-Powerful, am very protective of Jerusalem. ¹⁵ For a while I was angry with the nations, but now I am furious, because they have made things worse for Jerusalem and are not the least bit concerned. ¹⁶ And so, I will have pity on Jerusalem. The city will be completely rebuilt, and my temple will stand again. ¹⁷ I also promise that my towns will prosper — Jerusalem will once again be my chosen city, and I will comfort the people of Zion.

Second vision: animal horns

¹⁸ Next, I saw four animal horns.* 19-21 The angel who was sent to explain was there, and so I asked, "What do these mean?"

His answer was, "These horns are the nations that scattered the people of Judah, Israel, and Jerusalem, and took away their freedom."

Then the LORD showed me four blacksmiths, and I asked, "What are they going to do?"

He replied, "They are going to terrify and crush those horns."

Third vision: a measuring line

CHAPTER 2

¹ This time I saw someone holding a measuring line, ² and I asked, "Where are you going?"

"To measure Jerusalem," was the answer. "To find out how wide and long it is."

³ The angel who had spoken to me was leaving, when another angel came up to him ⁴ and said, "Hurry! Tell that man with the measuring line that Jerusalem won't have any boundaries. It will be too full of people and animals even to have a wall. ⁵ The LORD

---

*1.1 eighth month . . . second year . . . king of Persia: Bul, the eighth month of the Hebrew calendar, from about mid-October to mid-November; the second year of the rule of Darius was 520 BC.
*1.4 the earlier prophets: Those who preached before the fall of Jerusalem in either 587 or 586 BC.
*1.7-8 Shebat: The eleventh month of the Hebrew calendar, from about mid-January to mid-February.
*1.7-8 that same year: See verse 1 and the note there.
*1.7-8 myrtle trees: Evergreen shrubs, which in ancient times were symbols of fertility and renewal.
See also: 1.1: Ezra 4.24—5.1; 6.14. 1.8: a Rev 6.4; b Rev 6.2.

*1.18 animal horns: Horns, especially those of a bull, were symbols of power in ancient times. The number "four" would signal completeness, one representing each of the four directions.

himself has promised to be a protective wall of fire surrounding Jerusalem, and he will be its shining glory in the heart of the city."

A call to action

6 The LORD says to his people, "Run! Escape from the land in the north, where I scattered you to the four winds. 7 Leave Babylonia and hurry back to Zion."

8 Then the glorious LORD All-Powerful ordered me to say to the nations that had raided and robbed Zion:

Zion is as precious to the LORD as are his eyes. Whatever you do to Zion, you do to him. 9 And so, he will put you in the power of your slaves, and they will raid and rob you. Then you will know that I am a prophet of the LORD All-Powerful.

10 City of Zion, sing and celebrate! The LORD has promised to come and live with you. 11 When he does, many nations will turn to him and become his people. At that time you will know that I am a prophet of the LORD All-Powerful. 12 Then Judah will be his part of the holy land, and Jerusalem will again be his chosen city.

13 Everyone, be silent!
    The LORD is present
    and moving about
    in his holy place.

Fourth vision: Joshua and Satan

CHAPTER 3

1 I was given another vision. This time Joshua the high priest was standing in front of the LORD's angel. And there was Satan, standing at Joshua's right side, ready to accuse him. 2 But the LORD said, "Satan, you are wrong. Jerusalem is my chosen city, and this man was rescued like a stick from a flaming fire."

3 Joshua's clothes were filthy. 4 So the angel told some of the people to remove Joshua's filthy clothes. Then he said to Joshua, "This means you are forgiven. Now I will dress you in priestly clothes."

5 I spoke up and said, "Also put a clean priestly turban on his head." Then they dressed him in priestly clothes and put the turban on him, while the LORD's angel stood there watching.

6 After this, the angel encouraged Joshua by telling him that the LORD All-Powerful had promised:

7 If you truly obey me, I will put you in charge of my temple, including the courtyard around it, and you will be allowed to speak at any time with the angels standing beside me.* 8 Listen carefully, High Priest Joshua and all you other priests. You are a sign of things to come, because I am going to bring back my servant, the Chosen King.ʼ

9 Joshua, I have placed in front of you a stone with seven sides. I will engrave something on that stone, and in a single day I will forgive this guilty country. 10 Then each of you will live at peace and entertain your friends in your own vineyard and under your own fig trees.

Fifth vision: a lampstand and olive trees

CHAPTER 4

1 The angel who explained the visions woke me from what seemed like sleep. 2 Then he asked, "What do you see?"

"A solid gold lampstand with an oil container above it," I answered. "On the stand are seven lamps, each with seven flames. 3 One olive tree is on the right side and another on the left of the oil container. 4 But, sir, what do these mean?"

5 Then he asked, "Don't you know?"

"No sir," I replied.

6 So the angel explained that it was the following message of the LORD to Zerubbabel:*

I am the LORD All-Powerful. So don't depend on your own power or strength, but on my Spirit. 7 Zerubbabel, that mountain in front of you will be levelled to the ground. Then you will bring out the temple's most important stone and shout, "God has been very kind."ʼ

8 The LORD spoke to me again and said:

---

*3.7 with the angels . . . me: Or "with me". The angels are members of God's Council, who stand beside the throne of God in heaven and are allowed to speak with him and for him.
*4.6 Zerubbabel: Governor of Judah (see Haggai 1.1).

See also: 3.8: Jer 23.5; 33.15; Zech 6.12. 3.10: Mic 4.4.
4.3: Rev 11.4. 4.6: Ezra 5.2.

See also: 3.1: a Ezra 5.2; b Rev 12.10. 3.2: Jude 9.

⁹ Zerubbabel laid the foundation for the temple, and he will complete it. Then everyone will know that you were sent by me, the LORD All-Powerful. ¹⁰ Those who have made fun of this day of small beginnings will celebrate when they see Zerubbabel holding this important stone.ᴾ

Those seven lamps represent my eyes — the eyes of the LORD — and they see everything on this earth.

¹¹ Then I asked the angel, "What about the olive trees on each side of the lampstand? What do they represent? ¹² And what is the meaning of the two branches from which golden olive oilᴾ flows through the two gold pipes?"

¹³ "Don't you know?" he asked.

"No sir, I don't," was my answer.

¹⁴ Then he told me, "These branches are the two chosen leadersᴾ who stand beside the Lord of all the earth."

Sixth vision: a flying scroll

CHAPTER 5

¹ When I looked the next time, I saw a flying scroll,* ² and the angel asked, "What do you see?"

"A flying scroll," I answered. "About nine metres long and four and a half metres wide."

³ Then he told me:

This scroll puts a curse on everyone in the land who steals or tells lies. The writing on one side tells about the destruction of those who steal, while the writing on the other side tells about the destruction of those who lie.

⁴ The LORD All-Powerful has said, "I am sending this scroll into the house of everyone who is a robber or tells lies in my name, and it will remain there until every piece of wood and stone in that house crumbles."

Seventh vision: a woman in a basket

⁵ Now the angel who was there to explain the visions came over and said, "Look up and tell me what you see coming."

⁶ "I don't know what it is," was my reply.

"It's a big basket," he said. "And it shows what everyone in the land has in mind."ᴾ

⁷ The lead cover of the basket was opened, and in the basket was a woman. ⁸ "This woman represents evil," the angel explained. Then he threw her back into the basket and slammed the heavy cover down tight.

⁹ Straight after this I saw two women coming through the sky like storks with wings outstretched in the wind. Suddenly they lifted the basket into the air, ¹⁰ and I asked the angel, "Where are they taking the basket?"

¹¹ "To Babylonia,"ᴾ he answered, "where they will build a house for the basket and set it down inside."

Eighth vision: four chariots

CHAPTER 6

¹ Finally, I looked up and saw four chariots coming from between two bronze mountains. ² The first chariot was pulled by red horses, and the second by black horses; ³ the third chariot was pulled by white horses, and the fourth by spotted grey horses.

⁴ "Sir," I asked the angel. "What do these stand for?"

⁵ Then he explained, "These are the four windsᴾ of heaven, and now they are going out, after presenting themselves to the Lord of all the earth. ⁶ The chariot with black horses goes towards the north, the chariot with white horses goes towards the west,ᴾ and the one with spotted horses goes towards the south."

⁷ The horses came out eager to patrol the earth, and the angel told them, "Start patrolling the earth."

When they had gone on their way, ⁸ he shouted to me, "Those that have gone to the country in the north will do what the LORD's Spiritᴾ wants them to do there."

Mourning and celebrating

The chosen leader

⁹ The LORD said to me:

¹⁰⁻¹¹ Heldai, Tobijah, and Jedaiah have returned from Babylonia. Collect enough silver and gold from them to make a crown.ᴾ Then go with them to the house of Josiah son of Zephaniah and put the crown on the head of the high priest Joshua son of Jehozadak.ᴾ ¹²⁻¹³ Tell him that I, the

---

*5.1 scroll: A roll of paper or special leather used for writing on.

See also: 4.10: Rev 5.6. 4.11: Rev 11.4.

See also: 6.2: a Rev 6.4; b Rev 6.5. 6.3: Rev 6.2. 6.5: Rev 7.1. 6.12: Jer 23.5; 33.15; Zech 3.8.

LORD All-Powerful, say, "Someone will reach out from here like a branch and build a temple for me. I will name him 'Branch', and he will rule with royal honours. A priest will stand beside his throne,' and the two of them will be good friends. 14 This crown will be kept in my temple as a reminder and will be taken care of by Heldai,' Tobijah, Jedaiah, and Josiah."'

15 When people from distant lands come and help build the temple of the LORD All-Powerful, you will know that the LORD is the one who sent me. And this will happen, if you truly obey the LORD your God.

CHAPTER 7

A question about going without eating

1 On the fourth day of Chislev, the ninth month of the fourth year that Darius was king of Persia,* the LORD again spoke to me. 2-3 It happened after the people of Bethel had sent Sharezer with Regem-Melech and his men to ask the priests in the LORD's temple and the prophets to pray for them. So they prayed, "Should we mourn and go without eating during the fifth month,* as we have done for many years?"

4-5 It was then that the LORD All-Powerful told me to say to everyone in the country, including the priests:

For seventy years you have gone without eating during the fifth and seventh months of the year. But did you really do it for me? 6 And when you eat and drink, isn't it for your own enjoyment? 7 My message today is the same one I commanded the earlier prophets* to speak to Jerusalem and its villages when they were prosperous, and when all of Judah, including the Southern Desert and the hill country, was filled with people.

8-9 So once again, I, the LORD All-Powerful, tell you, "See that justice is done and be kind and merciful to one another! 10 Don't ill-treat widows or orphans or foreigners or anyone who is poor, and stop making plans to hurt each other."

11-12 But everyone who heard those prophets, stubbornly refused to obey. Instead, they turned their backs on everything my Spirit' had commanded the earlier prophets to preach. So I, the LORD, became angry 13 and said, "You people paid no attention when I called out to you, and now I'll pay no attention when you call out to me."

14 That's why I came with a whirlwind and scattered them among foreign nations, leaving their lovely country empty of people and in ruins.

CHAPTER 8

The LORD's promises to Zion

1 The LORD All-Powerful said to me:

2 I love Zion so much that her enemies make me angry. 3 I will return to Jerusalem and live there on Mount Zion. Then Jerusalem will be known as my faithful city, and Zion will be known as my holy mountain.

4 Very old people with walking sticks will once again sit around in Jerusalem, 5 while boys and girls play in the streets. 6 This may seem impossible for my people who are left, but it isn't impossible for me, the LORD All-Powerful. 7 I will save those who were taken to lands in the east and the west, 8 and I will bring them to live in Jerusalem. They will be my people, and I will be their God, faithful to bring about justice.

9 I am the LORD All-Powerful! So don't give up. Think about the message my prophets spoke when the foundation of my temple was laid. 10 Before that time, neither people nor animals were rewarded for their work, and no one was safe anywhere, because I had turned them against each other.

11 My people, only a few of you are left, and I promise not to punish you as I did before. 12 Instead, I will make sure that your crops are planted in peace and your vineyards are fruitful, that your fields are fertile and the dew falls from the sky. 13 People of Judah and Israel, you have been a curse to the nations, but I will save you and make you a blessing to them. So don't be afraid or lose courage.

14 When your ancestors made me angry, I decided to punish you with disasters, and

---

*7.1 Chislev . . . fourth year . . . king of Persia: Chislev, the ninth month of the Hebrew calendar, from about mid-November to mid-December; the fourth year of the rule of Darius was 518 BC.
*7.2–3 fifth month: Ab, the fifth month of the Hebrew calendar, from about mid-July to mid-August. The temple was destroyed by the Babylonians in the year 587 or 586 BC.
*7.7 the earlier prophets: See the note at 1.4.

I didn't hold back. [15] Now you no longer need to be afraid. I have decided to treat Jerusalem and Judah with kindness. [16] But you must be truthful with each other, and in court you must give fair decisions that lead to peace. [17] Don't ever plan evil things against others or tell lies under oath. I, the LORD, hate such things.

A time of celebration

[18] The LORD All-Powerful told me to say:

[19] People of Judah, I, the LORD, demand that whenever you go without food as a way of worshipping me, it should become a time of celebration. No matter if it's the fourth month, the fifth month, the seventh month, or the tenth month, you should have a joyful festival. So love truth and live at peace.

[20] I tell you that people will come here from cities everywhere. [21] Those of one town will go to another and say, "We're going to ask the LORD All-Powerful to treat us with kindness. Come and join us." [22] Many people from strong nations will come to Jerusalem to worship me and to ask me to treat them with kindness. [23] When this happens, ten people from nations with different languages will grab a Jew by his clothes and say, "Let us go with you. We've heard that God is on your side." I, the LORD All-Powerful, have spoken!

The Lord will rescue his people and punish their enemies

CHAPTER 9

Israel's enemies will be punished

[1] This is a message
    from the LORD:
His eyes are on everyone,
    especially the tribes of Israel.*
So he pronounces judgment
    against the cities
        of Hadrach and Damascus.*

---

*9.1 Hadrach and Damascus: Hadrach was north of both Damascus (the main city of Syria) and Hamath (verse 2).

See also: 8.16: Eph 4.25. 9.1: Isa 17.1–3; Jer 49.23–27; Amos 1.3–5. 9.1–4: Isa 23.1–18; Ezek 26.1–28.26; Joel 3.4–8; Amos 1.9–10; Matt 11.21–22; Luke 10.13–14.

Viewpoints

We have to uphold Jesus' reputation – even at the expense of our own

Contributed by Rachel P

'When this happens, ten people from nations with different languages will grab a Jew by his clothes and say, "Let us go with you. We've heard that God is on your side." I, the LORD All-powerful, have spoken!'

If you look at the passage in which this verse is found, it was a prophecy given to the people of Israel about when they would come out of exile. It promises that their reputation as a nation would be restored so much that people would come to them to find out about God and what he wanted them to do. We have to be radical Christians who are willing to uphold Jesus' reputation. We need to be so outwardly sure of our faith that people will be able to come to us when they need answers. Because Israel was in exile, many people thought that their God had deserted them and that he was not very powerful. However, God promised to give them back their dignity and their reputation. God has promised to be there for us too. We will probably be teased and mocked for standing up for our faith, but God will always be there for us and he will never let the devil throw anything at us that we can't handle if we lean on God.

More...

Living truthfully p.1070
Redemption p.292

Anorak corner

5 Lost Books of the Bible

The book of the prophet Nathan
The book of the prophet Gad
(both 1 Chronicles 29.29)
The book of the prophet Shemaiah
The book of the prophet Iddo
(both 2 Chronicles 12.15)
The letter of Paul to the Laodiceans
(Colossians 4.16)

2 Judgment will also fall
  on the nearby city of Hamath,
  as well as on Tyre and Sidon,*
  whose people are clever.
3 Tyre has built a fortress
  and piled up silver and gold,
  as though they were dust
  or mud from the streets.
4 Now the Lord will punish Tyre
  with poverty;
  he will sink its ships
  and send it up in flames.

5 Both Ashkelon and Gaza
  will tremble with fear;
  Ekron will lose all hope.
  Gaza's king will be killed,
  and Ashkelon emptied
  of its people.
6 A mob of half-breeds
  will settle in Ashdod,*
  and the Lord himself
  will rob Philistia of pride.

7 No longer will the Philistines
  eat meat with blood in it
  or any unclean food.*
  They will become part
  of the people of our God
  from the tribe of Judah.
  And God will accept
  the people of Ekron,
  as he did the Jebusites.*

8 God says, "I will stand guard
  to protect my temple from those
  who come to attack.
  I know what's happening,
  and no one will ill-treat
  my people ever again."

The LORD tells about the coming king

9 Everyone in Jerusalem,
  celebrate and shout!

Your king has won a victory,
  and he is coming to you.
He is humble
  and rides on a donkey;
he comes on the colt
  of a donkey.
10 I, the LORD, will take away
  war chariots and horses
  from Israel⁺ and Jerusalem.
Bows that were made for battle
  will be broken.
I will bring peace to nations,
  and your king will rule
  from sea to sea.
His kingdom will reach
  from the River Euphrates
  across the earth.

The LORD promises to rescue captives

11 When I made a sacred agreement
  with you, my people,
  we sealed it with blood.*
Now some of you are captives
  in waterless pits,
but I will come to your rescue
12 and offer you hope.
Return to your fortress,
  because today I will reward you
  with twice what you had.
13 I will use Judah as my bow
  and Israel⁺ as my arrow.
I will take the people of Zion
  as my sword
  and attack the Greeks.

The LORD will protect his people

14 Like a cloud, the LORD God
  will appear over his people,
  and his arrows will flash
  like lightning.
God will sound his trumpet
  and attack in a whirlwind
  from the south.
15 The LORD All-Powerful
  will protect his people,
  and they will trample down
  the sharpshooters
  and their slingshots.
They will drink and get rowdy;
  they will be as full as a bowl
  at the time of sacrifice.

*9.2 Tyre and Sidon: Phoenician cities.
*9.5–6 Ashkelon and Gaza . . . Ekron . . . Ashdod: Philistine cities.
*9.7 eat . . . food: The Philistines will become part of Judah and no longer eat meat with blood in it (see Genesis 9.4) or any other forbidden foods (see Leviticus 11.1–23; Deuteronomy 14.3–21).
*9.7 Jebusites: The original people of Canaan, who lived in Jerusalem before it was captured by David (see 2 Samuel 5.6–10) and were later accepted as part of Israel.
See also: 9.5–7: Isa 14.29–31; Jer 47.1–7; Ezek 25.15–17; Joel 3.4–8; Amos 1.6–8; Zeph 2.4–7. 9.9: Matt 21.5; John 12.15.

*9.11 agreement . . . blood: The agreement at Mount Sinai (see Exodus 24.7,8).
See also: 9.10: Psa 72.8. 9.11: Exod 24.8.

16 The LORD God will save them
    on that day,
        because they are his people,
    and they will shine on his land
        like jewels in a crown.
17 How lovely they will be.
    Young people will grow there
        like grain in a field
        or grapes in a vineyard.

CHAPTER 10

A bright future for Judah and Israel

1 I, the LORD, am the one
    who sends storm clouds
    and showers of rain
        to make fields produce.
    So when the crops need rain,
        you should pray to me.

2 You can't believe idols
    and fortune-tellers,
    or depend on the hope
        you receive from witchcraft
    and interpreters of dreams.
    But you have tried all of these,
    and now you are like sheep
        without a shepherd.

3 I, the LORD All-Powerful,
    am fiercely angry
    with you leaders,
        and I will punish you.
    I care for my people,
        the nation of Judah,
    and I will change
    this flock of sheep
        into charging war horses.

4 From this flock will come leaders
    who will be strong
        like cornerstones and tent pegs
        and weapons of war.
5 They will join in the fighting,
    and together they will trample
        their enemies like mud.
    They will fight,
    because I, the LORD,
        will be on their side.
    And they will crush
        the enemy cavalry.

6 I will strengthen
    the kingdoms of Judah and Israel.'
    And I will show mercy
    because I am the LORD, their God.
    I will answer their prayers
        and bring them home.

See also: 10.2: Matt 9.36; Mark 6.34.

Viewpoints

God promises us his power. So what is there to fear?

Contributed by Dave R

'I'll strengthen my people because of who I am, and they will follow me. I, the LORD, have spoken!'

God says, 'I have said I would do it, and I will.' God's word is final. What he has promised, he will do – and this is the seal on the end of this verse. God has spoken – it is a promise that will not be broken – WOW! It is not our power, it's God's.

Which is quite a good thing really, seeing as when we ever try to do anything by our strength we end up mucking up. But think of all that God has done – he parted the water of the Red Sea, destroyed cities in one day, sent a worldwide flood – this is the power of God, and he has promised this to us.

And it's God's authority, not ours. Authority is the right to do something, and the Bible says all authority has been given to Christ. The Almighty Creator God gives us his authority – when you think about it, it's mind blowing. So when you feel squashed by people opposing you and so weak, claim this verse for yourself – God will give you his strength and his authority. That's one amazing promise to claim, and it's yours. Don't do things in your own strength – it's only by God's that we'll get anything done. God will give us his strength. And if God is for us, who can stand against us?

More...
Trusting in Jesus p.1164

Then it will seem as though
I had never rejected them.
⁷ Israel' will be like a tribe of warriors
celebrating with wine.
When their children see this,
they will also be happy
because of me, the LORD.

⁸ I will give a signal
for them to come together
because I have rescued them.
And there will be as many
as ever before.
⁹ Although I scattered my people
in distant countries,
they won't forget me.
Once their children are raised,'
they will return —
¹⁰ I will bring them home
from Egypt and Assyria,
then let them settle
as far as Gilead and Lebanon,
until the land overflows with them.
¹¹ My people will go through
an ocean of troubles,
but I will overcome the waves
and dry up the deepest part
of the Nile.
Assyria's great pride
will be put down,
and the power of Egypt will disappear.
¹² I'll strengthen my people
because of who I am,
and they will follow me.
I, the LORD, have spoken!

CHAPTER 11

Trouble for Israel's enemies

¹ Lebanon, open your gates!
Let the fire come in
to destroy your cedar trees.
² Cry, you cypress trees!
The glorious cedars have fallen
and are rotting.
Cry, you oak trees of Bashan!
The dense forest
has been chopped down.
³ Listen! Shepherds are crying.
Their glorious pastures
have been ruined.
Listen! Lions are roaring.
The forests of the Jordan Valley
are no more to be found.

Israel's leaders are worthless shepherds

⁴ The LORD my God said to me:

Tend those sheep doomed for slaughter!
⁵ The people who buy and butcher them go
unpunished, while everyone who sells
them says, "Praise the LORD! I'm rich." Not
even their shepherds have pity on them.

⁶ Tend those sheep because I, the LORD,
will no longer have pity on the people of
this earth. I'll turn neighbour against
neighbour and make them slaves of a king.
They will bring disaster on the earth, and
I'll do nothing to rescue any of them.

⁷ So I became a shepherd of those sheep
doomed to be slaughtered by the sheep
dealers.' And I gave names to the two sticks I
used for tending the sheep: one of them was
named "Mercy" and the other "Unity". ⁸ In
less than a month, I became impatient with
three shepherds who didn't like me, and I got
rid of them. ⁹ Then I said, "I refuse to be your
shepherd. Let the sheep that are going to die,
go on and die, and those that are going to be
destroyed, go on and be destroyed. Then let
the others eat one another alive."

¹⁰ On that same day, I broke the stick
named "Mercy" to show that the LORD had
cancelled his agreement with all people.
¹¹ The sheep dealers who saw me knew
straight away that this was a message from
the LORD. ¹²⁻¹³ I told them, "Pay me my
wages, if you think you should; otherwise,
forget it." So they handed me my wages, a
measly thirty pieces of silver.

Then the LORD said, "Throw the money
into the treasury."' So I threw the money into
the treasury at the LORD's temple. ¹⁴ Then I
broke the stick named "Unity" and cancelled
the ties between Judah and Israel.

¹⁵ Next, the LORD said to me, "Act like a
shepherd again — this time a worthless
shepherd. ¹⁶ Once more I am going to let a
worthless nobody rule the land — one who
won't care for the strays or search for the
young or heal the sick or feed the healthy. He
will just dine on the fattest sheep, leaving
nothing but a few bones."

¹⁷ You worthless shepherd,
deserting the sheep!
I hope a sword
will cripple your arm
and blind your right eye.

See also: **11.12–13:** Matt 27.9–10. **11.12:** Matt 26.15.

Victory for Jerusalem

CHAPTER 12

[1] This is a message from the LORD about Israel:

I am the LORD! I stretched out the heavens; I put the earth on its foundations and gave breath to humans. [2] I have decided that Jerusalem will become a bowl of wine that makes the neighbouring nations drunk. And when Jerusalem is attacked, Judah will also be attacked.* [3] But I will turn Jerusalem into a heavy stone that crushes anyone who tries to lift it.

When all nations on earth surround Jerusalem, [4] I will make every horse panic and every rider confused. But at the same time, I will watch over Judah. [5] Then every clan in Judah will realize that I, the LORD All-Powerful, am their God, and that I am the source of their strength.

[6] At that time I will let the clans of Judah be like a ball of fire in a wood pile or a fiery torch in a hay stack. Then Judah will send the surrounding nations up in smoke. And once again the city of Jerusalem will be filled with people.

[7] But I will first give victory to Judah, so the kingdom of David and the city of Jerusalem in all their glory won't be thought of more highly than Judah itself. [8] I, the LORD God, will protect Jerusalem. Even the weakest person there will be as strong as David, and David's kingdom will rule as though my very own angel were its leader. [9] I am determined to wipe out every nation that attacks Jerusalem.

The people will mourn and return to the Lord

Mourning for the one pierced with a spear

[10] I, the LORD, will make the descendants of David and the people of Jerusalem feel deep sorrow and pray when they see the one they pierced with a spear. They will mourn and weep for him, as parents weep over the death of their only child or their firstborn. [11] On that day the people of Jerusalem will mourn as much as everyone did for Hadad Rimmon* on the flat lands near Megiddo. [12] Everyone of each family in the land will mourn, and the

men will mourn separately from the women. This includes those from the family of David, and the families of Nathan, [13] Levi, Shimei,* [14] and all other families as well.

CHAPTER 13

Getting rid of idols and false prophets

[1] In the future there will be a fountain, where David's descendants and the people of Jerusalem can wash away their sin and guilt.

[2] The LORD All-Powerful says:

When that time comes, I will get rid of every idol in the country, and they will be forgotten for ever. I will also do away with their prophets and those evil spirits that control them. [3] If any such prophets ever appear again, their own parents must warn them that they will die for telling lies in my name — the name of the LORD. If those prophets don't stop speaking, their parents must then kill them with a sword.

[4] Those prophets will be ashamed of their so-called visions, and they won't deceive anyone by dressing like a true prophet. [5] Instead, they will say, "I'm no prophet. I've been a farmer all my life."*

[6] And if any of them are asked why they are wounded,* they will answer, "It happened at the house of some friends."

A wounded shepherd and scattered sheep

[7] The LORD All-Powerful said:

My sword, wake up! Attack
    my shepherd and friend.
Strike down the shepherd!
Scatter the little sheep,
    and I will destroy them.
[8] Nowhere in the land
will more than a third of them be left alive.
[9] Then I will purify them
    and put them to the test,
just as gold and silver
    are purified and tested.
They will pray in my name,
    and I will answer them.
I will say, "You are my people,"
and they will reply,
    "You, LORD, are our God!"

---

*12.13 Shimei: A descendant of Gershon son of Levi (see Numbers 3.18).
*13.6 wounded: Probably from slashing themselves in the worship of a false god (see 1 Kings 18.28).
See also: 13.7: Matt 26.31; Mark 14.27.

See also: 12.10: John 19.37; Rev 1.7.   12.10–14: Matt 24.20; Rev 1.7.

1022

The final war and the Lord's victory

CHAPTER 14

¹ The LORD will have his day. And when it comes, everything that was ever taken from Jerusalem will be returned and divided among its people. ² But first, he will bring many nations to attack Jerusalem — homes will be robbed, women raped, and half of the population dragged off, though the others will be allowed to remain.

³ The LORD will attack those nations like a warrior fighting in battle. ⁴ He will take his stand on the Mount of Olives east of Jerusalem, and the mountain will split in half, forming a wide valley that runs from east to west. ⁵ Then you people will escape from the LORD's mountain, through this valley, which reaches to Azal.' You will run in all directions, just as everyone did when the earthquake struck* in the time of King Uzziah of Judah. Afterwards, the LORD my God will appear with his holy angels.

⁶ It will be a bright day that won't turn cloudy.' ⁷ And the LORD has decided when it will happen — this time of unending day.

⁸ In both summer and winter, life-giving streams will flow from Jerusalem, half of them to the Dead Sea in the east and half to the Mediterranean Sea in the west. ⁹ Then there will be only one LORD who rules as King and whose name is worshipped everywhere on earth.

¹⁰⁻¹¹ From Geba down to Rimmon* south of Jerusalem, the entire country will be turned into flat lands, with Jerusalem still towering above. Then the city will be full of people, from Benjamin Gate, Old Gate Place, and Hananel Tower in the north-east part of the city over to Corner Gate in the north-west and down to King's Wine Press in the south. Jerusalem will always be secure and will never again be destroyed.

¹² Here is what the LORD will do to those who attack Jerusalem: while they are standing there, he will make their flesh rot and their eyes fall from their sockets and their tongues drop out. ¹³ The LORD will make them go into a frenzy and start attacking each other, ¹⁴⁻¹⁵ until even the people of Judah turn against those in Jerusalem.' This same terrible disaster will also strike every animal nearby, including horses, mules, camels, and donkeys. Finally, everything of value in the surrounding nations will be collected and brought to Jerusalem — gold, silver, and piles of clothing.

¹⁶ Afterwards, the survivors from those nations that attacked Jerusalem will go there each year to worship the King, the LORD All-Powerful, and to celebrate the Festival of Shelters. ¹⁷ No rain will fall on the land of anyone in any country who refuses to go to Jerusalem to worship the King, the LORD All-Powerful. ¹⁸⁻¹⁹ This horrible disaster will strike the Egyptians and everyone else who refuses to go there for the celebration.

²⁰⁻²¹ At that time the words "Dedicated to the LORD" will be engraved on the bells worn by horses. In fact, every ordinary cooking pot in Jerusalem will be just as sacred to the LORD All-Powerful as the bowls used at the altar. Any one of them will be acceptable for boiling the meat of sacrificed animals, and there will no longer be a need to sell special pots and bowls.*

---

*14.20–21 special pots and bowls: Since all pots and bowls will be considered acceptable for use in the temple, there will be no more need for merchants to sell special ones to those people who come to offer sacrifices.

See also: 14.16: Lev 23.39–43.

Additional notes

'3.8 Chosen King: The Hebrew text has "Sprout" or "Branch", a term used of royalty (see Isaiah 11.1).
'4.7 God . . . kind: Or "What a beautiful stone."
'4.10 important stone: Or "measuring line (with a stone attached to the end)".
'4.12 golden olive oil: The Hebrew text has "gold", which possibly refers to the colour of the olive oil as it flows through the gold pipe.
'4.14 chosen leaders: The Hebrew text has "people of oil". In ancient times prophets, priests, and kings had olive oil poured over their heads to show that they had been chosen (see 1 Samuel 10.1; 16.13).
'5.6 what . . . mind: Hebrew; one ancient translation "the sin of everyone in the land".
'5.11 Babylonia: The Hebrew text has "Shinar", an ancient name for Babylonia.

---

*14.5 earthquake struck: See Amos 1.1.
*14.10–11 From Geba down to Rimmon: Approximately the northern and southern borders of Judah before the exile (see 2 Kings 23.8); Geba is about sixteen kilometres north of Jerusalem, and Rimmon is about sixteen kilometres north of Beersheba.

See also: 14.8: Ezek 47.1; John 7.38; Rev 22.1.
14.11: Rev 22.3.

'6.5 winds: Or "spirits". The Hebrew word may mean either.

'6.6 goes towards the west: Or "follows behind".

'6.8 LORD's Spirit: Or "LORD".

'6.10–11 a crown: Two ancient translations; Hebrew "some crowns".

'6.10–11 Heldai . . . Jehozadak: Or "Go to the house of Josiah son of Zephaniah, where you will find Heldai, Tobijah, and Jedaiah, who have returned from Babylonia. Collect enough silver and gold from them to make a crown. Then put it on the head of the high priest Joshua son of Jehozadak."

'6.12–13 stand beside his throne: Or "sit on a throne".

'6.14 Heldai: One ancient translation; Hebrew "Helem".

'6.14 Josiah: One ancient translation; Hebrew "Hen".

'7.11–12 my Spirit: Or "I".

'9.1 His . . . Israel: One possible meaning for the difficult Hebrew text.

'9.10 Israel: The Hebrew text has "Ephraim", the leading tribe of the northern kingdom of Israel, which sometimes stands for the whole kingdom.

'9.13 Israel: See the note at 9.10.

'10.6 Israel: The Hebrew text has "family of Joseph", the ancestor of Ephraim and Manasseh, the leading tribes of the northern kingdom (Israel).

'10.7 Israel: See the note at 9.10.

'10.9 Once . . . raised: One possible meaning for the difficult Hebrew text.

'11.7 by the sheep dealers: One ancient translation; Hebrew "especially the weak ones".

'11.12–13 Throw . . . treasury: Hebrew "Throw the money to the potter."

'12.2 Judah . . . attacked: One possible meaning for the difficult Hebrew text.

'12.11 Hadad Rimmon: Not mentioned elsewhere in the Old Testament.

'13.5 I've . . . my life: One possible meaning for the difficult Hebrew text.

'14.5 to Azal: One possible meaning for the difficult Hebrew text. The location of Azal is unknown.

'14.6 a bright . . . cloudy: One possible meaning for the difficult Hebrew text.

'14.13–15 each other . . . Jerusalem: Or "each other. 14-15 But the people of Judah will fight on the side of Jerusalem."

Malachi

The basics

What's the point? True religion is more than just attending services; it's being a servant.

What happens? Malachi reminds people of their purpose in God's plan and calls them to get their act together.

What should I remember? 4.2 'But for you who honour my name, victory will shine like the sun with healing in its rays, and you will jump around like calves at play.'

More details

Setting the scene It's Jerusalem after the return from exile. The temple has been rebuilt, sacrifices are being offered again, but people are simply going through the rituals...

What's it all about? The Jews have returned to Jerusalem from Babylon. After some difficulties, they have rebuilt the temple, but times are still hard. And no wonder: God's laws were being disobeyed, his instructions ignored, the people were once again suffering under a regime of injustice and greed. Malachi reminds the people that religious ritual is no good on its own. It's only valuable if it is sincere; if it really means something. It's one thing to talk about the law, or to guard it carefully; but they should also obey it.

Malachi reminds his listeners that God has a purpose for them. They should honour the Lord, do what is right, stay faithful to the promises. Then blessings would come.

Footsteps

God loves Israel: 1.1–5
The false priests: 1.6—2.9
The LORD will come: 3.1–4
Don't cheat God: 3.5–18

The Lord's love for Israel

CHAPTER 1

¹ I am Malachi. And this is the message that the LORD gave me for Israel.

The LORD's love for Israel

The LORD said:

² Israel, I, the LORD, have loved you. And yet you ask in what way have I loved you. Don't forget that Esau was the brother of your ancestor Jacob, but I chose Jacob ³ instead of Esau. And I turned Esau's hill country into a barren desert where jackals* roam. ⁴ Esau's descendants may say, "Although our nation Edom is in ruins, we will rebuild."

But I, the LORD All-Powerful, promise to tear down whatever they build. Then everyone will know that I will never stop being angry with them as long as they are so sinful.

⁵ Israel, when you see this, you will shout, "The LORD's great reputation reaches beyond our borders."

Against the priests

The LORD said:

⁶ I, the LORD All-Powerful, have something to say to you priests. Children respect their fathers, and servants respect their masters. I am your father and your master, so why don't you respect me? You priests have insulted me, and now you ask, "How did we insult you?"

---

*1.3 jackals: Desert animals related to wolves, but smaller.

See also: 1.2–3: Rom 9.13. 1.2–5: Isa 34.5–17; 63.1–6; Jer 49.7–22; Ezek 25.12–14; 35.1–15; Amos 1.11–12; Obad 1–14.

7 You embarrass me by offering worthless food on my altar. Then you ask, "How have we embarrassed you?" You have done it by saying, "What's so great about the LORD's altar?"

8 But isn't it wrong to offer animals that are blind, crippled, or sick? Just try giving those animals to your governor. That certainly wouldn't please him or make him want to help you. 9 I am the LORD God All-Powerful, and you had better try to please me. You have sinned. Now see if I will have mercy on any of you.

10 I wish someone would lock the doors of my temple, so you would stop wasting time building fires on my altar. I am not pleased with you priests, and I refuse to accept any more of your offerings. 11 From dawn until dusk my name is praised by every nation on this earth, as they burn incense and offer the proper sacrifices to me. 12 But even you priests insult me by saying, "There's nothing special about the LORD's altar, and these sacrifices are worthless."

13 You get so disgusted that you even make vulgar signs at me.' And for an offering, you bring stolen' animals or those that are crippled or sick. Should I accept these? 14 Instead of offering the acceptable animals you have promised, you bring me those that are unhealthy. I will punish you for this, because I am the great King, the LORD All-Powerful, and I am worshipped by nations everywhere.

CHAPTER 2

True and false priests

The LORD said:

1 I, the LORD All-Powerful, have something else to say to you priests. 2 You had better take seriously the need to honour my name. Otherwise, when you give a blessing, I will turn it into a curse. In fact, I have already done this, because you haven't taken to heart your duties as priests. 3 I will punish your descendants and rub your faces in the manure from your animal sacrifices, and then be done with you.'

4 I am telling you this, so I can continue to keep my agreement with your ancestor Levi. 5 I blessed him with a full life, as I had promised, and he kept his part of the

agreement by honouring me and respecting my name. 6 He taught the truth and never told lies, and he led a lot of people to turn from sin, because he obeyed me and lived right.

7 You priests should be eager to spread knowledge, and everyone should come to you for instruction, because you speak for me, the LORD All-Powerful. 8 But you have turned your backs on me. Your teachings have led others to do sinful things, and you have broken the agreement I made with your ancestor Levi. 9 So I caused everyone to hate and despise you, because you disobeyed me and failed to treat all people alike.

Broken agreements

10 Don't you know that we all have God as our Father? Didn't the one God create each of us? Then why do you cheat each other by breaking the agreement God made with your ancestors? 11 You people in Judah and Jerusalem have been unfaithful to the LORD. You have disgraced the temple that he loves, and you have committed the disgusting sin of worshipping other gods.' 12 I pray that the LORD will no longer let those who are guilty belong to his people, even if they eagerly decide to offer the LORD a gift.'

13 And what else are you doing? You cry noisily and flood the LORD's altar with your tears, because he isn't pleased with your offerings and refuses to accept them. 14 And why isn't God pleased? It's because he knows that each of you men has been unfaithful to the wife you married when you were young. You promised that she would be your partner, but now you have broken that promise. 15 Didn't God create you to become like one person with your wife?' And why did he do this? It was so you would have children, and then lead them to become God's people. Don't ever be unfaithful to your wife. 16 The LORD God All-Powerful of Israel hates anyone who is cruel enough to divorce his wife. So take care never to be unfaithful!

17 You have worn out the LORD with your words. And yet, you ask, "How did we do that?"

You did it by saying, "The LORD is pleased with evil and doesn't care about justice."

See also: 1.8: Deut 15.21. **2.4:** Num 3.11–13.
2.5: Num 25.12.

The Lord will come

CHAPTER 3

The promised messenger

[1] I, the LORD All-Powerful,
will send my messenger
    to prepare the way for me.
Then suddenly the Lord
you are looking for
    will appear in his temple.
The messenger you desire
is coming with my promise,
    and he is on his way.

A day of change

[2] On the day the Lord comes, he will be like a furnace that purifies silver or like strong soap in a washbasin. No one will be able to stand up to him. [3] The LORD will purify the descendants of Levi,* as though they were gold or silver. Then they will bring the proper offerings to the LORD, [4] and the offerings of the people of Judah and Jerusalem will please him, just as they did in the past.

Don't cheat God

[5] The LORD All-Powerful said:

I'm now on my way to judge you. And I will quickly condemn all who practise witchcraft or cheat in marriage or tell lies in court or rob workers of their pay or ill-treat widows and orphans or steal the property of foreigners or refuse to respect me.
[6] Descendants of Jacob, I am the LORD All-Powerful, and I never change. That's why you haven't been wiped out, [7] even though you have ignored and disobeyed my laws ever since the time of your ancestors. But if you return to me, I will return to you.
And yet you ask, "How can we return?"
[8] You people are robbing me, your God. And, here you are, asking, "How are we robbing you?"
You are robbing me of the offerings and of the ten per cent that belongs to me.*

[9] That's why your whole nation is under a curse. [10] I am the LORD All-Powerful, and I challenge you to put me to the test. Bring the entire ten per cent into the storehouse, so there will be food in my house. Then I will open the windows of heaven and flood you with blessing after blessing.* [11] I will also stop locusts* from destroying your crops and keeping your vineyards from producing. [12] Everyone of every nation will talk about how I have blessed you and about your wonderful land. I, the LORD All-Powerful, have spoken!

[13] You have said horrible things about me, and yet you ask, "What have we said?"

[14] Here is what you have said: "It's foolish to serve the LORD God All-Powerful. What do we get for obeying him and from going around looking sad? [15] See how happy those arrogant people are. Everyone who does wrong is successful, and when they put God to the test, they always get away with it."

The Lord will reward faithful people and punish those who are evil

Faithfulness is rewarded

[16] All those who truly respected the LORD and honoured his name started discussing these things, and when God saw what was happening, he had their names᾽ written as a reminder in his book.

[17] Then the LORD All-Powerful said:

You people are precious to me, and when I come to bring justice, I will protect you, just as parents protect an obedient child. [18] Then everyone will once again see the difference between those who obey me by doing right and those who reject me by doing wrong.

---

*3.3 descendants of Levi: The priests.
*3.8 the ten per cent . . . to me: The people of Israel were supposed to give a tenth of their harvests and of their flocks and herds to the LORD (see Leviticus 27.30–33; Deuteronomy 14.22–29).

See also: 3.1: Matt 11.10; Mark 1.2; Luke 1.76; 7.27.
3.2: Joel 2.11; Rev 6.17.

*3.10 open the windows . . . blessing: This may refer to rain, since there seems to have been a terrible drought at this time.
*3.11 locusts: A kind of grasshopper that comes in swarms and causes great damage to plant life.
See also: 3.10: Lev 27.30; Num 18.21–24; Deut 12.6; 14.22–29; Neh 13.12.

CHAPTER 4

The day of judgment

The LORD said:

¹ The day of judgment is certain to come. And it will be like a red-hot furnace with flames that burn up proud and sinful people, as though they were straw. Not a branch or a root will be left. I, the LORD All-Powerful, have spoken! ² But for you who honour my name, victory will shine like the sun with healing in its rays, and you will jump around like calves at play. ³ When I come to bring justice, you will trample those who are evil, as though they were ashes under your feet. I, the LORD All-Powerful, have spoken!

⁴ Don't ever forget the laws and teachings I gave my servant Moses on Mount Sinai.ʼ

⁵ I, the LORD, promise to send the prophet Elijah before that great and terrible day comes. ⁶ He will lead children and parents to love each other more, so that when I come, I won't bring doom to the land.

See also: 4.5: Matt 11.14; 17.10–13; Mark 9.11–13; Luke 1.17; John 1.21.

Additional notes

ʼ**1.13 me:** Or "the altar".
ʼ**1.13 stolen:** Or "injured".
ʼ**2.3 and then be done with you:** One possible meaning for the difficult Hebrew text.
ʼ**2.11 worshipping other gods:** Or "marrying the worshippers of other gods".
ʼ**2.12 even if . . . gift:** One possible meaning for the difficult Hebrew text.
ʼ**2.15 Didn't . . . wife:** One possible meaning for the difficult Hebrew text.
ʼ**3.16 names:** Or "deeds".
ʼ**4.4 Sinai:** Hebrew "Horeb".

Viewpoints

Why should we fear God?

Contributed by Dave H

'But for you that honour my name, victory will shine like the sun with healing in its rays, and you will jump around like calves at play.'

Before I had a real relationship with God, one of the things that really confused me was why you should 'fear' God. Surely being afraid of someone isn't a good thing – God isn't a bully, he's a nice bloke. After I really started talking to and hearing from God, it just clicked. The fear of God is a very powerful, and useful, thing. God is all-seeing, all-understanding, all-powerful. If there was a bully at school who could destroy the science block with one click of his fingers you'd probably listen to what he says and then do it, whatever your opinions were. Whereas if the class geek came up to you and asked to borrow some money, your response would probably be less submissive.

God hasn't got the same motives as the bullies at school, but the nice guy approach doesn't always work. God created us, saved us, gives us everything we have, and loves us more than we will ever be able to comprehend. Yet somehow, we think we're in a position to have a discussion with him about 'what would really be best'. God doesn't promise discipleship to be easy: sometimes it's just about doing it. If God is telling you to do something right now, put your selfish thoughts to one side, and obey your creator, saviour, sustainer, and one true love.

More...

God's love p.958
Staying committed p.1327

Holy history

Between the Testaments

By the end of the Old Testament the Israelites have re-established the kingdom of Israel after exile in Babylon. But between the last book of the Old Testament and the first book of the New there is a gap of about 400 years.

So what happened in between?

Although people like Nehemiah and Ezra rebuilt Israel, it was always a weak country, and for the next few centuries, the country was owned by a number of different empires. First there were the Greeks under their leader Alexander the Great. Alexander invented a policy known as Hellenisation, which is a posh word for turning everyone Greek. He tried to impose the Greek culture on all the lands he conquered.

When he died, his massive empire was split between his generals. Two of them – Ptolomy and Seleucis – founded families which each had a turn in ruling Israel. The Ptolomies went to Egypt and ruled Israel for about 100 years. Then the Seleucids had their turn – and here's where Hellenisation really started to kick in. Because a Seleucid ruler called Antiochus IV tried to completely wipe out the Jewish faith. He tried to destroy every copy of the Hebrew Scriptures and he forced people to make offerings to Zeus. He even marched into the temple, set up a statue of Zeus and sacrificed a pig – an unclean animal.

The Israelites were so revolted they... um... revolted. An uprising led by a soldier called Judas Maccabaeus drove out the Seleucids and led to 100 years of Jewish independence.

Which was fine until the Romans came along. In 63BC a Roman general called Pompey took Jerusalem after besieging Temple Mount for three months. He massacred priests and even marched into the Holy of Holies (which he was baffled to find completely empty).

And that's the situation at the beginning of the New Testament. Israel is under foreign occupation, controlled by the Romans with their vicious, brutal, irreligious and much hated army.

More...

Pharisees, Sadducees and the rest p.1097
Nehemiah p.522
Ezra p.517

 Anorak corner

10 Old Testament books most quoted in the New Testament

Isaiah (419 quotes)
Psalms (414 quotes)
Genesis (260 quotes)
Exodus (250 quotes)
Deuteronomy (208 quotes)
Ezekiel (141 quotes)
Daniel (133 quotes)
Jeremiah (125 quotes)
Leviticus (107 quotes)
Numbers (73 quotes)

 Anorak corner

Is it in the Bible?

1. Did three kings visit the baby Jesus?
2: Does the Bible say Jesus was born in a stable?
3. Did Adam and Eve eat an apple?
4. Did Salome ask Herod for the head of John the Baptist?
5. The Queen of Sheba married Solomon; True or false?
(Answers on p.1431)

The New
Testament

Big ideas

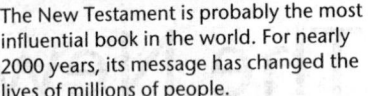

The New Testament

The New Testament is probably the most influential book in the world. For nearly 2000 years, its message has changed the lives of millions of people.

Jesus himself left no writings, but he was such an amazing figure that his most famous sayings and actions were remembered. These were passed on from person to person, and eventually collected and written down. The four gospels were not the only accounts of Jesus. There were probably other histories and collections of sayings.

 ## Anorak corner

Not all the sayings of Jesus made it into the gospels. Paul quotes Jesus in Acts 20.35: 'It is more blessed to give than to receive'; but it doesn't appear in any gospel, so he must have got it from another collection of Jesus's sayings.

So the gospels come from direct memories. In the case of John's Gospel, and the letters, there is also an element of divine inspiration. John had obviously spent many years thinking about and praying over what he had heard and seen. His gospel, therefore, includes reflections and comments from the writer himself, ideas which came to him direct from God, rather than from other sources.

When reading the New Testament we should bear in mind that they didn't have all that we have now. The early followers, therefore, saw Christianity as the fulfilment of Judaism. They didn't know they were founding a new religion; they thought they were completing the old one. That's why the New Testament is so full of references to the Old Testament: they weren't starting a new book, they were finishing the old one.

Gospels and Acts

These record the origins and early history of Christianity. Gospel means 'good news' and that is what Christians saw the content of these books to be – good news about Jesus.

Matthew, Mark and Luke are similar, covering many of the same events, using similar language, and in roughly the same order. They are sometimes called the synoptic Gospels because they see things together (syn = 'together' and optic = 'seeing'). John is very different. It focuses on fewer events in the life of Jesus, but looks at them in greater depth. Acts is a continuation of Luke's Gospel, taking us from the resurrection of Jesus through the foundation and spread of the early Church.

Letters for churches

The leaders of the early church – people like Peter and John and James and Paul – wrote to advise different churches in different cities. The letters answered questions, explained Jesus' teaching and reminded the followers of Jesus of what he had said. Gradually, the most important letters were collected together.

A vision of the future

The book of Revelation is neither a letter nor an historical account, but a vision of the future seen by John as a prisoner on the isle of Patmos. It's not really like anything else in the New Testament. Or the rest of the Bible, for that matter...

 ## Footsteps

Two weeks in the New Testament

Sermon on the mount: Matthew 5.1–16
The ideal prayer: Matthew 6.5–15
Good news for the poor: Luke 4.16–30
Born again: John 3.1–18
Loving your enemies: Luke 6.27–36
The servant king: John 13.1–20
The risen saviour: Matthew 28.1–20
The Holy Spirit: Acts 2.1–47
The conversion of Saul: Acts 9.1–31
OK with God: Romans 5.1–11
The Lord's Supper: 1 Corinthians 11.23–34
Many people, one body: Romans 12.1–8
Love: 1 Corinthians 13.1–13
Christ sets us free: Galatians 5.1–26

Matthew

tells the good news

The basics

What's the point? Jesus was the Messiah –
God's chosen one.

What happens? Matthew uses a lot of Old
Testament prophecies and language to show
that Jesus was the Messiah.

What should I remember? 28.19–20 'Go to
the people of all nations and make them my
disciples. Baptize them in the name of the
Father, the Son, and the Holy Spirit, and teach
them to do everything I have told you. I will be
with you always, even until the end of the
world.'

More details

Setting the scene As the early Church grew
and spread, it became important to write
down authentic accounts of Jesus' life.
Matthew is explaining to Jewish followers that
Jesus is the Messiah they were looking for...

What's it all about? Matthew's gospel
emphasises Old Testament prophecy and uses
a lot of Jewish terminology, such as calling
Jesus the 'Son of David', to prove to Jewish
readers that Jesus is the Messiah, the promised
one. His gospel uses more quotes from the Old
Testament than any other and begins with
Jesus' family tree to show Jesus' descent from
the great Jewish leader, King David.

Matthew wants to show that Jesus fulfilled the
Jewish faith. Christ is the true king of Jews:
Magi come to worship at his birth, he enters
Jerusalem in triumph, and the sign attached to
the cross says as much.

But he was a very different kind of king. The
Jews wanted a warrior prince to drive out the

Romans, but they were looking for the wrong
things. Jesus wasn't like that, but Matthew
shows how the prophecies all point to him.

Matthew talks a lot about Jesus' kingdom, too,
the 'kingdom of heaven'. This isn't a physical
place, but exists in the hearts of believers,
wherever two or three gather for prayer.

Any kingdom needs rules. So from the sermon
on the mount to the golden rule, 'Treat others
as you want them to treat you' (7.12), there's
lots here about how to be part of the kingdom.

Aimed at Jewish readers, Matthew's gospel is
not narrow: God's kingdom is open to people
from all nations. A series of parables show that
gentiles can follow this Messiah, and the
gospel finishes with 'the great commission',
where the disciples are told to spread the good
news throughout the world (28.18–20).

Footsteps

The birth of Jesus: 1.1–25
Jesus is baptised by John: 3.1–17
Temptation in the desert: 4.1–11
The rules of the kingdom: 5.1–48
How to pray: 6.1–21
Healing for sick people: 9.1–38
God's chosen servant: 12.1–50
True glory: 17.1–23
Last and first: 20.1–16
Triumphal entry: 21.1–11
The greatest commandment: 22.34–46
The last supper: 26.17–30
The death sentence: 27.15–56
Back for good: 28.1–20

Life files

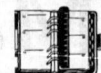

Jesus (a.k.a. Christ, Joshua, Immanuel, Matthew 1.23)

Background: Son of God

What's the story?

He was born into a poor family. His mother Mary had a teenage pregnancy and his adopted father, Joseph, married her after a dream. Soon after his birth the family fled abroad to escape being killed by Herod.

They returned a few years later. Little is known of his upbringing. He knew from an early age who his real father was, but he worked as a carpenter and builder in Nazareth, a trade he learnt from his father.

Around the age of 30, his teaching and preaching work began. After being baptised by his cousin John, he went into the desert to confront the devil. Then he set to work; teaching people, telling stories, changing lives. He taught with natural authority, answering the most difficult questions and summing up the law and the prophets in a few words. He healed the sick, raised the dead, cast out demons and miraculously provided food and drink. He controlled the weather and walked on water.

He had the power of God. He forgave sins, he even used one of God's sacred names to describe himself. Some of his closest disciples saw him talking with Moses and Elijah. Soon, they realised he was the Messiah, the one to rescue God's people.

Except he didn't act much like it. Far from driving out the Romans, Jesus told people to love their enemies. He preached forgiveness, peace and reconciliation. He spent time with the poor, the outcasts. He called the religious leaders hypocrites and liars. The authorities began to act. After a final meal with his disciples, one of his own followers betrayed him, and he was arrested. He was tried, beaten and abused. Despite the fact that there were no charges against him, they nailed him to a cross, where he died.

Three days later, strange rumours... His followers claimed he was back from the dead. His tomb was empty. People started to see him on roads, in rooms, by the lakeside, in the cemetery. News of his return spread like wildfire. They thought they'd killed him – but he was more alive than ever.

What's the point?

Jesus was the Messiah. The accounts of his life, written using the testimony of eyewitnesses, show that, as one onlooker put it, 'This man really was the Son of God!' (Mark 15.9). He preached a revolutionary gospel; he turned the values of the world on their head. In Jesus's kingdom, the poor were wealthy and enemies were friends. In the kingdom of God, servants were masters and only those who lost their lives would gain truly live. He called people to live for God and he gave people a way back to God. Through his life and death we can all be saved. All we have to do is believe in him and we will have eternal life.

Footsteps

Three weeks with Jesus

The very beginning: John 1.1
The birth of Jesus: Luke 2.1–21
Baptism and temptation: Luke 3.21—4.13
The work begins: Mark 1.14–45
The rules of the kingdom: Matthew 5.1–48
How to pray: Matthew 6.1–21
Walking the talk: Matthew 6.22—7.29
Born again: John 3.1–21
Feeding and water-walking: John 6.1–21
Who am I? Luke 8.22–38
The good samaritan: Luke 10.25–37
Healing for sick people: Matthew 9.1–38
Being a disciple: Luke 14.7–35
The great 'I am': John 8.12–59
Triumphal entry: Matthew 21.1–11
The key commandment: Matthew 22.34–46
Washing the feet: John 13.1–20
The arrest: Mark 14.27–72
The death: Luke 23.13–56
Resurrection: John 20.1–29
Back for good: Matthew 28.1–20

More...

Jesus' teaching p.1055
Jesus – the trials p.1160
Jesus' death p.1080
Messiah p.770
Resurrection p.1203

The ancestors and birth of Jesus

CHAPTER 1

The ancestors of Jesus

This is also told in Luke 3.23–38

¹ Jesus Christ came from the family of King David and also from the family of Abraham. And this is a list of his ancestors. ²⁻⁶ᵃ From Abraham to King David, his ancestors were:

Abraham, Isaac, Jacob, Judah and his brothers (Judah's sons were Perez and Zerah, and their mother was Tamar), Hezron;

Ram, Amminadab, Nahshon, Salmon, Boaz (his mother was Rahab), Obed (his mother was Ruth), Jesse, and King David.

⁶ᵇ⁻¹¹ From David to the time of the exile in Babylonia, the ancestors of Jesus were:

David, Solomon (his mother had been Uriah's wife), Rehoboam, Abijah, Asa, Jehoshaphat, Jehoram;

Uzziah, Jotham, Ahaz, Hezekiah, Manasseh, Amon, Josiah, and Jehoiachin and his brothers.

¹²⁻¹⁶ From the exile to the birth of Jesus, his ancestors were:

Jehoiachin, Shealtiel, Zerubbabel, Abiud, Eliakim, Azor, Zadok, Achim;

Eliud, Eleazar, Matthan, Jacob, and Joseph, the husband of Mary, the mother of Jesus, who is called the Messiah.

¹⁷ There were fourteen generations from Abraham to David. There were also fourteen from David to the exile in Babylonia and fourteen more to the birth of the Messiah.

The birth of Jesus

This is also told in Luke 2.1–7

¹⁸ This is how Jesus Christ was born. A young woman named Mary was engaged to Joseph from King David's family. But before they were married, she learnt that she was going to have a baby by God's Holy Spirit. ¹⁹ Joseph was a good man' and did not want to embarrass Mary in front of everyone. So he decided to call off the wedding quietly.

²⁰ While Joseph was thinking about this, an angel from the Lord came to him in a dream. The angel said, "Joseph, the baby that Mary will have is from the Holy Spirit.

See also: **1.11:** 2 King 24.14–15; 2 Chron 36.10; Jer 27.20. **1.18:** Luke 1.27.

Holy history

Jesus the Jew

Jesus was Jewish. In fact, he wasn't actually called Jesus. Jesus is the Greek version of Joshua. Really he was called Joshua ben Joseph – Joshua the son of Joseph (John 1.45). Joshua was a very common name in Israel; it's as if the son of God was called Dave or Joe. Raised in a Jewish home, and circumcised as a boy, Jesus was part of God's chosen people. Way back, God had promised Abraham that a great blessing would come through his descendants – and Jesus is the fulfilment of that promise. That's why Matthew opens his gospel with a list of Jesus' ancestors. He wanted to show to his readers that Jesus was the Messiah, a direct descendant of King David.

Jesus was brought up knowing Jewish law and tradition. He was called Rabbi by some of his followers, which means teacher. He knew the Jewish scriptures inside out. So much so that he managed to sum up the entire lot in a few words: 'Love the LORD your God with all your heart, soul, and mind' and 'Love others as much as you love yourself.' (Matthew 22.37–40). That's 600,000 words reduced to 20!

And because he was a Jew, he knew what he was saying. When he forgave people their sins, when he called himself 'I Am', he knew, as a Jew, that he was claiming to be God.

There's another thing as well. Over the centuries some Christians have persecuted Jews, or been anti-semitic. No Christian should be racist, because we're all children of God. But even more than that, no Christian should hate Jews. How can we when our own saviour was one – and most of the early church, too?

More...

Synagogues p.1123
Pharisees, Sadducees and the rest p.1097
Racism p.1308
Culture p.779

Go ahead and marry her. 21 Then after her baby is born, name him Jesus,* because he will save his people from their sins."

22 So the Lord's promise came true, just as the prophet had said, 23 "A virgin will have a baby boy, and he will be called Immanuel," which means "God is with us."

24 After Joseph woke up, he and Mary were soon married, just as the Lord's angel had told him to do. 25 But they did not sleep together before her baby was born. Then Joseph named him Jesus.

CHAPTER 2

The wise men

1 When Jesus was born in the village of Bethlehem in Judea, Herod was king. During this time some wise men* from the east came to Jerusalem 2 and said, "Where is the child born to be king of the Jews? We saw his star in the east' and have come to worship him."

3 When King Herod heard about this, he was worried, and so was everyone else in Jerusalem. 4 Herod brought together the chief priests and the teachers of the Law of Moses and asked them, "Where will the Messiah be born?"

5 They told him, "He will be born in Bethlehem, just as the prophet wrote,

6 'Bethlehem in the land
   of Judea,
  you are very important
     among the towns of Judea.
  From your town
    will come a leader,
  who will be like a shepherd
    for my people Israel.' "

7 Herod secretly called in the wise men and asked them when they had first seen the star. 8 He told them, "Go to Bethlehem and search carefully for the child. As soon as you find him, let me know. I want to go and worship him too."

9 The wise men listened to what the king said and then left. And the star they had seen in the east went on ahead of them until it stopped over the place where the child was. 10 They were thrilled and excited to see the star.

11 When the men went into the house and saw the child with Mary, his mother, they knelt down and worshipped him. They took out their gifts of gold, frankincense, and myrrh* and gave them to him. 12 Later they were warned in a dream not to return to Herod, and they went back home by another road.

The escape to Egypt

13 After the wise men had gone, an angel from the Lord appeared to Joseph in a dream and said, "Get up! Hurry and take the child and his mother to Egypt! Stay there until I tell you to return, because Herod is looking for the child and wants to kill him."

14 That night, Joseph got up and took his wife and the child to Egypt, 15 where they stayed until Herod died. So the Lord's promise came true, just as the prophet had said, "I called my son out of Egypt."

The killing of the children

16 When Herod found out that the wise men from the east had tricked him, he was very angry. He gave orders for his men to kill all the boys who lived in or near Bethlehem and were two years old and younger. This was based on what he had learnt from the wise men.

17 So the Lord's promise came true, just as the prophet Jeremiah had said,

18 "In Ramah a voice was heard
    crying and weeping loudly.
  Rachel was mourning
    for her children,
  and she refused
  to be comforted,
    because they were dead."

The return from Egypt

19 After King Herod died, an angel from the Lord appeared in a dream to Joseph while he was still in Egypt. 20 The angel said, "Get up and take the child and his mother back to Israel. The people who wanted to kill him are now dead."

21 Joseph got up and left with them for Israel. 22 But when he heard that Herod's son Archelaus was now ruler of Judea, he was

---

*1.21 name him Jesus: In Hebrew the name "Jesus" means "the Lord saves".
*2.1 wise men: People famous for studying the stars.
See also: 1.21: Luke 1.31. 1.23: Isa 7.14 (LXX). 1.25: Luke 2.21. 2.6: Mic 5.2.

*2.11 frankincense, and myrrh: Frankincense was a valuable powder that was burnt to make a sweet smell. Myrrh was a valuable sweet-smelling powder often used in perfume.
See also: 2.15: Hos 11.1. 2.18: Jer 31.15.

Viewpoints

Why did the magi come to visit Jesus?

Contributed by Marc W

'When the men went into the house and saw the child with Mary, his mother, they knelt down and worshipped him.'

It's the best question that you can have in a Christmas quiz: 'How many kings went to visit Jesus?' Matthew is the only gospel that mentions the visit of the 'three' kings/wise men/magi, and it doesn't mention once how many there were. It does say, though, that they had been looking for Jesus, with the intention of giving him gifts and worshipping him.

So who were they? I think these blokes were educated, and from 'the east'. They were there to show that Jesus was anticipated by people everywhere, not just from Israel, and shows that Jesus came for EVERYBODY, be they from Israel or wherever.

The Magi knew who Jesus was and what he was going to do, and came prepared to offer him very expensive gifts, and to worship him. They brought gold because it was of the highest value at the time; frankincense, a sacrificial incense for Jesus' sacrifice; and myrrh, for perfuming dead bodies.

They worshipped in the way they saw fit, which was giving what they had to him, sparing no cost, knowing that he had come to do the same. It should be the same today. We each have life, and gifts and talents. We can live for him, use our talents for him, to worship him, giving him glory.

More...

Worshipping God p.622

---

afraid to go there. Then in a dream he was told to go to Galilee, 23 and they went to live there in the town of Nazareth. So the Lord's promise came true, just as the prophet had said, "He will be called a Nazarene."*

The message of John the Baptist

CHAPTER 3

The preaching of John the Baptist

This is also told in Mark 1.1–8; Luke 3.1–18; John 1.19–28

1 Years later, John the Baptist started preaching in the desert of Judea. 2 He said, "Turn back to God! The kingdom of heaven› will soon be here."›

3 John was the one the prophet Isaiah was talking about, when he said,

> "In the desert someone
>   is shouting,
> 'Get the road ready
>   for the Lord!
> Make a straight path
>   for him.' "

4 John wore clothes made of camel's hair. He had a leather strap around his waist and ate grasshoppers and wild honey.

5 From Jerusalem and all Judea and from the River Jordan Valley crowds of people went to John. 6 They told how sorry they were for their sins, and he baptized them in the river.

7 Many Pharisees and Sadducees also came to be baptized. But John said to them:

You snakes! Who warned you to run from the coming judgment? 8 Do something to show that you have really given up your sins. 9 And don't start telling yourselves that you belong to Abraham's family. I tell you that God can turn these stones into children for Abraham. 10 An axe is ready to cut the trees down at their roots. Any tree that doesn't produce good fruit will be chopped down and thrown into a fire.

11 I baptize you with water so that you will give up your sins.› But someone more powerful is going to come, and I am not good enough even to carry his

---

*2.23 He will be called a Nazarene: The prophet who said this is not known.

See also: 2.23: Mark 1.24; Luke 2.39; John 1.45.
3.2: Matt 4.17; Mark 1.15. 3.3: Isa 40.3 (LXX). 3.4: 2 King 1.8.
3.7: Matt 12.34; 23.33. 3.9: John 8.33. 3.10: Matt 7.19.

Big ideas

Baptism

John the Baptist got his name because he baptised people. He dunked them in the river Jordan. It wasn't some kind of magic trick, or religious hocus-pocus; people were making a public sign that they were asking for forgiveness and going to start again.

Jesus also baptised people, and he told his followers to go into all he world, make disciples, baptise them and teach them to follow Jesus (Matthew 28.19–20). From the early days of the church, baptism was seen as the entry point. People believed in Jesus, were baptised, and became his followers.

Today, Christians are still baptised. Different churches do baptism in different ways, but the act itself symbolises two main things: washing away sins and new life.

Wash Away

If you ask God for forgiveness, he will wash you clean. Baptism shows others you have made a conscious decision to ask for forgiveness and that God has washed away all your sins.

New Life

Baptism also symbolises new life. Paul said that when people were baptised, they 'died and were buried with Christ' (Romans 6.4). In other words, baptism is like washing away the old life and starting a new one. The old you has been drowned; the new you has risen from the water.

Footsteps

A week with Baptism

John the Baptist at work: Matthew 3.1–12
Jesus is baptised: Matthew 3.13–17
Final orders: Matthew 28.16–20
Mass baptism in Jerusalem: Acts 2.29–41
Different types of baptism: Acts 19.1–7
Baptism – it's life and death: Romans 6.1–11
Baptised into the family: Ephesians 4.1–6

More...

John the Baptist p.1121
Forgiveness p. 614
Starting again p.1172

---

sandals.* He will baptize you with the Holy Spirit and with fire. ¹² His threshing fork is in his hand, and he is ready to separate the wheat from the husks.* He will store the wheat in a barn and burn the husks in a fire that never goes out.

The baptism and temptation of Jesus

The baptism of Jesus

This is also told in Mark 1.9–11; Luke 3.21–22

¹³ Jesus left Galilee and went to the River Jordan to be baptized by John. ¹⁴ But John kept objecting and said, "I ought to be baptized by you. Why have you come to me?"

¹⁵ Jesus answered, "For now this is how it should be, because we must do all that God wants us to do." Then John agreed.

¹⁶ So Jesus was baptized. And as soon as he came out of the water, the sky opened, and he saw the Spirit of God coming down on him like a dove. ¹⁷ Then a voice from heaven said, "This is my own dear Son, and I am pleased with him."

CHAPTER 4

Jesus and the devil

This is also told in Mark 1.12–13; Luke 4.1–13

¹ The Holy Spirit led Jesus into the desert, so that the devil could test him. ² After Jesus had gone without eating* for forty days and nights, he was very hungry. ³ Then the devil came to him and said, "If you are God's Son, tell these stones to turn into bread."

⁴ Jesus answered, "The Scriptures say:

'No one can live only on food.
People need every word
  that God has spoken.' "

---

*3.11 carry his sandals: This was one of the duties of a slave.

*3.12 His threshing fork is in his hand, and he is ready to separate the wheat from the husks: After Jewish farmers had trampled out the grain, they used a large fork to pitch the grain and the husks into the air. Wind would blow away the light husks, and the grain would fall back to the ground, where it could be gathered up.

*4.2 had gone without eating: The Jewish people sometimes went without eating (also called "fasting") to show their love for God or to show sorrow for their sins.

See also: 3.17: Gen 22.2; Psa 2.7; Isa 42.1; Matt 12.18; 17.5; Mark 1.11; Luke 9.35. 4.1: Heb 2.18; 4.15. 4.4: Deut 8.3.

⁵ Next, the devil took Jesus to the holy city and made him stand on the highest part of the temple. ⁶ The devil said, "If you are God's Son, jump off. The Scriptures say:

'God will give his angels
    orders about you.
They will catch you
    in their arms,
and you won't hurt
    your feet on the stones.' "

⁷ Jesus answered, "The Scriptures also say, 'Don't try to test the Lord your God!' "

⁸ Finally, the devil took Jesus up on a very high mountain and showed him all the kingdoms on earth and their power. ⁹ The devil said to him, "I will give all this to you, if you will bow down and worship me."

¹⁰ Jesus answered, "Go away Satan! The Scriptures say:

'Worship the Lord your God
    and serve only him.' "

¹¹ Then the devil left Jesus, and angels came to help him.

Jesus in Galilee

Jesus begins his work

This is also told in Mark 1.14–15; Luke 4.14–15

¹² When Jesus heard that John had been put in prison, he went to Galilee. ¹³ But instead of staying in Nazareth, Jesus moved to Capernaum. This town was beside Lake Galilee in the territory of Zebulun and Naphtali.* ¹⁴ So God's promise came true, just as the prophet Isaiah had said,

¹⁵ "Listen, lands of Zebulun
        and Naphtali,
    lands along the road
    to the sea and east
        of the Jordan!
    Listen Galilee,
        land of the Gentiles!
¹⁶ Although your people
        live in darkness,
    they will see a bright light.

Although they live
    in the shadow of death,
a light will shine on them."

¹⁷ Then Jesus started preaching, "Turn back to God! The kingdom of heaven will soon be here."

Jesus chooses four fishermen

This is also told in Mark 1.16–20; Luke 5.1–11

¹⁸ While Jesus was walking along the shore of Lake Galilee, he saw two brothers. One was Simon, also known as Peter, and the other was Andrew. They were fishermen, and they were casting their net into the lake. ¹⁹ Jesus said to them, "Come with me! I will teach you how to bring in people instead of fish." ²⁰ At once the two brothers dropped their nets and went with him.

²¹ Jesus walked on until he saw James and John, the sons of Zebedee. They were in a boat with their father, mending their nets. Jesus asked them to come with him too. ²² Straight away they left the boat and their father and went with Jesus.

Jesus teaches, preaches, and heals

This is also told in Luke 6.17–19

²³ Jesus went all over Galilee, teaching in the Jewish meeting places and preaching the good news about God's kingdom. He also healed every kind of disease and sickness. ²⁴ News about him spread all over Syria, and people with every kind of sickness or disease were brought to him. Some of them had a lot of demons in them, others were thought to be mad,* and still others could not walk. But Jesus healed them all.

²⁵ Large crowds followed Jesus from Galilee and the region around the ten cities known as Decapolis.* They also came from Jerusalem, Judea, and from across the River Jordan.

---

*4.13 Zebulun and Naphtali: In Old Testament times these tribes were in northern Palestine, and in New Testament times many Gentiles lived where these tribes had once been.

See also: 4.6: Psa 91.11–12.   4.7: Deut 6.16.
4.10: Deut 6.13.   4.12: Matt 14.3; Mark 6.17; Luke 3.19–20.
4.13: John 2.12.   4.15–16: Isa 9.1–2.

*4.24 thought to be mad: In ancient times people with epilepsy were thought to be mad.
*4.25 the ten cities known as Decapolis: A group of ten cities east of Samaria and Galilee, where the people followed the Greek way of life.
See also: 4.17: Matt 3.2.   4.23: Matt 9.35; Mark 1.39.

CHAPTER 5

The sermon on the mount

¹ When Jesus saw the crowds, he went up on the side of a mountain and sat down.*

Blessings

This is also told in Luke 6.20–23

Jesus' disciples gathered around him, ² and he taught them:

³ God blesses those people
   who depend only on him.
   They belong to the kingdom
      of heaven!ᐟ
⁴ God blesses those people
   who grieve.
   They will find comfort!
⁵ God blesses those people
   who are humble.
   The earth will belong
      to them!
⁶ God blesses those people
   who want to obey himᐟ
      more than to eat or drink.
   They will be given
      what they want!
⁷ God blesses those people
   who are merciful.
   They will be treated
      with mercy!
⁸ God blesses those people
   whose hearts are pure.
   They will see him!
⁹ God blesses those people
   who make peace.
   They will be called
      his children!
¹⁰ God blesses those people
   who are treated badly
      for doing right.
   They belong to the kingdom
      of heaven.ᐟ

¹¹ God will bless you when people insult you, ill-treat you, and tell all kinds of evil lies about you because of me. ¹² Be happy and excited! You will have a great reward in heaven. People did these same things to the prophets who lived long ago.

Salt and light

This is also told in Mark 9.50; Luke 14.34–35

Jesus continued:

¹³ You are like salt for everyone on earth. But if salt no longer tastes like salt, how can it make food salty? All it is good for is to be thrown out and walked on.

¹⁴ You are like light for the whole world. A city built on top of a hill cannot be hidden, ¹⁵ and no one would light a lamp and put it under a clay pot. A lamp is placed on a lampstand, where it can give light to everyone in the house. ¹⁶ Make your light shine, so that others will see the good that you do and will praise your Father in heaven.

The Law of Moses

Jesus continued:

¹⁷ Don't suppose that I came to do away with the Law and the Prophets.* I did not come to do away with them, but to give them their full meaning. ¹⁸ Heaven and earth may disappear. But I promise you that not even a full stop or comma will ever disappear from the Law. Everything written in it must happen.

¹⁹ If you reject even the least important command in the Law and teach others to do the same, you will be the least important person in the kingdom of heaven. But if you obey and teach others its commands, you will have an important place in the kingdom. ²⁰ You must obey God's commands better than the Pharisees and the teachers of the Law obey them. If you don't, I promise you that you will never get into the kingdom of heaven.

Anger

Jesus continued:

²¹ You know that our ancestors were told, "Do not murder" and "A murderer must be brought to trial." ²² But I promise you that if you are angry with someone,ᐟ you will have to stand trial. If you call someone a fool, you will be taken to court. And if you say that someone is worthless, you will be in danger of the fires of hell.

---

*5.1 sat down: Teachers in the ancient world, including Jewish teachers, usually sat down when they taught.

See also: 5.4: Isa 61.2.   5.5: Psa 37.11.   5.6: Isa 55.1–2.
5.8: Psa 24.3–4.   5.10: 1 Pet 3.14.   5.11: 1 Pet 4.14.
5.12: 2 Chron 36.16; Acts 7.52.

*5.17 the Law and the Prophets: The Jewish Scriptures, that is, the Old Testament.

See also: 5.13: Mark 9.50; Luke 14.34–35.   5.14: John 8.12;
9.5.   5.15: Mark 4.21; Luke 8.16; 11.33.   5.16: 1 Pet 2.12.
5.18: Luke 16.17.   5.21: Exod 20.13; Deut 5.17.

Big ideas

Sermon on the mount

Chapters 5 to 7 of Matthew contain what is known as the Sermon on the Mount.

It's Jesus' manifesto, his instructions for what the life of a follower should be like.

It's one of the most famous sections of the Bible and it includes things like the Lord's Prayer (Matthew 6.5–15), the blessings or beatitudes (Matthew 5.2–12), and what is known as 'the golden rule' (Matthew 7.12). It contains advice on praying and fasting; it contains Christ's commands on forgiveness and non-violence. It talks about integrity and anxiety and money and marriage and... well, let's just say there's a lot in there!

Moses went up a mountain and came down with the law; Jesus' sermon on a mount is a new law, a new foundation for life. We're citizens of a different kingdom and this is our declaration of Christian rights (and responsibilities).

High ideals

In the sermon on the mount, Jesus sets very high standards. Some people have argued that the standards are utterly unrealistic, but we should not be put off by the targets he's setting': Jesus always told his followers to aim high, and here he presents an ideal standard of human behaviour for us all to aim at.

Different values

The sermon on the mount draws a picture of a topsy-turvy world. This is a world where the poor are blessed, where enemies are not attacked by forgiven. The values in this sermon are totally different to those of the world. This is not a kingdom for the powerful and the rich, but for the poor and the humble.

Spirit not law

Jesus talks about the law in the sermon, but he says we should go beyond it. By Jesus' time, the law was a dead thing; a set of rules and rituals that imprisoned people. Jesus sums up the law in one sentence, almost completely ignoring the rules, and heading straight for the heart (7.12).

New relationships

'Everyone who asks will receive' (7.8). This sermon outlines a radical, loving God: a God who loves us and who cares for us, a God who knows everything about us. If we wholeheartedly turn to God, he will protect and bless us.

Different lives

Above all, the sermon on the mount is about real life. Its not some theory or nice statement. It's not something that looks good in a poster or on a fridge magnet (admittedly, you'd need a big fridge magnet).

It's a manifesto for action, a radical picture of the way we should live. Followers of Jesus should be like salt and light to the world; we should be getting out there and making a difference. The Sermon on the mount shows that God cares for the oppressed, the poor, the outcast. It shows that the values of the world are completely at odds with the values of the kingdom of God.

It points us to a new way of living.

Footsteps

A week with the sermon on the mount

Beginning with the blessings: 5.1–12
Salt and light: 5.13–16
Going beyond the ancestors: 5.17–37
Love your enemies: 5.38–48
Giving, praying, fasting: 6.1–18
Treasure for life: 6.19–34
Walking the talk: 7.1–29

More...

Money p.1043
Materialism p.1141
Politics p.1358
Incarnation p.1168

²³ So if you are about to place your gift on the altar and remember that someone is angry with you, ²⁴ leave your gift there in front of the altar. Make peace with that person, then come back and offer your gift to God.

²⁵ Before you are dragged into court, make friends with the person who has accused you of doing wrong. If you don't, you will be handed over to the judge and then to the officer who will put you in jail. ²⁶ I promise you that you will not get out until you have paid the last penny you owe.

Marriage

Jesus continued:

²⁷ You know the commandment which says, "Be faithful in marriage." ²⁸ But I tell you that if you look at another woman and want her, you are already unfaithful in your thoughts. ²⁹ If your right eye causes you to sin, poke it out and throw it away. It is better to lose one part of your body, than for your whole body to end up in hell. ³⁰ If your right hand causes you to sin, chop it off and throw it away! It is better to lose one part of your body, than for your whole body to be thrown into hell.

Divorce

This is also told in Matthew 19.9; Mark 10.11–12; Luke 16.18

Jesus continued:

³¹ You have been taught that a man who divorces his wife must write out divorce papers for her.* ³² But I tell you not to divorce your wife unless she has committed some terrible sexual sin.* If you divorce her, you will cause her to be unfaithful, just as any man who marries her is guilty of taking another man's wife.

*5.31 write out divorce papers for her: Jewish men could divorce their wives, but the women could not divorce their husbands. The purpose of writing these papers was to make it harder for a man to divorce his wife. Before this law was made, all a man had to do was to send his wife away and say that she was no longer his wife.
*5.32 some terrible sexual sin: This probably refers to the laws about the wrong kinds of marriages that are forbidden in Leviticus or to some serious sexual sin.
See also: 5.27: Exod 20.14; Deut 5.18. 5.29: Matt 18.9; Mark 9.47. 5.30: Matt 18.8; Mark 9.43. 5.31: Deut 24.1–4; Matt 19.7; Mark 10.4. 5.32: Matt 19.9; Mark 10.11,12; Luke 16.18; 1 Cor 7.10–11.

Promises

Jesus continued:

³³ You know that our ancestors were told, "Don't use the Lord's name to make a promise unless you are going to keep it." ³⁴ But I tell you not to swear by anything when you make a promise! Heaven is God's throne, so don't swear by heaven. ³⁵ The earth is God's footstool, so don't swear by the earth. Jerusalem is the city of the great king, so don't swear by it. ³⁶ Don't swear by your own head. You cannot make one hair white or black. ³⁷ When you make a promise, say only "Yes" or "No". Anything else comes from the devil.

Revenge

This is also told in Luke 6.29–30

Jesus continued:

³⁸ You know that you have been taught, "An eye for an eye and a tooth for a tooth." ³⁹ But I tell you not to try to get even with a person who has done something to you. When someone slaps your right cheek,* turn and let that person slap your other cheek. ⁴⁰ If someone sues you for your shirt, give up your coat as well. ⁴¹ If a soldier forces you to carry his pack one kilometre, carry it two kilometres.* ⁴² When people ask you for something, give it to them. When they want to borrow money, lend it to them.

Love

This is also told in Luke 6.27–28,32–36

Jesus continued:

⁴³ You have heard people say, "Love your neighbours and hate your enemies." ⁴⁴ But I tell you to love your enemies and pray for anyone who ill-treats you. ⁴⁵ Then you will be acting like your Father in heaven. He makes the sun rise on both good and bad people. And he sends rain for the ones who do right and for the ones who

*5.39 right cheek: A slap on the right cheek was a bad insult.
*5.41 two kilometres: A Roman soldier had the right to force a person to carry his pack as far as approximately one and a half kilometres.
See also: 5.33: a Lev 19.12; b Num 30.2; Deut 23.21. 5.34: a Jam 5.12; b Isa 66.1; Matt 23.22. 5.35: a Isa 66.1; b Psa 48.2. 5.38: Exod 21.24; Lev 24.20; Deut 19.21.

Real life

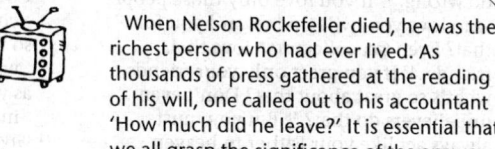

Money

Contributed by Credit Action

What comes first in your life? Is it God or money? People or possessions? Heaven or earth? Who of you, on your death bed, is going to wish your bank account had a few more thousands in it? When Jesus died for us on the cross, he took all our sin to make us spotless and thus able to enter heaven, where we will be for ever. Have you grasped what that means? Given that time on earth is but a blink of an eyelid, do you think we will be concerned about fashionable clothes in heaven?

Jesus tells us in Matthew 6.24 that we 'cannot serve both God and money.' Many Christians in Britain try, though. We buy things we don't need, with money we don't have, to impress people we don't even like! Do you recognize as Psalm 24.1 says that EVERYTHING is God's? If this is the case it doesn't matter what we can afford as it is not ours to be reckless with in the first place.

Think about your life, as you read Matthew 6.31–33, and ask yourself what your needs are? A need may be a bed-sit, a want may be a five bed-roomed detached house, and a desire may be that it is in Spain! Where are you going to spend 'your' money? Did you hear about the £50 note and the 50 pence coin talking in the bank? The note said 'I have a great time and often go to gyms and nice restaurants. How about you?' The coin didn't have to think very much. It replied 'I go to church quite a lot.'

Jesus brings us some great news. We can't take anything with us, but we are able to store up treasures in heaven, which we can never ever lose. Every time we feed the hungry, clothe the naked, or spend time with someone who is feeling lonely, that is what we are doing. Millions still die of starvation and preventable diseases in our world, and while we are not responsible for world hunger, we are called to do whatever we can to alleviate it. Look at Luke 16.10–12. When we start being financially responsible in the small things, God honours us with greater tasks to fulfil.

When Nelson Rockefeller died, he was the richest person who had ever lived. As thousands of press gathered at the reading of his will, one called out to his accountant 'How much did he leave?' It is essential that we all grasp the significance of the answer. The accountant replied 'Everything.'

Try and master money, and put it in its proper place – before it masters you.

Think

How does your income compare with your expenditure?
How does your giving to God's work compare with what you spend on little comforts and luxuries for yourself?
What great task would you like God to challenge you with? How might he be preparing you in the 'small things' you are doing at the moment?

Act

Find a good book on money management and work through it
Keep a journal of your spending for one month
Find out how far £10 will go in different parts of the world
Look out for charities who provide alternative ideas for gifts

Check

Psalm 24.1–6; Matthew 6.24–33;
Luke 16.10–12

More...

Debt p.697
Shopping p.973
Materialism p.1141

do wrong. ⁴⁶ If you love only those people who love you, will God reward you for that? Even tax collectors* love their friends. ⁴⁷ If you greet only your friends, what's so great about that? Don't even unbelievers do that? ⁴⁸ But you must always act like your Father in heaven.

CHAPTER 6

Giving

Jesus said:

¹ When you do good deeds, don't try to show off. If you do, you won't get a reward from your Father in heaven.

² When you give to the poor, don't blow a loud horn. That's what show-offs do in the meeting places and on the street corners, because they are always looking for praise. I can assure you that they already have their reward.

³ When you give to the poor, don't let anyone know about it.' ⁴ Then your gift will be given in secret. Your Father knows what is done in secret, and he will reward you.

Prayer

This is also told in Luke 11.2–4

Jesus continued:

⁵ When you pray, don't be like those show-offs who love to stand up and pray in the meeting places and on the street corners. They do this just to look good. I can assure you that they already have their reward.

⁶ When you pray, go into a room alone and close the door. Pray to your Father in private. He knows what is done in private, and he will reward you.

⁷ When you pray, don't talk on and on as people do who don't know God. They think God likes to hear long prayers. ⁸ Don't be like them. Your Father knows what you need before you ask.

⁹ You should pray like this:

Our Father in heaven,
help us to honour
your name.

¹⁰ Come and set up
your kingdom,
so that everyone on earth
will obey you,
as you are obeyed
in heaven.
¹¹ Give us our food for today.'
¹² Forgive us for doing wrong,
as we forgive others.
¹³ Keep us from being tempted
and protect us from evil.'

¹⁴ If you forgive others for the wrongs they do to you, your Father in heaven will forgive you. ¹⁵ But if you don't forgive others, your Father will not forgive your sins.

Worshipping God by going without eating

Jesus continued:

¹⁶ When you go without eating,* don't try to look gloomy as those show-offs do when they go without eating. I can assure you that they already have their reward. ¹⁷ Instead, comb your hair and wash your face. ¹⁸ Then others won't know that you are going without eating. But your Father sees what is done in private, and he will reward you.

Treasures in heaven

This is also told in Luke 12.33–34

Jesus continued:

¹⁹ Don't store up treasures on earth! Moths and rust can destroy them, and thieves can break in and steal them. ²⁰ Instead, store up your treasures in heaven, where moths and rust cannot destroy them, and thieves cannot break in and steal them. ²¹ Your heart will always be where your treasure is.

Light

This is also told in Luke 11.34–36

Jesus continued:

²² Your eyes are like a window for your body. When they are good, you have all the light you need. ²³ But when your eyes are bad, everything is dark. If the light inside you is dark, you are in the dark.

---

*5.46 tax collectors: These were usually Jewish people who paid the Romans for the right to collect taxes. They were hated by other Jews who thought of them as traitors to their country and to their religion.
See also: 5.48: Lev 19.2; Deut 18.13. 6.1: Matt 23.5. 6.5: Luke 18.10–14.

*6.16 without eating: See the note at 4.2.
See also: 6.14–15: Mark 11.25–26. 6.19: Jam 5.2–3.

Being christian

Going against the crowd

Matthew 6.21–33

When you become a Christian you turn your life around. Sometimes that will leave you travelling in the opposite direction to the world around you.

Being Christian will naturally make us stand out from the world around us. (At least it will if we're doing it right.)

Christians, you see, have different values. We live to serve others, not to 'look after number one'. We're supposed to love our enemies, not attack them. We believe in looking beyond the surface; the world likes to judge by appearances. The world likes the rich and famous; God loves the poor and humble. We trust in God, not in the insurance policies. In the kingdom of God, it's the last who are the first, and the servants who are the leaders.

The world might want you to believe that the main aim of life is to earn pots of money; sleep with whoever you like (whenever you like); eat, drink and be merry. But God's values are different. So we don't do what they do. We don't buy into the Hello lifestyle, or the macho posing of Hollywood.

We do things differently. We go God's way.

Being Christian: Going against the crowd

• Go against the tide. Don't do things just because the world says you should.
• Make a list of your core values. Write down how you think God wants you to live.
• Be careful of compromising with the world. It's easy to drift away from Jesus, without even realising it.
• Look beyond the surface. Don't just believe what the world wants you to believe. Look to the reality.
• Don't judge by appearances. Try to see things God's way.

Money

This is also told in Luke 16.13

Jesus continued:

²⁴ You cannot be the slave of two masters! You will like one more than the other or be more loyal to one than the other. You cannot serve both God and money.

Worry

This is also told in Luke 12.22–31

Jesus continued:

²⁵ I tell you not to worry about your life. Don't worry about having something to eat, drink, or wear. Isn't life more than food or clothing? ²⁶ Look at the birds in the sky! They don't plant or harvest. They don't even store grain in barns. Yet your Father in heaven takes care of them. Aren't you worth more than birds?

²⁷ Can worry make you live longer?ᵃ ²⁸ Why worry about clothes? Look how the wild flowers grow. They don't work hard to make their clothes. ²⁹ But I tell you that Solomon with all his wealth* wasn't as well clothed as one of them. ³⁰ God gives such beauty to everything that grows in the fields, even though it is here today and thrown into a fire tomorrow. He will surely do even more for you! Why do you have such little faith?

³¹ Don't worry and ask yourselves, "Will we have anything to eat? Will we have anything to drink? Will we have any clothes to wear?" ³² Only people who don't know God are always worrying about such things. Your Father in heaven knows that you need all these. ³³ But more than anything else, put God's work first and do what he wants. Then the other things will be yours as well.

³⁴ Don't worry about tomorrow. It will take care of itself. You have enough to worry about today.

---

*6.29 Solomon with all his wealth:** The Jewish people thought that Solomon was the richest person who had ever lived.

See also: 6.29: 1 King 10.4–7; 2 Chron 9.3–6.

CHAPTER 7

Judging others

This is also told in Luke 6.37–38,41–42

Jesus said:

¹ Don't condemn others, and God won't condemn you. ² God will be as hard on you as you are on others! He will treat you exactly as you treat them.

³ You can see the speck in your friend's eye, but you don't notice the log in your own eye. ⁴ How can you say, "My friend, let me take the speck out of your eye," when you don't see the log in your own eye? ⁵ You're nothing but show-offs! First, take the log out of your own eye. Then you can see how to take the speck out of your friend's eye.

⁶ Don't give to dogs what belongs to God. They will only turn and attack you. Don't throw pearls down in front of pigs. They will trample all over them.

Ask, search, knock

This is also told in Luke 11.9–13

Jesus continued:

⁷ Ask, and you will receive. Search, and you will find. Knock, and the door will be opened for you. ⁸ Everyone who asks will receive. Everyone who searches will find. And the door will be opened for everyone who knocks. ⁹ Would any of you give your hungry child a stone, if the child asked for some bread? ¹⁰ Would you give your child a snake if the child asked for a fish? ¹¹ As bad as you are, you still know how to give good gifts to your children. But your heavenly Father is even more ready to give good things to people who ask.

¹² Treat others as you want them to treat you. This is what the Law and the Prophets* are all about.

The narrow gate

This is also told in Luke 13.24

Jesus continued:

¹³ Go in through the narrow gate. The gate to destruction is wide, and the road that leads there is easy to follow. A lot of people go through that gate. ¹⁴ But the gate to life is very narrow. The road that leads there is so hard to follow that only a few people find it.

A tree and its fruit

This is also told in Luke 6.43–45

Jesus continued:

¹⁵ Watch out for false prophets! They dress up like sheep, but inside they are wolves who have come to attack you. ¹⁶ You can tell what they are by what they do. No one picks grapes or figs from thorn bushes. ¹⁷ A good tree produces good fruit, and a bad tree produces bad fruit. ¹⁸ A good tree cannot produce bad fruit, and a bad tree cannot produce good fruit. ¹⁹ Every tree that produces bad fruit will be chopped down and burnt. ²⁰ You can tell who the false prophets are by their deeds.

A warning

This is also told in Luke 13.26–27

Jesus continued:

²¹ Not everyone who calls me their Lord will get into the kingdom of heaven. Only the ones who obey my Father in heaven will get in. ²² On the day of judgment many will call me their Lord. They will say, "We preached in your name, and in your name we forced out demons and performed many miracles." ²³ But I will tell them, "I will have nothing to do with you! Get out of my sight, you evil people!"

Two builders

This is also told in Luke 6.47–49

Jesus continued:

²⁴ Anyone who hears and obeys these teachings of mine is like a wise person who built a house on solid rock. ²⁵ Rain poured down, rivers flooded, and winds beat against that house. But it did not fall, because it was built on solid rock.

²⁶ Anyone who hears my teachings and doesn't obey them is like a foolish person who built a house on sand. ²⁷ The rain poured down, the rivers flooded, and the winds blew and beat against that house. Finally, it fell with a crash.

---

*7.12 the Law and the Prophets: See the note at 5.17.
See also: 7.2: Mark 4.24. 7.12: Luke 6.31.

See also: 7.19: Matt 3.10; Luke 3.9. 7.20: Matt 12.33. 7.23: Psa 6.8.

²⁸ When Jesus finished speaking, the crowds were surprised at his teaching. ²⁹ He taught them like someone with authority, and not like their teachers of the Law of Moses.

CHAPTER 8

Jesus heals a man

This is also told in Mark 1.40–45; Luke 5.12–16

¹ As Jesus came down the mountain, he was followed by large crowds. ² Suddenly a man with leprosy* came and knelt in front of Jesus. He said, "Lord, you have the power to make me well, if only you wanted to."

³ Jesus put his hand on the man and said, "I want to! Now you are well." At once the man's leprosy disappeared. ⁴ Jesus told him, "Don't tell anyone about this, but go and show the priest that you are well. Then take a gift to the temple just as Moses commanded, and everyone will know that you have been healed."*

Jesus heals an army officer's servant

This is also told in Luke 7.1–10; John 4.43–54

⁵ When Jesus was going into the town of Capernaum, an army officer came up to him and said, ⁶ "Lord, my servant is at home in such terrible pain that he can't even move."

⁷ "I will go and heal him," Jesus replied.

⁸ But the officer said, "Lord, I'm not good enough for you to come into my house. Just give the order, and my servant will get well. ⁹ I have officers who give orders to me, and I have soldiers who take orders from me. I can say to one of them, 'Go!' and he goes. I can say to another, 'Come!' and he comes. I can say to my servant, 'Do this!' and he will do it."

¹⁰ When Jesus heard this, he was so surprised that he turned and said to the crowd following him, "I tell you that in all of Israel I've never found anyone with this much faith! ¹¹ Many people will come from everywhere to enjoy the feast in the

---

*8.2 leprosy: In biblical times the word "leprosy" was used for many different kinds of skin diseases.
*8.4 everyone will know that you have been healed: People with leprosy had to be examined by a priest and told that they were well (that is "clean") before they could once again live a normal life in the Jewish community. The gift that Moses commanded was the sacrifice of some lambs together with flour mixed with olive oil.

See also: 7.28–29: Mark 1.22; Luke 4.32. 8.4: Lev 14.1–32.
8.11: Luke 13.29.

Life files

Matthew a.k.a. Levi

Background: Son of Alphaeus

What's the story?

Matthew was a tax collector who lived in Capernaum near Galilee. Tax collectors were hated because they worked with the Roman authorities, and because they had a reputation as fraudsters and extortionists. With Matthew, it was even worse: he was a Jew working for the Roman government.

Jesus called him away from this life, and he became one of the twelve apostles – Jesus' core followers.

Matthew went on to write a gospel which is aimed primarily at Jewish readers.

What's the point?

Matthew was a sinner. He was a despised cheat who was collaborating with the authorities. Yet Jesus reached out to him, and his writing has gone on to influence millions of Christians throughout the centuries.

More...

Taxes p.1151
Apostles & disciples p.1094

 Anorak corner

Disciples

1. Which disciples asked to sit next to Jesus in heaven?
2. Which disciple walked on water – for a bit?
3. Which disciple was in charge of the money?
4. Which disciple was beheaded by Herod?
5. Which disciple was chosen by lots?
(Answers on p.1431)

kingdom of heaven with Abraham, Isaac, and Jacob. 12 But the ones who should have been in the kingdom will be thrown out into the dark. They will cry and grit their teeth in pain."

13 Then Jesus said to the officer, "You may go home now. Your faith has made it happen."

At once his servant was healed.

Jesus heals many people

This is also told in Mark 1.29–34; Luke 4.38–41

14 Jesus went to the home of Peter, where he found that Peter's mother-in-law was sick in bed with fever. 15 He took her by the hand, and the fever left her. Then she got up and served Jesus a meal.

16 That evening many people with demons in them were brought to Jesus. And with only a word he forced out the evil spirits and healed everyone who was sick. 17 So God's promise came true, just as the prophet Isaiah had said,

> "He healed our diseases
> and made us well."

Some who wanted to go with Jesus

This is also told in Luke 9.57–62

18 When Jesus saw the crowd,' he went across Lake Galilee. 19 A teacher of the Law of Moses came up to him and said, "Teacher, I'll go anywhere with you!"

20 Jesus replied, "Foxes have dens, and birds have nests. But the Son of Man doesn't have a place to call his own."

21 Another disciple said to Jesus, "Lord, let me wait till I bury my father."

22 Jesus answered, "Come with me, and let the dead bury their dead."*

A storm

This is also told in Mark 4.35–41; Luke 8.22–25

23 After Jesus left in a boat with his disciples, 24 a terrible storm suddenly struck the lake, and waves started splashing into their boat.

Jesus was sound asleep, 25 so the disciples went over to him and woke him up. They said, "Lord, save us! We're going to drown!"

26 But Jesus replied, "Why are you so afraid? You don't have much faith." Then he got up and ordered the wind and the waves to calm down. And everything was calm.

27 The men in the boat were amazed and said, "Who is this? Even the wind and the waves obey him."

Two men with demons in them

This is also told in Mark 5.1–20; Luke 8.26–39

28 After Jesus had crossed the lake, he came to shore near the town of Gadara' and started down the road. Two men with demons in them came to him from the tombs.* They were so fierce that no one could travel that way. 29 Suddenly they shouted, "Jesus, Son of God, what do you want with us? Have you come to punish us before our time?"

30 Not far from there a large herd of pigs was feeding. 31 So the demons begged Jesus, "If you force us out, please send us into those pigs!" 32 Jesus told them to go, and they went out of the men and into the pigs. All at once the pigs rushed down the steep bank into the lake and drowned.

33 The people taking care of the pigs ran to the town and told everything, especially what had happened to the two men. 34 Everyone in town came out to meet Jesus. When they saw him, they begged him to leave their part of the country.

CHAPTER 9

Jesus heals a crippled man

This is also told in Mark 2.1–12; Luke 5.17–26

1 Jesus got into a boat and crossed back over to the town where he lived.* 2 Some people soon brought to him a crippled man lying on a mat. When Jesus saw how much faith they had, he said to the crippled man, "My friend, don't worry! Your sins are forgiven."

3 Some teachers of the Law of Moses said to themselves, "Jesus must think he is God!"

4 But Jesus knew what was in their minds, and he said, "Why are you thinking such evil things? 5 Is it easier for me to tell this crippled man that his sins are forgiven or to tell him to get up and walk? 6 But I will show you that the Son of Man has the right to forgive sins here on earth." So Jesus said to

---

*8.22 let the dead bury their dead: For the Jewish people a proper burial of their dead was a very important duty. But Jesus teaches that following him is even more important.

See also: 8.12: Matt 22.13; 25.30; Luke 13.28. **8.17:** Isa 53.4.

*8.28 tombs: It was thought that demons and evil spirits lived in tombs and in caves that were used for burying the dead.
*9.1 where he lived: Capernaum. See 4.13.

the man, "Get up! Pick up your mat and go on home." [7] The man got up and went home. [8] When the crowds saw this, they were afraid' and praised God for giving such authority to people.

Jesus chooses Matthew

This is also told in Mark 2.13–17; Luke 5.27–32

[9] As Jesus was leaving, he saw a tax collector* named Matthew sitting at the place for paying taxes. Jesus said to him, "Come with me." Matthew got up and went with him.

[10] Later, Jesus and his disciples were having dinner at Matthew's house.' Many tax collectors and other sinners were also there. [11] Some Pharisees asked Jesus' disciples, "Why does your teacher eat with tax collectors and other sinners?"

[12] Jesus heard them and answered, "Healthy people don't need a doctor, but sick people do. [13] Go and learn what the Scriptures mean when they say, 'Instead of offering sacrifices to me, I want you to be merciful to others.' I didn't come to invite good people to be my followers. I came to invite sinners."

People ask about going without eating

This is also told in Mark 2.18–22; Luke 5.33–39

[14] One day some followers of John the Baptist came and asked Jesus, "Why do we and the Pharisees often go without eating,* while your disciples never do?"

[15] Jesus answered:

The friends of a bridegroom don't go without eating while he is still with them. But the time will come when he will be taken from them. Then they will go without eating.

[16] No one uses a new piece of cloth to patch old clothes. The patch would shrink and tear a bigger hole.

[17] No one pours new wine into old wineskins. The wine would swell and burst the old skins.* Then the wine would be lost, and the skins would be ruined. New wine must be put into new wineskins. Both the skins and the wine will then be safe.

A dying girl and a sick woman

This is also told in Mark 5.21–43; Luke 8.40–56

[18] While Jesus was still speaking, an official came and knelt in front of him. The man said, "My daughter has just died! Please come and place your hand on her. Then she will live again."

[19] Jesus and his disciples got up and went with the man.

[20] A woman who had been bleeding for twelve years came up behind Jesus and barely touched his clothes. [21] She had said to herself, "If I can just touch his clothes, I will get well."

[22] Jesus turned. He saw the woman and said, "Don't worry! You are now well because of your faith." At that moment she was healed.

[23] When Jesus went into the home of the official and saw the musicians and the crowd of mourners,* [24] he said, "Get out of here! The little girl isn't dead. She is just asleep." Everyone started laughing at Jesus. [25] But after the crowd had been sent out of the house, Jesus went to the girl's bedside. He took her by the hand and helped her up.

[26] News about this spread all over that part of the country.

Jesus heals two blind men

[27] As Jesus was walking along, two blind men began following him and shouting, "Son of David,* have pity on us!"

[28] After Jesus had gone indoors, the two blind men came up to him. He asked them, "Do you believe I can make you well?"

"Yes, Lord," they answered.

[29] Jesus touched their eyes and said, "Because of your faith, you will be healed." [30] They were able to see, and Jesus strictly warned them not to tell anyone about him. [31] But they left and talked about him to everyone in that part of the country.

---

*9.9 tax collector: See the note at 5.46.
*9.14 without eating: See the note at 4.2.
*9.17 swell and burst the old skins: While the juice from grapes was becoming wine, it would swell and stretch the skins in which it had been stored. If the skins were old and stiff, they would burst.

See also: 9.10–11: Luke 15.1–2. 9.13: a Matt 12.7; b Hos 6.6.

*9.23 the crowd of mourners: The Jewish people often hired mourners for funerals.
*9.27 Son of David: The Jewish people expected the Messiah to be from the family of King David, and for this reason the Messiah was often called the "Son of David".

Jesus heals a man who could not talk

³² As Jesus and his disciples were on their way, some people brought to him a man who could not talk because a demon was in him. ³³ After Jesus had forced the demon out, the man started talking. The crowds were so amazed that they began saying, "Nothing like this has ever happened in Israel!"

³⁴ But the Pharisees said, "The leader of the demons gives him the power to force out demons."

Jesus has pity on people

³⁵ Jesus went to every town and village. He taught in their meeting places and preached the good news about God's kingdom. Jesus also healed every kind of disease and sickness. ³⁶ When he saw the crowds, he felt sorry for them. They were confused and helpless, like sheep without a shepherd. ³⁷ He said to his disciples, "A large crop is in the fields, but there are only a few workers. ³⁸ Ask the Lord in charge of the harvest to send out workers to bring it in."

CHAPTER 10
Jesus chooses his twelve apostles

This is also told in Mark 3.13–19; Luke 6.12–16

¹ Jesus called together his twelve disciples. He gave them the power to force out evil spirits and to heal every kind of disease and sickness. ² The first of the twelve apostles was Simon, better known as Peter. His brother Andrew was an apostle, and so were James and John, the two sons of Zebedee. ³ Philip, Bartholomew, Thomas, Matthew the tax collector,* James the son of Alphaeus, and Thaddaeus were also apostles. ⁴ The others were Simon, known as the Eager One,* and Judas Iscariot,* who later betrayed Jesus.

Instructions for the twelve apostles

This is also told in Mark 6.7–13; Luke 9.1–6

⁵ Jesus sent out the twelve apostles with these instructions:

Stay away from the Gentiles and don't go to any Samaritan town. ⁶ Go only to the people of Israel, because they are like a flock of lost sheep. ⁷ As you go, announce that the kingdom of heaven will soon be here.* ⁸ Heal the sick, raise the dead to life, heal people who have leprosy,* and force out demons. You received without paying, now give without being paid. ⁹ Don't take along any gold, silver, or copper coins. ¹⁰ And don't carry* a travelling bag or an extra shirt or sandals or a walking stick. Workers deserve their food. ¹¹ So when you go to a town or a village, find someone worthy enough to have you as their guest and stay with them until you leave. ¹² When you go to a home, give it your blessing of peace. ¹³ If the home is deserving, let your blessing remain with them. But if the home isn't deserving, take back your blessing of peace. ¹⁴ If someone won't welcome you or listen to your message, leave their home or town. And shake the dust from your feet at them.* ¹⁵ I promise you that the day of judgment will be easier for the towns of Sodom and Gomorrah* than for that town.

Warning about trouble

This is also told in Mark 13.9–13; Luke 21.12–17

Jesus continued:

¹⁶ I am sending you like lambs into a pack of wolves. So be as wise as snakes and as innocent as doves. ¹⁷ Watch out for people who will take you to court and have you beaten in their meeting places. ¹⁸ Because of me, you will be dragged before rulers and kings to tell them and the Gentiles about your faith. ¹⁹ But when someone arrests you, don't worry about what you will say or how you will say it. At that time you will be

---

*10.3 tax collector: See the note at 5.46.
*10.4 known as the Eager One: The Greek text has "Cananaean", which probably comes from a Hebrew word meaning "zealous" (see Luke 6.15). "Zealot" was the name later given to the members of a Jewish group which resisted and fought against the Romans.
*10.4 Iscariot: This may mean "a man from Kerioth" (a place in Judea). But more probably it means "a man who was a liar" or "a man who was a betrayer".
See also: 9.34: Matt 10.25; 12.24; Mark 3.22; Luke 11.15. 9.35: Matt 4.23; Mark 1.39; Luke 4.44. 9.36: Num 27.17; 1 King 22.17; 2 Chron 18.16; Ezek 34.5; Mark 6.34. 9.37-38: Luke 10.2.

*10.8 leprosy: See the note at 8.2.
*10.14 shake the dust from your feet at them: This was a way of showing rejection. See Acts 13.51.
*10.15 Sodom and Gomorrah: During the time of Abraham the Lord destroyed these towns because the people there were so evil.
See also: 10.7-15: Luke 10.4-12. 10.10: 1 Cor 9.14; 1 Tim 5.18. 10.14: Acts 13.51. 10.15: a Matt 11.24; b Gen 19.24-28. 10.16: Luke 10.3. 10.17-20: Mark 13.9-11; Luke 12.11-12; 21.12-15.

given the words to say. [20] But you will not really be the one speaking. The Spirit from your Father will tell you what to say.

[21] Brothers and sisters will betray one another and have each other put to death. Parents will betray their own children, and children will turn against their parents and have them killed. [22] Everyone will hate you because of me. But if you remain faithful until the end, you will be saved. [23] When people ill-treat you in one town, hurry to another one. I promise you that before you have gone to all the towns of Israel, the Son of Man will come.

[24] Disciples are not better than their teacher, and slaves are not better than their master. [25] It is enough for disciples to be like their teacher and for slaves to be like their master. If people call the head of the family Satan, what will they say about the rest of the family?

The one to fear

This is also told in Luke 12.2–7

Jesus continued:

[26] Don't be afraid of anyone! Everything that is hidden will be found out, and every secret will be known. [27] Whatever I say to you in the dark, you must tell in the light. And you must announce from the housetops whatever I have whispered to you. [28] Don't be afraid of people. They can kill you, but they cannot harm your soul. Instead, you should fear God who can destroy both your body and your soul in hell. [29] Aren't two sparrows sold for only a penny? But your Father knows when any one of them falls to the ground. [30] Even the hairs on your head are counted. [31] So don't be afraid! You are worth much more than many sparrows.

Telling others about Christ

This is also told in Luke 12.8–9

Jesus continued:

[32] If you tell others that you belong to me, I will tell my Father in heaven that you are my followers. [33] But if you reject me, I will tell my Father in heaven that you don't belong to me.

Not peace, but trouble

This is also told in Luke 12.51–53; 14.26–27

Jesus continued:

[34] Don't think that I came to bring peace to the earth! I came to bring trouble, not peace. [35] I came to turn sons against their fathers, daughters against their mothers, and daughters-in-law against their mothers-in-law. [36] Your worst enemies will be in your own family.

[37] If you love your father or mother or even your sons and daughters more than me, you are not fit to be my disciples. [38] And unless you are willing to take up your cross and come with me, you are not fit to be my disciples. [39] If you try to save your life, you will lose it. But if you give it up for me, you will find it.

Rewards

This is also told in Mark 9.41

Jesus continued:

[40] Anyone who welcomes you welcomes me. And anyone who welcomes me also welcomes the one who sent me. [41] Anyone who welcomes a prophet, just because that person is a prophet, will be given the same reward as a prophet. Anyone who welcomes a good person, just because that person is good, will be given the same reward as a good person. [42] And anyone who gives one of my most humble followers a cup of cool water, just because that person is my follower, will be rewarded.

CHAPTER 11

John the Baptist

This is also told in Luke 7.18–35

[1] After Jesus had finished instructing his twelve disciples, he left and began teaching and preaching in the towns.'

[2] John was in prison when he heard what Christ was doing. So John sent some of his followers [3] to ask Jesus, "Are you the one we should be looking for? Or must we wait for someone else?"

[4] Jesus answered, "Go and tell John what you have heard and seen. [5] The blind are now

---

See also: **10.21:** Mark 13.12; Luke 21.16. **10.22:** a Matt 24.9; Mark 13.13; Luke 21.17; b Matt 24.13; Mark 13.13. **10.24:** a Luke 6.40; b John 13.16; 15.20. **10.25:** Matt 9.34; 12.24; Mark 3.22; Luke 11.15. **10.26:** Mark 4.22; Luke 8.17. **10.33:** 2 Tim 2.12.

See also: **10.35–36:** Mic 7.6. **10.38:** Matt 16.24; Mark 8.34; Luke 9.23. **10.39:** Matt 16.25; Mark 8.35; Luke 9.24; 17.33; John 12.25. **10.40:** a Luke 10.16; John 13.20; b Mark 9.37; Luke 9.48. **11.5:** a Isa 35.5–6; b Isa 61.1.

Being christian

Responding to God

Matthew 11.11–30
The first step in being Christian is, for many people, the biggest leap of all: acknowledging God for who he is.

Many people are happy to believe in 'God'. They don't mind believing in a vague, background figure; a being who hovers around just being all nice and fluffy and not interfering. But that's not who God is. That's not how he's shown in the Bible. God is a real being, with real emotions. He is angry, patient, sad, joyful; he is a living, feeling, real God.

More than that, he's a personal God. He wants to have an intimate relationship with you. He is not some distant, disinterested 'life-force', but a God who is described as our Father. Like all Fathers – well, like all the best Fathers – he wants a relationship with his children. He wants to carry your troubles for you. Like all the best Fathers, he loves his children. In fact, he loves them so much that, in the form of his son, Jesus Christ, he died for them.

Being Christian, therefore, is not a question of following some nice ideas or some neat philosophical theory. It's about being in a relationship with a God who is real, who is personal and who is loving.

All that we do as Christians, and all that we are, springs from this. Everything we do, we do as a response to the God who loves us.

Being Christian: Responding to God

• Understand that God is real and he wants a relationship with you
• God is described as a father. What does this mean for you?

able to see, and the lame can walk. People with leprosy* are being healed, and the deaf can hear. The dead are raised to life, and the poor are hearing the good news. 6 God will bless everyone who doesn't reject me because of what I do."

7 As John's followers were going away, Jesus spoke to the crowds about John:

What sort of person did you go out into the desert to see? Was he like tall grass blown about by the wind? 8 What kind of man did you go out to see? Was he someone dressed in fine clothes? People who dress like that live in the king's palace. 9 What did you really go out to see? Was he a prophet? He certainly was. I tell you that he was more than a prophet. 10 In the Scriptures God says about him, "I am sending my messenger ahead of you to get things ready for you." 11 I tell you that no one ever born on this earth is greater than John the Baptist. But whoever is least in the kingdom of heaven is greater than John.

12 From the time of John the Baptist until now, violent people have been trying to take over the kingdom of heaven by force. 13 All the Books of the Prophets and the Law of Moses* told what was going to happen up to the time of John. 14 And if you believe them, John is Elijah,* the prophet you are waiting for. 15 If you have ears, pay attention!

16 You people are like children sitting in the market and shouting to each other,

17 "We played the flute,
    but you would not dance!
We sang a funeral song,
    but you would not mourn!"

18 John the Baptist did not go around eating and drinking, and you said, "That man has a demon in him!" 19 But the Son of Man goes around eating and drinking, and you say, "That man eats and drinks too much! He is even a friend of tax collectors* and sinners." Yet Wisdom is shown to be right by what it does.

*11.5 leprosy: See the note at 8.2.
*11.13 the Books of the Prophets and the Law of Moses: See the note at 5.17.
*11.14 Elijah: Many of the Jewish people expected the prophet Elijah to prepare the way for the Messiah.
*11.19 tax collectors: See the note at 5.46.

See also: 11.10: Mal 3.1. 11.12–13: Luke 16.16. 11.14: Mal 4.5; Matt 17.10–13; Mark 9.11–13.

The unbelieving towns

This is also told in Luke 10.13–15

20 In the towns where Jesus had performed most of his miracles, the people refused to turn to God. So Jesus was upset with them and said:

21 You people of Chorazin are in for trouble! You people of Bethsaida are in for trouble too! If the miracles that took place in your towns had happened in Tyre and Sidon, the people there would have turned to God long ago. They would have dressed in sackcloth and put ashes on their heads.* 22 I tell you that on the day of judgment the people of Tyre and Sidon will get off easier than you will.

23 People of Capernaum, do you think you will be honoured in heaven? You will go down to hell! If the miracles that took place in your town had happened in Sodom, that town would still be standing. 24 So I tell you that on the day of judgment the people of Sodom will get off easier than you.

Come to me and rest

This is also told in Luke 10.21–22

25 At that moment Jesus said:

My Father, Lord of heaven and earth, I am grateful that you hid all this from wise and educated people and showed it to ordinary people. 26 Yes, Father, that is what pleased you.

27 My Father has given me everything, and he is the only one who knows the Son. The only one who truly knows the Father is the Son. But the Son wants to tell others about the Father, so that they can know him too.

28 If you are tired from carrying heavy burdens, come to me and I will give you rest. 29 Take the yoke* I give you. Put it on your shoulders and learn from me. I am gentle and humble, and you will find rest. 30 This yoke is easy to bear, and this burden is light.

---

*11.21 **sackcloth . . . ashes on their heads:** This was one way that people showed how sorry they were for their sins.

*11.29 **yoke:** Yokes were put on the necks of animals, so that they could pull a plough or wagon. A yoke was a symbol of obedience and hard work.

See also: **11.21:** Isa 23.1–18; Ezek 26.1–28.26; Joel 3.4–8; Amos 1.9–10; Zech 9.2–4. **11.23:** a Isa 14.13–15; b Gen 19.24–28. **11.24:** Matt 10.15; Luke 10.12. **11.27:** a John 3.35; b John 1.18; 10.15. **11.29:** Jer 6.16.

CHAPTER 12

A question about the Sabbath

This is also told in Mark 2.23–28; Luke 6.1–5

1 One Sabbath, Jesus and his disciples were walking through some wheat fields. His disciples were hungry and began picking and eating grains of wheat.* 2 Some Pharisees noticed this and said to Jesus, "Why are your disciples picking grain on the Sabbath? They are not supposed to do that!"

3 Jesus answered:

You must have read what David did when he and his followers were hungry. 4 He went into the house of God, and then they ate the sacred loaves of bread that only priests are supposed to eat. 5 Haven't you read in the Law of Moses that the priests are allowed to work in the temple on the Sabbath? But no one says that they are guilty of breaking the law of the Sabbath. 6 I tell you that there is something here greater than the temple. 7 Don't you know what the Scriptures mean when they say, "Instead of offering sacrifices to me, I want you to be merciful to others"? If you knew what this means, you would not condemn these innocent disciples of mine. 8 So the Son of Man is Lord over the Sabbath.

A man with a crippled hand

This is also told in Mark 3.1–6; Luke 6.6–11

9 Jesus left and went into one of the Jewish meeting places, 10 where there was a man whose hand was crippled. Some Pharisees wanted to accuse Jesus of doing something wrong, and they asked him, "Is it right to heal someone on the Sabbath?"

11 Jesus answered, "If you had a sheep that fell into a ditch on the Sabbath, wouldn't you lift it out? 12 People are worth much more than sheep, and so it is right to do good on the Sabbath." 13 Then Jesus told the man, "Hold out your hand." The man did, and it became as healthy as the other one.

14 The Pharisees left and started making plans to kill Jesus.

---

*12.1 **picking . . . grains of wheat:** It was the custom to let hungry travellers pick grains of wheat.

See also: **12.1:** Deut 23.25. **12.3,4:** 1 Sam 21.1–6. **12.4:** Lev 24.9. **12.5:** Num 28.9–10. **12.7:** a Matt 9.13; b Hos 6.6. **12.11:** Luke 14.5.

God's chosen servant

¹⁵ When Jesus found out what was happening, he left there and large crowds followed him. He healed all their sick, ¹⁶ but warned them not to tell anyone about him. ¹⁷ So God's promise came true, just as Isaiah the prophet had said,

¹⁸ "Here is my chosen servant!
  I love him,
    and he pleases me.
  I will give him my Spirit,
  and he will bring justice
    to the nations.
¹⁹ He won't shout or yell
    or call out in the streets.
²⁰ He won't break off a bent reed
    or put out a dying flame,
  but he will make sure
    that justice is done.
²¹ All nations will place
    their hope in him."

Jesus and the ruler of the demons

This is also told in Mark 3.20–30;
Luke 11.14–23; 12.10

²² Some people brought to Jesus a man who was blind and could not talk because he had a demon in him. Jesus healed the man, and then he was able to talk and see. ²³ The crowds were so amazed that they asked, "Could Jesus be the Son of David?"*

²⁴ When the Pharisees heard this, they said, "He forces out demons by the power of Beelzebul, the ruler of the demons!"

²⁵ Jesus knew what they were thinking, and he said to them:

Any kingdom where people fight each other will end up ruined. And a town or family that fights will soon destroy itself. ²⁶ So if Satan fights against himself, how can his kingdom last? ²⁷ If I use the power of Beelzebul to force out demons, whose power do your own followers use to force them out? Your followers are the ones who will judge you. ²⁸ But when I force out demons by the power of God's Spirit, it proves that God's kingdom has already come to you. ²⁹ How can anyone break into a strong man's house and steal his things,

unless he first ties up the strong man? Then he can take everything.

³⁰ If you are not on my side, you are against me. If you don't gather in the harvest with me, you scatter it. ³¹⁻³² I tell you that any sinful thing you do or say can be forgiven. Even if you speak against the Son of Man, you can be forgiven. But if you speak against the Holy Spirit, you can never be forgiven, either in this life or in the life to come.

A tree and its fruit

This is also told in Luke 6.43–45

Jesus continued:

³³ A good tree produces only good fruit, and a bad tree produces bad fruit. You can tell what a tree is like by the fruit it produces. ³⁴ You are evil snakes, so how can you say anything good? Your words show what is in your hearts. ³⁵ Good people bring good things out of their hearts, but evil people bring evil things out of their hearts. ³⁶ I promise you that on the day of judgment, everyone will have to account for every careless word they have spoken. ³⁷ On that day they will be told that they are either innocent or guilty because of the things they have said.

A sign from heaven

This is also told in Mark 8.11–12; Luke 11.29–32

³⁸ Some Pharisees and teachers of the Law of Moses said, "Teacher, we want you to show us a sign from heaven."

³⁹ But Jesus replied:

You want a sign because you are evil and won't believe! But the only sign you will get is the sign of the prophet Jonah. ⁴⁰ He was in the stomach of a big fish for three days and nights, just as the Son of Man will be deep in the earth for three days and nights. ⁴¹ On the day of judgment the people of Nineveh* will stand there with you and condemn you. They turned to God

---

*12.23 Could Jesus be the Son of David: Or "Does Jesus think he is the Son of David?" See the note at 9.27.

See also: **12.18–21:** Isa 42.1–4 (LXX).
12.24: Matt 9.34; 10.25.

*12.41 Nineveh: During the time of Jonah this city was the capital of the Assyrian Empire, which was Israel's worst enemy. But Jonah was sent there to preach, so that the people would turn to the Lord and be saved.

See also: **12.30:** Mark 9.40. **12.32:** Luke 12.10.
12.33: Matt 7.20; Luke 6.44. **12.34: a** Matt 3.7; 23.33;
Luke 3.7; **b** Matt 15.18; Luke 6.45. **12.38:** Matt 16.1;
Mark 8.11; Luke 11.16. **12.39:** Matt 16.4; Mark 8.12.
12.40: Jon 1.17. **12.41:** Jon 3.5.

Holy history

Jesus' teaching

Jesus spent a lot of his time teaching. He taught in synagogues, in fields, in a boat, on the side of a hill, in houses – wherever the opportunity afforded itself.

A lot of other teachers and scribes of his time backed up all their arguments with reference to other teachers and 'authorities', chucking in references and quotations to make their argument as impressive as they could. Jesus didn't. He might quote from the Scriptures, or refer to well known figures like Jonah, but mostly he just said things, simply and powerfully. Which is why people always said that Jesus taught 'with authority'.

Stories

Jesus told lots of stories. Loads and loads and loads of stories. In fact, he never taught without using parables.

Questions

Jesus' teaching was not just about making pronouncements, it was also about asking and answering questions, fuelling debate.

Demands

Jesus was not interested in making clever points or just winning the argument. He wanted people to actually change the way they behaved. He wanted to change lives.

Hmmmmm

Jesus gave a lot of people brainache. He made cryptic statements or told difficult stories without explanation. Some found it too demanding. But Jesus wanted people to think about what he said. He still does.

Direct

Jesus wasn't interested in theoretical debate. Several times in the gospels, he changes direction to avoid pointless argument.

Life

Jesus walked the talk. Most of all, he lived out what he taught.

when Jonah preached, and yet here is something far greater than Jonah. ⁴² The Queen of the South* will also stand there with you and condemn you. She travelled a long way to hear Solomon's wisdom, and yet here is something much greater than Solomon.

Return of an evil spirit

This is also told in Luke 11.24–26

Jesus continued:

⁴³ When an evil spirit leaves a person, it travels through the desert, looking for a place to rest. But when the demon doesn't find a place, ⁴⁴ it says, "I will go back to the home I left." When it gets there and finds the place empty, clean, and tidy, ⁴⁵ it goes off and finds seven other evil spirits even worse than itself. They all come and make their home there, and the person ends up in a worse state than before. That's how it will be with you evil people of today.

Jesus' mother and brothers

This is also told in Mark 3.31–35; Luke 8.19–21

⁴⁶ While Jesus was still speaking to the crowds, his mother and brothers came and stood outside because they wanted to talk with him. ⁴⁷ Someone told Jesus, "Your mother and brothers are standing outside and want to talk with you."▸

⁴⁸ Jesus answered, "Who is my mother and who are my brothers?" ⁴⁹ Then he pointed to his disciples and said, "These are my mother and my brothers! ⁵⁰ Anyone who obeys my Father in heaven is my brother or sister or mother."

CHAPTER 13

A story about a farmer

This is also told in Mark 4.1–9; Luke 8.4–8

¹ That same day Jesus left the house and went out beside Lake Galilee, where he sat down to teach.* ² Such large crowds gathered around him that he had to sit in a boat, while the people stood on the shore. ³ Then he taught them many things by using stories. He said:

---

*12.42 Queen of the South: Sheba, probably a country in southern Arabia.
*13.1 sat down to teach: See the note at 5.1.
See also: 12.42: 1 King 10.1–10; 2 Chron 9.1–12.
13.2: Luke 5.1–3.

A farmer went out to scatter seed in a field. ⁴ While the farmer was scattering the seed, some of it fell along the road and was eaten by birds. ⁵ Other seeds fell on thin, rocky ground and quickly started growing because the soil wasn't very deep. ⁶ But when the sun came up, the plants were scorched and dried up, because they did not have enough roots. ⁷ Some other seeds fell where thorn bushes grew up and choked the plants. ⁸ But a few seeds did fall on good ground where the plants produced a hundred or sixty or thirty times as much as was scattered. ⁹ If you have ears, pay attention!

Why Jesus used stories

This is also told in Mark 4.10–12; Luke 8.9–10

¹⁰ Jesus' disciples came to him and asked, "Why do you use nothing but stories when you speak to the people?"

¹¹ Jesus answered:

I have explained the secrets about the kingdom of heaven to you, but not to others. ¹² Everyone who has something will be given more. But people who don't have anything will lose even what little they have. ¹³ I use stories when I speak to them because when they look, they cannot see, and when they listen, they cannot hear or understand. ¹⁴ So God's promise came true, just as the prophet Isaiah had said,

"These people will listen
and listen,
but never understand.
They will look and look,
but never see.
¹⁵ All of them have
stubborn minds!
Their ears are stopped up,
and their eyes are covered.
They cannot see or hear
or understand.
If they could,
they would turn to me,
and I would heal them."

¹⁶ But God has blessed you, because your eyes can see and your ears can hear! ¹⁷ Many prophets and good people were eager to see what you see and to hear what you hear. But I tell you that they did not see or hear.

Jesus explains the story about the farmer

This is also told in Mark 4.13–20; Luke 8.11–15

Jesus continued:

¹⁸ Now listen to the meaning of the story about the farmer:

¹⁹ The seeds that fell along the road are the people who hear the message about the kingdom, but don't understand it. Then the evil one comes and snatches the message from their hearts. ²⁰ The seeds that fell on rocky ground are the people who gladly hear the message and accept it straight away. ²¹ But they don't have deep roots, and they don't last very long. As soon as life gets hard or the message gets them in trouble, they give up.

²² The seeds that fell among the thorn bushes are also people who hear the message. But they start worrying about the needs of this life and are fooled by the desire to get rich. So the message gets choked out, and they never produce anything. ²³ The seeds that fell on good ground are the people who hear and understand the message. They produce as much as a hundred or sixty or thirty times what was planted.

Weeds among the wheat

²⁴ Jesus then told them this story:

The kingdom of heaven is like what happened when a farmer scattered good seed in a field. ²⁵ But while everyone was sleeping, an enemy came and scattered weeds in the field and then left.

²⁶ When the plants came up and began to ripen, the farmer's servants could see the weeds. ²⁷ The servants came and asked, "Sir, didn't you scatter good seed in your field? Where did these weeds come from?"

²⁸ "An enemy did this," he replied.

His servants then asked, "Do you want us to go out and pull up the weeds?"

²⁹ "No!" he answered. "You might also pull up the wheat. ³⁰ Leave the weeds alone until harvest time. Then I'll tell my workers to gather the weeds and tie them up and burn them. But I'll order them to store the wheat in my barn."

See also: 13.12: Matt 25.29; Mark 4.25; Luke 8.18; 19.26. **13.14–15:** Isa 6.9–10 (LXX). **13.16–17:** Luke 10.23–24.

Fishing

Fishing isn't mentioned much in the Old Testament, mainly because the Israelites had limited access to the coast and they hadn't yet developed fishing in other waters. By the time of the New Testament, however, things were different, and the Sea of Galilee was home to a large number of fishing boats.

In Galilee most fishing was done at night, just before dawn. The main way of fishing was by throwing nets from the boats. The nets had clay or stone weights along the lower edge, and cork or wood floats along the top. Two teams of men then took hold of each end of the net and started to haul it in. As long as the hauling was continuous the fish would be unable to escape. Jesus compares the kingdom of heaven to this type of net (Matthew 13.47–48).

Another method of fishing was for a single fisherman to use a casting net, which he spun out over the water. As the net fell through the water, it would take on a dome-like shape, capturing the fish. The fisherman would draw the net in with a line attached to the centre.

Fishermen also used a hook and line – probably Peter used this method to catch the fish in Matthew 17.27.

In those days, of course, there were no fridges, so fish had to be salted and dried if it was going to be kept for any length of time.

More...

Farming p.494
Food and drink p.355
Work p.1343

Stories about a mustard seed and yeast
This is also told in Mark 4.30–32; Luke 13.18–21

[31] Jesus told them another story:

The kingdom of heaven is like what happens when a farmer plants a mustard seed in a field. [32] Although it is the smallest of all seeds, it grows larger than any garden plant and becomes a tree. Birds even come and nest on its branches.

[33] Jesus also said:

The kingdom of heaven is like what happens when a woman mixes a little yeast into three big batches of flour. Finally, all the dough rises.

The reason for teaching with stories
This is also told in Mark 4.33–34

[34] Jesus used stories when he spoke to the people. In fact, he did not tell them anything without using stories. [35] So God's promise came true, just as the prophet had said,

"I will use stories
  to speak my message
and to explain things
  that have been hidden
since the creation
  of the world."

Jesus explains the story about the weeds

[36] After Jesus left the crowd and went inside, his disciples came to him and said, "Explain to us the story about the weeds in the wheat field."

[37] Jesus answered:

The one who scattered the good seed is the Son of Man. [38] The field is the world, and the good seeds are the people who belong to the kingdom. The weeds are those who belong to the evil one, [39] and the one who scattered them is the devil. The harvest is the end of time, and angels are the ones who bring in the harvest.

[40] Weeds are gathered and burnt. That's how it will be at the end of time. [41] The Son of Man will send out his angels, and they will gather from his kingdom everyone who does wrong or causes others to sin. [42] Then he will throw them into a flaming furnace, where people will cry and grit

See also: 13.35: Psa 78.2.

their teeth in pain. ⁴³ But everyone who has done right will shine like the sun in their Father's kingdom. If you have ears, pay attention!

A hidden treasure

Jesus continued:

⁴⁴ The kingdom of heaven is like what happens when someone finds a treasure hidden in a field and buries it again. A person like that is happy and goes and sells everything in order to buy that field.

A valuable pearl

Jesus continued:

⁴⁵ The kingdom of heaven is like what happens when a shop owner is looking for fine pearls. ⁴⁶ After finding a very valuable one, the owner goes and sells everything in order to buy that pearl.

A fish net

Jesus continued:

⁴⁷ The kingdom of heaven is like what happens when a net is thrown into a lake and catches all kinds of fish. ⁴⁸ When the net is full, it is dragged to the shore, and the fishermen sit down to separate the fish. They keep the good ones, but throw the bad ones away. ⁴⁹ That's how it will be at the end of time. Angels will come and separate the evil people from the ones who have done right. ⁵⁰ Then those evil people will be thrown into a flaming furnace, where they will cry and grit their teeth in pain.

New and old treasures

⁵¹ Jesus asked his disciples if they understood all these things. They said, "Yes, we do." ⁵² So he told them, "Every student of the Scriptures who becomes a disciple in the kingdom of heaven is like someone who brings out new and old treasures from the storeroom."

The people of Nazareth turn against Jesus

This is also told in Mark 6.1–6; Luke 4.16–30

⁵³ When Jesus had finished telling these stories, he left ⁵⁴ and went to his home town. He taught in their meeting place, and the people were so amazed that they asked, "Where does he get all this wisdom and the power to perform these miracles? ⁵⁵ Isn't he

the son of the carpenter? Isn't Mary his mother, and aren't James, Joseph, Simon, and Judas his brothers? ⁵⁶ Don't his sisters still live here in our town? How can he do all this?" ⁵⁷ So the people were very unhappy because of what he was doing.

But Jesus said, "Prophets are honoured by everyone, except the people of their home town and their own family." ⁵⁸ And because the people did not have any faith, Jesus did not perform many miracles there.

CHAPTER 14

The death of John the Baptist

This is also told in Mark 6.14–29; Luke 9.7–9

¹ About this time Herod the ruler* heard the news about Jesus ² and told his officials, "This is John the Baptist! He has come back from death, and that's why he has the power to perform these miracles."

³⁻⁴ Herod had earlier arrested John and had him chained and put in prison. He did this because John had told him, "It isn't right for you to take Herodias, the wife of your brother Philip." ⁵ Herod wanted to kill John. But the people thought John was a prophet, and Herod was afraid of what they might do.

⁶ When Herod's birthday came, the daughter of Herodias danced for the guests. She pleased Herod ⁷ so much that he swore to give her whatever she wanted. ⁸ But the girl's mother told her to say, "Here on a dish I want the head of John the Baptist!"

⁹ The king was sorry for what he had said. But he did not want to break the promise he had made in front of his guests. So he ordered a guard ¹⁰ to go to the prison and cut off John's head. ¹¹ It was taken on a dish to the girl, and she gave it to her mother. ¹² John's followers took his body and buried it. Then they told Jesus what had happened.

Jesus feeds five thousand

This is also told in Mark 6.30–44; Luke 9.10–17; John 6.1–14

¹³ After Jesus heard about John, he crossed Lake Galilee* to go to some place where he could be alone. But the crowds found out and followed him on foot from the towns.

---

*14.1 Herod the ruler:** Herod Antipas, the son of Herod the Great (see 2.1).
*14.13 crossed Lake Galilee:** To the east side.
See also: **13.57:** John 4.44. **14.3–4:** Luke 3.19–20. **14.4:** Lev 18.16; 20.21.

[14] When Jesus got out of the boat, he saw the large crowd. He felt sorry for them and healed everyone who was sick.

[15] That evening the disciples came to Jesus and said, "This place is like a desert, and it is already late. Let the crowds leave, so they can go to the villages and buy some food."

[16] Jesus replied, "They don't have to leave. Why don't you give them something to eat?"

[17] But they said, "We have only five small loaves of bread* and two fish." [18] Jesus asked his disciples to bring the food to him, [19] and he told the crowd to sit down on the grass. Jesus took the five loaves and the two fish. He looked up towards heaven and blessed the food. Then he broke the bread and handed it to his disciples, and they gave it to the people.

[20] After everyone had eaten all they wanted, Jesus' disciples picked up twelve large baskets of leftovers.

[21] There were about five thousand men who ate, not counting the women and children.

Jesus walks on the water

This is also told in Mark 6.45–52; John 6.15–21

[22] Straight away, Jesus made his disciples get into a boat and start back across the lake.* But he stayed until he had sent the crowds away. [23] Then he went up on a mountain where he could be alone and pray. Later that evening, he was still there.

[24] By this time the boat was a long way from the shore. It was going against the wind and was being tossed around by the waves. [25] A little while before morning, Jesus came walking on the water towards his disciples. [26] When they saw him, they thought he was a ghost. They were terrified and started screaming.

[27] At once, Jesus said to them, "Don't worry! I am Jesus. Don't be afraid."

[28] Peter replied, "Lord, if it is really you, tell me to come to you on the water."

[29] "Come on!" Jesus said. Peter then got out of the boat and started walking on the water towards him.

[30] But when Peter saw how strong the wind was, he was afraid and started sinking. "Save me, Lord!" he shouted.

[31] Straight away, Jesus reached out his hand. He helped Peter up and said, "You don't have much faith. Why do you doubt?"

[32] When Jesus and Peter got into the boat, the wind died down. [33] The men in the boat worshipped Jesus and said, "You really are the Son of God!"

Jesus heals sick people in Gennesaret

This is also told in Mark 6.53–56

[34] Jesus and his disciples crossed the lake and came to shore near the town of Gennesaret. [35] The people found out that he was there, and they sent word to everyone who lived in that part of the country. So they brought all the sick people to Jesus. [36] They begged him just to let them touch his clothes, and everyone who did was healed.

CHAPTER 15

The teaching of the ancestors

This is also told in Mark 7.1–13

[1] About this time some Pharisees and teachers of the Law of Moses came from Jerusalem. They asked Jesus, [2] "Why don't your disciples obey what our ancestors taught us to do? They don't even wash their hands* before they eat."

[3] Jesus answered:

Why do you disobey God and follow your own teaching? [4] Didn't God command you to respect your father and mother? Didn't he tell you to put to death all who curse their parents? [5] But you let people get by without helping their parents when they should. You let them say that what they have has been offered to God.* [6] Is this any way to show respect to your parents? You ignore God's commands in order to follow your own teaching. [7] And you are nothing but show-offs! Isaiah the prophet was right when he wrote that God had said,

[8] "All of you praise me
    with your words,
but you never really
    think about me.

---

*14.17 small loaves of bread: These would have been flat and round or in the shape of a bun.
*14.22 back across the lake: To the west side.

---

*15.2 wash their hands: The Jewish people had strict laws about washing their hands before eating, especially if they had been out in public.
*15.5 has been offered to God: According to Jewish custom, when people said something was offered to God, it belonged to him and could not be used for anyone else, not even for their own parents.
See also: 15.4: a Exod 20.12; Deut 5.16; b Exod 21.17; Lev 20.9. 15.8–9: Isa 29.13 (LXX).

⁹ It is useless for you
  to worship me,
when you teach rules
  made up by humans."

What really makes people unclean

This is also told in Mark 7.14–23

¹⁰ Jesus called the crowd together and said, "Pay attention and try to understand what I mean. ¹¹ The food that you put into your mouth doesn't make you unclean and unfit to worship God. The bad words that come out of your mouth are what make you unclean."

¹² Then his disciples came over to him and asked, "Do you know that you insulted the Pharisees by what you said?"

¹³ Jesus answered, "Every plant that my Father in heaven did not plant will be pulled up by the roots. ¹⁴ Stay away from those Pharisees! They are like blind people leading other blind people, and all of them will fall into a ditch."

¹⁵ Peter replied, "What did you mean when you talked about the things that make people unclean?"

¹⁶ Jesus then said:

Don't any of you know what I am talking about by now? ¹⁷ Don't you know that the food you put into your mouth goes into your stomach and then out of your body? ¹⁸ But the words that come out of your mouth come from your heart. And they are what make you unfit to worship God. ¹⁹ Out of your heart come evil thoughts, murder, unfaithfulness in marriage, vulgar deeds, stealing, telling lies, and insulting others. ²⁰ These are what make you unclean. Eating without washing your hands will not make you unfit to worship God.

A woman's faith

This is also told in Mark 7.24–30

²¹ Jesus left and went to the territory near the cities of Tyre and Sidon. ²² Suddenly a Canaanite woman* from there came out shouting, "Lord and Son of David,* have pity on me! My daughter is full of demons."

²³ Jesus did not say a word. But the woman kept following along and shouting, so his disciples came up and asked him to send her away.

²⁴ Jesus said, "I was sent only to the people of Israel! They are like a flock of lost sheep."

²⁵ The woman came closer. Then she knelt down and begged, "Please help me, Lord!"

²⁶ Jesus replied, "It isn't right to take food away from children and feed it to dogs."*

²⁷ "Lord, that's true," the woman said, "but even dogs get the crumbs that fall from their owner's table."

²⁸ Jesus answered, "Dear woman, you really do have a lot of faith, and you will be given what you want." At that moment her daughter was healed.

Jesus heals many people

²⁹ From there, Jesus went along Lake Galilee. Then he climbed a hill and sat down. ³⁰ Large crowds came and brought many people who were crippled or blind or lame or unable to talk. They placed them, and many others, in front of Jesus, and he healed them all. ³¹ Everyone was amazed at what they saw and heard. People who had never spoken could now speak. The lame were healed, the crippled could walk, and the blind were able to see. Everyone was praising the God of Israel.

Jesus feeds four thousand

This is also told in Mark 8.1–10

³² Jesus called his disciples together and told them, "I feel sorry for these people. They have been with me for three days, and they don't have anything to eat. I don't want to send them away hungry. They might faint on their way home."

³³ His disciples said, "This place is like a desert. Where can we find enough food to feed such a crowd?"

³⁴ Jesus asked them how much food they had. They replied, "Seven small loaves of bread* and a few little fish."

³⁵ After Jesus had told the people to sit down, ³⁶ he took the seven loaves of bread and the fish and gave thanks. He then broke them and handed them to his disciples, who passed them around to the crowds.

³⁷ Everyone ate all they wanted, and the leftovers filled seven large baskets.

---

*15.22 Canaanite woman: This woman was not Jewish.
*15.22 Son of David: See the note at 9.27.
See also: 15.14: Luke 6.39. 15.18: Matt 12.34.

*15.26 feed it to dogs: The Jewish people sometimes referred to Gentiles as dogs.
*15.34 small loaves of bread: See the note at 14.17.

³⁸ There were four thousand men who ate, not counting the women and children.

³⁹ After Jesus had sent the crowds away, he got into a boat and sailed across the lake. He came to shore near the town of Magadan.*

CHAPTER 16

A demand for a sign from heaven

This is also told in Mark 8.11–13; Luke 12.54–56

¹ The Pharisees and Sadducees came to Jesus and tried to test him by asking for a sign from heaven. ² He told them:

If the sky is red in the evening, you say the weather will be good. ³ But if the sky is red and gloomy in the morning, you say it is going to rain. You can tell what the weather will be like by looking at the sky. But you don't understand what is happening now.' ⁴ You want a sign because you are evil and won't believe! But the only sign you will be given is what happened to Jonah.*

Then Jesus left.

The yeast of the Pharisees and Sadducees

This is also told in Mark 8.14–21

⁵ The disciples had forgotten to bring any bread when they crossed the lake.* ⁶ Jesus then warned them, "Watch out! Guard against the yeast of the Pharisees and Sadducees."

⁷ The disciples talked this over and said to each other, "He must be saying this because we didn't bring along any bread."

⁸ Jesus knew what they were thinking and said:

You don't have much faith! Why are you talking about not having any bread? ⁹ Don't you understand? Have you forgotten about the five thousand people and all those baskets of leftovers from just five loaves of bread? ¹⁰ And what about the four thousand people and all those baskets of leftovers from only seven loaves of bread? ¹¹ Don't

you know by now that I am not talking to you about bread? Watch out for the yeast of the Pharisees and Sadducees!

¹² Finally, the disciples understood that Jesus wasn't talking about the yeast used to make bread, but about the teaching of the Pharisees and Sadducees.

Who is Jesus?

This is also told in Mark 8.27–30; Luke 9.18–21

¹³ When Jesus and his disciples were near the town of Caesarea Philippi, he asked them, "What do people say about the Son of Man?"

¹⁴ The disciples answered, "Some people say you are John the Baptist or perhaps Elijah* or Jeremiah or some other prophet."

¹⁵ Then Jesus asked them, "But who do you say I am?"

¹⁶ Simon Peter spoke up, "You are the Messiah, the Son of the living God."

¹⁷ Jesus told him:

Simon, son of Jonah, you are blessed! You didn't discover this on your own. It was shown to you by my Father in heaven. ¹⁸ So I will call you Peter, which means "a rock". On this rock I will build my church, and death itself will not have any power over it. ¹⁹ I will give you the keys to the kingdom of heaven, and God in heaven will allow whatever you allow on earth. But he will not allow anything that you don't allow.

²⁰ Jesus told his disciples not to tell anyone that he was the Messiah.

Jesus speaks about his suffering and death

This is also told in Mark 8.31–9.1; Luke 9.22–27

²¹ From then on, Jesus began telling his disciples what would happen to him. He said, "I must go to Jerusalem. There the nation's leaders, the chief priests, and the teachers of the Law of Moses will make me suffer terribly. I will be killed, but three days later I will rise to life."

²² Peter took Jesus aside and told him to stop talking like that. He said, "God would never let this happen to you, Lord!"

*15.39 Magadan: The location is unknown.
*16.4 what happened to Jonah: Jonah was in the stomach of a big fish for three days and nights. See 12.40.
*16.5 crossed the lake: To the east side.
See also: 16.1: Matt 12.38; Luke 11.16. 16.4: Matt 12.39; Luke 11.29. 16.6: Luke 12.1. 16.9: Matt 14.17–21. 16.10: Matt 15.34–38.

*16.14 Elijah: See the note at 11.14.
See also: 16.14: Matt 14.1–2; Mark 6.14–15; Luke 9.7–8. 16.16: John 6.68–69. 16.19: Matt 18.18; John 20.23.

1061

23 Jesus turned to Peter and said, "Satan, get away from me! You're in my way because you think like everyone else and not like God."

24 Then Jesus said to his disciples:

If any of you want to be my followers, you must forget about yourself. You must take up your cross and follow me. 25 If you want to save your life,' you will destroy it. But if you give up your life for me, you will find it. 26 What will you gain, if you own the whole world but destroy yourself? What would you give to get back your soul?

27 The Son of Man will soon come in the glory of his Father and with his angels to reward all people for what they have done. 28 I promise you that some of those standing here will not die before they see the Son of Man coming with his kingdom.

CHAPTER 17

The true glory of Jesus

This is also told in Mark 9.2–13; Luke 9.28–36

1 Six days later Jesus took Peter and the brothers James and John with him. They went up on a very high mountain where they could be alone. 2 There in front of the disciples, Jesus was completely changed. His face was shining like the sun, and his clothes became white as light.

3 All at once Moses and Elijah were there talking with Jesus. 4 So Peter said to him, "Lord, it is good for us to be here! Let us make three shelters, one for you, one for Moses, and one for Elijah."

5 While Peter was still speaking, the shadow of a bright cloud passed over them. From the cloud a voice said, "This is my own dear Son, and I am pleased with him. Listen to what he says!" 6 When the disciples heard the voice, they were so afraid that they fell flat on the ground. 7 But Jesus came over and touched them. He said, "Get up and don't be afraid!" 8 When they opened their eyes, they saw only Jesus.

9 On their way down from the mountain, Jesus warned his disciples not to tell anyone what they had seen until after the Son of Man had been raised from death.

10 The disciples asked Jesus, "Don't the teachers of the Law of Moses say that Elijah must come before the Messiah does?"

11 Jesus told them, "Elijah certainly will come and get everything ready. 12 In fact, he has already come. But the people did not recognize him and treated him just as they wanted to. They will soon make the Son of Man suffer in the same way." 13 Then the disciples understood that Jesus was talking to them about John the Baptist.

Jesus heals a boy

This is also told in Mark 9.14–29; Luke 9.37–43a

14 Jesus and his disciples returned to the crowd. A man knelt in front of him 15 and said, "Lord, have pity on my son! He has a bad case of epilepsy and often falls into a fire or into water. 16 I brought him to your disciples, but none of them could heal him."

17 Jesus said, "You people are too stubborn to have any faith! How much longer must I be with you? Why do I have to put up with you? Bring the boy here." 18 Then Jesus spoke sternly to the demon. It went out of the boy, and at once he was healed.

19 Later the disciples went to Jesus in private and asked him, "Why couldn't we force out the demon?"

20-21 Jesus replied:

It is because you don't have enough faith! But I can promise you this. If you had faith no larger than a mustard seed, you could tell this mountain to move from here to there. And it would. Everything would be possible for you.'

Jesus again speaks about his death

This is also told in Mark 9.30–32; Luke 9.43b–45

22 While Jesus and his disciples were going from place to place in Galilee, he told them, "The Son of Man will be handed over to people 23 who will kill him. But three days later he will rise to life." All this made the disciples very sad.

Paying the temple tax

24 When Jesus and the others arrived in Capernaum, the collectors for the temple tax came to Peter and asked, "Does your teacher pay the temple tax?"

See also: **16.24:** Matt 10.38; Luke 14.27. **16.25:** Matt 10.39; Luke 17.33; John 12.25. **16.27:** a Matt 25.31; b Psa 62.12; Rom 2.6. **17.1–5:** 2 Pet 1.17–18. **17.5:** a Gen 22.2; Psa 2.7; Isa 42.1; Matt 3.17; 12.18; Mark 1.11; Luke 3.22; b Deut 18.15.

See also: **17.10:** Mal 4.5. **17.12:** Matt 11.14. **17.20:** Matt 21.21; Mark 11.23; 1 Cor 13.2. **17.24:** Exod 30.13–15; 38.26.

25 "Yes, he does," Peter answered.

After they had returned home, Jesus went up to Peter and asked him, "Simon, what do you think? Do the kings of this earth collect taxes and fees from their own people or from foreigners?"ʼ

26 Peter answered, "From foreigners."

Jesus replied, "Then their own peopleʼ don't have to pay. 27 But we don't want to cause trouble. So go and cast a line into the lake and pull out the first fish you hook. Open its mouth, and you will find a coin. Use it to pay your taxes and mine."

CHAPTER 18

Who is the greatest?

This is also told in Mark 9.33–37; Luke 9.46–48

1 About this time the disciples came to Jesus and asked him who would be the greatest in the kingdom of heaven. 2 Jesus called a child over and made the child stand near him. 3 Then he said:

I promise you this. If you don't change and become like a child, you will never get into the kingdom of heaven. 4 But if you are as humble as this child, you are the greatest in the kingdom of heaven. 5 And when you welcome one of these children because of me, you welcome me.

Temptations to sin

This is also told in Mark 9.42–48; Luke 17.1,2

Jesus continued:

6 It will be terrible for people who cause even one of my little followers to sin. Those people would be better off thrown into the deepest part of the sea with a heavy stone tied around their necks! 7 The world is in for trouble because of the way it causes people to sin. There will always be something to cause people to sin, but anyone who does this will be in for trouble.

8 If your hand or foot causes you to sin, chop it off and throw it away! You would be better off to go into life crippled or lame than to have two hands or two feet and be thrown into the fire that never goes out. 9 If your eye causes you to sin, poke it out and get rid of it. You would be better off to go into life with only one eye than to have two eyes and be thrown into the fires of hell.

See also: 18.1: Luke 22.24. 18.3: Mark 10.15; Luke 18.17. 18.8: Matt 5.30. 18.9: Matt 5.29.

The lost sheep

This is also told in Luke 15.3–7

Jesus continued:

10-11 Don't be cruel to any of these little ones! I promise you that their angels are always with my Father in heaven.ʼ 12 Let me ask you this. What would you do if you had a hundred sheep and one of them wandered off? Wouldn't you leave the ninety-nine on the hillside and go and look for the one that had wandered away? 13 I am sure that finding it would make you happier than having the ninety-nine that never wandered off. 14 That's how it is with your Father in heaven. He doesn't want any of these little ones to be lost.

When someone sins

This is also told in Luke 17.3

Jesus continued:

15 If one of my followers* sins against you, go and point out what was wrong. But do it in private, just between the two of you. If that person listens, you have won back a follower. 16 But if that one refuses to listen, take along one or two others. The Scriptures teach that every complaint must be proved true by two or more witnesses. 17 If the follower refuses to listen to them, report the matter to the church. Anyone who refuses to listen to the church must be treated like an unbeliever or a tax collector.*

Allowing and not allowing

Jesus continued:

18 I promise you that God in heaven will allow whatever you allow on earth, but he will not allow anything you don't allow. 19 I promise that when any two of you on earth agree about something you are praying for, my Father in heaven will do it for you. 20 Whenever two or three of you come together in my name,ʼ I am there with you.

*18.15 followers: The Greek text has "brother", which is used here and elsewhere in this chapter to refer to a follower of Christ.
*18.17 tax collector: See the note at 5.46.

See also: 18.11: Luke 19.10. 18.15: Luke 17.3. 18.16: Deut 19.15. 18.18: Matt 16.19; John 20.23.

An official who refused to forgive

²¹ Peter came up to the Lord and asked, "How many times should I forgive someone* who does something wrong to me? Is seven times enough?"

²² Jesus answered:

Not just seven times, but seventy-seven times!* ²³ This story will show you what the kingdom of heaven is like:

One day a king decided to call in his officials and ask them to give an account of what they owed him. ²⁴ As he was doing this, one official was brought in who owed him fifty million silver coins. ²⁵ But he didn't have any money to pay what he owed. The king ordered him to be sold, along with his wife and children and all he owned, in order to pay the debt.

²⁶ The official got down on his knees and began begging, "Have pity on me, and I will pay you every penny I owe!" ²⁷ The king felt sorry for him and let him go free. He even told the official that he did not have to pay back the money.

²⁸ As the official was leaving, he happened to meet another official, who owed him a hundred silver coins. So he grabbed the man by the throat. He started choking him and said, "Pay me what you owe!"

²⁹ The man got down on his knees and began begging, "Have pity on me, and I will pay you back." ³⁰ But the first official refused to have pity. Instead, he went and had the other official put in jail until he could pay what he owed.

³¹ When some other officials found out what had happened, they felt sorry for the man who had been put in jail. Then they told the king what had happened. ³² The king called the first official back in and said, "You're an evil man! When you begged for mercy, I said you did not have to pay back a penny. ³³ Don't you think you should show pity to someone else, as I did to you?" ³⁴ The king was so angry that he ordered the official to be tortured until he could pay back everything he owed. ³⁵ That is how

my Father in heaven will treat you, if you don't forgive each of my followers with all your heart.

Jesus goes from Galilee to Jerusalem

CHAPTER 19

Teaching about divorce

This is also told in Mark 10.1–12

¹ When Jesus finished teaching, he left Galilee and went to the part of Judea that is east of the River Jordan. ² Large crowds followed him, and he healed their sick people.

³ Some Pharisees wanted to test Jesus. They came up to him and asked, "Is it right for a man to divorce his wife for just any reason?"

⁴ Jesus answered, "Don't you know that in the beginning the Creator made a man and a woman? ⁵ That's why a man leaves his father and mother and gets married. He becomes like one person with his wife. ⁶ Then they are no longer two people, but one. And no one should separate a couple that God has joined together."

⁷ The Pharisees asked Jesus, "Why did Moses say that a man could write out divorce papers and send his wife away?"

⁸ Jesus replied, "You are so heartless! That's why Moses allowed you to divorce your wife. But from the beginning God did not intend it to be that way. ⁹ I say that if your wife has not committed some terrible sexual sin,* you must not divorce her to marry someone else. If you do, you are unfaithful."

¹⁰ The disciples said, "If that's how it is between a man and a woman, it's better not to get married."

¹¹ Jesus told them, "Only those people who have been given the gift of staying single can accept this teaching. ¹² Some people are unable to marry because of birth defects or because of what someone has done to their bodies. Others stay single for the sake of the kingdom of heaven. Anyone who can accept this teaching should do so."

---

*18.21 someone: Or "a follower". See the note at 18.15.

*18.22 seventy-seven times: Or "seventy times seven". The large number means that one follower should never stop forgiving another.

See also: 18.21–22: Luke 17.3,4. 18.22: Gen 4.24.

---

*19.9 some terrible sexual sin: See the note at 5.32.

See also: 19.4: Gen 1.27; 5.2. 19.5: Gen 2.24. 19.7: Deut 24.1–4; Matt 5.31. 19.9: Matt 5.32; 1 Cor 7.10–11.

Jesus blesses little children

This is also told in Mark 10.13–16; Luke 18.15–17

13 Some people brought their children to Jesus, so that he could place his hands on them and pray for them. His disciples told the people to stop bothering him. 14 But Jesus said, "Let the children come to me, and don't try to stop them! People who are like these children belong to God's kingdom."▸ 15 After Jesus had placed his hands on the children, he left.

A rich young man

This is also told in Mark 10.17–31; Luke 18.18–30

16 A man came to Jesus and asked, "Teacher, what good thing must I do to have eternal life?"

17 Jesus said to him, "Why do you ask me about what is good? Only God is good. If you want to have eternal life, you must obey his commandments."

18 "Which ones?" the man asked.

Jesus answered, "Do not murder. Be faithful in marriage. Do not steal. Do not tell lies about others. 19 Respect your father and mother. And love others as much as you love yourself." 20 The young man said, "I have obeyed all these. What else must I do?"

21 Jesus replied, "If you want to be perfect, go and sell everything you own! Give the money to the poor, and you will have riches in heaven. Then come and be my follower." 22 When the young man heard this, he was sad, because he was very rich.

23 Jesus said to his disciples, "It's terribly hard for rich people to get into the kingdom of heaven! 24 In fact, it's easier for a camel to go through the eye of a needle than for a rich person to get into God's kingdom."

25 When the disciples heard this, they were greatly surprised and asked, "How can anyone ever be saved?"

26 Jesus looked straight at them and said, "There are some things that people cannot do, but God can do anything."

27 Peter replied, "Remember, we have left everything to be your followers! What will we get?"

28 Jesus answered:

Yes, all of you have become my followers. And so in the future world, when the Son of Man sits on his glorious throne, I promise

that you will sit on twelve thrones to judge the twelve tribes of Israel. 29 All who have given up home or brothers and sisters or father and mother or children or land for me will be given a hundred times as much. They will also have eternal life. 30 But many who are now first will be last, and many who are last will be first.

CHAPTER 20

Workers in a vineyard

1 As Jesus was telling what the kingdom of heaven would be like, he said:

Early one morning a man went out to hire some workers for his vineyard. 2 After he had agreed to pay them the usual amount for a day's work, he sent them off to his vineyard.

3 About nine that morning, the man saw some other people standing in the market with nothing to do. 4 He said he would pay them what was fair, if they would work in his vineyard. 5 So they went.

At midday and again about three in the afternoon he returned to the market. And each time he made the same agreement with others who were lazing around with nothing to do.

6 Finally, about five in the afternoon the man went back and found some others standing there. He asked them, "Why have you been standing here all day long doing nothing?"

7 "Because no one has hired us," they answered. Then he told them to go and work in his vineyard.

8 That evening the owner of the vineyard told the man in charge of the workers to call them in and give them their money. He also told the man to begin with the ones who were hired last. 9 When the workers arrived, the ones who had been hired at five in the afternoon were given a full day's pay.

10 The workers who had been hired first thought they would be given more than the others. But when they were given the same, 11 they began complaining to the owner of the vineyard. 12 They said, "The ones who were hired last worked for only one hour. But you paid them the same that you did us. And we worked in the hot sun all day long!"

13 The owner answered one of them, "Friend, I didn't cheat you. I paid you

See also: **19.18: a** Exod 20.13; Deut 5.17; **b** Exod 20.14; Deut 5.18; **c** Exod 20.15; Deut 5.19. **d** Exod 20.16; Deut 5.20. **19.19: a** Exod 20.12; Deut 5.16; **b** Lev 19.18. **19.28: a** Matt 25.31; **b** Luke 22.30.

See also: **19.30:** Matt 20.16; Luke 13.30. **20.8:** Lev 19.13; Deut 24.15.

exactly what we agreed on. ¹⁴ Take your money now and go! What business is it of yours if I want to pay them the same that I paid you? ¹⁵ Don't I have the right to do what I want with my own money? Why should you be jealous, if I want to be generous?"

¹⁶ Jesus then said, "So it is. Everyone who is now first will be last, and everyone who is last will be first."

Jesus again tells about his death

This is also told in Mark 10.32–34; Luke 18.31–34

¹⁷ As Jesus was on his way to Jerusalem, he took his twelve disciples aside and told them in private:

¹⁸ We are now on our way to Jerusalem, where the Son of Man will be handed over to the chief priests and the teachers of the Law of Moses. They will sentence him to death, ¹⁹ and then they will hand him over to foreigners* who will make fun of him. They will beat him and nail him to a cross. But on the third day he will rise from death.

A mother's request

This is also told in Mark 10.35–45

²⁰ The mother of James and John' came to Jesus with her two sons. She knelt down and started begging him to do something for her. ²¹ Jesus asked her what she wanted, and she said, "When you come into your kingdom, please let one of my sons sit at your right side and the other at your left."*

²² Jesus answered, "Not one of you knows what you are asking. Are you able to drink from the cup* that I must soon drink from?"

James and John said, "Yes, we are!"

²³ Jesus replied, "You certainly will drink from my cup! But it isn't for me to say who will sit at my right side and at my left. That is for my Father to say."

²⁴ When the ten other disciples heard this, they were angry with the two brothers. ²⁵ But Jesus called the disciples together and said:

You know that foreign rulers like to order their people around. And their great leaders have full power over everyone they rule. ²⁶ But don't act like them. If you want to be great, you must be the servant of all the others. ²⁷ And if you want to be first, you must be the slave of the rest. ²⁸ The Son of Man did not come to be a slave master, but a slave who will give his life to rescue* many people.

Jesus heals two blind men

This is also told in Mark 10.46–52; Luke 18.35–43

²⁹ Jesus was followed by a large crowd as he and his disciples were leaving Jericho. ³⁰ Two blind men were sitting beside the road. And when they heard that Jesus was coming their way, they shouted, "Lord and Son of David,* have pity on us!"

³¹ The crowd told them to be quiet, but they shouted even louder, "Lord and Son of David, have pity on us!"

³² When Jesus heard them, he stopped and asked, "What do you want me to do for you?"

³³ They answered, "Lord, we want to see!"

³⁴ Jesus felt sorry for them and touched their eyes. Straight away they could see, and they became his followers.

Jesus' last week: his trial and death

CHAPTER 21

Jesus enters Jerusalem

This is also told in Mark 11.1–11; Luke 19.28–38; John 12.12–19

¹ When Jesus and his disciples came near Jerusalem, he went to Bethphage on the Mount of Olives and sent two of them on ahead. ² He told them, "Go into the next village, where you will at once find a donkey and her colt. Untie the two donkeys and bring them to me. ³ If anyone asks why you are doing that, just say, 'The Lord' needs them.' Straight away he will let you have the donkeys."

---

*20.19 foreigners: The Romans, who ruled Judea at this time.

*20.21 right side . . . left: The most powerful people in a kingdom sat at the right and left side of the king.

*20.22 drink from the cup: In the Scriptures a cup is sometimes used as a symbol of suffering. To "drink from the cup" is to suffer.

See also: 20.16: Matt 19.30; Mark 10.31; Luke 13.30. 20.25–26: Luke 22.25–26.

*20.28 rescue: The Greek word often, though not always, means the payment of a price to free a slave or a prisoner.

*20.30 Son of David: See the note at 9.27.

See also: 20.26–27: Matt 23.11; Mark 9.35; Luke 22.26.

⁴ So God's promise came true, just as the prophet had said,

⁵ "Announce to the people
of Jerusalem:
'Your king is coming to you!
He is humble
and rides on a donkey.
He comes on the colt
of a donkey.' "

⁶ The disciples left and did what Jesus had told them to do. ⁷ They brought the donkey and its colt and laid some clothes on their backs. Then Jesus got on.
⁸ Many people spread clothes in the road, while others put down branches* which they had cut from trees. ⁹ Some people walked ahead of Jesus and others followed behind. They were all shouting,

"Hooray* for the Son of David!*
God bless the one who comes
in the name of the Lord.
Hooray for God
in heaven above!"

¹⁰ When Jesus came to Jerusalem, everyone in the city was excited and asked, "Who can this be?"
¹¹ The crowd answered, "This is Jesus, the prophet from Nazareth in Galilee."

Jesus in the temple

This is also told in Mark 11.15–19; Luke 19.45–48; John 2.13–22

¹² Jesus went into the temple and chased out everyone who was selling or buying. He turned over the tables of the moneychangers and the benches of the ones who were selling doves. ¹³ He told them, "The Scriptures say, 'My house should be called a place of worship.' But you have turned it into a place where robbers hide."
¹⁴ Blind and lame people came to Jesus in the temple, and he healed them. ¹⁵ But the chief priests and the teachers of the Law of Moses were angry when they saw his miracles and heard the children

shouting praises to the Son of David.* ¹⁶ The men said to Jesus, "Don't you hear what those children are saying?"
"Yes, I do!" Jesus answered. "Don't you know that the Scriptures say, 'Children and infants will sing praises'?" ¹⁷ Then Jesus left the city and went out to the village of Bethany, where he spent the night.

Jesus puts a curse on a fig tree

This is also told in Mark 11.12–14,20–24

¹⁸ When Jesus got up the next morning, he was hungry. He started out for the city, ¹⁹ and along the way he saw a fig tree. But when he came to it, he found only leaves and no figs. So he told the tree, "You will never again grow any fruit!" At once the fig tree dried up.
²⁰ The disciples were shocked when they saw how quickly the tree had dried up. ²¹ But Jesus said to them, "If you have faith and don't doubt, I promise that you can do what I did to this tree. And you will be able to do even more. You can tell this mountain to get up and jump into the sea, and it will. ²² If you have faith when you pray, you will be given whatever you ask for."

A question about Jesus' authority

This is also told in Mark 11.27–33; Luke 20.1–8

²³ Jesus had gone into the temple and was teaching when the chief priests and the leaders of the people came up to him. They asked, "What right do you have to do these things? Who gave you this authority?"
²⁴ Jesus answered, "I have just one question to ask you. If you answer it, I will tell you where I got the right to do these things. ²⁵ Who gave John the right to baptize? Was it God in heaven or merely some human being?"
They thought it over and said to each other, "We can't say that God gave John this right. Jesus will ask us why we didn't believe John. ²⁶ On the other hand, these people think that John was a prophet, and we are afraid of what they might do to us. That's why we can't say that it was merely some human who gave John the right to baptize." ²⁷ So they told Jesus, "We don't know."
Jesus said, "Then I won't tell you who gave me the right to do what I do."

*21.8 spread clothes . . . put down branches: This was one way that the Jewish people welcomed a famous person.
*21.9 Hooray: This translates a word that can mean "please save us". But it is most often used as a shout of praise to God.
*21.9 Son of David: See the note at 9.27.
See also: 21.5: Zech 9.9. 21.9: Psa 118.25–26. 21.13: Isa 56.7; Jer 7.11.

*21.15 Son of David: See the note at 9.27.
See also: 21.16: Psa 8.2 (LXX). 21.21: Matt 17.20; 1 Cor 13.2.

A story about two sons

28 Jesus said:

I will tell you a story about a man who had two sons. Then you can tell me what you think. The father went to the elder son and said, "Go and work in the vineyard today!" 29 His son told him that he would not do it, but later he changed his mind and went. 30 The man then told his younger son to go and work in the vineyard. The boy said he would, but he didn't go. 31 Which one of the sons obeyed his father?

"The elder one," the chief priests and leaders answered.

Then Jesus told them:

You can be sure that tax collectors* and prostitutes will get into the kingdom of God before you ever will! 32 When John the Baptist showed you how to do right, you would not believe him. But these evil people did believe. And even when you saw what they did, you still would not change your minds and believe.

Tenants of a vineyard

This is also told in Mark 12.1–12; Luke 20.9–19

33 Jesus told the chief priests and leaders to listen to this story:

A land owner once planted a vineyard. He built a wall around it and dug a pit to crush the grapes in. He also built a lookout tower. Then he let his vineyard and left the country. 34 When it was harvest time, the owner sent some servants to get his share of the grapes. 35 But the tenants grabbed those servants. They beat up one, killed one, and stoned one of them to death. 36 He then sent more servants than he did the first time. But the tenants treated them in the same way.

37 Finally, the owner sent his own son to the tenants, because he thought they would respect him. 38 But when they saw the man's son, they said, "Some day he will own the vineyard. Let's kill him! Then we can have it all for ourselves." 39 So they grabbed him, threw him out of the vineyard, and killed him.

40 Jesus asked, "When the owner of that vineyard comes, what do you suppose he will do to those tenants?"

41 The chief priests and leaders answered, "He will kill them in some horrible way. Then he will let his vineyard to people who will give him his share of grapes at harvest time."

42 Jesus replied, "Surely you know that the Scriptures say,

'The stone that the builders
    tossed aside
is now the most important
    stone of all.
This is something
the Lord has done,
    and it is amazing to us.'

43 I tell you that God's kingdom will be taken from you and given to people who will do what he demands. 44 Anyone who stumbles over this stone will be crushed, and anyone it falls on will be smashed to pieces.'"

45 When the chief priests and the Pharisees heard these stories, they knew that Jesus was talking about them. 46 So they looked for a way to arrest Jesus. But they were afraid to, because the people thought he was a prophet.

CHAPTER 22

The great banquet

This is also told in Luke 14.15–24

1 Once again Jesus used stories to teach the people:

2 The kingdom of heaven is like what happened when a king gave a wedding banquet for his son. 3 The king sent some servants to tell the invited guests to come to the banquet, but the guests refused. 4 He sent other servants to say to the guests, "The banquet is ready! My cattle and prize calves have all been prepared. Everything is ready. Come to the banquet!"

5 But the guests did not pay any attention. Some of them left for their farms, and some went to their places of business. 6 Others grabbed the servants, then beat them up and killed them.

7 This made the king so furious that he sent an army to kill those murderers and burn down their city. 8 Then he said to the servants, "It is time for the wedding banquet, and the invited guests don't deserve to come. 9 Go out to the street corners and tell everyone you meet to come to the banquet." 10 They went out into the streets and brought in everyone they could find, good and bad

---

*21.31 tax collectors: See the note at 5.46.
See also: 21.32: Luke 3.12; 7.29–30. **21.33:** Isa 5.1–2.

See also: 21.42: Psa 118.22–23.

alike. And the banquet room was filled with guests.

¹¹ When the king went in to meet the guests, he found that one of them wasn't wearing the right kind of clothes for the wedding. ¹² The king asked, "Friend, why didn't you wear proper clothes for the wedding?" But the guest had no excuse. ¹³ So the king gave orders for that person to be tied hand and foot and to be thrown outside into the dark. That's where people will cry and grit their teeth in pain. ¹⁴ Many are invited, but only a few are chosen.

Paying taxes

This is also told in Mark 12.13–17; Luke 20.20–26

¹⁵ The Pharisees got together and planned how they could trick Jesus into saying something wrong. ¹⁶ They sent some of their followers and some of Herod's followers* to say to him, "Teacher, we know that you are honest. You teach the truth about what God wants people to do. And you treat everyone with the same respect, no matter who they are. ¹⁷ Tell us what you think! Should we pay taxes to the Emperor or not?"

¹⁸ Jesus knew their evil thoughts and said, "Why are you trying to test me? You show-offs! ¹⁹ Let me see one of the coins used for paying taxes." They brought him a silver coin, ²⁰ and he asked, "Whose picture and name are on it?"

²¹ "The Emperor's," they answered.

Then Jesus told them, "Give the Emperor what belongs to him and give God what belongs to God." ²² His answer surprised them so much that they walked away.

Life in the future world

This is also told in Mark 12.18–27; Luke 20.27–40

²³ The Sadducees did not believe that people would rise to life after death. So that same day some of the Sadducees came to Jesus and said:

²⁴ Teacher, Moses wrote that if a married man dies and has no children, his brother should marry the widow. Their first son would then be thought of as the son of the dead brother.

²⁵ Once there were seven brothers who lived here. The first one married, but

died without having any children. So his wife was left to his brother. ²⁶ The same thing happened to the second and third brothers and finally to all seven of them. ²⁷ At last the woman died. ²⁸ When God raises people from death, whose wife will this woman be? She had been married to all seven brothers.

²⁹ Jesus answered:

You are completely wrong! You don't know what the Scriptures teach. And you don't know anything about the power of God. ³⁰ When God raises people to life, they won't marry. They will be like the angels in heaven. ³¹ And as for people being raised to life, God was speaking to you when he said, ³² "I am the God worshipped by Abraham, Isaac, and Jacob."* He isn't the God of the dead, but of the living.

³³ The crowds were surprised to hear what Jesus was teaching.

The most important commandment

This is also told in Mark 12.28–34; Luke 10.25–28

³⁴ After Jesus had made the Sadducees look foolish, the Pharisees heard about it and got together. ³⁵ One of them was an expert in the Jewish Law. So he tried to test Jesus by asking, ³⁶ "Teacher, what is the most important commandment in the Law?"

³⁷ Jesus answered:

Love the Lord your God with all your heart, soul, and mind. ³⁸ This is the first and most important commandment. ³⁹ The second most important commandment is like this one. And it is, "Love others as much as you love yourself." ⁴⁰ All the Law of Moses and the Books of the Prophets* are based on these two commandments.

About David's son

This is also told in Mark 12.35–37; Luke 20.41–44

⁴¹ While the Pharisees were still there, Jesus asked them, ⁴² "What do you think about the Messiah? Whose family will he come from?"

---

*22.16 Herod's followers: People who were political followers of the family of Herod the Great (see 2.1) and his son Herod Antipas (see 14.1), and who wanted Herod to be king in Jerusalem.

See also: 22.13: Matt 8.12; 25.30; Luke 13.28. 22.23: Acts 23.8. 22.24: Deut 25.5.

*22.32 I am the God worshipped by Abraham, Isaac, and Jacob: Jesus argues that if God is worshipped by these three, they must still be alive, because he is the God of the living.
*22.40 the Law of Moses and the Books of the Prophets: See the note at 5.17.

See also: 22.32: Exod 3.6. 22.35–40: Luke 10.25–28. 22.37: Deut 6.5. 22.39: Lev 19.18.

They answered, "He will be a son of King David."*

⁴³ Jesus replied, "How then could the Spirit lead David to call the Messiah his Lord? David said,

⁴⁴ 'The Lord said to my Lord:
    Sit at my right side*
    until I make your enemies
    into a footstool for you.'

⁴⁵ If David called the Messiah his Lord, how can the Messiah be a son of King David?" ⁴⁶ No one was able to give Jesus an answer, and from that day on, no one dared ask him any more questions.

CHAPTER 23

Jesus condemns the Pharisees and the teachers of the Law of Moses

This is also told in Mark 12.38–40;
Luke 11.37–52; 20.45–47

¹ Jesus said to the crowds and to his disciples:

² The Pharisees and the teachers of the Law are experts in the Law of Moses. ³ So obey everything they teach you, but don't do as they do. After all, they say one thing and do something else.
    ⁴ They pile heavy burdens on people's shoulders and won't lift a finger to help. ⁵ Everything they do is just to show off in front of others. They even make a big show of wearing Scripture verses on their foreheads and arms, and they wear big tassels* for everyone to see. ⁶ They love the best seats at banquets and the front seats in the meeting places. ⁷ And when they are in the market, they like to have people greet them as their teachers.
    ⁸ But none of you should be called a teacher. You have only one teacher, and all of you are like brothers and sisters. ⁹ Don't call anyone on earth your father. All of you have the same Father in heaven. ¹⁰ None of

---

22.42 son of King David: See the note at 9.27.
22.44 right side: The place of power and honour.
23.5 wearing Scripture verses on their foreheads and arms . . . tassels: As a sign of their love for the Lord and his teachings, the Jewish people had started wearing Scripture verses in small leather boxes. But the Pharisees tried to show off by making the boxes bigger than necessary. The Jewish people were also taught to wear tassels on the four corners of their robes to show their love for God.

See also: 22.44: Psa 110.1.   23.5: a Matt 6.1; b Deut 6.8; c Num 15.38.

Being christian

Living truthfully

Matthew 23.1–22

Christians follow the true God. We believe that Jesus was the truth. Truth is the currency we deal in.

It follows that our lives should be truthful. Jesus reserved some of his strongest criticism for those who pretend to be something they're not. Especially people like the Pharisees, who were proud and made a big show of their religion, who said one thing and did another.

So none of that. No pretending to be the Holiest Person in Town. Our lives have to reflect the truth of what we believe. Few things do more damage to Christianity than people whose lives do not match up to their words. No living a lie.

And no speaking lies either. Watch your words. Jesus told us to keep our language simple and truthful (Matthew 5.37) and James warns us against lying – either as boasting or as a cover up. Don't be afraid to be honest. We're always tempted to try to make an impression. We don't exactly lie about things, but we don't mind if we give an impression that's not quite the truth.

Forget it. You're a child of God. You don't have to impress anyone. You just have to be yourself. God knows you better than anyone. He knows who you are; and he loves you.

Being Christian: Living truthfully

• Try not to lie to people.
• Walk the talk: let your actions match your words.
• Don't worry about what others think of you. Be truthful.

you should be called the leader. The Messiah is your only leader. 11 Whoever is the greatest should be the servant of the others. 12 If you put yourself above others, you will be put down. But if you humble yourself, you will be honoured.

13-14 You Pharisees and teachers of the Law of Moses are in for trouble! You're nothing but show-offs. You lock people out of the kingdom of heaven. You won't go in yourselves, and you keep others from going in.∗

15 You Pharisees and teachers of the Law of Moses are in for trouble! You're nothing but show-offs. You travel over land and sea to win one follower. And when you have done so, you make that person twice as fit for hell as you are.

16 You are in for trouble! You are supposed to lead others, but you are blind. You teach that it doesn't matter if a person swears by the temple. But you say that it does matter if someone swears by the gold in the temple. 17 You blind fools! Which is greater, the gold or the temple that makes the gold sacred?

18 You also teach that it doesn't matter if a person swears by the altar. But you say that it does matter if someone swears by the gift on the altar. 19 Are you blind? Which is more important, the gift or the altar that makes the gift sacred? 20 Anyone who swears by the altar also swears by everything on it. 21 And anyone who swears by the temple also swears by God, who lives there. 22 To swear by heaven is the same as swearing by God's throne and by the one who sits on that throne.

Jesus continued:

23 You Pharisees and teachers are show-offs, and you're in for trouble! You give God a tenth of the spices from your garden, such as mint, dill, and cumin. Yet you neglect the more important matters of the Law, such as justice, mercy, and faithfulness. These are the important things you should have done, though you should not have left the others undone either. 24 You blind leaders! You strain out a small fly but swallow a camel.

25 You Pharisees and teachers are show-offs, and you're in for trouble! You wash the outside of your cups and dishes,

while inside there is nothing but greed and selfishness. 26 You blind Pharisee! First clean the inside of a cup, and then the outside will also be clean.

27 You Pharisees and teachers are in for trouble! You're nothing but show-offs. You're like tombs that have been whitewashed.∗ On the outside they are beautiful, but inside they are full of bones and filth. 28 That's what you are like. Outside you look good, but inside you are evil and only pretend to be good.

29 You Pharisees and teachers are nothing but show-offs, and you're in for trouble! You build monuments for the prophets and decorate the tombs of good people. 30 And you claim that you would not have taken part with your ancestors in killing the prophets. 31 But you prove that you really are the relatives of the ones who killed the prophets. 32 So keep on doing everything they did. 33 You are nothing but snakes and the children of snakes! How can you escape going to hell?

34 I will send prophets and wise people and experts in the Law of Moses to you. But you will kill them or nail them to a cross or beat them in your meeting places or chase them from town to town. 35 That's why you will be held guilty for the murder of every good person, beginning with the good man Abel. This also includes Barachiah's son Zechariah,∗ the man you murdered between the temple and the altar. 36 I can promise that you people living today will be punished for all these things!

Jesus loves Jerusalem

This is also told in Luke 13.34-35

Jesus continued:

37 Jerusalem, Jerusalem! Your people have killed the prophets and have stoned the messengers who were sent to you. I have often wanted to gather your people, as a

---

*23.27 **whitewashed:** Tombs were whitewashed to keep anyone from accidentally touching them. A person who touched a dead body or a tomb was considered unclean and could not worship with the rest of the Jewish people.

*23.35 **Zechariah:** Genesis is the first book in the Jewish Scriptures, and it tells that Abel was the first person to be murdered. The Second Book of Chronicles is the last book in the Jewish Scriptures, and the last murder that it tells about is that of Zechariah.

See also: 23.27: Acts 23.3. 23.33: Matt 3.7; 12.34; Luke 3.7. 23.35: a Gen 4.8; b 2 Chron 24.20-21.

See also: 23.11: Matt 20.26-27; Mark 9.35; 10.43-44; Luke 22.26. 23.12: Luke 14.11; 18.14. 23.22: Isa 66.1; Matt 5.34. 23.23: Lev 27.30.

Holy history

Clothes

In Bible times clothes were valuable. Cloth took time to weave and sewing was laborious hard work. So people tended to keep their clothes simple.

In the Old Testament, they kept things very simple indeed. People generally wore a loin cloth, and then a simple tunic, tied at the waist with a belt. Everyone wore open leather sandals on their feet. And whereas today, clothes are often designed to reveal the shape of the body, or to accentuate a person's appearance or sexuality, things were totally different in Bible times. Women generally wore veils over their faces and covered their hair. Only prostitutes wore revealing garments.

Joseph's 'coat of many colours' attracted his brother's envy because it was a highly valuable gift, not only because it was brightly coloured. Sometimes these fine displays of clothing attract criticism. Isaiah criticises the finery of the women of his time, contrasting that with the poverty of people around them (Isaiah 3.18–23). Ezekiel likens Israel to a beautifully, and expensively dressed young woman, who then, unfortunately, behaved like a hooker (Ezekiel 16.10–14).

In New Testament times, both men and women wore a tight fitting, ankle-length, close-fitting tunic. This was tied at the waist with a belt. The belt would also have a purse or bag hanging to it for money. Over this, they wore a cloak. The Jewish cloak had tassels attached to the four corners.

The Pharisees wore impressive white linen tunics with dyed blue edges. You see, they really did look like whitewashed tombs (Matthew 23.27).

More...

Pharisees, Sadducees and the rest p.1097
Materialism p.1141

hen gathers her chicks under her wings. But you wouldn't let me. ³⁸ And now your temple will be deserted. ³⁹ You won't see me again until you say,

> "Blessed is the one who comes
> in the name of the Lord."

CHAPTER 24

The temple will be destroyed

This is also told in Mark 13.1–2; Luke 21.5–6

¹ After Jesus left the temple, his disciples came over and said, "Look at all these buildings!"

² Jesus replied, "Do you see these buildings? They will certainly be torn down! Not one stone will be left in place."

Warning about trouble

This is also told in Mark 13.3–13; Luke 21.7–19

³ Later, as Jesus was sitting on the Mount of Olives, his disciples came to him in private and asked, "When will this happen? What will be the sign of your coming and of the end of the world?"

⁴ Jesus answered:

Don't let anyone fool you. ⁵ Many will come and claim to be me. They will say that they are the Messiah, and they will fool many people.

⁶ You will soon hear about wars and threats of wars, but don't be afraid. These things will have to happen first, but that isn't the end. ⁷ Nations and kingdoms will go to war against each other. People will starve to death, and in some places there will be earthquakes. ⁸ But this is just the beginning of troubles.

⁹ You will be arrested, punished, and even killed. Because of me, you will be hated by people of all nations. ¹⁰ Many will give up and will betray and hate each other. ¹¹ Many false prophets will come and fool a lot of people. ¹² Evil will spread and cause many people to stop loving others. ¹³ But if you keep on being faithful right to the end, you will be saved. ¹⁴ When the good news about the kingdom has been preached all over the world and told to all nations, the end will come.

See also: **23.38:** Jer 22.5. **23.39:** Psa 118.26.
24.9: Matt 10.22. **24.13:** Matt 10.22.

Big ideas

End times

In his teaching, Jesus talks about the end times – the time when he will return and the world will end. Interpreting these passages is always very difficult and we should be wary of taking them too literally. Often the writers and speakers were using picture language, but we can unpack some of the features.

Jesus talks about the destruction of the temple, a prediction of the events of AD70, when the Romans destroyed the temple in Jerusalem. He links it to other events, such as wars, rumours of wars, earthquakes and darkness. He talks about false messiahs and false prophets, people who appear to miraculous powers but who are really fakes. We should wait for the real thing.

And the real thing will be obvious. Christ is pictured returning in a cloud of glory. All earth will see him return in triumph.

But we don't know when. Even though we might see some of the signs, the exact moment is hidden from us. Even Jesus doesn't know the exact timing (Matthew 24.36). So we should beware anyone who thinks they can predict exactly when the even will occur. Jesus has a job to do on his return. He will judge all people, and his judgement will be final. People will not be judged on how often they went to church or how clever their philosophy is, but on how their faith affected their lives. Did they really believe it and live it out? Or did they merely go through the motions?

Anorak corner

These are what are called 'apocalyptic' statements. Other apocalyptic writings in the Bible include Daniel and Revelation.

More...

Jesus' teaching p.1055
New heaven & new earth p.1427
Messiah p.770

The Horrible Thing

This is also told in Mark 13.14–23; Luke 21.20–24

Jesus continued:

15 Some day you will see that "Horrible Thing" in the holy place, just as the prophet Daniel said. Everyone who reads this must try to understand! 16 If you are living in Judea at that time, run to the mountains. 17 If you are on the roof* of your house, don't go inside to get anything. 18 If you are out in the field, don't go back for your coat. 19 It will be a terrible time for women who are expecting babies or nursing young children. 20 And pray that you won't have to escape in winter or on a Sabbath.* 21 This will be the worst time of suffering since the beginning of the world, and nothing this terrible will ever happen again. 22 If God doesn't make the time shorter, no one will be left alive. But because of God's chosen ones, he will make the time shorter.

23 Someone may say, "Here is the Messiah!" or "There he is!" But don't believe it. 24 False messiahs and false prophets will come and perform great miracles and signs. They will even try to fool God's chosen ones. 25 But I have warned you beforehand. 26 If you are told that the Messiah is out in the desert, don't go there! And if you are told that he is in some secret place, don't believe it! 27 The coming of the Son of Man will be like lightning that can be seen from east to west. 28 Where there is a corpse, there will always be vultures.*

---

*24.17 roof: In Palestine the houses usually had a flat roof. Stairs on the outside led up to the roof, which was made of beams and boards covered with packed earth.
*24.20 in winter or on a Sabbath: In Palestine the winters are cold and rainy and make travel difficult. The Jewish people were not allowed to travel much more than a kilometre on the Sabbath. For these reasons it was hard for them to escape from their enemies in the winter or on a Sabbath.
*24.28 Where there is a corpse, there will always be vultures: This saying may mean that when anything important happens, people soon know about it. Or the saying may mean that whenever something bad happens, curious people gather around and stare. But the word translated "vulture" also means "eagle" and may refer to the Roman army, which had an eagle as its symbol.

See also: 24.15: Dan 9.27; 11.31; 12.11.
24.17–18: Luke 17.31. 24.21: Dan 12.1; Rev 7.14.
24.26–27: Luke 17.23–24. 24.28: Luke 17.37.

When the Son of Man appears
This is also told in Mark 13.24–27; Luke 21.25–28

Jesus continued:

²⁹ Straight after those days of suffering,

"The sun will become dark,
and the moon
    will no longer shine.
The stars will fall,
and the powers in the sky*
    will be shaken."

³⁰ Then a sign will appear in the sky. And there will be the Son of Man.ᵇ All nations on earth will weep when they see the Son of Man coming on the clouds of heaven with power and great glory. ³¹ At the sound of a loud trumpet, he will send his angels to bring his chosen ones together from all over the earth.

A lesson from a fig tree
This is also told in Mark 13.28–31; Luke 21.29–33

Jesus continued:

³² Learn a lesson from a fig tree. When its branches sprout and start putting out leaves, you know that summer is near. ³³ So when you see all these things happening, you will know that the time has almost come.ᵇ ³⁴ I can promise you that some of the people of this generation will still be alive when all this happens. ³⁵ The sky and the earth won't last for ever, but my words will.

No one knows the day or time
This is also told in Mark 13.32–37; Luke 17.26–30,34–36

Jesus continued:

³⁶ No one knows the day or hour. The angels in heaven don't know, and the Son himself doesn't know.ᵇ Only the Father knows. ³⁷ When the Son of Man appears, things will be just as they were when Noah lived. ³⁸ People were eating, drinking, and getting married right up to the day that the flood came and Noah went into the big boat. ³⁹ They didn't know anything was happening until the flood came and swept

them all away. That is how it will be when the Son of Man appears. ⁴⁰ Two men will be in the same field, but only one will be taken. The other will be left. ⁴¹ Two women will be together grinding grain, but only one will be taken. The other will be left. ⁴² So be on your guard! You don't know when your Lord will come. ⁴³ Homeowners never know when a thief is coming, and they are always on guard to keep one from breaking in. ⁴⁴ Always be ready! You don't know when the Son of Man will come.

Faithful and unfaithful servants
This is also told in Luke 12.35–48

Jesus continued:

⁴⁵ Who are faithful and wise servants? Who are the ones the master will put in charge of giving the other servants their food supplies at the proper time? ⁴⁶ Servants are fortunate if their master comes and finds them doing their job. ⁴⁷ You may be sure that a servant who is always faithful will be put in charge of everything the master owns. ⁴⁸ But suppose one of the servants thinks that the master won't return until late. ⁴⁹ Suppose that evil servant starts beating the other servants and eats and drinks with people who are drunk. ⁵⁰ If that happens, the master will come on a day and at a time when the servant least expects him. ⁵¹ That servant will then be punished and thrown out with the ones who only pretended to serve their master. There they will cry and grit their teeth in pain.

CHAPTER 25

A story about ten girls
Jesus said:

¹ The kingdom of heaven is like what happened one night when ten girls took their oil lamps and went to a wedding to meet the groom.* ² Five of the girls were foolish and five were wise. ³ The foolish ones took their lamps, but no extra oil.

---

*24.29 the powers in the sky:** In ancient times people thought that the stars were spiritual powers.
See also: 24.29: a Isa 13.10; Joel 2.10,31; 3.15; Rev 6.12; **b** Isa 13.10; Ezek 32.7; Joel 2.10; 3.15; **c** Isa 34.4; Rev 6.13. **24.30:** Dan 7.13; Zech 12.10–14; Rev 1.7. **24.37:** Gen 6.5–8. **24.39:** Gen 7.6–24.

*25.1 to meet the groom:** Some manuscripts add "and the bride". It was the custom for the groom to go to the home of the bride's parents to get his bride. Young girls and other guests would then go with them to the home of the groom's parents, where the wedding feast would take place.
See also: 24.43–44: Luke 12.39–40. **25.1:** Luke 12.35.

4 The ones who were wise took along extra oil for their lamps.

5 The groom was late arriving, and the girls became drowsy and fell asleep. 6 Then in the middle of the night someone shouted, "Here's the groom! Come to meet him!"

7 When the girls got up and started getting their lamps ready, 8 the foolish ones said to the others, "Let us have some of your oil! Our lamps are going out."

9 The girls who were wise answered, "There's not enough oil for all of us! Go and buy some for yourselves."

10 While the foolish girls were on their way to get some oil, the groom arrived. The girls who were ready went into the wedding, and the doors were closed. 11 Later the other girls returned and shouted, "Sir, sir! Open the door for us!"

12 But the groom replied, "I don't even know you!"

13 So, my disciples, always be ready! You don't know the day or the time when all this will happen.

A story about three servants

This is also told in Luke 19.11–27

Jesus continued:

14 The kingdom is also like what happened when a man went away and put his three servants in charge of all he owned. 15 The man knew what each servant could do. So he handed five thousand coins to the first servant, two thousand to the second, and one thousand to the third. Then he left the country.

16 As soon as the man had gone, the servant with the five thousand coins used them to earn five thousand more. 17 The servant who had two thousand coins did the same with his money and earned two thousand more. 18 But the servant with one thousand coins dug a hole and hid his master's money in the ground.

19 Some time later the master of those servants returned. He called them in and asked what they had done with his money. 20 The servant who had been given five thousand coins brought them in with the five thousand that he had earned. He said, "Sir, you gave me five thousand coins, and I have earned five thousand more."

21 "Wonderful!" his master replied. "You are a good and faithful servant. I left you in charge of only a little, but now I will put you in charge of much more. Come and share in my happiness!"

22 Next, the servant who had been given two thousand coins came in and said, "Sir, you gave me two thousand coins, and I have earned two thousand more."

23 "Wonderful!" his master replied. "You are a good and faithful servant. I left you in charge of only a little, but now I will put you in charge of much more. Come and share in my happiness!"

24 The servant who had been given one thousand coins then came in and said, "Sir, I know that you are hard to get along with. You harvest what you don't plant and gather crops where you haven't scattered seed. 25 I was frightened and went out and hid your money in the ground. Here is every single coin!"

26 The master of the servant told him, "You are lazy and good-for-nothing! You know that I harvest what I don't plant and gather crops where I haven't scattered seed. 27 You could have at least put my money in the bank, so that I could have earned interest on it."

28 Then the master said, "Now your money will be taken away and given to the servant with ten thousand coins! 29 Everyone who has something will be given more, and they will have more than enough. But everything will be taken from those who don't have anything. 30 You are a worthless servant, and you will be thrown out into the dark where people will cry and grit their teeth in pain."

The final judgment

Jesus continued:

31 When the Son of Man comes in his glory with all his angels, he will sit on his royal throne. 32 The people of all nations will be brought before him, and he will separate them, as shepherds separate their sheep from their goats.

33 He will place the sheep on his right and the goats on his left. 34 Then the king will say to those on his right, "My father has blessed you! Come and receive the kingdom that was prepared for you before the world was created. 35 When I was hungry, you gave me something to eat,

and when I was thirsty, you gave me something to drink. When I was a stranger, you welcomed me, [36] and when I was naked, you gave me clothes to wear. When I was sick, you took care of me, and when I was in jail, you visited me."

[37] Then the ones who pleased the Lord will ask, "When did we give you something to eat or drink? [38] When did we welcome you as a stranger or give you clothes to wear [39] or visit you while you were sick or in jail?"

[40] The king will answer, "Whenever you did it for any of my people, no matter how unimportant they seemed, you did it for me."

[41] Then the king will say to those on his left, "Get away from me! You are under God's curse. Go into the everlasting fire prepared for the devil and his angels! [42] I was hungry, but you did not give me anything to eat, and I was thirsty, but you did not give me anything to drink. [43] I was a stranger, but you did not welcome me, and I was naked, but you did not give me any clothes to wear. I was sick and in jail, but you did not take care of me."

[44] Then the people will ask, "Lord, when did we fail to help you when you were hungry or thirsty or a stranger or naked or sick or in jail?"

[45] The king will say to them, "Whenever you failed to help any of my people, no matter how unimportant they seemed, you failed to do it for me."

[46] Then Jesus said, "Those people will be punished for ever. But the ones who pleased God will have eternal life."

CHAPTER 26

The plot to kill Jesus

This is also told in Mark 14.1–2; Luke 22.1–2; John 11.45–53

[1] When Jesus had finished teaching, he told his disciples, [2] "You know that two days from now will be Passover. That is when the Son of Man will be handed over to his enemies and nailed to a cross."

[3] At that time the chief priests and the nation's leaders were meeting at the home of Caiaphas the high priest. [4] They secretly planned to have Jesus arrested and put to death. [5] But they said, "We must not do it during Passover, because the people will riot."

At Bethany

This is also told in Mark 14.3–9; John 12.1–8

[6] Jesus was in the town of Bethany, eating at the home of Simon, who had leprosy.* [7] A woman came in with a bottle of expensive perfume and poured it on Jesus' head. [8] But when his disciples saw this, they became angry and complained, "Why such a waste? [9] We could have sold this perfume for a lot of money and given it to the poor."

[10] Jesus knew what they were thinking, and he said:

Why are you bothering this woman? She has done a beautiful thing for me. [11] You will always have the poor with you, but you won't always have me. [12] She has poured perfume on my body to prepare it for burial.* [13] You may be sure that wherever the good news is told all over the world, people will remember what she has done. And they will tell others.

Judas and the chief priests

This is also told in Mark 14.10–11; Luke 22.3–6

[14] Judas Iscariot* was one of the twelve disciples. He went to the chief priests [15] and asked, "How much will you give me if I help you arrest Jesus?" They paid Judas thirty silver coins, [16] and from then on he started looking for a good chance to betray Jesus.

Jesus eats the Passover meal with his disciples

This is also told in Mark 14.12–21; Luke 22.7–13; John 13.21–30

[17] On the first day of the Festival of Thin Bread, Jesus' disciples came to him and asked, "Where do you want us to prepare the Passover meal?"

[18] Jesus told them to go to a certain man in the city and tell him, "Our teacher says, 'My time has come! I want to eat the Passover meal with my disciples in your home.' " [19] They did as Jesus told them and prepared the meal.

[20-21] When Jesus was eating with his twelve disciples that evening, he said, "One of you will hand me over to my enemies."

---

*26.6 leprosy: See the note at 8.2.
*26.12 poured perfume on my body to prepare it for burial: The Jewish people taught that giving someone a proper burial was even more important than helping the poor.
*26.14 Iscariot: See the note at 10.4.

See also: 26.7: Luke 7.37–38. 26.11: Deut 15.11.
26.15: Zech 11.12.

See also: 25.46: Dan 12.2. 26.2: Exod 12.1–27.

²² The disciples were very sad, and each one said to Jesus, "Lord, you can't mean me!"

²³ He answered, "One of you men who has eaten with me from this dish will betray me. ²⁴ The Son of Man will die, as the Scriptures say. But it's going to be terrible for the one who betrays me! That man would be better off if he had never been born."

²⁵ Judas said, "Teacher, surely you don't mean me!"

"That's what you say!" Jesus replied. But later, Judas did betray him.

The Lord's Supper

This is also told in Mark 14.22–26; Luke 22.14–23; 1 Corinthians 11.23–25

²⁶ During the meal Jesus took some bread in his hands. He blessed the bread and broke it. Then he gave it to his disciples and said, "Take this and eat it. This is my body."

²⁷ Jesus picked up a cup of wine and gave thanks to God. He then gave it to his disciples and said, "Take this and drink it. ²⁸ This is my blood, and with it God makes his agreement with you. It will be poured out, so that many people will have their sins forgiven. ²⁹ From now on I am not going to drink any wine, until I drink new wine with you in my Father's kingdom." ³⁰ Then they sang a hymn and went out to the Mount of Olives.

Peter's promise

This is also told in Mark 14.27–31; Luke 22.31–34; John 13.36–38

³¹ Jesus said to his disciples, "During this very night, all of you will reject me, as the Scriptures say,

'I will strike down
    the shepherd,
and the sheep
    will be scattered.'

³² But after I am raised to life, I will go to Galilee ahead of you."

³³ Peter spoke up, "Even if all the others reject you, I never will!"

³⁴ Jesus replied, "I promise you that before a cock crows tonight, you will say three times that you don't know me." ³⁵ But Peter said, "Even if I have to die with you, I will never say I don't know you."

All the others said the same thing.

Jesus prays

This is also told in Mark 14.32–42; Luke 22.39–46

³⁶ Jesus went with his disciples to a place called Gethsemane. When they got there, he told them, "Sit here while I go over there and pray."

³⁷ Jesus took along Peter and the two brothers, James and John.ᵇ He was very sad and troubled, ³⁸ and he said to them, "I am so sad that I feel as if I am dying. Stay here and keep awake with me."

³⁹ Jesus walked on a little way. Then he knelt with his face to the ground and prayed, "My Father, if it is possible, don't make me suffer by making me drink from this cup.* But do what you want, and not what I want."

⁴⁰ He came back and found his disciples sleeping. So he said to Peter, "Can't any of you stay awake with me for just one hour? ⁴¹ Stay awake and pray that you won't be tested. You want to do what is right, but you are weak."

⁴² Again Jesus went to pray and said, "My Father, if there is no other way, and I must suffer, I will still do what you want."

⁴³ Jesus came back and found them sleeping again. They simply could not keep their eyes open. ⁴⁴ He left them and prayed the same prayer once more.

⁴⁵ Finally, Jesus returned to his disciples and said, "Are you still sleeping and resting?ᵇ The time has come for the Son of Man to be handed over to sinners. ⁴⁶ Get up! Let's go. The one who will betray me is already here."

Jesus is arrested

This is also told in Mark 14.43–50; Luke 22.47–53; John 18.3–12

⁴⁷ Jesus was still speaking, when Judas the betrayer came up. He was one of the twelve disciples, and a large mob armed with swords and clubs was with him. They had been sent by the chief priests and the nation's leaders. ⁴⁸ Judas had told them beforehand, "Arrest the man I greet with a kiss."*

⁴⁹ Judas walked right up to Jesus and said, "Hello, teacher." Then Judas kissed him.

⁵⁰ Jesus replied, "My friend, why are you here?"ᵇ

26.39 making me drink from this cup: See the note at 20.22.
26.48 the man I greet with a kiss: It was the custom for people to greet each other with a kiss on the cheek.

See also: 26.23: Psa 41.9. 26.28: a Exod 24.8; b Jer 31.31–34. 26.31: Zech 13.7. 26.32: Matt 28.16.

1077

The men grabbed Jesus and arrested him. [51] One of Jesus' followers pulled out a sword. He struck the servant of the high priest and cut off his ear.

[52] But Jesus told him, "Put your sword away. Anyone who lives by fighting will die by fighting. [53] Don't you know that I could ask my Father, and straight away he would send me more than twelve armies of angels? [54] But then, how could the words of the Scriptures come true, which say that this must happen?"

[55] Jesus said to the mob, "Why do you come with swords and clubs to arrest me like a criminal? Day after day I sat and taught in the temple, and you didn't arrest me. [56] But all this happened, so that what the prophets wrote would come true."

All Jesus' disciples left him and ran away.

Jesus is questioned by the council

This is also told in Mark 14.53–65; Luke 22.54–55,63–71; John 18.13–14,19–24

[57] After Jesus had been arrested, he was led off to the house of Caiaphas the high priest. The nation's leaders and the teachers of the Law of Moses were meeting there. [58] But Peter followed along at a distance and came to the courtyard of the high priest's palace. He went in and sat down with the guards to see what was going to happen.

[59] The chief priests and the whole council wanted to put Jesus to death. So they tried to find some people who would tell lies about him in court.* [60] But they could not find any, even though many did come and tell lies. At last, two men came forward [61] and said, "This man claimed that he would tear down God's temple and build it again in three days."

[62] The high priest stood up and asked Jesus, "Why don't you say something in your own defence? Don't you hear the charges they are making against you?" [63] But Jesus did not answer. So the high priest said, "With the living God looking on, you must tell the truth. Tell us, are you the Messiah, the Son of God?"*

---

*26.59 some people who would tell lies about him in court: The Law of Moses taught that two witnesses were necessary before a person could be put to death. See verse 60.
*26.63 Son of God: One of the titles used for the kings of Israel.
See also: 26.55: Luke 19.47; 21.37. 26.61: John 2.19.

[64] "That is what you say!" Jesus answered. "But I tell all of you,

'Soon you will see
    the Son of Man
sitting at the right side*
    of God All-Powerful
and coming on the clouds
    of heaven.' "

[65] The high priest then tore his robe and said, "This man claims to be God! We don't need any more witnesses! You have heard what he said. [66] What do you think?"

They answered, "He is guilty and deserves to die!" [67] Then they spat in his face and hit him with their fists. Others slapped him [68] and said, "You think you are the Messiah! So tell us who hit you!"

Peter says he doesn't know Jesus

This is also told in Mark 14.66–72; Luke 22.56–62; John 18.15–18,25–27

[69] While Peter was sitting out in the courtyard, a servant girl came up to him and said, "You were with Jesus from Galilee."

[70] But in front of everyone Peter said, "That isn't so! I don't know what you are talking about!"

[71] When Peter had gone out to the gate, another servant girl saw him and said to some people there, "This man was with Jesus from Nazareth."

[72] Again Peter denied it, and this time he swore, "I don't even know that man!"

[73] A little while later some people standing there walked over to Peter and said, "We know that you are one of them. We can tell it because you talk like someone from Galilee."

[74] Peter began to curse and swear, "I don't know that man!"

At once a cock crowed, [75] and Peter remembered that Jesus had said, "Before a cock crows, you will say three times that you don't know me." Then Peter went out and cried hard.

CHAPTER 27

Jesus is taken to Pilate

This is also told in Mark 15.1; Luke 23.1–2; John 18.28–32

[1] Early the next morning all the chief priests and the nation's leaders met and decided

---

*26.64 right side: See the note at 22.44.
See also: 26.64: Dan 7.13. 26.65–66: Lev 24.16. 26.67: Isa 50.6.

Life files

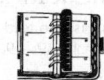

Judas

Background: Son of Simon. Probably from Kerioth in Judah

What's the story?

Judas was always the odd one out in the apostles. He was the treasurer, looking after the money, and money seems to have exercised a big influence over him. When Jesus was about to be anointed with expensive perfume, Judas argued that the perfume should be sold and the money given to the poor. He agreed to betray Jesus for thirty pieces of silver. When Jesus approached him on the Mount of Olives, Judas betrayed him with a kiss.

Later he was filled with remorse for what he had done. He returned the blood money he'd taken and went out and committed suicide (Matthew 27.3–5; Acts 1.18).

What's the point?

Why did he do it? How could this man, who had been so close to Jesus, betray him? How could it be that a man who had seen so much, could throw it all away for a handful of silver?

There have been many arguments over Judas's motives in betraying Jesus. Some see it as greed for money; others claim that Judas could not cope with the type of Messiah that Jesus was. The Bible points out that Satan had his claws into Judas.

Judas did the deed and Christ was crucified. But we should not lose sight of the fact that he died in his remorse for what he had done. Maybe he received forgiveness. Maybe he died in bitterness and despair. Whatever the case, Judas is a warning to us all: even the closest friends can be false.

 Footsteps

Five days with Judas

What about the poor? John 12.1–8
Thirty silver pieces: Matthew 26.1–5; 14–16
Someone at this table: John 13.21–30
Betrayed with a kiss: Luke 22.47–53
Remorse and suicide: Matthew 27.3–9

that Jesus should be put to death. ² They tied him up and led him away to Pilate the governor.

The death of Judas

This is also told in Acts 1.18–19

³ Judas had betrayed Jesus, but when he learnt that Jesus had been sentenced to death, he was sorry for what he had done. He returned the thirty silver coins to the chief priests and leaders ⁴ and said, "I have sinned by betraying a man who has never done anything wrong."

"So what? That's your problem," they replied. ⁵ Judas threw the money into the temple and then went out and hanged himself.

⁶ The chief priests picked up the money and said, "This money was paid to have a man killed. We can't put it in the temple treasury." ⁷ Then they had a meeting and decided to buy a field that belonged to someone who made clay pots. They wanted to use it as a graveyard for foreigners. ⁸ That's why people still call that place "Field of Blood". ⁹ So the words of the prophet Jeremiah came true,

> "They took
>   the thirty silver coins,
>   the price of a person
>   among the people of Israel.
> ¹⁰ They paid it
>   for a potter's field,*
>   as the Lord
>   had commanded me."

Pilate questions Jesus

This is also told in Mark 15.2–5; Luke 23.3–5; John 18.33–38

¹¹ Jesus was brought before Pilate the governor, who asked him, "Are you the king of the Jews?"

"Those are your words!" Jesus answered. ¹² And when the chief priests and leaders brought their charges against him, he did not say a thing.

¹³ Pilate asked him, "Don't you hear what crimes they say you have done?" ¹⁴ But Jesus did not say anything, and the governor was greatly amazed.

***27.10 a potter's field:** Perhaps a field owned by someone who made clay pots. But it may have been a field where potters came to get clay or to make pots or to throw away their broken pieces of pottery.
See also: 27.3–8: Acts 1.18–19. 27.9–10: Zech 11.12–13.

Holy history

Jesus' death

The moment of Jesus' death is attended by shattering noises and startling events.

The earth shakes, like an earthquake. Rocks split in two (Matthew 27.51). The sky grows unnaturally dark (Luke 23.44). It is as if nature itself is screaming in pain. Those watching the death of Jesus know that something unique has happened (Matthew 27.54; Mark 15.39; Luke 23.47).

And there are two, highly symbolic events. First, the earth opens and dead men walk around (Matthew 27.52–3). Jesus' death will defeat death itself; 'God's people' have been raised to life. Second, the curtain in the temple was torn. This was a huge curtain guarding the most holy place – the place where only the high priest could go, where it was believed that he met with God. This curtain rips in two from the top to the bottom – not a natural occurrence, for the curtain was too high for any human to reach the top (Matthew 27.51; Mark 15.38; Luke 23.45). Jesus' death has changed things completely – now anyone can have access to God, whenever they want.

Creation screamed out against it; imprisoned spirits were released; barriers were broken.

This was not an ordinary death.

Footsteps

Three days on Jesus' death
Darkness at noon: Luke 23.44–49
The return of God's people:
Matthew 27.45–53
The faith of the Roman soldier:
Mark 15.39–41

More...

Cross p.1112
Crucifixion p.1199
Suffering p.555
Grace p.1316
Sacrifice p.1368

The death sentence

This is also told in Mark 15.6–15; Luke 23.13–26; John 18.39–19.16

¹⁵ During Passover the governor always freed a prisoner chosen by the people. ¹⁶ At that time a well-known terrorist named Jesus Barabbas⁕ was in jail. ¹⁷ So when the crowd came together, Pilate asked them, "Which prisoner do you want me to set free? Do you want Jesus Barabbas or Jesus who is called the Messiah?" ¹⁸ Pilate knew that the leaders had brought Jesus to him because they were jealous.

¹⁹ While Pilate was judging the case, his wife sent him a message. It said, "Don't have anything to do with that innocent man. I have had nightmares because of him."

²⁰ But the chief priests and the leaders convinced the crowds to ask for Barabbas to be set free and for Jesus to be killed. ²¹ Pilate asked the crowd again, "Which of these two men do you want me to set free?"

"Barabbas!" they replied.

²² Pilate asked them, "What am I to do with Jesus, who is called the Messiah?"

They all yelled, "Nail him to a cross!"

²³ Pilate answered, "But what crime has he done?"

"Nail him to a cross!" they yelled even louder.

²⁴ Pilate saw that there was nothing he could do and that the people were starting to riot. So he took some water and washed his hands⁕ in front of them and said, "I won't have anything to do with killing this man. You are the ones doing it!"

²⁵ Everyone answered, "We and our own families will take the blame for his death!"

²⁶ Pilate set Barabbas free. Then he ordered his soldiers to beat Jesus with a whip and nail him to a cross.

Soldiers make fun of Jesus

This is also told in Mark 15.16–21; John 19.2–3

²⁷ The governor's soldiers led Jesus into the fortress⁕ and brought together the rest of the troops. ²⁸ They stripped off Jesus' clothes

---

⁕**27.24 washed his hands:** To show that he was innocent.
⁕**27.27 fortress:** The place where the Roman governor stayed. It was probably at Herod's palace west of Jerusalem, though it may have been Fortress Antonia north of the temple, where the Roman troops were stationed.
See also: 27.24: Deut 21.6–9.

and put a scarlet robe* on him. ²⁹ They made a crown out of thorn branches and placed it on his head, and they put a stick in his right hand. The soldiers knelt down and pretended to worship him. They made fun of him and shouted, "Hey, you king of the Jews!" ³⁰ Then they spat on him. They took the stick from him and beat him on the head with it.

Jesus is nailed to a cross

This is also told in Mark 15.22–32; Luke 23.27–43; John 19.17–27

³¹ When the soldiers had finished making fun of Jesus, they took off the robe. They put his own clothes back on him and led him off to be nailed to a cross. ³² On the way they met a man from Cyrene named Simon, and they forced him to carry Jesus' cross.

33 They came to a place named Golgotha, which means "Place of a Skull".* 34 There they gave Jesus some wine mixed with a drug to ease the pain. But when Jesus tasted what it was, he refused to drink it.

35 The soldiers nailed Jesus to a cross and gambled to see who would get his clothes. 36 Then they sat down to guard him. 37 Above his head they put a sign that told why he was nailed there. It read, "This is Jesus, the King of the Jews." 38 The soldiers also nailed two criminals on crosses, one to the right of Jesus and the other to his left.

39 People who passed by said terrible things about Jesus. They shook their heads and 40 shouted, "So you're the one who claimed you could tear down the temple and build it again in three days! If you are God's Son, save yourself and come down from the cross!"

41 The chief priests, the leaders, and the teachers of the Law of Moses also made fun of Jesus. They said, 42 "He saved others, but he can't save himself. If he is the king of Israel, he should come down from the cross! Then we will believe him. 43 He trusted God, so let God save him, if he wants to. He even said he was God's Son." 44 The two criminals also said cruel things to Jesus.

The death of Jesus

This is also told in Mark 15.33–41; Luke 23.44–49; John 19.28–30

⁴⁵ At midday the sky turned dark and stayed that way until three o'clock. ⁴⁶ Then about that time Jesus shouted, "Eli, Eli, lema sabachthani?"* which means, "My God, my God, why have you deserted me?"

47 Some of the people standing there heard Jesus and said, "He's calling for Elijah."* 48 One of them at once ran and grabbed a sponge. He soaked it in wine, then put it on a stick and held it up to Jesus. 49 Others said, "Wait! Let's see if Elijah will come* and save him." 50 Once again Jesus shouted, and then he died.

51 At once the curtain in the temple* was torn in two from top to bottom. The earth shook, and rocks split apart. 52 Graves opened, and many of God's people were raised to life. 53 Then after Jesus had risen to life, they came out of their graves and went into the holy city, where they were seen by many people.

54 The officer and the soldiers guarding Jesus felt the earthquake and saw everything else that happened. They were frightened and said, "This man really was God's Son!"

55 Many women had come with Jesus from Galilee to be of help to him, and they were there, looking on at a distance. 56 Mary Magdalene, Mary the mother of James and Joseph, and the mother of James and John' were some of these women.

Jesus is buried

This is also told in Mark 15.42–47; Luke 23.50–56; John 19.38–42

⁵⁷ That evening a rich disciple named Joseph from the town of Arimathea ⁵⁸ went and asked for Jesus' body. Pilate gave orders for it to be given to Joseph, ⁵⁹ who took the body and wrapped it in a clean linen cloth. ⁶⁰ Then

---

*27.28 scarlet robe: This was probably a Roman soldier's robe.

*27.33 Place of a Skull: The place was probably given this name because it was near a large rock in the shape of a human skull.

See also: 27.34: Psa 69.21.   27.35: Psa 22.18.
27.39: Psa 22.7; 109.25.   27.40: Matt 26.61; John 2.19.
27.43: Psa 22.8.

---

*27.46 Eli . . . sabachthani: These words are in Hebrew.

*27.47 Elijah: In Aramaic the name "Elijah" sounds like "Eli", which means "my God".

*27.49 Elijah will come: See the note at 16.14.

*27.51 curtain in the temple: There were two curtains in the temple. One was at the entrance, and the other separated the holy place from the most holy place that the Jewish people thought of as God's home on earth. The second curtain is probably the one that is meant.

See also: 27.46: Psa 22.1.   27.48: Psa 69.21.
27.51: Exod 26.31–33.   27.55–56: Luke 8.2–3.

Joseph put the body in his own tomb that had been cut into solid rock* and had never been used. He rolled a big stone against the entrance to the tomb and went away.

⁶¹ All this time Mary Magdalene and the other Mary were sitting across from the tomb.

⁶² On the next day, which was a Sabbath, the chief priests and the Pharisees went together to Pilate. ⁶³ They said, "Sir, we remember what that liar said while he was still alive. He claimed that in three days he would come back from death. ⁶⁴ So please order the tomb to be carefully guarded for three days. If you don't, his disciples may come and steal his body. They will tell the people that he has been raised to life, and this last lie will be worse than the first one."*

⁶⁵ Pilate said to them, "All right, take some of your soldiers and guard the tomb as well as you know how." ⁶⁶ So they sealed it tight and placed soldiers there to guard it.

Jesus is alive

CHAPTER 28

Jesus is alive

This is also told in Mark 16.1–8; Luke 24.1–12; John 20.1–10

¹ The Sabbath was over, and it was almost daybreak on Sunday when Mary Magdalene and the other Mary went to see the tomb. ² Suddenly a strong earthquake struck, and the Lord's angel came down from heaven. He rolled away the stone and sat on it. ³ The angel looked as bright as lightning, and his clothes were white as snow. ⁴ The guards shook from fear and fell down, as though they were dead.

⁵ The angel said to the women, "Don't be afraid! I know you are looking for Jesus, who was nailed to a cross. ⁶ He isn't here! God has raised him to life, just as Jesus said he would. Come, see the place where his body was lying. ⁷ Now hurry! Tell his disciples that he has been raised to life and is on his way to Galilee. Go there, and you will see him. That is what I came to tell you."

---

*27.60 tomb . . . solid rock: Some of the Jewish people buried their dead in rooms carved into solid rock. A heavy stone was rolled against the entrance.
*27.64 the first one: Probably the belief that Jesus is the Messiah.

See also: 27.63: Matt 16.21; 17.23; 20.19; Mark 8.31; 9.31; 10.33–34; Luke 9.22; 18.31–33.

Being christian

Sharing your faith

Matthew 28.11–20

Imagine that you found the cure for the common cold. What would you do? Would you hide it away and not talk to anyone about it? Or would you spread it around, publicise it and heal as many people as possible?

Of course you'd tell people. So why is it that we so often keep our faith to ourselves? After all, being a Christian means that you're loved, forgiven and will live with God forever. Isn't that the greatest news? Isn't that better than saving people from sneezing?

Jesus' final command to his disciples was for them to go into all the world and give them the good news. And that's a command which still applies to us. For some people that might mean speaking at events – or even on street corners! For others it might mean becoming a missionary. For most of us it will mean simply telling others about what we believe. Being Christian means telling people the good news. Why? Because it's the greatest news there has ever been. How can you keep that to yourself?

Being Christian: Sharing your faith

• Keep it simple. If you get the opportunity, tell people simply about your beliefs. You don't have to be the world's greatest speaker.

• Let your life speak. Actions speak louder than words. Practical love and Christian behaviour will say a lot about your faith.

• Be honest. If you don't know the answer to a question, admit it. Promise to find out and get back to the person.

8 The women were frightened and yet very happy, as they hurried from the tomb and ran to tell his disciples. 9 Suddenly Jesus met them and greeted them. They went near him, held on to his feet, and worshipped him. 10 Then Jesus said, "Don't be afraid! Tell my followers to go to Galilee. They will see me there."

Report of the guard

11 While the women were on their way, some soldiers who had been guarding the tomb went into the city. They told the chief priests everything that had happened. 12 So the chief priests met with the leaders and decided to bribe the soldiers with a lot of money. 13 They said to the soldiers, "Tell everyone that Jesus' disciples came during the night and stole his body while you were asleep. 14 If the governor* hears about this, we will talk to him. You won't have anything to worry about." 15 The soldiers took the money and did what they were told. Some of the Jewish people still tell each other this story.

What Jesus' followers must do

This is also told in Mark 16.14–18; Luke 24.36–49; John 20.19–23; Acts 1.6–8

16 Jesus' eleven disciples went to a mountain in Galilee, where Jesus had told them to meet him. 17 They saw him and worshipped him, but some of them doubted.

18 Jesus came to them and said:

I have been given all authority in heaven and on earth! 19 Go to the people of all nations and make them my disciples. Baptize them in the name of the Father, the Son, and the Holy Spirit, 20 and teach them to do everything I have told you. I will be with you always, even until the end of the world.

*28.14 governor: Pontius Pilate.
See also: 28.16: Matt 26.32; Mark 14.28. 28.19: Acts 1.8.

Additional notes

'1.19 good man: Or "kind man", or "man who always did the right thing".
'2.2 his star in the east: Or "his star rise".
'3.2 kingdom of heaven: In the Gospel of Matthew "kingdom of heaven" is used with the same meaning as "God's kingdom" in Mark and Luke.
'3.2 will soon be here: Or "is already here."

'3.11 so that you will give up your sins: Or "because you have given up your sins."
'4.17 The kingdom of heaven will soon be here: See the two notes at 3.2.
'5.3 They belong to the kingdom of heaven: Or "The kingdom of heaven belongs to them."
'5.6 who want to obey him: Or "who want to do right" or "who want everyone to be treated right".
'5.10 They belong to the kingdom of heaven: See the note at 5.3.
'5.22 someone: In verses 22–24 the Greek text has "brother", which may refer to people in general or to other followers.
'6.3 don't let anyone know about it: The Greek text has, "Don't let your left hand know what your right hand is doing."
'6.11 our food for today: Or "the food that we need" or "our food for the coming day."
'6.13 evil: Or "the evil one", that is, the devil. Some manuscripts add, "The kingdom, the power, and the glory are yours for ever. Amen."
'6.27 live longer: Or "grow taller".
'8.18 saw the crowd: Some manuscripts have "large crowd". Others have "large crowds".
'8.28 Gadara: Some manuscripts have "Gergesa". Others have "Gerasa".
'9.8 afraid: Some manuscripts have "amazed".
'9.10 Matthew's house: Or "Jesus' house".
'10.7 will soon be here: See the note at 3.2.
'10.9–10 Don't take along . . . don't carry: Or "Don't accept . . . don't accept".
'11.1 the towns: The Greek text has "their towns", which may refer to the towns of Galilee or to the towns where Jesus' disciples had lived.
'12.47 with you: Some manuscripts do not have verse 47.
'13.35 the prophet: Some manuscripts have "the prophet Isaiah".
'13.36 went inside: Or "went home".
'16.2,3 If the sky is red . . . what is happening now: The words of Jesus in verses 2 and 3 are not in some manuscripts.
'16.25 life: In verses 25 and 26 the same Greek word is translated "life", "yourself", and "soul".
'17.20–21 for you: Some manuscripts add, "But the only way to force out that kind of demon is by praying and going without eating."
'17.25 from their own people or from foreigners: Or "from their children or from others."
'17.26 From foreigners . . . their own people: Or "From other people . . . their children".
'18.10–11 in heaven: Some manuscripts add, "The Son of Man came to save people who are lost."
'18.20 in my name: Or "as my followers".
'19.14 People who are like these children belong to God's kingdom: Or "God's kingdom belongs to people who are like these children."
'20.20 mother of James and John: The Greek text has "mother of the sons of Zebedee". See 26.37.
'21.3 The Lord: Or "the master of the donkeys".
'21.44 pieces: Verse 44 is not in some manuscripts.

'23.13–14 from going in: Some manuscripts add, "You Pharisees and teachers are in for trouble! And you're nothing but show-offs! You cheat widows out of their homes and then pray long prayers just to show off. So you will be punished most of all."

'24.30 And there will be the Son of Man: Or "And it will be the Son of Man."

'24.33 the time has almost come: Or "he (that is, the Son of Man) will soon be here."

'24.36 and the Son himself doesn't know: These words are not in some manuscripts.

'26.37 the two brothers, James and John: The Greek text has "the two sons of Zebedee". See 27.56.

'26.45 Are you still sleeping and resting?: Or "You may as well keep on sleeping and resting."

'26.50 why are you here?: Or "do what you came for."

'27.16 Jesus Barabbas: Here and in verse 17 many manuscripts have "Barabbas".

'27.56 of James and John: The Greek text has "of Zebedee's sons". See 26.37.

Mark

tells the good news

The basics

What's the point? Jesus had an action-packed life, but it was also one of suffering and service.

What happens? Mark strips his gospel down to the bare essentials. All the core action is here, designed to explain to a largely Roman audience that Jesus was the son of God.

What should I remember? 16.6 'Don't be alarmed! You are looking for Jesus from Nazareth, who was nailed to a cross. God has raised him to life, and he isn't here.'

More details

Setting the scene

People are asking questions. They want to know who this Jesus was. Mark, who knows both Peter and Paul, decides to give them a simple, action-packed account...

What's it all about? Mark's is the busiest Gospel, mainly because it is the shortest. It was also probably the first gospel written, and is thought to have been written in Rome when Mark was working alongside Peter there.

Mark's aim is to get over the simple facts. So there is nothing in his gospel about Jesus' birth and upbringing, and no details about his age or the length of his ministry. The Gospel opens with a bang – with John the Baptist and Jesus' baptism. If it starts abruptly, it also ends rather quickly, with no resurrection appearance, just two women, an empty tomb and an angel with a message from God. (Although some versions of Mark include alternative, longer endings.)

The simple facts: Jesus Christ is the Son of God. Mark was probably writing for a mainly gentile, Roman audience. So he is careful to explain Jewish customs and translate Aramaic words and phrases and he includes testimonies from people like the Roman centurion when Christ was on the cross. There are also many accounts of healings and miracles – sure signs, according to Mark, that Jesus' power came from God. But he also emphasises the difficulties: the way that Jesus suffered. The new life that we get through Jesus isn't easy; it's a life of service and suffering.

Footsteps

The message of John the Baptist: 1.1–13
The work begins: 1.14–45
The crowds respond: 3.1–35
Seeds of faith: 4.13–41
Sending out the apostles: 6.1–13
Who am I? 8.22–38
True glory: 9.2–29
Who's the greatest? 9.33–50
Entering Jerusalem: 11.1–33
The key commandment: 13.28–37
The plot against Jesus: 14.1–26
The arrest: 14.27–72
The death: 15.6–41
The return: 16.1–8

The message of John the Baptist

CHAPTER 1

The preaching of John the Baptist

This is also told in Matthew 3.1–12; Luke 3.1–18; John 1.19–28

¹ This is the good news about Jesus Christ, the Son of God.' ² It began just as God had said in the book written by Isaiah the prophet,

> "I am sending my messenger
> to get the way ready
> for you.
> ³ In the desert
> someone is shouting,
> 'Get the road ready
> for the Lord!
> Make a straight path
> for him.' "

⁴ So John the Baptist appeared in the desert and told everyone, "Turn back to God and be baptized! Then your sins will be forgiven." ⁵ From all Judea and Jerusalem crowds of people went to John. They told how sorry they were for their sins, and he baptized them in the River Jordan. ⁶ John wore clothes made of camel's hair. He had a leather strap around his waist and ate grasshoppers and wild honey. ⁷ John also told the people, "Someone more powerful is going to come. And I am not good enough even to stoop down and untie his sandals.* ⁸ I baptize you with water, but he will baptize you with the Holy Spirit!"

The baptism and temptation of Jesus

The baptism of Jesus

This is also told in Matthew 3.13–17; Luke 3.21–22

⁹ About that time Jesus came from Nazareth in Galilee, and John baptized him in the River Jordan. ¹⁰ As soon as Jesus came out of the water, he saw the sky open and the Holy Spirit coming down to him like a dove. ¹¹ A voice from heaven said, "You are my own dear Son, and I am pleased with you."

---

*1.7 untie his sandals: This was the duty of a slave.
See also: 1.2: Mal 3.1. 1.3: Isa 40.3 (LXX). 1.6: 2 King 1.8. 1.11: Gen 22.2; Psa 2.7; Isa 42.1; Matt 3.17; 12.18; Mark 9.7; Luke 3.22.

Life files

Mark a.k.a. John Mark

Background: Son of Mary. Cousin of Barnabas.

What's the story?

John Mark – to give him his full name – lived in Jerusalem and was related to Barnabas. His mother Mary's house was a meeting place for the early church. Mark's father is never mentioned, and may have been dead by this date. Some people think Mark was the young man who fled at Jesus' arrest.

He became one of Paul's assistants, travelling with him and Barnabas from Antioch. Later, Mark returned home – causing a row between Paul and Barnabas. Mark then went with Barnabas to Cyprus.

The split was healed, because Mark joined Paul in Rome, going on various missions for him. Mark also worked with Peter, who views him as a 'son'. This may back up the tradition that Mark wrote his gospel from Peter's account.

What's the point?

Mark is one of the unsung heroes of the early church. He grew up among followers of Jesus, and put his faith into action from an early age. He served the greatest figures of the early church – Peter and Paul – and left a world-changing legacy in his gospel.

 Anorak corner

One early manuscript nicknames Mark *kolobodaktylos*, or 'stumpy fingered'.

 Footsteps

Five days with Mark

Mystery streaker? Mark 14.50–52
The church at Mark's home: Acts 12.6–19
The cause of an argument: Acts 15.36–41
Friend of Paul: 2 Timothy 4.11;
Colossians 4.10; Philemon 1.23–25
'Son' of Peter: 1 Peter 5.12–14

More...

Barnabas p.1228
Paul p.1222
Early church p.1212

Jesus and Satan

This is also told in Matthew 4.1–11; Luke 4.1–13

¹² Straight away God's Spirit made Jesus go into the desert. ¹³ He stayed there for forty days while Satan tested him. Jesus was with the wild animals, but angels took care of him.

Jesus in Galilee

Jesus begins his work

This is also told in Matthew 4.12–17; Luke 4.14–15

¹⁴ After John was arrested, Jesus went to Galilee and told the good news that comes from God.' ¹⁵ He said, "The time has come! God's kingdom will soon be here.' Turn back to God and believe the good news!"

Jesus chooses four fishermen

This is also told in Matthew 4.18–22; Luke 5.1–11

¹⁶ As Jesus was walking along the shore of Lake Galilee, he saw Simon and his brother Andrew. They were fishermen and were casting their nets into the lake. ¹⁷ Jesus said to them, "Come with me! I will teach you how to bring in people instead of fish." ¹⁸ At once the two brothers dropped their nets and went with him.

¹⁹ Jesus walked on and soon saw James and John, the sons of Zebedee. They were in a boat, mending their nets. ²⁰ At once Jesus asked them to come with him. They left their father in the boat with the hired workers and went with him.

A man with an evil spirit

This is also told in Luke 4.31–37

²¹ Jesus and his disciples went to the town of Capernaum. Then on the next Sabbath he went into the Jewish meeting place and started teaching. ²² Everyone was amazed at his teaching. He taught with authority, and not like the teachers of the Law of Moses. ²³ Suddenly a man with an evil spirit* in him entered the meeting place and yelled, ²⁴ "Jesus from Nazareth, what do you want with us? Have you come to destroy us? I know who you are! You are God's Holy One."

²⁵ Jesus told the evil spirit, "Be quiet and come out of the man!" ²⁶ The spirit shook him. Then it gave a loud shout and left.

²⁷ Everyone was completely surprised and kept saying to each other, "What is this? It must be some new kind of powerful teaching! Even the evil spirits obey him." ²⁸ News about Jesus quickly spread all over Galilee.

Jesus heals many people

This is also told in Matthew 8.14–17; Luke 4.38–41

²⁹ As soon as Jesus left the meeting place with James and John, they went home with Simon and Andrew. ³⁰ When they got there, Jesus was told that Simon's mother-in-law was sick in bed with fever. ³¹ Jesus went to her. He took hold of her hand and helped her up. The fever left her, and she served them a meal.

³² That evening after sunset,* all who were sick or had demons in them were brought to Jesus. ³³ In fact, the whole town gathered around the door of the house. ³⁴ Jesus healed all kinds of terrible diseases and forced out a lot of demons. But the demons knew who he was, and he did not let them speak.

³⁵ Very early the next morning, Jesus got up and went to a place where he could be alone and pray. ³⁶ Simon and the others started looking for him. ³⁷ And when they found him, they said, "Everyone is looking for you!"

³⁸ Jesus replied, "We must go to the nearby towns, so that I can tell the good news to those people. This is why I have come." ³⁹ Then Jesus went to Jewish meeting places everywhere in Galilee, where he preached and forced out demons.

Jesus heals a man

This is also told in Matthew 8.1–4; Luke 5.12–16

⁴⁰ A man with leprosy* came to Jesus and knelt down.' He begged, "You have the power to make me well, if only you wanted to."

⁴¹ Jesus felt sorry for' the man. So he put his hand on him and said, "I want to! Now you are well." ⁴² At once the man's leprosy disappeared, and he was well.

---

*1.23 evil spirit: A Jewish person who had an evil spirit was considered "unclean" and was not allowed to eat or worship with other Jewish people.
See also: 1.15: Matt 3.2. 1.22: Matt 7.28–29.

*1.32 after sunset: The Sabbath was over, and a new day began at sunset.
*1.40 leprosy: In biblical times the word "leprosy" was used for many different kinds of skin diseases.
See also: 1.39: Matt 4.23; 9.35.

43 After Jesus strictly warned the man, he sent him on his way. 44 He said, "Don't tell anyone about this. Just go and show the priest that you are well. Then take a gift to the temple as Moses commanded, and everyone will know that you have been healed."*

45 The man talked about it so much and told so many people, that Jesus could no longer go openly into a town. He had to stay away from the towns, but people still came to him from everywhere.

CHAPTER 2
Jesus heals a crippled man
This is also told in Matthew 9.1-8; Luke 5.17-26

1 Jesus went back to Capernaum, and a few days later people heard that he was at home.' 2 Then so many of them came to the house that there wasn't even standing room left in front of the door.

Jesus was still teaching 3 when four people came up, carrying a crippled man on a mat. 4 But because of the crowd, they could not get him to Jesus. So they made a hole in the roof* above him and let the man down in front of everyone.

5 When Jesus saw how much faith they had, he said to the crippled man, "My friend, your sins are forgiven."

6 Some of the teachers of the Law of Moses were sitting there. They started wondering, 7 "Why would he say such a thing? He must think he is God! Only God can forgive sins."

8 Straight away, Jesus knew what they were thinking, and he said, "Why are you thinking such things? 9 Is it easier for me to tell this crippled man that his sins are forgiven or to tell him to get up and pick up his mat and go on home? 10 I will show you that the Son of Man has the right to forgive sins here on earth." So Jesus said to the man, 11 "Get up! Pick up your mat and go on home."

12 The man got straight up. He picked up his mat and went out while everyone watched in amazement. They praised God and said, "We have never seen anything like this!"

Jesus chooses Levi
This is also told in Matthew 9.9-13; Luke 5.27-32

13 Once again, Jesus went to the shore of Lake Galilee. A large crowd gathered around him, and he taught them. 14 As he walked along, he saw Levi, the son of Alphaeus. Levi was sitting at the place for paying taxes, and Jesus said to him, "Come with me!" So he got up and went with Jesus.

15 Later, Jesus and his disciples were having dinner at Levi's house.' Many tax collectors* and other sinners had become followers of Jesus, and they were also guests at the dinner.

16 Some of the teachers of the Law of Moses were Pharisees, and they saw that Jesus was eating with sinners and tax collectors. So they asked his disciples, "Why does he eat with tax collectors and sinners?"

17 Jesus heard them and answered, "Healthy people don't need a doctor, but sick people do. I didn't come to invite good people to be my followers. I came to invite sinners."

People ask about going without eating
This is also told in Matthew 9.14-17; Luke 5.33-39

18 The followers of John the Baptist and the Pharisees often went without eating.* Some people came and asked Jesus, "Why do the followers of John and those of the Pharisees often go without eating, while your disciples never do?"

19 Jesus answered:

The friends of a bridegroom don't go without eating while he is still with them. 20 But the time will come when he will be taken from them. Then they will go without eating.

21 No one patches old clothes by sewing on a piece of new cloth. The new piece would shrink and tear a bigger hole.

---

*1.44 everyone will know that you have been healed: People with leprosy had to be examined by a priest and told that they were well (that is, "clean") before they could once again live a normal life in the Jewish community. The gift that Moses commanded was the sacrifice of some lambs together with flour mixed with olive oil.
*2.4 roof: In Palestine the houses usually had a flat roof. Stairs on the outside led up to the roof that was made of beams and boards covered with packed earth.
See also: 1.44: Lev 14.1-32.

*2.15 tax collectors: These were usually Jewish people who paid the Romans for the right to collect taxes. They were hated by other Jews who thought of them as traitors to their country and to their religion.
*2.18 without eating: The Jewish people sometimes went without eating (also called "fasting") to show their love for God or to show sorrow for their sins.

22 No one pours new wine into old wineskins. The wine would swell and burst the old skins.* Then the wine would be lost, and the skins would be ruined. New wine must be put into new wineskins.

A question about the Sabbath

This is also told in Matthew 12.1–8; Luke 6.1–5

23 One Sabbath Jesus and his disciples were walking through some wheat fields. His disciples were picking grains of wheat* as they went along. 24 Some Pharisees asked Jesus, "Why are your disciples picking grain on the Sabbath? They are not supposed to do that!"

25 Jesus answered, "Haven't you read what David did when he and his followers were hungry and in need? 26 It was during the time of Abiathar the high priest. David went into the house of God and ate the sacred loaves of bread that only priests are allowed to eat. He also gave some to his followers."

27 Jesus finished by saying, "People were not made for the good of the Sabbath. The Sabbath was made for the good of people. 28 So the Son of Man is Lord over the Sabbath."

CHAPTER 3

A man with a crippled hand

This is also told in Matthew 12.9–14; Luke 6.6–11

1 The next time that Jesus went into the meeting place, a man with a crippled hand was there. 2 The Pharisees* wanted to accuse Jesus of doing something wrong, and they kept watching to see if Jesus would heal him on the Sabbath.

3 Jesus told the man to stand up where everyone could see him. 4 Then he asked, "On the Sabbath should we do good deeds or evil deeds? Should we save someone's life or destroy it?" But no one said a word.

5 Jesus was angry as he looked around at the people. Yet he felt sorry for them because they were so stubborn. Then he

told the man, "Stretch out your hand." He did, and his bad hand was healed.

6 The Pharisees left. And straight away they started making plans with Herod's followers* to kill Jesus.

Large crowds come to Jesus

7 Jesus led his disciples down to the shore of the lake. Large crowds followed him from Galilee, Judea, 8 and Jerusalem. People came from Idumea, as well as other places east of the River Jordan. They also came from the region around the cities of Tyre and Sidon. All these crowds came because they had heard what Jesus was doing. 9 He even had to tell his disciples to get a boat ready to keep him from being crushed by the crowds.

10 After Jesus had healed many people, the other sick people begged him to let them touch him. 11 And whenever any evil spirits saw Jesus, they would fall to the ground and shout, "You are the Son of God!" 12 But Jesus warned the spirits not to tell who he was.

Jesus chooses his twelve apostles

This is also told in Matthew 10.1–4; Luke 6.12–16

13 Jesus decided to ask some of his disciples to go up on a mountain with him, and they went. 14 Then he chose twelve of them to be his apostles,' so that they could be with him. He also wanted to send them out to preach 15 and to force out demons. 16 Simon was one of the twelve, and Jesus named him Peter. 17 There were also James and John, the two sons of Zebedee. Jesus called them Boanerges, which means "Thunderbolts". 18 Andrew, Philip, Bartholomew, Matthew, Thomas, James son of Alphaeus, and Thaddaeus were also apostles. The others were Simon, known as the Eager One,* 19 and Judas Iscariot,* who later betrayed Jesus.

---

*2.22 swell and burst the old skins: While the juice from grapes was becoming wine, it would swell and stretch the skins in which it had been stored. If the skins were old and stiff, they would burst.
*2.23 picking grains of wheat: It was the custom to let hungry travellers pick grains of wheat.
*3.2 Pharisees: The Greek text has "they", but see verse 6.
See also: 2.23: Deut 23.25.   2.25–26: 1 Sam 21.1–6.
2.26: Lev 24.9.

*3.6 Herod's followers: People who were political followers of the family of Herod the Great and his son Herod Antipas.
*3.18 known as the Eager One: The Greek text has "Cananaean", which probably comes from a Hebrew word meaning "zealous" (see Luke 6.15). "Zealot" was the name later given to the members of a Jewish group which resisted and fought against the Romans.
*3.19 Iscariot: This may mean "a man from Kerioth" (a place in Judea). But more probably it means "a man who was a liar" or "a man who was a betrayer".
See also: 3.9–10: Mark 4.1; Luke 5.1–3.

Help! I'm the only Christian in my home

'It's so hard being the only Christian in my home. It feels like they're all waiting for me to fail, just so they can say "I thought you called yourself a Christian…"'

It can be tough to stand out in a family. Our families know us better than anyone else (except God). They know our ups and downs, our strengths and weaknesses. And they see us more than anyone else. Even Jesus' family seem to have had doubts about his work. So how do you show them that what you feel is real? How do you show them the love of Jesus?

Treat them with respect. Don't look down on them because 'you've been saved and they haven't'. Obey your parents. Be honest and open about your faith, but don't try to ram it down their throats.

And remember, sometimes we have more impact than we know. Sure, your family will notice the times when your behaviour doesn't match up to the ideal, but they'll also notice the times when it does.

Three things

Change

Change your behaviour. Try to 'walk the talk'. Practice forgiveness and always be prepared to make the first move.

Pray

Ask God to give you more of his Holy Spirit so that you can be a better witness. Pray for your family and their individual needs. Pray for opportunities to talk to them about Jesus.

Serve

Are there practical ways you can help around the house? Do so with a willing heart. Your parents will be astonished!

More…

Honour and obey God through our actions and he will be glorified p.382
Incarnation p.1168
Living truthfully p.1070

Jesus and the ruler of demons

This is also told in Matthew 12.22–32; Luke 11.14–23; 12.10

20 Jesus went back home, and once again such a large crowd gathered that there was no chance even to eat. 21 When Jesus' family heard what he was doing, they thought he was mad and went to get him under control.

22 Some teachers of the Law of Moses came from Jerusalem and said, "This man is under the power of Beelzebul, the ruler of demons! He is even forcing out demons with the help of Beelzebul."

23 Jesus told the people to gather around him. Then he spoke to them in riddles and said:

How can Satan force himself out?
24 A nation whose people fight each other won't last very long. 25 And a family that fights won't last long either. 26 So if Satan fights against himself, that will be the end of him.

27 How can anyone break into the house of a strong man and steal his things, unless he first ties up the strong man? Then he can take everything.

28 I promise you that any of the sinful things you say or do can be forgiven, no matter how terrible those things are. 29 But if you speak against the Holy Spirit, you can never be forgiven. That sin will be held against you for ever.

30 Jesus said this because the people were saying that he had an evil spirit in him.

Jesus' mother and brothers

This is also told in Matthew 12.46–50; Luke 8.19–21

31 Jesus' mother and brothers came and stood outside. Then they sent someone with a message for him to come out to them.
32 The crowd that was sitting around Jesus told him, "Your mother and your brothers and sisters are outside and want to see you."
33 Jesus asked, "Who is my mother and who are my brothers?" 34 Then he looked at the people sitting around him and said, "Here are my mother and my brothers.
35 Anyone who obeys God is my brother or sister or mother."

See also: 3.22: Matt 9.34; 10.25. **3.29:** Luke 12.10.

CHAPTER 4

A story about a farmer

This is also told in Matthew 13.1–9; Luke 8.4–8

¹ The next time Jesus taught beside Lake Galilee, a big crowd gathered. It was so large that he had to sit in a boat out on the lake, while the people stood on the shore. ² He used stories to teach them many things, and this is part of what he taught:

³ Now listen! A farmer went out to scatter seed in a field. ⁴ While the farmer was scattering the seed, some of it fell along the road and was eaten by birds. ⁵ Other seeds fell on thin, rocky ground and quickly started growing because the soil wasn't very deep. ⁶ But when the sun came up, the plants were scorched and dried up, because they did not have enough roots. ⁷ Some other seeds fell where thorn bushes grew up and choked out the plants. So they did not produce any grain. ⁸ But a few seeds did fall on good ground where the plants grew and produced thirty or sixty or even a hundred times as much as was scattered.

⁹ Then Jesus said, "If you have ears, pay attention."

Why Jesus used stories

This is also told in Matthew 13.10–17; Luke 8.9–10

¹⁰ When Jesus was alone with the twelve apostles and some others, they asked him about these stories. ¹¹ He answered:

I have explained the secret about God's kingdom to you, but for others I can use only stories. ¹² The reason is,

"These people will look
    and look, but never see.
They will listen and listen,
    but never understand.
If they did,
they would turn to God,
    and he would forgive them."

Jesus explains the story about the farmer

This is also told in Matthew 13.18–23; Luke 8.11–15

¹³ Jesus told them:

If you don't understand this story, you won't understand any others. ¹⁴ What the farmer is spreading is really the message

about the kingdom. ¹⁵ The seeds that fell along the road are the people who hear the message. But Satan soon comes and snatches it away from them. ¹⁶ The seeds that fell on rocky ground are the people who gladly hear the message and accept it straight away. ¹⁷ But they don't have any roots, and they don't last very long. As soon as life gets hard or the message gets them in trouble, they give up.

¹⁸ The seeds that fell among the thorn bushes are also people who hear the message. ¹⁹ But they start worrying about the needs of this life. They are fooled by the desire to get rich and to have all kinds of other things. So the message gets choked out, and they never produce anything. ²⁰ The seeds that fell on good ground are the people who hear and welcome the message. They produce thirty or sixty or even a hundred times as much as was planted.

Light

This is also told in Luke 8.16–18

²¹ Jesus also said:

You don't light a lamp and put it under a clay pot or under a bed. Don't you put a lamp on a lampstand? ²² There is nothing hidden that will not be made public. There is no secret that will not be well known. ²³ If you have ears, pay attention!

²⁴ Listen carefully to what you hear! The way you treat others will be the way you will be treated—and even worse. ²⁵ Everyone who has something will be given more. But people who don't have anything will lose what little they have.

Another story about seeds

²⁶ Again Jesus said:

God's kingdom is like what happens when a farmer scatters seed in a field. ²⁷ The farmer sleeps at night and is up and around during the day. Yet the seeds keep sprouting and growing, and he doesn't understand how. ²⁸ It is the ground that makes the seeds sprout and grow into plants that produce grain. ²⁹ Then when harvest season comes and the grain is ripe, the farmer cuts it with a sickle.*

---

*4.29 sickle: A knife with a long curved blade, used to cut grain and other crops.

See also: 4.21: Matt 5.15; Luke 11.33. **4.22:** Matt 10.26; Luke 12.2. **4.24:** Matt 7.2; Luke 6.38. **4.25:** Matt 13.12; 25.29; Luke 19.26. **4.29:** Joel 3.13.

See also: 4.1: Luke 5.1–3. **4.12:** Isa 6.9–10 (LXX).

A mustard seed

This is also told in Matthew 13.31–32; Luke 13.18–19

30 Finally, Jesus said:

What is God's kingdom like? What story can I use to explain it? 31 It is like what happens when a mustard seed is planted in the ground. It is the smallest seed in all the world. 32 But once it is planted, it grows larger than any garden plant. It even puts out branches that are big enough for birds to nest in its shade.

The reason for teaching with stories

This is also told in Matthew 13.34–35

33 Jesus used many other stories when he spoke to the people, and he taught them as much as they could understand. 34 He did not tell them anything without using stories. But when he was alone with his disciples, he explained everything to them.

A storm

This is also told in Matthew 8.23–27; Luke 8.22–25

35 That evening, Jesus said to his disciples, "Let's cross to the east side." 36 So they left the crowd, and his disciples started across the lake with him in the boat. Some other boats followed along. 37 Suddenly a storm struck the lake. Waves started splashing into the boat, and it was about to sink.

38 Jesus was in the back of the boat with his head on a pillow, and he was asleep. His disciples woke him and said, "Teacher, don't you care that we're about to drown?"

39 Jesus got up and ordered the wind and the waves to be quiet. The wind stopped, and everything was calm.

40 Jesus asked his disciples, "Why were you afraid? Don't you have any faith?"

41 Now they were more afraid than ever and said to each other, "Who is this? Even the wind and the waves obey him!"

CHAPTER 5

A man with evil spirits

This is also told in Matthew 8.28–34; Luke 8.26–39

1 Jesus and his disciples crossed Lake Galilee and came to shore near the town of Gerasa.▸ 2 When he was getting out of the boat, a man with an evil spirit quickly ran to him 3 from the graveyard* where he had been living. No one was able to tie the man up any more, not even with a chain. 4 He had often been put in chains and leg irons, but he broke the chains and smashed the leg irons. No one could control him. 5 Night and day he was in the graveyard or on the hills, yelling and cutting himself with stones.

6 When the man saw Jesus in the distance, he ran up to him and knelt down. 7 He shouted, "Jesus, Son of God in heaven, what do you want with me? Promise me in God's name that you won't torture me!" 8 The man said this because Jesus had already told the evil spirit to come out of him.

9 Jesus asked, "What is your name?"

The man answered, "My name is Lots, because I have 'lots' of evil spirits." 10 He then begged Jesus not to send them away.

11 Over on the hillside a large herd of pigs was feeding. 12 So the evil spirits begged Jesus, "Send us into those pigs! Let us go into them." 13 Jesus let them go, and they went out of the man and into the pigs. The whole herd of about two thousand pigs rushed down the steep bank into the lake and drowned.

14 The men taking care of the pigs ran to the town and the farms to spread the news. Then the people came out to see what had happened. 15 When they came to Jesus, they saw the man who had once been full of demons. He was sitting there with his clothes on and in his right mind, and they were terrified.

16 Everyone who had seen what had happened told about the man and the pigs. 17 Then the people started begging Jesus to leave their part of the country.

18 When Jesus was getting into the boat, the man begged to go with him. 19 But Jesus would not let him. Instead, he said, "Go home to your family and tell them how much the Lord has done for you and how good he has been to you."

20 The man went away into the region near the ten cities known as Decapolis* and began telling everyone how much Jesus had done for him. Everyone who heard what had happened was amazed.

---

*5.3 graveyard: It was thought that demons and evil spirits lived in graveyards.
*5.20 the ten cities known as Decapolis: A group of ten cities east of Samaria and Galilee, where the people followed the Greek way of life.

A dying girl and a sick woman
This is also told in Matthew 9.18–26; Luke 8.40–56

21 Once again Jesus got into the boat and crossed Lake Galilee.* Then as he stood on the shore, a large crowd gathered around him. 22 The person in charge of the Jewish meeting place was also there. His name was Jairus, and when he saw Jesus, he went over to him. He knelt at Jesus' feet 23 and started begging him for help. He said, "My daughter is about to die! Please come and touch her, so she will get well and live." 24 Jesus went with Jairus. Many people followed along and kept crowding around.

25 In the crowd was a woman who had been bleeding for twelve years. 26 She had gone to many doctors, and they had not done anything except cause her a lot of pain. She had paid them all the money she had. But instead of getting better, she only got worse.

27 The woman had heard about Jesus, so she came up behind him in the crowd and barely touched his clothes. 28 She had said to herself, "If I can just touch his clothes, I will get well." 29 As soon as she touched them, her bleeding stopped, and she knew she was well.

30 At that moment Jesus felt power go out from him. He turned to the crowd and asked, "Who touched my clothes?"

31 His disciples said to him, "Look at all these people crowding around you! How can you ask who touched you?" 32 But Jesus turned to see who had touched him.

33 The woman knew what had happened to her. She came shaking with fear and knelt down in front of Jesus. Then she told him the whole story.

34 Jesus said to the woman, "You are now well because of your faith. May God give you peace! You are healed, and you will no longer be in pain."

35 While Jesus was still speaking, some men came from Jairus' home and said, "Your daughter has died! Why bother the teacher any more?"

36 Jesus heard† what they said, and he said to Jairus, "Don't worry. Just have faith!"

37 Jesus did not let anyone go with him except Peter and the two brothers, James and John. 38 They went home with Jairus and saw the people crying and making a lot of noise.*

39 Then Jesus went inside and said to them, "Why are you crying and carrying on like this? The child isn't dead. She is just asleep." 40 But the people laughed at him.

After Jesus had sent them all out of the house, he took the girl's father and mother and his three disciples and went to where she was. 41-42 He took the twelve-year-old girl by the hand and said, "Talitha, koum!"* which means, "Little girl, get up!" The girl got straight up and started walking around. Everyone was greatly surprised. 43 But Jesus ordered them not to tell anyone what had happened. Then he said, "Give her something to eat."

CHAPTER 6

The people of Nazareth turn against Jesus
This is also told in Matthew 13.53–58; Luke 4.16–30

1 Jesus left and returned to his home town* with his disciples. 2 The next Sabbath he taught in the Jewish meeting place. Many of the people who heard him were amazed and asked, "How can he do all this? Where did he get such wisdom and the power to perform these miracles? 3 Isn't he the carpenter,† the son of Mary? Aren't James, Joseph, Judas, and Simon his brothers? Don't his sisters still live here in our town?" The people were very unhappy because of what he was doing.

4 But Jesus said, "Prophets are honoured by everyone, except the people of their home town and their relatives and their own family." 5 Jesus could not perform any miracles there, except to heal a few sick people by placing his hands on them. 6 He was surprised that the people did not have any faith.

Instructions for the twelve apostles
This is also told in Matthew 10.5–15; Luke 9.1–6

Jesus taught in all the neighbouring villages. 7 Then he called together his twelve apostles and sent them out two by two with power over evil spirits. 8 He told them, "You may take along a walking stick. But don't carry food or a travelling bag or any money. 9 It's all right to wear sandals, but don't take along

---

*5.41–42 Talitha, koum: These words are in Aramaic, a language spoken in Palestine during the time of Jesus.
*6.1 home town: Nazareth.
See also: 6.4: John 4.44. 6.8–11: Luke 10.4–11.

*5.21 crossed Lake Galilee: To the west side.
*5.38 crying and making a lot of noise: The Jewish people often hired mourners for funerals.

Big ideas 💡

Apostles & disciples

The 12 special followers of Jesus are called the disciples, or apostles.

The words mean different things. 'Disciples' followed a particular teacher and learned from them. Apostles comes from the Greek word for 'one who is sent'. After the resurrection, the twelve disciples are called the Apostles. No longer learners, they are now sent out as representatives of Jesus.

They were a mixed bag of individuals. They were often afraid, frequently baffled and, when the going got tough, they ran away. Yet they were also genuinely committed to Jesus and, after his resurrection, they took the message of the good news to all who would listen. Ultimately, this group of ordinary individuals was to change the world.

There were twelve core disciples, but there are minor differences about the actual names. The accounts agree on eleven of them. However, Matthew and Mark have Thaddeus, while Luke lists Judas, son of James. The likelihood is that these were the same person, and Thaddeus was his nickname (Matthew 10.2–4; Mark 3.16–19; Luke 6.13–16). John doesn't provide a list, but he does mention a 'Nathaniel', who was probably the same as Bartholomew.

Confused? Here they are, in order...

Simon Peter

A married fisherman from Bethsaida in Galilee. Brother of Andrew.

James

Son of Zebedee, brother of John, cousin of Jesus. Died in AD44 when he was beheaded by Herod Agrippa.

John

Brother of James. Cousin of Jesus. Originally a disciple of John the Baptist, he then followed and became very close to Jesus.

Andrew

Lived in Bethsaida. Brother of Simon Peter. It was Andrew who brought his brother Peter to see Jesus.

Philip

Philip's home was in Bethsaida, which means that he, too, may have been a fisherman, since the village was a well-known fishing village.

Bartholomew

Nothing much is known about him. He was probably the same as the Natahaniel mentioned by John.

Matthew

A tax collector from Capernaum, who is also known as Levi.

Simon

Described as a zealot – a member of a political group which was actively opposed to Roman occupation.

Thomas

Also known as Didymus, which is Greek for 'twin'. Anxious and a little sceptical, he did not believe the rest of the apostles when they said they'd seen Jesus, which is why he's known as 'doubting Thomas'. The moment he saw Jesus, all doubts disappeared.

James

Son of Alphaeus. Sometimes called 'James the less' or 'James the younger'.

Judas

Son of James. Probably the same as the Thaddeus listed by Matthew. Perhaps Matthew called him this to distinguish him from Judas Iscariot.

Judas Iscariot

The betrayer. The enigma. The question mark. Son of Simon who lived in Kerioth in Judah.

Matthias

The extra one. He was the replacement for Judas and was chosen by lot (Acts 1.23–26).

More...
Peter p.1169
John p.1396
Judas p.1079
Matthew p.1047
Jesus' teaching p.1055

a change of clothes. ¹⁰ When you are welcomed into a home, stay there until you leave that town. ¹¹ If any place won't welcome you or listen to your message, leave and shake the dust from your feet* as a warning to them."

¹² The apostles left and started telling everyone to turn to God. ¹³ They forced out many demons and healed a lot of sick people by putting olive oil* on them.

The death of John the Baptist
This is also told in Matthew 14.1–12; Luke 9.7–9

¹⁴ Jesus became so well-known that Herod the ruler* heard about him. Some people thought he was John the Baptist, who had come back to life with the power to perform miracles. ¹⁵ Others thought he was Elijah* or some other prophet who had lived long ago. ¹⁶ But when Herod heard about Jesus, he said, "This must be John! I had his head cut off, and now he has come back to life."

¹⁷⁻¹⁸ Herod had earlier married Herodias, the wife of his brother Philip. But John had told him, "It isn't right for you to take your brother's wife!" So, in order to please Herodias, Herod arrested John and put him in prison.

¹⁹ Herodias had a grudge against John and wanted to kill him. But she could not do it ²⁰ because Herod was afraid of John and protected him. He knew that John was a good and holy man. Even though Herod was confused by what John said,' he was glad to listen to him. And he often did.

²¹ Finally, Herodias got her chance when Herod gave a great birthday celebration for himself and invited his officials, his army officers, and the leaders of Galilee. ²² The daughter of Herodias' came in and danced for Herod and his guests. She pleased them so much that Herod said, "Ask for anything, and it's yours! ²³ I swear that I will give you as much as half of my kingdom, if you want it."

²⁴ The girl left and asked her mother, "What do you think I should ask for?"

Her mother answered, "The head of John the Baptist!"

²⁵ The girl hurried back and told Herod, "Straight away on a dish I want the head of John the Baptist!"

²⁶ The king was very sorry for what he had said. But he did not want to break the promise he had made in front of his guests. ²⁷ At once he ordered a guard to cut off John's head there in prison. ²⁸ The guard put the head on a dish and took it to the girl. Then she gave it to her mother.

²⁹ When John's followers learnt that he had been killed, they took his body and put it in a tomb.

Jesus feeds five thousand
This is also told in Matthew 14.13–21; Luke 9.10–17; John 6.1–14

³⁰ After the apostles returned to Jesus,* they told him everything they had done and taught. ³¹ But so many people were coming and going that Jesus and the apostles did not even have a chance to eat. Then Jesus said, "Let's go to a place* where we can be alone and get some rest." ³² They left in a boat for a place where they could be alone. ³³ But many people saw them leave and worked out where they were going. So people from every town ran on ahead and got there first.

³⁴ When Jesus got out of the boat, he saw the large crowd that was like sheep without a shepherd. He felt sorry for the people and started teaching them many things.

³⁵ That evening the disciples came to Jesus and said, "This place is like a desert, and it is already late. ³⁶ Let the crowds leave, so they can go to the farms and villages near here and buy something to eat."

³⁷ Jesus replied, "You give them something to eat."

But they asked him, "Don't you know that it would take almost a year's wages* to buy all these people something to eat?"

---

*6.11 shake the dust from your feet: This was a way of showing rejection.
*6.13 olive oil: The Jewish people used olive oil as a way of healing people. Sometimes olive oil is a symbol for healing by means of a miracle (see James 5.14).
*6.14 Herod the ruler: Herod Antipas, the son of Herod the Great.
*6.15 Elijah: Many of the Jewish people expected the prophet Elijah to come and prepare the way for the Messiah.
See also: 6.11: Acts 13.51. 6.13: Jam 5.14. 6.14–15: Matt 16.14; Mark 8.28; Luke 9.19. 6.17–18: Luke 3.19–20.

*6.30 the apostles returned to Jesus: From the mission on which he had sent them (see 6.7,12–13).
*6.31 a place: This was probably north-east of Lake Galilee (see verse 45).
*6.37 almost a year's wages: The Greek text has "two hundred silver coins". Each coin was the average day's wage for a worker.
See also: 6.34: Num 27.17; 1 King 22.17; 2 Chron 18.16; Ezek 34.5; Matt 9.36.

38 Then Jesus said, "How much bread do you have? Go and see!"

They found out and answered, "We have five small loaves of bread* and two fish." 39 Jesus told his disciples to make the people sit down on the green grass. 40 They sat down in groups of a hundred and groups of fifty.

41 Jesus took the five loaves and the two fish. He looked up towards heaven and blessed the food. Then he broke the bread and handed it to his disciples to give to the people. He also divided the two fish, so that everyone could have some.

42 After everyone had eaten all they wanted, 43 Jesus' disciples picked up twelve large baskets of leftover bread and fish.

44 There were five thousand men who ate the food.

Jesus walks on the water

This is also told in Matthew 14.22–33; John 6.15–21

45 Straight away, Jesus made his disciples get into the boat and start back across to Bethsaida. But he stayed until he had sent the crowds away. 46 Then he said goodbye to them and went up on the side of a mountain to pray.

47 Later that evening he was still there by himself, and the boat was somewhere in the middle of the lake. 48 He could see that the disciples were struggling hard, because they were rowing against the wind. Not long before morning, Jesus came towards them. He was walking on the water and was about to pass the boat.

49 When the disciples saw Jesus walking on the water, they thought he was a ghost, and they started screaming. 50 All of them saw him and were terrified. But at that same time he said, "Don't worry! I am Jesus. Don't be afraid." 51 He then got into the boat with them, and the wind died down. The disciples were completely confused. 52 Their minds were closed, and they could not understand the true meaning of the loaves of bread.

Jesus heals sick people in Gennesaret

This is also told in Matthew 14.34–36

53 Jesus and his disciples crossed the lake and brought the boat to shore near the town of Gennesaret. 54 As soon as they got out of the boat, the people recognized Jesus. 55 So they ran all over that part of the country to bring their sick people to him on mats. They brought them each time they heard where he was. 56 In every village or farm or market place where Jesus went, the people brought their sick to him. They begged him to let them just touch his clothes, and everyone who did was healed.

CHAPTER 7

The teaching of the ancestors

This is also told in Matthew 15.1–9

1 Some Pharisees and several teachers of the Law of Moses from Jerusalem came and gathered around Jesus. 2 They noticed that some of his disciples ate without first washing their hands.*

3 The Pharisees and many other Jewish people obey the teachings of their ancestors. They always wash their hands in the proper way before eating. 4 None of them will eat anything they buy in the market until it is washed. They also follow a lot of other teachings, such as washing cups, jugs, and bowls.

5 The Pharisees and teachers asked Jesus, "Why don't your disciples obey what our ancestors taught us to do? Why do they eat without washing their hands?"

6 Jesus replied:

You are nothing but show-offs! The prophet Isaiah was right when he wrote that God had said,

"All of you praise me
    with your words,
but you never really
    think about me.
7 It is useless for you
    to worship me,
when you teach rules
    made up by humans."

8 You disobey God's commands in order to obey what humans have taught. 9 You are good at rejecting God's commands so that you can follow your own teachings! 10 Didn't Moses command you to respect your father and mother? Didn't he tell you to put to death all who curse their parents? 11 But you let people get by without

---

*7.2 without first washing their hands:** The Jewish people had strict laws about washing their hands before eating, especially if they had been out in public.

See also: 7.6-7: Isa 29.13 (LXX); 7.10: a Exod 20.12; Deut 5.16; b Exod 21.17; Lev 20.9.

---

*6.38 small loaves of bread:** These would have been flat and round or in the shape of a bun.

Holy history

Pharisees, Sadducees and the rest

By the time of the New Testament, Orthodox Jews were split into two main factions, the Pharisees and the Sadducees. These two groups hated each other, except when they could both agree to hate someone else – such as Jesus.

Pharisees

The Pharisees were the local priesthood. They worked in the synagogues and placed a strong emphasis on observing the law, things like Sabbath-day observance, tithing and ritual cleanliness. Jesus criticised the Pharisees for their hypocrisy, but he had friends who were Pharisees and later, some Pharisees became Christians (Acts 15.5). Paul was a Pharisee before he met Jesus.

 Anorak corner

The word 'Pharisee' comes from a Hebrew word meaning 'to separate'.

Sadducees

The Sadducees were aristocratic traditionalists who occupied all the most powerful positions in the temple. They rejected all religious writings except the Pentateuch (Genesis to Deuteronomy). So they rejected theories that were not found there, such as the resurrection of the dead.

Scribes

The law always needed explanation and interpretation. This was the job of the Scribes. The Scribes built up a huge database of rules of conduct and expected people to obey them. They are sometimes referred to in the New Testament as 'lawyers' or 'teachers of law'.

Jesus was not like any of these groups. He didn't just obey the Law, or interpret the Law, or enforce the Law. He made the Law – and people were struck by his authority.

helping their parents when they should. You let them say that what they own has been offered to God.* ¹² You won't let those people help their parents. ¹³ And you ignore God's commands in order to follow your own teaching. You do a lot of other things that are just as bad.

What really makes people unclean

This is also told in Matthew 15.10–20

¹⁴ Jesus called the crowd together again and said, "Pay attention and try to understand what I mean. ¹⁵⁻¹⁶ The food that you put into your mouth doesn't make you unclean and unfit to worship God. The bad words that come out of your mouth are what make you unclean."›

¹⁷ After Jesus and his disciples had left the crowd and had gone into the house, they asked him what these sayings meant. ¹⁸ He answered, "Don't you know what I am talking about by now? Surely you know that the food you put into your mouth cannot make you unclean. ¹⁹ It doesn't go into your heart, but into your stomach, and then out of your body." By saying this, Jesus meant that all foods were fit to eat.

²⁰ Then Jesus said:

What comes from your heart is what makes you unclean. ²¹ Out of your heart come evil thoughts, vulgar deeds, stealing, murder, ²² unfaithfulness in marriage, greed, meanness, deceit, indecency, envy, insults, pride, and foolishness. ²³ All these come from your heart, and they are what make you unfit to worship God.

A woman's faith

This is also told in Matthew 15.21–28

²⁴ Jesus left and went to the region near the city of Tyre, where he stayed in someone's home. He did not want people to know he was there, but they found out anyway. ²⁵ A woman whose daughter had an evil spirit in her heard where Jesus was. And straight away she came and knelt down at his feet. ²⁶ The woman was Greek and had been born in the part of Syria known as Phoenicia. She begged Jesus to force the demon out of

---

*7.11 has been offered to God: According to Jewish custom, when anything was offered to God, it could not be used for anyone else, not even for a person's parents.

her daughter. ²⁷ But Jesus said, "The children must first be fed! It isn't right to take away their food and feed it to dogs."*

²⁸ The woman replied, "Lord, even dogs eat the crumbs that children drop from the table."

²⁹ Jesus answered, "That's true! You may go now. The demon has left your daughter." ³⁰ When the woman got back home, she found her child lying on the bed. The demon had gone.

Jesus heals a man who was deaf and could hardly talk

³¹ Jesus left the region around Tyre and went by way of Sidon towards Lake Galilee. He went through the land near the ten cities known as Decapolis.* ³² Some people brought to him a man who was deaf and could hardly talk. They begged Jesus just to touch him.

³³ After Jesus had taken him aside from the crowd, he stuck his fingers in the man's ears. Then he spat and put the spit on the man's tongue. ³⁴ Jesus looked up towards heaven, and with a groan he said, "Effatha!"* which means "Open up!" ³⁵ At once the man could hear, and he had no more trouble talking clearly.

³⁶ Jesus told the people not to say anything about what he had done. But the more he told them, the more they talked about it. ³⁷ They were completely amazed and said, "Everything he does is good! He even heals people who cannot hear or talk."

CHAPTER 8

Jesus feeds four thousand

This is also told in Matthew 15.32-39

¹ One day another large crowd gathered around Jesus. They had not brought along anything to eat. So Jesus called his disciples together and said, ² "I feel sorry for these people. They have been with me for three days, and they don't have anything to eat. ³ Some of them live a long way from here. If I send them away hungry, they might faint on their way home."

⁴ The disciples said, "This place is like a desert. Where can we find enough food to feed such a crowd?"

⁵ Jesus asked them how much food they had. They replied, "Seven small loaves of bread."*

⁶ After Jesus told the crowd to sit down, he took the seven loaves and blessed them. He then broke the loaves and handed them to his disciples, who passed them out to the crowd. ⁷ They also had a few little fish, and after Jesus had blessed these, he told the disciples to pass them around.

⁸⁻⁹ The crowd of about four thousand people ate all they wanted, and the leftovers filled seven large baskets.

As soon as Jesus had sent the people away, ¹⁰ he got into the boat with the disciples and crossed to the territory near Dalmanutha.*

A sign from heaven

This is also told in Matthew 16.1-4

¹¹ The Pharisees came out and started an argument with Jesus. They wanted to test him by asking for a sign from heaven. ¹² Jesus groaned and said, "Why are you always looking for a sign? I can promise you that you will not be given one!" ¹³ Then he left them. He again got into a boat and crossed over to the other side of the lake.

The yeast of the Pharisees and of Herod

This is also told in Matthew 16.5-12

¹⁴ The disciples had forgotten to bring any bread, and they had only one loaf with them in the boat. ¹⁵ Jesus warned them, "Watch out! Guard against the yeast of the Pharisees and of Herod."*

¹⁶ The disciples talked this over and said to each other, "He must be saying this because we don't have any bread."

¹⁷ Jesus knew what they were thinking and asked, "Why are you talking about not having any bread? Don't you understand? Are your minds still closed? ¹⁸ Are your eyes blind and your ears deaf? Don't you remember ¹⁹ how many baskets of leftovers

---

*7.27 feed it to dogs: The Jewish people often referred to Gentiles as dogs.

*7.31 the ten cities known as Decapolis: See the note at 5.20.

*7.34 Effatha: This word is in Aramaic, a language spoken in Palestine during the time of Jesus.

*8.5 small loaves of bread: See the note at 6.38.

*8.10 Dalmanutha: The place is unknown.

*8.15 Herod: See the note at 6.14.

See also: 8.11: Matt 12.38; Luke 11.16.   8.12: Matt 12.39; Luke 11.29.   8.15: Luke 12.1.   8.18: Jer 5.21; Ezek 12.2; Mark 4.12.

you picked up when I fed those five thousand people with only five small loaves of bread?"

"Yes," the disciples answered. "There were twelve baskets."

20 Jesus then asked, "And how many baskets of leftovers did you pick up when I broke seven small loaves of bread for those four thousand people?"

"Seven," they answered.

21 "Don't you know what I am talking about by now?" Jesus asked.

Jesus heals a blind man at Bethsaida

22 As Jesus and his disciples were going into Bethsaida, some people brought a blind man to him and begged him to touch the man. 23 Jesus took him by the hand and led him out of the village, where he spat into the man's eyes. He placed his hands on the blind man and asked him if he could see anything. 24 The man looked up and said, "I see people, but they look like trees walking around."

25 Once again Jesus placed his hands on the man's eyes, and this time the man stared. His eyes were healed, and he saw everything clearly. 26 Jesus said to him, "You may return home now, but don't go into the village."

Who is Jesus?

This is also told in Matthew 16.13-20; Luke 9.18-21

27 Jesus and his disciples went to the villages near the town of Caesarea Philippi. As they were walking along, he asked them, "What do people say about me?"

28 The disciples answered, "Some say you are John the Baptist or perhaps Elijah.* Others say you are one of the prophets."

29 Then Jesus asked them, "But who do you say I am?"

"You are the Messiah!" Peter replied.

30 Jesus warned the disciples not to tell anyone about him.

Jesus speaks about his suffering and death

This is also told in Matthew 16.21-28; Luke 9.22-27

31 Jesus began telling his disciples what would happen to him. He said, "The nation's leaders, the chief priests, and the teachers of the Law of Moses will make the Son of Man suffer terribly. He will be rejected and killed, but three days later he will rise to life." 32 Then Jesus explained clearly what he meant.

Peter took Jesus aside and told him to stop talking like that. 33 But when Jesus turned and saw the disciples, he corrected Peter. He said to him, "Satan, get away from me! You are thinking like everyone else and not like God."

34 Jesus then told the crowd and the disciples to come closer, and he said:

If any of you want to be my followers, you must forget about yourself. You must take up your cross and follow me. 35 If you want to save your life,' you will destroy it. But if you give up your life for me and for the good news, you will save it. 36 What will you gain, if you own the whole world but destroy yourself? 37 What could you give to get back your soul?

38 Don't be ashamed of me and my message among these unfaithful and sinful people! If you are, the Son of Man will be ashamed of you when he comes in the glory of his Father with the holy angels.

CHAPTER 9

Jesus continued:

1 I can assure you that some of the people standing here will not die before they see God's kingdom come with power.

The true glory of Jesus

This is also told in Matthew 17.1-13; Luke 9.28-36

2 Six days later Jesus took Peter, James, and John with him. They went up on a high mountain, where they could be alone. There in front of the disciples, Jesus was completely changed. 3 And his clothes became much whiter than any bleach on earth could make them. 4 Then Moses and Elijah were there talking with Jesus.

5 Peter said to Jesus, "Teacher, it is good for us to be here! Let us make three shelters, one for you, one for Moses, and one for Elijah." 6 But Peter and the others were terribly frightened, and he did not know what he was talking about.

7 The shadow of a cloud passed over and covered them. From the cloud a voice said, "This is my Son, and I love him. Listen to

---

*8.28 Elijah: See the note at 6.15.
See also: 8.28: Mark 6.14,15; Luke 9.7-8.
8.29: John 6.68-69.

See also: 8.34: Matt 10.38; Luke 14.27. 8.35: Matt 10.39; Luke 17.33; John 12.25. 9.2-7: 2 Pet 1.17-18. 9.7: Matt 3.17; Mark 1.11; Luke 3.22.

what he says!" [8] At once the disciples looked around, but they saw only Jesus.

[9] As Jesus and his disciples were coming down the mountain, he told them not to say a word about what they had seen, until the Son of Man had been raised from death. [10] So they kept it to themselves. But they wondered what he meant by the words "raised from death".

[11] The disciples asked Jesus, "Don't the teachers of the Law of Moses say that Elijah must come before the Messiah does?"

[12] Jesus answered:

Elijah certainly will come* to get everything ready. But don't the Scriptures also say that the Son of Man must suffer terribly and be rejected? [13] I can assure you that Elijah has already come. And people treated him just as they wanted to, as the Scriptures say they would.

Jesus heals a boy

This is also told in Matthew 17.14–20; Luke 9.37–43a

[14] When Jesus and his three disciples came back down, they saw a large crowd around the other disciples. The teachers of the Law of Moses were arguing with them.

[15] The crowd was really surprised to see Jesus, and everyone hurried over to greet him.

[16] Jesus asked, "What are you arguing about?"

[17] Someone from the crowd answered, "Teacher, I brought my son to you. A demon keeps him from talking. [18] Whenever the demon attacks my son, it throws him to the ground and makes him foam at the mouth and grit his teeth in pain. Then he becomes stiff. I asked your disciples to force out the demon, but they couldn't do it."

[19] Jesus said, "You people don't have any faith! How much longer must I be with you? Why do I have to put up with you? Bring the boy to me."

[20] They brought the boy, and as soon as the demon saw Jesus, it made the boy shake all over. He fell down and began rolling on the ground and foaming at the mouth.

[21] Jesus asked the boy's father, "How long has he been like this?"

The man answered, "Ever since he was a child. [22] The demon has often tried to kill him by throwing him into a fire or into water. Please have pity and help us if you can!"

[23] Jesus replied, "Why do you say 'if you can'? Anything is possible for someone who has faith!"

[24] Straight away the boy's father shouted, "I do have faith! Please help me to have even more."

[25] When Jesus saw that a crowd was gathering fast, he spoke sternly to the evil spirit that had kept the boy from speaking or hearing. He said, "I order you to come out of the boy! Don't ever bother him again."

[26] The spirit screamed and made the boy shake all over. Then it went out of him. The boy looked dead, and almost everyone said he was. [27] But Jesus took hold of his hand and helped him stand up.

[28] After Jesus and the disciples had gone back home and were alone, they asked him, "Why couldn't we force out that demon?"

[29] Jesus answered, "Only prayer can force out that kind of demon."

Jesus again speaks about his death

This is also told in Matthew 17.22–23; Luke 9.43b–45

[30] Jesus left with his disciples and started through Galilee. He did not want anyone to know about it, [31] because he was teaching the disciples that the Son of Man would be handed over to people who would kill him. But three days later he would rise to life. [32] The disciples did not understand what Jesus meant, and they were afraid to ask.

Who is the greatest?

This is also told in Matthew 18.1–5; Luke 9.46–48

[33] Jesus and his disciples went to his home in Capernaum. After they were inside the house, Jesus asked them, "What were you arguing about along the way?" [34] They had been arguing about which one of them was the greatest, and so they did not answer.

[35] After Jesus sat down and told the twelve disciples to gather around him, he said, "If you want the place of honour, you must become a slave and serve others!"

[36] Then Jesus made a child stand near him. He put his arm around the child and said, [37] "When you welcome even a child because of me, you welcome me. And when you welcome me, you welcome the one who sent me."

*9.12 Elijah certainly will come: See the note at 6.15.
See also: 9.11: Mal 4.5; Matt 11.14. 9.12: Luke 22.24.
1100

See also: 9.34: Luke 22.24. 9.35: Matt 20.26–27; 23.11; Mark 10.43–44; Luke 22.26. 9.37: Matt 10.40; Luke 10.16; John 13.20.

For or against Jesus

This is also told in Luke 9.49–50

38 John said, "Teacher, we saw a man using your name to force demons out of people. But he wasn't one of us, and we told him to stop."

39 Jesus said to his disciples:

Don't stop him! No one who performs miracles in my name is going to say something bad about me the next minute.
40 Anyone who isn't against us is for us.
41 And anyone who gives you a cup of water in my name, just because you belong to me, will surely be rewarded.

Temptations to sin

This is also told in Matthew 18.6–9; Luke 17.1–2

Jesus continued:

42 It will be terrible for people who cause even one of my little followers to sin. Those people would be better off thrown into the sea with a heavy stone tied around their necks. 43-44 So if your hand causes you to sin, cut it off! You would be better off to go into life crippled than to have two hands and be thrown into the fires of hell that never go out.▸ 45-46 If your foot causes you to sin, chop it off. You would be better off to go into life lame than to have two feet and be thrown into hell.▸ 47 If your eye causes you to sin, get rid of it. You would be better off to go into God's kingdom with only one eye than to have two eyes and be thrown into hell.
48 The worms there never die, and the fire never stops burning.

49 Everyone must be salted with fire.*

50 Salt is good. But if it no longer tastes like salt, how can it be made salty again? Have salt among you and live at peace with each other.*

Jesus goes from Galilee to Jerusalem

CHAPTER 10

Teaching about divorce

This is also told in Matthew 19.1–12; Luke 16.18

1 After Jesus left, he went to Judea and then on to the other side of the River Jordan. Once again large crowds came to him, and as usual, he taught them.

2 Some Pharisees wanted to test Jesus. So they came up to him and asked if it was right for a man to divorce his wife. 3 Jesus asked them, "What does the Law of Moses say about that?"

4 They answered, "Moses allows a man to write out divorce papers and send his wife away."

5 Jesus replied, "Moses gave you this law because you are so heartless. 6 But in the beginning God made a man and a woman. 7 That's why a man leaves his father and mother and gets married. 8 He becomes like one person with his wife. Then they are no longer two people, but one. 9 And no one should separate a couple that God has joined together."

10 When Jesus and his disciples were back in the house, they asked him about what he had said. 11 He told them, "A man who divorces his wife and marries someone else is unfaithful to his wife. 12 A woman who divorces her husband* and marries again is also unfaithful."

Jesus blesses little children

This is also told in Matthew 19.13–15; Luke 18.15–17

13 Some people brought their children to Jesus so that he could bless them by placing his hands on them. But his disciples told the people to stop bothering him.

14 When Jesus saw this, he became angry and said, "Let the children come to me! Don't try to stop them. People who are like these little children belong to the kingdom of God.▸ 15 I promise you that you cannot get into God's kingdom, unless you accept it the way a child does." 16 Then Jesus took the children

---

*9.49 salted with fire: Some manuscripts add "and every sacrifice will be seasoned with salt." The verse may mean that Christ's followers must suffer because of their faith.
*9.50 Have salt among you and live at peace with each other: This may mean that when Christ's followers have to suffer because of their faith, they must still try to live at peace with each other.
See also: 9.40: Matt 12.30; Luke 11.23. 9.41: Matt 10.42. 9.43: Matt 5.30. 9.47: Matt 5.29. 9.48: Isa 66.24. 9.50: Matt 5.13; Luke 14.34–35.

*10.12 A woman who divorces her husband: Roman law let a woman divorce her husband, but Jewish law did not let a woman do this.
See also: 10.4: Deut 24.1–4; Matt 5.31. 10.6: Gen 1.27; 5.2. 10.7-8: Gen 2.24. 10.11-12: Matt 5.32; 1 Cor 7.10–11. 10.15: Matt 18.3.

in his arms and blessed them by placing his hands on them.

A rich man

This is also told in Matthew 19.16–30; Luke 18.18–30

¹⁷ As Jesus was walking down a road, a man ran up to him. He knelt down, and asked, "Good teacher, what can I do to have eternal life?"

¹⁸ Jesus replied, "Why do you call me good? Only God is good. ¹⁹ You know the commandments. 'Do not murder. Be faithful in marriage. Do not steal. Do not tell lies about others. Do not cheat. Respect your father and mother.' "

²⁰ The man answered, "Teacher, I have obeyed all these commandments since I was a young man."

²¹ Jesus looked closely at the man. He liked him and said, "There's one thing you still need to do. Go and sell everything you own. Give the money to the poor, and you will have riches in heaven. Then come with me."

²² When the man heard Jesus say this, he went away gloomy and sad because he was very rich.

²³ Jesus looked around and said to his disciples, "It's hard for rich people to get into God's kingdom!" ²⁴ The disciples were shocked to hear this. So Jesus told them again, "It's terribly hard¹ to get into God's kingdom! ²⁵ In fact, it's easier for a camel to go through the eye of a needle than for a rich person to get into God's kingdom."

²⁶ Jesus' disciples were even more amazed. They asked each other, "How can anyone ever be saved?"

²⁷ Jesus looked at them and said, "There are some things that people cannot do, but God can do anything."

²⁸ Peter replied, "Remember, we left everything to be your followers!"

²⁹ Jesus told him:

You can be sure that anyone who gives up home or brothers or sisters or mother or father or children or land for me and for the good news ³⁰ will be rewarded. In this world they will be given a hundred times as many houses and brothers and sisters and mothers and children and pieces of land, though they will also be ill-treated. And in the world to come, they will have eternal life. ³¹ But many who are now first will be last, and many who are now last will be first.

Jesus again tells about his death

This is also told in Matthew 20.17–19; Luke 18.31–34

³² The disciples were confused as Jesus led them towards Jerusalem, and his other followers were afraid. Once again, Jesus took the twelve disciples aside and told them what was going to happen to him. He said:

³³ We are now on our way to Jerusalem where the Son of Man will be handed over to the chief priests and the teachers of the Law of Moses. They will sentence him to death and hand him over to foreigners,* ³⁴ who will make fun of him and spit on him. They will beat him and kill him. But three days later he will rise to life.

The request of James and John

This is also told in Matthew 20.20–28

³⁵ James and John, the sons of Zebedee, came up to Jesus and asked, "Teacher, will you do us a favour?"

³⁶ Jesus asked them what they wanted, ³⁷ and they answered, "When you come into your glory, please let one of us sit at your right side and the other at your left."*

³⁸ Jesus told them, "You don't really know what you're asking! Are you able to drink from the cup* that I must soon drink from or be baptized as I must be baptized?"*

³⁹ "Yes, we are!" James and John answered.

Then Jesus replied, "You certainly will drink from the cup from which I must drink. And you will be baptized just as I must! ⁴⁰ But it isn't for me to say who will sit at my right side and at my left. That is for God to decide."

⁴¹ When the ten other disciples heard this, they were angry with James and John. ⁴² But Jesus called the disciples together and said:

You know that those foreigners who call themselves kings like to order their people around. And their great leaders have full power over the people they rule. ⁴³ But don't act like them. If you want to be great, you

---

*10.33 **foreigners:** The Romans who ruled Judea at this time.

*10.37 **right side . . . left:** The most powerful people in a kingdom sat at the right and left side of the king.

*10.38 **drink from the cup:** In the Scriptures a "cup" is sometimes used as a symbol of suffering. To "drink from the cup" would be to suffer.

*10.38 **as I must be baptized:** Baptism is used with the same meaning that "cup" has in this verse.

See also: 10.38: Luke 12.50. 10.42,43: Luke 22.25–26. 10.43–44: Matt 23.11; Mark 9.35; Luke 22.26.

See also: **10.19: a** Exod 20.13; Deut 5.17; **b** Exod 20.14; Deut 5.18; **c** Exod 20.15; Deut 5.19; **d** Exod 20.16; Deut 5.20; **e** Exod 20.12; Deut 5.16. **10.31:** Matt 20.16; Luke 13.30.

1102

must be the servant of all the others. ⁴⁴ And if you want to be first, you must be everyone's slave. ⁴⁵ The Son of Man did not come to be a slave master, but a slave who will give his life to rescue* many people.

Jesus heals blind Bartimaeus

This is also told in Matthew 20.29–34; Luke 18.35–43

⁴⁶ Jesus and his disciples went to Jericho. And as they were leaving, they were followed by a large crowd. A blind beggar called Bartimaeus son of Timaeus was sitting beside the road. ⁴⁷ When he heard that it was Jesus from Nazareth, he shouted, "Jesus, Son of David,* have pity on me!" ⁴⁸ Many people told the man to stop, but he shouted even louder, "Son of David, have pity on me!"

⁴⁹ Jesus stopped and said, "Call him over!"

They called out to the blind man and said, "Don't be afraid! Come on! He is calling for you." ⁵⁰ The man threw off his coat as he jumped up and ran to Jesus.

⁵¹ Jesus asked, "What do you want me to do for you?"

The blind man answered, "Master,' I want to see!"

⁵² Jesus told him, "You may go. Your eyes are healed because of your faith."

Straight away the man could see, and he went down the road with Jesus.

Jesus' last week: his trial and death

CHAPTER 11

Jesus enters Jerusalem

This is also told in Matthew 21.1–11; Luke 19.28–40; John 12.12–19

¹ Jesus and his disciples reached Bethphage and Bethany near the Mount of Olives. When they were getting close to Jerusalem, Jesus sent two of them on ahead. ² He told them, "Go into the next village. As soon as you enter it, you will find a young donkey that has never been ridden. Untie the donkey and bring it here. ³ If anyone asks why you are doing that, say, 'The Lord' needs it and will soon bring it back.' "

⁴ The disciples left and found the donkey tied near a door that faced the street. While they were untying it, ⁵ some of the people standing there asked, "Why are you untying the donkey?" ⁶ They told them what Jesus had said, and the people let them take it.

⁷ The disciples led the donkey to Jesus. They put some of their clothes on its back, and Jesus got on. ⁸ Many people spread clothes on the road, while others went to cut branches from the fields.*

⁹ In front of Jesus and behind him, people went along shouting,

"Hooray!*
God bless the one who comes
    in the name of the Lord!
¹⁰ God bless the coming kingdom
    of our ancestor David.
Hooray for God
    in heaven above!"

¹¹ After Jesus had gone to Jerusalem, he went into the temple and looked around at everything. But since it was already late in the day, he went back to Bethany with the twelve disciples.

Jesus puts a curse on a fig tree

This is also told in Matthew 21.18–19

¹² When Jesus and his disciples left Bethany the next morning, he was hungry. ¹³ From a distance Jesus saw a fig tree covered with leaves, and he went to see if there were any figs on the tree. But there were not any, because it wasn't the season for figs. ¹⁴ So Jesus said to the tree, "Never again will anyone eat fruit from this tree!" The disciples heard him say this.

Jesus in the temple

This is also told in Matthew 21.12–17; Luke 19.45–48; John 2.13–22

¹⁵ After Jesus and his disciples reached Jerusalem, he went into the temple and began chasing out everyone who was selling and buying. He turned over the tables of the moneychangers and the benches of those who were selling doves. ¹⁶ Jesus would not let anyone carry things through the temple.

---

*10.45 rescue: The Greek word often, though not always, means the payment of a price to free a slave or a prisoner.

*10.47 Son of David: The Jewish people expected the Messiah to be from the family of King David, and for this reason the Messiah was often called the "Son of David".

*11.8 spread . . . branches from the fields: This was one way that the Jewish people welcomed a famous person.

*11.9 Hooray: This translates a word that can mean "please save us". But it is most often used as a shout of praise to God.

See also: 11.9: Psa 118.25–26.

17 Then he taught the people and said, "The Scriptures say, 'My house should be called a place of worship for all nations.' But you have made it a place where robbers hide!"

18 The chief priests and the teachers of the Law of Moses heard what Jesus said, and they started looking for a way to kill him. They were afraid of him, because the crowds were completely amazed at his teaching.

19 That evening, Jesus and the disciples went outside the city.

A lesson from the fig tree

This is also told in Matthew 21.20–22

20 As the disciples walked past the fig tree the next morning, they noticed that it was completely dried up, roots and all. 21 Peter remembered what Jesus had said to the tree. Then Peter said, "Teacher, look! The tree you put a curse on has dried up."

22 Jesus told his disciples:

Have faith in God! 23 If you have faith in God and don't doubt, you can tell this mountain to get up and jump into the sea, and it will. 24 Everything you ask for in prayer will be yours, if you only have faith.

25-26 Whenever you stand up to pray, you must forgive what others have done to you. Then your Father in heaven will forgive your sins.'

A question about Jesus' authority

This is also told in Matthew 21.23–27; Luke 20.1–8

27 Jesus and his disciples returned to Jerusalem. And as he was walking through the temple, the chief priests, the nation's leaders, and the teachers of the Law of Moses came over to him. 28 They asked, "What right do you have to do these things? Who gave you this authority?"

29 Jesus answered, "I have just one question to ask you. If you answer it, I will tell you where I got the right to do these things. 30 Who gave John the right to baptize? Was it God in heaven or merely some human being?"

31 They thought it over and said to each other, "We can't say that God gave John this right. Jesus will ask us why we didn't believe John. 32 On the other hand, these people think that John was a prophet. So we can't say that it was merely some human who gave John the right to baptize."

They were afraid of the crowd 33 and told Jesus, "We don't know."

Jesus replied, "Then I won't tell you who gave me the right to do what I do."

CHAPTER 12

Tenants of a vineyard

This is also told in Matthew 21.33–46; Luke 20.9–19

1 Jesus then told them this story:

A farmer once planted a vineyard. He built a wall around it and dug a pit to crush the grapes in. He also built a lookout tower. Then he let his vineyard and left the country.

2 When it was harvest time, he sent a servant to get his share of the grapes. 3 The tenants grabbed the servant. They beat him up and sent him away without a thing.

4 The owner sent another servant, but the tenants beat him on the head and insulted him terribly. 5 Then the man sent another servant, and they killed him. He kept sending servant after servant. They beat some of them and killed others.

6 The owner had a son he loved very much. Finally, he sent his son to the tenants because he thought they would respect him. 7 But they said to themselves, "Some day he will own this vineyard. Let's kill him! That way we can have it all for ourselves." 8 So they grabbed the owner's son and killed him. Then they threw his body out of the vineyard.

9 Jesus asked, "What do you think the owner of the vineyard will do? He will come and kill those tenants and let someone else have his vineyard. 10 Surely you know that the Scriptures say,

'The stone that the builders
    tossed aside
is now the most important
    stone of all.
11 This is something
    the Lord has done,
    and it is amazing to us.' "

12 The leaders knew that Jesus was really talking about them, and they wanted to arrest him. But because they were afraid of the crowd, they let him alone and left.

See also: **11.17:** a Isa 56.7; b Jer 7.11. **11.23:** Matt 17.20; 1 Cor 13.2. **11.25–26:** Matt 6.14–15.

See also: **12.1:** Isa 5.1–2. **12.10–11:** Psa 118.22–23.

Paying taxes

This is also told in Matthew 22.15–22; Luke 20.20–26

¹³ The Pharisees got together with Herod's followers.* Then they sent some men to trick Jesus into saying something wrong. ¹⁴ They went to him and said, "Teacher, we know that you are honest. You treat everyone with the same respect, no matter who they are. And you teach the truth about what God wants people to do. Tell us, should we pay taxes to the Emperor or not?"

¹⁵ Jesus knew what they were up to, and he said, "Why are you trying to test me? Show me a coin!"

¹⁶ They brought him a silver coin, and he asked, "Whose picture and name are on it?"

"The Emperor's," they answered.

¹⁷ Then Jesus told them, "Give the Emperor what belongs to him and give God what belongs to God." The men were amazed at Jesus.

Life in the future world

This is also told in Matthew 22.23–33; Luke 20.27–40

¹⁸ The Sadducees did not believe that people would rise to life after death. So some of them came to Jesus and said:

¹⁹ Teacher, Moses wrote that if a married man dies and has no children, his brother should marry the widow. Their first son would then be thought of as the son of the dead brother. ²⁰ There were once seven brothers. The first one married, but died without having any children. ²¹ The second brother married his brother's widow, and he also died without having children. The same thing happened to the third brother, ²² and finally to all seven brothers. At last the woman died. ²³ When God raises people from death, whose wife will this woman be? After all, she had been married to all seven brothers.

²⁴ Jesus answered:

You are completely wrong! You don't know what the Scriptures teach. And you don't know anything about the power of God. ²⁵ When God raises people to life, they won't marry. They will be like the angels in heaven. ²⁶ You know

about people being raised to life. You know that in the story about Moses and the burning bush, God said, "I am the God worshipped by Abraham, Isaac, and Jacob."* ²⁷ He isn't the God of the dead, but of the living. You Sadducees are all wrong.

The most important commandment

This is also told in Matthew 22.34–40; Luke 10.25–28

²⁸ One of the teachers of the Law of Moses came up while Jesus and the Sadducees were arguing. When he heard Jesus give a good answer, he asked him, "What is the most important commandment?"

²⁹ Jesus answered, "The most important one says: 'People of Israel, you have only one Lord and God. ³⁰ You must love him with all your heart, soul, mind, and strength.' ³¹ The second most important commandment says: 'Love others as much as you love yourself.' No other commandment is more important than these."

³² The man replied, "Teacher, you are certainly right to say there is only one God. ³³ It is also true that we must love God with all our heart, mind, and strength, and that we must love others as much as we love ourselves. These commandments are more important than all the sacrifices and offerings that we could possibly make."

³⁴ When Jesus saw that the man had given a sensible answer, he told him, "You are not far from God's kingdom." After this, no one dared ask Jesus any more questions.

About David's son

This is also told in Matthew 22.41–46; Luke 20.41–44

³⁵ As Jesus was teaching in the temple, he said, "How can the teachers of the Law of Moses say that the Messiah will come from the family of King David? ³⁶ The Holy Spirit led David to say,

'The Lord said to my Lord:
    Sit at my right side*
until I make your enemies
    into a footstool for you.'

---

*12.26 "I am the God worshipped by Abraham, Isaac, and Jacob"**: Jesus argues that if God is worshipped by these three, they must still be alive, because he is the God of the living.

*12.36 right side:** The place of power and honour.

See also: 12.28-34: Luke 10.25–28. 12.29,30: Deut 6.4–5. 12.31: Lev 19.18. 12.32: Deut 4.35. 12.33: Hos 6.6. 12.36: Psa 110.1.

*12.13 Herod's followers:** See the note at 3.6.

See also: 12.18: Acts 23.8. 12.19: Deut 25.5. 12.26: Exod 3.6.

[37] If David called the Messiah his Lord, how can the Messiah be his son?"*

The large crowd enjoyed listening to Jesus teach.

Jesus condemns the Pharisees and the teachers of the Law of Moses

This is also told in Matthew 23.1–36; Luke 20.45–47

[38] As Jesus was teaching, he said:

Guard against the teachers of the Law of Moses! They love to walk around in long robes and be greeted in the market. [39] They like the front seats in the meeting places and the best seats at banquets. [40] But they cheat widows out of their homes and pray long prayers just to show off. They will be punished most of all.

A widow's offering

This is also told in Luke 21.1–4

[41] Jesus was sitting in the temple near the offering box and watching people put in their gifts. He noticed that many rich people were giving a lot of money. [42] Finally, a poor widow came up and put in two coins that were worth only a few pennies. [43] Jesus told his disciples to gather around him. Then he said:

I tell you that this poor widow has put in more than all the others. [44] Everyone else gave what they didn't need. But she is very poor and gave everything she had. Now she doesn't have a penny to live on.

CHAPTER 13

The temple will be destroyed

This is also told in Matthew 24.1–2; Luke 21.5,6

[1] As Jesus was leaving the temple, one of his disciples said to him, "Teacher, look at these beautiful stones and wonderful buildings!"

[2] Jesus replied, "Do you see these huge buildings? They will certainly be torn down! Not one stone will be left in place."

Warning about trouble

This is also told in Matthew 24.3–14; Luke 21.7–19

[3] Later, as Jesus was sitting on the Mount of Olives across from the temple, Peter, James, John, and Andrew came to him in private. [4] They asked, "When will these things happen? What will be the sign that they are about to take place?"

[5] Jesus answered:

Watch out and don't let anyone fool you! [6] Many will come and claim to be me. They will use my name and fool many people. [7] When you hear about wars and threats of wars, don't be afraid. These things will have to happen first, but that isn't the end. [8] Nations and kingdoms will go to war against each other. There will be earthquakes in many places, and people will starve to death. But this is just the beginning of troubles.

[9] Be on your guard! You will be taken to courts and beaten with whips in their meeting places. And because of me, you will have to stand before rulers and kings to tell about your faith. [10] But before the end comes, the good news must be preached to all nations.

[11] When you are arrested, don't worry about what you will say. You will be given the right words when the time comes. But you will not really be the ones speaking. Your words will come from the Holy Spirit.

[12] Brothers and sisters will betray each other and have each other put to death. Parents will betray their own children, and children will turn against their parents and have them killed. [13] Everyone will hate you because of me. But if you keep on being faithful right to the end, you will be saved.

The Horrible Thing

This is also told in Matthew 24.15–21; Luke 21.20–24

Jesus continued:

[14] Some day you will see that "Horrible Thing" where it should not be.* Everyone who reads this must try to understand! If you are living in Judea at that time, run to the mountains. [15] If you are on the roof* of your house, don't go inside to get anything. [16] If you are out in the field, don't go back for your coat. [17] It will be an awful time for women who are expecting babies or nursing young children. [18] Pray that it won't happen in

---

*13.14 where it should not be:** Probably the holy place in the temple.
*13.15 roof:** See the note at 2.4.
See also: 13.9–11: Matt 10.17–20; Luke 12.11–12. 13.13: Matt 10.22. 13.14: Dan 9.27; 11.31; 12.11. 13.15–16: Luke 17.31.

---

*12.37 David . . . his son:** See the note at 10.47.

Viewpoints 👁

What happens to someone who's never heard about Jesus?

Contributed by Suzy W

'But before the end comes, the good news must be preached to all nations.'

Quick! Quick! If we tell everyone the Good News, Jesus will come sooner! That's what I thought when I read this verse. But what does it mean to 'preach to every nation'? Who is everyone?

Someone new has just been born, and another, and someone has just died as well. What about if they hadn't heard the Good News? Are they just going to Hell? So is 'everyone' all the people living on the earth this very second or is it every person from the beginning of time to the end? I am going to attempt to answer these questions according to the Bible.

Romans 2.14–16 tells us that those who don't have God's law, but still know what's right and wrong in their hearts and live according to what they think is right, shall be saved because Christ sees what is in their heart.

Everyone will be judged. That means that every person from the beginning to the end of time in the whole world will be judged. In Romans 3.25, Paul tells us that when Jesus died, he also forgave the sins of the people before Him, because they didn't know of the Good News. It is the same today.

More...

Sharing your faith p.1082
Language p.1208
Culture p.779

---

winter.* ¹⁹ This will be the worst time of suffering since God created the world, and nothing this terrible will ever happen again. ²⁰ If the Lord doesn't make the time shorter, no one will be left alive. But because of his chosen and special ones, he will make the time shorter.

²¹ If someone should say, "Here is the Messiah!" or "There he is!" don't believe it. ²² False messiahs and false prophets will come and perform miracles and signs. They will even try to fool God's chosen ones. ²³ But be on your guard! That's why I am telling you these things now.

When the Son of Man appears
This is also told in Matthew 24.29–31; Luke 21.25–28

Jesus continued:

²⁴ In those days, straight after that time of suffering,

"The sun will become dark,
   and the moon
      will no longer shine.
²⁵ The stars will fall,
   and the powers in the sky*
      will be shaken."

²⁶ Then the Son of Man will be seen coming in the clouds with great power and glory. ²⁷ He will send his angels to gather his chosen ones from all over the earth.

A lesson from a fig tree
This is also told in Matthew 24.32–35; Luke 21.29–33

Jesus continued:

²⁸ Learn a lesson from a fig tree. When its branches sprout and start putting out leaves, you know summer is near. ²⁹ So when you see all these things happening, you will know that the time has almost come.‣ ³⁰ You can be sure that some of the people of this generation will still be alive when all this happens. ³¹ The sky and the earth will not last for ever, but my words will.

---

*13.18 in winter: In Palestine the winters are cold and rainy and make travel difficult.
*13.25 the powers in the sky: In ancient times people thought that the stars were spiritual powers.
See also: 13.19: Dan 12.1; Rev 7.14. 13.24: a Isa 13.10; Joel 2.10,31; 3.15; Rev 6.12; b Isa 13.10; Ezek 32.7.
13.25: a Isa 34.4; Rev 6.13; b Joel 2.10. 13.26: Dan 7.13; Rev 1.7.

No one knows the day or time

This is also told in Matthew 24.36–44

Jesus continued:

³² No one knows the day or the time. The angels in heaven don't know, and the Son himself doesn't know. Only the Father knows. ³³ So watch out and be ready! You don't know when the time will come. ³⁴ It is like what happens when a man goes away for a while and places his servants in charge of everything. He tells each of them what to do, and he orders the guard to keep alert. ³⁵ So be alert! You don't know when the master of the house will come back. It could be in the evening or at midnight or before dawn or in the morning. ³⁶ But if he comes suddenly, don't let him find you asleep. ³⁷ I tell everyone just what I have told you. Be alert!

CHAPTER 14

A plot to kill Jesus

This is also told in Matthew 26.1–5; Luke 22.1–2; John 11.45–53

¹ It was now two days before Passover and the Festival of Thin Bread. The chief priests and the teachers of the Law of Moses were secretly planning to have Jesus arrested and put to death. ² They were saying, "We must not do it during the festival, because the people will riot."

At Bethany

This is also told in Matthew 26.6–13; John 12.1–8

³ Jesus was eating in Bethany at the home of Simon, who once had leprosy,* when a woman came in with a very expensive bottle of sweet-smelling perfume.' After breaking it open, she poured the perfume on Jesus' head. ⁴ This made some of the guests angry, and they complained, "Why such a waste? ⁵ We could have sold this perfume for more than three hundred silver coins and given the money to the poor!" So they started saying cruel things to the woman.

⁶ But Jesus said:

Leave her alone! Why are you bothering her? She has done a beautiful thing for me. ⁷ You will always have the poor with you. And whenever you want to, you can give to them. But you won't always have me here with you. ⁸ She has done all she could by pouring perfume on my body to prepare it for burial. ⁹ You may be sure that wherever the good news is told all over the world, people will remember what she has done. And they will tell others.

Judas and the chief priests

This is also told in Matthew 26.14–16; Luke 22.3–6

¹⁰ Judas Iscariot* was one of the twelve disciples. He went to the chief priests and offered to help them arrest Jesus. ¹¹ They were glad to hear this, and they promised to pay him. So Judas started looking for a good chance to betray Jesus.

Jesus eats with his disciples

This is also told in Matthew 26.17–25; Luke 22.7–14,21–23; John 13.21–30

¹² It was the first day of the Festival of Thin Bread, and the Passover lambs were being killed. Jesus' disciples asked him, "Where do you want us to prepare the Passover meal?"

¹³ Jesus said to two of the disciples, "Go into the city, where you will meet a man carrying a jar of water.* Follow him, ¹⁴ and when he goes into a house, say to the owner, 'Our teacher wants to know if you have a room where he can eat the Passover meal with his disciples.' ¹⁵ The owner will take you upstairs and show you a large room furnished and ready for you to use. Prepare the meal there."

¹⁶ The two disciples went into the city and found everything just as Jesus had told them. So they prepared the Passover meal.

¹⁷⁻¹⁸ While Jesus and the twelve disciples were eating together that evening, he said, "The one who will betray me is now eating with me."

¹⁹ This made the disciples sad, and one after another they said to Jesus, "Surely you don't mean me!"

²⁰ He answered, "It is one of you twelve men who is eating from this dish with me. ²¹ The Son of Man will die, just as the Scriptures say. But it is going to be terrible for the one who betrays me. That man would be better off if he had never been born."

---

*14.3 leprosy: See the note at 1.40.

See also: 13.32: Matt 24.36. 13.34: Luke 12.36–38. 14.1: Exod 12.1–27. 14.3: Luke 7.37–38. 14.7: Deut 15.11.

*14.10 Iscariot: See the note at 3.19.

*14.13 a man carrying a jar of water: A male slave carrying water could mean that the family was rich.
See also: 14.18: Psa 41.9.

The Lord's Supper

This is also told in Matthew 26.26–30; Luke 22.14–23; 1 Corinthians 11.23–25

22 During the meal Jesus took some bread in his hands. He blessed the bread and broke it. Then he gave it to his disciples and said, "Take this. It is my body."

23 Jesus picked up a cup of wine and gave thanks to God. He gave it to his disciples, and said, "Drink it!" So they all drank some. 24 Then he said, "This is my blood, which is poured out for many people, and with it God makes his agreement. 25 From now on I will not drink any wine, until I drink new wine in God's kingdom." 26 Then they sang a hymn and went out to the Mount of Olives.

Peter's promise

This is also told in Matthew 26.31–35; Luke 22.31–34; John 13.36–38

27 Jesus said to his disciples, "All of you will reject me, as the Scriptures say,

'I will strike down
    the shepherd,
and the sheep
    will be scattered.'

28 But after I am raised to life, I will go ahead of you to Galilee."

29 Peter spoke up, "Even if all the others reject you, I never will!"

30 Jesus replied, "This very night before a cock crows twice, you will say three times that you don't know me."

31 But Peter was so sure of himself that he said, "Even if I have to die with you, I will never say that I don't know you!"

All the others said the same thing.

Jesus prays

This is also told in Matthew 26.36–46; Luke 22.39–46

32 Jesus went with his disciples to a place called Gethsemane, and he told them, "Sit here while I pray."

33 Jesus took along Peter, James, and John. He was sad and troubled and 34 told them, "I am so sad that I feel as if I am dying. Stay here and keep awake with me."

35-36 Jesus walked on a little way. Then he knelt down on the ground and prayed, "Father,' if it is possible, don't let this happen to me! Father, you can do anything. Don't make me suffer by making me drink from this cup.* But do what you want, and not what I want."

37 When Jesus came back and found the disciples sleeping, he said to Simon Peter, "Are you asleep? Can't you stay awake for just one hour? 38 Stay awake and pray that you won't be tested. You want to do what is right, but you are weak."

39 Jesus went back and prayed the same prayer. 40 But when he returned to the disciples, he found them sleeping again. They simply could not keep their eyes open, and they did not know what to say.

41 When Jesus returned to the disciples the third time, he said, "Are you still sleeping and resting? Enough of that! The time has come for the Son of Man to be handed over to sinners. 42 Get up! Let's go. The one who will betray me is already here."

Jesus is arrested

This is also told in Matthew 26.47–56; Luke 22.47–53; John 18.3–12

43 Jesus was still speaking, when Judas the betrayer came up. He was one of the twelve disciples, and a mob of men armed with swords and clubs were with him. They had been sent by the chief priests, the nation's leaders, and the teachers of the Law of Moses. 44 Judas had told them beforehand, "Arrest the man I greet with a kiss.* Tie him up tight and lead him away."

45 Judas walked right up to Jesus and said, "Teacher!" Then Judas kissed him, 46 and the men grabbed Jesus and arrested him.

47 Someone standing there pulled out a sword. He struck the servant of the high priest and cut off his ear.

48 Jesus said to the mob, "Why do you come with swords and clubs to arrest me like a criminal? 49 Day after day I was with you and taught in the temple, and you didn't arrest me. But what the Scriptures say must come true."

50 All Jesus' disciples ran off and left him. 51 One of them was a young man who was wearing only a linen cloth. And when the men grabbed him, 52 he left the cloth behind and ran away naked.

*14.35–36 by making me drink from this cup: See the note at 10.38.
*14.44 greet with a kiss: It was the custom for people to greet each other with a kiss on the cheek.
See also: 14.49: Luke 19.47; 21.37.

See also: 14.24: a Exod 24.8; b Jer 31.31–34.
14.27: Zech 13.7.   14.28: Matt 28.16.

Jesus is questioned by the council

This is also told in Matthew 26.57–68;
Luke 22.54–55,63–71; John 18.13–14,19–24

53 Jesus was led off to the high priest. Then
the chief priests, the nation's leaders, and the
teachers of the Law of Moses all met together.
54 Peter had followed at a distance. And when
he reached the courtyard of the high priest's
house, he sat down with the guards to warm
himself beside a fire.

55 The chief priests and the whole council
tried to find someone to accuse Jesus of a
crime, so they could put him to death. But
they could not find anyone to accuse him.
56 Many people did tell lies against Jesus,
but they did not agree on what they said.
57 Finally, some men stood up and lied about
him. They said, 58 "We heard him say he
would tear down this temple that we built.
He also claimed that in three days he would
build another one without any help." 59 But
even then they did not agree on what they
said.

60 The high priest stood up in the council
and asked Jesus, "Why don't you say
something in your own defence? Don't you
hear the charges they are making against
you?" 61 But Jesus kept quiet and did not say a
word. The high priest asked him another
question, "Are you the Messiah, the Son of
the glorious God?"*

62 "Yes, I am!" Jesus answered.

> "Soon you will see
>   the Son of Man
> sitting at the right side*
>   of God All-Powerful,
> and coming with the clouds
>   of heaven."

63 At once the high priest ripped his robe
apart and shouted, "Why do we need more
witnesses? 64 You heard him claim to be God!
What is your decision?" They all agreed that
he should be put to death.

65 Some of the people started spitting on
Jesus. They blindfolded him, hit him with
their fists, and said, "Tell us who hit you!"
Then the guards took charge of Jesus and beat
him.

Peter says he doesn't know Jesus

This is also told in Matthew 26.69–75; Luke 22.56–62;
John 18.15–18,25–27

66 While Peter was still in the courtyard,
a servant girl of the high priest came up
67 and saw Peter warming himself by the fire.
She stared at him and said, "You were with
Jesus from Nazareth!"

68 Peter replied, "That isn't true! I don't
know what you're talking about. I don't have
any idea what you mean." He went out to the
gate, and a cock crowed.᾽

69 The servant girl saw Peter again and said
to the people standing there, "This man is
one of them!"

70 "No, I'm not!" Peter replied.

A little while later some of the people said
to Peter, "You certainly are one of them.
You're a Galilean!"

71 This time Peter began to curse and swear,
"I don't even know the man you're talking
about!"

72 Straight away the cock crowed a second
time. Then Peter remembered that Jesus had
told him, "Before a cock crows twice, you will
say three times that you don't know me." So
Peter started crying.

CHAPTER 15

Pilate questions Jesus

This is also told in Matthew 27.1–2,11–14;
Luke 23.1–5; John 18.28–38

1 Early the next morning the chief priests, the
nation's leaders, and the teachers of the Law
of Moses met together with the whole Jewish
council. They tied up Jesus and led him off to
Pilate.

2 He asked Jesus, "Are you the king of the
Jews?"

"Those are your words," Jesus answered.

3 The chief priests brought many charges
against Jesus. 4 Then Pilate questioned him
again, "Don't you have anything to say?
Don't you hear what crimes they say you
have done?" 5 But Jesus did not answer, and
Pilate was amazed.

The death sentence

This is also told in Matthew 27.15–26; Luke 23.13–25;
John 18.39–19.16

6 During Passover, Pilate always freed one
prisoner chosen by the people. 7 And at
that time there was a prisoner named
Barabbas. He and some others had been
arrested for murder during a riot. 8 The

---

*14.61 Son of the glorious God: "Son of God" was
one of the titles used for the kings of Israel.
*14.62 right side: See the note at 12.36.
See also: 14.58: John 2.19. 14.62: Dan 7.13.
14.64: Lev 24.16.

crowd now came and asked Pilate to set a prisoner free, just as he usually did.

⁹ Pilate asked them, "Do you want me to free the king of the Jews?" ¹⁰ Pilate knew that the chief priests had brought Jesus to him because they were jealous.

¹¹ But the chief priests told the crowd to ask Pilate to free Barabbas.

¹² Then Pilate asked the crowd, "What do you want me to do with this man you say is' the king of the Jews?"

¹³ They yelled, "Nail him to a cross!"

¹⁴ Pilate asked, "But what crime has he done?"

"Nail him to a cross!" they yelled even louder.

¹⁵ Pilate wanted to please the crowd. So he set Barabbas free. Then he ordered his soldiers to beat Jesus with a whip and nail him to a cross.

Soldiers make fun of Jesus
This is also told in Matthew 27.27–30; John 19.2–3

¹⁶ The soldiers led Jesus inside the courtyard of the fortress* and called together the rest of the troops. ¹⁷ They put a purple robe* on him, and on his head they placed a crown that they had made out of thorn branches. ¹⁸ They made fun of Jesus and shouted, "Hey, you king of the Jews!" ¹⁹ Then they beat him on the head with a stick. They spat on him and knelt down and pretended to worship him.

²⁰ When the soldiers had finished making fun of Jesus, they took off the purple robe. They put his own clothes back on him and led him off to be nailed to a cross. ²¹ Simon from Cyrene happened to be coming in from a farm, and they forced him to carry Jesus' cross. Simon was the father of Alexander and Rufus.

Jesus is nailed to a cross
This is also told in Matthew 27.31–44; Luke 23.27–43; John 19.17–27

²² The soldiers took Jesus to Golgotha, which means "Place of a Skull".* ²³ There

they gave him some wine mixed with a drug to ease the pain, but he refused to drink it.

²⁴ They nailed Jesus to a cross and gambled to see who would get his clothes. ²⁵ It was about nine o'clock in the morning when they nailed him to the cross. ²⁶ On it was a sign that told why he was nailed there. It read, "This is the King of the Jews." ²⁷⁻²⁸ The soldiers also nailed two criminals on crosses, one to the right of Jesus and the other to his left.'

²⁹ People who passed by said terrible things about Jesus. They shook their heads and shouted, "Ha! So you're the one who claimed you could tear down the temple and build it again in three days. ³⁰ Save yourself and come down from the cross!"

³¹ The chief priests and the teachers of the Law of Moses also made fun of Jesus. They said to each other, "He saved others, but he can't save himself. ³² If he is the Messiah, the king of Israel, let him come down from the cross! Then we will see and believe." The two criminals also said cruel things to Jesus.

The death of Jesus
This is also told in Matthew 27.45–56; Luke 23.44–49; John 19.28–30

³³ About midday the sky turned dark and stayed that way until around three o'clock. ³⁴ Then about that time Jesus shouted, "Eloi, Eloi, lema sabachthani?"* which means, "My God, my God, why have you deserted me?"

³⁵ Some of the people standing there heard Jesus and said, "He is calling for Elijah."* ³⁶ One of them ran and grabbed a sponge. After he had soaked it in wine, he put it on a stick and held it up to Jesus. He said, "Let's wait and see if Elijah will come* and take him down!" ³⁷ Jesus shouted and then died.

³⁸ At once the curtain in the temple* tore in two from top to bottom.

---

*15.34 Eloi . . . sabachthani: These words are in Aramaic, a language spoken in Palestine during the time of Jesus.
*15.35 Elijah: The name "Elijah" sounds something like "Eloi", which means "my God".
*15.36 see if Elijah will come: See the note at 6.15.
*15.38 curtain in the temple: There were two curtains in the temple. One was at the entrance, and the other separated the holy place from the most holy place that the Jewish people thought of as God's home on earth. The second curtain is probably the one which is meant.

See also: 15.24: Psa 22.18. 15.28: Isa 53.12.
15.29: a Psa 22.7; 109.25; b Mark 14.58; John 2.19.
15.34: Psa 22.1. 15.36: Psa 69.21. 15.38: Exod 26.31–33.

---

*15.16 fortress: The place where the Roman governor stayed. It was probably at Herod's palace west of Jerusalem, though it may have been Fortress Antonia, north of the temple, where the Roman troops were stationed.
*15.17 purple robe: This was probably a Roman soldier's robe.
*15.22 Place of a Skull: The place was probably given this name because it was near a large rock in the shape of a human skull.

See also: 15.21: Rom 16.13.

Big ideas

Cross

The cross is the most powerful symbol of Christianity. It reminds us of Jesus' death for us; of the way that he was willing to die the most painful death in order to bring humanity back to God. But why was it necessary for Jesus to die in this way? Why was it necessary for him to die at all?

Example

Jesus' death is an example we should follow. He was treated unfairly and brutally, but he did not fight back and he did not complain. Now all Christians are called to 'take up their cross' and follow his example.

Revolution

To the Romans, Jesus was a political agitator. To the Jewish leaders he was a false messiah, blaspheming against God and insulting their authority. The cross shows Jesus as a revolutionary, who stood against the oppression and injustice around him.

Sacrifice

We should be punished for our sin, but Jesus took our punishment for us. He has served our sentence, paid our fine. We will physically die, but if we have faith in Jesus, we won't suffer punishment, because someone has already done that for us.

Identification

Jesus' death means that there is nothing I can go through that he does not understand. We cannot accuse God of not knowing about suffering; through Jesus, he lived and died as a full part of humanity.

 Footsteps

A week on the Cross

Jesus is nailed to the cross: Mark 15.22–32
The cross cannot hold him: Luke 23.54—24.9
The miracle worker you killed: Acts 2.22–36
The world's folly: 1 Corinthians 1.18–28
Only the cross: Galatians 6.11–18
The charges wiped out: Colossians 2.9–15
Keep your eyes on Jesus: Hebrews 12.1–3

[39] A Roman army officer was standing in front of Jesus. When the officer saw how Jesus died, he said, "This man really was the Son of God!"
[40–41] Some women were looking on from a distance. They had come with Jesus to Jerusalem. But even before this they had been his followers and had helped him while he was in Galilee. Mary Magdalene and Mary the mother of the younger James and of Joseph were two of these women. Salome was also one of them.

Jesus is buried

This is also told in Matthew 27.57–61; Luke 23.50–56; John 19.38–42

[42] It was now the evening before the Sabbath, and the Jewish people were getting ready for that sacred day. [43] A man named Joseph from Arimathea was brave enough to ask Pilate for the body of Jesus. Joseph was a highly respected member of the Jewish council, and he was also waiting for God's kingdom to come.
[44] Pilate was surprised to hear that Jesus was already dead, and he called in the army officer to find out if Jesus had been dead very long. [45] After the officer told him, Pilate let Joseph have Jesus' body.
[46] Joseph bought a linen cloth and took the body down from the cross. He had it wrapped in the cloth, and he put it in a tomb that had been cut into solid rock. Then he rolled a big stone against the entrance to the tomb.
[47] Mary Magdalene and Mary the mother of Joseph were watching and saw where the body was placed.

Jesus is alive

CHAPTER 16

This is also told in Matthew 28.1–8; Luke 24.1–12; John 20.1–10

[1] After the Sabbath, Mary Magdalene, Salome, and Mary the mother of James bought some spices to put on Jesus' body. [2] Very early on Sunday morning, just as the sun was coming up, they went to the tomb. [3] On their way, they were asking one another, "Who will roll the stone away from the entrance for us?" [4] But when they looked, they saw that the stone had already been rolled away. And it was a huge stone!

See also: 15.40–41: Luke 8.2–3.

⁵ The women went into the tomb, and on the right side they saw a young man in a white robe sitting there. They were alarmed. ⁶ The man said, "Don't be alarmed! You are looking for Jesus from Nazareth, who was nailed to a cross. God has raised him to life, and he isn't here. You can see the place where they put his body. ⁷ Now go and tell his disciples, and especially Peter, that he will go ahead of you to Galilee. You will see him there, just as he told you."

⁸ When the women ran from the tomb, they were confused and shaking all over. They were too afraid to tell anyone what had happened.

Jesus appears to his followers

ONE OLD ENDING TO MARK'S GOSPEL›

Jesus appears to Mary Magdalene

This is also told in Matthew 28.9–10; John 20.11–18

⁹ Very early on the first day of the week, after Jesus had risen to life, he appeared to Mary Magdalene. Earlier he had forced seven demons out of her. ¹⁰ She left and told his friends, who were crying and mourning. ¹¹ Even though they heard that Jesus was alive and that Mary had seen him, they would not believe it.

Jesus appears to two disciples

This is also told in Luke 24.13–35

¹² Later, Jesus appeared in another form to two disciples, as they were on their way out of the city. ¹³ But when these disciples told what had happened, the others would not believe.

What Jesus' followers must do

This is also told in Matthew 28.16–20; Luke 24.36–49; John 20.19–23; Acts 1.6–8

¹⁴ Afterwards, Jesus appeared to his eleven disciples as they were eating. He scolded them because they were too stubborn to believe the ones who had seen him after he had been raised to life. ¹⁵ Then he told them:

Go and preach the good news to everyone in the world. ¹⁶ Anyone who believes me and is baptized will be saved. But anyone who refuses to believe me will be condemned. ¹⁷ Everyone who believes me will be able to do wonderful things. By using my name they will force out demons,

and they will speak new languages. ¹⁸ They will handle snakes and will drink poison and not be hurt. They will also heal sick people by placing their hands on them.

Jesus returns to heaven

This is also told in Luke 24.50–53; Acts 1.9–11

¹⁹ After the Lord Jesus had said these things to the disciples, he was taken back up to heaven where he sat down at the right side* of God. ²⁰ Then the disciples left and preached everywhere. The Lord was with them, and the miracles they performed proved that their message was true.

ANOTHER OLD ENDING TO MARK'S GOSPEL›

⁹⁻¹⁰ The women quickly told Peter and his friends what had happened. Later, Jesus sent the disciples to the east and to the west with his sacred and everlasting message of how people can be saved for ever.

---

*16.19 right side: See the note at 12.36.

See also: 16.19: Acts 1.9–11.

Additional notes

›1.1 the Son of God: These words are not in some manuscripts.
›1.14 that comes from God: Or "that is about God".
›1.15 will soon be here: Or "is already here".
›1.40 and knelt down: These words are not in some manuscripts.
›1.41 felt sorry for: Some manuscripts have "was angry with".
›2.1 at home: Or "in the house" (perhaps Simon Peter's home).
›2.15 Levi's house: Or "Jesus' house".
›3.14 to be his apostles: These words are not in some manuscripts.
›3.20 went back home: Or "entered a house" (perhaps the home of Simon Peter).
›3.32 and sisters: These words are not in some manuscripts.
›5.1 Gerasa: Some manuscripts have "Gadara", and others have "Gergesa".
›5.36 heard: Or "ignored".
›6.3 carpenter: The Greek word may also mean someone who builds or works with stone or brick.
›6.20 was confused by what John said: Some manuscripts have "did many things because of what John said".
›6.22 Herodias: Some manuscripts have "Herod".
›7.3 in the proper way: The Greek text has "with the fist", but the exact meaning is not clear. It could mean "to the wrist" or "to the elbow".

See also: 16.7: Matt 26.32; Mark 14.28. 16.15: Acts 1.8.

›**7.4 bowls:** Some manuscripts add "and sleeping mats".

›**7.15–16 unclean:** Some manuscripts add, "If you have ears, pay attention."

›**8.35 life:** In verses 35–37 the same Greek word is translated "life", "yourself", and "soul".

›**9.43–44 never go out:** Some manuscripts add, "The worms there never die, and the fire never stops burning."

›**9.45–46 thrown into hell:** See the note at 9.43–44.

›**10.14 People who are like these little children belong to the kingdom of God:** Or "The kingdom of God belongs to people who are like these little children."

›**10.24 hard:** Some manuscripts add "for people who trust in their wealth". Others add "for the rich".

›**10.51 Master:** A Hebrew word that may also mean "Teacher".

›**11.3 The Lord:** Or "The master of the donkey".

›**11.25–26 your sins:** Some manuscripts add, "But if you do not forgive others, God will not forgive you."

›**13.29 the time has almost come:** Or "he (that is, the Son of Man) will soon be here."

›**14.3 sweet-smelling perfume:** The Greek text has "perfume made of pure spikenard", a plant used to make perfume.

›**14.35–36 Father:** The Greek text has "Abba", which is an Aramaic word meaning "father".

›**14.41 Are you still sleeping and resting?:** Or "You may as well keep on sleeping and resting."

›**14.68 a cock crowed:** These words are not in some manuscripts.

›**15.12 this man you say is:** These words are not in some manuscripts.

›**15.27–28 left:** Some manuscripts add, "So the Scriptures came true which say, 'He was accused of being a criminal.' "

›**16.9 One old ending to Mark's Gospel:** Verses 9–20 are not in some manuscripts.

›**16.9–10 Another old ending to Mark's Gospel:** Some manuscripts and early translations have both this shorter ending and the longer one (verses 9–20).

Luke

tells the good news

The basics

What's the point? The good news is for the gentiles and for the poor and oppressed.

What happens? Luke makes a careful study of the facts, then he organises them and puts them together to form the case for Christ.

What should I remember? 1.3–4 'So I made a careful study of everything and then I decided to write and tell you exactly what took place... I have done this to let you know the truth about what you have heard.'

More details

Setting the scene Luke was an educated man, a doctor who had spent time working alongside Paul. He decides to write an account of Jesus' life, one based on a careful collection of all the sources...

What's it all about? Luke's aim is to write a proper history of what actually happened. The book is addressed to someone called Theophilus who may have been a high-ranking Roman official. Luke is making the case for Christ. He's looked at all the accounts, examined all the evidence, and this is his report. Luke's intention was to argue the case for Christianity; to counter ignorant and ill-founded reports. So he includes stories and songs that had been handed down among the early Church, such as the songs of Mary (1.46–55), Zechariah (1.68–79) and Simeon (2.29–32).

But the result is not some dry and stuffy history, rather a joyful, optimistic account. It's especially joyful because, in Luke's Gospel, it's the poor and the marginalised who get the full blast of the good news. Luke's account is

packed with tax collectors, prostitutes, lepers and thieves. The news of Jesus' birth comes not to the foreign 'wise men' as in Matthew, but to humble, despised shepherds. Significantly, Luke's Gospel also shows a respect for women that is highly unusual for the time. Luke's Gospel begins with two mothers celebrating and significant encounters of women with Jesus feature throughout. Here, women – who were also second-class citizens in Bible times, like the shepherds – play key roles.

Luke is also writing for a gentile audience. He was a gentile himself, probably from Antioch. So his gospel also features gentile 'heroes' such as Centurions and Samaritans. Like Matthew he includes a genealogy, but his goes back to Adam, the father of all.

Luke's gospel is the first part of a two-part work. He also wrote the book of Acts, which takes the story forward from the resurrection of Jesus through the spread of the early church.

Footsteps

Why Luke wrote this book

CHAPTER 1

[1] Many people have tried to tell the story of what God has done among us. [2] They wrote what we had been told by the ones who were there in the beginning and saw what happened. [3] So I made a careful study of everything and then decided to write and tell you exactly what took place. Honourable Theophilus,* [4] I have done this to let you know the truth about what you have heard.

The births of John the Baptist and Jesus

An angel tells about the birth of John

[5] When Herod was king of Judea, there was a priest called Zechariah from the priestly group of Abijah. His wife Elizabeth was from the family of Aaron.* [6] Both of them were good people and pleased the Lord God by obeying all that he had commanded. [7] But they did not have children. Elizabeth could not have any, and both Zechariah and Elizabeth were already old.

[8] One day Zechariah's group of priests were on duty, and he was serving God as a priest. [9] According to the custom of the priests, he had been chosen to go into the Lord's temple that day and to burn incense,* [10] while the people stood outside praying.

[11] All at once an angel from the Lord appeared to Zechariah at the right side of the altar. [12] Zechariah was confused and afraid when he saw the angel. [13] But the angel told him:

---

*1.3 Honourable Theophilus: Luke dedicated his Gospel and the Acts of the Apostles to this man, probably a high Roman official.
*1.5 Aaron: The brother of Moses and the first priest.
*1.9 burn incense: This was done twice a day, once in the morning and again in the late afternoon.
See also: 1.5: 1 Chron 24.10.

Life files

Mary a.k.a. The mother of Jesus

Background: Mother of Jesus, mother of 'the younger James, Joseph, Simon and Judas'.

What's the story?

Mary was a teenage bride. In those days, brides could be as young as 12, but she was probably a few years older.

From a poor family, she had a deep faith, as her reaction to the news from the angel shows. She endured a hard journey to Bethlehem and gave birth to Jesus among the animals. She, above all, knew who Jesus was, but she still had some doubts about his mission (Mark 3.21). But what mother doesn't worry about her child's career?

Even so, she was there at the end, standing by the cross while her son died a horrific death. She was also among the first to know of his resurrection, after she visited the tomb. She is known as 'the Virgin Mary' because Jesus was born by the Holy Spirit, but after Jesus' birth she seems to have had several more children.

What's the point?

Think of what Mary had to go through! The scandal of her pregnancy, the journey to Bethlehem, the birth amidst the filth of the animals. Yet she obeyed and trusted in God. This girl was given perhaps the greatest task any human has ever had: to give birth to and bring up the son of God. And she did it, with faith, humility and courage.

Anorak corner

She's really Miriam. Mary is the Greek version.

 Footsteps

A week with Mary

The announcement: Luke 1.26–38
Mary's song: Luke 1.27–56
Straw and shepherds: Luke 2.1–21
Where's he gone (part 1)? Luke 2.41–52
A family visit: Mark 3.20–35
At the death: John 19.17–27
Where's he gone (part 2)? Luke 24.1–12

Don't be afraid, Zechariah! God has heard your prayers. Your wife Elizabeth will have a son, and you must name him John. ¹⁴ His birth will make you very happy, and many people will be glad. ¹⁵ Your son will be a great servant of the Lord. He must never drink wine or beer, and the power of the Holy Spirit will be with him from the time he is born.

¹⁶ John will lead many people in Israel to turn back to the Lord their God. ¹⁷ He will go ahead of the Lord with the same power and spirit that Elijah* had. And because of John, parents will be more thoughtful of their children. And people who now disobey God will begin to think as they ought to. That is how John will get people ready for the Lord.

¹⁸ Zechariah said to the angel, "How will I know this is going to happen? My wife and I are both very old."

¹⁹ The angel answered, "I am Gabriel, God's servant, and I was sent to tell you this good news. ²⁰ You have not believed what I have said. So you will not be able to say a thing until all this happens. But everything will take place when it is supposed to."

²¹ The crowd was waiting for Zechariah and kept wondering why he was staying so long in the temple. ²² When he did come out, he could not speak, and they knew he had seen a vision. He motioned to them with his hands, but did not say a thing.

²³ When Zechariah's time of service in the temple was over, he went home. ²⁴ Soon after that, his wife was expecting a baby, and for five months she did not leave the house. She said to herself, ²⁵ "What the Lord has done for me will keep people from looking down on me."*

An angel tells about the birth of Jesus

²⁶ One month later God sent the angel Gabriel to the town of Nazareth in Galilee ²⁷ with a message for a virgin named Mary. She was engaged to Joseph from the family of King David. ²⁸ The angel greeted Mary and said, "You are truly blessed! The Lord is with you."

²⁹ Mary was confused by the angel's words and wondered what they meant. ³⁰ Then the angel told Mary, "Don't be afraid! God is pleased with you, ³¹ and you will have a son. His name will be Jesus. ³² He will be great and will be called the Son of God Most High. The Lord God will make him king, as his ancestor David was. ³³ He will rule the people of Israel for ever, and his kingdom will have no end."

³⁴ Mary asked the angel, "How can this happen? I am not married!"

³⁵ The angel answered, "The Holy Spirit will come down to you, and God's power will come over you. So your child will be called the holy Son of God. ³⁶ Your relative Elizabeth is also going to have a son, even though she is old. No one thought she could ever have a baby, but in three months she will have a son. ³⁷ Nothing is impossible for God!"

³⁸ Mary said, "I am the Lord's servant! Let it happen as you have said." And the angel left her.

Mary visits Elizabeth

³⁹ A short time later Mary hurried to a town in the hill country of Judea. ⁴⁰ She went into Zechariah's home, where she greeted Elizabeth. ⁴¹ When Elizabeth heard Mary's greeting, her baby moved within her.

The Holy Spirit came upon Elizabeth. ⁴² Then in a loud voice she said to Mary:

God has blessed you more than any other woman! He has also blessed the child you will have. ⁴³ Why should the mother of my Lord come to me? ⁴⁴ As soon as I heard your greeting, my baby became happy and moved within me. ⁴⁵ The Lord has blessed you because you believed that he will keep his promise.

Mary's song of praise

⁴⁶ Mary said:

With all my heart
I praise the Lord,
⁴⁷ and I am glad
because of God my Saviour.
⁴⁸ He cares for me,
his humble servant.
From now on,
all people will say
God has blessed me.

*1.17 Elijah: The prophet Elijah was known for his power to perform miracles.
*1.25 keep people from looking down on me: When a married woman could not have children, it was thought that the Lord was punishing her.
See also: 1.15: Num 6.3. 1.17: Mal 4.5–6. 1.19: Dan 8.16; 9.21. 1.27: Matt 1.18.

See also: 1.31: Matt 1.21. 1.32–33: 2 Sam 7.12–13,16; Isa 9.7. 1.37: Gen 18.14. 1.46–55: 1 Sam 2.1–10. 1.48: 1 Sam 1.11.

⁴⁹ God All-Powerful has done
   great things for me,
      and his name is holy.
⁵⁰ He always shows mercy
   to everyone
      who worships him.
⁵¹ The Lord has used
   his powerful arm
      to scatter those
      who are proud.
⁵² He drags strong rulers
   from their thrones
   and puts humble people
      in places of power.
⁵³ God gives the hungry
   good things to eat,
   and sends the rich away
      with nothing.
⁵⁴ He helps his servant Israel
   and is always merciful
      to his people.
⁵⁵ The Lord made this promise
   to our ancestors,
   to Abraham and his family
      for ever!

⁵⁶ Mary stayed with Elizabeth about three
months. Then she went back home.

The birth of John the Baptist

⁵⁷ When Elizabeth's son was born, ⁵⁸ her
neighbours and relatives heard how kind the
Lord had been to her, and they too were glad.

⁵⁹ Eight days later they did for the child
what the Law of Moses commands.* They
were going to name him Zechariah, after his
father. ⁶⁰ But Elizabeth said, "No! His name is
John."

⁶¹ The people argued, "No one in your
family has ever been named John." ⁶² So they
motioned to Zechariah to find out what he
wanted to name his son.

⁶³ Zechariah asked for a writing tablet.
Then he wrote, "His name is John." Everyone
was amazed. ⁶⁴ Straight away Zechariah
started speaking and praising God.

⁶⁵ All the neighbours were frightened
because of what had happened, and
everywhere in the hill country people kept
talking about these things. ⁶⁶ Everyone
who heard about this wondered what this

child would grow up to be. They knew
that the Lord was with him.

Zechariah praises the Lord

⁶⁷ The Holy Spirit came upon Zechariah, and
he began to speak:

⁶⁸ Praise the Lord,
   the God of Israel!
   He has come
      to save his people.
⁶⁹ Our God has given us
   a mighty Saviour*
   from the family
      of David his servant.
⁷⁰ Long ago the Lord promised
   by the words
      of his holy prophets
⁷¹ to save us from our enemies
   and from everyone
      who hates us.
⁷² God said he would be kind
   to our people and keep
      his sacred promise.
⁷³ He told our ancestor Abraham
⁷⁴ that he would rescue us
   from our enemies.
   Then we could serve him
      without fear,
⁷⁵ by being holy and good
   as long as we live.

⁷⁶ You, my son, will be called
   a prophet of God
      in heaven above.
   You will go ahead of the Lord
   to get everything ready
      for him.
⁷⁷ You will tell his people
   that they can be saved
   when their sins
      are forgiven.
⁷⁸ God's love and kindness
   will shine upon us
   like the sun that rises
      in the sky.›
⁷⁹ On us who live
   in the dark shadow
      of death
   this light will shine
   to guide us
      into a life of peace.

---

*1.59 what the Law of Moses commands: This refers
to circumcision. It is the cutting off of skin from the
private part of Jewish boys eight days after birth to
show that they belong to the Lord.
See also: 1.52: Job 5.11; 12.19. **1.55:** Gen 17.7.
1.59: Lev 12.3.

---

*1.69 a mighty Saviour: The Greek text has "a horn
of salvation". In the Scriptures animal horns are often
a symbol of great strength.
See also: 1.76: Mal 3.1. **1.79:** Isa 9.2.

80 As John grew up, God's Spirit gave him great power. John lived in the desert until the time he was sent to the people of Israel.

CHAPTER 2

The birth of Jesus

This is also told in Matthew 1.18–25

1 About that time Emperor Augustus gave orders for the names of all the people to be listed in record books.* 2 These first records were made when Quirinius was governor of Syria.*

3 Everyone had to go to their own home town to be listed. 4 So Joseph had to leave Nazareth in Galilee and go to Bethlehem in Judea. Long ago Bethlehem had been King David's home town, and Joseph went there because he was from David's family.

5 Mary was engaged to Joseph and travelled with him to Bethlehem. She was soon going to have a baby, 6 and while they were there, 7 she gave birth to her firstborn* son. She dressed him in baby clothes* and laid him on a bed of hay, because there was no room for them in the inn.

The shepherds

8 That night in the fields near Bethlehem some shepherds were guarding their sheep. 9 All at once an angel came down to them from the Lord, and the brightness of the Lord's glory flashed around them. The shepherds were frightened. 10 But the angel said, "Don't be afraid! I have good news for you, which will make everyone happy. 11 This very day in King David's home town a Saviour was born for you. He is Christ the Lord. 12 You will know who he is, because you will find him dressed in baby clothes* and lying on a bed of hay."

13 Suddenly many other angels came down from heaven and joined in praising God. They said:

14 "Praise God in heaven!
  Peace on earth to everyone
    who pleases God."

15 After the angels had left and gone back to heaven, the shepherds said to each other, "Let's go to Bethlehem and see what the Lord has told us about." 16 They hurried off and found Mary and Joseph, and they saw the baby lying on a bed of hay.

17 When the shepherds saw Jesus, they told his parents what the angel had said about him. 18 Everyone listened and was surprised. 19 But Mary kept thinking about all this and wondering what it meant.

20 As the shepherds returned to their sheep, they were praising God and saying wonderful things about him. Everything they had seen and heard was just as the angel had said.

21 Eight days later Jesus' parents did for him what the Law of Moses commands.* And they named him Jesus, just as the angel had told Mary when he promised she would have a baby.

Simeon praises the Lord

22 The time came for Mary and Joseph to do what the Law of Moses says a mother is supposed to do after her baby is born.*

They took Jesus to the temple in Jerusalem and presented him to the Lord, 23 just as the Law of the Lord says, "Each firstborn* baby boy belongs to the Lord." 24 The Law of the Lord also says that parents have to offer a sacrifice, giving at least a pair of doves or two young pigeons. So that is what Mary and Joseph did.

25 At this time a man named Simeon was living in Jerusalem. Simeon was a good man. He loved God and was waiting for God to save the people of Israel. God's Spirit came to him 26 and told him that he would not die until he had seen Christ the Lord.

---

*2.1 names . . . listed in record books: This was done so that everyone could be made to pay taxes to the Emperor.

*2.2 Quirinius was governor of Syria: It is known that Quirinius made a record of the people in AD 6 or 7. But the exact date of the record taking that Luke mentions is not known.

*2.7 firstborn: The Jewish people said that the firstborn son in each of their families belonged to the Lord.

*2.7,12 dressed him in baby clothes: The Greek text has "wrapped him in wide strips of cloth", which was how young babies were dressed.

---

*2.21 what the Law of Moses commands: See the note at 1.59.

*2.22 after her baby is born: After a Jewish mother gave birth to a son, she was considered "unclean" and had to stay at home until he was circumcised (see the note at 1.59). Then she had to stay at home for another 33 days, before offering a sacrifice to the Lord.

*2.23 firstborn: See the note at 2.7.

See also: 2.21: a Lev 12.3; b Luke 1.31.
2.22–24: Lev 12.6–8. 2.23: Exod 13.2,12.

27 When Mary and Joseph brought Jesus to the temple to do what the Law of Moses says should be done for a new baby, the Spirit told Simeon to go into the temple. 28 Simeon took the baby Jesus in his arms and praised God,

29 "Lord, I am your servant,
    and now I can die in peace,
    because you have kept
        your promise to me.
30 With my own eyes I have seen
    what you have done
        to save your people,
31 and foreign nations
    will also see this.
32 Your mighty power is a light
    for all nations,
    and it will bring honour
        to your people Israel."

33 Jesus' parents were surprised at what Simeon had said. 34 Then he blessed them and told Mary, "This child of yours will cause many people in Israel to fall and others to stand. The child will be like a warning sign. Many people will reject him, 35 and you, Mary, will suffer as though you had been stabbed by a dagger. But all this will show what people are really thinking."

Anna speaks about the child Jesus

36 The prophet Anna was also there in the temple. She was the daughter of Phanuel from the tribe of Asher, and she was very old. In her youth she had been married for seven years, but her husband had died. 37 And now she was eighty-four years old.' Night and day she served God in the temple by praying and often going without eating.*

38 At that time Anna came in and praised God. She spoke about the child Jesus to everyone who hoped for Jerusalem to be set free.

The return to Nazareth

39 After Joseph and Mary had done everything that the Law of the Lord commands, they returned home to Nazareth in Galilee. 40 The child Jesus grew. He became strong and wise, and God blessed him.

The boy Jesus in the temple

41 Every year Jesus' parents went to Jerusalem for Passover. 42 And when Jesus was twelve years old, they all went there as usual for the celebration. 43 After Passover his parents left, but they did not know that Jesus had stayed on in the city. 44 They thought he was travelling with some other people, and they went a whole day before they started looking for him. 45 When they could not find him with their relatives and friends, they went back to Jerusalem and started looking for him there.

46 Three days later they found Jesus sitting in the temple, listening to the teachers and asking them questions. 47 Everyone who heard him was surprised at how much he knew and at the answers he gave.

48 When his parents found him, they were amazed. His mother said, "Son, why have you done this to us? Your father and I have been very worried, and we have been searching for you!"

49 Jesus answered, "Why did you have to look for me? Didn't you know that I would be in my Father's house?"' 50 But they did not understand what he meant.

51 Jesus went back to Nazareth with his parents and obeyed them. His mother kept on thinking about all that had happened.

52 Jesus became wise, and he grew strong. God was pleased with him and so were the people.

The message of John the Baptist

CHAPTER 3

The preaching of John the Baptist

This is also told in Matthew 3.1–12; Mark 1.1–8; John 1.19–28

1 For fifteen years* Emperor Tiberius had ruled that part of the world. Pontius Pilate was governor of Judea, and Herod* was the ruler of Galilee. Herod's brother, Philip, was the ruler in the countries of Iturea and Trachonitis, and Lysanias was the ruler of

---

*2.37 without eating: The Jewish people sometimes went without eating (also called "fasting") to show their love for God or to show sorrow for their sins.
See also: 2.32: Isa 42.6; 49.6; 52.10. 2.39: Matt 2.23.

---

*3.1 For fifteen years: This was either AD 28 or 29, and Jesus was about thirty years old (see 3.23).
*3.1 Herod: Herod Antipas, the son of Herod the Great.
See also: 2.41: Exod 12.1–27; Deut 16.1–8. 2.52: 1 Sam 2.26; Prov 3.4.

Abilene. ² Annas and Caiaphas were the Jewish high priests.*

At that time God spoke to Zechariah's son John, who was living in the desert. ³ So John went along the Jordan Valley, telling the people, "Turn back to God and be baptized! Then your sins will be forgiven." ⁴ Isaiah the prophet wrote about John when he said,

> "In the desert
>   someone is shouting,
>   'Get the road ready
>   for the Lord!
> Make a straight path
>   for him.
> ⁵ Fill up every valley
>   and level every mountain
>   and hill.
> Straighten the crooked paths
>   and smooth out
>   the rough roads.
> ⁶ Then everyone will see
>   the saving power of God.' "

⁷ Crowds of people came out to be baptized, but John said to them, "You snakes! Who warned you to run from the coming judgment? ⁸ Do something to show that you really have given up your sins. Don't start saying that you belong to Abraham's family. God can turn these stones into children for Abraham.* ⁹ An axe is ready to cut the trees down at their roots. Any tree that doesn't produce good fruit will be cut down and thrown into a fire."

¹⁰ The crowds asked John, "What should we do?"

¹¹ John told them, "If you have two coats, give one to someone who doesn't have any. If you have food, share it with someone else."

¹² When tax collectors* came to be baptized, they asked John, "Teacher, what should we do?"

¹³ John told them, "Don't make people pay more than they owe."

---

*3.2 Annas and Caiaphas . . . high priests: Annas was high priest from AD 6 until 15. His son-in-law Caiaphas was high priest from AD 18 until 37.
*3.8 children for Abraham: The Jewish people thought they were God's chosen people because of God's promises to their ancestor Abraham.
*3.12 tax collectors: These were usually Jewish people who paid the Romans for the right to collect taxes. They were hated by other Jews who thought of them as traitors to their country and to their religion.
See also: 3.4–6: Isa 40.3–5 (LXX). 3.7: Matt 12.34; 23.33.
3.8: John 8.33. 3.9: Matt 7.19. 3.12: Luke 7.29.

Life files

John the Baptist

Background: Cousin of Jesus

What's the story?

John was the son of ageing parents, who thought that they would never have a child. He started his preaching work before Jesus. A wild man, living in the desert, he called people to repent of their sins, to say sorry to God and be baptised (hence the name). Jesus came to him for baptism, even though John realised that Jesus didn't need to say sorry for anything.

In the end, John's fiery preaching and outspoken courage got him into trouble. He criticised the king, Herod Antipas, for marrying his brother's wife, accusing him of incest. Herod imprisoned John and, after making a stupid, drunken vow, had to have the prophet beheaded.

What's the point?

John paved the way for Jesus. He was also one of the first people to recognise who Jesus really was: when Jesus came to John for baptism, John refused saying 'I ought to be baptized by you' (Matthew 3.14). John endured harsh conditions and was not afraid to speak out for what was right. Even though it cost him his life, he followed his mission from God to the end.

 Anorak corner

Some of Jesus' followers had been followers of John.

 Footsteps

A week with John the Baptist

A dumbstruck Dad: Luke 1.5–25
The birth of the Baptist: Luke 1.57–80
John's message: Matthew 3.1–12
The baptism of Jesus: Matthew 3.13–17
Jesus talks about John: Matthew 11.1–18
The death of John the Baptist: Mark 6.14–29
Herod confuses the two: Luke 9.7–9

More...

Baptism p.1038
Nazirites p.148

14 Some soldiers asked him, "And what about us? What do we have to do?"

John told them, "Don't force people to pay money to make you leave them alone. Be satisfied with your pay."

15 Everyone became excited and wondered, "Could John be the Messiah?"

16 John said, "I am just baptizing with water. But someone more powerful is going to come, and I am not good enough even to untie his sandals.* He will baptize you with the Holy Spirit and with fire. 17 His threshing fork* is in his hand, and he is ready to separate the wheat from the husks. He will store the wheat in his barn and burn the husks with a fire that never goes out."

18 In many different ways John preached the good news to the people. 19 But to Herod the ruler, he said, "It was wrong for you to take Herodias, your brother's wife." John also said that Herod had done many other bad things. 20 Finally, Herod put John in jail, and this was the worst thing he had done.

The baptism and temptation of Jesus

The baptism of Jesus

This is also told in Matthew 3.13–17; Mark 1.9–11

21 While everyone else was being baptized, Jesus himself was baptized. Then as he prayed, the sky opened up, 22 and the Holy Spirit came down upon him in the form of a dove. A voice from heaven said, "You are my own dear Son, and I am pleased with you."

The ancestors of Jesus

This is also told in Matthew 1.1–17

23 When Jesus began to preach, he was about thirty years old. Everyone thought he was the son of Joseph. But his family went back through Heli, 24 Matthat, Levi, Melchi, Jannai, Joseph, 25 Mattathias, Amos, Nahum, Esli, Naggai, 26 Maath, Mattathias, Semein, Josech, Joda;

27 Joanan, Rhesa, Zerubbabel, Shealtiel, Neri, 28 Melchi, Addi, Cosam, Elmadam, Er, 29 Joshua, Eliezer, Jorim, Matthat, Levi;

30 Simeon, Judah, Joseph, Jonam, Eliakim, 31 Melea, Menna, Mattatha, Nathan, David, 32 Jesse, Obed, Boaz, Salmon, Nahshon;

33 Amminadab, Admin, Arni, Hezron, Perez, Judah, 34 Jacob, Isaac, Abraham, Terah, Nahor, 35 Serug, Reu, Peleg, Eber, Shelah;

36 Cainan, Arphaxad, Shem, Noah, Lamech, 37 Methuselah, Enoch, Jared, Mahalaleel, Kenan, 38 Enosh, and Seth.

The family of Jesus went all the way back to Adam and then to God.

CHAPTER 4

Jesus and the devil

This is also told in Matthew 4.1–11; Mark 1.12–13

1 When Jesus returned from the River Jordan, the power of the Holy Spirit was with him, and the Spirit led him into the desert. 2 For forty days Jesus was tested by the devil, and during that time he went without eating.* When it was all over, he was hungry.

3 The devil said to Jesus, "If you are God's Son, tell this stone to turn into bread."

4 Jesus answered, "The Scriptures say, 'No one can live only on food.' "

5 Then the devil led Jesus up to a high place and quickly showed him all the nations on earth. 6 The devil said, "I will give all this power and glory to you. It has been given to me, and I can give it to anyone I want to. 7 Just worship me, and you can have it all."

8 Jesus answered, "The Scriptures say:

'Worship the Lord your God
    and serve only him!' "

9 Finally, the devil took Jesus to Jerusalem and had him stand on top of the temple. The devil said, "If you are God's Son, jump off. 10-11 The Scriptures say:

'God will tell his angels
    to take care of you.
They will catch you
    in their arms,
and you will not hurt
    your feet on the stones.' "

12 Jesus answered, "The Scriptures also say, 'Don't try to test the Lord your God!' "

---

*3.16 untie his sandals: This was the duty of a slave.
*3.17 threshing fork: After Jewish farmers had trampled out the grain, they used a large fork to pitch the grain and the husks into the air. Wind would blow away the light husks, and the grain would fall back to the ground, where it could be gathered up.

See also: 3.19–20: Matt 14.3–4; Mark 6.17–18.
3.22: Gen 22.2; Psa 2.7; Isa 42.1; Matt 3.17; Mark 1.11; Luke 9.35.

---

*4.2 went without eating: See the note at 2.37.
See also: 4.4: Deut 8.3. 4.8: Deut 6.13.
4.10–11: Psa 91.11–12. 4.12: Deut 6.16.

Holy history

Synagogues

The Jews were supposed to worship God in the temple, with animal sacrifices and elaborate rituals.

But when they were taken into exile in Babylon, there was no temple at which they could worship, no central point where they could gather to make sacrifices. So their faith became much more personal, and more focused on reading and discussion of the Scriptures. Instead of the elaborate rituals of sacrifice, they had to rely on personal prayer.

When they returned to Jerusalem, this attitude persisted. The Jewish faith became more simple. It could be practised anywhere there was a scroll and someone to read it.

This led to the establishment of synagogues, which were small, local meeting places, where Jews gathered to worship and study the Scriptures. These synagogues also served as schools where local boys were educated (girls didn't get educated, because, well, they were girls...)

The people sat on benches around the walls and and the synagogue leader or a rabbi would read a passage, talk about it and then answer questions.

Often a visiting teacher would be invited to choose a passage from the scriptures to talk about. Here Jesus, on a visit to his home town, chooses a classic passage of prophecy from Isaiah in order to explain who he was and what he was all about. And he upset quite a few people in the process...

More...

Pharisees, Sadducees and the rest p.1097
Temples and shrines p.296
Jesus' teaching p.1055

[13] After the devil had finished testing Jesus in every way possible, he left him for a while.

Jesus' ministry in Galilee

Jesus begins his work

This is also told in Matthew 4.12–17; Mark 1.14–15

[14] Jesus returned to Galilee with the power of the Spirit. News about him spread everywhere. [15] He taught in the Jewish meeting places, and everyone praised him.

The people of Nazareth turn against Jesus

This is also told in Matthew 13.53–58; Mark 6.1–6

[16] Jesus went back to Nazareth, where he had been brought up, and as usual he went to the meeting place on the Sabbath. When he stood up to read from the Scriptures, [17] he was given the book of Isaiah the prophet. He opened it and read,

> [18] "The Lord's Spirit
>   has come to me,
> because he has chosen me
>   to tell the good news
>   to the poor.
> The Lord has sent me
>   to announce freedom
>   for prisoners,
> to give sight to the blind,
> to free everyone
>   who suffers,
> [19] and to say, 'This is the year
>   the Lord has chosen.' "

[20] Jesus closed the book, then handed it back to the man in charge and sat down. Everyone in the meeting place looked straight at Jesus. [21] Then Jesus said to them, "What you have just heard me read has come true today."

[22] All the people started talking about Jesus and were amazed at the wonderful things he said. They kept on asking, "Isn't he Joseph's son?"

[23] Jesus answered:

You will certainly want to tell me this saying, "Doctor, first make yourself well." You will tell me to do the same things here in my own home town that you heard I did in Capernaum. [24] But you can be sure that no prophets are liked by the people of their own home town.

See also: 4.18–19: Isa 61.1–2 (LXX).   **4.24:** John 4.44.

Being christian

Resisting temptation

Luke 4.1–13

Wouldn't it be great if, when we became Christians, our minds were suddenly purified. If we were reprogrammed so that we could only think pure and good thoughts.

Not going to happen. I mean, apart from everything else, we'd be robots; brainwashed. As long as we have freedom, as long as we get to make choices, we'll be tempted.

And everyone is tempted. No-one escapes. Some people are tempted by lust; some by money; some by power; some by food or drink. Most of us are tempted by all of these – and more. Everyone gets tempted.

And here's the important thing to remember: temptation is not sin. Even Jesus was tempted. He went into the desert, where Satan offered Jesus power, he offered Jesus food, he offered Jesus all the wealth of the world. No, being tempted is not sin. Giving into temptation, acting on it: that's when it becomes sin.

The key thing is whether you can resist. Jesus rejected temptation. He didn't give in. Instead he rebutted Satan by quoting scripture. Which maybe gives us a helpful hint. When you're tempted, think what the Bible says on the subject. Let the word of God be your guide, rather than your own desires.

Being Christian: Resisting temptation

• Be aware of your own weaknesses. Be honest about yourself. What is it that really tempts you? How can you minimise or avoid being exposed to this temptation?
• Read the Bible. What passages or verses in the Bible could you use to resist temptation?
• Picture God. When you face temptation try to imagine what Jesus would say if he were physically present with you. What would he think?

25 Once during the time of Elijah there was no rain for three and a half years, and people everywhere were starving. There were many widows in Israel, 26 but Elijah was sent only to a widow in the town of Zarephath near the city of Sidon. 27 During the time of the prophet Elisha, many men in Israel had leprosy.* But no one was healed, except Naaman who lived in Syria.

28 When the people in the meeting place heard Jesus say this, they became so angry 29 that they got up and threw him out of town. They dragged him to the edge of the cliff on which the town was built, because they wanted to throw him down from there. 30 But Jesus slipped through the crowd and got away.

A man with an evil spirit

This is also told in Mark 1.21–28

31 Jesus went to the town of Capernaum in Galilee and taught the people on the Sabbath. 32 His teaching amazed them because he spoke with power. 33 There in the Jewish meeting place was a man with an evil spirit. He yelled out, 34 "Hey, Jesus of Nazareth, what do you want with us? Are you here to get rid of us? I know who you are! You are God's Holy One."

35 Jesus ordered the evil spirit to be quiet and come out. The demon threw the man to the ground in front of everyone and left without harming him.

36 They all were amazed and kept saying to each other, "What kind of teaching is this? He has power to order evil spirits out of people!" 37 News about Jesus spread all over that part of the country.

Jesus heals many people

This is also told in Matthew 8.14–17; Mark 1.29–34

38 Jesus left the meeting place and went to Simon's home. When Jesus got there, he was told that Simon's mother-in-law was sick with a high fever. 39 So Jesus went over to her and ordered the fever to go away. At once she was able to get up and serve them a meal.

40 After the sun had set, people with all kinds of diseases were brought to Jesus. He put his hands on each one of them and

*4.27 leprosy: In biblical times the word "leprosy" was used for many different kinds of skin diseases.
See also: 4.25: 1 King 17.1. 4.26: 1 King 17.8–16. 4.27: 2 King 5.1–14. 4.32: Matt 7.28–29.

healed them. ⁴¹ Demons went out of many people and shouted, "You are the Son of God!" But Jesus ordered the demons not to speak because they knew he was the Messiah.

⁴² The next morning Jesus went out to a place where he could be alone, and crowds came looking for him. When they found him, they tried to stop him from leaving. ⁴³ But Jesus said, "People in other towns must hear the good news about God's kingdom. That's why I was sent." ⁴⁴ So he kept on preaching in the Jewish meeting places in Judea.'

CHAPTER 5

Jesus chooses his first disciples
This is also told in Matthew 4.18–22; Mark 1.16–20

¹ Jesus was standing on the shore of Lake Gennesaret,* teaching the people as they crowded around him to hear God's message. ² Near the shore he saw two boats left there by some fishermen who had gone to wash their nets. ³ Jesus got into the boat that belonged to Simon and asked him to row it out a little way from the shore. Then Jesus sat down* in the boat to teach the crowd.

⁴ When Jesus had finished speaking, he told Simon, "Row the boat out into the deep water and let your nets down to catch some fish."

⁵ "Master," Simon answered, "we have worked hard all night long and have not caught a thing. But if you tell me to, I will let the nets down." ⁶ They did it and caught so many fish that their nets began ripping apart. ⁷ Then they signalled for their partners in the other boat to come and help them. The men came, and together they filled the two boats so full that they both began to sink.

⁸ When Simon Peter saw this happen, he knelt down in front of Jesus and said, "Lord, don't come near me! I am a sinner." ⁹ Peter and everyone with him were completely surprised at all the fish they had caught. ¹⁰ His partners James and John, the sons of Zebedee, were surprised too.

Jesus told Simon, "Don't be afraid! From now on you will bring in people instead of

fish." ¹¹ The men pulled their boats up on the shore. Then they left everything and went with Jesus.

Jesus heals a man
This is also told in Matthew 8.1–4; Mark 1.40–45

¹² Jesus came to a town where there was a man who had leprosy.* When the man saw Jesus, he knelt down on the ground in front of Jesus and begged, "Lord, you have the power to make me well, if only you wanted to."

¹³ Jesus put his hand on him and said, "I want to! Now you are well." At once the man's leprosy disappeared. ¹⁴ Jesus told him, "Don't tell anyone about this, but go and show yourself to the priest. Offer a gift to the priest, just as Moses commanded, and everyone will know that you have been healed."*

¹⁵ News about Jesus kept spreading. Large crowds came to listen to him teach and to be healed of their diseases. ¹⁶ But Jesus would often go to some place where he could be alone and pray.

Jesus heals a crippled man
This is also told in Matthew 9.1–8; Mark 2.1–12

¹⁷ One day some Pharisees and experts in the Law of Moses sat listening to Jesus teach. They had come from every village in Galilee and Judea and from Jerusalem.

God had given Jesus the power to heal the sick, ¹⁸ and some people came carrying a crippled man on a mat. They tried to take him inside the house and put him in front of Jesus. ¹⁹ But because of the crowd, they could not get him to Jesus. So they went up on the roof,* where they removed some tiles and let the mat down in the middle of the room.

---

*5.1 **Lake Gennesaret:** Another name for Lake Galilee.
*5.3 **sat down:** Teachers in the ancient world, including Jewish teachers, usually sat down when they taught.
See also: 5.1–3: Matt 13.1–2; Mark 3.9–10; 4.1.
5.5: John 21.3.   5.6: John 21.6.

*5.12 **leprosy:** See the note at 4.27.
*5.14 **everyone will know that you have been healed:** People with leprosy had to be examined by a priest and told that they were well (that is, "clean") before they could once again live a normal life in the Jewish community. The gift that Moses commanded was the sacrifice of some lambs together with flour mixed with olive oil.
*5.19 **roof:** In Palestine the houses usually had a flat roof. Stairs on the outside led up to the roof, which was made of beams and boards covered with packed earth. Luke says that the roof was made of (clay) tiles, which were also used for making roofs in New Testament times.
See also: 5.14: Lev 14.1–32.

20 When Jesus saw how much faith they had, he said to the crippled man, "My friend, your sins are forgiven."

21 The Pharisees and the experts began arguing, "Jesus must think he is God! Only God can forgive sins."

22 Jesus knew what they were thinking, and he said, "Why are you thinking that? 23 Is it easier for me to tell this crippled man that his sins are forgiven or to tell him to get up and walk? 24 But now you will see that the Son of Man has the right to forgive sins here on earth." Jesus then said to the man, "Get up! Pick up your mat and walk home."

25 At once the man stood up in front of everyone. He picked up his mat and went home, giving thanks to God. 26 Everyone was amazed and praised God. What they saw surprised them, and they said, "We have seen a great miracle today!"

Jesus chooses Levi

This is also told in Matthew 9.9–13; Mark 2.13–17

27 Later, Jesus went out and saw a tax collector* named Levi sitting at the place for paying taxes. Jesus said to him, "Come with me." 28 Levi left everything and went with Jesus.

29 In his home Levi gave a big dinner for Jesus. Many tax collectors and other guests were also there.

30 The Pharisees and some of their teachers of the Law of Moses grumbled to Jesus' disciples, "Why do you eat and drink with those tax collectors and other sinners?"

31 Jesus answered, "Healthy people don't need a doctor, but sick people do. 32 I didn't come to invite good people to turn to God. I came to invite sinners."

People ask about going without eating

This is also told in Matthew 9.14–17; Mark 2.18–22

33 Some people said to Jesus, "John's followers often pray and go without eating,* and so do the followers of the Pharisees. But your disciples never go without eating or drinking."

34 Jesus told them, "The friends of a bridegroom don't go without eating while he is still with them. 35 But the time will come when he will be taken from them. Then they will go without eating."

36 Jesus then told them these sayings:

No one uses a new piece of cloth to patch old clothes. The patch would shrink and make the hole even bigger.

37 No one pours new wine into old wineskins. The new wine would swell and burst the old skins.* Then the wine would be lost, and the skins would be ruined. 38 New wine must be put only into new wineskins.

39 No one wants new wine after drinking old wine. They say, "The old wine is better."

CHAPTER 6

A question about the Sabbath

This is also told in Matthew 12.1–8; Mark 2.23–28

1 One Sabbath when Jesus and his disciples were walking through some wheat fields, the disciples picked some wheat.* They rubbed the husks off with their hands and started eating the grain.

2 Some Pharisees said, "Why are you picking grain on the Sabbath? You're not supposed to do that!"

3 Jesus answered, "Surely you have read what David did when he and his followers were hungry. 4 He went into the house of God and took the sacred loaves of bread that only priests were supposed to eat. He not only ate some himself, but even gave some to his followers."

5 Jesus finished by saying, "The Son of Man is Lord over the Sabbath."

A man with a crippled hand

This is also told in Matthew 12.9–14; Mark 3.1–6

6 On another Sabbath⁾ Jesus was teaching in a Jewish meeting place, and a man with a crippled right hand was there. 7 Some Pharisees and teachers of the Law of Moses kept watching Jesus to see if he would heal the man. They did this because they wanted to accuse Jesus of doing something wrong.

---

*5.27 tax collector: See the note at 3.12.
*5.33 without eating: See the note at 2.37.
See also: 5.30: Luke 15.1–2.

*5.37 swell and burst the old skins: While the juice from grapes was becoming wine, it would swell and stretch the skins in which it had been stored. If the skins were old and stiff, they would burst.
*6.1 picked some wheat: It was the custom to let hungry travellers pick grains of wheat.
See also: 6.1: Deut 23.25. 6.3–4: 1 Sam 21.1–6.
6.4: Lev 24.9.

Helpline

Help! I want to pay someone back

'Just wait... I'm going to remember this and when the time comes, I'll get them back!'

Someone's done us wrong and we want revenge. It's like the final scene of an action movie, when the hero walks through the door and gives the villain a good kicking.

Doesn't have to be a physical payback. We'll bide our time; wait for the right moment to deliver the devastating put down, wait till they need something from us: then we can really rub their faces in it.

Wait. What about the wrong we've done in our lives? What about all the sins we committed against God... Maybe if we don't get what we deserve, we shouldn't dish it out to others. God is a God of mercy. He doesn't pay us back as we deserve, but tells us to forgive one another and love our enemies.

So let's change the ending to that movie: hero bursts in through the door and gives the villain a good old hug.

Three things

Mirror

Think first of the things that you've done that might deserve a bit of retribution. Why shouldn't people get their revenge on you?

Jesus

Jesus modelled a different way. He told us to love our enemies (Luke 6.27–36). Even on the cross he asked his father to forgive those who had put him there. God could have wiped them out in an instant, but Jesus chose to ask for mercy.

Forgive

Forgiveness is the key. It won't be easy. There will be times when you really want to stick the boot in; but try to hold back. Send a quick prayer to God. Forgive those who sin against you, and God will forgive you.

More...

Forgiveness p.614
Forgiving others p.1162

[8] Jesus knew what they were thinking. So he told the man to stand up where everyone could see him. And the man stood up. [9] Then Jesus asked, "On the Sabbath should we do good deeds or evil deeds? Should we save someone's life or destroy it?"

[10] After he had looked around at everyone, he told the man, "Stretch out your hand." He did, and his bad hand became completely well.

[11] The teachers and the Pharisees were furious and started saying to each other, "What can we do about Jesus?"

Jesus chooses his twelve apostles

This is also told in Matthew 10.1–4; Mark 3.13–19

[12] About that time Jesus went off to a mountain to pray, and he spent the whole night there. [13] The next morning he called his disciples together and chose twelve of them to be his apostles. [14] One was Simon, and Jesus named him Peter. Another was Andrew, Peter's brother. There were also James, John, Philip, Bartholomew, [15] Matthew, Thomas, and James the son of Alphaeus. The rest of the apostles were Simon, known as the Eager One,* [16] Jude, who was the son of James, and Judas Iscariot,* who later betrayed Jesus.

Jesus teaches, preaches, and heals

This is also told in Matthew 4.23–25

[17] Jesus and his apostles went down from the mountain and came to some flat, level ground. Many other disciples were there to meet him. Large crowds of people from all over Judea, Jerusalem, and the coastal cities of Tyre and Sidon were there too. [18] These people had come to listen to Jesus and to be healed of their diseases. All who were troubled by evil spirits were also healed. [19] Everyone was trying to touch Jesus, because power was going out from him and healing them all.

---

*6.15 known as the Eager One: The word "eager" translates the Greek word "zealot", which was a name later given to the members of a Jewish group that resisted and fought against the Romans.
*6.16 Iscariot: This may mean "a man from Kerioth" (a place in Judea). But more probably it means "a man who was a liar" or "a man who was a betrayer".

Blessings and troubles

This is also told in Matthew 5.1–12

20 Jesus looked at his disciples and said:

God will bless you people
who are poor.
His kingdom belongs to you!
21 God will bless
you hungry people.
You will have plenty
to eat!
God will bless you people
who are crying.
You will laugh!

22 God will bless you when others hate you
and won't have anything to do with you.
God will bless you when people insult you
and say cruel things about you, all because
you are a follower of the Son of Man.
23 Long ago your own people did these
same things to the prophets. So when this
happens to you, be happy and jump for
joy! You will have a great reward in
heaven.

24 But you rich people
are in for trouble.
You have already had
an easy life!
25 You well-fed people
are in for trouble.
You will go hungry!
You people
who are laughing now
are in for trouble.
You are going to cry
and weep!

26 You are in for trouble when everyone
says good things about you. That is what
your own people said about those prophets
who told lies.

Love for enemies

This is also told in Matthew 5.38–48; 7.12a

Jesus continued:

27 This is what I say to all who will listen
to me:

Love your enemies, and be good to
everyone who hates you. 28 Ask God to
bless anyone who curses you, and pray for
everyone who is cruel to you. 29 If someone
slaps you on one cheek, don't stop that
person from slapping you on the other
cheek. If someone wants to take your coat,
don't try to keep back your shirt. 30 Give to
everyone who asks and don't ask people to
return what they have taken from you.
31 Treat others just as you want to be
treated.

32 If you love only someone who loves
you, will God praise you for that? Even
sinners love people who love them. 33 If
you are kind only to someone who is kind
to you, will God be pleased with you for
that? Even sinners are kind to people who
are kind to them. 34 If you lend money only
to someone you think will pay you back,
will God be pleased with you for that? Even
sinners lend to sinners because they think
they will get it all back.

35 But love your enemies and be good to
them. Lend without expecting to be paid
back.‣ Then you will get a great reward,
and you will be the true children of God
in heaven. He is good even to people who
are unthankful and cruel. 36 Have pity on
others, just as your Father has pity on you.

Judging others

This is also told in Matthew 7.1–5

37 Jesus said:

Don't judge others, and God won't judge
you. Don't be hard on others, and God
won't be hard on you. Forgive others, and
God will forgive you. 38 If you give to
others, you will be given a full amount in
return. It will be packed down, shaken
together, and spilling over into your lap.
The way you treat others is the way you
will be treated.

39 Jesus also used some sayings as he spoke to
the people. He said:

Can one blind person lead another blind
person? Won't they both fall into a ditch?
40 Are students better than their teacher?
But when they are fully trained, they will
be like their teacher.

41 You can see the speck in your friend's
eye. But you don't notice the log in your
own eye. 42 How can you say, "My friend,
let me take the speck out of your eye,"
when you don't see the log in your own
eye? You show-offs! First, get the log out
of your own eye. Then you can see how
to take the speck out of your friend's eye.

See also: **6.22:** 1 Pet 4.14. **6.23:** 2 Chron 36.16; Acts 7.52.

See also: **6.31:** Matt 7.12. **6.39:** Matt 15.14.
6.40: Matt 10.24–25; John 13.16; 15.20.

A tree and its fruit

This is also told in Matthew 7.17–20; 12.34b–35

Jesus continued:

⁴³ A good tree cannot produce bad fruit, and a bad tree cannot produce good fruit. ⁴⁴ You can tell what a tree is like by the fruit it produces. You cannot pick figs or grapes from thorn bushes. ⁴⁵ Good people do good things because of the good in their hearts. Bad people do bad things because of the evil in their hearts. Your words show what is in your heart.

Two builders

This is also told in Matthew 7.24–27

Jesus continued:

⁴⁶ Why do you keep on saying that I am your Lord, when you refuse to do what I say? ⁴⁷ Anyone who comes and listens to me and obeys me ⁴⁸ is like someone who dug down deep and built a house on solid rock. When the flood came and the river rushed against the house, it was built so well that it didn't even shake. ⁴⁹ But anyone who hears what I say and doesn't obey me is like someone whose house wasn't built on solid rock. As soon as the river rushed against that house, it was smashed to pieces!

CHAPTER 7

Jesus heals an army officer's servant

This is also told in Matthew 8.5–13; John 4.43–54

¹ After Jesus had finished teaching the people, he went to Capernaum. ² In that town an army officer's servant was sick and about to die. The officer liked this servant very much. ³ And when he heard about Jesus, he sent some Jewish leaders to ask him to come and heal the servant.

⁴ The leaders went to Jesus and begged him to do something. They said, "This man deserves your help! ⁵ He loves our nation and even built us a meeting place." ⁶ So Jesus went with them.

When Jesus wasn't far from the house, the officer sent some friends to tell him, "Lord, don't go to any trouble for me! I am not good enough for you to come into my house. ⁷ And I am certainly not worthy to come to you. Just say the word, and my servant will get well. ⁸ I have officers who give orders to me, and I have soldiers who take orders from me. I can say to one of them, 'Go!' and he goes. I can say to another, 'Come!' and he comes. I can say to my servant, 'Do this!' and he will do it."

⁹ When Jesus heard this, he was so surprised that he turned and said to the crowd following him, "In all of Israel I've never found anyone with this much faith!"

¹⁰ The officer's friends returned and found the servant well.

A widow's son

¹¹ Soon Jesus and his disciples were on their way to the town of Nain, and a big crowd was going along with them. ¹² As they came near the gate of the town, they saw people carrying out the body of a widow's only son. Many people from the town were walking along with her.

¹³ When the Lord saw the woman, he felt sorry for her and said, "Don't cry!"

¹⁴ Jesus went over and touched the stretcher on which the people were carrying the dead boy. They stopped, and Jesus said, "Young man, get up!" ¹⁵ The boy sat up and began to speak. Jesus then gave him back to his mother.

¹⁶ Everyone was frightened and praised God. They said, "A great prophet is here with us! God has come to his people."

¹⁷ News about Jesus spread all over Judea and everywhere else in that part of the country.

John the Baptist

This is also told in Matthew 11.1–19

¹⁸⁻¹⁹ John's followers told John everything that was being said about Jesus. So he sent two of them to ask the Lord, "Are you the one we should be looking for? Or must we wait for someone else?"

²⁰ When these messengers came to Jesus, they said, "John the Baptist sent us to ask, 'Are you the one we should be looking for? Or are we supposed to wait for someone else?' "

²¹ At that time Jesus was healing many people who were sick or in pain or were troubled by evil spirits, and he was giving sight to a lot of blind people. ²² Jesus said to the messengers sent by John, "Go and tell John what you have seen and heard. Blind people are now able to see, and the lame can

---

See also: **6.44:** Matt 12.33.   **6.45:** Matt 12.34.

See also: **7.22:** a Isa 35.5–6; b Isa 61.1.

walk. People who have leprosy* are being healed, and the deaf can now hear. The dead are raised to life, and the poor are hearing the good news. ²³ God will bless everyone who doesn't reject me because of what I do."

²⁴ After John's messengers had gone, Jesus began speaking to the crowds about John:

What kind of person did you go out to the desert to see? Was he like tall grass blown about by the wind? ²⁵ What kind of man did you really go out to see? Was he someone dressed in fine clothes? People who wear expensive clothes and live in luxury are in the king's palace. ²⁶ What then did you go out to see? Was he a prophet? He certainly was! I tell you that he was more than a prophet. ²⁷ In the Scriptures, God calls John his messenger and says, "I am sending my messenger ahead of you to get things ready for you." ²⁸ No one ever born on this earth is greater than John. But whoever is least important in God's kingdom is greater than John.

²⁹ Everyone had been listening to John. Even the tax collectors* had obeyed God and had done what was right by letting John baptize them. ³⁰ But the Pharisees and the experts in the Law of Moses refused to obey God and be baptized by John.

³¹ Jesus went on to say:

What are you people like? What kind of people are you? ³² You are like children sitting in the market and shouting to each other,

"We played the flute,
    but you would not dance!
We sang a funeral song,
    but you would not cry!"

³³ John the Baptist did not go around eating and drinking, and you said, "John has a demon in him!" ³⁴ But because the Son of Man goes around eating and drinking, you say, "Jesus eats and drinks too much! He is even a friend of tax collectors and sinners." ³⁵ Yet Wisdom is shown to be right by what its followers do.

Simon the Pharisee

³⁶ A Pharisee invited Jesus to have dinner with him. So Jesus went to the Pharisee's home and got ready to eat.*

³⁷ When a sinful woman in that town found out that Jesus was there, she bought an expensive bottle of perfume. ³⁸ Then she came and stood behind Jesus. She cried and started washing his feet with her tears and drying them with her hair. The woman kissed his feet and poured the perfume on them.

³⁹ The Pharisee who had invited Jesus saw this and said to himself, "If this man really were a prophet, he would know what kind of woman is touching him! He would know that she is a sinner."

⁴⁰ Jesus said to the Pharisee, "Simon, I have something to say to you."

"Teacher, what is it?" Simon replied.

⁴¹ Jesus told him, "Two people were in debt to a moneylender. One of them owed him five hundred silver coins, and the other owed him fifty. ⁴² Since neither of them could pay him back, the moneylender said that they didn't have to pay him anything. Which one of them will like him more?"

⁴³ Simon answered, "I suppose it would be the one who had owed more and didn't have to pay it back."

"You are right," Jesus said.

⁴⁴ He turned towards the woman and said to Simon, "Have you noticed this woman? When I came into your home, you didn't give me any water so I could wash my feet. But she has washed my feet with her tears and dried them with her hair. ⁴⁵ You didn't greet me with a kiss, but from the time I came in, she has not stopped kissing my feet. ⁴⁶ You didn't even pour olive oil on my head,* but she has poured expensive perfume on my feet. ⁴⁷ So I tell you that all her sins are forgiven, and that is why she has shown great

*7.36 got ready to eat: On special occasions the Jewish people often followed the Greek and Roman custom of lying down on their left side and leaning on their left elbow, while eating with their right hand. This is how the woman could come up behind Jesus and wash his feet (see verse 38).
*7.44–46 washed my feet . . . greet me with a kiss . . . pour olive oil on my head: Guests in a home were usually offered water so they could wash their feet, because most people either went barefoot or wore sandals and would come into the house with very dusty feet. Guests were also greeted with a kiss on the cheek, and special ones often had sweet-smelling olive oil poured on their head.
See also: 7.37–38: Matt 26.7; Mark 14.3; John 12.3.

*7.22 leprosy: See the note at 4.27.
*7.29 tax collectors: See the note at 3.12.
See also: 7.27: Mal 3.1. 7.29–30: Matt 21.32; Luke 3.12.

love. But anyone who has been forgiven for only a little will show only a little love."

⁴⁸ Then Jesus said to the woman, "Your sins are forgiven."

⁴⁹ Some other guests started saying to one another, "Who is this who dares to forgive sins?"

⁵⁰ But Jesus told the woman, "Because of your faith, you are now saved.ᐟ May God give you peace!"

CHAPTER 8

Women who helped Jesus

¹ Soon after this, Jesus was going through towns and villages, telling the good news about God's kingdom. His twelve apostles were with him, ² and so were some women who had been healed of evil spirits and all sorts of diseases. One of the women was Mary Magdalene,* who once had seven demons in her. ³ Joanna, Susanna, and many others had also used what they owned to help Jesus* and his disciples. Joanna's husband Chuza was one of Herod's officials.*

A story about a farmer

This is also told in Matthew 13.1–9; Mark 4.1–9

⁴ When a large crowd from several towns had gathered around Jesus, he told them this story:

⁵ A farmer went out to scatter seed in a field. While the farmer was doing it, some of the seeds fell along the road and were stepped on or eaten by birds. ⁶ Other seeds fell on rocky ground and started growing. But the plants did not have enough water and soon dried up. ⁷ Some other seeds fell where thorn bushes grew up and choked the plants. ⁸ The rest of the seeds fell on good ground where they grew and produced a hundred times as many seeds.

When Jesus had finished speaking, he said, "If you have ears, pay attention!"

---

*8.2 Magdalene: Meaning "from Magdala", a small town on the western shore of Lake Galilee. There is no hint that she is the sinful woman in 7.36–50.
*8.3 used what they owned to help Jesus: Women often helped Jewish teachers by giving them money.
*8.3 Herod's officials: Herod Antipas, the son of Herod the Great.
See also: 8.2–3: Matt 27.55–56; Mark 15.40–41; Luke 23.49.

Big ideas

Demonic powers

Some time before the creation of the world – we don't know when – a group of angels rebelled against God. Their leader was an angel called Lucifer and they wanted to take over God's power and glory. Lucifer is also known as Satan or the Devil.

They were defeated in their rebellion and thrown out of heaven. But they continue to oppose God in whatever ways they can. The Bible tells us that there is a constant battle going on between the forces of good and the forces of evil. Christians are part of this battle; every time we resist temptation, every time we obey God or pray, we score a victory in this war.

The war manifests itself in different ways. Sometimes these fallen angels – or demons – attack or possess human beings. These are the spirits that are cast out by Jesus in the gospels, such as those cast into the pigs (Luke 8.26–39). Sometimes they tempt people or accuse them or attack them in other ways.

Although there is a war going on, the outcome is not in question. The Bible makes it clear that, after the final judgment, Satan and his rebellious angels will be consigned to punishment.

And we should also be clear that, if we pray to God, he will protect us. Have faith. If you're with God, then you're safe. As John says, the one who is in us, is greater than the powers that are in the world (1 John 4.4).

More...

Angels p.412
Heaven p.1412
Hell p.1148

Why Jesus used stories
This is also told in Matthew 13.10–17; Mark 4.10–12

⁹ Jesus' disciples asked him what the story meant. ¹⁰ So he answered:

I have explained the secrets about God's kingdom to you, but for others I can only use stories. These people look, but they don't see, and they hear, but they don't understand.

Jesus explains the story about a farmer
This is also told in Matthew 13.18–23; Mark 4.13–20

Jesus continued:

¹¹ This is what the story means: The seed is God's message, ¹² and the seeds that fell along the road are the people who hear the message. But the devil comes and snatches the message out of their hearts, so that they will not believe and be saved. ¹³ The seeds that fell on rocky ground are the people who gladly hear the message and accept it. But they don't have deep roots, and they believe only for a little while. As soon as life gets hard, they give up.

¹⁴ The seeds that fell among the thorn bushes are also people who hear the message. But they are so eager for riches and pleasures that they never produce anything. ¹⁵ Those seeds that fell on good ground are the people who listen to the message and keep it in good and honest hearts. They last and produce a harvest.

Light
This is also told in Mark 4.21–25

Jesus continued:

¹⁶ No one lights a lamp and puts it under a bowl or under a bed. A lamp is always put on a lampstand, so that people who come into a house will see the light. ¹⁷ There is nothing hidden that will not be found. There is no secret that will not be well known. ¹⁸ Pay attention to how you listen! Everyone who has something will be given more, but people who have nothing will lose what little they think they have.

Jesus' mother and brothers
This is also told in Matthew 12.46–50; Mark 3.31–35

¹⁹ Jesus' mother and brothers went to see him, but because of the crowd they could not

get near him. ²⁰ Someone told Jesus, "Your mother and brothers are standing outside and want to see you."

²¹ Jesus answered, "My mother and my brothers are those people who hear and obey God's message."

A storm
This is also told in Matthew 8.23–27; Mark 4.35–41

²² One day, Jesus and his disciples got into a boat, and he said, "Let's cross the lake."* They started out, ²³ and while they were sailing across, he went to sleep.

Suddenly a storm struck the lake, and the boat started sinking. They were in danger. ²⁴ So they went to Jesus and woke him up, "Master, Master! We are about to drown!"

Jesus got up and ordered the wind and waves to stop. They obeyed, and everything was calm. ²⁵ Then Jesus asked the disciples, "Don't you have any faith?"

But they were frightened and amazed. They said to each other, "Who is this? He can give orders to the wind and the waves, and they obey him!"

A man with demons in him
This is also told in Matthew 8.28–34; Mark 5.1–20

²⁶ Jesus and his disciples sailed across Lake Galilee and came to shore near the town of Gerasa.ᵇ ²⁷ As Jesus was getting out of the boat, he was met by a man from that town. The man had demons in him. He had gone naked for a long time and no longer lived in a house, but in the graveyard.*

²⁸ The man saw Jesus and screamed. He knelt down in front of him and shouted, "Jesus, Son of God in heaven, what do you want with me? I beg you not to torture me!" ²⁹ He said this because Jesus had already told the evil spirit to go out of him.

The man had often been attacked by the demon. And even though he had been bound with chains and leg irons and kept under guard, he smashed whatever bound him. Then the demon would force him out into lonely places.

³⁰ Jesus asked the man, "What is your name?"

He answered, "My name is Lots." He said this because there were 'lots' of demons in

See also: 8.10: Isa 6.9 (LXX). 8.16: Matt 5.15; Luke 11.33. 8.17: Matt 10.26; Luke 12.2. 8.18: Matt 25.29; Luke 19.26.

*8.22 cross the lake: To the eastern shore of Lake Galilee, where most of the people were not Jewish.
*8.27 graveyard: It was thought that demons and evil spirits lived in graveyards.

him. ³¹ They begged Jesus not to send them to the deep pit,* where they would be punished.

³² A large herd of pigs was feeding there on the hillside. So the demons begged Jesus to let them go into the pigs, and Jesus let them go. ³³ Then the demons left the man and went into the pigs. The whole herd rushed down the steep bank into the lake and drowned.

³⁴ When the men taking care of the pigs saw this, they ran to spread the news in the town and on the farms. ³⁵ The people went out to see what had happened, and when they came to Jesus, they also found the man. The demons had gone out of him, and he was sitting there at the feet of Jesus. He had clothes on and was in his right mind. But the people were terrified.

³⁶ Then all who had seen the man healed told about it. ³⁷ Everyone from around Gerasa▸ begged Jesus to leave, because they were so frightened.

When Jesus got into the boat to start back, ³⁸ the man who had been healed begged to go with him. But Jesus sent him off and said, ³⁹ "Go back home and tell everyone how much God has done for you." The man then went all over town, telling everything that Jesus had done for him.

A dying girl and a sick woman

This is also told in Matthew 9.18–26; Mark 5.21–43

⁴⁰ Everyone had been waiting for Jesus, and when he came back, a crowd was there to welcome him. ⁴¹ Just then the man in charge of the Jewish meeting place came and knelt down in front of Jesus. His name was Jairus, and he begged Jesus to come to his home ⁴² because his twelve-year-old child was dying. She was his only daughter.

While Jesus was on his way, people were crowding all around him. ⁴³ In the crowd was a woman who had been bleeding for twelve years. She had spent everything she had on doctors,▸ but none of them could make her well.

⁴⁴ As soon as she came up behind Jesus and barely touched his clothes, her bleeding stopped.

⁴⁵ "Who touched me?" Jesus asked.

While everyone was denying it, Peter said, "Master, people are crowding all around and pushing you from every side."▸

⁴⁶ But Jesus answered, "Someone touched me, because I felt power going out from me." ⁴⁷ The woman knew that she could not hide, so she came trembling and knelt down in front of Jesus. She told everyone why she had touched him and that she had been healed straight away.

⁴⁸ Jesus said to the woman, "You are now well because of your faith. May God give you peace!"

⁴⁹ While Jesus was speaking, someone came from Jairus' home and said, "Your daughter has died! Why bother the teacher any more?"

⁵⁰ When Jesus heard this, he told Jairus, "Don't worry! Have faith, and your daughter will get well."

⁵¹ Jesus went into the house, but he did not let anyone else go with him, except Peter, John, James, and the girl's father and mother. ⁵² Everyone was crying and weeping for the girl. But Jesus said, "The child isn't dead. She is just asleep." ⁵³ The people laughed at him because they knew she was dead.

⁵⁴ Jesus took hold of the girl's hand and said, "Child, get up!" ⁵⁵ She came back to life and got straight up. Jesus told them to give her something to eat. ⁵⁶ Her parents were surprised, but Jesus ordered them not to tell anyone what had happened.

CHAPTER 9

Instructions for the twelve apostles

This is also told in Matthew 10.5–15; Mark 6.7–13

¹ Jesus called together his twelve apostles and gave them complete power over all demons and diseases. ² Then he sent them to tell about God's kingdom and to heal the sick. ³ He told them, "Don't take anything with you! Don't take a walking stick or a travelling bag or food or money or even a change of clothes. ⁴ When you are welcomed into a home, stay there until you leave that town. ⁵ If people won't welcome you, leave the town and shake the dust from your feet* as a warning to them."

⁶ The apostles left and went from village to village, telling the good news and healing people everywhere.

---

*8.31 deep pit: The place where evil spirits are kept and punished.

*9.5 shake the dust from your feet: This was a way of showing rejection.
See also: 9.3–5: Luke 10.4–11. 9.5: Acts 13.51.

Herod is worried

This is also told in Matthew 14.1–12; Mark 6.14–29

7 Herod* the ruler heard about all that was happening, and he was worried. Some people were saying that John the Baptist had come back to life. 8 Others were saying that Elijah* had come or that one of the prophets from long ago had come back to life. 9 But Herod said, "I had John's head cut off! Who is this I hear so much about?" Herod was eager to meet Jesus.

Jesus feeds five thousand

This is also told in Matthew 14.13–21; Mark 6.30–44; John 6.1–14

10 The apostles came back and told Jesus everything they had done. He then took them with him to the village of Bethsaida, where they could be alone. 11 But a lot of people found out about this and followed him. Jesus welcomed them. He spoke to them about God's kingdom and healed everyone who was sick.

12 Late in the afternoon the twelve apostles came to Jesus and said, "Send the crowd to the villages and farms around here. They need to find a place to stay and something to eat. There is nothing in this place. It is like a desert!"

13 Jesus answered, "You give them something to eat."

But they replied, "We have only five small loaves of bread* and two fish. If we are going to feed all these people, we will have to go and buy food." 14 There were about five thousand men in the crowd.

Jesus said to his disciples, "Tell the people to sit in groups of fifty." 15 They did this, and all the people sat down. 16 Jesus took the five loaves and the two fish. He looked up towards heaven and blessed the food. Then he broke the bread and fish and handed them to his disciples to give to the people.

17 Everyone ate all they wanted. What was left over filled twelve baskets.

Who is Jesus?

This is also told in Matthew 16.13–19; Mark 8.27–29

18 When Jesus was alone praying, his disciples came to him, and he asked them, "What do people say about me?"

19 They answered, "Some say that you are John the Baptist or Elijah* or a prophet from long ago who has come back to life."

20 Jesus then asked them, "But who do you say I am?"

Peter answered, "You are the Messiah sent from God."

21 Jesus strictly warned his disciples not to tell anyone about this.

Jesus speaks about his suffering and death

This is also told in Matthew 16.20–28; Mark 8.30—9.1

22 Jesus told his disciples, "The nation's leaders, the chief priests, and the teachers of the Law of Moses will make the Son of Man suffer terribly. They will reject him and kill him, but three days later he will rise to life."

23 Then Jesus said to all the people:

If any of you want to be my followers, you must forget about yourself. You must take up your cross each day and follow me. 24 If you want to save your life,' you will destroy it. But if you give up your life for me, you will save it. 25 What will you gain, if you own the whole world but destroy yourself or waste your life? 26 If you are ashamed of me and my message, the Son of Man will be ashamed of you when he comes in his glory and in the glory of his Father and the holy angels. 27 You can be sure that some of the people standing here will not die before they see God's kingdom.

The true glory of Jesus

This is also told in Matthew 17.1–8; Mark 9.2–8

28 About eight days later Jesus took Peter, John, and James with him and went up on a mountain to pray. 29 While he was praying, his face changed, and his clothes became shining white. 30 Suddenly Moses and Elijah were there speaking with him. 31 They appeared in heavenly glory and talked about all that Jesus' death' in Jerusalem would mean.

---

*9.7 Herod: See the note at 3.1.
*9.8 Elijah: Many of the Jewish people expected the prophet Elijah to come and prepare the way for the Messiah.
*9.13 small loaves of bread: These would have been flat and round or in the shape of a bun.
See also: 9.7–8: Matt 16.14; Mark 8.28; Luke 9.19.

---

*9.19 Elijah: See the note at 9.8.
See also: 9.19: Matt 14.1–2; Mark 6.14–15; Luke 9.7–8.
9.20: John 6.68–69. 9.23: Matt 10.38; Luke 14.27.
9.24: Matt 10.39; Luke 17.33; John 12.25.
9.28–35: 2 Pet 1.17–18.

³² Peter and the other two disciples had been sound asleep. All at once they woke up and saw how glorious Jesus was. They also saw the two men who were with him.

³³ Moses and Elijah were about to leave, when Peter said to Jesus, "Master, it is good for us to be here! Let us make three shelters, one for you, one for Moses, and one for Elijah." But Peter did not know what he was talking about.

³⁴ While Peter was still speaking, a shadow from a cloud passed over them, and they were frightened as the cloud covered them. ³⁵ From the cloud a voice spoke, "This is my chosen Son. Listen to what he says!"

³⁶ After the voice had spoken, Peter, John, and James saw only Jesus. For some time they kept quiet and did not say anything about what they had seen.

Jesus heals a boy

This is also told in Matthew 17.14–18; Mark 9.14–27

³⁷ The next day Jesus and his three disciples came down from the mountain and were met by a large crowd. ³⁸ Just then someone in the crowd shouted, "Teacher, please do something for my son! He is my only child! ³⁹ A demon often attacks him and makes him scream. It shakes him until he foams at the mouth, and it won't leave him until it has completely worn the boy out. ⁴⁰ I begged your disciples to force out the demon, but they couldn't do it."

⁴¹ Jesus said to them, "You people are stubborn and don't have any faith! How much longer must I be with you? Why do I have to put up with you?"

Then Jesus said to the man, "Bring your son to me." ⁴² While the boy was being brought, the demon attacked him and made him shake all over. Jesus ordered the demon to stop. Then he healed the boy and gave him back to his father. ⁴³ Everyone was amazed at God's great power.

Jesus again speaks about his death

This is also told in Matthew 17.22–23; Mark 9.30–32

While everyone was still amazed at what Jesus was doing, he said to his disciples, ⁴⁴ "Pay close attention to what I am telling you! The Son of Man will be handed over to his enemies." ⁴⁵ But the disciples did not know what he meant. The meaning

was hidden from them. They could not understand it, and they were afraid to ask.

Who is the greatest?

This is also told in Matthew 18.1–5; Mark 9.33–37

⁴⁶ Jesus' disciples were arguing about which one of them was the greatest. ⁴⁷ Jesus knew what they were thinking, and he had a child stand there beside him. ⁴⁸ Then he said to his disciples, "When you welcome even a child because of me, you welcome me. And when you welcome me, you welcome the one who sent me. Whichever one of you is the most humble is the greatest."

For or against Jesus

This is also told in Mark 9.38–40

⁴⁹ John said, "Master, we saw a man using your name to force demons out of people. But we told him to stop, because he isn't one of us."

⁵⁰ "Don't stop him!" Jesus said. "Anyone who isn't against you is for you."

Jesus goes from Galilee to Jerusalem

A Samaritan village refuses to receive Jesus

⁵¹ Not long before it was time for Jesus to be taken up to heaven, he made up his mind to go to Jerusalem. ⁵² He sent some messengers on ahead to a Samaritan village to get things ready for him. ⁵³ But he was on his way to Jerusalem, so the people there refused to welcome him. ⁵⁴ When the disciples James and John saw what was happening, they asked, "Lord, do you want us to call down fire from heaven to destroy these people?"ᵖ

⁵⁵ But Jesus turned and corrected them for what they had said.ᶥ ⁵⁶ Then they all went on to another village.

Three people who wanted to be followers

This is also told in Matthew 8.19–22

⁵⁷ Along the way someone said to Jesus, "I'll go anywhere with you!"

See also: **9.35:** Isa 42.1; Matt 3.17; 12.18; Mark 1.11; Luke 3.22.

See also: **9.46:** Luke 22.24. **9.48:** Matt 10.40; Luke 10.16; John 13.20. **9.54:** 2 King 1.9–16.

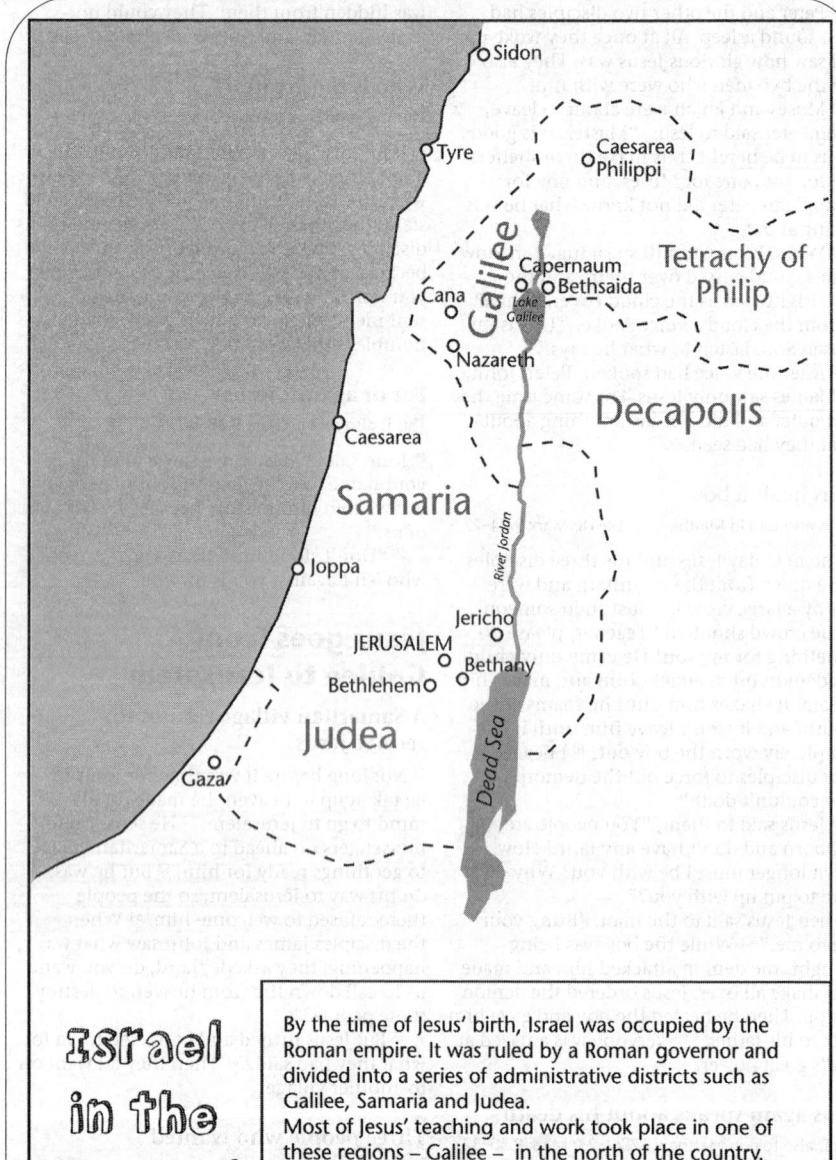

Sidon

Tyre

Caesarea
Philippi

Galilee

Capernaum
Bethsaida

Cana

Lake Galilee

Tetrachy of
Philip

Nazareth

Decapolis

Caesarea

Samaria

River Jordan

Joppa

Jericho

JERUSALEM

Bethany

Bethlehem

Judea

Dead Sea

Gaza

Israel in the time of Jesus

By the time of Jesus' birth, Israel was occupied by the
Roman empire. It was ruled by a Roman governor and
divided into a series of administrative districts such as
Galilee, Samaria and Judea.

Most of Jesus' teaching and work took place in one of
these regions – Galilee – in the north of the country.
Many of his disciples came from the towns of Bethsaida
and Capernaum. But Jesus also went to Samaria and to
Tyre and Sidon which were in a foreign country.

And, of course, he went to Jerusalem, where he spent
his final week.

58 Jesus said, "Foxes have dens, and birds have nests, but the Son of Man doesn't have a place to call his own."

59 Jesus told someone else to come with him. But the man said, "Lord, let me wait until I bury my father."*

60 Jesus answered, "Let the dead take care of the dead, while you go and tell about God's kingdom."

61 Then someone said to Jesus, "I want to go with you, Lord, but first let me go back and take care of things at home."

62 Jesus answered, "Anyone who starts ploughing and keeps looking back isn't worth a thing to God's kingdom!"

CHAPTER 10

The work of the seventy-two followers

1 Later the Lord chose seventy-two* other followers and sent them out two by two to every town and village where he was about to go. 2 He said to them:

A large crop is in the fields, but there are only a few workers. Ask the Lord in charge of the harvest to send out workers to bring it in. 3 Now go, but remember, I am sending you like lambs into a pack of wolves. 4 Don't take along a money bag or a travelling bag or sandals. And don't waste time greeting people on the road.* 5 As soon as you enter a home, say, "God bless this home with peace." 6 If the people living there are peace-loving, your prayer for peace will bless them. But if they are not peace-loving, your prayer will return to you. 7 Stay with the same family, eating and drinking whatever they give you, because workers are worth what they earn. Don't move around from house to house.

8 If the people of a town welcome you, eat whatever they offer. 9 Heal their sick and say, "God's kingdom will soon be here!"*

10 But if the people of a town refuse to welcome you, go out into the street and say, 11 "We are shaking the dust from our feet* as a warning to you. And you can be sure that God's kingdom will soon be here!"* 12 I tell you that on the day of judgment the people of Sodom will get off easier than the people of that town!

The unbelieving towns

This is also told in Matthew 11.20–24

Jesus continued:

13 You people of Chorazin are in for trouble! You people of Bethsaida are also in for trouble! If the miracles that took place in your towns had happened in Tyre and Sidon, the people there would have turned to God long ago. They would have dressed in sackcloth and put ashes on their heads.* 14 On the day of judgment the people of Tyre and Sidon will get off easier than you will. 15 People of Capernaum, do you think you will be honoured in heaven? Well, you will go down to hell!

16 My followers, whoever listens to you is listening to me. Anyone who says "No" to you is saying "No" to me. And anyone who says "No" to me is really saying "No" to the one who sent me.

The return of the seventy-two

17 When the seventy-two* followers returned, they were excited and said, "Lord, even the demons obeyed when we spoke in your name!"

18 Jesus told them:

I saw Satan fall from heaven like a flash of lightning. 19 I have given you the power to trample on snakes and scorpions and to defeat the power of your enemy Satan.

---

*9.59 bury my father: The Jewish people taught that giving someone a proper burial was even more important than helping the poor.

*10.1 seventy-two: Some manuscripts have "seventy". According to Jewish tradition there were seventy nations on earth. But the ancient Greek translation of the Old Testament has "seventy-two" in place of "seventy". Jesus probably chose this number of followers to show that his message was for everyone in the world.

*10.4 waste time greeting people on the road: In those days a polite greeting could take a long time.

See also: 9.61: 1 King 19.20. 10.2: Matt 9.37–38.
10.3: Matt 10.16. 10.4–11: Matt 10.7–14; Mark 6.8–11;
Luke 9.3–5. 10.7: 1 Cor 9.14; 1 Tim 5.18.

*10.11 shaking the dust from our feet: See the note at 9.5.

*10.13 dressed in sackcloth . . . ashes on their heads: This was one way that people showed how sorry they were for their sins.

*10.17 seventy-two: See the note at 10.1.

See also: 10.10–11: Acts 13.51. 10.12: a Gen 19.24–28;
Matt 11.24; b Matt 10.15. 10.13: Isa 23.1–18;
Ezek 26.1–28.26; Joel 3.4–8; Amos 1.9–10; Zech 9.2–4.
10.15: Isa 14.13–15. 10.16: Matt 10.40; Mark 9.37;
Luke 9.48; John 13.20. 10.19: Psa 91.13.

Nothing can harm you. ²⁰ But don't be happy because evil spirits obey you. Be happy that your names are written in heaven!

Jesus thanks his Father

This is also told in Matthew 11.25–27; 13.16–17

²¹ At that same time, Jesus felt the joy that comes from the Holy Spirit,' and he said:

My Father, Lord of heaven and earth, I am grateful that you hid all this from wise and educated people and showed it to ordinary people. Yes, Father, that is what pleased you.
²² My Father has given me everything, and he is the only one who knows the Son. The only one who really knows the Father is the Son. But the Son wants to tell others about the Father, so that they can know him too.

²³ Jesus then turned to his disciples and said to them in private, "You are really blessed to see what you see! ²⁴ Many prophets and kings were eager to see what you see and to hear what you hear. But I tell you that they did not see or hear."

The good Samaritan

²⁵ An expert in the Law of Moses stood up and asked Jesus a question to see what he would say. "Teacher," he asked, "what must I do to have eternal life?"
²⁶ Jesus answered, "What is written in the Scriptures? How do you understand them?"
²⁷ The man replied, "The Scriptures say, 'Love the Lord your God with all your heart, soul, strength, and mind.' They also say, 'Love your neighbours as much as you love yourself.' "
²⁸ Jesus said, "You have given the right answer. If you do this, you will have eternal life."
²⁹ But the man wanted to show that he knew what he was talking about. So he asked Jesus, "Who are my neighbours?"
³⁰ Jesus replied:

As a man was going down from Jerusalem to Jericho, robbers attacked him and grabbed everything he had. They beat him up and ran off, leaving him half dead. ³¹ A priest happened to be going down the same road. But when he saw the man,

he walked by on the other side. ³² Later a temple helper* came to the same place. But when he saw the man who had been beaten up, he also went by on the other side.
³³ A man from Samaria then came travelling along that road. When he saw the man, he felt sorry for him ³⁴ and went over to him. He treated his wounds with olive oil and wine* and bandaged them. Then he put him on his own donkey and took him to an inn, where he took care of him. ³⁵ The next morning he gave the innkeeper two silver coins and said, "Please take care of the man. If you spend more than this on him, I will pay you when I return."

³⁶ Then Jesus asked, "Which one of these three people was a real neighbour to the man who was beaten up by robbers?"
³⁷ The teacher answered, "The one who showed pity."
Jesus said, "Go and do the same!"

Martha and Mary

³⁸ The Lord and his disciples were travelling along and came to a village. When they got there, a woman named Martha welcomed him into her home. ³⁹ She had a sister named Mary, who sat down in front of the Lord and was listening to what he said. ⁴⁰ Martha was worried about all that had to be done. Finally, she went to Jesus and said, "Lord, doesn't it bother you that my sister has left me to do all the work by myself? Tell her to come and help me!"
⁴¹ The Lord answered, "Martha, Martha! You are worried and upset about so many things, ⁴² but only one thing is necessary. Mary has chosen what is best, and it will not be taken away from her."

CHAPTER 11

Prayer

This is also told in Matthew 6.9–13; 7.7–11

¹ When Jesus had finished praying, one of his disciples said to him, "Lord, teach us to pray, just as John taught his followers to pray."

---

*10.32 temple helper: A man from the tribe of Levi, whose job it was to work around the temple.
*10.34 olive oil and wine: In New Testament times these were used as medicine. Sometimes olive oil is a symbol for healing by means of a miracle (see James 5.14).
See also: 10.33–34: 2 Chron 28.15. 10.38–39: John 11.1.

See also: 10.22: a John 3.35; b John 10.15.
10.25–28: Matt 22.35–40; Mark 12.28–34. 10.27: a Deut 6.5;
b Lev 19.18. 10.28: Lev 18.5.

2 So Jesus told them, "Pray in this way:

'Father, help us
to honour your name.
Come and set up
your kingdom.
3 Give us each day
the food we need.'
4 Forgive our sins,
as we forgive everyone
who has done wrong to us.
And keep us
from being tempted.' "

5 Then Jesus went on to say:

Suppose one of you goes to a friend in the middle of the night and says, "Let me borrow three loaves of bread. 6 A friend of mine has dropped in, and I don't have a thing for him to eat." 7 And suppose your friend answers, "Don't bother me! The door is bolted, and my children and I are in bed. I cannot get up to give you something."

8 He may not get up and give you the bread, just because you are his friend. But he will get up and give you as much as you need, simply because you are not ashamed to keep on asking.

9 So I tell you to ask and you will receive, search and you will find, knock and the door will be opened for you. 10 Everyone who asks will receive, everyone who searches will find, and the door will be opened for everyone who knocks. 11 Which one of you fathers would give your hungry child a snake if the child asked for a fish? 12 Which one of you would give your child a scorpion if the child asked for an egg? 13 As bad as you are, you still know how to give good gifts to your children. But your heavenly Father is even more ready to give the Holy Spirit to anyone who asks.

Jesus and the ruler of demons

This is also told in Matthew 12.22–30; Mark 3.20–27

14 Jesus forced a demon out of a man who could not talk. And after the demon had gone out, the man started speaking, and the crowds were amazed. 15 But some people said, "He forces out demons by the power of Beelzebul, the ruler of the demons!"

16 Others wanted to put Jesus to the test. So they asked him to show them a sign from God. 17 Jesus knew what they were thinking, and he said:

A kingdom where people fight each other will end up in ruin. And a family that fights will break up. 18 If Satan fights against himself, how can his kingdom last? Yet you say that I force out demons by the power of Beelzebul. 19 If I use his power to force out demons, whose power do your own followers use to force them out? They are the ones who will judge you. 20 But if I use God's power to force out demons, it proves that God's kingdom has already come to you.

21 When a strong man arms himself and guards his home, everything he owns is safe. 22 But if a stronger man comes and defeats him, he will carry off all the weapons in which the strong man trusted. Then he will divide with others what he has taken. 23 If you are not on my side, you are against me. If you don't gather in the crop with me, you scatter it.

Return of an evil spirit

This is also told in Matthew 12.43–45

Jesus continued:

24 When an evil spirit leaves a person, it travels through the desert, looking for a place to rest. But when it doesn't find a place, it says, "I will go back to the home I left." 25 When it gets there and finds the place clean and tidy, 26 it goes off and finds seven other evil spirits even worse than itself. They all come and make their home there, and that person ends up in a worse state than before.

Being really blessed

27 While Jesus was still talking, a woman in the crowd spoke up, "The woman who gave birth to you and nursed you is blessed!"

28 Jesus replied, "That's true, but the people who are really blessed are the ones who hear and obey God's message!"

A sign from God

This is also told in Matthew 12.38–42; Mark 8.12

29 As crowds were gathering around Jesus, he said:

See also: 11.15: Matt 9.34; 10.25.

See also: 11.16: Matt 12.38; 16.1; Mark 8.11.
11.23: Mark 9.40.   **11.29:** Matt 16.4; Mark 8.12.

You people of today are evil! You keep looking for a sign from God. But what happened to Jonah* is the only sign you will be given. 30 Just as Jonah was a sign to the people of Nineveh, the Son of Man will be a sign to the people of today. 31 When the judgment comes, the Queen of the South* will stand there with you and condemn you. She travelled a long way to hear Solomon's wisdom, and yet here is something far greater than Solomon. 32 The people of Nineveh will also stand there with you and condemn you. They turned to God when Jonah preached, and yet here is something far greater than Jonah.

Light

This is also told in Matthew 5.15; 6.22–23

Jesus continued:

33 No one lights a lamp and then hides it or puts it under a clay pot. A lamp is put on a lampstand, so that everyone who comes into the house can see the light. 34 Your eyes are the lamp for your body. When your eyes are good, you have all the light you need. But when your eyes are bad, everything is dark. 35 So be sure that your light isn't darkness. 36 If you have light, and nothing is dark, then light will be everywhere, as when a lamp shines brightly on you.

Jesus condemns the Pharisees and teachers of the Law of Moses

This is also told in Matthew 23.1–36; Mark 12.38–40; Luke 20.45–47

37 When Jesus finished speaking, a Pharisee invited him home for a meal. Jesus went and sat down to eat.* 38 The Pharisee was surprised that he did not wash his hands* before eating. 39 So the Lord said to him:

You Pharisees clean the outside of cups and dishes, but on the inside you are

greedy and evil. 40 You fools! Didn't God make both the outside and the inside?' 41 If you would only give what you have to the poor, everything you do would please God.

42 You Pharisees are in for trouble! You give God a tenth of the spices from your gardens, such as mint and rue. But you cheat people, and you don't love God. You should be fair and kind to others and still give a tenth to God.

43 You Pharisees are in for trouble! You love the front seats in the meeting places, and you like to be greeted with honour in the market. 44 But you are in for trouble! You are like unmarked graves* that people walk on without even knowing it.

45 A teacher of the Law of Moses spoke up, "Teacher, you said cruel things about us." 46 Jesus replied:

You teachers are also in for trouble! You load people down with heavy burdens, but you won't lift a finger to help them carry the loads. 47 Yes, you are really in for trouble. You build monuments to honour the prophets your own people murdered long ago. 48 You must think that was the right thing for your people to do, or else you would not have built monuments for the prophets they murdered.

49 Because of your evil deeds, the Wisdom of God said, "I will send prophets and apostles to you. But you will murder some and ill-treat others." 50 You people living today will be punished for all the prophets who have been murdered since the beginning of the world. 51 This includes every prophet from the time of Abel to the time of Zechariah,* who was murdered between the altar and the temple. You people will certainly be punished for all this.

11.29 what happened to Jonah: Jonah was in the stomach of a big fish for three days and nights. See Matthew 12.40.
11.31 Queen of the South: Sheba, probably a country in southern Arabia.
11.37 sat down to eat: See the note at 7.36.
11.38 did not wash his hands: The Jewish people had strict laws about washing their hands before eating, especially if they had been out in public.
See also: 11.30: Jon 3.4. **11.31:** 1 King 10.1–10; 2 Chron 9.1–12. **11.32:** Jon 3.5. **11.33:** Matt 5.15; Mark 4.21; Luke 8.16.

11.44 unmarked graves: Tombs were whitewashed to keep anyone from accidentally touching them. A person who touched a dead body or a tomb was considered unclean and could not worship with other Jewish people.
11.51 from the time of Abel . . . Zechariah: Genesis is the first book in the Jewish Scriptures, and it tells that Abel was the first person to be murdered. The Second Book of Chronicles is the last book in the Jewish Scriptures, and the last murder that it tells about is that of Zechariah.
See also: 11.42: Lev 27.30. **11.51:** a Gen 4.8; b 2 Chron 24.20–21.

Real life

Materialism

Contributed by Soul Survivor

Whether it's obsessing over a new hairdo, drooling over a magazine of beautiful lifestyle shots, or being convinced that buying a Playstation will lift you out of a low spot, most people we know are quite keen on getting stuff.

And often this stuff is tied up with their identity. That's why TV adverts and everything about branding, products and lifestyle suggests that identity comes through what we own and what we wear.

But feeding your sense of identity through things like wearing hot new clothes is risky; it's fine when someone says, 'nice top!' – but get it wrong and your identity is in shreds on the floor. God is our provider, not just of clothes and stuff but the core of what we're really looking for: identity, acceptance, purpose, love.

This is where simplicity comes in. By simplicity, we mean living in a way where you are content with what you have and not being so attached to anything that giving it away would mean the end of the world. Simplicity starts with the attitude that everything is God's anyway. Simplicity is all about not making things more important than they truly are. If we get so in love with something that we fear the very thought of not having it, then maybe we have attached too much importance to it.

So how do we press on into the real security God has for us, and detox from the product junk? A bishop once said, 'Never underestimate or despise the power of the daily disciplines of sitting down, reading your Bible and praying.' That's the daily mirror we look into to find out who we are. The stuff about the birds and the flowers is Jesus saying not to worry about things but let God the Father look after you. So strip back the distractions where necessary to get you living at the foot of the cross as a child of God.

Think

'Tweet! Tweet!' What did Jesus mean in Matthew 6.26–30 and Luke 12.21–23? How much stuff have you got? If it was all put together in one place, would you be shocked? If you went camping, what would you take with you?

One sixth of the world lives on less than a dollar a day. What would you have to cut out if your finances were reduced to that?

Act

Ask God to show you anything you place too much value in. Try giving some money away to a charity. Stop wearing the labels for a while. If you think your identity is in your mobile phone or your CD player try giving them up for a week to rid yourself of the dependence.

If you feel insecure or low, remind yourself of what God says about you: keep reading the Bible. Tell trusted friends what you're doing; it may help you stay focused.

Give stuff away – just for fun. Do random acts of kindness by letting someone else have what you've got. Tell your possessions who's boss: God! Enjoy a worry-free lifestyle.

Cultivate simplicity. Keep asking, 'Do I need that?' set yourself a budget, occasionally fast from an item.

Check

Psalms 37.16–19; 119.33–40; Proverbs 3.13–15; 16.16; Isaiah 3.13—4.1; Luke 1.53; James 2.1–9

More...

Shopping p.973

52 You teachers of the Law of Moses are really in for trouble! You carry the keys to the door of knowledge about God. But you never go in, and you keep others from going in.

53 Jesus was about to leave, but the teachers and the Pharisees wanted to get even with him. They tried to make him say what he thought about other things, 54 so that they could catch him saying something wrong.

CHAPTER 12

Warnings

1 As thousands of people crowded around Jesus and were stepping on each other, he told his disciples:

Be sure to guard against the dishonest teaching* of the Pharisees! It is their way of fooling people. 2 Everything that is hidden will be found out, and every secret will be known. 3 Whatever you say in the dark will be heard when it is day. Whatever you whisper in a closed room will be shouted from the housetops.

The one to fear

This is also told in Matthew 10.28–31

Jesus continued:

4 My friends, don't be afraid of people. They can kill you, but after that, there is nothing else they can do. 5 God is the one you must fear. Not only can he take your life, but he can throw you into hell. God is certainly the one you should fear!

6 Five sparrows are sold for just two pennies, but God doesn't forget a single one of them. 7 Even the hairs on your head are counted. So don't be afraid! You are worth much more than many sparrows.

Telling others about Christ

This is also told in Matthew 10.32–33; 12.32; 10.19–20

Jesus continued:

8 If you tell others that you belong to me, the Son of Man will tell God's angels that you are my followers. 9 But if you reject me, you will be rejected in front of them.

10 If you speak against the Son of Man, you can be forgiven, but if you speak against the Holy Spirit, you cannot be forgiven.

11 When you are brought to trial in the Jewish meeting places or before rulers or officials, don't worry about how you will defend yourselves or what you will say. 12 At that time the Holy Spirit will tell you what to say.

A rich fool

13 A man in a crowd said to Jesus, "Teacher, tell my brother to give me my share of what our father left us when he died."

14 Jesus answered, "Who gave me the right to settle arguments between you and your brother?"

15 Then he said to the crowd, "Don't be greedy! Owning a lot of things won't make your life safe."

16 So Jesus told them this story:

A rich man's farm produced a big crop, 17 and he said to himself, "What can I do? I don't have a place large enough to store everything."

18 Later, he said, "Now I know what I'll do. I'll tear down my barns and build bigger ones, where I can store all my grain and other goods. 19 Then I'll say to myself, 'You have stored up enough good things to last for years to come. Live it up! Eat, drink, and enjoy yourself.' "

20 But God said to him, "You fool! Tonight you will die. Then who will get what you have stored up?"

21 "This is what happens to people who store up everything for themselves, but are poor in the sight of God."

Worry

This is also told in Matthew 6.25–34

22 Jesus said to his disciples:

I tell you not to worry about your life! Don't worry about having something to eat or wear. 23 Life is more than food or clothing. 24 Look at the crows! They don't plant or harvest, and they don't have storehouses or barns. But God takes care of them. You are much more important than any birds. 25 Can worry make you live longer? 26 If you don't have power over small things, why worry about everything else?

---

*12.1 **dishonest teaching:** The Greek text has "yeast", which is used here of a teaching that is not true. See Matthew 16.6,12.

See also: 12.1: Matt 16.6; Mark 8.15. 12.2: Mark 4.22; Luke 8.17.

See also: 12.10: Matt 12.32; Mark 3.29. 12.11-12: Matt 10.19–20; Mark 13.11; Luke 21.14–15.

²⁷ Look how the wild flowers grow! They don't work hard to make their clothes. But I tell you that Solomon with all his wealth* wasn't as well clothed as one of these flowers. ²⁸ God gives such beauty to everything that grows in the fields, even though it is here today and thrown into a fire tomorrow. Won't he do even more for you? You have such little faith!

²⁹ Don't keep worrying about having something to eat or drink. ³⁰ Only people who don't know God are always worrying about such things. Your Father knows what you need. ³¹ But put God's work first, and these things will be yours as well.

Treasures in heaven

This is also told in Matthew 6.19–21

Jesus continued:

³² My little group of disciples, don't be afraid! Your Father wants to give you the kingdom. ³³ Sell what you have and give the money to the poor. Make yourselves money bags that never wear out. Make sure your treasure is safe in heaven, where thieves cannot steal it and moths cannot destroy it. ³⁴ Your heart will always be where your treasure is.

Faithful and unfaithful servants

This is also told in Matthew 24.45–51

Jesus continued:

³⁵ Be ready and keep your lamps burning ³⁶ just like those servants who wait up for their master to return from a wedding feast. As soon as he comes and knocks, they open the door for him. ³⁷ Servants are fortunate if their master finds them awake and ready when he comes! I promise you that he will get ready and make his servants sit down so that he can serve them. ³⁸ Those servants are really fortunate if their master finds them ready, even though he comes late at night or early in the morning. ³⁹ You would not let a thief break into your home, if you knew when the thief was coming. ⁴⁰ So always be

---

*12.27 Solomon with all his wealth: The Jewish people thought that Solomon was the richest person who had ever lived.

See also: **12.27:** 1 King 10.4–7; 2 Chron 9.3–6.
12.35: Matt 25.1–13.   **12.36:** Mark 13.34–36.
12.39–40: Matt 24.43–44.

Helpline

Help! My parents oppose my faith

'My parents are dead against my faith. They think I've been abducted by a cult...'

When you become a Christian it's one of the best days of your life. But what if your parents aren't Christian? What if they actually feel threatened by your decision, instead of rejoicing in it?

Most parents want what's best for their children. When it comes to Christianity they might not see what's good about it. The only cure for this is lots of commitment, lots of communication and lots of perseverance.

In some extreme cases, parents might not allow you to go to church, or to spend time with Christian people. In that case, the best thing to do is get in touch with the pastor of your local church, or your local church youth leader. A visit from them may do a lot to persuade your parents that you have not signed your life away to a load of two-headed aliens from the planet Tharg.

Three things

Reassurance

Most parents are naturally concerned for their children, and sometimes they want reassurance. So spend time with them. Explain clearly and reasonably why you want to do what you want to do.

Attitude

Your parents will hink more of your faith if it really has changed you for the better. So get your act together. The better you are as a person, the better they'll think of your faith.

Perseverance

They might dismiss your Christianity as 'a phase you're going through'. So make sure it isn't. The more you persevere with it and the more impact it has on your life, the more seriously they will take it.

More...

Families p.1224
Living truthfully p.1070
Help! My parents have favourites p.42

ready! You don't know when the Son of Man will come.

⁴¹ Peter asked Jesus, "Did you say this just for us or for everyone?"
⁴² The Lord answered:

Who are faithful and wise servants? Who are the ones the master will put in charge of giving the other servants their food supplies at the proper time? ⁴³ Servants are fortunate if their master comes and finds them doing their job. ⁴⁴ A servant who is always faithful will be put in charge of everything the master owns.

⁴⁵ But suppose one of the servants thinks that the master won't return until late. Suppose that servant starts beating all the other servants and eats and drinks and gets drunk. ⁴⁶ If that happens, the master will come on a day and at a time when the servant least expects him. That servant will then be punished and thrown out with the servants who cannot be trusted.

⁴⁷ If servants are not ready or willing to do what their master wants them to do, they will be beaten hard. ⁴⁸ But servants who don't know what their master wants them to do will not be beaten so hard for doing wrong. If God has been generous with you, he will expect you to serve him well. But if he has been more than generous, he will expect you to serve him even better.

Not peace, but trouble

This is also told in Matthew 10.34–36

Jesus continued:

⁴⁹ I came to set fire to the earth, and I wish it were already on fire! ⁵⁰ I am going to be put to a hard test. And I will have to suffer a lot of pain until it is over. ⁵¹ Do you think that I came to bring peace to earth? No indeed! I came to make people choose sides. ⁵² A family of five will be divided, with two of them against the other three. ⁵³ Fathers and sons will turn against one another, and mothers and daughters will do the same. Mothers-in-law and daughters-in-law will also turn against each other.

Knowing what to do

This is also told in Matthew 16.2–3; 5.25–26

⁵⁴ Jesus said to all the people:

As soon as you see a cloud coming up in the west, you say, "It's going to rain," and it does. ⁵⁵ When the south wind blows, you say, "It's going to get hot," and it does. ⁵⁶ Are you trying to fool someone? You can predict the weather by looking at the earth and sky, but you don't really know what's going on right now. ⁵⁷ Why don't you understand the right thing to do? ⁵⁸ When someone accuses you of something, try to settle things before you are taken to court. If you don't, you will be dragged before the judge. Then the judge will hand you over to the jailer, and you will be locked up. ⁵⁹ You won't get out until you have paid the last penny you owe.

CHAPTER 13

Turn back to God

¹ About this same time Jesus was told that Pilate had given orders for some people from Galilee to be killed while they were offering sacrifices. ² Jesus replied:

Do you think that these people were worse sinners than everyone else in Galilee just because of what happened to them? ³ Not at all! But you can be sure that if you don't turn back to God, every one of you will also be killed. ⁴ What about those eighteen people who died when the tower in Siloam fell on them? Do you think they were worse than everyone else in Jerusalem? ⁵ Not at all! But you can be sure that if you don't turn back to God, every one of you will also die.

A story about a fig tree

⁶ Jesus then told them this story:

A man had a fig tree growing in his vineyard. One day he went out to pick some figs, but he didn't find any. ⁷ So he said to the gardener, "For three years I have come looking for figs on this tree, and I haven't found any yet. Chop it down! Why should it take up space?"

⁸ The gardener answered, "Master, leave it for another year. I'll dig around it and put some manure on it to make it grow. ⁹ Perhaps it will have figs on it next year. If it doesn't, you can have it cut down."

Healing a woman on the Sabbath

¹⁰ One Sabbath, Jesus was teaching in a Jewish meeting place, ¹¹ and a woman was there who had been crippled by an evil spirit for eighteen years. She was completely bent over and could not straighten up. ¹² When Jesus saw the woman, he called her over and said, "You are now well." ¹³ He placed his hands on her, and at once she stood up straight and praised God.

¹⁴ The man in charge of the meeting place was angry because Jesus had healed someone on the Sabbath. So he said to the people, "Each week has six days when we can work. Come and be healed on one of those days, but not on the Sabbath."

¹⁵ The Lord replied, "Are you trying to fool someone? Won't any one of you untie your ox or donkey and lead it out to drink on a Sabbath? ¹⁶ This woman belongs to the family of Abraham, but Satan has kept her bound for eighteen years. Isn't it right to set her free on the Sabbath?" ¹⁷ Jesus' words made his enemies ashamed. But everyone else in the crowd was happy about the wonderful things he was doing.

A mustard seed and yeast

This is also told in Matthew 13.31–33; Mark 4.30–32

¹⁸ Jesus said, "What is God's kingdom like? What can I compare it with? ¹⁹ It is like what happens when someone plants a mustard seed in a garden. The seed grows as big as a tree, and birds nest in its branches."

²⁰ Then Jesus said, "What can I compare God's kingdom with? ²¹ It is like what happens when a woman mixes yeast into three batches of flour. Finally, all the dough rises."

The narrow door

This is also told in Matthew 7.13–14,21–23

²² As Jesus was on his way to Jerusalem, he taught the people in the towns and villages. ²³ Someone asked him, "Lord, are only a few people going to be saved?"

Jesus answered:

²⁴ Do all you can to go in by the narrow door! A lot of people will try to get in, but will not be able to. ²⁵ Once the owner of the house gets up and locks the door, you will be left standing outside. You will knock on the door and say, "Sir, open the door for us!"

But the owner will answer, "I don't know a thing about you!"

²⁶ Then you will start saying, "We dined with you, and you taught in our streets."

²⁷ But he will say, "I really don't know who you are! Get away from me, you evil people!"

²⁸ Then when you have been thrown outside, you will weep and grit your teeth because you will see Abraham, Isaac, Jacob, and all the prophets in God's kingdom. ²⁹ People will come from all directions and sit down to feast in God's kingdom. ³⁰ There the ones who are now least important will be the most important, and those who are now most important will be least important.

Jesus and Herod

³¹ At that time some Pharisees came to Jesus and said, "You had better get away from here! Herod* wants to kill you."

³² Jesus said to them:

Go and tell that fox, "I am going to force out demons and heal people today and tomorrow, and three days later I'll have finished." ³³ But I am going on my way today and tomorrow and the next day. After all, Jerusalem is the place where prophets are killed.

Jesus loves Jerusalem

This is also told in Matthew 23.37–39

Jesus continued:

³⁴ Jerusalem, Jerusalem! Your people have killed the prophets and have stoned the messengers who were sent to you. I have often wanted to gather your people, as a hen gathers her chicks under her wings. But you wouldn't let me. ³⁵ Now your temple will be deserted. You won't see me again until the time when you say,

"Blessed is the one who comes
in the name of the Lord."

CHAPTER 14

Jesus heals a sick man

¹ One Sabbath, Jesus was having dinner in the home of an important Pharisee, and everyone was carefully watching Jesus. ² All

---

See also: 13.14: Exod 20.9–10; Deut 5.13–14.

*13.31 Herod:** See the note at 3.1.
See also: 13.27: Psa 6.8. 13.28: Matt 22.13; 25.30. 13.28–29: Matt 8.11–12. 13.30: Matt 19.30; 20.16; Mark 10.31. 13.35: Psa 118.26.

of a sudden a man with swollen legs stood up in front of him. ³ Jesus turned and asked the Pharisees and the teachers of the Law of Moses, "Is it right to heal on the Sabbath?" ⁴ But they did not say a word.

Jesus took hold of the man. Then he healed him and sent him away. ⁵ Afterwards, Jesus asked the people, "If your son or ox falls into a well, wouldn't you pull him out straight away, even on the Sabbath?" ⁶ There was nothing they could say.

How to be a guest

⁷ Jesus saw how the guests had tried to take the best seats. So he told them:

⁸ When you are invited to a wedding feast, don't sit in the best place. Someone more important may have been invited. ⁹ Then the one who invited you will come and say, "Give your place to this other guest!" You will be embarrassed and will have to sit in the worst place.

¹⁰ When you are invited to be a guest, go and sit in the worst place. Then the one who invited you may come and say, "My friend, take a better seat!" You will then be honoured in front of all the other guests. ¹¹ If you put yourself above others, you will be put down. But if you humble yourself, you will be honoured.

¹² Then Jesus said to the man who had invited him:

When you give a dinner or a banquet, don't invite your friends and family and relatives and rich neighbours. If you do, they will invite you in return, and you will be paid back. ¹³ When you give a feast, invite the poor, the crippled, the lame, and the blind. ¹⁴ They cannot pay you back. But God will bless you and reward you when his people rise from death.

The great banquet

This is also told in Matthew 22.1–10

¹⁵ After Jesus had finished speaking, one of the guests said, "The greatest blessing of all is to be at the banquet in God's kingdom!"

¹⁶ Jesus told him:

A man once gave a great banquet and invited a lot of guests. ¹⁷ When the banquet was ready, he sent a servant to tell the guests, "Everything is ready! Please come."

¹⁸ One guest after another started making excuses. The first one said, "I bought some land, and I've got to look it over. Please excuse me."

¹⁹ Another guest said, "I bought five teams of oxen, and I need to try them out. Please excuse me."

²⁰ Still another guest said, "I have just got married, and I can't be there."

²¹ The servant told his master what happened, and the master became so angry that he said, "Go as fast as you can to every street and alley in town! Bring in everyone who is poor or crippled or blind or lame."

²² When the servant returned, he said, "Master, I've done what you told me, and there is still plenty of room for more people."

²³ His master then told him, "Go out along the back roads and lanes and make people come in, so that my house will be full. ²⁴ Not one of the guests I first invited will get even a bite of my food!"

Being a disciple

This is also told in Matthew 10.37–38

²⁵ Large crowds were walking along with Jesus, when he turned and said:

²⁶ You cannot be my disciple, unless you love me more than you love your father and mother, your wife and children, and your brothers and sisters. You cannot come with me unless you love me more than you love your own life.

²⁷ You cannot be my disciple unless you carry your own cross and come with me.

²⁸ Suppose one of you wants to build a tower. What is the first thing you will do? Won't you sit down and figure out how much it will cost and if you have enough money to pay for it? ²⁹ Otherwise, you will start building the tower, but not be able to finish. Then everyone who sees what is happening will laugh at you. ³⁰ They will say, "You started building, but could not finish the job."

³¹ What will a king do if he has only ten thousand soldiers to defend himself against a king who is about to attack him with twenty thousand soldiers? Before he goes out to battle, won't he first sit down and decide if he can win? ³² If he thinks he won't be able to defend himself, he will

See also: 14.5: Matt 12.11.   **14.8–10:** Prov 25.6–7. **14.11:** Matt 23.12; Luke 18.14.

See also: 14.26: Matt 10.37.   **14.27:** Matt 10.38; 16.24; Mark 8.34; Luke 9.23.

send messengers and ask for peace while the other king is still a long way off. ³³ So then, you cannot be my disciple unless you give away everything you own.

Salt

This is also told in Matthew 5.13; Mark 9.50

Jesus continued:

³⁴ Salt is good, but if it no longer tastes like salt, how can it be made to taste salty again? ³⁵ It is no longer good for the soil or even for the manure pile. People simply throw it out. If you have ears, pay attention!

CHAPTER 15

One sheep

This is also told in Matthew 18.12–14

¹ Tax collectors* and sinners were all crowding around to listen to Jesus. ² So the Pharisees and the teachers of the Law of Moses started grumbling, "This man is friendly with sinners. He even eats with them."

³ Then Jesus told them this story:

⁴ If any of you has a hundred sheep, and one of them gets lost, what will you do? Won't you leave the ninety-nine in the field and go and look for the lost sheep until you find it? ⁵ And when you find it, you will be so glad that you will put it on your shoulder ⁶ and carry it home. Then you will call in your friends and neighbours and say, "Let's celebrate! I've found my lost sheep."

⁷ Jesus said, "In the same way there is more happiness in heaven because of one sinner who turns to God than over ninety-nine good people who don't need to."

One coin

⁸ Jesus told the people another story:

What will a woman do if she has ten silver coins and loses one of them? Won't she light a lamp, sweep the floor, and look carefully until she finds it? ⁹ Then she will call in her friends and neighbours and say, "Let's celebrate! I've found the coin I lost."

¹⁰ Jesus said, "In the same way God's angels are happy when even one person turns to him."

Two sons

¹¹ Jesus also told them another story:

Once a man had two sons. ¹² The younger son said to his father, "Give me my share of the property." So the father divided his property between his two sons.

¹³ Not long after that, the younger son packed up everything he owned and left for a foreign country, where he wasted all his money in wild living. ¹⁴ He had spent everything, when a bad famine spread through that whole land. Soon he had nothing to eat.

¹⁵ He went to work for a man in that country, and the man sent him out to take care of his pigs.* ¹⁶ He would have been glad to eat what the pigs were eating,* but no one gave him a thing.

¹⁷ Finally, he came to his senses and said, "My father's workers have plenty to eat, and here I am, starving to death! ¹⁸ I will go to my father and say to him, 'Father, I have sinned against God in heaven and against you. ¹⁹ I am no longer good enough to be called your son. Treat me like one of your workers.' "

²⁰ The younger son got up and started back to his father. But when he was still a long way off, his father saw him and felt sorry for him. He ran to his son and hugged and kissed him.

²¹ The son said, "Father, I have sinned against God in heaven and against you. I am no longer good enough to be called your son."

²² But his father said to the servants, "Hurry and bring the best clothes and put them on him. Give him a ring for his finger and sandals* for his feet. ²³ Get the best calf and prepare it, so we can eat and celebrate. ²⁴ This son of mine was dead, but has now come back to life.

---

*15.15 pigs: The Jewish religion taught that pigs were not fit to eat or even to touch. A Jewish man would have felt terribly insulted if he had to feed pigs, much less eat with them.
*15.16 what the pigs were eating: The Greek text has "(bean) pods", which came from a tree in Palestine. These were used to feed animals. Poor people sometimes ate them too.
*15.22 ring . . . sandals: These show that the young man's father fully accepted him as his son. A ring was a sign of high position in the family. Sandals showed that he was a son instead of a slave, since slaves did not usually wear sandals.

---

*15.1 Tax collectors: See the note at 3.12.
See also: 15.1–2: Luke 5.29–30.

Big ideas

Hell

Most of the statements about hell in the Bible are pictures. They're not necessarily literal descriptions. When Jesus talked of an 'outer darkness' with fire, weeping and lost, aimless people, he wasn't necessarily describing the physical details. He was painting a picture of a place of alienation, loneliness and despair.

There are three names for hell in the Bible.

Sheol

Sheol is the name used in the Old Testament. It meant the place where the soul went after the death of the individual. It was not a place where the dead enjoyed the presence of God, but it wasn't what we think of as 'Hell' (see below). There are several places where God promises to rescue those in Sheol and bring them into his presence (Psalms 16.9–11).

Hades

In the New Testament, Sheol is called Hades, the Greek term for the realm of the dead.

Gehenna

Jesus used the word Gehenna (Matthew 10.28; Luke 12.5) which was a real place – ge-hinnom, the valley of Hinnom – a valley outside Jerusalem. In Jesus' time it was the city's rubbish dump, where fires burned day and night. It had a horrible history, because it was in Gehenna that children were sacrificed to Molech (Jeremiah 7.31).

Gehenna was outside the sacred city, beyond the walls. So Gehenna symbolises a spiritual wasteland, a rubbish dump for lost souls, a place marked by the absence of God. The Bible is quite clear that there is a place where those who don't believe in Jesus will go. But people have a choice about whether or not they end up there.

More...

Heaven p.1412
Demonic powers p.1131
Resisting temptation p.1124

He was lost and has now been found." And they began to celebrate. ²⁵ The elder son had been out in the field. But when he came near the house, he heard the music and dancing. ²⁶ So he called one of the servants over and asked, "What's going on here?"

²⁷ The servant answered, "Your brother has come home safe and sound, and your father ordered us to kill the best calf." ²⁸ The elder brother got so angry that he would not even go into the house.

His father came out and begged him to go in. ²⁹ But he said to his father, "For years I have worked for you like a slave and have always obeyed you. But you have never even given me a little goat, so that I could give a dinner for my friends. ³⁰ This other son of yours wasted your money on prostitutes. And now that he has come home, you ordered the best calf to be killed for a feast."

³¹ His father replied, "My son, you are always with me, and everything I have is yours. ³² But we should be glad and celebrate! Your brother was dead, but he is now alive. He was lost and has now been found."

CHAPTER 16

A dishonest manager

¹ Jesus said to his disciples:

A rich man once had a manager to take care of his business. But he was told that his manager was wasting money. ² So the rich man called him in and said, "What is this I hear about you? Tell me what you have done! You are no longer going to work for me."

³ The manager said to himself, "What shall I do now that my master is going to fire me? I can't dig ditches, and I'm ashamed to beg. ⁴ I know what I'll do, so that people will welcome me into their homes after I've lost my job."

⁵ Then one by one he called in the people who were in debt to his master. He asked the first one, "How much do you owe my master?"

⁶ "A hundred barrels of olive oil," the man answered.

So the manager said, "Take your bill and sit down and quickly write 'fifty'."

7 The manager asked someone else who was in debt to his master, "How much do you owe?"

"A thousand sacks* of wheat," the man replied.

The manager said, "Take your bill and write 'eight hundred'."

8 The master praised his dishonest manager for looking out for himself so well. That's how it is! The people of this world look out for themselves better than the people who belong to the light.

9 My disciples, I tell you to use wicked wealth to make friends for yourselves. Then when it is gone, you will be welcomed into an eternal home. 10 Anyone who can be trusted in little matters can also be trusted in important matters. But anyone who is dishonest in little matters will be dishonest in important matters. 11 If you cannot be trusted with this wicked wealth, who will trust you with true wealth? 12 And if you cannot be trusted with what belongs to someone else, who will give you something that will be your own? 13 You cannot be the slave of two masters. You will like one more than the other or be more loyal to one than to the other. You cannot serve God and money.

Some sayings of Jesus

This is also told in Matthew 11.12–13; 5.31–32; Mark 10.11–12

14 The Pharisees really loved money. So when they heard what Jesus said, they made fun of him. 15 But Jesus told them:

You are always making yourselves look good, but God sees what is in your heart. The things that most people think are important are worthless as far as God is concerned.

16 Until the time of John the Baptist, people had to obey the Law of Moses and the Books of the Prophets.* But since God's kingdom has been preached, everyone is trying hard to get in. 17 Heaven and earth will disappear before the smallest letter of the Law does.

18 It is a terrible sin* for a man to divorce his wife and marry another woman. It is also a terrible sin for a man to marry a divorced woman.

Lazarus and the rich man

Jesus continued:

19 There was once a rich man who wore expensive clothes and every day ate the best food. 20 But a poor beggar named Lazarus was brought to the gate of the rich man's house. 21 He was happy just to eat the scraps that fell from the rich man's table. His body was covered with sores, and dogs kept coming up to lick them. 22 The poor man died, and angels took him to the place of honour next to Abraham.*

The rich man also died and was buried. 23 He went to hell* and was suffering terribly. When he looked up and saw Abraham far off and Lazarus at his side, 24 he said to Abraham, "Have pity on me! Send Lazarus to dip his finger in water and touch my tongue. I'm suffering terribly in this fire."

25 Abraham answered, "My friend, remember that while you lived, you had everything good, and Lazarus had everything bad. Now he is happy, and you are in pain. 26 And besides, there is a deep ditch between us, and no one from either side can cross over."

27 But the rich man said, "Abraham, then please send Lazarus to my father's home. 28 Let him warn my five brothers, so they won't come to this horrible place."

29 Abraham answered, "Your brothers can read what Moses and the prophets* wrote. They should pay attention to that."

30 Then the rich man said, "No, that's not enough! If only someone from the dead would go to them, they would listen and turn to God."

*16.18 a terrible sin: The Greek text uses a word that means the sin of being unfaithful in marriage.
*16.22 the place of honour next to Abraham: The Jewish people thought that heaven would be a banquet that God would give for them. Abraham would be the most important person there, and the guest of honour would sit next to him.
*16.23 hell: The Greek text has "hades", which the Jewish people often thought of as the place where the dead wait for the final judgment.
*16.29 Moses and the prophets: See the note at 16.16.
See also: 16.18: Matt 5.32; 1 Cor 7.10–11.

*16.7 a thousand sacks: The Greek text has "a hundred measures", and each measure is about 300 kilogrammes.
*16.16 the Law of Moses and the Books of the Prophets: The Jewish Scriptures, that is, the Old Testament.
See also: 16.13: Matt 6.24. 16.16: Matt 11.12–13. 16.17: Matt 5.18.

[31] So Abraham said, "If they won't pay attention to Moses and the prophets, they won't listen even to someone who comes back from the dead."

CHAPTER 17

Faith and service

This is also told in Matthew 18.6–7,21–22; Mark 9.42

[1] Jesus said to his disciples:

There will always be something that causes people to sin. But anyone who causes them to sin is in for trouble. A person who causes even one of my little followers to sin [2] would be better off thrown into the ocean with a heavy stone tied around their neck. [3] So be careful what you do.

Correct any followers* of mine who sin, and forgive the ones who say they are sorry. [4] Even if one of them ill-treats you seven times in one day and says, "I am sorry," you should still forgive that person.

[5] The apostles said to the Lord, "Make our faith stronger!"

[6] Jesus replied:

If you had faith no bigger than a tiny mustard seed, you could tell this mulberry tree to pull itself up, roots and all, and to plant itself in the ocean. And it would!

[7] If your servant comes in from ploughing or from taking care of the sheep, would you say, "Welcome! Come on in and have something to eat"? [8] No, you wouldn't say that. You would say, "Prepare me something to eat. Get ready to serve me, so I can have my meal. Then later on you can eat and drink." [9] Servants don't deserve special thanks for doing what they are supposed to do. [10] And that's how it should be with you. When you've done all you should, then say, "We are merely servants, and we have simply done our duty."

Ten men with leprosy

[11] On his way to Jerusalem, Jesus went along the border between Samaria and Galilee. [12] As he was going into a village, ten men with leprosy* came towards him. They stood at a distance [13] and shouted, "Jesus, Master, have pity on us!"

[14] Jesus looked at them and said, "Go and show yourselves to the priests."*

On their way they were healed. [15] When one of them discovered that he was healed, he came back, shouting praises to God. [16] He bowed down at the feet of Jesus and thanked him. The man was from the country of Samaria.

[17] Jesus asked, "Weren't ten men healed? Where are the other nine? [18] Why was this foreigner the only one who came back to thank God?" [19] Then Jesus told the man, "You may get up and go. Your faith has made you well."

God's kingdom

This is also told in Matthew 24.23–28,37–41

[20] Some Pharisees asked Jesus when God's kingdom would come. He answered, "God's kingdom isn't something you can see. [21] There is no use saying, 'Look! Here it is' or 'Look! There it is.' God's kingdom is here with you."

[22] Jesus said to his disciples:

The time will come when you will long to see one of the days of the Son of Man, but you will not. [23] When people say to you, "Look there," or "Look here," don't go looking for him. [24] The day of the Son of Man will be like lightning flashing across the sky. [25] But first he must suffer terribly and be rejected by the people of today. [26] When the Son of Man comes, things will be just as they were when Noah lived. [27] People were eating, drinking, and getting married right up to the day when Noah went into the big boat. Then the flood came and drowned everyone on earth.

[28] When Lot* lived, people were also eating and drinking. They were buying, selling, planting, and building. [29] But on the very day Lot left Sodom, fiery flames poured down from the sky and killed everyone. [30] The same will happen on the day when the Son of Man appears.

17.14 show yourselves to the priests: See the note at 5.14.

17.27–28 Noah . . . Lot: When God destroyed the earth by a flood, he saved Noah and his family. And when God destroyed the cities of Sodom and Gomorrah and the evil people who lived there, he rescued Lot and his family (see Genesis 19.1–29).

See also: 17.14: Lev 14.1–32. 17.26: Gen 6.5–8. 17.27: Gen 7.6–24. 17.28–29: Gen 18.20–19.25.

17.3 followers: The Greek text has "brothers", which is often used in the New Testament for followers of Jesus.

17.12 leprosy: See the note at 4.27.

See also: 17.3: Matt 18.15.

Holy history

Taxes

In Jesus' times, everyone hated the tax collectors. To be a tax collector in the time of Christ was to be completely despised and hated by your friends and neighbours. This seems a bit extreme. I mean, nobody enjoys paying tax, but that doesn't make all tax collectors the most evil, reviled people on earth.

The reason was that they were working for the Romans. They were working for the occupying power, collecting money from Jewish citizens and passing it on to the enemy. The Romans sent the money on to their headquarters in Rome.

That was bad enough. What really got up the noses of the Jewish people, however, was the fact that the tax collectors ripped them off. They would add a little bit more to the tax demands and cream off a percentage of the tax money for themselves. They were little more than criminals.

Which was why it was so shocking for all those 'virtuous' people that Jesus spent so much time with tax collectors. He talked to them. He went to their houses for parties. He even had an ex-tax-collector as part of his gang of followers! It was as if he was saying that anyone could be forgiven.

No wonder people were shocked.

More...

Matthew p.1047
Forgiveness p.614

 Anorak corner

Jesus

1. Who did Jesus meet on the mountain?
2. Jesus' family called him Jesus. True or false?
3. How many days was Jesus in the desert?
4. How did Jesus sum up all the laws in the Old Testament?
5. Where was Jesus brought up?
(Answers on p.1431)

³¹ At that time no one on a rooftop* should go down into the house to get anything. No one in a field should go back to the house for anything. ³² Remember what happened to Lot's wife.*

³³ People who try to save their lives will lose them, and those who lose their lives will save them. ³⁴ On that night two people will be sleeping in the same bed, but only one will be taken. The other will be left. ³⁵⁻³⁶ Two women will be together grinding wheat, but only one will be taken. The other will be left.'

³⁷ Then Jesus' disciples spoke up, "But where will this happen, Lord?"

Jesus said, "Where there is a corpse, there will always be vultures."*

CHAPTER 18

A widow and a judge

¹ Jesus told his disciples a story about how they should keep on praying and never give up:

² In a town there was once a judge who didn't fear God or care about people. ³ In that same town there was a widow who kept going to the judge and saying, "Make sure that I get fair treatment in court."

⁴ For a while the judge refused to do anything. Finally, he said to himself, "Even though I don't fear God or care about people, ⁵ I will help this widow because she keeps on bothering me. If I don't help her, she will wear me out."

⁶ The Lord said:

Think about what that crooked judge said. ⁷ Won't God protect his chosen ones who pray to him day and night? Won't he be

---

*17.31 rooftop: See the note at 5.19.
*17.32 what happened to Lot's wife: She turned into a block of salt when she disobeyed God (see Genesis 19.26).
*17.37 Where there is a corpse, there will always be vultures: This saying may mean that when anything important happens, people soon know about it. Or the saying may mean that whenever something bad happens, curious people gather around and stare. But the word translated "vulture" also means "eagle" and may refer to the Roman army, which had an eagle as its symbol.

See also: 17.31: Matt 24.17–18; Mark 13.15–16.
17.32: Gen 19.26. **17.33:** Matt 10.39; 16.25; Mark 8.35; Luke 9.24; John 12.25.

concerned for them? ⁸ He will hurry and help them. But when the Son of Man comes, will he find on this earth anyone with faith?

A Pharisee and a tax collector

⁹ Jesus told a story to some people who thought they were better than others and who looked down on everyone else:

¹⁰ Two men went into the temple to pray.* One was a Pharisee and the other a tax collector.* ¹¹ The Pharisee stood over by himself and prayed,ᵇ "God, I thank you that I am not greedy, dishonest, and unfaithful in marriage like other people. And I am really glad that I am not like that tax collector over there. ¹² I go without eating* for two days a week, and I give you one tenth of all I earn."

¹³ The tax collector stood off at a distance and did not think he was good enough even to look up towards heaven. He was so sorry for what he had done that he pounded his chest and prayed, "God, have pity on me! I am such a sinner."

¹⁴ Then Jesus said, "When the two men went home, it was the tax collector and not the Pharisee who was pleasing to God. If you put yourself above others, you will be put down. But if you humble yourself, you will be honoured."

Jesus blesses little children

This is also told in Matthew 19.13–15; Mark 10.13–16

¹⁵ Some people brought their little children for Jesus to bless. But when his disciples saw them doing this, they told the people to stop bothering him. ¹⁶ So Jesus called the children over to him and said, "Let the children come to me! Don't try to stop them. People who are like these children belong to God's kingdom.ᵇ ¹⁷ You will never get into God's kingdom unless you enter it like a child!"

A rich and important man

This is also told in Matthew 19.16–30; Mark 10.17–31

¹⁸ An important man asked Jesus, "Good Teacher, what must I do to have eternal life?" ¹⁹ Jesus said, "Why do you call me good? Only God is good. ²⁰ You know the commandments: 'Be faithful in marriage. Do not murder. Do not steal. Do not tell lies about others. Respect your father and mother.' "

²¹ He told Jesus, "I have obeyed all these commandments since I was a young man."

²² When Jesus heard this, he said, "There is one thing you still need to do. Go and sell everything you own! Give the money to the poor, and you will have riches in heaven. Then come and be my follower." ²³ When the man heard this, he was sad, because he was very rich.

²⁴ Jesus saw how sad the man was. So he said, "It's terribly hard for rich people to get into God's kingdom! ²⁵ In fact, it's easier for a camel to go through the eye of a needle than for a rich person to get into God's kingdom."

²⁶ When the crowd heard this, they asked, "How can anyone ever be saved?"

²⁷ Jesus replied, "There are some things that people cannot do, but God can do anything."

²⁸ Peter said, "Remember, we left everything to be your followers!"

²⁹ Jesus answered, "You can be sure that anyone who gives up home or wife or brothers or family or children because of God's kingdom ³⁰ will be given much more in this life. And in the future world they will have eternal life."

Jesus again tells about his death

This is also told in Matthew 20.17–19; Mark 10.32–34

³¹ Jesus took the twelve apostles aside and said:

We are now on our way to Jerusalem. Everything that the prophets wrote about the Son of Man will happen there. ³² He will be handed over to foreigners,* who will make fun of him, ill-treat him, and spit on him. ³³ They will beat him and kill him, but three days later he will rise to life.

³⁴ The apostles did not understand what Jesus was talking about. They could not understand, because the meaning of what he said was hidden from them.

---

*18.10 into the temple to pray: Jewish people usually prayed there early in the morning and late in the afternoon.
*18.10 tax collector: See the note at 3.12.
*18.12 without eating: See the note at 2.37.
See also: 18.14: Matt 23.12; Luke 14.11.

*18.32 foreigners: The Romans, who ruled Judea at this time.
See also: 18.20: a Exod 20.14; Deut 5.18; b Exod 20.13; Deut 5.17; c Exod 20.15; Deut 5.19; d Exod 20.16; Deut 5.20; e Exod 20.12; Deut 5.16.

Jesus heals a blind beggar

This is also told in Matthew 20.29–34; Mark 10.46–52

³⁵ When Jesus was coming close to Jericho, a blind man sat begging beside the road. ³⁶ The man heard the crowd walking by and asked what was happening. ³⁷ Some people told him that Jesus from Nazareth was passing by. ³⁸ So the blind man shouted, "Jesus, Son of David,* have pity on me!" ³⁹ The people who were going along with Jesus told the man to be quiet. But he shouted even louder, "Son of David, have pity on me!"

⁴⁰ Jesus stopped and told some people to bring the blind man over to him. When the blind man was getting near, Jesus asked, ⁴¹ "What do you want me to do for you?"

"Lord, I want to see!" he answered.

⁴² Jesus replied, "Look and you will see! Your eyes are healed because of your faith." ⁴³ Straight away the man could see, and he went with Jesus and started thanking God. When the crowds saw what happened, they praised God.

CHAPTER 19

Zacchaeus

¹ Jesus was going through Jericho, ² where a man named Zacchaeus lived. He was in charge of collecting taxes* and was very rich. ³⁻⁴ Jesus was heading his way, and Zacchaeus wanted to see what he was like. But Zacchaeus was a short man and could not see over the crowd. So he ran ahead and climbed up into a sycamore tree.

⁵ When Jesus got there, he looked up and said, "Zacchaeus, hurry down! I want to stay with you today." ⁶ Zacchaeus hurried down and gladly welcomed Jesus.

⁷ Everyone who saw this started grumbling, "This man Zacchaeus is a sinner! And Jesus is going home to eat with him."

⁸ Later that day Zacchaeus stood up and said to the Lord, "I will give half of my property to the poor. And I will now pay back four times as much* to everyone I have ever cheated."

⁹ Jesus said to Zacchaeus, "Today you and your family have been saved,* because you are a true son of Abraham.* ¹⁰ The Son of Man came to look for and to save people who are lost."

A story about ten servants

This is also told in Matthew 25.14–30

¹¹ The crowd was still listening to Jesus as he was getting close to Jerusalem. Many of them thought that God's kingdom would soon appear, ¹² and Jesus told them this story:

A prince once went to a foreign country to be crowned king and then to return. ¹³ But before leaving, he called in ten servants and gave each of them some money. He told them, "Use this to earn more money until I get back."

¹⁴ But the people of his country hated him, and they sent messengers to the foreign country to say, "We don't want this man to be our king."

¹⁵ After the prince had been made king, he returned and called in his servants. He asked them how much they had earned with the money they had been given. ¹⁶ The first servant came and said, "Sir, with the money you gave me I have earned ten times as much."

¹⁷ "That's fine, my good servant!" the king said. "Since you have shown that you can be trusted with a small amount, you will be given ten cities to rule."

¹⁸ The second one came and said, "Sir, with the money you gave me, I have earned five times as much."

¹⁹ The king said, "You will be given five cities."

²⁰ Another servant came and said, "Sir, here is your money. I kept it safe in a handkerchief. ²¹ You are a hard man, and I was afraid of you. You take what isn't yours, and you harvest crops you didn't plant."

²² "You worthless servant!" the king told him. "You have condemned yourself by what you have just said. You knew that I am a hard man, taking what isn't mine and harvesting what I haven't planted.

---

*18.38 Son of David: The Jewish people expected the Messiah to be from the family of King David, and for this reason the Messiah was often called the "Son of David".
*19.2 in charge of collecting taxes: See the note at 3.12.
*19.8 pay back four times as much: Both Jewish and Roman law said that a person must pay back four times the amount that was taken.

*19.9 saved: Zacchaeus was Jewish, but it is only now that he is rescued from sin and placed under God's care.
*19.9 son of Abraham: As used in this verse, the words mean that Zacchaeus is truly one of God's special people.
See also: 19.10: Matt 18.11. 19.11–27: Matt 25.14–30.

Holy history

Jesus – the last week

The events and sayings of Jesus' last week – sometimes called 'Holy Week' – take up about a third of all the gospels.

Why? Because it was the most important time of his physical life on earth. This was the time when he would die and rise again.

Sunday

The entry into Jerusalem. Lots of cheering and waving palm leaves and all that.

Monday

Jesus throws out the traders from the temple. The leaders begin to plot.

Tuesday

He teaches in the temple and on the mount of Olives. In the evening, at Bethany, Mary anoints his feet.

Wednesday

Judas begins to plot.

Thursday

The last supper. Jesus goes to Gethsemane and is arrested.

Friday

In the very early hours he faces trials and torture. At 9 in the morning he is crucified. At noon darkness covers the land. At 3 p.m. he dies. He is buried a few hours later.

Saturday

Not much happens. Everyone is in hiding.

Sunday

The women go to the tomb and find it empty. Mary Magdalene mistakes Jesus for the gardener. Jesus appears to two disciples on the road, to Peter and ten other disciples.

During the next forty days

Jesus appears to all the disciples, and to more than 500 people. He cooks his disciples breakfast in Galilee. Finally, he ascends to heaven.

23 Why didn't you put my money in the bank? On my return, I could have had the money together with interest."

24 Then he said to some other servants standing there, "Take the money away from him and give it to the servant who earned ten times as much."

25 But they said, "Sir, he already has ten times as much!"

26 The king replied, "Those who have something will be given more. But everything will be taken away from those who don't have anything. 27 Now bring me the enemies who didn't want me to be their king. Kill them while I watch!"

Jesus' last week: his trial and death

Jesus enters Jerusalem

This is also told in Matthew 21.1–11; Mark 11.1–11; John 12.12–19

28 When Jesus had finished saying all this, he went on towards Jerusalem. 29 As he was getting near Bethphage and Bethany on the Mount of Olives, he sent two of his disciples on ahead. 30 He told them, "Go into the next village, where you will find a young donkey that has never been ridden. Untie the donkey and bring it here. 31 If anyone asks why you are doing that, just say, 'The Lord⟩ needs it.' "

32 They went off and found everything just as Jesus had said. 33 While they were untying the donkey, its owners asked, "Why are you doing that?"

34 They answered, "The Lord⟩ needs it."

35 Then they led the donkey to Jesus. They put some of their clothes on its back and helped Jesus get on. 36 And as he rode along, the people spread clothes on the road* in front of him. 37 When Jesus was setting off down the Mount of Olives, his large crowd of disciples were happy and praised God because of all the miracles they had seen. 38 They shouted,

> "Blessed is the king who comes
>   in the name of the Lord!
> Peace in heaven
>   and glory to God."

---

*19.36 spread clothes on the road: This was one way that the Jewish people welcomed a famous person.

See also: 19.26: Matt 13.12; Mark 4.25; Luke 8.18. 19.38: Psa 118.26.

³⁹ Some Pharisees in the crowd said to Jesus, "Teacher, make your disciples stop shouting!"

⁴⁰ But Jesus answered, "If they keep quiet, these stones will start shouting."

⁴¹ When Jesus came closer and could see Jerusalem, he cried ⁴² and said:

Today your people don't know what will bring them peace! Now it is hidden from them. ⁴³ Jerusalem, the time will come when your enemies will build walls around you to attack you. Armies will surround you and close in on you from every side. ⁴⁴ They will level you to the ground and kill your people. Not one stone in your buildings will be left on top of another. This will happen because you did not see that God had come to save you.*

Jesus in the temple
This is also told in Matthew 21.12–17; Mark 11.15–19; John 2.13–22

⁴⁵ When Jesus entered the temple, he started chasing out the people who were selling things. ⁴⁶ He told them, "The Scriptures say, 'My house should be a place of worship.' But you have made it a place where robbers hide!"

⁴⁷ Each day, Jesus kept on teaching in the temple. So the chief priests, the teachers of the Law of Moses, and some other important people tried to have him killed. ⁴⁸ But they could not find a way to do it, because everyone else was eager to listen to him.

CHAPTER 20

A question about Jesus' authority
This is also told in Matthew 21.23–27; Mark 11.27–33

¹ One day, Jesus was teaching in the temple and telling the good news. So the chief priests, the teachers, and the nation's leaders ² asked him, "What right do you have to do these things? Who gave you this authority?"

³ Jesus replied, "I want to ask you a question. ⁴ Who gave John the right to baptize? Was it God in heaven or merely some human being?"

⁵ They talked this over and said to each other, "We can't say that God gave John this

right. Jesus will ask us why we didn't believe John. ⁶ And we can't say that it was merely some human who gave John the right to baptize. The crowd will stone us to death, because they think John was a prophet."

⁷ So they told Jesus, "We don't know who gave John the right to baptize."

⁸ Jesus replied, "Then I won't tell you who gave me the right to do what I do."

Tenants of a vineyard
This is also told in Matthew 21.33–46; Mark 12.1–12

⁹ Jesus told the people this story:

A man once planted a vineyard and let it. Then he left the country for a long time. ¹⁰ When it was time to harvest the crop, he sent a servant to ask the tenants for his share of the grapes. But they beat up the servant and sent him away without anything. ¹¹ So the owner sent another servant. The tenants also beat him up. They insulted him terribly and sent him away without a thing. ¹² The owner sent a third servant. He was also beaten terribly and thrown out of the vineyard.

¹³ The owner then said to himself, "What am I going to do? I know what. I'll send my son, the one I love so much. They will surely respect him!"

¹⁴ When the tenants saw the owner's son, they said to one another, "Some day he will own the vineyard. Let's kill him! Then we can have it all for ourselves." ¹⁵ So they threw him out of the vineyard and killed him.

Jesus asked, "What do you think the owner of the vineyard will do? ¹⁶ I'll tell you what. He will come and kill those tenants and let someone else have his vineyard."

When the people heard this, they said, "This must never happen!"

¹⁷ But Jesus looked straight at them and said, "Then what do the Scriptures mean when they say, 'The stone that the builders tossed aside is now the most important stone of all'? ¹⁸ Anyone who stumbles over this stone will get hurt, and anyone it falls on will be smashed to pieces."

¹⁹ The chief priests and the teachers of the Law of Moses knew that Jesus was talking about them when he was telling this story. They wanted to arrest him at once, but they were afraid of the people.

---

*19.44 that God had come to save you: The Jewish people looked for the time when God would come and rescue them from their enemies. But when Jesus came, many of them refused to obey him.
See also: **19.46:** Isa 56.7; Jer 7.11. **19.47:** Luke 21.37.

See also: **20.9:** Isa 5.1. **20.17:** Psa 118.22.

Paying taxes

This is also told in Matthew 22.15–22; Mark 12.13–17

20 Jesus' enemies kept watching him closely, because they wanted to hand him over to the Roman governor. So they sent some men who pretended to be good. But they were really spies trying to catch Jesus saying something wrong. 21 The spies said to him, "Teacher, we know that you teach the truth about what God wants people to do. And you treat everyone with the same respect, no matter who they are. 22 Tell us, should we pay taxes to the Emperor or not?"

23 Jesus knew that they were trying to trick him. So he told them, 24 "Show me a coin." Then he asked, "Whose picture and name are on it?"

"The Emperor's," they answered.

25 Then he told them, "Give the Emperor what belongs to him and give God what belongs to God." 26 Jesus' enemies could not catch him saying anything wrong there in front of the people. They were amazed at his answer and kept quiet.

Life in the future world

This is also told in Matthew 22.23–33; Mark 12.18–27

27 The Sadducees did not believe that people would rise to life after death. So some of them came to Jesus 28 and said:

Teacher, Moses wrote that if a married man dies and has no children, his brother should marry the widow. Their first son would then be thought of as the son of the dead brother.
29 There were once seven brothers. The first one married, but died without having any children. 30 The second one married his brother's widow, and he also died without having any children. 31 The same thing happened to the third one. Finally, all seven brothers married that woman and died without having any children. 32 At last the woman died. 33 When God raises people from death, whose wife will this woman be? All seven brothers had married her.

34 Jesus answered:

The people in this world get married. 35 But in the future world no one who is worthy to rise from death will either marry 36 or die. They will be like the angels and will be

God's children, because they have been raised to life.
37 In the story about the burning bush, Moses clearly shows that people will live again. He said, "The Lord is the God worshipped by Abraham, Isaac, and Jacob."* 38 So the Lord isn't the God of the dead, but of the living. This means that everyone is alive as far as God is concerned.

39 Some of the teachers of the Law of Moses said, "Teacher, you have given a good answer!" 40 From then on, no one dared to ask Jesus any questions.

About David's son

This is also told in Matthew 22.41–46; Mark 12.35–37

41 Jesus asked, "Why do people say that the Messiah will be the son of King David?* 42 In the book of Psalms, David himself says,

'The Lord said to my Lord,
    Sit at my right side*
43 until I make your enemies
    into a footstool for you.'

44 David spoke of the Messiah as his Lord, so how can the Messiah be his son?"

Jesus and the teachers of the Law of Moses

This is also told in Matthew 23.1–36; Mark 12.38–40; Luke 11.37–54

45 While everyone was listening to Jesus, he said to his disciples:

46 Guard against the teachers of the Law of Moses! They love to walk around in long robes, and they like to be greeted in the market. They want the front seats in the meeting places and the best seats at banquets. 47 But they cheat widows out of their homes and then pray long prayers just to show off. These teachers will be punished most of all.

---

*20.37 "The Lord is the God worshipped by Abraham, Isaac, and Jacob": Jesus argues that if God is worshipped by these three, they must be alive, because he is the God of the living.
*20.41 the son of King David: See the note at 18.38.
*20.42 right side: The place of power and honour.
See also: 20.37: Exod 3.6. 20.42–43: Psa 110.1.

CHAPTER 21

A widow's offering
This is also told in Mark 12.41–44

[1] Jesus looked up and saw some rich people tossing their gifts into the offering box. [2] He also saw a poor widow putting in two pennies. [3] And he said, "I tell you that this poor woman has put in more than all the others. [4] Everyone else gave what they didn't need. But she is very poor and gave everything she had."

The temple will be destroyed
This is also told in Matthew 24.1–2; Mark 13.1–2

[5] Some people were talking about the beautiful stones used to build the temple and about the gifts that had been placed in it. Jesus said, [6] "Do you see these stones? The time is coming when not one of them will be left in place. They will all be knocked down."

Warning about trouble
This is also told in Matthew 24.3–14; Mark 13.3–13

[7] Some people asked, "Teacher, when will all this happen? How can we know when these things are about to take place?"

[8] Jesus replied:

Don't be fooled by those who will come and claim to be me. They will say, "I am Christ!" and "Now is the time!" But don't follow them. [9] When you hear about wars and riots, don't be afraid. These things will have to happen first, but that isn't the end.

[10] Nations will go to war against one another, and kingdoms will attack each other. [11] There will be great earthquakes, and in many places people will starve to death and suffer terrible diseases. All sorts of frightening things will be seen in the sky.

[12] Before all this happens, you will be arrested and punished. You will be tried in your meeting places and put in jail. Because of me you will be placed on trial before kings and governors. [13] But this will be your chance to tell about your faith.

[14] Don't worry about what you will say to defend yourselves. [15] I will give you the wisdom to know what to say. None of your enemies will be able to oppose you or to say that you are wrong. [16] You will be betrayed

See also: **21.14–15:** Luke 12.11–12.

Holy history

The Last Supper
The meal we call 'the Last Supper' appears in all the Gospels. During the supper Jesus gives his disciples some important teaching concerning what is going to happen.

Exit Judas
Jesus knows he is going to die. He even indicates which disciple will betray him – and Judas Iscariot slips out halfway through.

Washing the feet
Before the meal, Jesus washes the feet of his disciples. In those days, the streets were filled with filth, there was animal dung – and worse – to be dodged, and people only wore sandals. So washing feet was the worst job. Jesus does this to indicate that his kingdom is one of service, not of prestige.

The bread and the wine
Jesus takes bread and wine. He says that the bread is his 'body' and the wine is his 'blood'. He asks that the disciples eat and drink these to remember him.

The early church created a celebration called the Eucharist or thanksgiving around this event, where they ate bread and wine and remembered what Jesus did. And Christians still do this today.

 Anorak corner

The earliest account of this event comes from Paul's first letter to the Corinthians, which was written before the gospels.

 Footsteps

A week with the Last Supper
The place to meet: Luke 22.7–13
Washing the feet: John 13.1–20
Bread and wine: Luke 22.14–23
The betrayer: John 13.21–30
The Holy Spirit: John 14.15–31
Servants not kings: Luke 22.24–30
Testing times ahead: Luke 22.31–38

by your own parents, brothers, family, and friends. Some of you will even be killed. ¹⁷ Because of me, you will be hated by everyone. ¹⁸ But don't worry!▸ ¹⁹ You will be saved by being faithful to me.

Jerusalem will be destroyed

This is also told in Matthew 24.15–21; Mark 13.14–19

Jesus continued:

²⁰ When you see Jerusalem surrounded by soldiers, you will know that it will soon be destroyed. ²¹ If you are living in Judea at that time, run to the mountains. If you are in the city, leave it. And if you are out in the country, don't go back into the city. ²² This time of punishment is what is written about in the Scriptures. ²³ It will be an awful time for women who are expecting babies or nursing young children! Everywhere in the land people will suffer horribly and be punished. ²⁴ Some of them will be killed by swords. Others will be carried off to foreign countries. Jerusalem will be overrun by foreign nations until their time comes to an end.

When the Son of Man appears

This is also told in Matthew 24.29–31; Mark 13.24–27

Jesus continued:

²⁵ Strange things will happen to the sun, moon, and stars. The nations on earth will be afraid of the roaring sea and tides, and they won't know what to do. ²⁶ People will be so frightened that they will faint because of what is happening to the world. Every power in the sky will be shaken.* ²⁷ Then the Son of Man will be seen, coming in a cloud with great power and glory. ²⁸ When all this starts happening, stand up straight and be brave. You will soon be set free.

A lesson from a fig tree

This is also told in Matthew 24.32–35; Mark 13.28–31

²⁹ Then Jesus told them a story:

When you see a fig tree or any other tree ³⁰ putting out leaves, you know that summer will soon come. ³¹ So, when you

see these things happening, you know that God's kingdom will soon be here. ³² You can be sure that some of the people of this generation will still be alive when all this takes place. ³³ The sky and the earth won't last for ever, but my words will.

A warning

Jesus continued:

³⁴ Don't spend all your time thinking about eating or drinking or worrying about life. If you do, the final day will suddenly catch you ³⁵ like a trap. That day will surprise everyone on earth. ³⁶ Watch out and keep praying that you can escape all that is going to happen and that the Son of Man will be pleased with you.

³⁷ Jesus taught in the temple each day, and he spent each night on the Mount of Olives. ³⁸ Everyone got up early and came to the temple to hear him teach.

CHAPTER 22

A plot to kill Jesus

This is also told in Matthew 26.1–5,14,16; Mark 14.1–2,10–11; John 11.45–53

¹ The Festival of Thin Bread, also called Passover, was near. ² The chief priests and the teachers of the Law of Moses were looking for a way to get rid of Jesus, because they were afraid of what the people might do. ³ Then Satan entered the heart of Judas Iscariot,* who was one of the twelve apostles.

⁴ Judas went to talk with the chief priests and the officers of the temple police about how he could help them arrest Jesus. ⁵ They were very pleased and offered to pay Judas some money. ⁶ He agreed and started looking for a good chance to betray Jesus when the crowds were not around.

Jesus eats with his disciples

This is also told in Matthew 26.17–25; Mark 14.12–21; John 13.21–30

⁷ The day had come for the Festival of Thin Bread, and it was time to kill the Passover lambs. ⁸ So Jesus said to Peter and John, "Go and prepare the Passover meal for us to eat." ⁹ But they asked, "Where do you want us to prepare it?"

---

*21.26 Every power in the sky will be shaken: In ancient times people thought that the stars were spiritual powers.

See also: 21.22: Hos 9.7. 21.25: Isa 13.10; Ezek 32.7; Joel 2.31; Rev 6.12–13. 21.27: Dan 7.13; Rev 1.7.

*22.3 Iscariot: See the note at 6.16.
See also: 21.37: Luke 19.47. 22.1: Exod 12.1–27.

¹⁰ Jesus told them, "As you go into the city, you will meet a man carrying a jar of water.* Follow him into the house ¹¹ and say to the owner, 'Our teacher wants to know where he can eat the Passover meal with his disciples.' ¹² The owner will take you upstairs and show you a large room ready for you to use. Prepare the meal there."

¹³ Peter and John left. They found everything just as Jesus had told them, and they prepared the Passover meal.

The Lord's Supper

This is also told in Matthew 26.26–30; Mark 14.22–26; 1 Corinthians 11.23–25

¹⁴ When the time came for Jesus and the apostles to eat, ¹⁵ he said to them, "I have very much wanted to eat this Passover meal with you before I suffer. ¹⁶ I tell you that I will not eat another Passover meal until it is finally eaten in God's kingdom."

¹⁷ Jesus took a cup of wine in his hands and gave thanks to God. Then he told the apostles, "Take this wine and share it with each other. ¹⁸ I tell you that I will not drink any more wine until God's kingdom comes."

¹⁹ Jesus took some bread in his hands and gave thanks for it. He broke the bread and handed it to his apostles. Then he said, "This is my body, which is given for you. Eat this as a way of remembering me!"

²⁰ After the meal he took another cup of wine in his hands. Then he said, "This is my blood. It is poured out for you, and with it God makes his new agreement. ²¹ The one who will betray me is here at the table with me! ²² The Son of Man will die in the way that has been decided for him, but it will be terrible for the one who betrays him!"

²³ Then the apostles started arguing about who would ever do such a thing.

An argument about greatness

²⁴ The apostles got into an argument about which one of them was the greatest. ²⁵ So Jesus told them:

Foreign kings order their people around, and powerful rulers call themselves

everyone's friends.* ²⁶ But don't be like them. The most important one of you should be like the least important, and your leader should be like a servant. ²⁷ Who do people think is the greatest, a person who is served or one who serves? Isn't it the one who is served? But I have been with you as a servant.

²⁸ You have stayed with me in all my troubles. ²⁹ So I will give you the right to rule as kings, just as my Father has given me the right to rule as a king. ³⁰ You will eat and drink with me in my kingdom, and you will each sit on a throne to judge the twelve tribes of Israel.

Jesus' disciples will be tested

This is also told in Matthew 26.31–35; Mark 14.27–31; John 13.36–38

³¹ Jesus said, "Simon, listen to me! Satan has demanded the right to test each one of you, as a farmer does when he separates wheat from the husks.* ³² But Simon, I have prayed that your faith will be strong. And when you have come back to me, help the others."

³³ Peter said, "Lord, I am ready to go with you to jail and even to die with you."

³⁴ Jesus replied, "Peter, I tell you that before a cock crows tomorrow morning, you will say three times that you don't know me."

Money bags, travelling bags, and swords

³⁵ Jesus asked his disciples, "When I sent you out without a money bag or a travelling bag or sandals, did you need anything?"

"No!" they answered.

³⁶ Jesus told them, "But now, if you have a money bag, take it with you. Also take a travelling bag, and if you don't have a sword,* sell some of your clothes and buy

---

*22.25 everyone's friends: This translates a Greek word that rulers sometimes used as a title for themselves or for special friends.

*22.31 separates wheat from the husks: See the note at 3.17.

*22.36 money bag . . . travelling bag . . . sword: These were things that someone would take on a dangerous journey. Jesus was telling his disciples to be ready for anything that might happen. They seem to have understood what he meant (see 22.49–51).

See also: 22.26: Matt 23.11; Mark 9.35.
22.27: John 13.12–15. 22.30: Matt 19.28.
22.35: Matt 10.9–10; Mark 6.8–9; Luke 9.3; 10.4.

---

*22.10 a man carrying a jar of water: A male slave carrying water would probably mean that the family was rich.

See also: 22.20: Jer 31.31–34. 22.21: Psa 41.9.
22.24: Matt 18.1; Mark 9.34; Luke 9.46.
22.25–26: Matt 20.25–27; Mark 10.42–44.

one. ³⁷ Do this because the Scriptures say, 'He was considered a criminal.' This was written about me, and it will soon come true."

³⁸ The disciples said, "Lord, here are two swords!"

"Enough of that!" Jesus replied.

Jesus prays

This is also told in Matthew 26.36–46; Mark 14.32–42

³⁹ Jesus went out to the Mount of Olives, as he often did, and his disciples went with him. ⁴⁰ When they got there, he told them, "Pray that you won't be tested."

⁴¹ Jesus walked on a little way before he knelt down and prayed, ⁴² "Father, if you will, please don't make me suffer by making me drink from this cup.* But do what you want, and not what I want."

⁴³ Then an angel from heaven came to help him. ⁴⁴ Jesus was in great pain and prayed so sincerely that his sweat fell to the ground like drops of blood.*

⁴⁵ Jesus got up from praying and went over to his disciples. They were asleep and worn out from being so sad. ⁴⁶ He said to them, "Why are you asleep? Wake up and pray that you won't be tested."

Jesus is arrested

This is also told in Matthew 26.47–56; Mark 14.43–50; John 18.3–11

⁴⁷ While Jesus was still speaking, a crowd came up. It was led by Judas, one of the twelve apostles. He went over to Jesus and greeted him with a kiss.*

⁴⁸ Jesus asked Judas, "Are you betraying the Son of Man with a kiss?"

⁴⁹ When Jesus' disciples saw what was about to happen, they asked, "Lord, should we attack them with a sword?" ⁵⁰ One of the disciples even struck at the high priest's servant with his sword and cut off the servant's right ear.

⁵¹ "Enough of that!" Jesus said. Then he touched the servant's ear and healed it.

⁵² Jesus spoke to the chief priests, the temple police, and the leaders who had come to arrest him. He said, "Why do you come

---

*22.42 making me drink from this cup: In the Scriptures "to drink from a cup" sometimes means to suffer.
*22.47 greeted him with a kiss: It was the custom for people to greet each other with a kiss on the cheek.
See also: 22.37: Isa 53.12.

Holy history

Jesus – the trials

On the night of his arrest, Jesus suffers three different trials.

Jesus first faces the religious leaders – the religious council and the high priest – over charges of blasphemy. This is an angry, emotional affair; the high priest screams and shouts and tears his robe in anger. Jesus is spat on and beaten. John's gospel adds details of a brief interrogation with Annas, the deposed high priest (John 18.12–14), but this is not a trial as such – just a prelude to the main meeting.

Jesus is taken to Pilate, the Roman governor. The charges against Jesus are incitement to riot, urging non-payment of taxes and claiming to be the king (Luke 23.1–2), but Pilate dismisses these charges. He even asks Jesus an important question: 'What is truth?' But he's not really interested in truth; he's interested in avoiding trouble. Pilate sends him to Herod, who happens to be in Jerusalem at the time (Luke 23.6–12). But Herod sends him back and, in the end, Pilate bottles it. He offers to free Jesus, but the crowd select a political prisoner called Barabbas to be freed instead. Fearful of a Jewish riot, or of bad reports going back to his superiors, Pilate sentences an innocent man to death.

King Herod is merely curious. He even hopes that Jesus will do a miracle for him, like some kind of performing magician. However, he was to be disappointed. Although Herod asks lots of questions, Jesus refuses to answer. Herod mocks Jesus and insults him, and sends him back to Pilate.

All three trials have different aims, but in the end, there is agreement between them: this Galilean trouble-maker is to be removed.

More...

Sacrifice p.1368
Cross p.1112
Crucifixion p.1199
Suffering p.555

out with swords and clubs and treat me like a criminal? 53 I was with you every day in the temple, and you didn't arrest me. But this is your time, and darkness* is in control."

Peter says he doesn't know Jesus

This is also told in Matthew 26.57–58,67–75; Mark 14.53–54,66–72; John 18.12–18,25–27

54 Jesus was arrested and led away to the house of the high priest, while Peter followed at a distance. 55 Some people built a fire in the middle of the courtyard and were sitting around it. Peter sat there with them, 56 and a servant girl saw him. Then after she had looked at him carefully, she said, "This man was with Jesus!"

57 Peter said, "Woman, I don't even know that man!"

58 A little later someone else saw Peter and said, "You are one of them!"

"No, I'm not!" Peter replied.

59 About an hour later another man insisted, "This man must have been with Jesus. They both come from Galilee."

60 Peter replied, "I don't know what you are talking about!" At once, while Peter was still speaking, a cock crowed.

61 The Lord turned and looked at Peter. And Peter remembered that the Lord had said, "Before a cock crows tomorrow morning, you will say three times that you don't know me." 62 Then Peter went out and cried hard.

63 The men who were guarding Jesus made fun of him and beat him. 64 They put a blindfold on him and said, "Tell us who struck you!" 65 They kept on insulting Jesus in many other ways.

Jesus is questioned by the council

This is also told in Matthew 26.59–66; Mark 14.55–64; John 18.19–24

66 At daybreak the nation's leaders, the chief priests, and the teachers of the Law of Moses got together and brought Jesus before their council. 67 They said, "Tell us! Are you the Messiah?"

Jesus replied, "If I said so, you wouldn't believe me. 68 And if I asked you a question, you wouldn't answer. 69 But from now on, the Son of Man will be seated at the right side of God All-Powerful."

70 Then they asked, "Are you the Son of God?"*

Jesus answered, "You say I am!"▸

71 They replied, "Why do we need more witnesses? He said it himself!"

CHAPTER 23

Pilate questions Jesus

This is also told in Matthew 27.1–2,11–14; Mark 15.1–5; John 18.28–38

1 Everyone in the council got up and led Jesus off to Pilate. 2 They started accusing him and said, "We caught this man trying to get our people to riot and to stop paying taxes to the Emperor. He also claims that he is the Messiah, our king."

3 Pilate asked Jesus, "Are you the king of the Jews?"

"Those are your words," Jesus answered.

4 Pilate told the chief priests and the crowd, "I don't find him guilty of anything."

5 But they all kept on saying, "He has been teaching and causing trouble all over Judea. He started in Galilee and has now come all the way here."

Jesus is brought before Herod

6 When Pilate heard this, he asked, "Is this man from Galilee?" 7 After Pilate learnt that Jesus came from the region ruled by Herod,* he sent him to Herod, who was in Jerusalem at that time.

8 For a long time Herod had wanted to see Jesus and was very happy because he finally had this chance. He had heard many things about Jesus and hoped to see him perform a miracle.

9 Herod asked him a lot of questions, but Jesus did not answer. 10 Then the chief priests and the teachers of the Law of Moses stood up and accused him of all kinds of bad things.

11 Herod and his soldiers made fun of Jesus and insulted him. They put a fine robe on him and sent him back to Pilate. 12 That same day Herod and Pilate became friends, even though they had been enemies before this.

---

*22.53 darkness: Darkness stands for the power of the devil.
See also: 22.53: Luke 19.47; 21.37.

*22.70 Son of God: This was one of the titles used for the kings of Israel.
*23.7 Herod: See the note at 3.1.

Being christian

Forgiving others

Luke 23.31–34

If we're Christians then we've asked God for forgiveness. And we've been forgiven.

Now, here's the next bit: we have to forgive others as well.

That's not so easy, is it? Yes, God has forgiven me, but, well, he's God isn't he? Forgiveness is one of the things he does best. Surely he's not expecting me to do the same?

Yes. He is. The Bible is really clear on this point: if you want to be forgiven, you have to forgive. You have to do what Jesus did. Even on the cross, even after all he had been through, Jesus asked God to forgive his killers. He could have zapped them, made them suffer. He could have taken revenge. But he forgave. And he expects us to do the same.

It's not easy. It requires a lot of willpower and loads of prayer. And it's not about 'feeling like forgiving them'. No-one ever feels like forgiving anyone. It's not something that comes naturally to us as sinful humans.

You've got to grit your teeth and do it. You've got to pray for the other person. You've got to deliberately say to yourself, 'I forgive them'. You may feel angry, hurt or wounded, but you can't afford to hold on to those feelings.

Give them away to God.

Forgive others, as he has forgiven you.

Being Christian: Forgiving others

• Has someone hurt or upset you? Don't bear grudges, and don't seek revenge.
• If you forgive someone, forgive them. If they're friends or people you know, don't keep bringing it up.
• Pray for those who have hurt you. Ask God to bless them. It's hard to hate someone if you're giving them a present.

The death sentence

This is also told in Matthew 27.15–26; Mark 15.6–15; John 18.39—19.16

13 Pilate called together the chief priests, the leaders, and the people. 14 He told them, "You brought Jesus to me and said he was a troublemaker. But I have questioned him here in front of you, and I have not found him guilty of anything that you say he has done. 15 Herod didn't find him guilty either and sent him back. This man doesn't deserve to be put to death! 16-17 I will just have him beaten with a whip and set free."

18 But the whole crowd shouted, "Kill Jesus! Give us Barabbas!" 19 Now Barabbas was in jail because he had started a riot in the city and had murdered someone.

20 Pilate wanted to set Jesus free, so he spoke again to the crowds. 21 But they kept shouting, "Nail him to a cross! Nail him to a cross!"

22 Pilate spoke to them a third time, "But what crime has he done? I have not found him guilty of anything for which he should be put to death. I will have him beaten with a whip and set free."

23 The people kept on shouting as loud as they could for Jesus to be put to death. 24 Finally, Pilate gave in. 25 He freed the man who was in jail for rioting and murder, because he was the one the crowd wanted to be set free. Then Pilate handed Jesus over for them to do what they wanted with him.

Jesus is nailed to a cross

This is also told in Matthew 27.31–44; Mark 15.21–32; John 19.17–27

26 As Jesus was being led away, some soldiers grabbed hold of a man from Cyrene named Simon. He was coming in from the fields, but they put the cross on him and made him carry it behind Jesus.

27 A large crowd was following Jesus, and in the crowd a lot of women were crying and weeping for him. 28 Jesus turned to the women and said:

Women of Jerusalem, don't cry for me! Cry for yourselves and for your children. 29 Some day people will say, "Women who never had children are really fortunate!" 30 At that time everyone will say to the mountains, "Fall on us!" They will say to the hills, "Hide us!" 31 If this can

See also: 23.30: Hos 10.8; Rev 6.16.

happen when the wood is green, what do you think will happen when it is dry?*

³² Two criminals were led out to be put to death with Jesus. ³³ When the soldiers came to the place called "The Skull",* they nailed Jesus to a cross. They also nailed the two criminals to crosses, one on each side of Jesus.

³⁴⁻³⁵ Jesus said, "Father, forgive these people! They don't know what they're doing."ᵛ

While the crowd stood there watching Jesus, the soldiers gambled for his clothes. The leaders insulted him by saying, "He saved others. Now he should save himself, if he really is God's chosen Messiah!"

³⁶ The soldiers made fun of Jesus and brought him some wine. ³⁷ They said, "If you are the king of the Jews, save yourself!"

³⁸ Above him was a sign that said, "This is the King of the Jews."

³⁹ One of the criminals hanging there also insulted Jesus by saying, "Aren't you the Messiah? Save yourself and save us!"

⁴⁰ But the other criminal told the first one off, "Don't you fear God? Aren't you getting the same punishment as this man? ⁴¹ We got what was coming to us, but he didn't do anything wrong." ⁴² Then he said to Jesus, "Remember me when you come into power!"

⁴³ Jesus replied, "I promise that today you will be with me in paradise."*

The death of Jesus
This is also told in Matthew 27.45–56; Mark 15.33–41; John 19.28–30

⁴⁴ Around midday the sky turned dark and stayed that way until the middle of the afternoon. ⁴⁵ The sun stopped shining, and the curtain in the temple* split down the middle. ⁴⁶ Jesus shouted, "Father, I put myself in your hands!" Then he died.

⁴⁷ When the Roman officer saw what had happened, he praised God and said, "Jesus must really have been a good man!"

⁴⁸ A crowd had gathered to see the terrible sight. Then after they had seen it, they felt brokenhearted and went home. ⁴⁹ All Jesus' close friends and the women who had come with him from Galilee stood at a distance and watched.

Jesus is buried
This is also told in Matthew 27.57–61; Mark 15.42–47; John 19.38–42

⁵⁰⁻⁵¹ There was a man named Joseph, who was from Arimathea in Judea. Joseph was a good and honest man, and he was eager for God's kingdom to come. He was also a member of the Jewish council, but he did not agree with what they had decided.

⁵² Joseph went to Pilate and asked for Jesus' body. ⁵³ He took the body down from the cross and wrapped it in fine cloth. Then he put it in a tomb that had been cut out of solid rock and had never been used. ⁵⁴ It was Friday, and the Sabbath was about to begin.*

⁵⁵ The women who had come with Jesus from Galilee followed Joseph and watched how Jesus' body was placed in the tomb. ⁵⁶ Then they went to prepare some sweet-smelling spices for his burial. But on the Sabbath they rested, as the Law of Moses commands.

Jesus is alive

CHAPTER 24
This is also told in Matthew 28.1–10; Mark 16.1–8; John 20.1–10

¹ Very early on Sunday morning the women went to the tomb, carrying the spices that they had prepared. ² When they found the stone rolled away from the entrance, ³ they went in.

---

*23.31 If this can happen when the wood is green, what do you think will happen when it is dry?: This saying probably means, "If this can happen to an innocent person, what do you think will happen to one who is guilty?"

*23.33 "The Skull": The place was probably given this name because it was near a large rock in the shape of a human skull.

*23.43 paradise: In the Greek translation of the Old Testament, this word is used for the Garden of Eden. In New Testament times it was sometimes used for the place where God's people are happy and at rest, as they wait for the final judgment.

See also: 23.34: Psa 22.18. 23.35: Psa 22.7. 23.36: Psa 69.21. 23.45: Exod 26.31–33.

*23.45 curtain in the temple: There were two curtains in the temple. One was at the entrance, and the other separated the holy place from the most holy place that the Jewish people thought of as God's home on earth. The second curtain is probably the one which is meant.
*23.54 the Sabbath was about to begin: The Sabbath begins at sunset on Friday.

See also: 23.46: Psa 31.5. 23.49: Luke 8.2–3. 23.56: Exod 20.10; Deut 5.14.

Being christian

Trusting in Jesus

Luke 24.11–52

For the disciples, those dark days after the crucifixion must have been hard. All Jesus' promises must have seemed a long way away. As these two guys trudged back from Jerusalem, they must have thought that they'd been fooled, that the person they thought had changed everything had changed nothing at all.

And then this stranger started walking alongside them, explaining everything. And when they sat down for a meal together, they realised that they hadn't been fooled after all. Jesus had done what he said he would do. He came back from the dead. He showed them that he was always going to be there.

If we've said sorry, and accepted Jesus, then we have to trust in him. He has saved us. And we're not alone. Jesus promised to send the Holy Spirit to his followers and, from the moment you accept him, the Holy Spirit enters your life. The Holy Spirit is the distinguishing characteristic of children of God. He will live in you, start to change you.

Sometimes life gets hard and scary. Sometimes we wonder whether all we have believed is true, or whether we're just fooling ourselves. Sometimes it feels like we're lost and alone.

But hold on. Trust Jesus. Jesus doesn't lie. He has said he will never leave us; and with the Holy Spirit in our lives, we can take him at his word.

Being Christian: Trusting in Jesus

• Whatever you're going through, trust in Jesus. Take your problems to him.
• If you're finding it difficult, talk to someone and pray with them. They can reassure you of God's presence.

But they did not find the body of the Lord⟩ Jesus, 4 and they did not know what to think.

Suddenly two men in shining white clothes stood beside them. 5 The women were afraid and bowed to the ground. But the men said, "Why are you looking in the place of the dead for someone who is alive? 6 Jesus isn't here! He has been raised from death. Remember that while he was still in Galilee, he told you, 7 'The Son of Man will be handed over to sinners who will nail him to a cross. But three days later he will rise to life.' " 8 Then they remembered what Jesus had said.

9-10 Mary Magdalene, Joanna, Mary the mother of James, and some other women were the ones who had gone to the tomb. When they returned, they told the eleven apostles and the others what had happened. 11 The apostles thought it was all nonsense, and they would not believe.

12 But Peter ran to the tomb. And when he stooped down and looked in, he saw only the burial clothes. Then he returned, wondering what had happened.⟩

Jesus appears. He is taken to heaven

Jesus appears to two disciples

This is also told in Mark 16.12–13

13 That same day two of Jesus' disciples were going to the village of Emmaus, which was about eleven kilometres from Jerusalem. 14 As they were talking and thinking about what had happened, 15 Jesus came near and started walking along beside them. 16 But they did not know who he was.

17 Jesus asked them, "What were you talking about as you walked along?"

The two of them stood there looking sad and gloomy. 18 Then the one named Cleopas asked Jesus, "Are you the only person from Jerusalem who didn't know what was happening there these last few days?"

19 "What do you mean?" Jesus asked. They answered:

Those things that happened to Jesus from Nazareth. By what he did and said he showed that he was a powerful prophet, who pleased God and all the people. 20 Then the chief priests and our leaders had him arrested and sentenced to die on a cross.

See also: 24.6–7: Matt 16.21; 17.22–23; 20.18–19; Mark 8.31; 9.31; 10.33–34; Luke 9.22; 18.31–33.

²¹ We had hoped that he would be the one to set Israel free! But it has already been three days since all this happened.

²² Some women in our group surprised us. They had gone to the tomb early in the morning, ²³ but did not find the body of Jesus. They came back, saying that they had seen a vision of angels who told them that he is alive. ²⁴ Some men from our group went to the tomb and found it just as the women had said. But they didn't see Jesus either.

²⁵ Then Jesus asked the two disciples, "Why can't you understand? How can you be so slow to believe all that the prophets said? ²⁶ Didn't you know that the Messiah would have to suffer before he was given his glory?" ²⁷ Jesus then explained everything written about himself in the Scriptures, beginning with the Law of Moses and the Books of the Prophets.*

²⁸ When the two of them came near the village where they were going, Jesus seemed to be going further. ²⁹ They begged him, "Stay with us! It's already late, and the sun is going down." So Jesus went into the house to stay with them.

³⁰ After Jesus sat down to eat, he took some bread. He blessed it and broke it. Then he gave it to them. ³¹ At once they knew who he was, but he disappeared. ³² They said to each other, "When he talked with us along the road and explained the Scriptures to us, didn't it warm our hearts?" ³³ So they got up at once and returned to Jerusalem.

The two disciples found the eleven apostles and the others gathered together. ³⁴ And they learnt from the group that the Lord was really alive and had appeared to Peter. ³⁵ Then the disciples from Emmaus told what happened on the road and how they knew he was the Lord when he broke the bread.

What Jesus' followers must do
This is also told in Matthew 28.16–20; Mark 16.14–18; John 20.19–23; Acts 1.6–8

³⁶ While Jesus' disciples were talking about what had happened, Jesus appeared and greeted them. ³⁷ They were frightened and terrified because they thought they were seeing a ghost.

³⁸ But Jesus said, "Why are you so frightened? Why do you doubt? ³⁹ Look at my

hands and my feet and see who I am! Touch me and find out for yourselves. Ghosts don't have flesh and bones as you see I have."

⁴⁰ After Jesus said this, he showed them his hands and his feet. ⁴¹ The disciples were so glad and amazed that they could not believe it. Jesus then asked them, "Do you have something to eat?" ⁴² They gave him a piece of baked fish. ⁴³ He took it and ate it as they watched.

⁴⁴ Jesus said to them, "While I was still with you, I told you that everything written about me in the Law of Moses, the Books of the Prophets, and in the Psalms* had to happen." ⁴⁵ Then he helped them understand the Scriptures. ⁴⁶ He told them:

The Scriptures say that the Messiah must suffer, then three days later he will rise from death. ⁴⁷ They also say that all people of every nation must be told in my name to turn to God, in order to be forgiven. So beginning in Jerusalem, ⁴⁸ you must tell everything that has happened. ⁴⁹ I will send you the one my Father has promised,* but you must stay in the city until you are given power from heaven.

Jesus returns to heaven
This is also told in Mark 16.19–20; Acts 1.9–11

⁵⁰ Jesus led his disciples out to Bethany, where he raised his hands and blessed them. ⁵¹ As he was doing this, he left and was taken up to heaven.› ⁵² After his disciples had worshipped him,› they returned to Jerusalem and were very happy. ⁵³ They spent their time in the temple, praising God.

*24.44 Psalms: The Jewish Scriptures were made up of three parts: (1) the Law of Moses, (2) the Books of the Prophets, and (3) the Writings, which included the Psalms. Sometimes the Scriptures were just called the Law or the Law (of Moses) and the Books of the Prophets.
*24.49 the one my Father has promised: Jesus means the Holy Spirit.
See also: 24.49: Acts 1.4. 24.50–51: Acts 1.9–11.

Additional notes
›1.3 a careful study: Or "a study from the beginning".
›1.78 like the sun that rises in the sky: Or "like the Messiah coming from heaven."
›2.37 And now she was eighty-four years old: Or "And now she had been a widow for eighty-four years."
›2.49 in my Father's house: Or "doing my Father's work".

*24.27 the Law of Moses and the Books of the Prophets: See the note at 16.16.

›**4.44 Judea:** Some manuscripts have "Galilee".

›**6.6 On another Sabbath:** Some manuscripts have a reading which may mean "the Sabbath after the next".

›**6.35 without expecting to be paid back:** Some manuscripts have "without giving up on anyone".

›**7.50 saved:** Or "healed". The Greek word may have either meaning.

›**8.26 Gerasa:** Some manuscripts have "Gergesa".

›**8.37 Gerasa:** See the note at 8.26.

›**8.43 She had spent everything she had on doctors:** Some manuscripts do not have these words.

›**8.45 from every side:** Some manuscripts add "and you ask, 'Who touched me?' "

›**9.24 life:** In verses 24–25 a Greek word which often means "soul" is translated "life" and "yourself".

›**9.31 Jesus' death:** In Greek this is "his departure", which probably includes his rising to life and his return to heaven.

›**9.54 to destroy these people:** Some manuscripts add "as Elijah did".

›**9.55 what they had said:** Some manuscripts add, "and said, 'Don't you know what spirit you belong to? The Son of Man did not come to destroy people's lives, but to save them.' "

›**10.9 will soon be here:** Or "is already here".

›**10.11 will soon be here:** See the note at 10.9.

›**10.21 the Holy Spirit:** Some manuscripts have "his spirit".

›**11.3 the food we need:** Or "food for today" or "food for the coming day".

›**11.28 "That's true, but the people who are really blessed . . . message":** Or " 'That's not true, the people who are blessed . . . message.' "

›**11.40 Didn't God make both the outside and the inside?:** Or "Doesn't the person who washes the outside always wash the inside too?"

›**12.25 live longer:** Or "grow taller".

›**17.21 here with you:** Or "in your hearts".

›**17.35–36 will be left:** Some manuscripts add, "Two men will be in the same field, but only one will be taken. The other will be left."

›**18.11 stood over by himself and prayed:** Some manuscripts have "stood up and prayed to himself".

›**18.16 People who are like these children belong to God's kingdom:** Or "God's kingdom belongs to people who are like these children."

›**19.31 The Lord:** Or "The master of the donkey".

›**19.34 The Lord:** See the note at 19.31.

›**21.18 But don't worry:** The Greek text has "Not a hair of your head will be lost", which means, "There's no need to worry".

›**22.43–44 Then an angel . . . like drops of blood:** Verses 43,44 are not in some manuscripts.

›**22.70 You say I am:** Or "That's what you say."

›**23.16–17 set free:** Some manuscripts add, "Pilate said this, because at every Passover he was supposed to set one prisoner free for the Jewish people."

›**23.34–35 Jesus said, "Father, forgive these people! They don't know what they're doing.":** These words are not in some manuscripts.

›**24.3 the Lord:** These words are not in some manuscripts.

›**24.12 what had happened:** Verse 12 is not in some manuscripts.

›**24.51 and was taken up to heaven:** These words are not in some manuscripts.

›**24.52 After his disciples had worshipped him:** These words are not in some manuscripts.

John

tells the good news

The basics

What's the point? Jesus is God. Faith in him will save all who believe.

What happens? John writes about not only what Jesus said and did, but who he really was and what it all means.

What should I remember? 3.16–17 'God loved the people of this world so much that he gave his only Son, so that everyone who has faith in him will have eternal life and never really die.'

More details

Setting the scene John's gospel was probably the last of the gospels to be written. The others had shown what Jesus did and said, John set out to explain what it all really means...

What's it all about? John's gospel is very different to the other three. There is more interpretation here, and times when the writer adds his own explanations. So it is more reflective than the other gospels. But there are historical details – including names and places that are missing from the other gospels, many of them confirmed by archaeology.

But John is different. Even with episodes that we find in the other gospels, John sees the same events from a different perspective. Mark, Matthew and Luke might tell us of Jesus' authority to forgive sins, John tells us where this authority came from. The other gospels show Jesus' claim to be God in human form through his actions. In John it is right there on page one, line one.

John, you see, is concerned with who Jesus is. He calls Jesus the Word, the power by which God created everything there is. Jesus is way more than a human being: he is and always has been God.

This theme recurs throughout the gospel, with Jesus on seven key occasions beginning by saying 'I am...' He says 'I am the light of the world', 'I am the good shepherd' and in one crucial incident he just calls himself, 'I am', which the Jews recognised as the most sacred name of God. Jesus also performs seven miraculous signs to show more of who he is.

John was with Jesus and knew him intimately. His gospel is clearly the work of one who, prayerfully and over many years, asked God what it all meant. And what it meant was life. Life in all its fullness, life everlasting.

Footsteps

In the beginning: 1.1–18
Sign 1 – the wedding at Cana: 2.1–12
Born again: 3.1–21
The woman at the well: 4.1–42
Signs 2 and 3: 4.43–5.18
Signs 4 and 5: 6.1–21
'I am the bread of life': 6.22–59
Two more 'I am's: 8.12–59
Sign 6 – the blind man sees: 9.1–41
And another two 'I am's: 10.1–42
Sign 7 – The raising of Lazarus: 11.1–43
'I am the one who raises the dead': 11.1–44
Washing the feet: 13.1–20
A new commandment: 14.15–31
'I am the way, the truth and the life': 14.1–31
'I am the true vine': 15.1–17
Pilate — and crucifixion: 18.28—19.42
Resurrection: 20.1–29

In praise of the Word

CHAPTER 1

The Word of life

1 In the beginning was the one
  who is called the Word.
  The Word was with God
  and was truly God.
2 From the very beginning
  the Word was with God.

3 And with this Word,
  God created all things.
  Nothing was made
  without the Word.
  Everything that was created
4   received its life from him,
  and his life gave light
  to everyone.
5 The light keeps shining
  in the dark,
  and darkness has never
  put it out.'
6 God sent a man named John,
7   who came to tell
  about the light
  and to lead all people
  to have faith.
8 John wasn't that light.
  He came only to tell
  about the light.

9 The true light that shines
  on everyone
  was coming into the world.
10 The Word was in the world,
  but no one knew him,
  though God had made the world
  with his Word.
11 He came into his own world,
  but his own nation
  did not welcome him.
12 Yet some people accepted him
  and put their faith in him.
  So he gave them the right
  to be the children of God.
13 They were not God's children
  by nature or because
  of any human desires.
  God himself was the one
  who made them his children.

14 The Word became
  a human being
  and lived here with us.

See also: 1.6: Matt 3.1; Mark 1.4; Luke 3.1–2.

Big ideas

Incarnation

The amazing thing about the Bible – OK, one of the many amazing things about the Bible – is that God took the form of a human being. Can you imagine what it was like for God, the ruler of the universe, to squeeze himself into human form?

What he did was called incarnation: it means simply, to appear in person. God took human form and lived among humans. And by doing so, he set an example that we have to follow. God could have just washed his hands of humanity, but he didn't. He came and lived alongside us. Christians have to learn from that lesson. If we want to tell people about Jesus, if we want to save people, we have to get alongside them.

And it means that God knows what it is like to be a human, because he has been one. Jesus was a human being like us. He knows what it is to be tempted, to be tired, to be lonely, to laugh, drink, sweat, die.

It also means that Jesus could demonstrate to us how we should live. Jesus didn't just issue a set of instructions, he lived it out. He provided a model that we should follow.

It's the job of Christians to make God known in the world. With the help of the Holy Spirit, Christians can make God real to people through our faith and actions.

God is still incarnate in the world. He walks this earth in the lives of his followers.

 Footsteps

Ten days on Incarnation

The word became human: John 1.14–8
Jesus is tempted: Luke 4.1–13
Washing the feet: John 13.3–17
Cooking breakfast for friends: John 21.1–14
Descendant of David: Romans 1.1–6
The image of his Father: Colossians 1.15–23
The attitude of Jesus: Philippians 2.1–13
Living letters: 2 Corinthians 2.14–3.3
He came as a human: 1 Timothy 3.16–4.10
Tempted like we are: Hebrews 4.14–16

More...

The Trinity p.1193
Serving others p.1190

We saw his true glory,
the glory of the only Son
   of the Father.
From him all the kindness
and all the truth of God
   have come down to us.

¹⁵ John spoke about him and shouted, "This is the one I told you would come! He is greater than I am, because he was alive before I was born."

¹⁶ Because of all that the Son is, we have been given one blessing after another.ᵇ ¹⁷ The Law was given by Moses, but Jesus Christ brought us undeserved kindness and truth. ¹⁸ No one has ever seen God. The only Son, who is truly God and is closest to the Father, has shown us what God is like.

The message of John the Baptist

John the Baptist tells about Jesus

This is also told in Matthew 3.1–12; Mark 1.1–8; Luke 3.15–17

¹⁹⁻²⁰ The Jewish leaders in Jerusalem sent priests and temple helpers to ask John who he was. He told them plainly, "I am not the Messiah." ²¹ Then when they asked him if he were Elijah, he said, "No, I am not!" And when they asked if he were the Prophet,* he also said "No!"

²² Finally, they said, "Who are you then? We have to give an answer to the ones who sent us. Tell us who you are!"

²³ John answered in the words of the prophet Isaiah, "I am only someone shouting in the desert, 'Get the road ready for the Lord!' "

²⁴ Some Pharisees had also been sent to John. ²⁵ They asked him, "Why are you baptizing people, if you are not the Messiah or Elijah or the Prophet?"

²⁶ John told them, "I use water to baptize people. But here with you is someone you don't know. ²⁷ Even though I came first, I am not good enough to untie his sandals."

²⁸ John said this as he was baptizing east of the River Jordan in Bethany.*

---

*1.21 the Prophet: Many of the Jewish people expected God to send them a prophet who would be like Moses, but with even greater power. See Deuteronomy 18.15,18.

*1.28 Bethany: An unknown village east of the Jordan with the same name as the village near Jerusalem.

See also: 1.21: a Mal 4.5; b Deut 18.15,18.
1.23: Isa 40.3 (LXX).

Life files

Peter (a.k.a. Simon/ Cephas, John 1.42)

Background: Son of John. Fisherman from Bethsaida in Galilee. Married (Mark 1.30).

What's the story?

Peter was a fisherman from Capernaum, in business with Andrew, James and John.

Jesus called Peter to be a 'fisher of men'. His real name was Simon, but when he met Jesus, Jesus called him the 'rock'. Petra is Greek for rock, from which we get Peter.

After the Holy Spirit came at Pentecost, he preached a sermon which led to 3000 people being converted. He was the first of the disciples to recognise that the gentiles had a part to play in the church. Tradition says that Peter went to Rome where he was put to death in AD64.

What's the point?

Peter did everything in a big way. Enthusiastic and committed, he jumped into things feet first. It was Peter who tried to walk on water, it was Peter who drew out his sword and charged at Jesus' arrest. It was Peter who called Jesus the Messiah. He even failed in a big way as when Jesus was being tried, Peter denied ever having known the man.

Later, of course, his relationship with Jesus was restored. Maybe this is the lesson of Peter's life. Enthusiasm and zeal are great, but only when they're linked with a close, personal relationship with Jesus. He had a big heart, and a big passion for God.

Footsteps

Ten days with Peter

Fishers of men: Luke 5.1–11
Walking on water: Matthew 14.22–32
Rocky: Matthew 16.13–20
Think before you speak: Matthew 8.31–38
Denial: Matthew 26.31–35,69–75
Restoration: John 21.1–19
Pentecost and preaching: Acts 2.1–42
Healing the lame: Acts 3.1–26
Arrest: Acts 4.1–31
Peter and Cornelius: Acts 10.1–48

The Lamb of God

29 The next day, John saw Jesus coming towards him and said:

Here is the Lamb of God who takes away the sin of the world! 30 He is the one I told you about when I said, "Someone else will come. He is greater than I am, because he was alive before I was born." 31 I didn't know who he was. But I came to baptize you with water, so that everyone in Israel would see him.

32 I was there and saw the Spirit come down on him like a dove from heaven. And the Spirit stayed on him. 33 Before this I didn't know who he was. But the one who sent me to baptize with water had told me, "You will see the Spirit come down and stay on someone. Then you will know that he is the one who will baptize with the Holy Spirit." 34 I saw this happen, and I tell you that he is the Son of God.

Jesus chooses his first disciples

35 The next day, John was there again, and two of his followers were with him. 36 When he saw Jesus walking by, he said, "Here is the Lamb of God!" 37 John's two followers heard him, and they went with Jesus.

38 When Jesus turned and saw them, he asked, "What do you want?"

They answered, "Rabbi, where do you live?" The Hebrew word "Rabbi" means "Teacher".

39 Jesus replied, "Come and see!" It was already about four o'clock in the afternoon when they went with him and saw where he lived. So they stayed on for the rest of the day.

40 One of the two men who had heard John and had gone with Jesus was Andrew, the brother of Simon Peter. 41 The first thing Andrew did was to find his brother and tell him, "We have found the Messiah!" The Hebrew word "Messiah" means the same as the Greek word "Christ".

42 Andrew brought his brother to Jesus. And when Jesus saw him, he said, "Simon son of John, you will be called Cephas." This name can be translated as "Peter".*

Jesus chooses Philip and Nathanael

43-44 The next day Jesus decided to go to Galilee. There he met Philip, who was from Bethsaida, the home town of Andrew and Peter. Jesus said to Philip, "Come with me."

45 Philip then found Nathanael and said, "We have found the one that Moses and the Prophets* wrote about. He is Jesus, the son of Joseph from Nazareth."

46 Nathanael asked, "Can anything good come from Nazareth?"

Philip answered, "Come and see."

47 When Jesus saw Nathanael coming towards him, he said, "Here is a true descendant of our ancestor Israel. And he isn't deceitful."*

48 "How do you know me?" Nathanael asked.

Jesus answered, "Before Philip called you, I saw you under the fig tree."

49 Nathanael said, "Rabbi, you are the Son of God and the King of Israel!"

50 Jesus answered, "Did you believe me just because I said that I saw you under the fig tree? You will see something even greater. 51 I tell you for certain that you will see heaven open and God's angels going up and coming down on the Son of Man."*

Jesus' seven special miracles

CHAPTER 2

Jesus at a wedding in Cana

1 Three days later Mary, the mother of Jesus, was at a wedding feast in the village of Cana in Galilee. 2 Jesus and his disciples had also been invited and were there.

3 When the wine was all gone, Mary said to Jesus, "They don't have any more wine."

---

*1.45 Moses and the Prophets: The Jewish Scriptures, that is, the Old Testament.
*1.47 Israel . . . isn't deceitful: Israel (meaning "a man who wrestled with God" or "a prince of God") was the name that the Lord gave to Jacob (meaning "cheater" or "deceiver"), the famous ancestor of the Jewish people.
*1.51 going up and coming down on the Son of Man: When Jacob (see the note at verse 47) was running from his brother Esau, he had a dream in which he saw angels going up and down on a ladder from earth to heaven. See Genesis 32.22-32.
See also: 1.51: Gen 28.12.

---

*1.42 Peter: The Aramaic name "Cephas" and the Greek name "Peter" each mean "rock".

4 Jesus replied, "Mother, my time hasn't yet come!* You must not tell me what to do."

5 Mary then said to the servants, "Do whatever Jesus tells you to do."

6 At the feast there were six stone water jars that were used by the people for washing themselves in the way that their religion said they must. Each jar held about a hundred litres. 7 Jesus told the servants to fill them to the top with water. Then after the jars had been filled, 8 he said, "Now take some water and give it to the man in charge of the feast."

The servants did as Jesus told them, 9 and the man in charge drank some of the water that had now turned into wine. He did not know where the wine had come from, but the servants did. He called the bridegroom over 10 and said, "The best wine is always served first. Then after the guests have had plenty, the other wine is served. But you have kept the best until last!"

11 This was Jesus' first miracle,* and he did it in the village of Cana in Galilee. There Jesus showed his glory, and his disciples put their faith in him. 12 After this, he went with his mother, his brothers, and his disciples to the town of Capernaum, where they stayed for a few days.

Jesus in the temple

This is also told in Matthew 21.12–13; Mark 11.15–17; Luke 19.45–46

13 Not long before the Jewish festival of Passover, Jesus went to Jerusalem. 14 There he found people selling cattle, sheep, and doves in the temple. He also saw moneychangers sitting at their tables. 15 So he took some rope and made a whip. Then he chased everyone out of the temple, together with their sheep and cattle. He turned over the tables of the moneychangers and scattered their coins.

16 Jesus said to the people who had been selling doves, "Get those doves out of here! Don't make my Father's house a market place."

17 The disciples then remembered that the Scriptures say, "My love for your house burns in me like a fire."

18 The Jewish leaders asked Jesus, "What miracle* will you perform to show us why you have done this?"

19 "Destroy this temple," Jesus answered, "and in three days I will build it again!"

20 The leaders replied, "It took forty-six years to build this temple. What makes you think you can rebuild it in three days?"

21 But Jesus was talking about his body as a temple. 22 And when he was raised from death, his disciples remembered what he had told them. Then they believed the Scriptures and the words of Jesus.

Jesus knows what people are like

23 In Jerusalem during Passover many people put their faith in Jesus, because they saw him perform miracles.* 24 But Jesus knew what was in their hearts, and he would not let them have power over him. 25 No one had to tell him what people were like. He already knew.

CHAPTER 3
Jesus and Nicodemus

1 There was a man named Nicodemus who was a Pharisee and a Jewish leader. 2 One night he went to Jesus and said, "Sir, we know that God has sent you to teach us. You could not perform these miracles, unless God were with you."

3 Jesus replied, "I tell you for certain that you must be born from above* before you can see God's kingdom!"

4 Nicodemus asked, "How can a grown man ever be born a second time?"

5 Jesus answered:

I tell you for certain that before you can get into God's kingdom, you must be born not only by water, but by the Spirit. 6 Humans give life to their children. Yet only God's Spirit can change you into a child of God. 7 Don't be surprised when I say that you must be born from above. 8 Only God's Spirit gives new life. The Spirit is like the wind that blows wherever it wants to. You can hear the wind, but you don't know where it comes from or where it is going.

*2.4 my time hasn't yet come!: The time when the true glory of Jesus would be seen, and he would be recognized as God's Son. See 12.23.
*2.11 miracle: The Greek text has "sign". In the Gospel of John the word "sign" is used for the miracle itself and as a way of pointing to Jesus as the Son of God.
See also: 2.12: Matt 4.13. 2.13: Exod 12.1–27. 2.17: Psa 69.9.

*2.18,23 miracle(s): See the note at 2.11.
*3.3 from above: Or "in a new way". The same Greek word is used in verses 7,31.
See also: 2.19: Matt 26.61; 27.40; Mark 14.58; 15.29.

Being christian

Starting again

John 3.1–8

In the night, a religious leader comes to talk to Jesus. He wants to find out more; he wants to know what Jesus is really about. During their conversation, Jesus gives him a surprising instruction: if he wants to see God's kingdom, he has to be born again.

Being Christian means starting a new life, wiping the slate clean and going back to the beginning. In the Bible this is sometimes symbolised by baptism: Christians are washed clean by the water. They kill off their old life and start a new one. Today, many Christians choose to be baptised as a sign of this new start.

Christianity is not a superficial change. It's not like wearing a new set of clothes or just a case of starting to go to church. It's a much more fundamental turn-around. We put to death the old ways of thinking, the old habits. Our lives are turned round to point in another direction. If you've accepted God's love, said sorry to him, then a miracle occurs: you've been born again, into a different family, with a different set of values. You have become a child of God. In your old life you followed the values set down by the world. But in your new life you're a child of God. You're starting again.

And this time we're going to do what our father wants us to do.

Being Christian: Starting again

• Commit your life to Jesus. Promise him that you're going to change your life.
• Talk to someone about this. Tell someone that you're starting anew.

More...

Baptism p.1038
Forgiveness p.614

[9] "How can this be?" Nicodemus asked. [10] Jesus replied:

How can you be a teacher of Israel and not know these things? [11] I tell you for certain that we know what we are talking about because we have seen it ourselves. But none of you will accept what we say. [12] If you don't believe when I talk to you about things on earth, how can you possibly believe if I talk to you about things in heaven?

[13] No one has gone up to heaven except the Son of Man, who came down from there. [14] And the Son of Man must be lifted up, just as that metal snake was lifted up by Moses in the desert.* [15] Then everyone who has faith in the Son of Man will have eternal life.

[16] God loved the people of this world so much that he gave his only Son, so that everyone who has faith in him will have eternal life and never really die. [17] God did not send his Son into the world to condemn its people. He sent him to save them! [18] No one who has faith in God's Son will be condemned. But everyone who doesn't have faith in him has already been condemned for not having faith in God's only Son.

[19] The light has come into the world, and people who do evil things are judged guilty because they love the dark more than the light. [20] People who do evil hate the light and won't come to the light, because it clearly shows what they have done. [21] But everyone who lives by the truth will come to the light, because they want others to know that God is really the one doing what they do.

Jesus and John the Baptist

[22] Later, Jesus and his disciples went to Judea, where he stayed with them for a while and was baptizing people.

[23–24] John had not yet been put in jail. He was at Aenon near Salim, where there was a lot of water, and people were coming there for John to baptize them.

---

*3.14 just as that metal snake was lifted up by Moses in the desert: When the Lord punished the people of Israel by sending snakes to bite them, he told Moses to hold a metal snake up on a pole. Everyone who looked at the snake was cured of the snake bites. See Numbers 21.4–9.

See also: 3.14: Num 21.9. 3.24: Matt 14.3; Mark 6.17; Luke 3.19–20.

²⁵ John's followers got into an argument with a Jewish man* about a ceremony of washing.* ²⁶ They went to John and said, "Rabbi, you spoke about a man when you were with him east of the Jordan. He is now baptizing people, and everyone is going to him."

²⁷ John replied:

No one can do anything unless God in heaven allows it. ²⁸ Surely you remember how I told you that I am not the Messiah. I am only the one sent ahead of him.

²⁹ At a wedding the groom is the one who gets married. The best man is glad just to be there and to hear the groom's voice. That's why I am so glad. ³⁰ Jesus must become more important, while I become less important.

The one who comes from heaven

John continued:

³¹ God's Son comes from heaven and is above all others. Everyone who comes from the earth belongs to the earth and speaks about earthly things. The one who comes from heaven is above all others. ³² He speaks about what he has seen and heard, and yet no one believes him. ³³ But everyone who does believe him has shown that God is truthful. ³⁴ The Son was sent to speak God's message, and he has been given the full power of God's Spirit.

³⁵ The Father loves the Son and has given him everything. ³⁶ Everyone who has faith in the Son has eternal life. But no one who rejects him will ever share in that life, and God will be angry with them for ever.

CHAPTER 4

¹ Jesus knew that the Pharisees had heard that he was winning and baptizing more followers than John was. ² But Jesus' disciples were really the ones doing the baptizing, and not Jesus himself.

Jesus and the Samaritan woman

³ Jesus left Judea and started for Galilee again. ⁴ This time he had to go through Samaria,

---

Holy history

Samaritans

In 722BC the northern kingdom, Israel, was wiped out by Assyria.

Samaria, the capital city of Israel, was captured and its citizens deported. Only the very poorest people were left in Israel. The Assyrians replaced the Israelites with people from other areas: Babylonians and other foreigners. These people moved in, settled down, married some of the remaining Israelites and became the Samaritans.

When the Jews eventually returned from exile in Babylon, they looked on this mixed race with horror. The Samaritans wanted to help with the rebuilding of Jerusalem, but were refused because of their mixed religion. The Jews regarded themselves as the pure race; the Samaritans were foreigners.

The Samaritans reacted to this attitude by building their own temple, on Mount Gerazim. This, they claimed, was the only true place of worship.

By Jesus' time, the Samaritans were living in the area between Judea and Galilee, and the antagonism between Jew and Samaritan was intense. When people wanted to insult Jesus, they called him a Samaritan. Jews were even forbidden to drink from the same vessels as Samaritans.

That didn't stop Jesus. He went into Samaria and spoke to a Samaritan woman. He told a story in which the good Samaritan was the hero. Jesus' love knew no boundaries, and in his new kingdom, old enemies were to become the best of friends.

More...

Racism p.1308
Canaanites p.241
Culture p.779
Sharing your faith p.1082

---

*3.25 **about a ceremony of washing:** The Jewish people had many rules about washing themselves and their dishes, in order to make themselves fit to worship God.

See also: 3.28: John 1.20. **3.35:** Matt 11.27; Luke 10.22.

⁵ and on his way he came to the town of Sychar. It was near the field that Jacob had long ago given to his son Joseph. ⁶⁻⁸ The well that Jacob had dug was still there, and Jesus sat down beside it because he was tired from travelling. It was midday, and after Jesus' disciples had gone into town to buy some food, a Samaritan woman came to draw water from the well.

Jesus asked her, "Would you please give me a drink of water?"

⁹ "You are a Jew," she replied, "and I am a Samaritan woman. How can you ask me for a drink of water when Jews and Samaritans won't have anything to do with each other?"*

¹⁰ Jesus answered, "You don't know what God wants to give you, and you don't know who is asking you for a drink. If you did, you would ask me for the water that gives life."

¹¹ "Sir," the woman said, "you don't even have a bucket, and the well is deep. Where are you going to get this life-giving water? ¹² Our ancestor Jacob dug this well for us, and his family and animals got water from it. Are you greater than Jacob?"

¹³ Jesus answered, "Everyone who drinks this water will get thirsty again. ¹⁴ But no one who drinks the water I give will ever be thirsty again. The water I give is like a flowing fountain that gives eternal life."

¹⁵ The woman replied, "Sir, please give me a drink of that water! Then I won't get thirsty and have to come to this well again."

¹⁶ Jesus told her, "Go and bring your husband."

¹⁷⁻¹⁸ The woman answered, "I don't have a husband."

"That's right," Jesus replied, "you're telling the truth. You don't have a husband. You have already been married five times, and the man you are now living with isn't your husband."

¹⁹ The woman said, "Sir, I can see that you are a prophet. ²⁰ My ancestors worshipped on this mountain,* but you Jews say Jerusalem is the only place to worship."

²¹ Jesus said to her:

Believe me, the time is coming when you won't worship the Father either on this mountain or in Jerusalem. ²² You Samaritans don't really know the one you worship. But we Jews do know the God we worship, and by using us, God will save the world. ²³ But a time is coming, and it is already here! Even now the true worshippers are being led by the Spirit to worship the Father according to the truth. These are the ones the Father is seeking to worship him. ²⁴ God is Spirit, and those who worship God must be led by the Spirit to worship him according to the truth.

²⁵ The woman said, "I know that the Messiah will come. He is the one we call Christ. When he comes, he will explain everything to us."

²⁶ "I am that one," Jesus told her, "and I am speaking to you now."

²⁷ The disciples returned about this time and were surprised to find Jesus talking with a woman. But none of them asked him what he wanted or why he was talking with her.

²⁸ The woman left her water jar and ran back into town. She said to the people, ²⁹ "Come and see a man who told me everything I have ever done! Could he be the Messiah?" ³⁰ Everyone in town went out to see Jesus.

³¹ While this was happening, Jesus' disciples were saying to him, "Teacher, please eat something."

³² But Jesus told them, "I have food that you don't know anything about."

³³ His disciples started asking each other, "Has someone brought him something to eat?"

³⁴ Jesus said:

My food is to do what God wants! He is the one who sent me, and I must finish the work that he gave me to do. ³⁵ You may say that there are still four months until harvest time. But I tell you to look, and you will see that the fields are ripe and ready to harvest.

³⁶ Even now the harvest workers are receiving their reward by gathering a harvest that brings eternal life. Then everyone who planted the seed and everyone who harvests the crop will celebrate together. ³⁷ So the saying proves true, "Some plant the seed, and others harvest the crop." ³⁸ I am sending you to harvest crops in fields where others have done all the hard work.

³⁹ A lot of Samaritans in that town put their faith in Jesus because the woman had said, "This man told me everything I have ever

---

*4.9 won't have anything to do with each other: Or "won't use the same cups". The Samaritans lived in the land between Judea and Galilee. They worshipped God differently from the Jews and did not get along with them.

*4.20 this mountain: Mount Gerizim, near the city of Shechem.

See also: 4.5: Gen 33.19; Josh 24.32. 4.9: Ezra 4.1–5; Neh 4.1–2.

done." 40 They came and asked him to stay in their town, and he stayed on for two days.

41 Many more Samaritans put their faith in Jesus because of what they heard him say. 42 They told the woman, "We no longer have faith in Jesus just because of what you told us. We have heard him ourselves, and we are certain that he is the Saviour of the world!"

Jesus heals an official's son

This is also told in Matthew 8.5–13; Luke 7.1–10

43-44 Jesus had said, "Prophets are honoured everywhere, except in their own country." Then two days later he left 45 and went to Galilee. The people there welcomed him, because they had gone to the festival in Jerusalem and had seen everything he had done.

46 While Jesus was in Galilee, he returned to the village of Cana, where he had turned the water into wine. There was an official in Capernaum whose son was sick. 47 And when the man heard that Jesus had come from Judea, he went and begged him to keep his son from dying.

48 Jesus told the official, "You won't have faith unless you see miracles and wonders!"

49 The man replied, "Lord, please come before my son dies!"

50 Jesus then said, "Your son will live. Go on home to him." The man believed Jesus and set off to return home.

51 Some of the official's servants met him along the road and told him, "Your son is better!" 52 He asked them when the boy got better, and they answered, "The fever left him yesterday at one o'clock."

53 The boy's father realized that at one o'clock the day before, Jesus had told him, "Your son will live!" So the man and everyone in his family put their faith in Jesus.

54 This was the second miracle* that Jesus performed after he left Judea and went to Galilee.

CHAPTER 5

Jesus heals a sick man

1 Later, Jesus went to Jerusalem for another Jewish festival.* 2 In the city near the Sheep

Gate was a pool with five porches, and its name in Hebrew was Bethzatha.*

3-4 Many sick, blind, lame, and crippled people were lying close to the pool.*

5 Beside the pool was a man who had been sick for thirty-eight years. 6 When Jesus saw the man and realized that he had been crippled for a long time, he asked him, "Do you want to be healed?"

7 The man answered, "Lord, I don't have anyone to put me in the pool when the water is stirred up. I try to get in, but someone else always gets there first."

8 Jesus told him, "Pick up your mat and walk!" 9 At once the man was healed. He picked up his mat and started walking around. The day on which this happened was a Sabbath.

10 When the Jewish leaders saw the man carrying his mat, they said to him, "This is the Sabbath! No one is allowed to carry a mat on the Sabbath."

11 But he replied, "The man who healed me told me to pick up my mat and walk."

12 They asked him, "Who is this man that told you to pick up your mat and walk?"

13 But he did not know who Jesus was, and Jesus had left because of the crowd.

14 Later, Jesus met the man in the temple and told him, "You are now well. But don't sin any more or something worse might happen to you." 15 The man left and told the leaders that Jesus was the one who had healed him. 16 They started making a lot of trouble for Jesus because he did things like this on the Sabbath.

17 But Jesus said, "My Father has never stopped working, and that is why I keep on working." 18 Now the leaders wanted to kill Jesus for two reasons. First, he had broken the law of the Sabbath. But even worse, he had said that God was his Father, which made him equal with God.

The Son's authority

19 Jesus told the people:

I tell you for certain that the Son cannot do anything on his own. He can do only what he sees the Father doing, and he does exactly what he sees the Father do. 20 The Father loves the Son and has shown him everything he does. The Father will show him even greater things, and you will be amazed. 21 Just as the Father raises the dead

---

*4.54 miracle: See the note at 2.11.
*5.1 another Jewish festival: Either the Festival of Shelters or Passover.

See also: 4.44: Matt 13.57; Mark 6.4; Luke 4.24.
4.45: John 2.23.   4.46: John 2.1–11.

See also: 5.10: Neh 13.19; Jer 17.21.

and gives life, so the Son gives life to anyone he wants to.

²² The Father doesn't judge anyone, but he has made his Son the judge of everyone. ²³ The Father wants all people to honour the Son as much as they honour him. When anyone refuses to honour the Son, that is the same as refusing to honour the Father who sent him. ²⁴ I tell you for certain that everyone who hears my message and has faith in the one who sent me has eternal life and will never be condemned. They have already gone from death to life.

²⁵ I tell you for certain that the time will come, and it is already here, when all the dead will hear the voice of the Son of God. And those who listen to it will live! ²⁶ The Father has the power to give life, and he has given that same power to the Son. ²⁷ And he has given his Son the right to judge everyone, because he is the Son of Man.

²⁸ Don't be surprised! The time will come when all the dead will hear the voice of the Son of Man, ²⁹ and they will come out of their graves. Everyone who has done good things will rise to life, but everyone who has done evil things will rise and be condemned.

³⁰ I cannot do anything on my own. The Father sent me, and he is the one who told me how to judge. I judge with fairness, because I obey him, and I don't just try to please myself.

Witnesses to Jesus

Jesus continued:

³¹ If I speak for myself, there is no way to prove I am telling the truth. ³² But there is someone else who speaks for me, and I know what he says is true. ³³ You sent messengers to John, and he told them the truth. ³⁴ I don't depend on what people say about me, but I tell you these things so that you may be saved. ³⁵ John was a lamp that gave a lot of light, and you were glad to enjoy his light for a while.

³⁶ But something more important than John speaks for me. I mean the things that the Father has given me to do! All of these speak for me and prove that the Father sent me.

³⁷ The Father who sent me also speaks for me, but you have never heard his voice or seen him face to face. ³⁸ You have not

See also: **5.29**: Dan 12.2. **5.33**: John 1.19–27; 3.27–30. **5.37**: Matt 3.17; Mark 1.11; Luke 3.22.

Big ideas

Judgment

God is a God of love. But he's also a God of judgment. At the end, everyone will be judged by Jesus. And the big question will be: have you accepted Christ and lived your life for him?

Some people find the idea of a God of judgment difficult. Surely if God loves everyone, he'd let everyone off? There has to be justice. If there is no judgment then those who commit evil deeds just get away with it. Do we really want to live in such a place? Would you really want the universe to be a place where evil is not punished, where people do not have to face up to their sins?

No, the Bible is clear: people have to pay for their sins. Or ask Jesus to pay the price.

And in the end, people choose their own fate. Because God does want to let everyone off. We can all start again with God: wipe away our sins, reboot the system. He's given everyone a chance to come to Christ, to ask for forgiveness, to say 'sorry' and come back to a relationship with him.

Mind you, the repentance has to be real. It has to result in changed lives and real, active faith. You cannot fool God. You cannot say 'sorry' and then carry on as before.

He is a God of justice. And his justice is perfect. There is no 'getting away with it', no slipping through a loophole; there is either real repentance or real punishment. No in betweens.

Footsteps

A week with Judgment

No excuses: Psalms 1.1–6
He is coming to judge: Psalms 98.1–9
God's servant brings justice: Isaiah 42.1–4
'I don't like to punish': Joel 2.10–13
What fruit do you bear? Matthew 7.15–23
The son will be the judge: John 5.19–30
He judges fairly: 2 Timothy 4.6–8

More...

Forgiveness p.614
Grace p.1316
Redemption p.292
Resurrection p.1203

believed his message, because you refused to have faith in the one he sent.

39 You search the Scriptures, because you think you will find eternal life in them. The Scriptures tell about me, 40 but you refuse to come to me for eternal life.

41 I don't care about human praise, 42 but I do know that none of you love God. 43 I have come with my Father's authority, and you have not welcomed me. But you will welcome people who come on their own. 44 How could you possibly believe? You like to have your friends praise you, and you don't care about praise that the only God can give!

45 Don't think that I will be the one to accuse you to the Father. You have put your hope in Moses, yet he is the very one who will accuse you. 46 Moses wrote about me, and if you had believed Moses, you would have believed me. 47 But if you don't believe what Moses wrote, how can you believe what I say?

CHAPTER 6

Feeding five thousand

This is also told in Matthew 14.13–21; Mark 6.30–44; Luke 9.10–17

1 Jesus crossed Lake Galilee, which was also known as Lake Tiberias. 2 A large crowd had seen him perform miracles to heal the sick, and those people went with him. 3-4 It was almost time for the Jewish festival of Passover, and Jesus went up on a mountain with his disciples and sat down.*

5 When Jesus saw the large crowd coming towards him, he asked Philip, "Where will we get enough food to feed all these people?" 6 He said this to test Philip, since he already knew what he was going to do.

7 Philip answered, "Don't you know that it would take almost a year's wages* just to buy only a little bread for each of these people?"

8 Andrew, the brother of Simon Peter, was one of the disciples. He spoke up and said, 9 "There is a boy here who has five small loaves* of barley bread and two fish. But what good is that with all these people?"

10 The ground was covered with grass, and Jesus told his disciples to make everyone sit down. About five thousand men were in the crowd. 11 Jesus took the bread in his hands and gave thanks to God. Then he passed the bread to the people, and he did the same with the fish, until everyone had plenty to eat.

12 The people ate all they wanted, and Jesus told his disciples to gather up the leftovers, so that nothing would be wasted. 13 The disciples gathered them up and filled twelve large baskets with what was left over from the five barley loaves.

14 After the people had seen Jesus perform this miracle,* they began saying, "This must be the Prophet* who is to come into the world!" 15 Jesus realized that they would try to force him to be their king. So he went up on a mountain, where he could be alone.

Jesus walks on the water

This is also told in Matthew 14.22–27; Mark 6.45–52

16 That evening, Jesus' disciples went down to the lake. 17 They got into a boat and set off for Capernaum. Later that evening Jesus had still not come to them, 18 and a strong wind was making the water rough.

19 When the disciples had rowed for five or six kilometres, they saw Jesus walking on the water. He kept coming closer to the boat, and they were terrified. 20 But he said, "I am Jesus!* Don't be afraid!" 21 The disciples wanted to take him into the boat, but suddenly the boat reached the shore where they were headed.

The bread that gives life

22 The people who had stayed on the east side of the lake knew that only one boat had been there. They also knew that Jesus had not left in it with his disciples. But the next day 23 some boats from Tiberias sailed near the place where the crowd had eaten the bread for which the Lord had given thanks. 24 They saw that Jesus and his disciples had left. Then they got into the boats and went to Capernaum to look for Jesus. 25 They found him on the west side of the lake and asked, "Rabbi, when did you get here?"

---

*6.3–4 sat down: Possibly to teach. Teachers in the ancient world, including Jewish teachers, usually sat down to teach.

*6.7 almost a year's wages: The Greek text has "two hundred silver coins". Each coin was worth the average day's wages for a worker.

*6.9 small loaves: These would have been flat and round or in the shape of a bun.

*6.14 miracle: See the note at 2.11.

*6.14 the Prophet: See the note at 1.21.

*6.20 I am Jesus: The Greek text has "I am". See the note at 8.24.

26 Jesus answered, "I tell you for certain that you are not looking for me because you saw the miracles,* but because you ate all the food you wanted. 27 Don't work for food that spoils. Work for food that gives eternal life. The Son of Man will give you this food, because God the Father has given him the right to do so."

28 "What exactly does God want us to do?" the people asked.

29 Jesus answered, "God wants you to have faith in the one he sent."

30 They replied, "What miracle will you perform, so that we can have faith in you? What will you do? 31 For example, when our ancestors were in the desert, they were given manna* to eat. It happened just as the Scriptures say, 'God gave them bread from heaven to eat.' "

32 Jesus then told them, "I tell you for certain that Moses wasn't the one who gave you bread from heaven. My Father is the one who gives you the true bread from heaven. 33 And the bread that God gives is the one who came down from heaven to give life to the world."

34 The people said, "Lord, give us this bread and don't ever stop!"

35 Jesus replied:

I am the bread that gives life! No one who comes to me will ever be hungry. No one who has faith in me will ever be thirsty. 36 I have told you already that you have seen me and still do not have faith in me. 37 Everything and everyone that the Father has given me will come to me, and I won't turn any of them away.

38 I didn't come from heaven to do what I want! I came to do what the Father wants me to do. He sent me, 39 and he wants to make certain that none of the ones he has given me will be lost. Instead, he wants me to raise them to life on the last day.* 40 My Father wants everyone who sees the Son to have faith in him and to have eternal life. Then I will raise them to life on the last day.

41 The people started grumbling because Jesus had said he was the bread that had come down from heaven. 42 They were asking each other, "Isn't he Jesus, the son of Joseph? Don't we know his father and mother? How can he say that he has come down from heaven?"

43 Jesus told them:

Stop grumbling! 44 No one can come to me, unless the Father who sent me makes them want to come. But if they do come, I will raise them to life on the last day. 45 One of the prophets wrote, "God will teach all of them." And so everyone who listens to the Father and learns from him will come to me.

46 The only one who has seen the Father is the one who has come from him. No one else has ever seen the Father. 47 I tell you for certain that everyone who has faith in me has eternal life.

48 I am the bread that gives life! 49 Your ancestors ate manna* in the desert, and later they died. 50 But the bread from heaven has come down, so that no one who eats it will ever die. 51 I am that bread from heaven! Everyone who eats it will live for ever. My flesh is the life-giving bread that I give to the people of this world.

52 They started arguing with each other and asked, "How can he give us his flesh to eat?"

53 Jesus answered:

I tell you for certain that you won't live unless you eat the flesh and drink the blood of the Son of Man. 54 But if you do eat my flesh and drink my blood, you will have eternal life, and I will raise you to life on the last day. 55 My flesh is the true food, and my blood is the true drink. 56 If you eat my flesh and drink my blood, you are one with me, and I am one with you.

57 The living Father sent me, and I have life because of him. Now everyone who eats my flesh will live because of me. 58 The bread that comes down from heaven isn't like what your ancestors ate. They died, but whoever eats this bread will live for ever.

59 Jesus was teaching in a Jewish place of worship in Capernaum when he said these things.

The words of eternal life

60 Many of Jesus' disciples heard him and said, "This is too hard for anyone to understand."

---

*6.26 miracles: The Greek text has "signs" here and "sign" in verse 30. See the note at 2.11.
*6.31 manna: When the people of Israel were wandering through the desert, the Lord gave them a special kind of food to eat. It tasted like a wafer and was called "manna", which in Hebrew means, "What is this?"
*6.39 the last day: When God will judge all people.
See also: 6.31: Exod 16.4,15; Psa 78.24.

*6.49 manna: See the note at 6.31.
See also: 6.45: Isa 54.13.

⁶¹ Jesus knew that his disciples were grumbling. So he asked, "Does this bother you? ⁶² What if you should see the Son of Man go up to heaven where he came from? ⁶³ The Spirit is the one who gives life! Human strength can do nothing. The words that I have spoken to you are from that life-giving Spirit. ⁶⁴ But some of you refuse to have faith in me." Jesus said this, because from the beginning he knew who would have faith in him. He also knew which one would betray him.

⁶⁵ Then Jesus said, "You cannot come to me, unless the Father makes you want to come. That is why I have told these things to all of you."

⁶⁶ Because of what Jesus said, many of his disciples turned their backs on him and stopped following him. ⁶⁷ Jesus then asked his twelve disciples if they were going to leave him. ⁶⁸ Simon Peter answered, "Lord, there is no one else that we can go to! Your words give eternal life. ⁶⁹ We have faith in you, and we are sure that you are God's Holy One."

⁷⁰ Jesus told his disciples, "I chose all twelve of you, but one of you is a demon!" ⁷¹ Jesus was talking about Judas, the son of Simon Iscariot.* He would later betray Jesus, even though he was one of the twelve disciples.

CHAPTER 7

Jesus' brothers don't have faith in him

¹ Jesus decided to leave Judea and to start going through Galilee because the Jewish leaders wanted to kill him. ² It was almost time for the Festival of Shelters, ³ and Jesus' brothers said to him, "Why don't you go to Judea? Then your disciples can see what you are doing. ⁴ No one does anything in secret, if they want others to know about them. So let the world know what you are doing!" ⁵ Even Jesus' own brothers had not yet become his followers.

⁶ Jesus answered, "My time hasn't yet come,* but your time is always here. ⁷ The people of this world cannot hate you. They hate me, because I tell them that they do evil things. ⁸ Go on to the festival. My time hasn't yet come, and I am not going." ⁹ Jesus said this and stayed on in Galilee.

Jesus at the Festival of Shelters

¹⁰ After Jesus' brothers had gone to the festival, he went secretly, without telling anyone.

¹¹ During the festival the Jewish leaders looked for Jesus and asked, "Where is he?" ¹² The crowds even got into an argument about him. Some were saying, "Jesus is a good man," while others were saying, "He is lying to everyone." ¹³ But the people were afraid of their leaders, and none of them talked in public about him.

¹⁴ When the festival was about half over, Jesus went into the temple and started teaching. ¹⁵ The leaders were surprised and said, "How does this man know so much? He has never been taught!"

¹⁶ Jesus replied:

I am not teaching something that I thought up. What I teach comes from the one who sent me. ¹⁷ If you really want to obey God, you will know if what I teach comes from God or from me. ¹⁸ If I wanted to bring honour to myself, I would speak for myself. But I want to honour the one who sent me. That is why I tell the truth and not a lie. ¹⁹ Didn't Moses give you the Law? Yet none of you obey it! So why do you want to kill me?

²⁰ The crowd replied, "You're mad! What makes you think someone wants to kill you?"

²¹ Jesus answered:

I performed one miracle,* and it amazed you. ²² Moses commanded you to circumcise your sons. But it wasn't really Moses who gave you this command. It was your ancestors, and even on the Sabbath you circumcise your sons ²³ in order to obey the Law of Moses. Why are you angry with me for making someone completely well on the Sabbath? ²⁴ Don't judge by appearances. Judge by what is right.

²⁵ Some of the people from Jerusalem were saying, "Isn't this the man they want to kill? ²⁶ Yet here he is, speaking for everyone to hear. And no one is arguing with him. Do you suppose the authorities know that he is the Messiah? ²⁷ But how could that be? No one knows where the Messiah will come from, but we know where this man comes from."

²⁸ As Jesus was teaching in the temple, he shouted, "Do you really think you know me

---

*6.71 Iscariot: This may mean "a man from Kerioth" (a place in Judea). But more probably it means "a man who was a liar" or "a man who was a betrayer".
*7.6 My time hasn't yet come: See the note at 2.4.
See also: 6.68–69: Matt 16.16; Mark 8.29; Luke 9.20.
7.2: Lev 23.34; Deut 16.13.

*7.21 one miracle: The healing of the lame man (5.1–18; see also the note at 2.11).
See also: 7.22: a Lev 12.3; b Gen 17.10. 7.23: John 5.9.

and where I came from? I didn't come on my own! The one who sent me is truthful, and you don't know him. 29 But I know the one who sent me, because I came from him."

30 Some of the people wanted to arrest Jesus there and then. But no one even laid a hand on him, because his time had not yet come.* 31 A lot of people in the crowd put their faith in him and said, "When the Messiah comes, he won't perform more miracles* than this man has done!"

Officers sent to arrest Jesus

32 When the Pharisees heard the crowd arguing about Jesus, they got together with the chief priests and sent some temple police to arrest him. 33 But Jesus told them, "I will be with you a little while longer, and then I will return to the one who sent me. 34 You will look for me, but you won't find me. You cannot go where I am going."

35 The Jewish leaders asked each other, "Where can he go to keep us from finding him? Is he going to some foreign country where our people live? Is he going there to teach the Greeks?* 36 What did he mean by saying that we will look for him, but won't find him? Why can't we go where he is going?"

Streams of life-giving water

37 On the last and most important day of the festival, Jesus stood up and shouted, "If you are thirsty, come to me and drink! 38 Have faith in me, and you will have life-giving water flowing from deep inside you, just as the Scriptures say." 39 Jesus was talking about the Holy Spirit, who would be given to everyone that had faith in him. The Spirit had not yet been given to anyone, since Jesus had not yet been given his full glory.*

The people take sides

40 When the crowd heard Jesus say this, some of them said, "He must be the Prophet!"* 41 Others said, "He is the Messiah!" Others

even said, "Can the Messiah come from Galilee? 42 The Scriptures say that the Messiah will come from the family of King David. Doesn't this mean that he will be born in David's home town of Bethlehem?" 43 The people started taking sides against each other because of Jesus. 44 Some of them wanted to arrest him, but no one laid a hand on him.

The leaders refuse to have faith in Jesus

45 When the temple police returned to the chief priests and Pharisees, they were asked, "Why didn't you bring Jesus here?"

46 They answered, "No one has ever spoken like that man!"

47 The Pharisees said to them, "Have you also been fooled? 48 Not one of the chief priests or the Pharisees has faith in him. 49 And these people who don't know the Law are under God's curse anyway."

50 Nicodemus was there at the time. He was a member of the council, and was the same one who had earlier come to see Jesus.* He said, 51 "Our Law doesn't let us condemn people before we hear what they have to say. We cannot judge them before we know what they have done."

52 Then they said, "Nicodemus, you must be from Galilee! Read the Scriptures, and you will find that no prophet is to come from Galilee."

CHAPTER 8

A woman caught in sin

53 Everyone else went home, 1 but Jesus walked out to the Mount of Olives. 2 Then early the next morning he went to the temple. The people came to him, and he sat down* and started teaching them.

3 The Pharisees and the teachers of the Law of Moses brought in a woman who had been caught in bed with a man who wasn't her husband. They made her stand in the middle of the crowd. 4 Then they said, "Teacher, this woman was caught sleeping with a man who isn't her husband. 5 The Law of Moses teaches that a woman like this should be stoned to death! What do you say?"

6 They asked Jesus this question, because they wanted to test him and bring some

---

*7.30 his time had not yet come: See the note at 2.4.
*7.31 miracles: See the note at 2.11.
*7.35 Greeks: Perhaps Gentiles or Jews who followed Greek customs.
*7.39 had not yet been given his full glory: In the Gospel of John, Jesus is given his full glory both when he is nailed to the cross and when he is raised from death to sit beside his Father in heaven.
*7.40 the Prophet: See the note at 1.21.
See also: 7.37: Lev 23.36. 7.38: Ezek 47.1; Zech 14.8.

*7.50 who had earlier come to see Jesus: See 3.1–21.
*8.2 sat down: See the note at 6.3–4.
See also: 7.42: 2 Sam 7.12; Mic 5.2. 7.50: John 3.1–2. 8.5: Lev 20.10; Deut 22.22–24.

charge against him. But Jesus simply bent over and started writing on the ground with his finger.

⁷ They kept on asking Jesus about the woman. Finally, he stood up and said, "If any of you have never sinned, then go ahead and throw the first stone at her!" ⁸ Once again he bent over and began writing on the ground. ⁹ The people left one by one, beginning with the oldest. Finally, Jesus and the woman were there alone.

¹⁰ Jesus stood up and asked her, "Where is everyone? Isn't there anyone left to accuse you?"

¹¹ "No sir," the woman answered.

Then Jesus told her, "I am not going to accuse you either. You may go now, but don't sin any more."▸

Jesus is the light for the world

¹² Once again Jesus spoke to the people. This time he said, "I am the light for the world! Follow me, and you won't be walking in the dark. You will have the light that gives life."

¹³ The Pharisees objected, "You are the only one speaking for yourself, and what you say isn't true!"

¹⁴ Jesus replied:

Even if I do speak for myself, what I say is true! I know where I came from and where I am going. But you don't know where I am from or where I am going. ¹⁵ You judge in the same way that everyone else does, but I don't judge anyone. ¹⁶ If I did judge, I would judge fairly, because I would not be doing it alone. The Father who sent me is here with me. ¹⁷ Your Law requires two witnesses to prove that something is true. ¹⁸ I am one of my witnesses, and the Father who sent me is the other one.

¹⁹ "Where is your Father?" they asked.

"You don't know me or my Father!" Jesus answered. "If you knew me, you would know my Father."

²⁰ Jesus said this while he was still teaching in the place where the temple treasures were stored. But no one arrested him, because his time had not yet come.*

You cannot go where I am going

²¹ Jesus also told them, "I am going away, and you will look for me. But you cannot go where I am going, and you will die with your sins unforgiven."

²² The Jewish leaders asked, "Does he intend to kill himself? Is that what he means by saying we cannot go where he is going?"

²³ Jesus answered, "You are from below, but I am from above. You belong to this world, but I don't. ²⁴ That is why I said you will die with your sins unforgiven. If you don't have faith in me for who I am,* you will die, and your sins will not be forgiven."

²⁵ "Who are you?" they asked Jesus.

Jesus answered, "I am exactly who I told you at the beginning. ²⁶ There is a lot more I could say to condemn you. But the one who sent me is truthful, and I tell the people of this world only what I have heard from him."

²⁷ No one understood that Jesus was talking to them about the Father.

²⁸ Jesus went on to say, "When you have lifted up the Son of Man,* you will know who I am. You will also know that I don't do anything on my own. I say only what my Father taught me. ²⁹ The one who sent me is with me. I always do what pleases him, and he will never leave me."

³⁰ After Jesus said this, many of the people put their faith in him.

The truth will set you free

³¹ Jesus told the people who had faith in him, "If you keep on obeying what I have said, you truly are my disciples. ³² You will know the truth, and the truth will set you free."

³³ They answered, "We are Abraham's children! We have never been anyone's slaves. How can you say we will be set free?"

³⁴ Jesus replied:

I tell you for certain that anyone who sins is a slave of sin! ³⁵ And slaves don't stay in the family for ever, though the Son will always remain in the family. ³⁶ If the Son gives you freedom, you are free! ³⁷ I know that you are from Abraham's family. Yet you want to kill me, because my message isn't really in your hearts. ³⁸ I am telling you what my Father has shown me, just as you are doing what your father has taught you.

---

*8.20 his time had not yet come: See the note at 2.4.
See also: 8.12: Matt 5.14; John 9.5. **8.13:** John 5.31.
8.17: Deut 19.15.

*8.24 I am: For the Jewish people the most holy name of God is "Yahweh", which may be translated "I am". In the Gospel of John "I am" is sometimes used by Jesus to show that he is that one.
*8.28 lifted up the Son of Man: See the note at 7.39.
See also: 8.33: Matt 3.9; Luke 3.8.

Real life

Addiction

Contributed by HopeUK

We live in a drug-taking society, where there is a 'pill for every ill'. If we go to the doctor we expect to be given something which will make us better. Certainly we can all benefit from the advances in medical science, and the wise use of drugs. But just as it is easy to depend on the doctor to make us better, it's easy to slip into the situation where we need a drink to relax or to cope with any new or uncomfortable situation.

The apostle Peter tells us we are free (1 Peter 3.16), but one person's freedom can be another person's prison. This is particularly so in the case of alcohol and other drug abuse. We may believe in liberty for all and jealously guard our individual freedom of choice, but for the person who is drug-dependent and addicted, there is little real freedom of choice. Some drugs are physically addictive, but all can cause powerful psychological dependence.

The cycle of addiction starts with a mounting desire to act in a certain way. If this desire is resisted or prevented, there is a growing anxiety and preoccupation with the act in question. Carrying out the act stills the tension, satisfies the desire and briefly eliminates the need. Many activities, apart from drug taking, fulfil this addictive sequence. People whose lives depend on their next shot of alcohol, nicotine or other drugs, face a frightening imprisonment which is unseen.

Jesus said 'If the Son sets you free you will be really free' (John 8.36). So what does it mean to be really free? (Check out John 8.34.) Peter says that, although we are free, we are also God's servants and that we must not use our freedom as an excuse for doing wrong (1 Peter 2.16).

Substance use ranges from experimentation through to regular recreational use and on to physical or psychological dependence. Whether through peer group influence, media indoctrination, parental example or sheer curiosity, many young people experiment with substance use. Christians have a responsibility to offer pastoral care, preventive education and realistic alternatives. Churches witness in a society where every young person will have to make choices regarding alcohol and other drugs. The most important decision we can make is to chose to 'live as free people' in Jesus Christ.

Think

Is it OK to experiment with drugs as long as you don't become addicted?
Are some people genetically predisposed to dependence or is it a result of human weakness and depravity?
Is the problem medical or moral? Or is there a spiritual dimension?

Act

Find out from Hope UK if there is a Christian rehab centre near you.

Check

John 8.31–36; 1 Peter 2.16; 3.16

More...

Alcohol p.700
Drugs p.1318
Help! I feel like I've failed p.837
Help! I've messed up really badly p.347
Help! I'm in trouble with the police p.378
Pornography p.952
Help! I can't stop masturbating p.1339

Your father is the devil

39 The people said to Jesus, "Abraham is our father!"

Jesus replied, "If you were Abraham's children, you would do what Abraham did. 40 Instead, you want to kill me for telling you the truth that God gave me. Abraham never did anything like that. 41 But you are doing exactly what your father does."

"Don't accuse us of having someone else as our father!" they said. "We just have one father, and he is God."

42 Jesus answered:

If God were your Father, you would love me, because I came from God and only from him. He sent me. I did not come on my own. 43 Why can't you understand what I am talking about? Can't you stand to hear what I am saying? 44 Your father is the devil, and you do exactly what he wants. He has always been a murderer and a liar. There is nothing truthful about him. He speaks on his own, and everything he says is a lie. Not only is he a liar himself, but he is also the father of all lies.

45 Everything I have told you is true, and you still refuse to have faith in me. 46 Can any of you accuse me of sin? If you cannot, why won't you have faith in me? After all, I am telling you the truth. 47 Anyone who belongs to God will listen to his message. But you refuse to listen, because you don't belong to God.

Jesus and Abraham

48 The people told Jesus, "We were right to say that you are a Samaritan* and that you have a demon in you!"

49 Jesus answered, "I don't have a demon in me. I honour my Father, and you refuse to honour me. 50 I don't want honour for myself. But there is one who wants me to be honoured, and he is also the one who judges. 51 I tell you for certain that if you obey my words, you will never die."

52 Then the people said, "Now we are sure that you have a demon. Abraham is dead, and so are the prophets. How can you say that no one who obeys your words will ever die? 53 Are you greater than our father Abraham? He died, and so did the prophets. Who do you think you are?"

54 Jesus replied, "If I honoured myself, it would mean nothing. My Father is the one

who honours me. You claim that he is your God, 55 even though you don't really know him. If I said I didn't know him, I would be a liar, just like all of you. But I know him, and I do what he says. 56 Your father Abraham was really glad to see me."

57 "You are not even fifty years old!" they said. "How could you have seen Abraham?"

58 Jesus answered, "I tell you for certain that even before Abraham was, I was, and I am."* 59 The people picked up stones to kill Jesus, but he hid and left the temple.

CHAPTER 9

Jesus heals a man born blind

1 As Jesus walked along, he saw a man who had been blind since birth. 2 Jesus' disciples asked, "Teacher, why was this man born blind? Was it because he or his parents sinned?"

3 "No, it wasn't!" Jesus answered. "But because of his blindness, you will see God perform a miracle for him. 4 As long as it is day, we must do what the one who sent me wants me to do. When night comes, no one can work. 5 While I am in the world, I am the light for the world."

6 After Jesus said this, he spat on the ground. He made some mud and smeared it on the man's eyes. 7 Then he said, "Go and wash off the mud in Siloam Pool." The man went and washed in Siloam, which means "One who is sent". When he had washed off the mud, he could see.

8 The man's neighbours and the people who had seen him begging wondered if he really could be the same man. 9 Some of them said he was the same beggar, while others said he only looked like him. But he told them, "I am that man."

10 "Then how can you see?" they asked.

11 He answered, "Someone named Jesus made some mud and smeared it on my eyes. He told me to go and wash it off in Siloam Pool. When I did, I could see."

12 "Where is he now?" they asked.

"I don't know," he answered.

The Pharisees try to find out what happened

13-14 The day when Jesus made the mud and healed the man was a Sabbath. So the people took the man to the Pharisees. 15 They asked

*8.58 I am: See the note at 8.24.
See also: 9.5: Matt 5.14; John 8.12.

*8.48 Samaritan: See 4.9 and the note there.

1183

him how he was able to see, and he answered, "Jesus made some mud and smeared it on my eyes. Then after I washed it off, I could see."

16 Some of the Pharisees said, "This man Jesus doesn't come from God. If he did, he would not break the law of the Sabbath."

Others asked, "How could someone who is a sinner perform such a miracle?"*

Since the Pharisees could not agree among themselves, 17 they asked the man, "What do you say about this one who healed your eyes?"

"He is a prophet!" the man told them.

18 But the Jewish leaders would not believe that the man had once been blind. They sent for his parents 19 and asked them, "Is this the son that you said was born blind? How can he now see?"

20 The man's parents answered, "We are certain that he is our son, and we know that he was born blind. 21 But we don't know how he got his sight or who gave it to him. Ask him! He is old enough to speak for himself."

22-23 The man's parents said this because they were afraid of the Jewish leaders. The leaders had already agreed that no one was to have anything to do with anyone who said Jesus was the Messiah.

24 The leaders called the man back and said, "Swear by God to tell the truth! We know that Jesus is a sinner."

25 The man replied, "I don't know if he is a sinner or not. All I know is that I used to be blind, but now I can see!"

26 "What did he do to you?" the Jewish leaders asked. "How did he heal your eyes?"

27 The man answered, "I have already told you once, and you refused to listen. Why do you want me to tell you again? Do you also want to become his disciples?"

28 The leaders insulted the man and said, "You are his follower! We are followers of Moses. 29 We are sure that God spoke to Moses, but we don't even know where Jesus comes from."

30 "How strange!" the man replied. "He healed my eyes, and yet you don't know where he comes from. 31 We know that God listens only to people who love and obey him. God doesn't listen to sinners. 32 And this is the first time in history that anyone has ever given sight to someone born blind. 33 Jesus could not do anything unless he came from God."

34 The leaders told the man, "You have been a sinner since the day you were born!

Do you think you can teach us anything?" Then they said, "You can never come back into any of our meeting places!"

35 When Jesus heard what had happened, he went and found the man. Then Jesus asked, "Do you have faith in the Son of Man?"

36 He replied, "Sir, if you will tell me who he is, I will put my faith in him."

37 "You have already seen him," Jesus answered, "and right now he is talking with you."

38 The man said, "Lord, I put my faith in you!" Then he worshipped Jesus.

39 Jesus told him, "I came to judge the people of this world. I am here to give sight to the blind and to make blind everyone who can see."

40 When the Pharisees heard Jesus say this, they asked, "Are we blind?"

41 Jesus answered, "If you were blind, you would not be guilty. But now that you claim to see, you will keep on being guilty."

CHAPTER 10

A story about sheep

1 Jesus said:

I tell you for certain that only thieves and robbers climb over the fence instead of going in through the gate to the sheep pen. 2-3 But the gatekeeper opens the gate for the shepherd, and he goes in through it. The sheep know their shepherd's voice. He calls each of them by name and leads them out.

4 When he has led out all his sheep, he walks in front of them, and they follow, because they know his voice. 5 The sheep will not follow strangers. They don't recognize a stranger's voice, and they run away.

6 Jesus told the people this story. But they did not understand what he was talking about.

Jesus is the good shepherd

7 Jesus said:

I tell you for certain that I am the gate for the sheep. 8 Everyone who came before me was a thief or a robber, and the sheep did not listen to any of them. 9 I am the gate. All who come in through me will be saved. Through me they will come and go and find pasture.

10 A thief comes only to rob, kill, and destroy. I came so that everyone would

---

*9.16 miracle: See the note at 2.11.

have life, and have it fully. ¹¹ I am the good shepherd, and the good shepherd gives up his life for his sheep. ¹² Hired workers are not like the shepherd. They don't own the sheep, and when they see a wolf coming, they run off and leave the sheep. Then the wolf attacks and scatters the flock. ¹³ Hired workers run away because they don't care about the sheep.

¹⁴ I am the good shepherd. I know my sheep, and they know me. ¹⁵ Just as the Father knows me, I know the Father, and I give up my life for my sheep. ¹⁶ I have other sheep that are not in this sheep pen. I must bring them together too, when they hear my voice. Then there will be one flock of sheep and one shepherd.

¹⁷ The Father loves me, because I give up my life, so that I may receive it back again. ¹⁸ No one takes my life from me. I give it up willingly! I have the power to give it up and the power to receive it back again, just as my Father commanded me to do.

¹⁹ The people took sides because of what Jesus had told them. ²⁰ Many of them said, "He has a demon in him! He is mad! Why listen to him?"

²¹ But others said, "How could anyone with a demon in him say these things? No one like that could give sight to a blind person!"

Jesus is rejected

²² That winter, Jesus was in Jerusalem for the Temple Festival. ²³ One day he was walking in that part of the temple known as Solomon's Porch,* ²⁴ and the people gathered all around him. They said, "How long are you going to keep us guessing? If you are the Messiah, tell us plainly!"

²⁵ Jesus answered:

I have told you, and you refused to believe me. The things I do by my Father's authority show who I am. ²⁶ But since you are not my sheep, you don't believe me. ²⁷ My sheep know my voice, and I know them. They follow me, ²⁸ and I give them eternal life, so that they will never be lost. No one can snatch them out of my hand. ²⁹ My Father gave them to me, and he is greater than all others.′ No one can snatch them from his hands, ³⁰ and I am one with the Father.

³¹ Once again the Jewish leaders picked up stones in order to kill Jesus. ³² But he said, "I have shown you many good things that my Father sent me to do. Which one are you going to stone me for?"

³³ They answered, "We are not stoning you because of any good thing you did. We are stoning you because you did a terrible thing. You are just a man, and here you are claiming to be God!"

³⁴ Jesus replied:

In your Scriptures doesn't God say, "You are gods"? ³⁵ You can't argue with the Scriptures, and God spoke to those people and called them gods. ³⁶ So why do you accuse me of a terrible sin for saying that I am the Son of God? After all, it is the Father who prepared me for this work. He is also the one who sent me into the world. ³⁷ If I don't do as my Father does, you should not believe me. ³⁸ But if I do what my Father does, you should believe because of that, even if you don't have faith in me. Then you will know for certain that the Father is one with me, and I am one with the Father.

³⁹ Again they wanted to arrest Jesus. But he escaped ⁴⁰ and crossed the Jordan to the place where John had earlier been baptizing. While Jesus was there, ⁴¹ many people came to him. They were saying, "John didn't perform any miracles, but everything he said about Jesus is true." ⁴² A lot of those people also put their faith in Jesus.

CHAPTER 11

The death of Lazarus

¹⁻² A man called Lazarus was sick in the village of Bethany. He had two sisters, Mary and Martha. This was the same Mary who later poured perfume on the Lord's head and wiped his feet with her hair. ³ The sisters sent a message to the Lord and told him that his good friend Lazarus was sick.

⁴ When Jesus heard this, he said, "His sickness won't end in death. It will bring glory to God and his Son."

⁵ Jesus loved Martha and her sister and brother. ⁶ But he stayed where he was for two more days. ⁷ Then he said to his disciples, "Now we will go back to Judea."

⁸ "Teacher," they said, "the people there want to stone you to death! Why do you want to go back?"

---

*10.23 Solomon's Porch: A public place with tall columns along the east side of the temple.
See also: 10.15: Matt 11.27; Luke 10.22.

See also: 10.33: Lev 24.16. 10.34: Psa 82.6.
10.40: John 1.28. 11.1: Luke 10.38–39. 11.2: John 12.3.

Big ideas

Miracles

By miracles, we mean God taking an active part in creation in a special way. However, Bible writers didn't really distinguish between God's 'normal' activity and his 'special' acts. They saw the whole of creation as miraculous. Psalm 135, for example, celebrates not only the miracles which rescued Israel from Egypt, but the clouds, the lightning and the rain.

Miracles are divine surprises which cannot be explained other than to say that God is at work. They display God's power. He is the only one who could do these things. His is the power to heal, to create, to destroy.

Miracles occur throughout the Bible, but there is a difference between the Testaments. In the Old, it is quite clearly God doing the miracles. He tells his servants what to say and do, and they follow his instructions. In the New, Jesus is God; he doesn't have to be instructed, he acts under his own authority.

Old Testament miracles are recorded, one by one, with no indication that there were more than were mentioned. But in the New Testament we are told that Jesus did masses of miracles, too many to record.

Jesus told his followers that they would do the same things that he had done. Christians today still pray for miracles – and Christians today still see miracles happen.

 Footsteps

Ten days with Miracles

The one true God: Deuteronomy 4.32–40
Remember miracles: 1 Chronicles 16.7–36
The power of God: Job 9.1–14
'You alone work miracles': Psalms 77.11–20
False miracles: Matthew 7.21–23
The fish and the bread: Matthew 15.13–21
The walking dead: John 11.1–46
Too many miracles: John 20.30–31
The man at the door: Acts 3.1–26
The open jail: Acts 16.16–40

More...

Holy Spirit p.1209

⁹ Jesus answered, "Aren't there twelve hours in each day? If you walk during the day, you will have light from the sun, and you won't stumble. ¹⁰ But if you walk during the night, you will stumble, because you don't have any light." ¹¹ Then he told them, "Our friend Lazarus is asleep, and I am going there to wake him up."

¹² They replied, "Lord, if he is asleep, he will get better." ¹³ Jesus really meant that Lazarus was dead, but they thought he was talking only about sleep.

¹⁴ Then Jesus told them plainly, "Lazarus is dead! ¹⁵ I am glad that I wasn't there, because now you will have a chance to put your faith in me. Let's go to him."

¹⁶ Thomas, whose nickname was "Twin", said to the other disciples, "Come on. Let's go, so we can die with him."

Jesus brings Lazarus to life

¹⁷ When Jesus got to Bethany, he found that Lazarus had already been in the tomb four days. ¹⁸ Bethany was less than three kilometres from Jerusalem, ¹⁹ and many people had come from the city to comfort Martha and Mary because their brother had died.

²⁰ When Martha heard that Jesus had arrived, she went out to meet him, but Mary stayed in the house. ²¹ Martha said to Jesus, "Lord, if you had been here, my brother would not have died. ²² Yet even now I know that God will do anything you ask."

²³ Jesus told her, "Your brother will live again!"

²⁴ Martha answered, "I know that he will be raised to life on the last day,* when all the dead are raised."

²⁵ Jesus then said, "I am the one who raises the dead to life! Everyone who has faith in me will live, even if they die. ²⁶ And everyone who lives because of faith in me will never really die. Do you believe this?"

²⁷ "Yes, Lord!" she replied. "I believe that you are Christ, the Son of God. You are the one we hoped would come into the world."

²⁸ After Martha said this, she went and privately said to her sister Mary, "The Teacher is here, and he wants to see you." ²⁹ As soon as Mary heard this, she got up and went out to Jesus. ³⁰ He was still outside the village where Martha had gone to meet him. ³¹ Many people had come to comfort Mary, and when they saw her quickly leave the

---

*11.24 the last day: See the note at 6.39.

house, they thought she was going out to the tomb to cry. So they followed her. 32 Mary went to where Jesus was. Then as soon as she saw him, she knelt at his feet and said, "Lord, if you had been here, my brother would not have died."

33 When Jesus saw that Mary and the people with her were crying, he was terribly upset 34 and asked, "Where have you put his body?"

They replied, "Lord, come and you will see." 35 Jesus started crying, 36 and the people said, "See how much he loved Lazarus."

37 Some of them said, "He gives sight to the blind. Why couldn't he have kept Lazarus from dying?"

38 Jesus was still terribly upset. So he went to the tomb, which was a cave with a stone rolled against the entrance. 39 Then he told the people to roll the stone away. But Martha said, "Lord, you know that Lazarus has been dead four days, and there will be a bad smell."

40 Jesus replied, "Didn't I tell you that if you had faith, you would see the glory of God?"

41 After the stone had been rolled aside, Jesus looked up towards heaven and prayed, "Father, I thank you for answering my prayer. 42 I know that you always answer my prayers. But I said this, so that the people here would believe that you sent me."

43 When Jesus had finished praying, he shouted, "Lazarus, come out!" 44 The man who had been dead came out. His hands and feet were wrapped with strips of burial cloth, and a cloth covered his face.

Jesus then told the people, "Untie him and let him go."

The plot to kill Jesus

This is also told in Matthew 26.1-5; Mark 14.1-2; Luke 22.1-2

45 Many of the people who had come to visit Mary saw the things that Jesus did, and they put their faith in him. 46 Others went to the Pharisees and told what Jesus had done. 47 Then the chief priests and the Pharisees called the council together and said, "What should we do? This man is performing a lot of miracles.* 48 If we don't stop him now, everyone will put their faith in him. Then the Romans will come and destroy our temple and our nation."*

49 One of the council members was Caiaphas, who was also high priest that year. He spoke up and said, "You people don't have any sense at all! 50 Don't you know it is better for one person to die for the people than for the whole nation to be destroyed?" 51 Caiaphas did not say this on his own. As high priest that year, he was prophesying that Jesus would die for the nation. 52 Yet Jesus would not die just for the Jewish nation. He would die to bring together all God's scattered people. 53 From that day on, the council started making plans to put Jesus to death.

54 Because of this plot against him, Jesus stopped going around in public. He went to the town of Ephraim, which was near the desert, and he stayed there with his disciples.

55 It was almost time for Passover. Many of the Jewish people who lived out in the country had come to Jerusalem to get themselves ready* for the festival. 56 They looked around for Jesus. Then when they were in the temple, they asked each other, "You don't think he will come here for Passover, do you?"

57 The chief priests and the Pharisees told the people to let them know if any of them saw Jesus. That is how they hoped to arrest him.

CHAPTER 12

At Bethany

This is also told in Matthew 26.6-13; Mark 14.3-9

1 Six days before Passover Jesus went back to Bethany, where he had raised Lazarus from death. 2 A meal had been prepared for Jesus. Martha was doing the serving, and Lazarus himself was there.

3 Mary took a very expensive bottle of perfume' and poured it on Jesus' feet. She wiped them with her hair, and the sweet smell of the perfume filled the house.

4 A disciple named Judas Iscariot* was there. He was the one who was going to betray Jesus, and he asked, 5 "Why wasn't this perfume sold for three hundred silver coins and the money given to the poor?" 6 Judas did not really care about the poor. He asked this because he carried the money bag and sometimes would steal from it.

7 Jesus replied, "Leave her alone! She has kept this perfume for the day of my burial. 8 You will always have the poor with you, but you won't always have me."

A plot to kill Lazarus

9 A lot of people came when they heard that Jesus was there. They also wanted to see Lazarus, because Jesus had raised him from death. 10 So the chief priests made plans to kill Lazarus. 11 He was the reason that many of the Jewish people were turning from them and putting their faith in Jesus.

Jesus enters Jerusalem

This is also told in Matthew 21.1–11; Mark 11.1–11; Luke 19.28–40

12 The next day a large crowd was in Jerusalem for Passover. When they heard that Jesus was coming for the festival, 13 they took palm branches and went out to greet him.* They shouted,

"Hooray!*
God bless the one who comes
    in the name of the Lord!
God bless the King
    of Israel!"

14 Jesus found a donkey and rode on it, just as the Scriptures say,

15 "People of Jerusalem,
    don't be afraid!
Your King is now coming,
    and he is riding
    on a donkey."

16 At first, Jesus' disciples did not understand. But after he had been given his glory,* they remembered all this. Everything had happened exactly as the Scriptures said it would.

17-18 A crowd had come to meet Jesus because they had seen him call Lazarus out of the tomb. They kept talking about him and this miracle.* 19 But the Pharisees said to each other, "There is nothing that can be done! Everyone in the world is following Jesus."

Some Greeks want to meet Jesus

20 Some Greeks* had gone to Jerusalem to worship during Passover. 21 Philip from Bethsaida in Galilee was there too. So they went to him and said, "Sir, we would like to meet Jesus." 22 Philip told Andrew. Then the two of them went to Jesus and told him.

The Son of Man must be lifted up

23 Jesus said:

The time has come for the Son of Man to be given his glory.* 24 I tell you for certain that a grain of wheat that falls on the ground will never be more than one grain unless it dies. But if it dies, it will produce lots of wheat. 25 If you love your life, you will lose it. If you give it up in this world, you will be given eternal life. 26 If you serve me, you must go with me. My servants will be with me wherever I am. If you serve me, my Father will honour you.

27 Now I am deeply troubled, and I don't know what to say. But I must not ask my Father to keep me from this time of suffering. In fact, I came into the world to suffer. 28 So Father, bring glory to yourself.

A voice from heaven then said, "I have already brought glory to myself, and I will do it again!" 29 When the crowd heard the voice, some of them thought it was thunder. Others thought an angel had spoken to Jesus.

30 Then Jesus told the crowd, "That voice spoke to help you, not me. 31 This world's people are now being judged, and the ruler of this world* is already being thrown out! 32 If I am lifted up above the earth, I will make everyone want to come to me." 33 Jesus was talking about the way he would be put to death.

34 The crowd said to Jesus, "The Scriptures teach that the Messiah will live for ever. How can you say that the Son of Man must be lifted up? Who is this Son of Man?"

---

*12.13 took palm branches and went out to greet him: This was one way that the Jewish people welcomed a famous person.
*12.13 Hooray: This translates a word that can mean "please save us". But it is most often used as a shout of praise to God.
*12.16 had been given his glory: See the note at 7.39.
*12.17–18 miracle: See the note at 2.11.
See also: 12.8: Deut 15.11. 12.13: Psa 118.25–26. 12.15: Zech 9.9.

*12.20 Greeks: Perhaps Gentiles who worshipped with the Jews. See the note at 7.35.
*12.23 be given his glory: See the note at 7.39.
*12.31 world: In the Gospel of John "world" sometimes refers to the people who live in this world and to the evil forces that control their lives.
See also: 12.25: Matt 10.39; 16.25; Mark 8.35; Luke 9.24; 17.33. 12.34: Psa 110.4; Isa 9.7; Ezek 37.25; Dan 7.14.

35 Jesus answered, "The light will be with you for only a little longer. Walk in the light while you can. Then you won't be caught walking blindly in the dark. 36 Have faith in the light while it is with you, and you will be children of the light."

The people refuse to have faith in Jesus

After Jesus had said these things, he left and went into hiding. 37 He had performed a lot of miracles* among the people, but they were still not willing to have faith in him. 38 This happened so that what the prophet Isaiah had said would come true,

> "Lord, who has believed
>   our message?
> And who has seen
>   your mighty strength?"

39 The people could not have faith in Jesus, because Isaiah had also said,

> 40 "The Lord has blinded
>   the eyes of the people,
> and he has made
>   the people stubborn.
> He did this so that they
>   could not see
>   or understand,
> and so that they
>   would not turn to the Lord
>   and be healed."

41 Isaiah said this, because he saw the glory of Jesus and spoke about him.▸ 42 Even then, many of the leaders put their faith in Jesus, but they did not tell anyone about it. The Pharisees had already given orders for the people not to have anything to do with anyone who had faith in Jesus. 43 And besides, the leaders liked praise from others more than they liked praise from God.

Jesus came to save the world

44 In a loud voice Jesus said:

Everyone who has faith in me also has faith in the one who sent me. 45 And everyone who has seen me has seen the one who sent me. 46 I am the light that has come into the world. No one who has faith in me will stay in the dark.

47 I am not the one who will judge those who refuse to obey my teachings. I came to save the people of this world, not to be their judge. 48 But everyone who rejects me and my teachings will be judged on the last day* by what I have said. 49 I don't speak on my own. I say only what the Father who sent me has told me to say. 50 I know that his commands will bring eternal life. That is why I tell you exactly what the Father has told me.

Jesus' last week: his trial and death

CHAPTER 13

Jesus washes the feet of his disciples

1 It was before Passover, and Jesus knew that the time had come for him to leave this world and to return to the Father. He had always loved his followers in this world, and he loved them to the very end.

2 Even before the evening meal started, the devil had made Judas, the son of Simon Iscariot,* decide to betray Jesus.

3 Jesus knew that he had come from God and would go back to God. He also knew that the Father had given him complete power. 4 So during the meal Jesus got up, removed his outer garment, and wrapped a towel around his waist. 5 He put some water into a large bowl. Then he began washing his disciples' feet and drying them with the towel he was wearing.

6 But when he came to Simon Peter, that disciple asked, "Lord, are you going to wash my feet?"

7 Jesus answered, "You don't really know what I am doing, but later you will understand."

8 "You will never wash my feet!" Peter replied.

"If I don't wash you," Jesus told him, "you don't really belong to me."

9 Peter said, "Lord, don't wash just my feet. Wash my hands and my head."

10 Jesus answered, "People who have bathed and are clean all over need to wash just their feet. And you, my disciples, are clean, except for one of you." 11 Jesus knew who would betray him. That is why he said, "except for one of you."

---

*12.37 miracles: See the note at 2.11.
See also: 12.38: Isa 53.1 (LXX).   12.40: Isa 6.10 (LXX).

*12.48 the last day: See the note at 6.39.
*13.2 Iscariot: See the note at 6.71.

Being christian

Serving others

John 13.1–20

Before the last supper, Jesus did an amazing thing. He took off his outer clothes, got a bowl of water and some towels, and washed his disciples' feet. The disciples were shocked. Only servants were supposed to do that. Here was their leader, their teacher, doing a dirty, menial task. This was not how leaders were supposed to behave.

The disciples always found it difficult to grasp how different Jesus' values were. They argued among themselves as to who would be the greatest, who would have the positions of honour. They thought that being a disciple gave them a better seat in the house. But Jesus didn't think that way. 'If you want to be great,' he told them, 'you have to be a servant.'

Jesus' actions showed the values of the kingdom of God. We're not here to rule people, but to serve them. In the kingdom of the world, people think it's great to have servants; in the kingdom of God, it's far better to serve. In the world, everyone wants to be a Very Important Person; but its amazing that the most important person ever was willing to serve – and die for – his friends.

So we should look for opportunities to serve others. Through serving them we will show them that God values them, that they are part of our family.

Being Christian: Serving others

• Look for opportunities to serve. How can you serve your community, your family, your friends?
• Don't go around thinking that you're better than other people. Walk humbly. We're all equal in God's sight.
• Find out about opportunities to serve with Christian organisations. How can you help them?

12 After Jesus had washed his disciples' feet and had put his outer garment back on, he sat down again.* Then he said:

Do you understand what I have done? 13 You call me your teacher and Lord, and you should, because that is who I am. 14 And if your Lord and teacher has washed your feet, you should do the same for each other. 15 I have set the example, and you should do for each other exactly what I have done for you. 16 I tell you for certain that servants are not greater than their master, and messengers are not greater than the one who sent them. 17 You know these things, and God will bless you, if you do them.

18 I am not talking about all of you. I know the ones I have chosen. But what the Scriptures say must come true. And they say, "The man who ate with me has turned against me!" 19 I am telling you this before it all happens. Then when it does happen, you will believe who I am.* 20 I tell you for certain that anyone who welcomes my messengers also welcomes me, and anyone who welcomes me welcomes the one who sent me.

Jesus tells what will happen to him

This is also told in Matthew 26.20–25; Mark 14.17–21; Luke 22.21–23

21 After Jesus had said these things, he was deeply troubled and told his disciples, "I tell you for certain that one of you will betray me." 22 They were confused about what he meant. And they just stared at each other.

23 Jesus' favourite disciple was sitting next to him at the meal, 24 and Simon motioned for that disciple to find out which one Jesus meant. 25 So the disciple leaned towards Jesus and asked, "Lord, which one of us are you talking about?"

26 Jesus answered, "I will dip this piece of bread in the sauce and give it to the one I was talking about."

Then Jesus dipped the bread and gave it to Judas, the son of Simon Iscariot.* 27 At once Satan took control of Judas.

---

*13.12 sat down again: On special occasions the Jewish people followed the Greek and Roman custom of lying down on their left side and leaning on their left elbow, while eating with their right hand.
*13.19 I am: See the note at 8.24.
*13.26 Iscariot: See the note at 6.71.

See also: 13.12–15: Luke 22.27. 13.16: Matt 10.24; Luke 6.40; John 15.20. 13.18: Psa 41.9. 13.20: Matt 10.40; Mark 9.37; Luke 9.48; 10.16.

Jesus said, "Judas, go quickly and do what you have to do." ²⁸ No one at the meal understood what Jesus meant. ²⁹ But because Judas was in charge of the money, some of them thought that Jesus had told him to buy something they needed for the festival. Others thought that Jesus had told him to give some money to the poor. ³⁰ Judas took the piece of bread and went out.

It was already night.

The new command

³¹ After Judas had gone, Jesus said:

Now the Son of Man will be given glory, and he will bring glory to God. ³² Then, after God is given glory because of him, God will bring glory to him, and God will do it very soon.

³³ My children, I will be with you for a little while longer. Then you will look for me, but you won't find me. I tell you just as I told the people, "You cannot go where I am going." ³⁴ But I am giving you a new command. You must love each other, just as I have loved you. ³⁵ If you love each other, everyone will know that you are my disciples.

Peter's promise

This is also told in Matthew 26.31–35; Mark 14.27–31; Luke 22.31–34

³⁶ Simon Peter asked, "Lord, where are you going?"

Jesus answered, "You can't go with me now, but later on you will."

³⁷ Peter asked, "Lord, why can't I go with you now? I would die for you!"

³⁸ "Would you really die for me?" Jesus asked. "I tell you for certain that before a cock crows, you will say three times that you don't even know me."

CHAPTER 14

Jesus is the way to the Father

¹ Jesus said to his disciples, "Don't be worried! Have faith in God and have faith in me.'
² There are many rooms in my Father's house. I wouldn't tell you this, unless it was true. I am going there to prepare a place for each of you. ³ After I have done this, I will come back and take you with me. Then we will be together. ⁴ You know the way to where I am going."

See also: **13.33:** John 7.34. **13.34:** John 15.12,17; 1 John 3.23; 2 John 5.

⁵ Thomas said, "Lord, we don't even know where you are going! How can we know the way?"

⁶ "I am the way, the truth, and the life!" Jesus answered. "Without me, no one can go to the Father. ⁷ If you had known me, you would have known the Father. But from now on, you do know him, and you have seen him."

⁸ Philip said, "Lord, show us the Father. That is all we need."

⁹ Jesus replied:

Philip, I have been with you for a long time. Don't you know who I am? If you have seen me, you have seen the Father. How can you ask me to show you the Father? ¹⁰ Don't you believe that I am one with the Father and that the Father is one with me? What I say isn't said on my own. The Father who lives in me does these things.

¹¹ Have faith in me when I say that the Father is one with me and that I am one with the Father. Or else have faith in me simply because of the things I do. ¹² I tell you for certain that if you have faith in me, you will do the same things that I am doing. You will do even greater things, now that I am going back to the Father. ¹³ Ask me, and I will do whatever you ask. This way the Son will bring honour to the Father. ¹⁴ I will do whatever you ask me to do.

The Holy Spirit is promised

¹⁵ Jesus said to his disciples:

If you love me, you will do as I command. ¹⁶ Then I will ask the Father to send you the Holy Spirit who will help' you and always be with you. ¹⁷ The Spirit will show you what is true. The people of this world cannot accept the Spirit, because they don't see or know him. But you know the Spirit, who is with you and will keep on living in you.

¹⁸ I won't leave you like orphans. I will come back to you. ¹⁹ In a little while the people of this world won't be able to see me, but you will see me. And because I live, you will live. ²⁰ Then you will know that I am one with the Father. You will know that you are one with me, and I am one with you. ²¹ If you love me, you will do what I have said, and my Father will love you. I will also love you and show you what I am like.

22 The other Judas, not Judas Iscariot,* then spoke up and asked, "Lord, what do you mean by saying that you will show us what you are like, but you will not show the people of this world?"

23 Jesus replied:

If anyone loves me, they will obey me. Then my Father will love them, and we will come to them and live in them. 24 But anyone who doesn't love me, won't obey me. What they have heard me say doesn't really come from me, but from the Father who sent me.

25 I have told you these things while I am still with you. 26 But the Holy Spirit will come and help▸ you, because the Father will send the Spirit to take my place. The Spirit will teach you everything and will remind you of what I said while I was with you.

27 I give you peace, the kind of peace that only I can give. It isn't like the peace that this world can give. So don't be worried or afraid.

28 You have already heard me say that I am going and that I will also come back to you. If you really love me, you should be glad that I am going back to the Father, because he is greater than I am.

29 I am telling you this before I leave, so that when it does happen, you will have faith in me. 30 I cannot speak with you much longer, because the ruler of this world is coming. But he has no power over me. 31 I obey my Father, so that everyone in the world might know that I love him.

It is time for us to go now.

CHAPTER 15

Jesus is the true vine

1 Jesus said to his disciples:

I am the true vine, and my Father is the gardener. 2 He cuts away every branch of mine that doesn't produce fruit. But he trims clean every branch that does produce fruit, so that it will produce even more fruit. 3 You are already clean because of what I have said to you.

4 Stay joined to me, and I will stay joined to you. Just as a branch cannot produce fruit unless it stays joined to the vine, you cannot produce fruit unless you stay joined to me. 5 I am the vine, and you are the branches. If you stay joined to me, and I stay joined to you, then you will produce lots of fruit. But you cannot do anything without me. 6 If you don't stay joined to me, you will be thrown away. You will be like dry branches that are gathered up and burnt in a fire.

7 Stay joined to me and let my teachings become part of you. Then you can pray for whatever you want, and your prayer will be answered. 8 When you become fruitful disciples of mine, my Father will be honoured. 9 I have loved you, just as my Father has loved me. So remain faithful to my love for you. 10 If you obey me, I will keep loving you, just as my Father keeps loving me, because I have obeyed him.

11 I have told you this to make you as completely happy as I am. 12 Now I tell you to love each other, as I have loved you. 13 The greatest way to show love for friends is to die for them. 14 And you are my friends, if you obey me. 15 Servants don't know what their master is doing, and so I don't speak to you as my servants. I speak to you as my friends, and I have told you everything that my Father has told me.

16 You did not choose me. I chose you and sent you out to produce fruit, the kind of fruit that will last. Then my Father will give you whatever you ask for in my name.▸ 17 So I command you to love each other.

The world's hatred

Jesus continued:

18 If the people of this world* hate you, just remember that they hated me first. 19 If you belonged to the world, its people would love you. But you don't belong to the world. I have chosen you to leave the world behind, and that is why its people hate you. 20 Remember how I told you that servants are not greater than their master. So if people ill-treat me, they will ill-treat you. If they do what I say, they will do what you say.

21 People will do to you exactly what they did to me. They will do it because you belong to me, and they don't know the one who sent me. 22 If I had not come and spoken to them, they would not be guilty of sin. But now they have no excuse for their sin.

---

*15.18 world: See the note at 12.31.

See also: 15.12: John 13.34; 15.17; 1 John 3.23; 2 John 5.
15.20: Matt 10.24; Luke 6.40; John 13.16.

Big ideas

The Trinity

In talking about the Trinity we mean that the Father, the Son and the Holy Spirit are one; that they are all, in fact, different aspects of God.

In fact, the Bible never uses the actual word 'Trinity'. But the idea is implied throughout the Bible. For Christians the Trinity is the best explanation for the facts.

Jesus claimed to be God

He forgave sins, God called him his 'son' and he used the phrase 'I Am' to describe himself. Every good Jew knew that 'I Am' was God's name, as revealed to Moses. Most of all, he defeated death and came back to life. When Thomas saw the risen Jesus, he said, 'My Lord and my God!' John's gospel makes it clear that Jesus was with God from the very start of all things.

The Holy Spirit came from God

After Jesus left earth, the Holy Spirit came to give power, energy, guidance. Christians were told he would be with them forever, so the early Church concluded that the Holy Spirit was equal with Jesus and the Father.

Linked together

There are plenty of occasions where the three names are linked together. At Jesus' baptism, God pronounced him his son and the Holy Spirit came down on him. In John 15.26, Jesus talks about the Spirit coming from the father. Paul links them together in passages like 2 Corinthians 13.14.

Footsteps

A week on the Trinity

Jesus, the Word: John 1.1–14
Together at the baptism: Matthew 3.13–17
'Jesus must think he's God!' Matthew 9.1–8
Jesus is 'I Am': John 8.52–59
One with the father: John 14.15–26
Baptise in the name of... Matthew 28.18–20
Christ in command: Ephesians 1.17–22

More...

Holy Spirit p.1209

---

23 Everyone who hates me also hates my Father. 24 I have done things that no one else has ever done. If they had not seen me do these things, they would not be guilty. But they did see me do these things, and they still hate me and my Father too. 25 That is why the Scriptures are true when they say, "People hated me for no reason."

26 I will send you the Spirit who comes from the Father and shows what is true. The Spirit will help' you and will tell you about me. 27 Then you will also tell others about me, because you have been with me from the beginning.

CHAPTER 16

Jesus continued:

1 I am telling you this to keep you from being afraid. 2 You will be chased out of the Jewish meeting places. And the time will come when people will kill you and think they are doing God a favour. 3 They will do these things because they don't know either the Father or me. 4 I am saying this to you now, so that when the time comes, you will remember what I have said.

The work of the Holy Spirit

Jesus continued:

I was with you at the first, and so I didn't tell you these things. 5 But now I am going back to the Father who sent me, and none of you asks me where I am going. 6 You are very sad from hearing all this. 7 But I tell you that I am going to do what is best for you. That is why I am going away. The Holy Spirit cannot come to help' you until I leave. But after I am gone, I will send the Spirit to you.

8 The Spirit will come and show the people of this world the truth about sin and God's justice and the judgment. 9 The Spirit will show them that they are wrong about sin, because they didn't have faith in me. 10 They are wrong about God's justice, because I am going to the Father, and you won't see me again. 11 And they are wrong about the judgment, because God has already judged the ruler of this world.

12 I have much more to say to you, but right now it would be more than you could understand. 13 The Spirit shows what is true and will come and guide you into the full truth. The Spirit doesn't speak on his own.

See also: 15.25: Psa 35.19; 69.4.

He will tell you only what he has heard from me, and he will let you know what is going to happen. ¹⁴ The Spirit will bring glory to me by taking my message and telling it to you. ¹⁵ Everything that the Father has is mine. That is why I have said that the Spirit takes my message and tells it to you.

Sorrow will turn into joy

¹⁶ Jesus told his disciples, "For a little while you won't see me, but after a while you will see me."

¹⁷ They said to each other, "What does Jesus mean by saying that for a little while we won't see him, but after a while we will see him? What does he mean by saying that he is going to the Father? ¹⁸ What is this 'little while' that he is talking about? We don't know what he means."

¹⁹ Jesus knew that they had some questions, so he said:

You are wondering what I meant when I said that for a little while you won't see me, but after a while you will see me. ²⁰ I tell you for certain that you will cry and be sad, but the world will be happy. You will be sad, but later you will be happy.

²¹ When a woman is about to give birth, she is in great pain. But after it is all over, she forgets the pain and is happy, because she has brought a child into the world. ²² You are now very sad. But later I will see you, and you will be so happy that no one will be able to change the way you feel. ²³ When that time comes, you won't have to ask me about anything. I tell you for certain that the Father will give you whatever you ask for in my name. ²⁴ You have not asked for anything in this way before, but now you must ask in my name.' Then it will be given to you, so that you will be completely happy.

²⁵ I have used examples to explain to you what I have been talking about. But the time will come when I will speak to you plainly about the Father and will no longer use examples like these. ²⁶ You will ask the Father in my name,' and I won't have to ask him for you. ²⁷ God the Father loves you because you love me, and you believe that I have come from him. ²⁸ I came from the Father into the world, but I am leaving the world and returning to the Father.

²⁹ The disciples said, "Now you are speaking plainly to us! You are not using examples. ³⁰ At last we know that you understand everything, and we don't have any more questions. Now we believe that you truly have come from God."

³¹ Jesus replied:

Do you really believe me? ³² The time will come and is already here when all of you will be scattered. Each of you will go back home and leave me by myself. But the Father will be with me, and I won't be alone. ³³ I have told you this, so that you might have peace in your hearts because of me. While you are in the world, you will have to suffer. But cheer up! I have defeated the world.*

CHAPTER 17

Jesus prays

¹ After Jesus had finished speaking to his disciples, he looked up towards heaven and prayed:

Father, the time has come for you to bring glory to your Son, in order that he may bring glory to you. ² And you gave him power over all people, so that he would give eternal life to everyone you give him. ³ Eternal life is to know you, the only true God, and to know Jesus Christ, the one you sent. ⁴ I have brought glory to you here on earth by doing everything you gave me to do. ⁵ Now, Father, give me back the glory that I had with you before the world was created.

⁶ You have given me some followers from this world, and I have shown them what you are like. They were yours, but you gave them to me, and they have obeyed you. ⁷ They know that you gave me everything I have. ⁸ I told my followers what you told me, and they accepted it. They know that I came from you, and they believe that you are the one who sent me. ⁹ I am praying for them, but not for those who belong to this world.* My followers belong to you, and I am praying for them. ¹⁰ All that I have is yours, and all that you have is mine, and they will bring glory to me.

¹¹ Holy Father, I am no longer in the world. I am coming to you, but my followers are still in the world. So keep

---

*16.33; 17.9 world: See the note at 12.31.

them safe by the power of the name that you have given me. Then they will be one with each other, just as you and I are one. ¹² While I was with them, I kept them safe by the power you have given me. I guarded them, and not one of them was lost, except the one who had to be lost. This happened so that what the Scriptures say would come true.

¹³ I am on my way to you. But I say these things while I am still in the world, so that my followers will have the same complete joy that I do. ¹⁴ I have told them your message. But the people of this world hate them, because they don't belong to this world, just as I don't.

¹⁵ Father, I don't ask you to take my followers out of the world, but keep them safe from the evil one. ¹⁶ They don't belong to this world, and neither do I. ¹⁷ Your word is the truth. So let this truth make them completely yours. ¹⁸ I am sending them into the world, just as you sent me. ¹⁹ I have given myself completely for their sake, so that they may belong completely to the truth.

²⁰ I am not praying just for these followers. I am also praying for everyone else who will have faith because of what my followers will say about me. ²¹ I want all of them to be one with each other, just as I am one with you and you are one with me. I also want them to be one with us. Then the people of this world will believe that you sent me.

²² I have honoured my followers in the same way that you honoured me, in order that they may be one with each other, just as we are one. ²³ I am one with them, and you are one with me, so that they may become completely one. Then this world's people will know that you sent me. They will know that you love my followers as much as you love me.

²⁴ Father, I want everyone you have given me to be with me, wherever I am. Then they will see the glory that you have given me, because you loved me before the world was created. ²⁵ Good Father, the people of this world don't know you. But I know you, and my followers know that you sent me. ²⁶ I told them what you are like, and I will tell them even more. Then the love that you have for me will become part of them, and I will be one with them.

Viewpoints

Are you like your Father?

Contributed by Robert A

'I have honoured my followers in the same way that you honoured me, in order that they may be one with each other, just as we are one.'

Jesus reflected his Father, just as, to some extent, I mirror my dad. The relationship between God and Jesus becomes the guide for us.

Over time we should be aiming to 'put on' Jesus. In doing that we should be developing closer relationships with the people around us, especially our local Christians. We are called to be a body, and the important thing about a body is that we work together for the same purpose, pushing forward for the same thing. We are not placed in a church to bring the church down, but to learn to live with our likenesses and our differences.

Other than just our human relationships, we should make sure that our relationship with God is developing. Remember, we are joint heirs with Christ, and as sons we should be reflecting as much as we can the absolute perfection that is God.

Why should we bother with trying to live this way? The answer is clear. We should live in a way that honours each other and God so that the world might know that God sent Jesus.

Anorak corner

Ages

1. Who lived to 969 years old?
2. How old was Noah when he took up sailing?
3. How old was Moses when he started to lead the Israelites?
4. How old was Jesus when he started preaching?
5. How old were the children massacred by Herod?
(Answers on p.1431)

CHAPTER 18

Jesus is betrayed and arrested

This is also told in Matthew 26.47–56; Mark 14.43–50; Luke 22.47–53

¹ When Jesus had finished praying, he and his disciples crossed the Kidron Valley and went into a garden.* ² Jesus had often met there with his disciples, and Judas knew where the place was.

³⁻⁵ Judas had promised to betray Jesus. So he went to the garden with some Roman soldiers and temple police, who had been sent by the chief priests and the Pharisees. They carried torches, lanterns, and weapons. Jesus already knew everything that was going to happen, but he asked, "Who are you looking for?"

They answered, "We are looking for Jesus from Nazareth!"

Jesus told them, "I am Jesus!"* ⁶ At once they all backed away and fell to the ground.

⁷ Jesus again asked, "Who are you looking for?"

"We are looking for Jesus from Nazareth," they answered.

⁸ This time Jesus replied, "I have already told you that I am Jesus. If I am the one you are looking for, let these others go. ⁹ Then everything will happen, just as I said, 'I did not lose anyone you gave me.' "

¹⁰ Simon Peter had brought along a sword. He now pulled it out and struck at the servant of the high priest. The servant's name was Malchus, and Peter cut off his right ear. ¹¹ Jesus told Peter, "Put your sword away. I must drink from the cup* that the Father has given me."

Jesus is brought to Annas

This is also told in Matthew 26.57,58; Mark 14.53–54; Luke 22.54

¹² The Roman officer and his men, together with the temple police, arrested Jesus and tied him up. ¹³ They took him first to Annas, who was the father-in-law of Caiaphas, the high priest that year. ¹⁴ This was the same Caiaphas

who had told the Jewish leaders, "It is better if one person dies for the people."

Peter says he doesn't know Jesus

This is also told in Matthew 26.69–70; Mark 14.66–68; Luke 22.55–57

¹⁵ Simon Peter and another disciple followed Jesus. That disciple knew the high priest, and he followed Jesus into the courtyard of the high priest's house. ¹⁶ Peter stayed outside near the gate. But the other disciple came back out and spoke to the girl at the gate. She let Peter go in, ¹⁷ but asked him, "Aren't you one of that man's followers?"

"No, I am not!" Peter answered.

¹⁸ It was cold, and the servants and temple police had made a charcoal fire. They were warming themselves around it, when Peter went over and stood near the fire to warm himself.

Jesus is questioned by the high priest

This is also told in Matthew 26.59–66; Mark 14.55–64; Luke 22.66–71

¹⁹ The high priest questioned Jesus about his followers and his teaching. ²⁰ But Jesus told him, "I have spoken freely in front of everyone. And I have always taught in our meeting places and in the temple, where all our people come together. I have not said anything in secret. ²¹ Why are you questioning me? Why don't you ask the people who heard me? They know what I have said."

²² As soon as Jesus said this, one of the temple police hit him and said, "That's no way to talk to the high priest!"

²³ Jesus answered, "If I have done something wrong, say so. But if not, why did you hit me?" ²⁴ Jesus was still tied up, and Annas sent him to Caiaphas the high priest.

Peter again denies that he knows Jesus

This is also told in Matthew 26.71–75; Mark 14.69–72; Luke 22.58–62

²⁵ While Simon Peter was standing there warming himself, someone asked him, "Aren't you one of Jesus' followers?"

Again Peter denied it and said, "No, I am not!"

²⁶ One of the high priest's servants was there. He was a relative of the servant whose ear Peter had cut off, and he asked, "Didn't I see you in the garden with that man?"

²⁷ Once more Peter denied it, and at once a cock crowed.

---

*18.1 garden: The Greek word is usually translated "garden", but probably referred to an olive orchard.
*18.3–5 I am Jesus: The Greek text has "I am". See the note at 8.24.
*18.11 drink from the cup: In the Scriptures a cup is sometimes used as a symbol of suffering. To "drink from the cup" is to suffer.

See also: 18.11: Matt 26.39; Mark 14.36; Luke 22.42.
18.14: John 11.49–50.

Jesus is tried by Pilate

This is also told in Matthew 27.1-2,11-14; Mark 15.1-5; Luke 23.1-5

²⁸ It was early in the morning when Jesus was taken from Caiaphas to the building where the Roman governor stayed. But the crowd waited outside. Any of them who had gone inside would have become unclean and would not be allowed to eat the Passover meal.*

²⁹ Pilate came out and asked, "What charges are you bringing against this man?"

³⁰ They answered, "He is a criminal! That's why we brought him to you."

³¹ Pilate told them, "Take him and judge him by your own laws."

The crowd replied, "We are not allowed to put anyone to death." ³² And so what Jesus said about his death* would soon come true.

³³ Pilate then went back inside. He called Jesus over and asked, "Are you the king of the Jews?"

³⁴ Jesus answered, "Are you asking this on your own or did someone tell you about me?"

³⁵ "You know I'm not a Jew!" Pilate said. "Your own people and the chief priests brought you to me. What have you done?"

³⁶ Jesus answered, "My kingdom doesn't belong to this world. If it did, my followers would have fought to keep me from being handed over to the Jewish leaders. No, my kingdom doesn't belong to this world."

³⁷ "So you are a king," Pilate replied.

"You are saying that I am a king," Jesus told him. "I was born into this world to tell about the truth. And everyone who belongs to the truth knows my voice."

³⁸ Pilate asked Jesus, "What is truth?"

Jesus is sentenced to death

This is also told in Matthew 27.15-31; Mark 15.6-20; Luke 23.13-25

Pilate went back out and said, "I don't find this man guilty of anything! ³⁹ And since I usually set a prisoner free for you at Passover, would you like me to set free the king of the Jews?"

---

*18.28 would have become unclean and would not be allowed to eat the Passover meal: Jewish people who came in close contact with foreigners just before Passover were not allowed to eat the Passover meal.

*18.32 about his death: Jesus had said that he would die by being "lifted up", which meant that he would die on a cross. The Romans killed criminals by nailing them on a cross, but they did not let the Jews kill anyone in this way.

See also: 18.32: John 3.14; 12.32.

⁴⁰ They shouted, "No, not him! We want Barabbas." Now Barabbas was a terrorist.*

CHAPTER 19

¹ Pilate gave orders for Jesus to be beaten with a whip. ² The soldiers made a crown out of thorn branches and put it on Jesus. Then they put a purple robe on him. ³ They came up to him and said, "Hey, you king of the Jews!" They also hit him with their fists.

⁴ Once again Pilate went out. This time he said, "I will have Jesus brought out to you again. Then you can see for yourselves that I have not found him guilty."

⁵ Jesus came out, wearing the crown of thorns and the purple robe. Pilate said, "Here is the man!"

⁶ When the chief priests and the temple police saw him, they yelled, "Nail him to a cross! Nail him to a cross!"

Pilate told them, "You take him and nail him to a cross! I don't find him guilty of anything."

⁷ The crowd replied, "He claimed to be the Son of God! Our Jewish Law says that he must be put to death."

⁸ When Pilate heard this, he was terrified. ⁹ He went back inside and asked Jesus, "Where are you from?" But Jesus did not answer.

¹⁰ "Why won't you answer my question?" Pilate asked. "Don't you know that I have the power to let you go free or to nail you to a cross?"

¹¹ Jesus replied, "If God had not given you the power, you couldn't do anything at all to me. But the one who handed me over to you did something even worse."

¹² Then Pilate wanted to set Jesus free. But the crowd again yelled, "If you set this man free, you are no friend of the Emperor! Anyone who claims to be a king is an enemy of the Emperor."

¹³ When Pilate heard this, he brought Jesus out. Then he sat down on the judge's bench at the place known as "The Stone Pavement". In Aramaic this pavement is called "Gabbatha". ¹⁴ It was about midday on the day before Passover, and Pilate said to the crowd, "Look at your king!"

¹⁵ "Kill him! Kill him!" they yelled. "Nail him to a cross!"

"So you want me to nail your king to a cross?" Pilate asked.

---

*18.40 terrorist: Someone who stirred up trouble against the Romans in the hope of gaining freedom for the Jewish people.

Real life

Sharing with your friends

Contributed by Discovery

One Monday evening, Lisa was sitting in a training session learning how to share her faith with teenagers that she might come into contact with. In her new job as a youth worker, it was important that she learnt how to communicate this very important truth that was so central to her life.

Later that week, full of nerves and excitement, she went into school equipped with her new training at the forefront of her mind and a tract to help her explain the gospel. After praying hard and asking the Holy Spirit to be with her, God sent along an 11 year old girl called Charlotte. She shared the gospel with her, and right there in school Charlotte prayed to ask Jesus into her life! The next day, Lisa met with Charlotte again, only to discover that she had gone home with the tract, gone through it with her friend and helped her to become a Christian too.

What an amazing testimony of how God can use a willing servant who simply goes out in the power of the Holy Spirit and leaves the results to God. Even a 1 day old Christian had grasped the importance of who God was and just couldn't keep it to herself.

Think

Read 1 Timothy 4.12–13. How does the 1 Timothy passage make you feel? What is your experience of this?
What helped Lisa go out and share her faith? How do you feel when you think about talking to your friends about Jesus?

Act

Have a go at writing down what you think the main points of the gospel message are. Maybe you could do this with a friend. Particularly think about your own story. Why are you following Jesus now? Why do you worship him on Sundays? What are you personally celebrating at Christmas/Easter/Pentecost?

Create an action plan of how to go about gaining confidence in sharing your faith with friends.
Pray for the Holy Spirit to give you extra confidence and sensitivity.
Look out for training days at your church or in your locality, if there are none, ask your pastor or youth worker to arrange something.
Read a book or watch a video on the subject.
Ask someone who seems to find it easy to give you some tips. Hang out with them and join in the conversation.
Spend a week over the summer as a helper on a Christian camp or holiday programme.
Suggest an event to your youth group which would help you all to reach out to friends.
Have a competition with a friend to see how many times you can bring God into the conversation in a day!

Check

Ezekiel 2.6–7; Matthew 10.16–20; Luke 19.1–10; John 4.7–42; Acts 3.1–26; 8.26–39; 11.19–21; 19.8–10; 2 Timothy 4.2&5

More...

Help! How do I stop my friends doing wrong? p.1312
Sharing your faith p.1082
School p.64
Help! People are saying horrible things about me p.822

The chief priests replied, "The Emperor is our king!" ¹⁶ Then Pilate handed Jesus over to be nailed to a cross.

Jesus is nailed to a cross

This is also told in Matthew 27.32–44; Mark 15.21–32; Luke 23.26–43

Jesus was taken away, ¹⁷ and he carried his cross to a place known as "The Skull".* In Aramaic this place is called "Golgotha". ¹⁸ There Jesus was nailed to the cross, and on each side of him a man was also nailed to a cross.

¹⁹ Pilate ordered the charge against Jesus to be written on a board and put above the cross. It read, "Jesus of Nazareth, King of the Jews." ²⁰ The words were written in Hebrew, Latin, and Greek.

The place where Jesus was taken wasn't far from the city, and many of the Jewish people read the charge against him. ²¹ So the chief priests went to Pilate and said, "Why did you write that he is King of the Jews? You should have written, 'He claimed to be King of the Jews.' "

²² But Pilate told them, "What is written will not be changed!"

²³ After the soldiers had nailed Jesus to the cross, they divided up his clothes into four parts, one for each of them. But his outer garment was made from a single piece of cloth, and it did not have any seams. ²⁴ The soldiers said to each other, "Let's not rip it apart. We will gamble to see who gets it." This happened so that the Scriptures would come true, which say,

> "They divided up my clothes
> and gambled
>   for my garments."

The soldiers then did what they had decided.

²⁵ Jesus' mother stood beside his cross with her sister and Mary the wife of Clopas. Mary Magdalene was standing there too.⸀ ²⁶ When Jesus saw his mother and his favourite disciple with her, he said to his mother, "This man is now your son." ²⁷ Then he said to the disciple, "She is now your mother." From then on, that disciple took her into his own home.

Holy history

Crucifixion

You were taken from the cell. You were beaten. You walked through the streets carrying a heavy crossbeam.

You were the lowest of the low. Scum of the earth.

This was why people found the crucifixion so disturbing. Of all methods of execution it was the most demeaning: it was reserved for the worst criminals.

Criminals had to carry the heavy crossbeam to the place of execution, which was usually a piece of waste ground outside the city. Sometimes the victim's offence was written on a board and hung around his neck.

At the execution site, the criminal was fixed to the crossbeam, and then hung on the stake. The victim's feet were just clear of the ground – Jesus was not high in the air as has often been depicted. They were not always nailed, sometimes they were tied there. They could bear some of their weight by straddling a small peg which stuck out from the upright post, but in the end, they all died, from loss of blood and sheer exhaustion. Often their legs were broken, so they could no longer support themselves and their heart would no longer stand the strain.

The cross was normally a 'T' shape, with a central stake stuck into the ground and a crossbeam on top. Jesus' cross was slightly different – it was what was known as the crux immissa, with an upright beam above his head, onto which the sign was pinned.

What most people could not cope with about Christianity was that the Son of God should have died in a way that was normally reserved for the scum of the earth. It was scandalous; it was unbelievable. It was real.

More...

Cross p.1112
Sacrifice p.1368
Jesus' death p.1080

---

*19.17 The Skull: The place was probably given this name because it was near a large rock in the shape of a human skull.

See also: 19.24: Psa 22.18.

The death of Jesus

This is also told in Matthew 27.45–56; Mark 15.33–41; Luke 23.44–49

[28] Jesus knew that he had now finished his work. And in order to make the Scriptures come true, he said, "I am thirsty!" [29] A jar of cheap wine was there. Someone then soaked a sponge with the wine and held it up to Jesus' mouth on the stem of a hyssop plant. [30] After Jesus drank the wine, he said, "Everything is done!" He bowed his head and died.

A spear is stuck in Jesus' side

[31] The next day would be both a Sabbath and the Passover. It was a special day for the Jewish people,* and they did not want the bodies to stay on the crosses during that day. So they asked Pilate to break the men's legs* and take their bodies down. [32] The soldiers first broke the legs of the other two men who were nailed there. [33] But when they came to Jesus, they saw that he was already dead, and they did not break his legs.

[34] One of the soldiers stuck his spear into Jesus' side, and blood and water came out. [35] We know this is true, because it was told by someone who saw it happen. Now you can have faith too. [36] All this happened so that the Scriptures would come true, which say, "No bone of his body will be broken" [37] and, "They will see the one in whose side they stuck a spear."

Jesus is buried

This is also told in Matthew 27.57–61; Mark 15.42–47; Luke 23.50–56

[38] Joseph from Arimathea was one of Jesus' disciples. He had kept it secret though, because he was afraid of the Jewish leaders. But now he asked Pilate to let him have Jesus' body. Pilate gave him permission, and Joseph took it down from the cross. [39] Nicodemus also came with about thirty kilogrammes of spices made from myrrh and aloes. This was the same Nicodemus who had

---

*19.31 a special day for the Jewish people: Passover could be any day of the week. But according to the Gospel of John, Passover was on a Sabbath in the year that Jesus was nailed to a cross.

*19.31 break the men's legs: This was the way that the Romans sometimes speeded up the death of a person who had been nailed to a cross.

See also: 19.28: Psa 69.21; 22.15. 19.36: Exod 12.46; Num 9.12; Psa 34.20. 19.37: Zech 12.10; Rev 1.7. 19.39: John 3.1–2.

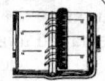

Life files

Mary Magdalene

Background: Not known. But she may well have had something of a dodgy past.

What's the story?

No one knows for sure. Mary was one of Jesus' closest followers. Indeed, Jesus had once cast seven demons out of her. She has sometimes been identified with the Mary who is the sister of Martha and Lazarus, but experts say that this is a different woman. Others identify her with the woman caught in adultery.

Whatever the case, she was obviously a close follower of Jesus, and someone who Jesus cared for greatly. It was Mary who was the first person to meet the risen Jesus. Even though she at first mistook him for the gardener...

 Anorak corner

Her name probably means that she came from the Galilean town of Magdala.

What's the point?

Mary obviously had a huge debt to Jesus. He had rescued her from the demons, and possibly from a life of sin and degradation. So it is no wonder that she stayed behind at the tomb when the others had fled in bewilderment; she wanted to find out what had happened. She was still looking for him, determined to find out the truth.

And she did.

 Footsteps

Three days with Mary Magdalene

Mary follows Jesus: Luke 8.1–3
Mary at the crucifixion: Mark 15.42–47
Mary at the tomb: John 19.11–18

More...

Demonic powers p.1131
Forgiveness p.614

visited Jesus one night.* ⁴⁰ The two men wrapped the body in a linen cloth, together with the spices, which was how the Jewish people buried their dead. ⁴¹ In the place where Jesus had been nailed to a cross, there was a garden with a tomb that had never been used. ⁴² The tomb was nearby, and since it was the time to prepare for the Sabbath, they were in a hurry to put Jesus' body there.

Jesus is alive

CHAPTER 20

This is also told in Matthew 28.1–10; Mark 16.1–8; Luke 24.1–12

¹ On Sunday morning while it was still dark, Mary Magdalene went to the tomb and saw that the stone had been rolled away from the entrance. ² She ran to Simon Peter and to Jesus' favourite disciple and said, "They have taken the Lord from the tomb! We don't know where they have put him."

³ Peter and the other disciple set off for the tomb. ⁴ They ran side by side, until the other disciple ran faster than Peter and got there first. ⁵ He bent over and saw the strips of linen cloth lying inside the tomb, but he did not go in.

⁶ When Simon Peter got there, he went into the tomb and saw the strips of cloth. ⁷ He also saw the piece of cloth that had been used to cover Jesus' face. It was rolled up and in a place by itself. ⁸ The disciple who got there first then went into the tomb, and when he saw it, he believed. ⁹ At that time Peter and the other disciple did not know that the Scriptures said Jesus would rise to life. ¹⁰ So the two of them went back to the other disciples.

Jesus appears to his disciples

Jesus appears to Mary Magdalene

This is also told in Mark 16.9–11

¹¹ Mary Magdalene stood crying outside the tomb. She was still weeping, when she stooped down ¹² and saw two angels inside. They were dressed in white and were sitting where Jesus' body had been. One was at the head and the other was at the foot. ¹³ The angels asked Mary, "Why are you crying?"

*19.39 **Nicodemus who had visited Jesus one night:** See 3.1–21.

Helpline

Help! I've got doubts about my faith

'I know I should be sure, but I've got all these questions. Am I sinning?'

There's an old proverb which says 'all doubt is the beginning of wisdom'. Doubting isn't wrong. In fact it's entirely natural. I mean, when you think about the claims of Christianity – that God became a man and died for all of us – that's a pretty amazing claim, isn't it?

Thomas, one of the disciples, wasn't there when Jesus first appeared to the disciples. So he doubted it had happened. And it's not just Thomas. People throughout the Bible have had doubts about God, questions they wanted to ask him, things they wanted to say. Look at some of the Psalms. Look at Job. They both had doubts about their faith.

And here's the thing: God doesn't mind. If it were wrong to ask questions about God, then no-one would ever find out anything about him. The key thing is not to allow your doubts to put you off exploring. Doubts and questions can lead us on to greater understanding, or they can lead us into a dead end.

Which direction will you go in?

Three things

Faith

Hold fast to what you can. Take the questions to God, but believe that God has the answers to your questions.

Explore

Continue to explore. The Christian faith is a journey and we're all travelling together.

Share

Don't keep your doubts to yourself. If Christianity is true, it's the most important thing ever, so you can't leave these things unsolved. Talk to others; they might have the answers you're searching for.

More...

Dealing with doubt p.554
Suffering p.555

She answered, "They have taken away my Lord's body! I don't know where they have put him."

¹⁴ As soon as Mary said this, she turned around and saw Jesus standing there. But she did not know who he was. ¹⁵ Jesus asked her, "Why are you crying? Who are you looking for?"

She thought he was the gardener and said, "Sir, if you have taken his body away, please tell me, so I can go and get him."

¹⁶ Then Jesus said to her, "Mary!"

She turned and said to him, "Rabboni." The Aramaic word "Rabboni" means "Teacher".

¹⁷ Jesus told her, "Don't hold on to me! I have not yet gone to the Father. But tell my disciples that I am going to the one who is my Father and my God, as well as your Father and your God." ¹⁸ Mary Magdalene then went and told the disciples that she had seen the Lord. She also told them what he had said to her.

Jesus appears to his disciples

This is also told in Matthew 28.16–20; Mark 16.14–18; Luke 24.36–49

¹⁹ The disciples were afraid of the Jewish leaders, and on the evening of that same Sunday they locked themselves in a room. Suddenly, Jesus appeared in the middle of the group. He greeted them ²⁰ and showed them his hands and his side. When the disciples saw the Lord, they became very happy.

²¹ After Jesus had greeted them again, he said, "I am sending you, just as the Father has sent me." ²² Then he breathed on them and said, "Receive the Holy Spirit. ²³ If you forgive anyone's sins, they will be forgiven. But if you don't forgive their sins, they will not be forgiven."

Jesus and Thomas

²⁴ Although Thomas the Twin was one of the twelve disciples, he wasn't with the others when Jesus appeared to them. ²⁵ So they told him, "We have seen the Lord!"

But Thomas said, "First, I must see the nail scars in his hands and touch them with my finger. I must put my hand where the spear went into his side. I won't believe unless I do this!"

²⁶ A week later the disciples were together again. This time, Thomas was with them. Jesus came in while the doors were still locked and stood in the middle of the group.

He greeted his disciples ²⁷ and said to Thomas, "Put your finger here and look at my hands! Put your hand into my side. Stop doubting and have faith!"

²⁸ Thomas replied, "You are my Lord and my God!"

²⁹ Jesus said, "Thomas, do you have faith because you have seen me? The people who have faith in me without seeing me are the ones who are really blessed!"

Why John wrote his book

³⁰ Jesus performed many other miracles* for his disciples, and not all of them are written in this book. ³¹ But these are written so that you will put your faith in Jesus as the Messiah and the Son of God. If you have faith inᵖ him, you will have true life.

CHAPTER 21

Jesus appears to seven disciples

¹ Jesus later appeared to his disciples along the shore of Lake Tiberias. ² Simon Peter, Thomas the Twin, Nathanael from Cana in Galilee, and the brothers James and John,ᵖ were there, together with two other disciples. ³ Simon Peter said, "I'm going fishing!"

The others said, "We will go with you." They went out in their boat. But they didn't catch a thing that night.

⁴ Early the next morning Jesus stood on the shore, but the disciples did not realize who he was. ⁵ Jesus shouted, "Friends, have you caught anything?"

"No!" they answered.

⁶ So he told them, "Let your net down on the right side of your boat, and you will catch some fish."

They did, and the net was so full of fish that they could not drag it up into the boat.

⁷ Jesus' favourite disciple told Peter, "It's the Lord!" When Simon heard that it was the Lord, he put on the clothes that he had taken off while he was working. Then he jumped into the water. ⁸ The boat was only about a hundred metres from shore. So the other disciples stayed in the boat and dragged in the net full of fish.

⁹ When the disciples got out of the boat, they saw some bread and a charcoal fire with fish on it. ¹⁰ Jesus told his disciples, "Bring some of the fish you have just caught."

¹¹ Simon Peter got back into the boat and

---

*20.30 miracles: See the note at 2.11.

See also: 21.3: Luke 5.5.   21.6: Luke 5.6.

See also: 20.23: Matt 16.19; 18.18.

dragged the net to shore. In it were one hundred and fifty-three large fish, but still the net did not rip.

¹² Jesus said, "Come and eat!" But none of the disciples dared ask who he was. They knew he was the Lord. ¹³ Jesus took the bread in his hands and gave some of it to his disciples. He did the same with the fish. ¹⁴ This was the third time that Jesus appeared to his disciples after he was raised from death.

Jesus and Peter

¹⁵ When Jesus and his disciples had finished eating, he asked, "Simon son of John, do you love me more than the others do?"▸

Simon Peter answered, "Yes, Lord, you know I do!"

"Then feed my lambs," Jesus said.

¹⁶ Jesus asked a second time, "Simon son of John, do you love me?"

Peter answered, "Yes, Lord, you know I love you!"

"Then take care of my sheep," Jesus told him.

¹⁷ Jesus asked a third time, "Simon son of John, do you love me?"

Peter was hurt because Jesus had asked him three times if he loved him. So he told Jesus, "Lord, you know everything. You know I love you."

Jesus replied, "Feed my sheep. ¹⁸ I tell you for certain that when you were a young man, you dressed yourself and went wherever you wanted to go. But when you are old, you will hold out your hands. Then others will tie your belt around you and lead you where you don't want to go."

¹⁹ Jesus said this to tell how Peter would die and bring honour to God. Then he said to Peter, "Follow me!"

Jesus and his favourite disciple

²⁰ Peter turned and saw Jesus' favourite disciple following them. He was the same one who had sat next to Jesus at the meal and had asked, "Lord, who is going to betray you?" ²¹ When Peter saw that disciple, he asked Jesus, "Lord, what about him?"

²² Jesus answered, "What is it to you, if I want him to live until I return? You must follow me." ²³ So the rumour spread among the other disciples that this disciple would not die. But Jesus did not say he would not die. He simply said, "What is it to you, if I want him to live until I return?"

See also: 21.20: John 13.25.

Big ideas

Resurrection

Christianity rests on one fact: that Jesus Christ rose from the grave.

If he didn't do that, he didn't defeat death. If he didn't defeat death, he can't help us. If he didn't rise from the grave, he wasn't who he claimed to be. 'If Christ wasn't raised to life,' wrote Paul, 'our message is worthless, and so is your faith'. So the resurrection is crucial to our faith.

But here's the good news: it happened. The evidence from the Bible is clear. Here were a load of scared, panicking people, who had seen their leader executed by the authorities. But suddenly they turn into a group of confident, alive, vibrant followers who perform miracles and tell everyone they have good news. What's changed them? What gave the early Church its power?

The answer is simple: they'd met Jesus. They'd seen the risen Christ. He'd been in rooms with them, talked to them on roads, cooked fish for them by the seashore. Paul says he appeared to more than 500 of his followers (1 Corinthians 15.5–7). They knew that he'd won. They realised he hadn't been lying, he was the truth. The person they'd put their faith was indeed God himself.

Jesus' resurrection proved he was the Messiah. It proved the claims that he made for himself. It proved he had the power to defeat death – for all of us. It was the most important day in history.

 ## Footsteps

A week on the Resurrection

The bribed guards: Matthew 28.11–15
Tell them what's happened: Luke 24.36–49
Walking the road: Luke 24.13–35
Mary meets the 'gardener': John 20.11–18
A barbecue on the beach: John 21.1–14
Jesus returns to heaven: Acts 1.1–11
Resurrection is proof: 1 Corinthians 15.3–24

More...

Cross p.1112
Crucifixion p.1199
Grace p.1316
Forgiveness p.614

²⁴ This disciple is the one who told all this. He wrote it, and we know he is telling the truth.

²⁵ Jesus did many other things. If they were all written in books, I don't suppose there would be room enough in the whole world for all the books.

Additional notes

›**1.5 put it out:** Or "understood it."
›**1.16 one blessing after another:** Or "one blessing in place of another."
›**3.25 a Jewish man:** Some manuscripts have "some Jewish men".
›**5.2 Bethzatha:** Some manuscripts have "Bethesda" and others have "Bethsaida".
›**5.3–4 pool:** Some manuscripts add, "They were waiting for the water to be stirred, because an angel from the Lord would sometimes come down and stir it. The first person to get into the pool after that would be healed."
›**8.11 don't sin any more:** Verses 1–11 are not in some manuscripts. In other manuscripts these verses are placed after 7.36 or after 21.25 or after Luke 21.38, with some differences in the text.
›**10.29 he is greater than all others:** Some manuscripts have "they are greater than all others."
›**12.3 very expensive bottle of perfume:** The Greek text has "expensive perfume made of pure spikenard", a plant used to make perfume.
›**12.41 he saw the glory of Jesus and spoke about him:** Or "he saw the glory of God and spoke about Jesus."
›**14.1 Have faith in God and have faith in me:** Or "You have faith in God, so have faith in me."
›**14.16 help:** The Greek word may mean "comfort", "encourage", or "defend".
›**14.26 help:** See the note at 14.16.
›**15.16 in my name:** Or "because you are my followers."
›**15.26 help:** See the note at 14.16.
›**16.7 help:** See the note at 14.16.
›**16.23–24 in my name . . . in my name:** Or "as my disciples . . . as my disciples."
›**16.26 in my name:** Or "because you are my followers".
›**19.5 "Here is the man!":** Or "Look at the man!"
›**19.25 Jesus' mother stood beside his cross with her sister and Mary the wife of Clopas. Mary Magdalene was standing there too:** The Greek text may also be understood to include only three women ("Jesus' mother stood beside the cross with her sister, Mary the mother of Clopas. Mary Magdalene was standing there too.") or merely two women ("Jesus' mother was standing there with her sister Mary of Clopas, that is, Mary Magdalene.") "Of Clopas" may mean "daughter of" or "mother of".

›**20.31 put your faith in . . . have faith in:** Some manuscripts have "keep on having faith in . . . keep on having faith in".
›**21.2 the brothers James and John:** Greek "the two sons of Zebedee".
›**21.15 more than the others do?:** Or "more than you love these things?"

The Acts

of the apostles

The basics

What's the point? To show how God's Spirit was at work in the world of the early Church.

What happens? The Holy Spirit comes to Jesus' followers, turning them from a small, scared huddle to a life-changing, world-altering church.

What should I remember? 2.33 'Jesus was taken up to sit at the right side of God, and he was given the Holy Spirit, just as the Father had promised. Jesus is also the one who has given the Spirit to us, and that is what you are now seeing and hearing.'

More details

Setting the scene After coming back from the dead, Jesus promised his followers that he would send them the Holy Spirit. He did, and the church exploded into growth...

What's it all about? Luke had written an account of Jesus' life; now he continues the story with the history of the early Church. Luke takes us from the resurrection of Jesus in Jerusalem to the imprisonment of Paul in Rome.

There are three key figures in Acts. The first is Peter, the enthusiastic, whole-hearted fisherman, who is transformed into the leader of the young church. In the months and years after the resurrection it is Peter who gives courage and leadership to the followers of Jesus.

And they needed courage, because the early years of Christianity were a period of huge conflict, as well as huge growth. The fact that the early Church grew so quickly brought it

into conflict with the Jewish and Roman authorities, and Acts features several episodes where followers of Jesus are martyred for their beliefs. Christianity was a dangerous, life-changing faith, and nothing illustrates that better than the conversion of Saul, who went from being Christianity's greatest enemy to its staunchest follower.

Saul – who became Paul – is the second major figure in Acts. He started out as an opponent of the faith, before an encounter with the risen Jesus changed his life completely. After that he took the good news to the gentiles; to the Greeks and Romans, to anyone who wasn't born a Jew.

Today, we're delighted if anyone set up churches in foreign lands, but to the early church this activity posed a problem. There were many arguments within the church itself as to what the Church should be like. Was the church a part of the Jewish faith, or was it something new? Should they try to recruit Gentiles – non-Jews – to the cause? And how should the church organise itself? Who should be in charge?

So Acts is the history of the first decades of the church. But Acts is also a kind of biography of the third key figure – the most key figure in Acts: the Holy Spirit. The Holy Spirit who is a constant figure in the background, inspiring, protecting, punishing, informing, pushing the first Christians to ever greater lengths as they spread the good news of Jesus Christ. It's the Holy Spirit who gives the church its courage, energy and passion.

It's the Holy Spirit who puts the acts in Acts!

Footsteps

Telling the good news in Jerusalem

CHAPTER 1

¹ Theophilus, I first wrote to you* about all that Jesus did and taught from the very first ² until he was taken up to heaven. But before he was taken up, he gave orders to the apostles he had chosen with the help of the Holy Spirit.

³ For forty days after Jesus had suffered and died, he proved in many ways that he had been raised from death. He appeared to his apostles and spoke to them about God's kingdom. ⁴ While he was still with them, he said:

> Don't leave Jerusalem yet. Wait here for the Father to give you the Holy Spirit, just as I told you he has promised to do. ⁵ John baptized with water, but in a few days you will be baptized with the Holy Spirit.

Jesus is taken to heaven

⁶ While the apostles were still with Jesus, they asked him, "Lord, are you now going to give Israel its own king again?"▸

⁷ Jesus said to them, "You don't need to know the time of those events that only the Father controls. ⁸ But the Holy Spirit will come upon you and give you power. Then you will tell everyone about me in Jerusalem, in all Judea, in Samaria, and everywhere in the world." ⁹ After Jesus had said this and while they were watching, he was taken up into a cloud. They could not see him, ¹⁰ but as he went up, they kept looking up into the sky.

Suddenly two men dressed in white clothes were standing there beside them. ¹¹ They said,

---

*1.1 I first wrote to you: The Gospel of Luke.

See also: 1.1: Luke 1.1–4. 1.4: Luke 24.49. 1.5: Matt 3.11; Mark 1.8; Luke 3.16; John 1.33. 1.8: Matt 28.19; Mark 16.15; Luke 24.47–48. 1.9: Mark 16.19; Luke 24.50–51.

Life files

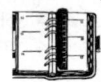

Luke (a.k.a. Doctor Luke)

What's the story?

Luke was a Greek doctor, probably a resident of Antioch. He was an educated man who wrote a history of Jesus and also a history of the early church.

Much of this he had seen first hand. He did not see Jesus, but he spoke to many of the people who had. He tells us that, like all good historians, he 'made a careful study of all that happened' (Luke 1.1–4).

He met many of the main characters in the gospel stories, through his close association and many journeys with Paul. He joined with Paul who joined with Paul and accompanied him on several of his missionary journeys. He went with Paul to Jerusalem where he met James and possibly Peter. So he would have been ideally placed to interview the main characters, listen to their stories and make notes for his history.

In fact Luke was among the most faithful of Paul's companions. In one of Paul's last messages, when he is imprisoned in Rome, Paul writes 'Only Luke has stayed with me' (2 Timothy 4.11).

What's the point?

Luke is an historian. His gospel draws on a number of sources and aims to give a complete picture of the life of Jesus from birth to death to resurrection.

 Anorak corner

Luke is the only non-Jewish writer in the New Testament.

More...

Paul p.1222
Barnabas p.1228
Timothy p.1346
Paul's Journeys p.1230

"Why are you men from Galilee standing here and looking up into the sky? Jesus has been taken to heaven. But he will come back in the same way that you have seen him go."

Someone to take the place of Judas

12-13 The Mount of Olives was about a kilometre from Jerusalem. The apostles who had gone there were Peter, John, James, Andrew, Philip, Thomas, Bartholomew, Matthew, James the son of Alphaeus, Simon, known as the Eager One,* and Judas the son of James.

After the apostles returned to the city, they went upstairs to the room where they had been staying.

14 The apostles often met together and prayed with a single purpose in mind.' The women and Mary the mother of Jesus would meet with them, and so would his brothers. 15 One day there were about a hundred and twenty of the Lord's followers meeting together, and Peter stood up to speak to them. 16-17 He said:

My friends, long ago by the power of the Holy Spirit, David said something about Judas, and what he said has now happened. Judas was one of us and had worked with us, but he brought the mob to arrest Jesus. 18 Then Judas bought some land with the money he was given for doing that evil thing. He fell head-first into the field. His body burst open, and all his insides came out. 19 When the people of Jerusalem found out about this, they called the place Akeldama, which in the local language means "Field of Blood".

20 In the book of Psalms it says,

"Leave his house empty,
and don't let anyone
live there."

It also says,

"Let someone else
have his job."

21-22 So we need someone else to help us tell others that Jesus has been raised from

death. He must also be one of the men who was with us from the very beginning. He must have been with us from the time the Lord Jesus was baptized by John until the day he was taken to heaven.

23 Two men were suggested: one of them was Joseph Barsabbas, known as Justus, and the other was Matthias. 24 Then they all prayed, "Lord, you know what everyone is like! Show us the one you have chosen 25 to be an apostle and to serve in place of Judas, who got what he deserved." 26 They drew names, and Matthias was chosen to join the group of the eleven apostles.

CHAPTER 2

The coming of the Holy Spirit

1 On the day of Pentecost* all the Lord's followers were together in one place. 2 Suddenly there was a noise from heaven like the sound of a mighty wind! It filled the house where they were meeting. 3 Then they saw what looked like fiery tongues moving in all directions, and a tongue came and settled on each person there. 4 The Holy Spirit took control of everyone, and they began speaking whatever languages the Spirit let them speak.

5 Many religious Jews from every country in the world were living in Jerusalem. 6 And when they heard this noise, a crowd gathered. But they were surprised, because they were hearing everything in their own languages. 7 They were excited and amazed, and said:

Don't all these who are speaking come from Galilee? 8 Then why do we hear them speaking our very own languages? 9 Some of us are from Parthia, Media, and Elam. Others are from Mesopotamia, Judea, Cappadocia, Pontus, Asia, 10 Phrygia, Pamphylia, Egypt, parts of Libya near Cyrene, Rome, 11 Crete, and Arabia. Some of us were born Jews, and others of us have chosen to be Jews. Yet we all hear them using our own languages to tell the wonderful things God has done.

12 Everyone was excited and confused. Some of them even kept asking each other, "What does all this mean?"

---

*1.12–13 known as the Eager One: The Greek text has "Zealot", a name later given to the members of a Jewish group which resisted and fought against the Romans.

See also: 1.13: Matt 10.2–4; Mark 3.16–19; Luke 6.14–16. **1.18–19:** Matt 27.3–8. **1.20: a** Psa 69.25; **b** Psa 109.8. **1.22: a** Matt 3.16; Mark 1.9; Luke 3.21; **b** Mark 16.19; Luke 24.51.

---

*2.1 Pentecost: A Jewish festival that came fifty days after Passover and celebrated the wheat harvest. Jews later celebrated Pentecost as the time when they were given the Law of Moses.
See also: 2.1: Lev 23.15–21; Deut 16.9–11.

Real life

Language

Contributed by Wycliffe

'Don't all these who are speaking come from Galilee?' said the surprised listeners in Acts 2. 'Then why do we hear them speaking our very own languages?' (Acts 2.7–8)

In Acts 2, the Holy Spirit descends. Most people look at this passage and focus on the amazing and sometimes controversial things that are the 'Holy Spirit' and 'the gift of tongues'.

But what was really going on that day? Was it an outpouring of the Spirit? Was it just about thousands of people coming to know the Lord? Or was it also about God doing an amazing miracle so that everyone in the world could understand him in their own language?

God was taking the initiative in communication. Why? Because he wants to have relationship with us in a form that we can understand; our 'mother tongue', the language of our everyday lives. God wants to communicate with us. He talks to us, he reveals himself to us through the Bible, and he uses words of knowledge, prophecy, and dreams.

That outpouring of different languages was just the start. Since then the Bible has been translated into many different languages – so we don't have to learn Hebrew or Greek to read the Bible any more!

Did you know that there are 6809 languages in the world? Only a creative God could do that! The sad thing is, at the time of writing, only 405 languages have got a complete Bible, and only another 350 have got a part of the Bible.

If they haven't got a Bible, how are they going to hear that God loves them? And that he sent Jesus to die for them so that they can have a relationship with the Father and go to heaven? God started something incredible in Jerusalem that day; WYnet is involved in continuing that by making God's word accessible to all nations, tribes and tongues.

6.3 billion people in the world.
6809 languages.
1 world. 1 God. 1 Gospel.

Think

Why do you think that there are so many languages in the world?
Why is it important for people to have the Bible in their own language?
What is the future of all these languages? (See Revelation 7.9–10)

Act

Find out about some of the people who don't have a Bible in their language. Where do they live?
Find out about the work of Bible translators. Pray for their work.
If you're interested in languages, put those skills to use and find out about becoming a translator.

Check

Genesis 11.1–9; Psalms 19.1–6; Matthew 28.16–20; Romans 10.14–17; Revelation 7.9–10

More...

Culture p.779
Sharing your faith p.1082

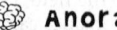 **Anorak corner**

The New Testament is written in what is called koine Greek. That is ordinary Greek, the language of the tradesmen and the shop-keepers. It wasn't written in Latin, the official language of the empire, or in classical Greek, the language of the philosophers and poets, or even in Hebrew, the language of the Jews.

It was written in the ordinary language that everyone could speak. Why? Because the gospel is for everyone.

13 Others made fun of the Lord's followers and said, "They are drunk."

Peter speaks to the crowd

14 Peter stood with the eleven apostles and spoke in a loud and clear voice to the crowd:

Friends and everyone else living in Jerusalem, listen carefully to what I have to say! 15 You are wrong to think that these people are drunk. After all, it is only nine o'clock in the morning. 16 But this is what God led the prophet Joel to say,

17 "When the last days come,
I will give my Spirit
to everyone.
Your sons and daughters
will prophesy.
Your young men
will see visions,
and your old men
will have dreams.
18 In those days I will give
my Spirit to my servants,
both men and women,
and they will prophesy.

19 I will perform miracles
in the sky above
and wonders
on the earth below.
There will be blood and fire
and clouds of smoke.
20 The sun will turn dark,
and the moon
will be as red as blood
before the great
and wonderful day
of the Lord appears.
21 Then the Lord
will save everyone
who asks for his help."

22 Now, listen to what I have to say about Jesus from Nazareth. God proved that he sent Jesus to you by having him perform miracles, wonders, and signs. All of you know this. 23 God had already planned and decided that Jesus would be handed over to you. So you took him and had evil men put him to death on a cross. 24 But God set him free from death and raised him to life. Death could not hold him in its power.

See also: 2.17–21: Joel 2.28–32 (LXX). 2.23: Matt 27.35; Mark 15.24; Luke 23.33; John 19.18. 2.24: Matt 28.5–6; Mark 16.6; Luke 24.5.

Big ideas

Holy Spirit

It's the basic, powerful energy which comes from God for us, the oxygen of the Christian life. Without the Holy Spirit, Christianity is just a set of ideas. With the Holy Spirit, Christianity is a living, powerful faith.

The Spirit is one aspect of God – the third person in the Trinity. In Old Testament times he didn't live permanently on earth. He descended on Jesus at his baptism. After Jesus finished his work, he promised that the Holy Spirit would live with his followers forever (John 14.16). So, at Pentecost, the Holy Spirit descended, turning the frightened, anxious followers of Jesus into a powerful, world-changing movement.

The Holy Spirit has a vital role:

Empowerer: Empowering the church, enabling Christians to love each other, to forgive, to be joyful, to be, in fact, what we ought to be.

Communicator: Giving messages from God, directly or in visions (Revelation 2.7).

Motivator: Inspiring Christians to get involved! The Holy Spirit sends people out and even tells them where to go (Acts 13.2).

Giver: Bringing gifts, such as healing, teaching, administration, helping others.

Teacher: Bringing wisdom and insight, so we can learn about God and each other.

Protector: Protecting us from sinful thoughts. The more of the Spirit that is in us, the less likely we are to stray.

Footsteps

Ten days with the Holy Spirit

Jesus' baptism: Matthew 3.1—4.10
Jesus promises the Spirit: John 14
The work of the Spirit: John 16
The Spirit at Pentecost: Acts 2
Victory in the Spirit: Romans 8
Wisdom from the Spirit: 1 Corinthians 2
Gifts of the Spirit: 1 Corinthians 12
Tongues & prophecy: 1 Corinthians 14
Life in the Spirit: Galatians 5
Unity and gifts: Ephesians 4

More...

Spiritual gifts p.1283

25 What David said are really the words of Jesus,

> "I always see the Lord
> near me,
> and I will not be afraid
> with him at my right side.
26 Because of this,
> my heart will be glad,
> my words will be joyful,
> and I will live in hope.
27 The Lord won't leave me
> in the grave.
> I am his holy one,
> and he won't let
> my body decay.
28 He has shown me
> the path to life,
> and he makes me glad
> by being near me."

29 My friends, it is right for me to speak to you about our ancestor David. He died and was buried, and his tomb is still here. 30 But David was a prophet, and he knew that God had made a promise he would not break. He had told David that someone from his own family would some day be king.

31 David knew this would happen, and so he told us that Christ would be raised to life. He said that God would not leave him in the grave or let his body decay. 32 All of us can tell you that God has raised Jesus to life!

33 Jesus was taken up to sit at the right side* of God, and he was given the Holy Spirit, just as the Father had promised. Jesus is also the one who has given the Spirit to us, and that is what you are now seeing and hearing.

34 David didn't go up to heaven. So he wasn't talking about himself when he said, "The Lord told my Lord to sit at his right side, 35 until he made my Lord's enemies into a footstool for him." 36 Everyone in Israel should then know for certain that God has made Jesus both Lord and Christ, even though you put him to death on a cross.

37 When the people heard this, they were very upset. They asked Peter and the other apostles, "Friends, what shall we do?"

38 Peter said, "Turn back to God! Be baptized in the name of Jesus Christ, so that your sins will be forgiven. Then you will be given the Holy Spirit. 39 This promise is for you and your children. It is for everyone our Lord God will choose, no matter where they live."

40 Peter told them many other things as well. Then he said, "I beg you to save yourselves from what will happen to all these evil people." 41 On that day about three thousand believed his message and were baptized. 42 They spent their time learning from the apostles, and they were like family to each other. They also broke bread* and prayed together.

Life among the Lord's followers

43 Everyone was amazed by the many miracles and wonders that the apostles performed. 44 All the Lord's followers often met together, and they shared everything they had. 45 They would sell their property and possessions and give the money to whoever needed it. 46 Day after day they met together in the temple. They broke bread* together in different homes and shared their food happily and freely, 47 while praising God. Everyone liked them, and each day the Lord added to their group others who were being saved.

CHAPTER 3

Peter and John heal a lame man

1 The time of prayer* was about three o'clock in the afternoon, and Peter and John were going into the temple. 2 A man who had been born lame was being carried to the temple door. Each day he was placed beside this door, known as the Beautiful Gate. He sat there and begged from the people who were going in.

3 The man saw Peter and John entering the temple, and he asked them for money. 4 But they looked straight at him and said, "Look up at us!"

5 The man stared at them and thought he was going to get something. 6 But Peter said, "I don't have any silver or gold! But I will give you what I do have. In the name of Jesus Christ from Nazareth, get up and start walking." 7 Peter then took him by the right hand and helped him up.

---

*2.33 right side: The place of honour and power.

See also: 2.25-28: Psa 16.8-11 (LXX). 2.30: Psa 132.11; 2 Sam 7.12-13. 2.34-35: Psa 110.1.

*2.42,46 broke bread: They ate together and celebrated the Lord's Supper.

*3.1 The time of prayer: Many of the Jewish people prayed in their homes at regular times each day (see Daniel 6.11), and on special occasions they prayed in the temple.

See also: 2.44: Acts 4.32-35.

At once the man's feet and ankles became strong, [8] and he jumped up and started walking. He went with Peter and John into the temple, walking and jumping and praising God. [9] Everyone saw him walking around and praising God. [10] They knew that he was the beggar who had been lying beside the Beautiful Gate, and they were completely surprised. They could not imagine what had happened to the man.

Peter speaks in the temple

[11] While the man kept holding on to Peter and John, the whole crowd ran to them in amazement at the place known as Solomon's Porch.* [12] Peter saw that a crowd had gathered, and he said:

Friends, why are you surprised at what has happened? Why are you staring at us? Do you think we have some power of our own? Do you think we were able to make this man walk because we are so religious? [13] The God that Abraham, Isaac, Jacob, and our other ancestors worshipped has brought honour to his Servant* Jesus. He is the one you betrayed. You turned against him when he was being tried by Pilate, even though Pilate wanted to set him free. [14] You rejected Jesus, who was holy and good. You asked for a murderer to be set free, [15] and you killed the one who leads people to life. But God raised him from death, and all of us can tell you what he has done. [16] You see this man, and you know him. He put his faith in the name of Jesus and was made strong. Faith in Jesus made this man completely well while everyone was watching.

[17] My friends, I am sure that you and your leaders didn't know what you were doing. [18] But God had his prophets tell that his Messiah would suffer, and now he has kept that promise. [19] So turn to God! Give up your sins, and you will be forgiven. [20] Then that time will come when the Lord will give you fresh strength. He will send you Jesus, his chosen Messiah. [21] But Jesus must stay in heaven until God makes all things new, just as his holy prophets promised long ago. [22] Moses said, "The Lord your God will choose one of your own people to be a

prophet, just as he chose me. Listen to everything he tells you. [23] No one who disobeys that prophet will be one of God's people any longer."

[24] Samuel and all the other prophets who came later also spoke about what is now happening. [25] You are really the ones God told his prophets to speak to. And you were given the promise that God made to your ancestors. He said to Abraham, "All nations on earth will be blessed because of someone from your family." [26] God sent his chosen Son* to you first, because God wanted to bless you and make each one of you turn away from your sins.

CHAPTER 4

Peter and John are brought in front of the council

[1] The apostles were still talking to the people, when some priests, the captain of the temple guard, and some Sadducees arrived. [2] These men were angry because the apostles were teaching the people that the dead would be raised from death, just as Jesus had been raised from death. [3] It was already late in the afternoon, and they arrested Peter and John and put them in jail for the night. [4] But a lot of people who had heard the message believed it. So by now there were about five thousand followers of the Lord.

[5] The next morning the leaders, the elders, and the teachers of the Law of Moses met in Jerusalem. [6] The high priest Annas was there, as well as Caiaphas, John, Alexander, and other members of the high priest's family. [7] They brought in Peter and John and made them stand in the middle while they questioned them. They asked, "By what power and in whose name have you done this?"

[8] Peter was filled with the Holy Spirit and told the nation's leaders and the elders:

[9] You are questioning us today about a kind deed in which a crippled man was healed. [10] But there is something we must tell you and everyone else in Israel. This man is standing here completely well because of the power of Jesus Christ from Nazareth. You put Jesus to death on a cross, but God raised him to life. [11] He is the stone that you builders thought was worthless, and now he is the most important stone of all.

---

*3.11 **Solomon's Porch:** A public place with tall columns along the east side of the temple.
See also: 3.13: Exod 3.15. **3.14:** Matt 27.15–23; Mark 15.6–14; Luke 23.13–23; John 19.12–15. **3.22:** Deut 18.15,18 (LXX).

See also: 3.23: Deut 18.19. **3.25:** Gen 22.18. **4.11:** Psa 118.22.

¹² Only Jesus has the power to save! His name is the only one in all the world that can save anyone.

¹³ The officials were amazed to see how brave Peter and John were, and they knew that these two apostles were only ordinary men and not well educated. The officials were certain that these men had been with Jesus. ¹⁴ But they could not deny what had happened. The man who had been healed was standing there with the apostles.

¹⁵ The officials commanded them to leave the council room. Then the officials said to each other, ¹⁶ "What can we do with these men? Everyone in Jerusalem knows about this miracle, and we cannot say it didn't happen. ¹⁷ But to keep this thing from spreading, we will warn them never again to speak to anyone about the name of Jesus." ¹⁸ So they called the two apostles back in and told them that they must never, for any reason, teach anything about the name of Jesus.

¹⁹ Peter and John answered, "Do you think God wants us to obey you or to obey him? ²⁰ We cannot keep quiet about what we have seen and heard."

²¹⁻²² The officials could not find any reason to punish Peter and John. So they threatened them and let them go. The man who was healed by this miracle was more than forty years old, and everyone was praising God for what had happened.

Peter and others pray for courage

²³ As soon as Peter and John had been set free, they went back and told the others everything that the chief priests and the leaders had said to them. ²⁴ When the rest of the Lord's followers heard this, they prayed together and said:

Master, you created heaven and earth, the sea, and everything in them. ²⁵ And by the Holy Spirit you spoke to our ancestor David. He was your servant, and you told him to say:

"Why are all the Gentiles
    so furious?
Why do people
    make foolish plans?
²⁶ The kings of earth
    prepare for war,
and the rulers
    join together

See also: 4.24: Exod 20.11; Neh 9.6; Psa 146.6.
4.25–26: Psa 2.1–2 (LXX).

Holy history

Early church

For the early Christians, 'church' didn't mean a large building with a pointy bit at one end, or a meeting on Sunday morning with a load of people in funny costumes.

Church meant people. The word 'church' comes from the Greek word ecclesia, which meant a gathering of people at the call of a herald. So, the first Christians saw themselves as people responding to a call.

The early church didn't have special buildings. It met in houses. Paul mentions several 'house churches', including those run by Priscilla and Aquila (Romans 16.5), Nympha (Colossians 4.15) and Philemon (Philemon 2). Since they met in houses, these churches were probably not more than 20–30 strong.

They probably met every day of the week, at least in the early days. They celebrated the Lord's Supper on the first day of the week (1 Corinthians 16.2). Their church services included prophecies, teaching, singing and readings. Sometimes there was a collection for those in need.

There were no official priests in the early Church. Instead, all believers were believed to be part of the priesthood (1 Peter 2.5,9). There was a leadership structure, however.

At the top were the apostles, the twelve chosen by Jesus. (Judas was replaced by Matthias.) Because they had known Jesus, they were held to be the ultimate authority of the church. At the local level there were elders, who were probably the strategic and spiritual leaders of the local Church. At Jerusalem there was a council of elders, including James. Along with the elders there were deacons, from the Greek word for 'servant'. Theymay have had a more practical role in the running of the church.

More...

Church p.1315
Communion p.1285
Meeting together p.1371

against the Lord
and his Messiah."

27 Here in Jerusalem, Herod* and Pontius Pilate got together with the Gentiles and the people of Israel. Then they turned against your holy Servant' Jesus, your chosen Messiah. 28 They did what you in your power and wisdom had already decided would happen.

29 Lord, listen to their threats! We are your servants. So make us brave enough to speak your message. 30 Show your mighty power, as we heal people and perform miracles and wonders in the name of your holy Servant' Jesus.

31 After they had prayed, the meeting place shook. They were all filled with the Holy Spirit and bravely spoke God's message.

Sharing possessions

32 The group of followers all felt the same way about everything. None of them claimed that their possessions were their own, and they shared everything they had with each other. 33 In a powerful way the apostles told everyone that the Lord Jesus was now alive. God greatly blessed his followers,' 34 and no one went in need of anything. Everyone who owned land or houses would sell them and bring the money 35 to the apostles. Then they would give the money to anyone who needed it.

36-37 Joseph was one of the followers who had sold a piece of property and brought the money to the apostles. He was a Levite from Cyprus, and the apostles called him Barnabas, which means "one who encourages others".

CHAPTER 5

Peter condemns Ananias and Sapphira

1 Ananias and his wife Sapphira also sold a piece of property. 2 But they agreed to cheat and keep some of the money for themselves.

So when Ananias took the rest of the money to the apostles, 3 Peter said, "Why has Satan made you keep back some of the money from the sale of the property? Why have you lied to the Holy Spirit? 4 The property was yours before you sold it, and even after you sold it, the money was still

yours. What made you do such a thing? You didn't lie to people. You lied to God!"

5 As soon as Ananias heard this, he dropped dead, and everyone who heard about it was frightened. 6 Some young men came in and wrapped up his body. Then they took it out and buried it.

7 Three hours later Sapphira came in, but she did not know what had happened to her husband. 8 Peter asked her, "Tell me, did you sell the property for this amount?"

"Yes," she answered, "that's the amount."

9 Then Peter said, "Why did the two of you agree to test the Lord's Spirit? The men who buried Ananias are by the door, and they will carry you out!" 10 At once she fell at Peter's feet and died.

When the young men came back in, they found Sapphira lying there dead. So they carried her out and buried her beside her husband. 11 The church members were afraid, and so was everyone else who heard what had happened.

Peter's unusual power

12 The apostles performed many miracles and wonders among the people. All the Lord's followers often met in the part of the temple known as Solomon's Porch.* 13 No one outside their group dared join them, even though everyone liked them very much.

14 Many men and women started having faith in the Lord. 15 Then sick people were brought out to the road and placed on stretchers and mats. It was hoped that Peter would walk by, and his shadow would fall on them and heal them. 16 A lot of people living in the towns near Jerusalem brought those who were sick or troubled by evil spirits, and they were all healed.

Trouble for the apostles

17 The high priest and all the other Sadducees who were with him became jealous. 18 They arrested the apostles and put them in the city jail. 19 But that night an angel from the Lord opened the doors of the jail and led the apostles out. The angel said, 20 "Go to the temple and tell the people everything about this new life." 21 So they went into the temple before sunrise and started teaching.

The high priest and his men called together their council, which included all Israel's leaders. Then they ordered the apostles to be brought to them from the jail.

---

*4.27 Herod:** Herod Antipas, the son of Herod the Great.

See also: 4.27: a Luke 23.7–11; b Matt 27.1–2; Mark 15.1; Luke 23.1; John 18.28–29   **4.32:** Acts 2.44–45.

*5.12 Solomon's Porch:** See the note at 3.11.

22 The temple police who were sent to the jail did not find the apostles. They returned and said, 23 "We found the jail locked tight and the guards standing at the doors. But when we opened the doors and went in, we didn't find anyone there." 24 The captain of the temple police and the chief priests listened to their report, but they did not know what to think about it.

25 Just then someone came in and said, "Now those men you put in jail are in the temple, teaching the people!" 26 The captain went with some of the temple police and brought the apostles back. But they did not use force. They were afraid that the people might start throwing stones at them.

27 When the apostles were brought before the council, the high priest said to them, 28 "We told you plainly not to teach in the name of Jesus. But look what you have done! You have been teaching all over Jerusalem, and you are trying to blame us for his death."

29 Peter and the apostles replied:

We don't obey people. We obey God. 30 You killed Jesus by nailing him to a cross. But the God our ancestors worshipped raised him to life 31 and made him our Leader and Saviour. Then God gave him a place at his right side,* so that the people of Israel would turn back to him and be forgiven. 32 We are here to tell you about all this, and so is the Holy Spirit, who is God's gift to everyone who obeys God.

33 When the council members heard this, they became so angry that they wanted to kill the apostles. 34 But one of the members was the Pharisee Gamaliel, a highly respected teacher. He ordered the apostles to be taken out of the room for a little while. 35 Then he said to the council:

People of Israel, be careful what you do with these men. 36 Not long ago Theudas claimed to be someone important, and about four hundred men joined him. But he was killed. All his followers were scattered, and that was the end of that. 37 Later, when the people of our nation were being counted, Judas from Galilee appeared. A lot of people followed him, but he was killed, and all his followers were scattered.

38 So I advise you to stay away from these men. Leave them alone. If what they are planning is something of their own doing, it will fail. 39 But if God is behind it, you cannot stop it anyway, unless you want to fight against God.

The council members agreed with what he said, 40 and they called the apostles back in. They had them beaten with a whip and warned them not to speak in the name of Jesus. Then they let them go.

41 The apostles left the council and were happy, because God had considered them worthy to suffer for the sake of Jesus. 42 Every day they spent time in the temple and in one home after another. They never stopped teaching and telling the good news that Jesus is the Messiah.

CHAPTER 6

Seven leaders for the church

1 A lot of people were now becoming followers of the Lord. But some of the ones who spoke Greek started complaining about the ones who spoke Aramaic. They complained that the Greek-speaking widows were not given their share when the food supplies were handed out each day. 2 The twelve apostles called the whole group of followers together and said, "We should not give up preaching God's message in order to serve at tables.* 3 My friends, choose seven men who are respected and wise and filled with God's Spirit. We will put them in charge of these things. 4 We can spend our time praying and serving God by preaching."

5 This suggestion pleased everyone, and they began by choosing Stephen. He had great faith and was filled with the Holy Spirit. Then they chose Philip, Prochorus, Nicanor, Timon, Parmenas, and also Nicolaus, who worshipped with the Jewish people* in Antioch. 6 These men were brought to the apostles. Then the apostles prayed and placed their hands on the men to show that they had been chosen to do this work. 7 God's message spread, and many

---

*6.2 to serve at tables: This may mean either that they were in charge of handing out food to the widows or that they were in charge of the money, since the Greek word "table" may also mean "bank".
*6.5 worshipped with the Jewish people: This translates the Greek word "proselyte" that means a Gentile who had accepted the Jewish religion.

---

*5.31 right side: See the note at 2.33.
See also: 5.28: Matt 27.25.

more people in Jerusalem became followers. Even a large number of priests put their faith in the Lord.

Stephen is arrested

⁸ God gave Stephen the power to perform great miracles and wonders among the people. ⁹ But some Jews from Cyrene and Alexandria were members of a group who called themselves "Free Men".* They started arguing with Stephen. Some others from Cilicia and Asia also argued with him. ¹⁰ But they were no match for Stephen, who spoke with the great wisdom that the Spirit gave him. ¹¹ So they talked some men into saying, "We heard Stephen say terrible things against Moses and God!"

¹² They turned the people and their leaders and the teachers of the Law of Moses against Stephen. Then they all grabbed Stephen and dragged him in front of the council.

¹³ Some men agreed to tell lies about Stephen, and they said, "This man keeps on saying terrible things about this holy temple and the Law of Moses. ¹⁴ We have heard him claim that Jesus from Nazareth will destroy this place and change the customs that Moses gave us." ¹⁵ Then all the council members stared at Stephen. They saw that his face looked like the face of an angel.

CHAPTER 7

Stephen's speech

¹ The high priest asked Stephen, "Are they telling the truth about you?"
² Stephen answered:

Friends, listen to me. Our glorious God appeared to our ancestor Abraham while he was still in Mesopotamia, before he had moved to Haran. ³ God told him, "Leave your country and your relatives and go to a land that I will show you." ⁴ Then Abraham left the land of the Chaldeans and settled in Haran.

After his father died, Abraham came and settled in this land where you now live. ⁵ God didn't give him any part of it, not even a square metre. But God did promise to give it to him and his family for ever, even though Abraham didn't have any children. ⁶ God said that Abraham's descendants

*6.9 Free Men: A group of Jewish men who had once been slaves, but had been freed.

See also: 7.2–3: Gen 12.1. 7.4: a Gen 11.31; b Gen 12.4.
7.5: Gen 12.7; 13.15; 15.18; 17.8. 7.6–7: Gen 15.13–14.

Holy history

Persecution

Early opposition to Christianity came from the Jews rather than from the Romans. The Jewish leaders saw Christians as blasphemers who rejected the Law, believed Jesus was the Messiah, and even ate unclean food. So they tried to hunt them down, with the death of Stephen starting a wave of persecution (Acts 6.14).

But it was a bit like throwing water on a blazing chip-pan: all it did was spread the fire all over the place. Forced out of Jerusalem, the Christians spread north, starting up churches as they went. Still the persecution continued. James the Apostle was executed by Herod Agrippa in AD44. Christians were banned from synagogues and took to meeting in their own homes.

Then the Romans got in on the act. The Romans realised that Christians had a completely different set of values. Christians refused to participate in pagan ceremonies or to worship the Roman emperor. It was even rumoured that they were cannibals who ate flesh and drank blood!

So, when Rome was ravaged by fire in AD64, Nero blamed the Christians. Both Peter and Paul are believed to have been martyred in Rome during this period. Later centuries saw a policy of torture, mass execution and the destruction of church buildings. Christians were often taken to the local stadia, where they were attacked by wild animals as a form of entertainment.

It was too late. Christianity had spread too far and was too well-established. The Christians' bravery in the face of torture and death only proved their cause. The fire was spreading and could not be put out.

More...
Persecuted church p.1220
Coping with suffering p.1391
Human rights p.707
Civil disobedience p.1247
Suffering p.555

would live for a while in a foreign land. There they would be slaves and would be ill-treated four hundred years. 7 But he also said, "I will punish the nation that makes them slaves. Then later they will come and worship me in this place."

8 God said to Abraham, "Every son in each family must be circumcised to show that you have kept your agreement with me." So when Isaac was eight days old, Abraham circumcised him. Later, Isaac circumcised his son Jacob, and Jacob circumcised his twelve sons. 9 These men were our ancestors.

Joseph was also one of our famous ancestors. His brothers were jealous of him and sold him as a slave to be taken to Egypt. But God was with him 10 and rescued him from all his troubles. God made him so wise that the Egyptian king Pharaoh* thought highly of him. Pharaoh even made Joseph governor over Egypt and put him in charge of everything he owned.

11 Everywhere in Egypt and Canaan the grain crops failed. There was terrible suffering, and our ancestors could not find enough to eat. 12 But when Jacob heard that there was grain in Egypt, he sent our ancestors there for the first time. 13 It was on their second trip that Joseph told his brothers who he was, and Pharaoh learnt about Joseph's family.

14 Joseph sent for his father and his relatives. In all, there were seventy-five of them. 15 His father went to Egypt and died there, just as our ancestors did. 16 Later their bodies were taken back to Shechem and placed in the tomb that Abraham had bought from the sons of Hamor.

Stephen continued:

17 Finally, the time came for God to do what he had promised Abraham. By then the number of our people in Egypt had greatly increased. 18 Another king was ruling Egypt, and he didn't know anything about Joseph. 19 He tricked our ancestors and was cruel to them. He even made

them leave their babies outside, so they would die.

20 During this time Moses was born. He was a very beautiful child, and for three months his parents took care of him in their home. 21 Then when they were forced to leave him outside, the king's daughter found him and raised him as her own son. 22 Moses was given the best education in Egypt. He was a strong man and a powerful speaker.

23 When Moses was forty years old, he wanted to help the Israelites because they were his own people. 24 One day he saw an Egyptian ill-treating one of them. So he rescued the man and killed the Egyptian. 25 Moses thought the rest of his people would realize that God was going to use him to set them free. But they didn't understand.

26 The next day Moses saw two of his own people fighting, and he tried to make them stop. He said, "Men, you are both Israelites. Why are you so cruel to each other?"

27 But the man who had started the fight pushed Moses aside and asked, "Who made you our ruler and judge? 28 Are you going to kill me, just as you killed that Egyptian yesterday?" 29 When Moses heard this, he ran away to live in the country of Midian. His two sons were born there.

Stephen continued:

30 Forty years later, an angel appeared to Moses from a burning bush in the desert near Mount Sinai. 31 Moses was surprised by what he saw. He went closer to get a better look, and the Lord said, 32 "I am the God who was worshipped by your ancestors, Abraham, Isaac, and Jacob." Moses started shaking all over and didn't dare to look at the bush.

33 The Lord said to him, "Take off your sandals. The place where you are standing is holy. 34 With my own eyes I have seen the suffering of my people in Egypt. I have heard their groans and have come down to rescue them. Now I am sending you back to Egypt."

35 This was the same Moses that the people rejected by saying, "Who made you our leader and judge?" God's angel had spoken to Moses from the bush. And God

*7.10 Pharaoh: A Hebrew word sometimes used for the title of the king of Egypt.

See also: 7.7: Exod 3.12. 7.8: a Gen 17.10–14; b Gen 21.2–4; c Gen 25.26; d Gen 29.31–35.18. 7.9: a Gen 37.11; b Gen 37.28; c Gen 39.2,21. 7.10: Gen 41.39–41. 7.11: Gen 42.1–2. 7.13: a Gen 45.1; b Gen 45.16. 7.14: a Gen 45.9–10,17–18; b Gen 46.27 (LXX). 7.15: a Gen 46.1–7; b Gen 49.33. 7.16: Gen 23.3–16; 33.19; 50.7–13; Josh 24.32. 7.17–18: Exod 1.7–8. 7.19: a Exod 1.10–11; b Exod 1.22.

See also: 7.20: Exod 2.2. 7.21: Exod 2.3–10. 7.23–29: Exod 2.11–15. 7.29: Exod 18.3–4. 7.30–34: Exod 3.1–10. 7.35: Exod 2.14.

had even sent the angel to help Moses rescue the people and be their leader.

³⁶ In Egypt and at the Red Sea* and in the desert, Moses rescued the people by performing miracles and wonders for forty years. ³⁷ Moses is the one who told the people of Israel, "God will choose one of your people to be a prophet, just as he chose me." ³⁸ Moses brought our people together in the desert, and the angel spoke to him on Mount Sinai. There he was given these life-giving words to pass on to us. ³⁹ But our ancestors refused to obey Moses. They rejected him and wanted to go back to Egypt.

⁴⁰ The people said to Aaron, "Make some gods to lead us! Moses led us out of Egypt, but we don't know what's happened to him now." ⁴¹ Then they made an idol in the shape of a calf. They offered sacrifices to the idol and were pleased with what they had done.

⁴² God turned his back on his people and left them. Then they worshipped the stars in the sky, just as it says in the Book of the Prophets, "People of Israel, you didn't offer sacrifices and offerings to me during those forty years in the desert. ⁴³ Instead, you carried the tent where the god Molech is worshipped, and you took along the star of your god Rephan. You made those idols and worshipped them. So now I will have you carried off beyond Babylonia."

Stephen continued:

⁴⁴ The tent where our ancestors worshipped God was with them in the desert. This was the same tent that God had commanded Moses to make. And it was made like the model that Moses had seen. ⁴⁵ Later it was given to our ancestors, and they took it with them when they went with Joshua. They carried the tent along as they took over the land from those people that God had chased out for them. Our ancestors used this tent until the time of King David.

⁴⁶ He pleased God and asked him if he could build a house of worship for the people▸ of Israel. ⁴⁷ And it was finally King Solomon who built a house for God.▸

⁴⁸ But the Most High God doesn't live in houses made by humans. It is just as the prophet said, when he spoke for the Lord,

⁴⁹ "Heaven is my throne,
    and the earth
        is my footstool.
    What kind of house
        will you build for me?
    In what place will I rest?
⁵⁰   I have made everything."

⁵¹ You stubborn and hardheaded people! You are always fighting against the Holy Spirit, just as your ancestors did. ⁵² Is there one prophet that your ancestors didn't ill-treat? They killed the prophets who told about the coming of the One Who Obeys God.* And now you have turned against him and killed him. ⁵³ Angels gave you God's Law, but you still don't obey it.

Stephen is stoned to death

⁵⁴ When the council members heard Stephen's speech, they were angry and furious. ⁵⁵ But Stephen was filled with the Holy Spirit. He looked towards heaven, where he saw our glorious God and Jesus standing at his right side.* ⁵⁶ Then Stephen said, "I see heaven open and the Son of Man standing at the right side of God!"

⁵⁷ The council members shouted and covered their ears. At once they all attacked Stephen ⁵⁸ and dragged him out of the city. Then they started throwing stones at him. The men who had brought charges against him put their coats at the feet of a young man named Saul.*

⁵⁹ As Stephen was being stoned to death, he called out, "Lord Jesus, please welcome me!" ⁶⁰ He knelt down and shouted, "Lord, don't blame them for what they have done." Then he died.

---

*7.36 Red Sea: This name comes from the Bible of the early Christians, a translation made into Greek about 200 BC. It refers to the body of water that the Israelites crossed and was one of the marshes or fresh water lakes near the eastern part of the Nile Delta, where they lived and where the towns of Exodus 13.17—14.9 were located.

See also: **7.36:** a Exod 7.3; b Exod 14.21; c Num 14.33. **7.37:** Deut 18.15,18. **7.38:** Exod 19.1—20.17; Deut 5.1–33. **7.40:** Exod 32.1. **7.41:** Exod 32.2–6. **7.42–43:** Amos 5.25–27 (LXX). **7.44:** Exod 25.9,40. **7.45:** Josh 3.14–17.

---

*7.52 One Who Obeys God: That is, Jesus.
*7.55 standing at his right side: The "right side" is the place of honour and power. "Standing" may mean that Jesus is welcoming Stephen (see verse 59).
*7.58 Saul: Better known as Paul, who became a famous follower of Jesus.

See also: **7.46:** 2 Sam 7.1–16; 1 Chron 17.1–14. **7.47:** 1 King 6.1–38; 2 Chron 3.1–17. **7.49–50:** Isa 66.1,2. **7.51:** Isa 63.10.

CHAPTER 8

1-2 Saul approved the stoning of Stephen. Some faithful followers of the Lord buried Stephen and mourned very much for him.

Saul makes trouble for the church

At that time the church in Jerusalem suffered terribly. All the Lord's followers, except the apostles, were scattered everywhere in Judea and Samaria. 3 Saul started making a lot of trouble for the church. He went from house to house, arresting men and women and putting them in jail.

The good news in Judea and Samaria

The good news is preached in Samaria

4 The Lord's followers who had been scattered went from place to place, telling the good news. 5 Philip went to the city of Samaria and told the people about Christ. 6 They crowded around Philip because they were eager to hear what he was saying and to see him perform miracles. 7 Many people with evil spirits were healed, and the spirits went out of them with a shout. A lot of crippled and lame people were also healed. 8 Everyone in that city was very glad because of what was happening.

9 For some time a man named Simon had lived in the city of Samaria and had amazed the people. He practised witchcraft and claimed to be somebody great. 10 Everyone, rich and poor, crowded around him. They said, "This man is the power of God called 'The Great Power'."

11 For a long time, Simon had used witchcraft to amaze the people, and they kept crowding around him. 12 But when they believed what Philip was saying about God's kingdom and about the name of Jesus Christ, they were all baptized. 13 Even Simon believed and was baptized. He stayed close to Philip, because he marvelled at all the miracles and wonders.

14 The apostles in Jerusalem heard that some people in Samaria had accepted God's message, and they sent Peter and John. 15 When the two apostles arrived, they prayed that the people would be given the Holy Spirit. 16 Before this, the Holy Spirit had not been given to anyone in Samaria, though some of them had been baptized in the name of the Lord Jesus. 17 Peter and John then placed their hands on everyone who had faith in the Lord, and they were given the Holy Spirit.

18 Simon noticed that the Spirit was given only when the apostles placed their hands on the people. So he brought money 19 and said to Peter and John, "Let me have this power too! Then anyone I place my hands on will also be given the Holy Spirit."

20 Peter said to him, "You and your money will both end up in hell if you think you can buy God's gift! 21 You don't have any part in this, and God sees that your heart isn't right. 22 Get rid of these evil thoughts and ask God to forgive you. 23 I can see that you are jealous and bound by your evil ways."

24 Simon said, "Please pray to the Lord, so that what you said won't happen to me."

25 After Peter and John had preached about the Lord, they returned to Jerusalem. On their way they told the good news in many villages of Samaria.

Philip and an Ethiopian official

26 The Lord's angel said to Philip, "Go south' along the desert road that leads from Jerusalem to Gaza."' 27 So Philip left.

An important Ethiopian official happened to be going along that road in his chariot. He was the chief treasurer for Candace, the Queen of Ethiopia. The official had gone to Jerusalem to worship 28 and was now on his way home. He was sitting in his chariot, reading the book of the prophet Isaiah. 29 The Spirit told Philip to catch up with the chariot. 30 Philip ran up close and heard the man reading aloud from the book of Isaiah. Philip asked him, "Do you understand what you are reading?"

31 The official answered, "How can I understand unless someone helps me?" He then invited Philip to come up and sit beside him.

32 The man was reading the passage that said,

"He was led like a sheep
    on its way to be killed.
He was silent as a lamb
    whose wool
        is being cut off,
    and he did not say
        a word.

See also: 8.3: Acts 22.4–5; 26.9–11.

See also: 8.32–33: Isa 53.7–8 (LXX).

Holy history

Eunuchs

The Ethiopian official was a eunuch.

Eunuchs were men who had been castrated. The reason for this barbaric act was so that the kings and court officials who employed eunuchs would feel confident that they would not enjoy themselves with the royal harem! Because of their trustworthiness, eunuchs were often given positions of high responsibility and authority in the land.

Jesus talks about three types of eunuchs: those who have a birth defect, those who have been mutilated, and those who stay single for the sake of the kingdom of heaven (Matthew 19.12).

Eunuchs, because of their distinctive anatomical feature, could not 'fully belong to the Lord's people' (Deuteronomy 23.1). That is why Philip's act in baptising a eunuch is so important: Philip is showing how the new relationship with Jesus breaks down these old boundaries, and how nobody is automatically excluded from Christ.

More...

Redemption p.292
Racism p.1308

 Anorak corner

Burials

1. Where were Abraham, Isaac and Jacob buried?
2. How long did embalming usually take in Egypt?
3. What two spices were used to anoint Jesus after his death?
4. Where was Elijah buried?
5. Whose tomb did Jesus borrow?
(Answers on p.1431)

33 He was treated like a nobody
and did not receive
a fair trial.
How can he have children,
if his life
is snatched away?"

34 The official said to Philip, "Tell me, was the prophet talking about himself or about someone else?" 35 So Philip began at this place in the Scriptures and explained the good news about Jesus.

36-37 As they were going along the road, they came to a place where there was some water. The official said, "Look! Here is some water. Why can't I be baptized?"* 38 He ordered the chariot to stop. Then they both went down into the water, and Philip baptized him.

39 After they had come out of the water, the Lord's Spirit took Philip away. The official never saw him again, but he was very happy as he went on his way.

40 Philip later appeared in Azotus. He went from town to town, all the way to Caesarea, telling people about Jesus.

CHAPTER 9

Saul becomes a follower of the Lord

This is also told in Acts 22.6–16; 26.12–18

1 Saul kept on threatening to kill the Lord's followers. He even went to the high priest 2 and asked for letters to the Jewish leaders in Damascus. He did this because he wanted to arrest and take to Jerusalem any man or woman who had accepted the Lord's Way.* 3 When Saul had almost reached Damascus, a bright light from heaven suddenly flashed around him. 4 He fell to the ground and heard a voice that said, "Saul! Saul! Why are you so cruel to me?"

5 "Who are you?" Saul asked.

"I am Jesus," the Lord answered. "I am the one you are so cruel to. 6 Now get up and go into the city, where you will be told what to do."

7 The men with Saul stood there speechless. They had heard the voice, but they had not seen anyone. 8 Saul got up from the ground, and when he opened his eyes, he could not see a thing. Someone then led him by the hand to Damascus, 9 and for three days he was blind and did not eat or drink.

*9.2 accepted the Lord's Way: In the book of Acts, this means to become a follower of the Lord Jesus.

Real life

Persecuted church

Contributed by Open Doors

A 15-year-old called Roy Pontoh was hacked to death on the island of Ambon by a frenzied mob. Roy stood up for his faith in Jesus right until the end. He entered heaven a hero.

Pure and simple, persecution is nasty, whatever form it takes: discrimination, bullying, oppression, torture, murder... Persecution hurts. Persecution reflects how bad our world is without Jesus; a world where people can commit unbelievable atrocities and acts of human rights abuse almost without blinking and showing little emotion. This is nothing new. Read through the Bible and you'll discover that persecution has been around for a long time. Right the way through, individuals and nations have faced persecution: the Israelites were persecuted in Egypt (Exodus 1); David, the giant slayer, was made an enemy of the state by King Saul (1 Samuel 19); in the book of Esther, the Jews faced extermination.

Now flick through the New Testament – see Acts 8.1–13 for starters – and you'll discover a church under fire, facing immense persecution for following Jesus 24/7. Today, over 2000 years on, around 200 million people still get hunted down, arrested, tortured, and disowned by their family and friends, simply for being a Christian. These are members of the persecuted church.

Truth is though, that there should be no distinction made between the persecuted church and the church living in freedom. There is only one church. If one part of the church is persecuted, then those living in freedom should respond and do whatever they can to help: the Bible makes that pretty clear. Read 1 Corinthians 12.26 and Galatians 6.10 and see that God's heart beats for justice, freedom, and peace...

It's highly likely that you have the freedom to worship God, and to own and read the Bible. Pause for a moment and think about the millions of Christians who can't meet openly, who don't have a Bible. Don't leave your action there, do whatever you can to stand up for the persecuted church: it pleases God big time. Take a look at Matthew 25.35–41. When Christians help each other, it's as if they're helping Jesus himself; just realising that fact is pretty mind blowing. So try it for yourself!

Questions

Where will you find the church being persecuted in today's world? And in what way?

What would you do if your Bible was taken from you? Or if you weren't allowed to go to church?

Action

Take a look at Psalm 89.14 and Isaiah 42.1–7. Read those verses through quietly and reflect on them, maybe write down your thoughts.

Make a difference for persecuted Christians by praying, campaigning, writing letters, giving time and money, and raising awareness right where you are. Remember: when you send a card, or when you pray for persecuted Christians, it's as if you're supporting Jesus himself!

Check

Matthew 25.35–41; 1 Corinthians 12.26; Galatians 6.10

More...

Persecution p.1215
Coping with suffering p.1391
Suffering p.555

10 A follower named Ananias lived in Damascus, and the Lord spoke to him in a vision. Ananias answered, "Lord, here I am."

11 The Lord said to him, "Get up and go to the house of Judas in Straight Street. When you get there, you will find a man named Saul from the city of Tarsus. Saul is praying, 12 and he has seen a vision. He saw a man named Ananias coming to him and putting his hands on him, so that he could see again."

13 Ananias replied, "Lord, a lot of people have told me about the terrible things this man has done to your followers in Jerusalem. 14 Now the chief priests have given him the power to come here and arrest anyone who worships in your name."

15 The Lord said to Ananias, "Go! I have chosen him to tell foreigners, kings, and the people of Israel about me. 16 I will show him how much he must suffer for worshipping in my name."

17 Ananias left and went into the house where Saul was staying. Ananias placed his hands on him and said, "Saul, the Lord Jesus has sent me. He is the same one who appeared to you along the road. He wants you to be able to see and to be filled with the Holy Spirit."

18 Suddenly something like fish scales fell from Saul's eyes, and he could see. He got up and was baptized. 19 Then he ate and felt much better.

Saul preaches in Damascus

For several days Saul stayed with the Lord's followers in Damascus. 20 Soon he went to the Jewish meeting places and started telling people that Jesus is the Son of God.

21 Everyone who heard Saul was amazed and said, "Isn't this the man who caused so much trouble for those people in Jerusalem who worship in the name of Jesus? Didn't he come here to arrest them and take them to the chief priests?"

22 Saul preached with such power that he completely confused the Jewish people in Damascus, as he tried to show them that Jesus is the Messiah.

23 Later some of them made plans to kill Saul, 24 but he found out about it. He learnt that they were guarding the gates of the city day and night in order to kill him. 25 Then one night his followers let him down over the city wall in a large basket.

Saul in Jerusalem

26 When Saul arrived in Jerusalem, he tried to join the followers. But they were all afraid of him, because they did not believe he was a true follower. 27 Then Barnabas helped him by taking him to the apostles. He explained how Saul had seen the Lord and how the Lord had spoken to him. Barnabas also said that when Saul was in Damascus, he had spoken bravely in the name of Jesus.

28 Saul moved about freely with the followers in Jerusalem and told everyone about the Lord. 29 He was always arguing with the Jews who spoke Greek, and so they tried to kill him. 30 But the followers found out about this and took Saul to Caesarea. From there they sent him to the city of Tarsus.

31 The church in Judea, Galilee, and Samaria now had a time of peace and kept on worshipping the Lord. The church became stronger, as the Holy Spirit encouraged it and helped it grow.

Peter heals Aeneas

32 While Peter was travelling from place to place, he visited the Lord's followers who lived in the town of Lydda. 33 There he met a man named Aeneas, who for eight years had been sick in bed and could not move. 34 Peter said to Aeneas, "Jesus Christ has healed you! Get up and make up your bed." Straight away he stood up.

35 Many people in the towns of Lydda and Sharon saw Aeneas and became followers of the Lord.

Peter brings Dorcas back to life

36 In Joppa there was a follower named Tabitha. Her Greek name was Dorcas, which means "deer". She was always doing good things for people and had given much to the poor. 37 But she became ill and died, and her body was washed and placed in an upstairs room. 38 Joppa wasn't far from Lydda, and the followers heard that Peter was there. They sent two men to say to him, "Please come with us as quickly as you can!" 39 Straight away, Peter went with them.

The men took Peter upstairs into the room. Many widows were there crying. They showed him the coats and clothes that Dorcas had made while she was still alive.

40 After Peter had sent everyone out of the room, he knelt down and prayed. Then he turned to the body of Dorcas and said, "Tabitha, get up!" The woman opened her

Life files

Paul (a.k.a. Saul of Tarsus)

Background: Born of Jewish parents in the city of Tarsus.

What's the story?

Paul was a Roman citizen from birth, implying that his parents had wealth and position. Like his father, he was a Pharisee (Acts 23.6) and was taught the trade of tent making (Acts 18.13). At an early age he went to Jerusalem, to study under the famous Rabbi Gamaliel (Acts 22.3).

Passionate about his religion, Paul was (though he says so himself) 'a much better Jew than anyone else my own age' and 'obeyed every law that our ancestors had given us' (Galatians 1.14). He put his passion to work, co-ordinating an anti-Christian campaign which included the murder of Stephen and arrests both in Jerusalem and in other cities.

Then, in a vision, he saw Jesus, and his life changed. He started preaching about what had happened, and had to be smuggled out of Damascus. He then went to Jerusalem, where Barnabas stood up for him amidst a great deal of suspicion.

After that he returned to Tarsus for a period of eight to ten years. Little is known of his activities, but he probably preached and taught (Galatians 1.23). Eventually Barnabas invited Paul to Antioch, and that was the start of Paul's missionary journeys. For the next twenty years or so, Paul travelled throughout the Mediterranean area, preaching, teaching, founding and organising churches. He took the gospel to the gentiles – the non-Jewish people – arguing that Christ had died for everyone.

In the end he was arrested by the authorities in Jerusalem. As a Roman citizen he was allowed to be tried in Rome, so he was shipped there, where he spent some time in house arrest. He was probably released eventually, but then re-arrested when a new wave of Christian persecution broke out. Tradition states that he was executed in Rome sometime around AD67.

What's the point?

As someone born in a Greek city, with Roman citizenship, and raised a Jew, Paul was ideally qualified to take the good news to different groups and people. Paul knew that Christ had died for all people; and he was determined that nothing should get in the way of those people hearing – and believing – the good news. He was not a great preacher (1 Corinthians 2.1–5; 2 Corinthians 10.10; 11.6), but he was a man to whom God had given immense wisdom and insight; insights that have shaped the church ever since.

Anorak corner

A Bishop in the second century described Paul as 'a man small of stature, with a bald head and crooked legs, in a good state of body, with eyebrows meeting and nose somewhat hooked, full of friendliness: for now he appears like man and now he had the face of an angel'. Perhaps this is backed up by his change of name. In Hebrew, Saul means 'asked for' while his Roman equivalent Paulos means 'little'.

Footsteps

Two weeks with Paul

The conversion of Saul: Acts 9. 1–31
Saul, Barnabas and Antioch: Acts 11.19–30
Sent on their way: Acts 13.1–12
Paul v Jerusalem: Acts 15.1–35
Scenes of missionary life: Acts 17.16–34
Paul's arrest: Acts 21.17–36
The case for the defence: Acts 26.1–32
Shipwreck! Acts 27.1–44
House arrest in Rome: Acts 28.16–31
Jews and Gentiles: Romans 3.1–31
Sin and the Spirit: Romans 7.7–8.17
Love: 1 Corinthians 13
Mission statement: Ephesians 3
The end of the race: 2 Timothy 4.1–22

More...

Pharisees, Sadducees and the rest p.1097
Gentiles p.1232
Paul's journeys p.1230
Luke p.1206
Timothy p.1346
Barnabas p.1228

eyes, and when she saw Peter, she sat up. ⁴¹ He took her by the hand and helped her to her feet.

Peter called in the widows and the other followers and showed them that Dorcas had been raised from death. ⁴² Everyone in Joppa heard what had happened, and many of them put their faith in the Lord. ⁴³ Peter stayed on for a while in Joppa in the house of a man named Simon, who made leather.

CHAPTER 10

Peter and Cornelius

¹ In Caesarea there was a man named Cornelius, who was the captain of a group of soldiers called "The Italian Unit". ² Cornelius was a very religious man. He worshipped God, and so did everyone else who lived in his house. He had given a lot of money to the poor and was always praying to God.

³ One afternoon at about three o'clock,* Cornelius had a vision. He saw an angel from God coming to him and calling him by name. ⁴ Cornelius was surprised and stared at the angel. Then he asked, "What is this all about?"

The angel answered, "God has heard your prayers and knows about your gifts to the poor. ⁵ Now send some men to Joppa for a man named Simon Peter. ⁶ He is staying with Simon the leather maker, who lives in a house near the sea." ⁷ After saying this, the angel left.

Cornelius called in two of his servants and one of his soldiers who worshipped God. ⁸ He explained everything to them and sent them off to Joppa.

⁹ The next day about midday these men were coming near Joppa. Peter went up on the roof* of the house to pray ¹⁰ and became very hungry. While the food was being prepared, he fell sound asleep and had a vision. ¹¹ He saw heaven open, and something came down like a huge sheet held up by its four corners. ¹² In it were all kinds of animals, snakes, and birds. ¹³ A voice said to him, "Peter, get up! Kill these and eat them." ¹⁴ But Peter said, "Lord, I can't do that! I've never eaten anything that is unclean and not fit to eat."*

¹⁵ The voice spoke to him again, "When God says that something can be used for food, don't say it isn't fit to eat."

¹⁶ This happened three times before the sheet was suddenly taken back to heaven.

¹⁷ Peter was still wondering what all this meant, when the men sent by Cornelius came and stood at the gate. They had found their way to Simon's house ¹⁸ and were asking if Simon Peter was staying there.

¹⁹ While Peter was still thinking about the vision, the Holy Spirit said to him, "Three men are here looking for you. ²⁰ Hurry down and go with them. Don't worry, I sent them."

²¹ Peter went down and said to the men, "I am the one you are looking for. Why have you come?"

²² They answered, "Captain Cornelius sent us. He is a good man who worships God and is liked by the Jewish people. One of God's holy angels told Cornelius to send for you, so he could hear what you have to say." ²³ Peter invited them to spend the night.

The next morning, Peter and some of the Lord's followers in Joppa left with the men who had come from Cornelius. ²⁴ The next day they arrived in Caesarea where Cornelius was waiting for them. He had also invited his relatives and close friends.

²⁵ When Peter arrived, Cornelius greeted him. Then he knelt at Peter's feet and started worshipping him. ²⁶ But Peter took hold of him and said, "Stand up! I am nothing more than a human."

²⁷ As Peter entered the house, he was still talking with Cornelius. Many people were there, ²⁸ and Peter said to them, "You know that we Jews are not allowed to have anything to do with other people. But God has shown me that he doesn't think anyone is unclean or unfit. ²⁹ I agreed to come here, but I want to know why you sent for me."

³⁰ Cornelius answered:

Four days ago at about three o'clock in the afternoon I was praying at home. Suddenly a man in bright clothes stood in front of me. ³¹ He said, "Cornelius, God has heard your prayers, and he knows about your gifts to the poor. ³² Now send to Joppa for Simon Peter. He is staying in the home of Simon the leather maker, who lives near the sea."

³³ I sent for you straight away, and you have been good enough to come. All of us are here in the presence of the Lord God, so that we can hear what he has to say.

---

*10.3 at about three o'clock: Probably while he was praying. See 3.1 and the note there.

*10.9 roof: In Palestine the houses usually had a flat roof. Stairs on the outside led up to the roof, which was made of beams and boards covered with packed earth.

*10.14 unclean and not fit to eat: The Law of Moses taught that some foods were not fit to eat.

³⁴ Peter then said:

> Now I am certain that God treats all people alike. ³⁵ God is pleased with everyone who worships him and does right, no matter what nation they come from. ³⁶ This is the same message that God gave to the people of Israel, when he sent Jesus Christ, the Lord of all, to offer peace to them.
>
> ³⁷ You know what happened’ everywhere in Judea. It all began in Galilee after John had told everyone to be baptized. ³⁸ God gave the Holy Spirit and power to Jesus from Nazareth. He was with Jesus, as he went around doing good and healing everyone who was under the power of the devil. ³⁹ We all saw what Jesus did both in Israel and in the city of Jerusalem.
>
> Jesus was put to death on a cross. ⁴⁰ But three days later, God raised him to life and let him be seen. ⁴¹ Not everyone saw him. He was seen only by us, who ate and drank with him after he was raised from death. We were the ones God chose to tell others about him.
>
> ⁴² God told us to announce clearly to the people that Jesus is the one he has chosen to judge the living and the dead. ⁴³ Every one of the prophets has said that all who have faith in Jesus will have their sins forgiven in his name.

⁴⁴ While Peter was still speaking, the Holy Spirit took control of everyone who was listening. ⁴⁵ Some Jewish followers of the Lord had come with Peter, and they were surprised that the Holy Spirit had been given to Gentiles. ⁴⁶ Now they were hearing Gentiles speaking unknown languages and praising God.

Peter said, ⁴⁷ "These Gentiles have been given the Holy Spirit, just as we have! I am certain that no one would dare stop us from baptizing them." ⁴⁸ Peter ordered them to be baptized in the name of Jesus Christ, and they asked him to stay on for a few days.

CHAPTER 11

Peter reports to the church in Jerusalem

¹ The apostles and the followers in Judea heard that Gentiles had accepted God's message. ² So when Peter came to Jerusalem, some of the Jewish followers started arguing with him. They wanted Gentile followers to be circumcised, and ³ they said, "You stayed in the homes of Gentiles, and you even ate with them!"

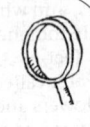

Holy history

Families

Families in the Bible – especially in Old Testament times – meant much more than just Mum, Dad and the kids.

In ancient society, and particularly in tribal societies, the family was a larger group. Today, we would call it an 'extended' family. A Biblical family would include the father, his wife (or wives), their children, various other dependent relatives and even the servants. Perhaps it is easier to imagine if we think about it in terms of the word 'household'; that is, those dwelling together under the same roof.

A New Testament household would include the slaves and employees of the family, as well as the core 'family' members. The household of Cornelius, for example, included Cornelius and his family, his servants and even some close friends (Acts 10.7,24).

Both Old Testament and New Testament societies were patriarchal, that is, the father was the undisputed head of the household. What he said, went; although there are plenty of examples in the Bible of women being able to get their own way.

The children generally remained under the father's control until they got married. Young children were looked after by their mother, but as soon as the boys were old enough, they started to work alongside their father.

The blood ties between members of the same family were strong – and members of the family had the right to expect protection and provision from their kinsfolk.

⁴ Then Peter told them exactly what had happened:

⁵ I was in the town of Joppa and was praying when I fell sound asleep and had a vision. I saw heaven open, and something like a huge sheet held by its four corners came down to me. ⁶ When I looked in it, I saw animals, wild beasts, snakes, and birds. ⁷ I heard a voice saying to me, "Peter, get up! Kill these and eat them."

⁸ But I said, "Lord, I can't do that! I've never taken a bite of anything that is unclean and not fit to eat."*

⁹ The voice from heaven spoke to me again, "When God says that something can be used for food, don't say it isn't fit to eat." ¹⁰ This happened three times before it was all taken back into heaven.

¹¹ Suddenly three men from Caesarea stood in front of the house where I was staying. ¹² The Holy Spirit told me to go with them and not to worry. Then six of the Lord's followers went with me to the home of a man ¹³ who told us that an angel had appeared to him. The angel had ordered him to send to Joppa for someone named Simon Peter. ¹⁴ Then Peter would tell him how he and everyone in his house could be saved.

¹⁵ After I started speaking, the Holy Spirit was given to them, just as the Spirit had been given to us at the beginning. ¹⁶ I remembered that the Lord had said, "John baptized with water, but you will be baptized with the Holy Spirit." ¹⁷ God gave those Gentiles the same gift that he gave us when we put our faith in the Lord Jesus Christ. So how could I have gone against God?

¹⁸ When they heard Peter say this, they stopped arguing and started praising God. They said, "God has now let Gentiles turn to him, and he has given life to them!"

The church in Antioch

¹⁹ Some of the Lord's followers had been scattered because of the terrible trouble that started when Stephen was killed. They went as far as Phoenicia, Cyprus, and Antioch, but they told the message only to the Jews.

²⁰ Some of the followers from Cyprus and Cyrene went to Antioch and started telling Gentiles' the good news about the Lord Jesus. ²¹ The Lord's power was with them, and many people turned to the Lord and put their faith in him. ²² News of what was happening reached the church in Jerusalem. Then they sent Barnabas to Antioch.

²³ When Barnabas got there and saw what God had been kind enough to do for them, he was very glad. So he begged them to remain faithful to the Lord with all their hearts. ²⁴ Barnabas was a good man of great faith, and he was filled with the Holy Spirit. Many more people turned to the Lord.

²⁵ Barnabas went to Tarsus to look for Saul. ²⁶ He found Saul and brought him to Antioch, where they met with the church for a whole year and taught many of its people. There in Antioch the Lord's followers were first called Christians.

²⁷ During this time some prophets from Jerusalem came to Antioch. ²⁸ One of them was Agabus. Then with the help of the Spirit, he told that there would be a terrible famine everywhere in the world. And it happened when Claudius was Emperor.* ²⁹ The followers in Antioch decided to send whatever help they could to the followers in Judea. ³⁰ So they asked Barnabas and Saul to take their gifts to the church leaders in Jerusalem.

CHAPTER 12

Herod causes trouble for the church

¹ At that time King Herod* caused terrible suffering for some members of the church. ² He ordered soldiers to cut off the head of James, the brother of John. ³ When Herod saw that this pleased the Jewish people, he had Peter arrested during the Festival of Thin Bread. ⁴ He put Peter in jail and ordered four squads of soldiers to guard him. Herod planned to put him on trial in public after the festival.

⁵ While Peter was being kept in jail, the church never stopped praying to God for him.

Peter is rescued

⁶ The night before Peter was to be put on trial, he was asleep and bound by two chains.

---

*11.8 unclean and not fit to eat: See the note at 10.14.
See also: 11.16: Acts 1.5.   11.19: Acts 8.1–4.

*11.28 when Claudius was Emperor: AD 41–54.
*12.1 Herod: Herod Agrippa I, the grandson of Herod the Great.
See also: 11.28: Acts 21.10.   12.4: Exod 12.1–27.

A soldier was guarding him on each side, and two other soldiers were guarding the entrance to the jail. ⁷ Suddenly an angel from the Lord appeared, and light flashed around in the cell. The angel poked Peter in the side and woke him up. Then he said, "Quick! Get up!"

The chains fell off his hands, ⁸ and the angel said, "Get dressed and put on your sandals." Peter did what he was told. Then the angel said, "Now put on your coat and follow me." ⁹ Peter left with the angel, but he thought everything was only a dream. ¹⁰ They went past the two groups of soldiers, and when they came to the iron gate to the city, it opened by itself. They went out and were going along the street, when all at once the angel disappeared.

¹¹ Peter now realized what had happened, and he said, "I am certain that the Lord sent his angel to rescue me from Herod and from everything the Jewish leaders planned to do to me." ¹² Then Peter went to the house of Mary the mother of John whose other name was Mark. Many of the Lord's followers had come together there and were praying.

¹³ Peter knocked on the gate, and a servant named Rhoda came to answer. ¹⁴ When she heard Peter's voice, she was too excited to open the gate. She ran back into the house and said that Peter was standing there.

¹⁵ "You are mad!" everyone told her. But she kept saying that it was Peter. Then they said, "It must be his angel."* ¹⁶ But Peter kept on knocking, until finally they opened the gate. They saw him and were completely amazed.

¹⁷ Peter motioned for them to keep quiet. Then he told how the Lord had led him out of jail. He also said, "Tell James* and the others what has happened." After that, he left and went somewhere else.

¹⁸ The next morning the soldiers who had been on guard were terribly worried and wondered what had happened to Peter. ¹⁹ Herod ordered his own soldiers to search for him, but they could not find him. Then he questioned the guards and had them put to death. After this, Herod left Judea to stay in Caesarea for a while.

Herod dies

²⁰ Herod and the people of Tyre and Sidon were very angry with each other. But their country got its food supply from the region that he ruled. So a group of them went to see Blastus, who was one of Herod's high officials. They convinced Blastus that they wanted to make peace between their cities and Herod, ²¹ and a day was set for them to meet with him.

Herod came dressed in his royal robes. He sat down on his throne and made a speech. ²² The people shouted, "You speak more like a god than a man!" ²³ At once an angel from the Lord struck him down because he took the honour that belonged to God. Later, Herod was eaten by worms and died.

²⁴ God's message kept spreading. ²⁵ And after Barnabas and Saul had done the work they were sent to do, they went back to Jerusalem* with John, whose other name was Mark.

Paul's first journey to tell the good news

CHAPTER 13

Barnabas and Saul are chosen and sent

¹ The church at Antioch had several prophets and teachers. They were Barnabas, Simeon, also called Niger, Lucius from Cyrene, Manaen, who was Herod's* close friend, and Saul. ² While they were worshipping the Lord and going without eating,* the Holy Spirit told them, "Appoint Barnabas and Saul to do the work for which I have chosen them." ³ Everyone prayed and went without eating for a while longer. Next, they placed their hands on Barnabas and Saul to show that they had been appointed to do this work. Then everyone sent them on their way.

Barnabas and Saul in Cyprus

⁴ After Barnabas and Saul had been sent by the Holy Spirit, they went to Seleucia. From there they sailed to the island of Cyprus. ⁵ They arrived at Salamis and began to preach God's message in the Jewish meeting places. They also had John* as a helper.

⁶ Barnabas and Saul went all the way to the city of Paphos on the other end of the island, where they met a Jewish man named

---

*12.17 James: The brother of the Lord.

*13.1 Herod's: See the note at 4.27.
*13.2 going without eating: The Jews often went without eating as a way of showing how much they loved God. This is also called "fasting".
*13.5 John: Whose other name was Mark (see 12.12,25).

Bar-Jesus. He practised witchcraft and was a false prophet. [7] He also worked for Sergius Paulus, who was very clever and was the governor of the island. Sergius Paulus wanted to hear God's message, and he sent for Barnabas and Saul. [8] But Bar-Jesus, whose other name was Elymas, was against them. He even tried to keep the governor from having faith in the Lord.

[9] Then Saul, better known as Paul, was filled with the Holy Spirit. He looked straight at Elymas [10] and said, "You son of the devil! You are a liar, a criminal, and an enemy of everything that is right. When will you stop speaking against the true ways of the Lord? [11] The Lord is going to punish you by making you completely blind for a while."

Suddenly the man's eyes were covered by a dark mist, and he went around trying to get someone to lead him by the hand. [12] When the governor saw what had happened, he was amazed at this teaching about the Lord. So he put his faith in the Lord.

Paul and Barnabas in Antioch of Pisidia

[13] Paul and the others left Paphos and sailed to Perga in Pamphylia. But John* left them and went back to Jerusalem. [14] The rest of them went on from Perga to Antioch in Pisidia. Then on the Sabbath they went to the Jewish meeting place and sat down.

[15] After the reading of the Law and the Prophets,* the leaders sent someone over to tell Paul and Barnabas, "Friends, if you have anything to say that will help the people, please say it."

[16] Paul got up. He motioned with his hand and said:

People of Israel, and everyone else who worships God, listen! [17] The God of Israel chose our ancestors, and he let our people prosper while they were living in Egypt. Then with his mighty power he led them out, [18] and for about forty years he took care of* them in the desert. [19] He destroyed seven nations in the land of Canaan and gave their land to our people. [20] All this happened in about 450 years.

Then God gave our people judges until the time of the prophet Samuel, [21] but the people demanded a king. So for forty years God gave them King Saul, the son of Kish from the tribe of Benjamin. [22] Later, God removed Saul and let David rule in his place. God said about him, "David the son of Jesse is the kind of person who pleases me most! He does everything I want him to do."

[23] God promised that someone from David's family would come to save the people of Israel, and that one is Jesus. [24] But before Jesus came, John was telling everyone in Israel to turn back to God and be baptized. [25] Then, when John's work was almost done, he said, "Who do you people think I am? Do you think I am the Promised One? He will come later, and I am not good enough to untie his sandals."

[26] Now listen, you descendants of Abraham! Pay attention, all you Gentiles who are here to worship God! Listen to this message about how to be saved, because it is for everyone. [27] The people of Jerusalem and their leaders didn't realize who Jesus was. And they didn't understand the words of the prophets that they read each Sabbath. So they condemned Jesus just as the prophets had said.

[28-29] They did exactly what the Scriptures said they would. Even though they couldn't find any reason to put Jesus to death, they still asked Pilate to have him killed.

After Jesus had been put to death, he was taken down from the cross' and placed in a tomb. [30] But God raised him from death! [31] Then for many days Jesus appeared to his followers who had gone with him from Galilee to Jerusalem. Now they are telling our people about him.

[32] God made a promise to our ancestors. And we are here to tell you the good news [33] that he has kept this promise to us. It is just as the second Psalm says about Jesus,

"You are my son because today
   I have become your Father."

[34] God raised Jesus from death and will never let his body decay. It is just as God said,

---

*13.13 John: See the note at 13.5.
*13.15 the Law and the Prophets: The Jewish Scriptures, that is, the Old Testament.
See also: 13.17: a Exod 1.7; b Exod 12.51.
13.18: Num 14.34; Deut 1.31. 13.19: a Deut 7.1; b Josh 14.1. 13.20: a Judg 2.16; b 1 Sam 3.20.

See also: 13.21: a 1 Sam 8.5; b 1 Sam 10.21.
13.22: a 1 Sam 13.14; b 1 Sam 16.12; Psa 89.20.
13.24: Mark 1.4; Luke 3.3. 13.25: a John 1.20; b Matt 3.11; Mark 1.7; Luke 3.16; John 1.27. 13.28: Matt 27.22–23; Mark 15.13–14; Luke 23.21–23; John 19.15.
13.29: Matt 27.57–61; Mark 15.42–47; Luke 23.50–56; John 19.38–42. 13.31: Acts 1.3. 13.33: Psa 2.7.
13.34: Isa 55.3 (LXX).

"I will make to you
the same holy promise
that I made to David."

³⁵ And in another psalm it says, "God will never let the body of his Holy One decay." ³⁶ When David was alive, he obeyed God. Then after he died, he was buried in the family grave, and his body decayed. ³⁷ But God raised Jesus from death, and his body did not decay.

³⁸ My friends, the message is that Jesus can forgive your sins! The Law of Moses could not set you free from all your sins. ³⁹ But everyone who has faith in Jesus is set free. ⁴⁰ Make sure that what the prophets have said doesn't happen to you. They said,

⁴¹ "Look, you people
who make fun of God!
Be amazed
and disappear.
I will do something today
that you won't believe,
even if someone
tells you about it!"

⁴² As Paul and Barnabas were leaving the meeting, the people begged them to say more about these same things on the next Sabbath. ⁴³ After the service, many Jews and a lot of Gentiles who worshipped God went with them. Paul and Barnabas begged them all to remain faithful to God, who had been so kind to them.

⁴⁴ The next Sabbath almost everyone in town came to hear the message about the Lord.' ⁴⁵ When the Jewish people saw the crowds, they were very jealous. They insulted Paul and spoke against everything he said.

⁴⁶ But Paul and Barnabas bravely said:

We had to tell God's message to you before we told it to anyone else. But you rejected the message! This proves that you don't deserve eternal life. Now we are going to the Gentiles. ⁴⁷ The Lord has given us this command,

"I have placed you here
as a light
for the Gentiles.
You are to take
the saving power of God
to people everywhere on earth."

See also: **13.35:** Psa 16.10. **13.41:** Hab 1.5 (LXX).
13.47: Isa 42.6; 49.6.

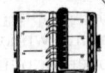

Life files

Barnabas (a.k.a. Joseph, Acts 4.36)

Background: Friend of Paul.

What's the story?

Barnabas was born in Cyprus. When he became a Christian he sold some property and gave the money to the early church (Acts 4.36). The apostles called him Barnabas, which means 'son of encouragement'.

And Barnabas was a very encouraging sort of bloke. When Paul became a Christian no-one in Jerusalem trusted him, but Barnabas spoke up for him, thus beginning a long friendship. He went to Antioch at the request of the Apostles, to look after the church there. It was Barnabas who recognised that the Antioch church really was a movement of God – and he called in Paul to help. Later Barnabas became one of Paul's most trusted travelling companions.

What's the point?

Luke describes Barnabas as 'a good man of great faith, and he was filled with the Holy Spirit'. His name indicates what he was like: a great, enthusiastic, encouraging man to have by your side. Even though he and Paul fell out at times, whenever Paul mentions Barnabas it is with affection and thankfulness.

 footsteps

A week with Barnabas

Barnabas sells a field: Acts 4.32–37
Barnabas speaks up for Saul: Acts 9.26–31
In Antioch: Acts 11.19–30
Travels with Saul: Acts 13.1–12
Worshipped then attacked: Acts 14.8–20
At Jerusalem: Acts 15.1–35
The split with Paul: Acts 15.36–41

More...

Early church p.1212
Paul p.1222
Sharing your faith p.1082
Mark p.1086

⁴⁸ This message made the Gentiles glad, and they praised what they had heard about the Lord.' Everyone who had been chosen for eternal life then put their faith in the Lord.

⁴⁹ The message about the Lord spread all over that region. ⁵⁰ But the Jewish leaders went to some of the important men in the town and to some respected women who were religious. They turned them against Paul and Barnabas and started making trouble for them. They even chased them out of that part of the country.

⁵¹ Paul and Barnabas shook the dust from that place off their feet* and went on to the city of Iconium.

⁵² But the Lord's followers in Antioch were very happy and were filled with the Holy Spirit.

CHAPTER 14

Paul and Barnabas in Iconium

¹ Paul and Barnabas spoke in the Jewish meeting place in Iconium, just as they had done at Antioch, and many Jews and Gentiles* put their faith in the Lord. ² But the Jews who did not have faith in him made the other Gentiles angry and turned them against the Lord's followers.

³ Paul and Barnabas stayed there for a while, having faith in the Lord and bravely speaking his message. The Lord gave them the power to perform miracles and wonders, and he showed that their message about his great kindness was true.

⁴ The people of Iconium did not know what to think. Some of them believed the Jewish group, and others believed the apostles. ⁵ Finally, some Gentiles and Jews, together with their leaders, decided to make trouble for Paul and Barnabas and to stone them to death.

⁶⁻⁷ But when the two apostles found out what was happening, they escaped to the region of Lycaonia. They preached the good news there in the towns of Lystra and Derbe and in the nearby countryside.

Paul and Barnabas in Lystra

⁸ In Lystra there was a man who had been born with crippled feet and had never been able to walk. ⁹ The man was listening to Paul speak, when Paul saw that he had faith in Jesus and could be healed. So he looked straight at the man ¹⁰ and shouted, "Stand up!" The man jumped up and started walking around.

¹¹ When the crowd saw what Paul had done, they yelled out in the language of Lycaonia, "The gods have turned into humans and have come down to us!" ¹² The people then gave Barnabas the name Zeus, and they gave Paul the name Hermes,* because he did the talking.

¹³ The temple of Zeus was near the entrance to the city. Its priest and the crowds wanted to offer a sacrifice to Barnabas and Paul. So the priest brought some bulls and flowers to the city gates. ¹⁴ When the two apostles found out about this, they tore their clothes in horror and ran to the crowd, shouting:

> ¹⁵ Why are you doing this? We are humans just like you. Please give up all this foolishness. Turn to the living God, who made the sky, the earth, the sea, and everything in them. ¹⁶ In times past, God let each nation go its own way. ¹⁷ But he showed that he was there by the good things he did. God sends rain from heaven and makes your crops grow. He gives food to you and makes your hearts glad.

¹⁸ Even after Paul and Barnabas had said all this, they could hardly keep the people from offering a sacrifice to them.

¹⁹ Some Jewish leaders from Antioch and Iconium came and turned the crowds against Paul. They hit him with stones and dragged him out of the city, thinking he was dead. ²⁰ But when the Lord's followers gathered around Paul, he stood up and went back into the city. The next day he and Barnabas went to Derbe.

Paul and Barnabas return to Antioch in Syria

²¹ Paul and Barnabas preached the good news in Derbe and won some people to the Lord. Then they went back to Lystra, Iconium, and Antioch in Pisidia. ²² They encouraged the followers and begged them to remain

---

*13.51 shook the dust from that place off their feet: This was a way of showing rejection.
*14.1 Gentiles: The Greek text has "Greeks", which probably means people who were not Jews. But it may mean Gentiles who worshipped with the Jews.
See also: 13.51: Matt 10.14; Mark 6.11; Luke 9.5; 10.11.

---

*14.12 Hermes: The Greeks thought of Hermes as the messenger of the other gods, especially of Zeus, their chief god.
See also: 14.15: Exod 20.11; Psa 146.6.

Paul's First Missionary Journey

Starting from **Antioch in Syria**, Paul goes to...
Cyprus, where a magician is blinded and the governor converted (Acts 13.4–12)
Perga, where John Mark leaves them, which later causes a row between Paul and Barnabas (Acts 13.13)
Pisidian Antioch, where even though Paul and Barnabas are chased out of the city, many Jews become converts (Acts 13.14–52)
Iconium, where, again, many people believe and, again, they are chased out of the city by a mob (Acts 14.1–6)
Lystra, where a man is healed, Paul and Barnabas are mistaken for gods and this time people chuck rocks at them, so they have to flee again (Acts 14.7–19)
Derbe, where some people are won for the Lord and no-one throws anything at anyone (Acts 14.21)

Paul's Second Missionary Journey

Starting from **Jerusalem**, Paul goes to...
Derbe, where he recruits Timothy (Acts 16.1–5)
Troas, where he is told to go to Macedonia by the Holy Spirit (Acts 16.6–10)
Philippi, where he converts Lydia, frees a demon-possessed slave girl and is thrown into prison. After a miraculous earthquake opens the jail, Paul converts the jailer's family and is escorted out of the city (Acts 16.11–30)
Thessalonica, where some Christians are arrested (Acts 17.1–9)
Berea, where people really think about the gospel (Acts 17.10–15)
Athens, where he goes to a pagan shrine and talks about the 'unknown god' (Acts 17.16–34)
Corinth, where he stays for two years, making tents and preaching the gospel despite opposition (Acts 18.1–17)

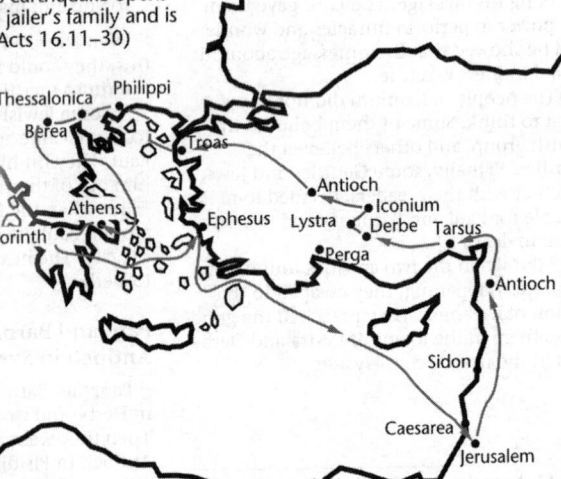

Paul's Third Missionary Journey

Starting from **Antioch**, Paul travels through Galatia, to...
Ephesus, where he advises the church and preaches about Jesus. This brings him into conflict with the silversmiths who make loads of money selling silver idols of the goddess Diana (Acts 19.1–41).

Troas, where a young man falls asleep, falls out of the window and dies. Paul prays for him, he comes back to life and Paul finishes his teaching (Acts 20.7–12)!
Back through Greece and across to **Miletus**, where he says goodbye to his friends from Ephesus (Acts 20.17–38)
Caesarea, where he receives a prophecy telling him that he will be imprisoned in Jerusalem. Paul returns to Jerusalem to be greeted by James and the Jerusalem church (Acts 21.1–16)

Paul's Journey to Rome

Starting from **Caesarea**, Paul sails to **Myra**, and then to **Cnidus**, from where they travel very slowly down to...
Fair Havens, where Paul warns against sailing. He is ignored (Acts 27.1–12).
Malta where, they are shipwrecked and Paul is bitten by a snake. When he survives the snakebite, the people of the island bring their sick to him for prayer and healing (Acts 28.1–10)
Rome, where they are met by local Christians and Paul is placed under house arrest (Acts 28.16–40)

Holy history

Gentiles

'Gentile' was a catch-all term for anyone who wasn't a Jew. They could be Greeks, Romans, Syrians, Egyptians – but if they weren't Jewish, they were gentiles.

Gentiles could become Jews and those who did were called proselytes. The Temple had a special Court of the Gentiles, where gentile worshippers of Israel's God could gather. Proselytes had to be circumcised, and undergo baptism, and make a sacrificial offering.

Some Jews of Jesus' time used the word 'gentile' as a term of abuse. After all, the Jews were the chosen people, Israel was the holy nation: to be a gentile was to be second best.

And to be fair, sometimes the Jews had a point. Many citizens of Roman and Greek cities had standards of behaviour which were scandalous and sinful and which the Jews were absolutely right to shun.

This is part of the reason why the early Church had so much discussion about gentiles. They didn't act like the Jews. They were part of a different culture. So shouldn't they have to become Jews, like the proselytes? The Jewish Christians were not against preaching the gospel to the gentiles, it's just they thought they should become more Jewish.

In the end, Paul won the day. He argued that Christ had changed the rules; that the law and outward observance had been superceded, that what mattered was faith in God, not what clothes you wore or what food you ate.

More...

Culture p.779
Paul p.1222
Circumcision p.1259
The Law p.127

faithful. They told them, "We have to suffer a lot before we can get into God's kingdom." [23] Paul and Barnabas chose some leaders for each of the churches. Then they went without eating* and prayed that the Lord would take good care of these leaders.

[24] Paul and Barnabas went on through Pisidia to Pamphylia, [25] where they preached in the town of Perga. Then they went down to Attalia [26] and sailed to Antioch in Syria. It was there that they had been placed in God's care for the work they had now completed.*

[27] After arriving in Antioch, they called the church together. They told the people what God had helped them do and how he had made it possible for the Gentiles to believe. [28] Then they stayed there with the followers for a long time.

An important decision in Jerusalem

CHAPTER 15

[1] Some people came from Judea and started teaching the Lord's followers that they could not be saved, unless they were circumcised as Moses had taught. [2] This caused trouble, and Paul and Barnabas argued with them about this teaching. So it was decided to send Paul and Barnabas and a few others to Jerusalem to discuss this problem with the apostles and the church leaders.

The church leaders meet in Jerusalem

[3] The men who were sent by the church went through Phoenicia and Samaria, telling how the Gentiles had turned to God. This news made the Lord's followers very happy. [4] When the men arrived in Jerusalem, they were welcomed by the church, including the apostles and the leaders. They told them everything God had helped them do. [5] But some Pharisees had become followers of the Lord. They stood up and said, "Gentiles who have faith in the Lord must be circumcised and told to obey the Law of Moses."

[6] The apostles and church leaders met to discuss this problem about Gentiles.

---

*14.23 went without eating: See the note at 13.2.
*14.26 the work they had now completed: See 13.1–3.
See also: 15.1: Lev 12.3.

7 They had talked it over for a long time, when Peter got up and said:

> My friends, you know that God decided long ago to let me be the one from your group to preach the good news to the Gentiles. God did this so that they would hear and obey him. 8 He knows what is in everyone's heart. And he showed that he had chosen the Gentiles, when he gave them the Holy Spirit, just as he had given his Spirit to us. 9 God treated them in the same way that he treated us. They put their faith in him, and he made their hearts pure.
>
> 10 Now why are you trying to make God angry by placing a heavy burden on these followers? This burden was too heavy for us or our ancestors. 11 But our Lord Jesus was kind to us, and we are saved by faith in him, just as the Gentiles are.

12 Everyone kept quiet and listened as Barnabas and Paul told how God had given them the power to perform a lot of miracles and wonders for the Gentiles.

13 After they had finished speaking, James* said:

> My friends, listen to me! 14 Simon Peter* has told how God first came to the Gentiles and made some of them his own people. 15 This agrees with what the prophets wrote,
>
> 16 "I, the Lord, will return
>   and rebuild
>   David's fallen house.
>   I will build it from its ruins
>   and set it up again.
> 17 Then other nations
>   will turn to me
>   and be my chosen ones.
>   I, the Lord, say this.
> 18   I promised it long ago."
>
> 19 And so, my friends, I don't think we should place burdens on the Gentiles who are turning to God. 20 We should simply write and tell them not to eat anything that has been offered to idols. They should be told not to eat the meat of any animal that has been strangled or that still has

Being christian

Fighting evil

Acts 16.11–40

We're Christian. We've moved out of the darkness and into the light.

But being Christian is not about getting saved and then doing nothing. We have to keep living in the light: we have to keep shining the light of Jesus into the dark places all around us.

When Paul and Silas were in Philippi they discovered a slave girl who was possessed. What's more, her owners were exploiting this by selling her fortune-telling services. Paul and Silas released this girl from the darkness she was in; not only from spiritual enslavement, but also from economic enslavement. They challenged all the forces that bound her. They shone the light of Jesus into her life.

We're called to do the same. We live in a world where a lot of people do a lot of evil things, a world where Satan and his forces are dedicated to opposing all that God stands for. If we're on God's side, we've got to fight. We can't just wash our hands of the battle; we have to get our armour on and get in there. Whether we're talking about spiritual darkness or economic slavery, whether we're talking about injustice or immorality, we have to join the fight.

Being Christian means fighting evil. It means fighting it with prayer, fighting it with action: confronting it and opposing it. Whatever form it takes.

Being Christian: Fighting evil

• Read the newspapers. Surf the internet. Find out what's going on in the world. Pray about it.
• Get info and prayer news from Christian organisations.
• See something that you know is wrong? Pray about it. What can you do about it?

---

*15.13 James: See the note at 12.17.
*15.14 Simon Peter: The Greek text has "Simeon", which is another form of the name "Simon". The apostle Peter is meant.

See also: 15.7: Acts 10.1–43. 15.8: Acts 10.44; Acts 2.4.
15.16–18: Amos 9.11–12 (LXX). 15.20: a Exod 34.15–17;
b Lev 18.6–23; c Lev 17.10–16.

blood in it. They must also not commit any terrible sexual sins.*

21 We must remember that the Law of Moses has been preached in city after city for many years, and every Sabbath it is read when we Jews meet.

A letter to Gentiles who had faith in the Lord

22 The apostles, the leaders, and all the church members decided to send some men to Antioch along with Paul and Barnabas. They chose Silas and Judas Barsabbas,* who were two leaders of the Lord's followers. 23 They wrote a letter that said:

We apostles and leaders send friendly greetings to all you Gentiles who are followers of the Lord in Antioch, Syria, and Cilicia.

24 We have heard that some people from here have terribly upset you by what they said. But we did not send them! 25 So we met together and decided to choose some men and to send them to you along with our good friends Barnabas and Paul. 26 These men have risked their lives for our Lord Jesus Christ. 27 We are also sending Judas and Silas, who will tell you in person the same things that we are writing.

28 The Holy Spirit has shown us that we should not place any extra burden on you. 29 But you should not eat anything offered to idols. You should not eat any meat that still has the blood in it or any meat of any animal that has been strangled. You must also not commit any terrible sexual sins. If you follow these instructions, you will do well.

We send our best wishes.

30 The four men left Jerusalem and went to Antioch. Then they called the church members together and gave them the letter. 31 When the letter was read, everyone was pleased and greatly encouraged. 32 Judas and Silas were prophets, and they spoke a long time, encouraging and helping the Lord's followers. 33 The men from Jerusalem stayed on in Antioch for a while. And when they left to

return to the ones who had sent them, the followers wished them well. 34-35 But Paul and Barnabas stayed on in Antioch, where they and many others taught and preached about the Lord.'

Paul's second journey to tell the good news

Paul and Barnabas go their separate ways

36 Some time later Paul said to Barnabas, "Let's go back and visit the Lord's followers in the cities where we preached his message. Then we will know how they are doing." 37 Barnabas wanted to take along John, whose other name was Mark. 38 But Paul did not want to, because Mark had left them in Pamphylia and had stopped working with them.

39 Paul and Barnabas argued, then each of them went his own way. Barnabas took Mark and sailed to Cyprus, 40 but Paul took Silas and left after the followers had placed them in God's care. 41 They travelled through Syria and Cilicia, encouraging the churches.

CHAPTER 16

Timothy works with Paul and Silas

1 Paul and Silas went back to Derbe and Lystra, where there was a follower named Timothy. His mother was also a follower. She was Jewish, and his father was Greek. 2 The Lord's followers in Lystra and Iconium said good things about Timothy, 3 and Paul wanted him to go with them. But Paul first had him circumcised, because all the Jewish people around there knew that Timothy's father was Greek.*

4 As Paul and the others went from city to city, they told the followers what the apostles and leaders in Jerusalem had decided, and they urged them to follow these instructions. 5 The churches became stronger in their faith, and each day more people put their faith in the Lord.

Paul's vision in Troas

6 Paul and his friends went through Phrygia and Galatia, but the Holy Spirit would not let

---

*15.20 not commit any terrible sexual sins: This probably refers to the laws about the wrong kind of marriages that are forbidden in Leviticus 18.6–18 or to some serious sexual sin.
*15.22 Judas Barsabbas: He may have been a brother of Joseph Barsabbas (see 1.23), but the name "Barsabbas" was often used by the Jewish people.

*16.3 had him circumcised . . . Timothy's father was Greek: Timothy would not have been acceptable to the Jews unless he had been circumcised, and Greeks did not circumcise their sons.
See also: 15.38: Acts 13.13.

Real life

Media

Contributed by Damaris

'The Matrix is everywhere. It is all around us... You can see it when you look out your window. Or when you turn on your television. You can feel it when you go to work. When you go to Church. When you pay your taxes. It is the world that has been pulled over your eyes to blind you from the truth.'

Today's media is similar to this description of the matrix. It is all around us, influencing what we say and do, subconsciously influencing our thoughts and actions.

There wasn't much media around in the Bible. Not as we know it, anyway. The closest biblical equivalent was probably the market place (Acts 17.16–18), where people exchanged ideas and debated their theories, like an internet chat room.

Today the media gives us a vast and valuable range of information, helping us at school, college or work. It communicates important ideas. It entertains. But it can also have a negative effect on our lives. The American Academy of Paediatrics says: 'Children and adolescents across the world are being exposed to increasing amounts of media violence, especially in television, movies, video games, and youth-oriented music. By age 18, the average young person will have viewed an estimated 200,000 acts of violence on television alone.'

So, how should Christians live in this media-rich world? Should we try to ignore it? That is not even possible. Perhaps the key is getting the balance right.

We should be people who live in the world. When Paul was in the market place in Acts 17, he didn't run and hide, he brought his message to the people by relating it to the culture of the time – the poets and philosophers.

But we should not be people of the world. In Philippians 1.27 and 4.8–9, Paul writes that we should conduct ourselves in a manner worthy of Christ.

Think

How much television do you think you watch? How much time do you spend on the internet, reading magazines, playing video games?

How much of what you see in the media is related to violence?

Act

Keep a record of the media you see/hear this week. What was it like? Why did you watch or listen to it? What did you expect it to do to/for you?

Evaluate its effect on your spiritual growth. Was it positive entertainment or did it offend God? What goes into your brain eventually comes out in the form of behaviour – and remember, the decisions you make today can have lifelong implications. Discernment isn't simple, but it's not impossible. Philippians 4.8 will help you.

Take the media really seriously – think about it. Have a look at some Christian websites that examine current secular media.

Check

Acts 17.16–18; Philippians 1.27; 4.8–9

More...

Movies p.1297
Culture p.779

them preach in Asia. [7] After they arrived in Mysia, they tried to go into Bithynia, but the Spirit of Jesus would not let them. [8] So they went on through' Mysia until they came to Troas.

[9] During the night, Paul had a vision of someone from Macedonia who was standing there and begging him, "Come over to Macedonia and help us!" [10] After Paul had seen the vision, we began looking for a way to go to Macedonia. We were sure that God had called us to preach the good news there.

Lydia becomes a follower of the Lord

[11] We sailed straight from Troas to Samothrace, and the next day we arrived in Neapolis. [12] From there we went to Philippi, which is a Roman colony in the first district of Macedonia.'

We spent several days in Philippi. [13] Then on the Sabbath we went outside the city gate to a place by the river, where we thought there would be a Jewish meeting place for prayer. We sat down and talked with the women who came. [14] One of them was Lydia, who was from the city of Thyatira and sold expensive purple cloth. She was a worshipper of the Lord God, and he made her willing to accept what Paul was saying.
[15] Then after she and her family were baptized, she kept on begging us, "If you think I really do have faith in the Lord, come and stay in my home." Finally, we accepted her invitation.

Paul and Silas are put in jail

[16] One day on our way to the place of prayer, we were met by a slave girl. She had a spirit in her that gave her the power to tell the future. By doing this she made a lot of money for her owners. [17] The girl followed Paul and the rest of us and kept yelling, "These men are servants of the Most High God! They are telling you how to be saved."

[18] This went on for several days. Finally, Paul got so upset that he turned and said to the spirit, "In the name of Jesus Christ, I order you to leave this girl alone!" At once the evil spirit left her.

[19] When the girl's owners realized that they had lost all chances for making more money, they grabbed Paul and Silas and dragged them into court. [20] They told the officials, "These Jews are upsetting our city! [21] They are telling us to do things we Romans are not allowed to do."

[22] The crowd joined in the attack on Paul and Silas. Then the officials tore the clothes off the two men and ordered them to be beaten with a whip. [23] After they had been badly beaten, they were put in jail, and the jailer was told to guard them carefully. [24] The jailer did as he was told. He put them deep inside the jail and chained their feet to heavy blocks of wood.

[25] About midnight Paul and Silas were praying and singing praises to God, while the other prisoners listened. [26] Suddenly a strong earthquake shook the jail to its foundations. The doors opened, and the chains fell from all the prisoners.

[27] When the jailer woke up and saw that the doors were open, he thought that the prisoners had escaped. He pulled out his sword and was about to kill himself. [28] But Paul shouted, "Don't harm yourself! No one has escaped."

[29] The jailer asked for a torch and went into the jail. He was shaking all over as he knelt down in front of Paul and Silas. [30] After he had led them out of the jail, he asked, "What must I do to be saved?"

[31] They replied, "Have faith in the Lord Jesus and you will be saved! This is also true for everyone who lives in your home."

[32] Then Paul and Silas told him and everyone else in his house about the Lord. [33] While it was still night, the jailer took them to a place where he could wash their cuts and bruises. Then he and everyone in his home were baptized. [34] They were very glad that they had put their faith in God. After this, the jailer took Paul and Silas to his home and gave them something to eat.

[35] The next morning the officials sent some police with orders for the jailer to let Paul and Silas go. [36] The jailer told Paul, "The officials have ordered me to set you free. Now you can leave in peace."

[37] But Paul told the police, "We are Roman citizens,* and the Roman officials had us beaten in public without giving us a trial. They threw us into jail. Now do they think they can secretly send us away? No, they cannot! They will have to come here themselves and let us out."

[38] When the police told the officials that Paul and Silas were Roman citizens, the officials were afraid. [39] So they came and apologized. They led them out of the jail and

---

*16.37 Roman citizens: Only a small number of the people living in the Roman Empire were citizens, and they had special rights and privileges.

asked them to leave town. ⁴⁰ But Paul and Silas went straight to the home of Lydia, where they saw the Lord's followers and encouraged them. Then they left.

CHAPTER 17

Trouble in Thessalonica

¹ After Paul and his friends had travelled through Amphipolis and Apollonia, they went on to Thessalonica. A Jewish meeting place was in that city. ² So as usual, Paul went there to worship, and on three Sabbaths he spoke to the people. He used the Scriptures ³ to show them that the Messiah had to suffer, but that he would rise from death. Paul also told them that Jesus is the Messiah he was preaching about. ⁴ Some of them believed what Paul had said, and they became followers with Paul and Silas. Some Gentiles* and many important women also believed the message.

⁵ The Jewish leaders were jealous and got some worthless louts who hung around the market place to start a riot in the city. They wanted to drag Paul and Silas out to the mob, and so they went straight to Jason's home. ⁶ But when they did not find them there, they dragged out Jason and some of the Lord's followers. They took them to the city authorities and shouted, "Paul and Silas have been upsetting things everywhere. Now they have come here, ⁷ and Jason has welcomed them into his home. All of them break the laws of the Roman Emperor by claiming that someone named Jesus is king."

⁸ The officials and the people were upset when they heard this. ⁹ So they made Jason and the other followers pay bail before letting them go.

People in Berea welcome the message

¹⁰ That same night the Lord's followers sent Paul and Silas on to Berea, and after they arrived, they went to the Jewish meeting place. ¹¹ The people in Berea were much nicer than those in Thessalonica, and they gladly accepted the message. Day after day they studied the Scriptures to see if these things were true. ¹² Many of them put their faith in the Lord, including some important Greek women and several men.

¹³ When the Jewish leaders in Thessalonica heard that Paul had been preaching God's message in Berea, they went there and caused trouble by turning the crowds against Paul.

¹⁴ Straight away the followers sent Paul down to the coast, but Silas and Timothy stayed in Berea. ¹⁵ Some men went with Paul as far as Athens, and then returned with instructions for Silas and Timothy to join him as soon as possible.

Paul in Athens

¹⁶ While Paul was waiting in Athens, he was upset to see all the idols in the city. ¹⁷ He went to the Jewish meeting place to speak to the Jews and to anyone who worshipped with them. Day after day he also spoke to everyone he met in the market. ¹⁸ Some of them were Epicureans* and some were Stoics,* and they started arguing with him.

People were asking, "What is this know-all trying to say?"

Some even said, "Paul must be preaching about foreign gods! That's what he means when he talks about Jesus and about people rising from death."

¹⁹ They brought Paul before a council called the Areopagus, and said, "Tell us what your new teaching is all about. ²⁰ We have heard you say some strange things, and we want to know what you mean." ²¹ More than anything else the people of Athens and the foreigners living there loved to hear and to talk about anything new. ²² So Paul stood up in front of the council and said:

People of Athens, I see that you are very religious. ²³ As I was going through your city and looking at the things you worship, I found an altar with the words, "To an Unknown God." You worship this God, but you don't really know him. So I want to tell you about him. ²⁴ This God made the world and everything in it. He is Lord of heaven and earth, and he doesn't live in temples built by human hands. ²⁵ He doesn't need help from anyone. He gives life, breath, and everything else to all people. ²⁶ From one person God made all nations who live on earth, and he decided when and where every nation would be.

²⁷ God has done all this, so that we will look for him and reach out and find him. He isn't far from any of us, ²⁸ and he gives

---

*17.18 **Epicureans:** People who followed the teaching of a man named Epicurus, who taught that happiness should be the main goal in life.
*17.18 **Stoics:** Followers of a man named Zeno, who taught that people should learn self-control and be guided by their consciences.
See also: 17.24–25: 1 King 8.27; Isa 42.5; Acts 7.48.

*17.4 **Gentiles:** See the note at 14.1.

us the power to live, to move, and to be who we are. "We are his children," just as some of your poets have said.

29 Since we are God's children, we must not think that he is like an idol made out of gold or silver or stone. He isn't like anything that humans have thought up and made. 30 In the past, God forgave all this because people did not know what they were doing. But now he says that everyone everywhere must turn to him. 31 He has set a day when he will judge the world's people with fairness. And he has chosen the man Jesus to do the judging for him. God has given proof of this to all of us by raising Jesus from death.

32 As soon as the people heard Paul say that a man had been raised from death, some of them started laughing. Others said, "We will hear you talk about this some other time." 33 When Paul left the council meeting, 34 some of the men put their faith in the Lord and went with Paul. One of them was a council member named Dionysius. A woman named Damaris and several others also put their faith in the Lord.

CHAPTER 18

Paul in Corinth

1 Paul left Athens and went to Corinth, 2 where he met Aquila, a Jewish man from Pontus. Not long before this, Aquila had come from Italy with his wife Priscilla, because Emperor Claudius had ordered the Jewish people to leave Rome.* Paul went to see Aquila and Priscilla 3 and found out that they were tent makers. Paul was a tent maker too. So he stayed with them, and they worked together.

4 Every Sabbath, Paul went to the Jewish meeting place. He spoke to Jews and Gentiles* and tried to win them over. 5 But after Silas and Timothy came from Macedonia, he spent all his time preaching to the Jews about Jesus the Messiah. 6 Finally, they turned against him and insulted him. So he shook the dust from his clothes* and told them, "Whatever happens to you will be your own fault! I am

not to blame. From now on I am going to preach to the Gentiles."

7 Paul then moved into the house of a man named Titius Justus, who worshipped God and lived next door to the Jewish meeting place. 8 Crispus was the leader of the meeting place. He and everyone in his family put their faith in the Lord. Many others in Corinth also heard the message, and all the people who had faith in the Lord were baptized.

9 One night, Paul had a vision, and in it the Lord said, "Don't be afraid to keep on preaching. Don't stop! 10 I am with you, and you won't be harmed. Many people in this city belong to me." 11 Paul stayed on in Corinth for a year and a half, teaching God's message to the people.

12 While Gallio was governor of Achaia, some of the Jewish leaders got together and grabbed Paul. They brought him into court 13 and said, "This man is trying to make our people worship God in a way that is against our Law!"

14 Even before Paul could speak, Gallio said, "If you were charging this man with a crime or some other wrong, I would have to listen to you. 15 But since this concerns only words, names, and your own law, you will have to take care of it. I refuse to judge such matters." 16 Then he sent them out of the court. 17 The crowd grabbed Sosthenes, the Jewish leader, and beat him up in front of the court. But none of this mattered to Gallio.

Paul returns to Antioch in Syria

18 After Paul had stayed for a while with the Lord's followers in Corinth, he said goodbye to them and sailed on to Syria with Aquila and Priscilla. But before he left, he had his head shaved* at Cenchreae because he had made a promise to God.

19 The three of them arrived in Ephesus, where Paul left Priscilla and Aquila. He then went into the Jewish meeting place to talk with the people there. 20 They asked him to stay longer, but he refused. 21 He said goodbye to them and told them, "If God lets me, I will come back."

---

*18.2 Emperor Claudius had ordered the Jewish people to leave Rome: Probably AD 49, though it may have been AD 41.
*18.4 Gentiles: Here the word is "Greeks". But see the note at 14.1.
*18.6 shook the dust from his clothes: This means the same as shaking dust from the feet. See the note at 13.51.

*18.18 he had his head shaved: Paul had promised to be a "Nazirite" for a while. This meant that for the time of the promise, he could not cut his hair or drink wine. When the time was over, he would have to cut his hair and offer a sacrifice to God.
See also: 18.18: Num 6.18.

Paul's third journey to tell the good news

22 Paul sailed to Caesarea, where he greeted the church. Then he went on to Antioch. 23 After staying there for a while, he left and visited several places in Galatia and Phrygia. He helped the followers there to become stronger in their faith.

Apollos in Ephesus

24 A Jewish man named Apollos came to Ephesus. Apollos had been born in the city of Alexandria. He was a very good speaker and knew a lot about the Scriptures. 25 He also knew much about the Lord's Way,* and he spoke about it with great excitement. What he taught about Jesus was right, but all he knew was John's message about baptism.

26 Apollos started speaking bravely in the Jewish meeting place. But when Priscilla and Aquila heard him, they took him to their home and helped him understand God's Way even better.

27 Apollos decided to travel through Achaia. So the Lord's followers wrote letters, encouraging the followers there to welcome him. After Apollos arrived in Achaia, he was a great help to everyone who had put their faith in the Lord Jesus because of God's kindness. 28 He got into fierce arguments with the Jewish people, and in public he used the Scriptures to prove that Jesus is the Messiah.

CHAPTER 19
Paul in Ephesus

1 While Apollos was in Corinth, Paul travelled across the hill country to Ephesus, where he met some of the Lord's followers. 2 He asked them, "When you put your faith in Jesus, were you given the Holy Spirit?"

"No!" they answered. "We have never even heard of the Holy Spirit."

3 "Then why were you baptized?" Paul asked.

They answered, "Because of what John taught."

4 Paul replied, "John baptized people so that they would turn to God. But he also told them that someone else was coming,

and that they should put their faith in him. Jesus is the one that John was talking about." 5 After the people heard Paul say this, they were baptized in the name of the Lord Jesus. 6 Then Paul placed his hands on them. The Holy Spirit was given to them, and they spoke unknown languages and prophesied. 7 There were about twelve men in this group.

8 For three months Paul went to the Jewish meeting place and talked bravely with the people about God's kingdom. He tried to win them over, 9 but some of them were stubborn and refused to believe. In front of everyone they said terrible things about God's Way. Paul left and took the followers with him to the lecture hall of Tyrannus. He spoke there every day 10 for two years, until every Jew and Gentile* in Asia had heard the Lord's message.

The sons of Sceva

11 God gave Paul the power to perform great miracles. 12 People even took handkerchiefs and aprons that had touched Paul's body, and they carried them to everyone who was sick. All the sick people were healed, and the evil spirits went out.

13 Some Jewish men started going around trying to force out evil spirits by using the name of the Lord Jesus. They said to the spirits, "Come out in the name of that same Jesus that Paul preaches about!"

14 Seven sons of a Jewish high priest named Sceva were doing this, 15 when an evil spirit said to them, "I know Jesus! And I have heard about Paul. But who are you?" 16 Then the man with the evil spirit jumped on them and beat them up. They ran out of the house, naked and bruised.

17 When the Jews and Gentiles* in Ephesus heard about this, they were so frightened that they praised the name of the Lord Jesus. 18 Many who were followers now started telling everyone about the evil things they had been doing. 19 Some who had been practising witchcraft even brought their books and burnt them in public. These books were worth about fifty thousand silver coins. 20 So the Lord's message spread and became even more powerful.

*18.25 the Lord's Way: See the note at 9.2.
See also: 19.4: Matt 3.11; Mark 1.4,7–8; Luke 3.4,16; John 1.26–27.

*19.10,17 Gentile(s): The text has "Greek(s)" (see the note at 14.1).

The riot in Ephesus

²¹ After all this had happened, Paul decided to visit Macedonia and Achaia on his way to Jerusalem. Paul had said, "From there I will go on to Rome." ²² So he sent his two helpers, Timothy and Erastus, to Macedonia. But he stayed on in Asia for a while.

²³ At that time there was serious trouble because of the Lord's Way.* ²⁴ A silversmith named Demetrius had a business that made silver models of the temple of the goddess Artemis. Those who worked for him earned a lot of money. ²⁵ Demetrius brought together everyone who was in the same business and said:

Friends, you know that we make a good living at this. ²⁶ But you have seen and heard how this man Paul is upsetting a lot of people, not only in Ephesus, but almost everywhere in Asia. He claims that the gods we humans make are not really gods at all. ²⁷ Everyone will start saying terrible things about our business. They will stop respecting the temple of the goddess Artemis, who is worshipped in Asia and all over the world. Our great goddess will be forgotten!

²⁸ When the workers heard this, they got angry and started shouting, "Great is Artemis, the goddess of the Ephesians!" ²⁹ Soon the whole city was in a riot, and some men grabbed Gaius and Aristarchus, who had come from Macedonia with Paul. Then everyone in the crowd rushed to the place where the town meetings were held. ³⁰ Paul wanted to go out and speak to the people, but the Lord's followers would not let him. ³¹ A few of the local officials were friendly to Paul, and they sent someone to warn him not to go.

³² Some of the people in the meeting were shouting one thing, and others were shouting something else. Everyone was completely confused, and most of them did not even know why they were there.

³³ Several of the Jewish leaders pushed a man named Alexander to the front of the crowd and started telling him what to say. He motioned with his hand and tried to explain what was going on. ³⁴ But when the crowd saw that he was Jewish, they all shouted for two hours, "Great is Artemis, the goddess of the Ephesians!"

³⁵ Finally, a town official made the crowd be quiet. Then he said:

People of Ephesus, who in the world doesn't know that our city is the centre for worshipping the great goddess Artemis? Who doesn't know that her image which fell from heaven is here? ³⁶ No one can deny this, and so you should calm down and not do anything foolish. ³⁷ You have brought men in here who have not robbed temples or spoken against our goddess.

³⁸ If Demetrius and his workers have a case against these men, we have courts and judges. Let them take their complaints there. ³⁹ But if you want to do more than that, the matter will have to be brought before the city council. ⁴⁰ We could easily be accused of starting a riot today. There is no excuse for it! We cannot even give a reason for this uproar.

⁴¹ After saying this, he told the people to leave.

CHAPTER 20

Paul goes through Macedonia and Greece

¹ When the riot was over, Paul sent for the followers and encouraged them. He then said goodbye to them and left for Macedonia. ² As he travelled from place to place, he encouraged the followers with many messages. Finally, he went to Greece* ³ and stayed there for three months.

Paul was about to sail to Syria. But some of the Jewish leaders plotted against him, so he decided to return by way of Macedonia. ⁴ With him were Sopater, son of Pyrrhus from Berea, and Aristarchus and Secundus from Thessalonica. Gaius from Derbe was also with him, and so were Timothy and the two Asians, Tychicus and Trophimus. ⁵ They went on ahead to Troas and waited for us there. ⁶ After the Festival of Thin Bread, we sailed from Philippi. Five days later we met them in Troas and stayed there for a week.

Paul's last visit to Troas

⁷ On the first day of the week* we met to break bread together.* Paul spoke to the people until midnight because he was leaving

---

*20.2 Greece: Probably Corinth.
*20.7 On the first day of the week: Since the Jewish day began at sunset, the meeting would have begun in the evening.
*20.7 break bread together: See the note at 2.46.

---

*19.23 the Lord's Way: See the note at 9.2.

the next morning. [8] In the upstairs room where we were meeting, there were a lot of lamps. [9] A young man called Eutychus was sitting on a window sill. While Paul was speaking, the young man got very sleepy. Finally, he went to sleep and fell three floors all the way down to the ground. When they picked him up, he was dead.

[10] Paul went down and bent over Eutychus. He took him in his arms and said, "Don't worry! He's alive." [11] After Paul had gone back upstairs, he broke bread, and ate with us. He then spoke until dawn and left. [12] Then the followers took the young man home alive and were very happy.

The voyage from Troas to Miletus

[13] Paul decided to travel by land to Assos. The rest of us went on ahead by ship, and we were to take him aboard there. [14] When he met us in Assos, he came aboard, and we sailed on to Mitylene. [15] The next day we came to a place near Chios, and the following day we reached Samos. The day after that we sailed to Miletus. [16] Paul had decided to sail on past Ephesus, because he did not want to spend too much time in Asia. He was in a hurry and wanted to be in Jerusalem in time for Pentecost.*

Paul says goodbye to the church leaders of Ephesus

[17] From Miletus, Paul sent a message for the church leaders at Ephesus to come and meet with him. [18] When they got there, he said:

You know everything I did during the time I was with you when I first came to Asia. [19] Some of the Jews plotted against me and caused me a lot of sorrow and trouble. But I served the Lord and was humble. [20] When I preached in public or taught in your homes, I didn't hold back from telling anything that would help you. [21] I told Jews and Gentiles to turn to God and have faith in our Lord Jesus.

[22] I don't know what will happen to me in Jerusalem, but I must obey God's Spirit and go there. [23] In every city I visit, I am told by the Holy Spirit that I will be put in jail and will be in trouble in Jerusalem. [24] But I don't care what happens to me, as

long as I finish the work that the Lord Jesus gave me to do. And that work is to tell the good news about God's great kindness.

[25] I have gone from place to place, preaching to you about God's kingdom, but now I know that none of you will ever see me again. [26] I tell you today that I am no longer responsible for any of you! [27] I have told you everything God wants you to know. [28] Look after yourselves and everyone the Holy Spirit has placed in your care. Be like shepherds to God's church. It is the flock that he bought with the blood of his own Son.'

[29] I know that after I am gone, others will come like fierce wolves to attack you. [30] Some of your own people will tell lies to win over the Lord's followers. [31] Be on your guard! Remember how day and night for three years I kept warning you with tears in my eyes.

[32] I now place you in God's care. Remember the message about his great kindness! This message can help you and give you what belongs to you as God's people. [33] I have never wanted anyone's money or clothes. [34] You know how I have worked with my own hands to make a living for myself and my friends. [35] By everything I did, I showed how you should work to help everyone who is weak. Remember that our Lord Jesus said, "More blessings come from giving than from receiving."

[36] After Paul had finished speaking, he knelt down with all of them and prayed. [37] Everyone cried and hugged and kissed him. [38] They were especially sad because Paul had told them, "You will never see me again." Then they went with him to the ship.

CHAPTER 21

Paul goes to Jerusalem

[1] After saying goodbye, we sailed straight to Cos. The next day we reached Rhodes and from there sailed on to Patara. [2] We found a ship going to Phoenicia, so we got on board and sailed off.

[3] We came within sight of Cyprus and then sailed south of it on to the port of Tyre in Syria, where the ship was going to unload its cargo. [4] We found the Lord's followers and stayed with them for a week. The Holy Spirit had told them to warn Paul not to go on to Jerusalem. [5] But when the week was over, we started on our way again. All the men,

---

*20.16 in time for Pentecost: The Jewish people liked to be in Jerusalem for this festival. See the note at 2.1.

See also: 20.24: 2 Tim 4.7.

together with their wives and children, walked with us from the town to the seashore. We knelt on the beach and prayed. 6 Then after saying goodbye to each other, we got into the ship, and they went back home.

7 We sailed from Tyre to Ptolemais, where we greeted the followers and stayed with them for a day. 8 The next day we went to Caesarea and stayed with Philip, the preacher. He was one of the seven men who helped the apostles, 9 and he had four unmarried᾽ daughters who prophesied.

10 We had been in Caesarea for several days, when the prophet Agabus came to us from Judea. 11 He took Paul's belt, and with it he tied up his own hands and feet. Then he told us, "The Holy Spirit says that some of the Jewish leaders in Jerusalem will tie up the man who owns this belt. They will also hand him over to the Gentiles." 12 After Agabus said this, we and the followers living there begged Paul not to go to Jerusalem.

13 But Paul answered, "Why are you crying and breaking my heart? I am not only willing to be put in jail for the Lord Jesus. I am even willing to die for him in Jerusalem!"

14 Since we could not get Paul to change his mind, we gave up and prayed, "Lord, please make us willing to do what you want."

15 Then we got ready to go to Jerusalem. 16 Some of the followers from Caesarea went with us and took us to stay in the home of Mnason. He was from Cyprus and had been a follower from the beginning.

Paul's arrest in Jerusalem

Paul visits James

17 When we arrived in Jerusalem, the Lord's followers gladly welcomed us. 18 Paul went with us to see James* the next day, and all the church leaders were present. 19 Paul greeted them and told how God had used him to help the Gentiles. 20 Everyone who heard this praised God and said to Paul:

My friend, you can see how many tens of thousands of the Jewish people have become followers! And all of them are eager to obey the Law of Moses. 21 But they have been told that you are teaching those who live among the Gentiles to disobey this Law. They claim that you are telling them not to circumcise their sons or to follow Jewish customs.

22 What should we do now that our people have heard that you are here? 23 Please do what we ask, because four of our men have made special promises to God. 24 Join with them and prepare yourself for the ceremony that goes with the promises. Pay the cost for their heads to be shaved. Then everyone will learn that the reports about you are not true. They will know that you do obey the Law of Moses.

25 Some while ago we told the Gentile followers what we think they should do. We instructed them not to eat anything offered to idols. They were told not to eat any meat with blood still in it or the meat of an animal that has been strangled. They were also told not to commit any terrible sexual sins.*

26 The next day Paul took the four men with him and got himself ready at the same time they did. Then he went into the temple and told when the final ceremony would take place and when an offering would be made for each of them.

Paul is arrested

27 When the period of seven days for the ceremony was almost over, some of the Jewish people from Asia saw Paul in the temple. They got a large crowd together and started attacking him. 28 They were shouting, "Friends, help us! This man goes around everywhere, saying bad things about our nation and about the Law of Moses and about this temple. He has even brought shame to this holy temple by bringing in Gentiles." 29 Some of them thought that Paul had brought Trophimus from Ephesus into the temple, because they had seen them together in the city.

30 The whole city was in an uproar, and the people turned into a mob. They grabbed Paul and dragged him out of the temple. Then suddenly the doors were shut. 31 The people were about to kill Paul when the Roman army commander heard that all Jerusalem was starting to riot. 32 So he quickly took some soldiers and officers and ran to where the crowd had gathered.

As soon as the mob saw the commander and soldiers, they stopped beating Paul.

---

*21.18 James: See the note at 12.17.
See also: 21.8: Acts 6.5; 8.5. 21.10: Acts 11.28.

*21.25 not to commit any terrible sexual sins: See the note at 15.20.
See also: 21.23–24: Num 6.13–21. 21.25: Acts 15.29. 21.29: Acts 20.4.

³³ The army commander went over and arrested him and had him bound with two chains. Then he tried to find out who Paul was and what he had done. ³⁴ Part of the crowd shouted one thing, and part of them shouted something else. But they were making so much noise that the commander could not find out a thing. Then he ordered Paul to be taken into the fortress. ³⁵ As they reached the steps, the crowd became so wild that the soldiers had to lift Paul up and carry him. ³⁶ The crowd followed and kept shouting, "Kill him! Kill him!"

Paul speaks to the crowd

³⁷ When Paul was about to be taken into the fortress, he asked the commander, "Can I say something to you?"

"How do you know Greek?" the commander asked. ³⁸ "Aren't you that Egyptian who started a riot not long ago and led four thousand terrorists into the desert?"

³⁹ "No!" Paul replied. "I am a Jew from Tarsus, an important city in Cilicia. Please let me speak to the crowd."

⁴⁰ The commander told him he could speak, so Paul stood on the steps and motioned to the people. When they were quiet, he spoke to them in Aramaic:

CHAPTER 22

¹ "My friends and leaders of our nation, listen as I explain what happened!" ² When the crowd heard Paul speak to them in Aramaic, they became even quieter. Then Paul said:

³ I am a Jew, born and raised in the city of Tarsus in Cilicia. I was a student of Gamaliel and was taught to follow every single law of our ancestors. In fact, I was just as eager to obey God as any of you are today.

⁴ I made trouble for everyone who followed the Lord's Way,* and I even had some of them killed. I had others arrested and put in jail. I didn't care if they were men or women. ⁵ The high priest and all the council members can tell you that this is true. They even gave me letters to the Jewish leaders in Damascus, so that I could arrest people there and bring them to Jerusalem to be punished.

⁶ One day about midday I was getting close to Damascus, when a bright light

from heaven suddenly flashed around me. ⁷ I fell to the ground and heard a voice asking me, "Saul, Saul, why are you so cruel to me?"

⁸ "Who are you?" I answered.

The Lord replied, "I am Jesus from Nazareth! I am the one you are so cruel to." ⁹ The men who were travelling with me saw the light, but did not hear the voice.

¹⁰ I asked, "Lord, what do you want me to do?"

Then he told me, "Get up and go to Damascus. When you get there, you will be told what to do." ¹¹ The light had been so bright that I couldn't see. And the other men had to lead me by the hand to Damascus.

¹² In that city there was a man named Ananias, who faithfully obeyed the Law of Moses and was well liked by all the Jewish people living there. ¹³ He came to me and said, "Saul, my friend, you can now see again!"

At once I could see. ¹⁴ Then Ananias told me, "The God that our ancestors worshipped has chosen you to know what he wants done. He has chosen you to see the One Who Obeys God* and to hear his voice. ¹⁵ You must tell everyone what you have seen and heard. ¹⁶ What are you waiting for? Get up! Be baptized, and wash away your sins by praying to the Lord."

¹⁷ After this I returned to Jerusalem and went to the temple to pray. There I had a vision ¹⁸ of the Lord who said to me, "Hurry and leave Jerusalem! The people won't listen to what you say about me."

¹⁹ I replied, "Lord, they know that in many of our meeting places I arrested and beat people who had faith in you. ²⁰ Stephen was killed because he spoke for you, and I stood there and cheered them on. I even guarded the clothes of the men who murdered him."

²¹ But the Lord told me to go, and he promised to send me far away to the Gentiles.

²² The crowd listened until Paul said this. Then they started shouting, "Get rid of this man! He doesn't deserve to live." ²³ They kept shouting. They waved their clothes around and threw dust into the air.

---

*22.4 followed the Lord's Way: See the note at 9.2.
See also: 22.3: Acts 5.34-39. 22.4-5: Acts 8.3; 26.9-11.

*22.14 One Who Obeys God: See the note at 7.52.
See also: 22.20: Acts 7.58.

Paul and the Roman army commander

24 The Roman commander ordered Paul to be taken into the fortress and beaten with a whip. He did this to find out why the people were screaming at Paul.

25 While the soldiers were tying Paul up to be beaten, he asked the officer standing there, "Is it legal to beat a Roman citizen before he has been tried in court?"

26 When the officer heard this, he went to the commander and said, "What are you doing? This man is a Roman citizen!"

27 The commander went to Paul and asked, "Tell me, are you a Roman citizen?"

"Yes," Paul answered.

28 The commander then said, "I paid a lot of money to become a Roman citizen."*

But Paul replied, "I was born a Roman citizen."

29 The men who were about to beat and question Paul quickly backed off. And the commander himself was frightened when he realized that he had put a Roman citizen in chains.

Paul is tried by the council

30 The next day the commander wanted to know the real reason why the Jewish leaders had brought charges against Paul. So he had Paul's chains removed, and he ordered the chief priests and the whole council to meet. Then he had Paul led in and made him stand in front of them.

CHAPTER 23

1 Paul looked straight at the council members and said, "My friends, to this day I have served God with a clear conscience!"

2 Then Ananias the high priest ordered the men standing beside Paul to hit him on the mouth. 3 Paul turned to the high priest and said, "You whitewashed wall!* God will hit you. You sit there to judge me by the Law of Moses. But at the same time you order men to break the Law by hitting me."

4 The men standing beside Paul asked, "Don't you know you are insulting God's high priest?"

5 Paul replied, "Oh! I didn't know he was the high priest. The Scriptures do tell us not to speak evil about a leader of our people."

6 When Paul saw that some of the council members were Sadducees and others were Pharisees, he shouted, "My friends, I am a Pharisee and the son of a Pharisee. I am on trial simply because I believe that the dead will be raised to life."

7 As soon as Paul said this, the Pharisees and the Sadducees got into a big argument, and the council members started taking sides. 8 The Sadducees do not believe in angels or spirits or that the dead will rise to life. But the Pharisees believe in all these, 9 and so there was a lot of shouting. Some of the teachers of the Law of Moses were Pharisees. Finally, they became angry and said, "We don't find anything wrong with this man. Perhaps a spirit or an angel really did speak to him."

10 The argument became fierce, and the commander was afraid that Paul would be pulled apart. So he ordered the soldiers to go in and rescue Paul. Then they took him back into the fortress.

11 That night the Lord stood beside Paul and said, "Don't worry! Just as you have told others about me in Jerusalem, you must also tell about me in Rome."

A plot to kill Paul

12-13 The next morning more than forty Jewish men got together and vowed that they would not eat or drink anything until they had killed Paul. 14 Then some of them went to the chief priests and the nation's leaders and said, "We have promised God that we would not eat a thing until we have killed Paul. 15 You and everyone in the council must go to the commander and pretend that you want to find out more about the charges against Paul. Ask for him to be brought before your court. Meanwhile, we will be waiting to kill him before he gets there."

16 When Paul's nephew heard about the plot, he went to the fortress and told Paul about it. 17 So Paul said to one of the army officers, "Take this young man to the commander. He has something to tell him."

18 The officer took him to the commander and said, "The prisoner named Paul asked me to bring this young man to you, because he has something to tell you."

---

*22.28 Roman citizen: See the note at 16.37.
*23.3 whitewashed wall: Someone who pretends to be good, but really isn't.
See also: 23.3: Matt 23.27-28. 23.5: Exod 22.28.

See also: 23.6: Acts 26.5; Phil 3.5. 23.8: Matt 22.23; Mark 12.18; Luke 20.27.

¹⁹ The commander took the young man aside and asked him in private, "What do you want to tell me?"

²⁰ He answered, "Some men are planning to ask you to bring Paul down to the Jewish council tomorrow. They will claim that they want to find out more about him. ²¹ But please don't do what they say. More than forty men are going to attack Paul. They have made a vow not to eat or drink anything until they have killed him. Even now they are waiting to hear what you decide."

²² The commander sent the young man away after saying to him, "Don't let anyone know that you told me this."

Paul is taken to Caesarea

Paul is sent to Felix the governor

²³ The commander called in two of his officers and told them, "By nine o'clock tonight have two hundred soldiers ready to go to Caesarea. Take along seventy men on horseback and two hundred foot soldiers with spears. ²⁴ Get a horse ready for Paul and make sure that he gets safely through to Felix the governor."

²⁵ The commander wrote a letter that said:

²⁶ Greetings from Claudius Lysias to the Honourable Governor Felix:

²⁷ Some Jews grabbed this man and were about to kill him. But when I found out that he was a Roman citizen, I took some soldiers and rescued him.

²⁸ I wanted to find out what they had against him. So I brought him before their council ²⁹ and learnt that the charges concern only their religious laws. This man isn't guilty of anything for which he should die or even be put in jail.

³⁰ As soon as I learnt that there was a plot against him, I sent him to you and told their leaders to bring charges against him in your court.

³¹ The soldiers obeyed the commander's orders, and that same night they took Paul to the city of Antipatris. ³² The next day the foot soldiers returned to the fortress and let the soldiers on horseback take him the rest of the way. ³³ When they came to Caesarea, they gave the letter to the governor and handed Paul over to him.

³⁴ The governor read the letter. Then he asked Paul and found out that he was from Cilicia. ³⁵ The governor said, "I will listen to your case as soon as the people come to bring their charges against you." After saying this, he gave orders for Paul to be kept as a prisoner in Herod's palace.*

CHAPTER 24

Paul is accused in the court of Felix

¹ Five days later Ananias the high priest, together with some of their leaders and a lawyer named Tertullus, went to the governor to present their case against Paul. ² So Paul was called in, and Tertullus stated the case against him:⸰

Honourable Felix, you have brought our people a long period of peace, and because of your concern our nation is much better off. ³ All of us are always grateful for what you have done. ⁴ I don't want to bother you, but please be patient with us and listen to me for just a few minutes.

⁵ This man has been found to be a real pest and troublemaker for Jews all over the world. He is also a leader of a group called Nazarenes. ⁶⁻⁸ When he tried to disgrace the temple, we arrested him.⸰ If you question him, you will find out for yourself that our charges are true.

⁹ The Jewish crowd spoke up and agreed with what Tertullus had said.

Paul defends himself

¹⁰ The governor motioned for Paul to speak, and he began:

I know that you have judged the people of our nation for many years, and I am glad to defend myself in your court. ¹¹ It was no more than twelve days ago that I went to worship in Jerusalem. You can find this out easily enough. ¹² Never once did the Jews find me arguing with anyone in the temple. I didn't cause trouble in the Jewish meeting places or in the city itself. ¹³ There is no way that they can prove these charges that they are now bringing against me.

¹⁴ I admit that their leaders think that the Lord's Way* which I follow is based on wrong beliefs. But I still worship the same God that my ancestors worshipped. And I believe everything written in the Law of

---

*23.35 Herod's palace: The palace built by Herod the Great and used by the Roman governors of Palestine.
*24.14 the Lord's Way: See the note at 9.2.

Moses and in the Prophets.* ¹⁵ I am just as sure as these people are that God will raise from death everyone who is good or evil. ¹⁶ And because I am sure, I try my best to have a clear conscience in whatever I do for God or for people.

¹⁷ After being away for several years, I returned here to bring gifts for the poor people of my nation and to offer sacrifices. ¹⁸ This is what I was doing when I was found going through a ceremony in the temple. I wasn't with a crowd, and there was no uproar.

¹⁹ Some Jews from Asia were there at that time, and if they have anything to say against me, they should be here now. ²⁰ Or ask the ones who are here. They can tell you that they didn't find me guilty of anything when I was tried by their own council. ²¹ The only charge they can bring against me is what I shouted out in court, when I said, "I am on trial today because I believe that the dead will be raised to life!"

²² Felix knew a lot about the Lord's Way.* But he brought the trial to an end and said, "I will make my decision after Lysias the commander arrives." ²³ He then ordered the army officer to keep Paul under guard, but not to lock him up or to stop his friends from helping him.

Paul is kept under guard

²⁴ Several days later Felix and his wife Drusilla, who was Jewish, went to the place where Paul was kept under guard. They sent for Paul and listened while he spoke to them about having faith in Christ Jesus. ²⁵ But Felix was frightened when Paul started talking to them about doing right, about self-control, and about the coming judgment. So he said to Paul, "That's enough for now. You may go. But when I have time I will send for you." ²⁶ After this, Felix often sent for Paul and talked with him, because he hoped that Paul would offer him a bribe.

²⁷ Two years later Porcius Festus became governor in place of Felix. But since Felix wanted to do the Jewish leaders a favour, he kept Paul in jail.

---

*24.14 Law of Moses . . . the Prophets: See the note at 13.15.
*24.22 the Lord's Way: See the note at 9.2.
See also: 24.17–18: Acts 21.17–28. 24.21: Acts 23.6.

CHAPTER 25

Paul asks to be tried by the Roman Emperor

¹ Three days after Festus had become governor, he went from Caesarea to Jerusalem. ² There the chief priests and some Jewish leaders told him about their charges against Paul. They also asked Festus ³ if he would be willing to bring Paul to Jerusalem. They begged him to do this because they were planning to attack and kill Paul on the way. ⁴ But Festus told them, "Paul will be kept in Caesarea, and I am soon going there myself. ⁵ If he has done anything wrong, let your leaders go with me and bring charges against him there."

⁶ Festus stayed in Jerusalem for eight or ten more days before going to Caesarea. Then the next day he took his place as judge and had Paul brought into court. ⁷ As soon as Paul came in, the Jewish leaders from Jerusalem crowded around him and said he was guilty of many serious crimes. But they could not prove anything. ⁸ Then Paul spoke in his own defence, "I have not broken the Law of my people. And I have not done anything against either the temple or the Emperor."

⁹ Festus wanted to please the leaders. So he asked Paul, "Are you willing to go to Jerusalem and be tried by me on these charges?"

¹⁰ Paul replied, "I am on trial in the Emperor's court, and that's where I should be tried. You know very well that I have not done anything to harm the Jewish nation. ¹¹ If I had done something deserving death, I would not ask to escape the death penalty. But I am not guilty of any of these crimes, and no one has the right to hand me over to these people. I now ask to be tried by the Emperor himself."

¹² After Festus had talked this over with members of his council, he told Paul, "You have asked to be tried by the Emperor, and to the Emperor you will go!"

Paul speaks to Agrippa and Bernice

¹³ A few days later King Agrippa and Bernice came to Caesarea to visit Festus. ¹⁴ They had been there for several days, when Festus told the king about the charges against Paul. He said:

Felix left a man here in jail, ¹⁵ and when I went to Jerusalem, the chief priests and the Jewish leaders came and asked me to find him guilty. ¹⁶ I told them that it isn't the Roman custom to hand a man over to people who are bringing charges against him. He must first have the chance to meet them face to face and to defend himself against their charges.

¹⁷ So when they came here with me, I wasted no time. On the very next day I took my place on the judge's bench and ordered him to be brought in. ¹⁸ But when the men stood up to make their charges against him, they did not accuse him of any of the crimes that I thought they would. ¹⁹ Instead, they argued with him about some of their beliefs and about a dead man named Jesus, who Paul said was alive.

²⁰ Since I did not know how to find out the truth about all this, I asked Paul if he would be willing to go to Jerusalem and be put on trial there. ²¹ But Paul asked to be kept in jail until the Emperor could decide his case. So I ordered him to be kept here until I could send him to the Emperor.

²² Then Agrippa said to Festus, "I would also like to hear what this man has to say."

Festus answered, "You can hear him tomorrow."

²³ The next day Agrippa and Bernice made a big show as they came into the meeting room. High ranking army officers and leading citizens of the town were also there. Festus then ordered Paul to be brought in ²⁴ and said:

King Agrippa and other guests, look at this man! Every Jew from Jerusalem and Caesarea has come to me, demanding for him to be put to death. ²⁵ I have not found him guilty of any crime deserving death. But because he has asked to be judged by the Emperor, I have decided to send him to Rome.

²⁶ I have to write some facts about this man to the Emperor. So I have brought him before all of you, but especially before you, King Agrippa. After we have talked about his case, I will then have something to write. ²⁷ It makes no sense to send a prisoner to the Emperor without stating the charges against him.

Real life

Civil disobedience

'Remind your people to obey the rulers and authorities and not to be rebellious,' Paul wrote (Titus 3.1). So why was he in jail?

Paul believed there were limits. Faced with unjust laws he made a real nuisance of himself. Jesus himself went into the temple and threw out all the rip-off traders. Christians refused to worship Caesar.

More recently, Christians helped with the 'Underground Railroad' – an escape route which saved the lives of thousands of American slaves. In World War 2, Christians organised shelter and escape for Jews threatened by the Nazis, including forging documents. Christians have fought apartheid, discrimination and war.

It's OK to fight evil. But check your motives. It's one thing to leave school to protest against war; it's another thing to join a protest because you fancy a day off. We fight for the rights of others; not for the benefit of ourselves.

So, use every lawful means first – write to your MP, vote in elections. And think about how you protest – marching, or chaining yourself to trees is one thing, acts of violence or spiteful hatred are another.

Think

Should Christians ever break the law?
What would you protest against?
If you have been involved in protest, were your motives pure?

Act

Start legitimate. Talk to your MP. Use your vote. Join an organisation.
Avoid hatred. You are protesting against sin, not hating sinners.

Check

A load of Biblical law-breakers!
Exodus 1.15—2.4; 1 Kings 18.3–4;
Daniel 3.16–18; John 2.13–22; Acts 5.29–42

More...

Politics p.1358
Persecution p.1215
Human rights p.707

CHAPTER 26

Paul's defence before Agrippa

¹ Agrippa told Paul, "You may now speak for yourself."

Paul stretched out his hand and said:

² King Agrippa, I am glad for this chance to defend myself before you today on all these charges that my own people have brought against me. ³ You know a lot about our religious customs and the beliefs that divide us. So I ask you to listen patiently to me.

⁴⁻⁵ All the Jews have known me since I was a child. They know what kind of life I have lived in my own country and in Jerusalem. And if they were willing, they could tell you that I was a Pharisee, a member of a group that is stricter than any other. ⁶ Now I am on trial because I believe the promise God made to our people long ago.

⁷ Day and night our twelve tribes have earnestly served God, waiting for his promised blessings. King Agrippa, because of this hope, the Jewish leaders have brought charges against me. ⁸ Why should any of you doubt that God raises the dead to life?

⁹ I once thought that I should do everything I could to oppose Jesus from Nazareth. ¹⁰ I did this first in Jerusalem, and with the authority of the chief priests I put many of God's people in jail. I even voted for them to be killed. ¹¹ I often had them punished in our meeting places, and I tried to make them give up their faith. In fact, I was so angry with them, that I went looking for them in foreign cities.

¹² King Agrippa, one day I was on my way to Damascus with the authority and permission of the chief priests. ¹³ About midday I saw a light brighter than the sun. It flashed from heaven on me and on everyone travelling with me. ¹⁴ We all fell to the ground. Then I heard a voice say to me in Aramaic, "Saul, Saul, why are you so cruel to me? It's foolish to fight against me!"

¹⁵ "Who are you?" I asked.

Then the Lord answered, "I am Jesus! I am the one you are so cruel to. ¹⁶ Now stand up. I have appeared to you, because I have chosen you to be my servant. You are to tell others what you have learnt about me and what I will show you later."

¹⁷ The Lord also said, "I will protect you from the Jews and from the Gentiles that I am sending you to. ¹⁸ I want you to open their eyes, so that they will turn from darkness to light and from the power of Satan to God. Then their sins will be forgiven, and by faith in me they will become part of God's holy people."

¹⁹ King Agrippa, I obeyed this vision from heaven. ²⁰ First I preached to the people in Damascus, and then I went to Jerusalem and all over Judea. Finally, I went to the Gentiles and said, "Stop sinning and turn to God! Then prove what you have done by the way you live."

²¹ That is why some men grabbed me in the temple and tried to kill me. ²² But all this time God has helped me, and I have preached both to the rich and to the poor. I have told them only what the prophets and Moses said would happen. ²³ I told them how the Messiah would suffer and be the first to be raised from death, so that he could bring light to his own people and to the Gentiles.

²⁴ Before Paul finished defending himself, Festus shouted, "Paul, you're mad! Too much learning has driven you out of your mind."

²⁵ But Paul replied, "Honourable Festus, I am not mad. What I am saying is true, and it makes sense. ²⁶ None of these things happened off in a corner somewhere. I am sure that King Agrippa knows what I am talking about. That's why I can speak so plainly to him."

²⁷ Then Paul said to Agrippa, "Do you believe what the prophets said? I know you do."

²⁸ Agrippa asked Paul, "In such a short time do you think you can talk me into being a Christian?"

²⁹ Paul answered, "Whether it takes a short time or a long time, I wish you and everyone else who hears me today would become just like me! Except, of course, for these chains."

³⁰ Then King Agrippa, Governor Festus, Bernice, and everyone who was with them got up. ³¹ But before they left, they said, "This man isn't guilty of anything. He doesn't deserve to die or to be put in jail."

³² Agrippa told Festus, "Paul could have been set free, if he had not asked to be tried by the Roman Emperor."

See also: 26.5: Acts 23.6; Phil 3.5. 26.9–11: Acts 8.3; 22.4–5.

See also: 26.20: Acts 9.20,28–29. 26.23: a 1 Cor 15.20; b Isa 42.6; 49.6.

Paul is taken to Rome

CHAPTER 27

¹ When it was time for us to sail to Rome, Captain Julius from the Emperor's special troops was put in charge of Paul and the other prisoners. ² We went aboard a ship from Adramyttium that was about to sail to some ports along the coast of Asia. Aristarchus from Thessalonica in Macedonia sailed on the ship with us.

³ The next day we came to shore at Sidon. Captain Julius was very kind to Paul. He even let him visit his friends, so they could give him whatever he needed. ⁴ When we left Sidon, the winds were blowing against us, and we sailed close to the island of Cyprus to be safe from the wind. ⁵ Then we sailed south of Cilicia and Pamphylia until we came to the port of Myra in Lycia. ⁶ There the army captain found a ship from Alexandria that was going to Italy. So he ordered us to board that ship.

⁷ We sailed along slowly for several days and had a hard time reaching Cnidus. The wind would not let us go any further in that direction, so we sailed past Cape Salmone, where the island of Crete would protect us from the wind. ⁸ We went slowly along the coast and finally reached a place called Fair Havens, not far from the town of Lasea.

⁹ By now we had already lost a lot of time, and sailing was no longer safe. In fact, even the Great Day of Forgiveness* was past. ¹⁰ Then Paul spoke to the crew of the ship, "Men, listen to me! If we sail now, our ship and its cargo will be badly damaged, and many lives will be lost." ¹¹ But Julius listened to the captain of the ship and its owner, rather than to Paul.

¹² The harbour at Fair Havens wasn't a good place to spend the winter. Because of this, almost everyone agreed that we should at least try to sail along the coast of Crete as far as Phoenix. It had a harbour that opened towards the south-west and north-west,' and we could spend the winter there.

*27.9 Great Day of Forgiveness: This Jewish festival took place near the end of September. The sailing season was dangerous after the middle of September, and it was stopped completely between the middle of November and the middle of March.

Viewpoints

Look around you – can you spot the people God is about to save?

Contributed by Zoë C

'The LORD also said, 'I will protect you from the Jews and from the Gentiles that I am sending you to.'

It's not rocket science that Britain is spiritually speaking, a very lost country. When we see so little fruit from trying to witness to our unsaved friends and family, it's easy for us to lose faith and begin to believe that Christianity is just another religion with no relevance to the 'real' world.

I tend to believe that only a certain type of person will get saved. The librarian type who wears a hand-knitted green woolly cardigan or the sort of human-rights-charity-shop type. Then there's people who I think will never get saved like a dark looking Goth or a trendy shopaholic. People who have got better things to do. But God wants to reach all people, not just the people we think are 'suitable'.

The Gentiles were a rather unsuitable bunch of people. They didn't behave according to the Jewish custom and they were seen as a threat to the Jewish way of life. The Jews would have avoided Gentiles. Yet God cared about them and God used people to reach out to them. God wants all people to be saved. In God's eyes there is no such thing as a geek or a punk rocker. So watch out, don't limit God. You never know whose heart God is working in, making them ready to be saved.

More...
Culture p.779
Gentiles p.1232
Racism p.1308
God's love p.958

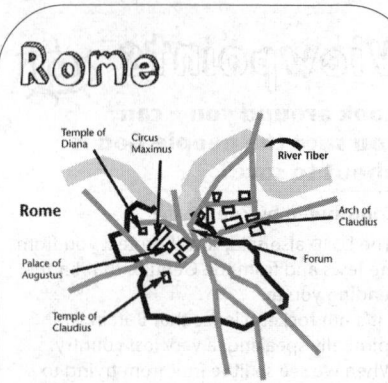

Rome

Capital of the empire and home to the emperor, Rome was the most famous city in the world.

It was a vast city for its time, crammed with people from all nations and faiths.

Some experts believe that it may have housed as many as 40,000 Jews. There were certainly enough Jews in the city to create a disturbance; in AD49 the emperor Claudius ordered them to be expelled because of fighting between the Jews and the Christians (Acts 18.2).

The heart of the city was the forum, where people would gather to exchange gossip, hear the latest news and do some shopping. Rome was also famous for its many buildings, including temples, palaces and amphitheatres, where the public entertainment included gladiator fighting and public executions.

Christians sometimes played the main role in these executions. After a fire destroyed part of the city in AD64, Nero blamed the Christians and had many publicly executed. It is during this wave of persecution that Paul and Peter are thought to have died.

Despite this persecution, the church in Rome continued to grow.

The storm at sea

13 When a gentle wind from the south started blowing, the men thought it was a good time to do what they had planned. So they pulled up the anchor, and we sailed along the coast of Crete. 14 But soon a strong wind called "The North-easter" blew against us from the island. 15 The wind struck the ship, and we could not sail against it. So we let the wind carry the ship.

16 We went along the island of Cauda on the side that was protected from the wind. We had a hard time holding the lifeboat in place, 17 but finally we got it where it belonged. Then the sailors tied ropes around the ship to hold it together. They lowered the sail and let the ship drift along, because they were afraid it might hit the sandbanks in the gulf of Syrtis.

18 The storm was so fierce that the next day they threw some of the ship's cargo overboard. 19 Then on the third day, with their bare hands they threw overboard some of the ship's gear. 20 For several days we could not see either the sun or the stars. A strong wind kept blowing, and we finally gave up all hope of being saved.

21 Since none of us had eaten anything for a long time, Paul stood up and told the men:

You should have listened to me! If you had stayed on in Crete, you would not have had this damage and loss. 22 But now I beg you to cheer up, because you will be safe. Only the ship will be lost.

23 I belong to God, and I worship him. Last night he sent an angel 24 to tell me, "Paul, don't be afraid! You will stand trial before the Emperor. And because of you, God will save the lives of everyone on the ship." 25 Cheer up! I am sure that God will do exactly what he promised. 26 But we will first be shipwrecked on some island.

27 For fourteen days and nights we had been blown around over the Mediterranean Sea. But about midnight the sailors realized that we were getting near land. 28 They measured and found that the water was about forty metres deep. A little later they measured again and found it was only about thirty metres. 29 The sailors were afraid that we might hit some rocks, and they let down four anchors from the back of the ship. Then they prayed for daylight.

30 The sailors wanted to escape from the ship. So they lowered the lifeboat into the water, pretending that they were letting down an anchor from the front of the ship. 31 But Paul said to Captain Julius and the soldiers, "If the sailors don't stay on the ship, you won't have any chance to save your lives." 32 The soldiers then cut the ropes that held the lifeboat and let it fall into the sea.

33 Just before daylight Paul begged the people to eat something. He told them, "For fourteen days you have been so worried that you haven't eaten a thing. 34 I beg you to eat something. Your lives depend on it. Do this and not one of you will be hurt."

35 After Paul had said this, he took a piece of bread and gave thanks to God. Then in front of everyone, he broke the bread and ate some. 36 They all felt encouraged, and each of them ate something. 37 There were 276 people on the ship, 38 and after everyone had eaten, they threw the cargo of wheat into the sea to make the ship lighter.

The shipwreck

39 Morning came, and the ship's crew saw a coast that they did not recognize. But they did see a cove with a beach. So they decided to try to run the ship aground on the beach. 40 They cut the anchors loose and let them sink into the sea. At the same time they untied the ropes that were holding the rudders. Next, they raised the sail at the front of the ship and let the wind carry the ship towards the beach. 41 But it ran aground on a sandbank. The front of the ship stuck firmly in the sand, and the rear was being smashed by the force of the waves.

42 The soldiers decided to kill the prisoners to keep them from swimming away and escaping. 43 But Captain Julius wanted to save Paul's life, and he did not let the soldiers do what they had planned. Instead, he ordered everyone who could swim to dive into the water and head for shore. 44 Then he told the others to hold on to planks of wood or parts of the ship. At last, everyone safely reached shore.

CHAPTER 28

On the island of Malta

1 When we came ashore, we learnt that the island was called Malta. 2 The local people were very friendly, and they welcomed us by building a fire, because it was rainy and cold.

Viewpoints 👁

Living the truth of God's power in your life

Contributed by Tim B

'But we would like to hear what you have to say. We understand that people everywhere are against this new group.'

The apostle Paul is in Rome. He's been shipwrecked, put in prison for two years, had various people trying to kill him and been held on trial in front of various corrupt rulers, who eventually, not wanting to take responsibility, send him off to Rome for Caesar to judge. The crimes he is accused of are completely false. So we would assume Paul might be a bit annoyed and slightly puzzled. He had been travelling round the known world telling the good news wherever he went, planting churches and doing God's will. Then all of a sudden he's put in jail indefinitely and there doesn't really seem to be anyone to spread the good news to except the odd corrupt ruler begging for bribes.

But God had a plan for Paul and has a plan for us. So Paul, trusting God's wisdom continues to live for God and when he is approached by some Jews in Rome he tells them what he knows, not grudgingly or because he has to but because he wants to. It's interesting that the only thing that the Jews knew of these Christians is that although nobody liked them they had heard no bad reports about them. How we come across to other people is important. It's not just us on our own, it's us as part of God's family, part of God's church and we should try and do everything we can to try and live like it.

More...

Civil disobedience p.1247
Sharing your faith p.1082
Living truthfully p.1070

³ After Paul had gathered some wood and had put it on the fire, the heat caused a snake to crawl out, and it bit him on the hand. ⁴ When the local people saw the snake hanging from Paul's hand, they said to each other, "This man must be a murderer! He didn't drown in the sea, but the goddess of justice will kill him anyway."

⁵ Paul shook the snake off into the fire and wasn't harmed. ⁶ The people kept thinking that Paul would either swell up or suddenly drop dead. They watched him for a long time, and when nothing happened to him, they changed their minds and said, "This man is a god."

⁷ The governor of the island was named Publius, and he owned some of the land around there. Publius was very friendly and welcomed us into his home for three days. ⁸ His father was in bed, sick with fever and stomach trouble, and Paul went to visit him. Paul healed the man by praying and placing his hands on him.

⁹ After this happened, everyone on the island brought their sick people to Paul, and they were all healed. ¹⁰ The people were very respectful to us, and when we sailed, they gave us everything we needed.

From Malta to Rome

¹¹ Three months later we sailed in a ship that had been docked at Malta for the winter. The ship was from Alexandria in Egypt and was known as "The Twin Gods".* ¹² We arrived in Syracuse and stayed for three days. ¹³ From there we sailed to Rhegium. The next day a south wind began to blow, and two days later we arrived in Puteoli. ¹⁴ There we found some of the Lord's followers, who begged us to stay with them. A week later we left for the city of Rome.

¹⁵ Some of the followers in Rome heard about us and came to meet us at the Market of Appius and at the Three Inns. When Paul saw them, he thanked God and was encouraged.

Paul in Rome

¹⁶ We arrived in Rome, and Paul was allowed to live in a house by himself with a soldier to guard him.

¹⁷ Three days after we got there, Paul called together some of the Jewish leaders and said:

> My friends, I have never done anything to hurt our people, and I have never gone against the customs of our ancestors. But in Jerusalem I was handed over as a prisoner to the Romans. ¹⁸ They looked into the charges against me and wanted to release me. They found that I had not done anything deserving death. ¹⁹ The Jewish leaders disagreed, so I asked to be tried by the Emperor.
>
> But I don't have anything to say against my own nation. ²⁰ I am bound by these chains because of what we people of Israel hope for. That's why I have called you here to talk about this hope of ours.

²¹ The leaders replied, "No one from Judea has written us a letter about you. And not one of them has come here to report on you or to say anything against you. ²² But we would like to hear what you have to say. We understand that people everywhere are against this new group."

²³ They agreed on a time to meet with Paul, and many of them came to his house. From early morning until late in the afternoon, Paul talked to them about God's kingdom. He used the Law of Moses and the Books of the Prophets* to try to win them over to Jesus. ²⁴ Some of the leaders agreed with what Paul said, but others did not. ²⁵ Since they could not agree among themselves, they started leaving. But Paul said, "The Holy Spirit said the right thing when he sent Isaiah the prophet ²⁶ to tell our ancestors,

> 'Go to these people
>   and tell them:
> You will listen and listen,
>   but never understand.
> You will look and look,
>   but never see.
> ²⁷ All of you
>   have stubborn hearts.
> Your ears are stopped up,
>   and your eyes are covered.
> You cannot see or hear
>   or understand.
> If you could,
> you would turn to me,
>   and I would heal you.' "

---

*28.11 known as "The Twin Gods": Or "carried on its bow a wooden carving of the Twin Gods." These gods were Castor and Pollux, two of the favourite gods among sailors.

*28.23 Law of Moses and the Books of the Prophets: See the note at 13.15.
See also: 28.19: Acts 25.11.   28.26–27: Isa 6.9–10 (LXX).

$^{28-29}$ Paul said, "You may be sure that God wants to save the Gentiles! And they will listen."›

^{30} For two years Paul stayed in a rented house and welcomed everyone who came to see him. ^{31} He bravely preached about God's kingdom and taught about the Lord Jesus Christ, and no one tried to stop him.

Additional notes

›**1.6 are you now going to give Israel its own king again?:** Or "Are you now going to rule Israel as its king?"

›**1.14 met together and prayed with a single purpose in mind:** Or "met together in a special place for prayer".

›**3.13 Servant:** Or "Son".

›**3.26 Son:** Or "Servant".

›**4.27 Servant:** See the note at 3.13.

›**4.30 Servant:** See the note at 3.13.

›**4.33 God greatly blessed his followers:** Or "Everyone highly respected his followers".

›**7.46 the people:** Some manuscripts have "God".

›**7.47 God:** Or "the people".

›**8.26 Go south:** Or "About midday go".

›**8.26 the desert road that leads from Jerusalem to Gaza:** Or "the road that leads from Jerusalem to Gaza in the desert."

›**8.36–37 Why can't I be baptized:** Some manuscripts add, "Philip replied, 'You can, if you believe with all your heart.' The official answered, 'I believe that Jesus Christ is the Son of God.' "

›**9.34 and make up your bed:** Or "and prepare something to eat."

›**10.19 Three:** One manuscript has "two"; some manuscripts have "some".

›**10.37 what happened:** Or "the message that went".

›**11.20 Gentiles:** This translates a Greek word that may mean "people who speak Greek" or "people who live as Greeks do". Here the word seems to mean "people who are not Jews". Some manuscripts have "Greeks", which also seems to mean "people who are not Jews".

›**12.15 his angel:** Probably meaning "his guardian angel".

›**12.25 went back to Jerusalem:** Some manuscripts have "left Jerusalem", and others have "went to Antioch".

›**13.18 took care of:** Some manuscripts have "put up with".

›**13.28–29 cross:** This translates a Greek word that means "wood", "pole", or "tree".

›**13.44 the Lord:** Some manuscripts have "God".

›**13.48 the Lord:** See the note at 13.44.

›**15.34–35** Verse 34, which says that Silas decided to stay on in Antioch, is not in some manuscripts.

›**16.8 went on through:** Or "passed by".

›**16.12 in the first district of Macedonia:** Some manuscripts have "and the leading city of Macedonia."

›**17.18 people rising from death:** Or "a goddess named 'Rising from Death'."

›**19.3 Then why were you baptized? . . . Because of what John taught:** Or "In whose name were you baptized? . . . We were baptized in John's name."

›**19.21 Paul decided:** Or "Paul was led by the Holy Spirit".

›**20.28 the blood of his own Son:** Or "his own blood."

›**21.9 unmarried:** Or "virgin".

›**24.2 Paul was called in, and Tertullus stated the case against him:** Or "Tertullus was called in and stated the case against Paul."

›**24.6–8 we arrested him:** Some manuscripts add, "We wanted to judge him by our own laws. But Lysias the commander took him away from us by force. Then Lysias ordered us to bring our charges against this man in your court."

›**27.12 south-west and north-west:** Or "north-east and south-east".

›**28.28–29 And they will listen:** Some manuscripts add, "After Paul said this, the people left, but they got into a fierce argument among themselves."

Romans

Paul's letter to the church in Rome

The basics

What's the point? We're all sinners but we can all be saved through faith in Jesus.

What happens? Paul writes to introduce himself. He describes himself as an apostle, chosen to spread the good news to the gentiles. And the message that he has been given is that all who put their faith in Jesus are saved.

What should I remember? 1.17 'The good news tells how God accepts everyone who has faith, but only those who have faith. It is just as the Scriptures say, "The people God accepts because of their faith will live".'

More details

Setting the scene Paul is in Corinth and planning to visit Rome. But he's never been there before, so he writes to introduce himself. And a whole lot more...

What's it all about? Faith. Faith in Jesus Christ. Although Paul is writing to introduce himself, he uses the letter to set out his core beliefs, his understanding of what the basis of Christianity is. Salvation, he argues, is not about what we do, but who we trust. It's God's forgiveness and love that rescues us, not our own efforts.

This theme recurs throughout Paul's letters. We've all fallen short of what is required and there's nothing we can do for ourselves to gain salvation. It is God's gift to us. That's not to say that it does not matter what we do. As followers of Jesus we are obliged to live lives of love, hope and sacrifice. But, Paul argues, we do this as a response to salvation, not in order to obtain it.

Footsteps

Paul the apostle: 1.1–15
The good news in two verses: 1.16–17
No one is good: 3.1–20
The great news: 3.21–31
New life: 5.1–11
Alive in Christ: 6.1–14
Live by the spirit: 8.1–17
A wonderful future 8.18–39
The chosen people: 11.1–36
Basic rules: 12.9–21

Paul and his message of good news

CHAPTER 1

[1] *From Paul, a servant of Christ Jesus.*

God chose me to be an apostle, and he appointed me to preach the good news [2] that he promised long ago by what his prophets said in the Holy Scriptures. [3-4] This good news is about his Son, our Lord Jesus Christ! As a human, he was from the family of David. But the Holy Spirit' proved that Jesus is the powerful Son of God,' because he was raised from death.

[5] Jesus was kind to me and chose me to be an apostle,' so that people of all nations would obey and have faith. [6] You are some of those people chosen by Jesus Christ.

Big ideas

Letters

The last section of the Bible consists of letters written to churches and individuals in the very early years of the church. The majority were written by Paul. But others are written by – or attributed to – other apostles, and one by an unnamed writer.

Paul's Letters

Romans, 1 and 2 Corinthians, Galatians, Ephesians, Philippians, Colossians, 1 and 2 Thessalonians, 1 and 2 Timothy, Titus, Philemon.

Most of these were written to churches, a few to individuals. Paul wrote mainly to churches where he'd had some involvement, either starting the church, or teaching there. He usually dictated to a secretary and just signed letters himself.

General letters

Hebrews, James, 1 and 2 Peter, Jude

These are general letters, not addressed to specific places, but to the Church in general. They deal with broader themes. Hebrews, for example, deals with the relationship of Christianity to the Old Testament Law, while James is a guide to living as a Christian.

Letters of John

1, 2 and 3 John, Revelation.

John's letters are much shorter than Paul's and deal mainly with false teaching. Revelation is not a letter at all. It's a powerful vision of the future, filled with mystical imagery and symbolic numbers.

 Footsteps

Ten days with the Letters

Paul introduces himself: Romans 1.1–15
Paul's building work: 1 Corinthians 3.10–23
Pulling no punches: Galatians: 3.1–20
Stop arguing: Philippians 4.2–9
Founded by Paul: 1 Thessalonians 2.1–20
A reminder to Timothy: 1 Timothy 6.11–21
Keep on being brave: Hebrews 10.19–39
No favourites: James 2.1–26
Paul is hard to understand: 2 Peter 3.1–18
The same commandment: 1 John 2.7–27

---

[7] This letter is to all of you in Rome. God loves you and has chosen you to be his very own people.

I pray that God our Father and our Lord Jesus Christ will be kind to you and will bless you with peace!

A prayer of thanks

[8] First, I thank God in the name of Jesus Christ for all of you. I do this because people everywhere in the world are talking about your faith. [9] God has seen how I never stop praying for you, while I serve him with all my heart and tell the good news about his Son.

[10] In all my prayers, I ask God to make it possible for me to visit you. [11] I want to see you and share with you the same blessings that God's Spirit has given me. Then you will grow stronger in your faith. [12] What I am saying is that we can encourage each other by the faith that is ours.

[13] My friends, I want you to know that I have often planned to come for a visit. But something has always kept me from doing it. I want to win followers to Christ in Rome, as I have done in many other places. [14-15] It doesn't matter if people are civilized and educated, or if they are uncivilized and uneducated. I must tell the good news to everyone. That's why I am eager to visit all of you in Rome.

The power of the good news

[16] I am proud of the good news! It is God's powerful way of saving all people who have faith, whether they are Jews or Gentiles. [17] The good news tells how God accepts everyone who has faith, but only those who have faith.' It is just as the Scriptures say, "The people God accepts because of their faith will live."'

Everyone is guilty

[18] From heaven God shows how angry he is with all the wicked and evil things that sinful people do to crush the truth. [19] They know everything that can be known about God, because God has shown it all to them. [20] God's eternal power and character cannot be seen. But from the beginning of creation, God has shown what these are like by all he has made. That's why those people don't have any excuse. [21] They know about God,

---

See also: **1.13:** Acts 19.21. **1.16:** Mark 8.38.
1.17: Hab 2.4. **1.21:** Eph 4.17–18.

but they don't honour him or even thank him. Their thoughts are useless, and their stupid minds are in the dark. ²² They claim to be wise, but they are fools. ²³ They don't worship the glorious and eternal God. Instead, they worship idols that are made to look like humans who cannot live for ever, and like birds, animals, and reptiles.

²⁴ So God let these people go their own way. They did what they wanted to do, and their filthy thoughts made them do shameful things with their bodies. ²⁵ They gave up the truth about God for a lie, and they worshipped God's creation instead of God, who will be praised for ever. Amen.

²⁶ God let them follow their own evil desires. Women no longer wanted to have sex in a natural way, and they did things with each other that were not natural. ²⁷ Men behaved in the same way. They stopped wanting to have sex with women and had strong desires for sex with other men. They did shameful things with each other, and what has happened to them is punishment for their foolish deeds.

²⁸ Since these people refused even to think about God, he let their useless minds rule over them. That's why they do all sorts of indecent things. ²⁹ They are evil, wicked, and greedy, as well as mean in every possible way. They want what others have, and they murder, argue, cheat, and are hard to get along with. They gossip, ³⁰ say cruel things about others, and hate God. They are proud, conceited, and boastful, always thinking up new ways to do evil.

These people don't respect their parents. ³¹ They are stupid, unreliable, and don't have any love or pity for others. ³² They know God has said that anyone who acts this way deserves to die. But they keep on doing evil things, and they even encourage others to do them.

CHAPTER 2

God's judgment is fair

¹ Some of you accuse others of doing wrong. But there is no excuse for what you do. When you judge others, you condemn yourselves, because you are guilty of doing the very same things. ² We know that God is right to judge everyone who behaves in this way. ³ Do you really think God won't punish you, when you behave exactly like the people you accuse? ⁴ You don't think much of God's

wonderful goodness or of his patience and willingness to put up with you. Don't you know that the reason God is good to you is because he wants you to turn to him?

⁵ But you are stubborn and refuse to turn to God. So you are making things even worse for yourselves on that day when he will show how angry he is and will judge the world with fairness. ⁶ God will reward each of us for what we have done. ⁷ He will give eternal life to everyone who has patiently done what is good in the hope of receiving glory, honour, and life that lasts for ever. ⁸ But he will show how angry and furious he can be with every selfish person who rejects the truth and wants to do evil. ⁹ All who are wicked are punished with trouble and suffering. It doesn't matter if they are Jews or Gentiles. ¹⁰ But all who do right will be rewarded with glory, honour, and peace, whether they are Jews or Gentiles. ¹¹ God doesn't have any favourites!

¹² Those people who don't know about God's Law will still be punished for what they do wrong. And the Law will be used to judge everyone who knows what it says. ¹³ God accepts those who obey his Law, but not those who simply hear it.

¹⁴ Some people naturally obey the Law's commands, even though they don't have the Law. ¹⁵ This proves that the conscience is like a law written in the human heart. And it will show whether we are forgiven or condemned, ¹⁶ when God appoints Jesus Christ to judge everyone's secret thoughts, just as my message says.

The Jews and the Law

¹⁷ Some of you call yourselves Jews. You trust in the Law and take pride in God. ¹⁸ By reading the Scriptures you learn how God wants you to behave, and you discover what is right. ¹⁹ You are sure that you are a guide for the blind and a light for all who are in the dark. ²⁰ And since there is knowledge and truth in God's Law, you think you can instruct fools and teach young people.

²¹ But how can you teach others when you refuse to learn? You preach that it is wrong to steal. But do you steal? ²² You say people should be faithful in marriage. But are you faithful? You hate idols, yet you rob their temples. ²³ You take pride in the Law, but you disobey the Law and bring shame to God. ²⁴ It

See also: 1.23: Deut 4.16–18. 2.1: Matt 7.1; Luke 6.37.

1256

See also: 2.6: Psa 62.12; Prov 24.12. 2.11: Deut 10.17. 2.24: Isa 52.5 (LXX).

is just as the Scriptures tell us, "You have made foreigners say insulting things about God."

²⁵ Being circumcised is worthwhile, if you obey the Law. But if you don't obey the Law, you are no better off than people who are not circumcised. ²⁶ In fact, if they obey the Law, they are as good as anyone who is circumcised. ²⁷ So everyone who obeys the Law, but has never been circumcised, will condemn you. Even though you are circumcised and have the Law, you still don't obey its teachings.

²⁸ Just because you live like a Jew and are circumcised doesn't make you a real Jew. ²⁹ To be a real Jew you must obey the Law. True circumcision is something that happens deep in your heart, not something done to your body. And besides, you should want praise from God and not from humans.

CHAPTER 3

¹ What good is it to be a Jew? What good is it to be circumcised? ² It is good in a lot of ways! First of all, God's messages were spoken to the Jews. ³ It is true that some of them did not believe the message. But does this mean that God cannot be trusted, just because they did not have faith? ⁴ No, indeed! God tells the truth, even if everyone else is a liar. The Scriptures say about God,

"Your words
    will be proved true,
and in court
    you will win your case."

⁵ If our evil deeds show how right God is, then what can we say? Is it wrong for God to become angry and punish us? What a foolish thing to ask. ⁶ But the answer is, "No." Otherwise, how could God judge the world? ⁷ Since your lies bring great honour to God by showing how truthful he is, you may ask why God still says you are a sinner. ⁸ You might as well say, "Let's do something evil, so that something good will come of it!" Some people even claim that we are saying this. But God is fair and will judge them as well.

No one is good

⁹ What does all this mean? Does it mean that we Jews are better off* than the Gentiles? No, it doesn't! Jews, as well as Gentiles, are ruled by sin, just as I have said. ¹⁰ The Scriptures tell us,

"No one is acceptable to God!
¹¹ Not one of them understands
    or even searches for God.
¹² They have all turned away
    and are worthless.
There isn't one person
    who does right.
¹³ Their words are like an open pit,
    and their tongues are good
        only for telling lies.
Each word is as deadly
    as the fangs of a snake,
¹⁴ and they say nothing
    but bitter curses.
¹⁵ These people quickly
    become violent.
¹⁶ Wherever they go,
    they leave ruin
        and destruction.
¹⁷ They don't know how
    to live in peace.
¹⁸ They don't even fear God."

¹⁹ We know that everything in the Law was written for those who are under its power. The Law says these things to stop anyone from making excuses and to let God show that the whole world is guilty. ²⁰ God doesn't accept people simply because they obey the Law. No, indeed! All the Law does is to point out our sin.

God's way of accepting people

²¹ Now we see how God does make us acceptable to him. The Law and the Prophets* tell how we become acceptable, and it isn't by obeying the Law of Moses. ²² God treats everyone alike. He accepts people only because they have faith in Jesus Christ. ²³ All of us have sinned and fallen short of God's glory. ²⁴ But God treats us much better than we deserve,* and because of Christ Jesus, he freely accepts us and sets us free from our sins. ²⁵⁻²⁶ God sent Christ to be our sacrifice. Christ offered his life's blood, so that by faith in him we could come to God. And God did

---

*3.21 The Law and the Prophets: The Jewish Scriptures, that is, the Old Testament.
*3.24 treats us much better than we deserve: The Greek word *charis*, traditionally rendered "grace", is translated here and in other places in the CEV to express the overwhelming kindness of God.

See also: 3.13: a Psa 5.9 (LXX); b Psa 140.3.
3.14: Psa 10.7 (LXX). 3.15–17: Isa 59.7–8. 3.18: Psa 36.1.
3.20: Psa 143.2; Gal 2.16. 3.22: Gal 2.16.

See also: 2.29: Deut 30.6. 3.4: Psa 51.4 (LXX).
3.10–12: Psa 14.1–3 (LXX); Psa 53.1–3 (LXX).

Being christian

Saying sorry

Romans 3.23

We're not very good at saying 'sorry' these days. Politicians never admit to getting things wrong; the media never apologises; no-one wants to admit to being a failure.

But being Christian means exactly that. We have to admit that we've failed, we have to say sorry to God.

There isn't anyone alive who hasn't let God down; who hasn't done something wrong. As Paul says in Romans, 'All of us have sinned and fallen short of God's glory.' At some time, all of us have sinned. We've lied or lost our temper, or gossiped or struck out at someone or cheated or... well, you can fill in the gaps.

And all those wrong things we've done come between us and God. Our sin means that we cannot come into his presence. It means that really we should all be punished. We should all die.

Unless...

The great news is that all we have to do is ask. Just say 'sorry' and God will take away our sins. We don't have to pay the price any more, because Jesus has died in our place. All we have to do to take advantage of that is say sorry to God and accept him into our lives.

Sometimes, you see, admitting failure is the most successful thing you'll ever do.

Being Christian: Saying sorry

• Say sorry to God for all you've done wrong. Wipe the past out and start again.
• Keep confessing your sins as you go forward in your Christian life. However 'good' we are at this Christianity stuff, we still muck up and we still do things wrong. God will always forgive us.

this to show that in the past he was right to be patient and forgive sinners. This also shows that God is right when he accepts people who have faith in Jesus.

²⁷ What is left for us to boast about? Not a thing! Is it because we obeyed some law? No! It is because of faith. ²⁸ We see that people are acceptable to God because they have faith, and not because they obey the Law. ²⁹ Does God belong only to the Jews? Isn't he also the God of the Gentiles? Yes, he is! ³⁰ There is only one God, and he accepts Gentiles as well as Jews, simply because of their faith. ³¹ Do we destroy the Law by our faith? Not at all! We make it even more powerful.

CHAPTER 4

The example of Abraham

¹ Well then, what can we say about our ancestor Abraham? ² If he became acceptable to God because of what he did, then he would have something to boast about. But he would never be able to boast about it to God. ³ The Scriptures say, "God accepted Abraham because Abraham had faith in him."

⁴ Money paid to workers isn't a gift. It is something they earn by working. ⁵ But you cannot make God accept you because of something you do. God accepts sinners only because they have faith in him. ⁶ In the Scriptures David talks about the blessings that come to people who are acceptable to God, even though they don't do anything to deserve these blessings. David says,

⁷ "God blesses people
　　whose sins are forgiven
　and whose evil deeds
　　are forgotten.
⁸ The Lord blesses people
　　whose sins are erased
　　from his book."

⁹ Are these blessings meant for circumcised people or for those who are not circumcised? Well, the Scriptures say that God accepted Abraham because Abraham had faith in him. ¹⁰ But when did this happen? Was it before or after Abraham was circumcised? Of course, it was before.

¹¹ Abraham let himself be circumcised to show that he had been accepted because of his faith even before he was circumcised. This makes Abraham the father of all who are acceptable to God because of their faith, even

See also: 3.30: Deut 6.4; Gal 3.20. 4.3: Gen 15.6; Gal 3.6.
4.7–8: Psa 32.1–2. 4.11: Gen 17.10.

though they are not circumcised. [12] This also makes Abraham the father of everyone who is circumcised and has faith in God, as Abraham did before he was circumcised.

The promise is for all who have faith

[13] God promised Abraham and his descendants that he would give them the world. This promise wasn't made because Abraham had obeyed a law, but because his faith in God made him acceptable. [14] If Abraham and his descendants were given this promise because they had obeyed a law, then faith would mean nothing, and the promise would be worthless.

[15] God becomes angry when his Law is broken. But where there isn't a law, it cannot be broken. [16] Everything depends on having faith in God, so that God's promise is assured by his great kindness. This promise isn't only for Abraham's descendants who have the Law. It is for all who are Abraham's descendants because they have faith, just as he did. Abraham is the ancestor of us all. [17] The Scriptures say that Abraham would become the ancestor of many nations. This promise was made to Abraham because he had faith in God, who raises the dead to life and creates new things.

[18] God promised Abraham a lot of descendants. And when it all seemed hopeless, Abraham still had faith in God and became the ancestor of many nations. [19] Abraham's faith never became weak, not even when he was nearly a hundred years old. He knew that he was almost dead and that his wife Sarah could not have children. [20] But Abraham never doubted or questioned God's promise. His faith made him strong, and he gave all the credit to God. [21] Abraham was certain that God could do what he had promised. [22] So God accepted him, [23] just as we read in the Scriptures. But these words were not written only for Abraham. [24] They were written for us, since we will also be accepted because of our faith in God, who raised our Lord Jesus to life. [25] God gave Jesus to die for our sins, and he raised him to life, so that we would be made acceptable to God.

Big ideas

Circumcision

Circumcision is a ritual operation which removes all, or part, of the foreskin from the penis. The practice dates back to very early times and has been practised by many cultures, including African, South American, Australian and Native American tribes. Generally it is used as a rite of passage, to mark the transition from being a boy to being a man.

For the Jews, however, it was not to do with becoming a man, or even belonging to a tribe. It was to do with belonging to God. The Jews circumcised their babies on the eighth day after their birth as a physical sign of the covenant between God and his people. God says that any male not circumcised 'hasn't kept his promise to me and cannot be one of my people' (Genesis 17.14).

Much later in Bible history, however, many Jews started to believe that circumcision was enough on it's own; that as long as they were circumcised, they were holy, they were OK. This attitude was criticised by prophets such as Jeremiah, who said to the people, 'Your bodies are circumcised, but your hearts are unchanged' (Jeremiah 9.26).

Later still, in New Testament times, the issue became the cause of conflict between Jewish and Greek Christians. Some Jewish Christians argued that everyone should be circumcised. Peter, and later Paul, fought this, arguing that Christians were justified by faith in Christ and did not need the physical act of circumcision (Romans 4.9–13).

 Footsteps

Five days on Circumcision

The First Instructions: Genesis 17.1–23
Not enough: Jeremiah 9.23–25
Christians and circumcision: Acts 15.1–21
Why Abraham was circumcised: Romans 4.11–17
Paul on circumcision: Galatians 6.11–16

More...

Gentiles p.1232
Holiness p.1386

See also: 4.13: Gen 17.4–6; 22.17–18; Gal 3.29.
4.14: Gal 3.18. **4.16:** Gal 3.7. **4.17:** Gen 17.5.
4.18: Gen 15.5. **4.19:** Gen 17.17. **4.25:** Isa 53.4–5.

A new life for God's people

CHAPTER 5

What it means to be acceptable to God

¹ By faith we have been made acceptable to God. And now, because of our Lord Jesus Christ, we live at peaceʼ with God. ² Christ has also introduced usʼ to God's undeserved kindness on which we take our stand. So we are happy, as we look forward to sharing in the glory of God. ³ But that's not all! We gladly suffer,ʼ because we know that suffering helps us to endure. ⁴ And endurance builds character, which gives us a hope ⁵ that will never disappoint us. All this happens because God has given us the Holy Spirit, who fills our hearts with his love.

⁶ Christ died for us at a time when we were helpless and sinful. ⁷ No one is really willing to die for an honest person, though someone might be willing to die for a truly good person. ⁸ But God showed how much he loved us by having Christ die for us, even though we were sinful.

⁹ But there is more! Now that God has accepted us because Christ sacrificed his life's blood, we will also be kept safe from God's anger. ¹⁰ Even when we were God's enemies, he made peace with us, because his Son died for us. Yet something even greater than friendship is ours. Now that we are at peace with God, we will be saved by his Son's life. ¹¹ And in addition to everything else, we are happy because God sent our Lord Jesus Christ to make peace with us.

Adam and Christ

¹² Adam sinned, and that sin brought death into the world. Now everyone has sinned, and so everyone must die. ¹³ Sin was in the world before the Law came. But no record of sin was kept, because there was no Law. ¹⁴ Yet death still had power over all who lived from the time of Adam to the time of Moses. This happened, though not everyone disobeyed a direct command from God, as Adam did.

In some ways Adam is like Christ who came later. ¹⁵ But the gift that God was kind enough to give was very different from Adam's sin. That one sin brought death to many others. Yet in an even greater way, Jesus Christ alone brought God's gift of kindness to many people.

¹⁶ There is a lot of difference between Adam's sin and God's gift. That one sin led to punishment. But God's gift made it possible for us to be acceptable to him, even though we have sinned many times. ¹⁷ Death ruled like a king because Adam had sinned. But that cannot compare with what Jesus Christ has done. God has been so kind to us, and he has accepted us because of Jesus. And so we will live and rule like kings.

¹⁸ Everyone was going to be punished because Adam sinned. But because of the good thing that Christ has done, God accepts us and gives us the gift of life. ¹⁹ Adam disobeyed God and caused many others to be sinners. But Jesus obeyed him and will make many people acceptable to God.

²⁰ The Law came, so that the full power of sin could be seen. Yet where sin was powerful, God's kindness was even more powerful. ²¹ Sin ruled by means of death. But God's kindness now rules, and God has accepted us because of Jesus Christ our Lord. This means that we will have eternal life.

CHAPTER 6

Dead to sin but alive because of Christ

¹ What should we say? Should we keep on sinning, so that God's wonderful kindness will show up even better? ² No, we should not! If we are dead to sin, how can we go on sinning? ³ Don't you know that all who share in Christ Jesus by being baptized also share in his death? ⁴ When we were baptized, we died and were buried with Christ. We were baptized, so that we would live a new life, as Christ was raised to life by the glory of God the Father.

⁵ If we shared in Jesus' death by being baptized, we will be raised to life with him. ⁶ We know that the persons we used to be were nailed to the cross with Jesus. This was done, so that our sinful bodies would no longer be the slaves of sin. ⁷ We know that sin doesn't have power over dead people.

⁸ As we died with Christ, we believe we will also live with him. ⁹ We know that death no longer has any power over Christ. He died and was raised to life, never again to die. ¹⁰ When Christ died, he died for sin once and for all. But now he is alive, and he lives only for God. ¹¹ In the same way, you must think of yourselves as dead to the power of sin. But Christ Jesus has given life to you, and you live for God.

See also: 5.12: Gen 3.6.

See also: 6.4: Col 2.12.

Big ideas

Sin

Sin has been a part of the world, hard-wired into creation, since the fall of Adam and Eve.

Their choice had consequences: it got them exiled from the garden. They couldn't live with God, because God is total holiness, and holiness and sin cannot coexist.

Adam and Eve made a choice to reject God's instructions, and to do things their way and we've been copying them ever since. Because that's what sin is; it's a deliberate choice to turn away from God and do what we want.

Through sin, death came into the world. Why? Because all who sin must die – that's the rule. We've all sinned; we must all die.

Except...

God sent Jesus to die for us. In his letter to Romans, Paul outlines the case. Adam's sin brought death to the world; Christ's death brings life. Because Adam disobeyed God we're all sinners; because Christ obeyed God we all have a shot at redemption.

Jesus has died in our place. So, if we ask him for forgiveness, if we turn round to follow him, our sins will be wiped away and we'll be able to live with God forever. Sin doesn't have to rule our lives; not if we give them to Jesus.

 Footsteps

Ten days on Sin

The first sin: Genesis 3.1–24
A lamb for a sin: Leviticus 4.27–35
Please wash me! Psalms 51.1–19
Not angry forever: Micah 7.18–20
Another lamb for sin: John 1.29–37
Has anyone seen me sin? John 8.31–47
From the inside: Matthew 15.10–20
Selfish desires: James 4.1–10
Jesus died for us: Romans 3.22–28
Sin's pay off is death: Romans 6.20–23

More...

Forgiveness p.614
Redemption p.292
Grace p.1316

[12] Don't let sin rule your body. After all, your body is bound to die, so don't obey its desires [13] or let any part of it become a slave of evil. Give yourselves to God, as people who have been raised from death to life. Make every part of your body a slave that pleases God. [14] Don't let sin keep ruling your lives. You are ruled by God's kindness and not by the Law.

Slaves who do what pleases God

[15] What does all this mean? Does it mean we are free to sin, because we are ruled by God's wonderful kindness and not by the Law? Certainly not! [16] Don't you know that you are slaves of anyone you obey? You can be slaves of sin and die, or you can be obedient slaves of God and be acceptable to him. [17] You used to be slaves of sin. But I thank God that with all your heart you obeyed the teaching you received from me. [18] Now you are set free from sin and are slaves who please God.

[19] I am using these everyday examples, because in some ways you are still weak. You used to let the different parts of your body be slaves of your evil thoughts. But now you must make every part of your body serve God, so that you will belong completely to him.

[20] When you were slaves of sin, you didn't have to please God. [21] But what good did you receive from the things you did? All you have to show for them is your shame, and they lead to death. [22] Now you have been set free from sin, and you are God's slaves. This will make you holy and will lead you to eternal life. [23] The reward for sin is death. But God's gift is eternal life given by Jesus Christ our Lord.

CHAPTER 7

An example from marriage

[1] My friends, you understand enough about law to know that laws only have power over people who are alive. [2] For example, the Law says that a man's wife must remain his wife as long as he lives. But once her husband is dead, she is free [3] to marry someone else. However, if she goes off with another man while her husband is still alive, she is said to be unfaithful.

[4] That is how it is with you, my friends. You are now part of the body of Christ and are dead to the power of the Law. You are free to belong to Christ, who was raised to life so that we could serve God. [5] When we thought

only of ourselves, the Law made us have sinful desires. It made every part of our bodies into slaves who are doomed to die. 6 But the Law no longer rules over us. We are like dead people, and it cannot have any power over us. Now we can serve God in a new way by obeying his Spirit, and not in the old way by obeying the written Law.

The battle with sin

7 Does this mean that the Law is sinful? Certainly not! But if it had not been for the Law, I would not have known what sin is really like. For example, I would not have known what it means to want something that belongs to someone else, unless the Law had told me not to do that. 8 It was sin that used this command as a way of making me have all kinds of desires. But without the Law, sin is dead.

9 Before I knew about the Law, I was alive. But as soon as I heard that command, sin came to life, 10 and I died. The very command that was supposed to bring life to me, instead brought death. 11 Sin used this command to trick me, and because of it I died. 12 Still, the Law and its commands are holy and correct and good.

13 Am I saying that something good caused my death? Certainly not! It was sin that killed me by using something good. Now we can see how terrible and evil sin really is. 14 We know that the Law is spiritual. But I am merely a human, and I have been sold as a slave to sin. 15 In fact, I don't understand why I act the way I do. I don't do what I know is right. I do the things I hate. 16 Although I don't do what I know is right, I agree that the Law is good. 17 So I am not the one doing these evil things. The sin that lives in me is what does them.

18 I know that my selfish desires won't let me do anything that is good. Even when I want to do right, I cannot. 19 Instead of doing what I know is right, I do wrong. 20 And so, if I don't do what I know is right, I am no longer the one doing these evil things. The sin that lives in me is what does them.

21 The Law has shown me that something in me keeps me from doing what I know is right. 22 With my whole heart I agree with the Law of God. 23 But in every part of me I discover something fighting against my mind, and it makes me a prisoner of sin that

controls everything I do. 24 What a miserable person I am. Who will rescue me from this body that is doomed to die? 25 Thank God! Jesus Christ will rescue me.

So with my mind I serve the Law of God, although my selfish desires make me serve the law of sin.

CHAPTER 8

Living by the power of God's Spirit

1 If you belong to Christ Jesus, you won't be punished. 2 The Holy Spirit will give you life that comes from Christ Jesus and will set you' free from sin and death. 3 The Law of Moses cannot do this, because our selfish desires make the Law weak. But God set you free when he sent his own Son to be like us sinners and to be a sacrifice for our sin. God used Christ's body to condemn sin. 4 He did this, so that we would do what the Law commands by obeying the Spirit instead of our own desires.

5 People who are ruled by their desires think only of themselves. Everyone who is ruled by the Holy Spirit thinks about spiritual things. 6 If our minds are ruled by our desires, we will die. But if our minds are ruled by the Spirit, we will have life and peace. 7 Our desires fight against God, because they do not and cannot obey God's laws. 8 If we follow our desires, we cannot please God.

9 You are no longer ruled by your desires, but by God's Spirit, who lives in you. People who don't have the Spirit of Christ in them don't belong to him. 10 But Christ lives in you. So you are alive because God has accepted you, even though your bodies must die because of your sins. 11 Yet God raised Jesus to life! God's Spirit now lives in you, and he will raise you to life by his Spirit.

12 My dear friends, we must not live to satisfy our desires. 13 If you do, you will die. But you will live, if by the help of God's Spirit you say "No" to your desires. 14 Only those people who are led by God's Spirit are his children. 15 God's Spirit doesn't make us slaves who are afraid of him. Instead, we become his children and call him our Father.* 16 God's Spirit makes us sure that we are his children. 17 His Spirit lets us know that together with Christ we will be given what

---

*8.15 our Father: The Greek text uses the Aramaic word "Abba" (meaning "father"), which shows the close relation between the children and their father.

See also: 7.7: Exod 20.17; Deut 5.21. 7.11: Gen 3.13. 7.15: Gal 5.17.

See also: 8.11: 1 Cor 3.16. 8.15-17: Gal 4.5-7. 8.15: Mark 14.36; Gal 4.6.

God has promised. We will also share in the glory of Christ, because we have suffered with him.

A wonderful future for God's people

18 I am sure that what we are suffering now cannot compare with the glory that will be shown to us. 19 In fact, all creation is eagerly waiting for God to show who his children are. 20 Meanwhile, creation is confused, but not because it wants to be confused. God made it this way in the hope 21 that creation would be set free from decay and would share in the glorious freedom of his children. 22 We know that all creation is still groaning and is in pain, like a woman about to give birth.

23 The Spirit makes us sure about what we will be in the future. But now we groan silently, while we wait for God to show that we are his children.' This means that our bodies will also be set free. 24 And this hope is what saves us. But if we already have what we hope for, there is no need to keep on hoping. 25 However, we hope for something we have not yet seen, and we patiently wait for it.

26 In certain ways we are weak, but the Spirit is here to help us. For example, when we don't know what to pray for, the Spirit prays for us in ways that cannot be put into words. 27 All our thoughts are known to God. He can understand what is in the mind of the Spirit, as the Spirit prays for God's people. 28 We know that God is always at work for the good of everyone who loves him.' They are the ones God has chosen for his purpose, 29 and he has always known who his chosen ones would be. He had decided to let them become like his own Son, so that his Son would be the first of many children. 30 God then accepted the people he had already decided to choose, and he has shared his glory with them.

God's love

31 What can we say about all this? If God is on our side, can anyone be against us? 32 God did not keep back his own Son, but he gave him for us. If God did this, won't he freely give us everything else? 33 If God says his chosen ones are acceptable to him, can anyone bring charges against them? 34 Or can anyone condemn them? No indeed! Christ died and was raised to life, and now he is at God's right side,* speaking to him for us.

---

*8.34 right side: The place of power and honour.
See also: 8.20: Gen 3.17–19.   8.23: 2 Cor 5.2–4.

Viewpoints

It's not in our nature to love or obey him. So what do we do?

Contributed by Hannah D

'Our desires fight against God, because they do not and cannot obey God's laws.'

A pretty dismal view of the world, don't you think? What makes it even worse is that it's true!

God and sin don't mix. They're two completely different things. When you start comparing a sinful nature to God it soon becomes clear that they have nothing in common.

Ever since Adam and Eve ate the fruit in the garden people down through the centuries have been born with sinful natures, and that includes us. We were born hostile to God. We were born separated from God because of our sinful nature. It's hopeless as far as we're concerned.

But not as far as God is concerned. God has made a way for us to be right with Him. Because God knew what a mess our world was in because of sin he gave us a solution, and that solution is Jesus. Now we no longer have to be slaves to our sinful nature. When Jesus went to the cross he took upon Himself our sin. He exchanged our sinful nature for his life. He opened up the way for us to walk into the Father's presence and be reconciled with Him.

We can't save ourselves, but God can. We're hopeless, but with God we have hope. We're slaves to sin, but through Jesus' death we can be alive in God.

More...

Sin p.1261
Forgiveness p.614
Cross p.1112
Redemption p.292
Grace p.1316

35 Can anything separate us from the love of Christ? Can trouble, suffering, and hard times, or hunger and nakedness, or danger and death? 36 It is exactly as the Scriptures say,

> "For you we face death
>   all day long.
> We are like sheep
>   on their way
>   to be butchered."

37 In everything we have won more than a victory because of Christ who loves us. 38 I am sure that nothing can separate us from God's love — not life or death, not angels or spirits, not the present or the future, 39 and not powers above or powers below. Nothing in all creation can separate us from God's love for us in Christ Jesus our Lord!

What about the people of Israel?

CHAPTER 9

God's choice of Israel

1 I am a follower of Christ, and the Holy Spirit is a witness to my conscience. So I tell the truth and I am not lying when I say 2 my heart is broken and I am in great sorrow. 3 I would gladly be placed under God's curse and be separated from Christ for the good of my own people. 4 They are the descendants of Israel, and they are also God's chosen people. God showed them his glory. He made agreements with them and gave them his Law. The temple is theirs and so are the promises that God made to them. 5 They have those famous ancestors, who were also the ancestors of Jesus Christ. I pray that God, who rules over all, will be praised for ever!▸ Amen.

6 It cannot be said that God broke his promise. After all, not all the people of Israel are the true people of God. 7-8 In fact, when God made the promise to Abraham, he meant only Abraham's descendants by his son Isaac. God was talking only about Isaac when he promised 9 Sarah, "At this time next year I will return, and you will already have a son."

10 Don't forget what happened to the twin sons of Isaac and Rebekah. 11-12 Even before they were born or had done anything good or bad, the Lord told Rebekah that her elder son would serve the younger one. The Lord said this to show that he makes his own choices and that it wasn't because of anything either of them had done. 13 That's why the Scriptures say that the Lord liked Jacob more than Esau.

14 Are we saying that God is unfair? Certainly not! 15 The Lord told Moses that he has pity and mercy on anyone he wants to. 16 Everything then depends on God's mercy and not on what people want or do. 17 In the Scriptures the Lord says to Pharaoh* of Egypt, "I let you become king, so that I could show you my power and be praised by all people on earth." 18 Everything depends on what God decides to do, and he can either have pity on people or make them stubborn.

God's anger and mercy

19 Someone may ask, "How can God blame us, if he makes us behave in the way he wants us to?" 20 But, my friend, I ask, "Who do you think you are to question God? Does the clay have the right to ask the potter why he shaped it the way he did? 21 Doesn't a potter have the right to make a fancy bowl and a plain bowl out of the same lump of clay?"

22 God wanted to show his anger and reveal his power against everyone who deserved to be destroyed. But instead, he patiently put up with them. 23 He did this by showing how glorious he is when he has pity on the people he has chosen to share in his glory. 24 Whether Jews or Gentiles, we are those chosen ones, 25 just as the Lord says in the book of Hosea,

> "Although they are not
> my people,
>   I will make them my people.
> I will treat with love
> those nations
>   that have never been loved.

26 "Once they were told,
>   'You are not my people.'
> But in that very place
> they will be called
>   children of the living God."

---

*9.17 **Pharaoh:** A Hebrew word sometimes used for the title of the king of Egypt.

See also: 9.12: Gen 25.23.   9.13: Mal 1.2–3.
9.15: Exod 33.19.   9.17: Exod 9.16 (LXX).   9.20: Isa 29.16;
45.9.   9.25: Hos 2.23.   9.26: Hos 1.10.

See also: 8.36: Psa 44.22.   9.4: Exod 4.22.   9.7: Gen 21.12.
9.9: Gen 18.10.

27 And this is what the prophet Isaiah said about the people of Israel,

> "The people of Israel
> are as many
> as the grains of sand
> along the beach.
> But only a few who are left
> will be saved.
> 28 The Lord will be quick
> and sure to do on earth
> what he has warned
> he will do."

29 Isaiah also said,

> "If the Lord All-Powerful
> had not spared some
> of our descendants,
> we would have been destroyed
> like the cities of Sodom
> and Gomorrah."*

Israel and the good news

30 What does all this mean? It means that the Gentiles were not trying to be acceptable to God, but they found that he would accept them if they had faith. 31-32 It also means that the people of Israel were not acceptable to God. And why not? It was because they were trying' to be acceptable by obeying the Law instead of by having faith in God. The people of Israel fell over the stone that makes people stumble, 33 just as God says in the Scriptures,

> "Look! I am placing in Zion
> a stone to make people
> stumble and fall.
> But those who have faith
> in that one will never
> be disappointed."

CHAPTER 10

1 Dear friends, my greatest wish and my prayer to God is for the people of Israel to be saved. 2 I know they love God, but they don't understand 3 what makes people acceptable to him. So they refuse to trust God, and they try to be acceptable by obeying the Law. 4 But Christ makes the Law no longer necessary' for those who become acceptable to God by faith.

Anyone can be saved

5 Moses said that a person could become acceptable to God by obeying the Law. He did this when he wrote, "If you want to live, you must do all that the Law commands."
6 But people whose faith makes them acceptable to God will never ask, "Who will go up to heaven to bring Christ down?"
7 Neither will they ask, "Who will go down into the world of the dead to raise him to life?"
8 All who are acceptable because of their faith simply say, "The message is as near as your mouth or your heart." And this is the same message we preach about faith. 9 So you will be saved, if you honestly say, "Jesus is Lord", and if you believe with all your heart that God raised him from death. 10 God will accept you and save you, if you truly believe this and tell it to others.
11 The Scriptures say that no one who has faith will be disappointed, 12 no matter if that person is a Jew or a Gentile. There is only one Lord, and he is generous to everyone who asks for his help. 13 All who call out to the Lord will be saved.
14 How can people have faith in the Lord and ask him to save them, if they have never heard about him? And how can they hear, unless someone tells them? 15 And how can anyone tell them without being sent by the Lord? The Scriptures say it is a beautiful sight to see even the feet of someone coming to preach the good news. 16 Yet not everyone has believed the message. For example, the prophet Isaiah asked, "Lord, has anyone believed what we said?"
17 No one can have faith without hearing the message about Christ. 18 But am I saying that the people of Israel did not hear? No, I am not! The Scriptures say,

> "The message was told
> everywhere on earth.
> It was announced
> all over the world."

19 Did the people of Israel understand or not? Moses answered this question when he told that the Lord had said,

> "I will make Israel jealous
> of people

---

*9.29 **Sodom and Gomorrah:** During the time of Abraham the Lord destroyed these two cities because their people were so sinful.
See also: 9.27-28: Isa 10.22-23 (LXX). 9.29: Isa 1.9 (LXX). 9.33: Isa 28.16 (LXX).

See also: 10.5: Lev 18.5. 10.6-8: Deut 30.12-14. 10.11: Isa 28.16 (LXX). 10.13: Joel 2.32. 10.15: Isa 52.7. 10.16: Isa 53.1 (LXX). 10.18: Psa 19.4 (LXX). 10.19: Deut 32.21.

who are a nation
  of nobodies.
I will make them angry
  with people
who don't understand
  a thing."

20 Isaiah was fearless enough to tell that the Lord had said,

"I was found by people
  who were not looking
  for me.
I appeared to the ones
  who were not asking
  about me."

21 And Isaiah said about the people of Israel,

"All day long the Lord
  has reached out
to people who are stubborn
  and refuse to obey."

CHAPTER 11

God has not rejected his people

1 Am I saying that God has turned his back on his people? Certainly not! I am one of the people of Israel, and I myself am a descendant of Abraham from the tribe of Benjamin. 2 God did not turn his back on his chosen people. Don't you remember reading in the Scriptures how Elijah complained to God about the people of Israel? 3 He said, "Lord, they killed your prophets and destroyed your altars. I am the only one left, and now they want to kill me."

4 But the Lord told Elijah, "I still have seven thousand followers who have not worshipped Baal." 5 It is the same way now. God was kind to the people of Israel, and so a few of them are still his followers. 6 This happened because of God's undeserved kindness and not because of anything they have done. It could not have happened except for God's kindness.

7 This means that only a chosen few of the people of Israel found what all of them were searching for. And the rest of them were stubborn, 8 just as the Scriptures say,

"God made them so stupid
  that their eyes are blind,
and their ears
  are still deaf."

9 Then David said,

"Turn their meals
  into bait for a trap,
so that they will stumble
  and be given
    what they deserve.
10 Blindfold their eyes!
  Don't let them see.
Bend their backs
  beneath a burden
    that will never be lifted."

Gentiles will be saved

11 Do I mean that the people of Israel fell, never to get up again? Certainly not! Their failure made it possible for the Gentiles to be saved, and this will make the people of Israel jealous. 12 But if the rest of the world's people were helped so much by Israel's sin and loss, they will be helped even more by their full return.

13 I am now speaking to you Gentiles, and as long as I am an apostle to you, I will take pride in my work. 14 I hope in this way to make some of my own people jealous enough to be saved. 15 When Israel rejected God,' the rest of the people in the world were able to turn to him. So when God makes friends with Israel, it will be like bringing the dead back to life. 16 If part of a batch of dough is made holy by being offered to God, then all the dough is holy. If the roots of a tree are holy, the rest of the tree is holy too.

17 You Gentiles are like branches of a wild olive tree that were made to be part of a cultivated olive tree. You have taken the place of some branches that were cut away from it. And because of this, you enjoy the blessings that come from being part of that cultivated tree. 18 But don't think you are better than the branches that were cut away. Just remember that you are not supporting the roots of that tree. Its roots are supporting you.

19 Perhaps you think those branches were cut away, so that you could be put in their place. 20 That's true enough. But they were cut away because they did not have faith, and you are where you are because you do have faith. So don't be proud, but be afraid. 21 If God cut away those natural branches, couldn't he do the same to you?

22 Now you see both how kind and how hard God can be. He was hard on those who fell, but he was kind to you. And he will keep on being kind to you, if you keep on trusting

See also: **10.20:** Isa 65.1 (LXX).   **10.21:** Isa 65.2 (LXX).
11.1: Phil 3.5.   **11.3:** 1 King 19.10,14.   **11.4:** 1 King 19.18.
11.8: Deut 29.4; Isa 29.10.

See also: **11.9–10:** Psa 69.22–23 (LXX).

Real life

Sport

Contributed by Christians in Sport

'Gazza picks it up midway in his own half. He jinks past one player, nutmegs the approaching anchor midfield man, and he's now well into his stride. He enters the opposing half, feigns to pass, cuts inside the centre half and, ping! He's drilled one past the advancing keeper straight into the top corner! Paul Gascoigne!'

It might be a different sport for you, and a different player, but I bet you've pretended to play your hero! What is it about sport that excites us and gets our juices flowing? What is it that inspires our thinking and imagination? Well, could it be that God, in his goodness, has given us hearts, minds and bodies, gifts, talents and abilities, to use them for his glory, to actually play for him?

So often when we think about God we relate him to specific areas of our life – our going to church, our prayer times, our meeting up with Christian mates.

Have you ever realised that God is as interested in you when you are in the swimming pool, on the tennis court, batting on the cricket square or running on the rugby pitch as when you are sitting in church? God is interested in every part of your life – your sport, social time, school, and church. He really cares about your sport as much as anything else and here's why....

Genesis 1.31 – after creating man, the pinnacle of all his creation, God looked down and saw that it was 'very good.' The creation reflects the character of the creator – his creation is good and so is God – that is important!

Psalm 139 – states that we have all been fearfully and wonderfully made. So it can only be right to enjoy the goodness of God's creation, to enjoy how our bodies work, to enjoy the ability to throw a Frisbee or flick a short corner. But we must realise that because Adam and Eve sinned, all that God made good has been scarred by sin and we see that in sport, and in us!! So we have a choice to make: play sport to glorify God, by using the good gifts he has given us, or play sport for our own selfish, sinful ways and trample on those good gifts.

Romans 12.1 – Because of Jesus, now you can offer your body as a living sacrifice! This is your act of worship! Don't think it's just about singing in church when we worship God – our whole life should be an act of worship and that includes when you're in the sports arena!

So, get out there and play for him... and let your light shine before others so that they too might come to know the creator of all good things!

Think

Ever thought of your sport as being an act of worship to God? You can make it that way, depending on your attitude towards it.
Why is sport that is exciting and inspirational? In what ways is it 'scarred by sin'?
Does your approach to sport, as a player or a supporter, shine a light towards God?

Act

Find a sport that interests you and follow it more closely. Notice the way people behave. Is it honouring to God?
Try a new sport and see what you learn about yourself in the process.

Check

Genesis 1.31; Psalms 139; Romans 12.1

More...

Finding God every day p.660
Incarnation p.1168

in his kindness. Otherwise, you will be cut away too.

²³ If those other branches will start having faith, they will be made a part of that tree again. God has the power to put them back. ²⁴ After all, it wasn't natural for branches to be cut from a wild olive tree and to be made part of a cultivated olive tree. So it is much more likely that God will join the natural branches back to the cultivated olive tree.

The people of Israel will be brought back

²⁵ My friends, I don't want you Gentiles to be too proud of yourselves. So I will explain the mystery of what has happened to the people of Israel. Some of them have become stubborn, and they will stay like that until the complete number of you Gentiles has come in. ²⁶ In this way all Israel will be saved, as the Scriptures say,

"From Zion someone will come
   to rescue us.
Then Jacob's descendants
   will stop being evil.
²⁷ This is what the Lord
   has promised to do
when he forgives their sins."

²⁸ The people of Israel are treated as God's enemies, so that the good news can come to you Gentiles. But they are still the chosen ones, and God loves them because of their famous ancestors. ²⁹ God doesn't take back the gifts he has given or forget about the people he has chosen.

³⁰ At one time you Gentiles rejected God. But now Israel has rejected God, and you have been shown mercy. ³¹ And because of the mercy shown to you, they will also be shown mercy. ³² All people have disobeyed God, and that's why he treats them as prisoners. But he does this, so that he can have mercy on all of them.

³³ Who can measure the wealth and wisdom and knowledge of God? Who can understand his decisions or explain what he does?

³⁴ "Has anyone known
   the thoughts of the Lord
   or given him advice?
³⁵ Has anyone loaned
   something to the Lord
   that must be repaid?"

³⁶ Everything comes from the Lord. All things were made because of him and will return to him. Praise the Lord for ever! Amen.

How to live the new life of love

CHAPTER 12

Christ brings new life

¹ Dear friends, God is good. So I beg you to offer your bodies to him as a living sacrifice, pure and pleasing. That's the most sensible way to serve God. ² Don't be like the people of this world, but let God change the way you think. Then you will know how to do everything that is good and pleasing to him.

³ I realize how kind God has been to me, and so I tell each of you not to think you are better than you really are. Use good sense and measure yourself by the amount of faith that God has given you. ⁴ A body is made up of many parts, and each of them has its own use. ⁵ That's how it is with us. There are many of us, but we are each part of the body of Christ, as well as part of one another.

⁶ God has also given each of us different gifts to use. If we can prophesy, we should do it according to the amount of faith we have. ⁷ If we can serve others, we should serve. If we can teach, we should teach. ⁸ If we can encourage others, we should encourage them. If we can give, we should be generous. If we are leaders, we should do our best. If we are good to others, we should do it cheerfully.

Rules for Christian living

⁹ Be sincere in your love for others. Hate everything that is evil and hold tight to everything that is good. ¹⁰ Love each other as brothers and sisters and honour others more than you do yourself. ¹¹ Never give up. Eagerly follow the Holy Spirit and serve the Lord. ¹² Let your hope make you glad. Be patient in time of trouble and never stop praying. ¹³ Take care of God's needy people and welcome strangers into your home.

¹⁴ Ask God to bless everyone who ill-treats you. Ask him to bless them and not to curse them. ¹⁵ When others are happy, be happy with them, and when they are sad, be sad.

See also: 11.26: Isa 59.20–21 (LXX).   11.27: Isa 27.9 (LXX). 11.33: Isa 55.8.   11.34: Isa 40.13 (LXX).   11.35: Job 41.11.

See also: 11.36: 1 Cor 8.6.   12.4–5: 1 Cor 12.12. 12.6–8: 1 Cor 12.4–11.   12.14: Matt 5.44; Luke 6.28.

Real life

Internet

Contributed by Exalt

The Internet has changed the way we live much of our lives. As a group of Christians designing and running websites, we often face criticism from fellow Christians thinking we have become sucked into a human invention that promised much but in essence was flawed.

'Don't be like the people of this world, but let God change the way you think. Then you will know how to do everything that is good and pleasing to him' Romans 12.2.

As Christians we have to avoid becoming so well adjusted to our culture that we fit into it without even thinking – and this is so true of the Internet. But the answer is not to withdraw from our culture, isolating ourselves and not relating to those around us.

Jesus had another radically different way. He sent his people into the culture of their time with a mission – not selling out to the culture but, in a divinely subversive way, infiltrating it with the kingdom of God, trying to redeem it for a higher agenda – God's agenda.

And that is surely what God wants for the Internet. It is a fantastic invention and God wants it to be used for good. The possibilities are endless and may include.

• Learning how to create websites for your local church or youth group

• Communicating with others on a personal, local, national or global scale – make new friends and look to bring the love of God into chat rooms, discussion forums and live gaming platforms

• Travel the world via the Internet – the Internet is making our a smaller place by giving us access to information, images and content that helps improve our understanding of each other and God's world

But we all have to be careful when using the Internet. Literally everything is available and accessible and there is much to be wary of including pornographic websites and unsafe chat rooms. Use the Internet safely and look to avoid temptation. If you do face temptation, be reassured that God is with you at these times and that you are not the only one to have faced them before (Hebrews 2.18).

Think

What are the good things about the internet? And what are the bad things? Are you being squeezed into an internet culture? What effect is the internet having on you?

The majority of the world's population have never used a telephone, never mind visited a web site. Is this fair?

Act

Don't stay on too long. The internet can help us to communicate better but it can also sap our time, our energy and our money and may leaves us less able to function in the real world.

Pray as you click. See something you know is wrong? Pray about it. Ask God to protect you.

Be careful out there. Not everything is what is seems and not everyone is who they claim to be.

Check

Friendship/chatroom behaviour:
Proverbs 18.24; Luke 6.31;
Hebrews 10.24–25
Avoiding temptation: Hebrews 2.18;
1 Corinthians 10.13; James 1, in particular verse 21

More...

Pornography p.952
Media p.1235
Finding God every day p.660
Work p.1343

[16] Be friendly with everyone. Don't be proud and feel that you are cleverer than others. Make friends with ordinary people.ᵈ [17] Don't ill-treat someone who has ill-treated you. But try to earn the respect of others, [18] and do your best to live at peace with everyone.

[19] Dear friends, don't try to get even. Let God take revenge. In the Scriptures the Lord says,

> "I am the one to take revenge
> and pay them back."

[20] The Scriptures also say,

> "If your enemies are hungry,
>   give them something to eat.
> And if they are thirsty,
>   give them something
>   to drink.
> This will be the same
>   as piling burning coals
>   on their heads."

[21] Don't let evil defeat you, but defeat evil with good.

CHAPTER 13

Obey rulers

[1] Obey the rulers who have authority over you. Only God can give authority to anyone, and he puts these rulers in their places of power. [2] People who oppose the authorities are opposing what God has done, and they will be punished. [3] Rulers are a threat to evil people, not to good people. There is no need to be afraid of the authorities. Just do right, and they will praise you for it. [4] After all, they are God's servants, and it is their duty to help you.

If you do something wrong, you ought to be afraid, because these rulers have the right to punish you. They are God's servants who punish criminals to show how angry God is. [5] But you should obey the rulers because you know it is the right thing to do, and not just because of God's anger.

[6] You must also pay your taxes. The authorities are God's servants, and it is their duty to take care of these matters. [7] Pay all that you owe, whether it is taxes and fees or respect and honour.

Love

[8] Let love be your only debt! If you love others, you have done all that the Law demands. [9] In the Law there are many commands, such as, "Be faithful in marriage. Do not murder. Do not steal. Do not want what belongs to others." But all these are summed up in the command that says, "Love others as much as you love yourself." [10] No one who loves others will harm them. So love is all that the Law demands.

The day when Christ returns

[11] You know what sort of times we live in, and so you should live properly. It is time to wake up. You know that the day when we will be saved is nearer now than when we first put our faith in the Lord. [12] Night is almost over, and day will soon appear. We must stop behaving as people do in the dark and be ready to live in the light. [13] So behave properly, as people do in the day. Don't go to wild parties or get drunk or be vulgar or indecent. Don't quarrel or be jealous. [14] Let the Lord Jesus Christ be as near to you as the clothes you wear. Then you won't try to satisfy your selfish desires.

CHAPTER 14

Don't criticize others

[1] Welcome all the Lord's followers, even those whose faith is weak. Don't criticize them for having beliefs that are different from yours. [2] Some think it is all right to eat anything, while those whose faith is weak will eat only vegetables. [3] But you should not criticize others for eating or for not eating. After all, God welcomes everyone. [4] What right do you have to criticize someone else's servants? Only their Lord can decide if they are doing right, and the Lord will make sure that they do right.

[5] Some of the Lord's followers think one day is more important than another. Others think all days are the same. But each of you should make up your own mind. [6] Any followers who count one day more important than another day do it to honour their Lord. And any followers who eat meat give thanks to God, just like the ones who don't eat meat.

See also: **12.16:** Prov 3.7.   **12.19:** Deut 32.35. **12.20:** Prov 25.21–22 (LXX).   **13.6–7:** Matt 22.21; Mark 12.17; Luke 20.25.

See also: **13.9: a** Exod 20.14; Deut 5.18; **b** Exod 20.13; Deut 5.17; **c** Exod 20.15; Deut 5.19; **d** Exod 20.17; Deut 5.21; **e** Lev 19.18.   **14.1–6:** Col 2.16.

7 Whether we live or die, it must be for God, rather than for ourselves. 8 Whether we live or die, it must be for the Lord. Alive or dead, we still belong to the Lord. 9 This is because Christ died and rose to life, so that he would be the Lord of the dead and of the living. 10 Why do you criticize other followers of the Lord? Why do you look down on them? The day is coming when God will judge all of us. 11 In the Scriptures God says,

> "I swear by my very life
> that everyone will kneel down
>   and praise my name!"

12 And so, each of us must give an account to God for what we do.

Don't cause problems for others

13 We must stop judging others. We must also make up our minds not to upset anyone's faith. 14 The Lord Jesus has made it clear to me that God considers all foods fit to eat. But if you think some foods are unfit to eat, then for you they are not fit.

15 If you are hurting others by the foods you eat, you are not guided by love. Don't let your appetite destroy someone Christ died for. 16 Don't let your right to eat bring shame to Christ. 17 God's kingdom isn't about eating and drinking. It is about pleasing God, about living in peace, and about true happiness. All this comes from the Holy Spirit. 18 If you serve Christ in this way, you will please God and be respected by people. 19 We should try' to live at peace and help each other have a strong faith.

20 Don't let your appetite destroy what God has done. All foods are fit to eat, but it is wrong to cause problems for others by what you eat. 21 It is best not to eat meat or drink wine or do anything else that causes problems for other followers of the Lord. 22 What you believe about these things should be kept between you and God. You are fortunate, if your actions don't make you have doubts. 23 But if you do have doubts about what you eat, you are going against your beliefs. And you know that is wrong, because anything you do against your beliefs is sin.

CHAPTER 15

Please others and not yourself

1 If our faith is strong, we should be patient with the Lord's followers whose faith is weak. We should try to please them instead of ourselves. 2 We should think of their good and try to help them by doing what pleases them. 3 Even Christ did not try to please himself. But as the Scriptures say, "The people who insulted you also insulted me." 4 And the Scriptures were written to teach and encourage us by giving us hope. 5 God is the one who makes us patient and cheerful. I pray that he will help you live at peace with each other, as you follow Christ. 6 Then all of you together will praise God, the Father of our Lord Jesus Christ.

The good news is for Jews and Gentiles

7 Honour God by accepting each other, as Christ has accepted you. 8 I tell you that Christ came as a servant of the Jews to show that God has kept the promises he made to their famous ancestors. Christ also came, 9 so that the Gentiles would praise God for being kind to them. It is just as the Scriptures say,

> "I will tell the nations
>   about you,
> and I will sing praises
>   to your name."

10 The Scriptures also say to the Gentiles, "Come and celebrate with God's people." 11 Again the Scriptures say,

> "Praise the Lord,
>   all you Gentiles.
> All you nations, come
>   and worship him."

12 Isaiah says,

> "Someone from David's family
>   will come to power.
> He will rule the nations,
> and they will put their hope
>   in him."

13 I pray that God, who gives hope, will bless you with complete happiness and peace because of your faith. And may the power of the Holy Spirit fill you with hope.

See also: 15.3: Psa 69.9.   15.9: 2 Sam 22.50; Psa 18.49.
15.10: Deut 32.43.   **15.11:** Psa 117.1.
15.12: Isa 11.10 (LXX).

See also: **14.10:** 2 Cor 5.10.   **14.11:** Isa 45.23 (LXX).

Paul's plans and personal greetings

Paul's work as a missionary

[14] My friends, I am sure that you are very good and that you have all the knowledge you need to teach each other. [15] But I have spoken to you plainly and have tried to remind you of some things. God was so kind to me! [16] He chose me to be a servant of Christ Jesus for the Gentiles and to do the work of a priest in the service of his good news. God did this so that the Holy Spirit could make the Gentiles into a holy offering, pleasing to him.

[17] Because of Christ Jesus, I can take pride in my service for God. [18] In fact, all I will talk about is how Christ let me speak and work, so that the Gentiles would obey him. [19] Indeed, I will tell how Christ performed miracles and wonders by the power of the Holy Spirit. I have preached the good news about him all the way from Jerusalem to Illyricum. [20] But I have always tried to preach where people have never heard about Christ. I am like a builder who doesn't build on anyone else's foundation. [21] It is just as the Scriptures say,

"All who haven't been told
about him
    will see him,
and those who haven't heard
about him
    will understand."

Paul's plan to visit Rome

[22] My work has always kept me from coming to see you. [23] Now there is nothing left for me to do in this part of the world, and for years I have wanted to visit you. [24] So I plan to stop off on my way to Spain. Then after a short, but refreshing, stay with you, I hope you will quickly send me on.

[25-26] I am now on my way to Jerusalem to deliver the money that the Lord's followers in Macedonia and Achaia collected for God's needy people. [27] This is something they really wanted to do. But sharing their money with the Jews was also like paying back a debt, because the Jews had already shared their spiritual blessings with the Gentiles. [28] After I have safely delivered this money, I will visit

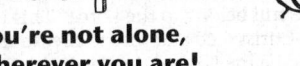

Viewpoints

You're not alone, wherever you are!

Contributed by Lucy C S

'My friends, by the power of the Lord Jesus Christ and by the love that comes from the Holy Spirit, I beg you to pray sincerely with me and for me.'

This is one big, big message to anyone who has ever felt alone or isolated in their love for God: your love for God has made you unified with however many thousands of Christians there are world-wide. So you can never be alone. It's like a huge and growing tribe, spread all across the world, where everyone loves everyone else, and everyone supports everyone else; and now for the best bit. It's the work of God, perfectly created to do his work.

We're always seeing the badness of this world.

All this evil – God's world-wide tribe is a bit of a contradiction really. But that's the whole point! We are the light of the world (Matthew 5.14) and the more unified we are, the brighter we shine, and the more people turn towards the light source: God Himself. Everything gets much more powerful when we do it together. Prayer... if each prayer is a deadly weapon, then the more the better! There's nothing to be embarrassed about in asking people to pray with you – Paul did in this verse. And you can pray for them in return – Paul starts the letter with a prayer for the Romans. So if you ever feel alone or unwanted or anything – then not only are you more special than anything to God, but you are also special to the how ever many thousands of other Christians in the world. Incredible!

More...

Help! I can't make friends p.714
Prayer p.1002
Praying to God p.1334
Sharing with your friends p.1198

See also: 15.21: Isa 52.15 (LXX). **15.22:** Rom 1.13.
15.25–26: 1 Cor 16.1–4. **15.27:** 1 Cor 9.11.

you and then go on to Spain. ²⁹ And when I do arrive in Rome, I know it will be with the full blessings of Christ.

³⁰ My friends, by the power of the Lord Jesus Christ and by the love that comes from the Holy Spirit, I beg you to pray sincerely with me and for me. ³¹ Pray that God will protect me from the unbelievers in Judea, and that his people in Jerusalem will be pleased with what I am doing. ³² Ask God to let me come to you and have a pleasant and refreshing visit. ³³ I pray that God, who gives peace, will be with all of you. Amen.

CHAPTER 16

Personal greetings

¹ I have good things to say about Phoebe, who is a leader in the church at Cenchreae. ² Welcome her in a way that is proper for someone who has faith in the Lord and is one of God's own people. Help her in any way you can. After all, she has proved to be a respected leader for many others, including me.

³ Give my greetings to Priscilla and Aquila. They have not only served Christ Jesus together with me, ⁴ but they have even risked their lives for me. I am grateful for them and so are all the Gentile churches. ⁵ Greet the church that meets in their home.

Greet my dear friend Epaenetus, who was the first person in Asia to have faith in Christ.

⁶ Greet Mary, who has worked so hard for you.

⁷ Greet my relatives' Andronicus and Junias', who were in jail with me. They are highly respected by the apostles and were followers of Christ before I was.

⁸ Greet Ampliatus, my dear friend whose faith is in the Lord.

⁹ Greet Urbanus, who serves Christ along with us.

Greet my dear friend Stachys.

¹⁰ Greet Apelles, a faithful servant of Christ. Greet Aristobulus and his family.

¹¹ Greet Herodion, who is a relative' of mine. Greet Narcissus and the others in his family, who have faith in the Lord.

¹² Greet Tryphaena and Tryphosa, who work hard for the Lord.

Greet my dear friend Persis. She also works hard for the Lord.

¹³ Greet Rufus, that special servant of the Lord, and greet his mother, who has been like a mother to me.

¹⁴ Greet Asyncritus, Phlegon, Hermes, Patrobas, and Hermas, as well as our friends who are with them.

¹⁵ Greet Philologus, Julia, Nereus and his sister, and Olympas, and all God's people who are with them.

¹⁶ Be sure to give each other a warm greeting.

All Christ's churches greet you.

¹⁷ My friends, I beg you to watch out for anyone who causes trouble and divides the church by refusing to do what all of you were taught. Stay away from them! ¹⁸ They want to serve themselves and not Christ the Lord. Their flattery and fancy talk fool people who don't know any better. ¹⁹ I am glad that everyone knows how well you obey the Lord. But still, I want you to understand what is good and not have anything to do with evil. ²⁰ Then God, who gives peace, will soon crush Satan under your feet. I pray that our Lord Jesus will be kind to you.

²¹ Timothy, who works with me, sends his greetings, and so do my relatives,' Lucius, Jason, and Sosipater.

²² I, Tertius, also send my greetings. I am a follower of the Lord, and I wrote this letter.*

²³⁻²⁴ Gaius welcomes me and the whole church into his home, and he sends his greetings.

Erastus, the city treasurer, and our dear friend Quartus send their greetings too.'

Paul's closing prayer

²⁵ Praise God! He can make you strong by means of my good news, which is the message about' Jesus Christ. For many ages this message was kept secret, ²⁶ but now at last it has been told. The eternal God commanded his prophets to write about the good news, so that all nations would obey and have faith. ²⁷ And now, because of Jesus Christ, we can praise the only wise God for ever! Amen.'

---

*16.22 I wrote this letter: Paul probably dictated this letter to Tertius.

See also: 16.21: Acts 16.1.

Additional notes

'1.4 the Holy Spirit: Or "his own spirit of holiness".
'1.4 proved that Jesus is the powerful Son of God: Or "proved in a powerful way that Jesus is the Son of God".

See also: 16.3: Acts 18.2. 16.13: Mark 15.21.

'1.5 Jesus was kind to me and chose me to be an apostle: Or "Jesus was kind to us and chose us to be his apostles".

'1.17 but only those who have faith: Or "and faith is all that matters."

'1.17 The people God accepts because of their faith will live: Or "The people God accepts will live because of their faith."

'3.9 better off: Or "worse off".

'5.1 we live at peace: Some manuscripts have "let us live at peace".

'5.2 introduced us: Some manuscripts add "by faith".

'5.3 We gladly suffer: Or "Let us gladly suffer".

'8.2 you: Some manuscripts have "me".

'8.23 to show that we are his children: These words are not in some manuscripts. The translation of the remainder of the verse would then read, "while we wait for God to set our bodies free."

'8.28 God is always at work for the good of everyone who loves him: Or "All things work for the good of everyone who loves God" or "God's Spirit always works for the good of everyone who loves God."

'9.5 Christ. I pray that God, who rules over all, will be praised for ever: Or "Christ, who rules over all. I pray that God will be praised for ever" or "Christ. And I pray that Christ, who is God and rules over all, will be praised for ever."

'9.31 because they were trying: Or "while they were trying" or "even though they were trying".

'10.4 But Christ makes the Law no longer necessary: Or "But Christ gives the full meaning to the Law".

'11.15 When Israel rejected God: Or "When Israel was rejected".

'12.16 Make friends with ordinary people: Or "Do ordinary jobs."

'14.19 We should try: Some manuscripts have "We try".

'16.7 relatives: Or "Jewish friends".

'16.7 Junias: Or "Junia". Some manuscripts have "Julia".

'16.11 relative(s): See the note at 16.7.

'16.21 relative(s): See the note at 16.7.

'16.23-24 send their greetings too: Some manuscripts add, "I pray that our Lord Jesus Christ will always be kind to you. Amen."

'16.25 about: Or "from".

'16.27 Amen: Some manuscripts have verses 25-27 after 14.23. Others have the verses here and after 14.23, and one manuscript has them after 15.33.

1 Corinthians

Paul's first letter to the church in Corinth

The basics

What's the point? Our actions should be guided by love.

What happens? Paul challenges the behaviour of the Corinthian church. He calls on them to stop arguing and stop trying to get one up on each other. He urges them to value the only thing that really counts: love.

What should I remember? 13.13 'For now there are faith, hope, and love. But of these three, the greatest is love.'

More details

Setting the scene Paul had already written to the Corinthian church once. And they'd written back asking him questions about marriage and food offered to idols. But Paul was also concerned about the splits and arguments in the church. So he wrote back...

What's it all about? Paul's relationship with the followers in Corinth was not an easy one. Part of it was due to the atmosphere of the city. Corinth was one of the most 'liberal' cities in the ancient world. It was a wealthy sea port with a reputation for sexual immorality, so much so that the Greeks used the word 'to corinth' as a verb: if someone was doing a bit of 'corinthing', they were sleeping around.

This atmosphere seeped into the church, turning it into a group of followers infected by wealth and exodus The Corinthian church had many of the signs of a true church, but they were behaving like spoilt brats, rather than children of God.

Paul was especially concerned with the amount of arguments and splits in the church.

They treated each other differently according to wealth and position; they split into different factions. So Paul encourages them to change their ways and worship God as he should be worshipped.

Above all, he talks about love. Love is the most important thing, he assures them. If they only loved one another, then the splits and the arguments would disappear.

And another thing

This is actually the second letter Paul wrote to the church at Corinth (and for all we know he might have slipped them the odd postcard as well). But this is the first letter we have, hence the name. Perhaps Paul's meaning in the first letter had not been clear, but there were still arguments in the church and accusations of sexual immorality. He wrote from Ephesus and dispatched Timothy to try to deal with the situation.

Footsteps

Paul's greeting and prayer

CHAPTER 1

¹ *From Paul, chosen by God to be an apostle of Christ Jesus, and from Sosthenes, who is also a follower.*

² *To God's church in Corinth.* Christ Jesus chose you to be his very own people, and you worship in his name, as we and all others do who call him Lord.

³ My prayer is that God our Father and the Lord Jesus Christ will be kind to you and will bless you with peace!

⁴ I never stop thanking my God for being kind enough to give you Christ Jesus, ⁵ who helps you speak and understand so well. ⁶ Now you are certain that everything we told you about our Lord Christ Jesus is true. ⁷ You are not missing out on any blessings, as you wait for him to return. ⁸ And until the day Christ does return, he will keep you completely innocent. ⁹ God can be trusted, and he chose you to be partners with his Son, our Lord Jesus Christ.

A call for unity

Taking sides

¹⁰ My dear friends, as a follower of our Lord Jesus Christ, I beg you to get along with each other. Don't take sides. Always try to agree in what you think. ¹¹ Several people from Chloe's family* have already reported to me that you keep arguing with each other. ¹² They have said that some of you claim to follow me, while others claim to follow Apollos or Peter* or Christ.

¹³ Has Christ been divided up? Was I nailed to a cross for you? Were you baptized in my name? ¹⁴ I thank God* that I didn't baptize any of you except Crispus and Gaius. ¹⁵ Not one of you can say that you were baptized in my name. ¹⁶ I did baptize the family* of Stephanas, but I don't remember if I baptized anyone else. ¹⁷ Christ did not send me to baptize. He sent me to tell the good news

---

*1.11 family: Family members and possibly slaves and others who may have lived in the house.
*1.12 Peter: The Greek text has "Cephas", which is an Aramaic name meaning "rock". Peter is the Greek name with the same meaning.
*1.16 family: See the note at 1.11.
See also: 1.2: Acts 18.1. 1.12: Acts 18.24. 1.14: a Acts 18.8; b Acts 19.29; Rom 16.23. 1.16: 1 Cor 16.15.

Viewpoints

Does church seem routine? Is this what God intends?

Contributed by Peter S

'My dear friends, as a follower of our Lord Jesus Christ, I beg you to get along with each other. Don't take sides. Always try to agree in what you think.'

So why should church just be this routine 'Baptism, communion, life'? Yes these are excellent things – we are commanded to do them, but should they just become like this to us?

The answer is no! How do you stop it? Paul tells these young believers that church should be where the fellowship is united in mind and judgement. If we are united together we seek to please each other and ultimately God together – and if this is our aim, these factors of church life will stop being just a routine. If we seek to be close to Jesus above all else then doing these things will stop being a chore because we will be doing them to keep his commandments – which should make us happy.

And if you ever do fall into this feeling of the routine of church, just think of the time when we will be united perfectly with Jesus, when it will not be a routine but it will be your whole existence – to have this communion with him.

More...
Church p.1315
Meeting together p.1371

Anorak corner

Donkeys

1. Who used a donkey's jawbone as a weapon?
2. Which king was found chasing lost donkeys?
3. Whose donkey spoke to him?
4. Who rode into Jerusalem on a donkey?
5. Who ate grass and lived among the wild donkeys?
(Answers on p.1431)

without using big words that would make the cross of Christ lose its power.

Christ is God's power and wisdom

18 The message about the cross doesn't make any sense to lost people. But for those of us who are being saved, it is God's power at work. 19 As God says in the Scriptures,

> "I will destroy the wisdom
> of all who claim
>   to be wise.
> I will confuse those
> who think they know
>   so much."

20 What happened to those wise people? What happened to those experts in the Scriptures? What happened to the ones who think they have all the answers? Didn't God show that the wisdom of this world is foolish? 21 God was wise and decided not to let the people of this world use their wisdom to learn about him.

Instead, God chose to save only those who believe the foolish message we preach. 22 Jews ask for miracles, and Greeks want something that sounds wise. 23 But we preach that Christ was nailed to a cross. Most Jews have problems with this, and most Gentiles think it is foolish. 24 Our message is God's power and wisdom for the Jews and the Greeks that he has chosen. 25 Even when God is foolish, he is wiser than everyone else, and even when God is weak, he is stronger than everyone else.

26 My dear friends, remember what you were when God chose you. The people of this world didn't think that many of you were wise. Only a few of you were in places of power, and not many of you came from important families. 27 But God chose the foolish things of this world to put the wise to shame. He chose the weak things of this world to put the powerful to shame.

28 What the world thinks is worthless, useless, and nothing at all is what God has used to destroy what the world considers important. 29 God did all this to keep anyone from boasting to him. 30 You are God's children. He sent Christ Jesus to save us and to make us wise, acceptable, and holy. 31 So if you want to boast, do what the Scriptures say and boast about the Lord.

CHAPTER 2

Telling about Christ and the cross

1 Friends, when I came and told you the mystery' that God had shared with us, I didn't use big words or try to sound wise. 2 In fact, while I was with you, I made up my mind to speak only about Jesus Christ, who had been nailed to a cross.

3 At first, I was weak and trembling with fear. 4 When I talked with you or preached, I didn't try to prove anything by sounding wise. I simply let God's Spirit show his power. 5 That way you would have faith because of God's power and not because of human wisdom.

6 We do use wisdom when speaking to people who are mature in their faith. But it isn't the wisdom of this world or of its rulers, who will soon disappear. 7 We speak of God's hidden and mysterious wisdom that God decided to use for our glory long before the world began. 8 The rulers of this world didn't know anything about this wisdom. If they had known about it, they would not have nailed the glorious Lord to a cross. 9 But it is just as the Scriptures say,

> "What God has planned
>   for people who love him
> is more than eyes have seen
>   or ears have heard.
> It has never even
>   entered our minds!"

10 God's Spirit has shown you everything. His Spirit finds out everything, even what is deep in the mind of God. 11 You are the only one who knows what is in your own mind, and God's Spirit is the only one who knows what is in God's mind. 12 But God has given us his Spirit. That's why we don't think the same way that the people of this world think. That's also why we can recognize the blessings that God has given us.

13 Every word we speak was taught to us by God's Spirit, not by human wisdom. And this same Spirit helps us teach spiritual things to spiritual people.' 14 That's why only someone who has God's Spirit can understand spiritual blessings. Anyone who doesn't have God's Spirit thinks these blessings are foolish. 15 People who are guided by the Spirit can make all kinds of judgments, but they cannot be judged by others. 16 The Scriptures ask,

See also: 1.19: Isa 29.14 (LXX).   **1.20: a** Job 12.17; Isa 19.12; 33.18; **b** Isa 44.25.   **1.31:** Jer 9.24.

See also: 2.3: Acts 18.9.   **2.9:** Isa 64.4. **2.16:** Isa 40.13 (LXX).

"Has anyone ever known
the thoughts of the Lord
or given him advice?"

But we understand what Christ is thinking.'

CHAPTER 3

Working together for God

[1] My friends, you are acting like the people of this world. That's why I could not speak to you as spiritual people. You are like babies as far as your faith in Christ is concerned. [2] So I had to treat you like babies and feed you milk. You could not take solid food, and you still cannot, [3] because you are not yet spiritual. You are jealous and argue with each other. This proves that you are not spiritual and that you are acting like the people of this world.

[4] Some of you say that you follow me, and others claim to follow Apollos. Isn't that how ordinary people behave? [5] Apollos and I are merely servants who helped you to have faith. It was the Lord who made it all happen. [6] I planted the seeds, Apollos watered them, but God made them sprout and grow. [7] What matters isn't those who planted or watered, but God who made the plants grow. [8] The one who plants is just as important as the one who waters. And each one will be paid for what they do. [9] Apollos and I work together for God, and you are God's garden and God's building.

Only one foundation

[10] God was kind and let me become an expert builder. I laid a foundation on which others have built. But we must each be careful how we build, [11] because Christ is the only foundation. [12-13] Whatever we build on that foundation will be tested by fire on the day of judgment. Then everyone will find out if we have used gold, silver, and precious stones, or wood, hay, and straw. [14] We will be rewarded if our building is left standing. [15] But if it is destroyed by the fire, we will lose everything. Yet we ourselves will be saved, like someone escaping from flames.

[16] All of you know that you are God's temple and that his Spirit lives in you. [17] Together you are God's holy temple, and God will destroy anyone who destroys his temple.

[18] Don't fool yourselves! If any of you think you are wise in the things of this world, you will have to become foolish before you can be truly wise. [19] This is because God considers the wisdom of this world to be foolish. It is just as the Scriptures say, "God catches the wise when they try to outsmart him." [20] The Scriptures also say, "The Lord knows that the plans made by wise people are useless." [21-22] So stop boasting about what anyone has done. Paul and Apollos and Peter* all belong to you. In fact, everything is yours, including the world, life, death, the present, and the future. Everything belongs to you, [23] and you belong to Christ, and Christ belongs to God.

CHAPTER 4

The work of the apostles

[1] Think of us as servants of Christ who have been given the work of explaining God's mysterious ways. [2] And since our first duty is to be faithful to the one we work for, [3] it doesn't matter to me if I am judged by you or even by a court of law. In fact, I don't judge myself. [4] I don't know of anything against me, but that doesn't prove that I am right. The Lord is my judge. [5] So don't judge anyone until the Lord returns. He will show what is hidden in the dark and what is in everyone's heart. Then God will be the one who praises each of us.

[6] Friends, I have used Apollos and myself as examples to teach you the meaning of the saying, "Follow the rules." I want you to stop saying that one of us is better than the other. [7] What is so special about you? What do you have that you were not given? And if it was given to you, how can you boast? [8] Are you already satisfied? Are you now rich? Have you become kings while we are still nobodies? I wish you were kings. Then we could have a share in your kingdom.

[9] It seems to me that God has put us apostles in the worst possible place. We are like prisoners on their way to death. Angels and the people of this world just laugh at us. [10] Because of Christ we are thought of as fools, but Christ has made you wise. We are weak and hated, but you are powerful and respected. [11] Even today we go hungry and thirsty and don't have anything to wear except rags. We are ill-treated and don't have

See also: 3.2: Heb 5.12–13.   **3.4:** 1 Cor 1.12.
3.6: a Acts 18.4–11; **b** Acts 18.24–28.   **3.16:** 1 Cor 6.19;
2 Cor 6.16.

*3.21–22 Peter: See the note at 1.12.
See also: 3.19: Job 5.13.   **3.20:** Psa 94.11.

a place to live. ¹² We work hard with our own hands, and when people abuse us, we wish them well. When we suffer, we are patient. ¹³ When someone curses us, we answer with kind words. Until now we are thought of as nothing more than the trash and rubbish of this world.

¹⁴ I am not writing to embarrass you. I want to help you, just as parents help their own dear children. ¹⁵ Ten thousand people may teach you about Christ, but I am your only father. You became my children when I told you about Christ Jesus, ¹⁶ and I want you to be like me. ¹⁷ That's why I sent Timothy to you. I love him like a son, and he is a faithful servant of the Lord. Timothy will tell you what I do to follow Christ and how it agrees with what I always teach about Christ in every church.

¹⁸ Some of you think I am not coming for a visit, and so you are boasting. ¹⁹ But if the Lord lets me come, I will soon be there. Then I will find out if the ones who are doing all this boasting really have any power. ²⁰ God's kingdom isn't just a lot of words. It is power. ²¹ What do you want me to do when I arrive? Do you want me to be hard on you or to be kind and gentle?

Problems in relationships

CHAPTER 5

Immoral followers

¹ I have heard terrible things about some of you. In fact, you are behaving worse than the Gentiles. A man is even sleeping with his own stepmother.ᵇ ² You are proud, when you ought to feel bad enough to chase away anyone who acts like that.

³⁻⁴ I am with you only in my thoughts. But in the name of our Lord Jesus I have already judged this man, as though I were with you in person. So when you meet together and the power of the Lord Jesus is with you, I will be there too. ⁵ You must then hand that man over to Satan. His body will be destroyed, but his spirit will be saved when the Lord Jesus returns.

⁶ Stop being proud! Don't you know how a little yeast can spread through the whole batch of dough? ⁷ Get rid of the old yeast! Then you will be like fresh bread made without yeast, and that is what you are. Our Passover lamb is Christ, who has already been sacrificed. ⁸ So don't celebrate the festival by being evil and sinful, which is like serving bread made with yeast. Be pure and truthful and celebrate by using bread made without yeast.

⁹ In my other letter* I told you not to have anything to do with immoral people. ¹⁰ But I wasn't talking about the people of this world. You would have to leave this world to get away from everyone who is immoral or greedy or who cheats or worships idols. ¹¹ I was talking about your own people who are immoral or greedy or worship idols or curse others or get drunk or cheat. Don't even eat with them! ¹² Why should I judge outsiders? Aren't we supposed to judge only church members? ¹³ God judges everyone else. The Scriptures say, "Chase away any of your own people who are evil."

CHAPTER 6

Taking each other to court

¹ When one of you has a complaint against another, do you take your complaint to a court of sinners? Or do you take it to God's people? ² Don't you know that God's people will judge the world? And if you are going to judge the world, can't you settle small problems? ³ Don't you know that we will judge angels? And if that is so, we can surely judge everyday matters. ⁴ Why do you take everyday complaints to judges who are not respected by the church? ⁵ I say this to your shame. Aren't any of you wise enough to act as a judge between one follower and another? ⁶ Why should one of you take another to be tried by unbelievers?

⁷ When one of you takes another to court, all of you lose. It would be better to let yourselves be cheated and robbed. ⁸ But instead, you cheat and rob other followers.

⁹ Don't you know that evil people won't have a share in the blessings of God's kingdom? Don't fool yourselves! No one who is immoral or worships idols or is unfaithful in marriage or is a pervert or behaves like a homosexual ¹⁰ will share in God's kingdom. Neither will any thief or greedy person or drunkard or anyone who curses and cheats others. ¹¹ Some of you used to be like that. But now the name of our

---

*5.9 other letter: An unknown letter that Paul wrote to the Christians at Corinth before he wrote this one.

See also: 4.12: Acts 18.3. 4.16: 1 Cor 11.1; Phil 3.17.
5.1: Deut 22.30. 5.6: Gal 5.9. 5.7: Exod 12.5.

See also: 5.8: Exod 13.7; Deut 16.3. 5.13: Deut 13.5;
17.7 (LXX).

Helpline

Help! I'm confused about my sexuality

'I'm really confused. I have these feelings that I think are wrong. People tell me they're wrong. What does the Bible say?'

Today's world is a sexual free market. Whatever your preference, whatever your fantasy, you're encouraged to indulge it. After all, they say, do what you want, as long as you don't harm anyone else.

The issue is, whether our urges actually harm ourselves. Are they really good for us? Or are we indulging in behaviour that is not what God wants?

This is difficult. The picture of sexuality in the Bible is heterosexual; of men having relationships with women. There are those who argue that this is to do with the culture of the time; there are others who argue that same sex relationships are always wrong.

Whatever the case, you need to control of your behaviour and your life. You need to honour God with your body.

So don't stay isolated. Talk about it. You may face difficult decisions; you will need their support and love.

Three things

Clarity

Don't get lost in confusion. Talk to your church or youth leader. They will help you make sense of the things you're feeling.

Control

'Some of you say, "We can do anything we want to." But I tell you that not everything is good for us,' writes Paul
(1 Corinthians 6.12). Think. Is it really what you want? Will it really be good for you?

Love

Whatever you feel, keep close to God. He is your father and he cares for you. Don't let your desires and feelings come between you and the creator who loves you.

More...

Sex p.727
Pornography p.952
God's love p.958

Lord Jesus Christ and the power of God's Spirit have washed you and made you holy and acceptable to God.

Honour God with your body

12 Some of you say, "We can do anything we want to." But I tell you that not everything is good for us. So I refuse to let anything have power over me. 13 You also say, "Food is meant for our bodies, and our bodies are meant for food." But I tell you that God will destroy them both. We are not supposed to do indecent things with our bodies. We are to use them for the Lord who is in charge of our bodies. 14 God will raise us from death by the same power that he used when he raised our Lord to life.

15 Don't you know that your bodies are part of the body of Christ? Is it right for me to join part of the body of Christ to a prostitute? No, it isn't! 16 Don't you know that a man who does that becomes part of her body? The Scriptures say, "The two of them will be like one person." 17 But anyone who is joined to the Lord is one in spirit with him.

18 Don't be immoral in matters of sex. That is a sin against your own body in a way that no other sin is. 19 You know that your body is a temple where the Holy Spirit lives. The Spirit is in you and is a gift from God. You are no longer your own. 20 God paid a great price for you. So use your body to honour God.

CHAPTER 7

Questions about marriage

1 Now I will answer the questions that you asked in your letter. You asked, "Is it best for people not to marry?" 2 Well, having your own husband or wife should keep you from doing something immoral. 3 Husbands and wives should be fair with each other about having sex. 4 A wife belongs to her husband instead of to herself, and a husband belongs to his wife instead of to himself. 5 So don't refuse sex to each other, unless you agree not to have sex for a little while, in order to spend time in prayer. Then Satan won't be able to tempt you because of your lack of self-control. 6 In my opinion that is what should be done, though I don't know of anything the Lord said about this matter. 7 I wish that all of you were like me, but God has given different gifts to each of us.

See also: **6.12:** 1 Cor 10.23. **6.16:** Gen 2.24.
6.19: 1 Cor 3.16; 2 Cor 6.16.

Real life

Divorce

Contributed by Soul Survivor

Imagine: it's a sleepish Sunday in late Autumn, where you probably got up at no fixed time. It's grey outside, and you're languishing around with your Space lego, wondering what would be a better way to set up the space station.

Your dad calls your name and slowly you make your way downstairs. The rest of your family are already sitting round the table. Strange. You sit down and wait.

Dad says it's time for a 'pow-wow.' And then he starts talking about not having been the best dad, or the best husband. You don't know where this is all going until you notice your mum's eyes looking all funny. She's crying. You've never seen her look like this before: pain brimming up, bloodshot and spoiling her mascara. Then you know something really bad is happening.

Dad says that he's thinking it's time for them to get divorced.

Your face flushes. You don't know what to feel: total shock, or acute embarrassment at the fact that you're in such intense pain with your whole family looking on. You run out of the kitchen and up the stairs to your room. Your whole world has changed.

Child Line say that 25% of children will see their parents divorce, and many need to adjust quickly to hugely changing circumstances. A different house, new relationships, a sense of isolation. Your parents getting divorced has a sort of underlying message. That you're not really that valuable, you can be discarded. And it profoundly changes your relationship with them. Suddenly, you can see that they aren't perfect, they too have problems and needs, and you end up feeling like you're the parent. But you're not. Hopefully your aunts, uncles and any friends your parents might have, should be there to help them. You might get some comfort from a new sort of friendship with your mum or your dad for a bit, but it's a weight you're not really meant to bear.

You may think you're supposed to cope with all this, and get on with life as though nothing had ever happened. No! Your world has been turned upside down and its not selfish or immature to want to cry into your pillow as you go to sleep. It's OK to be devastated, confused, lonely, angry and you don't have to cover any of that up. To have to fend for yourself prematurely is a big thing.

There aren't any easy answers for dealing with divorce. It can happen to us whether we, or our parents, are Christians or not. It doesn't necessarily make sense, and it just plain hurts: for you, your parents, for everyone – except perhaps the solicitors.

God IS with you. It won't feel like it. But when you're crying on your own he's there. It will get better. That isn't of any comfort if you're in the middle of it now, but the pain dies down a bit, and you learn to adjust. There will be a day when you're laughing again.

Think

What does God think about divorce? Angry? Sad? Indifferent?
Are your parents divorced? Do you have friends whose parents are divorced? How can you pray about the situation?

Act

Pray for people you know who are going through separation or divorce in the home. If this is happening to you, talk to your youth pastor, your pastor, or an older person that you can trust.

Check

Psalm 25; Proverbs 10.12; Isaiah 43.1–4; Ephesians 6.1–4;

More...

Help! My Dad's never around p.187
Fostering and adoption p.63

⁸ Here is my advice for people who have never been married and for widows. You should stay single, just as I am. ⁹ But if you don't have enough self-control, then go ahead and get married. After all, it is better to marry than to burn with desire.⁑

¹⁰ I instruct married couples to stay together, and this is exactly what the Lord himself taught. A wife who leaves her husband ¹¹ should either stay single or go back to her husband. And a husband should not leave his wife.

¹² I don't know of anything else the Lord said about marriage. All I can do is to give you my own advice. If your wife isn't a follower of the Lord, but is willing to stay with you, don't divorce her. ¹³ If your husband isn't a follower, but is willing to stay with you, don't divorce him. ¹⁴ Your husband or wife who isn't a follower is made holy by having you as a partner. This also makes your children holy and keeps them from being unclean in God's sight.

¹⁵ If your husband or wife isn't a follower of the Lord and decides to divorce you, then you should agree to it. You are no longer bound to that person. After all, God chose you and wants you to live at peace. ¹⁶ And besides, how do you know if you will be able to save your husband or wife who isn't a follower?

Obeying the Lord at all times

¹⁷ In every church I tell the people to stay as they were when the Lord Jesus chose them and God called them to be his own. Now I say the same thing to you. ¹⁸ If you are already circumcised, don't try to change it. If you are not circumcised, don't get circumcised. ¹⁹ Being circumcised or uncircumcised isn't really what matters. The important thing is to obey God's commands. ²⁰ So don't try to change what you were when God chose you. ²¹ Are you a slave? Don't let that bother you. But if you can win your freedom, you should. ²² When the Lord chooses slaves, they become his free people. And when he chooses free people, they become slaves of Christ. ²³ God paid a great price for you. So don't become slaves of anyone else. ²⁴ Stay what you were when God chose you.

Unmarried people

²⁵ I don't know of anything that the Lord said about people who have never been married.⁑ But I will tell you what I think. And you can trust me, because the Lord has treated me with kindness. ²⁶ We are now going through hard times, and I think it is best for you to stay as you are. ²⁷ If you are married, stay married. If you are not married, don't try to get married. ²⁸ It isn't wrong to marry, even if you have never been married before. But those who marry will have a lot of trouble, and I want to protect you from that.

²⁹ My friends, what I mean is that the Lord will soon come,⁑ and it won't matter if you are married or not. ³⁰ It will be all the same if you are crying or laughing, or if you are buying or are completely broke. ³¹ It won't make any difference how much good you are getting from this world or how much you like it. This world as we know it is now passing away.

³² I want all of you to be free from worry. An unmarried man worries about how to please the Lord. ³³ But a married man has more worries. He must worry about the things of this world, because he wants to please his wife. ³⁴ So he is pulled in two directions. Unmarried women and women who have never been married⁑ worry only about pleasing the Lord, and they keep their bodies and minds pure. But a married woman worries about the things of this world, because she wants to please her husband. ³⁵ What I am saying is for your own good — it isn't to limit your freedom. I want to help you to live right and to love the Lord above all else.

³⁶ But suppose you are engaged to someone old enough to be married, and you want her so much that all you can think about is getting married. Then go ahead and marry.⁑ There is nothing wrong with that. ³⁷ But it is better to have self-control and to make up your mind not to marry. ³⁸ It is perfectly all right to marry, but it is better not to get married at all.

³⁹ A wife should stay married to her husband until he dies. Then she is free to marry again, but only to a man who is a follower of the Lord. ⁴⁰ However, I think I am obeying God's Spirit when I say she would be happier to stay single.

See also: 7.10–11: Matt 5.32; 19.9; Mark 10.11–12; Luke 16.18.

Honouring God instead of idols

CHAPTER 8

Food offered to idols

¹ In your letter you asked me about food offered to idols. All of us know something about this subject. But knowledge makes us proud of ourselves, while love makes us helpful to others. ² In fact, people who think they know so much don't know anything at all. ³ But God has no doubts about who loves him.

⁴ Even though food is offered to idols, we know that none of the idols in this world are alive. After all, there is only one God. ⁵ Many things in heaven and on earth are called gods and lords, but none of them really are gods or lords. ⁶ We have only one God, and he is the Father. He created everything, and we live for him. Jesus Christ is our only Lord. Everything was made by him, and by him life was given to us.

⁷ Not everyone knows these things. In fact, many people have grown up with the belief that idols have life in them. So when they eat meat offered to idols, they are bothered by a weak conscience. ⁸ But food doesn't bring us any closer to God. We are no worse off if we don't eat, and we are no better off if we do.

⁹ Don't cause problems for someone with a weak conscience, just because you have the right to eat anything. ¹⁰ You know all this, and so it doesn't bother you to eat in the temple of an idol. But suppose a person with a weak conscience sees you and decides to eat food that has been offered to idols. ¹¹ Then what you know has destroyed someone Christ died for. ¹² When you sin by hurting a follower with a weak conscience, you sin against Christ. ¹³ So if I hurt one of the Lord's followers by what I eat, I will never eat meat as long as I live.

CHAPTER 9

The rights of an apostle

¹ I am free. I am an apostle. I have seen the Lord Jesus and have led you to have faith in him. ² Others may think that I am not an apostle, but you are proof that I am an apostle to you.

³ When people question me, I tell them ⁴ that Barnabas and I have the right to our food and drink. ⁵ We each have the right to marry one of the Lord's followers and to take her along with us, just as the other apostles and the Lord's brothers and Peter* do. ⁶ Are we the only ones who have to support ourselves by working at another job? ⁷ Do soldiers pay their own salaries? Don't people who raise grapes eat some of what they grow? Don't shepherds get milk from their own goats?

⁸⁻⁹ I am not saying this on my own authority. The Law of Moses tells us not to muzzle an ox when it is grinding grain. But was God concerned only about an ox? ¹⁰ No, he wasn't! He was talking about us. This was written in the Scriptures so that all who plough and all who grind the grain will look forward to sharing in the harvest.

¹¹ When we told the message to you, it was like planting spiritual seed. So we have the right to accept material things as our harvest from you. ¹² If others have the right to do this, we have an even greater right. But we haven't used this right of ours. We are willing to put up with anything to keep from causing trouble for the message about Christ.

¹³ Don't you know that people who work in the temple make their living from what is brought to the temple? Don't you know that a person who serves at the altar is given part of what is offered? ¹⁴ In the same way, the Lord wants everyone who preaches the good news to make a living from preaching this message.

¹⁵ But I have never used these privileges of mine, and I am not writing this because I want to start now. I would rather die than let someone rob me of the right to take pride in this. ¹⁶ I don't have any reason to boast about preaching the good news. Preaching is something God told me to do, and if I don't do it, I am doomed. ¹⁷ If I preach because I want to, I will be paid. But even if I don't want to, it is still something God has sent me to do. ¹⁸ What pay am I given? It is the chance to preach the good news free of charge and not to use the privileges that are mine because I am a preacher.

¹⁹ I am not anyone's slave. But I have become a slave to everyone, so that I can win as many people as possible. ²⁰ When I am with the Jews, I live like a Jew to win Jews. They are ruled by the Law of Moses, and I am not. But I live by the Law to win them. ²¹ And when I am with people who are not ruled by

---

*9.5 Peter: See the note at 1.12.

See also: 9.9: Deut 25.4; 1 Tim 5.18. 9.11: Rom 15.27. 9.13: Deut 18.1. 9.14: Matt 10.10; Luke 10.7.

the Law, I forget about the Law to win them. Of course, I never really forget about the law of God. In fact, I am ruled by the law of Christ. ²² When I am with people whose faith is weak, I live as they do to win them. I do everything I can to win everyone I possibly can. ²³ I do all this for the good news, because I want to share in its blessings.

A race and a fight

²⁴ You know that many runners enter a race, and only one of them wins the prize. So run to win! ²⁵ Athletes work hard to win a crown that cannot last, but we do it for a crown that will last for ever. ²⁶ I don't run without a goal. And I don't box by beating my fists in the air. ²⁷ I keep my body under control and make it my slave, so I won't lose out after telling the good news to others.

CHAPTER 10

Don't worship idols

¹ Friends, I want to remind you that all our ancestors walked under the cloud and went through the sea. ² This was like being baptized and becoming followers of Moses. ³ All of them also ate the same spiritual food ⁴ and drank the same spiritual drink, which flowed from the spiritual rock that followed them. That rock was Christ. ⁵ But most of them did not please God. So they died, and their bodies were scattered all over the desert.

⁶ What happened to them is a warning to keep us from wanting to do the same evil things. ⁷ They worshipped idols, just as the Scriptures say, "The people sat down to eat and drink. Then they got up to dance around." So don't worship idols. ⁸ Some of those people did shameful things, and in a single day about twenty-three thousand of them died. Don't do shameful things as they did. ⁹ And don't try to test Christ,' as some of them did and were later bitten by poisonous snakes. ¹⁰ Don't even grumble, as some of them did and were killed by the destroying angel. ¹¹ These things happened to them as a warning to us. All this was written in the Scriptures to teach us who live in these last days.

¹² Even if you think you can stand up to temptation, be careful not to fall. ¹³ You are tempted in the same way that everyone else is tempted. But God can be trusted not to let you be tempted too much, and he will show you how to escape from your temptations.

¹⁴ My friends, you must keep away from idols. ¹⁵ I am speaking to you as people who have enough sense to know what I am talking about. ¹⁶ When we drink from the cup that we ask God to bless, isn't that sharing in the blood of Christ? When we eat the bread that we break, isn't that sharing in the body of Christ? ¹⁷ By sharing in the same loaf of bread, we become one body, even though there are many of us.

¹⁸ Aren't the people of Israel sharing in the worship when they gather around the altar and eat the sacrifices offered there? ¹⁹ Am I saying that either the idols or the food sacrificed to them is anything at all? ²⁰ No, I am not! That food is really sacrificed to demons and not to God. I don't want you to have anything to do with demons. ²¹ You cannot drink from the cup of demons and still drink from the Lord's cup. You cannot eat at the table of demons and still eat at the Lord's table. ²² We would make the Lord jealous if we did that. And we are not stronger than the Lord.

Always honour God

²³ Some of you say, "We can do whatever we want to!" But I tell you that not everything may be good or helpful. ²⁴ We should think about others and not about ourselves. ²⁵ However, when you buy meat in the market, go ahead and eat it. Keep your conscience clear by not asking where the meat came from. ²⁶ The Scriptures say, "The earth and everything in it belong to the Lord."

²⁷ If an unbeliever invites you to dinner, and you want to go, then go. Eat whatever you are served. Don't cause a problem for someone's conscience by asking where the food came from. ²⁸⁻²⁹ But if you are told that it has been sacrificed to idols, don't cause a problem by eating it. I don't mean a problem for yourself, but for the one who told you. Why should my freedom be limited by someone else's conscience? ³⁰ If I give thanks for what I eat, why should anyone accuse me of doing wrong?

See also: **10.1:** a Exod 13.21–22; b Exod 14.22–29.
10.3: Exod 16.35.   **10.4:** Exod 17.6; Num 20.11.
10.5: Num 14.29–30. **10.6:** Num 11.4.   **10.7:** Exod 32.6.
10.8: Num 25.1–18. **10.9:** Num 21.5–6.
10.10: Num 16.41–49.

See also: 10.16: Matt 26.26–28; Mark 14.22–24;
Luke 22.19–20. **10.18:** Lev 7.6. **10.20:** Deut 32.17 (LXX).
10.22: Deut 32.21. **10.23:** 1 Cor 6.12. **10.26:** Psa 24.1.

[31] When you eat or drink or do anything else, always do it to honour God. [32] Don't cause problems for Jews or Greeks or anyone else who belongs to God's church. [33] I always try to please others instead of myself, in the hope that many of them will be saved.

CHAPTER 11

[1] You must follow my example, as I follow the example of Christ.

Guidance for worship and church life

Rules for worship

[2] I am proud of you, because you always remember me and obey the teachings I gave you. [3] Now I want you to know that Christ is the head over all men, and a man is the head over a woman. But God is the head over Christ. [4] This means that any man who prays or prophesies with something on his head brings shame to his head.

[5] But any woman who prays or prophesies without something on her head brings shame to her head. In fact, she may as well shave her head.* [6] A woman should wear something on her head. It is a disgrace for a woman to shave her head or cut her hair. But if she refuses to wear something on her head, let her cut off her hair.

[7] Men were created to be like God and to bring honour to God. This means that a man should not wear anything on his head. Women were created to bring honour to men. [8] It was the woman who was made from a man, and not the man who was made from a woman. [9] He wasn't created for her. She was created for him. [10] And so, because of this, and also because of the angels, a woman ought to wear something on her head, as a sign of her authority.*

[11] As far as the Lord is concerned, men and women need each other. [12] It is true that the first woman came from a man, but all other men have been given birth by women. Yet God is the one who created everything.

---

*11.5 she may as well shave her head: A woman's hair was a mark of beauty, and it was shameful for a woman to cut her hair short or to shave her head, so that she looked like a man.

*11.10 as a sign of her authority: Or "as a sign that she is under someone's authority."

See also: 11.1: 1 Cor 4.16; Phil 3.17.   **11.7:** Gen 1.26–27. **11.8–9:** Gen 2.18–23.

Big ideas

Communion

The night before he died, Jesus took bread and wine and told his disciples to eat it and drink it 'as a way of remembering me' (Luke 22.19). Jesus intended his followers to remember the new agreement that God was making with his people (Luke 22.20). He used ordinary bread and wine to make it easy for people to take part.

The early Church carried this tradition on through a celebration called 'Eucharist', which means 'thanksgiving', otherwise known as the 'Lord's Supper'. The Eucharist was just one part of a bigger, shared meal, which was known as the agape meal, or 'love feast'. This meal was open to anyone in the community, rich or poor, high-born or low, young or old. It was not a holy huddle, but a practical act of caring and sharing for the local community. As part of that meal, Christians would take the bread and the wine, and remember the person who had brought them all together in the first place.

It is mentioned first in Acts 3.42 and also by Paul in 1 Corinthians 11. The point of the meal, according to Paul, was to bring people together in shared remembrance (1 Corinthians 10.17).

This celebration gradually grew into the different forms of communion that are celebrated in churches today. Christians today, like Christians in the early church, join together in unity and equality to remember what Jesus had done for them, and to celebrate the new promise of forgiveness and salvation which God gave to them through Jesus' death.

 Footsteps

Three days on Communion

The first one: Luke 22.14–23
The early church breaks bread: Acts 2.42–47
Rules for the meal: 1 Corinthians 11.17–34

More...

The Last Supper p.1157
Early church p.1212

13 Ask yourselves if it is proper for a woman to pray without something on her head. 14 Isn't it unnatural and disgraceful for men to have long hair? 15 But long hair is a beautiful way for a woman to cover her head. 16 This is how things are done in all God's churches,' and that's why none of you should argue about what I have said.

Rules for the Lord's Supper

17 Your worship services do you more harm than good. I am certainly not going to praise you for this. 18 I am told that you can't get along with each other when you worship, and I am sure that some of what I have heard is true. 19 You are bound to argue with each other, but it is easy to see which of you have God's approval.

20 When you meet together, you don't really celebrate the Lord's Supper. 21 You even start eating before everyone gets to the meeting, and some of you go hungry, while others get drunk. 22 Don't you have homes where you can eat and drink? Do you hate God's church? Do you want to embarrass people who don't have anything? What can I say to you? I certainly cannot praise you.

The Lord's Supper

This is also told in Matthew 26.26–29; Mark 14.22–25; Luke 22.14–20

23 I have already told you what the Lord Jesus did on the night he was betrayed. And it came from the Lord himself.

He took some bread in his hands. 24 Then after he had given thanks, he broke it and said, "This is my body, which is given for you. Eat this and remember me."

25 After the meal, Jesus took a cup of wine in his hands and said, "This is my blood, and with it God makes his new agreement with you. Drink this and remember me."

26 The Lord meant that when you eat this bread and drink from this cup, you tell about his death until he comes.

27 But if you eat the bread and drink the wine in a way that isn't worthy of the Lord, you sin against his body and blood. 28 That's why you must examine the way you eat and drink. 29 If you fail to understand that you are the body of the Lord, you will condemn yourselves by the way you eat and drink. 30 That's why many of you are sick and weak

and why a lot of others have died. 31 If we carefully judge ourselves, we won't be punished. 32 But when the Lord judges and punishes us, he does it to keep us from being condemned with the rest of the world.

33 My dear friends, you should wait until everyone gets there before you start eating. 34 If you really are hungry, you can eat at home. Then you won't condemn yourselves when you meet together.

After I arrive, I will instruct you about the other matters.

CHAPTER 12

Spiritual gifts

1 My friends, you asked me about spiritual gifts. 2 I want you to remember that before you became followers of the Lord, you were led in all the wrong ways by idols that cannot even talk. 3 Now I want you to know that if you are led by God's Spirit, you will say that Jesus is Lord, and you will never curse Jesus.

4 There are different kinds of spiritual gifts, but they all come from the same Spirit. 5 There are different ways to serve the same Lord, 6 and we can each do different things. Yet the same God works in all of us and helps us in everything we do.

7 The Spirit has given each of us a special way of serving others. 8 Some of us can speak with wisdom, while others can speak with knowledge, but these gifts come from the same Spirit. 9 To others the Spirit has given great faith or the power to heal the sick 10 or the power to perform mighty miracles. Some of us are prophets, and some of us recognize when God's Spirit is present.* Others can speak different kinds of languages, and still others can tell what these languages mean. 11 But it is the Spirit who does all this and decides which gifts to give to each of us.

One body with many parts

12 The body of Christ has many different parts, just as any other body does. 13 Some of us are Jews, and others are Gentiles. Some of us are slaves, and others are free. But God's Spirit baptized each of us and made us part of the body of Christ. Now we each drink from that same Spirit.'

---

*12.10 and some of us . . . present: Or "and some of us recognize the difference between God's Spirit and other spirits."

See also: 11.25: a Exod 24.8; Jer 31.31–34; b Exod 24.6–8.
See also: 12.4–11: Rom 12.6–8. 12.12: Rom 12.4–5.

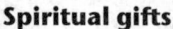

Big ideas

Spiritual gifts

A spiritual gift is simply a gift given to individuals by the Holy Spirit. Paul says that each Christian has been given 'a special way of serving others.'

Often when we think of these gifts, we think of the 'spectacular' ones, like prophecy or speaking in tongues. But the Bible lists around 15 different types of spiritual gift, including things like wisdom, evangelism, giving, encouragement and administration.

The spiritual gifts show that the Holy Spirit is working in our lives, that he is using us and changing us. The more we have of the Holy Spirit in our lives, the more encouraging, wise, helpful, hospitable and so on, we will be.

They also help us to serve others. Spiritual gifts are meant to be used to help others, they're not for selfish gain. Some people in the Corinthian church used their gifts to make other people feel second class Christians. Paul criticises this. They are above all, gifts – given to us by God so that we can share them out with other people.

Paul knew you need a whole range of different skills and abilities to run a church. And he likened churches to a body: each part of the body has different abilities and skills, but all parts are vital. As Paul put it, 'There are different kinds of spiritual gifts, but they all come from the same Spirit.' (1 Corinthians 12.4)

 Footsteps

Five days on Spiritual gifts

Many gifts, one spirit: 1 Corinthians 12.1–31
Want the best: 1 Corinthians 14.1–25
Many people, one body: Romans 12.1–8
United by faith: Ephesians 4.7–16
Serving others: 1 Peter 4.8–11

More...

Early church p.1212
Choices p.210
Worshipping God p.622
Serving others p.1190

¹⁴ Our bodies don't have just one part. They have many parts. ¹⁵ Suppose a foot says, "I'm not a hand, and so I'm not part of the body." Wouldn't the foot still belong to the body? ¹⁶ Or suppose an ear says, "I'm not an eye, and so I'm not part of the body." Wouldn't the ear still belong to the body? ¹⁷ If our bodies were only an eye, we couldn't hear a thing. And if they were only an ear, we couldn't smell a thing. ¹⁸ But God has put all parts of our body together in the way that he decided is best.

¹⁹ A body isn't really a body, unless there is more than one part. ²⁰ It takes many parts to make a single body. ²¹ That's why the eyes cannot say they don't need the hands. That's also why the head cannot say it doesn't need the feet. ²² In fact, we cannot get along without the parts of the body that seem to be the weakest. ²³ We take special care to dress up some parts of our bodies. We are modest about our personal parts, ²⁴ but we don't have to be modest about other parts.

God put our bodies together in such a way that even the parts that seem the least important are valuable. ²⁵ He did this to make all parts of the body work together smoothly, with each part caring about the others. ²⁶ If one part of our body hurts, we hurt all over. If one part of our body is honoured, the whole body will be happy.

²⁷ Together you are the body of Christ. Each one of you is part of his body. ²⁸ First, God chose some people to be apostles and prophets and teachers for the church. But he also chose some to perform miracles or heal the sick or help others or be leaders or speak different kinds of languages. ²⁹ Not everyone is an apostle. Not everyone is a prophet. Not everyone is a teacher. Not everyone can perform miracles. ³⁰ Not everyone can heal the sick. Not everyone can speak different kinds of languages. Not everyone can tell what these languages mean. ³¹ I want you to desire the best gifts.' So I will show you a much better way.

CHAPTER 13

Love

¹ What if I could speak
    all languages of humans
    and of angels?
If I did not love others,
    I would be nothing more

See also: 12.28: Eph 4.11.

than a noisy gong
or a clanging cymbal.
2 What if I could prophesy
and understand all secrets
and all knowledge?
And what if I had faith
that moved mountains?
I would be nothing,
unless I loved others.
3 What if I gave away all
that I owned
and let myself
be burnt alive?›
I would gain nothing,
unless I loved others.
4 Love is kind and patient,
never jealous, boastful,
proud, or 5 rude.
Love isn't selfish
or quick-tempered.
It doesn't keep a record
of wrongs that others do.
6 Love rejoices in the truth,
but not in evil.
7 Love is always supportive,
loyal, hopeful,
and trusting.
8 Love never fails!

Everyone who prophesies
will stop,
and unknown languages
will no longer
be spoken.
All that we know
will be forgotten.
9 We don't know everything,
and our prophecies
are not complete.
10 But what is perfect
will some day appear,
and what isn't perfect
will then disappear.
11 When we were children,
we thought and reasoned
as children do.
But when we grew up,
we stopped our childish ways.
12 Now all we can see of God
is like a cloudy picture
in a mirror.
Later we will see him
face to face.
We don't know everything,
but then we will,

just as God completely
understands us.
13 For now there are faith,
hope, and love.
But of these three,
the greatest is love.

CHAPTER 14

Speaking unknown languages and prophesying

1 Love should be your guide. Be eager to have the gifts that come from the Holy Spirit, especially the gift of prophecy. 2 If you speak languages that others don't know, God will understand what you are saying, though no one else will know what you mean. You will be talking about mysteries that only the Spirit understands. 3 But when you prophesy, you will be understood, and others will be helped. They will be encouraged and made to feel better.

4 By speaking languages that others don't know, you help only yourself. But by prophesying you help everyone in the church. 5 I am glad for you to speak unknown languages, although I would rather you prophesied. In fact, prophesying does much more good than speaking unknown languages, unless someone can help the church by explaining what you mean.

6 My friends, what good would it do, if I came and spoke unknown languages to you and didn't explain what I meant? How would I help you, unless I told you what God had shown me or gave you some knowledge or prophecy or teaching? 7 If all musical instruments sounded alike, how would you know the difference between a flute and a harp? 8 If a bugle call isn't clear, how would you know to get ready for battle?

9 That's how it is when you speak unknown languages. If no one can understand what you are talking about, you will only be talking to the wind. 10 There are many different languages in this world, and all of them make sense. 11 But if I don't understand the language that someone is using, we will be like foreigners to each other. 12 If you really want spiritual gifts, choose the ones that will be most helpful to the church.

13 When we speak languages that others don't know, we should pray for the power to explain what we mean. 14 For example, if I use an unknown language in my prayers, my spirit prays but my mind is useless. 15 Then what should I do? There are times

when I should pray with my spirit, and times when I should pray with my mind. Sometimes I should sing with my spirit, and at other times I should sing with my mind.

¹⁶ Suppose some strangers are in your worship service, when you are praising God with your spirit. If they don't understand you, how will they know to say, "Amen"? ¹⁷ You may be worshipping God in a wonderful way, but no one else will be helped. ¹⁸ I thank God that I speak unknown languages more than any of you. ¹⁹ But words that make sense can help the church. That's why in church I had rather speak five words that make sense than to speak ten thousand words in a language that others don't know.

²⁰ My friends, stop thinking like children. Think like mature people and be as innocent as tiny babies. ²¹ In the Scriptures the Lord says,

> "I will use strangers
> who speak unknown languages
>   to talk to my people.
> They will speak to them
>   in foreign languages,
> but still my people
>   won't listen to me."

²² Languages that others don't know may mean something to unbelievers, but not to the Lord's followers. Prophecy, on the other hand, is for followers, not for unbelievers. ²³ Suppose everyone in your worship service started speaking unknown languages, and some outsiders or some unbelievers come in. Won't they think you are mad? ²⁴ But suppose all of you are prophesying when those unbelievers and outsiders come in. They will realize that they are sinners, and they will want to change their ways because of what you are saying. ²⁵ They will tell what is hidden in their hearts. Then they will kneel down and say to God, "We are certain that you are with these people."

Worship must be orderly

²⁶ My friends, when you meet to worship, you must do everything for the good of everyone there. That's how it should be when someone sings or teaches or tells what God has said or speaks an unknown language or explains what the language means. ²⁷ No more than two or three of you should speak unknown languages during the meeting. You must take turns, and someone should always be there to

explain what you mean. ²⁸ If no one can explain, you must keep silent in church and speak only to yourself and to God.

²⁹ Two or three persons may prophesy, and everyone else must listen carefully. ³⁰ If someone sitting there receives a message from God, the speaker must stop and let the other person speak. ³¹ Let only one person speak at a time, then all of you will learn something and be encouraged. ³² A prophet should be willing to stop and let someone else speak. ³³ God wants everything to be done peacefully and in order.

When God's people meet in church, ³⁴ the women must not be allowed to speak. They must keep quiet and listen, as the Law of Moses teaches. ³⁵ If there is something they want to know, they can ask their husbands when they get home. It is disgraceful for women to speak in church. ³⁶ God's message did not start with you people, and you are not the only ones it has reached.

³⁷ If you think of yourself as a prophet or a spiritual person, you will know that I am writing only what the Lord has commanded. ³⁸ So don't pay attention to anyone who ignores what I am writing. ³⁹ My friends, be eager to prophesy and don't stop anyone from speaking languages that others don't know. ⁴⁰ But do everything properly and in order.

Christ's victory over death

CHAPTER 15

Christ was raised to life

¹ My friends, I want you to remember the message that I preached and that you believed and trusted. ² You will be saved by this message, if you hold firmly to it. But if you don't, your faith was all for nothing.

³ I told you the most important part of the message exactly as it was told to me. That part is:

> Christ died for our sins,
>   as the Scriptures say.
> ⁴ He was buried,
>   and three days later
> he was raised to life,
>   as the Scriptures say.
> ⁵ Christ appeared to Peter,*
>   then to the twelve.

---

*15.5 Peter: See the note at 1.12.

See also: 15.3: Isa 53.5–12. 15.4: Psa 16.8–10; Matt 12.40; Acts 2.24–32. 15.5: a Luke 24.34; b Matt 28.16–17; Mark 16.14; Luke 24.36; John 20.19.

See also: 14.21: Isa 28.11–12.

6 After this, he appeared
to more than five hundred
other followers.
Most of them are still alive,
but some have died.
7 He also appeared to James,
and then to all
the apostles.

8 Finally, he appeared to me, even though I am like someone who was born at the wrong time.⁾

9 I am the least important of all the apostles. In fact, I caused so much trouble for God's church that I don't even deserve to be called an apostle. 10 But God was kind! He made me what I am, and his wonderful kindness wasn't wasted. I worked much harder than any of the other apostles, although it was really God's kindness at work and not me. 11 But it doesn't matter if I preached or if they preached. All of you believed the message just the same.

God's people will be raised to life

12 If we preach that Christ was raised from death, how can some of you say that the dead will not be raised to life? 13 If they won't be raised to life, Christ himself wasn't raised to life. 14 And if Christ wasn't raised to life, our message is worthless, and so is your faith. 15 If the dead won't be raised to life, we have told lies about God by saying that he raised Christ to life, when he really did not.

16 So if the dead won't be raised to life, Christ wasn't raised to life. 17 Unless Christ was raised to life, your faith is useless, and you are still living in your sins. 18 And those people who died after putting their faith in him are completely lost. 19 If our hope in Christ is good only for this life, we are worse off than anyone else.

20 But Christ has been raised to life! And he makes us certain that others will also be raised to life. 21 Just as we will die because of Adam, we will be raised to life because of Christ. 22 Adam brought death to all of us, and Christ will bring life to all of us. 23 But we must each wait our turn. Christ was the first to be raised to life, and his people will be raised to life when he returns. 24 Then after Christ has destroyed all powers and forces, the end will come, and he will give the kingdom to God the Father.

25 Christ will rule until he puts all his enemies under his power, 26 and the last enemy he destroys will be death. 27 When the Scriptures say that he will put everything under his power, they don't include God. It was God who put everything under the power of Christ. 28 After everything is under the power of God's Son, he will put himself under the power of God, who put everything under his Son's power. Then God will mean everything to everyone.

29 If the dead are not going to be raised to life, what will people do who are being baptized for them? Why are they being baptized for those dead people? 30 And why do we always risk our lives 31 and face death every day? The pride that I have in you because of Christ Jesus our Lord is what makes me say this. 32 What do you think I gained by fighting wild animals in Ephesus? If the dead are not raised to life,

"Let's eat and drink.
Tomorrow we die."

33 Don't fool yourselves. Bad friends will destroy you. 34 Be sensible and stop sinning. You should be embarrassed that some people still don't know about God.

What our bodies will be like

35 Some of you have asked, "How will the dead be raised to life? What kind of bodies will they have?" 36 Don't be foolish. A seed must die before it can sprout from the ground. 37 Wheat seeds and all other seeds look different from the sprouts that come up. 38 This is because God gives everything the kind of body he wants it to have. 39 People, animals, birds, and fish are each made of flesh, but none of them are alike.

40 Everything in the heavens has a body, and so does everything on earth. But each one is very different from all the others. 41 The sun isn't like the moon, the moon isn't like the stars, and each star is different.

42 That's how it will be when our bodies are raised to life. These bodies will die, but the bodies that are raised will live for ever. 43 These ugly and weak bodies will become beautiful and strong. 44 As there are physical bodies, there are spiritual bodies. And our physical bodies will be changed into spiritual bodies.

See also: 15.8: Acts 9.3–6. **15.9:** Acts 8.3.

See also: 15.25: Psa 110.1. **15.27:** Psa 8.6.
15.32: Isa 22.13.

⁴⁵ The first man was named Adam, and the Scriptures tell us that he was a living person. But Jesus, who may be called the last Adam, is a life-giving spirit. ⁴⁶ We see that the one with a spiritual body did not come first. He came after the one who had a physical body. ⁴⁷ The first man was made from the dust of the earth, but the second man came from heaven. ⁴⁸ Everyone on earth has a body like the body of the one who was made from the dust of the earth. And everyone in heaven has a body like the body of the one who came from heaven. ⁴⁹ Just as we are like the one who was made out of earth, we will be like the one who came from heaven.

⁵⁰ My friends, I want you to know that our bodies of flesh and blood will decay. This means that they cannot share in God's kingdom, which lasts for ever. ⁵¹ I will explain a mystery to you. Not every one of us will die, but we will all be changed. ⁵² It will happen suddenly, quicker than the blink of an eye. At the sound of the last trumpet the dead will be raised. We will all be changed, so that we will never die again. ⁵³ Our dead and decaying bodies will be changed into bodies that won't die or decay. ⁵⁴ The bodies we now have are weak and can die. But they will be changed into bodies that are eternal. Then the Scriptures will come true,

> "Death has lost the battle!
> ⁵⁵ Where is its victory?
>   Where is its sting?"

⁵⁶ Sin is what gives death its sting, and the Law is the power behind sin. ⁵⁷ But thank God for letting our Lord Jesus Christ give us the victory!

⁵⁸ My dear friends, stand firm and don't be shaken. Always keep busy working for the Lord. You know that everything you do for him is worthwhile.

An offering for the poor

CHAPTER 16

A collection for God's people

¹ When you collect money for God's people, I want you to do exactly what I told the churches in Galatia to do. ² That is, each Sunday each of you must put aside part of what you have earned. If you do this, you won't have to take up a collection when I come. ³ Choose some followers to take the money to Jerusalem. I will send them on with the money and with letters which show that you approve of them. ⁴ If you think I should go along, they can go with me.

Paul's travel plans

⁵ After I have gone through Macedonia, I hope to see you ⁶ and stay with you for a while. I may even stay all winter, so that you can help me on my way to wherever I will be going next. ⁷ If the Lord lets me, I would rather come later for a longer visit than to stop off now for only a short visit. ⁸ I will stay in Ephesus until Pentecost, ⁹ because there is a wonderful opportunity for me to do some work here. But there are also many people who are against me.

¹⁰ When Timothy arrives, give him a friendly welcome. He is doing the Lord's work, just as I am. ¹¹ Don't let anyone ill-treat him. I am looking for him to return to me together with the other followers. So when he leaves, send him off with your blessings.

¹² I have tried hard to get our friend Apollos to visit you with the other followers. He doesn't want to come just now, but he will come when he can.

Personal concerns and greetings

¹³ Keep alert. Be firm in your faith. Stay brave and strong. ¹⁴ Show love in everything you do.

¹⁵ You know that Stephanas and his family were the first in Achaia to have faith in the Lord. They have done all they can for God's people. My friends, I ask you ¹⁶ to obey leaders like them and to do the same for all others who work hard with you.

¹⁷ I was glad to see Stephanas and Fortunatus and Achaicus. Having them here was like having you. ¹⁸ They made me feel much better, just as they made you feel better. You should appreciate people like them.

¹⁹ Greetings from the churches in Asia. Aquila and Priscilla, together with the church that meets in their house, send greetings in the name of the Lord.

²⁰ All the Lord's followers send their greetings.

See also: 15.45: Gen 2.7. 15.51–52: 1 Thes 4.15–17. 15.54: Isa 25.8. 15.55: Hos 13.14 (LXX). 16.1: Rom 15.25–26.

See also: 16.5: Acts 19.21. 16.8: Lev 23.15–21; Deut 16.9–11. 16.8–9: Acts 19.8–10. 16.10: 1 Cor 4.17. 16.15: 1 Cor 1.16. 16.19: Acts 18.2.

Give each other a warm greeting.

21 I am signing this letter myself: PAUL.

22 I pray that God will put a curse on everyone who doesn't love the Lord. And may the Lord come soon.

23 I pray that the Lord Jesus will be kind to you.

24 I love everyone who belongs to Christ Jesus.

Additional notes

›**1.14 I thank God:** Some manuscripts have "I thank my God".

›**2.1 mystery:** Some manuscripts have "testimony".

›**2.13 teach spiritual things to spiritual people:** Or "compare spiritual things with spiritual things."

›**2.16 we understand what Christ is thinking:** Or "we think as Christ does."

›**5.1 is even sleeping with his own stepmother:** Or "has even married his own stepmother."

›**7.1 people not to marry:** Or "married couples not to have sex."

›**7.9 with desire:** Or "in the flames of hell".

›**7.25 people who have never been married:** Or "virgins".

›**7.29 the Lord will soon come:** Or "there's not much time left" or "the time for decision comes quickly".

›**7.34 women who have never been married:** Or "virgins".

›**7.36 But suppose you are engaged . . . go ahead and marry:** Verses 36–38 may also be translated: 36"If you feel that you are not treating your grown-up daughter right by keeping her from getting married, then let her marry. You won't be doing anything wrong. 37But it is better to have self-control and make up your mind not to let your daughter get married. 38It is all right for you to let her marry. But it is better if you don't let her marry at all."

›**10.9 Christ:** Some manuscripts have "the Lord".

›**11.16 This is how things are done in all God's churches:** Or "There is no set rule for this in any of God's churches."

›**12.13 Some of us are Jews . . . that same Spirit:** Verse 13 may also be translated, "God's Spirit is inside each of us, and all around us as well. So it doesn't matter that some of us are Jews and others are Gentiles and that some are slaves and others are free. Together we are one body."

›**12.31 I want you to desire the best gifts:** Or "You desire the best gifts."

›**13.3 and let myself be burnt alive:** Some manuscripts have "so that I could boast."

›**15.8 who was born at the wrong time:** The meaning of these words in Greek is not clear.

2 Corinthians

Paul's second letter to the church in Corinth

The basics

What's the point? Times may be tough, but we should not lose heart, because God is at work with us.

What happens? Paul writes to correct rumours about himself and to encourage the church to deal with troublemakers.

What should I remember? 4.16 'We never give up. Our bodies are gradually dying, but we ourselves are being made stronger each day. These little troubles are getting us ready for an eternal glory that will make all our troubles seem like nothing at all.'

More details

Setting the scene There is still trouble in Corinth. Paul's opponents were accusing him of unreliability. They said he was not a real apostle and were even accusing him of pocketing the money he had collected for the Christians in Jerusalem. It was time for another letter...

What's it all about? Paul had only been able to visit Corinth for a short, and difficult, visit, not the 'long stay' he'd promised (1 Corinthians 16.6). He'd promised to return, but then decided that another painful visit would serve no purpose, so he returned to Asia. His opponents seized on this, claiming that Paul didn't live up to his promises.

The result is one of Paul's most personal letters. He asserts his integrity and honesty. He argues that he stayed away because he wanted to see if his instructions were being followed. He defends his work for the gospel and he promises to visit the Corinthians again.

Footsteps

Why didn't he come? 1.1–2.17
The new agreement: 3.1–18
Jars of clay: 4.1–18
Light and darkness: 6.14–7.16
Eager giving: 9.1–15
A true apostle: 10.1–18
Suffering for Christ: 11.16–12.10

Paul gives thanks to God

CHAPTER 1

[1] *From Paul, chosen by God to be an apostle of Jesus Christ, and from Timothy, who is also a follower.*

To God's church in Corinth and to all God's people in Achaia.

[2] I pray that God our Father and the Lord Jesus Christ will be kind to you and will bless you with peace!

Paul gives thanks

[3] Praise God, the Father of our Lord Jesus Christ! The Father is a merciful God, who always gives us comfort. [4] He comforts us when we are in trouble, so that we can share that same comfort with others in trouble. [5] We share in the terrible sufferings of Christ, but also in the wonderful comfort he gives. [6] We suffer in the hope that you will be comforted and saved. And because we are

See also: 1.1: Acts 18.1.

comforted, you will also be comforted, as you patiently endure suffering like ours. [7] You never disappoint us. You suffered as much as we did, and we know that you will be comforted as we were.

[8] My friends, I want you to know what a hard time we had in Asia. Our sufferings were so horrible and so unbearable that death seemed certain. [9] In fact, we felt sure that we were going to die. But this made us stop trusting in ourselves and start trusting God, who raises the dead to life. [10] God saved us from the threat of death,⁊ and we are sure that he will do it again and again. [11] Please help us by praying for us. Then many people will give thanks for the blessings we receive in answer to all these prayers.

The work of an apostle for God's people

Paul's change of plans

[12] We can be proud of our clear conscience. We have always lived honestly and sincerely, especially when we were with you. And we were guided by God's wonderful kindness instead of by the wisdom of this world. [13] I am not writing anything you cannot read and understand. I hope you will understand it completely, [14] just as you already partly understand us. Then when our Lord Jesus returns, you can be as proud of us as we are of you.

[15] I was so sure of your pride in us that I had planned to visit you first of all. In this way you would have the blessing of two visits from me. [16] Once on my way to Macedonia and again on my return from there. Then you could send me on to Judea. [17] Do you think I couldn't make up my mind about what to do? Or do I seem like someone who says "Yes" or "No" simply to please others? [18] God can be trusted, and so can I, when I say that our answer to you has always been "Yes" and never "No". [19] This is because Jesus Christ the Son of God is always "Yes" and never "No". And he is the one that Silas,⁊ Timothy, and I told you about.

[20] Christ says "Yes" to all of God's promises. That's why we have Christ to say "Amen"* for us to the glory of God. [21] And so

---

*1.20 Amen: The word "amen" is used here with the meaning of "yes".

See also: 1.8: 1 Cor 15.32. 1.16: Acts 19.21.
1.19: Acts 18.5.

Viewpoints

It's a simple choice: true or not?

Contributed by Joy G

'Christ says "Yes" to all of God's promises.' That's why we have Christ to say "Amen" for us to the glory of God.'

'It's just a book of stories', 'Why should I believe a book?', 'Everything's made up anyway'. Those are some of the excuses people make about the Bible. It can be hard to stand up against criticism, and sometimes it's easy to believe the lies others tell. It is often hard to trust that it is God's word and therefore truth. On the other hand, for me at least, it makes so much sense!

This verse states that 'Christ says "Yes" to all of God's promises.' The coming of Jesus fulfilled tons of prophecies which God has inspired years and years beforehand. God is not inconsistent. He never breaks promises. That consistency makes it hard for me to believe the Bible is untrue. In the same way, I don't see how the Bible could have been made up. It would have been an incredibly hard task to tie everything together perfectly. As we know, authors and screenplay writers sometimes make mistakes in keeping little details consistent in book series, movies, and TV shows. As uncommonly as it happens, it is so fun to find a mistake, isn't it? The fact that God's promises are faithful makes it much easier for me to accept the Bible as truth.

In the end, it is up to us to put our faith in God, and trust that everything isn't one big scam. No arguments or proof can give the same assurance simple trust gives. 'THE WORD OF GOD – STAND ON IT' or 'THE WORD OF GOD – REJECT IT'? It's your choice.

More...

Starting again p.1172
Prophecy p.730
Responding to God p.1052
Reading your Bible p.1354

God makes it possible for you and us to stand firmly together with Christ. God is also the one who chose us [22] and put his Spirit in our hearts to show that we belong only to him.

[23] God is my witness that I stayed away from Corinth, just to keep from being hard on you. [24] We are not bosses who tell you what to believe. We are working with you to make you glad, because your faith is strong.

CHAPTER 2

[1] I have decided not to make my next visit to you so painful. [2] If I make you feel bad, who would be left to cheer me up, except the people I had made to feel bad? [3] The reason I want to be happy is to make you happy. I wrote as I did because I didn't want to visit you and be made to feel bad, when you should make me feel happy. [4] At the time I wrote, I was suffering terribly. My eyes were full of tears, and my heart was broken. But I didn't want to make you feel bad. I only wanted to let you know how much I cared for you.

Forgiveness

[5] I don't want to be hard on you. But if one of you has made someone feel bad, I am not really the one who has been made to feel bad. Some of you are the ones. [6] Most of you have already pointed out the wrong that person did, and that is punishment enough for what was done.

[7] When people sin, you should forgive and comfort them, so they won't give up in despair. [8] You should make them sure of your love for them.

[9] I also wrote because I wanted to test you and find out if you would follow my instructions. [10] I will forgive anyone you forgive. Yes, for your sake and with Christ as my witness, I have forgiven whatever needed to be forgiven. [11] I have done this to keep Satan from getting the better of us. We all know what goes on in his mind.

[12] When I went to Troas to preach the good news about Christ, I found that the Lord had already prepared the way. [13] But I was worried when I didn't find my friend Titus there. So I left the other followers and went on to Macedonia.

[14] I am grateful that God always makes it possible for Christ to lead us to victory. God also helps us spread the knowledge about Christ everywhere, and this knowledge is like the smell of perfume. [15-16] In fact, God thinks of us as a perfume that brings Christ to everyone. For people who are being saved, this perfume has a sweet smell and leads them to a better life. But for people who are lost, it has a bad smell and leads them to a horrible death.

No one really has what it takes to do this work. [17] A lot of people try to get rich from preaching God's message. But we are God's sincere messengers, and by the power of Christ we speak our message with God as our witness.

Guided by the love of Christ

CHAPTER 3

God's new agreement

[1] Are we once again boasting about ourselves? Do we need letters to you or from you to tell others about us? Some people do need letters that tell about them. [2] But you are our letter, and you are in our' hearts for everyone to read and understand. [3] You are like a letter written by Christ and delivered by us. But you are not written with pen and ink or on tablets made of stone. You are written in our hearts by the Spirit of the living God.

[4] We are sure about all this. Christ makes us sure in the very presence of God. [5] We don't have the right to claim that we have done anything on our own. God gives us what it takes to do all that we do. [6] He makes us worthy to be the servants of his new agreement that comes from the Holy Spirit and not from a written Law. After all, the Law brings death, but the Spirit brings life.

[7] The Law of Moses brought only the promise of death, even though it was carved on stones and given in a wonderful way. Still the Law made Moses' face shine so brightly that the people of Israel could not look at it, even though it was a fading glory. [8] So won't the agreement that the Spirit brings to us be even more wonderful? [9] If something that brings the death sentence is glorious, won't something that makes us acceptable to God be even more glorious? [10] In fact, the new agreement is so wonderful that the Law is no longer glorious at all. [11] The Law was given with a glory that faded away. But the glory of the new agreement is much greater, because it will never fade away.

See also: 2.12–13: Acts 20.1.

See also: **3.3: a** Exod 24.12; **b** Jer 31.33; Ezek 11.19; 36.26. **3.6:** Jer 31.31. **3.7:** Exod 34.29.

¹² This wonderful hope makes us feel like speaking freely. ¹³ We are not like Moses. His face was shining, but he covered it to keep the people of Israel from seeing the brightness fade away. ¹⁴ The people were stubborn, and something still keeps them from seeing the truth when the Law is read. Only Christ can take away the covering that keeps them from seeing.

¹⁵ When the Law of Moses is read, they have their minds covered over ¹⁶ with a covering that is removed only for those who turn to the Lord. ¹⁷ The Lord and the Spirit are one and the same, and the Lord's Spirit sets us free. ¹⁸ So our faces are not covered. They show the bright glory of the Lord, as the Lord's Spirit makes us more and more like our glorious Lord.

CHAPTER 4

Treasure in clay jars

¹ God has been kind enough to trust us with this work. That's why we never give up. ² We don't do shameful things that must be kept secret. And we don't try to fool anyone or twist God's message around. God is our witness that we speak only the truth, so others will be sure that we can be trusted. ³ If there is anything hidden about our message, it is hidden only to someone who is lost.

⁴ The god who rules this world has blinded the minds of unbelievers. They cannot see the light, which is the good news about our glorious Christ, who shows what God is like. ⁵ We are not preaching about ourselves. Our message is that Jesus Christ is Lord. He also sent us to be your servants. ⁶ The Scriptures say, "God commanded light to shine in the dark." Now God is shining in our hearts to let you know that his glory is seen in Jesus Christ.

⁷ We are like clay jars in which this treasure is stored. The real power comes from God and not from us. ⁸ We often suffer, but we are never crushed. Even when we don't know what to do, we never give up. ⁹ In times of trouble, God is with us, and when we are knocked down, we get up again. ¹⁰⁻¹¹ We face death every day because of Jesus. Our bodies show what his death was like, so that his life can also be seen in us. ¹² This means that death is working in us, but life is working in you.

¹³ In the Scriptures it says, "I spoke because I had faith." We have that same kind of faith. So we speak ¹⁴ because we know that God raised the Lord Jesus to life. And just as God raised Jesus, he will also raise us to life. Then he will bring us into his presence together with you. ¹⁵ All this has been done for you, so that more and more people will know how kind God is and will praise and honour him.

Faith in the Lord

¹⁶ We never give up. Our bodies are gradually dying, but we ourselves are being made stronger each day. ¹⁷ These little troubles are getting us ready for an eternal glory that will make all our troubles seem like nothing. ¹⁸ Things that are seen don't last for ever, but things that are not seen are eternal. That's why we keep our minds on the things that cannot be seen.

CHAPTER 5

¹ Our bodies are like tents that we live in here on earth. But when these tents are destroyed, we know that God will give each of us a place to live. These homes will not be buildings that someone has made, but they are in heaven and will last for ever. ² While we are here on earth, we sigh because we want to live in that heavenly home. ³ We want to put it on like clothes and not be naked.

⁴ These tents we now live in are like a heavy burden, and we groan. But we don't do this just because we want to leave these bodies that will die. It is because we want to change them for bodies that will never die. ⁵ God is the one who makes all this possible. He has given us his Spirit to make us certain that he will do it. ⁶ So always be cheerful!

As long as we are in these bodies, we are away from the Lord. ⁷ But we live by faith, not by what we see. ⁸ We should be cheerful, because we would rather leave these bodies and be at home with the Lord. ⁹ But whether we are at home with the Lord or away from him, we still try our best to please him. ¹⁰ After all, Christ will judge each of us for the good or the bad that we do while living in these bodies.

Bringing people to God

¹¹ We know what it means to respect the Lord, and we encourage everyone to turn to him. God himself knows what we are like, and I hope you also know what kind of

Real life

Movies

Contributed by Damaris

A trip to the cinema might include seeing friends, popcorn, fizzy drinks, entertainment, thrills, laughter and maybe even tears – it's always an experience. But as the lights dim and we settle down to a couple of hours of audio-visual pleasure, what do we do with our brains?

It's all too easy to switch off when we go into amusement mode. The cinema often feels like a place to escape to, somewhere that we can forget about our own worries and get lost in another world. If everything we're watching isn't real, what is there to think about?

The stories told in films tell us a lot about where the world is at today. They are shaped by the beliefs and ideas of the writers and filmmakers, which may or may not be the same as our own. If we leave our brains in the ticket queue, we might miss the movie's message altogether. Paul writes that, 'The god who rules this world has blinded the minds of unbelievers' (2 Corinthians 4.4). This means that many of the ideas expressed in the movies will not reflect the truth of the Christian gospel. For instance, the overall message of a movie might be that belonging is related to how you look, or that putting yourself first is the only way to survive, or that freedom is about money and sex – all ideas that run counter to what Jesus taught. If we're not careful, such messages can lead us away from God's truth and begin to influence our sense of who we are.

In the rest of this verse, Paul explains that unbelievers 'cannot see the light, which is the good news about our glorious Christ, who shows what God is like.' So, although all artists may be able to communicate truth about humanity, if they don't know Jesus they are unlikely to convey an understanding of God and his creation. Many films truthfully reflect our human desires – for intimate relationships, for instance, or to be significant in an uncaring world – but they do not all offer examples to be followed, if you're trying to live God's way (2 Corinthians 10.3–5). From the American high school drama to the fantasy world of tomorrow, movies have the power to change the way we think about the world we live in. So keep the light on in your brain...

Think

Think about the last movie you saw. What were its themes and overall message? What did it say about how to live life? Which ideas rang true with what the Bible has to say on the subject? And which did not?

Act

Next time you see a movie ,have a conversation after it that isn't just about the actors' performances and the special effects. Ask, what did this movie mean to you?

Check

Read all of 2 Corinthians 4 and memorise verse 18!

More...

Media p.1235

people we are. ¹² We are not trying once more to boast about ourselves. But we want you to be proud of us, when you are with those who are not sincere and boast about what others think of them.

¹³ If we seem out of our minds, it is between God and us. But if we are in our right minds, it is for your good. ¹⁴ We are ruled by Christ's love for us. We are certain that if one person died for everyone else, then all of us have died. ¹⁵ And Christ did die for all of us. He died so we would no longer live for ourselves, but for the one who died and was raised to life for us.

¹⁶ We are careful not to judge people by what they seem to be, though we once judged Christ in that way. ¹⁷ Anyone who belongs to Christ is a new person. The past is forgotten, and everything is new. ¹⁸ God has done it all! He sent Christ to make peace between himself and us, and he has given us the work of making peace between himself and others.

¹⁹ What we mean is that God was in Christ, offering peace and forgiveness to the people of this world. And he has given us the work of sharing his message about peace. ²⁰ We were sent to speak for Christ, and God is begging you to listen to our message. We speak for Christ and sincerely ask you to make peace with God. ²¹ Christ never sinned! But God treated him as a sinner, so that Christ could make us acceptable to God.

CHAPTER 6

¹ We work together with God, and we beg you to make good use of God's kindness to you. ² In the Scriptures God says,

> "When the time came,
>   I listened to you,
> and when you needed help,
>   I came to save you."

That time has come. This is the day for you to be saved.

³ We don't want anyone to find fault with our work, and so we try hard not to cause problems. ⁴ But in everything and in every way we show that we truly are God's servants. We have always been patient, though we have had a lot of trouble, suffering, and hard times. ⁵ We have been beaten, put in jail, and hurt in riots. We have worked hard and have gone without sleep or food. ⁶ But we have kept ourselves pure and have been understanding, patient, and kind. The Holy Spirit has been

with us, and our love has been real. ⁷ We have spoken the truth, and God's power has worked in us. In all our struggles we have said and done only what is right.

⁸ Whether we were honoured or dishonoured or praised or cursed, we always told the truth about ourselves. But some people said we did not. ⁹ We are unknown to others, but well known to you. We seem to be dying, and yet we are still alive. We have been punished, but never killed, ¹⁰ and we are always happy, even in times of suffering. Although we are poor, we have made many people rich. And though we own nothing, everything is ours.

¹¹ Friends in Corinth, we are telling the truth when we say that there is room in our hearts for you. ¹² We are not holding back on our love for you, but you are holding back on your love for us. ¹³ I speak to you as I would speak to my own children. Please make room in your hearts for us.

The temple of the living God

¹⁴ Stay away from people who are not followers of the Lord! Can someone who is good get along with someone who is evil? Are light and darkness the same? ¹⁵ Is Christ a friend of Satan?* Can people who follow the Lord have anything in common with those who don't? ¹⁶ Do idols belong in the temple of God? We are the temple of the living God, as God himself says,

> "I will live with these people
>   and walk among them.
> I will be their God,
> and they will be
>   my people."

¹⁷ The Lord also says,

> "Leave them and stay away!
> Don't touch anything
>   that isn't clean.
> Then I will welcome you
> ¹⁸   and be your Father.
> You will be my sons
>   and my daughters,
> as surely as I am God,
>   the All-Powerful."

---

*6.15 Satan: The Greek text has "Beliar", which is another form of the Hebrew word "Belial", meaning "wicked" or "useless". The Jewish people sometimes used this as a name for Satan.

See also: 6.16: a 1 Cor 3.16; 6.19; b Lev 26.12; Ezek 37.27. 6.17: Isa 52.11. 6.18: 2 Sam 7.14; 1 Chron 17.13; Isa 43.6; Jer 31.9.

See also: 6.2: Isa 49.8. 6.5: Acts 16.23.

CHAPTER 7

¹ My friends, God has made us these promises. So we should stay away from everything that keeps our bodies and spirits from being clean. We should honour God and try to be completely like him.

The church makes Paul happy

² Make a place for us in your hearts! We haven't ill-treated or hurt anyone. We haven't cheated anyone. ³ I am not saying this to be hard on you. But, as I have said before, you will always be in our thoughts, whether we live or die. ⁴ I trust you completely.' I am always proud of you, and I am greatly encouraged. In all my trouble I am still very happy.

⁵ After we came to Macedonia, we didn't have any chance to rest. We were faced with all kinds of problems. We were troubled by enemies and troubled by fears. ⁶ But God cheers up people in need, and that is what he did when he sent Titus to us. ⁷ Of course, we were glad to see Titus, but what really made us glad is the way you cheered him up. He told how sorry you were and how concerned you were about me. And this made me even happier.

⁸ I don't feel bad any more, even though my letter* hurt your feelings. I did feel bad at first, but I don't now. I know that the letter hurt you for a while. ⁹ Now I am happy, but not because I hurt your feelings. It is because God used your hurt feelings to make you turn back to him, and none of you were harmed by us. ¹⁰ When God makes you feel sorry enough to turn to him and be saved, you don't have anything to feel bad about. But when this world makes you feel sorry, it can cause your death.

¹¹ Just look what God has done by making you feel sorry! You sincerely want to prove that you are innocent. You are angry. You are shocked. You are eager to see that justice is done. You have proved that you were completely right in this matter. ¹² When I wrote to you, it wasn't to accuse the one who was wrong or to stand up for the one who was hurt. I wrote, so that God would show you how much you do care for us. ¹³ And we were greatly encouraged.

Although we were encouraged, we felt even better when we saw how happy Titus was, because you had shown that he had nothing

to worry about. ¹⁴ We had told him how much we thought of you, and you did not disappoint us. Just as we have always told you the truth, so everything we told him about you has also proved to be true. ¹⁵ Titus loves all of you very much, especially when he remembers how you obeyed him and how you trembled with fear when you welcomed him. ¹⁶ It makes me really glad to know that I can depend on you.

Gifts for the poor

CHAPTER 8

Generous giving

¹ My friends, we want you to know that the churches in Macedonia* have shown others how kind God is. ² Although they were going through hard times and were very poor, they were glad to give generously. ³ They gave as much as they could afford and even more, simply because they wanted to. ⁴ They even asked and begged us to let them have the joy of giving their money for God's people. ⁵ And they did more than we had hoped. They gave themselves first to the Lord and then to us, just as God wanted them to do.

⁶ Titus was the one who got you started doing this good thing, so we begged him to help you finish what you had begun. ⁷ You do everything better than anyone else. You have stronger faith. You speak better and know more. You are eager to give, and you love us better.' Now you must give more generously than anyone else.

⁸ I am not ordering you to do this. I am simply testing how real your love is by comparing it with the concern that others have shown. ⁹ You know that our Lord Jesus Christ was kind enough to give up all his riches and become poor, so that you could become rich.

¹⁰ A year ago you were the first ones to give, and you gave because you wanted to. So listen to my advice. ¹¹ I think you should finish what you started. If you give according to what you have, you will prove that you are as eager to give as you were to think about giving. ¹² It doesn't matter how much you have. What matters is how much you are willing to give from what you have.

*7.8 my letter: There is no copy of this letter that Paul wrote to the church at Corinth.
See also: 7.5: 2 Cor 2.13.

*8.1 churches in Macedonia: The churches that Paul had started in Philippi and Thessalonica. The church in Berea is probably also meant.
See also: 8.1–4: Rom 15.26.

Being christian

Giving your money

2 Corinthians 8.1–5

Savings, pensions, mortgages – the amount of different ways of getting and saving money are enormous. And there are plenty of ways to spend it as well.

But what about giving it away?

You probably don't think you have much, but however much you have, you should still put aside some of it for God.

It's a basic Christian principle. All that we have comes from God; so we can't keep it all to ourselves. And as long as there are people in need in this world, we should do what we can for them. In the Bible there are plenty of accounts of people giving money and possessions to support either the work of the temple, or to provide for people in need.

Christians give their money away in different ways. Some people 'tithe' which means giving a set proportion of their earnings away. Others give different amounts whenever they see the need. If you're paying tax, you can covenant your giving, which means that Christian charities and your church can claim some money back from the tax man.

Whatever the case, the important thing is to give. God has given you all you have. Shouldn't you give some of it back? And, as Paul said, 'give because you want to, and not because you feel forced to.'

Being Christian: Giving your money

• How much do you earn? How much are you going to give away?
• What can you do to raise money for others in need?
• If you don't know where to give it, find out about Christian charities and aid agencies. Choose one which you feel particularly excited about.
• Give regularly to your church. Don't just be a taker.

13 I am not trying to make life easier for others by making life harder for you. But it is only fair 14 for you to share with them when you have so much, and they have so little. Later, when they have more than enough, and you are in need, they can share with you. Then everyone will have a fair share, 15 just as the Scriptures say,

> "Those who gathered
> too much
>   had nothing left.
> Those who gathered
> only a little
>   had all they needed."

Titus and his friends

16 I am grateful that God made Titus care as much about you as we do. 17 When we begged Titus to visit you, he said he would. He wanted to because he cared so much for you. 18 With Titus we are also sending one of the Lord's followers who is well known in every church for spreading the good news. 19 The churches chose this follower to travel with us while we carry this gift that will bring praise to the Lord and show how much we hope to help. 20 We don't want anyone to find fault with the way we handle your generous gift. 21 But we want to do what pleases the Lord and what people think is right.

22 We are also sending someone else with Titus and the other follower. We approve of this man. In fact, he has already shown us many times that he wants to help. And now he wants to help even more than ever, because he trusts you so much. 23 Titus is my partner, who works with me to serve you. The other two followers are sent by the churches, and they bring honour to Christ. 24 Treat them in such a way that the churches will see your love and will know why we boasted about you.

CHAPTER 9

The money for God's people

1 I don't need to write to you about the money you plan to give for God's people. 2 I know how eager you are to give. And I have proudly told the Lord's followers in Macedonia that you people in Achaia have been ready for a whole year. Now your desire to give has made them want to give. 3 That's why I am sending Titus and the two others to you. I want you to be ready, just as I promised. This will prove that we were not wrong to boast about you.

See also: 8.15: Exod 16.18.   8.21: Prov 3.4 (LXX).

⁴ Some followers from Macedonia may come with me, and I want them to find that you have the money ready. If you don't, I would be embarrassed for trusting you to do this. But you would be embarrassed even more. ⁵ So I have decided to ask Titus and the others to spend some time with you before I arrive. This way they can arrange to collect the money you have promised. Then you will have the chance to give because you want to, and not because you feel forced to.

⁶ Remember this saying,

> "A few seeds make
>   a small harvest,
> but a lot of seeds make
>   a big harvest."

⁷ Each of you must make up your own mind about how much to give. But don't feel sorry that you must give and don't feel that you are forced to give. God loves people who love to give. ⁸ God can bless you with everything you need, and you will always have more than enough to do all kinds of good things for others. ⁹ The Scriptures say,

> "God freely gives his gifts
>   to the poor,
> and always does right."

¹⁰ God gives seed to farmers and provides everyone with food. He will increase what you have, so that you can give even more to those in need. ¹¹ You will be blessed in every way, and you will be able to keep on being generous. Then many people will thank God when we deliver your gift.

¹² What you are doing is much more than a service that supplies God's people with what they need. It is something that will make many others thank God. ¹³ The way in which you have proved yourselves by this service will bring honour and praise to God. You believed the message about Christ, and you obeyed it by sharing generously with God's people and with everyone else. ¹⁴ Now they are praying for you and want to see you, because God used you to bless them so very much. ¹⁵ Thank God for his gift that is too wonderful for words!

Paul is a true apostle

CHAPTER 10

Paul defends his work for Christ

¹ Do you think I am a coward when I am with you and brave when I am far away? Well, I ask you to listen, because Christ himself was humble and gentle. ² Some people have said that we act like the people of this world. So when I arrive, I expect I will have to be firm and forceful in what I say to them. Please don't make me treat you that way. ³ We live in this world, but we don't act like its people ⁴ or fight our battles with the weapons of this world. Instead, we use God's power that can destroy fortresses. We destroy arguments ⁵ and every bit of pride that keeps anyone from knowing God. We capture people's thoughts and make them obey Christ. ⁶ And when you completely obey him, we will punish anyone who refuses to obey.

⁷ You judge by appearances.⸵ If any of you think you are the only ones who belong to Christ, then think again. We belong to Christ as much as you do. ⁸ Perhaps I boast a little too much about the authority that the Lord gave me to help you and not to hurt you. Yet I am not embarrassed to boast. ⁹ And I am not trying to scare you with my letters. ¹⁰ Some of you are saying, "Paul's letters are harsh and powerful. But in person, he is a weakling and has nothing worth saying." ¹¹ Those people had better understand that when I am with you, I will do exactly what I say in my letters.

¹² We won't dare compare ourselves with those who think so much of themselves. But they are foolish to compare themselves with themselves. ¹³ We won't boast about something we don't have a right to boast about. We will only boast about the work that God has sent us to do, and you are part of that work. ¹⁴ We are not boasting more than we should. After all, we did bring the message about Christ to you.

¹⁵ We don't boast about what others have done, as if we had done those things ourselves. But I hope that as you become stronger in your faith, we will be able to reach many more of the people around you.⸵ That has always been our goal. ¹⁶ Then we will be able to preach the good news in other lands where we cannot take credit for work someone else has already done. ¹⁷ The

---

See also: 9.9: Psa 112.9.   9.10: Isa 55.10.

See also: 10.17: Jer 9.24.

Scriptures say, "If you want to boast, then boast about the Lord." [18] You may boast about yourself, but the only approval that counts is the Lord's approval.

CHAPTER 11

Paul and the false apostles

[1] Please put up with a little of my foolishness. [2] I am as concerned about you as God is. You were like a virgin bride I had chosen only for Christ. [3] But now I fear that you will be tricked, just as Eve was tricked by that lying snake. I am afraid that you might stop thinking about Christ in an honest and sincere way. [4] We told you about Jesus, and you received the Holy Spirit and accepted our message. But you let some people tell you about another Jesus. Now you are ready to receive another spirit and accept a different message. [5] I think I am as good as any of those super apostles. [6] I may not speak as well as they do, but I know as much. And this has already been made perfectly clear to you.

[7] Was it wrong for me to lower myself and honour you by preaching God's message free of charge? [8] I robbed other churches by taking money from them to serve you. [9] Even when I was in need, I still didn't bother you. In fact, some of the Lord's followers from Macedonia brought me what I needed. I have not been a burden to you in the past, and I will never be a burden. [10] As surely as I speak the truth about Christ, no one in Achaia can stop me from boasting about this. [11] And it isn't because I don't love you. God himself knows how much I do love you.

[12] I plan to go on doing just what I have always done. Then those people won't be able to boast about doing the same things we are doing. [13] Anyway, they are no more than false apostles and dishonest workers. They only pretend to be apostles of Christ. [14] And it is no wonder. Even Satan tries to make himself look like an angel of light. [15] So why does it seem strange for Satan's servants to pretend to do what is right? Some day they will get exactly what they deserve.

Paul's sufferings for Christ

[16] I don't want any of you to think that I am a fool. But if you do, then let me be a fool and boast a little. [17] When I do all this boasting, I do it as a fool and not for the Lord. [18] Yet if others want to boast about what they have

done, so will I. [19] And since you are so clever, you will gladly put up with a fool. [20] In fact, you let people make slaves of you and cheat you and steal from you. Why, you even let them strut around and slap you in the face. [21] I am ashamed to say that we are too weak to behave in such a way.

If they can boast, so can I, but it is a foolish thing to do. [22] Are they Hebrews? So am I. Are they Jews? So am I. Are they from the family of Abraham? Well, so am I. [23] Are they servants of Christ? I am a fool to talk this way, but I serve him better than they do. I have worked harder and have been put in jail more times. I have been beaten with whips more and have been in danger of death more often.

[24] Five times the Jews gave me thirty-nine lashes with a whip. [25] Three times the Romans beat me with a big stick, and once my enemies stoned me. I have been shipwrecked three times, and I even had to spend a night and a day in the sea. [26] During my many travels, I have been in danger from rivers, robbers, my own people, and foreigners. My life has been in danger in cities, in deserts, at sea, and with people who only pretended to be the Lord's followers.

[27] I have worked and struggled and spent many sleepless nights. I have gone hungry and thirsty and often had nothing to eat. I have been cold from not having enough clothes to keep me warm. [28] Besides everything else, each day I am burdened down, worrying about all the churches. [29] When others are weak, I am weak too. When others are tricked into sin, I get angry.‣

[30] If I have to boast, I will boast about how weak I am. [31] God, the Father of our Lord Jesus, knows I am not lying. And God is to be praised for ever! [32] The governor of Damascus at the time of King Aretas had the city gates guarded, so that he could capture me. [33] But I escaped by being let down in a basket through a window in the city wall.

CHAPTER 12

Visions from the Lord

[1] I have to boast. There is nothing to be gained by it, but I must boast about the visions and other things that the Lord has shown me. [2] I know about one of Christ's followers who was taken up into the third

See also: 11.23: Acts 16.23.   **11.24:** Deut 25.3. **11.25: a** Acts 16.22; **b** Acts 14.19.   **11.26: a** Acts 9.23; **b** Acts 14.5.   **11.32–33:** Acts 9.23–25.

See also: 11.3: Gen 3.1–5,13.   **11.9:** Phil 4.15–18.

heaven fourteen years ago. I don't know if the man was still in his body when it happened, but God certainly knows.

³ As I said, only God really knows if this man was in his body at the time. ⁴ But he was taken up into paradise,* where he heard things that are too wonderful to tell. ⁵ I will boast about that man, but not about myself, except to say how weak I am.

⁶ Yet even if I did boast, I would not be foolish. I would simply be speaking the truth. But I will try not to say too much. That way, none of you will think more highly of me than you should because of what you have seen me do and say. ⁷ Of course, I am now referring to the wonderful things I saw. One of Satan's angels was sent to make me suffer terribly, so that I would not feel too proud.'

⁸ Three times I begged the Lord to make this suffering go away. ⁹ But he replied, "My kindness is all you need. My power is strongest when you are weak." So if Christ keeps giving me his power, I will gladly boast about how weak I am. ¹⁰ Yes, I am glad to be weak or insulted or ill-treated or to have troubles and sufferings, if it is for Christ. Because when I am weak, I am strong.

Paul's concern for the Lord's followers at Corinth

¹¹ I have been making a fool of myself. But you forced me to do it, when you should have been speaking up for me. I may be nothing at all, but I am as good as those super apostles. ¹² When I was with you, I was patient and worked all the powerful miracles and signs and wonders of a true apostle. ¹³ You missed out on only one blessing that the other churches received. That is, you didn't have to support me. Forgive me for doing you wrong.

¹⁴ I am planning to visit you for the third time. But I still won't make a burden of myself. What I really want is you, and not what you have. Children are not supposed to save up for their parents, but parents are supposed to take care of their children. ¹⁵ So I will gladly give all that I have and all that I am. Will you love me less for loving you too much? ¹⁶ You agree that I wasn't a burden to you. Perhaps that's because I was trying to

catch you off guard and trick you. ¹⁷ Were you cheated by any of those I sent to you?

¹⁸ I urged Titus to visit you, and I sent another follower with him. But Titus didn't cheat you, and we felt and behaved the same way he did.

¹⁹ Have you been thinking all along that we have been defending ourselves to you? Actually, we have been speaking to God as followers of Christ. But, my friends, we did it all for your good.

²⁰ I am afraid that when I come, we won't be pleased with each other. I fear that some of you may be arguing or jealous or angry or selfish or gossiping or insulting each other. I even fear that you may be proud and acting like a mob. ²¹ I am afraid God will make me ashamed when I visit you again. I will feel like crying because many of you have never given up your old sins. You are still doing things that are immoral, indecent, and shameful.

CHAPTER 13

Final warnings and greetings

¹ I am on my way to visit you for the third time. And as the Scriptures say, "Any charges must be proved true by at least two or three witnesses." ² During my second visit I warned you that I would punish you and anyone else who doesn't stop sinning. I am far away from you now, but I give you the same warning. ³ This should prove to you that I am speaking for Christ. When he corrects you, he won't be weak. He will be powerful! ⁴ Although he was weak when he was nailed to the cross, he now lives by the power of God. We are weak, just as Christ was. But you will see that we will live by the power of God, just as Christ does.

⁵ Test yourselves and find out if you really are true to your faith. If you pass the test, you will discover that Christ is living in you. But if Christ isn't living in you, you have failed. ⁶ I hope you will discover that we have not failed. ⁷ We pray that you will stop doing evil things. We don't pray like this to make ourselves look good, but to get you to do right, even if we are failures.

⁸ All we can do is to follow the truth and not fight against it. ⁹ Even though we are weak, we are glad that you are strong, and we pray that you will do even better. ¹⁰ I am writing these things to you before I arrive. This way I won't have to be hard on you when I use the authority that the Lord has given me. I was given this authority, so that I could help you and not destroy you.

---

*12.4 paradise: In the Greek translation of the Old Testament, this word is used for the Garden of Eden. In New Testament times it was sometimes used for the place where God's people are happy and at rest, as they wait for the final judgment.

See also: 13.1: Deut 17.6; 19.15.

Viewpoints

Should we ever challenge our own faith?

Contributed by Cia H

'Test yourselves and find out if you really are true to your faith.'

In my opinion faith is a tough thing... 'Faith is being sure of what we hope for and certain of what we do not see'. It isn't easy to believe in something even though we don't always have proof that it is there, or even though we can't see it at all.

This verse says that we have to examine ourselves and test ourselves, to see if our faith is genuine – how many of us do actually know that our faith is genuine? I know that sometimes I get doubts about what I believe such as, what if I've got the wrong religion, what if I've given my life to some one who doesn't exist? That's where the faith comes in, we need to have so much faith that those question don't even pop into our minds, and that we have NO doubt that there is a God in heaven who actually loves us so much and who is going to take us up to be with him eventually.

I think faith is one of the toughest things to keep, it's easy to give up on faith and to go with the crowd, so I challenge all of you who are reading this to find a way to challenge your faith, and do see if it is genuine, and to also help your faith grow.

Anorak corner

Ten notorious murders in the Bible

Cain kills Abel (Genesis 4.8)
Simeon and Levi kill the invalids at Shechem (Genesis 34.25)
The murder of Ishbosheth (2 Samuel 4.6)
David kills Uriah (2 Samuel 12.9)
Zimri kills Elah (1 Kings 16.9)
Nebuchadnezzar kills the King's sons (2 Kings 25.7)
Ishmael kills Gedaliah (Jeremiah 41.1)
Herod kills John the Baptist (Mark 6.21–8)
The crowd kill Stephen (Acts 7.56–60)
Herod kills James (Acts 12.1–2)

Final greetings

[11] Goodbye, my friends. Do better and pay attention to what I have said. Try to get along and live peacefully with each other.

Now I pray that God, who gives love and peace, will be with you. [12] Give each other a warm greeting. All God's people send their greetings.

[13] I pray that the Lord Jesus Christ will bless you and be kind to you! May God bless you with his love, and may the Holy Spirit join all your hearts together.

Additional notes

'**1.10 the threat of death:** Some manuscripts have "many threats of death".
'**1.19 Silas:** The Greek text has "Silvanus", which is another form of the name Silas.
'**3.2 our:** Some manuscripts have "your".
'**7.4 I trust you completely:** Or "I have always spoken the truth to you" or "I can speak freely to you."
'**8.7 you love us better:** Some manuscripts have "we love you better."
'**10.7 You judge by appearances:** Or "Take a close look at yourselves."
'**10.15 we will be able to reach many more of the people around you:** Or "you will praise us even more because of our work among you."
'**11.29 When others are tricked into sin, I get angry:** Or "When others stumble into sin, I hurt for them."
'**12.7 Of course . . . too proud:** Or "Because of the wonderful things that I saw, one of Satan's angels was sent to make me suffer terribly, so that I would not feel too proud."

Galatians

Paul's letter to the churches
in Galatia

The basics

What's the point? What matters is not outward show, but inner commitment.

What happens? Paul writes to combat the ideas of those who thought Christians still had to be circumcised. They need faith in Jesus, not outward shows of obedience.

What should I remember? 5.6 'If you are a follower of Christ Jesus, it makes no difference whether you are circumcised or not. All that matters is your faith that makes you love others.'

More details

Setting the scene The council in Jerusalem had agreed that gentile Christians did not need to obey all the laws of the Jews. But there were still Jewish followers who went around teaching that Christians must be circumcised.

When their teaching started to spread in Galatia, Paul decided that he had to write...

What's it all about? Some people were spreading false teaching. They argued that Paul was not a 'proper' apostle, and that he was toning down the requirements of the Jewish Law in order to make the gospel acceptable to gentiles.

Paul responded by asserting his right to be called an apostle and arguing that the gospel is a gospel of love and grace. In what is his most strongly worded letter, Paul states that it's no longer about laws and regulations, but faith in God.

Footsteps

True apostle: 1.1–24
True message: 2.1–21
True faith: 3.1–14
True freedom: 5.1–6.10

A true apostle and the true message

CHAPTER 1

¹⁻² *From the apostle Paul and from all the Lord's followers with me.*

I was chosen to be an apostle by Jesus Christ and by God the Father, who raised him from death. No mere human chose or appointed me to this work.

To the churches in Galatia.

³ I pray that God the Father and our Lord Jesus Christ will be kind to you and will bless you with peace! ⁴ Christ obeyed God our Father and gave himself as a sacrifice for our sins to rescue us from this evil world. ⁵ God will be given glory for ever and ever. Amen.

The only true message

⁶ I am shocked that you have so quickly turned from God, who chose you because of his wonderful kindness.' You have believed another message, ⁷ when there is really only one true message. But some people are causing you trouble and want to make you turn away from the good news about Christ. ⁸ I pray that God will punish anyone who

preaches anything different from our message to you! It doesn't matter if that person is one of us or an angel from heaven. 9 I have said it before, and I will say it again. I hope God will punish anyone who preaches anything different from what you have already believed.

10 I am not trying to please people. I want to please God. Do you think I am trying to please people? If I were doing that, I would not be a servant of Christ.

God chose Paul to be an apostle

How Paul became an apostle

11 My friends, I want you to know that no one made up the message I preach. 12 It wasn't given or taught to me by some mere human. My message came directly from Jesus Christ when he appeared to me.

13 You know how I used to live as a Jew. I was cruel to God's church and even tried to destroy it. 14 I was a much better Jew than anyone else my own age, and I obeyed every law that our ancestors had given us. 15 But even before I was born, God had chosen me. He was kind and had decided 16 to show me his Son, so that I would announce his message to the Gentiles. I didn't talk this over with anyone. 17 I didn't say a word, not even to the men in Jerusalem who were apostles before I was. Instead, I went at once to Arabia, and afterwards I returned to Damascus.

18 Three years later I went to visit Peter* in Jerusalem and stayed with him for fifteen days. 19 The only other apostle I saw was James, the Lord's brother. 20 And in the presence of God I swear I am telling the truth.

21 Later, I went to the regions of Syria and Cilicia. 22 But no one who belonged to Christ's churches in Judea had ever seen me in person. 23 They had only heard that the one who had been cruel to them was now preaching the message that he had once tried to destroy. 24 And because of me, they praised God.

Paul defends his message

CHAPTER 2

1 Fourteen years later I went to Jerusalem with Barnabas. I also took along Titus. 2 But I went there because God had told me to go, and I explained the good news that I had been preaching to the Gentiles. Then I met privately with the ones who seemed to be the most important leaders. I wanted to make sure that my work in the past and my future work would not be for nothing.

3 Titus went to Jerusalem with me. He was a Greek, but still he wasn't forced to be circumcised. 4 We went there because of those who pretended to be followers and had sneaked in among us as spies. They had come to take away the freedom that Christ Jesus had given us, and they were trying to make us their slaves. 5 But we wanted you to have the true message. That's why we didn't give in to them, not even for a second.

6 Some of them were supposed to be important leaders, but I didn't care who they were. God doesn't have any favourites! None of these so-called special leaders added anything to my message. 7 They realized that God had sent me with the good news for Gentiles, and that he had sent Peter with the same message for Jews. 8 God, who had sent Peter on a mission to the Jews, was now using me to preach to the Gentiles.

9 James, Peter,* and John realized that God had given me the message about his undeserved kindness. And these men are supposed to be the backbone of the church. They even gave Barnabas and me a friendly handshake. This was to show that we would work with Gentiles and that they would work with Jews. 10 They only asked us to remember the poor, and that was something I had always been eager to do.

Paul corrects Peter at Antioch

11 When Peter came to Antioch, I told him face to face that he was wrong. 12 He used to eat with Gentile followers of the Lord, until James sent some Jewish followers. Peter was afraid of the Jews and soon stopped eating with Gentiles. 13 He and the other Jews hid their true feelings so well that even Barnabas

---

*1.18 Peter: The Greek text has "Cephas", which is an Aramaic name meaning "rock". Peter is the Greek name with the same meaning.
See also: 1.13: Acts 8.3; 22.4–5; 26.9–11.   1.14: Acts 22.3.
1.15–16: Acts 9.3–6; 22.6–10; 26.13–18.   1.18: Acts 9.26–30.

*2.9 Peter: See the note at 1.18.
See also: 2.1: Acts 11.30; 15.2.   2.6: Deut 10.17.

Viewpoints

Ever been tempted to adjust the gospel to suit your audience?

Contributed by Austin A

'But we wanted you to have the true message. That's why we didn't give in to them, not even for a second.'

When you share about what Jesus did or about what Christians believe, do you tend to play around with it a little? Do you make Jesus more 'interesting', or skip over the fact that giving your life to Jesus means just that, giving up control of everything?

I know I feel like doing it sometimes, because I think that people around me think that the Bible is boring. The Bible is God's word; is God boring? No! Then what is boring them must be us, giving them our own 'improved' versions of the words which God designed to have maximum impact.

Quoting the Bible in every sentence isn't necessarily going to do you any good. But making sure that your answers to questions are reflecting what is said in the Bible is a necessary thing. And be ready to back up something you say from the Bible if someone asks 'Why?' Don't mess around with what the Bible message, tell it to those around you like it is, and then what you say will really be good news.

More...

Sharing your faith p.1082
Culture p.779
Living truthfully p.1070
Help! I'm the only Christian in my home p.1090

was fooled. [14] But when I saw that they were not really obeying the truth that is in the good news, I corrected Peter in front of everyone and said:

> Peter, you are a Jew, but you live like a Gentile. So how can you force Gentiles to live like Jews?

[15] We are Jews by birth and are not sinners like Gentiles. [16] But we know that God accepts only those who have faith in Jesus Christ. No one can please God by simply obeying the Law. So we put our faith in Christ Jesus, and God accepted us because of our faith.

[17] When we Jews started looking for a way to please God, we discovered that we are sinners too. Does this mean that Christ is the one who makes us sinners? No, it doesn't! [18] But if I tear down something and then build it again, I prove that I was wrong at first. [19] It was the Law itself that killed me and freed me from its power, so that I could live for God.

I have been nailed to the cross with Christ. [20] I have died, but Christ lives in me. And I now live by faith in the Son of God, who loved me and gave his life for me. [21] I don't turn my back on God's undeserved kindness. If we can be acceptable to God by obeying the Law, it was useless for Christ to die.

Faith is the only way to be saved

CHAPTER 3

[1] You stupid Galatians! I told you exactly how Jesus Christ was nailed to a cross. Has someone now put an evil spell on you? [2] I want to know only one thing. How were you given God's Spirit? Was it by obeying the Law of Moses or by hearing about Christ and having faith in him? [3] How can you be so stupid? Do you think that by yourself you can complete what God's Spirit started in you? [4] Have you gone through all this for nothing? Is it all really for nothing? [5] God gives you his Spirit and works miracles in you. But does he do this because you obey the Law of Moses or because you have heard about Christ and have faith in him?

See also: 2.16: a Psa 143.2; Rom 3.20; **b** Rom 3.22.

Real life

Racism

As long as there have been races, there has been racism. In the Bible there are people who hate the Jews and people who the Jews hate. There are plenty of examples of nations oppressed and enslaved.

But God doesn't care about racial or national boundaries. The Jews were the chosen nation, but frequently God chooses to work through another nation, or praise another nation for their worship. He instructed Jonah to go and call the Assyrians to repent – the nation who the Jews feared and hated. Elijah and Elisha performed miracles for foreigners, when their own people showed lack of faith. Jesus went to Samaria and told a story with a Samaritan hero (and the Jews and Samaritans absolutely detested one another).

Jesus Christ was good news for all humans. He died for Jew and Greek, slaves and free, men and women. If we belong to Christ we're all part of the same family. (Galatians 3.26–29).

There are no barriers to God's love. Everyone in the world is a child of God. We're all one family. We're all sinners. And we all have the same saviour.

Think

Why do different races hate one another? What does the Bible say about the origins of different nationalities?
Are there any ways in which you are racist?

Act

Challenge racist comments or racism when you encounter it.
Support those who are oppressed by racism.

Check

Jonah 4.1–11; John 4.3–30;
Colossians 3.10–11

More...

Jonah p.982
Refugees p.129
Gentiles p.1232
Other nations p.259
Samaritans p.1173

---

[6] The Scriptures say that God accepted Abraham because Abraham had faith. [7] And so, you should understand that everyone who has faith is a child of Abraham.* [8] Long ago the Scriptures said that God would accept the Gentiles because of their faith. That's why God told Abraham the good news that all nations would be blessed because of him. [9] This means that everyone who has faith will share in the blessings that were given to Abraham because of his faith.

[10] Anyone who tries to please God by obeying the Law is under a curse. The Scriptures say, "Everyone who doesn't obey everything in the Law is under a curse." [11] No one can please God by obeying the Law. The Scriptures also say, "The people God accepts because of their faith will live."◗

[12] The Law isn't based on faith. It promises life only to people who obey its commands. [13] But Christ rescued us from the Law's curse, when he became a curse in our place. This is because the Scriptures say that anyone who is nailed to a tree is under a curse. [14] And because of what Jesus Christ has done, the blessing that was promised to Abraham was taken to the Gentiles. This happened so that by faith we would be given the promised Holy Spirit.

The Law and the promise

[15] My friends, I will use an everyday example to explain what I mean. Once someone agrees to something, no one else can change or cancel the agreement.◗ [16] That is how it is with the promises God made to Abraham and his descendant.* The promises were not made to many descendants, but only to one, and that one is Christ. [17] What I am saying is that the Law cannot change or cancel God's promise that was made 430 years before the Law was given. [18] If we have to obey the Law in order to receive God's blessings, those blessings don't really come to us because of God's promise. But God was kind to Abraham and made him a promise.

---

*3.7 a child of Abraham: God chose Abraham, and so it was believed that anyone who was a child of Abraham was also a child of God. See the note at 3.29.
*3.16 descendant: The Greek text has "seed", which may mean one or many descendants. In this verse Paul says it means Christ.

See also: 3.6: Gen 15.6; Rom 4.3. 3.7: Rom 4.16.
3.8: Gen 12.3. 3.10: Deut 27.26 (LXX). 3.11: Hab 2.4.
3.12: Lev 18.5. 3.13: Deut 21.23. 3.17: Exod 12.40.
3.18: Rom 4.14.

19 What is the use of the Law? It was given later to show that we sin. But it was only supposed to last until the coming of that descendant* who was given the promise. In fact, angels gave the Law to Moses, and he gave it to the people. 20 There is only one God, and the Law did not come directly from him.

Slaves and children

21 Does the Law disagree with God's promises? No, it doesn't! If any law could give life to us, we could become acceptable to God by obeying that law. 22 But the Scriptures say that sin controls everyone, so that God's promises will be for anyone who has faith in Jesus Christ.

23 The Law controlled us and kept us under its power until the time came when we would have faith. 24 In fact, the Law was our teacher. It was supposed to teach us until we had faith and were acceptable to God. 25 But once a person has learnt to have faith, there is no more need to have the Law as a teacher.

26 All of you are God's children because of your faith in Christ Jesus. 27 And when you were baptized, it was as though you had put on Christ in the same way you put on new clothes. 28 Faith in Christ Jesus is what makes each of you equal with each other, whether you are a Jew or a Greek, a slave or a free person, a man or a woman. 29 So if you belong to Christ, you are now part of Abraham's family,* and you will be given what God has promised.

CHAPTER 4

1 Children who are under age are no better off than slaves, even though everything their parents own will some day be theirs. 2 This is because children are placed in the care of guardians and teachers until the time their parents have set. 3 That is how it was with us. We were like children ruled by the powers of this world.

4 But when the time was right, God sent his Son, and a woman gave birth to him. His Son obeyed the Law, 5 so he could set us free from the Law, and we could become God's children. 6 Now that we are his children, God has sent the Spirit of his Son into our hearts.

And his Spirit tells us that God is our Father. 7 You are no longer slaves. You are God's children, and you will be given what he has promised.

Paul's concern for the Galatians

8 Before you knew God, you were slaves of gods that are not real. 9 But now you know God, or better still, God knows you. How can you turn back and become the slaves of those weak and pitiful powers?* 10 You even celebrate certain days, months, seasons, and years. 11 I am afraid I have wasted my time working with you.

12 My friends, I beg you to be like me, just as I once tried to be like you. Did you ill-treat me 13 when I first preached to you? No you didn't, even though you knew I had come there because I was sick. 14 My illness must have caused you some trouble, but you didn't hate me or turn me away because of it. You welcomed me as though I were one of God's angels or even Christ Jesus himself. 15 Where is that good feeling now? I am sure that if it had been possible, you would have taken out your own eyes and given them to me. 16 Am I now your enemy, just because I told you the truth?

17 Those people may be paying you a lot of attention, but it isn't for your good. They only want to keep you away from me, so you will pay them a lot of attention. 18 It is always good to give your attention to something worthwhile, even when I am not with you. 19 My children, I am in terrible pain until Christ may be seen living in you. 20 I wish I were with you now. Then I would not have to talk this way. You really have me puzzled.

Hagar and Sarah

21 Some of you would like to be under the rule of the Law of Moses. But do you know what the Law says? 22 In the Scriptures we learn that Abraham had two sons. The mother of one of them was a slave, while the mother of the other one had always been free. 23 The son of the slave woman was born in the usual way. But the son of the free woman was born because of God's promise.

24 All this has another meaning as well. Each of the two women stands for one of the agreements God made with his people.

*3.19 that descendant: Jesus.
*3.29 you are now part of Abraham's family: Paul tells the Galatians that faith in Jesus Christ is what makes someone a true child of Abraham and of God. See the note at 3.7.
See also: 3.29: Rom 4.13. 4.5–7: Rom 8.15–17.

*4.9 powers: Spirits were thought to control human lives and were believed to be connected with the movements of the stars.
See also: 4.22: a Gen 16.15; b Gen 21.2.

Hagar, the slave woman, stands for the agreement that was made at Mount Sinai. Everyone born into her family is a slave. ²⁵ Hagar also stands for Mount Sinai in Arabia' and for the present city of Jerusalem. She' and her children are slaves.

²⁶ But our mother is the city of Jerusalem in heaven above, and she isn't a slave. ²⁷ The Scriptures say about her,

> "You have never had children,
>   but now you can be glad.
> You have never given birth,
>   but now you can shout.
> Once you had no children,
>   but now you will have
> more children than a woman
>   who has been married
>   for a long time."

²⁸ My friends, you were born because of this promise, just as Isaac was. ²⁹ But the child who was born in the natural way made trouble for the child who was born because of the Spirit. The same thing is happening today. ³⁰ The Scriptures say, "Get rid of the slave woman and her son! He won't be given anything. The son of the free woman will receive everything." ³¹ My friends, we are children of the free woman and not of the slave.

Guided by the Spirit and love

CHAPTER 5

Christ gives freedom

¹ Christ has set us free! This means we are really free. Now hold on to your freedom and don't ever become slaves of the Law again.

² I, Paul, promise you that Christ won't do you any good if you get circumcised. ³ If you do, you must obey the whole Law. ⁴ And if you try to please God by obeying the Law, you have cut yourself off from Christ and his wonderful kindness. ⁵ But the Spirit makes us sure that God will accept us because of our faith in Christ. ⁶ If you are a follower of Christ Jesus, it makes no difference whether you are circumcised or not. All that matters is your faith that makes you love others.

⁷ You were doing so well until someone made you turn from the truth. ⁸ And that person was certainly not sent by the one who chose you. ⁹ A little yeast can change a whole batch of dough, ¹⁰ but you belong to the Lord. That makes me certain that you will do what I say, instead of what someone else tells you to do. Whoever is causing trouble for you will be punished.

¹¹ My friends, if I still preach that people need to be circumcised, why am I in so much trouble? The message about the cross would no longer be a problem, if I told people to be circumcised. ¹² I wish that everyone who is upsetting you would not only get circumcised, but would cut off much more!

¹³ My friends, you were chosen to be free. So don't use your freedom as an excuse to do anything you want. Use it as an opportunity to serve each other with love. ¹⁴ All that the Law says can be summed up in the command to love others as much as you love yourself. ¹⁵ But if you keep attacking each other like wild animals, you had better watch out or you will destroy yourselves.

God's Spirit and our own desires

¹⁶ If you are guided by the Spirit, you won't obey your selfish desires. ¹⁷ The Spirit and your desires are enemies of each other. They are always fighting each other and keeping you from doing what you feel you should. ¹⁸ But if you obey the Spirit, the Law of Moses has no control over you.

¹⁹ People's desires make them give in to immoral ways, filthy thoughts, and shameful deeds. ²⁰ They worship idols, practise witchcraft, hate others, and are hard to get along with. People become jealous, angry, and selfish. They not only argue and cause trouble, but they are ²¹ envious. They get drunk, carry on at wild parties, and do other evil things as well. I told you before, and I am telling you again: no one who does these things will share in the blessings of God's kingdom.

²² God's Spirit makes us loving, happy, peaceful, patient, kind, good, faithful, ²³ gentle, and self-controlled. There is no law against behaving in any of these ways. ²⁴ And because we belong to Christ Jesus, we have killed our selfish feelings and desires.

See also: **4.27:** Isa 54.1.   **4.29:** Gen 21.9.   **4.30:** Gen 21.10.

See also: **5.9:** 1 Cor 5.6.   **5.14:** Lev 19.18.
5.17: Rom 7.15–23.

Real life

Food and eating

Contributed by Soul Survivor

'Did you have a good day, dear?' Once upon a time this sentence meant exactly that, but in some households today it means, 'How much chocolate did you consume, was your chicken sandwich at lunchtime low fat, how much snacking took place, did those evil people at work tempt you to a pub lunch?'

Have you noticed how much of our daily conversations revolve around food? 'I'd better not eat that, I'm trying to be good today', 'I know it's bad but I'm going to eat it anyway'. But for some of us it becomes more than just a matter of three meals a day. It becomes a real strain, thinking about food from the moment we wake up in the morning to when we go to bed at night. Very few of us would notice, admit it or want to confront it. But the Bible pulls no punches. It has something to say about our little obsession: Matthew 6.24.

No (wo)man can serve God and work, or God and shopping, or God and sport, or God and clothes, or God and Will Young, or God and food. None of these things is actually bad, in fact some are positively good, but God is clear in his calling for us to worship only him: Exodus 34.14.

Over recent years there has been a raised awareness for eating disorders – bulimia and anorexia. For any of us who have lived with these conditions, or watched any of our close friends battle with them, we will know how enslaving they are, how destructive, not just to our bodies but to our mind, soul and spirit. Galatians 5.1

And if you can't bear to look in the your bedroom mirror, look into God's mirror. He wants to show us where our self-image is malnourished: who we are, what our thought processes are like, and what wrong beliefs we hold. We may need to start having some honest conversations with God about food, to ask him to show us where we have become unbalanced. As the Lord and Master of all our lives he can help us make

this simple once again. John 10.10: 'I have come that they may have life, and have it to the full.'

God did not ever intend we would get our knickers in such a twist over our packed lunch. His intention was that food would nourish us and basically get the job done of fuelling our bodies to live life. But, like many other good gifts from God, he went beyond the functional and blessed us in creating an amazing variety of wonderful tastes. Think curry, Greek yoghurt, Turkish delight, or whatever your favourite food happens to be – what a wonderful God!

Think

Do you use food for comfort when you are sad and lonely, or if you've had a bad day? Do you like to be in control of the food you eat and stick to a rigid plan?
How can we enjoy our food without worshipping it?

Act

Read around the subject.
If you are struggling with more serious eating disorders, speak to your youth worker or GP. Alternatively you might find a professional counsellor or accountability group that could help you.

Check

Exodus 34.14; Psalms 139.13–16; Matthew 6.24; Galatians 5.1; John 8.36; 10.10

More...

Help! I hate myself! p.1332
Addiction p.1182

25 God's Spirit has given us life, and so we should follow the Spirit. 26 But don't be conceited or make others jealous by claiming to be better than they are.

CHAPTER 6

Help each other

1 My friends, you are spiritual. So if someone is trapped in sin, you should gently lead that person back to the right path. But watch out, and don't be tempted yourself. 2 You obey the law of Christ when you offer each other a helping hand.

3 If you think you are better than others, when you really aren't, you are wrong. 4 Do your own work well, and then you will have something to be proud of. But don't compare yourself with others. 5 We each must carry our own load.

6 Share every good thing you have with anyone who teaches you what God has said.

7 You cannot fool God, so don't make a fool of yourself! You will harvest what you plant. 8 If you follow your selfish desires, you will harvest destruction, but if you follow the Spirit, you will harvest eternal life. 9 Don't get tired of helping others. You will be rewarded when the time is right, if you don't give up. 10 We should help people whenever we can, especially if they are followers of the Lord.

Final warnings

11 You can see what big letters I make when I write with my own hand.

12 Those people who are telling you to get circumcised are only trying to show how important they are. And they don't want to get into trouble for preaching about the cross of Christ. 13 They are circumcised, but they don't obey the Law of Moses. All they want is to boast about having you circumcised. 14 But I will never boast about anything except the cross of our Lord Jesus Christ. Because of his cross, the world is dead as far as I am concerned, and I am dead as far as the world is concerned.

15 It doesn't matter if you are circumcised or not. All that matters is that you are a new person.

16 If you follow this rule, you will belong to God's true people. God will treat you with undeserved kindness and will bless you with peace.

Helpline

Help! How do I stop my friends doing wrong?

'My workmates keep swearing! My friends are drinking too much! I really don't agree with what they're doing.'

Christians follow a different set of rules to most of society, which can create conflict. So how do we confront other people? And should we even bother?

Jesus certainly wasn't afraid to confront people. But he also got alongside people. He went to parties. He hung out with 'sinners'. He knew you couldn't just go around lecturing people; you had to live with them as well. He loved people, as well as challenging them.

Certainly if friends are in danger – if they're into drugs or crime – then confronting them is right. If they can't see that you're trying to help, they're in deep trouble. But be gentle. 'So if someone is trapped in sin, you should gently lead that person back to the right path,' says Paul. But he adds, 'watch out, and don't be tempted yourself' (Galatians 6.1).

Three things

Sinner

Remember that you're not a saint yourself. So, no arrogance here. No pushing people down so that you can feel superior.

Gently

That word of Paul's – 'gently' – is important. You don't have to go in all guns blazing. Choose your words carefully. Walk humbly. Love in action.

Example

Do as much as you can through your own example. Let them see that you don't swear, that you don't sleep around, that you don't do the things that they do. Your example and the Holy Spirit working on them, might lead them to change their ways.

More...

Sin p.1261
Living truthfully p.1070

¹⁷ On my own body are scars that prove I belong to Christ Jesus. So I don't want anyone to bother me any more.

¹⁸ My friends, I pray that the Lord Jesus Christ will be kind to you! Amen.

Additional notes

›**1.6 his wonderful kindness:** Some manuscripts have "the wonderful kindness of Christ".

›**3.11 The people God accepts because of their faith will live:** Or "The people God accepts will live because of their faith."

›**3.15 Once someone . . . cancel the agreement:** Or "Once a person makes out a will, no one can change or cancel it."

›**4.25 Hagar also stands for Mount Sinai in Arabia:** Some manuscripts have "Sinai is a mountain in Arabia". This sentence would then be translated: "Sinai is a mountain in Arabia, and Hagar stands for the present city of Jerusalem."

›**4.25 She:** "Hagar" or "Jerusalem".

Ephesians

Paul's letter to the church in Ephesus

The basics

What's the point? All Christians are part of the same 'body'; we should all remain united in love.

What happens? Paul emphasises the need for unity. The walls of hatred between Jew and Gentile have been broken down.

What should I remember? 4.4–6 'All of you are part of the same body. There is only one Spirit of God, just as you were given one hope when you were chosen to be God's people. We have only one Lord, one faith, and one baptism. There is one God who is the Father of all people. Not only is God above all others, but he works by using all of us, and he lives in all of us.'

More details

Setting the scene Paul was probably in prison when he wrote this letter. He reflects on his role in the great plan that God has put into action, and he writes to the Ephesians to urge them to stay together...

What's it all about? The letter to the church at Ephesus brings together many of the major themes of Paul's teaching, as a kind of summary of his thought. It's a kind of general introduction to Paul's ideas, especially emphasising the need for unity.

As followers of Jesus we need to recognise that we are all joined together, and we should all work for and support one another. Christ has brought together Jew and Gentile, we all have our role to play, and no one is more important than another.

Paul has an almost breathless tone of wonder at God's kindness, wisdom and love. The overriding theme in this letter is the way in which God has planned all this from the start. Christ has died to give us freedom (1.7–8), and the same Christ now sits with God and rules over all things. Christ has given us life and he has given us a future (2.4–6). This is God's gift to us. There is nothing we can do to earn it.

Perhaps the most quoted passage from this book though is the one about 'the armour of God'. With Roman soldiers everywhere, with a clear and unassailable authority, the image of armour giving impregnability against attack was an obvious one for Paul to use. But it doesn't necessarily mean that truth is always belt-shaped or that peace can't reach above ankle-height: the point is that every part of us should be protected against attack with God's strength, and at the same time every part of us has its part to play in serving in God's army.

Footsteps

God's plan: 1.1–14
Unified by Christ: 2.11–22
New life: 4.1–24
Living for God: 5.6–20
The fight: 6.10–24

Greetings

CHAPTER 1

¹ *From Paul, chosen by God to be an apostle of Christ Jesus.*

To God's people who live in Ephesus and▸ are faithful followers of Christ Jesus.

² I pray that God our Father and our Lord Jesus Christ will be kind to you and will bless you with peace!

Christ brings spiritual blessings

³ Praise the God and Father of our Lord Jesus Christ for the spiritual blessings that Christ has brought us from heaven! ⁴ Before the world was created, God had Christ choose us to live with him and to be his holy and innocent and loving people. ⁵ God was kind▸ and decided that Christ would choose us to be God's own adopted children. ⁶ God was very kind to us because of the Son he dearly loves, and so we should praise God.

⁷⁻⁸ Christ sacrificed his life's blood to set us free, which means that our sins are now forgiven. Christ did this because God was so kind to us. God has great wisdom and understanding, ⁹ and by what Christ has done, God has shown us his own mysterious ways. ¹⁰ Then when the time is right, God will do all that he has planned, and Christ will bring together everything in heaven and on earth.

¹¹ God always does what he plans, and that's why he appointed Christ to choose us. ¹² He did this so that we Jews would bring honour to him and be the first ones to have hope because of him. ¹³ Christ also brought you the truth, which is the good news about how you can be saved. You put your faith in Christ and were given the promised Holy Spirit to show that you belong to God. ¹⁴ The Spirit also makes us sure that we will be given what God has stored up for his people. Then we will be set free, and God will be honoured and praised.

Paul's prayer

¹⁵ I have heard about your faith in the Lord Jesus and your love for all God's people. ¹⁶ So I never stop being grateful for you, as I mention you in my prayers. ¹⁷ I ask the

See also: 1.1: Acts 18.19–21; 19.1. 1.7: Col 1.14.

Big ideas

Church

Church doesn't mean the building, but the people. As one well-known saying puts it, 'Church isn't the building, it's what's left when the building burns down.'

When the New Testament talks about 'Church', it may be referring to all Jesus' followers, or a specific group, in a certain town or city.

A body

Paul likens the church to a body, with each member performing a different function, but all of them vital. (Ephesians 1.23)

A family

The church is a family of believers, because we are all brothers and sisters in Jesus (1 John 3.1). In some parts of the world this is especially true, where people who become Christians are thrown out of their real family. Like all the best families we should love and care for one another.

A worshipping group

The church is where we come together to worship God. Different people bring different gifts, so all can worship together (1 Corinthians 12).

A learning centre

Through church we learn more about God. From early times, travelling teachers and preachers would visit churches, teaching Christians more about God and Jesus.

A support group

Christians, no matter where they are, go through tough times. The church helps us with these times, prays for and supports us.

 Footsteps

A week with The Church

The first churches in Jerusalem: Acts 2.41–47
The church continues to grow: Acts 5.12–42
The church in Antioch: Acts 11.19–30
Hello Rome! Romans 15.22–16.5
Different gifts: 1 Corinthians 12.1–30
Christ is the head: Colossians 1.15–20
Requirements for church leaders: Titus 1.5–9

glorious Father and God of our Lord Jesus Christ to give you his Spirit. The Spirit will make you wise and let you understand what it means to know God. ¹⁸ My prayer is that light will flood your hearts and that you will understand the hope that was given to you when God chose you. Then you will discover the glorious blessings that will be yours together with all God's people.

¹⁹ I want you to know about the great and mighty power that God has for us followers. It is the same wonderful power he used ²⁰ when he raised Christ from death and let him sit at his right side* in heaven. ²¹ There Christ rules over all forces, authorities, powers, and rulers. He rules over all beings in this world and will rule in the future world as well. ²² God has put all things under the power of Christ, and for the good of the church he has made him the head of everything. ²³ The church is Christ's body and is filled with Christ who completely fills everything.'

CHAPTER 2

From death to life

¹ In the past you were dead because you sinned and fought against God. ² You followed the ways of this world and obeyed the devil. He rules the world, and his spirit has power over everyone who doesn't obey God. ³ Once we were also ruled by the selfish desires of our bodies and minds. We had made God angry, and we were going to be punished like everyone else.

⁴⁻⁵ But God was merciful! We were dead because of our sins, but God loved us so much that he made us alive with Christ, and God's wonderful kindness is what saves you. ⁶ God raised us from death to life with Christ Jesus, and he has given us a place beside Christ in heaven. ⁷ God did this so that in the future world he could show how truly good and kind he is to us because of what Christ Jesus has done. ⁸ You were saved by faith in God, who treats us much better than we deserve.* This is God's gift to you, and not anything you have done on your own. ⁹ It isn't something you have earned,

---

*1.20 right side: The place of power and honour.
*2.8 treats us much better than we deserve: The Greek word *charis*, traditionally rendered "grace", is translated here and in other places in the CEV to express the overwhelming kindness of God.

See also: 1.20: Psa 110.1.   1.22: Psa 8.6.
1.22–23: Col 1.18.   2.1–5: Col 2.13.

Big ideas

Grace

Grace means God's gift to us and it is the ultimate gift of God to us: salvation, not through anything we've done, but because Christ has died for us. Someone once defined Grace as 'God's Riches At Christ's Expense'. Because Christ has died for us, we can receive God's gift of eternal life.

It's not that we've done anything to deserve this. In fact, there was nothing we could do. No, God has given us this gift because he loves us. In his letter to Ephesians Paul writes 'You were saved by faith in God, who treats us much better than we deserve. This is God's gift to you, and not anything you have done on your own' (Ephesians 2.8).

That's what God's grace is all about. It's God's grace that makes us right with him. God's grace is patient. He does not want to punish people, he wants to give everyone the chance to receive this gift. But people do have to choose to receive it.

And the result of this grace is that we will live eternally with God. No matter how much we sin, if we turn to God and say sorry, his gift will still be there.

 footsteps

Five days on Grace

God's gift to us: Romans 5.14–21
From death to life: Ephesians 2.1–10
For all people: Titus 2.11–14
Undeserved kindness: John 1.16–18
All treated the same way: Acts 15.7–11

More...

Forgiveness p.614
Saying sorry p.1258
Redemption p.292

so there is nothing you can boast about.
[10] God planned for us to do good things and to live as he has always wanted us to live. That's why he sent Christ to make us what we are.

United by Christ

[11] Don't forget that you are Gentiles. In fact, you used to be called "uncircumcised" by those who take pride in being circumcised. [12] At that time you did not know about Christ. You were foreigners to the people of Israel, and you had no part in the promises that God had made to them. You were living in this world without hope and without God, [13] and you were far from God. But Christ offered his life's blood as a sacrifice and brought you near God.

[14] Christ has made peace between Jews and Gentiles, and he has united us by breaking down the wall of hatred that separated us. Christ gave his own body [15] to destroy the Law of Moses with all its rules and commands. He even brought Jews and Gentiles together as though we were only one person, when he united us in peace. [16] On the cross Christ did away with our hatred for each other. He also made peace᾽ between us and God by uniting Jews and Gentiles in one body. [17] Christ came and preached peace to you Gentiles, who were far from God, and peace to us Jews, who were near God. [18] And because of Christ, all of us can come to the Father by the same Spirit.

[19] You Gentiles are no longer strangers and foreigners. You are citizens with everyone else who belongs to the family of God. [20] You are like a building with the apostles and prophets as the foundation and with Christ as the most important stone. [21] Christ is the one who holds the building together and makes it grow into a holy temple for the Lord. [22] And you are part of that building Christ has built as a place for God's own Spirit to live.

CHAPTER 3

Paul's mission to the Gentiles

[1] Christ Jesus made me his prisoner, so that I could help you Gentiles. [2] You have heard about God's kindness in choosing me to help you. [3] In fact, this letter tells you a little about how God has shown me his mysterious ways.

[4] As you read the letter, you will also find out how well I really do understand the mystery about Christ. [5] No one knew about this mystery until God's Spirit told it to his holy apostles and prophets. [6] And the mystery is this: Because of Christ Jesus, the good news has given the Gentiles a share in the promises that God gave to the Jews. God has also let the Gentiles be part of the same body.

[7] God treated me with kindness. His power worked in me, and it became my job to spread the good news. [8] I am the least important of all God's people. But God was kind and chose me to tell the Gentiles that because of Christ there are blessings that cannot be measured. [9] God, who created everything, wanted me to help everyone understand the mysterious plan that had always been hidden in his mind. [10] Then God would use the church to show the powers and authorities in the spiritual world that he has many different kinds of wisdom.

[11] God did this according to his eternal plan. And he was able to do what he had planned because of all that Christ Jesus our Lord had done. [12] Christ now gives us courage and confidence, so that we can come to God by faith. [13] That's why you should not be discouraged when I suffer for you. After all, it will bring honour to you.

Christ's love for us

[14] I kneel in prayer to the Father. [15] All beings in heaven and on earth receive their life from him.᾽ [16] God is wonderful and glorious. I pray that his Spirit will make you become strong followers [17] and that Christ will live in your hearts because of your faith. Stand firm and be deeply rooted in his love. [18] I pray that you and all God's people will understand what is called wide or long or high or deep.* [19] I want you to know all about Christ's love, although it is too wonderful to be measured. Then your lives will be filled with all that God is.

[20-21] I pray that Christ Jesus and the church will for ever bring praise to God. His power at work in us can do far more than we dare ask or imagine. Amen.

---

*3.18 what is called wide or long or high or deep: This may refer to the heavenly Jerusalem or to God's love or wisdom or to the meaning of the cross.

See also: 3.4–6: Col 1.26–27.

See also: 2.15: Col 2.14.   2.16: Col 1.20.   2.17: Isa 57.19.

Real life

Drugs

Contributed by HopeUK

Although there are no references to drugs (other than alcohol) in the Bible, we are given important lifestyle guidelines. God asks us to live out a life that is pleasing to Him. 'You were taught with regard to your former way of life to put off your old self, which is being corrupted by its deceitful desires.' (Ephesians 4.22). We are told to leave behind our old habits and ways and to live out a new life.

There are two general principles which will help us decide whether we should use or agree with the use of drugs: the principles of caring for ourselves and caring for others. We can also ask ourselves two key questions: how will a drug affect our bodies? And how will it affect our relationship with God?

At Pentecost (Acts 2) Peter and the disciples were completely filled with the Holy Spirit and in control. The new testament encourages all Christians to be filled with the Holy Spirit (Ephesians 5.18). So is this consistent with using any drug which affects the mind? Drugs affect the mind in different ways – slowing it down, speeding it up or distorting it. They may give you different feelings, but the experience will be a short-lived illusion, however good it seems at the time. The apostle Peter says it is important to be clear-minded and self-controlled (1 Peter 4.7) because our bodies are the 'temple of the Holy Spirit' (1 Corinthians 3.16 & 17).

Christian teaching is also clear about the important role of personal example. We need to avoid actions which may cause others to 'fall' even if we might be all right ourselves (1 Corinthians 8.13). Jesus has set us free (1 Corinthians 10.23–11.1), but notice that where Paul writes 'so whether you eat or drink or whatever you do, do it all for the glory of God' (1 Corinthians 10.31), he qualifies this by saying 'do not cause anyone to stumble... for I am not seeking my own good, but the good of many, so that they may be saved' (1 Corinthians 10.32).

As one Christian youth worker said 'Young people no longer want to be told the truth, they want to be shown the truth. We must live lifestyles that back up our words and release the power of God through the very actions that we take.' Knowing the facts about drugs, and the effects they can have on us, should make us consider whether these substances encourage a lifestyle Jesus wants us to live.

Think

Do people of different ages have different attitudes towards drugs?
Will drugs help you have a spiritual experience?
How can Christians make a difference to the drug culture in our society?

Act

Design a short questionnaire to research different age groups' attitudes to drugs e.g. youth club, parents, church members. Test out the questionnaire and let people see the results of your findings.
Find out about becoming a youth representative with Hope UK.

Check

Acts 2; Ephesians 4.22; 5.18;
1 Corinthians 3.16–17; 8.13; 10.23—11.1;
1 Peter 4.7

More...

Addiction p.1182
Alcohol p.700
Forgiveness p.614
Help! I feel like I've failed p.837
Help! I'm in trouble with the police p.378

A new life in unity with Christ

CHAPTER 4

Unity with Christ

¹ As a prisoner of the Lord, I beg you to live in a way that is worthy of the people God has chosen to be his own. ² Always be humble and gentle. Patiently put up with each other and love each other. ³ Try your best to let God's Spirit keep your hearts united. Do this by living at peace. ⁴ All of you are part of the same body. There is only one Spirit of God, just as you were given one hope when you were chosen to be God's people. ⁵ We have only one Lord, one faith, and one baptism. ⁶ There is one God who is the Father of all people. Not only is God above all others, but he works by using all of us, and he lives in all of us.

⁷ Christ has generously divided out his gifts to us. ⁸ As the Scriptures say,

> "When he went up
>   to the highest place,
> he led away many prisoners
>   and gave gifts to people."

⁹ When it says, "he went up", it means that Christ had been deep in the earth. ¹⁰ This also means that the one who went deep into the earth is the same one who went into the highest heaven, so that he would fill the whole universe.

¹¹ Christ chose some of us to be apostles, prophets, missionaries, pastors, and teachers, ¹² so that his people would learn to serve and his body would grow strong. ¹³ This will continue until we are united by our faith and by our understanding of the Son of God. Then we will be mature, just as Christ is, and we will be completely like him.•

¹⁴ We must stop acting like children. We must not let deceitful people trick us by their false teachings, which are like winds that toss us around from place to place. ¹⁵ Love should always make us tell the truth. Then we will grow in every way and be more like Christ, the head ¹⁶ of the body. Christ holds it together and makes all its parts work perfectly, as it grows and becomes strong because of love.

The old life and the new life

¹⁷ As a follower of the Lord, I order you to stop living like stupid, godless people. ¹⁸ Their minds are in the dark, and they are stubborn and ignorant and have missed out on the life that comes from God. They no longer have any feelings about what is right, ¹⁹ and they are so greedy that they do all kinds of indecent things.

²⁰⁻²¹ But that isn't what you were taught about Jesus Christ. He is the truth, and you heard about him and learnt about him. ²² You were told that your foolish desires will destroy you and that you must give up your old way of life with all its bad habits. ²³ Let the Spirit change your way of thinking ²⁴ and make you into a new person. You were created to be like God, and so you must please him and be truly holy.

Rules for the new life

²⁵ We are part of the same body. Stop lying and start telling each other the truth. ²⁶ Don't get so angry that you sin. Don't go to bed angry ²⁷ and don't give the devil a chance.

²⁸ If you are a thief, stop stealing. Be honest and work hard, so you will have something to give to people in need.

²⁹ Stop all your dirty talk. Say the right thing at the right time and help others by what you say.

³⁰ Don't make God's Spirit sad. The Spirit makes you sure that some day you will be free from your sins.

³¹ Stop being bitter and angry with others. Don't yell at one another or curse each other or ever be rude. ³² Instead, be kind and merciful, and forgive others, just as God forgave you because of Christ.

CHAPTER 5

¹ Do as God does. After all, you are his dear children. ² Let love be your guide. Christ loved us• and offered his life for us as a sacrifice that pleases God.

³ You are God's people, so don't let it be said that any of you are immoral or indecent or greedy. ⁴ Don't use dirty or foolish or filthy words. Instead, say how thankful you are. ⁵ Being greedy, indecent, or immoral is just another way of worshipping idols.

See also: 4.2: Col 3.12–13. 4.8: Psa 68.18. 4.16: Col 2.19.

See also: 4.22: Col 3.9. 4.24: a Col 3.10; b Gen 1.26.
4.25: Zech 8.16. 4.26: Psa 4.4 (LXX). 4.32: Col 3.13.
5.2: Exod 29.18; Psa 40.6.

You can be sure that people who behave in this way will never be part of the kingdom that belongs to Christ and to God.

Living as people of the light

⁶ Don't let anyone trick you with foolish talk. God punishes everyone who disobeys him and says' foolish things. ⁷ So don't have anything to do with anyone like that.

⁸ You used to be like people living in the dark, but now you are people of the light because you belong to the Lord. So act like people of the light ⁹ and make your light shine. Be good and honest and truthful, ¹⁰ as you try to please the Lord. ¹¹ Don't take part in doing those worthless things that are done in the dark. Instead, show how wrong they are. ¹² It is disgusting even to talk about what is done in the dark. ¹³ But the light will show what these things are really like. ¹⁴ Light shows up everything,' just as the Scriptures say,

> "Wake up from your sleep
>   and rise from death.
> Then Christ will shine on you."

¹⁵ Act like people with good sense and not like fools. ¹⁶ These are evil times, so make every minute count. ¹⁷ Don't be stupid. Instead, find out what the Lord wants you to do. ¹⁸ Don't destroy yourself by getting drunk, but let the Spirit fill your life. ¹⁹ When you meet together, sing psalms, hymns, and spiritual songs, as you praise the Lord with all your heart. ²⁰ Always use the name of our Lord Jesus Christ to thank God the Father for everything.

Wives and husbands

²¹ Honour Christ and put others first. ²² A wife should put her husband first, as she does the Lord. ²³ A husband is the head of his wife, as Christ is the head and the Saviour of the church, which is his own body. ²⁴ Wives should always put their husbands first, as the church puts Christ first.

²⁵ A husband should love his wife as much as Christ loved the church and gave his life for it. ²⁶ He made the church holy by the power of his word, and he made it pure by washing it with water. ²⁷ Christ did this, so that he would have a glorious and holy church, without faults or spots or wrinkles or any other flaws.

See also: **5.16:** Col 4.5. **5.19–20:** Col 3.16–17.
5.22: Col 3.18; 1 Pet 3.1. **5.25:** Col 3.19; 1 Pet 3.7.

Helpline

Help! Why should I bother with marriage?

'It's just a bit of paper, isn't it? We don't need that to prove we love each other.'

Nowadays many people think marriage is just a chance to wear a nice dress; a photo-opportunity; an excuse for a party.

Wrong. Marrying – as opposed to just moving in together – is about making a public statement. You promise to stick together, to be faithful, to care for and support the other person. You make these promises before God and other people.

And you become one. Marriage, in God's eyes, is a gift, a mysterious, marvellous relationship when man and woman become one. Husband and wife loving each other as much as they love themselves. Husbands should love their wives as Christ loved the church. That means serving them, being willing to die for them. It's not just a convenient tax arrangement, nor a bit of paper. It's a lifelong, life-changing, life-giving commitment.

Three things

God

For Christians God is a part of every marriage. It's not just the two of you; it's the two of you and God. Getting married reminds you of who is the source of love.

Promises

The marriage service is about making a public act of commitment. It's not just the two of you deciding that it would be a nice idea; it's about making real promises that mean something, and allowing others to witness you making those vows.

Gift

The marriage service recognises that marriage is a gift from God. It's something that God has given us to allow people to live together in the best way.

More...

Sex p.727
Marriage p.205

²⁸ In the same way, a husband should love his wife as much as he loves himself. A husband who loves his wife shows that he loves himself. ²⁹ None of us hate our own bodies. We provide for them and take good care of them, just as Christ does for the church, ³⁰ because we are each part of his body. ³¹ As the Scriptures say, "A man leaves his father and mother to get married, and he becomes like one person with his wife." ³² This is a great mystery, but I understand it to mean Christ and his church. ³³ So each husband should love his wife as much as he loves himself, and each wife should respect her husband.

CHAPTER 6

Children and parents

¹ Children, you belong to the Lord, and you do the right thing when you obey your parents. The first commandment with a promise says, ² "Obey your father and your mother, ³ and you will have a long and happy life."

⁴ Parents, don't be hard on your children. Raise them properly. Teach them and instruct them about the Lord.

Slaves and masters

⁵ Slaves, you must obey your earthly masters. Show them great respect and be as loyal to them as you are to Christ. ⁶ Try to please them at all times, and not just when you think they are watching. You are slaves of Christ, so with your whole heart you must do what God wants you to do. ⁷ Gladly serve your masters, as though they were the Lord himself, and not simply people. ⁸ You know that you will be rewarded for any good things you do, whether you are slaves or free.

⁹ Slave owners, you must treat your slaves with this same respect. Don't threaten them. They have the same Master in heaven that you do, and he doesn't have any favourites.

The fight against evil

¹⁰ Finally, let the mighty strength of the Lord make you strong. ¹¹ Put on all the armour that God gives, so you can defend yourself against the devil's tricks. ¹² We are not fighting against humans. We are fighting against forces and authorities and against rulers of darkness and powers in the spiritual world. ¹³ So put on all the armour that God gives. Then when that evil dayᵇ comes, you will be able to defend yourself. And when the battle is over, you will still be standing firm.

¹⁴ Be ready! Let the truth be like a belt around your waist, and let God's justice protect you like armour. ¹⁵ Your desire to tell the good news about peace should be like shoes on your feet. ¹⁶ Let your faith be like a shield, and you will be able to stop all the flaming arrows of the evil one. ¹⁷ Let God's saving power be like a helmet, and for a sword use God's message that comes from the Spirit.

¹⁸ Never stop praying, especially for others. Always pray by the power of the Spirit. Stay alert and keep praying for God's people. ¹⁹ Pray that I will be given the message to speak and that I may fearlessly explain the mystery about the good news. ²⁰ I was sent to do this work, and that's the reason I am in jail. So pray that I will be brave and will speak as I should.

Final greetings

²¹⁻²² I want you to know how I am getting along and what I am doing. That's why I am sending Tychicus to you. He is a dear friend, as well as a faithful servant of the Lord. He will tell you how I am doing, and he will cheer you up.

²³ I pray that God the Father and the Lord Jesus Christ will give peace, love, and faith to every follower! ²⁴ May God be kind to everyone who keeps on loving our Lord Jesus Christ.

See also: **6.14:** a Isa 11.5; b Isa 59.17. **6.15:** Isa 52.7. **6.17:** Isa 59.17. **6.21:** Acts 20.4; 2 Tim 4.12. **6.21–22:** Col 4.7–8.

Additional notes

›**1.1 live in Ephesus and:** Some manuscripts do not have these words.
›**1.4–5 holy and innocent and loving people. ⁵ God was kind:** Or "holy and innocent people. God was loving ⁵ and kind."
›**1.23 and is filled with Christ who completely fills everything:** Or "which completely fills Christ and fully completes his work."
›**2.16 He also made peace:** Or "The cross also made peace".
›**3.15 receive their life from him:** Or "know who they really are because of him."

See also: **5.31:** Gen 2.24. **6.1:** Col 3.20. **6.2,3:** Exod 20.12; Deut 5.16. **6.4:** Col 3.21. **6.5–8:** Col 3.22–25. **6.9:** a Col 4.1; b Deut 10.17; Col 3.25.

›**4.13 and we will be completely like him:** Or "and he is completely perfect."

›**5.2 us:** Some manuscripts have "you".

›**5.6 says:** Or "does".

›**5.14 Light shows up everything:** Or "Everything that is seen in the light becomes light itself."

›**6.13 that evil day:** Either the present (see 5.16) or "the day of death" or "the day of judgment".

Philippians

Paul's letter to the church in Philippi

The basics

What's the point? We are moving towards heaven – so we have to keep going!

What happens? Paul thanks the Philippian church for their gift and urges them to keep running the race.

What should I remember? 3.13–14 'My friends, I don't feel that I have already arrived. But I forget what is behind, and I struggle for what is ahead. I run towards the goal, so that I can win the prize of being called to heaven. This is the prize that God offers because of what Christ Jesus has done.'

More details

Setting the scene Paul is in prison in Rome. The Philippians, hearing of Paul's imprisonment, have sent him a gift and Paul writes to thank them...

What's it all about? This is a thank you letter. The church at Philippi had had a long association with Paul and had always taken an active part in his work. This is reflected in their support for him while he is in prison. This, perhaps, is why his prayer for them is so full of joy (1.3–11). This church doesn't need correcting or rebuking; Paul encourages them to continue in their faith, despite the persecution they face.

But along the way Paul takes the opportunity to encourage the Philippians and to warn them about pitfalls. He encourages them to keep on running, because the race is not yet won. This race isn't the 100m sprint, though, with each of us competing against everyone else. It's more like a team endurance event or assault course, with all the members of the team responsible for supporting each other whether the running is smooth and flat or strewn with obstacles. There are times when the running is easy, but there are times too when it can be very hard.

And another thing

The Philippian church was always very special to Paul. He founded it on his first missionary journey and it was probably the first church founded on European soil.

Footsteps

Paul's prayer: 1.1–11
Prison life: 1.12–30
True humility: 2.1–18
Run the race: 3.1–21
How to be satisfied: 4.10–23

Greetings and a prayer

CHAPTER 1

¹ *From Paul and Timothy, servants of Christ Jesus.*

To all God's people who belong to Christ Jesus at Philippi and to all your church officials and officers.

² I pray that God our Father and the Lord Jesus Christ will be kind to you and will bless you with peace!

See also: 1.1: Acts 16.12.

Paul's prayer for the church in Philippi

3 Every time I think of you, I thank my God.
4 And whenever I mention you in my prayers, it makes me happy. 5 This is because you have taken part with me in spreading the good news from the first day you heard about it. 6 God is the one who began this good work in you, and I am certain that he won't stop before it is complete on the day that Christ Jesus returns.

7 You have a special place in my heart. So it is only natural for me to feel the way I do. All of you have helped in the work that God has given me, as I defend the good news and tell about it here in jail. 8 God himself knows how much I want to see you. He knows that I care for you in the same way that Christ Jesus does.

9 I pray that your love will keep on growing and that you will fully know and understand 10 how to make the right choices. Then you will still be pure and innocent when Christ returns. And until that day, 11 Jesus Christ will keep you busy doing good deeds that bring glory and praise to God.

What life means to Paul

12 My dear friends, I want you to know that what has happened to me has helped to spread the good news. 13 The Roman guards and all the others know that I am here in jail because I serve Christ. 14 Now most of the Lord's followers have become brave and are fearlessly telling the message.'

15 Some are preaching about Christ because they are jealous and envious of us. Others are preaching because they want to help. 16 They love Christ and know that I am here to defend the good news about him. 17 But the ones who are jealous of us are not sincere. They just want to cause trouble for me while I am in jail. 18 But that doesn't matter. All that matters is that people are telling about Christ, whether they are sincere or not. That is what makes me glad.

I will keep on being glad, 19 because I know that your prayers and the help that comes from the Spirit of Christ Jesus will keep me safe. 20 I honestly expect and hope that I will never do anything to be ashamed of. Whether I live or die, I always want to be as brave as I am now and bring honour to Christ.

See also: 1.13: Acts 28.30.

Viewpoints

How can we make God a priority?

Contributed by Lucy S

'Jesus Christ will keep you busy doing good deeds that bring glory and praise to God.'

Sometimes it feels like people around us are always making demands of us: our teachers are demanding us to produce our homework on time. Parents expect you to keep your room tidy, do work around the house, and to come out with straight As in school. Our friends, girlfriend/boyfriend also expect a certain amount of 'quality time' with you. It's easy to be left feeling completely over-awed by it all!

Then, when we think we've started to gain a bit of control, there's God, and he's also making demands of us. He asks us each day to do 'good things' for him, that means taking some of that valuable 'me time' that we've got and giving it to others in service to God. Yes it's the big S word, the one that fills us all with fear – Sacrifice!

Sometimes when I'm a over-stressed, sacrificing that little time for God is the hardest thing to do, but God gave us all talents and gifts and they're not just for our own enjoyment, they're for everyone else's too!

Yet there is a difference between the demands everyone else makes and the demands God makes of us. We don't have to try to cope all on our own. God actually helps us to give glory to him! So the next time someone asks something of you and you know you should do it but it's going to take a stretch – say yes, because with Jesus empowering you it will be no problem at all, and you'll be giving the glory straight back to him!

More...

Going against the crowd p.1045
Sacrifice p.1045
Forgiving others p.1162
Holy Spirit p.1209

²¹ If I live, it will be for Christ, and if I die, I will gain even more. ²² I don't know what to choose. I could keep on living and doing something useful. ²³ It is a hard choice to make. I want to die and be with Christ, because that would be much better. ²⁴⁻²⁵ But I know that all of you still need me. That's why I am sure I will stay on to help you grow and be happy in your faith. ²⁶ Then, when I visit you again, you will have good reason to take great pride in Christ Jesus because of me.ʼ

²⁷ Above all else, you must live in a way that brings honour to the good news about Christ. Then, whether I visit you or not, I will hear that all of you think alike. I will know that you are working together and that you are struggling side by side to get others to believe the good news.

²⁸ Be brave when you face your enemies. Your courage will show them that they are going to be destroyed, and it will show you that you will be saved. God will make all this happen, ²⁹ and he has blessed you. Not only do you have faith in Christ, but you suffer for him. ³⁰ You saw me suffer, and you still hear about my troubles. Now you must suffer in the same way.

Christ's example of true humility

CHAPTER 2

¹ Christ encourages you, and his love comforts you. God's Spirit unites you, and you are concerned for others. ² Now make me completely happy! Live in harmony by showing love for each other. Be united in what you think, as if you were only one person. ³ Don't be jealous or proud, but be humble and consider others more important than yourselves. ⁴ Care about them as much as you care about yourselves ⁵ and think the same way that Christ Jesus thought:ʼ

⁶ Christ was truly God.
　But he did not try to remainʼ
　　equal with God.
⁷ Instead he gave up everythingʼ
　and became a slave,
　when he became
　　like one of us.

⁸ Christ was humble.
　He obeyed God and even died
　　on a cross.

⁹ Then God gave Christ
　the highest place
　and honoured his name
　　above all others.
¹⁰ So at the name of Jesus
　everyone will bow down,
　those in heaven, on earth,
　　and under the earth.
¹¹ And to the glory
　of God the Father
　everyone will openly agree,
　　"Jesus Christ is Lord!"

Lights in the world

¹² My dear friends, you always obeyed when I was with you. Now that I am away, you should obey even more. So work with fear and trembling to discover what it really means to be saved. ¹³ God is working in you to make you willing and able to obey him.

¹⁴ Do everything without grumbling or arguing. ¹⁵ Then you will be the pure and innocent children of God. You live among people who are crooked and evil, but you must not do anything that they can say is wrong. Try to shine as lights among the people of this world, ¹⁶ as you hold firmly toʼ the message that gives life. Then on the day when Christ returns, I can take pride in you. I can also know that my work and efforts were not useless.

¹⁷ Your faith in the Lord and your service are like a sacrifice offered to him. And my own blood may have to be poured out with the sacrifice.* If this happens, I will be glad and rejoice with you. ¹⁸ In the same way, you should be glad and rejoice with me.

News about Paul's friends

Timothy and Epaphroditus

¹⁹ I want to be encouraged by news about you. So I hope the Lord Jesus will soon let me send Timothy to you. ²⁰ I don't have anyone else who cares about you as much as he does. ²¹ The others think only about what interests them and not about what concerns Christ Jesus. ²² But you know what kind of person Timothy is. He has worked with me like a son in spreading the good news. ²³ I hope to send

---

2.17 my own blood may have to be poured out with the sacrifice: Offerings of water or wine were sometimes poured out when animals were sacrificed on the altar.

See also: 1.30: Acts 16.19–40.　See also: 2.10–11: Isa 45.23 (LXX).　2.15: Deut 32.5.

him to you, as soon as I find out what is going to happen to me. 24 And I feel sure that the Lord will also let me come soon.

25 I think I ought to send my dear friend Epaphroditus back to you. He is a follower and a worker and a soldier of the Lord, just as I am. You sent him to look after me, 26 but now he is eager to see you. He is worried, because you heard he was sick. 27 In fact, he was very sick and almost died. But God was kind to him, and also to me, and he kept me from being burdened down with sorrow.

28 Now I am more eager than ever to send Epaphroditus back again. You will be glad to see him, and I won't have to worry any longer. 29 Be sure to give him a cheerful welcome, just as people who serve the Lord deserve. 30 He almost died working for Christ, and he risked his own life to do for me what you could not.

Being acceptable to God

CHAPTER 3

1 Finally, my dear friends, be glad that you belong to the Lord. It doesn't bother me to write the same things to you that I have written before. In fact, it is for your own good.

2 Watch out for those people who behave like dogs! They are evil and want to do more than just circumcise you. 3 But we are the ones who are truly circumcised, because we worship by the power of God's Spirit⟩ and take pride in Christ Jesus. We don't boast about what we have done, 4 although I could. Others may boast about themselves, but I have more reason to boast than anyone else. 5 I was circumcised when I was eight days old,* and I am from the nation of Israel and the tribe of Benjamin. I am a true Hebrew. As a Pharisee, I strictly obeyed the Law of Moses. 6 And I was so eager that I even made trouble for the church. I did everything the Law demands in order to please God.

7 But Christ has shown me that what I once thought was valuable is worthless. 8 Nothing is as wonderful as knowing Christ Jesus my Lord. I have given up everything else and count it all as rubbish. All I want is Christ 9 and to know that I belong to him. I could not make myself acceptable to God by

obeying the Law of Moses. God accepted me simply because of my faith in Christ. 10 All I want is to know Christ and the power that raised him to life. I want to suffer and die as he did, 11 so that somehow I also may be raised to life.

Running towards the goal

12 I have not yet reached my goal, and I am not perfect. But Christ has taken hold of me. So I keep on running and struggling to take hold of the prize. 13 My friends, I don't feel that I have already arrived. But I forget what is behind, and I struggle for what is ahead. 14 I run towards the goal, so that I can win the prize of being called to heaven. This is the prize that God offers because of what Christ Jesus has done. 15 All of us who are mature should think in this same way. And if any of you think differently, God will make it clear to you. 16 But we must keep going in the direction that we are now headed.

17 My friends, I want you to follow my example and learn from others who closely follow the example we set for you. 18 I often warned you that many people are living as enemies of the cross of Christ. And now with tears in my eyes, I warn you again 19 that they are headed for hell! They worship their stomachs and boast about the disgusting things they do. All they can think about are the things of this world.

20 But we are citizens of heaven and are eagerly waiting for our Saviour to come from there. Our Lord Jesus Christ 21 has power over everything, and he will make these poor bodies of ours like his own glorious body.

CHAPTER 4

1 Dear friends, I love you and long to see you. Please keep on being faithful to the Lord. You are my pride and joy.

Paul encourages the Lord's followers

2 Euodia and Syntyche, you belong to the Lord, so I beg you to stop arguing with each other. 3 And, my true partner,⟩ I ask you to help them. These women have worked together with me and with Clement and with the others in spreading the good news. Their names are now written in the book of life.*

---

*3.5 when I was eight days old: Jewish boys are circumcised eight days after birth.

See also: 3.5: a Rom 11.1; b Acts 23.6; 26.5. 3.6: Acts 8.3; 22.4; 26.9–11.

*4.3 the book of life: A book in which the names of God's people are written.

See also: 3.17: 1 Cor 4.16; 11.1.

⁴ Always be glad because of the Lord! I will say it again: be glad. ⁵ Always be gentle with others. The Lord will soon be here. ⁶ Don't worry about anything, but pray about everything. With thankful hearts offer up your prayers and requests to God. ⁷ Then, because you belong to Christ Jesus, God will bless you with peace that no one can completely understand. And this peace will control the way you think and feel.

⁸ Finally, my friends, keep your minds on whatever is true, pure, right, holy, friendly, and proper. Don't ever stop thinking about what is truly worthwhile and worthy of praise. ⁹ You know the teachings I gave you, and you know what you heard me say and saw me do. So follow my example. And God, who gives peace, will be with you.

Paul thanks the Philippians

¹⁰ The Lord has made me very grateful that at last you have thought about me once again. Actually, you were thinking about me all along, but you didn't have any chance to show it. ¹¹ I am not complaining about having too little. I have learnt to be satisfied with' whatever I have. ¹² I know what it is to be poor or to have plenty, and I have lived under all kinds of conditions. I know what it means to be full or to be hungry, to have too much or too little. ¹³ Christ gives me the strength to face anything.

¹⁴ It was good of you to help me when I was having such a hard time. ¹⁵ My friends at Philippi, you remember what it was like when I started preaching the good news in Macedonia.* After I left there, you were the only church that became my partner by giving blessings and by receiving them in return. ¹⁶ Even when I was in Thessalonica, you helped me more than once. ¹⁷ I am not trying to get something from you, but I want you to receive the blessings that come from giving.

¹⁸ I have been paid back everything, and with interest. I am completely satisfied with the gifts that you asked Epaphroditus to bring me. They are like a sweet-smelling offering or like the right kind of sacrifice that pleases

---

4.15 when I started preaching the good news in **Macedonia:** Paul is talking about his first visit to Philippi. See Acts 16.12–40.

See also: **4.15–16:** 2 Cor 11.9. **4.16:** Acts 17.1.
4.18: Exod 29.18.

Being christian

Staying committed

Philippians 4.11–21
Being Christian isn't easy. It requires self-discipline. It says you can't live in the same way as all those around you. You have to be honest; you have to walk the talk. You have to follow God's rules, rather than make up your own.

That requires commitment. It requires stickability. Several times, Paul compares following Jesus to running a race. It needs determination, hard work and commitment to reach the finishing line. You can't run a race 'part-time'.

And it's a marathon, not a sprint. Being Christian is not like taking up some hobby. It's not like being an angler, or playing football, or taking up dance. It's a life-long, demanding commitment. God doesn't want your spare time: he wants your life.

So being Christian means running the race with all our effort. When the times are tough we keep going. When we want to go one way, and God wants us to go another way; we go his way. We don't give up on it just because the going gets tough.

After all, we're just doing what Jesus did. We're following his examples.

Christ died for us all.

Now *that's* commitment.

Being Christian: Staying committed

• Don't be a part-time Christian. Stay close to God in all areas of your life.

• Share with others. Pray with them. Keep on track.

• Make someone your 'running partner'. Meet regularly with them to pray and read the Bible.

• Write down the rules you're going to follow in your life. What kind of behaviour is God demanding of you?

God. [19] I pray that God will take care of all your needs with the wonderful blessings that come from Christ Jesus! [20] May God our Father be praised for ever and ever. Amen.

Final greetings

[21] Give my greetings to all who are God's people because of Christ Jesus.

The Lord's followers here with me send you their greetings.

[22] All God's people send their greetings, especially those in the service of the Emperor.

[23] I pray that our Lord Jesus Christ will be kind to you and will bless your life!

Additional notes

›**1.1 church officials and officers:** Or "bishops and deacons".

›**1.14 the message:** Some manuscripts have "the Lord's message", and others have "God's message".

›**1.26 take great pride in Christ Jesus because of me:** Or "take great pride in me because of Christ Jesus."

›**2.5 think the same way that Christ Jesus thought:** Or "think the way you should because you belong to Christ Jesus".

›**2.6 remain:** Or "become".

›**2.7 he gave up everything:** Greek, "He emptied himself".

›**2.16 hold firmly to:** Or "offer them".

›**3.3 by the power of God's Spirit:** Some manuscripts have "sincerely".

›**4.3 partner:** Or "Syzygus", a person's name.

›**4.11 be satisfied with:** Or "get by on".

Colossians

Paul's letter to the church in Colossae

The basics

What's the point? We should fix our eyes on Jesus: he is all that matters.

What happens? Paul introduces himself to the church at Colossae. He tells them to forget all their false ideas and practices and focus on Jesus.

What should I remember? 3.10 'Each of you is now a new person. You are becoming more and more like your Creator, and you will understand him better.'

More details

Setting the scene Paul was in jail when he met a man called Epaphras. Epaphras told Paul about the faith of the Colossians. But he also told Paul that they were influenced by some very strange ideas...

What's it all about? The Colossians were confused. We can't be sure exactly what they believed, but it seems to have been some kind of mutant form of Judaism, combining Jewish dietary laws mixed with mystical pagan festivals.

The Colossians had a 'pick n' mix' religion, and they tried to simply mingle what they considered the best ideas from Christianity with other ideas they liked in other philosophies and religions, which were all viewed as equally true.

So Paul writes to put things right. He wants the Colossians to give up all their talk of angels and new moon festivals and all that, and to focus on directing their worship towards Christ.

Footsteps

Hello Colossae: 1.1–8
All about Jesus: 1.9–23
Suffering for the truth: 1.24—2.5
Don't let them tell you what to do: 2.6–19
New life in Christ: 2.20—3.17

Greetings

CHAPTER 1

¹ From Paul, chosen by God to be an apostle of Christ Jesus, and from Timothy, who is also a follower.
² *To God's people who live in Colossae and are faithful followers of Christ.*
I pray that God our Father will be kind to you and will bless you with peace!

A prayer of thanks

³ Each time we pray for you, we thank God, the Father of our Lord Jesus Christ. ⁴ We have heard of your faith in Christ and of your love for all God's people, ⁵ because what you hope for is kept safe for you in heaven. You first heard about this hope when you believed the true message, which is the good news.

⁶ The good news is spreading all over the world with great success. It has spread in that same way among you, ever since the first day

1329

you learnt the truth about God's wonderful kindness [7] from our good friend Epaphras. He works together with us for Christ and is a faithful worker for you.' [8] He is also the one who told us about the love that God's Spirit has given you.

The person and work of Christ

[9] We have not stopped praying for you since the first day we heard about you. In fact, we always pray that God will show you everything he wants you to do and that you may have all the wisdom and understanding that his Spirit gives. [10] Then you will live a life that honours the Lord, and you will always please him by doing good deeds. You will come to know God even better. [11] His glorious power will make you patient and strong enough to endure anything, and you will be truly happy.

[12] I pray that you will be grateful to God for letting you' have part in what he has promised his people in the kingdom of light. [13] God rescued us from the dark power of Satan and brought us into the kingdom of his dear Son, [14] who forgives our sins and sets us free.

[15] Christ is exactly like God,
     who cannot be seen.
He is the firstborn Son,
     superior to all creation.
[16] Everything was created by him,
     everything in heaven
     and on earth,
everything seen and unseen,
     including all forces
     and powers,
     and all rulers
     and authorities.
All things were created
     by God's Son,
and everything was made
     for him.

[17] God's Son was before all else,
     and by him everything
     is held together.
[18] He is the head of his body,
     which is the church.
He is the very beginning,
     the first to be raised
     from death,
     so that he would be
     above all others.

Viewpoints

We know it in our minds, but do we believe it in our hearts?

Contributed by Fiona H

'And the mystery is that Christ lives in you, and he is your hope of sharing in God's glory.'

We know it in our minds, but do we believe it in our hearts? Do we really believe that Christ lives in us, and as a result we have assurance that we will share in his glory? Believing will provoke a response. If we truly believe it, that hope will lead us to endure hardship, attack and mockery knowing that we will one day share in Christ's glory.

I certainly don't feel that I deserve to share Christ's glory. I don't have life sorted, and I most certainly am not perfect. Why then do I get to share in Christ's glory? I am not sure I know the answer to that other than God is amazing in his kindness!

Christ lives in you. He lives in me! Jesus Christ is real. Try that one on your friends at school next time they ask you how you know God's real. 'Because Jesus is right here in the room with us even now – he lives in me.' It would confuse them, wouldn't it? On a serious note however, how often do we stop to think about what it means to have Jesus Christ living in us? I think that sometimes it's easy, at least for me, to subconsciously almost treat Jesus as a fairy tale that I 'believe in strongly', or somehow forget just how real and alive he is. He's living in me! When I'm in a room, Jesus is in that room!

Persevere! The day when we share in his glory will come. And meanwhile, Jesus is living in you.

More...

Sharing your faith p.1082
School p.64
Holy Spirit p.1209
Grace p.1316

See also: 1.7: Col 4.12; Phlm 23.   1.14: Eph 1.7.
1.18: Eph 1.22–23.

19 God himself was pleased
  to live fully in his Son.
20 And God was pleased
  for him to make peace
  by sacrificing his blood
    on the cross,
  so that all beings in heaven
    and on earth
  would be brought back to God.

21 You used to be far from God. Your thoughts made you his enemies, and you did evil things. 22 But his Son became a human and died. So God made peace with you, and now he lets you stand in his presence as people who are holy and faultless and innocent. 23 But you must stay deeply rooted and firm in your faith. You must not give up the hope you received when you heard the good news. It was preached to everyone on earth, and I myself have become a servant of this message.

Paul's service to the church

24 I am glad that I can suffer for you. I am pleased also that in my own body I can continue' the suffering of Christ for his body, the church. 25 God's plan was to make me a servant of his church and to send me to preach his complete message to you. 26 For many ages this message was kept secret from everyone, but now it has been explained to God's people. 27 God did this because he wanted you Gentiles to understand his wonderful and glorious mystery. And the mystery is that Christ lives in you, and he is your hope of sharing in God's glory.

28 We announce the message about Christ, and we use all our wisdom to warn and teach everyone, so that all Christ's followers will grow and become mature. 29 That's why I work so hard and use the mighty power he gives me.

CHAPTER 2

1 I want you to know what a struggle I am going through for you, for God's people at Laodicea, and for all those followers who have never met me. 2 I do it to encourage them. Then as their hearts are joined together in love, they will be wonderfully blessed with complete understanding. And they will truly know Christ. Not only is he the key to God's mystery, 3 but all wisdom and knowledge are hidden away in him.

4 I tell you these things to keep you from being fooled by fancy talk. 5 Even though I am not with you, I keep thinking about you. I am glad to know that you are living as you should and that your faith in Christ is strong.

Christ brings real life

6 You have accepted Christ Jesus as your Lord. Now keep on following him. 7 Plant your roots in Christ and let him be the foundation for your life. Be strong in your faith, just as you were taught. And be grateful.

8 Don't let anyone fool you by using senseless arguments. These arguments may sound wise, but they are only human teachings. They come from the powers of this world* and not from Christ.

9 God lives fully in Christ. 10 And you are fully grown because you belong to Christ, who is over every power and authority. 11 Christ has also taken away your selfish desires, just as circumcision removes flesh from the body. 12 And when you were baptized, it was the same as being buried with Christ. Then you were raised to life because you had faith in the power of God, who raised Christ from death. 13 You were dead, because you were sinful and were not God's people. But God let Christ make you' alive, when he forgave all our sins.

14 God wiped out the charges that were against us for disobeying the Law of Moses. He took them away and nailed them to the cross. 15 There Christ defeated all powers and forces. He let the whole world see them being led away as prisoners when he celebrated his victory.

16 Don't let anyone tell you what you must eat or drink. Don't let them say that you must celebrate the New Moon festival, the Sabbath, or any other festival. 17 These things are only a shadow of what is to come. But Christ is real! 18 Don't be cheated by people who make a show of acting humble and who worship angels.' They boast about seeing visions. But it is all nonsense, because their minds are filled with selfish desires. 19 They are no longer part of Christ, who is the head of the whole body. Christ gives the body its strength, and he uses its joints and muscles to hold it together, as it grows by the power of God.

*2.8 **powers of this world:** Spirits and unseen forces were thought to control human lives and were believed to be connected with the movements of the stars.

See also: **2.12:** Rom 6.4. **2.13:** Eph 2.1–5. **2.14:** Eph 2.15. **2.16:** Rom 14.1–6. **2.19:** Eph 4.16.

See also: **1.20:** Eph 2.16.

New life with Christ

²⁰ You died with Christ. Now the forces of the universe* don't have any power over you. Why do you live as if you had to obey such rules as, ²¹ "Don't handle this. Don't taste that. Don't touch this."? ²² After these things are used, they are no longer good for anything. So why be bothered with the rules that humans have made up? ²³ Obeying these rules may seem to be the clever thing to do. They appear to make you love God more and to be very humble and to have control over your body. But they don't really have any power over our desires.

CHAPTER 3

¹ You have been raised to life with Christ. Now set your heart on what is in heaven, where Christ rules at God's right side.* ² Think about what is up there, not about what is here on earth. ³ You died, which means that your life is hidden with Christ, who sits beside God. ⁴ Christ gives meaning to your‸ life, and when he appears, you will also appear with him in glory.

⁵ Don't be controlled by your body. Kill every desire for the wrong kind of sex. Don't be immoral or indecent or have evil thoughts. Don't be greedy, which is the same as worshipping idols. ⁶ God is angry with people who disobey him by doing‸ these things. ⁷ And that is exactly what you did, when you lived among people who behaved in this way. ⁸ But now you must stop doing such things. You must stop being angry, hateful, and evil. You must no longer say insulting or cruel things about others. ⁹ And stop lying to each other. You have given up your old way of life with its habits.

¹⁰ Each of you is now a new person. You are becoming more and more like your Creator, and you will understand him better. ¹¹ It doesn't matter if you are a Greek or a Jew, or if you are circumcised or not. You may even be a barbarian or a Scythian,* and you may be a slave or a free person. Yet Christ is all that matters, and he lives in all of us.

---

*2.20 forces of the universe: See the note at 2.8.
*3.1 right side: The place of power and honour.
*3.11 a barbarian or a Scythian: Barbarians were people who could not speak Greek and would be in the lower class of society. Scythians were people who were known for their cruelty.

See also: 3.1: Psa 110.1.   3.9: Eph 4.22.   3.10: a Eph 4.24; b Gen 1.26.

Helpline

Help! I hate myself!

'I hate the way I look! I hate the sound of my voice! I'm not smart enough! No-one likes me!'

It's a sad fact that millions of people in this world think they're just not good enough.

If you feel like that, here's a message to you from God: you're special.

God took an interest in you before you were born. He made you unique. No-one is quite like you; no-one else in the world has your mix of abilities and attributes.

But look at Colossians 3.12: 'God loves you and has chosen you as his own special people...' it says. God has chosen you. You're special. And through Christ's death you have been made a member of his family. God thinks you're so special, he let his son die for you.

God doesn't care what you look like or how smart you are. He cares about how faithful you are. He cares about the relationship you have with him.

Three things

Special

Remember how special you are. You matter to God. He thinks you're great.

Talk

Sometimes we're a lot harder on ourselves than others are; we make more of our failings and inadequacies than others do. So, if you have these feelings, please, talk to someone you trust. They'll help you to see things more clearly.

Spirit

Buying new clothes, going on a diet, getting a new job; none of these can really change the way you feel about yourself. Only God's Holy Spirit can do that. Don't spend your money trying to feel better; spend your time getting more of God.

More...

Materialism p.114
Help! I can't make friends p.714

Real life

Worship in the real world

Contributed by Graham Kendrick

On the rare occasions I wash my car, a sponge is a great way to get clean soapy water onto dirty paintwork. Brains look a bit like sponges, and operate like them too: what you put into them is what you get out of them – something to remember with a magazine or TV remote control in your hand.

The lesson is simple and obvious; if we immerse ourselves in the message of Christ, allowing it to soak in properly, then when daily pressures squeeze us, Christ-like attitudes will flow out from us. There will be wisdom to speak (and for most of us this will be in conversation rather than from platforms or pulpits), and there will be fuel for thankfulness, to overflow in the 'psalms, hymns and spiritual songs' we sing.

Songs can be one of the best means to soak up the message of Christ, though some Christian songs don't have as clear or accurate a message as they ought to. What we sing, we remember, so maybe the most influential theologians today are the songwriters – the lyrics all combine to form our mental picture of what the message is and what it means to live it. This is a sobering thought for songwriters and for the planners of worship and choosers of songs. Songs are like house guests, and the longer they stay the more they influence your ethos, for better or worse. So, returning to that sponge analogy, let's check the contents of the bucket we choose to soak our thoughts in!

Think

What not-so-helpful things do you spend time reading and thinking about, and doing? And what helpful things?

Act

Try and edit out some of the things that might be unhelpful, and edit in some better ones.

Check

1 Colossians 3.16; 1 Thessalonians 5.16–18; Ephesians 5.1–21

12 God loves you and has chosen you as his own special people. So be gentle, kind, humble, meek, and patient. 13 Put up with each other, and forgive anyone who does you wrong, just as Christ has forgiven you. 14 Love is more important than anything else. It is what ties everything completely together.

15 Each one of you is part of the body of Christ, and you were chosen to live together in peace. So let the peace that comes from Christ control your thoughts. And be grateful. 16 Let the message about Christ completely fill your lives, while you use all your wisdom to teach and instruct each other. With thankful hearts, sing psalms, hymns, and spiritual songs to God. 17 Whatever you say or do should be done in the name of the Lord Jesus, as you give thanks to God the Father because of him.

Some rules for Christian living

18 A wife must put her husband first. This is her duty as a follower of the Lord.

19 A husband must love his wife and not abuse her.

20 Children must always obey their parents. This pleases the Lord.

21 Parents, don't be hard on your children. If you are, they might give up.

22 Slaves, you must always obey your earthly masters. Try to please them at all times, and not just when you think they are watching. Honour the Lord and serve your masters with your whole heart. 23 Do your work willingly, as though you were serving the Lord himself, and not just your earthly master. 24 In fact, the Lord Christ is the one you are really serving, and you know that he will reward you. 25 But Christ has no favourites! He will punish evil people, just as they deserve.

CHAPTER 4

1 Slave owners, be fair and honest with your slaves. Don't forget that you have a Master in heaven.

2 Never give up praying. And when you pray, keep alert and be thankful. 3 Be sure to pray that God will make a way for us to spread his message and explain the mystery

---

See also: 3.12–13: Eph 4.2. **3.13:** Eph 4.32. **3.16–17:** Eph 5.19,20. **3.18:** Eph 5.22; 1 Pet 3.1. **3.19:** Eph 5.25; 1 Pet 3.7. **3.20:** Eph 6.1. **3.21:** Eph 6.4. **3.22–25:** Eph 6.5–8. **3.25:** Deut 10.17; Eph 6.9. **4.1:** Eph 6.9.

Being christian

Praying to God

Colossians 4.1–4

Christians are people of prayer. To be Christian is to pray.

We often think of prayer as 'asking God for things'. But that's just one aspect of it. In our prayers sometimes we ask God for things; sometimes we just worship him; sometimes we tell him our concerns; sometimes we listen to him speak to us. Sometimes we think about passages we read in the Bible.

Prayer is a whole lot more than going to God with a shopping list. It's about spending time with him.

You don't have to put on any 'airs and graces'. You don't have to use posh language or religious terms. Just relax – this is your Dad you're talking to.

So spend some time with God. He's looking forward to hearing from you.

Being Christian: Prayer

• Look around you for things to pray about
• Keep a 'prayer diary' listing down things you're praying for, things you have prayed about and answers you've received
• Use all opportunities to pray. Standing at a bus stop, waiting for a lift, walking to the shops, clearing up your room; you can pray at all times.
• Use the Bible. Reading books like the Psalms is great – you'll find lots of thoughts about God that you'll be able to echo
• Use your imagination. Try to picture in your mind what you're praying for. Imagine what the answers to your prayers would look like.
• Use written prayers. If it helps, read a prayer from a prayer book or similar.

about Christ, even though I am in jail for doing this. ⁴ Please pray that I will make the message as clear as possible.

⁵ When you are with unbelievers, always make good use of the time. ⁶ Be pleasant and hold their interest when you speak the message. Choose your words carefully and be ready to give answers to anyone who asks questions.

Final greetings

⁷ Tychicus is the dear friend, who faithfully works and serves the Lord with us, and he will give you the news about me. ⁸ I am sending him to cheer you up by telling you how we are getting along. ⁹ Onesimus, that dear and faithful follower from your own group, is coming with him. The two of them will tell you everything that has happened here.

¹⁰ Aristarchus is in jail with me. He sends greetings to you, and so does Mark, the cousin of Barnabas. You have already been told to welcome Mark, if he visits you. ¹¹ Jesus, who is known as Justus, sends his greetings. These three men are the only Jewish followers who have worked with me for the kingdom of God. They have given me much comfort.

¹² Your own Epaphras, who serves Christ Jesus, sends his greetings. He always prays hard that you may fully know what the Lord wants you to do and that you may do it completely. ¹³ I have seen how much trouble he has gone through for you and for the followers in Laodicea and Hierapolis.

¹⁴ Our dear doctor Luke sends you his greetings, and so does Demas.

¹⁵ Give my greetings to the followers at Laodicea, especially to Nympha and the church that meets in her home.

¹⁶ After this letter has been read to your people, be sure to have it read in the church at Laodicea. And you should read the letter that I have sent to them.*

¹⁷ Remind Archippus to do the work that the Lord has given him to do.

¹⁸ I am signing this letter myself: PAUL. Don't forget that I am in jail.
I pray that God will be kind to you.

---

*4.16 the letter that I have sent to them: This is the only mention of the letter to the church at Laodicea.

See also: 4.5: Eph 5.16.   4.7: Acts 20.4; 2 Tim 4.12. 4.7–8: Eph 6.2–,22.   4.9: Phlm 10–12.   4.10: a Acts 19.29; 27.2; Phlm 24; b Acts 12.12,25; 13.13; 15.37–39. 4.12: Col 1.7; Phlm 23.   4.14: a 2 Tim 4.11; Phlm 24;

Additional notes

›**1.7 you:** Some manuscripts have "us".

›**1.12 you:** See the note at 1.7.

›**1.24 continue:** Or "complete".

›**2.13 you:** See the note at 1.7.

›**2.18 worship angels:** Or "worship with angels (in visions of heaven)."

›**3.4 your:** Some manuscripts have "our".

›**3.6 people who disobey him by doing:** Some manuscripts do not have these words.

1 Thessalonians

Paul's first letter to the church in Thessalonica

The basics

What's the point? Christ is going to return. So live as though you were expecting it.

What happens? Paul writes to encourage new converts to Christianity and explain a few key issues – especially about the future.

What should I remember? 5.10–11 'Christ died for us, so that we could live with him, whether we are alive or dead when he comes. That's why you must encourage and help each other, just as you are already doing.'

More details

Setting the scene Paul only stayed in Thessalonica for a short while on his first visit. He had to leave because of the fierce opposition. So he sent Timothy back to find out how the young church was doing. When Timothy returned with good news, Paul sat down to write...

What's it all about? Because Paul had had to leave in a hurry (Acts 17.5–10), the church in Thessalonica had been left without much support. So Paul sends them a letter, which deals with some issues which had arisen and repeats some of his teaching. Paul is writing to address two main issues: when the Lord will return and what to do while you're waiting.

The letter is full of Paul's delight in the church. He's like a father watching his child take those first, faltering steps. He's full of joy at their efforts, while still concerned that they don't fall over.

Footsteps

The Thessalonians' faith: 1.1–10
Paul's work: 2.1–20
The good life: 4.1–12
The Lord's return: 4.13—5.11
Final instructions 5.12–28

Greetings

CHAPTER 1

¹ *From Paul, Silas,* and Timothy.
To the church in Thessalonica, the people of God the Father and of the Lord Jesus Christ.
I pray that God will be kind to you and will bless you with peace!
² We thank God for you and always mention you in our prayers. Each time we pray, ³ we tell God our Father about your faith and loving work and about your firm hope in our Lord Jesus Christ.

The Thessalonians' faith and example

⁴ My dear friends, God loves you, and we know he has chosen you to be his people.
⁵ When we told you the good news, it was with the power and assurance that come

---

See also: 1.1: Acts 17.1.

from the Holy Spirit, and not simply with words. You knew what kind of people we were and how we helped you. [6] So, when you accepted the message, you followed our example and the example of the Lord. You suffered, but the Holy Spirit made you glad.

[7] You became an example for all the Lord's followers in Macedonia and Achaia. [8] And because of you, the Lord's message has spread everywhere in those regions. Now the news of your faith in God is known all over the world, and we don't have to say a thing about it. [9] Everyone is talking about how you welcomed us and how you turned away from idols to serve the true and living God. [10] They also tell how you are waiting for his Son Jesus to come from heaven. God raised him from death, and on the day of judgment Jesus will save us from God's anger.

CHAPTER 2

Paul's work in Thessalonica

[1] My friends, you know that our time with you wasn't wasted. [2] As you remember, we had been ill-treated and insulted at Philippi. But God gave us the courage to tell you the good news about him, even though many people caused us trouble. [3] We didn't have any hidden motives when we won you over, and we didn't try to fool or trick anyone. [4] God was pleased to trust us with his message. We didn't speak to please people, but to please God who knows our motives.

[5] You also know that we didn't try to flatter anyone. God himself knows that what we did wasn't a cover-up for greed. [6] We were not trying to get you or anyone else to praise us. [7] But as apostles, we could have demanded help from you. After all, Christ is the one who sent us. We chose to be like children or like a mother' nursing her baby. [8] We cared so much for you, and you became so dear to us, that we were willing to give our lives for you when we gave you God's message.

[9] My dear friends, you haven't forgotten our hard work and hardships. You remember how night and day we struggled to make a living, so that we could tell you God's message without being a burden to anyone. [10] Both you and God are witnesses that we were pure and honest and innocent in our dealings with you followers of the Lord. [11] You also know we did everything for you that parents would do for their own children.

See also: 1.6: Acts 17.5–9. **2.2: a** Acts 16.19–24; **b** Acts 17.1–9.

Viewpoints

You're living in a way that pleases God – but do your motives please him too?

Contributed by Rachel H

'God was pleased to trust us with his message. We didn't speak to please people, but to please God who knows our motives.'

Approved by God. Entrusted with life or death news. Messenger of the Most High. How many of us face our world with the confidence this implies?

Yet this is true: God – the almighty, unlimited One – has approved us to be entrusted with the most crucial message this world will ever hear. He could have proclaimed it through mighty angels or flashy miracles, but he chose me – weak, young, limited, so often wrong, so very fallible – me – and you – to spread his all-important words. WOW! What an honour. What a joy. And what an overwhelming responsibility! Yet I know that he will equip us with everything we need, if we simply obey Him. So what holds us back? Mostly just 4 little words: 'What will everyone think?' I love this verse's response: 'SO WHAT?' it screams, 'Big deal! Your purpose is to please God, not people.'

Our purpose, our vision, our entire reason for being is to please God. When I discard this purpose I find myself trapped, hurt, frustrated. We can never please everyone – I've tried and I felt like a pathetically superficial failure. But we can please God through the motives of our hearts, and there is freedom in embracing our purpose. You become a success – he's bursting with passionate love for you, just as you are right now!

This incredible freedom from others' ties releases us live life to the full and to reach out in confidence, spreading the freeing Good News, approved by God.

More...
Sharing your faith p.1082
Sharing with your friends p.1198
Going against the crowd p.1045

12 We begged, encouraged, and urged each of you to live in a way that would honour God. He is the one who chose you to share in his own kingdom and glory.

13 We always thank God that you believed the message we preached. It came from him, and it isn't something made up by humans. You accepted it as God's message, and now he is working in you. 14 My friends, you did just like God's churches in Judea and like the other followers of Christ Jesus there. And so, you were ill-treated by your own people, in the same way they were ill-treated by their people.

15 Those Jews killed the Lord Jesus and the prophets, and they even chased us away. God doesn't like what they do and neither does anyone else. 16 They keep us from speaking his message to the Gentiles and from leading them to be saved. The Jews have always gone too far with their sins. Now God has finally become angry and will punish them.

Paul wants to visit the church again

17 My friends, we were kept from coming to you for a while, but we never stopped thinking about you. We were eager to see you and tried our best to visit you in person. 18 We really wanted to come. I myself tried several times, but Satan always stopped us. 19 After all, when the Lord Jesus appears, who else but you will give us hope and joy and be like a glorious crown for us? 20 You alone are our glory and joy!

CHAPTER 3

1 Finally, we couldn't stand it any longer. We decided to stay in Athens by ourselves 2 and send our friend Timothy to you. He works with us as God's servant and preaches the good news about Christ. We wanted him to make you strong in your faith and to encourage you. 3 We didn't want any of you to be discouraged by all these troubles. You knew we would have to suffer, 4 because when we were with you, we told you this would happen. And we did suffer, as you well know. 5 At last, when I could not wait any longer, I sent Timothy to find out about your faith. I hoped that Satan had not tempted you and made all our work useless.

6 Timothy has come back from his visit to you and has told us about your faith and love. He also said that you always have happy memories of us and that you want to see us as much as we want to see you.

7 My friends, even though we have a lot of trouble and suffering, your faith makes us feel better about you. 8 Your strong faith in the Lord is like a breath of new life. 9 How can we possibly thank God enough for all the happiness you have brought us? 10 Day and night we sincerely pray that we will see you again and help you to have an even stronger faith.

11 We pray that God our Father and our Lord Jesus will let us visit you. 12 May the Lord make your love for each other and for everyone else grow by leaps and bounds. That's how our love for you has grown. 13 And when our Lord comes with all his people, I pray that he will make your hearts pure and innocent in the sight of God the Father.

A life that pleases God

CHAPTER 4

1 Finally, my dear friends, since you belong to the Lord Jesus, we beg and urge you to live as we taught you. Then you will please God. You are already living that way, but try even harder. 2 Remember the instructions we gave you as followers of the Lord Jesus. 3 God wants you to be holy, so don't be immoral in matters of sex. 4 Respect and honour your wife.' 5 Don't be a slave of your desires or live like people who don't know God. 6 You must not cheat any of the Lord's followers in matters of sex.' Remember, we warned you that he punishes everyone who does such things. 7 God didn't choose you to be filthy, but to be pure. 8 So if you don't obey these rules, you are not really disobeying us. You are disobeying God, who gives you his Holy Spirit.

9 We don't have to write to you about the need to love each other. God has taught you to do this, 10 and you already have shown your love for all his people in Macedonia. But, my dear friends, we ask you to do even more. 11 Try your best to live quietly, to mind your own business, and to work hard, just as we taught you to do. 12 Then you will be respected by people who are not followers of the Lord, and you won't have to depend on anyone.

See also: **2.14:** Acts 17.5. **2.15:** Acts 9.23,29; 13.45,50; 14.2,5,19; 17.5,13; 18.12. **3.1:** Acts 17.15. **3.6:** Acts 18.5.

1338

Help! I can't stop masturbating

'I feel so ashamed. I feel like it's a dirty secret. And I feel like I'm the only one who has this problem.'

Sex is a part of life. And for many people, the urge to masturbate is difficult to resist.

And it is an issue on which many Christians disagree. Some believe that the act is fundamentally wrong, and everyone should go to bed wearing boxing gloves. Others think masturbation is part of life and that it can provide a release.

Whatever you decide about this, don't let it get between you and God. Ask him for help. It isn't easy, but it really helps to share your difficulties with a trusted friend. Talk to them, talk to your youth leader.

Three things

Control

The more you do it, the more you want to do it, the more obsessed you become with it. So control it; don't let it control you. 'Don't be a slave of your desires, like people who don't know God' Paul writes (1 Thessalonians 4.5).

Reality

The fantasies can easily take over. You can end up spending a lot of time thinking about things that aren't very healthy for us to think about. But your fantasy life isn't real and shouldn't be allowed to get between you and the reality of your faith.

Secret

Nobody talks about it. It's embarrassing. But the result is that masturbation becomes a guilty secret between us and God. So it damages our ability to live for Jesus, because we think we're guilty. Try to talk about it with someone you trust. They'll understand.

More...

Sex p.727
Help! I feel like I've failed p.837
Help! I'm struggling with lust p.954
Internet p.1269
Pornography p.952

What to expect when the Lord returns

13 My friends, we want you to understand how it will be for those followers who have already died. Then you won't grieve over them and be like people who don't have any hope. 14 We believe that Jesus died and was raised to life. We also believe that when God brings Jesus back again, he will bring with him all who had faith in Jesus before they died. 15 Our Lord Jesus told us that when he comes, we won't go up to meet him ahead of his followers who have already died.

16 With a loud command and with the shout of the chief angel and a blast of God's trumpet, the Lord will return from heaven. Then those who had faith in Christ before they died will be raised to life. 17 Next, all of us who are still alive will be taken up into the clouds together with them to meet the Lord in the sky. From that time on we will all be with the Lord for ever. 18 Encourage each other with these words.

CHAPTER 5

1 I don't need to write to you about the time or date when all this will happen. 2 You know that the Lord's return▸ will be as a thief coming at night. 3 People will think they are safe and secure. But destruction will suddenly strike them like the pains of a woman about to give birth. And they won't escape.

4 My dear friends, you don't live in darkness, and so that day won't surprise you like a thief. 5 You belong to the light and live in the day. We don't live in the night or belong to the dark. 6 Others may sleep, but we should stay awake and be alert. 7 People sleep during the night, and some even get drunk. 8 But we belong to the day. So we must stay sober and let our faith and love be like a suit of armour. Our firm hope that we will be saved is our helmet.

9 God doesn't intend to punish us, but wants us to be saved by our Lord Jesus Christ. 10 Christ died for us, so that we could live with him, whether we are alive or dead when he comes. 11 That's why you must encourage and help each other, just as you are already doing.

See also: **4.15–17:** 1 Cor 15.51–52. **5.2:** Matt 24.43; Luke 12.39; 2 Pet 3.10. **5.8:** Isa 59.17; Eph 6.13–17.

Final instructions and greetings

[12] My friends, we ask you to be thoughtful of your leaders who work hard and tell you how to live for the Lord. [13] Show them great respect and love because of their work. Try to get along with each other. [14] My friends, we beg you to warn anyone who isn't living right. Encourage anyone who feels left out, help all who are weak, and be patient with everyone. [15] Don't be hateful to people, just because they are hateful to you. Rather, be good to each other and to everyone else.

[16] Always be joyful [17] and never stop praying. [18] Whatever happens, keep thanking God because of Jesus Christ. This is what God wants you to do.

[19] Don't turn away God's Spirit [20] or ignore prophecies. [21] Put everything to the test. Accept what is good [22] and don't have anything to do with evil.

[23] I pray that God, who gives peace, will make you completely holy. And may your spirit, soul, and body be kept healthy and faultless until our Lord Jesus Christ returns. [24] The one who chose you can be trusted, and he will do this.

[25] Friends, please pray for us.

[26] Give the Lord's followers a warm greeting.

[27] In the name of the Lord I beg you to read this letter to all his followers.

[28] I pray that our Lord Jesus Christ will be kind to you!

Additional notes

1.1 Silas: The Greek text has "Silvanus", which is another form of the name Silas.
2.7 like children or like a mother: Some manuscripts have "as gentle as a mother".
4.4 your wife: Or "your body".
4.6 in matters of sex: Or "in business".
5.2 the Lord's return: The Greek text has "the day of the Lord".

2 Thessalonians

Paul's second letter to the church
in Thessalonica

The basics

What's the point?   The Lord will return – and
justice will be done.

What happens?   Paul writes to encourage the
Thessalonian church to keep going.

What should I remember?   2.16 'God our
Father loves us. He is kind and he has given us
eternal comfort and a wonderful hope. We
pray that our Lord Jesus Christ and God our
Father will encourage you and help you always
to do and say the right thing.'

More details

Setting the scene   Someone in Thessalonica
claims to have a letter from Paul saying that
the Lord has already returned. So Paul writes to
them again...

What's it all about?   Someone is using Paul's
name to back up their own ideas. So Paul
writes again to the Thessalonians to go into
more detail about the second coming. He
warns them against laziness, and tells them to
guard against any followers who refuse to
obey what he's written.

He also assures them that the trials they are
going through are not punishments but tests
of their faith.

Footsteps

The Lord will bring justice: 1.1–12
He hasn't returned yet: 2.1–12
Be faithful and keep praying: 2.13—3.18

Greetings

CHAPTER 1

¹ *From Paul, Silas,* and Timothy.
   *To the church in Thessalonica, the people of
God our Father and of the Lord Jesus Christ.*

² I pray that God our Father and the Lord
Jesus Christ will be kind to you and will bless
you with peace!

The Lord's return will bring justice

³ My dear friends, we always have good
reason to thank God for you, because your
faith in God and your love for each other
keep growing all the time. ⁴ That's why we
boast about you to all God's churches. We
tell them how patient you are and how you
keep on having faith, even though you are
going through a lot of trouble and suffering.

⁵ All this shows that God judges fairly and
that he is making you fit to share in his
kingdom for which you are suffering. ⁶ It is
only right for God to punish everyone who is
causing you trouble, ⁷ but he will give you
relief from your troubles. He will do the same
for us, when the Lord Jesus comes from
heaven with his powerful angels ⁸ and with a
flaming fire.

   Our Lord Jesus will punish anyone who
doesn't know God and won't obey his
message. ⁹ Their punishment will be eternal
destruction, and they will be kept far from the
presence of our Lord and his glorious strength.

See also: 1.1: Acts 17.1.   **1.9:** Isa 2.10.

¹⁰ This will happen on that day when the Lord returns to be praised and honoured by all who have faith in him and belong to him. This includes you, because you believed what we said.

¹¹ God chose you, and we keep praying that God will make you worthy of being his people. We pray for God's power to help you do all the good things that you hope to do and that your faith makes you want to do. ¹² Then, because God and our Lord Jesus Christ are so kind, you will bring honour to the name of our Lord Jesus, and he will bring honour to you.

The Lord has not returned yet

CHAPTER 2

The Lord's return

¹ When our Lord Jesus returns, we will be gathered up to meet him. So I ask you, my friends, ² not to be easily upset or disturbed by people who claim that the Lord' has already come. They may say that they heard this directly from the Holy Spirit, or from someone else, or even that they read it in one of our letters. ³ But don't be fooled! People will rebel against God. Then before the Lord returns, the wicked' one who is doomed to be destroyed will appear. ⁴ He will boast and oppose everything that is holy or sacred. He will even sit in God's temple and claim to be God. ⁵ Don't you remember that I told you this while I was still with you?

⁶ You already know what is holding this wicked one back until it is time for him to come. ⁷ His mysterious power is already at work, but someone is holding him back. And the wicked one won't appear until that someone is out of the way. ⁸ Then he will appear, but the Lord Jesus will kill him simply by breathing on him. He will be completely destroyed by the Lord's glorious return.

⁹ When the wicked one appears, Satan will pretend to perform all kinds of miracles, wonders, and signs. ¹⁰ Lost people will be fooled by his evil deeds. They could be saved, but they will refuse to love the truth and accept it. ¹¹ So God will make sure that they are fooled into believing a lie. ¹² All of them will be punished, because they would rather do evil than believe the truth.

Viewpoints

Is God calling you to be a rebel?

Contributed by Helen C

'But don't be fooled! People will rebel against God. Then before the Lord returns, the wicked one who is doomed to be destroyed will appear.'

It's so amazing that God knows what the future holds; that he knew what the future would hold when this was written. This verse is such an accurate summary of society today. In the dictionary, it says rebellion is an 'organised, open resistance to authority.' Well, when that authority is God, we don't have to look far to see rebellion manifesting itself, both in the newspapers and in our personal experience. It doesn't take too long to find someone dabbling in the occult, getting plastered on Saturday night, or sleeping around. We live in a society where an 'eat, drink and be merry, for tomorrow I die' culture prevails. Sometimes it seems like the devil is winning. He's not.

God wants us to rebel for him, against conventions and authorities that oppose his will; to fight on the winning side. There's no denying that living as a Christian today is tough. It's inevitable that sometimes we'll wonder what we are doing when everyone else seems to think our beliefs and the way we live our lives are pretty dumb. But that's an amazing opportunity to grow stronger.

Powerful rebels who changed the course of history for the better mostly lived in societies that thought they were wrong. Lord Shaftesbury, Martin Luther King and Jesus spring to mind. I believe that God wants us to live as rebels for Him, surrendering everything to Him. And as we pray for those who are rebelling against God, so our lives will increasingly point them towards Jesus.

More...

Materialism p.1141
Going against the crowd p.1045
Civil disobedience p.1247
Politics p.1358

See also: 2.1: 1 Thes 4.15–17. **2.4:** Dan 11.36; Ezek 28.2. **2.8:** Isa 11.4. **2.9:** Matt 24.24.

Be faithful

¹³ My friends, the Lord loves you, and it is only natural for us to thank God for you. God chose you to be the first ones to be saved.' His Spirit made you holy, and you put your faith in the truth. ¹⁴ God used our preaching as his way of inviting you to share in the glory of our Lord Jesus Christ. ¹⁵ My friends, that's why you must remain faithful and follow closely what we taught you in person and by our letters.

¹⁶ God our Father loves us. He is kind and has given us eternal comfort and a wonderful hope. We pray that our Lord Jesus Christ and God our Father ¹⁷ will encourage you and help you always to do and say the right thing.

Pray and work

CHAPTER 3

Pray for us

¹ Finally, our friends, please pray for us. This will help the message about the Lord to spread quickly, and others will respect it, just as you do. ² Pray that we may be kept safe from worthless and evil people. After all, not everyone has faith. ³ But the Lord can be trusted to make you strong and protect you from harm. ⁴ He has made us sure that you are obeying what we taught you and that you will keep on obeying. ⁵ I pray that the Lord will guide you to be as loving as God and as patient as Christ.

Warnings against laziness

⁶ My dear friends, in the name of' the Lord Jesus, I beg you not to have anything to do with any of your people who waste their time and refuse to obey the instructions we gave you. ⁷ You know that you should follow our example. We didn't waste our time being lazy, ⁸ and we didn't accept food from anyone without paying for it. We didn't want to be a burden to any of you, so night and day we worked as hard as we could.

⁹ We had the right not to work, but we wanted to set an example for you. ¹⁰ We also gave you the rule that if you don't work, you don't eat. ¹¹ Now we learn that some of you waste your time and won't do any work, except the work of a busybody. ¹² So, for the sake of our Lord Jesus Christ, we ask and beg

these people to settle down and start working for a living. ¹³ Dear friends, you must never become tired of doing right.

¹⁴ Be on your guard against any followers who refuse to obey what we have written in this letter. Put them to shame by not having anything to do with them. ¹⁵ Don't consider them your enemies, but speak kindly to them as you would to any other follower.

A final prayer

¹⁶ I pray that the Lord, who gives peace, will always bless you with peace. May the Lord be with all of you.

¹⁷ I always sign my letters as I am now doing: PAUL.

¹⁸ I pray that our Lord Jesus Christ will be kind to all of you.

Additional notes

›**1.1 Silas:** The Greek text has "Silvanus", which is another form of the name Silas.
›**2.2 Lord:** The Greek text has "day of the Lord".
›**2.3 wicked:** Some manuscripts have "sinful".
›**2.13 God chose you to be the first ones to be saved:** Some manuscripts have "From the beginning God chose you to be saved."
›**3.6 in the name of:** Or "as a follower of".

1 Timothy

Paul's first letter to Timothy

The basics

What's the point? Walk the talk. Live what you teach.

What happens? Paul writes to instruct his 'son' on various aspects of church life and teaching.

What should I remember?

4.16 'Be careful about the way you live and about what you teach. Keep on doing this, and you will save not only yourself, but the people who hear you.'

More details

Setting the scene Paul had known Timothy for years and regarded him as a kind of son. Timothy was now at Ephesus, helping to lead the church there. But he was facing problems...

What's it all about? Timothy was one of Paul's most faithful companions, and became involved in church leadership at a very young age. He is mentioned in five of Paul's letters. Paul writes to Timothy at Ephesus giving him guidelines on how to choose church leaders and how to combat false teaching.

Footsteps

Greetings

CHAPTER 1

¹ *From Paul.*

God our Saviour and Christ Jesus commanded me to be an apostle of Christ Jesus, who gives us hope.

² Timothy, because of our faith, you are like a son to me. I pray that God our Father and our Lord Jesus Christ will be kind and merciful to you. May they bless you with peace!

Instructions for church life

Warning against false teaching

³ When I was leaving for Macedonia, I asked you to stay on in Ephesus and warn certain people there to stop spreading their false teachings. ⁴ You needed to warn them to stop wasting their time on senseless stories and endless lists of ancestors. Such things only cause arguments. They don't help anyone to do God's work that can only be done by faith.

⁵ You must teach people to have genuine love, as well as a good conscience and true faith. ⁶ There are some who have given up these for nothing but empty talk. ⁷ They want to be teachers of the Law of Moses. But they don't know what they are talking about, even though they think they do.

⁸ We know that the Law is good, if it is used in the right way. ⁹ We also understand that it wasn't given to control people who please God, but to control lawbreakers, criminals,

---

See also: 1.2: Acts 16.1.

Life files

Timothy

What's the story?

Timothy was a native of Lystra. His father was Greek and his mother, Eunice, a Jew. He was probably a convert of Paul's first missionary journey.

He became an assistant to Paul, and was confirmed in this work by a prophecy (1 Timothy 1.18; 4.14) and by Paul praying over him and laying his hands on him. From that time forward, Timothy was an evangelist and church leader.

Paul entrusted him with special missions, such as that to Thessalonica to encourage the persecuted Christians; and he went with Paul to Jerusalem. He supported Paul in prison and later may have become a prisoner himself (Hebrews 13.23). Probably he became a church leader in Ephesus, where he received letters from Paul full of advice on how to run his church. To Paul, Timothy was like a son.

What's the point?

Timothy was probably not a natural evangelist. He was shy and occasionally fearful (1 Corinthians 16.10–11; 2 Timothy 1.7); but he was also extremely loyal. He was often ill (1 Timothy 5.23). Most of all, he was young. Paul took him under his wing and saw in Timothy someone who could be taught. Timothy repaid this trust and belief with loyalty, hard work and years of service.

 Footsteps

Five days with Timothy

Paul meets Timothy: Acts 16.1–3
In Thessalonica: 1 Thessalonians 3.1–6
Timothy in Ephesus: 1 Timothy 1.1–20
'You belong to God': 1 Timothy 6.11–21
Last instructions: 2 Timothy 3.10–17

More...

Paul p.1222
Church p.1315
Early church p.1212

godless people, and sinners. It is for wicked and evil people, and for murderers, who would even kill their own parents. ¹⁰ The Law was written for people who are sexual perverts or who live as homosexuals or are kidnappers or liars or won't tell the truth in court. It is for anything else that opposes the correct teaching ¹¹ of the good news that the glorious and wonderful God has given me.

Being thankful for God's kindness

¹² I thank Christ Jesus our Lord. He has given me the strength for my work because he knew that he could trust me. ¹³ I used to say terrible and insulting things about him, and I was cruel. But he had mercy on me because I didn't know what I was doing, and I had not yet put my faith in him. ¹⁴ Christ Jesus our Lord was very kind to me. He has greatly blessed my life with faith and love just like his own.

¹⁵ "Christ Jesus came into the world to save sinners." This saying is true, and it can be trusted. I was the worst sinner of all! ¹⁶ But since I was worse than anyone else, God had mercy on me and let me be an example of the endless patience of Christ Jesus. He did this so that others would put their faith in Christ and have eternal life. ¹⁷ I pray that honour and glory will always be given to the only God, who lives for ever and is the invisible and eternal King! Amen.

¹⁸ Timothy, my son, the instructions I am giving you are based on what some prophets* once said about you. If you follow these instructions, you will fight like a good soldier. ¹⁹ You will be faithful and have a clear conscience. Some people have made a mess of their faith because they didn't listen to their consciences. ²⁰ Two of them are Hymenaeus and Alexander. I have given these men over to the power of Satan, so they will learn not to oppose God.

CHAPTER 2

How to pray

¹ First of all, I ask you to pray for everyone. Ask God to help and bless them all, and tell God how thankful you are for each of them. ² Pray for kings and others in power, so that we may live quiet and peaceful lives as we worship and honour God. ³ This kind of

---

*1.18 prophets: Probably the Christian prophets referred to in 4.14.
See also: 1.13: Acts 8.3; 9.4–5.

prayer is good, and it pleases God our Saviour. [4] God wants everyone to be saved and to know the whole truth, which is,

> [5] There is only one God,
> and Christ Jesus
>   is the only one
>   who can bring us
>   to God.
> Jesus was truly human,
>   and he gave himself
>   to rescue all of us.
> [6] God showed us this
>   at the right time.

[7] This is why God chose me to be a preacher and an apostle of the good news. I am telling the truth. I am not lying. God sent me to teach the Gentiles about faith and truth.

[8] I want everyone everywhere to lift innocent hands towards heaven and pray, without being angry or arguing with each other.

[9] I would like women to wear modest and sensible clothes. They should not have fancy hair styles, or wear expensive clothes, or put on jewellery made of gold or pearls. [10] Women who claim to love God should do helpful things for others, [11] and they should learn by being quiet and paying attention. [12] They should be silent and not be allowed to teach or to tell men what to do. [13] After all, Adam was created before Eve, [14] and the man Adam wasn't the one who was fooled. It was the woman Eve who was completely fooled and sinned. [15] But women will be saved by having children,* if they stay faithful, loving, holy, and modest.

CHAPTER 3

Church officials

[1] It is true that▸ anyone who desires to be a church official▸ wants to be something worthwhile. [2] That's why officials must have a good reputation and be faithful in marriage.▸ They must be self-controlled, sensible, well-behaved, friendly to strangers, and able to teach. [3] They must not be heavy drinkers or troublemakers. Instead, they must be kind and gentle and not love money.

[4] Church officials must be in control of their own families, and they must see that their children are obedient and always respectful. [5] If they don't know how to control their own families, how can they look after God's people?

[6] They must not be new followers of the Lord. If they are, they might become proud and be doomed along with the devil. [7] Finally, they must be well respected by people who are not followers. Then they won't be trapped and disgraced by the devil.

Church officers

[8] Church officers▸ should be serious. They must not be liars, heavy drinkers, or greedy for money. [9] And they must have a clear conscience and hold firmly to what God has shown us about our faith. [10] They must first prove themselves. Then if no one has anything against them, they can serve as officers.

[11] Women* must also be serious. They must not gossip or be heavy drinkers, and they must be faithful in everything they do.

[12] Church officers must be faithful in marriage.▸ They must be in full control of their children and everyone else in their home. [13] Those who serve well as officers will earn a good reputation and will be highly respected for their faith in Christ Jesus.

The mystery of our religion

[14] I hope to visit you soon. But I am writing these instructions, [15] so that if I am delayed, you will know how everyone who belongs to God's family ought to behave. After all, the church of the living God is the strong foundation of truth.

[16] Here is the great mystery of our religion:

> Christ▸ came as a human.
> The Spirit proved
>   that he pleased God,
> and he was seen by angels.
>
> Christ was preached
>   to the nations.
> People in this world
>   put their faith in him,
> and he was taken up to glory.

---

*2.15 **saved by having children:** Or "brought safely through childbirth" or "saved by the birth of a child" (that is, by the birth of Jesus) or "saved by being good mothers".

See also: 2.7: 2 Tim 1.11.   **2.9:** 1 Pet 3.3.   **2.13: a** Gen 2.7; **b** Gen 2.21–22.   **2.14:** Gen 3.1–6.   **3.2–7:** Titus 1.6–9.

---

*3.11 **Women:** Either church officers or the wives of church officers.

CHAPTER 4

People will turn from their faith

[1] God's Spirit clearly says that in the last days many people will turn from their faith. They will be fooled by evil spirits and by teachings that come from demons. [2] They will also be fooled by the false claims of liars whose consciences have lost all feeling. These liars [3] will forbid people to marry or to eat certain foods. But God created these foods to be eaten with thankful hearts by his followers who know the truth. [4] Everything God created is good. And if you give thanks, you may eat anything. [5] What God has said and your prayer will make it fit to eat.

Paul's advice to Timothy

[6] If you teach these things to other followers, you will be a good servant of Christ Jesus. You will show that you have grown up on the teachings about our faith and on the good instructions you have obeyed. [7] Don't have anything to do with worthless, senseless stories. Work hard to be truly religious.
[8-9] As the saying goes,

> "Exercise is good
>   for your body,
> but religion helps you
>   in every way.
> It promises life
>   now and for ever."

These words are worthwhile and should not be forgotten. [10] We have put our hope in the living God, who is the Saviour of everyone, but especially of those who have faith. That's why we work and struggle so hard.•

[11] Teach these things and tell everyone to do what you say. [12] Don't let anyone make fun of you, just because you are young. Set an example for other followers by what you say and do, as well as by your love, faith, and purity. [13] Until I arrive, be sure to keep on reading the Scriptures in worship, and don't stop preaching and teaching. [14] Use the gift you were given when the prophets spoke and the group of church leaders• blessed you by placing their hands on you. [15] Remember these things and think about them, so everyone can see how well you are doing. [16] Be careful about the way you live and about what you teach. Keep on doing this, and you will save not only yourself, but the people who hear you.

CHAPTER 5

How to act towards others

[1] Don't correct an older man. Encourage him, as you would your own father. Treat younger men as you would your own brother, [2] and treat older women as you would your own mother. Show the same respect to younger women that you would to your sister.

[3] Take care of any widow who is really in need. [4] But if a widow has children or grandchildren, they should learn to serve God by taking care of her, as she once took care of them. This is what God wants them to do. [5] A widow who is really in need is one who doesn't have any relatives. She has faith in God, and she keeps praying to him night and day, asking for his help.

[6] A widow who thinks only about having a good time is already dead, even though she is still alive.

[7] Tell all this to everyone, so they will do the right thing. [8] People who don't take care of their relatives, and especially their own families, have given up their faith. They are worse than someone who doesn't have faith in the Lord.

[9] For a widow to be put on the list of widows, she must be at least sixty years old, and she must have been faithful in marriage.• [10] She must also be well known for doing all sorts of good things, such as raising children, giving food to strangers, welcoming God's people into her home,* helping people in need, and always making herself useful.

[11] Don't put young widows on the list. They may later have a strong desire to get married. Then they will turn away from Christ [12] and become guilty of breaking their promise to him. [13] Besides, they will become lazy and get into the habit of going from house to house. Next, they will start gossiping and become busybodies, talking about things that are none of their business.

[14] I would prefer that young widows get married, have children, and look after their families. Then the enemy won't have any reason to say insulting things about us. [15] Look what's already happened to some of the young widows! They have turned away to follow Satan.

---

*5.10 welcoming God's people into her home: The Greek text has "washing the feet of God's people". In New Testament times most people either went barefoot or wore sandals, and a host would often wash the feet of special guests.

16 If a woman who is a follower has any widows in her family, she‣ should help them. This will keep the church from having that burden, and then the church can help widows who are really in need.

Church leaders

17 Church leaders‣ who do their job well deserve to be paid‣ twice as much, especially if they work hard at preaching and teaching. 18 It is just as the Scriptures say, "Don't muzzle an ox when you are using it to grind grain." You also know the saying, "Workers are worth their pay."

19 Don't listen to any charge against a church leader, unless at least two or three people bring the same charges. 20 But if any of the leaders should keep on sinning, they must be corrected in front of the whole group, as a warning to everyone else.

21 In the presence of God and Christ Jesus and their chosen angels, I order you to follow my instructions! Be fair with everyone, and don't have any favourites.

22 Don't be too quick to accept people into the service of the Lord‣ by placing your hands on them.

Don't sin because others do, but stay close to God.

23 Stop drinking only water. Take a little wine to help your stomach trouble and the other illnesses you always have.

24 Some people get caught in their sins straight away, even before the time of judgment. But other people's sins don't show up until later. 25 It is the same with good deeds. Some are easily seen, but none of them can be hidden.

CHAPTER 6

1 If you are a slave, you should respect and honour your owner. This will keep people from saying bad things about God and about our teaching. 2 If any of you slaves have owners who are followers, you should show them respect. After all, they are also followers of Christ, and he loves them. So you should serve and help them the best you can.

False teaching and true wealth

These are the things you must teach and tell the people to do. 3 Anyone who teaches something different disagrees with the correct

and godly teaching of our Lord Jesus Christ. 4 Those people who disagree are proud of themselves, but they don't really know a thing. Their minds are sick, and they like to argue over words. They cause jealousy, disagreements, unkind words, evil suspicions, 5 and nasty quarrels. They have wicked minds and have missed out on the truth.

These people think religion is supposed to make you rich. 6 And religion does make your life rich, by making you content with what you have. 7 We didn't bring anything into this world, and we won't‣ take anything with us when we leave. 8 So we should be satisfied just to have food and clothes. 9 People who want to be rich fall into all sorts of temptations and traps. They are caught by foolish and harmful desires that drag them down and destroy them. 10 The love of money causes all kinds of trouble. Some people want money so much that they have given up their faith and caused themselves a lot of pain.

Fighting a good fight for the faith

11 Timothy, you belong to God, so keep away from all these evil things. Try your best to please God and to be like him. Be faithful, loving, dependable, and gentle. 12 Fight a good fight for the faith and claim eternal life. God offered it to you when you clearly told about your faith, while so many people listened. 13 Now I ask you to make a promise. Make it in the presence of God, who gives life to all, and in the presence of Jesus Christ, who openly told Pontius Pilate about his faith. 14 Promise to obey completely and fully all that you have been told until our Lord Jesus Christ returns.

15 The glorious God
   is the only Ruler,
   the King of kings
   and Lord of lords.
At the time that God
   has already decided,
he will send Jesus Christ
   back again.

16 Only God lives for ever!
And he lives in light
   that no one can come near.
No human has ever seen God
   or ever can see him.
God will be honoured,
and his power
   will last for ever. Amen.

See also: **5.18:** a Deut 25.4; **b** Matt 10.10; Luke 10.7. **5.19:** Deut 17.6; 19.15.

See also: **6.13:** John 18.37.

1349

Helpline

Help! Other people are better Christians than me

'I bet other Christians don't struggle like me. I bet they read the Bible every day and pray for hours and never get tempted like I do...'

We're always comparing ourselves to others. Other people seem so much more, well, 'Christian'. They have an hour's Bible study every morning – we struggle to fit in ten minutes. They pray powerfully and at length – we struggle to fit more than 10 words together.

But they're probably looking at us and thinking 'I wish I was like them.' Every Christian finds different things tempting. Some can't resist chocolate, some lose their temper easily, some people struggle to control their tongue. And you might find some things easy that they consider hard. You might find it easy to share your faith, or forgive people or... whatever.

The truth is that everyone is different. We all have a unique relationship with God, we're all made uniquely and therefore we all have different gifts and abilities.

What matters is to be the best we can. Paul tells Timothy to try his best to be like God (1 Timothy 6.11). He doesn't ask him to be a superhero – just a good and faithful soldier.

Three things

Recognise

Recognise your own strengths as well as your weaknesses. It's not wrong to identify things we're good at – and to work at being even better at them.

Unique

Stop comparing yourself to others. Understand that you are unique and God loves you for who you are.

Improve

Pray for the areas where you feel you are weak, that the Holy Spirit will help you to improve and that you will get the strength to persevere.

[17] Warn the rich people of this world not to be proud or to trust in wealth that is easily lost. Tell them to have faith in God, who is rich and blesses us with everything we need to enjoy life. [18] Instruct them to do as many good deeds as they can and to help everyone. Remind the rich to be generous and share what they have. [19] This will lay a solid foundation for the future, so that they will know what true life is like.

[20] Timothy, guard what God has placed in your care! Don't pay any attention to that godless and stupid talk that sounds clever but really isn't. [21] Some people have even lost their faith by believing this talk.

I pray that the Lord will be kind to all of you!

Additional notes

'3.1 It is true that: These words may be taken with 2.15. If so, that verse would be translated: "It is true that women will be saved . . . holy, and modest." And 3.1 would be translated: "Anyone who desires . . . something worthwhile."

'3.1 church official: Or "bishop".

'3.2 be faithful in marriage: Or "be the husband of only one wife" or "have never been divorced".

'3.8 Church officers: Or "Deacons".

'3.12 be faithful in marriage: See the note at 3.2.

'3.16 Christ: The Greek text has "he", probably meaning "Christ". Some manuscripts have "God".

'4.10 struggle so hard: Some manuscripts have "are treated so badly".

'4.14 group of church leaders: Or "group of elders" or "group of presbyters" or "group of priests". This translates one Greek word, and it is related to the one used in 5.17,19.

'5.9 been faithful in marriage: Or "been the wife of only one husband" or "never been divorced".

'5.16 woman . . . she: Some manuscripts have "man or woman . . . that person".

'5.17 leaders: Or "elders" or "presbyters" or "priests".

'5.17 paid: Or "honoured" or "respected".

'5.22 to accept people into the service of the Lord: Or "to forgive people".

'6.7 we won't: Some manuscripts have "we certainly won't".

2 Timothy

Paul's second letter to Timothy

The basics

What's the point? The Bible teaches us the truth – and how to live it.

What happens? Paul asks for Timothy's help and encourages him to be strong in the faith.

What should I remember? 3.15–16 'Since childhood you have known the Holy Scriptures that are able to make you wise enough to have faith in Christ Jesus and be saved. Everything in the Scriptures is God's Word. All of it is useful for teaching and helping people and for correcting them and showing them how to live.'

More details

Setting the scene Paul is in jail. Facing the end of his life, he writes to Timothy to ask him a favour and give some final words of advice.

What's it all about? This is Paul's final letter, and is an intensely personal missive to one of his closest friends. Timothy is addressed as a 'dear child', a sign of the affection between the two men. Timothy was, in many ways, the son Paul never had.

Paul was lonely. In jail in Rome, Paul's friends had deserted him – only Luke remained faithful. At this time, more perhaps than any other, Paul missed his 'son'.

So Paul wrote to remind Timothy how he had laid hands on him and commissioned him for the special work he was to do and how he prays constantly for Timothy. Paul was also concerned for the churches, especially given the wave of persecution which was to be unleashed by Nero. So he encouraged Timothy

to continue in his work. Keep running, right until the point you reach the finishing line.

Footsteps
No shame: 1.1–18
Do your duty: 2.1–26
Keep running: 3.10—4.8

Greetings and prayer for Timothy

CHAPTER 1

[1] *From Paul, an apostle of Christ Jesus.*

God himself chose me to be an apostle, and he gave me the promised life that Jesus Christ makes possible.

[2] Timothy, you are like a dear child to me. I pray that God our Father and our Lord Christ Jesus will be kind and merciful to you and will bless you with peace!

Do not be ashamed of the Lord

[3] Night and day I mention you in my prayers. I am always grateful for you, as I pray to the God my ancestors and I have served with a clear conscience. [4] I remember how you cried, and I want to see you, because that will make me truly happy. [5] I also remember the genuine faith of your mother Eunice. Your grandmother Lois had the same sort of faith,

See also: 1.2: Acts 16.1. **1.5:** Acts 16.1.

Helpline

Help! I haven't been called

'I've heard Christians say that God has called them to do something. But I haven't felt called at all...'

God speaks to different people in different ways. Sometimes people feel that God has 'called' them. They feel that God has given them a specific instruction or message. That's what Paul is talking about here, when he remembers laying hands on Timothy (2 Timothy 1.6) and the way that Paul himself was called to be a preacher, apostle and teacher' (2 Timothy 1.11).

That's great. But it doesn't mean that you're a second class Christian if you haven't felt that call. Nor that it's wrong if you just want to do something.

You might want to serve God overseas; you might want to take up a certain career. Just because you don't feel 'called' doesn't mean God doesn't approve.

There are some tests that you can apply. What do you want to do? Why do you want to do it? Do you have the skills that are necessary? What do others think of the idea?

If there are no problems with any of the answers to these questions, then maybe you can take that as a sign that it's OK to pursue the idea. Whether you feel called or not.

Three things

Heart

Don't worry about specific calling; worry instead about bringing what's on your heart before God.

Ask

Ask yourself some questions and make sure that everything checks out OK.

Pray

Keep praying at every stage. Keep talking to trusted friends and leaders. And keep talking to God.

More...

Guidance p.685

and I am sure that you have it as well. ⁶ So I ask you to make full use of the gift that God gave you when I placed my hands on you.* Use it well. ⁷ God's Spirit' doesn't make cowards out of us. The Spirit gives us power, love, and self-control.

⁸ Don't be ashamed to speak for our Lord. And don't be ashamed of me, just because I am in jail for serving him. Use the power that comes from God and join with me in suffering for telling the good news.

⁹ God saved us and chose us
   to be his holy people.
We did nothing
   to deserve this,
but God planned it
   because he is so kind.
Even before time began
God planned for Christ Jesus
   to show kindness to us.

¹⁰ Now Christ Jesus has come
   to show us the kindness of God.
Christ our Saviour defeated death
   and brought us
   the good news.
It shines like a light
and offers life
   that never ends.

¹¹ My work is to be a preacher, an apostle, and a teacher.' ¹² That's why I am suffering now. But I am not ashamed! I know the one I have faith in, and I am sure that he can guard until the last day what he has trusted me with.' ¹³ Now follow the example of the correct teaching I gave you, and let the faith and love of Christ Jesus be your model. ¹⁴ You have been trusted with a wonderful treasure. Guard it with the help of the Holy Spirit, who lives within you.

¹⁵ You know that everyone in Asia has turned against me, especially Phygelus and Hermogenes.

¹⁶ I pray that the Lord will be kind to the family of Onesiphorus. He often cheered me up and wasn't ashamed of me when I was put in jail. ¹⁷ Then after he arrived in Rome, he searched everywhere until he found me. ¹⁸ I pray that the Lord Jesus will ask God to show mercy to Onesiphorus on the day of judgment. You know how much he helped me in Ephesus.

---

*1.6 when I placed my hands on you: Church leaders placed their hands on people who were being appointed to preach or teach. See 1 Timothy 4.14.
See also: 1.11: 1 Tim 2.7.

How to be a good soldier of Christ

CHAPTER 2

[1] Timothy, my child, Christ Jesus is kind, and you must let him make you strong. [2] You have often heard me teach. Now I want you to tell these same things to followers who can be trusted to tell others.

[3] As a good soldier of Christ Jesus you must endure your share of suffering. [4] Soldiers on duty don't work at outside jobs. They try only to please their commanding officer. [5] No one wins an athletic contest without obeying the rules. [6] And farmers who work hard are the first to eat what grows in their field. [7] If you keep in mind what I have told you, the Lord will help you understand completely.

[8] Keep your mind on Jesus Christ! He was from the family of David and was raised from death, just as my good news says. [9] And because of this message, I am locked up in jail and treated like a criminal. But God's good news isn't locked in jail, [10] and so I am willing to put up with anything. Then God's special people will be saved. They will be given eternal glory because they belong to Christ Jesus. [11] Here is a true message:

"If we died with Christ,
    we will live with him.
[12] If we don't give up,
    we will rule with him.
If we deny
    that we know him,
he will deny
    that he knows us.
[13] If we are not faithful,
    he will still be faithful.
Christ cannot deny
    who he is."

An approved worker

[14] Don't let anyone forget these things. And with God⸱ as your witness, you must warn them not to argue about words. These arguments don't help anyone. In fact, they ruin everyone who listens to them. [15] Do your best to win God's approval as a worker who doesn't need to be ashamed and who teaches only the true message.

[16] Keep away from worthless and useless talk. It only leads people further away from God. [17] That sort of talk is like a sore that won't heal. And Hymenaeus and Philetus have been talking this way [18] by teaching that the dead have already been raised to life. This is far from the truth, and it is destroying the faith of some people.

[19] But the foundation that God has laid is solid. On it is written, "The Lord knows who his people are. So everyone who worships the Lord must turn away from evil."

[20] In a large house some dishes are made of gold or silver, while others are made of wood or clay. Some of these are special, and others are not. [21] That's also how it is with people. The ones who stop doing evil and make themselves pure will become special. Their lives will be holy and pleasing to their Master, and they will be able to do all kinds of good deeds.

[22] Run from temptations that capture young people. Always do the right thing. Be faithful, loving, and easy to get along with. Worship with people whose hearts are pure. [23] Stay away from stupid and senseless arguments. These only lead to trouble, [24] and God's servants must not be troublemakers. They must be kind to everyone, and they must be good teachers and very patient.

[25] Be humble when you correct people who oppose you. Perhaps God will lead them to turn to him and learn the truth. [26] They have been trapped by the devil, and he makes them obey him, but God may help them escape.

What people will be like in the last days

CHAPTER 3

[1] You can be certain that in the last days there will be some very hard times. [2] People will love only themselves and money. They will be proud, stuck-up, rude, and disobedient to their parents. They will also be ungrateful, godless, [3] heartless, and hateful. Their words will be cruel, and they will have no self-control or pity. These people will hate everything that is good. [4] They will be sneaky, reckless, and puffed up with pride. Instead of loving God, they will love pleasure. [5] Even though they will make a show of being religious, their religion won't be real. Don't have anything to do with such people.

[6] Some men fool whole families, just to get power over those women who are slaves of sin and are controlled by all sorts of desires.

See also: **2.12:** Matt 10.33; Luke 12.9.

See also: **2.19:** Num 16.5.

Being christian

Reading your Bible

2 Timothy 3.11–17

The Bible. It's the rulebook, the manual. It contains the history of us all, the fundamental truth about life. It's packed with wisdom, inspiration, insight and emotion. It's the greatest book ever.

So how can we ignore it?

Christians are people of the Bible. We should read and study the scriptures, because that's one of the key ways that God speaks to us. The Bible gives us rules to live by and the strength to live right. It shares with us the experiences of some of the greatest humans who have ever lived.

It's not easy sometimes. There are some bits that are difficult for us to grasp. But the Bible is one of the ways that God speaks to us. So if we ignore it, we're ignoring him.

Paul advises Timothy to keep reading the scriptures. God's word, he says is 'useful for teaching and helping people and for correcting them and showing them how to live.'

So it's not just a nice collection of stories. It's not just some nice words and nice thoughts. It's the user's manual to eternal life.

If you want to hear from God, read the Bible. If you want to learn about God, read the Bible.

Being Christian: Reading your Bible

• Make time to read the Bible. Every day if you can.
• Try to learn some key bits. You'll find that they'll help you.
• Meet with others and read and discuss the Bible with them.

[7] These women always want to learn something new, but they never can discover the truth. [8] Just as Jannes and Jambres* opposed Moses, these people are enemies of the truth. Their minds are sick, and their faith isn't real. [9] But they won't get very far with their foolishness. Soon everyone will know the truth about them, just as Jannes and Jambres were found out.

Keep being faithful

Paul's last instructions to Timothy

[10] Timothy, you know what I teach and how I live. You know what I want to do and what I believe. You have seen how patient and loving I am, and how in the past I put up with [11] trouble and suffering in the cities of Antioch, Iconium, and Lystra. Yet the Lord rescued me from all those terrible troubles. [12] Anyone who belongs to Christ Jesus and wants to live right will have trouble from others. [13] But evil people who pretend to be what they are not will become worse than ever, as they fool others and are fooled themselves.

[14] Keep on being faithful to what you were taught and to what you believed. After all, you know who taught you these things. [15] Since childhood, you have known the Holy Scriptures that are able to make you wise enough to have faith in Christ Jesus and be saved. [16] Everything in the Scriptures is God's Word. All of it is useful for teaching and helping people and for correcting them and showing them how to live. [17] The Scriptures train God's servants to do all kinds of good deeds.

CHAPTER 4

[1] When Christ Jesus comes as king, he will be the judge of everyone, whether they are living or dead. So with God and Christ as witnesses, I command you [2] to preach God's message. Do it willingly, even if it isn't the popular thing to do. You must correct people and point out their sins. But also cheer them up, and when you instruct them, always be patient. [3] The time is coming when people

---

*3.8 Jannes and Jambres: These names are not found in the Old Testament. But many believe these were the names of the two Egyptian magicians who opposed Moses when he wanted to lead the people of Israel out of Egypt. See Exodus 7.11,22.

See also: 3.8: Exod 7.11.   3.11: a Acts 13.14–52; b Acts 14.1–7; c Acts 14.8–20.

won't listen to good teaching. Instead, they will look for teachers who will please them by telling them only what they are itching to hear. [4] They will turn from the truth and eagerly listen to senseless stories. [5] But you must stay calm and be willing to suffer. You must work hard to tell the good news and to do your job well.

[6] Now the time has come for me to die. My life is like a drink offering* being poured out on the altar. [7] I have fought well. I have finished the race, and I have been faithful. [8] So a crown will be given to me for pleasing the Lord. He judges fairly, and on the day of judgment he will give a crown to me and to everyone else who wants him to appear with power.

Personal instructions and final greetings

Personal instructions

[9] Come to see me as soon as you can. [10] Demas loves the things of this world so much that he left me and went to Thessalonica. Crescens has gone to Galatia, and Titus has gone to Dalmatia. [11] Only Luke has stayed with me.

Mark can be very helpful to me, so please find him and bring him with you. [12] I sent Tychicus to Ephesus.

[13] When you come, bring the coat I left at Troas with Carpus. Don't forget to bring the scrolls, especially the ones made of leather.*

[14] Alexander, the metalworker, has hurt me in many ways. But the Lord will pay him back for what he has done. [15] Alexander opposes what we preach. You had better watch out for him.

[16] When I was first put on trial, no one helped me. In fact, everyone deserted me. I hope it won't be held against them. [17] But the Lord stood beside me. He gave me the strength to tell his full message, so that all

Gentiles would hear it. And I was kept safe from hungry lions. [18] The Lord will always keep me from being harmed by evil, and he will bring me safely into his heavenly kingdom. Praise him for ever and ever! Amen.

Final greetings

[19] Give my greetings to Priscilla and Aquila and to the family of Onesiphorus.

[20] Erastus stayed at Corinth.

Trophimus was sick when I left him at Miletus.

[21] Do your best to come before winter.

Eubulus, Pudens, Linus, and Claudia send you their greetings, and so do the rest of the Lord's followers.

[22] I pray that the Lord will bless your life and will be kind to you.

See also: **4.19:** a Acts 18.2; **b** 2 Tim 1.16–17.
4.20: a Acts 19.22; Rom 16.23; **b** Acts 20.4; 21.29.

Additional notes

›**1.7 God's Spirit:** Or "God".
›**1.11 teacher:** Some manuscripts add "of the Gentiles".
›**1.12 what he has trusted me with:** Or "what I have trusted him with."
›**2.14 God:** Some manuscripts have "the Lord", and others have "Christ".

4.6 drink offering: Water or wine was sometimes poured out as an offering when an animal sacrifice was made.
***4.13 the ones made of leather:** A scroll was a kind of rolled up book, and it could be made out of paper (called "papyrus") or leather (that is, animal skin) or even copper.
See also: **4.10:** a Col 4.14; Phlm 24; **b** 2 Cor 8.23; Gal 2.3; Titus 1.4. **4.11:** a Col 4.14; Phlm 24; **b** Acts 12.12,25; 13.13; 15.37–39; Col 4.10; Phlm 24. **4.12:** Acts 20.4; Eph 6.21–22; Col 4.7–8. **4.13:** Acts 20.6. **4.14:** a 1 Tim 1.20; **b** Psa 62.12; Rom 2.6.

Titus

Paul's letter to Titus

The basics

What's the point? God has saved us and given us hope. Let us live lives that show that hope to others.

What happens? Paul writes to Titus with advice on church leadership, holiness and honesty.

What should I remember? 2.13–14 'We are filled with hope, as we wait for the glorious return of our great God and Saviour Jesus Christ. He gave himself to rescue us from everything that is evil and to make our hearts pure. He wanted us to be his own people and to be eager to do right.'

More details

Setting the scene Titus went with Paul on several of his journeys and worked alongside him in setting up new churches. Now Titus is leading the church in Crete, so Paul sends him some advice...

What's it all about? Paul appointed Titus to oversee the work in Crete and he is writing to encourage him and advise him. It's important to ensure that church leaders are people of good reputation and personal behaviour, because people will look to them as an example of how to live.

Arguments and disputes should be avoided. Above all, it matters how we conduct ourselves. We used to be evil and stupid and disobedient, but that behaviour should have gone now. We have been given new life through Jesus, and that means we need to adopt new ways of behaving, following Jesus rather than our own inclinations.

Footsteps

Church officials: 1.1–16
Setting examples: 2.1–15
Doing good: 3.1–15

Greetings and a prayer for Titus

CHAPTER 1

[1] *From Paul, a servant of God and an apostle of Jesus Christ.*

I encourage God's own people to have more faith and to understand the truth about religion. [2] Then they will have the hope of eternal life that God promised long ago. And God never tells a lie! [3] So, at the proper time, God our Saviour gave this message and told me to announce what he had said.

[4] Titus, because of our faith, you are like a son to me. I pray that God our Father and Christ Jesus our Saviour will be kind to you and will bless you with peace!

Instructions for church officials

What Titus was to do in Crete

[5] I left you in Crete to do what had been left undone and to appoint leaders* for the churches in each town. As I told you, [6] they must have a good reputation and be faithful in marriage.* Their children must

---

See also: 1.4: 2 Cor 8.23; Gal 2.3; 2 Tim 4.10.
1.6–9: 1 Tim 3.2–7.

be followers of the Lord and not have a reputation for being wild and disobedient. [7] Church officials' are in charge of God's work, and so they must also have a good reputation. They must not be bossy, quick-tempered, heavy drinkers, bullies, or dishonest in business. [8] Instead, they must be friendly to strangers and enjoy doing good things. They must also be sensible, fair, pure, and self-controlled. [9] They must stick to the true message they were taught, so that their good teaching can help others and correct everyone who opposes it.

[10] There are many who don't respect authority, and they fool others by talking nonsense. This is especially true of some Jewish followers. [11] But you must make them be quiet. They are after money, and they upset whole families by teaching what they should not. [12] It is like one of their own prophets once said,

> "The people of Crete
>   always tell lies.
> They are greedy and lazy
>   like wild animals."

[13] That is a true saying. And you should be hard on such people, so you can help them grow stronger in their faith. [14] Don't pay any attention to any of those senseless Jewish stories and human commands. These are made up by people who won't obey the truth.

[15] Everything is pure for someone whose heart is pure. But nothing is pure for an unbeliever with a dirty mind. That person's mind and conscience are destroyed. [16] Such people claim to know God, but their actions prove that they really don't. They are disgusting. They won't obey God, and they are too worthless to do anything good.

Instructions for church people

CHAPTER 2

Instructions for different groups of people

[1] Titus, you must teach only what is correct. [2] Tell the older men to have self-control and to be serious and sensible. Their faith, love, and patience must never fail.

[3] Tell the older women to behave as those who love the Lord should. They must not gossip about others or be slaves of wine. They must teach what is proper, [4] so the younger women will be loving wives and mothers. [5] Each of the younger women must be sensible and kind, as well as a good homemaker, who puts her own husband first. Then no one can say insulting things about God's message.

[6] Tell the young men to have self-control in everything. [7] Always set a good example for others. Be sincere and serious when you teach. [8] Use clean language that no one can criticize. Do this, and your enemies will be too ashamed to say anything against you.

[9] Tell slaves always to please their owners by obeying them in everything. Slaves must not talk back to their owners [10] or steal from them. They must be completely honest and trustworthy. Then everyone will show great respect for what is taught about God our Saviour.

God's kindness and the new life

[11] God has shown us how kind he is by coming to save all people. [12] He taught us to give up our wicked ways and our worldly desires and to live decent and honest lives in this world. [13] We are filled with hope, as we wait for the glorious return of our great God and Saviour Jesus Christ.' [14] He gave himself to rescue us from everything that is evil and to make our hearts pure. He wanted us to be his own people and to be eager to do right.

[15] Teach these things, as you use your full authority to encourage and correct people. Make sure you earn everyone's respect.

CHAPTER 3

Doing helpful things

[1] Remind your people to obey the rulers and authorities and not to be rebellious. They must always be ready to do something helpful [2] and not say cruel things or argue. They should be gentle and kind to everyone. [3] We used to be stupid, disobedient, and foolish, as well as slaves of all sorts of desires and pleasures. We were evil and jealous. Everyone hated us, and we hated everyone.

See also: 2.14: a Psa 130.8; **b** Exod 19.5; Deut 4.20; 7.6; 14.2; 1 Pet 2.9.

Real life

Politics

Nowadays we don't think much of our politicians. We listen to them all making strange noises during Prime Minister's questions; we watch them being grilled on the TV; we shrug our shoulders as we watch them call each other names.

A lot of people are turned off politics these days. But the truth is, that politics matters. Politics is about the way in which society is run. And, despite what we see on the media, many politicians are honest, committed individuals. We may not agree with their policies, but that doesn't mean that they're dishonest.

Christians have always been involved in politics, whether its people like Wilberforce, who persuaded Parliament to outlaw slavery; or Dietrich Bonhoeffer who stood up against the Nazis; or Martin Luther King Jr. who marched against racism in America.

They understood that Christians cannot stand aloof from the world. We have a duty to stand up for the oppressed, to see that our society is run justly and fairly – and that, believe it or not, is what politics is all about.

Think

What does 'politics' make you think of?
Do you know the name of your MP? Do you know any of their policies?
What kinds of things in your community
Would you like to see politicians doing something about?

Act

Find out who your MP is. Pray for them.
If there is something you want action on, write to them, or go and visit them.
Use your vote. Politics matters too much to be ignored.

Check

Amos 5.1–27; Isaiah 28.1–29;
Matthew 5.13–16; Mark 12.13–17;
Romans 13.1–7; Titus 3.1

More...

Civil disobedience p.1247
Incarnation p.1168

⁴ God our Saviour showed us
   how good and kind he is.
⁵ He saved us because
   of his mercy,
and not because
   of any good things
      that we have done.

God washed us by the power
   of the Holy Spirit.
He gave us new birth
   and a fresh beginning.
⁶ God sent Jesus Christ
   our Saviour
      to give us his Spirit.
⁷ Jesus treated us much better
   than we deserve.
He made us acceptable to God
and gave us the hope
   of eternal life.

⁸ This message is certainly true.

These teachings are useful and helpful for everyone. I want you to insist that the people follow them, so that all who have faith in God will be sure to do good deeds. ⁹ But don't have anything to do with stupid arguments about ancestors. And stay away from disagreements and quarrels about the Law of Moses. Such arguments are useless and senseless.

¹⁰ Warn troublemakers once or twice. Then don't have anything else to do with them. ¹¹ You know that their minds are twisted, and their own sins show how guilty they are.

Personal advice and final greetings

¹² I plan to send Artemas or Tychicus to you. After he arrives, please try your best to meet me at Nicopolis. I have decided to spend the winter there.

¹³ When Zenas the lawyer and Apollos get ready to leave, help them as much as you can, so they won't have need of anything.

¹⁴ Our people should learn to spend their time doing something useful and worthwhile.

¹⁵ Greetings to you from everyone here. Greet all our friends who share in our faith.

I pray that the Lord will be kind to all of you!

See also: **3.12:** Acts 20.4; Eph 6.21–22; Col 4.7–8;
2 Tim 4.12.   **3.13:** Acts 18.24; 1 Cor 16.12.

Additional notes

›**1.5 leaders:** Or "elders" or "presbyters" or "priests".
›**1.6 be faithful in marriage:** Or "be the husband of only one wife" or "have never been divorced".
›**1.7 Church officials:** Or "Bishops".
›**2.13 the glorious return of our great God and Saviour Jesus Christ:** Or "the glorious return of our great God and our Saviour Jesus Christ" or "the return of Jesus Christ, who is the glory of our great God and Saviour."

Philemon

Paul's letter to Philemon

The basics

What's the point? There is no discrimination in Christianity; all are children of God.

What happens? Paul is writing an appeal on behalf of a runaway slave.

What should I remember? 1.16 'Onesimus is much more to us than a slave. To me he is a dear friend, but to you he is even more, both as a person and as a follower of the Lord.'

More details

Setting the scene Onesimus was a slave who had stolen some money and run away to Rome. There , he met Paul and became a Christian. Now Paul is sending him back to his master, Philemon. And Paul wants Philemon to have mercy.

What's it all about? Under Roman law, Onesimus is a dead man. A runaway slave who had stolen money, he deserved to die. But Onesimus has become a Christian, like his master Philemon, who probably ran a church in his home in Colossae. So Paul tries to make peace between the two. Paul's letter is light-hearted and very personal. This is an appeal for mercy. The law says that Onesimus should die, but Paul offers to pay the money back himself.

Greetings to Philemon

[1] *From Paul, who is in jail for serving Christ Jesus, and from Timothy, who is like a brother because of our faith.*

Philemon, you work with us and are very dear to us. This letter is to you [2] *and to the church that meets in your home. It is also to our dear friend Apphia and to Archippus, who serves the Lord as we do.*

[3] I pray that God our Father and our Lord Jesus Christ will be kind to you and will bless you with peace!

Philemon's love and faith

[4] Philemon, each time I mention you in my prayers, I thank God. [5] I hear about your faith in our Lord Jesus and about your love for all God's people. [6] As you share your faith with others, I pray that they may come to know all the blessings Christ has given us. [7] My friend, your love has made me happy and has greatly encouraged me. It has also cheered the hearts of God's people.

Paul speaks to Philemon about Onesimus

[8] Christ gives me the courage to tell you what to do. [9] But I would rather ask you to do it simply because of love. Yes, as someone' in jail for Christ, [10] I beg you to help Onesimus!* He is like a son to me because I led him to Christ here in jail. [11] Before this, he was useless to you, but now he is useful both to you and to me.

[12] Sending Onesimus back to you makes me very sad. [13] I would like to keep him here with me, where he could take your place in

---

*v10 Onesimus: In Greek this name means "useful".
See also v2: Col 4.17. v10: Col 4.9.

Viewpoints 👁

Discover the 100% practicality of God's kind of love.

Contributed by John Mark C

'My friend, your love has made me happy and has greatly encouraged me. It has also cheered the hearts of God's people.'

Love's important, believe it or not! Love's not just a sentimental, romantic feeling; it's down-to-earth and it serves a purpose.

Let's look at where Paul was when he wrote this to Philemon. In prison, actually, and that's where Philemon's love comes in. In a place designed to make Paul miss out on the joys of life, he didn't lose out – he gained joy and comfort from Philemon's love. Paul doesn't seem surprised though; Philemon's love, Paul writes, had 'so often' had an impact on a practical level on the Christians around him.

We know that love can be the motivation for many great things. And what is talked about here is a perfect example of this: what love did was to 'refresh' (there isn't a better word for it!) Christians in what they were doing, giving them a spurt of energy and encouragement when they most needed it.

But let's not leave the loving and refreshing to just one or two super-sorted Christians. We all need a break at times, we all need someone to fall back on. As Christians, we've got to be there for each other, like Philemon was. It is just the best thing to know that when you're in a tough situation, you've got Christian mates looking out for you. I think we should be able to expect that from Christians around us and of ourselves.

More...

Civil disobedience p.1247
God's love p.958
Serving others p.1190

helping me while I am here in prison for preaching the good news. [14] But I won't do anything unless you agree to it first. I want your act of kindness to come from your heart, and not be something you feel forced to do.

[15] Perhaps Onesimus was taken from you for a little while so that you could have him back for good, [16] but not as a slave. Onesimus is much more than a slave. To me he is a dear friend, but to you he is even more, both as a person and as a follower of the Lord.

[17] If you consider me a friend because of Christ, then welcome Onesimus as you would welcome me. [18] If he has cheated you or owes you anything, charge it to my account. [19] With my own hand I write: I, PAUL, WILL PAY YOU BACK. But don't forget that you owe me your life. [20] My dear friend and follower of Christ our Lord, please cheer me up by doing this for me.

[21] I am sure you will do all I have asked, and even more. [22] Please get a room ready for me. I hope your prayers will be answered, and I can visit you.

Final greetings and a prayer

[23] Epaphras is also here in jail for being a follower of Christ Jesus. He sends his greetings, [24] and so do Mark, Aristarchus, Demas, and Luke, who work together with me.

[25] I pray that the Lord Jesus Christ will be kind to you!

See also **v23: a** Col 1.7; 4.12. **v24: a** Acts 12.12,25; 13.13; 15.37–39; Col 4.10; **b** Acts 19.29; 27.2; Col 4.10; **c** Col 4.14; 2 Tim 4.11; **d** Col 4.14; 2 Tim 4.11.

Additional notes

▸v9 someone: Greek "a messenger" or "an old man".

Hebrews

The letter to the Hebrews

The basics

What's the point? There is no longer anything between us and God: faith in Jesus brings us together.

What happens? The writer does a brief scan of Old Testament history to show that Jesus is the true fulfilment.

What should I remember? 11.1 'Faith makes us sure of what we hope for and gives us proof of what we cannot see.'

More details

Setting the scene Whoever wrote this letter was facing a major issue. The Jewish Christians knew the Scriptures, and may have been Christians for some time, but they were wondering whether they should turn back to Judaism. The Jews, after all, had history and heritage, a magnificent temple, rich worship services and a magnificently robed high price. And what did Christianity have?

What's it all about? We don't know who wrote Hebrews. But we know why he wrote it. He wrote it to persuade Jewish Christians that Christianity is the fulfilment of Judaism.

According to the writer of Hebrews, the Christian faith completes the picture, it finishes the puzzle. The rules and regulations have been superseded, the barriers torn down. The old system has found completion. The old promise or 'testament' has been replaced by the new.

To prove this, the writer fast-forwards through centuries of Jewish history, looking at all the great figures. The prophets, Aaron, Moses, Melchizedek, Abraham, angels, Joshua –

they're all brought into the picture, and they must all bow to their superior – the one true high priest, Jesus Christ.

So he shows how Jesus is the real, true high priest; and he shows how Jesus has made the one true, ultimate sacrifice. By dying for us, by sacrificing himself in our place, he has opened the way home to God.

In the end, the writer argues, it's all about faith. He shows how the great heroes of Jewish history were marked out by their faith. Abraham had the faith to set out on the journey. Noah had faith to build the boat. Even Moses' parents had faith to put him in a basket and bung him out on the river. They couldn't see the end of their journey, but they believed that God would keep his promises.

Faith makes us sure of what we hope for. Faith gives proof of things that we can't see. So we should learn from the faithful people of the past. We should keep our eyes on Jesus as we run the race.

And another thing

The Greek words for 'better' and 'superior' occur fifteen times in this letter. Why do you think that is?

Footsteps

Tempted as we were: 2.5–18
Greater than Moses: 3.1–19
The great high priest: 4.14—5.10
The better agreement: 8.1–13
No more need for sacrifice: 10.1–18
Faith makes us sure: 11.1–40
Keep your eyes on Jesus: 12.1–13

The greatness of God's Son

CHAPTER 1

¹ Long ago in many ways and at many times God's prophets spoke his message to our ancestors. ² But now at last, God sent his Son to bring his message to us. God created the universe by his Son, and everything will some day belong to the Son. ³ God's Son has all the brightness of God's own glory and is like him in every way. By his own mighty word, he holds the universe together.

After the Son had washed away our sins, he sat down at the right side* of the glorious God in heaven. ⁴ He had become much greater than the angels, and the name he was given is far greater than any of theirs.

Jesus is greater than angels

⁵ God has never said
    to any of the angels,
"You are my Son, because today
    I have become your Father!"
Neither has God said
    to any of them,
"I will be his Father,
    and he will be my Son!"

⁶ When God brings his firstborn Son* into the world, he commands all his angels to worship him.
⁷ And when God speaks about the angels, he says,

"I change my angels into wind
and my servants
    into flaming fire."

⁸ But God says about his Son,

"You are God,
and you will rule
    as King for ever!
Your' royal power
    brings about justice.
⁹ You loved justice
    and hated evil,
and so I, your God,
    have chosen you.

I appointed you
and made you happier
    than any of your friends."

¹⁰ The Scriptures also say,

"In the beginning, Lord,
    you were the one
who laid the foundation
    of the earth
    and created the heavens.
¹¹ They will all disappear
    and wear out like clothes,
    but you will last for ever.
¹² You will roll them up
    like a robe
    and change them
    like a garment.
But you are always the same,
    and you will live for ever."

¹³ God never said to any
    of the angels,
"Sit at my right side
    until I make your enemies
    into a footstool for you!"

¹⁴ Angels are merely spirits sent to serve people who are going to be saved.

CHAPTER 2

This great way of being saved

¹ We must give our full attention to what we were told, so that we won't drift away. ² The message spoken by angels proved to be true, and all who disobeyed or rejected it were punished as they deserved. ³ So if we refuse this great way of being saved, how can we hope to escape? The Lord himself was the first to tell about it, and people who heard the message proved to us that it was true. ⁴ God himself showed that his message was true by performing all kinds of powerful miracles and wonders. He also gave his Holy Spirit to anyone he chose to.

The one who leads us to be saved

⁵ We know that God did not put the future world under the power of angels. ⁶ Somewhere in the Scriptures someone says to God,

"What makes you care
    about us humans?
Why are you concerned
    for weaklings such as we?

---

*1.3 **right side:** The place of honour and power.
*1.6 **firstborn Son:** The first son born into a family had certain privileges that the other children did not have. In 12.23 "firstborn" refers to God's special people.

See also: 1.5: a Psa 2.7; b 2 Sam 7.14; 1 Chron 17.13.
1.6: Deut 32.43 (LXX). **1.7:** Psa 104.4 (LXX).
1.8–9: Psa 45.6–7.

See also: 1.10–12: Psa 102.25–27 (LXX). **1.13:** Psa 110.1.
2.6–8: Psa 8.4–6.

⁷ You made us lower
than the angels
for a while.
Yet you have crowned us
with glory and honour.'
⁸ And you have put everything
under our power!"

God has put everything under our power and has not left anything out of our power. But we still don't see it all under our power. ⁹ What we do see is Jesus, who for a little while was made lower than the angels. Because of God's wonderful kindness, Jesus died for everyone. And now that Jesus has suffered and died, he is crowned with glory and honour!

¹⁰ Everything belongs to God, and all things were created by his power. So God did the right thing when he made Jesus perfect by suffering, as Jesus led many of God's children to be saved and to share in his glory. ¹¹ Jesus and the people he makes holy all belong to the same family. That is why he isn't ashamed to call them his brothers and sisters. ¹² He even said to God,

"I will tell them your name
and sing your praises
when they come together
to worship."

¹³ He also said,

"I will trust God."

Then he said,

"Here I am with the children
God has given me."

¹⁴ We are people of flesh and blood. That is why Jesus became one of us. He died to destroy the devil, who had power over death. ¹⁵ But he also died to rescue all of us who live each day in fear of dying. ¹⁶ Jesus clearly did not come to help angels, but he did come to help Abraham's descendants. ¹⁷ He had to be one of us, so that he could serve God as our merciful and faithful high priest and sacrifice himself for the forgiveness of our sins. ¹⁸ And now that Jesus has suffered and was tempted, he can help anyone else who is tempted.

Jesus is greater than Moses and Joshua

CHAPTER 3

¹ My friends, God has chosen you to be his holy people. So think about Jesus, the one we call our apostle and high priest! ² Jesus was faithful to God, who appointed him, just as Moses was faithful in serving all' God's people. ³ But Jesus deserves more honour than Moses, just as the builder of a house deserves more honour than the house. ⁴ Of course, every house is built by someone, and God is really the one who built everything.

⁵ Moses was a faithful servant and told God's people what would be said in the future. ⁶ But Christ is the Son in charge of God's people. And we are those people, if we keep on being brave and don't lose hope.

A rest for God's people

⁷ It is just as the Holy Spirit says,

"If you hear God's voice today,
⁸   don't be stubborn!
Don't rebel like those people
who were tested
in the desert.
⁹⁻¹⁰ For forty years your ancestors
tested God and saw
the things he did.

"Then God got tired of them
and said,
'You people never
show good sense,
and you don't understand
what I want you to do.'
¹¹ God became angry
and told the people,
'You will never enter
my place of rest!' "

¹² My friends, watch out! Don't let evil thoughts or doubts make any of you turn from the living God. ¹³ You must encourage one another each day. And you must keep on while there is still a time that can be called "today". If you don't, then sin may fool some of you and make you stubborn. ¹⁴ We were sure about Christ when we first became his people. So let's hold tightly to our faith until the end. ¹⁵ The Scriptures say,

See also: **2.12:** Psa 22.22. **2.13:** a Isa 8.17 (LXX); b Isa 8.18. **2.16:** Isa 41.8–9.

See also: **3.2:** Num 12.7. **3.7–11:** Psa 95.7–11 (LXX). **3.15:** Psa 95.7–8 (LXX).

"If you hear his voice today,
don't be stubborn
like those who rebelled."

16 Who were those people that heard God's voice and rebelled? Weren't they the same ones that came out of Egypt with Moses? 17 Who were the people that made God angry for forty years? Weren't they the ones that sinned and died in the desert? 18 And who did God say would never enter his place of rest? Weren't they the ones that disobeyed him? 19 We see that those people did not enter the place of rest because they did not have faith.

CHAPTER 4

1 The promise to enter the place of rest is still good, and we must take care that none of you miss out. 2 We have heard the message, just as they did. But they failed to believe what they heard, and the message did not do them any good. 3 Only people who have faith will enter the place of rest. It is just as the Scriptures say,

"God became angry
and told the people,
'You will never enter
my place of rest!' "

God said this, even though everything has been ready from the time of creation. 4 In fact, somewhere the Scriptures say that by the seventh day, God had finished his work, and so he rested. 5 We also read that he later said, "You people will never enter my place of rest!" 6 This means that the promise to enter is still good, because those who first heard about it disobeyed and did not enter. 7 Much later God told David to make the promise again, just as I have already said,

"If you hear his voice today,
don't be stubborn!"

8 If Joshua had really given the people rest, there would not be any need for God to talk about another day of rest. 9 But God has promised us a Sabbath when we will rest, even though it has not yet come. 10 On that day God's people will rest from their work, just as God rested from his work.

11 We should do our best to enter that place of rest, so that none of us will disobey and miss going there, as they did. 12 What God has said isn't only alive and active! It is

See also: 3.16–18: Num 14.1–35.   **4.3:** Psa 95.11.
4.4: Gen 2.2.   **4.5:** Psa 95.11.   **4.7:** Psa 95.7–8 (LXX).
4.8: Deut 31.7; Josh 22.4.   **4.10:** Gen 2.2.

Viewpoints

God knows our secrets and thoughts. So how can we approach him?

Contributed by Naomi C

'So whenever we are in need, we should come bravely before the throne of our merciful God. There we will be treated with undeserved kindness, and we will find help.'

Have you ever seen an official royal event on TV where 'ordinary' people approach the queen or dignitary? When the person comes near they often have to kneel, or maybe bow and show respect. It's a tradition set in place because the monarch used to have absolute power, and if you weren't very careful when meeting them, you could find they would chop your head off! But in this verse we find out that God, although King of Kings, is different from any human ruler.

The thing that makes him so different is his grace. If we're honest, we know that no-one has any right to get close to the Almighty, Holy God because we've all done things wrong, and any drop of sin is unacceptable to God.

But we're told to go boldly to his throne, because God is gracious. We don't tend to hear very much about grace, especially outside the church, but it's an amazing concept. It just means getting good things we don't deserve. So maybe we don't feel like we ought to be in the presence of the Creator of the Universe, but because of the sacrifice of Jesus on the cross, taking the punishment for our sin, and the amazing love God has for us, we can be near to him. So go for it. Approach the throne of God, through prayer or worship, and go boldly!

More...

Grace p.1316
Cross p.1112
Sacrifice p.1368

sharper than any double-edged sword. His word can cut through our spirits and souls and through our joints and marrow, until it discovers the desires and thoughts of our hearts. [13] Nothing is hidden from God! He sees through everything, and we will have to tell him the truth.

Jesus is the great high priest

[14] We have a great high priest, who has gone into heaven, and he is Jesus the Son of God. That is why we must hold on to what we have said about him. [15] Jesus understands every weakness of ours, because he was tempted in every way that we are. But he did not sin! [16] So whenever we are in need, we should come bravely before the throne of our merciful God. There we will be treated with undeserved kindness, and we will find help.

CHAPTER 5

[1] Every high priest is appointed to help others by offering gifts and sacrifices to God because of their sins. [2] A high priest has weaknesses of his own, and he feels sorry for foolish and sinful people. [3] That is why he must offer sacrifices for his own sins and for the sins of others. [4] But no one can have the honour of being a high priest simply by wanting to be one. Only God can choose a priest, and God is the one who chose Aaron.

[5] That is how it was with Christ. He became a high priest, but not just because he wanted the honour of being one. It was God who told him,

> "You are my Son, because today
> I have become your Father!"

[6] In another place, God says,

> "You are a priest for ever
> just like Melchizedek."*

[7] God had the power to save Jesus from death. And while Jesus was on earth, he begged God with loud crying and tears to save him. He truly worshipped God, and God listened to his prayers. [8] Jesus is God's own Son, but still he had to suffer before he could learn what it really means to obey God. [9] Suffering made Jesus perfect, and now he can save for ever all who obey him. [10] This is because God chose him to be a high priest like Melchizedek.

Warning against turning away

[11] Much more could be said about this subject. But it is hard to explain, and all of you are slow to understand. [12] By now you should have been teachers, but once again you need to be taught the simplest things about what God has said. You need milk instead of solid food. [13] People who live on milk are like babies who don't really know what is right. [14] Solid food is for mature people who have been trained to know right from wrong.

CHAPTER 6

[1] We must try to become mature and start thinking about more than just the basic things we were taught about Christ. We shouldn't need to keep talking about why we ought to turn from deeds that bring death and why we ought to have faith in God. [2] And we shouldn't need to keep teaching about baptisms’ or about the laying on of hands* or about people being raised from death and the future judgment. [3] Let's grow up, if God is willing.

[4-6] But what about people who turn away after they have already seen the light and have received the gift from heaven and have shared in the Holy Spirit? What about those who turn away after they have received the good message of God and the powers of the future world? There is no way to bring them back. What they are doing is the same as nailing the Son of God to a cross and insulting him in public!

[7] A field is useful to farmers, if there is enough rain to make good crops grow. In fact, God will bless that field. [8] But land that produces only thorn bushes is worthless. It is likely to fall under God's curse, and in the end it will be set on fire.

---

*5.6 Melchizedek: When Melchizedek is mentioned in the Old Testament, he is described as a priest who lived before Aaron. Nothing is said about his ancestors or his death (see 7.3 and Genesis 14.17–20).

See also: 5.3: Lev 9.7.   5.4: Exod 28.1.   5.5: Psa 2.7.
5.6: Psa 110.4.   5.7: Matt 26.36–46; Mark 14.32–42;
Luke 22.39–46.

---

*6.2 laying on of hands: This was a ceremony in which church leaders and others put their hands on people to show that those people were chosen to do some special kind of work.

See also: 5.12–13: 1 Cor 3.2.   6.8: Gen 3.17–18.

⁹ My friends, we are talking this way. But we are sure that you are doing those really good things that people do when they are being saved. ¹⁰ God is always fair. He will remember how you helped his people in the past and how you are still helping them. You belong to God, and he won't forget the love you have shown his people. ¹¹ We wish that each of you would always be eager to show how strong and lasting your hope really is. ¹² Then you would never be lazy. You would be following the example of those who had faith and were patient until God kept his promise to them.

God's promise is sure

¹³ No one is greater than God. So he made a promise in his own name when he said to Abraham, ¹⁴ "I, the Lord, will bless you with many descendants!" ¹⁵ Then after Abraham had been very patient, he was given what God had promised. ¹⁶ When anyone wants to settle an argument, they make a vow by using the name of someone or something greater than themselves. ¹⁷ So when God wanted to prove for certain that his promise to his people could not be broken, he made a vow. ¹⁸ God cannot tell lies! And so his promises and vows are two things that can never be changed.

We have run to God for safety. Now his promises should greatly encourage us to take hold of the hope that is right in front of us. ¹⁹ This hope is like a firm and steady anchor for our souls. In fact, hope reaches behind the curtain* and into the most holy place. ²⁰ Jesus has gone there ahead of us, and he is our high priest for ever, just like Melchizedek.*

CHAPTER 7

The priestly family of Melchizedek

¹ Melchizedek was both king of Salem and priest of God Most High. He was the one who went out and gave Abraham his blessing, when Abraham returned from killing the kings. ² Then Abraham gave him a tenth of everything he had.

The meaning of the name Melchizedek is "King of Justice". But since Salem means "peace", he is also "King of Peace". ³ We are not told that he had a father or mother or ancestors or beginning or end. He is like the Son of God and will be a priest for ever.*

⁴ Notice how great Melchizedek is! Our famous ancestor Abraham gave him a tenth of what he had taken from his enemies. ⁵ The Law teaches that even Abraham's descendants must give a tenth of what they possess. And they are to give this to their own relatives, who are the descendants of Levi and are priests. ⁶ Although Melchizedek wasn't a descendant of Levi, Abraham gave him a tenth of what he had. Then Melchizedek blessed Abraham, who had been given God's promise. ⁷ Everyone agrees that a person who gives a blessing is greater than the one who receives the blessing.

⁸ Priests are given a tenth of what people earn. But all priests die, except Melchizedek, and the Scriptures teach that he is alive. ⁹ Levi's descendants are now the ones who receive a tenth from people. We could even say that when Abraham gave Melchizedek a tenth, Levi also gave him a tenth. ¹⁰ This is because Levi was born later into the family of Abraham, who gave a tenth to Melchizedek.

¹¹ Even though the Law of Moses says that the priests must be descendants of Levi, those priests cannot make anyone perfect. So there needs to be a priest like Melchizedek, rather than one from the priestly family of Aaron.* ¹² And when the rules for selecting a priest are changed, the Law must also be changed.

¹³ The person we are talking about is our Lord, who came from a tribe that had never had anyone to serve as a priest at the altar. ¹⁴ Everyone knows he came from the tribe of Judah, and Moses never said that priests would come from that tribe.

¹⁵ All this becomes clearer, when someone who is like Melchizedek is appointed to be a priest. ¹⁶ That person wasn't appointed because of his ancestors, but because his life can never end. ¹⁷ The Scriptures say about him,

---

*6.19 behind the curtain: In the tent that was used for worship, a curtain separated the "holy place" from the "most holy place", which only the high priest could enter.
*6.20 Melchizedek: See the note at 5.6.
See also: 6.14: Gen 22.16–17. 6.19: Lev 16.2.
6.20: Psa 110.4. 7.1–2: Gen 14.17–20.

*7.3 will be a priest for ever: See the note at 5.6.
*7.11 descendants of Levi . . . from the priestly family of Aaron: Levi was the ancestor of the tribe from which priests and their helpers (called "Levites") were chosen. Aaron was the first high priest.
See also: 7.5: Num 18.21. 7.17: Psa 110.4.

Big ideas

Sacrifice

Sacrifice was common among ancient religions. The idea of giving an offering to your god was widespread.

Sacrifices, were generally placed on an altar. They were offered as thanksgiving to God, or to honour him, or to make restitution for sins. After the Exodus, the sacrifices were organised into a complex system. Different sacrifices were done at different times, for different purposes.

After Jesus came, sacrifices under the Old Testament system were no longer necessary. He had paid the sacrifice for all of us. And anyway, there was a recognition among people that what God really wanted was not the old ritual, but meaningful sacrifice. Jesus pointed out that meaning was more important than amount. Amos pointed out that the sacrifice that God really wanted was a contrite heart.

Today, we don't have to perform sacrifices, but we do have to have a sacrificial attitude. The fundamental principle of sacrifice is to give something to God. Not our cast-offs, not something that means nothing to us, but something that costs.

That might mean that we have to sacrifice our own desires to follow what God wants. We sacrifice to God to show how much he means to us; to show how thankful we are; to show that he is the one who gives us everything in the first place.

Footsteps

A week with sacrifice

The first sacrifice: Genesis 4.1–16
Israelites bring sacrifices: Numbers 7.1–89
What God really wants: Psalms 50.1–23
Meaningless sacrifice: Hosea 8.11–14
The widow's offering: Mark 12.41–44
Once and for all: Hebrews 7.26–28
Our sacrifice today: Hebrews 13.15–16

More...

Cross p.1112
Redemption p.292

"You are a priest for ever,
   just like Melchizedek."

18 In this way a weak and useless command was put aside, 19 because the Law cannot make anything perfect. At the same time, we are given a much better hope, and it can bring us close to God.

20–21 God himself made a promise when this priest was appointed. But he did not make a promise like this when the other priests were appointed. The promise he made is,

"I, the Lord, promise that you
   will be a priest for ever!
And I will never
   change my mind!"

22 This means that Jesus guarantees us a better agreement with God. 23 There have been a lot of other priests, and all of them have died. 24 But Jesus will never die, and so he will be a priest for ever! 25 He is for ever able to save* the people he leads to God, because he always lives to speak to God for them.

26 Jesus is the high priest we need. He is holy and innocent and faultless, and not at all like us sinners. Jesus is honoured above all beings in heaven, 27 and he is better than any other high priest. Jesus doesn't need to offer sacrifices each day for his own sins and then for the sins of the people. He offered a sacrifice once for all, when he gave himself. 28 The Law appoints priests who have weaknesses. But God's promise, which came later than the Law, appoints his Son. And he is the perfect high priest for ever.

Jesus brings a better agreement

CHAPTER 8

1 What I mean is that we have a high priest who sits at the right side* of God's great throne in heaven. 2 He also serves as the priest in the most holy place* inside the real tent there in heaven. This tent of worship was set up by the Lord, not by humans.

3 Since all priests must offer gifts and sacrifices, Christ also needed to have something to offer. 4 If he were here on

*8.1 right side: See the note at 1.3.
*8.2 most holy place: See the note at 6.19.
See also: 7.21: Psa 110.4.   7.27: Lev 9.7.   8.1: Psa 110.1.

earth, he would not be a priest at all, because here the Law appoints other priests to offer sacrifices. ⁵ But the tent where they serve is just a copy and a shadow of the real one in heaven. Before Moses made the tent, he was told, "Be sure to make it exactly like the pattern you were shown on the mountain!" ⁶ Now Christ has been appointed to serve as a priest in a much better way, and he has given us much assurance of a better agreement.

⁷ If the first agreement with God had been all right, there would not have been any need for another one. ⁸ But the Lord found fault with it and said,

"I tell you the time will come,
  when I will make
  a new agreement
  with the people of Israel
  and the people of Judah.
⁹ It won't be like the agreement
  that I made
  with their ancestors,
  when I took them by the hand
  and led them out of Egypt.
They broke their agreement
  with me,
  and I stopped caring
  about them!

¹⁰ "But now I tell the people
  of Israel —
  this is my new agreement:
  'The time will come
  when I, the Lord,
  will write my laws
  on their minds and hearts.
I will be their God,
  and they will be
  my people.
¹¹ Not one of them
  will have to teach another
  to know me, their Lord.'

"All of them will know me,
  no matter who they are.
¹² I will treat them with kindness,
  even though they are wicked.
  I will forget their sins."

¹³ When the Lord talks about a new agreement, he means that the first one is out of date. And anything that is old and useless will soon disappear.

See also: 8.5: Exod 25.40. 8.8-12: Jer 31.31-34 (LXX).

CHAPTER 9

The tent in heaven

¹ The first promise that was made included rules for worship and a tent for worship here on earth. ² The first part of the tent was called the holy place, and a lampstand, a table, and the sacred loaves of bread were kept there.

³ Behind the curtain was the most holy place. ⁴ The gold altar that was used for burning incense was in this holy place. The gold-covered sacred chest was also there, and inside it were three things. First, there was a gold jar filled with manna.* Then there was Aaron's walking stick that sprouted.* Finally, there were the flat stones with the Ten Commandments written on them. ⁵ On top of the chest were the glorious creatures with wings* opened out above the place of mercy.*

Now isn't the time to go into detail about these things. ⁶ But this is how everything was when the priests went each day into the first part of the tent to do their duties. ⁷ However, only the high priest could go into the second part of the tent, and he went in only once a year. Each time he carried blood to offer for his sins and for any sins that the people had committed without meaning to.

⁸ All this is the Holy Spirit's way of saying that no one could enter the most holy place while the tent was still the place of worship. ⁹ This also has a meaning for today. It shows that we cannot make our consciences clear by offering gifts and sacrifices. ¹⁰ These rules are merely about such things as eating and drinking and ceremonies for washing

---

*9.4 manna: When the people of Israel were wandering through the desert, the Lord provided them with food that could be made into thin wafers. This food was called manna, which in Hebrew means "What is it?"

*9.4 Aaron's walking stick that sprouted: According to Numbers 17.1-11, Aaron's walking stick sprouted and produced almonds to show that the Lord was pleased with him and Moses.

*9.5 glorious creatures with wings: Two of these creatures (called "cherubim" in Hebrew and Greek) with outspread wings were on top of the sacred chest and were symbols of God's throne.

*9.5 place of mercy: The lid of the sacred chest, which was thought to be God's throne on earth.

See also: 9.2: a Exod 26.1-30; b Exod 25.31-40; c Exod 25.23-30. 9.3: Exod 26.31-33. 9.4: a Exod 30.1-6; b Exod 25.10-16; c Exod 16.33; d Num 17.8-10; e Exod 25.16; Deut 10.3-5. 9.5: Exod 25.18-22. 9.6: Num 18.2-6. 9.7: Lev 16.2-34.

ourselves. And rules about physical things will last only until the time comes to change them for something better. [11] Christ came as the high priest of the good things that are now here.* He also went into a much better tent that wasn't made by humans and that doesn't belong to this world. [12] Then Christ went once for all into the most holy place and freed us from sin for ever. He did this by offering his own blood instead of the blood of goats and bulls.

[13] According to the Law of Moses, those people who become unclean are not fit to worship God. Yet they will be considered clean, if they are sprinkled with the blood of goats and bulls and with the ashes of a sacrificed calf. [14] But Christ was sinless, and he offered himself as an eternal and spiritual sacrifice to God. That's why his blood is much more powerful and makes our* consciences clear. Now we can serve the living God and no longer do things that lead to death.

[15] Christ died to rescue those who had sinned and broken the old agreement. Now he brings his chosen ones a new agreement with its guarantee of God's eternal blessings! [16] In fact, making an agreement of this kind is like writing a will. This is because the one who makes the will must die before it is of any use. [17] In other words, a will doesn't go into effect as long as the one who made it is still alive.

[18] Blood was also used* to put the first agreement into effect. [19] Moses told the people all that the Law said they must do. Then he used red wool and a hyssop plant to sprinkle the people and the book of the Law with the blood of bulls and goats* and with water. [20] He told the people, "With this blood God makes his agreement with you."

[21] Moses also sprinkled blood on the tent and on everything else that was used in worship. [22] The Law says that almost everything must be sprinkled with blood, and no sins can be forgiven unless blood is offered.

Jesus' sacrifice is once and for all

[23] These things are only copies of what is in heaven, and so they had to be made holy by these ceremonies. But the real things in heaven must be made holy by something better. [24] This is why Christ did not go into a tent that had been made by humans and was only a copy of the real one. Instead, he went into heaven and is now there with God to help us.

[25] Christ did not have to offer himself many times. He wasn't like a high priest who goes into the most holy place each year to offer the blood of an animal. [26] If he had offered himself every year, he would have suffered many times since the creation of the world. But instead, near the end of time he offered himself once and for all, so that he could be a sacrifice that does away with sin.

[27] We die only once, and then we are judged. [28] So Christ died only once to take away the sins of many people. But when he comes again, it will not be to take away sin. He will come to save everyone who is waiting for him.

CHAPTER 10

[1] The Law of Moses is like a shadow of the good things to come. This shadow isn't the good things themselves, because it cannot free people from sin by the sacrifices that are offered year after year. [2] If there were worshippers who already have their sins washed away and their consciences made clear, there would not be any need to go on offering sacrifices. [3-4] But the blood of bulls and goats cannot take away sins. It only reminds people of their sins from one year to the next.

[5] When Christ came into the world, he said to God,

> "Sacrifices and offerings
>   are not what you want,
> but you have given me
>   my body.
> [6] No, you are not pleased
>   with animal sacrifices
>   and offerings for sin."

[7] Then Christ said,

> "And so, my God,
>   I have come to do
> what you want,
>   as the Scriptures say."

[8] The Law teaches that offerings and sacrifices must be made because of sin. But why did Christ mention these things and say that God did not want them? [9] Well, it was to do away with offerings and sacrifices and to replace

---

See also: 9.13: a Lev 16.15–16; b Num 19.9,17–19. 9.19–20: Exod 24.6–8. 9.21: Lev 8.15. 9.22: Lev 17.11.

See also: 9.28: Isa 53.12. 10.5–7: Psa 40.6–8 (LXX).

them. That is what he meant by saying to God, "I have come to do what you want." ¹⁰ So we are made holy because Christ obeyed God and offered himself once for all.

¹¹ The priests do their work each day, and they keep on offering sacrifices that can never take away sins. ¹² But Christ offered himself as a sacrifice that is good for ever. Now he is sitting at God's right side,* ¹³ and he will stay there until his enemies are put under his power. ¹⁴ By his one sacrifice he has for ever set free from sin the people he brings to God.

¹⁵ The Holy Spirit also speaks of this by telling us that the Lord said,

> ¹⁶ "When the time comes,
>   I will make an agreement
>   with them.
>   I will write my laws
>   on their minds and hearts.
> ¹⁷ Then I will forget
>   about their sins
>   and no longer remember
>   their evil deeds."

¹⁸ When sins are forgiven, there is no more need to offer sacrifices.

Encouragement and warning

¹⁹ My friends, the blood of Jesus gives us courage to enter the most holy place ²⁰ by a new way that leads to life! And this way takes us through the curtain that is Christ himself.

²¹ We have a great high priest who is in charge of God's house. ²² So let's come near God with pure hearts and a confidence that comes from having faith. Let's keep our hearts pure, our consciences free from evil, and our bodies washed with clean water. ²³ We must hold tightly to the hope that we say is ours. After all, we can trust the one who made the agreement with us. ²⁴ We should keep on encouraging each other to be thoughtful and to do helpful things. ²⁵ Some people have got out of the habit of meeting for worship, but we must not do that. We should keep on encouraging each other, especially since you know that the day of the Lord's coming is getting closer.

²⁶ No sacrifices can be made for people who decide to sin after they find out about the truth. ²⁷ They are God's enemies, and all they

---

Being christian

Meeting together

Hebrews 10.21–25

Being Christian is not a solitary pursuit. You need to meet with others.

Churches – which are, essentially, groups of Christians meeting together – come in all kinds of shapes and sizes, from the biggest, most traditional Cathedrals to a group of people just meeting in a house.

It's not so much where you meet, as why you're meeting and what you do. The early Church met together in houses to pray, to share the scriptures and to worship God. The writer of Hebrews lists some of the reasons why Christians should meet together: to worship God, 'to encourage one another and do helpful things.'

It's the same today. Meeting together gives us the chance to learn from each other, to pray together and to support each other in our Christian life. The Christian life can be a difficult journey. It's much easier to keep on walking in faith if there are others walking with you.

You choose which form of church is most helpful for you. No-one says you have to dress up smart and go to church; or even that you have to go and jump about in a warehouse. Don't let others tell you what church should be like; find the way of walking through life that is most helpful for your faith.

Being Christian: Meeting together

• Get together with other Christians. Support and encourage one another.
• If your church is not helping you, look for one which does; don't give up going to church.
• Meet regularly. Pray with each other; worship God together; study the Bible.
• Where you meet isn't important; what you do when you meet is. So make sure that you are focused on God.

---

*10.12 right side: See the note at 1.3.
See also: **10.11:** Exod 29.38. **10.12–13:** Psa 110.1.
10.16: Jer 31.33. **10.17:** Jer 31.34. **10.22:** Lev 8.30; Ezek 36.25. **10.27:** Isa 26.11 (LXX).

can look forward to is a terrible judgment and a furious fire. ²⁸ If two or more witnesses accused someone of breaking the Law of Moses, that person could be put to death. ²⁹ But it is much worse to dishonour God's Son and to disgrace the blood of the promise that made us holy. And it is just as bad to insult the Holy Spirit, who shows us mercy. ³⁰ We know that God has said he will punish and take revenge. We also know that the Scriptures say the Lord will judge his people. ³¹ It is a terrible thing to fall into the hands of the living God!

³² Don't forget all the hard times you went through when you first received the light. ³³ Sometimes you were abused and ill-treated in public, and at other times you shared in the sufferings of others. ³⁴ You were kind to people in jail. And you gladly let your possessions be taken away, because you knew you had something better, something that would last for ever.

³⁵ Keep on being brave! It will bring you great rewards. ³⁶ Learn to be patient, so that you will please God and be given what he has promised. ³⁷ As the Scriptures say,

"God is coming soon!
   It won't be very long.
³⁸ The people God accepts
   will live because
   of their faith.'
   But he isn't pleased
   with anyone
   who turns back."

³⁹ We are not like those people who turn back and get destroyed. We will keep on having faith until we are saved.

Some of God's people who had great faith

CHAPTER 11

¹ Faith makes us sure of what we hope for and gives us proof of what we cannot see. ² It was their faith that made our ancestors pleasing to God.

³ Because of our faith, we know that the world was made at God's command. We also know that what can be seen was made out of what cannot be seen.

⁴ Because Abel had faith, he offered God a better sacrifice than Cain did. God was pleased with him and his gift, and even though Abel is now dead, his faith still speaks for him.

⁵ Enoch had faith and did not die. He pleased God, and God took him up to heaven. That's why his body was never found. ⁶ But without faith no one can please God. We must believe that God is real and that he rewards everyone who searches for him.

⁷ Because Noah had faith, he was warned about something that had not yet happened. He obeyed and built a boat that saved him and his family. In this way the people of the world were judged, and Noah was given the blessings that come to everyone who pleases God.

⁸ Abraham had faith and obeyed God. He was told to go to the land that God had said would be his, and he left for a country he had never seen. ⁹ Because Abraham had faith, he lived as a stranger in the promised land. He lived there in a tent, and so did Isaac and Jacob, who were later given the same promise. ¹⁰ Abraham did this, because he was waiting for the eternal city that God had planned and built.

¹¹ Even when Sarah was too old to have children, she had faith that God would do what he had promised, and she had a son. ¹² Her husband Abraham was almost dead, but he became the ancestor of many people. In fact, there are as many of them as there are stars in the sky or grains of sand along the beach.

¹³ Every one of those people died. But they still had faith, even though they had not received what they had been promised. They were glad just to see these things from far away, and they agreed that they were only strangers and foreigners on this earth. ¹⁴ When people talk this way, it is clear that they are looking for a place to call their own. ¹⁵ If they had been talking about the land where they had once lived, they could have gone back at any time. ¹⁶ But they were looking forward to a better home in heaven. That's why God wasn't ashamed for them to call him their God. He even built a city for them.

¹⁷⁻¹⁸ Abraham had been promised that Isaac, his only son,* would continue his

---

11.17–18 his only son: Although Abraham had a son by a slave woman, his son Isaac was considered his only son, because he was born as a result of God's promise to Abraham.

See also: 11.4: Gen 4.3–10.   11.5: Gen 5.21–24 (LXX). 11.7: Gen 6.13–22.   11.8: Gen 12.1–5.   11.9: Gen 35.27. 11.11: Gen 18.11–14; 21.2.   11.12: Gen 15.5; 22.17; 32.12. 11.13: Gen 23.4; 1 Chron 29.15; Psa 39.12. 11.17–18: Gen 21.12; 22.1–14.

See also: 10.28: Deut 17.6; 19.15.   10.29: Exod 24.8. 10.30: a Deut 32.35; b Deut 32.36. 10.37–38: Hab 2.3–4 (LXX).   11.3: Gen 1.1; Psa 33.6,9; John 1.3.

Big ideas

Faith

Abraham had faith in God. Faith is one of the most important words in the Christian vocabulary, but what does it mean?

In the Old Testament the word 'faith' is only used twice (Deuteronomy 22.20 and Habakkuk 2.4, in case you're interested). But the topic is everywhere and is usually expressed where characters are said to 'trust' or 'believe' in God.

Faith is believing: Psalms 26.1 sums up the idea when David says: 'I have trusted you without doubting.' David trusts in God. To have faith in God means simply to trust that he will do what he says he will do. Not to doubt his promises, but to believe that he will do what he says.

Faith is acting. Abraham did not just trust in God, he acted on that trust. When God asked him to move, he moved.

Faith is demanding. To have faith in God means putting him first. If we believe that his way is best, then it means we reject the other ways. Abraham had such faith in God that he was prepared to sacrifice his most important possession – his son. Even Job, in the midst of all his suffering and questions, still trusts that God is just.

Faith in the Old Testament means believing that God will do what he promised. Faith in the New Testament means believing that God has done what he promised.

The Old Testament is full of God's promises of salvation, his promises that he will rescue his people. But in the New Testament we see those promises fulfilled in the person of Jesus. Faith in the New Testament means believing that God did it: that he sent his son to die for us on the cross.

Faith is factual. Faith is based on facts. It is based on the fact that Jesus died and rose again.

Faith is personal. It's not enough to believe the facts alone. James tells us that even demons believe there is only one God, 'and it makes them shake with fear.' James 2.19. What is important is what the facts mean.

It's the difference between believing that Jesus died on the cross; and believing that he died on the cross for me.

Faith is active. Jesus pointed out that people should be known by the fruits they bear. True faith issues out in actions.

Faith endures. True faith is not a temporary belief. It's a commitment. There will be times when our faith is tested; all Bible characters experienced those tough times. But trusting Jesus means just that: trusting him.

Faith is assisted. Jesus sends the Holy Spirit to help us. His Spirit reminds us that we are God's children, and that we 'will share in the glory of Christ' (Romans 8.16–17)

So when we say 'I have faith in God.' It means more than just a belief in his existence. It means that we believe God exists, that he cares for us, that he has kept his promises and that we live to put that faith into action.

 Footsteps

Five days with Old Testament faith

Abraham's Faith: Genesis 15.1–6
Be patient – trust the Lord: Psalms 37.1–40;
The Lord can be Trusted: Isaiah 26.1–15
Fools trust their strength: Jeremiah 16.5–11
God puts everything right: Micah 7.8–20

 Footsteps

Five days with New Testament faith

Faith brings healing: Matthew 9.18–31
The mountain mover: Matthew 21.18–22
Faith brings eternal life: John 3.16–18
Saved by faith: Romans 4.13–25
Faith and works: James 2.14–26

More...

Trusting in Jesus p.1164
Abraham p.14

family. But when Abraham was tested, he had faith and was willing to sacrifice Isaac, [19] because he was sure that God could raise people to life. This was just like getting Isaac back from death.

[20] Isaac had faith, and he promised blessings to Jacob and Esau. [21] Later, when Jacob was about to die, he leaned on his walking stick and worshipped. Then because of his faith he blessed each of Joseph's sons. [22] And just before Joseph died, he had faith that God would lead the people of Israel out of Egypt. So he told them to take his bones with them.

[23] Because Moses' parents had faith, they kept him hidden until he was three months old. They saw that he was a beautiful child, and they were not afraid to disobey the king's orders.* [24] Then after Moses grew up, his faith made him refuse to be called Pharaoh's* grandson. [25] He chose to be ill-treated with God's people instead of having the good time that sin could bring for a little while. [26] Moses knew that the treasures of Egypt were not as wonderful as what he would receive from suffering for the Messiah,' and he looked forward to his reward.

[27] Because of his faith, Moses left Egypt. Moses had seen the invisible God and wasn't afraid of the king's anger. [28] His faith also made him celebrate Passover. He sprinkled the blood of animals on the doorposts, so that the firstborn sons of the people of Israel would not be killed by the destroying angel.

[29] Because of their faith, the people walked through the Red Sea* on dry land. But when the Egyptians tried to do it, they were drowned.

[30] God's people had faith, and when they had walked around the city of Jericho for seven days, its walls fell down.

[31] Rahab had been a prostitute, but she had faith and welcomed the spies. So she wasn't killed with the people who disobeyed.

[32] What else can I say? There isn't enough time to tell about Gideon, Barak, Samson, Jephthah, David, Samuel, and the prophets. [33] Their faith helped them conquer kingdoms, and because they did right, God made promises to them. They closed the jaws of lions [34] and put out raging fires and escaped from the swords of their enemies. Although they were weak, they were given the strength and power to chase foreign armies away.

[35] Some women received their loved ones back from death. Many of these people were tortured, but they refused to be released. They were sure that they would get a better reward when the dead are raised to life. [36] Others were made fun of and beaten with whips, and some were chained in jail. [37] Still others were stoned to death or sawn in two' or killed with swords. Some had nothing but sheep skins or goat skins to wear. They were poor, ill-treated, and tortured. [38] The world did not deserve these good people, who had to wander in deserts and on mountains and had to live in caves and holes in the ground.

[39] All of them pleased God because of their faith! But still they died without being given what had been promised. [40] This was because God had something better in store for us. And he did not want them to reach the goal of their faith without us.

Follow the example of Jesus

CHAPTER 12

A large crowd of witnesses

[1] Such a large crowd of witnesses is all around us! So we must get rid of everything that slows us down, especially the sin that just won't let go. And we must be determined to run the race that is ahead of us. [2] We must keep our eyes on Jesus, who leads us and makes our faith complete. He endured the

---

*11.23 the king's orders: The king of Egypt ordered all Israelite baby boys to be left outside their homes, so they would die or be killed.
*11.24 Pharaoh: A Hebrew word sometimes used for the title of the king of Egypt.
*11.29 Red Sea: This name comes from the Bible of the early Christians, a translation made into Greek about 200 BC. It refers to the body of water that the Israelites crossed and was one of the marshes or fresh water lakes near the eastern part of the Nile Delta, where they lived and where the towns of Exodus 13.17—14.9 were located.

See also: 11.20: Gen 27.27–29,39–40. 11.21: a Gen 48.1–20; b Gen 47.31 (LXX). 11.22: Gen 50.24–25; Exod 13.19.
11.23: a Exod 2.2; b Exod 1.22. 11.24: Exod 2.10–12.
11.28: Exod 12.21–30. 11.29: Exod 14.21–31.

See also: 11.30: Josh 6.12–21. 11.31: a Josh 6.22–25; b Josh 2.1–21. 11.32: a Judg 6.11—8.32; b Judg 4.6—5.31; c Judg 13.2—16.31; d Judg 11.1—12.7; e 1 Sam 16.1—1 King 2.11; f 1 Sam 1.1—25.1.
11.33: Dan 6.1–27. 11.34: Dan 3.1–30.
11.35: 1 King 17.17–24; 2 King 4.25–37.
11.36: 1 King 22.26–27; 2 Chron 18.25–26; Jer 20.2; 37.15; 38.6. 11.37: 2 Chron 24.21.

shame of being nailed to a cross, because he knew that later on he would be glad he did. Now he is seated at the right side* of God's throne! ³ So keep your mind on Jesus, who put up with many insults from sinners. Then you won't get discouraged and give up.

⁴ None of you have yet been hurt' in your battle against sin. ⁵ But you have forgotten that the Scriptures say to God's children,

"When the Lord punishes you,
    don't make light of it,
    and when he corrects you,
    don't be discouraged.
⁶ The Lord corrects the people
    he loves
    and disciplines those
    he calls his own."

⁷ Be patient when you are being corrected! This is how God treats his children. Don't all parents correct their children? ⁸ God corrects all his children, and if he doesn't correct you, then you don't really belong to him. ⁹ Our earthly fathers correct us, and we still respect them. Isn't it even better to be given true life by letting our spiritual Father correct us?

¹⁰ Our human fathers correct us for a short time, and they do it as they think best. But God corrects us for our own good, because he wants us to be holy, as he is. ¹¹ It is never fun to be corrected. In fact, at the time it is always painful. But if we learn to obey by being corrected, we will do right and live at peace.

¹² Now stand up straight! Stop your knees from shaking ¹³ and walk a straight path. Then lame people will be healed, instead of getting worse.

Warning against turning from God

¹⁴ Try to live at peace with everyone! Live a clean life. If you don't, you will never see the Lord. ¹⁵ Make sure that no one misses out on God's wonderful kindness. Don't let anyone become bitter and cause trouble for the rest of you. ¹⁶ Watch out for immoral and ungodly people like Esau, who sold his future blessing* for only one meal. ¹⁷ You know how he later wanted it back. But there was

nothing he could do to change things, even though he begged his father and cried.

¹⁸ You have not come to a place like Mount Sinai* that can be seen and touched. There is no flaming fire or dark cloud or storm ¹⁹ or trumpet sound. The people of Israel heard a voice speak. But they begged it to stop, ²⁰ because they could not obey its commands. They were even told to kill any animal that touched the mountain. ²¹ The sight was so frightening that Moses said he shook with fear.

²² You have now come to Mount Zion and to the heavenly Jerusalem. This is the city of the living God, where thousands and thousands of angels have come to celebrate. ²³ Here you will find all God's dearest children,* whose names are written in heaven. And you will find God himself, who judges everyone. Here also are the spirits of those good people who have been made perfect. ²⁴ And Jesus is here! He is the one who makes God's new agreement with us, and his sprinkled blood says much better things than the blood of Abel.*

²⁵ Make sure that you obey the one who speaks to you. The people did not escape, when they refused to obey the one who spoke to them at Mount Sinai. Do you think you can possibly escape, if you refuse to obey the one who speaks to you from heaven? ²⁶ When God spoke the first time, his voice shook only the earth. This time he has promised to shake the earth once again, and heaven too.

²⁷ The words "once again" mean that these created things will some day be shaken and removed. Then what cannot be shaken will last. ²⁸ We should be grateful that we were given a kingdom that cannot be shaken. And in this kingdom we please God by worshipping him and by showing him great honour and respect. ²⁹ Our God is like a destructive fire!

---

*12.2 right side: See the note at 1.3.
*12.16 sold his future blessing: As the firstborn son, Esau had certain privileges that were known as a "birthright".

See also: 12.5-6: Job 5.17; Prov 3.11-12 (LXX).
12.12: Isa 35.3 (LXX). 12.13: Prov 4.26 (LXX).
12.15: Deut 29.18 (LXX). 12.16: Gen 25.29-34.
12.17: Gen 27.30-40.

*12.18 a place like Mount Sinai: The Greek text has "a place", but the writer is referring to the time that the Lord spoke to the people of Israel from Mount Sinai (see Exodus 19.16-25).
*12.23 all God's dearest children: The Greek text has "the gathering of the firstborn children". See the note at 1.6.
*12.24 blood of Abel: Cain and Abel were the two sons of Adam and Eve. Cain murdered Abel (see Genesis 4.1-16).

See also: 12.18-19: Exod 19.16-22; 20.18-21; Deut 4.11-12; 5.22-27. 12.20: Exod 19.12-13. 12.21: Deut 9.19.
12.24: Gen 4.10. 12.25: Exod 20.22. 12.26: Hag 2.6 (LXX).
12.29: Deut 4.24.

Viewpoints 👁

How could such an awesome God be interested in us?

Contributed by Noa P

'On this earth we don't have a city that lasts forever, but we are waiting for such a city.'

In trying to live a Christian life it can be easy to fall into the temptation of limiting ourselves to living in side the 'Christian bubble'. This may be because we feel we don't belong, which is fair enough, as this verse points out that we're not at home. We are not supposed to get all cosy here because it's only temporary. The Hebrews are being encouraged to think long term, to look ahead. And that's what we need to do as well. Sometimes we get all caught up in the technicalities of Christian life – to burn incense, or not to burn?

But we have to keep our focus. It's our job while here on earth to let other people have the opportunity to gain eternal life. This is too big a treasure to miss out on, and we have no right to leave others out. For this reason we must befriend people and show them Christ's love. We must not love the things of this world, but we should understand them. So that others can see the light of God through us.

When you want to give up, think about why you are living for Christ in the first place. Your reward is to go home with your Father in heaven. Surely, there can be nothing to look forward to more than that.

More...

Sharing with your friends p.1198
Sharing your faith p.1082
Culture p.779

CHAPTER 13

Service that pleases God

[1] Keep being concerned about each other as the Lord's followers should.

[2] Be sure to welcome strangers into your home. By doing this, some people have welcomed angels as guests, without even knowing it.

[3] Remember the Lord's people who are in jail and be concerned for them. Don't forget those who are suffering, but imagine that you are there with them.

[4] Have respect for marriage. Always be faithful to your partner, because God will punish anyone who is immoral or unfaithful in marriage.

[5] Don't fall in love with money. Be satisfied with what you have. The Lord has promised that he will not leave us or desert us. [6] That should make you feel like saying,

> "The Lord helps me!
> Why should I be afraid
> of what people
> can do to me?"

[7] Don't forget about your leaders who taught you God's message. Remember what kind of lives they lived and try to have faith like theirs.

[8] Jesus Christ never changes! He is the same yesterday, today, and for ever. [9] Don't be fooled by any kind of strange teachings. It is better to receive strength from God's undeserved kindness than to depend on certain foods. After all, these foods don't really help the people who eat them. [10] But we have an altar where even the priests who serve in the place of worship have no right to eat.

[11] After the high priest offers the blood of animals as a sin offering, the bodies of those animals are burnt outside the camp. [12] Jesus himself suffered outside the city gate, so that his blood would make people holy. [13] That's why we should go outside the camp to Jesus and share in his disgrace. [14] On this earth we don't have a city that lasts for ever, but we are waiting for such a city.

[15] Our sacrifice is to keep offering praise to God in the name of Jesus. [16] But don't forget to help others and to share your possessions with them. This too is like offering a sacrifice that pleases God.

See also: 13.2: Gen 18.1–8; 19.1–3.   **13.5:** Deut 31.6,8; Josh 1.5.   **13.6:** Psa 118.6 (LXX).   **13.11:** Lev 16.27.

¹⁷ Obey your leaders and do what they say. They are watching over you, and they must answer to God. So don't make them sad as they do their work. Make them happy. Otherwise, they won't be able to help you at all.

¹⁸ Pray for us. Our consciences are clear, and we always try to live right. ¹⁹ I especially want you to pray that I can visit you again soon.

Final prayers and greetings

²⁰ God gives peace, and he raised our Lord Jesus Christ from death. Now Jesus is like a Great Shepherd whose blood was used to make God's eternal agreement with his flock.* ²¹ I pray that God will make you ready to obey him and that you will always be eager to do right. May Jesus help you do what pleases God. To Jesus Christ be glory for ever and ever! Amen.

²² My friends, I have written only a short letter to encourage you, and I beg you to pay close attention to what I have said.

²³ By now you must know that our friend Timothy is out of jail. If he gets here in time, I will bring him with me when I come to visit you.

²⁴ Please give my greetings to your leaders and to the rest of the Lord's people.

His followers from Italy send you their greetings.

²⁵ I pray that God will be kind to all of you!›

---

*13.20 whose blood was used to make God's eternal agreement with his flock: See 9.18–22.

Additional notes

›1.8 Your: Some manuscripts have "His".
›2.7 and honour: Some manuscripts add "and you have placed us in charge of all you created."
›3.2 all: Some manuscripts do not have this word.
›6.2 baptisms: Or "ceremonies of washing".
›7.25 for ever able to save: Or "able to save for ever".
›9.11 that are now here: Some manuscripts have "that were coming".
›9.14 our: Some manuscripts have "your", and others have "their".
›9.18 Blood was also used: Or "There also had to be a death".
›9.19 blood of bulls and goats: Some manuscripts do not have "and goats".
›10.38 The people God accepts will live because of their faith: Or "The people God accepts because of their faith will live."
›11.26 the Messiah: Or "Christ".

›11.37 sawn in two: Some manuscripts have "tested" or "tempted".
›12.4 hurt: Or "killed".
›13.25 to all of you!: Some manuscripts add "Amen."

James

A letter from James

The basics

What's the point? What we believe is proved through what we do. What's the point of faith if it doesn't change the way we behave?

What happens? James urges Christians to put their faith into action.

What should I remember? 2.14 'My friends, what good is it to say you have faith, when you don't do anything to show that you really do have faith? Can that kind of faith save you?'

More details

Setting the scene James, the brother of Jesus, led the early church in Jerusalem. When people started to ask how the Christian faith should be lived practically, he wrote a letter...

What's it all about? The letter of James is about how we live out our faith. It was aimed at Jewish Christians and reflects a practical Jewish outlook. But it demands attention, whatever our background, as it addresses a crucial question: how should we live?

James challenges the reader to express faith in practical, loving ways. It champions the rights of the poor and criticises snobs and bigots. Actions are not a substitute for faith, but faith must result in practical, loving deeds, or there's something badly wrong with it.

Footsteps

Obey the Lord: 1.19–27
Look after the poor: 2.1–13
Faith and works: 2.14–26
Control your tongue: 3.1–18
Why do you fight? 4.1–5.6

Greetings

CHAPTER 1

¹ *From James, a servant of God and of our Lord Jesus Christ.*

Greetings to the twelve tribes scattered all over the world.*

A life of faith and wisdom

² My friends, be glad, even if you have a lot of trouble. ³ You know that you learn to endure by having your faith tested. ⁴ But you must learn to endure everything, so that you will be completely mature and not lacking in anything.

⁵ If any of you need wisdom, you should ask God, and it will be given to you. God is generous and won't correct you for asking. ⁶ But when you ask for something, you must have faith and not doubt. Anyone who doubts is like an ocean wave tossed around in a storm. ⁷⁻⁸ If you are that kind of person, you can't make up your mind, and you can't be trusted. So don't expect the Lord to give you anything at all.

Poor people and rich people

⁹ Any of God's people who are poor should be glad that he thinks so highly of them. ¹⁰ But

---

*1.1 twelve tribes scattered all over the world: James is saying that the Lord's followers are like the tribes of Israel that were scattered everywhere by their enemies.

See also: 1.1: Matt 13.55; Mark 6.3; Acts 15.13; Gal 1.19. **1.10–11:** Isa 40.6–7 (LXX).

Life files

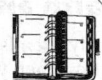

James

Background: Son of Mary, brother of Jesus.

What's the story?

James was the younger brother of Jesus. He became the leader of the church in Jerusalem. He may have become a Christian after Jesus' resurrection, because he is mentioned in the gospels as not believing in Jesus (John 7.2–5) and because Paul says that the Lord appeared to him (1 Corinthians 15.3–8).

Whatever the case, he became the leader of the Jerusalem church and was active in the council. According to early historians he was stoned to death in AD61.

What's the point?

James was the leader of the Jewish Christians, and the letter which he wrote reflects his upbringing, with its emphasis on practical action.

As the leader of the Jewish Christians he had a tricky task in balancing the views of those who believed that Christians should follow Jewish traditions and customs with those like Paul, who believed that Gentile Christians should not be bound by those laws. The respect in which he was held shows that he managed this job well.

More...

Early church p.1212
Faith p.1373
Gentiles p.1232

 Anorak corner

Priests

1. Who was Caiaphas?
2. Where was Eli a Priest?
3. Who was the first High Priest?
4. What tribe did Priests come from?
5. Who was the only Priest allowed into the most holy place?
(Answers on p.1431)

any who are rich should be glad when God makes them humble. Rich people will disappear like wild flowers [11] scorched by the burning heat of the sun. The flowers lose their blossoms, and their beauty is destroyed. That is how the rich will disappear, as they go about their business.

Trials and temptations

[12] God will bless you, if you don't give up when your faith is being tested. He will reward you with a glorious life,* just as he rewards everyone who loves him.

[13] Don't blame God when you are tempted! God cannot be tempted by evil, and he doesn't use evil to tempt others. [14] We are tempted by our own desires that drag us off and trap us. [15] Our desires make us sin, and when sin is finished with us, it leaves us dead.

[16] Don't be fooled, my dear friends. [17] Every good and perfect gift comes down from the Father who created all the lights in the heavens. He is always the same and never makes dark shadows by changing. [18] He wanted us to be his own special people,* and so he sent the true message to give us new birth.

Hearing and obeying God's message

[19] My dear friends, you should be quick to listen and slow to speak or to get angry. [20] If you are angry, you cannot do any of the good things that God wants done. [21] You must stop doing anything immoral or evil. Instead be humble and accept the message that is planted in you to save you.

[22] Obey God's message! Don't fool yourselves by just listening to it. [23] If you hear the message and don't obey it, you are like people who stare at themselves in a mirror [24] and forget what they look like as soon as they leave. [25] But you must never stop looking at the perfect law that sets you free. God will bless you in everything you do, if you listen and obey, and don't just hear and forget.

---

*1.12 a glorious life: The Greek text has "the crown of life". In ancient times an athlete who had won a contest was rewarded with a crown of flowers as a sign of victory.

*1.18 his own special people: The Greek text has "the first of his creatures". The Law of Moses taught that the firstborn of all animals and the first part of the harvest were special and belonged to the Lord.

²⁶ If you think you are being religious, but can't control your tongue, you are fooling yourself, and everything you do is useless. ²⁷ Religion that pleases God the Father must be pure and spotless. You must help needy orphans and widows and not let this world make you evil.

Don't favour the rich and powerful

CHAPTER 2

Warning against having favourites

¹ My friends, if you have faith in our glorious Lord Jesus Christ, you won't treat some people better than others. ² Suppose a rich person wearing fine clothes and a gold ring comes to one of your meetings. And suppose a poor person dressed in worn-out clothes also comes. ³ You must not give the best seat to the one in fine clothes and tell the one who is poor to stand at the side or sit on the floor. ⁴ That is the same as saying that some people are better than others, and you would be acting like a crooked judge.

⁵ My dear friends, pay attention. God has given a lot of faith to the poor people in this world. He has also promised them a share in his kingdom that he will give to everyone who loves him. ⁶ You ill-treat the poor. But isn't it the rich who boss you around and drag you off to court? ⁷ Aren't they the ones who make fun of your Lord?

⁸ You will do well, if you obey the most important law* in the Scriptures. It is the law that commands us to love others as much as we love ourselves. ⁹ But if you treat some people better than others, you have done wrong, and the Scriptures teach that you have sinned.

¹⁰ If you obey every law except one, you are still guilty of breaking them all. ¹¹ The same God who told us to be faithful in marriage also told us not to murder. So even if you are faithful in marriage, but murder someone, you have still broken God's Law.

¹² Speak and act like people who will be judged by the law that sets us free. ¹³ Do this, because on the day of judgment there will be no pity for those who have not had pity on others. But even in judgment, God is merciful!٠

Faith and works

¹⁴ My friends, what good is it to say you have faith, when you don't do anything to show that you really do have faith? Can that kind of faith save you? ¹⁵ If you know someone who doesn't have any clothes or food, ¹⁶ you shouldn't just say, "I hope all goes well for you. I hope you will be warm and have plenty to eat." What good is it to say this, unless you do something to help? ¹⁷ Faith that doesn't lead us to do good deeds is all alone and dead!

¹⁸ Suppose someone disagrees and says, "It is possible to have faith without doing kind deeds."

I would answer, "Prove that you have faith without doing kind deeds, and I will prove that I have faith by doing them." ¹⁹ You believe there is only one God. That's fine. Even demons believe this, and it makes them shake with fear.

²⁰ Does some stupid person want proof that faith without deeds is useless? ²¹ Well, our ancestor Abraham pleased God by putting his son Isaac on the altar to sacrifice him. ²² Now you see how Abraham's faith and deeds worked together. He proved that his faith was real by what he did. ²³ This is what the Scriptures mean by saying, "Abraham had faith in God, and God was pleased with him." That's how Abraham became God's friend.

²⁴ You can now see that we please God by what we do and not only by what we believe. ²⁵ For example, Rahab had been a prostitute. But she pleased God when she welcomed the spies and sent them home by another way.

²⁶ Anyone who doesn't breathe is dead, and faith that doesn't do anything is just as dead!

Wisdom and words

CHAPTER 3

The tongue

¹ My friends, we should not all try to become teachers. In fact, teachers will be judged more strictly than others. ² All of us do many wrong things. But if you can control your tongue, you are mature and able to control your whole body.

³ By putting a bit into the mouth of a horse, we can turn the horse in different directions. ⁴ It takes strong winds to move a

---

*2.8 most important law: The Greek text has "royal law", meaning the one given by the king (that is, God).

See also: 2.8: Lev 19.18. **2.11: a** Exod 20.14; Deut 5.18; **b** Exod 20.13; Deut 5.17.

See also: 2.21: Gen 22.1–14. **2.23: a** Gen 15.6; **b** 2 Chron 20.7; Isa 41.8. **2.25:** Josh 2.1–21.

large sailing ship, but the captain uses only a small rudder to make it go in any direction. [5] Our tongues are small too, and yet they boast about big things.

It takes only a spark to start a forest fire! [6] The tongue is like a spark. It is an evil power that dirties the rest of the body and sets a person's entire life on fire with flames that come from hell itself. [7] All kinds of animals, birds, reptiles, and sea creatures can be tamed and have been tamed. [8] But our tongues get out of control. They are restless and evil, and always spreading deadly poison.

[9-10] My dear friends, with our tongues we speak both praises and curses. We praise our Lord and Father, and we curse people who were created to be like God, and this isn't right. [11] Can clean water and dirty water both flow from the same spring? [12] Can a fig tree produce olives or a grapevine produce figs? Does fresh water come from a well full of salt water?

Wisdom from above

[13] Are any of you wise or sensible? Then show it by living right and by being humble and wise in everything you do. [14] But if your heart is full of bitter jealousy and selfishness, don't boast or lie to cover up the truth. [15] That kind of wisdom doesn't come from above. It is earthly and selfish and comes from the devil himself. [16] Whenever people are jealous or selfish, they cause trouble and do all sorts of cruel things. [17] But the wisdom that comes from above leads us to be pure, friendly, gentle, sensible, kind, helpful, genuine, and sincere. [18] When peacemakers plant seeds of peace, they will harvest justice.

Warning against friendship with the world

CHAPTER 4

[1] Why do you fight and argue with each other? Isn't it because you are full of selfish desires that fight to control your body? [2] You want something you don't have, and you will do anything to get it. You will even kill! But you still cannot get what you want, and you won't get it by fighting and arguing. You should pray for it. [3] Yet even when you do pray, your prayers are not answered, because you pray just for selfish reasons.

[4] You people aren't faithful to God! Don't you know that if you love the world, you are

See also: 3.9: Gen 1.26.

Helpline

Help! They're really annoying me

'I don't know what it is about him, but I just can't stand him! And she winds me up so much! I try to be patient, but they're just so irritating!'

The Bible is pretty honest about quarrels. It doesn't try to pretend that we all get along all the time. 'Why do you fight and argue with each other?' James asks. 'You want something you don't have, and you will do anything to get it.' (James 4.1–2)

Are we annoyed because we can't get what we want? Am I asking someone for something I have no right to expect? Am I annoyed because they don't agree with me? Like the Bible says, take the lump of wood out of your own eyes first.

Or maybe it's just a clash of personalities. Sometimes we just find people, well, annoying. It's nothing they can help, it's nothing we can help. It's just the way they are and the way we are. Even so, the Bible calls us to live in peace with each other. We are called to be patient and kind and long-suffering. Whether we like it or not.

Three things

Cause

Look at the cause of the annoyance. Is it you or the other person? Are you being reasonable, or unreasonable?

Honesty

Be honest about the situation. If it's a clash of personalities, try to bear it with patience. If possible get some time on your own away from the source of annoyance.

Resolve

Pray for an opportunity to resolve the issue. Don't speak out in anger. Pray for patience and wisdom and for the right words to say, at the right time.

More...

Forgiving others p.1162

God's enemies? And if you decide to be a friend of the world, you make yourself an enemy of God. 5 Do you doubt the Scriptures that say, "God truly cares about the Spirit he has put in us"? 6 In fact, God treats us with even greater kindness, just as the Scriptures say,

> "God opposes everyone
>   who is proud,
> but he is kind to everyone
>   who is humble."

7 Surrender to God! Resist the devil, and he will run from you. 8 Come near to God, and he will come near to you. Clean up your lives, you sinners. Purify your hearts, you people who can't make up your mind. 9 Be sad and sorry and weep. Stop laughing and start crying. Be gloomy instead of glad. 10 Be humble in the Lord's presence, and he will honour you.

Saying cruel things about others

11 My friends, don't say cruel things about others! If you do, or if you condemn others, you are condemning God's Law. And if you condemn the Law, you put yourself above the Law and refuse to obey either it 12 or God who gave it. God is our judge, and he can save or destroy us. What right do you have to condemn anyone?

Warning against boasting

13 You should know better than to say, "Today or tomorrow we will go to the city. We will do business there for a year and make a lot of money!" 14 What do you know about tomorrow? How can you be so sure about your life? It is nothing more than mist that appears for only a little while before it disappears. 15 You should say, "If the Lord lets us live, we will do these things." 16 Yet you are stupid enough to boast, and it is wrong to be so proud. 17 If you don't do what you know is right, you have sinned.

CHAPTER 5

Warning to the rich

1 You rich people should cry and weep! Terrible things are going to happen to you. 2 Your treasures have already rotted, and moths have eaten your clothes. 3 Your money has rusted, and the rust will be evidence

against you, as it burns your body like fire. Yet you keep on storing up wealth in these last days. 4 You refused to pay the people who worked in your fields, and now their unpaid wages are shouting out against you. The Lord All-Powerful has heard the cries of the workers who harvested your crops.

5 While here on earth, you have thought only of filling your own stomachs and having a good time. But now you are like fat cattle on their way to be butchered. 6 You have condemned and murdered innocent people, who couldn't even fight back.

Patience, kindness, and prayer

7 My friends, be patient until the Lord returns. Think of farmers who wait patiently for the spring and summer rains to make their valuable crops grow. 8 Be patient like those farmers and don't give up. The Lord will soon be here! 9 Don't grumble about each other or you will be judged, and the judge is just outside the door.

10 My friends, follow the example of the prophets who spoke for the Lord. They were patient, even when they had to suffer. 11 In fact, we praise the ones who endured the most. You remember how patient Job was and how the Lord finally helped him. The Lord did this because he is so merciful and kind.

12 My friends, above all else, don't take an oath. You must not swear by heaven or by earth or by anything else. "Yes" or "No" is all you need to say. If you say anything more, you will be condemned.

13 If you are having trouble, you should pray. And if you are feeling good, you should sing praises. 14 If you are sick, ask the church leaders' to come and pray for you. Ask them to put olive oil* on you in the name of the Lord. 15 If you have faith when you pray for sick people, they will get well. The Lord will heal them, and if they have sinned, he will forgive them.

16 If you have sinned, you should tell each other what you have done. Then you can pray for one another and be healed. The prayer of an innocent person is powerful, and it can help a lot. 17 Elijah was just as human

*5.14 olive oil: The Jewish people used olive oil for healing.

See also: 5.4: Deut 24.14–15. 5.11: a Job 1.21–22; 2.10; b Psa 103.8. 5.12: Matt 5.34–37. 5.14: Mark 6.13. 5.17: 1 King 17.1; 18.1.

See also: 4.6: Prov 3.34 (LXX). 4.13–14: Prov 27.1. 5.2–3: Matt 6.19.

1382

as we are, and for three and a half years his
prayers kept the rain from falling. [18] But
when he did pray for rain, it fell from the
skies and made the crops grow.

[19] My friends, if any followers have
wandered away from the truth, you should try
to lead them back. [20] If you turn sinners from
the wrong way, you will save them from
death, and many of their sins will be forgiven.

See also: **5.18:** 1 King 18.42–45.   **5.20:** Prov 10.12;
1 Pet 4.8.

Additional notes

ˈ**2.13 But even in judgment, God is merciful!:** Or
"So be merciful, and you will be shown mercy on the
day of judgment."

ˈ**4.5 God truly cares about the Spirit he has put in
us:** One possible meaning for the difficult Greek text;
other translations are possible, such as, "the Spirit
that God put in us truly cares."

ˈ**5.14 church leaders:** Or "elders" or "presbyters" or
"priests".

1 Peter

Peter's first letter

The basics

What's the point? Bad times will come, but God is always faithful.

What happens? Peter writes to encourage those who are suffering.

What should I remember? 2.9 'But you are God's chosen and special people. You are a group of royal priests and a holy nation. God has brought you out of darkness into his marvellous light. Now you must tell all the wonderful things that he has done.'

More details

Setting the scene The church is suffering. Christians are being persecuted because of their faith. So Peter writes to them, to encourage them to hold on...

What's it all about? It was tough being a Christian in Peter's day. Choose to follow Jesus and you were very often ostracised, mocked, or expelled from your family or work. In many cases Christians were killed. In the face of this suffering, Peter is realistic. Suffering comes with the territory; it is part and parcel of being a Christian. 'It's going to happen to you.' says Peter 'The question is, how will you respond?'

Peter's view is that our suffering is a prelude to glory. Peter urges his readers not to lose faith, but to remember that they are a special, holy people.

You may not be facing much persecution for your faith, but even today there are many societies where to be a Christian is to face danger and isolation. Peter argues that Christians are going to go through some tough testing, but it will bring rewards on the day

when Christ returns. In the meantime, they are called to love one another, and to use their God-given gifts wisely.

And another thing

There's some stuff here about husbands and wives and how women should dress that can seem pretty sexist today. But the encouragement to 'Be beautiful in your heart' rather than focussing on outward show isn't outdated in our appearance-oriented culture – what's changed, though, is that these days there are plenty of men too who spend far too long in front of the mirror, shopping for expensive clothes or getting their hair done!

Footsteps

Hope: 1.1–12
Living as God's people: 1.13—2.17
Don't be surprised: 3.12–19

Greetings and prayer

CHAPTER 1

¹ *From Peter, an apostle of Jesus Christ.*
    To God's people who are scattered like foreigners in Pontus, Galatia, Cappadocia, Asia, and Bithynia.
    ² God the Father decided to choose you as his people, and his Spirit has made you holy.

Big ideas

Holiness

'Holy' means 'set apart'. God is holy because he is set apart from the world and from sinful humanity. His holiness lies in the fact that he is absolutely, completely perfect.

For us, however, holiness means more than just being separated, it means being set apart for God. So, in the Old Testament you could have holy places which were specially set aside for worshipping God. You could even have holy time; the Sabbath, for example, was a day set apart and dedicated to God.

Or you could have holy people. Israel was supposed to be a holy nation; set apart from the rest of the people on earth, totally dedicated to God.

Christians are called to be holy. That doesn't mean being all pompous and sniffy about the world and the people around us. There's a difference between being righteous and being self-righteous. Just because you're holy, doesn't mean you have to be 'holier-than-thou'.

We have been set aside for God, to be used by him. Our values and our behaviour must be radically different to the world around us. We have been chosen by God to be different; to follow a different set of values, to obey God's rules, to put our faith in him. We are called to pursue purity. We are called, in fact, to be holy.

Footsteps

Ten days with holiness

A holy nation: Exodus 19.1–8
The holy Sabbath: Exodus 31.12–17
Be holy like I'm holy: Leviticus 19.1–3
How to be holy: Psalms 15.1–5
Who compares to God?: Isaiah 40.25–31
Not merely human: Hosea 11.8–11
Holy slaves: Romans 6.17–23
Chosen for holiness: 1 Corinthians 1.26–31
Made holy to do good: 2 Timothy 2.20–21
Live a holy life: 1 Peter 1.13–25

More...

Sabbath p.97
Living truthfully p.1070

You have obeyed Jesus Christ and are sprinkled with his blood.*

I pray that God will be kind to you and will keep on giving you peace!

A real reason for hope

³ Praise God, the Father of our Lord Jesus Christ. God is so good, and by raising Jesus from death, he has given us new life and a hope that lives on. ⁴ God has something stored up for you in heaven, where it will never decay or be ruined or disappear.

⁵ You have faith in God, whose power will protect you until the last day.* Then he will save you, just as he has always planned to do. ⁶ On that day you will be glad, even if you have to go through many hard trials for a while. ⁷ Your faith will be like gold that has been tested in a fire. And these trials will prove that your faith is worth much more than gold that can be destroyed. They will show that you will be given praise and honour and glory when Jesus Christ returns.

⁸ You have never seen Jesus, and you don't see him now. But still you love him and have faith in him, and no words can tell how glad and happy ⁹ you are to be saved. That's why you have faith.

¹⁰ Some prophets told how kind God would be to you, and they searched hard to find out more about the way you would be saved. ¹¹ The Spirit of Christ was in them and was telling them how Christ would suffer and would then be given great honour. So they searched to find out exactly who Christ would be and when this would happen. ¹² But they were told that they were serving you and not themselves. They preached to you by the power of the Holy Spirit, who was sent from heaven. And their message was only for you, even though angels would like to know more about it.

Living as God's holy people

¹³ Be alert and think straight. Put all your hope in how kind God will be to you when Jesus Christ appears. ¹⁴ Behave like obedient children. Don't let your lives be controlled by

---

*1.2 sprinkled with his blood: According to Exodus 24.3–8 the people of Israel were sprinkled with the blood of cows to show they would keep their agreement with God. Peter says that it is the blood of Jesus that seals the agreement between God and his people. See Hebrews 9.18–21.

*1.5 the last day: When God will judge all people.

your desires, as they used to be. ¹⁵ Always live as God's holy people should, because God is the one who chose you, and he is holy. ¹⁶ That's why the Scriptures say, "I am the holy God, and you must be holy too."

¹⁷ You say that God is your Father, but God doesn't have favourites! He judges all people by what they do. So you must honour God while you live as strangers here on earth. ¹⁸ You were rescued* from the useless way of life that you learnt from your ancestors. But you know that you were not rescued by such things as silver or gold that don't last for ever. ¹⁹ You were rescued by the precious blood of Christ, that spotless and innocent lamb. ²⁰ Christ was chosen even before the world was created, but because of you, he did not come until these last days. ²¹ And when he did come, it was to lead you to have faith in God, who raised him from death and honoured him in a glorious way. That's why you have put your faith and hope in God.

²² You obeyed the truth,' and your souls were made pure. Now you sincerely love each other. But you must keep on loving with all your heart. ²³ Do this because God has given you new birth by his message that lives on for ever. ²⁴ The Scriptures say,

"Humans wither like grass,
and their glory fades
    like wild flowers.
Grass dries up,
and flowers fall
    to the ground.
²⁵ But what the Lord has said
    will stand for ever."

Our good news to you is what the Lord has said.

CHAPTER 2

A living stone and a holy nation

¹ Stop being hateful! Stop trying to fool people, and start being sincere. Don't be jealous or say cruel things about others. ² Be like newborn babies who are thirsty for the pure spiritual milk that will help you grow and be saved. ³ You have already found out how good the Lord really is.

⁴ Come to Jesus Christ. He is the living stone that people have rejected, but which God has chosen and highly honoured. ⁵ And now you are living stones that are being used to build a spiritual house. You are also a group of holy priests, and with the help of Jesus Christ you will offer sacrifices that please God. ⁶ It is just as God says in the Scriptures,

"Look! I am placing in Zion
a choice and precious
    cornerstone.
No one who has faith
in that one
    will be disappointed."

⁷ You are followers of the Lord, and that stone is precious to you. But it isn't precious to those who refuse to follow him. They are the builders who tossed aside the stone that turned out to be the most important one of all. ⁸ They disobeyed the message and stumbled and fell over that stone, because they were doomed.

⁹ But you are God's chosen and special people. You are a group of royal priests and a holy nation. God has brought you out of darkness into his marvellous light. Now you must tell all the wonderful things that he has done. The Scriptures say,

¹⁰ "Once you were nobody.
    Now you are God's people.
At one time no one
    had pity on you.
Now God has treated you
    with kindness."

Live as God's servants should

¹¹ Dear friends, you are foreigners and strangers on this earth. So I beg you not to surrender to those desires that fight against you. ¹² Always let others see you behaving properly, even though they may still accuse you of doing wrong. Then on the day of judgment, they will honour God by telling the good things they saw you do.

¹³ The Lord wants you to obey all human authorities, especially the Emperor, who rules over everyone. ¹⁴ You must also obey governors, because they are sent by the Emperor to punish criminals and to praise good citizens. ¹⁵ God wants you to silence stupid and ignorant people by doing right.

---

*1.18 rescued: The Greek word often, though not always, means payment of a price to free a slave or prisoner.
See also: 1.16: Lev 11.44–45; 19.2.
1.24–25: Isa 40.6–8 (LXX). 2.3: Psa 34.8.

See also: 2.6: Isa 28.16 (LXX). 2.7: Psa 118.22.
2.8: Isa 8.14–15. 2.9: a Exod 19.5,6; Isa 43.20 (LXX);
b Exod 19.5; Deut 4.20; 7.6; 14.2; Titus 2.14; c Isa 43.21;
d Isa 9.2. 2.10: Hos 2.23.

Viewpoints 👁

Surprise! God sees you as a super-holy Priest...

Contributed by Esther S

'And now you are living stones that are being used to build a spiritual house. You are also a group of holy priests, and with the help of Jesus Christ you will offer sacrifices that please God.'

The first thing I felt when I read this verse was the encouragement of knowing that whether we're aware of it or not, God is building our lives into part of his amazing plan for the world he created. But I didn't get the full impact of the verse until I'd read the previous verse as well: 'Come to Jesus Christ. He is the living stone that people have rejected, but which God has chosen and highly honoured.'

Jesus is at the foundation of everything we believe. In the same way that God chose Jesus to reflect Him, we are also precious and chosen to be the dwelling place of God!

And as if that's not enough to blow your mind totally, God has also called us to be his holy priests – holy meaning 'pure; set apart for the service of God'. As well as being incredibly uplifting, this is an awesome responsibility. The Old Testament priests were chosen to reflect the holiness and purity of God, to intercede for man before God, and to represent God to those around them. As Christians we are given these same responsibilities – to be permanently inhabited by God, and to keep ourselves pure and set apart so he can be seen in us. It's a potentially life-changing challenge....

More...

Priests p.117
Holiness p.1386

---

16 You are free, but still you are God's servants, and you must not use your freedom as an excuse for doing wrong. 17 Respect everyone and show special love for God's people. Honour God and respect the Emperor.

The example of Christ's suffering

18 Servants, you must obey your masters and always show respect to them. Do this, not only to those who are kind and thoughtful, but also to those who are cruel. 19 God will bless you, even if others treat you unfairly for being loyal to him. 20 You don't gain anything by being punished for some wrong you have done. But God will bless you, if you have to suffer for doing something good.
21 After all, God chose you to suffer as you follow in the footsteps of Christ, who set an example by suffering for you.

> 22 Christ did not sin
> or ever tell a lie.
> 23 Although he was abused,
> he never tried to get even.
> And when he suffered,
> he made no threats.
> Instead, he had faith in God,
> who judges fairly.
> 24 Christ carried the burden
> of our sins.
> He was nailed to the cross,
> so that we would stop sinning
> and start living right.
> By his cuts and bruises
> you are healed.
> 25 You had wandered away
> like sheep.
> Now you have returned
> to the one
> who is your shepherd
> and protector.

Being a Christian and suffering

CHAPTER 3

Wives and husbands

1 If you are a wife, you must put your husband first. Even if he opposes our message, you will win him over by what you do. No one else

---

See also: 2.22: Isa 53.9. **2.23:** Isa 53.7.
2.24–25: Isa 53.5–6 (LXX). **3.1:** Eph 5.22; Col 3.18.

will have to say anything to him, ² because he will see how you honour God and live a pure life. ³ Don't depend on things like fancy hair styles or gold jewellery or expensive clothes to make you look beautiful. ⁴ Be beautiful in your heart by being gentle and quiet. This kind of beauty will last, and God considers it very special.

⁵ Long ago those women who worshipped God and put their hope in him made themselves beautiful by putting their husbands first. ⁶ For example, Sarah obeyed Abraham and called him her master. You are her true children, if you do right and don't let anything frighten you.

⁷ If you are a husband, you should be thoughtful of your wife. Treat her with honour, because she isn't as strong as you are, and she shares with you in the gift of life. Then nothing will stand in the way of your prayers.

Suffering for doing right

⁸ Finally, all of you should agree and have concern and love for each other. You should also be kind and humble. ⁹ Don't be hateful and insult people just because they are hateful and insult you. Instead, treat everyone with kindness. You are God's chosen ones, and he will bless you. The Scriptures say,

¹⁰ "Do you really love life?
    Do you want to be happy?
   Then stop saying cruel things
    and stop telling lies.
¹¹ Give up your evil ways
    and do right,
   as you find and follow
    the road that leads
     to peace.
¹² The Lord watches over
    everyone who obeys him,
   and he listens
    to their prayers.
   But he opposes everyone
    who does evil."

¹³ Can anyone really harm you for being eager to do good deeds? ¹⁴ Even if you have to suffer for doing good things, God will bless you. So stop being afraid and don't worry about what people might do. ¹⁵ Honour Christ and let him be the Lord of your life.

Always be ready to give an answer when someone asks you about your hope. ¹⁶ Give a kind and respectful answer and keep your conscience clear. This way you will make people ashamed for saying bad things about your good conduct as a follower of Christ. ¹⁷ You are better off to obey God and suffer for doing right than to suffer for doing wrong.

¹⁸ Christ died once for our sins.
   An innocent person died
    for those who are guilty.
   Christ did this
    to bring you to God,
   when his body
    was put to death
   and his spirit
    was made alive.

¹⁹ Christ then preached to the spirits that were being kept in prison. ²⁰ They had disobeyed God while Noah was building the boat, but God had been patient with them. Eight people went into that boat and were brought safely through the flood.

²¹ Those flood waters were like baptism that now saves you. But baptism is more than just washing your body. It means turning to God with a clear conscience, because Jesus Christ was raised from death. ²² Christ is now in heaven, where he sits at the right side* of God. All angels, authorities, and powers are under his control.

CHAPTER 4

Being faithful to God

¹ Christ suffered here on earth. Now you must be ready to suffer as he did, because suffering shows that you have stopped sinning. ² It means you have turned from your own desires and want to obey God for the rest of your life. ³ You have already lived long enough like people who don't know God. You were immoral and followed your evil desires. You went around drinking and feasting and carrying on. In fact, you even worshipped disgusting idols. ⁴ Now your former friends wonder why you have stopped running around with them, and they curse you for it. ⁵ But they will have to answer to God, who judges the living and the dead. ⁶ The good news has even been

See also: 3.3: 1 Tim 2.9. **3.6:** Gen 18.12. **3.7:** Eph 5.25; Col 3.19. **3.10–12:** Psa 34.12–16 (LXX). **3.14:** Matt 5.10. **3.14–15:** Isa 8.12–13.

*3.22 right side: The place of honour and power.
See also: 3.20: Gen 6.1–7.24.

preached to the dead,* so that after they have been judged for what they have done in this life, their spirits will live with God.

⁷ Everything will soon come to an end. So be serious and be sensible enough to pray.

⁸ Most important of all, you must sincerely love each other, because love wipes away many sins.

⁹ Welcome people into your home and don't grumble about it.

¹⁰ Each of you has been blessed with one of God's many wonderful gifts to be used in the service of others. So use your gift well. ¹¹ If you have the gift of speaking, preach God's message. If you have the gift of helping others, do it with the strength that God supplies. Everything should be done in a way that will bring honour to God because of Jesus Christ, who is glorious and powerful for ever. Amen.

Suffering for being a Christian

¹² Dear friends, don't be surprised or shocked that you are going through testing that is like walking through fire. ¹³ Be glad for the chance to suffer as Christ suffered. It will prepare you for even greater happiness when he makes his glorious return.

¹⁴ Count it a blessing when you suffer for being a Christian. This shows that God's glorious Spirit is with you. ¹⁵ But you deserve to suffer if you are a murderer, a thief, a criminal, or a busybody. ¹⁶ Don't be ashamed to suffer for being a Christian. Praise God that you belong to him. ¹⁷ God has already begun judging his own people. And if his judgment begins with us, imagine how terrible it will be for those who refuse to obey his message. The Scriptures say,

¹⁸ "If good people barely escape,
    what will happen to sinners
and to others
    who don't respect God?"

¹⁹ If you suffer for obeying God, you must have complete faith in your faithful Creator and keep on doing right.

Advice for church leaders

CHAPTER 5

Helping Christian leaders

¹ Church leaders,' I am writing to encourage you. I too am a leader, as well as a witness to Christ's suffering, and I will share in his glory when it is shown to us.

² Just as shepherds watch over their sheep, you must watch over everyone God has placed in your care. Do it willingly in order to please God, and not simply because you think you must. Let it be something you want to do, instead of something you do merely to make money. ³ Don't be bossy to those people who are in your care, but set an example for them. ⁴ Then when Christ the Chief Shepherd returns, you will be given a crown that will never lose its glory.

⁵ All you young people should obey your elders. In fact, everyone should be humble towards everyone else. The Scriptures say,

"God opposes proud people,
    but he helps everyone
    who is humble."

⁶ Be humble in the presence of God's mighty power, and he will honour you when the time comes. ⁷ God cares for you, so turn all your worries over to him.

⁸ Be on your guard and stay awake. Your enemy, the devil, is like a roaring lion, prowling around to find someone to attack. ⁹ But you must resist the devil and stay strong in your faith. You know that all over the world the Lord's followers are suffering just as you are. ¹⁰ But God shows undeserved kindness to everyone. That's why he appointed Christ Jesus to choose you to share in his eternal glory. You will suffer for a while, but God will make you complete, steady, strong, and firm. ¹¹ God will be in control for ever! Amen.

Final greetings

¹² Silvanus helped me write this short letter, and I consider him a faithful follower of the Lord. I wanted to encourage you and tell you how kind God really is, so that you will keep on having faith in him.

---

*4.6 the dead: Either people who died after becoming followers of Christ or the people of Noah's day (see 3.19).
See also: 4.8: Prov 10.12. 4.18: Prov 11.31 (LXX).

See also: 5.2: John 21.15–17. 5.5: Prov 3.34 (LXX).
5.6: Matt 23.12; Luke 14.11; 18.14. 5.12: Acts 15.22,40.

Being christian

Coping with suffering

Some people would like to believe that becoming a Christian makes everything right; that when you give your life to Jesus, 'all your troubles fade away.'

Not so. Being Christian solves a lot of things – the really important things. It puts you right with God, it gives you eternal life, it brings you into a relationship with Jesus.

But it doesn't insulate you from the world. It doesn't make all your problems magically disappear. It's not some kind of magic spell that makes everything in your life smooth and comfy. And it certainly doesn't mean you're going to be rich and healthy all your life – and anyone who claims that it does mean that is either a liar or a fool.

For one thing, many great Christians have suffered. Paul and Peter were probably executed for their faith. James the disciple was beheaded. Stephen was stoned to death. The early Church had to endure terrible suffering and persecution from those who were opposed to God's message. Throughout history, Christians have suffered. Even Jesus suffered.

No, being Christian is not about escaping suffering. It's about how you respond to it. Do you give up your faith and hope? Do you give into despair? Or do you trust in the love of God, believing that he will bring you through and that, whatever happens on this earth, one day you will be together?

Being Christian: Facing suffering

• Pray. Get together with others and pray about the situation you're facing.
• Trust in God. Believe that he is still there with you, still holding your hand.
• Persevere. Don't give up. Keep on with the race. Talk to others – they'll help you through these tough times.

---

13 Greetings from the Lord's followers in Babylon.* They are God's chosen ones.

Mark, who is like a son to me, sends his greetings too.

14 Give each other a warm greeting. I pray that God will give peace to everyone who belongs to Christ.﹜

*5.13 Babylon: This may be a secret name for the city of Rome.

See also: 5.13: Acts 12.12,25; 13.13; 15.37–39; Col 4.10; Phlm 24.

Additional notes

﹜1.22 You obeyed the truth: Some manuscripts add "by the power of the Spirit".
﹜5.1 Church leaders: Or "Elders" or "Presbyters" or "Priests".
﹜5.14 Christ: Some manuscripts add "Amen."

2 Peter

Peter's second letter

The basics

What's the point? We know what we should do; now we should get on and do it.

What happens? Christians are encouraged to live lives that please God.

What should I remember? 1.3 'We have everything we need to live a life that pleases God. It was all given to us by God's own power, when we learnt that he had invited us to share in his wonderful goodness.'

More details

Setting the scene False teachers and prophets are trying to lead Christians away from the truth. This letter reminds them to stick to their faith...

What's it all about? 2 Peter is a letter about how Christians should live. At a time when false teachers were corrupting the true message of God, the letter urges Christians to stick to their task. Keep to the real faith and put it into practice; look for understanding, self-control and patience, and wrap everything in love.

And another thing

The author of this letter finds Paul's letters hard to understand (3.15–16). So don't worry if you find them difficult to follow. You're not the only one...

Footsteps

Greetings and prayer

CHAPTER 1

¹ *From Simon Peter, a servant and an apostle of Jesus Christ.*

To everyone who shares with us in the privilege of believing that our God and Saviour Jesus Christ will do what is just and fair.'

² I pray that God will be kind to you and will let you live in perfect peace! May you keep learning more and more about God and our Lord Jesus.

How the Lord's followers should live

³ We have everything we need to live a life that pleases God. It was all given to us by God's own power, when we learnt that he had invited us to share in his wonderful goodness. ⁴ God made great and marvellous promises, so that his nature would become part of us. Then we could escape our evil desires and the corrupt influences of this world.

⁵ Do your best to improve your faith. You can do this by adding goodness, understanding, ⁶ self-control, patience, devotion to God, ⁷ concern for others, and love. ⁸ If you keep growing in this way, it will show that what you know about our Lord Jesus Christ has made your lives useful and meaningful. ⁹ But if you don't grow, you are like someone who is nearsighted or blind, and you have forgotten that your past sins are forgiven.

¹⁰ My friends, you must do all you can to show that God has really chosen and selected

you. If you keep on doing this, you won't stumble and fall. [11] Then our Lord and Saviour Jesus Christ will give you a glorious welcome into his kingdom that will last for ever.

[12] You are holding firmly to the truth that you were given. But I am still going to remind you of these things. [13] In fact, I think I should keep on reminding you until I leave this body. [14] And our Lord Jesus Christ has already told me that I will soon leave it behind. [15] That is why I am doing my best to make sure that each of you remembers all this after I am gone.

The glory of Christ

[16] When we told you about the power and the return of our Lord Jesus Christ, we were not telling clever stories that someone had made up. But with our own eyes we saw his true greatness. [17] God, our great and wonderful Father, truly honoured him by saying, "This is my own dear Son, and I am pleased with him." [18] We were there with Jesus on the holy mountain and heard this voice speak from heaven.

[19] All this makes us even more certain that what the prophets said is true. So you should pay close attention to their message, as you would to a lamp shining in some dark place. You must keep on paying attention until daylight comes and the morning star rises in your hearts. [20] But you need to realize that no one alone can understand any of the prophecies in the Scriptures. [21] The prophets did not think these things up on their own, but they were guided by the Spirit of God.

False prophets and teachers

CHAPTER 2

[1] Sometimes false prophets spoke to the people of Israel. False teachers will also sneak in and speak harmful lies to you. But these teachers don't really belong to the Master who paid a great price for them, and they will quickly destroy themselves. [2] Many people will follow their evil ways and cause others to tell lies about the true way. [3] They will be greedy and cheat you with smooth talk. But long ago God decided to punish them, and God doesn't sleep.

[4] God did not have pity on the angels that sinned. He had them tied up and thrown into the dark pits of hell until the time of judgment. [5] And during Noah's time, God did not have pity on the ungodly people of the world. He destroyed them with a flood, though he did save eight people, including Noah, who preached the truth.

[6] God punished the cities of Sodom and Gomorrah* by burning them to ashes, and this is a warning to anyone else who wants to sin.

[7-8] Lot lived right and was greatly troubled by the terrible way those wicked people were living. He was a good man, and day after day he suffered because of the evil things he saw and heard. So the Lord rescued him. [9] This shows that the Lord knows how to rescue godly people from their sufferings and to punish evil people while they wait for the day of judgment.

[10] The Lord is especially hard on people who disobey him and don't think of anything except their own filthy desires. They are reckless and proud and are not afraid of cursing the glorious beings in heaven. [11] Although angels are more powerful than these evil beings,' even the angels don't dare to accuse them to the Lord.

[12] These people are no better than senseless animals that live by their feelings and are born to be caught and killed. They speak evil of things they don't know anything about. But their own corrupt deeds will destroy them. [13] They have done evil, and they will be rewarded with evil.

They think it is fun to have wild parties during the day. They are immoral, and the meals they eat with you are spoilt by the shameful and selfish way they carry on.' [14] All they think about is having sex with someone else's husband or wife. There is no end to their wicked deeds. They trick people who are easily fooled, and their minds are filled with greedy thoughts. But they are headed for trouble!

[15] They have left the true road and have gone down the wrong path by following the example of the prophet Balaam. He was the son of Beor and loved what he got from being a criminal. [16] But a donkey corrected him for this evil deed. It spoke to him with a human voice and made him stop his foolishness.

---

*2.6 **Sodom and Gomorrah:** During the time of Abraham the Lord destroyed these cities because the people there were so evil. See Genesis 19.24.

See also: 2.5: Gen 6.1–7.24.   2.6: Gen 19.24.
2.7: Gen 19.1–16.   2.15–16: Num 22.4–35.

See also: 1.17–18: Matt 17.1–5; Mark 9.2–7; Luke 9.28–35.

¹⁷ These people are like dried-up water holes and clouds blown by a storm. The darkest part of hell is waiting for them. ¹⁸ They boast out loud about their stupid nonsense. And by being vulgar and crude, they trap people who have barely escaped from living the wrong kind of life. ¹⁹ They promise freedom to everyone. But they are merely slaves of filthy living, because people are slaves of whatever controls them.

²⁰ When they learnt about our Lord and Saviour Jesus Christ, they escaped from the filthy things of this world. But they are again caught up and controlled by these filthy things, and now they are in a worse state than they were at first. ²¹ They would have been better off if they had never known about the right way. Even after they knew what was right, they turned their backs on the holy commandments that they were given. ²² What happened to them is just like the true saying,

> "A dog will come back
> to lick up its own vomit.
> A pig that has been washed
> will roll in the mud."

The Lord's return is certain

CHAPTER 3

¹ My dear friends, this is the second letter I have written to encourage you to do some honest thinking. I don't want you to forget ² what God's prophets said would happen. You must never forget what the holy prophets taught in the past. And you must remember what the apostles told you our Lord and Saviour has commanded us to do.

³ But first you must realize that in the last days some people won't think about anything except their own selfish desires. They will make fun of you ⁴ and say, "Didn't your Lord promise to come back? Yet the first leaders have already died, and the world hasn't changed a bit."

⁵ They will say this because they want to forget that long ago the heavens and the earth were made at God's command. The earth came out of water and was made from water. ⁶ Later it was destroyed by the waters of a mighty flood. ⁷ But God has commanded the present heavens and earth to remain until the day of judgment. Then they will be set on fire, and ungodly people will be destroyed.

⁸ Dear friends, don't forget that for the Lord one day is the same as a thousand years, and a thousand years is the same as one day. ⁹ The Lord isn't slow about keeping his promises, as some people think he is. In fact, God is patient, because he wants everyone to turn from sin and no one to be lost.

¹⁰ The day of the Lord's return will surprise us like a thief. The heavens will disappear with a loud noise, and the heat will melt the whole universe.* Then the earth and everything on it will be seen for what they are.ʼ

¹¹ Everything will be destroyed. So you should serve and honour God by the way you live. ¹² You should look forward to the day when God judges everyone, and you should try to make it come soon.ʼ On that day the heavens will be destroyed by fire, and everything else will melt in the heat. ¹³ But God has promised us a new heaven and a new earth, where justice will rule. We are really looking forward to that!

¹⁴ My friends, while you are waiting, you should make certain that the Lord finds you pure, spotless, and living at peace. ¹⁵ Don't forget that the Lord is patient because he wants people to be saved. This is also what our dear friend Paul said when he wrote to you with the wisdom that God had given him. ¹⁶ Paul talks about these same things in all his letters, but part of what he says is hard to understand. Some ignorant and unsteady people even destroy themselves by twisting what he said. They do the same thing with other Scriptures too.

¹⁷ My dear friends, you have been warned beforehand! So don't let the errors of evil people lead you down the wrong path and make you lose your balance. ¹⁸ Let the wonderful kindness and the understanding that come from our Lord and Saviour Jesus Christ help you to keep on growing. Praise Jesus now and for ever! Amen.ʼ

---

*3.10 the whole universe: Probably the sun, moon, and stars, or the elements that everything in the universe is made of.

See also: 2.22: Prov 26.11. 3.3: Jude 18. 3.5: Gen 1.6–9. 3.6: Gen 7.11.

See also: 3.8: Psa 90.4. 3.10: Matt 24.43; Luke 12.39; 1 Thes 5.2; Rev 16.15. 3.13: Isa 65.17; 66.22; Rev 21.1.

Additional notes

'1.1 To everyone who . . . just and fair: Or "To everyone whose faith in the justice and fairness of our God and Saviour Jesus Christ is as precious as our own faith."

'2.11 evil beings: Or "evil teachers".

'2.13 and the meals they eat with you are spoilt by the shameful and selfish way they carry on: Some manuscripts have "and the meals they eat with you are spoilt by the shameful way they carry on during your feasts of Christian love."

'3.10 will be seen for what they are: Some manuscripts have "will go up in flames."

'3.12 and you should try to make it come soon: Or "and you should eagerly desire for that day to come."

'3.18 Amen: Some manuscripts do not have "Amen."

1 John

John's first letter

The basics

What's the point? Are you a child of God? Then live in the way that he wants you to live.

What happens? John writes to combat false teaching and call for pure lives.

What should I remember? 2.3–4 'When we obey God, we are sure that we know him. But if we claim to know him and don't obey him, we are lying and the truth isn't in our hearts.'

More details

Setting the scene The early church was being threatened by false beliefs. John writes to expose the false teachers and tell people the truth...

What's it all about? The early church had to counter the teachings of the Gnostics – a group of people who had changed the message of the Bible in several key ways. John exposes these false teachers and their lack of morality. He assures his readers that they have been saved. John had seen Christ, had known Christ, so he knows that Jesus wasn't some kind of spirit being, but a real man and a real God.

Footsteps

The Word that gives life

CHAPTER 1

¹ The Word that gives life
 was from the beginning,
and this is the one
 our message is about.

 Our ears have heard,
 our own eyes have seen,
and our hands touched
 this Word.

² The one who gives life appeared! We saw it happen, and we are witnesses to what we have seen. Now we are telling you about this eternal life that was with the Father and appeared to us. ³ We are telling you what we have seen and heard, so that you may share in this life with us. And we share in it with the Father and with his Son Jesus Christ. ⁴ We are writing to tell you these things, because this makes us⁾ truly happy.

God is light and Christ is our example

⁵ Jesus told us that God is light and doesn't have any darkness in him. Now we are telling you.

⁶ If we say that we share in life with God and keep on living in the dark, we are lying and are not living by the truth. ⁷ But if we live in the light, as God does, we share in life with each other. And the blood of his Son Jesus

See also: **1.1:** John 1.1. **1.2:** John 1.14.

Life files

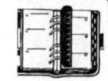

John (a.k.a. Son of thunder)

Background: Son of Zebedee, brother of James. Cousin of Jesus.

What's the story?

A fisherman by trade, John met Jesus when he was with the disciples of John the Baptist. He already knew Jesus, since his mother was Salome and Mary was his aunt (Matthew 27.56; Mark 16.1; John 19.25). He spent three years with Jesus. Jesus called him and his brother James 'sons of Thunder' maybe because he had a fiery temper.

With James and Peter he was one of Jesus' inner circle of followers. At his death, Jesus asked John to take care of his mother.

After the death and resurrection of Jesus he was with Peter in Rome for a while, and then he fades from the scene. Early church tradition has it that he went to Ephesus, where he wrote his gospel.

During the persecution of Christians under the Roman emperor Domitian, he was sent to the tiny isle of Patmos, where he had the visions which became the book of Revelation. He also wrote letters to the Church. In his gospel he rarely refers to himself by his name, preferring to use such phrases as 'Jesus' favourite disciple'.

What's the point?

John and James are described as the 'sons of Thunder', Later in life he seems to have mellowed: his letters are notable for their emphasis on love. His gospel shows this reflective character as well, since it is much more than just his recollection of what Jesus said and did. It also talks about the nature of Jesus himself; who he was and where he came from.

Footsteps

Five days with John

John joins Jesus: Mark 1.16–20
Not kings, but slaves: Mark 10.35–45
A new responsibility: John 19.25–27
Love one another: 1 John 3.11–24
A vision on an island: Revelation 1.1–20

washes all our sins away. ⁸ If we say that we have not sinned, we are fooling ourselves, and the truth isn't in our hearts. ⁹ But if we confess our sins to God, he can always be trusted to forgive us and take our sins away.

¹⁰ If we say that we have not sinned, we make God a liar, and his message isn't in our hearts.'

CHAPTER 2

Christ helps us

¹ My children, I am writing this so that you won't sin. But if you do sin, Jesus Christ always does the right thing, and he will speak to the Father for us. ² Christ is the sacrifice that takes away our sins and the sins of all the world's people.

³ When we obey God, we are sure that we know him. ⁴ But if we claim to know him and don't obey him, we are lying and the truth isn't in our hearts. ⁵ We truly love God only when we obey him as we should, and then we know that we belong to him. ⁶ If we say we are his, we must follow the example of Christ.

The new commandment

⁷ My dear friends, I am not writing to give you a new commandment. It is the same one that you were first given, and it is the message you heard. ⁸ But it really is a new commandment, and you know its true meaning, just as Christ does. You can see the darkness fading away and the true light already shining.

⁹ If we claim to be in the light and hate someone, we are still in the dark. ¹⁰ But if we love others, we are in the light, and we don't cause problems for them.' ¹¹ If we hate others, we are living and walking in the dark. We don't know where we are going, because we can't see in the dark.

¹² Children, I am writing to you,
   because your sins
   have been forgiven
   in the name of Christ.
¹³ Parents, I am writing to you,
   because you have known
   the one who was there
   from the beginning.
   Young people, I am writing to you,
   because you have defeated
   the evil one.

See also: 2.7: John 13.34.

¹⁴ Children, I am writing to you,
because you have known
the Father.
Parents, I am writing to you,
because you have known
the one who was there
from the beginning.
Young people, I am writing to you,
because you are strong.
God's message is firm
in your hearts,
and you have defeated
the evil one.

¹⁵ Don't love the world or anything that belongs to the world. If you love the world, you cannot love the Father. ¹⁶ Our foolish pride comes from this world, and so do our selfish desires and our desire to have everything we see. None of this comes from the Father. ¹⁷ The world and the desires it causes are disappearing. But if we obey God, we will live for ever.

The enemies of Christ and God's children

The enemy of Christ

¹⁸ Children, this is the last hour. You heard that the enemy of Christ would appear at this time, and many of Christ's enemies have already appeared. So we know that the last hour is here. ¹⁹ These people came from our own group, yet they were not part of us. If they had been part of us, they would have stayed with us. But they left, which proves that they did not belong to our group.

²⁰ Christ, the Holy One,' has blessed* you, and now all of you understand.' ²¹ I did not need to write to you about the truth, since you already know it. You also know that liars do not belong to the truth. ²² And a liar is anyone who says that Jesus isn't truly Christ. Anyone who says this is an enemy of Christ and rejects both the Father and the Son. ²³ If we reject the Son, we reject the Father. But if we say that we accept the Son, we have the

---

*2.20 blessed: This translates a word which means "to pour olive oil on (someone's head)". In Old Testament times it was the custom to pour olive oil on a person's head when that person was chosen to be a priest or a king. Here the meaning is not clear. It may refer to the ceremony of pouring olive oil on the followers of the Lord just before they were baptized or it may refer to the gift of the Holy Spirit which they were given at baptism (see verse 27).

Father. ²⁴ Keep thinking about the message you first heard, and you will always be one in your heart with the Son and with the Father. ²⁵ The Son' has promised us' eternal life.

²⁶ I am writing to warn you about those people who are misleading you. ²⁷ But Christ has blessed you with the Holy Spirit.' Now the Spirit stays in you, and you don't need any teachers. The Spirit is truthful and teaches you everything. So stay united in your heart with Christ, just as the Spirit has taught you to do.

Children of God

²⁸ Children, stay united in your hearts with Christ. Then when he returns, we will have confidence and won't have to hide in shame. ²⁹ You know that Christ always does right and that everyone who does right is a child of God.

CHAPTER 3

¹ Think how much the Father loves us. He loves us so much that he lets us be called his children, as we truly are. But since the people of this world did not know who Christ' is, they don't know who we are. ² My dear friends, we are already God's children, though what we will be hasn't yet been seen. But we do know that when Christ returns, we will be like him, because we will see him as he truly is. ³ This hope makes us keep ourselves holy, just as Christ' is holy.

⁴ Everyone who sins breaks God's law, because sin is the same as breaking God's law. ⁵ You know that Christ came to take away sins. He isn't sinful, ⁶ and people who stay united in their hearts with him won't keep on sinning. If they do keep on sinning, they don't know Christ, and they have never seen him.

⁷ Children, don't be fooled. Anyone who does right is good, just like Christ himself. ⁸ Anyone who keeps on sinning belongs to the devil. He has sinned from the beginning, but the Son of God came to destroy all that he has done. ⁹ God's children cannot keep on being sinful. His life-giving power' lives in them and makes them his children, so that they cannot keep on sinning. ¹⁰ You can tell God's children from the devil's children, because those who belong to the devil refuse to do right or to love each other.

See also: 3.1: John 1.12. **3.5:** John 1.29.

God's love and our love

Love each other

[11] From the beginning you were told that we must love each other. [12] Don't be like Cain, who belonged to the devil and murdered his own brother. Why did he murder him? He did it because his brother was good, and he was evil. [13] My friends, don't be surprised if the people of this world hate you. [14] Our love for each other proves that we have gone from death to life. But if you don't love each other, you are still under the power of death.

[15] If you hate each other, you are murderers, and we know that murderers do not have eternal life. [16] We know what love is because Jesus gave his life for us. That's why we must give our lives for each other. [17] If we have all we need and see one of our own people in need, we must have pity on that person, or else we cannot say we love God. [18] Children, you show love for others by truly helping them, and not merely by talking about it.

[19] When we love others, we know that we belong to the truth, and we feel at ease in the presence of God. [20] But even if we don't feel at ease, God is greater than our feelings, and he knows everything. [21] Dear friends, if we feel at ease in the presence of God, we will have the courage to come near him. [22] He will give us whatever we ask, because we obey him and do what pleases him. [23] God wants us to have faith in his Son Jesus Christ and to love each other. This is also what Jesus taught us to do. [24] If we obey God's commandments, we will stay united in our hearts with him, and he will stay united with us. The Spirit that he has given us is proof that we are one with him.

CHAPTER 4

God is love

[1] Dear friends, don't believe everyone who claims to have the Spirit of God. Test them all to find out if they really do come from God. Many false prophets have already gone out into the world, [2] and you can know which ones come from God. His Spirit says that Jesus Christ had a truly human body. [3] But when someone doesn't say this about Jesus, you know that person has a spirit that doesn't

Holy history

Gnosticism

One of the biggest problems the early Church had to face was a set of ideas called 'Gnosticism'.

The Gnostics claimed that they had secret knowledge about Jesus. They believed that God had kept some truth back and only allowed special people to be 'enlightened'.

They also believed that the material world, the stuff all around us, was evil. Some gnostics tried to punish their bodies and to live only eating and drinking a very few things. This appears to be the approach in Colossae. Others pretended that reality wasn't actually real. So they indulged in all kinds of sin in the belief that somehow it didn't affect them. This approach is condemned in 1 John.

If nature was evil, that meant changing their view of Jesus. 'If bodies are bad,' they argued, 'surely God's son wouldn't have used one?' So, the Gnostics claimed that Jesus wasn't really a human at all; he was a spirit who sort of rented out a human body and moved out just before the nasty death bit.

Apostles like Paul and John worked hard to combat these theories. Paul knew that Jesus had been a real man who had died a real death and rose to life again. And he knew that God was for everyone, not just the select few.

So, any time someone claims to have secret knowledge of God, stuff not revealed in the Bible, be on your guard. You might have met a Gnostic.

Anorak corner

'Gnostic' comes from the Greek word Gnosis meaning 'secret knowledge'. From this we get the word 'agnostic' for people who just don't know.

More...

John p.1396

See also: **3.11:** John 13.34.   **3.12:** Gen 4.8.
3.14: John 5.24.   **3.23:** John 13.34; 15.12,17.

1398

come from God and is the enemy of Christ. You knew that this enemy was coming into the world and now is already here.

⁴ Children, you belong to God, and you have defeated these enemies. God's Spirit' is in you and is more powerful than the one that is in the world. ⁵ These enemies belong to this world, and the world listens to them, because they speak its language. ⁶ We belong to God, and everyone who knows God will listen to us. But the people who don't know God won't listen to us. That is how we can tell the Spirit that speaks the truth from the one that tells lies.

⁷ My dear friends, we must love each other. Love comes from God, and when we love each other, it shows that we have been given new life. We are now God's children, and we know him. ⁸ God is love, and anyone who doesn't love others has never known him. ⁹ God showed his love for us when he sent his only Son into the world to give us life. ¹⁰ Real love isn't our love for God, but his love for us. God sent his Son to be the sacrifice by which our sins are forgiven. ¹¹ Dear friends, since God loved us this much, we must love each other.

¹² No one has ever seen God. But if we love each other, God lives in us, and his love is truly in our hearts.

¹³ God has given us his Spirit. That is how we know that we are one with him, just as he is one with us. ¹⁴ God sent his Son to be the Saviour of the world. We saw his Son and are now telling others about him. ¹⁵ God stays united with everyone who openly says that Jesus is the Son of God. That's how we stay united with God ¹⁶ and are sure that God loves us.

God is love. If we keep on loving others, we will stay united in our hearts with God, and he will stay united with us. ¹⁷ If we truly love others and live as Christ did in this world, we won't be worried about the day of judgment. ¹⁸ A real love for others will chase those worries away. The thought of being punished is what makes us afraid. It shows that we have not really learnt to love.

¹⁹ We love because God loved us first. ²⁰ But if we say we love God and don't love each other, we are liars. We cannot see God. So how can we love God, if we don't love the people we can see? ²¹ The commandment that God has given us is: "Love God and love each other!"

See also: **4.12:** John 1.18.

Victory over the world

CHAPTER 5

¹ If we believe that Jesus is truly Christ, we are God's children. Everyone who loves the Father will also love his children. ² If we love and obey God, we know that we will love his children. ³ We show our love for God by obeying his commandments, and they are not hard to follow.

⁴ Every child of God can defeat the world, and our faith is what gives us this victory. ⁵ No one can defeat the world without having faith in Jesus as the Son of God.

Who Jesus is

⁶ Water and blood came out from the side of Jesus Christ. It wasn't just water, but water and blood.* The Spirit tells about this, because the Spirit is truthful. ⁷ In fact, there are three who tell about it. ⁸ They are the Spirit, the water, and the blood, and they all agree.

⁹ We believe what people tell us. But we can trust what God says even more, and God is the one who has spoken about his Son. ¹⁰ If we have faith in God's Son, we have believed what God has said. But if we don't believe what God has said about his Son, it is the same as calling God a liar. ¹¹ God has also said that he gave us eternal life and that this life comes to us from his Son. ¹² And so, if we have God's Son, we have this life. But if we don't have the Son, we don't have this life.

Knowing about eternal life

¹³ All of you have faith in the Son of God, and I have written to let you know that you have eternal life. ¹⁴ We are certain that God will hear our prayers when we ask for what pleases him. ¹⁵ And if we know that God listens when we pray, we are sure that our prayers have already been answered.

¹⁶ Suppose you see one of our people commit a sin that isn't a deadly sin. You can pray, and that person will be given eternal

---

*5.6 Water and blood came out from the side of Jesus Christ. It wasn't just water, but water and blood: See John 19.34. It is also possible to translate, "Jesus Christ came by the water of baptism and by the blood of his death! He was not only baptized, but he bled and died." The purpose of the verse is to tell that Jesus was truly human and that he really died.
See also: **5.3:** John 14.15. **5.11:** John 3.36.

life. But the sin must not be one that is deadly. ¹⁷ Everything that is wrong is sin, but not all sins are deadly.

¹⁸ We are sure that God's children do not keep on sinning. God's own Son protects them, and the devil cannot harm them.

¹⁹ We are certain that we come from God and that the rest of the world is under the power of the devil.

²⁰ We know that Jesus Christ the Son of God has come and has shown us the true God. And because of Jesus, we now belong to the true God who gives eternal life.

²¹ Children, you must stay away from idols.

Additional notes

›1.4 us: Some manuscripts have "you".
›1.10 and his message isn't in our hearts: Or "because we have not accepted his message."
›2.10 and we don't cause problems for them: Or "and we can see anything that might make us fall."
›2.20 Christ, the Holy One: The Greek text has "the Holy One" which may refer either to Christ or to God the Father.
›2.20 now all of you understand: Some manuscripts have "you understand all things."
›2.25 The Son: The Greek text has "he" and may refer to God the Father.
›2.25 us: Some manuscripts have "you".
›2.27 Christ has blessed you with the Holy Spirit: The Greek text has "You received a pouring on of olive oil from him" (see verse 20). The "pouring on of olive oil" is here taken to refer to the gift of the Holy Spirit, and "he" may refer either to Christ or to the Father.
›3.1 Christ: The Greek text has "he" and may refer to God.
›3.3 Christ: The Greek text has "that one" and may refer to God.
›3.9 His life-giving power: The Greek text has "His seed".
›4.4 God's Spirit: The Greek text has "he" and may refer to the Spirit or to God or to Jesus.

2 John
John's second letter

The basics

What's the point?   Truth and love.

What happens?   Challenging false teaching.

What should I remember?   1.6 'Love means that we do what God tells us. And from the beginning he told you to love him.'

More details

Setting the scene   False teachers say Christ didn't have a real body. John answers them.

What's it all about?   The gospel was spread by travelling evangelists, but if they are teaching rubbish, they must be evicted.

Greetings and prayer

¹ *From the church leader.*ᐟ

*To a very special woman and her children.** I truly love all of you, and so does everyone else who knows the truth. ² We love you because the truth is now in our hearts, and it will be there for ever.

³ I pray that God the Father and Jesus Christ his Son will be kind and merciful to us! May they give us peace and truth and love.

Truth and love

⁴ I was very glad to learn that some of your children are obeying the truth, as the Father told us to do. ⁵ Dear friend, I am not writing to tell you and your children to do something you have not done before. I am writing to tell you to love each other, which is the first thing you were told to do. ⁶ Love means that we do what God tells us. And from the beginning, he told you to love him.

⁷ Many liars have gone out into the world. These deceitful liars are saying that Jesus Christ did not have a truly human body. But they are liars and the enemies of Christ. ⁸ So be sure not to lose what weᐟ have worked for. If you do, you won't be given your full reward. ⁹ Don't keep changing what you were taught about Christ, or else God will no longer be with you. But if you hold firmly to what you were taught, both the Father and the Son will be with you. ¹⁰ If people won't agree to this teaching, don't welcome them into your home or even greet them. ¹¹ Greeting them is the same as taking part in their evil deeds.

Final greetings

¹² I have much more to tell you, but I don't want to write it with pen and ink. I want to come and talk to you in person, because that will make usᐟ really happy.

¹³ Greetings from the children of your very special sister.*

*v13 sister: See the note at verse 1.

---

*v1 very special woman and her children: A group of the Lord's followers who met together for worship. "The children of your . . . sister" (see verse 13) is another group of followers. "Very special" (here and verse 13) probably means "chosen (by the Lord)".
See also: v5: John 13.34; 15.12,17.

Additional notes

ᐟv1 church leader: Or "elder" or "presbyter" or "priest".
ᐟv8 we: Some manuscripts have "you".
ᐟv12 us: Some manuscripts have "you".

3 John

John's third letter

The basics

What's the point? We should obey the truth, not false leaders.

What happens? John criticises a false leader, and urges true Christians to keep to the truth.

What should I remember? 1.4 'Nothing brings me greater happiness than to hear that my children are obeying the truth.'

More details

Setting the scene Diotrephes has been gossiping about John. Now John is going to come and sort things out...

What's it all about? John writes to a follower called Gaius, encouraging him to keep faithful and promising to come to sort out the split in the church. He urges him to keep supporting and welcoming those who speak the truth.

Greetings to Gaius

¹ *From the church leader.*
   To my dear friend Gaius.
   I love you because we follow the truth, ² dear friend, and I pray that all goes well for you. I hope that you are as strong in body, as I know you are in spirit. ³ It makes me very happy when the Lord's followers come by and speak openly of how you obey the truth. ⁴ Nothing brings me greater happiness than to hear that my children* are obeying the truth.

The importance of working together

⁵ Dear friend, you have always been faithful in helping other followers of the Lord, even the ones you didn't know before. ⁶ They have told the church about your love. They say you were good enough to welcome them and to send them on their mission in a way that God's servants deserve. ⁷ When they left to tell others about the Lord, they decided not to accept help from anyone who wasn't a follower. ⁸ We must support people like them, so that we can take part in what they are doing to spread the truth.

⁹ I wrote to the church. But Diotrephes likes to be the number-one leader, and he won't pay any attention to us. ¹⁰ So if I come, I will remind him of how he has been attacking us with gossip. Not only has he been doing this, but he refuses to welcome any of the Lord's followers who come by. And when other church members want to welcome them, he puts them out of the church.

¹¹ Dear friend, don't copy the evil deeds of others! Follow the example of people who do kind deeds. They are God's children, but those who are always doing evil have never seen God.

¹² Everyone speaks well of Demetrius, and so does the true message that he teaches. I also speak well of him, and you know what I say is true.

---

*v4 children: Probably persons that the leader had led to be followers of the Lord.

See also: v1: Acts 19.29; Rom 16.23; 1 Cor 1.14.

Final greetings

¹³ I have much more to say to you, but I don't want to write it with pen and ink. ¹⁴ I hope to see you soon, and then we can talk in person.

¹⁵ I pray that God will bless you with peace! Your friends send their greetings. Please give a personal greeting to each of our friends.

Additional notes

^b**v1 church leader:** Or "elder" or "presbyter" or "priest".

Jude

A letter from Jude

The basics

What's the point? Don't live by your own selfish desires; live in the way God wants.

What happens? Jude defends the true faith and rejects false teaching.

What should I remember? 1.20 'Dear friends, keep building on the foundation of your most holy faith, as the Holy Spirit helps you to pray.'

More details

Setting the scene The church is growing. New churches are being founded, new teachers coming forward. And some of those teachers have very different ideas about the Christian faith...

What's it all about? This letter is traditionally ascribed to Jude, brother of James and Jesus (Matthew 13.55). He's writing to combat false teaching that has arisen in the early Church. Jude says the offenders are more like animals than men. They are abusing their positions of leadership, by luring others into sexual acts – a feature of cults and false teaching down the ages.

Greetings

¹ *From Jude, a servant of Jesus Christ and the brother of James.*

To all who are chosen and loved by God the Father and are kept safe by Jesus Christ.

² I pray that God will greatly bless you with kindness, peace, and love!

Defending the faith against false teachers

³ My dear friends, I really wanted to write to you about God's saving power at work in our lives. But instead, I must write and ask you to defend the faith that God has once for all given to his people. ⁴ Some godless people have sneaked in among us and are saying, "God treats us much better than we deserve, and so it is all right to be immoral." They even deny that we must obey Jesus Christ as our only Master and Lord. But long ago the Scriptures warned that these godless people were doomed.

⁵ Don't forget what happened to those people that the Lord rescued from Egypt. Some of them did not have faith, and he later destroyed them. ⁶ You also know about the angels* who didn't do their work and left their proper places. God chained them with everlasting chains and is now keeping them in dark pits until the great day of judgment. ⁷ We should also be warned by what happened to the cities of Sodom and Gomorrah* and the nearby towns. Their people became immoral and did all sorts of sexual sins. Then God made an example of them and punished them with eternal fire.

---

*v6 angels: This may refer to the angels who liked the women on earth so much that they came down and married them (see Genesis 6.2).

*v7 Sodom and Gomorrah: During the time of Abraham the Lord destroyed these cities because the people there were so evil.

See also: v5: a Exod 12.51; b Num 14.29–30.
v7: Gen 19.1–24.

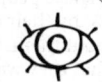

⁸ The people I am talking about are behaving just like those dreamers who destroyed their own bodies. They reject all authority and insult angels. ⁹ Even Michael, the chief angel, didn't dare to insult the devil, when the two of them were arguing about the body of Moses.* All Michael said was, "The Lord will punish you!"

¹⁰ But these people insult powers they don't know anything about. They are like senseless animals that end up getting destroyed, because they live only by their feelings. ¹¹ Now they are in for real trouble. They have followed Cain's example* and have made the same mistake that Balaam* did by caring only for money. They have also rebelled against God, just as Korah did.* Because of all this, they will be destroyed.

¹² These people are filthy minded, and by their shameful and selfish actions they spoil the meals you eat together. They are like clouds blown along by the wind, but never bringing any rain. They are like leafless trees, uprooted and dead, and unable to produce fruit. ¹³ Their shameful deeds show up like foam on wild ocean waves. They are like wandering stars for ever doomed to the darkest pits of hell.

¹⁴ Enoch was the seventh person after Adam, and he was talking about these people when he said:

Look! The Lord is coming with thousands and thousands of holy angels ¹⁵ to judge everyone. He will punish all those ungodly people for all the evil things they have done. The Lord will punish those ungodly sinners for every evil thing they have ever said about him.

---

*v9 Michael . . . the body of Moses:** This refers to what was said in an ancient Jewish book about Moses.
*v11 Cain's example:** Cain murdered his brother Abel.
*v11 Balaam:** According to the biblical account, Balaam refused to curse the people of Israel for profit (see Numbers 22.18; 24.13), though he led them to be unfaithful to the Lord (see Numbers 25.1–3; 31.16). But by New Testament times, some Jewish teachers taught that Balaam was greedy and did accept money to curse them.
*v11 just as Korah did:** Together with Dathan and Abiram, Korah led a rebellion against Moses and Aaron (see Numbers 16.1–35; 26.9,10).

See also: v9: a Dan 10.13,21; 12.1; Rev 12.7; b Deut 34.6; c Zech 3.2. v11: a Gen 4.3–8; b Num 22.1–35; c Num 16.1–35. v14: Gen 5.18,21–24.

Viewpoints

Remind yourself how to use prayer according to the maker's instructions

Contributed by Helen C

'Dear friends, keep building on the foundation of your most holy faith, as the Holy Spirit helps you to pray.'

It's really easy to underestimate what prayer is. Every time we speak to God, even if it is for the 25,789th time of our lives, we are coming before an awesome and powerful God. It's AMAZING that he wants to listen to us. It is wonderful that because of what Jesus has done we can talk to God as our friend, but we should never forget that he is also GOD. I reckon that when we really grasp that truth, this verse can become a reality for us. We WILL continue to pray, even when we can't see God at work, because we know that he will act in power.

However, God doesn't want us to come before him with our own agenda, but with his, being 'directed by the Holy Spirit'. It's easy to just run off a list of 'sorry', 'please' and 'thank you' to God without really listening to him. It's so great that we can pour out our hearts to God, but he wants us to pray according to his agenda. I guess that means saying, 'God, will you show me what you want me to be concerned about; what you want me to pray for?'

All of which might mean God telling you to pray for the seemingly 'impossible': the salvation of the hardest atheist you know or the healing of someone with an 'incurable' disease. However, your prayers will have maximum impact, because they're what God's concerned about. What's more, you'll come closer to his heart and have the opportunity to get involved in his radical plans. How exciting is that?

More...

Prayer p.1002
Praying to God p.1334
Holy Spirit p.1209

16 These people grumble and complain and live by their own selfish desires. They boast about themselves and flatter others to get what they want.

More warnings

17 My dear friends, remember the warning you were given by the apostles of our Lord Jesus Christ. 18 They told you that near the end of time, selfish and godless people would start making fun of God. 19 And now these people are already making you turn against each other. They think only about this life, and they don't have God's Spirit.

20 Dear friends, keep building on the foundation of your most holy faith, as the Holy Spirit helps you to pray. 21 And keep in step with God's love, as you wait for our Lord Jesus Christ to show how kind he is by giving you eternal life. 22 Be helpful to' all who may have doubts. 23 Rescue any who need to be saved, as you would rescue someone from a fire. Then with fear in your own hearts, have mercy on everyone who needs it. But hate even the clothes of those who have been made dirty by their filthy deeds.

Final prayer

24-25 Offer praise to God our Saviour because of our Lord Jesus Christ! Only God can keep you from falling and make you pure and joyful in his glorious presence. Before time began and now and for evermore, God is worthy of glory, honour, power, and authority. Amen.

See also: v18: 2 Pet 3.3.

Additional notes

'v22 Be helpful to: Some manuscripts have "Correct".

Revelation

The basics

What's the point? We have seen the future: God wins.

What happens? John sees a vision of the end times. And he writes to encourage certain churches to get their acts together.

What should I remember? 21.3–4 'I heard a loud voice shout from the throne: God's home is now with his people. He will live with them, and they will be his own. Yes, God will make his home among his people. He will wipe all tears from their eyes, and there will be no more death, suffering, crying or pain. These things of the past are gone for ever.'

More details

Setting the scene Towards the end of the first century AD, a prisoner on an island sees a marvellous vision of the end of all things...

What's it all about? The end. John is a prisoner on the isle of Patmos. There he sees a vision, and is told to write it down. (Let's face it; if you get a vision from God and you are told to write it down, you get on and do it.)

The vision gives a picture of the future. The church was facing huge persecution at the time that this book was written, but John's vision makes one thing completely clear: God wins. 'The battle is tough now,' he says, 'but I've seen the ending. And we win.'

Oceans of ink and forests of paper have been spent trying to 'decode' this difficult book. It's full of secret messages which would perhaps have been understood by the first Christians, but which present even today's experts with a number of problems. But, as someone very

wise once said, 'life can only be lived forwards and can only be understood backwards'. Revelation is a bit like this. It can really only be fully understood when we reach the end and look back.

So beware anyone who claims that they understand exactly what Revelation means. Revelation is not a timetable. It's a vision. The events may lead on from one another and they may appear exactly as described. Or the pictures may point to a different, but no less true, reality.

In a book like this – packed with obscure images and difficult details – it's probably best to concentrate on the big picture. This is a message about God's victory over evil. In the end, God will create a new heaven and a new earth and all evil will finally be defeated.

And another thing

Early church tradition held that John received this vision when he was imprisoned on the small isle of Patmos. He had been sent there by the Roman emperor Domitian, during widespread persecution of the church. Tradition also holds that John was in his nineties when he saw the things set down in Revelation.

Whatever the case, the background to Revelation is one of persecution and suffering. In the light of this, the core message of the book is even more important. Whatever the churches are enduring now, the victory of God is certain.

Footsteps

A prophecy from John

CHAPTER 1

¹ This is what God showed to Jesus Christ, so that he could tell his servants what must happen soon. Christ then sent his angel with the message to his servant John. ² And John told everything that he had seen about God's message and about what Jesus Christ had said and done.

³ God will bless everyone who reads this prophecy to others,* and he will bless everyone who hears and obeys it. The time is almost here.

⁴ From John to the seven churches in Asia.*

I pray that you
   will be blessed
with kindness and peace
from God, who is and was
   and is coming.
May you receive
   kindness and peace
from the seven spirits
   before the throne of God.
⁵ May kindness and peace
   be yours
from Jesus Christ,
   the faithful witness.

Jesus was the first
   to conquer death,
and he is the ruler
   of all earthly kings.
Christ loves us,
   and by his blood

he set us free
   from our sins.
⁶ He lets us rule as kings
and serve God his Father
   as priests.
To him be glory and power
   for ever and ever! Amen.
⁷ Look! He is coming
   with the clouds.
Everyone will see him,
even the ones who stuck
   a sword through him.
All people on earth
will weep because of him.
Yes, it will happen! Amen.

⁸ The Lord God says, "I am Alpha and Omega,* the one who is and was and is coming. I am God All-Powerful!"

A vision of the living Lord

⁹ I am John, a follower together with all of you. We suffer because Jesus is our king, but he gives us the strength to endure. I was sent to Patmos Island,* because I had preached God's message and had told about Jesus. ¹⁰ On the Lord's day the Spirit took control of me, and behind me I heard a loud voice that sounded like a trumpet. ¹¹ The voice said, "Write in a book what you see. Then send it to the seven churches in Ephesus, Smyrna, Pergamum, Thyatira, Sardis, Philadelphia, and Laodicea."*

¹² When I turned to see who was speaking to me, I saw seven gold lampstands. ¹³ There with the lampstands was someone who seemed to be the Son of Man.* He was wearing a robe that reached down to his feet, and a gold cloth was wrapped around his chest. ¹⁴ His head and his hair were white as wool or snow, and his eyes looked like flames of fire. ¹⁵ His feet were glowing like bronze

---

*1.3 who reads this prophecy to others: A public reading, in a worship service.
*1.4 Asia: The section 1.4–3.22 is in the form of a letter. Asia was in the eastern part of the Roman Empire and is present-day Turkey.
See also: 1.4: a Exod 3.14; b Rev 4.5. 1.5: a Isa 55.4; b Psa 89.27.

*1.8 Alpha and Omega: The first and last letters of the Greek alphabet, which sometimes mean "first" and "last".
*1.9 Patmos Island: A small island where prisoners were sometimes kept by the Romans.
*1.11 Ephesus . . . Laodicea: Ephesus was in the centre with the six other cities forming a half-circle around it.
*1.13 Son of Man: That is, Jesus.
See also: 1.6: Exod 19.6; Rev 5.10. 1.7: a Dan 7.13; Matt 24.30; Mark 13.26; Luke 21.27; 1 Thes 4.17; b Zech 12.10; John 19.34,37; c Zech 12.10; Matt 24.30. 1.8: a Rev 22.13; b Exod 3.14. 1.13: a Dan 7.13; b Dan 10.5. 1.14: Dan 7.9. 1.14–15: Dan 10.6. 1.15: Ezek 1.24; 43.2.

being heated in a furnace, and his voice sounded like the roar of a waterfall. [16] He held seven stars in his right hand, and a sharp double-edged sword was coming from his mouth. His face was shining as bright as the sun at midday.

[17] When I saw him, I fell at his feet like a dead person. But he put his right hand on me and said:

Don't be afraid! I am the first, the last, [18] and the living one. I died, but now I am alive for evermore, and I have the keys to death and the world of the dead.* [19] Write what you have seen and what is and what will happen after these things. [20] I will explain the mystery of the seven stars that you saw at my right side and the seven gold lampstands. The seven stars are the angels* of the seven churches, and the lampstands are the seven churches.

Letters to the seven churches

CHAPTER 2

The letter to Ephesus

The risen Lord said:

[1] This is what you must write to the angel of the church in Ephesus:

I am the one who holds the seven stars in my right hand, and I walk among the seven gold lampstands. Listen to what I say.

[2] I know everything you have done, including your hard work and how you have endured. I know you won't put up with anyone who is evil. When some people pretended to be apostles, you tested them and found out that they were liars. [3] You have endured and gone through hard times because of me, and you have not given up.

[4] But I do have something against you! And it is this: you don't have as much love as you used to. [5] Think about where you have fallen from, and then turn back and do as you did at first. If you don't turn

back, I will come and take away your lampstand. [6] But there is one thing you are doing right. You hate what the Nicolaitans* are doing, and so do I.

[7] If you have ears, listen to what the Spirit says to the churches. I will let everyone who wins the victory eat from the life-giving tree in God's wonderful garden.

The letter to Smyrna

The risen Lord continued:

[8] This is what you must write to the angel of the church in Smyrna:

I am the first and the last. I died, but now I am alive! Listen to what I say.

[9] I know how much you suffer and how poor you are, but you are rich. I also know the cruel things being said about you by people who claim to be Jews. But they are not really Jews. They are a group that belongs to Satan.

[10] Don't worry about what you will suffer. The devil will throw some of you into jail, and you will be tested and made to suffer for ten days. But if you are faithful until you die, I will reward you with a glorious life.*

[11] If you have ears, listen to what the Spirit says to the churches. Whoever wins the victory will not be hurt by the second death.*

The letter to Pergamum

The risen Lord continued:

[12] This is what you must write to the angel of the church in Pergamum:

I am the one who has the sharp double-edged sword! Listen to what I say.

[13] I know where you live where Satan has his throne.* But you have kept true to my name. There where Satan lives, my faithful

---

*1.18 keys to death and the world of the dead:** That is, power over death and the world of the dead.
*1.20 angels:** Perhaps guardian angels that represent the churches, or they may be church leaders or messengers sent to the churches.
See also: 1.17: Isa 44.6; 48.12; Rev 2.8; 22.13.

*2.6 Nicolaitans:** Nothing else is known about these people, though it is possible that they claimed to be followers of Nicolaus from Antioch (see Acts 6.5).
*2.10 a glorious life:** The Greek text has "a crown of life". In ancient times an athlete who had won a contest was rewarded with a crown of flowers as a sign of victory.
*2.11 second death:** The first death is physical death, and the "second death" is eternal death.
*2.13 where Satan has his throne:** The meaning is uncertain, but it may refer to the city as a centre of pagan worship or of Emperor worship.
See also: 2.7: a Gen 2.9; Rev 22.2; b Ezek 28.13; 31.8 (LXX). **2.8:** Isa 44.6; 48.12; Rev 1.17; 22.13. **2.11:** Rev 20.14; 21.8.

Big ideas

Dreams and visions

Dreams and visions – there's a difference between the two. Dreams occur when someone is asleep; visions when the person is awake.

In the Bible God uses both of these as methods of communication. Many visions deal with the future. Isaiah had visions of a future heaven and earth, where all suffering and pain had been taken away. Ezekiel had visions of heaven, filled with strange images and blinding lights. Paul was happily trotting along the road to Damascus when a vision of Jesus knocked him off his horse. Exiled on the tiny island of Patmos, John receives a series of startling visions about the end times.

The Holy Spirit gives people dreams and visions. God told Joel that one day he would give his spirit – along with dreams and visions – to everyone (Joel 2.28).

Significant Bible dreamers include Jacob (with a ladder stretching between heaven and earth) and Solomon (with God offering him whatever he wanted). Perhaps the most famous was Joseph, who received dreams from God, and also interpreted them for others.

God still uses dreams and visions to speak to his people. But we should be careful before attributing our dreams to God. Jeremiah warns about prophets who pass off their own dreams as something from God (Jeremiah 23.25–30).

So make sure. Test your dreams out with trusted, experienced leaders before standing up and announcing that 'God has given me a dream!'

 footsteps

A week with Dreams and visions

Jacob sees a ladder: Genesis 28.10–19
Unpopular dreams: Genesis 37.5–11
No fakers: Jeremiah 23.25–30
Dreams and visions: Joel 2.28–9
Paul's vision: Acts 9.3–9
Peter's vision: Acts 10.9–18
John's vision on the island:
Revelation 1.9–19

witness Antipas* was taken from you and put to death. Even then you did not give up your faith in me.

¹⁴ I do have a few things against you. Some of you are following the teaching of Balaam.* Long ago he told Balak to teach the people of Israel to eat food that had been offered to idols and to be immoral. ¹⁵ Now some of you are following the teaching of the Nicolaitans.* ¹⁶ Turn back! If you don't, I will come quickly and fight against these people. And my words will cut like a sword.

¹⁷ If you have ears, listen to what the Spirit says to the churches. To everyone who wins the victory, I will give some of the hidden food.* I will also give each one a white stone* with a new name* written on it. No one will know that name except the one who is given the stone.

The letter to Thyatira

The risen Lord continued:

¹⁸ This is what you must write to the angel of the church in Thyatira:

I am the Son of God! My eyes are like flames of fire, and my feet are like bronze. Listen to what I say.

¹⁹ I know everything about you, including your love, your faith, your service, and how you have endured. I know that you are doing more now than you have ever done

---

*2.13 Antipas: Nothing else is known about this man, who is mentioned only here in the New Testament.
*2.14 Balaam: According to Numbers 22—24, Balaam refused to disobey the Lord. But in other books of the Old Testament, he is spoken of as evil (see Deuteronomy 23.4–5; Joshua 13.22; 24.9–10; Nehemiah 13.2).
*2.15 Nicolaitans: See the note at 2.6.
*2.17 hidden food: When the people of Israel were going through the desert, the Lord provided a special food for them. Some of this was placed in a jar and stored in the sacred chest (see Exodus 16). According to later Jewish teaching, the prophet Jeremiah rescued the sacred chest when the temple was destroyed by the Babylonians. He hid the chest in a cave, where it would stay until God came to save his people.
*2.17 white stone: The meaning of this is uncertain, though it may be the same as a ticket that lets a person into God's banquet where the "hidden food" is eaten. Or it may be a symbol of victory.
*2.17 a new name: Either the name of Christ or God or the name of the follower who is given the stone.
See also: 2.14: a Num 22.5,7; 31.16; Deut 23.4; b Num 25.1–3. 2.17: a Exod 16.14–15; 16.33–34; John 6.48–50; b Isa 62.2; 65.15.

before. [20] But I still have something against you because of that woman Jezebel.* She calls herself a prophet, and you let her teach and mislead my servants to do immoral things and to eat food offered to idols. [21] I gave her a chance to turn from her sins, but she did not want to stop doing these immoral things.

[22] I am going to strike down Jezebel. Everyone who does these immoral things with her will also be punished, if they don't stop. [23] I will even kill her followers.⸆ Then all the churches will see that I know everyone's thoughts and feelings. I will treat each of you as you deserve.

[24] Some of you in Thyatira don't follow Jezebel's teaching. You don't know anything about what her followers call the "deep secrets of Satan". So I won't burden you down with any other commands. [25] But until I come, you must hold firmly to the teaching you have.

[26] I will give power over the nations to everyone who wins the victory and keeps on obeying me until the end. [27-28] I will give each of them the same power that my Father has given me. They will rule the nations with an iron rod and smash those nations to pieces like clay pots. I will also give them the morning star.*

[29] If you have ears, listen to what the Spirit says to the churches.

CHAPTER 3

The letter to Sardis

The risen Lord said:

[1] This is what you must write to the angel of the church in Sardis:

I have the seven spirits of God and the seven stars. Listen to what I say.

I know what you are doing. Everyone may think you are alive, but you are dead. [2] Wake up! You have only a little strength left, and it is almost gone. So try to become stronger. I have found that you are not completely obeying God. [3] Remember the teaching that you were given and that you heard. Hold firmly to it and turn from your sins. If you don't wake up, I will come when you least expect it, just as a thief does.

[4] A few of you in Sardis have not dirtied your clothes with sin. You will walk with me in white clothes, because you are worthy. [5] Everyone who wins the victory will wear white clothes. Their names will not be erased from the book of life,* and I will tell my Father and his angels that they are my followers.

[6] If you have ears, listen to what the Spirit says to the churches.

The letter to Philadelphia

The risen Lord continued:

[7] This is what you must write to the angel of the church in Philadelphia:

I am the one who is holy and true, and I have the keys that belonged to David.* When I open a door, no one can close it. And when I close a door, no one can open it. Listen to what I say.

[8] I know everything you have done. And I have placed before you an open door that no one can close. You were not very strong, but you obeyed my message and did not deny that you are my followers.⸆ [9] Now you will see what I will do with those people who belong to Satan's group. They claim to be Jews, but they are liars. I will make them come and kneel down at your feet. Then they will know that I love you.

[10] You obeyed my message and endured. So I will protect you from the time of testing that everyone in all the world must go through. [11] I am coming soon. So hold firmly to what you have, and no one will take away the crown that you will be given as your reward.

[12] Everyone who wins the victory will be made into a pillar in the temple of my God, and they will stay there for ever. I will write on each of them the name of my God and the name of his city. It is the new Jerusalem that my God will send down from heaven. I will also write on them my own new name.

---

*2.20 Jezebel: Nothing else is known about her. This may have been her real name or a name that was given to her because she was like Queen Jezebel, who opposed the Lord (see 1 Kings 19.1–2; 21.1–26).
*2.27–28 the morning star: Probably thought of as the star that signals the end of night and the beginning of day. In 22.16 Christ is called the "morning star".
See also: 2.20: 1 King 16.31; 2 King 9.22,30.   2.23: a Psa 7.9; Jer 17.10; b Psa 62.12.   2.26–27: Psa 2.8–9 (LXX).
3.3: Matt 24.43–44; Luke 12.39–40; Rev 16.15.

*3.5 book of life: The book in which the names of God's people are written.
*3.7 the keys that belonged to David: The keys stand for authority over David's kingdom.
See also: 3.5: a Exod 32.32–33; Psa 69.28; Rev 20.12; b Matt 10.32; Luke 12.8.   3.7: Isa 22.22; Job 12.14.
3.9: a Isa 49.23; 60.14; b Isa 43.4.   3.12: a Rev 21.2; b Isa 62.2; 65.15.

¹³ If you have ears, listen to what the Spirit says to the churches.

The letter to Laodicea

The risen Lord continued:

¹⁴ This is what you must write to the angel of the church in Laodicea:

I am the one called Amen!* I am the faithful and true witness and the source* of God's creation. Listen to what I say.

¹⁵ I know everything you have done, and you are not cold or hot. I wish you were either one or the other. ¹⁶ But since you are lukewarm and neither cold nor hot, I will spit you out of my mouth. ¹⁷ You claim to be rich and successful and to have everything you need. But you don't know how badly off you are. You are pitiful, poor, blind, and naked. ¹⁸ Buy your gold from me. It has been refined in a fire, and it will make you rich. Buy white clothes from me. Wear them and you can cover up your shameful nakedness. Buy medicine for your eyes, so that you will be able to see.

¹⁹ I correct and punish everyone I love. So make up your minds to turn away from your sins. ²⁰ Listen! I am standing and knocking at your door. If you hear my voice and open the door, I will come in and we will eat together. ²¹ Everyone who wins the victory will sit with me on my throne, just as I won the victory and sat with my Father on his throne.

²² If you have ears, listen to what the Spirit says to the churches.

A vision of worship in heaven

CHAPTER 4

¹ After this, I looked and saw a door that opened into heaven. Then the voice that had spoken to me at first and that sounded like a trumpet said, "Come up here! I will show you what must happen next." ² At once the Spirit took control of me, and there in heaven I saw a throne and someone sitting on it. ³ The one who was sitting there sparkled like precious stones of

---

*3.14 Amen: Meaning "Trustworthy".
*3.14 source: Or "beginning".
See also: 3.14: Prov 8.22. 3.19: Prov 3.12; Heb 12.6.
4.2–3: Ezek 1.26–28; 10.1.

Big ideas

Heaven

Heaven isn't some imaginary concept. It's not never-never land.

Heaven is the place where God lives. It's the place where Jesus came from, and where he returned to after his work on earth was done. It's a place of security and peace, where age and illness and pain will no longer have any part. It's a real destination to which we will actually go.

As to when we will go, well, there are different ideas about that. Some argue that we go there immediately after death; others argue that we sleep, and will all go there at the end of the world. The timing doesn't matter; what matters is that we'll get there.

Heaven gives Christians hope. If there were no final destination, no eventual meeting with God, what would be the point of what we're doing? If there's no place in heaven for us, then there's nothing to hope for on earth.

But don't worry. Heaven is real and it's waiting for us. Jesus talked about preparing a place for those who trusted him and the Bible is full of descriptions of heaven. Prophets caught glimpses of the glory that awaits us. They tried to describe it in words, but words can never give a full view.

Because the real feature of heaven is that it's a place where we will constantly be in the presence of God. No barriers any more; nothing but God and his people, together at last. That's difficult to describe, admittedly. But that doesn't make it any less real.

Footsteps

Ten days on Heaven

God's love: Psalms 103.1–22
Isaiah glimpses heaven: Isaiah 65.17–25
Ezekiel glimpses glory: Ezekiel 1.1–28
Jesus prepares a place: John 14.1–6
Stephen glimpses heaven: Acts 7.54–60
Heavenly bodies: 2 Corinthians 4.16–5.10
Citizens of heaven: Philippians 3.12–21
Jesus will return: 1 Thessalonians 4.13–18
John glimpses heaven: Revelation 4.1–11
New heaven, new earth: Revelation 21.1–7

jasper* and carnelian.* A rainbow that looked like an emerald* surrounded the throne.

⁴ Twenty-four other thrones were in a circle around that throne. And on each of these thrones there was an elder dressed in white clothes and wearing a gold crown. ⁵ Flashes of lightning and roars of thunder came out from the throne in the centre of the circle. Seven torches, which are the seven spirits of God, were burning in front of the throne. ⁶ Also in front of the throne was something that looked like a glass sea, clear as crystal.

Around the throne in the centre were four living creatures covered front and back with eyes. ⁷ The first creature was like a lion, the second one was like a bull, the third one had the face of a human, and the fourth was like a flying eagle. ⁸ Each of the four living creatures had six wings, and their bodies were covered with eyes. Day and night they never stopped singing,

"Holy, holy, holy is the Lord,
    Lord God All-Powerful,
who was and is
    and is coming!"

⁹ The living creatures kept praising, honouring, and thanking the one who sits on the throne and who lives for ever and ever. ¹⁰ At the same time the twenty-four elders knelt down before the one sitting on the throne. And as they worshipped the one who lives for ever, they placed their crowns in front of the throne and said,

¹¹ "Our Lord and God,
    you are worthy
to receive glory,
    honour, and power.
You created all things,
and by your decision they are
    and were created."

A scroll with seven seals

CHAPTER 5

The scroll and the Lamb

¹ In the right hand of the one sitting on the throne I saw a scroll* that had writing on the inside and on the outside. And it was sealed in seven places. ² I saw a mighty angel ask with a loud voice, "Who is worthy to open the scroll and break its seals?" ³ No one in heaven or on earth or under the earth was able to open the scroll or see inside it.

⁴ I cried hard because no one was found worthy to open the scroll or see inside it. ⁵ Then one of the elders said to me, "Stop crying and look! The one who is called both the 'Lion from the Tribe of Judah'* and 'King David's Great Descendant'* has won the victory. He will open the book and its seven seals."

⁶ Then I looked and saw a Lamb standing in the centre of the throne that was surrounded by the four living creatures and the elders. The Lamb looked as if it had once been killed. It had seven horns and seven eyes, which are the seven spirits* of God, sent out to all the earth.

⁷ The Lamb went over and took the scroll from the right hand of the one who sat on the throne. ⁸ After he had taken it, the four living creatures and the twenty-four elders knelt down before him. Each of them had a harp and a gold bowl full of incense,* which are the prayers of God's people. ⁹ Then they sang a new song,

"You are worthy
    to receive the scroll
and open its seals,
    because you were killed.
And with your own blood
    you bought for God

---

*4.3 **jasper:** Usually green or clear.
*4.3 **carnelian:** Usually deep-red or reddish-white.
*4.3 **emerald:** A precious stone, usually green.
See also: 4.5: a Exod 19.16; Rev 8.5; 11.19; 16.18; b Ezek 1.13; c Rev 1.4; Zech 4.2. 4.6: Ezek 1.22. 4.6–7: Ezek 1.5–10; 10.14. 4.8: a Ezek 1.18; 10.12; b Isa 6.2–3.

---

*5.1 **scroll:** A roll of paper or special leather used for writing on. Sometimes a scroll would be sealed on the outside with one or more pieces of wax.
*5.5 **'Lion from the Tribe of Judah':** In Genesis 49.9 the tribe of Judah is called a young lion, and King David was from Judah.
*5.5 **'King David's Great Descendant':** The Greek text has "the root of David" which is a title for the Messiah based on Isaiah 11.1,10.
*5.8 **incense:** A material that produces a sweet smell when burnt. Sometimes it is a symbol for the prayers of God's people.
See also: 5.1: Ezek 2.9,10; Isa 29.11. 5.5: a Gen 49.9; b Isa 11.1,10. 5.6: a Isa 53.7; b Zech 4.10. 5.8: Psa 141.2. 5.9: Psa 33.3; 98.1; Isa 42.10.

people from every tribe,
language, nation, and race.
[10] You let them become kings
and serve God as priests,
and they will rule on earth."

[11] As I looked, I heard the voices of a lot of angels around the throne and the voices of the living creatures and of the elders. There were millions and millions of them, [12] and they were saying in a loud voice,

"The Lamb who was killed
is worthy to receive power,
riches, wisdom, strength,
honour, glory, and praise."

[13] Then I heard all beings in heaven and on the earth and under the earth and in the sea offer praise. Together, all of them were saying,

"Praise, honour, glory,
and strength
for ever and ever
to the one who sits
on the throne
and to the Lamb!"

[14] The four living creatures said "Amen", while the elders knelt down and worshipped.

CHAPTER 6

Opening the seven seals

[1] At the same time that I saw the Lamb open the first of the seven seals, I heard one of the four living creatures shout with a voice like thunder. It said, "Come out!" [2] Then I saw a white horse. Its rider carried a bow and was given a crown. He had already won some victories, and he went out to win more.

[3] When the Lamb opened the second seal, I heard the second living creature say, "Come out!" [4] Then another horse came out. It was fiery red. And its rider was given the power to take away all peace from the earth, so that people would slaughter one another. He was also given a big sword.

[5] When the Lamb opened the third seal, I heard the third living creature say, "Come out!" Then I saw a black horse, and its rider had a balance scale in one hand. [6] I heard what sounded like a voice from somewhere among the four living creatures. It said, "A litre of wheat will cost you a whole day's wages! Three litres of barley will cost you a day's wages too. But don't ruin the olive oil or the wine."

[7] When the Lamb opened the fourth seal, I heard the voice of the fourth living creature say, "Come out!" [8] Then I saw a pale green horse. Its rider was named Death, and Death's Kingdom followed behind. They were given power over one fourth of the earth, and they could kill its people with swords, famines, diseases, and wild animals.

[9] When the Lamb opened the fifth seal, I saw under the altar the souls of everyone who had been killed for speaking God's message and telling about their faith. [10] They shouted, "Master, you are holy and faithful! How long will it be before you judge and punish the people of this earth who killed us?"

[11] Then each of those who had been killed was given a white robe and told to rest for a little while. They had to wait until the complete number of the Lord's other servants and followers would be killed.

[12] When I saw the Lamb open the sixth seal, I looked and saw a great earthquake. The sun turned as dark as sackcloth,* and the moon became as red as blood. [13] The stars in the sky fell to earth, just like figs shaken loose by a storm. [14] Then the sky was rolled up like a scroll,* and all mountains and islands were moved from their places.

[15] The kings of the earth, its famous people, and its military leaders hid in caves or behind rocks on the mountains. They hid there together with the rich and the powerful and with all the slaves and free people. [16] Then they shouted to the mountains and the rocks, "Fall on us! Hide us from the one who sits on the throne and from the anger of the Lamb! [17] That terrible day has come! God and the Lamb will show their anger, and who can face it?"

Worship in front of God's throne

CHAPTER 7

The 144,000 are marked for God

[1-2] After this I saw four angels. Each one was standing on one of the earth's four corners.

---

*6.12 sackcloth: A rough, dark-coloured cloth made from goat or camel hair and used to make grain sacks. It was worn in times of trouble or sorrow.
*6.14 scroll: See the note at 5.1.

See also: 6.8: Ezek 14.21. 6.12: a Rev 11.13; 16.18;
b Isa 13.10; Joel 2.10,31; 3.15; Matt 24.29; Mark 13.24–25;
Luke 21.25. 6.13–14: Isa 34.4. 6.14: Rev 16.20.
6.15: Isa 2.19,21. 6.16: Hos 10.8; Luke 23.30.
6.17: Joel 2.11; Mal 3.2. 7.1: Jer 49.36; Dan 7.2; Zech 6.5.

See also: 5.10: Exod 19.6; Rev 1.6. 5.11: Dan 7.10.
6.2: Zech 1.8; 6.3,6. 6.4: Zech 1.8; 6.2. 6.5: Zech 6.2,6.

The angels held back the four winds, so that no wind would blow on the earth or on the sea or on any tree. These angels had also been given the power to harm the earth and the sea. Then I saw another angel come up from where the sun rises in the east, and he was ready to put the mark of the living God on people. He shouted to the four angels, [3] "Don't harm the earth or the sea or any tree! Wait until I have marked the foreheads of the servants of our God."

[4] Then I heard how many people had been marked on the forehead. There were one hundred and forty-four thousand, and they came from every tribe of Israel:

[5] 12,000 from Judah,
    12,000 from Reuben,
    12,000 from Gad,
[6] 12,000 from Asher,
    12,000 from Naphtali,
    12,000 from Manasseh,
[7] 12,000 from Simeon,
    12,000 from Levi,
    12,000 from Issachar,
[8] 12,000 from Zebulun,
    12,000 from Joseph, and
    12,000 from Benjamin.

People from every nation

[9] After this, I saw a large crowd with more people than could be counted. They were from every race, tribe, nation, and language, and they stood before the throne and before the Lamb. They wore white robes and held palm branches in their hands, [10] as they shouted,

"Our God, who sits
    upon the throne,
has the power
    to save his people,
    and so does the Lamb."

[11] The angels who stood around the throne knelt in front of it with their faces to the ground. The elders and the four living creatures knelt there with them. Then they all worshipped God [12] and said,

"Amen! Praise, glory, wisdom,
    thanks, honour, power,
    and strength belong to our God
    for ever and ever! Amen!"

[13] One of the elders asked me, "Do you know who these people are that are dressed in white robes? Do you know where they come from?"

[14] "Sir," I answered, "you must know." Then he told me:

"These are the ones
who have gone through
    the great suffering.
They have washed their robes
    in the blood of the Lamb
    and have made them white.
[15] And so they stand
    before the throne of God
and worship him in his temple
    day and night.
The one who sits on the throne
    will spread his tent
    over them.
[16] They will never hunger
    or thirst again,
and they won't be troubled
    by the sun
    or any scorching heat.
[17] The Lamb in the centre
    of the throne
    will be their shepherd.
He will lead them to streams
    of life-giving water,
and God will wipe all tears
    from their eyes."

Seven trumpets

CHAPTER 8

The seventh seal is opened

[1] When the Lamb opened the seventh seal, there was silence in heaven for about half an hour. [2] I noticed that the seven angels who stood before God were each given a trumpet.

[3] Another angel, who had a gold container for incense,* came and stood at the altar. This one was given a lot of incense to offer with the prayers of God's people on the gold altar in front of the throne. [4] Then the smoke of the incense, together with the prayers of God's people, went up to God from the hand of the angel.

[5] After this, the angel filled the incense container with fire from the altar and threw it on the earth. Thunder roared, lightning flashed, and the earth shook.

---

*8.3 incense: See the note at 5.8.

See also: 7.14: Dan 12.1; Matt 24.21; Mark 13.19.
7.16: Isa 49.10.   7.17: a Psa 23.1; Ezek 34.23; b Psa 23.2;
Isa 49.10; c Isa 25.8.   8.3: a Amos 9.1; b Exod 30.1,3.
8.5: a Lev 16.12; Ezek 10.2; b Exod 19.16; Rev 11.19; 16.18.

See also: 7.3: Ezek 9.4,6.

The trumpets

⁶ The seven angels now got ready to blow their trumpets.

⁷ When the first angel blew his trumpet, hail and fire mixed with blood were thrown down on the earth. A third of the earth, a third of the trees, and a third of all green plants were burnt.

⁸ When the second angel blew his trumpet, something like a great fiery mountain was thrown into the sea. A third of the sea turned to blood, ⁹ a third of the living creatures in the sea died, and a third of the ships were destroyed.

¹⁰ When the third angel blew his trumpet, a great star fell from heaven. It was burning like a torch, and it fell on a third of the rivers and on a third of the springs of water. ¹¹ The name of the star was Bitter, and a third of the water turned bitter. Many people died because the water was so bitter.

¹² When the fourth angel blew his trumpet, a third of the sun, a third of the moon, and a third of the stars were struck. They each lost a third of their light. So during a third of the day there was no light, and a third of the night was also without light.

¹³ Then I looked and saw a lone eagle flying across the sky. It was shouting, "Trouble, trouble, trouble to everyone who lives on earth! The other three angels are now going to blow their trumpets."

CHAPTER 9

¹ When the fifth angel blew his trumpet, I saw a star* fall from the sky to earth. It was given the key to the tunnel that leads down to the deep pit. ² As it opened the tunnel, smoke poured out like the smoke of a great furnace. The sun and the air turned dark because of the smoke. ³ Locusts* came out of the smoke and covered the earth. They were given the same power that scorpions have.

⁴ The locusts were told not to harm the grass on the earth or any plant or any tree. They were to punish only those people who did not have God's mark on their foreheads. ⁵ The locusts were allowed to make them suffer for five months, but not to kill them.

The suffering they caused was like the sting of a scorpion. ⁶ In those days people will want to die, but they will not be able to. They will hope for death, but it will escape from them.

⁷ These locusts looked like horses ready for battle. On their heads they wore something like gold crowns, and they had human faces. ⁸ Their hair was like a woman's long hair, and their teeth were like those of a lion. ⁹ On their chests they wore armour made of iron. Their wings roared like an army of horse-drawn chariots rushing into battle. ¹⁰ Their tails were like a scorpion's tail with a sting that had the power to hurt someone for five months. ¹¹ Their king was the angel in charge of the deep pit. In Hebrew his name was Abaddon, and in Greek it was Apollyon.*

¹² The first horrible thing has now happened! But wait. Two more horrible things will happen soon.

¹³ Then the sixth angel blew his trumpet. I heard a voice speak from the four corners of the gold altar that stands in the presence of God. ¹⁴ The voice spoke to this angel and said, "Release the four angels who are tied up beside the great River Euphrates." ¹⁵ The four angels had been prepared for this very hour and day and month and year. Now they were set free to kill a third of all people.

¹⁶ By listening, I could tell there were more than two hundred million of these war horses. ¹⁷ In my vision their riders wore fiery red, dark blue, and yellow armour on their chests. The heads of the horses looked like lions, with fire and smoke and sulphur coming out of their mouths. ¹⁸ One-third of all people were killed by the three terrible troubles caused by the fire, the smoke, and the sulphur. ¹⁹ The horses had powerful mouths, and their tails were like poisonous snakes that bite and hurt.

²⁰ The people who lived through these terrible troubles did not turn away from the idols they had made, and they did not stop worshipping demons. They kept on worshipping idols that were made of gold, silver, bronze, stone, and wood. Not one of these idols could see, hear, or walk. ²¹ No one stopped murdering or practising witchcraft or being immoral or stealing.

---

*9.1 star: In the ancient world, stars were often thought of as living beings, such as angels.

*9.3 Locusts: A type of grasshopper that comes in swarms and causes great damage to crops.

See also: 8.7: Exod 9.23–25; Ezek 38.22. 8.10: Isa 14.12. 8.11: Jer 9.15. 8.12: Isa 13.10; Ezek 32.7; Joel 2.10,31; 3.15. 9.2: Gen 19.28. 9.3: Exod 10.12–15. 9.4: Ezek 9.4.

*9.11 Abaddon . . . Apollyon: The Hebrew word "Abaddon" and the Greek word "Apollyon" each mean "destruction".

See also: 9.6: Job 3.21; Jer 8.3. 9.7: Joel 2.4. 9.8: Joel 1.6. 9.9: Joel 2.5. 9.13: Exod 30.1–3. 9.20: Psa 115.4–7; 135.15–17; Dan 5.23.

Viewpoints

If money and fame won't outlast the world, what will?

Contributed by Michael D

'The angel said, "You won't have to wait any longer."'

For young people, living the Christian life has never been more difficult. We are encouraged to pursue nothing but fame and money. Shows like 'Sex and the City' tempt us into lust every time we turn on the TV, go to the cinema, or even read a magazine. Sometimes I am so afraid of my friends' patronising laughter that I'm scared even to tell them I spent last night at my church Youth Group or that I went away this summer on a Christian camp.

The good news in this verse, however, is that God will soon destroy this old, hostile world. The finishing line of our long and muddy cross-country run is in sight. In Revelations, God tells us how exactly this ending will take place and what will happen after it. Sinners will be punished by plagues and monsters, but, because we have trusted Jesus to take our punishment on Himself, Christians will be spared and will inherit a new creation, where there is no suffering or temptation.

This verse doesn't necessarily mean this will all happen tomorrow (though you never know). It is, after all, part of a prophesy of the future. However, it does mean this world and everything in it is only temporary. My friends are only interested in money, attractive partners and exam results, but these will not remain in God's new creation. So why pursue them now? It's better to work for what will outlast this world. This means building a relationship with God through prayer, learning more about him through the Bible and helping others to join us in God's new world, by telling them why they must put their trust in Jesus.

More...

Money p.1043
Media p.1235
Do we centre our dreams on God? p.712

CHAPTER 10

The angel and the little scroll

¹ I saw another powerful angel come down from heaven. This one was covered with a cloud, and a rainbow was over his head. His face was like the sun, his legs were like columns of fire, ² and with his hand he held a little scroll* that had been unrolled. He stood there with his right foot on the sea and his left foot on the land. ³ Then he shouted with a voice that sounded like a growling lion. Thunder roared seven times.

⁴ After the thunder stopped, I was about to write what it had said. But a voice from heaven shouted, "Keep it secret! Don't write these things."

⁵ The angel I had seen standing on the sea and the land then held his right hand up towards heaven. ⁶ He made a promise in the name of God who lives for ever and who created heaven, earth, the sea, and every living creature. The angel said, "You won't have to wait any longer. ⁷ God told his secret plans to his servants the prophets, and it will all happen by the time the seventh angel sounds his trumpet."

⁸ Once again the voice from heaven spoke to me. It said, "Go and take the open scroll from the hand of the angel standing on the sea and the land."

⁹ When I went over to ask the angel for the little scroll, the angel said, "Take the scroll and eat it! Your stomach will turn sour, but the taste in your mouth will be as sweet as honey." ¹⁰ I took the little scroll from the hand of the angel and ate it. The taste was as sweet as honey, but my stomach turned sour.

¹¹ Then some voices said, "Keep on telling what will happen to the people of many nations, races, and languages, and also to kings."

CHAPTER 11

The two witnesses

¹ An angel gave me a measuring stick and said:

Measure around God's temple. Be sure to include the altar and everyone worshipping there. ² But don't measure the courtyard outside the temple building. Leave it out. It has been given to those

---

*10.2 scroll: See the note at 5.1.

See also: **10.5–7:** Exod 20.11; Deut 32.40; Dan 12.7; Amos 3.7. **10.8–10:** Ezek 2.8—3.3. **11.1:** Ezek 40.3; Zech 2.1–2. **11.2:** Luke 21.24.

people who don't know God, and they will trample all over the holy city for forty-two months. ³ My two witnesses will wear sackcloth,* while I let them preach for one thousand two hundred and sixty days.

⁴ These two witnesses are the two olive trees and the two lampstands that stand in the presence of the Lord who rules the earth. ⁵ Any enemy who tries to harm them will be destroyed by the fire that comes out of their mouths. ⁶ They have the power to lock up the sky and to keep rain from falling while they are prophesying. And whenever they want to, they can turn water to blood and cause all kinds of terrible troubles on earth.

⁷ After the two witnesses have finished preaching God's message, the beast that lives in the deep pit will come up and fight against them. It will win the battle and kill them. ⁸ Their bodies will be left lying in the streets of the same great city where their Lord was nailed to a cross. And that city is spiritually like the city of Sodom or the country of Egypt.

⁹ For three and a half days the people of every nation, tribe, language, and race will stare at the bodies of these two witnesses and refuse to let them be buried. ¹⁰ Everyone on earth will celebrate and be happy. They will give gifts to each other, because of what happened to the two prophets who caused them so much trouble. ¹¹ But three and a half days later, God will breathe life into their bodies. They will stand up, and everyone who sees them will be terrified.

¹² The witnesses then heard a loud voice from heaven, saying, "Come up here." And while their enemies were watching, they were taken up to heaven in a cloud. ¹³ At that same moment there was a terrible earthquake that destroyed a tenth of the city. Seven thousand people were killed, and the rest were frightened and praised the God who rules in heaven.

¹⁴ The second horrible thing has now happened! But the third one will be here soon.

The seventh trumpet

¹⁵ At the sound of the seventh trumpet, loud voices were heard in heaven. They said,

"Now the kingdom
  of this world
belongs to our Lord
  and to his Chosen One!
And he will rule
  for ever and ever!"

¹⁶ Then the twenty-four elders, who were seated on thrones in God's presence, knelt down and worshipped him. ¹⁷ They said,

"Lord God All-Powerful,
  you are and you were,
    and we thank you.
You used your great power
  and started ruling.
¹⁸ When the nations got angry,
  you became angry too!
Now the time has come
  for the dead
    to be judged.
It is time for you to reward
  your servants the prophets
and all your people
who honour your name,
  no matter who they are.
It is time to destroy everyone
who has destroyed
  the earth."

¹⁹ The door to God's temple in heaven was then opened, and the sacred chest* could be seen inside the temple. I saw lightning and heard roars of thunder. The earth trembled and huge hailstones fell to the ground.

A dragon and two beasts

CHAPTER 12

The woman and the dragon

¹ Something important appeared in the sky. It was a woman whose clothes were the sun. The moon was under her feet, and a crown made of twelve stars was on her head. ² She was about to give birth, and she was crying because of the great pain.

³ Something else appeared in the sky. It was a huge red dragon with seven heads and ten horns, and a crown on each of its seven heads. ⁴ With its tail, it dragged a third of the

---

*11.3 sackcloth: See the note at 6.12.

See also: 11.4: Zech 4.3,11–14. 11.6: a 1 King 17.1; b Exod 7.17–19; c 1 Sam 4.8. 11.7: a Dan 7.7; Rev 13.5–7; 17.8; b Dan 7.21. 11.8: Isa 1.9–10. 11.11: Ezek 37.10. 11.12: 2 King 2.11. 11.13: Rev 6.12; 16.18. 11.15: Exod 15.18; Dan 2.44; 7.14,27.

*11.19 sacred chest: In Old Testament times the sacred chest was kept in the tent used for worship. It was the symbol of God's presence with his people and also of his agreement with them.

See also: 11.18: a Psa 2.5; 110.5; b Psa 115.13. 11.19: a Rev 8.5; 16.18; b Rev 16.21. 12.3: Dan 7.7. 12.4: Dan 8.10.

stars from the sky and threw them down to the earth. Then the dragon turned towards the woman, because it wanted to eat her child as soon as it was born.

⁵ The woman gave birth to a son, who would rule all nations with an iron rod. The boy was snatched away. He was taken to God and placed on his throne. ⁶ The woman ran into the desert to a place that God had prepared for her. There she would be taken care of for one thousand two hundred and sixty days.

Michael fights the dragon

⁷ A war broke out in heaven. Michael and his angels were fighting against the dragon and its angels. ⁸ But the dragon lost the battle. It and its angels were forced out of their places in heaven ⁹ and were thrown down to the earth. Yes, that old snake and his angels were thrown out of heaven! That snake, who fools everyone on earth, is known as the devil and Satan. ¹⁰ Then I heard a voice from heaven shout,

> "Our God has shown
> his saving power,
>   and his kingdom has come!
> God's own Chosen One
>   has shown his authority.
> Satan accused our people
> in the presence of God
>   day and night.
> Now he has been thrown out!

¹¹ Our people defeated Satan
    because of the blood›
of the Lamb
    and the message of God.
They were willing
    to give up their lives.
¹² The heavens should rejoice,
    together with everyone
        who lives there.
But pity the earth
    and the sea,
because the devil
    was thrown down
        to the earth.
He knows his time is short,
    and he is very angry."

¹³ When the dragon realized that it had been thrown down to the earth, it tried to make trouble for the woman who had given birth

to a son. ¹⁴ But the woman was given two wings like those of a huge eagle, so that she could fly into the desert. There she would escape from the snake and be taken care of for a time, two times, and half a time.

¹⁵ The snake then spewed out water like a river to sweep the woman away. ¹⁶ But the earth helped her and swallowed the water that had come from the dragon's mouth. ¹⁷ This made the dragon terribly angry with the woman. So it started a war against the rest of her children. They are the people who obey God and are faithful to what Jesus did and taught. ¹⁸ The dragon› stood on the beach beside the sea.

CHAPTER 13

The two beasts

¹ I looked and saw a beast coming up from the sea. This one had ten horns and seven heads, and a crown was on each of its ten horns. On each of its heads were names that were an insult to God. ² The beast that I saw had the body of a leopard, the feet of a bear, and the mouth of a lion. The dragon handed over its own power and throne and great authority to this beast. ³ One of its heads seemed to have been fatally wounded, but now it was well. Everyone on earth marvelled at this beast, ⁴ and they worshipped the dragon who had given its authority to the beast. They also worshipped the beast and said, "No one is like this beast! No one can fight against it."

⁵ The beast was allowed to boast and claim to be God, and for forty-two months it was allowed to rule. ⁶ The beast cursed God, and it cursed the name of God. It even cursed the place where God lives, as well as everyone who lives in heaven with God. ⁷ It was allowed to fight against God's people and defeat them. It was also given authority over the people of every tribe, nation, language, and race. ⁸ The beast was worshipped by everyone whose name wasn't written before the time of creation in the book of the Lamb who was killed.›

⁹ If you have ears,
    then listen!
¹⁰ If you are doomed
    to be captured,
        you will be captured.

See also: 12.5: a Isa 66.7; **b** Psa 2.9.   **12.7:** Dan 10.13,21; 12.1; Jude 9.   **12.9: a** Gen 3.1; **b** Luke 10.18. **12.10:** Job 1.9–11; Zech 3.1.

See also: 12.14: Dan 7.25; 12.7.   **13.1: a** Dan 7.3; **b** Rev 17.3,7–12.   **13.2:** Dan 7.4–6.   **13.5–6:** Dan 7.8,25; 11.36.   **13.7:** Dan 7.21.   **13.8:** Psa 69.28.   **13.10:** Jer 15.2; 43.11.

If you are doomed
    to be killed by a sword,
    you will be killed
    by a sword.

This means that God's people must learn to endure and be faithful!

¹¹ I now saw another beast. This one came out of the ground. It had two horns like a lamb, but spoke like a dragon. ¹² It worked for the beast whose fatal wound had been healed. And it used all its authority to force the earth and its people to worship that beast. ¹³ It performed mighty miracles, and while people watched, it even made fire come down from the sky.

¹⁴ This second beast fooled people on earth by performing miracles for the first one. Then it talked them into making an idol in the form of the beast that did not die after being wounded by a sword. ¹⁵ It was allowed to put breath into the idol, so that it could speak. Everyone who refused to worship the idol of the beast was put to death. ¹⁶ All people were forced to put a mark on their right hand or forehead. Whether they were powerful or weak, rich or poor, free people or slaves, ¹⁷ they all had to have this mark, or else they could not buy or sell anything. This mark stood for the name of the beast and for the number of its name.

¹⁸ You need wisdom to understand the number of the beast! But if you are clever enough, you can work this out. Its number is six hundred and sixty-six, and it stands for a person.

Visions of God's judgment and protection

CHAPTER 14

The Lamb and his 144,000 followers

¹ I looked and saw the Lamb standing on Mount Zion!* With him were a hundred and forty-four thousand, who had his name and his Father's name written on their foreheads. ² Then I heard a sound from heaven that was like a roaring flood or loud thunder or even like the music of harps. ³ And a new song was being sung in front of God's throne and in front of the four living creatures and the elders. No one could learn that song, except the one hundred and forty-four thousand

who had been rescued from the earth. ⁴ All these are pure virgins, and they follow the Lamb wherever he leads. They have been rescued to be presented to God and the Lamb as the most precious people* on earth. ⁵ They never tell lies, and they are innocent.

The messages of the three angels

⁶ I saw another angel. This one was flying across the sky and had the eternal good news to announce to the people of every race, tribe, language, and nation on earth. ⁷ The angel shouted, "Worship and honour God! The time has come for him to judge everyone. Kneel down before the one who created heaven and earth, the oceans, and every stream."

⁸ A second angel followed and said, "The great city of Babylon has fallen! This is the city that made all nations drunk and immoral. Now God is angry, and Babylon has fallen."

⁹ Finally, a third angel came and shouted:

Here is what will happen if you worship the beast and the idol and have the mark of the beast on your hand or forehead. ¹⁰ You will have to drink the wine that God gives to everyone who makes him angry. You will feel his mighty anger, and you will be tortured with fire and burning sulphur, while the holy angels and the Lamb look on.

¹¹ If you worship the beast and the idol and accept the mark of its name, you will be tortured day and night. The smoke from your torture will go up for ever and ever, and you will never be able to rest.

¹² God's people must learn to endure. They must also obey his commands and have faith in Jesus.

¹³ Then I heard a voice from heaven say, "Put this in writing. From now on, the Lord will bless everyone who has faith in him when they die."

The Spirit answered, "Yes, they will rest from their hard work, and they will be rewarded for what they have done."

---

*14.1 Mount Zion: Another name for Jerusalem.
See also: 14.1: Ezek 9.4; Rev 7.3.

*14.4 the most precious people: The Greek text has "the first people". The Law of Moses taught that the firstborn of all animals and the first part of the harvest were special and belonged to the Lord.

See also: 14.5: Zeph 3.13. 14.8: Isa 21.9; Jer 51.8; Rev 18.2. 14.10: a Isa 51.17; b Gen 19.24; Ezek 38.22. 14.11: Isa 34.10.

The earth is harvested

[14] I looked and saw a bright cloud, and someone who seemed to be the Son of Man* was sitting on the cloud. He wore a gold crown on his head and held a sharp sickle* in his hand. [15] An angel came out of the temple and shouted, "Start cutting with your sickle! Harvest season is here, and all crops on earth are ripe." [16] The one on the cloud swung his sickle and harvested the crops.

[17] Another angel with a sharp sickle then came out of the temple in heaven. [18] After this, an angel with power over fire came from the altar and shouted to the angel who had the sickle. He said, "All grapes on earth are ripe! Harvest them with your sharp sickle." [19] The angel swung his sickle on earth and cut off its grapes. He threw them into a pit* where they were trampled on as a sign of God's anger. [20] The pit was outside the city, and when the grapes were squashed, blood flowed out. The blood turned into a river that was about three hundred kilometres long and almost deep enough to cover a horse.

CHAPTER 15

The last of the terrible troubles

[1] After this, I looked at the sky and saw something else that was strange and important. Seven angels were bringing the last seven terrible troubles. When these are ended, God will no longer be angry.

[2] Then I saw something that looked like a glass sea mixed with fire, and people were standing on it. They were the ones who had defeated the beast and the idol and the number that tells the name of the beast. God had given them harps, [3] and they were singing the song that his servant Moses and the Lamb had sung. They were singing,

"Lord God All-Powerful,
  you have done great
    and marvellous things.
You are the ruler
  of all nations,
  and you do what is
    right and fair.

[4] Lord, who doesn't honour
    and praise your name?
  You alone are holy,
  and all nations will come
    and worship you,
  because you have shown
    that you judge with fairness."

[5] After this, I noticed something else in heaven. The sacred tent used for a temple was open. [6] And the seven angels who were bringing the terrible troubles were coming out of it. They were dressed in robes of pure white linen and wore belts made of pure gold. [7] One of the four living creatures gave each of the seven angels a bowl made of gold. These bowls were filled with the anger of God who lives for ever and ever. [8] The temple quickly filled with smoke from the glory and power of God. No one could enter it until the seven angels had finished pouring out the seven last troubles.

Seven bowls of God's anger

CHAPTER 16

[1] From the temple I heard a voice shout to the seven angels, "Go and empty the seven bowls of God's anger on the earth."

[2] The first angel emptied his bowl on the earth. At once ugly and painful sores broke out on everyone who had the mark of the beast and worshipped the idol.

[3] The second angel emptied his bowl on the sea. Straight away the sea turned into blood like that of a dead person, and every living thing in the sea died.

[4] The third angel emptied his bowl into the rivers and streams. At once they turned to blood. [5] Then I heard the angel, who has power over water, say,

"You have always been,
and you always will be
  the holy God.
You had the right
  to judge in this way.
[6] They poured out the blood*
  of your people
    and your prophets.
So you gave them blood
  to drink, as they deserve!"

---

*14.14 **Son of Man:** See the note at 1.13.
*14.14 **sickle:** A knife with a long curved blade, used to cut grain and other crops.
*14.19 **pit:** It was the custom to put grapes in a pit (called a wine press) and trample on them to make juice that would later turn to wine.
See also: 14.14: Dan 7.13. **14.15:** Joel 3.13.
14.20: Isa 63.3; Lam 1.15; Rev 19.15. **15.3:** Exod 15.1.

*16.6 **They poured out the blood:** A way of saying, "They murdered".

See also: 15.4: a Jer 10.7; b Psa 86.9. **15.5:** Exod 38.21.
15.8: Exod 40.34; 1 King 8.10–11; 2 Chron 5.13–14; Isa 6.4.
16.2: Exod 9.10. **16.4:** Exod 7.17–21; Psa 78.44.

7 After this, I heard
the altar shout,
"Yes, Lord God All-Powerful,
your judgments are honest
and fair."

8 The fourth angel emptied his bowl on the sun, and it began to scorch people like fire. 9 Everyone was scorched by its great heat, and all of them cursed the name of God who had power over these terrible troubles. But no one turned to God and praised him.

10 The fifth angel emptied his bowl on the throne of the beast. At once darkness covered its kingdom, and its people began biting their tongues in pain. 11 And because of their painful sores, they cursed the God who rules in heaven. But still they did not stop doing evil things.

12 The sixth angel emptied his bowl on the great River Euphrates, and it completely dried up to make a road for the kings from the east. 13 An evil spirit that looked like a frog came out of the mouth of the dragon. One also came out of the mouth of the beast, and another out of the mouth of the false prophet. 14 These evil spirits had the power to perform miracles. They went to every king on earth, to bring them together for a war against God All-Powerful. But that will be the day of God's great victory.

15 Remember that Christ says, "When I come, it will surprise you like a thief! But God will bless you, if you are awake and ready. Then you won't have to walk around naked and be ashamed."

16 Those armies came together in a place that in Hebrew is called Armageddon.*

17 As soon as the seventh angel emptied his bowl in the air, a loud voice from the throne in the temple shouted, "It's done!" 18 There were flashes of lightning, roars of thunder, and the worst earthquake in all history. 19 The great city of Babylon split into three parts, and the cities of other nations fell. So God made Babylon drink from the wine cup that was filled with his anger. 20 Every island ran away, and the mountains disappeared. 21 Hailstones, weighing about fifty kilogrammes each, fell

from the sky on people. Finally, the people cursed God, because the hail was so terrible.

God's enemies are defeated

CHAPTER 17

The prostitute and the beast

1 One of the seven angels who had emptied the bowls came over and said to me, "Come on! I will show you how God will punish that shameless prostitute who sits on many oceans. 2 Every king on earth has slept with her, and her shameless ways are like wine that has made everyone on earth drunk."

3 With the help of the Spirit, the angel took me into the desert, where I saw a woman sitting on a red beast. The beast was covered with names that were an insult to God, and it had seven heads and ten horns. 4 The woman was dressed in purple and scarlet robes, and she wore jewellery made of gold, precious stones, and pearls. In her hand she held a gold cup filled with the filthy and nasty things she had done. 5 On her forehead a mysterious name was written:

I AM THE GREAT CITY OF BABYLON,
THE MOTHER OF EVERY IMMORAL
AND FILTHY THING ON EARTH.

6 I could tell that the woman was drunk on the blood of God's people who had given their lives for Jesus. This surprising sight amazed me, 7 and the angel said:

Why are you so amazed? I will explain the mystery about this woman and about the beast she is sitting on, with its seven heads and ten horns. 8 The beast you saw is one that used to be and no longer is. It will come back from the deep pit, but only to be destroyed. Everyone on earth whose names were not written in the book of life* before the time of creation will be amazed. They will see this beast that used to be and no longer is, but will be once more.

9 Anyone with wisdom can work this out. The seven heads that the woman is sitting on stand for seven hills. These heads are also seven kings. 10 Five of the kings are dead. One is ruling now, and the other one has not yet come. But when he does, he will rule for only a little while.

---

*16.16 Armageddon: The Hebrew form of the name would be "Har Megiddo", meaning "Hill of Megiddo", where many battles were fought in ancient times (see Judges 5.19; 2 Kings 23.29–30).

See also: 16.10: Exod 10.21. **16.12:** Isa 11.15.
16.15: Matt 24.43–44; Luke 12.39–40; Rev 3.3.
16.16: 2 King 23.29; Zech 12.11. **16.18:** Rev 8.5; 11.13,19.
16.19: Isa 51.17. **16.20:** Rev 6.14. **16.21:** Exod 9.23;
Rev 11.19.

*17.8 book of life: See the note at 3.5.

See also: 17.1: Jer 51.13. **17.2:** Isa 23.17; Jer 51.7.
17.3: Rev 13.1. **17.4:** Jer 51.7. **17.8:** a Dan 7.7; Rev 11.7;
b Psa 69.28.

[11] You also saw a beast that used to be and no longer is. That beast is one of the seven kings who will return as the eighth king, but only to be destroyed.

[12] The ten horns that you saw are ten more kings, who have not yet come into power, and they will rule with the beast for only a short time. [13] They all think alike and will give their power and authority to the beast. [14] These kings will go to war against the Lamb. But he will defeat them, because he is Lord over all lords and King over all kings. His followers are chosen and special and faithful.

[15] The oceans that you saw the prostitute sitting on are crowds of people from all races and languages. [16] The ten horns and the beast will start hating the shameless woman. They will strip off her clothes and leave her naked. Then they will eat her flesh and throw the rest of her body into a fire. [17] God is the one who made these kings all think alike and decide to give their power to the beast. And they will do this until what God has said comes true.

[18] The woman you saw is the great city that rules over all kings on earth.

CHAPTER 18

The fall of Babylon

[1] I saw another angel come from heaven. This one had great power, and the earth was bright because of his glory. [2] The angel shouted,

> "Fallen! Powerful Babylon
>   has fallen
> and is now the home
>   of demons.
> It is the den
>   of every filthy spirit
> and of all unclean birds,
>   and every dirty
>   and hated animal.
> [3] Babylon's evil and immoral wine
>   has made all nations drunk.
> Every king on earth
>   has slept with her,
> and every merchant on earth
>   is rich because of
>   her evil desires."

[4] Then I heard another voice
  from heaven shout,

> "My people, you must escape
>   from Babylon.
> Don't take part in her sins
>   and share her punishment.
> [5] Her sins are piled
>   as high as heaven.
> God has remembered the evil
>   she has done.
> [6] Treat her as she
>   has treated others.
> Make her pay double
>   for what she has done.
> Make her drink twice as much
>   of what she mixed
>   for others.
> [7] That woman honoured herself
>   with a life of luxury.
> Reward her now
>   with suffering and pain.
>
> "Deep in her heart
> Babylon said,
>   'I am the queen!
> Never will I be a widow
> or know what it means
>   to be sad.'
> [8] And so, in a single day
> she will suffer the pain
>   of sorrow, hunger, and death.
> Fire will destroy
>   her dead body,
> because her judge
>   is the powerful Lord God."

[9] Every king on earth who slept with her and shared in her luxury will mourn. They will weep, when they see the smoke from that fire. [10] Her sufferings will frighten them, and they will stand at a distance and say,

> "Pity that great
>   and powerful city!
> Pity Babylon!
> In a single hour
>   her judgment has come."

[11] Every merchant on earth will mourn, because there is no one to buy their goods. [12] There won't be anyone to buy their gold, silver, jewels, pearls, fine linen, purple cloth, silk, scarlet cloth, sweet-smelling wood, fancy carvings of ivory and wood, as well as things made of bronze, iron, or marble. [13] No one will buy their cinnamon, spices, incense, myrrh,

See also: **17.12:** Dan 7.24. **18.2: a** Isa 21.9; Jer 51.8; Rev 14.8; **b** Isa 13.21; Jer 50.39. **18.3:** Isa 23.17; Jer 51.7. **18.4:** Isa 48.20; Jer 50.8; 51.6,45.

See also: **18.5:** Gen 18.20–21; Jer 51.9. **18.6:** Psa 137.8; Jer 50.29. **18.7–8:** Isa 47.7–9. **18.9–10:** Ezek 26.16–17. **18.11:** Ezek 27.31,36. **18.12–13:** Ezek 27.12–13,22.

frankincense,* wine, olive oil, fine flour, wheat, cattle, sheep, horses, chariots, slaves, and other humans.

¹⁴ Babylon, the things
    your heart desired
have all escaped
    from you.
Every luxury
and all your glory
    will be lost for ever.
You will never
    get them back.

¹⁵ The merchants had become rich because of her. But when they saw her sufferings, they were terrified. They stood at a distance, crying and mourning. ¹⁶ Then they shouted,

"Pity the great city
    of Babylon!
She dressed in fine linen
and wore purple
    and scarlet cloth.
She had jewellery
    made of gold
and precious stones
    and pearls.
¹⁷ Yet in a single hour
    her riches disappeared."

Every ship's captain and passenger and sailor stood at a distance, together with everyone who does business by travelling on the sea. ¹⁸ When they saw the smoke from her fire, they shouted, "This was the greatest city ever!"

¹⁹ They cried loudly, and in their sorrow they threw dust on their heads, as they said,

"Pity the great city
    of Babylon!
Everyone who sailed the seas
became rich
    from her treasures.
But in a single hour
    the city was destroyed.
²⁰ The heavens should be happy
    with God's people
        and apostles and prophets.
God has punished her
    for them."

²¹ A powerful angel then picked up a huge stone and threw it into the sea. The angel said,

"This is how the great city
    of Babylon
will be thrown down,
    never to rise again.
²² The music of harps and singers
    and of flutes and trumpets
        will no longer be heard.
No workers will ever
    set up shop in that city,
and the sound
    of grinding grain
        will be silenced for ever.
²³ Lamps will no longer shine
    anywhere in Babylon,
and couples will never again
    say wedding vows there.
Her merchants ruled
    the earth,
and by her witchcraft
    she fooled all nations.
²⁴ On the streets of Babylon
is found the blood
    of God's people
and of his prophets,
    and everyone else."

CHAPTER 19

¹ After this, I heard what sounded like a lot of voices in heaven, and they were shouting,

"Praise the Lord!
To our God belongs
    the glorious power to save,
² because his judgments
    are honest and fair.
That filthy prostitute
ruined the earth
    with shameful deeds.
But God has judged her
    and made her pay
the price for murdering
    his servants."

³ Then the crowd shouted,

"Praise the Lord!
Smoke will never stop rising
    from her burning body."

⁴ After this, the twenty-four elders and the four living creatures all knelt before the

---

*18.13 myrrh, frankincense: Myrrh was a valuable sweet-smelling powder often used in perfume. Frankincense was a valuable powder that was burnt to make a sweet smell.

See also: 18.15: Ezek 27.31,36. **18.17:** Isa 23.14; Ezek 27.26–30. **18.18:** Ezek 27.32. **18.19:** Ezek 27.30–34. **18.20:** Deut 32.43; Jer 51.48.

See also: 18.21: a Jer 51.63–64; **b** Ezek 26.21. **18.22:** Ezek 26.13; Isa 24.8. **18.22–23:** Jer 7.34; 25.10. **18.24:** Jer 51.49. **19.2:** Deut 32.43; 2 King 9.7. **19.3:** Isa 34.10.

throne of God and worshipped him. They said, "Amen! Praise the Lord!"

The marriage supper of the Lamb

⁵ From the throne a voice said,

"If you worship
and fear our God,
give praise to him,
no matter who you are."

⁶ Then I heard what seemed to be a large crowd that sounded like a roaring flood and loud thunder all mixed together. They were saying,

"Praise the Lord!
Our Lord God All-Powerful
now rules as king.
⁷ So we will be glad and happy
and give him praise.
The wedding day of the Lamb
is here,
and his bride is ready.
⁸ She will be given
a wedding dress
made of pure
and shining linen.
This linen stands for
the good things
God's people have done."

⁹ Then the angel told me, "Put this in writing. God will bless everyone who is invited to the wedding feast of the Lamb." The angel also said, "These things that God has said are true."

¹⁰ I knelt at the feet of the angel and began to worship him. But the angel said, "Don't do that! I am a servant, just like you and everyone else who tells about Jesus. Don't worship anyone but God. Everyone who tells about Jesus does it by the power of the Spirit."

The rider on the white horse

¹¹ I looked and saw that heaven was open, and a white horse was there. Its rider was called Faithful and True, and he is always fair when he judges or goes to war. ¹² He had eyes like flames of fire, and he was wearing a lot of crowns. His name was written on him, but he was the only one who knew what the name meant.

¹³ The rider wore a robe that was covered with⁺ blood, and he was known as "The Word of God". ¹⁴ He was followed by armies from heaven that rode on horses and were

dressed in pure white linen. ¹⁵ From his mouth a sharp sword went out to attack the nations. He will rule them with an iron rod and will show the fierce anger of God All-Powerful by trampling on the grapes in the pit where wine is made. ¹⁶ On the part of the robe that covered his thigh was written, "KING OF KINGS AND LORD OF LORDS".

¹⁷ I then saw an angel standing on the sun, and he shouted to all the birds flying in the sky, "Come and join in God's great feast! ¹⁸ You can eat the flesh of kings, rulers, leaders, horses, riders, free people, slaves, important people, and everyone else."

¹⁹ I also saw the beast and all kings of the earth come together. They fought against the rider on the white horse and against his army. ²⁰ But the beast was captured and so was the false prophet. This is the same prophet who had performed miracles for the beast, so that he could fool everyone who had the mark of the beast and worshipped the idol. The beast and the false prophet were thrown alive into a lake of burning sulphur. ²¹ But the rest of their army was killed by the sword that came from the mouth of the rider on the horse. Then birds stuffed themselves on the dead bodies.

CHAPTER 20

The thousand years

¹ I saw an angel come down from heaven, carrying the key to the deep pit and a big chain. ² He chained the dragon for a thousand years. It is that old snake, who is also known as the devil and Satan. ³ Then the angel threw the dragon into the pit. He locked and sealed it, so that a thousand years would go by before the dragon could fool the nations again. But after that, it would have to be set free for a little while.

⁴ I saw thrones, and sitting on those thrones were the ones who had been given the right to judge. I also saw the souls of the people who had their heads cut off because they had told about Jesus and preached God's message. They were the same ones who had not worshipped the beast or the idol, and they had refused to let its mark be put on their hands or foreheads. They will come to life and rule with Christ for a thousand years.

⁵⁻⁶ These people are the first to be raised to life, and they are especially blessed and

See also: **19.5:** Psa 115.13. **19.6:** a Ezek 1.24; b Psa 93.1; 97.1; 99.1. **19.9:** Matt 22.2–3. **19.11:** a Ezek 1.1; b Psa 96.13; Isa 11.4. **19.12:** Dan 10.6.

See also: **19.15:** a Psa 2.9; b Isa 63.3; Joel 3.13; Rev 14.20. **19.17–18:** Ezek 39.17–20. **19.20:** Rev 13.1–18. **20.2:** Gen 3.1. **20.4:** Dan 7.9,22.

holy. The second death* has no power over them. They will be priests for God and Christ and will rule with them for a thousand years.

No other dead people were raised to life until a thousand years later.

Satan is defeated

⁷ At the end of the thousand years, Satan will be set free. ⁸ He will fool the countries of Gog and Magog, which are at the far ends of the earth, and their people will follow him into battle. They will have as many followers as there are grains of sand along the beach, ⁹ and they will march all the way across the earth. They will surround the camp of God's people and the city that his people love. But fire will come down from heaven and destroy the whole army. ¹⁰ Then the devil who fooled them will be thrown into the lake of fire and burning sulphur. He will be there with the beast and the false prophet, and they will be in pain day and night for ever and ever.

The final judgment

The judgment at the great white throne

¹¹ I saw a great white throne with someone sitting on it. Earth and heaven tried to run away, but there was nowhere for them to go. ¹² I also saw all the dead people standing in front of that throne. Every one of them was there, no matter who they had once been. Several books were opened, and then the book of life* was opened. The dead were judged by what those books said they had done. ¹³ The sea gave up the dead people who were in it, and death and its kingdom also gave up their dead. Then everyone was judged by what they had done. ¹⁴ Afterwards, death and its kingdom were thrown into the lake of fire. This is the second death.* ¹⁵ Anyone whose name wasn't written in the book of life was thrown into the lake of fire.

A new heaven and a new earth

CHAPTER 21

¹ I saw a new heaven and a new earth. The first heaven and the first earth had disappeared, and so had the sea. ² Then I saw New Jerusalem, that holy city, coming down from God in heaven. It was like a bride dressed in her wedding gown and ready to meet her husband.

³ I heard a loud voice shout from the throne:

God's home is now with his people. He will live with them, and they will be his own. Yes, God will make his home among his people. ⁴ He will wipe all tears from their eyes, and there will be no more death, suffering, crying, or pain. These things of the past are gone for ever.

⁵ Then the one sitting on the throne said:

I am making everything new. Write down what I have said. My words are true and can be trusted. ⁶ Everything is finished! I am Alpha and Omega,* the beginning and the end. I will freely give water from the life-giving fountain to everyone who is thirsty. ⁷ All who win the victory will be given these blessings. I will be their God, and they will be my people.

⁸ But I will tell you what will happen to cowards and to everyone who is unfaithful or dirty-minded or who murders or is sexually immoral or uses witchcraft or worships idols or tells lies. They will be thrown into that lake of fire and burning sulphur. This is the second death.*

New Jerusalem

⁹ I saw one of the seven angels who had the bowls filled with the seven last terrible troubles. The angel came to me and said, "Come on! I will show you the one who will be the bride and wife of the Lamb." ¹⁰ Then with the help of the Spirit, he took me to the top of a very high mountain. There he showed me the holy city of Jerusalem coming down from God in heaven.

---

*20.5–6,14 second death: See the note at 2.11.
*20.12 book of life: See the note at 3.5.
See also: 20.8: a Ezek 7.2; b Ezek 38.2,9,15.
20.11–12: Dan 7.9–10.

*21.6 Alpha and Omega: See the note at 1.8.
*21.8 second death: See the note at 2.11.
See also: 21.1: Isa 65.17; 66.22; 2 Pet 3.13.   21.2: a Isa 52.1;
b Rev 3.12; c Isa 61.10.   21.3: Ezek 37.27; Lev 26.11–12.
21.4: a Isa 25.8; b Isa 35.10; 65.19.   21.6: Isa 55.1.
21.7: Psa 89.26–27.   21.10: Ezek 40.2.

¹¹ The glory of God made the city bright. It was dazzling and crystal clear like a precious jasper stone. ¹² The city had a high and thick wall with twelve gates, and each one of them was guarded by an angel. On each of the gates was written the name of one of the twelve tribes of Israel. ¹³ Three of these gates were on the east, three were on the north, three more were on the south, and the other three were on the west. ¹⁴ The city was built on twelve foundation stones. On each of the stones was written the name of one of the Lamb's twelve apostles.

¹⁵ The angel who spoke to me had a gold measuring stick to measure the city and its gates and its walls. ¹⁶ The city was shaped like a cube, because it was just as high as it was wide. When the angel measured the city, it was about two thousand four hundred kilometres high and two thousand four hundred kilometres wide. ¹⁷ Then the angel measured the wall, and by our measurements it was about sixty metres high.

¹⁸ The wall was built of jasper, and the city was made of pure gold, clear as crystal. ¹⁹ Each of the twelve foundations was a precious stone. The first was jasper,* the second was sapphire, the third was agate, the fourth was emerald, ²⁰ the fifth was onyx, the sixth was carnelian, the seventh was chrysolite, the eighth was beryl, the ninth was topaz, the tenth was chrysoprase, the eleventh was jacinth, and the twelfth was amethyst. ²¹ Each of the twelve gates was a solid pearl. The streets of the city were made of pure gold, clear as crystal.

²² I did not see a temple there. The Lord God All-Powerful and the Lamb were its temple. ²³ And the city did not need the sun or the moon. The glory of God was shining on it, and the Lamb was its light.

²⁴ Nations will walk by the light of that city, and kings will bring their riches there. ²⁵ Its gates are always open during the day, and night never comes. ²⁶ The glorious

---

*21.19 jasper: The precious and semi-precious stones mentioned in verses 19,20 are of different colours. *Jasper* is usually green or clear; *sapphire* is blue; *agate* has circles of brown and white; *emerald* is green; *onyx* has different bands of colour; *carnelian* is deep red or reddish-white; *chrysolite* is olive green; *beryl* is green or bluish-green; *topaz* is yellow; *chrysoprase* is apple green; *jacinth* is reddish-orange; and *amethyst* is deep purple.

See also: 21.12–13: Ezek 48.30–35. 21.15: Ezek 40.3.
21.18–21: Isa 54.11–12. 21.23: Isa 60.19–20.
21.24: Isa 60.3. 21.25–26: Isa 60.11.

Big ideas

New heaven & new earth

At the end, all things will be made anew.

Revelation reveals that, in the end, death and hell will be no more. In a way, God will take everything back to the beginning. He's going to reboot the system, shut down the old world and start again.

God and his people will live together. There is a new heaven and a new earth. As God says, 'I am making everything new' (Revelation 21.5).

In the centre of this new earth is the new Jerusalem, the new 'holy city', where God will live with his people. And here's an interesting detail – the city does not have a temple (Revelation 21.22). But why would it need one? God is everywhere and living with his people. The gates will always be open, because all the enemies have been defeated. There will be food for all, healing for all, peace for all.

The description of the new heaven and earth that we find in Revelation echoes the words and visions of previous writers. Prophets like Isaiah had seen glimpses of the perfect world that was to come. Isaiah had seen a world without pain, without tears, without death. He too had seen the world as it was going to be at the end.

God says that he is the alpha and the omega – the first and last letters of the Greek alphabet. He is the beginning and the end.

footsteps

Three days on New heaven and new earth
Isaiah sees the future: Isaiah 65.17–25
Looking forward: 2 Peter 3.1–13
The new city: Rev 21.1—22.5

More...

Heaven p.1412
Dreams and visions p.1410

treasures of nations will be brought into the city. [27] But nothing unworthy will be allowed to enter. No one who is dirty-minded or who tells lies will be there. Only those whose names are written in the Lamb's book of life* will be in the city.

CHAPTER 22

[1] The angel showed me a river that was crystal clear, and its waters gave life. The river came from the throne where God and the Lamb were seated. [2] Then it flowed down the middle of the city's main street. On each side of the river are trees* that grow a different kind of fruit each month of the year. The fruit gives life, and the leaves are used as medicine to heal the nations.

[3] God's curse will no longer be on the people of that city. He and the Lamb will be seated there on their thrones, and its people will worship God [4] and will see him face to face. God's name will be written on the foreheads of the people. [5] Never again will night appear, and no one who lives there will ever need a lamp or the sun. The Lord God will be their light, and they will rule for ever.

Christ will soon return

[6] Then I was told:

These words are true and can be trusted. The Lord God controls the spirits of his prophets, and he is the one who sent his angel to show his servants what must happen straight away. [7] Remember, I am coming soon! God will bless everyone who pays attention to the message of this book.

[8] My name is John, and I am the one who heard and saw these things. Then after I had heard and seen all this, I knelt down and began to worship at the feet of the angel who had shown it to me.

[9] But the angel said,

Don't do that! I am a servant, just like you. I am the same as a follower or a prophet or anyone else who obeys what is written in this book. God is the one you should worship.

[10] Don't keep the prophecies in this book a secret. These things will happen soon. [11] Evil people will keep on being evil, and everyone who is dirty-minded will still be dirty-minded. But good people will keep on doing right, and God's people will always be holy.

[12] Then I was told:

I am coming soon! And when I come, I will reward everyone for what they have done. [13] I am Alpha and Omega,* the first and the last, the beginning and the end.

[14] God will bless all who have washed their robes. They will each have the right to eat fruit from the tree that gives life, and they can enter the gates of the city. [15] But outside the city will be dogs, witches, immoral people, murderers, idol worshippers, and everyone who loves to tell lies and do wrong.

[16] I am Jesus! And I am the one who sent my angel to tell all of you these things for the churches. I am David's Great Descendant,* and I am also the bright morning star.*

[17] The Spirit and the bride say, "Come!" Everyone who hears this* should say, "Come!"

If you are thirsty, come! If you want life-giving water, come and take it. It's free!

[18] Here is my warning for everyone who hears the prophecies in this book:

If you add anything to them, God will make you suffer all the terrible troubles written in this book. [19] If you take anything away from these prophecies, God will not let you have part in the life-giving tree and in the holy city described in this book.

[20] The one who has spoken these things says, "I am coming soon!"

So, Lord Jesus, please come soon! [21] I pray that the Lord Jesus will be kind to all of you.

---

*22.13 Alpha and Omega:** See the note at 1.8.
*22.16 David's Great Descendant:** See the note at 5.5.
*22.16 the bright morning star:** Probably thought of as the brightest star. See 2.27-28.
*22.17 who hears this:** The reading of the book of Revelation in a service of worship.

See also: 22.11: Dan 12.10. 22.12: a Isa 40.10; 62.11; b Psa 28.4; Isa 40.10; Jer 17.10. 22.13: a Rev 1.8; b Isa 44.6; 48.12; Rev 1.17; 2.8. 22.14: Gen 2.9; 3.22. 22.16: Isa 11.1,10. 22.17: Isa 55.1. 22.18-19: Deut 4.2; 12.32.

---

*21.27 book of life:** See the note at 3.5.
*22.2 trees:** The Greek has "tree", which is used in a collective sense of trees on both sides of the heavenly river.

See also: 21.27: Isa 52.1; Ezek 44.9. 22.1: Ezek 47.1; Zech 14.8. 22.2: Gen 2.9. 22.3: Zech 14.11 (cp. Gen 3.17). 22.5: a Isa 60.19; b Dan 7.18.

Additional notes

›**2.23 her followers:** Or "her children".
›**3.8 did not deny that you are my followers:** Or "did not say evil things about me."
›**5.6 the seven spirits:** Some manuscripts have "the spirits".
›**12.11 blood:** Or "death".
›**12.18 The dragon:** The text has "he", and some manuscripts have "I".
›**13.8 wasn't written . . . was killed:** Or "wasn't written in the book of the Lamb who was killed before the time of creation."
›**19.13 covered with:** Some manuscripts have "sprinkled with".

Anorak corner

The Answers

Illness – p.148
1. He was lame in both feet (2 Samuel 4.4)
2. It was supposed to heal people (John 5.1–9)
3. One – and he was a foreigner from Samaria (Luke 17.11–19)
4. They bashed a hole in the roof and let him down through it (Mark 2.1–5)
5. A blind man healed by Jesus (Mark 8.22–26)

False Gods – p.241
1. Philistines (Judges 16.23)
2. Elijah (1 Kings 18.20–40)
3. The statue of their god was smashed and aplague broke out in the town (1 Samuel 5.1–7)
4. His worshippers sacrificed children to him (2 Kings 23.10)
5. Artemis or Diana (Acts 19.24–27)

Places – p.282
1. Spain (Jonah 1.3)
2. Damascus (Acts 9.3)
3. Jericho (Joshua 6.20)
4. David. He captured it from the Jebusites (2 Samuel 5.6–7)
5. In the Garden of Gethsemane (Mark 14.32–49)

The Temple – p.382
1. The sacred chest (1 Kings 6.19)
2. The stone tablets with the ten commandments on them (2 Chronicles 6.11)
3. The curtain separating the most holy place from the rest of the temple (Matthew 27.51)
4. Twelve (Luke 2.42–50)
5. Threw them out (John 2.13–16)

Rulers – p.468
1. 40 years (2 Samuel 5.4)
2. It split into two parts (1 Kings 12.15–19)
3. Uzziah or Azariah (2 Chronicles 26.10)
4. They wanted to be 'like the other nations' (1 Samuel 8.5)
5. Esther (Esther 2.17)

Big stuff – p.843
1. Heaven (Revelation 21.21)
2. Og (Deuteronomy 3.11)
3. Over nine feet (1 Samuel 17.4)
4. Ten of the spies sent in by Moses (Numbers 13.32–33)
5. A giant sea monster (Psalm 104.26)

Firsts – p.1001
1. Noah (Genesis 9.21)
2. Tubal Cain (Genesis 4.22)
3. Antioch (Acts 11.26)
4. Mary Magdalene (John 20.11–18)
5. False. It was Saul (1 Samuel 9.17)

Is it in the Bible? – p.1029
1. No. They were wise men and the Bible doesn't say how many there were (Matthew 2.1)
2. No. It says he was laid in some hay, but that could have been in a house (Luke 2.7).
3. They ate some fruit. The Bible doesn't say what kind (Genesis 2.16–17)
4. We don't know. The Bible just calls her the daughter of Herodias (Matthew 14.6–11)
5. False. She just visited him. (2 Chronicles 9.10)

Disciples – p.1047
1. James and John (Mark 10.35–40)
2. Peter (Matthew 14.29)
3. Judas (John 13.28–29)
4. James (Acts 12.2)
5. Matthias – the replacement for Judas (Acts 1.26)

Jesus – p.1151
1. Moses and Elijah (Matthew 17.3)
2. False. Jesus is the greek version of the name Joshua
3. Forty (Mark 1.13)
4. 'Love the Lord your God with all your heart, soul, and mind' and 'Love others as much as you love yourself.' (Matthew 22.37–40)
5. Nazareth (Luke 4.16)

Ages – p.1195
1. Methuselah (Genesis 5.25–27)
2. 600 years old (Genesis 7.5)
3. 80 years old (Exodus 7.6–7)
4. About thirty (Luke 3.23)
5. Under two (Matthew 2.16)

Burials – p.1219
1. Machpelah cave near Hebron (Genesis 49.29)
2. Forty days (Genesis 50.2–3)
3. Myrrh and Aloes (John 19.39)
4. He wasn't. He was taken away by God (2 Kings 2.11)
5. Joseph of Arimathea (Matthew 27.57–60)

Donkeys – p.1276

1. Samson – he killed 1,000 philistines with it (Judges 15.15)
2. Saul (1 Samuel 9.15–20)
3. Balaam (Numbers 22.21–33)
4. Jesus. (Matthew 21.5)
5. Nebuchadnezzar (Daniel 5.19–21)

Priests – p.1379

1. High Priest (Matthew 26.3)
2. Shiloh (1 Samuel 1.3)
3. Aaron (Exodus 28.3)
4. Levites (Numbers 3.8–10)
5. The High Priest, on the day of atonement (Hebrews 9.25)

Big index